FIFTEENTH EDITION

SCHROEDER'S
ANTIQUES
PRICE GUIDE

Edited by Sharon & Bob Huxford

COLLECTOR BOOKS
A Division of Schroeder Publishing Co., Inc.

The current values in this book should be used only as a guide. They are not intended to set prices, which vary from one section of the country to another. Auction prices as well as dealer prices vary greatly and are affected by condition as well as demand. Neither the Editors nor the Publisher assumes responsibility for any losses that might be incurred as a result of consulting this guide.

Searching For A Publisher?

We are always looking for knowledgable people considered experts within their fields. If you feel that there is a real need for a book on your collectible subject and have a large comprehensive collection, please contact Collector Books.

Additional copies of this book may be ordered from:

COLLECTOR BOOKS
P.O. Box 3009
Paducah, Kentucky 42002-3009

@$12.95. Add $2.00 for postage and handling.

Copyright: Schroeder Publishing Co., Inc. 1997

Introduction

As the editors and staff of *Schroeder's*, our goal is to compile the most useful, comprehensive, and accurate background and pricing information possible. Our guide encompasses nearly five hundred categories, many of which you will not find in other price guides. Our sources are varied; we use auction results, dealer lists, trade paper ads, and we consult with national collectors' clubs, recognized authorities, researchers, and appraisers. We have by far the largest Advisory Board of any similar publication on the market. Each year we add several new advisors and now have over 425 who cover almost all our categories. They go over our computer print-outs line by line, deleting listings that are misleading or too vague to be of merit; they often send background information and photos. We appreciate their assistance very much. Only through their expertise and experience in their special fields are we able to offer with confidence what we feel are useful, accurate evaluations that provide a sound understanding of the dealings in the market place today. Correspondence with so large an advisory panel adds months of extra work to an already monumental task, but we feel that to a very large extent this is the foundation that makes *Schroeder's* the success that it has become.

Our Directory, which you will find in the back of the book, lists each contributor by state. These are people who have allowed us to photograph various examples of merchandise from their show booths, sent us pricing information, or in any way have contributed to this year's book. If you happen to be traveling, consult the Directory for shops along your way. We also list clubs who have worked with us and auction houses who have agreed to permit us the use of photographs from their catalogs.

Our Advisory Board lists only names and home states, so check the Directory for addresses and telephone numbers should you want to correspond with one of our experts. Remember, when you do, always enclose a self-addressed, stamped envelope (SASE). Thousands of people buy our guide, and hundreds contact our advisors. The only agreement we have with our advisors is that they edit their categories. They are in no way obligated to answer mail. Some are dealers who do many shows a month. The time they spend at home may be very limited, and they may not be open to contacts. There's no doubt that the reason behind the success of our book is their assistance. We regret seeing them becoming more and more burdened by phone and mail inquiries. We have lost some of our good advisors for this reason, and when we do, the book suffers and consequently, so do our readers. Many of our listed reference sources report that they constantly receive long distance calls (at all hours) that are really valuation requests. If they are registered appraisers, they make their living at providing such information and expect a fee for their service and expertise.

If you find you need more information than *Schroeder's* provides, there are other sources available to you. Go to your local library; check their section on reference books. Museums are public facilities that are willing and able help you establish the origin and possibly even the value of your particular treasure. Check the yellow pages of your phone book. Other cities' phone books are available from either your library or from the telephone company office. Look under the heading Antique Dealers. Those who are qualified appraisers will mention this credit in their advertisement. But remember that if you sell to a dealer, he will expect to buy your merchandise at a price low enough that he will be able to make an appreciable profit when he sells it. Once you decide to contact one of these appraisers, unless you intend see them directly, you'll need to get photographs. Don't send photos that are under or over exposed, out of focus, or shot against a background that detracts from important details you want to emphasize. It is almost impossible for them to give you a value judgement on items they've not seen when your photos are of poor quality. Shoot the front, top, and the bottom; describe any marks and numbers (or send a pencil rubbing), explain how and when you acquired the article, and give accurate measurements and any further background information that may be helpful.

The auction houses listed in the Directory nearly all have a staff of appraisal experts. If the item you're attempting to research is of the caliber of material they deal with, they can offer extremely accurate evaluations. Of course, most have a fee. Be sure to send them only professional-quality photographs. Tell them if you expect to consign your item to their auction. If you disagree with the value they suggest, you are under no obligation to do so.

Nearly five hundred categories are included in our book. We have organized our topics alphabetically, following the most simple logic, usually either by manufacturer or by type of product. If you have difficulty in locating your subject, consult the index. Our guide is unique in that much more space has been allotted to background information than any other publication of this type, and it is easier to read due to the larger-than-average print. Our readers tell us that these are features they enjoy. To be able to do this, we have adopted a format of one-line listings wherein we describe the items to the fullest extent possible by using several common-sense abbreviations; they will be easy to read and understand if you will first take the time to quickly scan through them.

The Editors

Editorial Staff

Editors
Sharon and Bob Huxford

Research and Editorial Assistants
Michael Drollinger, Nancy Drollinger, Linda Holycross, Donna Newnum, Loretta Woodrow

Layout
Beth Ray, Karen Geary, and Michelle Dowling

Cover Design
Beth Summers

On the cover, clockwise from right:
Ambrina, vase with gold floral, heavy threading, 14", $350.00.

18" Belton-type doll with open/closed mouth and white space between. Has set glass eyes. On jointed French body with straight wrists, $2700.00. *Courtesy of Barbara Earnshaw-Cain.*

Coralene vase, 10¾" tall, mark 242, $900.00-1000.00.

Cardboard cut-out showing small boy peering around a door facing at Santa who's opening a bottle of Coca-Cola, easel back, 3-dimensional, 1950s, $175.00. *From the Mitchell collection.*

Frankart, Scotty bookends, 1920, repair to tip of tail, $75.00.

Listing of Standard Abbreviations

The following is a list of abbreviations that have been used throughout this book in order to provide you with the most detailed descriptions possible in the limited space available. No periods are used after initials or abbreviations. When two dimensions are given, height is noted first. If only one dimension is listed, it will be height, except in the case of bowls, dishes, plates, or platters, when it will be diameter. The standard two-letter state abbreviations apply.

For glassware, if no color is noted, the glass is clear. Hyphenated colors, for example blue-green, olive-amber, etc., describe a single color tone; colors divided by a slash mark indicate two or more colors, i.e. blue/white. Teapots, sugar bowls, and butter dishes are assumed to be 'with cover.' Condition is extremely important in determining market value. Common sense suggests that art pottery, china, and glassware values would be given for examples in pristine, mint condition, while suggested prices for utility wares such as Redware, Mocha, and Blue and White Stoneware, for example, reflect the probability that since such items were subjected to everyday use in the home they may show minor wear (which is acceptable) but no notable damage. Values for other categories reflect the best average condition in which the particular collectible is apt to be offered for sale without the dealer feeling it necessary to mention wear or damage. For instance, advertising items are assumed to be in excellent to near mint condition since mint items are scarce enough that when one is offered for sale the dealer will most likely make mention of that fact. The same holds true for Toys, Banks, Coin-Operated Machines, and the like. A basic rule of thumb is that an item listed as VG (very good) will bring 40% to 60% of its mint price — a first-hand, personal evaluation will enable you to make the final judgement; EX (excellent) is a condition midway between mint and very good, and values would correspond.

Am .... American	dtd ....dated	litho ....lithograph	rpl................................replaced
appl ....applied	dvtl ....dovetail	lt..light	rpr................................repaired
att............................attributed to	emb............embossed, embossing	M ....mint	rpt..............................repainted
bbl ....barrel	embr ....embroidered	mahog..........................mahogany	rstr................................restored
bk ....back	eng ....engraved, engraving	mc............................multicolor	rtcl..............................reticulated
bl ....blue	EPNS .electroplated nickel silver	MIB ....mint in box	rvpt ....reverse painted
blk ....black	etch ....etched, etching	MIG ....Made in Germany	s&p ....salt and pepper
brn.....................................brown	EX..............................excellent	mk ....mark	sgn ....signed
bulb ....bulbous	fr ....frame, framed	MOP ....mother-of-pearl	SP ....silverplated
bsk ....bisque	Fr ....French	mt, mtd............mount, mounted	sq ....square
b3m ....blown 3-mold	ft, ftd ....foot, feet, footed	NE ....New England	std ....standard
C ....century	G.......................................good	NM ....near mint	str ....straight
c ....copyright	gr......................................green	NP ....nickel plated	sz ....size
ca ....circa	grad............................graduated	opal............................opalescent	trn.....................turned, turning
can ....canister	grpt.....................grain painted	orig...................................original	turq...........................turquoise
cb ....cardboard	H..........................high, height	o/l......................................overlay	uphl ....upholstered
CI ....cast iron	hdl, hdld..........handle, handled	o/w..................................otherwise	VG.............................very good
compo...................composition	HP.........................hand painted	Pat ....patented	Vict ....Victorian
cr/sug ....creamer and sugar	illus .....illustration, illustrated by	pc ....piece	W ....width
c/s..................cup and saucer	imp................................impressed	ped...............................pedestal	wht ....white
cvd ....carved	ind.................................individual	pk ....pink	w/ ....with
cvg ....carving	int......................................interior	pnt.....................................paint	w/o................................without
dbl.....................................double	Invt T'print ..Inverted Thumbprint	porc ....porcelain	X, Xd....................cross, crossed
decor ....decoration	irid ....iridescent	prof...........................professional	yel ....yellow
dk ....dark	L............................length, long	re ....regarding	(+) ....has been reproduced
Dmn Quilt ......Diamond Quilted	lav ....lavender	rfn..............................refinished	
drw.....................................drawer	ldgl................................leaded glass	rnd ....round	

A B C Plates

Children's plates featuring the alphabet as part of the design were popular from as early as 1820 until after the turn of the century. The earliest English creamware plates were decorated with embossed letters and prim moralistic verses, but the later Staffordshire products were conducive to a more relaxed mealtime atmosphere, often depicting playful animals and riddles or scenes of pleasant leisure-time activities. They were made around the turn of the century by American potters as well. All featured transfer prints, but color was sometimes brushed on by hand to add interest to the design. Braille plates were made for the blind, but these are rather scarce and usually more valuable. You may also find an occasional bowl or mug. Our advisor for this category is Dr. Joan George; she is listed in the Directory under New Jersey.

Ceramic

Alpine shepherd, blk transfer w/mc, Staffordshire, 5" 65.00

American Sports — Base Ball, Pitcher, black transfer, ca 1870s, NM, $220.00.

Baby Bunting, kitten & dog, gold ABCs at rim 75.00
Birds on branch, brn transfer w/mc, unmk, 6¼" 115.00
Blind Girl, Victorian children, mc transfer, 5¾" 130.00
Bowl, None Are Wise or Safe..., bl transfer, 1840s 135.00
Boys Playing Cricket, dk red transfer, emb rim, 7" 60.00
Brighton Beach Bathing Pavilion, mc transfer, 8" 100.00
Catch It Carlo When I Throw, blk transfer w/mc, 5½", NM 110.00
Children frightened by goose, sign language, Aynsley, 6" 250.00
Children shooting firecrackers, ca 1870 ....65.00
Crusoe at Work, Staffordshire 125.00
Crusoe Making a Boat, pk transfer, printed rim, 6¼" 115.00
Crusoe on the Raft, mc transfer, printed rim, 8¼" 145.00
Dutch canal w/windmill, gr transfer, 7½" 140.00
Evening Bathing Scene at Manhattan Beach, mc transfer, 7½" ...90.00
Everybody Bids..., sheep & cow, blk transfer w/mc, 5¼" 90.00
Federal Generals, blk transfer w/brn & pk, rpr, 6⅛" 105.00
Flowers That Never Fade, Staffordshire, 7" 150.00
Football, blk transfer w/mc, Meakin, 6¼" 85.00
Fox hunt scene, brn transfer, emb rim, 7" 130.00
Graces, blk transfer w/burgundy rim, Godwin, 5" 165.00
Incidents of the War, brn transfer w/mc, 7⅛" 155.00
Iron Pier...Brighton Beach, bl transfer, Staffordshire, 6¾" 70.00
Major General Gillmore, blk transfer, Staffordshire 250.00
Make Hay While..., Franklin's Proverbs, blk transfer w/mc, 6" ...130.00
Men working at hearth, gr transfer, emb rim, 6¾" 120.00
Mug, GHI & children, Trap Bat & Ball transfer, Staffordshire ...150.00
Mug, L Is a Ladder..., kitten, blk transfer, Staffordshire 105.00
My Face Is My Fortune, bl-gr transfer, Staffordshire, 7½" 95.00
Now I Have a Sheep..., Franklin's Proverb, blk transfer, 7" 145.00
Old Mother Hubbard, brn transfer w/mc, printed rim, 5½" 145.00

Owls in classroom, pk transfer, Haynsley & Co, 6¼", NM 170.00
Pretty Child, blk transfer w/mc, Staffordshire, 8" 150.00
Punch & Judy, pk transfer, 7¼" 175.00
Queen Victoria & Prince Albert of Sax..., blk transfer, 7" 350.00
Rabbit-hunting scene, Staffordshire, ca 1860, 7¼" 75.00
Silks & Satins...& Velvets..., blk transfer w/mc, Meakin, 7¾" ...160.00
Stable yard, gray transfer w/mc, Staffordshire, 8¼" 85.00
That Girl Wants Pup Away, blk transfer, Staffordshire, 6" 90.00
Wooden dolls, gr transfer, red rim band, Staffordshire, 6" 185.00
2 cats in cherry tree, blk transfer, bl rim, 6" 155.00
3 Removes Are As Bad As a Fire, bl transfer w/lustre, 4¾" 115.00

Glass

Cane center, 6" 30.00
Clock, bl, ABC rim, 7" 65.00
Clock, Thousand Eye, amber, ABC rim 125.00
Ducks, ABC rim, 6" 60.00
Elephant w/howdah on bk, ABC rim, Ripley & Co, 6" 90.00
Flower bouquet, ABCs on stippled ground, frosted flowers, 6" 75.00
Garfield, ABC rim 100.00
Independence Hall, scalloped, 6¾" 110.00
Proud Dog, ABC rim 65.00
Quilted center, ABCs & numbers on stippled ground 105.00
Rooster, hen & chicks, ABC rim 65.00

Tin

ABCs & Arabic numbers, scrolled foliage, 7⅝" 40.00
Brownies, ca 1893, 8⅞" 160.00
Bust of Washington, dents, 6⅛" 170.00
Grinding Old Into Young, mini 165.00
Hey Diddle Diddle, cat & fiddle, 5½" 85.00
Jumbo, elephant, dk gray, 6½" 105.00
Mary Had a Little Lamb, 8" 135.00
Peter Rabbit, animals intertwined in ABC rim, 8½" 75.00
Who Killed Cock Robin?, emb ABC rim, 7⅞" 130.00

Abingdon

From 1934 until 1950, the Abingdon Pottery Co. of Abingdon, Ill., made a line of art pottery with a white vitrified body decorated with various types of glazes in many lovely colors. Novelties, cookie jars, utility ware, and lamps were made in addition to several lines of simple yet striking art ware. Fern Leaf, introduced in 1937, featured molded vertical feathering. La Fleur, in 1939, consisted of flowerpots and flower-arranger bowls with rows of vertical ribbing. Classic, 1939-40, was a line of vases, many with evidence of Chinese influence. Several marks were used, most of which employed the company name. In 1950 the company reverted to the manufacture of sanitary ware that had been their mainstay before the Art Ware Division was formed.

Highly decorated examples and those with black, bronze, or red glaze usually command at least 25% higher prices.

#116, vase, Classic, 10", from $18 to 22.50
#321, bookends, Cossack Dancer, blk, pr 95.00
#369, ashtray, guard, sq, 5x5" 20.00
#370, bookends, cactus, 6", pr 65.00
#382, bowl, wht w/yel decor, 12" 40.00
#386, ashtray, sunflower, gr, 4½" 15.00
#389, vase, geranium, 7" 25.00
#3902, Scarf Dancer, blk, 13" 250.00

#392, vase, morning glory, 5½" 20.00
#393, bowl, morning glory, 7" 35.00
#400, tea tile, geisha, sq, 5" 50.00
#402, vase, Box, 5½" 35.00
#408, bowl, leaf, beige, 1937, 6½" 40.00
#412, vase, Volute, wht, 1937-40, 15½" 125.00
#422, vase, Fern Leaf, wht, 10" 30.00
#423, bowl, Fern Leaf, 7" 25.00
#429, vase/candle holder, Fern Leaf, 8" 25.00
#431, wall pocket, Fern Leaf, 7½" 55.00
#435, wall pocket, Tri-Fern, 8", minimum value 135.00
#441, bookend, horse head, blk, pr 75.00
#444, bookend/planter, dolphin, decor, pr 50.00
#452, bowl, aster, 9x14½" 45.00
#453, vase, aster, 8" 25.00
#457, wall pocket, Ionic, 8¾" 45.00
#460, bowl, Panel, 8" 25.00
#463, vase, star, 7" 18.00
#476, vase, wreath, 8" 35.00
#485, vase, acanthus, 8" 20.00
#489, wall pocket, Dutch boy, 10", minimum value 75.00
#505, candle holder, shell, dbl, 4" 20.00
#513, vase, swirl, 9", from $15 to 25.00
#516, vase, Acadia, 7" 22.00

#520, Baden vase, decals and
gold on cream, 9", $40.00.

#562, gull, wht, 7" 45.00
#565, cornucopia, blk, 1942-47, 7" 25.00
#568, mint compote, pk, ftd, 1942-47, 6" dia 28.00
#569D, cornucopia, bl w/decor 27.50
#571, goose, blk, 5" 35.00
#573, penguin, decor, 5½" 40.00
#574, heron, no decor 35.00
#593, vase, bow knot, bl, 9" 25.00
#608, box, cigarette; elephant, 6" 65.00
#625, vase, ribbed, 6½" 25.00
#640, wall pocket, Triad, 5½" 35.00
#652, planter, puppy, decor, 6¾" 50.00
#657, swordfish, bl, 4½" 30.00
#681/#682, sugar bowl & creamer, daisy 27.50
#699, wall pocket, apron, 6" 50.00
#705, vase, Modern, bl gloss, 8" 28.00
#711, wall vase, carriage lamp, 10" 60.00
Cookie jar, #471, Little Old Lady, plain or decor, 1942 ....210.00
Cookie jar, #471, Little Old Lady, rare gr 195.00
Cookie jar, #495, Fat Boy 240.00

Cookie jar, #549, Hippo, decor, 1942 ....225.00
Cookie jar, #561, Baby, Blk decor 300.00
Cookie jar, #588, Money Bag, 1947 ....70.00
Cookie jar, #602, Hobby Horse 185.00
Cookie jar, #611, Jack-in-Box 255.00
Cookie jar, #622, Miss Muffet 205.00
Cookie jar, #651, Choo Choo (Locomotive) 150.00
Cookie jar, #653, Clock, 1949 ....85.00
Cookie jar, #663, Humpty Dumpty 250.00
Cookie jar, #664, Pineapple 60.00
Cookie jar, #665, Wigwam, minimum value 300.00
Cookie jar, #674, Pumpkin, 1949 ....310.00
Cookie jar, #677, Daisy, 1949 ....45.00
Cookie jar, #678, Windmill 185.00
Cookie jar, #692, Witch, minimum value 350.00
Cookie jar, #693, Little Girl 60.00
Cookie jar, #694, Bo Peep 240.00
Cookie jar, #695, Mother Goose 295.00
Cookie jar, #696, Three Bears 90.00

Adams

Wm. Adams, whose potting skills were developed under the tutelage of Josiah Wedgwood, founded the Greengates Pottery at Tunstall, England, in 1769. Many types of wares including basalt, ironstone, parian, and jasper were produced; and various impressed or printed marks were employed. Until 1800 'Adams Co.' or 'Adams' impressed in block letters identified the company's earthenwares and a fine type of jasper similar in color and decoration to Wedgwood's. The latter mark was used again from 1845 to 1864 on parian figures. Most examples of their product found on today's market are transfer-printed dinnerwares with ornate backstamps which often include the pattern name and the initials 'W.A. & S.' This type of product was made from 1820 until about 1920. After 1890 the word 'England' was included in the mark; 'Tunstall' was added after 1896. From 1914 through 1940, a printed crown with 'Adams, Estbd 1657, England' identified their products. From 1900 to 1965, they produced souvenir plates with transfers of American scenes, many of which were marketed in this country by Roth Importers of Peoria, Illinois. In 1965 the company affiliated with Wedgwood. Although there were other Adams potteries in Staffordshire, their marks incorporate either the first name initial or a partner's name and so are easily distinguished from those of this company. See also Spatter; Staffordshire; Adams Rose.

Bowl, Cries of London, Dr Syntax Reading His Tour, 9" 60.00
Bowl, soup; The Sea, blk transfer, 10¾" 75.00
Bowl, vegetable; Columbus Discovers Am, gr transfer, 11" L 195.00
Butter chip, Cries of London 22.00
Candlesticks, Cries of London, 3½", pr 80.00
Cup & saucer, handleless; The Pet, red transfer, EX 50.00
Jug, 4 Seasons, bl/wht Jasper w/metal lid, 10" 475.00
Plate, Columbia, red transfer, mk, 10¾" 40.00
Plate, Cupid & maiden, dk bl transfer, 9" 160.00
Plate, dinner; Currier & Ives, 10" 30.00
Plate, Palestine, red transfer border, gr center, 9½" 80.00
Plate, Seasons (Winter), pk transfer, 9½" 65.00
Plate, The Sea, pk transfer, rpr, 7½" 32.00
Sugar shaker, bl/wht Jasper 200.00
Urn, coat of arms, wht on cobalt, mini, 2½" 85.00

Adams Rose, Early and Late

In the second quarter of the 19th century, the Adams and Son

Pottery produced a line of hand-painted dinnerware decorated in large, red brush-stroke roses with green leaves on whiteware, which collectors call Adams Rose. Later, G. Jones and Son (and possibly others) made a similar ware with less brilliant colors on a gray-white surface.

Bowl, early, 2¾x5½", EX **55.00**
Bowl, late, mk Imperial Royal, Belgium, 3x5½" **35.00**
Bowl, vegetable; late, Staffordshire, England, oval, 8½" **80.00**
Bowl, vegetable; late, 11", M **130.00**
Coffeepot, early, scroll hdl, dome lid, Adams, 12", EX **575.00**
Creamer, early, 3", EX **150.00**
Creamer, late, mk Reg #6154, 5½", VG **70.00**
Cup plate, early, scalloped, mk Adams, 4", EX **95.00**
Pitcher, early, scalloped rim w/emb scrolls, Adams, 8", EX **450.00**
Pitcher, late, 6¾", M **325.00**
Plate, early, mk Adams, 9½", VG **45.00**
Plate, early, 9", M **195.00**
Plate, toddy; early, plain rim, mk Adams, 5", EX **120.00**
Platter, early, scalloped rim, Adams, 20x16½", NM **2,075.00**
Platter, late, unmk, 12½x9" **85.00**
Soup plate, early, plain rim, mk Adams, 10½", M **165.00**
Soup plate, early, plain rim, mk Adams, 9½", NM **90.00**
Sugar bowl, early, w/lid, M **350.00**
Tea bowl & saucer, late, M **125.00**
Teapot, early, dolphin hdl, 8x11", VG **475.00**
Teapot, early, rnd body, 5", VG **300.00**
Wash bowl, late, emb floral vine at rim, no mk, 14½" **160.00**

Advertising

The advertising world has always been a fiercely competitive field. In an effort to present their product to the customer, every imaginable gimmick was put into play. Colorful and artfully decorated signs and posters, thermometers, tape measures, fans, hand mirrors, and attractive tin containers (all with catchy slogans, familiar logos, and often-bogus claims) are only a few of the many examples of early advertising memorabilia that are of interest to today's collectors.

Porcelain signs were made as early as 1890 and are highly prized for their artistic portrayal of life as it was then . . . often allowing amusing insights into the tastes, humor, and way of life of a bygone era. As a general rule, older signs are made from a heavier gauge metal. Those with three or more fired-on colors are especially desirable.

Tin containers were used to package consumer goods ranging from crackers and coffee to tobacco and talcum. After 1880 can companies began to decorate their containers by the method of lithography. Though colors were still subdued, intricate designs were used to attract the eye of the consumer. False labeling and unfounded claims were curtailed by the Pure Food and Drug Administration in 1906, and the name of the manufacturer as well as the brand name of the product had to be printed on the label. By 1910 color was rampant with more than a dozen hues printed on the tin or on paper labels. The tins themselves were often designed with a second use in mind, such as canisters, lunch boxes, even toy trains. As a general rule, tobacco-related tins are the most desirable, though personal preference may direct the interest of the collector to peanut butter pails with illustrations of children, or talcum tins with irresistible babies or beautiful ladies. Coffee tins are popular, as are those made to contain a particularly successful or well-known product.

Perhaps the most visual of the early advertising gimmicks were the character logos, the Fairbank Company's Gold Dust Twins, the goose trademark of the Red Goose Shoe Company, Nabisco's ZuZu Clown and Uneeda Kid, the Campbell Kids, the RCA dog Nipper, and Mr. Peanut, to name only a few. Any example of these brings a high price on the market today.

Our listings are alphabetized by company name or, in lieu of that information, by word content or other pertinent description. When no condition is indicated, the items listed below are assumed to be in excellent condition, except glass and ceramic items, which are assumed mint. Remember that condition greatly affects value (especially true for tin items). For instance, a sign in excellent or mint condition may bring twice as much as the same one in only very good condition, sometimes even more. On today's market, items in good to very good condition are slow to sell, unless they are extremely rare. Mint (or near-mint) examples are high.

As a general rule, beer tip trays in near-mint condition are worth $150.00 to $250.00. Spool cabinets (depending on condition) may be evaluated at $100.00 to $150.00 per drawer.

We have several advertising advisors; see specific subheadings. For further information we recommend *Zany Characters of the Ad World* by Mary Jane Lamphier, *Advertising Character Collectibles* by Warren Dotz, *Value Guide to Advertising Memorabilia* by B.J. Summers, and *Huxford's Collectible Advertising* by Sharon and Bob Huxford. All of these books are available at your local bookstore or from Collector Books. See also Advertising Dolls; Advertising Cards; Automobilia; Coca-Cola; Banks; Calendars; Cookbooks; Paperweights; Posters; Sewing Items.

Key:
cb — cardboard	ps — porcelain sign
cl — celluloid	sf — self-framed
lcs — litho on canvas sign	tc — tin container
pp — pre-prohibition	ts — tin sign

AC Spark Plugs, tin box, old touring car, hinged lid, EX **70.00**
Alka Seltzer, apron, cloth w/red flames & To the Rescue, M **40.00**
Atlantic Refining, die-cut porc pump sign, 'fried egg' shape **550.00**
Aultman Co, paper sign, steam tractor/thresher, 24x17", EX **325.00**
Aunt Jemima Pancake Flour, cb sign, Aunt Jemima on swing, VG...**5,400.00**
Baby Diamond Dyes, cabinet, Wells & Hope front w/baby, 20", G ...**750.00**
Beadleston & Woerz Brewing, tray, lady at table, 13" sq, VG **200.00**
Belding Bros, wooden spool cabinet, brass/glass front, 39", VG ..**600.00**
Beverwyck Beer, coasters, horse & rider, series of 4, all **25.00**

Bevo Beer, tray, horse-drawn beer wagon, ca 1910-30, 13" long, minor rust spots, $95.00 (Bevo was produced by Anheuser-Busch).

Beymer-Bauman White Lead, tin string holder, Dutch boy, 28", G ..**2,800.00**
Big Buster Popcorn, tc, full, M **85.00**
Borden's, clock, Elsie in flower, electric, rnd, EX **400.00**
Borden's, Elsie the Cow punch-out train, M in pkg **22.50**
Borden's, tip tray, maid serving milk on tray, 4½" dia, G **85.00**
Borden's Malted Milk, store container, EX **200.00**
Brown Forman Distillers, ts, salesman at bar, 19x27"+fr, VG+ .**2,200.00**

Buck Skin Rubber Boots, ts, boy on swing, 16x22"+fr, G 225.00
Buckhorn Tobacco, pocket tin, NM 80.00
Budd's Baby Shoes, sf ts, 2 children, 1900-10, 20x15", EX 350.00
Budweiser, clock, w/Budman & bottle, lights up, 1990, M 180.00
Budweiser Barley Malt Syrup, milk glass shade, 4¾" dia, VG 250.00

Buster Brown

Buster Brown was the creation of cartoonist Richard Felton; his comic strip first appeared in the *New York Herald* on May 4, 1902. Since then Buster and his dog Tige (short for Tiger) have adorned sundry commercial products but are probably best known as the trademark for the Brown Shoe Company established early in this century. Today hundreds of Buster Brown premiums, store articles, and advertising items bring substantial prices from many serious collectors.

ABC plate 95.00
Bank, ceramic, bright color, 1950s, NM 295.00
Bill hook, cl, BB & Tige, c 1946, 2¼" dia 40.00
Book, BB & Company, 1907, EX 175.00
Book, BB & His Dog Tige, 1906, EX 250.00
Box, BB Stockings, 1905, EX 175.00
Camping kit, aluminum pan & bucket w/lid, 1930s, EX 120.00
Color book, 1940s, unused 55.00
Cup, mc BB, china, 3½x3¼" 200.00
Dealer's sign, 1950s, 15x15", MIB 150.00
Display, animated BB & Tige swimming, 54x60", VG 3,000.00
Display, cb standup, BB Socks, 1950s, 9x10", M 55.00
Display, tin litho diecut, BB & Tige, 2-pc, 39", 28", G 4,500.00
Doll pattern, BB & Tige, uncut cloth, 1924, NM 275.00
Hand puppet, cb, 1950s, EX 10.00
Handkerchief, early, EX 60.00
Key chain, 2" brn plastic fob w/emb image of BB & Tige, 1950s ..50.00
Kite, 1940s, NM 38.00
Paper dolls, 1910, EX 325.00
Party game, cloth, 1910 ....125.00
Pin-bk, BB Shoes, BB & Tige 35.00

Rocking horse, wood with metal springs, red logo on sides, 1950s, 30x32", EX with minor paint wear, $400.00.

Shaving mug 175.00
Shoe last, plastic 28.00
Shoes, BB & Tige Blue Ribbon, pr 20.00
Sign, pnt wood, BB & Tige, 1920s, EX 175.00
Sign, rvpt, BB Shoe Co, concave glass, 1905, orig fr 525.00
Sign, tin, BB & Tige, 20x28"+fr, VG 300.00
Sign, under glass, fr, counter standup, 1930s, NM 475.00
Standup, plastic, BB figure, early, 36", EX 135.00

C.D. Kenny

C.D. Kenny was determined to be a successful man, and he was.

Between 1890 and 1934, he owned seventy-five groceries in fifteen states. He realized his success in two ways: fair business dealings and premium giveaways. These ranged from trade cards and advertising mirrors to tin commemorative plates and kitchen items. There were banks and toys, clocks and tins. Today's collectors are finding scores of these items, all carrying Kenny's name.

Calendar, Pennant, 1919 ....35.00
Doll, pnt bsk, premium, pnt mk, 4", NM 90.00
Figurine, Indian in canoe, EX 22.50
Frame, Dutch motif 20.00
Pin-bk button, Welcome United Singers, 1900s, 1½" dia, VG 12.00
Plate, tin, child in snow scene 90.00
Plate, tin, Star Spangled Banner 40.00
Salt shaker, Geisha girl 15.00
Stamp holder, cl, Dutch waitresses 16.50
Strainer 45.00
Tape measure, retractable 48.00
Tin container, Tea Party, oval 150.00
Tip tray, lady in woods, flower border, M 120.00
Tip tray, raising flag 100.00
Tip tray, Thanksgiving Greetings, 5⅛" dia, EX 240.00

Capt Jack Oysters, tc, 1-gal, EX 40.00
Caravan, tc, camels & man, Tiger Skin Rubber Co NY, NM 125.00
Carnation Malted Milk, can, 1940, 25-lb, NM 120.00
Carson's Fine Ice Cream, bl porc arrow, 9x30", M 195.00
Case Tractors, dealer sign, 2-sided porc & neon, M in crate ...4,800.00
Chas Lutz...Brewers, tray, toasting scene, 13¼x10½", VG 50.00
City Club Crushed Cubes, upright pocket tin, 4½x3x¾", VG ...200.00
Columbia Ice Cream, tray, girl w/dog & horse, 16x13", VG 200.00
Connecticut Mutual, ts, office building & buggies, 18x24", VG .500.00
Corticelli, spool cabinet, 3-drw, gold stencil, 9x22x16", VG 225.00
Crawford's Puff Creams, cl sign, girl w/cookies, 11¼x11", VG ...400.00
Cremo Tobacco, tin trunk, 18½x28½x18½", G 225.00
Crush, bottle-cap thermometer, 1958, 12" dia, NM 250.00
Curtis Fresh Candies, counter-top display case, dbl doors, EX 225.00
Dad's Old Fashioned Root Beer, ts, bl/orange/red, 12x14", EX 75.00
De Laval Cream Separators, match safe, tin diecut, 6¼", G 350.00
De Laval Cream Separators, sf paper sgn, lady/child, 35x20", EX+ .725.00

De Laval Cream Separators, tin sign, original marked frame, 19x25", M, $4,000.00.

De Laval Cream Separators, ts, child w/bucket, 26" dia, G 725.00
Dial Tobacco, pocket tin, EX 45.00
Diamond Dyes, cabinet, baby in ornate fr, 20", G 1,200.00

Diamond Dyes, cabinet, children skipping rope, 24", VG **750.00**
Diamond Dyes, cabinet, children w/balloon, 24", VG **650.00**
Diamond Dyes, cabinet, children w/maypole, 30", VG **750.00**
Diamond Dyes, cabinet, court jester, 27", EX **1,300.00**
Diamond Dyes, cabinet, evolution of woman, 30", EX **900.00**
Diamond Dyes, cabinet, evolution of woman, 30", G **525.00**
Diamond Dyes, cabinet, fairies, 30", EX **2,600.00**
Diamond Dyes, cabinet, girl w/Kodak, 30", VG **1,250.00**
Diamond Dyes, cabinet, washer woman, 30", VG **1,200.00**
Diamond Dyes, case, glass top, stenciled front, VG **150.00**
Diamond Dyes, ts, All American Girls Use..., 14x26", G- **100.00**
Diet Rite Cola, ts, yel bkground, 12x31½", NM **90.00**
Double Cola, clock, sunburst logo, electric, rnd, '50s, EX **375.00**
Double Cola, thermometer, 18" dia, NM **175.00**
Dr AC Daniels' Veterinary Medicine, cabinet, horses, 29", G ...**2,700.00**
Dr Daniels' Dog & Cat Remedies, tin cabinet, lady, 20x13", VG ..**3,250.00**
Dr Daniels' Veterinary Medicine, cabinet, Dr/medicine, 28", G ..**1,350.00**
Dr Lesure's Remedies, cabinet, horse's head, 38½", VG/EX **3,200.00**
Dr Lyna's Hair Grower, cb sign, yel & blk, 1912, 10x14", EX **15.00**

Dr. Pepper

A young pharmacist, Charles C. Alderton, was hired by W.B. Morrison, owner of Morrison's Old Corner Drug Store in Waco, Texas, around 1884. Alderton, an observant sort, noticed that the drugstore's patrons could never quite make up their minds as to which flavor of extract to order. He concocted a formula that combined many flavors, and Dr. Pepper was born. The name was chosen by Morrison in honor of a beautiful young girl with whom he had once been in love. The girl's father, a Virginia doctor by the name of Pepper, had discouraged the relationship due to their youth, but Morrison had never forgotten her. On December 1, 1885, a U.S. patent was issued to the creators of Dr. Pepper. Our advisors for Dr. Pepper listings are Craig and Donna Stifter; they are listed in the Directory under Illinois.

Sign, porcelain with black and white raised lettering on red background with green and white border, 10½x26½", chips at mounting holes, $375.00.

Bottler, seltzer, 1920s-30s, EX+ **180.00**
Calendar, complete, 1942, 22x13½", EX **200.00**
Calendar, Donna Loren, complete, 1965, EX **15.00**
Calendar, full pad w/cover page, 1948, 22x13½", NM **110.00**
Calendar, girl in fur coat, 1948, 22x13½", NM **150.00**
Can, cone top, rare, 6-oz, EX **150.00**
Clock, Drink... on center band, 14" dia, VG **245.00**
Clock, neon, emphasis on 10-2-4, sq, EX **350.00**
Clock, Telechron, gr compo fr, electric, 1930s-40s, 15", EX **475.00**
Door pull, aluminum, mc bottle shape, 1940s, 10x3½", VG **210.00**
Menu board, emb tin, floor version, 33½x20½", EX **155.00**
Menu board, tin, oval above gr board, 28x20", NM **55.00**
Recipe book, Cookin' w/Dr Pepper, 1965, 15-pg, EX **5.00**
Sign, aluminum, Energy Up at 10, 2 & 4, 1930s, 10" dia, NM ...**600.00**
Sign, cb, Certainly & Drink..., lady in hat & stole, 1940s, NM ..**180.00**
Sign, cb, girl w/fishing pole, Smart Lift, 1940s, 16x25", EX+ **135.00**

Sign, horse soldiers, Harry Payne, 12x18", VG **350.00**
Sign, paper, Comic Books Given Away, 1930s-40s, 22x34", NM .**55.00**
Sign, paper, Try a Frosty Pepper..., 15x25", NM **15.00**
Sign, porc, For the Good Life on red, 1930s, 10x24", EX+ **375.00**
Sign, sf cb, Join Me!, girl in car, 1940s-50s, 15x25", NM **400.00**
Sign, tin, bottle, 10-2-4, late 1930s, 18x54", VG **175.00**
Sign, tin, For the Good Life, red/wht checked ground, 13x34", G+ ..**75.00**
Sign, tin, Good For Life!, late 1930s-early 1940s, 7x18", EX+ **150.00**
Sign, tin, lg bottle on wht, 1950s-60s, 48x14", VG+ **190.00**
Thermometer, tin, Good for Life, 1939, 17x5", EX+ **475.00**
Tray, You'll Like It Too!, girl w/2 bottles, vertical, EX **180.00**
Tumbler, glass, flared, 1910s, 3¾", NM **1,250.00**

Drewy's Beer, chalk statue, mountie riding bottle, 1955, 7", EX ...**75.00**
Driving Club Rye, ts, couples in carriage, 28x20", G **275.00**
Dy-O-La Dye, cabinet, tin face, 17x13½x8½", VG **60.00**
Edgeworth Jr Tobacco, pocket tin, NM **85.00**
Edgeworth Tobacco, pocket tin, NM **20.00**
Edgeworth Tobacco, pocket tin, sample sz, EX+ **60.00**
Edison Phonograph, cb sign, blk/wht portrait, 19x13"+fr, VG ...**220.00**
Edward Pure Rye, ts, bartender/waitress, 1890-1915, 33x23", EX ..**425.00**
Empire Female Regulating Pills, flat pocket tin, early, EX **35.00**
Equestrian Trail, porc flange sign, 2-sided, 16x15", EX **100.00**
Fan Tan Chewing Gum, tin tray, Oriental scene, 10½x13¼", VG ..**250.00**
Fehr Beer, chalk statue, polar bear, 1953, 15", NM **115.00**
Fehr's Ambrosia Non-Alcoholic..., tray, 3 Romans, 13" dia, EX ...**220.00**
Fern Glen Whiskey, sf ts, Blk man w/whiskey, 1890s, 23x33" ..**3,950.00**
Fleckenstein Brewing, ts, workmen at lunch, 19x14", EX/NM ...**450.00**
Forest & Stream Tobacco, pocket tin, duck, EX **85.00**
Fort Pitt Beer, clock, 1940s, EX+ **130.00**
Fort Pitt Beer, seltzer bottle, frosted/etched gr, 12¼" **185.00**
Fram Filter Service, tin thermometer, 1950s, 39x8", EX **95.00**
Frictionless Metal, sf ts, nude boy w/metal bar, 22x16", VG **500.00**
Friedman Keiler Distillers, ts, Brook Hill Dog, 39x29", VG **500.00**
Frisch's Big Boy Restaurant, die-cut menu, M **150.00**
Gander Brand Cooking Oil, ts, lady & servant, 13x19"+fr, VG ...**950.00**
Gold Dust Washing Powder, cb box, shows twins, lg sz, full **90.00**
Gold Dust Washing Powder, cb sign, twins on box, 21x14", VG ..**400.00**
Gold Dust Washing Powder, door push, NM **750.00**
Gold Dust Washing Powder, tc, twins, lg, full **95.00**
Gowans & Stover Soap, cb sign, boy washing, 26½x21"+fr, G ..**175.00**
Grace Graham Custom Corsetiere, rvpt sign w/gold, 15x39", G ...**45.00**
Grape-Nuts, sf ts, girl & St Bernard, 30x20", VG **900.00**
Grapette, cb trolley sign, Luscious, 1940s, EX **150.00**
Green River Whiskey, ts, Blk man/horse, 1900-20, 33x23", EX .**400.00**
Gretz Beer, Bakelite tap knob **40.00**
Gulf No-Nox, porc sign, mc enamel, 11x8¾", NM **130.00**
Gulf No-Nox Motor Fuel, porc flange sign, NM **425.00**
Gulf Supreme Auto Oil, porc flange sign, early, EX **675.00**
Hall Ice Cream, tray, mother w/desserts, 13¼x10½", EX **400.00**
Hamburger Helper, Helping Hand clock, MIB **45.00**
Hamilton Watch, sf ts, sm girl w/watch, 19x13", EX **500.00**
Heinz, tin string holder, pickle form, 57 Varieties, 15", G **3,250.00**
Helmar Cigarettes, sf ts, girl in straw hat, 39x22", VG **350.00**
Helmar Cigarettes, ts, girl in straw hat, 13½" dia, VG **350.00**
Henry George Cigars, ts, man's portrait, 19½x13½"+fr, EX+ .**1,750.00**
Hills Bros Coffee, measure, Bakelite **5.00**

Hires

Charles E. Hires, a drugstore owner in Philadelphia, became interested in natural teas. He began experimenting with roots and herbs and soon developed his own special formula. Hires introduced his product to his own patrons and began selling concentrated syrup to other soda fountains and grocery stores. Samples of his 'root beer' were offered for the public's approval at the 1876 Philadelphia Centennial. Today's collectors are often able to date their advertising items by observing the Hires boy on the logo. From 1891 to 1906, he wore a dress. From 1906 until 1914, he was shown in a bathrobe; and from 1915 until 1926, he was depicted in a dinner jacket. The apostrophe may or may not appear in the Hires name; this seems to have no bearing on dating an item. Our advisors for Hires are Craig and Donna Stifter; they are listed in the Directory under Illinois.

Bottle, clear w/orange & wht label, 1948, 8-oz, EX	8.50
Bottle topper, carnation logo, 6x3½", NM	25.00
Calendar, 2 girls w/kitten, 1893, rare	175.00
Display, cb diecut, syrup camp in woods, 28x22x7½", EX	1,800.00
Dixie cup, waxed paper, 1960s, 4x3" dia, EX	2.00
Door push, pnt tin, chrome fr, It's High Time..., 4x30", VG	35.00
Globe, milk glass w/brn lettering, Drink Hires, 8½", EX	185.00
Mug, boy in tuxedo, Villeroy & Boch, 1905, 5", EX+	185.00
Pin-bk button, Absolutely Pure..., log cabin, ⅞" dia, EX	21.00
Pocket mirror, lady w/mug & roses, oval, 2¾", EX	300.00
Pocketknife, Josh Slinger in wht, 1915, EX+	245.00
Punch bowl, boy in tuxedo holding mug, Villeroy & Boch, EX	35,500.00
Puzzle book, elephant dressed in clothing, EX	32.00
Sign, cb, girl w/glass in oval, 1900s, 21x15", EX	575.00
Sign, cb standup, bottle & fireplace, 18x12", EX	40.00
Sign, cl, 2 girls, 6½x10", VG	900.00
Sign, flange, Made w/Roots, Bark & Herbs..., EX+	200.00
Sign, metal diecut, bottle shape, 1940, 60", EX	425.00
Sign, paper, lady in wicker chair, fr, 11x20", VG	110.00
Sign, tin, Drink Hires in Bottles, 9¼x6¼", VG	350.00
Sign, tin, For Pleasure & Thirst, 1950s, 18x56", NM	675.00
Sign, tin, Josh Slinger, It Hits the Spot, 1914, 9x18", EX	650.00
Sign, tin, pointing Hires boy w/mug, sf, 20x24", EX	4,000.00
Sign, tin, R-J Root Beer, 1940s, 14x48", NM	500.00
Sign, tin, school girl, w/book & glass, colorful, 14x19", VG	225.00
Sign, tin, 2 girls w/glasses, sgn Meyers, '15, 23½x19½", EX	6,500.00
Spoon, SP brass, cabin finial, Souvenir...Golden Gate, 4½"	35.00
Syrup dispenser, hourglass style, orig pump, G	200.00
Syrup glass, dbl spout, clear w/name on red panel, 1940s, 2"	55.00
Thermometer, tin, bottle diecut, 1940s, 27x8", EX	200.00
Thermometer, tin, bottle diecut, 1950s-60s, 28", NM+	225.00
Thermometer, tin, rounded ends, 17x5", EX+	30.00
Trade card, lady in blk dress, 1890, EX	15.00
Tray, pointing Hires boy w/mug, Shonk, '30s-40s, 13½", VG	450.00
Tumbler, clear w/wht lettering & syrup line, 5", M	25.00

Hohenadel Beer, ts, John L Sullivan in ring, 23x17", VG	275.00
Holcome & Hoke Peanuts, boxes, kids & roaster, unfolded	6.00
Honeymoon Rum Flavored Tobacco, pocket tin, EX	135.00
Hood's Ice Cream, ts, emb cow & ice cream cone, 20x26", EX	500.00
Howel's Orange Julip, photo, 3 girls at table, 1900, 16x20"	475.00
Hush Puppies, whistle, molded plastic dog figural, M	5.00
Indian Motorcycles, pin, wings w/Indian head in center, EX	42.00
Iron Foreman, porc sign, robot center, 12" dia, NM	425.00
IW Harper Whiskey, vitrolite sign, lodge, 1909, 24x18", NM	700.00
Jas Pepper Whiskey, tray, Continental soldiers, 13¾x16½", G	125.00
Jersey-Creme, tray, girl in bonnet holds glass, 12" dia, G	50.00
Jersey-Creme, tray, girl w/feathers & straw hat, 12" dia, VG	100.00
John Deere, dealer sign, 2 disks, 1837-1937, NM	425.00
Jumbo Popcorn, tc, 10-lb, M	145.00
Kellogg's, aluminum sign, mounts on shelf, EX pnt, 5x15"	30.00
Life Cigarettes, sf ts, 1900s, 27x39", EX	595.00
Lily...Threads, spool cabinet, 30-compartment, slant front	100.00

Log Cabin Syrup

Log Cabin Syrup tins have been made since the 1890s in variations of design that can be attributed to specific years of production. Until about 1914, they were made with paper labels. These are quite rare and highly prized by today's collectors. Tins with colored lithographed designs were made after 1914. When General Foods purchased the Towle Company in 1927, the letters 'GF' were added.

A Cartoon series, illustrated with a mother flipping pancakes in the cabin window and various children and animals declaring their appreciation of the syrup in voice balloons, was introduced in the 1930s. A Frontier Village series followed in the late 1940s. A schoolhouse, jail, trading post, doctor's office, blacksmith shop, inn, and private homes were also available. Examples of either series today often command prices of $75.00 to $200.00 and up.

Bank, glass, cabin figural, EX	35.00
Can opener, Towle's, metal	14.00
Container, plastic wigwam, yel letters, 1950, 2x2" dia	7.50
Display, cb diecut, syrup camp scene, 28x22x7½", EX	1,600.00
Pin-bk, log cabin & lettering, ca 1896-98, ⅞" dia, EX	20.00
Syrup glass, dbl-spout, clear glass w/red panel, 2x1¾", EX	55.00
Syrup tin, bear in door, cartoon ends, Towle's, 5-lb	145.00
Syrup tin, blacksmith, 33-oz	140.00
Syrup tin, boy w/lasso, 1-lb	115.00

Syrup tin, child in the doorway, 4¾x3¼x4¾, $115.00.

Syrup tin, cartoon all sides, sm	115.00
Syrup tin, children, man by pump, Towle's, 33-oz	155.00
Syrup tin, children playing, Towle's, 33-oz, NM	145.00
Syrup tin, Dr RU Well, cartoon style, rare	255.00
Syrup tin, Express Office, coach, Towle's, 33-oz	155.00
Syrup tin, Frontier Inn, cowboys & horse, 5-lb	225.00
Syrup tin, Frontier Jail, 12-oz	155.00
Syrup tin, hand w/finger pointing on top, Towle's, med	165.00
Syrup tin, Home Sweet Home, 12-oz	155.00
Syrup tin, pancakes, VG	15.00
Syrup tin, paper label, sample sz, rare, 2x1½"	310.00
Syrup tin, red, 5-lb	55.00
Syrup tin, Stockade School, Towle's, 33-oz	155.00
Syrup tin, wigwam, 1-lb, very rare, 4x3¼x3½"	515.00

London Life Cigarettes, sf ts, cricket players, 39x28", EX	550.00
Louisville Slugger Bats, cb sign, easel bk, 15x20", EX	275.00
Lucky Brown Pressing Oil, tc, Famous Products, 1938, EX	25.00
Lucky Strike Cigarettes, cb sign, pack & leaf, 1934, 13x18", EX	100.00
Mail Pouch Tobacco, tin litho thermometer, 1920s, 9x3", NM	210.00
Mammy's Favorite Brand Coffee, tc, NM	400.00
Manhattan Cocktails, ts, man in wicker chair, 39x27"+fr, G	275.00
Manhattan Fire & Marine Insurance, rvpt sign, 24x18"+fr, NM	750.00

Marathon Ethyl, porc sign, 30" dia, NM 1,250.00
Massasoit Coffee, bag, full color, Indian chief, 1-lb, M 3.00
Mobil Oil, gargoyle porc sign, 19½x24", NM 495.00
Mother Goose Shoes, box, nursery rhyme characters 10.00

Moxie

The Moxie Company was organized in 1884 by George Archer of Boston, Massachusetts. It was at first touted as a 'nerve food' to improve the appetite, promote restful sleep, and in general to make one 'feel better!' Emphasis was soon shifted, however, to the good taste of the brew, and extensive advertising campaigns rivaling those of such giant competitors as Hires and Coca-Cola resulted in successful marketing through the 1930s. Today the term Moxie has become synonymous with courage and audacity, traits displayed by the company who dared compete with such well-established rivals. Our advisors for Moxie are Craig and Donna Stifter; they are listed in the Directory under Illinois.

Ashtray holders, butler & maid, wooden diecuts, 28½", pr 275.00
Blackboard, It's Always a Pleasure..., 28x19½", G 175.00
Bottle, rvpt label, Drink Moxie, 12x3", G 250.00
Clock, figure-8 regulator, pendulum face, Baird, 31", VG 6,250.00
Display, cb diecut, boy w/dog, 1928, 21x13", EX 325.00
Display, cb diecut, soda bottle, 29x11x5", G 70.00
Display, cb diecut girl w/glass, fan behind, '30s, 17x32", G- 300.00
Display, counter-top; Ted Williams at bat, 9x14", VG 500.00
Display, tin diecut, Frank Archer, Our Idol, 11½x6" dia, VG 650.00
Fan, cb diecut, girl on swing, 11x7", VG 145.00
Fan, cb diecut, Lillian MacKenzie, 10x8½", EX 60.00
Hydrometer, cb, girl & glass/Frank Archer, 11x11½", VG 1,000.00
Ice cooler, bottle form, 36x12", VG 750.00
Photograph, Moxie mobile & lg crowd, 7½x41"+fr, EX 95.00
Sign, cb, bathing beauty, 1930s, 50x30", VG 425.00
Sign, cb, 2-sided, Frank Archer/girl on verso, 16x16", G/VG 400.00
Sign, cb diecut, girl on swing, 40x26", G 150.00
Sign, cb diecut, girl w/tennis racquet, 39x27", G 135.00
Sign, cb diecut, Moxie man pointing, 8x8½", EX 175.00

Sign, embossed tin in wood frame, 5-color paint, very late, 30½x22", NM, $11,500.00.

Sign, rvpt, Ice Cream Soda 10¢/Moxie, 24x32"+fr, VG 775.00
Sign, tin, Drink Moxie, 19x27", VG 175.00
Sign, tin, Drink Moxie, 6¼x19", G 105.00
Sign, tin, Frank Archer pointing, 41½x15", G 275.00
Sign, tin, girl leans on chair w/bottle, early, 28x20", G- 550.00
Sign, tin, Hall of Fame, 53½x18½", G 350.00
Sign, tin, Horsemobile w/girl driving, 19x27", G 550.00
Sign, tin, To Eat Better...Very Healthful, mc, 22" dia, G 550.00
Sign, tin diecut, girl w/glass & bottle, 7x6¼", VG 300.00

Sign, tin sidewalk, Genuine 5 Cent Moxie, early, 36x20", G 800.00
Thermometer, tin, Frank Archer pointing, 26x9½", VG 300.00
Tray, glass, girl w/glass, 10" dia, EX 600.00

Munsingwear, oil on canvas, 2 girls & grandma, 22x30"+fr, VG .300.00
Munsingwear, sf ts, girl in underwear at mirror, 38x25½", G 400.00
Munyon's Homeopathic...Remedies, tin cabinet, 14½x13x12", EX ..600.00
Murad Turkish Cigarettes, ts, lady w/tray, 1900-25, 39x28", EX ...900.00
Murray Soda Water, tray, 2 men drinking, 12" dia, EX+ 100.00
National Cigars, matchbook holder, NP brass, EX 35.00
Nip Cigars, tin tray, dog & bale, 12" dia, VG+ 350.00
Noaker Ice Cream, tray, children share ice cream, 13" dia, G 125.00
None Such Mincemeat, ts, Indian chief, 28x20"+fr, EX+ 7,500.00
North American, ts, Rivals, man w/newspaper & girl, 27x18", VG ..3,000.00
Nucreme, porc sign, 2-sided, New Tonic Hair Cream, 18x24", VG ...100.00
NuGrape, clock, w/bottle, lights up, rnd 395.00
NuGrape, tin thermometer, old bottle, EX 75.00
Old Barbee Whiskey, tray, College Widow, 16x12¾", VG 150.00
Old Crow, leather dice cup, blk w/gold, EX 30.00
Old Overholt Rye, oilette, man pouring, 30x18½"+fr, VG 90.00
Old Town, typewriter tin, key wind, unopened 20.00
Orange Crush, clock, Pam, lights up, 15", M 585.00
Oretl's Beer, chalk statue, owl, 1954, 14½", NM 165.00
Orphan Boy Tobacco, cb sgn, mc pnt, 1930s, 9x13", M 25.00
Otto Huber Brewery, tray, interior scene, 16¾x13½", G 95.00
Oxygenated Bitters, rvpt sign, orig fr & wood bk, 6x12", EX 265.00
Paul Jones Whiskey, corner tin sign, Blk racist, 14x20", VG 650.00
Peerless Dyes, cabinet, gypsy girl/pack train, roll top, 32", G 450.00
Peerless Tobacco, flat pocket tin, florals, ¾x3¾x2½", NM 2,000.00

Pepsi-Cola

Pepsi-Cola was first served in the early 1890s to customers of Caleb D. Bradham, a young pharmacist who touted his concoction to be medicinal as well as delicious. It was first called 'Brad's Drink' but was renamed Pepsi-Cola in 1898. Various logos have been registered over the years. The familiar oval was first used in the early 1940s. At about the same time, the two 'dots' between the words Pepsi and Cola became one, though more recent items may carry the double-dot logo as well, especially when they're designed to be reminiscent of the old ones. The bottle cap logo came along in 1943 and with variations was used through the early sixties. Our advisors for Pepsi are Craig and Donna Stifter; they are listed in the Directory under Illinois.

Bank, compo, cooler shape, 3¾x3", G 55.00
Blotter, Drink 5¢...Delightful!, 1905, VG+ 300.00
Booklet, bottle on stage w/cityscape bkground, 1938, EX+ 90.00
Bottle, clear glass w/red & wht label, 16-oz, 1974, EX 8.50
Bottle, emb clear glass, ...LM Squires...NC, 1907-12, NM 55.00
Bottle, seltzer; clear glass, Jacksonville Fla, chips, VG 600.00
Bottle opener, emb metal, Pepsi-Cola in red, Starr, 3x2½", VG ...15.00
Cake carrier, metal, red/wht/bl w/logo, 9x11" dia, EX+ 50.00
Calendar, bare-shouldered lady by Armstrong, 1921, EX+ 2,400.00
Calendar, farm w/rolling hills, incomplete pad, 1942, VG 45.00
Calendar top, cl, lady w/hand on hip, 1954, 12x8", EX 60.00
Character glass, Mr Peabody, Ward Productions, 6¼", M 20.00
Checkers game, wood, Pepsi/Mtn Dew cans on brd, 1970s, NMIB 100.00
Clock, bottle cap, light-up, Think Young..., 1950s, NM 900.00
Clock, glass front w/metal fr, neon, sq, 1941, EX 850.00
Clock, masonite w/plastic lens, nonworking, 1940s, 14x14", VG 200.00
Clock, plastic lens, metal fr, 1960s, 18x14", EX+ 65.00
Clock, red/wht/bl logo, rnd, 1940s, VG 350.00
Cooler, gr Glascock type, 1920s-30s, 24x21x22", VG 1,200.00

Cooler, pnt metal, dbl-dotted, dbl-door, 33½x31x22", EX **650.00**
Display, cb die-cut standup, girl in shorts, 3-D, 1950s, 20", EX+ ..**75.00**
Display, cb die-cut standup, Pepsi & Pete, 1930s, 14x20", NM **3,300.00**
Display rack, metal, 2-case counter-top type, 1930s, EX **500.00**
Fan, paper, boy w/glass, rattan hdl, 1905, EX **1,350.00**
Fountain pen, plastic, red/wht/bl, 1930s, 5", NM **125.00**
Lighter, str-sided bottle shape, 1930s-40s, 2", NMIB **80.00**
Menu board, tin, red w/blk rope-like border, 30x19½", EX **175.00**
Menu board, tin, Special Today, 1950s, 30x19½", G **75.00**
Note pad, girl on front, couple on bk, 1920-21, NM **75.00**
Push bar, porc, modern logo, Prenez Un Pepsi, 3x30", EX **80.00**
Radio, Bakelite bottle on rnd base, rpt label, working **350.00**
Radio, upright vending machine form, 1964, 7", NMIB **275.00**
Sign, canvas, 2-sided, mid-1930s, 36x33", EX **275.00**
Sign, cb, bottle & 2 glasses, 1933, 10x16", EX **475.00**
Sign, cb hanger diecut, bottle hangs from oval, '40s, 16", M **300.00**
Sign, cl, crown, 1945, 9" dia, EX **176.00**
Sign, cl, More Bounce to the Ounce..., 1950s, 9" dia, EX+ **225.00**

Sign, embossed tin, 1930s, minor scratching and dents, 17½x55", EX, $600.00.

Sign, fiberboard, ...5¢...Worth a Dime..., 1930s, 15x13", EX **140.00**
Sign, paper, Light Refreshment Buy..., 19x11", NM **22.00**
Sign, plastic, light-up, red/wht/bl, 1950s, 16" dia, EX **425.00**
Sign, porc, red & wht w/blk border, 8x20", EX **385.00**
Sign, tin, bottle diecut, 1942, 30", NM **750.00**
Sign, tin, Keystone Cops, 1940, 3½x21", VG **215.00**
Sign, tin, slanted bottle cap on yel band, 1950s, 48x42", NM **100.00**
Sign, tin, Take Home a Carton..., w/6-pack, 12½x23", VG **395.00**
Sign, trolley; Where Fun Begins, 1940s, 12x30", VG+ **350.00**
Spoon holder, stoneware, cylindrical, w/lid, 1930s-40s, 6", VG ..**475.00**
Straw holder, stoneware, cylindrical, 1930s-40s, VG+ **325.00**
Thermometer, rvpt, Bigger & Better, metal fr, 1930s, EX **1,200.00**
Thermometer, tin, girl w/straw in bottle, 1941, 27", VG **375.00**
Thermometer, tin, Have a..., bottle cap on yel, 1957, 27", NM ..**175.00**
Tip tray, girl in gr at soda fountain, 6x4¼", EX+ **900.00**
Tip tray, girl w/roses lifts glass, 1908, 6x4", NM **2,500.00**
Toy truck, tin, van, friction, 1950s, 4", EX+ **250.00**
Tray, Coney Island scene, deep-dish, 1955, 12" dia, NM **30.00**
Tray, flower bouquet w/musical logo, 1940, 11x14", NM **50.00**
Tray, 3 singers under tree, red/wht/bl, 1930s, 11x14", G+ **50.00**
Vending machine, VMC-27, EX orig **1,750.00**

Perfection Dyes, cabinet, bright tin insert, 24x17x6", EX **900.00**
Peter Breidt...Brewing, tray, lady/bottles, 10½x13¼", VG **175.00**
Pilsner Beer, ts, bar maid w/mugs, 21x17", VG **185.00**
Pipe Major, upright pocket tin, 4½x3x¾", EX **175.00**

Planters Peanuts

Mr. Peanut, the dashing peanut man with the top hat, spats, monocle, and cane, has represented the Planters Peanut Company since 1916, although he took on a decidedly more modern appearance after the company was purchased by Standard Brands in 1961. He remains, however, perhaps the most highly recognized logo of any company in the world.

Mr. Peanut has promoted the company's products by appearing on premium giveaways, store displays, jars, and all company products, as well as in a special peanut costume at promotional events. Among the favored treasures of collectors today are the glass display jars which were sent to retailers nationwide to stimulate 'point-of-sale' trade. They come in a variety of shapes and styles — some are square, some hexagonal, some barrel shaped, and others round. The earliest, issued in the early 1920s, was a tall pedestal or apothecary jar, and it is unmarked except for a narrow paper label at the neck. In 1926 an octagonal jar was issued, and this is often called the 'Pennant Jar' or the 'eight-sided jar.' This jar has been widely reproduced (sometimes marked Made in Italy on the bottom; sometimes identified by the unusually wide space between the 'E' and R' in 'PLANTERS' on the jar neck), but most original jars of any shape are marked MADE IN USA on the bottom. In a second octagonal style, a paper label adorned one of the sides.

In 1930 a 'fishbowl' jar was introduced, and in 1932 a 'four-corner peanut' jar (arguably the most beautiful) with a blown-out peanut on each of the four corners was issued. Perhaps the rarest jar, the 'football' shape, was also introduced in the 1930s, as were the large 'barrel' jar, 'six-sided' jar with yellow decals, and 'square' jar. All of these early jars had glass lids, some with a peanut finial. In the 1940s, jars with tin lithographed lids were introduced, including the 'leap year,' 'clipper,' and 'streamline' models. Due to rusting, good tin lids are harder to find than the jars they covered. All told, at least fifteen different styles were developed, and several of these (octagon, barrel, four-corner, and clipper) have been recently reproduced in Asia.

In the late 1920s, the first premiums were introduced in the form of coloring/painting books, and in the 1930s, the wooden jointed doll and tin nut dishes (which were still made into the 1970s) were distributed. Post-WWII items were made of plastic: salt and pepper shakers, light switch pulls, drinking mugs, banks, mechanical pens and pencils, walking Mr. Peanuts, small cars and trucks, cookie cutters, and almost any other form and shape imaginable. In recent years, the company (now owned by RJR-Life Savers) has continued to make and distribute a wide variety of premiums. Today's collectors are able to find a treasure trove of advertising memorabilia depicting that debonair gentleman, Mr. Peanut. Our advisor for Planters Peanuts is Neil Williams; he is listed in the Directory under Massachusetts.

Bank, plastic, Mr Peanut figural, lt bl, MIB **25.00**
Bookmark, cb diecut Mr Peanut, 3-color, 8x3", EX **14.00**
Can, Planters Peanuts Pennant (brand), 10-lb **145.00**
Cook booklet, Planter's Oil, 1948, EX **22.00**
Cookie cutters, M in cb holder **90.00**
Costume, Mr Peanut, compo, 50x18x18", G **475.00**
Display, wood jtd Mr Peanut w/hat & cane, 1930s, 8½", NM **450.00**
Gift wrap, early Mr Peanut pictured, Hallmark **30.00**
Jar, Barrel, running Mr Peanut, EX paper label, orig lid **275.00**
Jar, Barrel, running Mr Peanut, no label, orig lid **200.00**
Jar, Clipper, orig tin lid, NM **150.00**
Jar, Fish Bowl, rectangular label, peanut finial lid, 13" **150.00**
Jar, Football, PLANTERS emb on orig lid **275.00**
Jar, Leap year, G orig tin lid, 1940 ....**50.00**
Jar, Octagon, VG paper label, orig lid **200.00**
Jar, Octagon, 6 sides emb, orig lid **125.00**
Jar, Octagon, 7 sides emb, orig lid **150.00**
Jar, Octagon, 8 sides emb, orig lid **250.00**
Jar, rnd, frosted label, orig knob-finial lid, 1950s **50.00**
Jar, Streamline, G orig tin lid **50.00**
Jar, supermarket; Chocolate...Cashews, label, tin lid, 1940s **25.00**
Jar, supermarket; Mixed Nuts, label, orig tin lid, 1940s **25.00**

Jar, supermarket; Peanut Butter, label, orig tin lid, 1950s 25.00
Jar, 4-corner, w/orig lid 225.00
Jar, 6-sided, yel decals, PLANTERS emb on orig lid 100.00
Paint book, Am presidents, 1960s, 32 pages, 11x8", NM 22.00
Paint book, Famous Men, 1935, EX 25.00
Paperweight, glass w/Mr Peanut & tennis player insert, 1938 ....75.00
Peanut bag, paper, Mr Peanut & dmn graphics, 80-oz, NM 15.00
Pencil, Mr Peanut floating at end, 6", EX 20.00
Pin, Wear a Lucky Mr Peanut, from 1939 World's Fair, 2", NM ...60.00
Pop gun, paper, Mr Peanut on oval grip, 5x8¾", VG 200.00
Popcorn popper, Mr Peanut, Wearever, 1½-qt, EX 75.00
Scales, Mr Peanut figural, 1¢ required, Hamilton, 45", VG ...15,000.00
Shakers, ceramic, Mr Peanut figures, worn pnt, 4½", pr 55.00
Sign, display; plastic, 1950s, 8½x35" 65.00
Sign, tin, Mr Peanut, The Name for Quality..., 13x24", VG 20.00
Straw, wht plastic w/3-D Mr Peanut mouthpc, 1960s, 8", NM 10.00
Tin, blk/bl/silver/red, pry lid, 10½", VG+ 85.00
Tin, mc on gr, pry lid, 1-lb, sq, ca 1920, VG 85.00
Tin, Pennant Brand Salted Peanuts, w/orig lid, 10-lb, EX 245.00
Toy, car, plastic, Mr Peanut driving, 2½x5", EX 500.00
Toy, walker, plastic Mr Peanut figure, 8½", VG+ 300.00
Vendor, Canadian, 10¢ coin operated, sheet metal case, 38", VG ...350.00

Poll Parrot Shoes, checkers, giveaway, M in 2½x5" box 30.00
Poplings Fresh Popped Old Fashioned Popcorn, tc, M 85.00
Prima Brewing, token for free beer, ca 1935 ....25.00
Prince Albert, tin charger, man smoking pipe, 24" dia, VG 375.00
Prince Albert, ts, Indian chief portrait, 25x19½", EX 700.00
Prince Albert Tobacco, glass humidor, NM 60.00
Purity Kiss, ts, children in wicker rocker, 8" dia, G 450.00
Q-Boid Tobacco, pocket tin, cabin, EX+ 230.00
Quaker Oats, tc, key open, EX 65.00
Queen Quality Shoes, pocket mirror, cl, oval, M 65.00
Queen Shoes, pocket mirror, cl, NM 65.00

RCA Victor

Nipper, the RCA Victor trademark, was the creation of Francis Barraud, an English artist. His pet's intent fascination with the music of the phonograph seemed to him a worthy subject for his canvas. Although he failed to find a publishing house who would buy his work, the Gramophone Co. in England saw its potential and adopted Nipper to advertise their product. The painting was later acquired and trademarked by the Victor Talking Machine Co., which was purchased by RCA in 1929. The trademark is owned today by EMI in England and by General Electric in the U.S. Nipper's image appeared on packages, accessories, in ads, brochures, and in three-dimensional form. You may find a life-size statue of him; but all are not old. They have been manufactured for the owner throughout RCA history and are marketed currently by licensees, BMG Inc. and Thomson Consumer Electronics (dba RCA). Except for the years between 1968 and 1976, Nipper has seen active duty, and with his image spruced up only a bit for the present day, the ageless symbol for RCA still listens intently to 'His Master's Voice.' Our advisor for RCA Victor is Roger R. Scott; he is listed in the Directory under Oklahoma.

Bank, flocked, metal, 9" 125.00
Buckle, His Master's Voice, brass, Nash Tiffany London 25.00
Clock, RCA Victor Records, w/Nipper 350.00
Curtains, RCA 40.00
Doll, Radiotron, G 500.00
Figure, Nipper, crystal, Fenton, 4" 50.00
Figure, Nipper, molded plastic, 36", EX 235.00

Nipper papier-mache figure, over-painting to body, usual cracks and chips, 36", $800.00.

Figure, Nipper, papier-mache, 14" 350.00
Figure, Nipper, papier-mache, 41" 1,000.00
Figure, Nipper, plaster, 12½x7½x5", VG 200.00
Pin-bk button, I Support Nipper, 1930s 45.00
Pin-bk button, Little Nipper Club Member, 1930s, 1½", EX 70.00
Plate, Nipper, Collector's Edition, 1980 ....50.00
Puzzle, assembled 100.00
Record brush, Nipper, 5½" L 25.00
Shakers, Nipper, Lenox, pr 50.00
Shakers, Radio Corp of Am, 1940s, pr 40.00
Sign, canvas, His Master's Voice, 26x19" 1,500.00
Sign, paper, His Master's Voice, texture, fr, 25x29", EX 675.00
Sign, plastic/metal, ...Radio, light-up, 1940s, 15x37", EX 180.00
Sign, tin, Nipper listening, fr, 13½x19", G 500.00
Snow dome, Nipper 50.00
Thermometer, porc, NM 485.00
Watch fob, EX 30.00

Raleigh Tobacco, door push, tin litho, 3x8¼", EX 75.00
Ranier Beer, tray, girl in fancy bonnet, 13¼" dia, VG 325.00
Ranier Beer, ts, girl & bear, rolled corners, 14½" sq, EX 250.00
Rawleigh's Aspen Pain & Ache, tc, early, EX 15.00
Red Cross Mills Coffee, cb container, paper label, 6x4¼", EX 75.00
Red Crown Gasoline, porc sign, 2-sided, 30" dia, VG 450.00

Red Goose Shoes

Realizing that his last name was difficult to pronounce, Herman Giesceke, a shoe company owner resolved to give the public a modified, shortened version that would be better suited to the business world. The results suggested the use of the goose trademark with the last two letters, 'ke,' represented by the key that this early goose held in his mouth. Upon observing an employee casually coloring in the goose trademark with a red pencil, Giesceke saw new advertising potential and renamed the company Red Goose Shoes. Although the company has changed hands down through the years, the Red Goose emblem has remained. Collectors of this desirable fowl increase in number yearly, as do prices. Beware of reproductions; new chalkware figures are prevalent.

Bank, plastic, Red Goose on red base, 1960s, 5", M 15.00
Dictionary, giveaway, w/Red Goose advertising, 1927 ....30.00
Display, cb goose appl to revolving shoe rack, 36x32x15", VG ..300.00
Display, goose on nest lays golden egg, electrified, NM 650.00
Display, plastic, red on gr base, 11", NM 100.00
Floor mirror, 21x14½", NM 150.00
Horn, cb w/wooden mouthpc, Half the Fun of Having Feet, 6" 8.50

School tablet, child & goose on cover, 8x10" 35.00
Sign, porc, dbl sided, neon, 1940s-50s, 108x48", EX 2,500.00
Souvenir of St Louis Zoo, punch-out Chimpanzee Show, NM 45.00
String holder, CI goose figural, mc pnt, 14½" L, VG 475.00
String holder, tin goose diecut, 26x18", VG+ 1,900.00
Thermometer, pnt wood, arched top, sq bottom, 1930s, 21x8", EX 200.00
Thermometer, porc, For Boys & Girls, 27x7", EX 260.00

Red Raven, tin tray, nude child reaching bottle, 12" dia, VG 300.00
Richardson's Silk, spool cabinet, 8-drw, 22x19x18", VG+ 575.00
Richfield Oil Corp-Kern Front..., porc sign, early, EX 225.00
Robinson's Sons Pilsner Beer, tray, rowboat scene, 12" dia, VG .250.00
Rockford Watch, ts, girl w/pocket watch, 23x17", G 550.00

Roly Poly

The Roly Poly tobacco tins were patented on November 5, 1912, by Washington Tuttle and produced by Tindeco of Baltimore, Maryland. There were six characters in all: Satisfied Customer, Storekeeper, Mammy, Dutchman, Singing Waiter, and Inspector. Four brands of tobacco were packaged in selected characters; some tins carry a printed tobacco box on the back to identify their contents. Mayo and Dixie Queen Tobacco were packed in all six; Red Indian and U.S. Marine Tobacco in only Mammy, Singing Waiter, and Storekeeper. Of the set, the Inspector is considered the rarest and in excellent condition may fetch more than $1,100.00 on today's market.

Dutchman, Mayo, EX 500.00
Dutchman, Mayo, NM 675.00
Inspector From Scotland Yard, EX 1,100.00
Mammy, 6½", EX 600.00
Satisfied Customer, Mayo, EX+ 700.00
Singing Waiter, Mayo, EX 600.00
Singing Waiter, US Marine, VG 450.00
Storekeeper, Mayo, NM 695.00
Storekeeper, VG 365.00

Roosevelt 5¢ Cigar, tin sign, DB Long & Co, very rare, 19½x13½", NM, $4,250.00.

Royal Crown Cola, clock, Pam, VG 80.00
Royal Crown Cola, ice chest, emb tin signs on sides, 31" L, G- ..250.00
Royal Crown Cola, tin menu chalkboard, ca 1950s, EX 85.00
Royal Crown Cola, tin thermometer, scale on arrow, '52, 26", EX ..90.00
Rubsam & Horrmann, tray, topless lady, 12½" dia, EX 650.00
Schenley Whiskey's, folding chair, decaled seat, 36x8", VG 95.00
Schlitz, stained glass window, banner & globe, 36x67"+sash, EX ...1,550.00

Schlitz Beer, paper sign, lady/dove, fr, 1910s, 39x28", EX 675.00
Schwinn-Built Bicycles, rvpt sign, 9x19"+fr, EX 90.00
Shedd's, peanut tin, animals & elves, bail hdl, 5-lb, EX 35.00
Silver Cup Chewing Tobacco, tin thermometer, 40", M 150.00
Sinclair Opaline, porc sign, EX colors, 19x46" 495.00
Sinclair Opaline, tc, 5-gal, VG 125.00
Sky Chief Supreme Texaco Gasoline..., porc sign, mc, 1959, EX ..170.00
Socony, paper cup, Pegasus logo 3.00
Squire's Pure Food..., sf ts, pig on bl, oval, G 285.00
Squirrel Peanut Butter, tc, Canadian version, 5", EX 150.00
Star Soap, corner porc sign, mc, 26x20½", G 550.00
Starlight Marshmallows, tc, 5-lb, NM 165.00
Stein's Face Powder, tc, For the Stage or Boudoir, EX 35.00
Sweet Georgia Brown Hairdressing Pomade, tc, Valmor, EX 10.00
Swift's Pride Soap, corner porc sign, mc, 14x10½x3", VG 350.00
Taka-Kola, tin tray, lady in toga w/bottle, 13" dia, VG 225.00
Thom McAn Shoes, Fortune Telling game, 1933, EX 15.00
Thomas Moore Whiskey, tray, Take...Moore, nude, 10" dia, G ..600.00
Tootsie Roll, mechanical pen, M 15.00
Turkish Dyes, cabinet, Turkish state seal, orig marquee, 28", G- .200.00
Union Leader Cut Plug, tc, eagle w/wings wide, 9x5", G 100.00
Union Leader Tobacco, cb victory pack, NM 45.00
Union Leader Tobacco, pocket tin, Sam, EX 55.00
Valley Brew, ts, girl w/glass at table, 13¾" dia, NM 400.00
Velvet Tobacco, ts, men w/child & dog, 28x22"+fr, EX 575.00
Velvet Tobacco, ts, 3 generations of men, 28x22"+fr, G 275.00
Virginia Dare, tray, Paul & Virginia, 13" dia, VG 50.00
Walter Baker, tip tray, serving girl/homestead, 6" dia, VG 150.00
Walter Baker LaBelle Chocolatier, sf ts, lady, 28x22", VG 650.00
Watta Pop, sucker holder, wht polar bear 365.00
Weber's Star Ginger Ale, tray, gypsy girl, 12" dia, EX 75.00
Welle-Boettler Bakery, porc sign, baby w/bread, 15x36", G 175.00
West End Brewing, tray, patriotic lady & eagle, 13" dia, VG 300.00
West Hair Net, display, multiple images, 18½x12½" sq, VG 300.00
Westminster Abbey, tc, Viscount Lascelles/Princess Mary, 6", G .25.00
Whistle, clock, bl on wht, electric, rnd, 1950s, EX 325.00
Wieland's Beer, tray, Indian princess, 13" dia, VG 300.00
Wildroot Hair Tonic, porc sign, pole on beige, 48x12", EX 235.00
Wishbone Coffee, tin, gr, blk & gold, sm 35.00
Wrangler Denim, banner, mc letters on bl denim, 39x74", NM .400.00
7-Up, compo bottle, 2-sided, 3-D, 14x4" dia, VG 650.00
7-Up, pencil clip, cl, M 30.00

Advertising Cards

Advertising trade cards enjoyed great popularity during the last quarter of the 19th century when the chromolithography printing process was refined and put into common use. The purpose of the trade card was to aquaint the public with a business, product, service, or event. Most trade cards range in size from 2" x 3" to 4" x 6"; however, many are found in both smaller and larger sizes.

There are two classifications of trade cards: 'private design' and 'stock.' Private design cards were used by a single company or individual; the images on the cards were designed for only that company. Stock cards were generics that any individual or company could purchase from a printer's inventory. These cards usually had a blank space on the front for the company to overprint their own name and product information. In these listings a stock card is indicated by 'stk.' If there is no such reference, it is assumed the card is a private design. Values are given for cards in near-mint condition.

Four categories of particular interest to collectors are:

Mechanical — a card which achieves movement through the use of a pull tab, fold-out side, or movable part.

Hold-to-light — a card that reveals its design only when viewed before a strong light.

Diecut — a card in the form of something like a box, a piece of clothing, etc.

Metamorphic — a card that by folding down a flap shows a transformed image, such as a white beard turning black after use of a product.

For a more thorough study of the subject, we recommend *Victorian Trade Cards* by Dave Cheadle; and *Reflections 1* and *Reflections 2* by Kit Barry; his address can be found in the Directory under Vermont.

A Wandering Minstrel I, cat on fence playing banjo, stk **16.00**
A Werner & Co, The America Champagne, lady draped in flag ... **15.00**
AC Yates...Popular Clotheirs, 2 men on horses, 1 jumping fence ... **5.00**
AE Lucas Shoes, diecut; boy & girl w/sled & dog, lg stk **36.00**
Armour's Extract of Beef, ladies pour soup, veggies on table **12.00**
Atmore's Mince Meat, man holds English plum pudding **4.00**
Ayer's Cherry Pectoral, 2 sm children try to get medicine **5.00**
Ayer's Sarsaparilla, Discovery of Am, men looking at shore **4.00**
Ayer's Sarsaparilla, Sunny Hours, lady in red w/baby on shoulder ... **7.00**
Beech-Nut, 4 children, 2 on table eating marmalade & bacon **38.00**
Boston Crystal Gelatin, 2 girls view ea other through gelatin **7.00**
Burdock Blood Bitters, girl holds doll & box of bitters **7.00**
CE Plummer clothing, 2 girls sew lg pants as Cupid watches **4.00**
Celluloid Collars & Cuffs, British Isle map, boys w/flyers **8.00**
Chase's Liquid Glue, children gluing cards in scrapbook **9.00**
Clark's ONT Spool Cotton, man roping steer w/thread **4.00**
Clark's ONT Spool Cotton, spool diecut, lady helps child walk **8.00**
Clark's ONT Spool Cotton, 2 boys fly kite, 1 off ground **3.00**
Colburn's Phila Mustard, diecut of owl's head w/bl collar **5.00**
Columbia Macaroni, Young American, boy eats pasta & holds box .. **46.00**
Corinne Merrie-Makers, buggy w/gold trim pulles by blk horses **9.00**
Corrugated Elbow Co, split, smoke w/elbow pcs, not w/corrugated .. **38.00**
Dr Buckland's...Essence, girl's head emerging from oat field **12.00**
Dr Morse's Indian Root Pills, 1883 vignette of Indian & bear **9.00**
Dwight's Soda, fr picture of cow in center of card **6.00**
Edward Kakas, manufacturer of furs, fox sees squirrel, Prang **3.00**
Enterprise Baking Powder, girl w/muff/pull toy/doll/etc **4.00**
Eureka Silk, dog swings baby in basket hanging from tree **7.00**
Excelsio Incubator & Wooden Hen, mechanical, hatching chick .**76.00**
Frank Miller's Crown Dressing, lady sits, maid shines shoes **35.00**
Gilbert S Graves Laundry Starch, 2 ladies hang wht laundry **8.00**
Goshen Sweeper Co, The Ladies' Friend, lady sweeping carpet **24.00**
Groff's Drug Store, cigars in box tied w/bl string **9.00**
Hasty Lunch Chocolate, Lucky find, well-dressed lady w/box **25.00**
Heide's Licorice Pastilles, boy w/candy boxes, crate beyond **45.00**
Huyler's Vanilla Chocolate, lady w/cup, granddaughter on lap **36.00**
I'm a Beet, What Are You?, parrot head, beet body, stk **10.00**
Imperial Granum, baby pictures, silver & bl card **25.00**
Ivorine, girl washes clothes in wooden tub w/washboard **5.00**
J&P Coats Spool Cotton, Gulliver & the Liliputians **6.00**
J&P Coats Spool Cotton, man kills golden goose/no treasure **4.00**
JS Kirk & Co's, Germany, women holding German flag & stamp ... **4.00**
Judge Publishing, Taken In, vol 9, no 222, Jan 16, 1886 .... **28.00**
Kellogg's Extract, 4 boys: 2 pouring vanilla & 2 watching **6.00**
Kendall's Spavin Cure, mule pulls man into post, dog bites pants **7.00**
Little Red Riding Hood in doorway w/basket on ground, stk **6.00**
Lydia E. Pinkham's Vegetable Compound, house & barn **6.00**
Magnetic Food, magnet diecut, lady feeds baby w/man at table **36.00**
Max Stadler & Co, well-dressed boy on pony led by stylish man ... **20.00**
McGibeny Family, railroad car w/flags on top, name on side **46.00**
Merchant's Gargling Oil, Hero of a Home Run, baseball player **16.00**
Moline Plow Co, metamorphic, winged man w/corn stands on stump .. **55.00**
Mrs Pott's Sad Irons, man pnts irons on fence, boy watches **28.00**
Mrs Pott's Sad Irons, man shows poster to couple in doorway **36.00**

Muzzy's Starch, child throws snowballs, pile at ft, stk **8.00**
New Home Sewing Machine Co, monkey sewing cat's paw **6.00**
Newark Machine Co, couple in clover, flowers in her apron, stk **5.00**
Noix De Coco, wht lady in hammock, boy w/fan, girl w/food **12.00**
Palmer Cox, The Brownies' Christmas Dinner **95.00**
Parker's Hair Balsam, family sits before a roaring fire **5.00**
Pearline Soap, Golly I B'leve Perline Make Dat Chile White **12.00**
People's Church, The Owner of This...Purchased One, red brick ... **6.00**
Pond's Extract, Bound for Donnybroiiok Fair, Irishman w/pipe **9.00**
Prudential Insurance, old lady knits, child sits at her ft **5.00**
Quaker Bitters, Rustic Beauty, girl in bbl **9.00**
Quaker Oats, girl on rocks in river holds box of oats **35.00**
Quaker Oats, Quaker man w/box of oats & paper w/Pure on it **38.00**
Reiger's Treble Extract, Lemon Sugar, 3 boys make lemonade **95.00**
Renolds Brothers Fine Shoes, 2 puppies playing w/slipper **8.00**
Reynolds Bros' Fine, 2 bullfrogs in suits look at flowers **7.00**
Rush's Pills, flowers surround inset of Rush's Pills **15.00**
Shaw, Applin & Co Manufacturers, fancy sofa on pk card **45.00**
Shiloh's Consumption Cure, steamship Shiloh, Silverlake NY **30.00**
Soapine, Soapine Did It, whale diecut, sailor washing whale **8.00**
Spencerian Pens, girl sits & writes at table, dog watches **15.00**
St. Jacobs Oil for Sprains, 3 horse riders, 1 falls, dogs run **7.00**
Standard Sewing Machine Co, boy pushes girl in wheelbarrow, stk ... **5.00**
Stecher Litho Co, 16 different fruit around edge, ad in center **10.00**
The Queen Self Measuring Tank, split, old & new way, pouring ... **95.00**
Thomson's Glove Fitting Corsets, Gilbert/Sullivan's 3 maidens **18.00**
Trix Breath Perfume, boy & girl pick up spilled Trix from lady **6.00**
WF Wheaton Printer & Stationer, 3 children roll lg egg, stk **3.00**
Women's Suffrage Stove Polish, girl sits in gr velvet chair **10.00**

Advertising Dolls

Whether your interest in ad dolls is fueled by nostalgia or strictly because of their amusing, often clever advertising impact, there are several points that should be considered before making your purchases. Condition is of utmost importance; never pay book price for dolls in poor condition, whether they are cloth or of another material. Restoring fabric dolls is usually unsatisfactory and involves a good deal of work. Seams must be opened, stuffing removed, the doll washed and dried, and then reassembled. Washing old fabrics may prove to be disastrous. Colors may fade or run, and most stains are totally resistant to washing. It's usually best to leave the fabric doll as it is.

Watch for new dolls as they become available. Save related advertising literature, extra coupons, etc., and keep these along with the doll to further enhance your collection. Old dolls with no marks are sometimes challenging to identify. While some products may use the same familiar trademark figures for a number of years (the Jolly Green Giant, Pillsbury's Poppin' Fresh, and the Keebler Elf, for example) others appear on the market for a short time only and may be difficult to trace. Most libraries have reference books with trademarks and logos that might provide a clue in tracking down your doll's identity. Children see advertising figures on Saturday morning cartoons that are often unfamiliar to adults, or other ad doll collectors may have the information you seek.

Some advertising dolls are still easy to find and relatively inexpensive, ranging in cost from $1.00 to $100.00. The hard plastic and early composition dolls are bringing the higher prices. Advertising dolls are popular with children as well as adults. For a more thorough study of the subject, we recommend *Advertising Dolls* by Joleen Robison and Kay Sellers. Our advisor for this category is Jim Rash; he is listed in the Directory under New Jersey.

A&W Root Beer, Great Root Bear, plush, 1975, 13", M **12.00**

Allied Van Lines, girl, litho cloth, 1970s, 17" 15.00
Am Beauty Macaroni, Roni Mac, cloth, premium, 1937, 11" 150.00
Arbuckle Bros, Jill, litho cloth, 1931, uncut, 14½" 200.00
Armour & Co, International doll, premium, 8", M 8.00
Atlas Van Lines, Atlas Annie, prestuffed cloth, 1977, 15½" 15.00
Aunt Jemima Pancake Flour, Aunt Jemima, cloth, 1924, 27" 200.00
Aunt Jemima Pancake Flour, Wade, cloth, 1905, 12" 175.00
Big Boy Restaurant, Big Boy, plastic, 1974-78, 10" 7.00
Bird's Eye Frozen Foods, Mike, cloth, 1953, uncut, 11" 50.00
Blue Ribbon Malt Extract, Lena, cloth, pre-1930s, 14" 175.00
Borden, Elsie, vinyl head w/plush, 1950s, 15" 40.00
Breck Hair Products, Bonnie Breck, vinyl, 1971, 9" 40.00
Brown's Chicken, Farmer Brown, litho cloth, 1978, 18" 25.00
Bumble Bee Tuna, Yum Yum Bumble Bee, inflatable, 24" 15.00
Campbell Soup Co, Campbell Cheerleader, 1957-61, 9½" 25.00
Campbell Soup Co, Campbell Kid, Horsman, 1910, 15½" 200.00
Canadian Club Whiskey, French Grenadier, felt, 19" 60.00
Chee•tos, Chee•tos Mouse Man, litho cloth, 1974, 12" 20.00
Chocks, Charlie Chocks, litho cloth, 1970-71, 20", VG 22.00
Choo Choo Charlie, 2 vinyl figures on ceramic train, '68, rare ..800.00
Concorde Confections, Andy Capp, foam rubber, 1972, 6½" 15.00
Cox Gelatin, Scottish child, litho cloth, 1973, uncut 175.00
Curad, Taped Crusader bank, plastic, 1977, 8" 60.00
Dak Meat Co, Thor (Viking), litho cloth, 14" 15.00
Duncan Hines...Brownie Mix, Brownie, cloth/felt, 1970, 26" 50.00
Eastman Kodak, Champion Retriever, litho cloth, 1971, 17" L 50.00
Eskimo Pie, Eskimo Pie Boy, litho cloth, 1964, unmk 10.00
Fanny Farmer Candy, Fanny Farmer, plastic & cloth 15.00
Final Touch, Snowman, plush, 1975, 11" 15.00
Franklin Life Insurance, Benjamin Franklin, litho cloth, 12" 20.00
Gasho Restaurant, chef plastic hand puppet, giveaway 3.00
General Mills, Betty Crocker, cloth, 1970s, 13" 35.00
Gerber, Gerber Baby, rubber, flannel sleeper, 1954, 12" 55.00
Glamour Kitty, vinyl, gold crown, 1977, rare 150.00
Gold Medal Flour, girl, litho cloth, ad on apron, 7½" 125.00
Hanes, Hanes Baby, vinyl & cloth, 1950s, 21" 75.00
HD Lee, Buddy Lee, hard plastic, dressed as cowboy 275.00
HD Lee, Buddy Lee, in 1-pc overalls, missing hat 175.00
Henderson Glove Co, Indian, litho cloth, 11" 75.00
IGA Stores, Tablerite Kid, litho cloth, 12" 20.00
Jack Frost Sugar, Jack Frost, litho cloth, 18" 25.00
Just Rite Restaurant, Li'l Miss Just Rite, vinyl, Dakin, 8" 75.00
Kellogg's, Dinkey the Dog, litho cloth, 1935, uncut 75.00

Kelly Services, Kelly Girl, prestuffed cloth, w/dress, 1978 ....35.00
Little Crow Foods, Groetchen, litho cloth, 1949-66, 13" 50.00
Malted Cereal, Gretchen, litho cloth, 1905, 8" 175.00
McDonald Corp, Grimace, purple plush w/vinyl ft 15.00
McDonald Corp, Ronald McDonald, litho cloth, 1971 ....10.00
MD Bathroom Toilet Tissue, Maisy, litho cloth, 1977 ....15.00
Mountain Dew, Hillbilly, vinyl & cloth, 18" 75.00
Munsingwear, penguin, hard vinyl, 7" 35.00
Nestle's, Little Hans, vinyl, mk AE, 1969, 12½" 65.00
Orange Crush, Orange Crush Man, bsk, 3½" 65.00
Peabody Overalls, man in overalls, litho cloth, 17" 250.00
Pillsbury, Doughboy, litho cloth, 1971, 16" 20.00
Post Cereals, Sugar Bear, plush & felt, 1972-76, 12½" 15.00
Procter & Gamble, Wizard of Oz finger puppet, vinyl 20.00
Razzles Dubble Bubble Gum, Razzie, litho cloth, 1970s, 13½" 15.00
Seiko Watches, Robot, inflatable, 21" 30.00
Shakey's Pizza Restaurant, Shakey Chef, litho cloth, 18" 20.00
Snoboy Apples, Snuggly Snoboy, plush & felt, 12" 20.00
Sony Boy, vinyl squeeze toy, 1960s, 4" 250.00
Speedy Alka Seltzer, vinyl, store display, 1960s, 8" 500.00
Sunbeam Bread, Miss Sunbeam, Eege, 1959, 17" 75.00
Tastee-Freez International, Tastee Dog, plush 15.00
Tillamook Cheese Co, Tillie the Cow, rubber, Remple, 1958 ......45.00
Travelodge International, Sleepy Bear, vinyl, 5" 40.00
Twinkie the Kid, inflatable vinyl, 28", M 45.00
Vigorine, Vigorine Pig, litho cloth, premium, 17" 20.00
Wurlitzer, Funmaker, litho cloth, 15" 25.00
Zee Toilet Tissue, Li'l Softee, vinyl & plastic, 1975, 5½" 15.00

African Art

African art does not consist of a single class of objects. Rather, these often-powerful sculptures are carved by many varying African tribes and groups across the central continent; each item represents specific cultural and spiritual functions and meanings. Many kinds of materials are used including wood, metal, fiber, ivory, and bone. Considerable numbers of these items are now being reproduced and sold to the tourist trade, but 'authentic' African art is generally considered to consist of objects which were used in cultural and religious activities. The items listed here are authentic, in good condition, and considered to be of average aesthetic quality. Scott Nelson, a collector of African art, is our advisor; his address is listed in the Directory under New Mexico.

Basket, Nigeria, open, fiber w/cowrie shells, 8x10" 125.00
Beads, trade, ceramic, string of 20 ....100.00
Bracelet, Ashanti, bronze, knobs 30.00
Cloth, Kuba, geometric design, 18" sq 175.00
Comb, Ashanti, bird's head surmount, 4" 200.00
Container, Luba, gourd, wooden figural stopper 600.00
Container, Warega, ivory, 15" 200.00
Divination board, Yoruba, animals, 20" dia 475.00
Doll, Ewe, pnt figure, 5" 175.00
Doll, Mossi, abstract human figure 275.00
Door, Dogon, granary, human figures, 26" 1,500.00
Drum, Hemba, geometric designs, 22" 275.00
Earrings, Massai, beaded, 6" 275.00
Figure, Baule, standing female, 14" 250.00
Figure, Dogon, crouched male, 10" 650.00
Figure, Yoruba, pnt Colonial, 12" 175.00
Goldweight, Ashanti, bronze turtle 125.00
Hat, Kuba, fiber, blk pnt 175.00
Headdress, Bamana, Tchi-wara (antelope), horizontal 475.00
Headrest, Luba, supporting human figure, 5" 375.00

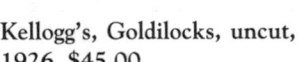
Kellogg's, Goldilocks, uncut, 1926, $45.00.

Kellogg's, Johnny Bear, litho cloth, mk, 12" 75.00
Kellogg's, Tony the Tiger, cloth head/plush body, 1970, 13" 25.00
Kellogg's, Toucan Sam, prestuffed cloth, 1964, 9x12" 20.00

Heddle pulley, Semifo, bird surmount, 5" 375.00
Ibejis, Yoruba, 9", pr 375.00
Knife, Kuba, throwing, str blade, 14" 125.00
Lock, Bamana, door, 2 figural surmounts, 14" 575.00
Mask, Bamana, N'Tomo, 14" 275.00
Mask, Dan, human face, 15" 375.00
Mask, Dogon, Kamaga, 26" 800.00
Mask, Karumba, polychrome, antelope, 21" 475.00
Mask, Mende, helmet, female initiation, 12" 675.00
Mask, Pende, human face, 8" 275.00
Pendant, Yoruba, ivory human figure, 4" 800.00
Pipe, Cameroons, elephant, brass, 14" 275.00
Ring, Dogon, bronze, horse & rider 275.00
Slingshot, Baule, animal head, 5" 85.00
Stool, Lega, human figural supports, 13" 475.00
Wisk, Yoruba, human figure, wood & horsehair, 12" 275.00

Agata

Agata is New England peachblow (the factory called it 'Wild Rose') with an applied metallic stain which produces gold tracery and dark blue mottling. The stain is subject to wear, and the amount of remaining stain greatly affects the value. It is especially valuable (and rare) when found on peachblow of intense color. Caution! Be sure to use only gentle cleaning methods.

Currently rare types of art glass have been realizing erratic prices at auction; until they stabilize, we can only suggest an average range of values. In the listings that follow, examples are glossy unless noted otherwise. Our advisors for this category are Betty and Clarence Maier; they are listed in the Directory under Pennsylvania. See also Green Opaque.

Bowl, ruffled, M mottling, 3x5¼" 800.00
Bowl, squatty, slightly ruffled, worn decor, 2¾x5½" 250.00
Celery vase, scalloped/sq rim, 6½" 1,950.00
Pitcher, sqd rim, tapered, 6" 2,750.00
Spooner, worn staining, sq top, 4½" 350.00
Toothpick holder, sqd rim, EX color, 2¼" 1,000.00
Toothpick holder, tricorner, 2¼" 1,300.00
Tumbler, EX color & mottling, 3¾x2¾" 1,050.00
Tumbler, worn mottling & gold, 3¾" 650.00
Vase, lily; EX color 950.00
Vase, stick neck w/doughnut ring, bulbous, dented sides, 10" .2,500.00
Vase, trumpet form, 7½" 1,350.00

Akro Agate

The Akro Agate Co., founded in 1914 primarily as a marble maker, operated in Clarksburg, West Virginia, until 1951. Their popular wares included children's dishes, powder jars, flowerpots, and novelty items along with the famous 'Akro Aggies.' Much of their glass was produced in the distinctive marbleized colors they called Red Onyx, Blue Onyx, etc.; solid opaque and transparent colors were also produced. Most of the wares are marked with their trademark, a crow flying through the letter 'A' holding an Aggie in its beak and one in each claw. Other marks include 'J.P.' on children's pieces, 'J.V. Co., Inc.,' 'Braun & Corwin,' 'N.Y.C. Vogue Merc Co. U.S.A.,' 'Hamilton Match Co.,' and 'Mexicali Pickwick Cosmetic Corp.' on novelty items. In 1936 Akro obtained the molds from the Balmer-Westite Co. of Weston, West Virginia. Westite produced a similar line of products for several years. Their ware is drab in color when compared to Akro and is generally unmarked. The embossed Westite logo does appear occasionally on the bottoms of some pieces. Westite is commonly accepted as a companion collectible of Akro.

For more information we recommend *The Collector's Encyclopedia of Children's Dishes* by Margaret and Kenn Whitmyer, available at your local bookstore. Our advisor for miscellaneous Akro Agate is Albert Morin; he is listed in the Directory under Massachusetts.

Chiquita

Chiquita, 12-piece set, transparent cobalt, $100.00.

Creamer, gr opaque, 1½" 5.00
Creamer, opaque colors other than gr, 1½" 18.00
Cup, baked-on color, 1½" 7.50
Plate, baked-on colors, 3¾" 3.00
Saucer, cobalt transparent, 3⅛" 4.00
Set, cobalt transparent, 16-pc, MIB 130.00
Set, gr opaque, 16-pc, MIB 58.00
Sugar bowl, gr opaque, 1½" 5.00
Sugar bowl, opaque colors other than gr, 1½" 18.00
Tablecloth, w/4 napkins, set 35.00

Concentric Rib

Creamer, sm, gr or wht opaque, 1¼" 8.00
Cup, sm, gr or wht opaque, 1¼" 5.00
Plate, gr or wht opaque, 3¼" 3.50
Plate, opaque colors other than gr or wht, 3¼" 7.00
Set, sm, gr or wht opaque, 16-pc, MIB 70.00
Teapot, opaque colors other than gr or wht, 3⅜" 18.00

Concentric Ring

Cup, lg, any opaque color, 1⅜" 30.00
Cup, lg, cobalt transparent, 1⅜" 35.00
Plate, sm, any opaque color, 3¼" 6.00
Plate, sm, bl marbleized, 3¼" 22.00
Set, sm, solid opaque colors, 16-pc, MIB 150.00
Sugar bowl, lg, cobalt transparent, w/lid, 1⅜" 55.00
Sugar bowl, sm, any opaque color, 1¼" 18.00
Sugar bowl, sm, bl marbleized, 1¼" 40.00
Teapot, sm, transparent cobalt, 3⅜" 50.00

Interior Panel, Stippled Interior Panel

Cereal, lg, red & wht, 3⅜" 37.00
Creamer, lg, gr transparent, 1⅜" 25.00
Creamer, lg, topaz transparent, 1⅜" 22.00
Creamer, sm, azure bl, 1¼" 32.00
Creamer, sm, yel, 1¼" 32.00
Cup, lg, bl & wht, 1⅜" 30.00

Cup, sm, bl & wht, 1¼" 28.00
Cup, sm, gr lustre, 1¼" 10.00
Cup, sm, pk lustre, 1¼" 12.00
Cup, sm, red & wht, 1¼" 25.00
Plate, lg, azure bl, 4¼" 10.00
Plate, lg, pk lustre, 4¼" 8.00
Plate, lg, yel opaque, 4¼" 10.00
Plate, sm, gr lustre, 3¾" 4.00
Plate, sm, pk lustre, 3¾" 6.00
Plate, sm, topaz transparent, 3¾" 4.00
Plate, sm, yel opaque, 3¾" 10.00
Set, lg, gr transparent, 21-pc, MIB 200.00
Set, lg, topaz transparent, 21-pc, MIB 200.00
Set, sm, aqure bl, 16-pc, MIB 285.00
Set, sm, pk lustre, 16-pc, MIB 175.00
Sugar bowl, lg, bl & wht, w/lid, 1⅞" 50.00
Sugar bowl, lg, gr transparent, w/lid, 1⅞" 32.00
Sugar bowl, lg, lemonade & oxblood, w/lid, 1⅞" 50.00
Sugar bowl, lg, yel opaque, w/lid, 1⅞" 50.00
Sugar bowl, sm, bl & wht, 1¼" 30.00
Sugar bowl, sm, pk lustre, 1¼" 27.00
Sugar bowl, sm, topaz transparent, 1¼" 20.00
Teapot, lg, topaz transparent, w/lid, 3¾" 40.00
Teapot, sm, gr lustre, w/lid, 3⅜" 22.00
Teapot, sm, topaz transparent, w/lid, 3⅜" 22.00
Tumbler, sm, gr transparent, 2" 9.50
Tumbler, sm, topaz transparent, 2" 9.50

J.P. (Made for J. Pressman Company)

Creamer, lg, lt bl transparent, or crystal, 1½" 30.00
Cup, lg, cobalt transparent w/ribs, 1½" 14.00
Cup, lg, lt bl transparent, 1½" 20.00
Plate, lg, gr transparent, 4¼" 12.00
Set, lg, baked-on color, 17-pc, MIB 110.00
Set, lg, brn transparent, 17-pc, MIB 400.00
Sugar bowl, lg, lt bl transparent, or crystal, 1½" 32.00
Teapot, lg, lt bl transparent, w/lid, 2¾" 85.00

Miss America

Creamer, forest gr, 1¼" 65.00
Cup, decal, 1⅝" 50.00
Cup, orange & wht, 1⅝" 50.00
Plate, decal or forest gr, 4½" 45.00
Saucer, forest gr, 3⅝" 15.00
Set, forest gr, 17-pc, MIB 650.00
Set, wht, 17-pc, MIB 500.00
Set, wht w/decal, 17-pc, MIB 650.00
Sugar bowl, decal, w/lid, 2" 85.00
Sugar bowl, orange & wht, w/lid, 2" 85.00
Teapot, decal, w/lid, 3¼" 140.00
Teapot, forest gr, w/lid, 3¼" 140.00

Octagonal

Cereal, lg, beige or pumpkin, 3⅜" 20.00
Cereal, lg, lemonade & oxblood, 3⅜" 27.00
Creamer, sm, any opaque color, open hdl, 1¼" 16.00
Pitcher, sm, any opaque color, open hdl, 2⅞" 18.00
Plate, sm, lime gr, 3⅜" 6.00
Set, lg, lemonade & oxblood, 21-pc, MIB 450.00
Sugar bowl, lg, beige or pumpkin, closed hdl, w/lid, 1½" 18.00
Sugar bowl, lg, lemonade & oxblood, closed hdl, 1½" 50.00

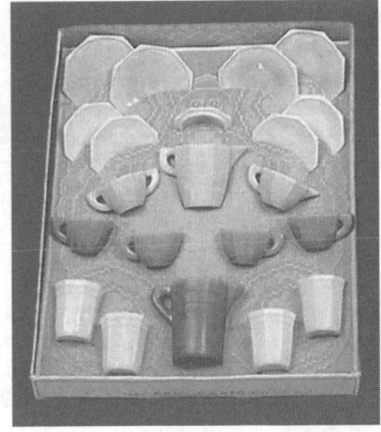

Octagonal, 21-piece set, mixed opaque colors, small, MIB, $195.00.

Tumbler, sm, any opaque color, 2" 12.00

Raised Daisy

Creamer, sm, yel, 1¼" 50.00
Cup, sm, bl, 1¾" 45.00
Cup, sm, gr, 1¾" 18.00
Plate, sm, bl, 3" 14.00
Saucer, sm, yel, 2½" 10.00
Sugar bowl, sm, yel, 1¾" 50.00
Teapot, sm, gr, no lid, 2⅜" 35.00
Tumbler, sm, beige, 2" 35.00
Tumbler, sm, yel, 2" 27.00

Stacked Disc

Creamer, sm, gr or wht, 1¼" 10.00
Cup, sm, any opaque color other than gr or wht, 1¼" 12.00
Cup, sm, gr or wht, 1¼" 6.00
Plate, sm, any opaque color other than gr or wht, 3¼" 5.00
Saucer, sm, any opaque color other than gr or wht, 2¾" 4.00
Saucer, sm, gr or wht, 2¾" 3.00
Set, sm, gr or wht, 21-pc, MIB 120.00
Sugar bowl, sm, gr or wht, 1¼" 10.00
Teapot, sm, gr or wht, w/lid, 3⅜" 15.00
Tumbler, sm, any opaque color other than gr or wht, 2" 14.00
Tumbler, sm, gr or wht, 2" 8.50

Stacked Disc and Interior Panel

Cereal, lg, any solid color, 3⅜" 25.00
Cereal, lg, bl marbleized, 3⅜" 45.00
Creamer, lg, cobalt transparent, 1⅜" 32.00
Creamer, sm, gr transparent, 1¼" 28.00
Cup, sm, bl marbleized, 1¼" 37.00
Cup, sm, cobalt transparent, 1¼" 22.00
Plate, lg, any solid color, 4¾" 12.00
Plate, lg, cobalt transparent, 4¾" 15.00
Set, lg, any solid color, 21-pc, MIB 370.00
Set, sm, bl marbleized, 16-pc, MIB 490.00
Set, sm, cobalt transparent, 16-pc, MIB 290.00
Sugar bowl, lg, cobalt transparent, w/lid, 1⅞" 55.00
Sugar bowl, sm, gr transparent, 1¼" 28.00
Teapot, lg, cobalt transparent, w/lid, 3¾" 75.00
Teapot, lg, gr transparent, w/lid, 3¾" 55.00
Teapot, sm, gr transparent, w/lid, 3⅜" 35.00
Tumbler, sm, cobalt transparent, 2" 18.00
Tumbler, sm, gr transparent, 2" 14.00

Stippled Band

Creamer, lg, amber transparent, 1½"	25.00
Creamer, lg, gr transparent, 1½"	25.00
Creamer, sm, amber transparent, 1¼"	40.00
Cup, sm, amber transparent, 1¼"	7.00
Plate, lg, azure transparent, 4¼"	16.00
Plate, lg, gr transparent, 4¼"	6.00
Plate, sm, amber transparent, 3¼"	6.00
Set, lg, azure transparent, 17-pc, MIB	355.00
Set, sm, amber transparent, 16-pc, MIB	145.00
Sugar bowl, lg, azure transparent, w/lid, 1½"	45.00
Sugar bowl, lg, gr transparent, w/lid, 1½"	32.00
Teapot, sm, amber transparent, w/lid, 3⅜"	22.00

Miscellaneous

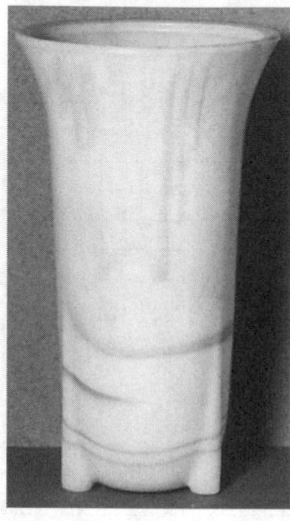

Vase, Graduated Dart, green/ivory marbleized, smooth top, #316, $125.00.

Ashtray, bl, Akroite advertising, 3" sq, rare	750.00
Ashtray, bl, Hotel Edison	65.00
Ashtray, blk, Hamilton Match	85.00
Ashtray, Kiwanis, 1935, rare	650.00
Ashtray, orange/wht, for car, w/suction cup	60.00
Ashtray, satin finish, Heinz 57	75.00
Ashtray, smoker's set, MIB	95.00
Ashtray, tire; bl/gray marbleized, Goodrich	48.00
Basket, bl/wht, 2-hdl	38.00
Basket, orange/wht, 1-hdl	275.00
Bell, ivory	65.00
Bowl, blk, tab hdls, #321	125.00
Bowl, orange, Dart, #340	24.00
Bowl, yel, Stacked Disc, #322	38.00
Brochure, Akroite Floral Ware, color, orig	150.00
Brochure, J Vivaudou, fold-out, orig	35.00
Brochure, Westite Ware, blk/wht, orig	125.00
Candlesticks, gr, 3¼", pr	250.00
Cornucopia, Niagara Falls scene, #765	35.00
Flowerpot, bl, w/saucer, #299	20.00
Flowerpot, bl/wht, ribbed top, #292	10.00
Flowerpot, blk, Banded Dart, #300	75.00
Flowerpot, ivory, #1308	195.00
Flowerpot, orange, #1310	165.00
Flowerpot, orange, ribbed top, #294	24.00
Flowerpot, orange, Ribs & Flutes, #307	35.00
Flowerpot, orange/wht, Ribs & Flutes, #305	28.00
J Vivaudou, apothecary jar, blk	45.00

J Vivaudou, puff box, wht, #334	24.00
Jardiniere, factory decor, tab hdls, #314	75.00
Jardiniere, gr/wht, Ribs & Flutes, #306CF	65.00
Knife, gr, grid style, #739	75.00
Lamp, gr, 3-pc	125.00
Lamp, orange/ivory, 5-pc	75.00
Lamp, wall; ivory, 3-pc	48.00
Marbles, tin, #150, in box	275.00
Marbles, yel, Popeye, #116, in box	900.00
Marbles, 100 #00 glassies, in box	175.00
Planter, factory decor, #654	38.00
Planter, orange/wht, Lily, #658, 5¼"	12.00
Powder jar, bl/wht, Concentric Ring, 3-ftd, #760	45.00
Powder jar, ivory, Mexicali	95.00
Powder jar, orange/wht marbleized, Ribbed	65.00
Urn, Grecian Urn, Niagara Falls scene, #764	35.00
Urn, orange/wht, floral, NYC Vogue Merc	15.00
Vase, bl/wht, Lily, #657, 4¼"	12.00
Westite, ashtray, bl, hexagonal	20.00
Westite, candlesticks, orange/beige, 8¼", pr	65.00
Westite, flowerpot, bl, #300	24.00
Westite, Japanese planter, gr/wht	150.00

Alamo Pottery

Operating for only a few years during the middle of the 20th century, Alamo Pottery Inc. was located in Texas where they produced dinnerware as well as some commercial art ware.

Vase, maroon, 13½"	90.00
Vase, wht, 9"	55.00

Alexandrite

Alexandrite is a type of art glass introduced around the turn of the century by Thomas Webb and Sons of England. It is recognized by its characteristic shading, pale yellow to rose and blue at the edge of the item. Although other companies produced glass they called alexandrite, only examples made by Webb possess all the described characteristics and command premium prices. Amount and intensity of blue determines value. Our advisors for this category are Betty and Clarence Maier; they are listed in the Directory under Pennsylvania.

Cup & saucer, handleless; tree-bark design, Webb	1,100.00
Finger bowl, ruffled, peacock-eye pattern, 2¾", +plate	2,100.00
Goblet, honeycomb, amber stem, 4½"	745.00
Punch cup, bbl shape, 2¾"	550.00
Vase, Optic Honeycomb, Webb, incurvate cylinder, 4"	1,950.00
Wine, bl-to-purple rim, lt amber body, stem & base, 4½"	1,650.00

Alhambra China

A line of dinnerware made in Vienna during this century, the Alhambra pattern is strongly geometric with bold colors and gold trim. It is marked with the line name and the country of origin.

Candy bowl, folded rim, 4 shell ft, 8½x6"	55.00
Compote, scalloped, 5x8½"	135.00
Compote, sm	85.00
Creamer & sugar bowl, w/lid, 2½", 4¾"	125.00
Demitasse pot	295.00

Jam jar, w/lid & underplate 110.00
Pitcher, 8½x4¼" 155.00
Plate, 7½" 15.00

Almanacs

The earliest evidence indicates that almanacs were used as long ago as Ancient Egypt. Throughout the Dark Ages they were circulated in great volume and were referred to by more people than any other book except the Bible. *The Old Farmer's Almanac* first appeared in 1793 and has been issued annually since that time. Usually more of a pamphlet than a book (only a few have hard covers), the almanac provided planting and harvesting information to farmers, weather forecasts for seamen, medical advice, household hints, mathematical tutoring, postal rates, railroad schedules, weights and measures, 'receipts,' and jokes. Before 1800 the information was unscientific and based entirely on astrology and folklore. The first almanac in America was printed in 1639 by William Pierce Mariner; it contained data of this nature. One of the best-known editions, Ben Franklin's *Poor Richard's Almanac*, was introduced in 1732 and continued to be printed for twenty-five years.

By the 19th century, merchants saw the advertising potential in a publication so widely distributed, and the advertising almanac evolved. These were distributed free of charge by drug stores and mercantiles and were usually somewhat lacking in information, containing simply a calendar, a few jokes, and a variety of ads for quick remedies and quack cures.

Today their concept and informative, often amusing, text make almanacs popular collectibles that may usually be had at reasonable prices. Because they were printed in such large numbers and often saved from year to year, their prices are still low. Most fall within a range of $4.00 to $15.00. Very common examples may be virtually worthless; those printed before 1860 are especially collectible. Quite rare and highly prized are the Kate Greenaway 'Almanacks,' printed in London from 1883 to 1897. These are illustrated with her drawings of children, one for each calendar month.

1812, Howe's, Greenwich, 30-pg, VG 22.00
1815, Robert B Thomas, illus frontispc, Boston, VG 10.00
1831, New England Anti-Masonic, Boston, Marsh & Co, VG 30.00
1837, Centennial Revolving...1800-1900, 2nd edition, 8½x11" ..175.00
1844, Franklin Almanac, blk & wht cover, 35-pg, 6½x8", EX 15.00
1861, Great Western Almanac, paddle-wheeler front, EX 17.50
1883, Hazeltine's Pocket Book, 1¼x2", EX 6.00
1884, Dr Harter's 8.00
1885, Green's Diary, Woodbury NJ, color, 18-pg, VG 12.00

1890, Warner's Safe Cure Almanac, some water stains, colorful cover, $90.00.

1890, Dr Ayer's American, EX 10.00
1891, Capitol Almanac, blk & wht illus, 1891, 40-pg, EX 20.00

1898, Poor Richard's, Century Co, EX 30.00
1905, Dr Herrick's, VG 7.50
1922, Dr Morse's Indian Root Pills, Indian & bear cover, EX 12.00
1922, Watkins...Home Doctor & Cook Book, 5¾x8¾", G 15.00
1923, Spalding Official Athletic, EX 8.00
1936, Lum & Abner, EX 22.50
1937, Ford's Home Almanac & Facts Book, 1937, EX 8.00
1938, Housewife's, Kellogg's, EX 25.00
1940, Dr Jayne's 5.00
1944, Flying Red Horse 7.00
1947, Indiana Botanic Gardens, The Herbalist, EX 15.00

Aluminum

Aluminum, though being the most abundant metal in the earth's crust, always occurs in combination with other elements. Before a practical method for its refinement was developed in the late 19th century, articles made of aluminum were very expensive. After the process for commercial smelting was perfected in 1916, it became profitable to adapt the ductile, non-tarnishing material to many uses.

By the late thirties, novelties, trays, pitchers, and many other tableware items were being produced. They were often handcrafted with elaborate decoration. Russel Wright designed a line of lovely pieces such as lamps, vases, and desk accessories that are becoming very collectible. Many who crafted the ware marked it with their company logo, and these signed pieces are attracting the most interest. Wendell August Forge (Grove City, PA) is a mark to watch for; this firm produced some particularly nice examples and upwardly mobile market values reflect their popularity with today's collectors. In general, 'spun' aluminum is from the thirties or early forties, and 'hammered' aluminum is from the fifties.

For further information, refer to *Hammered Aluminum, Hand Wrought Collectibles*, by our advisor for this category, Danny Woodard (listed in the Directory under Texas), and *Collectible Aluminum, An Identification and Value Guide*, by Everett Grist.

Ashtray, emb sailboat on water, W August Forge, 4½" sq 40.00
Ashtray, Knott's Berry Park in Buena Vista CA, 4x5" 15.00
Basket, emb fruits & flowers, twist hdl, Cromwell, 11" 35.00
Basket, Everlast, sm 12.00
Basket, floral pattern, sawtooth rim, loop hdl, Japan, 7x10x8" 10.00
Basket, fruit & flowers, dbl-loop hdl, unmk, 11x11" dia 15.00
Beverage server, concentric circles, Kromex, 11x5" dia 25.00
Bowl, Deco style, plain, Kensington, 5" dia 16.00
Bowl, flared, plain, Kensington, 9" 18.00
Bowl, medallion hdls & base, Kensington, 5" 21.00
Bowl, Pine Cone, serrated rim, Everlast, 2x10" 15.00
Bowl, 7-petal daisies decor, flower form, Buenilum, 6½" 10.00
Box, Apple Blossom, tube hdl, Wendell August Forge, 2½x5x4" ..90.00
Bread tray, floral spray, unmk, 7x12" 20.00
Bread tray, hammered, rectangular, loop hdl, Buenilum 20.00
Butter dish, Chrysanthemum, flower finial, glass base, 8¾" 25.00
Candle holders, w/Lucite ball, Kensington, 4", pr 75.00
Candy dish, hammered look, beaded rim, S hdl, Buenilum, 8" dia .25.00
Casserole, hammered, beaded edges, w/lid, Buenilum, 6x8" 15.00
Casserole holder, sailing ships, clip-type hdls, Forman, 3x9" 20.00
Coaster, angelfish, unmk, 5" dia 10.00
Coasters, plain, Kensington, set of 8 ....30.00
Compote, hammered, ped ft, unmk, 5x6" 10.00
Compote, over Lucite ball, Kensington, 13" 150.00
Gravy boat, plain w/serrated lip & base rim, Buenilum, 3x6" dia ..20.00
Lazy susan, fruit & flowers, fluted edge, Cromwell, 18" dia 10.00

Pitcher, Deco hdl, Kensington, 8" 40.00
Pitcher, gold anodized w/ice lip, +6 mc tumblers 45.00
Pitcher, tulips, ice lip, ear-shaped hdl, Rodney Kent, 9" ...35.00
Sherbet, anodized color base w/glass insert, unmk 10.00
Silent butler, acorn & leaf pattern, Continental, 7" dia 25.00
Spoon, Short'ning & Ice Cream, gold anodized, unmk, 8" 2.00
Syrup, hammered, blk plastic hdl, Stratford-On-Avon, 6x4" 15.00
Tidbit tray, acorns, short T hdl, serrated rim, unmk, 9" dia 15.00
Tidbit tray, gold Moire, Kensington, 10" 15.00
Tray, hammered, Bakelite hdls, MW Guildcraft, 10x13" 85.00
Tray, hammered, flower decor, 12" 20.00
Tray, Rodney Kent, w/2 powder jars & lids 25.00
Tray, roses, appl rose emb hdls, Continental, 18x13" 35.00
Tray, sandwich; berries & leaves, hammered, Farberware, 11" dia .10.00
Tray, serving; flower spray, appl hdl, unmk, 14" dia 20.00
Tray, serving; Morning Glory, china insert, Limoges/Cromwell ...40.00
Tray, serving; Poinsettia, wire loop hdls, unmk, 18x11" 10.00
Tray, snack; flower spray, unmk, 4x6" 8.00
Trivet, Pine Cone, Everlast, 11x8" 15.00
Tumbler, ftd, Kensington, 7¼" 15.00
Vase, gold laurel-leaf base, Kensington, 10" 50.00
Vase, Kensington, bl glass w/aluminum base, 10" 165.00
Waste basket, Pine Cone, scalloped rim, W August Forge, 11x11" ...150.00

AMACO, American Art Clay Co.

AMACO is the logo of the American Art Clay Co. Inc., founded in Indianapolis, Indiana, in 1919, by Ted O. Philpot. They produced a line of art pottery from 1931 through 1938 that is today beginning to interest collectors. The company is still in business but now produces only supplies, implements, and tools for the ceramic trade.

Values for AMACO have risen sharply, especially those for figurals, items with Art Deco styling, and pieces with uncommon shapes. Our advisor for this category is Virginia Heiss; she is listed in the Directory under Indiana.

Bowl, #127, oval w/sea horses, wht, 5½x10" 75.00
Candy dish, #183, gold gloss, w/lid, 8" 115.00
Ewer, #70, gold spray/rose, 10½" 175.00
Figure, male dancer, #156, wht gloss, 15" 275.00
Figure, puma, seated, bl gloss, 4¾" 120.00
Temple jar, #132, bl gloss, w/lid, 6" 75.00
Vase, #20, gray gloss w/silver, hdls, 11" 115.00
Vase, #4, gr w/silver, 4¾" 35.00
Vase, #74, dk bl matt, stick form, 8" 95.00
Vase, #86, gr matt w/silver, 9x8½" 165.00
Vase, S-5, yel gloss, 4½" 30.00

Amberina

Amberina, one of the earliest types of art glass, was developed in 1883 by Joseph Locke of the New England Glass Company. The trademark was registered by W.L. Libbey, who often signed his name in script within the pontil.

Amberina was made by adding gold powder to the batch, which produced glass in the basic amber hue. Part of the item, usually the top, was simply reheated to develop the characteristic deep red or fuchsia shading. Early amberina was mold-blown, but cut and pressed amberina was also produced. The rarest type is plated amberina, made by New England for a short time after 1886. It has been estimated that less than 2,000 pieces were ever produced. Other companies, among them Hobbs and Brockunier, Mt. Washington Glass Company, and Sowerby's Elli-

son Glassworks of England, made their own versions, being careful to change the name of their product to avoid infringing on Libbey's patent. Prices realized at auction seem to be erratic, to say the least, and dealers appear to be 'testing the waters' with prices that start out very high only to be reduced later if the item does not sell at the original asking price. Lots of amberina glassware is of a more recent vintage — look for evidence of an early production, since the later wares are worth much less than glassware that can be attributed to the older makers. Generic amberina with hand-painted flowers will bring lower prices as well. Our values are taken from auction results and dealer lists, omitting the extremely high and low ends of the range.

Basket, Daisy & Button; orig SP fr, 11x5¾" 650.00
Basket, swirled, wide crimped rim, amber hdl, 7x6" 250.00
Bottle, whiskey; inside swirled ribs, 8", +faceted stopper 195.00
Bowl, Daisy & Button, Hobbs, 2⅛x7⅛" sq 575.00
Bowl, Dmn Quilt, NE Glass, 1⅝x4⅝", +7" underplate 485.00
Bowl, flared rim, NE Glass, 2¾x5¼" 385.00
Bowl, heavy gold florals, 6-crimp, amber ft, 3⅜x5¾" 325.00
Bowl, Hobnail, 20-crimp ruffled edge, 3x5" 78.00
Bowl, Invt T'print, appl floral branch/3 branch ft, 5x8" 300.00
Bowl, Invt T'print, ornate appl legs, ruffled, NE Glass, 8" 450.00
Bowl, lt ribbing, wide ruffled rim, NE Glass, 3x5½" 375.00
Bowl, lt ribbing, Mt WA, 1½x5x4½" 425.00
Bowl, slightly iridized, fluted, 3¼x7½" 135.00
Carafe, Dmn Quilt, amber rigaree/HP flowers, dimpled, 9x6" 375.00
Celery vase, Dmn Quilt, sqd scalloped rim, EX color, 6½" 275.00
Celery vase, Invt T'print, scalloped, 6" 200.00
Celery vase, Venetian Dmn, NE Glass, 7½" 435.00
Creamer, Dmn Quilt, clear hdl, 2¾x5½" 110.00
Creamer, Invt T'print, sq top, reeded hdl, 4" 350.00
Creamer, Invt T'print, 2½" 165.00
Creamer, Swirl, bulbous, amber appl hdls, 5x3½" 135.00
Cruet, faceted amber stopper, tricorn spout, NE Glass, 6" 370.00
Cruet, Invt T'print, amber faceted stopper, 6" 450.00
Cruet, Invt T'print, amber hdls, bubble stopper, 6x3½" 250.00
Cruet, Swirl, flattened invt goblet form, 6" 545.00
Finger bowl, Dmn Quilt, 3x5¼" 200.00
Finger bowl, Invt T'print, ruffled, 2½x5½", +7" plate 350.00
Finger bowl, ruffled side, 2½x6½" 110.00
Goblet, water; emb ribs, amber stem, 6⅛x3⅜" 295.00
Mug, emb swirls, amber hdl, 3¾x3" 235.00
Nut dish, Daisy & Button, Gillinder, 1¾x6⅛x4¼" 365.00
Pitcher, Honeycomb, bl rope twist hdl, 6" 135.00
Pitcher, Invt T'print, amber hdl, 10½x5½" 400.00
Pitcher, Invt T'print, bulbous w/sq top, amber hdl, 6" 365.00
Pitcher, melon shape w/HP floral, clear reeded hdl, 9" 550.00
Pitcher, sq-top amber reeded hdl, att Mt WA, 4½" 325.00
Pitcher, Sunburst, molded, 10" 125.00
Pitcher, Swirl, rnd mouth, amber hdl, 6¾x5¾" 200.00
Pitcher, tankard, Dmn Quilt, NE Glass, 6¾" 1,200.00
Pitcher, tankard, 10-panel, amber hdl, 6¾" 650.00
Plate, Optic Panel, scalloped rim, NE Glass, 8½" 195.00
Punch cup, Dmn Quilt, amber ribbed hdl, 2¾" 115.00
Salt shaker, emb ribs, NE Glass, 3½" 225.00
Salt shaker, Invt T'print, NE Glass, 4" 185.00
Shade, Dmn Quilt, ruffled, 4¼x5" 575.00
Spooner, Dmn Quilt, sqd scalloped rim, 4¾" 250.00
Sugar bowl, Daisy & Button, amber base, 5½" 550.00
Sugar shaker, HP florals, w/pewter lid & collar 195.00
Toothpick holder, Baby Invt T'print, sqd top, NE Glass, 2¼" 285.00
Toothpick holder, Daisy & Button, 2¾" 365.00
Toothpick holder, Venetian Dmn, tricorner, NE Glass, 2¼x3" .350.00
Toothpick holder, Venetian Dmn, urn shape, in Aurora SP fr ...295.00

Tray, Daisy & Button, sq, 5¾" 90.00
Tumbler, Dmn Quilt, NE Glass, 3¾" 165.00
Tumbler, faint ribs, amber reeded hdl, 3¾x2½" 365.00
Tumbler, Herringbone, 4" 145.00
Tumbler, Swirl, 3⅞x2⅝" 150.00
Tumbler, Venetian Dmn, Mt WA, EX color, 4" 135.00
Vase, amber rigaree collar, dimpled/bulbous/ruffled, 5" ...550.00
Vase, appl crystal spiral decor, 8⅛x2½" 200.00
Vase, lily; EX color, flint, 15" 800.00
Vase, lily; NE Glass, 8" 665.00
Vase, lily; ribbed, scalloped rim, 10" 285.00
Vase, lily; ribbed, 7" 235.00
Vase, posy; Invt T'print, mini, 3x2¼" 350.00
Vase, ribbed, ball stem, raised rnd base, oversized, 32" ...650.00

Vase, ruffled top, 9½", $200.00.

Vase, ruffled top, sgn Libbey, 10¼" 475.00
Vase, trumpet form w/wide amber edge, 20" 975.00

Plated Amberina

Bowl, incurvate, 2¾x5¼" 6,000.00
Bowl, loosely ruffled rim, 3x8" 3,750.00
Creamer, squat w/cylinder neck, amber hdl, 3¾" 7,250.00
Creamer, squatty, looped amber hdl, 2¼" 9,000.00
Cruet, bulbous, stick neck, tricorn spout, amber hdl, 6¾" ...7,000.00
Pitcher, bulbous w/tricorn rim, dk amber hdl, 6¼" ...10,000.00
Pitcher, tankard, amber hdl, 7" 12,000.00
Punch cup, amber loop hdl, 2½" 2,350.00
Shaker, cylindrical, 4" 1,500.00
Tumbler, lemonade; amber hdl, 4¾" 3,200.00
Tumbler, 4" 2,200.00

American Bisque

The American Bisque Pottery operated in Williamstown, West Virginia, from 1919 to 1982. The company was begun by Mr. B.E. Allen and remained an Allen-family business until its sale in 1982. Figural pottery was produced from approximately 1937 until about the time the pottery sold in 1982.

American Bisque pottery is often identified by the 'wedges' or dry-footed cleats on the bottom of the ware. Many cookie jar designs are unique to the American Bisque Company, such as cookie jars with blackboards and magnets, cookie jars with lids that doubled as serving trays, and cookie jars with 'action pieces' which show movement.

American Bisque pieces are very collectible and are available in a broad variety of color schemes; some items are decorated with 22-24k gold. Many items are modeled after highly popular copyrighted characters.

For further information, we recommend *American Bisque, Collector's Guide With Prices*, by our advisor Mary Jane Giacomini; she is listed in the Directory under California.

Ashtray, Flintstones, mk Arrow Houseware Prod Inc, ea **125.00**
Bank, Attitude Momma (pig w/nose up), mk USA, 8½" **90.00**
Bank, Diaper Pin Pig, gold trim, mk USA, 9" **175.00**
Bank, Dimples (girl pig), unmk, 6" **32.00**
Bank, Donkey on Drum, laughing **60.00**
Bank, Figaro, unmk, 6¾" **75.00**
Bank, Humpty Dumpty, Alice in Philcoland mk, 6" **120.00**
Bank, Little Audrey, center stopper, unmk, 8¼" **775.00**
Bank, Popeye, center stopper, 7" **450.00**
Cookie jar, Bear & Beehive, corner jar, mk 804 USA, 10" **375.00**
Cookie jar, Boy Lamb, sitting, mk USA, 13" **165.00**
Cookie jar, Clown (Clown on Stage), mk 805 USA, 9¾" **285.00**
Cookie jar, Collegiate Owl, gold trim, mk USA, 11½" **85.00**
Cookie jar, Dog on the Quilt, mk USA, 13" **125.00**
Cookie jar, Peasant Girl, unmk, 10½" **375.00**
Cookie jar, Popeye, mk USA, 10½" (+) **1,000.00**
Cookie jar, Rabbit & Log (Tortoise & Hare), mk 803 USA, 9¾" ..**525.00**
Cookie jar, Santa Claus, winking **400.00**
Cookie jar, SS Kookie, sailor elephant, unmk, 11¾" **175.00**
Cookie jar, TV Bedtune (Sandman Cookies), mk 801 USA, 9¾" ..**285.00**
Cookie jar, Wilma on phone, mk USA, 12", minimum value .**1,200.00**
Pitcher, Figaro (cat) beside 'yarn-wrapped' pitcher **250.00**
Pitcher, Santa Claus figural **350.00**
Pitcher, strawberries, cold pnt, mk USA, 6¾" **35.00**
Planter, Bear w/Beehive, gold trim **28.00**
Planter, Boy Davy Crockett, mk w/c in circle, 4½" **50.00**
Planter, Circus Horse, unmk, 7" **32.00**
Planter, Dalmatians, unmk, 5½" **32.00**
Planter, Farmer Pig w/corn, made by APCO, unmk, 6½" **8.00**
Planter, Lovebirds, unmk, 6½" **14.00**
Planter, Mushrooms & Tree Stump, unmk, 4½" **14.00**
Planter, Sailfish, unmk, 8x10½" **50.00**
Planter, Stork w/Bassinet, unmk, 6¼" **10.00**
Planter, Winter Couple, unmk, 7½" **30.00**
Tea set, windmill forms, gold trim, 8½" pot+cr/sug **70.00**
Vase, Philodendron Leaves, gold decor by Shafer, unmk, 7¼" **28.00**

American Encaustic Tiling Co.

A.E. Tile was organized in 1879 in Zanesville, Ohio. Until its closing in 1935, they produced beautiful ornamental and architectural tile equal to the best European imports. They also made vases, figurines, and novelty items with exceptionally fine modeling and glazes.

Box, Oriental scene emb on orange crystalline matt, 7½" **200.00**
Figurine, snail, stylized, yel & brn w/bl, 6" sq **80.00**
Plaque, cavalier w/sword, pk majolica, fr, 5x18" **325.00**
Plaque, HP, pastel scenic, 9x6", orig fr **325.00**
Tile, Autumn, Bacchus scene, gr majolica, sgn HM, 12x18"+fr ..**2,200.00**
Tile, blossom relief under clear gr, sq frieze, 6", NM **60.00**
Tile, cherubs w/musical instruments, gr gloss, fr, 5½" **230.00**
Tile, classic lady w/horn on teal, Greek Key border, 6x18" **360.00**
Tile, hdld vase, F Rhead, bl-gr drip on mirror brn, 6x4¼" **250.00**
Tile, Oriental landscape, gold lustre on dk bl matt, mk, 6" **385.00**
Tile, stag emb in silver on blk matt, AETCo/F.445, 6"+fr **225.00**
Tile, Wm McKinley, 1896 election commemorative, bl crackle, 3" ..**195.00**

Trivet, AETCo logo in center, 8-sided, mc, 6" dia 125.00
Vase, olive/bl crystalline, gourd form, 9½" 160.00
Vase, red-brn semigloss, 4 full-length buttresses, 8", NM 325.00
Vase, yel-gr crystalline w/lav-bl, hdls, long neck, 9" 210.00

American Indian Art

That time when the American Indian was free to practice the crafts and culture that was his heritage has always held a fascination for many. They were a people who appreciated beauty of design and colorful decoration in their furnishings and clothing; and because instruction in their crafts was a routine part of their rearing, they were well accomplished. Several tribes developed areas in which they excelled. The Navajo were weavers and silversmiths, the Zuni, lapidaries. Examples of their craftsmanship are very valuable. Today even the work of contemporary Indian artists — weavers, silversmiths, carvers, and others — is highly collectible. For a more thorough study we recommend *Arrowheads and Projectile Points*, *Indian Axes*, and *Indian Artifacts of the Midwest*. All three have been written by our advisor, Lar Hothem; you will find his address in the Directory under Ohio.

Key:
bw — beadwork   S — Southern
dmn — diamond   s-s — sinew sewn
E — Eastern   W — Western
NE — Northeastern   x — cross
p-h — prehistoric

Apparel and Accessories

Before the white traders brought the Indian women cloth from which to sew their garments and beads to use for decorating them, clothing was made from skins sewn together with sinew, usually made of animal tendon. Porcupine quills were dyed bright colors and woven into bags and armbands and used to decorate clothing and moccasins. Examples of early quillwork are scarce today and highly collectible.

Early in the 19th century, beads were being transported via pony pack trains. These 'pony' beads were irregular shapes of opaque glass imported from Venice. Nearly always blue or white, they were twice as large as the later 'seed' beads. By 1870 translucent beads in many sizes and colors had been made available, and Indian beadwork had become commercialized. Each tribe developed its own distinctive methods and preferred decorations, making it possible for collectors today to determine the origin of many items. Soon after the turn of the century, the craft of beadworking began to diminish.

Apron, Chippewa, velvet w/bw floral, 1890, 16x5" 300.00
Belt, Flathead, full bw w/'fish' design, 1920, 1½x37" 275.00
Belt, Nez Perce, full bw florals, 1920, 3x39" 700.00
Cuffs, Sioux, fully quilled, w/geometrics, fringe, 1890, 5x3" 660.00
Dance outfit, full bw geometrics, 1950, 8-pc 585.00
Dress, Cheyenne, hide w/fringe, 2-color line bw, 1900, 41" 580.00
Dress, Gros Ventre girl's, bw yoke/fringed buckskin, 1920 ....550.00
Dress, Plateau girl's, gr velvet w/bw & sequins, 1920, 31" 85.00
Dress yoke, Plateau, full linear bw on canvas, 1900, 35x9" 440.00
Gauntlets, Athabascan, high-top wht buckskin w/embr floral 110.00
Gloves, Bannock, floral/star bw on buckskin, fringed, 1920s, 13" ...330.00
Hat, Haida, plaited basketry w/blk pnt eagle, 1910, 6x15" 600.00
Hat, Hupa woman's, basketry w/geometrics, 1910, 4x6" 275.00
Jacket, Cree, moosehide buckskin w/floral bw, 1935 ....150.00
Jacket, Nez Perce, leather w/bw, orig tribal label, 1940 ....275.00
Leggings, Nez Perce, geometric bw panels on canvas, 1925, 23" .165.00
Leggings, Nez Perce, red stroud cloth w/contour bw, 1890 ....400.00

Leggings, Plateau, red cloth panels, star bw, 1910, 12" 495.00
Leggings, Plateau woman's, bl trade cloth w/bw Vs, 1910, 15" ...385.00
Leggings, Sioux, full bw geometrics, buffalo hide, 1880, 12" 935.00
Leggings, Umatilla, cut bead swastika/etc panels, 1920, 28" 600.00
Mittens, Athabascan, silk-embr/fur-trim buckskin 1930, 12" 65.00
Moccasins, Apache, high-tops, buffalo hide, bw lines, 1890 ....770.00
Moccasins, Cree, mtn sheep/buffalo hide w/EX bw, cuffed, 1870 ..935.00
Moccasins, Hopi, ceremonial w/pnt lightning motif, 1940 ....120.00
Moccasins, Nez Perce, full bw, cut bead dmn motif, 1900, 11" .2,200.00
Moccasins, Shoshone child's, full bw toe, 1910, 5x2½" 220.00
Moccasins, Sioux, full bw, s-s, parfleche soles, 1890, VG 600.00
Moccasins, Sioux, full feather-like bw/parfleche soles, 1880 ....1,150.00
Moccasins, Tlingit, embr cloth w/fur trim, hide soles, 1920 ....95.00
Moccasins, Winnebago woman's, high-tops, cut bw floral, 1950 .165.00
Shawl, Osage, ribbonwork strips on red trade cloth blanket 220.00
Shirt, Chippewa, floral bw velvet strip on red cloth, 1900 ....385.00
Shirt, war; Plains style, pony beads, gr pnt, ermine, 20th C 1,100.00
Shirt, war; Sioux, buckskin, dragonfly bw panels/pnt, 1880 .....4,950.00
Shirt & apron, Kwakiutl ceremonial, button-work totems, 1965 ....275.00
Vest, Piegan, full bw, muslin lined, bw red stroud bk, 1800s 8,800.00
Vest, Sioux, full wht-ground bw on s-s buffalo, 1900, 23x20" ..2,090.00

Arts and Crafts

Blanket strip, Arapaho, full bw w/disks on trade blanket 525.00
Cvg, argillite raven/whale transformation, Joseph Ilg, 17" 385.00
Cvg, Kwakiutl, post top, bear, cvd/pnt w/copper mouth, 1880 ...440.00
Etching, cowboy on bucking horse, Edward Borien, 1935, 10x8" .195.00
Sand pnt, Hunchback Kachina, by Gray Squirrel, 1960, lg 55.00
Tapestry, Navajo, Yeibeichai, vegetal, framed, 1960, 12x15" 300.00
Watercolor, doe & fawn, sgn Kai-Sa (Percy Sandy), 1935, 7x5" ..165.00

Bags and Cases

The Indians used bags for many purposes, and most display excellent form and workmanship. Of the types listed below, many collectors consider the pipe bag to be the most desirable form. Pipe bags were long, narrow, leather and bead or quillwork creations made to hold tobacco in a compartment at the bottom and the pipe, with the bowl removed from the stem, in the top. Long buckskin fringe was used as trim and complemented the quilled and beaded design to make the bag a masterpiece of Indian Art.

Apache, shoulder pouch, beaded and fringed hide with red wool broadcloth shoulder strap, ca 1900, 30", $500.00.

Apache, medicine flask, full bw 3-color design, 1880, 5x3" 165.00
Apache, quiver, hide, w/orig bow, 1870, 38" 1,375.00

Apache, star/etc bw on pnt hide, beaded fringe, 1910, 16x6" **385.00**
Arapaho, dispatch, full bw, s-s hard leather, 1800s, 8x15" **1,400.00**
Arapaho, pnt bag, bw/fringe, s-s, 1870, 9" **600.00**
Blackfoot, pipe bag, bw, fringe w/wire twists, 1870, 31" **3,410.00**
Crow, full bw, s-s, long fringe, 1800s, 12" **330.00**
Crow, suitcase, pnt rawhide w/geometrics, 1900, 13x27" **550.00**
Nez Perce, belt case, corn husk w/9-color geometrics, 5x4" **275.00**
Nez Perce, corn husk, fine mc geometrics, 1900, 12x13" **880.00**
Nez Perce, corn husk, twined w/mc geometrics ea side, 1910, 8" .**495.00**
Nez Perce, medicine case, pnt parfleche, fringe, 1900, 7x12" **385.00**
Plains, pipe, hide w/bw, quilled bottom, fringe, 20th C, 42" **465.00**
Plateau, bw florals/geometric, pnt bottom, 1920, 25x10" **220.00**
Plateau, carrying bag, floral contour bw, 1910, 10x12" **770.00**
Plateau, carrying bag, full bw florals, 1935, 28x10" **275.00**
Plateau, carrying bag, mc floral/foliate bw, 1930, 10" dia **165.00**
Plateau, contour bw w/red rose design, 1930, 5x9" **250.00**
Plateau, full bw eagle & Am shield, fringe, 1960, 24x13" **275.00**
Plateau, purse, allover commercial bw on bl, 1880, 7x5", EX **330.00**
Plateau, 3-elk pictorial by Yakima, 1940, 18x17" **525.00**
Salish, violin case, imbricated hexagons, 1900, rare, 29" **1,100.00**
Ute, strike-a-lite, geometric bw/tin cones, 1890, 6x4" **495.00**
Winnebago, pipe bag, geometric bw, twist fringe, 1860, 22x4" ..**1,100.00**
Woodlands, bandolier, bw floral on wht, 1900, 35x12" **900.00**
Yakima, pictorial: man w/appl conchos, brass necklace, 1910 ....**935.00**
Yakima, portrait bag, full contour bw, #16 beads, 1930, 7x7" **165.00**

Baskets

In the following listings, examples are basket form and coiled unless noted otherwise.

Apache, bowl, line motif, 1910, 3x9" **385.00**
Apache, burden, pnt motif/twined/fringe, 1880, 14x17" **990.00**
Apache, canteen, pnt design, pitched, willow hdls, 1880, 7x5" ..**350.00**
Apache, tray, radiating stars w/stick-figure dogs, 1920, 12" **1,210.00**
Apache, tray, 4 bugs, clouds in rim, tight weave, 1940, 11" **1,045.00**
Chehalis, bowl, twined w/line design, rim loops, 1910, 3x6" **120.00**
Hopi, 2nd Mesa; bowl, allover horses, 1935, 3x8" **135.00**
Hopi, 2nd Mesa; lg Kachina figures/corn, 1940, 12x14" **1,045.00**
Hopi, 6 animal figures/geometrics, 1800s, 7x10", VG **330.00**
Hupa, acorn meal basket, twined, thunderbirds, 1890, 6x17" **550.00**
Hupa, burden, twined/tight weave, conical, 1900, 22x23" **495.00**
Hupa, mc geometrics on base & lid, fine quality, 1930, 3x4" **250.00**
Hupa, mush bowl, 3-color geometrics, fine weave, 1900, 6x5" **660.00**
Hupa, tobacco basket, tight weave/twined, by Amy Smoker, 3" ..**1,300.00**
Klamath, bowl, twined, brn line/rattlesnakes, 1900, 6x24" **1,925.00**
Klikitat, mc Vs, leather lugs, braid rim, 1900, 13x12" **770.00**
Madiu, bowl, red geometrics, 1910, 3x9" **220.00**
Makah, treasure, twined, arrow motif, mc lid, 1920, 4x16" **135.00**
Maricopa, olla, arrow/zigzag motif, 1910, 11x10" **275.00**
Mission, bowl, connecting arrowheads, 1880, 4x8" **330.00**
Mission, bowl, mc geometrics, 1880, 6x10" **600.00**
Mono, bowl, mc stair-step motif, 1920, 16½x17" **825.00**
Mono, 2 lines of parallel Vs, 1920, 3x5" **700.00**

Navajo, coiled, 4 figures between
4 stylized zigzags, black on beige,
ca 1970, 23½", $575.00.

Panamint, mc motif, shouldered form, fine weave, 1910, 5x6" ..**2,145.00**
Papago, horsehair w/geometric Paiute bw, 1975, 2½x6" **500.00**
Papago, olla, 2 rows of bird figures, w/lid, 1935, 13x11" **275.00**
Pima, bowl, classic fret design, 1900, 6x9" **220.00**
Pima, bowl, fret motif, 1910, 5x19" **2,035.00**
Pima, bowl, row of men gathering cactus fruit, 1920, 4x8" **385.00**
Pima, bowl, 2 rows human figures, 1920, 6x12" **825.00**
Pima, mat, star design, 1935, 8" dia **135.00**
Pima, olla, connecting dmns, finely coiled, 1920, 10x9" **700.00**
Pima, storage, swastika design, 1890, dirty, 13x12" **550.00**
Pomo, miniature, beaded, fine weave, contemporary, ½" dia **165.00**
Pomo, miniature, fully feathered, contemporary, 1¼x¾" **110.00**
Salish, sewing tray, imbricated, rim loops, 1930, 14" dia **85.00**
Salish, storage, fine imbricated Vs, w/lid, 1910, 20x12x8" **1,045.00**
Salish, storage, imbricated, w/lid, 1900, 14x14" **440.00**
Salish, tray, Frazer River, imbricated, 1920, 9x4" **110.00**
Salish, tray, imbricated, w/hdls, 1920, 15" dia **245.00**
San Jacinto Mission, olla, geometrics, w/lid, 1920, 15x11" **330.00**
Tlingit, bottle cover, orange/brn triangles, 1920, 10" **550.00**
Tulare, bowl, mc outline dmn & 'I' motif, 1935, 4½x11" **770.00**

Blades and Points

Relics of this type usually display characteristics of a general area, time period, or a particular location. With study, those made by the Plains Indians are easily discerned from those of the West Coast. Because modern man has imitated the art of the Indian by reproducing these artifacts through modern means, use caution before investing your money in 'too good to be authentic' specimens.

Adena, Beavertail, striped/swirled gray, 2" **5.00**
Adena, blk, slender w/sm point, 2" **5.00**
Adena, blk, wide/long base, 2½" **15.00**
Adena, Flint Ridge flint, reds/rusts, 2½" **15.00**
Adena, striped grays, 3" **10.00**
Antler, hollowed out, eng lines, point broken, 2½" **20.00**
AR, translucent smoky gray, stemmed, 2½" **6.00**
AR, wht, stemmed, widely barbed, needle point, 2½" **8.00**
Archaic, AZ, wht/gray translucent flint, 5" **90.00**
Archaic, midwestern US, stemmed, 2½", NM **20.00**
Corner notch, wht flint, 1¾", NM **20.00**
Corner tang, AR, 2½" **45.00**
Curved, wht chert, 4½", M **60.00**
Dovetail, KY, gray, well-beveled, indented base, polished, 4" **65.00**
Fish spear, lt grays, slight side notches, 2¼" **10.00**
NV, obsidian, bevelled, 2½", VG **18.00**
Paleo, brn, wide, 3" **75.00**
Paleo, IL, tan chert, EX flaking, fluted channels, 1½" **275.00**
Paleo, KY, grays, eared, 1¾" **6.00**
Paleo, lt gray, eared, VG quality, 3¾" **20.00**
Paleo, petrified wood, brn, semi-translucent, 4" **200.00**
Pentagonal, corner notch, str sides, 1¼" **15.00**
Petrified wood, red tones, med sz, M **10.00**
Rowan (Dalton) Paleo, IN, gray-tan, fishtail variant, 2" **15.00**
Spear head, AZ, blk flint, 3" **30.00**
Spear head, notched flint, p-h, w/provenance, 2½x4" **135.00**
Spear head, UT, obsidian, unusual shape, 3" **20.00**
War point, translucent gray-brn, 1" **2.00**
Willow leaf, brn, bi-pointed, 2", NM **15.00**

Blankets, Navajo

Pueblo Indians first made blankets centuries ago, but today most are made by Navajo Indians. Pendleton and Hudson's Bay blankets became widely available in the 1800s; around the turn of the century, rugs were developed because tourists were more likely to buy them as floor coverings and wallhangings. Rugs or blankets are made in various regional styles; an expert can usually identify the area where it was made, sometimes even the individual who made it. The colors of wool are natural (gray-white, brown-black), vegetal (from plant dyes), or artificial (aniline, from synthetic chemicals). Value factors include size, tightness of weave, artistry of design, and condition. Examples by artists whose names are well known command the higher prices.

Chief's, dbl saddle, mc, 1935, 64x29" 165.00
Child's wearing, museum quality, 1870-80, 32x54" 4,675.00
Child's wearing, red/blk terraces, 1890, 37x31" 135.00
Chimayo, blk w/swastikas, 1930, 82x48" 350.00
Chimayo Revival w/Valero stars, 1940, 78x51" 220.00
Eye Dazzler, Transitional, mc serrated dmns, 1910, 86x54" 660.00
Saddle, terraces, very fine weave, 1920, 24x20" 85.00
Transitional, banded, braided edges, 1910, 60x47" 495.00

Ceremonial Items

Dance bustle, N Plains, turkey feathers, 1950s, lg, VG 150.00
Dance crown, Yakima Princess, geometric bw, 1950, well used 85.00
Drum, Pueblo, 3-color pnt, 1940s, 4x4½" dia 225.00
Fetish, Crow warrior's, beaded deer tail, quilled drops, 10" 495.00
Fetish, hide turtle w/full bw geometrics, 20th C, 6x3" 135.00
Fetish, Plains, lizard, bw/tin cones/hair strands, 20th C, 8" 110.00
Fetish, Sioux, bw lizard on tan hide w/tin cones, 1920, 5" 165.00
Mask, Iroquois False Face, corn husk, much fringe, 1900, 20" 990.00
Medicine, Nez Perce, ermine w/beads & feathers, 1870 ....110.00
Medicine balls, Sioux, w/quills & feathers, 1870, 17", pr 385.00
Paint palette, Hohokam, slate w/decor, bails broken, 5" 285.00
Rattle, Kiowa, German silver peyote by Julius Ceasar, 1960, 3½" ..110.00
Rattle, Kiowa, gourd peyote, beaded tip/hdl, fringe, 1975, 20" 85.00
Rattle, Pueblo, pnt gourd, 1931, 15x5" 75.00
Rattle, turtle shell w/hawk bells, beaded neck is hdl, 20th C 220.00
Rattles, Hopi, pnt gourds, 1935, man's, woman's, pr 85.00

Dolls

Kachina, Butterfly Maid, 1-pc, sgn Frankie Howard, 1980, 20" ..195.00
Kachina, Mana, 1-pc, sgn Mike Hanns, 1980, 20" 135.00
Kachina, Ogre, Wm James, 1960, 11" 95.00
Kachina, Shalako, cvd/pnt cottonwood root, 20th C, 23" 110.00
Kachina, Whipper, sgn Silas Roy, 1-pc, 1980, rare, 14x5" 660.00
Kachina, Wht Ahote, Bob Gibbs, 1982, 21x7" 400.00
Nez Perce, bw dress (shell yoke)/leggings/shoes, 1880, 10" 1,760.00
Plains, buckskin w/hair, full bw ceremonial suit, 1900, 14" 220.00
Plains, hide w/pnt dress & bw moccasins, 20th C, 18" 300.00

Domestics

Cradle, Apache, willow, yel canvas covering, 1950, 35" 65.00
Cradle, Mesquakie, wood w/cutouts & brass tacks, 1900, 42" 330.00
Cradle, Sioux, full-quill buffalo w/EX mc geometrics, 1870 ...15,000.00
Cradleboard, Apache, slat bk/saguaro hood/canvas trim, 1958 ...135.00
Spoon, bent horn w/beaded & tacked hdl, 20th C, 13x3" 110.00
Toy cradle, Plains, full bw w/brass-tacked brds, 20th C, 20" 495.00

Jewelry and Adornments

As early as 500 A.D., Indians in the Southwest drilled turquoise nuggets and strung them on cords made of sinew or braided hair. The Spanish introduced them to coral, and it became a popular item of jewelry; abalone and clam shells were favored by the Coastal Indians. Not until the last half of the 19th century did the Indians learn to work with silver. Each tribe developed its own distinctive style and preferred design, which until about 1920 made it possible to determine tribal origin with some degree of accuracy. Since that time, because of modern means of communication and travel, motifs have become less distinct.

Quality Indian silver jewelry may be antique or contemporary. Age, though certainly to be considered, is not as important a factor as fine workmanship and good stones. Pre-1910 silver will show evidence of hammer marks, and designs are usually simple. Beads have sometimes been shaped from coins. Stones tend to be small; when silver wire was used, it is usually square. To insure your investment, choose a reputable dealer.

Beads, hand-wrought/hand-stamped silver, graduated, 20th C 95.00
Beads, Navajo, hand-stamped silver, handmade, 2 strings, 18" ...135.00
Beads, Navajo, heavy/graduated/stamped silver, 1970, 24" 165.00
Belt, Navajo, silver w/14 conchos, contemporary, 48" 300.00
Belt, Navajo, 6 conchos, 7 butterflies, hand hammered, 1935 ....660.00
Belt, Navajo, 9 conchos+buckle, 1st Phase style, 20th C 275.00
Belt, Santo Domingo, tooled brass conchos by Robert Lavato 150.00

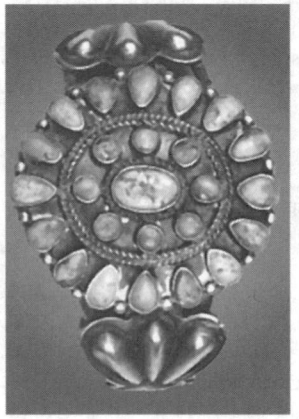

Bracelet, Zuni, silver and clusterwork turquoise, stamp and repousse decorated wire cuff, 1⅞", $250.00.

Bolo, Zuni, butterfly, turq/coral/jet/shell inlay, 1980s, 3" 190.00
Bracelet, Navajo, lg Blue Gem turq, 1935, 6½x2½" 200.00
Bracelet, Navajo, 14k gold w/coral+2 turq, sgn, 1978, 7x2" 330.00
Bracelet, Navajo man's, 5 lg turq, heavy, 1950, 8x1½" 220.00
Bracelet, Zuni, many turq, sgn Betty Etsaty, 1970, 6x2" 110.00
Breast plate, Plateau youth's, brass/glass beads, 1920, 14x9" 165.00
Drop, Sioux, quilled, horsehair/quill braids w/tin cones, 33" 495.00
Fetish, Zuni, 3-strand w/lg mc fetishes, 1960 ....275.00
Fetish, 3-strand coral heishi+coral birds by Calabaza, 1978 ....495.00
Fetish, 3-strand heishi w/birds by Leekya Dycee, 1950, 32" 1,500.00
Necklace, lg wht heart beads, 13 strands, 1800s, 30" 220.00
Necklace, Navajo, 26 Xs, handmade beads, dbl naja, 1920, 33" .440.00
Necklace, Navajo, 8 turq/silver leaves w/9th as drop, +earrings .165.00
Necklace, Nez Perce, hair pipes/brass beads, moon shell, 1880 ..1,200.00
Necklace, Pueblo, 18 sm Xs/lg dbl-bar X on beads, 1920, 32" 495.00
Necklace, Santo Domingo, lg turq slabs w/4 tooled bbls, 1980 .....95.00
Necklace, Santo Domingo, 2-strand nuggets on heishi+jacklas ..165.00
Necklace, 10-strand coral beads w/turq nuggets+silver cones 165.00
Necklace, 8-strand coral w/nuggets+silver beads/Xs, 1935, 32" ..395.00
Roach, Plains, porcupine/deer hair, 1800s, 17" 135.00
Roach, Sioux, quilled Am flag w/bw, bells & hair, 1910, 14" 275.00
Squash blossom, Navajo, box-&-bow style w/10 blossoms, 1975 ..330.00
Trade beads, blk Venetians w/bl & pk dots, 1840, 26" 65.00
Trade beads, chevrons, very lg, 1800, rare, 18" 465.00
Trade beads, cobalt Peking glass, 1890, 31" 110.00
Trade beads, red Venetians w/wht dots, rare, 1840, 24" 85.00
Trade beads, Russian cobalt faceted & Hudson Bay, 1800s 130.00

Pipes

Pipe bowls were usually carved from soft stone, such as catlinite or pipestone, an argilaceous sedimentary rock composed mainly of clay. Granite was also used. Some ceremonial pipes were simply styled, while others were intricately designed naturalistic figurals, sometimes in bird or frog forms called effigies. Their stems, made of wood and often covered with leather, were sometimes nearly a yard in length.

Blk L-bowl w/outer inlay, pnt wood stem, 20th C, 28x4" **165.00**
Hupa Cloud Blower, cvd stone/wood stem, 1870, 7x1½" **500.00**
Mimbres, brn stone, 2" **70.00**
Mound Builder, fish effigy, blk, Hardin Co OH, p-h, 8x2" **220.00**
Mound Builder, human face effigy, p-h, 4x3" **85.00**
Mound Builder, owl effigy, p-h, 7x3" **140.00**

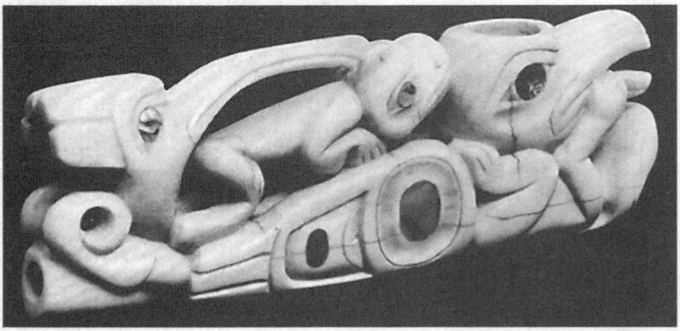

Northwest Coast ivory paneled pipe, carved with intertwined birds, animals, and shaman, inset abalone shell details, 8¼", $1,300.00.

Plains, blk stone T-bowl w/inlay, bw stem w/swastikas, 20th C ..**165.00**
Plains, blk w/pewter & catlinite, tacked/bw stem, 20th C, 32" ...**150.00**
Plains, catlinite, 20th C, 8" **55.00**
Plains, catlinite horse effigy, 1800s, 3¾x8½" **220.00**
Plains, pewter-inlay T-bowl, men/snakes/bw on stem, 20th C **330.00**
Sioux, catlinite claw form, lg tacked rtcl stem, 1890, 3x2x37"..**1,875.00**

Pottery

Indian pottery is nearly always decorated in such a manner as to indicate the tribe that produced it or the pueblo in which it was made. For instance, the designs of Cochiti potters were usually scattered forms from nature or sacred symbols. The Zuni preferred an ornate repetitive decoration of a closer configuration. They often used stylized deer and bird forms, sometimes in dimensional applications.

Acoma, jar, classic mc motif, very thin, 1915, 10x12" **990.00**
Acoma, jar, umber hatched curvilinear decor on wht, 6½x8¼" .**135.00**
Acoma, olla, intricate 3-color pnt w/bird etc, 20th C, 10x11" **440.00**
Acoma, olla, pnt bird/plants, 20th C, 10x12" **300.00**
Acoma, seed jar, Gila Monsters, sgn Emma Lewis, 1975, 5" **220.00**
Acoma, water jar, blk on wht, traditional form, 20th C, 8x8" **250.00**
Acoma, wedding jar, umber geometrics w/red-orange, 2-spout, 9" .**165.00**
Acoma, wedding vase, sgn Eva Histia, 1975, 11x7" **165.00**
Anasazi, canteen, 3-lobed, no rstr, excavated, 14x5" **770.00**
Casas Grandes, snake effigy pot, blk on blk, sgn Quezada, 9" **195.00**
Chaco, bowl, blk geometrics on wht, p-h, 4x9", ...**300.00**
Cochiti, dough bowl, blkware, 1930, well used, 6x14" **550.00**
Cochiti, story-teller w/8 children, att Cordero, 1960, 8x4" **250.00**
Gila, bowl, mc motif, from Four Mile Ruin, p-h, 3x8" **165.00**
Hopi, bowl, fine line w/in, 1935, 2x7" **110.00**

Hopi, bowl, sun face inside, sgn K CallaTewa, 1975, 4x9" **110.00**
Hopi, jar, intricate pnt motif, Rayvin Nampeyo, 1975, 8x5" **400.00**
Hopi, jar, redware w/'fingernail' motif, sgn Pavatea, 1960, 7" **120.00**
Hopi, urn, stylized birds, sgn Clinton Nampeyo, 1985, 5x3" **110.00**
Hopi, vase, butterflies, Annie Nampeyo Healing, 1935, 12x6" ...**330.00**
Mimbres, bowl, gray w/blk & brn fine lines w/in, p-h, 4x8" **440.00**
Mojave, human face jar, red/buff, turq-bead jewelry, 1870, 9" .**2,200.00**
Papago, cooking pot, plainware w/lugs, 1900, 9x7" **85.00**
Santa Clara, jar, polished redware w/cvd avanyu, Rose, '60, 12" ...**880.00**
Santa Clara, jar, twisted redware, Dalarita Patrocina, 8x6" **220.00**
Santa Clara, vase, blk, sgn Christiana Naranjo, 1950, 12x9" **385.00**
Santo Domingo, dough bowl, blk/cream geometrics, 1900, 15" ..**1,100.00**
Zuni, jar, mc rosettes/deer/heartline, 1940, 6x7" **440.00**
Zuni, Kiva bowl, terraced rim, w/birds/frogs/etc, 1940, 3x8" **495.00**

Pottery, San Ildefonso

The pottery of the San Ildefonso pueblo is especially sought after by collectors today. Under the leadership of Maria Martinez and her husband Julian, experiments began about 1918 which led to the development of the 'black-on-black' design achieved through exacting methods of firing the ware. They discovered that by smothering the fire at a specified temperature, the carbon in the smoke that ensued caused the pottery to blacken. Maria signed her work (often 'Marie') from the late teens to the 1960s; she died in 1980. Today a piece with her signature may bring prices in the $500.00 to $4,500.00 range.

Bowl, blkware, geometrics, Marie & Julian, 1930s, 3x4½" **600.00**
Bowl, blkware, matt, Blue Corn, 1980, 2x2½" **125.00**
Bowl, blkware matt design, Desideria, 1930, 5x4" **250.00**
Bowl, blkware, matt design, Susana, 1940s, 3½x6½" **75.00**
Bowl, blkware, scallops, Rose, ca 1935, 3x5¼" **195.00**
Bowl, blkware, triangles, Santana, 1940s, 4x5" **225.00**
Bowl, blkware, water serpent, Rose, 1930s, 3x4¾" **220.00**
Bowl, geometrics, red/blk on tan, Martha Quezada, modern, 6" ...**80.00**
Bowl, red w/blk serpent, Tonita, 1920, 3x8" **300.00**
Jar, blkware, curvilinears, Tonita/Juan Cruz Roybal, 6x9" **990.00**
Jar, blkware, feathers, Donica Tafoya, 3¼x4⅜" **75.00**
Jar, blkware, water serpent, Marie & Julian, '30s, 4¼x5⅞" **1,265.00**
Jar, blkware, water serpent, Ramona, 1935, 9x9" **330.00**
Jar, blkware, wing feathers, Marie, 9x6" **600.00**
Jar, polychrome, water serpent in wht, rstr, 9x10½" **110.00**
Jar, redware, geometrics, Rose, ca 1935, 3¼x4¼" **195.00**
Plate, blkware, feather decor, Maria/64, 6" **335.00**
Plate, blkware, geometrics, Blue Corn, 1960, 5" **225.00**
Plate, blkware, plain, Marie & Julian, 1930s, 11" **900.00**
Plate, blkware, plain, Marie & Julian, 1930s, 6½" **525.00**
Plate, blkware, plain/polished, Marie, 1923, 7" **440.00**
Plate, blkware, plain/polished, Marie & Julian, 1926, 4½" **495.00**
Pot, blkware, water serpent, Marie, wear, 5¾x11" **250.00**
Vase, blkware, band w/horned creature, Maria, 7½x7½" **3,000.00**
Vessel, redware, water serpent at shoulder, Rose, 4½x7¼" **500.00**

Rugs, Navajo

Checkerboard, blk/wht natural wool, 1935, 62x38" **440.00**
Chief's, fine weave, modern, 39x35" **165.00**
Chinle, hourglass design, natural wool, 1935, 38x35" **250.00**
Crystal, central dmn & X, 1920, 65x39" **600.00**
Crystal, 2 stylized Xs, natural wool, 1935, 60x38" **715.00**
Crystal classic Revival, vegetal, line design, 1930, 66x42" **245.00**
Eye Dazzler, sawtooth motif, 1910, 71x43", VG **220.00**
Eye Dazzler, Transitional, 4-color, 1910, 80x54" **825.00**
Ganado, central dmn & X, 1935, 86x53" **1,500.00**

Ganado pictorial, arrows/Xs in storm pattern, 1940, 47x37" **550.00**
Ganado Red, lozenge/crooked arrows, 1935, 65x48" **495.00**
Geometric, natural wool, 1950s, 120x120" **4,400.00**
Homespun/natural wool, lg star w/Xs, 1940, 47x36" **220.00**
Klagetoh, allover dmns, hand-spun wool, 1950, 59x30", M **385.00**
Klagetoh, central lozenge, 1940, 51x35" **275.00**
Klagetoh, feathers in center & border, 1935, 98x49" **1,500.00**
Klagetoh, soft weave w/central lozenge, 1935, 56x36" **330.00**
Optical checks w/central X, 1925, 64x42" **200.00**
Parallelogram in line design, natural wool, 1935, 50x27" **200.00**
Pictorial, corn stalks/feathers/birds/eagles, 1930, 100x45" **880.00**
Red Line Mesa, ½-dmn serrated motif, 1920, 58x35", VG **300.00**
Regional, red/blk geometrics on ivory, 1920, 56x36", VG **165.00**
Serrated dmns, heavy, 1920, 59x38" **275.00**
Serrated dmns on natural gray, 1920, 80x50" **700.00**
Storm, soft weave/colors, 1935, 70x45" **600.00**
Storm pictorial w/corn & arrows, fine weave, 1935, 57x36" **1,300.00**
Teec Nos Pos, intricate outline geometrics, 1940, 60x34" **440.00**
Teec Nos Pos, outline waterbugs, 1935, 37x32" **330.00**
Thunderbirds, arrows & feathers, EX color, 1935, 67x38" **3,750.00**
Transitional, mc geometrics, 1910, 91x55" **1,385.00**
Triple dmns, 1930, 62x36" **200.00**
Western Reservation, dmns/waterbirds, 1920, 74x53" **365.00**
Western Reservation, EX color/quality, 1935, 36x24" **550.00**
Western Reservation, jagged line design, 1920, 58x40" **385.00**
Western Reservation, stripes/waterbugs, 1950, 70x45" **495.00**
Wide Ruins, bows/arrows/t'birds, vegetal, 1940, 56x40" **275.00**
Wide Ruins, line/waterbug motif, vegetal, 1975, 50x53" **385.00**
Yei, fine weave, EX color, 1940, 58x37" **385.00**
2 Gray Hills, fine weave/natural, lozenge, modern, 52x29" **300.00**
2 Gray Hills, near-tapestry quality, natural, 1935, 66x37" **1,600.00**
2 Gray Hills, tapestry weave, 1960, 30x19" **550.00**

Stone Artifacts

Bannerstone, saddle; IN, red granite, 3", NM **900.00**
Bowl, incised lines, 2½" **85.00**
Fetish, Hohokam, 3½" **45.00**
Pestle, Northern Plains, quartzite, 8¾" **95.00**
Pestle, phallic shape, Columbia River, p-h, 8x4" **200.00**
Pestle, thick, 8" **45.00**
Plummet, MI, dbl, pnt, p-h, 6x1" **40.00**
Ring, Hohokam, 2¼" dia **40.00**

Tools

Awl, Hohokam, bone, 4" **5.00**
Axe, Columbia River, dk gray, ¾-grooved, p-h, 7x3" **165.00**
Axe, fully grooved, ridges, 7" **100.00**
Axe, Hohokam, polished, 9", M **225.00**
Axe, Hohokam, 5", EX **95.00**
Axe, Mimbres, polished, 6", M **125.00**
Axe, 5" **5.00**
Celt, OH, 3½", M **20.00**
Drill, 3", NM **25.00**
Hammer stone, grooved, high ridges, once an axe, 6" **40.00**
Hammer stone, hafted, 5", M **25.00**
Hammer stone, Hohokam, grooved, porous lava stone, 5½" **15.00**
Hide scraper, Plains, bone, 1890, 5x10" **100.00**
Hoe, Mimbres, 4x7", M **55.00**
Mace, speckled gray stone 'eagle claw,' 3x14" **385.00**
Maul, Hohokam, 3" **35.00**
Needle, stone, w/eye, from AR, p-h, 8x1" **20.00**
Pick, TN, slate, 3½" **25.00**

Weapons

Arrow, Plains, sinew-wrapped stone-tipped, fletched, 23" **45.00**
Club, blk w/pewter & catlinite inlay, bw hdl, 20th C, 30x8" **220.00**
Club, fish killing; Vancouver, p-h, 9x3" **50.00**
Club, flop knob; cvd stone w/full bw hdl, 20th C, 44x2" **2,200.00**
Club, Great Lakes, tacked/beaded, bird hdl, 1870, 29x7½" **660.00**
Club, Iroquois, ball head, cvd effigy face, 1840, 12x10x8" **440.00**
Club, natural wood, 1860, 19x6" **165.00**
Club, Sioux, hide-wrapped wood hdl w/quills, 1870, 28x6" **1,045.00**
Club, 4" oval stone head on beaded/hide-covered hdl, 20th C ...**300.00**
War axe, metal head, wood hdl, from MI, 1840, 25x9" **100.00**

Miscellaneous

Bridle, Navajo, hand-stamped silver, turq in brow band, 1935 ...**550.00**
Bridle, red horse hair w/Fleming silver bit from Pine Ridge **495.00**

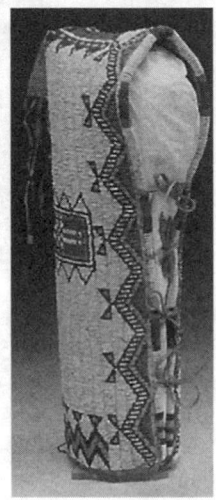

Cradle cover, Sioux, sinew-stitched with allover multicolor beadwork, beaded and fringed hide tab attachment at crown, 15", $3,100.00.

Fan, paddle; Omaha, elk effigy, cvd wood, 1880, 16x10" **1,100.00**
Flute, Sioux, hand cvd/playable, eagle form, modern, 26" **300.00**
Martingale, Nez Perce, red cloth w/bw florals, bells, 1880 ....**700.00**
Mirror, courting; Omaha, horse-head effigy fr, 1880, 13x7" **990.00**
Peace medal, Andrew Johnson, sterling on bl beads, 1865, 3" **440.00**
Peace medal, brass, Grover Cleveland, 1884, 2½x3" **55.00**
Peace medal, silver, wide rim band, 1841, 3" dia **1,200.00**
Peace medal, Treaty of Greenville, silver w/eagle, 1795, 4x3" **220.00**
Photogravure, Acoma Belfry, ES Curtis, rpl fr, 12x16" **700.00**
Photogravure, Jemez Architecture, ES Curtis, rpl fr, 12x16" **400.00**
Post office, Tlingit, beaded hide wall hanging for mail, 1920 ....**95.00**
Quirt, Blackfoot, braided rawhide, wood hdl, 1890, 60" **85.00**
Quirt, Plateau, leather w/bead-wrapped hdl, 1890, 31" **195.00**
Quirt, Sioux, brass tacks/pnt motif, 1900, 22x1" **600.00**
Saddle drape, Plateau, hide w/bw & fringe, 1950, 92x10" **465.00**
Spurs, Navajo, hand-stamped silver w/turq stones, 1930 ....**1,100.00**
Trade kettle, CI, from Browning Mt Blackfoot reservation, 6" **110.00**

Amethyst Glass

    The term amethyst simply describes the rich color of this glassware, made by many companies both here and abroad since the 19th century.

Bottle, cut panels, scalloped base, cut bubble stopper, 11x4" **150.00**
Bowl, pressed Sunburst base, scalloped rim, 1¼x6", NM **35.00**
Jar, mc autumn mtn scene w/gold, ped ft, 6½x4⅞" **150.00**

Tumbler, HP florals & scrolls, 3⅞x2¾" 20.00
Vase, flint, tulip form, early, 9¾" 375.00
Vase, hyacinth w/swirled ribs, 7½" 75.00

Amphora

The Amphora Porcelain Works in the Teplitz-Turn area of Bohemia produced Art Nouveau-styled vases and figurines during the latter part of the 1800s through the first few decades of the 20th century. They marked their wares with various stamps, some incorporating the name and location of the pottery with a crown or a shield. Because Bohemia was part of the Austro-Hungarian empire prior to WWI, some examples are marked Austria; items marked with the Czechoslovakia designation were made after the war. Our advisor for this category is Jack Gunsaulus; he is listed in the Directory under Michigan.

Bowl, cvd floral/bird band, mc on teal/gold mottle, 5x10" 275.00
Bowl, Deco birds/florals on tan/wht mottle, ftd, w/lid, 5x7" 180.00
Bowl, high-relief ghost-like females/daisies, 3x8", NM 550.00
Figurine, camel driver, 13" 600.00
Figurine, rearing stallion, beige w/gr & gold base, 16" 350.00
Figurine, 3 nude children gather pk roses in baskets, 8x11" 400.00
Jar, duck reserve on ball form, fox finial, 10½" 400.00
Jardiniere, appl berry clusters, 3 3-D infants, 18", EX 1,000.00
Jardiniere, mc fruit, 3 low hdls, blk trim, 6½" 220.00
Jug, rose/brn mottle w/3 floral panels, over-top hdl, 15" 350.00
Lamp, Deco-style, portrait reserve, 4 arms support globe, 21" 395.00
Lamp base, birds/flowers band, mc inlay, #508/710, wood base ...350.00
Pitcher, webby ribs, gr matt w/mc highlights, wide base, 14" ...1,200.00
Planter, floral in high relief, pk/gr/gold, split hdls, 6x13" 575.00
Vase, blk-lined mc floral on gr/wht crackle, 4 hdls, #3888, 7" 200.00
Vase, cvd floral/modern design set w/cabachon jewels, 7x5" 125.00
Vase, cvd stylized tree, bk: cvd bird, mc, hdls, 12" 325.00

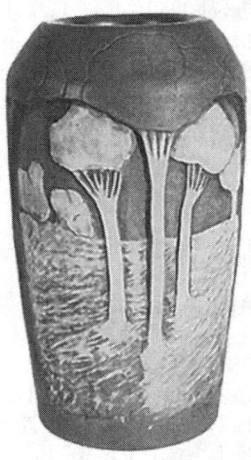

Vase, deeply carved trees, peasant farmers on reverse, cream, olive green, and purple, crown mark, #1155314, 18x10", $1,300.00.

Vase, Egyptian figure in reserve on brn, 13⅝" 350.00
Vase, emb Deco trees, bk: peasant couple, mc gloss, 18" 650.00
Vase, floral, bl w/cobalt rim, hdls, 8¾" 165.00
Vase, floral/geometrics, jeweled/HP/gilt on wht matt, 4x5" 750.00
Vase, gold leaves on cobalt & gr, gold lustre top, 6x6" 325.00
Vase, high-relief octopus, tenacle hdls, crab on base, 20" 1,725.00
Vase, jeweled band on jeweled spider-web ground, w/gold, 5x6" ...260.00
Vase, jeweled flowers, salamander hdls, crown mk, 9¾" 400.00
Vase, lady's portrait w/much enameling & jeweling, 6" 950.00
Vase, lg high-relief bat, olive-brn/dk amber mottle, 10" 4,000.00
Vase, mc drip glaze, twisted w/closed shoulder hdls, 8" 140.00
Vase, pine needles, gold/gr/wht on pitted matt, 2-neck, 5x5" 250.00

Vase, Sarah Bernhardt w/jewels in hair, 6" 850.00
Vase, slave girl/forest scene, hdls, crown mk, #2118, 8" 180.00
Vase, sqd basket form w/oak leaves, w/gilt, #12025, 10", EX 345.00
Vase, 2 mc floral bands, narrow ribs on gold/wht mottle, 12" 300.00
Vase, 3 emb female heads on cvd swirls, flower-petal rim, 16" 800.00
Vase, 3 3-D sea horses support geometric bowl, 5x7" 300.00

Animal Dishes with Covers

Covered animal dishes have been produced for nearly two centuries and are as varied as their manufacturers. They were made in many types of glass (slag, colored, clear, and milk glass) as well as china and pottery. On bases of nests and baskets, you will find animals and birds of every sort. The most common was the hen.

Some of the smaller versions made by McKee, Indiana Tumbler and Goblet Company, and Westmoreland Specialty Glass of Pittsburgh, Pennsylvania, were sold to food-processing companies who filled them with prepared mustard, baking powder, etc. Occasionally one will be found with the paper label identifying the product and processing company still intact.

Many of the glass versions produced during the latter part of the 19th century have been recently reproduced. As early as the 1960s, the Kemple Glass Company made the rooster, fox, lion, cat, lamb, hen, horse, turkey, duck, dove, and rabbit on split-ribbed or basketweave bases. They were made in amethyst, blue, amber, and milk glass, as well as a variegated slag. It is sometimes necessary to compare items in question to verified examples of older glass in order to recognize reproductions. Reproduction is continued today.

For more information, we recommend *Covered Animal Dishes* by our advisor, Everett Grist, whose address is in the Directory under Tennessee. In the listings below, when only one dimension is given, it is the greater one, usually length.

Boar's head, milk glass, Atterbury, Pat May 29, 1888, 9½" 1,500.00
Bull's head mustard jar, purple slag, no ladle, LG Wright 35.00
Chicken, Dbl-Headed; milk glass, unmk McKee, 5½" 600.00
Chicks in oblong basket, milk glass, pnt details, 2¼x4¼" 325.00
Dog, bl opaque, Westmoreland Specialty, 5½" 60.00
Dog (Chow), milk glass, mk McKee, 5½" 500.00
Dog (Pekingese) on base, milk glass, att Sandwich, 4¾" 800.00
Dog on wide-rib base, amber, Westmoreland, 5½" 65.00
Dolphin on sauce dish, milk glass, att Westmoreland, 7¼" 65.00
Dolphin on sawtooth base, milk glass, Kemple or St Clair repro ...75.00
Duck on cattail base, milk glass, 5½" 85.00
Duck on wavy base, milk glass, Challinor Taylor & Co, 8" 125.00
Duck soap dish, clear, pnt bill 15.00
Eagle mother, milk glass, Westmoreland reissue w/WG mk 100.00
Elephant, milk glass, mk McKee, 5½" 1,500.00
Fish, Entwined; milk glass, lacy base, dtd lid, 6" dia 200.00
Fish, Flat; gr transparent 75.00
Fish on collared base, clear frosted, Central Glass 150.00

Hen, milk glass with blue opaque head, Westmoreland Specialty, 5½", $65.00.

Hen, amberina, LE Smith, 5½" **75.00**
Hen, milk glass, Fenton, 8" **150.00**
Hen, milk glass, Westmoreland Specialty, 5½" **35.00**
Hen, Straight Headed; clear, att Indiana Glass, 5½" **15.00**
Hen on cattail base, milk glass, 5½" **85.00**
Hen on sleigh, milk glass, Westmoreland, 5½" **85.00**
Hen w/chicks, milk glass, pnt comb, ea pc mk McKee, 5½" **350.00**
Horse on split-rib base, milk glass, repro, 5½" **75.00**
Lamb, milk glass, ea pc mk McKee, 5½" **450.00**
Lion, British; milk glass, 6¼" **125.00**
Quail on scroll base, milk glass, 5½" **65.00**
Rabbit emerging from horizontal egg, pnt milk glass **100.00**
Rabbit on wheat base, milk glass, Flaccus **350.00**
Rooster on basketweave base, bl opaque, Westmoreland, lg **125.00**
Snail on strawberry, milk glass, Vallerysthal, 5¼" **150.00**
Swan, Block; milk glass, Challinor Taylor & Co, 7" **200.00**
Swan, Closed-Neck; milk glass, Westmoreland Specialty **75.00**
Swan, milk glass, unmk McKee, 5½" **220.00**
Swan, Raised-Wing; milk glass, molded eyes, Westmoreland **85.00**
Turkey, Standing; clear, US Glass, lg **250.00**
Turtle, clear, knobby bk forms lid, LG Wright, lg **75.00**

Anna Pottery

Founded in 1859 near a town in Illinois by the same name, the Anna Pottery operated for about thirty-five years, producing stoneware items and small animal figures as well as brick and tile from the native clay. They are best known for their whimsey jugs decorated with writhing snakes and flasks modeled as pigs. Examples are rare and expensive today.

Nodder, Tweed hatching from egg, Tweed Never Counts..., 2⅞" ..**3,200.00**
Pig, brn Albany slip, St Louis The Future Capital..., 8", EX **1,800.00**

Antiquities

The ancient Egyptians, Romans, and the early craftsmen of India and China have left us with exquisite treasures bearing mute witness of their esthetic convictions that even a water carrier, a knife, or a rug should be a thing of beauty. Though time and the elements have taken their toll on the more fragile works of these ancient artisans, it is incredible that many remain intact to this day. The thin-walled tear and scent bottles blown by Roman artisans from the last century A.D., and examples of the red or black predynastic potteries of Egypt, though understandably quite rare, can yet occasionally be found on the market today. Jewelry, often interred with the dead, has survived the centuries well; figurines of marble and terra cotta, ceremonial masks, earthenware vessels, and other relics such as these offer us of the 20th century the only tangible link possible to the ancient world. Our advisor for this category is Alex G. Malloy; he is listed in the Directory under New York.

Key:
cyl — cylinder
Dy — Dynasty

Mil — millennium

Amulets

Coptic Period, 4th-6th C AD, bird pr, MOP, ⅝x⅞" **250.00**
Late Period, 1085-333 BC, Isis, gr faience, detailed, 2" **200.00**
Ptolemaic, 332-30 BC, Harpocrates, ivory, nude figure, 1⅜" **400.00**

Roman Period, 1st-4th C AD, Isis, bl/gr faience, 2½" **125.00**
Sumerian, 3rd Mil BC, serpentine, stylized bird, 1" L **85.00**
1085-333 BC, Duatmutef, gr faience, jackal head, crude, 2⅜" **80.00**
18th Dy, 1567-1320 BC, glass heart, bl w/wht opaque, 1⅜" **175.00**
26th-30th Dys, 664-343 BC, papyrus sceptre, faience, 1" **100.00**

Bronze

Assyrian, 8th C BC, human arm figural, 1½x⅞" **125.00**
Luristan, 10th-7th C BC, brooch, antelope's head, 1⅜" **60.00**
Parthian, 300-200 BC, bell, horse finial, iron clapper, 1⅛" **65.00**
Roman, hairpin, decor on top, 2 beadwork bands, 4" **100.00**
Roman, 1st-3rd C AD, nail, curved end, flat head, 2½" **75.00**
Roman, 1st-3rd C AD, sewing pin, 2 holes for thread, 5⅛" **150.00**
Uratu, 800 BC, bell, truncated, cast rosettes, 2⅛" **165.00**
Visigothic, 6th-7th C AD, box, gilt, punched decor, 1⅝x1⅛" ...**225.00**
Visigothic, 6th-7th C AD, buckle, oval, thick tongue, 1⅛" **50.00**

Cunieform Tablet Fragments

Akkadian, 2334-2145 BC, red terra cotta, text, 1½" W **150.00**
Old Babylonian, 1900-1600 BC, economic text **350.00**
Syrian, 1200 BC, contract of sale, 1¾x1¼" **200.00**

Glass

Byzantine, 4th-5th C AD, flask, lt gr, sq shape, 2¾", VG **200.00**
Roman, 1st-2nd C AD, flask, dk bl, cyl neck, 4½" **875.00**
Roman/Byzantine, 4th-6th C AD, mirror, terra cotta fr, 3" **750.00**

Jewelry and Adornments

Coptic/Byzantine, 4th-7th C AD, sq & tubular beads/3 amulets .**100.00**
Greco/Roman, 1st C BC-2nd C AD, bronze, griffin bezel **125.00**
Greek, 6th-5th C BC, ring, silver, Zeus intaglio, incomplete **75.00**
Greek/Hellenistic, 1st C BC-1st C AD, gold loop earrings **500.00**
Judean, 10th C BC, earring, lunate, silver drop, ½" **100.00**
Roman, 2nd-3rd C AD, low arch fibula, bronze, 1⅞" **125.00**
Roman, 5th-6th C AD, bracelet, bronze, incised decor, 2½" **110.00**
Roman Republic, 2nd-1st C BC, high-arch fibula, bronze, 1⅞" .**400.00**
Visigothic, 6th-7th C AD, bracelet, bronze, stamped birds **135.00**
27th-30th Dy, 663-341 BC, necklace, mc faience beads, 19½" **40.00**

Pottery

Apulian, mid-4th C BC, blkware dish w/slip decor, 3⅞" **125.00**
Attic, 520-510 BC, blk satyr amphora fragment, 1⅜x1¾" **275.00**
Ayyubid to Seljuq, 11th-13th C AD, saucer oil lamp, buffware **75.00**
Coringh, 575-550 BC, buff cothon w/orange & slip, 5¼" dia **350.00**
Holy Land, 1st-2nd C AD, Judean cooking pot, 6" H **475.00**
Holy Land, 586-300 BC, jar, globular, brnware, 2½" **175.00**
Holy Land, 600-300 BC, ovoid flask, slip on grayware, 3¾" **150.00**
Holy Land, 731-530 BC, Ammonite mug, buffware, 2½" **200.00**
Holy Land, 800-586 BC, wheel-made bowl, redware, 5⅜" dia **175.00**
Ptolemaic, 3rd-1st C BC, mini votive lamp, terra cotta, 1⅜" **50.00**
Umayyad, 7th-8th C AD, lamp, terra cotta, wheel-made, rnd **85.00**
Western Asia Minor, 4th-3rd C BC, terra cotta lamp filler **250.00**

Scarabs (Egyptian)

Libyan Dy, 935-730 BC, Sashanq V, ¾x½" **175.00**
18th Dy, 1567-1320 BC, bl faience, Thotmoses III, ¾" **125.00**
22nd Dy, 93-730 BC, buff, cvd steatite, lion/gazelles, ½" **750.00**
26th Dy, 664-525 BC, cvd steatite, Psemthek I, ½x⅜" **175.00**

Stamp and Cylinder Seals

Early Dynastic, 2600-2500 BC, limestone cyl, hero/lion, ½" **225.00**
Mesopotamian, 1730-1600 BC, blk serpentine, lion/combat scene, 1" ..**450.00**
Mesopotamian, 1800-1650 BC, blk geothite, deity, chip, 1" **275.00**
Mesopotamian, 1900-1600 BC, blk hematite, 2 figures/alter, 1" .**300.00**
Mesopotamian, 3500-3000 BC, dk gray serpentine button, ⅝" **65.00**
Neo-Assyrian, 9th-8th C, bl faience, hunting contest, ⅞" **75.00**
Old Babylon, 2nd Mil BC, alabaster, cvd king/figure, 1¼" **500.00**
Old Hittite, 1600-1400 BC, red jasper ovoid stamp, 1x⅝" **175.00**

Appliances, Electric

Antique electric appliances represent a very diverse field and are always being sought after by collectors. There were literally hundreds of different companies making appliances in the early part of the 20th century. The most collectible of these are toasters, percolators, vacuums, waffle irons, and electric irons.

Prices listed below are for examples in very good to excellent condition and in good working order. Be sure to check any old appliances for safety before plugging in. If you have any questions regarding antique appliances, please contact our advisor, Jim Barker; he is listed in the Directory under Pennsylvania.

Toaster, Gold Seal, 1924, EX, $90.00.

Beater, Vidrio, paneled custard slag container, 1930s **60.00**
Biscuit baker, K-M #150-9 ....**55.00**
Chafing dish, Chase #17087 ....**125.00**
Chafing dish, Simplex #1203 ....**75.00**
Chafing dish, Universal, E-940 ....**85.00**
Coffee maker, Edicraft Menlo Siphonator, 9-cup, 1930 ....**65.00**
Coffee urn, Universal, copper, dtd, lg, EX **95.00**
Corn popper, Dominion **75.00**
Corn popper, Excel **65.00**
Fan, Dayton, brass blade **125.00**
Fan, Emerson, oscillating, 12" **130.00**
Fan, Emerson-Trojan, brass table-top, EX **125.00**
Fan, GE, brass blades, coin-op, 19x14x10", EX **300.00**
Fan, Knapp #145, battery **150.00**
Fan, Menominee, #562, cast base, steel blades, 9¼" dia **95.00**
Fan, Polar Cub, oscillating, 10" **75.00**
Fan, Signal Cool Spot Junior, 7" blade, EX **60.00**
Fan, Victron, oscillating, chrome blades, 10", EX **70.00**
Frappe mixer, Hamilton Beach, tan porc, EX+ **90.00**
Fudge sauce warmer, Johnston's, 1930s **45.00**
Hair dryer, metal, Universal, EX **15.00**
Hot chocolate warmer, Magic Whirl, chrome w/windmill **100.00**
Ice cream freezer, Hamilton Beach Iceless..., ca 1934, w/box **40.00**
Ice cream mixer, Smoothie, bullet shape, MIB **95.00**

Mixer, Sunbeam Model FC4, many attachments, ca 1930 ....**95.00**
Mixer, Whip-All, Air-O-Mix, cast & sheet metal, ca 1920s, rare ..**100.00**
Percolator/urn set, Hold Heet 220's **65.00**
Percolator/urn set, Universal E-9269 ....**90.00**
Popcorn popper, Dominion Electric, metal, 1930s **50.00**
Refrigerator, Freeze-Pak, blk metal, chrome tube legs, 39" **650.00**
Toaster, Auto-Toastmaker, Bersted Mfg, chrome, 1930 ....**40.00**
Toaster, Bersted #68 ....**65.00**
Toaster, Bersted #87 ....**40.00**
Toaster, Breakfaster T-2, Calkins Appliance **75.00**
Toaster, Electra Hot #38 ....**55.00**
Toaster, Excel Toastoy **85.00**
Toaster, General Electric #119T41 ....**85.00**
Toaster, General Electric #119T46 ....**55.00**
Toaster, General Electric #119T48 ....**65.00**
Toaster, General Electric #129T77 ....**55.00**
Toaster, General Electric D-12 ....**375.00**
Toaster, Majestic, 2-slice, tip-out style **75.00**
Toaster, Manning Bowman **50.00**
Toaster, Merit Made, auto pop-up style **85.00**
Toaster, Merit Made, Deco flip-side style, EX **75.00**
Toaster, Pelouze **200.00**
Toaster, Samson Long Slot **75.00**
Toaster, Samson Tri Matic **85.00**
Toaster, Toast-O-Later Model J, Alfredo DeMateeis, 1940, 11" .**175.00**
Toaster, Westinghouse TK-14, Deco pop-up style **65.00**
Toaster Hotpoint #114T5 ....**80.00**
Toaster stove, Westinghouse, rectangular, cabriole legs, early **65.00**
Vacuum cleaner, Airway, 1922, w/orig bag **145.00**
Vacuum cleaner, Electric Renovator, Skinner, 1905, EX **150.00**
Vacuum cleaner, Gurelle Guild Electrolux, EX **175.00**
Vacuum cleaner, Hoover Model I, tin & wood, 1908, EX **200.00**
Vacuum cleaner, Universal Supreme Model No E440, ca 1942 ..**125.00**
Washing machine, Maytag, dbl wringer, on casters, ca 1914 ......**150.00**
Washing machine, Minier, wringer style, on casters, ca 1924 .....**155.00**

Arequipa

The Arequipa Pottery operated from 1911 until 1918 at a sanitorium near Fairfax, California. Its purpose was two-fold: therapy for the patients and financial support for the institution. Frederick H. Rhead was the originator and director. The ware, made from local clays, was often hand thrown, simply styled and decorated. Marks were varied but always incorporated the name of the pottery and the state. A circular arrangement encompassing the negative image of a vase beside a tree is most common.

Examples are evaluated according to quality of artwork; size and shape are less important. Those done by Rhead himself are most desirable.

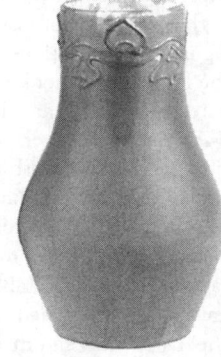

Vase, purple matt with Arts & Crafts squeezebag decoration at top, impressed mark, 6", $850.00.

Bowl, brn matt, incurvate rim, 1¾x6" **325.00**
Bowl, cvd floral on bl matt, 2 hairlines, 2¼x6½" **200.00**
Bowl, gr gloss w/blk streak geometrics, #703/14, 2¼x7½" **200.00**
Bowl, simple cvd floral, bl-gray gloss to dk brn, #558, 2½" **400.00**
Bowl, slip-trailed Aztec band, brn/bl on gr, 1912, 9", NM **800.00**
Bowl, stylized stars on shoulder, dk brn on aqua, sgn HH, 2x8" ..**200.00**
Bowl vase, bl/gray streaked, #550/9, 2¾x4¾" **200.00**
Vase, blade leaves on wht, #288, shouldered, 7¼x4¼" **750.00**
Vase, cvd iris/leaves, gr on brn matt, sgn BR, 7¾x3¼" **3,750.00**
Vase, cvd leaves encircle top, bl matt, 3¼x3" **300.00**
Vase, cvd pansies, dk bl on speckled bl-gray, 4¾x3¾" **500.00**
Vase, cvd stylized flowers/grass blades on bl matt, 7¾x5¾" **650.00**
Vase, floral branch relief, terra cotta, long neck, 8x6" **975.00**
Vase, gray-purple matt, bulbous top, incurvate, #201, 6x5" **350.00**
Vase, plum semimatt, ribbed/shouldered w/petal rim, 6x4" **350.00**
Vase, sculpted grapevines on shoulder, dk bl matt, 5x6", EX **300.00**
Vase, sky bl matt, cylindrical, #1115, 6x3¼" **300.00**
Vase, slip-trailed wht grapes under rim on teal matt, 6" **2,100.00**

Argy-Rousseau, G.

Gabriel Argy-Rousseau produced both fine art glass and quality commercial ware in Paris, France, in 1918. He favored Art Nouveau as well as Art Deco and in the twenties produced a line of vases in the Egyptian manner, made popular by the discovery of King Tut's tomb. One of the most important types of glass he made was pate-de-verre. Most of his work is signed. Items listed below are pate-de-verre unless noted otherwise.

Bowl vase, floral border on tan/brn mottle, 3⅛" H **4,300.00**
Lamp, ovoid-in-dish shade; wrought-iron base, sgn 2X, 13" ..**16,000.00**
Night light, leaves/vines, cylindrical shade, iron base, 8" **4,800.00**
Night light, V panels w/florals on ovoid, iron base, 8½" **5,750.00**
Paperweight block, 2 blk moths on mottled red, 3" **5,400.00**
Pendant, Bouquet des Fleurs, purple/gr/red/brn, 2½" dia **1,265.00**
Pendant, flowers, pk/wine w/blk centers, sgn G A-R, 2½" dia ..**1,380.00**
Pendant, parrot & floral, red/pk, 2½" dia, on silk cord **3,680.00**
Pendant, Pomme de Pin, pine cones, gr/wines, sq, 2⅜" **1,265.00**
Tray, sunflower to side, petal rim, 3½" dia **2,645.00**
Vase, emb swirling foliage on purple/bl/blk mottle, 5x5" **3,100.00**
Vase, heads of 3 long-haired maids, red/brn/gray mottle, 8" ..**16,000.00**
Vase, violets w/charcoal stems on cream & lt gr, ovoid, 6" **3,700.00**

Art Deco

To the uninformed observer, 'Art Deco' evokes images of chrome and glass, streamlined curves and aerodynamic shapes, mirrored prints of pink flamingos, and statues of slender nudes and greyhound dogs. Though the Deco movement began in 1925 at the Paris International Exposition and lasted to some extent into the 1950s, within that period of time the evolution of fashion and taste continued as it always has, resulting in subtle variations.

The French Deco look was one of opulence — exotic inlaid woods, rich material, lush fur and leather. Lines tended toward symmetrical curves. American designers adapted the concept to cover every aspect of fashion and home furnishings from small inexpensive picture frames, cigarette lighters, and costume jewelry to high-fashion designer clothing and exquisite massive furniture with squared or circular lines. Vinyl was a popular covering, and chrome-plated brass was used for chairs, cocktail shakers, lamps, and tables. Dinnerware, glassware, theaters, and train stations were designed to reflect the new 'Modernism.'

The Deco movement made itself apparent into the fifties in wrought iron lamps with stepped pink plastic shades and Venetian blinds. The sheer volume of production during those twenty-five years provides collectors today with fine examples of the period that can be bought for as little as $10.00 or $20.00 up to the thousands. Chrome items signed 'Chase' are prized by collectors, and blue glass radios and tables with blue glass tops are high on the list of desirability in many areas.

Those interested in learning more about this subject will want to read *Collector's Guide to Art Deco* by our advisor, Mary Frank Gaston. She is listed in the Directory under Texas. See also Bronzes; Chase; Frankart; Furniture; Jewelry; Lalique; Radios; etc.

Ashtray, cast-bronze dancing nude on onyx base, 10½" **100.00**
Bookends, Scottie dogs, brass-finished metal, Frankart, 7", pr **275.00**
Bottle, scent; blk glass w/silver lattice work, Fr **125.00**
Bottle, scent; Yardley, 8-point star, brass cap, Austria, 3" **65.00**
Cigarette holder, brass stick man w/'valises,' 1935, 10" **175.00**
Cigarette lighter, airplane form, chrome, working, EX **60.00**

Clock set, onyx and marble, ca 1930, 11½x16½" clock with candle holders, 3-piece, $750.00.

Clock, blk Bakelite skyscraper, w/calendar, Hammond, NM **75.00**
Clock, digital; bronze case, Silvercrest, 1930s, 19" L **250.00**
Clock, kitchen; red & chrome, stepped circles, Hammond, EX ..**100.00**
Clock, mantel; metal cougar atop gr/blk marble case, 17" L **375.00**
Coffee table, marble top, hammered iron scrolled base, 48" **2,300.00**
Figure, metal nude supports basin, 25" **500.00**
Figure, nude in long pleated drape, pottery, matt gr, 20" **500.00**
Fish tank, wrought iron/glass, 3-side cone, stepped base, 21" **475.00**
Grille, wrought iron, strapwork panel+4 w/bars, 38x55" **1,000.00**
Hairbrush, brn plastic, stepped design **25.00**
Incense burner, CI, emb florals, geometric form, Fr, 6½" **175.00**
Incense burner, girl w/flowers by basket, bronzed metal, 5½" **75.00**
Inkwell, hammered copper & cast brass, rnd shape **150.00**
Lamp, boudoir; dancing nude, gr pot metal, Beaver, rpl shade **350.00**
Lamp, boudoir; seated nude by gr crackle glass ball, Kelly, 8" **550.00**
Lamp, chrome & bl glass airplane w/silver trim **200.00**
Lamp, chrome gazelles on blk glass base, cone shade, 9" **125.00**
Lamp, leopard-skin Bakelite/aluminum, WD Teague, #100, 13" .**425.00**
Lamp, lighthouse form w/gr globe, 1920s, 15", NM **135.00**
Lamp, mc 'stain glass' enamel on glass, electric, Leune, 7" **1,300.00**
Lamp, nude on stomach w/arms up holds light, bronzed metal ..**250.00**
Lamp, seated nude w/marble ball, 15", EX **450.00**
Lamp, table; bronze lady holds up lg shell, Germany, 19x4" **700.00**
Lamp, table; tubular aluminum/chrome construction, 29", pr **400.00**
Lamp, 2 standing nudes w/light in center, 1930s, NM **300.00**
Luminaire, fan form w/wrought-iron cobra base, Fr, 22½" **1,200.00**
Magazine rack, nude & greyhound, bronze w/silver finish, 15½" .**850.00**
Mirror, hand; chromed metal w/blk enameling, 13¾" **85.00**
Place card holder, lustreware, bird w/long beak, Germany **35.00**
Plaque, nude w/2 greyhounds, heavy metal, 9x12¾" **150.00**

Poster, Peter Max, Love, psychedelic, sgn/#d, 38x25" 230.00
Ring/jewelry holder, girl w/drape figural, SP, c USA, 9½" 150.00
Smoker's stand, blk Bakelite top/base, chrome band support 425.00
Table, Lucite legs/scrolled braces, copper mirror 24x14" top 300.00
Toothpick holder, stylized swan form, chrome, unmk 25.00
Torchiere, alabaster bowl on std w/4 scrolled ft, 65" 3,450.00
Torchiere, chrome base, 3 stacked flared rims, 19x6" 450.00
Torchiere, tapered mahog shaft w/vertical mirror panel 250.00
Torchieres, ribbed globe shade, chrome base, 67x14", pr 865.00
Tray, rvpt geometrics, metal fr w/wood hdls, 12x19", VG 300.00
Vase, copper, pk/wine arches on silver, Faure/Limoges, 6" 2,000.00
Vase, HP florals on yel matt, sgn Swultmont Belgium, 13" 350.00

Art Glass Baskets

A popular novelty and gift item during the Victorian era, these one-of-a-kind works of art were produced in just about any type of art glass in use at that time. They were never marked, since these were not true production pieces but 'whimsies' made by glassworkers to relieve the tedium of the long work day. Some were made as special gifts. The more decorative and imaginative the design, the more valuable the basket.

Amber w/cream & brn spatter, gold mica, amber hdl, 6½x4½" ..355.00
Amberina overshot, ruffled thorn hdl, 7½" dia 225.00
Amethyst to clear, fine ribs, ornate rim, thorn hdl, 8" 195.00
Bl, openwork rim, amber rope hdl, rectangular, 4½x5x6½" 135.00
Bl MOP Herringbone, yel int, melon ribs, S&W, 5x4" 275.00
Bl opal to vaseline, appl pk florals, vaseline hdl, 7x4" 165.00
Bl spangle o/l, clear rim & hdl, 4¾x5¾" 145.00
Cranberry, sq, clear ruffle, sq thorn hdl, 6x5½" 165.00
Cranberry o/l, reverse swirl, crimped 4-lobe rim, 7½x6½" 225.00

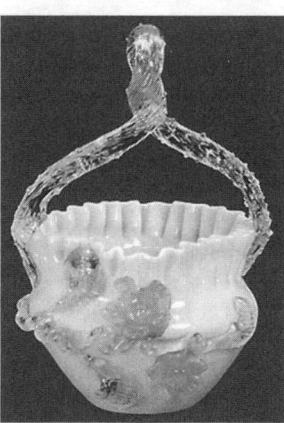

Creamy white with green twist handle, applied flowers and leaves, ruffled rim, 8½", $195.00.

Gr opal to red spatter, clear twist hdl, 6½x6" 150.00
Lemon yel to clear, Dmn Quilt, pk int, thorn hdl, 10x12" 225.00
Lime gr opal, ruffled, emb swirled ribs, clear hdl, 6½x6" 135.00
Mc spangle w/silver mica, clear hdl, 11x6½" 145.00
Pk MOP Herringbone, frosted hdl, mini 300.00
Pk o/l w/appl florals & amber leaves, amber hdl, 7½" 355.00
Pk opal, sq vaseline hdl, 5½" 140.00
Pk opal, 8-crimp rose bowl shape, 5⅜x4½" 115.00
Pk striped opal, appl flowers, vaseline twist hdl, 6x5" 165.00
Powder bl satin w/emb basketweave, satin thorn hdl, 5x7" 225.00
Rainbow, 4-color, cased, camphor trim, ruffled, 7x6" 800.00
Rainbow stripes, wht cased, twist hdl, 5½" W 250.00
Rainbow w/spangles, melon ribs, sqd/crimp rim, V hdl, 10x8" 900.00
Red Dmn Quilt, wht appl berries by clear hdl, 4 gr ft, 7" 425.00
Rose o/l, amber ruffle, amber crisscross hdl, 8x6¼" 215.00

Rose o/l, sq ruffled/hobnail rim, thorn hdl, 5x6½" 235.00
Rubena shaded w/wht spatter, scalloped, 6½" H 215.00
Spatter, emb shells, swirled crimp-rim collar, spatter hdl, 7" 260.00
Spatter, swirl ribs, ruffled 4-lobe rim, sq spatter hdl, 7x7" 210.00
Spatter, wht int, ruffled rim, clear thorn hdl, 5½x6¼" 175.00
Spatter on gr, gr thorn hdl, 6¼" L 185.00
Vaseline opal Dmn Quilt, appl spatter flowers, 7½" 225.00
Wht w/appl amber branch & 2 red cherries, ruffled, 6x3¾" 180.00
Wht w/rose int, crystal edge, thorn hdl, 9x9x10½" 245.00
Yel o/l satin, sq ruffled form, frosted braid hdl, 6" 155.00
Yel swirl, red int, red scalloped rim, 7x5½" 235.00

Art Nouveau

From the famous 'L'Art Nouveau' shop in the Rue de Provence in Paris, 'New Art' spread across the continent and belatedly arrived in America in time to add its curvilineal elements and asymmetrical ornamentations to the ostentatious remains of the Rococo revival of the 1800s. Nouveau manifested itself in every facet of decorative art. In glassware Tiffany turned the concept into a commercial success that lasted well into the second decade of this century and created a style that inspired other American glassmakers for decades. Furniture, lamps, bronzes, jewelry, and automobiles were designed within the realm of its dictates. Today's market abounds with lovely examples of Art Nouveau, allowing the collector to choose one or several areas that hold a special interest. Our advisor for this category is Steven Whysel; he is listed in the Directory under Arkansas. See also Bronzes; Galle; Jewelry; Loetz; Tiffany; Silver; specific manufacturers.

Ash stand, Secar, bronze, sea horse on hdl, fluted std, EX 250.00
Ashtray, Bergman, #5301, brass lily pad w/molded face 125.00
Cache pot, L Kann, gilt-bronze, leafy rim, rose-emb ft, 5½" 825.00
Candelabrum, Ceribelli, bronze, 5-arm, oak tree w/root base 985.00
Chandelier, 7-light, gilt bronze, tendril arms, 55x36" 5,400.00
Ewer, Marsch (att), ceramic w/nude hdl, emb grapevines, 18" ...690.00
Ewer, nude woman encircles top, mk Ernst Wahlis, 7" 700.00
Figure, lady holds skirt to form tray, bronze, 6½" 100.00
Lamp, Austrian, copper, tooled florals & red 'stones,' 16x10" .1,800.00
Lamp, bronze, maid by lg leafy flower w/burner atop, 23" 2,450.00
Lamp, bronze frog w/long arms lifts jeweled dome shade, 15" ..3,165.00
Lamp, gilt metal lady figural base, gr slag panel shade, 19" 165.00
Lamp, Le Faguays, maid-emb pnt/bronze base, alabaster shade ...750.00
Lamp, metal, lady stands beside flowering vine, 26" 300.00
Mirror, Argentor, behind head of SP metal maid std, 37" 2,875.00
Paperweight, bronze lizard figural, realistic, 1880s, 8¾" L 325.00
Plaque, bronzed metal, lady's profile, rtcl & scrollwork, 14" 100.00
Ring, 14k gold w/sm ruby lily pad flower 300.00
Sconce, brass, openwork/molded man's face, mirrored, 17", pr ...350.00
Seal, bronze bust of woman, cold pnt, 2½" 95.00
Vase, Bouval, cast bronze w/nudes & swirling water, 9x9" 865.00
Vase, bronze, nude holds bottle, appl grapes, 14" 500.00
Vase, Londe, bronze w/emb floral, slim w/long hdls, 8½" 250.00
Vase, nude on side w/flowers, Royal Dux, 15½" 800.00

Arts and Crafts

The Arts and Crafts movement began in England during the last quarter of the 19th century, and its influence was soon felt in this country. Among its proponents in America were Elbert Hubbard (see Roycroft) and Gustav Stickley (see Stickley). They rebelled against the mechanized mass production of the Industrial Revolution and against the cumulative influence of hundreds of years of man's changing taste.

They subscribed to a theory of purification of the styles: that designs be geared strictly to necessity. At the same time they sought to elevate these basic ideals to the level of accepted 'art.' Simplicity was their virtue; to their critics it was a fault.

The type of furniture they promoted was squarely built, usually of heavy oak, and so simple was its appearance that as a result many began to copy the style which became known as 'Mission.' Soon factories had geared production toward making cheap copies of their designs. In 1915 Stickley's own operation failed, a victim of changing styles and tastes. Hubbard lost his life that same year on the ill-fated *Lusitania*. Within the decade the style had lost its popularity.

Metalware was produced by numerous crafts people, from experts such as Dirk van Erp and Albert Berry to unknown novices. Prices for Arts and Crafts accessories rose dramatically in 1988, but by the beginning of 1991 leveled off and (in some cases) dropped. Metal items or hardware should not be scrubbed or scoured; to do so could remove or damage the rich, dark patina typical of this period. Our advisor for this category is Bruce Austin; he is listed in the Directory under New York. See also Furniture; Roycroft; Silver; Stickley; specific manufacturers.

Key: h/cp — hammered copper

Basket, J Hoffman, pnt metal w/sq grillwork, 10x3" 800.00
Basket, Van Erp, h/cp, tall w/riveted loop hdl, 13x5x6" 750.00
Basket, willow, vase shape, h/cp trim, 12x10" 225.00
Book holder, CW Faulkner, oak, pnt men on fold-down ends 80.00
Bookends, att Hurley, bronze, 1 lg+2 sm sea horses on book 550.00
Bookends, h/cp w/raised rnd center, no mk, 5¾x5" 50.00
Bookends, tooled leather, abstracts, rnded tops, 4½x7" 30.00
Bookends, Van Erp, stitched border, orig patina, 3½x4½" 300.00
Bowl, Dixon, h/cp, red/brn patina, 16½" 2,200.00
Bowl, Fred Brosi, h/cp, sgn, rfn, 2x13" 600.00
Bowl, fruit; Dixon, h/cp w/textured edge, rfn, 2½x9" 700.00
Bowl, Jarvie, h/cp, cleaned, 3¼x6½", VG 250.00
Bowl, Kalo, h/cp w/appl silver W, incurvate, 3½x8½", EX 1,000.00
Bowl, KSIA, h/cp w/emb maple leaf, flared, rfn, 6" 150.00
Bowl, Tudric, inscr band/rose bushes, hdls, 4½x12" 900.00
Box, Benedict (no mk), copper, 4 curly legs/hdl curves, 10" 150.00
Box, copper w/simple floral, wood lined, 3½x4½x3¼" 60.00
Box, ET Hurley, bronze w/2 cvd sea horses, sgn, 5" L 650.00
Box, Heintz, silver facing peacocks on bronze, wood int, 4" 200.00
Box, jewelry; McClelland Barclay, bronze, 3-D penguin, 8" L 375.00

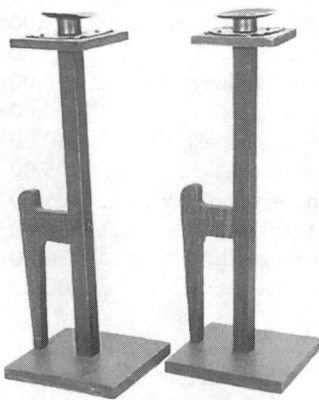

Candlesticks, Charles Rohlfs, brass bobeches riveted to oak platforms, branded mark, minor wear, 20½x7", $650.00 for the pair.

Candlestick, h/cp, 4 curved straps, 6-sided base, 8½x5" 200.00
Candlesticks, bronze, pencil std w/petal tops, 14½", pr 300.00
Candlesticks, ET Hurley, 2 sea horse arms, 12½", pr 800.00
Candlesticks, Karl Kipp, h/cp, 2 riveted straps as std, 8", pr 950.00
Chafing dish, Shreve Crump & Low, curled ft, tagged, 14", VG .. 250.00

Chocolate set, KPM, stylized floral, yel/gold/gr, sgn/#795 .... 600.00
Cigarette box/match safe set, Van Erp, h/cp, box 4" L 150.00
Coin purse, leather w/emb coat-of-arms, 3x3" 40.00
Firewood basket, Van Erp, h/cp, rfn, 20x18" 150.00
Flowerpot holder, Chas Rohlfs, h/cp, 3 tall legs, 8x7½" 400.00
Frame, h/cp & brass w/rivets & bl enamel, 11x9" 500.00
Frame, h/cp w/tooled florals at corners, wood bk, 6x4½" 450.00
Frame, hammered brass w/florals, 12x9" 125.00
Frame, Heintz, silver o/l geometrics on bronze, 3½x4¾" 125.00
Gong, h/cp w/blk geometric, leather straps, rfn, 9" 150.00
Jardiniere, Austrian, h/cp w/leaves, tall curved ft, 7x13" 200.00
Jardiniere, Van Erp, gr 'warty' patina, very rare, 11x12" 3,500.00
Jardiniere, Van Erp, h/cp, sides flare/braid hdls, 8x9", NM 800.00
Lamp, Benedict Studios, mica-panel shade, vase std, 20x21" .. 3,000.00
Lamp, desk; Van Erp, h/cp & brass, rfn, 16x17x7" 1,200.00
Lamp, Kopperkraft, h/cp, std: 4 twisted rods, 15x7" 900.00
Lamp, Prairie School, sq oak & slag glass shade w/metal o/l 650.00
Lamp, sq oak base, slag glass shade, 24x15x15" 425.00
Lamp, Van Erp, cone shade w/4 mica panels, bulbous base, 11" .. 4,500.00
Lamp, Van Erp, cone shade w/4 mica panels, trumpet base, 19" . 7,500.00
Match holder, Apollo Studios, hammered brass w/forest, 4x4" ... 125.00
Match holder, Frost, hammered brass w/appl windmill, 7x4" 70.00
Match holder, Van Erp, h/cp, 5" dia base, 3" 450.00
Mirror, oak, wall hanging, simple style, rfn, 29x35" 225.00
Pedestal, sq top, 4 long corbels at base, rfn, 27x12" 225.00
Pen tray, Craftsman, h/cp, emb/pnt holly, no mk, 9" 100.00
Pen tray, Van Erp, hammered brass, initials on lid, 14" L 375.00
Pie carrier, Van Erp, h/cp, 4-part scroll finial, new patina 1,000.00
Pillow, embr red roses/gr leaves on dk brn linen, 23x17" 200.00
Pillow, embr 3-color floral on blk, 13x18" 125.00
Pillow, Royal Society, att; 3-color floral/geometrics, 27x16" 250.00
Pitcher, Liberty & Co, hammered pewter w/bl enamel, 6", EX ... 275.00
Plant stand, Limbert, #244, bowed legs w/lower shelf, VG 1,500.00
Plate rack, oak, 2-shelf, card suits cutouts/shaped top, rfn 125.00
Print, woodblock; Ernest Watson, Last Load, 8½x11" 275.00
Print, woodblock; Eva Watson, Peony Decoration, 10x10" 200.00
Purse, Meeker, tooled leather w/strap, 8x5" 80.00
Spoon, baby's, silver w/cut-out hdl, 4" 80.00
Sugar cube rack, Kalo, sterling trough, rtcl, 7½" L 425.00
Table scarf, embr 3-color floral on ecru, fringe 74x32", EX 200.00
Tablecloth, embr wht lilies on wht, fringe, 33" dia, EX 350.00
Tongs, Kalo, hammered silver, 4½" 225.00
Travel kit, tooled leather case, compete, 10x8" 80.00
Tray, EA Brown, h/cp w/etched Miss Muffet, rfn, 12" 350.00
Tray, h/cp, riveted hdls, wavy edge, unsgn, 4x16x10" 175.00
Tray, h/cp w/acid-etched pine cone, no mk, 8" dia 100.00
Tray, Joseph Heinrich, h/cp w/silver border, 21" dia 900.00
Tray, Van Erp, h/cp, rim extensions w/raised hdls, 13" 500.00
Tray, Van Erp, h/cp w/emb closed hdls, rfn, no mk, 12x21" 600.00
Vase, Avon Coppersmith, h/cp, wide ruffle rim, 4½x5" 70.00
Vase, Dixon, h/cp, bulbous w/serrated edge, rfn, 3¾x4" 325.00
Vase, Dixon, h/cp w/lobe designs, rfn, 15x10" 1,900.00
Vase, Dixon, hammered brass, flared neck, rfn, 8x4" 400.00
Vase, h/cp, flared rim, shouldered, rfn, 12x5" 175.00
Vase, h/cp, rolled rim, lg hdls, no mk, 7¾x12" 150.00
Vase, Heintz, silver o/l cattail on bronze, 4¾x2½" 150.00
Vase, Heintz, silver o/l cattails, orig gr patina, 6x3" 250.00
Vase, Heintz, silver o/l floral branch, cylinder, rfn, 12x4" 300.00
Vase, Jarvie, ceramic, dk gr drip matt glaze, 6x6" 270.00
Vase, Jarvie, h/cp, flaring toward base, 9" 1,100.00
Vase, Karl Kipp, h/cp strap on sq base holds glass tube, 8" 300.00
Vase, Silvercrest, bronze w/gold finish & o/l, #8004, 10x5" 50.00
Vase, Silvercrest, silver o/l vines on bronze, incurvate, 12" 65.00
Vase, Tiesselinck, h/cp, GGI Expo sticker, 6½" 1,500.00

Vase, Van Erp, h/cp, cylindrical w/rolled rim, 5x9" 1,000.00
Vase, Van Erp, h/cp, rolled rim, San Fran mk, rfn, 3½x4½" 500.00
Wall planter, K Kipp, h/cp 4" copper pot, 12" stem hanger 100.00
Wastebasket, oak, 9-slat sides, flared, rfn, 22½x13x13" 225.00
Wastebasket, sq, 9 thin slats ea side, 4-point top, 17x11" 225.00
Whisk brush, in floral-emb leather case, 7½x3½" 40.00

Attwell, Mabel Lucie

Born in London in 1879, Mabel Lucie Attwell put her talent in illustration and design toward many outlets. Merchandise ranging from children's books and dinnerware, postcards, advertising, dolls, calendars, and greeting cards were marketed under her direction. She also designed a line of china called Nursery Ware for the Shelley China Company (see also Shelley). Our advisor for this category is David Ehrhard; he is listed in the Directory under California.

Book, Alice in Wonderland, L Carroll, Tuck & Sons, 12 plates..135.00
Calendar, Never Forget If the World Goes Wry...Standing By ..130.00
Figurine, BooBoo on a puppy, Shelley, 4"......................................300.00
Figurine, BooBoo w/mushroom...465.00
Figurine, Bride..625.00
Figurine, Little Mermaid...465.00
Figurine, Toddler, girl w/doll in hand, Shelley, from $600 to........800.00
Hanky set, Lucie Attwell Hanky Book...215.00
Nursery Ware, bowl, Look at This Wee Jolly...Shelley 195.00
Nursery Ware, plate, We've Just Come From..., oval, Shelley 235.00
Nursery Ware, teapot, flying plane scene & verse, Shelley..........150.00
Print, Evacuation of School Children...August 1939, from book..80.00
Print, Fairies Are Mischiefing Dorothy Dell, 4x6"..........................40.00
Print, Muvver's Pretty Pet 65.00
Tea set, mushroom house pot+BooBoo, creamer+toadstool sugar bowl.600.00

Austrian Glass

Many examples of fine art glass were produced in Austria during the time of Loetz and Moser that cannot be attributed to any glasshouse in particular, though much of it bears striking similarities to the products of both artists.

Basket, olive irid, clear hdl w/blossom prunts, 19" 230.00
Bowl, amethyst irid, ruffled, affixed to metal base, 5½" 300.00
Humidor, gr swirl on bright bl, 4 lg dents, rtcl silver mts 400.00
Vase, cobalt w/bl irid, amber rim wrap/ribbed hdls, 7½" 550.00
Vase, combed red/gold irid, rim trn down 3X, 13x6" 260.00
Vase, emerald gr w/appl gold threading, swollen cylinder, 9" 285.00
Vase, gold, 3-neck tree trunk, 4¾" 400.00
Vase, gr irid w/random int gr threading, 14x6" 345.00
Vase, irid loops/swags, rim w/4 3-D bronze bats, 8", EX 985.00
Vase, oil spots, gold-amber on clear, swollen cylinder, 10" 175.00
Vase, purple irid on diagonal ridges, dents, 4-lobe rim, 9" 285.00
Vase, silver o/l pond lilies/striations on bl irid, 5x4" 1,265.00
Vase, waves, purple/bl irid on lt yel, metal mt w/owls, 10" 635.00

Austrian Ware

From the late 1800s until the beginning of WWI, several companies were located in the area known at the turn of the century as Bohemia. They produced hard-paste porcelain dinnerware and decorative items primarily for the American trade. Today examples bearing the marks of these firms are usually referred to by collectors as Austrian ware, indicating simply the country of their origin. Of those various companies, these marks are best known: M.Z. Austria; Victoria, Carlsbad, Austria (Schmidt and Company); and O. & E.G. (Royal) Austria.

Though most of the decorations were transfer designs which were sometimes signed by the original artist, pieces marked Royal Austria were often hand painted and so indicated alongside the backstamp.

Of these three companies, Victoria, Carlsbad, Austria, is the most highly valued. Collectors should note that in our listings transfer decorations showing 'signatures' (sgn), such as 'Wagner,' 'Kauffmann,' 'LeBrun,' etc., were not actually painted by those artists but were merely based on their original paintings.

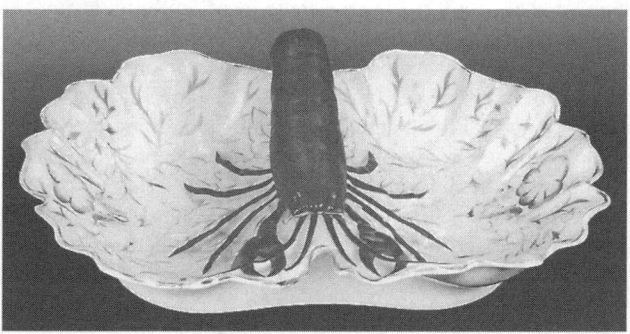

Lobster dish, red lobster forms center handle, gold trim, marked Victoria Carlsbad, 13", $175.00.

Bowl, violets etc, Schwartzburg, w/lid, 6½x5½" 55.00
Bust, serene maid, slate bl/lt gr w/gold, Doebrich, 14" 1,495.00
Centerpc, 2 maids, arms up, support rtcl basket, 2-pc, 15" 450.00
Creamer, dbl; bl HP cornflowers, MZ Austria 45.00
Figurine, seated lady, Wiener Werkstatte, rpr, 6½" 500.00
Fish set, gold trim/red rim, platter+8 plates+sauce w/tray 995.00
Hair receiver, roses 55.00
Hatpin holder, HP florals, 5½" 65.00
Plate, HP nasturtiums, artist sgn, 1907, 6", 9 for 120.00
Vase, appl 3-D nude in gold on bl/wht, Carlsbad, #1785, 9" 260.00
Vase, emb organic swirls, irid mc, hdls, Carlsbad, 3¾x5" 200.00
Vase, Nouveau lady w/flowers in relief, 6" 595.00
Vase, nude clings to rim of ovoid, rose/gr lustre, 4½" 275.00
Vase, rtcl/gilt leafy top/hdls, irid pillow body, Carlsbad, 9" 260.00

Autographs

Autograph collecting, also known as 'philography' or 'love of writing,' used to be a hobby shared by a few thousand dedicated collectors. But in recent years, autograph collecting has become a serious pursuit for more than 2,000,000 collectors worldwide. And in the past decade, more investors are adding rare and valuable autograph portfolios to their traditional investments. One reason for this sudden interest in autograph investing relates to the simple economic law of supply and demand. Rare autographs have a 'fixed' supply, meaning that unlike diamonds, gold, silver, stock certificates, etc., no more are being produced. There are only so many Abraham Lincoln, Marilyn Monroe, and Charles Lindbergh autographs available. In the meantime, it's estimated that more than 20,000 new collectors enter the market each year, thus creating an ever-increasing demand. Hence, the rare autographs generally rise steadily in value each year. Because of this scarcity, a serious collector will pay over $10,000.00 for a photograph signed by both Wilbur and Orville Wright, or as much as $25,000.00 for a handwritten letter of George Washington.

But by far, the majority of autograph collectors in the country do it for the love of the hobby. A polite letter and self-addressed, stamped envelope sent to a famous person will often bring the desired result. And occasionally one receives not only an autograph but a nice handwritten letter thanking the fan as well!

In terms of value, there are five general types of autographs: 1) mere signatures on an album page or card; 2) signed photographs; 3) signed documents; 4) typed letters signed; and 5) handwritten letters. The signatures are the least valuable, and handwritten letters the most valuable. The reasoning here is simple: with a handwritten letter, not only do you get an autograph but the handwritten message of the person as well. And this content can sometimes increase the value many times over. A handwritten letter of Babe Ruth thanking a fan for a gift might fetch a few thousand dollars. But if the letter were to mention Ruth's feelings on the day he retired, it could easily sell for $10,000.00 or more.

There are several major autograph collector organizations where members can exchange celebrity addresses or buy, sell, and trade their autographed wares. Philography can be a fun and rewarding hobby. And who knows! In ten or twenty years, those autographs you got for free could be worth a small fortune!

In the listings below, photos are assumed black and white unless noted color. Our advisor for autographs is Tim Anderson; he is listed in the Directory under Utah.

Key:
ADS — handwritten document signed
ALS — handwritten letter signed
ANS — handwritten note signed
AQS — autograph quotation signed
CS — counter signed
DS — document signed
ins — inscription
ISP — inscribed signed photo
LH — letterhead
LS — signed letter, typed or written by someone else
PLH — personal letterhead
sig — signature
SP — signed photo

Adams, John Quincy; ALS, re: widow's pension, 1844 ....**1,750.00**
Agassi, Andre; SP, color, 8x10" **35.00**
Ali, Muhammed; sig on card **25.00**
Ameche, Don; SP, sepia toned, 8x10" **50.00**
Anderson, John B; LS, views of Nixon's pardon, 8x10" **16.00**
Armstrong, Neil; SP, color, in space suit, 8x10" **265.00**
Ashe, Arthur; bold sig on card **27.50**
Astaire, Fred; ISP, blk/wht glossy, 8x10" **90.00**
Bacall, Lauren; SP, color portrait, 1940s **17.50**
Barnum, PT; ALS, re: travel plans, 1890, 1-pg **500.00**
Barrymore, Drew; SP, color, 8x10" **45.00**
Bassinger, Kim; SP, color, 8x10" **45.00**
Bernhardt, Sarah; AQS, 4 lines in French, 1881 ....**180.00**
Bird, Larry; SP, color, 8x10" **25.00**
Bolton, Michael; SP, color, 8x10" **50.00**
Bradshaw, Terry; SP, color, 8x10" **20.00**
Brinkley, Christy; SP, in swimsuit, 8x10" **20.00**
Budd, Zola; SP, color, 4x5" **8.00**
Burr, Aaron; ADS, signed cashier's check, Bank of Albany, 1800 ..**695.00**
Bush, George; ANS on personal card, 6x4" **200.00**
Carter, Jimmy & Rosalyn; SP, color, 8x10" **145.00**
Cash, Roseanne; ISP, color, 8x10" **17.50**
Checker, Chubby; ISP, blk/wht glossy, 8x10" **25.00**
Cobb, Ty; sig on personal check **455.00**
Coolidge, Calvin; sig on White House card, 2¾x4¼" **250.00**
Copperfield, David; SP, 4x5" **10.00**
Costner, Kevin; SP, color, 8x10" **60.00**
Davis, Bette; ISP, bold sig, early, blk/wht, 8x10" **75.00**
DeNiro, Robert; SP, color, Taxi Driver portrait **90.00**
DiMaggio, Joe; sig on vintage 3x5" card **75.00**

Dylan, Bob; SP, color, 8x10" **295.00**

Thomas Edison, cabinet photo signed with bold signature, Falk Photo, NY, EX, $550.00.

Edison, Thomas; DS, minutes of meeting, 1926 ....**650.00**
Edwards, Turk; sig on 3x5" card **125.00**
Eisenhower, Dwight D; LS on personal LH, re: party, 1963 ....**275.00**
Fairbanks, Douglas Jr; SP, blk/wht, early, 3½x5" **22.50**
Feinstein, Jeff; ALS, sending autograph, 1975, 1-pg **42.50**
Feller, Bob; sig on photo postcard in pitching pose **40.00**
Ford, Harrison; SP, color, 8x10" **125.00**
Gibson, Debbie; SP, color, 8x10" **22.50**
Grable, Betty; ISP, matt finish, 8x10" **110.00**
Gray, Coleen; SP, blk/wht glossy, 8x10" **22.50**
Griffey, Ken Jr; SP, color, 8x10" **35.00**
Harrison, Benjamin; ALS, hotel LH, 1899 ....**725.00**
Hearst, Patty; sig in book: Patty Hearst Her Own Story **45.00**
Holyfield, Evander; bold sig on card **15.00**
Horne, Lena; ISP, blk/wht glossy, 8x10" **20.00**
Jackson, Andrew; sig on eng vellum land grant, 1830s, EX **550.00**
Jackson, Michael; SP, color, 8x10" **225.00**
Jefferson Airplane, DS, publishing agreement, 1970 ....**365.00**
Johnson, Magic; SP, 8x10" in ball uniform **45.00**
Jordan, Michael; SP, color, 8x10" **75.00**
Kissinger, Henry; SP, color, 8x10" **22.50**
LaGuardia, Fiorello; LS, note of appreciation, 1933, 1-pg **70.00**
Letterman, David; SP, color, 8x10" **45.00**
Liszt, Franz; ALS in German, receipt of composition, 1880 .....**1,450.00**
Lombardi, Ernie; sign on 3x5" card **40.00**
Lombardi, Vince; sig on Packers' check **250.00**
Loren, Sophia; clipped bold signature matted w/topless print **40.00**
Lynn, Loretta; ISP, color, 8x10" **22.00**
Marino, Dan; SP, color, 8x10" **35.00**
Michener, James A; sig on card, 3x5" **37.50**
Miller, Henry; ANS, on personal stationery, 1978, 1-pg **225.00**
Olivier, Lawrence; sig on photo postcard, Clash of Titans **55.00**
Pauling, Linus; bold sig on 8x10" card **48.00**
Pickford, Mary; SP, sepia tone, 1920, 8x10" **88.00**
Prentis, Paula; SP, blk/wht glossy, 8x10" **18.00**
Quayle, Dan; sig on card **25.00**
Ray, James Earl; LS, from prison **150.00**
Rickenbacker, Eddie; sig on card, matted w/portrait, 1933 ....**80.00**
Robinson, Edward G; SP, closeup portrait **75.00**
Robinson, Sugar Ray; sig on magazine photo, 7½x4½" **65.00**
Roosevelt, Eleanor; LS, as First Lady, party plans, 1938 ....**180.00**
Roosevelt, Theodore; sig on 2½x3" card as Governor of NY **250.00**
Savich, Jessica; ISP, color, 8x10" **75.00**
Schiffer, Claudia; SP, in swimsuit, 8x10" **45.00**
Selleck, Tom; SP, color, in tuxedo, 8x10" **50.00**
Shatner, William; SP, as Captain Kirk **48.00**
Speilberg, Steven; SP, color, 8x10" **75.00**

Springsteen, Bruce; SP, color, 8x10" 100.00
Stanwyck, Barbara; SP, candid shot at home, 1940s 60.00
Taft, Wm H; sig on card 120.00
Thorpe, Jim; SP, 8x10" 1,200.00
Toscanini, Arturo; sig on 3x5" card 235.00
Youngman, Henny; ISP, 8x10" 18.00

Automobilia

While some automobilia buffs are primarily concerned with restoring vintage cars, others concentrate on only one area of collecting. For instance, hood ornaments were often quite spectacular. Made of chrome or nickel plate on brass or bronze, they were designed to represent the 'winged maiden' Victory, flying bats, sleek greyhounds, soaring eagles, and a host of other creatures. Today they often bring prices in the $75.00 to $200.00 range. R. Lalique glass ornaments go much higher!

Horns, radios, clocks, gear shift knobs, and key chains with company emblems are other areas of interest. Generally, items pertaining to the classics of the thirties are most in demand. Paper advertising material, manuals, and catalogs in excellent condition are also collectible.

License plate collectors search for the early porcelain-on-cast-iron examples. First year plates (e.g., Massachusetts, 1903; Wisconsin, 1905; Indiana, 1913) are especially valuable. The last of the states to issue regulation plates were South Carolina and Texas in 1917, and Florida in 1918. While many northeastern states had registered hundreds of thousands of vehicles by the 1920s making these plates relatively common, those from the southern and western states of that period are considered rare. Naturally, condition is important. While a pair in mint condition might sell for as much as $100.00 to $125.00, a pair with chipped or otherwise damaged porcelain may sometimes be had for as little as $25.00 to $30.00.

For more information we recommend *American Automobilia: An Illustrated History and Price Guide* by our advisors for this category, Jim and Nancy Schaut. They are listed in the Directory under Arizona. See also Gas Globes and Panels.

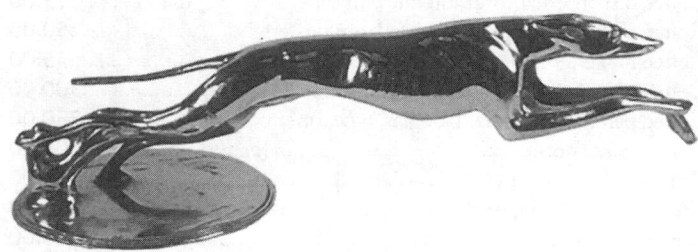

Hood ornament, Lincoln greyhound, chromed brass, 8¾" long, EX, $100.00.

Badge, chauffeur's, IA, 1941 ....16.00
Badge, chauffeur's, MO, 1914 ....130.00
Badge, chauffeur's, VA, 1931 ....40.00
Badge, chauffeur's, VT, 1927 ....30.00
Badge, Licensed Driver, PA, 1913 ....60.00
Blotter, Amoco, Rockwell illus, 1939, EX 24.00
Book, Automobile Quarterly, Summer 1968, 8½x10½" 12.00
Booklet, Kansas Motor Vehicle Laws, 1919 ....30.00
Box, Victor Tire Patches, mc pnt tin, counter-top type 275.00
Brochure, Hudson, color, 1932, 24-pg 35.00
Calendar, desk; Mobil, w/Pegasus 220.00
Calendar, perpetual; Chrysler Corp, logo on brass, '62, 2" sq 27.50
Catalog, Buick, 1942, 32-pg, 13½x9½" 60.00
Catalog, Cadillac, blk & wht, 1909, 32-pg, 6x9½", EX+ 145.00

Catalog, King Midget, blk & wht, 1968, 32-pg, 5x7" 16.00
Catalog, LaSalle, 1939, spiral bound, 28-pg, 12x9¼" 88.00
Catalog, Mercury, color, 1953, 28-pg, 6½x16" 27.50
Catalog, Oldsmobile, 1952, 16-pg, 11x8½" 30.00
Clock, Goodyear Tires, tire form 65.00
Compass, Taylor Navigator, self-illuminated, MIB 38.00
Folder, Desoto, color illus, 1950, 28x20" 7.50
Folder, Ford, color illus, 1920, 7½x20" 18.00
Gear shift knob, gr & cream swirl 50.00
Hood emblem, Frazer, enameled, 1948, M 65.00
Hood emblem, Hudson, 1949 ....90.00
Horn, Gesaco, 3 horns joined at stem, Germany, 15½" 35.00
Hub caps, Pontiac, chief's head in circle, 6½" dia, 4 for 85.00
Hub caps, Willys-Knight, 7¾" outside dia, NM, 5 for 125.00
Ink blotter, Have a Good Time on Time...w/Ford, 1920, 9x4" 25.00
Key holder, Dodge, emb early car on brn leather, 2¾x1½" 20.00
Key holder, Nash script, gr & wht plastic 8.00
Lapel pin, Henry Ford profile in gold, screw bk 55.00
Lapel pin, Studebaker, enameled birds & crown logo 37.50
License plate, motorcycle, MN, 1955, EX 40.00
License plate, motorcycle, WI, 1925 ....57.50
License plate, 1911, NY, lt rust 145.00
License plate, 1926, IA, pr 25.00
License plate attachment, Phillips 66 shield, Safety Pays 55.00
Light, side; Hupmobile 70.00
Magazine, Car Classics, Dec 1973, 82-pg, EX 3.00
Manual, Chevrolet owner's, 1951, 32-pg, M 12.00
Manual, Fiat owner's, 1974 Anniversary 8.00
Manual, Ford Mustang owner's, 1965, M 20.00
Manual, Ford owner's, 1951, lt wear on cover 12.00
Manual, Harley-Davidson owner's, 1941, M 85.00
Manual, Saab Model 93 owner's, 68-pg 18.00
Medallion, Ford Motor Co, brass, 30-yr 37.50
Opener, 1957 Chevrolet Sweet, Smooth & Sassy, bow-tie logo 22.00
Pail, Run Easy Axle Grease, tin, EX graphics 50.00
Pencil, mechanical; Dodge Plymouth logo, M 10.00
Pencil, mechanical; Ford-Mercury-Lincoln-Zephyr, V-8, 1940 .....22.50
Pin, lapel; Packard Work To Win wings award, mc enameling 55.00
Radiator cap, Chevrolet, eagle, 1932 ....85.00
Radiator cap, Chevrolet, Viking, 1929 ....185.00
Radiator cap, Mack Truck, NP bulldog, 1930s 20.00
Running board steps, for Model A, aluminum, fancy logo 80.00
Spark plug, Bethlehem Five Point, used, EX 8.00
Spark plug, Champion Gas Engine Special, NMIB 20.00
Spark plug, Wizard Twin Fire, MIB 5.00
Steering wheel knob, simulated Roman coin in center 15.00
Tie bar, General Motors Suggestion Plan, 25 Years 12.00
Tie clasp, Exxon 10.00
Tire gauge, Peerless gold eagle w/raised wings logo, dial type 88.00
Tire gauge, Pierce-Arrow, Schrader, tubular, NP brass, EX 150.00
Token, Chevrolet, Free Winter Inspection, bow-tie logo 6.50
Tool check, Fordson 17.50
Valve grinder, Model T Ford, EX 38.00
Watch chain, Dodge Bros, enamel & gold 88.00
Windshield scraper, 1957 Pontiac 5.00
Wrench, Ford script 8.00

Autumn Leaf

In 1933 the Hall China Company designed a line of dinnerware for the Jewel Tea Company, who offered it to their customers as premiums. Although you may hear the ware referred to as 'Jewel Tea,' it was officially named 'Autumn Leaf' in the 1940s. In addition to the dinnerware, frosted Libbey glass tumblers, stemware, and a Melmac service with the orange and gold bittersweet pod were available over the years, as were tablecloths, plastic covers for bowls and mixers, and metal items such as cake safes, hot pads, coasters, wastebaskets, and canisters. Even shelf paper and playing cards were made to coordinate. In 1958 the International Silver Company designed silverplated flatware in a pattern called 'Autumn' which was to be used with dishes in the Autumn Leaf pattern. A year later, a line of stainless flatware was introduced. These accessory lines are prized by collectors today.

One of the most fascinating aspects of collecting the Autumn Leaf pattern has been the wonderful discoveries of previously unlisted pieces. Among these items are two different bud-ray lid one-pound butter dishes; most recently a one-pound butter dish in the 'Zephyr' or 'Bingo' style; a miniature set of the 'Casper' salt and pepper shakers; coffee, tea, and sugar canisters; a pair of candlesticks; an experimental condiment jar; and a covered candy dish. All of these china pieces are attributed to the Hall China Company. Other unusual items have turned up in the accessory lines as well and include a Libbey frosted tumbler in a pilsner shape, a wooden serving bowl, and an apron made from the oilcloth (plastic) material that was used in the 1950s tablecloth. These latter items appear to be professionally done, and we can only speculate as to their origin. Collectors believe that the Hall items were sample pieces that were never meant to be distributed.

Hall discontinued the Autumn Leaf line in 1978. At that time the date was added to the backstamp to mark ware still in stock in the Hall warehouse. A special promotion by Jewel saw the reintroduction of basic dinnerware and serving pieces with the 1978 backstamp. These pieces have made their way into many collections. Additionally, in 1979 Jewel released a line of enamel-clad cookware and a Vellux blanket made by Martex which were decorated with the Autumn Leaf pattern. They continued to offer these items for a few years only, then all distribution of Autumn Leaf items was discontinued.

It should be noted that the Hall China Company has produced several limited edition items for the National Autumn Leaf Collectors Club (NALCC): a New York-style teapot (1984); an Edgewater vase (1987, different than the original shape); candlesticks (1988); a Philadelphia-style teapot, creamer, and sugar set (1990); a tea-for-two set and a Solo tea set (1991), a donut jug, and a large oval casserole. New items for the NALCC include: small ball jug, 1-cup French teapot, and a set of four chocolate mugs. The NALCC has also given their club members special items over the past few years made for them by Hall China: a sugar packet holder, a chamberstick, and an oyster cocktail. Other items are scheduled for production. All of these are plainly marked as having been made for the NALCC and are appropriately dated. A few other pieces have been made by Hall as limited editions for an Ohio company, but these are easily identified: the Airflow teapot and the Norris refrigerator pitcher (neither of which was previously decorated with the Autumn Leaf decal), a square-handled beverage mug, and the new-style Irish mug. A production problem with the square-handled mugs halted their production. The company then issued a regular conic-style mug with a round handle. Additional items available now are a covered onion soup, tall bud vase, china kitchen memo board, and egg drop-style salt and pepper shakers with a mustard pot. They have also issued a deck of playing cards and Libbey tumblers.

Our advisor for this category is Gwynne Harrison; she is listed in the Directory under California.

Baker, oval, Fort Pitt	150.00
Batter bowl, Saf-Hdl	2,500.00
Bean pot, 1-hdl	800.00
Bean pot, 2-hdl, 2¼-qt	225.00
Bowl, cereal; 6"	10.00
Bowl, coupe soup	12.00
Bowl, cream soup; 2-hdl	30.00
Bowl, fruit; 5½"	6.00
Bowl, metal, enamelware, set of 3	450.00
Bowl, mixing; set of 3: 6¼", 7½", 9"	65.00
Bowl, Royal Glas-Bake, set of 4	100.00
Bowl, salad	20.00
Bowl, stackette; set of 3: 18-oz, 24-oz, 34-oz, w/lid	75.00
Bowl, vegetable; divided, 10½"	90.00
Bowl, vegetable; oval, w/lid, 10"	50.00
Bowl, vegetable; oval, 10½"	15.00
Bowl, vegetable; rnd, 9"	90.00
Bowl cover set, plastic, 8-pc: 7 assorted covers in pouch	50.00
Bread box, metal	350.00
Butter dish, 1-lb	450.00
Butter dish, ¼-lb	150.00
Butter dish, ¼-lb, Square Top, rare	1,000.00
Butter dish, ¼-lb, Wings	1,400.00
Cake plate, 9½"	12.00
Cake safe, metal, motif on top & sides, 5"	35.00
Cake safe, metal, side decor only, 4½x10½"	30.00
Cake stand, metal base, orig box	175.00
Candy dish	400.00
Canister, metal, rnd, w/coppertone lid, set of 4	200.00
Canister, metal, rnd, w/ivory plastic lid	10.00
Canister, metal, rnd, w/matching lid, 6"	15.00
Canister, metal, rnd, w/matching lid, 7"	25.00
Canister, metal, rnd, w/matching lid, 8¼"	35.00
Canister, metal, sq, set of 4: 8½" & 4½"	175.00
Casserole, Royal Glas-Bake, deep, w/clear glass lid	25.00
Casserole, Royal Glas-Bake, shallow, w/clear glass lid	20.00
Casserole, Tootsie-hdl, w/lid	22.00
Casserole/souffle, swirl, 3-pt	15.00
Casserole/souffle, 10-oz	10.00
Casserole/souffle, 2-pt	85.00
Cleanser can, metal, sq, 6", M	700.00
Clock, orig works	400.00
Coaster, metal, 3⅛"	4.00
Coffee dispenser/canister, metal, wall type, 10½x19" dia	175.00
Coffee maker, 5-cup, all china, w/china insert	250.00
Coffee maker, 9-cup, w/metal dripper, 8"	35.00
Coffee percolator, electric, all china	300.00
Coffee percolator/carafe, Douglas, w/warmer base, MIB	250.00
Cookie jar, Tootsie	200.00
Creamer, New Style	8.00
Creamer, Old Style, 4¼"	15.00
Cup & saucer	8.00
Cup & saucer, St Denis	22.00
Custard cup	4.00
Flatware, silverplate, ea	30.00
Flatware, stainless, ea	25.00
Fruit cake tin, metal	10.00
Golden Ray base, to use w/candy dish or cake plate, pr	50.00
Gravy boat	18.00
Hot pad, metal, red or gr felt-like bking, rnd	15.00
Hot pad, oval	12.00
Hurricane lamp, Douglas, w/metal base, pr	400.00
Kitchen utility chair, metal	450.00
Marmalade jar, 3-pc	55.00
Mixer cover, Mary Dunbar, plastic	50.00
Mug, beverage	55.00
Mug, Irish coffee	95.00
Mustard jar, 3½"	55.00
Napkin, ecru muslin	35.00
Pickle dish or gravy liner, oval, 9"	18.00
Picnic thermos, metal	325.00

Pie baker, 9½" 18.00
Pitcher, utility; 2½-pt, 6" 15.00
Place mat, paper, scalloped 25.00
Place mat, set of 8, M in orig package 325.00
Plate, 10" 12.00
Plate, 6" or 7", ea 4.00
Plate, 8" 8.00
Plate, 9" 10.00
Platter, 11½" 15.00
Platter, 13½" 18.00
Playing cards, regular or Pinochle, dbl deck 160.00
Range set, shakers & covered drippings jar 35.00
Sauce dish, serving; Douglas, Bakelite hdl 150.00
Shakers, Casper, pr 18.00
Shakers, range, hdl, pr 18.00
Sugar bowl, New Style 12.00
Sugar bowl, Old Style, 3½" 18.00
Tablecloth, cotton sailcloth w/gold stripe, 54x54" 100.00
Tablecloth, cotton sailcloth w/gold stripe, 54x72" 110.00
Tablecloth, ecru muslin, 56x81" 300.00
Tablecloth, plastic 150.00
Teakettle, metal enamelware 200.00
Teapot, Aladdin 38.00
Teapot, long spout, 7" 45.00

Teapot, Newport shape, rectangular lid, 7¾", $185.00.

Teapot, Newport, dtd 1978 ....150.00
Toaster cover, plastic, fits 2-slice toaster 25.00
Towel, dish; pattern & clock motif 45.00
Towel, tea; cotton, 16x33" 35.00
Trash can, metal, red 250.00
Tray, glass, wood hdl, 19½x11¼" 95.00
Tray, metal, oval 55.00
Tray, red w/allover red & yel design, red border 65.00
Tray, tidbit; 2-tier 75.00
Tray, tidbit; 3-tier 100.00
Tumbler, Brockway, 13-oz 30.00
Tumbler, Brockway, 16-oz 35.00
Tumbler, Brockway, 9-oz 35.00
Tumbler, frosted, 14-oz, 5½" 12.00
Tumbler, frosted, 9-oz, 3¾" 30.00
Tumbler, gold frost etched, flat, 10-oz 40.00
Tumbler, gold frost etched, flat, 15-oz 50.00
Tumbler, gold frost etched, ftd, 10-oz 60.00
Tumbler, gold frost etched, ftd, 6½-oz 45.00
Vase, bud; 6" 175.00
Warmer base, oval 150.00
Warmer base, rnd 110.00
Warmer base, rnd, w/4 orig candles, orig mk box 125.00

Aviation

Aviation buffs are interested in any phase of flying, from early developments with gliders, balloons, airships, and flying machines to more modern innovations. Books, catalogs, photos, patents, lithographs, ad cards, and posters are among the paper ephemera they treasure alongside models of unlikely flying contraptions, propellers and rudders, insignia and equipment from WWI and WWII, and memorabilia from the flights of the Wright Brothers, Lindbergh, Earhart, and the zeppelins. See also Militaria. Our advisor for this category is John R. Joiner; he is listed in the Directory under Georgia.

Badge, Alaska Flight Attendant, gold-tone metal w/enamel, 1" ...**20.00**
Badge, cap; Western Airlines, wings w/W center, silvered, 2¼" ...**75.00**
Badge, celluloid button shows blimp, 2" tin airship below **65.00**
Badge, hat; Airline Freight Line Inc, silver-tone eagle, 2½" **35.00**
Badge, hat; Am Eagle, wht metal, 1¼" **45.00**
Badge, hat; Northwest Airlink Airlines, gold-tone w/red, 1½" **45.00**
Coffee mug, Burlington Air Express **6.00**
Coffee mug, Seko Air Freight **6.00**
Golf ball, Flying Tigers logo, M **4.00**
Highball, Continental Airlines, clear glass, 3" **5.00**
Photo, Lindbergh, blk & wht, NP brass fr, 2¼x2¾" **95.00**
Pin, lapel; Douglas Aircraft 10-Year Service, gold filled **25.00**
Pin-bk, Amelia Erhart's Frendship, Bond Bread, 1½" **15.00**
Pin-bk, Boeing 5 Years' Service, 10k gold top, ½" **35.00**
Pin-bk, Gone Again, blk & wht photo of Corrigan, 1¼" dia **25.00**
Pin-bk, Lindbergh, bust portrait, Hero of 1927, EX **35.00**
Pin-bk, Lindbergh, Pride of USA, celluloid, 1¼" dia **25.00**
Pin-bk, 1960 United DC-8 Inaugural Flight, sterling, VG **15.00**
Plaque, United Airlines 100,000 Miles, 1956, M **35.00**
Plate, Lindbergh 1927 commemorative **50.00**
Program, National Air Race, Cleveland, 1931, EX **120.00**
Ring, Jr stewardess or pilot, American Airlines, early, ea **15.00**
Roly poly, United Air lines, oval logo on clear glass **5.00**
Ruler, ABC Air Freight, golden metal, M **9.00**
Sheet music, ...Uncle Sam Takes Hat Off, Lindbergh photo **25.00**
Sherbet, Western Airlines, clear & frosted glass, ftd, 3¼x3½" **6.00**
Souvenir, zeppelin shape cut from actual fabric covering, 7" **35.00**
Tapestry, Lindy/plane, Statue of Liberty etc, French, 54x19" **250.00**
Timetable, American Airlines, packet & maps, 1955 ....**20.00**
Travel kit, Ozark Airlines, M **6.00**
Trophy, Cessna 1st Solo Flight, metal figure on wood base, '60s ..**30.00**
Tumbler, water; Mexicana, clear glass, 4½" **5.00**
Wine, Braniff, clear glass, stemmed, 5½" **5.00**
Wings, Braniff Airlines, gold-tone wings, 3" L **55.00**
Wings, Continental Airlines, SP w/enameling, 3½" **40.00**

Avon

The California Perfume Company, the parent of the Avon Co., was founded in 1886. Although an 'Avon' line was introduced by the company in the mid-twenties, not until 1939 did it become known as Avon Products, Inc. Collectible Avon items include not only figural bottles and jars but jewelry, awards, product samples, magazine ads, and catalogs as well. For more information concerning the Avon Collectors Club, see the Clubs, Newsletters, and Catalogs section of the Directory. See also California Perfume Company.

For more information, we recommend *Hastin's Avon Collector's Price Guide, 14th Edition,* by Bud Hastin.

Avon Talc for Men, sq tin, 1928 ....**35.00**

Mini perfumes: Gardenia, Sweet Pea, Cotillion, and Trailing Arbutis, front labels and blue caps, each 1¾", in miniature hat box marked Fair Lady, NM, $60.00.

Avon Trio Set, 1934 ....100.00
Bath Duet, Daphne Talc & Bath Salts, 1939 ....50.00
Colonial Set, 1 dram perfume & face powder, 1939 ......75.00
Commodore Set, 1934, 3-pc, boxed 75.00
Country Club Set, 1940, boxed 75.00
Facial Set, 1935, 5-pc 100.00
Gift Set, face powder & perfume, 1936 ....100.00
Hair Treatment Set for Women, 1931-35, 4-pc 150.00
Jaguar, 1973 ....5.00
Jolly Holly Day Men's Set, 1963, 3-pc 10.00
Little Doll Set, doll, cologne, lipstick & lotion, 1954 ......100.00
Little Folks Gift Box, 4 perfumes, 1932 ....200.00
Men's Traveling Set, 1944, 5-pc 100.00
Miss Fluffy Puff Cologne & Powder Set, 1954 ....50.00
Olympic Men's Set, 1946-49, 3-pc 100.00
Perfume Handkerchief Set, 1934-36, M in Christmas box 135.00
Petal of Beauty Orchard Blossom Set, 1942 ....100.00
Strawberry Bath Foam Pitcher, ruby red, 1971, 4-oz 7.00
Swan Lake Body Powder, 1947, 9-oz 30.00
Young Hearts Bubble Bath, w/cat head, 1952 ....50.00

Baccarat

The Baccarat Glass company was founded in 1765 near Luneville, France, and continues to this day to produce quality crystal tableware, vases, perfume bottles, and figurines. The firm became famous for the high-quality millefiori and caned paperweights produced there from 1845 until about 1860. Examples of these range from $300.00 to as much as several thousand. Since 1953 they have resumed the production of paperweights on a limited edition basis. Our advisors for this category are Randall Monsen and Rod Baer; their address is listed in the Directory under Virginia. See also Bottles, Commercial Perfume; Paperweights.

Bottle, scent; metal filigree bands w/Grecian ladies, 6" 125.00
Bottle, scent; Rose Tiente Sunburst, 6x2½" 70.00
Bottle, scent; Rose Tiente Swirl, swirl stopper, 6¾x2¾" 65.00
Candelabra, 5-arm, silver knop, spear prisms, att, 26", pr 1,800.00
Candlesticks, leaf shaft w/ladybug, snake at base, 8½", pr 425.00
Champagne flute, Prestige, 24k gold decor, 9¼", M, pr 600.00
Compote, canary yel, Swirl, 2¼x5¾" 60.00
Compote, pk, swirled w/gilt rim, 2¼x5¾" 75.00
Cruet, Rose Tiente Swirl, matching stopper, 10¼x5" 225.00
Dresser set, Rose Tiente Swirl, 2 bottles+ring tree+box+tray 350.00
Ice bucket, Rose Tiente Swirl, bronze rim & bail hdl, 5¼" 325.00
Sculpture, City, 9½x7" 565.00
Sculpture, Crouching Panther, 21", +display case/wood crate .8,000.00
Sculpture, Iceberg, gr glass, sgn/dtd 1969-25, 12x11" 800.00
Tumbler, Harcourt, 5¼" 50.00
Vase, Fr opal w/HP children, sgn, 15x7" 300.00
Vase, kite-shape facets front & bk, Paris Expo 1937, 10x10" ...1,150.00
Vase, thick walls, octagonal bucket form, modern, 9x8" 345.00

Wine, Colbert, 5⅛" 65.00
Wine decanter, Rose Tiente Swirl, swirl stopper, 11x5" 195.00

Badges

The breast badge came into general usage in this country about 1840. Since most are not marked and styles have changed very little to the present day, they are often difficult to date. The most reliable clue is the pin and catch. One of the earliest types, used primarily before the turn of the century, involved a 't-pin' and a 'shell' catch. In a second style, the pin was hinged with a small square of sheet metal, and the clasp was cylindrical. From the late 1800s until about 1940, the pin and clasp were made from one continuous piece of thin metal wire. The same type, with the addition of a flat back plate, was used a little later. There are exceptions to these findings, and other types of clasps were also used. Hallmarks and inscriptions may also help pinpoint an approximate age.

Badges have been made from a variety of materials, usually brass or nickel silver; but even solid silver and gold were used for special orders. They are found in many basic shapes and variations — stars with five to seven points, shields, disks, ovals, and octagonals being most often encountered. Of prime importance to collectors, however, is that the title and/or location appear on the badge. Those with designations of positions no longer existing (City Constable, for example) and names of early western states and towns are most valuable.

Badges are among the most commonly-reproduced (and faked) types of antiques on the market. At any flea market, ten fakes can be found for every authentic example. Genuine law badges start at $30.00 to $40.00 for recent examples (1950-1970); earlier pieces (1910-1930) usually bring $50.00 to $90.00. Pre-1900 badges often sell for more than $100.00. Authentic gold badges are usually priced at a minimum of scrap value (karat, weight, spot price for gold); fine gold badges from before 1900 can sell for $400.00 to $800.00, and a few will bring even more. A fire badge is usually valued at about half the price of a law badge from the same time and material. Our advisor for this category is Gene Matzke; he is listed in the Directory under Wisconsin.

Alaskan US Marshal, NP w/eagle & scrollwork border, 1920s, EX ...125.00
Austin Patrol Service, eagle atop shield, enamel/silver metal 30.00
Central Truck Lines, arrowhead shape, orange/blk enamel 20.00
Chief of Police, Thompson CT, eagle atop rnd shield, EX 60.00
City of NY Auxilliary Police Patrolman, pierced NP, 1960s 40.00
Confederate Reunion, bronze, 3-pc, dtd 1895 & 1896 ....175.00
Deputy Constable, CO, brass, 6-point star, sm 25.00
Deputy Sheriff, Laramie, 5-point star, silver metal 25.00
Deputy Sheriff, NJ, NP shield w/eagle atop, 1950s, EX 50.00
Detective Sergeant Chicago, star, presentation, '20s, EX in box ...165.00
Federal US Police Officer, bl letters, hollow, 2-pc 160.00
NYC Police, NP star w/scrolled inscription/copper #16, 1940s 80.00
Police, NP octagon w/blk letters, pin-bk, 1920s, EX 75.00
Private Detective, pierced NP shield w/center star, 1920s, EX 40.00
Security Officer, PA, NP eagle atop shield, mc enamel, 1980s, M ..20.00
Special Police, Indianapolis IN, 1950, M 30.00
Special Police, SP brass star w/blk enamel, 1930s, 2½" 45.00
Sterling Secret Service Police, NP shield, pin-bk, EX 175.00
Toledo Newsboy's Assoc, NP shield, 1912 ....20.00

Banks

This year the continuing impact of auctions shows in the listings. Again, condition is what is driving the market. The spread between a bank in good condition and an excellent or original condition example continues to widen. It is imperative that you realize the importance of paint and the completeness of a bank. Also some banks have a wide margin of value based on color variations. It becomes more and more important that you attend as many shows and auctions as possible. Direct contact with collectors and knowledgeable dealers is the only way you can get a feel for prices and the desirability of banks, both mechanical and still. Banks continue to hold their value. However, it is becoming extremely important for collectors to understand the market.

Let's take a look at the price variations possible on an Uncle Sam mechanical bank. If you find one with considerable paint missing but with some good color showing, the price would be around $1,000.00. If it has repairs or restoration, the value would drop to something like $800.00 or less. If you had another example, and it had two thirds of its original paint and no repairs, it would be priced around $1,800.00. One with minor nicks and 90% of the original paint could go as high as $3,500.00. Or if you find one that is in near-original paint and has no repairs, $5,000.00 would not be out of line. This should help you see what causes price variations. After considering all of these factors, remember the final price is always determined by what a willing buyer and seller agree on for a specific bank.

The category of mechanical banks is unique. Along with cast-iron toys, they are among the most outstanding products of the Industrial Revolution and are recognized as some of the most successful of the mass-produced products of the 19th century. The earliest mechanicals were made of wood or lead; but when John Hall introduced Hall's Excelsior, a cast-iron mechanical bank, it was an immediate success. J. & E. Stevens produced the bank for Hall and soon began to make their own designs. Several companies followed suit, most of which were already in the hardware business. They used newly developed iron-molding techniques to produce these novelty savings devices for the emerging toy market. Mechanical banks reflect the social and political attitudes of the times, racial prejudices, the excitement of the circus, and humorous everyday events. Their designers made the most of simple mechanics to produce banks with captivating actions that served not only to amuse but to promote the concept of thrift among children. The quality of detail in the castings are truly remarkable. The most collectible examples were made during the period of 1870 to 1900; however, they continued to be made until the early days of World War II. J. & E. Stevens, Shepard Hardware, and Kyser and Rex are some of the more well-known manufacturers; most made still banks as well.

Still banks are widely collected, and you can literally choose from thousands of banks. No one knows exactly how many different banks were made, but at least three thousand have been identified in the various books published on the subject. Cast-iron examples still dominate the market, but the lead banks from Europe are growing in value. Tin and early pottery banks are drawing more interest as well. American pottery banks which were primarily collected by Americana collectors are becoming more important in the still bank field. This market has not been as volatile as the mechanical banks, but the number of collectors is growing. The auction market on still banks is not as extensive as with the mechanicals, but some nice examples do turn up. Collectors and dealers are still the best source.

Book of Knowledge Banks were produced by John Wright (Pennsylvania) from circa 1950 until 1975. Of the thirty models they made during those years, a few continued to be made in very limited numbers until the late 1980s; these they referred to as the 'Medallion' series. (Today the Medallion banks command the same prices as the earlier Book of Knowledge series.) Each bank was a handcrafted, hand-painted duplicate of an original as was found in the collection of The Book of Knowledge, the first children's encyclopedia in this country. Because the antique banks are often priced out of the range of many of today's collectors, these banks are being sought out as an affordable substitute for their very expensive counterparts.

As both value and interest continue on the increase, it becomes even more important to educate one's self to the fullest extent possible. We recommend these books for your library: *The Dictionary of Still Banks* by Long and Pitman, *The Penny Bank Book* by Moore, and *The Bank Book* by Norman. If you are primarily interested in mechanicals, *Penny Lane*, a book by Davidson, is considered the most complete reference available. It contains a cross reference listing of numbers from all other publications on mechanical banks.

In the listings that follow, banks are identified by L for Long, G for Griffith, M for Moore, N for Norman, D for Davidson, and W for Whiting.

Our advisors for this category are Diane Patalano, listed in the Directory under New Jersey, and Dan Iannotti (for Book of Knowledge), listed under Michigan.

Key:
CI — cast iron   NPCI — nickel-plated cast iron
EPCI — electroplated cast iron

Advertising

Admiral Appliance, Admiral figure, vinyl, 1980s, 7", MIB 50.00
Boker Coffee, can shape, tin, 1970s, NM 15.00
Burma Shave, tin & glass, 1920s 50.00
Chocolate Cow, cow pnt on tin 40.00
Count Chocula, vinyl 40.00
Crown Premium Motor Oil, can shape, 3", EX 18.00
Del Monte, clown figure, 1985, EX 28.00
Donald Duck Orange Juice, Donald litho, cb/metal, 4", NM 5.00
Esso Tiger, gr plastic, bust form, M 40.00
Frisch's Big Boy, boy figure, vinyl, 1973, 9", EX 28.50
General Mills Cinnamon Toast Crunch Cereal, plastic, musical ..12.00
Hamm's Beer, bear figural, ceramic, 1980s, 11", M 25.00
Heinz 57, 1913 Model-T van form, metal, Ertl, 1970s, NMIB 75.00
Hershey's Syrup, can shape, pottery, silver/brn pnt, NM 50.00
Hush Puppy, dog figural, plastic 20.00
Kool-Aid, pitcher form, plastic, mechanical, 1970s, 7" 25.00
Lennox Furnace Co, Lennie Lennox, ceramic, 1949, 7½" 150.00

Metz Premium Beer, keg form, ceramic, brown and black with red and white lettering, 6¼x4½", EX, $25.00.

Nash Mustard, Donald Duck figure, pnt glass, tin lid, 4½" 95.00
Nestle Quik, Bunny Money 15.00
Oscar Mayer Weiner Mobile, M 45.00
Pepto Bismol, bug form, soft plastic, 7½" 65.00
Starkist, Charlie Tuna on coins, tuna can base, ceramic, 9½" 20.00
Sunmaid Raisins, raisin figure, hard vinyl, CALRAB, 1987, EX ...50.00
Taco Bell, bus form, M 15.00
Tootsie Roll, Tootsie Roll shape, tin & cb, EX 15.00
Trop-Artic All-Weather Motor Oil, can shape, shield logo, EX ...12.00
Wonder Bread, loaf shape, mini, G 35.00

Book of Knowledge Banks

Always Did 'Spise a Mule, B-39, jockey, M **265.00**
Always Did 'Spise a Mule, B-40, boy on bench, M **395.00**
Bulldog Bank, B-85, EX/NM **220.00**
Cabin Bank, B-65, NM **385.00**
Creedmoor Bank, B-54, NM **375.00**
Leap Frog, B-179, Special Medallion series, NM **395.00**
Milking Cow, B-44, NM **335.00**
Owl, B-32, turns head, unique colors, M **295.00**
Paddy & the Pig, B-137, NM **385.00**
Tammany Bank, B-149, NM **250.00**
Uncle Remus, B-5, Blk cop chases Remus into hen house, NM .**395.00**
Uncle Sam, B-19, EX **250.00**
US & Spain, B-97, w/orig cannonball, NM **295.00**
World's Fair, B-3, bronze, M **425.00**

Mechanical

Acrobat, J&E Stevens, pnt CI, kicks clown's head, EX **7,500.00**
Always Did 'Spise a Mule, Stevens, pnt CI, boy on bench, VG+ ..**1,320.00**
Artillery Bank, Stevens, copper-pnt CI, soldier shoots, EX **745.00**
Bad Accident, Stevens, pnt CI, boy darts before cart, EX **1,200.00**
Boy on Trapeze, Barton & Smith, pnt CI, boy revolves, VG ...**1,425.00**
Bulldog, Stevens, pnt CI, glass eyes, swallows coin, EX **1,100.00**
Cabin, Stevens, pnt CI, Blk man at door of cabin, 3½", VG **415.00**

Chief Big Moon, painted cast iron, J. & E. Stevens, Pat. 1899, NM, $4,500.00.

Clown, Chein, tin litho, tongue receives coin, ca 1939, VG **75.00**
Clown on Globe, Stevens, pnt CI, tan base, 9", VG **2,100.00**
Darktown Battery, Stevens, pnt CI, 3 players on rectangle, EX ...**4,500.00**
Eagle & Eaglets, Stevens, pnt CI, oval base, EX **1,850.00**
Elephant Swings Trunk, Williams, pnt CI, trunk moves, G **60.00**
Football Park, Harper, pnt CI, player kicks coin into net, VG ..**2,550.00**
Frog on Rnd Base, Stevens, pnt CI, swallows, rolls eyes, VG **950.00**
Humpty Dumpty, Shepard Hdw, pnt CI, clown bust, 7½", VG+ ...**1,450.00**
Jolly 'N' Starkies, pnt aluminum, coin flips, eyes roll, NM **500.00**
Leap Frog, Shepard Hdw, pnt CI, VG **2,200.00**
Magic Bank, Stevens, pnt CI, door opens/reveals cashier, G **525.00**
Mason, Shepard Hdw, rpt CI, 2 bricklayers on base, G- **220.00**
Monkey & Coconut, Stevens, pnt CI, coin goes into coconut, EX+ ...**2,200.00**
Monkey Tips Hat, Chein, tin litho, EX **100.00**
Organ Bank, Kyser & Rex, pnt CI, boy & girl, 7½", VG **600.00**
Owl, Kilgore, pnt CI, slot in book, 1920s, EX **500.00**
Paddy & Pig, Stevens, coin flips into Paddy's mouth, 1885, G+ ..**1,500.00**
Pig in Highchair, Stevens, NPCI, pig catches/swallows coin, EX ..**770.00**
Rabbit in Cabbage, Kilgore, pnt CI, ca 1925, VG **155.00**

Santa Claus, Shepard Hdw, pnt CI, coin enters chimney, VG ..**1,650.00**
Stump Speaker, Shepard Hdw, pnt CI, Blk w/satchel, G+ **745.00**
Teddy & Bear, Stevens, pnt CI, coin is shot/bear appears, EX ..**2,850.00**
Trick Dog, Hubley, pnt CI, dog leaps through hoop, EX+ **600.00**
Trick Dog, N-5630A, CI, varnished pnt, rpl figure, 8¾" **165.00**
Uncle Remus, Kyser & Rex, Blk cop chases Remus, 1890s, G ..**2,400.00**
Uncle Tom, N-5760E, pnt CI, EX **850.00**
Vending Machine, Hatwig & Vogels/Flora, tin litho/glass, EX ...**900.00**
William Tell, N-5940, CI, worn mc pnt, no trap, 10½" **990.00**
Zoo, Kyser & Rex, pnt CI, lion, tiger & monkey, EX **1,200.00**

Registering

Bean Pot, M-951, 5¢ registering, pnt CI, NP top, 4", EX **175.00**
Liberty Dime Safe, pnt CI, 3", EX **225.00**
Little Orphan Annie, 10¢ registering, 1936, EX **300.00**
Lucky Savings, Am Can Co, tin litho cash register, 5", EX **35.00**
Pail, 1¢ register, M-912, pnt CI, 2¾", EX **350.00**
Park-O-Meter, Zell, plastic meter, 1950s, MIB **35.00**
Prince Valiant, 10¢ registering, c KFS, 1959, M **150.00**
Prudential, pnt CI, 25¢ registering, orig label, 7⅜", NM **425.00**
Save for Victory, 10¢ registering, pnt tin & wood, 4¾", EX **200.00**
Trunk, M-947 variant, 10¢ registering, pnt CI, 3¾", EX **90.00**
Wee Folks Money Box, tin litho, sq, English, 5" **60.00**

Still

Air Mail Bank on Base, M-848, pnt CI, 6⅜", EX **900.00**
Baseball on 3 Bats, M-1608, NP CI, 5¼", EX+ **1,800.00**
Battleship Maine, M-1440, CI, gold japanning & trim, 4¾", EX ..**300.00**
Battleship Oregon, M-1450, CI, brn japanning w/gold, 5" L, EX ..**330.00**
Bay Window Building, M-1213, CI, worn old rpt, 5" **475.00**
Bear Stealing Honey, M-1308, pnt CI, 7", EX **500.00**
Bear Stealing Pig, M-693, pnt CI, 5½", EX **1,100.00**
Beauty on Oval Base, M-514, pnt CI, 4¾", EX **300.00**
Billiken, M-76, pnt wht metal, 3¾", EX **150.00**
Billy Bounce, M-14, pnt CI, 4¾", EX **1,300.00**
Bird on Stump, M-664, pnt CI, 4¾", EX **550.00**
Black Boy in Straw Hat, M-172 variant, pnt aluminum, 5", EX ...**120.00**
Blackpool Tower, M-984, pnt CI, 7⅜", EX **375.00**
Boston Bull Terrior, M-421, pnt CI, 5¼", EX **300.00**
Boston Bulldog, M-413, pnt CI, 4⅜", EX **275.00**
Boxer Head, M-400, lead, 2⅝", EX **275.00**
Bulldog, M-396, CI, worn gold pnt, 4" **95.00**
Bungalow, M-999, pnt CI & tin, rpl bkplate, 3¾", EX **140.00**
Cabin w/Shake Roof, M-1024, pnt CI, hairline, 3⅜" **275.00**
Camel, M-767, pnt CI, 7¼", NM **400.00**
Camel Resting, M-770, pnt CI, 2½", EX **600.00**
Captain Kidd, M-38, pnt CI, rpl screw, 5⅝", EX **225.00**
Cat & Ball, M-352, CI, worn gold pnt, 5⅝" **270.00**
Chimney Slot, M-997, pnt CI, 2⅞", EX **550.00**
Christian Police Assoc Hat, M-1390, pnt tin, 4½", NM **105.00**
Circus Elephant, M-462, pnt CI, 3⅞", NM **285.00**
City Bank w/Teller, M-1099, pnt CI, 5¼", EX **525.00**
Clown w/Crooked Hat, M-210, pnt CI, rpr ft, 6¾", EX **375.00**
Clown w/Pointed Nose, M-233, pnt lead, 2⅞", NM **2,400.00**
Columbia, M-1070, pnt CI (worn), combo trap, 5¾" **325.00**
Columbia, M-1077, rpt CI, 7", EX **135.00**
Columbia Magic, M-1065, pnt CI, casting flaw, 5" **200.00**
Coon Bank (Man on Cotton Bale), M-37, pnt CI, no trap, 4⅞" ..**1,400.00**
Country Bank, M-1110, pnt CI, 4¼", EX **175.00**
Crosley Radio, M-820, CI & tin, red pnt, 4¼" **150.00**
Crown Bank, M-1226, pnt CI, 3", EX **90.00**
Crown Bank on Legs, M-1151, pnt CI, 4⅞", EX **3,300.00**

Cupola, M-1145, pnt CI, 5½", EX 375.00
Cupola, M-1146, pnt CI, mica flakes on roof, 4⅛", EX 150.00
Cupola, M-1147, pnt CI, 3¼", EX 250.00
Dime Barrel, M-921, pnt CI, 4", EX 200.00
Do You Know Me, M-75, CI, gold & red pnt, lt wear, 6" 275.00
Dog at Phonograph, M-386, pnt lead & tin, 3¾", NM 850.00
Dog w/Drum, M-389, pnt lead & tin, 1¾", NM 275.00
Dolphin, M-33, pnt CI, 4½", EX 800.00
Donkey, M-500, pnt CI, 6¼", EX 250.00
Duck on Tub, M-616, pnt CI, 5⅜", EX 250.00
Dutch Boy on Barrel, M-180, pnt CI, EX 175.00
Eiffel Tower, M-1074, pnt CI, 8¾", EX 750.00
Elephant on Wheels, M-446, pnt CI, 4⅛", EX 475.00
Elephant w/Howdah, M-474, CI, gold pnt, 4¾", EX 115.00
Elsie the Cow, M-538, pnt aluminum, 6¾", EX 130.00
Every Copper Helps, M-71, pnt CI, 4¾", EX 600.00
Fidelity Trust Vault, M-901, pnt CI, 4⅞" EX 500.00
Fidelity Trust Vault, M-902, pnt CI, 6½", NM 900.00
Flat Iron Building, M-1161, pnt CI, 5½", EX 165.00
Football Player, M-11, pnt CI, 5⅞", EX 425.00
Four-Tower Bank, M-1121, pnt CI, 5¾", EX 675.00
Gas Pump, M-1485, pnt CI, 6", EX 550.00
General Pershing, M-140, pnt CI (worn), 7¾", VG 80.00
Girl w/Lamb, M-164, CI, worn wht & red pnt, 4½" 525.00
Give Me a Penny, M-167, pnt CI, 5⅝", EX 575.00
Globe, M-765, CI, worn mc pnt, 4⅝" 140.00
Globe, M-812, pnt CI, 5", EX 190.00
Globe on Arc, M-789, pnt CI, 5¼", EX 175.00
Globe on Wire Arc, M-785, pnt CI, 4⅝", EX 135.00
Golliwog, M-85, pnt CI, 6¼", EX 500.00
Good Luck Horseshoe, M-508, pnt CI, 4¼", VG 200.00
Goodyear Zeppelin Hanger, M-1430, pnt aluminum, 2¼", NM ..375.00
GOP Deco Elephant, M-450, pnt CI, 4⅜", EX 375.00
Graf Zeppelin on Wheels, M-1431, CI, worn overpnt, 2¼" 170.00
Hall Clock, M-1540, pnt CI & tin, 5⅝", EX 350.00
Hen on Nest, M-546, CI, worn gold pnt, rpl screw, 3" 830.00
High Rise, M-1217, pnt CI, 5½", EX 200.00
Holstein Cow, M-544, pnt CI, 2½", EX 275.00
Home Bank, M-1019, pnt CI, 4", EX 450.00
Home Savings Bank, M-1126, pnt CI, 5⅞", EX 800.00
Home Savings Bank, M-1237, pnt CI, 5¾", EX 475.00
Honey Bear, M-606, pnt CI, 2½", NM 1,600.00
Humpty Dumpty, M-338, pnt tin, 5¼", NM 165.00
Independence Hall, M-1211, pnt CI, 6⅜", EX 2,300.00
Independence Hall, M-1244, pnt CI, 8⅞", EX 675.00
Indian Bust, M-221, pnt lead, 3½", EX 275.00
Indian w/Tomahawk, M-228, pnt CI, 5⅞" 275.00
Kitty, M-349, pnt CI, 4¾", EX 80.00
Labrador Retriever, M-412, pnt CI, 4½", EX 185.00
Lion on Wheels, M-760, pnt CI, 4½", EX 225.00
Log Cabin, M-1023 variant, pnt CI, 2½", EX 200.00
Main Street Trolley (empty), M-1469, pnt CI, rpl wheels, 3" 160.00
Main Street Trolley (w/people), M-1471, pnt CI, 3", EX 325.00
Maine, M-1441, pnt CI, rstr, 5¼" 375.00
Mammy w/Basket, M-175, pnt wht metal, 5¼", EX 250.00
Mammy w/Hands on Hips, M-176, pnt CI, 5¼", EX 250.00
Mammy w/Spoon, M-168, pnt CI, 5⅞", EX 450.00
Marietta Silo, M-1246, rpt CI, 5½", EX 275.00
Mary & Little Lamb, M-164, pnt CI, much wear, 4⅜" 400.00
Mean Standing Bear, M-713, pnt CI, 5½", EX 175.00
Mermaid, M-34, pnt CI, 9¾", EX 675.00
Minuteman, M-44, pnt CI, 6", EX 275.00
Mulligan, M-177, pnt CI, 5¾", EX 185.00
My Pet (horse), M-531, pnt CI, 4⅛", EX 160.00
North Pole Freezer, M-1373, pnt CI, 4¼", EX 525.00
Old South Church, M-990, CI, wht w/metallic trim, 9¼", NM ..3,000.00
One-Car Garage, M-1009, pnt CI, 2½", EX 500.00
Owl, Be Wise Save Money; M-498, CI, worn gold & red pnt, 5" ..195.00
Owl, M-597, pnt CI, 4¼", EX 250.00
Palace, M-1116, pnt CI, 7½", NM 2,400.00
Parlor Stove, M-1357, pnt CI (worn), 6⅞" 180.00
Pelican, M-679, pnt CI, 4¾", EX 950.00
Penthouse, M-1234, pnt CI, rpl turnpin, 5⅞", EX 800.00
Pig w/Bow, M-606, pnt CI, 3", EX 160.00
Pocahantas Bust, M-226, pnt lead, 3⅛", EX 300.00
Policeman, M-182, pnt CI, 5½", NM 600.00
Porky Pig, M-264, pnt CI, 5¾", EX 275.00
Possum, M-561, pnt CI, 2⅜", EX 525.00
Potato, M-1612, pnt CI, 2⅛", NM 1,350.00
Prancing Horse w/Belly Band, M-506, CI, 4½", EX 175.00
Punch & Judy, M-1298, pnt tin, 2⅞", EX 105.00
Rabbit on oval base, M-569, CI, mc pnt, 2¼", EX 990.00
Radio Bank, M-831, pnt CI & tin, 3⅜", EX 140.00
Radio w/Combo Door, M-833, CI & tin, gr pnt, 4½", EX 100.00
Red Goose School Shoes, M-628, pnt CI, 3¾", EX 210.00
Retriever w/Pack, M-436, pnt CI, 4¾", EX 110.00
Rhino, M-721, pnt CI, 2⅝", EX 475.00
Roly Poly Monkey, M-1277, pnt tin, 6", NM 600.00
Roof Bank, M-1122, CI, brn japanning w/gold, 5½", VG+ 160.00
Roosevelt 'New Deal,' M-148, pnt CI, 5", EX 650.00
Rooster, M-548, pnt CI, 4¾", EX+ 175.00
Roper Stove, M-1341, pnt CI & tin, 3¾", NM 225.00
Rose Window, M-1170, pnt CI, 2⅜", EX 450.00
Round Duck, M-619, pnt CI, 4", EX 270.00
Royal Bank, M-1329, pnt CI, 5¼", EX 375.00
Santa in Chimney, M-82, pnt wht metal, casting flaw, 5", VG ..200.00
SBCCA Rocking Horse, M-515, pnt CI, 5⅝", NM 325.00
Scottie, M-419, pnt CI, 4⅞", EX 130.00
Scottie, M-425, pnt CI, 4", EX 240.00
Seated Royal Lion, M-751, pnt CI (possible rpt), 5", EX 90.00
Shell Out, M-1622, pnt CI, 2½", EX 500.00
Six-Sided Building, M-1007, pnt CI, rpl turnpin, 2⅜", EX 50.00
Space Heater (birds), M-1087, pnt CI, 6½", EX 110.00
Space Heater (flowers), M-1094, pnt CI, 6½", EX 425.00
Spaniel, M-418, CI, wht & blk pnt, lt rust/wear, 6" 115.00
Spaniel, M-418 variant, pnt CI, trap in stomach, 3¾", EX 135.00
Spaniel Begging, M-361, pnt lead, 4⅜", NM 325.00
Spitz, M-409, pnt CI, 4¼", EX 350.00
Squirrel w/Nut, M-660, pnt CI, 4⅛", EX 625.00
Standing Mailbox, M-841, pnt CI, 5½", EX 145.00
State Bank, M-1078, CI, brn japanning w/bronze, 8½", M 770.00
State Bank, M-1080, CI, brn japanning w/bronze & gold, 6", EX ..250.00
State Bank, M-1083, CI, brn japanning/bronze/gold, 4¼", EX ...200.00
Statue of Liberty, M-1166, CI, gr pnt, 9⅝", NM 3,000.00
Steamboat, M-1459, pnt CI, 2½", EX 310.00
Street Clock, M-1548, pnt CI & tin, rpl bk plate, 6", EX 175.00
Tally-Ho, M-535, pnt CI, 4½", EX 45.00
Teddy Bear, M-698, CI, worn gold pnt, 3⅞" 165.00
Teddy Roosevelt, M-120, CI, worn mc pnt, 5⅛" 195.00
Three Monkeys, M-743, pnt CI, 3¼", EX 450.00
Time Is Money, M-1555, pnt CI & tin, rpl hands, 4⅞" 150.00
Tower Bank, M-1208, pnt CI, 9¼", EX 275.00
Town Hall, M-998, pnt CI, chip in base, 4⅝", VG+ 400.00
Triangular Building, M-1235, pnt CI, 6", EX 425.00
Trolley, M-1472, pnt CI, 4", EX 475.00
Turkey, M-587, pnt CI, 3⅜", EX 125.00
Two Kids, M-594, pnt CI, casting flaw in base, 4½", NM 875.00
Two-Car Garage, M-1010, pnt CI, 2½", EX 475.00

Two-Faced Devil, M-31, pnt CI, 4¼", EX 625.00
Two-Story House, M-1002, pnt CI, 3⅛", EX 150.00
US Mail, M-834, pnt CI, 6⅞", EX 390.00
US Tank, M-1438, pnt CI, 1¾", EX 150.00
Victorian House, M-1142, pnt CI, 4½", EX 500.00
Victorian House, M-1143, pnt CI, 3¼", EX 275.00
Washington Bell, M-786, pnt CI, 2¾", EX 350.00
Washington Monument, M-1048, pnt CI, 6⅛", NM 250.00
Westminster Abbey, M-973, pnt CI, 6¼", EX 425.00
Young 'N,' M-170, CI, worn mc pnt/rust, rpl screw, 4⅝" 225.00
1876 Bank, M-1012, pnt CI, 2⅞", EX 250.00
1882 Villa Bank, M-959, pnt CI, 5⅞", EX 650.00

Barber Shop Collectibles

Even for the stranger in town, the local barber shop was easy to find, its location vividly marked with the traditional red and white striped barber pole that for centuries identified such establishments. As far back as the 12th century, the barber has had a place in recorded history. At one time he not only groomed the beards and cut the hair of his gentlemen clients but was known as the 'blood-letter' as well, hence the red stripe for blood and the white for bandages. Many early barbers even pulled teeth! Later, laws were enacted that divided the practices of barbering and surgery.

The Victorian barber shop reflected the charm of that era with fancy barber chairs upholstered in rich wine-colored velvet; rows of bottles made from colored art glass held hair tonics and shaving lotion. Backbars of richly carved oak with beveled mirrors lined the wall behind the barber's station. During the late 19th century, the barber pole with a blue stripe added to the standard red and white as a patriotic gesture came into vogue.

Today the barber shop has all but disappeared from the American scene, replaced by modern unisex salons. Collectors search for the barber poles, the fancy chairs, and the tonic bottles of an era gone but not forgotten. See also Bottles; Razors; Shaving Mugs.

Blade bank, frog figural, ceramic, Listerine advertising 18.50
Cabinet, Eastlake Victorian, marble top/rfn cherry, 104x39x16" ...1,800.00
Cabinet, pnt wood w/glass door & shelves, sm 275.00
Chair, child's, fire engine w/ladders, rstr 2,000.00
Chair, child's, orig wooden horse's head 1,600.00
Chair, Eugene Burninghaus, swan arms, 2-pc, VG 950.00
Chair, Hercules, gr velour, ornate castings/cvd oak, EX 1,900.00
Chair, Koch's, oak & iron, 48x26x36", VG 550.00
Chair, Koken, wht porc w/leather, 52x24x36", VG 300.00
Chair, mahog w/brass-plated hardware, hydraulic, 49x47x35", EX ..850.00
Chair, red velvet uphl, porc base, hydraulic, unmk 275.00
Chair, walnut w/cvd gargoyle heads, 1890, rstr 1,000.00
Clippers, Shapleigh Hardware, St Louis, hand held, EX 35.00
Curling iron, mustache; scarce 20.00
Jar, Antiseptic in gold on cobalt w/orange & wht flag 175.00
Pole, cvd & pnt wood, 19th C, sm losses, 60" 750.00
Pole, electric, metal & glass, revolves, 3-color, 1930s, 26" 295.00
Pole, pnt porc, dome top lights up, 48x12" dia, VG 300.00
Pole, pnt wood, red/wht stripes, early, 84x10", VG 800.00
Pole, pnt wood, wall mt, rpt, 36x14½", EX 155.00
Pole, sheet metal on wood, red/wht/bl spiral, 48", EX 235.00
Pole, trn wood, red & wht rpt, 66", EX 350.00
Rack, mug, oak, 10-compartment, 7x28x8½" 200.00
Rack, mug; oak, 40-compartment, 48x48", EX 525.00
Sharpener, razor; glass, Glix Blades, Glix Always Clicks 8.00
Shoeshine bench, marble & oak, brass ftrests, 85" L, VG 1,900.00
Shoeshine stand, bent-wire highchair w/shelf & shoe rest 250.00

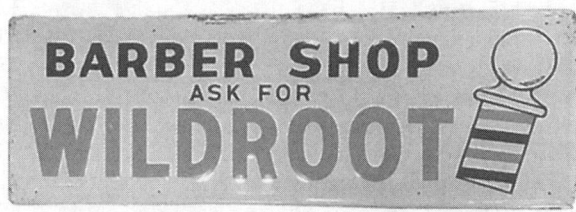

Sign, Ask for Wildroot, red, white, and blue painted metal, small chips and scratches, 14x40", $50.00.

Sterilizer, glove style, NP on brass, porc base, 60x20" dia 200.00
Sterilizer, Herpicide, Bakelite fr & lids, 2 glass containers 125.00
Sterilizer, porc, 9-compartment, DeWitt-Steri Tool, EX 95.00

Barometers

Barometers are instruments designed to measure the weight or pressure of the atmosphere in order to anticipate approaching weather changes. They have a glorious history. Some of the foremost thinkers of the 17th century developed the mercury barometer, as the discovery of the natural laws of the universe progressed. Working in 1644 from experiments by Galileo, Evangelista Torrecelli used a glass tube and a jar of mercury to create a vacuum and therefore prove that air has weight. Four years later, Rene Descartes added a paper scale to the top of Torrecelli's mercury tube and created the basic barometer. Blaise Pascal, working with Descartes, used it to determine the heights of mountains; indeed, only later was the correlation between changes in air pressure and changes in the weather observed and the term 'weather-glass' applied. Robert Boyle introduced it to England, and Robert Hook modified the form and designed the wheel barometer.

The most common barometer is the wheel or banjo type. Second is the stick type. Modifications of the plain stick would be the marine gimballed type, followed by the laboratory or kew or Fortin type. Others are the Admiral Fitzroys of which there are twelve or more types. The above all have mercury contained in either glass tubing or wood-box cisterns.

Another type of barometer is the aneroid, working on atmospheric pressure changes. They come in all sizes ranging from 1" in diameter to 12" or larger. They may be in metal or wood cases. There is a Barograph which records on a graph that rotates around a drum powered by a 7-day clock mechanism. Pocket barometers (altimeters) vary in sizes from 1" diameter up to 6" diameter. One final type of barometer is the sympiesometer, a modification of the stick barometer used for a limited time and not as accurate as a conventional marine barometer.

Our advisor for this category is Bob Elsner; he is listed in the Directory under Florida.

Aneroid, Negretti & Zambra, ca 1915, watch sz 200.00
Aneroid, pocket type, in standing case, ca 1885 ....200.00
Aneroid, Salom & Co, marine, open dial, ca 1875 ....300.00
Aneroid, ship's, oak case, ca 1885 ....200.00
Barograph, oak, ca 1920 ....875.00
Fitzroy type, ME Solomons, Dublin, ca 1900 ....2,500.00
Fitzroy type, Royal Polytechnic, Joseph Davis & Co, 1880 ......2,500.00
Kew Fortin, Chancellor & Son, Dublin, ca 1840 ....1,200.00
Stick type, Adam Routledge, mahog, bulb cistern, ca 1820 .....2,000.00
Stick type, H Hughes, London, mahog, cistern, ca 1825 ....2,000.00
Stick type, Jones, London, cistern, mahog, ca 1810 ....2,000.00
Stick type, Mathew Woller, mahog, bulb cistern, ca 1805 ....2,000.00
Sympiesometer, A Adie, Edinburgh, ca 1825 ....4,500.00
Sympiesometer, J Hughes, London, ca 1840 ....4,000.00

Wheel or banjo type, A Gilardino, ca 1840, 8" wheel **900.00**
Wheel or banjo type, C Maspolli, ca 1840, 12" wheel **1,100.00**
Wheel or banjo type, F Amadio & Son, ca 1840, 4½" wheel ..**1,300.00**
Wheel or banjo type, rosewood w/MOP inlay, ca 1840 ....**1,200.00**

Barware

Back in the thirties when social soirees were very elegant affairs thanks to the influence of Hollywood in all its glamour and mistique, cocktails were often served up in shakers styled as miniature airplanes, zeppelins, skyscrapers, lady's legs, penguins, roosters, bowling pins, etc. Some were by top designers such as Norman Bel Geddes and Russel Wright. They were made of silverplate, glass, and chrome, often trimmed with colorful Bakelite handles. Today these are hot collectibles, and even the more common Deco-styled chrome cylinders are often priced at $25.00 and up. Ice buckets, trays, and other bar accessories are also included in this area of collecting. Our advisor for this category is Stephen Visakay, who is listed in the Directory under New Jersey.

Book, The Savoy Cocktail Book, H Craddock, 1930, M **150.00**
Bottle, syphon; Norman Bel Geddes Soda King, chrome, bl top ...**160.00**
Cocktail shaker, lady's leg, clear frosted, chrome trim, 15" **350.00**
Cocktail shaker, SP, penguin form, Napier, 12" **1,000.00**
Dispenser, Blk bartender, France, 6½x6", NM **750.00**
Dispenser, seltzer; Soda King Syphon, ca 1938, 9½x3⅞" **200.00**
Ice bucket, aluminum, emb penguins, West Bend Alum Co, 1944 ..**35.00**
Ice bucket, chrome-plated copper, Keystone, 1930s, +tray **95.00**
Picks, bottle forms in wood 'bar' w/chrome, 4½x5" **45.00**
Pinch bottle, SP w/3 eng roosters, Meriden, 1927, 9" **400.00**
Rack, tumbler; gyroscopic, 20x4¼" dia rings, +4 tumblers **125.00**
Shaker, aluminum, Chicago Century of Progress, 1933 ....**45.00**
Shaker, chrome, pitcher form, ped base, Farberware **40.00**
Shaker, chrome & plastic w/glass insert, mk Ritz, 1930s **75.00**
Shaker, chrome w/Catalin lid, Revere, 1937, 12⅛" **350.00**
Shaker, clear glass, w/strainer, horse's head lid, Heisey **200.00**
Shaker, clear glass w/chrome, hourglass form, Maxwell Phillip **75.00**
Shaker, clear glass w/emb dmns, plastic lid, 1928, 12½" **40.00**
Shaker, cobalt glass w/silver o/l, 1920s, 11", +8 tumblers **350.00**
Shaker, cobalt glass w/wht silk-screened recipes, 10½" **38.00**
Shaker, cobalt w/wht angel-fish, chrome top, Hazel Atlas, 10" **28.00**
Shaker, frosted glass dumbbell w/SP trim, Nat'l, +12 martinis **500.00**
Shaker, polished aluminum, skyscraper inspired, 13x3½" **95.00**
Shaker, Revere Copper & Brass Co, 1938, +rnd tray/6 tumblers ..**900.00**
Shaker, ruby glass w/silver hunt scene, chrome lid, 1-qt **175.00**
Shaker, SP penguin form, Napier, rare **800.00**
Shaker, Tippler, West Bend Aluminum Co, ca 1934, +recipes **60.00**
Travel bar, SP plane breaks apart for shaker, etc, '28, 17½" **5,000.00**
Tray, flappers w/drinks, Here's How, rectangular, NM **100.00**
Tray, gyroscopic, glass/chrome, 24" dia, +shaker & 8 tumblers ...**750.00**

Basalt

Basalt is a type of unglazed black pottery developed by Josiah Wedgwood and copied by many other companies during the late 18th and early 19th centuries. It is also called 'Egyptian Black.' See also Wedgwood.

Coffeepot, emb motif, dome lid w/Widow Washburton, 10", VG ..**300.00**
Creamer, Prince of Wales Feathers, att Turner, 4" **110.00**
Jug, swags/ribbons, engine-trn bands, att Yates, 1790, 5" **180.00**
Pitcher, paneled, lady finial, mk Keeling Toft, 5", EX **135.00**
Teapot, molded classical design, sliding lid, 6½", EX **150.00**

Baskets

Basket weaving is a craft as old as ancient history. Baskets have been used to harvest crops, for domestic chores, and to contain the catch of fishermen. Materials at hand were utilized, and baskets from a specific region are often distinguishable simply by analyzing the natural fibers used in their construction. Early Indian baskets were made of corn husks or woven grasses. Willow splint, straw, rope, and paper were also used. Until the invention of the veneering machine in the late 1800s, splint was made by water-soaking a split log until the fibers were softened and flexible. Long strips were pulled out by hand and while still wet and pliable woven into baskets in either a crosshatch or hexagonal weave.

Most handcrafted baskets on the market today were made between 1860 and the early 1900s. Factory baskets with a thick, wide splint cut by machine are of little interest to collectors. The more popular baskets are those designed for a specific purpose, rather than the more commonly found utility baskets that had multiple uses. Among the most costly forms are the Nantucket Lighthouse baskets, which were basically copied from those made there for centuries by aboriginal Indians. They were designed in the style of whale-oil barrels and named for the South Shoal Nantucket Lightship where many were made during the last half of the 19th century. Cheese baskets (used to separate curds from whey), herb-gathering baskets, and finely woven Shaker miniatures are other highly-prized examples of the basket weaver's art.

In the listings that follow, assume that each has a center bentwood handle (unless handles of another type are noted) that is not included in the height. Unless another type of material is indicated, assume that each is made of splint.

For further information we recommend *Collector's Guide to Country Baskets* by Don and Carol Raycraft, available from Collector Books. See also American Indian; Eskimo; Sewing; Shaker.

Nantucket, swing handle, 3¾x8½x6½", usual wear, VG, $625.00.

Apple, dbl wood bottom, bail hdl, 12" dia, EX **125.00**
Apple, wht oak, old dk gr pnt, bowl shape, 1850s, 9x13½" **125.00**
Apple, wooden, dbl bottom, dk red pnt, 15" dia, EX **195.00**
Buttocks, EX age & color, well shaped, 4x8½x7¼" **200.00**
Buttocks, EX color & age, 9x11" **215.00**
Buttocks, faded gr & natural, well made, 9x18x13" **135.00**
Buttocks, lt natural patina, 3½x7x6" **130.00**
Buttocks, old patina, rare sz, 2½x5½x5" **300.00**
Buttocks, well made, orig label: Mammoth Cave KY 1908, 4x8x8" ..**110.00**
Buttocks, 2-tone design, 4½x8x7" **130.00**
Cheese, dk patina, lt wear, 26" **225.00**
Cheese, weathered gray, worn, 27" dia **250.00**
Cheese, well made, 19" dia, EX **250.00**
Cheese, well made, 8x12½", NM **325.00**

Egg, stationary bentwood hdl, 5⅛x8" **140.00**
Feed, hanging, ca 1900, 16" H **400.00**
Field, bentwood hdl, Stanley Smith, PA, 1930s, 10x28x17" **200.00**
Gathering, flared sides, 3 sm arched wooden hdls, 8x16", EX **115.00**
Goose feather, dome lid, hdls, 25" **225.00**
Goose feather, worn orange pnt, w/lid, 20" H, G **125.00**
Laundry, lg weave, rim hdls, dk finish, damage, 16x16" **50.00**
Laundry, lt natural patina, bentwood hdls, 11x21x26" **75.00**
Laundry, scrubbed, minor damage, 31" L **50.00**
Laundry, woven hdls, minor damage, 7x29x17" **110.00**
Loom, dk patina w/blk & faded red, hanging, 8½x11½" **75.00**
Market, arched wood hdl, 5½x12⅝x9⅜" **80.00**
Market, wicker, rnd bottom, wrapped hdl, gold pnt, 6x14x11" **35.00**
Melon shape, Eye-of-God hdl, oval, 3¼x7¼x7¼" **200.00**
Melon shape, 2 rows of dbl ribs on bottom, 5x10" dia **150.00**
Melon shape, 5 rows of dbl ribs on bottom, 6½x12" dia **165.00**
Miniature, buttocks, EX age & color, 1-egg sz, 2½" **250.00**
Miniature, buttocks, EX color, some age, 2⅜" **165.00**
Miniature, gathering, reed & splint, EX patina, 1x3½x6" **220.00**
Miniature, market, EX age & color, minor damage, 2x3¼" **525.00**
Nantucket, dtd 1977, 9½x18½x12", EX **865.00**
Nantucket, ivory pins, 20th C, 14½x19", EX **800.00**
Nantucket, late 1800s, 5½" dia, EX+ **1,150.00**
Nantucket, swing hdl, early 1900s, 5¾", EX **635.00**
Nantucket, swing hdl, early 1900s, 6½x6¾", EX **745.00**
Nantucket, swing hdl, incised base, ca 1900, 5x11", VG- **600.00**
Nantucket, swing hdl, 1800s, 6x5½", VG- **315.00**
Nantucket basket purse, leather & ivory fittings, 6½x7¼" **260.00**
Painted, bl, reed & splint, Eye-of-God hdl, 5x14x8" **225.00**
Painted, gr, wooden bottom, wood/wire bale hdl, 6x10" dia **530.00**
Painted, mustard-brn, oval, 5x14x11½" **200.00**
Painted, orig yel, oval w/rim hdls, 7" L **415.00**
Painted, wht w/gr trim, 3¾x11½", EX **140.00**
Pea picking, old wht pnt, rectangular, 6" L **85.00**
Picnic, hinged lid, swivel hdl, old gr pnt, 14" L, EX **200.00**
Picnic, splint appl over wooden liner, bentwood hdls, 8x13x9" ..**110.00**
Rye straw & splint, arched woven-in hdls, 8¾x16½" dia **110.00**
Splint, EX age & patina, 9½x15" dia **225.00**
Splint, G age, worn finish, 6½x11" **75.00**
Splint, old patina, 9x22" **180.00**
Splint, old varnish, hdl dtd 1934, oval, 4½x12½x9½" **85.00**
Splint & cane, swivel hdl, EX patina, 4½x7" **275.00**
Splint & coiled rye straw, ftd, woven-in hdls, 5½x12" **75.00**
Splint & sweet grass, 4x3" **30.00**
Splint & wicker, stationary wrapped hdl, 3½x7½" **30.00**
Truncated, rim hand holds, 17½x15x15" **140.00**

Batchelder

Ernest A. Batchelder was a leading exponent of the Arts and Crafts movement in the United States. His influential book, *Design in Theory and Practice*, was originally published in 1910. He is best known, however, for his artistic tiles which he first produced in Pasedena, California, from 1909 to 1916. In 1916 the business was relocated to Los Angeles where it continued until 1932, closing because of the Depression.

In 1938 Batchelder resumed production in Pasedena under the name of 'Kinneola Kiln.' Output of the new pottery consisted of delicately cast bowls and vases in an Oriental style. This business closed in 1951. Tiles carry a die-stamped mark; vases and bowls are hand incised. Our advisor for this category is Jack Chipman, author of *Collector's Encyclopedia of California Pottery*; he is listed in the Directory under California.

Bookends, emb floral on rectangular form, lt gray/bl bsk, EX **250.00**

Soap dish, ivory bsk w/cvd lines, 5¾x6½" **100.00**
Tile, cartoonish hunter & dog, red clay on yel matt, mk, 4" **125.00**
Tile, cherub in tree, bl semi-matt, 5¾x2½" **175.00**
Tile, knight on horsebk, buff on lt bl, unglazed, 4" **120.00**
Tile, knight on horsebk w/castle, 3-color engobe, 8" **375.00**

Tile, La Mayan, terra cotta, 3½" square, EX, $125.00.

Tile, mission bells in tower, dk tan w/bl hints, 14x10" **650.00**
Tile, stag, bl engobe on terra cotta, 4" **95.00**
Tile, stylized thistle, lt tan/bl bsk, 2¾" **70.00**
Tile fireplace surround, emb animals/leaves on bl-gr, 48x63" ..**5,750.00**
Vase, blk satin gloss, shouldered, 4x6½" **450.00**
Vase, Chinese bl mottle, cylinder neck, 6¼x4" **600.00**
Vase, dk bl mottled gloss, incurvate rim, 5½x5¼" **325.00**

Battersea

Battersea is a term that refers to enameling on copper or other metal. Though originally produced at Battersea, England, in the mid-18th century, the craft was later practiced throughout the Staffordshire district. Boxes are the most common examples. Some are figurals, and many bear an inscription. Values are given for examples with only minimal damage, which is normal. Our advisor for this category is John Harrigan; he is listed in the Directory under Minnesota.

Bonbonniere, florals/pnt-on 'hdls,' basketweave ground, 2" L **650.00**
Box, maid & lamb, bk: cherubs & lady w/fan, 1¾" dia **500.00**
Box, patch; bluebird on foliage on wht lid, bl base, 1⅝x1½" **285.00**
Box, snuff; Fr/English naval battle, 2" L **750.00**
Mirror holder, eagle/E Pluribus Unum, mc, rpr, 2", VG, pr **450.00**
Needle case, gold floral/pastoral scene on pk, 4½" L **425.00**
Opera glasses, children hunting & fishing, 4" W, in case **425.00**

Bauer

Originally founded in Paducah, Kentucky, in 1885, the J.A. Bauer Company moved to Los Angeles where it was re-established in 1909. Until the 1920s, their major products were terra-cotta gardenware, flowerpots, and stoneware and yellow ware bowls. During prohibition they produced crocks for home use. A more artful form of product began to develop with the addition of designer Louis Ipsen to the staff in 1915. Some of his work, a line of molded vases, flowerpots, bowls, etc., was awarded a bronze medal at the Pacific International Exposition the following year.

In 1930 the first of many dinnerware lines was tested on the market. Their initial pattern, Plain Ware, was well accepted and led the way to the introduction of the most popular dinnerware in their history and with today's collectors, Ring Ware. It was produced from 1932 into the early 1960s in solid colors of jade green, royal blue, Chinese yellow, light blue, orange-red, and (in very limited quantities) black or white. Its simple pattern was a design of closely-spaced concentric ribs, either convex or concave. Over the years, more than one hundred shapes were available. Some were made in limited quantities, resulting in rare items to whet the appetites of Bauer buffs today. Other patterns were La Linda, produced during the 1940s and 1950s, and Monterey Moderne, introduced in 1948 and remaining popular into the 1950s (made in pink, black, gray, brown, and green).

After WWII a flood of foreign imports drastically curtailed their sales, and the pottery began a steady decline that ended in failure in 1962. Prices listed below reflect the California market. For more information, we recommend *The Collector's Encyclopedia of California Pottery* by Jack Chipman, our advisor for this category. Mr. Chipman's address may be found in the Directory under California.

Ashtray, plain, blk, 4" sq 100.00
Ashtray, Ring, blk, 3" dia 75.00
Beater, for beating bowl, metal 50.00
Beverage server/storage, Monterey, all colors 150.00
Bowl, cereal; Brusche Al Fresco, speckled grs & gray, 5½" 10.00
Bowl, dessert; Monterey Moderne, blk, 5" 25.00
Bowl, fruit; Monterey, all colors but wht, 6" 15.00
Bowl, fruit; Monterey Moderne, all colors but blk, 4¼" ...12.50
Bowl, mixing; La Linda, gr, yel or turq, #36, 1-pt 12.00
Bowl, mixing; Ring, olive, chartreuse, or red-brn, #24, 1-qt ...30.00
Bowl, mixing; Ring, yel, lt bl or gr, #12, ½-gal 50.00
Bowl, ramekin, La Linda, all matt colors 10.00
Bowl, salad; Ring, blk, 9" 145.00
Bowl, salad; Ring, burgundy, dk bl or wht, low, 9" 65.00
Bowl, serving; Monterey Moderne, blk, 8½" 60.00
Bowl, vegetable; Brusche Al Fresco, speckled colors, 9½" ...15.00
Bowl, vegetable; Contempo, all colors, 9½" 20.00
Bowl, vegetable; Ring, olive, gray or red-brn, oval, 8" 50.00
Butter dish, Monterey Moderne, all colors but blk, rnd 45.00
Butter dish, Ring, dk bl, burgundy or wht, oblong 200.00
Canister, grease; Brusche Al Fresco, coffee brn or Dubonnet ...25.00
Casserole, La Linda, burgundy or dk brn, 1-qt 45.00
Casserole, Ring, dk bl, ivory or burgundy, 6½" 80.00
Casserole, Ring, dk bl, ivory or wht, w/lid, ind 80.00
Coffee server, plain, all colors but blk, open 40.00
Coffeepot, Ring, ivory, burgundy or wht, 8-cup 300.00
Cookie jar, Brusche Al Fresco, speckled colors 50.00
Creamer, Brusche Al Fresco, coffee brn or Dubonnet 10.00
Creamer, Ring, chartreuse, olive or turq, 12-oz 20.00
Cup, jumbo coffee; La Linda, all matt colors 35.00
Cup & saucer, El Chico, all colors 45.00
Cup & saucer, Monterey, all colors 30.00
Custard cup, Gloss Pastel Kitchenware, burgundy or dk brn ...10.00
Flowerpot, Ring Gardenware, blk, rolled rim, 6" 50.00
Gravy boat, La Linda, all colors 20.00
Gravy bowl, Monterey Moderne, all colors but blk 27.50
Hostess tray & cup, speckled colors 15.00
Jar, refrigerator; Ring, yel, lt bl or orange, w/lid 65.00
Jardiniere, Ring Gardenware, dk bl or wht, 8" 150.00
Mug, plain, blk, 8-oz 85.00
Pickle dish, Ring, all colors but blk 45.00
Pitcher, Brusche Al Fresco, coffee brn or Dubonnet, ½-pt ...15.00
Pitcher, Ring, dk bl, ivory or burgundy, bbl style 300.00
Plate, Brusche Al Fresco, coffee brn or Dubonnet, 10" 10.00
Plate, dinner; plain, blk, 10½" 100.00
Plate, El Chico, all colors, 9" 35.00
Plate, grill; Monterey Moderne, rnd 20.00
Plate, Monterey, all colors, 6" 8.50
Plate, Ring, blk, 9" 75.00

Platter, Brusche Contempo, all colors 15.00
Platter, Monterey, all colors but wht, oval, 12" 30.00
Platter, Monterey Moderne, all colors but blk, oval, 12" ...25.00
Platter, Ring, blk, oval, 9" 65.00
Platter, Ring, dk bl, burgundy or wht, oval, 12" 60.00
Shaker, La Linda, all matt colors 6.00
Shakers, Ring, dk bl, ivory or wht, bbl form, pr 30.00
Soup plate, Ring, yel, jade gr or turq, 7½" 60.00
Sugar bowl, Monterey, wht, w/lid 30.00
Sugar bowl, plain, all colors but blk, w/lid 45.00
Teapot, La Linda, lt brn, ivory or olive gr, 6-cup 35.00
Teapot, Monterey, wht, 6-cup 85.00
Tumbler, La Linda, burgundy or dk brn, 8-oz 20.00
Tumbler, Monterey, all colors but wht, 8-oz 15.00
Tumbler, Monterey Moderne, all colors but blk 12.00
Tumbler, Ring, lt bl or olive, raffia-wrapped hdl, 6-oz 35.00
Vase, blk gloss, hdls at top, Matt Carlton, 14x9" 700.00
Vase, Ring Gardenware, blk, ruffled, 7" 100.00
Vase, Ring Gardenware, turq or jade gr, ruffled, 7" 50.00

Bavaria

Bavaria, Germany, was long the center of that country's pottery industry; in the 1800s, many firms operated in and around the area. Chinaware vases, novelties, and table accessories were decorated with transfer prints as well as by hand by artists who sometimes signed their work. The examples here are marked with 'Bavaria' and the logos of some of the various companies which were located there.

Cabinet plate, lady's portrait within floral and gilt border, ca 1890, 9¾", $150.00.

Bonbon, floral transfer w/gold scrolls, 2-pc, 4x8¼" 40.00
Bowl, Chateau, Schumann, ped ft, 7" 45.00
Bowl, youth & maiden in garden, rtcl octagonal rim, 8½" 25.00
Box, lady w/rose bouquet figural, 9" 135.00
Mug, floral, lizard hdl, 6¼" 75.00
Plate, fairy scene w/much gold, hdls 250.00
Plate, lady's portrait, lacy gold rim, 6½" 35.00
Plate, Siamese cat's head, gold rim, sgn/mk, 8" 65.00
Tea set, demitasse; wht w/gold & cobalt, 1960s, 27-pc, M 275.00
Teapot, alternating panels w/gold, +6 c/s 200.00
Teapot, pk roses w/gold, ribbed, ZS&Co, +c/s 85.00

Beer Cans

When the flat-top can was first introduced in 1934, it came with printed instructions on how to use the triangular punch opener. Cone-top cans, which are rare today, were patented in 1935 by the Continental Can Company. By the 1960s, aluminum cans with pull tabs had made both types obsolete.

The hobby of collecting beer cans has been rapidly gaining momentum over the past ten years. Series types, such as South African Brewery, Lion, and the Cities Series by Schmit and Tucker, are especially popular.

Condition is an important consideration when evaluating market price. Grade 1 must be in like-new condition with no rust. However, the triangular punch hole is acceptable. Grade 2 cans may have slight scratches or dimples but must be free of rust. For Grade 3, light rust, minor scratching, and some fading may be acceptable. When these defects are more pronounced, a can is defaulted to Grade 4. Those in less-than-excellent condition devaluate sharply. In the listings that follow, cans are arranged alphabetically by brand name, not by brewery.

Ballantine Draft Beer, red, aluminum, flat top, 12-oz, M 2.50
Billy Beer, aluminum, 12-oz, M 2.00
Blatz Pilsner Beer, cone top, 12-oz, NM 40.00
Blue 'N Gold, gold/bl/wht, flat top, 12-oz, NM 150.00
Boston Stock Ale, cone top, 1-qt, NM 495.00
Brucks Jubilee, 86 Years of Brewing, cone top, 12-oz, EX 30.00
Burgermeister, cone top, 16-oz, NM 110.00
Canadian Ace, cone top, silver, 12-oz, M 30.00
Champagne Velvet, cone top, full, 12-oz, EX+ 65.00
E&B Special, cone top, 12-oz, M 40.00
Edelweiss, cone top, full, 1-qt, M 85.00
Edelweiss Light Beer, cone top, 12-oz, EX 30.00
Falstaff Draft, wht/gold/maroon, 12-oz, M 10.00
Fitzgerald's Lager Beer, blk around logo, cone top, 12-oz, EX 40.00
Frankenmuth Bock Beer, brn & yel, tab top, 12-oz, NM 38.00
Gibbons Beer, oval logo, cone top, 12-oz, M 65.00
Goebel Extra Dry Private Stock Beer, flat top, 12-oz, EX 30.00
Golden Glow, cone top, 16-oz, EX+ 175.00
Grand Select Cream Ale, gr & yel, flat top, 12-oz, EX+ 40.00
Groetz Country Club, cone top, 12-oz, NM 30.00
Grossvater Beer, cone top, 12-oz, EX 165.00
Hudepohl Beer, flat top, 12-oz, M 30.00
Imperial Extra Dry Pale Beer, gold, flat top, 12-oz, NM 65.00
Jennings Deluxe Beer, bl on gold, tab top, 12-oz, NM 175.00
Lucky Light Draft, tab top, 7-oz, NM 15.00
Maier Pale Dry Beer, gold & red, flat top, 12-oz, EX 100.00
Meister Brau Real Draft Beer, woodgrain, flat top, 12-oz, NM 30.00

Old Crown Bock Beer, brown, gold & cream, 12-oz, EX, $10.00.

Old Crown Light Dry Beer, flat top, 12-oz, EX 15.00
Old Dutch Brand, gold & brn, cone top, 12-oz, VG 250.00
Old Export Premium Beer, red, tab top, 12-oz, NM 2.50
Olde Virginia, red & blk, cone top, 12-oz, NM 60.00
Ortels '92, cone top, 12-oz, EX+ 35.00

Pabst Blue Ribbon, gold & wht, flat top, 12-oz, NM 27.50
Penguin Extra Dry Beer, wht & bl, flat top, 12-oz, M 40.00
Rainier, red, flat top, w/hdl, 12-oz, NM 30.00
Rainier Ale, oval logo on gr, flat top, 12-oz, EX 25.00
Rainier Beer, ...So Light, wht on bl, flat top, 12-oz, EX+ 25.00
Rainier Exposition Ale, brn & gold, flat top, 12-oz, EX 165.00
Rheingold Bock, combative rams, flat top, 12-oz, NM 140.00
Ruppiner Dark Beer, tan & brn, flat top, 12-oz, EX+ 90.00
Sierra, silver & bl, flat top, 12-oz, EX 75.00
Standard Premium Beer, wht, tab top, 12-oz, NM 20.00
Stegmaier's Gold Medal Beer, cone top, 12-oz, NM 75.00
Storz Gold Crest Beer, red & wht, flat top, 12-oz, EX 28.00
Tavern, cone top, 12-oz, NM 120.00
Walter's Premium Quality Beer, gold & red, flat top, 12-oz, M 18.00
20 Grand Ale, cone top, 12-oz, NM 120.00

Bellaire, Marc

Marc Bellaire was born in Toledo, Ohio. He studied at the Toledo Museum of Art while employed as a designer for the Libbey Glass Company. During World War II, while serving in the Navy, he traveled extensively throughout the Pacific resulting in his enriched sense of design and color.

Marc settled in California in the 1950s where his work attracted the attention of national buyers and agencies who persuaded him to create ceramic lines of his own, employing hand-decorating techniques throughout. This resulted in the building of a studio in Culver City. He produced high-quality ceramics, often decorated with ultra-modern figures or geometric patterns. His work was executed with a distinctive flair. His most famous line was Mardi Gras, decorated with slim dancers of spattered and striped colors of black, blue, pink and white.

During the period of 1951-1956, Mark was named one of the top ten artware designers by *Giftwares Magazine*. After 1956 he taught and lectured on art, design, and ceramic decorating techniques from coast to coast. Many pieces were one of a kind, commissioned throughout the United States.

During the 1970s he set up a studio in Marin County, California, and eventually moved to Palm Springs where he opened his final studio/gallery. There he produced large pieces with a Southwest style. Mr. Bellaire died in 1994. Our advisor for this category is Marty Webster; he is listed in the Directory under Michigan.

Ashtray, Bird Isle, blk on cream, 8" 85.00
Ashtray, Clown, mc on cream, 7" 45.00
Ashtray, Jamaica, musicians on brn, 10x14" 85.00
Ashtray, Mardi Gras, figures on blk, 14x14" 225.00
Ashtray, Still Life, matt fruits & leaves, 10x15" 100.00
Compote, Cave Painting, 4-ftd, 6x12" 125.00
Compote, Woman w/Blue Bird, 4-ftd, 8x17" 125.00
Ewer, Mardi Gras, figures on blk, hdl, 18" 400.00
Figurine, Mardi Gras, reclining man, very slim, 18" 1,000.00
Figurine, Mardi Gras, standing man, very slim, 24" 1,000.00
Figurine, Polynesian, standing man 400.00
Platter, Mardi Gras, figures on blk, 12x18" 250.00
Platter, Polynesian Dancer, egg shape, 11x15" 125.00
Platter, Polynesian People, 3 figures on orange, 7x13" 125.00
Tray, Polynesian Man, blk & gr, 12" dia 200.00
Vase, Balinese Women, hourglass shape, 8" 125.00
Vase, Mardi Gras, hourglass shape, 3-ftd, 11" 125.00

Belleek, American

From 1883 until 1930, several American potteries located in New Jersey and Ohio manufactured a type of china similar to the famous

Irish Belleek soft-paste porcelain. The American manufacturers identified their porcelain by using 'Belleek' or 'Beleek' in their marks. American Belleek is considered the highest achievement of the American porcelain industry. Production centered around artistic cabinet pieces and luxury tablewares. Many examples emulated Irish shapes and decor with marine themes and other naturalistic styles. While all are highly collectible, some companies' products are rarer than others. The best-known manufacturers are Ott and Brewer, Willets, The Ceramic Art Company (CAC), and Lenox. You will find more detailed information in those specific categories. Our advisor for this category is Mary Frank Gaston; you will find her address in the Directory under Texas.

Key:
AAC — American Art China Company
ABC — American Beleek Works
CAP — Columbian Art Pottery Works

Cream soup, Bouquet, Coxon, w/underplate 225.00
Creamer, floral border, sponged gold, ornate hdl, AAC, 4" 300.00
Cup & saucer, demitasse; wht w/pk int & saucer, gold trim, CAP ..200.00
Cup & saucer, floral reserves in red border, Morgan 250.00
Plate, peacocks & mixed florals w/gold, Gordon, 7" 85.00
Plate, workers in wheat field, man at gate, AAC, 6¼" 250.00
Teapot, dragon form, gold paste leaves, CAP, 7½x9" 1,500.00
Vase, florals on wht, gold emb hdls, AAC, 12" 1,000.00

Belleek, Irish

Belleek is a very thin translucent porcelain that takes its name from the village in Ireland where it originated in 1859. The glaze is a creamy ivory color with a pearl-like lustre. The tablewares, baskets, figurines, and vases that have always been made there are being crafted yet today. Shamrock, Tridacna, Echinus, and Thorn are but a few of the many patterns of tableware which have been made during some periods(s) of the pottery's history. Throughout the years, their most popular pattern has been Shamrock.

It is possible to date an example to within twenty to thirty years of crafting by the mark. Pieces with an early stamp often bring prices nearly triple that of a similar but current item. With some variation, the marks have always incorporated the Irish wolfhound, Celtic round tower, harp, and shamrocks. The first three marks (usually in black) were used from 1863 to 1946. A series of green marks identified the pottery's offerings from 1946 until the seventh mark (in gold/brown) was introduced in 1980 (it was discontinued in 1992). The most current mark, the eighth, is blue. Belleek Collector's International Society limited edition pieces are designated with a special mark in red. In the listings below, numbers designated with the prefix 'D' relate to the book *Belleek, The Complete Collector's Guide and Illustrated Reference, Second Edition*, published by Wallace-Homestead Book Company, One Chilton Way, Radnor, PA 19098-0230. The author, Richard K. Degenhardt, is our advisor for Belleek; he is listed in the Directory under North Carolina.

Key:
A — plain (glazed only)
B — cob lustre
C — hand tinted
D — hand painted
E — hand-painted shamrocks
F — hand gilted
G — hand tinted and gilted
H — hand-painted shamrocks and gilted

I — 1863-1890
II — 1891-1926
III — 1926-1946
IV — 1946-1955
V — 1955-1965
VI — 1965-3/31/1980
VII — 4/1/1980-12/22/1992
VIII — 1/4/1993-current

J — mother-of-pearl
K — hand painted and gilted
L — bisque and plain
M — decalcomania
N — special hand-painted decoration
T — transfer design

Further information concerning Periods of Crafting (Baskets):
1 — 1865-1890, BELLEEK (three-strand)
2 — 1865-1890, BELLEEK CO. FERMANAGH (three-strand)
3 — 1891-1920, BELLEEK CO. FERMANAGH IRELAND (three-strand)
4 — 1921-1954, BELLEEK CO. FERMANAGH IRELAND (four-strand)
5 — 1955-1979, BELLEEK® CO. FERMANAGH IRELAND (four-strand)
6 — 1980-1985, BELLEEK® IRELAND (four-strand)
7 — 1985-1989, BELLEEK® IRELAND 'ID NUMBER' (four-strand)
8-12 — 1990 to present (Refer to *Belleek, The Complete Collector's Guide and Illustrated Reference, 2nd Edition*, Chapter 5)

Acorn Covered Jam Pot, D1501-I, D, 4" 1,300.00
Bearded Mask Cream, D1294-I, A, sm 185.00
Blarney Tea Ware Bread Plate, D574-II, G, 10" dia 400.00
Blarney Tea Ware Tea & Saucer, D567-II, G 300.00
Bust of Joy, D1129-IV, A, 11" 750.00
Celtic Fruit Dish, D1512-II, K, 9⅝" 450.00
Chinese Tea Ware Dejeuner Tray, D487-I, K 2,500.00
Cleary Cream, D249-IV (cr), B, 8" 55.00
Diamond Flower Pot, D225-VI, A, 3½" 75.00
Dolphin Candlestick, D343-I, K, 7½" 1,800.00
Dolphin Spill, D189-III, J, 6½" 240.00
Echinus Footed Bowl, D1521-I, B, 8¼" 1,075.00
Egg Frame & Cups (6), D621-VI, G 350.00
Feather Vase, D155-V, B, sm 40.00
Figure of Meditation, D20-II, L, 14½" 2,400.00
Five O'Clock Tea Ware Teapot, D1943-II, D, 4½" 800.00
Gaelic Coffee Cup, D2007-VII, E, 4" 65.00
Gladstone Chamber Pot, D2082-I, T 1,250.00
Harp Shamrock Tea Ware Teapot, D525-VI, E, 4½" 200.00

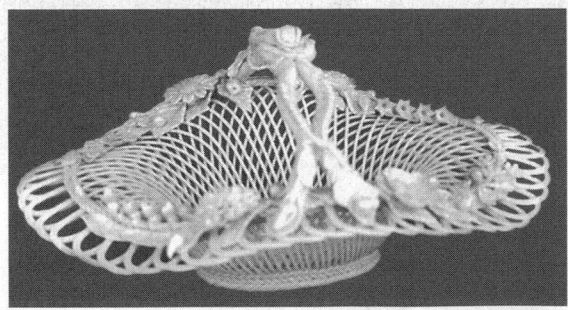

Henshall's Twig Basket, D1261-10, 10", $2,700.00.

Hexagon Tea Ware Tea & Saucer, D391-II, A 175.00
Indian Corn Spill, D190-I, A, 6¼" 300.00
Irish Independent Tray, earthenware, D2090-II, 7½" L 275.00
Ivy Tea Ware Cream, D240-III, B, med 85.00
Lace Tea Ware Cream, D810-II, K, lg, 3¾" 775.00
Lace Tea Ware Sugar, D809-II, K, lg, 4" 725.00
Lace Tea Ware Teapot, D2055-II, K, lg, 5¼" 1,400.00
Lattice Ashtray, D2092-VI, B, 4" dia 30.00
Lily of the Valley Frame, D1534-I, A, lg, 16" L 3,700.00
Limpet Tea Ware Plate, D1374-VI, B, dinner sz, 10½" 75.00

Limpet Tea Ware Teapot, D565-III, B 350.00
Man w/Cat & Puppies, D1143-II, A, 7¾" 2,600.00
Mask Tea Ware Cream, Tall Shape, D1483-II, A, lg 150.00
Neptune Tea Ware Teapot, D415-II, C, 5" 525.00
Oval Basket, flowered, D1270-6, 4-strand, D, 6¾" 600.00
Primrose Butter Plate, D1554-III, G, 4¾" 85.00
Quiver Vase, D152-I, K, 8" 2,400.00
Rathmore Vase, D1219-VI, B, 7½" 80.00
Richard K Degenhardt Basket, 1995, D1696-14, D, 8" L 400.00
Rock Spill, D162-II, C, med, 5" 275.00
Saint Spill, D1223-III, A, 4½" 400.00
Shamrock Basket, D109-6, 4-strand, A, sm 380.00
Shamrock Tea Ware Biscuit Jar, D531-VI, E, 6½" 135.00
Shamrock Tea Ware Coffeepot, D1319-III, E, 7" 375.00
Shamrock Tea Ware Milk Jug, rnd, D1327-III, E, 7" 125.00
Shamrock Tea Ware Tea & Saucer, low shape, D366-III, E 110.00
Shamrock Tea Ware Teapot, D384-VI, E, lg 260.00
Shell Tea Ware Tea & Saucer, D587-II, D 425.00
St Patrick's Day Plate,1986, D1890-VII, E&M 85.00
Sycamore Plate, D641-V, B, 4½" 35.00
Thistle Tea Ware Cake Plate, 2-tier, D2061-VII 150.00
Thorn Tea Ware Dejeuner Set (complete), D763-II, K 6,000.00
Tridacna Tea Ware Cream, D474-II, B, 5½" 150.00
Tridacna Tea Ware Shakers, D1350/D1351-unmk, B, 2¾", pr 70.00
Tridacna Tea Ware Teapot, D475-II, B, lg 375.00
Vase of Masks, D1233-II, J 1,900.00
Vine Tankard Jug, D1314-VI, D, 5½" 140.00
Water Lily Vase on Rocks, D1235-I, D, 10" dia 3,500.00

Bells

Some areas of interest represented in the study of bells are history, religion, and geography. Since Biblical times, bells have announced morning church services, vespers, deaths, christenings, school hours, fires, and community events. Countries have used them en masse to peal out the good news of Christmas, New Year's, and the endings of World Wars I and II. They've been rung in times of great sorrow, such as the death of Abraham Lincoln.

Dorothy Malone Anthony is the author of a series of nine books entitled *World of Bells*. Her address is in the Directory under Kansas. All have over two hundred colored pictures covering many bell categories. See also Nodders; Schoolhouse Collectibles.

Brass, embossed Saicnelecier 1878, 4½", $125.00.

Brass, crowned bear w/shield forms hdl, Hemony, 5⅝" 250.00
Brass, Fr lady w/fan, 5½" 80.00
Brass, Jacobean head forms finial, emb figures on sides, 4" 110.00
Brass, lady in hoop dress & bonnet figural, 5" 65.00
Brass, lady w/hat & fan figural, heavy, 5⅝x2½" 75.00
Brass, Lucy Locket, fancy clothes & hat, 4¾" 85.00
Brass, peasant girl w/pitcher figural, 6¼" 88.00
Brass, Queen Elizabeth I, high ruff collar & crown, 5½" 65.00

Brass, servant's, marble base, push on hdl/release to ring, 4" 125.00
Brass, Tony Weller figural 70.00
Brass, trn wood hdl, 11½x6¾" 45.00
Brass, warrior figural, Hemony, 6½x3" 125.00
Brass, warrior's head emb ea side, 4" 75.00
China, lady figural, gold lustre, Germany 40.00
CI, turtle figural, tap on head or tail to ring, 6½" 225.00
Door, cast brass w/ornate design, iron bk plate, 5" dia 90.00
Farm type, CI, upright, Crystal Metal #2 ....115.00
Glass, cranberry w/crystal hdl, England, 12" 165.00
Glass, cranberry w/wht opaque edge, clear hdl, 15" 215.00
Glass, custard, smocking pattern, orig clapper 125.00
Gong, brass, on stand w/wooden striker, 7" 15.00
Metal w/wrought & CI fittings, GW Coffin/Cincinnati, 28x16" ..360.00
Sheep, brass, 3 on leather strap 45.00
Silver, cherub figural, hallmk 150.00
Silver, pilgrim figural hdl, Udall & Ballou, 4 troy ozs 115.00
Sleigh, brass, 1¼" dia, 23 on orig leather strap, EX 200.00
Sleigh, brass, 25 grad bells on rpl 84" leather strap 150.00
Sleigh, brass, 4 on arched metal strap 45.00
Sterling, Red Riding hood figural hdl, chrome bell, 4½" 30.00
Stork & wolf hdl (from La Fontaine poem), ormolu, Fr, 4½" 425.00
Tap, SP, mushroom, CI 8-sided base, Pat 1883, 6" 60.00
Tea, silver, winged angel figural hdl, mk 800 ....75.00

Bennett, John

Bringing with him the knowledge and experience he had gained at the Doulton (Lambeth) Pottery in England, John Bennett opened a studio in New York City around 1877, where he continued his methods of decorating faience under the glaze. Early wares utilized imported English biscuit, though subsequently local clays (both white and cream-colored) were also used. His first kiln was on Lexington Avenue; he built another on East Twenty-Fourth Street. Pieces are usually signed 'J. Bennett, N.Y.,' often with the street address and date. Later examples may be marked 'West Orange, N.J.,' where he retired. The pottery was in operation approximately six years in New York. Pieces signed with other initials are usually worth less. Our advisor for this category is Robert Tuggle; he is listed in the Directory under New York.

Charger, floral branch/5 insects on apple gr, sgn/1878, 14½" ..4,625.00
Vase, crab apple blossoms on cobalt mottle, sgn/1880s, 20" 5,300.00
Vase, floral on mustard, bottle shape w/neck ring, 9x4¾" 2,200.00
Vase, peonies on cobalt mottle, sgn/1882, 26" 22,000.00

Bennington

Although the term has become a generic one for the mottled brown ware produced there, Bennington is not a type of pottery, but rather a town in Vermont where two important potteries were located. The Norton Company, founded in 1793, produced mainly redware and salt-glazed stoneware; only during a brief partnership with Fenton (1845-47) was any Rockingham attempted. The Norton Company endured until 1894, operated by succeeding generations of the Norton family. Fenton organized his own pottery in 1847. There he manufactured not only redware and stoneware, but more artistic types as well — graniteware, scroddled ware, flint enamel, a fine parian, and vast amounts of their famous Rockingham. Though from an esthetic standpoint his work rated highly among the country's finest ceramic achievements, he was economically unsuccessful. His pottery closed in 1858.

It is estimated that only one in five Fenton pieces were marked; and although it has become a common practice to link any fine piece of

Rockingham to this area, careful study is vital in order to be able to distinguish Bennington's from the similar wares of many other American and Staffordshire potteries. Although the practice was without the permission of the proprietor, it was nevertheless a common occurrence for a potter to take his molds with him when moving from one pottery to the next, so particularly well-received designs were often reproduced at several locations. Of eight known Fenton marks, four are variations of the '1849' impressed stamp: 'Lyman Fenton Co., Fenton's Enamel Patented 1849, Bennington, Vermont.' These are generally found on examples of Rockingham and flint enamel. A raised, rectangular scroll with 'Fenton's Works, Bennington, Vermont,' was used on early examples of porcelain. From 1852 to 1858, the company operated under the title of the United States Pottery Company. Three marks — the ribbon mark with the initials USP, the oval with a scrollwork border and the name in full, and the plain oval with the name in full — were used during that period.

Among the more sought-after examples are the bird and animal figurines, novelty pitchers, figural bottles, and all of the more finely-modeled items. Recumbent deer, cows, standing lions with one forepaw on a ball, and opposing pairs of poodles with baskets in their mouths and 'coleslaw' fur were made in Rockingham, flint enamel, and occasionally in parian. Numbers in the listings below refer to the book *Bennington Pottery and Porcelain* by Barret. Our advisors for Bennington (except for parian and stoneware) are Barbara and Charles Adams; they are listed in the Directory under Massachusetts.

Key: c/s — cobalt on salt glaze

Book flask, Departed Spirits, flint enamel, 5½" 875.00
Book flask, Departed Spirits G, Rockingham, 5½" ....500.00.
Book flask, Ned Buntline's Bible, flint enamel, 6" 2,500.00
Bottle, Coachman, Rockingham, 11", EX 695.00
Bowl, brn & yel Rockingham, shallow, 7⅛" dia 400.00
Bowl, vegetable; yel & brn Rockingham, octagonal, mk, 13" ..1,265.00
Candlestick, flint enamel, 6¾" 800.00
Candlestick, flint enamel, 8¼" 880.00
Candlestick, flint enamel, 9⅝" 900.00
Candlesticks, flint enamel, baluster form, 9¼", att, pr 925.00
Creamer, ribbed, Rockingham, 5½" 600.00
Pie plate, brn & yel Rockingham, 11¾" 150.00
Pie plate, brn & yel Rockingham, 9" 150.00
Pitcher, flint enamel, ribbed, 1849 mk, lt wear, 9¾" 600.00
Pitcher, flint enamel, swirled ribs, chip, 9½" 1,200.00
Poodle, flint enamel, appl fur, basket in jaws, rstr, 9", pr 3,000.00

Stoneware

Churn, butter; flowers in compote, c/s, w/dasher, J&E, 6-gal, EX ...4,100.00
Crock, bird on plume, c/s, E&LP, chip/hairline, 10½" 450.00
Crock, bird on plume (thick), c/s, E&LP, 2-gal, 10¾", EX 725.00
Crock, cake; stylized design, c/s, J&E, 2-gal, 7½", EX 275.00
Crock, chicken on dotted ground, J Norton & Co, 5-gal, NM ..2,250.00
Crock, chicken pecking corn, c/s, J Norton, 2-gal 800.00
Crock, floral, c/s, J Norton & Co, 2-gal, 9", NM 300.00
Crock, floral, c/s, ovoid, J Norton, 2-gal, 10¾", EX 525.00
Crock, floral (stylized/blurred), c/s, E&LP, 13", NM 400.00
Crock, floral (stylized/sm), c/s, E Norton & Co, 6-gal, 13", NM .200.00
Crock, leafy floral, c/s, ovoid, L Norton & Co, 1-gal, EX 180.00
Jar, bird on plume, c/s, E&LP, crack, 4-gal, 14" 300.00
Jar, floral spray, c/s, E&LP, ovoid, hdl chip, 14" 400.00
Jar, preserve; bird, c/s, J&E, 1½-gal, 11", EX 525.00
Jar, preserve; floral, c/s, J Norton, chip, 2-gal, 11½" 260.00
Jar, preserve; plume, c/s, E Norton & Co, 1½-gal, 10¾", EX 230.00
Jug, bird on branch (quilled/blurred), c/s, J&E, 11" 450.00

Jug, floral (stylized), c/s, E&LP, stain/chip, 2-gal 190.00
Jug, floral (stylized), c/s, J&E, 3-gal, 15", EX 550.00
Jug, hawk landing, c/s, J&E, 3-gal, 15½", EX 6,250.00
Jug, parrot on branch, c/s, J Norton, 11" 600.00
Jug, peacock on stump, c/s, J&E, prof rstr, 2-gal 775.00
Jug, plume, c/s, E Norton & Co, 1-gal, 10½", EX 210.00
Jug, pr lg birds on tree, tails Xd, c/s, J&E, 3-gal, EX 4,500.00
Pitcher, Albany slip, E&LP, 1½-gal 250.00

Beswick

In the early 1890s, James Wright Beswick operated a pottery in Longston, England, where he produced fine dinnerware as well as ornamental ceramics. Today's collectors are most interested in the figurines made since 1936 by a later generation Beswick firm, John Beswick, Ltd. They specialize in reproducing accurately detailed bone-china models of authentic breeds of animals. Their Fireside Series includes dogs, cats, elephants, horses, the Huntsman, and an Indian figure, which measure up to 14" in height. The Connoisseur line is modeled after the likenesses of famous racing horses. Beatrix Potter's characters and some of Walt Disney's are charmingly recreated and appeal to children and adults alike. Other items, such as character Tobys, have also been produced. The Beswick name is stamped on each piece. The firm was absorbed by the Doulton group in 1973.

Character jug, Barnaby Rudge 75.00
Character jug, Scrooge 55.00
Creamer, Tony Weller 24.00
Figurine, Appaloosa pony, #1516, 5¼" 295.00
Figurine, beagle, #1939, 3" 26.00
Figurine, bulldog, #965, 5½" 120.00

Figurine, cat, standing, white with green eyes, 7", $100.00.

Figurine, foal, Palomino, recumbent, #915 ....60.00
Figurine, Great Dane, standing, glossy, #968, 7" 80.00
Figurine, Jemima Puddleduck, Beatrix Potter, gold stamp 160.00
Figurine, Mr Alderman Ptolemy, brn stamp, no date 75.00
Figurine, Mr Benjamin Bunny & Peter Rabbit, brn stamp 130.00
Figurine, Persian cat, standing, glossy, #1898 ....42.00
Figurine, Peter Rabbit, Beatrix Potter, gold stamp 145.00
Figurine, Sir Isaac Newton, brn stamp 395.00
Figurine, Tom Kitten, Beatrix Potter, gold stamp 145.00
Figurine, Yorkshire terrier, seated, #3083 ....65.00
Flask, squirrel 30.00
Mug, Jeremy Fisher 55.00
Mug, Old Mr Brown 60.00

Big Little Books

The first Big Little Book was published in 1933 and copyrighted in 1932 by the Whitman Publishing Company of Racine, Wisconsin. Its hero was Dick Tracy. The concept was so well accepted that others soon followed Whitman's example; and though the 'Big Little Book' phrase became a trademark of the Whitman Company, the formats of his competitors (Saalfield, Goldsmith, Van Wiseman, Lynn, and World Syndicate) were exact copies. Today's Big Little Book buffs collect them all.

These hand-sized sagas of adventure were illustrated with full-page cartoons on the right-hand page and the story narration on the left. Colorful cardboard covers contained hundreds of pages, usually totaling over an inch in thickness. Big Little Books originally sold for 10¢ at the dime store; as late as the mid-1950s when the popularity of comic books caused sales to decline signaling an end to production, their price had risen to a mere 20¢. Their appeal was directed toward the pre-teens who bought, traded, and hoarded Big Little Books. Because so many were stored in attics and closets, many have survived. Among the super heroes are G-Men, Flash Gordon, Tarzan, the Lone Ranger, and Red Ryder; in a lighter vein, you'll find such lovable characters as Blondie and Dagwood, Mickey Mouse, Little Orphan Annie, and Felix the Cat.

In the early to mid-'30s, Whitman published several Big Little Books as advertising premiums for the Coco Malt Company, who packed them in boxes of their cereal. These are highly prized by today's collectors, as are Disney stories and super-hero adventures. Our advisor for this category is Ron Donnelly; he is listed in the Directory under Alabama.

Ace Drummond, Whitman #1177, 1935, VG 23.00
Adventures of Dick Tracy Detective, Whitman #707, VG 135.00
Adventures of Pete the Tramp, Saalfield #1082, 1935, VG 32.00
Air Fighters of America, Whitman #1448, 1941, EX 22.00
Alice in Wonderland, Whitman #759, 1934, EX 45.00

Alley Oop and Dinny in the Jungles of Moo, 1936, EX, $35.00.

Andy Panda & the Pirate Ghosts, Whitman #1459, 1947, EX 26.00
Andy Panda's Vacation, Whitman #1485, EX 30.00
Arizona Kid on the Bandit Trail, Whitman #1192, 1936, EX 35.00
Beasts of Tarzan, #1410, 1937, EX 57.00
Believe It or Not, Whitman #760, hardcover, 1931, VG 17.50
Big Chief Wahoo & the Great Gusto, Whitman #1443, 1938, EX .28.00
Billy the Kid, Whitman #773, 1935, EX 25.00
Blondie, Papa Knows Best, Whitman #1446, 1945, EX 35.00
Bob Stone the Young Detective, Whitman #1432, 1937, EX 28.00
Bringing Up Father, Whitman #1133, 1934, EX 35.00
Buccaneer, Whitman #1470, 1938, EX 28.00
Buck Jones in Ride 'Em Cowboy, Whitman #1116, 1937, EX 46.00
Buck Rogers in City Below the Sea, hardbk, Whitman #765, EX .80.00

Buck Rogers 25th Century AD, #742, 1933, EX 100.00
Buffalo Bill Plays a Lone Hand, Whitman #1194, EX 35.00
Captain Midnight & Secret Squadron, Whitman #1488, 1941, EX ..26.00
Charlie Chan Solves a New Mystery, Whitman #1459, 1940, EX ..44.00
Chester Gump Finds...Treasure, hardbk, Whitman #776, 1934, VG ..13.00
Cowboy Stories, Whitman #724, 1933, EX 38.00
Dan Dunn & the Underworld Gorillas, Whitman #1417, 1941, VG+ ...28.00
Danger Trails in Africa, Whitman #1151, 1935, VG+ 22.00
Desert Eagle Rides Again, Whitman #1458, 1941, EX 35.00
Dick Tracy & the Hotel Murders, Whitman #1420, 1937, VG+ ..28.00
Dick Tracy & the Spider Gang, Whitman #1446, 1936, EX 60.00
Don O'Daire Finds War, Whitman #1438, 1940, VG+ 10.00
Don Wilson, USN Lt Commander, Whitman #1107, 1935, VG+ ..17.00
Donald Duck Gets Fed Up, Whitman #1462, 1938, EX 55.00
Donald Duck Hunting for Trouble, Whitman #1478, 1938, VG ..23.00
Donald Duck Sees Stars, Whitman #1422, 1941, VG+ 38.00
Erik Noble & the Forty-Niners, Whitman #772, 1934, EX 24.00
Flame Boy & the Indians' Secret, Whitman #1464, 1938, EX+ 34.00
Flash Gordon & Power Men of Mongo, Whitman #1469, VG 45.00
Flash Gordon & Water World of Mongo, Whitman #1407, 1937, EX ..64.00
Flash Gordon & Witch Queen of Mongo, Whitman #1190, 1936, NM .100.00
Frank Merriwell at Yale, Whitman #1121, 1935, VG+ 25.00
Freckles & the Lost Diamond Mine, #1164, EX 45.00
G-Man on the Crime Trail, Whitman #1118, 1936, EX+ 39.00
Gang Busters Step In, Whitman #1433B, 1939, VG+ 28.00
George O'Brien & the Hooded Riders, Whitman #1457, 1940, NM 48.00
Green Hornet Returns, Whitman #1496, 1941, EX 80.00
Hall of Fame of the Air, Whitman #1150, 1936, EX 38.00
Hockey Spare, Saalfield #1125, 1937, VG 8.50
In the Name of the Law, Whitman #1155, 1937, NM 44.00
Invaders, Whitman #2012, 1967, G 3.50
Jack Armstrong & Ivory Treasure, Whitman #1435B, 1937, EX ..50.00
Jackie Cooper in Gangster Boy, Whitman #1402, 1939, VG+ 28.00
Jane Arden & Vanished Princess, Whitman #1498, 1938, VG+ ..23.00
Jane Withers in This Is the Life, Whitman #1179, 1938, EX 38.00
Jim Starr of the Border Patrol, Whitman #1428, 1937, EX 28.00
Jungle Jim, Whitman #1138, 1936, VG+ 33.00
Just Kids, Saalfield #1052, 1934, G 18.00
Kayo in the Land of Sunshine, Whitman #1105, 1937, VG+ 28.00
Kazan, King of the Pack, Whitman #1471, 1940, EX 33.00
Laughing Dragon of Oz, Whitman #1126, 1934, G 150.00
Little Annie Rooney, hardbk, Saalfield #1054, 1934, VG 15.00
Little Men, Whitman #1150, 1934, EX 24.00
Little Orphan Annie & Sandy, Whitman #716, 1933, VG+ 78.00
Little Women, Whitman #757, 1934, G+ 15.00
Lone Ranger & Red Renegades, Whitman #1489, 1943, VG+ 28.00
Lost Patrol, Whitman #753, 1934, VG 18.00
Mandrake the Magician, Whitman #1167, EX 60.00
Men of the Mounted, Whitman #755, 1934, VG+ 24.00
Mickey Mouse & Pluto the Racer, Whitman #1128, 1936, VG ...33.00
Mickey Mouse & the Dude Ranch Bandit, Whitman #1471, EX+ .50.00
Mickey Mouse & the Pirate Submarine, Whitman #1463, 1939, EX ..48.00
Mickey Mouse Runs His Own Newspaper, Whitman #1409, 1937, EX .50.00
Mickey Mouse the Mail Pilot, Whitman #731, 1933, VG 38.00
Mutt & Jeff, Whitman #1113, 1936, G 38.00
Pat Nelson, Ace of the Test Pilots, Whitman #1937, EX 34.00
Peggy Brown & the Mystery Basket, Whitman #1411, 1941, EX ..28.00
Perry Winkle & the Rinkeydinks, Whitman #1199, 1937, VG+ ..21.00
Pluto the Pup, Whitman #1467, 1936, EX 54.00
Popeye, Whitman #5755, 1967, VG 3.50
Popeye & the Deep Sea Mystery, Whitman #1499, 1939, G 15.00
Popeye Sees the Sea, Whitman #1163, 1936, VG 30.00
Powder Smoke Range, Whitman #1176, 1935, EX 38.00
Radio Patrol, Trailing Safeblowers, Whitman #1173, 1937, VG ..25.00

Red Death on the Range, Whitman #1449, 1940, VG 18.00
Red Ryder in War on the Range, Whitman #1473, 1942, VG+ ...24.00
Return of Tarzan, Whitman #1102, 1936, VG+ 28.00
Rex Beach's Jaragu of the Jungle, Whitman #1424, 1937, EX 38.00
Robinson Crusoe, Whitman #719, 1934, G+ 24.00
Scrappy, Whitman #1122, VG+ 20.00
Sequoia, Whitman #1161, 1935, VG+ 18.00
Silver Streak, Whitman #1155, 1935, VG+ 18.00
Smilin' Jack, Speed Pilot, Whitman #1473, 1941, VG+ 28.00
SOS Coast Guard, Whitman #1191, 1936, VG 22.00
Spy, Whitman #768, 1936, VG+ 19.00
Story of Charlie McCarthy & Edgar Bergen, 1938, EX 35.00
Tailspin Tommy & Hooded Flyer, Whitman #1423, EX 55.00
Tailspin Tommy Hunting...Pirate Gold, Whitman #1172, '35, VG+ ...21.00
Tarzan & the Golden Lion, Whitman #1448, 1943, G 18.00
Tarzan of the Apes, Whitman #744, 1933, VG+ 48.00
Terry & the Pirates, hardbk, Whitman #1156, 1935, EX 38.00
Texas Kid, Whitman #1429, 1937, EX 28.00
Three Musketeers, Whitman #1131, 1936, VG+ 35.00
Tiny Tim & the Mechanical Men, Whitman #1172, 1937, VG+ ...28.00
Tom Beatty, Ace of the Service, Whitman #1165, 1937, G 15.00
Tom Beatty & the Big Brain Gang, Whitman #1420, 1939, VG+ .18.00
Tom Mix & Tony Jr in Terror Trail, Whitman #762, 1935, G 22.00
Tom Mix in the Fighting Cowboy, Whitman #1144, VG 30.00
Two-Gun Montana, Whitman #1104, 1936, EX 24.00
Wash Tubs in Pandemonia, Whitman #751, 1934, G 15.00
Wells Fargo, Whitman #1471, 1938, NM 55.00
West Point Five, hardbk, Saalfield #1124, 1937, G 7.50
West Point of the Air, Whitman #1164, 1935, G+ 12.00
Wings of the USA, Whitman #1407, 1940, VG 18.00
Zane Grey's King of the Royal Mounted, Whitman #1103, 1936, EX ...**44.00**
Zane Grey's Tex Throne Comes...West, Whitman #1440, 1937, VG+ .18.00

Bing and Grondahl

In 1853 brothers M.H. and J.H. Bing formed a partnership with Frederick Vilhelm Grondahl in Copenhagen, Denmark. Their early wares were porcelain plaques and figurines designed by the noted sculptor Thorvaldsen of Denmark. Dinnerware production began in 1863, and by 1889 their underglaze color 'Copenhagen Blue' had earned them worldwide acclaim. They are perhaps most famous today for their Christmas plates, the first of which was made in 1895. See also Limited Edition Plates.

Bowl, vegetable; Offenbach, oval 120.00
Cup & saucer, Offenbach 40.00
Figurine, Boston terrier, 32330, 7½" 150.00
Figurine, boy & dog, #1747 ....120.00
Figurine, boy w/accordion, #1991 ....275.00
Figurine, girl & cat, #1779 ....120.00
Figurine, girl & cat sitting, #2329 ....180.00
Figurine, girl crying, #2246 ....135.00
Figurine, girl kissing boy, 7" 125.00
Figurine, mandolin player, #1600, lg 275.00
Figurine, monkey family, #1581, 4¾" 120.00
Figurine, Pekingese, #2114 ....75.00
Figurine, sm girl w/purse, #1574, 6½" 145.00
Pitcher, Offenbach, 36-oz 160.00
Plate, dinner; Offenbach 45.00
Platter, Offenbach, oval, 10" 90.00
Platter, Offenbach, oval, 16¼" 180.00
Teapot, Offenbach 165.00
Tray, 2 egrets & nes ···/babies, 1940, 5" sq 40.00

Binoculars

There are several types of binoculars, and the terminology used to refer to them is not consistent or precise. Generally, 'field glasses' refer to simple Galilean optics, where the lens next to the eye (the ocular) is concave and dished away from the eye. By looking through the large lens (the objective), it is easy to see that the light goes straight through the two lenses. These are lower power, have a very small field of view, and do not work nearly as well as prism binoculars. In a smaller size, they are opera glasses, and their price increases if they are covered with mother-of-pearl (fairly common but very attractive), abalone shell (more colorful), ivory (quite scarce), or other exotic materials. Field glasses are not valuable unless very unusual or by the best makers, such as Zeiss or Leitz. Prism binoculars have the objective lens offset from the eyepiece and give a much better view. This is the standard binocular form, called Porro prisms, and dates from around 1900. Another type of prism binocular is the roof prism, which at first resembles the straight-through field glasses, with two simple cylinders or cones, here containing very small prisms. These can be distinguished by the high quality views they give and by a thin diagonal line that can be seen when looking backwards through the objective. In general, German binoculars are the most desirable, followed by American, English, and finally French, which can be of good quality but are very common unless of unusual configuration. Japanese optics of WWII or before are often of very high quality. 'Made in Occupied Japan' binoculars are very common, but collectors prize those by Nippon Kogaku (Nikon). Some binoculars are center focus (CF), with one central wheel that focuses both sides at once. These are much easier to use but more difficult to seal against dirt and moisture. Individual focus (IF) binoculars are adjusted by rotating each eyepiece and tend to be cleaner inside in older optics. Each type is preferred by different collectors. Very large binoculars are always of great interest. All binoculars are numbered according to their magnifying power and the diameter of the objective in millimeters. 6 x 30 optics magnify six times and have 30 millimeter objectives.

Prisms are easily knocked out of alignment, requiring an expensive and difficult repair. If severe, this misalignment is immediately noticeable on use by the double-image scene. Minor damage can be seen by focusing on a small object and slowly moving the binoculars away from the eye, which will cause the images to appear to separate. Overall cleanliness should be checked by looking backwards (through the objective) at a light or the sky, when any film or dirt on the lenses or prisms can easily be seen. Pristine binoculars are worth far more than when dirty or misaligned, and broken or cracked optics lower the value far more. Cases help keep binoculars clean but do not add materially to the value. The following listings assume a very good overall condition, with generally clean and alligned optics.

Our advisor for this category is Peter Abrahams, who studies and collects binoculars and other optics. Please contact, especially to exchange reference material. Mr. Abrahams is listed in the Directory under Oregon.

Field Glasses

Folding, modern, hinged flat case, oculars outside 10.00
Folding or telescoping, no bbls, old 125.00
Goerz 5x40, military drab gr, WWI, IF, many other makers 40.00
Ivory covered, various sm szs & makers 180.00
LeMaire, bl leather/brass, various szs, other Fr makers same 25.00
Metal, emb hunting scene, various sm szs & makers 35.00
Pearl covered, various sm szs & makers 90.00
Porc covered, delicate painting, various sm szs & makers 175.00
US Naval Gun Factory Optical Shop 6x30 ....75.00
Zeiss 'Galan' 2x5x34, modern fringe design look, early 1920s 80.00

Prism Binoculars (Porro)

Barr & Stroud 7x50, Porro II prisms, IF, WWII 110.00
Bausch & Lomb Zephyr, 7x35 & other, CF 100.00
Bausch & Lomb 6x30, IF, WWI, Signal Corps 40.00
Bausch & Lomb 7x50, IF, WWII, other makers same 45.00
Bausch & Lomb/Zeiss, Pat 1897, 8x17, CF 140.00
Crown Optical, 6x30, IF, WWI, filters 45.00
France, various makers & szs, if not unusual 45.00
Goerz Trieder Binocle, various szs, unusual adjustment 65.00
Leitz 6x30 Dienstglas, IF, good optics 65.00
Leitz 8x30 Binuxit, CF, outstanding optics 150.00
Nikon 9x35, 7x35, CF, 1950s 65.00
Nippon Kogaku 7x50, IF, Made in Occupied Japan 85.00
Ross Stephada 7x30, CF, wide angle, 1930s 90.00
Sard 6x42, IF, very wide angle, WWII 750.00
Toko (Tokyo Opt Co) 7x50, IF, Made in Occupied Japan 45.00
Universal Camera 6x30, IF, WWII, other makers same 40.00
US Naval Gun Factory Optical Shop 6x30, IF, filters, WWI 70.00
US Naval Gun Factory Optical 10x45, IF, WWI 140.00
US Navy 20x120, various makers, WWII & later 2,000.00
Warner & Swasey (important maker) 8x20, CF, 1902 ....250.00
Zeiss, Starmobi 12/24/42x60, turret eyepcs, 1920s 2,000.00
Zeiss Deltrintem 8x30, CF, 1930s 95.00
Zeiss Teleater 3x13, CF, bl, leather 85.00
Zeiss 15x60, CF or IF, various models 600.00
Zeiss 8x40 Delactis, CF or IF, 1930s 150.00

Roof Prism Binoculars

Hensoldt, Dialyt, long tapered bbl, varous szs, 1930s-80s 110.00
Hensoldt Universal Dialyt, 6x26, 2.5x26, cylindrical, 1930s 80.00
Leitz Trinovid 7x42 & other, CF, 1960s-80s, EX 375.00
Zeiss Dialyt 8x30, CF, 1960s 400.00

Birdcages

Birdcages can be found in various architectural styles and in a range of materials such as wood, wicker, brass, and gilt metal with ormolu mounts. Those that once belonged to the wealthy are sometimes inlaid with silver or jewels. In the 1800s, it became fashionable to keep birds, and some of the most beautiful examples found today date back to that era. Musical cages that contained automated bird figures became popular; today these command prices of several thousand dollars. In the latter 1800s, wicker styles came into vogue. Collectors still appreciate their graceful lines and find they adapt easily to modern homes.

Pine/wire, Fr Provincial, arched bonnet, 18x24x11" 465.00
Polychromed, cvd & metal mtd, octagonal, Oriental, 34x28" 450.00
Tin, minor pitting & rust, 19¼" H 220.00
Walnut & wire pavilion form, Continental, 19th C, 22", EX 500.00
Walnut w/wire bars, poplar bk, worn patina, rprs, 23"+base 250.00
Wire pavilion, ebony finial, floral-inlay walnut base 22" 500.00

Bisque

Bisque is a term referring to unglazed earthenware or porcelain that has been fired only once. During the Victorian era, bisque figurines became very popular. Most were highly decorated in pastels and gilt and demonstrated a fine degree of workmanship in the quality of their modeling. Few were marked. See also Heubach; Nodders; Dolls; Piano Babies.

Boy, colonial dress, #d, sgn, 10" 125.00
Boy & girl in fancy chairs, much gold, 6½", pr 165.00
Boy & girl w/baskets, floral attire, Germany, 15", pr 450.00
Boy carrying basket, bl shorts/lav shirt, Germany, 14" 235.00
Boy w/book, pack on bk, #d, 9" 120.00
Bust, lad, hat w/flowers, pk/bl coat, flowered shirt, 11" 245.00
Bust, youthful blond man w/gray hat, mk MB, 11x6½" 295.00
Cherubs support rtcl vase, gold trim, 9" 195.00
Girl w/basket, gold trim, HP florals & birds, Germany, 7" 72.00
Girl w/dog in apron, boy w/feeding dish, mc, 13x4", pr 395.00
Lamp, boy & girl w/dancing bear figural, Germany, 11" 190.00
Musicians, mc, Germany, 5", 6-pc set 120.00
Planter, fox in boots w/musket & pipe, Germany 160.00
Vase, boy in hat holds tennis racquet/stands by tree trunk, 8" 90.00
Vase, figure of girl w/team of horses, Germany, 7¾" 75.00
Wall pocket, boy & girl in balcony, scrolling, mc, 7" 75.00

Black Americana

Black memorabilia is without a doubt a field that encompasses the most widely exploited ethnic group in our history. But within this field there are many levels of interest: arts and achievements such as folk music and literature, caricatures in advertising, souvenirs, toys, fine art, and legitimate research into the days of their enslavement and enduring struggle for equality. The list is endless.

In the listings below are some with a derogatory connotation. Thankfully, these are from a bygone era and represent the mores of a culture that existed nearly a century ago. They are included only to convey the fact that they are a part of this growing area of collecting interest. Black Americana catalogs featuring a wide variety of items for sale are available; see the Directory under Clubs, Newsletters, and Catalogs for more information. See also Cookie Jars; Postcards; Posters; Sheet Music.

Fishing lure, Sprinkling Sambo, plastic, MIB, $125.00.

Apron, couple pulling mule applique 45.00
Apron, golliwogg image, mc, child's pinafore style 115.00
Ashtray, butler holding tray figural, CI, on stand, 32x10x8" 500.00
Ashtray, Coon Chicken Inn, smiling face, glass, 1950s, NM 25.00
Ashtray, shanty form, ceramic 40.00
Biscuit jar, Mammy figural, basket hdl, Japan 800.00
Book, Little Black Sambo, Whitman, 1959, M 32.00
Book, Nights w/Uncle Remus, JC Harris, 1881, G- 50.00
Book, Selected Slave Songs, Hampton (Institute), 1881, EX 40.00
Book, Uncle Tom's Cabin, 5 color plates, England, 1920s, NM ...85.00
Bookends, boys eating watermelons, chalkware, pr 200.00
Coffee can, Luzianne Mammy Coffee & Chicory wht label, 1-lb ..35.00
Condiment set, ceramic, boys & hut on tray, Japan, 1950s 125.00
Cookbook, Mammy on wooden cover 45.00
Cookie jar, Aunt Jemima, F&F 400.00

Corn bread pan, Aunt Jemima Meal stamped on bottom, 5-stick ...175.00
Cracker jar, Chef, Cream of Wheat, Japan, 10" 850.00
Creamer & sugar bowl, Aunt Jemima, F&F 150.00
Doll, baby, bsk, jtd arms & legs, Japan, 4" 65.00
Doll, plush felt/wool hair/glass eyes, N Wellings, '30s, 15" 195.00
Dolls, Mammy & Mose, pnt corn husks, old & well made, 8", pr ..350.00
Doorstop, Mammy w/hands in washtub, pnt lead, ca 1910 ....235.00
Dresser scarf, embr girl eating watermelon 45.00
Figurine, baby emerging from egg w/rabbit, bsk, 3¾" 150.00
Figurine, boy on fence w/watermelon, pnt lead, 3" 75.00
Figurine, Mammy, CI, 3" 100.00
Grocery peg board, wooden Mammy figural, EX pnt 60.00
Gunny sack, Mammy printed on front 42.50
Handkerchief, people eating watermelon, silk, 10¼" sq 45.00
Hitching post, CI stable boy, mc pnt, att Fiske, 43", pr, EX 4,750.00
Humidor, Blk girl, bsk, Germany 335.00
Humidor, man w/pipe, Germany, 1930s, sm 390.00
Lamp, figure of a Blk man, ceramic, ca 1940, 14", M 125.00
Match holder, dbl; Mammy, tin & pnt copper, 4½x5" 245.00
Menu, Club Plantation, souvenir, 1930s, 5x6" 25.00
Menu, list & child's face pnt on wooden paddle 75.00
Mug, Sambo's Restaurants, US flag motif, rare 65.00
Nodder, Mammy holding watermelon, ceramic, Japan, NM 295.00
Note pad holder, Mammy figural, chalkware 85.00
Pancake mold, Aunt Jemima , aluminum 145.00
Pancake shaker, Aunt Jemima, yel bottom, ceramic, 9½", EX 65.00
Pancake shaker; Aunt Jemima, yel plastic, F&F, NM 100.00
Paperweight, Mammy, lead, 1920 ....250.00
Plate, Famous & Dandy, 6" 175.00
Poster, Harlem on the Prairie, 1st Blk western, 1-sheet, EX 465.00
Print, Types of African Races, color litho, 1880s 60.00
Program, Follies Bergere, Josephine Baker, 1927, EX 198.00
Program, Nat'l Assoc of Negro Musicians, 1941, 20-pg, VG 25.00
Recipe box, Mammy, plastic, Fosta, EX 125.00
Recipe box, Mammy, plastic, unmk F&F 125.00
Shakers, Al Jolson & wht gloves, ceramic, pr 195.00
Shakers, Aunt Jemima & Uncle Mose, F&F, 3½", pr 45.00
Shakers, Aunt Jemima & Uncle Mose, F&F, 5", pr 75.00
Shakers, boy & girl in yel aprons w/red spoons, ceramic, pr 45.00
Shakers, boy riding alligator (2nd shaker), ceramic, unmk, pr 45.00
Shakers, boy sits/holds watermelon slice (shaker), ceramic, pr 75.00
Shakers, Butler & Mammy w/plaid dress, ceramic, pr 110.00
Shakers, Jonah & the Whale, ceramic, unmk, pr 95.00
Shakers, Mammy, Luzianne, F&F, pr 150.00
Shakers, Mammy, pnt wood, Japan, 5", pr 35.00
Shakers, Mammy & Chef, yel clothes, Pearl China, 7½", pr 150.00
Shakers, Mammy & Pappy, pnt chalkware, NM, pr 30.00
Shakers, porter carrying suitcases (shakers), ceramic, pr 125.00
Shakers, singer & horn player, ceramic, unmk, 1990, 3½", pr 30.00
Shakers, 2 children sit in yel basket, ceramic, pr 65.00
Sheet music, Rastus on Parade, Civil War Battalion, 1896, M 45.00
Sheet music, Whitewash Man, 1908, EX 7.50
Sheet music, 5 Early Louisiana Songs of Slavery, EX 28.00
Soda bottle, Mammy figural, early, M 100.00
Spice jar, Ginger; Aunt Jemima, plastic, NM 65.00
Spice set, Aunt Jemima, copper rack, w/orig containers, NM .1,100.00
Spice set, w/red plastic rack, F&F 495.00
Spoon rest, Mammy face, Rockingham 195.00
String holder, ceramic, Chef, yel hat, brn face, Fredricksburg 385.00
String holder, ceramic, full-bodied Mammy, slot for scissors 375.00
String holder, ceramic, Mammy face, 1940s, rare 300.00
Swizzle sticks, Zulu ladies, 1950s, M on card 25.00
Syrup, Aunt Jemima figural, plastic, F&F 60.00
Tablecloth, Mammy w/market basket, hanging laundry, & w/pie 160.00

Toaster cover, Mammy, youthful w/oilcloth face 40.00
Toothpick holder, boys w/melons on cotton bale, pot metal, pr ...75.00
Toothpick holder, Coon Chicken Inn 250.00
Toothpick holder, Mammy in rocker, bsk, mc pnt, 4x5x2¾" 130.00
Towel, linen, boy w/watermelon 40.00
Towel, linen, Mammy w/pie 40.00
Toy, Shuffling Sambo, pnt wood, Bakers in Seattle, 14", NM 185.00
Tumbler, Aunt Fannies' Cabin Restaurant 20.00
Tumbler, Coon Chicken Inn 65.00
Tumbler, Old Folks at Home song 10.00
Wall pocket, Blk Chef, ceramic, 7" 245.00
Wall pocket, Mammy, gr scarf 250.00
Whistle, man's face form, pnt tin, ca 1900, EX 95.00

Black Cats

Made in Japan during the fifties, these novelty cats may be found bearing the labels of several different importers, all with their own particular characteristics. The best known and most collectible of these cats are from the Shafford line. Even when unmarked, they are easily identified by their red bows, green eyes, and white whiskers, eyeliners, and eyebrows. Relco/Royal Sealy cats are tall and slender, and their bow ties are gold with red dots. Wales is a wonderful line with yellow eyes and gold detailing; Enesco cats have blue eyes, and there are other lines as well. When evaluating your black cats, be sure to inspect their paint and judge them accordingly. 50% paint should relate to 50% of our suggested values, which are given for cats in mint (or nearly mint) paint.

Ashtray, flat face shape, Shafford, 4½x4½" 18.00
Ashtray, head-shape w/open mouth, Shafford, 3" 18.00
Cigarette lighter, Shafford, 5½" 150.00
Condiment set, 2 heads, J&M bows w/spoons, Shafford, 4" 65.00
Cookie jar, lg cat head, Shafford 85.00
Creamer & sugar bowl, cat-head lids are shakers, 5⅜" 45.00
Creamer & sugar bowl, Shafford, pr 45.00
Cruet, oil & vinegar; co-joined cats, 1-pc, Royal Sealy 40.00
Cruet, slender form, gold collar & tie, tail hdl 12.00
Cruets, he w/O eyes, she w/V eyes & hair bow, Shafford, pr 50.00
Decanter, upright cat holds bottle w/cork stopper, Shafford 50.00
Demitasse pot, tail hdl, bow finial, Shafford, 7½" 95.00
Desk caddy, pen forms tail, spring body holds letters, 6½" 8.00
Egg cup, cat face on bowl, ped ft, Shafford 30.00
Grease jar, sm cat head, Shafford 75.00
Measuring cup, 4 cups on wood rack w/cat's face, Shafford 150.00
Mug, Shafford, rare lg sz 40.00
Mug, Shafford, 3½" 30.00
Pincushion, cushion on bk, tongue measure 22.50

Pitcher, Shafford, hard to find, mid-size, 5", $50.00. (This can be found in 3 sizes, all are scarce.)

Pitcher, milk; upright, Shafford 85.00
Pot holder caddy, 'teapot' cat, 3-hook, Shafford 85.00
Shaker, long cat, salt in 1 end, pepper in other end, Shafford 75.00
Shakers, rnd-bodied teapot cat, Shafford, pr 40.00
Shakers, seated, bl eyes, Enesco label, 5¾", pr 15.00
Spice rack, wireware face w/marble eyes, 4 shakers, Shafford 165.00
Spice set, gr eyes, 6 sq shakers w/appl red bows, wood rack 125.00
Spice set, yel eyes, 9 sq shakers w/appl red bows, wood rack 125.00
Stacking tea set, mamma pot, kitty creamer & sugar bowl, yel eyes ...60.00
Strainer, w/cat face, long wood hdl, Shafford 60.00
Teapot, bulbous body, head lid, gr eyes, Shafford, 6½" 45.00
Teapot, dbl-chamber, Shafford 95.00
Teapot, panther-like, gold eyes, sm 20.00
Teapot, upright, ovoid body (not ball-shaped), Shafford, 7" 150.00
Teapot, upright cat, paw spout, yel eyes, red bow, Wales, 8¼" 60.00
Toothpick holder, cat by vase atop book, Occupied Japan 12.00
Wall pocket, flattened 'teapot' cat, Shafford, scarce 85.00
Wall rack, long flat cat w/hooks for utensils, Shafford 85.00
Wine, emb cat's face, gr eyes, Shafford, sm 20.00

Black Glass

Black glass is a type of colored glass that when held to strong light usually appears deep purple, though since each glasshouse had its own formula, tones may vary. It was sometimes etched or given a satin finish; and occasionally it was decorated with silver, gold, enamel, coralene, or any of these in combination. The decoration was done either by the glasshouse or by firms that specialized in decorating glassware. Crystal, jade, colored glass, or milk glass was sometimes used with the black as an accent. Black glass has been made by many companies since the 17th century. Contemporary glasshouses produced black glass during the Depression, seldom signing their product. It is still being made today.

To learn more about the subject, we recommend *A Collector's Guide to Black Glass*, written by our advisor, Marlena Toohey; she is listed in the Directory under Colorado. Look for her newly updated value guide. See also Tiffin, L.E. Smith, and other specific manufacturers.

Ashtray, elephant stands in center, Greensburg, 1920s, 6" 28.00
Bowl, crimped, 12", +flower frog 40.00
Bowl, flared, unknown mfg, 1920s, 10" 17.50
Candelabrum, 3-light, US Glass, 1930s, 6½x7" 110.00
Candlestick, Ellen, unknown mfg, pr 27.50
Candlestick, hexagonal std, rnd base, 7", pr 50.00
Compote, paneled, flared rim, ftd, 6x8¾" 45.00
Creamer & sugar bowl, Octagon Scroll, US Glass, 1930s 22.50
Creamer & sugar bowl, Ovide, silver decor, Hazel-Atlas 26.00
Epergne, unknown maker, ca 1915-30, 9¾x7½" 160.00

Hatpin holder with powder-box base, Mary Gregory-style stork painting, 7¾", $65.00.

Ladle, mayonnaise; 1920s 24.00
Pitcher, cylindrical, unknown mfg, 1920s, 1-pt 20.00
Planter box, emb nude dancers, LE Smith 50.00
Plate, maple leaf form 38.00
Shakers, floral sterling o/l, Hazel Atlas, pr 28.00
Vase, classic form, att Sinclaire, 9" 38.00
Vase, dancers in relief, 7½" 40.00
Vase, HP herons among swamp grass, triangular, 7½" 175.00
Vase, ped ft, hdls, 5¾" 24.00
Vase, Poppy, satin finish, US Glass, #16255, 1930 ....80.00
Vase, silver florals on trophy shape, 8" 35.00
Vase, slim w/wide flared rim, unknown mfg, 10½" 42.50
Wall vase, crackle, US Glass, 1920s, 5¾" 48.00

Blown Glass

Blown glass is rather difficult to date; 18th and 19th century examples vary little as to technique or style. It ranges from the primitive to the sophisticated, but the metallic content of very early glass caused tiny imperfections that are obvious upon examination, and these are often indicative of age.

In America, Stiegel introduced the English technique of using a patterned, part-size mold, a practice which was generally followed by many glasshouses after the Revolution. From 1820 to about 1850, glass was blown into full-size three-part molds. In the listings below, glass is assumed clear unless color is mentioned. Numbers refer to a standard reference book, *American Glass* by Helen McKearin. See also Bottles and specific manufacturers. Our advisor for this category is Mark Vuono; he is listed in the Directory under Connecticut.

Bowl, amethyst, 16 ribs, flared rim w/folded lip, 3x4¼" 1,265.00
Bowl, aqua, flared rim, appl ft, 2½x7¼" 85.00
Bowl, aqua, folded rim, rare sz, 1¼x3¾" 220.00
Bowl, deep puce, lily pad decor, ftd, 3x3¼" 3,200.00
Bowl, dk violet, 16 deep ribs, 3½x4¾" 880.00
Bowl, Pillar Mold, bulbous, ground pontil, 8" 275.00
Bowl, 16 broken-rib swirl, appl cobalt rim, 3½x5½" 550.00
Canister, tin lid, 11¼" 105.00
Chestnut flask, cobalt, 18 swirled ribs, pontil, 3" 440.00
Compote, emerald gr w/gilt bands, hollow ft, 8¼x8" 75.00
Creamer, amethyst, appl hdl & folded lip, 4¼" 330.00
Creamer, cobalt, 16 vertical ribs, appl ft & hdl, 4¼" 1,800.00
Creamer, cobalt, 20-dmn, appl ft & hdl, 3⅞" 990.00
Creamer, cobalt, 24 ribs & 23 dmns, appl ft & hdl, 3½" 935.00
Creamer, Dmn Quilt, cobalt, appl hdl, 3¼" 65.00
Creamer, sapphire bl, 16 ribs, appl hdl, wht opaque lip, 4" 275.00
Cruet, vertical ribs, purple amethyst, pontil, 6⅞" 400.00
Cruet, 15 vertical ribs, appl hdl, 9"+stopper 75.00
Egg cup, amethyst, 3½" 60.00
Goblet, wafer stem, wide ft, 5⅛" 70.00
Mug, amethyst, 16-broken-rib swirl, appl hdl, 2⅝" 1,650.00
Mug, cobalt, cylindrical w/hdl, 5⅞" 990.00
Pan, amethyst, swirled color, folded lip, 2x5½" 1,750.00
Pan, aqua, folded lip, 4½" 220.00
Pan, golden amber, folded rim, 4x10½" 1,125.00
Pan, olive-yel, folded rim, 2¾x8½" 770.00
Pan, sapphire bl, 16-broken-rib swirl, folded rim, 6" 55.00
Pitcher, aqua, appl ft & fancy hdl, 3⅜" 330.00
Pitcher, aqua, lily pad decor, threaded neck, 7" 5,500.00
Pitcher, dk olive gr, crooked appl hdl, 5¼", NM 880.00
Pitcher, lily pad decor, appl threading, 5½" 1,100.00
Pitcher, root beer-amber, pontil, appl hdl & base, 8" 325.00
Pitcher, sapphire bl, lily pad decor, appl hdl, 7⅜" 2,750.00

Pitcher, 2 appl chain-like rings & hdl, flint, 6½" 850.00
Salt cellar, amethyst, 14-dmn, chip, 1⅜x3" 275.00
Salt cellar, amethystine, vining foliage eng, ftd, 2½" 195.00
Salt cellar, cobalt, checkered dmns, appl ft, 2¾" 1,700.00
Salt cellar, cobalt, 12 ribs, appl ft, 2⅞" 330.00
Salt cellar, violet, knop stem, flared rim, 2⅝x2⅞" 1,100.00
Sugar bowl, folded rim on lid w/facet-cut finial, 10¼" 140.00
Sugar bowl, peacock bl w/dk slag swirl, 10-dmn, ftd, 2¾x4" 1,265.00
Syllabub glass, cut panels, dmn-point band, Anglo-Irish, 4" 18.00
Vase, baluster stem, folded rim, appl ft, stain, 9" 125.00
Vase, dk amethyst w/opal swirls, 9½" 45.00
Walking stick, aqua-amber twist, 34½" 75.00
Whimsy rolling pin, blk, pontil, 13" 75.00

Blown Three-Mold Glass

A popular collectible in the 1920s, '30s, and '40s, blown three-mold glass has again gained the attention of many. Produced from approximately 1815 to 1840 in various New York, New England, and Midwestern glasshouses, it was a cheaper alternative to the expensive imported Irish cut glass.

Distinguishing features of blown three-mold glass are the three distinct mold marks and the concave-convex appearance of the glass. For every indentation on the inner surface of the ware, there will be a corresponding protuberance on the outside. Blown three-mold glass is most often clear with the exception of inkwells and a few known decanters. Any colored three-mold glass commands a premium price.

The numbers in the listings that follow refer to the book *American Glass* by George and Helen McKearin. Our advisor for this category is Mark Vuono; he is listed in the Directory under Connecticut.

Bottle, scent; GII-18, flared lip, residue, 3⅞" 250.00
Bottle, scent; GIII-12, 2¾"+orig stopper 300.00
Bottle, toilet water; cobalt, GI-3, type 1, 5¾"+stopper 300.00
Bottle, toilet water; GI-7, type 4, cobalt, 5½" 300.00
Bottle, toilet water; GI-7, type 4, purple, 5⅜" 235.00
Bowl, GII-18, appl ft, folded rim, broken blister, 5½x9" 3,600.00

Bowl, GIII-8, folded rim, footed, open pontil, rare, 3x5⅜", $2,500.00.

Creamer, GI-21, 4½" 290.00
Creamer, GI-29, sapphire bl, appl hdl, 4½", NM 2,300.00
Creamer, GII-18, 3⅝" 275.00
Creamer, GIII-12, appl rib hdl, tooled lip, 4¼" 150.00
Creamer, GIII-24, cobalt, appl hdl (glued), 3" 250.00
Creamer, GIII-6, pontil scar, appl hdl, 4⅜" 325.00
Decanter, GII-18, 3 appl rings, 8⅜"+stopper 195.00
Decanter, GIII-21, 4"+wheel stopper 300.00
Decanter, GV-9, pontil scar, tooled mouth, 8⅞" 200.00
Flip hat, GIII-23, pontil scar, folded rim, 2½" 110.00
Hat whimsy, GII-18, cobalt, folded rim, 2" 475.00
Pan, GIII, folded rim, 2⅛x7¼" 140.00
Pitcher, GIII-5, appl hdl, 6½" 1,450.00
Pitcher, GIII-12, appl hdl, 2⅛" 550.00

Salt cellar, GII-24, cobalt, 2⅝" 1,075.00
Salt cellar, GII-25, cobalt, lip flake, 1¾x2½" 415.00
Tumbler, GII-18, 3⅜" 220.00
Tumbler, GII-22, 3¼" 225.00
Tumbler, GIII-16, 4¾" 100.00
Vase, GII-18, appl ft, flared lip, 7¼" 1,450.00
Vase, GV-21, appl ft, stem & flared rim, 8¼" 1,375.00
Wine, GII-19, 4", EX, pr 60.00
Wine, GII-19 (bowl), appl ft & stem, 3⅞" 440.00

Blue and White Stoneware

Blue and white stoneware, much of which was decorated with such in-mold designs as grazing cows and Dutch children, was made by practically every American pottery from the turn of the century until the mid-1930s. Crocks, pitchers, wash sets, rolling pins, and canisters are only a few of the items that may be found in this type of 'country' pottery that has become one of today's popular collectibles.

Roseville, Brush-McCoy, Uhl Co., and Burley Winter were among those who produced it; but very few pieces were ever signed. Naturally, condition must be a prime consideration, especially if one is buying for resale; pieces with good, strong color and fully molded patterns bring premium prices. Normal wear and signs of age are to be expected since this was utility ware and received heavy use in busy households. In the listings that follow, crocks and jars are assumed without lids unless noted otherwise. For further information we recommend *Blue and White Stoneware* by Kathryn McNerny. See also specific manufacturers.

Batter jar, Wildflower, thick appl hdl, 8x7" 275.00
Bean pot, Boston Baked Beans, Swirl, heavy diffused pattern 300.00
Beer cooler, Elves, brass spigot, 18x14" 850.00
Bowl, Apricot, 9½" 85.00
Bowl, batter; Wildflower, w/hdl 400.00
Bowl, Daisy on Waffle, 10¾" 95.00
Bowl, Gadroon Arches (Feather Panels), 4½x9½" 150.00
Bowl, mixing; Flying Bird, 4x7½" 225.00
Bowl, Reverse Pyramids w/Reverse Picket Fence, 2½x4½" 150.00
Bowl, Wildflower, 4½x7" 100.00
Butter crock, Butterfly, orig lid & bail, 6½" 225.00
Butter crock, Daisy & Trellis, orig lid & bail, 4½" 200.00
Butter crock, Eagle, orig lid & bail, M 450.00
Butter crock, Grapes & Leaves, dbl ring around rim, 3x6½" 175.00
Canister, Basketweave, Cereal, orig lid, 7½" 350.00
Canister, Basketweave, Cloves, orig lid, 5" 250.00
Canister, Basketweave, Coffee, orig lid, 7½" 250.00
Canister, Basketweave, Pepper, orig lid, 5" 250.00
Canister, Basketweave, Put Your Fist In, orig lid, 7½" 700.00
Canister, Basketweave, Sugar, orig lid, 7½" 250.00
Canister, Basketweave, Tobacco, orig lid, 7½" 500.00
Canister, Snowflake, rpl lid, 6½x5¾" 150.00
Chamberpot, Wildflower, stenciled pattern, 6x11" 135.00
Coffeepot, Oval, Diffused Bl, bl-tipped knob, str sides, 11x4" 250.00
Coffeepot, Swirl, 'spurs' on hdl, acorn finial, 11½x6" 450.00
Cookie jar, Brickers, flat button finial, 8x8" 325.00
Cookie jar, Turkey Eye color drip, Diffused Bl bands, 9x8" 250.00
Cookie/biscuit jar, Flying Bird, orig lid, 9x6¾" 650.00
Cup, Bow Tie, bird transfer, 3¾x3½" 95.00
Cup, Wildflower w/emb Ribbon & Bow, 4½x2½" 85.00
Custard cup, Fishscale, 5x2½" 75.00
Egg storage crock, Barrel Staves, bail hdl, 5½x6" 185.00
Footwarmer, Diffused Bl, A Warm Friend, 12½x6½" 275.00
Grease jar, Flying Bird, orig lid 650.00
Ice crock, Barrel Staves, rope/tongs/ice block emb, 4½x6" 225.00

Iced tea cooler, Bl Band, flat lid, complete, 13x11" 295.00
Measuring cup, Spearpoint & Flower Panels, 6x6¾" 150.00
Milk crock, Daisy & Lattice, 4x8", NM 125.00
Milk crock, Lovebird, rstr bail & handgrip, 5½x9" 145.00
Mug, Basketweave & Flower, 5x3" 125.00
Mug, beer; advertising, Diffused Bl, sqd hdl 150.00
Mug, Cattails 150.00
Mug, Flying Bird, 5x3" 225.00
Mug, plain 65.00
Mug, Windy City (Fannie Flagg), Robinson Clay Products 200.00
Pickle crock, Bl Band, advertising, recessed lid, 12x9" 225.00
Pickle crock, Heart Band, advertising, rolled rim, 8x8" 225.00
Pie plate, Bl-Walled Brick-Edge, star-emb base, 10½" 100.00
Pitcher, Acorns, stenciled, 8x6½" 135.00
Pitcher, American Beauty Rose, 10" 350.00
Pitcher, Apricot, 8" 250.00
Pitcher, Avenue of Trees, allover bl, 9x7" 200.00
Pitcher, Barrel, +6 mugs 395.00
Pitcher, Basketweave & Flower, 9" 225.00
Pitcher, Bl Band, plain 100.00
Pitcher, Bl Band Scroll 160.00
Pitcher, Bl Sawtooth, Wht Hall 150.00
Pitcher, Bluebird, 9x7" 250.00
Pitcher, Butterfly, 9x7" 250.00
Pitcher, Castle & Fishscale, 8" 195.00
Pitcher, Cattails, 7½" 150.00
Pitcher, Cattails, 9" 185.00
Pitcher, Cherries & Leaves, w/printing, 9½" 350.00
Pitcher, Cherry Cluster, 7½" 195.00
Pitcher, Cherry Cluster & Basketweave, 10" 175.00
Pitcher, Cosmos 195.00
Pitcher, Cow, 8½" 250.00
Pitcher, Doe & Fawn, EX color 250.00
Pitcher, Doe & Fawn, sparce bl, 8½" 185.00
Pitcher, Dutch Boy & Girl by Windmill, 9" 225.00
Pitcher, Dutch Landscape, stenciled, tall 200.00
Pitcher, Eagle 450.00
Pitcher, Eagle w/Shield & Arrows, rare 500.00
Pitcher, Edelweiss, metal thumb rest, 9x5" 300.00
Pitcher, Fishscale & Wild Rose, 10" 160.00
Pitcher, Flying Bird, 9" 700.00
Pitcher, Grape Cluster on Trellis, allover bl, 7x7" 200.00
Pitcher, Hunting Scene, rare, 7x8" 400.00
Pitcher, Indian Boy & Girl, 6" 350.00
Pitcher, Indian Good Luck, stenciled 250.00
Pitcher, Indian Head in War Bonnet, dl bl, waffled body, 9" 435.00
Pitcher, Iris, 9" 225.00
Pitcher, Lady w/Harp, deep cobalt 200.00
Pitcher, Leaping Deer, 8½" 175.00
Pitcher, Lincoln, allover deep bl, 10x7" 600.00
Pitcher, Lincoln, allover deep bl, 4¾x4¾" 175.00
Pitcher, Lincoln, allover deep bl, 6x4" 250.00
Pitcher, Lincoln, allover deep bl, 7x5" 300.00
Pitcher, Lincoln, allover deep bl, 8x6" 350.00
Pitcher, Lincoln w/Log Cabin 525.00
Pitcher, Lovebird, arc bands, deep color, 8½" 450.00
Pitcher, Lovebird, pale color, 8½", EX 300.00
Pitcher, Peacock, 7¾x6½" 450.00
Pitcher, Pine Cone, 9½" 200.00
Pitcher, Poinsettia, 6½" 275.00
Pitcher, Rose & Fishscale, 6" 165.00
Pitcher, Rose on Trellis 165.00
Pitcher, Scroll & Leaf, advertising, 8" 250.00
Pitcher, Stag & Pine Trees, 9" 295.00

Pitcher, Swan, long beak, arched neck, deep color, 8½" 275.00
Pitcher, Swan, lt bl, 8½" 295.00
Pitcher, tavern scene, Flemish Jugs...Kinney & Levan, 9" 165.00
Pitcher, Tulip, 8x4" 275.00
Pitcher, Wild Rose, sponged bands, 9" 295.00
Pitcher, Wild Rose, 9x6" 185.00
Pitcher, Wildflower, stenciled 250.00
Pitcher, Windmill & Bush, 9" 225.00
Pitcher, Windy City (Fannie Flagg), Robinson Clay, 8½" 450.00
Pitcher, 2 old men w/canes, dog's-head spout, Germany, 11" 200.00
Roaster, Diffused Bl, appl hdls, flat finial, 9x19" 225.00
Roaster, Wildflower, domed lid, 8½x12" 195.00
Rolling pin, Bl Band, advertising, 14x4" 350.00
Rolling pin, Swirl, orig wooden hdls, 13" 475.00
Rolling pin, Wildflower, w/advertising, 15x4½" 450.00
Salt crock, Apricot, orig lid 200.00
Salt crock, Butterfly, orig lid 185.00
Salt crock, Daisy on Snowflakes, orig lid, 6½x6" 220.00
Salt crock, Flying Bird, orig lid, 9" 350.00
Salt crock, Grapevine on Fence, pale bl, orig lid, 6½x6¾" 225.00
Soap dish, Beaded Rose 125.00
Soap dish, cat's head 150.00
Soap dish, Indian in War Bonnet 150.00
Syrup dispenser, Pep-So, rpl lid, 12x9" 325.00
Teapot, Swirl, dbl wire bail hdl, ball shape, 9x6½" 450.00
Toothbrush holder, Bow Tie, stenciled flower 50.00
Vase, Swirl, cone shape 300.00
Wash set, Rose on Trellis, 2-pc 300.00
Water cooler, Apple Blossom, brass spigot, 17x15" 700.00
Water cooler, Bl Band, orig lid 175.00
Water cooler, Cupid, brass spigot, patterned lid, 15x12" 700.00
Water cooler, Polar Bear, brass NP spigot, rare, 17x15" 700.00
Water jug, Diffused Bl, cork affixed to stopper, 7x7" 195.00

Blue Ridge

Blue Ridge dinnerware was produced by Southern Potteries of Erwin, Tennessee, from the late 1930s until 1956 in twelve basic styles and two thousand different patterns, all of which were hand decorated under the glaze. Vivid colors lit up floral arrangements of seemingly endless variation, fruit of every sort from simple clusters to lush assortments, barnyard fowl, peasant figures, and unpretentious textured patterns. Although it is these dinnerware lines for which they are best known, collectors prize the artist-signed plates from the forties and the limited line of character jugs made during the fifties most highly. Examples of the French Peasant pattern are valued at double the prices listed below; very simple patterns will bring 25% to 50% less.

Our advisors, Betty and Bill Newbound, have compiled two lovely books, *Blue Ridge Dinnerware, Revised Third Edition,* and *The Collector's Encyclopedia of Blue Ridge,* both with beautiful color illustrations and current market values. They are listed in the Directory under Michigan. For information concerning the National Blue Ridge Newsletter, see the Clubs, Newsletters, and Catalogs section of the Directory.

Ashtray, advertising, w/rest 65.00
Ashtray, ind 12.00
Basket, aluminum edge, 10" 20.00
Bonbon, divided, center hdl 85.00
Bowl, divided, 8" 20.00
Bowl, fruit; 5" 6.00
Bowl, mixing; lg 35.00
Bowl, mixing; sm 15.00
Bowl, salad; 10½" 50.00

Bowl, soup; flat 15.00
Bowl, vegetable; divided, oval, 9" 25.00
Bowl, vegetable; Premium, w/lid 80.00
Box, candy; rnd w/lid, rare 100.00
Box, Dancing Nudes, rare 375.00
Box, Mallard, rare 500.00
Box, powder; rnd 125.00
Butter dish, Woodcrest 60.00
Cake tray, Maple Leaf 55.00
Carafe, w/lid 60.00
Casserole, w/lid 40.00
Celery, leaf shape, china 35.00
Child's cereal bowl 30.00
Child's feeding dish 30.00
Child's mug 25.00
Child's plate 35.00
Coffeepot 125.00
Counter sign 200.00
Creamer, Colonial shape, no hdls 15.00
Creamer, Fifties shape 12.00
Creamer, pedestal 55.00
Creamer, regular 8.00
Cup, dessert; glass 12.00
Cup & saucer, Holiday 40.00
Cup & saucer, Premium 45.00
Cup & saucer, regular 10.00
Custard cup 12.00
Deviled egg dish 32.50
Dish, baking; 13x8", w/metal stand 35.00
Egg cup, Premium 30.00
Gravy boat 25.00
Jug, character; china, rare 600.00
Jug, syrup; w/lid 85.00
Lamp, china 135.00
Lazy Susan, complete 600.00
Leftover, w/lid, lg 30.00
Pitcher, fancy, china 95.00
Pitcher, Sculptured Fruit, china 80.00
Pitcher, Spiral shape, 7" 65.00
Plate, aluminum edge, 12" 25.00
Plate, Christmas Tree 65.00
Plate, dinner; 9½" 15.00
Plate, divided 20.00
Plate, party; w/cup well & cup 25.00
Plate, rnd, 6" 5.00
Plate, sq, novelty pattern, 6" 45.00
Plate, 11½" 40.00
Platter, Thanksgiving Turkey 200.00
Platter, Turkey w/Acorns 200.00
Platter, 11" 15.00
Ramekin, w/lid, 7½" 32.00
Relish, Charm House 125.00
Relish, crescent shape, ind 15.00
Relish, heart shape, sm 45.00
Relish, loop handle, china 80.00
Relish, Maple Leaf, china 65.00
Relish, shell shape, deep, china 60.00
Salad spoon 35.00
Server, center hdl 25.00
Shakers, Apple, pr 15.00
Shakers, Blossom Top, pr 35.00
Shakers, Charm House 95.00
Shakers, chickens, pr 95.00
Shakers, ftd, china, tall, pr 50.00

Shakers, Palisades, pr 30.00
Shakers, regular, short, pr 15.00
Sherbet 22.00
Sugar bowl, Charm House, china 70.00
Sugar bowl, demitasse; china 35.00
Sugar bowl, Rope hdl, w/lid 20.00
Sugar bowl, Waffle, w/lid 20.00
Sugar bowl, Woodcrest, w/lid 20.00
Teapot, Chevron hdl 90.00
Teapot, Colonial 90.00
Teapot, demitasse; china 125.00
Teapot, demitasse; earthenware 95.00
Teapot, Fine Panel, china 125.00
Teapot, Mini Ball, china 95.00
Teapot, Piecrust 95.00
Tidbit, 2-tier 25.00
Tidbit, 3-tier 30.00
Tile, rnd or sq, 6" 35.00
Tray, for chocolate pot, china 425.00
Tray, for demitasse, Skyline shape, 9½x7⅝" 90.00
Tray, flat shell, china 80.00
Tray, snack; Martha 95.00
Vase, boot, 8" 80.00
Vase, rnd, china, 5½" 75.00
Vase, tapered, china 90.00

Bluebird China

Made from 1910 to 1934, Bluebird china is lovely ware decorated with bluebirds flying among pink flowering branches. It was inexpensive dinnerware and reached the height of its popularity in the second decade of this century. Several potteries produced it; shapes differ from one manufacturer to another, but the decal remains basically the same. Among the backstamps you'll find W.S. George, Cleveland, Carrolton, Homer Laughlin, Limoges China of Sebring, Ohio; and there are others.

Because examples of this line are relatively scarce, we seldom find new listings. If you have some to add, let us hear from you.

Bowl, deep; 5" 25.00
Bowl, fruit; Deerwood, 5½" 12.50
Bowl, gravy; w/saucer, Hopewell China 50.00
Bowl, sauce; SP Co, 4½" 12.50
Butter dish, 4½" holder w/in 7" dia dish, Steubenville 85.00
Casserole, Royal China Internat'l, 7x11½" 125.00
Casserole, w/lid, Ostro China, 10½" dia 95.00

Creamer, 4¼", $20.00.

Creamer & sugar bowl, w/lid, Homer Laughlin 45.00
Cup, coffee; unmk, 3½" 25.00
Cup, ftd, 3½" 35.00
Cup, tea; unmk 15.00

Ladle, sauce; gold scrolling 40.00
Plate, dessert; Limoges, 6" 8.00
Plate, Homer Laughlin, 8½" 15.00
Plate, rtcl, sq, unmk, 9" 35.00
Plate, Steubenville China, 9" 15.00
Platter, Hopewell China, 13x10" 75.00
Platter, Hopewell China, 17½x13" 100.00
Platter, unmk, 9x7" 45.00
Syrup, unmk, 4" 35.00
Teapot, ELP Co, 8½x8½" 125.00

Boch Freres

Founded in the early 1840s in La Louviere, Boch Freres Keramis became the foremost producer of art pottery in Belgium. Though primarily they served a localized market, in 1844 they earned worldwide recognition for some of their sculptural works on display at the International Exposition in Paris.

In 1907 Charles Catteau of France was appointed head of the art department. Before that time, the firm had concentrated on developing glazes and perfecting elegant forms. The style they pursued was traditional, favoring the re-creation of established 18th-century ceramics. Catteau brought with him to Boch Freres the New Wave (or Art Nouveau) influence in form and decoration. His designs won him international acclaim at the Exhibition d'Art Decoratif in Paris in 1925, and it is for his work that Boch Freres is so highly regarded today. He occasionally signed his work as well as that of others who under his direct supervision carried out his preconceived designs. He was associated with the company until 1950 and lived the remainder of his life in Nice, France, where he died in 1966. The Boch Freres Keramis factory continues to operate today, producing bathroom fixtures and other utilitarian wares. A variety of marks have been used, most incorporating some combination of 'Boch Freres,' 'Keramis,' 'BFK,' or 'Ch Catteau.' A shield topped by a crown and flanked by a 'B' and an 'F' was used as well.

Jardiniere, wide floral band, Boch Freres Gres Keramis, ca 1890, 11x9⅜", $375.00; Vases, stylized floral on crackle, 10½" and 9¼", $245.00 for the pair.

Bowl, geometrics, bl/cobalt on wht crackle, #10L9/#1187, 10" ...435.00
Lamp, upright floral ribs, mc on cream crackle, bulbous, 13" 375.00
Vase, aqua crackle gloss, #879, 10½" 110.00
Vase, diving birds/waves, HP, Catteau, 9½x7" 1,000.00
Vase, floral band at waisted neck, blk lines on yel, 8x8" 300.00
Vase, lg allover florals, mc on lt yel, #23, 13½x8", EX 400.00
Vase, lg Deco floral sprays on wht crackle, spherical, 8" 750.00
Vase, lg wht cranes stand in water, red bsk ground, 10x10" 1,100.00
Vase, sunray checkerbrd, stepped neck/str sides, Keramis, 15" 600.00
Vase, swirled ribs, mc on cream crackle, #806, 11x5" 300.00
Vase, vertical scrolls, yel/blk/turq on wht crackle, 11" 700.00
Vase, wavy bars & ovals, aqua/blk on wht crackle, 9½x9" 400.00
Vase, wide/scalloped floral top over vertical stripes, 11" 450.00
Vase, zigzag ribs/neck band, brn/blk on crackle, Catteau, 8x8" ...460.00
Vase, 3 deer, bl/gr/blk on wht crackle, Catteau, 12x6", pr 1,400.00
Vase, 3 wht crackle panels, ea w/lg mc floral, Catteau, 11" 400.00

Boehm

Boehm sculptures were the creation of Edward Marshall Boehm, a ceramic artist who coupled his love of the art with his love of nature to produce figurines of birds, animals, and flowers in lovely background settings accurate to the smallest detail. Sculptures of historical figures and those representing the fine arts were also made and along with many of the bird figurines, have established secondary-market values many times their original prices. His first pieces were made in the very early 1950s in Trenton, New Jersey, under the name of Osso Ceramics. Mr. Boehm died in 1969, and the firm has since been managed by his wife. Today known as Edward Marshall Boehm, Inc., the private family-held corporation produces not only porcelain sculptures but collector plates as well. Both limited and non-limited editions of their works have been issued. Examples are marked with various backstamps, all of which have incorporated the Boehm name since 1951. 'Osso Ceramics' in upper case lettering was used in 1950 and 1951.

In our descriptions, those ending in (A) are auction values. All others are dealer's asking prices. As you can see, there is a wide variance.

African Elephant, #20044 ....475.00
American Bald Eagle, Bicentennial commemorative, 1976, 9¼" (A) ...500.00
Baby Bluebird, 4¾" (A) 95.00
Baby Ocelot, 5¾x9" 350.00
Baby Robin, #437 ....175.00
Baby Wood Thrush, #444 ....250.00
Ballet Dancer, bsk, 10" 190.00
Barn Owl, on fungus branch, wht feather on base, 19x26" (A) 1,600.00
Bluebird, #40256 ....125.00
Common Tern, #497 ....3,500.00
Daisies, #3002 ....695.00
Deer Mouse, #400-89 ....100.00
Fox, recumbent, 1952, rare 2,500.00
Foxhound, reclining, ltd ed, 1953 ....1,800.00
Giant Panda Cub, 6x8" 325.00
Global Peace Dove, #40347 ....285.00
Green Jays, #486, pr 2,000.00
Hummingbird, #440 ....700.00
Kestrels, #492 ....2,200.00
Mallards, #406 ....1,200.00
Mockingbird, #40380 ....150.00
Mute Swan w/Chicks, limited edition, 1980, 9½" (A) 1,000.00
Mute Swan w/Water Foliage, limited ediiton, 1980, 17¾" (A) ..1,250.00
Northern Water Thrush, #409 ....1,000.00
Owl, limited edition, 1980, 18⅜" (A) 865.00
Parula Warblers, #484 ....2,000.00
Pascali Rose, #30093 ....1,295.00
Pieta Madonna, lg 225.00
Poodle, #133, sm 235.00
Ptarmigans, #463 ....1,800.00
Rabbit, newborn, #40217 ....70.00
Raccoon, #HS6 ....95.00
Red Shouldered Hawk, #40251, 1954, 26½" 900.00
Red Squirrels, #4004, Malverne Studios, 13" 1,850.00
Royal Terns, limited issue, 1983, 31¾", EX (A) 450.00
Snow Buntings, #400-21 ....1,500.00
Soaring Eagle, #40276B 700.00
Trumpeter Swan, sgn edition, 1958, 14¼" (A) 450.00

Whiteface Scops Owl, #40114	1,025.00
Young & Spirited Eagles, #40049	1,650.00

Bohemian Glass

The term 'Bohemian glass' has come to refer to a type of glass developed in Bohemia in the late 16th century at the Imperial Court of Rudolf II, the Hapsburg Emperor. The popular artistic pursuit of the day was stone carving, and it naturally followed to transfer familiar procedures to the glassmaking industry. During the next century, a formula was discovered that produced a glass with a fine crystal appearance which lent itself well to deep, intricate engraving, and the art was further advanced.

Although many other kinds of art glass were made there, collectors today use the term 'Bohemian glass' to most often indicate clear glass overlaid or stained with color through which a design is cut or etched. (Unless otherwise described, the items in the listing that follows are of this type.) Red or yellow on clear glass is common, but other colors may also be found. Another type of Bohemian glass involves cutting through and exposing two layers of color in patterns that are often very intricate. Items such as these are sometimes further decorated with enamel and/or gilt work.

Basket, red, deer & trees, 5⅜"	90.00
Bottle, scent; red, matching red stopper, 9"	90.00
Bowl, red, naturalistic scenes, 5x6"	110.00
Bread plate, bl, deer & pine tree, 13x8"	100.00
Decanter, red, vintage, 9¼", NM	85.00
Goblet, red, view of Battle Monument Baltimore, 7"	465.00
Pokal, red, floral, 15¾"	200.00
Stein, red, Der Niagara Falls, 5"	325.00
Stein, red, dog in forest, pewter mts, 5½x3¼"	325.00
Vase, amber, floral panels, HP portrait panel, Wortia, 15"	600.00
Vase, amber, florals, 1920s, 11"	200.00
Vase, red, bird/trees/buildings, 6"	95.00
Vase, red, deer & stag gaze at pheasant, trees, 6"	125.00
Vase, red, dmns & ovals, flared, 5"	100.00

Bookends

Though a few were produced before 1880, bookends became a necessary library accessory and a popular commodity after the printing industry was revolutionized by Mergenthaler's invention, the linotype. Books became abundantly available at such affordable prices that almost every home suddenly had need for bookends. They were carved from wood, cast in iron, bronze, or brass, or cut from stone. Today's collectors may find such designs as ships, animals, flowers, and children. Patriotic themes, art reproductions, and those with Art Nouveau and Art Deco styling provide a basis for a diverse and interesting collection.

Recently, figural cast-iron pieces have been in demand, especially examples with good original polychrome paint. This has driven the value of painted cast-iron bookends up considerably. See also Bradley and Hubbard.

Ann Hathaway's Cottage, cast bronze	40.00
Aviator, CI w/bronze finish	50.00
Basset hound, wht metal w/bronze pnt, 3"	40.00
Boston terrier head on base, heavy bronze finish	90.00
Buffalo, cast bronze, 5"	75.00
Bulldog, CI, 5⅜", EX	65.00
Bulldog head, cast bronze, EX detail, 4⅝"	85.00
Camel, CI, mc pnt, #1153, 5¼"	95.00
Cat w/lg ears, gold-pnt metal	48.00

Cathedral, CI w/mc pnt, VG	60.00
Cathedral, CI w/mc pnt, 5⅜", EX	85.00
Coach, CI w/mc pnt, 7"	85.00
Conestoga wagon, CI, mc pnt, Hubley #378	65.00
Cowboy on bronco, CI w/old gold pnt, mk CFW, 5½"	50.00
Cowboy roping cow, CI w/bronze pnt, 4⅞"	45.00
Dog, full body, CI, silver pnt, 3"	45.00
Elephant, CI, red w/mc trim, #112, 4"	80.00
Elves, cast metal w/red pnt & wht faces, onyx base, 5", pr	140.00
End of Trail, Indian on horse, CI w/mc pnt, 3¾"	65.00
English hunt scene w/jumping horse, CI w/bronze finish, 5"	65.00
George Washington, CI, Copr 1923, 4¾"	50.00
German shepherd, bronzed metal	45.00
Horse head, silvered metal	45.00
Horse w/saddle, CI w/mc pnt, #110, 4⅝"	60.00
Indian chief, CI w/red & gold pnt, 4¾"	50.00
Indian's head in relief, cast metal, 3¼x4½"	35.00
Indian w/bow, cast bronze, mk WB, 5⅝"	75.00
Lady (Doulton style), 1 w/book,/1 w/fan, pnt porc, #d, 6"	150.00
Library shelf & quote from Browning, CI, bronze finish	65.00
Lincoln, Abraham, cast bronze, 3¾"	45.00
Lincoln, CI w/bronze & gr pnt, 5⅞"	50.00
Lincoln, seated, CI, Jennings Bros	150.00
Lincoln & Victory, The Emancipator, bronze, c 1925, 5⅝"	50.00
Lindbergh, CI w/bronze finish, 5⅝"	40.00
Lion, cast brass, 5½"	140.00
Log cabin, CI w/mc pnt	50.00
Longfellow, CI w/dk bronze finish & gilt, 5¾"	85.00

Old Ironsides, cast iron, worn paint, copyright 1929, 5¾", $35.00.

Owl, CI w/bronze finish, 5¾"	45.00
Physicians/owl, CI, Germany, pr	75.00
Pirate, bronze, EX	45.00
Plaque w/quotes, CI w/worn bronze finish, 7"	65.00
Punch & Judy, cast bronze, 7¼"	100.00
Quail, CI, mc pnt, 5½"	150.00
Rooster, CI, blk pnt, #1122, 6¾"	65.00
Scottie dog at fence, cast bronze, 6½"	120.00
Setter, bronze, red & gr pnt traces, mk Real 9656 Bronze, 3½"	35.00
Shepherdess, bronze, ca 1925, pr	125.00
Sphinx, CI, worn gold pnt, 3½"	35.00
Terrier, CI w/brass finish, Copr 1930, 5¾"	35.00
Thinker, CI, worn gilt pnt, 5¾"	25.00
Trekking West, Conestoga wagon, CI, worn pnt, 6"	85.00
Venus Rising From the Sea, CI, old gold pnt, 4½"	45.00
War Horse, NP on CI, Copr 1930	65.00
Wirehaired fox terrier in relief, brass, 1929	85.00
Wolfhound, CI, wht & gold pnt, 2⅝"	45.00

Bootjacks and Bootscrapers

Bootjacks were made from metal or wood. Some were fancy figural shapes, others strictly business! Their purpose was to facilitate the otherwise awkward process of removing one's boots. Bootscrapers were handy gadgets that provided an effective way to clean the soles of mud and such. Our advisor for this category is Louis Picek; he is listed in the Directory under Iowa.

Bootjacks

Beetle, CI, openwork bk, 11¾x5x2", EX 110.00
Boss emb on shaft, lacy CI, 15" L 135.00
CI, openwork between hexagonal supports, blk pnt, 6" L 65.00
Heart figural, CI, scalloped sides, 13" L 135.00
Hickory, bentwood hdl, hinged/folds, use w/out bending over 85.00
Lee Riders advertising, wood w/leather trim, EX 75.00
Naughty Nelly, CI, EX pnt, no rust, 9¾" 200.00
Pine w/sq nails, early, lg 150.00
Stylized fish, cvd wood, worn finish, 22" L 115.00
Sunflower, brass, Musselman's Plug advertising 150.00
V-shape, ornate CI, VG 48.00

Bootscrapers

CI, scrolled harp shape, 7⅞x7¼" 40.00
CI, spool & ball post ea corner, sq, orig pnt, JW Fiske, NY 140.00
Dachshund, CI, worn wht pnt, 1900s, 7x22x5" 225.00
Duck, full bodied, scraper on bk, CI, 14½" L 350.00
Pig silhouette, cut-out eye, CI, 8½x12" 200.00
Pointer on 'bridge,' brushes in base at 1 time, CI/rpt, 16" 330.00
Scottie dog, CI, orig pnt, EX 65.00
Wrought iron, scrolled & twisted design, side mt, 8x8½" 125.00
Wrought iron w/detailed scroll finial, 21x24" 500.00
Wrought iron w/scrolled ends in marble block, 13x11x12" 385.00

Boru, Sorcha

Sorcha Boru was the professional name used by California ceramist Claire Stewart. She was a founding member of the Allied Arts Guild of Menlo Park (California) where she maintained a studio from 1932 to 1938. From 1938 until 1955, she operated Sorcha Boru Ceramics, a production studio in San Carlos. Her highly acclaimed output consisted of colorful, slip-decorated figurines, salt and pepper shakers, vases, wall pockets, and flower bowls. Most production work was incised 'S.B.C.' by hand.

Figurine, dancing girls (2) 165.00
Figurine, fawn, Penelope 55.00
Figurine, shepherdess 155.00
Jar, peasant lady, w/lid 75.00
Pitcher, lt bl, 4½x3½" 60.00
Shakers, chicks, pr 35.00
Shakers, elephants, pr 45.00
Shakers, King & Queen, lg, pr 150.00
Vase/planter, appl flowers, 3½" 60.00

Bossons Artware

Bossons artware has been on the international market since 1948 when the first high-relief wall plaques were made to depict English scenes and floral subjects. Though floral plaques are still produced with many new releases becoming popular, it is Bossons character wall masks (life-like sculptures) and figurines that have been so popular as gift-store items since they were introduced in 1958-59. Today's collectors appreciate their extremely fine modeling and artistry, and interest is on the increase on an international basis. Masks most often found are usu-

ally subjects of men from all nations and walks of life (women are rare, two of the three 'Children Studies,' 1968, are extremely rare), and some of the larger wall figurines include an animal. Nearly all are made of a strong plaster medium that is easily chipped or scuffed. Mint or mint-in-box discontinued examples are few.

In most every case, Bossons have the sculpture name incised under the collar (Smuggler is one exception), or at the base of the figurine, with a date indicating when the mold was created. Also, on the reverse side of these sculptures will appear the following incision: 'Bossons Copyright Reserved,' and often 'Congleton, England,' with date. **Those dates will not change though that model may be issued for years,** but collectors seek out the variations in color and particularly sculptural changes that often occur during the mask's span of production. Collectors and dealers must be aware of many directly molded illegal copies, e.g., 'Pancho and Rawhide,' or 'fakes' and 'look-alikes' cast in everything from plaster, rubber, and even metal. There are some **English** character masks of good quality produced by Naturecraft and the Legend Company. They can have a striking resemblance to Bossons in that Fred Wright, principal sculptor for Bossons from 1957 to 1972, left Bossons was then employed at the Legend factory. The Bossons resident sculptor/artist several years before Wright and since 1972 is Mrs. Alice Brindley, who retired in December of 1995. Mr. W. Ray Bossons, son of the founder, W.H. Bossons, is chairman and managing director of the company. He has sculpted several Bossons including the Shakespeare collection and a Santa Claus.

Being molded in plaster, Bossons are frequently found in deplorable condition, and avid collectors pay the premium prices mentioned here for only the most perfect examples, either in factory 'mint' states or perfectly returned to their original structural and coloring beauty by a restoration artist recommended by Bossons.

Bossons also made a series of both domestic animals and wildlife in plaster as well as a hard plastic called 'Stonite.' This Fraser-Art Division of Bossons has temporarily been discontinued as of December, 1995. Full-length plaster Oriental figures and the 12" Afghan and Berber figures were made in a limited number as were clocks, mirrors, and other decorative items. Bossons also produces their 'Ivorex' plaques, formerly Osborne Editions. All Bossons products are hand painted by individual artists and highly collectible. The discontinued editions and some of the rarer examples in perfect condition command prices in excess of $1,000.00.

Our advisor for this category is Dr. Don Hardisty; he is recommended by Bossons to restore their products and is listed in the Directory under New Mexico.

Key:
DC — Dickens Character Series   DS — Dog of Distinction

Basset Hound, DS, 1969, 5", current retail 27.00
Betsy Trotwood, bl collar, DC, 1964, $100 to 250.00
Betsy Trotwood, pk collar, DC, ca 1965, current retail 42.00
Black Panther, same mold as Golden Puma, 1964, 16" 250.00
British Military Mask, orig w/eyes, 1965, extremely rare 600.00
British Military Mask, w/out eyes, 1968, $200 to 400.00
Cheyenne Indian, red fringed jacket, 1967-92 ....100.00
Desert Hunters, 2nd edition (dog's mouth open), 7" 175.00
Dog, Series II, Alsatian, 4¾", current retail 38.00
Dog, Series II, Double Terriers 100.00
Dog (Mac, Pooch, Patch, etc), ceramic, unmk, ea, $300 to 600.00
Dogs & Cats, Series I & II, 1959-61, 3" to 4", $75 to 200.00
Eagle, Bossons Ceramic, 1963, 12", $150 to 175.00
Koalas, orig model, 10½", $150 to 300.00
Series A, Bengali, 10½", very rare, $2,200 to 3,500.00
Series A, Coolie, c 1963, 8", from $150 to 175.00
Series A, Coolie, 8", $150 to 175.00
Series A, Deccan Hunters, brn-eyed cat, 8½", $175 to 250.00

Series A, Deccan Hunters, gr-eyed cat, 8½", $150 to 200.00
Series A, Eskimo, 8½", $75 to 125.00
Series A, Kassem, c 1966, 8", $100 to 225.00
Series A, Nigerian Man, c 1959, 5½", $165 to 185.00
Series A, Saracen, wht hat, 8" 185.00
Series A, Saracen, yel hat, 8" 165.00
Series A, Snake Charmer, 1958-59, 10", $150 to 400.00
Series B, Corsican, c 1959, 5½", $85 to 125.00
Series B, Paddy, 5½", current retail 38.00
Series B, Tibetan, 5½", $75 to 125.00
Shelf ornament, Berber, 1959 Reg Design, 12", $400 to 900.00
Shelf ornament, Himalayan, 1 of 4, $100 to 300.00
Shelf ornament, Sikh, unmk, 1963, 6", $100 to 300.00
Wall figure, Peon, full length, $150 to 275.00
Wall figure, Pony Girl, c 1968, 7", $400 to 600.00
Wall figure, Sherpa, full length, 15", $175 to 250.00
Warrier panel, Zulu or Sioux, 17x11", ea, $350 to 500.00
Warrior panel, Afridi or Berber, 17x11", ea, $350 to 500.00
Wildlife Studies, Birds & Sunflowers, c 1968, 7", $200 to 500.00
Wildlife Studies, Chaffinches, c 1971, 8", current retail 62.00
Wildlife Studies, Eagle (not Fraser-Art), 1963, 12", $150 to ...175.00
Wildlife Studies, Golden Puma, c 1959, 16" L, $100 to 250.00
Yorkshire Terrier, bl hair bow, DS, 5", current retail 27.00

Bottle Openers

Around the turn of the century, manufacturers began to seal bottles with a metal cap that required a new type of bottle opener. Now the screw cap and the flip top have made bottle openers nearly obsolete. There are many variations, some in combination with other tools. Many openers were used as means of advertising a product. Various materials were used including silver and brass.

A figural bottle opener is defined as a figure designed for the sole purpose of lifting a bottle cap. The actual opener must be an integral part of the figure itself. A base-plate opener is one where the lifter is a separate metal piece attached to the underside of the figure. The major producers of iron figurals were Wilton Products, John Wright Inc., Gadzik Sales, and L & L Favors. Openers may be free-standing and three-dimensional, wall hung or flat. They can be made of cast iron (often painted), brass, bronze, or aluminum.

Numbers within the listings refer to a reference book printed by the FBOC (Figural Bottle Opener Collectors) organization. Those seeking additional information are encouraged to contact FBOC, whose address can be found in the Directory under Clubs, Newsletters, and Catalogs.

Amish boy, F-31, pnt CI, rare, 1953, 4x2" 225.00
Billy goat, F-74, pnt CI, J Wright 150.00
Canadian goose, F-105, CI, worn pnt 35.00
Clown head, F-417, CI, rpt, 4½" 45.00
Cocker spaniel, F-80, brass 18.00
Cowboy w/guitar, F-27, aluminum, M 15.00
Donkey, F-60, brass, sm 40.00
Donkey, F-60, CI, pnt traces 20.00
Drunk & Palm Tree, F-19, CI, mc pnt, EX 48.00
Elephant, F-49, CI, gray pnt, EX 45.00
False teeth, F-420, pnt CI, common, 1954, 2⅜x3⅜" 75.00
Fish, F-154, aluminum, EX 18.00
Fish, F-162, pot metal, no pnt 20.00
Hand, F-201, brass 48.00
Jimmy Carter, 1975, M 55.00
Lamppost Drunk, F-2, CI, worn pnt 10.00
Lobster, F-167, CI, EX pnt 32.00

Negro w/indented pupils, CI, rpt, 4⅛" 70.00
Negro w/smooth pupils, F-402c, brass 45.00
Old Snifter, 1933 ....160.00
Palm tree, F-21, brass 18.00
Parrot, F-116b, brass 65.00
Peacock, F-103, brass 40.00
Pelican, F-129, CI, EX pnt 32.00

Rooster, F-97, cast iron with multicolor paint, light wear, 3¼", $75.00.

Sailor, F-17, pnt CI, 1950s, 3¾" 65.00
Sea horse, F-140, brass 35.00
Setter, F-79, CI, EX mc pnt 65.00
Shovel, F-221, brass 20.00
Signpost Drunk, F-11, CI, VG pnt 18.00

Bottles and Flasks

As far back as the 1st century B.C., the Romans preferred blown glass containers for their pills and potions. Though you're not apt to find many of those, you will find bottles of every size, shape, and color made to hold perfume, ink, medicine, soda, spirits, vinegar, and many other liquids. American business firms preferred glass bottles in which to package their commercial products and used them extensively from the late 18th century on. Bitters bottles contained 'medicine' (actually herb-flavored alcohol), and judging from the number of these found today, their contents found favor with many! Because of a heavy tax imposed on the sale of liquor in 17th-century England by King George, who hoped to curtail alcohol abuse among his subjects, bottlers simply added 'curative' herbs to their brew and thus avoided taxation. Since gin was taxed in America as well, the practice continued in this country. Scores of brands were sold; among the most popular were Dr. H.S. Flint & Co. Quaker Bitters, Dr. Kaufman's Anti-Cholera Bitters, and Dr. J. Hostetter's Stomach Bitters. Most bitters bottles were made in shades of amber, brown, and aquamarine. Clear glass was used to a lesser extent, as were green tones. Blue, amethyst, red-brown, and milk glass examples are rare. (Please note that color is a strong factor when pricing bottles. For example, an amber Hostetter's bitters sells for $25.00 or less, but a green variant can bring hundreds of dollars. An aqua scroll flask may bring $50.00, but a cobalt blue variation will command over $1,000.00.)

Perfume or scent bottles were produced abroad by companies all over Europe from the late 16th century on. Perfume making became such a prolific trade that as a result beautifully decorated bottles were fashionable. In America they were produced in great quantities by Stiegel in 1770 and by Boston and Sandwich in the early 19th century. Cologne bottles were first made in about 1830 and toilet-water bottles in the 1880s. Rene Lalique produced fine scent bottles from as early as the turn of the century. The first were one-of-a-kind creations done in the cire perdue method. He later designed bottles for the Coty Perfume Company with a different style for each Coty fragrance. Prices for commercial perfumes hinge on condition. Their values appreciate according to these factors: are they still sealed or full; do they retain all factory labels; is the original box or packing included? Deluxe versions bring premium prices. Example: blue flat

Dans la Nuite cologne by Rene Lalique, value for 6" size, $250.00. Dans la Nuit, enameled with stars by Rene Lalique, 3" round ball, $900.00.

Spirit flasks from the 19th century were blown in specially designed molds with varied motifs including political subjects, railroad trains, and symbolic devices. The most commonly used colors were amber, dark brown, and green.

From the 20th century, early pop and beer bottles are very collectible as is nearly every extinct commercial container. Dairy bottles are a relatively new area of interest; look for round bottles in good condition with both city and state as well as a nice graphic relating to the farm or the dairy.

Bottles may be dated by the methods used in their production. For instance, a rough pontil indicates a date before 1845. After the bottle was blown, a pontil rod was attached to the bottom, a glob of molten glass acting as the 'glue.' This allowed the glassblower to continue to manipulate the extremely hot bottle until it was finished. From about 1845 until approximately 1860, the molten glass 'glue' was omitted. The rod was simply heated to a temperature high enough to cause it to afix itself to the bottle. When the rod was snapped off, a metallic residue was left on the base of the bottle; this is called an 'iron pontil.' A seam that reaches from base to lip marks a machine-made bottle from after 1903, while an applied or hand-finished lip points to an early mold-blown bottle. The Industrial Revolution saw keen competition between manufacturers, and as a result, scores of patents were issued. Many concentrated on various types of closures; the crown bottle cap, for instance, was patented in 1892. If a manufacturer's name is present, consulting a book on marks may help you date your bottle.

Among our advisors for this category are Madeleine France (see the Directory under Florida), Mark Vuono (Connecticut), Steve Ketcham (Minnesota), Monsen and Baer (Virginia), and John Tutton (Virginia). In the listings that follow (most of which have been taken from auction catalogs), glass is assumed to be clear unless color is indicated. Numbers refer to a standard reference book, *American Glass*, by George and Helen McKearin. See also Advertising, various companies; Avon; Barber Shop Collectibles; Blown Glass; Blown Three-Mold Glass; California Perfume Company; Czechoslovakia; De Vilbiss; Fire Fighting; Lalique; Medical Collectibles; Steuben.

Key:

am — applied mouth	grd — ground pontil
bbl — barrel	GW — Glass Works
bt — blob top	ip — iron pontil
b3m — blown 3-mold	ps — pontil scar
cm — collared mouth	rm — rolled mouth
fl — filigree	sb — smooth base
fm — flared mouth	sl — sloping
gm — ground mouth	sm — sheared mouth
gp — graphite pontil	tm — tooled mouth

Apothecary (Druggist)

Cobalt, gold/red/blk label: P Myrist, ps, fm, early, 8½" 160.00
Cobalt, label: Syr Tolu, ps, tm, ca 1850-70, 7¾" 80.00
Cobalt, red/gold/blk label: Morph AC, ps, fm, stopper, 4⅛" 160.00
Cobalt w/orange & wht enamel: Tinct Opii Poison, sb, 5⅝" 170.00
Dk gr-aqua, ps, rm, German ½-post method, 13" 350.00
Powder bl opal, gold & blk label: Caix Sulphurata, ps, 4¼" 170.00
Sapphire bl, wht/blk label: Etr Cocae Fluid, tm, tin lid, 6¾" 60.00
Sapphire bl, 4-color label under glass, tin lid, 8½" 80.00
Yel-gr, 3-color label under glass, sb, tm, 6¾" 75.00

Barber Bottles

Bl opaque w/HP bird & flowers, 8¾" 445.00

Cobalt w/orange & wht daisies 200.00
Cranberry w/pk floral decor & inside ribs 250.00
Hobnail, amber, Hobbs 230.00
Hobnail, cranberry opal, Hobbs 370.00
Hobnail, cranberry w/clear rigaree, 7" 180.00
Lav cut o/l, pewter top, 5½" 65.00
Sapphire bl, HP flowers & leaves w/gold, bbl shape 200.00
Wht opal reversed raised swirls, am 135.00

Bitters Bottles

A Lambert...Phila, olive-gr, cylinder, ip, am, 11" 2,850.00
Benders...Cincinnati O, med amber, semicabin, 10¼" 5,000.00
Big Bill Best..., red-amber, sb, tm, 1900-10, 12" 150.00
Brown & Lyon's Blood...Binghampton NY, yel-amber, am/sb, 10" ..135.00
Brown's Celebrated Indian Herb..., golden to yel-amber, 12" 700.00
BT 1865 SC Smith's Druid, dk cherry-puce, sb, am, bbl, 9½" ..1,000.00
Canton, med amber, lady's leg, am, sb, ca 1865, 12¼" 240.00
CH Swain's Bourbon, med orange-amber, sb, am, whittled, 9⅛" ..140.00
Clarke's Vegetable Sherry Wine, aqua, sb, am, 1855-65, 14" 350.00
Cokamoke Bitters Co..., amber, sb, am, 1875-80, 9⅝" 220.00
Dimmitt's 50 Cts..., amber, strap-side flask, sb, am, 6½" 375.00
Dr AS Hopkins Union Stomach, amber, 9¾" 150.00
Dr CW Roback's Stomach...Cincinnati O, med amber, bbl, 9⅜" ...230.00

Doctor Fisch's Bitters, W.H. Ware Patented 1866, medium amber, fish form, 11½", minor dullness on 1 side, $160.00.

Dr Flint's Quaker, aqua, sb, am, 1885-95, 9½" 75.00
Dr Forest's Tonic...Bacon & Miller..., amber, sb, am, 9½" 350.00
Dr Gillmore's Laxative Kidney & Liver, med amber, 10¼" 85.00
Dr HA Jackson's, aqua, ps, am, crude, 1845-55, 7⅜" 90.00
Dr Hoff's German Stomach..., yel-amber, sb, am, 8⅞" 350.00
Dr J Hostetter's Stomach, amber, sb, am, 8⅞" 25.00
Dr John Bull's Cedron..., olive-amber, semicabin, 10" 1,250.00
Dr Langley's Root & Herb, amber, sb, am, NM label, 8½" 180.00
Dr Langley's Root & Herb, aqua, sb, am, 1870-80, 6⅛" 130.00
Dr Langley's Root & Herb, yel-olive, sb, am, crude, 6½" 2,400.00
Dr Loew's Celebrated Stomach..., bright yel-gr, sb, tm, 9¼" 350.00
Dr Mowe's Vegetable, aqua, sb, am, 1865-70, 10" 160.00
Dr S/Beltzhoover's-Dispeptic...PA, yel-amber, am, sb, 9¼" 325.00
Dr Skinner's Celebrated 25 Cent..., aqua, ps, am, 8½" 100.00
Dr Soule's Hop...1872, lt golden amber, semicabin, 7¾" 135.00
Dr Soule's Hop...1872, med apricot-puce, semicabin, 9½" 160.00
Eagle Angostura Bark...Pat Feb 4th 1902, amber, NM labels 75.00
EE Hall New Haven Hall's...1842, yel w/amber tones, bbl, 9¼" ..300.00
ER Clarke's Sarsaparilla..., aqua, ps, am, stain, 1840s, 7⅜" 150.00
German Hop...1880 DR CD Warner's..., amber, semicabin, 10" ..450.00
Great Universal Compound Stomach...1870..., clear, 10½" 4,900.00
Greeley's Bourbon, med puce, bbl, am, 1860-70, 9⅛" 240.00
Greeley's Bourbon, med to dk puce, sb, am, bbl, G- label, 9" 150.00
Green Mountain JH&L Cider, aqua, sb, am, 1875-85, 10¼" 135.00

Greer's Eclipse, amber, sb, am, 1870-80, sm stain, 8¾" **50.00**
Hartwid Kantorowicz Nach Berlin, olive-amber, sb, tm, 9⅛" **70.00**
Herkules...1 Quart, yel-gr, sb, tm, stain/bruise, 7⅛" **275.00**
Hertrich's Gesundheits..., olive gr, sb, am, 1875-90, 12" **450.00**
Holtzermann's Pat Stomach, med amber, 2-roof cabin, 9½" ...**1,450.00**
Holtzermann's Pat Stomach, med red-amber, 4-roof cabin, 10" ...**175.00**
Home Bitters Jas A Jackson..., yel-amber, sb, am, 9⅛" **140.00**
Hop & Iron...Utica NY, amber, sb, NM labels, 8½" **190.00**
Hops & Malt...Trade Mark..., amber, semicabin, 9⅞" **1,000.00**
Jenkin's Stomach, red-amber, sb, am, some crudeness, 9⅜" **775.00**
John Moffatt & Co Pheonix...$1.00, aqua, sb, NM labels, 6⅜" ...**1,400.00**
John W Steele's Niagara Star..., amber, semicabin, 10" **200.00**
Kelvy's Stomach, aqua, sb, am, 1870s, 8⅞" **275.00**
Khoosh, amber, sb, am, NM labels, 1880-90, 12½" **210.00**
Koehler & Hinrich's Red Star Stomach, amber, sb, tm, 11¼" **150.00**
Lorimer's Juniper Tar, yel-gr, sb, am, 9⅜", NM **700.00**
Malarion Bitters Snyder Gue & Condell, amber, sb, am, 9¼" **140.00**
Mishler's Herb...Tablespoon..., yel-amber, crude, 8¾" **130.00**
National, yel w/amber tone, ear of corn, sb, am, 1867, 12½" **950.00**
Old Sachem & Wigwam Tonic, gr-aqua, bbl, sb, am, 9½" **4,400.00**
Old Sachem & Wigwam Tonic, med copper-puce, bbl, sb, 9¼", EX ..**700.00**
Old Sachem & Wigwam Tonic, med golden amber, bbl, rpr, 9¼" ..**160.00**
Old Sachem & Wigwam Tonic, med yel-amber, bbl, sb, am, 9¼" ...**300.00**
Pat 1884 Dr Petzold's Genuine German...1862, med amber, 10½" ..**750.00**
Patd Dr RT Hylton's 1867 Wild Cherry Tonic, milk glass, 8¾" ...**1,600.00**
PDH Co Sazerac Aromatic, amber, sb, am, lady's leg, 12" **925.00**
Penn's Pony HW Long MD & Co, root beer-amber, sb, tm, 9" ..**525.00**
Peruvian Tonic, med amber, sb, tm, NM label, bruise, 9½" **450.00**
Phoenix...Price 2 Dollars, yel-olive, ps, am, 1835-45, 7⅞" **1,400.00**
Prof Leonard's Celebrated Nectar, amber, sb, am, 9¼" **240.00**
RC Ridgeway & Co Phila, olive-amber, lady's leg, ip, am, 11" ...**100.00**
Red Jacket Bennett Pieters & Co, yel-amber, sb, am, 9⅝" **160.00**
Royal Italian Registered Trade Mark..., pk-amethyst, 13½" **525.00**
RS Gardner & Co..., med yel-amber, Chinaman figural, 11¼" ..**3,100.00**
Sarracenia Life...Tucker Mobile Ala, amber, sb, am, 9" **140.00**
Schroeder's German, med amber, sb, tm, 1880-90, 10½" **1,100.00**
Sol Frank's Panacea...NY, med amber, lighthouse, sb, am, 10" ...**250.00**
ST Drake's 1860 Plant'n X Pat 1862, dk chocolate amber, 10" ..**325.00**
ST Drake's 1860 Plant'n X Pat 1862, yel w/puce tints, 10" **425.00**
ST Drake's 1860 Plant'n X Pat 1862, yel-amber, cabin, 10" **235.00**
Steinfeld's French Cognac...1st Prize...1867, amber, 9¾" **275.00**
The Fish...WH Ware Pat 1866, amber, fish, 11⅝" **140.00**
The Fish...WH Ware Pat 1866, yel-root beer-amber, fish, 12" ...**190.00**
Travelers (emb man w/cane), yel-amber, sb, am, 1870-80, 10½" ...**2,100.00**
Walton's...Saml W Walton & Co..., med amber, sb, am, 9⅜" **180.00**
Wampoo...Siegel & Bro New York, amber, sb, am, 1870-80, 9⅝" ..**130.00**
WC...Brobst & Rentschler..., med amber, bbl, sb, 10⅜" **600.00**
White's Stomach, golden amber, sb, am, 1865-75, 9½" **140.00**

Black Glass Bottles

Many early European and American bottles are deep, dark green, or amber in color. Collectors refer to such coloring as black glass, since unless held to light, the glass is so dark it appears to be black.

Mallet, dk olive-amber, ps, am, sm chip, 1840-50, 7x4½" **275.00**
Mallet, olive gr, ps, am, short neck, 1745-60, 7" **300.00**
Mallet, olive gr, ps on deep kick-up, am, 1740-60, 8½x4" **90.00**
Onion, bl-gr, ps, am, bubbles, 1720-40, 7x4¼" **160.00**
Onion, dk bl-gray, ps, am, 1690-1710, 5½x4½" **325.00**
Onion, med to dk gr, ps, am, 1720-40, 6¾x4¾" **85.00**
Onion, olive gr, str sides, European, ca 1710-25, 7¾x4½" **100.00**
Onion, olive-amber, seal: greyhound's head & coronet, 6½" ..**2,000.00**
Onion, yel-olive-amber, ps, am, horse's hoof type, 1700-30, 8" ...**100.00**

Seal: crown above letter C, dk olive-amber, ps, am, 8¾" **175.00**
Seal: H Rickets GW Bristol, yel-olive gr, ps, ca 1882, 8¾" **275.00**
Seal: HC & hand, olive-amber, ps, am, 1780-1800, 10¾" **350.00**
Seal: M below royal crown, dk olive amber, sb, am, 11⅝" **275.00**
Seal: WA, olive-amber, ps, am, 1790-1800, 10⅞" **190.00**
Wine, yel olive-amber, ps, am, Dutch, 1760-80, 11½" **100.00**

Blown Glass Bottles and Flasks

Chestnut flask, aqua, expanded ogival pattern, 4⅜", NM **110.00**
Chestnut flask, aqua, 15-dmn, ps, sm, bubbly, 5" **165.00**
Chestnut flask, golden amber, ps, am, 1800-20, 6¾" **100.00**
Chestnut flask, med yel-olive-amber, ps, rm, 1790-1810, 5⅜" **160.00**
Chestnut flask, olive gr, ps, rm, Am, 1780-1820, 5⅜" **85.00**
Chestnut flask, olive-amber, HP decor, ps, am, 1780-1810, 7" ...**75.00**
Chestnut flask, yel w/olive tones, ps, rm, 1790-1810, 10" **220.00**
Chestnut flask, yel-olive, ps, am w/dbl collar, 1790-1810, 8" **90.00**
Nursing, clear, 14-dmn, ps, tm, wear/scratches, 7" **25.00**
Nursing, lt amethyst, swirled, ps, sm, wear/stain, 8" **45.00**
Nursing, yel-gr w/blk-amber neck & shoulders, stain, 7" **225.00**
Pitkin flask, amber, 16 swirled ribs, ½-post neck, ps, 5½" **275.00**
Pitkin flask, amber, 36-broken-rib swirl, ps, sm, 6⅛" **600.00**
Pitkin flask, amber, 36-broken-rib swirl, ½-post neck, 6" **775.00**
Pitkin flask, cobalt, 24 vertical ribs, pinched center, 8⅛" **200.00**
Pitkin flask, golden olive-amber, 36-broken-rib swirl, 5¾" **880.00**
Pitkin flask, olive, 36-rib swirl, ½-post neck, ps, 4⅞" **275.00**
Snuff, yel-olive gr, ps, sm, bubbles, 1800-25, 4¼" **90.00**
Storage, dk olive-amber, ps, rm, stain, heavy, 1800s, 14¼" **210.00**
Storage, dk yel-olive-amber, ps, s&tm, expanded shoulders, 12" ...**120.00**
Storage, yel-olive gr, sb w/deep kick-up, tm, 1870-90, 9½" **100.00**
Utility, yel-olive-amber, sb, tm, sq w/beveled corners, 11⅜" **100.00**

Cologne, Perfume, and Toilet Water Bottles

Clear w/cranberry, wht & gold metallic twist, 4⅜" **85.00**
Cranberry, cut panels, lay-down, screw-on/hinged caps, 4" **185.00**
Cranberry frost to clear w/gold bands, clear cut stopper, 5¼" **70.00**
Cranberry w/gold florals, squatty, bulbous, faceted top, 5½" **165.00**
Gr satin w/HP florals, sterling screw-on top, lay-down, 4¾" **385.00**
Invt T'print, amber w/HP decor, bl bubble stopper, 7¾x3" **88.00**
Pearly wht w/HP decor & gold, clear stopper, 7¾x3" **118.00**

Porcelain lay-down type, ovoid with hand-painted Oriental lady in a kimono, hallmarked silver cap, ca 1904, 2¼", $200.00.

Rubena, allover cuttings, faceted stopper, 5¾x2¼" **95.00**
Ruby, cut panels, gold trim, cut ruby stopper w/gold, 7" **140.00**

Commercial Perfume Bottles

Abano, Matchabelli, metal crown stopper, gold label, 4½", MIB .**55.00**

Armour Sauvage, Ybry, blk w/silver overcap, 2½", MIB **2,900.00**
Ayer Muguet, H Hubbard, fan form w/flower band, gold label, 3" ..**130.00**
Beverly Hills 273, F Hayman, triangular w/gold collar, 12¼" **145.00**
Bond Street, Yardley, clear shouldered form, unopened, MIB **55.00**
Carnation, Vertra, decanter, emb flower top, Baccarat, 3⅜" **220.00**
Carnegie, Hattie Carnegie, pk w/wht cap, label, 1⅜", +box **145.00**
Castel, Lucien Lelong, 4 mini bottles w/plastic caps, MIB **230.00**
Casuma, Coty, emb florals on ball, ball stopper, 2⅜" **200.00**
Chanel No 1, apothecary shape, red & wht label, empty, 3¾" ...**660.00**
Chu Chin Chow, Bryenne, fat Oriental figure w/enameling, 2⅜" ...**1,400.00**
Cyclamen, E Arden, wht & clear fan w/gold, Baccarat, 6⅜", MIB ..**6,050.00**
Danger, Ciro, geometric rectangles, blk cap, Baccarat, 3", +box ...**90.00**
Dans la Nuite, Worth, bl ball, name & moon on stopper, 1¾" **55.00**
de Beaulieu, Beaulieu, gold metal fl, metal cap, 1⅝", +box **50.00**
Diorama, C Dior, bl & clear amphora shape, Baccarat, 7" **660.00**
Discovery, Moneau, 6-pointed star form, globe stopper, 4¾" **165.00**
Dorissimo, C Dior, clear urn form w/bronze dore flower top, 9" ...**770.00**
Ecusson, Jean d'Albret, clear shield w/gold cap, 1½", MIB **110.00**
Extase, Rygel, clear, rose intaglio top, gold label, 2½", MIB **25.00**
Fame, Corday, oblong w/PC emb in stopper, 3¼", MIB **45.00**
Femme, Marcel Rochas, milk glass, gold ball cap, 1¾", MIB **240.00**
Femme de Jour, Corday, blk flask w/gold, Baccarat, 4" **130.00**
Fete des Roses, Caron, gold crosshatching on clear, 4" **300.00**
Fleur de Feu, Guerlain, molded scallops, label, 7⅛" **495.00**
Fleuve Bleue, Lionceau, blk w/abstract swirls, 3¾" **385.00**
Heaven Sent, H Rubenstein, frosted star, metal cap, 1½" **220.00**
Impromptu, L Lelong, futuristic shape, clear/frost, 6½" **145.00**
Intoxication, D'Orsay, pleated star-like shape, 4¼", MIB **100.00**
It's You, E Arden, hand/vase, clear/frosted, Baccarat, 6¼" **850.00**
Jasmin de Corse, Coty, gold label, Baccarat, 3¼", +box **80.00**
Jean Lanvin, clear boule, gold logo, ball stopper, 6" **495.00**
Jouir, Floret, sphere w/inner stopper, brass overcap, 2¼" **195.00**
Kadine, Guerlaine, floriform stopper, Baccarat, 3¾", MIB **415.00**
Kobako, Bourjois, snuff bottle shape, gold label, 3¼" **75.00**
Le Roy Soleil, Schiaparelli, lg sunburst overcap, 6¾", +box .**10,000.00**
Liu, Gerlain, blk stepped form, gold/blk labels, 2¼", MIB **550.00**
Loin de Tout, Guerlain, dk topaz modern shape, Baccarat, 6" **440.00**
Lune d'Amour, Brissac, emb nude on frosted oval, no label, 4½" ...**385.00**
Memoire Cherie, E Arden, lady form, frosted, France, 7" **935.00**
Oellet Fane, Grenovile, clear w/metal cap, label, 2", +box **155.00**
Parfum Max, Max, decanter shape, bl enamel, Baccarat, 4¼", NM ..**385.00**
Parfum Militair Amunita, Pinaud, bullet shape, 2½", +box **55.00**
Pois de Senteur, Joubert, lady w/fan, frosted stopper, 4½" **200.00**
Quand, Corday, blk glass, label (rubbed), w/stopper, 2⅛" **100.00**
Sequoia, Pierre Dune, seated nude frosted stopper, 4¼" **300.00**
Sleeping, Schiaparelli, candle form w/red Bakelite cap, 3" **275.00**
Strategy, Mary Chess, chess castle form, 3", MIB **120.00**
Subtilite, Houbigant, seated Buddha form, Baccarat, 3½" **300.00**
Surrender, Ciro, faceted gemstone form, 4", MIB **100.00**
Sweet Pea Ambree, Renaud, gr opaque, gr stopper, 2⅜", MIB **165.00**
Tabac Doux-Cloche de Liberte, Edria, Liberty Bell form, MIB ...**120.00**
Toujours Moi, Corday, emb vegetal decor, gold label, 3", MIB ...**100.00**
Tsigane (Gypsy), Corday, violin shape w/gold, 3" **100.00**
Vrai Narcisse, Jardin, decanter shape, metallic label, 5½" **110.00**
White Lilac, Mary Chess, factice sz, M in gold-foil box **175.00**

Dairy

Adohr Milk Farm, yel & red pyro, ½-pt **25.00**
Clover Farms, Norwalk CT, gr pyro, 1-qt **20.00**
Dmn Dairy..., Bridgewater MA, red pyro, cream top, 1-qt, EX **25.00**
Fargo's Dairy, Batavia NY, red pyro, cream top, 1-qt **30.00**
Gail Borden Eagle Brand... emb on clear, w/cap & closure, 1-qt ...**75.00**
Guernsey Milk, Champaign IL, cow's head, red pyro, 1-gal **35.00**

Johnstown Sanitary Dairy, Johnstown PA, red pyro, 1-qt **15.00**
Meadow Gold Milk, shield, red pyro, 1-qt **22.50**
Melrose Dairy, Ormond FL, bl pyro, 1-qt **25.00**
Oakhurst Dairy, Bath ME, children in scene, orange pyro, 1-qt ..**22.50**
Perry Creamer Tuscaloosa AL, blk pyro, 1-qt **45.00**
Reed Bros...US Is a Democracy..., red pyro, 1-qt, EX **85.00**
Registered Liquid Peoples Milk Co..., amber, 1920-35, 1-qt **75.00**
Registered...Empire State Dairy..., sb, tm, 1900-20, 9" **60.00**
Robinson & Woolworth...NY, sb, tm, orig metal lid, 8½" **90.00**
Sanitary Best by Test Milk, red & bl pyro, cream top, ½-pt **28.50**
Seeman's Pasteurized...Safety, Loyal WI, orange pyro, 1-qt **20.00**

Titusville Dairy Products Co., black and red pyro, 1-qt, $75.00.

Twilley's Dairy, Cambridge MD, red pyro, 1-qt **18.00**
Woods Dairy..., Petersburg-Hopewell VA, orange pyro, 1-qt **35.00**

Figurals

Atterbury Duck, milk glass, sm, sb, 1860-80, 11⅝" **250.00**
Bell, Gaynor GW Salem NY..., clear, ABM, wood hdl, 6¼" **130.00**
Bullet, Pat Appl For, cobalt, sb, tm, EX label, ca 1900, 3⅞" **100.00**
Bust, Beecher Pat June 9th 1874, clear, sb, tm, 6¾" **70.00**
Busts of lady & 2 men on ped, bright yel-gr, fm, sb, 13⅛" **60.00**
Cherub w/medallion, emerald gr, tm, w/stopper, 11" **175.00**
Cherub w/medallion, med purple-amethyst, tm, w/stopper, 11" .**180.00**
Cigar, amber, s&tm, 1890-1900, 5⅜" **30.00**
Cucumber, med sapphire bl, 10-rib, ps, 1880-90, 7¾" **70.00**
Eiffel Tower, clear, sb, tm, ca 1895-1910, Fr, 7⅜" **60.00**
Fat Dutchman, milk glass, gm, sb, sm flake, 10" **850.00**
Grant's Tomb, milk glass, gm, sb, Am, 1880-1900, 8" **500.00**
Hand holding bottle, med yel-amber, ps, tm, stain, 7⅛" **160.00**
Man smoking pipe, amber, sb, tm, 1890-1910, 11½" **750.00**
Mermaid, brn Albany slip, 1870-90, 7½" L **95.00**
Revolver, purple-amethyst, gm, screw cap, 1890-1900, 7¾" **250.00**
Revolver, turq-bl, tm, ca 1890s, 10" **300.00**
Statue of Liberty, milk glass, gm, sb, 1880-1900, 9¼" **90.00**

Flasks

Adams & Jefferson..., GI-14, lt gr-aqua, ps, sm, 1-pt **240.00**
Anchor, GXIII-64, amber, sb, am, 9½" **55.00**
Benjamin Franklin/Dyott, GI-98, aqua, ps, sm, Wheeling, 6⅜" ..**2,750.00**
Clasped Hands/Eagle, GXII-21, amber, sb, am, whittled, ½-pt ...**120.00**
Clyde GW NY, GXV-I, golden amber, sb, am, haze/crude, 1-pt .**100.00**
Coffin & Hay.../Eagle, GII-48, lt citron, ps, sm, 1-qt **220.00**
Corn for the World/Ear of Corn-Monument, GVI-4, aqua, 1-pt ..**150.00**
Cornucopia-Urn, GII-13, lt to med yel-gr, ps, sm, ½-pt **525.00**
Dbl Eagle, GII-103, dk olive-amber, sb, am, 1860-70, 1-qt **130.00**

Dbl Eagle, GII-106, med yel-olive gr, sb, am, crude, 1-pt 120.00
Dbl Eagle, GII-2, gr-aqua, ps, sm, 1830-35, 1-pt 150.00
Dbl Eagle, GII-24, amber, ip, sm, 6¾", NM 880.00
Dbl Eagle, GII-24, dk aqua, ps, sm, 1825-35, 1-pt 120.00
Dbl Eagle, GII-24, med yel-gr, ps, sm, 1840-45, 1-pt, NM 325.00
Dbl Eagle, GII-4a, aqua, ps, sm, broken blisters, 6⅝" 165.00
Dbl Eagle, GII-40, lt yel-gr, ps, sm, 1825-35, 1-pt 185.00
Dbl Eagle, GII-71, yel-olive-amber, ps, sm, ½-pt 120.00
Deer Good Game/Willow Tree, GX-1, aqua, ps, sm, 1-pt 150.00
Eagle JR/Gen Washington, GI-6a, palest gr, ps, sm, 6⅜" 1,100.00
Eagle/Cornucopia, GII-14, lt gr, sm, ½-pt, 5½" 2,300.00
Eagle/Cornucopia, GII-15a, aqua, ps, sm, ½-pt, 6" 385.00
Eagle/Cornucopia, GII-69, dk aqua, ps, sm, 5⅜" 385.00
Eagle/Cornucopia, GII-72, olive-amber, ps, sm, 7" 165.00
Eagle/Masonic, GIV-14, lt gr, ps, polished lip, 5¾" 440.00
Eagle/Masonic, GIV-7a, aqua, ps, tm, 7½" 225.00
Eagle/Masonic Arch, GIV-32, golden amber, ps, sm, 1-pt 475.00
Eagle/Washington, GI-11, aqua, ps, sm, ground base, 7" 385.00
Father of His Country..., GI-46, blk, sb, am, 1850-60, 1-pt 1,650.00
For Pike's Peak Prospector/Eagle, GXI-7, dk olive-amber, 1-qt 75.00
For Pike's Peak Prospector/Eagle, GXI-8, aqua, 1-qt 75.00
For Pike's Peak Prospector/Hunter, GXI-46, dk bl-aqua, 1-qt 160.00
For Pike's Peak/Hunter, GXI-50, olive gr, am, stain, 7⅝" 550.00
Genl Taylor/Little More Grape, GX-4, olive gr, ps, 7⅛" 2,800.00
Hunter/Fisherman, GXIII-4, med bl-gr, sb, am, calabash 325.00
Hunter/Fisherman, GXIII-4, med strawberry puce, calabash 275.00
Hunter/Fisherman, GXIII-4, yel-amber, ip, am, calabash 210.00
Hunter/Hound, GXIII-16, bright yel w/olive tone, ip, am, 1-qt ..400.00
Isabella Anchor GW/Sheaf of Grain, GXIII-56, aqua, ps, 1-pt ...220.00
Jenny Lind/Glass Factory, GI-102, aqua, ip, am, calabash, NM ..110.00
Jenny Lind/Glass House, GI-104, sapphire bl, calabash, 9½" ..4,850.00
Lafayette/Coventry/Liberty..S&S, GI-87, olive, ps, sm, 6" 4,400.00
Lafayette/S&C Dewitt Clinton CT, GI-81, med yel-olive, ½-pt ..800.00
Louis Kossuth/Paddlewheel Schooner, GI-112, aqua, calabash ...210.00
Masonic Arch/Eagle, GIV-21, med yel-olive-amber, ps, sm, 1-pt ..140.00
Rough & Ready/Corn for World, GI-74, aqua, ps, sm, 7¼" 330.00
Rough & Ready/Corn for World, GI-75, olive gr, ps, sm, 7¼" .5,100.00
Rough & Ready/Eagle Masterson, GI-77, aqua, ps, sm, 8¼" 990.00
Rough & Ready/Major Ringold, GI-71, aqua, ps, sm, 1-pt 85.00
Rough & Ready/Major Ringold, GI-71, gray-clear, ps, sm, 1-pt ..110.00
Scroll, GIX-1, clambroth w/lav tinge, ps, sm, 1-qt 525.00
Sheaf/Traveler's Companion, GXIV-1, olive-amber, sb, am, 9" .100.00
Sunburst, GVIII-16, med olive gr, ps, sm, 1815-25, ½-pt 375.00
Sunburst, GVIII-18, yel-amber w/hint of olive, ps, ½-pt 325.00
Sunburst, GVIII-3, olive-amber, sb, sm, 7½" 600.00
Sunburst/Keen-P&W, GVIII-8, med yel-olive-amber, ps, sm, 1-pt ..475.00
Tree, Winter/Summer, GX-19, golden olive-amber, am, 8¼" 775.00
Union/Eagle, GXII-30, amber, sb, am, ½-pt 300.00
Washington/Eagle, GI-11, aqua, ps, sm, stain, 7" 360.00
Washington/Taylor, GI-52, yel-golden amber, ps, sm, 1-pt 400.00
Westford Glass/Sheaf of Grain, GXIII-35, olive-amber, 1-pt 60.00
Willington Glass/Eagle & Liberty, GII-64, olive gr, 7½" 110.00

Food Bottles and Jars

Mince meat, Wendell & Espy...Philada, aqua, ps, rm, 8⅛" 325.00
Mustard, emb battleship Maine & Morro Castle, sb 110.00
Mustard, emb battleship Maine & Morro Castle, milk glass, sb ..275.00
Pickle, bright bl-gr, cathedral, Gothic arches, 11½" 550.00
Pickle, dk gr-aqua, cathedral, hexagonal w/Gothic arches, 13" ..235.00
Pickle, EHVB (on shoulder), dk aqua, cathedral, 6-sided, 9¼" ..600.00
Pickle, lt gr, cathedral, sb, rm, EX+ orig label, 13" 200.00
Pickle, TB Smith & Co Philada, aqua, cathedral, ps/rm, 9¼" 200.00
Pickle, WK Lewis & Co Boston, aqua, 5 lobed panels, 10½" 275.00

Prunes, A Doufour A C Bordeaux, apple gr, orig label, 4¾" 65.00

Ink Bottles

Butler's Ink Cincinnati, aqua, 12-sided, ps, rm, stain, 2⅜" 100.00
Butler's Ink Cincinnati, lt apple gr, 12-sided, ps, rm, 2¼" 275.00
Carter, cathedral, cobalt, sb, tm, NM labels/stopper, 9¾" 160.00
Estes NY, aqua, 8-sided, ps, am, crude/whittled, master, 6¾" 250.00
Geometric, dk olive-amber, ps, appl disk rim, 1810-20, 1⅝" 170.00
Golden Treasure, aqua, bbl, sb, am, crude, 1855-65, 4⅞" 80.00
Harrison's Columbian, aqua, 12-sided, ps, am, 1840-55, 7⅛" 400.00
J&IEM, bright bl, igloo, sb, gm, overall stain, 1⅝" 800.00
J&IEM, citron, igloo, sm, sb, lt haze, 1⅝" 500.00
J&IEM, lt golden amber, igloo, sb, flake, 1½" 120.00
J&IEM, med bl-gr, igloo, haze, 1½" 110.00
J&IEM, yel w/gr tones, igloo, sm, sb, flake, 1½" 500.00
JS Mason Philada, med emerald gr, ps, fm, sm chip, 4⅜" 230.00
JW Ely Cincinnati, aqua, ps, rm, milky stain, 1845-55, 2⅝" 275.00
Lady's slipper, fiery opal, gm, sb, 3¼" 425.00
Paul's Inks NY Chicago, cobalt, sb, tm, cleaned, master, 9¼" 110.00
RF, blk amethyst, ps, rm, Fr, 1835-60, 2⅛" 100.00
Stoneware, Boss Bros & Co Binghampton NY, Albany slip 85.00
Stoneware, Ross Bros & Co Binghampton NY, salt glaze, 7⅛", EX ...55.00
Teakettle, aqua, sb, sm, 1875-90, 2⅛" 275.00
Teakettle, bright canary yel, sb, gm, spider/stain, 2⅛" 230.00
Teakettle, bright yel-gr, sb, sm, crude, 1875-95, 1⅞" 450.00
Teakettle, honey-amber, sb, gm, orig brass collar/lid, 2½" 210.00

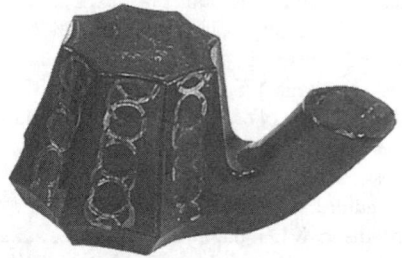

**Teakettle, dark green with gilt decoration, smooth
base, ground lip, tiny stress crack in base, 2", $350.00.**

Teakettle, lt to med gr-aqua, sb, gm, beehive form, 2¼" 625.00
Teakettle, powder bl opaque, sb, polished lip, 1875-95, 2⅝" 525.00
Umbrella, blk amethyst, sb, am, 1860-70, 2¼" 450.00
Umbrella, emerald gr, 12-sided, ps, rm, seed bubbles, 2¼" 325.00
Umbrella, JS Dunham & Co, bl-aqua, 12-sided, ps, rm, 2⅜" 450.00
Umbrella, root beer-amber, 8-sided, ps, sm, 1840-55, 2⅜" 160.00
Umbrella, yel-amber, 8-sided, ps, rm, 1840-55, 2¼" 250.00

Medicine Bottles

A Grandjeans Compositon for the Hair, clear, ps, fm, 3" 160.00
AT&SF Chemical Dept, clear, stain, 1890-1900, 10¾" 190.00
Budd's Wound Nerve & Bone Liniment..., aqua, ps, crude, 5⅜" ..475.00
Carter's Spanish Mixture, yel-olive gr, ip, am, 8¼" 250.00
D Mitchell's Tonic for Hair..., dk bl-aqua, ps, am, 6¼" 85.00
Dr SF Stowe's Ambrosial Nectar...1866, lt yel-gr, sb, am, 8" 65.00
From the Laboratory of GW Merchant..., emerald gr, ps, 5½" 275.00
Gargling Oil Lockport NY, emerald gr, sb, am, 7⅛" 325.00
GW Merchant Chemist Lockport NY, emerald gr, ip, am, 7⅜" .200.00
GW Stone's Cough Elixer Boston MA, aqua, ps, flake, 6¼" 50.00
HH Warner & Co Tippecanoe, amber, sb, am, 1885-95, 9" 80.00
Hyatt's Infallible Life Balsam NY, yel-gr, ip, chip, 9½" 1,050.00

JW Bull's Compound Pectoral Baltimore, aqua, ps, am, 5½" **85.00**
LQC Wishart's Trade Mark Pine...Cordial, bl-gr, 10¼" **150.00**
Myer's Rock Rose New Haven, aqua, ps, am, crude, 9" **235.00**
Phelp's Arcanum Worcester MA, dk olive-amber, ps, am, 8¾" **1,150.00**
Rohrer's Wild Cherry Tonic..., amber, ip, am, 1855-70, 10⅝" ...**240.00**
Selden's Magic Fluid, aqua, ps, am, 1840-55, 7⅜" **140.00**
Shaker Fluid Extract Valerian, aqua, ps, fm, 1835-50, 3¾" **140.00**
Warner's Safe Cure..., dk olive gr, sb, am, German, 9⅛" **400.00**
Warner's Safe Rheumatic Cure, chocolate-amber, sb, am, 9⅝" **65.00**
WE Hagan & Co Troy NY, med cobalt, 8-sided, sb, am, 6¾" **130.00**
WH Brown & Bro Druggist Baltimore, aqua, ps, am, 11⅝" **75.00**

Mineral Water and Soda Bottles

AD Schnackenberg...NY, amber, sb, am, cleaned, 1-pt, 7¾" **250.00**
Boardman, med sapphire bl, ip, am, flake, 7" **90.00**
C Whittemore NY, med emerald gr, ip, am, str shoulders, 8⅛" ..**190.00**
CB Owen...Cincinnati CBO & Co, dk sapphire bl, ip, am, 7½" ..**300.00**
Champion Spouting Spring..., aqua, sb, am, 1-pt, 7½" **85.00**
Clarke & Co NY, dk olive-amber, sb, am, 7½" **60.00**
Clarke & Wht NY, dk olive gr, high shoulder, sb, am, 1-qt **170.00**
Clarke & Wht NY, med yel-olive gr, ps, am, whittled, 1-qt **70.00**
Congress & Empire Spring...Saratoga NY, yel-olive gr, ½-pt **175.00**
Craven Unino GW Phila, sapphire bl, ip, am, stain, 7¼" **100.00**
DA Knowton Saratoga NY, dk olive gr, sb, am, whittled, 1-qt **55.00**
Darien Mineral Springs...NY, aqua, sb, am, 1-pt, 7⅝" **350.00**
Deep Rock Spring...Oswego NY, aqua, sb, am, lt haze, 1-qt **275.00**
Diehl's...Pat, med gr, ps, am, stain, 1830-40, 6½" **150.00**
E Roussell Philada, emerald gr, ip, am, 7⅜" **80.00**
E Smith Elmira NY, dk cobalt, sb, am, whittled, 7⅜" **130.00**
GW Felix Harrisburg, cobalt, ip, am, 1845-55, 7¼" **425.00**
GW Weston & Co Saratoga NY, dk olive gr, sb, am, 7⅝" **130.00**
GW Weston & Co Saratoga NY, dk olive-amber, sb, crude, 7½" ..**110.00**
Highrock Congress Spring, chocolate-amber, sb, 7⅞" **130.00**
Highrock Congress Spring, root beer-amber, flake, 7¾" **80.00**
I Brownell New Bedford...Never Sold, med cobalt, ip, 7½" **170.00**
IA Lindestram Madison WI, aqua, ip, am, 7¼" **110.00**
J Boardman...Is Never Sold, emerald gr, 8-sided, ip, 7¾" **450.00**
John Clarke NY, yel-olive-amber, ps, am, 7⅜", NM **170.00**
John H Gardner & Son..., bl-gr, sb, am, 1-pt, 7⅝" **220.00**
John S Baker...Is Never Sold, emerald gr, 8-sided, ip, 7¼" **150.00**
LJ Miday...Canton OH, aqua, sb, am, orig metal closure, 1-qt **90.00**
Luke Beard, med emerald gr, tenpin, sb, am, 7¼" **200.00**
Middleton Healing Springs..., golden yel-amber, sb, 9½" **500.00**
Pavilion & United States Spring..., dk bl-gr, sb, am, 7½" **240.00**
Phoenix GW Brooklyn, aqua, ip, am, lt wear, 7¼" **140.00**
Phoenix GW Brooklyn, lt gr, ip, am, lt stain, 7⅛" **150.00**
S Grossman Soda Mineral..., yel-gr, mug-based Hutch, 7½", EX ..**250.00**
Saratoga Spring, yel-amber, sb, am, potstone, 1-pt, 7⅝" **55.00**
Southwick & Tupper NY, cobalt, 10-sided, ip, am, 7⅜" **450.00**
Wm Betz & Co..., dk aqua, 10-sided, ps, am, 7⅞" **120.00**

Poison Bottles

Caution Not To Be Taken, yel-gr, sb, tm, 1890-1910, 3½" **140.00**
CLC & Co Pat Applied For, med moss gr, sb, tm, 5½" **110.00**
Diamond Antiseptics...(NM label), yel-amber, sb, tm, 10⅛" **110.00**
Excelsior Preservative..., clear, sb, tm, 1890-1910, 6⅝" **140.00**
HK Mulford Co Chemists/skull & crossbones, cobalt, 3⅛" **125.00**
Jacobs' Bichloride Tablets/skull & crossbones, amber, 2¼" **700.00**
Lattice & Dmn pattern, dk moss gr, sb, tm, 4½" **375.00**
Melvin & Badger Apothecaries..., cobalt, sb, tm, 5" **50.00**
Poison, amber, triangular, sb, tm, sm stain, 1890-1910, 3⅞" **350.00**
Poison/Pat App'd For NB & Co, amber, sb, stain, 2½" **75.00**

Poison - Poison, yellow-amber, smooth base, tooled mouth, American, 1890-1910, 7⅞" (rare size), $240.00.

Poison/Poison, yel-amber, sb, tm, Am, 1890-1910, 3¼" **70.00**

Sarsaparilla Bottles

Dr Myer's Vegetable Extract..., aqua, am, ip, 9¾" **230.00**
Dr Townsend's Albany NY, emerald gr, ps, am, scratches, 9⅝" **80.00**
Dr Townsend's Albany NY, root beer-amber, ps, am, 9⅛" **250.00**
Dr Townsend's Albany NY, yel-olive-amber, ps, bubbles, 10" ...**155.00**
Old Dr Jacob Townsend's...Blood Purifier, ice bl, ip, am, 9½" **400.00**
Turner's, aqua, oval, am, sb, lt stain, 12½" **275.00**

Spirits Bottles

AM Bininger & Co, olive gr, sb, am, VG label, crude, 9¾" **825.00**
AM Bininger No 19 Broad St NY, dk olive gr, sb, am & hdl, 8" ..**1,350.00**
Bennett & Carrol..., med yel-amber, bbl, ip, am, 9½" **550.00**
Bennett & Carrol..., yel-amber, flattened chestnut, ip, 8⅜" **825.00**
Bininger's Knickerbocker AM..., med golden amber, ps, 6½" .**1,300.00**
Bininger's Old KY Bourbon..., med amber, sb, am, 9⅝" **85.00**
Bininger's Peep-O-Day..., med amber to yel-amber, flask, 7¾" ...**350.00**
Bininger's Regulator..., amber, clock, ps, am, 1860-70, 6" **325.00**
Bininger's Travelers..., yel-amber, teardrop flask, 6⅝" **235.00**
Casper's Whiskey Made By..., cobalt, sb, tm, 1880-95, 12" **350.00**
Cognac W & Co, med amber, ps, am & hdl, sealed, 5¾" **275.00**
Forest Lawn JVH, olive gr, ip, am, 1860-70, 7½" **375.00**
Good Samaritan Brandy..., olive-amber, ip, am, 1865-75, 7" **900.00**
H Pharazyn Phila Right Secured, yel-amber, Indian Queen, 12" ..**1,050.00**
Imperial Levee J Noves..., yel-root beer-amber, ip, 9⅜" **1,900.00**
JFT & Co Philad, golden yel-amber, ps, am & hdl, crude, 7" **650.00**
JN Kline...Aromatic...Cordial, amber, teardrop flask, 5½" **250.00**
JN Kline...Aromatic...Cordial, cobalt, teardrop flask, 5½" **240.00**
Mohawk Whiskey Pure...1868, yel-amber, Indian Queen, 12⅜" ..**1,000.00**
Old London Dock Gin AM Bininger..., yel-olive-amber, 9⅝" ...**140.00**
Pure Malt Whiskey Bourbon Co KY, amber, sb, am & hdl, 8⅝" .**525.00**
RB Cutter Louisville KY, root beer-amber, ps, am & hdl, 8⅝" ...**210.00**
RB Cutter Pure Bourbon, med smoky pk-puce, ip, am & hdl, 8⅜" ..**600.00**
RB Cutter Pure Bourbon, med yel-amber, ps, am & hdl, 8½" **375.00**
Star Whiskey...Crowell Jr, golden yel-amber, ps, am & hdl, 8" **425.00**
Turner Bros New York, yel-olive, bbl, sb, am, 9⅞" **425.00**
Wharton's Whiskey..., med amber, teardrop flask, 5⅛" **325.00**
Wharton's Whiskey..., med cobalt, teardrop flask, 5⅛" **325.00**
Wm H Daly Sole Importer..., olive gr, bell, ps, am, 9¼" **850.00**

Miscellaneous

Lavender Salts, Goetting & Co, See California Perfume Co.

Boxes

Boxes have been used by civilized man since ancient Egypt and

Rome. Down through the centuries, specifically designed containers have been made from every conceivable material. Precious metals, papier-mache, Battersea, Oriental lacquer, and wood have held riches from the treasuries of kings, snuff for the fashionable set of the last century, China tea, and countless other commodities. See also Toleware; specific manufacturers.

Band, wallpaper-covered (geometrics), 1873 newspaper lined, 10" L ...**250.00**
Band, wallpaper-covered (griffin-pulled chariots), 18" L **500.00**
Band, wallpaper-covered cb (hunt scene), 16¼" L, EX **775.00**
Band, wallpaper-covered cb (mythological), 1800s, 11x18", EX .**975.00**
Bentwood, Harvard type, 1-finger w/iron tacks, yel rpt, 5" dia **145.00**
Bentwood, lapped & nailed seam, dk brn stain, 7" dia **55.00**
Bentwood, lapped & nailed seam, old bl pnt, 10¾" **400.00**
Bentwood, lapped & nailed seam, orig gray pnt, 6½" dia **260.00**
Bentwood, lapped & nailed seams, old bl pnt, 7" dia **260.00**
Bentwood, scratch-cvd & wood-burned decor, 11" L **300.00**
Brass, inlaid wood lid, mk Germany, 1920s, 4¾" **85.00**
Bride's, bentwood, mc florals & bands, soldier litho, 8x19x12" ..**850.00**
Bride's, bentwood, mc florals on wht, laced seams, 19", VG **195.00**
Bride's, pine w/mc florals on bl, laced seams, 14½" L **415.00**
Bride's, pine w/orig mc pnt, laced seam, 17" L, EX **675.00**
Candle, dvtl oak, beveled edge lid, hanging, 19" L **300.00**
Candle, fine-grained softwood w/sliding lid, 4x11x5" **275.00**
Candle, pine, chamfered sliding lid, ca 1800, 6x9x11" **275.00**
Candle, poplar w/curly maple, dvtl, wall mt, 14" L **500.00**
Chip cvd, step-cut ft, sliding lid, 1-pc, 4½" L **225.00**
Document, dvtl pine w/old brn pnt, 1800s, 10x15" **165.00**
Document, maple w/figured walnut lid, brass hdls, 13" L **220.00**
Dome top, dvtl pine, brn vinegar grpt, 30" **110.00**
Dome top, sponge pnt, baskets of flowers sides/top, 18x9x7½" ...**550.00**
Enameled copper w/bridal couple & other scenes, 3" dia **95.00**
Glass, lime gr w/flowers & gilt, 4¾x5½" **165.00**
Glass, turq bl w/mc floral, ormolu ft/mts, 5½" dia **265.00**
Grpt on red, compartments, 1830s, 11x28x23" **175.00**
Gum, poplar w/dk stain, chip cvd, rpl lid, 5½" **150.00**

Hat box, covered with classical figured landscape paper, American, ca 1840, 10¾x15½x12", EX, $1,000.00.

Inlaid marquetry, geometric foliage bands, 9" H **85.00**
Knife, dvtl walnut, cut-out hdl, old mellow rfn, 14x10" **195.00**
Knife, pnt (wear), divided, 1800s, 23½" **285.00**
Mahog, cvd edges, bracket ft, bronze bail, 1800s, 8¾" L **250.00**
Pantry, unpnt wood, pointed laps, 6½" dia **110.00**
Pantry, wood, pointed laps, dk mustard pnt, 7½" dia **145.00**
Pine, dvtl, red stain, slant-top lift lid, compartments, 14" L **225.00**
Pine w/red flame graining, mc florals on lid, att OH, 15" L **550.00**
Pipe, pine, orig bl pnt, scalloped edges/crest, drw, 18x7" **325.00**
Poplar, dvtl, worn red pnt, brass hdl, 14" L **150.00**
Saffron, treenware, urn-shaped finial, 4⅜x2⅝" **210.00**
Satinwood w/fan inlay, oval panels in front, 1800s, 7½" L **475.00**
Spice, dvtl poplar, pnt traces, 6-section, sgn lid, 8½" L **225.00**
Spice, dvtl walnut, sliding lid, 4-part interior, 8½" **725.00**
Walnut, star inlay lid, rpl bottom, 12" dia **80.00**
Walnut w/appl moldings, dvtl, lt wear, 14" L **110.00**
Writing, bird's-eye veneer w/abalone shell inlay, 15" L **100.00**

Writing, orig grpt imitates exotic wood, fitted int, 13" L **55.00**
Writing, pine, bl pnt, slant-top lift lid, molding, 21" L **385.00**
Writing, rosewood w/brass & ivory inlay, 11¼" L, EX **100.00**
Writing, smoke grpt, slant lid, 19th C, 10¼x21½", EX **515.00**
Writing, walnut veneer w/gold, fitted interior, 11½" L **60.00**

Boyd Crystal Art Glass

Boyd Crystal Art Glass is a small but productive glass factory located in Cambridge, Ohio. It was established in 1978 when the Boyd family bought out the Degenhart factory. Over the years Boyd has produced more than two hundred molds; while many were their own design, they acquired others from glasshouses no longer in business. All the Boyd pieces are marked with a distinct logo of a 'B' in diamond. Further dating is possible because a line was added under the diamond in 1983, and an additional line was added above the diamond in 1988. In September 1993 another line was added, this one on the right of the diamond. Boyd's glass is prized because of the colors they formulated and the fact that once a piece is produced in a particular color it will not be produced in that color again, even if that color is brought back years later. All pieces are hand pressed from glass that is from a single-day tank. Colors are made for about eight weeks or less, thus limiting the number of pieces that can be produced in that color. More than three hundred different colors have been used and developed by the Boyds. Much like Degenhart glass, the colors can be confusing and difficult to identify. Exceptional slags and hand-painted pieces can command up to 50% higher prices. Satin glass variations are priced 10% to 30% higher when they can be found.

In the following listings, (N) indicates a mold that was new in 1995-96. (R) indicates a yearly special edition of a retired piece. Our advisor for this category is Joyce Pringle; she is listed in the Directory under Texas.

Airplane, Cashmere Pink, 4x3¼" **18.50**
Airplane, Vaseline, 4x3¼" **25.00**
Angel, Mint Julep Carnival **16.50**
Angel, Vaseline (N) **20.00**
Artie the Penguin, Aqua Diamond **8.50**
Bow Slipper, Furr Green **12.50**
Bow Slipper, Ruby **20.00**
Bow Slipper, Waterloo **9.00**
Brian Bunny, Sunkist Carnival (R) **7.50**
Bunny Salt, Buckeye **6.25**
Bunny Salt, Cashmere Pink **8.50**
Bunny Salt, Skytop Blue **20.00**
Bunny Salt, Thistlebloom **15.00**
Cat Slipper, Classic Black Slag **11.00**
Cat Slipper, Platinum Carnival **22.50**
Cat Slipper, Waterloo (Blue) **10.50**
Chick, Bermuda (Red) **18.00**
Chick, Enchantment, 1" **20.00**
Chick, Nile Green **8.50**
Chick, Robin Egg Blue **20.00**
Chick, Royalty, 1" **50.00**
Chicken Covered Dish, Cardinal Red, 3" **11.50**
Chuckles the Clown, Confetti **12.50**
Duck Salt, Lt Peach **8.00**
Elizabeth, mini doll, Lime Carnival **30.00**
Elizabeth, mini doll, Teal, 2" **8.50**
Forget-Me-Not Toothpick, John's Surprise **21.50**
Forget-Me-Not Toothpick, Teal Swirl **15.00**
Fuzzy Bear, Ritz Blue **17.50**
Hand Dish, Snow **15.00**

Hand Dish, Vaseline Carnival 6.50
Heart Jewel Box, Opaline Blue Swirl 38.50
Heart Jewel Box, Vaseline 15.00
Hen Covered Dish, Chocolate, 5" 40.00
JB Scotty, Cobalt Carnival (R) 10.50
JB Scotty, Mulberry Mist 26.00
JB Scotty, Ruby 50.00
Jeremy Frog, Cobalt, 2¼" 7.25
Joey the Horse, Alexandrite Carnival, 4" 16.50
Joey the Horse, Chocolate (1st color in this mold) 22.50
Kitten on Pillow, Firefly 25.00
Kitten on Pillow, Sandpiper 13.50
Louise Doll, Delphinium 22.00
Lucky the Unicorn, Peridot 35.00
Mini Vase, Dk Tangerine Slag 12.50
Mini Vase, Smoke 12.00
Miss Cotton (Kitten Not on Pillow), Celery 8.00
Nancy Doll, Cobalt 8.25
Patrick Balloon Bear, Enchantment 24.50
Patrick Balloon Bear, Spinnaker Blue 10.00
Patrick Balloon Bear, Sunkist Carnival (R) 8.50
Sammy Squirrel, Crown Tuscan Carnival, 3" 10.00
Skate Boot, Heather 12.50
Skate Boot, Snow Slag, 4" 42.50
Tall Boot, Nile Green 10.00
Taxi, Alexandrite 12.50
Tucker (Car), Grape Parfait 12.50
Willie the Mouse, Primrose 7.00
Zak the Elephant, Cobalt 38.00
Zak the Elephant, Crystal 45.00
Zak the Elephant, Flame (1st color in this mold), 3¼x4½" 45.00
Zak the Elephant, Lemonade 35.00

Bradley and Hubbard

The Bradley and Hubbard Mfg. Company was a firm which produced metal accessories for the home. They operated from about 1860 until the early part of this century, and their products reflected both the Arts and Crafts and Art Nouveau influence. Their logo was a device with a triangular arrangement of the company name containing a smaller triangle and an Aladdin lamp. Our advisor for this category is Daniel Batchelor; he is listed in the Directory under New York.

Lamps

Banquet, HP globe w/flowers, cast base, sgn, 37" 450.00
Bracket, milk glass w/pansies, fancy CI mts, mercury reflector 125.00
Slag glass 15" 8-side shade w/metal floral fr; columnar std 575.00
Table, hammered copper 12" shade; Nouveau bronze base, 17" ..635.00
Table, rvt 22" 8-panel tulip shallow dome shade; 3-leg std 950.00

Miscellaneous

Andirons, brass, dmn-shaped motif, att, 22" 275.00
Bookends, dancing girl, CI w/gold pnt, mk, 5¾", pr 125.00
Bookends, eagle, bronze, mk, pr 100.00
Bookends, Franz Liszt, CI w/bronze finish, mk, pr 100.00
Bookends, gate, CI w/bronze pnt, mk, 5¾", pr 115.00
Bookends, girl w/umbrella, CI, mk, pr 110.00
Bookends, Harvard University, CI, pr 100.00
Bookends, lions, CI, bronze pnt, 3¼", pr 110.00
Bookends, monk reading book, seated, CI w/cold pnt, pr 135.00
Bookends, President T Roosevelt bust, pnt CI, mk, 6⅛", pr 100.00

Bookends, Priscilla & John Alden, CI, mc pnt, mk, 5⅞", pr 95.00
Bookends, seascape in oval, CI, mk, pr 85.00
Bookends, Study (nun w/book), CI, mk, pr 95.00

Fireplace set, wrought iron, includes large andirons, 4-piece tool set and large fire fender, unmarked, $1,400.00.

Fireplace tools, iron w/brass wash, 3-pc, in stand, 31" 600.00
Pen & ink stand, brass, 2 wells, w/drw, angular base, 10" 220.00

Brass

Brass is an alloy consisting essentially of copper and zinc in variable proportions. It is a medium that has been used for both utilitarian items and objects of artistic merit. Today, with the inflated price of copper and the popular use of plastics, almost anything made of brass is collectible. Our advisor, Mary Frank Gaston, has compiled a lovely book, *Antique Brass and Copper*, with full-color photos; you will find her address in the Directory under Texas. See also Candlesticks.

Bowl, stylized animals & foliage, sm split, 4½" dia 10.00
Box, cast oval, incised line decor, hinged lid, 2x7x3¼" 50.00
Candle reflector, cast, scalloped edges, tripod base, 7x4½" 155.00
Chamberstick, heart shape, England, 7¼" 225.00
Cup & saucer, demitasse; w/abalone shell inlay 25.00
Dresser bench, crewel uphl top, 34" L 60.00
Kettle, dvtl, simple scrolling, in fr w/burner, 12½" 140.00
Kettle, iron hdl, Am Brass Kettle Mfgs, 9x12½" 125.00
Kettle, iron hdl, HW Hayden's...1861...Waterbury..., 11x17" 175.00
Kettle, spun, iron hdl, Am Brass Kettle, 17" dia, VG 225.00
Kettle, spun, iron hdl, Miller & Co, Meriden Conn, 18" dia 250.00
Kettle, spun, paw ft & lion-head ring hdls, Waterbury, 8x11" 275.00
Kettle, spun, wire bale hdls, Hayden's Pat, 11½" dia 175.00
Kettle shelf, wrought-iron fr w/grate hooks, rstr, 10" 30.00
Ladle, copper rivets, wrought-iron hdl, 17½" 45.00
Ladle, inlaid hearts/circles in iron hdl, 5⅞" dia, 3½" hdl 180.00
Ladle, tasting; wrought hdl w/loop, J Schmidt, 11¼" 400.00
Ladle, wrought hdl w/heart-shape design & hook, 6" dia, 20" L .145.00
Ladle, wrought-iron hdl, 20" 35.00
Lamp, table; slag glass inserts in fringed shade, electric 255.00
Match holder, cast florals & scrolls, 5¾x2½" 45.00
Pail, Hayden's Patent label, 10" dia 165.00
Paper holder, hand shape, stamped Radcliff, Pat 1885..., 4" 50.00
Pie crimper, ivory lady's leg hdl w/boot, 6", EX 330.00
Salver, eng arabesque, cvd base, Middle Eastern, 29" dia 220.00
Saucepan, copper rivets, 1800s, 8"+9" iron hdl 110.00
Spatula, wrought hdl, sgn FBS Canton, Pat Jan 26 86, 15" 110.00
Spittoon, weighted bottom, 8x7" 75.00
Stand, plant; legs cast w/children's heads etc, Victorian, 32" 250.00
Stand, 3-tier, girls heads top corners, 27x11x11", NM 100.00
Statuette, fighting cocks, EX detail, 1900s, 11" W, pr 235.00
Teakettle, gooseneck copper spout, English, 10x12" 265.00
Teakettle, gooseneck spout, trn hdl, handmade/polished, 8" 240.00
Tie back, rnd w/flower center, 3" dia, pr 75.00

Umbrella stand, raised dragons, resoldered bottom, 25" 115.00
Wall brackets, ornamental, hinged, 10½", pr 45.00

Brastoff, Sascha

The son of immigrant parents, Sascha Brastoff was encouraged to develop his artistic talents to the fullest, encouragement that was well taken, as his achievements aptly attest. Though at various times he was a dancer, sculptor, Hollywood costume designer, jeweler, and painter, it is his ceramics that are today becoming highly regarded collectibles.

Sascha began his career in the United States in the late 1940s. In a beautiful studio built for him by his friend and mentor, Winthrop Rockefeller, he designed innovative wares that even then were among the most expensive on the market. All designing was done personally by Brastoff; he also supervised the staff which at the height of production numbered approximately 150. Wares signed with his full signature (not merely backstamped 'Sascha Brastoff') were personally crafted by him and are valued much more highly than those signed 'Sascha B.,' indicating work done under his supervision. Until his death in 1993, he continued his work in Los Angeles, in his latter years producing 'Sascha Holograms,' which were distributed by the Hummelwerk Company.

Though the resin animals signed 'Sascha B.' were neither made nor designed by Brastoff, collectors of these pieces value them highly. According to the first book cited in the last paragraph, after he left the factory in the 1960s, the company retained the use of the name to be used on reissues of earlier pieces or merchandise purchased at trade shows.

In the listings that follow, items are ceramic and signed 'Sascha B.' unless 'full signature' or another type of medium is indicated.

For further information we recommend *The Collector's Encyclopedia of Sascha Brastoff* by Steve Conti, A. DeWayne Bethany, and Bill Seay; available from Collector Books or your local book store. Our advisor for this category is Jack Chipman, author of *Collector's Encyclopedia of California Pottery*, another source of valuable information for Brastoff collectors. Mr. Chipman is listed in the Directory under California.

Ashtray, Pagoda, matt, 9x12" 65.00
Ashtray, Star Steed (horse) decor, 8" 55.00
Bowl, Alaska Line, Eskimo face, 6x11" 85.00
Bowl, centerpc; birds & floral on gr, full sgn, 10x16½" 1,200.00
Bowl, Jeweled Bird, 7" 45.00
Coffee set, Surf Ballet Line, wht/lav swirl w/gold o/l, 4-pc 250.00
Compote, Alaska Line, polar bear 85.00
Dish, Jeweled Bird, rolled edge, 10" 65.00
Dish, Rooftops Line, scene of houses, free-form, 10" 65.00
Dish, sq, abstract angular lineation, style 06, 8" 60.00
Dish, wht circus elephant on bl, 3-sided, 10" 100.00
Figurine, Foo Dog, blk matt w/gold factory decal, 16" 425.00
Figurine, owl, gr resin, 14" 350.00
Figurine, shoe, high-button, ceramic, Surf Ballet, 10" 200.00

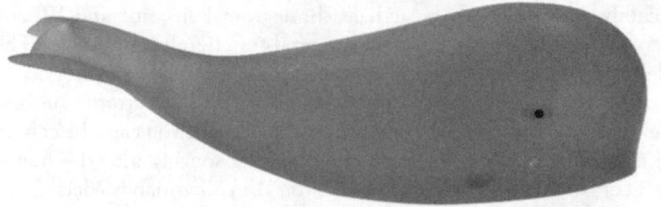

Figure of whale, amber resin with black glass eyes, 12" long, $375.00.

Pendant, gold tree design, MIB w/orig label 500.00
Piggy bank, abstract decor on sides, style S14, 5" 95.00

Pipe/cigarette holder, pipe shape, 8" 95.00
Pitcher, fruit decor, hdld, 7" 85.00
Plate, alien amphibious creature in gold, full sgn/dtd, 8" 900.00
Plate, chop; bl & gray abstract rings, style 053, 17" 175.00
Plate, Fall of the House of Usher, full sgn on front, 10" 850.00
Plate, fruit, 11" 65.00
Plate, 2 figures outlined in gold on bl matt, full sgn, 10" 1,000.00
Plate, 3 natives dancing, wht bkground, full sgn, 10" 875.00
Shaker, egg shape, Alaskan scene, hdld, 3" 25.00
Switch plate, horse's head, shiny brass finish, sgn, 10" 100.00
Tankard, Jeweled Bird, hdld, style 070, 5" 45.00
Tankards, different types of fruit depicted on ea, 5", set of 6 ....300.00
Tile, abstract animal, paper label only, 6x6" 175.00
Tile, Temple Towers in orig custom fr, sgn, 21x9" 375.00
Tray, sq, Fiesta Pools, sgn, 15" 125.00
Urn, gold finish, w/lid, 7" 150.00
Vase, Alaska Line, walrus, #082 ....85.00
Vase, candlestick; lady w/arms raised, full sgn/label, 13" 850.00
Vase, horse & gold foliage on charcoal, spherical, 8" 100.00
Vase, Jeweled Bird, 6" 65.00
Vase, wht ballerina on bl, sq, 9" 175.00
Wall pocket, Alaskan scene, full sgn, 12" 575.00

Brayton, Laguna

Durlin E. Brayton made handcrafted vases, lamps, and dinnerware in a small kiln at his Laguna Beach, California, home in 1927. He soon married, and with his wife, Ellen Webster Grieve, as his partner, the small business became a successful commercial venture. They are most famous for their amusing, well-detailed figurines, some of which were commissioned by Walt Disney Studios. Though very successful even through the Depression years, with the influx of imported novelties that deluged the country after WWII, business began to decline. By 1968 the pottery was closed. For more information on this as well as many other potteries in the state, we recommend *The Collectors Encyclopedia of California Pottery* by Jack Chipman; he is listed in the Directory under California.

Cigarette box, Dahlias 45.00
Cookie jar, Christina (Swedish Maiden) 425.00
Cookie jar, Gingerbread House 250.00
Cookie jar, Matilda, bl & gr skirt 475.00
Cookie jar, Provincial Lady 295.00
Cookie jar, Wedding Ring Granny (Grandma), mk (+) 475.00
Creamer & sugar bowl, Calico Cat & Plaid Dog 75.00
Dealer sign, rare 400.00
Figurine, Ann, seated, 4" 85.00
Figurine, ballerina 85.00
Figurine, Blackamoor, kneeling, gold & jewels, 10" 225.00
Figurine, blk panther, jeweled gold collar & gold ankle cuff 175.00
Figurine, Calico Dog, 8" 85.00
Figurine, cat, stylized, recumbent, crackle eyes, 16" 125.00
Figurine, clown, stylized, 1950s, lg 150.00
Figurine, duck, orange, stylized, 1950s 75.00
Figurine, Ellen, pigtails & hat, 7" 85.00
Figurine, Gay '90s bartender, bar scene w/3 figures 125.00
Figurine, Hanson Cab, lovers inside, Gay '90s series 250.00
Figurine, horse, 12x10" 175.00
Figurine, island girl in sarong 150.00
Figurine, Italian man w/push cart 75.00
Figurine, Olds, car w/man, woman & dog riders, Gay '90s 195.00
Figurine, peasant lady, early 65.00
Figurine, penguin, 1950s, 7½" 75.00
Figurine, Petunia, Blk child, 6" 175.00

Figurine, pheasant, aqua **75.00**
Figurine, Pluto, Disney, 1930s **125.00**
Figurine, Purple Cow **125.00**
Figurine, quail, mc, 1950s **55.00**
Figurine, Seashore Honeymoon, beach couple, Gay '90s series **75.00**
Figurine, swan, turq, sm **65.00**
Figurines, Hillbilly Wedding, 11" Pa & 9" Ma+4 figures, mk ..**1,000.00**
Flower holder, Sally **40.00**
Head vase, Blk lady **125.00**
Planter, baby on pillow, bl **65.00**
Planter, girl w/wolfhounds **65.00**
Shakers, Calico Cat & Plaid Dog, pr **50.00**
Shakers, Mammy & Chef, sm, pr **125.00**
Vase, seafoam bl w/lupines, 15½" **150.00**
Vase, Swiss peasant woman w/basket **75.00**

Bread Plates and Trays

Bread plates and trays have been produced not only in many types of glass but in metal and pottery as well. Those considered most collectible were made during the last quarter of the 19th century from pressed glass with well-detailed embossed designs, many of them portraying a particularly significant historical event. A great number of these plates were sold at the 1876 Philadelphia Centennial Exposition by various glass manufacturers who exhibited their wares on the grounds. Among the themes depicted are the Declaration of Independence, the Constitution, McKinley's memorial 'It Is God's Way,' Rememberance of Three Presidents, the Purchase of Alaska, and various presidential campaigns, to mention only a few.

'L' numbers correspond with a reference book by Lindsey. Our advisor for this category is Darlene Yohe; she is listed in the Directory under Arkansas.

Actress, Miss Nelson, 13x9" **90.00**
Balky Mule **85.00**
Barley, cable edging, stippled **65.00**
Bates, L-375 ....**65.00**
Bishop, L-201 ....**200.00**
Bunker Hill, L-44, 13¼x9" **75.00**
California Bear, 1894 Expo, L-104 ....**140.00**
Chain Variant **25.00**
Classic Warrior, frosted center, 11" dia **155.00**
Columbus, amber, L-54 ....**165.00**
Continental Hall, Give Us This Day..., oval **85.00**
Cupid & Venus, 10½" dia **37.50**
Eggs in Sand, 12¼x7¾" **50.00**
Egyptian, Cleopatra center, 13" L **50.00**
Frosted Lion, Give Us This Day..., 12" **175.00**
Frosted Stork **50.00**
GAR, L-505, 11" L **90.00**
Garfield Drape, We Mourn, L-303, 11½" **75.00**
Garfield 101, frosted, L-300 ....**85.00**
Heroes of Bunker Hill **75.00**
Horseshoe, single hdls, 13" L **60.00**
In Remembrance **50.00**
It Is Pleasant To Labor, vintage decor, 12¾" dia **55.00**
Jewel Band **25.00**
Kansas, motto **48.00**
Knights of Labor, amber, L-512 ....**145.00**
Last Supper **40.00**
Liberty Bell, John Hancock, oval, 13" **50.00**
Liberty Bell, Signers, L-43 ....**85.00**
Maltese Cross, 10" **26.00**

Maple Leaf, vaseline, oval, 13x9½" **85.00**
McCormick Reaper **160.00**
McKinley, Gold Standard, 10½" **250.00**
McKinley, His Will Be Done, clear/frosted **55.00**
McKinley, Protection, L-333 ....**45.00**
Memorial Hall **65.00**
Nelly Bly, L-136, 12" L **200.00**
Niagara Falls, milk glass, 2 American flags **55.00**
Old State House, L-31 ....**25.00**
Old State House, sapphire bl, L-31, rare **195.00**
Polar Bear, ship, L-486, 16" **165.00**
Queen Victoria, 10" dia **45.00**
Railroad, L-134 ....**95.00**
Retriever, milk glass **80.00**
Rock of Ages, dtd milk glass center, oval **175.00**
Rose & Snow, 11¼x8¾" **135.00**
Scroll w/Flowers, 12" dia **35.00**
Stippled Cherry, Our Daily Bread, 9½" **25.00**
Tam-O'-Shanter, purple slag, L-412, 12x8½" **250.00**
Teddy Roosevelt, dancing bears, L-357, 10" L **145.00**
Texas Centennial, Alamo center **90.00**
Train, L-134 ....**75.00**
Union Pacific Railroad **85.00**
US Grant, L-291, 10" sq **115.00**
US Grant, Let Us Have Peace, vaseline, L-289 ....**90.00**
Victoria Jubilee 1887 ....**65.00**
Westward Ho **95.00**
Wildflower, sq **28.00**
William J Bryan, milk glass **45.00**

Bretby

The Bretby Art Pottery was an English firm whose roots can be traced to the 1880s, an offspring of the earlier Tooth & Company Ltd. The Bretby mark was first used circa 1885. 'England' was added in later years of the 19th century, and by the 1920s, 'Made in England, Bretby,' was the standard mark.

Vase, blk woodgrain w/emb floral, suspended ring hdls, 11" **110.00**
Vase, brn matt w/relief jeweled 'copper' bands & straps, 9" **250.00**

Bride's Baskets and Bowls

Victorian brides were showered with gifts, as brides have always been; one of the most popular gift items was the bride's basket. Art glass inserts from both European and American glasshouses, some in lovely transparent hues with dainty enameled florals, others of Peachblow, Vasa Murrhina, satin, or cased glass, were cradled in complementary silverplated holders. While many of these holders were simply engraved or delicately embossed, others such as those from Pairpoint and Wilcox were wonderfully ornate, often with figurals of cherubs or animals. The bride's basket was no longer in fashion after the turn of the century.

Watch for 'marriages' of bowls and frames. To warrant the best price, the two pieces should be the original pairing. If you can't be certain of this, at least check to see that the bowl fits snugly into the frame. Beware of later-made bowls (such as Fenton's) in Victorian holders.

In the listings that follow, if no frame is described, the price is for a bowl only.

Aqua shaded to wht, cased, ruffled, 6" **95.00**
Bl cased, butterflies & floral; orig SP ftd fr, 12x10" **395.00**
Bl o/l satin, ruffled: rstr Victor SP fr, 13x13" **450.00**

Bl opal, Stevens & Wms; SP fr w/swans 550.00
Bl shaded to wht, cased, ruffled, 6½" 75.00
Cranberry opal lattice, ruffled, sq; 9½x6" ftd Simpson fr 595.00
Dk ruby to pk w/floral, 11"; ornate gilt ft, 10" 350.00
Gr satin w/berries & scrolls, crimped, 13"; fruit-appl ft 600.00
Hobnail, pk frost w/bl-accented crimped/folded rim, 4x9" 225.00
Hobnail, pk opal w/bl crimped rim; branch/leaf-trim fr, 5x11" ...500.00
Lt gr w/tiny wht floral, pleated rim, 10¾x3" 300.00
Maroon to cream w/floral & emb decor, 3x11" 225.00
MOP gr Dmn Quilt, gold pheasant etc; fr w/3 3-D maids, 19" 850.00
MOP zipper-emb yel, pk int, bl rim; cherries ea side fr, 10" 250.00
Opal w/peach int, bl trim, ribbed/ruffled, att S&W, 5x12" 160.00
Peach o/l satin, mc floral, scalloped, 2¼x10" 235.00
Peach shaded, pleated clear rim, flowers on bail; SP fr, 10" 350.00
Peachblow, ruffled w/crystal edging, 12"; ftd metal ft, 15" 160.00
Peachblow w/ruffled rim, mc & gold floral; SP fr, 9½" 100.00

Pink Herringbone mother-of-pearl with melon ribs, hand-painted florals, and gold, chartreuse interior, 3 silverplated cherubs at base which sits on tricorner plateau mirror, 15x10", $2,800.00.

Pk o/l satin, mc flowers w/gold; orig SP fr, 7¼x10½" 500.00
Pk o/l w/mc florals, 3¼x11¼" 250.00
Pk o/l w/mica veins, 10½"; emb birds on ftd fr, 8" 395.00
Pk to frost Dmn Quilt, ruffle w/yel trim, 3 sides dented, 10" 250.00
Purple shaded satin w/floral, 3½x10¾" 265.00
Red o/l w/clear ruffled rim; Rogers SP fr, 11x9½" 350.00
Red to yel w/gold daisies & forget-me-nots; SP fr 650.00
Robin's egg bl satin w/floral & gold coraleine, 4¾x8x6" 350.00
Rubena w/floral & gold, ruffled; orig SP fr 465.00
Wht, pk int, amber ruffle; tall stand w/8" lady, EX 750.00
Wht cased w/peach floral, gr scalloped rim, 12" 275.00
Wht satin w/floral, rose-shaded glossy int, Mt WA, 5x11" 350.00

Bristol Glass

Bristol is a type of semi-opaque opaline glass whose name was derived from the area in England where it was first produced. Similar glass was made in France, Germany, and Italy. In this country, it was made by the New England Glass Company and to a lesser extent by its contemporaries. During the 18th and 19th centuries, Bristol glass was imported in large amounts and sold cheaply, thereby contributing to the demise of the earlier glasshouses here in America. It is very difficult to distinguish the English Bristol from other opaline types. Style, design, and decoration serve as clues to its origin; but often only those well versed in the field can spot these subtle variations.

Biscuit jar, turq w/floral, resilvered top/rim/hdl, 6¾" 195.00
Biscuit jar, turq w/herons/trees, SP trim, 7x5" 195.00
Bottle, scent; bl w/floral, w/stopper, 5⅜x2¼" 110.00
Bottle, scent; wht w/floral, tulip stopper, 11½" 110.00
Cheese dish, wht w/floral, scalloped base, 7¾x9½" 195.00
Dresser set, floral, 2 ftd 10" bottles & powder jar 80.00
Lamp, amethyst w/floral, Krono Model 1914, 2-pc, 23¾" 150.00

Mug, cobalt bl w/grapes & gold, ftd, appl hdl, 4x3¼" 25.00
Sweetmeat, pk o/l w/bird scene, SP top, 4½x5½" 195.00
Vase, pk w/birds & floral, spear-cut can top, ftd, 15" 110.00
Vase, turq w/floral & gold, melon ribs, ped ft, 9⅜" 75.00
Wine, clear, mc floral & gold, 4½" 25.00

British Royalty Commemoratives

Royalty commemoratives have been issued for royal events since Edward VI's 1547 coronation through modern-day events, so it's possible to start collecting at any period of history. Many collectors begin with Queen Victoria's reign, collecting examples for each succeeding monarch and continuing through modern events.

Some collectors identify with a particular royal personage and limit their collecting to that era, ie., Queen Elizabeth's life and reign. Other collectors look to the future, expanding their collection to include the heir apparents Prince Charles, Princess Diana, and their first-born son, Prince William.

Royalty commemorative collecting is often further refined around a particular type of collectible. Nearly any item with room for a portrait and a description has been manufactured as a souvenir. Thus royalty commemoratives are available in glass, ceramic, metal, fabric, plastic, and paper. This wide variety of material lends itself to any pocketbook. The range covers expensive limited edition ceramics to inexpensive souvenir key chains, puzzles, matchbooks, etc.

Many recent royalty headline events have been commemorated in a variety of souvenirs. Buying some of these modern commemoratives at the moderate issue prices could be a good investment. After all, today's events are tomorrow's history.

For further study we recommend *British Royal Commemoratives* by our advisor for this category, Audrey Zeder; she is listed in the Directory under California.

Key:
anniv — anniversary
chr — christening
com — commemorative
cor — coronation
ILN — Illustrated London News

inscr — inscribed
jub — jubilee
LE — limited edition
mem — memorial
wed — wedding

Album, press pass cards, complete set 85.00
Bank, Elizabeth II 1953 cor, CI crown shape w/gold pnt 45.00
Bank, William 1983 birth, Bunnykins design, Royal Doulton 60.00
Beaker, Charles/Diana betrothal, mc portrait, Caverswall 125.00
Beaker, Edward VII 1902 cor, portrait, Bournemouth giveaway ...95.00
Beaker, George V cor, gr portrait, ships of war, Whitley 150.00
Beaker, George VI cor, mc portraits, Official Design 55.00
Bell, Anne 1973 wed, mc portrait, china, Aynsley, 5¼" 65.00
Bottle, Alexandra 1901 baby feeder, gr glass 60.00
Bottle, whiskey; 1981 wed, mini 45.00
Bowl, Princess Charlotte 1828 mem, pk lustre, 2½x5" 250.00
Bowl, Victoria, 1851, pk lustre w/mc accent 275.00
Button, Edward VII 1902 cor, gold-tone bezel w/mc portrait, ½" ..35.00
Coin, Edward I, silver penny, ca 1272 ....85.00
Coin, George VI, sterling silver crown, 1821 ....100.00
Coin, 7 bronze farthings, 1860-1950, in hard plastic case 60.00
Compact, Edward VII 1937 cor, mc portrait on gold-tone, 2" 75.00
Compact, George V 1911 cor, blk/wht portrait on chrome, 1¾" ..50.00
Covered dish (cheese), George VI cor, mc transfer, 7x5x3" 150.00
Covered dish (Rington tea jar), George VI cor, mc transfer 195.00
Cup & saucer, George VI 1939 Canada visit, child sz 35.00
Doll, Diana w/20-pc wardrobe, Danbury Mint 600.00
Egg cups, George VI 1911 cor, mc king/queen, pr 135.00

Ephemera, Elizabeth II 1953 cor stand ticket & instructions **30.00**
Ephemera, George VI, bridge tallies, 1930s, unused, pr **45.00**
Ephemera, George VI 1949 garden party invitation & instructions ...**45.00**
Ephemera, Victoria cigar band, mc w/gold, 1900 ....**15.00**
First Day cover, Charles/Diana 1981 wed, St Paul's, 3 stamps **20.00**
Glass, Edward VIII, frosted profile, crystal, 1930s, 5" **75.00**
Glass, Prince William 10th birthday, beaker, etched, w/hdl **45.00**
Glass, Victoria 1887, plate, pressed amber, domed lid **195.00**
Horsebrass, Elizabeth II 1953 cor, portrait, cutouts, 3¼" **30.00**
Horsebrass, George VI 1937 cor, relief portrait, cutouts, 3½" **35.00**
Horsebrass, Victoria, cross design w/relief head, 3x4" **60.00**
Jewelry, Edward VII 1902 cor pendant, mc portrait, 2-sided **45.00**
Jewelry, Elizabeth II bracelet, cut-out royal portrait **60.00**
Jewelry, Elizabeth II cuff links, mc pastel portrait **35.00**
Jewelry, Elizabeth II 1953 cor pin, mc portrait, M on card **25.00**
Jewelry, George V 1910 cor brooch, mc portrait **55.00**
Loving cup, Charles/Diana wed, Royal Doulton, LE, 5x3", +box .**125.00**
Magazine, Graphic, Prince of Wales Visits..., Jan 1907 ....**20.00**
Magazine, ILN, George V 1935 jub, May 1935 ....**35.00**
Magazine, ILN, Victoria Visits Chatsworth, Dec 1843 ....**25.00**
Magazine, Tatler, Princess Elizabeth 1947 wed **30.00**
Magnet, Charles 1995 Cairo visit, mc portrait, 2½" **5.00**
Magnet, Diana in pretty hats, mc portrait, 2½", set of 3 ....**15.00**
Matches, Edward VII cor, Bakelite vespa, book form w/portrait ...**95.00**
Matches, Elizabeth II 1953, matchbook cover, mc portrait, M **10.00**
Matches, Geo V 1935 jub, matchbook cover, blk/wht portrait, M .**20.00**
Matches, Geo VI 1937 cor, matchbook cover, mc portrait, M **15.00**
Medal, Edward VIII Empire day, brass, emb profile, 1¼" **45.00**
Medal, George V 'King's Medal,' for School Attendance, brass **35.00**
Medal, George V 1914-18 WWI Service, sterling silver **60.00**
Medal, George V 1935 jub, emb design, 8-sided, 1½" **45.00**
Medal, Victoria 1887 jub, 4 triangles w/photo center **65.00**
Medal, Victoria 1901 mem, w/late queen & Edward VII **50.00**
Miniature, Elizabeth II basket, mc portrait, ftd, China, 2½" **25.00**
Miniature, George V cor jug, mc portrait, 2" **60.00**
Mug, Charles 1981 wed, ear hdl, Carlton Ware **75.00**
Mug, Edward VII 1902 cor, brn design, Royal Doulton **175.00**
Mug, Edward VII 1910 mem, blk portrait & border, SFCo, 3½" ..**175.00**
Mug, Edward VIII, blk/wht portrait, mc buildings, Aynsley **50.00**
Mug, Elizabeth II 1953, sepia portrait, E hdl, Royal Doulton **85.00**
Mug, Elizabeth 1992 Annus Horribulus, mc portrait, w/events **35.00**
Mug, George V cor, mc portrait in uniform, child sz, 2½" **65.00**
Mug, Victoria 1897 jub, bl/gray overall transfer, JC&N **195.00**
Newspaper, Enfield Gazette, George VI 1937 cor **25.00**
Newspaper, Hamilton Spectator, Princess Elizabeth '51 Canada Visit .**20.00**
Newspaper, NY Post, George V decorated Lindbergh, May 1927 .**45.00**
Newspaper, Queen Mary mem pg sponsored by Eaton store **15.00**
Paperweight, Willam 1982 birth, mc parents/baby, acrylic, 2" **30.00**
Pin-bk, Edward VII 1902 cor, bl w/mc portrait, 1¼" **40.00**
Pin-bk, Edward VII 1937, blk/wht military portrait, 1½" **35.00**
Pitcher, Caroline 1820, relief portrait, mc enamel, 6" **325.00**
Pitcher, Edward Prince of Wales 1888 wed anniv, MIG **175.00**
Pitcher, Victoria 1897, blk w/gold portrait & mc enamel, 6" **225.00**
Pitcher, Victoria 1897 jub, royal bl stoneware, Doulton, 9" **875.00**
Plate, Charles/Di 1981 wed, portrait, Crown Staffordshire, 7½" ..**175.00**
Plate, Diana, mc portrait receiving flowers, Danbury, 8" **85.00**
Plate, Edward VIII 1937 cor, lt gr w/mc, Aynsley, 5" **55.00**
Plate, Edward VIII 1937 cor, sq, Meakin, 5x5" **30.00**
Plate, Elizabeth II 1953 cor, mc portrait, Royal Crown Derby, MIB ..**80.00**
Plate, George VI cor, sepia family portrait, 6¼" **50.00**
Plate, George VI cor, sepia portrait w/mc, scalloped, 5x4" **30.00**
Plate, Princess Margaret 1930 birth, Paragon, 7" **120.00**
Plate, Victoria 1897, blk transfer, gold rim, 7" **175.00**

Plate, Victoria 1897, blk transfer, mc details, 9" **195.00**
Pocketknife, Edward Prince of Wales 1863 wed, horn hdl, 3" **80.00**
Pocketknife, Elizabeth II cor, 1-blade, MOP hdl **35.00**
Pocketknife, George V 1911 cor, 2-blade, 3", leather case **65.00**
Pocketknife, George VI 1937 cor, 2-blade, bone hdl, Sheffield **75.00**
Postcard, Edward VII 1910 mem, 18 worldwide mourners, blk/wht ...**20.00**
Postcard, George VI 1937 cor, w/queen & children, Beagles **15.00**
Postcard, George VI 1939 Canada visit banquet, blk/wht, EX **20.00**
Poster stamp, George VI 1937 cor, cor regalia, 12-pc **35.00**
Poster stamp, Victoria 1897 jub, 4-pc heir apparents **60.00**
Print, George VI 1937 cor, mc portrait in cor robes, 10x14" **25.00**
Print, George VI 1939 visit, mc portrait, Eaton Dept Store **40.00**
Print, Princess Elizabeth 1937, mc pastel, 10x14" **25.00**
Print, Queen Elizabeth 1937, holding baby Elizabeth, 10x14" **20.00**
Print, Victoria 1887 jub, brn, 10x7", set of 3 different **55.00**
Print, Victoria 1902, as drawn by daughter in 1882, 8x11" **15.00**
Program, George V 1935 jub, Collegiate Church of St Mary **15.00**
Program, George V 1935 jub, Official Procession **45.00**
Spoon, Charles/Diana 1983 Canada visit, mc portrait, SP **30.00**
Spoon, Prince William 1982 birth & chr, SP, pr **45.00**
Stamps, Diana 21st birthday, 12 different on souvenir pg **15.00**
Teapot, Elizabeth II 1953 cor, chrome crown shape, 2-cup **75.00**
Teapot, George V 1911 cor, mc Naval portrait, 1-cup **145.00**
Teapot, Queen Mother/Margaret/Ann 1990 royal birthdays **75.00**
Teapot, Royal Year 1993, bl events & design, 2-cup **65.00**
Teapot stand, Elizabeth II jub, emb portrait on chrome **25.00**
Textile, Diana yardage to make stuffed doll **50.00**
Textile, Edward VIII, vivid mc portrait & design, 8x11" **45.00**
Textile, Elizabeth II 1950s Canada visit handkerchief, rayon **30.00**
Textile, Elizabeth II 1953 cor ribbon, 1¾x36" **5.00**
Textile, Elizabeth II 1977 jub towel, newspaper design, linen **25.00**
Textile, George V cor handkerchief, mc portrait, 12x12" **60.00**
Textile, George VI cor handkerchief, bl portrait, 18x18" **65.00**
Textile, George VI 1939 visit, mc portrait on red, 15" L **40.00**
Thimble, Prince Wm 1982 birth/chr, bl design, Royal Worcester ..**40.00**
Tiles, Edward VII cor, king & queen portraits on gr, pr **350.00**
Tin, Charles/Diana wed, portrait on royal bl, upright, 5½x4" **35.00**
Tin, Edward VII 1936 accession to throne, mc portrait, 4x3" **65.00**
Tin, Elizabeth II 1953 cor, 1 yel/1 blk w/portrait, Cadbury, pr **50.00**
Tin, George V 1911 cor, mc portrait on dk gr, 2½" dia **80.00**
Tin, George VI 1937 cor, mc portrait on gold, Mackintosh **45.00**
Tin, George VI 1939 Canada visit, family, Huntley-Palmer **95.00**
Tin, George VI 1939 Canada visit, mc portrait, flat, 8-sided **50.00**
Tin, Prince Albert 1860s tin, portrait on brass, 1½x¼" **80.00**
Tin, Prince of Wales 1930s, w/2 brothers, mc portraits **85.00**
Toby mug, George V & Queen Mary, pr **495.00**
Tray, Charles/Diana 1981 wed, uniform/formal clothes, 12" dia ...**35.00**
Tray, Elizabeth II 1977 jub, emb decor, silver-tone, 12x15" **25.00**
Tray, George V cor, mc portrait on red, 5" **55.00**

Broadmoor

In the October of 1933, the Broadmoor Art Pottery was formed and space rented at 217 East Pikes Peak Avenue, Colorado Springs, Colorado. Most of the pottery produced would not be considered elaborate and only a handful was decorated. Many pieces were signed by P.H. Genter, J.B. Hunt, Eric Hellman, and Cecil Jones. It is reported that this plant closed in 1936, and Genter moved his operations to Denver.

Broadmoor pottery is marked in several ways: a Greek or Egyptian-type label depicting two potters (one at the wheel and one at a tile-pressing machine) and the word Broadmoor; an ink-stamped 'Broadmoor Pottery, Colorado Springs (or Denver), Colorado'; and an incised version of the latter.

The bottoms of all pieces are always white and can be either glazed or unglazed. Glaze colors are turquoise, green, yellow, cobalt blue, light blue, white, pink, pink with blue, maroon red, black, and a copper lustre. Both matt and high gloss finishes were used.

The company produced many advertising tiles, novelty items, coasters, ashtrays, and vases for local establishments around Denver and as far away as Wyoming. An Indian head was incised into many of the advertising items, which also often bear a company or a product name. A series of small animals (horses, dogs, elephants, lamb, squirrels, a toucan bird, and a hippo), each about 2" high, are easily recognized by the style of their modeling and glaze treatments, though all are unmarked. Our advisors for this category are Carol and Jim Carlton, authors of *Collector's Encyclopedia of Colorado Pottery*; they are listed in the Directory under Colorado.

Ashtray, Bamboo Room, yel, Denver mk 30.00
Ashtray, leaf form, 3", 4-pc set 25.00
Cigarette holder, squirrel finial 45.00
Creamer & sugar bowl, bl, Denver mk 35.00
Figurine, squirrel, brn, stamped mk, 2" 40.00
Pitcher, cobalt, slim form, 12" 110.00
Relish tray, 3-petal flower form, 10" 45.00
Vase, blk, incurvate rim, 3" 30.00
Vase, bud; mauve, 6" 25.00

Vase, embossed figure on turquoise in the Arts & Crafts style, marked, dated 1936, 12x7", $500.00.

Vase, cobalt w/shiny pyrite flecks, 12" 125.00
Vase, copper-glazed pillow form, Denver mk, 6x9" 55.00
Vase, pk crackle, bulbous, sm hdls, 8" 95.00
Vase, wht bsk, longhorn steer relief on hdls, 12" 150.00

Broadsides

Webster defines a broadside as simply a large sheet of paper printed on one side. During the 1880s, they were the most practical means of mass-communication. By the middle of the century, they had become elaborate and lengthy with information, illustrations, portraits, and fancy border designs. Those printed on coated stock are usually worth more.

American verse, religious warnings, Boston, 1739, 8x11½" ...2,000.00
Comic romantic poem, crude woodcut artwork, 1790s, 7x11" 750.00
Fair to benefit orphan's home, moving poem, 1840s, 8x12" 18.50
Kansas Emigration Society, pro-slavery, 1856, 9x11", EX 1,375.00
Liberty Songs, 3-column, w/border, ca 1850s, 10x12" 395.00
Morman news of resettling in Rocky Mtns, 1846, 12x9" 4,250.00
Notice of criminal's execution, Boston, 1773, 19x15", EX 4,000.00
Revolutionary War call for reinforcements, MA, 1778, 8x14" ..1,200.00
Reward for runaway slave, MD, 1853, 9½x12" 750.00
Select Hymns for Religious Circles, 1810s, 18x11", EX 130.00

Temperance verse, Thomas Ward, MA, ca 1850, 11x8", VG 95.00
War of 1812, Constitution & Guerriere, 10¼x8⅝" 225.00

Bronzes

Thomas Ball, George Bessell, and Leonard Volk were some of the earliest American sculptors who produced figures in bronze for home decor during the 1840s. Pieces of historical significance were the most popular, but by the 1880s a more fanciful type of artwork took hold. Some of the fine sculptors of the day were Daniel Chester French, Augustus St. Gaudens, and John Quincy Adams Ward. Bronzes reached the height of their popularity at the turn of the century. The American West was portrayed to its fullest by Remington, Russell, James Frazier, Hermon MacNeil, and Solon Borglum. Animals of every species were modeled by A.P. Proctor, Paul Bartlett, and Albert Laellele, to name but a few.

Art Nouveau and Art Deco influenced the medium during the twenties, evidenced by the works of Allen Clark, Harriet Frismuth, E.F. Sanford, and Bessie P. Vonnoh.

Be aware that recasts abound. While often esthetically satisfactory, they are not original and should be priced accordingly. In much the same manner as prints are evaluated, the original castings made under the direction of the artist are the most valuable. Later castings from the original mold are worth less. A recast is not made from the original mold. Instead, a rubber-like substance is applied to the bronze, peeled away and filled with wax. Then, using the same 'lost wax' procedure as the artist uses on completion of his original wax model, a clay-like substance is formed around the wax figure and the whole fired to vitrify the clay. The wax, of course, melts away, hence the term 'lost wax.' Recast bronzes lose detail and are somewhat smaller than the original due to the shrinkage of the clay mold.

Allen, MN; girl in short flared dress looks into mirror, 37" 5,635.00
Alonzo, Dutch girl holds bucket, rock base, ivory mts, 9" 1,150.00
Austrian, Arab pets cat, robe lifts, erotic, Bergman, 5" 635.00
Austrian, Arab rug merchant displays wares, Bergman, 5" 345.00
Austrian, Arab snake charmer, Bergman, 2¾" 400.00
Austrian, Arab tailor seated on rug, Bergman, 2½" 460.00
Austrian, Arab warrior, kneeling/praying on rug, Bergman, 4" ...345.00
Austrian, concubine sleeps, lift-off blanket, Bergman, 2x7" 865.00
Austrian, pheasant, cold pnt, Bergman, 8", pr 690.00
Barillot, angel skating on 1 leg, mortarboard hat, 10" 800.00
Bayre, lion attacking horse, 8" 700.00
Bouchard, bust: Diane w/Laurel Chaplet, octagonal plinth, 20" ..5,750.00
Busch, WPA-style garmet worker, ca 1930s, 20x6" 850.00
Chiparus, Afghan on marble base behind seated girl, 13½x30" 3,700.00
Chiparus, dancer atop arched onyx base, ivory mts, rstr, 23" 5,700.00
Chiparus, girl in hooded cloak, bk to wind, ivory mts, 7½" 1,725.00
Chiparus, Lazzarone, boy w/concertina, ivory mts, 9½" 2,875.00
Chiparus, seated draped nude holds shell, silvered, 13" 1,265.00
Chiparus, 3 girls w/umbrella, rock base, ivory mts/gilt, 9" 7,400.00
Chiparus, 4 children at blindman's bluff, ivory mts/gilt, 8" 9,775.00
Colin, Egyptian lady dances w/snake about legs, 23" 1,380.00
Colinet, juggler, ball balanced on extended hand/ft, 23" 1,380.00
Colinet, juggler, nude w/head bowed, legs Xd, 23" 1,495.00
Daumier, Viennet, bust of a gentleman, #d, 7½" 6,600.00
Dearly, jockey, bent forward, looking right, ivory mts, 12½" 635.00
Delagrange, scarf dancer, wearing long drape, 17¾" 4,300.00
Delue, Eve, kneeling, head in hand, right arm up, 11x11x6" ...4,000.00
Delue, Leda & Swan, Modern Art Foundry, 8x11" 4,000.00
Eberle, seated scribe, scroll outstretched, c 1913, 7x7" 1,725.00
Fatori, dancer w/ivory face/midriff/arms/legs, 13" 5,400.00
Fayral, feather dancer kneels, extends leg bk, 1930, 20x21" 920.00

Fenton, The Acrobat, sgn/1926, 5½" **3,450.00**
Ferarri, blindfolded girl, arms out, stepped base, 8" **690.00**
Fratin, charging wild boar, 10x18" **2,750.00**
Gamacelli, Kneeling Female, nude gazing upward, 19" **600.00**
Gory, dancer, on tiptoe, left leg bent, arms bk, 24¾" **2,875.00**
Gory, kneeling female nude, arms arched over bent head, 24" .**1,495.00**
Guery, seated nude balances sm faun on knees, 1925, 7" **1,000.00**
Haupt, Matti; voluptous nude on sq base, 20" **350.00**
Jonchery, scarf dancer, arms stretched above head, 22" **800.00**
Kelety, seminude in low-rise exotic dance pants, unsgn, 19" .**13,800.00**
Larche, lamp: Satyr et Escargot, w/lg hollyhock, 14" **2,300.00**
Le Faguays, Spring Dance, dancer w/roses, 21" **975.00**
Lemo, maid sits on onyx plinth, looks down at Afghan, 18x24" .**2,875.00**
Lorenzl, seated girl in party dress, 12" **1,150.00**
Lorenzl, snake charmer, snake coiled about legs, 25" **4,000.00**
Lorenzl, 2 nude children (girl sits w/book), dog aside, 4¾" **690.00**
Lovet-Lorski, poodle, silvered patina, gr marble plinth, 3¾" ...**1,000.00**
MacLeary, Ouch, Gorham Co, 6⅜" **1,150.00**
Macmonnies, Bacchante & Infant Faun, Rouard, 17½" **1,950.00**
Manship, seated nude, 12½" **5,750.00**
Moreau, urn, putto on shoulder, stepped red marble base, 8½" ...**400.00**
Muller, cymbalist, cold pnt, ivory head/arms/legs, 18" **6,300.00**
Omerth, little girl in knitted cap/short coat, ivory mts, 6" **800.00**
Paris, Roland; bookends, seated man (1 w/bird), ivory mts, 7" ...**1,600.00**
Perl, satyr & nymph embracing, 14" **1,265.00**
Philippe, dancer on 1 ft, arms wide, twisted right, 23½" **1,725.00**
Philippe, Mischievous, female nude, 25" **1,950.00**
Plazzotta, Dynamic Torso #45, 1970, 24½" **950.00**
Poertzel, girl riding lg ostrich, silvered, 20½" **1,495.00**
Preiss, Balancing, girl leans bk/lifts ball, ivory mts, 15" **9,775.00**
Preiss, ballerina, arms extended, ivory head/arms, 7" **1,150.00**
Preiss, Red Dancer, on tiptoe, 1 arm up/1 down, 15" **690.00**
Renaud, night light, girl w/butterfly wings, mc, 10" **2,760.00**
Rosin, Bust of Young Woman, 1938, 16½" **400.00**
Sandoz, Poisson, curled gasping fish, gilt accents, 10½" **2,000.00**
Simard, nude, 1 arm across body, 1 behind head, on 1 ft, 26" ...**900.00**
Tereszczuk, boy/girl kiss, girl peeks from bk of screen, 7" **2,185.00**
Tremo, boy (& girl), animal fur on shouders, w/rifle, 8", pr **1,900.00**
Unmk, nude child sits on pillow by oval mirror, gilt, 5½" **800.00**
Villanis, maiden: Sapho, holding lyre, 28" **3,100.00**
Zach, ballet dancer, onyx base, 17¾" **975.00**
Zach, Broken Heart, female figure, 24" **6,300.00**
Zach, erotic seated female, removable dress, 2½" **1,265.00**
Zach, female fencer, 15¾" **1,265.00**
Zach, girl w/winged hat, 14" **1,380.00**
Zach, male dancer, 19" **1,095.00**
Zinsky, dancer, squatting w/1 leg extended, arms wide, 13" **800.00**

Brouwer

Theophilis A. Brouwer, an accomplished artist even before his interests turned to the medium of pottery, started a small one-man operation in 1894 in East Hampton, New York. Two years later he relocated in Westhampton, where he perfected the technique of fire-painting, learning to control the effects of the kiln to produce the best possible results. In 1925 he founded the Ceramic Flame Company in New York, but it is for his earlier work that he is best known. Brouwer died in 1932.

Vase, burgundy/gr/gold irid, sm collar rim, mk Flame, 5½x5" .**1,600.00**
Vase, gun-metal/brn/yel metallic, 3½x4" **450.00**
Vase, orange/gold/yel/vermillion, mk Flame, 3¾x6½" **2,300.00**
Vase, streaky mc irid, bulbous w/long flaring neck, 7½" **1,500.00**

Brownies by Palmer Cox

Created by Palmer Cox in 1883, the Brownies charmed children through the pages of books and magazines, as dolls, on their dinnerware, in advertising material, and on souvenirs. Each had his own personality, among them The Bellhop, The London Bobby, The Chairman, and Uncle Sam. But the oversized, triangular face with the startled expression, the protruding tummy, and the spindlelegs were characteristics of them all. They were inspired by the Scottish legends related to Cox as a child by his parents, who were of English descent. His introduction of the Brownies to the world was accomplished by a poem called *The Brownies Ride*. Books followed in rapid succession, thirteen in the series, all written as well as illustrated by Palmer Cox.

By the late 1890s, the Brownies were active in advertising. They promoted such products as games, coffee, toys, patent medicines, and rubber boots. 'Greenies' were the Brownies' first cousins, created by Cox to charm and to woo through the pages of the advertising almanacs of the G.G. Green Company of New Jersey. Perhaps the best-known endorsement in the Brownies' career was for the Kodak Brownie, which became so popular and sold in such volume that their name became synonymous with this type of camera. Our advisor for this category is Anne Kier; she is listed in the directory under Ohio.

Book, Another Brownie Book, Appleton Century, 1941, w/jacket **35.00**
Book, Brownie Clown of Brownietown, Century, 1908, EX **200.00**
Book, Brownies at Home, 1891, EX **60.00**
Book, Brownies at Home, 1942, w/dust jacket, VG **35.00**
Book, Little Goody Two Shoes, 1903, EX **40.00**
Brownie Portrait Cubes, McLoughlin Bros, c Palmer Cox 1892, VG ...**300.00**
Calendar, Ramon's Pills advertising, EX **75.00**
Candlestick, Bobby, majolica, 7½" **275.00**

Candlestick, Uncle Sam, majolica, 7½", $325.00 at auction.

Candy dish, 15 Brownies, Tufts SP, ball ft, 7x5½" **195.00**
Chocolate mold, 2-pc **120.00**
Cigar holder/ashtray, Brownie figural, Pairpoint SP **335.00**
Crate label, 1930s, 10x12", NM **15.00**
Cup & saucer, 4 action Brownies, 2¾x3½", 5" dia **115.00**
Doll, Brownie, Palmer Cox, orig clothes & top hat, 37", EX **300.00**
Figurine, Chinaman, papier-mache head, 9", EX **450.00**
Game, Brownie Horseshoes, early, complete in box **50.00**
Game, 9-Pins, 1883, G **1,495.00**
Game pc, Policeman, from 9-Pins, litho paper, 12½", EX **140.00**
Hand mirror, pewter fr w/emb Brownies **195.00**
Humidor, Bobby, 6" **175.00**
Knife, silver, deeply molded hdl **85.00**
Napkin ring, SP, Brownie climbs up side **175.00**
Paper doll, Lion Coffee, Indian Brownie, EX **40.00**

Paperweight, Brownie figural, SP 110.00
Plate, porc, mk La Francaise, 7" 85.00
Plate, 10 action Brownies on rim, china, 10" 75.00
Puzzle, Brownies skating, 20-pc, early, fr, 10½x12½" ...65.00
Rubber stamps, set of 12 ....100.00
Sheet music, Dance of the Brownies 25.00
Sheet music, The Brownie Rag, Brownie cover, 1907 ......35.00
Sign, Howell's Root Beer, emb Brownies on tin, EX 175.00
Spoon, SP 60.00
Spoon, sterling w/enameled Brownie man finial, demitasse ...60.00
Tea tile, 6 dancing Brownies, 6¼" 95.00

Brush

George Brush began his career in the pottery industry in 1901 working for the J.B. Owens Pottery Co. in Zanesville, Ohio. He left the company in 1907 to go into business for himself, only to have fire completely destroy his pottery less than one year after it was founded. Brush became associated with J.W. McCoy in 1909 and for many years served in capacities ranging from general manager to president. (From 1911 until 1925, the firm was known as The Brush-McCoy Pottery Co.; see that section for information.) After McCoy died, the family withdrew their interests, and in 1925 the name of the firm was changed to The Brush Pottery. The era of hand-decorated art pottery had passed for the most part and would soon be completely replaced by the production of commercial lines. Of all the wares bearing the later Brush script mark, their figural cookie jars are the most collectible, and several have been reproduced.

For additional information we recommend *The Collector's Encyclopedia of Brush McCoy Pottery* (recently revised) by Sharon and Bob Huxford. Information on Brush cookie jars (as well as confusing reproductions) can be found in *The Collector's Encyclopedia of Cookie Jars* by Joyce and Fred Roerig; they are listed in the Directory under South Carolina. See also Brush-McCoy for information on a second reference book.

Cookie Jars

Old Clock, #W20, $165.00; Little Girl, #017, $550.00.

Antique Touring Car, minimum value 700.00
Boy w/Balloons, minimum value 850.00
Chick in Nest 300.00
Cinderella Pumpkin, #W32 ....200.00
Circus Horse, gr 950.00
Clown, yel pants 250.00
Clown Bust, #W49, minimum value 250.00
Cookie House, #W31 ....85.00
Covered Wagon, dog finial, #W30 ....550.00
Cow w/Cat on Bk, brn 110.00
Cow w/Cat on Bk, purple, minimum value 1,000.00
Davy Crockett, gold trim, minimum value 800.00
Davy Crockett, no gold, mk USA 300.00
Dog & Basket 250.00
Donkey w/Cart, ears down, #W33, gray 400.00

Donkey w/Cart, ears up, #W33, minimum value 800.00
Elephant w/Baby Bonnet & Ice Cream Cone, wht 500.00
Elephant w/Monkey on Bk, minimum value 5,000.00
Fish, #W52 ....500.00
Formal Pig, gr hat & coat (+) 300.00
Gas Lamp, K1 ....75.00
Granny, pk apron, bl dots on skirt 325.00
Granny, plain skirt, minimum value 400.00
Happy Bunny, wht, #W25 ....225.00
Hen on Basket, unmk 125.00
Hillbilly Frog, minimum value (+) 4,500.00
Humpty Dumpty, w/beany & bow tie 275.00
Humpty Dumpty, w/peaked brn hat & shoes 250.00
Laughing Hippo, #W27 ....650.00
Little Angel 800.00
Little Boy Blue, gold trim, K25 USA, sm 700.00
Little Boy Blue, K24 Brush USA, lg 800.00
Little Red Riding Hood, gold trim, mk, lg, minimum value ...750.00
Little Red Riding Hood, no gold, K24 USA, sm 550.00
Nite Owl 115.00
Old Shoe, #W23 ....95.00
Panda, #W21 ....250.00
Peter, Peter Pumpkin Eater, #W24 ....300.00
Peter Pan, gold trim, lg 800.00
Peter Pan, sm 600.00
Puppy Police 585.00
Raggedy Ann, #W16 ....350.00
Sitting Hippo, #W45 ....400.00
Sitting Pig 400.00
Smiling Bear, #W46 ....350.00
Squirrel on Log, #W26 ....100.00
Squirrel w/Top Hat, blk coat & hat 275.00
Squirrel w/Top Hat, gr coat 250.00
Stylized Owl 250.00
Stylized Siamese, #W41 ....400.00
Teddy Bear, feet apart 250.00
Teddy Bear, feet together 200.00
Treasure Chest, #W28 ....150.00
3 Bears 100.00

Miscellaneous

Carafe, Bronze Line, #928, palette mk, 9" 45.00
Cornucopia planter, dbl; Bittersweet, #754, 4½x11½" 95.00
Ewer, pk, slim form, emb rings, 1950s, 7" 20.00
Figurine, animal miniature, ca 1939-40, ea, from $10 to ...20.00
Flowerpot, wht, #320 USA, 4" 17.50
Hanging basket, bl 3-ftd flower form, 1940, 4" 30.00
Lawn ornament, rooster, brn w/red details, 1956, lg 250.00
Pitcher, emb florals on tan, 1940s, 5½" 35.00
Planter, baby carriage form, bl, 1956 ....15.00
Planter, donkey beside stump, 1956 ....17.50
Planter, emb gazelle decor on cream, W5, USA, 1950s, 13½" L ..25.00
Planter, horse & carriage form, 1958 ....35.00
Vase, Glo Art, pk, #769, 8" 65.00
Vase, pagoda on sq shape, #225, USA, 7½" 30.00
Vase, pk florals on blk, #75, early 1940s, 7" 30.00
Vase, Stardust, wht linear decor on gray, #601, USA, 8" ...65.00
Vase, wht w/red & bl linear decor, #514 Brush USA, 18½" ...95.00

Brush-McCoy

The Brush-McCoy Pottery was formed in 1911 in Zanesville,

Ohio, an alliance between George Brush and J.W. McCoy. Brush's original pottery had been destroyed by fire in 1907; McCoy had operated his own business in Roseville, Ohio, since 1899. After the merger, the company expanded and produced not only their staple commercial wares but also fine artware. Lines such as Navarre, Venetian, Oriental, and Sylvan were of fine quality equal to that of their larger competitors. Because very little of the ware was marked, it is often mistaken for Weller, Roseville, or Peters and Reed.

In 1918 after a fire in Zanesville had destroyed the manufacturing portion of that plant, all production was contained in their Roseville (Ohio) plant #2. A stoneware type of clay was used there; and as a result, the artware lines of Jewel, Zuniart, King Tut, Florastone, Jetwood, Krakle-Kraft, and Panelart are so distinctive that they are more easily recognizable. Examples of these lines are unique and very beautiful, also quite rare and highly prized!

The Brush-McCoy Pottery operated under that name until after 1925 when it became the Brush Pottery. The Brush-Barnett family retained their interest in the pottery until 1981 when it was purchased by the Dearborn Company. For more information we recommend *The Guide to Brush-McCoy Pottery*, written by Martha and Steve Sanford and edited by David P. Sanford, our advisors for this category. They are listed in the Directory under California. See also Brush.

Bank, frog figural, gr, #068, 1916, 3½"	85.00
Bowl, Dandyline, gold, 1916, 3½x7½"	45.00
Candlestick, King Tut, #032, 10½"	1,300.00
Candlesticks, Onyx, 10½", pr	165.00
Fern dish, Onyx, w/liner, #055, 2½x5"	65.00
Jardiniere, bl birds on wht, #228, 1915, 7½"	350.00
Jardiniere, floral swags on ivory, 1915, 9"	375.00
Jardiniere, Pastel Ware, #248, 10"	225.00
Pitcher, Corn, #44, 1910, 6"	225.00
Umbrella stand, Bl Onyx, 1920s, 20½"	650.00
Umbrella stand, Liberty Bell, #73, 22½"	650.00
Vase, Navarre, wht decor on blk, integral hdls, 9"	350.00
Vase, Vogue, blk geometrics on wht, cylindrical, 10"	225.00

Buffalo Pottery

The founding of the Buffalo Pottery in Buffalo, New York, in 1901, was a direct result of the success achieved by John Larkin through his innovative methods of marketing 'Sweet Home Soap.' Choosing to omit 'middle-man' profits, Larkin preferred to deal directly with the consumer and offered premiums as an enticement for sales. The pottery soon proved a success in its own right and began producing advertising and commemorative items for other companies, as well as commercial tableware. In 1905 they introduced their Blue Willow line after extensive experimentation resulted in the development of the first successful underglaze cobalt achieved by an American company. Between 1905 and 1909, a line of pitchers and jugs were hand decorated in historical, literary, floral, and outdoor themes. Twenty-nine styles are known to have been made. These have been found in a wide array of color variations.

Their most famous line was Deldare Ware, the bulk of which was made from 1908 to 1909. It was hand decorated after illustrations by Cecil Aldin. Views of English life were portrayed in detail through unusual use of color against the natural olive green cast of the body. Today the 'Fallowfield Hunt' scenes are more difficult to locate than 'Scenes of Village Life in Ye Olden Days.' A Deldare calendar plate was made in 1910. These are very rare and are highly valued by collectors. The line was revived in 1923 and dropped again in 1925. Every piece was marked 'Made at Ye Buffalo Pottery, Deldare Ware Underglaze.' Most are dated, though date has no bearing on the value. Emerald Deldare, made with the same olive body and on standard Deldare Ware

shapes, featured historical scenes and Art Nouveau decorations. Most pieces are found with a 1911 date stamp. Production was very limited due to the intricate, time-consuming detail. Needless to say, it is very rare and extremely desirable.

Abino Ware, most of which was made in 1912, also used standard Deldare shapes, but its colors were earthy and the decorations more delicately applied. Sailboats, windmills, and country scenes were favored motifs. These designs were achieved by overpainting transfer prints and were often signed by the artist. The ware is marked 'Abino' in hand-printed block letters. Production was limited, and as a result, examples of this line are scarce today. Prices only slightly trail those of Emerald Deldare Ware.

The many uncataloged items that have been found over the years indicate that Buffalo Pottery decorators were free to use their own ideas and talents to create many beautiful one-of-a-kind pieces.

Our advisors for this category are Fred and Lila Shrader; they are listed in the Directory under California.

Abino

Ashtray/matchbox holder, windmills	875.00
Bowl, lakeside & windmills, 9"	865.00
Candlestick, sailing scene, 9½"	675.00
Creamer, sailing scene, 4½"	485.00
Cup & saucer, demitasse; sailing scene	375.00
Pitcher, windmill & pond, 10"	1,100.00
Plate, pastoral scene, 8"	350.00
Tankard, lighthouse, wht int, 7½"	800.00
Vase, cylindrical, sm boats & pond, 9"	875.00

Deldare

Vase, Kingfisher, J. Gerhardt, green and white on olive green, 1911, 7¾x6½", $2,645.00.

Bowl, Emerald, Dr Syntax Reading His Tour, 9½"	1,000.00
Bowl, nut; Ye Lion Inn, 8"	525.00
Bowl, sauce; Ye Olden Days, 5"	150.00
Bowl, The Fallowfield Hunt, Breakfast...Three Pigeons, 12"	975.00
Bowl, The Fallowfield Hunt, The Death, 9"	650.00
Candlestick, The Fallowfield Hunt, untitled, 9", pr	965.00
Candlestick, Ye Village Scenes, 9"	375.00
Chocolate pot, Ye Village Street	2,000.00
Creamer, Emerald, Dr Syntax w/the Dairymaid	375.00
Creamer & sugar bowl, Scenes of Village...Olden Days, w/lid	425.00
Cup, punch; Fallowfield, untitled	250.00
Cup & saucer, chocolate; Ye Village Street	400.00
Cup & saucer, Emerald, Dr Syntax at Liverpool/Bookseller	385.00
Hair receiver, Emerald, allover geometric & floral decor	785.00
Jardiniere & pedestal, Ye Lion Inn, 9x12", 14x14"	3,500.00
Mug, Breaking Cover, 3½"	325.00
Mug, Dr Syntax in the Cellar w/the Maid, 3½"	550.00
Mug, Emerald, allover geometric & floral decor, wht int, 4½"	525.00
Mug, Scenes of Village Life in Ye Olden Days, 2½"	335.00

Mug, The Fallowfield Hunt, untitled, 2½" 450.00
Pitcher, Emerald, Dr Syntax Stopt by Highway Men, 6" 845.00
Pitcher, Fallowfield Hunt, 8" 435.00
Pitcher, The Fallowfield Hunt, The Death, 10" 825.00
Pitcher, The Fallowfield Hunt, The Return, 8" 695.00
Pitcher, Ye Olde English Village, 10" 640.00
Plaque, The Fallowfield Hunt, Breakfast at Three Pigeons, 12" ..675.00
Plaque, Ye Lion Inn, 12" 500.00
Plate, At Ye Lion Inn, 6¼" 95.00
Plate, chop; An Evening at Ye Lion Inn, 14" 625.00
Plate, Deldare salesman's sample, 6½" 1,025.00
Plate, Emerald, calendar for 1910, 9½" 1,600.00
Plate, Emerald, Misfortune at Tulip Hall (Dr Syntax), 8" 560.00
Plate, The Fallowfield Hunt, Breaking Cover, 10" 295.00
Plate, The Fallowfield Hunt, The Start, 8¼" 200.00
Plate, Ye Olden Times, 9½" 195.00
Relish dish, Ye Olden Times, 6x9" 450.00
Sugar bowl, Emerald, 6-sided, 3¼" 475.00
Tankard, Emerald, To Becky's Hand... (Dr Syntax), 10" 1,400.00
Tankard, The Great Controversy, 12½" 925.00
Tea tile, Breaking Cover, 6¼" dia 375.00
Tea tile, Traveling in Ye Olden Days, 6" 325.00
Teapot, Emerald, Art Nouveau flowers & vines, 5¾" 1,420.00
Teapot, The Fallowfield Hunt, Breaking Cover, 3¾" 475.00
Toothpick holder, The Fallowfield Hunt, untitled, 2¼" 325.00
Tray, calling card; The Fallowfield Hunt, untitled, 7¾" 410.00
Tray, dresser; Dancing Ye Minuet, 9x12" 645.00
Tray, pin; Emerald, Beatrice, 6½x3¼" 500.00
Tray, tea; The Fallowfield Hunt, The Hunt Supper, 12x10½" ...925.00
Vase, The Fallowfield Hunt, hourglass shape, 9" 870.00

Miscellaneous

Ashtray/matchbox holder, LAAC 35.00
Bowl, berry; pk & gr roses w/gold trim, 10½" 72.00
Bowl, berry; pk & gr roses w/gold trim, 5½" 12.00
Bowl, rimmed soup; Blue Willow, 9" 77.00
Bowl, sq sauceboat; Blue Willow, 11½" 165.00
Bowl, vegetable; Blue Lune, Lucca's, Los Angeles, 8" 35.00
Butter pat, Blue Willow 25.00
Butter pat, Brown Derby, Hollywood 65.00
Butter pat, copper teakettle, Dayton 25.00
Butter pat, geraniums, mc, reverse: 1907 ....45.00
Butter pat, Hollywood Tavern 35.00
Butter pat, Hotel del Coronado 30.00
Butter pat, LAAC 35.00
Butter pat, The Tacoma 28.00
Canister, wht w/gold trim, Pepper in blk, w/lid, 3" 42.00
Canister, wht w/gold trim, Tea in blk, no lid, 7½" 25.00
Child's feeding dish, Campbell Kids w/ABC rim, VG color 85.00
Children's dishes, Violets, 14 pcs including teapot w/lid 185.00
Chocolate pot, sprays of roses w/gold trim, 11" 160.00
Cowboy hat, Blue Lune, 4½x2¾" 35.00
Creamer, Blue Willow, ind, 2½" 25.00
Creamer, Blue Willow, 5½" 65.00
Creamer, Bonrea, 5½" 38.00
Creamer, Vienna, rich bl & gold, 4½" 45.00
Cup & saucer, bouillon; Blue Willow 55.00
Cup & saucer, Gaudy Willow 135.00
Egg cup, Blue Willow, 2¾" 32.00
Mug, Celebration, Vacation, Meditation, etc, 4½", ea 65.00
Mug, Friar sipping brew, 4½" 65.00
Pitcher, Blue Willow, bulbous, 7" 195.00
Pitcher, Blue Willow, Chicago style, cobalt w/gold, 8" 255.00

Pitcher, Buffalo Hunt, teal & gold, 6" 395.00
Pitcher, Cinderella, mc w/gold, 6¼" 550.00

Pitcher, Gaudy Willow, 6¾", $495.00.

Pitcher, Geranium, bl & wht w/gold, 6½" 325.00
Pitcher, Geranium, teal & wht, 6½" 200.00
Pitcher, Hounds & Stag, mc, 6½" 585.00
Pitcher, Rip Van Winkle, mc, 6½" 775.00
Pitcher, Wild Ducks, teal w/gold, 6" 385.00
Plate, Blue Willow, 10½" 55.00
Plate, Blue Willow, 6" 22.00
Plate, cake; roses w/gold trim, open hdls, 12" 65.00
Plate, chop; Blue Willow, 13" 185.00
Plate, Christmas, 1950-60, ea 50.00
Plate, Commemorative, Hudson Terminal Buildings, NY City, 7½" ..85.00
Plate, Commemorative, Washington's Home at Mt Vernon, mc .75.00
Plate, fish set, 9", ea 65.00
Plate, Gaudy Willow, 10½" 165.00
Plate, Gaudy Willow, 6" 75.00
Plate, historical scene w/floral border, teal or bl, 10", ea 75.00
Plate, Japan, 8" 35.00
Plate, USBF, 5½" 25.00
Platter, Blue Willow, 16x13" 195.00
Platter, Bonrea, 14x11" 145.00
Platter, Buffalo Hunt, teal border, 15x11" 300.00
Platter, fish set, 14x11" 175.00
Teapot, Blue Willow, sq, 5½" 185.00
Toilet set, Cairo, pitcher+bowl+soap dish w/lid+shaving mug ...450.00
Vase, Chrysanthemum, teal & wht, 5½" 35.00
Vase, Multifleure Lamelle, 4" 45.00

Buggy Steps

Buggies were sold and distributed throughout the United States by over forty-six different registered companies. A majority of these manufacturies consolidated by forming the Carriage Manufactures Association in 1880. However, many iron buggy step makers sales were not exclusive to one company. The name steps, produced in the early 1900s, are found on many different wheeled vehicles. These were sold and distributed by many different companies of that period. Name steps are so rare that they command elevated prices. An original identically matched pair (one left, one right) of an Overland Stagecoach, would easily cost $1,000.00 for the set. Our advisor for this category is John Waddell; he is listed in the Directory under Texas.

Beebe Cart, sq, bolt on, 3x3" 38.00
Cole, eared oval, slot mt, 3½x2¼" 45.00
CWCo, sq, shield, bolt on, 3½x3½" 38.00
Dean & Co, oval, tee mt, 5¼x3½" 65.00
Deere, brass insert, rectangle, trifork mt, 4½x3" 70.00
Folding w/spring offset, open mt 36.00
Henny Buggy Co, oval, trifork mt, 15x3½" 60.00

Moon Bros, oval, trifork mt, 4½x3½" 60.00
NWS Co, open pad, bolt on, 5x2½" 40.00
Open grate, trifork mt, 4½x4" 60.00
Ornamental, w/scraper & scroll, trifork mt 75.00
Studebaker, rectangle, trifork mt, 5x3¼" 60.00
Surry step, oval, branch arm mt, 8½x6½" 130.00
Thompson Wagon Co, rectangle w/shield & branch 65.00

Burmese

Burmese glass was patented in 1885 by the Mount Washington Glass Co. It is typically shaded from canary yellow to a rosy salmon color. The yellow is produced by the addition of uranium oxide to the mix. The salmon color comes from the addition of gold salts and is achieved by reheating the object (partially) in the furnace. It is thus called 'heat sensitive' glass. Thomas Webb of England was licensed to produce Burmese and often added more gold, giving an almost fuchsia tinge to the salmon in some cases. They called their glass 'Queen's Burmese,' and this is sometimes etched on the base of the object. This is not to be confused with Mount Washington's 'Queen's Design,' which refers to the design painted on the object. Both companies added decoration to many pieces. Mount Washington-Pairpoint produced some Burmese in the late 1920s and Gunderson and Bryden in the '50s and '70s, but the color and shapes are different. Our advisors for this category are Dolli and Wilfred Cohen; they are listed in the Directory under California. In the listings that follow, examples are assumed to have the satin finish unless noted 'shiny.' See also Lamps, Fairy.

Bowl, appl yel-drip edge trim, folded-in sides, 2½x6" 475.00
Bowl, crimped ped ft, scalloped edge, 3½x4¼" 330.00
Bowl, ruffled rim, Gunderson, 2½x6" 295.00
Bowl, shiny, ruffled, Mt WA, 3½x12" 275.00
Compote, shiny, wavy bowl on ped ft, Pairpoint, 4½x7" 550.00
Creamer, Burmese hdl, Mt WA, 2½x1⅜" 450.00
Creamer & sugar bowl, burmese hdls, shiny, Pairpoint, 3¾" 415.00
Cruet, ribbed, squat/bulbous, w/ribbed stopper, Mt WA, 6" 1,200.00
Cup, shiny, flared rim, 2⅞x2½" 445.00
Epergne, ruffled cone w/silver petal ft in ruffled base, 4½" 250.00
Finger bowl, 9-crimp, Mt WA, 2⅛x4½" 225.00
Jar, ginger; Mt WA, 5¼" 400.00
Jar, gold floral; Pairpoint floral-emb rim/lid, 2½x4" 300.00
Marmalade, shiny, floral sprigs & blk-dotted bands, Webb 450.00
Pitcher, appl yel hdl, Mt WA, 7x6½" 1,100.00
Pitcher, cider; bulbous, Mt WA, 5¾" 600.00
Pitcher, shiny, Hobnail, Mt WA, 5¾" 1,450.00
Plate, floral, Mt WA, 12" 1,650.00
Plate, Gunderson, 9" 650.00
Plate, shiny, Pairpoint, 8" 225.00
Rose bowl, asters/vines, opal int, Mt WA, 4" 350.00
Rose bowl, 8-crimp, unmk Webb, 2⅝x2⅞" 250.00
Rose jar, florals, Mt WA, w/lid, 4¾" 1,500.00
Shakers, ribbed, Mt WA, 3¾", pr in SP fr w/sunflowers 550.00
Sherbet, Mt WA, 2½x2⅞" 445.00
Spooner, Dmn Quilt, Mt WA, 4½x2¾" 500.00
Toothpick holder, collared, 6-sided, 3" 395.00
Toothpick holder, faint Dmn Quilt, sq top, Mt WA, 2½x2" 450.00
Toothpick holder, forget-me-nots, Mt WA, ovoid, 2¾" 495.00
Tumbler, juice; Mt WA, 3¾x2⅛" 275.00
Tumbler, Mt WA, 3¾x2¾" 265.00
Tumbler, shiny, Mt WA, 3¾" 275.00
Vase, ball shape, widely flared ruffled top, Webb, 3x3¼" 275.00
Vase, egg form w/scalloped ft, Mt WA, 4" 250.00
Vase, fish/plants/gold netting, stick neck, Mt WA, 10" 3,500.00

Vase, flower form w/foliage & berries, Webb, 2¾x3½" 650.00
Vase, forget-me-nots on long stems, stick neck, Mt WA, 8" ...1,100.00
Vase, gourd shape, Mt WA, 10x5½" 750.00
Vase, gourd shape, Mt WA, 12x6½" 800.00
Vase, gourd shape, Mt WA, 4x8" 645.00
Vase, ivy/Dickens verse, tapered, hdls, Mt WA, 7" 700.00
Vase, jack-in-pulpit; bl dots/oak leaves, Mt WA, 12½" 1,700.00
Vase, jack-in-pulpit; crimped rim, 12½" 850.00
Vase, jack-in-pulpit; ruffled rim, 7¼" 650.00
Vase, King Tut, mc cranes/pyramids/palm, scroll hdls, 11" 1,000.00
Vase, lg dotted blossoms, cylindrical, 4¼" 635.00
Vase, lily; Gunderson, 9½" 375.00
Vase, nasturtiums, gourd shape, Webb's Queens, 8" 1,250.00
Vase, Queen's design, Egyptian style, bulbous/hdls, Mt WA, 6" ..2,750.00
Vase, ruffled top, Webb, 3⅞x3" 225.00
Vase, ruffled trumpet form on ped ft, Bryden, 10" 285.00
Vase, shiny, bl forget-me-nots, Webb, 3½x3½" 245.00
Vase, shiny, scalloped rim, 6¾" 525.00
Vase, shiny, wild roses, petal top, Webb Queen's, 3½" 475.00
Vase, squat, w/petal top, Webb Queen's, 3¼" 275.00
Vase, trumpet form, refired lip, 8¼" 675.00
Whiskey taster, Webb, 2⅞x2½" 335.00
Whiskey taster, 2⅞x2½", +4" saucer 445.00

Butter Molds and Stamps

The art of decorating butter began in Europe during the reign of Charles II. This practice was continued in America by the farmer's wife who sold her homemade butter at the weekly market to earn extra money during hard times. A mold or stamp with a special design, hand carved either by her husband or a local craftsman, not only made her product more attractive but also helped identify it as hers. The pattern became the trademark of Mrs. Smith, and all who saw it knew that this was her butter. It was usually the rule that no two farms used the same mold within a certain area, thus the many variations and patterns available to the collector today. The most valuable are those which have animals, birds, or odd shapes. The most sought-after motifs are the eagle, cow, fish, and rooster. These works of early folk art are quickly disappearing from the market.

Molds

Acorn, 1 in ea of 2 sqs, trn hdl, 4x7" 140.00
Cow, EX cvg, ca 1820, w/plunger, 5" dia 365.00

Cow, primitive carving, 2¼x8", $350.00.

Dbl sheaf of wheat & letter G, wood & NP brass, 6½x5¾" sq ...100.00
Ferns, 1-pc, 4⅝" dia 50.00
Fruit & vegetables in compote, EX detail, 4x5" 250.00
Geometric, deep cvg, cherry wood, 4½x7", EX 100.00

Heart, delicately cvd, age cracks, 3¾" dia 195.00
Rosette, 4⅝" dia 55.00
Sheaf of wheat, w/hdl, 4" dia 55.00
Strawberry, staved hexagonal case w/pewter bands, 4", VG 125.00
Swan, EX cvg, maple, ca 1830, 4" dia 235.00
Thistle, stylized, 2-pc, 4¾" dia 60.00
Tulip, no hdl, 4½" dia 165.00
2 houses, primitive, 2-pc, red pnt exterior, 10¾" L 100.00
8 sqs w/cvd leaves/acorns/sheaves of wheat/etc, ftd, 5½x11" 185.00

Stamps

Acorn & oak leaves, 1-pc trn hdl, 3½" dia 100.00
Bird looking bk, primitive cvg, 1-pc trn hdl, 4" dia 165.00
Eagle, 1-pc trn hdl, 4" dia 385.00
Eagle & acorn, EX cvg, 2⅞x4½" 300.00
Eagle & shield, 1-pc trn hdl, 3" dia 165.00
Eagle w/shield & stars, hdl missing, 4½" dia 225.00
Fish, 1-pc trn hdl, 2⅛" dia 225.00
Flower, stylized, scrubbed, 1-pc trn hdl, 3⅞" dia 60.00
Flower, stylized, w/paisley, hdl gone/edge damage, 4" dia 75.00
Foliage, rayed rim, 1-pc trn hdl, 3½" dia 115.00
Geometric, worn, scrubbed, w/hdl, 4" dia 95.00
Heart, primitive cvg, dtd 1829, worn, 4" dia 300.00
Heart w/foliage & crosshatching, semicircular, EX patina, 7" L ..365.00
Lamb w/cross, well cvd, 3⅛" 200.00
Pineapple, EX cvg, 1850s, 4¼" dia 135.00
Pineapple, stylized, scrubbed, 1-pc trn hdl, 4" dia 85.00
Pineapple & foliage, scrubbed, hand grip on bk, 3¾x4½" 145.00
Pinwheel, deep cvg, 3¾" dia 120.00
Pinwheel, EX worn patina, 4¼" dia 150.00
Prince of Wales Feather, 3¼" dia 85.00
Roman numerals, short hdl, 4¾" dia 35.00
Rosette, 3¾" dia+hdl 35.00
Sheaf & foliage, semicircular, inserted hdl, 7" L 440.00
Sheaf of wheat, leaf border, 3⅜" dia, 3" hdl 80.00
Sheaf of wheat, rectangular, 1x4⅝x2⅜", rstr hdl 30.00
Star, simple, burl, 1-pc trn hdl, scrubbed, 3¾" dia 330.00
Starflower, 3⅜" dia 35.00
Strawberries & leaves, detailed cvg, knob hdl, 2½" dia 185.00
Thistle, 4" dia, 2¼" hdl 50.00
Thistle w/in circles, 3¾" dia, 2¾" hdl 35.00
Tulip, primitive cvg, rectangular, dk patina, 3¼x4⅞" 85.00
Tulip, stylized, deeply cvd, scrubbed, 1-pc trn hdl, 3½" dia 360.00
3 leaves w/in concentric circle border, 1-pc trn hdl, 4" dia 65.00
6-point star, fine cvg, 4¾" dia 135.00

Buttonhooks

The earliest known written reference to buttonhooks (shoe hooks, glove hooks, or collar buttoners) is dated 1611. They became a necessary implement in the 1850s when tight-fitting high-button shoes became fashionable. Later in the 19th century, ladies' button gloves and men's button-on collars and cuffs dictated specific types of buttoners, some with a closed wire loop instead of a hook end. Both shoes and gloves used as many as twenty-four buttons each. Usage began to wane in the late 1920s following a fashion change to low-cut laced shoes and the invention of the zipper. There was a brief resurgence of use following the 1948 movie *High Button Shoes*. For a simple, needed utilitarian device, buttonhook handles were made from a surprising variety of materials: natural wood, bone, ivory, agate, and mother of pearl to plain steel, celluloid, aluminum, iron, lead and pewter, artistic copper, brass, silver, gold, and many other materials, in lengths that varied from under

2" to over 20". Many designs folded or retracted, and buttonhooks were often combined with shoehorns and other useful implements. Stamped steel buttonhooks often came free with the purchase of shoes, gloves, or collars. Material, design, workmanship, condition, and relative scarcity are the primary market value factors. Prices range from $1.00 to over $100.00. Buttonhooks are fairly easy to find, and they are interesting to display. Our advisor for this category is Richard Mathes; he is listed in the Directory under Ohio.

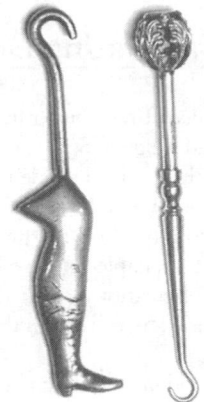

Lady's leg, lead, $40.00; Sterling with faux gem, $45.00.

Buttonhook/penknife, ivory side plates, man's 40.00
Glove hook, gold plated, retractable, 3" 75.00
Glove hook, loop end, agate hdl, 2½" 35.00
Shoe hook, colored celluloid hdl, 8" 10.00
Shoe hook, faux ivory celluloid hdl, 8" 5.00
Shoe hook, stamped steel, advertising, 5" 8.00
Shoe hook, wooden hdl, 8" 8.00
Shoe hook/shoehorn combination, steel & celluloid, 9" 20.00

Byrdcliffe

An outgrowth of a pottery class held at an art colony near Woodstock, New York, in 1903, the Birdcliffe Pottery produced handmade artware that they fired in open-air kilns. Their glazes were outstanding, and as a result the pottery was highly regarded in the field. They remained in production until 1928.

Bowl, gr/bl matt flambe, crude, ftd, 5½x8" 325.00
Bowl, stylized floral band, purple/gr on pk-brn mottle, 8" 425.00
Tile, floral, 5-color, wide oak fr, 5½" 200.00
Vase, gr/bl mottle, heavy walls, spherical, 8x9½" 1,200.00
Vase, heavy lt gr to raspberry mottled matt, sq rim, 6¾x4½" 325.00
Vase, purple mottle satin, flared rim, 8¼x4" 325.00

Cabat

Vase, aqua/caramel/tan drip over brn matt, 3" 200.00
Vase, blk/blk/wht drip over dk gray, 3" 210.00

Vase, porcelain feelie, yellow, orange, and black, marked, 5", $350.00; Vase, porcelain feelie, green, brown, and turquoise, $400.00.

Vase, dk bl metallic/gr flambe, 4", NM 225.00
Vase, ivory/cocoa drip over brn matt, 3½" 210.00
Vase, pk/lav/lt gr drip w/vivid bl highlghts over brn, 3½" 275.00
Vase, thick bl drip w/brn/gold highlights over brn/gold, 3" 150.00
Vase, thick lav drip w/bl highlights over blk matt, 3½" 170.00
Vase, thick lt gr drip w/tan highlights over brn matt, 3" 160.00
Vase, vivid aqua w/brn & gold highlights over brn matt, 3" 110.00
Vase, vivid deep violet/bl drip w/aqua over dk brn, 2x2½" 250.00
Vase, vivid yel drip over gunmetal, pear form, 4½" 375.00

Calculating Devices

Calculating, computing, and adding devices come in many shapes, sizes, and weights. Some are complex machines with many moving parts while others, such as slide rules, are quite simple in construction. These devices were used by scientists, accountants, engineers, and many other professionals when mathematical computations and exactness were required. Examples of devices and machines with early patent dates are usually of greatest interest to collectors. Our advisor for this category is Dale Beeks; he is listed in the Directory under Iowa.

Adder, addometer, 7 numbered wheels, in case, EX 35.00
Adder, Gem, chain drive, pocket sz 45.00
Adder, Webb, Pat 1867, wooden base, EX 350.00
Adder, Webb, Pat 1889, all metal, EX 165.00
Adder, Webb type, unsgn, all metal, EX 110.00
Curta, pepper-grinder type, w/case, EX 250.00
Machine, Burroughs, push button, glass sides, lg 95.00
Machine, Comptometer, copper case, push button 45.00
Machine, Comptometer, wooden case, G 350.00
Machine, Millionaire, metal case, heavy, lg, VG 1,200.00
Machine, Monroe, push button, suitcase sz 75.00
Slide rule, beginner's, w/case, EX 12.00
Slide rule, circular, Gilson, w/case, EX 35.00
Slide rule, demonstration, Pickett, 7-ft long, EX 120.00
Slide rule, Keuffel & Esser NY, typical, EX 22.00
Slide rule, Thacher's, cylindrical, Pat 1882, w/case, EX 1,100.00

Calendar Plates

Calendar plates were advertising giveaways most popular from about 1906 until the late 1920s. They were decorated with colorful underglaze decals of lovely ladies, flowers, animals, birds and, of course, the twelve months of the year of their issue. During the 1950s they came into vogue again, but never to the extent they were originally. Those with exceptional detailing or those with scenes of a particular activity are most desirable; so are any from before 1906 or after 1930.

Our advisor for this category is Elizabeth M. Stout; she is listed in the Directory under Missouri.

1908, dog, 8½" 48.00
1908, lady, Detroit MI 40.00
1909, cherry transfer, mk Carnation, McNicol, 9½" 30.00
1909, Friars w/fruit & goose, Sterling China, 9¼", EX 45.00
1909, fruit & flowers, 7" 30.00
1909, scenic, 8½" 30.00
1910, irises, 8" 30.00
1910, St Bernard dog 38.00
1911, harbor scene, MA 38.00
1911, Old Acquaintance 30.00
1912, airplanes, Peterson Bros, Hawley MN 45.00
1912, balloon w/basket & 2 people, EX gold 50.00

1912, biplane, Cincinnati grocery 68.00
1913, boy in rags under arch, 8" 35.00
1913, early airplane w/village below, EX gold, 8¼" 50.00
1913, farm boy 40.00
1915, Panama Canal & Am flag, 6" 35.00
1916, birds, Family Liquor Store, Steelton PA 40.00

1920, WWI Victory, 8¼", $40.00.

1921, dove & Allied flags, 7½" 40.00
1923, fish 45.00
1924, flowers, holly berries & leaves along border, 9" 45.00
1924, Happy New Year, Asbury Park 45.00
1928, deer scene, 8¾" 50.00
1930, Dutch boy & dog, 9" 70.00

Calendars

Calendars are collected for their colorful prints, often attributed to a well-recognized artist of the period. Advertising calendars from the turn of the century often have a double appeal when representing a company whose tins, signs, store displays, etc., are also collectible. See also Parrish, Maxfield.

1893, Buckeye, factories/equipment, 7¼x6½", VG 50.00
1894, Youth's Companion, Dainty Calendar for..., mc, EX 12.50
1897, Reymann Brewing, frothing mug/wheat/hops, 22x14", NM ..1,050.00
1899, Sweet Violets, sgn E Nister, wall hanging, sm, EX 25.00
1904, Hood's Sarsaparilla, lady, complete, 15x4", NM 225.00
1904, Playing, Maud Humphrey art, 6 sheets, 10x13", EX 500.00
1905, Gibson Girls, Armour advertising, EX 95.00
1905, Hill's Quinine, Child in Danger w/Train, mc, EX 75.00
1906, Harrington & Richardson Arms, pheasant, 24x12", NM ..400.00
1906, Wild West Warriors, 14½x10½"+fr, G 50.00
1907, Deering Binder, girl in pk, full pad, 24x12", VG 175.00
1907, Winchester, hunting dogs, partial pad, 14½x13½", EX 600.00
1907, Youth's Companion, Humphrey/Moran/etc art, 8x12", EX .45.00
1910, De Laval Cream Separators, milking scene, 20x10", NM .600.00
1910, Hazard Smokeless Powder, Return of Hunters, 17x17", VG ...250.00
1910, Kimmel Seeds, girl in red w/cane & dog, 26x12", NM 475.00
1910, Peter Cartridge Co, bull moose, partial pad, 26x16", EX .1,250.00
1912, Penn Beer, stylish lady, 30½x15½"+fr, EX 425.00
1912, The Greeting, CM Russel, 10½x6", EX 35.00
1913, Berkshire Brewery, girl & horse, partial pad, 20x16", VG ..1,100.00
1913, Marble City Garage, couple/open touring car, 20x15", VG ...95.00
1913, Winchester, hunter w/horses & rams on hill, 22x14", EX ..2,050.00
1914, Singer Sewing Machines, flowers, DeLongpre, 7x10", EX ...40.00
1917, De Laval Cream Separators, farm girl & collie, 24x12", EX ...700.00
1920, Chevrolet Motor Cars, open touring car, 28x15", VG 200.00
1927, Harrington & Richardson Arms, setter dog, 16x9", NM ...450.00
1930, Indian Maiden, by A Hieble, full pad, 16x10", NM 85.00

1931, lady w/horse, by A Hieble, full pad, 16x10", NM 80.00
1931, Pontiac, Chief Pontiac, partial pad, 27x19", G 300.00
1932, Abraham Lincoln, Brown & Bigelow, lg, EX 200.00
1932, Hercules Powder, Stowaways, full pad, 29½x13", EX 275.00
1934, On the Beam, R Armstrong, complete, M 125.00
1935, Franklin Roosevelt, Louis F Dow, St Paul, lg, EX 300.00
1937, Hi-Plane Tobacco, Indians, 30x17½", EX 100.00
1939, Batchelder Bros, baseball teams, 28x21", EX 160.00
1939, St John Motors, Indian princess, full pad, 45x22", EX 375.00
1940, Dionne Quintuplets, M in orig envelope 15.00
1942, Gloria by Earl Moran, EX 65.00
1947, Bewley's Flour, full pad, 18x12", NM 40.00
1947, Lucky Dog by Zoe Mozert, EX 55.00

Caliente

Caliente was a line of colored dinnerware made by the Paden City Pottery Company in Paden City, West Virginia. It was produced during the 1930s and 1940s in tangerine, yellow, blue, green, and cobalt blue.

Bowl, salad; 10" 25.00
Bowl, 5¼" 10.00
Bowl, 9" 20.00
Candle holder 15.00
Creamer 14.00
Cup & saucer 15.00
Plate, dinner; 10" 17.50
Plate, 6" 5.00
Plate, 9½" 10.00
Platter, 14" 25.00
Shakers, pr 25.00
Sugar bowl, w/lid 18.00
Teapot 45.00

California Faience

California Faience was the trade name used by William V. Bragdon and Chauncy R. Thomas on vases, bowls, and other artware produced at their pottery known as 'The Tile Shop' in Berkeley, California, from 1920 to 1930. Faience tile was the principal product of the business during these years and is the favorite with today's collectors. Items in a glossy glaze are rare and therefore more valuable. Tiles were marked 'California Faience' with a die stamp.

Ashtray, stylized dog spans length, orange-yel matt, 6x5x4" 225.00
Bowl, bl matt, ftd/flared, 3x10" 250.00
Bowl, bl matt, str rim, 3x5½" 200.00
Bowl, burgundy gloss, incurvate, 3¾x6½" 250.00
Bowl, lt bl matt, 2¼x5½" 150.00
Bowl, purple matt, shouldered, 1¾x5¼" 300.00
Bowl, yel/turq gloss, octagonal, 2½x11" 105.00
Bust, Awakening, lady, red clay under turq gloss, rstr, 12" 700.00
Tile, abstract pine tree, bl/yel gloss, 5¼" dia 250.00
Tile, galleon, mustard on dk bl, mk, 5¼" 450.00
Tile, griffin, bl on yel, red clay outline, mk, 5¼" sq 425.00
Tile, stylized goose, mustard/gr/lt bl matt, 6" dia 375.00
Vase, bl matt, sm ring mouth, shouldered, 7¼" 600.00
Vase, gr-turq matt, squat, incurvate rim, 2¾x4" 275.00
Vase, mustard matt, trumpet shape, 6¾x5", EX 200.00
Vase, pomegranates, bl, 11" 700.00
Vase, sgraffito flowers, wht & turq gloss, sgn Tize, 3¾" 400.00
Vase, stylized floral, wht slip trail on turq gloss, sgn, 4x4" 900.00

Vase, stylized floral band, mc on yel gloss, 8x3¾" 1,200.00

California Perfume Company

D.H. McConnell, Sr., founded the California Perfume Company (C.P. Company; C.P.C.) in 1886 in New York City. He had previously been a salesman for a book company, which he later purchased. His door-to-door sales usually involved the lady of the house, to whom he presented a complimentary bottle of inexpensive perfume. Upon determining his perfume to be more popular than his books, he decided that the manufacture of perfume might be more lucrative. He bottled toiletries under the name 'California Perfume Company' and a line of household products called 'Perfection.' In 1928 the name 'Avon' appeared on the label, and in 1939 the C.P.C. name was entirely removed from the product. The success of the company is attributed to the door-to-door sales approach and 'money back' guarantee offered by his first 'Depot Agent,' Mrs. P.F.E. Albee, known today as the 'Avon Lady.'

The company's containers are quite collectible today, especially the older, hard-to-find items. Advanced collectors seek bottles and other items labeled Goetting & Co., New York; Goetting's; or Savoi Et Cie, Paris. Such examples date from 1871 to 1896. The Goetting Company was purchased by D.H. McConnell; Savoi Et Cie was a line which they imported to sell through department stores. Also of special interest are packaging and advertising with the Ambrosia or Hinze Ambrosia Company label. This was a subsidiary company whose objective seems to have been to produce a line of face creams, etc., for sale through drugstores and other such commercial outlets. They operated in New York from about 1875 until 1954. Because very little is known about these companies and since only a few examples of their product containers and advertising material have been found, market values for such items have not yet been established. Other items sought by the collector include products marked Gertrude Recordon, Marvel Electric Silver Cleaner, Easy Day Automatic Clothes Washer, pre-1915 catalogs, and California Perfume Company 1909 and 1910 calendars.

There are hundreds of local Avon Collector Clubs throughout the world that also have C.P.C. collectors in their membership. If you are interested in joining, locating, or starting a new club, contact the National Association of Avon Collectors, Inc., listed in the Directory under Clubs, Newsletters, and Catalogs. Those wanting a National Newsletter Club or price guides may contact Avon Times, listed in the same section. See also Avon. Inquiries concerning California Perfume Company items and the companies or items mentioned in the previous paragraphs should be directed toward our advisor, Dick Pardini, whose address is given under California. (Please send a large SASE; not interested in Avons, 'Perfection' marked C.P.C.'s, or Anniversary Keepsakes.)

American Ideal Lipstick, 1929, CPC on tube, M 45.00
American Ideal Perfume, wood box, introductory sz, 1910, M 200.00
American Ideal perfume, 1929, gr satin box, 1-oz, MIB 140.00

**Baby Set, 1916, 3-piece,
1916, MIB, $350.00.**

Bandolene Hair Dressing, 1923, 4-oz, M **40.00**
Bay Rum, 1908, 4-oz, M **80.00**
Boudoir Manicure Set, 1929, 4-pc, w/booklet, M **80.00**
California Tooth Tablet, metal lid, glass bottom, ca 1900, M **60.00**
Catalog, color, w/tabs, 1915-29, M **60.00**
Cut Glass Perfume, sq label, 1915, MIB **225.00**
Daphne Bath Salts, glass jar w/gold label, 1925, 10-oz, MIB **70.00**
Daphne Talcum Powder, tin container, gr can, 1923, 4-oz, M **65.00**
Depilatory, 1915, 1-oz, M **100.00**
Eau De Quinine, 1923, 6-oz, M **75.00**
Elite Powder, Perfect Foot Powder, oval can, 1923, sm, M **25.00**
Elite Powder, Perfect Foot Powder, tin can, 1923, 1-lb, M **50.00**
Gentleman's Shaving Set, 1917, 7-pc, MIB **400.00**
Gertrude Recordon's Introductory Facial Treatment Set, MIB ...**300.00**
Juvenile Set, 1915, MIB **435.00**
Lavender Salts, gr glass, 1910, MIB **225.00**
Lemonal Cleansing Cream, jar, 1926, M **50.00**
Lilac Vegetal, ribbed glass, 1925, 2-oz, M **50.00**
Liquid Shampoo, 1923, 6-oz, M **60.00**
Little Folks Set, 4-bottles, 1905, MIB **250.00**
Lotus Cream, 1917, 12-oz, MIB **160.00**
Lotus Cream, 1924, 4-oz, MIB **90.00**
Mission Garden Dbl Compact, brass, 1922, M **45.00**
Nail Cream, tin container, 1924, M **10.00**

Calling Cards, Cases, and Receivers

The practice of announcing one's arrival with a calling card borne by the maid to the mistress of the house was a social grace of the Victorian era. Different messages (condolences, a personal visit, or a good-by) were related by turning down one corner or another. The custom was forgotten by WWI. Fashionable ladies and gents carried their personally engraved cards in elaborate cases made of such materials as embossed silver, mother-of-pearl with intricate inlay, tortoise shell, and ivory. Card receivers held cards left by visitors who called while the mistress was out or 'not receiving.' Calling cards with fringe, die-cut flaps that cover the name, or an unusual decoration are worth about $3.00 to $4.00, while plain cards usually sell for around $1.00.

Cases

Abalone & pearl w/cameo, minor damage, 4" **40.00**
Ivory, cvd birds & flowers, Oriental, 3¾" L **185.00**
MOP, dmn-shaped panels, SP center & corners **80.00**
Silver w/eng & cast cherubs, w/chain, 4" **100.00**
Sterling, chinoiserie relief, grapevines, 3¾" **215.00**
Tortoise shell w/detailed emb florals, 4" **85.00**

Receivers

Brass, Nouveau nude on shell, Lo-Mar Works **65.00**
Bronze, ornate w/low ped, Victorian, Oudry, 12½" **350.00**
Gilt-bronze, pond w/lily pads, 2 heads emerge/look at nude, 7" ..**750.00**
Pewter-like metal, lady w/flowing hair, 4½x7" **85.00**
Porcelain, bust of armored knight, Derby, 3¾x5" **90.00**
Sapphire bl glass teardrop shape in SP fr, 6x4x3½" **325.00**
SP, ped base w/leaf decor, Reed & Barton **70.00**
SP, Victorian cherubs, Barbour, 3x6½" dia **150.00**

Camark

The Camden Art and Tile Company (commonly known as

Camark) of Camden, Arkansas, was organized in the fall of 1926 by Samuel J. 'Jack' Carnes. Using clays from Arkansas, John Lessell, who had been hired as art director by Carnes, produced the initial lustre and iridescent Lessell wares for Camark ('CAM'den, 'ARK'ansas) before his death in December 1926. Before the plant opened in the spring of 1927, Carnes brought John's wife, Jeanne, and stepdaughter Billie to oversee the art department's manufacture of Le-Camark. Production by the Lessell family included variations of J.B. Owens' Soudanese and Opalesce and Weller's Marengo and Lamar. Camark's version of Marengo was called Old English. They also made wares identical to Weller's LaSa. Pieces made by John Lessell back in Ohio were signed 'Lessell,' while those made by Jeanne and Billie in Arkansas during 1927 were signed 'Le-Camark.' By 1928 Camark's production centered on traditional glazes. Drip glazes similar to Muncie Pottery were produced, in particular the green drip over pink. In the 1930s commercial castware with simple glossy and matt finishes became the primary focus and would continue so until Camark closed in the early 1960s. Between the 1960s and 1980s the company operated mainly as a retail store selling existing inventory, but some limited production occurred. In 1986 the company was purchased by the Ashcraft family of Camden, but no pottery has yet been made at the factory.

Our advisor for this category is David Edwin Gifford. He is listed in the Directory under Arkansas. Mr. Gifford is starting an Arkansas Pottery Collector's Society (Camark, Niloak, and others) and seeks those who are interested in joining to write him.

Flower ashtray, blue, 8", $8.00.

Ashtray, leaf form, #88, 10" **25.00**
Bottle, water bottle; #365, 7½x8x2" **95.00**
Pitcher, cat figural, HP features, tail forms hdl, #145, 8" **90.00**
Planter, turkey figural, #381, 8x8½" **50.00**
Planter/bowl, melon ribs, #620, 3x6" **22.50**
Sign, Arkansas shape, paper label **60.00**
Vase, emb & HP cornflowers, hdls, #563, 7½" **50.00**

Cambridge Glass

The Cambridge Glass Company began operations in 1901 in Cambridge, Ohio. Primarily they made crystal dinnerware and well-designed accessory pieces until the 1920s when they introduced the concept of color that was to become so popular on the American dinnerware market. Always maintaining high standards of quality and elegance, they produced many lines that became bestsellers; through the twenties and thirties they were recognized as the largest manufacturer of this type of glassware in the world.

Of the various marks the company used, the 'C in triangle' is the most familiar. Production stopped in 1958. For a more thorough study of the subject, we recommend *Colors in Cambridge Glass* by the National Cambridge Collectors, Inc.; their address may be found in the Directory under Clubs. *Glass Animals and Figural Flower Frogs of the Depression Era* by Lee Garmon and Dick Spencer is a wonderful source for an in-depth view of their particular aspect of glass collecting. They are both listed in the Directory under Illinois. See also Carnival Glass; Glass Animals.

Apple Blossom, crystal, bowl, cereal; 6" 15.00
Apple Blossom, crystal, bowl, finger; #3025, ftd, w/underplate 30.00
Apple Blossom, crystal, bowl, 4-ftd, 12" 40.00
Apple Blossom, crystal, candlestick, keyhole, 2-light 22.50
Apple Blossom, crystal, cup, AD 40.00
Apple Blossom, crystal, plate, dinner; 9½" 45.00
Apple Blossom, crystal, shakers, pr 37.50
Apple Blossom, crystal, stem, parfait; #1066 ....65.00
Apple Blossom, crystal, tumbler; #3130, ftd, 5-oz 11.00
Apple Blossom, crystal, vase, 5" 25.00
Apple Blossom, pk or gr, bowl, baker; 10" 85.00
Apple Blossom, pk or gr, bowl, bonbon; hdls, 5¼" 25.00
Apple Blossom, pk or gr, bowl, console; 12½" 55.00
Apple Blossom, pk or gr, comport, tall, 7" 65.00
Apple Blossom, pk or gr, pitcher, waisted, loop hdl, 67-oz 300.00
Apple Blossom, pk or gr, plate, dinner; sq 75.00
Apple Blossom, pk or gr, stem, sherbet; #3130, low, 6-oz 16.00
Apple Blossom, pk or gr, stem, water; #3130, 8-oz 30.00
Apple Blossom, pk or gr, sugar bowl, ftd, tall 22.50
Apple Blossom, pk or gr, tumbler, #3135, ftd, 8-oz 27.50
Apple Blossom, pk or gr, tumbler, #3400, ftd, 2½-oz 65.00
Apple Blossom, yel or amber, ashtray, heavy, 6" 150.00
Apple Blossom, yel or amber, bowl, oval, 4-ftd, 12" 60.00
Apple Blossom, yel or amber, bowl, pickle; 9" 32.00
Apple Blossom, yel or amber, candy box, w/lid, 4-ftd 85.00
Apple Blossom, yel or amber, mayonnaise, ftd, w/liner & ladle 50.00
Apple Blossom, yel or amber, plate, sandwich; tab hdld, 11½" 32.50
Apple Blossom, yel or amber, platter, 11½" 60.00
Apple Blossom, yel or amber, stem, sherbet; #3025, high, 7-oz 18.00
Apple Blossom, yel or amber, stem, sherbet; #3400, ftd, 6-oz 15.00
Apple Blossom, yel or amber, tumbler, #3130, ftd, 12-oz 35.00
Candlelight, crystal, bowl, #3900/54, 4-toed, flared, 10" 55.00
Candlelight, crystal, bowl, #3900/62, 4-toed, flared, 12" 62.50
Candlelight, crystal, candle holder, #3900/72, 2-light, 6" 37.50
Candlelight, crystal, comport, #3121, blown, 5⅜" 57.50
Candlelight, crystal, cup, #3900/17 ....27.50
Candlelight, crystal, hurricane lamp, #1603, keyhole, w/bobeche ..175.00
Candlelight, crystal, pitcher, #3400/141, Doulton shape 300.00
Candlelight, crystal, plate, #3900/26, 4-toed, 12" 55.00
Candlelight, crystal, relish tray, #3900/125, 3-part, 9" 42.50
Candlelight, crystal, relish tray, #3900/126, 3-part, 12" 52.50
Candlelight, crystal, stem, cocktail; #3111, 3-oz 27.50
Candlelight, crystal, stem, cordial; #3776, 1-oz 65.00
Candlelight, crystal, stem, oyster cocktail; #3111, 4½-oz 27.50
Candlelight, crystal, stem, sherbet; #3776, low, 7-oz 16.50
Candlelight, crystal, stem, water; #3776, 9-oz 30.00
Candlelight, crystal, sugar bowl, #3900/40, ind 17.50
Candlelight, crystal, tumbler, #3900/115, 13-oz 35.00
Candlelight, crystal, vase, #1299, ftd pedestal, 11" 105.00
Candlelight, crystal, vase, #6004, ftd, 6" 35.00
Caprice, bl or pk, ashtray, #215, 4" 14.00
Caprice, bl or pk, bonbon, #133, ftd, 6" sq 40.00
Caprice, bl or pk, bowl, #49, 4-ftd, 8" 115.00
Caprice, bl or pk, bowl, #60, crimped, 4-ftd, 11" 115.00
Caprice, bl or pk, bowl, #62, bell shape, 4-ftd, 12½" 90.00
Caprice, bl or pk, bowl, #66, crimped, 4-ftd, 13" 125.00
Caprice, bl or pk, bowl, pickle; #102, 9" 60.00
Caprice, bl or pk, cigarette holder, #204, triangular, 3x3" 55.00
Caprice, bl or pk, creamer, #38, med 22.00
Caprice, bl or pk, marmalade jar, #89, w/lid, 6-oz 210.00

Caprice, bl or pk, nut dish, #94, divided, 2½" 45.00
Caprice, bl or pk, pitcher, #183, ball shape, 80-oz 310.00
Caprice, bl or pk, plate, #30, 16" 110.00
Caprice, bl or pk, plate, bread & butter; #21, 6½" 24.00
Caprice, bl or pk, plate, cabaret; #32, 4-ftd, 11" 75.00
Caprice, bl or pk, plate, cake; #36, ftd, 13" 325.00
Caprice, bl or pk, saucer, #17 ....5.50
Caprice, bl or pk, stem, parfait; #300, blown, 5-oz 245.00
Caprice, bl or pk, sugar bowl, #38, med 20.00
Caprice, bl or pk, tumbler, #15, str sides, 12-oz 90.00
Caprice, bl or pk, vase, #238, ball shape, 6½" 155.00
Caprice, bl or pk, vase, #244, 4½" 150.00
Caprice, bl or pk, vase, #249, 3½" 195.00
Caprice, crystal, ashtray, #216, 5" 10.00
Caprice, crystal, bowl, #52, crimped, 4-ftd, 9½" 40.00
Caprice, crystal, bowl, #81, shallow, 4-ftd, 11½" 35.00
Caprice, crystal, bowl, #95, almond shape, 4-ftd, 2" 25.00
Caprice, crystal, bowl, bell shape, 4-ftd, 10½" 35.00
Caprice, crystal, bowl, salad; #84, shallow, 15" 50.00
Caprice, crystal, candlestick, #74, 3-light 35.00
Caprice, crystal, cigarette box, #207, w/lid, 3½x2¼" 20.00
Caprice, crystal, comport, #130, ftd, low, 7" 24.00
Caprice, crystal, decanter, #187, w/stopper, 35-oz 150.00
Caprice, crystal, mustard jar, #87, w/lid, 2-oz 55.00
Caprice, crystal, pitcher, #178, Doulton style, tall, 90-oz 700.00
Caprice, crystal, plate, #28, 4-ftd, 14" 40.00
Caprice, crystal, shakers, #91, ball shape, pr 40.00
Caprice, crystal, stem, cocktail; #3, 3½-oz 25.00
Caprice, crystal, stem, cocktail; #300, blown, 3-oz 22.00
Caprice, crystal, stem, wine; #301, blown, 2½-oz 27.50
Caprice, crystal, tumbler, #10, ftd, 10-oz 18.00
Caprice, crystal, tumbler, iced tea; #300, ftd, 12-oz 20.00
Caprice, crystal, tumbler, old-fashioned; #310, flat, 7-oz 35.00
Caprice, crystal, vase, #242, ftd, 6" 35.00
Caprice, crystal, vase, #252, blown, 4½" 40.00
Caprice, crystal, vase, #339, crimped top, 8½" 60.00
Caprice, crystal, vase, rose bowl; #236, ftd, 8" 60.00

Chantilly, sherbet, $17.50; water stem, $20.00; water tumbler, $22.00.

Chantilly, crystal, bowl, cereal/relish; 3-part, 9" 25.00
Chantilly, crystal, bowl, oval, 4-ftd, 11" 37.50
Chantilly, crystal, bowl, tab hdld, ftd, 11½" 35.00
Chantilly, crystal, butter dish, w/lid, rnd 125.00
Chantilly, crystal, candy box, w/lid, ftd 125.00
Chantilly, crystal, comport, blown, 5⅜" 37.50
Chantilly, crystal, comport, 5½" 30.00
Chantilly, crystal, decanter, ball shape 185.00
Chantilly, crystal, hurricane lamp, keyhole base w/prisms 150.00
Chantilly, crystal, pitcher, Doulton style 265.00
Chantilly, crystal, plate, service; 4-ftd, 12" 30.00

Chantilly, crystal, plate, torte; 14" 35.00
Chantilly, crystal, shakers, hdld 30.00
Chantilly, crystal, stem, claret; #3600, 4½-oz 40.00
Chantilly, crystal, stem, claret; #3775, 4½-oz 40.00
Chantilly, crystal, stem, claret; #3779, 4½-oz 40.00
Chantilly, crystal, stem, cocktail; #3600, 2½-oz 24.00
Chantilly, crystal, stem, cordial; #3625, 1-oz 50.00
Chantilly, crystal, stem, cordial; #3779, 1-oz 60.00
Chantilly, crystal, stem, oyster cocktail; #3625, low, 4½-oz 16.00
Chantilly, crystal, stem, sherbet; #3600, low, 7-oz 15.00
Chantilly, crystal, stem, sherbet; #3775, low, 6-oz 15.00
Chantilly, crystal, stem, wine; #3775, 2½-oz 30.00
Chantilly, crystal, sugar bowl, #3900, ind, scalloped edge 11.00
Chantilly, crystal, tumbler, iced tea; #3600, ftd, 12-oz 20.00
Chantilly, crystal, tumbler, iced tea; #3625, ftd, 12-oz 22.00
Chantilly, crystal, tumbler, juice; #3779, ftd, 5-oz 15.00
Chantilly, crystal, tumbler, water; #3775, ftd, 10-oz 15.00
Chantilly, crystal, vase, flower; ftd, high, 8" 30.00
Chantilly, crystal, vase, flower; ftd, 11" 45.00
Chantilly, crystal, vase, globe shape, 5" 30.00
Chantilly, crystal, vase, keyhole base, 12" 55.00
Cleo, bl, basket, upturned sides, hdls, Decagon, 11" 50.00
Cleo, bl, bowl, oval, 11½" 95.00
Cleo, bl, bowl, soup; tab hdls, 7½" 45.00
Cleo, bl, comport, #3115, tall, 7" 75.00
Cleo, bl, creamer, ftd 30.00
Cleo, bl, ice tub 110.00
Cleo, bl, plate, dinner; Decagon, 9½" 95.00
Cleo, bl, sugar bowl, ftd 30.00
Cleo, bl, tumbler, #3077, ftd, 2½-oz 95.00
Cleo, colors other than bl, bowl, comport; 4-ftd, 6" 35.00
Cleo, colors other than bl, bowl, finger; #3077, w/liner 30.00
Cleo, colors other than bl, bowl, vegetable; w/lid, 9" 150.00
Cleo, colors other than bl, bowl, 8½" 40.00
Cleo, colors other than bl, candlestick, 3-light 65.00
Cleo, colors other than bl, mayonnaise, ftd 35.00
Cleo, colors other than bl, pitcher, #3077, w/lid, 63-oz 275.00
Cleo, colors other than bl, salt cellar, 1½" 70.00
Cleo, colors other than bl, stem, #3115, 9-oz 30.00
Cleo, colors other than bl, tumbler, #3077, ftd, 8-oz 25.00
Cleo, colors other than bl, tumbler, #3115, ftd, 8-oz 25.00
Cleo, colors other than bl, vase, 5½" 65.00
Cleo, colors other than bl, wafer tray 225.00
Decagon, pastel colors, bowl, cereal; flat rim, 6" 10.00
Decagon, pastel colors, bowl, cranberry; bell shape, 3½" 15.00
Decagon, pastel colors, bowl, vegetable; oval, 9½" 12.00
Decagon, pastel colors, creamer, ftd 9.00
Decagon, pastel colors, cruet, oil; hdld, stopper, tall, 6-oz 50.00
Decagon, pastel colors, ftd, 8-oz 12.00
Decagon, pastel colors, mayonnaise, hdls, w/ladle/underplate 25.00
Decagon, pastel colors, plate, salad; 8½" 6.00
Decagon, pastel colors, plate, service; 12½" 9.00
Decagon, pastel colors, saucer 1.00
Decagon, pastel colors, stem, sherbet; low, 6-oz 9.00
Decagon, pastel colors, sugar bowl, w/lightning hdls 7.00
Decagon, pastel colors, tray, celery; 11" 10.00
Decagon, pastel colors, tray, pickle; flat, hdls, 8" 10.00
Decagon, pastel colors, tray, service; hdls, 13" 20.00
Decagon, red or bl, bowl, bouillon; w/liner 15.00
Decagon, red or bl, bowl, fruit; bell shape, 5½" 10.00
Decagon, red or bl, bowl, soup plate; flat rim, 8½" 25.00
Decagon, red or bl, bowl, vegetable; oval, 10½" 30.00
Decagon, red or bl, comport, ftd, low, 6½" 25.00
Decagon, red or bl, creamer, ftd, tall, lg 22.00

Decagon, red or bl, gravy boat, w/hdls liner 110.00
Decagon, red or bl, plate, hdls, 7" 15.00
Decagon, red or bl, relish tray, w/6 inserts 110.00
Decagon, red or bl, server, center hdl 20.00
Decagon, red or bl, stem, sherbet; high, 6-oz 20.00
Decagon, red or bl, sugar bowl, scalloped edge 20.00
Decagon, red or bl, tumbler, ftd, 12-oz 35.00
Decagon, red or bl, tumbler, ftd, 2½-oz 25.00
Diane, crystal, basket, hdls, ftd, 6" 16.00
Diane, crystal, bowl, bonbon; 2-hdld, ftd, 6" 17.00
Diane, crystal, bowl, cream soup; #3400, w/underplate 27.50
Diane, crystal, bowl, flared, 4-ftd, 12" 40.00
Diane, crystal, bowl, pickle (like corn dish), 9½" 22.00
Diane, crystal, bowl, relish; 3-part, 6½" 20.00
Diane, crystal, bowl, relish/pickle; 7" 22.00
Diane, crystal, bowl, tab hdld, ftd, 11½" 40.00
Diane, crystal, bowl, w/'ear' hdls, oval, 4-ftd, 12" 50.00
Diane, crystal, bowl, 2-hdld, 11" 35.00
Diane, crystal, cabinet flask 225.00
Diane, crystal, candelabrum, 2-light, keyhole 22.50
Diane, crystal, candlestick, 3-light, 6" 35.00
Diane, crystal, cocktail shaker, glass top 135.00
Diane, crystal, comport, blown, 5⅜" 35.00
Diane, crystal, creamer, #3400, scroll hdl 15.00
Diane, crystal, creamer, #3500, pie-crust edge, ind 15.00
Diane, crystal, cruet, oil; w/stopper, 6-oz 115.00
Diane, crystal, decanter, cordial; short ftd 195.00
Diane, crystal, decanter, ftd, lg 165.00
Diane, crystal, hurricane lamp, keyhole base w/prisms 195.00
Diane, crystal, mayonnaise, sherbet type w/ladle 32.50
Diane, crystal, pitcher, martini 600.00
Diane, crystal, plate, bread & butter; 6½" 5.00
Diane, crystal, plate, hdls, 13½" 30.00
Diane, crystal, plate, salad; 8" 10.00
Diane, crystal, plate, service; 4-ftd, 12" 35.00
Diane, crystal, shakers, glass tops, ftd, pr 32.00
Diane, crystal, stem, cocktail; #1066, tall, 3½" 17.50
Diane, crystal, stem, cocktail; #3122, 3-oz 14.00
Diane, crystal, stem, cordial; #1066, 1-oz 55.00
Diane, crystal, tumbler, iced tea; #3106, ftd, 12-oz 20.00
Diane, crystal, tumbler, juice; ftd, 5-oz 27.00
Diane, crystal, tumbler, 13-oz 30.00
Diane, crystal, vase, flower; 11" 60.00
Elaine, crystal, bowl, bouillon; hdls, 5¼" 13.00
Elaine, crystal, bowl, celery & relish; 3-part, 12" 30.00
Elaine, crystal, bowl, pickle (like corn dish); 9½" 22.00
Elaine, crystal, bowl, pickle/relish; 2-part, 7" 16.00
Elaine, crystal, candlestick, 2-light, 6" 27.50
Elaine, crystal, comport, #3500 stem, 5⅜" 39.00
Elaine, crystal, hurricane lamp, candlestick base 115.00
Elaine, crystal, pitcher, ball shape 135.00
Elaine, crystal, plate, bread & butter; 6½" 7.00
Elaine, crystal, plate, service; 4-ftd, 12" 25.00
Elaine, crystal, shakers, hdld, pr 35.00
Elaine, crystal, stem, claret; #3121, 4½-oz 30.00
Elaine, crystal, stem, claret; #3500, 4½-oz 30.00
Elaine, crystal, stem, cocktail; #1402, 3½-oz 20.00
Elaine, crystal, stem, cordial; #3104, 1-oz 135.00
Elaine, crystal, stem, goblet; #3104, 9-oz 95.00
Elaine, crystal, stem, roemer; #3105, 5-oz 75.00
Elaine, crystal, stem, sherbet; #1402, tall 15.00
Elaine, crystal, stem, sherbet; #3500, tall, 7-oz 15.00
Elaine, crystal, stem, water; #3121, 10-oz 21.00
Elaine, crystal, tumbler, juice; #3121, ftd, 5-oz 19.00

Elaine, crystal, vase, ftd, keyhole, 9" 55.00
Gloria, crystal, bowl, bonbon; flattened, ftd, 5½" 12.00
Gloria, crystal, bowl, finger; ftd 15.00
Gloria, crystal, bowl, flared rim, 13" 55.00
Gloria, crystal, bowl, flared rim, 4-ftd, 12" 22.00
Gloria, crystal, bowl, relish; figure-8 shape w/hdls, 8¾" 20.00
Gloria, crystal, comport, 4-ftd, 6" 19.00
Gloria, crystal, creamer, tall, ftd 11.00
Gloria, crystal, cruet, oil; w/stopper, hdl, ftd, tall 90.00
Gloria, crystal, cup, demitasse; rnd or sq, ea 60.00
Gloria, crystal, plate, 8½" 9.00
Gloria, crystal, saucer, AD; rnd 8.00
Gloria, crystal, stem, claret; #3035, 4½-oz 30.00
Gloria, crystal, stem, sherbet; #3120, low, 6-oz 10.00
Gloria, crystal, stem, water; #3135, 8-oz 18.00
Gloria, crystal, stem, water; #3180, 8-oz 18.00
Gloria, crystal, tumbler, #3035, ftd, 10-oz 12.00
Gloria, crystal, tumbler, #3115, ftd, 12-oz 17.00
Gloria, crystal, tumbler, #3130, ftd, 5-oz 12.00
Gloria, crystal, vase, sq top, 12" 50.00
Gloria, crystal, vase, 4-indent, oval, 9" 75.00
Gloria, gr, pk or yel, bowl, cereal; sq, 6" 22.00
Gloria, gr, pk or yel, bowl, hdls, 10" 70.00
Gloria, gr, pk or yel, bowl, nut; ind, 4-ftd, 3" 65.00
Gloria, gr, pk or yel, butter dish, hdls, w/lid 285.00
Gloria, gr, pk or yel, comport, tall, 7" 75.00
Gloria, gr, pk or yel, cup, sq, 4-ftd 65.00
Gloria, gr, pk or yel, icer, w/insert 85.00
Gloria, gr, pk or yel, pitcher, w/lid, 64-oz 310.00
Gloria, gr, pk or yel, plate, bread & butter; sq 9.00
Gloria, gr, pk or yel, stem, cordial; #3135, 1-oz 135.00
Gloria, gr, pk or yel, stem, water; #3035, 9-oz 30.00
Gloria, gr, pk or yel, stem, water; #3120, 9-oz 25.00
Gloria, gr, pk or yel, stem, wine; #3035, 2½-oz 40.00
Gloria, gr, pk or yel, tray, relish; 2-part, center hdl 37.50
Gloria, gr, pk or yel, tray, relish; 4-part, center hdl 45.00
Gloria, gr, pk or yel, tumbler, #3115, ftd, 8-oz 20.00
Gloria, gr, pk or yel, tumbler, #3120, ftd, 10-oz 20.00
Gloria, gr, pk or yel, vase, neck indent, 11" 125.00
Imperial Hunt Scene, colors, bowl, cereal; 6" 26.50
Imperial Hunt Scene, colors, comport, #3085, 5½" 35.00
Imperial Hunt Scene, colors, ice bucket 75.00
Imperial Hunt Scene, colors, stem, claret; #3085, 4½-oz ..67.50
Imperial Hunt Scene, colors, stem, parfait; #3085, 5½-oz ..60.00
Imperial Hunt Scene, colors, tumbler, #3085, ftd, 12-oz ..35.00
Imperial Hunt Scene, crystal, candlestick, keyhole, 2-light ..17.50
Imperial Hunt Scene, crystal, creamer, ftd 15.00
Imperial Hunt Scene, crystal, plate, 8" 12.00
Imperial Hunt Scene, crystal, stem, #1402, 14-oz 50.00
Imperial Hunt Scene, crystal, stem, sherbet; #1402, 6½-oz ..35.00
Imperial Hunt Scene, crystal, stem, wine; #1402, 2½-oz ..45.00
Imperial Hunt Scene, crystal, tumbler, #1402, flat, 10-oz ..23.00
Imperial Hunt Scene, crystal, tumbler, #1402, flat, 2½-oz ..25.00
Mt Vernon, amber or crystal, ashtray, #68, 4" 12.00
Mt Vernon, amber or crystal, bottle, bitters; #62, 2½-oz ..55.00
Mt Vernon, amber or crystal, bowl, #118, oblong, crimped, 12" ..32.50
Mt Vernon, amber or crystal, bowl, #121, flared, 12½" ..35.00
Mt Vernon, amber or crystal, bowl, #135, oval, 11" 25.00
Mt Vernon, amber or crystal, bowl, #43, 10½" 30.00
Mt Vernon, amber or crystal, bowl, #61, shallow cupped, 11½" ..30.00
Mt Vernon, amber or crystal, bowl, cereal; #32, 6" 12.50
Mt Vernon, amber or crystal, bowl, pickle; #65, 8" 17.50
Mt Vernon, amber or crystal, box, #17, w/lid, sq, 4" 30.00
Mt Vernon, amber or crystal, butter tub, #73, w/lid 65.00

Mt Vernon, amber or crystal, candlestick, #130, 4" 10.00
Mt Vernon, amber or crystal, candy box, #9, w/lid, ftd, 1-lb ..65.00
Mt Vernon, amber or crystal, celery tray, #79, 12" 20.00
Mt Vernon, amber or crystal, coaster, #70, ribbed, 3" 5.00
Mt Vernon, amber or crystal, comport, #33, 4½" 12.00
Mt Vernon, amber or crystal, comport, #81, 8" 25.00
Mt Vernon, amber or crystal, cup, #7 ....6.50
Mt Vernon, amber or crystal, honey jar (marmalade), #74, w/lid .30.00
Mt Vernon, amber or crystal, hurricane lamp, #1607, 9" ..70.00
Mt Vernon, amber or crystal, mug, #84, stein shape, 14-oz ..27.50
Mt Vernon, amber or crystal, pitcher, #13, 66-oz 85.00
Mt Vernon, amber or crystal, pitcher, #91, 86-oz 115.00
Mt Vernon, amber or crystal, plate, salad; #5, 8½" 7.00
Mt Vernon, amber or crystal, relish tray, #104, 5-part, 12" ..30.00
Mt Vernon, amber or crystal, relish tray, #200, 3-part, 11" ..25.00
Mt Vernon, amber or crystal, shakers, #88, short, pr 20.00
Mt Vernon, amber or crystal, stem, claret; #25, 4½-oz ..13.50
Mt Vernon, amber or crystal, stem, water; #1, 10-oz 15.00
Mt Vernon, amber or crystal, stem, wine; #27, 3-oz 13.50
Mt Vernon, amber or crystal, sugar bowl, #86 ....10.00
Mt Vernon, amber or crystal, tumbler, #21, ftd, 5-oz 12.00
Mt Vernon, amber or crystal, tumbler, #59, tall, 14-oz ..22.00
Mt Vernon, amber or crystal, tumbler, water; #3, ftd, 10-oz ..15.00
Mt Vernon, amber or crystal, tumbler, whiskey; #55, 2-oz ..10.00
Mt Vernon, amber or crystal, vase, #50, ftd, 6" 25.00
Mt Vernon, amber or crystal, vase, #54, ftd, 7" 35.00
Nude stem, amber, brandy 95.00
Nude stem, amber, bud vase, egg shape 650.00
Nude stem, amber, champagne 135.00
Nude stem, amber, cigarette holder, oval 650.00

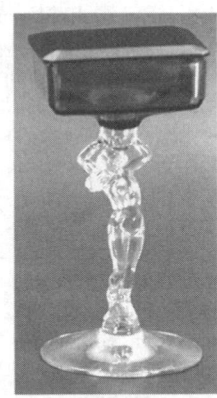

Nude stem, amethyst and clear, box, $295.00.

Nude stem, amethyst, claret 100.00
Nude stem, amethyst, cocktail 95.00
Nude stem, amethyst, goblet, water 125.00
Nude stem, amethyst, ivy ball 250.00
Nude stem, amethyst, shell compote, tall 180.00
Nude stem, carmen, brandy 145.00
Nude stem, carmen, compote, cupped 145.00
Nude stem, carmen, goblet, water 135.00
Nude stem, cobalt, ashtray 400.00
Nude stem, cobalt, bud vase, egg shape 900.00
Nude stem, cobalt, candlestick 950.00
Nude stem, cobalt, cigarette box, short 375.00
Nude stem, cobalt, cigarette box, tall 900.00
Nude stem, cobalt, cocktail, tulip shape 525.00
Nude stem, cobalt, cocktail, V shape 525.00
Nude stem, cobalt w/frosted stem, ivy ball 350.00
Nude stem, Crown Tuscan, candle holders, 9", pr 400.00
Nude stem, Crown Tuscan, compote, flared, 7" 175.00

Nude stem, Crown Tuscan/yel, cocktail 130.00
Nude stem, Crystal Optic, brandy 115.00
Nude stem, Crystal Optic, ivy ball 200.00
Nude stem, crystal w/blk stem, cocktail 120.00
Nude stem, Dianthis, ashtray 500.00
Nude stem, Dianthis, cocktail 160.00
Nude stem, dk gr, brandy 95.00
Nude stem, dk gr, cocktail 95.00
Nude stem, dk gr, goblet, water 115.00
Nude stem, Gold Crystol, brandy 100.00
Nude stem, Heatherbloom, claret 195.00
Nude stem, Mocha, cocktail 135.00
Nude stem, Moonlight, ashtray 475.00
Nude stem, Moonlight, cocktail 200.00
Nude stem, Pistachio, ashtray 600.00
Nude stem, Pistachio, cocktail 165.00
Nude stem, Royal Bl, claret 150.00
Nude stem, Royal Bl, goblet, water 300.00
Nude stem, Smoke, ashtray 500.00
Nude stem, Smoke, champagne 350.00
Nude stem, Smoke, goblet, water 560.00
Nude stem, Smoke, ivy ball 500.00
Nude stem, Smoke, shell compote, short 560.00
Nude stem, Smoke crackle, goblet, table sz 800.00
Nude stem, Tahoe Bl, claret 165.00
Nude stem, Tahoe Bl, cocktail 160.00
Portia, crystal, bottle, cologne; ball shape, w/stopper, hdld, 2-oz ..85.00
Portia, crystal, bowl, celery & relish; 5-part, 12" 37.50
Portia, crystal, bowl, cranberry; 3½" 22.50
Portia, crystal, bowl, flared, 4-ftd, 10" 40.00
Portia, crystal, bowl, grapefruit or oyster; 6" 17.00
Portia, crystal, cigarette holder, urn shape 55.00
Portia, crystal, cocktail shaker, w/stopper 90.00
Portia, crystal, creamer, ball shape, hdld 27.50
Portia, crystal, cup, ftd, sq 18.00
Portia, crystal, mayonnaise, w/ladle & liner 40.00
Portia, crystal, pitcher, Doulton shape 300.00
Portia, crystal, plate, salad; 8" 12.50
Portia, crystal, plate, sq, 8½" 15.00
Portia, crystal, saucer, rnd or sq 3.00
Portia, crystal, shakers, flat, pr 25.00
Portia, crystal, stem, claret; #3121, 4½-oz 37.50
Portia, crystal, stem, goblet; #3124, 10-oz 18.00
Portia, crystal, stem, wine; #3130, 2½-oz 25.00
Portia, crystal, sugar bowl, ind 11.50
Portia, crystal, tumbler, #3124, 3-oz 13.00
Portia, crystal, tumbler, #3126, 2½-oz 30.00
Portia, crystal, tumbler, iced tea; #3126, 12-oz 22.00
Portia, crystal, vase, bud; 10" 40.00
Portia, crystal, vase, flower; 13" 95.00
Portia, crystal, vase, globe shape, 5" 40.00
Rosalie, amber, bowl, basket shape, 2-hdld, 11" 35.00
Rosalie, amber, bowl, finger; w/liner 25.00
Rosalie, amber, bowl, soup; 8½" 30.00
Rosalie, amber, candy dish, w/lid, 6" 65.00
Rosalie, amber, creamer, ftd 12.00
Rosalie, amber, marmalade jar 75.00
Rosalie, amber, plate, 8⅜" 10.00
Rosalie, amber, relish tray, 2-part, 9" 15.00
Rosalie, amber, stem, sherbet; #3077, low, 6-oz 12.00
Rosalie, amber, tray, center hdl, 11" 20.00
Rosalie, bl, pk or gr, bottle, French dressing 110.00
Rosalie, bl, pk or gr, bowl, console; 13" 50.00
Rosalie, bl, pk or gr, bowl, flanged, oval, 15" 65.00

Rosalie, bl, pk or gr, bowl, fruit; 5½" 15.00
Rosalie, bl, pk or gr, bowl, 10" 37.50
Rosalie, bl, pk or gr, candlestick, 2 styles, 4", ea 30.00
Rosalie, bl, pk or gr, comport, 5¾" 30.00
Rosalie, bl, pk or gr, gravy boat, dbl, w/platter 135.00
Rosalie, bl, pk or gr, pitcher, #955, 62-oz 215.00
Rosalie, bl, pk or gr, platter, 12" 65.00
Rosalie, bl, pk or gr, saucer 5.00
Rosalie, bl, pk or gr, stem, goblet; #801, 10-oz 30.00
Rosalie, bl, pk or gr, tumbler, #3077, ftd, 8-oz 25.00
Rosalie, bl, pk or gr, vase, ftd, 5½" 27.50
Rosalie, bl, pk or gr, vase, 6" 55.00
Rose Point, crystal, ashtray, #3500/126, 4" 40.00
Rose Point, crystal, basket, #3500/52, hdld, 6" 245.00
Rose Point, crystal, basket, #3500/56, wide, 7" 50.00
Rose Point, crystal, bowl, #3400/1, flared, 13" 67.50
Rose Point, crystal, bowl, #3400/34, hdls, 9½" 67.50
Rose Point, crystal, bowl, #3500/16, ftd, 11" 100.00
Rose Point, crystal, bowl, #3500/17, ftd, 12" 110.00
Rose Point, crystal, bowl, #3500/28, hdls, 10" 77.50
Rose Point, crystal, bowl, cereal; #3500/11, 6" 77.50
Rose Point, crystal, bowl, fruit; #3500/10, 5" 42.50
Rose Point, crystal, bowl, salad; Pristine #427, 10" 135.00
Rose Point, crystal, candlestick, #3121, 7" 70.00
Rose Point, crystal, candlestick, #3500/31, 6" 87.50
Rose Point, crystal, candlestick, #628, 3½" 35.00
Rose Point, crystal, candy box, #3900/165, rnd, w/lid 100.00
Rose Point, crystal, celery tray, #3500/652, 12" 47.50
Rose Point, crystal, cigarette box, #747, w/lid 150.00
Rose Point, crystal, comport, #3500/111, 6" 140.00
Rose Point, crystal, comport, #3900/135, 5" 42.50
Rose Point, crystal, creamer, #3400/68 ....20.00
Rose Point, crystal, cruet, oil; #3400/193, hdld, 6-oz 90.00
Rose Point, crystal, cup, punch; #488, 5-oz 37.50
Rose Point, crystal, decanter, #1372, tall, 28-oz 575.00
Rose Point, crystal, hat, #1704, 5" 425.00
Rose Point, crystal, hurricane lamp, #1613, w/prisms 325.00

Rose Point, pitcher, Doulton, 80-oz, $275.00.

Rose Point, crystal, pitcher, martini; #1408, 60-oz 1,850.00
Rose Point, crystal, plate, #242, 13½" 145.00
Rose Point, crystal, plate, #3500/4, 7½" 15.00
Rose Point, crystal, plate, bread & butter; #3400/60, 6" 13.50
Rose Point, crystal, punch bowl, Martha #478, 15" 3,250.00
Rose Point, crystal, relish tray, #3500/67, 6-pc, 12" 215.00
Rose Point, crystal, relish tray, #3500/85, hdls, 10" 70.00
Rose Point, crystal, saucer, AD; #3400/69 ....55.00
Rose Point, crystal, shakers, #395, chrome tops, pr 165.00
Rose Point, crystal, stem, cordial; #3106, 1-oz 110.00
Rose Point, crystal, stem, wine; #3500, 2½-oz 57.50
Rose Point, crystal, sugar bowl, #3500/14 ....20.00

Rose Point, crystal, tray, #3500/67, rnd, 12" 150.00
Rose Point, crystal, tumbler, #3106, ftd, 12-oz **32.00**
Rose Point, crystal, tumbler, #3400/38, 12-oz **50.00**
Rose Point, crystal, tumbler, #498, str sides, 10-oz **45.00**
Rose Point, crystal, tumbler, water; #3500, ftd, low, 10-oz **50.00**
Rose Point, crystal, vase, #572, 6" 130.00
Rose Point, crystal, vase, #6004, ftd, 12" **85.00**
Rose Point, crystal, vase, sweet pea; #629 ....250.00
Valencia, crystal, ashtray, #3500/124, rnd, 3¼" **10.00**
Valencia, crystal, bowl, #1402/88, 11" **35.00**
Valencia, crystal, bowl, cereal; #3500/37, 6" **20.00**
Valencia, crystal, candy dish, #3500/103, w/lid **90.00**
Valencia, crystal, cigarette holder, #1066, ftd **38.00**
Valencia, crystal, creamer, #3500/14 ....**15.00**
Valencia, crystal, nut dish, #3400/71, 4-ftd, 3" **55.00**
Valencia, crystal, pitcher, #3400/141, Doulton style, 80-oz 275.00
Valencia, crystal, plate, torte; #3500/38, 13" **25.00**
Valencia, crystal, stem, claret; #3500, 4½-oz **40.00**
Valencia, crystal, stem, cordial; #1402 ....**65.00**
Valencia, crystal, stem, goblet; #1402 ....**20.00**
Valencia, crystal, stem, wine; #1402 ....**30.00**
Valencia, crystal, sugar bowl, #3500/14 ....**15.00**
Valencia, crystal, tumbler, #3500, ftd, 10-oz **14.00**
Valencia, crystal, tumbler, #3500, ftd, 3-oz **14.00**
Wildflower, crystal, bowl, #3900/54, flared, 4-ftd, 10" **37.50**
Wildflower, crystal, bowl, bonbon; hdls, ftd, 6" **17.50**
Wildflower, crystal, bowl, relish; #3900/123, 7" **18.00**
Wildflower, crystal, butter dish, #3400/52, 5" 115.00
Wildflower, crystal, candy box, #3900/165, w/lid **70.00**
Wildflower, crystal, pitcher, #3400/141, Doulton style 295.00
Wildflower, crystal, plate, dinner; #3900/24, 10½" **67.50**
Wildflower, crystal, plate, salad; #3900/22, 8" **17.50**
Wildflower, crystal, plate, torte; #3900/65, 14" **37.50**
Wildflower, crystal, saucer, #3900/17 or #3400/54 ....**3.50**
Wildflower, crystal, stem, wine; #3121, 3½-oz **30.00**
Wildflower, crystal, sugar bowl, #3900/41 ....**12.50**
Wildflower, crystal, vase, flower; #6004, ftd, 8" **55.00**

Cambridge Pottery

The Cambridge Art Pottery operated in Cambridge, Ohio, from 1900 until 1909. During that time, several lines of artware were developed under the direction of C.B. Upjohn, an established ceramic artist of the period. Their standard brown-glazed line was Terrhea, examples of which are often found bearing the signature of the artist responsible for the underglaze decoration. Oakwood was a second brown-glazed line, without the slip painting. Other lines were Acorn (introduced in 1904) and Otoe, a matt green ware (introduced in 1907) that utilized already existing shapes from earlier lines. However, their most successful product was a line of cookware called Gurnsey, made from a red-brown clay with a white-glazed interior. Sales proved to be so profitable that by 1908 all artware was discontinued in favor of its exclusive production. By the following year, the firm had elected to change the name of their pottery to the Gurnsey Earthenware Company. Marks varied, but all incorporated a device comprised of the letters 'CAP'; with the cojoined 'AP' usually contained within a larger-scale 'C.'

Note: Cambridge's brown-glazed artware is compatible in value to Roseville's Rozane line or Weller's Louwelsa.

Ewer, Terrhea, elaborate floral, sgn, ruffled/ornate hdl, 8" 200.00
Ewer, Terrhea, wild roses, ruffled rim, bulbous, 8½" 115.00
Mug, gr matt, mk Otoe/#362, 5x5" 110.00
Pitcher, berries/leaves emb on dk gr matt, 6", NM 80.00

Vase, portrait of a young girl on orange to green background, signed A. Williams, #211, 24", NM, $3,750.00.

Vase, irises cvd on thick dk gr matt, shouldered, no mk, 5" 100.00
Vase, Terrhea, nasturtiums, long incurvate neck, 11½" **170.00**
Vase, Terrhea, pansies, squat w/sm opening, 5½" 100.00
Vase, Terrhea, portrait of girl, Williams, #211, 24", NM **3,750.00**

Cameo

The technique of glass carving was perfected 2,000 years ago in ancient Rome and Greece. The most famous ancient example of cameo glass is the Portland Vase, made in Rome around 100 A.D. After glass blowing was developed, glassmakers devised a method of casing several layers of colored glass together, often with a light color over a darker base, to enhance the design. Skilled carvers meticulously worked the fragile glass to produce incredibly detailed classic scenes. In the 18th and 19th centuries, Oriental and Near-Eastern artisans used the technique more extensively. European glassmakers revived the art during the last quarter of the 19th century. In France, Galle and Daum produced some of the finest examples of modern times, using as many as five layers of glass to develop their designs, usually scenics or subjects from nature. Hand carving was supplemented by the use of a copper engraving wheel, and acid was used to cut away the layers more quickly.

In England, Thomas Webb and Sons used modern machinery and technology to eliminate many of the problems that plagued early glass carvers. One of Webb's best-known carvers, George Woodall, is credited with producing over four hundred pieces. Woodall was trained in the art by John Northwood, famous for reproducing the Portland Vase in 1876. Cameo glass became very popular during the late 1800s, resulting in a market that demanded more than could be produced, due to the tedious procedures involved. In an effort to produce greater volume, less elaborate pieces with simple floral or geometric designs were made, often entirely acid etched with little or no hand carving. While very little cameo glass was made in this country, a few pieces were produced by James Gillinder, Tiffany, and the Libbey Glass Company. Though some continued to be made on a limited scale into the 1900s (and until about 1920 in France), for the most part, inferior products caused a marked reduction in its manufacture by the turn of the century. Beware of new 'French' cameo glass from Romania and Taiwan. Some of it is very good and may be signed with 'old' signatures. Watch for stencil-cut designs that are 'disconnected' and segmented. Know your dealer! Our advisor for this category is Don Williams; he is listed in the Directory under Missouri. See also specific manufactures.

Key: fp — fire polished

English

Bottle, scent; lay-down, dahlias/ferns, wht on red, 6¼" **1,500.00**

Bottle, scent; lay-down, floral, wht on gr, emb silver mts, 5" **900.00**
Box, morning glories, wht on citron, rpl SP lid, 5¼" dia **685.00**
Cracker bbl, morning glories, wht on red, SP mts, 5x5" **2,000.00**
Pendant, 3 angel musicians, wht on bl opaque, gilt fr, 2" **1,100.00**
Rose bowl, floral, wht on sapphire bl, ftd, 4" **1,850.00**
Rose bowl, scroll chain, zigzag rim band, wht on citron, 3½" ..**1,600.00**
Sweetmeat, crisscross branches, wht on lt bl, 2½x6" **1,200.00**
Vase, buttercups/spear rim, wht on citron, 7½" **1,600.00**
Vase, fuchsia/elaborate borders, olive on wht w/gold, 7" **1,600.00**
Vase, geometric/floral bands, wht on med bl, 10½x5" **1,050.00**
Vase, pansies, bk: fern, red/wht on citron, stick neck, 8½" **3,400.00**
Vase, passion flower/butterfly, wht on wht-cased red, 2¼" **800.00**
Vase, thistles ea sides, wht on citron, stick neck, 2¾" **500.00**
Vase, 1 morning glory, wht on med bl, tapered, #d, 5½" **700.00**

French

Cracker bbl, grapes/leaves, gr/rose on opal/rose, sgn VS **1,000.00**
Lamp, spiked foliage, wine on red 8" shade/vase std, Riger **1,150.00**
Lamp base, berries/leaves, brn on lime, Veler, 16x7" **345.00**
Vase, cyclamen, red on amber, St Louis, 6¾x3½" **800.00**
Vase, floral, purple on frost, cylindrical, Portusot, 4" **175.00**
Vase, floral vines, red on rose/frost, Vessiere Nancy, 3¼" **300.00**
Vase, florals cascade from rim, lilac on frost, Portusot, 4" **200.00**
Vase, fuchsia, gr/pk on pk-tint opal frost, ovoid, 12" **375.00**
Vase, fuchsia, teal on frosty gold-yel, Pantin, 3½" **600.00**
Vase, horse chestnuts on pk/gr tinged frost, Weis, 5x3½" **460.00**
Vase, lg irises, rust/orange on pk to frost, Arsall, 16½" **950.00**
Vase, poppies, tan/brn on frost, sgn Arsall, 10" **500.00**
Vase, sailboats/trees, brn/orange, T Michel, stick neck, 10" **865.00**
Vase, thistles/butterfly, gr on frost, TVS&Co Pantin, 3½" **175.00**
Vase, trees/pond, cut/pnt, pillow form, Lamartine, 5x6", NM **450.00**
Vase, wild roses, violet on lav/wht, shouldered, Weis, 3½" **250.00**

Canary Ware

Canary ware was produced from the late 1700s until about the mid-19th century in the Staffordshire district of England. It was potted of yellow clay and the overglaze was yellow as well. More often than not, copper or silver lustre trim was added. Decorations were usually black-printed transfers, though occasionally hand-painted polychrome designs were also used.

Mug, Harp for Elisabeth, 2¼" **255.00**
Mug, lady & 2 children, purple transfer, 2⅛", EX **225.00**
Mug, lady w/goat, blk transfer, 2x1⅞", M **250.00**
Mug, Whip & Top for Richard, red transfer, 2½", EX **150.00**
Mug, 2 sheep, blk transfer, silver lustre top rim, NM **350.00**
Pitcher, emb Bacchus faces & vintage, mc enamel, rstr, 5¼" **325.00**
Pitcher, silver lustre resist foliage, wear, 5⅜" **300.00**
Pitcher, 3-color floral, brn striping, leaf hdl, rpr, 4½" **200.00**
Teapot, blk transfer, rprs, 19th C, 5¾" **575.00**
Teapot, emb weave-like texture, appl bl rim, rstr, child's, 4" **300.00**

Candle Holders

The earliest type of candlestick, called a pricket, was constructed with a sharp point on which the candle was impaled. The socket type, first used in the 16th century, consisted of the socket and a short stem with a wide drip pan and base. These were made from sheets of silver or other metal; not until late in the 17th century were candlesticks made by casting. By the 1700s, styles began to vary from the traditional fluted

column or baluster form and became more elaborate. A Rococo style with scrolls, shellwork, and naturalistic leaves and flowers came into vogue that afforded the individual silversmith the opportunity to exhibit his skill and artistry. The last half of the 18th century brought a return to fluted columns with neoclassic motifs. Because they were made of thin sheet silver, weighted bases were used to add stability. The Rococo styles of the Regency period were heavily encrusted with applied figures and flowers. Candelabra with six to nine branches became popular. By the Victorian era when lamps came into general use, there was less innovation and more adaptation of the earlier styles. See also Silver; Tinware; specific manufacturers.

Key: QA — Queen Anne

Bell metal, capstan type, hex base, dtd 1611, 11x7" dia, pr **650.00**
Bell metal, Queen Anne, scalloped base, 7¼" **300.00**
Brass, Ace of Diamonds, w/pushup, Victorian, 14", pr **375.00**
Brass, beehive detail, w/pushup, Victorian, 12", pr **170.00**
Brass, beehive detail, 1800s, 10¾", pr **120.00**
Brass, Diamond Princess, w/pushup, Victorian, 10¾", pr **165.00**
Brass, dmn & beehive details, pushups, 11¾", pr **200.00**
Brass, drum base, baluster stem, early, rpr, 5" **250.00**
Brass, King of Diamonds, w/pushup, Victorian, 12⅜", pr **300.00**
Brass, Louis XV style, scroll decor, 12", pr **600.00**
Brass, neoclassical, w/pushup, 10¾", pr **200.00**
Brass, octagonal base, early, 5" **165.00**
Brass, octagonal base & stem, early, 6⅞" **300.00**
Brass, Queen Anne, petal base, 18th C, 7⅞", pr **1,265.00**
Brass, Queen Anne, quatrefoil base, oversz socket, 8" **220.00**
Brass, Queen Anne, sq base, inverted corners, 6¾", pr **550.00**
Brass, Queen Anne, w/pushup, 8¼" **220.00**
Brass, Queen Anne, 1750s, 9⅞", pr **750.00**
Brass, Queen Anne style, ca 1900, 7⅝", pr **145.00**
Brass, Queen of Diamonds, w/pushup, 11⅜", pr **275.00**
Brass, rectangular base, cast finger hdl, w/pushup, 4⅝" **150.00**
Brass, saucer base w/cast hdl, w/pushup, 4x4¾" **75.00**
Brass, sq base, baluster stem, early, rprs, 5" **85.00**
Brass, sq base, baluster stem, w/pushup, 9⅜", pr **185.00**
Brass, sq base w/cut corners, early, 7⅛" **95.00**
Brass, tripod base w/paw ft, baluster stem, drip pan, 11½" **330.00**

Gilt bronze, Gothic style, electrified, ca 1870s, 26½", **$990.00** for the pair.

Bronze, exotic birds behind floral shaft, marble base, 9", pr **170.00**
Candelabra, church; brass, 18-arm, Italianate style, 60", pr **550.00**
Candelabra, Louis XVI style, gilt bronze, 4-light, 19", pr **2,600.00**
Glass, bl & wht opaque, crucifix form, 11¼" **85.00**
Glass, canary, hexagonal, made in 1 pc, 7⅝", pr **210.00**
Glass, cut/eng rock crystal w/appl ribbed vase cups, 11", pr **200.00**
Glass, Loop & Petal, canary, 7¼", EX, pr **350.00**
Glass, pressed base, free-blown deep socket & extension, 9" **140.00**
Glass, pressed 6-sided base, flint, brass collar, 11" **120.00**

Glass, wht opaque, crucifix form, flint, 11¼" 85.00
Hogscraper, brass, side pushup mk Bingham, 7¾" 220.00
Hogscraper, brass wedding band, w/pushup, lip hanger, 9", pr 900.00
Hogscraper, CI, triple brass-ringed band, w/ejector, 8½" 625.00
Hogscraper, CI, w/ejector, mk Smith, 5⅛x4" 140.00
Hogscraper, sheet steel w/worn tin plate, hanger, 6½" 95.00
Hogscraper, steel, w/pushup mk Shaw's, blk pnt, 7⅛" 145.00
Hogscraper, tin, w/pushup & lip hanger, worn pnt, 5" 127.50
Hogscraper, tin, w/pushup mk Pat 1853, lip hdl, 5⅛" 145.00
Hogscraper, wrought iron, triple wedding ring, 7¾x4⅜" 350.00
Pewter, unmk American, 7⅝", pr 185.00
Pewter, w/pushup, old rpr, 8¼", pr 125.00
Sconce, brass, lyre bk, 3 removable candle arms, 1800s, 10" 140.00
Sconce, brass w/gilt, 2-arm w/griffins, 7", pr 275.00
Sconce, bronze, 3 bird-head arms, urn/floral/masks, 24", pr 1,600.00
Sconce, sheet iron, heavy, primitive, 10½" 140.00
Sheffield silver, rnd weighted bases, unmk, 12x5⅜", pr 270.00
Ship's gimbal, sheet metal w/long curved hdl, 12" 270.00
Silver, jester holds cup in ea hand, Continental, 8", pr 825.00
Sticking tommy, wrought steel, w/match compartment, 12" 385.00
Wrought, adjustable spiral, trn wooden base, 7", EX 190.00
Wrought, trammel style, adjustable ratchet, hanging, 34" 115.00
Wrought & wood spiral w/adjust mechanism, hanger, 7⅜x3¾" .230.00

Candlewick

Candlewick crystal was made by the Imperial Glass Corporation, a division of Lenox Inc., Bellaire, Ohio. It was introduced in 1936, and though never marked except for paper labels, it is easily recognized by the beaded crystal rims, stems, and handles inspired by the tufted needlework called candlewicking, practiced by our pioneer women. During its production, more than 741 items were designed and produced. In September 1982 when Imperial closed its doors, thirty-four pieces were still being made.

Identification numbers and mold numbers used by the company help collectors recognize the various styles and shapes. Most of the pieces are from the #400 series, though other series numbers were also used. Stemware was made in eight styles — five from the #400 series made from 1941 to 1962, one from #3400 series made in 1937, another from #3800 series made in 1941, and the eighth style from the #4000 series made in 1947. In the listings that follow, some #400 items lack the mold number because that information was not found in the company files.

A few pieces have been made in color or with a gold wash. At least two lines, Valley Lily and Floral, utilized Candlewick with floral patterns cut into the crystal. These are scarce today. Other rare items include gifts such as the desk calendar made by the company for its employees and customers; the dresser set comprised of a mirror, clock, puff jar, and cologne; and the chip and dip set.

Bowl, 3-section, 10½", $30.00; Champagne, $25.00; Goblet, $25.00.

Ashtray, #400/134/1, oblong, 4½" 6.00
Ashtray, #400/172, heart form, 4½" 9.00
Ashtray, #400/652, sq, 4½" 32.50
Basket, #400/273, beaded hdl, 5" 195.00
Bottle, bitters; #400/117, w/tube, 4-oz 60.00
Bowl, #400/183, 3-ftd, 6" 60.00
Bowl, #400/205, 3-toed, 10" 135.00
Bowl, #400/51H, heart w/hand, 6" 25.00
Bowl, float; #444/75F, incurvate rim, ftd, 11" 40.00
Bowl, fruit; #400/1F, 5" 12.00
Bowl, lily; #400/74J, 4-ftd, 7" 65.00
Bowl, nappy, #400/74B, 4-ftd, 8½" 45.00
Bowl, pickle/celery; #400/57, 7½" 25.00
Bowl, relish; #400/217, oval, hdls, 10" 40.00
Butter & jam set, #400/204, 5-pc 245.00
Cake stand, #400/103D, high ft, 11" 67.50
Candle holder, #400/100, 2-light 20.00
Candle holder, #400/147, 3-light 25.00
Candle holder, #400/66C, flower form, 2-bead stem, 4½" 60.00
Candle holder, #400/86, mushroom shape 22.00
Candy box, #400/110, partitioned, w/lid, 7" 65.00
Candy box, #400/245, sq w/rnd lid, 6½" 150.00
Clock, rnd, 4" 265.00
Coaster, #400/78, 4" 6.00
Creamer, #400/18, domed ft 115.00
Creamer, #400/31, plain ft 9.00
Cup, punch; #400/211 ....7.50
Cup, tea; #400/35 ....7.50
Decanter, #400/163, w/stopper, 26-oz 295.00
Deviled egg server, #400/154, center hdl, 12" 100.00
Egg cup, #400/19, beaded ft 47.50
Fork & spoon set, #400/75 ....35.00
Ice tub, #400/168, hdls, 7" 195.00
Icer, seafood/fruit cocktail; #400/53/3, 2-pc 95.00
Knife, butter; #4000 ....250.00
Ladle, marmalade; #400/130, 3-bead stem 10.00
Lamp, hurricane; #400/79, candle base, 2-pc 120.00
Mayonnaise set, #400/52/3, tray, bowl & ladle 45.00
Mirror, rnd, standing, 4½" 95.00
Mustard jar, #400/156, w/spoon 30.00
Oil, #400/279, bulbous, hdl, 6-oz 80.00
Pitcher, #400/16, plain, 20-oz 40.00
Pitcher, #400/424, plain, 80-oz 55.00
Plate, #400/266, triangular, 7½" 85.00
Plate, #400/34, 4½" 6.00
Plate, #400/52C, crimped, hdls, 6¾" 25.00
Plate, #400/62D, hdls, 8½" 12.00
Plate, #400/72E, upturned sides, hdls, 10" 22.50
Plate, canape; #400/35, off-center indent, 6" 11.00
Plate, serving; #400/92V, cupped edge, 13½" 37.50
Plate, torte; #400/20D, 17" 45.00
Punch set, #400/20, bowl on base+12 cups & ladle 235.00
Sauce boat liner, #400/169 ....35.00
Shakers, #400/109, ind, pr 10.00
Shakers, #400/96, bulbous, beaded ft, chrome tops, pr 15.00
Stem, brandy; #3800 ....27.50
Stem, champagne/sherbet; #3800, 6-oz 25.00
Stem, cocktail; #3400, 4-oz 14.00
Stem, cocktail; #400/190, 4-oz 18.00
Stem, parfait; #3400, 6-oz 50.00
Stem, water; #400/190, 10-oz 18.00
Sugar bowl, #400/18, domed ft 115.00
Tidbit server, #400/2701, cupped, 2-tier 45.00
Tray, lemon; #400/221, center hdl, 5½" 30.00

Tumbler, #3400, ftd, 12-oz **16.00**
Tumbler, #3800, 9-oz **25.00**
Tumbler, #400/19, 12-oz **22.00**
Tumbler, sherbet; #400/18, 6-oz **40.00**
Tumbler, water; #400/18, 9-oz **40.00**
Vase, #400/198, 6" dia **195.00**
Vase, #400/22, str sides, beaded ft, 10" **150.00**
Vase, #400/27, incurvate rim, beaded ft, 8½" **125.00**
Vase, #400/87 R, rolled rim, beaded hdls, 7" **35.00**
Vase, mini bud; #400/107, beaded ft, 5¾" **40.00**

Candy Containers

Figural glass candy containers were first created in 1876 when ingenious candy manufacturers began to use them to package their products. Two of the first containers, the Liberty Bell and Independence Hall, were distributed for our country's centennial celebration. Children found these toys appealing, and an industry was launched that lasted into the mid-1960s.

Figural candy containers include animals, comic characters, guns, telephones, transportation vehicles, household appliances, and many other intriguing designs. The oldest (those made prior to 1920) were usually hand painted and often contained extra metal parts in addition to the metal strip or screw closures. During the 1950s these metal parts were replaced with plastic, a practice that continued until candy containers met their demise in the 1960s. While predominately clear, they are found in nearly all colors of glass including milk glass, green, amber, pink, emerald, cobalt, ruby flashed, and light blue. Usually the color was intentional, but leftover glass was used as well and resulted in unplanned colors. Various examples are found in light or ice blue, and new finds are always being discovered. Production of the glass portion of candy containers was centered around the western Pennsylvania city of Jeannette. Major producers include Westmoreland Glass, West Bros., Victory Glass, J.H. Millstein, J.C. Crosetti, L.E. Smith, Jack Stough, and T.H. Stough. While 90% of all glass candies were made in the Jeannette area, other companies such as Eagle Glass, Play Toy, and Geo. Borgfeldt Co. have a few to their credit as well.

Buyer beware! Many candy containers have been reproduced. Some, including the Camera and the Rabbit Pushing Wheelbarrow, come already painted from distributors. Others may have a slick or oily feel to the touch. The following list may also alert you to possible reproductions:

E&A #149/L #12 Chicken on Nest

E&A #184/L #17 Scottie Dog (repro has a ice-like color and is often slick and oily)

E&A #180/L #24 Dog (clear and cobalt)

E&A #566/L #37, Owl (original in clear only, often painted. Repro found in clear, blue, green and pink with a higher threaded base and less detail)

E&A #539/L #38 Mule and Waterwagon (original marked Jeannette, PA)

E&A #601/L #47 Rabbit Pushing Wheelbarrow (eggs are speckled on the repro; solid on the original)

E&A #618/L #55 Peter Rabbit

E&A #651/L #58 Rocking Horse (original in clear only)

E&A #342/L #76 Independence Hall (original is rectangular; repro has offset base with red felt-lined closure)

E&A #137/L #83 Charlie Chaplin (original has 'Geo. Borgfeldt' on base; reproduction comes in pink and blue)

E&A #208/L #89 Happifats on Drum (no notches on repro for closure to hook into)

E&A #345/L #90 Jackie Coogan (marked inside 'B')

E&A #349/L #91 Kewpie (must have Geo. Borgfeldt on base to be original)

E&A #546/L #94 Naked Child

E&A #674/L #103 Santa (original has plastic head; repro is all glass and opens at bottom)

E&A #162/L #114 Mantel Clock (originally in ruby flashed, milk glass, clear and frosted only)

#144 Amber Pistol (first sold full in the 1970s, not listed in E&A)

E&A #303/L #168 Uncle Sam's Hat

E&A #111/L #233 Santa's Boot

E&A #121/L #238 Camera (original says 'Pat Apld For' on bottom, (reproduction says 'B. Shakman' or is ground off)

E&A #132/L #242 Carpet Sweeper (currently being sold with no metal parts)

E&A #133/L #243 Carpet Sweeper (currently being sold with no metal parts)

E&A #177/L #246 Display Case

E&A #521/L #254 Mailbox

E&A #543/L #255 Drum Mug

E&A #661/L #268 Safe (original in clear, ruby flashed, and milk glass only)

E&A #577/L #289 Piano (original in only clear and milk glass, both painted)

E&A #60/L #356 Auto

E&A #33/L #377 Auto

E&A #56/L #378 Station Wagon

E&A #213/L #386 Fire Engine

Others are possible. If in doubt, don't buy without a guarantee from the dealer and a return privilege in writing.

Our advisor for glass containers is Jeff Bradfield; he is listed in the Directory under Virginia. You may contact him with questions, if you will include an SASE. See Clubs, Newsletters, and Catalogs for the address of the Candy Container Collectors of America. A bimonthly newsletter offers insight into new finds, reproductions, updates, and articles from over four hundred collectors and members, including all authors of books on candy containers. Advise on papier-mache and composition candy containers comes from Jenny Tarrant; she is listed in the Directory under Maryland.

'L' numbers used in this guide refer to a standard reference series, *An Album of Candy Containers*, Vols 1 and 2, by Jennie Long. 'E&A' numbers correlate with *The Compleat American Glass Candy Containers Handbook* by Eikelberner and Agadjanian, revised by Adele Bowden. Values are given for undamaged examples with original paint and metal parts when applicable or unless noted otherwise. Repaired pieces (often repainted) are worth only a small fraction of one that is perfect. The symbol (+) at the end of some of the following lines was used to indicate items that have been reproduced. See also Christmas; Halloween.

Acorn, L #221 ....**375.00**
Airplane, Army Bomber, w/paper label prop, L #328 (E&A #6) ..**32.00**
Airplane, P-51; L #327 (E&A #5) **45.00**
Amos & Andy, G pnt, L #77 (E&A #21) **450.00**
Auto w/Tassels #2, L #361 (E&A #64) **150.00**
Auto w/Tassels #3, L #362 (E&A #39) **175.00**
Baby Dear Bottle, L #64 (E&A #555) **20.00**
Barney Google by Barrel, L #79 (E&A #71) **700.00**
Baseball Player w/Glove, L #81 (E&A #78) **800.00**
Battleship, L #337 (E&A #97) **25.00**
Battleship on Waves, L #335 (E&A #96) **175.00**
Bear in Auto, L #2 (E&A #84) **175.00**
Bear on Circus Tub, orig blades, L #1 (E&A #83) **375.00**
Bird Cage, L #230 (E&A #94) **225.00**
Black Cat for Luck, L #4 (E&A #136-1) **800.00**
Boat, w/photograph, L #594 ....**115.00**
Bottle, Round Nurser; L #70 (E&A #549) **25.00**
Boy Wearing Cap (Kayo), L #522 ....**30.00**

Bulldog, screw-on closure, G pnt, L #15 (E&A #189) 55.00
Bureau, G pnt, L #125 (E&A #112) 200.00
Bus, Rapid Transit; no pnt, L #345 (E&A #116) 550.00
Bus, San Francisco-New York, L #346 (E&A #118) 300.00
Candelabrum, L #202 (E&A #174-1) 50.00
Cannon, cobalt bbl, rpl carriage, L #534 (E&A #122) 300.00
Cannon, Rapid Fire, L #143 (E&A #129) 335.00
Cannon, sm bbl, orig carriage, L #535 ....600.00
Car, Electric Coupe #2, closure, L #356 (E&A #47) (+) 60.00

Coupe with Long Hood #1, L #359 (E&A #51), 5¼", $110.00.

Cat, glass head, L #470 ....15.00
Chick in Eggshell Auto, G pnt, L #7 (E&A #144) 350.00
Chicken on Oblong Basket, closure, gr, L #10 (E&A #147) 45.00
Circus Dog w/Hat, L #478 ....30.00
Coal Car w/Tender, orig closure, L #402 (E&A #170) 300.00
Darner, Amster, L #245 ....90.00
Dirigible, Los Angeles, L #322 (E&A #176) 175.00
Dog, Mutt, L #20 (E&A #194) 55.00
Dog, Poodle; glass head, L #471 ....15.00
Dog by Barrel, orig pnt & closure, L #13 (E&A #190) 225.00
Dog w/Top Hat, L #480 ....32.00
Dog w/Umbrella, L #19 (E&A #194-2) 30.00
Dolly's Bathtub, L #226 (E&A #82) 2,500.00
Don't Park Here, L #314 (E&A #196) 200.00
Esther Coach, all orig, L #397 (E&A #165) 400.00
Fannie Farmer, cowboy, L #528 ....150.00
Felix on Pedestal, L #87 (E&A #211-1) 3,000.00
Fire Engine, Little Boiler, L #383 (E&A #217) 75.00
Flatiron, orig pnt, no closure, L #249 (E&A #344) 325.00
Flatiron, orig pnt & closure, L #249 (E&A #344) 385.00
Flossie Fisher Side Board, L #130 (E&A #237) 700.00
Frog, milk glass, L #36 (E&A #238) 825.00
Gun, cork closure, L #540 ....25.00
Gun, Indian head, L #539 (E&A #254) 85.00
Gun, Millstein's, plastic, L #154 (E&A #261) 45.00
Gun, Victory Glass Co, L #149 (E&A #255) 35.00
Horn, Stough's Musical Toy #1, L #283 (E&A #310) 20.00
Horn, 3-valve, w/mouthpiece, L #281 (E&A #312) 175.00
House of Glass, L #75 (E&A #324) 175.00
Ice Truck, all orig, L #458 (E&A #784) 700.00
Iron, Electric; w/cord & plug, L #248 (E&A #343) 50.00
Jack-o'-lantern, str eyes, L #160 (E&A #347) 200.00
Jeep Scout Car, L #390 (E&A #350) 35.00
Kewpie By Barrel, L #91 (E&A #359) (+) 125.00
Lamp, Hobnail, orig shade, L #209 (E&A #365) 175.00
Lamp, Hurricane; mini, L #211 (E&A #366) 75.00
Lantern, barn type #1, L #177 (E&A #426) 75.00
Lantern, beveled glass w/gilt & ruby stain, L #175 (E&A #396) ...85.00
Lantern, domed closure, L #576 ....45.00
Lantern, glass reflector, L #185 ....30.00
Lantern, high base, L #189 ....30.00

Lantern, magnifying lens, L #176 (E&A #438) 115.00
Lantern, oval panels, L #570 ....35.00
Library Lamp, orig fringe, L #207 (E&A #372) 500.00
Locomotive, Little Gem, L #587 (E&A #474) 500.00
Locomotive, rectangle windows, w/closure, L #413 (E&A #496) .85.00
Locomotive 888, man in window, L #419 (E&A #486) 175.00
Lucky Lindy Candy Air Mail, L #666 ....300.00
Mantel Clock #1, w/paper face, L #115 (E&A #164) 150.00
Model Cruiser, orig closure, L #339 (E&A #98) 22.00
Mr Rabbit w/Hat, no pnt, L #39 (E&A #610) 1,100.00
Mug, screw cap, L #257 (E&A 542) 20.00
Naked Child, Kewpie type, L #93 (E&A #545) 65.00
Naked Child, Victory Glass, L #94 (E&A #546) 40.00
Opera Glass, brass fr, L #260 (E&A #559) 125.00
Pencil, paper label, L #263 (E&A #567) 65.00
Pocket Watch, 'Jeannette' on paper face, L #457 (E&A #825) ..400.00
Powder Horn, L #265 (E&A #589) 40.00
Pumpkin Head Policeman, L #163 (E&A #592) 825.00
Puss in Boots, L #468 ....85.00
Rabbit Family, G pnt, L #43 (E&A #604) 825.00
Rabbit in Eggshell, gold pnt, L #48 (E&A #608) 75.00
Rabbit Pushing Cart, G pnt, L #44 (E&A #602) 285.00
Rabbit w/Collar, G pnt, L #51 (E&A #612) 100.00
Rabbit w/Layed-Back Ears, EX pnt, L #40 (E&A #616) 100.00
Radio, orig closure, G pnt, L #290 (E&A #643) 125.00
Santa Claus, banded coat, L #97 (E&A #669) 215.00
Santa Claus w/Double Cuff, L #101 (E&A #671) 115.00
Sedan, 4-door, orig tin wheels, no pnt, L #370 (E&A #57) 85.00
Soldier on Monument, L #107 (E&A #682) 825.00
Tank, 2 guns, L #438 (E&A #723) 30.00
Telephone, lg glass receiver, bl glass, L #580 (E&A #754) 80.00
Telephone, Victory Glass #6, L #303 (E&A #738) 45.00
Truck, Bakery; L #605 (E&A #782) 700.00
Trunk, L #218 (E&A #789) 90.00
Turkey, L #61 (E&A #790) 135.00
Ugly Duckling, left, L #28 (E&A #199) 150.00
Uncle Sam by Barrel, L #112 (E&A #801) 400.00
Wagon, tin, L #442 (E&A #820) 150.00
Watch w/Fob, complete w/fob, L #122 (E&A #823) 350.00
Watch w/Fob, watch only, L #122 (E&A #823) 200.00
Windmill, pewter top, all orig, L #443 (E&A #840) 450.00
Witch's Kettle, L #629 ....25.00
World Globe, tin, L #275 ....45.00

Papier-Mache, Composition

Chick, mc pnt, wire legs, on cb drum, Germany, 1900s, 5" 150.00
Chinaman sitting on log, Germany, 4" 165.00
Dog, wht rabbit fur, glass eyes, head removes, 9" 350.00
Football player, jtd limbs, wooden base, lt wear, 8½" 465.00
Gnome, compo face, cotton clothes, Germany, 3¾" 140.00
Hen on nest, Drake Process...1924...FN Burt, 6½", EX 55.00
Rabbit, appl eyes, Germany, 7¾", VG 325.00
Rabbit, upright, wht plaster ext, glass eyes, red tie, 8" 145.00
Rabbit pulling wooden cart w/cb wheels, 8½" L, NM 200.00
Stump w/cherries, leaves & hatchet, 4¼", VG 85.00
Turkey, baked; EX 60.00
Turkey, compo, hair waddle, head removes, Germany, 7½" 225.00

Canes

Fancy canes and walking sticks were once the mark of a gentleman. Hand-carved examples are collected and admired as folk art from the past. The glass canes that never could have been practical are unique whimseys of the glass-blower's profession. Gadget and container sticks, which were produced in a wide variety, are highly desirable. Character, political, and novelty types are also sought after as are those with handles made of precious metals.

For more information we recommend *American Folk Art Canes, Personal Sculpture,* by George H. Meyer, Sandringham Press, 100 West Long Lake Rd., Suite 100, Bloomfield Hills, MI 48304. Other possible references are *Canes in the United States* by Catherine Dike and *Canes From the 17th – 20th Century* by Jeffrey Snyder. Our advisor for this category is Bruce Thalberg.

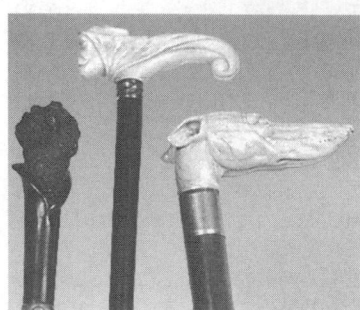

Carved and ebonized handle in form of French poodle on rosewood shaft with metal collar and horn tip, $400.00; Carved ivory handle in form of Middle-Eastern man's head, silver collar, $400.00; Carved ivory handle in form of greyhound's head, metal collar, horn tip, $500.00.

Alligator holding Blk boy, cvd horn/wood hdl 1,600.00
Bamboo, cvd screaming ape hdl, sgn Brigg, 1-pc, late 1800s 450.00
Blk man's head of Meissen porc on palisander shaft 1,300.00
Breech-load gun curio, pnt metal, Belgium, ca 1890, 34" 750.00
Cigarette case inside bamboo shaft, Pat Aug 23 '87, 1890s 650.00
Civil war symbols in overall cvgs, sgn DR Fogle 1,815.00
Cvd hunting themes along shaft, bent hdl, metal tip, 36" 675.00
Cvd military figures & Am flag along w/deer/goat/etc, 36" 775.00
Ebony folk-cvd Blk man hdl w/glass eyes, 1-pc, 1880s, 33" 800.00
Ebony shaft w/wht metal ferrule, sterling Tiffany eagle hdl 2,250.00
Folk art, cvd Indian heads/flowers/eagles/etc, 38" 225.00
Hazelnut shaft w/cvd/pnt parrot hdl, sterling collar, 1900s 350.00
Ivory fist & ball finial on ebonized hardwood shaft, 1880s 500.00
Mahog shaft, cvd whale ivory Naughty Nellie leg hdl, 35", VG ...350.00
Polychromed (exceptional) cvd circus type w/multiple figures .11,000.00
Porc hdl w/HP scene, ivorene mts, hardwood shaft, 1900s 450.00
Rosewood shaft w/pnt porc ball finial, gilt mts, 1920s 425.00
Rosewood w/whale ivory tortoise-inlay hdl, 33" 150.00
Spitting Chinaman silver hdl, working, bamboo shaft, 1890s .3,200.00
Stiletto in partridge wood shaft, cvd ivory 7" hdl, 1850s 600.00
Triple-fold traveling, mahog w/marquetry inlay, 1870s 475.00
Tropical Island wood w/cvd ivory eagle head, 33" 250.00
Walnut shaft w/sterling hdl w/repousse roses, 1910s, 36" 650.00
Whalebone, cvd/inlaid w/baleen & MOP geometrics, 1800s, EX .2,450.00
Whalebone shaft w/cvd walrus ivory clenched-fist hdl, 32", EX ..650.00
Whalebone w/walrus ivory hdl, baleen separators, 35", EX 350.00
Wood w/faceted whale ivory hdl w/silver inlay at top, 36" 300.00
Wood w/ivory, Blk man's head finial, hidden sword, rare 1,100.00
Zebra wood, sterling rabbit hdl w/1894 London hallmks, G 600.00
3-draw telescope in hardwood shaft, brass ferrule, 1860s, EX ..1,000.00

Canton

Canton is a blue and white porcelain that was first exported in the 1790s by clipper ships from China to the United States, a practice that continued into the 1920s. Canton became very popular along the East Coast where the major ports were located. Its popularity was due to several factors: it was readily available, inexpensive, and (due to the fact that it came in many different forms) appealing to the housewife.

The porcelain's blue and white color and simple motif (teahouse, trees, bridge, and a rain-cloud border) have made it a favorite of people who collect early American furniture and accessories. Buyers of Canton should shop at large outdoor shows and up-scale antique shows. Collections are regularly sold at auction. Collectors usually prefer a rich, deep tone rather than a lighter blue. Cracks, large chips, and major repairs will substantially affect values. Prices of Canton have escalated sharply over the last twenty years, and rare forms are highly sought after by advanced collectors. Our advisor for this category is Hobart D. Van Deusen; he is listed in the Directory under Connecticut.

Bowl, fruit; rtcl sides, oval, 10" L, +underplate 925.00
Bowl, salad; 19th C, 9¾" 865.00
Bowl, vegetable; rectangular, 8¾" 330.00
Bowl, 2x11", NM 400.00
Bowl, 4½x10¼" 1,000.00
Box, rectangular, 3x7x3¾" 1,200.00
Candlesticks, 8", EX, pr 2,800.00
Mug, twisted hdl, 4¼x3¾" 600.00
Plate, 8¾" 100.00
Platter, hairline, 19¼" 545.00
Platter, octagonal, orig insert, 17x14" 1,100.00
Platter, octagonal, 17x14" 690.00
Shrimp dish, glaze flaws, 9¼x10¼" 700.00
Teapot, sq, 4", EX+ 1,500.00
Teapot, tapered cylinder, Xd branch hdl, fruit finial, 5" 750.00
Undertray, rtcl rim, 11", NM 315.00

Capo-Di-Monte

Established in 1743 near Naples and sponsored by Charles II, who was King of Naples at that time, Capo-Di-Monte produced soft-paste porcelain figurines and dinnerware usually marked with a 'crown over N' device, though a fleur-de-lis was used on occasion. The factory was closed throughout the 1760s but reopened in 1771 in the city of Naples. There both hard- and soft-paste porcelains were made, sometimes decorated with applied florals in high relief. Their technique as well as their marks were blatantly copied. As a result, this type of encrusted decoration is often referred to today as Capo-Di-Monte. The original factory closed in 1821. Some of their molds were purchased by the Docceia Porcelain factory in Florence which continues to operate to the present time. Most examples on the market today are of fairly recent manufacture. Capo-Di-Monte type wares have been made in Hungary and Germany as well as France and Italy. Many of these pieces continue to bear the 'crown over N' gold stamp. As more collectors recognize and appreciate the quality of the older ware, buyer demand drives prices higher.

Box, cherubs ride goat in landscape, quatrefoil shape, 4" 145.00
Box, cupids engaged in various activities, 4x7x7" 200.00
Box, people in landscape, oval, hinged, late, ½x3½" 75.00
Box, warriors & mythological reserves, hinged dome lid, 10" ..1,200.00
Cup & saucer, demitasse; harvesting scene, late 22.00
Figurine, Chestnut Vendor, Armani, 10" 265.00
Figurine, girl arranges ponytail, sgn, on wood base, 7½" 50.00
Figurine, man holds bag w/shell & pearl, Bonalberti, 10x8" 265.00
Figurine, Pan, seated on plinth w/emb bat's head, w/gold, 8½" ..300.00
Plate, floral center, cherubs border, late, 10" 75.00
Tazza, shaped rim, crest, mermaids as support, 5" 350.00
Tray, floral sprays in center, scroll & floral rim, 14" 225.00
Urn, ladies & floral swags, w/lid & hdls, late, 9" 85.00
Urn, Roman bath scenes, ornate scroll hdls, w/lid, 13", pr 800.00
Vase, figures/florals, slim/ftd, w/lid, late, 15" 150.00

Carlton Ware

Carlton Ware was the product of Wiltshaw and Robinson, who operated in the Staffordshire district of England from about 1890. During the 1920s, they produced ornamental ware with enameled and gilded decorations such as flowers and birds, often on a black background. In 1958 the firm was renamed Carlton Ware Ltd. Their trademark was a crown over a circular stamp with 'W & R, Stoke on Trent' surrounding a swallow. 'Carlton Ware' was sometimes added by hand.

Ashtray, Deco-shaped, card suits, set of 4 ....125.00
Coffeepot, Royal Rouge, pagoda scenic, 7¾" 375.00
Creamer & sugar bowl, foxglove on gr 55.00
Creamer & sugar bowl, Nautilus, Rouge Royale, gold trim 95.00
Jam pot, Foxglove on gr 45.00
Tray, maple leaf, 10" 195.00
Vase, birds & flowers, mc w/gold on maroon lustre, label, 7" 240.00
Vase, Deco geometric floral on peacock ground, 10x7½" 950.00
Vase, lg open bl/tan blossoms on pk & cream, 8x9" 200.00
Vase, Oriental scene, mc & gold on cobalt, 3½x2½" 75.00

Carnival Collectibles

Carnival items from the early part of this century represent the lighter side of an America that was alternately prospering and sophisticated or devastated by war and domestic conflict. But whatever the country's condition, the carnival's thrilling rides and shooting galleries were a sure way of letting it all go by — at least for an evening.

For further information on chalkware figures, we recommend *The Carnival Chalk Prize* by Thomas G. Morris, who is listed in the Directory under Oregon. Our advisors for shooting gallery targets are Richard and Valerie Tucker; their address is listed in the Directory under Texas.

Baseball toss figure, Boston player, pnt wood, 75", EX 3,000.00
Baseball toss figure, kicking donkey, canvas/wood, 1920s, 62" ..1,200.00
Baseball toss figure, lady, pnt wood, ca 1915, 53", EX 1,000.00

Chalkware figure, Sugar, JY Jenkins, 1948, 13", NM, $120.00.

Chalkware figure, Air Raid Warden w/flag, 1940s, 14" 75.00
Chalkware figure, Alice the Goon, 1930s, 10" 120.00
Chalkware figure, Amos & Andy, 1930s, 12", pr 300.00
Chalkware figure, Apache Dancer, 1940s, 13" 45.00
Chalkware figure, Bathing Beauty, HP, 1920s, 12" 95.00
Chalkware figure, Bellhop, mk Rainwater, 1936, 14½" 95.00
Chalkware figure, Betty Boop, 1930-40, 14½" 265.00
Chalkware figure, Charlie McCarthy, 1930s, 9½" 55.00
Chalkware figure, cowboy ashtray, 1930-40, 8¼" 35.00

Chalkware figure, El Matador, mk 1939, 14" 95.00
Chalkware figure, girl in horseshoe, 1947, 10½" 75.00
Chalkware figure, girl sits w/flower, HP, '20s, 11" 120.00
Chalkware figure, girl w/goat, 1930s, 9½" 45.00
Chalkware figure, Hollywood Actress, 1930s, 11½" 65.00
Chalkware figure, Indian w/drum, KC Art Statuary, 1940s, 13" ...55.00
Chalkware figure, Jackie Coogan, My Boy, 1930s, 17" 165.00
Chalkware figure, Little Egypt, 1915-20, rare, 14½" 220.00
Chalkware figure, Little Mail Boy, 1940s, 7" 25.00
Chalkware figure, Mae West, mk Jenkins, 1934, 13" 100.00
Chalkware figure, Maggie & Jiggs, 1930s, 11½" 250.00
Chalkware figure, Pluto, 1930s, 6" 30.00
Chalkware figure, Popeye w/pipe, 1930s, 21" 120.00
Chalkware figure, Tom & Jerry, 1939, 8½" 45.00
Chalkware figure, Uncle Scrooge, 1940s, 8" 35.00
Chalkware figure, US Soldier, Jenkins, 1942, 13" 95.00
Chalkware figure, Wimpy, 1930s, 8" 45.00
Chalkware figure, 3 Little Pigs, 1930s-50s, 5x5½" 20.00
Game, Bean Toss, folky Blk man in bbl, 45x22" 900.00
Shooting gallery target, animal, CI, Evans, about 5" W, ea 125.00
Shooting gallery target, battleship, wht pnt, 11½" 175.00
Shooting gallery target, bird, CI, pnt traces, 4¼" 75.00
Shooting gallery target, card suit, pnt CI, Terpening, 13", ea ..2,000.00
Shooting gallery target, clown w/hat, turnover, CI, Evans, 14" ..800.00
Shooting gallery target, clown w/mask, pnt CI, Evans, 21" 7,500.00
Shooting gallery target, dog running, pnt CI, Hoffman, 30" W ..2,500.00
Shooting gallery target, duck, CI, 5½" 70.00
Shooting gallery target, gorilla, pnt CI, HC Evans, 13" 750.00
Shooting gallery target, Hitler head, CI, orig pnt, 10½" 425.00
Shooting gallery target, jumping lion, CI, 1900s, 11x7" 195.00
Shooting gallery target, moose, CI, bl pnt, 7x5x¼" 95.00
Shooting gallery target, rabbit, CI, rusted red pnt, 4½" 90.00
Shooting gallery target, rooster, CI, pnt traces 88.00
Shooting gallery target, rooster w/star, pnt CI, 14" 3,200.00
Shooting gallery target, squirrel, wht pnt, HC Evans, 7¾" 75.00
Shooting gallery target, Tom turkey, CI, mk Evans, 7" 175.00
Shooting gallery target, WWI soldier w/rifle, wht pnt, 7½" 145.00

Carnival Glass

Carnival glass is pressed glass that has been coated with a sodium solution and fired to give it an exterior lustre. First made in America in 1905, it was produced until the late 1920s and had great popularity in the average American household; for unlike the costly art glass produced by Tiffany, carnival glass could be mass produced at a small cost. Colors most found are marigold, green, blue, and purple; but others exist in lesser quantities and include white, clear, red, aqua opalescent, peach opalescent, ice blue, ice green, amber, lavender, and smoke.

Companies mainly responsible for its production in America include the Fenton Art Glass Company, Williamstown, West Virginia; the Northwood Glass Company, Wheeling, West Virginia; the Imperial Glass Company, Bellaire, Ohio; the Millersburg Glass Company, Millersburg, Ohio; and the Dugan Glass Company (Diamond Glass), Indiana, Pennsylvania. In addition to these major manufacturers, lesser producers included the U.S. Glass Company, the Cambridge Glass Company, the Westmoreland Glass Company, and the McKee Glass Company.

Carnival glass has been highly collectible since the 1950s and has been reproduced for the last twenty-five years. Several national and state collectors' organizations exist, and many fine books are available on old carnival glass, including *The Standard Encyclopedia of Carnival Glass* by Bill Edwards.

Acanthus (Imperial), plate, marigold, 10" 200.00

Acorn (Fenton), bowl, peach opal, 7-8½" **290.00**
Acorn (Millersburg), compote, gr, rare **1,900.00**
Acorn & File, compote, vaseline, ftd, rare **1,500.00**
Acorn Burrs (Northwood), butter dish, gr, w/lid **950.00**

Acorn Burrs (Northwood), pitcher, amethyst, water size, $600.00.

Acorn Burrs (Northwood), punch bowl & base, marigold **550.00**
African Shield (English), toothpick holder, marigold **115.00**
Amaryllis (Northwood), compote, wht, sm **450.00**
Apple & Pear Intaglio (Northwood), bowl, marigold, 5" **60.00**
Apple Blossom Twigs (Dugan), bowl, amethyst **165.00**
Apple Blossom Twigs (Dugan), plate, bl **200.00**
Apple Blossoms (Dugan), bowl, gr, 7½" **70.00**
April Showers (Fenton), vase, amethyst **110.00**
Arcadia Baskets, plate, marigold, 8" **50.00**
Arched Fleur-De-Lis (Higbee), mug, marigold, rare **250.00**
Asters, compote, marigold **90.00**
Aurora Pearls, bowl, marigold, decor, 2 szs, ea **400.00**
Autumn Acorns (Fenton), bowl, vaseline, 8¼" **220.00**
Aztec (McKee), pitcher, marigold, rare **1,300.00**
Aztec (McKee), sugar bowl, marigold **250.00**
Baker's Rosette, ornament, marigold **75.00**
Balloons (Imperial), perfume atomizer, marigold **60.00**
Balloons (Imperial), plate, cake; smoke **110.00**
Bamboo Bird, jar, marigold, complete **800.00**
Banded Diamonds (Crystal), bowl, marigold, 10" **100.00**
Banded Diamonds (Crystal), pitcher, water; marigold, rare **900.00**
Banded Diamonds & Bars, tumbler, marigold, rare **550.00**
Banded Grape (Fenton), pitcher, water; gr **500.00**
Banded Rib, pitcher, marigold **125.00**
Basketweave (Fenton), bowl, bl, open edge, 5" **50.00**
Basketweave (Fenton), plate, bl, open edge, 10" **1,600.00**
Beaded Acanthus (Imperial), pitcher, milk; gr **260.00**
Beaded Band & Octagon, lamp, kerosene; marigold **250.00**
Beaded Cable (Northwood), candy dish, gr **80.00**
Beaded Hearts (Northwood), bowl, gr **90.00**
Beaded Panels (Imperial), bowl, marigold, 8" **45.00**
Beaded Shell (Dugan), butter dish, amethyst, w/lid **150.00**
Beaded Shell (Dugan), tumbler, marigold **60.00**
Beaded Spears (Crystal), tumbler, amethyst, rare **200.00**
Bells & Beads (Dugan), gravy boat, peach opal, hdld **140.00**
Bells & Beads (Dugan), nappy, marigold **60.00**
Birds & Cherries (Fenton), bonbon, amethyst **65.00**
Birds & Cherries (Fenton), bowl, bl, rare, 9½" **375.00**
Blackberry, Miniature (Fenton), compote, marigold, sm **125.00**
Blackberry (Fenton), plate, bl, rare **400.00**
Blackberry (Fenton), vase, whimsey; marigold, rare **750.00**
Blackberry Banded (Fenton), hat, bl **45.00**
Blackberry Spray (Fenton), compote, bl **50.00**
Blackberry Wreath (Millersburg), bowl, gr, 7-9" **90.00**
Blackberry Wreath (Millersburg), bowl, ice cream; marigold, 10" ...**100.00**

Blocks & Arches (Crystal), tumbler, marigold, rare **75.00**
Blossoms & Band (Imperial), bowl, amethyst, 5" **30.00**
Border Plants (Dugan), bowl, amethyst, flat, 8½" **125.00**
Boutonniere (Millersburg), compote, marigold **280.00**
Broken Arches (Imperial), punch bowl, marigold, w/base **365.00**
Brooklyn Bridge (Dugan), bowl, marigold, rare **350.00**
Bull's Eye (US Glass), lamp, oil; marigold **210.00**
Bull's Eye & Loop (Millersburg), vase, marigold, 7-11" **400.00**
Bumblebees, hatpin, amethyst **70.00**
Butterflies (Fenton), bonbon, gr **75.00**
Butterflies (Fenton), card tray, marigold **55.00**
Butterflies & Bells (Crystal), compote, marigold **220.00**
Butterflies & Waratah (Crystal), compote, amethyst, lg **300.00**
Butterfly (Northwood), bonbon, marigold, regular **65.00**
Butterfly (US Glass), tumbler, gr, rare **6,000.00**
Butterfly & Berry (Fenton), bowl, gr, ftd, 10" **250.00**
Butterfly & Berry (Fenton), bowl, whimsey; marigold **850.00**
Butterfly & Berry (Fenton), creamer, bl, w/lid **170.00**
Butterfly & Berry (Fenton), hatpin holder, marigold, rare **1,200.00**
Butterfly & Berry (Fenton), plate, whimsey; bl, ftd **1,500.00**
Butterfly & Berry (Fenton), sugar bowl, gr, w/lid **200.00**
Butterfly & Fern (Fenton), pitcher, amethyst **575.00**
Butterfly Bower (Crystal), compote, marigold **115.00**
Buttons & Daisy (Imperial), hat, clambroth, old only **70.00**
Buzz Saw (Cambridge), cruet, marigold, rare, lg, 6" **550.00**
Cane & Daisy Cut (Jenkins), vase, marigold **150.00**
Cane & Scroll (Sea Thistle), creamer, marigold **45.00**
Capitol (Westmoreland), mug, marigold, sm **140.00**
Captive Rose (Fenton), plate, gr, 9" **500.00**
Carnival Honeycomb (Imperial), bonbon, gr **60.00**
Carnival Honeycomb (Imperial), sugar bowl, marigold **35.00**
Caroline (Dugan), banana bowl, peach opal **210.00**
Cartwheel #411 (Heisey), goblet, marigold **75.00**
Cathedral (Sweden), bowl, marigold, 10" **50.00**
Cathedral (Sweden), pitcher, bl, rare **3,700.00**
Chain & Star (Fostoria), tumbler, marigold, rare **900.00**
Chatelaine (Imperial), pitcher, amethyst, rare **3,700.00**
Checkerboard (Westmoreland), cruet, clear, rare **750.00**
Checkerboard (Westmoreland), wine, marigold, rare **295.00**
Cherry (Dugan), bowl, amethyst, ftd, 8½" **310.00**
Cherry (Dugan), bowl, marigold, flat, 5" **40.00**
Cherry (Millersburg), bowl, bl, 4" **1,100.00**
Cherry (Millersburg), bowl, gr, rare, 7" **130.00**
Cherry (Millersburg), bowl, ice cream; amethyst, 10" **375.00**
Cherry (Millersburg), butter dish, marigold, w/lid **250.00**
Cherry (Millersburg), compote, gr, rare, lg **1,600.00**
Cherry (Millersburg), tumbler, marigold, 2 styles, ea **145.00**
Cherry Chain (Fenton), bonbon, marigold **50.00**
Cherry Chain (Fenton), plate, bl, 7"-9" **140.00**
Cherry Smash (US Glass), tumbler, marigold **190.00**
Chippendale Souvenir, creamer, amethyst **80.00**
Chrysanthemum (Fenton), bowl, bl, flat, 9" **80.00**
Circle Scroll (Dugan), bowl, amethyst, 5" **45.00**
Circle Scroll (Dugan), hat, marigold, rare **60.00**
Cobblestones (Dugan), bowl, amethyst, 5" **80.00**
Cobblestones (Imperial), bonbon, marigold **45.00**
Coin Dot (Fenton), tumbler, gr, rare **265.00**
Coin Dot VT (Westmoreland), bowl, gr **70.00**
Coin Dot VT (Westmoreland), compote, marigold **60.00**
Colonial (Imperial), creamer, marigold, open **47.00**
Columbia (Imperial), vase, gr **50.00**
Columbus, plate, marigold, 8" **45.00**
Concave Diamond, tumbler, vaseline **190.00**
Corinth (Dugan), bowl, peach opal, 9" **200.00**

Cosmos & Cane, compote, marigold, rare, tall 350.00
Cosmos & Cane, pitcher, marigold, rare 750.00
Cosmos & Cane, rose bowl, whimsey; marigold 1,700.00
Cosmos VT (Fenton), bowl, bl, 9-10" 75.00
Country Kitchen (Millersburg), butter dish, marigold 650.00
Country Kitchen (Millersburg), creamer, vaseline 900.00
Crab Claw (Imperial), bowl, fruit; marigold, w/base 110.00
Crab Claw (Imperial), bowl, gr, 5" 40.00
Crab Claw (Imperial), cruet, marigold, rare 950.00
Crackle (Imperial), auto vase, marigold 30.00
Crackle (Imperial), bowl, amethyst, 9" 35.00
Crackle (Imperial), candlestick, marigold, 7" 30.00
Crackle (Imperial), punch bowl, marigold, w/base 55.00
Crackle (Imperial), wall vase, marigold 40.00
Crocus VT, tumbler, marigold 45.00
Cut Arcs (Fenton), compote, marigold 55.00
Cut Cosmos (Millersburg), tumbler, marigold, rare 450.00
Cut Ovals (Fenton), candlesticks, pastel, pr 210.00
Dahlia (Dugan), sugar bowl, amethyst 100.00
Dahlia (Fenton), twist epergne (1 lily), wht 300.00
Daisy (Fenton), bonbon, marigold, scarce 250.00
Daisy & Plume (Northwood), candy dish, marigold 70.00
Daisy & Plume (Northwood), rose bowl, bl, 2 shapes, ea 110.00
Daisy Block (English), rowboat, amethyst, scarce 250.00
Daisy Dear (Dugan), bowl, marigold 40.00
Daisy Squares, rose bowl, marigold 600.00
Daisy Web (Dugan), hat, peach opal, rare 750.00
Dandelion (Northwood), mug, aqua opal 550.00
Dandelion (Northwood), pitcher, gr 1,700.00
Dandelion (Northwood), vase, whimsey; amethyst, rare 850.00
Deep Grape (Millersburg), compote, marigold, rare 1,200.00
Diamond & Daisy Cut (US Glass), pitcher, marigold, rare 400.00
Diamond & Rib (Fenton), vase, gr, 7-14" 90.00
Diamond & Sunburst (Imperial), cruet, oil; gr, rare 900.00
Diamond & Sunburst (Imperial), decanter, marigold 110.00
Diamond Band (Crystal), float set, marigold 400.00
Diamond Checkerboard, bowl, marigold, 9" 40.00
Diamond Lace (Imperial), bowl, marigold, 5" 30.00
Diamond Ovals (English), creamer, marigold 40.00
Diamond Ovals (English), sugar bowl, marigold 40.00
Diamond Point Columns (Imperial), bowl, marigold, 4½" 20.00
Diamond Point Columns (Imperial), creamer, marigold 40.00
Diamond Point Columns (Imperial), vase, amethyst 55.00
Diamond Points (Northwood), vase, amethyst, 7-14" 90.00
Diamond Top (English), creamer 40.00
Diamonds (Millersburg), pitcher, gr 350.00
Diamonds (Millersburg), tumbler, gr 85.00
Dogwood Sprays (Dugan), bowl, amethyst, 9" 270.00
Dots & Curves, hatpin, amethyst 55.00
Double Dolphins (Fenton), bowl, pastel, ftd, 9-11" 115.00
Double Loop (Northwood), creamer, gr 170.00
Double Scroll (Imperial), bowl, marigold 45.00
Double Scroll (Imperial), candlesticks, gr, pr 80.00
Double Star (Cambridge), tumbler, marigold, scarce 280.00
Double Stem Rose (Dugan), bowl, peach opal, dome base, 8½" .190.00
Dragon & Lotus (Fenton), bowl, amethyst, flat, 9" 150.00
Dragon & Strawberry (Fenton), bowl, marigold, ftd, scarce, 9" ..400.00
Drapery (Northwood), rose bowl, aqua opal 700.00
Drapery (Northwood), vase, marigold 45.00
Dreibus Parfait Sweets (Northwood), plate, amethyst, 6" 550.00
Dugan Fan (Dugan), gravy boat, peach opal, ftd 210.00
Dugan's Many Ribs, vase, marigold 60.00
Elks (Fenton), bowl, Atlantic City; bl 1,325.00
Elks (Fenton), bowl, Detroit; marigold, scarce 1,300.00

Elks (Fenton), plate, Atlantic City; gr, rare 1,800.00
Elks (Millersburg), bowl, amethyst, rare 1,750.00
Elks (Millersburg), paperweight, gr, rare 1,700.00
Embroidered Mums (Northwood), bowl, marigold, 9" 475.00
Emu (Crystal), bowl, marigold, rare, 5" 175.00
Enameled Panel, goblet, marigold 190.00
English Hob & Button (English), bowl, gr, 7-10" 95.00
English Hob & Button (English), epergne, marigold, metal base .125.00
Engraved Grapes (Fenton), pitcher, marigold, squat 120.00
Estate (Westmoreland), vase, bud; marigold, 6" 50.00
Evelyn (Fostoria), bowl, gr, 1940s 1,000.00
Fanciful (Dugan), bowl, marigold, 8½" 90.00
Fancy Cut (English), pitcher, marigold, rare, mini 225.00
Fantail (Fenton), bowl, bl, ftd, 9" 275.00
Fantail (Fenton), bowl, marigold, ftd, 5" 80.00
Fashion (Imperial), creamer, marigold 42.00
Fashion (Imperial), pitcher, marigold 250.00
Fashion (Imperial), rose bowl, gr, rare 950.00
Feather & Heart (Millersburg), tumbler, gr, scarce 200.00
Feather Swirl (US Glass), butter dish, marigold 165.00
Feathered Serpent (Fenton), bowl, gr, 5" 45.00
Fentonia, bowl, marigold, ftd, 5" 30.00
Fentonia, pitcher, bl 600.00
Fentonia Fruit (Fenton), bowl, marigold, ftd, 6" 45.00
Fern Panels (Fenton), hat, gr 60.00
Field Flower (Imperial), pitcher, bl, rare 400.00
Field Thistle (US Glass), bowl, marigold, 6-10" 45.00
Field Thistle (US Glass), plate, marigold, rare, 6" 180.00
File (Imperial & English), bowl, amethyst, 7-10" 50.00
File (Imperial & English), vase, marigold 75.00
Fine Cut & Roses (Northwood), rose bowl, amethyst, ftd 200.00
Fine Cut Flowers & Vt (Fenton), compote, marigold 50.00
Fine Cut Rings (English), bowl, marigold, oval 140.00
Fine Cut Rings (English), butter dish, marigold 170.00
Fish Net (Dugan), epergne, peach opal 360.00
Fishscale & Beads (Dugan), bowl, peach opal, 6-8" 150.00
Five Hearts (Dugan), bowl, amethyst, dome base, 8¾" 110.00
Flannel Flower (Crystal), compote, marigold, lg 120.00
Flared Wide Panel, atomizer, marigold, 3½" 90.00
Flora (English), float bowl, bl 175.00
Floral & Grape (Dugan), hat, whimsey; marigold 40.00
Floral & Grape (Dugan), pitcher, amethyst 200.00
Floral & Wheat (Dugan), bonbon, peach opal, stemmed 155.00
Floral & Wheat (Dugan), compote, marigold 40.00
Floral Oval (Higbee), plate, marigold, rare, 7" 90.00
Flower & Beads, plate, marigold, 6-sided, 7½" 95.00
Flowering Dill (Fenton), hat, gr 45.00
Flowering Vine (Millersburg), compote, amethyst, rare, tall ...8,500.00
Flowers & Spades (Dugan), bowl, peach opal, 10" 210.00
Flute (British), sherbet, marigold, mk British 50.00
Flute (Millersburg), bowl, amethyst, 4" 45.00
Flute (Millersburg), punch bowl, amethyst, w/base, rare 320.00
Flute (Northwood), creamer, amethyst 85.00
Flute (Northwood), pitcher, gr, rare 600.00
Flute #3 (Imperial), bowl, custard; gr, 11" 300.00
Flute #3 (Imperial), butter dish, gr, w/lid 210.00
Flute #3 (Imperial), punch bowl, marigold, w/base 295.00
Fluted Scrolls (Imperial), rose bowl, amethyst, ftd, rare 975.00
Folding Fan (Dugan), compote, bl 85.00
Footed Rib (Northwood), vase, bl 75.00
Formal (Dugan), hatpin holder, marigold, rare 800.00
Four Flowers, bowl, peach opal, 10" 220.00
Four Flowers, plate, gr, 6½" 200.00
Four Flowers Vt, plate, amethyst, rare, 10½" 450.00

Four Pillars (Northwood & Dugan), vase, marigold 50.00
French Knots (Fenton), hat, bl 45.00
Frosted Block (Imperial), butter dish, marigold, w/lid 70.00
Frosted Block (Imperial), vase, smoke, 6" 100.00
Frosted Ribbon, pitcher, marigold 85.00
Fruit & Flowers (Northwood), bowl, amethyst, 5" 50.00
Fruit & Flowers (Northwood), plate, gr, 9½" 260.00
Garden Mums (Northwood), bowl, amethyst, 8½-10" 75.00
Garden Path (Dugan), plate, peach opal, rare, 6" 985.00
Garden Path Vt (Dugan), rose bowl, marigold, rare 400.00
Georgia Belle (Dugan), compote, peach opal, ftd 140.00
Golden Cupids (Crystal), bowl, pastel, rare, 9" 500.00
Golden Grapes (Dugan), bowl, marigold, 7" 35.00
Golden Harvest (US Glass), decanter, marigold, w/stopper 125.00
Good Luck (Northwood), bowl, marigold, 8¼" 235.00
Good Luck Vt (Northwood), bowl, amethyst, rare, 8¼" 400.00
Gooseberry Spray, bowl, marigold, 10" 55.00
Gooseberry Spray, compote, bl, rare 250.00
Graceful (Northwood), vase, marigold 60.00
Grape, Heavy (Dugan), bowl, marigold, rare, 5" 160.00
Grape, Heavy (Imperial), plate, amethyst, 6" 160.00
Grape (Fenton's Grape & Cable), bowl, marigold, ftd, 8¾" 65.00
Grape (Fenton's Grape & Cable), bowl, orange; gr, ftd 240.00
Grape (Fenton's Grape & Cable), plate, gr, ftd, 9" 200.00
Grape (Imperial), bowl, amethyst, 5" 40.00
Grape (Imperial), bowl, gr, 10" 65.00
Grape (Imperial), decanter, gr, w/stopper 170.00
Grape (Imperial), goblet, amethyst, rare 75.00
Grape (Imperial), pitcher, gr 175.00
Grape (Northwood's Grape & Cable), bonbon, gr 105.00
Grape (Northwood's Grape & Cable), bowl, centerpc; bl, ftd ..1,250.00
Grape (Northwood's Grape & Cable), bowl, gr, ftd 105.00
Grape (Northwood's Grape & Cable), hat, marigold 40.00
Grape (Northwood's Grape & Cable), pin tray, gr 250.00
Grape (Northwood's Grape & Cable), shade, amethyst 180.00
Grape (Northwood's Grape & Cable), tumbler, marigold, reg 50.00
Grape & Cherry (English), bowl, marigold, rare, 8½" 75.00
Grape & Gothic Arches (Northwood), bowl, marigold, 10" 80.00
Grape Arbor (Dugan), bowl, marigold, ftd, 9½-11" 150.00
Grape Arbor (Northwood), tumbler, amethyst 70.00
Grape Delight (Dugan), rose bowl, bl, ftd, 6" 70.00
Grape Wreath (Millersburg), bowl, amethyst, 5" 55.00
Grapevine Lattice (Dugan), bowl, gr, 8½" 52.00
Grapevine Lattice (Fenton), pitcher, marigold, rare 325.00
Harvest Flower (Dugan), pitcher, marigold, rare 1,250.00
Harvest Flower (Dugan), tumbler, bl 365.00
Harvest Poppy, compote, marigold 320.00
Hawaiian Lei (Higbee), sugar bowl, marigold 75.00
Headdress, bowl, gr, 9" 60.00
Heart & Trees (Fenton), bowl, marigold, 8¾" 165.00
Heart Band Souvenir (McKee), mug, marigold, lg 90.00
Hearts & Flowers (Northwood), bowl, marigold, 8½" 525.00
Hearts & Flowers (Northwood), plate, gr, rare, 9" 2,500.00
Heavy Diamond (Imperial), compote, gr 55.00
Heavy Prisms (English), vase, celery; marigold, 6" 85.00
Heavy Shell (Fenton), candle holder, pastel 100.00
Heisey #357, tumbler, marigold 65.00
Heisey Cartwheel, compote, pastel 85.00
Hex Base, candlesticks, marigold, pr 75.00
Hobnail (Millersburg), butter dish, bl, rare 800.00
Hobnail (Millersburg), rose bowl, gr, scarce 595.00
Hobnail (Millersburg), tumbler, marigold, rare 775.00
Hobnail Soda Gold (Imperial), spittoon, gr, lg 75.00
Hobnail Vt (Millersburg), jardiniere, bl, rare 1,100.00

Hobstar (Imperial), bowl, berry; pastel, 5" 35.00
Hobstar (Imperial), bride's basket, marigold, complete 75.00
Hobstar (Imperial), sugar bowl, gr, w/lid 90.00
Hobstar & Cut Triangles (English), plate, marigold 70.00
Hobstar & Cut Triangles (English), rose bowl, gr 70.00
Hobstar & Feather (Millersburg), creamer, gr, rare 800.00
Hobstar & Feather (Millersburg), spooner, amethyst, rare 800.00
Hobstar & File, pitcher, marigold, rare 1,700.00
Hobstar & Fruit (Westmoreland), bowl, peach opal, rare, 10" ...195.00
Hobstar Flower (Northwood), compote, gr, scarce 270.00
Hobstar Reversed (English), spooner, marigold 45.00
Hobstar Whirl (Whirligig), compote, marigold, 4½" 50.00
Holly, Panelled (Northwood), bowl, amethyst 75.00
Holly, Panelled (Northwood), spooner, marigold 50.00
Holly (Fenton), compote, gr, 5" 225.00
Holly & Berry (Dugan), bowl, gr, 7-9" 50.00
Holly Sprig or Whirl (Millersburg), bowl, gr, rnd, 7-10" 60.00
Holly Sprig or Whirl (Millersburg), nappy, gr, tricornered 120.00
Honeycomb (Dugan), rose bowl, marigold 190.00
Honeycomb & Clover (Fenton), bonbon, gr 60.00
Honeycomb & Clover (Fenton), compote, marigold 35.00
Horses' Heads (Fenton), bowl, gr, flat, 7½" 300.00
Horses' Heads (Fenton), plate, marigold, 6½-8½" 500.00
Horses' Heads (Fenton), rose bowl, marigold, ftd 170.00
Idyll (Fenton), vase, marigold, rare 550.00
Illinois Daisy (English), bowl, marigold, 8" 40.00
Illusion (Fenton), bowl, marigold 60.00
Imperial Grape (Imperial), shade, marigold 85.00
Inca, vase, amethyst, rare, 7" 950.00
Intaglio Ovals (US Glass), bowl, aqua opal, 7" 70.00
Intaglio Ovals (US Glass), plate, aqua opal, 7½" 90.00
Intaglio Stars, tumbler, marigold, rare 600.00
Interior Swirl, vase, marigold, ftd, 9" 40.00
Inverted Coin Dot (Northwood-Fenton), pitcher, amethyst 450.00
Inverted Feather (Cambridge), cracker jar, gr, w/lid 395.00
Inverted Feather (Cambridge), cup, marigold, rare 60.00
Inverted Strawberry, bowl, amethyst, 5" 55.00
Inverted Strawberry, candlesticks, marigold, rare, pr 300.00
Inverted Strawberry, compote, whimsey; marigold 500.00
Inverted Strawberry, spittoon, lady's, marigold, rare 900.00
Inverted Strawberry, tumbler, gr, rare 350.00
Inverted Thistle (Cambridge), butter dish, gr, rare 700.00
Iris, Heavy (Dugan), pitcher, peach opal 1,000.00
Iris (Fenton), compote, gr 60.00
Jack-in-the-Pulpit (Dugan), vase, marigold 45.00
Jacob's Ladder Vt (US Glass), rose bowl, marigold 90.00
Jacobean Ranger (Czechoslovakian & English), bowl, marigold ...60.00
Jeweled Heart (Dugan), plate, marigold, 6" 195.00
Jewels (Imperial-Dugan), bowl, bl 185.00
Jewels (Imperial-Dugan), vase, amethyst 150.00
Kingfisher & Variant (Australian), bowl, amethyst, 5" 125.00
Kingfisher & Variant (Australian), bowl, marigold, 9½" 175.00
Kittens (Fenton), bowl, cereal; bl, scarce 500.00
Kittens (Fenton), toothpick holder, vaseline, 3" 300.00
Knight Templar (Northwood), mug, advertising; marigold, rare ..600.00
Kokomo (English), rose bowl, bl, ftd 50.00
Lacy Dewdrop (Westmoreland), creamer, pastel 160.00
Large Kangaroo (Australian), bowl, marigold, 10" 295.00
Late Enameled Bleeding Hearts, tumbler, marigold 175.00
Lattice & Daisy (Dugan), tumbler, bl 50.00
Lattice & Grape (Fenton), pitcher, amethyst 425.00
Lattice & Points (Dugan), vase, amethyst 45.00
Lattice Heart (English), bowl, marigold, 10" 50.00
Lattice Heart (English), compote, amethyst 90.00

Laurel Band, tumbler, marigold 40.00
Laurel Leaves (Imperial), plate, amethyst 55.00
Leaf & Beads (Northwood-Dugan), bowl, amethyst, 9" 275.00
Leaf & Beads (Northwood-Dugan), candy dish, pastel, ftd 425.00
Leaf Chain (Fenton), bonbon, marigold 60.00
Leaf Column (Fenton), vase, amethyst 45.00
Leaf Rays (Dugan), nappy, marigold 30.00
Leaf Swirl (Westmoreland), compote, amber 70.00
Leaf Tiers (Fenton), bowl, marigold, ftd, 10" 60.00
Leaf Tiers (Fenton), creamer, marigold, ftd 85.00
Leaf Tiers (Fenton), tumbler, bl, ftd, rare 95.00
Lined Lattice (Dugan), vase, gr, 7-14" 190.00
Lion (Fenton), bowl, marigold, scarce, 7" 150.00
Little Daisies (Fenton), bowl, bl, 8-9½" 1,350.00
Little Fishes (Fenton), bowl, amethyst, flat or ftd, 5½" 290.00
Little Flowers (Fenton), bowl, gr, rare, 5½" 70.00
Little Stars (Millersburg), bowl, marigold, rare, 10½" 600.00
Log, paperweight, marigold, rare, 3x1¼" 150.00
Loganberry (Imperial), vase, amethyst, scarce 525.00
Long Thumbprint (Dugan), sugar bowl, marigold 40.00
Long Thumbprint (Dugan), vase, bl, 7-11" 40.00
Lotus & Grape (Fenton), bonbon, marigold 145.00
Louisa (Westmoreland), rose bowl, amethyst 65.00
Lucille, pitcher, marigold, rare 1,200.00
Lucky Bell, bowl, marigold, rare, 8¾" 80.00

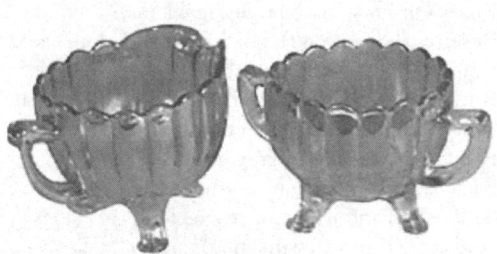

Lustre and Clear (Imperial), creamer and sugar bowl, marigold, $40.00 each.

Lustre & Clear (Imperial), tumbler, marigold 40.00
Lustre & Flute (Fenton), cup, marigold 15.00
Lustre Flute (Northwood), compote, gr 45.00
Lustre Rose (Imperial), bowl, gr, ftd, 9-12" 70.00
Lustre Rose (Imperial), butter dish, marigold 60.00
Magpie (Australian), bowl, amethyst, 6-10" 560.00
Maize (Libbey), syrup jug, clambroth, rare 235.00
Malaga (Dugan), bowl, amethyst, scarce, 9" 185.00
Many Stars (Millersburg), bowl, bl, ruffled, scarce, 9" 2,700.00
Maple Leaf (Dugan), bowl, bl, stemmed, 9" 95.00
Maple Leaf (Dugan), tumbler, amethyst 50.00
Marilyn (Millersburg), pitcher, marigold, rare 750.00
Mayflower, bowl, marigold, 7½" 30.00
Mayflower, bowl, peach opal, 7½" 160.00
Mayflower, hat, marigold 40.00
Melon Rib (Imperial), shakers, marigold, pr 35.00
Memphis (Northwood), bowl, gr, 10" 200.00
Memphis (Northwood), punch bowl, amethyst, w/base 550.00
Milady (Fenton), tumbler, amethyst 140.00
Miniature Intaglio (Westmoreland), nut cup, wht, stemmed 700.00
Mirrored Lotus (Fenton), bowl, gr, 7-8½" 90.00
Mitered Ovals (Millersburg), vase, amethyst, rare 7,500.00
Moonprint (English), creamer, marigold 45.00
Moonprint (English), vase, marigold 50.00
Multi-Fruits & Flowers (Millersburg), cup, amethyst, rare 75.00
Multi-Fruits & Flowers (Millersburg), tumbler, gr, rare 1,400.00
Mystic (Cambridge), vase, marigold, ftd, rare 165.00

Near Cut Souvenir (Cambridge), mug, marigold, rare 190.00
Nesting Swan (Millersburg), bowl, gr, tricornered, rare 1,200.00
Nesting Swan (Millersburg), rose bowl, marigold, rare 3,000.00
Nippon (Northwood), bowl, marigold, 8½" 250.00
Nippon (Northwood), plate, bl, 9" 700.00
Northern Star (Fenton), card tray, marigold, 6" 40.00
Northwood's Poppy, bowl, bl, 7-8¾" 140.00
Northwood's Poppy, tray, amethyst, oval, rare 300.00
Nu-Art (Imperial), plate, marigold, scarce 850.00
Number 2351 (Cambridge), bowl, gr, rare, 9" 350.00
Octagon (Imperial), butter dish, gr 475.00
Octagon (Imperial), decanter, gr, complete 750.00
Octagon (Imperial), toothpick holder, marigold, rare 170.00
Octet (Northwood), bowl, amethyst, 8½" 150.00
Ohio Star (Millersburg), compote, marigold, rare 1,100.00
Oklahoma (Mexican), tumbler, marigold, rare 500.00
Open Flower (Dugan), bowl, amethyst, flat or ftd, 7" 45.00
Open Rose (Imperial), bowl, amethyst, flat, 9" 40.00
Open Rose (Imperial), bowl, fruit; marigold, 7-10" 40.00
Optic (Imperial), bowl, amethyst, 6" 50.00
Optic & Buttons (Imperial), pitcher, marigold, rare, sm 185.00
Optic Flute (Imperial), bowl, amethyst, 10" 80.00
Orange Peel (Westmoreland), cup, amethyst 30.00
Orange Tree (Fenton), bowl, gr, flat, 8-10" 325.00
Orange Tree (Fenton), bowl, marigold, ftd, 5½" 40.00
Orange Tree (Fenton), hatpin holder, gr 350.00
Orange Tree (Fenton), plate, bl, 8-9½" 450.00
Orange Tree (Fenton), sugar bowl, marigold 65.00
Orange Tree Orchard (Fenton), tumbler, marigold 40.00
Ostrich (Australian), cake stand, amethyst, rare 350.00
Oval & Round (Imperial), plate, amber, 10" 90.00
Oval Star & Fan (Jenkins), rose bowl, marigold 50.00
Pacifica (US Glass), tumbler, marigold 400.00
Palm Beach (US Glass), banana bowl, marigold 100.00
Palm Beach (US Glass), bowl, marigold, 9" 55.00
Palm Beach (US Glass), spooner, marigold 75.00
Panelled Diamond & Bows (Fenton), vase, amethyst, 7-14" 140.00
Panelled Hobnail (Dugan), vase, pastel, 5-10" 95.00
Panelled Palm (US Glass), mug, marigold, rare 95.00
Panelled Tree Trunk (Dugan), vase, amethyst, rare, 7-12" 90.00
Panels & Ball (Fenton), bowl, marigold, 11" 60.00
Pansy (Imperial), bowl, marigold, 8¾" 40.00
Pansy (Imperial), plate, marigold, ruffled, rare 80.00
Panther (Fenton), bowl, marigold, ftd, 10" 135.00
Parlor Panels, vase, gr, 4-11" 250.00
Pastel Panels (Imperial), tumbler, pastel 75.00
Peach (Northwood), pitcher, bl 650.00
Peach & Pear (Dugan), banana bowl, marigold 90.00
Peacock, Fluffy (Fenton), tumbler, gr 260.00
Peacock, Strutting (Westmoreland), creamer, amethyst 65.00
Peacock (Millersburg), bowl, ice cream; gr, 5" 600.00
Peacock (Millersburg), bowl, ice cream; marigold, rare, 10" 500.00
Peacock (Millersburg), bowl, marigold, 5" 90.00
Peacock & Dahlia (Fenton), bowl, gr, 7½" 125.00
Peacock & Grape (Fenton), bowl, bl, flat or ftd, 7¾" 150.00
Peacock & Urn (Fenton), bowl, marigold, 8½" 150.00
Peacock & Urn (Fenton), goblet, amethyst, rare 100.00
Peacock & Urn (Northwood), bowl, gr, 5" 800.00
Peacock & Urn (Northwood), bowl, marigold, 9" 200.00
Peacock & Urn (Northwood), plate, marigold, rare, 6" 450.00
Peacock & Urn & Vts (Millersburg), bowl, gr, 9½" 375.00
Peacock & Urn & Vts (Millersburg), bowl, ice cream; bl, 6" 750.00
Peacock & Urn & Vts (Millersburg), bowl, ice cream; gr, 10" ..2,600.00
Peacock at the Fountain (Northwood), bowl, bl, 5" 75.00

Peacock at the Fountain (Northwood), bowl, gr, 9" 145.00
Peacock at the Fountain (Northwood), creamer, amethyst 100.00
Peacock at the Fountain (Northwood), tumbler, amethyst 650.00
Peacock Tail (Fenton), bonbon, marigold 75.00
Peacock Tail (Fenton), plate, bl, 6" 870.00
Pearl #37 (Northwood), shade, peach opal 100.00
Perfection (Millersburg), tumbler, gr, rare 650.00
Persian Garden (Dugan), bowl, berry; peach opal, 5" 80.00
Persian Garden (Dugan), plate, amethyst, rare, 6" 450.00
Persian Medallion (Fenton), bonbon, marigold 75.00
Persian Medallion (Fenton), bowl, marigold, 8¾" 60.00
Persian Medallion (Fenton), punch cup, gr 40.00
Petal & Fan (Dugan), bowl, marigold, 10" 275.00
Petals (Dugan), banana bowl, peach opal 110.00
Pillar & Flute (Imperial), celery vase, marigold 60.00
Pillar & Flute (Imperial), compote, marigold 50.00
Pine Cone (Fenton), bowl, marigold, 6" 125.00
Pineapple, Heavy (Fenton), bowl, bl, ftd, rare, 10" 950.00
Pineapple (English), butter dish, marigold 85.00

Pineapple (English), bowl, amethyst, 7", $70.00.

Pinwheel (Dugan), bowl, marigold, 6" 50.00
Pinwheel (English), vase, marigold, 8" 120.00
Plaid (Fenton), bowl, gr, 8¾" 350.00
Plain Jane, paperweight, marigold 90.00
Plume Panels, vase, bl, 7-12" 90.00
Plums & Cherries (Northwood), spooner, bl, rare 1,750.00
Poinsettia (Imperial), pitcher, milk; marigold 170.00
Pony (Dugan), bowl, marigold, 8½" 120.00
Poppy (Millersburg), compote, amethyst, scarce 695.00
Poppy Show (Imperial), vase, marigold, old only, 12" 450.00
Premium (Imperial), bowl, marigold, 12" 55.00
Premium (Imperial), underplate, pastel, 14" 120.00
Primrose (Millersburg), bowl, ice cream; amethyst, 9" 190.00
Prism, shakers, marigold, pr 60.00
Prism & Daisy Band (Imperial), compote, marigold 35.00
Prism & Daisy Band (Imperial), creamer, marigold 35.00
Prism Band (Fenton), tumbler, bl, decor 55.00
Prisms (Westmoreland), compote, amethyst, scarce, 5" 90.00
Propeller (Imperial), bowl, marigold, rare, 9½" 80.00
Propeller (Imperial), vase, marigold, stemmed, rare 90.00
Pulled Loop (Dugan), vase, bl 110.00
Puzzle (Dugan), bonbon, marigold, stemmed 40.00
Puzzle (Dugan), compote, bl 85.00
Queen's Jewel, goblet, marigold 55.00
Quill (Dugan), pitcher, amethyst, rare 3,500.00
Quill (Dugan), tumbler, marigold 400.00
Ragged Robin (Fenton), bowl, amethyst, scarce, 8¾" 100.00
Rainbow (Northwood), plate, amethyst, 9" 135.00
Raindrops (Dugan), bowl, marigold, 9" 65.00
Rambler Rose (Dugan), pitcher, amethyst 250.00
Ranger (Mexican), sugar bowl, marigold 150.00

Ranger Toothpick, toothpick holder, marigold 95.00
Raspberry (Northwood), bowl, gr, 5" 40.00
Raspberry (Northwood), sauce boat, marigold, ftd 90.00
Raspberry (Northwood), tumbler, gr 60.00
Rays & Ribbons (Millersburg), banana bowl, gr, rare 1,100.00
Rex, tumbler, marigold 60.00
Rib & Panel (Fenton), vase, bl 65.00
Ribbed Holly (Fenton), compote, marigold 50.00
Ribbon & Fern, atomizer, marigold, 7" 90.00
Ribbon Tie (Fenton), bowl, marigold, 8¾" 190.00
Ribs (Czechoslovakian), puff box, marigold 95.00
Ripple (Imperial), vase, gr 190.00
Rising Sun (US Glass), butter dish, marigold 175.00
Rising Sun (US Glass), sugar bowl, marigold 125.00
Robin (Imperial), tumbler, marigold, old only, scarce 60.00
Rococo (Imperial), bowl, smoke, 5" 160.00
Roll, cordial set, marigold, complete 350.00
Rosalind (Millersburg), bowl, marigold, scarce, 10" 275.00
Rosalind (Millersburg), compote, gr, rare, 6" 500.00
Rose Garden (Sweden), bowl, amethyst, 8¾" 80.00
Rose Garden (Sweden), butter dish, marigold, rare 450.00
Rose Garden (Sweden), letter vase, bl 190.00
Rose Panels (Australian), compote, marigold, lg 145.00
Rose Show (Northwood), bowl, amethyst, 8¾" 850.00
Rose Show Variant (Northwood), plate, marigold, 9" 1,800.00
Rose Tree (Fenton), bowl, bl, rare, 10" 1,200.00
Rose Windows, tumbler, marigold, rare 400.00
Rosettes (Northwood), bowl, marigold, dome base, 9" 50.00
Round-Up (Dugan), bowl, bl, 8¾" 230.00
Royalty (Imperial), punch bowl, marigold, w/base 140.00
Rustic (Fenton), vase, funeral; marigold, 15-20" 625.00
Rustic (Fenton), vase, gr, various szs, ea 70.00
Sacic (English), ashtray, marigold 70.00
Sailboats (Fenton), plate, marigold, 8" 775.00
Sailboats (Fenton), wine, marigold 35.00
Sawtooth Band, tumbler, marigold, rare 400.00
Scale Band (Fenton), pitcher, bl 400.00
Scales (Westmoreland), bonbon, marigold 40.00
Scotch Thistle (Fenton), compote, bl 115.00
Scottie, powder jar, marigold, w/lid 35.00
Scroll & Flower Panels (Imperial), vase, bl, old only, 10" 150.00
Scroll Embossed (Imperial), plate, gr, 9" 200.00
Scroll Embossed (Imperial), sauce boat, marigold 35.00
Seacoast (Millersburg), pin tray, amethyst, rare 550.00
Seaweed (Millersburg), bowl, marigold, rare, 9" 275.00
Serrated Ribs, shaker, marigold, ea 60.00
Shell (Imperial), bowl, marigold, 7-9" 45.00
Shell & Balls, perfume, marigold, 2½" 65.00
Shell & Jewel (Westmoreland), creamer, gr, w/lid 60.00
Shell & Jewel (Westmoreland), sugar bowl, marigold, w/lid 55.00
Shrine (US Glass), toothpick holder, clear 200.00
Singing Birds (Northwood), bowl, gr, 10" 85.00
Singing Birds (Northwood), butter dish, marigold 185.00
Singing Birds (Northwood), creamer, gr 125.00
Single Flower (Dugan), hat, amethyst 40.00
Single Flower Framed (Dugan), bowl, marigold, 8¾" 65.00
Six Petals (Dugan), bowl, amethyst, 8½" 125.00
Ski-Star (Dugan), bowl, amethyst, 8-10" 95.00
Ski-Star (Dugan), rose bowl, peach opal, rare 600.00
Small Rib (Dugan), compote, gr 45.00
Smooth Panels (Imperial), plate, clear, 9¼" 90.00
Smooth Panels (Imperial), vase, red 250.00
Smooth Rays (Northwood), bonbon, marigold 30.00
Smooth Rays (Northwood-Dugan), plate, marigold, 7-9" 60.00

Snow Fancy (McKee), creamer, marigold 50.00
Soda Gold (Imperial), candlestick, smoke, 3½" 60.00
Southern Ivy, wine, marigold, 2 szs, ea 45.00
Spiderweb (Northwood), candy dish, smoke, w/lid 40.00
Spiralex (English), vase, marigold, various szs, ea 50.00
Spiralled Diamond Point, vase, marigold, 6" 90.00
Split Diamond (English), creamer, marigold, sm 40.00
Spring Basket (Imperial), basket, smoke, 5" 65.00
Springtime (Northwood), bowl, amethyst, 9" 200.00
Springtime (Northwood), bowl, marigold, 5" 40.00
Springtime (Northwood), creamer, gr 400.00
Stag & Holly (Fenton), bowl, amethyst, ftd, 9-13" 350.00
Stag & Holly (Fenton), plate, bl, ftd, 9" 1,800.00
Star (English), bowl, marigold, 8" 50.00
Star & Fan, vase, bl, rare, 9½" 200.00
Star & File (Imperial), creamer, marigold 30.00
Star & File (Imperial), pickle dish, marigold 40.00
Star & File (Imperial), wine, marigold 75.00
Star Center (Imperial), bowl, pastel, 8½" 50.00
Star Center (Imperial), plate, amethyst, 9" 80.00

**Star Medallion (Imperial),
milk pitcher, green, $95.00.**

Star Medallion (Imperial), pickle dish, marigold 40.00
Star Medallion (Imperial), plate, pastel, 5" 45.00
Star Medallion (Imperial), spooner, marigold 60.00
Star of David (Imperial), bowl, marigold, scarce, 8¾" 70.00
Star Spray (Imperial), plate, marigold, 7½" 75.00
Starbright, vase, bl, 6½" 50.00
Starlyte (Imperial), shade, marigold 40.00
Stippled Acorns, candy dish, amethyst, ftd, w/lid 95.00
Stippled Petals (Dugan), bowl, amethyst, 9" 75.00
Stippled Rambler Rose (Dugan), nut bowl, bl, ftd 90.00
Stippled Rays (Fenton), bonbon, amethyst 45.00
Stippled Rays (Fenton), creamer, marigold 30.00
Stippled Rays (Imperial), sugar bowl, marigold, stemmed 40.00
Stippled Rays (Northwood), bowl, gr, 8-10" 65.00
Stippled Strawberry (Jenkins), bowl, amethyst, rare, 9" 200.00
Stippled Strawberry (Jenkins), creamer, marigold 35.00
Stork & Rushes (Dugan), butter dish, marigold, rare 145.00
Stork & Rushes (Dugan), cup, marigold 20.00
Stork & Rushes (Dugan), tumbler, amethyst 60.00
Strawberry (Fenton), bonbon, gr 65.00
Strawberry (Millersburg), bowl, gr, tricornered, 9½" 450.00
Strawberry (Millersburg), bowl, marigold, 6½" 90.00
Strawberry (Millersburg), compote, gr, rare 450.00
Strawberry (Northwood), plate, gr, stippled, 7" 1,500.00
Strawberry Intaglio (Northwood), bowl, marigold, 9½" 65.00
Strawberry Scroll (Fenton), tumbler, marigold, rare 275.00
Stream of Hearts (Fenton), goblet, marigold, rare 200.00
Stretched Diamonds & Dots, tumbler, marigold 175.00
Sunflower (Northwood), bowl, marigold, 8½" 50.00
Sunflower (Northwood), plate, gr, rare 400.00

Sunk Diamond Band (US Glass), tumbler, marigold, rare 50.00
Sunray, compote, amethyst 40.00
Swirl (Imperial), candlestick, marigold 35.00
Swirl (Northwood), pitcher, marigold 250.00
Swirl Hobnail (Millersburg), vase, bl, rare, 7-10" 500.00
Swirl Vt (Imperial), vase, marigold, 6½" 35.00
Swirled Threads, goblet, marigold 95.00
Taffeta Lustre (Fostoria), console bowl, gr, rare, 11" 150.00
Ten Mums (Fenton), bowl, amethyst, 8-11" 125.00
Texas Headdress (Westmoreland), punch cup, marigold 45.00
Thin Rib (Fenton), candlesticks, marigold, pr 80.00
Thin Rib & Drape (Fenton), vase, gr, 5-14" 255.00
Thistle (Fenton), bowl, gr, 8-10", ea 160.00
Thistle & Thorn (English), bowl, marigold, ftd, 6" 50.00
Three Flowers (Imperial), tray, marigold, center hdl, 12" 60.00
Three Fruits (Northwood), plate, gr, rnd, 9" 290.00
Three Fruits Vt (Dugan), plate, marigold, 12-sided 150.00
Three-in-One (Imperial), bowl, amethyst, 8¾" 40.00
Three-in-One (Imperial), rose bowl, marigold, rare 200.00
Thumbprint & Spears, creamer, marigold 50.00
Tiger Lily (Imperial), pitcher, marigold 125.00
Tiger Lily (Imperial), tumbler, gr 40.00
Tobacco Leaf (US Glass), champagne, clear 160.00
Tornado (Northwood), vase, bl, ribbed, 2 szs, ea 1,150.00
Tornado Vt (Northwood), vase, marigold, rare 1,450.00
Tracery (Millersburg), bonbon, gr, rare 650.00
Tree of Life (Imperial), perfumer, marigold, w/lid 40.00
Tree of Life (Imperial), tumbler, marigold 25.00
Tree Trunk (Northwood), vase, funeral; marigold, 15-20" 950.00
Triands (English), butter dish, marigold 65.00
Triplets (Dugan), bowl, gr, 6-8" 45.00
Triplets (Dugan), hat, marigold 30.00
Tulip (Millersburg), compote, marigold, rare, 9" 750.00
Tulip & Cane (Imperial), goblet, marigold, rare, 8-oz 75.00
Tulip Scroll (Millersburg), vase, amethyst, rare, 6-12" 400.00
Twins (Imperial), bowl, marigold, 5" 25.00
Twitch (Bartlett-Collins), cup, marigold 30.00
Two Flowers (Fenton), bowl, amethyst, ftd, 5-8" 70.00
Two Fruits (Fenton), bowl, gr, divided, scarce, 5½" 190.00
Umbrella Prisms, hatpin, amethyst, lg 70.00
Unshod, pitcher, marigold 85.00
Valentine (Northwood), bowl, marigold, rare, 10" 500.00
Venetian (Cambridge), butter dish, marigold, rare 950.00
Venetian (Cambridge), creamer, marigold, rare 550.00
Vineyard Harvest (Australian), tumbler, marigold, rare 250.00
Vining Twigs (Dugan), bowl, amethyst, 7½" 45.00
Vintage (Dugan), tray, dresser; marigold, 7-11" 85.00
Vintage (Fenton), bowl, amethyst, 6½" 40.00
Vintage (Fenton), compote, gr 55.00
Vintage (Fenton), epergne, marigold, 1-lily, 2 szs, ea 100.00
Vintage (Fenton), plate, marigold, 7¾" 300.00
Vintage (Millersburg), bowl, gr, rare, 5" 1,000.00
Vintage (US Glass), wine, marigold 40.00
Vintage Banded (Dugan), mug, marigold 35.00
Violet, basket, amethyst, 2 styles, ea 65.00
Votive Light (Mexican), candle vase, marigold, rare, 4½" 450.00
Waffle Block (Imperial), parfait glass, pastel, stemmed 45.00
Waffle Block (Imperial), shakers, marigold, pr 75.00
Waffle Block & Hobstar (Imperial), basket, marigold 250.00
Washboard, creamer, marigold, 5½" 45.00
Water Lily & Cattails (Fenton), bowl, bl, 5" 50.00
Water Lily & Cattails (Fenton), spooner, marigold 75.00
Water Lily & Cattails (Fenton), toothpick whimsey, marigold 75.00
Wavy Satin, hatpin, amethyst 95.00

Weeping Cherry (Dugan), bowl, peach opal, flat base 220.00
Western Daisy (Westmoreland), bowl, amethyst 60.00
Westmoreland Jester's Cap, vase, amethyst 50.00
Wheels (Imperial), bowl, marigold, 9" 50.00
Whirling Hobstar, pitcher, marigold 290.00
Whirling Star (Imperial), bowl, marigold, 9-11" 40.00
Wickerwork (English), bowl, marigold, w/base, complete 275.00
Wide Panel (Westmoreland), bowl, teal, 7½" 70.00
Wide Panel Vt (Northwood), pitcher, marigold, tankard style ...200.00
Wild Blackberry (Fenton), bowl, amethyst, scarce, 8½" 115.00
Wild Rose, syrup, marigold, rare 700.00
Wild Rose (Millersburg), lamp, marigold, sm 1,000.00
Windmill (Imperial), bowl, amethyst, 9" 55.00
Windmill (Imperial), bowl, fruit; gr, 10½" 40.00
Windmill (Imperial), pitcher, marigold, lg 70.00
Windsor (Imperial), flower arranger, marigold, rare 90.00
Wine & Roses (Fenton), wine, bl 95.00
Wishbone (Northwood), epergne, gr, rare 1,850.00
Wishbone (Northwood), plate, marigold, flat, rare, 10" 2,500.00
Wishbone (Northwood), tumbler, gr, scarce 200.00
Wishbone & Spades (Dugan), plate, peach opal, rare, 6" 300.00
Wreath Cherry (Dugan), bowl, amethyst, oval, 10½" 140.00
Wreath of Roses (Fenton), bonbon, gr, stemmed 50.00
Wreath of Roses (Fenton), bonbon, marigold, flat 40.00
Wreath of Roses (Fenton), cup, amethyst 30.00
Wreath of Roses Vt (Dugan), compote, marigold 55.00
Wreathed Cherry (Dugan), spooner, marigold 65.00
Zig Zag (Millersburg), bowl, amethyst, rnd or ruffled, 9½" 420.00
Zipper Loop (Imperial), lamp, marigold, rare, med 600.00
Zippered Heart, bowl, amethyst, 5" 50.00
474 (Imperial), pitcher, milk; marigold, scarce 225.00
474 (Imperial), punch bowl, gr, w/base 600.00
474 (Imperial), tumbler, gr, scarce 65.00

Carousel Figures

For generations of Americans, visions of carousel horses revolving majestically around lively band organs rekindle wonderful childhood experiences. These nostalgic memories are the legacy of the creative talent from a dozen carving shops that created America's carousel art. Skilled craftsmen brought their trade from Europe where American carvers took the carousel animal from a folk art creation to a true art form. The 'Golden Age of Carousel Art' lasted from 1880 to 1929.

There are two basic types of American carousels. The largest and most impressive is the 'park style' carousel built for permanent installation in major amusement centers. These were created in Philadelphia by Gustav and William Dentzel, Muller Brothers, and E. Joy Morris who became the Philadelphia Toboggan Company in 1902. A more flamboyant group of carousel animals was carved in Coney Island, New York, by Charles Looff, Marcus Illions, Charles Carmel, and Stein & Goldstein's Artistic Carousel Company. These park-style carousels were typically three, four, and even five rows with forty-five to sixty-eight animals on a platform. Collectors often pay a premium for the carvings by these men. The outside row animals are larger and more ornate and command higher prices. The horses on the inside rows are smaller, less decorated and of lesser value.

The most popular style of carousel art is the 'country fair style.' These carousels were portable affairs created for mobility. The horses are smaller and less ornate with leg and head positions that allow for stacking and easy loading. These were built primarily for North Tonawanda, New York, near Niagara Falls, by Armitage Herschell Company, Herschell Spillman Company, Spillman Engineering Company, and Allen Herschell. Charles W. Parker was also well known for his portable merry-go-rounds. He was based in Leavenworth, Kansas. Parker and Herschell Spillman both created a few large park-style carousels as well, but they are better known for their portable models.

Horses are by far the most common figure found, but there are two dozen other animals that were created for the carousel platform. Carousel animals, unlike most other antiques, are oftentimes worth more in a restored condition. Figures found with original factory paint are extraordinarily rare and bring premium amounts. Typically, carousel horses are found in garish, poorly applied 'park paint' and oftentimes are missing legs or ears. Carousel horses are hollow. They were glued up from several blocks for greater strength and lighter weight. Bass and poplar woods were used extensively.

If you have an antique carousel animal you would like to have identified, send a clear photograph and description along with a LSASE to our advisor, William Manns, who is listed in the Directory under New Mexico. Mr. Manns is the author of *Painted Ponies*, containing many full-color photographs, guides, charts, and directories for the collector.

Key:
IR — inside row   OR — outside row
MR — middle row   PTC — Philadelphia Toboggan
                                               Company

Coney Island-Style Horses

Carmel, IR jumper, unrstr 7,000.00
Carmel, MR jumper, unrstr 12,500.00
Carmel, OR jumper w/cherub, rstr 52,000.00
Illions, MR stander, rstr 18,000.00
Illions, OR stander, eagle saddle, rstr 44,000.00
Illions IR jumper, rstr, from $5,000 to 6,500.00
Looff, IR jumper, unrstr 6,000.00
Looff, OR jumper, unrstr 21,500.00
Stein & Goldstein, IR jumper, unrstr 4,900.00
Stein & Goldstein, MR jumper, rstr 17,000.00
Stein & Goldstein, OR stander w/bells, unrstr 38,000.00

European Horses

Anderson, English, unrstr 4,200.00
Bayol, French, unrstr 3,400.00
Heyn, German, unrstr 4,500.00
Hubner, Belgian, unrstr 3,000.00
Savage, English, unrstr 3,500.00

Menagerie Animals (Non-Horses)

Dentzel, bear, unrstr 28,000.00
Dentzel, cat, unrstr 38,000.00
Dentzel, lion, unrstr 55,000.00
Dentzel, pig, unrstr 9,000.00
Dentzel, rabbit, unrstr 45,000.00
E Joy Morris, deer, unrstr 16,500.00
Herschell Spillman, cat, unrstr 18,000.00
Herschell Spillman, chicken, portable, unrstr 9,500.00
Herschell Spillman, dog, portable, unrstr 10,000.00
Herschell Spillman, frog, unrstr 29,000.00
Looff, camel, unrstr 9,000.00
Looff, goat, rstr 20,000.00
Muller, tiger, rstr 37,000.00

Philadelphia-Style Horses

Dentzel, IR 'topknot' jumper, unrstr 7,000.00

Dentzel, MR jumper, unrstr 14,000.00
Dentzel, OR stander, rstr 45,000.00
Dentzel, prancer, rstr 9,500.00
Morris, IR prancer, rstr 7,000.00
Morris, MR stander, unrstr 9,500.00
Morris, OR stander, rstr 20,000.00
Muller, IR jumper, rstr 8,900.00

Muller, middle row jumper, ca 1905, $13,000.00 to $16,000.00.

Muller, OR stander, rstr 48,000.00
Muller, OR stander w/military trappings 75,000.00
PTC, chariot (bench-like seat), rstr 8,900.00
PTC, IR jumper, rstr 6,000.00
PTC, MR jumper, rstr 15,500.00
PTC, OR stander, armored, rstr 58,000.00
PTC, OR stander, unrstr 29,500.00

Portable Carousel Horses

Allan Herschell, all aluminum, ca 1950 ....700.00
Allan Herschell, half & half, wood & aluminum head 1,500.00
Allan Herschell, IR Indian pony, unrstr 2,900.00
Allan Herschell, OR, rstr 3,200.00
Allan Herschell, OR Trojan-style jumper 4,500.00
Armitage Herschell, track machine jumper 3,200.00
Dare, jumper, unrstr 3,500.00
Herschell Spillman, chariot (bench-like seat) 3,500.00
Herschell Spillman, IR jumper, unrstr 3,000.00
Herschell Spillman, MR jumper, unrstr 3,200.00
Herschell Spillman, OR, eagle decor 6,000.00
Herschell Spillman, OR, park machine 18,000.00
Parker, MR jumper, unrstr 4,500.00
Parker, OR jumper, park machine, unrstr 14,000.00
Parker, OR jumper, rstr 7,000.00

Cartoon Art

Collectors of cartoon art are interested in many forms of original art — animation cels, sports, political or editorial cartoons, syndicated comic strip panels, and caricature. To produce even a short animated cartoon strip, hundreds of original drawings are required, each showing the characters in slightly advancing positions. Called 'cels' because those made prior to the 1950s were made from a celluloid material, collectors often pay hundreds of dollars for a frame from a favorite movie. Prices of Disney cels with backgrounds vary widely. Background paintings, model sheets, storyboards, and preliminary sketches are also collectible — so are comic book drawings executed in India ink and signed by the artist. Daily 'funnies' originals, especially the earlier ones portraying super heroes, and Sunday comic strips, the early as well as the later ones, are collected. Cartoon art has become recognized and valued as a novel yet valid form of contemporary art.

Key:
ab — airbrushed   cel — celluloid
C — Courvosier   wc — watercolor

Animation Cels, Full Color

Bedknobs & Broomsticks, Disney, Mr Codfish, 7x6" 285.00
Black Cauldron, Disney, Creeper w/robe, 10x12" 265.00
Brown Hornet, Filmation, closeup, 1972 ....100.00
Bugs Bunny, Warner Bros, cut paper ground, 1970s, 10x11" ...1,000.00
Buzz Buzzard, Walter Lantz, w/mouse, ca 1960, 7x5½" 500.00
Daffy & Elmer, Warner Bros, print bkground, 1940s, 5x7" 2,550.00
Dino, Hanna-Barbera, print bkground, 6x12" 600.00
Duck Tales, Disney, Donald Duck, color repro ground, 9x13" ..3,335.00
Fat Albert, Filmation, Rudy, full figure, 1972 ....55.00
Fred Flintstone, Hanna-Barbera, w/sunglasses, 1970s, 5x4" 155.00
Jerry & Tuffy, MGM, as musketeers, hand inked, matted 400.00
Jungle Book, Disney, Baloo in stream, 7x11" 500.00
Laurel & Hardy, Hanna-Barbera, production bkground, 1966 ....200.00
Marvin Martian, Warner Bros, profile, 1952, 5½x3" 2,800.00
Mickey's Xmas Carol, Disney, Scrooge, nightclothes, 9x7" 425.00
Oliver & Co, Disney, Georgette at mirror, repro ground, 11x17" ...285.00
Peter Pan, Disney, w/Lost Boys, production ground, 9x12½" ..1,500.00
Rescuers, Disney, Penny, 6x4" 285.00
Robin Hood, Disney, closeup w/lg smile, 10x14" 795.00
Robin Hood, Disney, removing disguise, 7x6" 300.00
Scooby Doo & Friends, Hanna-Barbera, Scrappy Doo, full figure .38.00
Sleeping Beauty, Disney, Flora w/wand, sparkles, '59, 6x6" 900.00
Sport Goofy, Disney, spinning ball on finger, mc ground, 12x15" ..500.00
Tom & Jerry, MGM Studios, Jerry on keyboard, 1947, 2¼x2" ..585.00
Winnie the Pooh, Disney, w/Eeyore, 1983, 4x8½" 700.00

Animation Drawings

Betty Boop, Fleischer Studios, no details, 1977, 10x7" 500.00
Betty Boop & Pudgy, Fleischer Studios, pencil, 1930s, 5x5" 300.00
Birds, conceptual for Bambi, Walt Disney, mc pencils 235.00
Black Cauldron, Disney, Taran, ¾-image w/apple, 6x5" 135.00
Bugs Bunny, Warner Bros, as Super Rabbit, 1943, very rare 900.00
Dognapper, Disney, Mickey & Minnie, pencil, '34, 3½x5½" ..2,200.00
Dude Duck, Disney, Donald in derby, pencil, 1951, 5x4¼" 300.00
Dudley Do-Right, Jaw Ward, graphite, 6x2½" 325.00
Elmer Fudd, Warner Bros, red & graphite, 1950s, 5-peg paper ...425.00
Flintstones, figures w/grownup & baby Pebbles/Bamm-Bamm, 16x9" .800.00
Jungle Book, Disney, Bagheera, pencil w/red, 1967, 5x11" 185.00
Jungle Book, Disney, Baloo, pencil, 1967, 6x6½" 200.00
Lady & Tramp, Disney, Lady w/muzzle, 1955, 12½x15½" 675.00
Lady & Tramp, Disney, Peg, pencil, 1955, 7x8" 400.00
Magician Mickey, Disney, canaries/Donald, mc, '37, 4½x10" .3,350.00
Mickey's Circus, Disney, Mickey on high wire, 1936x, 4x11½" .850.00
Mickey's Fire Brigade, Disney, as fireman, pencil, '35, 3x2" 300.00
Mumbly, Hanna-Barbera, as detective, full figure 30.00
Pebbles, Hanna-Barbera, baby playing, 1950s 175.00
Pinocchio, Disney, Blue Fairy, pencil, 1936, 8x4" 600.00
Pinocchio, Disney, Geppetto/Figaro, mc pencils, 1940, 10x12" ..525.00
Robin Hood, Disney, Sir Hiss w/evil face 165.00
Screwy Squirrel, MGM, up on toes, rare 215.00
Skeleton Dance, Disney, Skeleton, Ub Iwerks, 1928, 5x3½" 335.00
Superman, Hanna-Barbera, knees up, full figure 25.00
Tom & Jerry, MGM, chase scene, red pencil, notations 200.00
Winnie the Pooh, Disney, waist-up view, mc 100.00

Woody Woodpecker, Walter Lantz, eyes closed 65.00
Yel Submarine, Beatles on hill, 1968, 1x1¼" 135.00

Daily Newspaper Comic Strips

Bugs & Elmer, Armstrong, 1979 ....235.00
Dick Tracy, Chester Gould, w/villian, 1953 ....485.00
Doonesbury, G Trudeau, Elvis theme, 1978, rare 1,225.00
Mickey Mouse, Disney, cooking theme w/Minnie, 1977 ....400.00
Mutt & Jeff, Fischer, baseball theme, 1922 ....600.00
Napoleon, McBride, 1938 ....300.00

Miscellaneous

Model layout, Sam the Sheepdog, Warner Bros, red pencil, 1947 ..325.00
Model layout, Wile E Coyote, mc, notations, 1953, 2-peg sheet .1,000.00
Model sheet, Daffy as Musketeer, graphite & bl pencil, 6x8" 335.00
Model sheet, Tweetie birds, 6 images, graphite, 8½x13" 900.00
Model sheet, Yosemite Sam as in Rabbitson Crusoe, 1956, 10x14" ..1,200.00
Pastel on blk sheet, Fantasia, flowers, 1938, 6x10" 895.00
Pastel on gr paper, Fantasia, Appatasauri, 1940, 7x9" 1,000.00
Production layout, Daffy Duck & Yosemite Sam, mc pencil, 6x8" ..665.00
Publicity layout, Bugs Bunny as Cowboy Bugs, 1990, 11x7" 235.00
Storyboard, Tasmanian Devil, 4 scenes, image szs: 3x4" 185.00
Storyboard, 8-panel scenes of DJ Buzzard, 14x15" 180.00

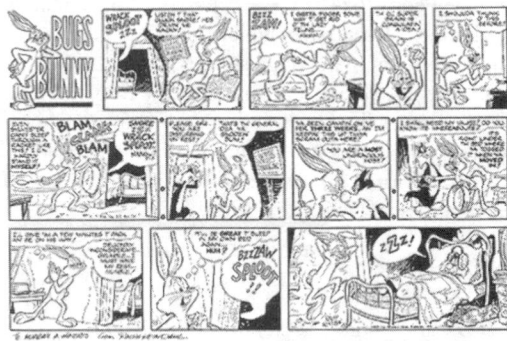

Sunday page original of Bugs Bunny, September, 1965, signed and inscribed by Ralph Heimdahl, 15½x24", $250.00.

Sunday strip, Nancy, E Bushmiller, 1947 ....400.00

Cartoon Books

'Books of cartoons' were printed during the first decade of the 20th century and remained popular until the advent of the modern comic book in the late thirties. Cartoon books, printed in both color and black and white, were merely reprints of current newspaper comic strips. The books, ranging from thirty to seventy pages and in sizes from 3½" x 8" up to 11" x 17", were usually bound with cardboard covers and were often distributed as premiums in exchange for coupons saved from the daily paper. One of the largest of the companies who printed these books was Cupples and Leon, producer of nearly half of the two hundred titles on record. Among the most popular sellers were *Mutt and Jeff, Bringing Up Father,* and *Little Orphan Annie.*

Bringing Up Father, #12, Cupples & Leon, NM 125.00
Bringing Up Father, #2, Cupples & Leon, EX 80.00
Charlie Chaplin in the Movies, NM 265.00

Dick Tracy & Dick Tracy Jr, Cupples & Leon, EX+ 85.00
Famous Comics, Captain Easy & Wash Tubbs, Whitman, EX 50.00
Henry, McKay, 1935, 52-pg, NM 50.00
Little Annie Rooney, McKay, 1943, 48-pg, NM 60.00
Little Orphan Annie, #1, Cupples & Leon, 1926, NM 125.00
Little Orphan Annie Willing Helper, Cupples & Leon, 1932, VG ..30.00
Mutt & Jeff Big Book, Cupples & Leon, hardcover, 1926, NM ..175.00
Popeye, Saalfield, 1934, 40-pg, EX+ 400.00
Skeezix & Uncle Walt, Reilly & Lee, 1924, NM 65.00
Skeezix Out West, Reilly & Lee, hardcover, 1928, NM 75.00
Smitty at Military School, 1933, VG 20.00
Tillie the Toiler, #2, Cupples & Leon, 52-pg, NM 40.00
Tricks of the Katzenjammer Kids, 1905, NM 150.00
Winnie Winkle, #1, Cupples & Leon, NM 65.00

Cash Registers

By 1970 antique cash registers had risen to become blue chip collectibles, joining the ranks of fine paintings, bronzes, firearms, clocks, and other categories having permanent, established worth. Some extremely scarce and elegant cash registers will command up to $25,000.00 on today's market.

Register prices are determined by make, model, size, desirability of pattern and accessories such as add-on clocks, topsigns, and personalized nameplates (which may be cast as topsigns, or 'lid ovals' and on occassion cast into the register's front or back plates). Of immense consideration is the register's condition.

This column uses 'mint' condition (M) to indicate registers which have been cleaned, oiled, polished, and lacquered by a professional and have perfect glass, keytops, and indicators. Some restorers will replace the velvet underneath the lid (where applicable), which is an added touch of elegance. 'Very good' condition (VG) describes unrestored, unpolished registers which are complete and operating. Their values are usually about half of the restored model's value. All prices may vary as much as 20%, depending on geography and demand. The brass cash registers have seen a slight upward trend this year. It is harder to find good unrestored models in complete and working condition. Rare models are getting quite scarce. Next year should see continuing upward prices.

For further information we recommend the highly informative books *Antique Cash Registers, 1880-1920,* by Bartsch and Sanchez (Mr. Bartsch's address may be found in our Directory under Oregon); and *The Incorruptible Cashier,* Vols. I & II, currently available from our other advisor, John Apple, listed in our Directory under Wisconsin.

NCR #1, American detail adder, VG 2,650.00
NCR #1000, glass autographic box attachment, 1910-16, M ..1,200.00
NCR #1000, glass autographic box attachment, 1910-16, VG ...650.00
NCR #129-130, bronze, VG 850.00
NCR #13 or #14, Ionic CI, 1899, G 750.00
NCR #130, Art Nouveau cabinet, M 1,600.00
NCR #135, Art Nouveau pattern, CI, 31-key, 1905, VG 600.00
NCR #2 or #3, detail adder, scroll pattern, VG 900.00
NCR #2 or #3, inlaid oak or mahog, scarce 2,250.00
NCR #215 or #216, bronze fleur-de-lis, VG 950.00
NCR #226, rare bilingual topsign, EX orig 900.00
NCR #250 or #251, bronze, VG 900.00
NCR #3, mahog inlay, deep wood drw, ca 1886 ....4,500.00
NCR #30, bronze, total adder, VG 1,400.00
NCR #312, #313, or #317, dolphin pattern, M 1,500.00
NCR #312, #313, or #317, dolphin pattern, VG 800.00
NCR #322, #323, or #327, marble 3 sides, extended base, M ..1,800.00
NCR #322, #323, or #327, marble 3 sides, extended base, VG ..1,050.00
NCR #324, or #325 Woolworth sz, M 1,050.00

NCR #33, $5 maximum, CA, 1903, VG 900.00
NCR #332, #333, #349 or #356, orig topsign, M 1,150.00
NCR #332, #333, #349 or #356, orig topsign, VG 550.00
NCR #337, dolphin design, M 1,150.00
NCR #338, dogwood pattern, English numerals, CA, 1910-16, VG 475.00
NCR #356, 33 keys, rings to $20, 1908-16, M 1,300.00
NCR #360, 37 keys, rings to $60, 1908-9, M 1,500.00
NCR #441-#442, Empire design w/quartered-oak base, M 1,750.00
NCR #441-#452, Empire pattern, M 1,750.00
NCR #441-#452, Empire pattern, VG 800.00
NCR #441E-#452E, electric, M 2,250.00
NCR #441E-#452E, electric, VG 950.00
NCR #442E-L, EX orig 950.00
NCR #47, oak or mahog inlay, up to $6, VG 2,250.00
NCR #5, narrow scroll, glass topsign, EX orig 2,750.00
NCR #50, Renaissance design, orig clock, EX orig 2,500.00
NCR #50 or #51, Renaissance pattern, VG 1,350.00
NCR #52, Renaissance design, orig clock, extended base, M ..3,800.00
NCR #52 or #52¼, Renaissance design, extended base, VG ...2,900.00
NCR #52¼, dolphin design, extended base, M 2,200.00
NCR #522, 2-drw, electric bar model, 1910-16, M 2,500.00
NCR #522, 2-drw, electric bar model, 1910-16, VG 1,800.00
NCR #64, Bohemian pattern, iron, 25-key, 1901, VG 600.00

National Cash Register #78, custom built in 1902 to eliminate the back window (adding to collectibility), nickel plated, VG, $950.00.

NCR #7 or #8, detail adder, fleur-de-lis, VG 850.00
NCR #711-#717, mahog-grain finish on steel, M 275.00

Cast Iron

In the mid-1800s, the cast-iron industry was raging in the United States. It was recognized as a medium extremely adaptable for uses ranging from ornamental architectural filigree to actual building construction. It could be cast from a mold into any conceivable design that could be reproduced over and over at a relatively small cost. It could be painted to give an entirely versatile appearance. Furniture with openwork designs of grapevines and leaves and intricate lacy scrollwork was cast for gardens as well as inside use. Figural doorstops of every sort, bootjacks, trivets, and a host of other useful and decorative items were made before the 'ferromania' had run its course. Our advisor for this category is J.M. Ellwood; he is listed in the Directory under Arizona. See also Kitchen, Cast-Iron Bakers, and Kettles; and other specific categories.

Armchair, fern design, EX detail, rust/pitting, 36" 550.00
Cookie mold, bird on branch designs w/5 stars, 3¼x5" 75.00
Cookie mold, fraternal symbols, 5x6⅞" 75.00
Cuspidor, ft-activated, sheet steel lid, blk pnt, 14" 95.00
Figure, rabbit, full body, worn wht rpt, 10½" 220.00
Fire dogs, brass finial, ca 1890, 9", pr 30.00
Flowerpot holder, floral crests & ring for pot, blk pnt, 22" 60.00

Footstool, pierced apron, cabriole legs, needlepoint uphl 365.00
Hitching post, Blk boy on sq base, EX detail, 46", EX 3,300.00
Hitching post, jockey on sq base, Champion, rust/losses, 50" 700.00
Hitching post, tree-like w/branches, incomplete base, 49" 360.00
Kettle, gypsy; 9½x12" dia 95.00
Letter holder, camel figural 75.00
Memo clip, dolphin head, worn gold pnt, 6¼" L 40.00
Paperweight, turtle, Hoosier advertising, 2½" 65.00
Plant stand, scrolled openwork on rnd top & ft, 32x15" dia 175.00
Planter, old blk rpt, 19½x21½" dia 140.00
Plaque, pig face in relief, scalloped, hdls, 9½" 475.00
Posset pot, 6¼" dia, 5" hdl 55.00
Rosette cookie maker, card suits, ca 1900, set of 4 ....85.00
Shoeshine footrest, camel figural, chrome plated, 8x8x3½" 90.00
Stove plate, scrolls & foliage, Berkshire Furnace, 25x31", EX 100.00
Teakettle, wrought hdl & tilter, 24" 415.00
Umbrella stand, EX floral detail on center std, rpt, 27" 125.00
Urn, cherub on plinth holds bowl on head, rpt, 45", pr 6,000.00
Urn, scrolled ear hdls, fluted, tall base, 49", EX, pr 2,200.00
Wick trimmers, scissors shape, ca 1870 ....40.00

Castor Sets

Castor sets became popular during the early years of the 18th century and continued to be used through the late Victorian era. Their purpose was to hold various condiments for table use. The most common type was a circular arrangement with a center handle on a revolving pedestal base that held three, four, five, or six bottles. Some had extras; a few were equipped with a bell for calling the servant. Frames were made of silverplate, glass, or pewter. Though most bottles were of pressed glass, some of the designs were cut, and on rare occasion, colored glass with enameled decorations was used as well. To maintain authenticity and value, castor sets should have matching bottles. Prices listed below are for those with matching bottles and in frames with plating that is in excellent condition (unless noted otherwise).

Watch for new frames and bottles in both clear and colored glass; these have recently been appearing on the market.

Key: D&B — Daisy and Button

3-bottle, Am Shield; pewter fr w/eagle, mini, child sz 150.00
3-bottle, D&B, blown; pressed glass fr w/toothpick on bail 150.00
4-bottle, cranberry, orig stoppers; pressed glass holder 265.00
4-bottle, cut dots/etch; rectangular/ftd fr w/figures, Rogers 175.00
4-bottle, Log & Star, amber; orig ped-base fr 145.00
4-bottle, pressed, SP tops, orig SP fr w/rnd base, 6½" 65.00
5-bottle, etched & wheel cut; orig SP fr, EX 250.00
5-bottle, etched floral w/cutting, much decor; Meriden fr 295.00
5-bottle, Honeycomb; ornate Wilcox fr 295.00
6-bottle, D&B, pressed; oversz 18" decor Meriden fr 395.00
6-bottle, etched & cut, sq; ornate 18" fr w/call bell, Tufts 450.00
6-bottle, pressed; 18" Simpson-Hall-Miller fr w/EX SP 295.00
6-bottle, Sawtooth; ornate Meriden fr, call bell, dtd 1888, EX ...450.00
7-bottle, cut crystal; lg ped-ft Gleason fr w/doors 1,550.00
7-bottle+vase on figural std, Redfield & Rice SP, 1865, 21" 525.00

Catalina Island

Catalina Island pottery was made on the island of the same name, which is about twenty-six miles off the coast of Los Angeles. The pottery was started in 1927 at Pebbly Beach, by Wm. Wrigley, Jr., who was instrumental in developing and using the native clays. Its principal products were brick and tile to be used for construction on the island. Garden pieces were first produced, then vases, bookends, lamps, ashtrays, novelty items, and finally dinnerware. The ware became very popular and was soon being shipped to the mainland as well.

Some of the pottery was hand thrown; some was made in molds. Most pieces are marked Catalina Island or Catalina with a printed incised stamp or handwritten with a pointed tool. Cast items were sometimes marked in the mold; a few have an ink stamp, and a paper label was also used.

The color of the clay can help to identify approximately when a piece was made: 1927 to 1932, brown to red clay; 1931 to 1932, an experimental period with various colors; 1932 to 1937, mainly white clay, but tan to brown were also used on occasion.

Items marked Catalina Pottery are listed in Gladding McBean. For further information we recommend *The Collector's Encyclopedia of California Pottery* by our advisor, Jack Chipman; he is listed in the Directory under California.

Dinnerware

Catalina Island, bowl, berry 25.00
Catalina Island, bowl, cereal 45.00
Catalina Island, bowl, vegetable; rnd, 8½" 65.00
Catalina Island, candle holder, low 75.00
Catalina Island, cup, coffee/tea 45.00
Catalina Island, custard cup 25.00
Catalina Island, mug, 6" 45.00
Catalina Island, pitcher, squat base 125.00
Catalina Island, plate, bread & butter; coupe design, 6" 15.00
Catalina Island, plate, dinner; wide rim, 10½" 30.00
Catalina Island, plate, rolled rim, 12½" 75.00
Catalina Island, sugar bowl, w/lid 50.00
Catalina Island, teapot, traditional English style 250.00
Catalina Island, tumbler, 4" 22.50
Catalina Island, wine cup, hdld 25.00
Rope Edge, casserole, w/lid 50.00
Rope Edge, chop plate, 13½" 60.00
Rope Edge, creamer 25.00
Rope Edge, cup & saucer 35.00
Rope Edge, plate, dinner; 10½" 25.00
Rope Edge, plate, salad; 8½" 20.00
Rope Edge, sugar bowl 35.00
Rope Edge, teapot 150.00

Miscellaneous

Vase, early, marked Catalina Island, 9", $850.00.

Bowl, Indian design, rare 375.00
Candelabrum, turq, 3-hole, str 200.00
Charger, HP Mexican scene, mk, ca 1932, 11½" 600.00

Charger, swordfish, HP on lt bl, 14" 500.00
Flower frog, pelican 245.00
Shakers, tulip, pr 65.00
Tile, mc Spanish design, 6x6" 165.00
Tray, turq, rolled edge, 14½", w/forged iron hdl 125.00
Vase, Monterey Brn, flowerpot form, old mk, 5½" 125.00
Vase, orange, urn shape w/hdls, 8" 250.00
Vase, red-orange, squat base, conical neck, 8" 235.00
Vase, stepped design w/hdls, 5" 350.00
Vinegar bottle, bl matt, gourd shape 100.00
Wall pocket, basketweave, 9" 200.00

Catalogs

Catalogs are not only intriguing to collect on their own merit, but for the collector with a specific interest, they are often the only remaining source of background information available, and as such they offer a wealth of otherwise unrecorded data. The mail-order industry can be traced as far back as the mid-1800s. Even before Aaron Montgomery Ward began his career in 1872, Laacke and Joys of Wisconsin and the Orvis Company of Vermont, both dealers in sporting goods, had been well established for many years. The E.C. Allen Company sold household necessities and novelties by mail on a broad scale in the 1870s. By the end of the Civil War, sewing machines, garden seed, musical instruments, even medicine, were available from catalogs. In the 1880s Macy's of New York issued a 127-page catalog; Sears and Spiegel followed suit in about 1890. Craft and art supply catalogs were first available about 1880 and covered such varied fields as china painting, stenciling, wood burning, brass embossing, hair weaving, and shellcraft. Today some collectors confine their interests not only to craft catalogs in general but often to just one subject. There are several factors besides rarity which make a catalog valuable: age, condition, profuse illustrations, how collectible the field is that it deals with, the amount of color used in its printing, its size (format and number of pages), and whether it is a manufacturer's catalog verses a jobber's catalog (the former being the most desirable). Our advisor for this category is Richard M. Bueschel; he is listed in the Directory under Illinois.

Abercombie & Fitch, Servicemen gifts, 1943, 24-pg, EX 32.00
AC Gilbert Co, Erector set instructions, 1938, 38-pg, VG 35.00
Albert Pick & Co, fountain supplies, 1934, 322-pg, G 350.00
Albert Pick & Co, saloon supplies, 1907-08, 234-pg, G 400.00
Allis-Chalmers Hoistong Engines, 1901, 127-pg, EX 20.00
American Flyer, trains & accessories, color, 1933, 8-pg, VG+ 25.00
American Mechanical Toy Co, model building, 1915, 80-pg, G ..31.00
American Sawmill & Woodworking Machinery, 1921, 208-pg, EX ..25.00
American Woodworking Machine Co, hardbk, 1898, 364-pg, EX ..60.00
Armstrong Tool Co, 1915, 126-pg, EX 15.00
Bing's Constructor, toy building sets, 1920, 125-pg, G- 35.00
Bliss Co Special Machinery, hardbk, 1906, 578-pg, EX 15.00
Bradley Knitting, knitted items, 1922-23, 24-pg, VG 40.00
Brown & Sharp, sm tools, 1916, 375-pg 25.00
Carson, Pirie, Scott & Co Gift Book, 1929, EX 40.00
Carter Ink, 71 products, illus, 1921, EX 75.00
Carter Tru-Scale Machine, metal miniatures, 1961, 16-pg, VG ...35.00
Charles C Merzback, trains & accessories, 1968, 56-pg, VG+ 32.00
Chicago Millwork Supply, housing material, 1927, 96-pg, G 35.00
Cincinnati Butcher's Supply, 1895, 160-pg, EX 40.00
Clark Hutchinson, shoe store equipment, 48-pg, VG 30.00
Crane Hand & Power Pumps, hardbk, 1920, 247-pg, EX 20.00
Daisy Mfg, air rifles, 1930, 128-pg, 4½x5¼", G- 50.00
Ducommun Mechanics Tools, 1925, 1,248-pg, EX 60.00

Dunham Carrigan Hardware, loose leaf, 1880, 83-pg, EX 45.00
E Butterick, clothing, Winter 1887-88, 32-pg, 8x11", EX 60.00
Evans Mfg, bob sleighs, no date, 12-pg, 3½x6¼", G 30.00
Fulton, Conway & Co, auto/wagon items, 1924, 228-pg, VG+ ..200.00
Hall & Brown Woodworking Machinery, hardbk, 1900, 398-pg ..30.00
Hartz Mountain Products, animal care, 1920s, 30-pg, VG 30.00
HC Evans & Co, gambling goods, 1946, 44-pg, VG 35.00
Henry Disston Handbook for Lumbermen, 1902, 176-pg, EX 20.00
Henry Disston Saws, 1918, 143-pg, EX 20.00
Hibbard, Spencer & Bartlet, hardware store, 1935, 54-pg, G 15.00
Holcomb & Hoke, Butter-Kist popcorn machines, 1921, 16-pg, VG ..120.00
Huffy Mfg, bicycles, 1961, color, 9-pg, 8½x11", VG 35.00
Hunt, Helm & Ferris & Co, hardware items, 1908, 24-pg, VG 36.00
Indian Motorcycles, color, 1911, 24-pg, M 150.00
J Lynn & Co, jewelry, silver & pocketknives, 80-pg, VG 40.00
Komp Natural Wood Ornaments, 1886, 16-pg, EX 20.00
Landis, holiday issue, children's vehicles, '37, 22-pg, VG+ 40.00
Lane Bryant, women's fashion, Summer 1942, 58-pg, VG+ 30.00
LB Ramsdell Co, children's furniture/toys, 1927, 40-pg, G 48.00
Lionel Corp, trains accessories, 1962, 40-pg, 8¼x11", VG 22.00
Lionel Toys, trains & accessories, 1958, 54-pg, G 37.00
Lutheran Church Supplies, 1963, color, 24-pg, EX 35.00
Macoy Publishing-Masonic Supply, Masonic goods, '05, 64-pg, VG ..75.00
McArthur, Wirth & Co, store fixtures etc, 1900, 8x10", 84-pg 25.00
Metropolitan Fashions, clothing, Nov 1886, 8-pg, 11x16", EX 45.00
Meyer-Wise-Kaichen, 25th Anniversary, clothes, '20, 122-pg, VG ...40.00
Mills Novelty Co, coin machines, 1918, 24-pg, EX 175.00
Mills Novelty Co, coin machines (Spanish), 1933, 40-pg, VG ...125.00
Monarch Theatre Supply, 1929, 16-pg, 8½x11¼", G 50.00
Montgomery Wards, Christmas book, 1943, 144-pg, 8x11", G+ 50.00
Montgomery Wards, 1931, 64-pg, 6½x9½", EX 35.00
Mueller & Co, surgical supplies, 1948, 680-pg, EX 145.00
Nash & Brothers, farming equipment, 1884, 48-pg, VG 45.00
National Cloak & Suit Co, clothing, 1917, 94-pg, G 35.00
National Cloak & Suit Co NY, Christy cover, 1909, M 70.00
National Clothier Service, store supplies, 1956, 162-pg, VG 30.00
Palmer Penmanship Pointers, better penmanship, 1919, 20-pg, G ..35.00
Paramount Supplies, general merchandise, 1938, 96-pg, VG 50.00
Parker Brothers, games, 1929, 12-pg, 6x9", G 40.00
Paul H Gesswein, jewelry supplies, 1948, 79-pg, VG 35.00
Pep Boys-Manny, Moe & Jack, auto equipment, '57, 86-pg, VG ..35.00
Pfleuger, tackle, 1941, EX 65.00
Philadelphia Bird Food, cages/bird items, 1890s, 32-pg, NM 30.00
Phoenix Mfg, horseshoes, tools, etc, 1920s, 26-pg, VG 45.00
Playskool Mfg, learning toys, 1931, 38-pg, 3¼x7¼", G 45.00
Pratt & Whitney Small Tools, hardbk, 1944, 443-pg, EX 25.00
Ranger Bicycles, color cover, Mead Cycle Co, 1920, 57-pg 75.00
Roucher Playthings, model shipbuilding, 1939, 68-pg, VG+ 15.00
Samuel Kirk & Sons, flatware, 1931, 64-pg, 6x9¼", EX 38.00
Sears, Roebuck, Christmas book, 1949, 268-pg, 8½x11", G 72.00
Sears, Roebuck, pressure cooker uses, 1920s, 32-pg, G 15.00
Smith-Worthington, wholesale auto supplies, 1918, 12-pg, VG+ 125.00
South Bend, tackle, 1942, EX 45.00
Spear & Co, home furnishings, 1928, 16-pg, G 35.00
Spiegel-May-Stern, general merchandise, 1920s, 12-pg, VG 25.00
Stanley Tools, 1939, 240-pg, EX 20.00
Stockman-Farmer Supply, Spring/Summer 1935, 64-pg, VG 70.00
TF Memmen Co, soda fountain/stove/bar supplies, '18, 180-pg, G ..150.00
Tracy-Wells, holiday goods, 1927, 64-pg, 9x11¾", G+ 43.00
Vick's Floral Guide, seeds & plants supplies, '81, 112-pg, VG 60.00
Watson Mfg Co, sliding blinds/screens, 1886, 36-pg, G 35.00
Whitehead & Hoag Co, badges/honors/ribbons, 1899, 24-pg, VG ..175.00
Winchester-Western, guns & ammo, 1962, 32-pg, 10x7", EX 25.00
Wm K Walthers, HO & O ga trains, 1948, 100+pgs, 6x9", VG 35.00

Caughley Ware

The Caughley Coalport Porcelain Manufactory operated from about 1775 until 1799 in Caughley, near Salop, Shropshire, in England. The owner was Thomas Turner, who gained his potting experience from his association with the Worcester Pottery Company. The wares he manufactured in Caughley are referred to as 'Salopian.' He is most famous for his blue-printed earthenwares, particularly the Blue Willow pattern, designed for him by Thomas Minton. For a more detailed history, see Coalport.

Creamer, flowers/butterflies, underglaze bl, w/lid, 6", VG 230.00
Creamer, Grecian women, brn transfer, scalloped, 3", VG 38.00
Cup, bird, mc, 1⅞" 150.00
Cup, deer & cottage, bl & wht, NM 50.00
Cup, man/lady/cottage, floral int border, EX 80.00
Cup & saucer, bird, mc, NM 250.00
Cup & saucer, Brittania, brn transfer w/mc 110.00
Cup & saucer, exotic bird w/fruits & flowers, VG 110.00
Cup & saucer, mc HP stylized florals, vine band, mk 100.00
Jug, Cabbage Leaf, mask spout, chinoiserie transfer, 8½" 775.00
Mug, fruit & flower clusters, bl transfer, 1790, 5¾" 325.00
Plate, soup; elephant scene, 9⅞", EX 115.00
Saucer, Cupid on goat, mc, EX 130.00
Saucer, fallow deer, mc 115.00
Teapot, fruit clusters, bl transfer, bulbous, 1790, 4½" 500.00
Waste bowl, red & bl Oriental decor, pearlware, 2⅝x5⅝" 80.00

Ceramic Art Company

Jonathan Coxon, Sr., and Walter Scott Lenox established the Ceramic Art Company in 1889 in Trenton, New Jersey, where they produced fine belleek porcelain. Both were experienced in its production, having previously worked for Ott and Brewer. They hired artists to hand paint their wares with portraits, scenes, and lovely florals. Today artist-signed examples bring the highest prices. Several marks were used, three of which contain the 'CAC' monogram. A green wreath surrounding the company name in full was used on special-order wares, but these are not often encountered. Coxon eventually left the company, and it was later reorganized under the Lenox name. See also Lenox. Our advisor for this category is Mary Frank Gaston; she is listed in the Directory under Texas.

Ink blotter holder, hand-painted pink floral designs with butterflies and gold trim, brown mark, 6", $195.00.

Buttonhook, mc florals w/gold, factory decor, unmk, 7¾" 275.00
Creamer & sugar bowl, floral, gold on ivory, palette mk 195.00
Cup, chocolate; bl beading & gold on ivory, ped ft 65.00
Mug, ears of corn on brn, bbl shape, 5" 75.00
Mug, pomegranates, 1890 palette mk, 5½" 195.00
Mug, strawberries, emb hdl & base, palette mk, 6" 85.00
Pitcher, cider; 3-color grapes, beaded hdl, lg 155.00
Pitcher, lemonade; roses, red on gr, sgn Durr, 5½" 175.00
Pitcher, tankard, pines & full moon on dk gr, gr mk 255.00
Stein, 3 boys playing football, sgn, 5¼" 325.00

Vase, mums, mc on blended ground, mk, 10x4" 275.00
Vase, roses w/gold on purple, hdls, flat bell top, 16x7" 500.00
Vase, 3 heron reserves, iris on blk at neck, mk, 22" 550.00

Ceramic Arts Studio, Madison

The Ceramic Arts Studio Company began operations sometime prior to the 1940s, but it was about then that Betty Harrington started marketing her goods through this company. Betty Harrington is the designer primarily responsible for creating the line of figurines and knick-knacks that has become so popular with collectors. There were two others — Ulli Rebus, who not only designed several of the animals and various other pieces but taught Betty the art of mold-making as well, and Ruth Planter, who's work may have been very limited. About 65% of these items are marked, but even unmarked items become easily recognizable after only a brief study of their distinctive styling and glaze colors. At least eight different marks were used, among them the black ink stamp and the incised mark: 'Ceramic Arts Studio, Madison, Wisc.' A paper sticker was used in the early years.

After the 1955 demise of the company in Madison, the owner (Ruben Sand) went to Japan where he continued production under the same name using many of the same molds. After a short time, the old molds were retired, and new and quite different items were produced. Most of the Japan pieces can be found with a Ceramic Arts Studio backstamp. The Japan identification was on a paper label and is often missing. Japan pieces are never marked Madison, Wisc., but not all Madison pieces are either. Red or blue backstamps are exclusively Japanese.

Another company that also produced figurines operated at about the same time as the Madison studio. It was called Ceramic Art (no 's') Studio; do not confuse the two.

A second and larger building in the C.A.S. complex in Madison was for the exclusive production of metal accessories. The creator and designer of this related line was Zona Liberace, Liberace's stepmother, who was art director for the line of figurines as well. These pieces are rising fast in value and because they weren't marked can sometimes be found at bargain prices. They were so popular that other ceramic companies bought them to complement their own lines, so they may also be found with ceramic figures other than C.A.S.'s.

For those seeking additional information, video tapes (Series 1 and 2) are available from the author, BA Wellman, whose address can be found under Massachusetts. 1996-1997 price guides are also available. Mr. Wellman encourages collectors to write him with any new information concerning company history and/or production. He sends Vera a 'thank you' for helping us with this year's updates.

Figurine, Archibald the dragon, 8", $195.00.

Bank, Skunky, 4" 85.00
Bell, Summer Belle, 5¼" 68.00
Bowl, Bonita, 3¾" 40.00
Bowl, shallow, scalloped, 2¼" 28.00
Candle holder, bedtime boy & girl, 4¾" 85.00

Figurine, accordion lady, standing, 8½" 145.00
Figurine, Adam & Eve (1-pc), 12" 565.00
Figurine, Alice & wht rabbit, 4½", 6", pr 185.00
Figurine, angel singing, 3½" 26.00
Figurine, Autumn Andy, 5" 50.00
Figurine, Bali-Gong, 5½" 48.00
Figurine, Bali-Lao, topless, 8½" 95.00
Figurine, Balinese dance couple, 9½", pr 195.00
Figurine, Balky & Frisky (horses), 3¾", pr 125.00
Figurine, Bashful, 4¾" 65.00
Figurine, birch bark canoe, 8" 95.00
Figurine, Bobby sitting, blk, 3¼" 125.00
Figurine, Bruce & Beth, gr, 6½", 5", pr 75.00
Figurine, Burmese woman, 5" 50.00
Figurine, camel standing, 5½" 95.00
Figurine, charger left (no rider), 5½" 115.00
Figurine, Chinese lantern holders, 6", pr 125.00
Figurine, chipmunk, 2" 24.00
Figurine, Cinderella & Prince Charming, 6½", pr 145.00
Figurine, Colonial boy & girl, 5", 5¼", pr 75.00
Figurine, dachshunds, standing & lying, 2½", 3½", pr 75.00
Figurine, Dawn, stylized, 6½" 125.00
Figurine, donkeys, 3¼", 2⅞", pr 65.00
Figurine, drum girl, 4½" 50.00
Figurine, Dutch Love boy & girl, 5", pr 45.00
Figurine, Egyptian man & woman, 9½", pr 285.00
Figurine, elephant, trunk down, sm 25.00
Figurine, Elsie (elephant), 5" 65.00
Figurine, Fire man & woman, 11¼", pr 225.00
Figurine, flute lady, standing, 8½" 165.00
Figurine, French horn man, sitting, 6½" 165.00
Figurine, Frisky lamb w/garland, 2¾" 18.00
Figurine, frog, 2" 16.00
Figurine, gremlin boy & girl, 4", 2½", pr 185.00
Figurine, guitar boy, 5" 60.00
Figurine, Hans & Katinka, on pedestal, 5½", pr 50.00
Figurine, harem girl, sitting, 4½" 45.00
Figurine, Harry & Lillibeth, 6½", pr 85.00
Figurine, Hiawatha, 3½" 95.00
Figurine, Indian boy, 3" 20.00
Figurine, Kabuki dancers, 8¾", 5½", pr 425.00
Figurine, kitten, scratching, wht, 2" 18.00
Figurine, leopards, fighting, 8½", 6", pr 145.00
Figurine, Little Miss Muffett #2, 4½" 55.00
Figurine, Lu Tang & Wing Sang, 6¼", pr 45.00
Figurine, Lucindy & Col Jackson, 7", 7¼", pr 85.00
Figurine, Lutist & Flutust, 12", pr 235.00
Figurine, Madonna & Child (1-pc), 6½" 85.00
Figurine, mermaid baby on tummy, 2½" 35.00
Figurine, mermaid mother on rocks, 4" 65.00
Figurine, Mexican man w/cactus & Senorita, 7", 6½", pr 68.00
Figurine, Minnehaha, 6½" 110.00
Figurine, modern colt, 7½" 95.00
Figurine, modern fox, 3" 95.00
Figurine, modern jaguar, 5" 125.00
Figurine, mouse, 3" 35.00
Figurine, Muff & Puff, 3", pr 65.00
Figurine, Palomino colt, 5¾" 75.00
Figurine, panda w/hat, 2½" 35.00
Figurine, Peter Pan & Wendy, 5¼", pr 125.00
Figurine, Peter Rabbit, 3¾" 40.00
Figurine, Petrov & Petrushka, 5¼", 5", pr 45.00
Figurine, Piper boy, in sailor suit, 3½" 38.00
Figurine, Piper girl singing, 3" 38.00

Figurine, pixie boy on toadstool, 4" 22.00
Figurine, pixie girl kneeling, 2½" 25.00
Figurine, Pomeranian, sitting & standing, 2¼", 2¾", pr 65.00
Figurine, Promenade man & woman, 7¾", pr 125.00
Figurine, Ralph the goat w/flower, 4" 35.00
Figurine, red devil imp reclining 62.00
Figurine, saxophone boy, 5¼" 60.00
Figurine, shepherd & shepherdess, 8½", 8", pr 175.00
Figurine, snuggle seal mother & pup, 6" overall, pr 185.00
Figurine, Sonny & Honey, 5¾", pr 125.00
Figurine, Spaniel, mom & pup, sitting, 2¼", 1¾", pr 45.00
Figurine, Spring Sue, 5" 50.00
Figurine, Squeaky the squirrel, 3¼" 20.00
Figurine, St Francis w/2 birds, 9½" 65.00
Figurine, St George on charger, 8½" 165.00
Figurine, sultan, 4½" 55.00
Figurine, Sun-Li & Sun-Lin, 5½", pr 38.00
Figurine, Swan Lake man & woman, 7" overall, pr 225.00
Figurine, temple dancers, 6¾", pr 185.00
Figurine, toadstool, 3" 20.00
Figurine, Tom cat, blk, 4¾" 65.00
Figurine, tortoise w/cane, 3¼" 32.00
Figurine, Violet, ballerina, sitting, 3" 65.00
Figurine, violin lady, standing, 8½" 145.00
Figurine, Willing, 4¾" 50.00
Figurine, zebra, 5" 65.00
Figurine, Zulu man & woman #2, 6", 7¼", pr 295.00
Jug, Miss Forward, 4" 42.00
Lamp, Fire man on base 225.00
Lamp, flutist on base 195.00
Planter, bamboo, 2" 25.00
Planter, Becky, 5¼" 65.00
Planter, ivy pot, rectanglar, 4x2½" 18.00

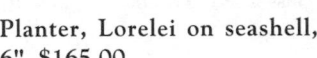

Planter, Lorelei on seashell, 6", $165.00.

Plaque, Attitude & Arabesque, gr, 9½" 95.00
Plaque, Chinese lantern man & woman, 8" 125.00
Plaque, cockatoo A&B, 8", pr 65.00
Plaque, Comedy & Tragedy mask, 5½", pr 95.00
Plaque, Dutch boy & girl, 8" 75.00
Plaque, G Gander & M Contrary, 4½", 5", pr 145.00
Plaque, Grace & Greg, 9½", 9", pr 80.00
Plaque, Hamlet & Ophelia, 8¼", pr 195.00
Plaque, Jack & the beanstalk, 6½" 125.00
Plaque, Neptune, 6" 135.00
Plaque, striped fish, mom & baby 55.00
Plaque, water sprite (fish up), 4¼" 38.00
Plaque, Zor & Zorina, 9", pr 95.00
Shakers, bunnies kissing, 4", 2½", pr 150.00
Shakers, bunnies running, 4½", 3½", pr 195.00
Shakers, Butch & Billy (pups), 3", 2", pr 95.00
Shakers, Chinese boy & girl, 4¼", 4", pr 25.00

Shakers, Chinese wee boy & girl, 3", pr 20.00
Shakers, cocks fighting, 3¾", pr 45.00
Shakers, donkeys, 3¼", 2⅞", pr 125.00
Shakers, Dutch wee boy & girl, 3", pr 22.00
Shakers, Fifi & Fufu, 3", 2½", pr 125.00
Shakers, fish (swimming), 3½", pr 45.00
Shakers, fox & goose, 3¼", 2¼", pr 125.00
Shakers, French wee boy & girl, 3", pr 32.00
Shakers, Gingham Dog & Calico Cat, 2¾", 3", pr 32.00
Shakers, giraffes, mother & baby, 6½", 5½", pr 195.00
Shakers, leopards, 2 fighting, 3½", 5¼", pr 195.00
Shakers, lion & lioness, ea 5¼", pr 225.00
Shakers, Minnehaha & Hiawatha, 6½", 3½", pr 225.00
Shakers, pixie boy & toadstool, 2½", 3", pr 38.00
Shakers, ram & ewe (modern), 2", 1¾", pr 65.00
Shakers, Scottish wee boy & girl, 3¼", pr 38.00
Shakers, Siamese cats, mom & baby, 4¼", 3¼", pr 65.00
Shakers, snuggle bears, mom & baby, blk, 4¾" overall, pr 225.00
Shakers, snuggle bears, mom & baby, brn, 4¼" overall, pr 65.00
Shakers, snuggle bears, mom & baby, wht, 4¼" overall, pr 75.00
Shakers, snuggle bunnies, mom & baby, 4½" overall, pr 95.00
Shakers, snuggle dog in doghouse, 1¾" overall, pr 75.00
Shakers, snuggle kangaroos, mom & child, 4¾" overall, pr ...65.00
Shakers, Tembino & Tembo (elephants), 2½", 6½", pr 245.00
Shelf sitter, Angels, Sleeping girl & Pray boy, 4¼", pr 75.00
Shelf sitter, Bali boy & girl, 5½", pr 125.00
Shelf sitter, banjo girl, 4" 50.00
Shelf sitter, Colonial man & woman, ea 5", pr 70.00
Shelf sitter, fishing boy & farm girl, w/pole, 4¾", pr 95.00
Shelf sitter, Fluffy (cat), wht, 4¾" 48.00
Shelf sitter, harmonica boy, 4" 50.00
Shelf sitter, Jack & Jill, 4¾", 5", pr 48.00
Shelf sitter, Little Jack Horner, 4½" 45.00
Shelf sitter, Maurice & Michele, 7", pr 85.00
Shelf sitter, Nip & Tuck, 4¼", 4", pr 45.00
Shelf sitter, Pierrot & Pierette, 6½", pr 135.00
Shelf sitter, setter, prone, paws hang, 5" 65.00
Shelf sitter, Willy, ball down, wht, 4½" 135.00
Vase, Chinese, sq, 2" 18.00
Vase, duck motif, rnd, 2" 22.00
Vase, Wing Sang on bamboo bud, 7" 28.00

Metal Accessories

Arched window for Madonna & Child, 14" 45.00
Artist palette w/shelves, left/right 65.00
Birdcage w/perch for birds, 14" 65.00
Diamond shadow box, for Attitude & Arabesque, 15½x13¾" 55.00
Frame w/shelf, 22½" sq 24.00
Holder for planter 18.00
Pyramid shelves, ea 35.00
Sofa for Maurice & Michele, 10x3¾" 65.00
Triple ring shelves 65.00

Chalkware

Chalkware figures were a popular commodity from approximately 1860 until 1890. They were made from gypsum or plaster of Paris formed in a mold and then hand painted in oils or watercolors. Items such as animals and birds, figures, banks, toys, and religious ornaments modeled after more expensive Staffordshire wares were often sold door to door. Their origin is attributed to Italian immigrants. Today regarded as a form of folk art, 19th-century American pieces bring prices in the hundreds of dollars. Carnival chalkware from this century is also collectible, especially figures that are personality related. For those, see Carnival Collectibles.

Bank, bull, standing, emb fur & horns, blk pnt, 15" L 2,650.00
Bird on plinth, worn 2-color pnt, 6½" 200.00
Cat, ball between front paws, worn mc pnt, solid, 9" 125.00
Cat, seated, wht w/orig red/blk/yel pnt, lt wear, 6⅝" 1,150.00
Cat, seated w/pipe in mouth, worn mc pnt, 10" 265.00
Dog, free-standing, worn mc pnt, 8" 300.00
Eagle on ball, 2-color pnt, sq base, 8½", NM 485.00
Garniture, fruit compote, bright mc pnt, rpr, 13", pr 985.00
Madonna & Child, orig mc pnt, 10" 450.00
Rooster, mc pnt on yel, 5½" 550.00
Squirrel, acorn in mouth, worn mc pnt, rprs, 6" 350.00
Stag, recumbent, gr pnt, England, rpr, 10x8", facing pr 460.00
Stag w/antlers, recumbent, mc pnt on yel, 10x8" 1,650.00

Chase Brass & Copper Company

Americans were shocked in 1923 when an invitation to stage an exhibit at the first major postwar fair, *The 1925 Exposition des Arts Decoratifs et Industriels,* was declined by the American government because the U.S. could not comply with the exposition's requirement that only original work would be exhibited. Even though American industry produced a vast quantity of varied goods, there was very little 'original American' to show, since most design ideas were being brought in from Europe.

This blow to American prestige and the uproar that resulted prompted a dispatch of designers (among them Donald Deskey, Walter Dorwin Teague, and Russel Wright) to the Paris exhibition. They were to determine what steps would be necessary in order for U.S. designs to compete with European standards. They returned championing the new modernist style. By the mid-1930s, products were being designed and marketed that were attractive to the reluctant consumer insistent upon buying a streamline style that was uniquely American. During the decade of the thirties, the Chase Brass & Copper Company offered lamps, smoking acessories, and housewares similar to those Americans were seeing on the Hollywood screen at prices the average buyer could afford. These products are highly valued today not only because of their superior quality but also because of those who created them. Walter von Nessen, Gerth & Gerth, Rockwell Kent, Russel Wright, Laurelle Guild, and Dr. A. Reimann were some of Chase's well-known designers. Emily Post, who served as spokesperson for Chase, promoted a trend away from expensive silver and toward chromium serving pieces.

Besides chromium, Chase manufactured many products in brass, copper, nickel plate, or a combination of these metals; all are equally collectible. Some items had glass inserts which collectors also seek.

Nearly all Chase products were marked, either on the item itself or on a screw or rivet. On sets containing several pieces, the trademark may appear on only one. Be cautious. Check unmarked items to make sure they measure up to Chase's standard of quality, and lighting fixtures that are unmarked may be compared with pictures of verified examples. For safety's sake, replace both cords and internal wiring before attempting to use any electrical product. Not only will you be protected against possible loss from fire, but you will enhance the value of your collectible as well.

For more thorough study we recommend *Art Deco Chrome, The Chase Era,* and *Art Deco Chrome, Book 2, A Collector's Guide, Industrial Design in the Chase Era.* Both are authored by Richard J. Kilbride; Mrs. Kilbride is listed in the Directory under Connecticut. In the listings that follow, examples are polished unless noted satin. For further information contact the Chase Collector's Society, listed in the Directory under Clubs, Newsletters, and Catalogs.

Ash receiver, Cube, blk, red, chrome, #17069, 2" 350.00
Ash receiver, Flip-top, chrome, 1939 World's Fair logo, #871 ....275.00
Ashtray, Golfers, chrome w/golf club rests, #890, 4" 45.00
Ashtrays, chrome, #839, ind, 2¾", set of 4 ....30.00
Bar caddy, chrome, #90141, 6⅛" 10.00
Bell, Canterbury, brass w/gr plastic hdl, #13008, 3¾" 45.00
Bell, Cuckoo, chrome w/blk nickel bird hdl, #13004, 2½" 75.00
Bookends, Arch, satin brass/copper, #17020, 5½x4", pr 350.00
Bookends, Horse, satin nickel/blk, #17044, 6½x4", pr 525.00
Bookends, Ring, satin brass/copper, #17019, 5x5", pr 275.00
Bowl, ice; chrome w/curved hdl, #28002, 7", +tongs 70.00
Bowl, nut; chrome & walnut, #90084, 10x6¾", +4 picks 60.00
Box, cigarette; Connoisseur, satin copper, #842, 7" L 75.00
Box, cigarette; Rockwell Kent, bronze, #847, 6½" L 1,050.00
Box, cigarette; Rollaround, satin nickel, 5" L 90.00
Box, Dolphin, antique brass top w/ivory base, #856, 3¾x3" 45.00
Box, Iris, ivory plastic base, brass lid, #90074 ....65.00
Bud holder, chrome, 4-tube, #11230, 9" 30.00
Buffet warming oven, chrome & walnut, #90096, 10½x7⅛" 120.00
Candlestick, Disk, chrome, dbl candles, 4¾x8½", ea 170.00
Candlesticks, Bubble, chrome/bl glass, #17063, 2½", pr 75.00
Candlesticks, Dee-Handle, by Reimann, brass, #21006, pr 1,450.00
Candlesticks, Diana, chrome/walnut, #24009, 1⅞x3½", pr 45.00
Candlesticks, Fiesta, chrome/blk base, #29001, 8⅜x8", pr 175.00
Candy dish, brass w/fruit finial on lid, glass insert, 7" 25.00
Cigarette server, Cube, 2-compartment, red/wht, #17070 ....270.00
Cocktail ball, chrome w/red rubber base, #90071, 3⅜" 25.00
Cocktail shaker, Blue Moon, chrome w/bl top, #90066 ....100.00
Cocktail shaker, Gaiety, chrome w/blk rings, #90034 ....45.00
Coffee service, Continental, chrome, #17054, 3-pc 200.00
Coffee service, Diplomat, chrome w/tray, #17029, 4-pc 600.00
Coffee set, chrome w/wht plastic, #90073, ind, 6¼" 95.00
Cup, Blue Moon Cocktail, chrome w/bl glass, #90067, 3½" 30.00
Cup, Cocktail, chrome hemisphere, #26002, 2¾" 5.00
Cup, Doric Cocktail, chrome w/bl plastic base, #90101, 3" 28.00
Cup, Iced Drink, chrome w/leaf hdl stirrer, 5½" 30.00
Cup, Old-Fashioned Cocktail, chrome w/muddler, 2⅞" 30.00
Doorstop, stylized cat form, copper & brass, #90035 ....280.00
Duplex Jelly Dish, chrome basket w/glass insert, 5½" 30.00

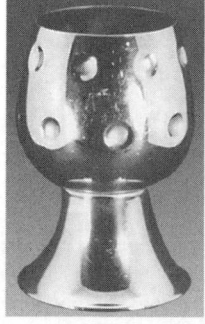

Goblet, Bacchus, embossed 'thumbprints,' footed, #90032, 6", $30.00.

Lamp, Circle, chrome, rpl shade, 14½" 75.00
Lamp, Desk, chrome, C-shape, rpl shade, 14½" 75.00
Lighter, Automatic Table, chrome/bl, #825, 3¼" 75.00
Lighter, Fireball, chrome, 1939 World's Fair logo, #851, 2⅜" 225.00
Lotus Sauce Bowl, chrome w/blk hdl, ladle & tray, #17045 ....50.00
Mint & Nut Dish, chrome, twin bowls, loop hdl, #29003 ....30.00
Olympia Saucer, chrome, #90072, 6⅜" 12.00
Pancake & Corn Set, chrome w/cobalt glass, #28003, 4-pc 225.00
Pitcher, Sparta Water, chrome, wht plastic hdl, #90055, 8" 70.00
Pretzelman, copper, #90038, 18" H 70.00
Salt & Pepper Spheres, chrome, #28004, 1¾", 1⅛", pr 45.00

Serving Fork & Spoon, chrome w/wht plastic hdl, #90076 ....30.00
Silent Butler, chrome w/wht plastic hdl, #17111 ....40.00
Smoke Stand, Lazy Boy, chrome & red, #17031, 27" 445.00
Smokers' Stand, Pelican, blk & wht, #17056, 21" 450.00
Sugar Sphere, chrome shaker, #90078, 2⅝" 40.00
Teapot, non-electric, chrome w/wht hdl, spherical, #17082 ....100.00
Tray, Cocktail, chrome, #09013, 15⅞x5⅝" 30.00
Tray, Ring, chrome, etched circular design, #90058, 12" 45.00
Tray, Triple, chrome folding, all metal, #09001 ....25.00
Vase, Ring, chrome w/blk, #17039, 9½" 45.00
Wall sconce, Dolphin, chrome w/frosted glass shade, #M531 .....525.00
Watering can, Sunshine, brass & copper, 8½" L 45.00
Wine cooler, chrome, Rockwell Kent, #27015, 9¼" 425.00

Chelsea

The Chelsea Porcelain Works operated in London from the middle of the 18th century, making porcelain of the finest quality. In 1770 it was purchased by the owner of the Derby Pottery and for about twenty years operated as a decorating shop. Production periods are indicated by trademarks: 1745-1750 — incised triangle, sometimes with 'Chelsea' and the year added; early 1750s — raised anchor mark on oval pad; 1752-1756 — small painted red anchor, only rarely found in blue underglaze; 1756-1769 — gold anchor; 1769-84 — Chelsea Derby mark with the script 'D' containing a horizontal anchor. Many reproductions have been made; be suspicious of any anchor mark larger than ¼".

Clock, brass w/cvd ivory panel, Wannamaker/Caldwell, 17" ...7,500.00
Dish, floral w/insect, brn-trimmed wavy rim, 7", EX 600.00
Figurine, spotted dog & pup, gold anchor mk, 1700s, 3" 285.00
Plate, fruit & nuts, wavy brn-trimmed rim, mk, 8" 500.00
Tray, butterflies/insects, mc on wht, leaf shape, 10" 650.00

Chelsea Dinnerware

Made from about 1830 to 1880 in the Staffordshire district of England, this white dinnerware is decorated with lustre embossings in the grape, thistle, sprig, or fruit and cornucopia patterns. The relief designs vary from lavender to blue, and the body of the ware may be porcelain, ironstone, or earthenware. Because it was not produced in Chelsea as the name would suggest, dealers often prefer to call it 'Grandmother's Ware.'

Grape, teapot, octagonal, 10", $130.00.

Grape, bowl, 8" 30.00
Grape, coffeepot, stick hdl, 2-cup, 7" 65.00
Grape, creamer 35.00
Grape, cup & saucer 25.00
Grape, egg cup 25.00
Grape, pitcher, milk; 40-oz 50.00
Grape, plate, 6" 12.00
Grape, plate, 7" 18.00

Grape, plate, 8" 20.00
Grape, sauce boat 30.00
Grape, sugar bowl, w/lid 50.00
Grape, teacup 25.00
Grape, teapot, 2-cup 65.00
Grape, waste bowl 40.00
Sprig, cake plate, 9" 40.00
Sprig, cup & saucer 40.00
Sprig, pitcher, milk 45.00
Sprig, plate, dinner 25.00
Sprig, plate, 7" 18.00
Thistle, butter pat 15.00
Thistle, cup & saucer 35.00
Thistle, plate, 7" 15.00

Chelsea Keramic Art Works

The Chelsea Keramic Art Works Robertson and Sons Pottery was established in 1872 in Chelsea, MA, by several members of the Robertson family, including Hugh C. Robertson who later formed the Dedham Pottery. Though their very early artware utilized a redware body, by the late 1870s it was replaced with yellow or buff-burning clay. A line called Bourg-la-Reine (underglazed slip-decorated ware with primarily blue and green backgrounds) was produced, though not to any great extent. Other pieces were designed in imitation of Asian metalware, even to the extent that surfaces were 'hammered' to further enhance the effect. Occasionally live flora was pressed into the damp vessel walls to leave a decorative impression. They also made glazed plaques and tiles. Hugh C. Robertson ran the pottery alone after 1884 and labored to re-create the ancient Ming-Era blood red glaze. Although world acclaim greeted his rediscovery of what he then called 'Robertson's Blood,' his red-glazed vases cost too much to produce and bankruptcy followed in 1889. Supported by wealthy Boston art patrons, Hugh's pottery reopened in 1891 as the Chelsea Pottery U.S., and began using his other 1880s rediscovery, the crackle glaze, producing cobalt blue-decorated dinnerware. When this firm moved to Dedham in 1895 the ware became known as Dedham Pottery. From 1875 to 1880 the pottery was marked Chelsea Keramic Art Works Robertson and Sons in either two or three impressed lines. Earlier pieces were not marked. The impressed mark CKAW in a diamond formation was also used between 1875 and 1889. From 1891 through 1895, the impressed letters CPUS in a clover leaf was utilized for the new firm. After the move to Dedham, only new Dedham Pottery marks were used. Our advisor for this category is James D. Kaufman; he is listed in the Directory under Massachusetts. See the Clubs, Newsletters, and Catalogs section for Dedham/Chelsea Newletter information. See also Dedham Pottery.

Cup, bl w/brn streaks, 4 lion's head & paw ft, CKAW, 3x3" 375.00
Pitcher, emb cascading floral branch, mc, HCR, 6x6", EX 700.00
Plate, pineapple band, bl on crackle gloss, sgn HCR, 10" 475.00
Plate, Rabbit, bl on crackle, CPUS, 8¾" 250.00
Plate, Rabbit, bl on wht crackle, CPUS, 9¾" 350.00
Plate, Upside Down Dolphin, cobalt on crackle, CPUS, 10" 600.00
Tile, emb floral on bl, 3-line mk, 12x6", pr 1,035.00
Tile, Longfellow portrait relief, yel & olive, HCR, 6" 285.00
Vase, bl/brn/gr gloss, 4-sided, scroll base/rim, CKAW, 12½" 500.00
Vase, mustard satin matt, 5 cylindrical necks, CKAW, 6¾" ...1,300.00
Vase, sang-de-boeuf, orange-peel texture, dbl gourd, 8x3½" ...2,100.00
Vase, sang-de-boeuf flambe w/gold overlustre, pitted, 6" 1,200.00

Chicago Crucible

For only a few years during the 1920s, the Chicago (IL) Crucible

Company made a limited amount of decorative pottery in addition to their regular line of architectural wares. Examples are very scarce today; they carry a variety of marks, all with the company name and location.

Vase, olive/aqua matt mottle, 4-lobed, bulbous bottom, 8" 425.00
Vase, yel/gr matt on seafoam, 4-lobed, 5x3½" 350.00

Children's Books

Children's books, especially those from the Victorian era, are charming collectibles. Colorful lithographic illustrations that once delighted little boys in long curls and tiny girls in long stockings and lots of ribbons and lace have lost none of their appeal. Some collectors limit themselves to a specific subject, while others may be far more interested in the illustrations. First editions are more valuable than later issues, and condition and rarity are very important factors to consider before making your purchase.

A Apple Pie ABC, CE Graham & Co, 12-pg, 5x6½", EX 15.00
Adventure of Walter & Rabbits, Cupples & Leon, 1908, 32-pg, EX ..25.00
Alice in Wonderland, Bessie Pease color plates, 1930s, EX 125.00
Boat for Peppe, Politi, Scribner, 1940, 1st ed, EX 24.00
Botany for Young People, Asa Gray MD, Am Book Co, 1858, VG ...18.00
Celery Stalks at Midnight, J Howe, Atheneum/1st ed, 1983 ....30.00
Child's Garden of Verses, RL Stevenson, 1945, w/dust jacket 22.50
Children of Dickens, Jessie Willcox Smith illus, 1930, EX 45.00
Christmas Day Kitten, J Herriot, St Martin Press, 1986, EX 12.00
Christmas Time in Action, pop-up book, 1949, EX 48.00
Daddy Long Legs, Webster, Century, 1912, 304-pg, EX 30.00
Dear Sooky, Crosby, Putnam, color illus, 1929, 124-pg, VG 35.00
Donald Duck, linen, #1, Disney, Whitman, 1935, EX 165.00
Elmer Elephant, linen book, Disney, 1938, 9x12", EX 78.00
Eskimo Twins, LF Perkins, Houghton, 1914, 192-pg, VG 22.50
Five Little Peppers, H Lathrop ed, EX 30.00

Flash Gordon, Tournament of Death, 3 pop-up pictures, ca 1935, NM, $475.00.

Flash Gordon Tournament of Death, 3 pop-ups, Raymond, 1935, G..160.00
Forest Pool, LA Armer, NY/Toronto, 1st ed, 1938 ....42.50
Four Wee Mice, Ullman's Blue Line Series, 1908, 16-pg, G 20.00
Freddy the Pilot, Brooks, Knopf, 1st ed, 1952, w/jacket 32.00
Ghost Wore White, B Allen, Grosset & Dunlap, w/jacket, EX 24.00
Gingerbread Boy & Other Stories, Piper, Eulalie illus, G 45.00
Golden Egg Book, Big Golden Book, 1947, EX 10.00
Happy Hours, Baker & Hayes, mc illus, 1885, 8-pg, EX 12.00
Henny Penny, McLoughlin Bros, 1938, EX 12.00
House on the Cliff, Dixon, Grosset & Dunlap, 1935 printing, NM ..145.00
Jolly Jump Up, pop-up book, 1939, EX 75.00
Jungle River, H Pease, Doubleday Doran, 1939, w/jacket, EX 15.00
Just So Stories, Kipling, Garden City, 1912, EX 37.50
Knock at the Door, Coatsworth, Macmillan, 1st ed, 1931 ....40.00
Little Brown Monkey, E Upham, Platt & Monk, 1st ed, '49 ....18.00
Little Colonel, Burt, Shirley Temple ed, 1935, VG 27.50

Little Goody Two-Shoes, Goldsmith, Saalfield, VG 35.00
Magic Flutes, Kozisek, Mates illus, 1929, G 100.00
Marvelous Land of Oz, Baum, Easton Press, leatherette, 1989 ......55.00
Merry Time Stories, McLoughlin Bros, ca 1890, EX 35.00
Orphan Annie Book, James W Riley, 1908, EX 38.00
Penny Fiddle, R Graves, Doubleday, 1960, 1st ed, w/jacket 22.50
Perfect Zoo, E Farjeon, McKay, 1929, G 100.00
Peter Pan, color illus by Best, Whitman, 1931, EX 58.00
Peter Rabbit & His Pa, Field & Albert, 1916, w/jacket, NM 27.50
Peter Rabbit Goes to School, Saalfield, EX 85.00
Pinocchio, C Colliqi, Ginn & Co, 1904, G 25.00
Princess of Dozeytown, RP Thompson, Volland, 1922, EX 75.00
Raggedy Andy Stories, Gruelle, Donohue, 1920, EX 20.00
Rebecca Mary, AH Donnell, Harper, 1904, 194-pg, VG 27.50
Rolf in Woods, ET Seton, Doubleday Page, 1911, 437-pg, EX 40.00
Shire Colt, Z&J Gay, Doubleday Doran, 1931, w/jacket, EX 45.00
Snoopy & the Red Baron, 1st ed, 1966, EX 15.00
Snow White's Last Call for Dinner, NY Graphic Society, 1947 ...85.00
Sonny Elephant, M Bigham, Little Brown & Co, 1930, G 28.00
Story of Our Gang, Hal Roach comedies, Whitman, 1929, VG ...35.00
Tale of Peter Rabbit, Potter, MA Donohue, 16 color illus, EX 32.00
Treasure Island, RL Stevenson, University Press, 1929, EX 48.00
Twelve Months Make a Year, Coatsworth, Macmillan, 1943, EX ..30.00
Visit to the White Farm, H Alban, Nister & Dutton, 1st ed, EX ..40.00
W Disney's Version of Pinocchio, Random House, '39, w/jacket ..45.00
While the Clock Ticked, Dixon, Grosset & Dunlap, 1941, EX 80.00
Wizard of Oz, linen, Baum, 1939, EX 35.00

Children's Things

Nearly every item devised for adult furnishings has been reduced to child size — furniture, dishes, sporting goods, even some tools. All are very collectible. During the late 17th and early 18th centuries, miniature china dinnerware sets were made both in China and in England. They were not intended primarily as children's playthings, however, but instead were made to furnish miniature rooms and cabinets that provided a popular diversion for the adults of that period. By the 19th century, the emphasis had shifted, and most of the small-scaled dinnerware and tea sets were made for children's play.

Late in the 19th century and well into the 20th, toy pressed glass dishes were made, many in the same pattern as full-scale glassware. Today these toy dishes often fetch prices in the same range as those for the 'grown-ups'!

Authorities Margaret and Kenn Whitmyer have compiled a lovely book, *The Collector's Encyclopedia of Children's Dishes*, with full-color photos and current market values; you will find their address in the Directory under Ohio. We also recommend *Children's Glass Dishes, China, and Furniture*, by Doris Anderson Lechler, available at your local bookstore or public library. See also A B C Plates; Canary Lustre; Clothing; Stickley; Willow Ware; etc.

Key:
ds — doll size   Fr — French
Emp — Empire

China

Bowl, Tommy Tucker, Shenango 24.00
Creamer, Butterfly, Japan, 2¼" 7.50
Creamer & sugar bowl, hunt scene, pk lustre, Germany, w/lid 55.00
Cup & saucer, pk lustre w/gr band & leaf decor, EX 25.00
Cup & saucer, Punch & Judy, 1⅞", 4¼" 42.50
Mug, blacksmith scene, Staffordshire 125.00

Mug, children fishing, bird whistle hdl, Germany, 1900s 50.00
Mug, For My Dear Girl, blk transfer, pk lustre rim, 2¼" 170.00
Mug, hunters, mulberry transfer, Edge Malkin, 3" 100.00
Mug, pig feeding, pigs, house, fence, 2¾" 95.00
Mug, sleeping boy w/drum & dog, red transfer on yel, 2¼", EX ..120.00
Plate, Bottle Is Brought..., lt bl transfer, English, 5½" 145.00
Plate, Dost Thou Love Life..., Franklin's Maxims, 6½", NM 110.00
Plate, Hansel & Gretel, pk lustre, Germany, 5" 24.00
Plate, How Glorious Is Our..., blk w/mc, Staffordshire, 5⅜" 65.00
Plate, Rev J Wesley blk transfer w/pk lustre, 6" 150.00
Plate, Those Who Dainties Love..., blk transfer w/mc, 5" 55.00
Tea set, Blue Willow, Japan, 23-pc, MIB 325.00
Tea set, Chinaman figural, Germany, 1900s, pot+cr/sug+6 c/s ...475.00
Tea set, Circus Tricks, lustre on porc, Germany, 4-place 175.00
Tea set, floral on tan lustre, Japan, 2-place 30.00
Tea set, Moss Rose, Japan, 26-pc 215.00
Tea set, pk roses on wht porc, 1930s, 4-place, MIB 150.00
Teapot, Blue Onion, ironstone 22.50
Teapot, Cat's Thanksgiving, Germany, +cr/sug 225.00
Teapot, Dutch figures, Japan 8.50
Teapot, tan lustre, Occupied Japan 12.00

Furniture

Examples with no dimensions given are child size unless noted doll size.

Armchair, English Windsor, sack-bk, spindle legs, rpr, 28" 350.00
Armchair, hardwood w/cane seat (damaged), 24" 200.00
Armchair, sausage trn w/mushroom cap arms, 1700s, 23" 350.00
Armchair, Sheraton w/bamboo trn, brn rpt, worn rust seat 350.00
Armchair, Victorian cvd walnut, medallion bk, plank seat, 29" .125.00

Bed, George IV, mahogany, ca 1820, 63x29", $1,000.00.

Bed, pine Country, sq posts, old red-brn finish, 16x39x20" 275.00
Bed, recessed arch-panel headbrd, cvd rosette, 24x12x20" 165.00
Bed, rope, ball & bell trn post, wood stain, 12x20x15" 215.00
Bed, rosewood Am Gothic, trefoil shaped rails, 1840s, 39" H .1,400.00
Bureau, Sheraton-style, 2 short drw over 2, trn ft, 11x9½" 150.00
Chair, captain's; oak & hardwoods, rprs, rfn, 18¾" 85.00
Chair, EX trn detail, old blk pnt, front rung broken, 15" 135.00
Chair, Morris; Prairie School, rpl leather seat/bk, 32" 1,800.00
Chair, oak English, removable baby guard, rush seat, rpr, 20" 225.00
Chair, PA pnt Empire style, plank seat, trn posts, 18⅝" 250.00
Chair, side; Limbert #1939, 2-slat bk, plank seat, brand, 24" 175.00
Chair, Windsor, bamboo turnings, spindle bk, mc foliage, 25" .1,200.00
Chairs, bentwood w/orig red pnt w/yel stripes, 18", 4 for 200.00
Chest, Hplwht mahog, 12½x11x7½" 665.00
China closet, walnut, glazed doors, cvd crest, 16x10" 100.00
Couch, wooden fr, old blk leatherized cloth uphl, 14" L 935.00
Cradle, bentwood, spindle construction, worn varnish, 38" L 95.00
Cradle, pine, worn cream-wht pnt, minor damage, 14½" L 95.00

Cradle, pine Country, cut-out rockers, 36" L, EX 165.00
Cradle, pine Country w/old red-brn pnt, 47" L 715.00
Cradle, pine w/worn dk red, mortised & pinned, 39" L, EX 225.00
Cradle, poplar, trn spindles/posts/finials, 40" L 140.00
Cradle, red pnt wood w/arched ends, dvtl, 19" L, EX 105.00
Cradle, softwood, arched head/ft brds, 18" L 45.00
Cradle, softwood, shaped head/ft brds, dvtl, 18" L 95.00
Cupboard, hardwood, 2 drws, scrolled crest, wire nails, 8x5" 140.00
Cupboard, pine/poplar, wire nails, 4 doors, 2-pc, 36x25" 220.00
Cupboard, pnt wood, 4 flat-panel doors, stencil, 45" 825.00
Cupboard, step-bk; poplar w/old red, appl moldings, 24", VG 500.00
Highchair, ash & hardwood, caned seat, bentwood crest, 36" 200.00
Highchair, bamboo Windsor, arrow-bk, red traces, wear, 34" 330.00
Highchair, Co Windsor, 3-spindle, stenciling, 36", EX 145.00
Highchair, oak, hinged shelf, cane seat, CI wheels, rfn, 37" 165.00
Highchair, Windsor, kitchen type, yel striping/cane seat, 35" 175.00
Potty chair, cherry, wingbk, 27", EX 440.00
Rocker, Limbert #874, 2-slat bk, no mk, all orig, 21x14" 475.00
Rocker, oak, pressed bk, cane seat, w/arms, rfn, 28" 100.00
Rocker, pnt ladderbk, woven splint seat, trn finials, 24" 80.00
Rocker, pnt PA style, spindle bk, plank seat, 23½" 300.00
Rocker, Windsor, 3-spindle bk, bamboo-trn posts, grpt, 21" 140.00
Stroller, wood w/steel springs/CI fittings, old pnt, 34" 165.00
Table, pine Hplwht w/pnt, rpl dvtl drw, 19x16x21" 195.00

Glass

Acorn, creamer 125.00
Amazon, spooner 34.00
Austrian, creamer 70.00
Bead & Scroll, creamer 70.00
Begging Dog, mug 40.00
Bucket, creamer 52.50
Button Panel, spooner 70.00
Buzz Saw, creamer 25.00
Buzz Saw, sugar bowl, w/lid 30.00
Colonial, butter dish, Cambridge 25.00
Cupid & Venus, mug 45.00
Dog Medallion, cup & saucer 140.00
Drum, butter dish 125.00
Fine Cut Star & Fan, butter dish 35.00
Galloway, pitcher 32.00
Hawaiian Lei, cake stand 48.00
Hearts & Vines, mug 32.00
Jackson, epergne, clear opal, toy sz 160.00
Lacy Daisy, berry set, 7-pc 70.00
Lamb, butter dish 195.00
Liberty Bell, creamer 95.00
Liberty Bell, mug, 1⅞" 140.00
Lion, creamer 65.00
Lion, cup & saucer 65.00
Little Bo Peep, mug 130.00
Menagerie, spooner, fish, amber 145.00
Menagerie, spooner, fish, bl 125.00
Michigan, pitcher, gold trim 38.00
Monk, stein, milk glass, 2" 25.00
Nursery Rhyme, butter dish 85.00
Nursery Rhyme, creamer 50.00
Nursery Rhyme, punch bowl, milk glass, +6 cups 275.00
Oval Star, pitcher, water 60.00
Oval Star, punch bowl 48.00
Oval Star, tumbler 9.00
Pennsylvania, creamer, clear w/gold 50.00
Portland, pitcher, water; gold trim 28.00

Rex, creamer 25.00
Rex, pitcher, +6 tumblers 175.00
Rex, spooner 30.00
Rex, sugar bowl, w/lid 40.00
Rexford, creamer 18.00
Ribbon Candy, cake stand, gr 75.00
Sawtooth, creamer 35.00
Stippled Leaf & Grape, cup & saucer 35.00
Sunbeam, creamer 65.00
Sunbeam, spooner 120.00
Swan, mug 22.50
Tulip & Honeycomb, sugar bowl, w/lid 40.00
Tumble-up, amethyst, plain, 5⅜" 265.00
Tumble-up, cobalt, Mary Gregory style, 1½" 325.00
Wild Rose, butter dish, milk glass 80.00
Wild Rose, creamer, milk glass 55.00
Wild Rose, punch bowl, clear 95.00
Wild Rose, punch bowl, milk glass, +6 cups 185.00
Wild Rose, punch cup, milk glass 15.00

Miscellaneous

Bicycle, Schwinn Phantom, complete 1,300.00
Bicycle horn, metal, battery-operated, push button & light 22.50
Buggy, leather w/gold & red stencil, blk pnt, all orig, 41" 500.00
Buggy, wooden wheels & fr, folding leather top, 54" L 798.00
Clothespins, wooden, 1930s, mini, set of 36, MIB 16.00
Desk, Chautauqua Industrial Art Deck, wall type, 1930s, MIB ...125.00
Horse, glider, pnt wood, missing eyes/tail, 1890s, VG 465.00
Horse, glider, rpt wood, glass eyes, 49x52x18", EX 1,085.00
Horse, glider, Whitney Reed MA, dapple gray, 30x36" 435.00
Horse, rocking, cvd wood, old gray pnt, rpl tail, rprs, 45" 440.00
Measuring cup, aluminum, 1930s 6.00
Muffin tin, makes 4, 1930s 11.00
Pencil sharpener, red rocketship, Admiration, ca 1940, EX 25.00
Potato masher, wooden, 1930s, EX 8.00
Rattle, tin w/emb designs, stick whistle hdl 90.00
Sled, steel fr & runners w/CI finials, wood top w/orig pnt, 36" ...195.00
Sled, wood w/steel-tipped runners, blk rpt & varnished, 35", EX ..60.00
Sulky, wire w/rubber tires, blk w/yel striping, 12x30x9" 80.00
Symmetroscope (old kaleidoscope), 1899 ....200.00
Trunk, wood w/brn pnt, metal trim, 10½x18x10¼", EX 70.00
Wagon, pnt wood, Heider Coaster, 40", EX 225.00
Wagon, wood w/steel fittings, worn gray pnt, 31"+tongue 990.00
Wheelbarrow, varnished wood w/red striping, 34" L 195.00

Chocolate Glass

Jacob Rosenthal developed chocolate glass, a rich shaded opaque brown sometimes referred to as caramel slag, in 1900 at the Indiana Tumbler and Goblet Company of Greentown, Indiana. Later, other companies produced similar ware. Only the latter is listed here. See also Greentown. Our advisors for this category are Jerry and Sandi Garrett; they are listed in the Directory under Indiana.

Bowl, Shield w/Daisy & Button, 8⅜" 1,300.00
Butter dish, Chrysanthemum Leaf 1,400.00
Butter dish, Touching Squares 2,650.00
Compote, jelly; Majestic 750.00
Compote, Melrose, 6" 250.00
Creamer, Aldine 1,300.00
Creamer, Chrysanthemum Leaf 650.00
Creamer, Geneva 225.00

Creamer, Strigal, tankard-shape 165.00
Glove box, Venetian, w/lid, 9½x3½" 675.00
Nappy, Beaded Triangle, hdld 325.00
Nappy, Masonic, hdld 175.00
Nappy, Navarre, hdld 250.00
Pickle dish, Aurora, violin shape 200.00
Pickle jar, Pioneer's Victoria, w/lid 850.00
Pitcher, milk; Feather 1,300.00
Pitcher, Rose Garland 2,850.00
Salt dip, Honeycomb, ind, 1¾" 450.00
Sauce dish, Shield w/Daisy & Button 450.00
Spooner, File 400.00
Spooner, Wild Rose w/Scrolling, child sz 275.00
Syrup jug, Chrysanthemum Leaf, w/metal lid 1,000.00
Tray, celery; Jubilee, 10" 350.00
Tumbler, Geneva 150.00
Vase, Wild Rose w/Bowknot, 10½" 400.00

Christmas Collectibles

Christmas past . . . lovely mementos from long ago attest to the ostentatious Victorian celebrations of the season.

St. Nicholas, better known as Santa, has changed much since 300 A.D. when the good Bishop Nicholas showered needy children with gifts and kindnesses. During the early 18th century, Santa was portrayed as the kind gift-giver to well-behaved children and the stern switch-bearing disciplinarian to those who were bad. In 1822 Clement Clark Moore, a New York poet, wrote his famous *Night Before Christmas*, and the Santa he described was jolly and jovial — a lovable old elf who was stern with no one. Early Santas wore robes of yellow, brown, blue, green, red, white, or even purple. But Thomas Nast, who worked as an illustrator for *Harper's Weekly*, was the first to depict Santa in a red suit instead of the traditional robe and to locate him the entire year at the North Pole headquarters.

Today's collectors prize early Santa figures, especially those in robes of fur or mohair or those dressed in an unusual color. Some early examples of Christmas memorabilia are the pre-1870 ornaments from Dresden, Germany. These cardboard figures — angels, gondolas, umbrellas, dirigibles, and countless others — sparkled with gold and silver trim. Late in the 1870s, blown glass ornaments were imported from Germany. There were over 6,000 recorded designs, all painted inside with silvery colors. From 1890 through 1910, blown glass spheres were often decorated with beads, tassels, and tinsel rope.

Christmas lights, made by Sandwich and some of their contemporaries, were either pressed or mold-blown glass shaped into a form similar to a water tumbler. They were filled with water and then hung from the tree by a wire handle; oil floating on the surface of the water served as fuel for the lighted wick.

Kugels are glass ornaments that were made as early as 1820 and as late as 1890. Ball-shaped examples are more common than the fruit and vegetable forms and have been found in sizes ranging from 1" to 14" in diameter. They were made of thick glass with heavy brass caps, in cobalt, green, gold, silver, red, and occasionally in amethyst.

Although experiments involving the use of electric light bulbs for the Christmas tree occured before 1900, it was 1903 before the first manufactured socket set was marketed. These were very expensive and often proved a safety hazard. In 1921 safety regulations were established, and products were guaranteed safety approved. The early bulbs were smaller replicas of Edison's household bulb. By 1910 G.E. bulbs were rounded with a pointed end, and until 1919 all bulbs were hand blown. The first figural bulbs were made around 1910 in Austria. Japan soon followed, but their product was never of the high quality of the Austrian wares. American manufacturers produced their first machine-made figurals after 1919. Today figural bulbs (especially character-related examples) are very popular collectibles. Bubble lights were popular from about 1945 to 1960 when miniature lights were introduced. These tiny lamps dampened the public's enthusiasm for the bubblers, and manufacturers stopped providing replacement bulbs.

Feather trees were made from 1850 to 1950. All are collectible. Watch for newly manufactured feather trees that have lately been reintroduced.

For further information concerning Christmas collectibles, we recommend these highly informative books, *Christmas Collectibles* by Margaret and Kenn Whitmyer and *Christmas Ornaments, Lights, and Decorations, A Collector's Identification and Value Guide,* by George Johnson. All books are available from Collector Books or your local bookstore.

Note: bulbs termed 'mini' measure no larger than 1½".

Bulbs

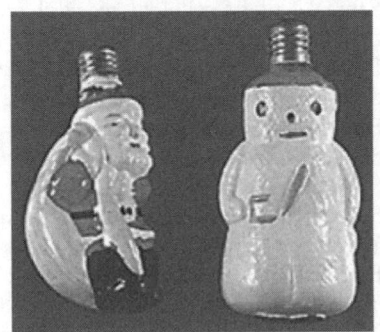

Hump-backed Santa, Japan, 4", $25.00; Snowman with a stick, Japan, 4", $25.00.

Andy Gump, EX mc pnt, 1930s-50s	110.00
Ape w/rifle sits on mound, mc pnt, milk glass, rare	150.00
Aviator, purple coat, pk hat, gold trim, milk glass, EX	40.00
Ball w/stars, red	18.00
Beach ball, mc pnt, 1930s-50s, Japan, mini	30.00
Bell w/emb Santa face, mc details	18.00
Betty Boop, EX pnt	95.00
Birdcage w/2 red birds, milk glass	20.00
Bulldog, pnt details, 1930s-50s, mini	28.00
Canadian Mountie, milk glass, mc pnt	60.00
Candy cane, red & wht, 3", EX	32.00
Cat & the Fiddle, mc pnt, milk glass, ca 1930s, NM	30.00
Chick in egg, yel & pk pnt, milk glass, 2¾", NM	150.00
Chinese schoolgirl, milk glass, mc pnt, rare	50.00
Choir girl, mc pnt, milk glass, EX	45.00
Clown on ball, bl suit w/yel ruffle, milk glass, 3"	85.00
Cross, pk pnt, milk glass, 3"	35.00
Dick Tracy, milk glass, worn mc pnt	110.00
Dog in a clown suit, milk glass, mc pnt, rare	150.00
Dog in basket, mc pnt, milk glass, EX	50.00
Dog on ball, pnt details, 1930s-50s, Japan, mini	45.00
Drum, gr w/blk details, 1930s-50s, Japan, mini	35.00
Drummer boy, mc pnt, milk glass, EX	55.00
Ducklings, mc pnt on milk glass, sm, NM	48.00
Dutch girl, milk glass, mc pnt, full figure	60.00
Elephant, mc pnt, milk glass, 3", EX	50.00
Flapper girl, milk glass, red & blk details	60.00
Flower, peach to gold shaded, 1930s-50s, Japan, mini	30.00
Frog, lt gr pnt, milk glass, EX	30.00
Fruit basket, mc pnt, milk glass, lg, NM	45.00
Grapes, mc w/gr leaves, milk glass, 3¼"	15.00
Grapes, red & gr, 1930s-50s, Japan, mini	20.00
Hound dog, pnt details, 1930s-50s, Japan, mini	85.00
Humpty Dumpty (bust), milk glass, mc pnt	45.00
Humpty Dumpty (full figure), milk glass, mc pnt	65.00

Indian chief, clear w/mc pnt, full figure, '10, Germany, 3¾"	375.00
Indian head, pnt details, 1930s-50s, mini	110.00
Jackie Coogan, milk glass, mc pnt, Japan, rare	75.00
Jester head, milk glass w/red & blk details, ca 1910, Germany	165.00
Jester points to playing card, milk glass, mc pnt	90.00
Kewpie, pnt details, 1930s-50s, Japan, mini	35.00
Keystone Cop, mc pnt, milk glass, EX	95.00
Lady w/cross, mc pnt, milk glass, 3½"	50.00
Lantern, VG pnt, milk glass, Japan, sm	12.00
Lemon, worn pnt on clear	30.00
Little Boy Blue, milk glass, bl suit, blond hair	35.00
Little Orphan Annie, EX mc pnt, milk glass, c 1935, 3⅛"	165.00
Minstrel, yel & wht w/orange & red horn, Germany	60.00
Moon Mullins, EX mc pnt, 1930s-50s	110.00
Mother Goose, milk glass, mc pnt	50.00
Owl, mc pnt, clear glass, Germany	75.00
Peewee, EX mc pnt, 1930s-50s	85.00
Rose, open, EX red pnt, milk glass, lg	50.00
Rose, red pnt, milk glass, sm	30.00
Santa, mc pnt, milk glass, 9"	185.00
Santa in oval, mc pnt, milk glass, 3¾", NM	45.00
Santa w/pack, mc pnt, milk glass, full figure, EX	35.00
Smitty, EX mc pnt, 1930s-50s	95.00
Snowman on skis, milk glass, mc details	45.00
Snowman w/beret, milk glass, EX	35.00
Snowman w/shovel, mc pnt, milk glass, VG	35.00
Teddy bear, red pnt, milk glass, EX	110.00
Three men in a tub, milk glass, mc pnt	150.00
Tom the Piper's Son, mc pnt, milk glass, EX	245.00
Tulip, pk w/gr leaves, milk glass, EX	35.00

Candy Containers

Barrel, Dresden, brn & tan, 2¼"	165.00
Boy in snowball, bsk & cloth, 5½", VG	110.00
Cornucopia, crepe paper, die-cut decor, EX	85.00
Drum, Dresden, red/wht/bl w/gold stripe, 2⅛", NM	75.00
Elf, compo, stands, detailed face, Germany, 8", EX	365.00
House, cb litho, 1930s, Japan, 5x4x3"	45.00
House w/cotton Santa on cotton roof, mk Japan	95.00
Opera glasses, Dresden, dbl, old resilvering, 2x3"	195.00
Santa, cb w/gold flecks, mk Germany on base, 15", EX	230.00
Santa, clay face, flannel suit, Japan, 1930s, 7"	130.00
Santa, papier-mache, flannel suit/fur beard, '20s, Germany, 8"	300.00
Santa, red flannel coat, rabbit beard, plaster pants, 7", EX	265.00
Santa face, celluloid, on foil cornucopia container	40.00
Santa in basket, plaster hands, Japan, 5"	125.00
Santa in boot, plaster face, cotton beard, Japan, 7"	100.00
Santa in sleigh, papier-mache, EX pnt, lg	215.00
Santa on deer, compo & metal, Dresden trim, Germany, 10"	625.00
Santa w/tree, papier-mache, wht robe w/yel trim, 12", EX	800.00
Snowball, celluloid, 2"	65.00
Snowman, coated cb, head attached w/spring, Japan, 7"	35.00
Snowman, mica-coated cb, cotton carrot nose, Germany, 9"	70.00
Snowman, papier-mache, blk eyes, gr hat, 8"	95.00
Top hat, Dresden, red silk w/silver rosettes, 2", EX	265.00
Turtle, Dresden, mc pnt, EX	425.00
Walnut, Dresden, natural colors, 2½"	90.00
Wreath, Dresden, 4½", EX	200.00

Ornaments

Accordion, blown, mc pnt, 2¾", M	65.00
Angel, molded wax, spun glass wings, brn hair, 7", EX	180.00

Angel, Tuck diecut, in spun glass circle, 4¼" 85.00
Animal, pressed cotton, Germany, pre-WWI 35.00
Baby Jesus' head, mold blown, pnt details, 3" 85.00
Balloon, wire wrapped, scrap angel w/Am flag w/in, 1910, 6" 85.00
Bear w/extended legs, mold blown, pnt details, 1900s, 3" 200.00
Bear w/stick, blown, matt pnt, 2½" 98.00
Beetle, blown, pk w/gr wings, 3" 165.00
Bell, red crepe-paper honeycomb type, Doubl-Glo...USA, 7" 15.00
Bell w/clapper, blown, silver w/holly decor, 1900, 2½" 50.00
Bird, blown, silver, spun glass tail, annealed hanger, 2½" 37.50
Bird, celluloid, on ring, Japan, 6" 50.00
Bird on branch emb on ball ornament, early 1900s, 2" 35.00
Brownie, blown, gr pants, pk tie, blk hat, unsilvered, 5" 300.00
Brownie w/extended legs, red coat/silver pants, 1900s, 5" 225.00
Butterfly, mold blown w/gr spun glass wings, 3½x3" 180.00
Candle, mold blown, wht w/red, on clip, pre-1940, 5" 125.00
Candy cane, red & wht twisted chenille, 12" 10.00
Cart, Sebnitz w/Dresden wheels, wax figure w/in, EX 235.00
Cat in slipper, blown, pearly wht/pk/yel, 3½" 155.00
Chandelier, wire wrapped, 5" 140.00
Clam shell, Dresden, gold 140.00
Clown's head, mold blown, pearly wht/red/blk/gold, 3" 50.00
Clown w/500,000 on stomach, mold blown, early 1900s, 4, EX 100.00
Coach, Dresden, 3-D, silver, 4x6¼" 300.00
Cock Robin, molded milk glass, worn pnt, on clip, 4", EX 195.00
Cockatoo, blown, mc pnt, spun glass tail, clip, 4", M 40.00
Crane, blown, bl body, pre-1940, 4½" 50.00
Devil's head, mold blown, sneering, mc pnt, pre-1940, 4" 275.00
Donkey pulling sleigh, Dresden, 4" 550.00
Eagle flying, Dresden, tan & brn, 5½" wingspan, NM 295.00
Elephant on ball, blown, yel-gold w/red trim, 3½", EX 150.00
Elf in house, mold blown, mc pnt, 1920s, 3½" 65.00
Elf w/shovel, blown, mc w/silver, frosted beard, 3", EX 140.00
Father Christmas, blown, pk robe, lt wear, 5" 165.00
Father Christmas, scrap, in heart shape w/tinsel, 6" 25.00
Father Christmas, scrap, w/spun glass 'skirt,' 9½" 80.00
Father Christmas head, mold blown, pearly wht w/mc pnt, 2½" ...50.00
Flower girl, blown, flesh face, gold hair, mc flowers, 4" 150.00
Football, mold blown, gold pnt, early 1900s 125.00
Fox, mold blown, milk glass, on clip, 3" 50.00
Fruit basket, blown, mc fruits, 3" 65.00
Girl, scrap, in wreath w/spun glass skirt, 5½" 45.00
Girl in bag, molded, pearly wht/pk/bl, ca 1920, 3", VG 80.00
Girl's head, mold blown, silver hair, pre-1940, 4" 110.00
Goldilocks' head, blown, mc pnt, ca 1910, 3x2½", EX 225.00
Goldilocks, mold blown, mc pnt, 1930s, 3½", EX 85.00
Hansel & Gretel, mold blown, mc pnt, 3¾", EX, pr 200.00
Happy Hooligan, blown, peach coat, yel legs, 4½", EX 315.00
House w/turkey, blown, mc pnt, 1910s, 3" 40.00
Hummingbird, mold blown, mc pnt, spun glass wings 25.00
Ice skate, Dresden, 3-D, silver, 2½" 200.00
Icicle, mold blown, pk, 1950s, 14" 35.00
Indian bust, mold blown, mc pnt, 1920s, 3½", EX 295.00
Jester head, mold blown, mc pnt, 1960s, 4½" 35.00
Jockey on horse, Dresden, 3-D, EX mc pnt, 3x3" 395.00
Kugel imitation, ltweight thinner version, Japan, 1⅛" 20.00
Lady Liberty, mold blown, attached real hair, 1920s, 6½" 175.00
Lady on urn, blown, silver matt w/gold, 3½" 30.00
Lady's face in flower, mold blown, mc pnt, 2½" 35.00
Little Miss Muffett, mold blown, pnt details, 1920s, 4" 85.00
Lord Fauntleroy, blown, pearly wht w/red tie, 3" 375.00
Man in the Moon, mold blown crescent shape, mc pnt, 4¾" 85.00
Mandolin, cb w/scrap flowers & angels, tinsel strings, 9" 40.00
Mrs Claus, molded, pearly wht & red, 4½" 200.00

Mushroom, mold blown, unsilvered, mc pnt, 1920s, on clip, 3" 30.00
Ostrich, Dresden, 3-D, blk & tan, 4x3¾", EX 215.00
Patriotic shield, Dresden, mc pnt, 3x1½", VG 110.00
Peacock, mold blown, mc pnt, 1920s-50s 30.00
Pear, pressed cotton, yel & orange, 1" 25.00
Pig w/flower on stomach, mold blown, mc pnt, pre-1940, 4" 80.00
Policeman w/billy club, mold blown, worn mc pnt, 4½" 150.00
Popcorn head, molded, frosty wht w/blk & red details, 4½" 300.00
Rail car, blown, silver matt w/orange & gr, 3" 65.00
Roadster, mold blown, red pnt, ca 1920s, 3" 125.00
Santa, blown, gold & red suit, frosted beard, 5¼", EX 165.00
Santa, cotton batting w/scrap face, w/feather tree, 6" 90.00
Santa head, scrap, on Victorian wire-wrapped airplane, 7" 80.00
Santa in car, celluloid, red/wht/gr, 3x4½" 110.00
Santa in chimney, mold blown, mc pnt, 1930s, 3" 45.00
Santa in stocking, mold blown, red pnt, 3½" 110.00
Santa w/lantern, celluloid, red w/silver, 2" 75.00
Santa w/tennis racket, celluloid, EX 55.00
Santa w/tree, mold blown, mc pnt, 1920s-30s, 3" 35.00
Scrap angel in tinsel wreath, 6½" 20.00
Scrap figure in wire-wrapped red balloon, 6½" 70.00
Shoe, mold blown, silver w/red & gr trim, 4¾" 100.00
Snow child, molded, pearly gold w/pnt details, 1920s, 3¾" 95.00
Snowman, mold blown, pearly wht w/red, on clip, 3¾" 80.00
Street lamp, blown, pk, gr & red panels, 4" 30.00
Sunburst, spun glass & Dresden w/wax baby center, on clip, 5" 60.00
Table lamp, blown, pearly wht/red/gold/gr/silver, 4", VG 45.00
Trumpet flower, mold blown, mc pnt, on clip, 3¼" 85.00
Umbrella, wire wrapped, Germany, early 100.00
Windmill, blown, mc pnt, silver Dresden blades, 2½" 80.00
Witch, blown, 4-colored pnt, unsilvered, 5" 265.00
Woodpecker on tree trunk, molded, EX pnt, glass tail, 3¼" 195.00

Miscellaneous

Bank, Santa on chimney, chalkware, recent, 11", M 30.00
Book, Night Before Christmas, McLoughlin Bros, 1896, EX 40.00
Bubble light, Noma, red & gr 5.00
Cake pan, tin, Christmas tree form w/rolled rim, 10x11" 35.00
Charm, boot w/hinged top opens, Santa pops up, 14k gold 150.00
Cow, Putz, brn, 2½x3½", EX 50.00
Cup & saucer, Father Christmas w/toys, bsk, Germany 70.00

Decoration, Santa in sleigh with reindeer, embossed diecut with mica accents, Germany, 1930s, 15½" long, $45.00.

Decoration, Santa on chimney, ceramic, EX pnt, 1950s, EX 50.00
Father Christmas, Belsnickle, bl w/gold, w/tree, Japan, 11½" 275.00
Father Christmas, Belsnickle, dk yel, w/tree, Japan, 11" 255.00
Father Christmas, Belsnickle, gold w/red, w/tree, Japan, 6" 145.00
Father Christmas, Belsnickle, gr robe, Germany, 9½" 825.00

Father Christmas, clockworks nodder, felt robe, 1900s, 26", EX ..1,900.00
Father Christmas, molded cb, Germany, 1920s, 9", EX 325.00
Fence, twig style w/gate, Germany, lg, EX 155.00
Fence, wood, red & gr pickets, red gate, 18" sq, EX 175.00
Garland, fuchsia beads, 96" 25.00
Garland, gr w/1½" beads, 96", EX 50.00
Garland, mixed oval & rnd mc glass beads, 1920s-30s, 28" 30.00
Kugel, ball, pk-red, orig metal cap, 2" 70.00
Kugel, ball w/ribs, burnt orange, orig metal cap, 4¼" 375.00
Kugel, ball w/ribs, silver, orig metal cap, 2" 85.00
Kugel, grapes, burnt orange, orig metal cap, 8" 800.00
Kugel, grapes, cobalt, orig metal cap, 8" 450.00
Kugel, grapes, cranberry, orig metal cap, 7" 800.00
Kugel, grapes, dk ruby, orig metal cap, 2¾" 300.00
Kugel, grapes, purple, orig metal cap, 8" 900.00
Kugel, grapes, turq, orig metal cap, 8" 475.00
Kugel, grapes, yel-olive gr, orig metal cap, 8" 475.00
Kugel, pear, ribbed pattern, emerald gr, orig metal cap, 2½" 110.00
Kugel, pear, turq, orig metal cap, 2½" 65.00
Kugel, pear, yel-amber, orig metal cap, 2¾" 110.00
Kugel, raspberry, cobalt, orig metal cap, 5" 1,000.00
Light, bust of King Edward, bright yel-gr, Regd..., 4⅛" 400.00
Light, bust of Queen Victoria, cobalt, Hearn Wright, 4" 350.00
Light, Expanded Dmn, bl, folded rim, 3½" 110.00
Light, Expanded Dmn, cranberry red, Pains Pat, 3⅜" 150.00
Light, Expanded Dmn, deep root beer-amber, crude, 3" 95.00
Light, Expanded Dmn, dk red-amber, pontil scar, 2⅜" 150.00
Light, Expanded Dmn, golden yel-amber, Registered..., 3⅝" 140.00
Light, Expanded Dmn, pk-amethyst, folded rim, 3¼" 180.00
Light, Expanded Dmn, Stiegel type, amethyst, folded rim, 2½" 65.00
Light, Expanded Dmn, Stiegel type, lt amber, 2¾x3" 50.00
Light, Expanded Dmn, wht opal, pontil scar, 3¼", pr 55.00
Light, Fern pattern, dk yel-amber, Hearn..., 3⅝" 350.00
Light, Harlequin pattern, bl opaque, 3½" 100.00
Light, Harlequin pattern, copper-puce, orig hanger, 3⅜" 190.00
Light, Harlequin pattern, purple amethyst, wire hanger, 3½" 100.00
Light, Ogival pattern, dk amethyst, pontil scar, 2¾" 75.00
Light, strawberry, clear, 1870-1900, 3¾" 200.00
Light, Thumbprint or Seeing Eye, yel-amber, sm chip, 4⅛" 350.00
Light, tulip form, med gr, Hearn Wright, 3½" 325.00
Lights, Fantasia, Mazda, England, 1940, set of 12, MIB 235.00
Night light, Santa, plastic, hole in bk for bulb, 17" 20.00
Postcard, Kind Wishes for Christmas, hold-to-light, EX 35.00
Reindeer, lead, Germany, 2x1¾" 42.00
Santa, ceramic, wearing rabbit-fur hula skirt, 1959, NM 60.00
Santa, cloth face/satin suit/shredded beard, Am, '40s, 20", EX ...125.00
Santa, doll, stuffed body, brn rubber head, Knickerbocker, 13" 45.00
Santa, felt w/rubber face, jtd body, 9", EX 35.00
Santa, papier-mache & clay, felt coat, Japan, 1950s, 5¼" 20.00
Santa, plastic, red & wht, Irving, 4" 70.00
Santa, plastic, red & wht w/gr, lights up, lg, EX 75.00
Santa, spring-head ceramic figure, M pnt, 8" 35.00
Santa & reindeer, celluloid, in cb sleigh, 10½" L 75.00
Santa w/lamb, clay face, flannel suit, 1930s, Japan, 6", EX 75.00
Tree, cellophane, gr, 1950s, 55", EX 40.00
Tree, feather; gr, candle clips, wood base, 22" 215.00
Tree, feather; gr w/red berries & poinsettias, 1900s, 36" 285.00
Tree, feather; gr w/red compo berries & candle clips, 19" 75.00
Tree, feather; paper flower tip branches, 6½" 55.00
Tree, feather; red holly, w/candle clips, wht sq base, 29" 250.00
Tree, feather; wht w/red berries, well made, 1930s, 32" 250.00
Tree stand, cast cement, Santa's head form, 1920s, 12" 200.00
Tree stand, CI, gr pnt, gold star on ea leg (4), 3" opening 55.00
Tree stand, Echardt, musical, key wind, Pat 1878, EX 600.00

Chrysanthemum Sprig, Blue

This is the blue opaque version of Northwood's popular pattern, Chrysanthemum Sprig. It was made at the turn of the century and is today very rare, as its values indicate. Prices are influenced by the amount of gold remaining on the raised designs. Our advisors for this category are Betty and Clarence Maier; they're listed in the Directory under Pennsylvania.

Bowl, berry; sm 325.00
Bowl, master fruit; 10½" W 600.00
Butter dish 850.00
Compote, jelly 600.00
Condiment tray, rare, VG gold 750.00
Creamer 385.00
Cruet, 6½" 1,250.00
Pitcher, water 1,100.00
Shakers, pr 450.00
Spooner 450.00
Sugar bowl, w/lid 600.00
Toothpick holder 450.00
Tumbler 350.00

Circus Collectibles

The 1890s — the golden age of the circus. Barnum and Bailey's parades transformed mundane city streets into an exotic never-never land inhabited by trumpeting elephants with jeweled gold headgear strutting by to the strains of the calliope that issued from a fine red- and gilt-painted wagon extravagantly decorated with carved wooden animals of every description. It was an exciting experience. Is it any wonder that collectors today treasure the mementos of that golden era? See also Posters.

Key:
B&B — Barnum & Bailey   RB — Ringling Bros.

Banner, Downie Bros, Buried Alive sideshow, 91x119" 400.00
Banner, Jolly Joe (fat man), oil on canvas, early 1900s 1,000.00
Banner, Milliard & Bulsterbaum, Prof Kloss Punch & Judy, 96" ..1,500.00
Banner, Nieman Studios, Shackles the Great, escape artist 1,000.00
Pin, celluloid, blk & wht, B&B, ⅞", EX 40.00
Pin, celluloid, lady on trapeze w/umbrella, brn/wht, 1¼" 45.00
Poster, Al G Branes, Bert Nelson's lion-taming act, 27x41", EX ...200.00
Poster, B&B, Mister Mistin Jr Child Wonder, mc, ca 1930, lg ...110.00
Poster, Christy Bros, monkeys/policemen/clowns/etc, 79x80", G- ..800.00
Poster, Christy Bros 5 Ring Wild Animal Show, 34x48" 150.00
Poster, Cole Bros, Mrs Jean Allen...Horsewoman, 27x41", EX ...200.00
Poster, Knie, abstract of a woman w/2 snakes, 1988, 50x35½" ...375.00
Poster, RB, Dorothy Herbet on horse jumping, 40x27½", EX 50.00
Poster, RB B&B, chimps pay elephant 2 nuts admission, 28x41" .150.00
Poster, RB B&B, leopard, 1950, 40x28", NM 1,250.00
Poster, RB B&B, pigmy elephants/clowns/etc, 1920s, 27x41", EX ...395.00

Clambroth

Clambroth is a term that refers to a type of glass popular in the Victorian period. It was semiopaque and gray-white in color, said to resemble the broth of the clam. See also Sandwich.

Bowl, scalloped, 3x12" 38.00

Candlestick, crucifix form, 9¾", pr, NM **65.00**
Cruet, lt bl cuttings in paneled body, step-cut lip, 7" **725.00**
Epergne, 1-lily, ftd/ruffled bowl: 6¼x4½" **135.00**
Toothpick holder, Button Arches **24.00**
Vase, blk horizontal lines, 9x4¾" **35.00**

Clarice Cliff

Between 1928 and 1935 in Burslem, England, as the director and part owner of Wilkinson and Newport Pottery Companies, Clarice Cliff and her 'paintresses' created a body of hand-painted pottery whose influence is felt to the present time.

The name for the oevre was Bizarre Ware, and the predominant sensibility, style, and appearance was Deco. Almost all pieces are signed and include the pattern names. There were over 160 patterns and more than 400 shapes, all of which are illustrated in *A Bizarre Affair — the Life and Work of Clarice Cliff*, published by Harry N. Abrams, Inc., written by Len Griffen and our advisors, Susan and Louis Meisel, whose address is listed in the Directory under New York.

Clarice Cliff died in 1972, shortly after the Victoria and Albert Museum showed her work in retrospect, and collectors (primarily in England) began seeking and admiring her work. In September of 1982, the Metropolitan Museum of Art in New York acquired and placed on view a selection of six pieces.

Note: Non-hand-painted work (transfer printed) was produced after World War II and into the 1950s. Some of the most common names are 'Tonquin' and 'Charlotte.' These items, while attractive and enjoyable to own, have no value in the collector market.

Biscuit jar, Latona Trees Bizarre, cane-wrapped hdl, #300, 6" **315.00**
Bowl, Blue Chintz Bizarre Hiawatha, #515, 11" **525.00**
Bowl, Gibraltar Bizarre Odilon, #526, 8¼" **875.00**
Bowl, Red Trees & House Fantasque Bizarre, #485, 8" **350.00**
Charger, Summerhouse, #718, 17¾" dia **7,000.00**
Charger, Sunray Bizarre, #721, 16½" dia **8,750.00**
Honey pot, Orange Capri Bizarre Beehive, w/lid, #154, 2⅝" **335.00**
Jardiniere, Dover, Sliced Fruit Bizarre, #309, 8½" **560.00**
Jug, Athens, Orange Roof Cottage, Fantasque Bizarre, #354, 8" .**615.00**
Jug, Conical, Orange Trees & House Fantasque Bizarre, #353, 6" ...**665.00**
Jug, Coronet, Broth Fantasque Bizarre, #331, 6¼" **440.00**
Jug, Daffodil, Honolulu Bizarre, #360, 2 sm chips, 6¾" **700.00**
Jug, Lotus, Inspiration Caprice Bizarre, 1-hdl, #566, 11¾" **1,665.00**
Jug, Lotus, Latona Dahlia Bizarre, #561, hairline, 11½" **790.00**
Jug, Lotus, Rudyard Fantasque Bizarre, 1-hdl, #573, 11⅜" **1,575.00**
Pitcher, Spring Crocus, 2½" **70.00**
Plate, Pansies Delicia on drip-glaze, Bizarre, 10", EX **110.00**
Plate, Viscaria, landscape, 9¾" **345.00**
Shaker, orange-roof cottage/trees, strong colors, 5" **375.00**
Sugar sifter, Conical, Coral Firs Bizarre, #279, 5½" **315.00**

Teapot, Bizarre in Autumn Crocus pattern, Athens shape, marked, 6½", $550.00; Handled jug, Bizarre in Autumn Crocus pattern, 2 marks, 9⅞", $770.00; Vase, Bizarre in Gay Day pattern, cylindrical with everted rim, 2 marks, 8¾", $440.00.

Vase, Autumn Fantasque Bizarre, shape #264, #648, chip, 8" **490.00**
Vase, Isis, Umbrellas & Rain Fantasque Bizarre, #537, 9½", NM **840.00**

Vase, Melon Fantasque Bizarre, shape #205, #650, 8¼", NM **560.00**
Wall plaque, Latona Red Roses Bizarre, #709, 13" dia **615.00**

Cleminson

A hobby turned to enterprise, Cleminson is one of several California potteries whose clever hand-decorated wares are attracting the attention of today's collectors. The Cleminsons started their business at their El Monte home in 1941 and were so successful that eventually they expanded to a modern plant that employed more than 150 workers. They produced not only dinnerware and kitchen items such as cookie jars, canisters, and accessories, but novelty wall vases, small trays, plaques, etc., as well. Though nearly always marked, Cleminson wares are easy to spot as you become familiar with their distinctive glaze colors. Their grayed-down blue and green, berry red, and dusty pink say 'Cleminson' as clearly as their trademark. Unable to compete with foreign imports, the pottery closed in 1963. Our advisor for this category is Jack Chipman, author of *The Collector's Encyclopedia of California Pottery*; he is listed in the Directory under California.

Appetizer bird, Gala Gray **37.50**
Ashtray, fish, 7½" **25.00**
Bell, French maid **65.00**
Bowl, vegetable; Distlefink, 12½" **20.00**
Cleanser shaker, lady figural, 5 holes **30.00**
Coffee canister, Cherry **35.00**
Cookie jar, Christmas house **150.00**
Cookie jar, Gingerbread house **200.00**
Creamer & sugar bowl, King & Queen **75.00**
Cup & saucer, No Grounds for Divorce **25.00**
Drippings jar, cherry decor **35.00**
Egg cup, Distlefink, brn **25.00**
Gravy boat, Distlefink, wht **30.00**
Lazy Susan, Distlefink, brn **85.00**
Match safe, Cherry **28.00**
Mug, Morning After, ice-pack lid **30.00**
Mug, Now Is the Hour, w/man & woman **30.00**
Pitcher, Distlefink, brn **65.00**
Pitcher, Gala Gray, 7" **35.00**
Plaque, Tom Sawyer **30.00**
Ring holder, bulldog **25.00**
Salt box, Cherry **45.00**
Shakers, country lady w/apron, yel/brn, 6", pr **60.00**
Spoon rest, Cherry **20.00**
String holder, heart shape, You'll Always Have a Pull... ....**35.00**
Toothbrush holder, Pinocchio, MIB **55.00**
Toothpick holder, Mom's **25.00**
Tray, Distlefink, gr/brn **35.00**
Trivet, floral decor **35.00**
Wall pocket, Tea Time **50.00**

Clewell

Charles Walter Clewell was a metal worker who perfected the technique of plating an entire ceramic vessel with a thin layer of copper or bronze treated with an oxidizing agent to produce a natural deterioration of the surface. Through trial and error, he was able to control the degree of patina achieved. In the early stages, the metal darkened and, if allowed to develop further, formed a natural turquoise-blue or green corrosion. He worked alone in his small Akron, Ohio, studio from about 1906, buying undecorated pottery from several Ohio firms, among them Weller, Owens, and Cambridge. His work is usually marked.

Clewell died in 1965, having never revealed his secret process to others.

Prices for Clewell have advanced rapidly during the past few years along with the Arts and Crafts market in general. Right now, good examples are bringing whatever the traffic will bear.

Bowl, appl copper-clad leaves on rim, no mk, 2x7½" 200.00
Bowl, gr/cream/yel/brn patina, incurvate, #364-1, 4x9" 325.00
Bowl, rust/gr patina, wide form on narrow ft, 3x9½", EX 250.00
Bowl, stylized brass monogram in reserve, 1½x4", EX 120.00
Candlesticks, copper & gr patina, #414-2-6, 9½", pr 1,200.00
Candlesticks, gunmetal patina w/gold, hdls, 7", pr 475.00
Cider set, riveted, pitcher: 10x9", +6 4¼" mugs 650.00
Jardiniere, no mk, rfn, 8¾x12" 500.00
Mug, riveted straps, raised oval w/monogram & 1908, 4½" 120.00
Teacup, riveted copper o/l, 3x4" 100.00
Vase, brn patina, emb leaves/stems, pencil neck, 5" 375.00
Vase, brn to gr patina, flared base/rim, #322-2-6, 8½x3¾" 425.00
Vase, brn/blk patina, Greek Revival form, ribbing, hdls, 8" 550.00
Vase, brn/lt gr/aqua/lt bl patina, narrow neck, #368-2-6, 6½" 450.00
Vase, cvd floral top, base w/emb floral, 6½x6" 600.00
Vase, cylindrical, no mk, rfn, 9x3¾" 375.00
Vase, cylindrical w/short flared neck, rfn, 16x6" 800.00
Vase, dk rust/gr/brn patina, simple form, #444-224, 6½" 550.00
Vase, EX gr-red patina, bulbous, #323-2-6, 8x7" 950.00
Vase, EX orange & gr patina, #418-2-9, 5½x6½" 700.00
Vase, futuristic form w/4 fin-like buttress at base, 20" 3,250.00
Vase, gr/bl patina, cylindrical, ftd, #412-6, 9" 500.00
Vase, gr/brn patina, bulbous w/4 lobes & 2 integral hdls, 3" 850.00
Vase, gr/brn patina, shoulder hdls, tapering w/wide ft, 9" 1,200.00
Vase, gr/bronze patina, #91, 10x6" 550.00
Vase, gr/orange patina, trumpet neck, #290-211, 7½" 650.00
Vase, lt gr/aqua/rust/brn patina, sm neck, #369, 5½", EX 375.00
Vase, orange to bright gr patina, #445-211, 7x4¼" 400.00
Vase, orange to gr patina, ovoid w/sm collar neck, 11x6" 700.00
Vase, orange to gr patina, sm flaring neck, #363-210, 5½" 700.00
Vase, orange/gr patina, #418-246, 5x6½" 475.00
Vase, orig patina, tiny ring neck, 5¼x5¼" 300.00
Vase, pear shape, #252-6, int crack, 4x3½" 125.00
Vase, rtcl shoulder, 3 relief poppy pods, stems/leaves, 13½" 2,600.00
Vase, rust/brn/lt gr patina, short collar neck, 5½x5½" 550.00

Clews

Brothers Ralph and James Clews were potters who operated in Cobridge in the Staffordshire district from 1817 to 1835. They are best known for their blue and white transfer-printed earthenwares, which included American Views, Moral Maxims, Picturesque Views, and English Views. A series called *Three Tours of Dr. Syntax* contained thirty-one different scenes with each piece bearing a descriptive title. Another popular series was *Pictures of Sir David Wilkie* with seven prints. (Though we once thought that the Don Quixote series was made by Clews, new information seems to indicate that it was made instead by Davenport.) Both printed and impressed marks were used, often incorporating the pattern name as well as the pottery. See also Staffordshire, Historical.

Bowl, Meeting of Sancho Panza & Dapple, dk bl, rstr, 3x11¾" ..400.00
Bowl, Water Girl, dk bl transfer, 3¾" 120.00
Creamer, Christmas, Wilkie's Designs, dk bl transfer, 5½" 250.00
Cup & saucer, Water Girl, dk bl transfer 200.00
Cup plate, Dr Syntax Bound to a Tree by Highwayman 325.00
Cup plate, Mosaic Tracery, dk bl transfer, 3⅞", EX 75.00
Plate, Don Quixote Curious Impertinent, dk bl transfer, 5¼" 165.00
Plate, Dr Syntax Reading His Tour, dk bl, emb rim, 8⅝", EX 100.00

Plate, Meeting of Sancho & Dapple, dk bl transfer, 9" 200.00
Plate, Sancho Panza's Debate w/Teresa, dk bl transfer, 9½" 195.00
Plate, Valentine, Wilkie's Designs, dk bl transfer, 9" 100.00
Sugar bowl, Stag & Hound, dk bl, mismatched lid, 5¾" 135.00

Clifton

Clifton Art Pottery of Clifton, New Jersey, was organized about 1903. Until 1911 when they turned to the production of wall and floor tile, they made artware of several varieties. The founders were Fred Tschirner and William A. Long. Long had developed the method for underglaze slip painting that had been used at the Lonhuda Pottery in Steubenville, Ohio, in the 1890s. Crystal Patina, the first artware made by the small company, utilized a fine white body and flowing, blended colors, the earliest a green crystalline. Indian Ware, copied from the pottery of the American Indians, was usually decorated in black geometric designs on red clay. (On the occasions when white was used in addition to the black, the ware was often not as well executed; so even though two-color decoration is very rare, it is normally not as desirable to the collector.) Robin's Egg Blue, pale blue on the white body, and Tirrube, a slip-decorated matt ware, were also produced.

Bank, seated monkey figural, dk brn bsk, #278, 6x4" 450.00
Bowl, Crystal Patina, gunmetal gray, 5½" 75.00
Bowl, Indian Ware, blk on red, Florida/#184, 1¾x4" 125.00
Lamp base, celadon crystalline over clear amber, 1906, 5x7¾" ..325.00
Teapot, Crystal Patina, #277, squat w/lg hdl, 3¾" 150.00
Teapot, Crystal Patina, lt/olive gr, bulbous shoulder, 6" 150.00
Vase, Crystal Patina, celadon, hdls, #116, 5x6" 125.00
Vase, Crystal Patina, celadon/cream, organic hdls, 11x7" 300.00
Vase, Crystal Patina, gr/olive, bottle shape, 1905, 11x4½" 350.00
Vase, Crystal Patina, olive/brn, dbl gourd, hdls, 4x3¾" 200.00
Vase, Crystal Patina, olive/lt gold matt, 4-sided neck, 7x5" 200.00
Vase, Crystal Patina, yel-gr drip w/tan & bl, 9½" 350.00
Vase, Indian Ware, blk/wht on red, no mk/#213, 3x4" 60.00

Vase, Indian Ware, geometrics in black and beige on terra cotta, #190, 9x14½", $750.00.

Vase, Indian Ware, geometrics, Four Mile/#102, 2¾x3" 125.00
Vase, Indian Ware, stair-step band, Four Mile Ruin, 3½x4" 200.00
Vase, Indian Ware, wht/blk on red, Chevlon AZ/#2-7, 3½x5" ..150.00
Vase, Indian Ware, 4 Mile Ruin #105, 2¼x4" 125.00
Vase, tan/gray drip over lt gr, closed hdls, #135, 4½" 250.00

Clocks

In the early days of our country's history, clock makers were influenced by styles imported from Europe. They copied the European's cabinets and reconstructed their movements — needed materials were in short supply; modifications had to be made. Of necessity was born mainspring motive power and spring clocks. Wooden movements were made on a mass-production basis as early as 1808. Before the middle of the century, metal movements had been developed.

Today's collectors prefer clocks from the 18th and 19th centuries with pendulum-regulated movements. Bracket clocks made during this period utilized the shorter pendulum improvised in 1658 by Fromentiel, a prominent English clock maker. These smaller square-face clocks usually were made with a dome top fitted with a handle or a decorative finial. The case was usually walnut or ebony and was sometimes decorated with pierced brass mountings. Brackets were often mounted on the wall to accommodate the clock, hence the name. The banjo clock was patented in 1802 by Simon Willard. It derived its descriptive name from its banjo-like shape. A similar but more elaborate style was called the lyre clock.

The first electric novelty clocks were developed in the 1940s. Lux, who was the major producer, had been in business since 1912, making wind-up novelties during the '20s and '30s. Another company, Mastercrafter Novelty Clocks, first obtained a patent to produce these clocks in the late 1940s. Other manufacturers were Keebler, Westclox, and Columbia Time. The cases were made of china, Syroco, wood and plastic; most were animated and some had pendulettes. Prices vary according to condition and rarity.

Except for the novelty clocks whose values are on the increase, clock prices have been stable for several years. Unless noted otherwise, values are given for clocks in excellent condition. Clocks that have been altered, damaged, or have had parts replaced are worth considerably less.

Our advisor is Bruce A. Austin; he is listed in the Directory under New York. Our novelty clock advisors are DLK Nostalgia and Collectibles; their address is given under Pennsylvania.

Key:
br — brass	reg — regulator
dl — dial	rswd — rosewood
esc — escapement	T — time only
mcr — mercury	wt — weight
mvt — movement	vnr — veneer
og — ogee	2nds — seconds
pnd — pendulum	

Novelty Clocks

Ballerina dancing, United, M	140.00
Beer Barrel Drinkers, non-animated, Lux Pendulette, minimum value	350.00
Bird swinging, Mastercrafters	225.00
Blacksmith beating anvil, flickering fire, Mastercrafters	125.00
Bobbing chicks, plastic house, red & wht roof, United	50.00
Bobbing chicks, w/rare hanging weights, United, NM	100.00
Boy Scout, Lux Pendulette, non-animated	400.00
Care Bear, animated, Bradley, MIB (unopened)	135.00
Cat, animated, Spartus, rstr	75.00
Church w/bell ringer & cross, gold, Mastercrafters	140.00
Covered wagon, driver's arm moves, NM	60.00
Cowboy w/horse & twirling lasso, United	200.00
Dixie Boy, Lux, EX	800.00
Enchanted Forest, animated, Lux Pendulette	200.00
Fireplace, animated, Mastercrafters, newer style, NM	45.00
Fish & ship's wheel, United, M	145.00
Fishing boy, United, M	130.00
Girl on swing, Mastercrafters, NM	65.00
God Bless America, flag moves, 1940, NM	200.00
Happy Time, bum at lamppost, Mastercrafters, MIB	160.00
Home Sweet Home, old lady rocking, Haddon, compo	110.00

Hula girl & drummer, United, wood	165.00
Hunting scene, non-animated, Lux Pendulette	95.00
Joe Lewis, United, 1939, M	800.00
Lighthouse w/sailing ships scene, United	200.00
Owl, eyes move, Oswald, compo	350.00
Owl, eyes move, United, metal owl on wood base	90.00
Panda bear, eyes move, Spartus, plastic	80.00
Perky, red percolating coffeepot, Mastercrafters	120.00
Rancho cowboy on bronco, Haddon, M	185.00
Ship Ahoy, sailing ship bounces in waves, Haddon, NM	300.00
Smurf, animated, Bradley, MIB	125.00
Swinging couple, fancy case, United	200.00
Swinging playmates, boy & girl, Mastercrafters	135.00
Water wheel, Spartus, rstr	50.00
Waterfall, Mastercrafter	95.00
Windmill, Chronoart, 1930s, rstr	175.00
Windmill scene, pk & gold, United, rare	165.00
Woman working, moving spinning wheel, Lux, 1950s	65.00

Shelf Clocks

Eli Terry & Sons, Federal mahogany Pillar and Scroll, ca 1830s, repairs, 32x18x4½", $1,495.00; Silas Hoadley, carved and mahogany veneered, ca 1825, old restored finish, 27x12x5", $1,840.00.

Ansonia, blk iron Fr-style w/ormolu, porc dl, 1890, 12"	200.00
Ansonia, Etruscan (3-pc set), spelter urn w/2 ewers, 13½"	450.00
Birge Mallory, mahog vnr Emp w/gilt, 2 rvpt, 38", VG	800.00
Blk Forest, cvd w/eagle & mtn goats, unmk mvt, 40x34"	3,450.00
Boston, br/glass, tandem wind, porc dl, 1920s, 10"	500.00
Eli Terry, mahog vnr Empire, wood works/face, VG rvpt, 28"	600.00
Eli Terry Jun'r Empire mahog, rvpt, paw ft, rprs, 37"	600.00
Forrestville Empire mahog flame grain vnr, rvpt, 28", VG	375.00
Fr Atmos by JJ Reutter, sgn Tiffany, mcr tube in drum, '20s	1,150.00
Fr china w/ormolu, HP floral sgn Roche, sm rnd mvt, porc dl, 7"	400.00
Fr Zappler, sgn Roia a'Paris, butterfly pnd, orig dome, 15"	450.00
Gilbert, ebonized walnut w/cherubs ea side, all orig, 1890	285.00
Ingraham, mini Venetian, rnd top, 30-hr T/alarm, rare sz, 12"	300.00
Iron front, 8-day, paper dl, runs & strikes, 1860	225.00
Ithaca, Farmer's, walnut, dbl dl/calendar, ornate crest, 9½"	625.00
Ithaca, Granger #4, walnut, dbl dl/calendar, 1875, 26"	775.00
LF & WW Carter, rswd, 8-day & Lewis 'Y' mvt, calendar	650.00
New Haven, gilt metal case w/cherubs, porc face, 10"	115.00
New Haven, kitchen, walnut & poplar, key & pnd, alarm, 22"	100.00
New Haven, polished oak, octagon top, 30-hr, bbl pnd, 18"	130.00
Seth Thos, Athens, 8-day/T/strike & alarm, all orig, 1890	300.00

Seth Thos, Fashion #3, walnut, 8-day T/strike, 3 finials 1,650.00
Seth Thos, Lincoln, walnut, 2-wt, floor-mt gong, rpt dl 650.00
Seth Thos, mahog vnr, br works, alarm, rvpt, 15½", VG 250.00
Seth Thos, mini 8-day cottage, rswd, 'F' mvt w/alarm, 9½" 360.00
Seth Thos, Parlor #5, dbl dl/calendar, rstr dl/rfn, 1970 ....725.00
Statue of female on park bench, Fr, marble, 1960, 16" 300.00
Statue of man, ormolu paw ft, marble case/base, 1860s, 17" 175.00
Terry & Andrews, rswd 8-day cottage, orig dl/tablet, 1850 ....200.00
Waterbury, mahog vnr w/gilt, br works, pnd, 17" 185.00
Waterbury, Parlor #0, rose porc w/emb scrolls, 1890, 11", VG ...185.00
Welch, Italian #3, dbl dl w/BB Lewis calendar (no cover) 475.00
Winterhalder & Hoffmeier, mahog vnr bracket, 2-fusee, 5 gongs ...450.00

Tall Case Clocks

Aaron Willard, Chpndl mahog, old finish, ca 1790, 91", VG .10,350.00
Aaron Willard, mahog Fed w/inlay, fretwork, 3 finials, 97", EX .20,000.00
Benjamin Swan, mahog & bird's-eye maple, 1850s, 92", EX ...4,000.00
Classical mahog w/inlay, Boston, ca 1820, old finish, 90", EX .6,325.00
E Batchelder Jr, 8-day mvt, old rfn, early 19th C, 90" 11,000.00
Fed mahog w/inlay, 8-day mvt, old finish, ca 1790, 90", EX 8,625.00
Lebbeus Bailey, ME, 8-day mvt, old rfn, ca 1800, 94½" 31,000.00
Levi & Abel Hutchins, Fed maple, 8-day mvt, ca 1800, 92", EX .4,850.00
M Egerton Jr, Fed mahog w/inlay, 8-day mvt, 1830s, 97", VG ...6,325.00
Mahog, 2nd hand, date/moon phase, bonnet top, HP face, 90" 2,400.00
Mahog, 2nd hand, date/moon phase, Geo III, 94x19" 3,000.00
S Hoadly, CT, 30-hr wooden mvt, grpt case, 1830s, 89", EX ...3,750.00
Walnut, 8-day mvt, old rfn, att PA, late 18th C, 80" 4,025.00

Wall Clocks

Seth Thomas, regulator, maple case, time only, seconds dial (repainted), 1 weight, 50", EX, $865.00.

Ansonia, oak vnr short-drop school clock, 11" dl, T, 1890 ....300.00
Ansonia, rswd short drop w/Terry's calendar, orig dl, 1870 ....825.00
Atkins, rswd vnr reg w/18" dl, 2-wt rolling pinion mvt, 54" 1,500.00
Baird, figure-8 w/cigar ad, rfn/rpt, 1890, 30" 1,200.00
Banjo, mahog, rvpt door & waist: sea battle, eagle finial, 33" ..1,500.00
Banjo, mahog vnr on pine w/gilt facade, rstr/rpl, 40" 445.00
Dent, br, 8" dia w/5" dl, English platform mvt w/rear wind 375.00
E Howard, watchman's reg, walnut, T/1-wt/2nds dl, 76" 2,300.00
English, mahog w/br inlay, drop-dl fusee, dl 11" chapter 525.00
Fr, walnut cartel w/10" porc dl, gold #s etc, ornate, 22" 180.00
German, cvd walnut, rpt 11" silvered dl, 1890, 35x17" 325.00
German, walnut reg, 2-wt, mvt w/maintaining power/2nd bit, 43" ..475.00
Gothic Revival, solid block of cvd oak w/clock inset, 17" 200.00
Ingraham, pressed oak, short-drop octagon, new dl/rfn, 1900 .....200.00
Ingraham, Treasure Island banjo, eagle w/rpr, 1910 ....400.00
New Haven, br works, calendar mvt, 30-day, rstr case, 48" 600.00

New Haven, Whitney banjo, all orig w/label, rod strike, 30" 125.00
SB Terry, 30-hr ogee, T/strike & alarm, floral rvpt, 26" 300.00
Sessions, Bim-Bam banjo #805, 1920 ....160.00
Sessions, pressed oak store reg, wheat & stars design, '20s 300.00
Seth Thos, #6 re-issue by Tally Ind, 1975, 48", M 500.00
Seth Thos, calendar, mahog vnr, Pat 1876, 26½", G 715.00
Seth Thos, calendar, mahog vnr case, Pat 1876, 30½", VG 900.00
Seth Thos, gallery, walnut, 24" rpt dl on orig pan, 1880 ....1,375.00
Seth Thos, long-drop reg, oak, T/1 wt, worn dl, 36" 750.00
Seth Thos, office calendar/reg, walnut, dbl dl, T, 50" 3,335.00
Seth Thos, ship's, brass, 24-hr dl/center 2nds, 1950, M 200.00
Seth Thos, Walnut World long drop, T/15-day mvt, orig, 1890 .450.00
Standard Time, Empire reg, rfn mahog vnr, pnd, 66" 965.00
Vienna, reg, ebonized case/top trim, 1-wt, 4" dl, 33" 450.00
Waterbury, Willard #6 banjo w/wts, NM naval rvpt, EX gilt, 42" ..1,600.00

Cloisonne

Cloisonne is a method of decorating metal with enameling. Fine metal wires are soldered onto the metal body following the lines of a predetermined design. The resulting channels are filled in with enamels of various colors, and the item is fired. The final step is a smoothing process that assures even exposure of the wire pattern. The art is predominately Oriental and has been practiced continuously, except during war years, since the 16th century. The most excellent examples date from 1865 until the turn of the century. The early 20th century export variety is usually lightweight and the workmanship inferior. Modern wares are of good quality and are produced in Taiwan as well as China.

Several variations of the basic art include plique-a-jour, achieved by removing the metal body after firing, leaving only the transparent enamel work; foil cloisonne, using transparent or semitranslucent enameling over a layer of embossed silver covering the metal body of the vessel; wireless cloisonne, made by removing the wire dividers prior to firing; and cloisonne executed on ceramic, wood, or lacquer rather than metal.

Bowl, dragons, mc on dk bl, wear, China, 3x10" 80.00
Box, blk/wht/red bird on cloudy sky, Jeiji, 3⅜" L 8,625.00
Charger, dragon w/in floral borders, shaped rim, 12" 315.00
Compote, floral, mc on bl, ped ft, scalloped, 5½x9½" 195.00
Jar, Buddha & foo dog in relief, mc, hdls, Made in Japan, 12" 105.00
Jar, butterfly/phoenix panels on brn aventurine, 6x5" 460.00
Jar, dragon, mc on midnight bl, paneled, Japan, 14¼", NM 185.00
Jar, dragons, mc on bl ground, China, 9", pr 150.00
Jar, dragons & flowers, mc on blk, melon ribs, China, 12¾" 175.00
Jar, florals, mc on translucent red, Japan, 12" 385.00
Jar, florals, mc on yel, w/lid, China, 7½" 125.00
Jar, wisteria, purple on cobalt, hdls, Japan, 4" 150.00
Pencil pot, floral, mc on bl, cylindrical, 6½x3¼" 85.00
Plate, bird among mc flowers on turq, 12" 350.00
Plate, chrysanthemums & butterfly on bl, Japan, 11¾", EX 175.00
Plate, exotic birds & dragon, mc, Japan, 11¾" 225.00
Plate, warriors practice martial arts by river, Japan, 12" 235.00
Plate, 2 geese w/flowers, mc on bl, Japan, 12" 165.00
Tray, lg temple in mtns, ornate border, 1880s, 18" 1,900.00
Vase, birds in panels on lt bl, bottle form, 20" 365.00
Vase, butterflies/mythical beasts/flowers, 12x4½", pr 690.00
Vase, cherry blossoms/gilt branches on blk, 2¾" 125.00
Vase, floral/butterfly on dk ground w/allover scrolls, 6" 300.00
Vase, lg carp on bl, morning-glory border, mk, 15" 1,200.00
Vase, prunus tree on royal bl, 10x6" 225.00
Vase, roses/palm trees/birds on hammered red, 9½" 235.00

Clothing and Accessories

'Second-hand' or 'vintage?' It's all a matter of opinion. But these days it's considered good taste (downright fashionable) to wear clothing from Victorian to styles from the sixties. Jackets with padded shoulders from the thirties are 'trendy.' Jewelry from the Art Deco era is just as beautiful and often less expensive than current copies. But why settle for new when the genuine article can be bought for the same price with exquisite lace that no reproduction can rival! When once the 'style' of the day was so strictly obeyed, today, in New York and the larger cities of California and Texas, in particular, nothing well-designed and constructed is 'out of style.' And though costumes by such designers as Chanel, Fortuny, and Lanvin may bring four-figure prices at fine auction houses, as a general rule, prices are very modest considering the wonderful fabrics one may find in vintage clothing, many of which are no longer available. Cashmere coats, elegant furs, and sequined or beaded gowns can be bought for only a small fraction of today's retail. Though some are strictly collectors, many do buy their clothes to wear. Care must be given to alterations, and gentle cleaning methods employed to avoid damage that would detract from their value. For any valuable garment requiring more than minimal repair, consult a professional restorer.

Prices in vintage clothing depend on condition, basic materials, trims, label (if available), construction, where found, scarcity of type, and desirability as a collectible item or a wearable historic artifact. Our advisor for this category is Maryanne Dolan; she is listed in the Directory under California.

Key:
cap/s — cap sleeves
embr — embroidery
hs — hand sewn
lgth — length
l/s — long sleeves
ms — machine sewn

n/s — no sleeves
plt — pleated
s/p — shoulder pads
s/s — short sleeves
/s — sleeves

Apron, wht cotton w/hand-sewn embr & eyelet, long, VG 35.00
Bathrobe, Indian motif cotton blanket-like material 30.00
Bed jacket, silk, shoulders smocked w/much lace, ribbon closure ..35.00
Bloomers, cotton, split style, lace edged, 1890s, EX 125.00
Blouse, blk velvet, bows & mc embr, l/s, 1900s, EX 10.00
Blouse, lace inserts, wht embr, pin tucks, 1900s 55.00
Blouse, wht, l/s, lace trim, 1920s 30.00
Boating outfit, bl plaid, 1910, EX 115.00
Bonnet, infant's, Broiderie Anglaise, M 50.00
Boots, blk, lace-up, 1900s, pr 120.00
Boots, child's, brn leather, lace-up, 1900s, MIB, pr 200.00
Camisole, crocheted yoke, 1900s, EX 50.00
Camisole, drawstring, crocheted yoke, 1890s 60.00
Camisole, gauze-like w/lace front, neck w/rosettes & ribbons 30.00
Cape, opera; blk velvet, Victorian, 1900s, EX 175.00
Chemise, crocheted yoke, s/s, 1900s 75.00
Christening gown, wht lawn, lace trim 45.00
Coat, velvet brocade w/fur trim, bustle bk, full length, EX 285.00
Coat, wht cotton car style w/amber lens driving glasses 60.00
Dress, calico cotton print, w/bustle, EX 65.00
Dress, child's, Fairy Tale by Loomcraft, 1948, unworn 20.00
Dress, child's, gabardine sailor suit, w/cap, 1940s, sm 65.00
Dress, child's, pin tucked, ca 1860, EX 60.00
Dress, child's, wht cotton pinafore style, scoop neck, cap/s 30.00
Dress, child's, wht cotton sheeting w/crochet trim, s/s, VG 50.00
Dress, evening; bl crepe w/bugle beads allover, long, 1950s 65.00
Dress, flapper style w/red beads allover, n/s, 1930s, NM 175.00

Dress, silk, wrap style w/applique lapel & s/s, 1930s, EX 45.00
Dressing gown, wht cotton, button front, l/s, VG 40.00
Fur stole, autumn haze mink, EX 60.00
Gloves, wht kid leather, pr 18.00
Gown, christening; l/s, much lace, ca 1880, EX 115.00
Hat, allover feathered cloche, 1920s, 5¾x8" 60.00
Hat, beaver top hat, NM 150.00
Hat, child's, straw, ca 1880s, EX 65.00
Hat, fur, beaver skin, feather trim, handmade, 1890s 150.00
Hat, Gibson-girl style, blk velvet, 1900s, EX 100.00
Hat, man's, blk seal 15.00
Hat, satin toque, feathers 62.00
Hat, straw, wide brim w/flowers, Edwardian, EX 125.00
Hat, wide brim, lg moire bow, feathers, Edwardian, EX 95.00
Jacket, leather, Harley-Davidson, 1970s 395.00
Pantaloons, cotton w/embr edges, 1900s, NM 125.00
Pantaloons, wht cotton w/eyelet trim, VG 25.00
Panties, side-button style w/flared legs, cotton waistband 15.00
Parasol, pleated silk, folding hdl, sm 95.00
Petticoat, full length w/embr & lace, EX 75.00
Shawl, blk & gray wool, 132x64"+fringe, VG 90.00
Shawl, paisley, wool, woven center w/embr border, 80x72" 415.00
Shawl, paisley, woven wool, rpr, 60x62" 100.00
Shirt, brn & wht homespun, l/s, machine sewn, 36" L 140.00
Shirt, child's, drawstring neck w/embr trim, s/s, ca 1910s, VG 25.00
Shirt, denim, Levi Deluxe Western, l/s, EX 85.00

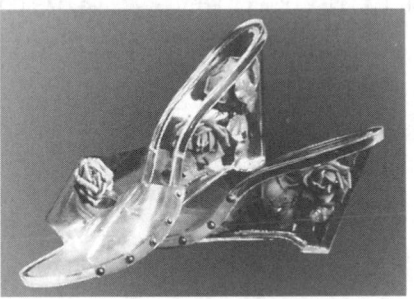

Shoes, clear Lucite with roses, late 1940s-early 1950s, $125.00 for the pair.

Shoes, boy's, blk high-tops, lace up, M, pr 75.00
Shoes, brn leather, ribbon ties, 1890s, pr 100.00
Shoes, wht leather high-tops, M, pr 125.00
Skirt, wht net, 3 rows of lace, 1900s, EX 100.00
Suit, baby's, wool knit, pants/sweater/cap/mittens, 1930s, NM 25.00
Suit, child's, brn linen, 1910, 2-pc 60.00
Suit, child's sailor, button-on pants, sm 45.00
Sweater, baby's, crocheted wool, 1930s, NM 15.00
Undershirt, baby's, E-Z, rib knit, long sleeves, M 5.00

Cluthra

The name Cluthra is derived from the Scottish word 'clutha,' meaning cloudy. Glassware by this name was first produced by J. Couper and Sons, England. Frederick Carder developed Cluthra while at the Steuben Glass Works, and similar types of glassware were also made by Durand and Kimball. It is found in both solid and shaded colors and is characterized by a spotty appearance resulting from small air pockets trapped between its two layers. See also Steuben.

Vase, gr, morning-glory form w/squatty body, att Kimball, 6" 100.00
Vase, lt bl & orange, Kimball, 4¼" 300.00
Vase, wht, Kimball, 6" 225.00
Vase, yel/opal mottle, ftd cylinder, Kimball, 12½" 250.00

Vase, 4-color, bulbous, Kimball, 6½" 1,225.00

Coalport

In 1745 in Caughley, England, Squire Brown began a modest business fashioning crude pots and jugs from clay mined in his own fields. Tom Turner, a young potter who had apprenticed his trade at Worcester, was hired in 1772 to plan and oversee the construction of a 'proper' factory. Three years later he bought the business, which he named Caughley Coalport Porcelain Manufactory. Though the dinnerware he produced was meant to be only everyday china, the hand-painted florals, birds, and landscapes used to decorate the ware were done in exquisite detail and in a wide range of colors. In 1780 Turner introduced the Willow pattern which he produced using a newly perfected method of transfer printing. (Wares from the period between 1775 and 1799 are termed 'Caughley' or 'Salopian'; see section on Caughley.) John Rose purchased the Caughley factory from Thomas Turner in 1799, adding that holding to his own pottery which he had built two years before in Coalport. (It is from this point in the pottery's history that the wares are termed 'Coalport.') The porcelain produced there before 1814 was unmarked with very few exceptions. After 1820 some examples were marked with a '2' with an oversize top loop. The term 'Coalbrookdale' refers to a fine type of porcelain decorated in floral bas relief, similar to the work of Dresden.

After 1835 highly decorated ware with rich ground colors imitated the work of Sevres and Chelsea, even going so far as to copy their marks. From about 1895 until the 1920s, the mark in use was 'Coalport' over a crown with 'England A.D. 1750' indicating the date claimed as the founding, not the date of manufacture. From the 1920s until 1945, 'Made in England' over a crown and 'Coalport' below was used. Later, the mark was 'Coalport' over a smaller crown with 'Made in England' in a curve below.

Each of the major English porcelain companies excelled in certain areas of manufacture. Coalport produced the finest 'jeweled' porcelain, made by picking up a heavy mixture of slip and color and dropping it onto the surface of the ware. These 'jewels' are perfectly spaced and are often graduated in size with the smaller 'jewels' at the neck or the base of the vase. Some ware was decorated with very large 'jewels' resembling black opals or other polished stones. Such pieces are in demand by the advanced collector.

It is common to find considerable crazing on old Coalport, since the glaze was thinly applied to increase the brilliance of the colors. Many early vases had covers; look for a flat surface that would have supported a lid (just because it is gilted does not mean the vase never had one). Pieces whose lids are missing are worth about 40% less. Most lids had a finial which has been broken and restored. You should deduct about 10% for a professional restoration on a finial.

In 1926 the Coalport Company moved to Shelton in Staffordshire and today belongs to a group headed by the Wedgwood Company. Our advisors for this category are Henry and Geneva Tyler; they are listed in the Directory under Florida. See also Indian Tree.

Plate, hand-painted castle landscape, signed A. Bowdler, late 19th century, 9½", $95.00.

Box, jeweled, #V1838, ca 1895, 3¼x5¼" 1,650.00
Box, jeweled, #V2535, 3" sq 1,400.00
Box, powder; jeweled, w/lid, #V1838, 5" dia 2,200.00
Cup & saucer, jeweled, clover shape, 1½" 750.00
Ewer, lg jewels on jeweled gilt ground, #2446, 1895, 11¾" 6,500.00
Shoe, jewels on gilt, 2½x5" 1,750.00
Sugar bowl, jewels, hdls, open, #5488, 3" 600.00
Tea set, Willow, Auld Lang Syne verse, for Tiffany, 10-pc 900.00
Vase, hdls, w/lid, #VC200, 6¾" 1,450.00
Vase, jewels, ped ft, #V2591, 10" 2,500.00
Vase, jewels on pk, stick shape, #V1259, 6⅝" 1,000.00
Vase, Plant, yel & cobalt, claw ft, hdls, #6798, 16¾" 6,000.00

Coca-Cola

J.S. Pemberton, creator of Coca-Cola, originated his world-famous drink in 1886. From its inception the Coca-Cola Company began an incredible advertising campaign which has proven to be one of the most successful promotions in history. The quantity and diversity of advertising material put out by Coca-Cola in the last one hundred years is literally mind-boggling. From the beginning, the company has projected an image of wholesomeness and Americana. Beautiful women in Victorian costumes, teenagers and schoolchildren, blue- and white-collar workers, the men and women of the Armed Forces and even Santa Claus, have appeared in advertisements with a Coke in their hands. Some of the earliest collectibles include trays, syrup dispensers, gum jars, pocket mirrors, and calendars. Many of these items fetch prices in the thousands of dollars. Later examples include radios, signs, lighters, thermometers, playing cards, clocks, and toys — particularly toy trucks.

In 1970 the Coca-Cola Company initialed a multimillion-dollar 'image-refurbishing campaign,' which introduced the new 'Dynamic Contour' logo, a twisting white ribbon under the Coca-Cola and Coke trademarks. The new logo often serves as a cut-off point to the purist collector. Newer and very ardent collectors, however, relish the myriad of items marketed since that date, as they often cannot afford the high prices that the vintage pieces command. For more information we recommend *Petretti's Coca-Cola Collectibles Price Guide*, 1994 edition (available from Nostalgia Publications whose address you will find under Auctions in the Directory); *Huxford's Collectible Advertising, Second Edition*, and *Collectible Coca-Cola Toy Trucks* by our advisor Gael deCourtivron, who is listed in the Directory under Florida. For further information call the Cocaholics Hotline: 941-355-COLA or 941-359-COLA.

Key:
b/o — battery operated   tm — trademark

Reproductions and Fantasies

Beware of reproductions! Prices are given for the genuine original articles, but the symbol (+) at the end of some of the following lines indicate items that have been reproduced. Warning! The 1924, 1925, and 1935 calendars have been reproduced. They are identical in almost every way; only a professional can tell them apart. They are *very* deceiving! Watch for frauds: genuinely old celluloid items ranging from combs, mirrors, knives, and forks to doorknobs that have been recently etched with a new double-lined trademark. Still another area of concern deals with reproduction and fantasy items. A fantasy item is a novelty made to appear authentic with inscriptions such as 'Tiffany Studios,' 'Trans Pan Expo,' 'World's Fair,' etc. In reality, these items never existed as originals. For instance, don't be fooled by a Coca-Cola cash register; no originals are known to exist! Large mirrors for bars are being reproduced and are often selling for $10.00 to $50.00.

Of the hundreds of reproductions (designated 'R' in the following examples) and fantasies (designated 'F') on the market today, these are the most deceiving.

Belt buckle, no originals thought to exist (F), up to 10.00
Bottle, dk amber, w/arrows, heavy, narrow spout (R) 10.00
Bottle carrier, wood, yel w/red logo, holds 6 bottles (R) 10.00
Cooler, Glascock Jr, made by Coca-Cola USA (R) 325.00
Doorknob, glass etched w/tm (F) 3.00
Knife, bottle shape, 1970s, many variations (F), ea 5.00
Knife, fork or spoon w/celluloid hdl, newly etched tm (F) 5.00
Letter opener, stamped metal, Coca-Cola for 5¢ (F) 3.00
Pocketknife, yel & red, 1933 World's Fair (F) 2.00
Sign, cb, lady w/fur, dtd 1911, 9x11" (F) 3.00
Soda fountain glass holder, word 'Drink' not on orig (R) 5.00
Thermometer, bottle shape, orig must say Robertson, 17" (R) 10.00
Trade card, copy of 1905 'Bathtub' foldout, emb 1978 (R) 45.00
Watch, pocket; often old watch w/new face (R) 10.00

The following items have been reproduced and are among the most deceptive of all:

Pocket mirrors from 1905, 1906, 1908, 1909, 1910, 1911, 1916, and 1920.

Trays from 1899, 1910, 1913, 1914, 1917, 1920, 1923, 1925, 1926, 1934, and 1937.

Tip trays from 1907, 1909, 1910, 1913, 1914, 1917, and 1920.

Knives: many versions of the German brass model.

Cartons: wood versions, yellow with logo.

Calendars: 1924, 1925, and 1935.

These items are currently being marketed:

Brass button, Taiwan, 18", (R)

Brass thermometer, bottle shape, Taiwan, 24"

Cast-iron toys (none ever made)

Cast-iron door pull, bottle shape, made to look old

Poster, Yes Girl (R)

Button sign, has 1 round hole while original has 4 slots, most have bottle logo, 12", 16", 20" (R)

Bullet trash receptacles (old cans with decals)

Paperweight, rectangular, with Pepsin Gum insert

1949 cooler radio (reproduced with tape deck)

Straw holders (no originals exist)

Countless trays — most unauthorized (must read 'American Art-works; Coshocton, OH.')

Centennial Items

1986 was the year for the Coca-Cola Company to celebrate its 100th birthday, and amidst all the fanfare came many new collectible items, all sporting the 100th-anniversary logo. These items are destined to become an important part of the total Coca-Cola collectible spectrum. The following pieces are among the most popular centennial items.

Bottle, gold dipped, in velvet sleeve, 6½-oz 60.00
Bottle, Hutchinson, amber, Root Co, ½-oz, 3 in case 325.00
Bottle, International, set of 9 in plexiglas case 350.00
Bottle, lead crystal, 100th logo, 6½-oz, MIB 150.00
Medallion, bronze, 3" dia, w/box 85.00
Pin set, wood fr, 101 pins, MIB 500.00
Scarf, silk, 30x30" 40.00
Thermometer, glass cover, 14" dia, M 25.00

Coca-Cola Originals

Ashtray, 1940s, Drink CC in Bottles, Bakelite, rnd, NM 35.00
Bat, 1958, wood, EX 125.00

Bingo card, many variations, 1940s, EX 30.00
Blotter, 1938, policeman, Stop..., EX 18.00
Blotter, 1942, girl on blanket, NM 10.00
Bottle, amber, Indiana PA, EX 50.00
Bottle, amber, Painesville Mineral Springs, NM 100.00
Bottle, clear, Nussbaum Bros, Bainbridge GA, EX+ 75.00
Bottle, flavor; lt gr, Big Chief, emb Indian head 18.00
Bottle, seltzer; ACL lettering, CC script, Cairo IL, complete 425.00
Bottle, seltzer; block lettering, complete, $250 to 450.00
Bottle, syrup; 1900s, label under glass (variations), EX, $750 to ...1,500.00
Bottle, syrup; 1920s, foil label, EX 600.00
Bottle carrier, 1950s, plastic, for 6 bottles, M 12.00
Bowl, gr opaque glass, Drink CC Ice Cold emb, folded rim 375.00
Calendar, 1903, Hilda Clark, w/calendar page, 15x7¾", EX 4,000.00
Calendar, 1906, Juanita, w/calendar page, 15¼x7¾", EX 2,750.00
Calendar, 1908, lady in red on gr, Good to Last..., 14x7", EX ..3,750.00
Calendar, 1912, Hamilton King girl on gray, 19¾x9¾", NM 4,500.00
Calendar, 1935, Rockwell boy on stump fishing, 24½x12", EX (+) ..500.00
Can, syrup; 1930s, cylindrical, EX 300.00
Carrier, 6-pack; 1930s, Seasons Greetings, cb, wood hdl, EX 200.00
Carrier, 6-pack; 1940s, aluminum (many variations), EX 85.00
Case, 1950s, wood, EX yel pnt 22.00

Clock, 1970s, pocketwatch shape, red, green, and beige face, gold-colored frame, electric, 18x14", NM, $80.00 to $100.00.

Clock, counter; 1930s, neon light-up, It's Time..., EX 3,800.00
Clock, 1903-05, Ingraham, octagon schoolhouse type, NM 2,000.00
Clock, 1970s, battery operated, pendulum, 27x12", EX+ 300.00
Clock, 1972, plastic, octagon schoolhouse style, NM 65.00
Cooler, picnic; 1950s, Acton, 17x12x19", EX 85.00
Cooler, picnic; 1950s, Acton Jr, 11½x9x14", EX 175.00
Cooler, picnic; 1950s, Cavalier Sr, 19¼x13¼x18", EX 125.00
Cooler, picnic; 1950s, Progress A4, 18x8¾x14⅜", EX 75.00
Cooler, picnic; 1950s, stainless, red w/wht letters, NM 150.00
Cooler, picnic; 1950s, vinyl, red w/wht letters (variations), NM ..50.00
Cooler, 1940s, Westinghouse Master, electric, holds 140, EX 400.00
Cooler bag, 1950s, wht vinyl w/red lettering, NM 50.00
Cup, 1950s, paper, Drink..., M 3.00
Diecut, 1922, cb, bathing beauty w/glass, 40x23", EX 2,600.00
Diecut, 1932, cb, Loretta Young, easel bk, Niagara Litho, VG ...800.00
Diecut, 1940s, cb, nurse serving glasses, 3-D, 22x19", NM 650.00
Diecut, 1948, cb, girl w/veil & glass, 3-D, 18x17", EX 450.00
Diecut, 1949, cb, lady w/daisies & glass, 3-D, 18x14", EX 500.00
Dispenser, ceramic, Wheeling Pottery, 4-pc, 18", EX (+) 4,000.00
Dispenser, 1950s-60s, barrel shape, EX 500.00
Display, window; 1939, cb, brunette w/bottle, 42x32", EX 750.00
Display, 1936, cb, Santa w/bottle & toys, 40x36", EX 500.00
Doll, Buddy Lee, 1950s, compo, orig uniform (+), 12", EX 850.00
Doll, Santa, 1960s, stuffed body, wht boots, Rushton Co, NM 80.00
Fan, 1950s, cb, hand holds bottle, NM 25.00
Festoon, 1922, Autumn Leaves, EX 1,000.00
Glass, 1927, modified flared shape, trademk in C's tail 100.00
Glass, 1929-40, bell shape, trademk in C's tail 35.00

Glass, 35th Anniversary, Cape Cod 10.00
Ice pick, 1950s, wooden hdl, M (+) 10.00
Jigsaw puzzle, 1950s, Sprite boy & bottle, NM 245.00
Jug, syrup; 1930s, amber glass, jug shape, paper label, EX 385.00
Jump rope, 1920s, Pure as Sunlight on hdl, NM 300.00
Menu, 1904, Lillian Nordica, 6½x4⅛", EX 600.00
Menu board, 1950s, cb, 6-pack & Take Home at bottom, EX 150.00
Mug, 1920, ceramic, emb letters, EX 600.00
Music box, 1950s, cooler form, figure turns on top, rare, EX ...1,500.00
Opener, 1905, Handy Pocket Companion, 3-purpose, EX 155.00
Opener, 1920-50s, Vaughan's Special, block letters, NM 20.00
Opener, 1930-40s, Never Slip, Drink..., EX 30.00
Pin-bk button, 1980s, Have a Good Day, M 2.00
Sheet music, 1906, The Palms, Juanita cover, EX 600.00
Sign, trolley; 1912, Hamilton King ladies, rare, 11x20½", EX .2,800.00
Sign, trolley; 1927, couple toasting, Good Company, M 1,250.00
Sign, 1897, Victorian girl in pk, Ideal Brain..., 10½x6½", EX .10,000.00
Sign, 1901, paper, Hilda Clark, 15x20"+fr, NM 6,500.00
Sign, 1902, paper, girl in feathered hat, 19½x14¾", EX 8,500.00
Sign, 1920s, paper, boy w/hot dog, 20x12", EX 600.00
Sign, 1926, tin, girl offers bottle, oval, 8x11", EX 1,500.00
Sign, 1927, paper, silhouettes, Refresh Yourself, 16x10", EX 100.00
Sign, 1928, paper, flapper w/bottle, 20x12", EX 600.00
Sign, 1928, paper, girl w/bottle, Refresh Yourself, 20x12", EX 600.00
Sign, 1929, paper, man w/hot dog & bottle, 30x10", EX 1,000.00
Sign, 1930, cb, girl in swimsuit on blanket w/bottle, 50x29", EX ..850.00
Sign, 1930s, flange, Ice Cold...Sold Here, 12x16", NM 600.00
Sign, 1932, rvpt, Please Pay Cashier, 10x22", NM 1,600.00
Sign, 1934, cb, Wallace Beery w/bottle, 30x14", VG 1,000.00
Sign, 1939-41, rvpt, lights up & has motion, rnd, EX 925.00
Sign, 1940s, girl in chaise lounge, Mind Reader!, 27x56", M 750.00
Sign, 1940s, neon, Drink Coca-Cola, 18x28", NM 1,450.00
Sign, 1942, cb, girl in rowboat, Wherever Thirst..., 27x56", M ..750.00
Sign, 1945, cb, cheerleader w/megaphone, 20x36", EX 350.00
Sign, 1945, cb, girl w/bottle, The Answer to Thirst, 10x26", NM ..350.00
Sign, 1946, cb, lady w/mask & bottle, Refreshing, 27x56", EX ..425.00
Sign, 1946, cb, Santa stands w/bottle, 12x6", M 175.00
Sign, 1950, cb, bottle diecut, 59x16", EX 300.00
Sign, 1950, plastic, Work Safely, paper cup, 12x14", EX 75.00
Sign, 1950, tin, Serve...at Home, 6-pack, vertical, 54x18", EX ...350.00
Sign, 1950s, cb, bottle & hand, easel bk, 18", NM 115.00
Sign, 1950s, cb, dancing couple w/masks, 27x16" w/fr, EX 425.00
Sign, 1950s, paper, Hamburger Sandwich, hanging, 15x12", EX ..25.00
Sign, 1950s, paper, picnic fixings, Good w/Food, 11x24", M 35.00
Sign, 1950s, plastic front, lights up/hanging, 28x36", EX 200.00
Sign, 1950s, porc, Fountain Service (variations), mc, 12x28", NM ..350.00
Sign, 1950s, porc, Stop Here Drink..., 36x26", NM 250.00
Sign, 1951, cb, cowgirl, Play Refreshed, 20x36", EX 225.00
Sign, 1955, tin, diecut of 12-bottle carton, 13x20", EX 575.00
Sign, 1956, cb, Travel Girl, 50x29", EX 300.00
Sign, 1957, cb, snowman w/lg bottle on dolly, 27x16", EX 300.00
Sign, 1959, cb, Ricky Nelson in red sweater, 18¼x14", NM 550.00
Sign, 1960s, plastic, Sno-ee, lights up, 18" sq, NM 100.00
Sign, 1960s, tin, paper cup, Ice Cold, vertical, 28x20", EX 175.00
Sign, 1970s, cb, girl w/purse high, huge bottle, 27x16", M 15.00
Thermometer, 1923s, tin, bottle form, Dec 25, 17", NM 285.00
Thermometer, 1939, tin, Pause..., bottle, variations, 9" dia, EX ..1,000.00
Thermometer, 1950s, glass front, many variations, 12" dia, NM ..195.00
Thermometer, 1950s, tin, Refresh Yourself, 17x3¼", EX 400.00
Tip tray, 1903, Hilda Clark, 6" dia, EX 1,200.00
Tip tray, 1909, lady w/glass, bay beyond, 6x4¼", EX 400.00
Toy, plane, 1930s, celluloid & wood, MIB 475.00
Toy, telescope, 1950s, EX 110.00
Yo-Yo, 1970s, Duncan Imperial, M 5.00

Trays

Values are given for trays in excellent condition (C8). Those that have been reproduced are marked with a (+). The 1934 Weismuller and O'Sullivan tray has been reproduced at least three times. To be original, it must have a black back and must say 'American Artworks, Coshocton, Ohio.' It was not reproduced by Coca-Cola in the 1950s.

All 10½x13½" original serving trays produced from 1910-42 are marked with a date, Made in USA, and the American Artworks Inc., Coshocton Ohio. All original trays of this format (1910-40) had REG TM in the tail of the C.

Tray, 1950, Girl with Wind in Hair, screened backbround, 10½x13¼", EX, $60.00 (beware of reproductions).

1897, Victorian lady, 9¼" dia, EX+ 12,500.00
1901, Hilda Clark, 9¾" dia, EX+ 4,500.00
1903, Hilda Clark, oval, 18½x15", EX+ 6,000.00
1905, Lillian Russel, glass or bottle, 10½x13¾" 3,500.00
1906, Juanita, oval, 13¼x10¾" 2,200.00
1907, Relieves Fatigue, 10½x13¼", EX+ 2,800.00
1907, Relieves Fatigue, 13½x16½" 3,500.00
1908, Topless, Ginger Ale..., 12¼" dia, NM, $6,500 to 7,500.00
1909, St Louis Fair, 10½x13¼" 1,800.00
1909, St Louis Fair, 13½x16½" 3,000.00
1910, Girl in Lg Hat, Hamilton King, 10½x13¼" (+) 850.00
1913, Girl in Lg Hat, Hamilton King, oval, 12¼x15¼" (+) 650.00
1914, Betty, oval, 12¼x15¼" (+) 575.00
1914, Betty, 10½x13¼" (+) 600.00
1916, Elaine, 8½x19" (+) 325.00
1920, Garden Girl, oval, 12¼x15¼" 800.00
1921, Autumn Girl, 10½x13¼" 800.00
1922, Summer Girl, 10½x13¼" 750.00
1923, Flapper, 10½x13¼" 400.00
1924, Smiling Girl, brn rim, 10½x13¼" 650.00
1924, Smiling Girl, maroon rim, 10½x13¼" 850.00
1925, Party, 10½x13¼" (+) 400.00
1926, Golfers, 10½x13¼" (+) 700.00
1927, Curbside Service, 10½x13¼" 750.00
1928, Bobbed Hair, 10½x13¼" 650.00
1928, Soda Jerk, 10½x13¼" 650.00
1929, Girl in Swimsuit w/Glass, 10½x13¼" 450.00
1930, Swimmer, 10½x13¼" 425.00
1930, Telephone, 10½x13¼" 400.00
1931, Boy w/Sandwich & Dog, 10½x13¼" 750.00
1932, Girl in Swimsuit, Hayden, 10½x13¼" 625.00
1933, Francis Dee, 10½x13¼" 500.00
1934, Weismuller & O'Sullivan, 10½x13¼" (+) 900.00
1935, Madge Evans, 10½x13¼" 375.00
1936, Hostess, 10½x13¼" 350.00
1937, Running Girl, 10½x13¼" (+) 300.00
1938, Girl in Afternoon, 10½x13¼" 275.00
1939, Springboard Girl, 10½x13¼" 285.00

1940, Sailor Girl, 10½x13¼" 285.00
1941, Ice Skater, 10½x13¼" 300.00
1942, Roadster, 10½x13¼" 325.00
1950, Girl w/Wind in Hair, solid bkground, 10½x13¼" (+) 125.00
1955, Menu, 10½x13¼" 65.00
1957, Birdhouse, 10½x13¼" 100.00
1957, Rooster, 10½x13¼" 275.00
1957, Umbrella Girl, 10½x13¼" 275.00
1961, Pansy Garden, 3 varieties, 10½x13¼" 20.00

Vendors

Though interest in Coca-Cola machines of the 1949 – 1959 era rose dramatically over the last few years, values currently seem to have leveled off and actually dropped 15% to 20%. The major manufacturers of these curved-top, 5¢ and 10¢ machines were Vendo (V), Vendorlator (VMC), Cavalier (C or CS), and Jacobs. Prices are for machines in excellent or better condition, complete and working. They vary greatly according to geographical location.

Cavalier, model #CS72, EX orig 900.00
Cavalier, model #CS72, M rstr 2,500.00
Cavalier, model #C27, EX orig 1,500.00
Cavalier, model #C27, M rstr 3,000.00
Cavalier, model #C51, EX orig 650.00
Cavalier, model #C51, M rstr 2,000.00
Jacobs, model #26, EX orig 1,500.00
Jacobs, model #26, M rstr 3,000.00
Vendo, model #23, EX orig 650.00
Vendo, model #23, M rstr 1,500.00
Vendo, model #39, EX orig 850.00
Vendo, model #39, M rstr 2,250.00
Vendo, model #44, EX orig 1,800.00
Vendo, model #44, M rstr 3,500.00
Vendo, model #56, EX orig 1,500.00
Vendo, model #56, M rstr 3,000.00
Vendo, model #80, EX orig 650.00
Vendo, model #80, M rstr 1,600.00
Vendo, model #81, EX orig 1,500.00
Vendo, model #81, M rstr 3,000.00
Vendorlator, model #27, EX orig 1,800.00
Vendorlator, model #27, M rstr (on stand) 2,500.00
Vendorlator, model #27A, EX orig 800.00
Vendorlator, model #27A, M rstr 2,000.00
Vendorlator, model #33, EX orig 800.00
Vendorlator, model #33, M rstr 2,250.00
Vendorlator, model #44, EX orig 1,800.00
Vendorlator, model #44, M rstr 3,200.00
Vendorlator, model #72, EX orig 1,200.00
Vendorlator, model #72, M rstr 2,500.00

Coffee Grinders

The serious collector of kitchenwares and country store items rank coffee mills high on the list of desirable examples. A trend is developing toward preferring items whose manufacturers are easily identifiable. Names to look for include Adams, Arcade, Baldwin Bros., Daisy, Elgin National, Elma, Enterprise, Lane Bros., Parker, Regal, and Sun Mfg. Co.; there are many others. Any of these marks found on coffee mills represent companies who were in business at or before the turn of the century.

Side mills usually have a brass tag located on the tin hopper. If the hopper was made of cast iron, the name was usually cast into the metal. Some of the less expensive versions had no identification. Decals were often used on the front of lap mills and table styles, though sometimes you will find these decals on the inside of the drawer. Because decals are prone to flake off and fade, and since they are often destroyed when the mill is being refinished, lap and table mills are the most difficult types to attribute to a specific manufacturer. Canister mills had names and patent dates molded into the cast-iron housing or on the canister itself. Commercial mills used in country and general stores were made of cast iron. Important information such as manufacture and patent dates was usually cast into the wheels, housing, or base of the mill. Such identification contributes considerably toward value.

Good examples of early coffee mills are rapidly becoming difficult to find. Beware of the many imported imposters that are on the market today.

Key: adj — adjustment

Adams Pat, lap, pewter hopper, wood box, porc knob 135.00
American Beauty, canister, CI & tin, orig cup & papers 65.00
American Duplex, coffeepot shape, electric 1,200.00
American Duplex Model No 50, electric 50.00
American Duplex No 47, electric 25.00
Arcade, Crystal No 44, CI w/glass hopper, Arcade lid & cup 95.00
Arcade, Favorite No 47, wood box, CI hopper 155.00
Arcade, Favorite No 74, CI hopper, wood box 155.00
Arcade, Imperial, lap, CI closed hopper, wood box, EX 110.00
Arcade, IXL, table, ornate CI hopper, hdl on side, 1-lb, EX 225.00
Arcade, Jewel, canister, rectangular glass hopper, w/lid, EX 225.00
Arcade, table, w/decal, Pat 6-5-1884, 1-lb 95.00
Arcade, Telephone, canister, CI front, Pat Sept 25 '88 ....495.00
Arcade, Telephone, Hoffman's advertising 895.00
Arcade No 3, canister, CI w/glass hopper, orig lid 95.00
Arcade No 4, canister, CI, glass hopper, orig lid, wall mt 175.00
Arcade No 40, canister, CI/glass 95.00
Arcade No 5, side, CI, Pat June '94 ....75.00
Belmont, Lightning No 23, canister 250.00
Blksmith-made, funnel shape, 1-hdl, open hopper, wall mt 225.00
Bronson-Walton Ever Ready No 2, canister, Pat 1905 ....95.00
Bronson-Walton Monitor, table, tin, ca 1909 ....55.00
Bronson-Walton, Silver Lake, canister, glass hopper 150.00
C Ibach stamp on hdl, dvtl walnut, CI hopper 145.00
Cannon No 2, table, CI box & drw, brass hopper 185.00
Cavanaugh Bros, table, front fill, 1-lb 175.00
Citizen's Golden Rule, coffee bin 275.00
Clark & Clawson No 1, CI, dbl grind, Pat 1886, 6" wheel 495.00
Coles Mfg No 7, counter, CI, Pat 1887, 16" wheels, 27", EX 695.00
Cowboy, cylinder, carried in saddle bag 270.00
Crescent, Rutland VT, CI, 15" wheels 225.00
Daisy No 667, miniature, CI top, wood box & drw, orig decal 80.00
Dwinel Wright Co, coffee bin, VG 250.00
Elgin Nat'l, floor, silver hopper, 24" wheels 1,100.00
Elgin Nat'l No 44, CI/red pnt, w/eagle & pan, 5" wheels, 24" 525.00
Elma, counter, CI, closed hopper, 10" single wheel, 17" 165.00
Elma No 0, CI, single wheel, 9¼" 110.00
Elma No 2, CI, single wheel, 12½" 140.00
Elma No 3, CI, single wheel, 15½" 160.00
Enterprise, Baby No 2, orig pnt, 2 wheels, 7½" 600.00
Enterprise, Champion No 1, single wheel, 19½" 650.00
Enterprise, floor, CI, CI hopper, Pat 1898, 39" wheels, VG 2,500.00
Enterprise No 1, CI w/CI drw, hdl, covered hopper 225.00
Enterprise No 116½, floor, Pat 1873, 39" wheels, 72", EX 3,675.00
Enterprise No 12½, 24¾" wheels 650.00
Enterprise No 16, floor, CI, orig pnt, CI hopper 4,100.00

Enterprise No 212, floor, CI, 2 wheels, 30½" **2,700.00**
Enterprise No 3, counter, CI w/wood drw, orig decals/pnt **575.00**
Enterprise No 300, very heavy, wall mt, w/catcher **750.00**
Enterprise No 9, CI, brass eagle, Pat 1898, 19" wheels, 28", VG ..**750.00**
Euclid No 4, counter, aluminum hopper, 10" wheels, VG **395.00**
Golden Rule, canister, w/orig glass, CI front, wood box, EX **395.00**
Grand Union Tea, table, CI sq base, rnd hopper, mfg Griswold .**495.00**
Griswold, counter, CI, 2 wheels, Pat 1897 ....**675.00**
Husqvrna No 7, Swedish made, single wheel, 16½" **525.00**
J Fisher, dvtl mahog, pewter hopper, handmade **195.00**
Japy Freres, ornate woodwork, brass hopper, ftd **135.00**
L&S, side, CI, on orig brd **75.00**
Landers, Frary & Clark, CI, rnd, sq base, ornate, Pat 1875 ....**425.00**
Landers, Frary & Clark, Regal, canister, wall mt **150.00**
Landers, Frary & Clark, Regal No 44, canister, CI/tin, orig **95.00**
Landers, Frary & Clark, Standard, lap, 1878 ....**145.00**
Landers, Frary & Clark, Universal No 14, table, Pat 1905, VG **85.00**
Lap, CI, brn pnt, octagon base & hopper, cup in base, 4x4x4" ...**135.00**
Lees, canister, CI works, rnd glass hopper, EX **70.00**
Logan & Strobridge, Franco-American, lap, ornate CI hopper ...**125.00**
Luther, side, CI, tin hopper, brass plate, Pat 1843 ....**175.00**
Nat'l, coffee & spice counter, CI, 12" wheels, 25", VG **525.00**
Nat'l, counter, CI works, covered hopper, wood drw, 1-wheel **95.00**
Nat'l Specialty No 0, table clamp-on, CI, covered hopper **95.00**
New Home, table, CI top, enclosed hopper, wood box, 1-lb, EX+ ..**80.00**
Parker, side, Pat 1876, CI, on orig brd, grind adj front **75.00**
Parker No 2, counter, CI w/orig decals, 9" wheels, EX **575.00**
Parker No 400 Series, lap, split covered top, ornate **135.00**
Parker No 49, side, tin hopper w/brass eagle, tin lid **95.00**
Parker No 5005, counter, CI, 12½" wheels, 17", EX **575.00**
Parker No 560, table, side crank, wood drw **375.00**
Parker No 700, counter, CI, wood drw, 17" wheels **675.00**
Peck, Stow & Wilcox International #360, lap, unusual **155.00**
Peugot Freres, lap, wood box, tin-covered hopper, Fr **45.00**
Primitive, lap, dvtl, red buttermilk pnt, orig drw, pewter **175.00**
PS&W No 3500, side, CI, orig lid, Britannia hopper **85.00**
Queen, miniature, CI hopper & drw front, wood box, decal **80.00**
Russell & Erwin, Diamond, CI, bronze finish, rare **350.00**
Russell & Erwin, Diamond, lap, CI, sloped sides **340.00**
Russell & Erwin Mfg Co, lap, top adj, CI hopper, wood box **95.00**
School Bell, canister, similar to Golden Rule, CI & wood **375.00**
Simmons Hardware Co, Delmar Coffee, table, CI cover **295.00**
Standard Cabinet Co, spice cabinet w/mill **400.00**
Star, counter, tin drw, blk, 1-wheel, sm, VG **325.00**
Star No 7, counter, CI, w/pan, 2-wheel, VG **475.00**
Steinfield, canister, CI works, glass jar **100.00**
Sun No 1050 Improved, lap, wood, tin hopper **85.00**
Swift, side, CI, Pat 1845, Pat Aug 16, 1859, top missing **95.00**
Swift No 12, Lane Brothers, 9" wheel **550.00**
Swift No 16, red w/lg decal, 2-wheel **795.00**
Swift No 26, Lane Brothers, floor, CI, 2 wheels **2,500.00**
Thomas Robert & Co, coffee bin **300.00**
Vandegrift, side, CI, hinged, ca 1870 ....**95.00**
W Cross & Sons, lap, CI w/orig CI drw, brass hopper & pull **85.00**
Walton, Bronson, canister, tin & CI, Pat 1911 ....**85.00**
Wilson, Increase, side, CI & tin **60.00**
Wrightsville Hdwe Co, Peerless No 200, canister, CI/glass **95.00**

Coin-Operated Machines

Coin-operated machines may be the fastest-growing area of collector interest in today's market. Many machines are bought, restored, and used for home entertainment. Older examples from the turn of the century and those with especially elaborate decoration and innovative accessories are most desirable.

Vending machines sold a product or a service. They were already in common usage by 1900 selling gum, cigars, matches, and a host of other commodities. Peanut and gumball machines are especially popular today. The most valuable are those with their original finish and decals. Older machines made of cast iron are especially desirable, while those with plastic globes have little or no collector value. When buying unrestored peanut machines, beware of salt damage.

The coin-operated phonograph of the early 1900s paved the way for the jukeboxes of the twenties. Seeburg was first on the market with an automatic 8-tune phonograph. By the 1930s Wurlitzer was the top name in the industry with dealerships all over the country. As a result of the growing ranks of competitors, the forties produced the most beautiful machines made. Wurlitzers from this era are probably the most popularly sought-after models on the market today. The model #1015 of 1946 is considered the all-time classic and often brings prices in excess of $7,000.00.

Coin-Op Newsletter; Jukebox Collectors' Newsletter; Antique Amusements, Slot Machine, and Jukebox Gazette; and *Classic Amusements Magazine* are all excellent publications for those interested in coin-operated machines; see the Clubs, Newsletters, and Catalogs section of the Directory for publishing information.

Jackie and Ken Durham are our advisors (for all but jukeboxes); they are listed in the Directory under the District of Columbia. Our advisor for jukeboxes is Norman Nelson; he is listed in the Directory under Ohio.

Arcade Machines

Buckley Jewel Box Digger, floor model, EX orig **1,900.00**
Cail-o-scope Peep Show, oak & CI, floor model, EX orig **1,500.00**
Caille Electric Wave, ca 1905, EX orig **3,250.00**
Caille Mickey Finn Strength Tester, rstr **4,600.00**
Chicago Coin, Speedway, rstr **950.00**
ESCo Rotary Merchandiser, EX orig **1,500.00**
Exhibit Supply, Love Tester, EX orig **1,600.00**
Exhibit Supply Crystal Palace Digger, EX orig **1,600.00**
Exhibit Supply Grandfather's Clock, ca 1925, VG orig **2,500.00**
Exhibit Supply Kiss-O-Meter, EX orig **715.00**
Exhibit Supply Mauser Gun Game, EX orig **350.00**
Exhibit Supply Streamline Digger, rstr **2,700.00**
Exhibit Supply 1¢ Five Ball Shooter, rstr **1,200.00**
Exhibit Supply 12-column Astrology Card Machine, EX orig .**1,300.00**
Golden Arm Strength Tester, EX orig **400.00**
Gottlieb Strength Test, hold grip to test, 15x8¼", EX **350.00**
Groetchen Pike's Peak, skill game, 1940, EX rstr **550.00**
Gypsy Grandma 5¢ Fortune Teller, 1920s, EX **4,600.00**
Hi Fly Coin Toss, baseball coin toss, 21", EX **450.00**
Jennings Sportsman Payout Pinball, hunter & game, 42x43x23", G ...**1,600.00**
Kicker & Catcher, 5 balls for 5¢, G- **400.00**
Mercury Strength Tester, rstr **600.00**
Mills Wizard Fortune Teller, ca 1920s, EX orig **1,400.00**
Mills 5-reel Fortune-Jumbo Success, rstr **1,275.00**
Mutoscope, tin, 1940s style, EX orig **1,100.00**
Mutoscope Clam Shell, CI, ca 1895, EX rstr **4,500.00**
Mutoscope Punching Bag, quartersawn oak, rstr **2,650.00**
Rockola World Series, pinball, EX **1,350.00**
Uncle Sam Grip Test, ca 1910, VG **12,000.00**
Watling 1¢ Fortune Telling, porc top, 66½x17x25½", G **400.00**
Whiting Sculptoscope, EX orig **700.00**

Jukeboxes

AMI #200, 1957, NM **1,500.00**

AMI F-120, 1954, EX orig 800.00
AMI F-80, 1954, EX orig 1,000.00
Packard Manhattan, 1946, EX orig 5,500.00
Rockola #1422, rstr 4,000.00
Rockola #1422, 1946, EX orig 3,600.00

Rockola #1426, walnut-veneered case with Bakelite panels, ca 1946, 56", EX original, $3,000.00.

Rockola #1426, rstr 4,350.00
Rockola #1428, 45 rpm, rstr 4,650.00
Rockola #1448, 1955, EX orig 1,550.00
Rockola #1454, 1956, EX orig 1,500.00
Rockola #484, EX orig 550.00
Rockola Rocket, 1951, EX orig 975.00
Scopitone, 1962, EX orig 3,500.00
Seeburg #100, rstr cabinet, EX working 1,100.00
Seeburg #100B, 1950, NM 1,000.00
Seeburg #147MA, rstr 3,300.00
Seeburg #148SL, EX orig 2,200.00
Seeburg #222, 1959, rstr 2,800.00
Seeburg A, plays 45s, 1948, VG orig 850.00
Seeburg B, 1951, rstr 2,500.00
Seeburg DS-100, 1962, EX orig 1,250.00
Seeburg G, 1953, EX orig 1,700.00
Seeburg R, 1954, EX orig 2,000.00
Seeburg V-200, G orig 2,000.00
Western Electric Selectraphone, 1928, EX orig 4,000.00
Wurlitzer #1015 (Bubbler), rstr 10,000.00
Wurlitzer #1050, 1973, EX orig 5,000.00
Wurlitzer #1100, M rstr 8,500.00
Wurlitzer #1700, 1954, EX orig 2,600.00
Wurlitzer #1700, 1954, G orig 1,650.00
Wurlitzer #2150, 1957, EX orig 1,700.00
Wurlitzer #500, ca 1938, EX orig 2,250.00
Wurlitzer #600, 1938, EX orig 3,000.00
Wurlitzer #71, 1941, EX orig 5,000.00
Wurlitzer #750, G orig 5,000.00
Wurlitzer Americana #3100, 1967, EX orig 365.00
Wurlitzer Americana #3800, 1974, EX orig 800.00

Slot Machines

Aristocrat Fiesta 5¢, EX orig 650.00
Bally 5¢ Reliance, M rstr 4,695.00
Bally 5¢/25¢ Double Bell, EX orig 3,600.00
Big Bertha Dollar, 96", EX orig 3,500.00
Buckley 25¢ Criss Cross, G orig 1,600.00

Caille 1¢ Baseball, CI, EX orig 9,700.00
Caille 10¢ Superior, EX orig 1,100.00
Caille 5¢ Center Pull, w/vendor, EX orig 4,600.00
Jennings $1 Prospector, rstr, in stand 4,500.00
Jennings $1 Standard Chief, EX orig 1,800.00
Jennings Victoria Silent 1932 Peacock, rstr 3,500.00
Jennings 1¢ Little Duke, w/vendor, rstr 2,400.00
Jennings 10¢ Sun Chief, G orig 1,600.00
Jennings 25¢ Golf Ball, floor model, rstr 5,000.00
Jennings 25¢ Light-Up Governor 1,900.00
Jennings 25¢ Silver Club, rstr 1,900.00
Jennings 25¢ Silver Moon Chief, EX orig 1,600.00
Jennings 25¢ Standard Chief, EX orig 2,000.00
Jennings 5¢ Club Chief, rstr 2,500.00
Jennings 5¢ Dutch boy & girl, rstr 1,400.00
Jennings 5¢ Peacock, rstr 2,300.00
Jennings 5¢ Standard Chief, EX orig 1,400.00
Jennings 5¢ Sun Chief, EX orig 1,750.00
Jennings 5¢ Torch Front, rstr 1,400.00
Jennings 50¢ Standard Chief, rstr 2,250.00
Mills Silent Gooseneck Lion's Head, G orig 2,000.00
Mills Vest Pocket, rstr 450.00
Mills 10¢ Castle front, hand load, rstr 2,000.00
Mills 10¢ Hi Top, EX orig 1,800.00
Mills 25¢ Black Cherry, EX orig 1,875.00
Mills 25¢ Golden Nugget, rstr 2,400.00
Mills 25¢ Hi Top, rstr 2,200.00
Mills 25¢ Operator Bell, EX orig 1,800.00
Mills 5¢ Black Cherry, EX orig 1,100.00
Mills 5¢ Diamond Front, rstr 1,800.00
Mills 5¢ Futurity, rstr 3,000.00
Mills 5¢ Golden Falls, M rstr 2,395.00
Mills 5¢ Hi Top, VG orig 950.00
Mills 5¢ Horse Head Bonus, rstr 2,500.00
Mills 5¢ Silent War Eagle, G orig 2,500.00
Mills 5¢ Skyscraper, rstr 1,800.00
Mills 5¢/25¢ Double Dewey, rstr 27,500.00
Pace $1 Harrah's Club, G orig 1,500.00
Pace 10¢ Kitty, rstr 4,000.00
Pace 25¢ Comet, EX orig 1,650.00
Pace 5¢ Chrome Deluxe, rstr 1,400.00
Watling 1¢ Gum Ball Slot, rstr 2,200.00
Watling 1¢ Treasury, rstr 4,500.00
Watling 5¢ Baby Lincoln, rstr 1,800.00
Watling 5¢ Rol-A-Top, gold plated, rstr 4,000.00
Watling 5¢ Rol-A-Top Bird, rstr 4,695.00
Watling 5¢ Torch Front, EX orig 1,600.00

Trade Stimulators

Buckley Horses, 1935, EX orig 600.00
Caille Puritan Bell, CI, EX orig 850.00
Daval Am Eagle, EX orig 350.00
Daval Buddy, ca 1940, EX orig 550.00
Daval Clearing House, 3-reel, 1936, VG 495.00
Daval Reel Dice, 1936 ....450.00
Daval Reel Spot, 1937, EX orig 450.00
Daval 1¢ Penny Pack, 3-reel, ca 1939, 9x11x9", EX 450.00
Gottlieb 1¢ Indian Dice, 1937, EX orig 950.00
Groetchen Dandy, w/vendor, 1932, EX orig 750.00
Groetchen Mercury, EX orig 325.00
Groetchen Yankee, ca 1941, NM 350.00
Jennings Grandstand, EX orig 500.00
Jennings 1¢ Target Indian Front, coin drop, EX orig 625.00

Marvel 1¢, cigarettes & gum, 3-reel, 9½x8x11", EX orig 365.00
Mills New Target Practice, 1925, VG 600.00
Mills Upright Perfection, 1901, EX orig 2,000.00
Pace New Deal, 5-reel, 1935, EX orig 650.00
Pierce Whirlwind, disk model, 1933, EX orig 1,200.00
Puritan 1¢ Confection, Chicago Mint Co, EX orig 575.00
Rockola Hold & Draw, ca 1934, EX orig 950.00
Scramball Gambling, mc balls on ramps, 19", EX 300.00
Stephens Magic Beer Barrel, pretzels, 3-reel, EX orig 950.00
Whitney Seven Grand, ca 1939, EX orig 700.00
Wings, 5-reel, EX orig 365.00

Vendors

Advance #11 Big Mouth, peanuts, 1923, rstr 225.00
Advance 1¢, matches, orig glass dome, oak case, 18x11x10", G .350.00
Atlas 1¢ Matchbox, ca 1915, 17", EX orig 800.00
Bluebird 1¢, gumball, rpl decal, rstr, 1920s, 14x7" dia 300.00
Collar buttons, 10¢, CI base, glass sides, 10½x5½", EX 600.00
Columbus #21, EX orig 400.00
Columbus M, hexagonal globe, EX orig 250.00
Dixie-Fortex 1¢, Dixie cups, long glass dome, 36x4x5", NM 650.00
Doremus, cigars, ca 1907, VG 3,000.00
Ford, gumball, chrome, w/orig base, marque top, rstr 95.00
Hance 1¢, peanuts, porc on CI, 18x8x9", G 1,100.00
Masters 1¢, bulk, 16x8½x9", G 200.00
Masters 1¢, gumball, vertical sq w/cast mechanism, 16", VG 200.00

Mills 1¢ Perfume Your Handkerchief, painted cast iron, ca 1916, 17", EX original, $3,500.00.

National Hunter, gumball, EX orig 400.00
Peerless Bluebird 1¢, gumball & penny drop, 1920s, 21", G 575.00
Pulver, Policeman, gum, red porc, 1931, 21", EX 800.00
Schermack 5¢, postage stamps, Uncle Sam marque, 21", G 375.00
Scoopy Gum, clockwork, man drops gum from scoop, 20", EX .2,000.00
Victor 1¢ Topper, gumball, metal w/glass, 16x6¼x6¼", EX 95.00
Zeno 1¢, gum, w/CI, clockworks, 17x10x8½", EX orig 850.00

Comic Books

For almost sixty years, the American public has been thrilled by the monthly adventures of everyone's favorite comic book heroes such as Superman, Captain Marvel, and Spiderman. Each 10¢ comic book issue, featuring a new saga of adventure and mystery, were usually met with excitement and anticipation by the youngsters who eagerly purchased them from their neighborhood candy store or newsstand. Unfortunately, the vast majority of these comic books were eventually discarded in favor of other worldly pursuits. Due to this fact, most comic books from the '30s and '40s did not survive, making them a very scarce

and desirable collectible in today's world. Many comic books are worth very little, a few of the better examples are listed here.

Action Comics, #96, Superman cover, 1946, NM, $500.00;
Detective Comics, #113, Batman cover, 1946, NM, $250.00.

Abbott & Costello, #1, Feb 1948, EX 80.00
Archie's Madhouse, #2, Archie Publications, 1959, EX 30.00
Blackhawk, #9, Comic Magazines, 1944, VG 115.00
Bonanza, #37, Gold Key, 1970, EX 5.00
Bronco Bill, #5, United Features Syndicate, 1948, EX 85.00
Campus Romance, #1, Avon Periodicals, 1949, NM 84.00
Catwoman, #1, DC Comics, Feb 1989, NM 15.00
Cheyenne, #6, Dell, EX+ 30.00
Clue Comics, #2, Hillman Periodicals, 1943, VG 52.00
Dagwood, #2, Harvey Comics, 1950, EX 13.00
Daktari, #1, Dell, 1967, NM 19.00
Dale Evans Queen of the West, #5, Dell, NM 40.00
Dearly Beloved, #1, Ziff-Davis, 1952, EX 28.00
Dennis the Menace, #2, Standard, 1953, EX 39.50
Eagle, #3, Fox Features, 1941, EX 96.00
Etta Kett, #11, King Features, 12/48, NM 42.00
Falling in Love, #1, Arleigh Publishing, 1955, NM 108.00
Fighting American, #2, Headline Publications, 1954, EX 122.00
Flippity & Flop, #2, National Periodical, 1952, EX 43.00
Gene Autry, #54, Dell, EX+ 25.00
Ghost, #2, Fiction House, 1951, EX 48.00
Goofy Comics, #2, Nedor Publications, 1943, NM 82.00
Gunsmoke, #679, Dell Four Color, NM 80.00
Haunted Thrills, #1, Ajax/Farrell Publications, 1952, EX 46.00
Hot Rod Racers, #2, Charlton Comics, 1951, NM 8.00
Invaders, #4, Gold Key, 1968, NM 25.00
Johnny Quest, #1, Gold Key, 1964, EX 38.00
Justice League of America, #20, National Periodical, 1962, VG 8.00
Kelly's, #23, Marvel, 1950, EX 22.00
Kid Colt, #5, Marvel, G 18.00
Little Lotta, #3, Harvey Publications, 1956, EX 28.00
Lone Ranger, #24, Dell, 1950, EX 45.00
Mad Follies, #2, EC Comics, 1964, EX 20.00
Marge's Little Lulu, #166, Dell, 1962, EX 15.00
Marvel Family, #47, Fawcett, 1951, NM 60.00
Maverick, #9, Dell, EX 25.00
Men in Action, #9, Atlas Comics, 1952, EX 6.00
Minute Man, #3, Fawcett, 1942, EX 185.00
New Warriors, #1, Marvel, 1990, NM 6.00
Nurses, #2, Ziff-Davis, 1950, EX 4.00
Our Fighting Forces, #3, National Periodical, 1955, EX 46.00
Outlaw Kid, #18, Atlas, 1958, EX 15.00
Pawnee Bill, #1, Story Comics, 1951, EX 38.00
Pixie & Dixie & Mr Jinx, #1, Gold Key, 1963, EX 16.00
Private Eye, #8, Atlas Comics, 1952, VG 6.00

Real Hit, #1, Fox Features, 1944, VG **10.00**
Restless Gun, #934, Dell Four Color, 1st issue, G+ **25.00**
Return of the Outlaw, #1, Toby Press, 1953, EX **15.00**
Rex Allen, #16, Dell, NM **28.00**
Rifleman, #3, Dell, 1960, EX **29.00**
Romantic Love, #4, Quality Comics Group, 1950, VG **4.00**
Roy Rogers, #27, Dell, VG+ **25.00**
Saint, #9, Avon Periodicals, 1950, EX **83.00**
Select Detective, #2, DS Publishing, 1949, VG **8.00**
Sgt Preston, #22, Dell, EX **18.00**
Shorty Shriner, #1, Dandy Magazine, 1956, EX **11.00**
Smash Comics, #4, Quality Comics Group, 1940, EX **72.00**
Space Squadron, #5, Marvel, 1952, EX **56.00**
Spin & Marty, #714, Dell, Mickey Mouse Club, 1956, EX **17.00**
Strange Terrors, #10, Atlas, 1957, EX **16.00**
Sugar & Spice, #3, National Periodical, 1956, VG **34.00**
Super Duper, #11, Harvey, 1941, VG **9.50**
Superspook, #4, Ajax/Farrell, 1958, EX **9.00**
Tales of the Beanworld, #1, Eclipse Comics, 1985, NM **13.00**
Tell It to the Marines, #3, Toby Press, 1953, EX **13.00**
Tex Ritter Western, #33, Fawcett/Charlton, EX **28.00**
Three Stooges, #1, Dell, 1959, EX **29.00**
Top Cat, #1, Dell, 1962, NM **24.00**
Treasure Comics, #5, Prize Publications, 1946, EX **30.00**
True Love Confessions, #1, Premier Magazines, 1954, EX **18.00**
Underworld Crime, #1, Fawcett, 1952, EX **47.00**
Vampirella, #2, Warren Publishing, 1969, VG **16.00**
Virginian, #1, Gold Key, 1963, EX **9.00**
Wagon Train, #3, Gold Key, color photo cover, EX **15.00**
Wedding Bells, #19, Quality Comics Group, 1956, EX **11.00**
Zane Grey's Stories of the West, #632, Dell Four Color, NM **25.00**

Compacts

The use of cosmetics before WWI was looked upon with disdain. After the war women became liberated, entered the work force, and started to use cosmetics. The compact, a portable container for cosmetics, became a necessity. The basic compact contains a mirror and a powder puff.

The vintage compacts were fashioned in a myriad of shapes, styles, materials, and motifs. They were made of precious metals, fabrics, plastics, and in almost any other conceivable medium imaginable. Commemorative, premium, patriotic, figural, Art Deco, plastic, and gadgetry compacts are just a few of the most sought-after types available today. Those that are combined with other accessories (music/compact, watch/compact, cane/compact) are also very much in demand. Vintage compacts are an especially desirable collectible since the workmanship, design, techniques, and materials used in their execution would be very expensive and virtually impossible to duplicate today.

Our advisor, Roselyn Gerson, has written three highly informative books, *Ladies' Compacts of the 19th and 20th Centuries*; *Vintage Vanity Bags and Purses*, the first book devoted solely to bags and purses that incorporate compacts; and *Vintage Ladies' Compacts*. She is listed in the Directory under the state of New York. See Clubs and Newsletters for information concerning the compact collectors' club and their periodical publication, *The Powder Puff*.

Army officer's cap form, M **85.00**
Ball shape, gold-tone metal, M, unused **95.00**
Bliss Bros, blk enamel on gold-tone, 2⅞" dia **75.00**
Butterfly encased under lid, wrist cord, mirror/puff/rouge **195.00**
Clarice Jane, flower in gr circle on blk enamel, 2½x2½" **100.00**
Dorothy Gray, moon & stars on gold-tone, ca 1947, 3¼" dia **80.00**

Dorothy Gray, Sunbonnet, mirror, no puff **185.00**
EBMCo, Art Moderne lightning on wht metal, vanity, 2¼" L **80.00**
Elgin, Eastern Star enameled emblem on lid **45.00**
Elizabeth Arden, gold-tone metal, fr mirror, 2" octagon **65.00**
Evans, basketweave heart shape w/gold-plate trim **175.00**
Evans, gold trunk shape w/watch in lid, M, unused **150.00**
Evans, gold-tone, blk enamel lid w/crest, 3" dia **60.00**
Evans, Mayfair, vanity w/finger ring/rouge/etc, unused **235.00**
Evans, orchid relief on gold-tone, 2½" dia **45.00**
Evans, rhinestones on silver-tone o/l case, 3¼" sq **175.00**
Faberge, wht & blk enamel, fr mirror, 2½" triangle **80.00**
Fitch, wht metal w/Nouveau lady, triple vanity, 2⅝" **150.00**
Foto Kompak, enameled flag, picture fr, WWII era, M **98.00**
Fr celluloid w/fabric flowers, cream w/gold, mirror **100.00**
Harlequin, blk & gold, Elizabeth Arden **145.00**

Italy, 800 silver vermeil with swirled enamel, 3" diameter, $275.00.

La Bara, gold-tone metal, pressed powder can type, 2½" **150.00**
Langois, gr enamel on gold-tone, triple vanity, 3¾x2" **100.00**
Lentheric, wht enamel & mc florals on gold-tone, 3¼x2¼" **75.00**
Majestic, MOP on gold-tone, w/lipstick & perfume, 3x2" **60.00**
Marhill, padded wht leather lid w/gilt, 2¾x2⅜" **45.00**
Max Factor, gold-tone flapjack w/emb sq & ribbing, 3¾" dia **90.00**
Naval officer's cap, red/wht/bl, M **85.00**
Norida, gold-tone metal, loose powder can form, 2½" dia **85.00**
Norida, wht metal, concentric circles, vanity case, 2" dia **65.00**
Norida, wht metal, hammered finish, 1920s, 2⅛" dia **60.00**
Novelty, Oh Please Don't Kiss Me on red, 1940s **85.00**
Revlon, moire on gold-tone, fr mirror, 2¼x3¼" **65.00**
Rex 5th Ave, rhinestone-trimmed blk moire, w/lipstick, M **45.00**
Rex 5th Ave, SP w/Dmn Cut ribbon, lunette case, 1940s, 5¼" L ..**175.00**
Rhinestones in celluloid, w/strap, no tassel, NM **235.00**
Richard Hudnut, champleve on gold-tone, w/lipstick, 3¼" L **90.00**
Tussy, hunting scene relief on SP, fr mirror, 3¼" dia **90.00**
Vanity, silver metal w/enamel, finger chain, ca 1925 ....**65.00**
Volupte, gold-tone, Swing-Lok swag closure w/stones, 3" sq **65.00**
Volupte, lattice relief on gold-tone, 2⅜" sq **35.00**
Wht metal w/walnut veneer & Scotty dogs relief on lid, 3" sq **65.00**
Wht porc domed lid w/mc transfer, unmk, 2½" dia **40.00**
Zell, gold-tone, cloisonne scrolls, mirror, 2⅛" sq **150.00**

Consolidated Lamp and Glass

The Consolidated Lamp and Glass Company of Coraopolis, Pennsylvania, was incorporated in 1894. For many years their primary business was the manufacture of lighting glass such as oil lamps and shades for both gas and electric lighting. The popular 'Cosmos' line of lamps and tableware was produced from 1894 to 1915. (See also Cosmos.) In 1926 Consolidated introduced their Martele line, a type of 'sculptured' ware closely resembling Lalique glassware of France. (Compare Consolidated's 'Lovebirds' vase with the Lalique 'Perruches' vase.) It is this line of vases, lamps, and tableware which is often mistaken for a very similar type of glassware produced by the Phoenix Glass Company, located nearby in Monaca, Pennsylvania. For example, the so-called Phoenix 'Grasshopper' vases are actually Consolidated's 'Katydid' vases.

Items in the Martele line were produced in blue, pink, green, crystal, white, or custard glass decorated with various fired-on color treatments or a satin finish. For the most part, their colors were distinctively different from those used by Phoenix. Although not foolproof, one of the ways of distinguishing Consolidated's wares from those of Phoenix is that most of the time Consolidated applied color to the raised portion of the design, leaving the background plain, while Phoenix usually applied color to the background, leaving the raised surfaces undecorated. This is particularly true of those pieces in white or custard glass.

In 1928 Consolidated introduced their Ruba Rombic line, which was their Art Deco or Art Moderne line of glassware. It was only produced from 1928-1932 and is quite scarce. Today it is highly sought after by both Consolidated and Art Deco collectors.

Consolidated closed its doors for good in 1964. Subsequently a few of the molds passed into the hands of other glass companies that later reproduced certain patterns; one such reissue is the 'Chickadee' vase, found in avocado green, satin-finish custard, or milk glass. Our advisor for this category is Jack D. Wilson, author of *Phoenix and Consolidated Art Glass, 1926 - 1980*; he is listed in the Directory under Illinois.

Key: mg — milk glass

Bird of Paradise, fan vase, gr wash, 7"	105.00
Bird of Paradise, plate, yel wash, 8¼"	45.00
Bird of Paradise, vase, lt bl, fancy ormolu mts, 9"	275.00
Bittersweet, vase, ruby stain on crystal, 9½"	150.00
Blackberry, vase, amber wash, 18"	500.00
Catalonian, vase, yel, top hat form, 7"	55.00
Catalonian, vase, yel, tricornered, 6"	35.00
Catalonian, violet vase, ruby stain, 4"	75.00
Catalonian, whiskey, amethyst, 2-oz	10.00
Chickadee, vase, red, rare, 6½"	425.00
Chickadee, vase, tricolor on custard, 6½"	100.00
Chrysanthemum, vase, 3-color, lamp form	105.00
Cockatoo, vase, 3-color on mg, 9½"	275.00

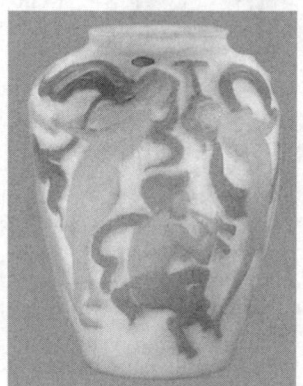

Dancing Girls, vase, 3-color highlighting on satin custard, 12", $550.00.

Dancing Girls, vase, bl highlights on satin mg, 12"	350.00
Dancing Nymph, fan vase, ruby stain on crystal, 7"	320.00
Dancing Nymph, goblet, pk frosted	125.00
Dancing Nymph, platter, wht wash, 16"	500.00
Dogwood, vase, yel cased, 11"	300.00
Dragon-Fly, vase, blk satin, rare, 7"	350.00
Dragon-Fly, vase, yel wash, 6"	100.00

Dragon-Fly, vase, 3-color on custard, ormolu mt, 7"	200.00
Five Fruits, goblet, purple wash	30.00
Five Fruits, plate, sepia wash, 12"	95.00
Hummingbird, vase, bl on custard, 5x5"	80.00
Iris, tumbler, purple wash	35.00
Katydid, vase, brn wash, ovoid, 7"	150.00
Katydid, vase, purple wash, tumbler shape, 8½"	170.00
Lamp, Cone, pk cased, 5"	125.00
Lamp, elk figural, 12", EX	1,100.00
Lamp, lovebirds figural, 10", EX	700.00
Lamp, owl figural, 8", EX	325.00
Lamp, parrot figural, 13", EX	325.00
Lamp, Santa Claus, 9", EX	1,100.00
Line 700, candlestick, crystal	40.00
Line 700, fan vase, brn wash, 6½"	45.00
Line 700, fan vase, Fr crystal, 6½"	75.00
Line 700, vase, bl on crystal, 11"	525.00
Line 700, vase, red, 10"	425.00
Lovebird, vase, gold highlights on straw opal, 10½"	400.00
Lovebird, vase, gold on custard, minor wear, 11"	170.00
Lovebird, vase, milk glass (no color), 11"	60.00
Nuthatch, planter vase, purple wash, 10x5"	175.00
Nuthatch, planter vase, ruby stain on crystal, 10x5"	250.00
Nuthatch, planter vase, 2-color on custard, 10x5"	100.00
Olive, planter vase, 2-color on custard, 8x4"	175.00
Regent Line, cookie jar, ash-rose pk over wht opal cased	250.00
Ruba Rombic, bowl, jade w/lt opal, no mk, 3½x9x8", NM	800.00
Ruba Rombic, candlesticks, wht opal, rare, pr	650.00
Ruba Rombic, cigarette box, Sunshine	400.00
Ruba Rombic, creamer, jungle gr	75.00
Ruba Rombic, plate, jungle gr, 15"	325.00
Ruba Rombic, tray for whiskey set, wht opal, rare	650.00
Ruba Rombic, vase, jade gr, 9¼x7"	1,800.00
Ruba Rombic, vase, smoky topaz, 9½"	1,700.00
Ruba Rombic, whiskey glass, jungle gr	25.00
Santa Maria, cigarette holder, crystal	175.00
Sea Gulls, vase, gold highlighting on red, rare, 11"	550.00
Sea Gulls, vase, yel cased, 11"	375.00
Tropical Fish, vase, straw opal, 9"	225.00
Tropical Fish, vase, yel wash on crystal, 9"	210.00

Cookbooks

Cookbooks from the 19th century, though often hard to find, are a delight to today's collectors both for their quaint formats and printing methods as well as for their outmoded, often humorous views on nutrition. Recipes required a 'pinch' of salt, butter 'the size of an egg' or a 'walnut,' or a 'handful' of flour. Collectors sometimes specialize in cookbooks issued as advertising premiums. Especially desirable are the figurals that were shaped like a jar, a slice of bread, or some other form relative to the product. Others with unique features such as illustrations by well-known artists or references to famous people or places are priced in accordance. Cookbooks written earlier than 1874 are the most valuable and when found command prices as high as $200.00; figurals usually sell in the $10.00 to $15.00 range.

As is true with all other books, if the original dust jacket is present and in nice condition, a cookbook's value goes up by at least $5.00. Right now, books on Italian cooking from before circa 1940 are in demand, and bread-baking is important this year. For further information we recommend *A Guide to Collecting Cookbooks* by Col. Bob Allen and *Price Guide to Cookbooks and Recipe Leaflets* by Linda Dickinson. Our advisor for this category is Charlotte Safir; she is listed in the Directory under New York.

Jell-O, The Bride and Her Task,
1916, 6½x4½", EX, $80.00.

All About Home Baking, Calumet, HB, 1937, 144-pg, VG 18.00
Armour's Extract of Beef Culinary Wrinkles, Ida M Palmer, VG ...3.00
Aunt Bee's Mayberry Cookbook, Ken Beck, PB, '91, 246-pg, VG ..7.50
Aunt Sammy's Radio Recipes Revised, 1931, VG+ 20.00
Big Chocolate Cookbook, Gertrude Parke, 325-pg, HB, 1968, VG .12.00
Bird's Eye Cookbook, 1941, VG 4.00
Briggs, Richard; New Art of Cookery..., 1798, 444-pg, EX 500.00
Carnation Milk, Mary Blake, 1932, EX 4.00
College Woman's Cookbook, 1st ed, 1923, 96-pg, EX 10.00
Cook Until Done, G Bradshaw, HB, 1962, 181-pg, VG 7.00
Cookie Jar, Culinary Arts, PB, 1978, 96-pg, VG 8.00
Cooking for Two, M Cavendish, 151-pg, HB, 1978, VG 10.00
Cooking w/an Accent, I Gaylord, 1950, w/dust jacket, VG 20.00
Cooking w/Style, Charlotte Adams, 1967, 248-pg, VG 6.00
Dr Chase's Recipes...for Everybody, 1880, 400-pg, EX 25.00
Dumpling Cookbook, M Polushkin, 200-pg, PB, 1977, VG+ 8.00
Every Lady's Cookbook..., Mrs TJ Crowen, 1st ed, 1854, EX 250.00
Experienced Am Housekeeper of Domestic Cookery, NY, 1823, EX ...240.00
Fannie Farmer Chafing Dish Possibilities, Brown, 1912, VG+ 30.00
Fast & Fancy Cookery, J Cranwell, 239-pg, HB, 1959, VG 7.00
Frugal Housewife, Susannah Carter, 1802, 132-pg, VG 500.00
Good Housekeeping Book of Meals, HB, 1927, 256-pg, EX 17.00
Good Ways To Serve Woodcock Macaroni, 1919, 50-pg, leaflet 5.00
Holland's Cookbook, from Holland's Magazine, 1937, 335-pg, VG ..15.00
International Cookbook, Betty Crocker, 372-pg, HB, 1980, VG ..14.00
Kate Smith Cookbook, PB, 1940, EX 25.00
Kitchen Primer, C Claiborne, 258-pg, HB, 1975, VG 15.00
Lippincott's Housewifery, Balderston, 1919, EX 35.00
Low Calorie Recipes, Culinary Arts, PB, 1955, 68-pg, EX 3.00
Menus For Every Occasion, E Tipton, 217-pg, HB, 1927, VG 20.00
Merry Christmas Cookbook, Peter Pauper, HB, 1955, 64-pg, VG ..8.00
Moody's Household Advisor & Cookbook, 1st ed, 1884, EX 360.00
Nut Cookbook, William Kaufman, HB, 1964, 194-pg, VG 8.50
Practical Cooking & Dinner Giving, Henderson, 1881, 376-pg, EX ..25.00
Practical Cooking & Serving, Janet Hill, HB, 1902, 731-pg, VG ..23.00
Principles of Domestic Engineering, M Pattison, 1915, EX 35.00
Simplified Hospitality, Servel, PB, 1932, 47-pg, EX 4.00
Soups & Salads, S Cooper, PB, 84-pg, 1982, VG 6.00
Spicy Food, Stendahl, HB, 1979, 304-pg, VG 14.00
Stillmeadow Cookbook, Gladys Taber, 335-pg, HB, 1965, VG 20.00
System of Domestic Cookery, Rundell, London, 1836, VG 180.00
Theory...Good Cooking, James Beard, HB, 1977, 468-pg, VG 10.00

Tropical Cooking, Gladys Graham, HB, 1947, 130-pg, VG- 20.00
WD Collector's Cookbook, Woman's Day, 519-pg, HB, 1973, VG ..17.00
What To Have for Luncheon, Mary J Lincoln, 1904, VG 35.00
White House Cookbook, Hugo Ziemann, 605-pg, HB, 1929, VG ..35.00
10,000 Snacks, Browns, HB, 1948, 593-pg, VG 17.50
1001 Dairy Dishes, Sealtest, 288-pg, PB, 1963, VG 6.00
200 Main Course Dishes, Marian Tracy, 219-pg, HB, 1964, VG 8.00

Cookie Cutters

Early hand-fashioned cookie cutters have recently been commanding stiff prices at country auctions, and the ranks of interested collectors are growing steadily. Especially valuable are the figural cutters; and the more complicated the design, the higher the price. A follow-up of the carved wooden cookie boards, the first cutters were probably made by itinerant tinkers from leftover or recycled pieces of tin. Though most of the 18th-century examples are now in museums or collections, it is still possible to find some good cutters from the late 1800s when changes in the manufacture of tin resulted in a thinner, less expensive material. The width of the cutting strip is often a good indicator of age; the wider the strip, the older the cutter. While the very early cutters were 1" to 1½" deep, by the twenties and thirties, many were less than ½" deep. Crude, spotty soldering indicates an older cutter, while a thin line of solder usually tends to suggest a much later manufacture. The shape of the backplate is another clue. Later cutters will have oval, round, or rectangular backs, while on the earlier type the back was cut to follow the lines of the design. Cookie cutters usually vary from 2" to 4" in size, but gingerbread men were often made as tall as 12". Birds, fish, hearts, and tulips are common; simple versions can be purchased for as little as $12.00 to $15.00. The larger figurals, especially those with more imaginative details, often bring $75.00 and up. The cookie cutters listed here are tin and handmade unless noted otherwise.

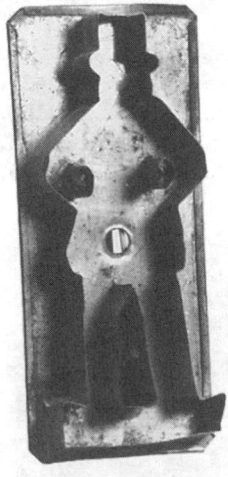

Man wearing hat, simple design,
7¼", $95.00.

Acorn, notched around entire 'cap,' folded rim, 4x4¾" 220.00
Boot, flat bk, 4" 30.00
Boy w/hat in profile, flat bk, resoldered, 5¾" 40.00
Bugle, flat bk, 4" 30.00
Dbl tulip & leaf in crimped oval, strap hdl, 3¾x2¾" 25.00
Dutch man & lady, flat bk, 6¾", pr 385.00
Dutchman w/lg head, strap hdl, 7¼" 170.00
Eagle, stylized, flat bk, 5½" 90.00
Fish, strap hdl, 4" 20.00
Hatchet, strap hdl, 7" 55.00
Heart, strap hdl, 6½" 50.00
Heart & hand, flat bk, 3½" 220.00

Horse, inset pcs to define right legs from left, 5½x6½"	75.00
Horse, rearing, flat back, 4½"	40.00
Horse, stylized, flat bk, w/hdl, 5⅝x8⅝"	50.00
Horse, stylized, no hdl, 6½x6¼"	65.00
Horse, very detailed, flat bk, 7¼" L	250.00
Lady, very primitive, 4x3"	18.00
Lady in long skirt, strap hdl, 4½"	50.00
Lady's head, 4"	30.00
Lady w/full skirt, flat bk, lt rust, 11"	115.00
Man in moon, flat bk, 4"	60.00
Man on horse, very simple, flat bk, 4"	40.00
Man w/coat tails, strap hdl, 6¼"	66.00
Man wearing hat, simple outline shape, 7¼x2½"	95.00
Man wearing hat, very detailed, no hdl, 5x2¾"	200.00
Parrot, 3⅜x7"	45.00
Pea hen, strap hdl, 4x2⅞"	20.00
Rabbit, flat bk, 8½"	50.00
Rabbit, jumping, 7¾"	40.00
Reindeer, insert missing from front legs, no hdl, 5½x5"	110.00
Reindeer, lg antlers, leg detail, flat bk, 7½"	330.00
Reindeer, stylized antlers, 5¾x6¼"	140.00
Rooster, flat bk, 7"	80.00
Star, flat bk, 7"	30.00
Star, 5-pointed inset, crimped edge, w/hdl, 3x3⅛"	45.00
Turkey, galvanized, flat bk, 4½"	65.00

Cookie Jars

The appeal of the cookie jar is universal; folks of all ages, both male and female, love to collect 'em! The early thirties' heavy stoneware jars of a rather nondescript nature quickly gave way to figurals of every type imaginable. Those from the mid to late thirties were often decorated over the glaze with 'cold paint,' but by the early forties underglaze decorating resulted in cheerful, bright, permanent colors and cookie jars that still have a new look fifty years later.

Because many cookie jars have become so expensive, reproductions abound. Though some are obviously inferior, others are harder to spot — beware. One of the most troublesome is the Little Red Riding Hood jar marked McCoy. See the McCoy category for more information. Several Brush jars are being reproduced, and because the old molds are being used, these are especially deceptive. In addition to these reproductions we've also been alerted to watch for cookie jars marked Brush-McCoy made from molds that Brush never used. Remember that none of Brush's cookie jars were marked Brush-McCoy, so any bearing the compound name is fraudulent. For more information on cookie jars and reproductions, we recommend *The Collector's Encyclopedia of Cookie Jars* by Fred and Joyce Roerig; they are listed in the Directory under South Carolina. Another good source is *An Illustrated Guide to Cookie Jars* by Ermagene Westfall. Our advisors for this category are Charlie and Rose Snyder; they are listed in the Directory under Kansas.

The examples listed below were made by companies other than those found elsewhere in this book; see also specific manufacturers.

'57 Chevy, Applause	80.00
Airplane, North American Ceramics, minimum value	500.00
Albert Apple, Pitman-Dreitzer & Co	125.00
Alien Pig, Pomona Pacific Stoneware	50.00
Barney Rubble, Certified Int'l	40.00
Bartender, Pan American Art	225.00
Batman Forever, Warner Bros	125.00
Bear, Fredricksburg Art Pottery	45.00
Bear on Blocks, Starnes	200.00
Betsy Ross, Enesco	225.00

Betty Boop (standing), Vandor	500.00
Big Bird, Demand Marketing	42.00
Black Cat, North American Ceramics	45.00
Bugs Bunny, Certified Int'l	40.00
C-3PO, Roman Ceramics	500.00
Candy Shack, Twin Winton	50.00
Care Bear Tenderheart, American Greetings	300.00
Castle, WH Hirsch	325.00
Chef, gold trim, Robinson-Ransbottom, #411	275.00
Chef (Blk), Artistic Potteries	400.00
Chinese man wearing coolie hat, Twin Winton	150.00
Church, Twin Winton, rare, minimum value	300.00
Cinderella, NAPCO	250.00
Coach, brn w/yel & wht flower wheels, gr leaves, Twin Winton	175.00
Cookie Barn, Twin Winton, #41	50.00
Cookie Jarrin's Little Angel, 1992, limited edition	395.00
Cookie Monster, Newcor	45.00
Corvette, North American Ceramics	175.00
Cowboy, Lane (+)	450.00
Dale Evans, McMe	175.00
Darth Vader, Sigma	150.00
Donald Duck, Dan Brechner	450.00
Donatello (TMNT), Int'l Silver	40.00
Dutch Boy, unmk Robinson-Ransbottom	250.00
Elephant, Cumberland Ware	60.00

Fancy Cat, solid color, Doranne of California, marked J5 USA, $35.00 (multicolor will be slightly higher).

Fortune Cookie, DeForest of California	25.00
Frosty the Snowman, Robinson-Ransbottom, minimum value	500.00
Giraffe, Hearth & Home	45.00
Grandma Bell, JC Miller	80.00
Grandma w/Rolling Pin, NS Gustin	125.00
Hi Diddle Diddle, gold trim, Robinson-Ransbottom, #317	375.00
Hopalong Cassidy, Happy Memories	300.00
Hortense, Sigma	175.00
Hot Rod, Omnibus, scarce	145.00
Hotei, brn, Twin Winton, #78	95.00
Howdy Doody Head, Vandor	350.00
Humpty Dumpty, Clay Art	70.00
Jocko the Monkey, Robinson-Ransbottom	325.00
Kliban Mama Cat, Sigma	250.00
Kookie Clown, cold pnt	175.00
Kookie Clown, under glaze	285.00
Kooky-K-Egg, Newhauser	125.00
Lion King, Treasure Craft	55.00
Little Red Riding Hood, Pottery Guild	195.00
Mail Box, Doranne of California, $70 to	85.00
Mammy, National Silver	200.00

Mammy, Pearl China 650.00
Man in the Moon, Alfano Pottery 125.00
Mary Had a Little Lamb, JC Penney 45.00
Mona Lisa, Vandor 65.00
Mother Goose, Dayton Hudson 45.00
Mother-in-the-Kitchen, Enesco 275.00
Noah's Ark, Twin Winton USA 75.00
Oscar the Grouch, Demand Marketing 75.00
Owl, Holiday Designs 40.00
Panda, Holiday Designs 50.00
Panda, Morton 85.00
Persian Kitten, Twin Winton, #44 ....175.00
Peter Max, Sigma 385.00
Pig, Terrace Ceramics 65.00
Pig Turnabout, American Pottery 175.00
Pinocchio w/Glass Bowl, Treasure Craft 80.00
Pirate, Starnes 300.00
Police Car, Henry Cavanagh 350.00
Polka Dot Witch, Fitz & Floyd 275.00
Raggedy Andy, Twin Winton, Collectors' Series 175.00
Ranger Bear, brn, Twin Winton, #84 ....40.00
Rocking Horse, Hirsch 300.00

Rooster, Gilner, #622, $35.00.

Roy Rogers, McMe 175.00
R2-D2, Roman Ceramics 125.00
Safari Truck, Omnibus 45.00
Sailor Elephant, Twin Winton, #60 ....75.00
Santa Calls, '94 Saks Fifth Ave ltd ed 150.00
Santa on Motorcycle, Fitz & Floyd 500.00
Scottie Dog, Marcia Ceramics 55.00
Smokey Bear, 50th Anniversery, ltd ed 450, Cookie Jarrin' 295.00
Snoopy, Holiday Designs, gr/brn tones, not licensed 55.00
Snowman, BC 65.00
Soldier, Cardinal 200.00
Someone's in the Kitchen, Dept 56 ....140.00
Spaceship, Sierra Vista, minimum value 500.00
Squirrel, Twin Winton, #74 ....50.00
Squirrel Stump, Gilner 35.00
Stage Coach, Sierra Vista, c 1956, $250 to 300.00
Tasmanian Devil, Certified Int'l 40.00
Taxi, Neiman Marcus, $175 to 225.00
Tepee, brn w/yel details, Twin Winton USA 250.00
Thunderbird, North American Ceramics 200.00
Tiger, Holt Howard 75.00
Toy Soldier, Marsh 90.00
Train, Maurice of California 75.00
Train, smiling face, Sierra Vista 105.00

Transformer, Hasbro, Portugal 125.00
Woody Woodpecker, NAPCO 400.00

Cooper, Susie

A 20th-century ceramic designer whose works are now attracting the attention of collectors, Susie Cooper was first affiliated with the A.E. Gray Pottery in Henley, England, in 1922 where she designed in lustres and painted items with her own ideas as well. (Examples of Gray's lustreware is rare and costly.) By 1930 she and her brother-in-law, Jack Beeson, had established a family business. Her pottery soon became a success and she was subsequently offered space at Crown Works, Burslem. In 1940 she received the honorary title of Royal Designer for Industry, the only such distinction ever awarded by the Royal Society of Arts solely for pottery design. Miss Cooper received the Order of the British Empire in the New Year's Honors List of 1979. She was the chief designer for the Wedgwood group from 1966 until she resigned in 1972. After 1980 she worked on a free-lance basis until her death in July 1995.

Bowl, Cockerel, 4-color w/copper lustre, Gray's Period, 9" 400.00
Bowl, Cubist pattern, Gray's Period, 8" dia 380.00
Bowl, sgraffito squirrels, 4½" 450.00
Coffee set, red-brn w/sgraffito, Faenza Kestrel, 7¾" pot 350.00
Coffeepot, orange & gray bands, Gray's Period, 8" 220.00

Cups and saucers, orange, yellow, or turquoise with black circles, $45.00 each; Hand-painted vase, Jazz Age design, 7½", $380.00; Jug, Cubist pattern, Paris shape, 4¼", $280.00.

Cup & saucer, dk gr w/sgraffito leaves, 2½" 45.00
Cup & saucer, Ferndown, 2½" 40.00
Cup & saucer, Wild Strawberry 15.00
Egg cup, Gray Leaves, gr wash 35.00
Jug, Crocus, turq, 6" 185.00
Meat dish, Dresden Spray, gr wash border, 14" L 80.00
Plaque, maroon leaves, 14" dia 175.00
Plate, Leaf & Vine, bl scroll border, 9" 40.00
Plate, turq sgraffito pineapple, 9" 60.00
Sauce boat, Gray Leaf w/gr wash 45.00
Tureen, sauce; brn-wash bands, w/lid, 4" H 75.00
Vase, aerographed brn/gr/yel, 7½" 225.00
Vase, appl buttons at top, pk, 7½" 400.00

Coors

The firm that became known as Coors Porcelain Company in

1920 was founded in 1908 by John J. Herold, originally of the Roseville Pottery in Zanesville, Ohio. Though still in business today, they are best known for their artware vases and Rosebud dinnerware produced before 1939.

Coors vases produced before the late thirties were made in a matt finish; by the latter years of the decade, high-gloss glazes were also being used. Nearly fifty shapes were in production, and some of the more common forms were made in three sizes. Typical colors in matt are white, orange, blue, green, yellow, and tan. Yellow, blue, maroon, pink, and green are found in high gloss. All vases are marked with a triangular arrangement of the words 'Coors Colorado Pottery' enclosing the word 'Golden.' You may find vases (usually 6" to 6½") marked with the Colorado State Fair stamp and dated 1939. For such a vase, add $10.00 to the suggested values given below.

For further information we recommend *Collector's Encyclopedia of Colorado Pottery, Identification and Values*, by Carol and Jim Carlton, who provide miscellaneous listings. Our Rosebud advisor is Jo Ellen Winther. All are listed in the Directory under Colorado.

Rosebud

Covered mixing bowl, 3½-pint, $50.00.

Apple baker, w/lid, 4¾" dia	45.00
Bake pan, 10¼x8¼"	65.00
Baker, oval, deep, sm	25.00
Baker, 11¼"	55.00
Bowl, mixing; 1½-pt	40.00
Bowl, oatmeal	25.00
Bowl, pudding; 7-pt	45.00
Bowl, vegetable; deep	35.00
Cake plate	35.00
Casserole, Dutch; w/lid, lg	95.00
Casserole, Fr	65.00
Casserole, str sides, 7"	55.00
Cookie jar, Deluxe	95.00
Cup & saucer	35.00
Honey pot, no spoon	150.00
Honey pot, w/spoon	250.00
Loaf pan	40.00
Pie plate	35.00
Pitcher, w/lid, lg	150.00
Plate, 8"	25.00
Refrigerator set	110.00
Shakers, sm, pr	35.00
Shirred egg dish	35.00
Sugar bowl, w/lid	40.00
Sugar shaker	50.00
Teapot, lg, 6-cup	145.00
Tumbler, hdl	95.00
Water server, w/stopper	120.00

Miscellaneous

Vases, Trinidad: White matt with turquoise interior, 12", $100.00; Tan matt with turquoise interior, 8", $70.00; Orange matt, 6", $45.00.

Bank, clown	150.00
Cookie jar	95.00
Creamer & sugar bowl, Mello-Tone	25.00
Malted milk container, porc	300.00
Malted milk container, tin lid	150.00
Pie plate, Coorado	55.00
Shakers, Rockmount, pr	15.00
Tip tray, malted milk	95.00
Trivet, cobalt	100.00
Vase, Aspen, tan matt, flared rim, ftd, 12"	125.00
Vase, matchless, gr matt, ribbed body, 8"	70.00
Water server, Open Window, decalcomania	150.00

Copper

Handcrafted copper was made in America from early in the 18th century until about 1850, with the center of its production in Pennsylvania. Examples have been found signed by such notable coppersmiths as Kidd, Buchanan, Babb, Bently, and Harbeson. Of the many utilitarian items made, teakettles are the most desirable. Early examples from the 18th century were made with a dovetailed joint which was hammered and smoothed to a uniform thickness. Pots from the 19th century were seamed. Coffeepots were made in many shapes and sizes and along with mugs, kettles, warming pans, and measures are easiest to find. Stills ranging in sizes of up to fifty-gallon are popular with collectors today. Our advisor, Mary Frank Gaston, has compiled a lovely book, *Antique Brass and Copper*, with many full-color photos and current market values; you will find her address in the Directory under Texas.

Fruit bowl, hammered, oval with flared and curled rim, Marie Zimmerman (unsigned), #22, 1921-22, 6x18", $2,200.00.

Boiler, dvtl, 3 wrought-iron legs, 9¾x5½" dia 300.00
Coal hod, dvtl helmet shape, wooden hdls, 10" L 100.00
Coffeepot, rnd w/lid attached w/copper chain, 13x10" dia 225.00
Cowboy boot, mk Made in USA Moulded 9, 14¼" 85.00
Funnel, wine; rolled rim, brass loop hanger, 4½x3¼" dia 50.00
Glue pot, copper insert, brass wire hdl, 2¼x2⅞", EX 75.00
Glue pot w/copper insert, cast brass hdl mts, 4x4⅝" 90.00
Kettle, dvtl, brass trim, swivel hdl, brass spigot, 17" H 275.00
Kettle, dvtl, CI hdls, w/lid, J Van Range Co, 13x15" dia 250.00
Kettle, dvtl, copper over iron rim, 16x26" 275.00
Kettle, dvtl, iron bale hdl, 14½x22" 225.00
Kettle, dvtl, iron bale hdl, 36" dia 325.00
Kettle, dvtl, iron hdl, 10x14" dia 225.00
Ladle, tasting; 2" dia bowl attached to iron hdl w/rivets, 8" 280.00
Mug, appl hdl, 5" 20.00
Pitcher, bbl shape, strap hdl, 9½x6½" 60.00
Snuff box, dragon on lid 65.00

Teakettle, D. Grauel, Philadelphia, brass finial, early 1800s, 6", EX, $825.00.

Teakettle, brass hinged hdl w/wood grip, mk 20-oz, 7x9" 150.00
Teakettle, dvtl, hdl mk F Clark Harrisburg, 12x14" (w/hdl) 700.00
Teakettle, dvtl, hinged hdl mk J Lyne, 14x13" (w/hdl) 375.00
Teakettle, gooseneck, dvtl, arched hdl, orig lid, 6½x6½" 190.00
Teakettle, Revere, acorn finial, wood hdl grip, 9" dia 95.00

Copper Lustre

Copper lustre is a term referring to a type of pottery made in Staffordshire after the turn of the 19th century. It is finished in a metallic rusty-brown glaze resembling true copper. Pitchers are found in abundance, ranging from simple styles with dull bands of color to those with fancy handles and bands of embossed, polychromed flowers. Bowls are common; goblets, mugs, teapots, and sugar bowls much less so. It's easy to find, but not in good condition. Pieces with hand-painted decoration and those with historical transfers are the most valuable.

Creamer, girl w/horse, blk transfer, lustre trim, 4¾" 55.00
Creamer, wide band flanked by bl striping, scroll hdl, 4⅛" 40.00
Flowerpot, birds emb in bl band, lion head/ring hdls, 6" 200.00
Mug, mc floral emb in wide bl band, scroll hdl, 3½", NM 60.00
Mug, Seal of US/house w/tree, bl band, 3¼" 160.00
Mug, 4-color floral in wide wht band, beaded rim, 2¾" 50.00

Pitcher, dancers, bl scroll trim, 5½x3½" 75.00
Pitcher, dancers, bl scroll trim, 7¼x4⅝" 95.00
Pitcher, emb rose & yel flowers w/gr leaves ea side, 8½" 135.00
Pitcher, emb sheepherder in lustre on yel band, 6", EX 60.00
Pitcher, Faith, purple transfer on wht, 4", VG 40.00

Pitchers: Blue floral band at top, 6", $75.00; Stripe and flowers on ochre bands, 4½", $50.00.

Pitcher, floral, orange/pk lustre on bl band, 5¾" 75.00
Pitcher, London scenes, 7½" 85.00
Pitcher, 2 fishing vignette pk transfers, 8" 85.00
Pitcher, 2-color floral vines on pk lustre band, 6", NM 65.00
Pitcher, 3-color emb roses in wide orange band, 4", NM 50.00
Pitcher, 5-color figures & urn relief in wide bl band, 4½" 60.00
Pot, florals & bl bands, 6½" 75.00
Salt cellar, floral in copper on wide brn band, ftd, 2x3" 45.00
Shaker, bl band, 4½" 75.00
Teapot, floral spray, bl trim, faceted sides, 7", NM 125.00
Tumbler, floral, copper & yel on wide bl band, 2⅞" 50.00
Vase, floral decor w/mc details, bl band, 3" 50.00

Coralene Glass

Coralene is a unique type of art glass easily recognized by the tiny grains of glass that form its decoration. Lacy allover patterns of seaweed, geometrics, and florals were used, as well as solid forms such as fish, plants, and single blossoms. (Seaweed is most commonly found and not as valuable as the other types of decoration.) It was made by several glasshouses both here and abroad. Values are based to a considerable extent on the amount of beading that remains. Our advisors for this category are Betty and Clarence Maier; they are listed in the Directory under Pennsylvania.

Basket, wht w/pk/gr ruffle w/seaweed, 3 amber hdl/ft, 10" 1,500.00
Creamer, orange w/fruit motif, amber hdl, mk Pat, 3¾" 250.00
Pitcher, orange-red w/water lilies motif, 6¼x4" 225.00
Pitcher, rose glossy Dmn Quilt MOP w/seaweed motif, 9" 350.00
Vase, acid peachblow w/seaweed motif, camphor rigaree, 6½" ...425.00
Vase, apricot Herringbone MOP w/fleur-de-lis motif, 6x6" 600.00
Vase, bl Herringbone MOP w/alternating flowers & vines, 7" 200.00
Vase, bl Herringbone MOP mc flower/insects, bk: goose, 11" 300.00
Vase, bl satin w/mc branch/berry motif, ruffled, bulbous, 6" 400.00
Vase, ivory/wht vertical stripes w/floral & insect motif, 8" 150.00
Vase, pk Raindrop MOP w/bl & gr floral motif, stick neck, 6" ...135.00
Vase, pk Snowflake MOP w/snowflake motif, tapered, 7½" 200.00
Vase, yel MOP w/horizontal lines, 3-repeat floral branch, 7" 400.00
Vase, yel shaded, dmn/fleur-de-lis between beading, 4x4" 300.00

Cordey

The Cordey China Company was founded in 1942 in Trenton, New Jersey, by Boleslaw Cybis. The operation was small with less than a dozen workers. They produced figurines, vases, lamps, and similar wares, much of which was marketed through gift shops both nationwide and abroad. Though the earlier wares were made of plaster, Cybis soon developed his own formula for a porcelain composition which he called 'Papka.' Cordey figurines and busts were characterized by old-world charm, Rococo scrolls, delicate floral appliques, ruffles, and real lace which was dipped in liquified clay to add dimension to the work.

Although on rare occasions some items were not numbered or signed, the 'basic' figure was cast both with numbers and the Cordey signature. The molded pieces were then individually decorated and each marked with its own impressed identification number as well as a mark to indicate the artist-decorator. Their numbering system began with 200 and in later years progressed into the 8000s. As can best be established, Cordey continued production until sometime in the mid-1950s. Boleslaw Cybis died in 1957, his wife in 1958. Our advisor for this category is Sharon A. Payne; she is listed in the Directory under Washington.

Key: ff — full figure

#325, Chinese wood duck, intricate base, EX colors, rare **400.00**
#4004, lamp, bust on metal fr, orig shade, pr **180.00**
#4153, man, ff, much lace, 14" **185.00**

Lamp, #4524-25A, Cupid, blue wings, roses, rare, $175.00.

#5029, Elizabeth, high ruffled collar, Raleigh group, 7½" **85.00**
#5041, man, ff, gray coat, rose & pk trim, 11½" **125.00**
#5045, Neopolitan boy w/basket of breadsticks, 9½" **105.00**
#5054, lady w/flowers in hair, bustle, skirt forms base, 9¼" **95.00**
#5089, lady, ringlets, lace, lg bustle, 10¾" **150.00**
#6004, bluebird on stump, lg **150.00**
#6029, box, oval **65.00**
#6046, ashtray **18.00**
#7006, bowl, 2 appl roses, rtcl, gold trim, 8½x6" **82.00**
#7028, wall shelf, Nouveau nude w/cornucopia, 8x6½" **100.00**
#7094, vase, Oriental figures & florals, gourd form, 9x8" **165.00**
#902, plaque, lady's face, ringlets, 10" **200.00**
#909, clock, bird & roses, rococo, wall hanging, 14½" **150.00**

#914, clock, mantel; rococo, Lanshire Electric, 9½" **165.00**

Corkscrews

The history of the corkscrew dates back to the mid-1600s, when wine makers concluded that the best-aged wine was that stored in smaller containers, either stoneware or glass. Since plugs left unsealed were often damaged by rodents, corks were cut off flush with the bottle top and sealed with wax or a metal cover. Removing the cork cleanly with none left to grasp became a problem. The task was found to be relatively simple using the worm on the end of a flintlock gun rod. So the corkscrew evolved. Endless patents have been issued for mechanized models. Handles range from carved wood, ivory, and bone to porcelain and repousse silver. Exotic materials such as agate, mother-of-pearl, and gold plate were also used on occasion. Celluloid lady's legs are popular.

In the following descriptions, values are for examples in excellent condition, unless noted otherwise. Our advisor for this category is Roger Baker; he is listed in the Directory under California.

Anheuser-Busch, bottle shape, EX **55.00**
Black bulldog, Syroco wood, 1920-30s **45.00**
Brubaker, T-shaped, twisted wire shaft, wood hdl, 4¼" **15.00**
Champion, CI w/emb vines overall, wood hdl, bar mt **125.00**
England, champagne tap, screw in cork, hdls make faucets, ca 1890s ..**60.00**
England, Farrow & Jackson Ltd..., sq shaft, wire helix, 1885 ....**85.00**
England, pearl hdls, scent & medicine bottle puller, 3½" **60.00**
England, steel w/gold finish, cube-shaped ends, 3" **130.00**
England, Sulgrave Manor, 2-finger style, bronze, EX **30.00**
England, 4-finger pull, w/button, ca 1895 ....**27.50**
Germany, Hercules, wood hdl **40.00**
Germany, legs figural (gr stripes), ca 1910, EX **300.00**
Germany, pocket style, plated lifter & worm, silver sleeve **88.00**
Germany, swivel over collar, rubber ring on fr, mid-1900s **25.00**
Haff Pat, brass ring mk Pat Appl For Apr/May 1885 ....**100.00**
Italy, bar man figural, dbl-lever style, 10½" **48.00**
Italy, swivel-over collar type, NP brass, VG **25.00**
John Watts Sheffield England, NP w/center worm, ca 1909 ....**37.50**
London, John Dewar & Son Distillery, bottle type **35.00**
Man w/straw hat figural, modern dbl-lever type, 8½" **20.00**
Perpetual, dbl-threaded shaft, automatic reverse, unmk **75.00**
Plastic duplex (dbl worm), picnic type, modern **5.00**
Sommerlier, dbl lever, chrome **30.00**
Staghorn hdl, mk sterling cap, 7½" **85.00**
US, brass band on boar's tooth hdl, 6", EX **85.00**
US, H&B Mfg Co, rosewood hdl w/brush & ivory plug on end **49.00**
US, Hollwig, advertising Pabst Milwaukee, 1891 ....**125.00**
US, NP steel worm, cap lifter & wire breaker, EX **150.00**
US, rnd steel shaft w/2" worm, wooden hdl **35.00**
US, roundlet style, bullet shape, EX **50.00**
US, staghorn hdl, sterling silver cap ea end, 1900s **115.00**
US, Woodward Tool Pat Aug 24, 1875, 10 tools in 1, EX **60.00**
Walker, 1900 mechanism, wooden hdl **30.00**
Walrus tusk hdl w/sterling ends, SP worm & lifter, Pat 1906 ......**155.00**
Weir's Pat 12804 25, Sept 1884, VG bronze finish **125.00**

Cosmos

Cosmos, sometimes called Stemless Daisy, is a patterned glass tableware produced from 1894 through 1915 by Consolidated Lamp and Glass Company. Relief-molded flowers on a finely crosscut background were painted in soft colors of pink, blue, and yellow. Though nearly all were made of milk glass, a few items may be found in clear glass with the designs painted on. In addition to the tableware, lamps were also made.

Bottle, cologne; orig stopper, rare 150.00
Butter dish, 6x8" 235.00

Creamer and sugar bowl, $150.00 each.

Lamp, banquet; kerosene, 24" 475.00
Lamp, banquet; slender base, rnd globe, all orig, 16" 525.00
Lamp, mini, 7" 365.00
Lamp, 10" 400.00
Pickle castor, mk SP fr 500.00
Pitcher, milk; 5" 170.00
Pitcher, syrup; 6" 200.00
Pitcher, water 250.00
Shakers, tall, orig lids, pr 100.00
Spooner 125.00
Sugar bowl, w/lid 185.00
Sugar shaker 230.00
Tumbler, 3¾" 65.00

Cottageware

You'll find a varied assortment of novelty dinnerware items, all styled as cozy little English cottages or huts with cone-shaped roofs; some may have a waterwheel or a windmill. Marks will vary. English-made Price Brothers or Beswick pieces are valued in the same range as those marked Occupied Japan, while items marked simply Japan are considered slightly less pricey. Our advisor for this category is Grace Klender; she is listed in the Directory under Ohio. In the listings, unless noted otherwise, prices are for items with either the English or Occupied Japan marks.

Biscuit jar, Maruhon Ware, Occupied Japan, 6½" 65.00
Bowl, salad; English 65.00
Breakfast set: 2 ftd egg cups, s&p on 5¼" sq hdld tray 60.00
Butter dish, English 45.00
Butter pat, emb cottage, rectangular, Occupied Japan 18.00
Chocolate pot, English 135.00
Condiment set, mustard, 2½" s&p, on 5" hdld leaf tray 75.00
Condiment set, mustard pot, s&p, tray, row arrangement, 6" 45.00
Condiment set, mustard pot, s&p, tray, row arrangement, 7¾" 45.00
Condiment set, 3-part cottage on shaped tray w/appl bush, 4½" ..75.00
Cookie jar, pk/brn/gr, sq, Japan, 8½x5½" 65.00
Cookie jar/canister, cylindrical, English 125.00
Cookie or biscuit jar, Occupied Japan 85.00
Creamer (post-like hdl) & sugar (no hdls) on 8" tray 65.00

Creamer & sugar bowl, English, 2½", 4½" 45.00
Cup & saucer, chocolate; str-sided cup: 3½x2¾", saucer: 5½" 40.00
Cup & saucer, English, 2½", 4½" 45.00
Demitasse pot, English 100.00
Egg cup set, 4 on 6" sq tray, English 60.00
Grease jar, Occupied Japan 25.00
Marmalade, English 40.00
Marmalade & jelly, 2 cojoined houses, Price Bros 85.00
Mug, Price Bros 50.00
Pin tray, English, 4" dia 20.00
Pitcher, tankard, rnd, 7⅞" 125.00
Pitcher, water; English 150.00

Platter, 11¾x7½", $45.00.

Sugar box, for cubes, English, 5¾" L 45.00
Tea set, Japan, child's, serves 4 ....150.00
Teapot, English, rare sz, 7¼" 75.00
Teapot, English, 5" 45.00
Teapot, English or Occupied Japan, 6½" 65.00
Teapot, Keele Street, +cr/sug 95.00
Toast rack, 3-slot, 3½" 65.00
Toast rack, 4-slot, 5½" 75.00
Tumblers, Occupied Japan, 3½", set of 6 ....60.00

Coverlets

The Jacquard attachment for hand looms represented a culmination of weaving developments made in France. Introduced to America by the early 1820s, it gave professional weavers the ability to easily create complex patterns with curved lines. Those who could afford the new loom adaptation could now use hole-punched pasteboard cards to weave floral patterns that before could only be achieved with intense labor on a draw-loom.

Before the Jacquard mechanism, most weavers made their coverlets in geometric patterns. Use of indigo-blue and brightly colored wools often livened the twills and overshot patterns available to the small-loom home weaver. Those who had larger multiple-harness looms could produce warm double-woven, twill-block, or summer-and-winter designs.

While the new floral and pictorial patterns' popularity had displaced the geometrics in urban areas, the mid-Atlantic, and the Midwest by the 1840s, even factory production of the Jacquard coverlets was disrupted by cotton and wool shortages during the Civil War. A revived production in the 1870s saw a style change to a center-medallion motif, but a new fad for white 'Marseilles' spreads soon halted sales of Jacquard-woven coverlets. Production of Jacquard carpets continued to the turn of the century.

Rural and frontier weavers continued to make geometric-design coverlets through the 19th century, and local craft revivals have continued the tradition through this century. All-cotton overshots were factory produced in Kentucky from the 1940s, and factories and professional weavers made cotton-and-wool overshots during the past decade. Many Jacquard-woven coverlets have dates and names of places and people (often the intended owner — not the weaver) woven into corners or borders. In the listings that follow, examples are blue and white unless noted otherwise. When dates are included, they appear on the coverlet itself as part of the woven design.

Jacquard

Boston town design with vintage borders, blue and white, double weave, 1-piece, minor wear and stains, 74x62", $385.00.

Floral medallion/stars/birds, OH, 1856, 2-pc, 96x84"	465.00
Floral medallions, border w/eagle corners, 2-pc, 86x75"	200.00
Floral medallions on checkerboard, 4-color, 2-pc, 72x69"	550.00
Floral medallions/bird/trees, PA, 4-color, 1-pc, 88x79"	550.00
Floral medallions/stags/flower border, 4-color, 2-pc, 92x80"	880.00
Floral medallions/stars/etc, 4-color, 2-pc, 86x78"	445.00
Floral w/bird borders, 1-pc, 84x67", VG	150.00
Floral w/star borders, 4-color, 2-pc, 1853, 88x82", EX-	300.00
Geometric floral, star corners, 4-color, 2-pc, 90x82"	500.00
Geometric floral medallion/schoolhouse, 2-pc, 1842, 91x76"	745.00
Snowflake & pine tree, 2-pc, appl fringe, 96x70"	220.00
Washington Hail, red/bl/gr, 1869, 76x76", EX	575.00
4 rose medallions, vintage border, 1-pc, 81x72"	150.00
4 rose medallions/stars, 2-pc, 1833, 76x93"	385.00

Overshot

Optical, red/bl/wht, 2-pc, 94x79"	180.00
Optical, 2-pc, no fringe, 84x66"	150.00

Cowan

Guy Cowan opened a small pottery near Cleveland, Ohio, ca 1909, where he made tile and artware on a small scale from the natural red clay available there. He developed distinctive glazes — necessary, he felt, to cover the dark red body. After the war and a temporary halt in production, Cowan moved his pottery to Rocky River, where he made a commercial line of artware utilizing a highly-fired white porcelain. Although he acquiesced to the necessity of mass production, every effort was made to insure a product of highest quality. Fine artists, among them Waylande Gregory, Thelma Frazier, and Viktor Schreckengost, designed pieces which were often produced in limited editions,

some of which sell today for prices in the thousands. Most of the ware was marked 'Cowan' or 'Lakewood Ware,' not to be confused with the name of the 1930 mass-produced line called 'Lakeware.' Falling under the crunch of the Great Depression, the pottery closed in 1931.

The use of an asterisk (*) in the listing below indicates a nonfactory name that is being provided as a suggested name for the convenience of present-day collectors. One example is the glaze *Original Ivory, which is a high-gloss white that resembles undecorated porcelain. It was used on many of Cowan's lady 'flower figures' (Cowan's more graceful term for what some collectors call frogs). Our advisor for this category is Mark Bassett; he is listed in the Directory under Ohio.

Ashtray, unicorn, Oriental Red, Waylande Gregory, #925	75.00
Bookends, Kicking Horses, Egyptian Bl, W Gregory, #E-1, 9", pr	1,200.00
Bowl, ftd console; Hyacinth, #741-B, 17"	75.00
Bowl, Larkspur w/mc oil spots, #538, 3½x12", +#610 frog	100.00
Box, emb flowers, Special Ivory, flame finial, #X-14, R Josset	225.00
Cake plate, Caramel, scalloped edge, ftd, #X-1	75.00
Candlesticks, Foliage, grape hdls, W Gregory, #959, 7", pr	175.00
Candlesticks, Marigold, dbl hdls, #528, 3½", pr	35.00
Candlesticks, Orange Velour, 8-sided base, #692, 3", pr	35.00
Candlesticks, sea horse, April Gr, R Guy Cowan, #716, pr	50.00
Candlesticks, Special Ivory, floral, triangular base, #782, 3", pr	45.00
Comport, Apple Blossom, floriform ft, W Gregory, #779, 3½x6"	75.00
Flower frog, *Awakening, Special Ivory, arms bent, RG Cowan, 9"	375.00
Flower frog, *Duet, Special Ivory, RG Cowan, #685, 6½"	450.00
Flower frog, *Scarf Dancer, Special Ivory, #686, 6"	250.00
Flower frog, nude scarf dancer, wht, Walter Sinz, no mk, 6"	160.00
Flower frog, Pavlova, *Orig Ivory, Cowan &Y Sinz, #698, 8"	175.00
Lamp, based on Chinese Bird vase #747, October, RG Cowan	750.00

Lamp, Oriental Red, bulbous ribbed base on V-44, with metal and parchment shade simulating mica, ca 1930, 19½", $1,200.00.

Pitcher, Delphinium, bulbous, #623, 5"	125.00
Plate, nudes/birds, Guava Yel, T Frazier, 8-sided, 13"	800.00
Sculpture, Mary, kneeling, M Postgate, ltd ed, #861	3,500.00
Trivet, fish & Deco flowers, hand decor, T Frazier, 6-sided	400.00
Vase, Antique Gr, Oriental-look, fan form, RG Cowan, #801, 5½"	125.00
Vase, emb nudes/geometrics, hand decor, T Frazier, 1930, 9½"	3,000.00
Vase, Foliage, flared cylinder, bulbous ribbed base, #V-53, 6"	175.00
Vase, Marigold, bulbous shoulder, #664, 5"	65.00
Vase, Oriental Red, flared/ribbed neck, rnd base, V-75, 8"	225.00
Vase, Oriental Red, ribbed, short lip, RG Cowan, V-45, 9½"	650.00
Wall plaque, dancer & dog, Guava & Egyptian Bl, rpr	550.00

Cracker Jack

Kids have been buying Cracker Jack since it was first introduced in the 1890s. By 1912 it was packaged with a free toy inside. Before the first kernel was crunched, eager fingers had retrieved the surprise from the depth of the box — actually no easy task, considering the care required to keep the contents so swiftly displaced from spilling over the side! Though a little older, perhaps, many of those same kids still are looking — just as eagerly — for the Cracker Jack prizes. Point of sale, company collectibles, and the prizes as well have over the years reflected America's changing culture. Grocer sales and incentives from around the turn of the century — paper dolls, postcards, and song books — were often marked Rueckheim Brothers (the inventors of Cracker Jack) or Reliable Confections. Over the years the company made some changes, leaving a trail of clues that often help collectors date their items. The company's name changed in 1922 from Rueckheim Brothers & Eckstein to The Cracker Jack Company. Their Brooklyn office was open from 1914 until it closed in 1923, and the first time the sailor Jack logo was used on their packaging was 1919. For packages and 'point of sale' dating, note that the word 'prize' was used from 1912 to 1925, 'novelty' from 1925 to 1932, and 'toy' from 1933 on.

The first loose-packed prizes were toys made of wood, clay, tin, metal, and lithographed paper. Plastic toys were introduced in 1946. Paper wrapped for safety purposes in 1948, subjects echo the 'hype' of the day — yo-yos, tops, whistles, and sports cards in the simple, peaceful days of our country, propaganda and war toys in the forties, games in the fifties, and space toys in the sixties. Few of the estimated 15 billion prizes were marked. Advertising items from Angelus Marshmallow and Checkers Confections (cousins of the Cracker Jack family) are also collectible. When no condition is indicated, the items listed below are assumed to be in excellent condition. 'CJ' indicates that the item is marked. Note: An often-asked question concerns the tin Toonerville Trolley called 'CJ.' No data has been found in the factory archives to authenticate this item; it is assumed that the 'CJ' merely refers to its small size. Our advisor for this category is Wes Johnson; he is listed in the Directory under Kentucky.

Cast Metal Prizes

Badge, shield, CJ Jr Detective, silver, 1931, 1¼" 40.00
Badge, 6-point star, mk CJ Police, silver, 1931, 1¼" 44.00
Button, stud bk, Me for Cracker Jack, boy & dog, oval 44.00
Button, stud bk, Xd bats & ball, CJ pitcher/etc series, 1928 ....110.00
Chair, T (Tootsie), 3 different sectional pcs, pnt, mini, ea 12.00
Coins, Presidents, 31 series, CJ, 1933, ea 8.00
Dollhouse items: lantern, mug, candlestick, etc; no mk, ea 6.50
Horse & wagon, CJ, 3-D, silver or gold, early, 2½", ea 250.00
Pistol, soft lead, inked, CJ on barrel, early, rare, 2⅛" 180.00
Ring, alphabet letter setting (series), unmk, ea 4.00
Rocking horse, no rider, 3-D, inked, early, 1⅛" 10.00
Rocking horse w/boy, 3-D, inked, early, 1½" 29.00
Spinner, early pkg in center, 'More You Eat...,' CJ, rare 295.00
Tootsietoy series: boats, cars, animals; '31, ¾"-1½", ea 7.00

Dealer Incentives and Premiums

Golf Tee set, wood tees in paper 'matchbook' folder, CJ, 1920s, $725.00.

Badge, pin-bk, celluloid, pretty lady w/CJ label, 1905, 1¼" 65.00
Bat, baseball; wood, Hillerich & Bradsby, CJ, full sz 125.00
Blotter, CJ question mk box, yel, 7¾x3¾" 285.00
Book, pocket; jester on cover, CJ Riddles 73.00
Book, pocket; riddle/sailor boy/dog on cover, RWB, CJ, 1919 ......60.00
Book, recipe; Angelus, 1930s 22.00
Book, Uncle Sam Song Book, CJ, 1911, ea 60.00
Cart w/2 movable wheels, wood dowel tongue, CJ 75.00
Corkscrew/opener, metal plated, CJ/Angelus, 3" 79.00
Corkscrew/opener, metal plated, CJ/Angelus, 3¾" tube case 79.00
Harmonica, full scale, emb CJ, early, 5⅛" 385.00
Jigsaw puzzle, CJ or Checkers, 1 of 4, 7x10", in envelope 35.00
Marbles, Akro set of 12 in box w/instructions, CJ, 1929 ....950.00
Mask, Halloween; paper, CJ, series, 10" or 12", ea 22.00
Match holder, hinged, eng gold-tone case, CJ, 2½x1⅞" 650.00
Mirror, oval, Angelus (redhead or blond) on box 89.00
Palm puzzle, mirror bk, CJ, mk Germany/RWB, 1910-14, 1½" ...110.00
Pen, ink; w/nib, tin litho bbl, CJ 650.00
Pencil top clip, metal/celluloid, oval boy & dog logo 210.00
Pencil top clip, metal/celluloid, tube shape w/package 190.00
Postcard, bear, 1 of 16, CJ, 1907, ea 30.00
Puzzle, metal, CJ/Angelus, 1 of 15, '34, in envelope, ea 14.00
Riddle card, 2 series of 20, w/package/from factory, CJ, '07, ea 7.00
Tablet, school; CJ, 1929, 8x10" 195.00
Thimble, aluminum, CJ Co/Angelus, red pnt, rare, ea 165.00
Wings, air corps type, silver or blk, stud-bk, CJ, '30s, 3", ea 80.00

Packaging

Box, popcorn; Question Mark box end for CJ 'Toy,' 1923-27 ....85.00
Box, popcorn; red scroll border, CJ 'Prize,' 1912-25, ea 95.00
Box, popcorn; store display, CJ 'Novelty,' 1925-32, ea 90.00
Canister, tin, CJ Candy Corn Crisp, 10-oz 75.00
Canister, tin, CJ Coconut Corn Crisp, 1-lb 55.00
Canister, tin, CJ Coconut Corn Crisp, 10-oz 65.00
CJ Commemorative canister, mc scene, 1990s, ea 9.00
CJ Commemorative canister, wht w/red scroll, 1980s, ea 6.50
Crate, shipping; wood, CJ, Rueckheim Bros Eck, 1902-22, lg 150.00

Paper Prizes

Baseball CJ score counter, 3⅜" L 145.00
Book, Animals (or Birds), to color, Makatoy, 1949, mini 35.00
Book, Bess & Bill on CJ Hill, series of 12, 1937, mini 95.00
Book, Birds We Know, CJ, 1928, mini 75.00
Book, Chaplin flip book, CJ, 1920s, ea 115.00
Book, drawing w/tracing paper, CJ, 1920s, mini 110.00
Book, Twigg & Sprigg, CJ, 1930, mini 95.00
Booklet, stickers/wise cracks/riddles, Borden, CJ, 1965 on 2.50
Decal, cartoon or nursery rhyme figure, 1947-49, CJ 12.00
Disguise, ears, red (out of carrier, 1950, pr 30.00
Disguise, ears, red (still in carrier, CJ, 1950, pr 110.00
Disguise, glasses, hinged, cello lenses, CJ Where Ever..., '33 ....145.00
Disguise, glasses, hinged, w/eyeballs, unmk, 1933 ....6.00
Disguise, mustache, blk/brn, in carrier, CJ, 1949 ....60.00
Fortune Teller, boy/dog on film in envelope, CJ, '20s, 1¾x2½" ...75.00
Fortune wheel, 2-pc litho, turn for fortune, CJ, 1¾" 70.00
Game, Midget Auto Race, wheel spins, CJ, 1949, 3⅜" H 45.00
Game spinner, ...baseball at home, rectangle, CJ, 2¾" W 125.00
Game spinner, ...baseball at home, unmk, 1946, 1½" dia 40.00
Hat, fold out, More You Eat/More You Want, CJ, early 75.00
Hat, Indian headdress, CJ, 1931, 2½" H 110.00
Hat, Indian headdress, CJ, 1950s, 5⅜" H 275.00
Hat, Me for CJ, early, ea 105.00

Hat visor, baseball, tie-on string, red or gr, CJ, 1931 ....120.00
Magic game book, erasable slate, series of 13, 1946, ea 35.00
Movie, boy at blkboard, turn wheel: draws/erases, CJ, '31, 2" 185.00
Movie, Goofy Zoo, turn wheel(s): change animals, 1939 ....17.00
Movie, pull tab for 2nd picture, series, CJ, 1943, 1¼", ea 82.00
Movie, pull tab for 2nd picture, yel, early, 3", in envelope 125.00
Sand toy pictures, pours for action, series of 14, 1967, ea 9.00
Top, golf game, wood stick center, CJ, 1933 ....57.00
Transfer, iron on, sport figure or patriotic, CJ, 1939, ea 18.00
Whistle, Blow for More, CJ box/boy/dog, yel, 1931, ea 55.00
Whistle, Blow for More, CJ/Angelus packages, 1928, '31 or '33, ea ..45.00
Whistle, pressed paper, series of 10, 1948-49, CJ, 1¼x2", ea 34.00
Whistle, Razz Zooka, C Carey Cloud design, CJ, 1949 ....32.00

Plastic Prizes

Animals, standup, letter on bk, series of 26, Nosco, 1953, ea 3.50
Animals, standup on base, assorted, Nosco or CJ, 1947 on, ea 1.50
Baseball players, 3-D, bl or gray team, 1958, 1½", ea 7.00
Disc, emb comic character, series of 12, 1954, 1½" dia 16.00
Disc, emb fish plaque, oval, series of 10, 1956, ea 14.00
Dog, 3-D, hollow base, series of 10, CJCO, 1954, ea 4.50
Figure, circus; stands on base, 1 of 12, Nosco, 1951-54 ....1.75
Figure on rocking base, semi-flat, 1 of 9, Cloud design, '56 ....3.00
Fob, alphabet letter w/loop on top, 1 of 26, 1954, 1½" 2.25
Magnifying glass, many designs/shapes, from 1961, ea 1.00
Palm puzzle, ball(s) roll into holes, plastic dome, from 1966 ....2.50
Palm puzzle, ball(s) roll into holes, rectangle, CJ, 1920s, ea 37.00
Palm puzzle, ball(s) roll into holes, sq, CJ, 1920s, ea 22.00
Pinball game, lever shoots ball/score in holes, 1964 to recent 5.00
Ships in a bottle, 6 different, 1960, ea 5.00
Signs, road; Stop, Caution, etc, yel, series of 10, 1954-60, ea 3.00
Spinner, tops varied colors, 10 designs, from 1948, ea 1.50
Toys, take apart/assemble, variety, from '62, assembled, ea 1.00
Toys, take apart/assemble, variety, from '62, unassembled, ea 3.00
Whistle, tube w/animals on top, CJ, series, 1950-53, 1⅜" 6.50

Tin Prizes

Badge, boy & dog diecut, complete w/bend-over tab, CJ 150.00
Badge, boy & dog diecut, w/o tab at top 85.00
Badge, emb/plated CJ officer, 2⅜" or 1⅝", early, ea 110.00
Badge, litho, red/wht/bl, boy/dog, CJ, 1920s, 1¼" dia 150.00
Bank, 3-D book form, red/gr/or blk, CJ Bank, early, 2" 95.00
Bookmark, dogs, 4 different, 1941, 3", ea 22.00
Brooch or pin, various designs on card, CJ/logo, early, ea 125.00
Cash register, litho, More You Eat, CJ, early, 1⅞" 275.00
Clicker, 'Noisy CJ Snapper,' pear shape, aluminum, 1949 ....32.00
Clicker, CJ Telegraph, Pat 1897, inked, 1¾" dia, ea 145.00
Doll dishes, tin plated, CJ, '31, 1¾", 1⅞", & 2⅛" dia, ea 35.00
Fortune Wheel, 2-pc litho, CJ, 1939-41, 1¾" 55.00
Helicopter, yel propeller, wood stick, unmk, 1937, 2⅝" 24.00
Horse & wagon, litho diecut, CJ & Angelus, 2⅛" 65.00
Horse & wagon, litho diecut, gray/red mks, CJ, 1914-23, 3⅛" ...395.00
Model T Ford, License: NY 1915 #999, blk/wht, CJ, rare, 2" 410.00
Pocket watch, silver gold, CJ as numerals, 1931, 1½" 55.00
Sled, tin plated, CJ, 1931, 2" L 39.00
Small box shape: Elect Alarm Clock, litho, unmk, 1⅛" 85.00
Small box shape: electric stove litho, unmk, 1⅛" 90.00
Small box shape: garage litho, unmk, 1⅛" 85.00
Small box shape: radio litho, bl, unmk, 1⅛" 80.00
Soldier, litho, die-cut standup, officer/private/etc, unmk, ea 17.00
Spinner, wood stick, Always on Top, red/wht/bl, 1½" dia 25.00
Spinner, wood stick, Fortune Teller Game, red/wht/bl, CJ, 1½" ..105.00

Spinner, wood stick, Question Mark Box at center 50.00
Spinner, wood stick, 2 Toppers, red/wht/bl, Angelus/Jack, 1½" ...70.00
Stand up, comic character, 1 of 10, CJ, 1936-46, ea 125.00
Stand up, oval Am flag, series of 4, unmk, 1936-45, ea 35.00
Stand up, rectangle litho, boy & dog, ca 1916, lg or sm, ea 145.00
Tall box shape: Frozen Foods locker freezer, '47, unmk, 1¾" 65.00
Tall box shape: grandfather clock, unmk, 1947, 1¾" 55.00
Tall box shape: radio, Tune in w/CJ, brn/yel, 1939, 1¾" 120.00
Tall box shape: Refrigerator Car, CJ 2006, 1947, 1¾" L 155.00
Train, engine & tender, litho, CJ Line/512 ....125.00
Train, litho coach only, red, unmk, 1941 ....24.00
Train, litho engine only, red, 1941, unmk 20.00
Tray, emb, litho w/early package, smaller version 115.00
Tray, emb, litho w/early package, 2¼x1¾" 95.00
Truck, litho, RWB, CJ/Angelus, 1931, ea 65.00
Wagon shape: Caterpillar tractor, unmk, 1931, 1¾" L 29.00
Wagon shape: CJ Shows, yel circus wagon, series of 5, ea 135.00
Wagon shape: Playtime Trailer (auto trailer), unmk, 1947 ....40.00
Wagon shape: tank, orange/red/gr camouflage, unmk 65.00
Wagon shape: Tank Corps No 57, gr & blk, 1941 ....30.00
Wheelbarrow, tin plated, bk leg in place, CJ, 1931, 2½" L 40.00

Miscellaneous

Ad, comic book, CJ, ea 9.00
Ad, Saturday Evening Post, mc, CJ, 1919, 11x14" 18.00
Hat, ball park vendor cap, CJ, 1930s 30.00
Lunch box, tin, 2 hdls, CJ, 1980s, 4½x5x6" 25.00
Lunch box, tin emb, CJ, 1970s, 4x7x9" 30.00
Medal, CJ salesman award, brass, 1939, scarce 125.00
Sign, bathing beauty, 5-color cb, CJ, early, 17x22" 350.00
Sign, boy or girl w/box of CJ, 5-color cb, early, 17x22", ea 350.00
Sign, Jack & Bingo, die-cut litho, easel standup, CJ, early 310.00
Sign, Jack & Bingo, standing on early CJ pkg, mc cb, rare 385.00
Sign, Santa & prizes, mc cb, Angelus, early, lg 200.00
Sign, Santa & prizes, mc cb, Checkers, early, lg 1,000.00
Sign, Santa & prizes, mc cb, CJ, early, lg 250.00

Cranberry

    Cranberry glass is named for its resemblance to the color of cranberry juice. It was made by many companies both here and abroad, becoming popular in America soon after the Civil War. It was made in free-blown ware as well as mold-blown. Today cranberry glass is being reproduced, and it is sometimes difficult to distinguish the old from the new. Ask a reputable dealer if you are unsure.

    For further information we recommend *American Art Glass* by John A. Shuman III, available from Collector Books or your local bookstore. See also Cruets; Salts; Sugar Shakers; Syrups.

Bottle, gold florals, matching bubble stopper, 6½x2¼" 145.00
Bottle, scent; wht floral on front, ringed neck, 6x3", pr 375.00
Bowl/vase, clear rigaree at rim, 4¾x6" 95.00
Box, HP sheep & foliage w/gold, hinged, 3¼x5¼" dia 295.00
Box, tulips/scrolls, melon ribs, ormolu mts, 4" dia 290.00
Candle holders, Dmn Quilt, 3x4½" dia, pr 150.00
Creamer & sugar bowl, clear hdls, 3¼", 2⅝x3¾" 95.00
Creamer & sugar bowl, clear rim/hdl/ft, 3½", 2½" 175.00
Cruet, HP florals w/gold, clear bubble stopper, 8½x3¾" 195.00
Decanter, flattened bulb w/star-cut base, 10x5" 150.00
Decanter, gold stars, clear bubble stopper, 9¾x4½" 155.00
Decanter, mc flowers/garlands w/gold, appl hdl, 11½" 200.00
Liqueur set, gold trim, 8¾" decanter+6 shots+9" tray 295.00

Pitcher, allover network patterning, clear hdl, 6⅜" 70.00
Pitcher, bulbous w/longer neck, clear hdl, ice bladder, 10" 195.00
Pitcher, Dmn Quilt, clear lasso extends into twist hdl, 9" 225.00
Pitcher, gold florals on frost, gold on hdl, 4x2⅜" 75.00
Pitcher, HP florals, ruffled top, clear hdl, 9" 175.00
Pitcher, Invt T'print, clear hdl, triangular top, 6¼" 110.00
Pitcher, Invt T'print, mc florals, 5¼" dia 325.00
Pitcher, Invt T'print, sq mouth, tapered, reeded hdl, 7½" 140.00
Pitcher, Optic, bulbous, rnd mouth, clear hdl, 7⅜x4¾" 95.00
Pitcher, rippled t'print, bulbous, clear hdl, 6¼x4¼" 95.00
Pitcher, sq bulbous shape w/rnd mouth, clear hdl, 6⅝x3¾" 95.00
Rose bowl, intaglio-cut flowers, crimped top, ball ft, 3x3⅜" 265.00
Stein, pewter mt & thumbpc, clear hdl, ½-liter, 6½" 225.00
Urn, appl clear flowers & leaves, w/lid, 9x7" 450.00

Vase, applied clear 'icicles' and rigaree at neck, Sandwich, 9", $850.00.

Vase, appl florals, tricorner top, wafer ft, 5⅛x3¾" 165.00
Vase, Dmn Quilt, appl crystal ruffle & hdl, 4⅝x3½" 135.00
Vase, Hobnail, ruffled, 3 appl wishbone ft, 7⅝x2¼" 85.00

Creamware

Creamware was a type of earthenware developed by Wedgwood in the 1760s and produced by many other Staffordshire potteries, including Leeds. Since it could be potted cheaply and was light in weight, it became popular abroad as well as in England, due to the lower freight charges involved in its export. It was revived at Leeds in the late 19th century, and the type most often reproduced was heavily reticulated or molded in high relief. These later wares are easily distinguished from the originals since they are thicker and tend to craze heavily. See also Leeds; Wedgwood.

Plate, Christ's Baptism by John in flesh and black, orange border with multicolor flowers, EX, 10", $200.00.

Coffeepot, bl sprigs/striping, dome lid, ftd, 11", EX 250.00
Coffeepot, iron red floral, late 1700s, mini, 3½", EX 500.00
Fruit basket, rtcl shaped oblong form, rstr, 10", +tray 495.00
Mold, lion form, early 1800s, chip/stain, 8", pr 400.00
Mug, Industry transfer, England, 1800s, rpr, 3½" 200.00
Mug, verse & floral border, early 1800s, chips, 3⅛" 275.00
Plate, blk botanical transfer w/mc, emb rim, 5½", NM 60.00
Plate, Jesus & woman at well, mc enamel, orange/bl rim, 9¾", EX ..200.00
Plate, rtcl basketweave border, 8½" 100.00
Soup plate, ship w/British flag, florals on rim, 10", VG 335.00

Crown Milano

Crown Milano was introduced in 1894 by the Mt. Washington Glass Company of New Bedford, Massachusetts. Along with Burmese, it was their bestselling line. The glass is very pale, almost ivory. It was blown, free-form or in molds, highly decorated with flowers and colored enamels, and fired. Made to compete with the English Porcelain Companies, Crown Milano required only about half as many steps to produce as the porcelain (for which it is often mistaken, especially when viewed from a distance). This enabled Mt. Washington to make very attractive pieces at competitive prices. Some of the very early pieces are referred to as 'Albertine'; these had a glossy finish. Satin pieces were marked 'CM,' and some were shipped with paper labels. One of the most outstanding Crown Milano decorators was Frank Guba, who preferred subjects such as flying ducks or other birds. Pieces decorated by him command very high prices.

Our advisors for this category are Henry and Geneva Tyler; they are listed in the Directory under Florida. In the descriptions that follow, the glassware is assumed to be satin unless noted glossy.

Biscuit jar, bamboo, amber/gr/gold on opal, SP floral lid 575.00
Biscuit jar, violets/gold scrolls, emb lid w/appl butterfly 900.00
Bowl, apple blossoms, gold on yel/peach, sgn SP fr, 11" H 675.00
Bride's bowl, floral/gold scrolls on pnt Burmese, 2¾x10" 875.00
Cracker bbl, bamboo, gold/brn on pnt Burmese, SP mts, 6" 895.00
Cracker bbl, floral branches on wht w/ivory swirl, 4x6" 850.00
Cracker bbl, lotus, gr/gold, melon ribs, gilt lid, 6x7" 700.00
Cracker bbl, mums/shadow mums on smooth wht, SP lid, 4x7½" ...1,400.00
Cracker bbl, raspberries/shadow leaves, melon ribs, crab on lid ...1,400.00
Creamer, leaves on ivory, melon ribs, emb silver rim & hdl 650.00
Creamer & sugar bowl, mc florals/gold ribbons 1,250.00
Cup & saucer, handleless; wild rose/gold on pk to wht, 2½" 950.00
Ewer, floral/gold netting/scrolls, bulbous/squat, 5½x7" 1,600.00
Lamp, florals/appl gold ribbons on wht, ball shade, 37" 12,650.00
Pansy dish, mc lg florals, triangular, 2 rolled-in edges 475.00
Pitcher, blown-out panels w/gold & silver floral, 8x7" 1,800.00
Pitcher, brn snipes at water's edge, gold scrolls at rim, 9½" 8,250.00
Pitcher, gold lilies, silver/gr trim, snake hdl, #d, 8" 2,450.00
Rose jar, florals w/in scrollwork, steeple stopper, 12x7" 3,250.00
Sweetmeat, floral, mc/gold on shaded yel, melon ribs, 2¾" 900.00
Tumbler, gold flower garlands & bows, glossy, 3¾x2¾" 575.00
Vase, apple blossoms, gold/silver/beading on yel mottle, 8x8" 800.00
Vase, beaded wild roses on pk/tan shadow leaves, hdls, 5x5" 575.00
Vase, cactus flowers, squat w/stick neck, label, 9" 950.00
Vase, floral branches on yel w/beige shadows, 6x7" 520.00
Vase, floral on wht w/pk, rose/gold shoulder band, 9x6" 1,800.00
Vase, floral/gold scrolls, gold hdls, 4 sides w/dents, 8x8" 1,250.00
Vase, gold florals on beige, spiral stick on pillow base, 7¾" 895.00
Vase, gold leaves over gold/pk scrolls & dbl eagle, 6x8" 800.00
Vase, ivy, red/brn/gr/gold on creamy ground w/scrolls, 8x7" 750.00
Vase, lily; baby roses/gold on ribbed wht gloss, 15", pr 2,750.00

Vase, oak leaves/acorns w/shadows, sqd/bulbous, hdls, 8" 920.00
Vase, pansies/gilt, 3-sided, stick neck w/open petals, 8" 1,100.00
Vase, roses on ribbing, shouldered w/bulbous top, 8½" 1,200.00
Vase, wild roses, shadows/gold beads, hdls, turret lid, 15" 3,700.00

Cruets

    Cruets, containers made to hold oil or vinegar, are usually bulbous with tall, narrow throats and a stopper. During the 19th century and for several years after, they were produced in abundance in virtually every type of glassware available. Those listed below are assumed to be with stopper and mint unless noted otherwise. Our advisor for this category is Elaine Ezell; she is listed in the Directory under Maryland.

Arched Ovals, gr 130.00
Argonaut Shell, wht opal 395.00
Beaded Swirl & Lens, ruby stained 195.00
Berkshire, cut, faceted stopper, 8-oz 90.00
Broken Column, ruby stained 260.00
Burmese, ribbed, squat/bulbous, ribbed stopper, Mt WA, 6" ...1,050.00
Button Arches, ruby stained 195.00
Cactus, chocolate, orig chocolate stopper, Fenton, 7" 175.00
Cathedral, amber 110.00
Champion, amber stained 165.00
Coin, amber, Fostoria 75.00
Cone, bl satin, opaque faceted stopper, 6" 300.00
Cornucopia, pk stain, orig stopper 80.00
Cranberry, threaded, clear reed hdl/bubble stopper, 7x3½" 195.00
Cranberry Invt Swirl, bulbous, clear hdl/stopper, 5½" 75.00
Cranberry w/floral & gold, clear hdl/bubble stopper, 9x3½" 195.00
Cut Log, lg 65.00
Daisy & Button w/Crossbar, bl 150.00
Daisy & Fern, Apple Blossom mold, bl opal 225.00
Delaware Rose, EX gold, rare 565.00
Dmn Quilt, wht to peach opal, ca 1885 ....195.00
Dmn Quilt MOP, shaded bl, frosted hdl/stopper, Mt WA, 5¾" .400.00
Empress, gr w/gold 315.00
Esther, emerald gr, matching stopper, lg 350.00
Everglades, vaseline opal 495.00
Flora, gr w/gold 200.00
Florette, pk satin, frosted hdl & stopper 235.00
Galloway, Maiden Blush 295.00

Gemel type, threaded glass, hallmarked silver stoppers, Stevens and Williams, $125.00.

Georgia Gem, custard 245.00
Guttate, cranberry 495.00
Herringbone, wht opal 200.00

Hobnail, amber w/med bl reeded hdl, amber stopper, 7" 90.00
Hobnail, rubena verde, Hobbs & Brockunier 595.00
Hobnail, vaseline 450.00
Idyll, clear w/gold 70.00
Illinois 75.00
Invt T'print, amberina, faceted amber stopper, NE Glass, 6" 395.00
Invt T'print, amberina, HP decor 450.00
Invt T'print, cranberry 265.00
Iowa 90.00
Ivy Scroll, gr 125.00
Jackson, vaseline opal 250.00
Kalana Poppy, faceted stopper, Dorflinger, 8-oz 175.00
Lime gr w/floral, gr hdl/bubble stopper, 8x3½" 100.00
Majestic, ruby stained, pressed faceted stopper 175.00
Manhattan 55.00
Millefiori, ftd, camphor hdl, millefiori ball stopper, 7½" 350.00
Missouri, emerald gr 265.00
New Hampshire, rose stained 290.00
Paneled Thistle 80.00
Peachblow, amber reeded hdl/faceted stopper, bulbous, Wheeling ..1,200.00
Radiant Daisy, frosted w/amber stain 100.00
Ribbed Drape, custard w/decor 695.00
Ribbed Opal Lattice, clear opal, cut stopper 165.00
Riverside's Ranson, vaseline 240.00
Royal Crystal, ruby stain, sm 495.00
Satina Swirl, swan's bill, amber 895.00
Seaweed, Northwood's cranberry opal 850.00
Swirl, amberina, bulbous w/stick neck, 6" 400.00
Thousand Eye, amber, 3-knob 175.00
Tiny Optic, amethyst w/HP decor 95.00
Truncated Cube, ruby flashed & clear, pressed cube stopper 235.00
Verre de soie, Hawkes eng, fancy hollow stopper, Steuben, 7" ...600.00
Windows, cranberry opal, oval, scarce, 6½" 600.00
Winged Scroll, emerald gr w/gold, cut faceted stopper, Heisey ...335.00

Cup Plates, Glass

    Before the middle 1850s, it was socially acceptable to pour hot tea into a deep saucer to cool. The tea was sipped from the saucer rather than the cup, which frequently was handleless and too hot to hold. The cup plate served as a coaster for the cup. It is generally agreed that the first examples of pressed glass cup plates were made about 1826 at the Boston and Sandwich Glass Co. in Sandwich, Cape Cod, Massachusetts. Other glassworks in three major areas (New England, Philadelphia, and the Midwest, especially Pittsburgh) quickly followed suit.

    Antique glass cup plates range in size from 2⅝" up to 4¼" in diameter. The earliest plates had simple designs inspired by cut glass patterns, but by 1829 they had become more complex. The span from then until about 1845 is known as the 'Lacy Period,' when cup plate designs and pressing techniques were at their peak. To cover pressing imperfections, the backgrounds of the plates were often covered with fine stippling which endowed them with a glittering brilliance called 'laciness.' They were made in a multitude of designs — some purely decorative, others commemorative. Subjects include the American eagle, hearts, sunbursts, log cabins, ships, George Washington, the political candidates Clay and Harrison, plows, beehives, etc. Of all the patterns, the round George Washington plate is the rarest and most valuable — only four are known to exist today.

    Authenticity is most important. Collectors must be aware that contemporary plates which have no antique counterparts and fakes modeled after antique patterns have had wide distribution. Condition is also important, though it is the exceptional plate that does not have some rim roughness. More important considerations are scarcity of design and color.

Our advisor for this category is John Bilane; he is listed in the Directory under New Jersey. The book *American Glass* by George and Helen McKearin has a section on glass cup plates. The definitive book is *American Glass Cup Plates* by Ruth Webb Lee and James H. Rose. Numbers in the listings that follow (computer sorted) refer to the latter. When no condition is indicated, the examples listed below are assumed to have only minor rim roughness as is normal. See also Staffordshire; Pairpoint.

R-100-A, scarce, G 41.00
R-102, G- 25.00
R-136-A, rare, VG- 70.00
R-145-C, G+ 28.00
R-149, VG 33.00
R-150, G- 28.00
R-150-X-1, VG- 33.00
R-151, VG+ 35.00
R-154-B, VG 33.00
R-159-B, VG 34.00
R-160-B, G+ 30.00
R-162-A, VG 34.00
R-162-B, VG+ 35.00
R-165, VG 35.00
R-172-A, EX 40.00
R-172-B, VG+ 35.00
R-176-B, VG- 32.00
R-208, VG- 48.00
R-216-A, VG+ 67.00
R-217-A, VG 64.00
R-22, EX 32.00
R-230-B, VG 50.00
R-232, rare, G- 47.00
R-233-A, VG- 32.00
R-235, G 26.00
R-242-A, VG 34.00
R-243, VG+ 37.00
R-256-A, rare, VG- 80.00
R-257-A, VG 34.00
R-262, VG+ 28.00
R-27, VG 30.00
R-271, G 24.00
R-272, VG+ 31.00
R-275, VG+ 35.00
R-277, VG 48.00
R-28, VG 30.00
R-280, VG 35.00
R-29-X-1, VG 30.00
R-324, G+ 17.00
R-324, honey amber, G 65.00
R-328, G- 12.00
R-330, G 17.00
R-332, G 18.00
R-332-A, G+ 18.00
R-333, VG 19.00
R-341, VG+ 21.00
R-364, EX- 18.00
R-365, VG 16.00
R-37, VG 41.00
R-370, G+ 13.00
R-371, VG- 14.00
R-377-A, EX- 14.00
R-389, VG 17.00
R-39, VG+ 33.00
R-391, VG 13.00
R-392, VG- 13.00

R-403, VG 12.00
R-416, G- 8.00
R-417, VG- 12.00
R-439-C, G- 22.00
R-440-B, VG- 32.00
R-441, VG 43.00
R-441-A, VG- 32.00
R-444, EX- 36.00
R-45, VG 64.00
R-455-B, G+ 26.00
R-458-A, VG- 28.00
R-459-Q, G- 14.00
R-465-A-V-1, G 18.00
R-465-F, bl opal, scarce, VG 60.00
R-465-J, VG 19.00
R-467, VG 19.00
R-467-B, G 13.00
R-477, G 16.00
R-479, VG 20.00
R-48, G- 23.00
R-49, VG 30.00
R-500, very rare, G 46.00
R-522, G 10.00
R-523, G 11.00
R-531, G 18.00
R-531, VG 20.00
R-537, G 12.00
R-54, G+ 45.00
R-55, VG- 80.00
R-56, VG+ 52.00
R-562-A, very rare, VG 300.00
R-564, G+ 26.00
R-569, G+ 38.00
R-595, VG- 45.00
R-596, VG 45.00
R-612-A, rare, G 185.00
R-640, VG+ 21.00
R-641, G+ 11.00
R-641-A, G- 9.00
R-643, VG 25.00
R-643-A, VG+ 25.00
R-645-A, G+ 18.00
R-65, VG- 49.00
R-666-A, VG+ 50.00
R-670-A, VG 41.00
R-680, VG- 32.00
R-691, VG 85.00
R-95, VG 36.00

Currier & Ives by Royal

During the 1950s dinnerware decorated with transfer-printed scenes taken from prints by Currier and Ives was manufactured by Royal China and given as premiums through A&P stores. Though it was also made in pink and green, the blue is by far the most popular. Pie plates in black and brown can be found, but no china sets in these colors have been reported. Today it is readily available at reasonable prices, and it has become a very popular collectible at malls and flea markets around the country. Included this year in our listings are pieces from Hostess sets, which should be of great interest to collectors. New pieces which have been added to the price list include tall cup (9"), snack plate, spoon rest, second-type gravy and underplate, and sugar bowl with no handles. Our advisors for this category are Treva and Jack Hamlin; they are listed in the Directory under Ohio.

Ashtray, 5½"	13.00
Bowl, cereal; tab hdl, 6¼"	30.00
Bowl, cereal; 6¼"	10.00
Bowl, cereal; 6⅝"	10.00
Bowl, dessert; 5½"	3.50
Bowl, soup; 8"	10.00
Bowl, vegetable; deep, 10"	25.00
Bowl, vegetable; 9"	20.00
Butter dish, Fashionable	35.00
Butter dish, Road Winter	30.00
Casserole, angle hdls	85.00
Casserole, tab hdls	150.00

Creamer and sugar bowl, with lid, $20.00.

Creamer, angle hdl	6.00
Cup, angle hdl	3.50
Cup, rnd hdl, tall, 9"	6.00
Gravy boat, pour spout	15.00
Gravy boat, tab hdl	20.00
Ladle, gravy	30.00
Lamp, candle; w/globe	75.00
Mug, coffee	25.00
Pie baker, 7 decals, 10"	25.00
Plate, bread; 6½"	3.50
Plate, calendar; 10"	15.00
Plate, chop; 11½"	25.00
Plate, chop; 12¼"	25.00
Plate, dinner; 10"	6.00
Plate, luncheon; 9"	13.00
Plate, salad; 7¼"	10.00
Plate, snack; w/cup & well, 9"	25.00
Platter, oval, 13"	30.00
Platter, tab hdls, 10½"	25.00
Platter, 13" dia	40.00
Saucer, 6⅛"	1.50
Shakers, pr	30.00
Spoon rest, wall hanging	30.00
Sugar bowl, hdld, w/lid	15.00
Sugar bowl, no hdls, w/lid	25.00
Teapot	125.00
Tidbit tray, 3-tier	65.00
Tray, gravy boat; 7¼"	15.00
Tray, gravy; like 7" plate	30.00
Tumbler, iced tea; 5½"	15.00
Tumbler, juice; 3½"	15.00
Tumbler, old-fashioned; 3¼"	15.00
Tumbler, water; 4¾"	15.00

Hostess Set Pieces

Cake plate, flat, 10"	25.00
Cake plate, ftd, 10"	50.00

Candy bowl, 7¾"	25.00
Dip bowl, 4⅜"	15.00
Pie baker, 11"	30.00
Plate, serving; 7"	10.00
Tray, deviled egg	50.00

Custard Glass

As early as the 1880s, custard glass was produced in England. Migrating glassmakers brought the formula for the creamy ivory ware to America. One of them was Harry Northwood, who in 1898 founded his company in Indiana, Pennsylvania, and introduced the glassware to the American market. Soon other companies were producing custard, among them Heisey, Tarentum, Fenton, and McKee. Not only dinnerware patterns but souvenir items were made. Today custard is the most expensive of the colored pressed glassware patterns. The formula for producing the luminous glass contains uranium salts which imparts the cream color to the batch and causes it to glow when it is examined under a black light.

Argonaut Shell, bowl, master berry; gold & decor, 10½" L	265.00
Argonaut Shell, butter dish, gold & decor	350.00
Argonaut Shell, butter dish, no gold	275.00
Argonaut Shell, compote, jelly; gold & decor, scarce	145.00
Argonaut Shell, creamer, gold & decor	135.00
Argonaut Shell, cruet, gold & decor	700.00
Argonaut Shell, pitcher, water; gold & decor	435.00
Argonaut Shell, shakers, gold & decor, pr	345.00
Argonaut Shell, spooner, gold & decor	135.00
Argonaut Shell, sugar bowl, w/lid, gold & decor	200.00

Argonaut Shell, tumbler, gold and decoration, 3¾", $110.00.

Bead Swag, goblet, floral & gold	65.00
Bead Swag, tray, pickle; floral & gold, rare	260.00
Bead Swag, wine, floral & gold	60.00
Beaded Circle, bowl, master berry; floral & gold	245.00
Beaded Circle, butter dish, floral & gold	450.00
Beaded Circle, cruet, floral & gold, rare	1,175.00
Beaded Circle, pitcher, water; floral & gold	675.00
Beaded Circle, shakers, floral & gold, pr	800.00
Beaded Circle, spooner, floral & gold	175.00
Beaded Circle, sugar bowl, w/lid, floral & gold	275.00
Beaded Circle, tumbler, floral & gold, very rare	100.00
Cane Insert, berry set, 7-pc	450.00
Cane Insert, table set, 4-pc	450.00
Cherry & Scales, bowl, master berry; nutmeg stain	130.00
Cherry & Scales, butter dish, nutmeg stain	225.00

Cherry & Scales, creamer, nutmeg stain 115.00
Cherry & Scales, pitcher, water; nutmeg stain, scarce 325.00
Cherry & Scales, sugar bowl, w/lid, nutmeg stain, scarce 125.00
Cherry & Scales, tumbler, nutmeg stain, scarce 50.00
Chrysanthemum Sprig, bowl, master berry; gold & decor 275.00
Chrysanthemum Sprig, bowl, master berry; no gold 175.00
Chrysanthemum Sprig, butter dish, gold & decor 300.00
Chrysanthemum Sprig, celery vase, gold & decor, rare 600.00
Chrysanthemum Sprig, compote, jelly; gold & decor 135.00
Chrysanthemum Sprig, compote, jelly; no decor 95.00
Chrysanthemum Sprig, creamer, gold & decor 125.00
Chrysanthemum Sprig, cruet, gold & decor, 6¾" 365.00
Chrysanthemum Sprig, pitcher, water; gold & decor 470.00
Chrysanthemum Sprig, shakers, gold & decor, pr 300.00
Chrysanthemum Sprig, spooner, gold & decor 130.00
Chrysanthemum Sprig, toothpick holder, gold & decor 300.00
Chrysanthemum Sprig, toothpick holder, no decor 165.00
Chrysanthemum Sprig, tray, condiment; gold & decor, rare 595.00
Chrysanthemum Sprig, tumbler, gold & decor 65.00
Dandelion, mug, nutmeg stain 165.00
Delaware, bowl, sauce; pk stain 65.00
Delaware, creamer, breakfast; pk stain 70.00
Delaware, tray, pin; gr stain 75.00
Diamond w/Peg, bowl, master berry; roses & gold 215.00
Diamond w/Peg, bowl, sauce; roses & gold 40.00
Diamond w/Peg, butter dish, roses & gold 235.00
Diamond w/Peg, creamer, ind; souvenir 45.00
Diamond w/Peg, creamer, roses & gold 75.00
Diamond w/Peg, napkin ring, roses & gold, rare 150.00
Diamond w/Peg, pitcher, roses & gold, 5½" 260.00
Diamond w/Peg, shakers, souvenir, pr 175.00
Diamond w/Peg, sugar bowl, w/lid, roses & gold 160.00
Diamond w/Peg, toothpick holder, roses & gold 150.00
Diamond w/Peg, tumbler, roses & gold 60.00
Diamond w/Peg, water set, souvenir, 7-pc 650.00
Diamond w/Peg, wine, roses & gold 55.00
Everglades, bowl, master berry; gold & decor 215.00
Everglades, bowl, sauce; gold & decor 60.00
Everglades, butter dish, gold & decor 395.00
Everglades, creamer, gold & decor 155.00
Everglades, shakers, gold & decor, pr 375.00
Everglades, spooner, gold & decor 160.00
Everglades, sugar bowl, w/lid, gold & decor 235.00
Everglades, tumbler, gold & decor 100.00
Fan, bowl, sauce; good gold 55.00
Fan, butter dish, good gold 225.00
Fan, ice cream set, good gold, 7-pc 500.00
Fan, pitcher, water; good gold 275.00
Fan, spooner, good gold 100.00
Fan, sugar bowl, w/lid, good gold 150.00
Fan, tumbler, good gold 75.00
Fan, water set, good gold, 7-pc 700.00
Fine Cut & Roses, rose bowl, fancy int, nutmeg stain 100.00
Fine Cut & Roses, rose bowl, plain int 85.00
Geneva, bowl, master berry; floral decor, ftd, oval, 9" L 90.00
Geneva, bowl, master berry; floral decor, rnd, 9" 130.00
Geneva, bowl, sauce; floral decor, oval 45.00
Geneva, bowl, sauce; floral decor, rnd 45.00
Geneva, butter dish, floral decor 225.00
Geneva, butter dish, no decor 135.00
Geneva, compote, jelly; floral decor 95.00
Geneva, cruet, floral decor 465.00
Geneva, pitcher, water; floral decor 250.00
Geneva, shakers, floral decor, pr 280.00

Geneva, spooner, floral decor 100.00
Geneva, sugar bowl, open, floral decor 85.00
Geneva, sugar bowl, w/lid, floral decor 150.00
Geneva, syrup, floral decor 475.00
Geneva, toothpick holder, floral w/M gold 375.00
Georgia Gem, bowl, master berry; good gold 135.00
Georgia Gem, bowl, master berry; gr opaque 115.00
Georgia Gem, butter dish, good gold 190.00
Georgia Gem, celery vase, good gold 145.00
Georgia Gem, creamer, good gold 100.00
Georgia Gem, mug, good gold 45.00
Georgia Gem, powder jar, w/lid, good gold 80.00
Georgia Gem, shakers, good gold, pr 160.00
Georgia Gem, sugar bowl, w/lid, no gold 95.00
Grape (& Cable), bottle, scent; orig stopper, nutmeg stain 600.00
Grape (& Cable), bowl, master berry; nutmeg stain, ftd, 11" 375.00
Grape (& Cable), bowl, nutmeg stain, 7½" 60.00
Grape (& Cable), bowl, sauce; nutmeg stain, ftd 50.00
Grape (& Cable), butter dish, nutmeg stain 275.00
Grape (& Cable), compote, jelly; open, nutmeg stain 145.00
Grape (& Cable), compote, nutmeg stain, 4½x8" 300.00
Grape (& Cable), cracker jar, nutmeg stain 800.00
Grape (& Cable), creamer, breakfast; nutmeg stain 80.00
Grape (& Cable), humidor, nutmeg stain, rare 900.00
Grape (& Cable), nappy, nutmeg stain, rare 60.00
Grape (& Cable), pitcher, water; nutmeg stain 400.00
Grape (& Cable), plate, nutmeg stain, 7" 50.00
Grape (& Cable), plate, nutmeg stain, 8" 65.00
Grape (& Cable), powder jar, nutmeg stain 350.00
Grape (& Cable), punch bowl, w/base, nutmeg stain 1,750.00
Grape (& Cable), spooner, nutmeg stain 145.00
Grape (& Cable), sugar bowl, breakfast; open, nutmeg stain 75.00
Grape (& Cable), sugar bowl, w/lid, nutmeg stain 195.00
Grape (& Cable), tray, dresser; nutmeg stain, scarce, lg 350.00
Grape (& Cable), tray, pin; nutmeg stain 135.00
Grape & Gothic Arches, bowl, master berry; pearl w/gold 200.00
Grape & Gothic Arches, bowl, sauce; pearl w/gold, rare 80.00
Grape & Gothic Arches, butter dish, pearl w/gold 235.00
Grape & Gothic Arches, creamer, pearl w/gold, rare 100.00
Grape & Gothic Arches, favor vase, nutmeg stain 80.00
Grape & Gothic Arches, pitcher, water; pearl w/gold 300.00
Grape & Gothic Arches, spooner, pearl w/gold 85.00
Grape & Gothic Arches, sugar bowl, w/lid, pearl w/gold 135.00
Grape & Gothic Arches, tumbler, pearl w/gold 65.00
Grape Arbor, vase, hat form 90.00
Heart w/T'print, creamer 85.00
Heart w/T'print, lamp, good pnt, scarce, 8" 435.00
Heart w/T'print, sugar bowl, ind 80.00
Honeycomb, wine 65.00
Horse Medallion, bowl, gr stain, 7" 80.00
Intaglio, bowl, master berry; gold & decor, ftd, 9" 250.00
Intaglio, butter dish, gold & decor, scarce 300.00
Intaglio, compote, jelly; gold & decor 125.00
Intaglio, creamer, gold & decor 125.00
Intaglio, cruet, gold & decor 475.00
Intaglio, pitcher, water; gold & decor 395.00
Intaglio, shakers, gold & decor, pr 235.00
Intaglio, spooner, gold & decor 125.00
Intaglio, sugar bowl, w/lid, gold & decor 165.00
Inverted Fan & Feather, bowl, master berry; gold & decor 250.00
Inverted Fan & Feather, bowl, sauce; gold & decor 65.00
Inverted Fan & Feather, butter dish, gold & decor 350.00
Inverted Fan & Feather, compote, jelly; gold & decor, rare 500.00
Inverted Fan & Feather, cruet, gold & decor, scarce, 6½" 1,100.00

Inverted Fan & Feather, pitcher, water; gold & decor 600.00
Inverted Fan & Feather, punch cup, gold & decor 250.00
Inverted Fan & Feather, shakers, gold & decor, pr 600.00
Inverted Fan & Feather, spooner, gold & decor 145.00
Inverted Fan & Feather, sugar bowl, w/lid, gold & decor 225.00
Inverted Fan & Feather, tumbler, gold & decor 95.00
Jackson, bowl, master berry; good gold, ftd 135.00
Jackson, creamer, good gold 85.00
Jackson, pitcher, water; good gold 250.00
Jackson, pitcher, water; no decor 175.00
Jackson, shakers, good gold, pr 195.00
Jackson, tumbler, good gold 50.00

Jefferson Optic, master berry bowl, $95.00; Individual berry bowl, $30.00.

Louis XV, berry set, w/nutmeg, 7-pc 375.00
Louis XV, bowl, master berry; good gold 165.00
Louis XV, bowl, sauce; good gold, ftd 47.00
Louis XV, butter dish, good gold 200.00
Louis XV, cruet, good gold 365.00
Louis XV, pitcher, water; good gold 225.00
Louis XV, spooner, good gold 80.00
Louis XV, sugar bowl, w/lid, good gold 150.00
Louis XV, tumbler, good gold 65.00
Maple Leaf, bowl, master berry; gold & decor, scarce 335.00
Maple Leaf, bowl, sauce; gold & decor, scarce 95.00
Maple Leaf, butter dish, gold & decor 350.00
Maple Leaf, compote, jelly; gold & decor, rare 455.00
Maple Leaf, cruet, gold & decor, rare 3,000.00
Maple Leaf, pitcher, water; gold & decor 400.00
Maple Leaf, shakers, gold & decor, very rare, pr 800.00
Maple Leaf, spooner, gold & decor 155.00
Maple Leaf, sugar bowl, w/lid, gold & decor 230.00
Panelled Poppy, lamp shade, nutmeg stain, scarce 800.00
Peacock & Urn, bowl, ice cream; nutmeg stain, sm 80.00
Peacock & Urn, bowl, ice cream; nutmeg stain, 10" 350.00
Punty Band, shakers, pr 175.00
Punty Band, spooner, floral decor 100.00
Punty Band, tumbler, floral decor, souvenir 65.00
Ribbed Drape, butter dish, scalloped, roses & gold 375.00
Ribbed Drape, compote, jelly; roses & gold, rare 200.00
Ribbed Drape, creamer, roses & gold, scarce 180.00
Ribbed Drape, cruet, roses & gold, rare 650.00
Ribbed Drape, pitcher, water; roses & gold, rare 365.00
Ribbed Drape, shakers, roses & gold, rare, pr 360.00
Ribbed Drape, spooner, roses & gold 180.00
Ribbed Drape, toothpick holder, roses & gold 475.00
Ribbed Thumbprint, wine, floral decor 80.00
Ring Band, bowl, master berry; roses & gold 150.00
Ring Band, butter dish, roses & gold 250.00

Ring Band, compote, jelly; roses & gold, scarce 195.00
Ring Band, creamer, roses & gold 115.00
Ring Band, cruet, roses & gold 450.00
Ring Band, pitcher, roses & gold, 7½" 335.00
Ring Band, shakers, roses & gold, pr 155.00
Ring Band, syrup, roses & gold 465.00
Ring Band, toothpick holder, roses & gold 135.00
Ring Band, tray, condiment; roses & gold 200.00
Singing Birds, mug, nutmeg stain 75.00
Tarentum's Victoria, bowl, master berry; gold & decor 200.00
Tarentum's Victoria, butter dish, gold & decor, rare 300.00
Tarentum's Victoria, celery vase, gold & decor, rare 275.00
Tarentum's Victoria, pitcher, water; gold & decor, rare 375.00
Tarentum's Victoria, spooner, gold & decor 135.00
Tarentum's Victoria, sugar bowl, w/lid, gold & decor 160.00
Tarentum's Victoria, tumbler, gold & decor 70.00

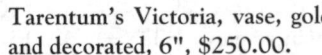

Tarentum's Victoria, vase, gold and decorated, 6", $250.00.

Vermont, butter dish, bl decor 195.00
Vermont, toothpick holder, bl decor 155.00
Vermont, vase, floral decor, jeweled 95.00
Wide Band, bell, roses 195.00
Wild Bouquet, butter dish, gold & decor, rare 700.00
Wild Bouquet, creamer, no gold 145.00
Wild Bouquet, cruet, no decor, w/clear stopper 995.00
Wild Bouquet, spooner, gold & decor 160.00
Wild Bouquet, tumbler, no decor 95.00
Winged Scroll, bowl, master berry; gold & decor, 11" L 175.00
Winged Scroll, bowl, sauce; good gold 45.00
Winged Scroll, butter dish, good gold 200.00
Winged Scroll, butter dish, no decor 150.00
Winged Scroll, celery vase, good gold, rare 400.00
Winged Scroll, cigarette jar, scarce 195.00
Winged Scroll, compote, ruffled, rare, 6¾x10¾" 495.00
Winged Scroll, cruet, good gold, clear stopper 375.00
Winged Scroll, pitcher, water; bulbous, good gold 350.00
Winged Scroll, shakers, bulbous, good gold, rare, pr 400.00
Winged Scroll, shakers, str sides, good gold, pr 195.00
Winged Scroll, sugar bowl, w/lid, good gold 150.00
Winged Scroll, syrup, good gold 395.00

Cut Glass

The earliest documented evidence of commercial glass cutting in the United States was in 1810; the producers were Bakewell and Page of Pittsburgh. These first efforts resulted in simple patterns with only a moderate amount of cutting. By the middle of the century, glass cutters began experimenting with a thicker glass which enabled them to use deeper cuttings, though patterns remained much the same. This period is usually referred to as Rich Cut. Using three types of wheels — a flat edge, a mitered edge, and a convex edge — facets, miters, and depressions were combined to produce various designs. In the late 1870s, a curved miter was developed which greatly expanded design potential. Patterns became more elaborate, often covering the entire surface. The Brilliant Period of cut glass covered a span from about 1880 until 1915. Because of the pressure necessary to achieve the deeply cut patterns, only glass containing a high grade of metal could withstand the process. For this reason and the amount of handwork involved, cut glass has always been expensive. Bowls cut with pinwheels may be either foreign or of a newer vintage, beware! Identifiable patterns and signed pieces that are well cut and in excellent condition bring the higher prices on today's market. See also Dorflinger; Hawkes; Libbey; Tuthill; Val St. Lambert; other specific manufacturers.

Key:
dmn — diamonds   X-cut — crosscut
strw — strawberry   X-hatch — crosshatch

Basket, brilliant allover florals, 17" 575.00
Basket, brilliant cut, eng floral/bird, thick ft, 12x8" 220.00
Basket, cut floral, cut/eng hdl, ped base, 10x7" 350.00
Basket, floral & wheat cuttings, 10x10x8" 250.00
Boat, elaborate geometrics, str bk/pointed prow, 3x13" 150.00
Bowl, allover lace-like pattern, sq, 2¼x7" 140.00
Bowl, allover pinwheels, sterling rim, 4½x9" 100.00
Bowl, allover stars w/lace-like qualities, well cut, 4x8" 200.00
Bowl, eggnog; hobstars/pinwheels/snowflakes, Clarke, 2-pc, 9" ..450.00
Bowl, fruit; hobstars/notches, lg hobstar base, 5x9" 275.00
Bowl, geometrics, ¾" thick, 5x11" 350.00
Bowl, Harvard, hobstar & ovals, feather base border, 5x9" 225.00
Bowl, Harvard-like variant, scalloped top, 2x9" 275.00
Bowl, Jubilee, 9" dia 225.00
Bowl, orange; Harvard variant, oval, 5x7" 135.00
Bowl, Propeller, blown blank, hdls, 12" 225.00
Bowl, salad; Russian, EX/sharp cuttings, 2¾x13½" 1,100.00
Bowl, starflowers & strw bars, scalloped rim, 4x9¼" 100.00
Bowl, vintage & geometric cuttings, 1¼x11¼" 145.00
Bowl, 12 points at rim, ea w/lg hobstar, star bottom, 4x9" 250.00
Bowl, 5-point flower center, 3x12" 300.00
Box, glove; butterfly in lid, chamfered corners, SP mts, 11" 475.00
Butter tub, Pluto, hdls, J Hoare & Co, 5¾x5½" 300.00
Cake stand, Russian, allover Pat-cut base, 3x9" 450.00
Cake stand, strw dmn/fan, strw-cut rnd base, 10x10" 300.00
Candelabrum, 4-arm, pinwheels/tulip-cut stem, SP top, 20" 400.00
Candlesticks, Viscaria, teardrop stems, Pairpoint, 9" pr 225.00
Candy jar, crossed ovals & hobstars, w/lid, 5x5" 235.00
Canoe, allover hobstars, 3¼x11x4½" 200.00
Champagne, hobstars/fan & cane, rayed base, 3½x3¾" 20.00
Cheese & cracker, band of stars/fans, 3x9" dia 150.00
Cheese dish, Monarch, J Hoare & Co, w/Gorham plate & finial ..350.00
Compote, Harvard, notched stem, Bergen, 8x9" 220.00
Compote, hobstars & fine checkering, teardrop stem, 8" 175.00
Compote, 4 hobstars+4 more w/canes, teardrop stem, 9x6" 350.00
Creamer & sugar bowl, hobstars & fans, Clarke, sm 350.00
Creamer & sugar bowl, lg star, hobstar base, ped ft, 3½" 400.00
Creamer & sugar bowl, starflowers, 3" 75.00
Creamer & sugar bowl, strw dmns & fans, sm 225.00
Decanter, fans, mitre cuts, etc, faceted stopper, 11" 140.00
Decanter, hobstars/strw dmns/honeycomb, cut stopper, Hoare, 17" ...450.00
Decanter, starflowers, panels in neck, 7"+stopper, pr 135.00
Doughnut stand, strw dmn & fan variant, 3x7¾" 100.00
Flower center, hobstars, cut neck, 9" 350.00

Horseradish jar, hobstars & fans, 5½" 160.00
Humidor, hobstar/ovals, mk silver neck band, 9½", NM 690.00

Jar, Hobstar and Oval, rose-decorated silver-plated rim, 9x7", $750.00.

Knife rest, hobnail ends, 5½" L 165.00
Mustard jar, prisms & fans 85.00
Nappy, hobstars, heart shape, center hdl 125.00
Pitcher, cider; lg expanding star, notched hdl, 6x6" 200.00
Pitcher, dmns & fans, slim, appl hdl, 11½" 80.00
Pitcher, flowers & stars, leaves cut in hdl, cream sz 55.00
Pitcher, hobstars/expanding stars, notched hdl, flared, 8" 200.00
Pitcher, Hunt's Royal, blown blank, 10" 325.00
Pitcher, intricate florals, 8¼" 120.00
Pitcher, lemonade; expanding star w/cane & fan, 12x6" 300.00
Pitcher, stars, floral-chased silver rim/collar, 10x4" 400.00
Pitcher, strw dmns & fans, bulbous, cut hdl, 8" 275.00
Pitcher, tankard; Harvard, notched hdl, 10x4" 300.00
Pitcher, tankard; 3-dmn panels, ea w/lg swirl, Clarke, 15" 750.00
Pitcher, wine; Persian cut, notched hdl, rayed base, 6x16" 295.00
Plate, ice cream; Baker's Gothic, 7" 325.00
Powder jar, fans, rayed bottom, SP lid, 3¼x5" 80.00

Punch bowl on stand, fan and buzz star motifs, sawtooth rim, 13½x14½", $900.00.

Punch bowl, allover hobstar bands, 6 points/6 petals, 8x14" 700.00
Punch bowl, daisies & dmns, 10x13" 145.00
Rose bowl, hobstars/strw dmns, hobstar ft, 7x6" 225.00
Tray, celery; dbl mitres, hobstars, fans, Clarke, 12" L 145.00
Tray, ice cream; allover hobstars, J Hoare & Co, 2¾x17½" L .2,300.00
Tray, ice cream; allover hobstars/lace, cane panel, 14" 1,100.00
Tray, ice cream; hobstars, canes, X-hatching, heavy, 15" 1,100.00
Tumbler, allover Persian cut, 10 for 295.00
Vase, allover hobstars/prisms, flared notched rim, 10x5" 280.00
Vase, butterflies/daisies/herringbone, w/eng, goblet form, 15" 690.00
Vase, fish w/bubbles & 'waves,' heavy/well cut, 12x7" 600.00

Vase, pinwheels/pineapple, wide cut rim, trumpet neck, 16" ...**1,000.00**
Vase, starflowers & fans, scalloped rim, slim, 12" **145.00**
Vase, starflowers & fans w/vertical bars, slim, 12" **185.00**
Vase, stars, strw dmns, zippers, 16", NM **300.00**
Vase, sunflowers on elongated stalks, flared cylinder, 24" **400.00**

Cut Overlay Glass

Glassware with one or more overlying colors through which a design has been cut is called 'Cut Overlay.' It was made both here and abroad.

Bowl, cobalt cut to clear, t'prints/fantails/bull's eyes, 8" **235.00**

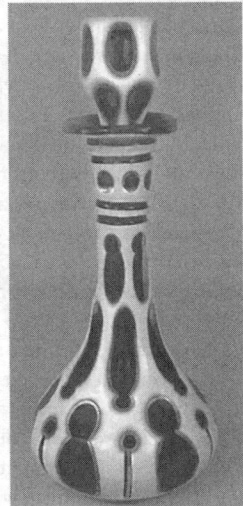

Cologne bottle, white to ruby with gold trim, ground pontil, 6½", $200.00.

Compote, wht cut to cranberry w/gold, goblet shape, 8⅞" **170.00**
Compote, wht cut to gr w/gold, 6x7" dia **475.00**
Decanter, amethyst cut to wht to clear, 16" **350.00**
Rose bowl, gr o/l, fans etc, 4¼x4½" **140.00**
Vase, cranberry cut to clear, lady's portrait, gold hdls, 12" **250.00**
Vase, cranberry o/l, geometric canes/fans, scalloped, 12x5" **475.00**

Cut Velvet

Cut Velvet glassware was made during the late 1800s. It is characterized by the effect achieved through the execution of relief-molded patterns, often ribbing or diamond quilting, which allows its white inner casing to show through the outer layer.

Bottle, Dmn Quilt, bl, 7½x3½" **145.00**
Bowl, Dmn Quilt, bl, appl thorny vases form ft, 4¾x6½" **400.00**
Bowl, Dmn Quilt, bl, 3-crimp, 4½x4⅛" **145.00**
Bowl, Ribbon, golden-yel, SP rim, 4x8", +SP fork & spoon **850.00**
Celery vase, Dmn Quilt, bl, box-pleat top, Mt WA, 6½" **700.00**
Pickle castor, butterscotch; orig SP fr, w/tongs **325.00**
Pitcher, Dmn Quilt, pk, camphor branch hdl, 6x4½" **300.00**
Pitcher, Dmn Quilt, pk, sq rim, bulbous, camphor hdl, 7x7" **525.00**
Pitcher, Dmn Quilt, yel, sq rim, clear reeded hdl, Mt WA, 7" **200.00**
Pitcher, Honeycomb, pk, crimped tricorn rim, camphor hdl, 8" .**375.00**
Rose bowl, Dmn Quilt, bl, 3-crimp top, 4¼x3⅝" **135.00**
Rose bowl, Dmn Quilt, pk, egg shape, 4½x 3½" **175.00**
Vase, Dmn Quilt, bl, bottle form, 6x3⅛" **110.00**
Vase, Dmn Quilt, bl, trumpet neck, 6½x3¾" **145.00**

Vase, Dmn Quilt, bl, waisted neck, 3½" **110.00**
Vase, Dmn Quilt, bl, 6¼x2¾" **110.00**
Vase, Dmn Quilt, chartreuse w/HP flowers & butterfly, 7½" **200.00**
Vase, Dmn Quilt, lt gr, stick neck, 7" **145.00**
Vase, Dmn Quilt, pk, cylinder neck, 9" **150.00**
Vase, Rib, bl, 6⅛x3⅛" **100.00**
Vase, Rib, pk, 9⅜x4½" **125.00**

Cybis

Boleslaw Cybis was a graduate of the Academy of Fine Arts in Warsaw, Poland, and was well recognized as a fine artist by the time he was commissioned by his government to paint murals in the Polish Pavillion's Hall of Honor at the 1939 World's Fair. Finding themselves stranded in America at the outbreak of WWII, the Cybises founded an artists' studio, first in Astoria, New York, and later in Trenton, New Jersey, where they made fine figurines and plaques with exacting artistry and craftsmanship entailing extensive handwork. The studio still operates today producing exquisite porcelains on a limited edition basis.

Allegra **295.00**
Bacchus, carafe **250.00**
Ballerina on Cue, wht, on wood stand, 12½" **400.00**
Bear Cub, brn **175.00**
Bicentennial, heart box **95.00**
Bunny, Mr Snowball, 4" L **75.00**
Burro, Fitzgerald, 7¼" **200.00**
Calla Lily, #427, 16" **750.00**
Carousel Pony, Sugar Plum **1,250.00**
Carousel Tiger **750.00**
Christmas Bell, 1983 ....**75.00**
Chrysanthemum, bud vase **195.00**
Cinderella at the Ball **350.00**
Clematis, wht **350.00**
Columbine **1,650.00**
Council Fire **3,500.00**
Dahlia **685.00**
Dakota, Minnehaha **2,250.00**
Edward & Victoria, pr **750.00**
Egg, 1983 or 1984, ea **195.00**
Elizabeth Ann **250.00**
First in Flight, girl w/bluebird **285.00**
Folk Singer **495.00**

Goldilocks with 3 panda bears, 6¼x4", $500.00.

Guinevere Bust	950.00
Harp Seal	95.00
Head of Girl, wht, w/wooden pedestal, 9½"	450.00
Heidi, 8"	400.00
Hermit Thrush	1,000.00
Holiday Child, w/panda bear, 6¼"	195.00
Horse	1,675.00
Iris, compote, wht	95.00
Jennifer Bust	250.00
Kitten Chelsea	150.00
Little Boy Blue, 9"	450.00
Little Miss Muffet, 7"	300.00
Lucy Locket	295.00
Madonna, w/bird	375.00
Madonna, w/crown of roses, pastels, bl eyes, 11"	495.00
Madonna Angelica	225.00
Musician, mandolin player	350.00
Narcissus	295.00
Oriental Boy or Girl Bust, ea	250.00
Pandora w/Box, 5"	495.00
Pegasus Colts	850.00
Peter Pan's Wendy, w/doll	295.00
Pollyanna, seated on chair, 7½"	350.00
Portia	1,800.00
Queen Esther, #98, 13"	1,100.00
Rebecca, kneeling w/flowers, 6½"	600.00
Ring-Neck Pheasant	1,000.00
Romance, heart box	95.00
Shoshone, Sacajawea	2,250.00
Thumbelina	295.00
Turtle the Baron	195.00
Wee Willie Winkie	250.00
Wendy w/Doll	550.00
Wood Duck	650.00
Yankee Doodle Dandy, 9"	900.00

Czechoslovakian Collectibles

Czechoslovakia came into being as a country in 1918. Located in the heart of Europe, it was a land with the natural resources necessary to support a glass industry that dated back to the mid-14th century. The glass that was produced there has recently captured the attention of today's collectors, and for good reason. There are beautiful vases — cased, ruffled, applied with rigaree or silver overlay — fine enough to rival those of the best glasshouses. Czechoslovakian art glass baskets are quite as attractive as Victorian America's, and the elegant cut glass perfumes made in colors as well as crystal are unrivaled. There are also pressed glass perfumes, molded in lovely Deco shapes, of various types of art glass. Some are overlaid with gold filigree set with 'jewels.' Jewelry, lamps, porcelains, and fine art pottery are also included in the field.

More than seventy marks have been recorded, including those in the mold, ink stamped, acid etched, or on a small metal nameplate. The newer marks are incised, stamped 'Royal Dux Made in Czechoslovakia' (see Royal Dux), or printed on a paper label which reads 'Bohemian Glass Made in Czechoslovakia.' (Communist controlled from 1948, Czechoslovakia once again was made a free country in December 1989. Today it no longer exists; since 1993 it has been divided to form the world's two newest countries, the Czech Republic and the Slovak Republic.) For a more thorough study of the subject, we recommend you refer to the books *Made in Czechoslovakia* and *Made in Czechoslovakia, Book 2,* by Ruth A. Forsythe; she is listed in the Directory under Ohio. Another fine book is *Czechoslovakian Glass & Collectibles* by Dale and Diane Barta. In the listings that follow, when one dimension is given, it refers to height; decoration is enamel unless noted otherwise. See also Erphila.

Candy Baskets

Bl w/blk ruffled rim, clear hdl, 6½"	200.00
Blk w/silver mica, bl int, simple blk hdl, 8"	350.00
Hobnail, red w/blk rim, plain crystal hdl, 6½"	200.00
Lt gr w/bl stripes, gr hdl, 8"	190.00
Mc mottle w/twisted clear thorn hdl, 6½"	225.00
Red & yellow mottle w/ruffled rim, simple clear hdl, 6½"	175.00

Cased Art Glass

Bowl, mottled autumn colors, amber cased, 3-footed, 4⅛"	200.00
Box, mc mottle w/4 blk buttressed ft, w/lid, 8"	300.00
Candlestick, blk vining cameo decor on orange, 12½"	650.00
Cocktail shaker, enameled rooster on gr, metal top, 8¾"	125.00
Goblet, wine; red bowl w/silver trim, tall blk stem, 7½"	55.00
Pitcher, HP exotic bird on orange w/blk trim, 11½"	285.00
Vase, blk serpentine decor on yel, ruffled rim, slim, 10"	145.00
Vase, dk orange bulbous form, bl rim/3 bl angle hdls, 5½"	450.00
Vase, gr trumpet form w/appl gr ornaments, 5½"	85.00
Vase, jack-in-the-pulpit; yel w/mc mottling at base, 7½"	95.00
Vase, mottled colors, thick form w/flared base, 8½"	55.00
Vase, pk w/canes & partial red opaque o/l, pk hdls, 7"	375.00
Vase, red w/gr aventurine, gourd shape, 7¼"	180.00
Vase, silver birds o/l on orange, bulbous, 7¾"	95.00
Vase, silver o/l on blk, classic shape, 7¼"	95.00
Vase, varicolored ball form, 6"	95.00
Vase, varicolored swirl, dbl cased, bulbous, 5½"	120.00
Vase, varicolored trumpet form w/gr aventurine, 7"	150.00
Vase, wht waisted form w/appl bl ornament, 7¾"	120.00

Cut Glass Perfume Bottles

Harem Dancer colorless and frosted glass stopper on clear pink base, very rare, 6⅛", $2,860.00 at auction.

Amber half-circle base w/figure intaglio stopper, 5½"	250.00
Blk opaque w/gold jewels at shoulder, clear cut stopper, 4⅛"	250.00
Crystal, faceted pillow, amber crane intaglio stopper, 7½"	350.00
Crystal, flared base, tall amber prism stopper, 6½"	155.00
Crystal, geometric arched base, firebird intaglio stopper, 6½"	275.00
Crystal, Indian & bird intaglio, bird-form stopper, 6"	600.00

Crystal, shouldered form, red lovebird intaglio stopper, 4⅜" 300.00
Crystal, stepped hexagon, lady's face intaglio stopper, 7" 350.00
Crystal, stepped sides, intaglio dbl-cut stopper, 6⅜" 495.00
Crystal, stepped sides, lt bl intaglio girl/bird stopper, 7" 500.00
Crystal, stepped/faceted, lg butterfly intaglio stopper, 8½" 500.00
Crystal w/gr ft, gr frosted flower stopper, 6" 300.00
Gr, ball shape w/gr flower stopper, 5⅛" 155.00
Gr, stepped form w/clear intaglio floral stopper, 5¾" 130.00
Gr w/gold jewels, gr cut stopper, 4¾" 225.00
Pk, pyramid w/metalwork/jewels, dancer intaglio top, 6½" 1,000.00
Pk, stepped base (low), clear triangular stopper, 5⅝" 150.00
Pk w/clear harem dancer stopper, 6⅛" 2,860.00
Violet, faceted slim form w/pyramidal stopper, 6" 200.00
Violet, hexagonal form w/tiara-form intaglio stopper, 6" 415.00
Violet, 8-sided star shape w/8-point fan-shaped stopper, 4⅞" 285.00
Yel, shouldered form w/cut pleats, intaglio nude stopper, 6" 500.00
Yel w/ornate facets, Spanish dancers intaglio stopper, 5½" 220.00

Lamps

Basket, crystal beads, bl flowers, 8½" 500.00
Basket, crystal beads, glass fruit, 10¾" 650.00
Boudoir, brass peacock w/beaded tail, onyx base, 12¼" 1,200.00
Boudoir, lady figural, flower skirt, 10¼" 950.00
Desk, Deco figure by crystal bubbly paperweight lamp, 9" 900.00
Milk glass w/pnt pk & gold decor, kerosene burner, 12¾" 185.00
Student, acid-cut shade w/floral decor, 21" 900.00
Table, Deco-style geometric decor on wht, 9" 1,200.00
Table, dk bl lustre, rpl shade, 13¼" 175.00
Table, mottled satin base & shade, 12½" 450.00
Wall sconce, crystal w/prisms, 2-light, 14½" 250.00

Mold-Blown and Pressed Bottles

Bl w/emb nude & butterfly, fan stopper, 5¼" 1,000.00
Blk w/gold decor at shoulder, atomizer, 9½" 170.00
Cranberry opal Hobnail, wht opal stopper, cologne, 5½" 85.00
Crystal, sq w/jeweled stopper, 4" 85.00
Crystal, w/jeweled cap, 2¼" 45.00
Crystal & frosted, waffled cuts, butterfly stopper, 5½" 120.00
Crystal & frosted w/enamel floral decor, cylindrical, 5¼" 45.00
Jeweled overall decor on crystal, 2¼" 95.00
Mc mottled satin, cased, Mar Franc Paris, atomizer, 6½" 125.00
Orange cased w/blk stopper & base, 6¼" 55.00

Opaque, Crystal, Colored Transparent Glass

Bowl, pk lustre w/bl lustre King Tut decor, 3½" 2,500.00
Candy jar, gr w/3 apricot buttressed ft, w/lid, 6" 250.00
Decanter, topaz tinted, HP scene by Borokistol, 10¼" 140.00
Pitcher, amber waffled body w/yel o/l, amber hdl, 11½" 650.00
Shakers, pk transparent, cut decor, 4¾", pr 165.00
Tumbler, HP exotic bird on bl, 5¾" 80.00
Vase, bl lustre, tall ft, flared rim, 5⅞" 100.00
Vase, blk w/orange spirals, cylindrical w/sm ft & rim, 6½" 75.00
Vase, clear w/canes, mottled colors & red decor, hdls, 7" 325.00
Vase, dk bl cut to clear, 10¼" 350.00
Vase, floral coralene decor on bl to wht, 7½" 85.00
Vase, orange fan form w/yel o/l, 8" 165.00
Vase, pk lustre w/lustre threads at top, ftd cylinder, 9⅜" 275.00
Vase, pk opaque w/bl streaks, mottled colors at base, 9¼" 125.00
Vase, red & wht opaque mottling, slim, 5⅞" 50.00
Vase, wht opaque w/HP decor, 8⅛" 110.00
Wine, gr bubbly glass w/HP decor, 4¼" 65.00

Pottery, Porcelain, Semiporcelain

Box, Deco HP decor on scarlet, 2½x4" 350.00
Box, dresser; bl, mirrored lid w/HP scene & gold, 3¼" 45.00
Creamer, cow figural, tail hdl, open mouth, mc, 6¼" 60.00
Creamer, duck figural, mc, 3¾" 35.00
Creamer, pk lustre, 3¼" 30.00
Creamer, wht w/cat hdl, 4⅜" 25.00
Figurine, Deco-style lady, wht, 9¾" 185.00
Figurine, dog, sitting, brn & wht, 5" 35.00
Flower holder, bird perched on open log, mc, 3½" 25.00
Napkin ring, girl figural, 4" 25.00

Pitcher, multicolor Deco-style flowers with black on cream, 5¾", $180.00.

Plate, HP yel chicks on wht, 6½" 30.00
Teapot, girl w/basket figural, EX details, 8" 150.00
Vase, Egyptian chariot decor w/head hdls, 8½" 350.00
Vase, Egyptian figures on tan, squat, 9⅛" 300.00
Wall pocket, bird & birdhouse, mc, 5½" 45.00
Wall pocket, woodpecker on tree trunk, mc, 7¾" 85.00

D'Argental

D'Argental cameo glass was produced in France from the 1870s until about 1920 in the Art Nouveau style. Browns and tans were favored colors used to complement florals and scenic designs developed through acid cuttings. Our advisor for this category is Don Williams; he is listed in the Directory under Missouri.

Lamp, 3 butterflies among leafy-stemmed flowers, orange and brown on yellow-amber, signed, 19" with 8⅞" shade, $5,175.00.

Cameo

Box, morning glories, wine on peach, 5¼" dia 1,600.00
Box, orchids/ferns, red/gr on citron, 2x5" dia 1,600.00
Vase, anemones/stalks, distant lake, brn/shaded tan, 12x4" 1,450.00
Vase, aquatic scene w/fish, orange/brn on red-amber, 14x7" ...1,700.00
Vase, berry branch, brn/wine on shaded amber, 7½" 865.00
Vase, floral branches, orange/brn on amber frost, 8x4" 1,380.00
Vase, gooseberries, wine/red on citron, stick neck, 8" 625.00
Vase, long seed pods/branches, amber/gr on gr/brn, ovoid, 7¾" .865.00
Vase, orchids/ferns, wine on red-amber, 4½x8½" 1,300.00
Vase, poppies, royal bl on yel frost, shouldered, 4¼" 425.00
Vase, trees, red-wine on amber, ovoid, 6" 920.00
Vase, trees/meadows, olive on gold-amber, slender/ftd, 12" 1,050.00

Daum Nancy

Daum was an important producer of French cameo glass, operating from the late 1800s until after the turn of the century. They used various techniques — acid cutting, wheel engraving, and handwork — to create beautiful scenic designs and nature subjects in the Art Nouveau manner. Virtually all examples are signed. Our advisor for this category is Don Williams; he is listed in the Directory under Missouri.

Key: fp — fire polished

Cameo

Bowl, berries/leaves, cut/pnt on amber w/gilt, oval, 11½" 1,000.00
Bowl, floral, cvd/pnt on yel, 2½x4½" 600.00
Bowl, floral, pk/gray-gr on pk/yel mottle, 4-fold rim, 3x6" 1,300.00
Bowl, trees/bridge, dk gr-blk on pastel mottle, 6x7" 2,500.00
Bowl, trees/river, blk-amethyst on bl w/yel, sqd, 4½x6" 1,950.00
Bowl, winter trees, cut/pnt on pastel mottle, scalloped, 4½" ...1,200.00
Inkstand, oak leaves, 3 foil-bkd cvd acorns/insects, 5x4x4" 8,000.00
Lamp, trees/lake, wine on orange 14" shaped dome/vase std ...8,000.00
Lamp, winter trees on yel/rust, cone shade, slim std, 17" 14,900.00
Rose bowl, thistles, gold on textured opal w/red glow, 2¾" 450.00
Salt cellar, pine cones on branches, blk & wht on yel, 1¾" 495.00
Toothpick holder, winter scene, blk/wht on orange/yel, 2" 550.00
Tray, lotus/leaves, gray/gilt on bl, 2-line verse, hdl, 6" 1,700.00

Vase, Dutch winter landscape at sunset, clear walls mottled with white opaque, pink and orange, baluster form, 7", $2,700.00; Vase, blackberries on leafy stems, gray with green, violet, sea green, and amber, fire polished, cylindrical form, 8½", $1,800.00.

Vase, autumn leaves, yel/amber on yel/brn, int decor, 22" 8,000.00
Vase, bell flowers, red/gr on yel/gr mottle, sqd rim, 7x4" 1,350.00
Vase, berries/leaves, violet/orange/red on yel mottle, sq, 4" 700.00
Vase, bleeding hearts, cut/pnt on yel/orange, ovoid, 4" 1,380.00
Vase, blk birds/evergreens/moon on yel, wht ftd base, 10" 2,800.00
Vase, boats, purple/blk on gr/red/lime, shouldered, 5¾" 1,850.00
Vase, exotic flowers, wine on red/yel mottle, hdls, 7x6½" 4,000.00
Vase, floral branch, cut/pnt on opal, bulbous, 3¾" 1,100.00
Vase, floral spire, cut/pnt on yel mottle, cylindrical, 4¾" 1,380.00
Vase, floral spires cut/pnt on gr/amber mottle, bun ft, 19" 5,300.00
Vase, floral spires/spiked leaves, red/gr on yel/wine, 7" 1,000.00
Vase, fuchsia vines, red/purple/gr on purple/frost, 3¾" 1,500.00
Vase, grape clusters, blk on yel/gr/red mottle, ftd, 13½" 1,600.00
Vase, grapevines, blk-gr on gr w/red mottle, ftd, 15½" 2,750.00
Vase, insects on yel to brn, sqd/incurvate, 20" 4,000.00
Vase, lg blossoms/blade leaves, lav/violet on yel, 12" 3,750.00
Vase, lg rampant lion, dbl-etched/gilt on emerald, 11½" 1,725.00
Vase, nasturtiums, purple on pastel mottle, wide hex rim, 9" ..3,000.00
Vase, pond lilies, dk gr/orange on opal martelle, 9½x4" 5,175.00
Vase, stylized grapes/geometric bands, orange on opaque, 7½" ...300.00
Vase, summer trees cut/pnt on yel-gr & bl, 9½x7" 7,500.00
Vase, sweet peas, raspberry on wht/orange mottle, squat, 2" 500.00
Vase, sweet peas/vines, rose/gr on amber/wht, ftd, 12" 2,700.00
Vase, thistles, cut/pnt/gilt on amber opal, stick neck, 5" 400.00
Vase, thistles, cvd/pnt/gilt on banded pk/yel, hdls, 9½" 4,600.00
Vase, trees, cut/pnt on gray & yel, ogee sides, 23" 8,500.00
Vase, trees fr lake, dk gray/gr/brn on yel, bun ft, 16" 2,600.00
Vase, trees/mtns, burgundy on yel to tan, ftd U-form, 6", NM 450.00
Vase, trees/water/sailboats on mottle, tooled rim, 5½x5" 1,265.00
Vase, trumpet flowers, red/wine on red/yel mottle, ftd, 7" 2,800.00
Vase, vines/buds, rose/pk/gr on wht w/yel, gr bun base, 16" 2,700.00
Vase, violets, cut/pnt on purple/wht frost, 3¾x4" 2,750.00
Vase, violets, cut/pnt/gilt on wht/purple, str sides, 7" 3,700.00
Vase, winter sunset, cut/pnt on red to yel, bulb base, 10" 4,000.00
Vase, winter trees, cut/pnt on yel to orange, cylinder, 4½" 1,200.00
Vase, 4 appl disks w/hunting scenes on etched gray, 6½x5" 7,000.00

Miscellaneous

Bowl, etched geometrics on topaz texture, 12" 500.00
Bowl, gr mottle blown into rtcl ftd iron Marjorelle mt, 7x10" .3,000.00
Chandelier, etched bands on topaz w/chipped ice motif, 23" ..1,600.00
Chandelier, 3-color mottled bowl shape, 3 chains, 18" 975.00
Sculpture, bird, pate-de-verre bl/amber body, 1980s, 12x14" 575.00
Shade, mottled colors, sqd flared-edge bowl form, 6½x9½" 485.00
Tray, pate-de-verre, owl aside, 6½x9" 4,600.00
Vase, Berluze, etched metallic mottle, long slim neck, 18½" 690.00
Vase, Dutch village, HP bls on frost, rectangular ovoid, 4" 1,950.00
Vase, etched disks/scales on amber w/foil, 9½x10" 3,000.00
Vase, etched dmns on amber, shouldered cylinder, 7" 575.00
Vase, etched fretwork at shoulder on amber, ovoid, 14" 900.00
Vase, etched lav w/abstract lines, spherical, 10" 500.00
Vase, etched ribs, 3 bulging ribs at sq base, gray, 9½" 345.00
Vase, etched zigzags/circles on gray, bulbous ovoid, 8" 345.00
Vase, int latticework w/dots, brn in bl, thick, ovoid, 16" 2,875.00
Vase, millefiori, tangerine/wine w/4 opal inclusions, 8" 800.00
Vase, mottled/foil inclusions, in ribbed Marjorelle mt, 10" 2,300.00
Vase, waterway scenes, blk on opal mottle, stick neck, 6", pr 600.00
Vase, windmills/trees, blk enamel on etched wht, hdls, 11" 2,875.00

Davenport

W. Davenport and Company were Staffordshire potters operating in that area from 1793 to 1887, producing earthenware, creamware, porcelain, and ironstone. Many different stamps, all with 'Davenport,' were used to mark the various types of ware. See also Mulberry; Flow Blue.

Compote, Imari, 9" 100.00
Creamer & sugar bowl, mc roses, 5", VG 250.00
Fruit basket, gr transfer floral, 11¼", +undertray 230.00
Jug, Japan, serpent hdls, diapering, 1820s, 4" 225.00
Platter, exotic birds & flowers, dk bl transfer, 19½" 195.00
Tureen, sauce; Flute Player, bl transfer, anchor mk 150.00

De Vez

De Vez was a type of acid-cut French cameo glass produced by Cristallerie de Pantin in Paris around the turn of the century. Our advisor for this category is Don Williams; he is listed in the Directory under Missouri.

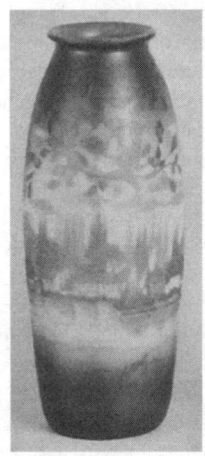

Vase, lake with fisherman, village along shore, framed with large branches, 4-color, baluster form, 10½", $1,700.00.

Cameo

Vase, cranes/aquatic plants, brn on mustard, spherical, 6" 600.00
Vase, desert oasis, distant mtns, invt baluster, 10" 1,100.00
Vase, exotic flowers, red/maroon on chartreuse, stick neck, 7½" ..950.00
Vase, moonlit harbor w/boats, lav w/bl mtns, cylindrical, 9" 950.00
Vase, pond lilies, pk/gr on opal, squat bottle form, 6" 635.00
Vase, river/mtns/trees, brn to purple-pk, 7¾x3¼" 1,400.00
Vase, trees/river, gr on rose/citron, ftd ovoid, 9" 900.00
Vase, wisteria, amethyst on wht, cylinder neck/bun base, 16" .1,000.00

De Vilbiss

Perfume bottles, atomizers, and dresser accessories marketed by the De Vilbiss Company are appreciated by collectors today for the various types of lovely glassware used in their manufacture as well as for their pleasing shapes. Various companies provided the glass, while De Vilbiss made only the metal tops. They marketed their merchandise not only here but in Paris, England, Canada, and Havana as well. Their marks were acid stamped, ink stamped, in gold script, molded in, or on paper labels. One is no more significant than another. For more information we recommend *Bedroom and Bathroom Glassware of the Depression Years* by Margaret and Kenn Whitmyer; their address is listed in the Directory under Ohio. Our advisor for this category is Randy Monsen; he is listed in the Directory under Virginia.

Atomizer, bl, on Deco-style brass base, 5⅞" 350.00

Atomizer, bl transparent, 3" 55.00
Atomizer, blk, gold Deco design, Bakelite crown top, 6½" 550.00

Atomizer, clear with silver-resist decoration, blue base, signed on top of bulb, 3¾", $300.00.

Atomizer, clear, cut floral decor 175.00
Atomizer, clear frosted flatiron shape w/ridges, 2¼" 45.00
Atomizer, cranberry stain, gold decor, mesh bulb & cord, 7" 115.00
Atomizer, enameled dk gr w/blk florals, octagonal, 5½" 65.00
Atomizer, French opal, Coin Dot, ball form, by Fenton 45.00
Atomizer, King Tut, bl-gr irid on gr opaque, Durand, 7½" 770.00
Atomizer, lt amber, eng decor, 7" 175.00
Atomizer, lt gr, Opalescent Windows, 5" 95.00
Atomizer, orange stain on crystal base, 6" 85.00
Atomizer, ruby stain w/gold lustre, 8" 325.00
Bottle, amber irid, ftd, 6½", MIB 175.00
Bottle, Imperial Line, bl to yel opal w/gold & pk stones, 7" 2,000.00
Bottle, irid, blk enamel top, stemmed ft, mk 90.00
Box, acid-cut gr w/gold kingfisher bird on lid 150.00
Dresser set, HP florals w/gold, mk, 7-pc 425.00
Dresser set, orange enamel w/blk & gold decor, 3-pc 195.00
Lamp, perfume; nude figure on glass insert, 7" 250.00
Perfume dropper, crystal w/bl florals 25.00
Pin tray, orange enamel w/blk & gold decor, 3¼x5⅝" 30.00

Decanters

Ceramic whiskey decanters were brought into prominence in 1955 by the James Beam Distilling Company. Few other companies besides Beam produced these decanters during the next ten years or so; however, other companies did eventually follow suit. At its peak in 1975, at least twenty prominent companies and several on a lesser scale made these decanters. Beam stopped making decanters in mid-1992. Now only a couple of companies are still producing these collectibles.

Liquor dealers have told collectors for years that ceramic decanters are not as valuable, and in some cases worthless, if emptied or if the federal tax stamp has been broken. Nothing is further from the truth. Following are but a few of many reasons you should consider emptying ceramic decanters:

1) If the thin glaze on the inside ever cracks (and it does in a small percentage of decanters), the contents will push through to the outside. It is then referred to as a 'leaker' and worth a fraction of its original value.

2) A large number of decanters left full in one area of your house poses a fire hazard.

3) A burglar, after stealing jewelry and electronics, may make off with some of your decanters just to enjoy the contents. If they are empty, chances are they will not be bothered.

4) It is illegal in most states for collectors to sell a full decanter without a liquor license.

Unlike years ago, few collectors now collect all types of decanters. Most now specialize. For example, they may collect trains, cars, owls, Indians, clowns, or any number of different things that have been depicted on or as a decanter. They are finding exceptional quality available at reasonable prices, especially when compared with many other types of collectibles.

We have tried to list those brands that are the most popular with collectors. Likewise, individual decanters listed are the ones (or representative of the ones) most commonly found. The following listing is but a small fraction of the thousands of decanters that have been produced.

These decanters come from all over the world. While Jim Beam owned its own china factory in the U.S., some of the others have been imported from Mexico, Taiwan, Japan, and elsewhere. They vary in size from miniatures (approximately 2 oz.) to gallons. Values range from a few dollars to more than $3,000.00 per decanter.

Most collectors and dealers define a 'mint' decanter as one with no chips, no cracks, and label intact. A missing federal tax stamp or lack of contents have no bearing on value. All values are given for 'mint' decanters. A 'mini' behind a listing indicates a miniature. All others are fifth or 750 ml unless noted otherwise. Our advisor for this category is Roy Willis; he is listed in the Directory under Kentucky.

Aesthetic Specialties (ASI)

Golf, Bing Crosby 41st	50.00
Truck, Ice Cream	75.00
Truck, Telephone	65.00

Beam

International Petroleum, Regal China Co., 1972, 14½", $12.00.

Casino Series, Binion's Horseshoe	12.00
Casino Series, Harold's Club Covered Wagon (1969)	7.00
Casino Series, Smith's North Shore	15.00
Centennial Series, Alaska Purchase	10.00
Centennial Series, Cheyenne	6.00
Centennial Series, Chicago Fire	18.00
Centennial Series, Edison Light Bulb	15.00
Centennial Series, San Diego	5.00
Centennial Series, Yellowstone	7.00

Executive Series, 1973 Phoenician	12.00
Executive Series, 1974 Twin Cherubs	15.00
Executive Series, 1975 Reflections	12.00
Executive Series, 1976 Floro de Oro	15.00
Executive Series, 1977 Golden Jubilee	15.00
Executive Series, 1978 Yellow Rose	15.00
Foreign Series, Boys Town, Italy	10.00
Foreign Series, Fiji Islands	7.00
Foreign Series, Germany, Hansel & Gretel	10.00
Foreign Series, Germany, Pied Piper	10.00
Foreign Series, Germany, Wiesbaden	10.00
Foreign Series, Thailand	5.00
Foreign Series, 1970	10.00
Organization Series, Ducks Unlimited #1, 1974	40.00
Organization Series, Ducks Unlimited #2, 1975	48.00
Organization Series, Ducks Unlimited #3, 1977	45.00
Organization Series, Ducks Unlimited #4, 1978	45.00
Organization Series, Ducks Unlimited #5, 1979	40.00
Organization Series, Telephone #1, Wall	30.00
Organization Series, Telephone #2, Candlestick	35.00
Organization Series, Telephone #3, French Cradle	18.00
Organization Series, Telephone #4, 1919 Dial	50.00
Organization Series, Telephone #5, Pay Phone	50.00
Organization Series, Telephone #6, Battery	42.00
Organization Series, Telephone #7, 100 Digit	55.00
People Series, Buffalo Bill	18.00
People Series, General Stark	15.00
People Series, Hatfield, Devil Anse	20.00
People Series, Indian Chief	20.00
People Series, John Henry	28.00
People Series, McCoy, Randolph	28.00
State Series, Florida Shell	7.00
State Series, Illinois	12.00
State Series, Michigan	8.00
State Series, Nebraska	7.00
State Series, Pennsylvania	12.00
Wheel Series, Bass Boat	30.00
Wheel Series, Corvette, 1953, wht	200.00
Wheel Series, Corvette, 1954, bl	100.00
Wheel Series, Corvette, 1955, bronze	100.00
Wheel Series, Corvette, 1963, red or silver	80.00
Wheel Series, Corvette, 1978, yel or red	75.00
Wheel Series, Ford, 1903 Model A, red or blk	45.00
Wheel Series, Ford, 1964 Mustang, blk	130.00
Wheel Series, Ford, 1964 Mustang, red	85.00
Wheel Series, Ford, 1964 Mustang, wht	75.00
Wheel Series, Golf Car	45.00
Wheel Series, Harold's Club Covered Wagon (1974)	35.00
Wheel Series, Locomotive, Grant	90.00
Wheel Series, Locomotive, JB Turner	150.00
Wheel Series, Mack Fire Engine	130.00
Wheel Series, Tender, Wood for General	125.00
Wheel Series, Train, Caboose, gray	70.00
Wheel Series, Train, Caboose, red	65.00
Wheel Series, Train, Locomotive, General	125.00
Wheel Series, Train, Tender, Coal for Grant	70.00
Wheel Series, Train, Tender, Wood for Turner	75.00
Wheel Series, Train, Tender, yel	85.00
Wheel Series, 1913 Model T, blk or gr	50.00

Brooks

American Legion, Hawaii, 1973	12.00
American Legion, Miami Beach, 1974	10.00

Bird Series, Quail, Heritage China, dated 1970, $10.00.

Car, Auburn 25.00
Car, Corvette Indy Pacecar 45.00
Car, Thunderbird, 1956 .... 70.00
Dollar, Silver 8.00
Equestrienne 12.00
Goldpanner 9.00
Greensboro Open, 1973 .... 28.00
Hereford 16.00
Jug, 1.75 Liter 20.00
Keystone Cops 55.00
Motorcycle 15.00
Nugget Classic, 1970 .... 12.00
Penguin 10.00
Pirate 9.00
Shrine, Clown 18.00
Shrine, Sphinx 12.00
Tank, Military 40.00
Tecumseh 9.00
Totem Pole #1, 1972 .... 12.00
Totem Pole #2, 1973 .... 15.00
Trout & Fly 10.00
West Virginia Mountain Lady 20.00
West Virginia Mountain Man 60.00

Dant, J.W.

Field Birds, 8 different, ea 12.00
Ft Sill 10.00
Mt Rushmore 8.00

Dickel

Gold Club (glass) 12.00
Powder Horn 12.00
Powder Horn, qt 15.00

Famous Firsts

Balloon 34.00
Cable Car 45.00
Hurdy Gurdy 18.00
Racer, Marmon Wasp #32 .... 75.00
Racer, Marmon Wasp #32, mini 35.00
Racer, Renault #3A 75.00

Hoffman

Aesop's Fables, 6 different, ea 18.00
College Series, Helmet, Georgia 40.00
College Series, Helmet, LSU 35.00
College Series, Helmet, Nebraska 45.00
College Series, Helmet, Tennessee 40.00
College Series, Mascot, Kentucky 40.00
College Series, Mascot, Mississippi State .. 45.00
Mr Lucky Series, Mr Barber 35.00
Mr Lucky Series, Mr Barber, mini 15.00
Mr Lucky Series, Mr Cobbler 30.00
Mr Lucky Series, Mr Cobbler, mini 15.00
Mr Lucky Series, Mr Sandman 28.00
Mr Lucky Series, Mr Sandman, mini 14.00
Racecar, Donahue Sunoco #66 .... 120.00
Racecar, Rutherford #3 .... 110.00
Wildlife Series, Bobcat & Pheasant 50.00
Wildlife Series, Wolf & Raccoon 50.00

Kontinental

Editor 30.00
Editor, mini 18.00
Gunsmith 30.00
Gunsmith, mini 18.00
Prospector 42.00
Prospector, mini 18.00
Saddle Maker 32.00
Saddle Maker, mini 18.00

Lionstone

Annie Christmas 18.00
Baseball Players 80.00
Belly Robber 18.00
Blacksmith 30.00
Boxers 70.00
Buccaneer 25.00
Calamity Jane 25.00
Dancehall Girl 45.00
Dancehall Girl, mini 15.00
European Workers, 6 different, ea 35.00
Hockey Players 55.00
Jesse James 20.00
Madame 45.00
Meadowlark 28.00
OK Corral Shootout, mini, 3-pc set 125.00
OK Corral Shootout, 3-pc set 400.00
Oriental Workers, 6 different, ea 40.00
Professor 45.00
Professor, mini 22.00
Riverboat Captain 22.00
Roadrunner 25.00
Roadrunner, mini 10.00
Rose Parade 20.00
Stage Drive 22.00
Tinker 25.00
Trapper 25.00
Wells Fargo Man 20.00

McCormick

Bicentennial, mini, set of 8 .... 170.00

Bicentennial, set of 8	200.00
Buffalo Bill	65.00

Elvis #1, white, '77, $85.00.

Elvis, #1, 1977, wht, mini	48.00
Elvis, #2, 1955, pk	75.00
Elvis, #2, 1955, pk, mini	42.00
Elvis, #3, 1968, blk	85.00
Elvis, #3, 1968, blk, mini	48.00
Gunfighters, mini, set of 8	125.00
Gunfighters, 8 different, ea	35.00
King Arthur's Court, Guinevere	30.00
King Arthur's Court, King Arthur	45.00
King Arthur's Court, Merlin	35.00
King Arthur's Court, Sir Lancelot	30.00
Louis Armstrong	80.00
Muhammad Ali	150.00
Ozark Ike	35.00
Ozark Ike, mini	15.00
Pocahontas	90.00
Roosevelt, Eleanor	25.00
Shrine, Dune Buggy	40.00
Shrine, Midian	12.00
Thelma Lu	35.00
Thelma Lu, mini	15.00

O.B.R.

Balloon	10.00
Football Player #7	25.00
River Queen	12.00
WC Fields, Bank Dick	45.00
WC Fields, Top Hat	40.00

Old Commonwealth

Coal Miner #1, w/Shovel	75.00
Coal Miner #1, w/Shovel, mini	25.00
Coal Miner #2, w/Pick	45.00
Coal Miner #2, w/Pick, mini	20.00
Coal Miner #3, w/Lump of Coal	40.00
Coal Miner #3, w/Lump of Coal, mini	20.00
Coal Miner #4, Lunch Time	45.00

Coal Miner #4, Lunch Time, mini	22.00
Coal Miner #5, Coal Shooter	30.00
Coal Miner #5, Coal Shooter, mini	20.00

Old Crow

Chess Set, Pawns	22.00
Chess Set, Rug	100.00
Chest Set, Castle, Bishop, Knight, Queen, King, ea	20.00

Old Mr. Boston

Anthony Wayne	8.00
Molly Pitcher	6.00
Mooseheart	10.00
Polish Legion	15.00
Racecar #9, red or yel	38.00
Town Crier	10.00

Ski Country

Antelope	45.00
Badger Family	35.00
Badger Family, mini	22.00
Barnum, PT	45.00
Barnum, PT; mini	20.00
Bassett Hound	35.00
Bassett Hound, mini	25.00
Bluebirds Wall Plaque	60.00
Bluebirds Wall Plaque, mini	28.00
Clown	65.00
Clown, mini	25.00
Coyote Family	38.00
Coyote Family, mini	25.00
Ducks Unlimited, Mallard, 1980	50.00
Ducks Unlimited, Mallard, 1980, mini	40.00
Ducks Unlimited, Oldsquaw, 1992	65.00
Ducks Unlimited, Oldsquaw, 1992, mini	35.00
Ducks Unlimited, Wood Duck, 1982	75.00
Ducks Unlimited, Wood Duck, 1982, mini	35.00
Eagle, Harpy	100.00
Eagle, Harpy, mini	65.00
Falcon, Peregrine	90.00
Falcon, Peregrine, mini	20.00
Falcon, Peregrine, 1-gal	300.00
Goat, Mountain	65.00
Goat, Mountain, mini	30.00
Goat, Mountain, 1-gal	700.00
Indian, End of the Trail	225.00
Indian, End of the Trail, mini	85.00
Indian, Great Spirit	90.00
Indian, Great Spirit, mini	20.00
Indian, Lookout	50.00
Indian, Lookout, mini	25.00
Labrador w/Duck	90.00
Labrador w/Duck, mini	30.00
Labrador w/Pheasant	75.00
Labrador w/Pheasant, mini	25.00
Owl, Barn	70.00
Owl, Barn; mini	20.00
Owl, Spectacled	65.00
Owl, Spectacled; mini	40.00
Pheasant, Fighting	40.00
Pheasant, Fighting, mini	40.00

Pheasant, Fighting, ½-gal 150.00
Pheasant, in Corn 60.00
Pheasant, in Corn, mini 25.00
Raccoon 45.00
Raccoon, mini 30.00
Raccoon Wall Plaque 60.00
Raccoon Wall Plaque, mini 40.00
Sea Gull Wall Plaque 50.00
Sea Gull Wall Plaque, mini 30.00
Woodpecker, Gila 45.00
Woodpecker, Gila; mini 20.00

Wild Turkey

Series I, #1, #2, #3, or #4, mini, ea 15.00
Series I, #1, 1971 ....260.00
Series I, #2 ....160.00
Series I, #3 ....70.00
Series I, #4 ....70.00
Series I, #5 ....30.00
Series I, #6 ....25.00
Series I, #7 ....25.00
Series I, #8 ....45.00
Series I, set of #5, #6, #7 & #8, mini 130.00

Series II, Lore #1, 1979, $25.00.

Series II, Lore #2 ....35.00
Series II, Lore #3 ....45.00
Series II, Lore #4 ....50.00
Series III, #1, In Flight 110.00
Series III, #1, In Flight, mini 45.00
Series III, #2, Turkey & Bobcat 140.00
Series III, #2, Turkey & Bobcat, mini 45.00
Series III, #3, Fighting Turkeys 150.00
Series III, #3, Fighting Turkeys, mini 50.00
Series III, #4, Turkey & Eagle 90.00
Series III, #4, Turkey & Eagle, mini 80.00
Series III, #5, Turkey & Raccoon 90.00
Series III, #5, Turkey & Raccoon, mini 45.00
Series III, #6, Turkey & Poults 90.00
Series III, #6, Turkey & Poults, mini 45.00
Series III, #7, Turkey & Red Fox 90.00
Series III, #7, Turkey & Red Fox, mini 50.00
Series III, #8, Turkey & Owl 90.00
Series III, #8, Turkey & Owl, mini 50.00
Series III, #9, Turkey & Bear Cubs 90.00

Series III, #9, Turkey & Bear Cubs, mini 50.00
Series III, #10, Turkey & Coyote 90.00
Series III, #10, Turkey & Coyote, mini 45.00
Series III, #11, Turkey & Falcon 90.00
Series III, #11, Turkey & Falcon, mini 45.00
Series III, #12, Turkey & Skunks 90.00
Series III, #12, Turkey & Skunks, mini 45.00

Decoys

American colonists learned the craft of decoy making from the Indians who used them to lure birds out of the sky as an important food source. Early models were carved from wood such as pine, cedar, balsa, etc., and a few were made of canvas or papier-mache. There are two basic types of decoys: water floaters and shorebirds (also called 'stick-ups'). Within each type are many different species, ducks being the most plentiful since they migrated along all four of America's great waterways. Market hunting became big business around 1880, resulting in large-scale commercial production of decoys which continued until about 1910 when such hunting was outlawed by the Migratory Bird Treaty.

Today decoys are one of the most collectible types of American folk art. The most valuable are those carved by such artists as Laing, Crowell, Ward, and Wheeler, to name only a few. Each area, such as Massachusetts, Connecticut, Maine, the Illinois River, and the Delaware River, produces decoys with distinctive regional characteristics. Examples of commercial decoys produced by well-known factories — among them Mason, Stevens, and Dodge — are also prized by collectors. Though mass-produced, these nevertheless required a certain amount of hand carving and decorating. Well-carved examples, especially those of rare species, are appreciating rapidly, and those with original paint are more desirable. Writer Carl F. Luckey has compiled a fully illustrated identification and value guide, *Collecting Antique Bird Decoys*; you will find his address in the Directory under Alabama. In the listings that follow, all decoys are solid-bodied unless noted hollow.

Key:
CG — Challenge Grade	RP — repaint
MDF — Mason's Decoy Factory	SG — Standard Grade
OP — original paint	WDF — Wildfowler Decoy Factory
ORP — old repaint	WOP — worn original paint
OWP — original working paint	WRP — working repaint
PG — Premier Grade	

Baird Sandpiper, E Crowell, lt pnt shrinkage on head, o/w M .1,450.00
Barrows Goldeneyes pr, B White, Delaware River style, M 1,500.00
Blk Brant, J McLellan, EX WRP, bill loose, 1940s 200.00
Blk Duck, CG, MDF, NM OP, hollow, sgn 2,400.00
Blk Duck, Chas Hart, EX wing/feather cvg, EX OP, 1900s 4,400.00
Blk Duck, Robbins Bros, branded, EX OP 100.00
Blk Duck, WDF, inlet head, EX OP, sm dents in body 200.00
Bluebill drake, Blair School, Mackey tag cvd, 2 pcs 600.00
Bluebill drake, Sam Barnes, EX+ OP, EX structure, 1910-15 ......650.00
Bluebill drake, Verity family, Long Island form, ORP 275.00
Bluebill pr, Charles Birdsall, sgn & branded, M 350.00
Bluewing Teal, X Bourg, exhibit mk, tack eyes, EX OP 500.00
Bluewing Teal pr, SG, MDF, glass eyes, EX OP 1,250.00
Brant, Henry Grant, ORP in Jersey style, VG structure 325.00
Brant, J Pichney, VG OP, hollow redwood, G structure, 1940s ..150.00
Brant, swimming, Mitchell, EX OP, trn head, sgn, 1968 ....600.00
Bufflehead drake, Doug Jester, EX OP, lightly shot 500.00
Canada Goose, feeding, Ward Bros, EX OP, ¼-sz 400.00
Canada Goose, flying, Dave Watson, EX cvg, EX OP, mini 275.00
Canada Goose, Roy Conklin, G feather pnt, cvd bill, EX OP 500.00

Canvasback Drake, Elmer Crowell, turned head, extensive wing and tail feather carving, structurally perfect, NM paint, $9,750.00.

Canvasbk drake, M Whipple, exhibit stamps, EX ORP/varnish 500.00
Coot, A Carmadel, pnt mk WER, EX OP, EX form, 1915 ....600.00
Coot, M Whipple, EX OP, sm pc of bill missing, 1910 ....475.00
Goldeneye drake, Wm Bowman, EX OP, age lines, shot mks 200.00
Greenwing Teal, SG, MDF, glass eyes, very sm cracks & chips ..650.00
Killdeer, mini, Crowell, slight pnt shrinkage on head, M 800.00
Mallard drake, M Mitchell, EX OP, EX structure, sgn, 1958 ....200.00
Mallard hen, Paul Gibson, EX feather pnt, NM OP, tiny dents ..175.00
Mallard hen, PG, MDF, EX+ OP, snakey head style 525.00
Mallard pr, Dolph Hall, R Horner-style cvg, branded, M 400.00
Mallard pr, WDF, hen w/tucked head, VG+ OP, sm dents, shot .225.00
Merganser drake, G Huey, slightly trn head, cvd eyes, EX OP 900.00
Merganser drake, Joel Salmon, RP in orig style, VG structure 200.00
Pintail drake, M LaFrance, exhibit mk, Minnow Chaser style 500.00
Pintail drake, PG, MDF, extra fine patina & form, NM OP 8,500.00
Pintail drake, Ward Bros, ORP prof stripped, EX OP, 1920s ...2,000.00
Pintail pr, J Holloway, hollow, NM 200.00
Redhead hen, CG, MDF, EX+ OP 850.00
Redhead hen, Ira Hudson, ORP down to OP, G structure 500.00
Redhead pr, James T Holly, both branded, EX OP 5,000.00
Ringneck drake, RA Roussel, superb cvg, EX OP, EX structure ..600.00
Ruddy Duck, Capt Ben Dye, Mackey tag, EX OP, shot mks 8,500.00
Ruddy Ducks pr, B White, McLoughlin cvg, NM OP, sgn, 1986 ..750.00
Sanderling, E Crowell, underside pnt blk, bill flakes, o/w M ...1,550.00
Sea gull, Robert Bates, EX+ OP, sgn, ca 1948 ....600.00
Sea gull, WDF, EX OP, EX structure, circular stamp 275.00
Swan, M Mitchell, clear varnish over OP, sgn, 1972, ¼-sz 500.00
Widgeon hen, J McLoughlin, slightly trn head, NM OP, '83 ......500.00
Widgeon pr, D Marshall, sgn, 1991, M 325.00
Wood Duck, Ken Harris, never weighted, NM 600.00

Dedham Pottery

Originally founded in Chelsea, Massachusetts, as the Chelsea Keramic Works, the name was changed to Dedham Pottery in 1895 after the firm relocated in Dedham, near Boston, Massachusetts. The ware utilized a gray stoneware body with a crackle glaze and simple cobalt border designs of flowers, birds, and animals. Decorations were brushed on by hand using an ancient Chinese method which suspended the cobalt within the overall glaze. There were thirteen standard patterns, among them Magnolia, Iris, Butterfly, Duck, Polar Bear, and Rabbit, the latter of which was chosen to represent the company on their logo. On the very early pieces, the rabbits face left; decorators soon found the reverse position easier to paint, and the rabbits were turned to the right. In addition to the standard patterns, other designs were produced for special orders. These and artist-signed pieces are highly valued by collectors today.

Though their primary product was the blue-printed, crackle-glazed dinnerware, two types of artware were also produced: crackle glaze and flambe. Their notable volcanic ware was a type of the latter. The mark is incised and often accompanies the cipher of Hugh Robertson. The firm was operated by succeeding generations of the Robertson family until it closed in 1943. Our advisor for this category is Dale MacLean; he is listed in the Directory under Massachusetts. See also Chelsea Keramic Art Works.

Dinnerware

Rabbit, left to right: Pitcher, unmarked, 1-qt, 7x6", $700.00; Chocolate pot, minor restoration, ink mark, 8¾", $600.00; Covered nappy, minor restoration, 2½x10½", $500.00; Tray, ink mark, 13¼", $900.00; Covered nappy, hairlines and chip to lid, ink mark, $400.00.

Ashtray, Azalea, stamped registered, 3¾" 150.00
Bacon rasher, Rabbit, stamped registered, 1½x9½" dia 350.00
Bacon rasher, Rabbit, stamped/impressed, 9x6" 375.00
Bowl, Chick, #6, hand thrown, stamped, rstr line, 2x4½" 800.00
Bowl, fruit; Rabbit, stamped, 4x9" 300.00
Bowl, Grape, #3, stamped, 3x6¾" 375.00
Bowl, Lotus Leaf, custom order, stamped registered, 2x5" 450.00
Bowl, nappy; Rabbit, #3, stamped, 2x9" 175.00
Bowl, nappy; Rabbit, #5, stamped, 1½x5¾" 175.00
Bowl, nappy; Rabbit, w/lid, stamped, 2½x9" 400.00
Bowl, Rabbit, #6, stamped registered, +NM 6" underplate 200.00
Bowl, swans/cattails band, stamped registered, 2x5" 300.00
Candlestick, Azalea, paper label, 1¾x3½" dia 250.00
Chocolate pot, Horse Chestnut, stamped registered, chip, 9" 700.00
Creamer, Rabbit, bulbous mid-section, #1, registered, 3¼" 275.00
Creamer, Swan, #1, stamped registered, 3½x6" 450.00
Cup & saucer, demitasse; Rabbit, stamped, cup: 2⅛" H 250.00
Cup & saucer, Rabbit, stamped, 2", 6" 175.00
Cup plate, Horse Chestnut, stamped registered, 4¼" 150.00
Knife rest, rabbit figural, 1½x2½" 350.00
Pickle dish, Rabbit, stamped registered, 1¾x10" dia 350.00
Pitcher, night & morning: birds/moon, chickens/sun, #10, 5" 750.00
Pitcher, Rabbit, floral band, #7, tapered, minor peppering, 9" 650.00
Plate, Azalea, stamped/imp, 10" 575.00
Plate, Bending Poppy, brushed bl ground/rim, stamped/imp, 6" .550.00
Plate, Birds in Orange tree, stamped/imp, 8½" 450.00
Plate, Coat of Arms/crest, Rabbit border, registered, 8½" 800.00
Plate, Crab, stamped/imp, 8½" 750.00
Plate, Dbl Turtle, stamped/imp, 9¾" 1,000.00
Plate, Dolphin, stamped/imp, 8¾" 800.00
Plate, Duck, Davenport rebus, stamped/imp, 6" 225.00

Plate, Duck, Davenport rebus, stamped/imp, 8½" 325.00
Plate, Grape, Davenport rebus, 8¼" 300.00
Plate, Grape, stamped/imp, 8¾" 250.00
Plate, Horse Chestnut, Davenport rebus, stamped/imp, 8½" 300.00
Plate, Horse Chestnut, stamped/imp, 10" 400.00
Plate, Iris, Davenport rebus, stamped/imp, 6" 175.00
Plate, lg crab at side, ink mk, 8½" 600.00
Plate, Lion Tapestry, stamped/imp, 8½" 1,200.00
Plate, Magnolia, Davenport rebus, stamped/imp, 6" 280.00
Plate, Magnolia, stamped, 6" 150.00
Plate, Magnolia, stamped/imp, 8½" 350.00
Plate, Moth, Davenport rebus, stamped, minor rim pitting, 8" ...800.00
Plate, Moth, gr tint, stamped/imp, 6" 550.00
Plate, Polar Bear, Davenport rebus, stamped/imp, 10" 750.00
Plate, Polar Bear, stamped registered/imp, 9¾" 750.00
Plate, Pond Lily, Davenport rebus, stamped/imp, 6" 290.00
Plate, Pond Lily, stamped, 10", EX 350.00
Plate, Pond Lily, stamped/imp, 7½" 225.00
Plate, Poppy Bud, stamped/imp, 8½" 650.00
Plate, Rabbit, stamped, 10" 240.00
Plate, Rabbit, stamped registered/imp, 8" 200.00
Plate, Rabbit, stamped/imp, 6" 150.00
Plate, Snow Tree, Davenport rebus, stamped/imp, 6" 300.00
Plate, Snow Tree, Davenport rebus, stamped/imp, 8¼" 350.00
Plate, Tiger Lily, stamped/imp, 8½" 950.00
Plate, Turkey, stamped, 8¼" 325.00
Plate, Turtle, stamped/imp, 6" 600.00
Plate, Wht Day Lily w/Lily Pod border, Davenport rebus, 8½" .1,400.00
Shakers, Rabbit, floral shoulder bands, 3", NM, pr 400.00
Soup plate, Rabbit, coupe style, stamped, 1½x7" 250.00
Soup plate, Rabbit, stamped registered/imp, 8½" 250.00
Stein, Rabbit, floral band, sgn/stamped, minor peppering, 5" 450.00
Tea stand, Rabbit, stamped, 7½" 400.00
Tile, elephants in circular band, stamped registered, 5¾" sq 600.00

Miscellaneous

Figurine, rabbit, cream crackle w/bl highlights, 2½x3½" 350.00
Pitcher, bubbly mc irid, experimental, rabbit mk, 8x7", NM ...1,300.00

Vase, blue painted florals on white crackle, stamped mark, rare, 6", $1,000.00.

Vase, brn/tan/dk bl/blk cratered drip glaze, shouldered, 8x6" ..1,200.00
Vase, floral on scroll stems, bl on crackle gloss, HR, 7x3" 1,400.00
Vase, gr/gray/teal drip on tan/brn, mk/sgn, 9x6" 750.00
Vase, sang-de-boeuf irid, HCR, 6x5" 920.00
Vase, sang-de-boeuf w/thick red mottle, 4½" 650.00
Vase, thick gr/bl-gray flambe, can neck, HCR, 7x4" 700.00
Vase, thick volcanic dk brn over khaki w/wht drips, 10x4¾" ..1,500.00

Degenhart

The Crystal Art Glass factory in Cambridge, Ohio, opened in 1947 under the private ownership of John and Elizabeth Degenhart. John had previously worked for the Cambridge Glass Company and was well known for his superior paperweights. After his death in 1964, Elizabeth took over management of the factory, hiring several workers from the defunct Cambridge Company, including Zack Boyd. Boyd was responsible for many unique colors, some of which were named for him. From 1964 to 1974, more than twenty-seven different moulds were created, most of them resulting from Elizabeth Degenhart's work and creativity, and over 145 official colors were developed. Elizabeth died in 1978, requesting that the ten moulds she had built while operating the factory were to be turned over to the Degenhart Museum. The remaining moulds were to be held by the Island Mould and Machine Company, who (complying with her request) removed the familiar 'D in heart' trademark. The factory was eventually bought by Zack's son, Bernard Boyd. He also acquired the remaining Degenhart moulds, to which he added his own logo.

In general, slags and opaques should be valued 15% to 20% higher than crystals in color.

Key: HS — hand stamped

Baby Shoe (Hobo) Toothpick, Dark Custard Slag 35.00
Baby Shoe (Hobo) Toothpick, Mint Green 12.00
Basket Toothpick, Amethyst 15.00
Basket Toothpick, Sparrow Slag 22.50
Beaded Oval Toothpick, Bittersweet Slag, 1976 ....45.00
Beaded Oval Toothpick, Maverick 45.00
Beaded Oval Toothpick, Rubena 65.00
Beaded Oval Toothpick, Toffee 25.00
Bicentennial Bell, Caramel Opal 25.00
Bicentennial Bell, Crown Tuscan 16.00
Bicentennial Bell, Pearl Gray 20.00
Bird Salt & Pepper Shakers, Bernard Boyd's Ebony, pr 60.00
Bird Salt & Pepper Shakers, Mint Green Opal Slag, rare, pr 95.00
Bird Salt & Pepper Shakers, Taffeta, pr 60.00
Bird Salt & Pepper Shakers, Teal, pr 32.50
Bird Salt w/Cherry, Blue & White Slag 30.00
Bird Salt w/Cherry, Blue Fire 25.00
Bird Salt w/Cherry, Concorde Grape 25.00
Bird Salt w/Cherry, Ivory 25.00
Bird Toothpick, Blue Green Marble 45.00
Bird Toothpick, Ruby 30.00
Bow Slipper, Blue Jay Slag 27.50
Bow Slipper, Custard w/Slag, Dark 45.00
Bow Slipper, End of Blizzard 22.50
Bow Slipper, Gold 17.50
Bow Slipper, Pigeon Blood 27.50
Bow Slipper, Willow Green 25.00
Bow Slipper, Wondor Blue 25.00
Buzz Saw Wine, Carnival (Pink) 45.00
Buzz Saw Wine, Desert Sun 40.00
Chick Salt, 2", Aqua 32.50
Chick Salt, 2", Cambridge Pink 20.00
Chick Salt, 2", Honey Amber 25.00
Chick Salt, 2", Lemon Custard 60.00
Colonial Drape Toothpick, Aqua 22.50
Colonial Drape Toothpick, Custard 27.50
Colonial Drape Toothpick, Taffeta 30.00
Daisy & Button Creamer & Sugar Bowl, Cobalt Carnival, HS ..125.00
Daisy & Button Salt, Delft Blue 15.00
Daisy & Button Salt, Sunset 15.00

Daisy & Button Toothpick, Baby Blue Slag 27.50
Daisy & Button Toothpick, Forest Green 15.00
Daisy & Button Toothpick, Pink 15.00
Elephant Head Toothpick, Gray Slag 45.00
Elephant Head Toothpick, Honey Amber 27.50
Elephant Head Toothpick, Milk Blue 40.00
Forget-Me-Not Toothpick, Amethyst w/White 45.00
Forget-Me-Not Toothpick, Baby Pink Slag 30.00
Forget-Me-Not Toothpick, Charcoal 20.00
Forget-Me-Not Toothpick, Cobalt 25.00
Forget-Me-Not Toothpick, Honey 16.00
Forget-Me-Not Toothpick, Misty Green 22.50
Gypsy Pot Toothpick, Apple Green 25.00
Gypsy Pot Toothpick, Bloody Mary 50.00
Hand, Amberina 14.00
Hand, Brown 6.00
Hand, Gray Slag 25.00
Hand, Sapphire 7.00
Heart & Lyre Cup Plate, Apple Green 13.50
Heart Jewel Box, Antique Blue 30.00

Heart Jewel Box, Bittersweet, $50.00.

Heart Jewel Box, Fawn 22.50
Heart Toothpick, Blue Jay Slag 35.00
Heart Toothpick, Frosted Milk Blue, unsigned, rare 30.00
Heart Toothpick, Sea Foam 22.50
Hen Covered Dish, 3", Baby Green 30.00
Hen Covered Dish, 3", Light Caramel, unsigned 55.00
Hen Covered Dish, 3", Willow Green 25.00
Hen Covered Dish, 5", Cobalt 60.00
Hen Covered Dish, 5", Milk Blue 65.00
Hen Covered Dish, 5", Opalescent 65.00
High Boots, Crystal Frosted 16.00
High Boots, Emerald Green 25.00
High Boots, Milk White 30.00
Kat Slipper, Blue & Brown Slag 60.00
Kat Slipper, Tiger 40.00
Lamb Covered Dish, 5", Bernard Boyd's Ebony 125.00

Lamb Covered Dish, Crown Tuscan, 5", $80.00.

Lamb Covered Dish, 5", Pine Green 65.00
Mini Pitcher, Chocolate Slag 22.50
Mini Pitcher, Nile Green 21.00
Mini Slipper w/o Sole, Rose Marie 16.00
Mini Slipper w/Sole, Champagne 35.00
Mini Slipper w/Sole, Vaseline 35.00
Owl, Antique Blue 40.00
Owl, April Day 40.00
Owl, Blue Jay 50.00
Owl, Buttercup 50.00
Owl, Caramel, dark 125.00
Owl, Daffodil 40.00
Owl, Ebony Slag 125.00
Owl, Jim Dandy 175.00
Owl, Pea Green Jade 150.00
Owl, Spice Brown 50.00
Pooch, Blue Marble Slag 40.00
Pooch, Fantastic 45.00
Pooch, Ivory Opal 40.00
Pooch, Orchid 25.00
Pottie Salt, Chocolate Creme Slag 17.50
Pottie Salt, Nile Green 16.00
Priscilla Doll, Amber 90.00
Priscilla Doll, Blue Lady 125.00
Priscilla Doll, Powder Blue 125.00
Robin Covered Dish, 5", Milk Blue 65.00
Robin Covered Dish, 5", Tomato 125.00
Roller Skate (Skate Shoe), Crown Tuscan 60.00
Roller Skate (Skate Shoe), Dark Sapphire 35.00
Seal of Ohio Cup Plate, Heliotrope 25.00
Star & Dewdrop Salt, Amberina 25.00
Star & Dewdrop Salt, Elizabeth's Lime Ice 25.00
Star & Dewdrop Salt, Forest Green 15.00
Star & Dewdrop Salt, Ivory 25.00
Stork & Peacock Child's Mug, Blue Green 25.00
Stork & Peacock Child's Mug, Light Caramel, unsigned 45.00
Texas Boot, Baby Green 22.00
Texas Boot, Milk White 16.00
Texas Boot, Peach (clear) 15.00
Turkey Covered Dish, 5", Peach Blo 50.00
Turkey Covered Dish, 5", Unique Blue 100.00
Wildflower Candle Holder, Ruby 60.00
Wildflower Candy Dish, Bloody Mary 80.00
Wildflower Candy Dish, Persimmon 45.00

Delatte

Delatte was a manufacturer of French cameo glass. Founded in 1921, their style reflected the influence of the Art Deco era with strong color contrasts and bold design. Our advisor for this category is Don Williams; he is listed in the Directory under Missouri.

Cameo

Lamp, sea gulls on shade, ships on std, seaweed base, 18" 3,450.00
Vase, morning glories, brn on gray/yel, spherical, 7¾" 600.00
Vase, river landscape, maroon/rose on wht, hdls, 9" 1,300.00
Vase, Venetian cityscape, rose on pk/wht, frost hdls, 6x7" 1,250.00

Delft

Old Delftware, made as early as the 16th century, was originally a low-fired earthenware coated in a thin opaque tin glaze with painted-on blue or polychrome designs. It was not until the last half of the 19th century, however, that the ware became commonly referred to as Delft, acquiring the name from the Dutch village that had become the major center of its production. English, German, and French potters also produced Delft, though with noticeable differences both in shape and decorative theme.

In the early part of the 18th century, the German potter, Bottger, developed a formula for porcelain; in England, Wedgwood began producing creamware — both of which were much more durable. Unable to compete, one by one the Delft potteries failed. Soon only one remained. In 1876 De Porcelyne Fles reintroduced Delftware on a hard white body with blue and white decorative themes reflecting the Dutch countryside, windmills by the sea, and Dutch children. This manufacturer is the most well known of several operating today. Their products are now produced under the Royal Delft label. Examples listed here are blue on white unless noted otherwise. See also specific manufacturers.

Vase, river landscape with Oriental figures fishing from terrace, scrolling motifs, floral lappet border, octagonal shape, lambrequin-bordered baluster finial (restored), ca 1700, 20½", $5,400.00.

Bottle, Liverpool, floral, ca 1760, 10¼" 450.00
Bowl, Bristol, Oriental decor, scalloped, 11¾" 550.00
Bowl, Dutch, floral w/leafy border, ca 1750, 11¾" 350.00
Bowl, Irish, florals, berry border, shallow, 1760, 11" 250.00
Bowl, Lambeth, floral & fence, ca 1760, 6¾", VG 125.00
Charger, Dutch, allover florals, sgn MQ, 18th C, 14", EX 500.00
Charger, Dutch, dragon & branches, 1700s, 13¾", EX 600.00
Charger, Dutch, floral, shaped rim, 18th C, chips, 14" 525.00
Charger, Dutch, floral landscape, ca 1760, 13½", EX 400.00
Charger, Dutch, landscape, floral border, 1750s, 13", EX 350.00
Charger, Dutch, Oriental landscape, manganese, 1750s, 13", EX ..450.00
Charger, England, Oriental scene, 1740s, 13", EX 350.00
Charger, Lambeth, floral, ca 1750, 13⅛", EX 400.00
Charger, Liverpool, Oriental coastal scene, 1750s, 13½", EX 250.00
Deep dish, Dutch, berries & flowers, ca 1770, 12¼" 450.00
Deep dish, Dutch, Wm of Orange portrait, mc, 1690s, 12" 1,200.00
Flower arranger, English, floral, 7" 550.00
Flower brick, English, floral panels, ca 1750, 5", EX 800.00
Ink stand, Bristol, Oriental decor, rpr, 6" 560.00
Jar, English, landscape w/flowers, bl & wht, 6½" 250.00
Lobed dish, Dutch, Oriental landscape, 18th C, 13¾", EX 300.00
Lobed dish, Dutch, Oriental landscape, 18th C, 14", NM 900.00
Novelty, clock, crest/landscape/figures, 12¼" 210.00
Plaque, flow bl w/Dutch lady's portrait, 16¼" dia 395.00
Plate, Bristol, floral, bl w/red & gr enamel & gold, 9" dia 195.00
Plate, Dutch, crown/monogram/Xd branches, 1740, 8⅝", EX ...300.00
Plate, Dutch, Oriental landscape, mc, 1750s, 8¾", pr 550.00

Plate, Dutch, verse, floral border, ca 1760, 9", EX 350.00
Plate, English, floral, 9", EX 140.00
Plate, English, landscape, 8⅞" 935.00
Plate, English, Oriental decor, bl & red w/gold, 9⅛" 225.00
Plate, English, Oriental landscape, bl/yel/purple, 8½" 440.00
Plate, Lambeth, house in landscape, bl & purple, 8½" 275.00
Posset pot, Dutch, bird & flowers, chips, 18th C 140.00
Tankard, Continental, dog & houses, pewter lid, 4¾", EX 250.00
Vase, Lambeth, floral, bottle form, 1740s, 10", EX 900.00

Denver

The Denver China and Pottery Company began production in 1901 in Denver, Colorado. The founder, William A. Long, used materials native to Colorado to produce underglaze-decorated brownware as well as other artware lines. Several marks were used: an impressed 'Denver' (often with the Lonhuda Faience cipher inside a shield), an imprinted 'Denaura,' and an arrow mark.

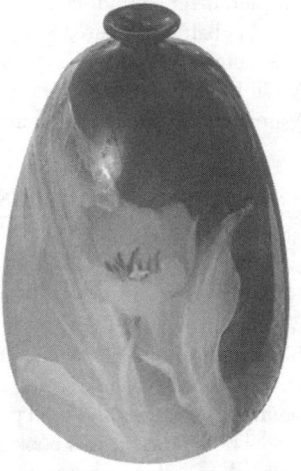

Vase, tulip, signed Wm Long, Lonhuda mark, 9½", $600.00.

Cigar ashtray, blk gargoyle, EX 75.00
Planter, frog, gr, terra cotta 175.00
Vase, cvd lines at shoulder, bl satin w/dk bl int, 4½x3" 150.00
Vase, long-stem poppies on gr matt, mushroom shape, 6x5" ...1,400.00
Vase, nasturtiums on gr matt, Denaura, mushroom form, 6" 1,200.00

Denver White

In 1894 Frederick and Frank White settled in Denver, Colorado, and formed the F.J. White & Son pottery company. They located at 1434 Logan Street. After the death of Frederick in 1919, Frank moved the pottery to 1560 South Logan, where he remained until the company closed. He had a kiln set up at home and worked each day on the pottery, often selling his products in his front yard. On many occasions he was commissioned to produce specialty items for customers.

Each piece is hand thrown and many are dated. They are usually incised with the name Denver and the letter 'W' inside the capital 'D.' Many items are decorated with Colorado scenery. Though most pieces are matt glazed with a glossy interior, some later examples were completely glossy. The Whites would also add a small band to some of the ware, similar to what you see on Wedgwood pottery today. They created a line with swirled colors as well. On March 6, 1960, Frank White died at the age of 91.

Our advisors for this category are Jim and Carol Carlton, authors of *Collector's Encyclopedia of Colorado Pottery*; they are listed in the Directory under Colorado.

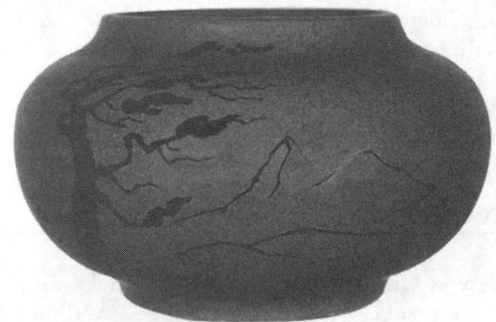

Bowl, dark red tree and mountain scene on rose red, 6x10", minimum value $200.00.

Jar, bl bsk w/wht geometric band, mk Denver, w/lid, 5½" 225.00
Pitcher, dk gr, cylindrical, 7" 95.00
Vase, cobalt, shouldered form w/hdls, 10" 125.00
Vase, emb rim band, cream w/aqua int, 4" 30.00
Vase, linear band imp at shoulder, bl w/lav int, 5" 140.00
Vase, wht decor band on bl matt, 4¼x3¼" 85.00

Depression Glass

Depression glass is defined by Gene Florence, author of several bestselling books on the subject, as 'the inexpensive glassware made primarily during the Depression era in the colors of amber, green, pink, blue, red, yellow, white, and crystal.' This glass was mass produced, sold through five-and-dime stores and mail-order catalogs, and given away as premiums with gas and food products.

The listings in this book are far from being complete. If you want a more thorough presentation of this fascinating glassware, we recommend *The Collector's Encyclopedia of Depression Glass*, *The Pocket Guide to Depression Glass*, *Elegant Glassware of the Depression Era*, and *Very Rare Glassware of the Depression Years* by Gene Florence, whose address is listed in the Directory under Kentucky.

Key:
AOP — allover pattern   PAT — pattern at top

Adam, gr, bowl, no lid, 9" 38.00
Adam, gr, butter dish, w/lid 310.00
Adam, gr, pitcher, 32-oz, 8" 42.50
Adam, gr, plate, dinner; sq, 9" 28.00
Adam, gr, tumbler, iced tea; 5½" 50.00
Adam, pk, bowl, cereal; 5¾" 37.50
Adam, pk, plate, cake; ftd, 10" 25.00
Adam, pk, plate, sherbet; 6" 7.50
Adam, pk, sugar bowl 16.00
American Pioneer, crystal or pk, bowl, hdld, 5" 20.00
American Pioneer, crystal or pk, goblet, cocktail; 3-oz, 3¾" 40.00
American Pioneer, crystal or pk, lamp, ball shape, rnd, 5½" 75.00
American Pioneer, crystal or pk, saucer 5.00
American Pioneer, crystal or pk, sugar bowl, 2¾" 20.00
American Pioneer, gr, bowl, w/lid, 9¼" 125.00
American Pioneer, gr, cheese & cracker set 57.50
American Pioneer, gr, goblet, water; 8-oz, 6" 42.00
American Pioneer, gr, mayonnaise, 4¼" 90.00

American Pioneer, gr, sherbet, 3½" 19.00
American Sweetheart, bl, creamer, ftd 115.00
American Sweetheart, bl, sugar bowl, ftd, open 115.00
American Sweetheart, cremax, bowl, cereal; 6" 8.00
American Sweetheart, monax, saucer 3.00
American Sweetheart, monax, sugar bowl lid only 300.00
American Sweetheart, pk, bowl, cream soup; 4½" 75.00
American Sweetheart, pk, platter, oval, 13" 45.00
American Sweetheart, pk, tumbler, 9-oz, 4¼" 75.00
American Sweetheart, red, tidbit, 8", 12" & 15½" tiers 575.00
American Sweetheart, smoke & other trims, plate, salad; 6" 25.00
Aunt Polly, bl, bowl, 1-hdl, 5½" 20.00
Aunt Polly, bl, plate, luncheon; 8" 18.00
Aunt Polly, bl, vase, ftd, 6½" 45.00
Aunt Polly, gr or irid, bowl, berry; 4¾" 8.00
Aunt Polly, gr or irid, creamer 26.00
Aunt Polly, gr or irid, sugar bowl 23.00
Aurora, bl or pk, bowl, cereal; 5⅜" 15.00
Aurora, bl or pk, tumbler, 10-oz, 4¾" 19.00
Avocado, crystal, bowl, relish; ftd, 6" 9.00
Avocado, gr, creamer, ftd 35.00
Avocado, pk, bowl, 3¼x9½" 100.00
Avocado, pk, plate, luncheon; 8¼" 17.00
Beaded Block, gr, bowl, lily; rnd, 4½" 9.50
Beaded Block, irid, bowl, pickle; hdls, 6½" 19.00
Beaded Block, pk, bowl, rnd, flared, 7¼" 11.50
Beaded Block, pk, bowl, rnd, 6¼" 8.00
Beaded Block, red, bowl, hdl, 5½" 12.00
Beaded Block, red, vase, bouquet; 6" 24.00
Beaded Block, vaseline, bowl, rnd, plain edge, 7½" 23.00
Block Optic, gr, bowl, 4¼" 7.50
Block Optic, gr, butter dish lid only 20.00
Block Optic, gr, goblet, cocktail; 4" 32.00
Block Optic, gr, saucer, w/cup ring, 5¾" 10.00
Block Optic, gr, tumbler, flat, 12-oz, 4⅞" 24.00
Block Optic, gr, tumbler, flat, 9½-oz, 3¼" 14.00
Block Optic, pk, bowl, cereal; 5¼" 22.50
Block Optic, pk, candy jar, w/lid, 2¼" 45.00
Block Optic, pk, ice tub, open 90.00
Block Optic, pk, tumbler, flat, 15-oz, 5¼" 30.00
Block Optic, pk, tumbler, 3-oz, 2⅝" 21.00
Block Optic, pk or gr, tumbler, ftd, 10-oz, 6" 24.00
Block Optic, yel, goblet, thin, 9-oz, 7¼" 32.00
Block Optic, yel, sherbet, 5½-oz, 3¼" 9.00
Block Optic, yel or gr, creamer, 3 styles, ea 13.00
Block Optic, yel or pk, shakers, ftd, pr 70.00
Bowknot, gr, bowl, berry; 4½" 14.00
Bowknot, gr, sherbet, low ftd 14.00
Bowknot, gr, tumbler, ftd, 10-oz, 5" 20.00
Cameo, crystal, decanter, w/stopper, 10" 195.00
Cameo, gr, bowl, cream soup; 4¾" 29.00
Cameo, gr, comport, mayonnaise; 5" wide 27.00
Cameo, gr, jam jar, w/lid, 2" 160.00
Cameo, gr, plate, cake; 3-legged, 10" 19.00
Cameo, gr, tumbler, juice; 5-oz, 3¾" 26.00
Cameo, gr or yel, plate, sherbet; 6" 4.00
Cameo, gr or yel, plate, w/closed hdls, 10½" 11.00
Cameo, pk, bowl, berry; lg, 8¼" 150.00
Cameo, pk, candy jar, w/lid, low, 4" 475.00
Cameo, pk, creamer, 4¼" 110.00
Cameo, pk, plate, luncheon; 8" 30.00
Cameo, pk, sherbet, blown, 3⅛" 75.00
Cameo, pk, tumbler, juice; ftd, 3-oz 125.00
Cameo, yel, bowl, vegetable; oval, 10" 38.00

Cameo, yel, plate, grill; 10½" 6.00
Cherry Blossom, any color, saucer 6.00
Cherry Blossom, delphite, bowl, hdls, 9" 23.00
Cherry Blossom, delphite, plate, dinner; 9" 18.00
Cherry Blossom, gr, coaster 12.00
Cherry Blossom, gr, plate, grill; 10" 85.00
Cherry Blossom, gr, tumbler, rnd ft, AOP, 9-oz, 4½" 18.00
Cherry Blossom, pk, bowl, cereal; 5¾" 35.00
Cherry Blossom, pk, platter, oval, 11" 35.00
Cherry Blossom, pk, sugar bowl lid only 15.00
Cherry Blossom, pk or delphite, bowl, berry; 4¾" ...14.00
Cherry Blossom, pk or delphite, cup 16.00
Cherry Blossom, pk or gr, bowl, fruit; 3-legged, 10½" 80.00
Cherry Blossom, pk or gr, creamer 17.00
Cherry Blossom, pk or gr, pitcher, flat, PAT, 42-oz, 8" 50.00
Cherry Blossom, pk or gr, plate, sherbet; 6" 7.00
Cherryberry, crystal, bowl, berry; 4" 6.50
Cherryberry, irid, plate, sherbet; 6" 6.00
Cherryberry, pk or gr, bowl, salad; deep, 6½" 20.00
Cherryberry, pk or gr, creamer, lg, 4⅝" 35.00
Chinex Classic, castle decal, bowl, vegetable; 9" 32.50
Chinex Classic, castle decal, creamer 18.00
Chinex Classic, floral decal, bowl, soup; 7¾" 17.50
Chinex Classic, floral decal, sherbet, low ftd 11.00
Chinex Classic, ivory, bowl, cereal; 5¾" 5.50
Chinex Classic, ivory, butter dish, w/lid 55.00
Chinex Classic, ivory, plate, sherbet; 6¼" 2.50
Chinex Classic, ivory, sugar bowl, open 5.50
Circle, gr or pk, bowl, 4½" 8.00
Circle, gr or pk, bowl, 8" 15.00
Circle, gr or pk, decanter, hdld 45.00
Circle, gr or pk, pitcher, 80-oz 27.50
Circle, gr or pk, plate, luncheon; 8¼" 4.00
Circle, gr or pk, sherbet, 3⅛" 4.00
Circle, gr or pk, tumbler, water; 4-oz, 3½" 9.00
Cloverleaf, blk, ashtray, w/match holder in center, 4" 67.50
Cloverleaf, blk, cup 18.00
Cloverleaf, gr, bowl, dessert; 4" 18.00
Cloverleaf, gr, creamer, ftd, 3⅝" 10.00
Cloverleaf, gr, sugar bowl, ftd, 3⅝" 10.00
Cloverleaf, pk, sherbet, ftd, 3" 6.00
Cloverleaf, pk, tumbler, flat, flared, 10-oz, 3¾" 19.00
Cloverleaf, yel, plate, grill; 10¼" 20.00
Cloverleaf, yel, plate, sherbet; 6" 7.00
Colonial, crystal, bowl, soup; low, 7" 22.00
Colonial, crystal, goblet, cordial; 1-oz, 3¾" 18.00
Colonial, crystal, pitcher, 54-oz, 7" 28.00
Colonial, crystal, platter, oval, 12" 15.00
Colonial, crystal, tumbler, 11-oz, 5⅛" 20.00

Colonial, goblets, all in green: Water, $28.00; Claret, $25.00; Cordial, $27.00; Cocktail, $25.00.

Colonial, gr, butter dish, w/lid 55.00
Colonial, gr, goblet, wine; 2½-oz, 4½" 25.00

Colonial, gr, pitcher, milk/cream; 16-oz, 5" 20.00
Colonial, gr, sherbet, 3⅜" 14.00
Colonial, gr, tumbler, lemonade; 15-oz 75.00
Colonial, pk, bowl, berry; 3¾" 42.50
Colonial, pk, butter dish, w/lid 600.00
Colonial, pk, tumbler, iced tea; 12-oz 42.00
Colonial, pk or gr, shakers, pr 130.00
Colonial Block, pk or gr, bowl, 7" 16.00
Colonial Block, pk or gr, butter dish, w/lid 45.00
Colonial Block, pk or gr, butter tub 37.50
Colonial Block, wht, creamer 7.00
Colonial Block, wht, sugar bowl 5.50
Colonial Fluted, gr, bowl, salad; deep, 6½" 18.00
Colonial Fluted, gr, cup 5.00
Colonial Fluted, gr, plate, luncheon; 8" 5.00
Colonial Fluted, gr, sugar bowl 5.00
Columbia, crystal, bowl, cereal; 5" 15.00
Columbia, crystal, bowl, salad; 8½" 17.00
Columbia, crystal, butter dish, w/lid 20.00
Columbia, crystal, tumbler, juice; 4-oz, 2⅞" 17.50
Columbia, pk, cup 18.00
Columbia, pk, plate, luncheon; 9½" 27.50
Coronation, gr, bowl, no hdls, 8" 150.00
Coronation, gr, sherbet 65.00
Coronation, pk, bowl, berry; 4¼" 4.50
Coronation, pk, plate, sherbet; 6" 2.00
Coronation, royal ruby, bowl, berry; hdl, lg, 8" 15.00
Coronation, royal ruby, plate, luncheon; 8½" 8.00
Cremax, decal decor, cup 5.00
Crow's Foot, amber, bowl, console; rnd, 3-ftd, 11½" 42.50
Crow's Foot, amber, sandwich server, rnd, center hdl 32.50
Crow's Foot, bl or blk, bowl, ftd, 10" 75.00
Crow's Foot, bl or blk, candle, mushroom shape, sq 42.50
Crow's Foot, bl or blk, platter, 12" 32.50
Crow's Foot, pk, plate, dinner; rnd, sm, 9¼" 15.00
Crow's Foot, pk, vase, flared, 11¾" 65.00
Crow's Foot, red, bowl, sq, 4⅞" 25.00
Crow's Foot, red, gravy boat, flat 85.00
Crow's Foot, red, sugar bowl, flat 11.00
Cube, gr, bowl, salad; 6½" 14.00
Cube, gr, candy jar, w/lid, 6½" 30.00
Cube, gr, cup 9.00
Cube, gr, tumbler, 9-oz, 4" 65.00
Cube, pk, bowl, dessert; 4½" 6.50
Cube, pk, creamer, 2⅝" 2.00
Cube, pk or gr, butter dish, w/lid 60.00
Cube, pk or gr, powder jar, w/lid, 3-legged 23.00
Cube, pk or gr, saucer 3.00
Cupid, pk or gr, bowl, rolled edge, 10½" 135.00
Cupid, pk or gr, comport, 6¼" 75.00
Cupid, pk or gr, creamer, ftd, 5" 90.00
Cupid, pk or gr, plate, cake; ftd, 2" 150.00
Cupid, pk or gr, plate, 10½" 100.00
Cupid, pk or gr, sugar bowl, ftd, 4¼" or 5", ea 90.00
Diamond Quilted, bl or blk, candlesticks, 2 styles, pr 47.50
Diamond Quilted, bl or blk, creamer 16.50
Diamond Quilted, bl or blk, ice bucket 83.00
Diamond Quilted, bl or blk, sandwich server, center hdl 50.00
Diamond Quilted, pk or gr, bowl, console; rolled edge, 10½" 18.00
Diamond Quilted, pk or gr, bowl, cream soup; 4¾" 8.00
Diamond Quilted, pk or gr, goblet, wine; 2-oz 11.00
Diamond Quilted, pk or gr, pitcher, 64-oz 47.50
Diamond Quilted, pk or gr, plate, luncheon; 8" 6.00
Diamond Quilted, pk or gr, tumbler, ftd, 6-oz 8.50

Diamond Quilted, pk or gr, tumbler, water; 9-oz 9.00
Diamond Quilted, pk or gr, whiskey, 1½-oz 8.00
Diana, amber, coaster, 3½" 10.00
Diana, amber, plate, bread & butter; 6" 2.00
Diana, amber, shakers, pr 100.00
Diana, crystal, bowl, scalloped edge, 12" 7.00
Diana, crystal, cup 3.00
Diana, pk, bowl, cream soup; 5½" 20.00
Diana, pk, cup (2-oz) & saucer (4½") set, demitasse 45.00
Diana, pk, platter, oval, 12" 25.00
Diana, pk, sherbet 11.00
Dogwood, gr, creamer, thin, flat, 2½" 42.00
Dogwood, gr, pitcher, decor, 80-oz, 8" 495.00
Dogwood, gr, sugar bowl, thin, flat, 2½" 42.00
Dogwood, pk, cup, thick 16.00
Dogwood, pk, plate, bread & butter; 6" 8.00
Dogwood, pk, plate, cake; solid ft, heavy, 13" 100.00
Dogwood, pk, plate, dinner; 9¼" 35.00
Dogwood, pk, tumbler, molded band 20.00
Dogwood, pk or gr, bowl, cereal; 5½" 30.00
Dogwood, pk or gr, plate, grill; AOP, 10½" 19.00
Doric, delphite, bowl, berry; lg, 8¼" 125.00
Doric, gr, bowl, cereal; 5½" 65.00
Doric, gr, butter dish, w/lid 85.00
Doric, gr, sugar bowl 12.00
Doric, gr, tumbler, 9-oz, 4½" 95.00
Doric, pk, butter dish, w/lid 65.00
Doric, pk, cup 8.00
Doric, pk, plate, grill; 9" 12.50
Doric, pk, shakers, pr 32.50
Doric, pk, tray, hdld, 10" 12.50
Doric, pk or gr, plate, cake; 3-legged, 10" 21.00

Doric and Pansy, dinner plate, teal, 9", $30.00.

Doric & Pansy, gr or teal, bowl, berry; 4½" 15.00
Doric & Pansy, gr or teal, butter dish, w/lid 495.00
Doric & Pansy, gr or teal, plate, sherbet; 6" 10.00
Doric & Pansy, gr or teal, tray, hdld, 10" 22.50
Doric & Pansy, pk or crystal, bowl, hdld, 9" 14.00
Doric & Pansy, pk or crystal, plate, dinner; 9" 7.50
English Hobnail, ice bl, ashtray, 4½" 21.00
English Hobnail, ice bl, bottle, toilet; 5-oz 45.00
English Hobnail, ice bl, bowl, finger; ftd, sq, 4½" 35.00
English Hobnail, ice bl, bowl, hdls, hexagonal ftd, 8" 110.00
English Hobnail, ice bl, creamer, ftd, hexagonal 45.00
English Hobnail, ice bl, puff box, w/lid, rnd, 6" 77.50
English Hobnail, ice bl, stem, sherbet; rnd, low ftd 12.00
English Hobnail, pk or gr, ashtray, 3" 20.00
English Hobnail, pk or gr, bowl, celery; 9" 30.00

English Hobnail, pk or gr, bowl, grapefruit; 6½" 18.00
English Hobnail, pk or gr, bowl, nappy; rnd, 7" 20.00
English Hobnail, pk or gr, candlestick, rnd base, 9" 32.50
English Hobnail, pk or gr, compote, honey; rnd ftd, 6" 30.00
English Hobnail, pk or gr, pitcher, rnd, 23-oz 145.00
English Hobnail, pk or gr, plate, rnd, 5½" 9.50
English Hobnail, pk or gr, stem, cocktail; rnd ftd, 3-oz 20.00
English Hobnail, pk or gr, tumbler, water; 8-oz 22.00
Floral, delphite, bowl, salad; 7½" 60.00
Floral, delphite, tumbler, water; ftd, 7-oz, 4¾" 185.00
Floral, gr, butter dish, w/lid 85.00
Floral, gr, lamp 265.00
Floral, gr, plate, grill; 9" 175.00
Floral, gr, tray, for dresser set, oval, 9¼" 185.00
Floral, pk, candy dish/sugar bowl lid only 15.00
Floral, pk, plate, sherbet; 6" 6.00
Floral, pk, relish dish, oval, 2-part 15.00
Floral & Diamond Band, gr, bowl, berry; lg, 8" 13.50
Floral & Diamond Band, gr, creamer, sm 11.00
Floral & Diamond Band, gr, tumbler, iced tea; 5" 35.00
Floral & Diamond Band, pk, butter dish, w/lid 130.00
Floral & Diamond Band, pk, plate, luncheon; 8" 40.00
Floral & Diamond Band, pk, sugar bowl lid only 47.50
Florentine No 1, cobalt, cup 85.00
Florentine No 1, cobalt, sugar bowl, ruffled 55.00
Florentine No 1, crystal or gr, ashtray, 5½" 22.00
Florentine No 1, crystal or gr, creamer 9.50
Florentine No 1, crystal or gr, pitcher, ftd, 36-oz, 6½" 40.00

Florentine No. 1, all green: Butter dish, $125.00; Tumbler, 4¾", $22.00; Sherbet, $10.00.

Florentine No 1, gr, comport, ruffled, 3½" 22.00
Florentine No 1, pk, bowl, berry; 5" 12.00
Florentine No 1, pk, platter, oval, 11½" 19.00
Florentine No 1, yel, bowl, cereal; 6" 22.00
Florentine No 1, yel, tumbler, iced tea; 12-oz, 5¼" 29.00
Florentine No 2, amber, cup 50.00
Florentine No 2, amber, saucer 15.00
Florentine No 2, crystal, butter dish, w/lid 100.00
Florentine No 2, crystal or gr, bowl, berry; lg, 8" 20.00
Florentine No 2, crystal or gr, bowl, berry; 4½" 11.00
Florentine No 2, crystal or gr, plate, salad; 8½" 8.50
Florentine No 2, crystal or gr, vase, 6" 29.00
Florentine No 2, pk, bowl, cream soup; 4¾" 15.00
Florentine No 2, pk, candy dish, w/lid 120.00
Florentine No 2, pk, plate, dinner; 10" 15.00
Florentine No 2, pk, relish dish, 3-part or plain, 10" 24.00
Florentine No 2, pk, tumbler, ftd, 5-oz, 3¼" 15.00
Florentine No 2, yel, bowl, vegetable; w/lid, oval, 9" 65.00
Florentine No 2, yel, bowl, 5½" 37.50
Florentine No 2, yel, platter, oval, 11" 18.00

Florentine No 2, yel, tumbler, iced tea; 12-oz, 5" 42.00
Flower Garden w/Butterflies, amber, candlesticks, 4", pr 42.50
Flower Garden w/Butterflies, amber or crystal, plate, 7" 16.00
Flower Garden w/Butterflies, blk, candlesticks, 8", pr 275.00
Flower Garden w/Butterflies, blk, comport, ftd, 7" 175.00
Flower Garden w/Butterflies, pk or gr, cup 60.00
Flower Garden w/Butterflies, pk or gr, sugar bowl 65.00
Fortune, pk or crystal, bowl, berry; 4" 3.50
Fortune, pk or crystal, candy dish, w/lid, flat 22.50
Fortune, pk or crystal, plate, sherbet; 6" 3.00
Fortune, pk or crystal, tumbler, juice; 5-oz, 3½" 7.00
Fruits, gr, plate, luncheon; 8" 6.50
Fruits, gr, sherbet 8.00
Fruits, pk, tumbler, juice; 3½" 17.50
Georgian, gr, bowl, deep, 6½" 62.50
Georgian, gr, bowl, vegetable; oval, 9" 60.00
Georgian, gr, butter dish, w/lid 70.00
Georgian, gr, creamer, ftd, 3" 11.00
Georgian, gr, lid for 3" sugar bowl 35.00
Georgian, gr, plate, sherbet; 6" 6.00
Georgian, gr, sugar bowl, ftd, 3" 9.50
Georgian, gr, tumbler, flat, 12-oz, 5¼" 110.00
Hex Optic, pk or gr, bowl, berry; ruffled, 4¼" 5.50
Hex Optic, pk or gr, bowl, mixing; 8¼" 17.50
Hex Optic, pk or gr, pitcher, ftd, 48-oz, 9" 45.00
Hex Optic, pk or gr, plate, luncheon; 8" 5.50
Hex Optic, pk or gr, refrigerator stack set, 3-pc 47.50
Hex Optic, pk or gr, tumbler, ftd, 5¾" 10.00
Hobnail, crystal, goblet, iced tea; 13-oz 7.50
Hobnail, crystal, tumbler, cordial; ftd, 5-oz 5.50
Hobnail, crystal, tumbler, iced tea; 15-oz 7.00
Hobnail, pk, cup 4.50
Hobnail, pk, plate, luncheon; 8½" 3.50
Hobnail, pk, sherbet 3.50
Homespun, pk or crystal, bowl, closed hdls, 4½" 10.00
Homespun, pk or crystal, creamer, ftd 10.00
Homespun, pk or crystal, plate, dinner; 9¼" 15.00
Homespun, pk or crystal, saucer 4.00
Homespun, pk or crystal, tumbler, ftd, 15-oz, 6¼" 24.00
Homespun, pk or crystal, tumbler, iced tea; 13-oz, 5¼" 27.50
Indiana Custard, bowl, berry; 5½" 8.00
Indiana Custard, bowl, soup; flat, 7½" 29.00
Indiana Custard, cup 37.50
Indiana Custard, plate, bread & butter; 5¾" 6.50
Indiana Custard, plate, dinner; 9¾" 25.00
Indiana Custard, plate, salad; 7½" 15.00

Iris and Herringbone, pitcher, 9½", $37.50.

Iris, crystal, bowl, berry; beaded edge, 4½" 38.00
Iris, crystal, bowl, fruit; str edge, 11" 55.00
Iris, crystal, candlesticks, pr 40.00
Iris, crystal, goblet, cocktail; 4-oz, 4½" 24.00
Iris, crystal, plate, dinner; 9" 50.00
Iris, crystal, sherbet, ftd, 4" 20.00
Iris, crystal, tumbler, flat, 4" 130.00
Iris, gr or pk, sugar bowl 110.00
Iris, irid, bowl, soup; 7½" 55.00
Iris, irid, creamer, ftd 12.00
Iris, irid, goblet, wine; 4" 30.00
Iris, irid, goblet, 8-oz, 5½" 165.00
Iris, irid, saucer 11.00
Jubilee, pk, plate, salad; 7" 22.50
Jubilee, pk, sugar bowl 35.00
Jubilee, yel, bowl, fruit; hdld, 9" 125.00
Jubilee, yel, candlesticks, pr 185.00
Jubilee, yel, saucer, 2 styles 8.00
Jubilee, yel, tumbler, juice; ftd, 6-oz, 5" 85.00
Lace Edge, pk, bowl, cereal; 6⅜" 17.50
Lace Edge, pk, bowl, plain or ribbed, 9½" 18.00
Lace Edge, pk, butter dish, w/lid 60.00
Lace Edge, pk, candlesticks, pr 180.00
Lace Edge, pk, comport, w/lid, ftd, 7" 45.00
Lace Edge, pk, plate, dinner; 10½" 25.00
Lace Edge, pk, plate, salad; 8¼" 20.00
Lace Edge, pk, plate, 4-part, solid lace, 13" 28.00
Lace Edge, pk, sherbet, ftd 77.50
Lace Edge, pk, tumbler, flat, 9-oz, 4½" 16.00
Laced Edge, opal, bowl, fruit; 4⅜"-4¾", ea 27.00
Laced Edge, opal, bowl, vegetable; 9" 85.00
Laced Edge, opal, bowl, 5½" 35.00
Laced Edge, opal, plate, bread & butter; 6½" 18.00
Laced Edge, opal, plate, dinner; 10" 80.00
Laced Edge, opal, platter, 13" 155.00
Lake Como, wht, bowl, cereal; 6" 22.00
Lake Como, wht, bowl, soup; flat 90.00
Lake Como, wht, cup, St Denis 25.00
Lake Como, wht, saucer 11.00
Laurel, bl, bowl, vegetable; oval, 9¾" 45.00
Laurel, bl, plate, salad; 7½" 14.00
Laurel, gr, bowl, berry; 5" 6.50
Laurel, gr, bowl, 11" 27.00
Laurel, gr, sugar bowl, short 8.50
Laurel, gr or ivory, plate, grill; 9⅛" 11.00
Laurel, gr or ivory, plate, sherbet; 6" 5.00
Laurel, ivory, cheese dish, w/lid 55.00
Laurel, ivory, platter, oval, 10¾" 25.00
Laurel, ivory, sherbet 11.00
Lincoln Inn, bl or red, ashtray 17.50
Lincoln Inn, bl or red, bowl, olive; hdld 15.00
Lincoln Inn, bl or red, candy dish, ftd, oval 22.50
Lincoln Inn, bl or red, shakers, pr 250.00
Lincoln Inn, bl or red, sugar bowl 20.00
Lincoln Inn, bl or red, vase, ftd, 12" 145.00
Lincoln Inn, colors other than bl or red, bonbon, hdld, sq 12.00
Lincoln Inn, colors other than bl or red, creamer 14.50
Lincoln Inn, colors other than bl or red, plate, 8" 7.50
Lincoln Inn, colors other than bl or red, sherbet, 4¾" 12.50
Lorain, crystal or gr, bowl, vegetable; oval, 9¾" 16.00
Lorain, crystal or gr, plate, dinner; 10¼" 40.00
Lorain, yel, bowl, berry; deep, 8" 140.00
Lorain, yel, plate, sherbet; 5½" 11.00
Madrid, amber, ashtray, 6" sq 200.00

Madrid, amber, butter dish, w/lid 65.00
Madrid, amber, pitcher, sq, 60-oz, 8" 45.00
Madrid, amber, shakers, ftd, 3½", pr 90.00
Madrid, amber, tumbler, ftd, 5-oz, 4" 24.00
Madrid, bl, bowl, vegetable; oval, 10" 38.00
Madrid, bl, plate, luncheon; 8⅞" 18.00
Madrid, gr, bowl, salad; 8" 17.50
Madrid, gr, creamer, ftd 11.00
Madrid, gr, hot dish coaster 37.50
Madrid, gr, pitcher, ice lip, 80-oz, 8½" 225.00
Madrid, gr, tumbler, 5-oz, 3⅞" 32.00
Madrid, pk, candlesticks, 2¼", pr 20.00
Madrid, pk, plate, relish; 10¼" 12.50
Madrid, pk or gr, bowl, sauce; 5" 6.50
Manhattan, crystal, relish tray, 4-part, 14" 18.00
Manhattan, crystal or pk, bowl, berry; hdld, 5⅜" 17.50
Manhattan, crystal or pk, comport, 5¾" 30.00
Manhattan, pk, pitcher, tilted, 80-oz 60.00

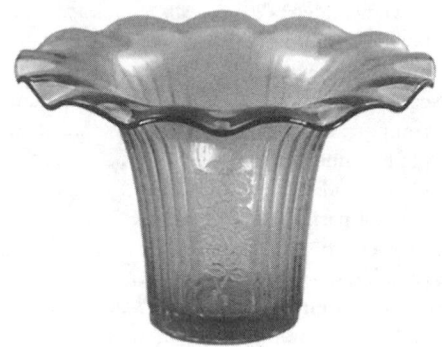

Mayfair, vase, blue, ruffled rim, 5½", $110.00.

Mayfair, bl, bowl, cereal; 5½" 45.00
Mayfair, bl, bowl, vegetable; 10" 65.00
Mayfair, bl, cup 50.00
Mayfair, bl, plate, cake; hdld, 12" 70.00
Mayfair, bl, sandwich server, center hdl 75.00
Mayfair, gr, plate, cake; ftd, 10" 100.00
Mayfair, gr, tumbler, water; 11-oz, 4¾" 200.00
Mayfair, gr or yel, relish dish, 4-part, 8⅜" 165.00
Mayfair, pk, cookie jar, w/lid 47.50
Mayfair, pk, plate, luncheon; 8½" 24.00
Mayfair, pk or gr, goblet, 2½-oz, 4⅛" 900.00
Mayfair, yel, bowl, vegetable; 7" 120.00
Mayfair, yel, pitcher, 37-oz, 6" 500.00
Mayfair, yel, tumbler, ftd, 10-oz, 5¼" 180.00
Mayfair Federal, amber, creamer, ftd 13.00
Mayfair Federal, amber, plate, dinner; 9½" 12.50
Mayfair Federal, amber, saucer 4.50
Mayfair Federal, crystal, bowl, cream soup; 5" 11.00
Mayfair Federal, crystal, cup 5.00
Mayfair Federal, crystal, sugar bowl, ftd 11.00
Mayfair Federal, gr, bowl, cereal; 6" 20.00
Mayfair Federal, gr, platter, oval, 12" 29.00
Mayfair Federal, gr, tumbler, 9-oz, 4½" 27.00
Miss America, crystal, candy jar, w/lid, 11½" 57.50
Miss America, crystal, goblet, water; 10-oz, 5½" 21.00
Miss America, crystal, saucer 4.00
Miss America, gr, shakers, pr 290.00
Miss America, gr, tumbler, water; 10-oz, 4½" 18.00
Miss America, ice bl, celery dish, oblong, 10½" 100.00

Miss America, pk, butter dish, w/lid 550.00
Miss America, pk, pitcher, ice lip; 65-oz, 8½" 135.00
Miss America, pk, plate, grill; 10¼" 22.00
Miss America, royal ruby, cup 225.00
Miss America, royal ruby, sherbet 125.00
Miss America, tumbler, juice; 5-oz, 4" 16.50
Moderntone, amethyst, plate, sherbet; 5⅞" 5.00
Moderntone, amethyst, tumbler, 9-oz 25.00
Moderntone, cobalt, plate, luncheon; 7¾" 12.50
Moderntone, cobalt, platter, oval, 12" 75.00
Moderntone, cobalt, sugar bowl 11.00
Moderntone, cobalt, whiskey, 1½-oz 40.00
Moderntone, cobalt or amethyst, bowl, berry; 5" 22.50
Moderntone, cobalt or amethyst, bowl, cereal; 6½" 67.50
Moondrops, bl or red, bowl, casserole; w/lid, 9¾" 185.00
Moondrops, bl or red, bowl, pickle; 7½" 22.00
Moondrops, bl or red, butter dish, w/lid 430.00
Moondrops, bl or red, plate, dinner; 9½" 25.00
Moondrops, bl or red, sherbet, 2⅝" 16.00
Moondrops, bl or red, tumbler, juice; ftd, 3-oz, 3¼" 16.00
Moondrops, colors other than bl or red, gravy boat 90.00
Moondrops, colors other than bl or red, plate, 5⅞" 8.00
Mt Pleasant, amethyst, blk or cobalt, cup 12.00
Mt Pleasant, amethyst, blk or cobalt, plate, grill; 9" 11.00
Mt Pleasant, amethyst, bowl, scalloped, ftd, 9" 28.00
Mt Pleasant, pk or gr, bowl, hdls, sq, 6" 13.00
Mt Pleasant, pk or gr, candlesticks, single, pr 20.00
New Century, gr or crystal, ashtray/coaster, 5⅜" 28.00
New Century, gr or crystal, plate, salad; 8½" 8.50
New Century, gr or crystal, shakers, pr 35.00
New Century, pk, cobalt or amethyst, cup 19.00
Newport, amethyst, bowl, cereal; 5¼" 25.00
Newport, amethyst, plate, luncheon; 8½" 11.00
Newport, amethyst, platter, oval, 11¾" 32.00
Newport, cobalt, cup 11.00
Newport, cobalt, plate, dinner; 8¾" 27.50
Newport, cobalt, sherbet 15.00
No 610 Pyramid, gr, ice tub 90.00
No 610 Pyramid, pk, tumbler, ftd, 2 styles, 8-oz, ea 35.00
No 610 Pyramid, yel, relish tray, hdld, 4-part 60.00

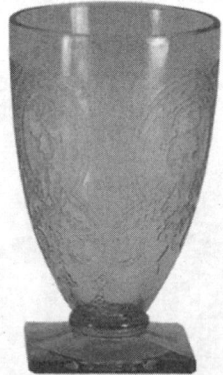

No. 612, Tumbler, green, footed, 4¾", 12-oz, $150.00.

No 612 Horseshoe, gr, creamer, ftd 15.00
No 612 Horseshoe, gr, sherbet 14.00
No 612 Horseshoe, yel, bowl, salad; 7½" 23.00
No 612 Horseshoe, yel, bowl, vegetable; oval, 10½" 27.50
No 612 Horseshoe, yel, pitcher, 64-oz, 8½" 300.00
No 612 Horseshoe, yel, tumbler, ftd, 12-oz 150.00
No 616 Vernon, crystal, creamer, ftd 12.00
No 616 Vernon, crystal, sugar bowl, ftd 11.00

No 616 Vernon, yel, plate, sandwich; 11½" 25.00
No 616 Vernon, yel, tumbler, ftd, 5" 32.00
No 618 Pineapple & Floral, amber, platter, closed hdls, 11" 18.00
No 618 Pineapple & Floral, amber or red, bowl, salad; 7" 10.00
No 618 Pineapple & Floral, crystal, ashtray, 4½" 17.50
No 618 Pineapple & Floral, crystal, plate, sandwich; 11½" 15.00
No 618 Pineapple & Floral, crystal, sugar bowl, dmn shape 7.50
Nora Bird, pk or gr, candlesticks, pr 80.00
Nora Bird, pk or gr, creamer, rnd hdl, 4½" 42.50
Nora Bird, pk or gr, ice tub, 6" 110.00
Nora Bird, pk or gr, tumbler, ftd, 4¾" 60.00
Normandie, amber, plate, dinner; 11" 28.00
Normandie, amber, tumbler, juice; 5-oz, 4" 25.00
Normandie, irid, saucer 3.00
Normandie, pk, creamer, ftd 11.00
Normandie, pk, platter, 11¾" 23.00
Old Cafe, crystal, pk or royal ruby, candy dish, low, 8" 11.00
Old Cafe, crystal or pk, pitcher, 36-oz, 6" 70.00
Old Cafe, royal ruby, bowl, cereal; 5½" 10.00
Old Cafe, royal ruby, lamp 25.00
Old Cafe, royal ruby, sherbet, low ftd, ¾" 10.00
Old English, pk, gr or amber, bowl, flat, 4" 16.00
Old English, pk, gr or amber, candlesticks, 4", pr 32.50
Old English, pk, gr or amber, compote, hdls, 3½x6⅜" 21.00
Old English, pk, gr or amber, pitcher 65.00
Old English, pk, gr or amber, sherbet, 2 styles, ea 19.00
Old English, pk, gr or amber, tumbler, ftd, 5½" 32.00
Ovide, Art Deco, cup 50.00
Ovide, gr, candy dish, w/lid 22.00
Ovide, gr, sugar bowl, open 4.00
Oyster & Pearl, crystal or pk, bowl, hdld, 5½" 7.00
Oyster & Pearl, royal ruby, bowl, deep, hdld, 6½" 19.00
Parrot, amber, hot plate, pointed, 5" 875.00
Parrot, gr, bowl, berry; 5" 22.00

Parrot, sugar bowl, green, $35.00.

Parrot, gr, creamer 50.00
Parrot, gr or amber, saucer 15.00
Patrician, amber, crystal or pk, plate, salad; 7½" 15.00
Patrician, amber, crystal or pk, sherbet 13.00
Patrician, amber or crystal, platter, oval, 11½" 30.00
Patrician, amber or crystal, tumbler, 5-oz, 4" 28.00
Patrician, gr, bowl, cereal; 6" 24.00
Patrician, gr, plate, luncheon; 9" 11.00
Patrician, gr, sugar bowl lid only 52.00
Patrician, pk, bowl, vegetable; oval, 10" 12.00
Patrician, pk, gr, amber or crystal, bowl, berry; 5" 11.00
Patrician, pk, tumbler, 14-oz, 5½" 50.00
Patrician, pk or gr, butter dish, w/lid 100.00

Patrick, pk, cheese & cracker set 150.00
Patrick, pk, mayonnaise set, 3-pc 195.00
Patrick, yel, candlesticks, pr 150.00
Patrick, yel, goblet, cocktail; 4" 80.00
Patrick, yel, sugar bowl 37.50
Petalware, cobalt, sherbet, low ftd, 4½" 30.00
Petalware, crystal, bowl, cereal; 5¾" 4.00
Petalware, crystal, tumbler, 12-oz, 4⅝" 35.00
Petalware, pk, bowl, berry; lg, 9" 15.00
Petalware, pk, plate, salver; 11" 10.00
Petalware, plain monax, plate, salver; 12" 18.00
Petalware, red trim floral, saucer 8.00
Primo, yel or gr, bowl, 4½" 9.50
Primo, yel or gr, plate, dinner; 10" 16.00
Primo, yel or gr, plate, 7½" 7.50
Princess, gr, ashtray, 4½" 67.50
Princess, gr, tumbler, water; 9-oz, 4" 25.00
Princess, gr or pk, pitcher, 60-oz, 8" 55.00
Princess, gr or pk, plate, grill; 10¼" 12.00
Princess, gr or pk, platter, closed hdls, 12" 21.00
Princess, gr or pk, sherbet, ftd 20.00
Princess, pk, bowl, salad; octagonal, 9" 30.00
Princess, pk, cake stand, 10" 26.00
Princess, topaz/apricot, butter dish, w/lid 650.00
Princess, topaz/apricot, shakers, 4½", pr 70.00
Princess, topaz/apricot, tumbler, ftd, 10-oz, 5¼" 20.00
Queen Mary, crystal, bowl, berry; 4½" 4.00
Queen Mary, crystal, bowl, cereal; 6" 6.50
Queen Mary, crystal, butter dish, w/lid 25.00
Queen Mary, crystal, plate, serving; 14" 12.00
Queen Mary, pk, celery/pickle dish, 5x10" 21.00
Queen Mary, pk, plate, dinner; 9¾" 50.00
Queen Mary, pk, relish tray, 4-part, 14" 16.00
Queen Mary, pk, tumbler, water; 9-oz, 4" 11.00
Radiance, amber, bowl, bonbon; w/lid, 6" 45.00
Radiance, amber, bowl, celery; 10" 18.00
Radiance, amber, candlesticks, 2-light, pr 70.00
Radiance, amber, plate, punch bowl liner, 14" 45.00
Radiance, amber, tray, oval 24.00
Radiance, ice bl or red, bowl, crimped, 12" 42.00
Radiance, ice bl or red, bowl, pickle; 7" 25.00
Radiance, ice bl or red, candlesticks, ruffled, 6", pr 160.00
Radiance, ice bl or red, comport, 5" 27.50
Radiance, ice bl or red, creamer 22.00
Radiance, ice bl or red, mayonnaise set, 3-pc 75.00
Raindrops, gr, plate, luncheon; 8" 5.50
Raindrops, gr, sugar bowl 6.50
Raindrops, gr, tumbler, 9½-oz, 4⅛" 9.00
Raindrops, gr, whiskey, 1-oz, 1⅞" 7.00
Ribbon, blk, bowl, berry; lg, 8" 35.00
Ribbon, blk, plate, luncheon; 8" 12.50
Ribbon, blk, shakers, pr 45.00
Ribbon, gr, bowl, berry; 4" 9.50
Ribbon, gr, cup 5.00
Ribbon, gr, sugar bowl, ftd 12.00
Ring, crystal, bowl, berry; 5" 3.50
Ring, crystal, bowl, divided, 5¼" 9.50
Ring, crystal, pitcher, 80-oz, 8½" 18.00
Ring, crystal, tumbler, 9-oz, 4¼" 4.50
Ring, crystal, vase, 8" 16.00
Ring, gr, goblet, cocktail; 3½-oz, 3¾" 16.00
Ring, gr, plate, sandwich; 11¾" 11.00
Ring, gr, tumbler, juice; ftd, 3½" 7.50
Rock Crystal, crystal, bonbon, scalloped edge, 7½" 18.00

Rock Crystal, crystal, bowl, salad; scalloped edge, 10½" 24.00
Rock Crystal, crystal, butter dish, w/lid 335.00
Rock Crystal, crystal, salt cellar 35.00
Rock Crystal, red, bowl, ftd, 12½" 295.00
Rock Crystal, red, bowl, relish; 2-part, 11½" 75.00
Rock Crystal, red, bowl, scalloped edge, 5" 40.00
Rock Crystal, red, plate, scalloped edge, 10½" 65.00
Rose Cameo, gr, bowl, berry; 4½" 8.50
Rose Cameo, gr, bowl, str sides, 6" 17.50
Rose Cameo, gr, tumbler, ftd, 2 styles, 5", ea 20.00
Rosemary, amber, plate, grill 7.50
Rosemary, gr, bowl, cereal; 6" 29.00
Rosemary, gr, platter, oval, 12" 20.00
Rosemary, pk, creamer, ftd 15.00
Rosemary, pk, sugar bowl, ftd 17.00
Roulette, crystal, saucer 1.50
Roulette, crystal, tumbler, iced tea; 12-oz, 5⅛" 16.00
Roulette, pk or gr, tumbler, juice; 5-oz, 3¼" 20.00
Roulette, pk or gr, whiskey, 1½-oz, 2½" 14.00
Round Robin, gr or irid, plate, luncheon; 8" 4.00
Round Robin, irid, creamer, ftd 6.50
Roxana, wht, bowl, 4½x2⅜" 13.00
Roxana, yel, bowl, cereal; 6" 13.00
Royal Lace, bl, bowl, 3-legged, rolled edge, 10" 300.00
Royal Lace, bl, butter dish, w/lid 600.00
Royal Lace, bl, plate, sherbet; 6" 12.00
Royal Lace, bl, saucer 12.50
Royal Lace, bl, tumbler, 9-oz, 4⅛" 40.00
Royal Lace, crystal, bowl, vegetable; oval, 11" 20.00
Royal Lace, crystal, candlesticks, str edge, pr 30.00
Royal Lace, crystal, pitcher, no lip, 64-oz, 8" 45.00
Royal Lace, crystal, plate, dinner; 9⅞" 12.50

Royal Lace, cookie jar, green, $80.00.

Royal Lace, gr, bowl, 3-legged, str edge, 10" 40.00
Royal Lace, gr, butter dish, w/lid 260.00
Royal Lace, gr, pitcher, w/lip, 96-oz, 8½" 145.00
Royal Lace, gr, platter, oval, 13" 38.00
Royal Lace, gr, tumbler, 5-oz, 3½" 28.00
Royal Lace, pk, butter dish, w/lid 140.00
Royal Lace, pk, candlesticks, ruffled edge, pr 65.00
Royal Lace, pk, plate, grill; 9⅞" 20.00
Royal Lace, pk, sugar bowl lid only 45.00
S Pattern, amber, plate, cake; heavy, 13" 70.00
S Pattern, amber, yel or crystal w/colored trim, cup 4.50
S Pattern, crystal, pitcher, 80-oz 60.00
S Pattern, crystal, plate, grill 6.50
S Pattern, crystal, sherbet, low ftd 4.50

S Pattern, red, plate, luncheon; 8¼" 40.00
Sharon, amber, bowl, berry; 5" 8.50
Sharon, amber, pitcher, no ice lip, 80-oz 130.00
Sharon, amber, sherbet, ftd 12.00
Sharon, gr, bowl, vegetable; oval, 9½" 30.00
Sharon, gr, plate, dinner; 9½" 21.00
Sharon, gr, tumbler, thin, 9-oz, 4⅛" 70.00
Sharon, pk, bowl, soup; flat, 1⅞" deep, 7¾" 45.00
Sharon, pk, butter dish, w/lid 50.00
Sharon, pk, candy jar, w/lid 50.00
Sharon, pk, jam dish, 7½" 210.00
Sharon, pk, shakers, pr 47.50
Sharon, pk, sugar bowl lid only 28.00
Ships, bl & wht, pitcher, no ice lip, 86-oz 45.00
Ships, bl & wht, plate, dinner; 9" 27.50
Ships, bl & wht, tumbler, old fashioned; 8-oz, 3⅜" 15.00
Sierra, gr, bowl, vegetable; oval, 9¼" 110.00
Sierra, gr, pitcher, 32-oz, 6½" 110.00
Sierra, gr, tumbler, ftd, 9-oz, 4½" 75.00
Sierra, pk, creamer 18.00
Sierra, pk, platter, oval, 11" 38.00
Sierra, pk, sugar bowl 16.00
Spiral, gr, pitcher, 58-oz, 7⅝" 30.00
Spiral, gr, preserve, w/lid 30.00
Spiral, gr, tumbler, water; 9-oz, 5" 7.50
Starlight, crystal or wht, bowl, 2¾" deep, 12" 24.00
Starlight, crystal or wht, sugar bowl, oval 5.00
Starlight, pk, bowl, cereal; closed hdls, 5½" 8.50
Starlight, pk, plate, sandwich; 13" 14.00
Strawberry, crystal or irid, butter dish, w/lid 135.00
Strawberry, crystal or irid, creamer, lg, 4⅝" 22.50
Strawberry, crystal or irid, sugar bowl, open, sm 12.00
Strawberry, pk or gr, bowl, salad; deep, 6½" 18.00
Strawberry, pk or gr, butter dish, w/lid 150.00
Strawberry, pk or gr, pitcher, 7¾" 150.00
Strawberry, pk or gr, tumbler, 8-oz, 3⅝" 30.00
Sunflower, gr, creamer 18.00
Sunflower, opaque, cup 75.00
Sunflower, pk, plate, dinner; 9" 14.00
Sunflower, pk, trivet, 3-legged, turned-up edge, 7" 285.00

Swirl, cup & saucer, ultramarine, $20.00.

Swirl, delphite, candle holders, single branch, pr 115.00
Swirl, delphite, cup 10.00
Swirl, delphite, plate, 10½" 18.00
Swirl, pk, butter dish, w/lid 180.00
Swirl, pk, plate, sherbet; 6½" 4.50
Swirl, ultramarine, bowl, console; ftd, 10½" 26.00
Swirl, ultramarine, bowl, salad; rimmed, 9" 25.00
Swirl, ultramarine, candle holders, dbl-branch, pr 45.00
Swirl, ultramarine, plate, salad; 8" 13.00
Tea Room, gr, bowl, finger 47.50
Tea Room, gr, candlesticks, low, pr 48.00
Tea Room, gr, ice bucket 57.50

Tea Room, gr, shakers, pr 55.00
Tea Room, gr, sugar bowl, rectangular 20.00
Tea Room, gr, vase, str, 11" 95.00
Tea Room, pk, bowl, celery; 8¼" 26.00
Tea Room, pk, creamer, rectangular 17.00
Tea Room, pk, parfait 70.00
Tea Room, pk, tray, center hdl 155.00
Tea Room, pk, tumbler, ftd, 11" 40.00
Thistle, gr, cup, thin 24.00
Thistle, pk, bowl, cereal; 5½" 20.00
Thistle, pk, plate, grill; 10¼" 17.50
Tulip, amber, crystal or gr, cup 10.00
Tulip, amethyst or bl, bowl, oval, oblong, 13¼" 50.00
Twisted Optic, bl or yel, bowl, 9" 22.50
Twisted Optic, bl or yel, cologne bottle, w/stopper 65.00
Twisted Optic, bl or yel, sandwich server, open center hdl 35.00
Twisted Optic, pk, gr or amber, basket, tall, 10" 40.00
Twisted Optic, pk, gr or amber, pitcher, 64-oz 30.00
Twisted Optic, pk, gr or amber, tumbler, 9-oz, 4½" 6.00
US Swirl, gr, butter dish, w/lid 110.00
US Swirl, gr, pitcher, 48-oz, 8" 50.00
US Swirl, pk, candy dish, w/lid, hdls 32.00
US Swirl, pk, vase, 6½" 19.00
US Swirl, pk or gr, shakers, pr 42.50
US Swirl, pk or gr, sugar bowl, w/lid 32.00
Victory, amber, pk or gr, bonbon, 7" 11.00
Victory, amber, pk or gr, creamer 15.00
Victory, amber, pk or gr, plate, luncheon; 8" 7.00
Victory, bl or blk, candlesticks, 3", pr 95.00
Victory, bl or blk, plate, bread & butter; 6" 16.00
Vitrock, wht, bowl, berry; 4" 4.50
Vitrock, wht, bowl, cereal; 7½" 6.00
Vitrock, wht, plate, salad; 7¼" 2.50
Vitrock, wht, sugar bowl 4.50

Waterford, tumbler, crystal, 4⅞", $12.00.

Waterford, crystal, ashtray, 4" 7.50
Waterford, crystal, butter dish, w/lid 25.00
Waterford, crystal, lamp, spherical base, 4" 26.00
Waterford, crystal, plate, salad; 7⅛" 6.00
Waterford, crystal, sherbet, ftd 4.00
Waterford, pk, bowl, berry; 5½" 16.00
Waterford, pk, plate, sandwich; 13¾" 25.00
Waterford, pk, plate, sherbet; 6" 6.00
Waterford, pk, tumbler, ftd, 10-oz, 4⅞" 19.00
Windsor, bl, plate, dinner; 9" 65.00
Windsor, crystal, plate, cake; ftd, 10¾" 8.50
Windsor, crystal, tray, hdld, sq, 4" 5.00

Windsor, crystal, tumbler, ftd, 7¼" 15.00
Windsor, gr, bowl, hdls, 8" 20.00
Windsor, gr, cup 11.00
Windsor, gr, saucer 6.00
Windsor, pk, bowl, pointed edge, 10½" 120.00
Windsor, pk, coaster, 3¼" 12.50
Windsor, pk, platter, oval, 11½" 19.00
Windsor, red, tumbler, 9-oz, 4" 55.00

Derby

William Duesbury operated in Derby, England, from about 1755, purchasing a second establishment, The Chelsea Works, in 1769. During this period fine porcelains were produced which so impressed the King that in 1773 he issued the company the Crown Derby patent. In 1810, several years after Duesbury's death, the factory was bought by Robert Bloor. The quality of the ware suffered under the new management, and the main Derby pottery closed in 1848. Within a short time, the work was revived by a dedicated number of former employees who established their own works on King Street in Derby.

The earliest known Derby mark was the crown over a script 'D'; however this mark is rarely found today. Soon after 1782, that mark was augmented with a device of crossed batons and six dots, usually applied in underglaze blue. During the Bloor period, the crown was centered within a ring containing the words 'Bloor' above and 'Derby' below the crown, or with a red printed stamp — the crowned Gothic 'D.' The King Street plant produced figurines that may be distinguished from their earlier counterparts by the presence of an 'S' and 'H' on either side of the crown and crossed batons.

In 1876 a new pottery was constructed in Derby, and the owners revived the earlier company's former standard of excellence. The Queen bestowed the firm the title Royal Crown Derby in 1890; it still operates under that name today. See also Royal Crown Derby.

Bowl, garden landscape, Imari palette, scalloped, 1800s, 12" **200.00**

Cup and saucer, Oriental shrubs below a cracked-ice border in famille verte palette, minor wear, 1755-60, $600.00.

Plate, game birds, urn & leaf border, gold trim, 1810, 8½" **300.00**

Desert Sands

As early as the 1850s, the Evans family living in the Ozark Mountains of Missouri produced domestic clay products. Their small pot shop was passed on from one generation to the next. In the 1920s it was moved to North Las Vegas, Nevada, where the name Desert Sands was adopted. Succeeding generations of the family continued to relocate, taking the business with them. From 1937 to 1962 it operated in Boulder City, Nevada; then it was moved to Barstow where it remained until it closed in the late 1970s.

Desert Sands pottery is similar to Mission Ware by Niloak. Various mineral oxides were blended to mimic the naturally occuring sand formations of the American West. A high-gloss glaze was applied to add intensity to the colorful striations that characterize the ware. Not all examples are marked, making it sometimes difficult to attribute. Marked items carry an ink stamp with the Desert Sands designation. Paper labels were also used.

Ashtray, 6½" **20.00**
Bowl, console; hand thrown, 9½" **45.00**
Bowl, 3" **15.00**
Butter dish **45.00**
Shakers, pr **25.00**

Tumbler, $20.00.

Vase, cactus ink mk, 7" **30.00**
Vase, slim inverted cylinder, 5" **25.00**
Vase, 3½x3" **25.00**

Documents

Although the word 'document' is defined in the general sense as 'anything printed or written, etc., relied upon to record or prove something. . .,' in the collectibles market, the term is more diversified with broadsides, billheads, checks, invoices, letters and letterheads, land grants, receipts, and waybills some of the most sought after. Some documents in demand are those related to a specific subject such as advertising, mining, railroads, military, politics, banking, slavery, nautical, or legal (deeds, mortgages, etc.). Other collectors look for examples representing a specific period of time such as colonial documents, Revolutionary or Civil War documents, early western documents or those from a specific region, state, or city.

Aside from supply and demand, there are five major factors which determine the collector-value of a document. These are:

1) Age — Documents from the eastern half of the country can be found that date back to the 1700s or earlier. Most documents sought by collectors usually date from 1700 to 1900. Those with 20th-century dates are still abundant and not in demand unless of special significance or beauty.

2) Region of origin — Depending on age, documents from rural and less-populated areas are harder to find than those from major cities and heavily populated states. The colonization of the West and Mid-West did not begin until after 1850, so while an 1870s billhead from New York or Chicago is common, one from Albuquerque or Phoenix is not, since most of the Southwest was still unsettled.

3) Attractiveness — Some documents are plain and unadorned, but collectors prefer colorful, profusely illustrated pieces. Additional artwork and engravings add to the value.

4) Historical content — Unusual or interesting content, such as a letter written by a Civil War soldier giving an eye-witness account of the Battle of Gettysburg or a western territorial billhead listing numerous animal hides purchased from a trapper, will sell for more than one with mundane information.

5) Condition — Through neglect or environmental conditions, over many decades paper articles can become stained, torn, or deteriorated. Heavily damaged or stained documents are generally avoided altogether. Those with minor problems are more acceptable, although their value will decrease anywhere from 20% to 50%, depending upon the extent of damage. Avoid attempting to repair tears with scotch tape — sell 'as is' so that the collector can take proper steps toward restoration.

Foreign documents are plentiful; and though some are very attractive, resale may be difficult. The listings that follow are generalized; prices are variable depending entirely upon the five points noted above. Values here are based upon examples with no major damage. Common grade documents without significant content are found in abundance and generally have little collector value. These usually date from the late 1800s and early 1900s. It should be noted that the items listed below are examples of those that meet the criteria for having collector value. There is little demand for documents worth less than $5.00. For more information we recommend *Owning Western History* by our advisor Warren Anderson. His address and ordering information may be found in the Directory under Utah.

Key:
illus — illustrated   vgn — vignette

Affidavit, CO Territory Mining, handwritten, 1864, 1½-pg **55.00**
Appointment, ME Militia, partly printed, 1840s, G **20.00**
Assay certificate, Silverton Smelting & Mining Co, 5x8" **25.00**
Bank draft, NM Territory, preprinted, from Las Vegas, 1890 ....**30.00**
Bank draft, Pima Co, Tombstone AZ, orange stamp, 1881 ....**30.00**
Bill of sale, New Orleans, cotton, printed script, 1878, 8x11" **30.00**
Birth certificate, Am, 19th Oct Anno Domini 1837, 14x12" **750.00**
Bus card, Truxal & Dunmeyer Mfg, Chattanooga TN, 1895, EX ..**12.00**
Card, honary citizen; Boy's Town, 1945, 2¼x3¾", EX **5.00**
Certificate of health, MA, ship's crew, handwritten, 1808 ....**12.50**
Check, Wells Fargo Co, UT Territory, 1870s, 8x11", EX **25.00**
Currency, 15¢ fractional note, Columbia & eagle, 1863, EX **21.00**
Deed, AL, land in Randolph County, 1882, 8x12½", EX **25.00**
Diary, Civil war soldiers, war campaigns/etc, 1864-67, VG **650.00**
Discharge, Continental Army, sgn Lt Col E Gray, 1780, EX **125.00**
Discharge, NJ, Revolutionary drummer boy, 1780, fr, EX **135.00**
Draft, of bill to present to Congress, 1844, 8x12", EX **6.50**
Envelope, Arms of IA w/eagle & arrows, ca 1861 ....**10.00**
Envelope, Major General JE Wool portrait & flags, 1860s **10.00**
Envelope, Wells Fargo logo, 4¢ stamp, 1870s **12.50**
Estate sale list, GA, Blk man to new owner, 1836, 5x8" **200.00**
General orders, Civil War, daily activities, 1862, 4½x7" **20.00**
Indenture, calligraphy on vellum, sgn by lady, 1817, 17x22" **20.00**
Insurance policy, Sam Cook, whaling, MA, 1874, 9x12", VG **65.00**
Invoice, Ft Wadsworth, clothing & equipage, sgn GA Hull, 1875 .**15.00**
Land deed, MA, partly printed & handwritten, w/seal, 1801, G ...**22.50**
Land grant, MI Territory, sgn A Jackson by secretary, 1834 ....**25.00**
Lease, CO Territory gold mine, machinery & mill, 1869, EX **65.00**
Letter, camp near WA, capture of Jeff Davis, 1865, w/envelope ...**24.00**
Letter, IL, business trip out West by rail, 1867, 2-pg **20.00**
Letter, military appointment, 1833, 8x10" **35.00**
Letter, OK Territory, Indian's guardianship, from judge, 1905 ......**30.00**
Letter, SC, wine shipment from Madeira, 1838, 2-pg **195.00**
Letter, settling of army accounts, Revolutionary War era, EX **55.00**
Letter, soldier's wife to mother, 1885, 6-pg, 5x8" **40.00**
Letter, TX, Christmas holiday news, typed, 1915, 2-pg **15.00**
Letterhead, cigar maker, burning cigar/band, HN Heusner, PA **5.00**

Letterhead, Territory of AK, Officer of Auditor, Juneau, 1933 .....20.00
Marriage license, partly handwritten, MS, 1865, 8x7", EX 27.50
Mining Prospectus, NM, US Copper CO, w/photos, 1916, 22-pg .30.00
Oath of office, AL Justice of the Peace, printed, 1866, EX 75.00
Orders, NH Cavalry to report for duty, 1838, EX 12.00
Pay order, CT Revolutionary War, full manuscript, 7x6" 25.00
Payment on debt, Revolutionary War, Wolcott, 1789, 3⅝x7" 30.00
Promissory note, handwritten using Ye/etc, 1776, EX 15.00
Prospectus, Silver King Mining, 1920, 8-pg, 3x6" 20.00
Receipt, articles published, WI, 1869, 5x9", EX 78.00
Receipt, gun & bayonet for Minute Man, Apr 1777 ....50.00
Receipt, lg amount of sugar, PA, 1786, 3½x7", VG 7.50
Receipt, payment of special income tax, 1863, 4x8", EX 12.50
Receipt, UP Express, printed/handwritten, 1875, 3x8", EX 35.00
Record book, Civil War military election, 1860s, 12x17" 85.00
Report, ordnance; money spent on weapons & munitions, 1839 ....8.00
Sermon, handwritten, dtd 1838, 7-pg, EX..............................15.00
Summons, partly printed on bl, OH, 1846, 8x6", VG 15.00
Surrender of property, widow so ordered, 1754, 14x15" 70.00
Tax form, preprinted, lists property, including slaves, 1860 ....15.00
Voucher, expenses leading to arrest, preprinted, 1886, 9x14" 40.00
Way bill, Baltimore & OH RR, preprinted, 1852, EX 6.00

Dollhouses and Furnishings

Dollhouses were introduced commercially in this country late in the 1700s by Dutch craftsmen who settled in the East. By the mid-1800s, they had become meticulously detailed, divided into separate rooms, and lavishly furnished to reflect the opulence of the day. Originally intended for the amusement of adults of the household, by the latter 1800s their status had changed to that of a child's toy. Though many early dollhouses were lovingly hand-fashioned for a special little girl, those made commercially by such companies as Bliss and Schoenhut are highly valued.

Furniture and furnishings in the Biedermeier style featuring stenciled Victorian decorations often sell for several hundred dollars each. Other early pieces made of pewter, porcelain, or papier-mache are also quite valuable. Certainly less expensive but very collectible, nonetheless, is the quality, hallmarked plastic furniture produced during the forties by Renwal and Acme, and the 1960s Petite Princess line produced by Ideal. In the listings that follow, dollhouses are litho paper on wood, unless otherwise noted. When no manufacturer or country of origin is noted, examples are German, turn of the century. For more information, see *Schroeder's Collectible Toys, Antique to Modern*. Our advisor for this category is Barbara Rosen; she is listed in the Directory under New Jersey. See also Miniatures.

Furniture

Andirons, brass, Tynietoy, pr 20.00
Basin, gr pnt, Strombecker, EX+ 12.00
Bathinet, pk or bl, Renwal 10.00
Bathroom scales, ivory w/printed dial, Renwal, VG 12.50
Bathtub, pk w/bl fixtures, Renwal, 1⅜x4x2", EX 8.00
Bed, brn w/molded ivory spread, single sz, Renwal 6.00
Chair, bbl type, Renwal 7.50
Chair, club; red pnt, Strombecker 9.00
Chair, dining; w/2 hostess chairs, Petite Princess 45.00
Chair, drum style, dk gold, Petite Princess 15.00
Chair, side; Federal style, brn Bakelite w/bl seats, Ideal 5.00
Chair, wingbk; bl & brn, Renwall 12.00
Chair, wingbk; red w/brn legs, Little Hostess 12.00
Chair, wingbk; wht brocade w/flowers, Petite Princess 16.00

Chest of drws, pk, 2 sm drws over 4, Renwal, 3⅛x2¼" 6.50
Clock, hump-bk mantel, ivory w/printed dial, Renwal, ⅝" 18.00
Decanter, porc, for tea cart, Petite Princess 6.00
Dresser, Chippendale, brn Bakelite, mirror, Renwal, 4¼" 7.50
End table, brn Bakelite, 2-drw, Renwal, 1½x⅞x⅞" 6.00
Footstool, walnut wood w/tan flocking, Strombecker 5.00
Hamper, pk, Renwal, 2x1¾" 3.00
Ice cube tray, Petite Princess 5.00

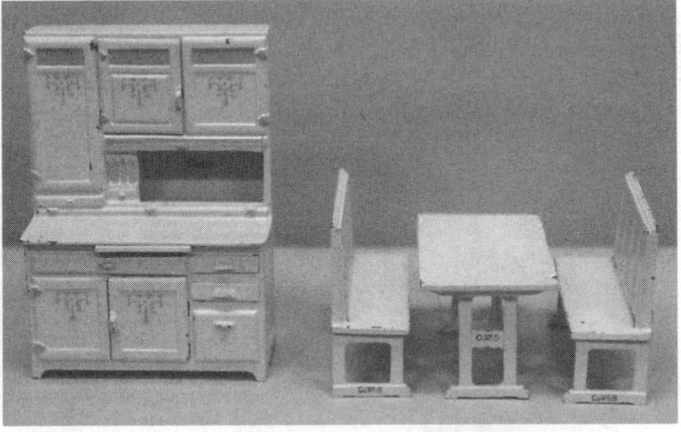

Kitchen set, painted cast iron, Arcade, NM, $750.00.

Lamp, table; brass, Petite Princess 10.00
Mirror, gilt fr, hanging, Little Hostess 12.50
Piano, baby grand; brn w/yel tufted bench, Little Hostess 16.00
Piano, grand; brn Bakelite, Renwal, 2¼x3⅝x3", VG 5.00
Playpen, pk w/bl, Renwal, #118 ....14.00
Radio, brn Bakelite, pull-out phonograph, Renwal, 2⅛" 10.00
Rocking chair, tall bk, brn, Little Hostess 12.00
Sideboard, Hplwht, brn mottled Bakelite, Ideal, VG 6.50
Sink, bathroom; pk w/bl, ped style, Renwal, 2¼" 7.50
Sofa, cream & gold, Petite Princess, EX 35.00
Stool, kitchen; cream pnt, Strombecker, VG 4.00

Table set, Heirloom Petite Princess Fantasy Furniture set by Ideal, MIB, $28.50.

Table, dining; walnut wood w/6 trn legs, Strombecker 18.00
Table, dressing; ivory w/triple mirror, Little Hostess 12.00

Table, kitchen; ivory, Renwal **7.50**
Table, side; Sheraton half-moon style, mahog, Tynietoy, VG **40.00**
Table, tilt top, ped ft, rnd, Petite Princess **12.00**
Table/stand, brn Bakelite, 3-ftd base, Renwal **6.50**
Tea cart, walnut wood, 3 shelves, Strombecker **18.00**
Telephone, French type, gold trim, Petite Princess **10.00**
Wicker set, ivory pnt, 13", 4-pc, EX **250.00**

Houses, Shops, and Single Rooms

Barn, Roosevelt Stock Farm, 2½-story, 20x19½x10⅜", EX **275.00**
Bliss, paper on wood, metal lattice, hinged door, 17", G **600.00**
Bliss, paper on wood, 2-story/2-room, early 1900s, 16", EX **850.00**
Bliss, paper on wood, 2-story/4-room, trn columns, 21", VG **950.00**
Cabin, 1-story, pnt wood, 8x9x8", VG **150.00**
Converse, Red Robin Farm, 1½-story, dbl doors, 17x20x10" **300.00**
Converse, 1-story w/porch, pnt wood, hinged front, 12x14x12" .**350.00**
Germany, bake shop, papered wood/glass, 10x26", +80 pcs **650.00**
Germany, kitchen, pnt wood, wood/tin pcs, 14x28x12", EX ...**1,200.00**
Germany, stable, litho on pnt wood, horses & cart, 9", VG **250.00**
Germany, wrapping counter, desk/cabinet/papers, 21x18", EX ...**575.00**

Mansard-roof house, 3-floor/6-room, central hall and staircase, late 19th century, 51x53x19", with assorted furniture from later years, $1,000.00.

Marklin, kitchen, HP, fully furnished, 1900s, 19x37x20", EX .**9,900.00**
Marx, Ranch, 1-story w/porch, furniture, 33x10x9", MIB **95.00**
Marx, suburban Colonial, 2-story w/carport, furniture, 38", MIB .**165.00**
McLoughlin Bros, folding, 4-room, Pat 1894, 12x12", EX **400.00**
Parker Bros, grocery, pnt/unfinished wood, furnished, 17", EX ...**425.00**
Unmk, pnt wood, appl wood trim, 2-story, opens 2 sides, 62", G+ ..**1,050.00**
Unmk, pnt/varnished wood, collapsible, folding roof, 21", VG **25.00**
Unmk, stable, litho on wood, w/2 horses, 8½", VG **250.00**
Unmk, Victorian, 4 rooms/staircase, furniture, 1930s, 35", G **600.00**
Unmk, Victorian tobacco shop, paper on wood, furnished, EX ..**475.00**

Dolls

Collecting dolls of any sort is one of the most rewarding hobbies in the United States. The rewards are in the fun, the search, and the finds — plus there is a built-in factor of investment. No hobby, be it dolls, glass, or anything else, should be based completely on investment; but any collector should ask: 'Can I get my money back out of this item if I should ever have to sell it?' Many times we buy on impulse rather than with logic, which is understandable; but by asking this question we can save ourselves a lot of 'buyer's remorse' which we have all experienced at one time or another.

Since we want to learn to invest our money wisely while we are having fun, we must become aware of defects which may devaluate a doll. In bisque, watch for eye chips, hairline cracks and chips, or breaks on any part of the head. Composition should be clean, not crazed or cracked. Vinyl and plastic should be clean with no pen or crayon marks. Though a quality replacement wig is acceptable for bisque dolls, composition and hard plastics should have their originals in uncut condition. Original clothing is a must except in bisque dolls, since it is unusual to find one in its original costume.

A price guide is only that — a guide. It suggests the average price for each doll. Bargains can be found for less-than-suggested values, and 'unplayed-with' dolls in their original boxes may cost more. Dealers must become aware of condition so that they do not overpay and therefore overprice their dolls — a common occurrence across the country. Quantity does not replace quality, as most find out in time. A faster turnover of sales with a smaller margin of profit is far better than being stuck with an item that does not sell because it is overpriced. It is important to remember that prices are based on condition and rarity. When no condition is noted, dolls are assumed to be in excellent condition with the exceptions of Armand Marseille, Madame Alexander, and Cabbage Patch dolls, which are priced in mint condition. In relation to bisque dolls, excellent means having no cracks, chips, or hairlines, being nicely dressed, shoed, wigged, and ready to to be placed into a collection. For a more thorough study of the subject, we recommend you refer to the many lovely doll books written by authority Pat Smith, available at your favorite bookstore or public library. If you're interested in Liddle Kiddles we recommend *Liddle Kiddles* (Collector Books) by Paris Langford.

Key:
bjtd — ball-jointed	OC — original clothes
blb — bent limb body	o/m — open mouth
bsk — bisque	p/e — pierced ears
c/m — closed mouth	pnt — painted
hh — human hair	pwt — paperweight eyes
hp — hard plastic	RpC — replaced clothes
jtd — jointed	ShHd — shoulder head
MIG — Made In Germany	ShPl — shoulder plate
NC — no clothes	SkHd — socket head
o/c — open closed eyes	str — straight
o/c/m — open closed mouth	trn — turned

American Character

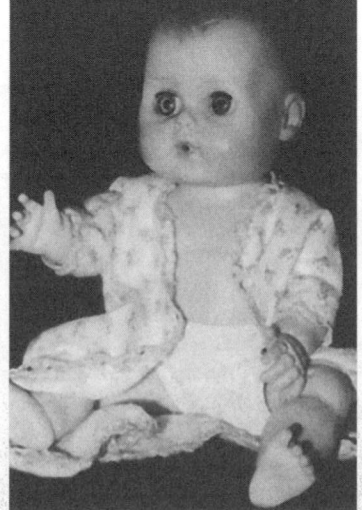

Tiny Toodles, all vinyl with molded and painted hair, blue sleep eyes, open mouth/nurser, 1956, M, $165.00.

Baby, compo/cloth, mk AC, 1930s-40s, 16", EX **200.00**
Baby Lou, plastic (1-pc mold), molded hair, RpC, 1950, 8" **15.00**
Campbell Kid, compo toddler, mk Petite, 1929-31, 12", M **325.00**

Child, compo, mk AC, OC, 14" 165.00
Chuckles, vinyl, elastic strung legs, pnt brn eyes, 1961, 23" 175.00
Cricket, magic grow hair, orig sweater outfit, 1961, 9" 35.00
Little Joe Cartwright, rigid vinyl, molded clothes, 8" 100.00
Little Miss Echo, talker, 1964, OC, 30", M 250.00
Marie Ann, plastic/vinyl, dk red hair, sleep eyes, 1966, 13" 20.00
Marie Lee, plastic & vinyl, sleep eyes, redressed, 13" 20.00
Pouty Miss Marie, plastic & vinyl, sleep eyes, 1965, 13" 30.00
Puggy, compo, pnt eyes, frown, mk Petite, OC, 12", M 500.00
Sally Says, plastic/vinyl, talker, 1954, OC, 19", M 90.00
Sweet Sue, hp, OC (red ball gown), 14" 285.00
Sweet Sue, hp, walker, OC, 18", minimum value 45.00
Talking Marie, vinyl/plastic, battery operated, 1963, 18", M 95.00
Toodles, vinyl, brn flirty eyes, curly hair, 1956, RpC, 22" 250.00
Tressy, magic grow hair, in Miss Am Character clothes, 1963 ......50.00
Wee Girl, compo, brn pnt eyes, pnt blk hair, 1940, 10" 85.00
Whimette, hp/vinyl, pnt eyes, red hair, RpC, 1963, 18" 35.00

Annalee

Aerobic dancer, 1984, 10" 75.00
Be My Honey Bear, 1985, 18" 110.00
Caroller boy, 1989, 7" 35.00
Caroller girl, 1974, 18" 100.00
Choir boy, w/blk eye, gr robe, 1964, 10" 175.00
Choir girl, red or orange hair, 1972, 10" 85.00
Clown, pk & wht, 1984, 10" 65.00
Elephant or donkey w/pins, 1972, 10", ea 300.00
Elf skier, 1986, 10" 65.00
Gingerbread man, 1984, 18" 125.00
Gnome, 1979, 7" 50.00
Leprechaun, 1979, 10" 70.00
Reindeer w/Santa hat & pipe cleaner antlers, 1982, 10" 30.00

Santa and Mrs. Claus on couch, 9", 1971 on tag, $95.00.

Santa & Mrs Claus w/potbelly stove, 1980, 7" 150.00
Santa chef, 1989, 18" 50.00
Santa frog w/bag, 1987, 10" 55.00
Santa in rocking chair, 1986, 18" 60.00
Santa monkey w/o bag, 1981, 7" 100.00
Santa w/reindeer, 1984, 5" 75.00
Santa w/stocking, 1984, 7" 35.00
Slingshot angel, 1984, 12" 75.00
Snowman, 1979, 10" 55.00
Stork w/baby in basket, 10" 125.00
Workshop elf w/tools, red or wht, 1982, 10" 60.00

Armand Marseille

Alma, ShHd, 15" 250.00
AM, baby, flange neck, 1907, 16" 650.00
AM, Floradora, ShHd, 20" 350.00
AM, Floradora, SkHd, 12" 150.00
AM, Floradora, SkHd, 27" 500.00
AM, Floradora 3748, ShHd, 21" 385.00
AM, Kiddiejoy, ShHd, cloth body, c/m, girl, 20" 1,600.00
AM, My Dearie, SkHd, 1908, 14" 300.00
AM, Rosebud, ShHd, 1902, 15" 300.00
AM, ShHd, boy, 14" 250.00
AM, SkHd, o/c eyes, 7" 185.00
AM, SkHd, 16" 275.00
AM, SkHd, 26" 525.00
AM, Sunshine, ShHd, 1910, 24" 525.00
AM 1894, ShPl, 26" 650.00
AM 210, SkHd, googly eyes, 6" 1,850.00
AM 248, mk GB (Geo Brogfeldt), o/m, 1912, 10" 325.00
AM 252, SkHd, googly eyes, 10" 1,100.00
AM 253, SkHd, googly eyes, 1915, 16" 2,100.00
AM 253, SkHd, googly eyes, 8" 900.00
AM 255, SkHd, intaglio eyes, 7½" 900.00
AM 300n, adult, SkHd, 15½" 1,200.00
AM 320, SkHd, c/m, googly eyes, 6½" 650.00
AM 3200, ShHd, some trn, 1898, 14" 265.00
AM 3200, ShHd, some trn, 22" 450.00
AM 323, SkHd, googly eyes, 11" 1,200.00
AM 324, googly eyes, 7" 465.00
AM 327, SkHd, 1914, 12" 325.00
AM 328, baby, SkHd, closed dome, 1922, 14" 275.00
AM 341, My Dream Baby, flange, c/m, wht, 8" 185.00
AM 341, My Dream Baby, flange, c/m, 18" 550.00
AM 341, My Dream Baby, flange, c/m, 21" 625.00
AM 347, SkHd, 1909, 16" 365.00
AM 351, My Dream Baby, flange, o/m, wht, 22" 625.00
Am 351, My Dream Baby, flange, o/m, 6" 150.00
AM 352, Baby Love, flange, 1914, 19" 675.00
AM 362, Teenie Weenie, baby, closed dome, wht, 15" 550.00
AM 370, 12" 185.00
AM 370, 16½" 275.00
AM 370n, 12" 185.00
AM 375, Kiddiejoy, girl, SkHd, c/m, molded hair, 20" 2,600.00
AM 390, My Dearie, 23" 465.00
AM 390, pnt bsk, 9" 145.00
AM 390, SkHd, 16" 300.00

AM 390, socket-head, brown sleep eyes, mohair wig on composition body with stick legs, original clothes, 21", M, $750.00.

AM 390n, SkHd, 1915, 27" **550.00**
AM 390n, 1915, 11" **200.00**
AM 402, SkHd, pnt bsk, 14" **300.00**
AM 500, Infant Berry, molded hair, 1908, 10" **450.00**
AM 500, Infant Berry, molded hair, 1908, 8" **265.00**
AM 560a, Dorothy, 1912, 15" **350.00**
AM 600, SkHd, flange, c/m, 1910, 10" **1,200.00**
AM 917, Mobi, baby, Germany, SkHd, 1921, 16" **525.00**
AM 966, baby, SkHd, flirty eyes, 14" **350.00**
AM 975, Sadie, baby, Otto Gans, 1914, 17" **500.00**
AM 975, Sadie, baby, SkHd, 1914, 9" **250.00**
AM 985, baby, SkHd, 13½" **400.00**
AM 990, Happy Tot, baby, SkHd, 1910, 16" **450.00**
AM 990, Happy Tot, baby, SkHd, 8" **200.00**
AM 992, baby, SkHd, 1914, 22" **700.00**
AM 996, baby, SkHd, 15" **425.00**
Columbia, ShHd, 1904, 24" **385.00**
Mabel, ShHd, 1898, 15" **300.00**
Queen Louise, SkHd, 1910, 22" **400.00**
Queen Louise, 100, SkHd, 1910, 18½" **425.00**

Arranbee

Baby Nancy, compo/cloth, bl-gr o/c eyes, o/m w/teeth, OC, 26" ..**325.00**
Bessie Toddler, Blk, compo, jtd, pnt eyes, c/m, dimples, OC, 14"..**75.00**
Carolyn Lee, blk pnt molded hair, pnt eyes, c/m, nude, 8½" **65.00**
Cloth w/compo head, arms & legs, bl sleep eyes, all orig, MIB ...**125.00**
Happy Time, hp head/cloth body/compo limbs, rpl wig, RpC, 15" ..**30.00**
Miss Internat'l, compo, bl o/c eyes, o/m/4 teeth, OC, 16½" **275.00**
Nancy, compo, jtd limbs, pnt hair/eyes, '30s, 12", M, +trunk **300.00**
Swiss Girl, compo, bl o/c eyes, OC, 1946, 18" **200.00**

Barbie Dolls and Related Dolls

Though the face has changed three times since 1959, Barbie is still as popular today as she was when she was first introduced. Named after the young daughter of the first owner of the Mattel Company, the original Barbie had a white iris but no eye color. These dolls are nearly impossible to find, but there is a myriad of her successors and related collectibles just waiting to be found. When no condition is indicated, the dolls listed below are assumed to be complete and in mint condition (without original box) unless otherwise specified. For further information we recommend *The World of Barbie Dolls* and *The Wonder of Barbie, 1976 — 1986,* by Paris & Susan Manos; *The Collector's Encyclopedia of Barbie Dolls and Collectibles* by Sibyl DeWein and Joan Ashabraner, *Barbie Exclusives* by Margo Rana, and *Barbie, The First Thirty Years,* by Stefanie Deutsch. *Barbie Fashion, Vol I, 1959 — 1967,* by Sarah Sink Eames, gives a history of the wardrobes of Barbie, her friends, and her family. Many of Patricia Smith's books contain chapters on Barbie dolls as well as other dolls by Mattel. Our advisor for Barbie dolls is Karen Martin; she is listed in the Directory under Michigan.

Allan, 1965, bendable legs, bl trunks/red jacket **350.00**
Allan, 1964, 12" **95.00**
Barbie, Bob Mackie, Masquerade **225.00**
Barbie, Golden Dream **40.00**
Barbie, Golden Jubilee **1,500.00**
Barbie, 1958-59, #1, doll only, 11½", M **2,500.00**
Barbie, 1961, #4, bubble cut, 11½", minimum value **140.00**
Barbie, 1961, Friday Nite Date, 11½" **250.00**
Barbie, 1961, Ponytail **500.00**
Barbie, 1962, Airline Stewardess, 11½", minimum value **400.00**
Barbie, 1963, Movie Date, 11½" **225.00**
Barbie, 1963, Swinging Easy, 11½" **300.00**

Barbie, 1960, Solo in the Spotlight, bubble-cut hairdo, MIB, $550.00 minimum value.

Barbie, 1963-65, Baby Sits **250.00**
Barbie, 1964, Guinevere, 11½" **400.00**
Barbie, 1965, bendable legs **700.00**
Barbie, 1967, Hair Fair Set, #4042 ....**100.00**
Barbie, 1967, Spanish Talking, MIB, minimum value **400.00**
Barbie, 1967-69, standard doll, #1190 ....**300.00**
Barbie, 1967-69, standard doll, #1190, nude **35.00**
Barbie, 1972, Growing Pretty Hair, 11½" **175.00**
Barbie, 1972, Walk Lively, pale blond hair, MIB **125.00**
Barbie, 1973, Action Barbie, M in plastic sack, minimum value ..**100.00**
Barbie, 1975, Free Moving, 11½" **65.00**
Barbie, 1975, Gold Medal Winter Sports, #9042, MIB **40.00**
Barbie, 1975, Hawaiian, #7470, MIB **50.00**
Barbie, 1976, Ballerina, wht tutu, w/stand, MIB **50.00**
Barbie, 1976, Beautiful Bride, #9599, MIB **300.00**
Barbie, 1977, Super Star, 11½" **50.00**
Barbie, 1982, Magic Curl, 11½" **35.00**
Barbie, 1982, Oriental, 11½" **110.00**
Barbie, 1987, Star Dream, Sears, MIB **75.00**
Barbie, 1991, Gay Parisienne **195.00**
Barbie, 35th Anniversary, brunette, MIB **90.00**
Brad, 1968, Talking, 12", minimum value **125.00**
Brad, 1970, bendable legs, MIB **80.00**
Cara, 1976, Ballerina, pk tutu, w/stand, MIB **100.00**
Casey, 1975, Baggie, swimsuit, MIB **45.00**
Christie, 1971, Live Action, #1175, MIB **75.00**
Francie, 1966, str legs, pnt lashes, #1140, MIB **200.00**
Francie, 1966, 11½", minimum value **100.00**
Francie, 1967-70, Twist 'N Turn, nude **20.00**
Francie, 1970, Growin' Pretty Hair, bendable knees, M **50.00**
Francie, 1971, Twist 'N Turn, MIB **600.00**
Julia, 1970, Twist 'N Turn, 1-pc uniform, MIB **100.00**
Ken, flocked hair, minimum value **125.00**
Ken, Malibu, minimum value **25.00**
Ken, 1962, Dr Ken, MIB, minimum value **200.00**
Ken, 1965, bendable legs, #1020, MIB **350.00**
Ken, 1970, bendable legs, brn pnt hair, #1124, MIB **125.00**
Ken, 1970, Talking, MIB **75.00**
Ken, 1971-73, Malibu, MIB **35.00**
Ken, 30th Anniversary, MIB **195.00**
Midge, 1963, str legs, MIB **200.00**
Midge, 1965, bendable legs, MIB **500.00**
Midge, 30th Anniversary, MIB **195.00**
PJ, 1975, Free Moving, #7281, MIB **75.00**

PJ, 1976, Deluxe Quick Curl, MIB 75.00
PJ, 1976, Quick Curl, 11½" 40.00
Ricky, 1965, str legs, red hair & freckles, MIB 100.00

Skipper, red hair, dated 1963, MIB, $100.00 minimum value.

Skipper, 1963, minimum value 85.00
Skipper, 1967, Growing Up, OC, MIB 45.00
Skipper, 1972, Pose 'N Play, w/gym, MIB 250.00
Skipper, 1975, Growing Up, lt blond hair, MIB 50.00
Skooter, 1976, Funtime, dk red hair, bl swimsuit, MIB 150.00
Stacey, 1968, Talking, M in plastic box 150.00
Steffie, 1972, Busy, pnt lashes, #3312, MIB 150.00
Todd, 1965, #3590, MIB 100.00
Truly Scrumptious, 1969, str legs, #1108, MIB 400.00
Tutti, 1966, jtd at neck, blond or brunette, #3550, MIB 100.00
Tutti, 1967, Cookin' Goodies, #3559, MIB 300.00

Barbie Gifts Sets and Related Accessories

When no condition is indicated, the items listed below are assumed to be mint and in the original box or package (if one was issued). Items in only excellent condition may be worth 40% to 60% less.

Clothes, Beautiful Bride, ca 1964-66, M 800.00
Clothes, Bride's Dream, early, M 175.00
Clothes, Drum Majorette, early, M 150.00
Clothes, Enchantment, ca 1964-66, M 475.00
Clothes, Holiday Dance, ca 1964-66, M 395.00
Clothes, Oscar de la Renta series, 1980-90, M (sealed), minimum .45.00
Clothes, Outdoor Life, ca 1964-66, M 200.00
Clothes, Suburban Shopper, early, M 200.00
Country Camper, 1970, #4994, NMIB 35.00
Display set, Francie & Casey Fashion Boutique, 1969, M 800.00
Gift set, Barbie & Ken Little Theatre, MIB (sealed) 2,800.00
Gift set, Barbie Perfectly Plaid, Sears, MIB (sealed) 350.00
Gift set, Barbie Sparkling Pink, MIB (sealed) 950.00
Gift set, Mix & Match, ponytail or bubble cut, MIB (sealed) .1,000.00
Gift set, Walking Jamie Strollin' in Style, 1972, M 1,000.00
Horse, Dallas, palomino, M 60.00
Miss America Beauty Center, #7893, 1974, M 15.00
Sun 'N Fun Buggy, 1971-72, #1158, M 75.00
Tutti Playcase, #3001, M 25.00
Tutti Playhouse, 1967, #3300, M 75.00

Belton

Concave head, 2 or 3 hole, EX bsk, o/c/m or c/m w/wig, 10" ...1,300.00

Concave head, 2 or 3 hole, EX bsk, o/c/m or c/m w/wig, 13" ...1,800.00
Concave head, 2 or 3 hole, EX bsk, o/c/m or c/m w/wig, 15" .2,300.00
Concave head, 2 or 3 hole, EX bsk, o/c/m or c/m w/wig, 16" .2,500.00
Concave head, 2 or 3 hole, EX bsk, o/c/m or c/m w/wig, 17" .2,800.00
Concave head, 2 or 3 hole, EX bsk, o/c/m or c/m w/wig, 20" .3,200.00
Concave head, 2 or 3 hole, EX bsk, o/c/m or c/m w/wig, 22" .3,400.00
Concave head, 2 or 3 hole, EX bsk, o/c/m or c/m w/wig, 23" .3,500.00
Concave head, 2 or 3 hole, EX bsk, o/c/m or c/m w/wig, 26" .4,000.00
Concave head, 2 or 3 hole, EX bsk, o/c/m or c/m w/wig, 8" 1,000.00

Bru

Closed mouth, all kid body, bsk lower arms, Bru, 16" 9,200.00

Closed mouth, kid body with bisque lower arms and legs, blue paperweight eyes, human hair wig, pierced ears, redressed, original marked shoes, Bru Jne, 21½", $20,000.

Closed mouth, all kid body, bsk lower arms, Bru, 21" 19,000.00
Closed mouth, kid/wood body, bsk lower arms, Bru Jne, 12" .16,000.00
Closed mouth, kid/wood body, bsk lower arms, Bru Jne, 16" .20,000.00
Closed mouth, kid/wood body, bsk lower arms, Bru Jne, 25" .26,000.00
Closed mouth, kid/wood body, bsk lower arms, Bru Jne, 32" .35,000.00
Closed mouth, mk Bru, circle dot, 23" 26,000.00
Open mouth, compo walker's body, throws kisses, 18" 7,600.00
Open mouth, compo walker's body, throws kisses, 26" 9,400.00

Cabbage Patch

Babyland General Hospital, A (bl edition), 1978, minimum ..1,600.00
Babyland General Hospital, Champagne edition, 1983-84 ....800.00
Babyland General Hospital, E (bronze edition), 1979, minimum ..500.00
Babyland General Hospital, Grand edition, 1980, minimum 750.00
Babyland General Hospital, Oriental edition, 1983 ....900.00

Coleco, 1986 brunette #10 with 2 bottom teeth, popcorn hairdo, and toothbrush, M, $45.00; 1986 #11 clown with gold popcorn hair, tongue exposed, M, $50.00.

Coleco, bald baby, 1983, minimum 125.00
Coleco, Blk boy or girl w/freckles, 1983, minimum 195.00
Coleco, brunette w/ponytail, gr signature stamp, 1984 ....165.00
Coleco, popcorn hairdo, bl signature stamp, 1985 ....200.00
Coleco, powder scent, blk stamp, boy or girl, 1983 ....125.00
Coleco, w/pacifier, 1983, from $50 to 175.00

Celebrity

Charlie Chaplin, Lewis Amberg & Sons, 1915, EX 750.00
Desi Arnez as Ricky Ricardo, Applause, 1988, 17", MIB 40.00
Dolly Parton, plastic/vinyl, red dress, Goldberger, '87, 17" 75.00
Dorothy Hamill, Olympic, Ideal, 1977, 11½", MIB (sealed) 75.00
Elizabeth Taylor, from Cat on Hot Tin Roof, World, 11½", M 50.00
Elvis Presley, The Phoenix (blk clothes), World, 18", M 185.00
Engelbert Humperdink, bsk, intaglio eyes, NIADA, 1972, 17" ..500.00
Farrah Fawcett (as Jill), Hasbro, 1977, 8½", M on card 35.00
Harlem Globetrotter, vinyl, posable, Lakeside, 9", M 12.50

Marilyn Monroe, Seven Year Itch, 20th Century Fox, 1982, 11½", MIB, $75.00.

Marilyn Monroe, musical, revolves, 8½", MIB 125.00
Marilyn Monroe, vinyl, 7 Year Itch, Tri-Star, 1982, 16½", MIB ..75.00
Marilyn Monroe, wht sequin gown, World, M 475.00
Michael Jackson, jtd waist, bendable knees, LJN, '84, 11½", M ...45.00
Michael of Mary Poppins, plastic/vinyl, Horsman, 1965, OC, 8" ..30.00
Mr T, plastic/vinyl, Galoob, 1983, OC, 12" 32.00
OJ Simpson, Shindana, 1975, 9½", VG 200.00
Pee Wee Herman, cloth/vinyl, talker, Matchbox, 18", M 95.00
Prince Charles, American Character, M 65.00
Princess Diana, as bride, Danbury Mint, MIB 150.00
Redd Foxx, stuffed cloth, talker, Shindana, 1977, MIB 50.00
Sally Field as Flying Nun, Hasbro, 1967, 12", MIB (sealed) 200.00
Sonja Henie, Madame Alexander, all orig, 18", M 325.00
Sylvester Stallone as Lincoln Hawks, Lewco, 1986, M 17.50
Wayne Gretzky, Mattel, MIB 135.00
6 Million Dollar Man, as astronaut, Kenner, 13", M 65.00

China, Unmarked

Adelina Patti, center part, curls at temples, 1860s, 14" 275.00
Adelina Patti, center part, curls at temples, 1860s, 18" 450.00
Adelina Patti, center part, curls at temples, 1860s, 22" 485.00
Biedermeier or Bald Head, takes wig, RpC, 14" 625.00
Biedermeier or Bald Head, takes wig, RpC, 20" 875.00
Brown Eyes (pnt), any hairstyle or date, 16" 575.00
Brown Eyes (pnt), any hairstyle or date, 20" 950.00
Common Hairdo, blond or blk hair, RpC, after 1905, 12" 145.00

Common Hairdo, blond or blk hair, RpC, after 1905, 23" 285.00
Common Hairdo, blond or blk hair, RpC, after 1905, 8" 80.00
Covered Wagon Style, sausage curls, RpC, 1840s-70s, 12" 285.00
Covered Wagon Style, sausage curls, RpC, 1840s-70s, 24" 900.00
Curly Top, loose ringlet curls, RpC, 1845-60s, 16" 500.00
Curly Top, loose ringlet curls, RpC, 1845-60s, 20" 700.00

Curly Top, loose ringlet curls, redressed, 1845-60, 27", $550.00; Flat Top, black hair with mid-part and short curls, redressed, ca 1860, 18", $350.00.

Dolly Madison, modeled ribbon & bow, RpC, 1870-80s, 14" 250.00
Dolly Madison, modeled ribbon & bow, RpC, 1870-80s, 18" 475.00
Dolly Madison, modeled ribbon & bow, RpC, 1870-80s, 21" 550.00
Flat Top, blk hair, mid-part/short curls, RpC, ca 1860, 17" 300.00
Flat Top, blk hair, mid-part/short curls, RpC, ca 1860, 20" 350.00
Glass Eyes, various hairstyles, RpC, 1840s-70s, 14" 1,400.00
Japanese, blk or blond hair, mk or unmk, RpC, 1910-20s, 14" 185.00
Japanese, blk or blond hair, mk or unmk, RpC, 1910-20s, 17" 250.00
Man or Boy, glass eyes, side part, RpC, 14" 2,200.00
Man or Boy, pnt eyes, side part, RpC, 14", EX 1,200.00
Man or Boy, pnt eyes, side part, RpC, 16" 1,400.00
Man or Boy, pnt eyes, side part, RpC, 21½" 2,400.00
Peg Wood Body, early hairdo, 1840s, 16", EX 2,200.00
Pet Name, molded shirtwaist w/name on front, RpC, 1905, 8" ...125.00
Pierced Ears, various hairstyles, RpC, 14" 475.00
Pierced Ears, various hairstyles, RpC, 18" 675.00
Snood/Combs, any appl hair decor, RpC, 14" 650.00
Snood/Combs, any appl hair decor, RpC, 17" 800.00
Spill Curls, w/or w/out head band, RpC, 14" 400.00
Spill Curls, w/or w/out head band, RpC, 22" 850.00
Wood Body, articulated/slim hips, RpC, 1840s-50s, 12" 1,500.00
Wood Body, articulated/slim hips, RpC, 1840s-50s, 17" 3,200.00
Wood Body, jtd hips, covered-wagon hairdo, 1840s-50s, 12" 985.00
Wood Body, jtd hips, covered-wagon hairdo, 1840s-50s, 15" ..1,800.00

Cloth

Honey Lou, vinyl face mask, Gund, 1951, OC minus bonnet, 18" .45.00
Little Lulu, pressed face, felt OC, Georgene Novelties, 15½" 165.00
Nancy, printed, Knickerbocker, 1973, 6¼" 20.00
Scarecrow, from Wizard of Oz, Knickerbocker, 1939, 23½" 185.00
Tiny Tim, felt features, wires in limbs for posing, 18" 50.00

Eegee

Ballerina Sherry, vinyl, 1-pc body, o/c eyes, OC, 8½" 20.00

Susan Stroller, hard plastic with rooted hair and sleep eyes, 1962, all original, 20", $45.00.

Bonnie Ballerina, plastic/vinyl, jtd, o/c eyes, OC, 31" 185.00
Buster, plastic/vinyl, o/c/m, molded hair, RpC, 17" 45.00
Chickie, compo, tin o/c eyes, o/m/teeth, molded hair, OC, 16" ..285.00
Early, stuffed vinyl, 1-pc body, disk jtd arms, RpC, 29" 40.00
Gemette, plastic/vinyl, 1963, OC, 15" 45.00
Granny type, plastic/vinyl, wht hair in bun, OC, 14" 80.00
Kiss Me, plastic/vinyl, raise arm for kiss, OC, 17" 25.00
Lovable Baby/Sherry Lou, vinyl 1-pc body, o/c eyes, OC, 15" 15.00
Rose Red Flowerkin, plastic/vinyl, o/c eyes, OC, 16" 90.00
Sleepy Time Girl, vinyl/latex, bl o/c eyes, RpC, 18" 15.00

Effanbee

Bernard Fleischaker and Hugo Baum became business partners in 1910, and after two difficult years of finding toys to buy and a retail market to sell them in, they decided to manufacture dolls of their own. Their lovely dolls were a decided success largely because of their dedication to their work and the mutual trust and respect they held for each other. This is reflected in the Effanbee trademark — Eff stands for Fleischaker and bee for Baum. The company still exists today.

Baby Cup Cake, plastic/vinyl, o/c eyes, dimples, RpC, 12" 20.00
Baby Tinyette, compo, str or bent legs, OC, 8" 245.00
Baby Wonder, compo, tin o/c eyes, o/c/m, holds bottle, OC, 13" ..165.00
Button Nose, compo, pnt eyes, molded hair, OC, 8" 185.00
Candy Walker, vinyl/hp, head turns, rooted hair, OC, 24" 200.00
Lil Darlin', vinyl/cloth, cry box, o/c eyes, OC, 16" 95.00
Mary Lee, compo, o/c eyes, o/m/teeth/felt tongue, RpC, 16" 265.00

Effanbee Patsy-Ann, composition head and 5-piece body, blue tin sleep eyes, original clothes, 19", $465.00.

Patsy Baby, compo/cloth/celluloid, o/c eyes, OC, 10" 265.00
Patsy Jr, compo, pnt/molded hair, pnt eyes, OC, 11½" 285.00
Patsy Ruth, compo/cloth, brn o/c eyes, hh wig, OC, 27" 850.00
Plymouth Colony Historical, compo, pnt brn eyes, OC, 14" 650.00

Half Dolls

Half dolls, lovely porcelain figures awaiting attachment to secure bases, were never meant to be objects of play. Most of these lovely ladies were firmly sewn into pincushion bases that were beautifully decorated and served as the skirt of their gown. Other skirts were actually covers for items on milady's dressing table. Some were used for parasol or brush handles or for tops to candy containers or perfume bottles. Most popular from 1900 to about 1930, they will most often be found marked with the country of their origin — Bavaria, Germany, France, and Japan. You may also find some fine quality pieces marked Goebel, Dressel and Kester, and Heubach.

Germany, arms & hands attached, common type, 3" 25.00
Germany, arms & hands attached, common type, 5" 35.00
Germany, arms & hands attached, common type, 8" 55.00
Germany, arms & hands completely away, 12", $200 to 950.00
Germany, arms & hands completely away, 3", $85 to 145.00
Germany, arms & hands completely away, 5", $100 to 285.00
Germany, arms & hands completely away, 8", $165 to 650.00
Germany, arms extended, hands attached, 3" 50.00
Germany, arms extended, hands attached, 5" 85.00
Germany, arms extended, hands attached, 8" 125.00

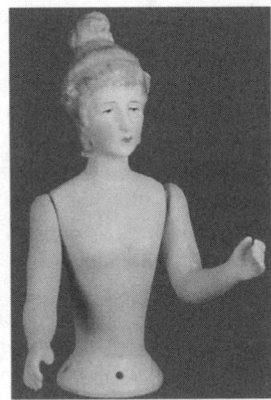

Germany, bisque with jointed shoulders, gray hair, #3536, 5½", $300.00.

Japan mk, 3" 20.00
Japan mk, 5" 30.00
Japan mk, 8" 50.00

Heubach

#1017, baby-faced toddler, bsk head, o/m, RpC, 18" 1,600.00
#2850, bsk head, o/c/m w/teeth, molded braids, RpC, 16" 9,400.00
#5636, laughing child, intaglio pnt eyes, 2 teeth, RpC, 9" 850.00
#7129, laughing character, ShHd, cloth body, RpC, 11" 675.00
#7603, pouty ShHd, intaglio eyes, cloth body, RpC, 18" 995.00
#7644, ShHd, chubby cheeks, kid body, bsk arms, RpC, 16" 800.00
#7701, pouty, intaglio eyes, RpC, 16" 1,500.00
#7959, intaglio eyes, molded-on bonnet & hair, RpC, 17" 3,500.00
#9141, winking glass eyes, RpC, 9" 1,500.00

Horsman

Campbell Kid, compo, pnt-on shoes & socks, all orig, 12" 350.00
Compo & cloth, brn tin o/c eyes, curly molded hair, OC, 14½" ..185.00

Fairy Skin Doll, plastic/vinyl, 1-pc body, molded hair, OC, 18" ...20.00

Hansel and Gretel, soft vinyl, rooted hair, sleep eyes, all original, unmarked but tagged Horsman Doll Co., 1963, 15", $245.00 each.

Jody, vinyl/plastic, bl o/c eyes, 1964, OC, 15" 30.00
Linda, vinyl/plastic, rooted hair, o/c eyes, 1959, OC, 36" 200.00
Mary Poppins, plastic/vinyl walker, o/c eyes, 1966, OC, 26" 245.00
Patty Duke, plastic/vinyl, posable, pnt eyes, 1965, OC, 12" 75.00
Pudgie, vinyl, lg pnt eyes, OC, 12½" 15.00
Sherry, vinyl/cloth, gr o/c eyes, rooted red hair, OC, 19" 20.00
Vinyl w/1-pc vinyl body, crying face, pnt eyes, OC, 7" 8.00
Vinyl w/1-pc vinyl stuffed body, brn o/c eyes, 1955, OC, 22" 30.00
Zodiac Baby, vinyl, rooted pk hair, o/c/m, OC, 6" 15.00

Ideal

Tammy, in school outfit, 1962, 12", M, $60.00.

Bonnie Walker, hp, cryer, pin-hip walker, o/c eyes, RpC, 17" 90.00
Carol Brent, hp, pnt eyes, OC, 15" 50.00
Cousin Sue, vinyl/cloth, o/c eyes, o/c/m w/teeth, RpC, 18" 85.00
Dr Evil, action figure, 1965, OC, 11" 45.00
Fannie Brice as Baby Snooks, flexy wire w/compo, 1939, 12½" ..275.00
Ginger, compo, brn o/c eyes, o/m, OC, 1939, 15" 185.00
Honeysuckle, vinyl, 1-pc body, o/c eyes, o/c/m, 1955, OC, 20" 75.00
Magic Squeezums, plastic/latex, o/c eyes, molded hair, OC, 30" ...50.00
Mary Jane, compo, flirty o/c eyes, mohair wig, OC, 18" 265.00
Mortimer Snerd, flexy wire w/compo, OC, 1939, 13" 275.00
Posie, vinyl/hp walker, o/c eyes, OC, 1954, 17", MIB 165.00
Rub-A-Dub Baby, plastic/vinyl, o/c/m, OC, 17" 20.00
Snow White, compo/cloth, red pnt bow, OC, 18" 450.00

Madame Alexander

Beatrice Alexander founded the Alexander Doll company in 1923 using a lovely doll that was designed after her daughter Mildred. With the help of her three sisters, the company prospered; and by the late 1950s there were three factories with over six hundred employees making Madame Alexander dolls. The company still produces these lovely dolls today.

Active Miss, hp, Violet/Cissy, 1954 only, 18" 725.00
Alexander-Kins, hp, bend-knee nonwalker, 1965-72, nude, 8" 85.00
Alexander-Kins, hp, bend-knee walker, 1956-64, carcoat, 8" 425.00
Alexander-Kins, hp, nonwalker, Wendy Ann, nightgown, 8" 300.00
Alexander-Kins, hp, walker, 1955 only, school dress, 7½-8" 300.00
Alice in Wonderland, compo, Little Betty, 1930s, 9" 350.00
Ana McGuffey, compo, Betty, 1935-37, 15" 600.00
Anastasia, Portrette, Cissette, #1125, 1988-89, 10" 78.00
Antoinette, compo, Wendy Ann, 1946, 21" 1,900.00
Astor, vinyl, toddler, 1953 only, gold organdy outfit, 9" 100.00
Austria Girl, hp, str legs, Wendy Ann, 1973-75, 8" 60.00
Baby Clown, hp, pnt face, Wendy Ann, #464, '55, 8", minimum 1,200.00
Bali, hp, #533, 1993 only, 8" 54.00
Ballerina, bend-knee walker, 1954-60, #564, yel clothes, 8" 500.00
Barbary Coast, hp, Portrette, Cissette, 1962-63, 10", minimum ...1,200.00
Belle Brummel, cloth, 1930s 650.00
Betty, compo, 1934-43, 7" 325.00
Black Forest, Wendy Ann, 1989-90, #512, 8" 60.00
Bonnie Walker, hp, skater, 1955 only, 15" 550.00
Bride, compo, Little Betty, 1936-41, 9-11" 325.00
Bride, hp, Margaret, 1949, 1952-55, 23" 675.00
Bride, porc, 1989-90, satin & lace, 21" 570.00
Bridesmaid, hp, Maggie, 1952, 15" 425.00
Brigetta of Sound of Music, Cissette, 1971-72, 10" 200.00
Butch, compo/cloth, 1942-46, 11-12" 150.00
Carmen, compo, Tiny Betty, 1938-43, 7" 325.00
Carnival in Rio, porc, 1989-90, 21" 450.00
Christening Baby, cloth/vinyl, 1951-54, 11-13" 75.00
Cinderella, compo, Princess Elizabeth, 1935-39, 16" 475.00
Cinderella, hp, Wendy Ann, #402, 1955 only, 8" 950.00
Cissette, hp, jtd elbows & knees, 1947-63, ball gown, 10" 400.00
Colleen, Portrait, Cissette, #1121, 1988 only, 10" 60.00
Country Cousins, cloth, 1940s, 10" 725.00
Cowgirl, hp, bend-knee, Wendy Ann, #724, 1967-70, 8" 350.00
Cynthia, hp, Blk Margaret, 1952 only, 15", minimum 750.00
Dearest, vinyl baby, 1962-64, 12" 125.00
Denmark, hp, bend-knee, Wendy Ann, #769, 1970-72, 8" 145.00
Ding Dong Bell, compo, Tiny Betty, 1937-42, 7" 325.00
Dolly Dryper, vinyl, 1952 only, 11", w/7-pc layette 280.00
Dr DeFoe, compo, 1937-39, 15-16" 1,600.00
Dutch, compo, Tiny Betty, 1935-39, 7" 325.00
Easter Doll, hp, Wendy Ann, 1968, yel dress, 8", minimum 1,200.00
Elaine, hp, Cissy, 1954 only, bl organdy, 18" 1,500.00
Enchanted Evening, Portrait, Cissy, 1991-92, 21" 250.00
Evangeline, cloth, 1930s, 18", minimum 700.00
Fairy Queen, compo, Wendy Ann, 1940-46, 14½" 600.00
Finnish, compo, Tiny Betty, 1935-37, 7" 245.00
France, compo, Tiny Betty, 1936-43, 7" 265.00
Funny, cloth, 1963-77, 18" 50.00
Geranium, vinyl toddler, 1953 only, red dress/bonnet, 9" 95.00
Glamour Girl, hp, Margaret or Maggie, 1953 only, 18" 1,300.00
Goldilocks, cloth, 1930s, 18", minimum 750.00
Gretel, compo, Tiny Betty, 1935-42, 7" 275.00
Groom, bend-knee, #477, 1956, 8" 425.00
Groom, compo, Margaret, 1946-47, 18-21" 900.00

Hansel, compo, Little Betty, 1938-40, 9" 325.00
Holly, Portrette, Cissette, #1135, 1990-91, 10" 85.00
Huckleberry Finn, hp, Wendy Ann, #490, 1989-91, 8" 60.00
Hulda, hp, lamb's wool wig, Blk Margaret, 1949, 18" 1,500.00
Ida McKinley, First Ladies Series, Louisa, 1988 ....85.00
India, hp, bend-knee walker, Wendy Ann, #775, 1965, 8" 225.00
Isolde, Opera Series, Mary Ann, #1413, 1985-86, 14" 90.00
Jack & Jill, compo, Little Betty, 1939, 9", ea 300.00
Jane Withers, compo, c/m, 1937, 12-13½", minimum 950.00
Jasmine, Portrait, Cissette, burnt orange, 1987-88, 10" 75.00
Jeannie Walker, compo, jtd legs, 1940s, 13-14" 400.00
Juliet, compo, Portrait, Wendy Ann, 1945-46, 21", minimum .2,600.00
June Wedding, hp, 1956, 8" 600.00
Kate Greenaway, cloth, 1936-38, 16" 900.00

Kathy Tears, vinyl, closed mouth, 1959, 15", M, $85.00.

Kathy Tears, vinyl, c/m, 1959-62, 11" 50.00
Korea, hp, bend-knee, Wendy Ann, #772, 1968-70, 8" 225.00
Lady in Waiting, hp, Wendy Ann, #487, 1955, 8", minimum .1,400.00
Lazy Mary, compo, Tiny Betty, 1936-38, 7" 265.00
Lion Tamer, Americana Series, Wendy Ann, #306, 1990, 8" 80.00
Little Bo Peep, hp, bend-knee walker, Wendy Ann, 1962-64, 8" .375.00
Little Cherub, compo, 1945-46, 11" 300.00
Little Genius, compo/cloth, 1935-40, 1942-46, 12-14" 125.00
Little Jack Horner, compo, Tiny Betty, 1937-43, 7" 325.00
Little Madeline, hp, Madeline, 1953-54, 8", minimum 625.00
Little Shaver, cloth, 1940-44, 15" 485.00
Little Women, compo, Tiny Betty, 1935-44, 7", ea 275.00
Little Women, hp, 1-pc arms & legs, Lissy, 1959-68, 12", ea .225.00
Lively Huggums, knob makes limbs & head move, 1963, 25" 125.00
Lovey Dove, hp/latex, 1950-51, 19" 95.00
Lucinda, plastic/vinyl, Janie, 1969-70, 12", minimum 345.00
Madame (Alexander), 1984, 1-pc pk skirt, 21" 400.00
Madeline, hp, jtd elbows & knees, 1950-53, 17-18", minimum ..950.00
Maggie Mixup, hp/vinyl, Elise body, 1960 only, 16½" 425.00
Maggie Walker, Cissy, 1951-53, 23-25" 650.00
Maid of Honor, compo, Wendy Ann, 1940-44, 18", minimum ..700.00
Margaret O'Brien, compo, 1946-48, 14½" 700.00
Marine, compo, Wendy Ann, 1943-44, 14" 750.00
Mary Mine, cloth/vinyl, 1977-89, 21" 125.00
Melanie, Jacqueline, #2173, 1967, bl dress w/rickrack 575.00
Mimi, hp, jtd, 1961 only, formal, 30" 800.00
Mommy & Me, compo, Margaret, 1948-49, 14", set, minimum ..1,500.00
Mrs Buck Rabbit, cloth/felt, mid-1930s 600.00
Muffin, cloth, 1966 only, 19" 100.00

Nancy Ann, hp, 1950 only, 17-18", minimum 800.00
Nicole, Portrait, Cissette, #1139, 1989-90, 10" 70.00
Nina Ballerina, compo, Tiny Betty, 1940, 7" 285.00
Nurse, compo, Tiny Betty, 1936-39, 7" 285.00
Oliver Twistail, cloth/felt, 1930s 700.00
Patty, plastic/vinyl, 1965 only, 18" 225.00
Peter Pan, hp, Margaret, 1953-54, 15", minimum 800.00
Polly, plastic/vinyl, 1965, ballgown, 17" 325.00
Pollyana, rigid vinyl, Marybel, 1960-61, 16" 350.00
Poodles, standing/sitting, named Ivy, 1940s, 14-17", minimum ..250.00
Prince Charles, hp, Wendy Ann, #397, 1957, 8", minimum 700.00
Princess Elizabeth, compo, o/m, 1938-39, 28", minimum 1,800.00
Priscilla, cloth, mid-1930s, 18" 650.00
Pussy Cat, cloth/vinyl, 1965-85, 14" 95.00
Queen, hp/vinyl, Jacqueline, 1965, wht brocade, 21", minimum .950.00
Queen Alexandrine, compo, Wendy Ann, 1939-41, 21" 1,700.00
Rebecca, compo, Wendy Ann, 1940-41, 21" 950.00
Renoir, compo, Wendy Ann, 1945-46, 21" 1,800.00
Riding Habit, Americana Series, Wendy Ann, #571, 1956, 8" ...425.00
Romeo, compo, Wendy Ann, 1949, 18", minimum 1,200.00
Rosebud, cloth/vinyl, 1952-53, 16-19" 135.00
Rusty, cloth/vinyl, 1967-68, 20" 350.00

Sarah Polk, Presidents' Ladies, 2nd set, 1979-81, #1511 with Martha face, 14", M, $90.00.

Scarlett O'Hara, compo, Tiny Betty, 1937-42, 7" 425.00
Scarlett O'Hara, hp, bend-knee, #760, 1963, 8", minimum 700.00
Scarlett O'Hara, hp, Margaret, 1950s, 20", minimum 1,400.00
Scarlett O'Hara, hp/vinyl, Jacqueline, #2152, 1965, 21" 1,200.00
Seven Dwarfs, compo, 1937 only, ea, minimum 450.00
Sleeping Beauty, compo, Princess Elizabeth, 1938-40, 15-16" 400.00
So Big, cloth/vinyl, pnt eyes, 1968-75, 22" 250.00
Sonja Henie, compo, Little Betty, 1940-41, 9" 450.00
South American, compo, Tiny Betty, 1938-43, 7" 285.00
Spanish Girl, str leg, #595, 1976-82, 3-tiered skirt, 8" 85.00
Spanish Matador, Wendy Ann, #530, 1992-93, 8" 55.00
Sugar Tears, vinyl baby, Honeybea, 1964 only, 12" 95.00
Sunbonnet Sue, compo, Little Betty, 1937-40, 9" 300.00
Swedish, compo, Tiny Betty, 1936-40, 7" 265.00
Teeny Twinkle, cloth, flirty eyes, 1946 only 500.00
Tippy Toe, cloth, 1940s, 16" 625.00
Turkey, hp, bend-knee, Wendy Ann, #787, 1968-72, 8" 125.00
Tyrolean Boy & Girl, hp, bend-knee, 1965-72, 8", ea 135.00
Victoria, baby, 1967-89, 20" 75.00
Victoria, compo, Wendy Ann, 1939, 1941, 21", minimum 1,800.00
Violetta, Cissette, #1116, 1987-88, 10" 60.00
WAAC (Army), compo, Wendy Ann, 1943-44, 14", minimum .750.00

Wendy Bride, compo, Wendy Ann, 1944-45, 14" 285.00
Yolanda, Brenda Star, 1965 only, 12" 325.00

Mattel

Chatty Cathy, pull-string talker, blond with blue eyes, 20", MIB, $185.00 minimum value.

Black Chatty Cathy, RpC, 10" 300.00
Bugs Bunny, plush/vinyl, pull-string talker, 1969, 19" 35.00
Chatty Baby, hexagon open grill, dtd 1960/1961/1962 ....175.00
Chatty Cathy, cloth covered speaker grill, mk, dtd 1960 ....300.00
Chatty Cathy, open speaker grill, dtd 1960/1961 ....250.00
Chester O'Chimp, plush/vinyl, wired fingers, 15" 30.00
Gentle Ben, plush, pull-string talker, felt tongue, 1967, 18" 25.00
Mama Beans, cloth/vinyl, 1974, OC, 10", w/4" twins 20.00
Sexed Girl, plastic/vinyl, bl o/c eyes, all orig, 11" 40.00
Slugger, vinyl/cloth, rooted red hair, 1975, 5½" 15.00
T-Bone (dog), pull-string talker, vinyl/cloth, 1964, 11" 25.00
Tangie, cloth/vinyl/yarn, pnt eyes, OC, 3½" 15.00

Mollye

Angel Face, compo/cloth, cry box, RpC, 24" 100.00
Baby Fun, compo toddler, orig wig, OC, 20" 150.00
Cloth w/pressed mask face, wht fur hair, all orig, 24" 225.00
Debbie Deb, compo, o/c eyes w/eyeshadow, c/m, 18" on music box .300.00
International series, all orig, 15", ea 150.00
Lone Ranger, hp & latex, OC, 22" 200.00
Margaret Rose Bride, hp, bl o/c eyes, o/m, OC, 20" 325.00
Mollye, cloth, OC w/wide brimmed bonnet, 1920s, 12" 85.00
Peggy Rose the Royal Bride, hp, bl o/c eyes, o/m, OC, 16" 265.00
Perky, vinyl, freckles, molded hair, 11", minimum value 25.00
Royal Wedding, compo, bl o/c eyes w/eyeshadow, c/m, OC, 21" .465.00

Schoenhut

Albert Schoenhut left Germany in 1866 to go to Pennsylvania to work as a repairman for toy pianos. He eventually applied his skills to wooden toys and later designed an all-wood doll which he patented on January 17, 1911. These uniquely jointed dolls were painted with enamels and came with a metal stand. Some of the later dolls had stuffed bodies, voice boxes, and hollow heads; some were made with heads of imitation bisque. These innovations influenced the development of the popular Bye-Lo Baby which was introduced in 1924. Due to the changing economy and fierce competition, the company closed in the mid-1930s.

Baby head, on regular body, wig, decal eyes, 12", EX 565.00
Child, character face, wig, intaglio eyes, o/c/m, OC, 14" 1,600.00
Child w/cvd hair, c/m, 14", EX 2,500.00
Child w/cvd hair, some wear, 17" 1,750.00

Compo, molded curly hair, Patsy-style body, 13" 550.00
Dolly face, o/c/m w/teeth, pnt eyes, OC, 14" 675.00
Man w/cvd hair, 19", minimum 2,700.00
Sleep eyes, o/m w/teeth, OC, 14" 1,200.00
Toddler, 12", EX 900.00
Tootsie Wootsie, molded/pnt hair, o/c/m w/teeth, OC, 14" 1,900.00
Walker, pnt eyes, o/c or o/m, OC, 15", EX 900.00

SFBJ

By 1895 Germany was producing dolls of good quality at much lower prices than the French dollmakers because of lower wages in German factories. This was a serious threat to the French companies, and in a supreme effort to save the doll industry, several leading French manufacturers united to form one large company in the hope they could combine their strengths to save the French market. Bru, Raberry and Delphieu, Pintel and Godshaux, Fleischman and Bodel, and Jumeau united to form the company today known as SFBJ. Their dolls did well while Germany was otherwise occupied with WWII, but after the war German doll production proved to be too strongly competitive, and SFBJ closed in 1958.

Tete Jumeau, p/e, o/m w/teeth, o/c eyes, jtd wrists, 22" 2,000.00
20, molded pnt shoes & eyes, 5-pc body, Paris/12, 10" 365.00
215, bsk swivel on compo, c/m, inset eyes, 15" 1,800.00
227, brn swivel closed dome head, animal skin wig, 15" 1,900.00
227, closed dome, o/m, inset eyes, pnt hair, 15" 2,100.00
229, compo w/swivel head, o/c/m, inset eyes, 18" 5,000.00

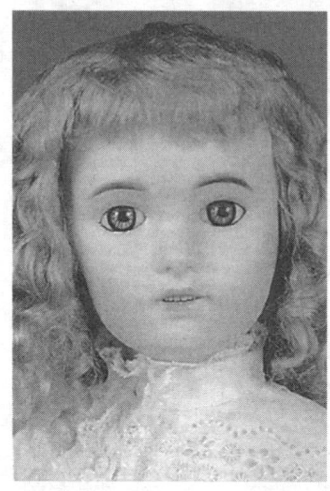

#230, bisque socket head with blue paperweight eyes, open mouth with 6 teeth, mohair wig, jointed wood and composition body, nicely redressed, 24", EX, $1,000.00.

230, compo walker, p/e, o/m, inset eyes, 16" 1,600.00
235, closed dome, molded hair, o/c/m & eyes, 16" 1,700.00
236, laughing Jumeau, o/m, o/c eyes, dbl chin, 12" 1,300.00
236, laughing Jumeau, o/m, o/c eyes, dbl chin, 20" 2,200.00
238, compo w/swivel head, o/m, inset eyes, Paris 6, 15" 3,800.00
239, Poulbot, c/m, street urchin, red wig, 17" 9,500.00
245, boy, o/c mouth, lg glass googly eyes, pnt shoes, 8" 1,400.00
247, toddler, o/c/m w/2 inset teeth, 20" 2,900.00
247, Twirp, SkHd, o/c/m & eyes, 2 teeth, 21" 3,000.00
252, pouty, c/m, inset eyes, papier-mache body, 11" 2,800.00
252, pouty, c/m, inset eyes, papier-mache body, 22" 7,800.00
266, character, bsk head, closed dome, o/c/m, 20" 4,200.00
301, bsk SkHd on compo, o/m, inset eyes, 22" 1,200.00
301, bsk SkHd on compo, o/m, inset eyes, 22" 1,200.00
301, bsk SkHd on compo, o/m, inset eyes, 28" 1,700.00
60, French WWI nurse, 5-pc body, SFBJ/13/0, 8½" 475.00
60, o/m w/teeth, o/c eyes, hh wig, RpC, 12" 450.00

60, SkHd, compo w/str legs, o/m, curved arms, 15" 650.00

Shirley Temple

Prices are suggested for dolls complete and in mint conditon. Add from 25% to 50% (depending on her outfit) if the original box is present.

Bsk, 6", pnt, molded hair, Japan 250.00
Celluloid, 5", Japan 185.00
Celluloid, 8", Japan 245.00
Compo, 11", cowgirl 850.00
Compo, 11", 1934 to late '30s 900.00
Compo, 13" 700.00
Compo, 15-16" 800.00
Compo, 16", Germany, o/c eyes, o/m smile, 1936, minimum 600.00
Compo, 17-18" 950.00
Compo, 20" 1,100.00

Composition, 22", hazel sleep eyes, open mouth with 6 teeth and molded tongue, original mohair wig, 5-piece child body, all original clothing including blue organdy dress, M, $1,250.00.

Compo, 25", cowgirl 1,500.00
Compo, 7-8", Japan 300.00
Plastic/vinyl, 12", 1982-83 ....35.00
Plastic/vinyl, 8", 1982-83 ....30.00
Vinyl, 12", 1950s 165.00
Vinyl, 15", 1950s 265.00
Vinyl, 16", 1973 ....125.00
Vinyl, 17", Montgomery Ward, 1972 ....165.00
Vinyl, 17", 1950s 325.00
Vinyl, 19", 1950s 400.00
Vinyl, 36", 1950s 1,600.00

Simon and Halbig

Simon and Halbig was a large German doll firm that operated from ca 1870 until the 1930s. They were a popular supplier of bisque heads to French dollmakers of the 1870s and 1880s. This company made dolls for such famous companies as Gimbel Bros., Jumeau, Kammer and Reinhardt, as well as many others. Halbig became the sole owner of the company in 1895 but did not register 'S&H' as his trademark until ten years later.

#1073, o/m, flirty eyes, teeth, hh wig, p/e, OC, 24½" 900.00
Baby Blanche, SkHd, o/m baby, S&H, 16" 600.00
CM Bergmann, SkHd, o/m, Simon & Halbig, 3½, 18" 625.00

CM Bergmann, SkHd, o/m, 1897, S&H6, 12" 350.00
CM Bergmann, SkHd, o/m w/teeth, Simon & Halbig, RpC, 32" ...1,500.00
G68, SkHd, flirty eyes, 1908, S&H/K*R, 16" 550.00
Handwerck, SkHd, o/m, o/c eyes, rpt jtd body, RpC, 33" 1,400.00
Handwerck, SkHd, o/m, 1893, 16" 450.00
Handwerck, SkHd, o/m, 1895, G/S&H/1, 16" 450.00
Handwerck, SkHd, o/m w/teeth, o/c eyes, p/e, RpC, 38" 1,700.00
S&H3, all bsk, c/m, inset eyes, molded-on shoes, 6" 350.00
10, SkHd, o/m, G/Halbig/S&H, 19" 800.00
10, SkHd, o/m, G/Halbig/S&H, 22" 900.00
10½, SkHd, o/m, flirty o/c eyes, S*H, 18" 900.00
100, SkHd, o/m, Simon & Halbig/S&C/G, 22" 725.00
1039, SkHd, o/m w/teeth, p/e, jtd arms/wrists, hh, 22" 900.00
1159, SkHd, adult, 1905, G/Simon & Halbig/S&H7, 14" 1,400.00
1159, SkHd, adult, 1905, G/Simon & Halbig/S&H7, 24" 2,600.00

1159, socket head, adult lady, brown eyes, open mouth with teeth, mohair wig, S&H DEP, nicely dressed, 26", $2,900.00.

1160, bsk ShHd, Little Women type, cloth body, S&H, 7" 400.00
1249 Santa, bsk head, jtd compo, o/m, o/c eyes, p/e, 20" 1,400.00
1329, SkHd, o/m, olive, G/Simon & Halbig/SH, 14" 1,900.00
151, SkHd, o/c/m, pnt eyes, S&H/1, 16" 5,300.00
159, SkHd, o/m, Simon & Halbig, 16" 550.00
179, SkHd, o/m, Simon & Halbig S11H DEP, 20" 700.00
282, SkHd, o/m, SH, 14" 500.00
282, SkHd, o/m, SH, 22" 725.00
409, SkHd, o/m, S&H, 24" 685.00
409, SkHd, o/m, S&H, 30" 1,400.00
530, SkHd, o/m, G/Simon & Halbig, 21" 800.00
540, SkHd, swivel on bsk ShPl, o/m, S&H, G, 16" 600.00
570, SkHd, o/m, Halbig S&H/G, 18" 700.00
576, SkHd, o/m, Simon & Halbig, 16" 600.00
719, SkHd, bjtd, o/m, S12H/Dep, rpl wig, RpC, 20" 3,300.00
719, SkHd, swivel, ShPl, c/m, S&H, DEP, 20" 2,600.00
739, SkHd, c/m, brn, S 5 H DEP, 18" 2,400.00
759, SkHd, o/m, brn, S 10 H, DEP, rare, 20" 8,500.00
905, SkHd, swivel on ShPl, c/m, SH, 21" 3,000.00
929, SkHd, c/m, S&H, DEP, 20" 4,000.00
939, SkHd, c/m, S 11H DEP, 17" 2,700.00
939, SkHd, o/m, o/c eyes, S16H, 30" 4,200.00
940, SkHd, swivel on ShPl, o/c/m, S 2 H, 14" 1,500.00
949, ShHd, o/m, o/c eyes, S 10 H, bride clothes, 19½" 2,600.00

Terri Lee

Jerri Lee, in Spring Coat outfit 250.00
Jerri Lee, orig Davy Crockett outfit 300.00

Jerri Lee, w/chaps & gun belt, all orig 300.00
Terri Lee, Bridesmaid, pk gown, flower headband 350.00
Terri Lee, Brownie uniform, incomplete accessories 385.00
Terri Lee, Cowgirl, dk gr satin shirt/leather skirt & vest 300.00
Terri Lee, early pk coat w/lt bl piping 325.00
Terri Lee, Hawaiian outfit w/hula skirt 400.00
Terri Lee, lt rose formal w/pk net skirt 325.00
Terri Lee, mink coat, 16" 1,000.00
Terri Lee, pedal-pusher outfit 250.00
Terri Lee, pk & wht pinafore 285.00
Terri Lee, pk terry cloth bathrobe 250.00
Terri Lee, red & wht checked sundress 275.00
Terri Lee, red school dress w/wht collar 300.00
Terri Lee, wht fur coat & hat 350.00
Terri Lee, wht lace blouse & navy pleated skirt 300.00
Terri Lee, wht short blouse & bl jeans 250.00
Tiny Terri Lee, OC, 10", M in red/wht cb case 185.00

Uneeda

Am Gem Collection, various costumes, 8½", ea 10.00
Baby Dana, plastic/vinyl, o/c eyes, nurser, grows hair, OC, 20" 25.00

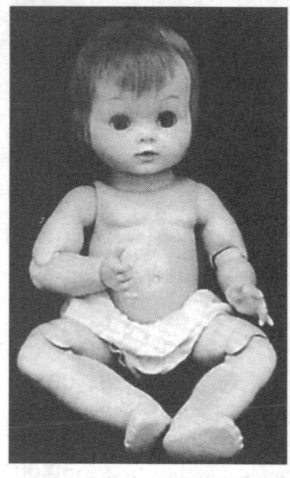

Baby Dollikins, rooted red hair, blue sleep eyes, open mouth/nurser, pin-jointed elbows and knees, 20", $50.00.

Chubby Toddler, plastic/vinyl, o/c eyes, c/m, OC, 16½" 20.00
Clover, plastic/vinyl, Hong Kong, OC, 10" 5.00
Grannykins, plastic/vinyl, gray hair, pnt eyes, OC, 6" 15.00
Little Coquette, plastic/vinyl, o/c eyes, o/m, OC, 18" 35.00
Serenade, plastic/vinyl, talker, c/m, ponytail, OC, 21" 50.00
Suzette, vinyl, molded & pnt lashes, OC, 10", MIB 65.00
Tiny Penelope, vinyl, orange rooted hair, Hong Kong, OC, 6" 3.00
Twin, plastic/vinyl, molded hair, o/c eyes, nurser, OC, 11" 10.00
Twinkle Tears, vinyl, squeeze body for tears, OC, 12" 20.00

Vogue

Baby Dear One, vinyl/cloth, bl o/c eyes, o/c/m w/teeth, OC, 23" .165.00
Baby Dear Too, vinyl & hp, bl o/c eyes, c/m, OC, 1963, 17" 185.00
Boy & Girl Toodles, compo, complete & all orig in trunk 450.00
Ginny, hp, brn caracul wig, o/c eyes, OC, 8" 365.00
Ginny, hp, brn eyes, bent legs, wool wig, orig bunny suit, rare .1,400.00
Ginny, hp, in riding habit, 8" 325.00
Ginny, hp, pnt eyes, gold velveteen coat w/hood, 8" 375.00
Ginny, hp, pnt eyes, OC, 1949, 7½" 375.00
Ginny as Davy Crockett, 1953, 8" 400.00
Ginny as Nan Bridesmaid, hp, 1953, 8" 375.00
Hansel, hp, OC, 1953 ....385.00

Toodles, compo, dressed as Hansel, 1940s, 8" 300.00
Toodles, compo, pnt bl eyes, in Mexican dress, 1940s, 8" 300.00
Toodles Baby, compo, pnt eyes, orig dress/coat/bonnet, 7" 265.00
Toodles Boy, compo, orig striped outfit, 8" 365.00

Door Knockers

Door knockers, those charming precursors of the doorbell, come in an intriguing array of shapes and styles. The very rare ones come from England. Cast-iron examples made in this country were often produced in forms similar to the more familiar doorstop figures.

Amish man, CI, eyes open & close 45.00
Cat, arched bk, bronze, England, 1900s, 3½" 55.00
Couple kissing against roses, brass, 5½" 90.00
Devil's head, brass, old 65.00
Flower basket on oval, CI w/mc & cream pnt, 4x3" 95.00
Girl knocking at door, pnt CI, 3½" 150.00
Girl watering flowers, CI w/MOP 85.00
Indian head, brass, 7½" 165.00
Lady's head, brass, foliate bkplate, 10" 225.00
Morning glory, CI, wht & yel w/gr leaves, 3x3", NM 125.00
Oliver Twist, brass 30.00
Owl, pnt CI, oval bk, 4½" 175.00
Parrot on perch on oval, CI w/EX mc pnt, 4¾x2¾" 185.00
Rooster on oval, CI w/EX mc pnt, 4½x3" 155.00
Rose & buds among leaves on oval, CI w/EX mc pnt, 4½x3" 155.00
Sailing ship, CI w/EX mc pnt, 4x2¾" 75.00
Spider hanging from web w/bee, CI, EX pnt, 3½" 150.00
Woodpecker, tree bkplate, pnt CI 85.00

Doorstops

Although introduced in England in the mid-1800s, cast-iron doorstops were not made to any great extent in this country until after the Civil War. Once called 'door porters,' their function was to keep doors open to provide better ventilation. They have been produced in many shapes and sizes, both dimensional and flat backed, and in the past few years have become a popular, yet affordable collectible. While cast-iron examples are the most common, brass, wood, and chalk were also used. An average price is in the $100.00 to $200.00 range, though some are valued at more than $400.00. Doorstops retained their usefulness and appeal well into the thirties.

The prices below reflect market values in the East where doorstops are at a premium. For other areas of the country, it may be necessary to adjust prices down about 25%. In the listings below, when no condition code is present, items are assumed to be in excellent original condition, flat backed unless noted full figured, and cast iron unless another material is mentioned. For further information we recommend *Doorstops, Identification and Values*, by Jeanne Bertoia.

Key:
B&H — Bradley & Hubbard   ff — full figured

Basket of Kittens, M Rosenstein, 1932, 10x7" 375.00
Basset Hound, Hubley, ff, sitting, 7x6½" 325.00
Bellhop, mk #1244, bl uniform w/red trim, 8⅞x4⅝" 300.00
Bird of Prey, English, blk pnt, 16¾x10½" 175.00
Blowfish, Hubley, ff, cream over pk, 8x7¼" 325.00
Bobby Blake, Hubley #46, holding teddy, 9½x5¼" 450.00
Boston Terrier, Hubley, ff, 10x10" 100.00
Boxer, Hubley, ff, brn, 8½x9" 300.00

Bulldog, Boston; Greenblatt, glass eyes, 13x5½" 225.00
Bulldog, English; B&H, 9½x5½" 375.00
Cat, blk pnt, glass eyes, 9¾x4⅜" 150.00
Cat, Eastern Specialty MFG #62, 7x4½" 250.00
Cat, Fireside; Hubley/Littco, ff, 5⅝x10¾" 200.00
Cat, Halloween; Greenblatt Studios #19, 1927, 9¼x6" 225.00
Cat, Hunchback; Hubley, ff, 10⅝x7½" 150.00
Cat, Modernistic; Hubley, ff, 9¾x5" 375.00
Cat, Sculptured Metal Studios, 1928, 13x9" 250.00
Cat, Sleeping; Hubley, ff, 7½x8" 350.00
Cats, Twin; Hubley #73/National #57, 7x5¼" 325.00
Charleston Dancers, Hubley, #270 FISH, 8⅞x5⅝", minimum 500.00
Cockatoo, White; National #82, 11¾x5¼" 150.00
Colonial Dame, Hubley #37, bl shaw, pk dress, 8x4½" 225.00
Colonial Woman, Littco Products, pk dress, 10¼x5¾" 150.00
Cow, New Holland Machine Co, bronze color, 12½x8½" 375.00
Dachshund, Taylor #8, 1930, 5½x7¼" 375.00
Dog & Duck, Greenblatt, 1925, 10x8¾", minimum 500.00
Dolly, Hubley #45, holding doll, 9½x5½" 450.00
Dolly Dimple, Hubley, ff, yel dress, bl hat, 7¾x3¾" 300.00
Duck w/Top Hat, blk hat, bl pants, yel duck, 7½x4¼" 275.00
Ducks, Hubley #291, 8¼x6¼" 325.00
Dutch Girl, ff, 6x3¾" 175.00
Dutch Girl, Littco Products, #33, w/2 water buckets, 13x10" 400.00
Elephant, mk S-117, cream on gr base, 6½x8¼" 200.00
Elephant (on base), B&H, 10x11¾" 200.00
Elephant w/o Tree, National #9, 10x9⅞" 225.00
Fawn, Taylor Cook #6, 1930, 10x6" 225.00
Fish, Fantail; Hubley #464, brass color, 9¾x5⅞" 175.00
Frog, mk 'I Croak for the Jackson Wagon,' ff, 5x2½" 150.00
Geisha, Hubley, ff, lute player, 7x6" 250.00
George Washington, hat off, leaning on post, 12¼x6⅜" 475.00
Giraffe, mk S-110, wedge, 13½x5¼" 275.00
Girl Holding Bouquet, Albany Foundry, ff, 7⅝x4¾" 200.00
Girls, Reading; sitting bk-to-bk, 5x8⅝" 475.00
Horse, National #12, blk horse w/red saddle, 8x10" 175.00
Horse Jumping Fence, Eastern #79, w/rider, 7⅞x11¾" 350.00
Huckleberry Finn, Littco, bl overalls, yel hat, 12½x9½" 500.00
Humpty Dumpty, mk #661, ff, 4½x3½" 300.00
Japanese Spaniel, mk #1267, begging, 9x4½" 275.00
Jill, Hubley #226, silver dress & bonnet, w/pail, 8¾x5¾" 375.00
Kitten, Hubley #38/National #37, 8x6" 150.00
Kitten, Reclining; National, ff, 8⅛x4" 225.00
Koala, Taylor Cook, #5, 1930, 7¼x5½" 425.00
Lafayette, blk coat, yel pants, sword at side, 11⅝x6⅜" 475.00
Little Boy w/Bear, Albany, ff, 5¼x3½" 175.00
Little Girl by Wall, Albany, ff, 5¼x3¼" 175.00
Marigolds, Hubley #315, mk Made in USA, 7½x8" 150.00
Messenger Boy, Hubley, mk #249 FISH, 10x5⅜" 450.00
Monkey on Barrel, Taylor #3, 1930, 8⅜x4⅞" 350.00
Old Fashion Lady, Hubley #296, yel over gr dress, 7¾x4" 275.00
Old Woman, B&H 7796, 11x7" 500.00
Organ Grinder, w/monkey, 9⅞x5¾" 350.00
Ostrich (on base), mk #120, 8½x9" 275.00
Owl, B&H #7797, glass eyes, 15½x5", minimum 500.00
Owl, Hubley #254, on flowered perch, 10x4½" 225.00
Owl on Books, Eastern, brn owl, red & bl books, 9¼x6½" 475.00
Parlor Maid, Hubley, mk #268 FISH, 9¼x3½", minimum value .500.00
Parrot, Blodgett Studios, #1010, 12½x6½" 250.00
Parrot, mk #1269, on perch, mc pnt, 8x3⅞" 200.00
Parrot, National, glass eyes, 10¾x6¾" 175.00
Peacock by Urn, Hubley #208, 7½x4¼" 225.00
Peasant Girl, Hubley #5, bl dress, basket on head, 8¾x5" 200.00
Pekingese, Hubley, ff, 14½x9" 450.00
Pelican on Dock, Albany #113, 8x7¼" 250.00
Penguin, Taylor Cook #1, 1930, 9½x5¼" 500.00
Peter Rabbit, Hubley #96, eating carrot, 9½x4¾" 400.00
Pheasant, Hubley #458 (Fred Everett), 8½x7½" 275.00
Polly, Hubley #180, mc pnt, 8⅛x5¼" 150.00
Poppies & Cornflowers, Hubley #265, 7¼x6½" 125.00
Punch, English, w/dog, 12x9" 500.00
Puppies in a Basket, M Rosenstein, 7x7⅜" 350.00
Quail, Hubley #459 (Fred Everett), 7¼x6¼" 350.00
Rabbit by Fence, Albany, 6⅞x8⅛" 350.00
Rabbit w/Top Hat, Albany #94, red tux, blk hat, 9⅞x4¾" 400.00
Rooster, Spencer, 13¼x11", minimum 500.00
Setter (at point), Hubley, ff, blk & wht, 8¾x15⅞" 175.00
Silhouette Girl, Albany Foundry #5, 11¼x10¼" 475.00
Southern Belle, National Foundry #72, 11¼x6" 150.00
Spanish Girl, Hubley #192, w/fan & shawl, 9x5" 225.00
Squirrel, mk EMIG #1382, blk pnt, 8x5½" 175.00
Stork, Hubley, wht, blk tail feathers, red beak & legs, 12¼x7" ..375.00
Swallows (in berry bush), Hubley #480, 8½x7½" 350.00
Terrier, Wirehaired Fox; Hubley #467, 10½x12¾" 450.00
Terrier (on base), Holest Rubber, rubber, 12¾x11" 200.00
Terrier (running), Spencer/Guilford, wedge, 4x7" 175.00
Terrier w/Bushes, mk copt c 1929 PAL, 8x7" 175.00
Terrior, Fox (on base); wht w/blk spots, 10⅜x10½" 250.00
Topsy, Hubley, wedge, 6x4" 275.00

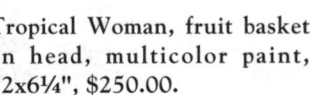

Tropical Woman, fruit basket on head, multicolor paint, 12x6¼", $250.00.

Warrior, B&H 7795, blk overall w/wht beard, 13¼x7¼" 425.00
Welsh Corgi (on base), B&H, 8¼x5⅞" 225.00
Whimsical Man, mk #1258, wood wedge, 7x3½" 325.00
Woman w/Muff, ff, brn pnt, 9¼x5" 225.00
Woman w/Ruffled Dress, gray w/blk bows, holding fan, 6¼x4¾" ..175.00

Dorchester Pottery

Taking its name from the town in Massachusetts where it was organized in 1895, the Dorchester Pottery Company made primarily utilitarian wares, though other types of items were made as well. By 1940 a line of decorative pottery was introduced, some of which was painted by hand with scrollwork or themes from nature. The buildings were destroyed by fire in the late 1970s, and the pottery was never rebuilt. In the listings that follow, the decorations described are all in cobalt unless otherwise noted. Our advisor for this category is Dale MacLean; he is listed in the Directory under Massachusetts.

Bowl, cereal; Pine Cone, 6" 40.00
Bowl, Sea Horse (int), sgn CAH, 2x5½" 100.00
Bowl, Whale, sgn CAH, 2¼x5½", +swirled bl underplate 100.00

Casserole, signed under handle by decorator Ronald Brake, signed on bottom by potter Ernesto Ricci, 6x12", $950.00.

Casserole, Blueberry, w/lid, mk, 1-qt, 4x6" dia 200.00
Casserole, Pine Cone, sgn CAH, 4½x7½" 150.00
Coffeecup, Pine Cone 40.00
Dish, Tear Drop, sgn CAH, 1⅛x6¼" 225.00
Mug, Apple, sgn CAH, 3", set of 4 ....175.00
Mug, Bell, striped hdl, paper label, 4½x3⅜" 130.00
Mug, Clown, Happy Day, sgn CAH, 2¾" 125.00
Mug, Full Scroll, sgn CAH, 4½" 75.00
Mug, Grape, striped buttressed hdl, cylindrical, CAH, 4½" 75.00
Mug, Whale, sgn CAH, 3", +6" saucer 70.00
Plate, Pine Cone, sgn CAH, 7¼" 120.00
Plate, Whale, sgn CAH, 10¼" 250.00
Syrup, Grape, sgn CAH, stamped, 5½x5" 140.00
Syrup, Half Scroll, bulbous, 5¼x4½" 125.00

Dorflinger

C. Dorflinger was born in Alsace, France, and came to this country when he was ten years old. When still very young, he obtained a job in a glass factory in New Jersey. As a young man, he started his own glassworks in Brooklyn, New York, opening new factories as profits permitted. During that time he made cut glass articles for many famous people including President and Mrs. Lincoln, for whom he produced a complete service of tableware with the United States Coat of Arms. In 1863 he sold the New York factories because of ill health and moved to his farm near White Mills, Pennsylvania. His health returned, and he started a plant near his home. It was there that he did much of his best work, making use of only the very finest materials. Christian died in 1915, and the plant was closed in 1921 by consent of the family.

Dorflinger glass is rare and often hard to identify. Very few pieces were marked — many only carried a small paper label which was quickly discarded.

Cruet, Heavy Flutes, cranberry to clear, cut stopper, att 265.00
Decanter, gr to clear, Dmn Point & oval cuttings, w/stopper 295.00
Plate, cranberry to clear, Vintage, 8" 495.00
Plate, oyster; Kalana Art #17, etched, 9", 8 for 275.00
Relish, Dmn & Fan cutting w/stars, triple-cut hdl, 2-part 500.00
Sherbet, Calla Lily, 4x4½" 75.00
Sherbet, Renaissance, bl to clear, stemmed, pr 175.00

Waste bowl, Mitre, cobalt to clear 110.00
Wine, cranberry to clear, Renaissance 185.00
Wine, Kalana Lily, 5", set of 6 ....90.00

Dragon Ware

Dragon ware is fairly accessible and is still being made today. The new Dragon ware is distinguishable by the lack of detail in the dragon. In the older pieces, much care is given to the slipwork dragon's eyes, scales, and wings. In the new ware, the dragon is flat and lacks detail.

Colors are primary, referring to background color, not the color of the dragon. The primary color of a new piece has more shine than the older ware. Old colors are vibrant but for the most part not shiny (except for the lustre colors). New colors include green, lavender, yellow, pink, blue, pearlized, and orange as well as the classic blue/black. Old colors include orange, green, yellow, blue, pearlized, and blue/black. In addition to lustre finishes, you will find some background colors that are applied unevenly (and without shine), producing a 'cloud' effect behind the dragon.

Many Dragon ware cups have lithophanes in the bottoms, often the face of a geisha girl. Nude lithophanes are more scarce but can sometimes be found in cups and saki cups. New pieces may also have lithophanes, but they are lacking in detail and tend to be flat.

Items listed below are unmarked unless noted otherwise. Our advisor for this category is Suzi Hibbard; she is listed in the Directory under California.

Vase, can form with small handles, Nippon mark, 4¼", $65.00.

Biscuit jar, gray, wicker hdl, mk MIJ, 4" 25.00
Box, dmn shape, mk MIJ, 4" 35.00
Children's cup & saucer, bl 15.00
Children's cup & saucer, teapot, cr/sug, orange 45.00
Children's cup & saucer, 5-sided, souvenir (Catalina) 12.50
Children's set, lustre, 1950s, mk MIJ, 15-pc, in box 125.00
Cigarette box, gray, mk MIOJ, +2 ashtrays 35.00
Condiment set, shakers/mustard/toothpick/plate, red, Nippon ...175.00
Cookie jar, gray, wicker hdl, mk MIJ 75.00
Cup & saucer, bl, mk Orton China 17.50
Cup & saucer, gr & yel cloud 20.00
Dinner set, gray, mk Kutani, 5-pc place setting 125.00
Ewer, gray, mk Nippon, 6¾" 225.00
Ferner, orange, mk MIJ, 9" W 75.00
Incense jar, gray, mk MIJ, 5" 35.00
Lamp, gray, 9" 125.00
Match holder, coal hod; bl, mk MIJ 17.50
Match holder, gray, mk Nippon, 5" 175.00
Nut bowl, orange 25.00
Nut dish, 3 bowls w/hdl, gray 50.00

Plate, bl/brn, mk MIJ, 8" **25.00**
Saki cup, gray bbl, orange hdl **15.00**
Saki set, gr cloud, +6 cups w/lithophane, mk MIJ **60.00**
Saki set, orange cloud, +6 cups w/lithophane, mk MIOJ **75.00**
Shakers, gray, mk MIJ, pr+tray **25.00**
Tea set, bl cloud, gr eyes, mk MIJ, 21-pc **325.00**
Tea set, bl/wht, dragon spouts, lithophanes, 21-pc **275.00**
Tea set, gray/yel, lustre interior, mk MIOJ, 21-pc **275.00**
Tea set, wht/red, dragon spout, lithophanes, 21-pc **225.00**
Teapot, blk/yel, lustre int, +cr/sug **150.00**
Teapot, red, dragon spout, mk Kutani, 8" **75.00**
Vase, bl cloud, mk MIOJ, 8" **50.00**
Vase, gray, jewel eyes, mk Nippon, 6" **200.00**
Vase, gray, 6-sided, mk MIJ, 3" **17.50**
Vase, orange, 6", pr **75.00**
Wall pocket, gray, pr **80.00**

Dresden

The term Dresden is used today to indicate the porcelains that were produced in Meissen and Dresden, Germany, from the very early 18th century well into the next. John Bottger, a young alchemist, discovered the formula for the first true porcelain in 1708 while being held a virtual prisoner at the palace in Dresden because of the King's determination to produce a superior ware. Two years later a factory was erected in nearby Meissen with Bottger as director. There fine tableware, elaborate centerpieces, and exquisite figurines with applied details were produced. In 1731, to distinguish their product from the wares of such potters as Sevres, Worcester, Chelsea, and Derby, the Meissen company adopted their famous crossed swords trademark. During the next century, several potteries were producing porcelain in the 'Meissen style' in Dresden itself. Their wares were often marked with imitations of Meissen's crossed swords.

The Carl Theime factory produced dinnerware as well as decorative pieces in the Meissen style from 1872 until 1972. Openwork pieces were their specialty. Their mark was an intertwined 'SP' with the word Dresden below. Other companies followed suit, and in 1883 began using the crown mark along with the Dresden indication. There were several variations of this mark employed over the years. Many of these companies produced Meissen-type wares well into the 20th century. See also Meissen.

Biscuit jar, lovers scenes, bl latticework at top, gold trim **250.00**
Bonbon, mc flowers on wht, 2-part, hdls, late, 6½" **85.00**
Bowl, centerpc; appl florals, trunk support w/Eros & girl, 15" **525.00**
Bowl, cherubs & flowers w/gold, mk, 10⅝", NM **165.00**
Bowl, mc floral w/gold, deep, mk, late, 4⅝" **45.00**
Cake stand, mc floral w/gold, Schumann, openwork, 4¾x12" **400.00**

Centerpiece, 6 putti support frame of flower garland, late 1800s, 12x13", $600.00.

Cake stand, mc florals w/gold, Schumann, openwork, 6x10½" **300.00**
Compote, bl florals, rtcl scalloped rim, late, lg **150.00**
Compote, rtcl/oval, 2 cherubs on flower-appl stump base, 12" **440.00**
Egg dish, mc floral w/gold, late, 8¾" **60.00**
Figurine, ballerina, pk/wht lace dress w/appl flowers, 7½" **235.00**
Figurine, chess players, couple at table, much gold **345.00**
Figurine, courting couple w/dachshund, 7" **260.00**
Figurine, peasant & sleeping lover, lamb/kid/children/bee, 10" **650.00**
Figurine, 2 male musicians, lady at piano, ftd base, 10x11" **1,000.00**
Figurine, 3-pc cat family, brn/wht w/bl collar, 11" **2,500.00**
Inkwell, dbl; pastel flowers w/gold, ca 1905 ....**300.00**
Mint basket, appl roses & forget-me-nots, HP floral int, 2½" **250.00**
Monkey band & singer, 18th-C attire, 3¾" to 6", 5 pcs **700.00**
Plate, courting scene, rtcl border w/gold, 9", pr **340.00**
Reamer, HP decor, Franziska Hirsch, ca 1890 ....**350.00**
Vase, courting scenes, much gold, long neck w/scenes, 12¾" **250.00**

Dresser Accessories

Dresser sets, ring trees, figural or satin pincushions, manicure sets — all those lovely items that graced milady's dressing table — were at the same time decorative as well as functional. Today they appeal to collectors for many reasons. The Victorian era is well represented by repousse silver-backed mirrors and brushes and pincushions that were used to display ornamental pins for the hair, hats, and scarves. The hair receiver — similar to a powder jar but with an opening in the lid — was used to hold long strands of hair retrieved from the comb or brush. These were wound around the finger and tucked in the opening to be used later for hair jewelry and pictures, many of which survive to the present day. (See Hair Weaving.)

Celluloid dresser sets were popular during the late 1800s and early 1900s. Some included manicure tools, pill boxes, and buttonhooks, as well as the basic items. Because celluloid tends to break rather easily, a whole set may be hard to find today. (See also Plastics.) With the current interest in anything Art Deco, sets from the thirties and forties are especially collectible. These may be made of crystal, Bakelite, or silver, and the original boxes just as lavishly appointed as their contents.

Box, clear frosted egg shape w/gold & cream, 4¾x2⅜" **185.00**
Box, greyhound, chrome on blk glass base w/compartments **550.00**
Box, stylized antelope, chrome on blk glass, w/compartments **550.00**
Brush & comb, silver w/emb florals, mk Sterling **75.00**
Curling iron, wrought scissors type w/sq box joint, 10⅛" **50.00**

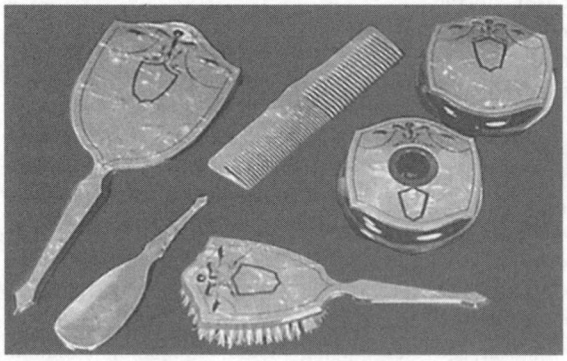

Dresser set, sea green Mother-of-Pearl celluloid, brush, comb, mirror, pick, hair clip (not shown) and 2 honey-amber dishes, 7 pieces in all, $100.00.

Hair pin, sterling, 1893 on top, 4" **35.00**
Hairbrush, gilt metal w/portrait on bk, +hand mirror **230.00**
Patch box, blk amethyst glass w/HP florals, hinged, 1½x2" **95.00**
Patch box, gr glass w/lacy brass filigree, hinged, 1⅜x2⅜" **110.00**
Patch box, wht opaque glass w/HP bird, hinged, 1x1½" **75.00**
Ring tree, cobalt glass w/HP florals **45.00**
Set, celluloid, gr marbleized, 10 pcs in case **125.00**
Set, sterling, emb shells/scrolls, mirror/tray/2 brushes+3 pcs **260.00**
Set, sterling, Old Colony repousse, Gorham, 3-pc+case **200.00**
Set, unmk German china, mc roses on turq w/gold, 5-pc+tray ...**275.00**

Dryden

Dryden Pottery was founded fifty years ago in Ellsworth, Kansas, by Jim Dryden, WWII veteran with financing from a G.I. loan. A mention on the front page of the Wall Street Journal resulted in substantial orders from Macy's of New York and Fred Harvey Restaurants and gift shops in all the stations of the Santa Fe Railroad.

In the late 1940s and early 1950s, some six hundred stores stocked Dryden pottery. Stiff competition from occupied Japan and Europe forced wholesale prices so low that the only profit from the pottery was from direct sales to the traveling public. Tourists watched potters at work. These sales were profitable, but in 1955, the new transcontinental highway 70 through Kansas missed Ellsworth. The pottery had to move. Hot Springs, Arkansas, with its hundreds of thousands of tourists was chosen as the new location.

Since 1970 more and more of the production is wheel thrown and hand-sculpted originals in an all-out attempt to follow the example of the world-famous Rookwood Pottery (1880-1967). Beautiful matt and gloss glazes plus one-of-a-kind originals make Dryden Pottery highly collectible.

Ashtray, #17A, souvenir **16.00**
Ashtray, #7B, yel **19.00**
Bookends, #80, Scotty **30.00**
Boot, #19, blk **20.00**
Bowl, #7C, mauve **32.00**
Bowl, #7D, gr **21.00**
Candle holders, #42, maroon, pr **24.00**
Flowerpot, #86, maroon **24.00**
Jug, #H3, A1955, blk **24.00**
Mug, #6, Clovis, New Mexico, gr **16.00**
Mug, #7, Kansas Univ, blk **24.00**
Mug, #8, Ells G Tourney **19.00**
Pitcher, #12, Lawrence KS **26.00**
Pitcher, #49, blk **48.00**
Pitcher, #8P, bbl, gr **32.00**
Pitcher, Kensington KS, #H7 ....**21.00**
Planter, #80, low, blk **28.00**
Planter, #87, Madonna **38.00**
Planter, Rooster, #Y, gr **29.00**
Shakers, #70, Junction City KS, pr **22.00**
Shakers, #73, Wichita KS, mauve, pr **24.00**
Tumbler, #4, blk **12.00**
Vase, #16, tan, sq **18.00**
Vase, #6A, yel **21.00**
Vase, #7K, Bridal Cave **24.00**
Vase, #7M, fish, yel **18.00**
Vase, #7X, deer, souvenir **28.00**

Duncan and Miller

The firm that became known as the Duncan and Miller Glass Com-

pany in 1900 was organized in 1874 in Pittsburgh, Pennsylvania, a partnership between George Duncan, his sons Harry and James, and his son-in-law Augustus Heisey. John Ernest Miller was hired as their designer. He is credited with creating the most famous of all Duncan's glassware lines, Three Face. (See Pattern Glass.) The George Duncan and Sons Glass Company, as it was titled, was only one of eighteen companies that merged in 1891 with U.S. Glass. Soon after the Pittsburgh factory burned in 1892, the association was dissolved, and Heisey left the firm to set up his own factory in Newark, Ohio. Duncan built his new plant in Washington, Pennsylvania, where he continued to make pressed glassware in such notable patterns as Bagware, Amberette, Duncan Flute, Button Arches, and Zippered Slash. The firm was eventually sold to U.S. Glass in Tiffin, Ohio, and unofficially closed in August 1955.

In addition to the early pressed dinnerware patterns, today's Duncan and Miller collectors enjoy searching for opalescent vases in many patterns and colors, frosted 'Satin Tone' glassware, acid-etched designs, and lovely stemware such as the Rock Crystal cuttings. Milk glass was made in limited quantity and is considered a good investment. Ruby glass, Ebony (a lovely opaque black glass popular during the twenties and thirties), and, of course, the glass animal and bird figurines are all highly valued examples of the art of Duncan and Miller.

Expect to pay at least 25% more than values listed for other colors, for ruby and cobalt, as much as 50% more in the Georgian, Pall Mall, and Sandwich lines. Pink, green, and amber Sandwich is worth approximately 30% more than the same items in crystal. Milk glass examples of American Way are valued up to 30% higher than color, 50% higher in Pall Mall. Add approximately 40% to listed prices for opalescent items. Etchings, cuttings, and other decorations will increase values by about 50%. For further study we recommend *The Encyclopedia of Duncan Glass*, by Gail Krause; she is listed in the Directory under Pennsylvania. Several Duncan and Miller lines are shown in *Elegant Glassware of the Depression Era* by Gene Florence. Also refer to *Glass Animals and Figural Flower Frogs of the Depression Era* by Lee Garmon and Dick Spencer; they are both listed under Illinois. See also Glass Animals.

Canterbury, crystal, ashtray, 3" **6.00**
Canterbury, crystal, basket, oval, hdld, 3½" **25.00**
Canterbury, crystal, bowl, fruit nappy; 5" **9.00**
Canterbury, crystal, bowl, oval, 11½x8¼" **30.00**
Canterbury, crystal, bowl, 8½x4" **22.00**
Canterbury, crystal, candleholder, low, 3" **12.50**
Canterbury, crystal, candy dish, w/5" lid, 6½" **32.50**
Canterbury, crystal, cheese box, w/lid, 3½x4½" **18.00**
Canterbury, crystal, cup **10.00**
Canterbury, crystal, mayonnaise, 6x3¼" **17.50**
Canterbury, crystal, plate, dinner; 11¼" **25.00**
Canterbury, crystal, rose bowl, 5" **20.00**
Canterbury, crystal, saucer **3.00**
Canterbury, crystal, stem, cocktail; 3½-oz, 4¼" **10.00**
Canterbury, crystal, urn, 4½x4½" **17.00**
Canterbury, crystal, vase, crimped, 5½" **20.00**
Canterbury, crystal, vase, oval, 4" **17.50**

Caribbean, blue: Punch bowl, $425.00; Punch underliner, 18", $90.00; Punch cup, $22.50; Ladle, $95.00.

Caribbean, bl, ashtray, 4 indents, 6" 32.50
Caribbean, bl, bowl, hdld, 7" 45.00
Caribbean, bl, pitcher, syrup; 9-oz, 4¼" 145.00
Caribbean, bl, plate, luncheon; 8½" 32.50
Caribbean, bl, saucer 8.00
Caribbean, bl, sugar bowl 22.00
Caribbean, bl, tumbler, flat, 11½-oz, 5¼" 40.00
Caribbean, crystal, bowl, finger; 4½" 16.00
Caribbean, crystal, candy dish, w/lid, 4x7" 40.00
Caribbean, crystal, oblong, 9½" 27.50
Caribbean, crystal, plate, salad; 7½" 10.00
Caribbean, crystal, vase, ftd, 10" 52.50
Caribbean, crystal, wine goblet, ball stem, 3-oz, 4¾" 22.00
Caribbean, crystal, wine goblet, 3½-oz, 3½" 22.00
First Love, crystal, ashtray, #111, 3½" sq 17.50
First Love, crystal, bottle, oil; #5200, w/stopper, 8" 60.00
First Love, crystal, bowl, #115, 8½x4" 37.50
First Love, crystal, bowl, #30, 11x1¾" 55.00
First Love, crystal, butter or cheese dish, #111, 7" sq 125.00
First Love, crystal, candle holder, #30, 2-light, 6" 40.00
First Love, crystal, cigarette box, w/lid, 4x4¼" 32.00
First Love, crystal, comport, #111, 3½x4¾" 20.00
First Love, crystal, cruet, #25 ....90.00
First Love, crystal, ice bucket, #30, 6" 70.00
First Love, crystal, mayonnaise, #115, 5½x2¾" 30.00
First Love, crystal, perfume tray, #5200, 8x5" 30.00
First Love, crystal, plate, #111, 7½" 18.00
First Love, crystal, plate, egg; #30, 12" 115.00
First Love, crystal, relish tray, #115, 11¾" 40.00
First Love, crystal, relish tray, oblong, 3-part, 10" 27.50
First Love, crystal, shakers, #115, pr 40.00
First Love, crystal, stem, claret; #5111½, 4½-oz 45.00
First Love, crystal, sugar bowl, #111, 10-oz, 3" 15.00
First Love, crystal, urn, #111, 4½x4½" 27.50
First Love, crystal, vase, #505, 11x5¼" 135.00
First Love, crystal, vase, #509, 9" 90.00

Sandwich, crystal, candy box with lid, 5", $40.00.

Sandwich, crystal, ashtray, rectangular, 2½x3¾" 7.00
Sandwich, crystal, basket, w/loop hdl, 11½" 195.00
Sandwich, crystal, bonbon, w/lid, ftd, 7½" 40.00
Sandwich, crystal, bottle oil; 5¾" 30.00
Sandwich, crystal, bowl, finger; 4" 12.50
Sandwich, crystal, bowl, fruit salad; 6" 17.00
Sandwich, crystal, bowl, fruit; 3-part, 10" 70.00
Sandwich, crystal, bowl, nappy; 2-part, 5" 12.00

Sandwich, crystal, cake stand, rolled edge, ftd, 11½" 110.00
Sandwich, crystal, candlestick, 1-light, 4" 14.00
Sandwich, crystal, candlestick, 2-light, 5" 30.00
Sandwich, crystal, candy dish, 6" sq 350.00
Sandwich, crystal, coaster, 5" 12.00
Sandwich, crystal, cup, tea; 6-oz 10.00
Sandwich, crystal, plate, hostess; 16" 80.00
Sandwich, crystal, plate, salad; 9½" 42.00
Sandwich, crystal, plate, service; 13" 50.00
Sandwich, crystal, shakers, w/glass tops, 2½", pr 18.00
Sandwich, crystal, stem, cocktail; 3-oz, 4¼" 12.50
Sandwich, crystal, urn, ftd, w/lid, 12" 125.00
Sandwich, crystal, vase, ftd, 10" 60.00
Spiral Flutes, amber, gr or pk, bowl, almond; 2" 11.00
Spiral Flutes, amber, gr or pk, bowl, grapefruit; ftd 20.00
Spiral Flutes, amber, gr or pk, bowl, mayonnaise; 4" 17.50
Spiral Flutes, amber, gr or pk, bowl, nappy, 8" 17.50
Spiral Flutes, amber, gr or pk, bowl, nappy; hdld, 6" 22.00
Spiral Flutes, amber, gr or pk, candle holder, 11½" 90.00
Spiral Flutes, amber, gr or pk, candle holder, 3½" 15.00
Spiral Flutes, amber, gr or pk, cigarette holder, 4" 30.00
Spiral Flutes, amber, gr or pk, creamer, oval 8.00
Spiral Flutes, amber, gr or pk, cup, demitasse 20.00
Spiral Flutes, amber, gr or pk, ice tub, hdld 45.00
Spiral Flutes, amber, gr or pk, oil, w/stopper, 6-oz 100.00
Spiral Flutes, amber, gr or pk, plate, salad; 7½" 4.00
Spiral Flutes, amber, gr or pk, plate, torte; 13⅝" 27.50
Spiral Flutes, amber, gr or pk, platter, 13" 50.00
Spiral Flutes, amber, gr or pk, saucer, demitasse 10.00
Spiral Flutes, amber, gr or pk, sugar bowl, oval 8.00
Spiral Flutes, amber, gr or pk, tumbler, soda; flat, 7-oz, 4¾" 32.50
Spiral Flutes, amber, gr or pk, vase, 6½" 12.00
Spiral Flutes, bowl, lily pond; 10½" 40.00
Tear Drop, crystal, ashtray, ind, 3" 8.00
Tear Drop, crystal, bowl, finger; 4¼" 7.00
Tear Drop, crystal, bowl, fruit nappy; 7" 7.00
Tear Drop, crystal, bowl, nappy; hdls, 9" 20.00
Tear Drop, crystal, bowl, salad; 12" 40.00
Tear Drop, crystal, butter dish, hdls, w/lid, ¼-lb 22.00
Tear Drop, crystal, candlestick, 4" 9.00
Tear Drop, crystal, candy dish, heart shape, 7½" 22.00
Tear Drop, crystal, celery tray, 3-part, 12" 22.00
Tear Drop, crystal, comport, ftd, 4¾" 12.00
Tear Drop, crystal, creamer, 3-oz 5.00
Tear Drop, crystal, cup, tea; 6-oz 6.00
Tear Drop, crystal, flower basket, loop hdl, 12" 115.00
Tear Drop, crystal, mustard jar, w/lid, 4¼" 35.00
Tear Drop, crystal, nut dish, 2-part, 6" 10.00
Tear Drop, crystal, pickle dish, 6" 15.00
Tear Drop, crystal, pitcher, ice lip, 8½" 125.00
Tear Drop, crystal, plate, canape; 6" 10.00
Tear Drop, crystal, plate, torte; 14" 35.00
Tear Drop, crystal, relish tray, 3-part, 12" 27.50
Tear Drop, crystal, shakers, 5" 25.00
Tear Drop, crystal, stem, sherry; 1¾-oz, 4½" 30.00
Tear Drop, crystal, sugar bowl, 3-oz 5.00
Tear Drop, crystal, tumbler, hi-ball; flat, 10-oz, 4¾" 10.00
Tear Drop, crystal, tumbler, whiskey; ftd, 3-oz, 3" 12.00
Tear Drop, crystal, vase, fan shape, ftd, 9" 25.00

Durand

Durand Art Glass was a division of Vineland Flint Glass Works in

Vineland, New Jersey. This division was geared toward the manufacture of fine hand-blown art glass in the style of Tiffany and Steuben. Lustered glass and opal glass were used as a basis to create such patterns as King Tut, Heart and Vine, Peacock Feather, and Egyptian Crackle. Crystal, cased and overlay glass were used to produce cut designs. Production began in 1924 and continued until 1931. Early art glass was unmarked. Later pieces were generally signed Durand, often written across a large 'V,' all in script. The numbers that sometimes appear along with the signature indicate shape and height of the object. Owner Victor Durand employed several employees as well as the owner of the failed Quezal Art Glass and Decorating Company, which explains why early Durand is often mistaken for Quezal. Note: Examples listed below are all signed unless noted otherwise. Our advisor for this category is Edward J. Meschi; he is listed in the Directory under New Jersey.

Candlesticks, petals, pk/wht on amber/ruby, yel ft, 3", pr **635.00**
Candlesticks, red flanged rim w/wht pulled feather, 3", pr **650.00**
Compote, heart & vine, lav irid on cobalt irid, w/lid, 4x5" **950.00**
Dish, ambergris trimmed w/gr, 8" **100.00**
Dish, bl w/wht pulled feather, 8" **200.00**
Dish, ruby trimmed w/wht, 8" **125.00**
Ginger jar, King Tut, royal bl swirls on marigold irid, 11" **2,750.00**
Goblet, pulled feather on gr cup, ambergris stem, 6" **225.00**
Jar, heart & vine, wht on bl/violet irid, att, w/lid, 9x10" **1,300.00**
Lamp base, King Tut, platinum on gr irid, 9" **375.00**
Night light, King Tut, invt vase on scrolled wood base, 11" **900.00**
Shade, torchiere; marigold irid w/bl random coils, 8¼" **335.00**
Torchiere, wht-cased red, 11x13" vasiform shade, ornate std ..**1,500.00**
Tumbler, emerald cut to crystal, 5" **165.00**
Tumbler, ruby cut to crystal, 5" **165.00**
Vase, ambergris w/milk wht pulls, 7" **450.00**
Vase, bl irid, irid yel ft, long trumpet neck, 9½x4" **850.00**
Vase, bl irid, lav/gold hues on shoulder, trumpet neck, 5" **450.00**
Vase, bl irid, trumpet neck, #1716-14, 14" **1,250.00**
Vase, coil, bl irid w/wht overall decor, #1707, 7" **850.00**
Vase, coil, marigold irid w/bl overall decor, 1971, 6" **850.00**

Vase, Egyptian crackle, blue and white on amber-gris, 6", $950.00.

Vase, Egyptian crackle, bl/wht o/l, ambergris base, #1812, 10" ..**1,100.00**
Vase, emerald gr ribbed over opal base, gold int, #1812, 7" **3,000.00**
Vase, feathers, bl on opal, gold threads, 9x5" **1,150.00**
Vase, feathers, opal/gr on marigold irid, gold threading, 10" **900.00**
Vase, gold irid, classic form, #1710, 6½" **575.00**
Vase, heart & vine, marigold irid w/gr overall decor, #1710, 6" .**925.00**
Vase, heart & vine, opal on bl irid, ftd, 10" **1,100.00**
Vase, intaglio daisies in Vs, 3-layer: bl/wht/gr, 8x8" **1,400.00**
Vase, King Tut, bl irid swirls on Apple Gr, #1995, ovoid, 3¾" ...**700.00**
Vase, King Tut, bl irid swirls on coral, yel irid int, 13" **2,350.00**

Vase, King Tut, bl on marigold, shouldered cylinder, 7¾" **950.00**
Vase, King Tut, gold w/mc highlights & wht swirls, 9½" **1,100.00**
Vase, King Tut, gr irid on marigold, opal casing, 8x8" **1,000.00**
Vase, King Tut, royal bl swirls on marigold irid, 10" **1,200.00**
Vase, King Tut, wht on gold irid, flared rim, 7" **675.00**
Vase, King Tut, wht over bl irid, baluster, no mk, 7" **865.00**
Vase, lg rayed stars/kite forms, opal cut to bl, 7x6" **2,500.00**
Vase, marigold irid, closed rim, spherical, #1995, 6" **400.00**
Vase, marigold irid w/allover gold threading, trumpet neck, 7" ..**600.00**
Vase, Moorish crackle, ruby over ambergris, 6" **800.00**
Vase, ruby cut to crystal, floral design, #1812, 10" **1,250.00**

Durant Kilns

The Durant Pottery Company operated in Bedford Village, New York in the early 1900s. Its founder was Mrs. Clarence Rice; she was aided by L. Volkmar to whom she assigned the task of technical direction. (See also Volkmar.) The artware and tableware they produced was simple in form and decoration. The creative aspects of the were carried on almost entirely by Volkmar himself, with only a minimal crew to help with production. After Mrs. Rice's death in 1919, the property was purchased by Volkmar, who chose to drop the Durant name by 1930. Prior to 1919 the ware was marked simply 'Durant' and dated. After that time a stylized 'V' was added.

Bowl, blk drip, bl int, flared, dtd 1914, 6x4" **395.00**
Candlestick, maroon gloss, sgn Durant, 1916, 10x3" **100.00**
Candlestick, petals top & base, stems up column, wht, 12" **265.00**
Vase, cobalt, exposed ft, flanged U-form, 1917, 6x7½" **175.00**
Vase, Persian bl matt, base/neck tapers, Volkmar/1927, 11x7" .**1,100.00**

Egg Cups

Egg cups, one of the fastest growing collectibles of the 1990s, have been traced back to the ruins of Pompeii. Since then, they have been made in almost every country in almost every conceivable material (ceramics, glass, metal, papier-mache, plastic, wood, ivory, even rubber and straw). Popular categories include Art Deco, Black Memorabilia, Chintz, Characters/Personalities, Golliwoggs, Railroadiana, Steamship, Souvenir Ware, etc.

Still being produced today in most countries, egg cups appeal to collectors on many levels. Prices can range from quite inexpensive to many thousands of dollars. Those made prior to 1840 are scarce and sought after, as are the character/personality egg cups of the 1930s.

For a more thorough study of egg cups we recommend that you refer to *Egg Cups: An Illustrated History and Price Guide* by Brenda Blake, our advisor for this category. You will find her address listed in the Directory under Maine.

Key:
bkt — bucket, a single cup without a foot
dbl — 2-sided, with small end for eating egg in shell, large end for mixing egg with toast and butter
fig — figural, an egg cup actually molded into the shape of an animal, bird, car, person, etc.
hoop — hoop, a single open cup with waistline
set — tray or cruet (stand, frame or basket) with 2 to 8 cups
sgl — single, with a foot; goblet shaped

Black Memorabilia

Fig, earrings, lg red lips, gr bow, collar, Germany, ca 1910 ....**150.00**

Fig, man sits w/ft out, yel hat, gr coat, Japan, 1930s 110.00

Characters/Personalities

Bkt, Lone Ranger, Clayton Moore's face, Keele St Pottery, 1961 ...100.00
Bkt, Tonto, Jay Silverheels' face, Keele St Pottery, 1961 ....85.00
Fig, Betty Boop, lustreware, face w/earrings, Japan, 1930s 325.00
Fig, Popeye, squatting, smoking pipe, red or bl cap, Japan 125.00
Fig, Ronald Reagan, Spitting Image face, Luck & Flaw, 1980s 75.00
Set, Beatles, 4 bkts, blk & wht, names on bk, KSP mk 180.00
Sgl, Holly Hobbie, at kitchen counter w/cat, Japan, 1960-70 ....15.00

Chintz

Bkt, Majestic, Royal Winton 55.00
Dbl, Old Cottage, Royal Winton 85.00
Dbl, Summertime, Royal Winton 85.00
Set, Nantwich, 4 bkts w/matching tray, Royal Winton 325.00

Glass

Dbl, amberina, clear on sm end, att Hobbs & Brockunier, 1890s .200.00
Dbl, jadite, Depression era, Anchor Hocking 8.00
Fig, chicken, wings support cup, pnt details, Vallerysthal 40.00
Sgl, blown, cobalt w/appl wht threaded rim, ca 1815 ....250.00
Sgl, Continental, Heisey, #339, ca 1905, 5-oz 70.00

Golliwoggs

Bkt, pointing to kitchen, Regd...J Robertson & Sons, 1960s 50.00
Fig, standing, appl to orange lustreware cup, Japan, 1930s 225.00

Metal

Hoop, graniteware, wht w/bl rim trim, 1930s 80.00
Set, christening; silver, cup/ring/spoon, England, '31, +case 100.00
Set, Sheffield SP, Georgian style, urn finial, 6 cups, 1790s 985.00
Set, SP, sq tray, 4 ftd cups, 4 spoons, Dixon, ca 1910 ....200.00
Sgl, silver, short ft, Spratling, Made in Mexico, 1930s, 1¼" 110.00
Sgl, wire, blk twisted coat-hanger style, recent 8.00

Plastic

Fig, soldier, colorful, Registered Design, Hong Kong, 1980 ....5.00
Sgl, Bakelite, brn cup sits on 3 prongs, England, 1940s 8.00

Railroad

Dbl, Baltimore & Ohio, Bl Centenary, bl transfer 95.00
Dbl, MKT, Katy Ornaments, no bottom stamp 75.00
Sgl, CMStP&P, Traveler, 1940s 60.00
Sgl, Great Northern, Oriental 125.00
Sgl, Southern Pacific Lines, Sunset, gr & wht florals 250.00

Souvenir

Sgl, Cambridge, colorful coat of arms, Goss, 1900s 60.00
Sgl, Channel Tunnel, 1988-94, transfer, 1994 ....15.00
Sgl, Soldier's Monument...Gettysburg, transfer, Germany, 1900s .35.00
Sgl, World's Fair, St Louis 1904, transfer scene, 1904 ....90.00

Staffordshire

Dbl, Ferrara, red boats transfer, Wedgwood, Etruria England 22.00

Dbl, Friendly Village, red barn transfer, fluting, Johnson Bros 12.00
Dbl, Harebell, Shelley 45.00
Dbl, Singapore Bird, Calyx Ware on lt gr, Adams, England 15.00
Fig, Harrods' Doorman, gr outfit, Wade, 1990-94 ....32.00
Set, Amherst Japan, cobalt/orange/gold, Minton, 1830s, 6 for .1,300.00
Set, Cottage Ware, 4 bkt cups on sq tray, Price Bros, 1930s 60.00
Sgl, blk basalt, unglazed, engine-trn body, reeded, 1790s 500.00
Sgl, Bunnykins, scenes #3 and #6, Royal Doulton, ca 1940 ....28.00
Sgl, Crocus, HP Bizarre Ware by Clarice Cliff, 1930s 120.00
Sgl, Mansfield, pierced, bl & wht, Worcester, 1760-65 ....1,200.00

Steamship/Cruiseship

Bkt, SAL, Swedish Am Line, flag on yel, Lidkoping, ALP 15.00
Hoop, Rotterdamsche Lloyd, rnd logo w/blk flag, ca 1900 ....75.00
Hoop, Union-Castle Line, bl band at rim & base, logo, 1900 ....65.00

Miscellaneous

Bkt, Elfinware, Dresden, ca 1910-30s 95.00
Dbl, Gingham, gr & yel plaid, Vernon Kilns, 1949-58 ....22.00
Dbl, Old Ivory, Silesia, ca 1890 ....85.00
Dbl, Tuxedo, gold crisscross border on cream, Lenox, 1930s 35.00
Fig, Friar Tuck, Goebel, stylized bee mk 45.00
Set, 4 bkts on rnd tray, HP floral on cream, mk Poole, 1930s 175.00
Sgl, faience, Terre de Lorraine, Count Custine mk, ca 1775 ......450.00
Sgl, Kingfisher, bl, integral saucer, Longpark, Torquay, 1920s 55.00
Sgl, Limpet, Belleek, 3rd gr mk 30.00
Sgl, Nan King, river scene, ca 1870 ....225.00
Sgl, Tartan Ware, plaid of McDuff clan 140.00

Elfinware

Made in Germany from about 1920 until the 1940s, these miniature vases, boxes, salt cellars, and miscellaneous novelty items are characterized by the tiny applied flowers that often cover their entire surface. Pieces with animals and birds are the most valuable, followed by the more interesting examples such as diminutive grand pianos, candle holders, etc. Items covered in 'spinach' (applied green moss) can be valued at 75% to 100% higher than pieces that are not decorated in this manner. See also Salts, Open.

Basket, loop hdl, sm 35.00
Basket, moss, high hdls, 3" 60.00

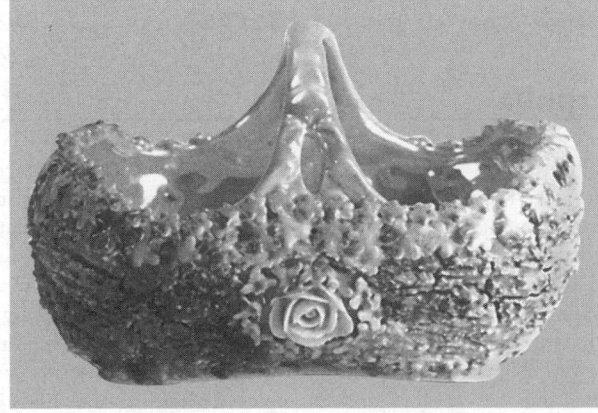

Basket, green 'spinach' decoration and applied rose, 3½x5", $110.00.

Box, w/lid 25.00
Candlestick, sm ring hdl, 2½" 50.00
Card holder, fan shape 25.00
Cradle, much spinach, 3½" 75.00
Dutch shoe 30.00
Lady's shoes, fused, iridized, 2" 36.00
Slipper 25.00
Slippers (attached) 45.00
Swan 40.00
Vase, 3" 45.00
Watering can, 6" 60.00

Epergnes

Popular during the Victorian era, epergnes were fancy centerpieces often consisting of several tiers of vases (called lilies), candle holders, or dishes, or a combination of components. They were made in all types of art glass, and some were set in ornate plated frames.

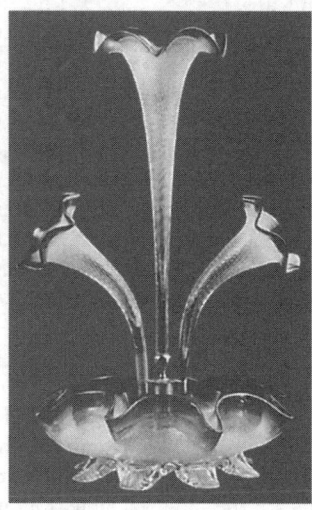

Diamond Quilted white opalescent with cranberry ruffled rims, 12" bowl and 3 lilies, 20", $350.00.

Bl o/l w/florals, lg lily in ruffled compote base, 16x11" 495.00
Bl opal, HP florals, 2-pc, child sz 135.00
Bl opal w/gold enamel, 5" bowl in Victorian brass fr 370.00
Bl w/opal trim, appl threading, 3-lily, 16½" 325.00
Cranberry-trim opal, 3 lg canes center 3 baskets, 4-lily 1,100.00
Peach o/l, mc florals w/gold, 1-lily, NP ft & center, 13½" 325.00
Wht w/rainbow int, lg lily+3, trilobe mirrored paw-ftd base 600.00
Yel irid opal, 5½" ribbed lily in gold twig fr w/2 cups 125.00
3-color opal trumpet & 4 lilies, ca 1890, 21" 595.00

Erphila

Ebeling and Ruess, an importing company in Philadelphia, began operations in 1886. The acronym 'Erphila' was frequently substituted for the manufacturer's mark on the imported items. It appears that the Erphila mark was used through the late 1930s and then again after WW II on products from U.S. Zone Germany as well as from other areas. The company imported from factories such as Fustenberg, W. Goebel, Villeroy and Boch, Heinrich, Keramos, and Schumann, to name a few. Figurines, art pottery, and some utilitarian items can be found bearing the Erphila mark. Examples are hard to find. Early German marks (those prior to 1900) often contain the word 'Fayence.' After the turn of the century, a rectangular mark in green ink was used. Following WW I, porcelain items were imported from Czechoslo-

vakia. These sometimes carried gold and silver labels. A small variety of marks were used in the 1920s and 1930s, but they all contained the name Erphila. Sticker labels were also used. 'Bavaria,' 'Black Forest,' and 'Italy' are sometimes found in combination with 'Erphila.'

Ebeling and Reuss continue the importing business, but it appears that since the 1940s they are also using an 'E' and 'R' on a bell-shaped mark. Because this mark does not contain the name 'Erphila,' we do not consider it to be such. We assume that they stopped using this name sometime in the 1950s.

Basket, porc, desert scene w/sphinx, Czech 56.00
Basket, rust, sm, MIG, 4½" 30.00
Bookends, man/woman, mc, MIG 75.00
Bottle, cologne; courting scenes, Dresden style, mk, 6½" 60.00
Box, fruit decor on tan, gr hdls & trim, w/lid, 6¼" 140.00
Candlesticks, bl & wht, ea dbl, Czech, pr 45.00
Charger, majolica, gr grapes in center, bl forest mk 120.00
Compote, majolica, gr grapes in center, bl forest mk 156.00
Cookie jar, drinking scene on wht, 9½" 115.00
Creamer, blk silhouette scene on yel, blk hdl, w/lid, 5½" 125.00
Creamer, gr & wht, dog hdl, MIG 75.00
Creamer & sugar bowl, floral, Czech 44.00
Dresser doll, lady w/pk dress, MIG 115.00
Dresser doll, Nancy Pert, bl, MIG 140.00
Dresser doll, Nancy Pert, yel, MIG 145.00
Figurine, airdale, standing, MIG, 6" 75.00
Figurine, birds (2), gr on wht base, MIG, 5" 30.00
Figurine, brn, MIG, 15x15" 450.00
Figurine, bull terrier dog, MIG, 5" L 40.00
Figurine, cat, gray & blk, MIG, 3" 45.00
Figurine, cherub & donkey, MIG, 5½" 100.00
Figurine, cockatoo on limb, mc, MIG, 7" 55.00
Figurine, elephant, gray, 5" L 45.00
Figurine, fox, wht & tan, MIG, pr 55.00
Figurine, Pekingese dog, blk & wht, MIG, 3" 33.50
Inkwell, Ink Girls, 2 figures on 1 base, MIG 300.00
Leaf dish, wht, sm, MIG 15.00
Match holder, book matches, boy stands on top, MIG, 5¼" 40.00
Pitcher, bird figural, blk/yel/red, Czech 170.00
Planter, lady in pleated dress, Czech, 8" 45.00
Planter, red flowers, ring hdls, Czech, 4" 30.00
Sprinkling can, wht, orange & gr flowers, 6½" 40.00
Teapot, rabbit form, brn & blk, MIG, 7¾" 140.00
Vase, blk silhouette scene on yel, urn form, 8⅛" 90.00
Vase, wht w/yel rings, 3-leg, 4" 12.50

Eskimo Artifacts

While ivory carvings made from walrus tusks or whale teeth have been the most emphasized articles of Eskimo art, basketry and woodworking are other areas in which these Alaskan Indians excell. Their designs are effected through the application of simple yet dramatic lines and almost stark decorative devices. Though not pursued to the extent of American Indian art, the unique work of these northern tribes are beginning to attract the serious attention of today's collectors.

Basket, coiled, red dogs/humans, w/lid, 1920, 10x12" 33.00
Basket, dyed seal gut design, w/lid, Yupik, 1940s, 10x11" 125.00
Basket, storage; alternating Xs & birds, w/lid, 1890, 20x20" 465.00
Basket, woven grass w/trade yarn decor, breaks, 7x8⅞" 220.00
Cribbage board, fossil ivory, sgn, 1950, 13x1½" 165.00
Cribbage board, 2 seals atop, cvd from tusk, 1930, 18" 350.00
Cvg, human head atop 3 stacked stones, cvd stone, 1930, 13x7" .250.00

Cvg, men in kayaks, soapstone on baleen slab, sgn, 1950, 9" 85.00
Cvg, Nunivak human-form doll, fossil ivory, pre-historic, 13" 600.00
Cvg, seal, cvd stone, minor flakes, 5¼x9¾" 75.00
Cvg, seal on iceberg, ivory, 1930s, 1x4" 100.00
Cvg, sled dog, ivory, 1920, 3½" 150.00
Cvg, umbilical figure, ivory, 1930, 2½" 90.00
Cvg, walrus, gr banded jadeite, sgn on base, 2¾x4" 55.00
Doll, cvd ivory in worn fur costume, 5" 320.00
Fossil ivory (Bering Sea), w/scrimshaw pictograph, 1x2" 110.00
Pipe, cvd ivory w/seals overlaid w/circles, 1880, 8x1½" 825.00
Tusk, diorama cvg of walrus & Eskimos in boat, 10" L 175.00

Fairings

Fairings, small chinaware figural groups that portray amusing (if not risque) scenes of courting couples, marital woes, and family feuds, were popular purchases and prizes at 19th-century English fairs. From 1840 through the 1850s, their bases were embossed with marks that identified the manufacturer as well as the artist who applied the polychrome enameling. From 1860 until 1870, they were no longer marked and became smaller in size. During the 1870s they retained their smaller size but once again were marked in relief, indicating manufacturer and artisan. Through the 1880s all marks were omitted; but the bases were much more shallow than those from the 1860s. About 1890 the Staffordshire potters sold the molds to German manufacturers who marked their product with the name of their country until about 1900. Examples from this period are most commonly encountered. Fairings made in Germany in the early 20th century often have two holes in their bases.

Generally, the more complex groups and those that are marked bring the higher prices. Earlier examples from the sixties and seventies are of better quality. Similar items such as small boxes and match holders with much the same type of theme and figural decoration are also listed here.

Returning at One O'Clock in the Morning, series #3, 1870s, 3¼", $300.00.

Baby & dog pull at doll, gold trim, 2¾x2½x5" 175.00
Before Marriage, couple on sofa 245.00
Box, baby asleep on pillow, ruffled edge, 2½" 250.00
Box, baby in cradle, bsk, unmk Germany, 2¾x4¼" 165.00
Box, cat w/frog, English, 3" 90.00
Box, child on bed pulls on pajama bottoms, Elbogen mk, 4" 120.00
Box, child on sideboard taking grapes, 1880s 250.00
Box, child w/trumpet, doll in basket, Staffordshire, 3¾" 175.00
Box, fireplace, child looks into mirror, 4¼" 85.00
Box, girl w/mama dog & 2 puppies on lid, some gold, 4½" 150.00
Box, monkey playing instrument 200.00
For Heaven's Sake Maria..., lady by man in bed, German mk 210.00
I Am Starting for a Long Journey, man w/satchel & book 175.00

Now Ma — mm Say When, lady being lifted on stagecoach 200.00
O Do Leave Me a Drop, 2 cats at box 175.00
Oysters Sir, lady at bench, w/match striker 255.00
Watch stand, kneeling child ea side of wreath 145.00
Wedding Night, man on knee to lady, gold trim, Germany 180.00
12 Months of Marriage, unmk, 3½x3½" 265.00

Fans

The Japanese are said to have invented the fan. From there it went to China, and Portuguese traders took the idea to Europe. Though usually considered milady's accessory, even the gentlemen in 17th-century England carried fans! More fashionable than practical, some were of feathers and lovely hand-painted silks with carved ivory or tortoise sticks. Some French fans had peepholes. There are mourning fans, calendar fans, and those with advertising.

Fine antique fans (pre-1900) of ivory or mother-of-pearl have recently escalated in value. Those from before 1800 often sell for upwards of $1,000.00. Examples with mother-of-pearl sticks are most desirable; least desirable are those with sticks of celluloid. Our advisor for this category is Vicki Flanigan; she is listed in the Directory under Virginia.

Aristocratic scenes on Fr paper, rtcl, MOP sticks, 14x8" 265.00
Blk Chantilly lace, ornate cvd/gilt MOP sticks, 1870s, 10½" 565.00
Brise, ivory, 4 cvd/pierced vignettes, Canton, 1790s, 10" 2,000.00
Brise, pierced ivory, 3 HP vignettes w/gilt, 1720s, 9" 2,000.00
Cabriolet, HP scene w/putti & gilt, ivory sticks, 1750s, 10" 1,400.00
Chicken-skin leaf, Neoclassical decor, ivory sticks, 1780s, 11" .2,000.00
Flowers HP on silk, ivory sticks, Fr, in 30" W fr 375.00
Gauze w/embr sequins, cvd/pierced ivory sticks, 1790s, 10" 1,400.00
Gilt abalone shell & paper, hand-colored Fr garden litho, 22" ...250.00
HP figures, landscape verso, MOP sticks, Fr, 1750s, 10" 1,400.00
Ivory w/HP fabric covering ribs, in fr, 11½x19½" 250.00
Lace & HP tulle, tortoise shell sticks, Fr, 26" W 165.00
Lace/gorgette/ivory, pierced & MOP sticks, Victorian, 13" 145.00
MOP panels, HP lovers scene, ivory sticks, 1760, +provenance ..1,250.00
Oriental scene on silk, tortoise shell sticks, 1890s 215.00
Ostrich feathers, bl on celluloid base, EX 45.00

Farm Collectibles

Country living in the 19th century entailed plowing, planting, and harvesting; gathering eggs and milking; making soap from lard rendered on butchering day; and numerous other tasks performed with primitive tools of which we in the 20th century have had little first-hand knowledge. Our advisor for this category is Lar Hothem; his address is listed in the Directory under Ohio. See also Cast Iron; Woodenware; Wrought Iron.

Bee smoker, tin w/red leather bellows, EX 40.00
Bull blinder, 2 leather pcs in lg harness, Pat Apr 15, 1898 ....95.00
Curry comb, CI, w/open-letter logo in hdl, 3½" 65.00
Fork, shaking; wooden, 3-prong, sgn GH Leicy on hdl, 60" 150.00
Hook, iron, 4 prongs, w/hanging ring 25.00
Implement seat, Adriance, CI w/openwork, 19x20x16", EX 30.00
Implement seat, Grand Detour IL, CI, 1900s, 16x15x4" 135.00
Implement seat, Hayes, CI, EX 175.00
Implement seat, Stoddard, CI, EX 85.00
Lantern, barn; tin & copper, Buhl #575, EX 100.00
Lard press, wood, heavy iron hinge, ca 1900 ....125.00
Pump, wooden w/CI spout/hdl pivot, stencil mfg mk, 72", EX 95.00
Rope maker, 5-strand 325.00
Sausage grinder, blades remove, porc int, ca 1860, 6x6½" 45.00

Sausage stuffer & lard press, Simmons Hdw, 4-qt, EX 85.00
Scoop, grain; metal w/trn wood hdl 32.50
Seed grader, 2 tin grooved pcs w/varied hole szs in wood fr 55.00
Strainer, milk; tin, on heavy wire stand 25.00
Threshing flail, hickory & ash, 2-part, 1880s, EX 65.00
Tractor, John Deere Model R, diesel, EX 3,500.00
Washtub, wood w/iron bands, pnt traces, 1850s, minimum 125.00
Yoke, water carrying; ltweight wood w/2 hooks, sm 50.00

Fenton

Frank and John Fenton were brothers who founded the Fenton Art Glass Company in 1906 in Martin's Ferry, Ohio. The venture, at first only a decorating shop, began operations in July of 1905 using blanks purchased from other companies. This operation soon proved unsatisfactory, and by 1907 they had constructed their own glass factory in Williamstown, West Virginia. John left the company in 1909 and organized his own firm in Millersburg, Ohio.

The Fenton Company produced over 130 patterns of carnival glass. They also made custard, chocolate, opalescent, and stretch glass. This company has always been noted for its various colors of glass and has continually changed its production to stay attune with current tastes in decorating. In 1925 they produced a line of 'handmade' items that incorporated the techniques of threading and mosaic work. Because the process proved to be unprofitable, the line was discontinued by 1927. Even their glassware made in the past twenty-five years is already regarded as collectible. Various paper labels have been used since the 1920s; only since 1970 has the logo been stamped into the glass. For information concerning Fenton Art Glass Collectors of America, Inc., see the Clubs, Newsletters, and Catalogs section of the Directory. See also Carnival Glass; Custard Glass; Stretch Glass.

Amber Crest, center epergne lily, 5½" 20.00
Apple Tree, vase, milk glass, 9" 110.00
Aqua Crest, bonbon, ruffled, 6" 20.00
Aqua Crest, compote, ftd, #7228 ....45.00
Aqua Crest, vase, cone shape, sq flared top, 4" 22.00
Basket, plate, gr opal, 7½" 18.00
Basketweave, candlesticks, crystal, 3-toed, pr 30.00
Beaded Melon, creamer, gold o/l, #711 ....38.00
Beaded Melon, rose bowl, gr o/l, 3½" 35.00
Beaded Melon, vase, gr cased, tulip form, sm 36.00
Beaded Melon/Peach Crest, basket, 10" 165.00
Beaded Melon/Peach Crest, jug, hdld, 8" 75.00
Beaded Melon/Peach Crest, vase, 5" 55.00
Bicentennial, paperweight, eagle, Independence Bl, #8470 ....45.00
Bicentennial, Patriot Planter, purple carnival, #8499 ....45.00
Bicentennial, stein, milk wht, #8446 ....65.00
Black Crest, basket, low 125.00
Blue Overlay, jug, hdl, #192, 6" 40.00
Blue Overlay, vanity set, 3-pc 90.00
Burmese, basket, rose decor, #7437 ....60.00
Burmese, fairy lamp, maple leaf decor, #7492, 2-pc 65.00
Burmese, vase, #7251, 11" 95.00
Burmese, vase, #7457, 5" 50.00
Butterfly, bonbon, rosalene 40.00
Coin Dot, bowl, Fr opal, dbl-crimp, 10½" 45.00
Coin Dot, bowl, gr opal, 6" 75.00
Coin Dot, creamer, cranberry opal, #1924, 4" 55.00
Coin Dot, lamp, Fr opal, w/chimney, 11" 215.00
Coin Dot, vase, cranberry opal, #194, 8¾" 130.00
Coin Dot, vase, Fr opal, #1450, 5" 40.00
Coin Dot, vase, Fr opal, #1925 ....52.50

Crystal Crest, basket, 7" 145.00
Crystal Crest, fan vase, #7357, 6½" 95.00
Daisy & Button, basket, amber, #1936, 6" 55.00
Daisy & Button, bonbon, Fr opal, 5" 15.00
Daisy & Button, shakers, milk glass, ftd, pr 27.50
Daisy & Button, vase, bl pastel, fan form, #1959, 8" 55.00
Daisy & Button, vase, gr pastel, 8½" 45.00
Dancing Ladies, bowl, cobalt, #900, 12" 150.00
Dancing Ladies, vase, Mongolian gr, ftd, 9" 345.00
Diamond Lace, bowl, bl opal, #1949, 12" 45.00
Diamond Lace, candle holders, Fr opal, pr 40.00
Diamond Lace, console set, Fr opal, #1948, 3-pc 85.00
Diamond Optic, basket, mulberry, #192, 10½" 475.00
Diamond Optic, basket, ruby o/l, 4½" 45.00
Diamond Optic, bowl, Fr opal, triangular, 8" 55.00
Diamond Optic, ice bucket, gr, #1614 ....35.00
Dolphin, bonbon, ruby, #1621 ....38.00
Dolphin, bowl, moonstone, oval, #1608, 10" 95.00
Dolphin, vase, topaz stretch, fan form, 5" 65.00
Dot Optic, pitcher, gr opal, 80-oz 170.00
Dot Optic, pitcher, water; ruby o/l 195.00
Emerald Crest, compote, low std, #7329 ....35.00
Emerald Crest, jug, #711, 6" 42.00
Emerald Crest, nut dish, ftd, #7229, 6" 35.00
Emerald Crest, vase, fan form, 4½" 30.00
Georgian, claret, ruby, #1611, 4½-oz 20.00
Georgian, cup & saucer, red, ftd 35.00
Georgian, goblet, ruby, #1611 ....12.50
Georgian, tumbler, red, ftd, 5½" 18.00
Gold Crest, bonbon, 6" 18.00
Heart, fairy light, rosalene 60.00
Hobnail, ashtray, Fr opal, fan shape, 6" 30.00
Hobnail, ashtray, topaz opal, fan shape, #3872 ....38.00
Hobnail, basket, bl marble, #3736, 6½" 50.00
Hobnail, basket, bl opal, 4" 50.00
Hobnail, basket, bl opal, 7" 50.00
Hobnail, basket, lime opal, rare, 4" 95.00
Hobnail, basket, milk glass, #3734, 12" 45.00
Hobnail, basket, yel opal, 4" 65.00
Hobnail, bonbon, bl opal, dbl-crimp 22.00
Hobnail, bonbon, Fr opal, crimped rim 15.00
Hobnail, bonbon, topaz opal, flared, 6" 25.00
Hobnail, bowl, bl opal, #3802, 9½" 40.00
Hobnail, bowl, bl opal, dbl-crimp, 10" 65.00
Hobnail, bowl, bl opaque, sq 30.00
Hobnail, bowl, fruit; bl opaque 30.00
Hobnail, bowl, gr opal, #3824, 11" 70.00
Hobnail, bowl, peachblow, #3924, 9" 50.00
Hobnail, bowl, rose pastel, #3924, 9" 35.00
Hobnail, candle bowl, milk glass, #3872 ....25.00
Hobnail, candle holder, topaz opal, cornucopia form, #3874 ....40.00
Hobnail, candle holders, bl opal, low, pr 60.00
Hobnail, candle holders, Fr opal, 3¼", pr 50.00
Hobnail, cat slipper, bl opal 33.00
Hobnail, cologne, Fr opal, w/stopper 30.00
Hobnail, creamer & sugar bowl, bl opal 28.00
Hobnail, creamer & sugar bowl, bl opal, star shape 55.00
Hobnail, creamer & sugar bowl, w/tray, milk glass 25.00
Hobnail, crescent dish, yel opal, 6½" 38.00
Hobnail, cruet, bl opal, 4" 32.00
Hobnail, epergne, bl pastel, apartment sz 100.00
Hobnail, goblet, milk glass, #3845, 5½" 18.00
Hobnail, goblet, water; bl opal, 6" 35.00
Hobnail, hat vase, bl opal, 3½" 37.50

Hobnail, ivy bowl, milk glass, #3757	20.00
Hobnail, lamp, courting; amber, electric, #3792	85.00
Hobnail, lamp, table; cranberry opal	265.00
Hobnail, mayonnaise, bl opal, w/underplate & spoon	70.00
Hobnail, mustard jar, bl opal, w/lid	25.00
Hobnail, nappy, yel opal, dbl-crimp, 6"	32.00
Hobnail, pitcher, juice; yel opal, squat, +6 tumblers	195.00
Hobnail, puff box, Fr opal, w/lid	35.00
Hobnail, toothpick holder, Fr opal, top hat shape, 1¾"	18.00
Hobnail, top hat, bl opal, 2¾"	30.00
Hobnail, top hat, yel opal, 2½"	45.00
Hobnail, tray, bl opal, fan form, 10½"	32.00
Hobnail, tray, yel opal, fan shape, 10"	57.00
Hobnail, tumbler, cranberry opal, 12-oz	35.00
Hobnail, vase, bl opal, dbl-crimp, 8"	50.00
Hobnail, vase, bl opal, triangular, 3½"	18.00
Hobnail, vase, bud; yel opal, ftd, 8"	40.00
Hobnail, vase, cranberry opal, mini, 4"	35.00
Hobnail, vase, Fr opal, flared, 4½"	38.00
Hobnail, vase, gold o/l, #3856, 5½"	42.00
Hobnail, vase, gr opal, 4½"	45.00
Hobnail, vase, Mandarin Red, flared rim, #621, 6"	60.00
Hobnail, vase, plum opal, #3759, 15½"	185.00
Hobnail, vase, yel opal, 5"	60.00
Ivory Crest, bowl, 7"	60.00
Ivory Crest, cornucopia candlesticks, 6", pr	70.00
Ivory Crest, plate, 8½"	30.00
Ivory Crest, vase, #201, 5" sq	55.00
Ivory Crest, vase, sq top, 5"	45.00
Ivy, vase, gr & wht, #1925, 6¼"	65.00
Jade, candy dish, ftd	40.00
Jade, vase, str sides, 8"	35.00
Jadite, bowl, #848, 9"	25.00
Leaf, plate, milk glass, #5108, 11"	22.50
Leaf/Orange Tree, bowl, rosalene	60.00
Lilac, biscuit jar, #1681, rare	350.00
Lincoln Inn, see Depression Glass	
Mandarin Red, bowl, centerpc; cornucopia form, #950	110.00
Mandarin Red, flip vase, #621	85.00
Mandarin Red, ginger jar, #893, rare	285.00
Peach Crest, bowl, shell shape, #9020, 10"	65.00
Peach Crest, bowl, 10"	55.00
Peach Crest, candlestick, single, #7370	25.00
Polka Dot, butter dish, cranberry opal, milk glass base	125.00
Polka Dot, hat, Fr opal, 6"	110.00
Polka Dot, shakers, cranberry opal, pr	55.00
Polka Dot, vase, cranberry opal, dbl-crimp, #2251, 7¾"	135.00

Rib Optic, vase, lime opal, #184	85.00
Rib Optic, wine, gr opal, #1647, 4"	65.00
Rib Optic, wine bottle, cranberry opal, #667, w/stopper	175.00
Rosalene, swan, open, #5217	35.00
Rose, candy box, Colonial pk, #9282	45.00
Rose, candy dish, amber, ftd, w/lid, #9284	35.00
Rose, comport, Colonial bl, 7½"	30.00
Rose, compote, orange, #9222	35.00
Rose Crest, bowl, #192, 11"	50.00
Rose Crest, center epergne flower, 5¾"	20.00
Rose Crest, vase/pitcher, hdld, lg	65.00
Ruby Overlay, bottle, scent; #192A	40.00
Silver Crest, banana bowl, low	50.00
Silver Crest, basket, #3736, 6½"	45.00
Silver Crest, basket, #7233, 13"	90.00
Silver Crest, bowl, ftd, #7427, lg & tall	75.00
Silver Crest, bowl, shallow, 10"	30.00
Silver Crest, bowl, 5"	14.00
Silver Crest, cake salver, #5813, 13"	45.00
Silver Crest, chip & dip set	65.00
Silver Crest, compote, ftd, #7228, 8"	20.00
Silver Crest, compote, ftd, #7429, 8"	36.00
Silver Crest, compote, 3½" H	16.00
Silver Crest, epergne, 4-pc, 12"	145.00
Silver Crest, plate, 12"	40.00
Silver Crest, plate, 6½"	14.00
Silver Crest, plate, 8½"	27.50
Silver Crest, relish, 2-part, 9¼" dia	35.00
Silver Crest, tidbit, 2-tier	48.00
Silver Crest, tidbit, 3-tier	45.00
Silver Crest, vase, fan form, 12"	110.00
Silver Crest/Spanish Lace, cake stand, low ft	40.00
Silver Crest/Spanish Lace, candlesticks, low, pr	25.00
Silver Rose, cake stand	55.00
Silver Rose, heart bowl, hdld	25.00
Silvertone, bowl, crystal, ftd cup shape, 5"	35.00
Silvertone, bowl, crystal, triangular, ftd	35.00
Snow Crest, hat vase, gr, #1921, 4"	75.00
Snow Crest, top hat, emerald gr, 6"	75.00
Snow Crest, vase, amber, #3005, 7½"	45.00
Snow Crest, vase, amber, 5"	35.00
Spiral Optic, vase, cranberry opal, #3253, 6½"	68.00
Spiral Optic, vase, Fr opal, flared, 7½"	65.00
Strawberry, bell, crystal velvet, #9465	35.00
Stretch, bonbon, bl, w/lid, #634	55.00
Stretch, candle holder, gr, single, #316	22.50
Swirl, ginger jar, cranberry opal, 10½"	180.00
Vasa Murrhina, basket, gr/bl aventurine, 11½"	110.00
Vasa Murrhina, vase, bl/orange aventurine, tall	85.00
Violets in Snow, bonbon	20.00
Violets in Snow, compote, ftd, #7429, 8"	45.00
Violets in Snow/Silver Crest, vase, #7451, 5½"	45.00
Water Lily, candlesticks, lime satin, pr	35.00
Water Lily, candlesticks, rosalene, pr	85.00
Water Lily, candy box, rosalene	85.00
Water Lily, compote, Lime Sherbet, #8429, lg	28.00
Water Lily, rose bowl, custard satin, 38429	20.00
Wild Strawberry, candy box, custard satin, w/lid, #9088	35.00
Wistaria, pitcher, crystal satin, #1355, lg	130.00

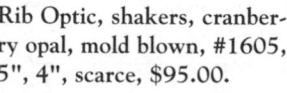
Rib Optic, shakers, cranberry opal, mold blown, #1605, 5", 4", scarce, $95.00.

Fiesta

Fiesta is a line of dinnerware produced by the Homer Laughlin

China Company of Newell, West Virginia, from 1936 until 1973. It was made in eleven different solid colors with over fifty pieces in the assortment. The pattern was developed by Frederick Rhead, an English Stoke-on-Trent potter who was an important contributor to the art-pottery movement in this country during the early part of the century. The design was carried out through the use of a simple band-of-rings device near the rim. Fiesta Red, a strong red-orange glaze color, was made with depleted uranium oxide. It was more expensive to produce than the other colors and sold at higher prices. Today's collectors still pay premium prices for Fiesta Red pieces. During the fifties the color assortment was gray, rose, chartreuse, and dark green. These colors are relatively harder to find and along with Fiesta Red and medium green (new in 1959) command the higher prices.

Fiesta Kitchen Kraft was introduced in 1939; it consisted of seventeen pieces of kitchenware such as pie plates, refrigerator sets, mixing bowls, and covered jars in four popular Fiesta colors.

As a final attempt to adapt production to modern-day techniques and methods, Fiesta was restyled in 1969. Of the original colors, only Fiesta Red remained. This line, called Fiesta Ironstone, was discontinued in 1973.

Two types of marks were used: an ink stamp on machine-jiggered pieces and an indented mark molded into the hollowware pieces.

In 1986 HLC reintroduced a line of Fiesta dinnerware in five colors: black, white, pink, apricot, and cobalt (darker and denser than the original shade). Since then yellow, turquoise, seafoam green, 'country' blue, lilac, and persimmon have been added. Collectors have found that the new line poses no theat to their investments.

In the listings below, 'original colors' indicates only three of the original six — light green, turquoise, and yellow (or those remaining after specific original colors have been priced). Red, ivory, and cobalt values are listed separately. For more information we recommend *The Collector's Encyclopedia of Fiesta, Harlequin, and Riviera* (values updated in 1996) by Sharon and Bob Huxford, available at your local bookstore or from Collector Books.

Dinnerware

Covered onion soup bowl, light green, $465.00; Dessert bowl, cobalt, 6", $48.00; Individual salad bowl, red, 7½", $75.00; Fruit bowl, yellow, 5½", $25.00; Fruit bowl, rose, 4¾", $32.00.

Ashtray, '50s colors	75.00
Ashtray, orig colors	42.00
Ashtray, red, cobalt or ivory	50.00
Bowl, covered onion soup; cobalt or ivory	550.00
Bowl, covered onion soup; red	600.00
Bowl, covered onion soup; turq, minimum value	2,200.00
Bowl, cream soup; '50s colors	70.00

Bowl, cream soup; med gr, minimum value	3,200.00
Bowl, cream soup; orig colors	40.00
Bowl, cream soup; red, cobalt or ivory	55.00
Bowl, dessert; '50s colors, 6"	48.00
Bowl, dessert; med gr, 6"	325.00
Bowl, dessert; orig colors, 6"	35.00
Bowl, dessert; red, cobalt or ivory, 6"	48.00
Bowl, fruit; '50s colors, 4¾"	32.00
Bowl, fruit; '50s colors, 5½"	35.00
Bowl, fruit; med gr, 4¾"	375.00
Bowl, fruit; med gr, 5½"	65.00
Bowl, fruit; orig colors, 11¾"	190.00
Bowl, fruit; orig colors, 4¾"	24.00
Bowl, fruit; orig colors, 5½"	25.00
Bowl, fruit; red, cobalt or ivory, 11¾"	235.00
Bowl, fruit; red, cobalt or ivory, 4¾"	30.00
Bowl, fruit; red, cobalt or ivory, 5½"	32.00
Bowl, ftd salad; orig colors	220.00
Bowl, ftd salad; red, cobalt or ivory	275.00
Bowl, ind salad; med gr, 7½"	95.00
Bowl, ind salad; red, turq or yel, 7½"	75.00
Bowl, nappy; '50s colors, 8½"	50.00
Bowl, nappy; med gr, 8½"	110.00
Bowl, nappy; orig colors, 8½"	35.00
Bowl, nappy; orig colors, 9½"	48.00
Bowl, nappy; red, cobalt or ivory, 8½"	45.00
Bowl, nappy; red, cobalt or ivory, 9½"	60.00
Bowl, Tom & Jerry; ivory w/gold letters	250.00
Bowl, unlisted salad; red, cobalt, or ivory	310.00
Bowl, unlisted salad; yel	90.00
Candle holders, bulb; orig colors, pr	85.00
Candle holders, bulb; red, cobalt or ivory, pr	110.00
Candle holders, tripod; orig colors, pr	385.00
Candle holders, tripod; red, cobalt or ivory, pr	485.00
Carafe, orig colors	180.00
Carafe, red, cobalt or ivory	225.00
Casserole, '50s colors	265.00
Casserole, French; standard colors other than yel	475.00
Casserole, French; yel	245.00
Casserole, med gr	500.00
Casserole, orig colors	125.00
Casserole, red, cobalt or ivory	180.00
Coffeepot, '50s colors	265.00
Coffeepot, demi; orig colors	250.00
Coffeepot, demi; red, cobalt or ivory	300.00
Coffeepot, orig colors	165.00
Coffeepot, red, cobalt or ivory	210.00
Compote, orig colors, 12"	130.00
Compote, red, cobalt or ivory, 12"	165.00
Compote, sweets; orig colors	68.00
Compote, sweets; red, cobalt or ivory	80.00
Creamer, '50s colors	38.00
Creamer, ind; red	200.00
Creamer, ind; turq	295.00
Creamer, ind; yel	60.00
Creamer, med gr	68.00
Creamer, orig colors	20.00
Creamer, red, cobalt or ivory	28.00
Creamer, stick hdld, orig colors	38.00
Creamer, stick hdld, red, cobalt or ivory	50.00
Cup, demi; '50s colors	270.00
Cup, demi; orig colors	56.00
Cup, demi; red, cobalt or ivory	62.00
Egg cup, '50s colors	145.00

Egg cup, orig colors 50.00
Egg cup, red, cobalt, or ivory 60.00
Lid, for mixing bowl #1-#3, any color, minimum value 600.00
Lid, for mixing bowl #4, any color, minimum value 650.00
Marmalade, orig colors 190.00
Marmalade, red, cobalt or ivory 225.00
Mixing bowl, #1, orig colors 130.00
Mixing bowl, #1, red, cobalt, or ivory 150.00
Mixing bowl, #2, orig colors 85.00
Mixing bowl, #2, red, cobalt or ivory 100.00
Mixing bowl, #3, orig colors 95.00
Mixing bowl, #3, red, cobalt or ivory 110.00
Mixing bowl, #4, orig colors 110.00
Mixing bowl, #4, red, cobalt or ivory 125.00
Mixing bowl, #5, orig colors 130.00
Mixing bowl, #5, red, cobalt or ivory 145.00
Mixing bowl, #6, orig colors 165.00
Mixing bowl, #6, red, cobalt or ivory 185.00
Mixing bowl, #7, orig colors 220.00
Mixing bowl, #7, red, cobalt or ivory 260.00
Mug, Tom & Jerry; '50s colors 90.00
Mug, Tom & Jerry; ivory w/gold letters 65.00
Mug, Tom & Jerry; orig colors 55.00
Mug, Tom & Jerry; red, cobalt or ivory 75.00
Mustard, orig colors 180.00
Mustard, red, cobalt or ivory 220.00
Pitcher, disk juice; gray 2,000.00
Pitcher, disk juice; red 345.00
Pitcher, disk juice; yel 42.00
Pitcher, disk water; '50s colors 225.00
Pitcher, disk water; med gr 950.00
Pitcher, disk water; orig colors 105.00
Pitcher, disk water; red, cobalt or ivory 145.00
Pitcher, ice; orig colors 110.00
Pitcher, ice; red, cobalt or ivory 135.00
Pitcher, jug, 2-pt; '50s colors 130.00
Pitcher, jug, 2-pt; orig colors 70.00
Pitcher, jug, 2-pt; red, cobalt or ivory 100.00
Plate, '50s colors, 10" 50.00
Plate, '50s colors, 6" 9.00
Plate, '50s colors, 7" 13.00
Plate, '50s colors, 9" 22.00
Plate, cake; orig colors 620.00
Plate, cake; red, cobalt or ivory 700.00
Plate, calendar; 1954 or 1955, 10" 38.00
Plate, calendar; 1955, 9" 42.00
Plate, chop; '50s colors, 13" 85.00
Plate, chop; '50s colors, 15" 100.00
Plate, chop; med gr, 13" 175.00
Plate, chop; orig colors, 13" 35.00
Plate, chop; orig colors, 15" 42.00
Plate, chop; red, cobalt or ivory, 13" 45.00
Plate, chop; red, cobalt or ivory, 15" 62.00
Plate, compartment; '50s colors, 10½" 65.00
Plate, compartment; orig colors, 10½" 35.00
Plate, compartment; orig colors, 12" 52.00
Plate, compartment; red, cobalt or ivory, 10½" 38.00
Plate, compartment; red, cobalt or ivory, 12" 55.00
Plate, deep; '50s colors 50.00
Plate, deep; med gr 110.00
Plate, deep; orig colors 38.00
Plate, deep; red, cobalt or ivory 48.00
Plate, med gr, 10" 100.00
Plate, med gr, 6" 18.00

Plate, med gr, 7" 30.00
Plate, med gr, 9" 42.00
Plate, orig colors, 10" 30.00
Plate, orig colors, 6" 5.00
Plate, orig colors, 7" 9.00
Plate, orig colors, 9" 12.00
Plate, red, cobalt or ivory, 10" 40.00
Plate, red, cobalt or ivory, 6" 7.00
Plate, red, cobalt or ivory, 7" 10.00
Plate, red, cobalt or ivory, 9" 18.00
Platter, '50s colors 55.00
Platter, med gr 120.00
Platter, orig colors 32.00
Platter, red, cobalt or ivory 44.00
Sauce boat, '50s colors 70.00
Sauce boat, med gr 130.00
Sauce boat, orig colors 40.00
Sauce boat, red, cobalt or ivory 60.00
Saucer, '50s colors 6.00
Saucer, demi; '50s colors 85.00
Saucer, demi; orig colors 16.00
Saucer, demi; red, cobalt or ivory 20.00
Saucer, med gr 10.00
Saucer, orig colors 4.00
Saucer, red, cobalt or ivory 5.00
Shakers, '50s colors, pr 40.00
Shakers, med gr, pr 115.00
Shakers, orig colors, pr 20.00
Shakers, red, cobalt or ivory, pr 28.00
Sugar bowl, ind; turq 310.00
Sugar bowl, ind; yel 95.00
Sugar bowl, w/lid, '50s colors, 3¼x3½" 65.00
Sugar bowl, w/lid, med gr, 3¼x3½" 130.00
Sugar bowl, w/lid, orig colors, 3¼x3½" 40.00
Sugar bowl, w/lid, red, cobalt or ivory, 3¼x3½" 52.00
Syrup, orig colors 260.00
Syrup, red, cobalt or ivory 310.00
Teacup, '50s colors 35.00
Teacup, med gr 55.00
Teacup, orig colors 25.00
Teacup, red, cobalt or ivory 32.00
Teapot, lg; orig colors 150.00
Teapot, lg; red, cobalt or ivory 190.00
Teapot, med; '50s colors 260.00
Teapot, med; med gr 625.00
Teapot, med; orig colors 140.00
Teapot, med; red, cobalt or ivory 165.00
Tray, figure-8; cobalt 75.00
Tray, figure-8; turq 230.00
Tray, figure-8; yel 230.00
Tray, relish; mixed colors, no red 238.00
Tray, utility; orig colors 35.00
Tray, utility; red, cobalt or ivory 38.00
Tumbler, juice; chartreuse, Harlequin yel or dk gr 375.00
Tumbler, juice; orig colors 35.00
Tumbler, juice; red, cobalt or ivory 40.00
Tumbler, juice; rose 55.00
Tumbler, water; orig colors 55.00
Tumbler, water; red, cobalt or ivory 65.00
Vase, bud; orig colors 62.00
Vase, bud; red, cobalt or ivory 80.00
Vase, orig colors, 10" 610.00
Vase, orig colors, 12" 785.00
Vase, orig colors, 8" 450.00

Vase, red, cobalt or ivory, 10" 680.00
Vase, red, cobalt or ivory, 12" 900.00
Vase, red, cobalt or ivory, 8" 520.00

Kitchen Kraft

Bowl, mixing; lt gr or yel, 10" 85.00
Bowl, mixing; lt gr or yel, 6" 55.00
Bowl, mixing; lt gr or yel, 8" 72.00
Bowl, mixing; red or cobalt, 10" 95.00
Bowl, mixing; red or cobalt, 6" 65.00
Bowl, mixing; red or cobalt, 8" 82.00
Cake plate, lt gr or yel 48.00
Cake plate, red or cobalt 52.00
Cake server, lt gr or yel 100.00
Cake server, red or cobalt 125.00
Casserole, ind; lt gr or yel 135.00
Casserole, ind; red or cobalt 145.00
Casserole, lt gr or yel, 7½" 75.00
Casserole, lt gr or yel, 8½" 90.00
Casserole, red or cobalt, 7½" 85.00
Casserole, red or cobalt, 8½" 100.00

Covered jar, yellow, large, $250.00.

Covered jar, lg; lt gr or yel 250.00
Covered jar, lg; red or cobalt 275.00
Covered jar, med; lt gr or yel 220.00
Covered jar, med; red or cobalt 240.00
Covered jar, sm; lt gr or yel 225.00
Covered jar, sm; red or cobalt 250.00
Covered jug, lt gr or yel 200.00
Covered jug, red or cobalt 220.00
Fork, lt gr or yel 90.00
Fork, red or cobalt 100.00
Metal frame for platter 26.00
Pie plate, lt gr or yel, 10" 40.00
Pie plate, lt gr or yel, 9" 40.00
Pie plate, red or cobalt, 10" 45.00
Pie plate, red or cobalt, 9" 45.00
Platter, lt gr or yel 68.00
Platter, red or cobalt 78.00
Platter, spruce gr 300.00
Shakers, lt gr or yel, pr 85.00
Shakers, red or cobalt, pr 95.00
Spoon, lt gr or yel 95.00
Spoon, red or cobalt 110.00
Stacking refrigerator lid, ivory 180.00
Stacking refrigerator lid, lt gr or yel 58.00
Stacking refrigerator lid, red or cobalt 68.00

Stacking refrigerator unit, ivory 180.00
Stacking refrigerator unit, lt gr or yel 40.00
Stacking refrigerator unit, red or cobalt 45.00

Fifties Modern

Postwar furniture design is marked by organic shapes and lighter woods and forms. New materials from war research such as molded plywood and fiberglass were used extensively. For the first time, design was extended to the mass and the baby-boomer generation grew up surrounded by modern shape and color, the perfect expression of postwar optimism. The top designers in America worked for Herman Miller and Knoll Furniture Company. These include Charles Eames, George Nelson, and Eero Saarinen.

Italian glass from the fifties represents some of the most beautiful designs of the period. The color and expressive forms that came from the island of Murano during this time were the perfect expression of Italian style and flair.

This information was provided to us by Richard Wright. See also Italian Glass.

Key:
uphl — upholstered   vnr — veneer

Armchair, Cherner, laminated 8-shaped bk/seat, bentwood arms ..575.00
Armchair, McCobb, cubist molded orange fiberglass 375.00
Bed, Nelson, Thin Edge, woven rattan headbrd, 35x38x76" ...1,800.00
Bench, Frankl, lacquered cork top, mahog legs, 70", VG 1,600.00
Bench, Maloof, walnut fr w/orig rope seat, 16½x16½x29" 600.00
Bench, Risley, wire-built whimsical seated couple, 51x34" 900.00
Bookcase, Rohde, East Indian Laurel series, 1-door, 2-tone 1,700.00
Bowl, German, hand-wrought brass oval on disk ft, mk, 14" L ...150.00
Buffet, Heywood Wakefield, birch, 48", EX 350.00
Bust, Kent Art Ware, stylized woman, wht glaze, 11" 130.00
Cabinet, Geo Nelson, oak w/glass sliding doors, V legs, 29x34" .1,100.00
Carpet, sunburst design, machine-woven wool, 96x138", EX 80.00
Chair, Bertoia, child's, wht-coated wire, yel cushions, VG 100.00
Chair, Chas Eames, metal fr, blk wood seat/bk, 26x22", VG 300.00
Chair, Jacobsen, uphl sculptural 'egg' shell, tilting, G 650.00
Chair, Knorr, conical metal body w/snap-on uphl, 23" dia 900.00
Chair, LeCorbusier, Petit Comfort, chrome fr, leather pads 2,500.00
Chair, lounge; Rietveld, geometric mc wood fr, rpr, VG 400.00
Chair, lounge; Vladimir, cvd walnut fr, seat tilts, EX 2,000.00
Chair, McArthur, folding, uphl bk/arms/seat, metal tube fr 650.00
Chair, Nakasima, Windsor style, walnut, spindle curved bk, VG ..600.00
Chair, Nelson, triangular uphl-metal 'coconut,' chrome legs, VG ..1,900.00
Chair, P Paulin/Airfort, orange-uphl sculpted foam 'tongue' 900.00
Chair, Paulin/Airfort, uphl sculpted foam 'ribbon,' wood base ..1,300.00
Chair, Saarinen/Knoll, molded plastic, disk base, set of 6 ....750.00
Chair set, Rohde, birch w/red & gold uphl, 6 side+2 arm 425.00
Chest, Nelson, Steelframe, blk/lt bl/gray, wht top, 34" W 110.00
Chest, Nelson, 5-drw, Primavera finish, blk legs, 39x40", G 750.00
Chest, Rohde/Miller, 5-drw, Macassar/blonde burl, 18" mirror .1,600.00
China cabinet, Heywood Wakefield, sliding glass, 67x34x18" 275.00
China cabinet, Rohde, 2-door, Lucite hdls, rfn, 36x50" 700.00
Clock, desk; Rohde/Miller, chrome sq fr, wht face, 6½x8" 210.00
Clock, Frankl, telchron, chrome/pnt ray-section case, 8x5" 425.00
Clock, Nelson/Miller, Italian ceramic, orange tones, 14" dia 110.00
Clock, Nelson/Miller, openwork wood 'sunflower,' 28" dia 400.00
Clock, Nelson/Miller, radiating rods w/blk wood balls, 13", VG .325.00
Clock, Nelson/Miller, sheet metal dmn, blk/wht/red, 21", VG .1,300.00
Clock, Nelson/Miller, walnut w/blk spokes & string, 19", VG ...550.00
Desk, Heywood Wakefield, streamlined maple roll-top, 32" 1,200.00

Desk, Rohde, E Indian Laurel vnr, tubular chrome leg, 44" **1,600.00**
Desk, Steelframe, 3-drw, blk/bl/cream, wht top, 42", VG **120.00**
Dresser, Robsjohn-Gibbings, 3-drw, mahog, rattan hdls, 32x34" .**800.00**
Figure, Waylande Gregory, ceramic mc hollow macaw, 11x10" ...**100.00**
Figures, Shienkona, ceramic women, 14", set of 5, EX **260.00**
Footstool, Sori Yanagi, rosewood vnr 'butterfly' w/brass mts **1,800.00**
Lamp, floor; Arteluce, 3-arm, blk cone shades, Italy, 59" **950.00**
Lamp, floor; German, pivoting brass stand w/dbl-cone shade **900.00**
Lamp, floor; Italian, 1 arm upright/2nd adjusts, cone shades **200.00**
Lamp, Sottass/Stilnovo, Sinus, wht plastic sculpture, 13x3" **500.00**

Lounge (#670) and ottoman, Charles and Ray Eames for Herman Miller, rosewood veneer on laminated wood shell, original black upholstery, 1956, 32⅜x32½", $1,850.00.

Mobile, Alexander Calder's style, aluminum w/pnt metal shapes ...**500.00**
Ottoman, Paulin/Airfort, uphl rnd foam & metal fr, 20" dia **400.00**
Rocker, Eames/Miller, naugahyde shell, wirework base, EX **425.00**
Rug, biomorphic shapes, 4-color, hand-hooked, 97x99", VG **400.00**
Rug, Matisse Mimosa, hooked, 5-color, ltd edition, 36x58", VG ..**1,800.00**
Sideboard, Robsjohn-Gibbings, walnut 3-door, 72" L **1,300.00**
Sofa, Nelson, 9 'marshmallow' disks form bk/seat, rstr, VG ...**10,000.00**
Sofa, Studio 65/Gurfram, Marilyn, molded foam lips, 81", VG ..**1,900.00**
Stool, Nakashima, Mira, walnut, 3-leg, spindle bk, ftrest **850.00**
Storage unit, Castelli/Beylerian, cylindrical plastic, 49" **575.00**
Table, bed; Nelson, Primavera finish, 2-shelf+pull-out tray **800.00**
Table, coffee; Noguchi/Miller, triangular glass top, 50x36" **1,000.00**
Table, coffee; Otmar, walnut, sculptural legs, 60" **375.00**
Table, coffee; 30" dia top, arched aluminum legs w/ball spacers ...**500.00**
Table, console; McArthur, 30" blk oval top on aluminum tube fr ..**5,000.00**
Table, dining; Frankl, fluted gold/cream ped, 71" 'marble' top ...**1,600.00**
Table, dining; Rohde, walnut vnr, aluminum legs, 66", VG **700.00**
Table, Eames, blk plywood 'surfboard,' wire cage legs, 90" **2,600.00**
Table, Eames, child's, gray laminate top w/wood edge, folding .**2,000.00**
Table, Eames, molded plywood 34" dia top, pencil legs **950.00**
Table, Moderne, burled vnr, rectangle top/base, 68x42" **1,100.00**
Table, Noguchi/Knoll, child's, 10 wire supports, 23" dia **1,800.00**
Table, occasional; Aalto/Artek, 29" dia top, bentwood legs, G ..**350.00**
Table, occasional; Nakashima, sq walnut vrn top, 16x30", pr .**1,500.00**
Table, occasional; Weber, blk laminate, chrome band frwork **500.00**
Table, Saarinen/Knoll, 22" oval wht laminate top, molded base ..**250.00**
Table, side; Nelson, Steelframe, lower shelf, 17" sq, EX, pr **700.00**
Table, Teague, walnut vnr 50" oval, 2-leg, 3 oval stretchers ...**1,700.00**
Table, tray; Nelson/Miller, wood-vnr top w/curled edge, G **325.00**
Vanity, Rohde/Miller, rnd 3-drw unit ea side mirror, rfn, 85" .**2,100.00**
Vase, Fantoni/Raymor, textured gr/yel/brn, ftd cylinder, 15" **70.00**
Vase, Fantoni/Raymor, wht w/blk & purple brush strokes, 12" **70.00**
Vase, Fantoni/Raymor, woman walking dog, cvd/mc, 10" **325.00**

Vase, Gamboni, orange/bl bands, cylinder w/waisted neck, 21" ..**550.00**
Vase, Raymor, blk/purple rings w/etched vertical lines, 13" **90.00**
Vase, Raymor, horizontal mc stripes, can neck, wider base, 11" ..**125.00**
Wall abstract, Weinberg, Swingtime, wht w/squiggles, 27x39" ...**800.00**

Finch, Kay

Kay Finch and her husband, Braden, operated a small pottery in Corona Del Mar, California, from 1939 to 1963. The company remained small, employing from twenty to sixty local residents who Kay trained in all but the most requiring tasks, which she herself performed. The company produced animal and bird figurines, most notably dogs, Kay's favorites. Figures of 'Godey' type couples were also made, as were tableware (consisting of breakfast sets) and other artware. Most pieces were marked. Kay Finch died on June 21, 1993. Prices for her work have been climbing.

Our advisor for this category is Jack Chipman, author of *The Collector's Encyclopedia of California Pottery*; he is listed in the Directory under California. Another source of information is *Collectible Kay Finch* by Richard Martinez, Devin and Jean Frick. Original model numbers are included in the following descriptions — three-digit numbers indicate pre-1946 models. After 1946 they were assigned four-digit numbers, the first two digits representing the year of initial production. *Kay Finch Ceramics Identification Guide* (published in 1992), containing many reprints of original catalog pages, is available from Frances Finch Webb; she is also listed in the Directory under California.

Ashtray, dog's head (outline) **55.00**
Figurine, Ambrosia, cat, #155, pastels, 11" **450.00**
Figurine, angel, #114, pk w/pastels, 4¾" **65.00**
Figurine, bunny, #152, pastels, 2½" **85.00**
Figurine, bunny, listening, upright, #452, 8½" **375.00**
Figurine, choir boys, #210 & #211, pr **150.00**
Figurine, dog, Airedale, brn w/blk spots, #4832 ....**375.00**
Figurine, donkey, #4768, pastels, sm **95.00**
Figurine, ducks, Peep & Jeep, #178, 4", pr **120.00**
Figurine, elephant, Peanuts, #191, 8¾" **275.00**
Figurine, elephant, Popcorn, #192, pastels, 6¾" **195.00**
Figurine, Godey man & lady, #122, 9½", pr **135.00**
Figurine, hippo, #5019, pastels, 6x6½" **385.00**
Figurine, kitten, Muff, pastels/gold, mini, 2" **200.00**
Figurine, kittens, Muff & Puff, #182 & #183, pastels, pr **150.00**
Figurine, lamb, prancing, #168, pastels, 10½" **600.00**
Figurine, Madonna & Child, #5594 & #4900A, pr **250.00**
Figurine, monkey, seated, #4903, 10½" **650.00**
Figurine, owl, Hoot, pastels, 8¾" **200.00**
Figurine, owl, Toot, pastels, 5¾" **100.00**
Figurine, owl, Tootsie, pastels, 3¾" **45.00**
Figurine, peasant boy, #113, & girl, #117, pastels, 6¾", pr **125.00**
Figurine, pekingese, #156, sm **175.00**
Figurine, penguin family, 3¾" to 7½", 3-pc set **550.00**
Figurine, Percheron (horse), 4¾" **145.00**
Figurine, pig, Smiley or Grumpy, #164 or #165, 6¾" H, ea **225.00**
Figurine, pig, Winkie or Sassy, #166 or #185, pastels, 3¾", ea **100.00**
Figurine, rooster & hen, Butch & Biddy, #177/#176, he: 8½", pr ..**250.00**
Figurine, rooster & hen, #4843 & #4844, sm, pr **145.00**
Figurine, Scandie boy & girl, #127 & #126, 5¼", pr **100.00**
Figurine, swan, w/pk leaf, #3948, sm **75.00**
Figurine, Yorky pups, #170 & #171, pastels, 5½", 6", pr **500.00**
Planter, lamb attached to block, #6031 ....**75.00**
Plaque, Now I Lay Me Down To Sleep **200.00**
Plate, horse decor **35.00**
Vase/candle holder, pk **65.00**

Wall decoration, sea horse, pk, 16" 250.00

Findlay Onyx and Floradine

Findlay, Ohio, was the location of the Dalzell, Gilmore, and Leighton Glass Company, one of at least sixteen companies that flourished there between 1886 and 1901. Their most famous ware, Onyx, is very rare. It was produced for only a short time beginning in 1889 due to the heavy losses incurred in the manufacturing process.

Onyx is layered glass, usually found in creamy white with a dainty floral pattern accented with metallic lustre that has been trapped between the two layers. Other colors found on rare occasions include a light amber (with either no lustre or with gilt flowers), light amethyst (or lavender), and rose. Although old tradepaper articles indicate the company originally intended to produce the line in three distinct colors, long-time Onyx collectors report that aside from the white, production was very limited. Other colors of Onyx are very rare, and the few examples that are found tend to support the theory that production of colored Onyx ware remained for the most part in the experimental stage. Even three-layered items have been found (they are extremely rare) decorated with three-color flowers. As a rule of thumb, using white Onyx prices as a basis for evaluation, expect to pay two to five times more for colored examples.

Floradine is a separate line that was made with the Onyx molds. A single-layer rose satin glassware with white opal flowers, it is usually priced in the general range of colored Onyx.

Chipping around the rims is very common, and price is determined to a great extent by condition. Our advisors for this category are Betty and Clarence Maier; they are listed in the Directory under Pennsylvania.

Floradine

Bowl, fluted, squat bulbous base, 4" 950.00
Celery vase, fluted cylinder neck, bulbous body, 6½", EX 1,000.00
Celery vase, NM 1,800.00
Creamer, bulbous, 4⅝" 950.00
Mustard pot, NM 1,550.00
Mustard pot, 3¾", EX 600.00
Spooner 1,000.00
Sugar bowl, bulbous, w/lid, 5½" 1,200.00
Sugar shaker 900.00
Syrup pitcher 1,750.00
Toothpick holder, 2½" 1,500.00
Tumbler, slightly bulbous, 3⅝" 1,000.00

Onyx

Bowl, wht w/raspberry decor, fluted top, 2½x4½" 1,300.00
Creamer, wht w/silver decor, opal hdl, 4¾" 400.00
Shaker, wht w/silver decor, Pat 3/23/1889, 2⅝" 800.00
Spooner, wht w/silver decor, 4½x4" 525.00
Sugar bowl, wht w/silver decor, 5½", EX 475.00
Sugar shaker, wht w/silver decor, 5½" 545.00
Syrup pitcher, wht w/silver decor, pale opal hdl, 7¾", M 850.00
Toothpick holder, minor sm rim chips, 2½" 400.00
Tumbler, bbl shape, 3½" 450.00

Fire Marks

The earliest American fire marks date back to 1752 when 'The Philadelphia Contributionship For the Insurance of Houses From Loss By Fire' (the official name of this company, still in business) used a plaque to identify property they insured. The first fire marks were made of cast iron; later, sheet brass, lead, copper, tin, and zinc were also used. The insignia of the insurance company appeared on each mark, and they would normally reward the volunteer fire department who managed to be the first on the scene to battle the fire. (Altercations occasionally broke out between firefighting companies vying for the chance to earn the reward!)

Fire marks were first used in Great Britain about 1780 and were more elaborate than U.S. marks. The first English examples were made of lead and carried a policy number. They were used to identify insured property to the fire brigades maintained by the insurance companies.

During the latter half of the 19th century, municipalities replaced the volunteer fire companies and fire brigades with paid fire departments. No longer was there a need for fire marks, so the companies discontinued their use. Some companies still use fire marks for advertising purposes. Reproductions may be purchased for decorative purposes. Our Advisor for fire marks is Glenn Hartley, Sr.; he is listed in the Directory under Georgia. See also *The Fire Mark Circle of America*, listed under Clubs, Catalogs, and Newsletters in the Directory.

Eagle Hose No 2, CI, lt rust, 11" H 35.00
FA, hydrant w/hose, CI, dk gr pnt, 10¾x7½" 85.00
FA (Fire Association)), CI, gr pnt, EX 180.00
Fire Assurance of Philadelphia, CI, oval, 11x7½" 85.00
German Freeport Ill, tin, lt pnt wear, 2½x7", EX 150.00
Insured Home New York, tin, 5¼x8⅛", VG 80.00
Insured Mutual Hartford, brass 50.00
Invicta & famous wht horse of Kent, lead, 8¾x6½" 350.00
London Assurance Co AD 1720, tin, 10x11¾", EX 75.00
Northwestern National Service Strength Safety, tin, 3" 55.00
Phoenix Hartford, tin, lt pnt loss/rust, 8⅜x4¼" 250.00

UF (United Fireman's Insurance), steam engine relief, cast iron, $110.00.

United Fireman's Ins Co Phila PA, CI, 11⅜x8¾", VG 100.00
4 clasped hands & #906, 7x10½" 365.00

Firefighting Collectibles

Firefighting collectibles have always been a good investment in terms of value appreciation. Many times the market will be temporarily affected by wild price swings caused by the 'supply and demand principle' as related to a small group of aggressive collectors. These collectors will occasionally pay well over market value for a particular item they need or want. Once their desires are satisfied, prices seem to return to their normal range. It has been noticed that during these periods of high prices, many items enter the marketplace that otherwise would remain in collections. This may (it has in the past) cause a price depression (due again to the 'supply and demand principle' of market behavior). But when all is said and done, the careful purchase of quality, well-documented firefighting items has been an enjoyable hobby and an excellent investment opportunity.

Today there is a large, active group of collectors for fire department antiques (items over 100 years old) and an even larger group seeking related collectibles (those less than 100 years old). Our advisors for this category (except grenades) are H. Thomas and Patricia Laun; they are listed in the directory under New York.

Fire grenades preceded the pressurized metal fire extinguishers used today. They were filled with a mixture of chemicals and water and made of glass thin enough to shatter easily when thrown into the flames. Many varieties of colors and shapes were used. Not all the grenades listed contain salt-brine solution, some, such as the Red Comet, contain carbon tetrachloride, a powerful solvent that is also a health hazard and an environmental threat. (It attacks the ozone layer.) It is best to leave any contents inside the glass balls. The source of grenade prices are mainly auction results; current retail values. Our fire grenades advisor is Larry Meyer; he is listed in the Directory under Illinois.

Key:
ALF — American LaFrance   s&a — soda & acid
CCL4 — carbon tetrachloride

Apparatus bell with spotlight, Dietz, NY, 12", $475.00.

Alarm box, Autocall, industrial style, EX 35.00
Alarm box, break glass front, CI, complete mechanism, 6" dia 45.00
Alarm box, Gamewell, cottage type, red/silver pnt CI, 17", EX ..125.00
Alarm box, Gamewell, Harrington Signal, CI on rpl ped, 66" 350.00
Alarm box, Gamewell #4 sector box, half-glass door, EX 325.00
Alarm box, Gamewell Vita-Guard, aluminum, EX 95.00
Alarm box, Gamewell 1951 type, aluminum, complete, EX 135.00
Alarm box, Pearce Jones, Albany...Telegraph Station, CI, VG ..650.00
Alarm box, SAFA #6945, aluminum, complete 135.00
Alarm box back plate, CI, mk fire 65.00
Alarm indicator, Gamewell, oak case, flat top, 27", EX 1,750.00
Alarm indicator, Gamewell, open pediment top w/finial, walnut ..3,750.00
Alarm indicator, Gamewell, vibrating 8½" bell atop oak case ..3,200.00
Alarm mechanism, Gamewell, Peerless type, CI or porc case 40.00
Alarm mechanism, Gamewell, 3-fold type, alunimum case 35.00
Alarm mechanism, SAFA, aluminum, 2-door case 35.00
Alarm rattle, metal w/4 wooden reeds, crank hdl, 6¾", VG 155.00
Alarm rattle, wood w/brass weighted end, single reed, EX 70.00
Alarm rattle, wood w/weighted iron end, dbl reed, VG 50.00
Alarm tapper, Gamewell, brass, umbrella, captain's, oak, unmk .350.00
Alarm tapper, Gamewell, brass on slate base, captain's, 4¼" 395.00
Annunciator, Automatic Sprinkler..., 4 indicators, oak case, 9" .100.00
Axe, presentation; silver metal head w/eng, 1928, 17", NM 475.00
Badge, AM 2 Hose Co NFD, nickel, VG 95.00
Badge, Athol H&L CO 1-FD, w/hook & ladder, VG 75.00
Badge, CFD 4 w/hose carriage/etc in wreath, silver-tone 80.00
Badge, Conshonoken 2 Fire Co E Davis, nickel, hanging, 1⅝" 80.00

Badge, EX President Elmont NY, gold-tone metal, NM 35.00
Badge, Foreman Hose 4 RFD, GA Twitchell, silver-tone, EX 110.00
Badge, Gen Putnam Danielson & steamer, nickel 50.00
Badge, Pathogue 1 FD, hand-pumper on silver-tone, EX 90.00
Badge, presentation; Battalion Chief LA, gold-tone/enamel 180.00
Badge, President Narangansett No 1 Peacedale, gold-tone 45.00
Badge, Volunteer Assoc NY City w/eagle, nickel & brass, EX 80.00
Badge, WA 4 Chemical Co, Braxmar, nickel, EX 50.00
Badge, 1 Volunteer/trumpets/shield, nickel 15.00
Ballot box, walnut, w/blk & wht marbles, EX orig 85.00
Banner, Welcome Firemen w/panoply & equipment, early, EX 70.00
Bell, ALF apparatus, w/eagle, complete 625.00
Bell, brass muffin style, trn wood hdl w/iron ring, 5" dia, EX 350.00
Bell, muffin type w/trn wood hdl, 4" dia, VG 215.00
Bell, Seagrave, apparatus, w/bracket 550.00
Bell, 15" brass bell only, for firehouse gong, w/bracket 250.00
Bell, 8" brass w/CI fr, manual, w/pull rope 125.00
Belt, parade; felt covered w/metal letters, EX 100.00
Belt, parade; red & wht leather w/Liberty, VG 70.00
Book, Footprints of Assurance, EX 35.00
Bucket, leather, from hand tub, no pnt, early, VG 260.00
Bucket, leather, gr pnt w/gold stenciling, 11¾x7¾", EX 270.00
Bucket, leather, much pnt decor & name, EX 350.00
Bucket, leather, SFDI & decor on blk pnt, EX+ 800.00
Bucket, leather w/old gr rpt, wear, damaged hdl, 12" H 385.00
Bucket, leather w/old tan pnt w/#1 in oval, 12", EX 395.00
Buckle, Director in blk on nickeled brass, 2¾x6¼" 210.00
Button, uniform; fireman at fire, Brooklyn FD, NM 15.00
Cord, trumpet tassle; wrapped in metallic thread, EX 50.00
Extinguisher, ALF, cartridge type, copper/brass, 2½-gal, EX 35.00
Extinguisher, apparatus; ALF Foamite Corp, complete, 25½" 140.00
Extinguisher, Badger's Pony Nautilus Water..., copper/brass, EX .100.00
Extinguisher, Fireen Allentown PA, dry chemicals, 12x3", G 35.00
Extinguisher, Foamite, s&a, 5-gal, EX 250.00
Extinguisher, General Quick Aid, copper, 2½-gal, EX 35.00
Extinguisher, Holloway...MD, copper, s&a, 2½-gal, VG 275.00
Extinguisher, Homestead, copper, s&a, pony sz, G 75.00
Extinguisher, Knight & Thomas, brass/copper, s&a, 2½-gal, EX ..35.00
Extinguisher, Pacific, brass, CCL4 pump, VG 50.00
Extinguisher, Phillex, red w/blk letters, dry chemicals, 10" 25.00
Extinguisher, Ranger, tubular cb, dry powder, EX 20.00
Foam generator, red opaque glass, rnd, mk Fire, 8" 85.00
Frontispc, leather, #10 & initials, 7½", EX 150.00
Frontispc, leather, New Utrect Exempt FA, 8", EX 50.00
Frontispc, low front, modern, various lettering 18.50
Frontispc holder, brass eagle (new old stock) 88.00
Generator, Fomite Foam, w/loading hopper, ALF on gauge, 23" ..250.00
Globe, red glass, for alarm pole, 12", EX 180.00
Gong, General Fire Ext Co, electro-mechanical, steel, 6" 75.00
Gong, station, captain's, Excelsior, flat-top oak case, 6" 750.00
Gong, station, Gamewell, feather & ball top walnut, orig, 15" ..3,300.00
Gong, station, Gamewell, feather & ball top walnut, orig, 18" ..4,000.00
Gong, station, Gamewell, feather-top oak case, 8½", EX 1,700.00
Gong, station, Gamewell, flat-top oak case, orig, 15" 2,850.00
Gong, station, Gamwell, ball-top oak case, rfn, 15" 3,600.00
Gong indicator, Gamewell, oak case, open pediment top, 15", EX ...6,800.00
Gong indicator, Gamewell, oak case, open pediment top, 18", EX ...7,800.00
Gong indicator, Gamewell, walnut case, feather top, 15", EX .7,200.00
Gong indicator, Gamewell, walnut case, feather top, 8", EX ..4,800.00
Grenade, Dri-Gas...Chattanooga TN, clear, emb dmns, EX 160.00
Grenade, Grenades Du Progress..., golden amber, pontiled, 5⅛" ..950.00
Grenade, Harden's Hand Fire..., lt cobalt, ftd base, 4¾" 180.00
Grenade, Harden's Improved..., med amber, smooth base, 6⅝" .1,050.00
Grenade, Hayward Hand Grenade..., clear, rolled lip, 6½" 100.00

Grenade, Haywards...NY, lt yel-gr, smooth base, 6⅛" 185.00
Grenade, Hazelton's High Pressure..., amber, wire hdl, empty ...275.00
Grenade, Hazelton's High Pressure..., yel-amber, bbl, 11" 240.00
Grenade, HNS monogram, amber, smooth base, lt stain, 7⅛" 300.00
Grenade, HNS monogram, amber, w/label, EX+ 200.00
Grenade, HNS monogram, clear, smooth base, stain, 7⅛" 200.00
Grenade, Kalamazoo Automatic..., med cobalt, stain, 11½" 250.00
Grenade, Magic, yel-amber, smooth base, Am, 1880s, 6¼" 475.00
Grenade, Prevoyante Extincteur..., Fr, 1890, EX 200.00
Grenade, unemb, cobalt, smooth base, crude, 6" 190.00
Hat, parade; felt w/much pnt decor/gold, sgn Woodside, EX ...4,000.00
Helmet, aluminum, Cairns, high eagle, complete, w/frontispc, EX ...250.00
Helmet, aluminum, Cairns, Senator, BFD on front, EX 95.00
Helmet, aluminum, Cairns, Senator, Captain, Watertown, EX 95.00
Helmet, aluminum, Cairns, Senator, Norwell 2 FD, VG 85.00
Helmet, brass, Defiance Hook & Ladder, spiked style, VG 475.00
Helmet, fiber glass composite, Cairns (flint flex) 40.00

Helmet, leather, unusual Derby style, Protection 1 on front, brim damage (restorable), $225.00.

Helmet, leather, Cairns, greyhound holder, metal frontispc, VG ..375.00
Helmet, leather, Cairns, high eagle, w/frontispc, EX 240.00
Helmet, leather, Cairns, high eagle, 8-comb, cut letter front 325.00
Helmet, leather, Cairns, New Yorker, blk, old cut letters 165.00
Helmet, leather, Cairns, New Yorker, Honorary Chief..., wht, EX ..250.00
Helmet, leather, Cairns, War Baby type, VG 140.00
Helmet, leather, high eagle, Foreman 5 WN, EX 300.00
Helmet, leather, high eagle, Sheffan & Cheever..., 8-comb, G ..350.00
Helmet, leather, high eagle, Trent-n EFA-JN, 8-comb, VG 350.00
Helmet, leather, high eagle, 4-comb, Am #2, Roxbury, early, VG ..800.00
Helmet, leather, jockey style, Fire King 1 Hose, EX 500.00
Helmet, leather, jockey style, Washington FA 1825 frontispc 600.00
Helmet, leather, Olson, high eagle, Asst Engineer MFD, EX 550.00
Helmet, leather, South Am style, wht w/blk front 500.00
Helmet, leather, Wilson, red, 8-comb, lion holder, 1850s, VG ..300.00
Helmet, leather, Wilson jockey style, brass frontispc, EX 500.00
Helmet, plastic, Fireman's Fund advertising, full sz, EX 150.00
Helmet, presentation; leather, Chief, HP front, serpent holder ..2,000.00
Hose, riveted leather, fittings on ends, 48" L 425.00
Hose carriage jumper on spring, brass, 8", w/bracket 425.00
Hose clamp, Akron, steel or aluminum 65.00
Hose jacket, Cooper, aluminum, 2½" sz 85.00
Hose strainer, suction, nickel/brass, 6" 110.00
Hydrant, CI, fancy, Victorian 325.00
Hydrant, CI, Mueller, Kennedy, Victorian, or other common 65.00
Lamp, engine; Gen B McClellan on 2 bl glass panels, 16" 2,100.00
Lantern, Adams & Westlake, brass, gr/clear globe, 11½", EX .1,100.00
Lantern, Dietz Chief, cold blast style, NP/brass, EX 400.00
Lantern, Dietz Fire King, all brass, EX 300.00
Lantern, Dietz Fire King Dept, brass, slide-over cage, EX 350.00
Lantern, Dietz King, steel w/NP tank, Pat...07, VG 175.00
Lantern, Dietz Queen, brass, bl cobalt globe 800.00
Lantern, Fire Dept Tubular, brass, slide-over cage, EX 350.00

Lantern, Ham's (Boston Woven Hose), NP/brass w/shield, EX ..425.00
Lantern, Porter, brass, Union Hose #1 on globe 650.00
Lantern, presentation; NP/brass, Chief, red on clear globe 800.00
Lantern, Sangster, clear globe, pole-mtd, Pat 10 June 1861 ....225.00
Letter opener, Gamewell...Co, brass, alarm box at hdl, 9" 200.00
Letter opener, German Am Ins Co of NY, celluloid, 10¾" 15.00
Life belt, fabric & leather, Pompier, EX 50.00
Log book, Fairfield Co Fire Ins...CT, 1878-86, 18x12", EX 35.00
Marker, auto; aluminum, AFD w/helmet, 5½" dia, EX 35.00
Match safe, Presented by Home Ins...NY, steamer, sterling, EX .375.00
Nozzle, Akron, booster, chrome 35.00
Nozzle, Akron, chrome/brass playpipe w/hard rubber hdls, 2½" .150.00
Nozzle, ALF Foamite, NP/brass play pipe, leather hdls, VG/EX .235.00
Nozzle, booster; Seagrave Corp, NP/brass 75.00
Nozzle, Callaghan, brass, playpipe w/leather hdls, 2½", VG 185.00
Nozzle, Larkin, NP/brass, playpipe w/leather hdls, 2½", G 135.00
Nozzle, low velocity applicator for 1½" Rockwood nozzle 45.00
Nozzle, NP brass, Montrois Pat 1897, 22", VG 100.00
Nozzle, Rockwood, brass, combination, 1½", EX 45.00
Nozzle, Silsby, str pipe, brass, steamer, 36", VG 275.00
Nozzle, tip only, various sizes, common styles, ea 20.00
Nozzle, Wooster, NP brass, playpipe w/hdls, 2½", VG 135.00
Nozzle-piercing applicator for ½" Rockwood nozzle 45.00
Pitcher, presentation; eng SP, w/liner/stand, 1890s+2 goblets .1,500.00
Play pipe, brass, Fabric Hose Co, 30", EX 120.00
Play pipe, hand pumper, dvtl copper, 63", VG 680.00
Play pipe, leather-covered brass, early, 25", G 100.00
Play pipe, string over copper, Underwriter, short, 17" 85.00
Pole, solid brass w/railing & hand bar, 96", 44" dia rail 750.00
Punch register & take-up reel, Gamewell, EX 180.00
Rack, CI, fancy, for stand pipe hose 75.00
Ribbon, convention; Veteran...Assoc of NY, ca 1902, 15", NM ...50.00
Shirt, parade; red wool, lg metal 8 on bibbed front, G 150.00
Siren, Sterling Siren Fire Horn, hand cranked, EX 450.00
Spotlight, apparatus, chrome, 12" dia, EX 75.00
Steering wheel, iron, from bk of ladder truck, 24" dia, EX 100.00
Switch, Gamewell Automatic Light..., brass front, wind-up, EX ..300.00
Ticket, fireman's ball, Good Will Stream..., 1880, EX 12.50
Tintype, 2 firemen w/parade attire, hand-colored shirts, EX 100.00
Torch, apparatus; nickel/brass, acorn finial, 11½", EX 150.00
Torch, brass, trn & ebonized wood hdl, 28" 220.00
Torch, brass, whale oil burner, from hose carriage, 1880s, VG ...200.00
Torch, parade; NP, hand held, 19", EX 75.00
Torch, pewter, mtd on wooden pole, Am, early, G 60.00
Toy helmet, Texaco Fire Chief, plastic, MIB 175.00
Trumpet, presentation; emb sterling w/scenes & flowers, 20", M .3,600.00
Trumpet, presentation; eng SP, 21", VG 650.00
Trumpet, presentation; eng SP, 1881, 21", NM 1,000.00
Trumpet, speaking; tin, red w/gold trim, 70", VG 100.00
Trumpet, tin, red & cream pnt, 2 tassel mts, flaking, 17", VG 225.00
Whistle, Acme City Police of Fire Whistle, Pat NY & England ..100.00

Fireglow

Fireglow is a type of art glass that first appears to be an opaque cafe au lait, but glows with rich red 'fire' when held to a strong source of light.

Creamer & sugar bowl, floral, 3" 155.00
Epergne, 1-lily, floral, crimped, ornate silver fr, 19" 275.00
Pitcher, bird & apple blossoms, reeded hdl, 7½" 225.00
Tumbler, narrow ribs 115.00
Vase, flowers & bird, satin w/concave base, 9x4½", pr 285.00
Vase, stick neck, 7½" 115.00

Fireplace Implements

In the colonial days of our country, fireplaces provided heat in the winter and were used year round to cook food in the kitchen. The implements that were a necessary part of these functions were varied and have become treasured collectibles, many put to new use in modern homes as decorative accessories. Gypsy pots may hold magazines; copper and brass kettles, newly polished and gleaming, contain dried flowers or green plants. Firebacks, highly ornamental iron panels that once reflected heat and protected masonry walls, are now sometimes used as wall decorations. By Victorian times the cookstove had replaced the kitchen fireplace, and many of these early utensils were already obsolete; but as a source of heat and comfort, the fireplace continued to be used for several more decades. See also Wrought Iron.

Andirons, brass, ball finial, early, 14¾", pr 275.00
Andirons, brass, ball finial steeple, slipper ft, 1820s, 16" 350.00
Andirons, brass, ball finials, att Boston, 14¾", pr 450.00
Andirons, brass, ball finials, att Wm Hunneman, 1830s 500.00
Andirons, brass, ball finials, rpl dogs, 1800s, 17", +2 tools 260.00
Andirons, brass, belted ball finials, slipper ft, 1820s, 15" 300.00
Andirons, brass, lemon tops, ball & claw ft, 20" 1,400.00

Andirons, brass, steeple tops, early 1800s, 22", together with matching shovel and tongs, $1,550.00.

Andirons, bronze, lions/devil's heads/cherubs, griffin ft, 35" 2,100.00
Andirons, wrought iron, scrollwork & twists, 20th C, 24", pr 75.00
Bellows, HP floral on wood, worn leather, 18" 160.00
Bellows, mc sponging/blk stripes on wood, brass nozzle, 17" 95.00
Bellows, pnt & smoke decor on wood w/gold stenciling, 17", VG ..110.00
Bellows, stenciled floral on wood, worn leather, 18" 75.00
Bellows, turtle bk, mc mourning scene, worn leather, 19", EX ..2,100.00
Broiler, wrought iron, overall scroll decor, ftd, 20x30" 360.00
Broiler, wrought iron, rnd w/grease trap in hdl, 24" dia 300.00
Broiler, wrought iron, sq w/rnd end, hole on hdl 235.00
Broiler, wrought iron & wire, folding front, penny ft, 17" 195.00
Broom, trn hdl w/mc pnt scrolls, horsehair bristles, 25" 160.00
Chestnut roaster, brass & copper, 5½" dia, 15" hdl 150.00
Coffee roaster, CI, w/sliding door, trn wood hdl, 42" L 155.00
Fender, brass, emb tulips, paw ft, England, 1840s, 10x45" 460.00
Fender, brass, pierced front, Am, 1830s, 7x45", EX 400.00
Fender, brass w/rtcl leaf design, 8x40x10" 250.00
Fender, wire w/brass rail, 24x12x42" 165.00
Fire back, CI w/cast deer & flowers, 26x20", VG 250.00
Fork, wrought steel, FBS Canton O Pat Jan 26 '86, 17" L 85.00
Fry pan, wrought iron, 12" dia w/flared rim, 38" hdl w/loop 135.00
Insert, CI, neoclassical, brass rosettes, Wheeler, 29x40x14" 85.00
Insert cover, CI, musicians decor, 26x24" 95.00
Mantel, pine/poplar w/orig blk & brn grpt, 50x43" 385.00
Meat hook, wrought iron, 3-prong 45.00
Meat or fish cooker, wrought, skewers/hooks/grease tray, 21"+hdl .500.00
Pot holders, for crane, wrought iron, 12x9" w/loop top, pr 70.00

Roaster, bird or fish; wrought iron, crescent shape, 18½" L 160.00
Roasting oven, tin, used for quail etc, rare, 9x8" 700.00
Roasting oven, tin, 13x10" 400.00
Roasting oven, tin, 18x14" 375.00
Spider pan, wrought iron, W Foster on hdl, 13⅝" dia, EX 600.00
Spit rack, wrought iron, dbl headed, 21½" L 140.00
Toaster, dbl; wrought iron, penny ft, 12x14", 13" hdl 450.00
Toaster, dbl; wrought iron, swivels, sq legs, rattail hdl 450.00
Toaster, kick; wrought iron, scrolled ft, 6x15½x17½" 275.00
Toaster, wrought iron, scrolled racks, tripod base, 10½" hdl 185.00
Toaster, wrought iron, tacks on tripod base, 14" hdl 525.00
Toaster, wrought iron, twist detail, shaped hdl, 19x14" 250.00
Tongs, brass, 29" 65.00
Tongs, wrought iron, ram's head finial, 18" 80.00
Tongs, wrought iron w/brass hdle, 31" +matching poker 95.00
Trammel, wrought-iron ratchet type, sawtooth design, 47" 85.00
Utensil rack, brass, w/tongs, shovel & 4 tools, 28" 365.00
Waffle iron, wrought iron, folding, 6x4" waffle, 22" L 65.00

Fisher, Harrison

Harrison Fisher (1875-1934), noted illustrator and creator of the Fisher Girl, was the son of landscape artist, Hugh Antoine Fisher. His career began in his teens in San Francisco where he did artwork for the Hearst papers. Later in New York his drawings of beautiful American women attracted much attention and graced the covers of the most popular magazines of the day such as *Puck*, *Ladies' Home Journal*, *Saturday Evening Post*, and *Cosmopolitan*. He also illustrated novels, and his art books are treasured. His drawings appeared on thousands of postcards and posters. His creation of the Fisher Girl and his panel of six scenes of the *Greatest Moments in a Woman's Life* made him the most sought-after and well-paid illustrator of his day.

Banner, Red Cross, nurse, w/Foringer's Madonna, 41½x8½", EX ..110.00
Book, Am Beauties, c 1909, 21 color illus, EX 350.00
Book, Bachelor Bells, 1908, EX 185.00
Book, Song of Hiawatha, Fisher illus, Bobbs-Merrill, 1906, G- 55.00
Magazine cover, Ladies' Home Journal, ea 25.00
Magazine cover, lady in bathing suit, Cosmopolitan 25.00
Magazine cover, lady in flowered shawl, Cosmopolitan 25.00
Magazine cover, lady w/hankie to face, Cosmopolitan 25.00
Postcard, Following the Race, EX 25.00
Postcard, Greatest Moments, set of 6 in orig matting & fr 165.00
Postcard, Her Future, VG 55.00
Print, Dumb Luck, matted print: 6½x10½", fr: 11x15" 30.00

Fishing Collectibles

Collecting old fishing tackle is becoming more popular every year. Though at first most interest was geared toward old lures and some reels, rods, advertising, and miscellaneous items are quickly gaining ground. Values are given for examples in excellent or better condition and should be used only as a guide. For more information contact our advisor Randy Hilst, an appraiser and collector whose address and phone number are listed in the Directory under Illinois.

Key:
BE — bead eyes   PE — painted eyes
GE — glass eyes   TE — tack eyes

Catalog, Heddon, tackle, color, 1964, 63-pg, EX- 70.00
Catalog, Makinen, tackle, color, 1947, 16-pg, NM 30.00

Catalog, Shakespeare #37D, dealer tackle, 1936, 56-pg, EX 120.00
Catalog, Shakespeare Fine Fishing Tackle, 1951, booklet sz 20.00
Catalog, South Bend, tackle, 1935, 108-pg, NM 45.00
Fly reel, Heddon #37, MIB 65.00
Fly rod, Granger Champion, bamboo, 9' 275.00
Fly rod, South Bend #290, bamboo, 7½' 115.00
Fly rod, South Bend #359, bamboo 125.00
Fly rod, South Bend #47, bamboo, 9' 95.00
Fly rod, South Bend #59, bamboo 85.00
Lure, Creek Chub Crawdad #300, BE, 1916, 2¾", EX 25.00
Lure, Creek Chub Pollywiggle #1700, BE, 1924, 1¾", EX 50.00
Lure, Creek Chub Wiggler #100, GE, HP gills, 3½", EX 35.00
Lure, Heddon, Crab Wiggler #1800, U-shape collar, 1916, 4", EX ..40.00
Lure, Heddon, Dowagiac #2, sloping nose, 1903, 4½", EX 625.00
Lure, Heddon, RH #1001 Woodpecker, no eyes, 1916, 5", EX ...300.00
Lure, Jamison, Nemo Bass Bait, rotating head, 1910, 2⅜", EX ...125.00
Lure, Paw Paw, Feather Minnow #1500, flat sloping bk, 1½", EX ...75.00
Lure, Paw Paw, Moonlight #3354, concave face, GE, '25, 3½", EX ..25.00
Lure, Paw Paw, Musky Mouse, TE, hair tail, 1930, 4¾", EX 100.00
Lure, Shakespeare, Shiner #23, nose prop, feathered tail, EX 85.00

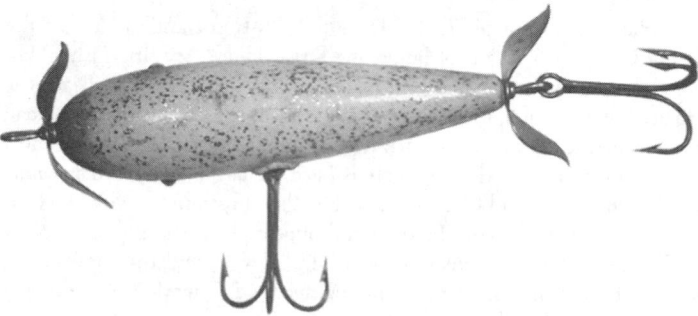

Lure, South Bend, Best-O-Luck Wounded Minnow, brown and orange, 4", $25.00.

Reel, South Bend, #666, free cast, level winding, EX 10.00

Flags of the United States

The brevity and imprecise language of the first Flag Act of 1777 allowed great artistic license for America's early flag makers. This resulted in a rich variety of imaginative star formations which coexisted with more conventional union patterns. In 1912 inviolate design standards were established for the new 48-star flag, but the banners of our past history continue to survive:

The 'Great Star' pattern — configured from the combined stars of the union, appeared in various star denominations for about 50 years, then gradually disappeared in the post-Civil War years.

The utilitarian 'scatter' pattern — created through the random placement of stars, is traceable to the formative years of our nation and remained a design influence through most of the 19th century.

The 'wreath' pattern — first appearing in the form of simple single-wreath formations, eventually evolved into the elegant double- and triple-wreath medallion patterns of the Centennial period.

Acquisition of specific star denominations is also a primary consideration in the collecting process. Pre-Civil War flags of 33 stars or less are very scarce and are typically treated as 'blue chip' items. Civil War-era flags of 34 and 35 stars also stand among the most sought-after denominations. Market demand for 36-, 37- and 38-star flags is strong but less broad-based, while interest in the unofficial 39-, 40-, 41- and 42-star examples is largely confined to flag aficionados. The very rare 43

remains in a class by itself and is guaranteed to attract the attention of the serious collector.

Row-patterned flags of 44, 45, and 46 stars still turn up with some frequency and serve as a source of more modestly priced vintage flags. Ordinary 48-star flags flood the flea markets and are priced accordingly, while the short-lived 49 is regarded as a legitimate collectible. 13-star flags, produced over a period of more than 200 years, surface in many forms and must be assessed on a case-by-case basis.

Many flag buffs favor sizes that are manageable for wall display while others are attracted to the more monumental proportions. Allowances are typically made for the normal wear and tear — it goes with the territory. But severe fabric deterioration and other forms of excessive physical damage are legitimate points of negotiation.

The dollar value of a flag is by no means based upon age alone. The wide price swings in the listing below have been influenced by a variety of determining factors related to age, scarcity, and aesthetic merit. In fact, almost any special feature that stands out as unusual or distinctive is a potential asset. Imprinted flags and inscribed flags; 8-point stars, gold stars, and added stars; extra stripes, missing stripes, tri-color stripes, and war stripes are all part of the pricing equation. And while political and military flags may rank above all others in terms of prestige and price, any flag with a significant and well-documented historical connection has 'star' potential (pardon the pun). Our advisor for this category is Robert Banks; he is listed in the Directory under Maryland.

11 stars, wreath pattern, hand-sewn flannel, 1840s, 31x40" 560.00
13 stars, (4-5-4), sea captain's, ca 1860s, 74x140" 380.00
13 stars, hand/machine sewn, Centennial, 60x86" 175.00
13 stars, in semi-wreath, hand sewn, 1870s, 54x102" 240.00
13 stars, printed glazed muslin, 1880s, 7x11" 20.00
13 stars, 3rd MD pattern, hand sewn, 1840s, 32x45" 750.00
13 stars, 9 stripes, hand sewn, 1860s, 27x50" 525.00
16 stars, naval ensign, hand sewn, CW era, 44x60" 800.00
19 stars, 16 orig+3, sewn scrap fabric, 39x66" 1,200.00
20 stars, hand-embr into Great Star, rare, 24x32" 1,325.00
24 stars, folk art, hand-tatted construction, 12x18" 250.00
25 stars, stenciled burlap on 24" wood tripod pole, 5x7" 300.00
26 stars, Great Star, embr on sewn silk, 30x43" 730.00
29 stars, entirely hand sewn, poor condition, 43x68" 575.00
30 stars, gold stars/fringe, silk, delicate, 52x68" 550.00
31 stars, Great Star, Lincoln related, printed, 11x14" 285.00
31 stars, row pattern, hand-stitched bunting, 104x247" 850.00
32 stars, dbl wreath of inset stars, hand sewn, 36x48" 600.00
33 stars, Great Star, hand-sewn muslin, 60x96" 825.00
33 stars, hand-/machine-sewn wool bunting, 66x92" 550.00
33 stars, wreath w/10 stripes, hand sewn, 77x127" 600.00
34 stars, dbl-wreath pattern, printed silk, 18x28" 250.00
34 stars, Great Star, mixed fabrics, sewn, 91x154" 800.00
34 stars, printed linen, 3 sewn sections, 22x48" 220.00
34 stars, random pattern, hand sewn, 66x140" 710.00
35 stars, dbl-wreath pattern, printed, sized muslin, 19x28" 190.00
35 stars, recruiting flag, sewn bunting, 50x116" 625.00
35 stars, row pattern, hand/machine sewn, 96x180" 570.00
36 stars, in 6 rows, hand-sewn wool bunting, 71x114" 310.00
36 stars, inscr parade flag, muslin print, 6x9" 90.00
36 stars, sailing ship's, inscr & dtd, 75x142" 350.00
37 stars, medallion pattern, printed/sewn muslin, 48x87" 280.00
37 stars, printed silk, 32x40" 85.00
37 stars, row pattern, hand-sewn silk, poor, 60x80" 230.00
37 stars, row pattern, stitched bunting, 30x48" 300.00
38 stars, from SS America, hand sewn, 68x108" 520.00
38 stars, Great Star, printed silk, gold fringe, 12x17" 110.00
38 stars, medallion-wreath pattern, printed cotton, 12x17" 90.00
38 stars, printed silk w/ribbon ties, 30x47" 100.00

38 stars, row pattern, clamp dyed in 3 sections, 60x120" 220.00
38 stars, row pattern, hand/machine-stitched bunting, 71x116" .225.00
38 stars, 1776-1876 pattern, printed linen, 27½x46" 480.00
39 stars, row pattern, all machine-stitched bunting, 40x84" 250.00
39 stars, row pattern variation, printed silk, 12x24" 65.00
39 stars (6-5 pattern), printed gauze bunting, 19x34" 55.00
40 stars, row pattern, hand-sewn bunting, lg, 98x204" 270.00
40 stars, row pattern, printed/sewn British import, 55x106" 185.00
41 stars (rare), printed cotton sheeting, 15x24" 140.00
42 stars, row pattern, printed silk/fringe, poor, 24x36" 70.00
42 stars, sewn cotton, from Ft Hamilton NY, 120x177" 225.00
42 stars, 7-row pattern, printed cotton, 27x47" 80.00
43 stars, machine-sewn bunting, extremely rare, 29x70" 550.00
44 stars, machine-sewn cotton bunting, 53x82" 90.00
44 stars, triple-wreath pattern, printed cotton, 23x26" 100.00
45 stars, HP w/sewn stripes, 38x70" 120.00
45 stars, machine-sewn cotton bunting, 80x108" 55.00
45 stars, printed silk w/red ribbon ties, 32x46" 45.00
45 stars, row pattern variant, printed muslin, 9x13" 25.00
45 stars, 5-row pattern, machine sewn, poor, 79x112" 35.00
46 stars, machine-sewn wool bunting, 72x138" 50.00
46 stars, printed silk, GAR Post in gold, 32x45" 310.00
47 stars, unofficial, sewn bunting, 108x137" 200.00
48 stars, machine-sewn cotton bunting, 60x96" 30.00
48 stars, printed cotton w/GAR surprint, 11x16" 25.00
48 stars, sewn to form 'USA,' unauthorized WWI, 45x69" 240.00
48 stars, staggered rows (early), printed muslin, 13x23" 15.00
48 stars, Whipple Peace Flag, printed silk, 14x24" 260.00
48 stars in gold, sewn WWII casket flag, 58x118" 150.00
49 stars, embr, sewn stripes, 36x60" 45.00
49 stars, 3 uncut flags, printed cotton sheet, 37x36" 20.00
50 stars, hand-knitted coverlet w/fringe, 30x51" 30.00
50 stars, printed & sewn, ecology gr & wht, 34x60" 90.00
51 stars, printed flaglette for DC statehood, 4x6" 15.00

Florence Ceramics

Figurines marked 'Florence Ceramics' were produced in the forties and fifties in Pasadena, California. The quality of the ware and the attention given to detail are prompting a growing interest among today's collectors. The names of these lovely ladies, gents, and figural groups are nearly always incised into their bases. The company name is ink-stamped. Because this is a relatively new area of collecting and the rarity of many items has yet to be determined, examples are evaluated by size and intricacy of design. For more information we recommend *The Florence Collectibles* by Doug Foland, our advisor for this category. You will find him listed in the Directory under Oregon. Another source is *The Collector's Encyclopedia of California Pottery* by Jack Chipman; he is listed in the Directory under California.

Story Hour, with boy and girl, 1-piece, rare, $800.00.

Abigail, bl/gr/tan, 8½" 150.00
Abigail, burgundy/gray, 8½" 150.00
Abigail, rose, 8½" 125.00
Amber, 9¼" 425.00
Amelia, brn, 8¼" 200.00
Amelia, burgundy/gray, 8¼" 175.00
Angel, 7¾" 85.00
Ann, tan, 6" 125.00
Annabella, 8" 350.00
Annette, 8¼" 400.00
Belle, 8" 125.00
Blue Boy, 12" 350.00
Bride, rare, 8¾" 500.00
California quail, wht matt 350.00
Cardinal 325.00
Catherine on couch, burgundy, 6¾x7¾" 400.00
Catherine on couch, teal, rare, 6¾x7¾" 525.00
Charles, lamp, wht 300.00
Charmaine, 8½" 350.00
Chinese boy & girl, wht/gold, 7", 7½", pr 110.00
Choir boy, 6" 85.00
Cindy, 8" 325.00
Clarissa, 7¾" 375.00
Colleen, gr, 8" 200.00
David, wht/gold, 7½" 200.00
David & Betsy, lamps, pr 460.00
Dear Ruth, lamp, rare 650.00
Delia, bl w/blond hair, 7¼" 160.00
Delia, rose, hand showing, 8½" 250.00
Douglas, beige & gr, 8" 175.00
Douglas, wht, 8" 230.00
Edward, gray suit, bl chair, 7" 430.00
Elaine, gr, 6" 85.00
Elaine, rose, 6" 75.00
Elaine, wht, 6" 75.00
Elizabeth, bl dress, gray sofa, 8¼x7" 425.00
Fair Lady, rare, 11¾" 900.00
Gary, gr, 8½" 230.00
Gary, pk, 8½" 260.00
Georgette, w/hatbox, royal red, 10" 375.00
Grace, bl, plain, 10" 230.00

Grandmother and I, 1-piece, rare, $1,200.00.

Haru & Misha, red, 11", pr 550.00
Irene, burgundy & gray, 6" 85.00
Jeannette, 8" 160.00
Jennifer, pk, 8½" 280.00
Jim, wht, 6" 75.00
Josephine, 9" 200.00
Laura, gr, 7½" 150.00
Leading Man & Prima Donna, pk & lace, lg, pr 800.00

Lillian, burgundy & gr, 7" 125.00
Lillian, gray, 7" 110.00
Lillian, rose, 7" 100.00
Linda Lou, 7¾" 100.00
Louis XV, 10" 300.00
Louise, burgundy & gray, 7" 175.00
Madame Pompadour, burgundy, 12" 600.00
Madame Pompadour bust, wht, 7" 300.00
Madeline, 9" 135.00
Madonna, 10½" 190.00
Madonna & Child, 10½" 400.00
Man pushing cart, planter 200.00
Marie Antoinette, 10" 430.00
Marilyn, carrying hat box, violet, 8" 150.00
Mark Antony & Cleopatra, 13½", 12", pr 1,600.00
Martin, gr, 10½" 250.00
Mary, gray dress, mauve chair, 7½" 400.00
Master David, 8" 150.00
Matilda, 8½" 250.00
Melanie, rose, 7½" 125.00
Memories, 5¼x6½" 550.00
Mermaid 200.00
Mike & Pat, 6", pr 300.00
Mockingbird (young) 200.00
Mockingbird family 350.00
Nell Given, rare, 10" 550.00
Pinky, 11" 350.00
Princess, rare, 10¼" 500.00
Rebecca, bl, 7" 200.00
Rebecca, gr, 7" 150.00
Rhett, 9" 395.00
Sarah, bl, 7½" 125.00
Sarah, gray, 7½" 105.00
Sarah, pk, 7½" 135.00
Scarlett, hand showing, 8¾" 500.00
She-Ti & Kiu, wht, 11", pr 400.00
Shirley, 8" 200.00
Sue, teal, 6" 105.00
Sue Ellen, tan & gr, 8¼" 125.00
Victoria on couch, turq, 8¼x7" 400.00
Vivian, 10" 400.00
Winkin & Blynkin, fancy, 8½", pr 300.00
Yvonne, burgundy, 8¾" 300.00

Florentine Cameo

Although the appearance may look much like English cameo, the decoration on this type of glass is not wheel cut or acid etched. Instead a type of heavy paste — usually a frosty white — is applied to the face to create a look very similar to true cameo. It was produced in France as well as England; it is sometimes marked 'Florentine.'

Pitcher, bird/grasses, med bl, w/camphor hdl, 7" 180.00
Vase, flower w/leafy stem, red, squatty body, 4" 100.00
Vase, trumpet flowers & grasses, red, waisted, 6" 200.00

Flow Blue

Flow Blue ware was produced by many Staffordshire potters; among the most familiar were Meigh, Podmore and Walker, Samuel Alcock, Ridgway, John Wedge Wood (who often signed his work Wedgewood), and Davenport. It was popular from about 1825

through 1860 and again from 1880 until the turn of the century. The name describes the blurred or flowing effect of the cobalt decoration, achieved through the introduction of a chemical vapor into the kiln. The body of the ware is ironstone, and Oriental motifs were favored. Later issues were on a lighter body and often decorated with gilt.

Our advisor, Mary Frank Gaston, has compiled a lovely book, *The Collector's Encyclopedia of Flow Blue China*, with full-color illustrations and current market values; you will find her address in the Directory under Texas.

Abbey, bowl, cereal 150.00
Abbey, cup & saucer 40.00
Adelphi, sauce tureen, w/lid & underplate, Furnival 250.00
Albany, bowl, vegetable; w/lid 250.00
Albany, plate, Johnson Bros, 7½" 32.00
Alton, sauce tureen, Grindley, w/ladle, lid & tray 495.00
Amoy, bowl, vegetable; 9x6¼" 340.00
Amoy, cup plate, Davenport 125.00
Amoy, plate, Davenport, 10½" 175.00
Amoy, plate, 9½" 150.00
Amoy, platter, Davenport, 16" 550.00
Amoy, sugar bowl, Davenport, w/lid 550.00
Amoy, teapot, full panel Gothic, Davenport, 10" 995.00
Arabesque, platter, 20¼" 1,100.00
Arabesque, sugar bowl, w/lid 500.00
Argyle, bowl, vegetable; Ford, w/lid 175.00
Argyle, plate, Ford, 9¼" 60.00
Argyle, relish, Ford 125.00
Argyle, sauce tureen, Ford, w/underplate 125.00
Ashburton, bowl, dessert; Grindley, 5¾" 38.00
Ashburton, creamer, Grindley 75.00
Ashburton, plate, Grindley, 10" 55.00
Ashburton, plate, Grindley, 9" 45.00
Baltic, bowl, vegetable; w/lid, Burgess & Leigh 275.00
Bamboo, sauce plate, Dimmock 115.00
Bamboo, soup tureen, Alcott 1,550.00
Beaufort, bowl, vegetable; Grindley, lg 80.00
Beaufort, platter, 14x10" 175.00
Belmont, plate, Meakin, 8" 65.00
Bentick, cup & saucer, bouillon; Cauldon 110.00
Brooklyn, bowl, vegetable; w/lid 350.00
Brooklyn, plate, 8" 80.00
Brooklyn, platter, 13x9" 300.00
Brushstroke-Scroll, platter, Morely, 15½" 350.00
Burleigh, platter, Burgess & Leigh, 16" 250.00
Byronia, teapot, twig hdls, Villeroy & Boch 525.00
Byzantium, plate, 10" 60.00
Carlton, soup plate, 10½" 150.00
Cashmere, plate, dinner; Ridgway & Morley, 10½" 250.00
Cashmere, platter, 19x15½" 1,850.00
Chapoo, bowl, soup; Wedge Wood, 8⅜" 150.00
Chapoo, creamer, Wedge Wood 700.00
Chapoo, plate, Wedge Wood, 8⅜" 115.00
Chapoo, teapot, Wedge Wood 850.00
Chinese, platter, Dimmock, 15¾" 400.00
Chinese, sugar bowl, Dimmock 375.00
Chinese, teapot, Dimmock 775.00
Chrysanthemum, chocolate pot 350.00
Chusan, pitcher, milk sz, 8" 550.00
Chusan, tea cup, hdld, Holdcroft, ca 1830 ....195.00
Claremont, cup & saucer, demitasse 95.00
Clarence, cup & saucer 70.00
Clarence, sugar bowl, w/lid, Johnson Bros 100.00

Conway, bowl, vegetable; New Wharf Pottery, 9" 115.00
Conway, bowl, 9" 95.00
Conway, platter, 10½" 115.00
Conway, soup, 9" 70.00
Cyprus, honey dish, Davenport 85.00
Delft, plate, Petrus Regout, 7¼" 25.00
Delph, teapot, Minton 375.00
Duchess, bowl, Grindley, w/lid, 5½x11" 165.00
Duchess, plate, Grindley, 9½" 70.00
Dundee, plate, Ridgway, 9" 50.00
Evangeline, portrait plate, 9⅝" 125.00
Floral, cake stand, Minton 450.00
Florida, bowl, vegetable; Johnson Bros 185.00
Florida, bowl, vegetable; Johnson Bros, w/lid 420.00
Florida, butter pat, Johnson Bros 50.00
Florida, cup plate, Johnson Bros 195.00
Florida, gravy ladle, Johnson Bros 450.00
Florida, plate, Johnson Bros, 8" 65.00
Florida, plate, Johnson Bros, 9" 70.00
Florida, platter, Johnson Bros, 16" 595.00
Florida, relish, Grindley 98.00
Florida, sugar bowl, Johnson Bros 300.00
Florida, waste bowl, Johnson Bros 215.00
Formosa, bowl, potato; Mayer, 12" 995.00
Formosa, platter, Mayer, rare, 10" 235.00
Genevese, pitcher, Minton, 6½" 180.00
Georgia, bowl, berry; Johnson Bros, ind 35.00
Georgia, platter, Meakin, 12¼x9¼" 145.00
Grace, bowl, vegetable; w/lid, Grindley 275.00
Grace, platter, Grindley, 21" 350.00
Halford, bowl, soup; Ford & Sons, 9½" 50.00
Hamilton, creamer, Maddock 130.00
Harrington, soup tureen 275.00
Hindustan, creamer, Maddock 325.00
Hindustan, relish, Maccock 275.00
Holland, platter, Johnson Bros, 10½", NM 80.00
Holland, platter, Johnson Bros, 14" 150.00
Hong Kong, bowl, vegetable; Meigh, w/lid 600.00
Hong Kong, chamber pot, w/lid (sm chip) 600.00
Hong Kong, pitcher, water; 11½" 400.00
Hong Kong, platter, 15¼" 525.00
Hong Kong, sugar bowl, w/lid 750.00
Hong Kong, waste bowl 450.00
Hudson, bowl, vegetable; w/lid, Meakin 255.00
Idris, bone dish, Grindley 55.00
Idris, casserole 200.00
Indian, plate, Pratt, 7¼" 75.00
Indian, waste bowl, Meigh 300.00
Iris, platter, Wilkinson, 14½" 225.00
Jenny Lind, bowl, vegetable; Wilkinson, 7½" 225.00
Keswick, bowl, oval, Wood, 12" 185.00
La Belle, charger, 11" 185.00
La Belle, charger, 12½" 225.00
La Belle, chop plate, Wheeling, 11" 175.00
La Belle, plate, 9½" 85.00
La Belle, platter, 12" 165.00
La Francaise, bowl, soup; 9" 50.00
La Francaise, cup & saucer 40.00
Lahore, plate, Phillips & Son, 8½" 115.00
Lakewood, bowl, vegetable; oblong, w/lid 250.00
Lancaster, creamer, New Wharf Pottery 165.00
Lancaster, cup & saucer, New Wharf Pottery 115.00
Lancaster, platter, New Wharf Pottery, 12x9" 150.00
Le Pavot, pitcher, milk; Grindley 275.00

Le Pavot, platter, 16x11" 285.00
Le Pavot, soup tureen, Grindley, 12" 275.00
Linda, bone dish 65.00
Linda, teapot, +cr/sug 1,195.00
Lonsdale, bowl, cereal; Ford, 6⅛" 48.00
Lonsdale, bowl, Ridgway, 5¼" 45.00
Lonsdale, bowl, vegetable; w/lid, Ridgway 225.00
Lonsdale, plate, Ridgway, 7" 50.00

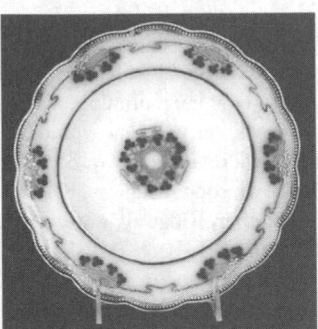

Lorne, soup bowl,
Grindley, 9", $45.00.

Lorne, bowl, vegetable; oval, w/lid 295.00
Lorne, gravy boat, Grindley 110.00
Lorne, platter, Grindley, 18x13" 350.00
Madras, cup & saucer, hdld, Alcock, oversz 175.00
Madras, pitcher, Doulton, milk sz 450.00
Madras, platter, Doulton, 18x14" 350.00
Magnolia, gravy boat, 2-spout, attached underplate, Johnson 165.00
Manilla, gravy boat, Podmore Walker 345.00
Manilla, platter, Podmore Walker, 13½x10½" 395.00
Manilla, platter, Podmore Walker, 17¾" 695.00
Manilla, teapot, Podmore Walker 950.00
Manilla, waste bowl, Podmore Walker 275.00
Marechal Neil, bone dish 60.00
Marechal Neil, bowl, vegetable; w/lid 245.00
Marechal Neil, platter, 16" 225.00
Marguerite, bone dish, Grindley 40.00
Marguerite, bowl, vetetable; Grindley, w/lid 250.00
Marie, bowl, vegetable; w/lid 250.00
Marie, butter pat, Grindley 32.00
Marsaille, plate, ZS&C, 8" 35.00
Meissen, bowl, soup; Libertas, 7¼" 50.00
Melbourne, gravy boat, Grindley, w/underplate 210.00
Melbourne, platter, 16" 265.00
Monarch, bowl, rimmed soup; Myott, 9" 40.00
Mongolia, bowl, berry 55.00
Mongolia, bowl, soup; 9" 110.00
Mongolia, cup & saucer 105.00
Mongolia, plate, 10" 105.00
Mongolia, plate, 8" 80.00
Mongolia, platter, 14" 320.00
Morning Glory, platter, Ashworth, 11x8½" 95.00
Morning Glory, sugar bowl, Ashworth 395.00
Nankin, cake plate, Ashworth 150.00
Nankin, platter, Doulton, 15½x12½" 265.00
Non Pareil, bone dish 75.00
Non Pareil, bowl, vegetable; Burgess & Leigh, w/lid 550.00
Non Pareil, cake plate 225.00
Non Pareil, charger, 11½" 395.00
Non Pareil, plate, dinner; 10" 100.00
Non Pareil, plate, flanged soup 100.00
Non Pareil, plate, 6¾" 65.00
Non Pareil, plate, 9¾" 110.00

Non Pareil, soup tureen 750.00
Norfolk, plate, Royal Doulton, 10" 98.00
Normandy, bowl, cereal; Johnson Bros 30.00
Normandy, plate, Johnson Bros, 8" 65.00
Normandy, plate, 10" 85.00
Normandy, teacup & saucer, Johnson Bros ...105.00
Oregon, cup & saucer, Mayer 175.00
Oregon, pitcher, water; 12½", EX 800.00
Oregon, plate, 9½" 110.00
Oriental, bowl, soup; Ridgway, 9" 125.00
Oriental, bowl, vegetable; Ridgway 125.00
Oriental, bowl, vegetable; Ridgway, w/lid ...350.00
Oriental, shaving mug, unmk 120.00
Osborne, bowl, berry; Ridgway, ind 35.00
Osborne, bowl, oval, Ridgway, 8" 55.00
Osborne, bowl, soup; Ridgway, 8⅞" 50.00
Osborne, pitcher, Ridgway, water sz 150.00
Ovando, drainer, 13½x9¼" 400.00
Ovando, platter, Meakin, 12½" 165.00
Oxford, bowl, vegetable; Johnson Bros, 7x9½" ...95.00
Oxford, sugar bowl, Johnson 140.00
Paisley, bowl, soup; Mercer, 8⅞" 80.00
Paisley, bowl, vegetable; w/lid, Mercer 200.00
Paris, bowl, New Wharf Pottery, 8" 40.00
Paris, plate, New Wharf Pottery, 8" 55.00
Pekin, bowl, soup; Davenport, 10¼" 150.00
Pekin, bowl, soup; Wilkinson 115.00
Persian Spray, flower holder, Doulton, 3x7" ...165.00
Portsmouth, bowl, soup; New Wharf Pottery, 9" ...50.00
Raleigh, bowl, vegetable; Grindley, w/lid 325.00
Regal, bowl, vegetable; w/lid 150.00
Richfield, platter, Ridgeway, bk stain, 11½x8" ...85.00
Richmond, sugar bowl, w/lid 135.00
Sabraon, creamer 215.00
Sabraon, plate, 6¼" 95.00
Sabraon, sauce tureen 595.00
Savoy, sugar bowl, Stoke, w/lid 120.00
Scinde, bowl, dessert; 5" 50.00
Scinde, bowl, soup; Alcock, 10½" 140.00
Scinde, creamer, pumpkin shape, Alcock 495.00
Scinde, gravy boat, Alcock 475.00
Scinde, mitten relish, Alcock 185.00
Scinde, plate, Alcock, 10¼" 130.00
Scinde, platter, Alcock, 13x10⅓" 395.00
Scinde, platter, Alcock, 16" 800.00
Scinde, platter, Alcock, 17¾" 900.00
Scinde, platter, Walker, 11" 275.00
Scinde, platter, 14x10¼" 595.00
Seville, sugar bowl, Wood & Son 175.00
Sevres, butter pat, Wood & Son 20.00
Shanghai, cookie plate, Grindley, 9¾" 135.00
Spinach, cup & saucer 75.00
St Louis, plate, Johnson Bros, 7" 35.00
Temple, creamer, Podmore Walker 250.00
Temple, cup & saucer, Podmore Walker 150.00
Ting Hae, tea cup & saucer, hdl, Holdcroft ...195.00
Togo, platter, 14½x10¼" 175.00
Touraine, bowl, vegetable; Alcock 200.00
Touraine, bowl, vegetable; Alcock, w/lid 375.00
Touraine, bowl, vegetable; oval, Alcock, child sz ...55.00
Touraine, creamer, Stanley 235.00
Touraine, cup & saucer, Alcott 100.00
Touraine, cup & saucer, Stanley 95.00
Touraine, gravy boat, Alcott 185.00

Touraine, gravy boat, w/underplate 250.00
Touraine, plate, Alcock, 10" 80.00

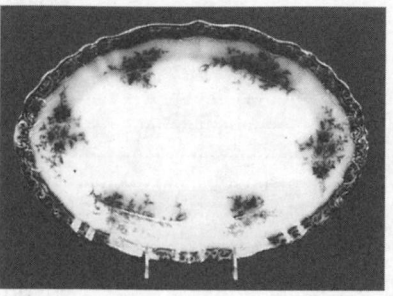

Touraine, platter, Stanley, 15x10", $225.00.

Touraine, platter, Stanley, 12½" 165.00
Touraine, platter, Stanley, 17" 250.00
Touraine, sauce dish, Alcott 45.00
Trent, cup & saucer, New Wharf Pottery 65.00
Venice, bone dish, Johnson Bros 55.00
Venice, bowl, berry; Johnson Bros, 5" 45.00
Venice, toothbrush jar, Grimwades 85.00
Verona, creamer, Ridgways 135.00
Verona, waste bowl, Wood & Son, 3x5¼" 125.00
Virginia, bowl, serving; Maddock 175.00
Wagon Wheel, teapot, child sz 250.00
Waldorf, bowl, vegetable; New Wharf Pottery, 9" ...160.00
Waldorf, plate, New Wharf Pottery, 9" 77.50
Waldorf, waste bowl, New Wharf Pottery 180.00
Watteau, plate, Doulton, 6½" 75.00
Watteau, plate, 10" 125.00
Watteau, platter, 13½" 325.00
Waverly, bowl, vegetable; oval, Maddock, w/lid ...275.00
Waverly, butter pat, Maddock 45.00
Waverly, plate, Maddock, 6¼" 42.50
Wentworth, plate, J&G Meakin, 8" 50.00
Yeddo, plate, dinner; Ashworth, 10⅜" 95.00
Yeddo, plate, flanges soup; Ashworth, 10¼" ...110.00
Yeddo, plate, soup; Ashworth, 10" 110.00

Flue Covers

When spring housecleaning started and the heating stove was taken down for the warm weather season, the unsightly hole where the stovepipe joined the chimney was hidden with an attractive flue cover. They were made with a colorful litho print behind glass with a chain for hanging. In a 1929 catalog, they were advertised at 16¢ each or six for 80¢. Although scarce today, some scenes were actually reverse painted on the glass itself. The most popular motifs were florals, children, animals, and lovely ladies. Occasionally flue covers were made in sets of three — one served a functional purpose, while the others were added to provide a more attractive wall arrangement. They range in size from 7" to 14", but 9" is the average. Our advisor for this category is Cara J. Washburn; her address is in the Directory under Wisconsin.

Blond lady in bl dress, shoulder up, bl-gr bkground, 4" dia, EX ...125.00
Brunette in jeweled dress & helmet, 8½", EX 85.00
Father Christmas w/doll & child litho, 7" dia 70.00
Greek scenic w/couple in foreground, 8½" 25.00
Ladies (2) in bl & gr on gray in gold-tone fr, 9", G 22.50
Oriental boy w/bouquet, tin border, orig chain, 8½x7½", EX 125.00
Victorian girl in wht dress w/dog, 8" dia, EX 100.00

Folk Art

That the creative energies of the mind ever spark innovations in functional utilitarian channels as well as toward playful frivolity is well documented in the study of American folk art. While the average early settler rarely had free time to pursue art for its own sake, his creative energy exemplified itself in fashioning useful objects carved or otherwise ornamented beyond the scope of pure practicality. After the advent of the Industrial Revolution, the pace of everyday living became more leisurely, and country folk found they had extra time. Not accustomed to sitting idle, many turned to carving, painting, or weaving. Whirligigs, imaginative toys for the children, and whimsies of all types resulted. Though often rather crude, this type of early art represents a segment of our heritage and as such has become valued by collectors.

Values given for drawings, paintings, and theorems are 'in frame' unless noted otherwise. See also Baskets; Decoys; Frakturs; Samplers; Trade Signs; Weathervanes; Wood Carvings.

Basket, mc wallpaper fragments w/appl straw sections, 8" 115.00
Birdhouse, wooden, church w/steeple, dtd 1887 on door, 12" 95.00
Box, cvd flowers/stars/trees, nailed, yel pnt, 5x15x6" 260.00

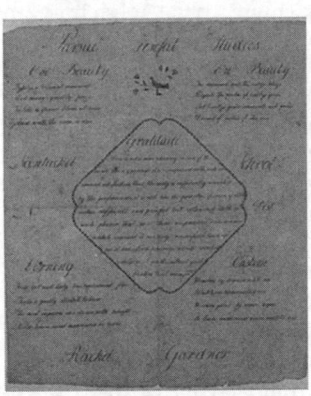

Calligraphy, penmanship exercises including verses, watercolor flowers and doves, signed, 19th century, 16x13½", $700.00.

Calligraphic drawing, Am eagle, sgn/dtd 1891, fr, 20x27" 500.00
Calligraphic drawing, rampant lion, ink, 19th C, 22x18", EX 975.00
Calligraphic drawing, stag, ink on paper, 1800s, 20x30" 400.00
Drawing, charcoal on paper, horses in storm, fr, 20x29" 195.00
Drawing, pencil on paper, country landscape, fr, 14x18" 165.00
Ferris wheel, cvd wood, orig mc pnt, hand crank, 1900s, 22" 125.00
Ladle, cvd dmn shapes & geometrics, sunburst in bowl, 10" 75.00
Painting, lady's portrait, oil on board, Prior School, 20x18" 775.00
Picture, rvpt tinsel, cornucopia w/flowers, old fr, 10x18" 50.00
Sculpture, Blk man's head, pnt clay, mtd on base, 19", EX 1,000.00
Theorem on paper, fruit & foliage, water-color, fr, 9x11" 500.00
Theorem on paper, fruit compote, outstanding, fr, 14x16" 1,650.00
Theorem on velvet, berry basket, outstanding, fr, 11x9" 1,750.00
Theorem on velvet, flower basket, water-color, 1800s, 19x23" ...435.00
Theorem on velvet, fruit basket, outstanding, 1800s, 11x14" ..3,175.00
Theorem on velvet, fruit w/in floral wreath, old fr, 20x20" 500.00
Theorem on velvet, literary scene, watercolor, fr, 20x24" 400.00
Whirligig, man fishing in boat, tin/wood/wire, 1930s, 13", EX ...150.00
Whirligig, men sawing wood, pnt wood, 17x10x26½" 375.00
Whirligig, Uncle Sam in airplane, pnt wood, 11x19", EX 650.00
Whirligig, windmill w/windows & door, pnt wood, '30s, 26", EX ..200.00

Fostoria

The Fostoria Glass Company was built in 1887 at Fostoria, Ohio, but by 1891 it had moved to Moundsville, West Virginia. During the next two decades, they produced many lines of pressed patterned tableware and lamps. Their most famous pattern, American, was introduced in 1915 and was produced continuously until 1986 in well over two hundred different pieces. From 1920 to 1925, top artists designed tablewares in colored glass — canary (vaseline), amber, blue, orchid, green, and ebony — in pressed patterns as well as etched designs. By the late thirties, Fostoria was recognized as the largest producer of handmade glassware in the world. The company ceased operations in Moundsville in 1986.

Many items from both the American and Coin Glass lines are currently being reproduced by Lancaster Colony. In some cases the new glass is superior in quality to the old. Since the 1950s, Indiana Glass has produced a pattern called 'Whitehall' that looks very much like Fostoria's American, though with slight variations. Because Indiana's is not handmade glass, the lines of the 'cube' pattern and the edges of the items are sharp and untapered in comparison to the fire-polished originals. Three-footed pieces lack the 'toe' and instead have a peg-like foot, and the rays on the bottoms of the American examples are narrower than on the Whitehall counterparts. The Home Interiors Company currently offers several pieces of American look-alikes which were not even produced in the United States. Be sure of your dealer and study the books suggested below to become more familiar with the original line.

Coin Glass reproductions are flooding the market. Among items you may encounter are an 8" round bowl, 9" oval bowl, 8¼" wedding bowl, 4½" candlesticks, urn with lid, 6¼" candy jar with lid, footed comport, sugar and creamer; there could possibly be others. Colors in production are crystal, green, blue, and red. The red color is very good, but the blue is not the original color, nor is the emerald green. Buyer beware!

For further information see *Elegant Glassware of the Depression Era* by Gene Florence; *Fostoria, the Popular Years, Third Edition Price Guide*, by Jo Ann Schliesman; and *Fostoria, An Identification and Value Guide of Pressed, Blown & Hand Molded Shapes*, by Ann Kerr. *Glass Animals and Figural Flower Frogs of the Depression Era* by Lee Garmon and Dick Spencer offers an in-depth look at that particular aspect of Fostoria's production. (See also Glass Animals.) Their addresses are listed in the Directory under Illinois. Items with (+) at the end of the lines are currently being reproduced; prices are for original issues.

Alexis, crystal, bowl, finger 12.00
Alexis, crystal, butter dish, w/lid 55.00
Alexis, crystal, pickle tray 14.00
Ambassador, crystal, tumbler, juice; #88, ftd, 6-oz, 4⅝" 10.00
American, amber, bl or yel, cologne bottle, 6-oz 150.00
American, amber, bl or yel, puff box, w/lid, sq 440.00
American, crystal, almond dish, oval, 4½" 17.50
American, crystal, ashtray, 2⅞" sq 8.00
American, crystal, bowl, cupped, 7" 62.50
American, crystal, bowl, shrimp; 12¼" 300.00
American, crystal, candle holder, 7" 65.00
American, crystal, candy tray, 7x5" 250.00
American, crystal, centerpc, 15" 150.00
American, crystal, coaster, cube bottom 9.00
American, crystal, cocktail, oyster; 4½" 15.00
American, crystal, creamer, 9½" 18.00
American, crystal, floating garden, 10" 65.00
American, crystal, glove box, w/lid 350.00
American, crystal, goblet, cordial; 1-oz 55.00
American, crystal, ice bucket, metal hdl 60.00
American, crystal, jam jar, w/lid 52.50
American, crystal, jelly jar, flared, ftd 35.00
American, crystal, jug, 1-qt, 7¼" 50.00
American, crystal, lamp, hurricane 180.00
American, crystal, marmalade jar, w/lid & spoon 65.00

American, crystal, mug, beer; 4½" 40.00
American, crystal, nappy, cupped, 7¼" 45.00
American, crystal, nappy, regular, 4¼" 11.00
American, crystal, nappy, regular, 7" 28.00
American, crystal, nappy, shallow, 10" 53.00
American, crystal, picture fr 15.00
American, crystal, plate, salad; 7" 12.00
American, crystal, plate, sandwich; 9" 15.00
American, crystal, platter, oval, 12" 55.00
American, crystal, relish tray, oval, 4-part 65.00
American, crystal, saucer 5.00
American, crystal, spoon, crushed fruit 350.00
American, crystal, syrup, metal screw top, 6-oz 250.00
American, crystal, tankard 50.00
American, crystal, tray, oval, 12x8½" 75.00
American, crystal, tray, pin; oval, 5¼" 125.00
American, crystal, tumbler, iced tea; 12-oz 15.00
American, crystal, urn, 7½" sq 50.00
American, crystal, vase, str, 10" 85.00
American, gr, gravy boat, 12" 30.00
American, red, bowl, salad; 10" 110.00
American, red, candy dish, ftd, w/lid, 7" 95.00
American, red, plate, torte; 14" 70.00
Astrid, crystal, bowl, dessert/finger; #495 ....8.00
Baroque, bl, ashtray 15.00
Baroque, bl, bowl, fruit; 5" 25.00
Baroque, bl, bowl, jelly; w/lid, 7½" 85.00
Baroque, bl, bowl, relish; 3-part, 10" 30.00
Baroque, bl, candelabrum, 2-light, 16-lustre, 8¼" 95.00
Baroque, bl, comport, 4¾" 30.00
Baroque, bl, cup, punch; 6-oz 30.00
Baroque, bl, pitcher, ice lip; 7" 650.00
Baroque, bl, plate, torte; 14" 37.50
Baroque, bl, sugar bowl, ftd, 3½" 15.00
Baroque, crystal, bowl, flared, 12" 21.50
Baroque, crystal, bowl, hdld, 10" 15.00
Baroque, crystal, bowl, punch; ftd 350.00
Baroque, crystal, bowl, 2-part, 6½" 9.00
Baroque, crystal, candlestick, 3-light, 6" 17.50
Baroque, crystal, mustard jar, w/lid 22.00
Baroque, crystal, sherbet, 5-oz, 3¾" 10.00
Baroque, crystal, vase, 7" 40.00
Baroque, yel, bowl, celery; 11" 25.00
Baroque, yel, bowl, hdld, 8½" 30.00
Baroque, yel, creamer, ftd, 3¾" 14.00
Baroque, yel, plate, 8½" 17.50
Baroque, yel, tumbler, old-fashioned; 6½-oz, 3½" 50.00

Baroque, yellow, vase, handles, 7", $85.00.

Brazilian, crystal, celery tray 20.00
Brazilian, crystal, jug 75.00
Brazilian, crystal, pickle jar, w/lid 42.50

Buttercup, crystal, bowl, baked apple; #2364, 6" 16.00
Buttercup, crystal, candlestick, #2324, 4" 15.00
Buttercup, crystal, celery tray, #2350, 11" 27.50
Buttercup, crystal, cup, #2350½, ftd 15.00
Buttercup, crystal, plate, #2337, 6" 7.00
Buttercup, crystal, plate, torte; #2364, 16" 75.00
Buttercup, crystal, stem, cocktail; #6030, 3½-oz, 5¼" ..22.50
Buttercup, crystal, syrup, sani-cut, #2586 ....225.00
Buttercup, crystal, vase, #2614, 10" 120.00
Century, crystal, ashtray, 2¾" 10.00
Century, crystal, bowl, flared, 12" 35.00
Century, crystal, bowl, flared, 8" 25.00
Century, crystal, bowl, hdld, oval, 10" 32.50
Century, crystal, bowl, salad; 8½" 25.00
Century, crystal, candlestick, 4½" 17.50
Century, crystal, comport, cheese; 2¾" 15.00
Century, crystal, cracker plate, 10¾" 30.00
Century, crystal, ice bucket 65.00
Century, crystal, pickle tray, 8¾" 15.00
Century, crystal, pitcher, 48-oz, 7⅛" 95.00
Century, crystal, plate, dinner; 10½" 30.00
Century, crystal, plate, luncheon; 8½" 12.50
Century, crystal, plate, salad; 7½" 8.00
Century, crystal, relish tray, 2-part, 7⅜" 15.00
Century, crystal, shakers, 3⅛", pr 20.00
Century, crystal, stem, cocktail; 3½-oz, 4⅛" 20.00
Century, crystal, stem, sherbet; 5½-oz, 4½" 12.00
Century, crystal, sugar bowl, ind 9.00
Century, crystal, tray, utility; hdld, 9⅛" 25.00
Century, crystal, tumbler, juice; ftd, 5-oz, 4¾" 22.50
Century, crystal, vase, bud; 6" 18.00
Chintz, crystal, bottle, salad dressing; #2083, 6½" 300.00
Chintz, crystal, bowl, #2496, tricornered, 4⅝" 20.00
Chintz, crystal, bowl, #6023, ftd 37.50
Chintz, crystal, bowl, bonbon; #2496, 7⅝" 32.50
Chintz, crystal, bowl, vegetable; #2496, 9½" 70.00
Chintz, crystal, candlestick, #2496, 5½" 30.00
Chintz, crystal, comport, cheese; #2496, 3¼" 25.00
Chintz, crystal, cup, #2496, ftd 21.00
Chintz, crystal, jelly dish, #2496, w/lid, 7½" 82.50
Chintz, crystal, plate, dinner; #2496, 9½" 50.00
Chintz, crystal, relish tray, #2496, 2-part, 6" sq 32.50
Chintz, crystal, saucer, #2496 ....5.00
Chintz, crystal, stem, claret/wine; #6026, 4½-oz, 5⅜" ..40.00
Chintz, crystal, tray, #2375, center hdld, 11" 40.00
Chintz, crystal, vase, #4108, 5" 85.00
Coin, amber or olive gr, bowl, #189, oval, 9" 45.00
Coin, amber or olive gr, compote, #199, ftd, 8½" 54.00
Coin, amber or olive gr, cup, punch; #615, 3½" 17.00
Coin, amber or olive gr, tumbler, iced tea; #58, 14-oz ..35.00
Coin, amber or olive gr, vase, bud; #799, 8" 19.00
Coin, crystal, ashtray, #114, rnd, 7½" 22.00
Coin, crystal, bowl, #179, 8" 45.00
Coin, crystal, creamer, #680, 3½" 16.00
Coin, crystal, decanter, #400, w/stopper 90.00
Coin, Empire gr, red or bl, ashtray, #124, 10" 75.00
Coin, Empire gr, red or bl, candle holder, #316, 4½", pr ..125.00
Coin, Empire gr, red or bl, condiment tray, #738, 9⅝" ..105.00
Coin, Empire gr, red or bl, pitcher, #453, 32-oz, 6½" ..195.00
Coin, Empire gr, red or bl, vase, bud; #799, 8" 45.00
Colony, crystal, bowl, finger; 4¾" 14.00
Colony, crystal, bowl, fruit; 14" 40.00
Colony, crystal, bowl, oval, 10½" 30.00
Colony, crystal, bowl, rnd, 4½" 7.00

Colony, crystal, bowl, salad; 7¾" 22.50
Colony, crystal, candlestick, w/8 prisms, 7½" 60.00
Colony, crystal, candlestick, 9" 30.00
Colony, crystal, cigarette box 40.00
Colony, crystal, comport, 4" 15.00
Colony, crystal, ice bucket 65.00
Colony, crystal, lamp, electric 135.00
Colony, crystal, plate, dinner; 9" 25.00
Colony, crystal, plate, torte; 18" 80.00
Colony, crystal, platter, 12" 45.00
Colony, crystal, rose bowl, 6" 25.00
Colony, crystal, shakers, 3⅝", pr 12.50
Colony, crystal, stem, sherbet; 5-oz, 3⅝" 9.00
Colony, crystal, sugar bowl, 3½" 5.00
Colony, crystal, tumbler, tea; 12-oz, 4⅞" 25.00
Colony, crystal, vase, flared, 7½" 40.00
Coronet, crystal, cheese & cracker set 25.00
Coronet, crystal, lunch tray, hdld, 11½" 28.00
Coronet, crystal, tidbit, flat, 3-toed 13.00
Essex, crystal, celery tray 20.00
Essex, crystal, creamer 15.00
Essex, crystal, spooner 15.00
Fairfax, amber, bowl, centerpc; 15" 20.00
Fairfax, amber, bowl, dessert; hdld, lg 12.00
Fairfax, amber, bowl, fruit; 5" 5.00
Fairfax, amber, cheese & cracker set, 2 styles, ea 20.00
Fairfax, amber, comport, 7" 10.00
Fairfax, amber, mayonnaise 9.00
Fairfax, amber, plate, cake; 10" 13.00
Fairfax, amber, sauce boat 20.00
Fairfax, amber, stem, wine; 3-oz, 5½" 18.00
Fairfax, amber, tumbler, ftd, 2½-oz 10.00
Fairfax, gr or yel, bonbon 10.00
Fairfax, gr or yel, bowl, nappy; rnd, 8" 14.00
Fairfax, gr or yel, candlestick, flattened top 10.00
Fairfax, gr or yel, platter, oval, 12" 25.00
Fairfax, gr or yel, sugar bowl, flat 12.00
Fairfax, rose, bl or orchid, ashtray, 5½" 20.00
Fairfax, rose, bl or orchid, bowl, bouillon; ftd 11.00
Fairfax, rose, bl or orchid, bowl, centerpc; 12" 25.00
Fairfax, rose, bl or orchid, bowl, grapefruit 30.00
Fairfax, rose, bl or orchid, plate, salad; 8¾" 10.00
Fairfax, rose, bl or orchid, saucer 4.00
Fairfax, rose, bl or orchid, whipped cream pail 45.00
Flemish, crystal, basket, 11" 50.00
Flemish, crystal, bowl, punch 60.00
Flemish, crystal, vase, bud; 6" 9.00
Glacier, crystal, creamer, ftd 8.00
Glacier, crystal, saucer 2.00
Hartford, crystal, butter dish 68.00
Hartford, crystal, syrup, nickel top 45.00
Heather, crystal, bowl, cereal; 6" 22.00
Heather, crystal, bowl, flared, 12" 35.00
Heather, crystal, bowl, salad; 10½" 30.00
Heather, crystal, candlestick, 4½" 15.00
Heather, crystal, comport, 4⅜" 17.50
Heather, crystal, creamer, 4¼" 8.00
Heather, crystal, cup, ftd, 6-oz 15.00
Heather, crystal, pitcher, 48-oz, 7⅛" 95.00
Heather, crystal, plate, bread & butter; 6" 5.00
Heather, crystal, plate, luncheon; 8½" 12.50
Heather, crystal, platter, 12" 47.50
Heather, crystal, shakers, 3⅛", pr 17.50
Heather, crystal, stem, cordial; #6037, 1-oz, 4" 35.00

Heather, crystal, stem, goblet; #6037, 9-oz, 7⅞" 22.00
Heather, crystal, sugar bowl, ftd, 4" 8.00
Heather, crystal, tray, center hdl, 11½" 27.50
Heather, crystal, tray, muffin; hdld, 9½" 25.00
Heather, crystal, vase, #2470, ftd, 10" 85.00
Heather, crystal, vase, bud; 6" 17.50
Hermitage, amber, decanter, #2449, w/stopper, 28-oz 50.00
Hermitage, amber, gr or yel, ashtray, #2449 ....5.00
Hermitage, amber, gr or yel, bowl, soup; #2449½, 7" 12.00
Hermitage, amber, gr or yel, ice tub, #2449, 6" 35.00
Hermitage, amber, gr or yel, pitcher, 16-oz 35.00
Hermitage, amber, gr or yel, plate, #2449½, 8" 10.00
Hermitage, amber, gr or yel, plate, #2449½, 9" 20.00
Hermitage, amber, gr or yel, relish/celery tray, #2449, 11" 15.00
Hermitage, amber, gr or yel, vase, ftd, 6" 32.50
Hermitage, amber, stem, high sherbet; #2449, 5½-oz, 3¼" 11.00
Hermitage, amber or gr, tumbler, #2449½, 5-oz, 3⅞" 8.00
Hermitage, bl, tumbler, cocktail; #2449, ftd, 4-oz, 3" 12.00
Hermitage, bl or Wisteria, candle holder, #2449, 6" 35.00
Hermitage, bl or Wisteria, creamer, #2449, ftd 10.00
Hermitage, bl or Wisteria, plate, ice dish liner; 7" 10.00
Hermitage, bl or Wisteria, shaker, #2449, ind 10.00
Hermitage, bl or Wisteria, shakers, #2449, 3⅜", pr 55.00
Hermitage, crystal, bowl, #2449, ftd, 10" 20.00
Hermitage, crystal, bowl, finger; #2449½, 4½" 4.00
Hermitage, crystal, mayonnaise, #2449, ftd, 9-oz 20.00
Hermitage, crystal, mug, #2449, ftd, 12-oz 15.00
Hermitage, crystal, relish tray, #2449, 3-part, 7¼" 8.00
Hermitage, crystal, stem, water goblet; #2449, 9-oz, 5¼" 10.00

Hermitage, green,
creamer, $6.00.

Hermitage, gr or yel, tray, condiment; #2449, 6½" 10.00
June, crystal, bowl, bonbon 12.50
June, crystal, bowl, centerpc; 12" 25.00
June, crystal, bowl, 10" 30.00
June, crystal, celery tray, 11½" 25.00
June, crystal, ice bucket 47.50
June, crystal, plate, canape 10.00
June, crystal, plate, dinner; 10¼" 35.00
June, crystal, plate, salad; 7½" 5.00
June, crystal, saucer 4.00
June, pk or bl, bowl, mint; 5" 22.00
June, pk or bl, candlestick, 2" 25.00
June, pk or bl, comport, #2400, 5" 55.00
June, pk or bl, goblet, water; 10-oz, 8¼" 55.00
June, pk or bl, mayonnaise, w/liner 65.00
June, pk or bl, plate, grill; 10" 80.00
June, pk or bl, sugar pail 210.00
June, pk or bl, tray, center hdl, 11" 45.00
June, yel, bowl, finger; w/liner 25.00
June, yel, bowl, soup; 7" 110.00
June, yel, candlestick, 5" 30.00

June, yel, creamer, tea 40.00
June, yel, pitcher 300.00
June, yel, plate, dinner; sm, 9½" 22.00
June, yel, platter, 12" 60.00
June, yel, shakers, ftd, pr 110.00
June, yel, tray, center hdl, 11" 35.00
Kashmir, bl, ashtray 30.00
Kashmir, bl, bowl, pickle; 8½" 30.00
Kashmir, bl, candy dish, w/lid 95.00
Kashmir, bl, creamer, ftd 20.00
Kashmir, bl, pitcher, ftd 375.00
Kashmir, bl, plate, grill; 10" 50.00
Kashmir, bl, plate, salad; 7" sq 7.00
Kashmir, bl, plate, sandwich; center hdl 40.00
Kashmir, bl, stem, juice; ftd, 5-oz 25.00
Kashmir, bl, stem, parfait; 5½-oz 40.00
Kashmir, bl, stem, wine; 2½-oz 40.00
Kashmir, bl, sugar bowl lid (only) 75.00
Kashmir, yel or gr, bowl, finger 15.00
Kashmir, yel or gr, bowl, grapefruit 50.00
Kashmir, yel or gr, bowl, pickle; 8½" 25.00
Kashmir, yel or gr, candlestick, 5" 22.50
Kashmir, yel or gr, plate, dinner; 10" 40.00
Kashmir, yel or gr, saucer, AD; rnd 7.50
Kashmir, yel or gr, stem, claret; 4-oz 35.00
Kashmir, yel or gr, stem, ftd, 2½-oz 25.00
Kashmir, yel or gr, stem, tea; ftd, 13-oz 25.00
Kashmir, yel or gr, stem, water; ftd, 10-oz 22.00
Kashmir, yel or gr, stem, 11-oz 22.50
Kashmir, yel or gr, vase, 8" 85.00
Lafayette, crystal, bowl, 10" 14.00
Lafayette, Wisteria, platter, 12" 44.00
Lincoln, crystal, cracker jar, w/lid 50.00
Lincoln, crystal, punch bowl 70.00
Moon Ring, crystal, tumbler, iced tea; #60, ftd, 13-oz, 9⅛" 11.00
Navarre, crystal, bowl, finger; #869, 4½" 42.50
Navarre, crystal, bowl, nut; #2496, 3-ftd, 6¼" 18.50
Navarre, crystal, candlestick, #2496, 4" 20.00
Navarre, crystal, candlestick, dbl; #2472, 5" 42.50
Navarre, crystal, candy dish, #2496, w/lid, 3-part 115.00
Navarre, crystal, celery tray, #2496, 11" 40.00
Navarre, crystal, comport, #2496, 4¾" 30.00
Navarre, crystal, cup, #2440 ....18.00
Navarre, crystal, dinner bell 45.00
Navarre, crystal, pickle dish, #2496, 8" 27.50
Navarre, crystal, pitcher, #5000, ftd, 48-oz 325.00
Navarre, crystal, plate, cake; #2496, hdld, 10" 47.50
Navarre, crystal, plate, cracker; #2496, 11" 42.50
Navarre, crystal, plate, salad; #2440, 7½" 15.00
Navarre, crystal, plate, torte; #2496, 14" 57.50
Navarre, crystal, relish tray, #2496, 4-part, 10" 52.50
Navarre, crystal, sauce dish, #2496, 6½x5¼" 125.00
Navarre, crystal, shakers, #2396, flat, 3¼", pr 57.50
Navarre, crystal, stem, wine; #6106, 3¼-oz, 5½" 35.00
Navarre, crystal, sugar bowl, #2440, ftd, 3⅝" 18.00
Navarre, crystal, tumbler, juice; #6106, ftd, 5-oz, 4⅝" ..25.00
Navarre, crystal, vase, #4121, 5" 85.00
Niagara, crystal, butter dish 40.00
Priscilla, crystal, egg dish 20.00
Priscilla, crystal, toothpick holder 18.00
Rambler, crystal, custard 9.00
Romance, crystal, bowl, salad; #2364, 10½" 42.50
Romance, crystal, bowl, salad; #2364, 9" 37.50
Romance, crystal, candlestick, #2596, 5" 22.50

Romance, crystal, candlestick, #2596, 5½" 25.00
Romance, crystal, comport, #6030, 5" 22.50
Romance, crystal, creamer, #2350½, ftd, 3¼" 17.50
Romance, crystal, cup, #2350½, ftd 20.00
Romance, crystal, plate, #2337, 6" 8.00
Romance, crystal, plate, #2337, 8" 15.00
Romance, crystal, plate, torte; #2364, 16" 60.00
Romance, crystal, saucer, #2350 ....5.00
Romance, crystal, shakers, #2364, 2⅝", pr 50.00
Romance, crystal, stem, claret; #6017, 4-oz, 5⅞" 32.50
Romance, crystal, sugar bowl, #2350½, ftd, 3⅛" 16.50
Romance, crystal, tumbler, #6017, ftd, 9-oz, 5½" 20.00
Romance, crystal, vase, #2614, 10" 75.00
Romance, crystal, vase, #4121, 5" 39.50
Romance, crystal, vase, #4143, ftd, 7½" 60.00
Rosby, crystal, plate, serving; 10" 26.00
Rosby, crystal, spooner 18.00
Royal, amber or gr, ashtray, #2350, 3½" 22.50
Royal, amber or gr, bottle, cologne; #2323, short 25.00
Royal, amber or gr, bowl, #2297, deep, 12" 22.00
Royal, amber or gr, bowl, fruit; #2350, 5½" 12.00
Royal, amber or gr, bowl, salad; #2350, 10" 35.00
Royal, amber or gr, candy dish, #2331, w/lid, 3-part 60.00

Royal, green, cologne/powder jar combination, $200.00.

Royal, amber or gr, comport, #2327, 7" 28.00
Royal, amber or gr, creamer, flat 14.00
Royal, amber or gr, plate, bread & butter; #2350, 6" ..3.00
Royal, amber or gr, shakers, #5100, pr 60.00
Royal, amber or gr, sugar bowl, w/lid, flat 155.00
Royal, amber or gr, vase, #2292, flared 90.00
Royal, bl or blk, bowl, #2267, ftd, 7" 45.00
Royal, bl or blk, candlestick, #2324, 4" 21.00
Royal, bl or blk, cup, #2350, flat 18.00
Royal, bl or blk, ice bucket, #2378 ....72.00
Royal, bl or blk, pickle tray, #2350, 8" 30.00
Royal, bl or blk, plate, chop; #2350, 15" 60.00
Royal, bl or blk, plate, soup; w/underplate, deep, 8½" ..52.00
Royal, bl or blk, saucer, demitasse; #2350 ....7.50
Royal, bl or blk, stem, wine; #869, 2¾-oz 42.00
Royal, bl or blk, tumbler, #5000, ftd, 5-oz 21.00
Royal, bl or blk, tumbler, #869, flat, 5-oz 34.00
Seville, amber, bowl, cream soup; #2350, flat 14.50
Seville, amber, bowl, fruit; #2350, 5½" 10.00
Seville, amber, bowl, vegetable; #2350 ....20.00
Seville, amber, candlestick, #2324, 2" 15.00
Seville, amber, creamer, #2315½, flat, ftd 13.50
Seville, amber, egg cup, #2350 ....30.00

Seville, amber, ice bucket, #2378 ....50.00
Seville, amber, pitcher, #5084, ftd 235.00
Seville, amber, platter, #2350, 12" 35.00
Seville, amber, platter, #2350, 15" 70.00
Seville, amber, stem, wine; #870 ....22.50
Seville, amber, tumbler, #5084, ftd, 2-oz 35.00
Seville, gr, bowl, nappy; #2350, 9" 35.00
Seville, gr, bowl, salad; #2350, 10" 35.00
Seville, gr, celery tray, #2350, 11" 17.50
Seville, gr, cup, AD; #2350 ....30.00
Seville, gr, plate, dinner; #2350, 9½" 13.50
Seville, gr, plate, salad; #2350, 7½" 5.50
Seville, gr, saucer, #2350 ....3.00
Seville, gr, stem, cordial; #870 ....70.00
Seville, gr, urn, #2324, sm 95.00
Simplicity, crystal, mayonnaise, #477, w/plate & ladle 27.00
Sun-Ray, crystal, bowl, bonbon; 3-toed 11.00
Sun-Ray, crystal, jug, 2-qt 60.00
Sun-Ray, crystal, tray, hdld, oval 16.00
Tea Room, crystal, ice bucket 45.00
Tea Room, crystal, shakers, w/glass tops, pr 40.00
Trojan, pk, bowl, #2395, 10" 90.00
Trojan, pk, bowl, lemon; #2375 ....18.00
Trojan, pk, candlestick, #2394, 2" 18.00

Trojan, pink, cup, $20.00; saucer, $6.00.

Trojan, pk, goblet, claret; #5099, 4-oz, 6" 120.00
Trojan, pk, goblet, wine; #5099, 3-oz, 5½" 55.00
Trojan, pk, parfait, #5099 ....70.00
Trojan, pk, plate, cake; #2375, hdld, 10" 35.00
Trojan, pk, platter, #2375, 15" 135.00
Trojan, pk, sweetmeat tray, #2375 ....15.00
Trojan, pk, whipped cream pail, #2378 ....135.00
Trojan, yel, ashtray, #2350, sm 25.00
Trojan, yel, bowl, bonbon; #2375 ....13.00
Trojan, yel, celery tray, #2375, 11½" 27.50
Trojan, yel, comport, #2375, 7" 40.00
Trojan, yel, ice bucket, #2375 ....65.00
Trojan, yel, plate, chop; #2375, 13" 45.00
Trojan, yel, plate, salad; #2375, 7½" 8.00
Trojan, yel, sauce plate, #2375 ....40.00
Trojan, yel, shakers, #2375, ftd, pr 75.00
Trojan, yel, vase, #2417, 8" 120.00
Tuxedo, crystal, bowl, fruit 15.00
Tuxedo, crystal, butter dish, w/lid 50.00
Tuxedo, crystal, pickle dish 12.00
Valencia, crystal, bowl, 7" 15.00
Valencia, crystal, salver, 10" 42.00
Versailles, bl, bowl, cereal; #2375, 6½" 35.00
Versailles, bl, bowl, fruit; #2375, 5" 25.00
Versailles, bl, candlestick, #2395, 3" 27.50
Versailles, bl, comport, #2375, 7" 55.00
Versailles, bl, mayonnaise ladle 40.00
Versailles, bl, plate, dinner; #2375, 10¼" 85.00

Versailles, bl, sugar bowl, #2375½, ftd 20.00
Versailles, bl, tumbler, #5098 or #5099, ftd, 2½-oz, ea 50.00
Versailles, pk or gr, bowl, #2394, ftd, 12" 35.00
Versailles, pk or gr, comport, #5098, 3" 25.00
Versailles, pk or gr, ice bucket; #2451 ....30.00
Versailles, pk or gr, sauce boat, #2375 ....75.00
Versailles, pk or gr, tray, #2375, center hdl, 11" 30.00
Versailles, pk or gr, vase, #4100, 8" 125.00
Versailles, yel, ashtray, #2350 ....25.00
Versailles, yel, bowl, whipped cream 13.00
Versailles, yel, candy dish, #2394, w/lid, ½-lb 160.00
Versailles, yel, decanter, #2439, 9" 600.00
Versailles, yel, plate, salad; #2375, 7½" 7.00
Vesper, amber, ashtray, #2350, 4" 30.00
Vesper, amber, bowl, #2267, low, ftd, 7" 25.00
Vesper, amber, butter dish, #2350 ....800.00
Vesper, amber, pitcher, #5100, ftd 325.00
Vesper, amber, vase, #2292, 8" 90.00
Vesper, bl, bowl, baker; #2350, oval, 9" 85.00
Vesper, bl, candlestick, #2394, 3" 35.00
Vesper, bl, candlestick, #2394, 9" 90.00
Vesper, bl, comport, 6" 40.00
Vesper, bl, plate, luncheon; #2350, 8½" 17.50
Vesper, bl, saucer, #2350 ....5.00
Vesper, bl, stem, cocktail; #5093, 3-oz 40.00
Vesper, gr, bowl, #2371, oval, 13" 40.00
Vesper, gr, bowl, cream soup; #2350, flat 25.00
Vesper, gr, bowl, 8" 30.00
Vesper, gr, celery tray, #2350 ....17.00
Vesper, gr, cup, #2350 ....14.00
Virginia, crystal, ice jug, ½-gal 65.00
Virginia, crystal, sugar bowl, w/lid 25.00

Frakturs

Fraktur is a German style of black letter text type. To collectors the fraktur is a type of hand-lettered document used by the people of German descent who settled in the areas of Pennsylvania, New Jersey, Maryland, Virginia, North and South Carolina, Ohio, Kentucky, and Ontario. These documents recorded births and baptisms and were used as bookplates and as certificates of honor. They were elaborately decorated with colorful folk-art borders of hearts, birds, angels, and flowers. Examples by recognized artists and those with an unusual decorative motif bring prices well into the thousands of dollars, in fact, some have sold at major auction houses in excess of $5,000.00. Frakturs made in the late 1700s after the invention of the printing press provided the writer with a prepared text that he needed only to fill in at his own discretion. The next step in the evolution of machine-printed frakturs combined woodblock-printed decorations along with the text which the 'artist' sometimes enhanced with color. By the mid-1800s, even the coloring was done by machine. The vorschrift was a handwritten example prepared by a fraktur teacher to demonstrate his skill in lettering and decorating. These are often considered to be the finest of frakturs. Those dated before 1820 are most valuable.

The practice of fraktur art began to diminish after 1830 but hung on even to the early years of this century among the Pennsylvania Germans ingrained with such customs. Our advisor for this category is Frederick S. Weiser; he is listed in the Directory under Pennsylvania. Note: Our values are low average compared to the East where values will be noticeably higher.

Key:
lp — laid paper   wc — watercolored
pr — printed   wp — wove paper
p/i — pen and ink

Birth Record

P/i/wc, family register, floral wreaths, PA, 1820s-70s, EX 2,600.00
P/i/wc, fox/peacock/flowers, NJ, 1784, orig fr, 8x10" 2,500.00
P/i/wc, heart/tulips/moon/etc, sgn C Mertel, 1793, EX+ 1,950.00
P/i/wc/lp, flowers/hearts/vines, PA, 1808, rprs, 13x16" 5,450.00
P/i/wc/lp, hearts/birds/tulips/text, no date, 7x4½" 400.00
P/i/wc/lp, Lancaster Co/1790, 12x17", EX 500.00
P/i/wc/lp, lions/star/crown, sgn Beigen, 18x16", EX 4,850.00
P/i/wc/lp, printed hearts, drawn birds/etc, 1788, 17x14" 350.00

Watercolor on wove paper, large ornamental strapwork decoration with birth statistics, ornate borders with hearts, crowns, flowers, etc., PA, 1774, 12x14¾", EX, $2,500.00.

P/i/wc/wp, flowers/1817/PA, fr, 11x9" 3,850.00
P/i/wc/wp, tulips, mc, 1827, fr, 10x12" 385.00
P/i/wc/wp, tulips & flowers, PA, 11x16" 440.00
Pr/wc, angels & birds, Blumer & Busch, 1845, fr, 22x17" 125.00
Pr/wc, angels/cherubs/text, Ritter, PA, 1921, 16x13", VG 55.00
Pr/wc, birds/flowers/cherub/etc, 1776, 13¾x16¾", EX 4,000.00
Pr/wc/lp, angels/cherub/text, PA, 1821, foxing, 16x13" 55.00
Pr/wc/lp, cherub/florals/text, Otto/Ephrata Cloister, 13x16" 250.00
Pr/wood engr/lp, florals, Johann Herman, OH, 1817, 15x13", VG ..230.00

Miscellaneous

Art work, bird, p/i/wc, PA, 19th C, fr, 3½x4" 260.00
Art work, bird, p/i/wc/lp, unsgn, PA, ca 1900, 6¼x4¼" 545.00
Art work, rooster, p/i/wc/lp, PA, 19th C, fr, 3½x3¼" 375.00
Bookplate, Das Eigenthum..., tulips, dtd 1861, 7⅞x3⅝" 100.00
Bookplate, p/i/wc, ABCs/cherub/A Springer/1819, 6¼x3⅞" 200.00
Bookplate, p/i/wc, PA, 1791 & 1830, pr 375.00
Bookplate, p/i/wc/lp, flower/name/1810, fr, 6x4⅝" 635.00
Marriage record, p/i/wc, swags, PA, 15½x10⅜", EX 1,400.00
Reward of merit, p/i/wc/lp, Holmes Co, OH, 1849, EX, 3 for 575.00
Urn of flowers, wc, Mary Hoover, PA, late 1800s, 7½x10½" 300.00

Frames

Styles in picture frames have changed with the fashion of the day, but those that especially interest today's collectors are the deep shadow boxes made of fine woods such as walnut or cherry, those with Art Nouveau influence, and the oak frames decorated with molded gesso and gilt from the Victorian era. Our advisor for this category is Michael Hinton; he is listed in the Directory under Pennsylvania.

Alligator hide, brn w/blk edges, 7½x6½" 50.00

Beveled pine w/red rosewood grpt, 12x16" 125.00
Brass filigree, stand-up type, Victorian, 5½x8" 55.00
Brass-plated CI, pierced foliage, Victorian, 13x9½" 65.00
Brushed aluminum, beveled glass, 14x12½" 50.00
Ceramic, rococo scrolls, lt gr & gold w/pastel flowers, 20x17" 125.00
Cherry, worn, 2" W, 19x16" 75.00
Chip cvd, old red pnt & natural, easel bk, 7x6" 250.00
Chrome & brass, Commaso Barbi/Made in Italy, 15x13" 60.00
Mahog Federal 2-part architectural, orig house rvpt, 21x14" 300.00
Mahog veneer fr, 2⅛" W, 16x18" 45.00
Molded plaster w/scroll design, gilt pnt, Victorian, 15x11" 50.00
Molded walnut w/ebonized & gilt borders, Victorian, 16x14" 65.00
Murano glass, red & blk canes alternate, blk corners, 10x8" 500.00
Pine w/orig blk pnt & gold stenciling, 14x18" 165.00
Plaster over wood, oval shadow box, Victorian, 20x17x4" 75.00
Poplar, mortised & pinned corners, red flame grpt, 18x14" 300.00
Sterling w/etched flowers in corners, standing, 2x3" 75.00
Walnut crisscross, cvd leaves at corners, Victorian, 22x18" 165.00
Walnut, gilt inner border, cvd rim, 13x15" 85.00
Walnut w/gilt & marbleized inner borders, 15x17" 90.00

Frances Ware

Frances Ware, produced in the 1880s by Hobbs, Brockunier and Company of Wheeling, West Virginia, is either clear or frosted with amber-stained rim bands. The most often found pattern is Hobnail, but Swirl was also made.

Hobnail, clear; bowl, 7½" 65.00
Hobnail, clear; butter dish 95.00
Hobnail, clear; creamer 60.00
Hobnail, clear; finger bowl, 4" 35.00
Hobnail, clear; pitcher, 8½" 125.00
Hobnail, clear; spooner 40.00
Hobnail, frosted; bowl, ftd, berry pontil, 6x10" 150.00
Hobnail, frosted; bowl, oblong, 8" 75.00
Hobnail, frosted; bowl, sq, 7½" 70.00
Hobnail, frosted; bowl, 2½x5½" 40.00
Hobnail, frosted; bowl, 4½" 30.00
Hobnail, frosted; bowl, 8" dia 75.00
Hobnail, frosted; bowl, 9" 85.00
Hobnail, frosted; butter dish 120.00

Hobnail, frosted; celery vase, 6", $75.00.

Hobnail, frosted; chandelier, amber font, brass fr, 14" dia 950.00
Hobnail, frosted; creamer & sugar bowl, amber rims, lg 250.00
Hobnail, frosted; cruet 550.00

Hobnail, frosted; marmalade 125.00
Hobnail, frosted; pitcher, milk 150.00
Hobnail, frosted; pitcher, water; sq top, 8½" 175.00
Hobnail, frosted; plate, sq, 5¾" 25.00
Hobnail, frosted; sauce dish, sq, 4" 28.00
Hobnail, frosted; shakers, very rare, pr 180.00
Hobnail, frosted; spooner 70.00
Hobnail, frosted; sugar bowl, w/lid 80.00
Hobnail, frosted; syrup, pewter lid 165.00
Hobnail, frosted; toothpick holder 60.00
Hobnail, frosted; tray, cloverleaf, 12" 125.00
Hobnail, frosted; tray, oblong, 14" 150.00
Hobnail, frosted; tumbler, water 45.00
Swirl, clear; shakers, pr 55.00
Swirl, clear; syrup 90.00
Swirl, frosted; bowl, 3¾" H 40.00
Swirl, frosted; cruet 175.00
Swirl, frosted; cruet, orig stopper, mini 295.00
Swirl, frosted; mustard jar 140.00
Swirl, frosted; shakers, pr 105.00
Swirl, frosted; sugar shaker, orig lid 125.00
Swirl, frosted; syrup, Pat dtd 145.00
Swirl, frosted; tumbler 35.00

Franciscan

Franciscan is a trade name used by Gladding McBean and Co., founded in northern California in 1875. In 1923 they purchased the Tropico plant in Glendale where they produced sewer pipe, gardenware, and tile. By 1934 the first of their dinnerware lines, El Patio, was produced. It was a plain design made in bright, attractive colors. El Patio Nouveau followed in 1935, glazed in two colors — one tone on the inside, a contrasting hue on the outside. Coronado, a favorite of today's collectors, was introduced in 1936. It was styled with a wide, swirled border and was made in pastels, both satin and glossy. Before 1940 fifteen patterns had been produced. The first hand-decorated lines were introduced in 1937, the ever-popular Apple pattern in 1940, Desert Rose in 1941, and Ivy in 1948. Many other hand-decorated and decaled patterns were produced there from 1934 to 1984.

Dinnerware marks before 1940 include 'GMcB' in an oval, 'F' within a square, or 'Franciscan' with 'Pottery' underneath (which was later changed to 'Ware'). A circular arrangement of 'Franciscan' with 'Made in California USA' in the center was used from 1940 until 1949. At least forty marks were used before 1975; several more were introduced after that. At one time, paper labels were used.

The company merged with Lock Joint Pipe Company in 1963, becoming part of the Interpace Corporation. In July of 1979 Franciscan was purchased by Wedgwood Limited of England, and the Glendale plant closed in October, 1984.

Our advisors for this category are Mick and Lorna Chase (Fiesta Plus); they are listed in the Directory under Tennessee. Authority Delleen Enge has compiled an informative book, *Franciscan Ware*. You will find her address in the Directory under California. See also Gladding McBean.

Coronado

Bowl, cereal 12.00
Bowl, cream soup 23.00
Bowl, vegetable; serving, oval 20.00
Bowl, vegetable; serving, rnd 15.00
Candlesticks, pr 28.00

Coronado, Teapot, $65.00; Butter dish, $45.00; Demitasse coffeepot, $95.00; Creamer and sugar bowl, with lid, $30.00.

Casserole, w/lid 35.00
Cigarette box 40.00
Cup & saucer 12.00
Cup & saucer, demitasse 22.00
Gravy boat, w/attached plate 28.00
Nut cup, ftd 16.00
Plate, chop; 12" 25.00
Plate, chop; 14" 35.00
Plate, 6½" 8.00
Plate, 7½" 10.00
Plate, 8½" 12.00
Platter, 11½" 25.00
Platter, 15½" 35.00
Saucer, cream soup 35.00
Shakers, pr 15.00
Sherbet 10.00

Desert Rose

Ashtray, ind 20.00
Ashtray, oval 125.00
Ashtray, sq, no established value
Bell, Danbury Mint 125.00
Bell, dinner 125.00
Bowl, bouillon; w/lid 325.00
Bowl, cereal; 6" 15.00
Bowl, divided vegetable 45.00
Bowl, fruit 12.00
Bowl, mixing; lg 195.00
Bowl, mixing; med 175.00
Bowl, mixing; sm 125.00
Bowl, rimmed soup 28.00
Bowl, salad; 10" 115.00
Bowl, soup; ftd 32.00
Bowl, vegetable; 8" 32.00
Bowl, vegetable; 9" 40.00
Box, cigarette 125.00
Box, egg 195.00
Box, heart shape 165.00
Box, rnd 165.00
Butter dish 45.00
Candle holders, pr 75.00
Candy dish, oval, no established value
Casserole, 1½-qt 85.00
Casserole, 2½-qt 195.00
Coffeepot 95.00
Coffeepot, ind 395.00
Compote, lg 75.00
Compote, low, no established value

Desert Rose, cookie jar, $295.00.

Creamer, ind 40.00
Creamer, regular 22.00
Cup & saucer, coffee; no established value
Cup & saucer, demitasse 55.00
Cup & saucer, jumbo 65.00
Cup & saucer, tall 45.00
Cup & saucer, tea 18.00
Egg cup 35.00
Ginger jar 225.00
Goblet, ftd 165.00
Gravy boat 32.00
Heart 145.00
Hurricane lamp, no established value
Jam jar 75.00
Long 'n narrow 495.00
Microwave dish, oblong, 1½-qt 275.00
Microwave dish, sq, 1-qt 215.00
Microwave dish, sq, 8" 245.00
Mug, bbl, 12-oz 50.00
Mug, cocoa; 20-oz 135.00
Mug, 7-oz 25.00
Napkin ring 35.00
Piggy bank 250.00
Pitcher, jug; no established value
Pitcher, milk 95.00
Pitcher, syrup 75.00
Pitcher, water; 2½-qt 125.00
Plate, chop; 12" 75.00
Plate, chop; 14" 175.00
Plate, coupe dessert 75.00
Plate, coupe party 295.00
Plate, coupe steak 195.00
Plate, divided; child sz 195.00
Plate, grill 125.00
Plate, salad; ind 40.00
Plate, TV 175.00
Plate, 10½" 25.00
Plate, 6½" 6.00
Plate, 8½" or 9½", ea 18.00
Platter, turkey; 19" 295.00
Platter, 12¾" 45.00
Platter, 14" 65.00
Porringer, no established value
Shaker & pepper mill, pr 295.00
Shakers, rose bud, pr 24.00
Shakers, tall, pr 65.00
Sherbet 25.00
Soup ladle, no established value

Sugar bowl, open, ind 125.00
Sugar bowl, regular 32.00
Tea canister 225.00
Teapot 85.00
Thimble 45.00
Tidbit tray, 2-tier 195.00
Tile, in fr 75.00
Tile, rnd, fluted 195.00
Tile, sq 65.00
Toast cover 195.00
Trivet, fluted, rnd 125.00
Tumbler, juice; 6-oz 35.00
Tumbler, 10-oz 32.00
Tureen, soup; flat bottom 495.00
Tureen, soup; ftd, either style 695.00
Vase, bud 75.00

Apple Pieces Not Available in Desert Rose

Bowl, batter 395.00
Bowl, str sides, lg 55.00
Bowl, str sides, med 45.00
Casserole, hdls, ind 65.00
Celery, divided, 3-part 75.00
Celery, 10" 35.00
Jam jar, redesigned 125.00
Porringer, lg, no established value
Shaker & pepper mill, wooden top, pr, no established value
½-apple baker, from $195 to 225.00

For other hand-painted patterns, we recommend the following general guide for comparable pieces:

Cafe Royal	-30%
Daisy	-20%
October	-20%
Forget-Me-Not	-10%
Meadow Rose	-10%
Desert Rose	Base Line Values
Apple	+10%
Ivy	+20%
Strawberry Fair	+20%
Strawberry Time	+20%
Fresh Fruit	+20%
Bountiful	+20%
Poppy	+35%
Original (small) Fruit	+50%
Wild Flower	+100% to 200%

There is not an active market in Bouquet, Rosette, or Twilight Rose, as these are scarce, having been produced only a short time. Our estimate would place Bouquet and Rosette in the October range (-20%) and Twilight Rose in the Ivy range (+20%).

El Patio

Bowl, cereal 12.00
Bowl, fruit 12.00
Bowl, salad; 3-qt 25.00
Bowl, vegetable; oval 30.00
Butter dish 40.00
Creamer 10.00
Cup 10.00
Cup, jumbo 18.00
Cup & saucer, demitasse 40.00

Gravy boat, w/attached underplate 35.00
Plate, bread & butter 7.00
Plate, 10½" 15.00
Plate, 8½" 12.00
Platter, 13" 45.00
Saucer 4.00
Saucer, jumbo 8.00
Sherbet 10.00
Sugar bowl, w/lid 18.00
Teapot, w/lid, 6-cup 65.00

Franciscan Fine China

The main line of fine china was called Masterpiece. There were at least four marks used during its production from 1941 to 1977. Almost every piece is clearly marked. This china is true porcelain, the body having been fired at a very high temperature. Many years of research and experimentation went into this china before it was marketed. Production was temporarily suspended during the war years. More than 170 patterns and many varying shapes were produced. All are valued about the same with the exception of the Renaissance group, which is 25% higher.

Bowl, vegetable; serving, oval 50.00
Cup 20.00
Plate, bread & butter 18.00
Plate, dinner 30.00
Plate, salad 25.00
Saucer 12.00

Frankart

During the 1920s Frankart, Inc., of New York City, produced a line of accessories that included figural nude lamps, bookends, ashtrays, etc. These white metal composition items were offered in several finishes including verde green, jap black, and gun-metal gray. The company also produced a line of caricatured animals, but the stylized nude figurals have proven to be the most collectible today. With few exceptions, all pieces were marked 'Frankart, Inc.' with a patent number or 'pat. appl. for.' All pieces listed are in very good original condition unless otherwise indicated. Our advisor for this category is Walter Glenn; he is listed in the Directory under Georgia.

Aquarium, nude sits atop wrought-iron stand, aqua, sq, 14" 650.00
Ashtray, ballet girl in center of 8" rnd onyx tray, 10" 475.00
Ashtray, dachshund (stylized) spans 4½" sq ashtray, 5" 200.00
Ashtray, duck (stylized) holds tray in outstretched wings, 5" 225.00
Ashtray, nude dancer holds tray on hip, box on base, 10" 450.00
Ashtray, nude kneels on cushion, holds 3" pottery tray, 6" 325.00
Ashtray, nude stands on chrome ball, holds 6" tray, 24" 675.00
Ashtray, 3 nudes joined at hips hold 6" pottery ball, 25" 1,150.00
Bookends, female heads (futuristic, long-necked), 7", pr 250.00
Bookends, nude dancers, frog on base, 10", pr 425.00
Bookends, nude sits atop human skull, 8", pr 375.00
Bookends, nude stands, arm bk to support books, 7½", pr 325.00
Bookends, nude stands & peeks around books, 8", pr 325.00
Bookends, polar bear (stylized), seated, 6½", pr 175.00
Bookends, Roman-inspired masks, 7½", pr 375.00
Clock, nude stands ea side of rectangular glass clock, 10½" 1,500.00
Lamp, nude kneels before 4" bubble ball, 8" 700.00
Lamp, nude seated, legs extended, 3" globes on sides, 7" 900.00
Lamp, nude stands, arms bk, glass butterfly wings, 10¼" 1,500.00
Lamp, seated 'debutante' gazes into 3" globe, 6½" 550.00
Lamp, seated nude silhouettes against 3" sq glass cylinder, 12" ...950.00

Lamp, 2 nudes kneel & embrace 8" crackle glass globe, 9" 750.00
Match holder, burro w/pack (holder) on bk, 8" 175.00
Vase, nude dancer holds flower vase on hip, 10" 725.00

Frankoma

The Frank Pottery, founded in Oklahoma in 1933 by John Frank, became known as Frankoma in 1934. The company produced decorative figurals, vases, and such, marking their ware from 1936-38 with a pacing leopard 'Frankoma' mark. These pieces are highly sought. The entire operation was destroyed by fire in 1938, and new molds were cast — some from surviving pieces — and a similar line of production was pursued. The body of the ware was changed in 1955 from a honey tan (called 'Ada clay,' referring to the name of the town near the area where it was dug) to a red brick clay (known as Sapulpa), and this, along with the color of the glazes (over fifty have been used), helps determine the period of production. A Southwestern theme has always been favored in design as well as in color selection.

In 1965 they began to produce a limited-edition series of Christmas plates, followed by a bottle vase series in 1969. Considered very collectible are their political mugs, bicentennial plates, Teenagers of the Bible plates, and the Wildlife series. Their ceramic Christmas cards are also very popular items with today's collectors.

Frankoma celebrated their 50th Anniversary in 1983. On September 26 of that same year, Frankoma was again destroyed by fire. Because of a fire-proof wall, master molds of all 1983 production items were saved, allowing plans for rebuilding to begin immediately.

Frankoma filed for Chapter 11 in April, 1990, and eventually sold to a Maryland investor in February of 1991, thereby ending the family-ownership era. For a more thorough study of the subject, we recommend that you refer to *Frankoma Treasures* and *Frankoma and Other Oklahoma Potteries* by Phyllis and Tom Bess, our advisors; you will find their address in the Directory under Oklahoma.

Baker, Lazybones, 2-qt 25.00
Bank, Boot 8.50
Bolo tie, 4-leaf clover 30.00
Bookends, Rearing Clydesdale, #431, pr 350.00

Bookends, Charger Horses, Black Onyx, Ada clay, $250.00.

Chop plate, 15" 35.00
Christmas card, Donna Frank, 1952 ....60.00
Christmas card, 1944 ....105.00
Christmas card, 1947-48 ....85.00
Christmas card, 1949 ....65.00
Christmas card, 1950-51 ....75.00
Christmas card, 1952 ....85.00
Christmas card, 1953-56 ....75.00

Christmas card, 1957 ....70.00
Christmas card, 1958-60 ....65.00
Christmas card, 1961-66 ....60.00
Christmas card, 1967-68 ....50.00
Christmas card, 1969-71 ....40.00
Christmas card, 1972 ....35.00
Christmas card, 1973-75 ....30.00
Christmas card, 1976-77 ....85.00
Christmas card, 1980-82 ....25.00
Christmas plate, 1965 ....310.00
Christmas plate, 1967 ....70.00
Christmas plate, 1977-82 ....35.00
Flower frog, Mermaid, 7" 1,200.00
Flower holder, Hobby Horse, #182, 1942, 3½" 165.00
Flowerabrum, #58, 1942, 11½" 85.00
Ivy bowl, #27, 5⅞" 40.00
Jug, Uncle Slug, #10, 2¼" 20.00
Lazy susan, #94FC, 1947-63, 15" 75.00
Mask, Comedy 15.00
Mask, Oriental Man, #134, 5½" 185.00
Medallion, lady's profile, oval 100.00
Pitcher, Aztec, #551, mini 10.00
Pitcher, Mayan, #82 ....20.00
Pitcher, Widow Maker 85.00
Plaque, Will Rogers, borderless, 1934-35, 4x4¾" 50.00
Plate, Conestoga Wagon 75.00
Plate, Helen Keller 40.00
Plate, Will Rogers Centennial 20.00
Plate, 50th Anniversary 30.00
Platter, 17" 20.00
Political mug, Elephant, 1968 ....100.00
Political mug, Elephant, 1972-73 ....50.00
Political mug, Elephant or Donkey, 1975-76 ....35.00
Sculpture, Amazon Woman, mk Taylor, 6¼x8" 500.00
Sculpture, Circus Horse, Wht Sand 195.00
Sculpture, Coyote Pup, #105 ....450.00
Sculpture, English Setter 185.00
Sculpture, English Setter, #163, 2⅞" 65.00
Sculpture, Fan Dancer, Ada clay, #113, 1934-69, 8½x13½" 350.00
Sculpture, Swan, #168, 3" 45.00
Sculpture, Swan, Norman glaze, #168, 3" 55.00
Sculpture, Torch Singer, #126, ca 1934, 13½" 1,200.00
Sculpture, Walking Ocelot 350.00
Shakers, Dutch Shoe, pr 40.00
Shakers, Puma, #165H, 3", pr 60.00
Teapot, Plainsman, 6-cup 40.00
Teapot, 8-cup 60.00
Tie tac 20.00
Toby mug, Uncle Sam, 1976 ....20.00
Trivet, Cherokee Alphabet, Flame 6.50
Tumbler, Ada clay, 12-oz 15.00
Vase, #503, mini, 2½" 25.00
Vase, bud; blk onyx, glossy, 1933 ....35.00
Vase, bud; Flame, brn int, 6¼" 50.00
Vase, collector; V-1, 1969, 15" 100.00
Vase, collector; V-10, 11½" 50.00
Vase, collector; V-12, 1980 ....55.00
Vase, collector; V-14, 1972 ....80.00
Vase, collector; V-14, 1981, 13" 85.00
Vase, collector; V-15, 2-pc, last of series 60.00
Vase, collector; V-3, 1971, 12" 75.00
Vase, collector; V-8, 1976 ....70.00
Vase, Flying Goose, #60B, 6" 25.00
Vase, leaf hdls, early glaze, #71, 1942, 10" 100.00

Vase, Ram's Head, #38, 6" 40.00
Vase, scalloped rim, #79, ca 1934-38, 7" 200.00
Vase, stepped hdls, 341, 7" 75.00
Vase, Thunderbird, #506, 3½" 30.00
Wall mask, Maiden, Ada clay 65.00
Wall masks, Comedy & Tragedy, pr 65.00
Wall pocket, Acorn, Woodland Moss, #190, lg 40.00
Wall pocket, Leaf, #197, 8½" 40.00
Wall pocket, Phoebe, #730, 1948-49, 7½" 85.00

Fraternal Organizations

Fraternal memorabilia is a vast and varied field. Emblems representing the various organizations have been used to decorate cups, shaving mugs, plates, and glassware. Medals, swords, documents, and other ceremonial paraphernalia from the 1800s and early 1900s are especially prized. Our advisor for Odd Fellows is Greg Spiess; he is listed in the Directory under Illinois. Information on Masonic and Shrine memorabilia has been provided by David Smies, who is listed under Kansas.

Elks

Sign, reverse painting on glass, inscription on back, dated 1908, 22x16", EX, $90.00.

Charm, watch; gold enameling 30.00
Cuff links, enameled, pr 4.50
Inkwell, elk's-head base, rack is pen holder, O of E, 1800s 150.00
Plaque, cvd wood, stag w/clock & scroll, 21x24", VG 125.00
Stein, pottery, hunter on ground, elk, We Are Bros, 10" 95.00

Masons

Apron, embr silk, w/sash, 1800s, some discoloration 150.00
Ashtray, G center eye at top, hammer & trowel, 5½" dia 20.00
Cuff links & tie bar, sterling, 1940s, MIB 25.00
Cup & saucer, handleless; soft paste, floral 15.00
Handbook, 1890, EX 20.00
Linen spread, copper-plate Masonic symbols, late 1700s, VG 465.00
Medal, presentation; 18k gold, London, 1880 ....350.00
Paperweight, glass, symbols, mushroom cap, Pittsburgh Glass 110.00
Plate, ceramic, Jerusalem Chapter, lady in hat w/fan, 1907 ....38.00
Tie tack, 14k gold 18.00
Tintype, man in Masonic garb, EX 50.00
Wall shelf, Victorian, cvd walnut, sm, EX 50.00

Odd Fellows

Book, Code of General Laws, 1916, EX 10.00
Catalog, Costumes, Regalia & Paraphernalia, Lilley OH, EX 17.50
Collar, cream w/red trim, 4 rosettes, VG 2.50

Cookie mold, symbols, CI, 1820s, 5x6½" 250.00
Robe, ceremonial, bl & blk w/gold braid, ca 1900, EX 90.00
Staff, wood w/hand & heart, EX 265.00
Torch, ceremonial, tin & wood, 1890s, 22", EX 75.00
Turban, EX 5.00
Watch fob, symbols, EX 20.00

Shrine

Champagne, alligators, New Orleans, 1910, M 90.00
Fez, Arab, rhinestone tassel pin, EX 45.00
Goblet, ruby stain, St Paul MN, 1908 ....32.50
Pendant, gold & silver scimitar, cross w/dmns 265.00
Shaving mug, symbol & name in gold, TV Limoges 195.00
Tumbler, Pittsburgh, 1900 ....58.00

Fraunfelter

Charles Fraunfelter organized his company in Zanesville, Ohio, in 1915. It was known as the Ohio Pottery Company until 1923. During this period their main product was a line of utilitarian articles for chemical laboratories made of hard-paste porcelain. In 1918 they used the same body to produce a brown and white line called 'Petruscan.' By 1920 a line of hotel ware was added. The company organized in 1923 and became known as Fraunfelter China Company; but after the death of Fraunfelter in 1925, the business fell into hard times and eventually closed altogether in 1939.

Candlesticks, 8½", $15.00 for the pair.

Casserole, Petruscan, floral transfer, orig chrome holder 55.00
Teapot, brn & cream w/gold transfers, ribbed body 35.00
Vase, bl lustre, 6¼" 22.00
Vase, lovebirds, gold/silver details on gray, sgn/mk, 10" 195.00

Fruit Jars

As early as 1829, canning jars were being manufactured for use in the home preservation of foodstuffs. For the past twenty-five years, they have been sought as popular collectibles. At the last estimate, over four thousand fruit jars and variations were known to exist. Some are very rare, perhaps one-of-a-kind examples known to have survived to the present day. Among the most valuable are the black glass jars, the amber Van Vliet, and the cobalt Millville. These often bring prices in excess of $3,000.00 when they can be found. Aside from condition, values are based on age, rarity, color, and special features. Our advisor for this category is John Hathaway; he is listed in the Directory under Maine.

Acme Seal (script), regular mouth, clear, pt 145.00
Air Tight, clear, qt 48.00
Almy, aqua, qt 128.00
Am (flag & eagle), lt gr, ½-gal 150.00
Atlas Mason Improved Pat'd, lt emerald gr, qt 35.00
Atlas Strong Shoulder Mason, lt cornflower bl, pt 25.00
Ball (3 L loop) Mason, med emerald gr, qt 35.00
Ball Pat Apl'd For, aqua, qt 198.00
Ball Perfect Mason, med olive gr, pt 125.00
Ball Perfect Mason (block letters), lt gr, qt 28.00
Ball Perfect Mason (dbl-lined letters), clear, qt, sm chip 73.00
Best, lt sun-colored amethyst, qt 35.00
Bosco Dbl Seal, clear, qt 53.00
Bostwich Perfect Sealer (in script), clear, pt 50.00
Buckeye 3, aqua, qt, lt lid stain 198.00
Canton Domestic Fruit Jars, clear, qt 83.00
CK Hale & Co 121 Water St Cleveland OH, aqua, qt 298.00
Clarke Fruit Jar Co, Cleveland OH, aqua, qt, no closure 38.00
Cohansey (arched), aqua, qt 25.00
Cohansey Mfg Co, Pat 3/20/77, aqua, bbl form, ½-gal 128.00
Columbia, clear, pt 28.00
Cross Mason's Improved (ghost gem), aqua, ½-gal 20.00
Daisy Jar, clear, qt, repro clamp 188.00
Doolittle, aqua, qt, no closures 38.00
Easy Trade VJC Co (mono), mk Vacuum Jar, aqua, pt 30.00
Eclipse Jar, aqua, qt 448.00
Erie Lightning Co, clear, qt 60.00
Everlasting (jar in flag), aqua, ½-gal 30.00
Excelsior Improved, aqua, ½-gal 48.00
Favorite Trade Mark, aqua, qt, correct insert, edge bruise 48.00
Fruit Keeper GCCO, aqua, qt or pt 42.00
Geo D Brown & Co, clear, pt 48.00
Globe, amber, pt 90.00
Haines Combination, aqua, qt, no lid, sm inner lip chip 138.00
Hamilton, clear qt 68.00
Hero (over cross), aqua, qt 48.00
Heroine, aqua, pt, 2-pc zinc lid 120.00
Heroine, aqua, qt, 2-pc zinc lid 58.00
Howe Jar, Scranton PA, clear, qt or ½-gal 85.00
Ideal, aqua, qt or ½-gal 18.00
Independent Jar, clear, ½-gal, lid Pat 12/17/1878 ....38.00
Jewell Jar (block letters in fr), clear, qt 15.00
K (in star) Stark Jar Pat'd, clear, qt 123.00
King, Pat 11/2/1869, aqua, qt, lid chip 248.00
Knowltown Vacuum (star) Fruit Jar, bl, pt 43.00
Lafayette (script), aqua, qt 123.00
Leader (1-line), clear, ½-gal 65.00
Mason Jar of 1872, aqua, ½-gal 45.00
Mason Porcelain Lined, aqua, qt or ½-gal, ea 150.00
Mason's Crystal Jar, clear, glass screw-on lid, ½-gal 40.00
Putnam (base), amber, pt 75.00
Sierra Mason Jar Made in California, clear, pt 60.00
Star Below Star (curled R), clear, qt 48.00
Swayzee's Improved Mason, med emerald gr, ½-gal 55.00
TM Lightning (base) Putnam, aqua, 1½-pt 45.00
Valve Jar Co PA, aqua, repro wire, qt or ½-gal, glass lid 238.00

Fry

Henry Fry established his glassworks in 1901 in Rochester, Pennsylvania. There, until 1933 when it was sold to the Libbey Company, he produced glassware of the finest quality. In the early years they produced beautiful cut glass; and when it began to wane in popularity, Fry turned to the manufacture of occasional pieces and oven glassware. He is perhaps most famous for the opalescent pearl glass called 'Foval.' It was sometimes made with blue or jade green trim in combination. Because it was in production for only a short time in 1926 and 1927, it is hard to find. Our advisor for this category is Ron Damaska; he is listed in the Directory under Pennsylvania. See also Kitchen Collectibles, Glassware.

Ashtray, Rose (pk), 4 buttressed ft	25.00
Baker, pearl ovenware, oval, 13"	35.00
Basket, jade gr w/festooning, 12"	600.00
Bean pot, pearl ovenware, w/lid, 1924, 1-qt	120.00
Bowl, ivy; blk, clear swirl connector, blk ft	40.00
Bowl, salad; pearl opal w/jade gr rim & ft, 5½x9"	275.00
Cake pan, pearl ovenware, 9" dia	25.00
Candle holder, amber, HP floral trim	15.00
Candlesticks, Foval, bl spiral threaded stems/wafers, 11", pr	250.00
Candy dish, pearl opal, bl ft & stem, 4¾"	160.00
Casserole, pearl ovenware, oval, w/lid, 10"	45.00
Casserole, pearl ovenware, w/lid, 7" dia	35.00

Clock, Pershing pattern, 10" long, $550.00.

Coffeepot, Foval, w/stem & basket, 10"	250.00
Compote, Foval, bl stem/trim/festooning, low, #2502, 5½"	250.00
Compote, Foval, wht & gr, 7x5¾"	275.00
Coquette, pearl ovenware, 6"	30.00
Creamer & sugar bowl, Vienna cutting, sawtooth rim	230.00
Cup & saucer, coffee; Foval	75.00
Egg cup, Foval, conical jade ft, #2300	55.00
Finger bowl, Grapes etching	20.00
Goblet, Quilted, Rose (pk), no connector, sm ft	15.00
Goblet, Wild Rose etching, cut stem	20.00
Jug, floral intaglio, scalloped rim, 4-pt	200.00
Jug, whiskey; Poppy cutting allover, orig cut stopper, 8"	345.00
Loaf pan, pearl ovenware, rectangular, 9"	30.00
Mug, lemonade; Foval, jade gr hdl	75.00
Percolator, Foval, glass insert	400.00
Pitcher, Orient cutting	265.00
Plate, grill; amber, 3-part	25.00
Relish, Asteroid etching, oblong, 13"	150.00
Roaster, clear opal, w/lid, 1946, 14" L	75.00
Shaker, unnamed cut pattern, metal top	85.00
Spice tray, Rose (pk), 3-compartment, center hdl	35.00
Teapot, gold enamel bands, #2000, 6-cup	225.00
Tray, ice cream; Elsie cutting, 14" L	385.00
Tray, sandwich; emerald gr, center hdl	35.00
Tumble up, Thistle etching	60.00
Tumbler, floral cutting	55.00
Tumbler, Foval w/Delft Bl appl rim, 2½"	65.00
Tumbler, lemonade; Foval, jade hdl, #9416	75.00

Vase, Anemone etching, #804 line, 16"	85.00
Vase, cut, Vardin, trumpet form, 9"	120.00
Vase, Ivy cutting, slim form, 14"	275.00
Vase, Poppy cutting on lower half, 4"	75.00
Vase, reeded crystal w/emerald threading	90.00
Vase, violet; Foval, 3 bl ft, #823, 4"	250.00

Fulper

The Fulper Pottery was founded in 1899, after nearly a century of producing utilitarian stoneware under various titles and managements. Not until 1909 did Fulper venture into the art pottery field. Vasekraft, their first art line, utilized the same heavy clay body used for their utility ware. Although shapes were unadorned and simple, the glazes they developed were used with such flair and imagination (alone and in unexpected combined harmony) that each piece was truly a work of art. Graceful Oriental shapes were produced to complement the important 'famille rose' glaze developed by W.H. Fulper, Jr. Other shapes and glazes were developed in line with the Arts and Crafts movement of the same period.

During WWI, doll's heads and Kewpies were made to meet the demand for hard-to-find imports. Figural perfume lamps and powder boxes were made both in bisque and glazed ware. Examples prized most highly by collectors today are those made before a devastating fire destroyed the plant in 1929, resulting in an operations takeover by Martin Stangl later that same year.

Several marks were used: a vertical 'Fulper' in a line reserve, a horizontal mark, a Vasekraft paper label, 'Rafco,' 'Prang,' and 'Flemington.' Fulper values are to a major degree determined by the desirability of the glazes and forms. And, of course, larger examples command higher prices. Lamps with colored glass inserts are rare and highly prized. Our advisor for this category is Douglass White; he is listed in the Directory under Florida.

Bottle, dk bl w/metallic, 3-sided, racetrack mk, 8x4"	125.00
Bowl, bl/gr/mahog flambe, 1¾x6"	40.00
Bowl, emb peacock feather reserves, bl/gr/yel flambe, 6x10"	700.00
Bowl, gr w/tan streaks, sky bl flambe int, 2¾x12½"	230.00
Bowl, gray/bl/lt brn flambe, shouldered, 5x12"	500.00
Bowl vase, bl, 5x10"	100.00
Candlestick, gr/pk drip, rim-to-width hdls, 3x5"	90.00
Decanter, brn/caramel flambe w/silver o/l & lid, 11x6"	400.00
Figurine, dog, copper/bl gloss, #492, no mk, 8x5", EX	375.00
Flower frog, mushroom shape, ivory/brn flambe, #92, 2"	40.00
Jug, Flemington gr, musical, hexagonal, 8"	195.00
Jug, musical; copperdust crystalline, 8x5"	225.00
Lamp, perfume; cockatoo, bl/yel feathers, no mk, 13x5½"	350.00
Lamp, perfume; robin, red chest/brn feathers, mk, 8x5"	500.00
Pitcher, mustard/brn speckled matt, widens at base, lg	300.00
Temple jar, bl flambe, w/lid, #566C, racetrack mk, 12"	950.00
Vase, bl crystalline, raised ft, hdls, 6¾x6½"	70.00
Vase, bl speckled matt, slim w/1 long hdl, 5x4"	75.00
Vase, cat's eye/bl flambe, tall cylinder neck, 8x5"	250.00
Vase, Chinese Bl flambe, angle shoulder, collar rim, 4¾x3½"	100.00
Vase, Chinese Bl to mahog/ivory flambe, 7-sided, 10x5½"	475.00
Vase, copperdust crystalline, buttressed hdls, 4½x5¾"	425.00
Vase, copperdust crystalline to gr flambe, hdls, 9¾x7"	400.00
Vase, cucumber crystalline, bulbous w/2 sqd hdls, 7x9½"	800.00
Vase, dk bl gloss over bl matt, scroll hdls, #486, 10¾"	700.00
Vase, dk gr flambe on tan-brn matt, collar rim, 5x6"	250.00
Vase, dk purple matt, 3 sm rim hdls, #564, 6½x8"	275.00
Vase, emb cattails, med/dk olive matt, cylindrical, 13", NM	1,400.00
Vase, gr flambe, flask form, ornate shoulder hdls, 10"	375.00

Vase, gr gloss over dk bl crystalline matt, ftd urn, 9x8" 550.00
Vase, gr gloss over speckled purple matt, #567, 7x5" 250.00
Vase, gr lustre, rolled rim, 6x3½" 125.00
Vase, gr matt, in-body straps at hdl terminals, #587, 9x9" 600.00
Vase, gray matt over speckled bl, bulbous, akimbo hdls, 5x6" 200.00
Vase, ivory-to-gr flambe, 3-neck, spherical, 8x5¼" 800.00
Vase, leopard skin crystalline, 17x7" 1,500.00
Vase, lt brn w/mirror blk overglaze, hdls, 8" 175.00
Vase, med brn/mahog flambe, ridged beehive w/hdls, 10x9" 325.00
Vase, micro crystalline pk/bl/gr, 2¼x1¾" 50.00
Vase, mint gr crystalline leopard skin, hdls, #490, 12x12" 850.00
Vase, mirror blk, sq hdls w/uprights, can neck, 9½x8" 650.00
Vase, mirror blk speckled, rim-to-body hdls, #642, 6x6" 275.00
Vase, olive-gr flambe, incurvate, #26, 9½x5" 300.00
Vase, olive/Chinese Bl flambe on bl matt, 3x4½" 175.00
Vase, purple/bl matt, bulbous shoulder, 2 sqd hdls, 8½x5" 350.00
Vase, rouge flambe, bulbous w/cylinder neck, 8x5" 275.00
Vase, sage gr lustre drips on tan, short buttresses, 5x6" 225.00
Vase, wisteria matt, flat shoulder, ring neck, 6¾x7" 375.00
Vase, wisteria matt, squat ovoid, #657, 6x9" 300.00

Furniture

American 17th- and 18th-century furniture played an important role in its environment. Aside from the utility, furniture was a symbol indicating wealth, taste, and station in life of the owner. Each period brought about distinct design changes that created a recognizable form for that particular time frame. Our earliest furniture was handmade by the cabinetmaker with apprentices and journeymen who learned every phase of the craft of the master cabinetmaker. The end of the Civil War brought the Industrial Revolution and mechanization of furniture manufacturing. With it came the ornate Victorian period and the many revival styles. These were followed in the 20th century by Art Deco and Art Nouveau and more revival of our earliest periods.

It is important for the buyer of antique and collectible furniture to approach each piece from the point of view of the prevailing taste of that particular time frame. Pieces from lesser cabinetmakers should be recognized simply as makers of old furniture, as age alone does not equal value.

The marketplace is showing a definite recovery from the recession, however some categories are still selling below their market value. Because of this, items that have sold at auction for at least 25% lower than their normal market values will be designated with (*). Items listed in the lines that are designated with (**) are pieces in the best of form and of museum quality. Traditional mahogany furniture from the 20th century and machine made in the style of Hepplewhite, Sheraton, and Duncan Phyfe is still enjoying great popularity as are their English counterparts. Turn-of-the-century European inlaid and carved furniture is also rising in value. Commonplace oak furniture is still selling well below its highs of a few years ago.

Condition is the most important factor to consider in determining value. It is also important to remember that *where* a piece sells has a definite bearing on the price it will realize, due simply to regional preference. Our advisor for this category is Suzy McLennan Anderson, ISA, of Heritage Antiques, whose address is listed in the Directory under New Jersey. To learn more about furniture, we recommend *The Collector's Encyclopedia of American Furniture* by Robert and Harriet Swedberg. See also Fifties Modern; Stickley.

Note: When only one dimension is given for blanket chests, dry sinks, tables, settees, and sofas, it is length.

Key:

Am — American	Geo — Georgian
bj — bootjack	grpt — grainpainted
brd — board	hdbd — headboard
Chpndl — Chippendale	hdw — hardware
Co — Country	Hplwht — Hepplewhite
cvd — carved	mar — marriage
cvg — carving	NE — New England
c&b — claw and ball	QA — Queen Anne
do — door	trn — turning
drw — drawer	uphl — upholstered/upholstery
Emp — Empire	vnr — veneer
Fed — Federal	Vict — Victorian
Fr — French	W/M — William and Mary
ftbd — footboard	: — over (example: 1 do:2 drw —
G — good	1 door over 2 drawers)

Beds

Four poster, carved mahogany, attributed to Prudent Mallard of New Orleans, shell and scroll crest, Gothic-inspired panels, 1850-60s, 92x71x62", ** (museum quality), $7,000.00.

Canopy, Fed Cherry tall post, New England, 1810, rfn, 81x52x70" ..3,100.00
Day, Limbert #850, angled headrest, brand, new leather, 80" ..1,000.00
Day, oak Co, pencil post legs, pine apron, 13x68x26" 50.00
Hired man's, ash & pine, old red wash, New England, 1800s 400.00
Hired man's, red pnt, early 19th C, 40x76x40", EX 525.00
Iron w/brass trim, wht rpt, single sz w/rails, 60" H 145.00
Mahog Emp sleigh w/flame vnr, dk finish, 44x64" 600.00
Mahog Traditional style, rfn, ca 1900, full sz w/rails 40.00
Murphy (disguised as sidebrd), oak, rprs, 67x55x19" 800.00
Poplar Co Emp tall post, rfn, rpl rails, 84x72x55" 110.00
Rope, curly maple, trn posts, shaped hdbd, rfn, 32x72x52" 715.00
Rope, curly maple/poplar, trn posts, blanket bar, 56x49" 550.00
Rope, hardwood/poplar, cannonball posts, 50x68x52" 495.00
Rope, hardwood/poplar, trn posts, old red, 33x68x53" 800.00
Rope, maple Co Sheraton, tall trn posts, canopy fr, 65x70x42" ..1,650.00
Rope, poplar w/orig grpt & stencil, trn posts, 46x68x51" 220.00
Walnut Vict Eastlake, cvd flowers, burl vnr, full sz 350.00

Benches

Bucket, primitive pine, old mellow finish, 48x48x12" 330.00
Cobbler's, primitive, pine, whittled legs, rpl drws, 47" 580.00
Fireside settle, Pine English or Irish, 2-do base, 70x68" 935.00
Hardwood/pine, 3 shelves+top, end cutouts, wire nails, 44x34" ...550.00
Piano, rosewood & mahog Edwardian w/inlay, uphl seat, 23" 165.00

Poplar Co, 1-brd top, rnded corners, cut-out ft, rpt, 18x54" **195.00**
Primitive pine, mortised plank ends, bj cutouts, 21x38x10", VG .**250.00**
Renaissance style, trn legs, reuphl top, 44" L **120.00**
Settle, arrowbk, trn legs, scroll arms, plank seat, 75" **1,300.00**
Settle, Arts & Crafts, 10-slat bk/3-slat sides, reuphl, 79" **2,300.00**
Settle, bird's-eye maple, 1830-40, 31x77½x21", EX **800.00**
Settle, fireside; pine English, curved, rpt, early, 55x72" **1,300.00**
Settle, Limbert #649½, 14-slat bk, spade cutouts, reuphl **2,400.00**
Settle, PA, orig flame grpt w/gr & wht stripes & gold, 76" **1,875.00**
Settle, pine Co, 1-brd ends, folding seat, old pnt, 72" L **495.00**
Settle, scrolled arms, ½-spindle bk, plain crest, rfn, 81" **225.00**
Settle, ½-spindle bk, scroll arms, shaped crest, rpt, 72" **770.00**
Water, pine, primitive, att New England, 37x50x10" **360.00**

Blanket Chests, Coffers, Trunks, and Mule Chests

Cherry, dvtl drw, cvd fruit pulls, breadbrd top, rfn, 38x34" **600.00**
Cherry, paneled ends & sides, rpl till, rfn, 40" **450.00**
Cherry Co Emp, 3 dvtl drw, till w/lid, rfn, 31x49x22" **1,300.00**
Cherry Co w/ash panels, till w/lid, late, 38x24x19" **225.00**
OH, old red grpt over yel, dvtl drw, till, 38x27x16" **950.00**
OH, orig compass star pnt on lid, 1851, 23x42" **1,980.00**
PA pine, floral decor (rstr), dvtl case, 51x23x23" **385.00**
Pine, old red pnt w/blk trim, dvtl, w/till, 25x38x19" **550.00**
Pine, orig red pnt, 6-brd type, appl molding, 23x44x18", EX **475.00**
Pine Co, 6-brd, red traces, cut-out ft, 72", EX **250.00**
Pine w/old grpt on red, 6-brd, cut-out lid, 23x44x18" **300.00**
Pine/poplar, dvtl case, trn ft, worn gr pnt, 25" L **1,200.00**
Poplar, dvtl, bracket ft, till w/lid, 26x38x20" **300.00**
Poplar, dvtl, worn blk pnt, strap hinge, w/till, 38" **175.00**
Poplar/cherry, red-brn pnt w/gr panels, OH, 25x43x20" **660.00**
Poplar/pine PA decor, blk grpt on orange, 1852, 27x45x20" ...**2,000.00**
Sea, English, rpt portraits on blk, rprs, 46½" L **330.00**
Southern pine w/rpt red grpt, dvtl case, 41" L **275.00**
Sugar, cherry Co, 1-brd sides & ends, rfn, 25x33x18" **1,155.00**
Walnut Co Chpndl, 2 dvtl drw w/beading, rprs/rfn, 25x50x23" ..**1,485.00**
Walnut PA Chpndl w/inlay, 2 dvtl drw, rprs/rpl, 28x49x22" ...**3,000.00**
Walnut w/sulfur inlay, dvtl drws, PA, 1768, 25x52x25" ** ...**15,400.00**

Bookcases

Ebonized Vict Eastlake, 3-drw base, shelves, gallery, 61" * **360.00**
Hardwood, stacked, cornice, short legs, 3-shelf, 50" **330.00**
Limbert #322, 3-do, ea w/ldgl at top, label, rfn, 54x60" **3,500.00**
Limbert #340, 2-do, 2 sq panes top of ea, label, orig, 46" **2,000.00**
Limbert #358, 2-do w/2 long panel ea, splay legs, 57x48" **3,250.00**
Mahog Emp, 2-pc stepbk, 8-pane do:2 panel do, 91x50" **1,150.00**
Mahog Emp style, paw ft, dbl do w/wood o/l, 1900s, 58x55" **660.00**
Quarter-sawn oak, stacked, cornice, 3-shelf, 51x34x11" **360.00**
Quarter-sawn oak, stacked, drw in base, cornice, 6-shelf, 81" **770.00**
Quarter-sawn oak, stacked, drw in base, 4-shelf, 53" **440.00**
Walnut Vict Eastlake w/burl vnr, 3-shelf, 63x31x12" **250.00**

Bureaus, See Chests

Cabinets

Cellarette, Limbert #752, pull-out tray w/glass insert, mk **6,000.00**
China, Limbert #452, 1-door w/3 panes, side shelves, EX **6,500.00**
China, mahog Fr style w/ormolu trim, 20th C, 66½" **1,500.00**
Curio, gilt Fr style, 2 glass shelves, ca 1900, 55x32x13" **935.00**
Curio, gilt Fr w/ormolu & pnt garden scenes, 20th C, 57x28" .**1,450.00**
Curio, inlaid wood w/ormolu, Fr-style repro, 68x30" **330.00**
Curio, mahog acrylic curved panels, Fr-style, repro, 60x27" **275.00**

Hoosier, ash, porc top, pull-down do, 1925 ....**500.00**
Hoosier, oak, porc dop, pull-down do, 1920s **950.00**
Mahog Fr Emp style, brass inlay, ormolu trim, 2-pc, 50x40x20" .**660.00**
Marjorelle, marquetry flowers, appl fruit, glass top do, 71" ** .**9,775.00**
Oak, bowfront w/2 do, 2-shelf, side posts form ft, 54x36" **485.00**

Candlestands

Bleached walnut Co Emp, tripod base, 1-brd top, 28x22" dia **220.00**
Cherry Chpndl, tripod base, snake ft, 2-brd top, 26x15x15" **935.00**
Cherry Co Chpndl, tilt top, tripod base, snake ft, 37x22" dia **300.00**
Cherry Co Chpndl, 1-brd, tripod base w/snake ft, 27x17" dia **935.00**
Cherry Co Emp, tilt top, tripod base, trn column, 30x22" dia **330.00**
Cherry/curly maple Co New England Hplwht, tilt top, 17x18" sq ..**3,600.00**

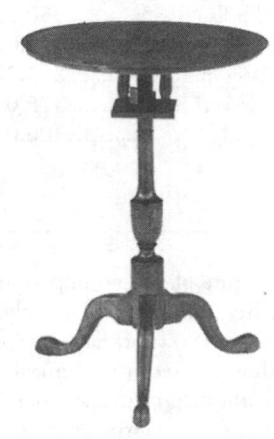

Maple candlestand with dished
top, swivel birdcage construction,
snake feet, American, late
1700s, 29x20", $2,500.00.

Mahog English Chpndl, tilt top, tripod base, snake ft, 22" dia **600.00**
Oak/mahog English, rpr ft, 27x15" dia **220.00**
Primitive, hardwood w/weathered gray surface, 36" **550.00**
Walnut Hplwht, tripod base w/spider legs, rpr/rfn, 30x20" dia **825.00**
Walnut PA Chpndl tilt top, 2 brd/snake ft/trn column, 38x22" ...**5,225.00**

Chairs

Armchair, bamboo Windsor, 7-spindle, H stretcher, rfn, 37" **330.00**
Armchair, Baroque style, early 1900s, 56" **220.00**
Armchair, bowbk Windsor, 7-spindle, saddle seat, rfn, 37" **880.00**
Armchair, bowbk Windsor, 7-spindle, trn posts, blk rpt, 38" ..**2,200.00**
Armchair, Co, 3-slat, trn details, rpl splint seat, rfn, 40" **140.00**
Armchair, combbk Windsor, brn rpt w/gold striping, CT, 44" ** ..**11,000.00**
Armchair, combbk Windsor, early 20th C repro, 45", EX **300.00**
Armchair, combbk Windsor, 7-spindle, gr rpt, 44¾" **550.00**
Armchair, Fr style, cvd fr w/old rpt, old uphl, 1900s, 38" **195.00**
Armchair, Fr style, open arms, cvd fr, reuphl, 20th C, 36" **250.00**
Armchair, mahog Emp, much cvg, rfn/reuphl, 39" **1,150.00**
Armchair, mahog Nouveau style, vinyl seat, simple crest, 34" **140.00**
Armchair, New England bowbk Windsor, saddle seat, 37" **6,600.00**
Armchair, overstuffed Vict, Rococo Revival legs, reuphl, 39" **165.00**
Armchair, QA style w/decor, damaged rush seat, repro, 42" **250.00**
Armchair, walnut Baroque Revival, old uphl, much cvg, 51" **745.00**
Armchair, walnut Eastlake Vict, cvd details, reuphl, 38" **85.00**
Armchair, walnut Louis XV style, needlepoint uphl, 1800s **500.00**
Armchair, walnut Vict, burl vnr, uphl/tufted bk, rfn, 37" **165.00**
Armchair, walnut Vict Rococo Revival, rose crest, worn uphl ...**145.00**
Armchair, walnut Vict w/spiral posts/spindles, uphl seat **75.00**
Armchair, Windsor, sack bk, red pnt, saddle seat, early, 37x25" .**850.00**
Armchair, wingbk, Chpndl style, modern repro, 41" **225.00**
Armchair, wingbk, mahog Hplwht, worn uphl, 43" **1,200.00**
Armchair, wingbk, Sheraton style, modern repro, 44" **600.00**

Armchair writing, Co lowbk Windsor, rprs/rpl/rfn, 30x17" * 225.00
Corner, cherry Am Co Chpndl, rpl arm rail, rush seat, 30" 300.00
Corner, Co, bentwood bk forms arms, trn legs/rush seat, 27" 325.00
Hall, Limbert #80, spade cutouts, shaped seat, mk, 39" 500.00
Limbert, ebony inlay on legs, 5-slat bk, open arms, EX 1,600.00
Limbert #693, 4-slat bk, long corbels, mk, new leather, 36" ...1,100.00
Mahog Vict Rococo Revival, cvd fr, worn uphl, 42" 165.00
Morris, JM Young #471, 5-slat sides, rfn, new vinyl, 35" 1,800.00
Rocker, Boston, orig red & blk grpt, foliage crest, 39", EX 165.00
Rocker, golden oak, pressed crest/spindle bk, reuphl, 36" 175.00
Rocker, Limbert #1964, 3-slat bk, open arms, wood seat 230.00
Rocker, Limbert #934, 3-slat bk, open arms w/corbels, VG 350.00
Rocker, oak, wide pressed headpc, 7-spindle, saddle seat, 35" 185.00
Rocker/arm, Co, high half-arrow spindle bk, rfn, 42" 250.00
Rocker/arm, walnut, Sleepy Hollow, old reuphl, 41" 75.00
Rocker/arm, walnut Vict Eastlake platform, rfn/reuphl * 250.00
Rocker/arm, worn orig red & blk grpt w/stencil, rprs, 43" 55.00
Rocker/arm, 3-slat bk, splint seat, old rfn, 32" 195.00
Rocker/arm, 4 arched slats, tape seat, red rpt, 42" 225.00
Rocker/arm, 4-slat bk, splint seat, blk pnt, ca 1900, 43" 440.00
Rocker/arm, 5 grad arched slats, wicker seat, 47" 545.00
Side, bamboo bowbk Windsor, heavy blk pnt, old rprs, 35x16" ..220.00
Side, bamboo Windsor, step-down crest, old blk pnt, 34" 250.00
Side, bamboo Windsor, 7-spindle, rpr splayed seat, 34" 195.00
Side, curly maple Co Sheraton, cane seat, slat bk, rfn, 33" 185.00
Side, fanbk Windsor, yoke crest, spindle bk, rpt, 37" 275.00
Side, fanbk Windsor, 7-spindle, shaped crest, saddle seat, rfn 325.00
Side, hardwood/mahog Windsor, trn spindles, reeded bow, repro .150.00
Side, Limbert #79, bicycle seat, loose leather bk rpl, mk 900.00
Side, mahog English Chpndl, rpl seat, 38" 50.00
Side, mahog Hplwht style, uphl seats, 20th C, 35", 4 for 300.00
Side, mahog veneer Emp, sabre leg, rfn, 33½" 220.00
Side, Michigan Chair Co, narrow, 3-slat bk, label, rfn, 40x15" ...250.00
Side, New England fanbk Windsor, 7-spindle, saddle seat, 37" ...770.00
Side, oak, loop bk w/trn spindles, rpl cane seat, 33" 75.00
Side, RI bracebk Windsor, 9-spindle, saddle seat, rpt, 36" 825.00
Side, walnut Euro QA, cabriole legs, slip seat, rfn, 44" 775.00

Chair Sets

English Jacobean style, Wainscot bk/leather seat, 2 side+2 arm .600.00
Louis XV style, cvd & wht pnt fr, worn uphl, 20th C, 3 for 330.00
Mahog Chpndl style, uphl seat, rprs, 2 arm+6 side 975.00
Mahog Chpndl style w/cvg, uphl seat, 20th C, 38", 2 arm+4 side .1,800.00
Mahog Chpndl style w/EX cvg, reuphl/rfn, 2 arm+6 side 3,960.00
Mahog Hplwht style w/cvd details, best repro, 2 arm+4 side ...1,600.00
Oak English Jacobean style, cvd, uphl seat, 20th C, 38", pr 200.00
Side, banister bk, rpl rush seat, rpt, 40½", pr 500.00
Side, Co New England Chpndl, rush seat/ribbon slats, 5 for ...1,100.00
Side, curly maple, lyre splat, shaped crest, cane seat, 6 for * 925.00
Side, curly maple Co Sheraton, caned seat, rfn, 33", 5 for 440.00
Side, half-arrow bk, rpt grpt w/stencils & stripes, 4 for 650.00
Side, hardwood Chpndl-style, high bk, floral uphl, 37", pr 220.00
Side, Hitchcock-type Sheraton, stenciled, repro, 34", 4 for 285.00
Side, Limbert, 2-slat bk, mk, rfn, new leather, 36", 4 for 550.00
Side, mahog English Regency, medallion bks, uphl, 33", 4 for * ..575.00
Side, mahog English Regency, much cvg, reuphl, 34", 4 for 1,430.00
Side, oak, press-cvd bk, central splat, saddle seat, 4 for 600.00
Side, oak English Co QA, rpl rush seat, worn finish, pr * 220.00
Side, PA, lyre splat, brn rpt w/florals/gold, 33", 6 for 675.00
Side, PA, rpt w/striping & mc fruit decor, 32¼", pr 440.00
Side, quarter-sawn golden oak, slip seats, 38", 6 for * 300.00
Side, quarter-sawn golden oak era, figure in splats, 38", 6 for * ..300.00
Side, rabbit-ear Windsor, spindle bk, rpt grpt, 32", 6 for 525.00

Side, rosewood Vict, rose-cvd crest, needlework seat, 35", pr 400.00
Side, Standard Co, 4-spindle bk w/sq cutouts, new leather, 6 ..2,000.00
Side, walnut QA style, new uphl, repro, 39", 4 for 575.00
Side, walnut Vict, floral crest/uphl seat/rprs/rfn, 3 for 500.00
Side, walnut Vict sabre leg, cvd bks, reuphl seats, 4 for 450.00
Side, walnut w/burl veneer English QA, uphl seat, 38", pr 465.00
Walnut Eastlake Vict w/burl vnr, fr only, 2 arm+4 side 360.00

Chests

Classical mahogany and bird's-eye maple bureau, old refinish, New England, ca 1835-50, 51x41x20", $1,850.00.

Birch/mahog NH Sheraton, bowfront, step-bk secretary top, 64" ..6,000.00
Bird's eye maple vnr/mahog Fed, high trn ft, rfn, 42x44" ...2,300.00
Cherry Chpndl, 5 dvtl drw w/beading, rpr/rfn/rpl, 38x39" 3,650.00
Cherry Chpndl serpentine, 4 dvtl drw, rpl/rfn, 41x39" 4,070.00
Cherry Chpndl serpentine, 4 dvtl drw w/beading, rstr, 37x38" ...8,000.00
Cherry Chpndl w/exaggerated serpentine, 4-drw, rfn, 34x36" ** ..11,000.00
Cherry Co, 4 dvtl drw, trn ft, simple crest, 41x42x19" 220.00
Cherry Co Emp, 4 dvtl drw, trn ft & pilasters, rfn, 48x42" * 250.00
Cherry Co Fed, 4 dvtl drw w/beading, rpl/rfn, 52x44" 1,100.00
Cherry Co Sheraton, 2 sm dvtl drw:4, paneled ends, 53x42" ..1,500.00
Cherry Co Sheraton, 4 dvtl drw, rpl brasses, rfn, 46x38" 935.00
Cherry Hplwht, 3 sm drw:3 sm drw:6 grad drw, rstr, 71x44" ...8,250.00
Cherry RI Sheraton, 4 dvtl drw, rpl brasses, rfn, 38x42x22" ...1,200.00
Cherry/curly maple Emp, 4 dvtl drw, cvd pilasters, rfn, 43x41" * ..900.00
Cherry/curly maple/mahog Co Emp, 3 dvtl drw, rstr, 44x39x21" * .635.00
Cherry/poplar Hplwht, 4 dvtl drw w/beading, rfn, 38x38" 1,750.00
Cherry/walnut Co, 3 short drw:2:4 grad drws, rfn, 64x40" 2,200.00
Cherry/walnut Hplwht, 4 grad dvtl drw, Fr ft, rfn, 42x39" 990.00
Curly cherry Co Emp, 4 dvtl drw, trn pilasters, rfn, 45x42" 770.00
Curly maple Chpndl, 6 dvtl grad drws, 2 orig locks, 59x36" ** ...13,000.00
Curly maple Co Emp, 4 dvtl drw w/beading, rfn, 44x40" 770.00
Curly maple/pine Chpndl, 3 dvtl drw, rpl/rfn, 38x37x19" 4,300.00
Curly walnut Chpndl, 9 dvtl drw (3 arched tops), rstr, 62x38" ...9,900.00
Drexel, mahog Hplwht style, serpentine, 7-drw, 20th C, 54x36" 450.00
Hardwood/mahog vnr Co Emp, 6 dvtl drw, ornaments, 47x45" ..250.00
Heywood Wakefield, 5-drw, long wood pulls, 96x33", VG 275.00
Mahog Chpndl-style serpentine, 6-drw, 20th C, 53x36x21" 250.00
Mahog Hplwht bowfront w/inlay, 4-drw w/decor, 38x42x23" .1,650.00
Mahog MA Hplwht, 4 grad dvtl drw, rpl pulls, Fr ft, 34x38" ...1,375.00
Mahog veneer Hplwht bowfront w/inlay, 4 grad drw, 39x37" .3,300.00
Mahog veneer NY Emp, rnded dvtl drw:2 flat, grpt, 60x42" 1,425.00
Mahog veneer transitional Hplwht to Sheraton, 4-drw, 40x44" .195.00
Maple Co Chpndl w/some curl, 6 dvtl drw, rfn, 51x40x20" 1,650.00
Mule, hardwood/pine Co, 6-brd, 2-drw, sq nails, 45x22x22" 660.00
Russel Wright, blk lacquer 5-drw, rfn, mk, 46x32" 575.00
Walnut Chpndl, 3 sm drw:2:4 grad, cornice, rpr/rpl, 63x38" ...1,200.00

Walnut Eastlake Vict w/burl vnr, 6 dvtl drw, 55"+gallery **990.00**
Walnut PA Chpndl, 4 dvtl drw, rpl brasses, ornate ft, 34x36" .**7,700.00**
Walnut vnr English W/M w/inlay, 2 drw:3, rstr, 33x36" **3,000.00**
Walnut vnr Sheraton style, chest on chest, repro, 50x36" **165.00**
Walnut Vict, appl cvgs/trns, 2 drw:3, mirror, 74x41" * **385.00**
Walnut/pine Chpndl, 4 dvtl drw, bracket ft, rfn, 40x36" **880.00**

Cupboards (See Also Pie Safes)

Apothecary, walnut, 2 6-pane do:3 drw:18 sm drw, 81x43x22" ..**4,400.00**
Cherry Co, 2 1-pane do:drw:2 panel do, cornice, 2-pc, 90x58" .**2,150.00**
Cherry Co, 2 5-pane do:3 drw:2 panel do, 2-pc, rfn, 54" W **6,050.00**
Cherry Co, 2 8-pane do:shelf:2 arched panel do, 1-pc, 87x46" .**1,600.00**
Cherry Co Chpndl, 12-pane do:2 panel do, 2-pc, 86x42" **9,000.00**
Cherry Co Vict, 4 long raised panel do:4 short, rstr, 86x75" ..**1,980.00**
China, Lifetime #6478, 2-do, copper hdw, label, 56x42" **1,100.00**
Corner, cherry Co, 2 panel do, cornice, 1-pc, 85x49" **2,100.00**
Corner, cherry Co, 2 panel do:2 drw:2 panel do, 2-pc, 85x40" .**2,300.00**
Corner, cherry Co, 2 1-pane do:drw:2 panel do, 2-pc, 82x48" .**1,750.00**
Corner, cherry Co, 2 8-pane do:2 drw:2 panel do, 1-pc, 93" ..**2,800.00**
Corner, cherry Co, 2 8-pane do:2 panel do, 1-pc, 86x52" **2,000.00**
Corner, cherry Co, 4 raised panel do, scrolled apron, 70x37" ..**1,750.00**
Corner, cherry Hplwht, 2 8-pane do:2 drw:2 panel do, 88" **6,400.00**
Corner, hanging, curly maple, drw, panel do, repro, 29" **165.00**
Corner, hanging, oak English, panel do w/arch, rpr, 48x32" **440.00**
Corner, hanging, pine English, gray rpt, 39x28" **525.00**
Corner, oak English, dk finish, 8-pane do:panel do, 2-pc, 87" .**1,450.00**
Corner, pine/poplar, 9-pane do:panel do, grpt, 1-pc, 72x36" ..**1,650.00**
Corner, walnut, open shelves:2 panel do, 1-pc, 20th C, 80" **385.00**
Corner, walnut, 2 panel do:2, scalloped apron, 2-pc, 85x43" ..**1,870.00**
Corner, walnut architectural, arched 15-pane do:panel do, 88" ..**2,750.00**
Corner, walnut Co, panel do top, nailed apron, rfn, 79x50" **825.00**
Corner, walnut Co, 2 panel do:rpl drw:2 panel do, 1-pc, 87" ..**1,870.00**
Corner, walnut Co, 9-pane do:2 panel do, 1-pc, 85x48" **2,750.00**
Court, oak Jacobean Revival, 2-pc+mirror, 1900s, 79x48x22" ...**600.00**
Court, quarter-sawn oak Gothic Revival, refitted int, 65x55" **400.00**
Euro, hardwood, 2 panel do:2 dvtl drw, 2-part, 85x45x22" **2,200.00**
Hanging, butternut/mixed woods, panel do, rfn, sm, 17" H **150.00**
Hanging, cherry, 1 4-pane do:dvtl drw w/locks, 37x26" **600.00**
Hanging, mahog, 1-pane do, 1-shelf, old finish, 18x22x8" **165.00**
Hanging, poplar, 4 wire-nailed drw, open shelves, 28x14x8" **200.00**
Hanging, walnut, cornice molding, beaded edge, rfn, 32x27" **440.00**
Jelly, pine Co, old red, dvtl drw:panel do, CI hdl, 55x36" **880.00**
Jelly, pine Co, 1-brd top w/crest, panel do, 55x31x16" **825.00**
Jelly, pine Co, 2 raised panel do, old red rpt, 64x38" **2,500.00**
Jelly, poplar Co, 2 panel do, 5 shelves, old red pnt, 68x42" **600.00**
Pewter, pine Co, 1-brd ends, open step-bk top, 1-pc, 79x40x16" .**2,100.00**
Pewter, pine/poplar Co, 2 1-brd do, open shelf, old red, 70x41" **3,500.00**
Pewter, walnut Co, open front:drw:2 drw, 1-pc, 75x36x19" **525.00**
Pewter, walnut/birch Co, open shelves, 1-brd do, 1-pc, 79" **880.00**
Pine architectural, 4 raised-panel do, 1-pc, rfn, 94x50" **880.00**
Pine Co, dbl do:open shelf, cornice, old bl-gr pnt, 70x48" **990.00**
Pine Co, 1-brd ends, open top:panel do, 2-pc, 74x32x18" **1,980.00**
Pine Co, 2 panel do:pie shelf:panel do, old rpt, 79x44" **1,980.00**
Pine Co Euro, 2-pc, rfn, 70x35x17" **165.00**
Pine Co step-bk, 1-brd ends, 20-pane do:panel do, rfn, 94x36" ..**2,000.00**
Pine/poplar Co, 4 panel do:shelf:4 drw:4 panel do, 85x107" ..**4,300.00**
Poplar Co, 1-brd ends, apron, old gr pnt, 2-pc, 70x34x19" **1,400.00**
Poplar step-bk, 2 6-pane do:shelf:3 drw:2 do, orig pnt, 83" ** .**24,000.00**
Walnut, 2 6-pane do:shelf:2 drw:2 panel do, OH, 2-pc, 83x47" ..**2,200.00**
Walnut Co, 2 8-pane do: 3 drw:2 panel do, 2-pc, rfn, 85x58" ..**2,650.00**
Walnut Co step-bk, 2 6-pane do:2 panel do, rfn, 93x48" **1,200.00**
Walnut OH, 2 6-pane do:shelf:2 drw:2 panel do, 2-pc, 87" **3,500.00**
Walnut/poplar Co, 2 1-pane do:shelf:2 drw:2 panel do, 85x48" ..**825.00**

Welsh, oak, open shelves:5 dvtl drw, rpl hdw, rprs, 83x64" **1,925.00**
Whatnot corner, Walnut Vict, jigsaw work, trn details, 68x38" ..**300.00**
Wht oak Euro Baroque Revival, 2-pc, ca 1900, 99x63" **2,300.00**

Desks

Chippendale mahogany
slant-lid desk, restored
brass, refinished,
42x41x20", $5,000.00.

Blk lacquer, kneehole, 1952, 53", VG **1,495.00**
Butler's, cherry/curly maple Fed, 3 dvtl drw, 47x44x23" **1,100.00**
Cherry Chpndl, slant front, hinged lid, fitted int, 43x36" * **3,200.00**
Clerk's, cherry Co Hplwht, dvtl drw/lift lid/gallery, 36x22x22" ..**685.00**
Clerk's, walnut Co, 3-section, dvtl drws, slant top, 72x56" **715.00**
Lady's, mahog Fr style w/inlay, clock, drws, 1890s, 42" **900.00**
Lady's, mahog Hplwht, dbl do:tambour top:4 drw, 2-pc, 76x39" .**5,600.00**
Lady's, mahog Hplwht, 2 do:fold-down top:3 drw, 2-pc, 51x41" **1,600.00**
Lady's, mahog Sheraton, trn rope-cvd legs, dvtl drw, 36x30x18" ...**1,100.00**
Lifetime #8564, drop-front, 1-drw, decal, 40x27x16" **450.00**
Lifetime #8603, Puritan drop-front, label, rfn, 43x32x16" **800.00**
Limbert #142, fitted drw, rpl pc, brand, rfn, 30" L **800.00**
Mahog English kneehole style, 9 dvtl drw, rprs, 30x48x28" **1,650.00**
Mahog veneer transitional Chpndl/Hplwht, slant front, 44x39" ...**7,590.00**
Oak Arts & Crafts, kneehole, center drw, 2 ea side, 50", VG **400.00**
Oak English Chpndl, 4 dvtl drw, slant lid, rprs, 44x50x21" **600.00**
Pine English Chpndl, slant front, rprs/frn, 41x36x20" **550.00**
Rock maple QA style, 20th C repro, 31x42x20"+crest **150.00**
Roll top, oak, C roll, 2 ped w/3 drw, plain **750.00**
Roll top, oak, S roll, fitted int, 4-drw ea ped, 60" **1,000.00**
Roll top, walnut, S roll, fitted int, 53x69x33" **2,000.00**
Tiger maple Chpndl, slant lid, rpl brasses/rfn, 42x36x19" **4,500.00**
Walnut/cherry/mahog Am Chpndl style, 3-drw, repro, 43" **715.00**

Dressers

Cherry Am Emp w/flame grpt vnr, 1 dvtl/2 step-bk drws, 40x39" **415.00**
Hardwood w/mahog finish, step-bk top w/2 drw:3, mirror, 67x43" ..**150.00**
Heywood Wakefield, 2 banks of 4 drw, long wood pulls, 54" W .**275.00**
Mahog Vict, 3 dvtl drw, 2 step-bk drw, 43x41x19"+mirror **275.00**
Sheraton, cherry/maple vnr, 5 grad drw, 40" **1,500.00**
Vict Eastlake walnut & walnut burl, 3-drw, marble top, 48x43" ..**300.00**
Walnut Vict, burl medallions, 2 drw:2 do, marble top, 92x50" .**1,800.00**
Walnut Vict w/walnut vnr, 3-drw, marble top, 80x44" **385.00**

Dry Sinks

Co, cut-out ft, panel do, nailed well, 33x46x18", EX **825.00**
Grained pine, dvtl drw, dbl panel do, shelf, 38⅝x44x20" **420.00**
Pine, sm shelf, nailed drw:2 panel do, rfn, 30x45x19" **450.00**
Pine, trn legs, pegged construction, rfn, 33x54x24" **240.00**
Poplar Co, cleaned down to old red, 2-brd do, crest, 33x40x16" ..**580.00**

Poplar co, cut-out ft, 2 panel do, dvtl drw, rfn, 54x48x21" **1,375.00**
Softwood, 3 dvtl drw, porc pulls, 2 shelves, 51x39x19", EX **500.00**

Hall Pieces

Hall tree, oak Eastlake Vict, mirror/rack/hooks, 85", EX **450.00**
Hall tree, quarter-sawn golden oak, beveled glass, rfn, 86" **880.00**
Hat rack, reeded oak fr w/spindles, center mirror, hanging **165.00**
Walnut Vict w/wht marble top, mirror bk, drw, 84x40x15", EX * ..**600.00**

Highboys

Curly maple Chpndl style, 20th-C repro, 55x33x20" **500.00**
Curly maple Delaware QA, 5 tiers of dvtl drws, married, 76" ..**2,300.00**
Maple Chpndl of Dunlap School, 5 drw:2, cabriole legs, 80x36" ** ...**25,300.00**
Maple QA style w/inlay, 2 short drw:4 drw top, rprs/rfn, 70" ...**1,400.00**
Maple w/some curl QA, 4-drw top, cornice: 18½x38", 36" W ..**9,625.00**
Walnut English Chpndl w/burl vnr, 8-drw, rprs, 65x38" **6,875.00**

Lowboys

Mahog Chpndl style, cvd details, repro, 30x33x18" **425.00**
Mahog English Chpndl, 3 dvtl drw, rpr/rpl, 27x29x19" **1,045.00**
Mahog QA style, old finish, 20th-C repro, 30x36x20" **385.00**
Oak English Co Chpndl, sq legs, 3 dvtl drw, rprs, 28x30" **385.00**

Pie Safes

Hardwood/poplar, 2 do w/10 punched panels, nailed drw, 58x39" ..**550.00**
Poplar Co, 2 do w/punched tin, 5-drw, 64x45" **1,500.00**
Walnut Co w/mellow finish, panel do, tin panels, 60x74x16" .**2,050.00**

Secretaries

Ash/poplar Co, dbl do:3 drw: fall-front lid:panel do, 89x42" **525.00**
Curly maple Co Emp w/figured vnr, dvtl drw, 66x14x25" **2,200.00**
Mahog Hplwht style w/inlay, 2 do:fold-down shelf:4 drw, 82" ..**1,150.00**
Pine Co w/orig grpt, 2 do:2 do:fold-down shelf:6 drw, 76x42" .**3,575.00**
Walnut Co, 2 3-pane do:lid:3 drw:2 do, 2-pc, 83x41x20" **1,650.00**
Walnut Vict, 2-pc w/bookcase, 3 dvtl drw, 82x41x22" **550.00**

Settees

Louis XVI style, cvd fr w/worn blond finish, old uphl, 49" **150.00**
Mahog Chpndl style, much cvg, damask uphl, 41" **660.00**
Walnut Fr-style, reuphl, early 20th C, 55" **195.00**
Walnut Vict Eastlake, flower cvg, burl vnr, uphl, 58" **250.00**

Shelves

Hanging, bird's-eye maple, 3-shelf, scalloped ends, 30x19x7" **300.00**
Hanging, poplar, 3-shelf, orig brn pnt, tapered ends, 28x20" **550.00**
Hanging, 3-shelf, old gray pnt w/gr & blk sponging, 22x11" **550.00**
Hanging corner, pine, scalloped sides, 3 grad shelves, 30" **550.00**
Poplar, scalloped ends, scroll finial, 3-shelf, 34x21x8" **775.00**
Poplar, worn dk pnt, 5-shelf, scrolled ends, 32x30x9" **330.00**

Sideboards

Ash Arts & Crafts, 5-drw+2 side do, copper hdw, rfn, 42x66" ..**2,200.00**
Burl vnr Euro w/inlay, 3-do/3-drw/ marble top, 59x49" **600.00**
Cherry Co, 3 drw:3 do, removable top shelf, worn, 43x65" **1,980.00**
Cherry Co Sheraton, 2-drw/gallery/shelf, rfn, 34x39x18" **1,650.00**
Heywood Wakefield, birch, 4 drw+2 do, 48", EX **350.00**

Limbert #1443½, arched bk w/mirror, side shelves, 60" **7,500.00**
Mahog Am Hplwht w/inlay, serpentine case, repro, 42x70x25" ..**1,800.00**
Mahog English Hplwht bowfront w/inlay, 3-drw, 36x66x26", EX ..**2,000.00**
Mahog Fr style, 3 bays/3-do/pull-out shelves, 40x86" **385.00**
Mahog Hplwht, serpentine top:3-drw, 2-do/2-drw base, 76" ..**4,750.00**
Mahog Hplwht style w/grain vnr & inlay, repro, 39x72x26" ...**1,450.00**
Mahog vnr Emp, 4 panel do, 3 curved front drws, 43x66" **450.00**
Quarter-sawn golden oak, 4-drw/dbl do, mirror bk, 64x56x25" * .**385.00**

Sofas

Chpndl style camel bk, red/bl uphl, modern repro, 70" **330.00**
Duncan Phyfe, serpentine fr, brass paw ft, uphl, repro, 82" **80.00**
Emp, old blk rpt w/gilt, caned seat, reuphl seat/arms, 78" **715.00**
English Chpndl-style camelbk, 6 c&b legs, reuphl, 81" **1,200.00**
Fr Louis XVI style, cvd fr w/wht rpt, reuphl, 63" **470.00**
Loveseat, walnut fr w/burl vnr, Eastlake Vict, rstr, 63" **275.00**
Mahog Classical Revival w/marquetry inlay, reuphl, 100" L **3,300.00**
Mahog Co Hplwht, sq legs, reuphl, rprs, 72" **575.00**
Mahog Emp, lyre-shaped fr, cvd ft, worn uphl, 95" **880.00**
Mahog Fed, cvd bows/wheat sheaves, reeded arms/legs, 78" **3,450.00**
Mahog Fr-style w/velvet uphl & pillows, 20th C, 78" L **360.00**
Rosewood Vict Revival, worn uphl & finish, 76" **500.00**
Settee, Limbert, Ebon-Oak, 2-chair bk, new leather, 45" **2,300.00**
Settee, Old Hickory, twig fr w/arms, rpl woven seat/bk, 45" **550.00**
Tiger maple Fed, trn arm supports, rfn, 73" **4,600.00**
Walnut & walnut burl Vict Eastlake, reuphl, rprs, 53" **475.00**
Walnut Baroque Revival, much cvg/velvet reuphl, 1800s, 72" ...**550.00**
Walnut Rococo Revival w/flame vnr apron, EX uphl, 75" **550.00**
Walnut Vict Rococo Revival, finger cvg, reuphl/rfn, 70" **415.00**
Walnut Vict w/cvd medallion bk, old uphl, rprs, sm **300.00**

Stands

Birch/poplar Co Hplwht, 1-drw, 1-brd top, rpt, 38x14x16" **825.00**
Cherry Co, cut-out shoe ft, sq posts, 1-brd top, 29x24x16" **475.00**
Cherry Sheraton w/birch/mahog inlay, dvtl drw, rfn, 28x16x15" ..**825.00**
Cherry/walnut Co, dvtl drw, 1-brd top, tapered legs, 30x21x19" ...**770.00**
Corner, pine w/old brn finish, 4 grad shelves, primitive, 34" **110.00**
Curly maple Co, 2-brd top, scrolled apron, rfn, 29x21x21" **445.00**
Hardwood/pine Windsor, 1-brd top, trn legs, rprs, 27x18x18" **550.00**

Federal mahogany inlaid chamber
stand, old refinish, Mas-
sachusetts, ca 1790, 42x23x16",
$935.00.

Mahog English, cylindrical, curved do, marble inset, 18x15" **385.00**
Mahog English Hplwht w/inlay, dvtl drw, 27x20x12"+leaves **550.00**

Pine English Co, 1-drw, apron w/cvd fans, old red rpt, 32" **200.00**
Quarter-sawn oak, stepped oblong base, 2 sq colums, 33x24x13" ..**200.00**
Sewing, chinoiserie decor, lyre base, lacquered, 25x17" **425.00**
Sewing, figured wood vnr Dutch style, 2 dvtl drw, 30" **275.00**
Shaving, quarter-sawn oak Arts & Crafts, lift lid, 69" **385.00**
Telephone, Limbert #261, 30x18x15" **375.00**
Walnut Italian Rococo, 12" shaped triangle top, arched legs **800.00**
Walnut Vict, marble top, trn details, 32x22" dia **330.00**
Walnut/poplar Co, trn legs, dvtl drw, rpl top, rfn, 39x17x22" **165.00**

Stools

Victorian upholstered ottoman, suede velvet with tasseled fringe, late 1800s, 19½x21" diameter, $425.00.

Footstool, Lakeside Crafts, Arts & Crafts, all wood, 7" L **150.00**
Footstool, Paine, Arts & Crafts, metal tag, new leather, 20" **350.00**
Footstool, quarter-sawn oak, reuphl, cvd paw ft, 22x14" **140.00**
Footstool, Windsor, brn pnt w/florals & gold stripes, 14" **385.00**
Footstool, Windsor, muslin-covered oval top, splayed base, 16" .**110.00**
Footstool, Windsor, trn legs, chamfered top, orig pnt, 13" **195.00**

Tables

Banquet, Fed mahog, banded, 3 cvd peds, opens to 112" **4,000.00**
Banquet, mahog Hplwht, sq legs, 29x94x54" (open), pr **2,300.00**
Breakfast, oak Arts & Crafts, X stretchers, 42" dia **800.00**
Card, mahog Hplwht style w/inlay, repro, 30x36x18", pr **1,100.00**
Card, mahog Hplwht-style demilune, rprs, old rfn, 29x36x18" ...**440.00**
Card, walnut Co Vict, swing top, serpentine apron, 29x36x18" .**275.00**
Console, Deco, 5-strap wrought-iron support, marble top/ft **3,700.00**
Dining, Arts & Crafts, 5-leg, 42", EX **450.00**
Dining, mahog Duncan Phyfe style, 20th C, opens to 92x40" **150.00**
Dining, mahog vnr Hplwht style w/inlay, 50x44"+2 leaves **580.00**
Dining, oak, lg ped w/c&b ft, some cvg, rnd **1,200.00**
Dining, oak, lg ped w/4 cut-out scroll legs, rnd **650.00**
Dressing, mahog Oriental Export Chpndl style, 3-drw, 34x43" ..**385.00**
Dressing, mahog/cherry Sheraton w/flame vnr, 38x28x16" **1,265.00**
Dressing, mahog/oak English Chpndl, dvtl drw, 27x30x19" **440.00**
Dressing, pine English Co Sheraton, 5-drw, rfn, 32x26x16" **635.00**
Dressing, pine Sheraton w/red & blk grpt, dvtl drw, 31x34" **550.00**
Dressing, walnut Hplwht style w/inlay, 4-drw, rstr, 31x38" **660.00**
Drop-leaf, Cherry New England Chpndl, 1-brd, 28x42x15"+leaves ..**1,650.00**
Drop-leaf, hardwood Co, trn legs, rpl top, 30x43x16+leaves **195.00**
Drop-leaf, mahog English Regency, 1-drw, castors, 42"+leaves ..**400.00**
Drop-leaf, mahog Hplwht Pembroke, dvtl drw, 28x36x18"+leaves ...**990.00**
Drop-leaf, mahog Hplwht style w/inlay, repro, 39x30x21"+leaves **330.00**
Drop-leaf, maple QA w/swing legs, rprs, 27x42x12"+leaves **2,300.00**
Drop-leaf, walnut Hplwht, 6-leg, old finish, 28x42x18" **550.00**
Drop-leaf, walnut PA QA, cabriole legs, 2-brd top, 43"+leaves .**2,750.00**
Drop-leaf, walnut Phyfe style, worn, 29x66x38"+leaf **195.00**
Drop-leaf, walnut QA, cabriole legs, rprs/rfn, 46"+leaves **1,700.00**

Gate-leg, oak English W/M style, 1800s, 28x36x16"+leaves **600.00**
Gate-leg, walnut w/scalloped edge, repro, 30x35x12"+2 leaves ..**175.00**
Harvest, poplar Co, old gr pnt, 3-brd top, 30x85x27" **660.00**
Hunt, mahog English drop-leaf, 8-leg, 28x75x15"+leaves **5,700.00**
Hunt, mahog Irish Chpndl, 8-leg, rprs, 29x83x15"+leaves **2,100.00**
Hutch, cherry/maple, shoe ft, rpt, Hudson Valley, 45" dia ** .9,350.00**
Hutch, pine Co, sq legs, nailed drw under seat, rpt, 53" dia **1,980.00**
Hutch, poplar Co, 1 nailed drw, 4-brd top, 28x56" **835.00**
Library, Arts & Crafts, octagonal w/lower shelf, 48" **1,500.00**
Library, Limbert #1141, 2-drw, long corbels, brand, 48" **2,300.00**
Library, Limbert #172, 2-drw, 2 corbels ea leg, 1 new drw **2,400.00**
Library, oak, lyre pillars & scroll ft, 1920s, 30x40" **245.00**
Library, walnut, brass griffins/lion ft, drw, rfn, 40" L **575.00**
Library, walnut burl w/leather top English style, repro, 45" **275.00**
Library, walnut Vict w/vnr, dvtl drw, 30x36x24" **250.00**
Limbert #146, oval top, slab sides w/cutouts, 45" **2,100.00**
Mahog English Regency w/line inlay, 2 dvtl drw, 38x31x16" **165.00**
Mahog Fr-style w/inlay & ormolu, drw, repro, 37x21x16" **195.00**
Parlor, bleached walnut Vict, marble top, 30x29x21" **325.00**
Parlor, Eastlake Vict, cvd/trn details, granite top, 29x30x20" **220.00**
Parlor, walnut Vict, oval marble top, old finish/stains, 34" **440.00**
Parlor, walnut Vict style, oval marble top, 20th C, 38" **250.00**
Parlor, walnut w/burl vnr Vict, marble top, 1-drw, 38", EX **400.00**
Pine Co, sq legs, T apron, 1-brd ½-circle top, rfn, 32x18x36" **525.00**
Sawbuck, pine, old dk patina, scrubbed 2-brd top, 48x45x28" **550.00**
Side, Old Hickory, twig legs w/X stretcher, rfn 24" top **375.00**
Taborette, oak Arts & Crafts, through tenons, 19x14" dia **375.00**
Tavern, hardwood/pine, butterfly supports, drw, 28"L+leaves .**1,300.00**
Tavern, maple Co Hplwht, 2-brd top, rfn, 28x35x26" **600.00**
Tavern, maple QA, 2-brd top, apron, tapered legs, 38x44x28" .**3,900.00**
Tavern, maple w/some curl, dvtl drw, 3-brd top, 29x34x28" ...**1,400.00**
Tea, curly maple QA, porringer 2-brd top, 26x37x25" ** **19,800.00**
Tea, mahog Chpndl-style, 2-tier, 1900s, 32x29" **55.00**
Tea, maple QA, cabriole legs, apron, tray top, rfn, 35x28x22" .**2,800.00**
Turtle-top, cvd, crane legs, rpr marble insert, repro, 33" L **415.00**
Walnut Co Eastlake Vict, 4-part base w/cvgs, rfn, 37" dia **350.00**
Walnut Emp-style, tilt top, urn ped, scroll ft, rfn, 32" dia **140.00**
Work, maple Co QA, bread-brd top, trn legs, rfn, 25x32x45" .**1,600.00**
Work, maple Co w/some curl, 2 dvtl drw, weathered, 73" L **850.00**
Work, mixed woods Co Chpndl, bread-brd top, drw, 25x47x26", VG ..**225.00**
Work, walnut Canadian, trn legs, 2 dvtl drw, rprs, 30x60x34" .**6,800.00**
Work, walnut Co Hplwht, 2 dvtl drw, old rpt, 38x60x36" **1,650.00**
Work, walnut Co QA, 2 dvtl drw, removable top, rstr, 30x58x33" ..**600.00**

Wardrobes

Figured walnut vnr Continental, 3 panel do, 73x78x25½" **660.00**
Kas, cherry Co w/line inlay, 2 panel do:2 dvtl drw, 86x58" **600.00**
Kas, walnut QA, 2 arched panel do:3 drw, cornice, 80x58" **8,800.00**
Poplar Co, 2-panel do, pintel hinges, 1-brd ends, rfn, 78x48" **495.00**
Quarter-sawn oak English, dbl do:dvtl drw, 2-pc, 20th C, 89" **225.00**
Walnut Co Vict, 2 dvtl drw, dbl do, cornice, 86x55" **715.00**
Walnut English Renaissance Revival w/burl vnr, 83x48" **500.00**

Washstands

Cherry Co Sheraton, base drw, cutout w/ironstone bowl, 17" W .**175.00**
Cherry Emp, 2 sm dvtl drw:2 panel do, gallery, 38x39x23" **475.00**
Corner, mahog English Hplwht w/inlay, bowfront, gallery, 44x24" .**360.00**
Curly maple Co Sheraton, dvtl drw, towel bars, rfn, 33x35x16" ...**1,045.00**
Hplwht Co, red flame grpt, base drw, shaped gallery, 21" W **600.00**
Oak, sm mirror in lyre fr, simple press cvg, drw:2 do, sm **350.00**
Oak, sm mirror in lyre fr/towel bar, 1 drw:2+do, lg **400.00**
Oak, 3-drw, towel bar, reeded posts, brass pulls, 53x30" **265.00**

Walnut Co, dvtl drw, scalloped base shelf, rprs, 39x24" 140.00
Walnut Victorian Eastlake style, marble top, 37x28x15" 825.00

Miscellaneous

Armoire, Fr style, herringbone inlay, drw, crest, 94x48" 825.00
Armoire, olive vnr Euro w/marquetry inlay, 98x74" 2,750.00
Armoire, pine Continental, 2-tone rpt w/flowers, 2-drw, 70x37" ..525.00
Armoire/desk, oak Continental, 2-pc, worn finish, 79x75" 2,100.00
Breakfront w/pull-out desk, Martinsville, 20th C, 76"+crest 525.00
Chaise lounge, Thonet, caned bentwood, unsgn, ca 1910 ....2,185.00
Credenza, ebony vnr Fr w/boule inlay, marble top, 45x76" 2,750.00
Etagere, oak w/quarter-sawn shelves, ca 1900, 36x42x22", pr ...500.00
Linen press, mahog English Edwardian, 3 sections, 91x99½" 990.00
Linen press, pine Euro w/marquetry inlay, on base, 68x55x18" .1,870.00
Magazine stand, Arts & Crafts, 5-shelf, 1 wide slat ea side 550.00
Magazine stand, Brooks, cut-out panels in sides, 4-shelf 950.00
Magazine stand, Limbert #321, cutout w/spindle ea side, #d 950.00
Screen, cvd teak, Indian, 4-section, ea: 75x20", EX 220.00
Screen, Dutch floral oil on canvas, 3-part, ea: 73x22" 1,750.00
Screen, pole; mahog vnr Emp, needlework scene, 53" 900.00

Galle

Emile Galle was one of the most important producers of cameo glass in France. His firm, founded in Nancy in 1874, produced beautiful cameo in the Art Nouveau style during the 1890s, using a variety of techniques. He also produced glassware with enameled decoration, as well as some fine pottery — animal figurines, table services, vases, and other objets d' art. In the mid-1880s he became interested in the various colors and textures of natural woods and as a result began to create furniture which he used as yet another medium for expression of his artistic talent. Marquetry was the primary method Galle used in decorating his furniture, preferring landscapes, Nouveau floral and fruit arrangements, butterflies, squirrels, and other forms from nature. It is for his furniture and his cameo glass that he is best known today. All Galle is signed.

In the listings below, 'fp' indicates items that have been fire polished. Our advisor for this category is Don Williams; he is listed in the Directory under Missouri.

Cameo

Atomizer, exotic flowers/vines, red on citron, no bulb, 8" 1,000.00
Atomizer, floral, violet on lav, conical, 8" 425.00
Chandelier, floral, red on amber, 22" bowl shade+8 lilies 20,000.00
Compote, leaves, yel/gr on pk, int: pods, pointed rim, 5x8" 1,100.00
Lamp base/vase, lilies, lav on yel, drilled, 19x7" 3,335.00
Vase, berries/vines, red on bone, fp, tall slim neck, 12½" 3,750.00
Vase, butterfly/floral, red on frost, flattened U-form, 9½" 2,300.00
Vase, church steeple/village/prominent trees, ftd, 17x6½" 10,000.00
Vase, clematis/tendrils, purple on gray frost, can neck, 6¾" 750.00
Vase, exotic flowers, brn on amber frost, trumpet form, 4" 550.00
Vase, ferns, wine/rose on peach, cylinder w/bun base, 9½" 1,400.00
Vase, floral, gr/lav on shaded olive-yel, stick neck, 17" 1,950.00
Vase, floral, olive/gr on amber frost w/pk, shouldered, 18" 7,500.00
Vase, floral, peach on wht frost, bulbous w/stick neck, 6½" 600.00
Vase, floral, pk/olive on olive/wht w/bl frost, sqd rim, 9" 900.00
Vase, floral, violet on yel/wht, 8x3" 800.00
Vase, floral, wine on rose frost, stick neck, 6x6" 600.00
Vase, floral vines, amber on frost, fp, 7½x5" 1,600.00
Vase, floral vines, brn on yel, tapered cylinder, 4½" 550.00
Vase, fuchsia, violet on yel/wht frost, can neck, 6" 700.00

Vase, fuchsia, wine/red on citron, tapered, flared rim, 5" 850.00
Vase, gloxinias, lav-bl on yel/frost, conical, 4¼" 700.00
Vase, grapevines, brn on gray/rose/tan frost, boat rim, 9" 2,300.00
Vase, irises, lav on frost, goblet form, 6" 690.00
Vase, leaves/pods, red on yel/wht frost, stick neck, 12" 2,000.00
Vase, leaves/pods, violet on lt lav & violet, shouldered, 3" 550.00
Vase, leaves/pods, yel-gr on frost, stick neck, 8½" 800.00
Vase, lilies, pk/orange on yel/frost, squat w/long neck, 9" 700.00
Vase, lily pads/leaves, violet on yel/bl, shouldered, 9x3" 1,400.00

Vase, magnolia blossoms, red on frosted yellow, oviform, 18", $7,475.00.

Vase, maple leaves, orange on frost, star mk, ovoid, 5" 650.00
Vase, morning glories, gray on lt gr, fp, ftd ball form, 10" 3,750.00
Vase, mums, lav/purple on yel/peach, ftd/flattened, 14x10" 8,500.00
Vase, pine cones/needles, brn on shaded yel, stick neck, 14" ..1,495.00
Vase, poppies, rose/pk/red/wht on yel frost, 6x5" 4,250.00
Vase, seed pods, gr/brn on gr to frost, bun ft, 18" 1,725.00
Vase, ships, tan/brn on pastels, cylinder w/bun base, 21" 4,750.00
Vase, thistles, gr on pk/wht, bun base, cylinder neck, 13" 1,100.00
Vase, thistles/tendrils, violet on frost, stick neck, 11" 1,900.00
Vase, trees/lake, brn on frost to yel, invt cone, 9½" 1,200.00
Vase, trees/man on bridge, amber/gr-brn on shaded pk, 11x3" ...2,645.00
Vase, vines/3 appl flowers, hammered/fp, pulled rim, 9½" 9,200.00
Vase, water lilies in pond, pk/amber on frost, 9⅜" 2,990.00
Vase, wisteria, lav on shaded gray/purple, can neck, 13" 1,380.00
Vase, wisteria, purple on apricot/frost, 3½" 425.00

Enameled Glass

Bottle, twigs, blk w/gold & wine insects on clear, 7x6" 4,150.00
Claret jug, leaves/flowers on ribbed amber, baluster, 12" 900.00
Decanter, lg floral spray, mc/gilt on ribbed amber, 7" 2,300.00
Decanter, sm flowers w/in leafy scrolls on amber cone, 13" 800.00
Decanter, topaz, etch/mc Persian reserve w/equestrians, 7½" ..9,775.00
Flask, winged griffin/crown on ribbed bl, 6x5" 2,185.00
Tumbler, motto/whimsical peasant on ribbed clear, 4½" 200.00
Vase, amber w/etched leaves, jewel-appl flower centers, 12" ...2,185.00
Vase, eng hunter/dog/prey, red/blk/wht on clear, ftd, 5" 1,265.00
Vase, etch/eng flowers & stars, pk/wht/gold on peacock, 6½" .2,300.00
Vase, floral, pk/red/wht w/gold on lt gr, sqd w/rnd ped ft, 2" 350.00
Vase, nasturtiums, mc on amber frost, hexagonal, 10" 1,950.00
Vase, scene in blk, mc insects/etc, etched florals, 9x3" 8,000.00

Marquetry, Wood

Music stand, gladiolas, scalloped top+2 tiers, rtcl notes, 34" ...2,000.00
Table, floral, half-reeded legs, 16x31x18" 4,485.00
Table, leaves on scalloped top & sm tier, 3-leg, 32x16" 2,185.00

Table, sunflowers on top & lower tier, 3-leg, 29x35" **3,100.00**

Pottery

Bowl, duck form, bl/red/orange w/gilt, 7x8" **1,200.00**
Cat, seated, smiling expression, pnt w/hearts, 13" **3,000.00**
Ewer, poppies front/bk on dk bronze, bulbous/pinched, 7" **1,500.00**
Flagon, man's portrait, lid w/3-D cherries, rope hdl, 13" **1,200.00**
Lions, ea holds coat of arms, scroll base, 26", pr **5,175.00**
Pitcher, serpent spout, ribbed/bulbous, scroll hdl, 9" **900.00**
Pitcher, 2 men on bench, 3rd w/bagpipes on bronze C-shape, 8" ..**1,500.00**
Plate, Oriental in landscape, floral border, 9¾", pr **600.00**
Plate, surrealistic mc motif, scalloped, 1 side folded up **700.00**
Tray, bachelor buttons emb/pnt on wht, 3x6" **200.00**
Vase, man's portrait, pillow form w/dbl ring hdls, sgn, 12" **1,600.00**
Wall vase, lady's hat w/insects, ribbons & flowers, 12" **1,600.00**

Gambling Memorabilia

Gambling memorabilia from the infamous casinos of the West and items that were once used on the 'Floating Palace' riverboats are especially sought after by today's collectors.

Book, Am Card Player, 1866, 154-pg, worn **85.00**
Book, Complete Poker Player, J Blackbridge, 1880, EX **275.00**
Book, Gambler's Tricks w/Cards Exposed & Explained, 1850, EX ..**900.00**
Book, How To Beat the Game, G Brown, 1903, 117-pg, VG **130.00**
Book, New Book of Hoyle's Games, 1889, 159-pg, VG **55.00**
Box, card; blk walnut & mahog w/aces inlay, 1885, 4½x8x2½" ...**60.00**
Box, chip; celluloid, pnt/emb aces, lined, 1900s, 7x8½x2½" **160.00**
Card press, maple w/turq inlay roses, EX **275.00**
Card trimmer, shears style, unmk, ca 1910, 12¾x6½" **1,200.00**
Chips, clay, assorted advertising, 1900s, 30 for **150.00**
Chips, cvd ivory, natural/red or bl stain, 10½" dia, 10 for **200.00**
Chips, ivory w/fancy numeral cvgs, set of 5 ....**210.00**
Dice, celluloid, ea w/different number (1-5), set of 5 ....**260.00**
Dice cage, Chuck-A-Luck, w/dice, ca 1930 ....**75.00**
Dice cup, leather **40.00**
Pharo casekeeper, Cowper, celluloid strips/maple, 1910, EX **550.00**
Pharo casekeeper, Mason & Co Chicago, veneer, 1900, EX **400.00**
Roulette watch, Roulette Ideal, beveled crystal, 1890s, EX **350.00**
Roulette watch, 17 jewels, outer wheel spins freely, M **250.00**
Table, bridge; inlaid woods, suit sign ea corner, 1940s, 31" sq **200.00**
Wheel, roulette; wood w/old mc pnt, 36" dia, EX **175.00**
Wheel, roulette; 8" dia, w/12x24" felt layout, dtd 1941, MIB **125.00**
Wheel, wooden floor model, worn pnt, 73x42" dia, G **300.00**
Whist scorer, cvd ivory hand w/pointing finger, 1870s, 7 for **850.00**

Game Calls

Those interested in hunting and fishing collectibles are beginning to take notice of the finer specimens of game calls available on today's market. Our advisor for this category is Randy Hilst; he is listed in the Directory under Illinois.

Crow, C Perdew, Pat 1900, sm, EX **375.00**
Duck, AM Bowles, Olt-style toneboard, walnut bbl, EX **150.00**
Duck, att Dick Burns, checkered, walnut, rare, VG **2,000.00**
Duck, C Perdew, Cedar IL River, 2 bands, G **450.00**
Duck, Duc-Em, MIB **35.00**
Duck, Grubbs Perfection Tone, walnut bbl, G **1,000.00**
Duck, J Marsh, checkered w/walnut bbl, cocobola insert, EX **750.00**

Duck, Skippy Barto, after Perdew's cedar call, crack in bbl **1,200.00**
Pintail whistle, T Turpin, rosewood, VG **170.00**
Suzie call, WC Cowaan, walnut bbl, cedar stopper, rare, M **150.00**

Gameboards

Gameboards, the handmade ones from the 18th and 19th century, are collected more for their folk art quality than their relation to games. Excellent examples of these handcrafted 'playthings' sell well into the thousands of dollars; even the simple designs are often expensive. If you are interested in this field, you must study it carefully. The market is always full of 'new' examples. Well-established dealers are often your best sources; they are essential if you do not have the expertise to judge the age of the boards yourself. Our advisor for this category is Louis Picek; he is listed in the Directory under Iowa.

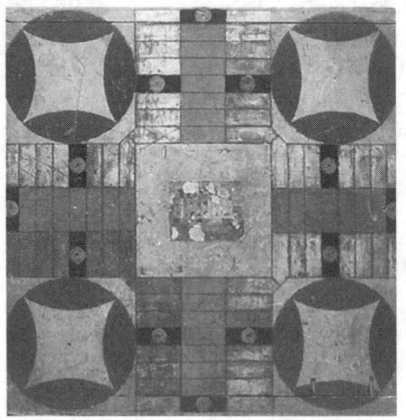

Parcheesi, orange, green, and black painted squares with gold trim, black and white checkerboard on reverse, American, 1800s, 18½x19½", $880.00.

Checkers, laminated panel in pine fr, mc pnt, sgn/1927, 19" sq **88.00**
Checkers, maroon/yel, gilt scrolls on blk border, 1880s **1,350.00**
Checkers, pine, old patina & blk sqs, compartment, 16x10" **115.00**
Checkers, plywood & pine, red & blk pnt, 18½" sq **50.00**
Checkers, pnt slate w/faux marble, wide border, 22" **260.00**
Checkers, pnt slate w/faux-marble pnt border, 22" sq, EX **265.00**
Checkers, pnt wood, appl gallery rim, dtd 1861, 16x19" **425.00**
Checkers, pnt wood w/gold bands, 16¾x17", EX **425.00**
Checkers, red & blk w/molded gilt edge, 20th C, 12x12" **145.00**
Checkers, walnut w/brn & blk sqs, 29x18" **440.00**
Checkers/bkgammon, folding, pine w/orig 3-color pnt, 16x8" **450.00**
Fox & Geese, maple, rim holds 32 clay marbles, 10¾" dia **135.00**
Oil on canvasboard, cattle in landscape on bk, 1880s, 19x25" ...**400.00**
Parcheesi, red/yel/blk pnt, HP castle & marine scenes, 17" sq .**2,850.00**

Games

Collectors of antique games are finding it more difficult to find their treasures at shows and flea markets. Most of the action these days seems to be through specialty dealers and auctions. The appreciation of the art on the boards and boxes continues to grow. You see many of the early games proudly displayed as art, and they should be. The period from the 1850s to 1910 continues to draw the most interest. Many of the games of that period were executed by well-known artists and illustrators. The quality of their lithography cannot be matched today. The historical value of games made before 1850 has caused interest in this period to increase. While they may not have the graphic quality of the later period, their insights into the social and moral character of the early 19th century are interesting.

20th-century games invoke a nostalgic feeling among collectors who recall looking forward to a game under the Christmas tree each year. They search for examples that bring back those Christmas-morning memories. While the quality of their lithography is certainly less than the early games, the introduction of personalities from the comic strips, radio, and later TV created new interest. Every child wanted a game that featured their favorite character. Monopoly, probably the most famous game ever produced, was introduced during the Great Depression.

For further information, we recommend *Schroeder's Collectible Toys, Antique to Modern,* available from Collector Books. Our advisor for personality-related games in Norm Vigue; he is listed in the Directory under Massachusetts.

Miscellaneous

ABC Magnetic Board, Toy Guidance, EX 10.00
All American Football, Cadaco, 1958, VG 25.00
American Logs, Halsam, 1940s, EX (G box) 15.00
Baseball, Parker Bros, 1967, M 20.00
Bingo, Milton Bradley, 1934, VG 18.00
Bingo, Whitman, 1941, VG 15.00
Careers, Parker Bros, 1971, EX 15.00
Chinese Checkers/Checkers, Ohio Art, rnd tin, M 10.00
Chutes & Ladders, Milton Bradley, 1956, EX 50.00
Circle-X, Marietta Games, 1940s, EX 10.00
Climb the Mountains, Parker Bros, 1951, VG 18.00
Cross Over the Bridge, Kohner, 1970, VG 10.00
Daytona 500, Milton Bradley, 1990, M 18.00
Drew Pearson's Predict-A-Word, Deejay Products, 1949, VG 12.00
Easy Money, Milton Bradley, 1935, EX 35.00
Electronic Football, Tudor, 1950s, VG 20.00
Formula 1, Parker Bros, 1963, EX (VG box) 18.00
Funny Bones, Parker Bros, 1968, EX 10.00

Game of Golf, Clark and Sowdon, early 1900s, EX, $525.00.

Game of the States, Milton Bradley, 1960, EX 18.00
Game of Who?, Parker Bros, 1951, EX 20.00
Going to Jerusalem, Parker Bros, 1965, NM (G box) 65.00
Gold Medal Krokay, Transogram, 1948, EX 30.00
Handicap Golf, Sports Illustrated, 1971, no instructions, EX 40.00
Happy Little Train, Milton Bradley, 1957, EX 20.00
Hi-Q Double Master Set, Tryne Games, 1960, VG 10.00
Jr Combo Games, Milton Bradley, 1955, EX 15.00
Kooky Carnival, Milton Bradley, 1967, NM 45.00
Lotto, Milton Bradley, 1932, EX 22.00
Magic Dots, Milton Bradley, 1938, VG 20.00
Milles Bornes, Parker Bros, 1971, VG 8.00
Monopoly, Parker Bros, 1946, EX 18.00
Monopoly, Parker Bros, 1961, VG 12.00
Old Maid (jumbo cards), Milton Bradley, 1978, EX 8.00

Operation, Milton Bradley, 1965, M 15.00
Parcheesi, Selchow & Righter, 1938, EX 20.00
Peggity, Parker Bros, 1953, VG 15.00
Pit, Parker Bros, 1919, EX 10.00
Quiz Kids Cards, LG Cowan, 1941, EX (no box) 15.00
Ranger Commandos, Parker Bros, 1942, NM (VG box) 40.00
Road Race, Whitman, 1960, EX 23.00
Scrabble, Selchow & Righter, 1953, VG 10.00
Screaming Eagles, Milton Bradley, 1987, M 10.00
Shoot the Moon, 1958, EX 40.00
Solitaire, Kingsbridge, 1950, EX 15.00
Sorry, Parker Bros, 1939, M 20.00
Stratego, Milton Bradley, 1961, EX 18.00
Strategy Poker, Milton Bradley, 1968, M 12.00
Sub Attack, Milton Bradley, 1965, EX 15.00
Ten-Q, KT Games, 1955, VG 12.00
Tiddley Winks, Whitman, 1963, EX 15.00
Tiger Island, Ideal, 1965, EX 40.00
Twister, Milton Bradley, 1974, EX 12.00
Varsity Football, Cadaco, 1942, VG 30.00
Wacky Racers, 1945, M 65.00
Whirling Words, Bodell, 1942, EX 20.00

Personalities, Movies, and TV Shows

Barney Miller, board game, Four D Prod, VG 15.00
Barney Miller, Parker Bros, 1977, M 15.00
Beat the Clock, Milton Bradley, 1969, M 30.00
Ben Casey MD, board game, Transogram, M (G box) 30.00
Cannonball Run, board game, 1981, M (sealed) 17.00
Captain Kangaroo, card game, Old Maid version, 1960s, M 20.00
Casper, card game, EduCards, M 8.00
Charlie's Angels, Milton Bradley, 1977, M 20.00
Chilly Willy, card game, Fairchild, 1964, M 12.00
Columbo, board game, Milton Bradley, 1973, M 20.00
Dallas, card game, Mego, 1980, M 8.00
Dallas, Lorimar, 1980, M 20.00
Daniel Boone, card game, EduCards, 1965, M 15.00
Donald Duck, board game, 1938 ....150.00
Donald Duck, card game, WDP, EduCards, M 4.00
Dr Dolittle, Mattel, 3-D game, 1967, EX 40.00
Dragnet, Transogram, 1955, M 50.00
Dynomutt, Milton Bradley, 1977, EX 12.00
ET, card game, Parker Bros, 1982, M 12.00
ET the Extra-Terrestrial, board game, Parker Bros, G 10.00
Flintstones, card game, EduCards, 1961, MIP 15.00
Good Ol' Charlie Brown, board game, Parker Bros, M 35.00
Hank Aaron Baseball, M 35.00
Harlem Globetrotters, board game, Milton Bradley, 1972, M 30.00
Hollywood Squares, Milton Bradley, 1986, M 12.00
Honeymooners, board game, 1986, M 10.00
Jack & the Beanstalk, 1957, M 25.00
Jack Be Nimble, Embossing Comp, 1920s, VG 30.00
James Bond, Goldfinger, 1966 ....28.00
Johnny Quest, card game, 1965, EX 39.00
Laurel & Hardy, card game, EduCards, 1972, M 10.00
Little Orphan Annie's Treasure Hunt, cb board, Ovaltine, 1933 .65.00
Love Boat, Aaron Spelling, 1980, EX 15.00
M*A*S*H, board game, Milton Bradley, 1981, NM 18.00
Marlin Perkins Zoo Parade, M 20.00
Mary Poppins, Parker Bros, 1964, M 25.00
Mating Game (NBC), Hasbro, 1969, EX 20.00
Miami Vice, Pepper Lane, 1984, NM 20.00
Mickey Mouse Library of Card Games, 1946, EX 65.00

Mork & Mindy, Parker Bros, 1979, M **18.00**
Mr T, board game, Milton Bradley, 1983, M **18.00**
Paladin Have Gun Will Travel, 1959, EX **50.00**
Partridge Family, board game, Milton Bradley, 1971, M **20.00**
Password, Milton Bradley, 1963, EX **10.00**
Paul Winchell/Jerry Mahoney, Chuggedy Chug, 1955, M **40.00**
Peter Pan, Transogram, 1950s, EX **30.00**
Quick Draw McGraw, card game, EduCards, 1961, M **15.00**
Raggedy Ann, Magic Pebble Game, 1941, EX **49.00**
Raiders of the Lost Ark, Kenner, 1981, M **16.00**
Ruff & Ready, spelling game, 1959, EX **25.00**
Six Million Dollar Man, Bionic Crisis, Parker Bros, 1975, NM **18.00**
Space 1999, Milton Bradley, 1976, M **15.00**
Star Wars Adventures of R2D2, board game, Kenner, 1977, EX ..**18.00**
Superman Match II, M **35.00**
Tammy, card game, Whitman, 1964, M **12.00**

G. A. R. Memorabilia

The 'The Grand Army of the Republic' was first conceived by Chaplain W.J. Rutledge and Major B.J. Stephenson early in 1864 when they were tent-mates during our own Civil War. These men vowed to each other that if they were spared they would establish an organization that would preserve friendships and memories formed during this time. Shortly after the war ended, Rutledge and Stephenson made their desires a reality. The first National Convention of the Grand Army of the Republic was held in Indianapolis, Indiana, on November 20, 1866. The purpose of the organization was to provide aid and assistance to the widows and orphans of the fallen Union dead and to care for the hospitalized veterans as needed. The last comrade of the G.A.R. died in 1949.

Many items are surfacing from the early encampments which were held on both state and national levels, resulting in a wide variety of souvenir items having been made. Our advisor for this category is Richard Haussmann; he is listed in the Directory under Illinois.

Badge, delegate's, 28th Annual Encampment, PA, 2-pc **35.00**
Badge, membership; cannon bronze, eagle/flag/star, 3rd issue **30.00**
Badge, 1892 Annual Encampment, WA DC, 2-pc, EX **40.00**
Badge, 1897 Annual Encampment, PA, 3-pc, w/red ribbon, M **45.00**
Cane, cvd wood w/cast pewter knob hdl w/GAR mk, Grant finial .**75.00**
Cane, Washington, Grant's bust at top, 1892, EX **65.00**
Flask, canteen; china, mk Gettysburgh PA, July 1863, 1913 ......**165.00**
Goblet, pressed glass, souvenir **50.00**
Medal, Ladies of the GAR, 1886, M in orig box **40.00**
Medal, made from captured cannon **32.00**
Medal, 6th Annual Reunion, 1889 Dept of Kansas, EX **35.00**
Pin, bimetal, Grant Monument, frayed ribbon, Chicago, 1900 .....**38.00**
Pin-bk button, brass, bl & gold enameling, old, EX **18.00**
Pin-bk button, celluloid, 40th Encampment, IL, 1906 ....**45.00**
Pin-bk button, 31st Nat'l Encampment, Buffalo NY, 1¼" **30.00**
Ribbon, red/wht/bl, 37th Encampment, Los Angeles, 1908 ....**85.00**
Ribbon, 9th annual reunion, NY Volunteers, yel w/flags, VG **200.00**
Spoon, National Encampment, 1892 ....**55.00**
Sword, brass hilt w/eagle/flags/etc, 30" blade, VG **65.00**
Teaspoon, rifle figural hdl, SP, 1894, EX **35.00**

Gas Globes and Panels

Gas globes and panels, once a common sight, have vanished from the countryside but are being sought by collectors as a unique form of advertising memorabilia. Early globes from the 1920s (some date back to as early as 1912), now referred to as 'one-piece globes,' were made of

molded milk glass and were globular in shape. The gas company name was etched or painted on the glass. Few of these were ever produced, and this type is valued very highly by collectors today.

A new type of pump was introduced in the early 1930s; the old 'visible' pumps were replaced by 'electric' models. Globes were changing at the same time. By the mid-teens a three-piece globe consisting of a pair of inserts and a metal body was being produced in both 15" and 16½" sizes. Collectors prefer to call globes that are not one-piece or plastic 'three-piece glass' (Type 2) or 'metal body, glass inserts' (Type 3). Though metal-body globes (Type 3) were popular in the 1930s, they were common in the 1920s, and some were actually made as early as 1915. Though rare in numbers, their use spans many years. In the 1930s Type 2 and Type 3 globes became the replacements of the one-piece globe. The most recently manufactured gas globes are made with a plastic body that contains two 13½" glass lenses. These were common in the fifties but were actually used as early as 1932.

Note: Standard Crowns with raised letters are one-piece globes that were made in the 1920s; those made in the 1950s (no raised letters), though one-piece, are not regarded as such by today's collectors. Both variations are listed below. Our advisor for this category is Scott Benjamin; he is listed in the Directory under Ohio.

Type 1, Plastic Body, Glass Inserts (Inserts 13½"), 1931-1950s

Ashland Diesel **200.00**
D-X Marine, rare **650.00**
DX Ethyl **250.00**
DX Lubricating Gasoline, tan body **250.00**
Falcon **650.00**
Hornet, Capcolite body, 13½", NM **225.00**
Kendal Deluxe, Capcolite body w/red pnt, 13½" **250.00**
Kendall Polly Power, Capcolite body, 13½" dia, NM **225.00**
Marine, sea horse, EX color **550.00**
Never Nox Ethyl **275.00**
Shamrock, oval body **250.00**
Spur, oval body **250.00**
Texaco Sky Chief **250.00**
Viking, pictures Viking ship **400.00**
66 Flite Fuel, Phillips, shield shape, all plastic **400.00**

Type 2, Glass Frame, Glass Inserts (Inserts 13½"), 1926-1940s

Atlantic Imperial Globe, gill body, 13½", EX, $400.00.

American, gill body, 12½", NM **350.00**
Amoco, gill body, 13½", NM **350.00**
Amoco, glass body, 12½", NM **350.00**
Derby **375.00**

Esso 325.00
Golden 97 Ethyl, hull glass body, 12½", NM 350.00
Gulf, hull body, 13½", NM 400.00
Indian Gas, Red Dot 575.00
Kanotex, w/sunflower, gill body 450.00
Koolmotor, clover shape 1,000.00
Pitman Streamlined, bl gill rippled body, 13½", NM 4,500.00
Pure 400.00
Sinclair Dino, milk glass, EX 250.00
Sinclair Pennant 800.00
Sky Chief, gill body, 13½", NM 400.00
Standard Crown, gr or orange, ea 800.00
Standard Flame 300.00
Texaco Diesel Chief 750.00
Texaco Ethyl 1,500.00
White Flash, gill body 375.00
WNAX, w/radio station pictured 1,500.00

Type 3, Metal Frame, Glass Inserts (Inserts 15" or 16½"), 1915-1930s

Atlantic Ethyl, 16½" 600.00
Blue Sunoco, 15" 475.00
Cities Services Oils, 1929, 15" fr 500.00
Crown, crown figural, 16½", EX 1,200.00
General Ethyl, 15" fr, complete 700.00
Kendal Gasoline, airplane, metal body, rare, 15", NM 4,000.00
Mobil Gas, winged horse, 15" or 16½" metal fr, NM 600.00
Oil Creek Gas, drake well & derrick, 15" dia, NM 2,500.00
Pure, porc body, 15" 650.00
Purol Pep, porc body 750.00
Richfield, w/eagle 600.00
Signal, old stoplight, 15", VG 3,500.00
Socony, milk glass inserts on metal 1,200.00
Stanolined Aviation, rare, 16½", EX 4,000.00
Sunland Ethyl, 15" 550.00
Texaco Leaded, glass panels, pr 4,500.00
Tidex, 16½" 475.00

Type 4, One-Piece Glass Globes, No Inserts, Co. Name Etched, Raised or Enameled, 1912-1931

Atlantic, chimney cap 2,800.00
Iowa Gas 1,800.00
Musgo 4,800.00
Red Crown, rnd, etched 3,500.00
Republic, 3-sided 1,800.00
Shell, rnd, etched 750.00
Sinclair Aircraft, etched 4,500.00
Skelly 750.00
Super Shell, clam shape 1,800.00
Super Shell, rnd, etched 3,500.00
Texaco, milk glass, emb letters, brass collar 1,000.00
Texaco Ethyl 2,000.00
White Rose, boy pictured, pnt 2,500.00

Gaudy Dutch

Inspired by Oriental Imari wares, Gaudy Dutch was made in England from 1800 to 1820. It was hand decorated on a soft-paste body with rich underglaze blues accented in orange, red, pink, green, and yellow. It differs from Gaudy Welsh in that there is no lustre (except on Water Lily). There are seventeen patterns, some

of which are: War Bonnet, Grape, Dahlia, Oyster, Urn, Butterfly, Carnation, Single Rose, Double Rose, and Water Lily. Values are given for mint condition examples unless otherwise.

Butterfly, pitcher, milk; 4" 825.00
Butterfly, plate, butterfly on side, 8¼" 900.00
Butterfly, sugar bowl 1,700.00

Butterfly Variant, deep dishes, 9⅞" and 10", $1,000.00 each.

Carnation, cup plate 650.00
Carnation, plate, 8⅜" 775.00
Carnation, soup plate, 8½" 700.00
Dahlia, plate, 8⅜" 900.00
Dahlia, tea bowl & saucer 750.00
Dahlia, teapot, body checks 600.00
Double Rose, cup, handleless; NM 335.00
Double Rose, cup & saucer 525.00
Double Rose, plate, 9¾" 775.00
Double Rose, platter, 10½", NM 2,700.00
Double Rose, platter, 17" 3,100.00
Double Rose, sugar bowl 800.00
Dove, cup & saucer, bl band 560.00
Dove, plate, 8½", NM 715.00
Dove, plate, 9¾" 800.00
Dove, teapot, NM 800.00
Dove, waste bowl, 2¾x5⅝", NM 715.00
Grape, cream pitcher 695.00
Grape, plate, toddy; 5¾" 300.00
Grape, plate, 9¾" 600.00
Grape, soup, deep, 9¾", NM 425.00
Grape, teapot 700.00
Leaf, sugar bowl, w/lid 1,000.00
Oyster, cup & saucer, NM 285.00
Oyster, plate, 8½" 475.00
Oyster, waste bowl, 6¼" 1,100.00
Primrose, sugar bowl 900.00
Primrose, waste bowl 750.00
Single Rose, creamer 875.00
Single Rose, cup & saucer 475.00
Single Rose, plate, flakes, 6⅜" 300.00
Single Rose, plate, 5¼" 375.00
Single Rose, plate, 9½" 550.00
Single Rose, sugar bowl, shell hdls, beehive finial, stain 375.00
Single Rose, teapot 1,500.00
Starflower, plate, mk Riley, 8¼" 475.00

Strawflower, plate, toddy; mk Riley, chip, 4¾" 525.00
Strawflower, plate, 8½" 825.00
Sunflower, creamer 450.00
Sunflower, plate, 8¼" 600.00
Urn, creamer 550.00
Urn, plate, sm stain, 7¼" 500.00
Urn, plate, toddy; 5⅝", EX+ 360.00
War Bonnet, creamer, 4½", EX+ 965.00
War Bonnet, cup & saucer, handleless; NM 600.00
War Bonnet, cup plate 650.00
War Bonnet, plate, 5¼", EX 250.00
War Bonnet, waste bowl, 5" 1,000.00
Zinnia, plate, mk Riley, rare, 8¾" 475.00
Zinnia, plate, 6⅜" 600.00

Gaudy Ironstone

Gaudy Ironstone was produced in the mid-1800s in Staffordshire, England. Some of the ware was decorated in much the same colors and designs as Gaudy Welsh, while other pieces were painted in pink, orange, and red with black and light blue accents. Lustre was used on some designs, omitted on others. The heavy ironstone body is its most distinguishing feature.

Key:
pc — polychrome   ug bl — underglaze blue

Bowl, Seeing Eye, paneled sides, lustre decor, 3⅜x5½" 220.00
Coffeepot, Seeing Eye, Walley, Niagara shape, 11", EX 650.00
Cup & saucer, Morning Glory, ug bl w/gr 120.00
Mug, rabbits & frogs w/floral, blk transfer+4 colors, 5⅜" 1,325.00
Pitcher, molded design, ug bl w/bl highlights & lustre, 8" 165.00
Plate, blackberries/leaves in yel & orange, E Walley, 8½" 100.00
Plate, Morning Glory, ug bl/red, 2-tone gr pnt, 9½" 125.00
Plate, Pinwheel, mk Ironstone, EX 50.00
Plate, Seeing Eye, wear, 9½" 90.00
Plate, Strawberry, gold lustre, mk, 10", NM 325.00
Plate, Strawberry, ug bl, pc enamel & lustre, 8½" 150.00
Plate, Urn of Flowers, ug bl, flaking, 9⅜" 250.00
Plate, vintage, ug bl w/red & gr & lustre, 9" 115.00
Platter, rose, 4-color, mk England, 13" 200.00
Platter, Strawberry & Rose, 3-color, wear/stains, 14¾" 325.00
Teapot, Morning Glory, ug bl w/gr, 8-sided, mk D, 9" 875.00
Waste bowl, Strawberry, stain/edge chips, 5½" 150.00

Gaudy Welsh

Gaudy Welsh was an inexpensive hand-decorated ware made in both England and Wales from 1820 until 1860. It is characterized by its colors — principally underglaze blue, orange-rust, and copper lustre — and by its uninhibited patterns. Accent colors may be yellow and green. (Pink lustre may be present, since lustre applied to the white areas appears pink. A copper tone develops from painting lustre onto the dark colors.) The body of the ware may be heavy ironstone, creamware, earthenware, or porcelain; even style and shapes vary considerably. Patterns, while usually floral, are also sometimes geometric and may have trees and birds. Beware! The Wagon Wheel pattern has been reproduced.

Our advisor for this category is Cheryl Nelson; she is listed in the Directory under Minnesota.

Bryn Pistyll, jug, 5" 175.00

Buckle, plate, 10" 135.00
Cambrian Rose, mug, 8" 425.00
Chain, jug, flow bl, 7¼" 385.00
Chinoiserie, mug, 2" 180.00
Columbine, cup & saucer 85.00
Columbine, teapot 275.00
Feather, cup & saucer 95.00
Flower Basket, plate, 8" 225.00
Glamorgan, mug, 7" 375.00
Grape, jug, 7" 150.00
Grape, plate, 10" 110.00
Grape & Lily, cup & saucer 145.00
Grape & Lily, plate, 10" 175.00
Grape & Lily, sugar bowl 185.00
Gwent, jug, 5" 295.00
Herald, cup & saucer 175.00
Herald, plate, 10" 215.00
Hexagon, plate, 10" 135.00
Japan, jug 475.00
Japan, teapot 425.00
Morning Glory, creamer, 5" 165.00
Oyster, cup & saucer 85.00
Oyster, jug, 7" 100.00
Oyster, teapot 295.00
Pagoda, bowl, 10" 785.00
Pot de Fleurs, vase, 7" 575.00
Rainbow, plate, 10" 275.00
Rhondda, jug, 5" 395.00
Rhondda, jug, 7¼" 475.00
Strawberry, teapot 495.00

Sugar bowl, Basket of Flowers, large fancy handles, ring finial, 6-footed base, 7", $145.00.

Tulip, creamer, 5" 150.00
Tulip, mug, 2½" 125.00
Tulip, plate, 10" 95.00
Tulip, waste bowl 90.00
Village, cup & saucer 185.00
Village, plate, 7½" 215.00
Welsh War Bonnet, cup & saucer 235.00

Geisha Girl

Geisha Girl Porcelain was one of several key Japanese china production efforts aimed at the booming export markets of the U.S., Canada, England, and other parts of Europe. The wares feature colorful, kimono-clad Japanese ladies in scenes of everyday Japanese life, surrounded by exquisite flora, fauna, and mountain ranges. Nonetheless, the forms in which the wares were produced reflected the late 19th- and early 20th-century Western dining and decorating preferences: tea and coffee services, vases, dresser sets, children's items, planters, etc.

Over a hundred manufacturers were involved in Geisha Girl production. This accounts for the several hundred different patterns, well over a dozen border colors and styles, and several methods of design execution. Geisha Girl Porcelain was produced in wholly hand-painted versions, but most were hand painted over stencilled outlines. Be wary of Geisha ware executed with decals. Very few decalled examples came out of Japan. Rather, most were Czechoslovakian attempts to hone in on the market. Czech pieces have stamped marks in broad, pseudo-Oriental characters. Items with portraits of Oriental ladies in the bottom of tea or sake cups are *not* Geisha Girl Porcelain, unless the outside surface of the wares are decorated as described above. These lovely faces are formed by varying the thickness of the porcelain body and are called lithophanes.

The height of Geisha Girl production was between 1910 and the mid-1930s. Some post-World War II production has been found marked Occupied Japan. The ware continued in minimal production through the 1980s, but point of origin for the latest reproductions was Hong Kong. Modern productions are discerned by the pure whiteness of the porcelain; even, unemotional borders; lack of background washes and gold enameling; and overall sparseness of detail. Our advisor for this category is Elyce Litts; she is listed in the Directory under New Jersey.

Key:
#2 — Torii	#68 — SGK China, Occupied
#4 — T in Cherry Blossom	Japan
#11 — diaper mk	J #1 — Yachi
#12 — Royal Kaga	J #6 — Tashiro
#16 — SNB	J #16 — Kutani
#19 — Japan	J #19 — Ozan
#20 — Made in Japan	J #36 — Made by Kato
#35 — Plum Blossom	J #46 — Yasutera
#42 — Vantine	

Basket vase, Bamboo Trellis, gr hdl & brn ft w/gold, 8½" **150.00**
Berry set, Dragon Boat, cobalt w/gold, master+5 ind **85.00**
Biscuit jar, Basket of Mums B, melon ribs, red w/gold **65.00**
Biscuit jar, Court Lady, cobalt w/blk-outlined reserves, J#1 ....**75.00**
Biscuit jar, Flower Gathering B, red w/gold, 6½" **55.00**
Biscuit jar, Gardening, cobalt waved & circled border, ftd **65.00**
Bowl, berry; Fan A, cobalt/brick red/gold, scalloped, mk **22.00**
Bowl, berry; River's Edge, gr/orange/gold, ind **20.00**
Bowl, Boy's Processional, red-orange w/yel, 9½" **55.00**
Bowl, Chinese Coin, Battledore/etc scenes, hdls, mk, 10" **85.00**
Bowl, dessert; Garden Bench H, cobalt w/blk-outlined reserves ...**15.00**
Bowl, nut; Feather Fan, ladies w/uchiwa & fans, ftd, #12 ....**48.00**
Box, Garden Bench B, red sides, 6-sided, #20, 6" **35.00**
Cocoa pot, Basket A, 4 ladies gather shells at river, 8" **55.00**
Cocoa pot, Battledore, conical, yel-gr, 8" **55.00**
Cocoa pot, To the Teahouse, gold rim, #2 ....**65.00**
Cocoa set, Bamboo Trellis, red-orange, pot+6 c/s **125.00**
Cocoa set, Child's Play, red w/gold, pot+6 c/s **150.00**
Compote, Boat Festival, river scene, #4, 6" H **55.00**
Creamer, Chrysanthemum Garden, red, toy sz **15.00**
Creamer, Lantern A, J #16 ....**25.00**
Creamer, Long-Stemmed Peony, bl w/gold, slim, #20 ....**15.00**
Creamer, Paper Carp, red-orange w/gold, J #16 ....**20.00**
Creamer, Porch, red-orange, modern **10.00**
Creamer, Rokkasen (Six Poets), red-orange, leaf shape, mk **30.00**
Cup, bouillon; Garden Bench J, w/lid & drip plate, mk **55.00**
Cup & saucer, AD; Basket B, 4 ladies, none pointing **20.00**
Cup & saucer, AD; Temple A, mc, J #16, toy sz **25.00**
Cup & saucer, cocoa; Fan D, ladies w/uchiwa, gold border **25.00**
Cup & saucer; AD; Flower Gathering D, wisteria, J #6, ...**18.00**

Dresser tray, Blind Man's Bluff, cobalt blue ground, $85.00.

Egg cup, Cherry Blossom Ikebana, flowers in pot, cobalt **18.00**
Egg cup, dbl; Duck Watching, gold border, mk **22.00**
Egg cup, dbl; Mother & Son A, bl-gr **20.00**
Hair receiver, Footbridge A **35.00**
Jug, Garden Bench Q, red-orange/mint/pine gr/gold, mk, 6½" **55.00**
Lemonade set, Bellflower, brn w/gr, #19, pitcher+5 mugs **125.00**
Luncheon set, Garden Bench D, mc border, pot+6 c/s+6 plates .**175.00**
Marmalade, Cloud A, red-orange w/yel, ribs, w/tray, J #6, 5" **55.00**
Match holder, Garden Bench A, bl-gr, hanging **30.00**
Muffineer, Parasol C, wavy red, bulbous, #20 ....**35.00**
Pancake server, So Big, boy gesturing, J #16, 9½x3½" **150.00**
Pin tray, Duck Watching B, pine gr w/wht, mk **10.00**
Plate, Battledore, red-orange, scalloped swirl, 6¼" **15.00**
Plate, Fan w/Fan Dance reserves, red-orange, toy, #19, 4¼" **20.00**
Plate, Greeting Grandma, red w/gold, scalloped, 8½" **25.00**
Plate, Parasol & Basket, cobalt w/gold, 3 reserves, mk, 7" **25.00**
Plate, Writing A, scalloped cobalt w/gold lacing, #20, 7⅜" **28.00**
Sauce dish, Mother & Son, red w/gold, emb leaves, #19, 6" **16.00**
Shaker, Child Reaching for Butterfly, bl top/red border **10.00**
Sugar bowl, Blue Hoo, bl bird on branch, red-orange, J#36 ....**25.00**
Tea set, Fan Dance B, red-orange/cobalt/gr/wht/gold, mk, 15-pc ..**125.00**
Tea set, Visitor to the Court, cobalt w/gold trim, #19, 3-pc **65.00**
Teacup, Garden Bench C, apple gr w/gold, patterned int **4.00**
Teacup & saucer, Bamboo Tree, pine gr border **10.00**
Teacup & saucer, Child Reaching for Butterfly, red-orange, #20 ....**8.00**
Teapot, Fan Dance A, pk bkground, gold trim, J#16 ....**125.00**
Toothpick holder, Court Lady, 3 blk-lined reserves, melon shape ...**28.00**

German Porcelain

Unless otherwise noted, the porcelain listed in this section is marked simply 'Germany.' Products of other German manufactures are listed in specific categories. See also Bisque; Pink Pigs; Elfinware.

Box, jewel; Victorian couple transfer on pk, Kalk Co **120.00**
Candelabrum, 3-arm, appl floral, mother/child std, 20" **120.00**
Candle holders, lady (& man), floral boscage, 10", NM, pr **325.00**
Chocolate set, floral on rainbowl pearl ground, pot+4 c/s **250.00**
Figurine, bathing beauty, legs up, gold trim, D&K, 7" **650.00**
Figurine, dancing couple, 18th-C attire, all wht, 9¾" **250.00**
Figurine, lady in chair sewing, EX detail & color, 8⅞" **235.00**
Figurine, lady w/tambourine & man w/horn, Fr style, 12¼", pr ..**325.00**
Figurine, nude lying in clam shell, mc irid, unmk **100.00**
Figurine, nude on horsebk, wht, sgn Kunst, oval vase, 10¾" **150.00**
Figurine, Victorian lady stands w/basket in hand, 11" **145.00**
Mirror, 2 appl cherubs & flowers, 14½", pr **425.00**
Plaque, Der Ersten Rosen, seated maid, after Bernard, 7x5" **2,250.00**
Plate, floral transfer w/gold, emb scroll & poppy rim, 12¼" **35.00**
Plate, hummingbird & flowers on bl lustre, 10" **48.00**

Gladding McBean and Company

This company was established in 1875 in Lincoln, California. They first produced only clay drainage pipes, but in 1883 architectural terra cotta was introduced, which has been used extensively in the United States as well as abroad. Sometime later a line of garden pottery was added. They soon became the leading producers of tile in the country. In 1923 they purchased the Tropico Pottery in Glendale, California, where in addition to tile they also produced huge garden vases. Their line was expanded in 1934 to included artware and dinnerware.

At least fifteen lines of art pottery were developed between 1934 and 1942. For a short time they stamped their wares with the Tropico Pottery mark; but the majority was signed 'GMcB' in an oval. Later the mark was changed to 'Franciscan' with several variations. After 1937 'Catalina Pottery' was used on some lines. (All items marked 'Catalina Pottery' were made in Glendale.) For further information we recommend *The Collector's Encyclopedia of California Pottery*, by our advisor for this category, Jack Chipman. He is listed in the Directory under California.

Candle holder, Tropico Art Ware, wht	20.00
Compote, Avalon Art Ware, turq & ivory, 8"	22.50
Cup & saucer, Ruby Art Ware	30.00
Figurine, Samoan woman w/child, satin wht, 13"	150.00
Pitcher, Tropico Art Ware, bl, 5¾"	18.00
Tile, Mexican in serape on burro, Hermosa, 1937, 4¼" sq	35.00
Vase, Coronado Art Ware, satin ivory, bulbous base, 8½"	30.00
Vase, Ox Blood Art Ware, bulbous w/waisted neck, 4¾x3¾"	75.00
Vase, Ox Blood Art Ware, 11"	200.00

Glass Animals and Figurines

These beautiful glass sculptures have been produced by many major companies in America, in fact, some are still being made today. Heisey, Fostoria, Duncan and Miller, Imperial, Paden City, Tiffin, and Cambridge made the vast majority, but there were many others involved on a lesser scale. Some, but not all, marked their animals.

As many of the glass companies went out of business, molds were often sold to others still active who used them to reproduce their own line of animals. While some are easy to recognize, others can be very confusing. For example, Summit Art Glass now owns Cambridge's 6½", 8½", and 10" swan molds. We recommend *Glass Animals of the Depression Era* by Lee Garmon and Dick Spencer, if you're thinking of starting a collection or wanting to identify and evaluate the glass animals you already have. Both are our advisors for this category and are listed in the Directory under Illinois.

Note: Heisey Collectors of America stopped using the plug horse as a mascot last year and have adoped the rabbit paperweight as the new yearly mascot. In our descriptions, unless a color is mentioned, values are for clear examples.

Cambridge

Bashful Charlotte, flower frog, gr, 11½"	375.00
Bashful Charlotte, flower frog, moonlight bl, 11½"	525.00
Bashful Charlotte, flower frog, 11½"	175.00
Bird, crystal satin, 2¾" L	30.00
Blue jay, flower holder	125.00
Buddha, amber, 5½"	225.00
Draped Lady, flower frog, crystal frost, 13¼"	175.00
Draped Lady, flower frog, gr frost, 8½"	115.00
Draped Lady, flower frog, lt pk, 8½"	125.00
Draped Lady, flower frog, pk frost, 8½"	150.00

Frog, crystal satin	25.00
Heron, sm, 9"	75.00
Mandolin Lady, flower frog	250.00
Mandolin Lady, flower frog, gr	400.00
Owl, lamp, ivory w/brn enamel, ebony base, 13½"	1,100.00
Rose Lady, flower frog, crystal satin, tall base, 9½"	225.00
Rose Lady, flower frog, dk pk, 8½"	190.00
Rose Lady, flower frog, gr, 8½"	200.00
Rose Lady, flower frog, tall base, 9½"	200.00
Scottie, crystal frost, hollow, ea	75.00
Swan, candlestick, milk glass, 4½"	175.00
Swan, carmen, 8½"	250.00
Swan, Crown Tuscan, 8½"	125.00
Swan, ebony, 12½"	300.00
Swan, ebony, 8½"	165.00
Swan, emerald, 8½"	125.00
Swan, milk glass, 6½"	125.00
Turkey, bl, w/lid	550.00
Turkey, pk, w/lid	400.00
Two Kids, flower frog, 9½"	200.00

Duncan and Miller

Bird of paradise	700.00
Dove, head down, 11½" L	175.00
Duck, cigarette box, red, 6"	170.00
Heron, crystal satin, 7"	120.00
Ruffled grouse, very rare	1,750.00
Swan, bl opal, W&F, spread wings, 10x12½"	245.00
Swan, chartreuse, open bk, 7"	30.00
Swan, open, 7"	45.00
Swan, solid, 5"	30.00
Swan, wheat cutting, 11"	75.00
Swordfish	300.00
Sylvan swan, bl or pk, 6½"	125.00
Sylvan swan, yel opal, 7½"	100.00
Tropical fish, ashtray, pk opal, 3½"	50.00

Fenton

Alley cat, teal marigold, 11"	85.00
Bear, carnival, sitting	20.00
Boy, blk, praying	12.00
Bunny, pale yel	20.00
Cardinal head, ruby, 6½"	95.00
Donkey, custard, HP daisies, 4½"	45.00
Elephant, flower bowl, blk satin, 6½x9"	400.00
Fish, paperweight, red carnival, ltd ed	65.00
Fish, vase, milk glass w/blk tail & eyes, 7"	425.00
Peacock, bookends, crystal satin, 5¾", pr	175.00

Fostoria

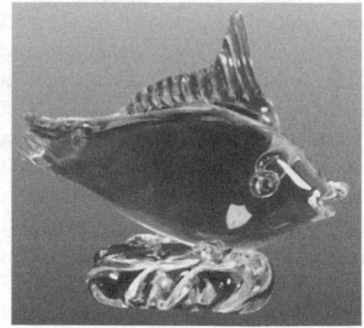

Goldfish, horizontal, rare, $125.00.

Bird, candle holder, 1½" 20.00
Cardinal head, Silver Mist, 6½" 125.00
Chanticleer, blk, 10¾" 600.00
Colts, standing, Silver Mist 45.00
Deer, sitting or standing, milk glass 55.00
Dolphin, bl, 4¾" 25.00
Duck w/3 ducklings, amber, set 50.00
Duckling, head down (+) 20.00
Eagle, bookend, Silver Mist, NM 150.00
Elephant, bookend, ebony, 6½", ea 125.00
Goldfish, vertical 95.00
Madonna, Silver Mist, orig issue, 10" (+) 50.00
Mermaid, 11½" 125.00
Pelican, amber, 1991 commemorative 55.00
Penguin, crystal frost, sq base, 4½" 85.00
Polar bear, topaz, 4⅝" 125.00
Sea horse, bookend, 8", ea 115.00
Squirrel, amber, running 35.00
St Francis, Silver Mist, orig issue, 13½" (+) 325.00

Heisey

Airdale 550.00
Asiatic pheasant, 7½" L 300.00
Bunny, head down, 2½" 200.00
Clydesdale, 7½x7" 400.00
Colt, kicking, amber 650.00
Colt, rearing 200.00
Colt, rearing, cobalt 1,200.00
Colt, standing, amber 550.00
Cygnet, baby swan, 2½" 200.00
Dolphin, candlesticks, #110, pr 250.00
Donkey 275.00
Duck, ashtray, Flamingo 160.00
Duck, flower block 140.00
Duck, flower block, Hawthorne 295.00
Elephant, amber, sm 1,600.00
Elephant, sm 195.00
Fish, bookend, ea 135.00
Fish, candlestick, 5" 175.00
Flying mare 3,000.00
Frog, cheese plate, Flamingo, #1210 ....145.00
Gazelle, 10¾" 1,500.00
Giraffe, head forward 200.00
Goose, wings down 425.00
Goose, wings up 100.00
Horse head, bookend 165.00
Horse head, box, 6½" 85.00
Horse head, cocktail shaker 135.00
Irish setter, ashtray, Flamingo 45.00
Kingfisher, flower block, Flamingo 175.00
Mallard, wings down 325.00
Mallard, wings up 150.00
Piglet, standing 100.00
Plug horse, amber 600.00
Pouter pigeon, 7½" L 700.00
Rabbit mother, 4½x5½" 800.00
Ringneck pheasant, 11¾" 140.00
Rooster, Fighting; crystal frost, 7½x5½" 200.00
Rooster, 5½x5" 325.00
Rooster head, cocktail shaker, 1-qt 75.00
Scotty 125.00
Show horse 1,250.00
Sparrow 120.00

Swan, master nut, #1503 ....45.00
Swan, 7x8½" 800.00
Wood duck 600.00

Imperial

Angelfish, bookend, amber (crystal or frosted) 150.00
Bull, amber, very rare, 4" 685.00
Champ terrier, caramel slag, 5¾" 95.00
Chick, head up, milk glass 10.00
Clydesdale, Salmon 275.00
Colt, balking, amber 140.00
Colt, kicking, Horizon Bl 35.00
Colt, standing, Sunshine Yel 85.00
Cygnet, caramel slag 55.00
Dog, Airedale, caramel slag 95.00
Donkey, caramel slag 55.00
Donkey, Ultra Bl 110.00

Dragon candle holder, crystal and frosted, 1949 original issue, $200.00.

Duck, standing, Ultra Bl, 2⅝" 45.00
Elephant, Meadow Gr Carnival, #674, med 110.00
Filly, head bkward, Verde Gr 145.00
Filly, head forward, crystal satin 75.00
Fish, canape plate, cobalt 30.00
Fish, candlestick, Sunshine Yel, 5" 50.00
Flying Mare, amber, NI mk, extremely rare 1,800.00
Giraffe, amber, ALIG mk, extremely rare 400.00
Jack, gr carnival, #506 ....110.00
Mallard, wings down, lt bl satin 35.00
Mallard, wings up, caramel slag 40.00
Owl, Hootless; caramel slag 50.00
Owl, purple slag, shiny 85.00
Piglet, standing, amber 75.00
Plug horse, pk, HCA, 1978 ....40.00
Ringneck pheasant, amber, extremely rare 260.00
Rooster, fighting, pk 175.00
Scolding bird, Cathay Crystal 175.00
Swan, purple slag, glossy 95.00
Terrier pup, amethyst carnival, 3½" 45.00
Tiger, paperweight, jade marbleized, 8" L 150.00
Wood duck, caramel slag 45.00
Wood duckling, floating, Sunshine Yel satin 20.00
Wood duckling, standing, Ultra Bl 45.00

L.E. Smith

Camel, recumbent, amber, 4½x6" 60.00
Elephant, 1¾" 12.00
Goose girl, gr or flame, 6", ea 50.00
Horse, bookend, rearing, amber, ea 38.00

Horse, bookend, rearing, ea 25.00
Horse, bookend, rearing, ruby, ea 40.00
King fish, aquarium, gr, 7¼x15" 265.00
Rooster, butterscotch slag, ltd ed, #208 ....85.00
Sparrow, head up, 3½" 15.00
Swan, milk glass w/decor, 8½" 45.00
Thrush, bl frost 20.00

New Martinsville

Bear, baby, head trn or str, 3" 60.00
Bear, papa, 4x6½" 250.00
Duck, standing, Viking's Epic Line, 9" 35.00
Elephant, bookend, 5½", ea 85.00
German shepherd, 5" 75.00
Horse, head up, 8" 95.00
Nautilus shell, bookend, crystal frost, 6", ea 35.00
Piglet, standing 125.00
Rabbit, mama 350.00
Seal, candlesticks, lg, pr 150.00
Seal w/ball, candle holder, 4½" 70.00
Swan, ruby, candle holders, pr 45.00
Tiger, head down, crystal frost, 7¼" 200.00
Wolfhound, 7" 95.00

Paden City

American eagle head, bookends, crystal frost, 7½", pr 300.00
Bunny, cotton-ball dispenser, ears bk, crystal frost 60.00
Bunny, cotton-ball dispenser, ears up, pk frost 150.00
Goose, lt bl, 5" 115.00
Pheasant, Chinese; med bl, 13¾" 150.00
Polar Bear on ice, 4½" 65.00
Pony, 12" 100.00
Rooster, Barnyard; 8¾" 85.00
Rooster, Elegant; lt bl, 11" 225.00
Squirrel on curved log, 5½" 65.00

Tiffin

Cat, Sassy Susie, blk satin w/pnt decor, #9448, 11" 175.00
Fish, solid, 8¾x9" 350.00
Owl, lamp, cobalt, 1934-29 ....1,250.00

Viking

Angelfish, blk, 6½" 150.00
Bird, med dk bl, 9½" 25.00
Bird, Orchid, 9½" 30.00
Duck, dk teal, Viking's Epic Line, 9" 35.00
Duck, vaseline, 5" 25.00
Horse, aqua bl, 11½" 95.00
Rabbit, amber, 6½" 35.00
Rooster, Epic; red, 9½" (+) 60.00

Westmoreland

Bird in flight, Amber Marigold, wings out, 5" W 25.00
Butterfly, Gr Mist, 2½" 22.00
Cardinal, Gr Mist 20.00
Penguin on ice floe, Brandywine Bl Mist 35.00
Pouter pigeon, any color, 2½", ea 25.00
Robin, red, 5⅛" 27.50
Robin, 5⅛" 20.00

Turtle, ashtray 10.00
Turtle, paperweight, Gr Mist, no holes, 4" L 25.00
Wren on perch, lt bl on wht, 2-pc 40.00

Miscellaneous

Horse head, bookends, milk glass, Indiana, 6", pr 45.00
Mopey dog, Federal, 3½" 10.00
Pouter pigeon, bookend, Indiana, 5½" 40.00
Turtle, amber, LG Wright, 10" L 85.00

Glass Knives

Glass knives were manufactured from about 1920 to 1950, with distribution at its greatest in the late thirties and early forties. Colors generally followed Depression glass dinnerware: crystal, light blue, light green, pink (originally called rose), and more rarely amber, forest green, and white (opal). Many glass knives were hand painted in fruit or flower designs. Knife blades were ground to a sharp edge. Today knives are usually found with blades nicked through years of use or bumping in silverware drawers or reground, which is acceptable to collectors as long as the original knife shape is maintained.

Many glass knives were engraved for gift-giving, personalized with the recipient's name and occasionally with a greeting. Originally presented in boxes, most glass knives were accompanied by a paper insert extolling the virtues of the knife and describing its care.

Boxes printed with World's Fair logos are fun to find, though not rare. Butter knives, which are smaller than other glass knives, typically were made in Czechoslovakia and sometimes match the handle patterns of glass salad sets. Knife lengths often vary slightly because the knives were snapped off the molded glass during manufacture.

Our advisor for this category is Adrienne Escoe; she is listed in the Directory under California. For information concerning the Glass Knife Collectors Club, see the Clubs, Newsletters, and Catalogs section of the Directory.

Values reflect knives with minor blade roughness or resharpening.

Aer-Flo (Grid), forest gr, 7½" 200.00
Block, pk, Atlantic City eng, 8¼" 30.00

Buffalo Knife (B.K. Co.), clear with hand-painted floral handle, $25.00.

Butter, gr/crystal, 6¼" 25.00
Dagger, crystal, 9¼" 75.00
Dur-X (3-Leaf), crystal, 8½" 12.00
Dur-X (5-Leaf), bl, 9¼" 20.00
Dur-X (5-Leaf), crystal, 8½" 12.00
Plain hdl, gr, 9" 30.00
Plain hdl, lt pk, 9" 25.00
Rose Spray, gr, 8½" 70.00
Steel-ite, crystal, 8½" 20.00
Stonex, amber, 8½" 110.00
Stonex, opal, 8½" 135.00
Vitex (3-Star), bl, 9¼", w/world's fair box 25.00
Vitex (3-Star), crystal, MIB 12.00
Vitex (3-Star), crystal, 8½" 10.00
Vitex (3-Star), pk, 9¼" 25.00

Glass Shoes

Little shoes made of glass can be found in hundreds of styles, shapes, and colors. They've been made since the early 1800s by nearly every glasshouse, large and small, in America. To learn more about them, we recommend *Shoes of Glass* by our advisor Libby Yalom, who is listed in the Directory under Maryland. Numbers in the listings refer to her book.

English Sowerby shoes, 1880s, 2½x5⅞": #100, blue and white slag, $145.00; #99, purple and white slag, $145.00; #98, blue, $70.00.

#101, cane, crystal, high front, mesh sole, plain toe, 4⅝" L 40.00
#11, Daisy & Button, wht opal, Duncan, Patd Oct 19/86 ....120.00
#116, bow on front, milk glass, scrolls on toe & bk, 4¾" L 45.00
#128, Hobnail atop ea rib, crystal, scalloped, 4⅜x4¼" 65.00
#13, Finecut, crystal, front opening, 3 lace holes ea side 48.00
#136, cuffed boot w/spur, blk, att Challinor-Taylor, 3¼x4" 52.00
#139, left buttons, crystal, ribbed, hollow sole, 4¼" 50.00
#171, high top, crystal w/gold, 4 bottons/solid heel, 4¼" 48.00
#184, Finecut bottle holder, vaseline, mk B&H, 5½" 57.00
#2, Daisy & Button, clear, mesh sole, lg 45.00
#203, baby's, frosted crystal w/gold laces & bow, 2⅜x3⅞" 30.00
#227, baby's, milk glass w/pk bow, Lornita label, 2¼x4⅛" 38.00
#262, scalloped near top, bl, mesh sole, 6 lace holes, 6" L 80.00
#276, crystal, stippled finish, sm flat bow, 2½x4⅜" 26.00
#294, beading on toe & vamp, gr, souvenir, 2⅝x4⅜" 30.00
#320, boot, milk glass, appl flower/leaves/rigaree, 3¾x4⅞" 145.00
#353, 3-color millefiori on red w/clear heel, Murano, 2¾" L 85.00
#359, burmese coloring (frosted/shaded), ruffled, 2½x6⅜" 100.00
#386, dmn-patterned bk w/plain front, crystal, 3½x7½" 165.00
#427, Dutch shoe, crystal, 1⅞x4" 40.00
#523, bootee, milk glass, knitted look, pk pnt w/gold, 2¾" L 60.00
#53, Finecut, amber, no laces, unmk, 2⅜x4⅜" 35.00
#566, boot, ruby cut to crystal, ca 1980, 7¾x5½" 130.00
#581, lady's shoe-&-leg bottle on hassock, crystal, 12¾" 225.00
#602, Daisy & Button, bl, 2¼x4⅜" 35.00
#64, sandal, Daisy & Button, crystal, att Bryce Bros, 4½" L 42.00
#87, cat, milk glass, no pnt, ca 1900, 3½x4" 52.00

Glidden

Genius designer Glidden Parker established Glidden Pottery in 1940 in Alfred, New York, having been schooled at the unrivaled New York State College of Ceramics at Alfred University. Glidden pottery is characterized by a fine stoneware body, innovative forms, outstanding hand-milled glazes, and hand decoration which make the pieces individual works of art. Production consisted of casual dinnerware, artware, and accessories that were distributed internationally.

In 1949 Glidden Pottery became the second ceramic plant in the country to utilize the revolutionary Ram pressing machine. This allowed for increased production and for the most part eliminated the previously used slip-casting method. However, Glidden stoneware continued to reflect the same superb quality of craftsmanship until the factory closed in 1957. Although the majority of form and decorative patterns were Mr. Parker's personal designs, Fong Chow and Sergio Dello Strologo also designed award-winning lines.

Glidden will be found marked on the unglazed underside with a signature that is hand incised, mold impressed, or ink stamped. Interest in this unique stoneware is growing as collectors discover that it embodies the very finest of Mid-Century High Style. Our advisor is David Pierce; he is listed in the Directory under Ohio.

Ashtray, Alfred Stoneware, #821, 6¾x6" 20.00
Ashtray, Fish (Fred Press), #275 ....20.00
Ashtray, Green Mesa, #274-U, 5½" 35.00
Ashtray, Leaves (Fred Press), #274, 5½" 20.00
Ashtray, Loop Artware, #904-U, 6½x3¾" 65.00
Ashtray, Safex, dbl sq 20.00
Bowl, blk & wht w/gold stripes, #207, 8x8" 55.00
Bowl, cobalt, #23, 2x10x10" 35.00
Bowl, Counterpane, #622, 7½" 20.00
Bowl, Early Pink, oval, #38, 2x7¼x4¾" 35.00
Bowl, Plaid, #27, 1¼x5¾x5¾" 25.00
Bowl, Turquoise Matrix, #21, 4½" 15.00
Bowl, Turquoise Matrix, #26, 1¼x6½x5" 15.00
Bowl, Viridian, lug soup, #467, 3½x7½x6" 20.00
Bowl, Viridian, oval, #417, 4x9½x8" 20.00
Candle bench, Afrikans, 2x8¾x3¾" 40.00
Canister, Garden, w/lid & bail, #601, 5x5½" 45.00
Casserole, Pear, w/lid, #165, 8½x5½" 35.00
Casserole, Ric Rac, yel, #167, 4¼x5¼" 15.00
Casserole, Turquoise Matrix, #162, 6½x8½" 20.00
Casserole, Viridian, #165, 5½x8½" 20.00
Casserole, Will o' the Wisp, #167, 4¼x5¼" 15.00
Coaster, Mexican Cock, #19, 4" sq 6.00
Creamer & sugar bowl, Feather, w/lid, #144/#133 ....30.00
Creamer & sugar bowl, Pear, w/lid, #144/#143 ....55.00
Creamer & sugar bowl, Turquoise Matrix, w/lid, #1430/#1440 .....20.00
Creamer & sugar bowl, Yellowstone, w/lid, #1430/#1440 ....20.00
Cup & saucer, Boston Spice, #441A/#442 ....15.00
Cup & saucer, Feather, #441A/#442 ....12.00
Cup & saucer, Turquoise Matrix, #141/#142 ....12.00
Pitcher, Turquoise Matrix, #617 ....40.00
Planter, Charcoal & Rice, bird form 100.00
Planter, Sage & Sand, #122, 2x6" 10.00
Plate, Marine Fantasia Lucent Green, #431, 11½x10¼" 50.00
Plate, Mexican Cock, #35, 5½" 15.00
Plate, salad; Plaid, #65, 7x7" 20.00
Plate, Turn of the Century, #35, 5½" 40.00
Teapot, Flourish, #140, 5¼x9x4¼" 60.00
Teapot, Yellowstone, #240, 3½x7x5¼" 45.00
Tumbler, bl, #1127 ....20.00
Vase, cobalt, ball form, #49, 7x5¾" 50.00
Vase, Early Pink, pillow form, #128, 4½x5¼x2½" 25.00

Goebel

F.W. Goebel founded the Hummelwork Porcelain Manufactory in 1871, located in Rodental, West Germany. They produced porcelain figurines, plates, and novelties, the most famous of which are the Hummel figurines (these are listed in a separate section). There were many other series produced by Goebel — Disney characters, birds, animals,

Art Deco figurines, and the Friar Tuck Monks that are especially popular. Our advisors for this category are Gale and Wayne Bailey; they are listed in the Directory under Georgia.

Cardinal Tuck (Red Monk)

Pitcher, S141-2/0, stylized bee mk, 2½" **75.00**
Pitcher, S141/0, stylized bee mk, 4" **125.00**
Shakers, P153, stylized bee mk, 2", pr **85.00**
Sugar bowl, Z37, stylized bee mk, 4" **125.00**

Friar Tuck (Brown Monk)

Ashtray, RF142, stylized bee mk **65.00**
Ashtray, ZF43/II, 3-line mk **50.00**
Bank, SD29, full bee mk **65.00**
Calendar holder, KF55, stylized bee mk **65.00**
Cigarette holder, RX110, stylized bee mk **75.00**
Condiment set, mustard, shakers & tray, stylized bee mk **85.00**
Cookie jar, K29, full bee mk **250.00**
Decanter, KL92, toes, full bee mk **100.00**
Decanter, KL95, 3-line mk **75.00**
Egg timer, dbl, E96, stylized bee mk **65.00**
Egg timer, single, E104, 3-line mk **50.00**
Liquor tot, KL94, stylized bee mk **20.00**
Mug, T74/0, stylized bee mk, 4" **35.00**
Mug, T74/1, stylized bee mk, 5" **45.00**
Mustard, S183, full bee mk **40.00**
Pitcher, S141-2/0, full bee mk, 2½" **30.00**
Pitcher, S141/0, cross-eyed, full bee mk, 4" **45.00**
Shakers, P153, toes, 2⅜", pr **30.00**
Sugar bowl, Z37, toes, full bee mk, 4½" **35.00**

Miscellaneous

Ashtray, RT133, Scottie dogs, crown mk **65.00**
Ashtray, RT894, yel duck, dbl crown mk **65.00**
Bank, chimney sweep, Goebel bee mk, 5" **45.00**
Figurine, chimney sweep, Goebel bee mk, 5" **45.00**
Figurine, Victorian couple, FR624 A&B, 9", pr **75.00**
Pitcher, S130/1, crown mk, 6" **65.00**
Pretzel holder, blk cat, KT123, full bee mk **50.00**
Shakers, P154, bear & beehive, stylized bee mk **25.00**
Teacup & saucer, Santa Claus, T73D, full bee mk **75.00**
Vases, man & lady, VB110 A&B, crown mk, pr **85.00**
Wine glasses, no TMK, set of 6 ....**125.00**

Goldscheider

The Goldscheider family operated a pottery in Vienna for many generations before seeking refuge in the United States following Hitler's invasion of their country. They settled in Trenton, New Jersey, in the early 1940s where they established a new corporation and began producing objects of art and tableware items. (No mention was made of the company in the Trenton City Directory after 1950, and it is assumed that by this time the influx of foreign imports had taken its toll.) In 1946 Marcel Goldscheider established a pottery in Staffordshire where he manufactured bone china figures, earthenware, etc., marked with a stamp of his signature. Larger artist-signed examples are the most valuable with the Austrian pieces bringing the higher prices.

A wide variety of marks has been found. Listed here are several of that correspond with numbers in the listings that follow. Our advisors are Randy and Debbie Coe; they're listed under Oregon.

Key:
1 — Goldscheider USA Fine China
2 — Original Goldscheider Fine China
3 — Goldscheider USA
4 — Goldscheider-Everlast Corp.
5 — Goldscheider Everlast Corp. in circle
6 — Goldscheider Inc. in circle
7 — Goldcrest Ceramics Corp. in circle
8 — Goldcrest Fine China
9 — Goldcrest Fine China USA
10 — A Goldcrest Creation
11 — Created by Goldscheider USA

Anne Boleyn, Dorier, #1199, mk #7 or #8, 10½" **250.00**
Ashtray, German shepherd, 5½x7½" **85.00**
Bust, Bali head, pk turban, Barbara Baldwin, 12¾" **275.00**
Butterfly, lady holding butterfly, Lindhoff, #851, mk #1 or #5 ....**175.00**
Butterfly maid, arms extended, Austria, #5960, 16" **1,200.00**
Butterfly maid, arms extended, sgn VW, 19" **2,800.00**
Chinese princess, Lindloff, #8950, 12" **150.00**
Dancer, split skirt held wide, bends bk, Dakon/Austria, 9" **490.00**

Exotically dressed dancer holding cape wide, signed Laurenzl, raised circular base, Austria, #5500 36 8, 20½", $1,800.00.

Great Dane, USA **85.00**
Harem girl, stepping forward, arms out, #380, 21" **1,800.00**
Henry VII, Dorier, mk #7 or #8, #1198, 10½" **250.00**
Horse, stylized, orange w/rust highlights, #5821/Austria, 8" **400.00**
Juliet w/doves, mk #7 or #9, 12¼" **350.00**
Lady in hat w/muff, 8¼" **95.00**
Lady walking in bl floral dress, Dakon, 19" **1,650.00**
Mask, face/hand of turbaned lady, necklace/bracelet, 14", VG ...**300.00**
Mask, Medusa-style hair, 12" **1,200.00**
Music box, colonial girl, 7" **140.00**
New Blue Bonnet **145.00**
Nude dancer, plumed headpc, cape, Thumasch, 19" **2,500.00**
Old Virginia, sgn Polly Porcher, 8½" **115.00**
Oriental lady dancing, #823, mk #3 or #5, 10¼" **125.00**
Oriental man playing mandolin, #822, mk #3 or #5, 10¾" **125.00**
Prince of Wales, Peggy Poacher, 6¾" **85.00**
Royal Blackamoors, B Loveday, 15" **195.00**
Sing Lo, 7¼" **60.00**
Yankee Doodle Dandy, 7" **125.00**

Gonder

Lawton Gonder grew up with clay in his hands and fire in his eyes. Gonder's interest in ceramics was greatly influenced by his parents who worked for Weller and a close family friend and noted ceramic authority, John Herold. In his early teens Gonder launched his ceramic career at the Ohio Pottery Company while working for Herold. He later gained valuable experience at American Encaustic Tile Company, Cherry Art Tile, and the Florence Pottery. Gonder was plant manager at the Florence Pottery until fire destroyed the facility in late 1941.

After years of solid production and management experience, Lawton Gonder established the Gonder Ceramic Art Company, formerly the Peters and Reed plant, in South Zanesville, Ohio. Gonder Ceramic Arts produced quality art pottery with beautiful contemporary designs which included human and animal figures and a complete line of Oriental pottery. Accentuating the beautiful shapes were unique and innovative glazes developed by Gonder such as flambe (flame red with streakes of yellow), 24k gold crackle, antique gold, and Chinese crackle.

All Gonder is marked with the company name and mold number. They include 'Gonder U.S.A' in block letters, 'Gonder' in script, 'Gonder Original' in script, and 'Gonder Ceramic Art' in block letters. Paper labels were also used. Some of the early Gonder molds closely resemble RumRill designs that had been manufactured at the Florence Pottery; and because some RumRill pieces are found with similar (if not identical) shapes, matching mold numbers, and Gonder glazes, it is speculated that some RumRill was produced at the Gonder plant. In 1946 Gonder started another company which he named Elgee (chosen for his initials LG) where he manufactured lamp bases until a fire in 1954 resulted in his shifting lamp production to the main plant. Operations ceased in 1957.

Basket, shell form, lt yel, #674, 8" 25.00
Bookends, horse's head, dk warm brn, #582, pr 40.00
Console bowl, shell form, #505, 8x16" 50.00
Cookie jar, rnd w/swirls, plain lid 48.00

Ewer, shell form, gray with pinkish-gray interior, 13", $35.00.

Figurine, elephant, stylized, pale gray, #108, 7½x10" 250.00
Figurine, lady water carrier, yel, complete w/buckets, 14¼" 45.00
Figurine, ram, wht crackle, 6" 18.00
Teapot, La Gonda, #914, 7½" 55.00
Vase, aqua, hdls, #E-48, 6½" 30.00
Vase, bl, twisted form, 6" 18.00
Vase, fan form, brn mottle on yel, J-60, 9" 30.00
Vase, fish figural, brn shaded to aqua gr, #522, 9" 60.00
Vase, rim-to-shoulder hdls, yel, H-5, 9" 18.00
Vase, shaped rim, gr, E-1 ....18.00
Vase, sq sides, yel, H-74, 8½" 20.00
Vase, trumpet neck, up-trn hdls, gold crackle, #604, 10" 40.00
Vase, trumpet neck w/scalloped rim, E-49 ....16.00
Vase, upright cornucopia shape w/integral hdls, yel, #419, 8" 20.00

Goofus Glass

Goofus was an inexpensive type of lustre-painted pressed glassware made by many companies during the first two decades of the 20th century. Bowls and trays are most common, and red and gold combinations are found more often than blues and greens. Note: Values are given for examples that are in excellent condition.

Bottle, perfume; Tulips, pk & gr orig pnt, w/stopper, 3½" 35.00
Bowl, Pine Cones & Leaves, ruffled edge, orig pnt, 10", M 60.00
Coasters, Flower, red & gold orig pnt, 3", M 15.00
Compote & saucer set, Poppy, crackle glass, orig pnt, 6", M 40.00
Decanter, La Belle, red & gold, w/stopper, 9½", M 70.00
Lamp, fairy; flash-fired gr, perfectly shaped roses, 7", NM 45.00
Lamp, oil; Cabbage Rose, amethyst, w/chimney, 15", NM 120.00
Nut dish, Cherry, hdl, flash-fired, scalloped rim, 6½", M 50.00
Picture fr, Cabbage Rose, bl glass, 10½x6½", M 60.00
Plate, Morning Glory, red & gold, rpt, 12" 40.00
Plate, Rose & Lattice, red & gold orig pnt, 6" 30.00
Powder box, Love Birds, satin glass, 4½x3", NM 35.00
Sauce dish, Rose, crackle glass, orig pnt, 5½" 35.00
Sugar shaker, Grape, milk glass, orig pnt & top, 4½" 45.00
Syrup pitcher, Strawberry, orig pnt, no top, 6½", M 55.00
Tray, bread; Last Supper, red & gold orig pnt, 7x11" 90.00
Tray, dresser; Rose, heart form, amethyst, 1½" deep, 6" W 70.00
Tray, pin; Basketweave, rose decor, rpt, 4x2" 30.00
Vase, Bird Sitting in Grapevine, satin glass, 9" 15.00
Vase, Dogwood Blossoms, satin glass, design front & bk, 6½" 12.00
Vase, Four Daisies, sm hdls in mold, orig pnt, 12" 55.00
Vase, Grape, crackle glass, str sides, amethyst, 9" 15.00
Vase, Grapes on Basketweave, hourglass form, no pnt, 10" 20.00
Vase, Single Rose, design front & bk, orig pnt, thin, 9½" 40.00
Water bottle, Basketweave, rose decor, amethyst, 10" 30.00
Water bottle, Grape, crackle glass, bulbous form, 7½" 60.00

Goss and Crested China

William Henry Goss received his early education at the Government School of Design at Somerset House, London, and as a result of his merit was introduced to Alderman William Copeland, who owned the Copeland Spode Pottery. Under the influence of Copeland from 1852 to 1858, Goss quickly learned the trade and soon became their chief designer. Little is known about this brief association, and in 1858 Goss left to begin his own business. After a short-lived partnership with a Mr. Peake, Goss opened a pottery on John Street, Stoke-on-Trent, but by 1870 he had moved to his business to a location near London Road. This pottery became the famous Falcon Works. Their mark was a spread-wing falcon (goshawk) centering a narrow, horizontal bar with 'W.H. Goss' printed below.

Many of the early pieces made by Goss were left unmarked and are difficult to discern from products made by the Copeland factory, but after he had been in business for about fifteen years, all of his wares were marked. Today unmarked items do not command the prices of the later marked wares.

Adolphus William Henry Goss (Goss's eldest son) joined his father's firm in the 1880s. He introduced cheaper lines, though the more expensive lines continued in production. Shortly after his father's death in 1906, Adolphus retired and left the business to his two younger brothers. The business suffered from problems created by a war economy, and in 1936 Goss assets were held by Cauldon Potteries Ltd. These were eventually taken over by the Coalport Group, who retained the right to use the Goss trademark. Messrs. Ridgeway Potteries bought all the assets in 1954 as well as the right to use the Goss trademark and name. In 1964 the group was known as Allied English Potteies Ltd. (A.E.P.), and in 1971 A.E.P. merged with the Doulton Group. Now it remains to be seen if Goss ware will ever be produced again. Our advisor for this category is Patrick Herley; he is listed in the Directory under New York.

Abbots cup, Fountains Abbey **16.00**
Beer barrel, Burton **18.00**
Bowl, Christ Church **13.50**
Bucket, milk; Swiss **18.00**
Bust, Dickens, parian, 8" **75.00**
Candle snuffer, Aseroovy crest on wht, 2¼" **75.00**

Cow and sheep group, parian, $950.00.

Creamer, Yarmouth, sm **24.00**
Jug, Firg Grate, Valleta **20.00**
Look Out House **110.00**
Mocha Cup, Egyptian, Egypt **11.00**
Mortar, Bideford **14.00**
Mortar, Hythe Gromwellian **15.00**
Night light, R Burns Cottage, 6" **150.00**
Old Salt Pot, Crystal Palace Crest, #403422 ....**18.00**
Rufus Stone **18.00**
Shakespeare bust, sm **35.00**
St Nicholas Chapel **170.00**
Tyg, 1-hdl **9.00**
Urn, Minister **16.00**
Vase, amphora, 1911 Coronation, 4" **42.50**
Vase, Exeter, Sheffield **24.00**
Wall pocket, Christ Church, lg **30.00**
Welsh Jack, Llanberis, 4" **15.00**
Welsh Lady Jug, Ychydig Olagth, 3¾" **35.00**

Crested China

Arcadian, bottle, whiskey; '1 Special Irish,' Arms of Wicklow **25.00**
Arcadian, ewer, Wembly **18.00**
Arcadian, milk churn, Chippenham Ancient, 2¼" **10.00**
Arcadian, officer's cap, Yorking, 2¾" L **7.00**
Carlton, bust, Tommy on Sentry Duty **57.50**
Carlton, bust of Edward VII **75.00**
Carlton, figurine, Fisher girl **50.00**
Carlton, pot, hdls, w/lid **22.50**
Willow, figure, Burns at the plough **75.00**
Willow, model of Hay Castle, 3½" **47.50**
Willow, pig, City of St Andrews, 3¼" L **28.00**
Willow, Shakespeare Cottage, lg **75.00**

Gouda

Since the 18th century the main center of the pottery industry in

Holland was in Gouda. One of its earliest industries, the manufacture of clay pipes, continues to the present day. The artware so easily recognized by collectors today was first produced about 1885. It was decorated in the Art Nouveau manner. Stylized florals, birds, and geometrics were favored motifs; only rarely are they naturalistic. The Nouveau influence was strong until about 1915. Art Deco was attempted but with less success. Though most of the ware is finished in a matt glaze, glossy pieces in both pastels and dark colors are found on occasion and command higher prices. Decoration on the glossy ware is usually very well executed. Most of the workshops failed during the Depression, though earthenware is still being made in Gouda and carries the Gouda mark. Until very recently Regina was still making a limited amount of the old Gouda-style pottery in a matt finish. Watch for the Gouda name, which is usually a part of the backstamp of the various manufacturers.

Ashtray, glossy, w/matchbook holder, Ponseau, date tree, 6" dia ..**300.00**
Bowl, glossy, incurvate rim, Oriental, house mk, 2½x7¾" **300.00**
Bowl, 8-petal flower w/in, Barbara, house mk, 1926, 2½x12" **600.00**
Candlestick, glossy, spiral stem w/in 4 hdls, dome ft, 8½" **300.00**
Candlestick, mc on cream, Gandia, house mk, drilled, 18" **375.00**
Candlesticks, hdl arches over rim, flared base, Gluck, 14½", pr .**635.00**
Candlesticks, scrolls/floral, Blanca, house mk, 15", pr **575.00**
Decanter, floral/appl beads, Madeleine, house mk, 1928, 10" **230.00**
Ewer, bl w/wht paisley, angle hdl, Royal Plazuid, 1950s, 11" **70.00**
Inkwell, Ivora & mc florals on wht, attached tray, 10½" L **275.00**
Jar, cobwebs/butterflies, mc on wht gloss, Plateel, 21x6", EX **460.00**
Jar, geometrics, flat lid, Krias/Koninklyk, 6½x5" **430.00**
Lantern, rtcl cylinder, cone top w/4 sm appl cones, Kelat, 12" ...**700.00**
Lantern, rtcl cylinder, cone top w/4 sm appl cones, 9" **300.00**

Vase, large stylized multicolor florals along shoulder, #0123, 16⅜x10", NM, $1,000.00.

Vase, floral, mc on gr gloss, blk rim/ft, NEMO, rstr, 10", pr **575.00**
Vase, floral band, hdls, shouldered, Percy, 1923, 10", pr **375.00**
Vase, floral band, mc on blk, short collar neck, ovoid, 7x5" **300.00**
Vase, floral in reserve, geometric bands, Oud, 14x5" **400.00**
Vase, geometrics: dmns/circles/Vs, mc on dk brn, 6x5" **230.00**
Vase, horse-drawn cart/woods, glossy, Paijace, house mk, 13" **500.00**
Vase, leaves, slim w/low hdls, Corona, tree/house mk, 14", pr **690.00**
Vase, Nouveau design by Zuid, glossy, ca 1896, 11" **650.00**
Vase, stylized leafy band/geometrics, mc on blk, 10½" **450.00**
Vase, 3 wavy floral bands, Majja, house mk, 10x7" **375.00**

Grand Feu

The Grand Feu Art Pottery existed from 1912 until about 1918 in Los Angeles, California. It was owned and operated by Cornelius Brauckman, who developed a method of producing remarkably artistic glaze effects achieved through extremely high temperatures during the firing process. The body of the ware, as a result of the intense heat (2500 degrees), was vitrified as the glaze matured. Brauckman signed his ware either with his name or 'Grand Feu Pottery, L.A. California.' His work is regarded today as being among the finest art pottery ever produced in the United States. Examples are rare and command high prices on today's market.

Vase, brn matt mottle, bottle shape, Brauckman Art, 5½x3" 950.00
Vase, complex dk gr/burgundy glossy flambe, flared neck, 5½" .2,200.00
Vase, feathered silver-gr/brn w/mirror gloss, 4½x4¼" 3,000.00
Vase, grs/brns/rabbit's fur flambe, cup neck, bulb bottom, 11" .7,750.00
Vase, mustard/lt gr/mahog matt flambe on brn/bl gloss, 9" 6,750.00
Vase, pocked bl/gr/gray/blk crystalline, cylinder w/wide ft, 7" .3,500.00

Graniteware

Graniteware, made of a variety of metals with enamel coatings, derives its name from its appearance. The speckled, swirled, or mottled effect of the vari-colored enamels may look like granite — but there the resemblance stops. It wasn't especially durable! Expect at least minor chipping if you plan to collect.

Graniteware was featured in 1876 at Phily's Expo. It was massproduced in quantity, and enough of it has survived to make at least the common items easily affordable. Condition, color, shape, and size are important considerations in evaluating an item; cobalt blue and white, green and white, brown and white, and old red and white swirled items are unusual, thus more expensive. Pieces of heavier weight, seam constructed, riveted, and those with wooden handles and tin or matching graniteware lids are usually older.

For further study we recommend *The Collector's Encyclopedia of Graniteware, Colors, Shapes, and Values*, Books I and II, by our advisor, Helen Greguire. Both are available from the author. For information on how to order, see her listing in the Directory under New York. For the address of the National Graniteware Society, see the section on Clubs, Newsletters, and Catalogs.

Ashtray, red, Polar Ware advertising, ca 1928, M 185.00
Baking pan, cobalt & wht lg mottle w/blk, wht int, oblong, EX .150.00
Baking pan, gr & wht lg swirl w/cobalt, Emerald Ware, hdls, M .295.00
Baking pan, gray med mottle, molded hdls, oblong, EX 40.00
Batter jug, gray med mottle, bail hdl, spout lid, L&G Mfg, NM .310.00
Bed pan, bl & wht fine mottle w/cobalt, wht top, NM 85.00
Bowl, cereal; bl & wht relish w/pewter trim, M 165.00
Bowl, mixing; bl & wht lg mottle w/blk trim, wht int, NM 95.00
Bowl, serving; brn & wht lg swirl w/blk trim, wht int, M 135.00
Bread box, wht w/blk trim & letters, rnd, vented lid, EX 125.00
Bread pan, bl solid, wht int, oblong, ring for hanging, EX 60.00
Bread riser, bl & wht med mottle w/blk, wht int, domed lid, NM .425.00
Bucket, berry; Chrysolite swirl w/matching lid, bail hdl, M 600.00
Bucket, cobalt & wht lg swirl, w/lid, med, M 425.00
Bucket, gr & wht med mottle, Elite Austria, w/lid, M 185.00
Butter carrier, gray med mottle, strap hdl, med, NM 250.00
Canister, sugar; wht w/dk bl trim, recessed strap hdl, EX 95.00
Canister set, orange solid w/blk, Elite Czeclo..., 5-pc, M 350.00
Chamber pail, wht w/bl mottling, wooden bail, w/lid, lg, NM 185.00
Chamber pot, cobalt & wht lg swirl, blk trim, w/lid, lg, M 325.00
Churn, gr shading to ivory, floor model, complete, EX 750.00
Coffee biggin, cobalt & wht checkered w/red trim, 3-pc, M 425.00
Coffee biggin, red & wht med swirl w/red trim, 4-pc, M 595.00
Coffee biggin, solid yel w/blk trim, 5-pc, M 195.00
Coffee biggin, wht w/blk trim, 4-pc, M 125.00
Coffee boiler, Chrysolite lg swirl w/dk bl trim, M 495.00
Coffee boiler, lav & wht lg swirl, NM 350.00
Coffee carrier, bl & wht checks w/red, wire ears, tin lid, EX 265.00
Coffeepot, gr & wht lg swirl (Emerald Ware), NM 550.00

Coffeepot, med brn & wht mottle, brass-plated lid, wood hdl, M .395.00

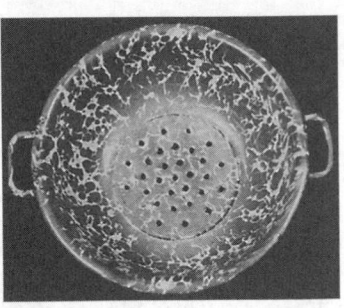

Colander, blue and white large mottle inside and out, 4½" from handle to handle, M, $325.00.

Colander, cobalt & wht lg swirl w/blk, wht int, deep, M 395.00
Colander, gr shaded to ivory w/blk, Old Ivory Ware, NM 135.00
Colander, wht w/cobalt trim, fancy perforations, NM 45.00
Cream can, bl & wht lg swirl w/blk, wire bail, EX 525.00
Cream can, lav-bl & wht lg swirl, wire bail, NM 395.00
Creamer, bl & wht lg mottle, bl strap hdl, squatty, EX 395.00
Cup, Azure Marble Enamel, wht w/bl marbling, blk trim, NM 55.00
Cup & saucer, cream w/gr trim, Golden Rule..., M 75.00
Cup & saucer, lt bl & wht lg mottle w/blk, EX 135.00
Dinner bucket, gray lg mottle, seamed, oval, complete, NM 395.00
Dipper, bl & wht lg mottle w/bl, flared, hdl, M 110.00
Dipper, cobalt & wht lg swirl w/blk, flat hook hdl, M 135.00
Dipper, cocoa; bl shaded, wht int, blk trim, Bluebelle Ware, EX ..295.00
Dishpan, brn & wht lg swirl w/brn, wht int, 1970s, M 55.00
Double boiler, bl & wht lg swirl, Lava Ware, EX 395.00
Double boiler, cobalt & wht lg swirl w/blk, seamless, M 525.00
Dustpan, dk bl w/blk appl hdl, seamless, NM 225.00
Egg cup, wht w/blk trim, M 95.00
Egg dish, bl & wht lg mottle w/blk, wht int, 4⅞" dia, NM 285.00
Fish poacher, lt bl & wht mottle, w/insert, Elite Austria, NM 325.00
Foot tub, cobalt & wht lg swirl w/blk, oval, eyelet, EX 225.00
Fruit jar filler, gray lg mottle, riveted strap hdl, EX 35.00
Fry pan, bl & wht lg swirl w/blk, wht int, sm, EX 135.00
Fry pan, Emerald Ware, gr & wht lg swirl, wht int, lg, EX 395.00
Fry pan, lav-bl & wht lg swirl w/blk, wht int, med, EX 185.00
Funnel, brn shaded to lt brn, wht int, squatty, NM 115.00
Funnel, gray solid, squatty, pierced hanging ear, EX 40.00
Funnel, old red & wht lg mottle w/red trim, foreign, EX 210.00
Grater, bl & wht med mottle, EX 325.00
Grater, cobalt solid, lg, NM 120.00
Grater, wht w/lt bl chicken wire, revolving type, NM 195.00
Griddle, gray lg mottle, oval, riveted hdl, L&G Mfg, EX 295.00
Kettle, bl & wht lg swirl w/blk, Maslin style, Azure Ware, M 210.00
Kettle, preserving; bl & wht lg mottle w/blk, lipped, NM 265.00
Ladle, soup; gr & wht lg swirl w/dk bl hdl, wht int, EX 300.00
Ladle, soup; gray med mottle, blk wooden trn hdl, NM 125.00
Lunch bucket, brn & wht lg swirl, oval, 3-pc 1,800.00
Measure, bl & wht lg mottle w/dk bl, seamed lip, sm, EX 165.00
Measure, brn & wht lg swirl w/dk bl, riveted lip, lg, NM 625.00
Measure, gray lg mottle, seamed, strap hdl, sm, M 195.00
Measure, old red & wht med mottle, seamless, foreign, med, EX ...425.00
Milk can, bl & wht fine mottle w/dk bl, bail hdl, lg, NM 295.00
Milk can, brn & wht lg swirl w/blk, wire bail, NM 995.00
Milk can, gr & wht lg swirl w/bl trim, Emerald Ware, NM 1,195.00
Milk can, reddish-brn & wht relish, Boston style, EX 125.00
Mold, bl & wht fine mottle int/ext, rnd tube style, M 225.00
Mold, fish form, wht solid, ring for hanging, lg, NM 175.00
Mold, gray lg mottle, ribbed tube style, M 95.00
Mold, ice cream; scalloped, wht, ring for hanging, EX 60.00
Mold, shell form, wht solid, oblong, ring for hanging, EX 85.00

Muffin pan, bl & wht lg mottle, wht int, 8-cup, EX 295.00
Muffin pan, gray lg mottle, deep, 12-cup, NM 75.00
Muffin pan, gray mottle, wire fr, strap hdls, 12-cup, EX 195.00
Muffin pan, lg gray mottle, Turk's turban style, 12-cup, EX 150.00
Mug, bl & wht lg swirl w/blk trim, NM 65.00
Mug, cobalt & wht lg swirl, 2-cup, NM 95.00
Mug, gr & wht lg swirl w/blk trim, Emerald Ware, lg, EX 150.00
Pail, water; bl & wht lg mottle w/blk, wooden bail, sm, M 150.00
Pail, water; bl & wht lg swirl w/blk, wht int, bail hdl, NM 200.00
Pail, water; Chrysolite lg swirl, w/lid, 9⅛x4¾", NM 1,000.00
Pie plate, cobalt & wht lg swirl w/blk, wht int, deep, EX 85.00
Pitcher, molasses; brn shaded, wht int, NM 295.00
Pitcher, water; bl & wht lg swirl w/blk, EX 140.00
Pitcher, water; bl & wht wavy mottling w/blk, 3-coated, M 650.00
Pitcher, water; brn & wht relish w/dk bl, NM 195.00
Pitcher, water; brn/cobalt/wht lg swirl w/bl flecks & trim, EX 175.00
Pitcher, water; gr shaded to lt gr, blk hdl & trim, NM 150.00
Pitcher, water; gray lg mottle, welded hdl, Nesco Ware, M 225.00
Pitcher & bowl, red solid w/blk trim & hdl, squatty, EX 200.00
Plate, aqua & wht lg swirl, cobalt trim, wht int, 6½", EX 110.00
Plate, cobalt & wht lg swirl w/blk trim, wht int, M 125.00
Plate, soup; red & wht lg swirl w/bl trim, ltweight, 1960s, M 45.00
Platter, bl & wht lg swirl, wht int, oval, M 395.00
Rack, utensil; solid blk w/3 gray utensils w/blk hdls, M 300.00
Roaster, Bl Dmn Ware, bl & wht lg swirl w/blk, 3-pc, NM 375.00
Roaster, cobalt & wht lg swirl, w/insert, flat lid, lg, NM 295.00
Roaster, gray med mottle, oval, 2-pc, sm, M 195.00
Rolling pin, wht w/gray screw-on hdls, CI base, M 975.00
Salt box, solid red, Genuine Swedish... on bottom, M 225.00
Salt box, wht w/lt bl chicken wire, hanging, EX 225.00
Saucepan, bl & wht lg swirl w/blk, wht int, convex, EX 160.00
Saucer, bl & wht med mottle w/bl trim, wht int, NM 60.00
Scoop, candy; gray med mottle, NM 275.00
Scoop, thumb; gray lg mottle, M 195.00
Skimmer, cobalt & wht med mottle w/gr veins, blk hdl, NM 195.00
Skimmer, gray med mottle, preforated, sm, NM 55.00
Soap dish, bl solid, fluted bottom, hole for hanging, EX 60.00
Soap holder, red solid, SABE (soap) in wht, EX 85.00
Spatula, gray med mottle, NM 85.00
Spatula or turner, wht w/brick red hdl, perforated, EX 55.00
Spoon, cream & gr, hole in hdl, NM 25.00
Spoon, mixing; bl & wht lg mottle w/blk hdl, wht int, EX 75.00
Spoon, tasting; wht w/bl lg mottled veins, side hdl, NM 60.00
Stew pan, bl & wht lg mottle w/blk, wht int, deep, EX 115.00
Stew pan, cobalt & wht lg mottle w/blk, wht int, shallow, EX ...225.00
Strainer, wht w/bl chicken wire, hdl w/kettle hook, EX 130.00
Sugar bowl, morning glories on wht, pewter lid/hdls/trim, M 395.00
Syrup, gr & wht lg swirl (Chrysolite), pewter lid, M 995.00
Tea steeper, gr & wht lg swirl (Chrysolite), w/granite lid, NM ...375.00
Tea strainer, wht w/cobalt rim, perforated, M 55.00
Teakettle, bl & wht fine mottle, lg, EX 235.00
Teakettle, bl & wht lg swirl w/blk, wht int, lg, EX 310.00
Teakettle, gr & wht lg mottled Snow on Mountain, lg, EX 155.00
Teakettle, gray mottle, L&G Mfg, sm, NM 225.00
Teapot, dk bl & wht relish, copper-plated lid, L&G Mfg, EX 295.00
Teapot, gray mottle w/pewter trim, scalloped top edge, lg, M 295.00
Teapot, gray mottle w/pewter trim, squatty, metal bottom, M 395.00
Teapot, Iris swirl, bulbous, gooseneck spout, NM 750.00
Teapot, pk roses on wht enameling, pewter trim, lg, M 295.00
Teapot, red & wht med swirl, 1960s, M 125.00
Teapot, 3-color sponged effect, hexagon, Elite, NM 175.00
Toothbrush holder, solid wht, wall type, holds 3, EX 145.00
Tray, cobalt & wht lg swirl w/blk trim, wht int, oblong, NM 295.00
Tray, gray med mottle, grooved bottom, rnd, NM 110.00

Tray, red & wht swirl w/dk bl trim, rnd, ltweight, 1960s, NM 65.00
Trivet, aqua bl w/3 molded ft on CI, F&W ETI mk, M 75.00
Tumbler, bl & wht lg mottle w/blk trim, M 65.00
Tumbler, dk bl solid w/blk trim, Ski Bl label, M 110.00
Tureen, soup; wht w/bl chicken wire, rnd, ftd, w/lid, M 295.00
Wash basin, cobalt & wht lg swirl, w/eyelet, EX 125.00
Wash basin, lt bl & wht med swirl, w/eyelet, child sz, M 195.00

Green Opaque

Introduced in 1887 by the New England Glass Company, this ware is very scarce due to the fact that it was produced for less than one year. It is characterized by its soft green color and a wavy band of gold reserving a mottled blue metallic stain. It is usually found in satin; examples with a shiny finish are extremely rare.

Bowl, 4x8", M 1,150.00
Box, powder; NM gold mottling on bowl & lid, 4x6¼" 1,150.00
Cruet, orig stopper 1,150.00
Mug, 2¼" 500.00
Punch cup 350.00
Punch cup, worn decor, 2½" 225.00
Toothpick holder, gold trim 1,150.00
Tumbler, EX gold & mottling 665.00
Tumbler, lemonade; w/hdl, 5" 900.00

Tumbler, M mottling, 3½", $800.00.

Vase, flared, M gold & mottling, 6" 900.00
Vase, 14-rib ovoid w/flaring rim, VG gold & mottling, 6" 500.00

Greenaway, Kate

Kate Greenaway was an English artist who lived from 1846 to 1901. She gained worldwide fame as an illustrator of children's books, drawing children clothed in the styles worn by proper English and American boys and girls of the very early 1800s. Her book, *Under the Willow Tree*, published in 1878, was the first of many. Her sketches appeared in leading magazines, and her greeting cards were in great demand. Manufacturers of china, pottery, and metal products copied her characters to decorate children's dishes, tiles, and salt and pepper shakers as well as many other items. See also Almanacs; Napkin Rings.

Almanac, Almanack for 1886, London, Routledge, 1st ed, EX+ ..175.00
Almanac, 1886, wht leather, Sangorski/Sutcliffe 475.00
Biscuit jar, ceramic, boy w/tinted features, w/lid 165.00
Book, A Apple Pie, muslin, Saalfield, 1907, VG+ 200.00
Book, April Baby's Book of Tunes, Macmillan, 1st ed, 1900, EX .450.00

Book, Birthday Book for Children, Greenaway illus, 1880, VG .145.00
Book, Kate Greenaway's Alphabet, London, 1880, EX 175.00
Book, Language of Flowers, Greenaway illus, Morocco cover, VG ..250.00
Book, Pied Piper of Hamlin, Greenaway illus, NM 75.00
Book, pnt; Little Folks, hardcover, early, EX 65.00
Book, Under the Willow, Routledge, 1st edition, orig cloth 150.00
Butter pat, children playing 40.00
Inkwell, boy & girl, bronze 195.00
Match holder, ornate SP, girl in fancy clothes, Tufts 195.00
Pencil holder, pnt porc 20.00
Pickle castor, bl, in SP fr w/2 girls, blown-out florals 455.00
Plate, ABC, girl in lg hat, Staffordshire, 7" 95.00
Scarf, Greenaway illus on silk, early, EX 65.00
Stickpin holder, SP, girl figural, Meriden, 4" 125.00
Toothpick holder, bsk, girl sits on stump, basket on bk 40.00
Wall pocket, ceramic, 6 girls on open book form, 6x9x3" 125.00

Greentown Glass

Greentown glass is a term referring to the product of the Indiana Tumbler and Goblet Company of Greentown, Indiana, ca 1894 to 1903. Their earlier pressed glass patterns were #11, a pseudo-cut glass design; #137, Pleat Band; and #200, Austrian. Another line, Dewey, was designed in 1898. Many lovely colors were produced in addition to crystal. Jacob Rosenthal, who was later affiliated with Fenton, developed his famous chocolate glass in 1900. The rich, shaded opaque brown glass was an overnight success. Two new patterns, Leaf Bracket and Cactus, were designed to display the glass to its best advantage, but previously existing molds were also used. In only three years Rosenthal developed yet another important color formula, golden agate. The Holly Amber pattern was designed especially for its production. The Dolphin covered dish with a fish finial is perhaps the most common and easily recognized piece ever produced. Other animal dishes were also made; all are highly collectible. There have been many repros — not all are marked! The symbol (+) at the end of some of the following lines was used to indicate items that have been reproduced.

Our advisors for this category are Jerry and Sandi Garrett; they are listed in the Directory under Indiana. See the Pattern Glass section for clear pressed glass; only colored items are listed here.

Animal dish, bird w/berry, amber (+) 325.00
Animal dish, bird w/berry, cobalt 400.00
Animal dish, bird w/berry, Nile gr 1,950.00
Animal dish, cat on hamper, amber or teal bl, tall 325.00
Animal dish, cat on hamper, canary, low 700.00
Animal dish, cat on hamper, chocolate, tall 425.00
Animal dish, cat on hamper, wht opaque, tall 475.00
Animal dish, dolphin, beaded; emerald gr 625.00
Animal dish, dolphin, beaded; Nile gr 2,850.00
Animal dish, dolphin, sawtooth; chocolate (+) 250.00
Animal dish, dolphin, sawtooth; teal bl (+) 550.00
Animal dish, fighting cocks, emerald gr 1,250.00
Animal dish, fighting cocks, teal bl 1,250.00
Animal dish, hen on nest, chocolate 800.00
Animal dish, hen on nest, cobalt 450.00
Animal dish, hen on nest, emerald gr 200.00
Animal dish, rabbit, emerald gr (+) 250.00
Animal dish, rabbit, teal bl 225.00
Austrian, bowl, canary, 8" 300.00
Austrian, butter dish, canary 425.00
Austrian, compote, canary, low ped 225.00
Austrian, cordial, amber 250.00
Austrian, creamer, amber, child sz 225.00
Austrian, creamer, canary, no rim, lg 185.00

Austrian, creamer, emerald gr, 4¼" 200.00
Austrian, nappy, canary, w/lid 265.00
Austrian, punch cup, bluish-purple 300.00
Austrian, spooner, chocolate, child sz 225.00
Austrian, sugar bowl, canary, w/lid, child sz 225.00
Austrian, sugar bowl, chocolate, w/lid, 2½" 175.00
Austrian, wine, emerald gr 200.00
Beehive, tumbler, chocolate 550.00
Brazen Shield, butter dish, bl 265.00
Brazen Shield, creamer, bl 125.00
Brazen Shield, goblet, bl 175.00
Brazen Shield, sugar bowl, bl, w/lid 185.00
Cactus, butter dish, chocolate 200.00
Cactus, creamer, Nile gr, 2¼" 300.00
Cactus, nappy, chocolate 165.00
Cactus, sugar bowl, canary, w/lid 275.00
Cord Drapery, bowl, amber, 8" 165.00
Cord Drapery, bowl, bl, hand fluted, ftd, 6¼" 200.00
Cord Drapery, bowl, emerald gr, oval, 2 szs, ea 165.00
Cord Drapery, compote, canary, hand fluted, 10" 550.00
Cord Drapery, pitcher, bl 275.00
Cord Drapery, tumbler, chocolate 275.00
Cupid, creamer, wht opaque 100.00
Cupid, spooner, chocolate 325.00
Cupid, sugar bowl, Nile gr, w/lid 375.00
Dewey, bowl, amber, 8" 85.00
Dewey, butter dish, canary, 4" 100.00
Dewey, butter dish, Nile gr, 5" 400.00
Dewey, creamer, emerald gr, 4" 50.00
Dewey, cruet, amber, w/stopper 175.00
Dewey, mug, canary 85.00
Dewey, pitcher, emerald gr 150.00
Dewey, sauce, amber 40.00
Dewey, sauce dish, canary, ...50.00
Dewey, serpentine tray, canary, sm 65.00
Dewey, spooner, Nile gr, 5" 250.00
Early Diamond, pitcher, emerald gr 200.00
Early Diamond, tumbler, bl 150.00
Fleur-de-lis, celery holder, chocolate, 5¾" 365.00
Fleur-de-lis, creamer, chocolate 210.00
Fleur-de-lis, nappy, chocolate, 2-hdld 450.00
Fleur-de-lis, sugar bowl, chocolate, w/lid 250.00
Greentown Daisy, butter dish, chocolate 270.00
Greentown Daisy, creamer, wht opaque, w/lid 60.00
Greentown Daisy, sugar bowl, frosted emerald gr, w/lid 85.00
Herringbone Buttress, bowl, amber, 6¼" 275.00
Herringbone Buttress, butter dish, emerald gr 345.00
Herringbone Buttress, cordial, amber, 3" 365.00
Herringbone Buttress, cracker jar, emerald gr 375.00
Herringbone Buttress, nappy, emerald gr 225.00
Herringbone Buttress, wine, olive gr 175.00
Holly, toothpick, Rose Agate 4,500.00
Holly, tumbler, chocolate, beads on rim 5,800.00
Holly Amber, bowl, 7½" 675.00

**Holly Amber, creamer,
$800.00.**

Holly Amber, cake stand 2,400.00
Holly Amber, compote, jelly; low ped base, w/lid, 4¼" 1,450.00
Holly Amber, compote, w/lid, 7¼" 1,750.00
Holly Amber, mug, 4" (+) 425.00
Holly Amber, nappy, hdld 600.00
Holly Amber, shaker 475.00
Holly Amber, spooner 750.00
Holly Amber, toothpick holder, lg 725.00
Leaf Bracket, bowl, chocolate, 8" 100.00
Leaf Bracket, cruet, chocolate, w/stopper 225.00
Leaf Bracket, relish tray, chocolate, 7¼x4½" 95.00
Leaf Bracket, tumbler, chocolate 70.00
Mug, deer & oak tree, chocolate 450.00
Mug, indoor drinking scene, Nile gr, no hdl 435.00
Mug, outdoor drinking scene, lt cobalt 340.00
Mug, pepper box, chocolate 325.00
Mug, Serenade; amber, 4¾" 135.00
Mug, Serenade; deep bl, 4¾" 350.00
Novelty, cuff set, teal bl 400.00
Novelty, dustpan, canary 175.00
Novelty, mitted hand, Nile gr 600.00
Novelty, scotch thistle, chocolate 1,000.00
Novelty, wheelbarrow, amber 150.00
Novelty, wheelbarrow, chocolate (+) 875.00
Pattern #11, goblet, clear 35.00
Pattern #11, plate, gr, 8" sq 80.00
Pattern #11, vase, gr, 6" 60.00
Pleat Band, compote, chocolate, plain stem, smooth rim, 4¼" ...175.00
Pleat Band, shaker, canary 65.00
Pleat Band, shaker, teal bl 65.00
Pleat Band, wine, canary 150.00
Scalloped Flange, tumbler, chocolate 150.00
Shuttle, mug, chocolate 85.00
Shuttle, spooner, chocolate 400.00
Teardrop & Tassel, bowl, emerald gr, 8¼" 185.00
Teardrop & Tassel, butter dish, amber 275.00
Teardrop & Tassel, compote, Nile gr, w/lid, 6½" 450.00
Teardrop & Tassel, creamer, bl 175.00
Teardrop & Tassel, goblet, emerald gr 300.00
Teardrop & Tassel, spooner, chocolate 300.00
Toothpick holder, dog's head, frosted bl 350.00
Toothpick holder, picture fr, teal bl 300.00
Toothpick holder, sheaf of wheat, bl 275.00
Toothpick holder, sheaf of wheat, Nile gr 325.00
Toothpick holder, witch's head, chocolate (+) 800.00
Tumbler, Paneled, chocolate 500.00

Grueby

William Henry Grueby joined the firm of the Low Art Tile Works at the age of fifteen and in 1894, after several years of experience in the production of architectural tiles, founded his own plant, the Grueby Faience Company, in Boston, Massachusetts. Grueby began experimenting with the idea of producing art pottery and had soon perfected a fine glaze (soft and without gloss) in shades of blue, gray, yellow, brown, and his most successful, cucumber green. In 1900 his exhibit at the Paris Exposition Universelle won three gold medals.

Grueby pottery was hand thrown and hand decorated in the Arts and Crafts style. Vertically thrust stylized leaves and flowers in relief were the most common decorative devices. Tiles continued to be an important product, unique (due to the matt glaze decoration) as well as durable. Grueby tiles were often a full inch thick. Obviously incompatible with the Art Nouveau style, the artware was discontinued soon after

1910. The ware is marked in one of several ways: 'Grueby Pottery, Boston, USA'; 'Grueby, Boston, Mass.'; or 'Grueby Faience.' The artware is often artist signed. Our advisor for this category is David Rago; he is listed in the Directory under New Jersey.

Bowl, alligatored deep cucumber gr, ochre/blk int, 5½x9" 700.00
Bowl, gr, rnd ft, 3x4½" 345.00
Bowl, gr, 2 rows overlapping leaves, sgn ER, 3x6" 1,380.00
Bowl, heavy rust drip on bsk, gr gloss int, 2½x8" 300.00
Bowl, lt bl, 1¼x4" 250.00
Bowl vase, gr, 3x7" 800.00
Paperweight, scarab, gr, 2¼" 325.00
Paperweight, scarab, gr, sm rpr to base, 4" L 375.00
Paperweight, scarab, silvery gr, 4", EX 600.00
Tile, candle, yel on gr, hammered copper mt, unmk, 6" 1,500.00
Tile, candle in chamberstick, gr/wht on bl, sgn DC, fr, 6x6" ...1,600.00
Tile, fountain in garden, 5-color, fr, 4x4" 450.00
Tile, geometrics, ivory over brn clay bkground, fr, 4" 175.00
Tile, horses, 5-color, sgn DC, 6x6" 1,000.00
Tile, house/trees/clouds, 5-color, fr, 4x4" 650.00
Tile, lg tree/clouds, from Greenwald installation, 6½x6" 2,400.00
Tile, lg turtle, brns/cream/gr/yel, sgn KC, 6x6" 800.00
Tile, mermaid, curdled oatmeal on gr, oak fr, 6x6" 1,000.00
Tile, mermaid, ochre, red clay exposed, #657, 6" 285.00
Tile, molded bunny, terra cotta, wide oak fr, 4" 300.00
Tile, monk playing cello, bl/brn, no mk, 6x6" 450.00
Tile, sailing vessel, 5-color, sgn MD, 4x4" 260.00
Tile, Spanish galleon, brn/wht on bl, new fr, 6x6" 900.00
Tile, stylized pine trees, 4-color, no mk, 6x6", NM 1,800.00
Tile, swans/stylized trees, 5-color, 4", EX 325.00
Tile, winged beast/sun, 3-color, oak fr, 6" 500.00
Tile, 2 winged angels/family crest, brn/wht, no mk, 6x6" 325.00
Vase, bl, cream lily buds at rim, leaves at base, sgn RE, 14" 3,700.00
Vase, cream, bulbous w/long neck, 3x2¼" 300.00
Vase, cucumber gr, vertical ribbing, collar rim, 5½x3¾" 750.00
Vase, cucumber gr w/speckles, 9 leaf panels, RE, 4¾x5½" 1,300.00
Vase, curdled lt bl, arches/ribbing, sgn RE, sm rpr, 5x3" 750.00
Vase, dk gr mottle, shouldered, 3" 425.00
Vase, dk gr w/lg area of exposed clay, cylindrical, 8" 1,000.00
Vase, gr, cylinder w/bun base w/2 rows leaves, Erickson, 13" ...3,500.00
Vase, gr, ivory/mint gr wide leaves & buds alternate, 7x12" 6,500.00

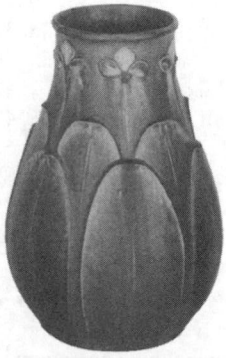

Vase, green, overlapping leaves and trefoil yellow flowers, 13x8", $13,200.00.

Vase, gr, leaves & buds, sgn Erickson, 10x9" 2,645.00
Vase, gr, leaves at wide base, long-stem yel buds, 4¾" 2,900.00
Vase, gr, leaves on bulbous base, sgn ERF, 7x4½" 1,400.00
Vase, gr, leaves on bulbous body, can neck, sgn Post, 7x8" 1,700.00
Vase, gr, lg upright leaves w/yel buds, sgn Post, 12x6" 6,300.00
Vase, gr, overlapping leaves & trefoil yel florals, 13x8", M ...13,200.00
Vase, gr, tooled 'razor clam' leaves, 7½x4¼" 2,200.00
Vase, gr, tooled panels, bulbous w/cylinder neck, 6½x4½" 1,000.00

Vase, gr, 10 leaves (5 end in open scrolls at rim), 9", EX 5,000.00
Vase, gr, 3 repeats: yel (3rd is ecru) bud/4 leaves, 8½" 4,000.00
Vase, gr, 4 lg leaves on ovoid, sgn Seaman, 8x4" 1,950.00
Vase, gr, 5 tooled thin leaves, sgn R Erickson, 3½" 495.00
Vase, gr, 5 wide leaves, sm ring neck, sgn MS, 5x3¾" 750.00
Vase, gr, 7x3½" 545.00
Vase, leathery dk bl, full-length leaves, sgn MCJ, 8½x4¾" 1,600.00
Vase, leathery gr, waisted neck, ftd, w/lid, #1279, 7", EX 1,500.00
Vase, lt bl, lt ribbing, sgn Post, ovoid w/waisted neck, 8" 900.00
Vase, lt bl, 4½x3½" 345.00
Vase, lt gr/chalk wht, cylinder w/short collar neck, 4" 350.00
Vase, mustard w/flecks, prominent finger rings, 2x4" 650.00
Vase, oatmeal, bulbous, sm rpr, 4½" 375.00
Vase, ochre, no mk, 3x3½" 460.00
Vase, warty bl, wide-rib sphere, sgn Ellen Farrington, 3½" 900.00

Gustavsberg

Gustavsberg Pottery, founded near Stockholm, Sweden, in the late 1700s, manufactured faience, creamware, and porcelain in the English taste until the end of the 19th century. During the 20th century, the factory has produced some inventive modernistic designs, often signed by their artists. Wilhelm Kage (1889-1960) is best remembered for Argenta, a stoneware body decorated in silver overlay, introduced in the 1930s. Usually a mottled green, Argenta can also be found in cobalt blue and white. Other lines included Cintra (an exceptionally translucent porcelain), Farsta (copper-glazed ware), and Farstarust (iron oxide geometric overlay). Designer Stig Lindberg's work, which dates from the 1940s through the early 1970s, includes slab-built figures and a full range of tableware. Some pieces of Gustavsberg are dated.

Bowl, Argenta, silver o/l fish on gr, stoneware, 6½" 315.00
Bowl, Argenta, silver o/l lion on gr mottle, anchor mk 9½" 365.00
Bowl, wht crystalline, 2 parts of rim folded in, 4x7x11" 275.00
Cat, cvd/pnt stripes, bl/blk on gray, 12" L 375.00
Pitcher, leaves, gr on wht, Stig Lindberg, earthenware, 5x6" 40.00
Plate, Argenta, silver o/l fruit basket, scalloped, 7" 260.00
Vase, Argenta, silver o/l fish on gr matt, #1042, 5x5" 375.00
Vase, Argenta, silver o/l nude seated on log, sqd/bulbous, 9" 650.00
Vase, cvd flowers, bl on turq, sgn JE, angle shoulder, 5x5½" 250.00

Hagen-Renaker

Best known for their line of miniature animal figures, Hagen-Renaker was founded in Monrovia, California, in 1946. In addition to the animals, they made replicas of characters from several popular Disney films under license from the Disney Studio. The firm relocated in San Dimas in 1966, where they remain active to the present time. Their wares are sometimes marked with an incised 'HR,' a stamped 'Hagen-Renaker' or part of the name, or paper labels. For more information, we recommond *The Collector's Encyclopedia of California Pottery* by Jack Chipman. Another source of information is Hagen-Renaker Collectors Club (HRCC) listed in the Directory under Clubs, Newsletters, and Catalogs.

Bank, Thumper 350.00
Figurine, basset hound, Pedigree Dog 70.00
Figurine, blackbird, mini 8.00
Figurine, Bonnie, collie, Pedigree Dog, recumbent, 2" 65.00
Figurine, cat & kitten w/spilled pail of milk, mini 26.00
Figurine, Ching Wu, Siamese cat, 1954, 6½" 75.00
Figurine, Choo Choo, Pekinese puppy, sitting, 2" 25.00
Figurine, fox, sgn, 1950s, mini 20.00

Figurine, Lady, dog, Disney (later issues not Disney much less) 48.00
Figurine, lamb, 1950s, mini 15.00
Figurine, Marc, Heather, Designer's Workshop, 1954, 5" 200.00
Figurine, Masterson drafter horse 50.00
Figurine, Miss Pepper, foal, recumbent, brn 125.00
Figurine, Mops, English sheep dog, 3½" 25.00
Figurine, Patsy, Cocker Spaniel puppy, 2¾" 45.00
Figurine, Pekinese Ming Toy, Pekinese dog, 3" 40.00
Figurine, Persian cat, 6½" 35.00
Figurine, Robbie, Scottie dog, 2½" 35.00
Figurine, Sealyham terrier, 2" 25.00
Figurine, skunk, 1950s, mini, set of 3 ....25.00
Figurine, Sparkle, Persian kitten on bk, 2½" 25.00
Figurine, Starlight, Persian cat, 9½" 45.00
Figurine, Winston, English bulldog, 1954, 3½" 75.00

Hagenauer

Carl Hagenauer founded his metal workshops in Vienna in 1898. He was joined by his son Karl in 1919. They produced a wide range of stylized sculptural designs in both metal and wood.

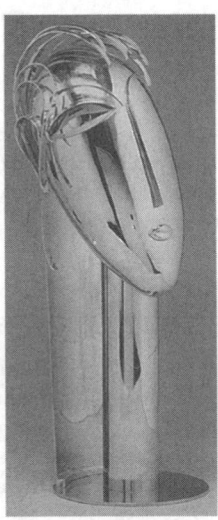

Head of a woman, chromium-plated metal, on circular base, signed, 16¾", $4,000.00.

African native w/bow & arrow, blk/gold, 7" 500.00
African native w/spear & shield, blk w/grass skirt, 7" 450.00
African w/spear & shield, blk/gold, 5½" 390.00
Angel (& devil), blk & brass, 2½", pr 140.00
Bowl, stylized goose w/curved neck form, hammered, 8x10" 920.00
Boy w/spear & shield, seated, blk/gold, 3½" 160.00
Bunnies w/long ears, bronzed patina, 1½", set of 4 ....350.00
Bust of bare-breasted lady, elongated features, hammered, 19" ..3,680.00
Bust of lady w/long hair & necklace, hammered brass, 18" 750.00
Candlestick/match holder, geometrics, hammered brass, 6" 460.00
Candlesticks, 4-arm, ea tube w/right angle, metal, 20", pr 3,680.00
Dachshund, nose to ground, curled strap ft, metal, 17" L 975.00
Dish, stylized fish form, metal, 19½" 690.00
Dish, stylized mouse, curly tail, metal, 21" L 975.00
Female bust, in profile, windblown hair, brass, no mk, 19½" ...5,500.00
Flowering branch, stylized, hammered brass, 29" 6,775.00
Giraffe lopes on hind legs, blk/gold, 7½" 690.00
Golfer in knickers (& lady), blk/gold, 3½", pr 550.00
Ink stand, figural male tennis player, metal/glass, 8½" 690.00
Javelin thrower, metal, 11¼" 345.00
Lady golfer, club swung back over shoulder, brass, 15" 2,300.00
Lady golfer, preparing to tee off, brass, 15¾" 1,380.00

Lamp, seated stylized monkey gripping tree trunk, brass, 20" ...**3,700.00**
Mask, stylized boy, center fold, pointed chin, metal, 13½" **1,150.00**
Monkey, bronze, walking/scratching head, 4¾" **200.00**
Native girl kneels on oval, bronze w/brass arm bands, att, 11" **800.00**
Native girl w/hair in lg knot, dancer's pose, blk, 9½" **590.00**
Nude, brass/copper neck rings, kneeling/arms behind head, 10" .**900.00**
Nude, knee bent, 1 arm over head, metal, 16½" **3,200.00**
Nude seated, w/copper ankle & wrist bracelets, 7x7" **800.00**
Nudes, she standing/in dance pose, he on 1 knee, brass, 44" ...**6,670.00**
Stag, cvd wood w/brass antlers, 1925, 15½" L **635.00**
Teapot, copper/brass/teak, open J-hdl, flaring, 6⅜", pr **490.00**
Tropical bird, by Rena Rosenthal, blk, 1½" **130.00**

Hair Weaving

A rather unusual craft became popular during the mid-1800s. Human hair was used to make jewelry (rings, bracelets, lockets, etc.) by braiding and interlacing fine strands of hair into hollow forms with pearls and beads added for effect. Hair wreaths were also made, often using hair from deceased family members as well as the living. They were displayed in deep satin-lined frames along with mementoes of the weaver or her departed kin. The fad was abandoned before the turn of the century. See also Mourning Collectibles.

Bracelet, woven hair, gold mts, gold suspended heart, EX **485.00**
Brooch, woven hair tube formed as bow, 18k gold mts, 1860s **335.00**
Cross, sterling & jet w/glass enclosure w/woven hair, 1860s **175.00**
Earrings, woven bell shape w/gold clappers, 18k gold wires **300.00**
Watch chain, mc braid w/gold eng mts **95.00**
Wreath, ornate floral design, mc hair, shadow-box fr, 16x14" **110.00**

Hall

The Hall China Company of East Liverpool, Ohio, was established in 1903. Their earliest product was whiteware toilet seats, mugs, jugs, etc. By 1920 their restaurant-type dinnerware and cookingware had become so successful that Hall was assured of a solid future. They continue today to be one of the country's largest manufacturers of this type of product.

Hall introduced the first of their famous teapots in 1920; new shapes and colors were added each year until about 1948, making them the largest teapot manufacturer in the world. These and the dinnerware lines of the thirties through the fifties have become popular collectibles. For more thorough study of the subject, we recommend *The Collector's Encyclopedia of Hall China* by Margaret and Kenn Whitmyer; their address may be found in the Directory under Ohio.

Blue Bouquet, creamer and sugar bowl, with lid, $32.00.

Acacia, bowl, Radiance, 7½" **19.00**
Acacia, custard, Radiance **8.00**
Beauty, casserole, rnd knob hdld **32.00**

Beauty, marmite, w/lid **35.00**
Blue Blossom, batter jug, Sundial **225.00**
Blue Blossom, canister, Radiance **150.00**
Blue Blossom, leftover, loop hdld **95.00**
Blue Blossom, teapot, Airflow **225.00**
Blue Bouquet, ball jug, #3 ....**65.00**
Blue Bouquet, bowl, cereal; D-style, 6" **10.00**
Blue Bouquet, bowl, salad; 9" **16.00**
Blue Bouquet, canister, pnt metal **11.00**
Blue Bouquet, coaster, pnt metal **5.00**
Blue Bouquet, creamer, Boston **12.00**
Blue Bouquet, electric percolator **225.00**
Blue Bouquet, pie baker **30.00**
Blue Bouquet, plate, cake **11.00**
Blue Bouquet, plate, D-style, 8¼" **9.50**
Blue Bouquet, pretzel jar **150.00**
Blue Bouquet, spoon **110.00**
Blue Garden, bowl, Thick Rim, 7½" **24.00**
Blue Garden, butter dish, Zephyr, 1-lb **300.00**
Blue Garden, jug, loop hdld **124.00**
Blue Willow, bowl, finger; 4" **25.00**
Blue Willow, teapot, Boston, 2-cup **185.00**
Cactus, bowl, onion soup; ind **50.00**
Cactus, cookie jar, Five Band **175.00**
Cactus, creamer, New York **25.00**
Cameo Rose, bowl, vegetable; w/lid **42.50**
Cameo Rose, gravy boat, w/underplate **30.00**
Cameo Rose, plate, 8" **8.00**
Cameo Rose, platter, oval, 13¼" **17.00**
Cameo Rose, teapot, 8-cup **55.00**
Carrot/Golden Carrot, ball jug, #3 ....**100.00**
Carrot/Golden Carrot, cookie jar, Zeisel **150.00**
Carrot/Golden Carrot, shakers, hdld, ea **20.00**
Carrot/Golden Carrot, teapot, Windshield **165.00**
Christmas Tree & Holly, bowl, plum pudding; 4½" **15.00**
Christmas Tree & Holly, cup **18.00**
Christmas Tree & Holly, mug, Irish coffee; 3-oz **20.00**
Clover/Golden Clover, casserole, Thick Rim **35.00**
Clover/Golden Clover, jug, #5, Radiance **45.00**
Crocus, bowl, fruit; D-style, 5½" **8.00**
Crocus, bowl, salad; 9" **20.00**
Crocus, casserole, Radiance **35.00**
Crocus, coffee dispenser, pnt metal **25.00**
Crocus, coffeepot, Meltdown **100.00**
Crocus, cup, D-style **12.00**
Crocus, custard **20.00**
Crocus, drip jar w/lid, Radiance **25.00**
Crocus, leftover, sq **65.00**
Crocus, mug, tankard style **45.00**
Crocus, plate, D-style, 9" **14.00**
Crocus, platter, D-style, oval, 13¼" **28.00**
Crocus, shakers, teardrop style, pr **50.00**
Crocus, soup tureen, w/clover lid **275.00**
Crocus, sugar bowl, w/lid, Meltdown **50.00**
Crocus, teapot, Aladdin **500.00**
Crocus, teapot, Streamline **350.00**
Eggshell, baker, fish-shape, Plaid pattern, 13½" **45.00**
Eggshell, bowl, salad; Red Dot, 9¾" **24.00**
Eggshell, custard, Red Dot **8.00**
Eggshell, mustard jar, Red Dot **32.00**
Fantasy, ball jug, #4 ....**125.00**
Fantasy, custard, Thick Rim **18.00**
Fantasy, syrup, Sundial **150.00**
Five Band, carafe, red or cobalt **125.00**

Five Band, cookie jar, colors other than red or cobalt 60.00
Five Band, syrup, red or cobalt 65.00
Flamingo, casserole, Radiance 40.00
Flamingo, shakers, hdld, ea 20.00
Floral Lattice, bowl, onion soup; ind 35.00
Floral Lattice, tea tile, rnd, 6" 65.00
Game Bird, creamer 16.00
Game Bird, mug, coffee; china 12.00
Game Bird, saucer 4.00
Golden Glo, bowl, salad; 9¾" 15.00
Golden Glo, creamer, Boston 12.00
Golden Glo, mug, #343 ....12.00
Heather Rose, bowl, fruit; 5¼" 6.00
Heather Rose, gravy boat, w/underplate 25.00
Heather Rose, pickle dish, 9" 18.00
Heather Rose, plate, cake 14.00
Heather Rose, sugar bowl, w/lid 15.00
Homewood, bowl, fruit; D-style, 5½" 6.00
Homewood, coffeepot, Terrace 50.00
Meadow Flower, canister, Radiance 115.00
Meadow Flower, jug, Five Band 55.00
Medallion, bowl, gr, #4, 7¼" 12.00
Medallion, casserole, ivory 12.00
Medallion, jug, ice lip, colors other than gr or ivory; 4-pt 30.00
Medallion, leftover, sq, ivory 18.00
Medallion, sugar bowl, w/lid, gr 15.00
Morning Glory, bowl, str sides, 6" 16.00
Morning Glory, casserole, Thick Rim 35.00
Mums, casserole, Radiance 35.00
Mums, custard, Medallion 16.00
Mums, plate, D-style, 6" 8.00
No 488, bowl, D-style, rnd, 9¼" 35.00
No 488, bowl, Radiance, 9" 25.00
No 488, coffeepot, Meltdown 125.00
No 488, drip jar, w/lid, Medallion 25.00
No 488, shirred egg dish 35.00
Orange Poppy, bowl, cereal; C-style, 6" 16.00
Orange Poppy, bowl, salad; 9" 20.00
Orange Poppy, bread box, pnt metal 40.00

Orange Poppy, casserole, oval, with lid, 8", $45.00.

Orange Poppy, casserole, oval, 11¾" 85.00
Orange Poppy, custard 8.00
Orange Poppy, leftover, loop hdl 45.00
Orange Poppy, match safe, pnt metal 25.00
Orange Poppy, plate, C-style, 6" 8.00
Orange Poppy, saucer, C-style 4.00
Orange Poppy, sifter, pnt metal 40.00
Orange Poppy, spoon 75.00
Orange Poppy, teapot, Melody 250.00
Orange Poppy, teapot, Windshield 250.00
Pastel Morning-Glory, bowl, Radiance, 9" 20.00
Pastel Morning-Glory, bowl, soup; D-style, flat, 8½" 18.00

Pastel Morning-Glory, casserole, Radiance 35.00
Pastel Morning-Glory, cup, St Denis 35.00
Pastel Morning-Glory, plate, D-style, 6" 6.00
Pastel Morning-Glory, shakers, Teardrops, ea 16.00
Pastel Morning-Glory, tea tile 50.00
Pastel Morning-Glory, teapot, Aladdin 150.00
Pert, Cadet, casserole, tab-hdld 18.00
Pert, Cadet, jug, 7½" 12.00
Pert, Chinese red, bean pot, tab-hdld 45.00
Pert, Chinese red, drip jar, tab-hdld 25.00
Pert, Chinese red, sugar bowl 12.00
Radiance, bowl, red or cobalt, #2, 5¼" 18.00
Radiance, canister, colors other than red, cobalt or ivory, 2-qt 90.00
Radiance, drip jar, ivory 8.00
Radiance, stack set, red or cobalt 110.00
Red Poppy, bowl, fruit; D-style, 5½" 6.00
Red Poppy, bowl, salad; 9" 18.00
Red Poppy, coffee dispenser, pnt metal 25.00
Red Poppy, coffeepot, Daniel 45.00
Red Poppy, cutting board, wooden 35.00
Red Poppy, hot pad, pnt metal 12.00
Red Poppy, jug, milk/syrup; Daniel, 4" 35.00
Red Poppy, mixer cover, plastic 25.00
Red Poppy, pie baker 28.00
Red Poppy, plate, D-style, 8¼" 8.00
Red Poppy, shakers, hdld, ea 13.00
Red Poppy, teapot, Aladdin 100.00
Red Poppy, tumbler, glass, clear 25.00
Red Poppy, waste can, oval, pnt metal, 12½" 32.00
Ribbed, bowl, russet/red, 8¼" 15.00
Ribbed, casserole, russet/red, 8" 26.00
Ribbed, ramekin, colors other than russet/red, 6-oz 6.00
Rose Parade, creamer, Pert 15.00
Rose Parade, jug, Pert, 7½" 35.00
Rose White, bowl, salad; 9" 22.00
Rose White, drip jar, w/lid, tab-hdld 24.00
Royal Rose, casserole, Thick Rim 30.00
Royal Rose, shakers, hdld, ea 15.00
Rx, butter dish, ¼-lb· 50.00
Rx, gravy boat, w/underplate 22.00
Sears' Arlington, bowl, oval, 9¼" 15.00
Sears' Arlington, plate, 10" 8.00
Sears' Arlington, platter, oval, 15½" 18.00
Sears' Fairfax, bowl, fruit; 5¼" 4.00
Sears' Fairfax, cup 3.50
Sears' Fairfax, sugar bowl, w/lid 15.00
Sears' Monticello, bowl, soup; flat, 8" 12.00
Sears' Monticello, bowl, vegetable; w/lid 30.00
Sears' Monticello, pickle dish, 9" 16.00
Sears' Monticello, saucer 2.00
Sears' Mount Vernon, casserole, w/lid, E-style 30.00
Sears' Mount Vernon, plate, E-style, 6½" 5.00
Sears' Mount Vernon, platter, E-style, oval, 11¼" 15.00
Sears' Richmond, creamer 8.00
Sears' Richmond, cup 5.00
Sears' Richmond, teapot, Aladdin (Brown-Eyed Susan) 70.00
Serenade, ball jug, #3 ....60.00
Serenade, bowl, D-style, oval 18.00
Serenade, casserole, Radiance 25.00
Serenade, custard 8.00
Serenade, pretzel jar 88.00
Shaggy Tulip, pretzel jar 125.00
Shaggy Tulip, shirred egg dish, 5¼" 25.00
Silhouette, bowl, flared, 7¾" 35.00

Silhouette, bowl, fruit; D-style, 5½" 8.00
Silhouette, bread box, pnt metal 70.00
Silhouette, coaster, pnt metal 8.00
Silhouette, coffee-pot, Five Band 50.00
Silhouette, jug, #3, Medallion 25.00
Silhouette, mirror 70.00
Silhouette, mug, beverage 50.00
Silhouette, platter, D-style, oval, 13¼" 28.00
Silhouette, teapot, New York 175.00
Silhouette, waffle iron, metal 125.00
Springtime, bowl, cereal; D-style, 6" 6.00
Springtime, pie baker 20.00
Springtime, plate, cake 16.00
Springtime, plate, D-style, 9" 8.50
Stonewall, juicer, Medallion 500.00
Stonewall, leftover, rectangular 45.00
Sundial, batter jug, red or cobalt 125.00
Sundial, casserole, colors other than red or cobalt, #4, 8" 25.00
Sundial, teapot, red or cobalt, ind 55.00
Teapot, Airflow, teal w/EX gold, 6-cup 65.00
Teapot, Aladdin, ivory, 6-cup 50.00
Teapot, Albany, Chinese red, 6-cup 225.00
Teapot, Albany, rose, 6-cup 65.00

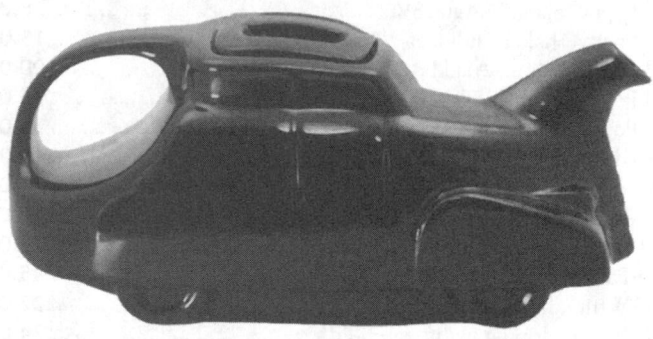

Teapot, Automobile, cobalt, 6-cup, $650.00.

Teapot, Baltimore, Dresden, 6-cup 50.00
Teapot, Baltimore, yel, 6-cup 50.00
Teapot, Basketball, red, 6-cup 750.00
Teapot, Bird Cage, marine bl, 6-cup 400.00
Teapot, Boston, red, 2-cup 125.00
Teapot, Cleveland, pk, 6-cup 75.00
Teapot, Football, delphinium, 6-cup 650.00
Teapot, Globe, emerald gr, 6-cup 90.00
Teapot, Globe, turq w/gold, 6-cup 95.00
Teapot, Hollywood, red, 8-cup 225.00
Teapot, Hookcover, cobalt, 6-cup 90.00
Teapot, Illinois, maroon w/gold, 6-cup 175.00
Teapot, Indiana, Cadet, 6-cup 250.00
Teapot, Indiana, stock brn or gr, 6-cup 150.00
Teapot, Kansas, delphinium, 6-cup 300.00
Teapot, Kansas, emerald gr w/gold, 6-cup 275.00
Teapot, Moderne, Dresden, 6-cup 30.00
Teapot, Nautilus, camellia, 6-cup 225.00
Teapot, New York, pk, 6-cup 35.00
Teapot, Ohio, canary, 6-cup 175.00
Teapot, Parade, cobalt, 6-cup 75.00
Teapot, Philadelphia, camellia, 6-cup 40.00
Teapot, Saf-Handle, turq, 6-cup 95.00
Teapot, Sani Grid, maroon w/gold, 6-cup 75.00
Teapot, Star, ivory, 6-cup 100.00

Teapot, Surfside, canary, 6-cup 100.00
Teapot, Teataster, turq w/gold, 6-cup 135.00
Teapot, Washington, marine, 12-cup 65.00
Teapot, Windshield, cobalt w/gold, 6-cup 75.00
Teapot, Windshield, delphinium w/gold, 6-cup 100.00
Tulip, bowl, fruit; D-style, 6" 10.00
Tulip, bowl, salad; 9" 18.00
Tulip, canister set, metal, 4-pc 45.00
Tulip, coffeepot, Perk 55.00
Tulip, gravy boat, D-style 25.00
Tulip, tidbit, 3-tier, D-style 40.00
Tulip, waffle iron, metal 70.00
Wild Poppy, casserole, #103, oval 95.00
Wild Poppy, shirred egg dish, 6½" 35.00
Wild Poppy, tea tile, 6" 45.00
Wildfire, bowl, Thick Rim, 6" 14.00
Wildfire, plate, D-style, 6" 6.00
Wildfire, sugar bowl, Pert 24.00
Wildfire, tidbit, 3-tier, D-style 45.00
Yellow Rose, bowl, Radiance, 6" 12.00
Yellow Rose, bowl, vegetable; D-style, rnd, 9¼" 20.00
Yellow Rose, creamer, Norse 14.00

Eva Zeisel Designs

Arizona, ashtray 6.00
Arizona, bowl, baker; open, 11-oz 14.00
Arizona, creamer 10.00
Arizona, jug, 3-qt 24.00
Bouquet, bowl, coupe soup; 9" 12.00
Bouquet, candlestick, 8" 35.00
Bouquet, coffeepot, 6-cup 80.00
Bouquet, egg cup 20.00
Bouquet, ladle 15.00
Buckingham, ashtray 7.50
Buckingham, bowl, baker; open, 11-oz 15.00
Buckingham, casserole, 1¼-qt 32.00
Buckingham, cup, AD 15.00
Buckingham, plate, 6" 4.50
Caprice, marmite, w/lid 25.00
Caprice, vase 25.00
Caprice, vinegar bottle 30.00
Fantasy, butter dish 50.00
Fantasy, jug, 3-qt 25.00
Fantasy, onion soup, w/lid 25.00
Fantasy, platter, 17" 25.00
Fern, ashtray 6.00
Fern, bowl, vegetable; 10½" 16.00
Fern, creamer 8.00
Fern, plate, 8" 6.00
Frost Flowers, ashtray 7.50
Frost Flowers, candlestick, 4½" 30.00
Frost Flowers, egg cup 20.00
Frost Flowers, gravy boat 20.00
Frost Flowers, platter, 12¼" 18.00
Harlequin, bowl, baker; open, 11-oz 16.00
Harlequin, cup, AD 15.00
Harlequin, plate, 6" 6.00
Harlequin, platter, 17" 25.00
Harlequin, teapot, Thorley 75.00
Holiday, bowl, fruit; 5¾" 5.00
Holiday, ladle 12.00
Holiday, marmite, w/lid 20.00
Holiday, shakers, ea 8.00

Holiday, vase	25.00
Lyric, ashtray	6.00
Lyric, bowl, fruit; ftd, lg	25.00
Lyric, egg cup	20.00
Lyric, platter, 12¼"	15.00
Mulberry, bowl, vegetable; open, sq, 8¾"	15.00
Mulberry, cup, AD	15.00
Mulberry, ladle	15.00
Peach Blossom, ashtray	7.50
Peach Blossom, bowl, celery; oval	15.00
Peach Blossom, casserole, 1¼-qt	32.00
Peach Blossom, gravy boat	24.00
Peach Blossom, saucer, AD	2.50
Pine Cone, bowl, celery; oval	14.00
Pine Cone, bowl, fruit; 5¾"	5.00
Pine Cone, gravy boat	20.00
Pine Cone, plate, E-style, 6"	5.00
Pine Cone, plate, 11"	10.00
Spring, bowl, celery; oval	12.00
Spring, bowl, fruit; 5¾"	6.00
Spring, casserole, 2-qt	25.00
Spring, egg cup	20.00
Spring, marmite, w/lid	20.00
Spring, vinegar bottle	30.00
Sunglow, bowl, fruit; 5¾"	4.00
Sunglow, bowl, vegetable; 10½"	15.00
Sunglow, casserole	20.00
Sunglow, gravy boat	18.00
Sunglow, plate, 10¼"	7.00
Sunglow, shakers, ea	8.00

Hallmark

Hallmark introduced a line of artplas (molded plastic) ornaments in 1973 that have quickly become popular with collectors. They also have produced miniature ornaments since 1988, which are very collectible, as well as limited edition ornaments produced for members of the Hallmark Keepsake Ornament Collectors' Club.

'Merry Miniatures' is a line of artplas 'Table Trimmers' made in 1973 which have become quite collectible as well, and collectors are avidly searching for these tiny figures in closets, children's toy boxes, and at flea markets.

The magazine, *The Ornament Collector,* edited by Rosie Wells, our advisor for this category, is available if you want more information on ornament collecting. Rosie also publishes a yearly official Secondary Market Price Guide on Hallmark Ornaments, Merry Miniatures, Stocking Hangers, Lapel Pins, Cookie Cutters, etc. Her address is listed in the Directory under Clubs, Newsletters, and Catalogs and again under Illinois. Values are for ornaments in mint condition and with their original boxes, while Merry Miniatures are assumed to be mint.

1980, Frosty Friends: A Cool Yule, QX137-4, 1st in series, handcrafted, MIB, $600.00.

1978, Holiday Highlights: Nativity, QX309-6, acrylic	85.00
1979, Holiday Highlights: Santa, QX307-6, acrylic	80.00
1980, Here Comes Santa: Santa's Express, QX143-4, 2nd in series	185.00
1980, Rockwell: Santa's Visitors, QX306-1, 1st in series, 2¼"	35.00
1981, Frosty Friends: Eskimo & Puppy, QX433-5, 2nd in series, 2"	410.00
1981, Rocking Horse, QX422-2, 1st in series, handcrafted, 2"	650.00
1981, Starship Enterprise, QLX719-9, blinking lights	325.00
1982, Holiday Wildlife: Cardinals, QX313-3, wood/decofoam, 4"	375.00
1982, Rocking Horse, QX502-3, 2nd in series, handcrafted, 2"	400.00
1982, Tin Locomotive, QX460-3, 1st in series, dtd, 3⅝"	600.00
1983, Tin Locomotive, QX404-9, 2nd in series, dtd, 3"	280.00
1984, Nostalgic Houses: Victorian Dollhouse, QX448-1, 3½"	45.00
1985, Nostalgic Houses: Toy Shop, QX497-5, 2nd in series, 2½"	110.00
1986, Mr & Mrs Claus: Merry Mistletoe Time, QX402-6, dtd	110.00
1988, Mary's Angels: Buttercup, QX407-4, 1st in series, 2¼"	45.00
1989, Mary's Angels: Bluebell, QX454-5, 2nd in series, 3"	52.00
1995, Football Legends: Kansas City-Joe Montana	150.00
1995, Football Legends: San Francisco-J Montana, 1st in series	65.00

Halloween

The origin of Halloween can be traced back to the ancient practices of the Druids of Great Britain who began their New Year on the 1st of November. The Druids were pagans, and their New Year's celebrations involved pagan rites and superstitions. They believed that as the old year came to an end the devil would gather up all the demons and evil in the world and take them back to Hell with him. Witches were women who had sold their souls to the devil and, with their black cat in attendance, flew up through their chimneys on brooms. When the Roman Catholic Church came into power in 700 A.D., they changed the holiday into a religious event called 'All Saints Day' or 'Allhallows.' The evening before, October 31, became 'Allhallow's Eve' or 'Halloween.' Today Halloween is strictly a fun time, and Halloween items are fun to collect. Pumpkin-head candy containers of papier-mache or pressed cardboard, noisemakers, postcards with black cats and witches, costumes, and decorations are only a sampling of the variety available.

Our advisor for this category is Jenny Tarrant; she is listed in the Directory under Missouri. See also Candy Containers.

Candy cup, cat, owl, or pumpkin name plates, paper, 3 for	15.00
Costume, Bart Maverick, Collegeville, 1959, MIB	85.00
Costume, Dick Dastardly, Ben Cooper, 1969, MIB	35.00
Costume, Lily Munster, lifelike hair, Ben Cooper, MIB	200.00
Costume, Quick Draw McGraw, Ben Cooper, 1959, M in VG box	55.00
Costume, Secret Squirrel, Ben Cooper, 1967, NM	30.00
Costume, The Flash, DC Comics, Ben Cooper, 1966, NM	35.00
Costume, Touche Turtle, Ben Cooper, 1965, MIB	175.00
Decoration, cat w/horn, papier-mache, wire neck, 7"	35.00
Decoration, pumpkin w/horn nose, metal, USA, 1950s, 6"	35.00
Decoration, witch, papier-mache, rnd, 6"	40.00
Diecut, cat on the moon, HE Lehrs, 14"	35.00
Diecut, scarecrow, w/honeycomb tissue, 7¾"	45.00
Hat, cb w/lg pumpkin face, 8"	45.00
Jack-o'-lantern, Germany, 1920s-40s, 3"	95.00
Jack-o'-lantern, Germany, 1920s-40s, 4"	125.00
Jack-o'-lantern, Germany, 1920s-40s, 5"	175.00
Jack-o'-lantern, Germany, 1920s-40s, 6"	225.00
Jack-o'-lantern, Germany, 1920s-40s, 7"	300.00
Jack-o'-lantern, molded tin w/cut-out face, Germany, 7", VG	495.00
Jack-o'-lantern, paper accordion type, Germany, 1910, 24", VG	80.00
Jack-o'-lantern, papier-mache pulp, USA, '40s-50s, 4", $65 to	85.00

Jack-o'-lantern, papier-mache pulp, USA, '40s-50s, 5", $55 to **75.00**
Jack-o'-lantern, papier-mache pulp, USA, '40s-50s, 5½", $85 to ..**95.00**
Jack-o'-lantern, papier-mache pulp, USA, '40s-50s, 7½" **135.00**
Lantern, cat, Germany, 1920s, 3" **125.00**
Lantern, cat, Germany, 1920s, 4" **150.00**
Lantern, cat, Germany, 1920s, 5" **275.00**
Lantern, cat, Germany, 1920s, 6" **350.00**
Lantern, cat, papier-mache pulp, USA, '40s-50s, $145 to **185.00**
Lantern, cat on fence, papier-mache pulp, USA, '40s-50s, $145 to ..**185.00**
Lantern, cat's head, orange papier-mache, 1930s, 3", NM **200.00**
Lantern, devil, cb, USA, 1950s-60s, 7" **95.00**
Lantern, devil, papier-mache, no insert, USA, 1930s, 9" **200.00**
Lantern, devil, papier-mache, w/insert, USA, 1930s, 9" **300.00**
Lantern, devil's head, papier-mache, Germany, 1930s, 5½", NM ..**350.00**
Lantern, owl's face, cb, dbl-sided, USA, 1930s, 8x11", EX **75.00**
Lantern, paper, cutout ea side (4), USA, '50s-70s, 6", $45 to **55.00**
Lantern, skull, cb, USA, 1950s-60s, 6" **75.00**
Lantern, skull, papier-mache, Germany, 3", VG **165.00**
Lantern, witch, cb, USA, 1950s-60s, 7" **110.00**
Marionette, skeleton, papier-mache, wire & cloth, 21" **195.00**
Mask, HP gauze, M **7.00**
Noisemaker, metal, pumpkin/witch/cat, wooden hdl, 4" dia **35.00**
Nut cup, papier-mache, resembles jack-o'lantern, USA, 2½" **35.00**

Candy Containers

Cat, blk mohair-covered papier-mache figure, glass eyes, 7½", EX .**450.00**
Cat, blk plastic, face on bk, 1950s, 3" **12.50**
Cat, common type, Germany, 1920s, 3" **125.00**
Cat, common type, Germany, 1920s, 3½" **175.00**
Cat, papier-mache pulp, USA, 1940s-50s, 7" **125.00**
Cat face w/carrot body, common type, Germany, 1920s, 5" **295.00**
Cat w/basket on bk, papier-mache pulp, USA, 1940s-50s, 9" **145.00**
Devil emerging from top hat, Germany, 1910s-20s, 3½" **350.00**
Devil's face, EX detail, Germany, 1910s-20s, 5" **425.00**
Goblin astride pumpkin w/cat, papier-mache, Germany, 6", EX ..**400.00**
Jack-o'-lantern, cb w/whimsical features, Ann-Dee, 4", EX- **60.00**
Owl, papier-mache pulp, USA, 1940s-50s, 4", $55 to **65.00**
Pear face, head only, Germany, 1910s-20s, 3½" **350.00**
Pear-head vegetable man, papier-mache, 6½", VG **700.00**
Pumpkin-head boy on orange, common type, Germany, '20s, 4" ..**225.00**
Pumpkin-head girl beside pumpkin, Germany, 1910s-20s, 4" **375.00**
Various figures, Germany, 1910s-20s, oversz, 7"-8", $550 to **650.00**
Witch, compo, orange & blk pnt, Germany, 1930s-40s, 3½" **95.00**
Witch, full figure, holding cat, Germany, 1910s-20s, 5" **425.00**
Witch, papier-mache, cone shape, W Germany, 7½" **45.00**
Witch, papier-mache, W Germany, 1950s, 7½" **45.00**
Witch on pumpkin, papier-mache pulp, 1940s-50s, 5" **95.00**
Witch riding blk cat, Germany, 1910s-20s, 7" **550.00**
Witch's head, papier-mache, MIG, 6" **8.00**

Hampshire

The Hampshire Pottery Company was established in 1871 in Keene, New Hampshire, by James Scollay Taft. Their earliest products were redware and stoneware utility items such as jugs, churns, crocks, and flowerpots. In 1878 they produced majolica ware which met with such success that they began to experiment with the idea of manufacturing art pottery. By 1883 they had developed a Royal Worcester type of finish which they applied to vases, tea sets, powder boxes, and cookie jars. It was also utilized for souvenir items that were decorated with transfer designs prepared from photographic plates.

Cadmon Robertson, brother-in-law of Taft, joined the company in 1904 and was responsible for developing their famous matt glazes. Colors included shades of green, brown, red, and blue. Early examples were of earthenware, but eventually the body was changed to semiporcelain. Some of his designs were marked with an M in a circle as a tribute to his wife, Emoretta. Robertson died in 1914, leaving a void impossible to fill. Taft sold the business in 1916 to George Morton, who continued to use the matt glazes that Robertson had developed. After a temporary halt in production during WWI, Morton returned to Keene and re-equipped the factory with the machinery needed to manufacture hotel china and floor tile. Because of the expense involved in transporting coal to fire the kilns, Morton found he could not compete with potteries of Ohio and New Jersey who were able to utilize locally available natural gas. He was forced to close the plant in 1923.

Interest is highest on examples in the monochrome glazes, and it is the glaze, not the size or form, that dictates value. The souvenir pieces are not particularly of high quality and tend to be passed over by today's collectors.

Bowl, blk veins on aqua to cobalt, artichoke form, 3½" **150.00**
Bowl, gr matt, emb leaves/buds, scroll rim, mk ST, 3x10" **300.00**
Bowl, wht mottle on cobalt, artichoke form, mk, 3½" **180.00**
Bowl vase, cobalt & wht mottle, emb floral, #19/1, 2¼" H **210.00**
Bowl vase, gr matt, emb lilies & waves, sgn King, mk, 2¼" H **180.00**
Candle holder, bl matt, att, 5x5½" **80.00**
Chamberstick, gr matt, #0029, 7x4" **200.00**
Chamberstick, mocha-mauve mottled matt, mk/label, 4½x6" **130.00**
Lamp, gr matt w/11 raised panels, glass shade, mk, 20x12" **800.00**
Lamp base, veined gr matt, long can neck, brass font, 15x8" ...**1,000.00**
Mug, gr mottle, imp leaf band at top, 5½" **120.00**
Tea set, cobalt gloss, 3½" teapot+cr/sug **100.00**

Urn, green matt with tub handles atop broad shoulders, circular lid rests inside rim, 8x8", $650.00.

Vase, aqua/gr/blk/gray mottle on dk aqua, squat, 3" **230.00**
Vase, bl-gr feathering, flat urn shape, 6" **250.00**
Vase, brn mottle on mauve-brn w/lustre, M in O mk, 9⅛" **55.00**
Vase, brn/bl/gr/gray mottle, Greek Key at shoulder, 5x5¾" **275.00**
Vase, copper & copper lustres on gunmetal blk, bulbous, 3¼" **130.00**
Vase, deep cocoa-red, emb blade-like leaves, ovoid, #1/11, 9" **450.00**
Vase, dk/med gr flambe, hand-thrown, 6x3¾" **250.00**
Vase, gr, brn & gray mottle, flared mouth, #91, mk, 9¼" **550.00**
Vase, gr & gray flecks on turq, ovoid, bulging waist, 3¾" **400.00**
Vase, gr matt, alternating buds & leaves, 7" **280.00**
Vase, gr matt, emb panels, #54, M in O mk, 3¼" **150.00**
Vase, gr matt, full-length leaves/buds, sgn MO/33, 7x4½" **425.00**
Vase, gr matt (smooth grain), tapering at base, 4¼x5" **175.00**
Vase, gray & blk mottle on aqua, cobalt int, #17/2, 5¼" **250.00**
Vase, gray flecks on aqua, emb crisscrossing, #152, 4" **220.00**
Vase, gray speckled matt, melon ribs, rolled rim, #119, 6x6" **375.00**
Vase, lt bl on dk bl, leaves at bulbous base, long neck, 10" **450.00**
Vase, lt gr/maroon matt, sculpted leaves, corseted, 3" **110.00**

Vase, lt gray mottle on gr matt, bulbous, inscr mk, 5" 190.00
Vase, ochre gloss, serpent-form hdls, detailed, mk, 6⅛" 160.00
Vase, sea gr mottle on dk aqua, ovoid, M in O mk, 7¼" 475.00
Vase, veined blk & gray mottle on shaded aqua, mk, 5¼" 450.00
Vase, wht mottle on brn, mocha int, #54, M in O mk, 3½" 140.00

Handel

Philip Handel was best known for the art glass lamps he produced at the turn of the century. His work is similar to the Tiffany lamps of the same era. Handel made gas and electric lamps with both leaded glass and reverse-painted shades. Chipped ice shades with a texture similar to overshot glass were also produced. Shades signed by artists such as Bailey, Palme, and Parlow are highly valued.

China and glassware decorated by Handel are rare and command high prices on today's market. Teroma is a term used to describe glassware decorated on the exterior with paint that has a sandy finish. Many of Handel's chinaware blanks were supplied by Limoges. Our advisor for this category is Daniel Batchelor; he is listed in the Directory under New York.

Key: chp — chipped/lightly sanded

Lamps

Base, bun ft w/emb foliage, slim emb std, bronzed, mk, 24" 575.00
Boudoir, rvpt/chp 7" windmill/moon dome shade; geometric std ..1,700.00
Desk, chp 8" moss gr cylinder shade; std w/curved arm, 12" 800.00
Desk, chp-ice 6-lobe flower-border shade, harp std, 18", EX 800.00
Desk, ldgl shell-form shade; curved neck on rnd-base std 1,300.00
Desk, rvpt 8" mtns/trees cylinder shade; leaf-cast base, EX 1,725.00
Floor, brn-pnt chp-ice 10" dome shade; harp std, 57" 1,250.00
Floor, palm tree o/l 23" shade; fluted column, 64" 10,000.00
Hanging, Hawaiian metal o/l on 6-panel bell-form 6" shade 400.00
Hanging, pnt 10" parrot orange-amber ball shade, +gr-pnt cap ..460.00
Shade, ceiling; ldgl 8x24" shaped dome w/fruit border 1,380.00
Shade, ceiling; rvpt/etched 18" dome w/floral & butterfly 11,500.00
Table, chp 18" #5342 shade w/brn loops band; vase std, 24" ...3,000.00
Table, chp-ice 16" floral-band shade; sgn bronze std 2,700.00
Table, chp/pnt 18" full-length peacocks shade; bronzed std ..19,550.00
Table, ldgl 14" nasturtium shade; 3-scroll std, 20" 1,950.00
Table, ldgl 16" bow-tie apron shade (att); bronzed metal std 875.00
Table, ldgl 16" shade w/leaf band on apron; Hampshire base ..1,265.00
Table, ldgl 18" floral-band shade; Tiffany std #533 ....2,750.00
Table, ldgl 20" floral cone shade; bronzed floral-emb std 5,175.00
Table, ldgl 20" triangle/oval-panel shade; swirled std, 24" 1,000.00
Table, ldgl 22" periwinkle shade; X-ftd Nouveau-emb std 4,450.00
Table, ldgl 26" iris cone shade w/apron (EX); slim std, VG 2,450.00
Table, palm tree o/l 18" curve-panel shade; Chinese-style std .5,500.00
Table, palm tree o/l 18" shade; std w/3 scrolls 2,100.00
Table, pnt/chp 15" winter trees shade; mk 6-side stick std 2,750.00
Table, pnt/rvpt 18" trees shade sgn WR; tree-trunk std, 24" 7,000.00
Table, rvpt 15" ribbed shade w/scenic apron panels; rib std 2,645.00
Table, rvpt 15" 4-color roses shade; 'wicker' brass std 2,300.00
Table, rvpt 16" trees/lake shade; copper-tone std (worn) 3,220.00
Table, rvpt 18" berry-band shade; base w/wide petal ft 5,000.00
Table, rvpt 18" birch trees/sunset shade; mk bronzed std 4,300.00
Table, rvpt 18" Elephantine Isle (faces right) shade; #6641 std ..5,750.00
Table, rvpt 18" floral-edge shade; copper-tone baluster std 1,800.00
Table, rvpt 18" medallions on orange shade; unmk base 1,600.00
Table, rvpt 18" scenic shade; mk std w/upright leaves 5,900.00
Table, rvpt 18" summer-scene ribbed shade; rtcl base 5,175.00
Table, rvpt 18" Treasure Isle shade; gray-patina swirl std 8,000.00

Table lamp, reverse-painted 16" Venetian scene shade, #7135; bronzed metal Arts & Crafts-style base with original green-brown patina, marked, 23", EX, $4,500.00.

Table, rvpt 18" trees/moon shade; leaf-emb std w/wide ft 6,000.00
Table, rvpt/chp 16" leafy shade w/int scenic; slim metal std 3,250.00
Table, rvpt/chp 18" birds of paradise shade; 3-scroll std 18,000.00
Table, rvpt/chp 18" CT River shade sgn HR; lily-pad std, 23" ..6,000.00
Table, rvpt/chp 18" jungle bird shade; bronzed step-ftd std ...15,500.00
Table, rvpt/chp 18" trees/mtns shade; bronzed metal base 6,000.00
Table, tam o'shanter 12" gr-cased wht shade (EX), leafy std ...1,150.00

Miscellaneous

Chocolate pot, china, parrot tulip on beige, 9½x6½" 375.00
Humidor, golfing pr on shaded ground, mk/#d, 8½x6", NM 900.00

Humidor, Indian scout painted on opalware, hinged rim, lid closure, signed P.J. Handel, 7½" high, $1,265.00.

Mug, monks reading newspaper on shaded turq, mini, 2¼" 150.00
Vase, acid-cut floral, amber on frost sgn Rouchett, 10", EX 1,495.00
Vase, Teroma, mtn town w/trees, artist sgn, #4221, 10x4" 1,300.00
Vase, Teroma, trees, 8x5", NM 1,200.00
Vase, Teroma, woodland/birds on frost, sgn Lockrow, ftd, 10" ..1,450.00

Harker

The Harker Pottery was established in East Liverpool, Ohio, in 1840. Their earliest products were yellow ware and Rockingham produced from local clay. After 1900 whiteware was made from imported materials. The plant eventually grew to be a large manufacturer of dinnerware and kitchenware, employing as many as three hundred people. It closed in 1972 after it was purchased by the Jeannette Glass Company. Perhaps their best-known lines were their Cameo wares, decorated with white silhouettes in a cameo effect on contrasting solid colors. Floral silhouettes are standard, but other designs were also used. Blue and pink are the most often found background hues; a few pieces are found in yellow. For further information we recommend *The Collector's Guide to Harker Pottery* by Neva Colbert.

Amy, hi-rise jug	22.00
Amy, plate, dinner	5.00
Antique Auto, cup & saucer, jumbo	15.00
Bamboo, plate, luncheon	8.00
Black-Eyed Susan, saucer, 6"	2.00
Black-Eyed Susan, tidbit tray, 3-tier	12.50
Calendar plate, Christmas 1907	65.00
Calendar plate, Heritance shape, 1960	3.00
Calico Tulip, condiment jar, metal lid	5.00

Cameo Rose, plate, 8½", $5.00.

Cherry Blossom, plate, dinner	6.00
Chesterton, cake/pie lifter, teal	12.50
Chesterton, cup	3.00
Chesterton, shaker	1.50
Chesterton, snack set, gray & pk, 12-pc	60.00
Colonial Lady, au gratin casserole	22.50
Colonial Lady, cup & saucer	7.50
Dainty Flower, casserole, Zephyr	25.00
Dainty Flower, cup & saucer, Swirl	10.00
Dainty Flower, rolling pin	70.00
Deco Dahlia, plate, Virginia, 6"	3.00
Deco Dahlia, scoop	26.00
Heritance, bowl, divided vegetable	4.00
Heritance, plate, dinner; 16-sided	3.00
Ivy, creamer & sugar bowl	12.50
Ivy, plate, dinner	6.00
Ivy, soup, oval, plain	3.50
Modern Tulip, creamer, Modern Age	7.50
Modern Tulip, custard	6.00
Monterey, casserole, w/lid	18.00
Oriental Poppy, mixing bowl	22.50
Oriental Poppy, platter, Melrose, 15"	18.50
Petit Point, fork & spoon	25.00
Petit Point, plate, dinner	6.00
Petit Point, rolling pin	75.00
Red Apple, bowl, Zephyr, 4"	8.00
Red Apple, drip jar, Skyscraper	15.00
Red Apple, plate, dinner	6.00
Shadow Rose, cup & saucer	9.00
Shadow Rose, plate, 6"	3.00
Shadow Rose, platter	13.00
Tulip, pie baker	15.00
Tulip, syrup jug	12.00
White Rose, cake/pie lifter	12.50

White Rose, plate, dinner	12.00

Harlequin

Harlequin dinnerware, produced by the Homer Laughlin China Company of Newell, West Virginia, was introduced in 1938. It was a lightweight ware made in maroon, mauve blue, and spruce green, as well as all the Fiesta colors except ivory (see Fiesta). It was marketed exclusively by the Woolworth stores, who considered it to be their all-time bestseller. For this reason they contracted with Homer Laughlin to reissue Harlequin to commemorate their 100th anniversary in 1979. Although three of the original glazes were used in the reissue, the few serving pieces that were made were restyled, and collectors found the new line to be no threat to their investments.

The Harlequin animals, including a fish, lamb, cat, penguin, duck, and donkey, were made during the early 1940s, also for the dime-store trade. Today these are very desirable to collectors of Homer Laughlin china.

In the listings that follow, use the values designated 'high' for all colors other than turquoise and yellow. For medium green, double the 'high' values on all items other than flat items and small bowls. *The Collector's Encyclopedia of Fiesta* (values updated in 1994) by Sharon and Bob Huxford contains a more thorough study of this subject. It is available from Collector Books or your local library.

Animals, maverick, gold trim	45.00
Animals, non-standard color	215.00
Animals, standard color	125.00
Ashtray, basketweave, high	50.00
Ashtray, basketweave, low	32.00
Ashtray, regular, high	50.00
Ashtray, regular, low	36.00
Bowl, '36s oatmeal; high	22.00
Bowl, '36s oatmeal; low	14.00
Bowl, '36s; high	34.00
Bowl, '36s; low	23.00
Bowl, cream soup; high	26.00
Bowl, cream soup; low	20.00
Bowl, fruit; high, 5½"	10.00
Bowl, fruit; low, 5½"	7.00
Bowl, ind salad; high	36.00
Bowl, ind salad; low	22.00
Bowl, mixing; Kitchen Kraft, mauve bl, 8"	110.00
Bowl, mixing; Kitchen Kraft, red or spruce gr, 6", ea	80.00
Bowl, mixing; Kitchen Kraft, yel, 10"	110.00
Bowl, nappy; high, 9"	35.00
Bowl, nappy; low, 9"	22.00
Bowl, oval baker, high	32.00
Bowl, oval baker, low	22.00

Butter dish, ½-lb, high, 115.00; low, $95.00.

Candle holders, high, pr	250.00

Candle holders, low, pr 210.00
Casserole, w/lid, high 140.00
Casserole, w/lid, low 88.00
Creamer, high lip, any color, ea 100.00
Creamer, ind; high 28.00
Creamer, ind; low 18.00
Creamer, novelty, high 32.00
Creamer, novelty, low 22.00
Creamer, regular, high 16.00
Creamer, regular, low 11.00
Cup, demitasse; high 100.00
Cup, demitasse; low 38.00
Cup, lg, any color, ea 170.00
Cup, tea; high 11.00
Cup, tea; low 8.50
Egg cup, dbl, high 24.00
Egg cup, dbl, low 16.00
Egg cup, single, high 30.00
Egg cup, single, low 22.00
Marmalade, any color, ea 165.00
Nut dish, basketweave, high 14.00
Nut dish, basketweave, low 10.00
Perfume bottle, any color, ea 100.00
Pitcher, service water; high 85.00
Pitcher, service water; low 65.00

Pitcher, 22-oz ball jug, high, $60.00; low, $35.00.

Plate, deep; high 25.00
Plate, deep; low 18.00
Plate, high, 10" 30.00
Plate, high, 6" 5.50
Plate, high, 7" 8.00
Plate, high, 9" 14.00
Plate, low, 10" 18.00
Plate, low, 6" 4.00
Plate, low, 7" 5.50
Plate, low, 9" 9.00
Platter, high, 11" 22.00
Platter, high, 13" 28.00
Platter, low, 11" 15.00
Platter, low, 13" 20.00
Sauce boat, high 28.00
Sauce boat, low 22.00
Saucer, demitasse; high 20.00
Saucer, demitasse; low 12.00
Saucer, high 4.00
Saucer, low 2.00
Saucer/ashtray, high 52.00
Saucer/ashtray, ivory 85.00
Saucer/ashtray, low 42.00

Shakers, high, pr 20.00
Shakers, low, pr 14.00
Sugar bowl, w/lid, high 28.00
Sugar bowl, w/lid, low 15.00
Syrup, any color 235.00
Teapot, high 120.00
Teapot, low 72.00
Tray, relish; mixed colors 280.00
Tumbler, high 50.00
Tumbler, low 40.00

Hatpin Holders

Most hatpin holders were made from 1860 to 1920 to coincide with the period during which hatpins were popularly in vogue. The taller types were required to house the long hatpins necessary to secure the large hats that were in style from 1890 to 1914. They were usually porcelain, either decorated by hand or by transfer with florals or scenics, although some were clever figurals. Glass examples are rare, and those of slag or carnival glass are especially valuable.

If you are interested in collecting or dealing in hatpins or hatpin holders, you will find that authority Lillian Baker has several fine books available on the subject, including her most recent publication, *Hatpins and Hatpin Holders,* complete with beautiful color illustrations and current market values. She is listed in the Directory under California. For information concerning the International Club for Collectors of Hatpins and Hatpin Holders, see the Clubs, Newsletters, and Catalogs section of the Directory. Our advisor for this category is Robert Larsen; he is listed in the Directory under Nebraska.

Bsk, bear & tower form, Schafer & Vater mk, 4¾x3½" 225.00
Bsk, pk & wht w/gr cameo ea side, 7-hole, 4½" 175.00

Carnival Glass, Formal pattern, attributed to Imperial Glass Co., found in marigold and purple, rare, $900.00 to $1,200.00.

China, dbl-face, lady 1 side/man on other, unmk 275.00
China, gr w/silver o/l, Rosenthal 225.00
China, Jewish symbol transfer, Willow Art, Jerusalem, 5½" 125.00
China, mc roses, artist sgn, Bavaria 125.00
China, roses on lustre, scalloped base, RS Prussia, 4¾" 285.00
China, slipper form, wall mt 360.00
China, windmill scene, bl & wht export, mk Japan, 4" 75.00
China w/silver floral decor, mk Bavaria, 4¾" 115.00
Chocolate glass, emb florals, ftd, 7⅞x2⅝" 550.00
Jasperware, bl w/wht Grecian figures 145.00
Jasperware, cameo on urn form, Schafer & Vater, 5¼" 275.00
Moriage, gold butterflies on wht, Nippon mk, 5⅛x2¾" 200.00
Pottery, brn shaded, GH Richards, London, ca 1890 ....115.00

Pottery, City of York crest, souvenir, WH Goss, 3½x2½"	100.00
Royal Bayreuth, lady's portrait tapestry, bl mk	650.00
RS Prussia, floral, hexagonal w/attached trinket box, mk	550.00
Silver, etched & eng, 16-hole, unmk, 1880s, 5½x2¾"	225.00

Hatpins

A hatpin was used to securely fasten a hat to the hair and head of the wearer. Hatpins, measuring from 4" to 12" in length, were worn from approximately 1850 to 1920. During the Art Deco period, hatpins became ornaments rather than the decorative functional jewels that they had been. The hatpin period reached its zenith in 1913 just prior to World War I, which brought about a radical change in women's headdress and fashion. About that time, women began to scorn the bonnet and adopt 'the hat' as a symbol of their equality. The hatpin was made of every natural and manufactured element in a myriad of designs that challenge the imagination. They were contrived to serve every fashion need and complement the milliner's art. Collectors often concentrate on a specific type: hand-painted porcelains, sterling silver, commemoratives, sporting activities, carnival glass, Art Nouveau and/or Art Deco designs, Victorian gothics with mounted stones, exquisite rhinestones, engraved and brass-mounted escutcheon heads, gold and gems, or simply primitive types made in the Victorian parlor. Some collectors prefer the long pin shanks while others select only those on tremblants or nodder-type pin shanks.

If you are interested in collecting or dealing in hatpins, see the information in the Hatpin Holders introduction concerning reference books and a national collectors' club. For further study we recommend *The Collector's Encyclopedia of Hatpins and Hatpin Holders*, available at your local bookstore or from Collector Books. Our advisor for this category is Robert Larsen; he is listed in the Directory under Nebraska.

Key: cab — cabochon

Amethyst faceted glass in silver alloy (oxidized) mt, ½"	125.00
Amethyst stone atop brass mt w/emb florals, 1¼x1¼"	160.00
Brass (oxidized), Nouveau style w/amethyst brilliant, 9½"	175.00

Compact with mirror, $750.00 to $1,500.00; Vinaigrette (holds smelling salts), $850.00 to $1,100.00; Compact with straight pins, $650.00 to $900.00.

Concentric rings on molded plastic, brass mts, 1920s, 2"	60.00
Cvd ivory chrysanthemum & flowers, hollow, 1" on 7⅜" pin	135.00
Gold-filled, oval openwork w/garnet ea side, 9½"	150.00
Horn, butterfly form w/mc rhinestones, 3⅜" on 9½" pin	175.00
Lady's portrait transfer w/overpnt on porc w/gold, 1½"	500.00
Mosaic, in brass button-sleeve mt w/gold, 1", on 8" pin	195.00
Nouveau flower form, enamel on copper, ca 1900, 1"	55.00

Peacock-eye glass, oval, ⅞" on 7½" steel pin	65.00
Porc, courting couple medallion w/gold o/l, 1890s, 1¾"	225.00
Satsuma, HP birds & leaves, 1½" on 10½" steel pin	225.00
Satsuma, HP robins, metallic mt, 1½", on 9" pin	300.00
Scorpion, brass on pearl w/brass filigree, 3", EX	200.00
Silver foil glass, peacock eye ea side, ¾" on 8" pin	80.00
Souvenir, sterling, Snoqualmie Falls, Seattle, 10¼"	65.00
Sterling Nouveau lady w/repousse work, 1", on 8¾" pin	175.00
Topaz stone w/in Nouveau brass lariat fr, 2¾" on 7½" pin	150.00
Vanity, red stone on brass mt, 2x1x1½" on 11½" pin	900.00

Haviland

The Haviland China Company was organized in 1840 by David Haviland, a New York china importer. His search for a pure white, non-porous porcelain led him to Limoges, France, where natural deposits of suitable clay had already attracted numerous china manufacturers. The fine china he produced there was translucent and meticulously decorated, with each piece fired in an individual sagger.

It has been estimated that as many as 60,000 chinaware patterns were designed, each piece marked with one of several company back-stamps. 'H. & Co.' was used until 1890 when a law was enacted making it necessary to include the country of origin. Various marks have been used since that time including 'Haviland, France'; 'Haviland & Co. Limoges'; and 'Decorated by Haviland & Co.' Various associations with family members over the years have resulted in changes in management as well as company name. In 1892 Theodore Haviland left the firm to start his own business. Some of his ware was marked 'Mont Mery.' Later logos included a horseshoe, a shield, and various uses of his initials and name. In 1941 this branch moved to the United States. Wares produced here are marked 'Theodore Haviland, N.Y.' or 'Made In America.'

Though it is their dinnerware lines for which they are most famous, during the 1880s and 1890s they also made exquisite art pottery using a technique of underglaze slip decoration called Barbotine, which had been invented by Ernest Chaplet. In 1885 Haviland bought the formula and hired Chaplet to oversee its production. The technique involved mixing heavy white clay slip with pigments to produce a compound of the same consistency as oil paints. The finished product actually resembled oil paintings of the period, the texture achieved through the application of the heavy medium to the clay body in much the same manner as an artist would apply paint to his canvas. Primarily the body used with this method was a low-fired faience, though they also produced stoneware. Numbers in the listings below refer to pattern books by Arlene Schleiger.

Mustard set, violets with gold trim, $80.00.

Berry set, violets, amateur decor, 6-pc	100.00
Bowl, vegetable; Yale, w/lid	50.00

Chocolate pot, pk florals w/gold, emb scallops, 1890s, 5¼" 115.00
Chocolate pot, scenic, bl transfer, anchor blank 175.00
Chocolate set, pk roses & ribbons, Limoges, 10" pot+4 c/s 425.00
Coffeepot, rose finial, ca 1876-1889, 10" 225.00
Coffeepot, Sandoz, bird figural, 1904-20s, 5½" 550.00
Cracker jar, HP violets, Rouen, from 1895-1903, 7¼" 185.00
Cracker jar, Rouen, HP violets, ca 1895-1903, 7¼" 150.00
Creamer & sugar bowl, wht w/gold band, 1850s-65 ....175.00
Cup & saucer, pk floral center, Ranson form 95.00
Cup & saucer, Yale 65.00
Humidor, bl ribbon bands w/pk flowers & gold, 7" 300.00
Jardiniere, wht w/gold decor, Marseille form, 4x9¾" 240.00
Pitcher, milk; Norma, Ranson form, 1893-1930, 7" 175.00
Plate, fish center, F Bracquemond, 1876-79, 8½", pr 200.00
Plate, oyster; floral, ca 1887, 10" 100.00
Plate, oyster; purple & gold on wht, 9" 75.00
Plate, Yale, dinner sz 25.00
Platter, Should Old Acquaintance..., man at doorway, gilt 175.00
Platter, Yale, 10" 40.00
Shaving mug, gold name & trim, 1876-78, 3¼" 135.00
Sugar bowl, emb florals, flower finial, gold trim, 1850s-60 ....95.00
Teapot, emb florals, flower finial, gold trim, 1850s-65 ....110.00
Teapot, Sandoz, penguin form, ca 1904-20s, 5¾" 600.00
Tray, Drop Rose, ca 1876-1930, 15¾x10¾" 550.00
Vase, birds on floral branches on bl/gr, 1880s, 16", EX 1,850.00
Vase, grapes, sgn, non-factory decor, hdls, 1893-1930, 12" 255.00
Vase, Terra Cotta, mc florals on brn, 3-ftd, 1873-82, 5" 550.00

Hawkes

Thomas Hawkes established his factory in Corning, New York, in 1880. He developed many beautiful patterns of cut glass, two of which were awarded the Grand Prize at the Paris Exposition in 1889. By the end of the century, his company was renowned for the finest in cut glass production. The company logo was a trefoil form enclosing a hawk in each of the two bottom lobes with a fleur-de-lis in the center. With the exception of some of the very early designs, all Hawkes was signed.

Bonbon, eng floral, silver finial, compartmented, 8" dia 285.00
Bowl, allover geometrics, scalloped rim, 2¾x8" 70.00
Bowl, hobstars, heavy blank, 3½x8" 215.00
Bowl, Napoleon pattern, 6" 350.00
Candy jar, Revere, w/lid, 10½" 325.00
Carafe, Venetian, flat bottom, 7¼" 175.00
Cheese & cracker, cut mitres, eng flower band, 3½x9½" 60.00
Cheese & cracker, eng roses, 4x9" 50.00
Compote, t'print cuttings, twisted stem, 7¼" 195.00
Decanter, eng thistles, silver cap, 11" 175.00
Lamp, Newport/stars on 12" mushroom shade/base, stepped std .2,400.00
Nappy, hobstars, wreaths & florals, ring hdl, 6½" dia 110.00
Oil bottle, Middlesex variation, w/stopper, 9½" 100.00
Plate, hobstars & fine cuttings, sgn, 7" dia 140.00
Plate, Marquis, hobstars, 10" 325.00
Punch bowl, Albion, hobstars/stars/fans/mitres, 7¼x15" 1,650.00
Tray, ice cream; Empress, 13" 1,000.00
Urn, relief dmns/X-cut dmns on amethyst, pleated rim, 8", pr 850.00
Vase, Brunswick, hobstar base, trumpet shape, 12" 325.00
Vase, cut, Teutonic, trumpet form, mk, 14" 625.00
Vase, cut/eng florals/ribbons, appl gr base, fan form, 11x8" 225.00
Vase, Dmn Point, cut rays & hobstars, 10x3½" 275.00
Vase, elaborate geometrics, 5-point flared rim, 11" 225.00
Vase, eng irises, bulbous w/flared neck, 10" 800.00
Vase, eng tiger lilies, ftd cylinder, 16½x3" 200.00

Vase, red o/l, turkey & stars, oval rim, sq ft, 12" 920.00

Head Vases

Vases modeled as heads of lovely ladies, delightful children, clowns, Madonnas — even some animals — were once popular as flower containers. Today they represent a growing area of collector interest. Most of them were imported from Japan, although some American potteries produced a few as well.

For more information, we recommend *Head Vases, Identification and Values*, by Kathleen Cole and *The World of Head Vase Planters* by Mike Posgay and Ian Warner.

Baby in bl blanket w/kitten, unmk, 6" 42.50
Baby w/pk bow in hair, Inarco #E3156, 5½" 42.50
Blond boy w/eyes to side, bsk, gold trim, unmk, 5½" 52.50
Blond girl in Christmas outfit, Napco #CS2348B, 5½" 47.50
Blond girl w/braids, lg bow on top of hair, #4796, 5¾" 37.50
Blond lady w/flip, pearl necklace, R/B paper label, 5½" 37.50
Blond w/flower in hair, blk glove, Inarco #E2104, 7" 42.50
Blond w/leaf on dress, pearl earrings, Napcoware #C7471, 4½" 27.50
Blond w/long hair & blk headband, Relpo #K1931, 8½" 95.00
Clown in red hat w/bl pompom, Inarco, not #d, 7" 37.50
Geisha in blk w/gold, Lee Wards label, 5" 37.50
Girl graduate, wht w/gold, Napco #C4072G, 1959, 6" 42.50
Girl in lg bl bonnet winking, Japan, 4½" 27.50
Girl in yel & wht, chin rests on hands, Napco #C4556B, 5" 37.50
Girl in yel holds blk telephone, Inarco #E3548, 5½" 32.50
Girl w/long hair, Love on necklace, Brinn's #2 TP-2444, 7½" 56.50
Girl w/ponytail on side, pearl earrings, Inarco #E3143, 7½" 67.50
Girl w/umbrella, flowers in hair, unmk, 4½" 52.50
Girl w/2 ponytails in gr hat, Reliable Glassware #K679C, 6" 32.50
Lady in bl hat w/wht bow, pearl earrings, Napco #C3342C, 4½" .32.50
Lady in blk, blk glove, pearl earrings, Napcoware #C347, 7" 42.50
Lady in blk hat, hand up, pearl jewelry, Inarco #E190/L, 7" 42.50
Lady in brn Derby-style hat, pearls, hand up, unmk, 6½" 37.50
Lady in draped scarf, Relpo #K162, 5½" 32.50
Lady in flat pk hat, pearl earrings, VCAGCO, 5¼" 32.50
Lady in gr & wht hat, pearl jewelry, Rubens #476, 5" 27.50
Lady in heart-shaped bonnet, Rubens label, #484, 5½" 37.50
Lady in pk pill-box hat, wht gloves, Relpo #A-1373S, 4½" 32.50
Lady in yel hat, wht gloves, Lefton's #1736, 5½" 37.50
Lady w/hand beside temple, wht w/gold, unmk, 5" 22.50
Lady w/lg brn curls, pearls, Brinn's #T1821, 7" 42.50
Lady w/lg curls, flower in hair, pearls, Inarco #E779, 6½" 42.50
Lady w/ornate curls, pk bow, pearl jewelry, Lark label, 7" 60.00
Lady w/sm tiara in hair, pearl jewelry, Inarco #E-1069, 10" 175.00
Lady w/3 flowers at neck, earrings, Napcoware #6429, 7½" 52.50

Man's face in clock surround, Lefton, 1956, 5½", $65.00.

Man in blk top hat, unmk, 4½" **27.50**
Man w/sm brn Derby hat & lg smile, Japan, 4" **27.50**
Royal Copley-style lady in pk hat, unmk, #214, 6¾" **42.50**

Heisey

A.H. Heisey began his long career at the King Glass Company of Pittsburgh. He later joined the Ripley Glass Company which soon became Geo. Duncan and Sons. After Duncan's death Heisey became half-owner in partnership with his brother-in-law, James Duncan. In 1895 he built his own factory in Newark, Ohio, initiating production in 1896 and continuing until Christmas of 1957. At that time Imperial Glass Corporation bought some of the molds. After 1968 they removed the old 'Diamond H' from any they put into use. In 1985 HCA purchased all of Imperial's Heisey molds with the exception of the Old Williamsburg line.

During their highly successful period of production, Heisey made fine handcrafted tableware with simple, yet graceful designs. Early pieces were not marked. After November 1901 the glassware was marked either with the 'Diamond H' or a paper label. Blown ware is often marked on the stem, never on the bowl or foot. For information concerning Heisey Collectors of America, see the Clubs, Newsletters, and Catalogs section of the Directory. See also Glass Animals.

Ipswich, green, candlestick centerpiece, footed vase with prisms, $450.00.

Charter Oak, crystal, comport, #3362, low ftd, 6" **50.00**
Charter Oak, gr, pitcher, #3362, flat **95.00**
Charter Oak, marigold, stem, parfait; #3362, 4½-oz **50.00**
Charter Oak, orchid, stem, cocktail; #3362, 3-oz **45.00**
Charter Oak, pk, plate, salad; #1246, Acorn & Leaves, 6" **10.00**
Chintz, crystal, bowl, floral; 2-hdld, ftd, 8½" **32.00**
Chintz, crystal, bowl, mint; ftd, 5½" **18.00**
Chintz, crystal, creamer, ind **12.00**
Chintz, crystal, plate, salad; sq, 7" **8.00**
Chintz, crystal, stem, water; #3389, 9-oz **15.00**
Chintz, crystal, stem, wine; #3389, 2½-oz **17.50**
Chintz, crystal, tumbler, water; #3389, ftd, 10-oz **13.00**
Chintz, yel, bowl, pickle/olive; 2-part, 7" **35.00**
Chintz, yel, bowl, relish; 3-part, 7" **35.00**
Chintz, yel, mayonnaise, dolphin ftd, 5½" **65.00**
Chintz, yel, plate, dinner; sq, 10½" **45.00**
Chintz, yel, plate, hdls, 12" **45.00**
Chintz, yel, stem, oyster/cocktail; #3389, 4-oz **20.00**
Chintz, yel, tray, sandwich; center hdl, sq, 12" **65.00**
Crystolite, crystal, ashtray, sq, 4½" **4.50**
Crystolite, crystal, bonbon, shell shape, 7" **17.00**

Crystolite, crystal, bottle, cologne; #108 stopper, 4-oz **65.00**
Crystolite, crystal, bowl, dressing; ruffled top, 5" **18.00**
Crystolite, crystal, bowl, floral; oval, deep, 13" **30.00**
Crystolite, crystal, bowl, nut; ind, hdld, 3" **15.00**
Crystolite, crystal, bowl, pickle; leaf shape, 9" **20.00**
Crystolite, crystal, candlestick, w/out vase, 3-light **20.00**
Crystolite, crystal, cigarette holder, ftd **17.50**
Crystolite, crystal, coaster, 4" **6.00**
Crystolite, crystal, cup **20.00**
Crystolite, crystal, mustard jar, w/lid **37.00**
Crystolite, crystal, pitcher, syrup; drip-cut top **100.00**
Crystolite, crystal, plate, buffet or punch liner, 20" **100.00**
Crystolite, crystal, plate, coupe; 7½" **20.00**
Crystolite, crystal, plate, salad; 7" **9.00**
Crystolite, crystal, plate, torte; 11" **24.00**
Crystolite, crystal, saucer **5.00**
Crystolite, crystal, tray, celery/olive; rectangular, 12" **35.00**
Crystolite, crystal, vase, ftd, 6" **22.50**
Empress, alexandrite, bowl, cream soup; w/sq liner **165.00**
Empress, alexandrite, bowl, floral; dolphin ftd, 11" **500.00**
Empress, alexandrite, sugar bowl, ind **210.00**
Empress, cobalt, plate, sq, 7" **55.00**
Empress, gr, bowl, floral; lion head, 10" **700.00**
Empress, gr, bowl, grapefruit; w/sq liner **35.00**
Empress, gr, bowl, lemon; w/lid, oval, 6½" **90.00**
Empress, gr, compotier, dolphin ftd, 6" **250.00**
Empress, gr, plate, sq, 8" **35.00**
Empress, gr, saucer **16.00**
Empress, pk, bowl, cream soup **26.00**
Empress, pk, bowl, nasturtium; dolphin ftd, 7½" **120.00**
Empress, pk, bowl, pickle/olive; 2-part, 13" **18.00**
Empress, pk, cup **27.00**
Empress, pk, marmalade, w/lid, dolphin ftd **70.00**
Empress, pk, plate, 10½" **100.00**
Empress, pk, sugar bowl, 3-hdld, dolphin ftd **35.00**
Empress, pk or gr, tumbler, ground bottom, 8-oz **40.00**
Empress, pk or yel, plate, 4½" **6.00**
Empress, yel, bowl, floral; rolled edge, 9" **38.00**
Empress, yel, bowl, preserve; hdls, 5" **22.00**
Empress, yel, candlestick, dolphin ftd, 6" **100.00**
Empress, yel, cup, bouillon; hdls **25.00**
Empress, yel, plate, hdls, sq, 13" **45.00**
Empress, yel, tray, celery; 10" **22.00**
Greek Key, crystal, bottle, oil; squat, w/#8 stopper, 6-oz **100.00**
Greek Key, crystal, bottle, oil; w/#6 stopper, 2-oz **110.00**
Greek Key, crystal, bowl, almond shape, ftd, 5" **35.00**
Greek Key, crystal, bowl, almond shape, ind, ftd **25.00**
Greek Key, crystal, bowl, nappy; 5½" **25.00**
Greek Key, crystal, bowl, nappy; 6½" **30.00**
Greek Key, crystal, bowl, orange; flared rim, 12" **115.00**
Greek Key, crystal, bowl, shallow, low ftd, 10" **85.00**
Greek Key, crystal, bowl, shallow, low ftd, 8" **75.00**
Greek Key, crystal, bowl, str, low ftd, 9" **50.00**
Greek Key, crystal, butter/jelly dish, w/lid, 2-hdld **180.00**
Greek Key, crystal, cheese & cracker set, 10" **80.00**
Greek Key, crystal, cup, punch; 4½-oz **20.00**
Greek Key, crystal, ice tub, tab hdld, lg **110.00**
Greek Key, crystal, jar, celery; tall **70.00**
Greek Key, crystal, jar, crushed fruit; w/lid, 1-qt **300.00**
Greek Key, crystal, plate, 10" **85.00**
Greek Key, crystal, plate, 6" **20.00**
Greek Key, crystal, shakers, pr **75.00**
Greek Key, crystal, sherbet, shallow, ftd, 4½-oz **15.00**
Greek Key, crystal, stem, low ftd, 9-oz **100.00**

Greek Key, crystal, stem, saucer champagne; 4½-oz 40.00
Greek Key, crystal, stem cordial; ¾-oz 250.00
Greek Key, crystal, sugar bowl, rnd, hotel sz 30.00
Greek Key, crystal, tray, French roll; 12½" 100.00
Greek Key, crystal, tumbler, flared rim, 12-oz 40.00
Greek Key, crystal, tumbler, flared rim, 13-oz 42.00
Greek Key, crystal, tumbler, flared rim, 5-oz 20.00
Ipswich, cobalt, candlestick, 1-light, 6" 350.00
Ipswich, crystal, bowl, floral; ftd, 11" 50.00
Ipswich, crystal, stem, schoppen; flat bottom, 12-oz 30.00
Ipswich, crystal, tumbler, soda; ftd, 12-oz 35.00
Ipswich, gr, creamer 90.00
Ipswich, gr, tumbler, soda; ftd, 5-oz 50.00
Ipswich, pk, bottle, oil; #86 stopper, ftd, 2-oz 185.00
Ipswich, pk, candy jar, w/lid, ½-lb 225.00
Ipswich, yel, sherbet, knob in stem, ftd, 4-oz 25.00
Lariat, crystal, basket, bonbon; 7½" 100.00
Lariat, crystal, bowl, nougat; flat, 8" 15.00
Lariat, crystal, bowl, nut; ind, 4" 20.00
Lariat, crystal, bowl, relish; oblong, 2-hdld, 11" 25.00
Lariat, crystal, candlestick, 1-light 15.00
Lariat, crystal, candy box, caramel; w/lid 55.00
Lariat, crystal, candy box, horse-head finial, w/lid, 8" 1,500.00
Lariat, crystal, compote, w/lid, 10" 100.00
Lariat, crystal, cup, punch 6.00
Lariat, crystal, plate, deviled egg; oval, 15" 185.00
Lariat, crystal, plate, salad; 8" 12.00
Lariat, crystal, saucer 5.00
Lariat, crystal, stem, cocktail; pressed, 3½-oz 15.00
Lariat, crystal, stem, oyster/cocktail; blown, 4½-oz 15.00
Lariat, crystal, stem, pressed, 9-oz 20.00
Lariat, crystal, stem, wine; pressed, 3½-oz 20.00
Lariat, crystal, tray (for sugar & creamer), hdls, 8" 20.00
Lariat, crystal, tumbler, iced tea; ftd, 12-oz 18.00
Lariat, crystal, vase, swung 125.00
Lodestar, dawn, bowl, crimped, 11" 95.00
Lodestar, dawn, bowl, mayonnaise; 5" 55.00
Lodestar, dawn, candlestick, 1-light centerpc, 2", pr 100.00
Lodestar, dawn, jar, #1626, w/lid, 8" 140.00
Lodestar, dawn, pitcher, #1626, 1-qt 150.00
Lodestar, dawn, sugar bowl 50.00
Lodestar, dawn, tray, celery; 10" 60.00
Lodestar, dawn, tray, relish; 3-part, 7½" 55.00
Lodestar, dawn, tumbler, juice; 6-oz 40.00
Lodestar, dawn, vase, #1626, crimped, 8" 175.00
New Era, crystal, bottle, rye; stopper 120.00
New Era, crystal, bowl, floral; 11" 35.00
New Era, crystal, cup 10.00
New Era, crystal, pilsner, 8-oz 25.00
New Era, crystal, plate, bread & butter; 5½x4½" 15.00
New Era, crystal, stem, claret; 4-oz 15.00
New Era, crystal, stem, cordial; 1-oz 45.00
New Era, crystal, stem, sherbet; low, 6-oz 10.00
New Era, crystal, tray, relish; 3-part, 13" 25.00
New Era, crystal, tumbler, low, ftd, 10-oz 10.00
New Era, crystal, tumbler, soda; ftd, 12-oz 12.50
New Era, crystal, tumbler, soda; ftd, 5-oz 7.00
Octagon, crystal, bowl, cream soup; 2-hdld 10.00
Octagon, crystal, mayonnaise, #1229, ftd, 5½" 10.00
Octagon, crystal, plate, sandwich; center hdl, 10½" 25.00
Octagon, dawn, tray, #500, 4-part, 12" 300.00
Octagon, gr, candlestick, 1-light, 3" 30.00
Octagon, gr, plate, 10½" 35.00
Octagon, marigold, bowl, mint; #1229, 6" 30.00

Octagon, orchid, cup, AD 42.00
Octagon, orchid, plate, 14" 50.00
Octagon, pk, bowl, jelly; #1229, 5½" 15.00
Octagon, pk, plate, cream soup liner 5.00
Octagon, pk or yel, plate, luncheon; 8" 10.00
Octagon, yel, bowl, grapefruit; 6½" 22.00
Octagon, yel, saucer, #1231 ....6.00
Octagon, yel or gr, tray, #500, oblong, 6" 12.00
Old Colony, crystal, bowl, finger; #3390, ftd 5.50
Old Colony, crystal, bowl, floral; dolphin ftd, 11" 32.00
Old Colony, crystal, cup 10.00
Old Colony, crystal, plate, sq, 6" 6.00
Old Colony, crystal, stem, short soda; #3380, 10-oz 7.00
Old Colony, crystal, sugar bowl, ind 12.50
Old Colony, gr, bottle, oil; ftd, 4-oz 120.00
Old Colony, gr, bowl, salad; hdls, rnd, 10" 65.00
Old Colony, gr, creamer, dolphin ftd 50.00
Old Colony, gr, plate, muffin; rnd, 2-hdld, 12" 75.00
Old Colony, gr, stem, parfait; #3380, 5-oz 17.00
Old Colony, gr, stem, water; #3390, low, 11-oz 30.00
Old Colony, gr, tumbler, soda; #3380, ftd, 8-oz 25.00
Old Colony, marigold, stem, claret; #3380, 4-oz 65.00
Old Colony, marigold, tumbler, bar; #3380, ftd, 2-oz 35.00
Old Colony, pk, bowl, mint; dolphin ftd, 6" 22.00
Old Colony, pk, bowl, pickle/olive; 2-part, 13" 20.00
Old Colony, pk, flagon, #3390, 12-oz 55.00
Old Colony, pk, plate, rnd, 8" 17.00
Old Colony, pk, saucer, sq 8.00
Old Colony, pk, stem, cocktail; #3390, 3-oz 15.00
Old Colony, pk, tray, celery; 13" 20.00
Old Colony, yel, bowl, grapefruit; #3380, ftd 18.00
Old Colony, yel, bowl, nappy; 8" 40.00
Old Colony, yel, comport, oval, ftd, 7" 80.00
Old Colony, yel, plate, rnd, 10½" 70.00
Old Colony, yel, stem, champagne; #3390, 6-oz 25.00
Old Colony, yel, stem, wine; #3380, 2½-oz 35.00
Old Colony, yel, tumbler, bar; #3380, ftd, 1-oz 42.50
Old Sandwich, cobalt, decanter, #98 stopper, 1-pt 425.00
Old Sandwich, crystal, creamer, 18-oz 40.00
Old Sandwich, crystal, mug, beer; 12-oz 35.00
Old Sandwich, crystal, plate, sq, 7" 10.00
Old Sandwich, gr, cigarette holder 65.00
Old Sandwich, gr, pitcher, ice lip, ½-gal 185.00
Old Sandwich, gr, stem, oyster/cocktail; 4-oz 32.00
Old Sandwich, gr, tumbler, 10-oz 45.00
Old Sandwich, pk, bottle, catsup; #3 stopper 200.00
Old Sandwich, pk, floral block, #22 ....25.00
Old Sandwich, pk, tumbler, bar; ground bottom, 1½-oz 130.00
Old Sandwich, pk or yel, tumbler, toddy; 6½-oz 22.00
Old Sandwich, yel, bowl, popcorn; cupped, ftd 75.00
Old Sandwich, yel, pilsner, 8-oz 32.00
Old Sandwich, yel, shakers, pr 75.00
Old Sandwich, yel, stem, low ftd, 10-oz 20.00
Old Sandwich, yel, stem, wine; 2½-oz 45.00
Orchid, crystal, basket, Lariat, 8½" 750.00
Orchid, crystal, bowl, dressing; oval, 2-part, Waverly, 6½" 47.50
Orchid, crystal, bowl, epergne; 9½" 500.00
Orchid, crystal, bowl, finger; #3309 or #5025 ....85.00
Orchid, crystal, bowl, flared, Queen Ann, 8½" 65.00
Orchid, crystal, bowl, floral; ftd, 11" 110.00
Orchid, crystal, bowl, floral; 11" 57.50
Orchid, crystal, bowl, gardenia; 13" 70.00
Orchid, crystal, bowl, jelly; ftd, 7" 40.00
Orchid, crystal, candlestick, 1-light, w/prisms, Queen Ann 125.00

Orchid, crystal, candlestick, 3-light, Cascade **75.00**
Orchid, crystal, candy box, w/lid, bowknot finial, 6" **165.00**
Orchid, crystal, chocolate box, w/lid, Waverly, 5" **185.00**
Orchid, crystal, cigarette holder, w/lid **125.00**
Orchid, crystal, cocktail shaker, #4036 or #4225, 1-qt **225.00**
Orchid, crystal, creamer, ftd **25.00**
Orchid, crystal, decanter, #4036, ftd, 1-pt **325.00**
Orchid, crystal, marmalade, w/lid **225.00**
Orchid, crystal, mayonnaise, 1-hdl, 5½" **40.00**
Orchid, crystal, mustard jar, w/lid, Queen Ann **135.00**
Orchid, crystal, pitcher, 73-oz **450.00**
Orchid, crystal, plate, cake or salver; ftd, 14" **275.00**
Orchid, crystal, plate, salad; 7" **18.00**
Orchid, crystal, stem, claret; #5022 or #5025, 4½-oz **135.00**
Orchid, crystal, stem, sherry; #5022 or #5025, 2-oz **120.00**
Orchid, crystal, stem, water; #5022 or #5025, low, 10-oz **35.00**
Orchid, crystal, tray, celery; 12" **47.50**
Orchid, crystal, vase, ftd, 7" **85.00**
Plantation, crystal, ashtray, 3½" **35.00**
Plantation, crystal, bottle, syrup; drip-cut top **80.00**
Plantation, crystal, bowl, celery; 13" **35.00**
Plantation, crystal, bowl, dressing; 2-part, 8½" **45.00**
Plantation, crystal, bowl, jelly; hdls, 6½" **35.00**
Plantation, crystal, butter dish, w/lid, oblong, ¼-lb **95.00**
Plantation, crystal, candlestick, 1-light **50.00**
Plantation, crystal, cheese dish, w/lid, ftd, 5" **90.00**
Plantation, crystal, coaster, 4" **50.00**
Plantation, crystal, cup **30.00**
Plantation, crystal, cup, punch **30.00**
Plantation, crystal, pitcher, ice lip, blown, ½-gal **400.00**
Plantation, crystal, plate, salad; 8" **25.00**
Plantation, crystal, plate, sandwich; 14" **65.00**
Plantation, crystal, shakers, pr **50.00**
Plantation, crystal, stem, claret; pressed, 4½-oz **65.00**
Plantation, crystal, stem, cocktail; pressed, 3½-oz **35.00**
Plantation, crystal, stem, pressed, 10-oz **50.00**
Plantation, crystal, tumbler, iced tea; pressed, ftd, 12-oz **75.00**
Pleat & Panel, crystal, bottle, oil; pressed stopper, 3-oz **20.00**
Pleat & Panel, crystal, bowl, bouillon; hdls, 5" **7.00**
Pleat & Panel, gr, compotier, w/lid, high ftd, 5" **70.00**
Pleat & Panel, gr, platter, oval, 12" **40.00**
Pleat & Panel, pk, bowl, grapefruit/cereal; 6½" **13.00**
Pleat & Panel, pk, plate, bouillon underliner; 6¾" **8.00**
Pleat & Panel, pk, vase, 8" **50.00**
Provincial, crystal, ashtray, sq, 3" **12.50**
Provincial, crystal, bowl, nut/jelly; hdls, 5" **12.00**
Provincial, crystal, bowl, relish; 4-part, 10" **40.00**
Provincial, crystal, candlestick, 3-light **60.00**
Provincial, crystal, coaster, 4" **10.00**
Provincial, crystal, mayonnaise set, plate, bowl & ladle, 7" **40.00**
Provincial, crystal, plate, torte; 14" **30.00**
Provincial, crystal, stem, 10-oz **15.00**
Provincial, crystal, vase, violet; 3½" **30.00**
Provincial, limelight gr, bonbon, upturned sides, 2-hdld, 7" **37.50**
Provincial, limelight gr, candy box, w/lid, ftd, 5½" **500.00**
Provincial, limelight gr, plate, luncheon; 8" **50.00**
Provincial, limelight gr, tumbler, juice; ftd, 5-oz **50.00**
Queen Ann, crystal, bowl, cream soup; w/sq liner **20.00**
Queen Ann, crystal, bowl, dessert; oval, 2-hdld, 10" **30.00**
Queen Ann, crystal, bowl, mint; dolphin ftd, 6" **14.00**
Queen Ann, crystal, candlestick, hdls, 4-ftd, low **15.00**
Queen Ann, crystal, cup, bouillon; hdls **16.00**
Queen Ann, crystal, plate, 10½" **40.00**
Queen Ann, crystal, plate, 4½" **5.00**

Queen Ann, crystal, saucer, sq **3.00**
Queen Ann, crystal, stem, Empress stemware, rare, 9-oz **30.00**
Queen Ann, crystal, tray, buffet relish; 4-part, 16" **30.00**
Ridgeleigh, crystal, ashtray, rnd, 4" **12.00**
Ridgeleigh, crystal, bowl, floral; 11½" **35.00**
Ridgeleigh, crystal, bowl, nappy; ball or cupped, 4½" **7.00**
Ridgeleigh, crystal, bowl, nappy; sq, 8" **45.00**
Ridgeleigh, crystal, candlestick, bobeche & A prisms, 2-light **70.00**
Ridgeleigh, crystal, cup **15.00**
Ridgeleigh, crystal, pitcher, ice lip, ball shape, ½-gal **190.00**
Ridgeleigh, crystal, stem, cocktail; pressed **22.00**
Ridgeleigh, crystal, stem, luncheon; low, 8-oz **25.00**
Ridgeleigh, crystal, tumbler, iced tea; blown, 13-oz **22.00**
Ridgeleigh, crystal, tumbler, juice; blown, 5-oz **24.00**
Rose, crystal, bowl, floral; Waverly, 11" **67.50**
Rose, crystal, bowl, lily; Queen Ann, 7" **50.00**
Rose, crystal, bowl, mint; ftd, 5½" **35.00**
Rose, crystal, creamer, ind, Waverly **25.00**
Rose, crystal, mayonnaise, ftd, Waverly, 5½" **60.00**

Rose, crystal, pitcher, #4164, 73-oz, $575.00.

Rose, crystal, stem, cordial; #5072, 1-oz **145.00**
Rose, crystal, tray, celery; Waverly, 13" **67.50**
Saturn, crystal, bowl, celery; 10" **15.00**
Saturn, crystal, bowl, finger **5.00**
Saturn, crystal, marmalade, w/lid **45.00**
Saturn, crystal, tumbler, soda; 12-oz **10.00**
Saturn, limelight gr, comport, 7" **550.00**
Saturn, limelight gr, plate, luncheon; 8" **55.00**
Stanhope, crystal, cup, w/ or w/o rnd knobs **15.00**
Stanhope, crystal, plate, 7" **7.50**
Stanhope, crystal, shakers, #60 top **45.00**
Stanhope, crystal, stem, claret; #4083, 4-oz **25.00**
Stanhope, crystal, tumbler, soda; #4083, 8-oz **22.50**
Twist, crystal, bottle, oil; #78 stopper, 4-oz **40.00**
Twist, crystal, sugar bowl, almond shape, ind, ftd **15.00**
Twist, gr, cheese dish, hdls, 6" **17.50**
Twist, gr, stem, saucer champagne; 2-block stem, 5-oz **22.00**
Twist, pk, bowl, nappy; ground bottom, 8" **25.00**
Twist, pk, plate, relish, 3-part, 13" **17.00**
Twist, yel, bowl, grapefruit; ftd **60.00**
Twist, yel, tray, celery; 10" **30.00**
Victorian, crystal, bowl, floral; 10½" **40.00**
Victorian, crystal, bowl, nappy; 8" **30.00**
Victorian, crystal, cigarette box, 4" **50.00**
Victorian, crystal, shakers, pr **40.00**
Victorian, crystal, sugar bowl **25.00**
Victorian, crystal, vase, 5½" **35.00**
Waverly, crystal, bowl, gardenia; 13" **25.00**
Waverly, crystal, bowl, salad; 7" **17.00**
Waverly, crystal, candle holder, flame center, 2-light **65.00**

Waverly, crystal, comport, oval, low ftd, 7" 40.00
Waverly, crystal, mayonnaise, w/ladle & liner, 5½" 50.00
Waverly, crystal, shakers, pr 50.00
Yeoman, crystal, bowl, finger 5.00
Yeoman, crystal, cruet, oil; 3-oz 20.00
Yeoman, gr, plate, bouillon underliner; 6" 10.00
Yeoman, marigold, cigarette box (ashtray) 100.00
Yeoman, orchid, bowl, vegetable; w/lid, 2-hdld, 9" 95.00
Yeoman, orchid, plate, finger-bowl underliner 11.00
Yeoman, pk, bowl, grapefruit; ftd 17.00
Yeoman, pk, bowl, lemon; oval, 5" 10.00
Yeoman, yel, bowl, vegetable; 6" 14.00
Yeoman, yel, parfait, 5-oz 20.00

Herend

Herend, Hungary, was the center of a thriving pottery industry as early as the mid-1800s. Decorative items as well as tablewares were made in keeping with the styles of the times. Items described in the following listings may be marked simply Herend, indicating the city, or with a manufacturer's backstamp.

Figurine, Belly Dancer, #5981, 13" 440.00
Figurine, nude w/snake, 10" 600.00
Tea set, bl floral w/gold, rose finials, 3-pc 350.00
Tureen, w/3¼" nymph finial 1,100.00

Heubach

Gebruder Heubach is a German porcelain company that has been in operation since the 1800s, producing quality figurines and novelty items. They are perhaps most famous for their doll heads and piano babies, most of which are marked with the circular rising sun device containing an 'H' superimposed over a 'C.' Our advisor for this category is Grace Ochsner; she is listed in the Directory under Illinois.

Angry baby w/clenched hands sits before open eggshell, 5" 450.00
Baby, crawling, molded hair, intaglio eyes, 7" L, NM 495.00
Baby in highchair, molded clothes, sm 525.00

Baby sitting in wicker high-chair removing socks, 7", $500.00 at auction.

Baby in wht gown sitting & reaching for toes, 8" 550.00
Baby seated before planter, 5½" 475.00
Batter & pitcher, solid-color jerseys, mk, 9", pr 1,200.00
Blond baby sits in tattered shoe, 12" 1,950.00
Boy (or girl) beside lg turkey, bl, gold trim, #3318, 5", pr 595.00
Boy in man's top hat & coat leans on umbrella, 13" 625.00
Boy in red hat & eyeglasses sits w/arms Xd on chair bk, 7" 675.00

Boy w/fish in baskets, on base, 7" 395.00
Bust of Victorian girl leaning on log, mk, 6" 625.00
Dog smoking pipe, polka-dot scarf around head, 6¼x8½" 595.00
Dutch boy, seated, eyes right, 4" 425.00
Dutch girl, seated, basket on bk, mk, 5" 425.00
Girl in bunny costume before lg pk egg, eyes to side, 7½" 695.00
Girl sitting, bl dress, wht cap, #3218, 5" 450.00
Lady sits & holds egg to side, gr dress, #5655, 4" 325.00
Man w/ax & lady w/baby, bsk, 12½", pr 895.00
Nude blond child sits w/hands to cheeks, 4" 450.00
Pup crouches over bowl, pipe in mouth, jaw tied w/cloth, 3" 625.00
Vase, lady's profile w/in Nouveau floral reserve on bl, 4½" 350.00

Hickman, Royal Arden

Born in Willamette, Oregon, Royal A. Hickman was a genius in all aspects of design interpretation. Mr. Hickman's expertise can be seen in the designs of the lovely Heisey figurines, Kosta crystal, Bruce Fox aluminum, Three Crowns aluminum, Vernon Kilns, and Royal Haeger Pottery (as well as handcrafted silver, furniture, and paintings).

Because Mr. Hickman moved around during much of his lifetime, his influence has been felt in all forms of the media. Designs from his independent companies include 'Royal Hickman Pottery and Lamps' (sold through Ceramic Arts Inc., of Chattanooga, Tennessee), 'Royal Hickman's Paris Ware,' 'Royal Hickman — Florida,' and 'California Designed by Royal Hickman.' The following listings will give examples of pieces bearing the various trademarks. Our advisors for this category are Lee Garmon and Doris Frizzell; both are listed in the Directory under Illinois. See also Royal Haegar; Vernon Kilns, Melinda pattern.

Bruce Fox Aluminum

Banana leaf, sgn Royal Hickman-RH 6, 22½" L 25.00
Dish, lobster, lg 50.00
Dish, 3-point leaf, sgn Royal Hickman, 15½" L 25.00
Ivy tray, #362, 13" 20.00
Platter, fish, EX detail, sgn Royal Hickman-RH 3, 13x9" 50.00
2-acorn oak tray, 14½" 25.00
5-point leaf tray, 14" 25.00
7-point leaf tray, sgn Royal Hickman, 14" 25.00

California, Designed by Royal Hickman

Bowl, red w/blk highlights, #607, 9½" 25.00
Figurine, deer, apple gr w/wht spots, appl eyes, 15" 45.00
Figurine, giraffe & young, pk w/blk spots 65.00

Lamp base, flying geese, 17", $200.00.

Punch bowl, Tom & Jerry, w/8 mugs 300.00
Swan, red w/blk highlights, #643, 17" 40.00

Miscellaneous Signatures

Sea horse vase, sgn Royal Hickman USA, #468, 8" 35.00
Vase, fish figurine, Petty Crystal Glaze, #467 ....25.00
Vase, lg heart, sgn Royal Hickman, Italy, #3774 ....45.00
Vase, rooster figurine, Petty Crystal Glaze, #565 ....95.00

Royal Hickman — Florida

Vase, free-form, #578, 14" 40.00
Vase, horse's head, gray w/wht mane, 13¾" 85.00
Vase, pouter pigeon, blk cascade, #599, 8½" 40.00
Vase, swan, head down, blk cascade, 3624-R, 14" 60.00

Royal Hickman — Guadalajara, Mexico

Vase, 3 dolphin figures, 13" 95.00

Higgins

Contemporary glass artists Frances and Michael Higgins have been designing high-quality glassware since the late 1940s. Their designs are often created by fusing layers of glass together, though sometimes colored ground glass is used to 'paint' the decoration onto the surface. Molds are used, and through a process called 'slumping,' the glass is fired to a very high temperature, causing it to soften and take on the predetermined shape. Their work is ultramodern and is more readily found in metropolitan areas.

The earliest mark was an etched signature on the bottom of the glass — either 'Frances Stewart Higgins' or 'Michael Higgins' or both, which was dropped in favor of just 'Higgins' with a raised 'Higgins Man' figure. From approximately 1957 to 1964, the Higgins signature was embossed in gold on top. After 1964 up to the present the signature again appears on the bottom and is etched in the glass. Our advisor is Dennis Hopp; he is listed in the Directory under Illinois.

Trays by Michael and Frances Higgins, all late 1950s and early 1960s; Enameled and applied glass with 2 pocket watches in yellow and orange, gilt enameled fobs, 7x5", $40.00; Green glass with internal stylized flower, 5x5", $40.00; Molded lavender iridescent with long blue and green triangles, 9½x9½", $130.00.

Ashtray, lt gr w/stylized yel/gr/gilt flower, 5" sq 40.00
Ashtray, Peacock, stylized feathers, gold tracing, 10x14" 125.00
Bowl, bl, sq, sgn, 2x7" 75.00
Bowl, int abstracts in gold/gr, conical w/wide rim, 5x10" 300.00

Charger, lime blobs w/coral-like branches on clear, 14" 145.00
Clock, fused 8" face, blk/gold hr markers, aluminum stand, EX ..400.00
Dish, 4-color geometrics, 3 slumped sections, 3x14x15" 375.00
Dish, 5-color decor, slumped compartments, 2x13½" dia 100.00
Plate, astors, gr w/gold trim, 8-sided, 12" 90.00
Platter, bl peacock feathers, 12" 85.00
Posey pocket, Roman Stripes, bl/lime, 2 fused planes, 10x7" 200.00
Tray, lav irid w/long triangles in bl & gr, 10" sq 130.00
Vase, wht & gold int decor, 7" 200.00

Historical Glass

Glassware commemorating particularly significant historical events became popular in the late 1800s. Bread trays were the most common form, but plates, mugs, pitchers, and other items were also pressed in clear as well as colored glass. It was sold in vast amounts at the 1876 Philadelphia Centennial Exposition by various manufacturers who exhibited their wares on the grounds. It remained popular well into the 20th century.

In the listings that follow, L numbers refer to a book by Lindsey, a standard guide used by many collectors. Our advisor for this category is Darlene Yohe; she is listed in the Directory under Arkansas. See also Bread Plates; Pattern Glass.

Bottle, Columbus, milk glass, w/stopper 600.00
Bottle, Grant's Tomb, milk glass, no stopper 250.00
Bust, Dewey, Manila 1898, 5" 145.00
Butter dish, American Shield 195.00
Butter dish, Garfield Drape 85.00
Calabash, Roosevelt-TVA, aqua, qt 60.00
Covered dish, Battleship Oregon, milk glass, L-469, 6½" L, EX ...75.00
Covered dish, Uncle Sam, milk glass, L-112 ....75.00
Creamer, Bullet Emblem 165.00
Cup, Harrison & Morton, bl 165.00
Cup, McKinley, w/lid, L-355 ....60.00
Cup plate, Bunker Hill 30.00
Flask, Blaine & Logan, oval, 6¾" 550.00
Flask, Cleveland & Stevenson side-by-side jugate, 7" 50.00
Glass, ale; Centennial 55.00
Goblet, Pittsburgh Centennial 95.00
Jar, Statue of Liberty, L-530 ....55.00
Lamp, Emblem, L-62 ....195.00
Mug, Bryan, The People's Money, no lid 55.00
Mug, Bumper to the Flag, sabers & 35-star flag 235.00
Mug, Christopher Columbus, L-1 ....45.00
Mug, Garfield Assassination, 2¼" 65.00
Mug, Liberty Bell, milk glass, mini 115.00
Mug, Liberty Bell, snake hdl, Gillinder 300.00
Mug, Martyrs Lincoln & Garfield 50.00
Mug, striped shields w/3 stars front & bk, dtd 1776-1876 ....110.00
Paperweight, Director Goshorn, 1876, Gillinder, L-449 ....155.00
Paperweight, Infant Samuel 110.00
Paperweight, Lincoln, clear/frost, L-275 ....165.00
Paperweight, Lincoln, clear/frost, oval, L-276 ....225.00
Paperweight, Lion, Gillinder, frosted, L-516 ....195.00
Paperweight, McKinley portrait, milk glass 125.00
Paperweight, Plymouth Rock, L-18 ....65.00
Paperweight, Washington, L-257 ....135.00
Paperweight, Washington Monument, milk glass, 5½" 175.00
Pitcher, Dewey, L-400 ....55.00
Plate, Abraham Lincoln w/backward C edge, milk glass 65.00
Plate, Battleship Maine, openwork border, 5½" 16.00
Plate, Bryan, flag/eagle/star border, milk glass, L-359 ....85.00

Plate, Columbia Shield, sapphire bl 225.00
Plate, Columbus, milk glass, 9½" 65.00
Plate, For President Winfield S Hancock, 8" 110.00
Plate, Harrison/Ft Meigs, amber 75.00
Plate, Indian, milk glass, L-14, 7½" 60.00
Plate, McKinley 35.00
Plate, Old Glory, openwork border, 5½" 32.00
Plate, Queen Victoria, L-435, 5¼" 25.00
Plate, Texan Campaign, lt bl, 9½" 195.00
Plate, We Mourn our Nation's Loss, Garfield, w/gold, 11" 55.00
Plate, Wm H Harrison, Tippecanoe, Fort Meigs, amber, 8" 225.00
Shaker, Benjamin Franklin, M-194 ....85.00
Shaker, Lighthouse 48.00
Spooner, Bullet Emblem, rare 115.00
Spooner, Log Cabin, L-184 ....115.00
Statue, Ruth the Gleaner, frosted, 1876 Phila Expo, Gillinder ...175.00
Toothpick holder, man w/hat, rare 225.00
Toothpick holder, Preparedness, soldier figural, L-483 ....145.00
Tumbler, Bust of McKinley in laurel wreath 75.00
Tumbler, Lord's Prayer, blown & etched 35.00
Tumbler, Louisiana Purchase, milk glass, M-193b 22.50
Tumbler, Philadelphia Sesquicentennial 18.00
Tumbler, Rock of Ages, L-227 ....25.00
Wine, Washington Centennial 65.00

Hobbs, Brockunier, & Co.

Hobbs and Brockunier's South Wheeling Glass Works was in operation during the last quarter of the 19th century. They are most famous for their peachblow, amberina, Daisy and Button, and Hobnail pattern glass. The mainstay of the operation, however, was druggist items and plain glassware — bowls, mugs, and simple footed pitchers with shell handles. See also Frances Ware.

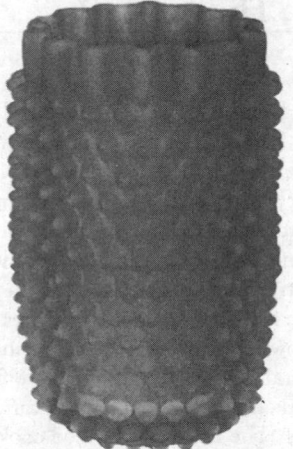

Vase, Hobnail, pink frost, ruffled rim, 6½", $150.00.

Berry set, Daisy & Button, amberina, sq forms, 7-pc, EX 345.00
Boat, Daisy & Button, amberina, 14" 850.00
Celery vase, Gonterman Swirl, bl rim, wht opal base, 5⅝x5" 245.00
Cruet, Hobnail, cranberry opal, faceted clear stopper, 7x4½" 485.00
Pitcher, milk; Hobnail, wht opal, sq top, 5¾x5" 235.00

Holt Howard

Novelty ceramics marked Holt Howard represent one of the newest areas of collectibles on today's market, and dealers report a good

amount of market activity. Made from the '50s into the '70s, they're not only marked, but most are dated as well. There are several lines to reassemble — the rooster, the white cat, figural banks, Christmas angels and Santas, to name only a few — but the one that most Holt Howard collectors seem to gravitate toward is the pixie line.

Ashtray, cat on sq plaid base, 4 corner rests 45.00
Bank, clown w/bobbing head figural 95.00
Bell, Christmas, w/holly decor 15.00
Candle holder, drunken snowman 20.00
Candle holders, angel & fawn, pr 28.00
Candle holders, Christmas angel, pr 35.00
Cherries jar, pixie-head finial w/cherry pick or spoon 65.00
Cookie jar, apples 40.00
Cookie jar, mice 50.00
Cookie jar, Santa, 3-pc 145.00
Cookie jar, wht cat head 45.00
Cottage cheese keeper, cat knob on lid 45.00
Creamer & sugar bowl, rooster 45.00
Desk set, chicken figures in wht w/gold & brn, 3-pc set 95.00
Egg cup, rooster figural 18.00
Hors d'oeuvre, pixie head, exaggerated tall hairdo, 7" 85.00
Instant coffee jar, brn-skinned blond pixie-head finial 100.00
Jam & jelly jar, emb rooster, yel/orange/brn on wht 35.00
Jam & jelly jar, pixie head on lid 45.00
Ketchup jar, orange pixie-head finial 40.00
Letter holder, cat w/coiled wire bk 20.00
Match holder, mouse 30.00
Mayonnaise jar, pixie-head finial 45.00
Memo holder, cat figural, legs cradle note pad 85.00
Mug, emb rooster, yel/orange/brn on wht 15.00
Napkin holder, rooster 20.00
Onion jar, flat onion-head pixie finial, 1958 ....45.00
Pitcher, Santa, 5" 25.00
Planter, mother deer & fawn, wht w/gold bow 24.00
Sewing box, cat figural, tape measure tongue on lid 65.00
Shakers, apple, pr 8.00
Shakers, cat's head, wht, pr 12.00
Shakers, cow, pr 35.00
Shakers, girl w/flower fan, pr 15.00
Shakers, rooster, lg, pr 30.00
Shakers, Santa, stackable, pr 25.00
Shakers, tomato, pr 15.00
Spoon rest, rooster figural, yel/orange/brn on wht 35.00
Vase, bud; cat figural 75.00
Wall pocket, cat's head, wht 34.00

Homer Laughlin

The Homer Laughlin China Company of Newell, West Virginia, was founded in 1871. The superior dinnerware they displayed at the Centennial Exposition in Philadelphia in 1876 won the highest award of excellence. From that time to the present, they have continued to produce quality dinnerware and kitchenware, many lines of which are becoming very popular collectibles. Most of the dinnerware is marked with the name of the pattern and occasionally with the shape name as well. The 'HLC' trademark is usually followed by a number series, the first two digits of which indicate the year of its manufacture. See also Fiesta; Harlequin; Riviera.

Amberstone, bowl, soup/cereal 8.00
Amberstone, butter dish 42.00
Amberstone, cup & saucer 8.00

Amberstone, platter, oval 15.00
Amberstone, sauce boat 22.00
Americana, bowl, cream soup 75.00
Americana, bowl, vegetable; 9" 26.00
Americana, sugar bowl, w/lid 18.00
Carnival, bowl, fruit; cobalt or ivory, sm 7.00
Carnival, plate, lt or dk gr, 6½" 2.00
Casualstone, bowl, rnd vegetable 15.00
Casualstone, cup & saucer 8.00
Casualstone, marmalade 45.00
Casualstone, plate, dinner 8.00
Casualstone, platter, rnd 15.00
Child's, Dick Tracy set, 3-pc 245.00
Child's, Ralston bowl 40.00
Conchita, batter jug, Kitchen Kraft, w/lid 152.00
Conchita, cake server, Kitchen Kraft 60.00
Dogwood, bowl, vegetable; oval, 9½" 20.00
Dogwood, cup & saucer 10.00
Dogwood, plate, 9" 8.00
Dogwood, teapot 70.00
Dreamland, plate, 10" 175.00
Dreamland, stein 150.00
Embossed Line, bowl, mixing; 7¼" 15.00
Embossed Line, bowl, soup; tab hdl, 7" 10.00
Embossed Line, casserole, 8½" 30.00
Epicure, casserole, ind 72.00
Epicure, ladle, 5½" 42.00
Epicure, teacup & saucer 22.00
Hacienda, butter dish, ½-lb 125.00
Hacienda, plate, 9" 20.00
Hacienda, teapot, rare 130.00
Harmony, bowl, nappy, 9" 15.00
Harmony, cup & saucer 10.00
Jubilee, casserole 32.00
Jubilee, egg cup 11.00
Jubilee, shakers, pr 9.00
Laughlin Art China, mug, American Beauty 100.00

Laughlin Art China pitcher, lady with birds, gold trim, 6", $85.00.

Laughlin Art China, pitcher, bulbous, Currant, 4½x5" 100.00
Laughlin Art China, rose bowl, Currant, 4" 150.00
Laughlin Art China, stein, White Pets 150.00
Laughlin Art China, vase, slim form, Currant, 16" 225.00
Max-i-cana, bowl, oatmeal; 6" 25.00
Max-i-cana, egg cup, rolled edge 40.00
Max-i-cana Fiesta, cup & saucer 40.00
Mexicana, bowl, lug soup; 4½" 35.00
Mexicana, casserole, Kitchen Kraft, w/lid, 8½" 75.00
Mexicana, pie plate, Kitchen Kraft 32.00
Mexicana, tumbler, fired-on design, 10-oz 18.00

Oven Serve, cake server, Kitchen Kraft 40.00
Oven Serve, shakers, Kitchen Kraft, pr 42.00
Oven Serve, stacking refrigerator unit, Kitchen Kraft 28.00
Pastel Nautilus, bowl, fruit; 5" 6.50
Pastel Nautilus, gravy boat 15.00
Pastel Nautilus, platter, 11" 12.00
Price list, Fiesta, 1930s through 1940s, ea 55.00
Price list, Harlequin 60.00
Price list, Jubilee 35.00
Priscilla, bowl, mixing; Kitchen Kraft, 8" 30.00
Priscilla, creamer 12.00
Priscilla, pitcher, water; Kitchen Kraft 30.00
Priscilla, plate, 9" 9.00
Rhythm, bowl, fruit; 5½" 6.50
Rhythm, cup & saucer 10.00
Rhythm, plate, 9" 9.00
Rhythm, shakers, pr 11.00
Rhythm Rose, bowl, mixing; Kitchen Kraft, lg 22.00
Rhythm Rose, coffeepot, Kitchen Kraft 35.00
Serenade, bowl, lug soup 20.00
Serenade, creamer 9.00
Serenade, plate, chop 17.00
Tango, bowl, oval baker, 9" 12.00
Tango, plate, 10" 11.00
Tango, sugar bowl, w/lid 11.00
Virginia Rose, bowl, deep, 5" 15.00
Virginia Rose, butter dish, ½-lb 100.00
Virginia Rose, egg cup, dbl 40.00
Virginia Rose, mug, coffee 35.00
Virginia Rose, plate, deep, no flange or 1" flange, ea 18.00
Wells Art Glaze, bowl, oatmeal '36s 18.00
Wells Art Glaze, cup & saucer, AD 24.00
Wells Art Glaze, plate, 9" 12.00
Wells Art Glaze, syrup 95.00

Hull

The A.E. Hull Pottery was formed in 1905 in Zanesville, Ohio, and in the early years produced stoneware specialities. They expanded in 1907, adding a second plant and employing over two hundred workers. By 1920 they were manufacturing a full line of stoneware, art pottery with both airbrushed and blended glazes, florist pots, and gardenware. They also produced toilet ware and kitchen items with a white semi-porcelain body. Although these continued to be staple products, after the stock market crash of 1929, emphasis was shifted to tile production. By the mid-thirties interest in art pottery production was growing, and over the next fifteen years, several lines of matt pastel floral-decorated patterns were designed, consisting of vases, planters, baskets, ewers, and bowls in various sizes.

The Red Riding Hood cookie jar, patented in 1943, proved so successful that a whole line of figural kitchenware and novelty items was added. They continued to be produced well into the fifties. (See also Little Red Riding Hood.) Through the forties their floral artware lines flooded the market, due to the restriction of foreign imports. Although best known for their pastel matt-glazed ware, some of the lines were high gloss. Rosella, glossy coral on a pink clay body, was produced for a short time only; and Magnolia, although offered in a matt glaze, was produced in gloss as well.

The plant was destroyed in 1950 by a flood which resulted in a devastating fire when the floodwater caused the kilns to explode. The company rebuilt and equipped their new factory with the most modern machinery. It was soon apparent that the matt glaze could not be duplicated through the more modern processes, however, and soon attention was concentrated on high-gloss artware lines such as Parchment and Pine and Ebb Tide. Figural planters and novelties, piggy banks, and dinnerware were produced in abundance in the late fifties and sixties. By the mid-seventies dinnerware and florist ware were the mainstay of their business. The firm discontinued operations in 1985.

Our advisor, Brenda Roberts, has compiled a lovely book, *The Collector's Encyclopedia of Hull Pottery*, with full-color photos and current values. You will find her address in the Directory under Missouri. Another informative book is *Collector's Guide to Hull Pottery, The Dinnerware Lines*, by Barbara Loveless Gick-Burke, available from Collector Books or your bookstore.

Blossom Flite, basket, pk/blk, T-2, 6" 70.00
Blossom Flite, candle holders, pk/blk, T-11, 3", pr 50.00
Blossom Flite, ewer, pk/blk, rope hdl, T-13, 13½" 155.00
Bow-Knot, candle holder, bl/gr, B-17, 4" 100.00

Bow-Knot, double cornucopia, B-13, 13", $285.00.

Bow-Knot, cornucopia, pk/turq, B-5, 7½" 145.00
Bow-Knot, jardiniere, bl/gr, hdls, B-19, 9⅜" 1,000.00
Bow-Knot, vase, pk/turq, shaped rim, B-11, 10½" 435.00
Bow-Knot, wall plaque, flat plate-like shape, B-28, 10" 1,100.00
Bow-Knot, wall pocket, pressing-iron form, unmk, 6¼" 265.00
Butterfly, ashtray, wht matt, heart shape, B-3, 7" 37.50
Butterfly, ewer, wht matt/turq, gold trim, B-15, 13½" 225.00
Butterfly, serving tray, wht matt/turq w/gold, B-23, 11½" 100.00
Butterfly, vase, wht matt, ftd, B-10, 7" 60.00
Calla Lily, bowl, emb florals, incurvate rim, #500/32, 10" 215.00
Calla Lily, vase, gr/pk, angle hdls, #500/33, 8" 160.00
Calla Lily, vase, gr/yel, angle hdls, #560/33, 13" 385.00
Camellia, basket, pk/bl, scalloped, simple hdl, #140, 10½" ...1,050.00
Camellia, ewer, pk/bl, scalloped lip, #106, 13¼" 775.00
Camellia, teapot, wht, squat, #110, 8½" 325.00
Camellia, vase, pk/bl, ornate hdls, #134, 6¼" 110.00
Camellia, wall pocket, pk/bl, scalloped rim, #125, 8½" 400.00
Cinderella Blossom or Bouquet, bowl, ink stamp, 9¾" 115.00
Cinderella Blossom or Bouquet, bowl, mixing; #20, 7½" 42.50
Cinderella Blossom or Bouquet, creamer, #28, 4½" 40.00
Cinderella Blossom or Bouquet, pitcher, #22, 64-oz 155.00
Cinderella Blossom or Bouquet, pitcher, #29, 32-oz 55.00
Classic, vase, floral on ivory swirled shape, #5, 6" 30.00
Continental, basket, Mtn Bl/Wht Haze, #55, 12¾" 175.00
Continental, candle holder/planter, dk bl, unmk, 4" 27.50
Continental, planter, Evergreen/Wht Haze, #41, 15½" 35.00
Continental, vase, Evergreen/Wht Haze, #53, 8½" 45.00
Debonair, cookie jar, yel, #0-8, 8¾" 110.00
Dogwood, candle holder, pk/bl, cornucopia form, #512, 3¾" 115.00
Dogwood, low bowl, scalloped, sm hdls, #521, 7" 150.00

Dogwood, vase, pk/bl, ornate hdls, #510, 10½" 310.00
Dogwood, vase, pk/bl, rim-to-base hdls, #513, 6½" 135.00
Early Art, jardiniere, semi-porc, emb trees on turq, #546, 7" 90.00
Early Art, vase, stoneware, mc splotches on cream, #40, mk, 7" ...75.00
Early Art, vase, stoneware, mc stripes, unmk, 5½" 60.00
Early Utility, bowl, brn band on yel, #106, 6" 21.50
Early Utility, canister, emb SUGAR on gr, 6½" 85.00
Early Utility, casserole, gr bands on cream, w/lid, #113, 7½" 60.00
Ebb Tide, basket, shell form, fish hdl, unmk, 6¼" 120.00
Ebb Tide, candle holder, shell form, E-13, 2¾" 26.00
Ebb Tide, ewer, shell form, fish hdl, E-10, 14" 250.00
Fiesta, basket, gr/yel, twist hdl, #51, 12½" L 85.00
Fiesta, cornucopia, yel, ruffled, #49, 8½" 65.00
Fiesta, flowerpot, blk, #40, 4¼" 25.00
Floral, grease jar, yel flowers, #43, 5¾" 40.00
Floral, pitcher, yel flowers, #45, 6" 47.50
Imperial, basket, dk gr, F-38, 6¾" 30.00
Imperial, leaf dish, dk gr, #63, 14" 30.00
Imperial, Madonna, wht, F-7, 7" 35.00
Imperial, planter, Carnation Pk, F-24, 12½" 28.00
Imperial, planter, pk squiggles on blk, unmk, 6¼" L 25.00
Imperial, urn vase, blk, #454, 5" 18.00
Imperial, vase, Carnation Pk, #413, 8¾" 20.00
Imperial, vase, Carnation Pk, F-28, 9½" 13.00
Imperial, vase, Daisy Chain decor, F-34, 5" 35.00
Imperial, window box, pk squiggles on blk, #82, 12½" 30.00
Iris, basket, pk/bl, simple hdl, #408, 7" 315.00
Iris, rose bowl, pk/bl, sm hdls, #412, 4" 85.00
Iris, vase, pk/bl, petal rim, hdls, #407, 4¾" 105.00
Iris, vase, yel/pk, ornate hdls, #403, 7" 185.00
Magnolia, glossy; basket, pk floral, H-14, 10½" 375.00
Magnolia, glossy; sugar bowl, bl floral, w/lid, H-22, 3¾" 35.00
Magnolia, glossy; vase, pk floral, ornate hdls, H-16, 12½" 260.00
Magnolia, matt; basket, yel/Dusty Rose, rare, #10, 10½" 400.00
Magnolia, matt; console bowl, Dusty Rose/yel, hdls, #26, 12" 180.00
Magnolia, matt; dbl cornucopia, Dusty Rose/yel, #6, 12" 175.00
Magnolia, matt; lamp base, Dusty Rose, 12½" 300.00
Magnolia, matt; vase, yel/Dusty Rose, hdls, #3, 8½" 115.00
Marcrest, ashtray, dk gr, 8½x4½" 17.50
Mardi Gras/Granada, basket, ivory/pk, emb florals, #32, 8" 170.00
Mardi Gras/Granada, ewer, ivory/pk, emb florals, #66, 10" 130.00
Mardi Gras/Granada, vase, ivory, low hdls, #49, 9" 47.50
Mardi Gras/Granada, vase, pk/ivory/bl, low hdls, #47, 9" 72.00
Mayfair, vase, hand holding vase, lt gr, #83, 7¾" 42.50
Mayfair, wall pocket, mandolin form, wht, #84, 7" 35.00
Mirror Almond, bowl, 6" 4.50
Mirror Almond, bud vase, 9" 20.00
Mirror Almond, creamer, 8-oz 14.00
Mirror Almond, jug, 2-qt 30.00
Mirror Almond, mug, 9-oz 5.00
Mirror Almond, plate, dinner, 10" 7.50
Mirror Almond, server, gingerbread man, 10" 60.00
Mirror Almond, snack set 22.50
Mirror Almond, sugar bowl, 12-oz 14.00
Mirror Brown, bean pot, 2-qt 35.00
Mirror Brown, bowl, divided vegetable; 10¾" 25.00
Mirror Brown, butter dish, ¼-lb 22.50
Mirror Brown, casserole w/duck lid, 2-qt 42.50
Mirror Brown, coffeepot, 8-cup 35.00
Mirror Brown, cookie jar, 94-oz 36.00
Mirror Brown, Dutch oven, 3-pt 35.00
Mirror Brown, gravy boat, 16-oz 42.50
Mirror Brown, leaf chip 'n dip, 15" 30.00
Mirror Brown, mug, 9-oz 5.00

Mirror Brown, pie plate, 9¼" 20.00
Mirror Brown, plate, 8½" 7.00
Mirror Brown, server w/chicken lid, 13⅜" 180.00
Mirror Brown, steak plate, 14" 22.50
Mirror Brown, teapot 25.00
Novelty, Basket Girl, bl/cream/yel, matt, #954, 8" 55.00
Novelty, colt figurine, blk w/wht tail, unmk, 5½" 55.00
Novelty, Corky Pig bank, Mirror Brown, 5" 45.00
Novelty, giraffe planter, maroon/dk gr, #115, 8" 47.50
Novelty, kitten planter, pk bow, #61, 7½" 37.50
Novelty, leaf dish, maroon/dk gr, #85, 13" 35.00
Novelty, lovebirds planter, turq/blk, #93, 6" 40.00
Novelty, pheasant planter, gr/yel, #61, 6x8" 40.00
Novelty, pig planter, open bk, smiling face, #60, 5" 37.50
Novelty, shrimp planter, curled shrimp form, yel, #210, 5" 35.00
Novelty, twin geese planter, gr/yel, #95, 6½" 40.00
Novelty, vase, maroon/dk gr, suspended, #108, 8" 55.00
Nuline Bak-Serv, custard cup, bl, B-14, 2¾" 10.00
Orchid, candle holder, cream/pk, low hdls, #315, 4" 105.00
Orchid, ewer, pk/bl, scalloped top, ornate hdl, #401, 13½" 650.00
Orchid, jardiniere, bl/pk, sm hdls, #317, 4¾" 115.00
Orchid, vase, pk/bl, hdls, #304, 10¼" 350.00
Parchment & Pine, basket, S-8, Pearl Gray, 16½" L 190.00
Parchment & Pine, cornucopia, Pearl Gray, S-2-R, 7¾" 52.50
Parchment & Pine, teapot, Pearl Gray, S-15, 8" 100.00
Pine Cone, vase, bl, hdls, #55, 6½" 155.00
Poppy, basket, cream/pk, simple hdl, ornate rim, #601, 9" 750.00
Poppy, planter, bl/pk, ornate rim, hdls, #602, 6½" 225.00
Rainbow, leaf dish, brn w/ivory edge, detailed, 12¼" 35.00
Rosella, lamp base, gr & wht floral on cream, L-3, 11" 440.00
Rosella, sugar bowl, gr/wht floral on cream, w/lid, R-4, 5½" 75.00
Rosella, vase, gr & wht floral on cream, R-14, 8½" 115.00
Rosella, wall pocket, emb floral on cream, R-10, 6½" 140.00
Royal Woodland, basket, turq, W-9, 8¾" 85.00
Royal Woodland, console bowl, turq/gray, W-29, 14½" 80.00
Royal Woodland, cornucopia, turq, W-10, 11" 65.00
Royal Woodland, ewer, pk, twig hdl, W-24, 13½" 225.00
Serenade, candle holders, bl w/yel int, S-16, 6½", pr 125.00
Serenade, candy dish, yel, ftd, loop finial, S-3, 8¼" 140.00
Serenade, sugar bowl, pk, w/lid, S-19, 3¼" 42.00
Serenade, vase, yel, S-1, 6½" 55.00
Sueno Tulip, ewer, pk/bl, curved hdl, #109-33, 13" 480.00
Sueno Tulip, flowerpot, yel/bl, w/saucer, #116-33, 4¼" 110.00
Sueno Tulip, vase, bud; pk/bl, #104-33, 6" 110.00
Sun-Glow, bowl, pk flower on yel, #50, 9½" 40.00
Sun-Glow, flowerpot, yel, #97, 5½" 35.00
Sun-Glow, pitcher, pk florals on yel, #52, 24-oz 40.00
Sun-Glow, shaker, yel flower on pk, #54, 2¾" 12.50
Sun-Glow, vase, dk pk gloss, #100, 6½" 50.00
Sun-Glow, wall pocket, iron form, yel, unmk, 6" 145.00
Thistle, vase, pk/bl, angle hdls, #52, 6½" 110.00
Tile, decorated border; 2⅞x6" 55.00
Tile, plain, 4¼x4¼" 17.50
Tokay, cornucopia, pk grapes on pk to lt gr, #10, 11" 65.00
Tokay, creamer, pk grapes on pk to gr, #17 ....65.00
Tokay, vase, pk grapes, pk/gr, twig hdls, #8, 10" 85.00
Tropicana, basket, Caribbean figure, #55, 12¾" 715.00
Tropicana, ewer, wht gloss/Tropic Gr trim, #56, 12½" 580.00
Tropicana, vase, Caribbean lady on wht, #54, 12½" 445.00
Tuscany, basket, gr grapes on milk wht, #11, 10½" 115.00
Tuscany, leaf dish, gr grapes on milk wht, #19 ....40.00
Tuscany, urn, gr grapes on milk wht, low hdls, #5, 5½" 50.00
Utility, bowl, tan & bl bands on cream, unmk, 7" 25.00
Water Lily, matt; console bowl, Sweet Pk/turq, L-21, 13½" 235.00

Water Lily, matt; cornucopia, Sweet Pk/turq, L-7, 6½" 110.00
Water Lily, matt; creamer, apricot/walnut, L-19, 5" 67.50
Water Lily, matt; dbl cornucopia, Sweet Pk/turq, L-27, 12" 225.00
Water Lily, matt; ewer, Sweet Pk/turq, L-17, 13½" 485.00
Water Lily, matt; jardiniere, apricot/walnut, L-24, 8½" 315.00
Wild Flower (# series), console bowl, low hdls, #70, 12" 385.00
Wild Flower (# series), cornucopia, pk/russet, 358, 6¼" 145.00
Wild Flower (# series), vase, pk/bl, hdls, #59, 10½" 265.00
Wild Flower (W series), candle holder, Dusty Rose/yel, 2½" 40.00
Wild Flower (W series), vase, Dusty Rose/bl, W-17, 12½" 260.00
Wild Flower (W series), vase, Dusty Rose/yel, W-1, 5½" 52.00
Wild Flower (W series), vase, yel/russet, hdls, W-12, 9½" 175.00

Woodland, matt; basket, Harvest Yellow, matt, W-9, 8¾", $250.00.

Woodland, glossy; basket, bl/gr, post-1950, W-22, 10½" 240.00
Woodland, glossy; vase, wht w/gold trim, W-1, 5½" 42.00
Woodland, glossy; window box, 2-tone gr, post-1950, W-14, 10" .65.00
Woodland, matt; candle holder, yel/gr, W-30, 3½" 110.00
Woodland, matt; cornucopia, Dawn Rose, W-10, 11" 145.00
Woodland, matt; dbl bud vase, Harvest Yel, W-15, 8½" 185.00
Woodland, matt; dbl cornucopia, yel/gr, W-23, 14" 565.00
Woodland, matt; ewer, Harvest Yel, W-6, 6½" 170.00
Woodland, matt; flowerpot/saucer, post-1950, W-11, 5¾" 135.00
Woodland, matt; vase, suspended, Dawn Rose, W-17, 7½" 325.00
Woodland, matt; vase, yel/gr, post-1950, W-16, 8½" 170.00
Woodland, matt; window box, Dawn Rose, W-14, 10" 150.00

Hummel

Hummel figurines were created through the artistry of Berta Hummel, a Franciscan nun called Sister M. Innocentia. The first figures were made about 1935 by Franz Goebel of Goebel Art Inc., Rodental, Germany. Plates, plaques, and candy dishes are also produced, and the older, discontinued editions are highly sought collectibles. Generally speaking, an issue can be dated by the trademark. The first Hummels, from 1934-1949, were either incised or stamped with the 'Crown WG' mark. The 'full bee in V' mark was employed with minor variations until 1959. At that time the bee was stylized and represented by a solid disk with angled symmetrical wings completely contained within the confines of the 'V.' The three-line mark, 1964-1972, utilized the stylized bee and included a three-line arrangement, 'c by W. Goebel, W. Germany.' Another change in 1970 saw the 'stylized bee in V' suspended between the vertical bars of the 'b' and 'l' of a printed 'Goebel, West Germany.' Collectors refer to this mark as the 'last bee' or 'Goebel bee.' The mark in use from 1979 to 1990 omits the 'bee in V.' The current mark, used since 1991, is a crown with 'WG' initials with a large 'Goebel' and a small 'Germany' signifying a united Germany. For a more thorough study of the subject, we recommend *Hummel, An Illustrated Handbook and Price Guide* by Ken Armke. A second source is *Hummel*

Figurines and Plates, A Collector's Identification and Value Guide, by Carl Luckey. Both books are available through your local book dealer. Idiosyncrasies in the numerical order of the following listings are due to computer sorting. See also Limited Edition Plates.

Key:

ce — closed edition	SB — stylized bee
CM — crown mark	LB — last bee
FB — full bee	MB — missing bee

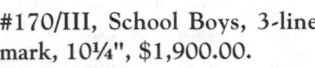
#170/III, School Boys, 3-line mark, 10¼", $1,900.00.

#II/111, Wayside Harmony, table lamp, SB, ce, 7½" 245.00
#II/112, Just Resting, table lamp, CM, ce, 7½" 455.00
#III/110, Let's Sing, candy box, LB, ce, 5¼" 112.00
#III/63, Singing Lesson, candy box, 3-line mk, ce, 4¾" 120.00
#1, Puppy Love, SB, ce, 5" 300.00
#101, To Market, table lamp, plain post, FB, ce, 7½" 4,200.00
#103, Farewell, table lamp, CM, ce, 7½" 5,600.00
#106, Merry Wanderer, plaque w/wood fr, CM, ce, 6x6" 3,500.00
#109/II, Happy Traveler, FB, ce, 7½" 525.00
#109/0, Happy Traveler, SB, ce, 4¾" 140.00
#11/0, Merry Wanderer, FB, ce, 4¾" 215.00
#110, Let's Sing, CM, ce, 4" 295.00
#111/I, Wayside Harmony, SB, ce, 5¼" 245.00
#111/3/0, Wayside Harmony, FB, ce, 4" 175.00
#112, Just Resting, CM, ce, 5½" 455.00
#114, Let's Sing, ashtray, CM, ce, 3½x6¼" 595.00
#118, Little Thrifty, bank, FB, ce, 5¼" 245.00
#119, Postman, CM, ce, 5" 385.00
#123, Max & Moritz, SB, ce, 5" 210.00
#124, Hello, CM, ce, 6½" 525.00
#124/I, Hello, FB, ce, 7" 280.00
#127, Doctor, CM, ce, 5" 295.00
#129, Band Leader, FB, ce, 5½" 225.00
#13/II, Meditation, SB, ce, 7" 2,100.00
#131, Street Singer, FB, ce, 5" 225.00
#131, Street Singer, LB, ce, 5" 135.00
#133, Mother's Helper, FB, ce, 5" 245.00
#134, Quartet, plaque, 3-line mk, ce, 5½x6¼" 210.00
#136, Friends, FB, ce, 10½" 1,400.00
#136/I, Friends, SB, ce, 5¼" 210.00
#139, Flitting Butterfly, plaque, SB, ce, 2½x2½" 70.00
#140, The Mail Is Here, plaque, SB, ce, 4¼x6¾" 210.00
#141/V, Apple Tree Girl, 3-line mk, ce, 10¼" 945.00
#141/3/0, Apple Tree Girl, FB, ce, 4" 175.00
#142/X, Apple Tree Boy, SB, ce, 33" 7,795.00
#142/3/0, Apple Tree Boy, SB, ce, 4" 140.00
#143, Boots, FB, ce, 6¾" 420.00
#143/0, Boots, SB, ce, 5" 195.00
#145, Little Guardian, 3-line mk, ce, 4" 125.00

#147, Angel Shrine, font, MB, ce, 3x5" 35.00
#150/0, Happy Days, LB, ce, 5" 215.00
#151, Madonna Holding Child, FB, bl, ce, 12½" 1,400.00
#152, Umbrella Boy, FB, ce, 8" 1,540.00
#154, Waiter, CM, ce, 6½" 560.00
#154/0, Waiter, CM, ce, 6" 385.00
#16, Little Hiker, CM, ce, 5½" 455.00
#163, Whitsuntide, LB, ce, 6¾" 215.00
#165, Swaying Lullaby, FB, ce, 4½x5¼" 350.00
#167, Angel w/Bird, font, 3-line mk, ce, 3¼x4⅛" 42.00
#169, Bird Duet, FB, ce, 4" 160.00
#171, Little Sweeper, MB, ce, 4¼" 100.00
#172/0, Festival Harmony (mandolin), 3-line mk, ce, 8" 245.00
#173/II, Festival Harmony (flute), LB, ce, 10½" 295.00
#173/0, Festival Harmony (flute), SB, ce, 8" 315.00
#174, She Loves Me, She Loves Me Not, SB, ce, 4¼" 175.00
#175, Mother's Darling, CM, pk & gr bags, ce, 5½" 385.00
#175, Mother's Darling, LB, bl bags, ce, 5½" 150.00
#176, Happy Birthday, FB, ce, 5½" 385.00
#177, School Girls, SB, ce, 9½" 1,470.00
#178, Photographer, 3-line mk, ce, 5" 225.00
#179, Coquettes, SB, ce, 5" 280.00
#18, Christ Child, LB, ce, 3¼x6" 105.00
#180, Tuneful Good Night, plaque, FB, ce, 5x4¾" 245.00
#183, Forest Shrine, CM, ce, 9" 910.00
#183, Forest Shrine, MB, ce, 9" 370.00
#185, Accordion Boy, FB, ce, 5½" 245.00
#186, Sweet Music, SB, ce, 5½" 195.00
#187, MI Hummel Plaque, English, 3-line mk, ce, 5½x4" 315.00
#188, Celestial Musician, SB, ce, 7" 280.00
#192, Candlelight, candle holder, FB, ce, 7" 490.00
#193, Angel Duet, candle holder, MB, ce, 5" 145.00
#193, Angel Duet, candle holder, SB, ce, 5" 210.00
#195/I, Barnyard Hero, LB, ce, 5½" 220.00
#195/2/0, Barnyard Hero, FB, ce, 4" 225.00
#197, Be Patient, CM, ce, 6¼" 525.00
#198/I, Home From Market, SB, ce, 5½" 210.00
#198/2/0, Home From Market, LB, ce, 4½" 105.00
#199/0, Feeding Time, 3-line mk, ce, 4½" 165.00
#201, Retreat to Safety, FB, ce, 6" 420.00
#201/2/0, Retreat to Safety, SB, ce, 4" 175.00
#203, Signs of Spring, FB, ce, 5¼" 385.00
#203/2/O, Signs of Spring, FB, 1 shoe, ce, 4" 280.00
#204, Weary Wanderer, CM, ce, 5¾" 455.00
#206, Angel Cloud, font, SB, ce, 3¼x4¾" 140.00
#208, MI Hummel Dealer's Plaque (in French), FB, ce, 5½x4" .3,500.00
#21/I, Heavenly Angel, 3-line mk, ce, 6¾" 195.00
#217, Boy w/Toothache, SB, ce, 5½" 210.00
#218/2/O, Birthday Serenade, FB, ce, 4¼" 405.00
#220, We Congratulate (w/base), 3-line mk, ce, 3¾" 130.00
#222, Madonna Plaque, SB, w/metal fr, ce, 4x5" 525.00
#224/I, Wayside Harmony, table lamp, FB, ce, 7½" 350.00
#224/II, Wayside Harmony, table lamp, LB, ce, 9½" 245.00
#225/I, Just Resting, table lamp, SB, ce, 7½" 265.00
#226, Mail Is Here, CM, ce, 4½x6¼" 735.00
#226, Mail Is Here, LB, ce, 4¼x6" 385.00
#228, Good Friends, table lamp, LB, ce, 7½" 210.00
#229, Apple Tree Girl, table lamp, 3-line mk, ce, 7½" 230.00
#230, Apple Tree Boy, table lamp, FB, ce, 7½" 560.00
#231, Birthday Serenade, table lamp, FB, ce, 9¾" 1,400.00
#232, Happy Days, table lamp, LB, ce, 9¾" 300.00
#235, Happy Days, table lamp, 3-line mk, ce, 7¾" 315.00
#238A, Angel w/Lute, SB, ce, 2¼" 65.00
#238C, Angel w/Trumpet, LB, ce, 2¼" 36.00

#239B, Girl w/Doll, 3-line mk, ce, 3½" 42.00
#239C, Boy w/Horse, SB, ce, 3½" 63.00
#24/III, Lullaby, candle holder, FB, ce, 6¼x8¾" 630.00
#240, Little Drummer, FB, ce, 4" 195.00
#241, Angel Lights, candle holder, LB, ce, 10½x8½" 210.00
#243, Madonna & Child, font, SB, ce, 3⅛x4" 63.00
#246, Holy Family, font, 3-line mk, ce, 3⅛x4½" 42.00
#248/I, Guardian Angel, font, SB, ce, 2¾x6¼" 700.00
#248/0, Guardian Angel, font, 3-line mk, ce, 2⅜x5⅜" 42.00
#25, Angelic Sleep, candle holder, CM, ce, 3½x5½" 350.00
#255, Stitch in Time, SB, ce, 6½" 350.00
#255/4/0, Stitch in Time, MB, ce, 3" 68.00
#256. Knitting Lesson, 3-line mk, ce, 7½" 420.00
#257, For Mother, 3-line mk, ce, 5" 170.00
#258, Which Hand?, MB, ce, 5¼" 135.00
#258, Which Hand?, SB, ce, 5¼" 420.00
#260, Nativity Set (lg), w/wooden stable, LB, ce, 16-pc 3,605.00
#260A, Madonna, LB, ce, 9¾" 365.00
#260D, Good Night, LB, ce, 5¼" 100.00
#260F, We Congratulate, 3-line mk, ce, 6¼" 270.00
#260J, Shepherd Boy, kneeling, LB, ce, 7" 210.00
#260L, Donkey, standing, 3-line mk, ce, 7½" 100.00
#260N, Moorish King, standing, LB, ce, 12¾" 350.00
#260O, King, standing, LB, ce, 12" 350.00
#260R, Sheep (single), lying, LB, ce, 3¼x4" 42.00
#261, Angel Duet, LB, ce, 5" 155.00
#262, Heavenly Lullaby, 3-line mk, ce, 3½x5" 420.00
#264, Heavenly Angel, Annual Plate, 1971, 3-line mk, ce, 7½" ...600.00
#266, Globe Trotter, Annual Plate, 1973, LB, ce, 7½" 140.00
#268, Rise Into Christmas, Annual Plate, 1975, LB, ce, 7½" 56.00
#27/3, Joyous News, FB, ce, 4¼x4¾" 700.00
#272, Singing Lesson, Annual Plate, 1979, LB, ce, 7½" 53.00
#275, Umbrella Girl, Annual Plate, 1982, LB, ce, 7½" 130.00
#29/0, Guardian Angel, font, FB, ce, 2⅞x6" 700.00
#3/1, Book Worm, FB, ce, 5½" 325.00
#300, Bird Watcher, SB, early sample, ce, 5" 1,400.00
#301, Christmas Angel, MB, ce, 6" 175.00
#303, Arithmetic Lesson, FB, early sample, ce, 5¼" 2,800.00
#304, Artist, 3-line mk, ce, 5½" 525.00
#305, Builder, SB, ce, 5½" 560.00
#306, Little Bookkeeper, SB, ce, 4¾" 700.00
#307, Good Hunting, SB, ce, 5" 560.00
#314, Confidentially, 3-line mk, ce, 5½" 630.00
#317, Not for You, SB, ce, 5½" 525.00
#32, Little Gabriel, LB, ce, 5" 100.00
#322, Little Pharmacist, SB, ce, 5¾" 385.00
#327, Run-A-Way, 3-line mk, ce, 5¼" 700.00
#340, Letter to Santa, LB, ce, 7¼" 250.00
#344, Feathered Friends, 3-line mk, ce, 4¾" 350.00
#35/I, Good Shepherd, font, CM, ce, 2¾x5¾" 245.00
#350, On Holiday, LB, ce, 4¼" 1,050.00

#353/I, Spring Dance, last bee mark, 6¾", $370.00.

#363, Big Housecleaning, 3-line mk, ce, 4" 700.00
#37, Herald Angels, candle holder, FB, ce, 2¾x4" 245.00
#396, Ride Into Christmas, LB, ce, 5¾" 330.00
#4, Little Fiddler, CM, ce, 4¾" 385.00
#406, Pleasant Journey, MB, ce, 7⅛x6½" 1,750.00
#415, Thoughtful, MB, ce, 4½" 155.00
#43, March Winds, SB, ce, 4¾x5½" 150.00
#431, The Surprise, MB, ce, 5½" 195.00
#437, Tuba Player, MB, ce, 6¼" 185.00
#44B, Out of Danger, table lamp, FB, ce, 8½" 280.00
#46/I, Madonna w/o Halo, CM, colored, ce, 11¼" 175.00
#48/0, Madonna, plaque, CM, ce, 3¼x4¼" 210.00
#50, Volunteers, CM, ce, 7" 840.00
#51 2/0, Village Boy, FB, ce, 5" 160.00
#55, Saint George, LB, ce, 6¾" 230.00
#56A, Culprits, FB, ce, 6¼" 315.00
#57/0, Chick Girl, FB, ce, 3½" 195.00
#58/0, Playmates, SB, ce, 4" 160.00
#59, Skier, SB, ce, 5" 210.00
#62, Happy Pastime, ashtray, FB, ce, 3½x6¼" 175.00
#64, Shepherd's Boy, 3-line mk, ce, 5½" 175.00
#66, Farm Boy, FB, ce, 5" 245.00
#70, Holy Child, SB, ce, 6¾" 160.00
#73, Little Helper, FB, ce, 4¼" 140.00
#75, White Angel, font, FB, ce, 3¼" 70.00
#78/VIII, Blessed Child, CM, ce, 13¼" 525.00
#8, Book Worm, FB, ce, 4" 260.00
#80, Little Scholar, SB, ce, 5½" 210.00
#83, Angel Serenade, w/lamb, CM, ce, 5½" 385.00
#86, Happiness, CM, ce, 4¾" 245.00
#89/I, Little Cellist, FB, ce, 5¾" 245.00
#92, Merry Wanderer, plaque, SB, ce, 4½x5" 150.00
#95, Brother, SB, ce, 5½" 190.00
#96, Little Shopper, CM, ce, 4¾" 260.00
#98, Sister, FB, ce, 5¾" 215.00

Hutschenreuther

The Porcelain Factory C.M. Hutschenreuther operated in Bavaria from 1814 to 1969. After the death of the elder Hutschenreuther in 1845, his son Lorenz took over operations, continuing there until 1857 when he left to establish his own company in the nearby city of Selb. The original manufactory became a joint stock company in 1904, absorbing several other potteries. In 1969 both Hutschenreuther firms merged, and that company still operates in Selb. They have distributing centers in both France and the United States. Our advisor for this category is Jack Gunsaulus; he is listed in the Directory under Michigan.

Bowl, centerpc; 2 cherub supports, appl flowers, ca 1900, 4" 175.00
Figurine, Deco nude running on gold ped ball, 8½" 225.00
Figurine, female dancer, male swordsman, Werner, 12½", pr 600.00
Figurine, Flame Dancer, 11½" 475.00
Figurine, girl w/borzoi (Russian wolfhound), 8½" 400.00
Figurine, moose, recumbent, head turned, Tutter, 8x9" 275.00
Figurine, nude w/deer, 9" 450.00
Figurine, Siamese cat, cream w/brn, bl eyes, 7½" 295.00
Figurine, 2 seated cats, MH Fritz, 6¾x7⅜x6" 145.00

Imari

Imari is a generic term which covers a broad family of wares. It was made in more than a dozen Japanese villages, but the name is that of the port from whence it was shipped to Europe. There are several types of Imari. The most common features a design with panels of birds, florals, or people surrounding a central basket of flowers. The colors used in this type are underglaze blue with overglaze red, gold, and green enamels. The Chinese also made Imari wares which differ from the Japanese type in several ways — the absence of spur marks, a thinner-type body, and a more consistent control of the blue. Imari-type wares were copied on the Continent by Meissen and by English potters, among them Worcester, Derby, and Bow. Unless noted otherwise, our values are for Japanese ware. Our advisor is Norma Angelo; she is listed in the Directory under New York.

Biscuit jar, florals, bbl form, 1800s, 6"	225.00
Bowl, dragon & phoenix, bl w/mc & gold, Meiji period, 14½"	2,070.00
Bowl, floral in bl/gr/gold, 1800s, 12½"	925.00
Bowl, vase of flowers, bronze mts, 2½x8½"	365.00
Charger, cranes in pine boughs, wht/red/gr/gold, Meiji, 18"	900.00
Charger, floral w/wht rim reserves, 25"	925.00
Charger, sages encircle floral medallion, Meiji period, 18"	1,265.00
Charger, scholars on parapet, Meiji/Taisho, 15½"	1,250.00
Dinner service, birds & clouds panels, 1900s, 20-place, NM	2,875.00
Ewer, phoenix & paulownia reserves, Meiji period, 9⅝"	690.00
Plate, buildings/flowers, foliate rims, 18th C, 8½", pr	460.00
Plate, mc florals, shaped rim, 12"	150.00
Tea caddy, silver lid, 4¾"	350.00
Teapot, China, 19th C, 1-cup, 4½", EX	635.00
Vase, birds in costumes, ladies, wood base, 1890s, 25"	950.00
Vase, birds/flowers reserve on dk bl w/gold, sgn, 12"	375.00

Imperial Glass Company

The Imperial Glass Company was organized in 1901 in Bellaire, Ohio, and started manufacturing glassware in 1904. Their early products were jelly glasses, hotel tumblers, etc., but by 1910 they were making a name for themselves by pressing quantities of carnival glass, the iridescent glassware that was popular during that time. In 1914 NuCut was introduced to imitate cut glass. The line was so popular that it was made in crystal and colors and was reintroduced as Collector's Crystal in the 1950s. From 1916 to 1920 they used the lustre process to make a line called Imperial Jewels. Free-Hand ware, art glass made entirely by hand using no molds, was made from 1922 to 1928.

The company entered bankruptcy in 1931 but was able to continue operations and reorganize as the Imperial Glass Corporation. In 1936 Imperial introduced the Candlewick line, for which it is best known. In the late thirties the Vintage Grape Milk Glass line was added, and in 1951 a major ad campaign was launched, making Imperial one of the leading milk glass manufacturers.

In 1940 Imperial bought the molds and assets of the Central Glass Works of Wheeling, West Virginia; in 1958 they acquired the molds of the Heisey Company; and in 1960 the molds of the Cambridge Glass Company of Cambridge, Ohio. Imperial used these molds, and after 1951 they marked their glassware with an 'I' superimposed over the 'G' trademark. The company became a subsidiary of Lenox in 1973; subsequently an 'L' was added to the 'IG' mark. In 1981 Lenox sold Imperial to Arthur Lorch, a private investor (who modified the L by adding a line at the top angled to the left, giving rise to the 'ALIG' mark). He in turn sold the company to Robert F. Stahl, Jr., in 1982. Mr. Stahl filed for Chapter 11 to reorganize, but in mid-1984 liquidation was ordered, and all assets were sold. The few items that had been made in '84 were marked with an 'N' superimposed over the 'I' for 'New Imperial.'

For more information, we recommend *Imperial Glass Encyclopedia, Vol I and II*, edited by James Measell. Our advisor is Joan Cimini; she is listed in the Directory under Ohio. See also Candlewick; Carnival Glass; Glass Animals and Figurines; Stretch Glass.

Baked apple, Cape Cod, crystal, #160/50x	8.00
Baked apple, Tradition, crystal	8.00
Bonbon, Pillar Flutes, bl, crimped, 7"	22.50
Bottle, cologne; Early American Hobnail, pk	45.00

Box, frosted, dove finial, #214, $90.00.

Butter dish, Cape Cod, crystal, hdls, #160	40.00
Cake stand, Cape Cod, crystal, ftd, #160/167D	55.00
Cake stand, Cape Cod, crystal, multi-server top, #160/93, 12"	110.00
Cake stand, Crochet Crystal, crystal, ftd	45.00
Candle cake plate, Cape Cod, crystal, #160/72	325.00
Candlesticks, Tradition, crystal, sq base, 3½", pr	28.00
Candy jar, Cape Cod, crystal, ftd, w/lid, #160/110, 10"	75.00
Celery tray, Cape Cod, crystal, #160/189, 10½"	65.00
Cigarette lighter, Cape Cod, milk glass, #1602	30.00
Claret, Cape Cod, Verde, #1602	18.00
Coaster/spoon rest, Cape Cod, crystal, #160/76	14.00
Cocktail, Reeded (Spun), teal, ftd	17.50
Compote, Cape Cod, crystal, ftd, #160/48B, 7"	45.00
Creamer & sugar bowl, Cape Cod, crystal, flat, #160/30	24.00
Creamer & sugar bowl, Cape Cod, crystal, ftd, #160/31	36.00
Cruet, Cape Cod, crystal, #160/119, 4-oz	30.00
Decanter, Cape Cod, crystal, #160/163, 30-oz	65.00
Decanter, Cape Cod, crystal, sq, #160/212, 24-oz	70.00
Decanter, Sure Shot, red w/EX gold	165.00
Finger bowl, Cape Cod, crystal, #1602	12.00
Goblet, Cape Cod, crystal, #160, 8-oz	9.00
Goblet, champagne; Cape Cod, Verde, #1602, 6-oz	16.50
Goblet, claret; Cape Cod, crystal, 5-oz	10.00
Goblet, Dew Drop opal, #1886	22.00
Goblet, Hoffman House, Heather, #46	14.00
Goblet, Turn O' the Century, Azalea, #612	18.00
Goblet, water; Cape Cod, crystal, #1602, 11-oz	10.00
Goblet, water; Cape Cod, ruby, #160	28.00
Ivy ball, Early American Hobnail, amber, ftd, #742	24.00
Ivy ball, Spun, teal w/crystal ft, reeded, 4"	65.00
Jar, Cathay Crystal, Ming, #5019	380.00
Jar, Ipswich, Heather, #1405, 2-pc	45.00
Jar, pokal, caramel slag, #464, 2-pc	85.00
Lamp, Dew Drop opal, #1886/350	160.00
Marmalade, Cape Cod, crystal, #160/89, 4-pc	45.00
Mayonnaise, Laurel, cut, Rose Pk, #256, w/ladle	30.00
Mug, Dumbo, gr, 1974	75.00
Mustard jar, Cape Cod, crystal, #160/156	30.00
Mustard jar, 3-in-1 Diamond, crystal, #1, lg	65.00
Nappy, Early American Hobnail, Ritz Bl, #7145B, 7" sq	26.00
Pepper mill, Cape Cod, crystal, #160/236	27.50
Pickle dish, Pillar Flutes, bl, hdl, #682	25.00
Pitcher, Early American Hobnail, crystal, #742, 55-oz	30.00
Pitcher, iced tea; Tradition, crystal, ice lip, #165, 54-oz	60.00
Pitcher, Reeded (Spun), teal, ice lip, 80-oz	95.00

Plate, Collector's Crystal, #5059D, 13" 30.00
Plate, Dmn Quilted, blk, 8" 15.00
Plate, Mum, Peacock carnival, #524, 10½" 45.00
Plate, Niagara, crystal, 9½" 10.00
Plate, Old English, crystal, 7" 16.00
Plate, Pillar Flutes, bl, 8" 18.00
Plate, salad; Cape Cod, crystal, 8" 10.00
Plate, torte; Provincial, amber, #1506, 13" 35.00
Plate, Tradition, crystal, 6¾" 6.00
Plate, Tradition, crystal, 8" 12.00
Punch bowl, Crocheted Crystal, +12 cups & ladle 130.00
Punch set, Cape Cod, crystal, #160/20, 15-pc 275.00
Punch set, Mt Vernon, crystal, complete 150.00
Relish, Cape Cod, crystal, oval, 3-part, #160/55, 9½" 35.00
Rose bowl, Reeded (Spun), red 45.00
Rose bowl, Spun, cobalt, metal fr 35.00
Saucer, Tradition, crystal, 5½" 6.00
Shakers, Cape Cod, crystal, #160/213, 3-pc set 55.00
Shakers, Cape Cod, crystal, ftd, #160/116, pr 22.50
Sherbet, Cape Cod, amber, #1602 ....12.00
Sherbet, Cape Cod, crystal, high std, #1603 ....45.00
Sherbet, Cape Cod, ruby, #160 ....20.00
Sherbet, Cape Cod, Verde, #1602, tall 20.00
Sherbet, Mt Vernon, crystal, low 7.00
Spider, Cape Cod, crystal, hdld, #160/180, 4½" 30.00
Trivet, milk glass, #1950/450, 4-pc set 35.00
Tumbler, Crown Concord decor, Grape, #995, 10-oz 18.00
Tumbler, Gypsy Rings, Azalea, #116, 16-oz 14.00
Tumbler, iced tea; Reeded (Spun), teal, 14-oz 20.00
Tumbler, juice; Cape Cod, amber, ftd, #1602 ....12.00
Tumbler, juice; Cape Cod, Azalea, ftd, #1602, 6-oz 16.00
Tumbler, Niagara, crystal, 10-oz 10.00
Tumbler, Shaeffer, cobalt, #4511, 9½-oz 12.50
Tumbler, Sure Shot; gr w/EX gold, #711 ....25.00
Tumbler, Voo Doo, bl/gold, #760, 16-oz 18.00
Tumbler, whiskey; Cape Cod, crystal, flat, 2½" 15.00
Tumbler, wine; Cape Cod, crystal, #160, 2½-oz 14.00
Vase, Cathay Crystal, Ku ribbon, #5012 ....800.00
Vase, Free-Hand, drape decor, wht on mustard, orange int, 8½" 160.00
Vase, Free-Hand, hearts/vines, cobalt on opal, 6½" 375.00
Vase, Free-Hand, hearts/vines, purple on gr-tint opal, 4" ...175.00
Vase, marigold irid, flared, 8" 125.00
Vase, Reeded (Spun), red, 5" 45.00

Imperial Porcelain

The Blue Ridge Mountain Boys were created by cartoonist Paul Webb and translated into figurines by the Imperial Porcelain Corporation of Zanesville, Ohio, in 1947. These figurines decorated ashtrays, vases, mugs, bowls, pitchers, planters, and other items. The Mountain Boys series were numbered 92 through 108, each with a different and amusing portrayal of mountain life. Imperial also produced American Folklore miniatures, twenty-three tiny animals one inch or less in size, and the Al Capp Dogpatch series. Because of financial difficulties, the company closed in 1960.

American Folklore Miniatures

Cat, 1½" 40.00
Cow, 1¾" 35.00
Hound dogs 50.00
Plaque, store ad, Am Folklore Porcelain Miniatures, 4½" 450.00
Sow 35.00

Blue Ridge Mountain Boys by Paul Webb

Ashtray, #101, man w/jug & snake 95.00
Ashtray, #103, hillbilly & skunk 95.00
Ashtray, #105, baby, hound dog, & frog 125.00
Ashtray, #106, Barrel of Wishes, w/hound 75.00
Ashtray, #92, 2 men by tree stump, for pipes 125.00
Box, cigarette; #98, dog atop, baby at door, sq 115.00
Dealer's sign, Handcrafted Paul Webb Mtn Boys, rare, 9" 650.00
Decanter, #100, outhouse, man, & bird 95.00
Decanter, #104, Ma leaning over stump, w/baby & skunk 95.00
Decanter, man, jug, snake, & tree stump, Hispch Inc, 1946 ....75.00
Figurine, #101, man leans against tree trunk, 5" 90.00
Figurine, man on hands & knees, 3" 95.00
Figurine, man sitting, 3½" 95.00
Figurine, man sitting w/chicken on knee, 3" 95.00
Jug, #101, Willie & snake 75.00
Mug, #94, Bearing Down, 6" 95.00
Mug, #94, dbl baby hdl, 4¼" 95.00
Mug, #94, ma hdl, 4¼" 95.00
Mug, #94, man w/bl pants hdl, 4¼" 95.00
Mug, #94, man w/yel beard & red pants hdl, 4¼" 95.00
Mug, #99, Target Practice, boy on goat, farmer, 5¾" 95.00
Pitcher, lemonade 200.00
Planter, #100, outhouse, man, & bird 75.00
Planter, #105, man w/chicken on knee, washtub 125.00
Planter, #110, man, w/jug & snake, 4½" 65.00
Planter, #81, man drinking from jug, sitting by washtub 75.00
Shakers, Ma & Old Doc, pr 95.00

Miscellaneous

Items in this section that are designated 'IP' are miscellaneous novelties made by Imperial Porcelain; the remainder are of interest to Paul Webb collectors, though made by an unknown manufacturer. Prints on calendars and playing cards are signed 'Paul Webb.'

Artist board, babies or mtn women, sgn Paul Webb, 30x30" 275.00
Artist board, mtn boys only, sgn Paul Webb, 30x30" 225.00
Calendar, 1954, 12 sgn scenes, Brown & Bigelow, complete 48.00
Figurine, cat in high-heeled shoe, 5½" L 40.00
Hot pad, Dutch boy w/tulips, rnd, IP 30.00
Ink blotters, sgn scenes, ea 12.00
Mug, #29, man hdl, sgn Paul Webb, 4¾" 45.00
Planter, #106, dog sitting by tub, IP 75.00
Playing cards, ad: Rafe Oiling Gun, Brown & Bigelow, MIB 75.00
Shakers, pigs, 5", pr 95.00
Shakers, standing pigs, IP, 8", pr 95.00

Indian Tree

Indian Tree is a popular dinnerware pattern produced by various potteries since the early 1800s to recent times. Although backgrounds and borders vary, the Oriental theme is carried out with the gnarled, brown branch of a pink-blossomed tree. Among the manufacturers' marks, you may find represented such notable firms as Coalport, S. Hancock and Sons, Soho Pottery, and John Maddock and Sons.

Bowl, cereal; gold trim, Maddock 9.00
Bowl, Myott, 8" 18.00
Bowl, rim soup; Maddock, 9" 20.00
Bowl, soup; Johnson Bros 13.00
Bowl, vegetable; oval, gold trim, Maddock 30.00

Bowl, vegetable; rnd, Morley 22.00
Cup & saucer, demitasse; Minton 18.00
Cup & saucer, gold trim, Maddock 16.00
Cup & saucer, Myott 12.00
Cup & saucer, Spode 32.00
Gravy boat, Maddock 32.00
Gravy boat, w/attached underplate, Spode 80.00
Gravy tureen, English, w/lid & ladle 85.00
Jar, Sadler, fancy shape, w/lid, 4½" 50.00
Plate, bread & butter; gold trim, Maddock, 7½" 9.00
Plate, gold trim, Maddock, 9⅞" 16.00
Plate, luncheon; Morley, 8" 7.00
Plate, Morley, 9½" 15.00
Platter, gold trim, Maddock, 12" 35.00
Platter, gold trim, Maddock, 13⅞" 55.00
Platter, Morley, 12" 28.00
Platter, Spode, 15" 165.00
Platter, well & tree, 21" 275.00
Relish, 2-part, 6" 35.00
Teapot, Burgess & Lee 60.00

Inkwells and Inkstands

Receptacles for various writing fluids have been used since ancient times. Through the years they have been made from countless materials — glass, metal, porcelain, pottery, wood, and even papier-mache. During the 18th century gold or silver inkstands were presented to royalty, the well-known silver inkstand by Philip Syng, Jr., was used for the signing of the Declaration of Independence, and impressive brass inkstands with wells and a pounce pot (sander) were proud possessions of men of letters. When literacy vastly increased in the 19th century, the dip pen replaced the quill pen; and inkwells and inkstands were widely used and produced in a broad range of sizes in functional and decorative forms from ornate Victorian to flowing Art Nouveau and stylized Art Deco designs. However, the acceptance of the ballpoint pen literally put inkstands and inkwells 'out of business.' But their historical significance and intriguing diversity of form and styling fascinate today's collectors. See also Bottles, Ink.

Bl glass w/controlled bubbles, hinged lid, brass mts, 4½" 300.00
Blk glass, sq base w/cut sides, clear well, Mt WA, 2½x2½" 210.00
Blown, amber, paneled pyramid form, 2½" 120.00
Blown, olive gr, conical, disk mouth, att Keene, 2¾" 275.00
Brass, cast in Roman style, w/eagle finial, 6¼" 45.00
Brass, Egyptian Revival, figural god as well, dish base 350.00
Brass, Johnny Griffin figure at side, ca 1910 ....395.00
Brass, 2 wells w/cut glass lids, pen holder, w/dip pen 135.00
Brass peacock feathers w/cvd ivory lady's face, Austria, 3x7" 400.00
Bronze, cockatoo figural, Austria, worn pnt, 3½x4" 195.00
Bronze, well ea side elephant, emb florals, w/tray, 10½" 150.00
Bronze, 3 pheasants above step-down tray, Cornik, 5x15" 375.00
Cast metal, rabbit nodder w/mandolin, mc pnt, glass well, 4" 195.00
Champleve, on onyx base, Fr, ca 1850 ....395.00
Charles X patinated & gilt bronze, rtcl case, 3¾" 650.00
CI, man eating turkey figural, mc pnt, late 1800s, 5", EX 330.00
Copper, Greek Key design, brn patina w/silver o/l, Heintz 195.00
Fr Empire gilt & patinated bronze, Doric column, 7¼" 400.00
Gilt bronze bell shape on marble base, ribbon finial, 6" 200.00
Glass, Memorial Hall 1876, NM 375.00
Loetz type, gr iridized w/emb decor, bronze mts, 4½" 250.00
Pewter, Nouveau emb w/enamel jewels, conical, English, 2x5" ..250.00
Porc, standing cat lady in yel dress, 5" 150.00
Silver w/hinged lid, ftd, clear insert, Walker & Hall, 3½x6" 165.00

Stoneware w/Albany slip, paneled base, rnd, 2½" 45.00

White-glazed graniteware phrenology head with black and gold details, F. Bridges Phrenologist, Bennington VT, ca 1855, 5½", EX, $1,850.00.

Wht metal & brass, Queen Victoria bust, 1897 Jubilee, 7¼" 350.00
2 fiery opal 'snail' wells in ornate CI revolving stand 350.00

Insulators

The telegraph was invented in 1844. The devices developed to hold the electrical transmission wires to the poles were called insulators. The telephone, invented in 1876, intensified their usefulness, and by the turn of the century, thousands of varieties were being produced in pottery, wood, and glass of various colors. Even though it has been rumored that red glass insulators exist, none have ever been authenticated. Many insulators are embossed with patent dates.

Of the more than 3,000 types known to exist, today's collectors evaluate their worth by age and rarity of color. Aqua and green are the most common colors in glass, dark brown the most common in ceramic. Threadless insulators, (for example, CD #701.1) made between 1850 and 1865, bring prices well into the hundreds, if in mint condition.

In the listings that follow, the CD numbers are from an identification system developed in the late 1960s by N.R. Woodward.

Those seeking additional information about insulators are encouraged to contact Line Jewels NIA #255 (whose address may be found in the Directory under Clubs, Newsletters, and Catalogs) or attend a club-endorsed show. For information, contact Len Linscott, listed in the Directory under Florida. In the listings that follow those stating 'no name' have no company identification, but have embossed numbers, dots, etc. Those stating 'no embossing' are without raised letters, dots, or any other markings.

Key:
* (asterisk) — Canadian   SDP — sharp drip points
CB — corrugated base   RB — rough base
CD — Consolidated Design   RDP — round drip points
SB — smooth base

Threaded Pin-type Glass Insulators

CD 102, Hawley, SB, ice gr 3.00
CD 106, Maydwell-9, SB, lt pk 5.00
CD 108, Whitall Tatum Co No 9, SB, lt straw 2.00
CD 112, Lynchburg 31, RDP, gr 5.00
CD 114, Hemingray No 11, SDP, lt bl 6.00
CD 115, Armstrong No 3, SB, clear 3.00
CD 117, no name, SB, dk aqua 15.00
CD 120, Pat/Dec 19, 1871, SB, ice bl 10.00
CD 121, C&P Tel Co, SB, gr 20.00
CD 123, EC&M Co, SB, gr aqua 75.00
CD 128, Hemingray, SB, off-clear 2.00
CD 133, BGM Co, SB, lt purple 40.00

CD 138, Brookfield Postal Tel Co, SB, lt aqua 12.00
CD 139, McLaughlin USLD, SB, aqua 125.00
CD 143.5, THE Co, SB, lt gr 60.00
CD 147, Hemingray Pat Oct 8, 1907, SB, aqua 1.00
CD 154, Gayner No 44, SB, bl aqua 2.00
CD 155, Kerr DP 1, SB, off-clear 3.00
CD 160, Armstrong's No 14, SB, clear 20.00
CD 162, Hamilton Glass Co, RDP, lt gr 40.00

CD 166, California, smooth base, purple, $10.00 to $12.00.

CD 168, Hemingray No 510, CB, carnival 30.00
CD 188, B, SB, gr 25.00
CD 196, HG Co, Pat May 2, 1893, SDP, ice aqua 75.00
CD 202, Hemingray 53, SDP, aqua 20.00
CD 213, Hemingray 43, RDP, bl 15.00
CD 230, Hemingray 512, SB, lt citrine 25.00
CD 235, Pyrex 662, SB, carnival 30.00
CD 240, Pyrex 131, SB, clear 15.00
CD 245, no name, 9200, SB, gr 300.00
CD 251, NEGM Co, SB, ice bl 20.00
CD 254, No 3 Cable, SB, lt bl 50.00
CD 257, Hemingray No 60, RDP, clear 15.00
CD 263, Columbia, SB, aqua 60.00
CD 269, Jumbo, SB, dk aqua 300.00
CD 282, Knowles Boston, SB, aqua 200.00
Cd 286, Locke, SB, lt bl 50.00
CD 294, NEGM Co, SB, aqua 40.00
CD 299.1, prism, SB, lt bl 250.00
CD 306, Lynchburg, SDP, aqua 200.00
CD 317, Chambers, SB, gr 300.00
CD 325, Pyrex 401, SB, clear 15.00

Threadless Pin-type Glass Insulators

CD 1032, Cutter, SB, aqua 200.00
CD 728, no embossing, SB, lt bl 125.00
CD 734, McMicking, SB, lt aqua 60.00
CD 742, no embossing, SB, lt gr 100.00

Irons

History, geography, art, and cultural diversity are all represented in the collecting of antique pressing irons. The progress of fashion and invention can be traced through the ages by relics left in the form of pressing devices used in earlier times. Goffering irons, once needed for the frills and ruffles of the Victorian age, have been out of use so long that they are seldom recognized today. The fluter, essential for producing the yards of crimped ruffles demanded by 19th-century ladies, is now a quaint curiosity. Industrial technology can be traced through records left by centuries of irons.

Some countries lacked iron, so they made their pressing devices of other materials. And because an iron foundry represents a high form of investment and technology, less-wealthy societies frequently used the easier-to-work brass.

A culture's priorities are reflected in the tools in daily use. Some value innovation while others are content with a standard generic product. There are degrees of ornamentation, depending on the country, the people, and their approach to life.

At times, to the pleasure of today's collectors, the work transcends proficiency and rises into the realm of art. Using a variety of materials — iron, brass, or wood — artisans built a monument to their inner vision. Their work survives, testifiying to the care, love, and attention lavished on household implements, elevating them in status to something that delights the eye.

In the listing that follows, prices are given for examples in very good to excellent condition. Damage, repairs, plating, excessive wear, rust, and missing parts can dramatically reduce value. For further information we recommend *Irons By Irons* by our advisor Dave Irons; his address and information for ordering the book are given in the Directory under Pennsylvania.

Charcoal, Chinese, decorative/bronze pan, ivory hdl, VG 175.00
Charcoal, Dutch, all brass, cut-work sides, EX 350.00
Charcoal, Eclipse, Aug 25, 1903, EX 125.00
Charcoal, German, dragon chimney, the Monster Iron, VG 850.00
Charcoal, The Marvel, Pat 1924, EX 140.00
Charcoal, WD Cummings, E Bless, 1852, EX 225.00
Cold hdl, detachable slant hdl, EX 180.00
Cold hdl, Dover Sad Iron, detachable hdl, EX 50.00
Cold hdl, Griswold Erie, detachable hdl, EX 200.00
Cold hdl, PW Weida's, Pat 1870, hdl flips bk, G 250.00
Electric, Eureka Cordless, 2-pc, EX 65.00
Electric, Proctor Never Lift, self-contained std, EX 75.00
Fluter, combination charcoal, side fluter plate, VG 250.00
Fluter, combination sad iron, Knapp, Aug 2, '70, EX 200.00
Fluter, machine, English, fine flutes, VG 275.00
Fluter, machine, The Original Knox 1877, 90% pnt 275.00
Fluter, rocker, The Best, all CI, EX 85.00
Fluter, roller, AM Machine Co Phila PA, VG 100.00
Goffering, English, brass Queen Anne tripod base, EX 350.00
Goffering, S-style upright, Kenrick, w/heater, VG 170.00
Heater, pyramid, cast, holds 3 irons, VG 175.00
Laundry stove, Tip Top, holds 8 irons, G 350.00
Liquid fuel, Comfort Iron, rear tank, VG 125.00
Liquid fuel, Jubilee Iron Oct 31, 1899, VG 150.00
Little, box, English, brass, 3½", EX 250.00
Little, Enterprise Mfg Co No 115, 3⅞", EX 120.00
Little, Geneva Fluter Pat 1866, VG 600.00
Little, goffering, S stand, 3½" bbl, EX 250.00
Little, Our Pet, wood grip, 3½", EX 130.00
Little, Star #10, Stevens Co, wood grip, VG 150.00
Little, tribump, 3⅜", VG 50.00
Little, Wapac #2, cast, 4", VG 90.00
Meta fuel, British Boudoir Iron, VG 80.00
Natural gas, Clark's Fairy Prince, bl enamel, VG 150.00
Natural gas, Uneedit Gas Iron, Rosenbaum Mfg Co, VG 110.00
Sad iron, dbl-point, Keystone #7, VG 150.00
Sad iron, Fr, Le Caiffa No 5, thin base, EX 75.00
Sad iron, Ober #6, Pat Mar 19, '12, ribbed hdl, VG 75.00
Slug, English, all brass, lift gate, EX 225.00
Slug, German, ox tongue, L hdl, lift gate, VG 160.00
Tailor's, Colebrookdale 20, C in shield, all cast, VG 40.00

Special-Purpose Irons

Egg, AK & Sons, all cast, standing, 2-pc, VG 200.00

Egg, long wood hdl, 2¼" egg, VG 90.00
Hat, tolliker, 2-groove bottom for brims, EX 125.00
Polisher, Carron #2, English, rnd bottom, EX 100.00
Polisher, MAB Cook, Dec 5, 1848, curved nose, VG 140.00
Polisher, Mahony Troy, dmn-grid bottom, EX 60.00
Sleeve, #1 Taylor, detachable hdl, EX 50.00
Sleeve, Grand Union Tea Co, detachable hdl, EX 55.00

Ironstone

During the last quarter of the 18th century, English potters began experimenting with a new type of body that contained calcinated flint and a higher china clay content, intent on producing a fine durable whiteware — heavy, yet with a texture that would resemble porcelain. To remove the last trace of yellow, a minute amount of cobalt was added, often resulting in a bluish-white tone. Wm and John Turner of Caughley and Josiah Spode II were the first to manufacture the ware successfully. Others, such as Davenport, Hicks and Meigh, and Ralph and Josiah Wedgwood, followed with their own versions. The latter coined the name 'Pearl' to refer to his product and incorporated the term into his trademark. In 1813 a 14-year patent was issued to Charles James Mason, who called his ware Patented Ironstone. Francis Morley, G.L. Asworth, T.J. Mayer, and other Staffordshire potters continued to produce ironstone until the end of the century. While some of these patterns are simple to the extreme, many are decorated with in-mold designs of fruit, grain, and foliage on ribbed or scalloped shapes. In the 1830s transfer-printed designs in blue, mulberry, pink, green, and black became popular; and polychrome versions of Oriental wares were manufactured to compete with the Chinese trade. See also Mason's Ironstone. Our advise for this category comes from Home Place Antiques, whose address is listed in the Directory under Illinois.

Bone dish, Crescent, Wilkinson, 3x6¼", EX 55.00
Bowl, soup; Flora, Wedgwood & Co, 9½" 35.00
Bowl, vegetable; Prairie, Clementson, 1¾x8¼x6⅝" 40.00
Bowl, vegetable; President, oval, w/lid 145.00
Bowl, vegetable; Sq Ridged, Wilkinson, 7⅝" 35.00
Bowl, waste; Lily of the Valley, Anthony Shaw, 4¾" dia 75.00
Butter dish, Daisy, sq, w/lid & liner, Shaw, EX 160.00
Coffeepot, Lily, Burgess 200.00
Creamer, Bamboo, Meakin, 5⅛", EX 95.00
Creamer & sugar bowl, Victor, Jones 265.00
Cup & saucer, demitasse; Western 55.00
Cup & saucer, handleless; Athens, Wedgwood 48.00
Cup & saucer, handleless; Niagara, Paris 50.00
Cup & saucer, handleless; Pomegranate Variant, 2⅝x3⅞" 60.00
Cup & saucer, handleless; Wheat, Cochran 45.00
Cup plate, Niagara Fan, Shaw, 3⅞", EX 70.00
Dish, honey; Gothic, Royal Ironstone China, 4¼", EX 80.00
Food mold, eagle, oval, Meakin, 5¼x7", EX 150.00
Food mold, man milking in relief, oval, fluted sides, 8" 110.00
Gravy boat, Ceres, Elsmore & Forster, EX 60.00
Gravy boat, Fuchsia, bulbous, 1860s, 5¼" 65.00
Pitcher, milk; Olympic, Elsmore & Forster, 9⅜" 110.00
Pitcher, President, water sz 165.00
Pitcher, Victor, Jones, ca 1865, 10" 175.00
Plate, Ceres, Turner & Goddard, 10" 35.00
Plate, dinner; Bellflower, Edwards, 9¾" 35.00
Plate, dinner; New York, Clementson, 10¾" 40.00
Plate, Sharon Arch, Wedgwood, 10⅝" 38.00
Plate, Western Shape, Hope & Carter, mini, 5" 20.00
Platter, Nosegay, Baker & Co, 13½" 50.00
Platter, Sharon Arch, Wedgwood, 16½" 55.00

Shaving mug, Berlin Swirl 85.00
Soap dish, Bordered Hyacinth, w/insert & lid, 4¼" 165.00
Sugar bowl, Pomegranate Variant, Niagara, Walley, 6¾" 185.00

Teapot, Wheat, 11", $150.00.

Teapot, Full Ribbed, unmk, mini, 5¾" 175.00
Tureen, sauce; Lily of the Valley, w/lid & underplate 195.00
Tureen, vegetable; Sq Ridged, Wedgwood, w/lid, 5¼" 135.00
Wash bowl, Hyacinth, unmk, 13" 120.00
Wash bowl, Victory, John Edwards 115.00
Wash bowl & pitcher, Sydenham, T&R Boote 285.00
Wash pitcher, Corn & Oats 175.00
Wash pitcher, Vintage, Challinor 150.00
Waste bowl, Tuscan, unmk, 5¼" dia 85.00

Patterned Ironstone

Bowl, vegetable; Abbeville, bl transfer, 9⅛x7⅞" 55.00
Bowl, vegetable; Carrare, pk transfer, unmk, 1⅝x7⅜x5⅞" 85.00
Bowl, vegetable; Fox Hunt, gr & purple transfer, 2x10x8" 60.00
Bowl, vegetable; No 21, purple transfer, 2x9⅜x6⅝" 45.00
Butter dish, Castle Scenery, bl transfer, Furnigal, 5½x7¼" 160.00
Coffeepot, Eon, purple & brn transfer, Wooliscroft, 9½", NM ...175.00
Coffeepot, Tyrol, purple transfer, Wedgwood, rpr, 10" 75.00
Creamer, Columbia, bl transfer, Registry mk, 5¾" 105.00
Creamer, Princess Feather, bl transfer, Challinor, 5¼" 120.00
Creamer, Rose, purple transfer, 5⅞" 70.00
Creamer & sugar bowl, Spray, bl transfer, JWP&Co, w/lid 90.00
Cup & saucer, Ailanthus, brn transfer, C&WHK 45.00
Cup & saucer, Cleopatra, brn transfer 25.00
Cup & saucer, Lucerne, bl transfer, Pankhurst 25.00
Cup & saucer, Pelew, blk, Challinor 55.00
Cup & saucer, Rose, purple transfer, Challinor 25.00
Cup & saucer, Roselle, pk transfer, Meir 50.00
Cup & saucer, Washington Vase, brn transfer, Podmore Walker .50.00
Cup & saucer, Zamara, red transfer 30.00
Cup plate, Floral Sprig, purple transfer w/mc decor, unmk, 4" ...35.00
Cup plate, Versailles, bl transfer, unmk, 4⅛" 40.00
Pitcher, milk; Tyrol, purple transfer, Wedgwood, 8¾", NM 60.00
Plate, #20, purple transfer w/bl, red & gr, 7¼" 35.00
Plate, Ailanthus, brn transfer, C&WHK, 6½", NM 30.00
Plate, Ailanthus, purple transfer, C&WHK, 6¼", pr 40.00
Plate, Canella, gr transfer, unmk, 10" 35.00
Plate, Coringh, bl transfer, Edwards, 10½", NM 30.00
Plate, Corinthia, pk transfer, Challinor, 10" 20.00
Plate, Eon, purple & brn transfer, Wooliscroft, 9", pr 35.00
Plate, Excelsior, purple transfer, Wooliscroft, 9⅞" 70.00
Plate, Medina, purple transfer, C&B, 8⅝" 30.00
Plate, Paradise, gr transfer, LP&Co, 8½" 25.00
Plate, Pastoral, purple transfer, England, 1790, 10⅜" 30.00
Plate, Priory, bl transfer, Challinor, 8¾" 30.00
Plate, Venus, purple transfer, Podmore Walker, 8⅝" 25.00

Plate, Vintage, bl transfer, Alcock, 8⅜" **23.00**
Plate, Washington Vase, brn transfer, Podmore Walker, 9" **25.00**
Plate, Yale College, lt bl transfer, England, 19th C, 9⅜" **60.00**
Platter, Corinthia, pk transfer, Challinor, 10⅛x7⅜" **50.00**
Platter, Eon, brn transfer, Wooliscroft, 13⅜x10½", NM **95.00**
Platter, Gipsy, bl transfer, 15x11¾" **80.00**
Platter, Gipsy, bl transfer, 17⅜x13½", NM **85.00**
Platter, Lozere, bl transfer, Challinor, 12⅜x9½" **80.00**
Platter, Palestine, bl transfer, Ridgeway, 13x10⅝" **105.00**
Platter, Tyrol, purple transfer, Wedgwood, 15½x12" **120.00**
Platter, Tyrol, purple transfer, Wedgwood, 18¼x14" **160.00**
Punch bowl, mc flower basket transfer w/gold, 1850s, 14¼" **250.00**
Relish, Tyrol, purple transfer, hdls, Wedgwood, 9¼x5½" **35.00**
Relish, Venus, bl transfer, Podmore Walker, 8¾x5½", pr **60.00**
Sugar bowl, Tyrol, purple transfer, w/lid, rpr, 8½" **85.00**
Toothbrush box, Missouri, bl transfer, unmk, 3x8x3½" **115.00**
Tureen, gravy; Rhine, bl transfer, 8½" L, +lid & tray **55.00**
Waste bowl, Roselle, pk transfer, Meir, 3¾x5½" **40.00**
Waste bowl, Seaweed, bl transfer, Ridgeway, 3⅜x5⅝" dia **35.00**

Italian Glass

Throughout the 20th century, one of the major glassmaking centers of the world was the island of Murano. From the Stile Liberte work of Artisi Barovier (1890-1920s) to the early work of Ettore Sottsass in the 1970s, they excelled in creativity and craftsmanship. The 1920s to 1940s featured the work of glass designers like Ercole Barovier for Barovier and Toso, and Vittorio Zecchin, Napoleone Martinuzzi, and Carlo Scarpa for Venini. Many of these pieces are highly prized by collectors.

The 1950s saw a revival of Italy as a world-reknown design center for all of the arts. Glass led the charge with the brightly colored work of Fulvio Bianconi for Venini, Dino Martens for Aureliano Toso, and Ercole Barovier for Barovier and Toso. The best of these pieces are extremely desirable. The '60s and '70s have also seen many innovative designs with work by the Finnish Tapio Wirkkala, the American Thomas Stearns, and many other designers.

Unfortunately, amongst the great glass, there was a plethora of commercial ashtrays, vases, and figurines produced that, though have some value, do not compare in quality and design as the great glass of Murano. These pieces are listed as 'Murano' glass rather than by maker.

Venini: The Venini company was founded in 1921 by Paolo Venini, and he led the company until his death in 1959. Major Italian designers worked for the firm, including Vittorio Zecchin, Napoleone Martinuzzi, Carlo Scarpa, and Fulvio Bianconi. After his death, his son-in-law, Ludovico de Santillana, ran the factory and employed designers like Toni Zucchieri, Tapio Wirkkala, and Thomas Stearns. The company is known for creative designs and techniques including Inciso (finely etched lines), Battuto (carved facets), Sommerso (controlled bubbles), Pezzato (patches of fused glass), and Fascie (horizontal colored lines in clear glass). Until the mid-'60s, most pieces were signed with acid-etched 'Venini Murano ITALIA.' In the '60s they started engraving the signatures. The factory still exists.

Barovier: In the late 1920s, Ercole Barovier took over the Artisti Barovier and started designing many different vases. In the 1930s he merged with Ferro Toso and became Barovier and Toso. He designed many different series of glass including the Barbarico (rough, acid-treated brown or deep blue glass), Eugenio (free-blown vases), Efeso, Rotallato, Dorico, Egeo (vases incorporating murrine designs), and Primavera (white etched glass with black bands). He designed until 1974. The company is still in existence. Most pieces were unsigned.

Aureliano Toso: The great glass designer Dino Martens was involved with the company from about 1938 to 1965. It was his work

that produced the very desirable Oriente vases. This technique consisted of free-formed patches of green, yellow, blue, purple, black, and white stars and pieces of zanfirico canes fused into brilliantly colored vases and bowls. His El Dorado series was based on the same technique but was not opaque. He also designed pieces with alternating groups of black and white filigrana lines. Pieces are unsigned.

Seguso: Flavio Poli became the artistic director of Seguso in the late 1930s and remained until 1963. He is known for his Corroso (acid-etched glass) and his Valve series (elegant forms of two to three layers of colored glass with a clear glass casing).

Archimede Seguso: In 1946 Archimede Seguso left the Seguso Vetri D'Arte to open a new company and designed many innovative pieces. His Merletto (thin white filigrana suspended three dimensionally) series is his most famous. The epitome of his work is where a colored glass (yellow or purple) is windowed in the merlotti. His Macchia Ambra Verde is yellow and spots on a gold base encased in clear glass. The A Piume series contained feathers and leaves suspended in glass. Pieces are unsigned.

Alfredo Barbini: Barbini was a designer known for his sculptures of sea subjects and his amorphic-shaped vases with an inner core of red or blue glass with a heavy layer of finely incised outer glass. He worked in the 1950s to 1960s, and some pieces are signed.

Vistosi: Although this glassworks was started in the 1940s, fame came in the 1960s and 1970s with the birds designed by Allesandro Pianon and the early work of the Memphis school designer, Ettorre Sottsass. Pieces may be signed.

AVEM: This company is known for its work in the 1950s and 1960s. The designer, Ansolo Fuga, did work using a solid white glass with inclusions of multicolored murrines.

Cenedese: This is a postwar company led by Gino Cenedese with Alfredo Barbini as designer. When Barbini left, Cenedese took over the design work and also used the free-lanced designs of Fulvio Bianconi. They are known for their figurines and vases with suspended murrines.

Cappellin: Venini's original partner (1921-25), Giacomo Cappellin, opened a short-lived company (1925-32) that was to become extremely important. His chief designer was the young Carlo Scarpa who was to create many masterpieces in glass both for Cappellin and then Venini.

Key: inc — inclusions

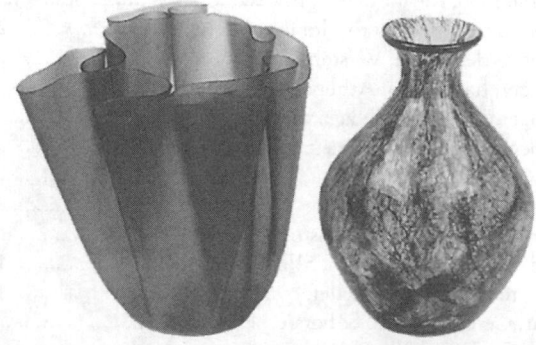

Fontana Arte fazzoletto vase, folded green body with satin finish, ca 1940, 10½x10", $1,400.00; Barovier & Toso crepuscolor vase, hair-like black inclusions in clear, Ercole Barovier, ca 1935, 10x8", $1,980.00.

Venini Glass

Birds, Corroso, clear glass, 7", pr **1,825.00**
Birds, doves, lt bl tessuto, appl wings, 4¾", pr, NM **1,495.00**

Birds, hen & rooster, mc & wht lattimo on blk bases, 7", pr ...9,200.00
Bottle, Incalmo, female form, teal/dk bl/gr, +5 bowls, 15" 1,870.00
Bottle, Morandi, red opaque w/gr clear top, red stopper, 14" 990.00
Bottle, red & gr vertical lines, w/stopper, 12¼" 690.00
Bottle vase, Pezzati, opaque wht/gr/red/bl patches, 14¼" 18,400.00
Bowl, Corroso, amber, sq base, 2¾x4" 250.00
Bowl, Fasce Orizzontali w/aqua & bl stripes on clear, 5" dia 330.00
Bowl, heavy clear w/spiraling wht filigrana, 1½x3½" 187.00
Bowl, Laguna, lt bl w/appl wht lattimo ft, 9x12" 750.00
Bowl, Sommerso, lt gr w/gold inclusions, sq, 3x5½" 355.00
Candlesticks, Inciso, 8¾", pr 1,160.00
Clock, leather face in clear fr w/orange inclusions, 9¾" 485.00
Figurine, Commedia Dell Arte series; Arlechinno, 5¾x10¼" .2,945.00
Figurine, Commedia Dell Arte series: Giangurgolo, 13" 2,795.00
Figurine, Commedia Dell Arte series: Pantalone, 13¼" 2,945.00
Figurine, Commedia Dell Arte series: Tartaglia, 12¼" 2,575.00
Figurine, Costume series: lady in pk skirt, topaz top, 13½" 2,530.00
Figurine, fish, clear w/turq bones & bl glass stripes, 12½" 920.00
Figurine, Grotteschi series: 4 wht lattimo male figures, 9¼" 920.00
Figurine, mermaid, gr torso vase w/Xd wht lines, 15½" 19,550.00
Figurine, seated lady, lav murrines, model #4868, 9x7" 37,950.00
Garniture bowl & 2 sticks, lav w/red flowers/gr leaves, 9¾" 5,750.00
Hourglass, bl & gr, 5¾" 365.00
Hourglass, orange, 10" 1,045.00
Lamp shade, wht w/Fasce Orizzontali border, hanging, 20" H 750.00
Mortar & pestle, aquamarine iridized free-form+gr irid bowl, 6" ..345.00
Obelisk, clear w/blk floral int core, 14½" 520.00
Vase, Battuto, wht w/vertical stripes, wheel-cvd, 3¾" 460.00
Vase, Bugne, heavy bl Corroso w/lg prunts, 12¼" 635.00
Vase, Canne red/gr/amethyst/amber vertical stripes, 10" 575.00
Vase, Con Macchie, yel w/abstracts in blk & bl, 10½" 6,900.00
Vase, Fasce Verticale, red & gr patches, cylindrical, 9½" 4,830.00
Vase, Fasce Verticale, red/bl/gr vertical lines, 14¼" 8,050.00
Vase, Forati, lt gr w/pierced center, 10¾" 800.00
Vase, Giada, red-cased w/copper inclusions & blk lines, 12" ...1,035.00
Vase, Incalmo, cobalt w/fused red band, cylindrical, 7½" 400.00
Vase, Inciso, int bl & amber layers, cylindrical, 10" 495.00
Vase, Penellatte, clear w/yel horizontal band, stain, 10½" 5,865.00
Vase, Pezzati, gr/dk gr/yel/clear patches, 5¼" 3,220.00
Vase, Scolpiti, blk w/clear intersecting bands, 8½" 660.00
Vase, Soffiati, pk/wht diagonals, Veronese shape, 11¾" 1,265.00

Other Italian Glassmakers

Archimede Seguso, bowl, shell shape, gr to purple 575.00
Archimede Seguso, clown, reclining, wht merletto w/blk trim ...12,650.00
Archimede Seguso, vase, clear w/gold incl & appl red bands ..1,030.00
Archimede Seguso Bullicante, vase, clear w/gold incl 615.00
Archimede Seguso Macchie Ambra Verde, basket 460.00
Archimede Seguso Merletto, bowl, bl w/wht merlotto base 310.00
Archimede Seguso Merletto, bowl, emerald w/wht merletto canes ..575.00
Archimede Seguso Merletto, vase, turq w/wht patches, asymetrical ...8,625.00
Artisti Barovier Murrine, vase, yel w/star murrines 2,875.00
Aureliano Toso, cornucopia, gr/wht filigrana, appl leaf base 135.00
Aureliano Toso, rooster, blk/wht wings, red crop, yel beak 635.00
Aureliano Toso, vase, wht parrot form w/mc wings, red crop 865.00
Aureliano Toso Bianca Nera, vase, appl clear ft 345.00
Aureliano Toso Bianca Nera, vase, gooseneck, mc spiral bands ..1,150.00
Aureliano Toso Bianca Nera, vase, 2-hdld 875.00
Aureliano Toso Bianca Nera Mezza, pitcher, filigrana 1,035.00
Aureliano Toso Oriente, bowl, crimped clear rim & ft 430.00
Aureliano Toso Oriente, bowl, ftd, lg 8,800.00
Aureliano Toso Oriente, vase, yel/aventurine/orange/gr patches .1,265.00
AVEM, rooster, red/pk/yel on clear base w/gold incl, EX 275.00

AVEM, vase, wht w/windows of red/yel & bl murrines 3,900.00
AVEM Anse Volante, vase, free-form, 2-prong, appl blobs/etc 2,415.00
Barbina Incalmo, vase, lt bl top w/yel body 575.00
Barbina Scavo, vases, pr 345.00
Barbini, figurine/sculpture, 2 carps 250.00
Barbini Inciso/Sommerso, vase, sculptured w/red core 6,250.00
Barbini Torso, female torso, amethyst Corroso 2,990.00
Barovier, att; tiger, clear w/gold incl & amethyst stripes 475.00
Barovier, figurine, monkey, amber w/blk eyes 5,980.00
Barovier Aborigeni, bowl, clear, random bubbles, gr/yel specks ..510.00
Barovier Ambrati, ewers, amber/caramel over wht cased, pr ...1,840.00
Barovier Barbarico Dorato, vase, donut shape, pinched snout .1,150.00
Barovier Christian Dior, flask, red/gr/violet, w/stopper 7,980.00
Barovier Crepsola, vase, clear w/hair-like blk incl 1,980.00
Barovier Diamontati, vase, blk-edged 5-color murrines 4,370.00
Barovier Dorico, bowl, aquamarine & lattimo 3,300.00
Barovier Egeo, bottle, purple & gr murrines, tall 3,095.00
Barovier Eugeneo, vase, bl irid w/single pierced hdl 4,125.00
Barovier Gemmata, vase 510.00
Barovier Lenti, vase, cobalt layer on heavy-wall cylinder 6,900.00
Barovier Neolitica, bowl 440.00
Barovier Neolitica, fish, pr 900.00
Barovier Oriente, vase, rectangular 1,725.00
Barovier Primavera, vase, sea horse 17,250.00
Barovier Rugiadoso, bowl, ltly fumed clear, pulled hdls, 1940s 1,430.00
Barovier Sidereo, vase, clear w/clear murrines, dbl gourd 1,400.00
Barovier Zebrati, vase, pk-specked gold incl, wht spiral, sq 1,300.00
Cappellin Fenicio, vase, lattimo/gr zigzags, #3887, w/label 12,150.00
Cenedese, att; aquarium, mc fish & grass, 3-panel 1,495.00
Cenedese, att; aquarium, red/yel/gr/wht marine forms, 4-panel ..925.00
Cenedese Patchwork, bowl, red/yel/gr/purple/bl/wht patches 550.00
Cenedese Scavo, bowl, yel w/metallic incl 490.00
Cenedese Sommerso, bowl, wht opaque w/bright red basin 165.00
Fratelli Toso, hat, red & wht bull's-eye murrines on clear 175.00
Fratelli Toso, vase, red & bl murrines 4,050.00
Fratellio Toso Sasso, egg, appl blk abstracts, +stand 220.00
SAIAR-Ferro-Toso, figurine, jumping gazelle on base, lt pk 9,200.00
Salviati, figure, stag, amber on clear rock-form base 245.00
Salviati Sommerso, vase, dk amber int layer, base w/bl island 825.00
Seguso Vetri D'Arte Siderale, bowl, lt gr, sm 1,645.00
Seguso Vetri D'Arte Sommerso, teardrop, gr/amber int layers .1,430.00
Unknown, chess set, frosted/polished sqs, blk/clear chess pcs ..3,220.00
Unknown, frame, red & blk canes alternate, blk ribbon corners ..550.00
Unknown, Soffiati, vase, red w/irid throughout, appl hdls 255.00
Unknown, tableware bowl, bl w/3 glass fruits 115.00
Unknown, tableware bowl, clear w/internal red & bl ring, NM .100.00
Unknown, tableware charger, clear w/11 glass fruits 365.00
Vistosi, vase, bl w/6 rows of red & bl murrines 1,475.00
Vistosi, vase, gray w/3 bands of purple & bl murrines 735.00
Vistosi Pulcino, bird, bl w/bands of bl & gr murrines 1,260.00
Vistosi Pulcino, bird, bl w/flat top & bronze legs, S-190 ....1,495.00
Vistosi Pulcino, bird, gr cubes, bl/red murrines, wire legs 1,870.00
Vistosi Pulcino, bird, gr w/red & bl murrines, J-form, copper legs .1,225.00
Vistosi Pulcino, bird, orange w/rnd body & wire legs 1,350.00
Zecchin-Martinuzzi Nero Rosso, vase, blk/silver inc/red trim ..1,265.00

Ivory

Technically, true ivory is the substance composing the tusk of the elephant; the finest type comes from Africa. However, tusks and teeth of other animals — the walrus, the hippopotamus, and the sperm whale, for instance — are similar in composition and appearance and have also been used for carving. The Chinese have used this substance for centuries, preferring it over bone because of the natural oil contained in its pores, which not only renders it easier to carve but also imparts a soft sheen to the finished product. Aged ivory usually takes on a soft caramel patina, but unscrupulous dealers sometimes treat new ivory to a tea bath to 'antique' it! A bill passed in 1978 reinforced a ban on the importation of whale and walrus ivory. All examples listed here are Oriental in origin unless noted otherwise.

Study of Ebisu on back of fish, horn-inlaid eyes, black pigment highlights, signed Masatomo, late 19th century, 1¾", $700.00.

Boy w/awahi shell forming himotoshi, blk stain, 1880s, 2" **460.00**
Brush pot, figures/trees/houses cvd in relief, 4¾" **195.00**
Chess set, pcs cvd as Europeans & (wood) Africans, no board ...**1,300.00**
Daikoku on rice bail, MOP inlay/sepia stain, Meiji, 1" **635.00**
Deity of Foo dog, 8¾" **500.00**
Dignitary, eng details w/blk wash, 11"+rosewood base **330.00**
Dr's lady, high heels & flowers, rests on wood bench, 6" **1,200.00**
Dr's lady, reclining on pallet, 6"L+wooden base **1,600.00**
Elegant lady w/child on her bk, Masatoshi, Meiji, 8¾", EX **1,265.00**
European trader in long tunic, blk stain, rstr, 18th C, 4¾" **575.00**
Farmer w/hoe & winnowing basket, Shugetsu, Meiji, rpr, 6½" ...**460.00**
Fox, inlaid eyes, tail forms himotoshi, sgn Bishu, 2⅜" **975.00**
Geisha w/open fan/parasol, sepia wash, Akayama, 1900s, 9½" ...**800.00**
Kwan-Tin figure, EX detail, 14"+wooden base **660.00**
Lady holding flowers, much detail, wooden base, 9¾" **385.00**
Lady in kimono on mat w/puppy, sepia wash, Tokuku/Meiji, 2" ..**345.00**
Lady musicians, seated, 5¾"+wooden baase, pr **550.00**
Lady w/fan, 10⅜", on wooden base **360.00**
Man & child w/chicken & eggs, 10¼", base missing **990.00**
Man seated & wrapped in robe, 4"+wooden base **275.00**
Mother in plain kimono drying sm son, Ryuichi, Meiji, 14½" ...**6,325.00**
Parasol hdl, allover cvg, 13", EX **160.00**
Plaque, elephant & 2 tigers in high relief, wood fr, 4x7½" **390.00**
Priest w/deer, blk & red highlights, 12"+base **330.00**
Rakkon w/Oni issuing from bowl held aloft, Shuzan, Meiji, 8" ...**700.00**
Ram, hunched over, joined hooves form himotoshi, 1900s, 1¾" ..**700.00**
Samurai on knoll, sepia wash, Koshun, Meiji, 18⅝" **3,735.00**
Shojo w/sake cup/dipper, blk stain, Gyokushun, Meiji, 1¾" **600.00**
Tusk, polished patina, 18" **250.00**
Vase, cvd figures, ring hdls w/grotesque heads, 6¾" **360.00**
Vegetable seller w/basket, sgn Yoshimitsu, Meiji, 8¾", EX **1,380.00**

Jack-in-the-Pulpit Vases

Popular novelties at the turn of the century, jack-in-the-pulpit vases were made in every type of art glass produced. Some were simple, others elaborately appliqued and enameled. They were shaped to resemble the lily for which they were named.

Frosted o/l w/ribs, appl gr leaves & ruby Xmas cactus, 13" **750.00**
Lt gr w/red-shaded rim, ruffled/crimped, 9x10½" **115.00**
Maroon & wht spatter, vaseline opal appl top, 11x6" **100.00**
Pk Hobnail, crimped rim, opal cased, 7" **125.00**

Pk opal to vaseline, 11¼x4⅞" **135.00**
Rainbow, tooled crimped camphor ft, ruffled rim, 8" **250.00**
Rubena verde opal, crimped rim, 12" **225.00**
Spangle, 3-color/silver on wht, clear edge, swirled, 6x3½" **250.00**
Wht w/pk int, ruffled top, 6⅝x6½" **115.00**

Japanese Lustreware

Imported from Japan during the 1920s, novelty tableware items, vases ashtrays, etc. — often in blue, tan, and mother-of-pearl lustre glazes — were sold through five-and-dime stores or given as premiums for selling magazine subscriptions. The Occupied Japan Club is listed in the Directory under Clubs, Newletters, and Catalogs.

Ashtray, conch shell form, caramel, pk int **15.00**
Bottle, perfume; lay-down style **35.00**
Cigarette holder/ashtray, elephant w/howdah figural, 4¼" **45.00**
Condiment set, Deco florals w/aqua trim, 4-pc **17.50**

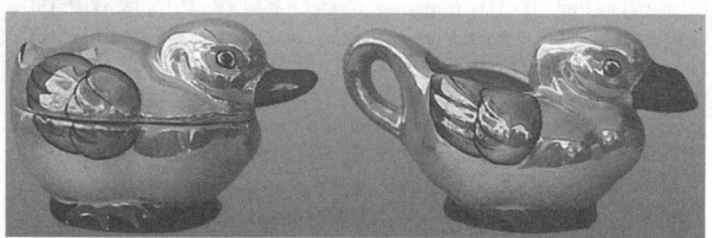

Creamer and sugar bowl, duck figurals in tan and blue lustre, hand-painted Japan mark, 3½", $50.00.

Creamer & sugar bowl, Deco florals, w/tray **27.50**
Flask, A Wee Scotch, tan lustre, 4" **40.00**
Lemon dish, flowers on bl, Occupied Japan **20.00**
Pincushion, boy reading book on tan lustre potty **25.00**
Pincushion, lady in bl lustre dress holds lg basket, 5¾" **35.00**
Sugar shaker, caramel top & base, mc florals **14.00**
Tea set, bluebird decor, child sz, 13-pc, serves 4 ....**75.00**
Teapot, mc floral on bl & wht lustre, 6½" **45.00**
Vase, duck figural, red & yel w/bl lustre, 7¼" **30.00**

Jervis

W.P. Jervis began his career as a potter in 1898. By 1908 he had his own pottery in Oyster Bay, New York. His shapes were graceful; often he decorated his wares with sgraffito designs over which he applied a matt glaze. Many piece were incised 'Jervis' in a vertical arrangement. The pottery closed around 1912.

Cup, sea gulls, wht on dk bl, 3-hdld, 4¾" **500.00**
Vase, bl matt/gr crackle, squat dbl gourd, Rose Valley, 4" **1,100.00**
Vase, textured bl matt, cylinder w/bulbed base, 7¾x4¼" **350.00**
Wall pocket, sea horses, bl/brn on speckled bl, Rhead, 6x6" **900.00**

Jewelry

Jewelry as objects of adornment has always been regarded with special affection. Whether it be a trinket or a costly ornament of gold, silver, or enameled work, jewelry has personal significance to the wearer. The art of the jeweler is valued as is any art object, and the names of

Lalique or Faberge on collectible pieces bring prices demanded by the signed works of Picasso. Once the province of kings and noblemen, jewelry now is a legacy of all strata of society. The creativity reflected in the jeweler's art has resulted in a myriad of decorative adornments for men and women, and the modern usage of 'lesser' gems and base metals has elevated the value and increased the demand for artistic merit, so that now it is considered by collectors to be on a par with intrinsic value. Luxuriously appointed pieces of Victorian splendor and Edwardian grandeur now compete with the unique, imaginative renditions of jewelry produced in the exciting Art Nouveau period as well as the adventurous translation of jewelry executed in man-made materials versus natural elements. Today prices for gems and gemstones crafted into antique and collectible jewelry are based on artistic merit, personal appeal, pure sentimentality, and intrinsic value. Note: Diamond prices vary greatly depending on color, clarity, etc. Values given here are for diamond jewelry with a standard commercial grade of diamonds that are most likely to be encountered.

Our advisor for this category is Rebecca Dodds; her address may be found in the Directory under Florida. If you are interested in collecting or dealing in jewelry, you will find that authority Lillian Baker has several fine books available on the subject — *100 Years of Collectible Jewelry: 1850-1950; Art Nouveau and Art Deco Jewelry;* and *Fifty Years of Collectible Fashion Jewelry: 1925-1975.* These books are complete with beautiful full-color illustrations and current market values. Mrs. Baker is listed in the Directory under California. Another fine source of information is *Christmas Pins, Past and Present* by Jill Gallina. (All books referenced are published by Collector Books.) See also Plastics.

Key:
cab — cabochon	gw — gold washed
ct — carat	k — karat
dmn — diamond	plat — platinum
dwt — penny weight	r/stn — rhinestone
Euro — European cut	stn — stone
fl — filigree	wg — white gold
gf — gold filled	yg — yellow gold
grad — graduated	ygf — yellow gold filled

Bracelet, Antonio, sterling w/moonstones, trapezoidal links 700.00
Bracelet, bangle, bl lapiz w/1" W hinge, eng, safety chain 425.00
Bracelet, bangle, gf w/chased decor 75.00
Bracelet, bangle, ivory w/dragon cvg 275.00
Bracelet, bangle, ygf, wide, Victorian 150.00
Bracelet, bangle, 10k yg w/eng floral, child's 100.00
Bracelet, bangle, 14k yg, 3 dmn melees: 1ct tw, 13.7 dwt 1,300.00
Bracelet, bangle, 14k yg w/emerald/garnet/sapphires, 1960s 750.00
Bracelet, charm; silver, w/18 charms, mk Sterling 125.00
Bracelet, charm; 14k yg w/10k, 14k & 18k yg charms 540.00
Bracelet, charm; 14k yg woven wire, ¼" W, w/8 charms 175.00
Bracelet, cuff; sterling, hexagon w/lg gr center turq, 1¼" 50.00
Bracelet, Geo Jensen, silver, scallop shell links, #77 ....485.00
Bracelet, Jondell, sterling, thick C-form, Mexican #925 ....60.00
Bracelet, sterling spiral, mk Denmark 95.00
Bracelet, 14k yg w/blk enamel & seed pearls, Victorian, pr 1,700.00
Bracelet, 14k yg w/2ct tw dmns, 1.5ct tw emeralds, link style .2,800.00
Bracelet, 14k yg w/5 lg Imperial topaz & tiny seed pearls 635.00
Bracelet, 18k yg, snake, sapphire/ruby cab eyes, 15.2 dwt 1,400.00
Cuff links, gf, enameled lodge symbols, Victorian, pr 20.00
Cuff links, sterling, ¾" dia cutwork, 2ct cab moonstones (2) 65.00
Cuff links, sterling horseman on 1" polished wood circle 28.00
Cuff links, 18k yg over sterling leaf w/8mm cultured pearl 38.00
Earrings, Geo Jensen, sterling doves, screw-bks, pr 175.00
Earrings, Kalo, sterling, flower bud, 1" 70.00
Earrings, yg, dmn studs, .77cts tw, prong set w/gold heads 600.00

Earrings, 14k yg, amethyst dangles w/seed pearls 325.00
Hair comb, celluloid, Nouveau style, gr w/blk stones, 8" L 105.00
Locket, solid yg, 3 inset dmns .35 tw 300.00
Necklace, Art Smith, sterling, glass ball in cup drop on links .1,100.00
Necklace, Chinese jade beads (med gr), 70 grad 350.00
Necklace, coral beads, wired to silver drop w/lg amethyst 125.00
Necklace, cultured pearls, 6½mm, 26½" strand 475.00
Necklace, lapis lazuli, 76 matched beads, vermeil clasp, 28" 140.00
Necklace, lapis lazuli+6 14k beads, 30" 275.00
Necklace, pearls, 9mm, blemishes, 14k yg clasp, 16" 1,500.00
Necklace, pearls, 9mm, fine quality, 14k yg clasp, 16" 4,000.00
Necklace, Persian turq nuggets, strand of 41 grad 110.00
Necklace, 10k yg hollow beads, 4mm, 10" L 60.00
Necklace, 18k yg 11mm beads, soft brushed finish, 55 grams 800.00
Necklace+bracelet, Hector Aguilar, sterling, beaded links 920.00
Pendant, ivory cvd elephant w/7 garnets in arch, 2¼" 275.00
Pendant, 14k yg cast cat, 1.1-troy oz, on 9k yg chain 440.00
Pill box pendant, Wm Spratling, sterling/amethyst, +chain ...1,100.00
Pin, brass, Nouveau snakes, birds & purple glass, 1910, 3" 110.00
Pin, cameo, tower & bridge landscape, 10k rose gold fr, 2" 95.00
Pin, cameo, w/chariot, 14k wg fl fr, oval, 2¼" 225.00
Pin, Carence Crafters (att), brass w/etch sea gull, 2½" 80.00
Pin, Ed Wiener, sterling, 2 oval disks, 1 w/emb animal, 2½" 700.00
Pin, Geo Gensen, sterling, O-shape fish w/agate cab, 1½" 400.00
Pin, Geo Jensen, sterling, buds/berries w/moonstones, #100 ....300.00
Pin, Geo Jensen, sterling, flower w/bl lapis center, #189 ....350.00
Pin, Geo Jensen, sterling, rtcl florals w/silver cabs, 2" 285.00
Pin, Geo Jensen, sterling, rtcl oval w/leaves & berries, 2" 375.00
Pin, Geo Jensen, sterling, 3-point star w/cut-out center, 3" 130.00
Pin, Kalo, sterling, berry & leaf design, 3", EX 375.00
Pin, Ledesma, sterling bar w/2 gr stn rectangles, 2½" 260.00
Pin, Liberty, silver, scarab w/enamel wings, mk, 1½", EX 300.00

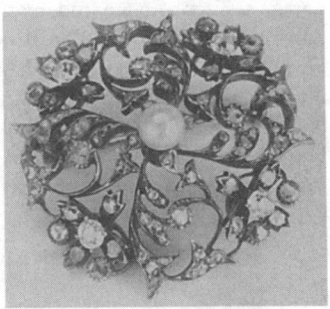

Pin, delicate silver and gold scrollwork with cut diamonds and central pearl, Victorian era, $750.00.

Pin, silver basket w/mc paste stns, early 110.00
Pin, sterling & marcasite ballerina figure 100.00
Pin, Taxco RIC, sterling, triangle w/turq cupped in free-form, 2" .80.00
Pin, 14k wg fl, sm onyx & dmn center 185.00
Pin/pendant, cameo, lady's portrait, 14k wg fl mts 235.00
Pin/pendant, Kalo, sterling, orchid, #183, 2½" dia 450.00
Ring, Cartier, plat, 5x25ct tourmaline fr w/dmn melees 1,650.00
Ring, Cire Perdu, 14k yg w/lg citron 65.00
Ring, Cire Perdu, 14k yg w/lg pearl 75.00
Ring, Geo Jensen, sterling, cut-out heart shape, Denmark 80.00
Ring, man's, 14k yg, malachite & 6 sm dmns 235.00
Ring, man's, 14k yg w/oval opal 225.00
Ring, plat, 1.6ct sapphire amid 2 dmn melees 650.00
Ring, plat Art Deco fl w/Euro 1.8ct dmn 2,600.00
Ring, plat Art Deco fl w/1.4ct dmn 1,850.00
Ring, plat Art Deco w/1.24ct dmn & 2 faux sapphires 1,500.00
Ring, yg, .53ct wht dmn & yel dmns, .80ct tw, prong mts 1,000.00
Ring, yg, 1ct oval sapphire amid 18 rnd/marquise dmns, '60s .2,000.00
Ring, 10k wg, 1.8ct dmn solitaire 2,500.00

Ring, 10k wg w/3 full-cut & 6 single-cut dmns, .45tw 165.00
Ring, 14k rose gold, blk onyx w/10 seed pearls & gold intaglio ..185.00
Ring, 14k wg, w/attached 10mm solid gold nugget atop 75.00
Ring, 14k wg, w/14 dmns in 2 clusters, .40tw 250.00
Ring, 14k wg fl w/3 .35 dmns, 6 sm sapphires, 1" mt 1,200.00
Ring, 14k wg w/5 .8 dmns in str line 350.00
Ring, 14k yg, 11.0x3.4mm jadeite gypsy cab, Kobrin Bros NY 975.00
Ring, 14k yg, 5 5mm cab gr jade stns 50.00
Ring, 14k yg lg oval jade stn in laurel-leaf mt 285.00
Ring, 14k yg openwork band w/6 mc oval jade stns 175.00
Ring, 14k yg Victorian band w/turq & seed pearls 135.00
Ring, 14k yg w/intaglio-cut blk onyx w/head of gladiator 30.00
Ring, 14k yg w/1.3ct dmn solitaire 1,850.00
Ring, 18k yg, w/1891 Indian head penny 75.00
Ring, 18k yg, 12ct amethyst in wg basket mt w/yg flowers 425.00
Slide chain w/cameo, 10k rose gold, Victorian 715.00
Stick pin, silver, question mk, paste stns outline, coral center 75.00
Stick pin, sterling Art Nouveau head 45.00
Stick pin, yg horseshoe, 3 heart-shaped opals & 1 ruby 120.00
Stick pin, 14k yg w/.20ct dmn 40.00

Costume Jewelry

Bracelet, Arpeggio, 22-section MOP expansion type, 1¾" W 50.00
Bracelet, D Anderson, pearlized wht enamel/HP flowers/silver ..325.00
Bracelet, Lisner, faux coral, w/orig tag 22.50
Bracelet, Trifari, brushed gold, hinged, 1¾" W 25.00
Brooch, Coro, flower form, gr stns 22.00
Brooch, Coro, r/stns, 3" 30.00
Brooch, Coro, 3-color stns, 5-levels, 2" dia 30.00
Brooch, Emmons, butterfly, mc stns/pearls, 2¼" 20.00
Brooch, Sarah Coventry, r/stns surround lg topaz, 5" dia 25.00
Earrings, Danescraft, sterling, leaf shape 22.00
Earrings, Eisenberg Ice, rnd, marquise & pave stns, pr 34.00
Earrings, Weiss, Aurora Borealis & wht glass flower 16.50
Earrings, Weiss, flower-petal shape, marquise & rnd stns 20.00
Necklace, Haskell, 4-strand pearl choker w/lg faux sapphire 125.00
Necklace, KJ Lane, 8-strand choker of 2-tone & gold beads 350.00
Pendant/brooch, Sarah Coventry, Aurora Borealis & faux pearls .12.50
Pin, Beau, sterling flowers & leaves on branch 15.00

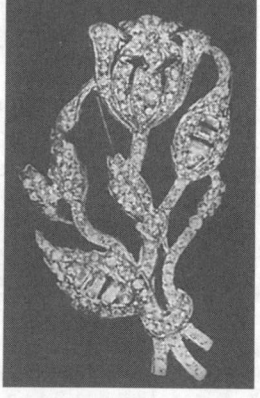

Pin, Coro, multicolored stone flower heads on spray, 1940s, $50.00.

Pin, Coro, enameled flower, 4" L 15.00
Pin, Coro, lt & dk bl stns, 3", +earrings 28.00
Pin, Expo, sterling circle w/flowers & wht r/stns, 2" 20.00
Pin, Kenneth J Lane, grasshopper 60.00
Pin, Made in Austria, bl & purple crystal flower, lg 25.00
Pin, Monet, enameled daisy, 2¼" L 8.00
Pin, Pat Pend, circle w/faux turq sapphires/dmns/rubies 20.00

Pin, Sarah Coventry, Santa figural 40.00
Pin, Trifari, enameled butterfly 25.00
Pin, Trifari, sterling, bird of paradise, w/enameling, 3½" 350.00
Pin, Var-Lou, sterling circle w/real pearl in rosette 25.00
Pin & earrings, Schiaparelli, irid red stns & rnd red beads 165.00

Josef Originals

Josef Original figurines were designed by Muriel Joseph George of Arcadia, California, from 1946 until she retired in 1982. (The spelling Josef was a printer error in the first labels for Pitty Sing. The first retail sale and time did not permit them to correct it, so it remains 'Josef Originals.') They were made in California until the early 1960s, at which time George Good (her representative and soon-to-be partner) convinced her to go to Japan to remain competive in the marketplace. All figures produced in Japan were made to her exact specifications, and the quality continued to be very high. After she retired, her partner, George Good, retained the Josef name and produced figurines until 1985 (she still designed some things for him), when he sold the company to Applause. They continue to make Josef figurines, though pieces are limited and not of the same quality. Examples below are from the period of the 1940s through the 1980s (before Muriel's retirement), when the girls were all made with black eyes and a glossy finish, the animals with a semigloss finish. Prices are for figurines in perfect condition; one with repair or damage is not considered collectible. Caution: we have found figurines that have Josef labels, but are not Josef Originals. All Josef Originals are marked with an oval sticker, either with the California or Japan designation, and all (except the animals) carry either an incised or ink-stamped mark, 'Josef Originals©'. Our advisors for this category are Jim and Kaye Whitaker (Eclectic Antiques), authors of *Josef Originals*; their address is in the Directory under Washington.

Birthday Girl #16, bl gown, blk eyes, Japan 36.00
Birthstone Doll, Japan 22.00

California Belles: Dinner Belle, blue gown, holds plate; Chapel Belle, pink gown, holds hymnal, California, bisque, 7", $32.00 each.

Camel, standing, Japan, 6¼" 60.00
Christmas Lady Music Box, fur collar, 6½" 85.00
Duck Family, Japan, 2" to 3", 3-pc set 58.00
Gigi series, w/tennis racket, wht & gray dress, Japan 90.00
Ladybug, Japan, 2½" 14.00
Little International, Japan, 4" 33.00
Love's Rendezvous, aqua gown & hat, Japan, 9" 100.00
Monkeys, various poses & szs, Japan, ea 18.00
Rabbits, various poses, 3" to 5", ea 16.00

Judaica

The items listed below are representative of objects used in both the secular and religious life of the Jewish people. They are evident of a culture where silversmiths, painters, engravers, writers, and metal workers were highly gifted and skilled in their art. Most of the treasures shown in recently displayed exhibits of Judaica were confiscated by the Germans during the late 1930s up to 1945; by then eight Jewish synagogues and fifty warehouses had been filled with Hitler's plunder. Judaica is currently available through dealers, from private collections, and the annual auction held in Israel.

Beaker, silver w/emb swags & birds, Goldberg, 1785, 3" **500.00**
Circumcision dish, Continental silver, repousse, 1900s, 8" **525.00**
Cup & saucer, enameled silver, phoenix/sun face, SB, 1895 ....**800.00**
Demitasse cup & saucer, enamel/silver-gilt, Zverev, +spoon ...**2,585.00**
Dish, 84 silver, fluted, reeded rim, Talberg, 1829, 10x14" **800.00**
Egg, enamel/84 silver, flower panels/geometrics, mk, 2½" **1,495.00**
Egg, enamel/84 silver-gilt, appl wire/beads, Alexayev, 2" **1,495.00**
Egg, enamel/925 silver, geometric flowers/scrolls, mk, 2" **635.00**
Ethrog container, Israeli silver gilt, oviform, 1940s, 8" **650.00**
Hanukkah lamp, Polish brass, stepped base, 1800s, 15½" **625.00**
Kovsh, enamel/gilt-silver, scrolls/bird etc, Ya B, 7", EX **2,300.00**
Kovsh, enamel/silver, foliage/beading, 11th Artel, 5", EX **2,000.00**
Kovsh, enamel/84 silver, fleur-de-lis hdl, bird w/in, 3½" **1,150.00**

Menorah, German 800 standard silver, decorated stepped base, baluster-form shaft surmounted by Star of David, 8 scroll and floral arms, 12¼", $1,265.00.

Menorah, Polish 800 silver, domed/sq base, plain, 13" **1,100.00**
Passover cloth, Palestinian silk, printed views, '20s, 18x23" **225.00**
Purim dish, Hungarian pnt porc, 1900s, 12¼" **875.00**
Shoe horn, 84 silver w/enamel hdl, appl drape, St Petersburg **865.00**
Snuff box, niello decor/84 silver, city/maid, FL, 1820, 2½" **800.00**
Spice container, Continental silver, fish form, 1800s, 9" **325.00**
Spice tower, German silver, 2-tier, gallery, 1790s, 6½" **1,775.00**
Teaspoons, gilt silver/champleve, 1900, Tiffany mk, in case **920.00**
Triptych, 84 silver, arched panel tops, PJL, 1900, 4" L **1,495.00**
Vase, sterling, ftd trumpet w/ornate hdls, Wood-Hughes, 9½" ...**800.00**
Yamulka (skull cap), blk velvet w/silver threads, 1890s, M **75.00**

Jugtown

The Jugtown Pottery was started about 1920 by Juliana and Jacques Busbee, in Moore County, North Carolina. Ben Owen, a young descendant of a Staffordshire potter, was hired in 1923. He was the master potter, while the Busbees experimented with perfecting glazes and supervising design and modeling. Preferred shapes were those reminiscent of traditional country wares and classic Oriental forms. Glazes were various: natural-clay oranges, buffs, 'tobacco-spit' brown, mirror black, white, 'frog-skin' green, a lovely turquoise called Chinese blue, and the traditional cobalt-decorated salt glaze. The pottery gained national recognition, and as a result of their success, several other local potteries were established. Jugtown is still in operation; however, they no longer use their original glaze colors which are now so collectible.

Bowl, olive gr speckled, repeated indents, ftd, 5½" **100.00**
Candlesticks, creamy wht, trumpet form, 11x4½", pr **175.00**
Dish, orange gloss, hand thrown, w/lid, hdls, 11" dia, NM **250.00**

Vase, Chinese blue dripping over red clay body, ovoid, circle mark, 7x4¾", $450.00.

Vase, Chinese bl, incurvate rim, 4" **220.00**
Vase, Chinese bl, ovoid, 6" **260.00**
Vase, Chinese red, bulbous, 4½" **800.00**
Vase, gray/wine gloss, bulbous w/waisted neck, hdls, 9½" **350.00**
Vase, red & gr mottling, bulbous, mk, 8¾x6¾" **775.00**

K. P. M. Porcelain

Under the tutelage of Frederick the Great, King of Prussia, porcelain manufacture was instituted in Berlin in 1751 by William K. Wegeley. In jealous competition with Meissen, hard-paste porcelain was produced (dinnerware, figurines, vases, etc.), some of which were undecorated while other pieces were hand painted in Watteau scenes, landscapes, or florals. It soon became evident that the factory was unable to offer serious competition. The King withdrew his support, and the factory failed in 1757. In 1761 Johann Ernst Gotzkowsky bought the rights and attempted a similar operation which soon failed due to financial difficulties. Still determined to gain the same recognition enjoyed by Meissen, the King bought the plant in 1763 and ruled the operation with an iron hand, often assuring his success by taking advantage of his position. The King died in 1786, but production has continued and quality tableware and decorative porcelains are still being made on a commercial basis. Earliest marks were simply 'G' or 'W,' followed by the scepter mark. After 1830 'K.P.M.' with an orb or eagle was adopted. Our advisor for this category is Don Williams; he is listed in the Directory under Missouri.

Charger, castle ruins, 19th C, 15½" **700.00**
Clock, Rococo form, cherub sits on side, shaped stand, 21" **2,500.00**
Ewer, continuous scene, orb & sceptre mk, 1800s, 20" **1,650.00**
Figurine, boy w/fur hat & ax, girl w/goat, late, 7" **250.00**
Figurine, monkey, glazed wht porc, 17" **750.00**
Jar, 2 couple portraits on wht, cobalt & gold trim, w/lid, 7" **395.00**
Plaque, Beggars, 2 barefoot boys, sgn Griener, 13x8" **7,500.00**
Plaque, Giovantine, lady w/flower in hat, sgn Wagner, 6x4" ...**1,000.00**
Plaque, maid in golden cap w/pearls, yel/red drape, 6x8" **2,500.00**
Plaque, maid w/nude twins, Chaule/Douguer, 8x12", +ornate fr .**1,500.00**

Plaque, Matter Dolorosa, sgn H Bucker, ca 1850s, mk, fr, 7" **950.00**
Plaque, mother & nude child, 8¾x12", ornate fr, 15x17" **3,000.00**
Plaque, youth dressed as cavalier w/lace collar, 10x8" **4,000.00**
Vase, lady's portrait w/cherubs, sgn, ca 1920, 6¼" **750.00**

Kayserzinn Pewter

J.P. Kayser Sohn produced pewter decorated with relief-molded Art Nouveau motifs in Germany during the late 1800s and into the 20th century. Examples are marked with 'Kayserzinn' and the mold number within an elongated oval reserve. Items with dimensional animals, insects, birds, etc., are valued much higher than bowls, plates, and trays with simple embossed florals, which are usually priced at $100.00 to about $200.00, depending on size.

Basket, floral decor, twisted 2-strap hdl, 8½x12" **345.00**
Beaker, poppies, #436, 4½" **130.00**
Bowl, cartouches, scroll legs, hdls, 16½" **395.00**
Box, blossoms/leaves, hdls, bud finial, #4036, 4x6" **150.00**
Candlesticks, floral, 3-sided w/tiny neck hdls, 12", pr **700.00**
Casserole, sunflowers on lid & ftd base, hdls, 8" **175.00**
Egg dish, ftd sq base tray, dome lid, emb design, 10" W **300.00**
Ewer, Nouveau snakes & ladies' heads, 10½" **265.00**
Flagon, acorns & leaves, squirrel finial, 13" **465.00**

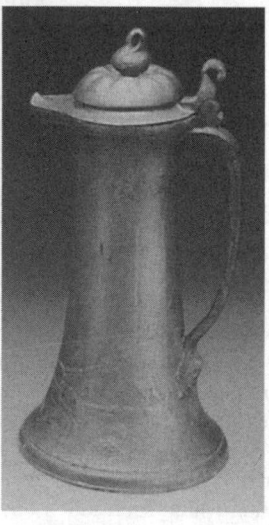

Flagon, stylized wheat stalks and hops in low relief, impressed mark, #4289, 16", $400.00.

Pitcher, bearded devil under petal spout, stem hdl, 12½" **450.00**
Platter, leaves & veins, organic hdl on dome lid, #4413, 21" **450.00**
Sugar bowl, dragon ship form, open, 8" **150.00**
Tankard, emb eagle & sheafs of wheat, 15" **450.00**
Tray, #322 ....**200.00**
Vase, emb vintage, #49, 12" **200.00**
Water can, fish relief, snail finial, leaf hdl, #7-4203, 11" **1,300.00**

Keeler, Brad

Keeler studied art for a time in the 1930s; later he be became a modeler for a Los Angeles firm. By 1939 he was working in his own studio where he created naturalistic studies of birds and animals which were marketed through giftware stores. They were decorated by means of the airbrush method and enhanced with hand-painted details. His flamingo figures were particularly popular. In the mid-forties, he developed a successful line of Chinese Modern housewares glazed in Ming Dragon Blood, a red color he personally developed. Keeler died of a

heart attack in 1952, and the pottery closed soon thereafter. For more information, we recommend *The Collector's Encyclopedia of California Pottery* by Jack Chipman.

Figurine, blue jay **65.00**
Figurine, canary, tail down, 6" **40.00**
Figurine, canary, tail up, 8¼" **40.00**
Figurine, cockatoo, 6" **75.00**
Figurine, Cocker spaniel pup, #735 ....**40.00**
Figurine, ducks, sm, pr **40.00**
Figurine, fawn, #879, 3x4" **45.00**
Figurine, flamingo, head down, #3, 7½" **80.00**
Figurine, peacock, Fantasy line, #717, 11" **165.00**
Figurine, penguin, 9½" **75.00**
Figurine, pheasant, 8½" **65.00**
Figurine, quail, pr **100.00**
Figurine, sea gull, 10½" **85.00**
Figurine, Siamese cat, #798 ....**50.00**
Lobster dish, 14" **65.00**
Lobster dish, 18" **85.00**

Keen Kutter

Keen Kutter was the brand name chosen in 1870 by the Simmons Firm for a line of high-grade tools and cutlery. The trademark was first applied to high-grade axes. A corporation was formed in 1874 called Simmons Hardware Company. In 1923 Winchester merged with Simmons and continued to carry a full line of hardware plus the Winchester brand. The merger dissolved. On July 1, 1940, the Simmons Company was purchased by Shapleigh Hardware Company. All Simmons Hardwar Co. trademark lines were continued, and the business operated successfully until closing in 1962. Today the Keen Kutter logo is owned by the Val-Test Company of Chicago, Illinois. For further study we recommend *Keen Kutter Collectibles*, an illustrated price guide by our advisors for this category, Jerry and Elaine Heuring, available at your favorite bookstore or public library. The Heurings are listed in the Directory under Missouri. See also Knives.

Paper holder with 12" roll of paper, $800.00; Without paper, $175.00.

Apple peeler **100.00**
Axe, w/logo **35.00**
Brace, K18, 8" sweep **30.00**
Broad axe, lg logo **200.00**
Broadhead hatchet, 3" to 4" **45.00**
Calendar, 1944, M **200.00**
Calipers, K46, outside **45.00**
Can opener **22.50**
Catalog, 1935, Simmons Hardware Co, yel **375.00**

Chisel, cold	15.00
Cigar box, wooden	300.00
Clock, electric, sq, 15x15"	875.00
Concrete groover, K01, brass	110.00
Display case, logo etched in glass, 72"	1,000.00
Draw knife, K8, 8" blade	35.00
Drill, electric; mk Shapleigh Model KK100, ¼"	45.00
File	12.00
Flashlight	65.00
Flint paper, KF2	30.00
Food chopper	12.00
Garden rake	30.00
Gauge, metal marking; K45	100.00
Gouge, 1"	35.00
Hammer, ball pein	55.00
Hammer, blacksmith shop	65.00
Hoe, mortar	30.00
Ice pick	75.00
Ice shaver, K33	125.00
Knife, cook's, K10, 8" blade	25.00
Knife steel, 12"	17.50
Lapel pin, Simmons, KK axe-head shape	100.00
Level, iron, K624, 24"	200.00
Level, wooden, KK0, 24"	32.50
Nail set	10.00
Padlock, logo shape	115.00
Pencil, carpenter's	20.00
Pipe vise	150.00
Pipe wrench, Keen Kutter on hdl, 12"	30.00
Plane, block; iron, adjustable/removable side fence, K140	225.00
Plane, block; K110	35.00
Plane, combination; K64, complete, in orig box	1,750.00
Plane, smooth, K5	50.00
Plane, wood bottom, K26, 2⅛" cutter, 15"	55.00
Pliers, combination; K180	30.00
Pliers, needle-nose; K66, 6"	35.00
Plumb bob, rnd, 18-oz	200.00
Postcard, advertising Keen Kutter lawn mower	175.00
Punch holder, red, logo shape	90.00
Ruler, 4-fold, brass bound, K620, 24"	65.00
Safety razor, in orig box	30.00
Saw, hack; adjustable, K48	45.00
Saw, handsaw; logo on blade, K88, 26"	50.00
Saw, keyhole; mk EC Simmons, 10"	40.00
Scissors, 7"	8.00
Screwdriver, brass ferrules, 5" blade	35.00
Shears, hedge; KS8½	20.00
Spatula, K646/7, 7" blade	22.50
Spoke shave, concave cutter, K95	85.00
Square, take-down	275.00
Tap & die set, K31, rare, M in wooden box	1,000.00
Waffle iron, 7¼" (beware of repros)	150.00
Wagon, KK, Rocket, ball bearings, 15½x34"	225.00
Wrench, adjustable, K4	180.00
Wrench, alligator; K40, combination bolt wrench	65.00

Kelva

Kelva was a trademark of the C.F. Monroe Company of Meriden, Connecticut; it was produced for only a few years after the turn of the century. It is distinguished from the Wave Crest and Nakara lines by its unique batik-like background, probably achieved through the use of a cloth or sponge to apply the color. Large florals are hand painted on the opaque milk glass, and ormolu and brass mounts were used for the boxes, vases, and trays. Most pieces are signed. Our advisors for this category are Dolli and Wilfred Cohen; they are listed in the Directory under California.

Box, Bishop's Hat, wild roses on gr w/grayed border, 3x4"	495.00
Box, blown-out rose on lid, hexagonal, 2½" dia	650.00
Box, floral, orange on gr, ftd base, sqd, 4" W	425.00
Box, floral, pk on gr mottle, mirror in lid, 4½"	525.00
Box, roses, pk on gr, fuchsia trim, wht dots, mk, 3½x6"	700.00
Box, wild rose on dk gr, 3¼x7"	1,000.00
Ferner, floral on pk, ogee sides, 7½" dia	575.00

Humidor, floral decoration with gold bands, 'Cigars' on front, 6¼x5¼", $650.00; Box, floral pastel panels, 6" diameter, $850.00.

Humidor, Cigars/floral on bl, oval	850.00
Match holder, floral, hexagonal, ormolu mts, 2½x7½"	500.00
Napkin ring, floral on waisted hexagonal form, rare	450.00
Tray, daisies on maroon, rnd w/emb metal rim, rope hdl, 3½"	300.00
Tray, floral on gr, unemb bowl form, ormolu bail, 3" dia	185.00
Vase, daisies, pk on gr, ormolu scroll hdls/rim, 9"	700.00
Vase, floral on rose, trumpet form w/4 ormolu ft, 6x2"	450.00
Vase, lg roses on gr, ornate ormolu hdls & 4-ftd base, 16"	1,450.00
Whisk broom holder, floral on red, ornate ormolu bkplate	1,250.00

Kenton Hills

Kenton Hills Porcelain was established in 1940 in Erlanger, Kentucky, by Harold Bopp, former Rookwood superintendent, and David Seyler, noted artist and sculptor. Native clay was used; glazes were very similar to Rookwood's of the same period. The work was of high quality, but because of the restrictions imposed on needed material due to the onset of the war; the operation failed in 1942. Much of the ware is artist signed and marked with the Kenton Hills name or cipher and shape number.

Bookends, aventurine orange/gunmetal/burgundy, #164, 6½"	250.00
Bowl, oxblood aventurine, 8"	300.00
Vase, bl gloss, mk, HB #111, 6"	200.00
Vase, Deco-style overlapping chevrons, W Hentchel, 1940, 5"	550.00
Vase, dk gr tiger-eye glaze, tiny rim, 8½"	465.00
Vase, mc abstract decor, W Hentchel, ca 1940, mk, 6½"	350.00

Kentucky Derby Glasses

Since the 1940s souvenir glasses have commemorated the famous Kentucky Derby; recently these have become popular collectibles, especially among race fans. Some of the most valuable are the plastic Beetleware tumblers from the forties, the shorter version made in 1945, and the 1950 tumbler which is now valued at around $350.00. On the Gold Cup glass from 1952, current winners are shown along with those from the previous year. There were two from 1958; one was the Gold Bar tumbler, and the other was called Iron Liege. Both were simply leftover '57 glasses with the 1958 winners added at the top. Our advisor for this category is Betty Hornback; she is listed in the Directory under Kentucky.

1941, aluminum	800.00
1941, Fr Lick	800.00
1941-44, Beetleware, from $2,500 to	4,000.00
1945, jigger	1,000.00
1945, regular	1,200.00
1945, tall	425.00
1946-47, ea	100.00
1948	180.00
1948, frosted bottom	200.00
1949	180.00
1950	350.00
1951	450.00

1952, Gold Cup, $180.00.

1953	135.00
1954	165.00
1955	135.00
1956, from $150 to	250.00
1957	110.00
1958, Gold Bar or Iron Leige, ea	175.00
1959-60, ea	80.00
1961	100.00
1962	65.00
1963	47.00
1964	45.00
1965	55.00
1966	50.00
1967-68, ea	45.00
1969	40.00
1970	55.00
1971	45.00
1972-73, ea	37.50
1974, mistake	18.00
1974, regular	16.00
1975	10.00
1976	14.00
1976, plastic	10.00
1977	10.00
1978-79, ea	12.00

1980	18.00
1981-82, ea	10.00
1983	9.00
1984	7.00
1985	9.00
1986	8.00
1986 (1985 copy)	18.00
1987-1988, ea	8.00
1989-91, ea	6.00
1992-94, ea	4.50
1995-96, ea	3.00

Kew Blas

Kew Blas was a trade name used by the Union Glass Company of Summerville, Massachusetts, for their iridescent, lustered art glass produced from 1893 until about 1920. The glass was made in imitation of Tiffany and achieved notable success. Some items were decorated with pulled leaf and feather designs, while others had a monochrome lustre surface. The mark was an engraved 'Kew Blas' in an arching arrangement.

Decanter, gold w/mc highlights, ribbed stopper, 15x5"	1,200.00
Salt cellar, gold irid	175.00

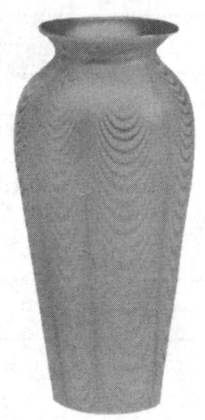

Vase, opal iridescent with pulled gold swagged design, signed, 7¾", $865.00.

Vase, feathers, gold on opal, bulbous shoulder, 8¾"	950.00
Vase, feathers, gr/wht/gold, orange irid int, 3¼x5¼"	550.00
Vase, gold, ribbed, bottle form, 8½x4"	750.00
Vase, gr/gold irid w/mc highlights, dents at shoulder, 10½"	650.00
Vase, pulled leaves, gold on golden opal, bottle neck, 4"	800.00

King's Rose

King's Rose is a soft-paste ware that was made in Staffordshire, England, from about 1820 to 1830. It is closely related to Gaudy Dutch in body type as well as the colors used in its decoration. The pattern consists of a full-blown, orange-red rose with green, pink, and yellow leaves and accents. When the rose is in pink, the ware is often referred to as Queen's Rose.

Coffeepot, dome lid, minor wear, 11¾"	950.00
Creamer, diapered, early prof rpr, mk W&B	150.00
Cup & saucer, Queen's, pk & gr w/mc floral border, unmk	90.00
Cup & saucer, Queen's, 4-color, reserves in border	190.00
Cup & saucer, solid border, M	250.00
Plate, orange rose, pk lustre bands w/X-hatching, 6¾", EX	65.00
Plate, orange rose, pk lustre X-hatched rim, 5¾", pr	100.00

Plate, Queen's, emb basketweave & mc floral reserves, 6⅝", EX ..70.00
Plate, Queen's, 4-color, vine border, scalloped, 8" 180.00
Plate, sectional border, lt wear, 9¾" 165.00
Plate, toddy; Queen's, scalloped, 5½" 110.00
Soup plate, sectional border, 9" 165.00
Sugar bowl, Queen's, vine border, scalloped, 5½" 185.00
Teapot, sectional border, lt wear, 5⅞" 425.00
Waste bowl, solid border, minor wear, 2¾x5⅝" 200.00

Kitchen Collectibles

During the last half of the 1850s, mass-produced kitchen gadgets were patented at an astonishing rate. Most were ingeniously efficient. Apple peelers, egg beaters, cherry pitters, food choppers, and such were only the most common of hundreds of kitchen tools well designed to perform only specific tasks. Today all are very collectible.

We should note here that cast-iron counterfeit production is on its way up. Phony production numbers, finishes, etc., are being made at this time. Many of these new pieces are the popular cornstick pans. Buyer beware! Our advisor for Cast Kitchen Ware is Denise Harned, who is the author of *Griswold Cast Collectibles*. She is listed in the Directory under Connecticut. We also recommend *Kitchen Glassware of the Depression Years* by Gene Florence and *Kitchen Antiques, 1790-1940*, by Kathryn McNerney. See also Appliances; Glass Knives; Molds; Primitives; Reamers; Tinware; Wooden Ware.

Cast Kitchen Ware

Note: To command the values given below, waffle irons must be complete with all three pieces and the handle.

Wheat stick pan, unmarked, 5½x12¾", $75.00.

Ashtray, #00, sm emblem, unused.......70.00
Ashtray, Griswold, sq, #770, 1950s 55.00
Ashtray, Griswold #570A 60.00
Brownie pan, Griswold #9, pattern #947 ....145.00
Bundt cake pan, Griswold 500.00
Coffee grinder, Griswold, orig pnt, EX+ 995.00
Cornstick pan, Griswold #21, 7-stick 100.00
Cornstick pan, Griswold #273, Erie, 7-stick 100.00
Cornstick pan, Griswold #280, 7 alternating ears 500.00
Cornstick pan, Jr Krusty Korn Kobs, Pat July 6, 1920 ....35.00
Dutch oven, chuck wagon; Griswold #10 ....145.00
Dutch oven, Griswold #13, w/glass lid 175.00
Dutch oven, Griswold #8 Tite Top, w/lid 80.00
Dutch oven, Griswold #9, w/trivet 95.00
Egg pan, Griswold #129, sq 40.00
Gem pan, Griswold #8, Erie USA 175.00
Grease pot, Griswold 75.00
Grill, utility; Wagner #8 ....60.00
Lid, Griswold #8, Washington Centennial 195.00

Lid, skillet; Griswold #468, self-basting 55.00
Loaf pan, Griswold #877 ....150.00
Long pan or iron heater, Griswold #8, Erie, deep oval 95.00
Long pan or iron heater, Griswold #9 ....110.00
Mold, lamb, Griswold #866 ....185.00
Mold, rabbit, Griswold 285.00
Mold, Turk's head, Griswold #140 ....200.00
Muffin pan, Griswold #17 ....75.00
Muffin pan, Griswold #19 ....185.00
Muffin pan, Griswold #262 ....125.00
Muffin pan, Griswold #283 ....150.00
Muffin pan, Wagner, Little Gem 100.00
Patty bowl, Griswold #871 ....85.00
Patty irons, Griswold #1, boxed 45.00
Platt pan, Griswold #34 ....50.00
Platter, Griswold #846, oval tree type, rare 100.00
Popover pan, Griswold #10, USN, 11-cup 75.00
Popover pan, Griswold #18, 6-cup 100.00
Roaster, Griswold #5, oval 120.00
Roaster, Wagner #3, oval 185.00
Roaster, Wagner #5, oval 225.00
Roaster, Wagner #9, oval 275.00
Scotch bowl, Griswold #3, Erie...USA 75.00
Skillet, Eagle Stove Works #12 ....300.00
Skillet, Erie #10, shallow, 3 holes in hdl 135.00
Skillet, Griswold #11, block logo, w/heat ring 150.00
Skillet, Griswold #13, Erie, w/heat ring 250.00
Skillet, Griswold #14, bail hdl 150.00
Skillet, Griswold #168, sq, corner hdl 75.00
Skillet, Griswold #3, Erie 50.00
Skillet, Griswold #57, sq 75.00
Skillet, Griswold #7, Erie PA USA, w/heat ring 45.00
Skillet, Griswold #8, chicken fryer, smooth bottom, w/lid 65.00
Skillet, Griswold #9, sm emblem, self-basting, w/lid 65.00
Skillet, Wagner #12 ....95.00
Skillet, Wagner #2 ....150.00
Skillet/griddle, Griswold #110 ....115.00
Vienna roll pan, Griswold #6 ....135.00
Wafer iron, Andersen Kornucopia 175.00
Wafer iron, Griswold 300.00
Waffle iron, Griswold #0, mini (many counterfeits, beware) 400.00
Waffle iron, Griswold #11, sq 150.00
Waffle iron, Griswold #18, Heart & Star, low base 135.00
Waffle iron, Griswold #7, May 21, 1901 ....125.00
Waffle iron, Griswold #8, low base, 1910 ....125.00
Waffle iron, Israel Deer Hamburg, 8½" dia, 22¾" L 610.00
Waffle iron, Wagner #11, sq, high fr, wood hdls 125.00
Waffle iron, Wagner #8, crescent 75.00
Waffle iron, Wagner #8, high fr, 1910 ....135.00
Wax ladle, Erie 95.00
Wax ladle, unmk 45.00
Wheat/cornstick pan, Griswold #280, Erie 200.00

Egg Beaters

Egg beaters are an unbeatable collectible. Ranging from hand-helds to rotary cranks, to squeeze power, to Archimedes up-and-down models, egg beaters are America's favorite kitchen gadget. A mainstay of any kitchenware collection, egg beaters in recent years have come into their own — nutmeg graters, spatulas, and can openers will have to scramble to catch up. At the turn of the century, everyone in America owned an egg beater. Every household did its own mixing and baking — there were no pre-processed foods. And every inventor thought he/she could make a better beater. Thus American ingenuity produced more than one thousand egg beater patents, dating back to 1856, with several hundred different models being manufactured over the years. As a true piece of Americana, egg beaters have risen in value over the past couple of years, with a half dozen mixers valued at $1,000.00. But the vast majority are under $40.00 in range. And just when you think you've seen them all, new ones always — always — turn up, usually at flea markets or garage sales. For further information, we recommend our advisor (author of the definitive book on egg beaters) Don Thornton, who is listed in the Directory under California. See also Clubs and Newsletters for Kollectors of Old Kitchen Stuff (KOOKS).

Another Androck Product Pat No 2210910, rotary crank, 10¾" .15.00
Biltrite...Pat Stuber & Kuck..., rotary crank, wood hdl, 10½" 30.00
Dover, CI, hotel model, 1870, 16½" 165.00
Dover, CI, 1870, rare, 12½" 200.00
Dover, flat wheel, 1870, 10" 75.00
Dover, Pat May 31st 1870, CI, beveled wheel, 10" 65.00
Dover, steel hdl, 9", 10", or 10½", ea 45.00
Jiffy Whip...Krasbert & Sons' Mfg, rotary crank turbine, 11¾" 25.00
Super Speed A&J Spinnit..., rotary turbine, wood hdl, 11½" 30.00
Vandeusen Egg Whip, CA Chapman...1894, all metal, hand held, 11" .15.00
Whipwell...USA Pat Mch 23, 1920..., rotary crank, wood hdl, 11" .20.00
Zip Whit S, J&H Dist...Cal, rotary crank, plastic hdl, 13½" 45.00

Glassware

Sugar canister, jadite, square, Jeannette, 48-oz, $50.00.

Ashtray, jadite, Jeannette 7.00
Ashtray holder, crystal, Cambridge 33.00
Batter jug, blk, McKee, w/metal lid 105.00
Batter jug, forest gr, New Martinsville, w/lid 70.00
Batter jug, gr, New Martinsville, w/lid 70.00
Bottle, oil; gr, Hawkes, w/stopper 80.00
Bottle, oil; pk, Party Line, Paden City, w/stopper 60.00
Bottle, oil; pk or gr, Paden City, w/stopper 55.00
Bottle, water; amber, drinking well etching 60.00
Bowl, cobalt, Hazel Atlas, 8½" 28.00
Bowl, cobalt, Hazel Atlas, 9⅝" 35.00
Bowl, custard, McKee, 6" 12.00
Bowl, Delphite bl, Jeannette, 9" 75.00
Bowl, mixing; amber, US Glass, 6" 16.00
Bowl, mixing; amber, US Glass, 7" 20.00
Bowl, mixing; amber, US Glass, 9" 33.00
Bowl, mixing; bl, Crisscross, 7⅝" 38.00
Bowl, mixing; bl or red dots on custard, McKee, 8" 16.50
Bowl, mixing; blk, McKee, 7⅜" 28.00
Bowl, mixing; Chalaine bl, ribbed, 9" 90.00
Bowl, mixing; Delphite bl, vertical ribs, 9" 70.00
Bowl, mixing; jadite, Hocking, 9" 13.00
Butter dish, amber, Federal, rectangular, 1-lb 33.00

Butter dish, amber, Federal, rnd 27.00
Butter dish, Chalaine bl, ribbed, tab hdls 315.00
Butter dish, cobalt, Hazel Atlas, emb Butter on lid 195.00
Butter dish, custard, McKee, w/lid 38.00
Butter dish, Delphite bl, McKee, w/lid 235.00
Butter dish, Delphite bl, rectangular, emb Butter on lid 240.00
Butter dish, gr, Crisscross, w/lid, 1-lb 38.00
Butter dish, wht, Hazel Atlas, emb lid 22.00
Canister, blk or gr dots on custard, McKee, screw lid, 48-oz 63.00
Canister, crystal, Dutch boy design, w/lid 18.00
Canister, dk amber, emb Tea, metal lid, sq 75.00
Canister, jadite, Jeannette, sq, 29-oz 38.00
Canister, peacock bl, emb Coffee, 40-oz 165.00
Casserole, amber, Cambridge, oval, w/lid 33.00
Casserole, wht clambroth, Pyrex, w/lid, oval 115.00
Cocktail shaker, blk, metal lid 55.00
Cocktail shaker, cobalt, metal lid, barbell shape 80.00
Cookie jar, peacock bl, LE Smith, ball form, metal lid 85.00
Creamer, ewer form, gr, Cambridge, tall, hdld 38.00
Crock, gr transparent, Hocking, w/lid, 8" 42.00
Decanter, peacock bl, Imperial, w/stopper 34.00
Drippings jar, Delphite bl, Jeannette, pnt letters, w/lid 110.00
Egg cup, Chalaine bl 14.00
Egg cup, dk amber, Paden City 9.00
Gravy boat, dk amber, Cambridge, 2-spout, 2-hdld 25.00
Grease jar, red dots on wht, Hazel Atlas 17.00
Ice bucket, blk, 2-hdld 55.00
Ice bucket, cobalt, Cambridge, metal hdl 115.00
Ice bucket, gr, Hex Optic, w/reamer top, hdl 42.00
Ice bucket, red, Plymouth, Fenton, hdl 55.00
Jar, gr, LE Smith, w/lid, lg 62.00
Ladle, amberina, Cambridge 38.00
Ladle, crystal, Candlewick 5.00
Marmalade, Emerald-glo, Rubel, w/spoon 19.00
Match holder, Delphite bl 80.00
Measuring cup, caramel, McKee, 4-cup 550.00
Measuring cup, Chalaine bl, no hdl, 4-cup 1,350.00
Measuring cup, gr, Cambridge, dry measure 235.00
Measuring cup, pk, Cambridge, 1-spout, 1-cup 210.00
Measuring pitcher, Chalaine bl, ftd, 4-cup 360.00
Measuring pitcher, Delphite bl, Jeannette, 2-cup 70.00
Measuring pitcher, Delphite bl, McKee, 2-cup 80.00
Measuring pitcher, wht w/dmn check, McKee, 2-cup 27.00
Mug, amber, Chesterfield, ftd 22.00
Mug, blk 25.00
Mug, forest gr, Cambridge 42.00
Mug, jadite, Hocking, 7-oz 5.00
Mug, pk, Colonial, Hocking 425.00
Mug, pk, Jeannette, ftd 27.00
Mug, Tom & Jerry; custard, McKee, gold lettering 14.00
Mustard pot, cobalt, w/spoon 22.00
Napkin holder, blk, Paramount 425.00
Napkin holder, blk, Party Line, Paden City 125.00
Napkin holder, crystal, LE Smith, horizontal ribs 42.00
Napkin holder, wht, Nar-O-Fold 40.00
Pitcher, amber, Chesterfield, glass lid 88.00
Refrigerator jar, cobalt, Hazel Atlas, rnd, 5¾" 70.00
Rolling pin, cobalt, all glass 425.00
Rolling pin, custard, McKee 300.00
Rolling pin, peacock bl, wood hdls 265.00
Salt box, gr, Jeannette, rnd, emb Salt on lid 170.00
Shaker, cinnamon; custard, McKee, w/metal lid 27.50
Shaker, pk, Hazel Atlas, emb Salt or Pepper, ea 42.00
Shakers, pk, Jennyware, flat, label, pr 68.00

Spoon holder, crystal, Pat 2-11-1913 ....17.00
Straw holder, blk, metal lid 650.00
Straw holder, crystal, Heisey, glass lid 250.00
Sugar shaker, amber, Paden City, hourglass form, Tilt-a-Spoon .165.00
Sugar shaker, cobalt, Paden City, metal lid 625.00
Sugar shaker, dk amber, metal lid 185.00
Sugar shaker, pk, Cambridge, #732, metal lid 120.00
Sugar shaker, pk, Heisey, Yeoman, metal lid 78.00
Syrup jug, amber, Cambridge, w/lid 52.00
Syrup pitcher, bl, Duncan & Miller, metal lid 165.00
Syrup pitcher, blk, Fenton, glass lid 70.00
Syrup pitcher, crystal, w/glass top, 2-pc 28.00
Syrup pitcher, gr, Cambridge, glass lid 63.00
Syrup pitcher, pk, Imperial, floral etching, glass lid 43.00
Syrup pitcher, pk, Imperial, slotted glass lid 73.00
Syrup pitcher, pk or gr, Fostoria, Mayfair, w/underliner 60.00
Toast rack, crystal 60.00
Tray, batter set; blk, oblong 27.00
Tumbler, blk, McKee 16.00
Tumbler, pk, Crisscross, 9-oz 70.00
Vase, Chalaine bl, scalloped rim, 12" 115.00
Water bottle, Royal Ruby, Hocking, ribbed or plain, w/lid 70.00
Water dispenser, cobalt, LE Smith, metal spout 375.00

Miscellaneous

Angel food cake pan, Swan's Down Cake Flour 27.50
Apple peeler, Baldwin, CI 125.00
Apple peeler, Gold Medal, CI, EX 165.00
Apple peeler, Goodell Improved Bay State, CI, EX 165.00
Apple peeler, Lightning, CI, geared quadrant 195.00
Apple peeler, Sargent & Foster, CI on wood base, 1850s 175.00
Apple peeler, Sinclair, Scott & Co, Baltimore, CI, clamps on ...110.00
Biscuit cutter, Rumford Yeast 15.00
Box, spice; bentwood, tin bands, 8 containers inside ...350.00
Bread maker, Universal #4, 1906, w/orig recipe book ...60.00
Butter curler, wood, curved wood pc w/wooden hdl 95.00
Can opener, CI bull form, tail forms hdl, 6¾" 95.00
Can opener, CI fish shape, ball-shaped hdl, 5½" 105.00
Cheese curd breaker, wooden crank hdl, old red pnt, 1860s 225.00
Cherry seeder, Buckwald's 1863 Pat, CI, horseshoe shape 155.00
Cherry seeder, Goodel's Dbl, Antrim NH, CI, EX 75.00
Cherry seeder, Mt Joye, CI, 4-station carousel 165.00
Cherry seeder, The Electric, CI, stands on 4 legs 65.00
Chopper, Starrett's Food Chopping Machine, sm 325.00
Chopper, wrought iron crescent-shaped blade, wood hdl, 7⅝x7"..50.00
Chopper, wrought iron oval blade w/wooden hdl, 9x8" 85.00
Chopper, wrought iron rectangular blade w/wood hdl, 6¾x7" 50.00
Chopper, wrought iron w/heart cutout, wood hdl, 6x6½" 135.00
Churn, Cyclone 140.00
Churn, Dazey, #10, 1-qt 1,250.00
Churn, Dazey, #30, 3-qt 165.00
Churn, Dazey, #40, 4-qt 110.00
Churn, Holt, 1-qt 125.00
Churn, Lightning, 1-qt 295.00
Churn, Lightning, 2-qt 95.00
Churn, Taplin Tumbler 75.00
Churn, Universal, glass, 1-qt 495.00
Churn, Universal, tin, 2-qt 375.00
Churn, Universal #125 ....450.00
Clothes sprinkler bottle, cat w/marble eyes, 9" 150.00
Clothes sprinkler bottle, Chinaman, bl/wht, hands folded, 8½" ...45.00
Clothes sprinkler bottle, Chinaman holding iron 145.00
Clothes sprinkler bottle, clothespin, 8" 60.00

Clothes sprinkler bottle, elephant, gray w/pk, seated ...55.00
Clothes sprinkler bottle, gourd shape, clear glass 35.00
Clothes sprinkler bottle, jar w/S-shaped pump 25.00
Clothes sprinkler bottle, Mammy, wht dress w/pk trim 225.00
Clothes sprinkler bottle, poodle, blk & wht 135.00
Clothes sprinkler bottle, sadiron, girl ironing 60.00
Clothes sprinkler bottle, Siamese cat 100.00
Cucumber/vegetable slicer; Universal, CI, clamps on ...55.00
Cutlery tray, pine, center divider, fancy hdl 95.00
Cutter, cabbage; nailed box w/2 iron blades, 8½x15x39", EX 60.00
Cutter, herb; Go Devil, CI, early, 10x16", EX 400.00
Cutting brd, slat construction, 16¾" dia 560.00
Flour sifter, handmade, wooden w/iron crank hdl, ca 1850 ....350.00
Grater, cheese; wooden box w/hdl, punched tin front 210.00
Grater, nutmeg; Gem, Caldwell, tin, mechanical, EX 125.00
Grater, nutmeg; mechanical, CI w/tin wheel, wire hdl, 1880s 185.00
Grater, nutmeg; The Edgar, CI, Pat 1891 ....65.00
Grater, nutmeg; tin, spring mechanism, crank hdl, 4⅝" 55.00
Ice cream freezer, Dandy, metal, 2-qt, 9" 35.00
Knife/fork scrubber, odd iron pc, orig paper label 125.00
Lemon reamer, wooden, hand cvd, hand held, 1-pc 125.00
Mixer, Lightning, 1-qt glass jar 265.00
Mixer, mayonnaise; Universal, EX, w/reproduction funnel 475.00
Mixer, New Keystone, 1-qt glass jar 155.00
Mixer, Super Whipper, rotary crank, attaches to jar ...150.00
Mixer, Universal Cake Mixer 50.00
Noodle cutter, Vitantonio's, CI, clamps to table 55.00
Nut grinder, Lorraine Metal #4, clamps to table, EX 60.00
Popover pan, aluminum, Griswold #949C, c 1935, 10-cup 25.00
Potato masher, old grid wire style w/wooden hdl 7.50
Raisin seeder, EZY, May 21, 1895, 6½" table clamp 250.00
Rolling pin, curly maple, trn stationary hdls, 18⅝" 60.00
Rolling pin, maple w/dbl-barred hdl 295.00
Spice cabinet, pine, hanging, 8 sm/11 lg drw, porc knobs 295.00
Thermometer, Kitchen Aid, w/baster, MIB 22.50
Whip, Fries Cream Whip 100.00
Whip/beater, Arthur Beck Co, operates w/1 hand, c 1948, EX 40.00

Knives

Knife collecting as a hobby began in earnest during the 1960s when government regulations required for the first time that knife companies mark their product with the country of origin. The few collectors and dealers cognizant of this change at once began stockpiling the older knives made before this law was enacted. Another impetus to the growing interest in this area came with the Gun Control Act of 1968, which severely restricted gun trading. Frustrated gun dealers transferred their attention to knives. Today there are collectors clubs in many of the states.

The most sought-after pocketknives are those made before WWII. However, Case, Schrade, and Primble knives of a more recent manufacture are also collected. Most collectors prefer knives 'as found.' Do not attempt to clean, sharpen, or in any way 'improve' on an old knife.

The prices quoted here are for knives in mint condition (except for those in the Miscellaneous section). If a knife has been used, sharpened, or blemished in any way, its value decreases. The newer the knife, the greater the reduction in value. For further information refer to *The Standard Knife Collector's Guide, 2nd Edition,* by Ron Stewart and Roy Ritchie and *Sargent's American Premium Guide to Knives and Razors, Identification and Values, 3rd Edition,* by Jim Sargent. Our advisor for this category is Bill Wright; he is listed in the Directory under Indiana.

Key:
bd — blade   p/b — push button
jack — jackknife   sb — switchblade
imi — imitation   wb — winterbottom
lp — long pull

Case, B1098, waterfall hdl, 1-bd, Tested XX, 1920-40, 5½" **500.00**
Case, B344PU, imi onyx hdl, 3-bd, Tested XX, 1920-30, 3¼" ...**200.00**
Case, C61050, red bone hdl, 1-bd, XX, 5⅜" **300.00**
Case, P2052, pyramite hdl, 2-bd, WR Case & Sons, 3½" **225.00**
Case, RM279, Xmas tree hdl, 2-bd, Tested XX, 1920-40, 3⅛" ...**225.00**
Case, R1049, candy-stripe hdl, 1-bd, Tested XX, 1920-40, 4" **400.00**
Case, R1093, celluloid hdl, 1-bd, Tested XX, 5" **350.00**
Case, R285, dr's, candy-stripe hdl, 2-bd, Case Brad PA, 3⅛" **500.00**
Case, 05247SP, stag hdl, 2-bd, Tested XX, 1920-40, 3⅞" **175.00**
Case, 2137, Sod Buster Jr, blk compo, 1-bd, 10 Dot, 1970, 3⅝" ...**35.00**
Case, 2207, slick blk hdl, 2-bd, Tested XX, 1920-40, 3½" **350.00**
Case, 2279½, slick blk hdl, 2-bd, Tested XX, 3¼" **125.00**
Case, 31213, yel compo hdl, 1-bd, Tested XX, 1920-40, 5⅜" **500.00**
Case, 4100SS, wht compo hdl, 1-bd, USA, 1965-69, 5½" **75.00**
Case, 5260, stag hdl, 2-bd, WR Case & Sons **225.00**
Case, 5265SAB, stag hdl, 2-bd, Tested XX, 1920-40, 5¼" **325.00**
Case, 5299½, stag hdl, 2-bd, USA, 1965-69, 4⅛" **80.00**
Case, 5332, stag hdl, 3-bd, Tested XX, 1920-40, 3⅝" **250.00**
Case, 61011, bone stag hdl, 1-bd, XX, 1940-64, 4" **65.00**
Case, 61011, hawkbill, bone hdl, 1-bd, Tested XX, 1920-40, 4" .**150.00**
Case, 61093, bone hdl, 1-bd, USA, 1965-69, 5" **85.00**
Case, 62001, bone hdl, 2-bd, Case in written script, 2⅝" **150.00**
Case, 62005, Barlow, gr bone hdl, 2-bd, Case Brad PA, 3⅜" **400.00**
Case, 62024SH, gr bone hdl, 2-bd, Tested XX, 1920-40, 3" **200.00**
Case, 62087, red bone hdl, 2-bd, XX, 1940-64, 3¼" **55.00**
Case, 62089, gr bone hdl, 2-bd, Case Brad PA, 3¾" **500.00**
Case, 62099, gr bone hdl, 2-bd, Case Brad PA, 4⅛" **350.00**

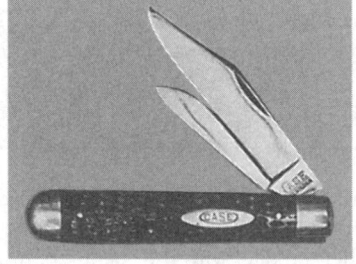

Case, #6214½, green bone handle, 2-blade, Tested XX, 3⅜", $130.00.

Case, 6214½, bone stag hdl, 2-bd, 10 Dot, 1970, 3⅜" **35.00**
Case, 6227, bone hdl, 2-bd, 10 Dot, 1970, 2¾" **35.00**
Case, 6240, penknife, gr bone hdl, 2-bd, Tested XX, 4½" **600.00**
Case, 6250, red bone hdl, 2-bd, XX, 1940-64, 4⅜" **250.00**
Case, 6251, hobo, gr bone hdl, 2-bd, Case Brad PA, 5¼" **600.00**
Case, 6279, gr bone hdl, 2-bd, Tested XX, 3⅛" **125.00**
Case, 6279, gr bone hdl, 2-bd, XX, 1940-55, 3⅛" **90.00**
Case, 6292, bone hdl, 2-bd, 10 Dot, 1970, 4" **35.00**
Case, 63067F, Rogers bone hdl, 3-bd, Case Brad PA, 3⅞" **400.00**
Case, 6345½, gr bone hdl, 3-bd, Tested XX, 1920-40, 3⅝" **225.00**
Case, 6347SHSP, gr bone hdl, 3-bd, XX, 1940-55, 3⅞" **200.00**
Case, 6366, gr bone hdl, 3-bd, Tested XX, 1920-40, 3⅛" **250.00**
Case, 6392, red bone hdl, 3-bd, XX, 1940-64, 4" **110.00**
Case, 6394½, bone hdl, 3-bd, XX, 1940-64, 4¼" **700.00**
Case, 6394½LP, bone hdl, 3-bd, XX, 1940-64, 4¼" **750.00**
Case, 640045R, Scout, blk plastic, 4-bd, XX, 1940-50, 3⅝" **30.00**

Case, 64052, bone hdl, 4-bd, XX, 1940-64, 3½" **90.00**
Case, 6488, bone hdl, 4-bd, USA, 1965-69, 4⅛" **90.00**
Case, 6488RP, rough blk hdl, 4-bd, Case XX, 4⅛" **400.00**
Case, 72006, tortoise-shell hdl, 2-bd, Case Brad PA, 2⅝" **300.00**
Case, 8151SAB, pearl hdl, 1-bd, Tested XX, 5¼" **1,000.00**
Case, 82058, pearl hdl, 2-bd, Case Bros Cutlery Co, 2⅞" **250.00**
Case, 8268, pearl hdl, 2-bd, Tested XX, 3¼" **250.00**
Case, 8269, pearl hdl, 2-bd, Tested XX, 1920-40, 3" **250.00**
Case, 8271LP, pearl hdl, 2-bd, XX, 3¼" **225.00**
Case, 83012SS, pearl hdl, 3-bd, XX, 1940-64, 2¾" **150.00**
Case, 8347LP, pearl hdl, 3-bd, Case & Sons Brad PA, 3⅞" **500.00**
Case, 8407F, pearl hdl, 4-bd, Case Brad PA, 3" **750.00**
Case, 92058, cracked-ice hdl, 2-bd, XX, 1940-50, 3¼" **125.00**
Case, 92131, cracked-ice hdl, 2-bd, Tested XX, 1920-40, 3⅝" ...**500.00**
Case, 9240SP, imi pearl hdl, 2-bd, Tested XX, 1920-40, 4½" **550.00**
Case, 9261F, imi pearl hdl, 2-bd, Tested XX, 1920-40, 2⅞" **120.00**
Case, 93047, cracked-ice hdl, 3-bd, Tested XX, 1920-40, 3⅞" ...**275.00**
Keen Kutter, Barlow, yel bone hdl, 2-bd, 3⅜" **60.00**
Keen Kutter, Coke bottle, ebony hdl, 1-bd, 5¼" **200.00**
Keen Kutter, dog-leg jack, walnut hdl, 1-bd, 3⅜" **30.00**
Keen Kutter, G1135, sleeveboard dog-leg, goldstone hdl, 2-bd, 3" ..**60.00**
Keen Kutter, K187, moose, brn bone hdl, 2-bd, 4" **175.00**
Keen Kutter, K196, dr's pill buster, brn bone hdl, 2-bd, 2⅞" **200.00**
Keen Kutter, peanut, brn bone hdl, 2-bd, 2⅞" **35.00**
Keen Kutter, 0388, Senator pen, pearl hdl, 2-bd, 2⅞" **45.00**
Keen Kutter, 0488, Senator pen, pearl hdl, 2-bd, w/bail, 2⅞" **40.00**
Keen Kutter, 218, peanut, ivory hdl, 2-bd, 2⅞" **20.00**
Keen Kutter, 2203, jack, brn bone hdl, 2-bd, 3⅞" **75.00**
Keen Kutter, 53¾, jack, brn bone hdl, 2-bd, 3⅜" **50.00**
Queen, 19, fisherman's, Rogers bone hdl, 2-bd, 5" **80.00**
Queen, 3, wb bone hdl, 2-bd, 3¼" **25.00**
Queen, 36, lockbk, Rogers bone hdl, 1-bd, 4½" **75.00**
Remington, bartender's knife, R4336, stag hdl, 2-bd, 3½" **225.00**
Remington, R105A, onyx hdl, 3-bd, 3⅜" **150.00**
Remington, R1123, brn bone hdl, bullet shield, 2-bd, 4½" **1,200.00**
Remington, R1241, Barlow, redwood hdl, 1-bd, 5" **285.00**
Remington, R1263, brn bone hdl, 2-bd, bullet shield, 5⅜" **1,500.00**
Remington, R1303, lockbk, bone hdl, 1-bd, bullet shield, 4½" ...**1,400.00**
Remington, R1379, metal hdl, 2-bd, 4¼" **250.00**
Remington, R1582, slick blk hdl, 2-bd, 3" **90.00**
Remington, R17, pull ball sb, wht compo hdl, 1-bd, 2¾" **150.00**
Remington, R173, jack, brn bone hdl, 2-bd, 3¾" **150.00**
Remington, R1825, imi tortoise hdl, 2-bd, lp, 3⅝" **125.00**
Remington, R2557, stockman, imi ivory hdl, 3-bd, 4" **250.00**
Remington, R2605, jack, red scale hdl, 2-bd, 3⅜" **110.00**
Remington, R293, brn bone hdl, 2-bd, lp, bullet shield, 5¼" ..**2,000.00**
Remington, R3173, bone hdl, 3-bd, acorn shield, 3½" **265.00**
Remington, R3273, cattle/equal end, brn bone hdl, 3-bd, 3¾" ..**250.00**
Remington, R3424, equal end, pearl hdl, 3-bd, 3⅜" **350.00**
Remington, R3580, horn hdl, 2-bd+punch, 4" **300.00**
Remington, R3853, utility knife, bone hdl, multi-bd, 4" **215.00**
Remington, R391, redwood hdl, 2-bd, acorn shield, 3⅜" **160.00**
Remington, R4133, stockman, bone hdl, 3-bd, 3⅜" **175.00**
Remington, R4273, Girl Scout, brn bone hdl, 2-bd, bail, 3¾" ...**200.00**
Remington, R4405, Christmas tree hdl, 3-bd, lp, 3⅜" **250.00**
Remington, R563, brn bone hdl, 2-bd, acorn shield, 3¼" **150.00**
Remington, R6043, Congress, brn bone hdl, 4-bd, 4⅛" **600.00**
Remington, R6195, equal end, brn mottled hdl, 2-bd, 3¼" **110.00**
Remington, R6499, metal hdl, 2-bd, 3" **60.00**
Remington, R703, hawkbill, stag hdl, 1-bd, 3⅝" **150.00**
Remington, R953, brn bone hdl, 1-bd, 5" **225.00**
Remington, R963, Scout/easy open, imi bone hdl, 2-bd, 4¼" **350.00**
Remington, R973, imi bone hdl, 2-bd, 4¼" **275.00**
Western States, S203B, gr sparkle hdl, 2-bd, w/bail, 2½" **25.00**

Western States, 6100, bone hdl, 1-bd, etching, 5⅜" 300.00
Winchester, 2059, Senator, celluloid hdl, 2-bd, 3¼" 100.00
Winchester, 2608, stabber, cocobolo hdl, 2-bd, 3⅝" 125.00
Winchester, 2847, pen, brn bone hdl, 2-bd, 3¼" 125.00
Winchester, 2910, lobster, bone hdl, 2-bd, 3½" 135.00
Winchester, 2945, Senator, bone hdl, 2-bd, 3⅜" 100.00
Winchester, 3016, cattle, celluloid hdl, 3-bd, 3¾" 300.00
Winchester, 3018, stockman, candy-stripe hdl, 3-bd, 4" 400.00
Winchester, 3345, whittler, pearl hdl, 3-bd, 3¼" 225.00
Winchester, 3382, lobster, pearl hdl, 3-bd, 3" 150.00
Winchester, 3959, stockman, brn bone hdl, 3-bd, 4" 250.00
Winchester, 4901, utility, brn bone hdl, 4-bd, 3⅜" 325.00

Miscellaneous

Bowie, etched bd, Wilson Hawksworth Ellison, Sheffield, 14" ...400.00
Bowie, 10" clip-point bd, Solingen 447 on side, stag grips, EX ...150.00
Bowie, 8" bd, silver hdl w/eng & inlay, 1910s, 13", +sheath 125.00
Case XX, bowie style, brass guard, plastic hdl, 9⅜", EX 95.00
Dagger, steel 5" bd, antler-crown hdl w/inlay, 10" 75.00
Folding, wrought blade mk LU, cvd deer-head hdl, 1790s, 10" ...150.00
Folding, 2-bd, stag grip w/silver caps, Am, 5¼" closed, G 55.00
Patch, curved bd mk IXL, wood grip, iron pommel, 1880s, 8½" ...65.00
US Army Trench Model 1917, mk knucklebow, 15", NM, +sheath .200.00
US Marine Corps medical corpsman's, 11½" bd, +sheath 80.00

Kosta

Kosta glassware has been made in Sweden since 1742. Today they are one of that country's leading producers of quality art glass. Two of their most important designers were Elis Bergh (1929-1950) and Vicke Lindstrand, artistic director from 1950 to 1973. Lindstrand brought to the company knowledge of important techniques such as Graal, fine figural engraving, Ariel, etc. He influenced new artists to experiment with these techniques and inspired them to create new and innovative designs. Today's collectors are most interested in pieces made during the 1950s and 1960s. Our advisor for this category is Abby Malowanczyk; she is listed in the Directory under Texas.

Bowl, cranberry, int wht webbing, Lindstrand/LH1036, 3½" 195.00
Bowl, int swirls/lines/dots, mc in clear, Lindstrand, 4x7¾" 400.00
Sculpture, chipped ice block w/polar bears, Lindstrand, 5x7" 150.00
Vase, bathers on bl to amber, Vallien/Unik #5279, 6x6x7" 950.00
Vase, clear w/lav to amber int layer, Lindstrand, #1438, 12" 300.00
Vase, eng feathers, lg oval rim/hourglass ft, Lindstrand, 9" 140.00
Vase, eng gondolier, U-form, Lindstrand, LG #155, 10½" 250.00
Vase, eng nude sits before mirror, flattened oval, #180, 8½" 375.00

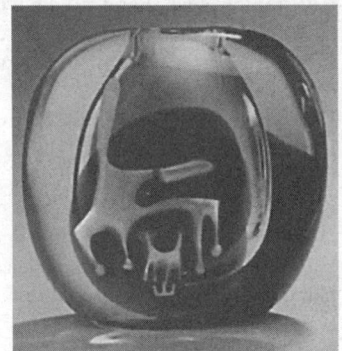

Vase, flattened ovoid with blue spots on front and back, deep engravings depict felines with young, Lindstrand, #46682, 5¾", $900.00.

Vase, heavy w/int blk dots & cut windows, Lindstrand, 6" 125.00

Vase, int blk trailing from rim to base, Lindstrand, 13x4" 650.00
Vase, int brn repeating lines, Lindstrand, 6x4x2" 210.00
Vase, int gr striations/bubbles, eng fish, Lindstrand, 9" 175.00
Vase, int swirling wht trails, Lindstrand, #1153, 1951, 12" 375.00

Labels

Before the advent of the cardboard box, wooden crates were used for transporting products. Paper labels were attached to the crates to identify the contents and the packer. These labels often had colorful lithographed illustrations covering a broad range of subjects. Eventually the cardboard box replaced the crate, and the artwork was imprinted directly onto the carton. Today these paper labels are becoming collectible — primarily for the art, but also for their advertising appeal. Our advisor for this category is Cerebro; their address is listed in the Directory under Pennsylvania.

Unless otherwise noted, values are given for examples in excellent to near-mint condition.

Apple, Bird Valley, bl crow on shield, 10½x9" 4.50
Apple, Chief Joseph, Indian Chief w/bl bkground, 10½x9" 7.50
Apple, Diving Girl, girl diving w/friends on pier, 10½x9" 30.00
Apple, Duckwall, wood duck by stone wall, 10½x9" 10.00
Apple, Swan, wht swan on blk bkground, 10½x9" 10.00
Apple, Wenoka, Indian profile on arrowhead, 10½x9" 10.00
Cigar box, El Gallo, rooster struting, 6x9" 300.00
Cigar box, Hidden Fortune, parrot & treasure chest, 6x9", M 2.00
Cigar box, Honeycomb, colorful peacock, 6x9" 50.00
Cigar box, JH, Indian maiden & tepees, 6x9" 50.00
Cigar box, Judge Kent, man, eagle & scales, 6x9", M 8.00
Cigar box, Key West Beauties, 2 women w/flowers, 6x9" 45.00
Cigar box, La Mareva, woman in feathered hat, 6x9", M 6.00
Cigar box, Lanista, scenes from ancient Rome, 6x9", M 45.00
Cigar box, Le Biplan, airplane, 6x9", M 35.00
Cigar box, Little African, nude Blk baby & alligator, 6x9" 60.00
Cigar box, London Spires, London skyline, 6x9" 8.00
Cigar box, Lucy Gray, girl wearing kilt, 6x9", M 65.00
Cigar box, Majestic, ocean liner, 6x9", M 60.00
Cigar box, National Club, lg estate w/fountain, 6x9", M 6.00
Cigar box, Nov 11th, Statue of Liberty, 6x9", M 16.00
Cigar box, Our Bird, Spirit of St Louis airplane, 6x9", M 5.00
Cigar box, Porto-Vana, tobacco plantation, 6x9", M 2.00
Cigar box, Salesmen Sample, 3 men holding suitcases, 6x9" 60.00
Cigar box, Single Kay, trotter horse, 6x9", M 20.00
Cigar box, Stalwart, lion, 6x9", M 20.00
Cigar box, Tom & Dick, 2 cats, blk & red, 6x9", M 125.00
Cigar box, Vale, gold eagle over red title, 6x9", M 3.00
Cigar box, Whip-Poor-Will, bird on branch, 6x9", M 40.00
Cigar box, Yellow Jack, lg bee & clover, 6x9", M 25.00
Citrus, Mike, crate of grapefruit w/gr bkground, 9x9" 4.00
Citrus, Orchid, 2 orchids & bowl of sliced grapefruit, 9x9" 3.00
Cranberry, Fenwick, red berries & gr leaves, 7x10" 2.00
Cranberry, Red Bell, lg red bell, 7x10" 3.00
Grapefruit, Barbara Worth, heroine of Harold Wright's, 10x11" ..75.00
Grapefruit, Collegiate, grapefruit w/golfers, 10x11" 9.00
Lemon, Bulldog, fierce wht dog, dk bl bkground, 9x12" 50.00
Lemon, By The Sea, coastal scene, 9x12" 10.00
Lemon, Montecito Valley, beautiful landscape, 9x12" 35.00
Lemon, Pet, girl w/St Bernard, 9x12" 15.00
Orange, California Dreams, mc castle & gold peacocks, 10x11" ...16.00
Orange, Hummingbird, red bird on bl bkground, 10x11" 60.00
Pear, Buy the Best, 3 pears & orchard scene 1.00
Pear, Out of the West, Spanish galleon 5.00

Vegetable, Bronco, cowboy riding bucking bronco, 8¾x9¾" **2.00**
Vegetable, Conestoga, ox pulling wagon in desert **2.00**
Whiskey, Old Crow, distillery scene in sepia, 3½x4½" **1.00**

Labino

Dominick Labino was a glass blower who until mid-1985 worked in his studio in Ohio, blowing and sculpting various items which he signed and dated. A ceramic engineer by trade, he was instrumental in developing the heat-resistant tiles used in space flights. His glassmaking shows his versatility in the art. While some of his designs are free-form and futuristic, others are reminiscent of the products of older glasshouses. Because of problems with his health, Mr. Labino became unable to blow glass himself; he died January, 10, 1987. Work coming from his studio since mid-1985 has been signed 'Labino Studios, Baker,' indicating ware made by his protegee, E. Baker O'Brien. In addition to her own compositions, she continues to use many of the colors developed by Labino.

Cup, smoky w/red rim, 1967, 3½" **450.00**
Decanter, amber w/4 prunts ea on bottle & stopper, 1977, 11½" ...**1,400.00**
Emergence, dbl veil, encased in clear, 1980, 6" **5,200.00**
Emergence, dbl veil & encased air, 1976, 6" **6,100.00**
Emergence, yel cascades over pk in crystal, 1977, 6" **3,000.00**
Emergence, 2 pinched & pulled rows in clear, 1983, 4½" **3,000.00**
Fountain, bl w/gold veil, twisted rim, 1969, 8½" **6,500.00**
Fountain, clear bl w/gold veil & colored design, 1970, 5¾" **3,500.00**
Goblet, clear w/encased topaz opal & twist air-trap stem, 9" **350.00**
Paperweight, opal, tulip, 1968 ....**450.00**
Paperweight, peach w/air bubbles & veil, 1971, lg **400.00**
Pitcher, clear bl to chartreuse, integral hdl, 1971, 8½" **300.00**
Rendezvous, w/veil, arrow piercing a bubble, 1979, 6" **2,000.00**
Saffron, female torso, 1968, 5½" **1,800.00**
Sea Kingdom, clear w/bl fish, 1979, 4" **4,800.00**
Spatial Movement, amber, 1983, 5½" **3,250.00**
Tumbler, smoky red, ribbed sides, 1976, 4" **200.00**
Vase, bl opal w/lt ruby swirls, ovoid, 1971, 5x4" **525.00**
Vase, bl w/cobalt & yel design, pear shape, 1969, 4½" **600.00**
Vase, bl w/horse-head prunts, bulbous, 1981, 6" **650.00**
Vase, bl w/orange looping festoons, 1970, 8" **1,300.00**
Vase, bud; pk swirled, 1968, 5½" **850.00**

Vase, clear, orange and gold striped design, signed, dated 1982, 5½", $850.00.

Vase, clear bl-gr, dbl gourd int w/2 bubbles, 1967, 5½" **750.00**
Vase, clear gr w/aventurine, bulbous, 1970, 4¾" **2,800.00**
Vase, clear w/appl purple, everted rim, 1966, 6½" **2,000.00**
Vase, clear w/incased bl irid w/mc, sq, 1984, 5" **950.00**
Vase, cobalt bl w/appl dripping ribs & tooling, 1981, 6½" **450.00**
Vase, lt milky bl, narrow base, 1966, 6" **375.00**
Vase, owl, amber irid, 1982, 3½" **400.00**

Vase, owl, clear salmon irid, 1981, 3¾" **325.00**
Vase, peach w/clear panelled sides, loop design, 1980, 6½" **750.00**
Vase, purple w/hobnail design, 1975, 5¼" **500.00**
Vase, ruby/yel, flat w/pulled corners, 2 sm openings, 5x5" **750.00**
Vase, silver schmeltz w/lav & gr swirls, wide mouth, 1968, 7½" ..**1,300.00**
Vase, silver schmeltz w/mc swirls, 1958, 7½" **1,600.00**
Vase, sqd form w/amethyst & purple core, mc inclusions, 4¼" ...**650.00**
Vase, upright 'ferns,' yel-rust on clear bl, ovoid, 1982, 4" **650.00**
Vase, yel 'ferns' on caramel w/int petal motif, 1982, 5½" **650.00**
Vase, yel/bl opal w/2 tan/opal flowers w/bubbles, 1968, 6½" **750.00**

Lace, Linens, and Needlework

Two distinct audiences vie for old lace and linens. Collectors seek out exceptional stitchery like philatelists and numismatists seek stamps or coins — simply to marvel at their beauty, rarity, and ties to history. Collectors judge lace and linens like figure skaters and gymnasts are judged: artistic impression is half the score, technical merit the other. How complex and difficult are the stitches, and how well are they done? The 'users' see lace and linens as recyclables. They seek pretty wearables or decorative materials. They want fashionable things in mint condition, and have little or no interest in technique. Both groups influence price.

Undiscovered and underpriced are the eighteenth-century masterpieces of lace and needle art in techniques which will never be duplicated. Their beauty is subtle. Amazing stitches often are invisible without magnification. To get the best value in any lace, linen, or textile item, learn to look closely at individual stitches, and study the design and technique. The finest pieces of any lace, linen, or textile are wonderfully constructed. The stitches are beautiful to look at and do a good job of holding the thing together. Our advisor for this category is Elizabeth M. Kurella; she is listed in the Directory under Michigan.

Key:
embr — embroidered   ms — machine sewn
hs — hand sewn

Bedspread, crochet, popcorn stitch, ecru, 104x80", VG **150.00**
Bedspread, crochet, scalloped edges, full sz **200.00**
Bedspread, embr homespun, scattered staining, 75x72" **375.00**
Bedspread, maroon & wht chenille, full sz, NM **50.00**
Bedspread, Victorian lace, 3 matching scarves, EX **450.00**
Blanket, bl & wht plaid wool, rolled hems, 86x77", EX **135.00**
Bonnet, baby; Ayrshire bk, needle lace & embr, ca 1830 ....**65.00**
Bonnet, baby; hand embr w/yel silk, 20th C **25.00**
Bonnet, baby; Hollie Point insert in bk, added lace, 18th C **175.00**
Bridal veil, 8" long teardrop, 14" needle-lace border, rprs **1,100.00**
Chair set, crochet, butterfly pattern, 3-pc **25.00**
Christening gown, Ayrshire whtwork, winged robe front, 1830s, 40" ..**575.00**
Christening gown, hand stitched, embr, 1920, 24" **75.00**
Christening gown, hand stitched, embr & tucks, 1890s, 30" **125.00**
Comforter, Log Cabin in mc prints w/red sqs, knotted, 78x74" ..**165.00**
Coverlet, crochet, ecru, 108x112" **200.00**
Doily, Battenburg, grapes & leaves, 10" dia **75.00**
Doily, crochet, pineapple, 14" dia **28.00**
Doily, crochet, star, 14" dia **38.00**
Handkerchief, Fr whtwork w/lace inserts, 19th C **150.00**
Handkerchief, 1" deep crochet edge, 20th C **3.00**
Handkerchief, 2" deep tatted edge, medallions w/picots, 20th C ..**25.00**
Handkerchief, 5" Point-de-Gaze needle lace, 1870s, 18" sq **350.00**
Lappet, Argentan needle lace, joined, ca 1740, G **475.00**
Lappet, Brussels bobbin lace, ca 1740, 22" ea, damaged, pr **650.00**
Lappet, Point-de-Gaze needle lace, joined, ca 1870, 32" **150.00**
Mattress cover, bl & wht homespun, hand sewn, 77x61" **330.00**

Napkin, linen, embr flower basket corners, crochet edge 14.00
Needlepoint panel, fruit/game birds/curtains, fr, 22x48" 220.00
Needlepoint/petit-point panel, 3 men in oval, fr, 34x29" 465.00
Needlework panel, church & tree, some fading, fr, 17x16" 100.00
Needlework panel, family register, MA, 1782-1824, 15x16", EX .700.00
Needlework panel, lady/boy/dog, silk on linen, sgn/1709, 17x15" .195.00
Needlework panel, wool on silk w/watercolor, landscape, 25x20" .600.00
Needlework panel, 3-masted Am ship, wool yarn, fr, 30x29" 600.00
Parasol, cream silk w/embr mc flowers & gold accents, 18th C .2,500.00
Pillow cover, bl & wht homespun w/tape ties & red embr, 28x21" ..165.00
Pillowcase, wht w/crochet edge, pr 30.00
Runner, Battenburg, 17x54" 135.00
Scarf, cotton w/cotton embr, 15x32" 15.00
Scarf, cotton w/wht embr, 8x14" 8.00
Scarf, nylon w/cotton embr, 32" L, M 10.00
Scarf, sheer nylon w/cotton embr, 10x15" 8.00
Sham, pieced design in mc calico w/pk ruffle, 34x14" 30.00
Shams, Battenburg, buttoned bk, lace edge, 16" sq, pr 165.00
Sheet, homespun linen, made from 2 pcs, hemmed, 80x74" 150.00
Show towel, red & bl embr, name/1844, 54x20", VG 145.00
Show towel, X-stitch flowers/animals/birds/name/1847, 8x18" ...170.00
Show towel, 4-color embr, rows of fringe, 62" 225.00
Strip of homespun, unhemmed, 185x39" 160.00
Tablecloth, Battenburg trim, 40x40", EX 135.00
Tablecloth, crochet, ecru, sq, 40x40" 65.00
Tablecloth, crocheted, 112x70" 120.00
Tablecloth, homespun linen, wht-on-wht stripes, hs, 62x44" 90.00
Tablecloth, Irish linen, 84x70", +10 napkins 70.00
Tablecloth, linen, tatting at edges & corners, 74x56" 95.00
Tablecloth, wht lawn, 82x65" +6 napkins w/cutwork & embr ...115.00
Towel, bl & wht homespun w/lace trim, 3 for 185.00
Towel, bl & wht plaid w/tied fringe on 1 end, 26x19" 60.00
Towel, finger; linen, embr children at play, hemstitched 16.50

Lacy Glassware

Lacy glass became popular in the late 1820s after the development of the pressing machine. It was decorated with allover patterns — hearts, lyres, sheaves of wheat, etc. — and backgrounds were completely stippled. The designs were intricate and delicate, hence the term 'lacy.' Although Sandwich produced this type of glassware in abundance, it was also made by other eastern glassworks as well as in the midwest. By 1840, its popularity on the wane and a depressed economy forcing manufacturers to seek less expensive modes of production, lacy glass began to be phased out in favor of pressed pattern glass.

Reference numbers correspond with *Sandwich Glass* by Ruth Webb Lee. When no condition is indicated, the items listed below are assumed to be without obvious damage; minor roughness is normal. See also Salts, Open.

Bowl, pattern resembling Princess Feather, Midwestern, 7½", NM, $80.00; Bowl, Heart pattern, New England type, shallow flake, 8", $110.00.

Bowl, Gothic Arch & Pineapple, 10" L, EX 300.00
Bowl, Hairpin, L-92, Midwestern, minor roughness, 2x7½" 60.00
Bowl, Rayed Peacock Eye, 11" L, VG 100.00
Bowl, Tulip & Acanthus Leaf, L-121-2, 9½", EX 50.00
Bowl, vegetable; Princess Feather/Basket of Flowers, 10½" 350.00
Bowl, vegetable; Scroll, mini, 3", EX 40.00
Compote, Princess Feather base, quatrefoil & zigzags in bowl 600.00
Creamer, Tulip & Scroll, flake/roughness, mini, 1⅝" 40.00
Honey dish, Scroll, amethyst, 4½" dia 50.00
Plate, Basket of Flowers, RB Curling & Sons, 7", EX 325.00
Plate, Pine Tree & Shield, opal, scalloped, 6" 350.00
Plate, Scroll, mini, 2⅛", EX 30.00
Plate, scrolls between bar terminals in rnd rim, 8" 35.00
Tea plate, Heart variant, L-107, opal, 6" 200.00
Tie back, opal, pewter posts, chips, 4½", pr 55.00
Whiskey taster, gray-bl, pontil, 1⅞" 105.00

Lalique

Beginning his lengthy career as a designer and maker of fine jewelry, Rene Lalique at first only dabbled in glass, making small panels of cire perdue (wax casting) to use in his jewelry. He also made small flacons of gold and silver with his glass inlays, which attracted the attention of M.F. Coty, who commissioned Lalique to design bottles for his perfume company. The success of this venture resulted in the opening of his own glassworks at Combs-la-Ville in 1909. In 1921 a larger factory was established at Wingen-sur-Moder in Alsace-Lorraine. By the thirties Lalique was world renown as the most important designer of his time.

Lalique glass is lead based, either mold blown or pressed. Favored motifs during the Art Nouveau period were dancing nymphs, fish, dragonflies, and foliage. Characteristically the glass is crystal in combination with acid-etched relief. Later some items were made in as many as ten colors (red, amber, and green among them) and were occasionally accented with enameling. These colored pieces, especially those in black, are highly prized by advanced collectors.

During the twenties and thirties, Lalique designed several vases and bowls reminiscent of American Indian art. He also developed a line in the Art Deco style decorated with stylized birds, florals, and geometrics. In addition to vases, clocks, automobile mascots, stemware, and bottles, many other useful objects were produced. Most items made before his death in 1945 were marked 'R. Lalique'; later the 'R' was deleted even though some of the original molds were still used. Numbers found on the bases of some pieces are catalog numbers. Beware of fraudulent pieces that have began to surface in increasing numbers. Our advisor for this category is John Danis; he is listed in the Directory under Illinois.

Key:
cl/fr — clear and frosted   RL — signed R. Lalique
L — signed Lalique   RLF — signed R. Lalique, France
LF — signed Lalique France

Ashtray, carp/bubbles, cl/fr, L, 6" dia 175.00
Atomizer, dancing nudes, gr stain on frost, RL, 2¾" 585.00
Bottle, scent; bl, flattened sphere, turq jade top, Worth, 4" 225.00
Bottle, scent; Cactus, fr ball shape w/protrusions, LF, 1¾" 180.00
Bottle, scent; Cactus, fr w/blk points, spherical, RLF, 4½" 500.00
Bottle, scent; Camille, gr opaque, shell-like shape, 2¼" 1,550.00
Bottle, scent; Clairefontaine, lily-of-valley stopper, 4⅝" 130.00
Bottle, scent; Lentiles, flower bands on cl flat disk, RL, 1¾" 880.00
Bottle, scent; Palerme, teardrop w/pearl strands, RL, 4½" 300.00
Bottle, scent; Pan, cl/fr, dk gray patina, RL, 5" 1,000.00
Bottle, scent; Trois Hirondelles, 3-bird stopper, RLF, 5" 8,000.00

Bottle, scent; 4 hearts, cl/fr, RL, 3¾" **225.00**
Bowl, Algues emb/beaded seaweed spirals, opal, RLF, 2½x14" **600.00**
Bowl, Calypso, 5 water sprites, cl/fr, RL, 1¾x14½" **1,495.00**
Bowl, Chevreuse, scalloped flat rim w/emb arches, LF, 10½" **175.00**
Bowl, Chiens, dogs in spiral race, fr, RL, 9½" **1,200.00**
Bowl, Coquilles, radiating clam shells, opal, RLF, 9½" **500.00**
Bowl, Farandole, dancing nude children, fr, RLF, 10½" **1,750.00**
Bowl, Poissons, fish/bubbling water, opal, RL, minor wear, 8" **500.00**
Bowl, Poissons, fish/bubbling water, opal, shallow, RL, 11¾" **600.00**
Box, Cleones, 10 scarabs, opal, RL, 6½" dia **400.00**
Box, Deux Sirenes, sea nymphs, opal, RL, 10" dia **690.00**
Box, powder; Scarabee, for Piver, emb beetle, sepia wash **575.00**
Box, Roger, grapevines/birds, blk enamel on fr, L, 5" dia **975.00**
Bracelet, Sophora, bl rectangle links w/foliage, RL **5,500.00**
Champagne, Ange, angel faces/wings, cl/fr, LF, 8" **75.00**
Chandelier, Dahlias, fr, invt dome on 4 chains, RLF, 12" dia ..**3,400.00**
Charger, Cote D'or, nudes in grape bower, cl/fr, LF, 16" **1,725.00**
Clock, mantel; Deux Colombes, lovebirds, opal, RLF, 8½" **2,000.00**
Decanter, Clos-Vougeot, orb-cluster stopper, L c, 12" **345.00**
Dish, etched bands lace about cl circles, RL, 2x4" **160.00**
Goblet/vase, Alger, foliate knop stem, LF, 9" **145.00**
Ice bucket, Fougeres, fern-leaf ribs, gr enamel, RLF, 9" **1,950.00**
Lamp, table; Saint Vincent, grapes on dome shade, RLF, 17" ...**9,775.00**
Lamp finial, 2 nudes/floral branches, fr, RL, 2⅛" dia **230.00**
Luminaire, Gros Poisson Algues, carp, bronze base, RLF, 15½" ..**6,300.00**
Mascot, Coc Nain, cl/fr amethyst, swivel metal mt, RLF, 9", EX ..**1,950.00**

Mascot, Grenouille, clear and frosted, engraved and molded R. Lalique, 2½", $10,000.00.

Mascot, Longchamp, horse head, blk base, RL, 6", EX **1,800.00**
Mascot, Tete D-Aigle, amber fr/cl **1,700.00**
Mascot, Victorie, face w/streaming hair, fr, RL, 9", NM **6,900.00**
Paperweight, Taureau Sacre, sacred cow, fr, RLF, 1938, 3½" **575.00**
Pendant, Muguet, lilies of the valley, opal, triangular, L **460.00**
Plaque, Vierge a L'Enfant, mother & child, wood base, RL, 14½" ...**460.00**
Sculpture, swan, fr, LF, 9½x12½" **1,400.00**
Smoking set, emb lions, ashtray/cigarette holder/lighter, L **200.00**
Statuette, Dancers, fr, 8" **650.00**
Statuette, Deux Tourterelles, doves/flowers, opal, RLF, 4¾" **690.00**
Statuette, Perdrix Couchee, crouching partridge, fr, LF, 4x6" **460.00**
Statuette, Perdux, partridge, fr, LF, 5¼x5¾" **460.00**
Statuette, Sainte Therese De L'Enfant Jesus, wood base, FL, 15" .**800.00**
Statuette, Sirene, seated mermaid, opal, RL, 4" **1,495.00**
Statuette, Source de La Fontaine Calliope, cl/fr, #403, RL, 20" .**9,625.00**
Statuette, Suzanne, nude w/drape, amber, bronze base, RL, 9" .**5,500.00**
Statuette, Suzanne, nude w/drape, fr, bronze base, RL, 9x8" ...**1,100.00**
Statuettes, Lion Family, fr, contemporary, LF, 3-pc **575.00**
Vase, Aras, parakeets/vines, opal, RLF, 9x12" **2,875.00**
Vase, Archers, nude males, amber, RL, 11¼" **2,500.00**
Vase, Bacchantes, in relief on textured fr, LF, 9½" **1,500.00**
Vase, Bagatelle, thick walled w/birds in recesses, LF, 6½" **260.00**

Vase, Borromee, peacocks, bl, RLF, 9½x7" **6,000.00**
Vase, Borromee, peacocks, opal w/gray wash, ovoid, RLF, 9" ..**1,725.00**
Vase, Bresse, roosters, turq, spherical, RLF, 4" **2,100.00**
Vase, Ceylan, lovebirds, opal, flared cylinder, RLF, 9¾" **2,500.00**
Vase, Coquilles, scallop shells, gray wash, RL, 7x6" **575.00**
Vase, Corinthe, protruding leaf-tip ribs, cl/fr, U-form, 7" **800.00**
Vase, Courges, repeating gourds, purple, RL, #417, 7½x7½" ..**2,400.00**
Vase, Courlis, sea gulls/ocean waves, red opal, RLF, 7x7" **2,900.00**
Vase, Eglantines, wild roses, fr/gray wash, bottle form, RL, 5" ...**345.00**
Vase, Formose, school of fish, bl wash, spherical, RL/F, 6¾" ...**1,000.00**
Vase, Fougeres, leaves w/tips in relief, fr, RLF, 6x8" **750.00**
Vase, Grenade, rows of lappets, blk/fr, spherical, RL, 4½" **4,250.00**
Vase, Grenade, rows of lappets, gray-bl enamel, RLF, 5" **865.00**
Vase, Le Mans, crowing roosters, honey, spherical, RLF, 4" **1,725.00**
Vase, Malines, 8 fern-like ribs, cornflower bl, RL, 54" **2,400.00**
Vase, Marguerite, daisies, cased wht w/blk enamel, RL, 8" **1,495.00**
Vase, Marisa, 4 bands of fish, fr, spherical, RLF, 9" **2,760.00**
Vase, Martins-Pecheurs, birds/branches, blk, ovoid, RL, 9½" .**4,600.00**
Vase, Myrrhis, intaglio ferns, bl wash, sqd, RLF, 7½" **550.00**
Vase, Nerfliers, floral, partial polish, RL, 5½x5½" **300.00**
Vase, Oleron, allover fish, fr, RLF/#1008, 3½" **800.00**
Vase, Ormeaux, elm leaves, opal, #984, RLF, 6½x5" **800.00**
Vase, Palmes, overlapping fern leaves, spherical, RL/MIF, 4½" ..**300.00**
Vase, Perruches, parakeets/limbs, RLF, 10" **6,000.00**
Vase, Pinsons, finches/cherry tree, opal, lg cone top, RL, 7" **920.00**
Vase, Rampillon, emb dmns/floral surface, opal, RL, 5" **690.00**
Vase, Saint Francois, 11 sparrows, opal, V-form, RLF, 7" **1,600.00**
Vase, Salmonides, salmon, fr, RLF, 12x12" **5,750.00**
Vase, Sauge, overlapping leaves, gr, spherical, RLF, 10" **1,725.00**
Vase, Sauterelles, grasshoppers, bl/gr wash, RL, 11", NM **1,725.00**
Vase, Tourbillons, Deco swirl, amber, ovoid, RLF, 8" **9,775.00**

Lamps

The earliest lamps were simple dish containers with a wick that hung over the edge or was supported by a channel or tube. Grease and oil from animal or vegetable sources were the first fuels used. Ancient pottery lamps, crusie, and Betty lamps are examples of these early types. In 1784 Swiss inventor Ami Argand introduced the first major improvement in lamps. His lamp featured a tubular wick and a glass chimney. During the first half of the 19th century, whale oil, burning fluid (a highly explosive mixture of turpentine and alcohol), and lard were the most common fuels used in North America. Many lamps were patented for specific use with these fuels.

Kerosene was the first major breakthrough in lighting fuels. It was demonstrated by Canadian geologist Dr. Abraham Gesner in 1846. The discovery and drilling of petroleum in the late 1850s provided an abundant and inexpensive supply of kerosene. It became the main source of light for homes during the balance of the 19th century and for remote locations until the 1950s.

Although Thomas A. Edison invented the electric lamp in 1879, it was not until two or three decades later that electric lamps replaced kerosene household lamps. Millions of kerosene lamps were made for every purpose and pocketbook. They ranged in size from tiny night or miniature lamps to tall stand or piano lamps. Hanging varieties for homes commonly had one or two fonts (oil containers), but chandeliers for churches and public buildings often had six or more. Wall or bracket lamps usually had silvered reflectors. Student lamps, parlor lamps (now called Gone-with-the-Wind lamps), and patterned glass lamps were designed to complement the popular furnishing trends of the day. Gaslight, introduced in the early 19th century, was used mainly in homes of the wealthy and public places until the early 20th century. Most fixtures were wall or ceiling mounted, although some table models were also used.

Few of the ordinary early electric lamps have survived. Many lamp manufacturers made the same or similar styles for either kerosene or electricity, sometimes for gas. Top-of-the-line lamps were made by Pairpoint, Phoenix, Tiffany, Bradley and Hubbard, and Handel. See also these specific sections.

When buying lamps that have been converted to electricity, inspect them very carefully for any damage that may have resulted from the alterations; such damage is very common, and when it does occur, the lamp's value may be lessened by as much as 50%. Lamps seem to bring much higher prices in some areas than others, especially the larger cities. Conversely, in rural areas they may bring only half as much as our listed values. One of our advisors for lamps is Carl Heck; he is listed in the Directory under Colorado. See also Stained Glass.

Key:
ab — acorn burner
hb — hornet burner
nb — nutmeg burner
Ob — O burner
pb — pinafore burner
SIA — Scenes in Action
Vb — P&A Victor burner

Aladdin Lamps, Electric

From 1908 Aladdin lamps with a mantle became the mainstay of rural America, providing light that compared favorably with the electric light bulb. They were produced by the Mantle Lamp Company of America in over eighteen models and more than one hundred styles. During the 1930s to the 1950s, this company was the leading manufacturer of electric lamps as well. Still in operation today, the company is now known as Aladdin Industries Inc., located in Nashville, Tennessee. For those seeking additional information on Aladdin Lamps, we recommend *Aladdin — The Magic Name in Lamps*; *Aladdin Electric Lamps*; and *A Collector's Manual and Price Guide*, all written by our advisor for Aladdins, J. W. Courter; he is listed in the Directory under Kentucky. Mr. Courter has also published a book called *Angle Lamps, Collector's Manual and Price Guide*.

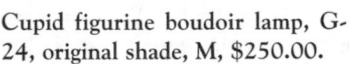
Cupid figurine boudoir lamp, G-24, original shade, M, $250.00.

Bed, #2021SS, Whip-o-lite shade, EX 75.00
Bed, B-45, Whip-o-lite shade, EX 85.00
Bedroom, P-52, ceramic, EX 30.00
Bedroom, P-68, ceramic, EX 35.00
Boudoir, G-10, glass, 1934, EX 40.00
Boudoir, G-15, floral base, crystal, EX 125.00
Boudoir, G-46, Cupid, Alacite, tall base, EX 165.00
Boudoir, G-92, Moonstone, 1937, EX 75.00
Bridge, #2079, wood, EX 300.00
Bridge, #7011, swing arm, wood, EX 200.00
Desk, M-238, plastic shade, EX 75.00
Figurine, G-24, Cupid, short base, EX 180.00
Figurine, G-79, Rooster, EX, minimum value 1,200.00

Floor, #3334, reflector, EX 175.00
Floor, #3356, type A, EX 275.00
Floor, #3690, reflector, candle arms, EX 200.00
Floor, #3994, Alacite ring, candle arms, night light, EX 300.00
Floor, #771, fluorescent, 2 15" tubes, EX 175.00
Glass Urn, G-375, Dancing Ladies, Alacite, EX 800.00
Glass Urn, G-379, Alacite tall ribbed urn w/top, EX 150.00
Magic Touch, MT-507, ceramic base, EX 350.00
Magic Touch, MT-520, cherry & brass base, EX 500.00
Pinup, G-351, wall medallion, Alacite, EX 85.00
Pinup, G-355C, Hoppy Gun in Holster, Alacite, EX 295.00
Ranch House, G335C, Topper horse head w/shade, Alacite, EX ...1,000.00
Table, E-203, Vogue ped, orange, EX 450.00
Table, E-303, Vogue Vase, orange, EX 350.00
Table, G-155, Moonstone, EX 60.00
Table, G-179, Opalique, EX 100.00
Table, G-19, EX 150.00
Table, G-223, Alacite, EX 50.00
Table, G-266, Alacite, EX 40.00
Table, G-322, Stanley, Alacite, w/shade, EX 30.00
Table, G-7, marble-like glass, EX 300.00
Table, G-77, Susie figurine, EX, minimum value 800.00
Table, M-1, metal, bronze color, EX 100.00
Table, M-446, ceramic pyramid, EX 25.00
Table, M-456, ceramic & metal, EX 30.00
Table, MM-7, metal & moonstone, EX 100.00
Table, P-402, ceramic, EX 40.00
Table, P-412, ceramic, lighted base, EX 70.00
Table, P-441, ceramic figural, EX 175.00
Torchier, #3760, EX 275.00
Torchier, #4512, wood & metal, EX 175.00
TV lamp, TV-382, ceramic, modern design, EX 40.00
TV lamp, TV-426, metal, foil shade, EX 25.00

Aladdin Lamps, Kerosene

Caboose Model #21C, B-400, aluminum font, w/shade, EX 100.00
Floor Model #12, Verde Antique, EX 175.00
Floor Model B, B-281, bronze & gold, EX 200.00
Floor Model B, B-294, bronze & gold lacquer 200.00
Hanging Model B, inside chain, parchment shade, EX 375.00
Hanging Model #23, aluminum hanger & font, wht paper shade, EX ...75.00
Parlour, Practicus, polished brass or Old English, EX, ea 600.00
Parlour Model #4, Old English or Jap bronze, EX, ea 600.00
Table Model #5, satin brass or nickel, EX 225.00
Table Model #11, nickel, EX 95.00
Table Model #23, B-2301, brass, EX 60.00
Table Model A, Venetian, #100, wht, EX 120.00
Table Model B, Beehive, B-82L, lt amber crystal, EX 150.00
Table Model B, Colonial, #105, gr crystal, EX 175.00
Table Model B, Corinthian, B-101, amber crystal, EX 125.00
Table Model B, Corinthian, B-126, wht & rose Moonstone, EX ..250.00
Table Model B, Majestic, B-121, rose Moonstone, EX 400.00
Table Model B, Oriental, B-130, ivory, EX 150.00
Table Model B, Queen, B-97, gr Moonstone, EX 350.00
Table Model B, Simplicity, B-30, wht, EX 150.00
Table Model B, Tall Lincoln Drape, B-75, Alacite (old), EX 175.00
Table Model B, Washington Drape, B-41, amber crystal, rnd, EX ..125.00
Table Model B, Washington Drape, B-52, amber crystal, EX 150.00
Wall bracket #6, complete, EX 200.00

Angle Lamps

The Angle Lamp Company of New York City developed a unique

type of kerosene lamp that was a vast improvement over those already on the market; they were sold from about 1896 until 1929 and were expensive for their time. Our Angle lamp advisor is J.W. Courter; he is listed in the Directory under Kentucky. See the narrative for Aladdin Lamps for information concerning popular books Mr. Courter has authored.

Classic hanging, dbl, Antique Gold, EX 1,400.00

Double hanging lamp, #252, polished brass fleur-de-lis pattern, reproduction milk glass shades, kerosene burning, EX, $350.00.

Gas adaptor, polished brass, no glass, EX 850.00
Hanging, dbl, #203, nickel, old glass, EX 425.00
Hanging, dbl, emb grapes, old glass, EX 625.00
Hanging, dbl, leaf & vine, nickel, EX 375.00
Hanging, Fleur-de-Lis, 4-burner, antique copper, old glass, EX ..925.00
Hanging, 3-burner, emb grapes, nickel, no glass, EX 675.00
Wall, #103, nickel, old glass, NM 265.00
Wall, #125, Pinwheel, nickel, no glass, EX 290.00
Wall, dbl, grape pattern, brass, old glass, EX 950.00
Wall, floral pattern, tin, no glass, EX 245.00
Wall cone, tin, blk pnt, no glass 265.00

Chandeliers

Bridgeport Brass Leader burners on 2-arm brass fixture 600.00
Brushed chrome Deco frwork w/5 saucer-shaped shades, 25" dia .700.00
Degue, frosted flower-emb bowl w/4 metal ribs+4 lilies 1,840.00

Empire-style, gilt bronze, 5-light style with cherubs holding torches, joined to acanthus leaf crown by twisted rope cables, electrified, 32½x20", $2,500.00.

Gilt brass, 18 branches depicting mythical serpents, prisms 2,750.00
Slag glass, metal windmill o/l in apron panels, sq, 16x22x22" 900.00
Wrought iron, 3 candle sockets, twist detail, 13" 360.00
Wrought-iron strap mts w/mottled glass 12" bowl, Fr 690.00

Decorated Kerosene Lamps

Bl cut to wht to clear, cylinder font, wht glass base, 9½" 565.00
Brn-lav MOP Swirl, ribbed clambroth ball shade, 21" 795.00
Cobalt cut to clear/frosted flowers, brass ft, 7" cut shade 900.00
Cranberry w/florals & gold, ruffled shade; metal ft, 12½" 650.00
Dot Optic, cranberry, 26½" 625.00
Gr opaque acanthus font, fire-gilt std, marble base, 12" 165.00

Rayo-type, CI base, HP milk glass dome shade w/floral, 20" 110.00
Triple cut o/l w/butterflies, wht stem/marble base, Sandwich 900.00
Wht cut to clear punties, brass stem, marble ft, 9" 250.00
Wht cut to clear w/circles, marble base, 9" 265.00
Wht cut to cranberry pear font, blk glass stem/ft, 18" 565.00

Fairy Lamps

Amber opal, pressed swirl, Clarke base, pyramid sz, 3⅝" 95.00
Apple gr frost emb swirl, clear Clarke base, pyramid sz, 3½" 100.00
Bl & wht nailsea, uptrn & ruffled base, 6x6½" 485.00
Bl & wht satin swirl, ruffled edge, 6½" 635.00
Bl Dmn Quilt MOP, clear Clarke flower-bowl vase, 6x5¾" 325.00
Bl shaded satin w/deep emb molding, 6½x6½" 480.00
Bl Swirl MOP, mk Clarke base, 4½x4" 245.00
Burmese, dbl, cut crystal 2-arm std w/silver mts, mk Clarke's 750.00
Burmese, 2¾" dome on metal 3-arm std w/griffins & mirror 600.00
Burmese, 3½" dome, 4-arm metal base w/4 ruffled holders 1,200.00
Burmese, 3½" dome shade, clear Clarke base, clear burner 250.00
Burmese, 5 3" shades+3 vases in ball-ftd ruffled 11" bowl 5,000.00
Chartreuse gr satin verre moire w/wht opaque pull-ups, 5⅛" 225.00
Cranberry nailsea, pinched/ruffled bowl base, 7x8" 795.00
Cranberry nailsea, 3" dome, clear Clarke base 165.00
Cranberry nailsea, 3" dome shade in pressed clear holder 125.00
Cranberry overshot, clear mk Clarke base, 3¾x3" 110.00
Cranberry swirl, crystal dripping on base, pyramid sz, 4¼" 420.00
Cranberry w/wht spiral threading, ribbed, Clarke base, 3" 400.00
Gr Eyewinker, modern 35.00
Mc spatter shade, pressed base, Clarke's Trademk Cricklite, 5" ..100.00
Owl's head, gr frosted, clear Clarke base, 4½x3⅜" 300.00
Pk overshot, Hobbs, clear Clarke base, pyramid sz, 3¾" 120.00
Pk satin swirl, clear mk Clarke base, 3¾x3" 125.00
Pk shaded/cased open-top ruffled shade w/4 inset jewels, 5½" ...200.00
Pk/wht/bl nailsea-type looped shade, clear base, 5" 125.00
Red nailsea, dome shade over 2nd tier of 4 on clear base 2,200.00
Red nailsea, 3" dome in ruffled triangular bowl, 6½", pr 3,000.00
Wht opal overshot, crown shape, clear Clarke base, 4¼x3" 165.00
Yel Swirl MOP, on matching crimped-edge holder, 4¾" 250.00

Gone-With-the-Wind and Banquet Lamps

Artichoke, pnt milk glass shade & font, ormolu ft, 24", EX 250.00
Cut/frosted pyriform shade, prisms, marble plinth, 20" 885.00
Floral, pk on aqua ball shade/base, brass set-in can, 22" 295.00
Floral on milk glass ball shade/shouldered font, 19" 300.00
Rose transfer/HP on milk glass ball shade/font, 18½" 175.00
Vaseline opal stripes on font & matching shade, 21¼" 750.00
Victoria, red satin, ball shade, ovoid font, ormolu ft, 27" 500.00

Hanging Lamps

Cranberry pear-shaped shade, brass fr w/pull-down base, 22" 300.00
Cranberry shade w/opal net, brass fr, clear prisms, 14" dia 1,155.00
Cranberry w/emb florals & rtcl ornate brass fr, 29" 500.00
Hall, pk shaded w/opal Dmn Quilt net, brass fr, 10" 195.00
Hall, wht opal w/pale coin spots, brass fr, electrified, 12" 115.00
Peachblow melon-rib 14" shade/font, rtcl brass fr, Sandwich ..2,000.00
Ruby o/l shade w/eng scenic panels, ornate sq brass fr, 33", VG .155.00
Ruby T'print 14" shade/chimney, clear font, prisms 800.00
Wht font/ball shade w/mc bird in rushes, CI fr mk Pat 1875 .....900.00

Lanterns

Barn, tin, triangular, oil burner, 27", EX 250.00

Brass/tin, rnd base, brass shade guard/hdl, w/chimney, 10" **180.00**
Candle, punched tin Revere type, worn blk hdl (rpl), 12" **175.00**
Carbide, Justrite, NP, bull's-eye lens, 9¼", G **100.00**
Carbide, NP, Toledo Acetylene Lantern Co, 11¾" **95.00**
Carriage, Dietz, USA, clear & red lens, Pat Feb 10-14, EX **125.00**
Hall, brass & beveled glass, rectangular, Am, 1875, 24" **500.00**
Skater's, Pat Dec 24 1867, brass w/clear globe, 8⅜" **125.00**
Skater's, Pat Dec 24 1887, brass & tin w/clear globe, 10" **165.00**
Skating, Dietz Sport, tin w/glass chimney-shape globe, 7¾" **140.00**
Tin w/bull's- eye lens, brn japanning w/gold, Peter Gray, 8½" ...**115.00**

Lard Oil/Grease Lamps

Betty, cast & wrought iron, brass spout extension, H Foker, 4" ..**440.00**
Betty, tin, weighted saucer base, 6½" **220.00**
Betty, wrought iron, bird on filler hole lid, 4" **415.00**
Betty, wrought iron, chicken finial, heart on arm, 7" **375.00**
Betty, wrought iron, heart finial on font lid, brass hanger, 4" **220.00**
Betty, wrought iron, knob on hinged lid, 4¾x3⅛x4½" **175.00**
Betty, wrought iron, tin lid, rpl hanger, 6" **99.00**
Betty, wrought iron, w/stand, 8¼" **385.00**
Betty, wrought iron w/brass tulips, 1770s, 4x2⅞x4¼", EX **370.00**
Crusie, dbl, sheet iron, cut-out finials, mk, 9" **100.00**
Crusie, wrought iron w/jamb spike of twisted design, 7⅜x4⅝" **70.00**
Loom, Continental, wrought iron w/brass rooster finial, 18x5¼" ..**350.00**
Pan, iron, twisted hanger, 1700s, 20" **220.00**
Pan, wrought iron, pendant, pinched corner, 4⅜x3¾x41" L **500.00**
Rush, iron, candle socket counterbalance, 7¾" **350.00**

Miniature Lamps, Kerosene

Amber Daisy & Cube, open-top scalloped shade, stemmed, 8" **75.00**

Amber, ribbed swirls, nutmeg burner, 8", EX, $450.00; Red satin, embossed acanthus leaves, 8¾", EX, $450.00.

Amethyst, wht/gold enamel flower band, 3" **58.00**
Banquet, gr to clear font w/floral, onyx/brass base, 12" **110.00**
Beaded Heart, clear, stemmed, w/chimney, ab, 5½" **250.00**
Bl, sqd ped base w/hdl, octagonal font, Vb, 7½" **120.00**
Bl Dmn Quilt MOP, vase-shaped shade, pinched base, ftd, 10" ..**1,000.00**
Bl Little Buttercup, nb, 7⅝" **125.00**
Bl opal Snowflake, finger lamp, #1 burner, 3" **425.00**
Bl opaque base, clear font, brass collar, 4⅜" **260.00**
Bl opaque Fleur-de-Lis, gold accents, wear, 5" **150.00**
Brass, plain font, ornate ftd base, 6" **175.00**
Bull's Eye, clear, ped ft, brass ABCO nb, +chimney, 11" **75.00**
Bull's Eye, clear w/HP bl flowers, 9½", pr **160.00**
Cameo, wht on red, U-shape shade, ftd squat base, Webb, 8½" ..**4,050.00**
Cosmos, clear, w/ornate punched-tin shade, 8" **75.00**
Cranberry, HP lily of the valley, 7¼" **1,070.00**
Cranberry Beaded Swirl, orig brass burner, 6½x4" **350.00**
Cranberry Beaded Swirl, orig burner, 8½x4½" **385.00**
Cranberry opal Swirl, dome shade/ball base, ab, LG Wright, 7" .**100.00**

Custard-color milk glass, Maltése Cross, Eagle Glass Co, 5½" **125.00**
Dk teal Bull's Eye, stemmed, w/clear chimney, ab, 5" **100.00**
Gone-With-the-Wind, bl Dmn Quilt MOP 2" shade, ftd base ...**700.00**
Gr, emb hairpin-like design, ped base, Scovill, no chimney, 9" ...**75.00**
Gr Raindrop MOP, ball shade/flared base, nb, 8" **1,050.00**
Honey amber Fishscale, stemmed, w/chimney, nb, 5" **250.00**
Improved Banner, Olmsted-type burner, wht Bristol shade, 5⅜" ..**45.00**
London Lamp, tin burner & reflector, 6", VG **40.00**
Lt bl Picket, stemmed, w/chimney, ab, 5¼" **90.00**
Milk glass Acanthus w/pk decor, ball shade/base, nb, 8½" **125.00**
Milk glass Artichoke, gr/pk, ribbed shouldered base, nb, 8" **100.00**
Milk glass Banner Improved, ftd base/chimney-shape shade, 6" **35.00**
Milk glass Kenova Night Lamp, worn gr/gold, emb base, ab, 6" ..**150.00**
Milk glass Nelly Bly w/HP floral, hb, no deflector, +chimney **50.00**
Milk glass Paneled Cosmos w/mc floral, ball shade, nb, 8½" **150.00**
Milk glass w/basketweave motif, wht/brn, 3½" **55.00**
Milk glass w/brn windmill, cylinder base, ball shade, ab, 7" **50.00**
Milk glass w/eagle, pk/gr/gold, squat w/ball shade, nb, 7¾" **400.00**
Milk glass w/eagle, rust/beige, wear, 5" **185.00**
Milk glass w/emb dots in panels, octagonal, matching shade, 7" .**185.00**
Milk glass w/emb floral/pk bands, bowl base w/short neck, 7" **75.00**
Milk glass w/pk & gr floral on ball shade, 7¼x3" **275.00**
Milk glass ½-shade w/Geo & Martha Washington, 5¾x3" **175.00**
Nutmeg, clear shade & chimney, brass band forms hdl, 7⅝" **55.00**
Nutmeg type, gr shade, clear chimney, brass band hdl, 7⅞" **80.00**
Pk Dmn Quilt MOP, sqd ruffled vase on sqd petal-ft base, 10" .**1,050.00**
Pk nailsea, ruffled shade/ftd base, nailsea chimney, 11½" **2,500.00**
Rainbow Dmn Quilt MOP, ruffled U-form shade, sqd base, NM .**1,250.00**
Rubena verde w/gold flowers & leaves, 6" **450.00**
Santa Claus, milk glass w/red & blk pnt, ab, 9½", EX **1,700.00**
Smoke Beaded Swirl, orig brass burner, 8¼x4" **325.00**
SP, ornate, sgn Standard Silver Co Canada, 2½" **275.00**
Spatter, red/yel Beaded Swirl, crimp-rim chimney, 10½" **85.00**
Teal bl cut-bk fuchsia-like florals, ball shade, 10½x4" **695.00**
Time & Light Pride of Am..., milk glass beehive shade, 6⅝" **65.00**
Vapo Cressoline, gilt CI fr, clear font, milk glass shade, 7" **65.00**

Motion Lamps

Animated motion lamps were popular from the 1920s to the early 1960s. They are characterized by action created by heat from a light bulb which causes a cylinder to revolve and create the illusion of an animated scene. Most were probably designed after the burning candle type in early days that rang bells and had hanging designs. Some of the better-known manufacturers were Econolite Corp., Scene in Action Corp., and L.A. Goodman Mfg. Company. As with many collectible items, prices are guided by condition, availibility, and collector demand, which seems to be more intense on the west and east coast, often resulting in higher prices there than in the midwest. Values are given for lamps in mint condition. Any damage or flaws seriously reduce the price. For further information we recommend *Animated Motion Lamps, A Price Guide 1920s to Present,* by Bill and Linda Montgomery (L-W Book Sales). Our advisors for motion lamps are Kaye and Jim Whitaker; they are listed in the Directory under Washington.

Airplanes, Econolite, plastic, 1958, 11" **125.00**
Antique cars, Econolite, gold wire base, 1947, 11" **140.00**
Christmas tree, Econolite, many colors, paper, 1951, 15" **120.00**
Fireplace, Econolite, gold wire base, 1958, 11" **120.00**
Forest fire, Econolite, gold wire base, 1955, 11" **120.00**
Forest fire, Scene in Action, glass & pot metal, 1931, 10" **195.00**
Fountain of Youth, Econolite (Roto-Vue Jr), gold, 1950, 10" **130.00**
Hopalong Cassidy, Econolite (Roto-Vue Jr), red, 1949, 10" **600.00**
Marine scene, SIA, ship/lighthouse, glass, 1930s **175.00**

Mtn waterfall/campers, LA Goodman, gold wire base, 1956, 11" ..130.00
Niagara Falls, Econolite, gold wire base, 1955, 11" 110.00
Niagara Falls, Econolite (Roto-Vue Jr), gold, 1950, 10" 115.00
Niagara Falls, Scene in Action, glass & pot metal, 1931, 10" 195.00
Ocean creatures, LA Goodman, plastic, 1955, 11" 125.00
Oriental fantasy, LA Goodman, plastic, 1957, 11" 115.00
Santa & reindeer, LA Goodman, plastic, 1955, 11" 130.00
Seattle World's Fair, Econolite, gold wire base, 1962, 11" 150.00
Serenader, Scene in Action, glass & pot metal, 1932, 13" 225.00
Ships, Rev-O-Lite, bronze & plastic, 1930s, 10" 125.00
Steamboats or riverboats, Econolite, gold wire base, '57, 11" 130.00
Truck & bus, Econolite, gold wire base, 1955, 11" 140.00
Water skiers, Econolite, plastic, 1957, 11" 150.00

Pattern Glass Lamps

Acanthus, bl opaque w/clambroth base, brass collar, 11", EX 775.00
Acanthus, jade gr font, clambroth base, brass collar, 11" 935.00
Acanthus, lime gr font, clambroth base, sanded, 11½" 1,450.00
Allover Bull's Eye, stand lamp 165.00
Ball Base Swirl, stand lamp, 8" 165.00
Beaded Dmn & Rib Bands, finger lamp, flat, dtd collar, 3" 50.00
Brick Band, finger lamp, flat, brass collar, 3" 70.00
Buckle, variation, stand lamp, 8" 40.00
Bull's Eye, finger lamp, flat 115.00
Bull's Eye, gr, hand lamp, flat 225.00
Bull's Eye, stand lamp, Safety hdl 130.00
Cable, finger lamp, flat, brass collar/burner, w/chimney 50.00
Central Sawtooth Panel w/Star & Cable Base, ftd, 14½" 100.00
Checkered Star Band, stand lamp, 6½" 185.00
Coin Dot, finger lamp, flat, dtd Taplin-Brn collar, chimney 325.00
Daisy & Bow Knot, finger lamp, ftd, 5" 165.00
Dbl Dotted Band, finger lamp, flat 135.00
Diagonal Rib & Pod, finger lamp, flat 165.00
Dmn Sawtooth & Sheath, finger lamp, flat 130.00
Duncan Bar Rayed Panel, brass collar & burner, 10⅜" 90.00
Ellipse w/T'print, finger lamp, ftd, 4½" 165.00
Empress, gr, finger lamp, ftd, Riverside 220.00
Erin Fan, gr, hand lamp, flat 200.00
Feathered Bull's Eye & Fleur-de-Lis, stand lamp 225.00
Grecian Key, gr, ped base, ab, 7⅝" 90.00
Hamilton w/Leaf, stand lamp, 7" 215.00
Heart, opaque custard, finger lamp, flat 495.00
Heart, opaque custard, finger lamp, ftd 425.00
Hearts & Stars, bl opaque font, wht base, 9½", VG 225.00
Hero, finger lamp, ftd, dbl-loop hdl, 5" 225.00
Honeycomb, stand lamp 200.00
Icicle & Panel, stand lamp 185.00
King Melon, lt bl w/opal spots, stand lamp, 7½", NM 400.00
Markham Swirl Band, wht optic, finger lamp, flat 650.00
Melon & Fine Rib, stand lamp 185.00
Palmette, #1 Queen Anne burner, w/chimney, 17½" 95.00
Paneled Bull's Eye, stand lamp 165.00
Plume, finger lamp, flat 165.00
Prince Edward, wht opaque, finger lamp, ftd, ear hdl 400.00
Princess Feather, brass collar & burner, w/chimney, 13" 125.00
Prisms & Dmn Point, finger lamp, flat 150.00
Prisms w/Plain Band, finger lamp, flat 160.00
Queen Heart, gr, finger lamp, flat 340.00
Queen Heart, gr w/wht opaque base, brass burner, 18", EX 125.00
Ring & Rib, stand lamp, 6½" 210.00
Ring Punty, stand lamp, 7" 200.00
Riverside Fern, gr font, clear beaded ft, stand lamp 200.00
Riverside Panel, gr font, clear beaded ft, stand lamp 200.00

Sharon Panel, finger lamp, flat, 2¾", EX 30.00
Shield & Star, finger lamp, flat 175.00
St Lawrence, finger lamp, flat rayed base, amber, w/chimney 140.00
Stippled Leaf, brass collar & burner, w/chimney, 16" 85.00
Sultan, finger lamp, ftd 400.00
Tapered Rib, finger lamp, flat 135.00
Triple Flute & Bar, stand lamp, 7" 250.00
Turkey Foot, bl, finger lamp, ftd 245.00
Vine & Rib, finger lamp, flat 175.00
Westmoreland, ftd, dtd 1883 brass burner, crimp-top chimney ..100.00
York, stand lamp 185.00
Zipper & Rib, finger lamp, flat 135.00

Peg Lamps

Blown, pewter collar, brass & pewter burner, 5¾" 235.00
Cranberry fluted shade/font, brass base, w/chimney, 15" 335.00
Cranberry w/floral shade/font, brass dmn-motif stick, 18x5" 550.00
Pk shaded satin w/emb swirled ribs, pleat-top shade, 11" 450.00
Pk Swirl MOP fluted shade, gold dore base, 13" 585.00
Ruby cut to clear, brass collar, dbl camphene burner, 6⅝" 110.00
Stippled cranberry w/gold cherries on shade/font, 11" 565.00

Reverse-Painted Lamps

Moe Bridges, 18" landscape
shade in blues and greens,
signed, #186, mounted on
metal base with applied green
patina, molded mark, 23",
$2,400.00.

Classique, 18" trees shade; gr-speckled blk hdld metal std 1,800.00
Jefferson, 16" trees/sun/boat shade; gilt fleur-de-lis emb std 1,000.00
Jefferson, 16" 6-panel scenic shade; ribbed metal std 1,000.00
Jefferson, 18" hollyhocks shade; bronze ribbed std, 22" 3,000.00
Moe Bridges, 15" chipped-ice trees shade; leaf-cvd std 2,300.00
Pittsburgh, 16" Lakes of Killarney shade; emb std, 23" 1,750.00
Pittsburgh-type 18" water lily shade; hdld metal vase std 1,750.00
Unmk, 16" leaf-etch mtn scene; cast metal std adjusts 1,265.00
Unmk, 16" village/rocky water scene shade; gilt-metal std 1,100.00
Unmk, 17" dome winter cottages shade; gilt metal std, 21" 1,100.00
Unmk, 18" trees/lake dome shade; emb lilies on bronzed std 950.00
Unmk, 18" winter house/windmill shade; glass std lights up 1,500.00

Student Lamps, Kerosene

Brass, dbl, repousse fluid font, Dardonville NY, 1850s 650.00
Brass, milk glass shade, Kosmose Brenner, 18" 365.00
Brass w/yel-cased umbrella shade, urn font, adjusts, 22" 600.00
Cast brass w/gilt, gr cased shade, electrified, 26" 850.00
NP brass, dbl, GA Kleemann, NY, 20" 565.00
NP brass, gr cased shade, 21", EX 200.00
NP brass w/repro 7" milk glass shade, Manhattan, 21" 300.00

SP brass, dbl, milk glass shades, Argand/1871, 21x19", EX 800.00

Whale Oil/Burning Fluid Lamps

Blown, bulbous font, sausage-trn stem, tin burner, 8½" 1,200.00
Blown, bulbous font w/button knop/saucer base, tin burner, 5" ..850.00
Brass, rnd base, acorn-shaped font, orig burner, 9⅜x4⅛" 150.00
Brass fluted shaft w/dolphin hdl, acorn font, 7x5" dia 150.00
Mold-blown corset form, pewter collar & burner, hdl, 5⅛" 180.00
Pressed, cobalt w/melon ribs, appl hdl, 4⅛"+burner 800.00
Pressed, corset-shaped font on hex base, pewter burner, 9" 120.00
Pressed, hex base, stem & font, heart pattern, 8" 185.00
Pressed, hex base & stem, ornate font, brass burner, 11" 150.00
Pressed, monument-form base w/Bigler pattern font, 11½" 200.00
Pressed, quatrefoil tiered base, bulb font, pewter burner, 7½" 125.00
Pressed, sq base w/lg blown knop & wafers, conical font, 8½" 110.00
Pressed, sq claw-ft & scroll base, globular font, 8¼" 210.00
Pressed, sq lacy base w/solid stem, bulb font, 8½" 100.00
Pressed, sq tiered base w/conical blown font, w/burner, 8½" 125.00
Pressed, sq tiered base w/knop, bulb font, smooth base, 9½" 175.00
Pressed, sq tiered base w/ringed knop, globular font, 6¼" 175.00
Pressed, tiered base w/globular font, w/burner, 5¾", EX 175.00
Pressed base w/lion & flowers, blown bulb font, 10", EX 150.00

Miscellaneous

Argand, B Gardiner, bronze, urn form, single arm, 14¼", pr ...1,100.00
Argand, brass, modified burner, eng floral, 17", EX 250.00
Argand, gilt brass, cut prisms, marble base, Cornelius, 15" 110.00
Argand, gilt bronze, frosted/etched shade, 15½", pr 1,200.00
Argand, JB Jones, gilt bronze urn fonts, etched shade, 16" 600.00
Bent-panel slag glass 20" shade/base w/bird & urn metal o/l 620.00
Bicycle, carbine, NP w/red & gr lenses, Solar, EX 30.00
Dyott Pat, glass font/int draft, Pat 1866, 13½", VG 45.00
Hand lamp, Little Butter Cup, appl brass collar, 2¾" 50.00
Lace maker's, blown, aqua, appl saucer base & hdl, 5¾" 900.00
Lace maker's, blown, bulb font, hollow stem w/appl ft/hdl, 10" ..300.00
Lace maker's, blown, cobalt flared base, clear font, 6¾" 4,100.00
Lace maker's, blown peg on stem w/flanged lip, rnd ft, 8" 500.00
Lace maker's, lacy base, blown spherical font, no burner, 11" 275.00
Night lamp, hexagonal, cranberry, brass collar & burner, 7¾" ...150.00
Rayo, NP brass, lt gr cased umbrella shade w/emb floral, 21" 110.00
Skaters, tin, clear globe, 7" 100.00
Southern Belle, lt gr glass, holds bouquet, other arm down 110.00
Southern Belle, pk glass, holds bouquet, other arm down 55.00
Sparking, pewter, single spout burner, Capen & Molineux, 2¼" .165.00
Store, B&H No 96, brass, in iron fr, hangs, Pat 1891, 34x20" 250.00

Lang, Anton

Anton Lang was a German studio potter and an actor in the Oberammergau Passion Plays early in the 20th century. Because he played the role of Christ three times, tourists brought his pottery back to the U.S. in suitcases, which accounts for the prevalence of smaller examples today. During 1923-1924 Anton Lang and the other 'Passion Players' toured the U.S. selling their crafts. Lang would occasionally throw pottery when the cast passed through a pottery center such as Cincinnati, where Rookwood was located. His pottery, marked with his name in script, is fairly scarce and highly valued for its artistic quality. His son Karl designed most of the Art Deco shapes and conducted glaze experiments. Only pieces bearing a hand-written signature (not a facsimile) are certain to be Anton Lang originals instead of the work of Karl or the Langs' assistants. Postcards, programs, and photographs depicting Lang are also collectible.

Book, Anton Lang, Aus Meinem Leben (Reminiscences), hardbk, 1938 .100.00
Figurine, cat & ball, gun-metal irid, Deco style, 8" 350.00
Figurine, pelican on oval base, natural colors, MIG, 6" 100.00
Pitcher, cobalt irid, HP Deco flowers & dots, yel int, 5" 125.00
Vase, brn drip on bl irid, hand signed, 10" 325.00
Vase, mc stripes on overall milky ground, mini, 2" 50.00

Le Verre Francais

Le Verre Francais was produced during the 1920s by Schneider at Epinay-sur-Seine in France. It was a commercial art glass in the cameo style composed of layered glass with the designs engraved by acid. Favored motifs were stylized leaves and flowers or geometric patterns. It was marked with the name in script or with an inlaid filigrane. Our advisor for this category is Don Williams; he is listed in the Directory under Missouri.

Key: fp — fire polished

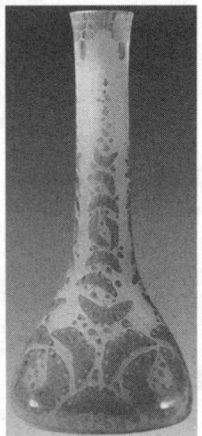

Vase, luna moths, Chinese red and sapphire blue on gray mottled with cream and turquoise, slim neck with ovoid body, ca 1925, 29", $4,125.00.

Cameo

Bowl, thorn-covered seed pods, brn/yel/orange, 5½x11" 865.00
Chandelier, grapes/vines, purple/violet on orange 16" bowl 3,250.00
Compote, floral branches, dk on med bl, bell form, 10x10" 1,250.00
Ewer, floral at wide bottom, leafy columns, Charder, 19" 1,500.00
Lamp base, mums/stylized stems, lav/purple/pk, slim, 14½" 375.00
Planter, 3 blossom-filled ball forms, cobalt on turq, 8" L 460.00
Vase, Deco floral, brn on yel, shouldered/bun base, 23" 2,070.00
Vase, fuchsia, rust/dk bl, tapered, ftd, 9¾" 800.00
Vase, geometrics/stylized flower stalks, amber/brn, 11x4" 800.00
Vase, lg scarabs/stacked geometrics, ovoid w/gourd neck, 12½" ..1,400.00
Vase, money-plant columns, brn/rust on blk/teal/rust, 13x11" ...1,100.00
Vase, mums on long stems, lav on pk/frost, ftd, 12x4" 900.00
Vase, optic ribs/leaves, gr to orange on yel, squat, 8" 375.00
Vase, stylized trees, orange/bl on yel, shouldered/bun ft, 7¾" 800.00
Vase, tiger lilies, ftd shouldered cone, Charder, 12" 1,500.00
Vase, upright berry clusters, rust to dk bl on yel-gold, 7½" 600.00
Vase, 3 scarabs/geometric borders, brn/orange, slim/ftd, 16" 1,000.00
Vase, 4 Deco blossom panels, sgn Charder, ftd ovoid, 13½" 865.00

Leach, Bernard

Bernard Leach was an artist who became a potter. From 1909 to 1920, he stayed in China and Japan where he became fascinated with traditional Oriental pottery and became a master of it. After returning to his native England, he became the most influential potter of the 20th century. Leach's methods and materials revolutionized modern art pottery. His ceramics are marked with a 'BL' seal and a 'S' seal for St. Ives, where his pottery was located in England.

Bowl, tenmoku w/rust, paneled sides, short ft, St Ives, 8"	1,250.00
Mug, brn w/clear-glazed rim band, concave, low hdl, 5x3½"	115.00
Vase, oatmeal glaze w/pnt salmon, stoneware, 15½"	1,875.00

Leeds, Leeds Type

The Leeds Pottery was established in 1758 in Yorkshire and under varied management produced fine creamware, often highly reticulated and transfer printed, shiny black-glazed Jackfield wares, polychromed pearlware, and figurines similar to those made in the Staffordshire area. Little of the early ware was marked; after 1775 the impressed 'Leeds Pottery' mark was used. From 1781 to 1820, the name 'Hartley Greens & Co.' was added. The pottery closed in 1898.

Today the term 'Leeds' has become generic and is used to encompass all polychromed pearlware and creamware, wherever its origin. Thus similar wares of other potters (Wood for instance) is often incorrectly called 'Leeds.' Unless a piece is marked or can be definitely attributed to Leeds by confirming the pattern to be authentic, 'Leeds-Type' would be a more accurate nomenclature.

Key:
cw — creamware   pw — pearlware

Tea caddy, creamware, cherubs decoration, lion finial, running inscription: Mrs D., Bickle, Creditor 1796, restorations, 6¼", $1,200.00.

Charger, mc floral, bl feather edge, pw, rpr, 13"	330.00
Coffeepot, strawberries, pw, imperfections, 10"	460.00
Creamer, gaudy mc floral, pw, 3⅝"	200.00
Loving cup, mc floral, pw, hairline, 5⅜"	300.00
Mug, mc pagoda & trees, pw, 6⅛", NM	600.00
Pitcher, leaves/bands, 4-color, cw, 1780s, 5"	250.00
Plate, toddy; bl feather edge, cw, 4⅜"	100.00
Plate, 4-color eagle, feather edge, pw, 8¼"	500.00
Potpourri jar, mc florals, urn shape, pw, 8¼"	1,980.00
Soup, Oriental in garden, bl diapered border, cw, 9½"	395.00
Sugar bowl, gaudy mc floral, lion-head hdls, pw, w/lid	250.00
Teapot, mc floral, pw, rpr, 6¾"	330.00

Lefton China

Lefton China is one of the most desirable, most sought-after col-

lectibles in the market place today. The company was founded in the early 1940s by Mr. Geo Zoltan Lefton who had migrated to the United States from Hungary. In the 1930s he was in the designing and manufacturing of sportswear, and his hobby of collecting fine china and porcelain led him to the creation of his own ceramic business.

When the bombing of Pearl Harbor occurred in December of 1941, Mr. Lefton befriended and helped a Japanese-American protect his property from being destroyed by groups of anti-Japanese. After this event Mr. Lefton became associated with a Japanese factory owned by Kowa Toki K.K. Up until 1980 this factory produced thousands of pieces that were sold by the Lefton Company, all bearing the initials KW before the item number. These items and many of the whimsical pieces from the Bluebirds, Dainty Miss, Miss Priss, Cabbage Cutie, Mr. Toodles, and Dutch Girl lines are eagerly sought by collectors today. As with any antique or collectible, the prices vary depending on location, condition, and availability. For the history of Lefton China, information about Lefton factories, marks, and other identification methods, we highly recommend the *Collector's Encyclopedia of Lefton China* by our advisor, Loretta DeLozier, listed in the Directory under Iowa. You may also contact her regarding the National Society of Lefton Collectors.

Ashtray, lilacs, stones & sponge gold, #194, 2¾"	18.00
Baby set (bowl & cup) Bluebirds, #435	65.00
Bank, owl, bsk, #479, 6½"	37.00
Bird, Bird of Paradise, #140, 6¾"	80.00
Bird, Bobwhite, #300, 5½"	38.00
Bird, Golden Pheasant, #1060, 11¾"	75.00
Bird, Long Tail Rooster, #1057, 10" L	135.00
Bowl, Sleigh, Green Holly, #1346, 8"	55.00
Box, Flower Garden Line, appl flowers on bsk, #2152, 3x5" dia	65.00
Box, jewels & appl flowers, #2748, w/lid, 4½"	70.00
Box, pin; pk w/flowers & stones, #90254, 2¼"	35.00
Bust, Franklin, #1146, 5½"	30.00
Butter dish, Mr Toodles, #3294, 6¾"	35.00
Cake plate, Green Heritage, #719, 9¼"	35.00
Canister set, Rustic Daisy, #4115	105.00
Cheese dish, Honey Bee, #1285	55.00
Coffeepot, Brown Heritage, Fruit, #20591, 8-cup	135.00
Coffeepot, Violet Chintz, #660, 8¾"	130.00
Cookie jar, Girlface, #40, 7½"	175.00
Cookie jar, Honey Bee, #1279	110.00
Cookie jar, Miss Priss, #1502	135.00
Cookie jar, Winking Santa Claus, #90148, 10½"	225.00
Creamer & sugar bowl, Dutch Girl, #2698	38.00
Creamer & sugar bowl, Green Holly, #1355	45.00
Creamer & sugar bowl, Miss Priss, #1508	45.00
Cup & saucer, Americana, #973	30.00
Cup & saucer, Rose Chintz, #662	35.00
Cup & saucer, tea; Blue Paisley, #2339	18.00
Cup & saucer, tea; Green Heritage, #3067	30.00
Cup & saucer, tea; To a Wild Rose, #2566	25.00
Dish, Rustic Daisy, 2-compartment, w/hdl, #4122, 13x7"	40.00
Egg cup, Bluebird, #286, 3¼"	20.00
Egg tray, Country Squire, #1601, 12½"	38.00
Figurine, Colonial man & woman, #2256, 10½", pr	275.00
Figurine, Don Quixote & Sancho Panza, #4721, 8"	110.00
Figurine, Napolean on horse, #4908, 11"	225.00
Figurine, Siamese dancers, #493, 6½", pr	95.00
Jam jar, Cabbage Cutie, #1282	40.00
Jam jar, Dutch girl, #2697	38.00
Jam jar, Grapes, #4852	27.00
Pitcher, Floral Bisque Bouquet, bsk, #4209, 7"	30.00
Plate, Americana, #963	32.00
Plate, Holly w/touches of Candy Cane Red, #2617	24.00

Plate, To a Wild Rose, #2573, 7½" 24.00
Shakers, Dainty Miss, #439, pr 27.00
Shakers, Green Holly, #1353, pr 28.00
Shakers, Miss Priss, #1511, pr 24.00
Snack set, Brown Heritage, Fruit, #20130 ....38.00
Snack set, different colors, #2759 ....22.00
Snack set, Forget-Me-Not, #4179 ....20.00
Snack set, Rose Heirloom, #1074, 9" 30.00
Teapot, Bluebirds, musical, #734 ....215.00
Teapot, Cabbage Cutie, #2123 ....85.00
Teapot, Fleur-de-Lis, #1799, 6-cup 80.00
Teapot, Grapes, #2663, 7" 85.00
Teapot, Green Holly, #1357 ....80.00
Teapot, Poinsettia, #4388, 6-cup 120.00
Teapot, Spring Violets, #2439 ....165.00
Tray, tidbit; Green Heritage, 2-tier, #1153 ....75.00
Tray, tidbit; Green Holly, 2-tier, #1364 ....75.00
Wall plaque, Home Sweet Home, #219, 7" 22.00
Wall plaque, 2 angels on oval, bsk, #1697, 6" 40.00

Legras

Legras and Cie was founded in St. Denis, France, in 1864. Production continued until the 1930s. In addition to their enameled wares, they made cameo art glass decorated with outdoor scenes and florals executed by acid cuttings through two to six layers of glass. Their work is signed 'Legras' in relief and in enamel. Our advisor for this category is Don Williams; he is listed in the Directory under Missouri.

Cameo

Bowl, honeysuckle, wine on textured frost, 2½x14" 550.00
Bowl, wild roses, lt bl/gr on gr, gold scroll rim, 10" 1,900.00
Vase, ivy on pk frost, 3-prong opening, 16½" 2,350.00
Vase, maple leaves, wine on red, ovoid, 11" 950.00
Vase, snow scene w/village & peasant, dk on gold-orange, 8½" .900.00
Vase, trees/river, wht/lime & dk gr on pk, ftd U-form, 7" 1,100.00
Vase, tulips, wine/yel-orange on orange-gr mottle, 4¾" 1,050.00
Vase, winter trees, brn on yel-rust, stick neck, flattened, 5" 550.00
Vase, 3-leaf device, gr/blk/lav on clear, 3-sided, 4¾" 300.00

Enameled Glass

Lamp, mantel; trees, earth tones, sqd, on metal base 8½" 500.00
Salt, winter trees, 1x1¾" 575.00
Vase, snowy trees/houses/ladies on frost, trefoil rim, 17" 800.00
Vase, trees/lake, cut/pnt on frost, flared top, 11x5½" 1,035.00
Vase, trees/river, cut/pnt, flared cylinder, 11" 950.00
Vase, waterfront HP on etched clear, flared sqd rim, 3½x5" 300.00
Vase, winter scene, yel/orange/brn/on clear, shaped rim, 13" ..1,000.00
Vase, wisteria, purple/brn on bl mottle, dbl bulb, 8" 690.00

Lenox

Walter Scott Lenox, former art director at Ott and Brewer, and Jonathan Coxon founded The Ceramic Art Company of Trenton, New Jersey, in 1889. By 1906 Cox had left the company and to reflect the change in ownership, the name was changed to Lenox Inc. Until 1930 when the production of American-made Belleek came to an end, they continued to produce the same type of high-quality ornamental wares that Lenox and Coxon had learned to master while in the employ of Ott and Brewer. Their superior dinnerware made the company famous, and since 1917 Lenox has been chosen the official White House china. Our advisor for this category is Mary Frank Gaston; she is listed in the Directory under Texas. See also Ceramic Art Company.

Perfume bottle, swan in relief, M in box (not shown), $85.00.

Ashtray, gold ship, Am Export 1960, 5½" 40.00
Bookends, Blk lady's torso, Deco, gr mk, pr 400.00
Bowl, Lenox Leaf, wht, shape #37 ....110.00
Bowl, rimmed soup; Kingsley 50.00
Bowl, rimmed soup; Lenox Rose, 9" 45.00
Bowl, rimmed soup; Westfield 35.00
Bowl, salad/cereal; Springdale 35.00
Bowl, vegetable; Eternal, oval 55.00
Bowl, vegetable; Lenox Rose, 9½" L 95.00
Bowl, vegetable; Wyndcrest, oval 75.00
Box, cigarette; Lenox Rose, +3 ashtrays 75.00
Bust of female, cascading hair, wht, gr mk, 8½" 325.00
Candlesticks, Westfield, pr 75.00
Candlesticks, wht ware, raised scalloped base, Belleek mk, pr 165.00
Chocolate pot, Autumn 225.00
Chocolate pot, mc daisies, Belleek, 11", +6 c/s 425.00
Coffeepot, floral garlands, silver o/l, Belleek mk, 11" 700.00
Creamer, Kingsley 85.00
Creamer, Westfield 45.00
Creamer & sugar bowl, Lenox Rose 100.00
Cup, demitasse; wht, sterling holder, gr mk 25.00
Cup & saucer, Amethyst 30.00
Cup & saucer, Ashley 35.00
Cup & saucer, Autumn 50.00
Cup & saucer, Black Royale 42.50
Cup & saucer, Blue Ridge 40.00
Cup & saucer, Brandywine 35.00
Cup & saucer, Charleston 42.50
Cup & saucer, Clarion 30.00
Cup & saucer, Country Garden 35.00
Cup & saucer, demitasse; Trent 45.00
Cup & saucer, Filigree 35.00
Cup & saucer, Fireflower 25.00
Cup & saucer, Lace Point 42.50
Cup & saucer, Lacquer 45.00
Cup & saucer, Moonlight Mood 42.50
Cup & saucer, Mystic 35.00
Cup & saucer, Solitaire 42.50
Cup & saucer, Twilight Dell 45.00
Cup & saucer, Weatherly 35.00
Cup & saucer, Westwind 25.00
Cup & saucer, Willow Tree 40.00
Cup & saucer, Wyndcrest 36.00
Figurine, Floradora, no decor 310.00
Figurine vase, blue jay in tree, 5-color, ink stamp 350.00

Lamp, boudoir; Deco lady w/hoop skirt & fan forms shade, 9" 410.00
Mug, bearded man w/mug & cigar, artist sgn, Belleek 200.00
Mug, monk scene on brn 125.00
Pitcher, cherries on gr/bl Belleek, 6½x7" 175.00
Pitcher, gold band w/6 red apples on olive, sgn McGrayhy, 6" ...200.00
Pitcher, silver o/l w/floral cameo, palette mk, 8" 600.00
Plate, bread & butter; Flirtation 20.00
Plate, bread & butter; Westwind 18.00
Plate, dessert; Moonlight Mood 15.00
Plate, dinner, Fairfield 30.00
Plate, dinner; Ashley 30.00
Plate, dinner; Autumn 50.00
Plate, dinner; Brandywine 40.00
Plate, dinner; Brookdale 35.00
Plate, dinner; Cinderella 30.00
Plate, dinner; Country Garden 35.00
Plate, dinner; Fantasies 25.00
Plate, dinner; Flirtation 30.00
Plate, dinner; Forever 20.00
Plate, dinner; Fountain, 20th C, USA, 9", set of 12 ....275.00
Plate, dinner; Goldenrod 35.00
Plate, dinner; Harrison 25.00
Plate, dinner; Lenox Rose 30.00
Plate, dinner; Midsummer 30.00
Plate, dinner; Moonlight Mood 35.00
Plate, dinner; Mystic 30.00
Plate, dinner; Noblesse 35.00
Plate, dinner; Rosemont 42.50
Plate, dinner; Sutton Place 42.50
Plate, dinner; Twilight Dell 45.00
Plate, dinner; Weatherly 30.00
Plate, dinner; Westwind 30.00
Plate, dinner; Willow Tree 35.00
Plate, mallard duck among rushes, gold trim, sgn Nosek, 10" 225.00
Plate, salad; Autumn 50.00
Plate, salad; Filigree 15.00
Plate, salad; Goldenrod 15.00
Plate, salad; Montclair 18.00
Plate, salad; Moonlight Mood 18.00
Platter, Westfield, oval, lg 135.00
Platter, Westfield, oval, sm 95.00
Punch bowl, bl plums on shaded ground, 2-part, Belleek, 15" 800.00
Relish plate, dbl, leaf-emb rim & int, center hdl, 15½" 125.00
Shaker, talcum; HP roses (nonfactory), Belleek mk, 6" 140.00
Sugar bowl, Westfield, w/lid 45.00
Swan, blk mk, 8½" 95.00
Swan, gold mk, 2" 35.00
Swan, wht, gr mk, 4x5" 50.00
Teapot, Virginian, gold hdls, 11", +cr/sug 450.00
Teapot, wide gold bands, squat, old mk, +cr/sug 125.00
Toby, William Penn, Indian hdl 250.00
Vase, Belleek, peacocks on bl, sgn Hipple on base, 12" 700.00
Vase, brn w/fan-shaped Nouveau leaves, brn mk, 4x3½" 225.00
Vase, Deco peacocks, HP, cylindrical, Belleek mk, 13" 450.00
Vase, lady in long wht gown/pk floral, cylinder, Lenox, 12" 500.00
Vase, poppies, sgn Wilcox, baluster, Belleek mk, 16" 600.00
Vase, roses, HP, mk Belleek, 18" 950.00
Vase, springer spaniel, sgn Baker, Belleek wreath mk, 8¼" 800.00
Vase, stylized upright florals, mc on ivory, Belleek, 12x4" 225.00

Letter Openers

Made in a wide variety of materials and designs, letter openers

make for an interesting collection that is easy to display and easy on the budget as well. Our advisor for this category is Ron Damaska; he is listed in the Directory under Pennsylvania.

Brass dagger, 9½", in red leather scabbard 20.00
Celluloid, doll figure on end 75.00
Celluloid, emb Indian head, souvenir of Montreal 25.00
Celluloid, owl 45.00
Celluloid, relief violets & leaves w/some color, 10" 18.00
Metal w/copper blade, CA state seal, emb hdl, 7" 15.00
Plastic, nude lady figural hdl, advertising 65.00
SP, Reed & Barton, cherubs in grape arbor hdl, ornate 40.00
Vegetable ivory, 4½", w/tassel 15.00
14k yel gold, Cartier, eng & monogramed, 5½x1", MIB 535.00

Libbey

The New England Glass Company was established in 1818 in Boston, Massachusetts. In 1892 it became known as the Libbey Glass Company. At Chicago's Columbian Expo in 1893, Libbey set up a ten-pot furnace and made glass souvenirs. The display brought them world-wide fame. Between 1878 and 1918 Libbey made exquisite cut and faceted glass, considered today to be the best from the brilliant period. The company is credited for several innovations — the Owens bottle machine that made mass production possible and the Westlake machine which turned out both electric light bulbs and tumblers automatically. They developed a machine to polish the rims of their tumblers in such a way that chipping was unlikely to occur. Their glassware carried the patented Safedge guarantee. Libbey also made glassware in numerous colors, among them cobalt, ruby, pink, green, and amber. Our advisor for this category is Mike Roscoe; he is listed in the Directory under Ohio. See also Amberina.

Maize, pitcher, iridized clear with amber stain, 8½", $500.00.

Bowl, cut, Ellsmere, 9" 550.00
Bowl, cut, Senora, triangle, 3x10", EX 500.00
Bowl, cut, starflowers, single lg flower in base, 4x8", NM 250.00
Bowl, cut, Wedgmere, att, 4½x10" 1,600.00
Bowl, ribbed swirls, sgn, bulbous, 8" 50.00
Candlesticks, cut, thistle blossoms & leaves, 10", pr 350.00
Chalice, cut, gr/frost, deer & foliage allover, 5½" 500.00
Claret, bear stem, opal 165.00
Compote, clear w/pk Optic Swirl, knob stem, Nash, 4x10" 450.00
Compote, pk nailsea-type loops, flared petal top, Nash, 4x12" ...450.00
Console compote, feathers, chartreuse on opal, 6x7", +6" sticks ..650.00
Cordial, crystal w/gr jade knop on stem, Nash, 5", set of 8 ....400.00
Cordial, etched, lime gr knobs, sgn, 6 for 300.00
Cordial, greyhound stem, opal 175.00
Creamer & sugar bowl, cut, Marcella, notched hdls, 3¼" 200.00
Creamer & sugar bowl, hobstars/prisms/strawberry dmns, 3" 110.00
Flower center, cut, Express, cut ring near top, 13x8" 950.00

Goblet, cat stem, opal 200.00
Maize, celery vase, clear w/amber staining & bl leaves, 6" 235.00
Maize, celery vase, gr husks on custard 180.00
Maize, condiment set, custard, 3 pcs on tray w/metal hdl 600.00
Maize, pickle castor, gr husks on custard, SP fr 500.00
Maize, pitcher, bl husks on clear w/amber irid, clear hdl, 9" 585.00
Maize, shakers, gold-edged bl husks on custard, pr 250.00
Maize, sugar shaker, yel/gold leaves on custard, 5¾" 300.00
Maize, toothpick holder, gold-edged gr husks on custard 400.00
Maize, tumbler, bl husks on irid 235.00
Pitcher, cut, Kingston, sgn, 9" 395.00
Pitcher, milk; cut hobstar & notched prims, bulbous, 7½" 300.00
Pitcher, Zenda, bulbous, 8" 375.00
Plate, cut, Holly & Snowflake, allover pattern, 7" 295.00
Plate, cut, Imperial, 7" 200.00
Punch bowl on stand, cut, star/zipper, mk, 11x12" 635.00
Saloon shaker, hobstars/X-hatching/fans, honeycomb neck, 5" ..165.00
Salt cellar, 1893 Columbian Exhibition, lay-down egg shape 225.00
Sherbet, blk rabbit stem, sgn 110.00
Sherbet, rabbit stem, opal, low ft 125.00
Sherbet, squirrel stem, opal, ftd 125.00
Sherry, monkey stem, opal 145.00
Tazza, intaglio flowers & leaves, twist stem, 5½x7½" 120.00
Tray, ice cream; cut hobstar band, ray/hobstar bottom, 14" 1,100.00
Urn, fuchsias & sunflowers intaglio, 9x6½" 550.00
Vase, cornucopia; Modern America, swirled, appl ft, 12" L 135.00
Vase, cut, floral/brilliant cuttings, scalloped, 13x5½" 400.00
Vase, Zipper, turq on clear, 10" 425.00
Whiskey, wheat/fern/leaves intaglio, 2¼", pr 90.00
Wine, kangaroo stem, 6" 165.00

Lightning Rod Balls

Used as ornaments on lightning rods, the vast majority of these balls were made of glass, but ceramic examples can be found as well. Their average diameter is 4½" but can vary from 3½" up to 5½". Only a few of the many available pattern-and-color combinations are listed here. The most common measure 4½" and are found in sun-colored amethyst and milk glass. Our advisor is Rod Krupka, author of a book on this subject. Anyone interested in receiving a hobby-related newsletter may write to him for more information; he is listed in the Directory under Michigan.

Amber, Hawkeye 100.00
Amber, Raised Quilt 100.00
Amethyst, sun-colored, plain, rnd 15.00
Bl opaque, Hawkeye 50.00
Bl opaque, Moon & Star 30.00
Bl opaque, 8-sided 20.00
Clear, swirl 200.00
Gray-gr, D&S 125.00
Orange, plain, rnd 400.00
Purple-blk, rnd 400.00
Red, Electra, rnd 250.00
Red, Flat Quilt 150.00
Silver mercury, rnd 75.00
Wht milk glass, Chestnut 24.00
Wht milk glass, Hawkeye 35.00
Wht swirl 40.00

Limited Edition Plates

Currently values of some limited edition plates have risen dramati-cally while others have drastically fallen. Prices charged by plate dealers in the secondary market vary greatly; we have tried to suggest an average.

Bing and Grondahl

1895, Behind the Frozen Window 6,250.00
1896, New Moon 1,950.00
1897, Christmas Meal of Sparrows 1,100.00
1898, Roses & Star 685.00
1899, Crows Enjoying Christmas 1,500.00
1900, Church Bells Chiming 850.00
1901, 3 Wise Men 425.00
1902, Gothic Church Interior 395.00
1903, Expectant Children 425.00
1904, View of Copenhagen From Fredericksberg Hill 225.00
1905, Anxiety of the Coming Christmas Night 195.00
1906, Sleighing to Church 155.00
1907, Little Match Girl 225.00
1908, St Petri Church 105.00
1909, Yule Tree 105.00
1910, Old Organist 105.00
1911, Angels & Shepherds 105.00
1912, Going to Church 105.00
1913, Bringing Home the Tree 105.00
1914, Amalienborg Castle 100.00
1915, Dog on Chain Outside Window 175.00
1916, Prayer of the Sparrows 105.00
1917, Christmas Boat 105.00
1918, Fishing Boat 105.00
1919, Outside the Lighted Window 95.00
1920, Hare in the Snow 95.00
1921, Pigeons 95.00
1922, Star of Bethlehem 95.00
1923, Hermitage 95.00
1924, Lighthouse 105.00
1925, Child's Christmas 95.00
1926, Churchgoers 95.00
1927, Skating Couple 145.00
1928, Eskimos 95.00
1929, Fox Outside Farm 105.00
1930, Tree in Town Hall Square 115.00
1931, Christmas Train 115.00
1932, Lifeboat at Work 115.00
1933, Korsor-Nyborg Ferry 105.00
1934, Church Bell in Tower 95.00
1935, Lillebelt Bridge 105.00
1936, Royal Guard 105.00
1937, Arrival of Christmas Guests 135.00
1938, Lighting the Candles 165.00
1939, Old Lock-Eye, The Sandman 225.00
1940, Delivering Christmas Letters 265.00
1941, Horses Enjoying Meal 315.00
1942, Danish Farm on Christmas Night 225.00
1943, Ribe Cathedral 155.00
1944, Sorgenfri Castle 115.00
1945, Old Water Mill 175.00
1946, Commemoration Cross 105.00
1947, Dybbol Mill 145.00
1948, Watchman 105.00
1949, Landsoldaten 170.00
1950, Kronborg Castle at Elsinore 175.00
1951, Jens Bang 145.00
1952, Old Copenhagen Canals & Thorsvaldsen Museum 145.00
1953, Royal Boat 145.00

1954, Snowman 145.00
1955, Kaulundborg Church 130.00
1956, Christmas in Copenhagen 160.00
1957, Christmas Candles 175.00
1958, Santa Claus 140.00
1959, Christmas Eve 155.00
1960, Village Church 170.00
1961, Winter Harmony 115.00
1962, Winter Night 85.00
1963, Christmas Elf 110.00
1964, Fir Tree & Hare 65.00
1965, Bringing Home the Tree 55.00
1966, Home for Christmas 55.00
1967, Sharing the Joy 47.00
1968, Christmas in Church 35.00
1969, Arrival of Guests 35.00
1970, Pheasants in Snow 28.00
1971, Christmas at Home 28.00
1972, Christmas in Greenland 25.00
1973, Country Christmas 29.00
1974, Christmas in the Village 28.00
1975, The Old Water Mill 28.00
1976, Christmas Welcome 27.00
1977, Copenhagen Christmas 27.00
1978, A Christmas Tale 27.00
1979, White Christmas 27.00
1980, Christmas in the Woods 32.00
1981, Christmas Peace 32.00
1982, The Christmas Tree 42.00
1983, Christmas in Old Town 42.00
1984, Christmas Letter 45.00
1985, Christmas Eve, Farm 45.00
1986, Silent Night 45.00
1987, Snowman's Christmas 55.00
1988, In King's Garden 45.00
1989, Christmas Anchorage 46.00
1990, Changing Guards 57.00
1991, Copenhagen Stock Exchange 73.00
1992, Pastor's Christmas 73.00
1993, Father Christmas in Copenhagen 73.00

M. I. Hummel

The last issue for M.I. Hummel annual plates was made in 1995. Values listed here are for plates in mint condition with original boxes.

1971, Heavenly Angel, $525.00; 1972, Hear Ye, Hear Ye, $50.00.

1973, Glober Trotter 95.00
1974, Goose Girl 50.00

1975, Ride Into Christmas 50.00
1976, Apple Tree Girl 50.00
1977, Apple Tree Boy 60.00
1978, Happy Pastime 45.00
1979, Singing Lesson 35.00
1980, School Girl 49.00
1981, Umbrella Boy 49.00
1982, Umbrella Girl 80.00
1983, The Postman 165.00
1984, Little Helper 60.00
1985, Chick Girl 75.00
1986, Playmates 140.00
1987, Feeding Time 105.00
1988, Little Goat Herder 95.00
1989, Farm Boy 110.00
1990, Shepherd's Boy 185.00
1991, Just Resting 115.00
1992, Meditation 130.00
1993, Doll Bath 160.00
1994, Doctor 200.00
1995, Come Back Soon 225.00

Royal Copenhagen

1908, Madonna & Child 3,400.00
1909, Danish Landscape 205.00
1910, Magi 160.00
1911, Danish Landscape 170.00
1912, Christmas Tree 155.00
1913, Frederik Church Spire 155.00
1914, Holy Spirit Church 170.00
1915, Danish Landscape 185.00
1916, Shepherd at Christmas 135.00
1917, Our Savior Church 135.00
1918, Sheep & Shepherds 125.00
1919, In the Park 125.00
1920, Mary & Child Jesus 125.00
1921, Aabenraa Marketplace 115.00
1922, 3 Singing Angels 115.00
1923, Danish Landscape 115.00
1924, Sailing Ship 150.00
1925, Christianshavn Street Scene 110.00
1926, Christianshavn Canal 105.00
1927, Ship's Boy at Tiller 175.00
1928, Vicar's Family 115.00
1929, Grundtvig Church 115.00
1930, Fishing Boats 140.00
1931, Mother & Child 135.00
1932, Frederiksberg Gardens 140.00
1933, Ferry & Great Belt 160.00
1934, Hermitage Castle 165.00
1935, Kronborg Castle 215.00
1936, Roskilde Cathedral 195.00
1937, Main Street of Copenhagen 265.00
1938, Round Church of Osterlars 325.00
1939, Greenland Pack Ice 415.00
1940, Good Shepherd 425.00
1941, Danish Village Church 375.00
1942, Bell Tower 415.00
1943, Flight Into Egypt 550.00
1944, Danish Village Scene 305.00
1945, Peaceful Scene 450.00
1946, Zealand Village Church 200.00
1947, Good Shepherd 255.00

1948, Nodebo Church 225.00
1949, Our Lady's Cathedral 245.00
1950, Boeslunde Church 235.00
1951, Christmas Angel 375.00
1952, Christmas in Forest 145.00
1953, Frederiksberg Castle 160.00
1954, Amalienborg Palace 175.00
1955, Fano Girl 195.00
1956, Rosenborg Castle 195.00
1957, Good Shepherd 145.00
1958, Sunshine Over Greenland 145.00
1959, Christmas Night 145.00
1960, Stag 155.00
1961, Training Ship 165.00
1962, Little Mermaid 225.00
1963, Hojsager Mill 85.00
1964, Fetching the Tree 65.00
1965, Little Skaters 74.00
1966, Blackbird 45.00
1967, Royal Oak 45.00
1968, Last Umiak 42.00

1969, Old Farmyard, $39.00.

1970, Christmas Rose & Cat 47.00
1971, Hare in Winter 27.00
1972, In the Desert 26.00
1973, Train Home Bound 32.00
1974, Winter Twilight 32.00
1975, Queen's Palace 26.00
1976, Danish Watermill 35.00
1977, Immervad Bridge 28.00
1978, Greenland Scenery 28.00
1979, Choosing the Tree 57.00
1980, Bringing Home the Tree 38.00
1981, Admiring the Tree 40.00
1982, Waiting for Christmas 85.00
1983, Merry Christmas 55.00
1984, Jingle Bells 52.00
1985, Snowman 65.00
1986, Wait for Me 59.00
1987, Winter Birds 65.00
1988, Christmas Eve Copenhagen 75.00
1989, Old Skating Pond 85.00
1990, Christmas in Tivoli 120.00
1991, St Lucia Basilica 52.00
1992, Royal Coach 70.00
1993, Arrival Guests by Train 70.00

Limoges

From the mid-18th century, Limoges was the center of the porcelain industry of France, where at one time more than forty companies utilized the local kaolin to make a superior quality china, much of which was exported to the United States. Various marks were used; some included the name of the American export company (rather than the manufacturer) and 'Limoges.' After 1891 'France' was added. Pieces signed by factory artists are more valuable than those decorated outside the factory by amateurs. For a more thorough study of the subject, we recommend you refer to *The Collector's Encyclopedia of Limoges Porcelain, 2nd Edition*, by our advisor, Mary Frank Gaston, who is listed in the Directory under Texas. Her book has beautiful color illustrations and current market values.

Bowl, fruit & grapes, sgn, gold border, 2½x10" 235.00
Cake plate, roses, gold hdls & trim, mk, 10½" 45.00
Dresser set, florals w/gold, hair receiver+box+9x13" tray 195.00
Dresser set, lilacs, tray+pin tray+ring tree+box+candlestick 160.00
Game set, various birds, gold rims, 20" platter+12 9" plates 1,250.00
Loving cup, floral/gold vines, emb decor, 5½" 175.00
Pitcher, tankard; 2 monks drinking, gold trim/hdl, sgn, 14" 325.00
Plaque, Dutch scene, sgn, gold rococo border, 12" 245.00
Plaque, Dutchman (may be Rubens), 7x9" 700.00
Plaque, seminude lady, sgn Baumy, B&H mk, 12" 500.00
Plate, bearded man in chair on cobalt, gold scroll edge, 10" 200.00
Plate, birds, sgn Lancy, 9½" 65.00
Plate, dessert; florals w/gold, bird mk, 6⅛", 6 for 80.00
Plate, floral, floral-emb gilt rim, Mirello, 10", set of 12 ....340.00
Plate, flying ducks, gold rococo border, unmk, 11¼" dia 225.00
Plate, fruit, sgn, gold border, 10" 135.00
Plate, fruit, sgn Golse, gold scroll edge, 13" 265.00
Plate, fruit, sgn Rosier, gold trim, mk, 12⅜" 235.00
Plate, game bird, gold scalloped rim, Coronet, 10¾", pr 325.00
Plate, hunter & dog, gold scalloped rim, mk, 13½" 325.00
Plate, lady w/lamb, suitor beside, gold trim, mk, 10" 155.00
Plate, orchid sprays, wide borders, T&V, 9½" 250.00
Plate, roses w/gold, irregular rim, mk, 10⅜", pr 275.00
Punch bowl, grapes w/gold, T&V, 14x6", +8 matching cups ...1,295.00
Punch bowl, leaf band, currants/gold bands w/in, T&V, 12" 200.00
Tea tile, autumn leaves & acorns, T&V, 6¾" dia 110.00
Tureen, floral sprigs w/gold, w/lid, 3¼x5¼x3¾" 75.00
Vase, bird w/much gold & bl, rtcl neck, hdls, ca 1885, 7½" 225.00

Lithophanes

Lithophanes are porcelain panels with relief designs of varying degrees of thickness and density. Transmitted light brings out the pattern in graduated shading, lighter where the procelain is thin and darker in the heavy areas. They were cast from wax models prepared by artists and depict views of life from the 1800s, religious themes, or scenes of historical significance. First made in Berlin about 1803, they were used as lampshade panels, window plaques, or candle shields. Later steins, mugs, and cups were made with lithophanes in their bases. Japanese wares were sometimes made with dragons or geisha lithophanes. Our advisor for this category is Lucille Malitz; she is listed in the Directory under New York. See also Dragon Ware; Steins.

Cup & saucer, pk w/moriage dragon, lady in bottom of cup 45.00
Lamp, open-top 13" dome shade w/3 panels, genre scenes 775.00
Lamp, 5-panel shade; figural cherub std, electrified, 16" 350.00
Panel, Emperor & Empress, MOP inlay fr on stand, 1850s 2,450.00
Panel, mother & child, cat & kittens, PPM #1362, 4¾x5½" 210.00
Panel, Petraca, KPM/235, 6x7½", in ftd gold dore emb fr 350.00
Stein, 2 girls read letter (in base), tavern scene ext, 10" 225.00
Tea warmer, 4 panels w/children, ornate fr/base mk S&S-12, 7" .250.00

Little Red Riding Hood

Though usually thought of as a product of the Hull Pottery Company, research has shown that a major part of this line was actually made by Regal China. The idea for this popular line of novelties and kitchenware items was developed and patented by Hull, but records show that to a large extent Hull sent their whiteware to Regal to be decorated. Little Red Riding Hood was produced from 1943 until 1957. Values have risen sharply over the past several months. For further information we recommend *Collecting Hull Pottery's Red Riding Hood* by Mark Supnick. Watch for the announcement of another book on this subject by Joyce and Fred Roerig, authors of *The Collector's Encyclopedia of Cookie Jars*. Our advisors for this category are Rose and Charlie Snyder; they are listed in the Directory under Kansas.

Note: Beware of reproductions.

Wolf jar, red basketweave base, $1,000.00.

Bank, standing	600.00
Bank, wall hanging	1,700.00
Batter pot	425.00
Butter dish	425.00
Canister, cereal	900.00
Canister, flour; tea; coffee; or sugar; ea	800.00
Canister, salt	850.00
Cookie jar, closed basket, minimum	360.00
Cookie jar, open, stars	350.00
Cookie jar, open basket, red shoes	575.00
Cookie jar, poinsettia, lg flowers	950.00
Cookie jar, red spray, gold bows, red shoes, rare	850.00
Cookie jar, wht	200.00
Cracker jar, unmk	900.00
Creamer, pours from head, no tab hdl	450.00
Creamer, pours from head, tab hdl	350.00
Creamer & sugar bowl, side pour	300.00
Grease jar, flower basket, gold trim	1,200.00
Lamp, rare	1,995.00
Match holder, wall hanging	800.00
Match holder, wall hanging, blank, EX	300.00
Mustard, no spoon	300.00
Mustard, w/spoon	400.00
Pitcher, batter	425.00
Pitcher, standing, milk sz, 8"	350.00
Planter, hanging	475.00
Shakers, lg, 5½", pr	175.00
Shakers, Pat Design 135889, med sz, pr	850.00
Shakers, 3¼", pr	125.00
Spice jar, sq base	750.00
String holder	3,000.00
Sugar bowl, crawling, unmk	275.00

Sugar bowl, side pour	175.00
Sugar bowl lid	225.00
Teapot	365.00
Vase, 2 hdls, poppy decals	95.00
Wall pocket	550.00
Wolf jar, yel	900.00

Liverpool

In the late 1700s Liverpool potters produced a creamy ivory ware, sometimes called Queen's Ware, which they decorated by means of the newly perfected transfer print. Made specifically for the American market, patriotic inscriptions, political portraits, or other state themes were applied in black with colors sometimes added by hand. (Obviously their loyalty to the crown did not inhibit the progress of business!) Before it lost favor in about 1825, other English potters made a similar product. Today Liverpool is a generic term used to refer to all ware of this type. Our advisor for this category is William Kurau; he is listed in the Directory under Pennsylvania.

Bowl, 3-masted ship/inscription dtd 1796, blk w/mc, 10½"	600.00
Jug, Admiral Nelson/Hibernia, 1800s, 7¾", NM	350.00
Jug, Am eagle, iron red transfer, 1800s, 8", EX	1,200.00
Jug, Am 2-masted ship/eagle, 1800s, rpr, 8"	920.00
Jug, Am 3-masted ship, bk: eagle, rpr, 9½"	450.00
Jug, Am 3-masted ship/Independence, mk Herculaneum, rpr, 8"	400.00
Jug, Am 3-masted ship/Masonic design, blk w/mc, 9¼"	1,495.00
Jug, Forester's Arms, red-brn transfer w/mc, 9"	250.00
Jug, Geo WA/Independence, blk w/gold, early 1800s, 8", EX	950.00
Jug, Jefferson cartoon, Apotheosis of WA, quote, 12", EX	3,700.00
Jug, Peace, Plenty & Independence, 1800s, rpr, 9"	500.00
Jug, ship w/Am flag, Geo WA under spout, mc/gilt, 9", NM	1,950.00
Jug, Success to Trade, bk: Militia, Jefferson quote, mc, 9"	1,840.00
Jug, Washington/Liberty, mk Herculaneum, wear, 8"	925.00
Jug, Washington/Virtue & Valor, early 1800s, 9¾"	1,725.00
Plate, Returning Hopes, 1800s, 9¾", EX	175.00
Plate, 3-masted ship, mk Herculaneum, 1800s, 10", EX	315.00
Plate, 3-masted ship, scalloped rim, 10", EX	125.00
Punch bowl, harbor scenes, ship inside, 1800s, 12¼" dia	2,415.00
Tureen, 3-masted ship, blk w/mc pnt, 1800s, 14½", +ladle	1,600.00

Lladro

Lladro porcelains are currently being produced in Labernes Blanques, Spain. Their retired and limited edition figurines are popular collectibles on the secondary market.

Boy w/Bass, #4615	435.00
Boy w/Comet, #1105	485.00
Bull, 7"	200.00
Court Jester, Rockwell, #1405	850.00
Dormouse	350.00
Dutch Girl, #4860	300.00
Fishing w/Gramps, #5215	575.00
Flower Song	700.00
Free As a Butterfly, #1483	425.00
Full Moon, #1438	600.00
Girl Manicuring, #1082	275.00
Girl w/Brush, #1081	275.00
Girl w/Chicken & Basket, #4591, 9⅜"	85.00
Girl w/Lamb, #4584, 10⅝"	110.00
Great Dane, #1068	280.00

Hebrew Student, LN4684	600.00
In the Garden, LN4978	800.00
Kangaroo	150.00
Koala Love	150.00
Little Traveler	1,500.00
Little Troubador, LN1314	1,200.00
Looking for Refuge, LN4891	2,500.00
Madonna, #4649	140.00
May Flowers, sgn	450.00
Monkey	130.00
Olympic Ball, #5945	160.00
Plaque, Don Quixote, bl signatures	175.00
Rain in Spain, #2077	400.00
School Days	900.00
Sign, Collector's Society, wht bsk, 5¾x4"	25.00
Sport Soccer Girl, #5134	450.00
Spring Bouquets	1,200.00
Torchbearer, #5151	285.00
Traveler, club pc	1,250.00
Valencian Boy, #1400	475.00
Victorian Girl on Swing, #1297	1,450.00
Wrath of Don Quixote, #1343	725.00

Lobmeyer

J. and L. Lobmeyer, contemporaries of Moser, worked in Vienna, Austria, during the last quarter of the 1800s. Most of the work attributed to them is decorated with distinctive enameling; favored motifs are people in 18th-century garb.

Bowl, cobalt w/mc horses/nudes, 2 portraits ea side, ftd, 8"	500.00
Bowl, 18th-C people, fluted, oval, 5" L, +oval underplate	350.00
Box, intaglio lid w/nude & cornucopias, clear, 6" dia	750.00
Chocolate cup, maid serving man, faceted, +undertray, att	230.00
Tumbler, gold, scrolls/mc beading, ftd, 5¼"	500.00
Vase, gr patina w/gold & mc enameling, sgn, 1890, 8"	725.00

Locke Art

Joseph Locke already had proven himself many times over as a master glassmaker, working in leading English glasshouses for more than seventeen years. He came to America where he joined the New England Glass Company. There he invented processes for the manufacture of several types of art glass — amberina, peachblow, pomona, and agata among them. In 1898 he established the Locke Art Glassware Co. in Mt. Oliver, Pittsburgh, Pennsylvania. Locke Art Glass was produced using an acid-etching process by which the most delicate designs were executed on crystal blanks. Most examples are signed simply 'Locke Art,' often placed unobtrusively near a leaf or a stem. Other items are signed 'Jo Locke,' some are dated, and some are unsigned. Most of the work was done by hand. The business continued into the 1920s. For further study we recommend *Locke Art Glass, Guide for Collectors,* by Joseph and Janet Locke, available at your local bookstore.

Cup, punch; Poppy, sgn	86.00
Fruit cup, Vintage, ftd, sgn, 4½x5"	135.00
Goblet, Ivy	145.00
Honey dish, chrysanthemum in center, 4 at top, ftd	115.00
Sherbet, Ivy	260.00
Sherbet, Vintage, saucer ft	145.00
Tray, ice cream; eng florals, 16x8"	435.00

Tumbler, Grape & Vine	110.00
Tumbler, Vintage, vertical lines, optic ribs, 5"	135.00
Vase, Peonies, ruffled rim, 5"	585.00
Vase, Poppy, 6x3"	265.00

Locks

The earliest type of lock in recorded history was the wooden cross bar used by ancient Egyptians and their contemporaries. The early Romans are credited with making the first key-operated mechanical lock. The ward lock was invented during the Middle Ages by the Etruscans of Northern Italy; the lever tumbler and combination locks followed at various stages of history with varying degrees of effectiveness. In the 18th century the first precision lock was constructed. It was a device that utilized a lever-tumbler mechanism. Two of the best known of the early 19th-century American lock manufacturers are Yale and Sargent, and today's collectors value Winchester and Keen Kutter locks very highly. Factors to consider are rarity, condition, and construction. Brass and bronze locks are generally priced higher than those of steel or iron. Our advisor for this section is Joe Tanner; he is listed in the Directory under Washington.

Key:
bbl — barrel   st — stamped

Brass Lever Tumbler

Ames Sword Co, Perfection st on shackle, 2¾"	65.00
Automatic, emb, flat key, 2⅛"	15.00
Bingham's Best Brand, BBB emb on front, 3¼"	150.00
Cleveland 4 Way, Cleveland 4 Way emb on front, 3⅝"	90.00
Cotterill, st High Security key, 5⅛x3⅛"	290.00
Crusader, shield, swords emb on body, 2¾"	45.00
Eagle Lock Co, word Eagle emb on front, scrolled, 3"	60.00
Jackson's, st Jackson's on front, 2½"	20.00
JWM, emb, bbl key, 2⅝"	25.00
Keen Kutter, shape of KK emblem, KK emb on front, 4¾"	125.00
Mercury, Mercury emb on body, 2¾"	75.00
Motor, Motor emb on body, 3¼"	35.00
Our Very Best, OVB emb on body, 2⅞"	150.00
Roeyonoc, Roeyonoc st on body, 3¼"	30.00
Romer & Co, Romer & Co st on dust cover, 3"	55.00
Ruby, Ruby emb in scroll on front, 2¾"	20.00
Safe, Safe emb in scroll on front, 2⅜"	20.00
Siberian, Siberian emb on shackle, 2½"	110.00
Sphinx, sphinx & pharaoh head emb on front, 2¾"	35.00
W Bohannan & Co, SW emb in scroll on front, 2⅜"	30.00
Watch, emb, flat key, 3"	30.00
Winchester, Winchester emb on front, 3"	160.00

Combinations

Chicago Combination Lock Co, st on front, brass, 2¾"	60.00
Corbin Sesamee 4-Dial Brass Lock, st Sesamee, 2¾"	15.00
Edwards Mfg Co No-Key, st on lock, brass, 2¾"	60.00
Junkunc Bros Mfrs, all st on bk, brass, 1⅞"	30.00
Karco st on body, 2½"	50.00
Number or letter disk type (4 disks), brass, 2¾"	130.00
Quaint Mfg Co, st on lock case, 4¼"	200.00
Sq lock case of steel, st Pat Germany, 4-wheel, 3¼"	110.00
Sutton Lock Co st on body, 3"	200.00
Vulcana Push Lock Corp, st on lock case, 3¼"	50.00
Your Own st on body, 3⅞"	325.00

Eight-Lever Type

Armory, brass, Armory 8-Lever st on front 30.00
Electric, steel, Electric st on front 30.00
Goliath, steel, Goliath 8-Lever st on front 25.00
Miller, steel, Miller 8-Lever st on front 18.00
Samson, brass, 8-Lever st on front 18.00

Iron Lever Tumbler

Bull, word Bull emb on front, 2⅝" 30.00
Bulldog, word Bulldog & face of dog emb on front, 2¾" 30.00
Dan Patch, Dan Patch emb on front, horseshoe on bk, 2¾" 130.00
Dragon, word Dragon & dragon emb on front, 2⅞" 25.00
Eagle, word Eagle emb on body, 4⅜" 40.00
Indian Head, Indian head emb on front, 3" 90.00
Jupiter, word Jupiter/star & moon emb on front, 3¼" 18.00
Karo, word Karo emb on front, CI, 3⅛" 25.00
King Korn, words King Korn emb on body, 2⅞" 40.00
Nineteen O Three, 1903 emb on front, iron, 3⅞" 90.00
Red Chief, words Red Chief emb on body, 3¾" 90.00
Rugby, football emb on body, 3" 20.00
Unique, word Unique emb on front, 3¼" 120.00
Yale & Towne, lion face emb on front, shackle mk Y&T, 3" 110.00

Lever Push Key

Aztec, emb 6-Lever, 2⅛" 50.00
Celtic Cross, emb cross on face, brass, 2¼" 125.00
Champion, emb Champion 6-Lever, brass push-key type, 2¼" 25.00
Climax, emb Climax 6-Lever, iron push-key type, 2¼" 35.00
Columbia, emb Columbia 6-Lever, brass push-key type, 2¼" 35.00
Dash, emb Dash 6-Lever, iron push-key type, 2¼" 25.00
Duke, emb 6-Lever, 2⅛" 45.00
Excelsior, emb Excelsior 6-Lever, brass push-key type, 2¼" 25.00
Harvard, emb Harvard 4-Lever, brass push-key type, 2" 50.00
IXL, emb IXL on body, 2¼" 75.00
Jewett Buffalo, emb, brass, 2¼" 150.00
Keystone, emb Keystone 6-Lever, brass push-key type, 2¼" 40.00
McIntosh, emb McIntosh on body, 2¼" 90.00
SB Co, emb SB Co on body, 3¼" 60.00
Smith & Egge Mfg Co, Smith & Egge stamped on front, 3" 75.00
Ten Star, emb Ten Star 6-Lever, 2¼" 45.00

Logo — Special Made

Brass pancake push key emb US Internal Revenue, 2¼" 185.00
Heart-shape brass lever type emb Shults Co, bbl key, 2¾" 55.00
Heart-shape brass lever type st Board Education, bbl key, 3½" 65.00
Sq brass pin-tumbler case st Regd US Mail, int counter, 2¾" 140.00
Sq Yale-type brass pin tumbler, emb w/Texaco & star, 3" 30.00
Sq Yale-type brass pin tumbler, st Shell Oil Co on body, 3⅛" 25.00
Sq Yale-type brass pin tumbler, st US/A/tree/Forest Svc, 2⅞" 125.00

Pin-Tumbler Type

Corbin, brass, Corbin in oval st on body, 3⅝" 25.00
Eagle, brass, Eagle st on body, 2⅞" 20.00
Fulton, emb Fulton on body, 2⅝" 30.00
Hope, brass, emb Hope on body, 2½" 20.00
Il-A-Noy, emb Il-A-Noy on body, 2½" 40.00
Pearl, brass, emb Pearl on body, 2⅛" 20.00
Sargent, brass, emb Sargent on body, 3" 15.00
Segal, iron, emb Segal on shackle, 3¾" 30.00

Shapleigh, emb Shapleigh on body, 2⅝" 30.00
Yale, brass, emb Yale on body, Made in England on shackle, 3" ...30.00
Yale, brass, emb Yale on body, Yale & Towne on shackle, 2⅝" 25.00

Scandinavian (Jail House) Type

JHW Climax Co, iron, 2⅞" 50.00
Star, emb line on bottom, iron, 3¾" 100.00
Star, iron, 2½" 70.00
99 Miller, emb 99, brass, 1¾" 80.00
999 Miller, emb 999, brass, 2½" 70.00

Six-Lever Type

Eagle, brass, Eagle 6- Lever st on body 18.00
Edwards, iron, Edwards st on body 18.00
Safe, brass, Safe st on body 18.00
Yale, brass, Yale emb on front 12.00

Story and Commemorative

Top row, all Story locks, left to right: US canteen, $500.00;
US canteen, $500.00; Eagle Liberty, $300.00; Commemorative, NY to Paris, $150.00; Bottom row: Pancake push key,
Harvard, 4-lever, $50.00; Story, NHCo., $150.00; Iron
lever, Crusader, $45.00; Story, Scroll, $170.00.

AYPEX Seattle (Alaska Yukon Pacific Expo), emb tin/iron, 3" .235.00
CI, emb ornate scroll motif throughout body of lock, 3½" 170.00
CI, emb skull/X-bones w/florals, NH Co on bk, 3¼" 200.00
CQD/sinking ship Titanic & SOS waves emb on brass, 2¾" 120.00
Mail Pouch, emb on lock, lock in shape of a mail pouch, 3⅛" ...225.00
1901 Pan Am Expo, brass, emb w/buffalo, 2⅝" 175.00

Warded Type

Army, iron pancake ward key, emb letters, 2½" 40.00
Globe, iron sq lock case, emb US on bk, 2⅜" 20.00
Hex, iron, sq lock case, emb US on bk, 2⅛" 95.00
Navy, iron pancake ward key, bk: scrolled emb letters, 2½" 40.00
Red Cross, brass sq case, emb letters, 2" 10.00
Rex, steel case, emb letters, 2⅝" 18.00
Safe, brass sq case, emb letters, 1⅞" 8.00
Safety First, brass pancake type, emb letters, 2¾" 15.00
Secure, iron pancake type, emb letters, 2⅝" 20.00
Sprocket, brass oval shape, emb letters, 2⅛" 50.00
Try Me, iron pancake type, emb letters, 2½" 25.00
Winchester, brass sq case, st letters, 2¾" 125.00

Wrought Iron Lever Type (Smokehouse Type)

DM&Co, bbl key, 4¼" 20.00
MW&Co, bbl key, 2⅝" 10.00
MW&Co, flat key, 3½" 20.00
S&Co, bbl key, 3" 8.00

Loetz

The Loetz Glassworks was established in Klostermule, Austria, in 1840. After Loetz's death the firm was purchased by his grandson, Johann Loetz Witwe. Until WWII the operation continued to produce fine artware, some of which made in the early 1900s bears a striking resemblance to Tiffany's, with whom Loetz was associated at one time. In addition to the iridescent Tiffany-style glass, he also produced threaded glass and some cameo. The majority of Loetz pieces will have a polished pontil. Our advisor for this category is Don Williams; he is listed in the Directory under Missouri.

Bowl, oil spots on dk bl, bl/gold irid int, att, 1x3" 90.00
Box, gr irid w/lav threading, crystal beveled lid, 1½x4½" 140.00
Vase, appl prunt-flowers, red/wht/clear on bl, threaded, 4x6" 575.00
Vase, bl irid, bell form w/dimples, 4½" 325.00
Vase, bl irid, gold-amber ft, trumpet form, att, 10" 800.00
Vase, bl irid atop dk yel, pocked/pinched abstract, att, 5" 230.00
Vase, bl/gold w/textured striations, dbl gourd, att, 9½" 250.00
Vase, blk irid, bronze 3-D maid aside, bronze crown rim, 11" 225.00
Vase, cameo Deco floral/dots, purple on wht frost, att, 6½" 200.00
Vase, cameo leaf/vine panels, gold on orange-amber, 8x4" 2,875.00
Vase, clear w/irid, tree trunk, 3 openings, irregular rim, 10" 460.00
Vase, cobalt, cylindrical w/ruffled top, dimpled body, 14" 375.00
Vase, cobalt w/allover mc wavy-textured irid, dented, 6" 400.00
Vase, dk gr w/mc irid, dimpled shoulder, 8½" 130.00
Vase, emerald irid, bark texture, sq rim, dimpled, 10" 195.00
Vase, emerald w/irid craquelle texture, reverse swirl, 15" 1,500.00
Vase, etched florals/swirls on yel, wide ruffled rim, 8½x7" 500.00
Vase, feathers, lav-bl on emerald, ftd, early mk, 13" 850.00

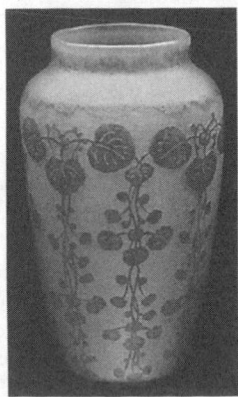

Vase, gold iridescent cameo-cut leaf and vine panels on orange-amber, 8", $2,825.00.

Vase, gold, appl daisy below folded rim ea side, 9" 550.00
Vase, gold, can neck, dented shoulder, ridged body, 6½" 285.00
Vase, gold, 3 tubes w/irregular openings on dome body, 5" 575.00
Vase, gr ribbed cylinder w/dimples, metal collar, 10" 450.00
Vase, jack-in-pulpit; emerald w/stretched bl irid, dented, 9" 350.00
Vase, lt gr w/mc irid, aqua coil about funnel neck, att, 6½" 230.00
Vase, lt gr/mc irid crackle, ruffled, triple gourd, 11" 200.00
Vase, lt yel, hooked/pulled decor in silver/bl, ovoid, 4½" 700.00
Vase, oil spots, bl/gold/lav irid, ruffled, tapering, 6" 600.00
Vase, oil spots, dk bl/aqua/gold on gr, pinched rim, att, 5" 500.00

Vase, oil spots, gold on amber, 3 pinched sides, 11" 865.00
Vase, oil spots, gold on amber irid, dented sides, 7" 865.00
Vase, oil spots, gold on gr, can neck, wide waist, 9" 575.00
Vase, oil spots, gold/platinum on clear, wide flat lip, 8¾" 460.00
Vase, oil spots, gr on pk irid, stick neck, petal rim, 13½" 600.00
Vase, oil spots, lav/gr irid, emb waves, crimped rim 6½" 600.00
Vase, oil spots, silver/bl on royal bl, flared U-form, 8" 800.00
Vase, oil spots on dk bl/mc irid, 4 long dents in sides, 14" 1,200.00
Vase, oil spots on gold, long neck, rim w/2 points, 9½" 1,300.00
Vase, oil spots on pk pearl, gold rim/ribbed hdls, 7" 900.00
Vase, oil spots on rubena verde, cylinder w/bulb bottom, 12" .1,000.00
Vase, oil spots on violet/gr/gold irid, 4-lobe rim, unmk, 8" 950.00
Vase, oil spots w/pulled & swirled lines, dbl bulb, 12x10" 2,000.00
Vase, oil spots w/pulled decor, dk bl/irid on yel, 6x8" 800.00
Vase, oil spots w/pulled decor, mc irid, crimped rim, 13x6" 1,200.00
Vase, orange w/irid bl & lav bands, wide invt cone, 6x8" 400.00
Vase, red-cased amber w/combed bl irid, shouldered, 7x7" 1,600.00
Vase, ruby w/textured silver craquelle pattern, waisted, 8" 425.00
Vase, ruby-pk w/irid gridwork, tooled tricorn rim, 11x5" 865.00
Vase, silver o/l floral on ruby irid, ftd, mk Pat, 4" 1,000.00
Vase, silver o/l leaves on bl/gr irid, royal bl int, att, 3½" 1,150.00
Vase, silver o/l lilies/leaves on emerald, int swirls, 7½" 2,750.00
Vase, silver o/l swan & lotus on bl irid, stick neck, 12" 3,250.00
Vase, threaded sqd pot, 4-leg metal base w/appl leaves, 10" 650.00
Vase, threading, gr on emerald, stick neck, flanged rim, 15" 375.00
Vase, waves, bl irid on ruby, squat w/stick neck, 11" 1,000.00
Vase, wht w/mc irid, appl bl irid vine, crimped top, 6" 130.00
Vase, yel irid w/mc highlights, wide crimped rim, 7½" 110.00

Lomonosov Porcelain

Founded in Leningrad in 1744, the Lomonosov porcelain factory produced exquisite porcelain miniatures for the Czar and other Russian nobility. One of the first factories of its kind, Lomonosov pieces consisted largely of vases and delicate sculptures. In the 1800s Lomonosov became closely involved with the Russian Academy of Fine Arts, a connection which has continued to this day as the company continues to supply the world with these fine artistic treasures. In 1992 the backstamp was changed to read 'Made in Russia,' instead of 'Made in USSR.' Some dealers may be pricing items marked 'Made in USSR' at 75% to 100% above prices listed below.

Bear, standing 13.00
Camel, young offspring 25.00
Cat 32.00
Collie (discontinued) 25.00
Doe 105.00
Fawn, mini (discontinued) 10.00
Foal, brn 23.00
Gazelle 10.00
Leopard Cub 15.00
Mongrel Dog, mini 5.00
Moose 125.00
Panda, sm 15.00
Raccoon 14.50
Rock Partridge #1 ....10.00
Seal 18.50
Snowbird 10.00
Snowbird Chick, mini 5.00
Terrier (discontinued) 24.00
Tiger Cub 28.00
Yakut Woman w/Fish 75.00

Longwy

The Longwy workshops were founded in 1798 and continue today to produce pottery in the north of France near the Luxembourg-Belgian border under the name 'Societe des Faienceries de Lonswy et Senelle.' The ware for which they are best known was produced during the Art Deco period, decorated in bold colors and designs. Earlier wares made during the first quarter of the 19th century reflected the popularity of Oriental art, cloisonne enamels in particular. The designs were executed by impressing the pattern into the moist clay and filling in the depressions with enamels. Examples are marked 'Longwy,' either impressed or painted under glaze.

Bowl, stylized berries on ivory crackle, w/gold, 7x10" 300.00
Box, semicircles/swirls, royal/med bl/aqua, #4029, 2x4" dia 210.00
Charger, floral, geometric border on aqua crackle, #5447, 12" 435.00
Charger, stylized deer in woods, blk on dk bl, 15" 365.00
Charger, 2 nudes & fawn, mc, Primavera, 14¾" 1,635.00
Charger, 2 seated nudes in desert garden, #1252, 15" 460.00
Pin dish, florals, pk on bl 65.00

Plaque, multicolor Limoges-style flowers with gold highlights, signed E. Killiert, Longwy D/1182, 17" diameter, $880.00.

Tile, Deco-style lady in garden, mk Primavera, 8" sq 400.00
Tile, 2 ladies gather flowers in meadow, mc, 8x8" 345.00
Vase, allover floral, red/wht/gr on scarlet, cylinder, 7", pr 425.00
Vase, grazing deer, bl/aqua/blk, #895, 11¾", pr 635.00

Lonhuda

William Long was a druggist by trade who combined his knowledge of chemistry with his artistic ability in an attempt to produce a type of brown-glazed slip-decorated artware similar to that made by the Rookwood Pottery. He achieved his goal in 1889 after years of long and dedicated study. Three years later he founded his firm, the Lonhuda Pottery Company. The name was coined from the first few letters of the last name of each of his partners, W.H. Hunter and Alfred Day. Laura Fry, formerly of the Rookwood company, joined the firm in 1892, bringing with her a license for Long to use her patented airbrush-blending process. Other artists of note, Sarah McLaughlin, Helen Harper, and Jessie Spaulding, joined the firm and decorated the ware with nature studies, animals, and portraits, often signing their work with their initials. Three types of marks were used on the Steubenville Lonhuda ware. The first was a linear composite of the letters 'LPCO' with the name 'Lonhuda' impressed above it. The second, adopted in 1893, was a die-stamp representing the solid profile of an Indian, used on ware patterned after pottery made by the American Indians. This mark was later replaced with an impressed outline of the Indian head with 'Lonhuda' arching above it. Although the ware was successful, the business floundered due to poor management. In 1895 Long became a partner of Sam

Weller and moved to Zanesville where the manufacture of the Lonhuda line continued. Less than a year later, Long left the Weller company. He was associated with J.B. Owens until 1899, at which time he moved to Denver, Colorado, where he established the Denver China and Pottery Company in 1901. His efforts to produce Lonhuda utilizing local clay were highly successful. Examples of Denver Lonhuda are sometimes marked with the LF (Lonhuda Faience) cipher contained within a canted diamond form.

Bowl, floral, sgn Jessie Spaulding, 3-ftd, mk/1899, 7" 265.00
Planter, floral, half-moon w/loop hdls ea end, ftd, 10" L 325.00
Plaque, lady's profile, ML McLaughlin, oval, #406, 3¼" 425.00
Vase, geraniums on shaded brn, bulbous w/3 splay ft, 6½x7" 325.00
Vase, gr leaves, bulbous w/long neck, sgn STR, 8¾" 170.00
Vase, pansy cvg, bl on dk brn, sgn MCL, 6x5", NM 3,250.00

Lotton

Charles Lotton is a contemporary glass artist. He began blowing glass and developing original designs nearly thirty years ago. He now has work on display in many major glass museums and collections, among them the Smithsonian, the Art Institute of Chicago, the Museum of Glass, and the Chrysler Museum. He has become famous for his unique lamps. Each piece is signed and dated. His three sons, David, Daniel, and John, each work in their own studios. All four artists produce distinctive work. They sell their glass at antique shows and in their showroom in Lansing, Illinois. For further information read *Lotton Art Glass* by Charles Lotton and Tom O'Conner; see the Directory under Illinois.

Bottle, scent; Multi-Flora, wht, 10" 700.00
Paperweight, 3 pk blossoms/curved bl stems/heart leaves, 2½" 60.00
Vase, Leaf & Vine, copper & bl, 10" 350.00
Vase, paperweight; Floral, cased cobalt, magnum, 10" 800.00
Vase, paperweight; Floral, on clear, 11" 450.00
Vase, Ruby Fern, cased gold, 8¾" 550.00
Vase, Zipper, bl irid, 6" 350.00

Lotus Ware

Isaac Knowles and Issac Harvey operated a pottery in East Liverpool, Ohio, in 1853 where they produced both yellow ware and Rockingham. In 1870 Knowles brought Harvey's interests and took as partners John Taylor and Homer Knowles. Their principal product was ironstone china, but Knowles was confident that American potters could produce as fine a ware as the Europeans. To prove his point, he hired Joshua Poole, an artist from the Belleek Works in Ireland. Poole quickly perfected a Belleek-type china, but fire destroyed this portion of the company. Before it could function again, their hotel china business had grown to the point that it required their full attention in order to meet market demands. By 1891 they were able to try again. They developed a bone china, as fine and thin as before, which they called Lotus. Henry Schmidt from the Meissen factory in Germany decorated the ware, often with lacy filigree applications or hand-formed leaves and flowers to which he added further decoration with liquid slip applied by means of a squeeze bag. Due to high production costs resulting from so much of the fragile ware being damaged in firing and because of changes in tastes and styles of decoration, the Lotus Ware line was dropped in 1896. Some of the early ware was marked 'KT&K China'; later marks have a star and a crescent with 'Lotus Ware' added. For further information we recommend *Collector's Encyclopedia of Knowles, Taylor & Knowles China*, by Mary Frank Gaston, our advisor for this category; she is listed in the Directory under Texas.

Bowl, prunus flowers emb on wht, beaded top, 4½" 350.00
Ewer, HP leafy sprigs w/gold, 9½" 375.00
Ewer, pk florals, gold-speckled twig hdl, 6½" 375.00
Ewer, Tiberian, pk & gr floral w/gold, dimpled body, 7" 1,100.00
Pitcher, leaves emb on wht, bulbous/squat, 5" 150.00
Pitcher, purple florals, H Schmidt, 5x7" 300.00
Shell dish, wht w/coral branch ft, 8" 165.00
Teapot, fishnet on wht, 4", +cr/sug, ea 4" 225.00
Vase, Cremonian, pk & wht flowers, gold trim, 6¼" 550.00
Vase, Egyptian, Victorian portraits, hdls, 15" 3,250.00
Vase, Etruscan, appl flowers, filigree hdls, whtware, 10" 1,350.00
Vase, Psyche HP in oval, baluster, hdls, 14½" 2,500.00
Vase, ruffled bowl form w/allover appl chains, 7½" 1,100.00
Vase, Tuscan, lav appl florals & fishscale work at rim, 8" 900.00
Vase, yel lily form w/mounded leafy base, gold trim, 8" 225.00

Lu Ray Pastels

Lu Ray Pastels dinnerware was introduced in the early 1940s by Taylor, Smith, and Taylor of East Liverpool, Ohio. It was offered in assorted colors of Persian Cream, Sharon Pink, Surf Green, Windsor Blue, and Gray in complete place settings as well as many service pieces. It was a successful line in its day and is once again finding favor with collectors of American dinnerware. For further information we recommend *Collector's Guide to Lu Ray Pastels* by Bill and Kathy Meehan.

Nut dish, embossed flower decoration, $35.00; Pitcher, bulbous with flat bottom, $45.00.

Bowl, '36s oatmeal 36.00
Bowl, coupe soup; flat 13.00
Bowl, cream soup 45.00
Bowl, fruit; Chatham Gray, 5" 12.50
Bowl, fruit; 5" 5.00
Bowl, lug soup; tab hdld 16.50
Bowl, mixing; 10" 75.00
Bowl, mixing; 7" 70.00
Bowl, salad 42.00
Bowl, vegetable; oval, 9½" 16.00
Bowl, 10¼" 85.00
Bowl, 7" 75.00
Bowl, 8¾" 75.00
Butter dish, Chatham Gray, rare color, w/lid 90.00
Calendar plates, 8", 9" & 10", ea 40.00
Casserole 70.00
Chocolate cup, AD; str sides 60.00
Chocolate pot, AD; str sides 360.00
Coaster/nut dish 65.00
Coffee cup, AD 18.00
Coffeepot, AD 135.00
Creamer 8.00
Creamer, AD, ind 40.00
Creamer, AD, ind, from chocolate set 92.00

Egg cup, dbl 18.00
Epergne 125.00
Gravy boat 13.00
Jug, water; ftd 75.00
Muffin cover 90.00
Muffin cover, w/8" underplate 115.00
Nappy, vegetable; rnd, 8½" 13.00
Pitcher, juice 135.00
Plate, cake 60.00
Plate, Chatham Gray, rare color, 7" 16.00
Plate, chop; 15" 25.00
Plate, grill; compartment 25.00
Plate, 10" 16.00
Plate, 6" 2.50
Plate, 8" 25.00
Plate, 9" 10.00
Platter, oval, 11½" 13.50
Platter, oval, 13" 16.00
Relish dish, 4-part 75.00
Sauce boat, fixed stand 23.00
Saucer, coffee; AD 8.50
Saucer, cream soup 22.50
Saucer, tea 2.00
Shakers, pr 13.00
Sugar bowl, AD; w/lid, from chocolate set 92.00
Sugar bowl, AD; w/lid, ind 40.00
Sugar bowl, w/lid 12.50
Teacup 8.00
Teapot, w/lid, curved spout 68.00
Teapot, w/lid, flat spout 75.00
Tray, pickle 24.00
Tumbler, juice 35.00
Tumbler, water 65.00
Vase, bud 215.00

Lunch Boxes

Early 20th-century tobacco companies such as Union Leader, Tiger, and Dixie sold their products in square, steel containers with flat, metal carrying handles. These were specifically engineered to be used as lunch boxes when they became empty. (See Advertising, specific companies.) By 1930 oval lunch pails with colorful lithographed decorations on tin were being manufactured to appeal directly to children. These were made by Ohio Art, Decoware, and a few other companies. In 1950 Aladdin Industries produced the first 'real' character lunch box — a Hopalong Cassidy decal-decorated steel container now considered the beginning of the kids' lunch box industry. The other big lunch box manufacturer, American Thermos (later King Seely Thermos Company) brought out its 'blockbuster' Roy Rogers box in 1953, the first fully lithographed steel lunch box and matching bottle. Other companies (ADCO Liberty; Landers, Frary & Clark; Ardee Industries; Okay Industries; Universal; Tindco; Cheinco) also produced character pails. Today's collectors often tend to specialize in those boxes dealing with a particular subject. Western, space, TV series, Disney movies, and cartoon characters are the most popular. There are well over five hundred different lunch boxes available to the astute collector. For further information we recommend *The Illustrated Encyclopedia of Metal Lunch Boxes* by Allen Woodall and Sean Brickell. Our advisor for this category is Allan Smith; he is listed in the Directory under Texas. In the following listings, lunch boxes are metal unless noted vinyl or plastic, and values include thermoses only when they are mentioned within the descriptions.

Annie Oakley & Tagg, Aladdin, 1955, EX 250.00
Ballet, Universal, vinyl, 1961, EX 700.00
Bang Bang, Thermos, plastic, 1982, EX 45.00
Barbie Lunch Kit, King Seeley, vinyl, w/thermos, 1962, EX 200.00
Black Hole, Aladdin, w/thermos, 1979, EX 80.00
Bond XX, Ohio Art, 1967, EX 200.00
Bozo, Aladdin, dome top, w/thermos, 1963, EX 400.00
Buck Rogers, Aladdin, w/thermos, 1979, EX 50.00
Care Bears, Aladdin, plastic, 1986, EX 15.00
Carousel, Aladdin, vinyl, w/thermos, 1962, EX 300.00
Cartoon Zoo, Universal, w/thermos, 1963, EX 440.00
Cowboy in Africa, King Seeley, 1968, EX 190.00
Curiosity Shop, Thermos, plastic, w/thermos, 1972, EX 75.00
Davy Crockett at Alamo, w/thermos, 1955, EX 330.00
Dawn, Aladdin, vinyl, 1971, EX 120.00
Dr Seuss, Aladdin, 1970, EX 110.00
Dudley Do-Right, Universal, w/thermos, 1962, EX 625.00
Dune, Aladdin, plastic, 1984, EX 40.00
Dutch Cottage, American Thermos, dome top, 1958, EX 480.00
Fat Albert, King Seeley, w/thermos, 1973, EX 50.00
Flintstones, Aladdin, w/thermos, 1964, EX 215.00
Frito Lay's, Thermos, plastic, 1982, EX 30.00
GI Joe, King Seeley, 1967, EX 125.00
Giant Eagle, Taiwan, plastic, 1978, EX 30.00
Girl & Poodle, Ardee, vinyl, w/thermos, 1960, EX 160.00
Great Wild West, Universal, 1959, EX 600.00
Hector Heathcote, Aladdin, w/thermos, 1964, EX+ 330.00
Hopalong Cassidy, Aladdin, 1952, EX 160.00
James Bond, Aladdin, 1966, EX 180.00
Jet Patrol, Aladdin, w/thermos, 1957, EX 375.00
Jr Miss Safari, Prepac, vinyl, 1962, EX 140.00
Jungle, unknown, plastic, 1990, EX 20.00
Kid Power, American Thermos, 1974, EX 45.00
Lance Link, King Seeley, 1971, EX 110.00
Lawman, King Seeley, w/thermos, 1961, EX 160.00
Little Orphan Annie, Thermos, plastic, 1973, EX 55.00
Lunch 'n Munch, American Thermos, vinyl, 1959, EX 480.00
Man From UNCLE, King Seeley, w/thermos, 1966, EX 230.00
Menuda, Thermos, plastic, w/thermos, 1984, EX 30.00
Miss Piggy's Safari Van, Superseal, plastic, 1989, EX 20.00
Mod Floral, Okay, w/thermos, 1975, EX 300.00
NFL Quarterback, Aladdin, 1964, EX 130.00
Open for Lunch, Taiwan, plastic, 1987, EX 30.00
Peanuts, King Seeley, w/thermos, 1966, EX+ 60.00
Popeye, King Seeley, w/thermos, 1964, EX 150.00
Porky's Lunch Wagon, American Thermos, dome top, 1959, EX .250.00
Rifleman, Aladdin, 1961, EX 330.00
Rocky, Thermos, plastic, 1977, EX 25.00

Roy Rogers, American Thermos Products, brown vinyl, 1960, NM, $195.00.

Roy Rogers (bl band), American Thermos, 1955, EX 110.00
School Days, Ohio Art, 1960, EX+ 120.00
Smurfs, Thermos (England), plastic, 1973, EX 15.00

Snoopy, King Seeley, dome top, w/thermos, 1968, EX 60.00
Snow White, unknown, vinyl, 1967, EX 285.00
Space 1999, King Seeley, w/thermos, 1976, EX+ 85.00
Star Trek Next Generation, Thermos, plastic, 1988, NM 25.00
Supercar, Universal, 1962, EX 300.00
Tom & Jerry, Aladdin, plastic, w/thermos, 1989, EX 45.00
Track King, Okay, 1975, EX 300.00
US Mail, Aladdin, dome top, 1961, EX 60.00
Waltons, Aladdin, 1973, EX 55.00
Wild Fire, Aladdin, plastic, 1986, EX 15.00
Winnie the Pooh, Aladdin, vinyl, 1967, EX 200.00
Zorro, Aladdin, red rim, 1966, EX 200.00

Maddux of California

One of the California-made ceramics now so popular with collectors, Maddux was founded in the late 1930s and during the years that followed produced novelty items, TV lamps, figurines, planters, and tableware accessories. Our advisor for this category is Doris Frizzell; she is listed in the Directory under Illinois.

#1019, swan console bowl (set), porc wht, 11½" 20.00
#1047, Contempo bowl (set), wht satin, 16½" 15.00
#1067, shell console bowl (set), pk, 16" 15.00
#2015, vase, Antique Gold, hdls, 12" 15.00
#206A, planter, Chinese Bell Tower, 8" 20.00
#2102, bowl, ftd 10.00
#221, vase, swan, wht, 12" 20.00
#225, vase, horse's head top, str-sided body, aqua, 12" 18.00
#3006, TV lamp/planter, half circle 25.00
#3017, seashell bowl, wht 15.00
#3095A, bowl, ped w/6 ind servers 25.00
#3251-L, tray, serving; 2-tier 20.00
#3275, gr pepper relish, w/lid 12.00
#3304, planter, bird 20.00
#400/#401, flamingo, pr 35.00
#510, planter, swan, blk, 11" 18.00
#515, planter, flamingo, pk, 10½" 45.00
#527, Chinese pheasant, 11½" 20.00
#528, planter, 2 birds in flight, pk & blk, 10" 20.00
#536, planter, bird in flight, 11½" H 20.00
#7001, ashtray, 12" dia 10.00
#7134, fish ashtray, 6" L 20.00
#809, TV lamp, shell, pearltone, 13" 20.00
#810, TV lamp, stallion, prancing, on base, 12" 20.00
#826, TV lamp, cockatiels 50.00
#828, TV lamp, swan planter, wht porc, 12½" 20.00
#829, TV lamp, deer (2), running, natural, 10½" 20.00
#839, TV lamp, mallard, flying, natural colors, 11½" 35.00
#841, TV lamp, head of Christ, 3-D planter 25.00
#844, TV lamp, prairie schooner (covered wagon), 11" 30.00
#846, TV lamp, nativity scene, 3-D planter, 12" 25.00
#859, TV lamp, Toro (bull), ft on mound, 11½" 20.00
#887, TV lamp, Persian Glory (horse head), 11½" 20.00
#889, TV lamp, Malibu shell, pearltone, 10¼" 20.00
#892, TV lamp, Colonial ship, 10½" 30.00
#894, TV lamp, Toro (bull), charging, walnut, 11½" 20.00
#896, TV lamp, bassett hound, 12½" 45.00
#897, TV lamp, mare & foal, wht porc 30.00
#907, doe, walnut, wht porc, tangerine, 12½" 15.00
#912/#913, Chinese pheasants, air-brushed colors, 11", pr 30.00
#914, stag, standing, natural colors, 12½" 15.00
#923, swans (2), blk matt, 10½" 25.00

#924, stag, standing, natural colors, 12½" 15.00
#925/#926, horses, rearing/charging, pr 20.00
#928/#929, mallards, male/female, natural colors, 9½", pr 40.00
#932, rooster, 10½" 30.00
#969, Early Birds, blk matt, tangerine, 14½", pr 25.00
#970, flamingo, flying, natural colors, 11" 45.00
#971, flamingo, winging, natural colors, 12" 45.00
#972/#973, bull, red, head up/head down, 11" L, pr 50.00
#982, horse, prancing 20.00
#984, elephant, sitting, 18" 25.00
Ashtray, red or yel, metal caddy w/6 ind trays 20.00
Cats, Deco style, blk matt, 12½", facing pr 45.00
Cockatiel, on branch w/appl flower, 11" 35.00
Cookie jar, #2101, Bear 50.00
Cookie jar, #2104, Queen 125.00
Cookie jar, #2108, Raggedy Andy 300.00
Cookie jar, #2110, Squirrel, Maddux of Calif 300.00
Cookie jar, #2113, Humpty Dumpty 300.00
Cookie jar, Beatrix Potter Rabbit, c Maddux of Calif 100.00
Cookie jar, Calory Hippy 50.00
Cookie jar, Cat, c Maddux of Calif 50.00
Cookie jar, clown, very lg 325.00
Cookie jar, Grape Cylinder 45.00
Cookie jar, Koala 75.00
Cookie jar, Scottie 75.00
Cookie jar, Snowman 75.00
Cookie jar, Strawberry 35.00
Cookie jar, Walrus 65.00
Deer & doe, stylized, elongated, 12", pr 30.00
Ducklings, 3 on grassy base 20.00
Flamingo Line, dbl flamingo vase, 5" 40.00
Flamingo Line, single flamingo planter, 6" 40.00
Planter, rearing horse, 10x7½" 22.00

Magazines

Magazines are collected for their cover prints and for the information pertaining to defunct companies and their products that can be gleaned from the old advertisements. In the listings that follow, items are assumed to be in very good condition unless noted otherwise. See also Movie Memorabilia; Parrish, Maxfield.

Key:
  M — mint condition, in original wrapper
  EX — excellent condition, spine intact, edges of pages clean and straight
  VG — very good condition, the average as-found condition

Boys' Life, 1913, October, EX, $15.00.

Avant Garde, 1969, November, John & Yoko cover, EX 10.00
Avant Garde, 1969, September, Picasso cover, EX 20.00
Esquire, 1941, April, Alberto Varga gatefold, EX 20.00
Harper's Bazaar, 1911, April, EX 25.00
House & Garden, 1939, November, Gone w/the Wind article, EX ..65.00
Illustrated London News, 1940, Christmas, EX 35.00
Jet, 1975, March 9, Florence Ballad cover article, EX 20.00
Ladies' Home Journal, 1903, February, Parrish cover, EX 15.00
Ladies' Home Journal, 1910, December, O'Neill cover, EX 15.00
Ladies' Home Journal, 1911, H Fisher cover, girl in fez, EX 35.00
Ladies' Home Journal, 1925, Wyeth City of Tyre cover 35.00
Ladies' World, 1913, June, Leyendecker cover, EX 35.00
Ladies' World, 1916, December, Underwood cover, lady & dog, EX 30.00
Life, 1937, January 4, FDR cover, EX 32.00
Life, 1937, May 3, Jean Harlow cover, EX 25.00
Life, 1939, May 1, Joe DiMaggio cover, NM 50.00
Life, 1940, September 1, Ted Williams cover, EX 45.00
Life, 1941, October 13, Lana Turner & Clark Gable, cover only .12.00
Life, 1943, July 12, Roy Rogers & Trigger cover, NM 35.00
Life, 1950, June 12, Hopalong Cassidy cover, NM 40.00
Life, 1950, May 8, Jackie Robinson cover, NM 35.00
Life, 1952, April 7, Marilyn Monroe cover, NM 45.00
Life, 1955, August 8, Ben Hogan cover, NM 60.00
Life, 1956, June 25, Mickey Mantle cover, NM 50.00
Life, 1956, March 26, Julie Andrews cover, EX 10.00
Life, 1961, August 18, M Mantle & R Maris cover, NM 45.00
Life, 1961, July 28, B Bardot cover, NM 15.00
Life, 1962, April 13, R Burton & E Taylor, w/insert, NM 125.00
Life, 1963, July 12, Steve McQueen cover, EX 16.00
Life, 1964, August 28, Beatles cover, NM 35.00
Life, 1964, December 18, Elizabeth Taylor cover, EX 12.50
Life, 1969, September 21, Woodstock Special Issue, NM 35.00
Life, 1971, June 25, Frank Sinatra cover, EX 15.00
Life, 1972, January 28, John Wayne cover, EX 26.00
Life, 1972, June 2, Racquel Welch cover, EX 7.00
Literary Digest, 1909, Leyendecker cover, EX 18.00
Look, 1943, April 6, Ingrid Bergman cover only, NM 5.00
Look, 1955, November 24, Dick Clark cover, VG 12.00
Look, 1956, February 7, Jackie Gleason cover, EX 12.50
Look, 1958, April 29, Churchill/Willie Mays articles, EX 20.00
Look, 1959, December 22, Arthur Godfrey cover, EX 12.00
Look, 1966, April 5, Barbra Streisand cover, EX 25.00
Look, 1971, September 7, Lucille Ball cover, EX 16.00
Playboy, 1953, 1st edition, Monroe nude cover, NM, $750 to ..1,000.00
Playboy, 1955, February, Jane Mansfield, EX 150.00
Playboy, 1956, November, Betty Blue, EX 60.00
Playboy, 1957, December, Linda Vargas, EX 34.00
Playboy, 1958, April, Felicia Atkins, EX 20.00
Playboy, 1959, November, Donna Lynn, EX 17.00
Playboy, 1960, May, Ginger Young, EX 17.00
Playboy, 1961, January, Connie Cooper, EX 32.00
Playboy, 1962, June, Merissa Mathes, EX 24.00
Playboy, 1963, August, Phyllis Sherwood, EX 24.00
Playboy, 1964, May, Terri Kimble, EX 26.00
Playboy, 1965, October, Allison Parks, EX 22.00
Rolling Stone, 1970, November 2, Hendrix cover, EX 50.00
Rolling Stone, 1971, August 5, Jim Morrison cover, EX 60.00
Saturday Evening Post, 1909, June 12, Boileau bride cover, EX 40.00
Saturday Evening Post, 1912, November 23, Boileau cover, EX ...20.00
Saturday Evening Post, 1964, June 13, Harry Truman cover, EX 7.00
Saturday Evening Post, 1964, October 31, LBJ cover, EX 7.00
Sports Illustrated, 1955, April 5, Ben Hogan cover, EX 25.00
Sports Illustrated, 1955, July 11, Yogi Berra cover, EX 20.00
Sports Illustrated, 1965, June 21, Mickey Mantle cover, EX 50.00

Teen, 1957, October, Jerry Lewis cover, EX 8.00
Teen, 1958, August, Dick Clark cover, VG 12.00
Teen, 1958, January, Pat Boone cover, EX 8.00
Time, 1939, December 25, V Leigh as Scarlett cover, EX 85.00
Time, 1947, April 14, Leo Durocher cover, M 50.00
Time, 1962, December 21, Vince Lombardi cover, EX 40.00
Time, 1980, September 29, Bear Bryant cover, M 20.00
TV Family, 1972, March, All in the Family cover, EX 16.00
TV Guide, 1953, July 3, Perry Como cover, NM 35.00
TV Guide, 1954, August 14, Martin & Lewis cover, NM 75.00
TV Guide, 1955, January 22, Ed Sullivan cover, EX 25.00
TV Guide, 1957, January 12, Lucille Ball cover, NM 95.00
TV Guide, 1958, May 3, Shirley Temple cover, NM 30.00
TV Guide, 1959, May 30, Steve McQueen cover, NM 45.00
TV Guide, 1960, March 12, Chuck Conners/Rifleman cover, NM ...35.00
TV Guide, 1961, October 14, Red Skelton cover, NM 9.00
TV Guide, 1962, September 8, Cast of Bonanza cover, NM 60.00
TV Guide, 1963, October 19, Judy Garland cover, NM 35.00
TV Guide, 1964, November 21, Gomer Pyle cover, NM 10.00
TV Guide, 1965, December 11, Cast of F Troop cover, NM 22.00
TV Guide, 1966, June 11, Cast of Gilligan's Island cover, NM 50.00
TV Guide, 1967, July 29, Rat Patrol cover, NM 42.00

Majolica

Majolica is a type of heavy earthenware, design-molded and decorated in vivid colors with either a lead or tin type of glaze. It reached its height of popularity in the Victorian era; examples from this period are found in only the lead glazes. Nearly every potter of note, both here and abroad, produced large majolica jardinieres, umbrella stands, pitchers with animal themes, leaf shapes, vegetable forms, and nearly any other design from nature that came to mind. Few, however, marked their ware. Among those who did were Minton, Wedgwood, Holdcroft, and George Jones in England; Griffin, Smith and Hill (Etruscan) in Phoenixville, Pennsylvania; and Chesapeake Pottery (Avalon and Clifton) in Baltimore.

Color and condition are both very important worth-assessing factors. Pieces with cobalt, lavender, and turquoise glazes command the highest prices. For further information we recommend *The Collector's Encyclopedia of Majolica* by Mariann Katz-Marks (see Directory, Pennsylvania). Values below are for pieces in mint condition. Our advisor for this category is Hardy Hudson; he is listed in the Directory under Florida.

Butter dish, musical instruments in relief, portrait medallions, 3-piece, Minton, 5½x10½", $7,000.00.

Basket, Bird & Fan, lav int, Wardles 580.00
Basket, florals on basketweave, arched hdl, 7⅝x8¼x5½" 350.00
Bowl, alternating lobster & vegetable panels, Wedgwood, 11" .1,000.00
Bowl, centerpc; Water Lily on Basketweave, G Jones, 2¼x14½" ..2,100.00
Bowl, dessert; Strawberry & Bow, Wedgwood, 6½" 125.00
Bowl, Lily, dolphin ftd, 9½x9½" 1,265.00

Bowl, Shell & Seaweed, Griffin-Smith-Hill, ca 1880, 8¼" 750.00
Butter dish, Shell, Seaweed & Waves, 7" 400.00
Butter pat, Aster, red w/gray & wht, Wedgwood 150.00
Butter pat, Morning Glory on Napkin, cobalt 195.00
Cake stand, Bird on Branch on yel, Eureka 350.00
Cake stand, Morning Glory on Napkin, 10" 275.00
Centerpc, 4 winged cherubs, ftd, lattice rim, Minton, 23" 4,000.00
Cheese keeper, Rope & Fern, 11½" 3,000.00
Cheese keeper, Swan & Lily on wht 1,500.00
Compote, bird in flight, Holdcroft, 2½x9½" 400.00
Compote, Classical Urn & Sunflower, Samuel Lear, 9¼" 385.00
Compote, Fish & Daisy on cobalt, Holdcroft, 6" 450.00
Compote, water lily held by nymph on dolphin, Holdcroft, 12" ..1,500.00
Condiment dish, bird on oak leaf, mc, Minton, 8¼" 1,200.00
Creamer, bird in flight, mc on cobalt 175.00
Creamer, Hawthorne, Etruscan, 3¾" 250.00
Creamer & sugar bowl, Dogwood on cobalt, G Gones, EX 550.00
Cup & saucer, Blackberry on turq 225.00
Cup & saucer, Cauliflower, Etruscan 375.00
Cup & saucer, Pineapple, yel w/gr leaves 275.00
Cup & saucer, Shell & Seaweed, Etruscan 350.00
Fish plate, mc mottle w/brn fins & tail, Minton, 10" L 330.00
Game dish, Oak Leaf & Basketweave, game on lid, Minton, 12½" .1,800.00
Gravy boat, Asparagus, gr & turq w/red & wht, attached plate ..360.00
Humidor, Indian princess w/mc floral headband, 6½" 250.00
Humidor, pug dog smoking cigar, 5½" 375.00
Match holder, Blk boy w/ear of corn on bridge, w/striker 600.00
Match holder, monk w/mug, w/striker, 12" 440.00
Mug, Bamboo, brn w/pk int, 4½" 175.00
Mug, Water Lily w/cobalt top, Etruscan 330.00
Mush bowl, Cauliflower, Etruscan 440.00
Nut bowl, water lily, w/frog, Minton, 4½x7" 450.00
Oyster plate, mc shells on agate body, Minton, 9" dia 550.00
Pitcher, Acorn, 7¼" 175.00
Pitcher, Basketweave & Floral, 6½" 175.00
Pitcher, birds feeding young in nest, English, 8" 350.00
Pitcher, Blackberry on Bark, Shorter & Son, 8" 200.00
Pitcher, English Rose, red on brn & yel, 7" 195.00
Pitcher, fish relief, cobalt & turq, Holdcroft, 7½" 450.00
Pitcher, flowers, mc on mottle, turq int, G Jones, 7½" 450.00
Pitcher, Hummingbird, 6¼" 225.00
Pitcher, milk; Fern, Etruscan, 8" 300.00
Pitcher, owl figural, cobalt hdl, 7½" 250.00
Pitcher, Shell & Seaweed, Etruscan, 5½" 550.00
Pitcher, Water Lily, mc, Samuel Lear, 5½" 225.00
Plate, Bamboo, Etruscan, 8" 175.00
Plate, Bird & Fan, Wedgwood, 9" 315.00
Plate, Blackberry, mc on wht, Wedgwood, 8" 175.00
Plate, butterfly/bee/floral, mc, Wedgwood, 9" 275.00
Plate, Cauliflower, Etruscan, 9" 275.00
Plate, Fan border, mc w/pk rim, Wedgwood, 9" 275.00
Plate, Fish & Daisy on cobalt, Holdcroft, 8½" 250.00
Plate, Maple Leaf on Basketweave, mottled, 9" 125.00
Plate, Running Stag & Dog on pk, bl band, brn border, 8¼" 150.00
Plate, Shell & Seaweed, Etruscan, 8" 325.00
Plate, Water Lily, yel border, Holdcroft, 8" 275.00
Platter, Asparagus, mottled leaves on wht, 13½x9½" 440.00
Platter, Banana Leaf, 9½x6½" 250.00
Platter, Begonia Leaf, mc, 11½x8½" 250.00
Platter, Corn & Floral, mc on wht, Wedgwood, 12½x9½" 350.00
Platter, Dog & Doghouse, 11" 195.00
Platter, Fish on Seaweed, mc on brn, 13x11" 440.00
Platter, Flying Crane & Fan, 13½x9" 300.00
Platter, Overlapping Leaf, mottled w/mc border, 11¼x8½" 225.00

Platter, Shell & Seaweed, Etruscan, 14x9½" 1,165.00
Platter, Sunflower, Wardles, 12½" 350.00
Punch bowl, Bird & Fan, mc on wht, Wedgwood, 7x12" 1,200.00
Punch bowl, Wheat & Ribbon, Samuel Lear, 6½x13½" 900.00
Salt cellar, sailor figural, Minton, 7½" 660.00
Sardine box, fish finial, leaves on base, G Jones, 7½x8½" 1,200.00
Sardine box, Pointed Leaves on cobalt, 4⅛x9¼x8¼" 775.00
Sardine box, Shell & Seaweed, Wedgwood, 1868, 7¼x8" 950.00
Spittoon, Shell & Seaweed, mc 800.00
Spooner, Shell & Seaweed, Etruscan 500.00
Sugar bowl, Shell & Seaweed, Wardles 440.00
Syrup, Pineapple, pewter top, 6½" 385.00
Syrup, Sunflower, Etruscan 660.00
Tea set, Cauliflower, Etruscan, 3-pc 750.00
Teapot, Bird & Fan, mc on yel, 6½" 330.00
Teapot, Dogwood on cobalt, G Jones, 6½" 770.00
Teapot, Pineapple, +cr/sug 500.00
Teapot, Rooster, turq int, G Jones, prof rpr 3,750.00
Teapot, Shell & Seaweed, Etruscan, 6" 800.00
Tray, bread; Pineapple, mc, 12½x10½" 330.00
Tray, Maple Leaf on lt bl, scalloped, 11¾x8¾" 275.00
Tray, Oak Leaf, Etruscan, 12" 325.00

Malachite Glass

Malachite is a type of art glass that exhibits strata-like layerings in shades of green, similar to the mineral in its natural form. Some examples have an acid-etched mark of Moser/Carlsbad, usually on the base. However, it should be noted that in the past fifteen years there have been reproductions from Czechoslovakia with a paper label.

Bottle, scent; 3 recessed leaves, metal cap, Bohemian, 4½" 230.00
Box, berries & bows, ca 1920, 3½" 210.00
Dish, Deco fish figural, Moser 145.00
Toothpick holder, emb putti 200.00
Vase, nude/vintage, faceted base, Moser, 9½" 250.00

Mantel Lustres

Mantel lustres are decorative vases or candle holders made from all types of glass, often highly decorated, and usually hung with one or more rows of prisms. In the listings that follow, values are given for a pair.

Apple gr Bristol w/gold decor, 7 cut prisms ea, 9⅝" 450.00
Gr w/enamel & gilt, 6" spear-cut prisms, Bohemian, 14½" 425.00
Gr w/florals & gold, 2 rows of prisms, 12¼x6½" 465.00
O/l, wht cut to cobalt w/HP florals & gilt, prisms, 9" 265.00
O/l, wht to cranberry, castellated rim, prisms, 10" 325.00
Pk Bristol w/gilt, scalloped, 8 prisms, 12" 595.00
Ruby w/gold decor, castellated rim, prisms, 11½" 435.00

Maps and Atlases

Maps are highly collectible, not only for historical value but also for their sometimes elaborate artwork, legendary information, or data that since they were printed has been proven erroneous. There are many types of maps including geographical, military, celestial, road, and railroad. The most valuable are those made before the mid-1800s. Geological condition is a major factor. Items with defects bring less than half the retail values listed below. Our advisor for this category is Murray Hudson; he is listed in the Directory under Tennessee.

Key:
CW — Civil War   hc — hand colored

Atlases

Colton's General Atlas, hc, 170 steel plate maps, 1857, EX 2,250.00
Cram's...of World, mc, 63 dbl-pg maps, 1887, sm folio 325.00
Johnson's New Illus Family, hc, 99 steel plate maps, 1863 ....1,450.00
Jones' Historical...of World, 41 dbl-pg maps, 1875, 20x15", EX .650.00
Middle TN Campaign of...1863, US Army, 1874, dbl folio, EX ..1,750.00
Tanner's Universal, 117 maps (32 of US), 1841, EX 4,750.00

Maps

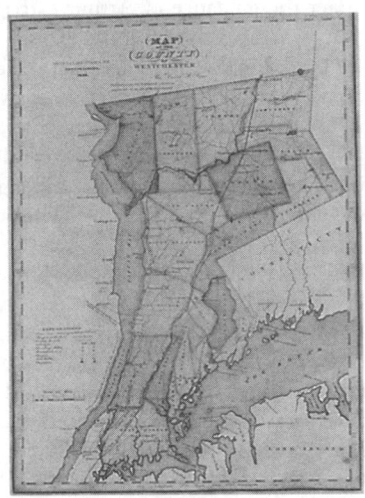

Westchester County of New York, David Burr, dated 1839, 18½x13" in frame, minor stains, $350.00.

AL, hc, steamer routes/canals/etc, Tanner, 1841, 14x11" 175.00
Alaska w/Klondike & goldfields, 1897, 24x36", EX 90.00
CA/NM/AZ/CO/UT/NV, hc, Johnson & Ward, ca 1861, 18x28", EX ..185.00
Chesapeake Bay Coast Chart #33, WA DC, 1862, 30x37½", EX ..175.00
Counties of KY & TN, hc, Mitchell, 9¼x12", EX 60.00
CT, hc, towns/railroads/canals, bright, Colton, 1855, 15x12" 60.00
DE/MD/VA/WV, hc, counties/towns/rivers, Mitchell, 1887, 15x22" ..35.00
IL, hc, vertical, Chicago inset, Mitchell, 1887, 15x22" 50.00
IN, hc, towns/railroads, Bradley, 1887, 12x15" 30.00
IN Territory, EX color, Indian lands/forts, 1887, 25x32" 75.00
Indian Reservations of US, w/forts/etc, dtd 1885, 22x33" 60.00
Indianapolis IN, streets, DF Dreher & Co, 1919, VG 20.00
Johnson's KY & TN, Johnson/Browning, NY, 1861, 17x24", VG .95.00
Johnson's MO & KS, hc, Johnson/Ward, 1862, 16x22", G 85.00
Johnson's PA & NJ, hc, AJ Johnson, 15¾x22½", G 60.00
KS &NB, hc, forts/railroads/towns/etc, Mitchell, 1887, 15x22" 45.00
KS/CO/Indian Territory, War Office, dtd 1867, 18x28", EX 90.00
LA/MS/AR/partial TX, hc, RC Smith, JB Lippincott, 12x10" 45.00
Louisville KY, Standard Printing, 1928, 34x28", G 18.00
MI/WI, hc, lakes/railroads/towns, Mitchell, 1887, 15x22" 35.00
Military posts, mc litho, forts/railroads/etc, 1907, 27x38" 30.00
NC/SC, hc w/insets, AJ Johnson, 1865, dbl folio 60.00
NH, hc, towns/railroads/etc, Colton, 1855, 16x12" 60.00
North Am, Chapman & Hall, 1843, 12x16½", EX 85.00
NY City/Brooklyn, hc, lg margins, Mitchell, 1887, 15x22" 40.00
OH, hc, towns/railroads, Milton Bradley/Mitchell, 1887, 12x15"..40.00
OR, Coos Bay area, tidal chart, 1865, 21x27" 55.00
Philadelphia City plan, hc, Bradley/Mitchell, 1887, 15x22" 35.00
Rocky Mtns to Pugent Sound, printed, J Davis, 1850s, 27x37" 85.00
St Louis MO, Chas Hoelscher, 1922, 39x28", VG 20.00
Transcontinental Main Travel Rtes, AAA, 1924, lg, VG 20.00

TX, forts/roads/Indian lands/etc, dtd 1857, War Dept, 18x28" ...100.00
US, hc, JH Daniels, S Walker, Boston, 1862, 9¼x15¼", EX 125.00
US, hc, towns/railroads/canals, Colton, 1855, 25x14", EX 250.00
US Touring Map, Texaco, ca 1920, VG 15.00
UT Territory, wagon roads/mtn ranges, dtd 1855, 19x22", EX 80.00
WA DC/Georgetown, hc, buildings/etc, Johnson, 1863, 15x12" ...65.00
WA Territory, trails/Indian areas/etc, Bien, 1859, 24x29" 75.00

Marblehead

What began as therapy for patients in a sanitarium in Marblehead, Massachusetts, has become recognized as an important part of the Arts and Crafts movement in America. Results of the early experiments under the guidance of Arthur E. Baggs in 1904 met with such success that by 1908 the pottery had been converted to a solely commercial venture. Simple vase shapes were often incised with stylized animal and floral motifs or sailing ships. Some were decorated in low relief; many were plain. Simple matt glazes in soft yellow, gray, wisteria, rose, tobacco brown, and their most popular, Marblehead blue, were used alone or in combination. The Marblehead logo is distinctive — a ship with full sail and the letters 'M' and 'P.' The pottery closed in 1936.

Bottle, scent; sarcophagus form, brn symbols on violet, 5", NM .375.00
Bowl, deep bl speckled, 2x8½" 200.00
Bowl, dk bl, incurvate, 2¾x5½" 250.00
Bowl, fruit; deep bl speckled, 3½x9½" 375.00
Bowl, gr gloss w/lt bl matt int, sgn AEB, minor bubbles, 4x12" ..375.00
Bowl, gray w/lt bl int, 2x6" 175.00
Bowl, lav, 4½x5½" 200.00
Bowl, lav speckled, closed rim, 2¾x5½" 200.00
Bowl, strawberry pk, 3½x5½" 325.00
Bowl, stylized cvd flowers, red/gr/bl on bl speckled, 5½" 1,400.00
Bowl, yel, 3¼x5" 250.00
Bowl vase, bl, 4¼x6½" 425.00
Bowl vase, lav, 3x5½" 325.00
Hanging basket, dk bl, 3 loop hdls, pointed bottom, 4x4½" 200.00
Inkwell, Arts & Crafts panels, gray on gr speckled, Tutt, 4" 2,600.00
Inkwell, geometrics, blk on dk gr, no liner, 3½x5" 1,000.00
Lamp, gray, hand thrown, 11½x7" 750.00
Pitcher, deep bl speckled gloss, bulbous, 6x6" 150.00
Tile, flower basket, peach/pk on dk brn, 6" 325.00
Tile, tree scene, brn/gr on bl, new fr, 4¼x4¼" 500.00
Tile, trees/clouds, 5-color, in oak fr, 4" 1,650.00
Vase, aqua/wine mottled shoulder/mid-section on lav, 4x5½" ...150.00
Vase, bl, bulbous (rare form), 5x6½" 375.00
Vase, bl, swollen cylinder, 7x3¾" 500.00
Vase, bl, tapering cylinder, 5x3" 300.00
Vase, bl speckled over lav, waisted, tapered neck, 6x3" 250.00
Vase, bud; deep bl speckled, elongated neck, 6" 225.00
Vase, bud; gray speckled, 5½" 150.00
Vase, bud; lav, elongated neck, 6" 150.00
Vase, bud; mauve, squat base, cylinder neck, 6x2½" 175.00
Vase, canary yel, waisted, 4¾" 250.00
Vase, cvd berries, lav on blk gloss, 4¼x4¾" 1,100.00
Vase, deep bl, ovoid, 3½x2½" 200.00
Vase, deep bl, waisted, 4½" 450.00
Vase, dk bl speckled, shouldered, 4x5½" 250.00
Vase, dk gr, shouldered w/short collar neck, 5" 325.00
Vase, floral, gray on bl, sea gull mk, 4" 1,100.00
Vase, floral at top, yel/bl/brn/gray-gr on tan, sgn HT, 3½" 950.00
Vase, floral w/long stems, bl on gray w/bl specks, 6x6", EX 1,000.00
Vase, floral w/long/narrow leaves, brn/olive, 7½x10" 16,000.00
Vase, fruit/leaves at rim, tan/bl/brn on gr, HT, 3x4½" 1,500.00
Vase, gray mottle, rnd base w/cylinder neck, 5½" 190.00
Vase, gray speckled, 3½x2¼" 125.00
Vase, heart leaves/stems, bl on gray speckled, 3½x3" 850.00

Vase, incised and painted Viking ships, blue, orange, and olive against light, medium, and navy blue, impressed mark, 14", $16,000.00.

Vase, lav, pear shape w/flared rim, 5x3¾" 425.00
Vase, lav/lt bl, shouldered, 2½x3¾" 175.00
Vase, leaves, simple/sytlized, lt gr on bl, Tutt, 3½x4½" 1,150.00
Vase, lt pk, squat, 1½x3½" 130.00
Vase, med gr flecked, cylindrical, 7½" 200.00
Vase, mustard, wht int, 3½" 220.00
Vase, panther stalking in panels, wht on bl, 8x9" 11,500.00
Vase, scalloped top band, gray on lt gray speckled, 3¾x4" 900.00
Vase, smoke bl speckled, swollen cylinder, 5¼x3¼" 225.00
Vase, trees, 3 repeats, navy/bl on gray, 6¾x4" 2,400.00
Vase, trees/leaves/berries, 4-color, EX contrast, 6¼x3¾" 2,000.00
Vase, 2-leaf stalks, gray on rose, AE Baggs, cylinder, 2½" 1,200.00
Wall pocket, bl speckled, ribbed, 5x4" 225.00
Wall pocket, turq speckled lustre, ribbed, 5x4" 250.00

Marbles

Marbles have been popular with children since the mid-1800s. They've been made in many types from a variety of materials. Among some of the first glass items to be produced, the earliest marbles were made from a solid glass rod broken into sections of the proper length which were placed in a tray of sand and charcoal and returned to the fire. As they were reheated, the trays were constantly agitated until the marbles were completely round. Other marbles were made of china, pottery, steel, and natural stones.

Below is a listing of the various types, along with a brief description of each. When size is not otherwise indicated, prices are listed for mint condition marbles of average size, ½" to 1".

Agates: stone marbles of many different colors — bands of color alternating with white usually encircle the marble; most are translucent.

Ballot Box: handmade (with pontils), opaque white or black, used in lodge elections.

Bloodstone: green chalcedony with red spots, a type of quartz.

China: with or without glaze, in a variety of hand-painted designs — parallel bands or bull's-eye designs most common.

Clambroth: opaque glass with outer evenly spaced swirls of one or alternating colors.

Clay: one of the most common older types; some are painted while others are not.

Comic Strip: a series of twelve machine-made marbles with faces of comic strip characters, Peltier Glass Factory, Illinois.

Crockery: sometimes referred to as Benningtons; most are either blue or brown, although some are speckled. The clay is shaped into a sphere, then coated with glaze and fired.

 End of the Day: single-pontil glass marbles — the colored part often appears as a multicolored blob or mushroom cloud.

 Goldstone: clear glass completely filled with copper flakes that have turned gold-colored from the heat of the manufacturing process.

 Indian Swirls: usually black glass with a colored swirl appearing on the outside next to the surface, often irregular.

 Latticinio Core Swirls: double-pontil marble with an inner area with net-like effects of swirls coming up around the center.

 Lutz Type: glass with colored or clear bands alternating with bands which contain copper flecks.

 Micas: clear or colored glass with mica flecks which reflect as silver dots when marble is turned. Red is rare.

 Onionskin: spiral type which are solidly colored instead of having individual ribbons or threads, multicolored.

 Peppermint Swirls: made of white opaque glass with alternating blue and red outer swirls.

 Ribbon Core Swirls: double-pontil marble — center shaped like a ribbon with swirls that come up around the middle.

 Rose Quartz: stone marble, usually pink in color, often with fractures inside and on outer surface.

 Solid Core Swirls: double-pontil marble — middle is solid with swirls coming up around the core.

 Steelies: hollow steel spheres marked with a cross where the steel was bent together to form the ball.

 Sulfides: generally made of clear glass with figures inside. Rarer types have colored figures or colored glass.

 Tiger Eye: stone marble of golden quartz with inclusions of asbestos, dark brown with gold highlights.

 Vaseline: machine-made of yellowish-green glass with small bubbles.

 For a more thorough study of the subject, we recommend *Antique and Collectible Marbles, 3rd Edition; Machine-Made and Contemporary Marbles, 2nd Edition;* and *Big Book of Marbles,* all by our advisor, Everett Grist; you will find his address in the Directory under Tennessee.

Agate, contemporary, carnelian, 1¾"	160.00
Banded Opaque, gr & wht, 2"	1,200.00
Banded Opaque, red & wht, 1¾"	1,200.00
Banded Opaque, red & wht, ¾"	95.00
Banded Transparent Swirl, bl, ¾"	75.00
Banded Transparent Swirl, lt gr, 1¾"	750.00
Bennington, bl, 1¾"	40.00
Bennington, bl, ¾"	3.00
Bennington, brn, 1¾"	30.00
Bennington, fancy, 1¾"	80.00
Bennington, fancy, ¾"	5.00
China, decorated, glazed, apple, 1¾"	800.00
China, decorated, glazed, rose, 1¾"	1,200.00
China, decorated, glazed, wht w/geometrics, 1¾"	125.00
China, decorated, unglazed, geometrics & flowers, ¾"	200.00
Clambroth, opaque, bl & wht, 1¾"	2,600.00
Clambroth, opaque, bl & wht, ¾"	250.00
Clambroth Swirl, red/wht, Germany, 1900, ⅞"	475.00
Comic, Andy Gump	100.00
Comic, Betty Boop	200.00
Comic, Cotes Bakery, advertising	700.00
Comic, Kayo, rare	400.00
Comic, Little Orphan Annie	100.00
Comic, Moon Mullins	300.00
Comic, set of 12	1,500.00
Comic, Skeezix	100.00
Comic, Tom Mix	2,500.00
Cork Screw, machine-made, common, ⅝"	5.00

End of Day, bl & wht, 1¾"	1,200.00
Goldstone, ¾"	35.00
Indian Swirl, 1¾"	2,500.00
Indian Swirl Lutz-type, gold flakes, ¾"	600.00
Line Crockery, clay, 1¾"	75.00
Mica, bl, ¾"	35.00
Mica, gr, 1¾"	800.00

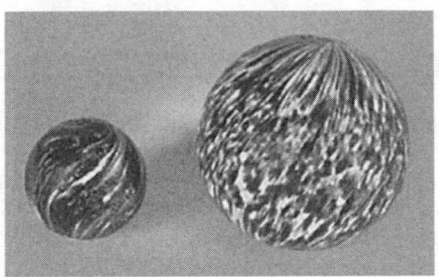

Onionskins: Green and white Lutz type, 1¼", EX+, $750.00; Red, white, and blue, 2¼", EX, $500.00.

Onionskin, w/mica, 1¾"	1,500.00
Onionskin, w/mica, ¾"	110.00
Onionskin, 16-lobe, unusual, 1¾"	1,800.00
Onionskin, ¾"	90.00
Onionskin, 4-lobe, 1¼"	450.00
Opaque Swirl, gr, ¾"	75.00
Opaque Swirl Lutz-type, bl, yel, gr, ¾"	325.00
Peppermint Swirl, opaque, red, wht, & bl, 1¾"	2,000.00
Peppermint Swirl, opaque, red, wht, & bl, ¾"	125.00
Pottery, 1¾"	75.00
Ribbon Core Lutz-type, red, 1¾"	1,800.00
Slag, machine-made, sm	3.00
Slag, machine-made, 1½"	150.00
Solid Opaque, gr, 1¾"	800.00
Solid Opaque, ¾"	75.00
Sulfide, alligator, 1¾"	250.00
Sulfide, bird, 2", EX	150.00
Sulfide, boar, 1⅞", EX	160.00
Sulfide, bust of George Washington, 2⅜", NM	1,000.00
Sulfide, cat, 1¼"	100.00
Sulfide, child sitting, 1¾"	600.00
Sulfide, child w/hammer, 1¾"	700.00
Sulfide, child w/sailboat, 1¾"	800.00
Sulfide, crucifix, 1¾"	800.00
Sulfide, dbl eagle, rare, 1¾"	675.00
Sulfide, dog, 1¾"	125.00
Sulfide, dog w/bird in mouth, 1¾"	900.00
Sulfide, dove, 1⅝", M	200.00
Sulfide, elephant, 1¾"	300.00
Sulfide, face of angel w/wings, 1¾"	1,000.00
Sulfide, fox, 1½", EX	130.00
Sulfide, goat, 1¾"	125.00
Sulfide, hen, 1⅛"	150.00
Sulfide, lamb, lt amber, 1¾"	1,600.00
Sulfide, lamb, 1¾", NM	125.00
Sulfide, lion, 2", NM	175.00
Sulfide, Little Boy Blue, 1¾"	700.00
Sulfide, owl w/wings spread, 1¾"	500.00
Sulfide, papoose, 1¾"	700.00
Sulfide, pig, 1¾"	150.00
Sulfide, pig, 2", M	180.00

Sulfide, pony, 1¾" 200.00
Sulfide, rabbit, 1¾" 150.00
Sulfide, raccoon, 2" 200.00
Sulfide, rooster, 1¾" 150.00
Sulfide, Santa Claus, 1¾" 800.00
Sulfide, sheep, 1¾" 150.00
Sulfide, squirrel, standing, 1¾", EX 170.00
Sulfide, squirrel w/nut, 2", EX 200.00

Marine Collectibles

See also Steamship Collectibles; Telescopes; Scrimshaw; Tools.

Binnacle, Chas Hutchinson Boston, 12", EX in orig dvtl case 275.00
Binnacle, Kelvin-White, brass, dome top, 11", VG 150.00

Binnacle, solid brass, made for a yacht by Hutchinson Boston, 10x3" diameter, complete with burner and wooden base, $825.00.

Chronometer, Hamilton Watch..., Model #22, brass/mahog, EX ...850.00
Chronometer, Negretti & Zambre London No 2081, 8-day, EX .3,600.00
Chronometer, Thomas Mercer Ltd, EX in case 925.00
Clock, Chelsea US Navy Deck Clock No 2, brass case, 5½", EX .175.00
Grappling hook, old wood hdl, 65" L 85.00
Harpoon, forged steel w/added rope, UDD on head, 32" 275.00
Harpoon, forged steel w/wood hdl, mk Cast Steel, 119" L 330.00
Harpoon, toggle type, Azorean, 20", EX 175.00
Horn, fog; Farraday, brass & metal, wooden hdl, 24" 300.00
Lantern, masthead; Elisha Webb...PA, brass, clear lens, 20", G ..200.00
Meter, current; W&LE Gurley Troy NY, NP brass, rare, EX 350.00
Octant, Hemsly Tower Hill London, ebony & brass, 12", w/case ..550.00
Octant, Spencer Barrett...London...NY, 1850s, eagle on case 600.00
Oil can, US Lighthouse Depot...NY, brass, rare, 5" 900.00
Periscope, Russian mks, hammer & sickle, 18", NM in case 200.00
Protractor, Negretti & Zambra, 8", in orig carrying case 130.00
Sailor's bag, pnt canvas, ship w/Am flags/fraternal, 47" 975.00
Sextant, Cassens & Plath Germany, brass fr, orig case 425.00
Sextant, H Lawrenson San Francisco, brass/silver, 6½" arm 325.00
Sextant, Owen Owens Liverpool, brass, 1800s, 9", w/case 525.00
Slate, ship's watch, folding, 1900s, 11x15" folded, EX 325.00
Sounder, Dobbie McInnes Glasgow, NM brass, 1800s, EX in box ..325.00
Sundial w/sm inset compass, wood w/paper dials, 3½x3¼" 300.00
Thermograph, L Maxant, pnt metal case, 1920s, 13½", EX 125.00
Wheel, bronze & aluminum w/wood grips, 30" dia 150.00
Wheel, Browner Grand Rapids, brass & mahog, 42" dia 500.00
Wheel, hardwoods w/inlay, brass hub, 36" 385.00
Wheel, teak & brass, old brn pnt, 49" dia 400.00
Wheel, yacht; bronze & mahog, 27", EX 200.00

Martin Bros.

The Martin Bros. were studio potters who worked from 1873 until 1914, first at Fulham and later at London and Southall. There were four brothers, each of whom excelled in their particular area. Robert, known as Wallace, was an experienced stonecarver. He modeled a series of grotesque bird and animal figural caricatures. Walter was the potter, responsible for throwing the larger vases on the wheel, firing the kiln, and mixing the clay. Edwin, an artist of stature, preferred more naturalistic forms of decoration. His work was often incised or had relief designs of seaweed, florals, fish, and birds. The fourth brother, Charles, was their business manager. Their work was incised with their names, place of production, and letters and numbers indicating month and year.

Bird vessel, brn beak, tooled feathers, sgn/1899, 11½" 6,900.00
Bird vessel, broad chest, narrow beak, sgn/1889, 10½" 6,300.00
Bird vessel, feathered neck ruffle, web ft, sgn/1900, 9" 4,000.00
Bird vessel, lg beak molded w/body, sgn/1884, 14" 8,620.00
Bird vessel, wide short beak, wide shoulders, sgn/1902, 9½" ...4,370.00
Bird vessel, wings behind, tooled feathers, sgn/1888, 13" 11,200.00
Bird vessel, 3 joined birds on oval base, sgn/1908, 8x7" 13,800.00
Figurine, seated Pan, ivory, 4½" 1,380.00
Jar, smiling face ea side, hat is lid, brn/tan/ivory, 8" 5,200.00
Jardiniere, monster head medallions, dragons/etc, 8½x11" 1,725.00
Jug, Eskimo face on wht w/gray & gr, silver rim, 12½" 900.00
Jug, fish on brn/ivory, sqd cylinder, 9½" 800.00
Jug, fish/octopus/sea-snail on ivory w/gr & brn, ovoid, 10½" ..1,600.00
Jug, smiling face ea side, tan/warm brn, 7" 3,680.00
Mug, smiling face, bk: doubtful face, brn/tan, 5¾" 1,800.00
Spoon warmer, creature w/gaping mouth, brn/gray, 5" 2,500.00
Spoon warmer, fish w/gaping mouth, blk/brn/ivory, 3½" 1,265.00
Vase, cvd winged lizards, wht/tan/dk brn on brn/blk, 9x5" 2,300.00
Vase, dragons, bees about rim, brn/ivory, drilled, 10" 1,150.00
Vase, dragons/snakes on caramel w/brn/ivory, flared neck, 18" ..2,300.00
Vase, gun-metal gloss, trn body, ring ft, mk, 1902, 8x3¼" 200.00
Vase, incised butterflies & leaves, RW Martin, 1881, 8¾" 500.00
Vase, sea creature on ivory w/pastels, sqd neck/body, 9½" 1,380.00
Vase, snake hdls arch down to bite rim, brns/gr, 6" 3,200.00
Vase, 4 dragons on brn/ivory, classic form, 9¾" 1,150.00
Wall plaque, fantastic creature w/open mouth, tan/brn, 6" 1,725.00

Mary Gregory

Mary Gregory glass, for reasons that remain obscure, is the namesake of a Boston and Sandwich Glass Company employee who worked for the company for only two years in the mid-1800s. Although no evidence actually exists to indicate that glass of this type was even produced there, the fine colored or crystal ware decorated with figures of children in white enamel is commonly referred to as Mary Gregory. The glass, in fact, originated in Europe and was imported into this country where it was copied by several eastern glasshouses. It was popular from the mid-1800s until the turn of the century. It is generally accepted that examples with all-white figures were made in the U.S.A., while gold-trimmed items and those with children having tinted faces or a small amount of color on their clothing are European. Though amethyst is rare, examples in cranberry command the higher prices. Blue ranks next; and green, amber, and clear items are worth the least. Watch for new glass decorated with screen-printed children and a minimum of hand painting. The screen effect is easily detected with a magnifying glass.

Bottle, liqueur; amber, boy w/kite, 9x3¾" 195.00
Bottle, scent; sapphire bl, girl in garden, 9½" 385.00
Box, bl, Dutch boy & wht flower sprays, w/lid, 2½x3½" dia 165.00
Box, jewel; lt amethyst, girl w/bag in garden, 2¼x3½" 375.00
Box, patch; cobalt, girl, hinged lid, 2" dia 200.00
Box, powder; gr, boy w/butterfly, lift-off lid, 6½x4" 200.00
Carafe, champagne color, boy w/butterfly net, 7⅝" 145.00

Cruet, amber, girl, amber stopper, 9x3½"	260.00
Cruet, dk amber, Optic, boy, amber hdl, 9½x3"	250.00
Cruet, gr, little boy, gr stopper, 8x3½"	265.00
Decanter, lime gr, boy on chair, bulbous, 10¼x5½"	235.00
Goblet, emerald gr, elk	135.00
Mug, amber, boy (& girl), bbl shape, 4", pr	145.00
Mug, liqueur; amber, boy (& gir), 1⅞", facing pr	125.00
Pitcher, emerald gr, girl w/tray, ribbed, 7"	195.00
Pitcher, sapphire bl, girl w/flowers, 2"	225.00
Pitcher, tankard; emerald gr, girl, clear hdl, 6x4"	165.00
Stein, amber, girl w/parasol & birds, w/metal lid, 6"	250.00
Tray, cranberry, boy w/butterfly, 10"	375.00
Tumbler, amber, girl, 4"	55.00
Tumbler, cranberry, girl, 3½"	125.00
Vase, amber/wht spatter, girl/foliage, 7x2½"	225.00
Vase, bl, boy on knee holds heart to girl, 11¾"	460.00
Vase, blk amethyst, girl in hat, 9¾x4"	195.00
Vase, chartreuse gr satin, boy feeding birds, 9¼"	165.00
Vase, cranberry, boy w/birdcage, flared rim/ftd, 11x4½"	425.00
Vase, gr, boy in suit, 11x3⅜"	85.00
Vase, gr opaque glossy Bristol, boy w/flowers, ped ft, 11"	225.00
Vase, lime gr, boy (& girl), clear rigaree on side, 11", pr	495.00
Vase, lt amber, girl in forest, bk: flowers, 6¾x3"	225.00
Vase, plum opaque, girl w/parasol (pnt features), ftd, 12"	250.00
Vase, sapphire bl, boy (& girl), 6¼x2¾", facing pr	195.00
Vase, sapphire bl, seated girl w/umbrella reads, 5x5"	245.00
Wine, gr, boy (& girl), gr stem & ft, 5¾x2½", pr	195.00
Wine, lime gr, boy (& girl), 5¾x2½", pr	170.00

Mason's Ironstone

In 1813 Charles J. Mason was granted a patent for a process said to 'improve the quality of English porcelain.' The new type of ware was in fact ironstone which Mason decorated with colorful florals and scenics, some of which reflected the Oriental taste. Although his business failed for a short time in the late 1840s, Mason re-established himself and continued to produce dinnerware, tea services, and ornamental pieces until about 1852 at which time the pottery was sold to Francis Morley. Ten years later, Geo. L. and Taylor Ashworth became owners. Both Morley and the Ashworths not only used Mason's molds and patterns but often his mark as well. Because the quality and the workmanship of the later wares do not compare with Mason's earlier product, collectors should take care to distinguish one from the other. Consult a good book on marks to be sure. The Wedgwood Company now owns the rights to the Mason patterns and is reproducing the Vista pattern under its Franciscan trademark. Note: Blue Vista is generally valued at 15% to 20% above prices for pink/red. Our advisor for this category is Susan Hirshman; she is listed in the Directory under Oregon.

Ashtray, Vista, bl, 4 for	50.00
Bowl, fruit; Regency, mc, 10"	250.00
Bowl, soup; Willow, bl, 9½"	100.00
Bowl, vegetable; Oriental scenes, mc, Ashworth, 9x7¼"	50.00
Bowl, Vista, bl, dragon head/tail hdls, 11"	250.00
Compote, Am Marine, red, 7"	250.00
Creamer, Watteau, mulberry, serpent hdl, 4½"	100.00
Ginger jar, Fruit Basket, mc, 5½"	40.00
Gravy boat, Fruit Basket, mc, 3x8"+tray	80.00
Jug, dragons & scrolls, mc, 8x4"	850.00
Jug, floral on cobalt, Fenton style, 8-sided, 5"	325.00
Jug, Oriental floral, mc, dragon hdl, 8½", EX	350.00
Jug, Oriental landscape, mc on dk orange, 8"	500.00
Jug, The Kill, dogs & wild boar, mc on cream, ca 1891, 7"	300.00

Jug, Vista, brn, serpent hdl, 7"	250.00
Jug, Vista, mulberry, serpent hdl, 6½"	225.00
Plate, Vista, bl, 10½", 6 for	200.00
Plate, Vista, brn, luncheon sz, 6 for	120.00
Plate, Vista, red, 10½", 6 for	200.00
Plate, Willow, mulberry, floral rim, 10½"	100.00
Platter, Bible, mc transfer w/HP flowers, 17" L	175.00
Platter, Regency, mc, 12x9½"	150.00
Platter, Vista, bl, scalloped rim, 16" L	300.00
Platter, Vista, red, 13" dia	195.00
Sugar bowl, Regency, mc, oval, w/lid	200.00
Teapot, Vista, brn, 9½", +trivet	295.00
Toothbrush holder, Bow, HP & mc transfer, 4x3"	60.00
Tureen, Vista, brn, w/lid, 11x14"+tray	550.00
Vase, red pheasant & floral, mc, 8x3½"	350.00

Massier

Clement Massier was a French artist-potter who in 1881 established a workshop at Golfe Juan, France, where he experimented with metallic lustre glazes. (One of his pupils was Jacques Sicardo, who brought the knowledge he had gained through his association with Massier to the Weller Pottery Company in Zanesville, Ohio.) The lustre lines developed by Massier incorporated nature themes with allover decorations of foliage or flowers on shapes modeled in the Art Nouveau style. The ware was usually incised with the Massier name, his initials, or the location of the pottery. Massier died in 1917.

Charger, tree on shoreline, mc irid, sgn/initialed, 12½"	1,800.00
Charger, 2 sailboats, mc irid, 13"	690.00

Plaque, profile of Ste. Cecilia, nacreous chartreuse, pink, blue, and gold, signed and marked, 21x15½", $5,000.00.

Plaque, stylized sunset, streaky irid, 18½"	1,800.00
Plaque, 2 men/nude on sea creature, gray w/mc irid, 13x11"	1,000.00
Vase, Chinese bl translucent gloss, hdls, 41x18", EX, pr	3,000.00
Vase, leaves/berries, lav/cream w/gold, sq rim w/hdls, 5½"	250.00
Vase, scallop shells, ivory/gold/dk red on sea gr, sq top, 12"	345.00
Vase, 3-leaf clovers, gold/gr irid, bulbous, 2¼"	285.00

Match Holders

Before the invention of the safety match in 1855, matches were kept in matchboxes and carried in pocket-size match safes because they ignited so easily. John Walker, an English chemist, invented the match more than one hundred years ago, quite by accident. Walker was working with a mixture of potash and antimony, hoping to make a combustible that could be used to fire guns. The mixture adhered to the end of the wooden stick he had used for stirring. As he tried to remove it by scraping the stick on the stone floor, it burst into flames. The invention of the match was only a step away! From that time to the present, match holders have been made in amusing figural forms as well as simple utilitarian styles and in a wide range of materials. Both table-top and wall-hanging models were made — all designed to keep matches conveniently at hand. Our advisor for this category is Ron Damaska; he is listed in the Directory under Pennsylvania. See also Advertising.

Advertising, American Brew Co., Rochester NY, Whites Utica, stoneware, 3x3⅜", $375.00.

Bsk, boy w/butterfly net 50.00
Bsk, girl in bonnet, Germany 35.00
China, cone-shaped holder on tray w/floral decor, Limoges 100.00
China, saucer type, box holder, Mayer 28.00
China chamberstick w/matchbox holder, Dresden 110.00
CI, alligator w/hinged bk forming lid, mc pnt, 8" L 65.00
CI, boy w/basket mtd on ashtray w/matchbox holder, Hubley 200.00
CI, C Parker, Pat Oct 1868, EX 215.00
CI, grape-cluster form 80.00
CI, rabbit & bird above single pocket, orig gold pnt, EX 200.00
CI, self closing, Pat 12/20/1864, rare sm version 90.00
CI, turtle w/urn on bk, 1850s, 3⅜" L 125.00
CI, urn, dbl; lacy, hanging, dtd 1867, 5½x7½" 80.00
CI, urn, dbl; mk Bradley & Hubbard, Pat 1/28/1868 ....100.00
CI, urn w/hdls, on sq saucer base, 3" 75.00
CI, wild game above 2 pockets, orig gold pnt, EX 200.00
CI, 2 urns with scrollwork 100.00
CI, 2-pocket, 4-ftd, arched hdl 80.00
CI, 2-pocket style w/scrollwork 80.00
Compo, Indian in full headdress, mc pnt, 7½x4⅞x3½" 50.00
Glass, lady's bloomers, 3" 145.00
Glass, Miss Liberty's head, 4½", NM 100.00
Lead, beatle figural, 4¼" 25.00
NP iron, hatchet, wall hanging, 1908 ....40.00
Parian, 2 owls on fallen tree, English, 8" 185.00
Pottery, saucer base on low stem, unglazed sides, 3½" 25.00
Redware, acorns & leaves, wht & gr, around pocket, 7" dia 165.00
Tin, crest w/crimped & cut-out decor, pnt traces, 4x7", EX 32.00

Match Safes

Match safes, aptly named cases used to carry matches in the days before cigarette lighters, were used during the last half of the 19th century until about 1920. Some incorporated added features (hidden compartments, cigar cutters, etc.), some were figural, and others were used by retail companies as advertising giveaways. They were made from every type of material, but silverplated styles abound. Both the advertising and common silverplated cases generally fall in the $50.00 to $100.00 price range. Our advisor for this category is Ron Damaska; he is listed in the Directory under Pennsylvania. See also Advertising.

Advertising, Arm & Hammer, gutta percha 55.00
Advertising, Gimball Printing, nickel, celluloid insets, NM 50.00
Domino figural, celluloid, 1⅛x1⅞" 110.00
Indian chief eng on MOP w/brass mts 95.00
Jockey on horse emb on NP brass horseshoe, 1¾x2" 155.00
Nouveau floral emb on SP, EX 75.00
Nouveau floral emb on sterling, inscr/dtd 1898 ....75.00
Nouveau foliage emb on wht metal w/sq center scene 75.00
Nouveau nude & 2 stallions in relief, Bristol Silver 155.00
Sea nymph emb on sterling 95.00
Shoe figural, lacquer, lift top 135.00
Sterling, plain, w/monogram, 2½" 80.00
Winged nude on diagonal stripes, German silver, 2½" 85.00

Mauchline Ware

Mauchline Ware is the generic name for small, well-made, and useful wooden souvenirs and giftware from Mauchline, Scotland, and nearby locations. It was made from the early 19th century into the 1930s. Snuff boxes were among the earliest items, and tea caddies soon followed. From the 1830s on, needlework, stationery, domestic, and cosmetic items were made by the thousands. Today, needlework items are the most plentiful and range from boxes of all sizes made to hold supplies to tiny bodkins and buttons. Napkin rings, egg cups, vases, and bowls are just a few of the domestic items available.

The wood most commonly used in the production of Mauchline Ware was sycamore. Finishes vary. Early items were hand decorated with colored paints or pen and ink. By the 1850s, perhaps even earlier, transferware was produced, decorated with views associated with the place of purchase. These souvenir items were avidly bought by travelers for themselves as well as for gifts. Major exhibitions and royal occasions were also represented on transferware. An alternative decorating process was initiated during the mid-1860s whereby actual photos replaced the transfers. Because they were finished with multiple layers of varnish, many examples found today are still in excellent condition.

Tartan ware's distinctive decoration was originally hand painted directly on the wood with inks, but in the 1840s machine-made paper in authentic Tartan designs became available. Except for the smallest items, each piece was stamped with the Tartan name. The Tartan decoration was applied to virtually the entire range of Mauchline ware, and because it was favored by Queen Victoria, it became widely popular. Collectors still value Tartan ware above other types of decoration, with transferware being their second choice. Other types of Mauchline decorations include Fern Ware and Black Lacquer with floral or transfer decoration.

When cleaning any Mauchline item, extreme care should be used to avoid damaging the finish! Mauchline ware has been reproduced for at least twenty-five years, especially some of the more popular pieces and finishes. Collectors should study the older items for comparison and to learn about the decorating and manufacturing processes.

Our advisor for this category is Marjorie Geddes; she is listed in the Directory under Oregon.

Bodkin case, Campbell Tartan..395.00
Bookmark, Bird's Eye View of World's Columbian Expo...1893, 9" ..45.00
Bookmark, Weymouth, 4½x¾" 45.00
Box, Alexandra Palace, 3¼x2¼" 58.00
Box, Hastings Pier, 3x2¼" 38.00
Box, spool; Llangollen..., orig label, spool pegs, 9¼x5" 225.00
Box, stationery; Lamont Tartan, fitted interior 650.00
Box, Weymouth, The Esplanade, oval, sm, 3" dia 75.00
Cotton holder, Clark & Co transferware..................................185.00
Darning needle case, Ryde Pier, Isle of Wight, 7¾" L 65.00
Flask holder, Present From Dunoon, Xmas scene, 3" 60.00

Glass holder, Trinity Church, Sheerness, 3" **55.00**
Hourglass, The Wish Tower Eastbourne, 2¾" **125.00**
Lap desk, Balmoral Castle+2 scenes, opens, mini, 7x9" **195.00**
Letter holder, Interior...Burns Cottage..., w/poem, 7½x4½" **125.00**
Monument thermometer, Burns Monument, 6½" **215.00**

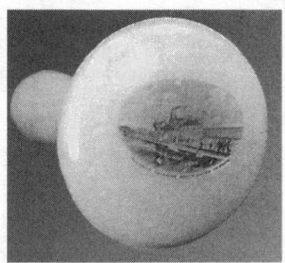

Needle case and darner, steamer entering South Haven, 4½", $65.00.

Needle case, Burns Cottage transfer **125.00**
Needle case, Loch Tay From Killin, cylindrical, 5½" L **67.00**
Needle case, Ruins of Old Abbey, Reading, cylindrical, 3½" **46.00**
Notebook, Prince Charlie Tartan, pnt panel view, 4" **225.00**
Pin disk, Glascow **165.00**
Pin disk, Tartan Ware, w/transfer view.....................................**265.00**
Pincushion, The Fountain Saltburn, 2" dia **42.00**
String holder, Burns Cottage Interior, 2" **125.00**
Tatting shuttle, McBeth Tartan...**345.00**
Tatting shuttle, McLean Tartan **345.00**
Thimble case, McDonald Tartan, egg shape...............................**265.00**
Watch holder, Church of Holy Trinity, Stratford on Avon, 3x4" ..**55.00**
Watch stand, Glasgow Green & Suspension Bridge, 5½" **150.00**
Whist marker, unnamed Tartan **115.00**

McCoy

The third generation McCoy potter in the Roseville, Ohio, area was Nelson, who with the aid of his father, J.W., established the Nelson McCoy Sanitary Stoneware Company in 1910. They manufactured churns, jars, jugs, poultry fountains, and foot warmers. By 1925 they had expanded their wares to include majolica jardinieres and pedestals, umbrella stands and cuspidors, and an embossed line of vases and small jardinieres in a blended brown and green matt glaze. From the late twenties through the mid-forties, a utilitarian stoneware was produced, some of which was glazed in the soft blue and white so popular with collectors today. They also used a dark brown mahogany color and a medium to dark green, both in a high gloss. In 1933 the firm became known as the Nelson McCoy Pottery Company. They expanded their facilities in 1940 and began to make the novelty artware, cookie jars, and dinnerware that today are synonomous with 'McCoy.' More than two hundred cookie jars of every theme and description were produced.

Stimulated by the high prices commanded by desirable cookie jars, a broad spectrum of 'new' cookie jars are flooding the marketplace in three categories: 1) Manufacturers have expanded their lines with exciting new designs to attract the collector market. 2) Limited editions and artist-designed jars have proliferated. 3) Reproductions, signed and unsigned, have pervaded the market, creating uncertainty among new collectors and inexperienced dealers.

More than a dozen different marks have been used by the company; nearly all incorporate the name 'McCoy,' although some of the older items were marked 'NM USA.' For further information consult *The Collector's Encyclopedia of McCoy Pottery* (with recently updated values) by Sharon and Bob Huxford, available at your local bookstore or public library. Numbers in listings below refer to this book.

Alert! It should be noted that the original Nelson McCoy Pottery

has closed its doors. Now an entrepreneur has emerged and has adopted the McCoy Pottery name and mark. This company is reproducing old McCoy designs as well as some classic designs of other defunct American potteries. Their wares are signed 'McCoy' with a mark which very closely approximates the old McCoy mark.

Cookie Jars

Animal Crackers **95.00**
Apollo Age, minimum value **1,000.00**
Apple, 1950-64 ....**40.00**
Apple on Basketweave **50.00**
Astronauts **650.00**
Bananas **95.00**
Barnum's Animals **350.00**
Baseball Boy **225.00**
Bear, cookie in vest, no 'Cookies' **75.00**
Betsy Baker **250.00**
Black Kettle, w/immovable bail, HP flowers **35.00**
Black Vase, w/flowers on lid **185.00**
Bobby Baker **85.00**
Bugs Bunny, cylinder **225.00**
Caboose **165.00**
Cat on Coal Scuttle **200.00**
Chairman of the Board, minimum value **400.00**
Chef **125.00**
Chinese Lantern **75.00**
Chipmunk **120.00**
Circus Horse **250.00**
Clown Bust **85.00**
Clown in Barrel **130.00**
Clyde Dog **150.00**
Coalby Cat **400.00**
Coffee Grinder **45.00**
Coffee Mug **40.00**
Colonial Fireplace **95.00**
Cookie Barrel **40.00**
Cookie Boy **225.00**
Cookie Cabin **125.00**
Cookie Jug, dbl loop **30.00**
Cookie Jug, single loop, 2-tone gr rope **25.00**
Cookie Jug, w/cork stopper, brn & wht **25.00**
Cookie Log **65.00**
Cookie Safe **65.00**
Cookstove **50.00**
Corn **150.00**
Covered Wagon **150.00**
Cylinder, w/red flowers **35.00**
Dalmatians in Rocking Chair **395.00**
Dog on Basketweave **85.00**
Drum **75.00**
Duck on Basketweave **75.00**
Dutch Boy **55.00**
Dutch Girl, boy on reverse, rare **150.00**
Dutch Treat Barn **50.00**
Elephant w/Split Trunk, rare, minimum value **425.00**
Engine, blk **175.00**
Flowerpot, plastic flower on top, minimum value **500.00**
Football Boy **225.00**
Forbidden Fruit **65.00**
Freddy Gleep **500.00**
Friendship **200.00**
Frontier Family **50.00**
Fruit in Bushel Basket **80.00**

Gingerbread Boy 75.00

Globe, $325.00.

Grandfather Clock 85.00
Granny 85.00
Granny, gold trim 125.00
Hamm's Bear 225.00
Happy Face 75.00
Hen on Nest 95.00
Hillbilly Bear, rare, minimum value 900.00
Hobby Horse 150.00
Honey Bear 85.00
Indian 350.00
Jack-O'-Lantern, minimum value 500.00
Kangaroo, bl 300.00
Kettle, jumbo sz 40.00
Kissing Penguins 85.00
Kitten on Basketweave 90.00
Kittens (2) on Low Basket, minimum value 800.00
Kittens on Ball of Yarn 120.00
Kookie Kettle, blk 35.00
Lamb on Basketweave 65.00
Leprechaun, minimum value 1,200.00
Liberty Bell 60.00
Little Clown 85.00
Lollipops 85.00
Mac Dog 95.00
Mammy, Cookies on base 225.00
Mammy w/Cauliflower, G pnt, minimum value 1,100.00
Modern 45.00
Monk 45.00
Mother Goose 150.00
Mr & Mrs Owl 110.00
Nursery, decal of Humpty Dumpty 100.00
Oaken Bucket 35.00
Old Churn 35.00
Pears on Basketweave 50.00
Pelican 175.00
Pepper, yel 40.00
Picnic Basket 75.00
Pineapple 65.00
Pineapple, Modern 60.00
Pirate's Chest 90.00
Popeye Cylinder 225.00
Potbelly Stove, blk 40.00
Puppy, w/sign 95.00
Quaker Oats, rare, minimum value 800.00
Red Barn, cow in door, rare, minimum value 350.00
Rooster, wht, 1970-1974 ....65.00
Rooster, 1955-1957 ....125.00
Round w/HP Leaves 55.00

Sad Clown 75.00
Snoopy on Doghouse 295.00
Snow Bear 85.00
Spaniel in Doghouse, pup finial 295.00
Stagecoach, minimum value 1,000.00
Strawberry, 1955-57 ....45.00
Strawberry, 1971-75 ....55.00
Teapot, 1971 ....50.00
Tepee, str top 325.00
Tilt Pitcher, blk w/roses 40.00
Tomato 35.00
Touring Car 125.00
Tudor Cookie House 125.00
Tulip on Flowerpot 185.00
Turkey, gr, rare color 300.00
Upside Down Bear, panda 75.00
WC Fields 225.00
Wedding Jar 110.00
Windmill 150.00
Wishing Well 45.00
Woodsy Owl 250.00
Wren House 150.00
Yosemite Sam, cylinder 225.00

Miscellaneous

Basket, Pine Cone, Rustic glaze, 1945 ....35.00
Bean pot, Kathy Kale, HP apple on yelware, 2-qt 75.00
Bowl, horizontal ribs on gr gloss, #11 in shield 40.00
Figurine, blk panther, no mk, 1950s, lg 40.00
Flowerpot, lg leaves emb at base of ribbed U-form, gr gloss 20.00
Grease jar, Cabbage, lg gr cabbage head on red base 55.00
Hanging basket, basketweave w/emb 'ring' hdls, aqua, 7½" ...32.50
Jardiniere, butterfly band, gr on tan matt, sm 30.00
Ladder pc, duck, head down, on tall base, no mk, sm 30.00
Ladder pc, hillbilly, seated, in lg hat, mk USA 75.00
Lamp base, rearing horse, textured gold 85.00
Loy-Nel Art, jug, ear of corn, 5½" 90.00
Pitcher, stylized chicken form, wht semigloss, ca 1943 ...25.00
Pitcher, tankard; Buccaneer, pirate emb on gr gloss 100.00
Pitcher, tilt type w/ice lip, yel gloss, no mk 30.00
Pitcher, Water Lily, fish hdl, gr gloss, no mk 55.00
Planter, Butterfly, lg figural, 1940 ....28.00
Planter, carriage w/separate umbrella, movable wheels ...90.00
Planter, cat w/gr bow, crouching, looking right, unmk, 1953 ...30.00
Planter, rolling pin, boy seated on top, no mk, 1952 ......65.00
Planter, spinning wheel, gr & tan gloss, 1953 ....20.00
Planter, stork by basket, 1956 ....40.00
Planter, stretch doggie, no mk, 1941, sm 100.00
Planter, 2 fawns, beige gloss w/blk accents, sm 20.00
Planter, 3 fawns by fence, trees in bkground, 1954, lg ...165.00
Planter bookends, hunting dog w/fowl in mouth, 1955, pr ...85.00
Tea set, Pine Cone, 3-pc 70.00
Tray, cupped hands w/leaves & berries at wrist, 1940s ...30.00
Vase, Blossomtime, appl flowers, 5" 25.00
Vase, emb birds, bk cherries, ftd, yel gloss, 8" 22.00
Vase, heart shape w/emb roses, pk gloss 25.00
Vase, leaf band emb at shoulder, closed hdls, yel, 9" 23.00
Vase, lily form, lg flower w/leaves at base, 1947 ....30.00
Vase, Onyx, bulbous w/hdls, 7" 65.00
Vase, poppies form, 3 lg flowers & leaves, 1955 ....100.00
Vase, Springwood, dogwood spray, wht on pk, pillow form ...25.00
Wall pocket, clock, weights on chains 55.00
Wall pocket, orange, leaf bkground 40.00

Wall pocket, owls on trivet **40.00**
Window planter, Grecian, gold swags w/gr highlights on wht **40.00**

McCoy, J. W.

The J.W. McCoy Pottery Company was incorporated in 1899. It operated under that name in Roseville, Ohio, until 1911 when McCoy entered into a partnership with George Brush, forming the Brush-McCoy Company. During the early years, McCoy produced kitchenware, majolica jardinieres and pedestals, umbrella stands, and cuspidors. By 1903 they had begun to experiment in the field of art pottery and, though never involved to the extent of some of their contemporaries, nevertheless produced several art lines of merit. Their first line was Mt. Pelee, examples of which are very rare today. Two types of glazes were used, matt green and an iridescent charcoal gray. Though the line was primarily mold formed, some pieces evidence the fact that while the clay remained wet and pliable it was pulled and pinched with the fingers to form crests and peaks in a style not unlike George Ohr.

The company rebuilt in 1904 after being destroyed by fire, and other artware was designed. Loy-Nel Art and Renaissance were standard brown lines, hand decorated under the glaze with colored slip. Shapes and artwork were usually simple but effective. Olympia and Rosewood were relief-molded brown-glaze lines decorated in natural colors with wreaths of leaves and berries or simple floral sprays. Although much of this ware was not marked, you will find examples with the die-stamped 'Loy-Nel Art, McCoy' or an incised line identification.

Corn, tankard, unmk, 1910 ....**350.00**
Loy-Nel-Art, bowl, floral, 3½" **225.00**
Loy-Nel-Art, jardiniere, Halley's Comet, 1910, 4" **400.00**
Loy-Nel-Art, jardiniere, iris, 1905, 5" **145.00**
Loy-Nel-Art, spittoon, floral, 1905, 6" **250.00**
Loy-Nel-Art, vase, floral, sm integral hdls, 9", minimum value ..**265.00**

Loy-Nel-Art, vase, floral on shaded brown, no mark, 1905, 8", $225.00.

Loy-Nel-Art, vase, pansies, hdls, 1905, 8" **250.00**
Mat Green, umbrella stand, unmk, 21" **500.00**
Olympia, pretzel bowl, unmk, 1905 ....**100.00**
Olympia, punch bowl, emb grapes, 1905 ....**495.00**
Olympia, vase, emb cattails, 1905, 8½" **295.00**
Olympia, vase, emb foliage, bulbous, angular hdls, 1905, 5" **250.00**
Onyx, clock, mk Jug-Time Novelty..., Pat Oct 21, 1924 ....**250.00**
Rosewood, vase, waisted form, unmk, pre-1903, 6" **150.00**

McKee

McKee Glass was founded in 1853 in Pittsburgh, Pennsylvania.

Among their early products were tablewares of both the flint and non-flint varieties. In 1888 the company relocated to avail themselves of a source of natural gas, thereby founding the town of Jeannette, Pennsylvania. One of their most famous colored dinnerware lines, Rock Crystal, was manufactured in the 1920s. During the thirties and forties, colored opaque dinnerware and kitchenware, Sunkist reamers, and 'bottoms up' cocktail tumblers were produced as well as a line of black glass vases, bowls, and novelty items. All are popular items with today's collectors. The company was purchased in 1916 by Jeannette Glass, under which name it continues to operate. Our advisor for this category is Lisa Rastello; she is listed in the Directory under Illinois. See also Animal Dishes with Covers; Depression Glass; Kitchen Collectibles; Reamers.

Batter jug, cobalt w/chrome trim **125.00**
Bottoms up, caramel **80.00**
Bottoms up, jadite, w/coaster **175.00**
Centerpiece, Honeycomb, pk, ftd **42.50**
Clock, Tambour Art Glass, pk or amber, 14" L **225.00**
Clock, Tambour Art Glass, Twin Ballerina, flashed color **150.00**
Dresser set, Shari, pk 7" base+2 metal compacts+2 perfumes+lid ...**190.00**
Lamp, Danse de Lumiere, gr frost, nude holds drape wide **750.00**
Lamp, Danse de Lumiere, pk frost, nude holds drape wide **700.00**
Lamp, pressed pattern, topaz w/clear prisms, electric **350.00**
Mug, jadite, Bottoms Down **185.00**
Pitcher, Prescutt, Yutec 'Eclipse' **45.00**
Punch bowl, Aztec, clear, w/base & 10 cups **300.00**
Stein, Serenade (Troubador), bl opaque, 4¾" **75.00**
Sugar bowl, Laurel, ivory **32.50**
Tumbler, custard **20.00**
Vase, Sarah, delphite, 12" **150.00**

Medical Collectibles

The field of medical-related items encompasses a wide area from the primitive bleeding bowl to the X-ray machines of the early 1900s. Other closely related collectibles include apothecary and dental items. Many tools that were originally intended for the pharmacist found their way to the doctor's office, and dentists often used surgical tools when no suitable dental instrument was available. A trend in the late 1700s toward self-medication brought a whole new wave of home-care manuals and 'patent' medical machines for home use. Commonly referred to as 'quack' medical gimmicks, these machines were usually ineffective and occasionally dangerous. Our advisor for this category is Jim Calison; he is listed in the Directory under New York.

Bleeder, brass, eng decor, EX in orig leather box **95.00**
Bleeder, folding, 2-blade, 3", w/brass case mk Borwick **85.00**
Blood pressure kit, Jarcho Pressometer, EX in 1½x14x5" case **30.00**
Bottle, apothecary; amber, Syr Simplex label, bl stopper, 8" **65.00**
Bottle, apothecary; amber, w/stopper, 1900s, 3½" **22.00**
Bullet probe, silver shaft w/porc tip, 1860s, 10" **325.00**
Dental drill, steel shaft w/sm driller head, ivory hdl, 5¼" **65.00**
Dose glass, cobalt, emb WR Warner & Co Phila, 1⅝" **22.50**
Dose glass, Enjoy Life Fismark Bitters Once a Day, 2½" **170.00**
Dr's bag, blk leather w/instruments & sm pill case, 1930s, EX **85.00**
Ear scoop, silver w/ebony hdl, dtd 1804 ....**265.00**
Ear trumpet, brass, 1860s, 3½" **335.00**
Eye cup, cobalt, emb Wyeth on 2 sides, 2 panels, 1¾", NM **14.00**
Eye cup, crystal, John Bull, 1917 ....**20.00**
Eye cup, gr, John Bull, 1917 ....**22.00**
Eye cup, gr glass, bulbous base, 2¼", NM **35.00**
Fleam, horn, 3-blade, ca 1830, EX **210.00**
Forceps, obstetric; steel blades, ebony hdls, 14½" **220.00**

Hammer, autopsy; unplated steel, ebony hdl, 1860s, 8¼" **70.00**
Inhaler, tin, Simplex Lamp Co, 1890s, 7", EX **20.00**
Knife, amputation; Liston type, blk hdl, John Wood, 14" **215.00**
Needle, arterial; S Maw, Son & Tompson, ivory hdl, 1860s, 7⅜" ..**50.00**
Pill-roller machine, hardwood w/brass bindings, 12½x7¼" **235.00**
Quack machine, Magneto-Electric...For Nervous..., 4x8x4", EX ..**55.00**
Spoon, glass, emb Phillips Milk of Magnesia, 4" **18.50**
Stethoscope, monaural, dk fruitwood, flat chest pc, 7" **265.00**
Surgical kit, 16 instruments in wooden box, 1840s, EX **350.00**
Syringe, irrigation; brass, Reynolds & Branson, 1890s, 8" **140.00**
Tongue scraper, tortoise shell & ivory, 1840s **185.00**

Meissen

The Royal Saxon Porcelain Works was established in 1710 in Meissen, Saxony. Under the direction of Johann Frederick Bottger, who in 1708 had developed the formula for the first true porcelain body, fine ceramic figurines with exquisite detail and tableware of the highest quality were produced. Although every effort was made to insure the secrecy of Bottger's discovery, others soon began to copy his ware; and in 1731 Meissen adopted the famous crossed swords trademark to identify their own work. The term 'Dresden ware' is often used to refer to Meissen porcelain, since Bottger's discovery and first potting efforts were in nearby Dresden. See also Onion Pattern.

Box, snuff; lady's leg form, pk shoe/wht stocking, 2½" **550.00**
Candlestick, gold-traced bl florals, 6-side top/base, 6" **175.00**
Chamberstick, red/pk flowers w/gilt, +cone-form snuffer **500.00**
Charger, wht w/emb gold foliage, Xd swords, 11" **325.00**
Compote, floral/bead-emb center, emb floral edge, gilt, 12" **575.00**
Cup & saucer, flowers in quatrefoils on yel, 1700s **325.00**
Desk set, red/pk flowers & vines w/gilt, tray+2 rnd pots **450.00**
Figurine, cherub, Coup Sur Coup, Xd swords, 5¾" **700.00**
Figurine, cherub tailor cuts cloth, Xd swords, 5" **265.00**
Figurine, cherub w/flower & bird beside birdcage, 5", EX **475.00**
Figurine, child kneels by fish trap, lobster in bag, 4¼" **525.00**
Figurine, Cupid by fluted column, Jes Les Unis, 5½", NM **450.00**
Figurine, Cupid holds heart, quiver on bk, 8½" **1,100.00**
Figurine, dog drinks from bowl, little girl sits beside, 3½" **500.00**
Figurine, falconer on plinth, Xd swords, 8" **265.00**
Figurine, lady card player, 6½", EX **425.00**
Figurine, lady sits at table listing her goods, rpr, 7" **1,300.00**
Figurine, lady w/grapes in apron, lg hat, 1880s, rprs, 6¾" **550.00**
Figurine, seated girl & cat, 1800s, 5" **900.00**
Figurine, Venus in bird-drawn chariot, cherub aside, 7", EX **650.00**
Medallion, Madonna del Sedia in panel, after Raphael, 2¾" **220.00**
Stein, HP porc, harbor scene, inlay lid, 1800s, mk, ¼-liter **3,100.00**
Vase, florals on cobalt, swan-head hdls, urn form, 20" **1,350.00**

Mercury Glass

Mercury glass was popular during the 1850s and enjoyed a short revival at the turn of the century. It was made with two thin layers, either blown with a double wall or joined in sections, with the space between the walls of the vessel filled with a mixture of tin, lead, bismuth, and mercury. The opening was sealed to prevent air from dulling the bright color. Though most examples are silver, blue and gold can be found on occasion. Remember that the value of this type of glass hinges greatly upon condition of the mercury lining. In the listings that follow, all examples are silver unless noted another color.

Bowl, clear appl ft, 4¾x9½" **90.00**

Candlestick, gold, dome base, 6", pr **85.00**
Goblet, gold wht enamel floral band, 5" **42.00**
Mug, clear hdl, 3" **30.00**
Reflector, tin mt on bk, 7" dia **35.00**
Spooner, HP floral **45.00**
Tie backs, emb flowers, pewter fittings, 3½" dia, pr **70.00**

Vase, hand-painted florals on silver, worn, 7¾", $40.00.

Vase, HP floral sprays in panel, 10", pr **225.00**
Witch ball, 18", +stand **195.00**

Merrimac

Founded in 1897 in Newburyport, Massachusetts, the Merrimac Pottery Company primarily produced gardenware. In 1901, however, they introduced a line of artware that is now attracting the interest of collectors. Marked examples carry an impressed die-stamp or a paper label, each with the firm name and the outline of a sturgeon, the Indian word for Merrimac.

Bowl, appl/cvd swirling leaves, dk gr mottled matt, 5x8½" **2,300.00**
Vase, cvd long-stem floral, feathered gr matt, 7x3¼" **3,750.00**
Vase, dk gr mottled, angle shoulder w/hdl, 3x6" **60.00**
Vase, feathered burnt orange/yel-gr matt, no mk, 4½x4½" **650.00**
Vase, thick lt bl w/yel-gr highlights at neck, flared rim, 9" **600.00**
Vase, volcanic oatmeal matt, doughnut collar, invt cone, 7" **250.00**
Vase, volcanic orange/gr matt, shouldered ovoid, label, 7½x3¾" ...**900.00**
Vase, 5 cvd/relief stylized trees on gr matt, 6x4¼" **1,000.00**

Metlox

Metlox Potteries was founded in 1927 in Manhattan Beach, California. Before 1934 when they began producing the ceramic housewares for which they have become famous, they made ceramic and neon outdoor advertising signs. The company went out of business in 1989.

Well-known sculptor Carl Romanelli designed artware in the late 1930s and early 1940s (and again briefly in the 1950s). His work is especially sought after today. Some dinnerware lines can be confusing. There are two 'rooster' lines, Red Rooster (red, orange, and brown) and California Provincial (dark green and burgundy), and there are two 'homestead' lines, Colonial Homestead (red, orange, and brown like the Red Rooster pieces) and Homestead Provincial (dark green and burgundy like California Provincial). For further information we recommend *Collector's Encyclopedia of Metlox Potteries* by our advisor Carl Gibbs, Jr.; he is listed in the Directory under Texas.

Cookie Jars

Raccoon, Cookie Bandit, $175.00.

Apple, Golden Delicious, 9½" 150.00
Apple, red, 3½-qt, 9½" 85.00
Apple Barrel, 3¾-qt, 11" 70.00
Barn, Mac's, minimum value 350.00
Barrel, gr apple finial 125.00
Basket, natural, w/gr apple finial 65.00
Bear, Ballerina 150.00
Bear, Circus, minimum value 350.00
Bear, Koala 125.00
Bear, Panda, no lollipop 100.00
Bear, Panda, w/lollipop, minimum value 350.00
Bear, Sombrero, Pancho 150.00
Bear, Teddy, bsk, brn, or wht, ea 45.00
Bear, Uncle Sam, minimum value 950.00
Bluebird on Pine Cone, glaze decor, 3-qt 175.00
Bluebird on Pine Cone, stain finish, 3-qt 90.00
Bluebird on Stump, glaze decor 200.00
Bucky Beaver 175.00
Calf, Ferdinand, minimum value 750.00
Calf, says 'moo,' 3½-qt, 10½" 375.00
Calico Cat, cream w/bl ribbon 150.00
Calico Cat, gr w/pk ribbon 225.00
Candy Girl, 9" 350.00
Clown, wht w/bl details, 3-qt 250.00
Cookie Barrel, 11" 125.00
Cookie Boy, 9" 350.00
Cow, purple w/mc trim 700.00
Cow, yel w/flowers, mc details 375.00
Cow, yel w/o flowers, mc details, minimum value 500.00
Dinosaur, any of 3 types, aqua, Fr bl, rose, or yel, ea 175.00
Dog, Bassett, minimum value 525.00
Dog, Gingham, bl 225.00
Dog, Scottie, wht 200.00
Drummer Boy, 2½-qt, minimum value 500.00
Duck, Francine 225.00
Dutch Boy 350.00
Dutch Girl, minimum value 350.00
Elephant, 11", minimum value 750.00
Fruit Basket, 4-qt 50.00
Grape 250.00
Hippo, Dottie, wht w/yel dots, minimum value 450.00
Humpty Dumpty, no ft, 11", minimum value 525.00
Humpty Dumpty, seated, w/ft 275.00
Lighthouse, minimum value 500.00
Little Red Riding Hood, minimum value 1,500.00
Mammy, Cook, bl 575.00
Mammy, Cook, red 850.00
Mammy, Cook, yel 500.00

Mammy, Scrub Woman, minimum value 2,000.00
Merry Go Round 225.00
Mother Hen, wht 150.00
Mushroom Cottage 350.00
Parrot, minimum value 350.00
Pig, Slenderella 175.00
Pinocchio, 11" 400.00
Pretzel Barrel, 11" 125.00
Rabbit, Easter Bunny, color glazed 325.00
Rabbit, Easter Bunny, solid brn, minimum value 550.00
Rabbit, Mrs Bunny, holding carrot 175.00
Rabbit on Cabbage, 3-qt, 10" 150.00
Rag Doll Girl, 2½-qt 175.00
Rocking Horse, 11", minimum value 500.00
Santa, standing, Blk man, minimum value 750.00
Santa, standing, solid brn, minimum value 900.00
Santa, standing, wht man 750.00
Santa Head, minimum value 450.00
Scout, Brownie or Cub, minimum value, ea 750.00
Space Rocket, 12⅞", minimum value 1,000.00
Squirrel & Nuts on a Basket 150.00
Squirrel Nut Barrel 175.00
Squirrel on Stump, glaze decor 175.00
Topsy, bl polka dots 575.00
Topsy, red polka dots, minimum value 800.00
Topsy, solid bl apron 550.00
Topsy, yel polka dots 575.00
Tulip, minimum value 500.00
Turtle, Flash, minimum value 900.00
Watermelon 325.00
Whale, bl, minimum value 500.00
Wheat Shock, 4-qt 125.00
Woodpecker on Acorn, 3-qt 400.00

Dinnerware

Aztec, beverage server w/juice cup lid 225.00
Aztec, bowl, fruit; 5¾" 16.00
Aztec, bowl, soup; 6¾" 22.00
Aztec, bowl, twin vegetable 180.00
Aztec, bowl, vegetable; 9⅜" 50.00
Aztec, cup & saucer 20.00
Aztec, jaw bone 115.00
Aztec, plate, dinner; 10¼" 20.00
Aztec, platter, 13" 65.00

California Ivy, creamer and sugar bowl, $45.00; Plate, 9¼", $11.00.

California Ivy, bowl, divided vegetable; 11" 45.00
California Ivy, bowl, salad; 11¼" 55.00
California Ivy, bowl, vegetable; w/lid, 11" 70.00
California Ivy, butter dish 50.00

California Ivy, celery, oval, 12" 40.00
California Ivy, chop plate, 13¼" 50.00
California Ivy, coaster, 3¾" 18.00
California Ivy, cream soup 28.00
California Ivy, cup & saucer 12.00
California Ivy, plate, dinner; 10¼" 13.00
California Ivy, platter, oval, 13" 40.00
California Ivy, platter, sm, 9" 30.00
California Ivy, shakers, pr 22.00
California Ivy, sugar bowl, w/lid 24.00
California Ivy, tumbler 22.00
California Provincial, bowl, basket vegetable; 8⅛" 45.00
California Provincial, bowl, divided vegetable; rectangular 60.00
California Provincial, bowl, rim soup, 8" 25.00
California Provincial, bowl, vegetable; w/lid 90.00
California Provincial, candlesticks, pr 80.00
California Provincial, carafe 135.00
California Provincial, coffeepot 125.00
California Provincial, creamer & sugar bowl, w/lid 55.00
California Provincial, cup & saucer 16.00
California Provincial, gravy 40.00
California Provincial, plate, dinner; 10" 18.00
California Provincial, plate, salad; 7½" 14.00
California Provincial, platter, lg, 13½" 50.00
California Provincial, shakers, hdld, pr 28.00
California Provincial, stein, w/lid 50.00
California Provincial, teapot 125.00
Colorstax, bowl, cereal; 6½" 12.00
Colorstax, bowl, fruit; 5½" 10.00
Colorstax, bowl, mixing; 3-pc set 85.00
Colorstax, bowl, vegetable; 9" 30.00
Colorstax, cup & saucer 12.00
Colorstax, flowerpot & saucer, 6" 28.00
Colorstax, plate, bread & butter; 6½" 7.00
Colorstax, plate, dinner; 10½" 12.00
Colorstax, plate, salad; 7¾" 9.00
Colorstax, platter, lg, 13⅛" 35.00
Della Robbia, bowl, vegetable; 10⅝" 40.00
Della Robbia, coffeepot 90.00
Della Robbia, cup & saucer 13.00
Della Robbia, plate, dinner; 10⅝" 13.00
Fruit Basket, bowl, baker; oval, 11¼" 40.00
Fruit Basket, coffeepot 80.00
Fruit Basket, cup & saucer 12.00
Fruit Basket, gravy w/attached tray 32.00
Fruit Basket, pitcher, med, 1-qt 40.00
Fruit Basket, plate, dinner; 10¾" 12.00
Fruit Basket, platter, med, 12⅜" 30.00
Golden Fruit, platter, med, 11⅛" 40.00
Golden Fruit, shakers, pr 24.00
Happy Time, bowl, fruit; 6" 14.00
Happy Time, bowl, lug soup; 5" 22.00
Happy Time, bowl, vegetable; 10" 50.00
Happy Time, bread tray, rectangular, 9½" 65.00
Happy Time, mug, cocoa; 8-oz 22.00
Happy Time, plate, bread & butter; 6⅜" 9.00
Happy Time, plate, dinner; 10" 15.00
Happy Time, plate, salad; 7½" 12.00
Homestead Provincial, ashtray, lg, 10" 35.00
Homestead Provincial, bowl, cereal; 7¼" 18.00
Homestead Provincial, bowl, fruit; 6" 15.00
Homestead Provincial, bowl, vegetable; sm, 7⅛" 45.00
Homestead Provincial, bread tray 70.00
Homestead Provincial, canister set, 4-pc 280.00

Homestead Provincial, cruet set, 5-pc w/wood base 180.00
Homestead Provincial, egg cup 30.00
Homestead Provincial, kettle casserole, w/lid 125.00
Homestead Provincial, pitcher, milk; 1-qt 65.00
Homestead Provincial, pitcher, water; 2¼-qt 85.00
Homestead Provincial, plate, chop 70.00
Homestead Provincial, salt & pepper mills, pr 85.00
Homestead Provincial, shakers, chickens, pr 56.00
Lotus, banana leaf, 11" 40.00
Lotus, banana leaf, 15" 50.00
Lotus, banana leaf, 20" 60.00
Lotus, banana leaf, 24" 75.00
Lotus, mug, 7-oz 22.00
Lotus, plate, dinner; 10½" 13.00
Lotus, shell chip & dip 55.00
Lotus, soup tureen, w/lid 160.00
Peach Blossom, bowl, divided vegetable; 10½" 50.00
Peach Blossom, celery 40.00
Peach Blossom, gravy boat, attached tray 40.00
Peach Blossom, jam & jelly 45.00
Red Rooster Provincial, bowl, lug soup; 5" 22.00
Red Rooster Provincial, bowl, salad; 11⅛" 75.00
Red Rooster Provincial, casserole, w/chicken lid 130.00
Red Rooster Provincial, coaster, 3¾" 18.00
Red Rooster Provincial, cookie jar, wooden lid 85.00
Red Rooster Provincial, creamer & sugar bowl, w/lid 48.00
Red Rooster Provincial, cup & saucer 14.00
Red Rooster Provincial, plate, bread & butter, 6⅛" 8.00
Red Rooster Provincial, plate, dinner; 10" 14.00
Red Rooster Provincial, plate, salad; 7½" 10.00
Red Rooster Provincial, platter, sm, 9½" 32.00
Red Rooster Provincial, tumbler 30.00
Sculptured Grape, bowl, soup; 8⅛" 20.00
Sculptured Grape, cup & saucer 16.00
Sculptured Grape, plate, dinner; 10½" 15.00
Sculptured Grape, plate, salad; 7½" 12.00
Sculptured Zinnia, bowl, cereal; 7⅜" 14.00
Sculptured Zinnia, bowl, divided vegetable; 9½" 45.00
Sculptured Zinnia, bowl, fruit; 6" 12.00
Sculptured Zinnia, cup & saucer 14.00
Sculptured Zinnia, mug 18.00
Sculptured Zinnia, shakers, pr 24.00

Miniatures

Aardvark 85.00
Bear, reclining, 5½" 65.00
Bee 25.00
Burro, standing or sitting, 3" 45.00
Caterpillar 25.00
Chimpanzee, ashtray 75.00
Dinosaur, 4½" 140.00
Duck, head up, forward or down, ea 35.00
Elephant, trunk up, stylized 50.00
Giraffe, 5¾" 85.00
Goose, head bk, forward or upright, ea 45.00
Indian elephant baby, sitting, 3¾" 85.00
Lizard, 9½" 85.00
Otter 75.00
Penguin, 3" 50.00
Scottie dog, either sz 65.00
Shark, 6" 75.00
Squirrel, 2" 35.00
Turtle, standing 50.00

Nostalgia Line

Amish figure **45.00**
Arabian horse, 7¾x8¾" **115.00**
Buggy **70.00**
Burro **60.00**
Circus horse, 6x6" **115.00**
Colt, prone, 4¼x3" **70.00**
Cutter sleigh, 8½" **85.00**
Dr's buggy, 9" **70.00**
Mail wagon **80.00**
Mama or Papa, ea **45.00**
Merrie Oldsmobile **85.00**
Mustang horse, 10x8" **125.00**
Piano & lid **80.00**
Saddle-bred horse, 6x6" **95.00**
Santa **65.00**
Trolley car **95.00**

Poppets

Alaskan girl, 5" **35.00**
Chimney Sweep, 7¾" **55.00**
Colleen, girl w/coiled hair, 7¼" **45.00**
Conchita, Mexican girl, 8¾" **60.00**
Eliza, flower vendor, 5⅝" **55.00**
Elizabeth, queen **45.00**
Emma the Cook, 8" **45.00**
Florence, nurse w/4" bowl **55.00**
Grover, w/4" bowl **65.00**
Molly, tambourine girl, 6⅜" **35.00**
Mother Nature, 6¾" **60.00**
Ronnie, choir boy #2 ....**45.00**
School Marm, w/4" bowl **65.00**
St Francis, 7¾" **60.00**

Mettlach

In 1836 Nicholas Villeroy and Eugene Francis Boch, both of whom were already involved in the potting industry, formed a partnership and established a stoneware factory in an old restored abbey in Mettlach, Germany. Decorative stoneware with in-mold relief was their specialty, steins in particular. Through constant experimentation, they developed innovative methods of decoration. One process, called chromolith, involved inlaying colorful mosaic designs into the body of the ware. Later underglaze printing from copper plates was used. Their stoneware was of high quality, and their steins won many medals at the St. Louis Expo and early world's fairs. Most examples are marked with an incised castle and the name 'Mettlach.' The numbering system indicates size, date, stock number, and decorator. Production was halted by a fire in 1921; the factory was not rebuilt. Our advisor for this category is Ron Fox; he is listed in the Directory under New York.

Key:
L — liter   PUG — print under glaze
POG — print over glaze   tl — thumb lift

#1010/1909, stein, PUG: dwarfs, pewter lid, ½-L **210.00**
#1024/2327, beaker, PUG: musician, ¼-L **80.00**
#1025/2327, beaker, PUG: woman in landscape, ¼-L **115.00**
#1028, stein, relief: couple at harvest/verse, inlaid lid, ½-L **175.00**
#1055/2271, stein, PUG: cavaliers & monkeys, pewter lid, ½-L ..**265.00**

#1093/2368, beaker, PUG: guitar player, ¼-L **100.00**
#1108, plaque, eched: castle on the Rhine, 17" dia **1,150.00**
#1108, plaque, etched: landscape w/bird, 16½", NM **1,100.00**
#1108, plaque, etched: landscape w/no bird, 17" **580.00**
#1108/1526, stein, PUG: castle, pewter lid, ½-L **220.00**
#1161, stein, etched: women & shield, pewter lid, 7-L **1,650.00**
#1187/2327, beaker, PUG: peasant lady, ¼-L **130.00**
#1212/1526, stein, PUG: man bowling, pewter lid, 1-L **440.00**
#1365, plaque, etched: castle on the Rhine, 17" dia **1,150.00**
#1370, stein, relief: couple & verse, inlaid lid, ½-L **165.00**
#1385, plaque, etched: man w/shield fighting, 1910, 14¾" **995.00**
#1526, stein, PUG: Der Dom Zu Trier, pewter lid, ½-L **300.00**
#1526, stein, PUG: Walsheim, no lid, 1-L, M body **55.00**
#1570, stein, glazed, mosaic, inlaid lid, sm rpr, ½-L, EX **265.00**
#1643, stein, tapestry: man drinking, pewter lid, .3-L, NM **400.00**
#171, stein, relief: farming people, inlaid lid, ¼-L, NM **175.00**
#1724, stein, etched: standing male figure, inlaid lid, ½-L **1,980.00**
#1733, stein, etched: jockey/rearing horse, inlaid lid, ½-L **2,200.00**
#1734, stein, etched: young couple, inlaid lid, 2.1-L **1,650.00**
#1801, stein, mosaic, floral, inlaid lid, ¼-L **265.00**
#1802, stein, mosaic: floral, inlaid lid, ½-L, NM **300.00**
#1856, stein, etched: eagle, inlaid lid, ½-L **1,550.00**
#1859, punch bowl, etched: drinking scene, rpr lid, 9-L **500.00**
#1909/1110, stein, PUG: drinking scene, pewter lid, ½-L **275.00**
#1909/1351, stein, PUG: portrait reserve, pewter lid, ½-L, NM .**445.00**
#1909/727, stein, PUG: dwarfs bowling, pewter lid, ½-L, NM ...**215.00**
#1932, stein, etched: cavaliers, bronze inlaid lid, ½-L **550.00**
#1997, stein, PUG/etched: portrait in shield, ½-L, M **695.00**
#2003, stein, etched: cavaliers, pewter inlaid lid, ½-L, EX **300.00**
#2041, plaque, etched: couple on horses at fence, lt wear, 15" **580.00**
#2049, stein, etched: chess, inlaid lid, ½-L, NM **3,400.00**
#2052, stein, etched: Munich Maid, inlaid lid, sm chip, ¼-L **160.00**
#2057, stein, etched: peasants dancing, inlaid lid, rpr, .3-L **200.00**
#2075, stein, etched; telegrapher, new lid, rprs, ½-L **715.00**
#2077, stein, relief: coat of arms, inlaid lid, .3-L **170.00**
#2077, stein, relief: 3 panels, inlaid lid, firing line, ½-L **175.00**
#2080, plaque, etched: 4 Kurassiers, 15" **1,300.00**
#2081, plaque, etched: horsemen, 15" **965.00**
#2082, stein, etched: Wilhelm Tell, inlaid lid, ½-L **1,265.00**
#2082, stein, etched: Wilhelm Tell, rpl inlay on lid, ½-L **695.00**
#2083, stein, etched: boar hunt, inlaid lid, ½-L **1,100.00**
#2090, stein, etched: man at table, inlaid lid, .3-L **750.00**
#2090, stein, etched: man at table, inlaid lid (cracked), ½-L **465.00**
#2100, stein, etched: warriors, inlaid lid, rprs, ½-L **280.00**
#2112, plaque, etched: gnome, lt wear on gold rim, 16" **850.00**
#2123, stein, etched: knight, inlaid lid, sm rpr, ½-L **850.00**
#2123, stein, etched: knight drinking, inlaid lid, ½-L **990.00**
#2133, stein, etched: gnome, inlaid lid, ½-L **2,850.00**
#2134, stein, etched: gnome, inlaid lid, ½-L **2,650.00**
#2134, stein, etched: gnome in nest, inlaid lid, rpr, .3-L **750.00**
#2140, stein, PUG: Yale baseball & football scenes, ½-L **1,045.00**
#2140/770, stein, PUG: Inft Regt Nr 96, new pewter lid, ½-L ...**300.00**
#2142, plaque, etched: military man on horse, 15" **600.00**
#2146, plaque, etched: infantry men, 15" **850.00**
#2176, stein, etched: cavaliers dining, inlaid lid, 1-L **745.00**
#2182, stein, relief: bowling scene, inlaid lid, ½-L **375.00**
#2211, stein, relief: dwarfs bowling on bl, inlaid lid, .3-L **160.00**
#2322, creamer, etched: Art Nouveau, 4½" **120.00**
#2322, plaque, etched: cavalier & barmaid, castle mk, 14½" ..**1,200.00**
#2327, beaker, PUG: Old Vienna, ¼-L **95.00**
#2327/1172, beaker, PUG: dwarf, ¼-L, NM **125.00**
#2358, stein, relief: dance scene, inlaid lid, sm chip, ½-L **180.00**
#2362, plaque, etched: Heidelberg castle, rim wear, 17½" **715.00**
#2368, beaker, PUG: elks, ¼-L **100.00**

#2373, stein, etched: St Augustine, old rpl pewter lid, ½-L 230.00
#2391, stein, etched: Lohengrin's wedding, inlaid lid, 1-L 2,300.00
#2401, stein, etched: Tannhauser, inlaid lid, 1-L 1,700.00
#2442, plaque, cameo: Roman soldiers in boat, 18" dia 1,300.00
#2443, plaque, cameo: Roman lady & servants, 18" dia 1,150.00
#2520, stein, etched: student & barmaid, inlaid lid, 1-L 825.00
#2533, plaque, etched: castle, 17½" 715.00
#2548, plaque, etched: Nouveau lady & flowers, 18" 1,485.00
#2561, plaque, etched: trees landscape, 17½" 850.00
#2563, plaque, etched: bicyclists, 17½" 4,290.00
#2581, stein, etched: singing women, inlaid lid, ½-L 635.00
#2585, stein, etched/relief: Munich Maid on world, 1-L 850.00
#2604, pitcher, etched: Art Nouveau, flake, 11" 850.00
#2622, plaque, etched: man making toast, 7¾" dia 275.00
#2624, plaque, etched: man smoking, 7¾" dia 275.00
#2632, stein, etched: drinking scene, inlaid lid, ½-L, NM 350.00
#2717, stein, etched: target, inlaid lid, ½-L 3,500.00
#2718, stein, etched: David & Goliath, inlaid lid, 1-l 2,550.00
#2718, stein, etched: David & Goliath, inlaid lid, ½-L 2,650.00
#2721, stein, etched: cabinetmaker, inlaid lid, sm rpr, ½-L 770.00
#2722, stein, etched: man on horse, inlaid lid, rpr, ½-L 850.00
#2722, stein, etched: man's portrait reserve, inlay rpr, ½-L 850.00
#2755, stein, cameo: drinking scenes, inlaid lid, ½-L, NM 440.00
#2764, stein, etched: knight on horse, inlaid lid, rpr, ⅝-L 3,400.00
#2765, stein, etched; knight on wht horse, inlaid lid, 1-L 3,625.00
#2796, stein, etched: Heidelberg scene, inlaid lid, 3-L 1,450.00
#2828, stein, decor relief: Wartburg on body & lid, ½-L 3,400.00
#2829, stein, decor relief: Rodenstein, inlaid lid, ½-L 2,550.00
#2842, beaker, PUG: dwarf drinking, sm rpr, ¼-L 55.00
#2842/1173, beaker, PUG: dwarf drinking, ¼-L 150.00
#2935, stein, etched: hops & barley, inlaid lid, flake, ½-L 600.00
#2947, pitcher, etched: Art Nouveau, 4½" 250.00
#2960, tray, etched: Art Nouveau, 15", NM 240.00
#3068, sugar bowl, etched: Art Nouveau, 4", NM 60.00
#3089, stein, etched: Diogenes, inlaid lid, 1-L 1,100.00
#3091, stein, etched: knight drinking, inlaid lid, 1-L 1,400.00
#3092, stein, etched: barrel man, inlaid lid, 1-L 880.00
#3093, stein, etched: troll, inlaid lid, strap rpr, ½-L 2,530.00
#3095, mug, PUG: Hires Root Beer, ¼-L 190.00
#3096, cup & saucer, etched: Art Nouveau, rare, 6½" 250.00

#3254, stein, etched Alpine couple and dog, inlaid lid, ½-L, poor repair, $300.00; #1786, stein, etched St. Florian, alligator head, poor repairs, ½-L, $275.00; #2394, stein, etched Siegfried, inlaid lid, factory glaze flaw, ½-L, M, $525.00.

#3321, plate, etched: Art Nouveau, 9" 66.00
#3435, stein, relief: child soldier, pewter lid, rare, ½-L 440.00
#377, ashtray, yel & platinum, early, 7½" dia 130.00
#38, vase, relief: florals, worn platinum 115.00
#421, stein, relief: tree trunk, inlaid lid (sm chip), 1-L 150.00

#589/1526, stein, PUG: drinking scene, inlaid lid, ½-L, NM 175.00
#6146/2327, beaker, Rookwood type, ¼-L, EX 85.00
#675, stein, relief: keg, inlaid lid (rpr), ½-L 110.00
#7032, plaque, cameo: lady's head, mk, 7½x9" 395.00
#979/1909, stein, PUG: Blk children in school, pewter lid, ½-L ..800.00

Microscopes

The microscope has taken on many forms during its 250-year evolutionary period. The current collectors' market primarily includes examples from England, those surplused from institutions, and continental beginner and intermediate forms which sold through Sears Roebuck & Company and other retailers of technical instruments. Earlier examples have brass maintubes which are unpainted. Later, more common examples are all black with brass or silver knobs and horseshoe-shaped bases. Early and more complex forms are the most valuable; these always had hardwood cases to house the delicate instruments and their accessories. Instruments were never polished during use, and those that have been polished to use as decorator pieces are of little interest to most avid collectors. Our advisor for this category is Dale Beeks; he is listed in the Directory under Idaho.

Acme, brass & iron, 14" case, EX 350.00
Bausch & Lomb, all brass, horseshoe base, 1897, 14", EX 350.00
Bausch & Lomb, blk, horseshoe base, 1915, EX 150.00
Bausch & Lomb, blk base, brass tube, 1897, 14", EX 275.00
Bausch & Lomb, brass, tripod base, 1876, 16", EX, +case 420.00
Bausch & Lomb, brass, tripod base, 1885, 16", EX, +case 350.00
Bausch & Lomb, dissecting, w/filters & holders 200.00
Bausch & Lomb, rack & pinion focus, triple nosepc, EX, +case .350.00
Bulloch, Chicago, brass, complex, Y base, 1880, 15", +case 1,100.00
English, professional, brass, 1876, 18", +case/accessories 950.00
English, student, brass, ca 1870, 12", +case/accessories 450.00
French, drum or furnace form, 5", EX, +case 65.00
French, student, ca 1910, 9", G, +case 65.00
German, student, rnd base, ca 1860, G, +case 125.00
Grundlach, brass, Y base, 1879, 14", EX 325.00
Grundlach Manhattan, student, all brass, 11", EX 165.00
Grunow, New Haven, iron & brass, 15", EX, +case 1,100.00
Hand-held, simple form, 1890, 3", G 45.00
McAllister, brass, chain-drive focus, 14", G, +case 325.00
McIntosh Battery & Optical, brass & iron, 12", G 550.00
Queen, brass & iron, Y base, 14", G, +case 325.00
Spencer Lens Co, brass, horseshoe base, 13", EX 155.00
Stamp magnifier, brass, 3-leg, 1½", G 40.00
Tighe, brass, 12", EX, +case 325.00
Tolles, Boston, brass, Y base, ca 1880, 16", G, +case 750.00
Watson, English binocular form, 1880, 18", EX, +case 950.00
Zentmeyer, brass, complex, dbl pillar, tripod base, 18", G 1,250.00

Midwestern Glass

As early as 1814, blown glass was made in Ohio. By 1835 glasshouses in Michigan were producing similar pattern-molded types that have long been highly regarded by collectors. During the latter part of the 19th century, all six of the states of the Northwest Territory were mass producing the pressed glass tableware patterns that were then in vogue. Various types of art glass were produced in the area until after the turn of the century. Items listed here are attributed to the Midwest by certain physical characteristics known to be indigenous to that part of the country. See also Findlay Onyx; Greentown Glass; Libbey;

Zanesville Glass. Our advisor for this category is Mark Vuono; he is listed in the Directory under Connecticut.

Bottle, amber, flared lip, mini, 4⅜" 240.00
Bottle, aqua, club shape w/16 vertical melon ribs, 8⅛" 150.00
Bottle, globular, amber, HP florals, folded lip, 3⅞" 385.00
Candlestick, canary, hexagonal, sm flakes, 7¾" 860.00
Chestnut flask, golden amber, 18-rib swirl, 6¼", EX 250.00
Chestnut flask, golden amber, 20 broken-rib swirl, 6¾" 935.00
Cruet, cobalt, 16 vertical ribs, hollow hdl, 7½"+stopper 1,200.00
Cuspidor, dk amber, 2¼x5" 275.00
Flask, Grandfather's, med amber, 24 vertical ribs, 8⅛", NM 825.00
Pear, amber, rough stem (where it was snapped), 4½" 275.00
Sweetmeat, triple band & sunburst design, 4⅛x7⅛" 135.00

Militaria

Because of the wide and varied scope of items available to collectors of militaria, most tend to concentrate mainly on the area or areas that interest them most or that they can afford to buy. Some items represent a major investment and because of their value have been reproduced. Extreme caution should be used when purchasing Nazi items. Every badge, medal, cap, uniform, dagger, and sword that Nazi Germany issued is being reproduced today. Some repros are crude and easily identified as fakes, while others are very well done and difficult to recognize as reproductions. Purchases from WWII veterans are usually your safest buys. Reputable dealers or collectors will normally offer a money-back guarantee on Nazi items purchased from them. There are a number of excellent Third Reich reference books available in bookstores at very reasonable prices. Study them to avoid losing a much larger sum spent on a reproduction. Our advisor for this category is Ron Willis; he is listed in the Directory under Oklahoma.

Key: insg — insignia

Imperial German

Badge, Navy wound; Xd swords/anchor/chain on blk, EX 48.00
Badge, wound; EX gilt finish, stamped construction, EX 115.00
Boots, mtd enlisted, WWI era, blk leather, high tops, EX 125.00
Buckle, Bavarian enlisted, nickel & brass, In Treue Fest, EX 22.50
Buckle, Navy officer, brass w/fire gilding, wreath border, EX 100.00
Canister, gas mask; rpt, G 15.00
Collar tabs, red w/dbltrees, gilt w/blk border, EX 16.50
Disk grenade, EX gray pnt, brass fittings, pull-ring, inert 90.00
Document, Prussian 25 Yr Service Cross Award, 1920, EX 30.00
Helmet, Artillery NCO, eagle frontplate/spike, dtd 1893, VG+ .800.00
Helmet, camo pnt on steel, 3-pad liner rstr, VG 300.00
Helmet, Guard Dragoon Regiment NCO, brass eagle/spike, EX .750.00
Helmet, Model 1918, field gray pnt steel, w/strap, dtd 1918, VG ..325.00
Helmet, Oldenburg officer, blk leather & brass w/spike, EX 750.00
Helmet, trench; Model 1916, old field gray pnt, w/liner, VG 75.00
Helmet, Uhlan Guard Regiment, pressed gray felt w/insg, EX 850.00
Insignia, sleeve; Medical Service, yel embr on dk bl wool, EX 20.00
Leggings, mtn troop, WWI era, padded, buckles, 1911, EX 34.00
Medal, Hessian Bravery, silver planchet, w/ribbon 30.00
Medal, Hessian Bravery, tarnished silver planchet, no ribbon 22.50
Medal, Iron Cross, 2nd class, silver, w/ribbon, VG 25.00
Medal, Marksmanship Assoc, aluminum, Prussian eagle/1888, EX .17.50
Medal, noncombattant campaign, steel, 1870 ....35.00
Overcoat, Army Model 1915, WWI era, gray wool, silver insg, VG ...495.00
Postcard, troops march near comrades graves, NM 17.50

Pouch, cartridge, Model 1889, blk leather w/brass fittings, EX 25.00
Shoulderbrds, Prussian Captain, silver bullion on yel wool, G 75.00
Stickpin, Bavarian Veteran Assoc, crest, gilt brass, EX 18.00
Sword knot, Bavarian officer, bl striped silver bullion strap 30.00
Tunic, Infantry officer, prewar, dk bl wool w/red trim, EX 110.00
Watch fob, Iron Cross commemorative, wht metal, 1914-15 ....27.50

Third Reich

Armband, Armed Forces worker, blk print on wht cotton, EX 30.00
Armband, Veteran Assoc, embr monument/swastika on bl wool ..32.00
Badge, Army Handwerker Proficiency, rose embr on gray wool 22.50
Badge, Hitler Youth Markmanship, dmn insg w/rifles, hallmk 45.00
Badge, Luftwaffe Ground Combat, gray metal, solid bk, worn 110.00
Badge, Luftwaffe Observer's Combat, hallmk, worn/tarnished 265.00
Badge, Navy Blockade Runner, silver eagle w/blued body, hallmk ..300.00
Badge, Navy Submarine Combat, worn gilt, solid bk, dk w/age ..135.00
Badge, Police Landwacht, silver-washed planchet, pin-bk 30.00
Badge, War Order of German Cross, star embr on cloth, G 110.00
Banner, blk silk swastika on wht silk w/red, 87x46", EX 200.00
Book, Kampf um Norwegen, 1940, EX 45.00
Book, Rommel the Desert Fox, illus, D Young, c 1950, EX 50.00
Booklet, foreign worker's ID, gr cover, complete w/photo, EX 48.00
Boots, ankle; Army, brn leather, brass grommets, wool top, EX 60.00
Boots, combat; Army, blk leather, pegged soles, cloth tabs, EX 40.00
Bread bag, Army, khaki canvas w/brn leather fittings, G 30.00
Breeches, Luftwaffe officer, gray wool, compo buttons, VG 135.00

Belt buckle, German Police, light metal with embossed insignia, with leather belt, EX, $95.00.

Buckle, Army, silver lacquered, brn leather tab, 1941 ....30.00
Buckle, Nat'l Railway officer, gray metal winged wheel w/gilt 24.00
Buckle, RAD enlisted, pebbled aluminum, hallmk, 1937 ....25.00
Card, SS official ID; complete w/photo, eagle ink stamp, EX 300.00
Coat, Army, camo w/hood, fur lining, 4 flap pockets, G 400.00
Collar tabs, Army Artillery, silver litzen on red wool, pr 30.00
Collar tabs, SS Unterscharfuhrer, embr gray SS runics, EX 45.00
Cup, drinking field; Army, aluminum, folding hdls, dtd 39, EX 20.00
Field pack, Army, gray w/fur flap, shoulder straps, 1940, EX 38.00
Gas mask, Army Luftschutz, gray rubberized canvas face, G 30.00
Gas mask, Luftschutz Civilian, gr rubber face w/filter, EX 24.00
Hand pump, Army, cylinder-style pump, field gray, G 35.00
Hat, visor; Army Administration, gray w/gr trim & silver insg ...450.00
Hat, visor; Luftwaffe Flak Artillery, summer, wht cotton, EX 300.00
Hat, visor; Postal Service, bl wool w/eagle/cockade insg, EX 125.00
Hat, visor; Waffen SS Mtn Troup, gray crusher w/eagle, EX ...1,000.00
Helmet, Army M35, desert camo, partial rpt, G 300.00
Helmet, Army M42 style, field gray w/tan camo & eagle insg, G ...175.00
Helmet, chicken wire; Army M35 pattern, EX gray camo pnt, EX .450.00
Helmet, Luftwaffe Model 42, eagle decal on bl-gray, EX 165.00
Helmet, Luftwaffe Paratrooper, late war style w/eagle, EX 750.00
Helmet, pith; Africa Corps, early pattern w/gr wool cover, EX ...200.00
Insignia, Army officer's breast eagle, silver on gr wool 48.00
Insignia, police visor hat eagle, aluminum w/prongs, hallmk 15.00

Insignia, sleeve; Army Russian Foreign Volunteer, unissued **32.40**
Insignia, sleeve; KSK Driver's Specialty, eagle on blk, G **25.00**
Insignia, TENO Gen officer's visor hat wreath, gilt aluminum **37.50**
Lanyard, rank; Hitler Youth Leader, lt bl braided cord, NM **50.00**
Medal, War Service Cross, 2nd class, bronze, no swords, VG **25.00**
Medal, West Wall Defense Honor, bronze, w/ribbon **18.00**
Mess fork, Luftwaffe, aluminum w/eagle, EX **15.00**
Overcoat, Army officer, gray wool w/gr, dbl-breasted, EX **300.00**
Parachute, gray & tan camo silk, in brn bag, EX **85.00**
Pennant, SS vehicle, 2-sided, SS runics/wht cotton, 13x11½" ..**1,150.00**
Pin, Handicap Assoc Membership, blk/wht enamel w/swastika **58.00**
Pin, NSKK Supporter, silvered eagle planchet, hallmk, EX **20.00**
Poster, Mein Kampf ad w/Hitler in uniform, 1920s, 18x12½", EX ..**60.00**
Rain cape, Hitler Youth, brn rubberized canvas, complete, EX ...**365.00**
Raincoat, navy U-Boat, blk rubberized, dbl-breasted, 1943, EX .**250.00**
Rifle cleaning kit, Army, tobacco tin style, pull chain, EX **30.00**
Rucksack, Army Tropical Mtn, tan canvas, web straps, 1943, EX ..**88.00**
Shoulder brds, Army Signal Troops Hauptmann, silver/yel wool ..**25.00**
Shoulder brds, Wachtmeister, silver/brn tresse on gr wool **25.00**
Sling, shoulder drag; Army Artillery, leather w/iron buckle **125.00**
Smock, Army, winter camo, pullover style w/hood, EX **165.00**
Snow goggles, Armi Ski Troop, slotted metal eye covers, EX **45.00**
Trousers, Army fatigue, natural linen, EX **50.00**
Trousers, Waffen SS, camo herringbone twill, VG **200.00**
Tunic, Hitler Youth Navy, wht cotton twill w/MOP buttons, EX ...**265.00**

Japanese

Air raid siren, WWII, EX khaki pnt, wood grips, scarce, EX **185.00**
Badge, WWII Military Veteran, silver w/gilt star insg, EX **75.00**
Breast star, Order of Rising Sun, silver/gold medallion, NM ...**2,650.00**
Buckle, WWII, NCO, NP brass, anchor/roped circle, 2-pc, G **65.00**
Camera, aerial; WWII, 'machine gun' style, pistol grip, G **225.00**
Canteen, WWII, aluminum, khaki pnt, web sling/harness, G **65.00**
Field light, WWII Army, flashlight w/hand-cranked generator, EX .**75.00**
Goggles, WWII pilot, folding frames, cotton mask, NM **100.00**
Helmet, WWII, Tanker, complete w/liner & strap, mk, EX **265.00**
Medal, Order of Golden Kite, 7th class, M in case **185.00**
Medal, Order of Sacred Treasure, 8th class, silver planchet, EX ..**60.00**
Medal, Red Cross Special membership, w/rosette, M in case **30.00**
Medal, WWII, Red Cross, silver planchet, w/ribbon, EX **25.00**
Medal, WWII era, Red Cross, silver planchet, w/ribbon, NM **35.00**
Postcard, WWII, artillery crew in jungle, EX **17.50**
Sake cup, China Incident, helmet/cherry blossoms on wht porc ...**17.50**
Sake cup, WWII, gold pawlonia leaf/pk cherry blossoms on porc .**18.00**
Shoulderbrds, WWII, Navy Ensign, gold bullion/purple on bl **38.00**
Tunic, Army, tropical, 1942, EX **40.00**
Wings, WWII, Army Air Corps, aluminum wire/gilt on bl **30.00**

United States

Badge, WWI, Air Service Pilot, winged shield, silver planchet ..**265.00**
Badge, WWII Ship Builder's ID, brass shield w/gr, pin-bk, EX **30.00**
Belt, WWI BAR Rifleman, 4-pocket, magazine pouch, khaki, EX ..**30.00**
Blanket, WWII Army, khaki wool, EX **30.00**
Box, cartridge; Indian War era, blk leather, ca 1876, EX **30.00**
Breeches, WWI Army, khaki cotton twill, metal buttons, VG **35.00**
Canteen, Civil War, bull's-eye pattern, pewter spout, 7½" **415.00**
Canteen, Civil War, wooden wagon type, w/strap, 10x10" dia ...**500.00**
Cap, militia forage; Civil War, high crown, blk wool, VG **1,950.00**
Cap, visor; WAAC enlisted, tan khaki cotton twill w/badge, G ...**50.00**
Cap, WWII, Army officer overseas, dk khaki wool w/piping, EX ..**18.00**
Chevron, WWII Army Sergeant Electrician, spark on khaki wool ..**22.00**
Coat, deck; WWII Navy, khaki twill, compo buttons, EX **85.00**

Great coat, Civil War Infantry, Federal issue, blue wool jersey, 5-button front, 6-button attached cape, lined body, EX, $3,000.00.

Collar disk, WWI Air Service, bronzed winged propeller, EX **22.50**
Collar disk, WWI Cavalry enlisted, bronzed, Xd swords, EX **17.50**
Flight suit, heated, WWII AAF, 1-pc khaki cotton twill, EX **175.00**
Hat, jungle; Vietnam War, khaki cotton, natural camo, M **17.50**
Hat, WWI, Army Campaign officer, khaki wool, leather strap, G ..**50.00**
Helmet, Army Armoured Vehicle Crew Member, compo, khaki pnt, EX **25.00**
Helmet, WWI, Infantry regiment, khaki w/pnt tree insg **70.00**
Helmet, WWI, Marine Corps, khaki finish, Indian head insg, EX ...**110.00**
Helmet, WWI, Tanks Corps, khaki sand finish, castle insg, EX ...**70.00**
Helmet liner, Vietnam War era, NM khaki pnt, webbed straps, EX .**15.00**
Insignia, collar; WWI Signal Corps, bronze, pin-bk, EX **18.00**
Insignia, collar; WWII Women's Army Corps officer, gilt, pr **37.50**
Jacket, deck; WWII Navy, khaki twill, fur lining, NM **65.00**
Jacket, field; WWII M1942 Paratrooper, khaki twill, EX **325.00**
Kepi, Indian War Era, Artillery enlisted, dk bl, blk visor, EX **275.00**
Leggings, Civil War, wht w/yel piping, brass buttons, 10", EX **200.00**
Medal, Daughters of Am Revolution Membership, 14k gold, 1930s ..**350.00**
Medal, Mexican Border Service, bronze planchet, rpl ribbon, VG ..**25.00**
Medal, Spanish-Am War, Admiral Dewey, bronze planchet, EX ..**135.00**
Medal, WWI, NH State Service, bronze planchet, w/ribbon, VG ..**25.00**
Medallion, Civil War, Gen Sherman, bronze, 1¼" dia **110.00**
Mess kit, Spanish-Am War, tinned iron, EX **22.50**
Mirror, hand signal; unissued, w/attachment cord, ca 1985, M **18.00**
Photo, early Airforce biplane on airfield, 1931, EX **20.00**
Photo, Space Shuttle Challenger crew, STS-7 misson, 10x7" **40.00**
Shako, Indian War-era Bandman, dk bl wool w/gold bullion, EX ...**235.00**
Shirt, Vietnam War Army, tiger-striped camo, shoulderbrds, EX .**22.50**
Surgeon's kit, Civil War, 10 tools in mahog case, EX **1,100.00**
Telescope, Civil War era, pocket sz **55.00**
Tunic, WWI Army Air Service enlisted, khaki wool, insg, EX ..**200.00**
Tunic, WWI Marine Corps, khaki wool, 4-pocket, chevrons, EX ..**425.00**
Wings, WWI Air Service Pilot, Dallas style, EX finish, pin-bk ...**1,250.00**
Wristwatch, Vietnam War era, Timex, blk dial/khaki finish, EX .**70.00**

Miscellaneous

Austria, medal, Imperial Era Signum Memorial, bronze, +ribbon .**20.00**
Canada, medallion, Sm Bore Rifle Assoc, silver, 1935, EX **30.00**
Dutch, helmet, WWII Army, khaki finish, rubberized lining, EX .**30.00**
E Germany, camo uniform: jacket & pants, EX **15.00**
E Germany, uniform: tunic/breeches/hat/shirt/tie, M **50.00**
England, Army beret, dk bl wool, blk cotton lining, 1955, EX **20.00**
England, badge, Lt Infantry Paratrooper, cloth chute w/wings **20.00**
England, helmet, WWII Mark III, EX khaki pnt, complete, EX ...**40.00**
England, medal, RAF Long Service & Good Conduct, silver, NM **95.00**
England, medal, Star, bronze, 1939-45, w/ribbon, EX **22.50**
France, badge, Air Force Radio Operator, gilt wings/silver **20.00**
France, cap, WWII Sailor, dk bl wool w/red trim, EX **50.00**
France, helmet, WWII Resistance Fighter, pnt steel, EX **40.00**

France, medal, Legion of Honor, Officer grade, silver/mc, VG ...200.00
Germany, badge, Shooting Assoc, bronze w/mc, 1978, EX 22.00
Italy, building insignia, WWII Fascist, iron fascio, 16", NM 400.00
Italy, emblem, WWII Fascist Mtn Climbing Assoc, eagle/shield ..40.00
Italy, hat, visor; WWII Fascist Party Minister, blk wool w/yel 225.00
Italy, helmet, WWII Army, VG khaki pnt, w/liner & strap 25.00
Italy, medal, Civil Valor, King Umberto I on bronze, 1890s 45.00
Italy, medal, WWI War Cross, bronze, w/ribbon 25.00
Italy, medallion, WWII, Mussolini, bronze portrait, 100mm dia ...70.00
Mexican, medal, Army 25 Yrs Long Service Cross, 2nd class, 1926 .65.00
Poland, Cross of Merit, type I, gilt w/mc, no swords, w/ribbon 65.00
Russia, book, Propoganda Posters 1918-41, c 1985, EX 25.00
Russia, cap, folding side; Navy Officer, bl wool w/wht, 1990, M ...25.00
Russia, cap, WWII Sailor, blk wool, silk ribbon, EX 100.00
Russia, helmet, Army Riot Control, camo w/clear visor, EX 250.00
Russia, ID Book, gilt on red cover, 1980s, unissued 18.00
Russia, medal, Capture of Berlin, bronze, w/ribbon, EX 30.00
Russia, medal, Civil War Awaloff, bronze, St George/dragon 60.00
Russia, medal, 30th Anniversary of Red Army, bronze, 1948, EX .20.00
Spain, hat, Guardia Civil Police, Bi-Corn pattern, EX 45.00
Spain, helmet, Civil War Army Model 1926, EX khaki pnt 35.00
Spain, helmet, WWII Tank Crew, blk padded leather, complete .70.00
West Germany, booklet, Army recruiting, Die Bundeswehr, EX ..17.50

Milk Glass

Milk glass is the current collector's name for milk-white opaque glass. The early glassmaker's term was Opal Ware. Originally attempted in England in the 18th century with the intention of imitating china, milk glass was not commercially successful until the mid-1800s. Pieces produced in the U.S.A., England, and France during the 1870-1900 period are highly prized for their intricate detail and fiery, opalescent edges.

For further information we recommend *Collector's Encyclopedia of Milk Glass, An Identification & Value Guide,* by Betty and Bill Newbound. Our advisor for this category is Rod Dockery; he is listed in the Directory under Texas. Several standard collectors' books have been referenced in our listings: Belknap (B), Collector's Encyclopedia by Newbound (CE), Ferson (F), Grist (G), Imperial's Vintage Milk Glass (I), Lindsey (L), Millard (M), and Warman (W). See also Animal Dishes with Covers; Bread Plates; Historical Glass; Westmoreland.

Bookends, bear, upright w/paws on book, CE-192, 8¾", pr 80.00
Bowl, Daisy, mc enamelling, Challinor, F-165, 8" 85.00
Bowl, fruit; floral center, lattice edge, ftd, B-106b 35.00
Bowl, trumpet vines, open latticework edge, CE-27a, 2x9½" 35.00
Box, Flatiron, CE-173b, 7" L 60.00
Butter dish, Melon w/Leaf & Net, Atterbury, M-120 ....85.00
Compote, Atlas, scalloped rim, B-103 ....80.00
Compote, Jenny Lind, F-380A, 7½" 110.00
Covered dish, Baseball, G-100 ....30.00
Covered dish, Battleship Newark, W-18b, 6" L 75.00
Covered dish, Dewey on Tile Base, M-296b, 6¾" L 85.00
Covered dish, Football, G-100, 5" 75.00
Covered dish, Picnic Basket, CE-167, 5" 45.00
Covered dish, Pope Leon XIII, F-127 ....225.00
Covered dish, Prairie Schooner, 5-rib fr, F-409, 5⅞" L 150.00
Covered dish, Royal Coach, LE Smith, B190c, 4¼x5" 85.00
Covered dish, Uncle Sam on Battleship, B-189, 6½" 75.00
Creamer, lacy top, M-206b 30.00
Creamer & sugar bowl, Twin Horn, M-207b 65.00
Goblet, Jewel & Dewdrop, Kemple, CE-218B, 5" 17.50
Honey jar, beehive form, worn pnt, B-181b 25.00

Jar, Queen Victoria, M-259a 150.00
Jar, Trumpeting Swan, W-79D 7.50
Knife rest, Triple Daisy, 4¼" L 15.00
Match holder, dog in house 40.00
Match holder, horse pulling cart 12.00
Match holder, Indian, F-587/M-204a, NM 95.00
Match holder, owl w/wings spread, M-164c 17.50
Match holder, Pillar & Panel, w/dbl strike, sq 27.50
Match holder, Rameses III, McKee, ca 1890s, F-630, EX 75.00
Mug, Bar & Swirl, 3⅝" 15.00
Novelty, sailor hat, M-181a 40.00
Pickle dish, boat shape, Atterbury, Pat 1874, B-62b, 9½" 40.00
Pin dish, Star of David w/bl florals & gold trim, 4" 22.50
Pitcher, grapes, branch hdl, I-1950/473, 8½", +4 tumblers 95.00
Pitcher, owl, red eyes, F-587, 8" 150.00
Plate, Audubon decal, Club & Shell border, Kemple, 9½" 35.00
Plate, California Bear, F-543 ....115.00
Plate, cherries, lacy edge, Kemple, 7¼" 12.00

Plate, Contrary Mule, worn paint, $40.00.

Plate, Cupid & Psyche, orig pnt, B-6b 40.00
Plate, Dutch girl, Sheaf of Wheat border, 6" 22.50
Plate, Eagle, Flag & Star border, B-6d 25.00
Plate, Easter Bunny & Egg, B-3c 68.00
Plate, floral decor, open latticework along rim, 10½" 50.00
Plate, Gothic, B-9b, 5½" 27.50
Plate, Gray Ghost Streamer (lure), Lacy Heart border, 6½" 12.00
Plate, H border, Atterbury, 1890, 7½" 22.50
Plate, heart border, B-13e, 8" 18.00
Plate, heart shape, 6" 20.00
Plate, Indian, lacy edge, B-4f 75.00
Plate, Leaf & Branch border, EX 22.50
Plate, Lotus Flower edge, 7⅝" 22.50
Plate, pears, Club & Shell border, Kemple, 7" 20.00
Plate, Rabbit & Horseshoe, Pat Appl For, B-7a, 7¼" 45.00
Plate, rose decal w/gold trim, scrolled edge, 12" 28.00
Plate, Serenade, B-9e, 6½" 40.00
Plate, Water Lilies, Dmn & Shell Border, mk HP, Kemple 20.00
Plate, wicker border, 7¼" 25.00
Plate, Woof Woof, B-13f 50.00
Plate, Yacht & Anchor, M-28b 30.00
Plate, 101 border, B-13c 20.00
Plate, 3 Kittens, B-10c 35.00
Plate, 3 Owls, Pat July 2, 1901, 7¼" 35.00
Platter, Clover, W-109C, 11½x7½" 18.00
Platter, Retriever (after bird), Lily Pad border, B-53 ....100.00
Platter, Rock of Ages, F-569 ....175.00
Relish, Double Fish, Atterbury, Pat dtd, F-333 ....60.00
Salt cellar, swan form, M-276b, Sandwich 65.00
Shakers, Fan & Scroll, W-139b, metal tops, 2½", pr 17.50
Smoke bell, plain edge, W-155A 25.00

Statuette, Dewey Bust, F-542 ....**120.00**
Stein, monk drinking, brn overspray w/transfer, 4" **50.00**
Sugar bowl, Blackberry, berry finial, dtd, F-250 ....**60.00**
Sugar bowl, Dahlia, M-152b, sm **35.00**
Toothpick holder, alligator, F-451, EX **90.00**
Tray, Barred Scrolls, W-106b, 10x6¾" **15.00**
Tray, Dahlias & Cosmos border, irregular shape, 7½x6½" **22.50**
Tray, pinwheel w/leaves, ftd, M-27b, 10½" dia **65.00**
Tray, relish; shell w/melon ribs, B-60c, 8¾x5" **18.00**
Tray, Roses & Poppies, M-33, 11¼x7½" **25.00**
Tumbler, emb Dutch boy w/wagon, 6" **22.00**
Urn, ribbed lid, M-148, 5¾" **27.50**
Vase, ear of corn, some old pnt, CE-381a, 4¼" **35.00**

Millefiori

Millefiori was a type of art glass first produced during the late 1800s. Literally, the term means 'thousand flowers,' an accurate description of its appearance. Canes, fused bundles of multicolored glass threads such as are often used in paperweights, were cut into small cross sections, arranged in the desired pattern, refired, and shaped into articles such as cruets, lamps, and novelty items. It is still being produced, and many examples found on the market today are of fairly recent manufacture. See also Paperweights.

Bottle, rose-cut o/l w/millefiori base & stopper, 6⅞x2¾" **1,100.00**
Cruet, ftd, camphor hdl, millefiori ball stopper, 7½" **410.00**
Cup & saucer, satin **85.00**
Pitcher, appl hdl, 6" **175.00**
Syrup pitcher, frosted hdl, shell thumb lift, SP top **225.00**

Tumbler, blue ground, 4", $110.00.

Vase, lg scroll hdls, stick neck, 7" **275.00**

Miniatures

There is some confusion as to what should be included in a listing of miniature collectibles. Some feel the only true miniature is the salesman's sample; other collectors consider certain small-scale children's toys to be appropriately referred to as miniatures, while yet others believe a miniature to be any small-scale item that gives evidence to the craftsmanship of its creator. For salesman's samples, see specific category; other types are listed below. See also Dollhouses and Furnishings; Children's Things.

Ranking at the top of today's leading collectibles, scaled 1:12" miniatures represent the work of hundreds of artisans who supply local shops with highly prized one-of-a-kind articles and specialties, all scaled one inch to the foot. Many leading producers and distributors of collectibles have entered the field as well. Clubs for miniature enthusiasts have sprung up throughout the United States, Canada, and abroad.

Bed warmer, brass w/trn hdl, 9" **130.00**
Bed warmer, copper, brass ferrule, trn wood hdl, 9" **195.00**
Blanket chest, dvtl case, appl moldings, varnish, 21" L **600.00**
Blanket chest, Empire, 1840, 8¾x12¾", EX **255.00**
Box, dome top, relief cvg, wire nails, 3" L **30.00**
Bureau, soft wood, 4 dvtl drw, trn knob pulls, 12x13x8" **850.00**
Bureau, walnut, 3 dvtl drws, brass knobs, 12x11⅜x6¼" **280.00**
Candlestick, cast brass, rnd base, 3x2½" **25.00**
Chair, side; orig gr pnt w/mc florals, PA, 12½" **1,100.00**
Chair, side; plank seat, old mellow rfn, 14½" **75.00**
Chest, cherry Empire, 3 nailed drws, paneled ends, 22" **440.00**
Chest, cherry Empire w/maple inlay, 3 dvtl drws, 18x15x8" **1,400.00**
Chest, mahog Sheraton, trn ft, reeded corners, 4-drw, 15" **625.00**
Chest, pine, 5-drw, cut-out ft, rpl knobs, rfn, 11½" **165.00**
Chest, pnt decor, 12¼x6¼", VG **300.00**
Cradle, yelware w/yel & brn sponging, 3x4⅜x2¼" **300.00**
Cupboard, pine, old finish, dvtl drw/porc pulls/wire nails, 18" ...**165.00**
Cupboard, poplar, orig red pnt w/mc stripes, 2-drw, 11" **1,500.00**
Cupboard, step-bk style, 1800s, 17", EX **345.00**
Dresser, pine, orig blk w/gold striping, 3-drw, mirror, 22" ...**165.00**
Ice box, oak, working hardware, 11x8½x6", EX **225.00**
Kettle, cast brass, iron bail hdl, polished, 2¾x5" **165.00**
Loving cup, 14k yel gold, w/monogram, 2¾" **400.00**
Spinning wheel, cvd wood w/EX details, works, 6" **60.00**
Spinning wheel, ivory, 3¾" **95.00**
Table, mahog Empire tilt-top; tripod base, inlay top, 8x11" **195.00**

Minton

Thomas Minton established his firm in 1793 at Stoke on Trent and within a few years began producing earthenware with blue-printed patterns similar to the ware he had learned to decorate while employed by the Caughley Porcelain Factory. The Willow pattern was one of his most popular. Neither this nor the porcelain made from 1798 to 1805 was marked (except for an occasional number series), making identification often impossible.

After 1805 until about 1816, fine tea services, beehive-shaped honey pots, trays, etc., were hand decorated with florals, landscapes, Imari-type designs, and neoclassic devices. These were often marked with crossed 'L's. It was Minton that invented the acid gold process of decorating (1863), which is now used by a number of different companies. From 1816 until 1823, no porcelain was made. Through the twenties and thirties, the ornamental wares with colorful decoration of applied fruits and florals and figurines in both bisque and enamel were usually left unmarked. As a result, they have been erroneously attributed to other potters. Some of the ware that was marked bears a deliberate imitation of Meissen's crossed swords. From the late twenties through the forties, Minton made a molded stoneware line (mugs, jugs, teapots, etc.) with florals or figures in high relief. These were marked with an embossed scroll with an 'M' in the bottom curve. Fine parian ware was made in the late 1840s, and in the 1850s Minton experimented with and perfected a line of quality majolica which they produced from 1860 until it was discontinued in 1908. Their slogan was 'Majolica for the Millions,' and for it they gained widespread recognition. Leadership of the firm was assumed by Minton's son Herbert sometime around the middle of the 19th century. Working hand in hand with Leon Arnoux, who was both a chemist and an artist, he managed to secure the company's financial future through constant, successful experimentation with both materials and decorating methods. During the Victorian era, M.L. Solon decorated pieces in the pate-sur-pate style, often signing his work; these examples are considered to be the finest of their type. After 1862 all wares were marked 'Minton' or 'Mintons,' with an impressed year cipher.

Many collectors today reassemble the lovely dinnerware patterns that have been made by Minton. Perhaps one of their most popular lines was Minton Rose, introduced in 1854. The company itself once counted forty-seven versions of this pattern being made by other potteries around the world. In addition to less expensive copies, elaborate hand-enameled pieces were also made by Aynsley, Crown Staffordshire, and Paragon China. Solando Ware (1937) and Byzantine Range (1938) were designed by John Wadsworth. Minton ceased all earthenware production in 1939.

Dinnerware values given in the following listings are for items that were produced from 1870 to 1950. Current production pieces bring lower prices on the resale market. See also Majolica; Pate-Sur-Pate.

Bouillon cup & saucer, Cockatrice, pk 60.00
Bowl, vegetable; Kent, oval 135.00
Cup & saucer, Ashton 55.00
Cup & saucer, Greenwich 55.00
Cup & saucer, Kent 60.00
Demitasse set, gilt florals, scrolled/ribbed, 1900s, 15-pc 230.00
Figurine, magpies on base, salt glaze, ca 1930, 21½", pr 900.00

Flask, cloisonne-enameled dragon masks and floral reserves with gilt, attributed to Dr. Christopher Dresser, 10¼", $1,200.00.

Plate, bread & butter; Buckingham 25.00
Plate, dinner; Ardmore 60.00
Plate, dinner; Ashton 45.00
Plate, dinner; Windsor, bl, #K396 ....60.00
Plate, salad; Ardmore 35.00
Platter, Kent, 14" 110.00
Teapot, Cheviot 165.00
Vase, allover floral, Persian style, hdld gourd form, 24" 225.00
Vase, pond lilies/cattails on yel, gilt ring 'hdls,' 11" 1,450.00
Vase, squeeze-bag vertical leaves/pods on purple gloss, 13" 800.00

Mirrors

The first mirrors were made in England in the 13th century of very thin glass backed with lead. Reverse-painted glass mirrors were made in this country as early as the late 1700s and remained popular throughout the next century. The simple hand-painted panel was separated from the mirrored section by a narrow slat, and the frame was either the dark-finished Federal style or the more elegant, often-gilded Sheraton.

Mirrors changed with the style of other furnishings; but whatever type you purchase, as long as the glass sections remain solid, even broken or flaking mirrors are more valued than replaced glass. Careful resilvering is acceptable if excessive deterioration has taken place. In the listings that follow, the term 'style' (example: Federal style) is used to indicate a mirror reminiscent of but made well after the period indicated. Obviously these repro styles are valued much lower than their original counterparts. Our advisor for this category is Michael Hinton; he is listed in the Directory under Pennsylvania.

Key:
Chpndl — Chippendale   Fed — Federal
Emp — Empire   QA — Queen Anne

Architectural, fruit & foliage cvg, trn columns, gilded, 33" 1,100.00
Architectural Emp 2-part, rvpt floral band, rpt, 27x14" 185.00
Architectural Fed 2-part gilt fr, rvpt scene, 35x18" 275.00
Architectural Fed 2-part mahog, rvpt country scene, 35x19" 715.00
Architectural Fed 2-part mahog veneer, Am, rstr, 33" 300.00
Architectural Fed 2-part pine w/old alligatored red, rvpt, 19" 300.00
Architectural 2-part pine w/old red, rvpt house, 22x14" 600.00
Arts & Crafts, oak w/coat hooks, trapezoidal, 26x37" 200.00
Cheval, Emp style, shield-shaped mirror, gr pnt, 20th C, 73" 385.00
Chpndl scroll mahog, molded, rfn, 17x12" 195.00
Chpndl scroll mahog, old finish, 21" 385.00
Chpndl scroll mahog, regilded ornament, rfn, 31x18" 2,400.00
Chpndl scroll mahog veneer on pine w/gilt, 25", EX 400.00
Chpndl scroll walnut, molded, glued rprs, 19½x12" 275.00
Chpndl-style scroll bird's-eye maple, handmade repro, 28" 165.00
Chpndl-style scroll cherry, 20th C repro, 46x26", pr 195.00
Chpndl-style scroll curly maple, handmade repro, 28x17" 150.00
Chpndl-style scroll flame veneer, old but not period, 32x18" 165.00
Courting, mahog veneer, rvpt scene in crest, 15x10", EX 385.00
Curly maple veneer w/ivory inlay & bone bars, 23x19" 5,500.00
English QA scroll, walnut w/figure, rstr/rpt, 37" 990.00
Florentine style, cvd & gilded, rpl mirror, 50x38" 1,500.00
Gilded gesso, beveled glass, ornate, 20th C, 54x34" 775.00
Gilded gesso, Classical girandole, ca 1820, 37x28", EX 2,650.00
Giltwood girandole, convex, w/eagle crest, 18th C, 44x29" 3,250.00
Giltwood Provincial Louis XVI, rtcl crest, 1780s, 40x70, EX ..3,450.00
Grpt, molded cornice, reeded half-columns, rvpt house, 24x14" ...550.00
Mahog/parcel gilt, cvd shell crest, gilt bezel, 1770, 33" 700.00
Over-the-mantle, gesso on wood w/dolphins & cattails, 54x57" ..220.00
Over-the-mantle, mahog w/gilt, eagle crest, ca 1900, 61x32" 225.00
Pier, Baroque Revival, gold rpt, EX rprs, on stand, 104x34" 150.00
Pier, walnut & walnut burl Victorian Eastlake, 96x30" 850.00
Pier, walnut Eastlake Victorian, marble shelf, 91x25" 550.00
Pier, walnut Eastlake Victorian, much cvg, marble shelf, 92" 825.00
Pier, wood/plaster Rococo Revival, marble shelf, rpt, 106" 1,100.00
Pine w/gesso & mc rpt w/gold, rpr, 14x11" 330.00
Shaving, mahog Hplwht w/inlay, bow front, 3 dvtl drw, 23" 110.00
Shaving, mahog Hplwht-style w/inlay, Fr ft, 2-drw, 23" 165.00
Shaving, mahog veneer Emp, dvtl drws, 22x15x7" 360.00
Shaving, mahog veneer Hplwht bowfront w/inlay, 2 drws, 17x17" ..220.00
Shaving, mahog veneer Hplwht w/line inlay, dvtl drw, 16x14" 75.00

Mocha

Mochaware is utilitarian pottery made principally in England (and to a lesser extent in France) between 1780 and 1840 on the then prevalent creamware and pearlware bodies. Initially, only those pieces decorated in the seaweed pattern were called 'Mocha,' while geometrically decorated pieces were referred to as 'Banded Creamware.' Other types of decorations were called 'Dipped Ware.' During the last thirty to forty years the term 'Mocha' has been applied to the entire realm of 'Industrialized Slipware' — pottery decorated by the turner on his lathe using coggle wheels and slip cups.

Mocha was made in numerous patterns — Tree, Seaweed or Dandelion, Rope (also called Worm or Loop), Cat's-Eye, Tobacco Leaf, Lollipop or Balloon, Marbled, Marbled and Combed, Twig, Geometric or Checkered, Banded, and slip decorations of rings, dots, flags, tulips, wavy lines, etc. It came into its own as a collectible in the latter half of the 1940s and has become increasingly popular as more and more people are exposed to the rich colorings and artistic appeal of its varied forms of abstract decoration.

The collector should take care not to confuse the early pearlware and creamware Mocha with the later kitchen yellow ware, graniteware, and ironstone sporting mocha-type decoration that was produced in America by such potters as J. Vodrey, George S. Harker, Edwin Bennett, and John Bell. This type was also produced in Scotland and Wales and was marketed well into the 20th century.

Bowl, blk & wht geometric rim, marbleized/combed band, 3x7½" .150.00
Bowl, mixing; seaweed, gr on cream band w/brn stripes, 5½x12" ..350.00
Bowl, seaweed, bl on wht band, 3⅜x6¾", EX 250.00
Bowl, seaweed, brn on wide wht band w/bl stripes, 3x6½" 265.00
Creamer, earthworm, 3-color on gray band, leaf hdl/spout, 3⅝" .1,375.00
Creamer, seaweed, dk brn on tan, molded gr band w/stripes, 2¾" ..440.00
Cup, handleless; seaweed, blk w/bl & blk stripes, hairlines 110.00
Egg cup, seaweed, blk w/brn & bl bands, blk stripes, 3" 330.00
Mug, cat's eyes, 3-color, w/stripes, rpr, 3" 330.00
Mug, earthworm, bl & wht w/3-color stripes, tan band, 4¼" 550.00
Mug, earthworm, brn & wht w/mc stripes & bands, 4¾", NM ...600.00
Mug, feathery designs, 3-color, mc stripes, leaf hdl, 4¾" 1,100.00
Mug, seaweed, blk w/brn stripes, leaf hdls, rpr, 2⅝" 330.00
Mug, seaweed, 3-color, gray band, 3⅝" 475.00
Mustard pot, seaweed, blk, brn stripes, leaf hdl, 2⅛x3" 385.00
Pepper pot, earthworm, 3-color on gray, w/stripes, 4½" 850.00
Pepper pot, earthworm, 3-color on gray band, bl dome, 5" 935.00
Pepper pot, earthworm, 3-color on yel ochre band, 2⅝" 1,100.00
Pepper pot, earthworm, 3-color on yel-orange w/stripes, 4" 1,100.00
Pepper pot, seaweed, blk, brn stripes, orange band, 3⅝" 990.00
Pepper pot, seaweed, blk on gray, brn/wht stripes, rpr, 4½" 385.00
Pepper pot, seaweed, blk on orange band w/stripes, 3⅝" 990.00
Pitcher, bl & gr bands w/stripes & wavy lines, leaf hdl, 5" 550.00
Pitcher, bl & teal bands, blk/wht stripes, leaf hdl, 6¼", EX 140.00
Pitcher, earthworm, 2-color, blk/wht stripes, mc bands, rpr, 6" ..175.00
Pitcher, earthworm, 2-color, brn & wht stripes, rpr, 7" 550.00
Pitcher, earthworm, 3-color, brn stripes, leaf hdl, 5⅛" 1,150.00
Pitcher, earthworm, 3-color, brn stripes, leaf hdl, 6⅝" 1,925.00
Pitcher, earthworm, 3-color, brn/wht stripes, leaf hdl, 8", EX .1,425.00
Pitcher, earthworm, 4-color, brn/tan stripes, rpr, 5⅝" 715.00
Pitcher, earthworm & cat's eye, 3-color w/mc emb bands, 7" ..1,500.00
Pitcher, mc stripes & bands on wht, 8¾" 360.00
Pitcher, polka dot & leaf design in wht, mc bands, 6" 935.00
Pitcher, seaweed, blk w/mc bands, prof rpr, 7⅝" 825.00
Pitcher, zigzags, 3-color w/bl/wht/gray bands, rprs, 8" 385.00
Pitcher, 2-color stripes, bl & wht band w/blk rim, 6⅝", EX 250.00
Salt cellar, seaweed, blk on wht, emb gr band w/mc stripes, NM .220.00
Waste bowl, earthworm, bl & wht w/2-color stripes, 4¾" 385.00
Waste bowl, earthworm, 3-color, beige band, 2⅝x4½", EX 220.00
Waste bowl, earthworm, 3-color w/brn & blk stripes, 6½", VG .165.00

Molds

Food molds have become popular as collectibles — not only for their value as antiques, but because they also revive childhood memories of elaborate ice cream Santas with candy trim or barley sugar figurals adorning a Christmas tree. Ice cream molds were made of pewter and came in a wide variety of shapes and styles. Chocolate molds were made in fewer shapes but were more detailed. They were usually made of tin, copper, and occasionally of pewter. Hard candy molds were usually metal, although primitive maple sugar molds (usually simple hearts, rabbits, and other animals) were carved from wood. (Unless otherwise indicated, those in our listings are cast aluminum or stainless steel.) Cake molds were made of cast iron or cast aluminum and were most

common in the shape of a lamb, a rabbit, or Santa Claus. Our advisors for this category are Dale and Jean Van Kuren; they are listed in the Directory under New York.

Chocolate Molds

Angel w/harp, Jaburg Bros, 2-pc, 3 clips, 4¾" 50.00
Bear, NY, hinged, 5" 95.00
Charlie Chaplin, 7½" 125.00
Chick w/hat, 2-pc, w/clip, USA, 3½" 40.00
Clown, 5¾" 85.00
Comic man w/top hat & glasses, 2-part, 1 clip, 4½" 45.00
Cottage w/witch & Hansel & Gretel, 4¾x6" 100.00
Cowboy, Holland, 2-pc, 1 clip, 4⅝" 45.00

Cupid, 2-piece with clamps, 5", $95.00.

Donkey, Made in Germany, 3 clamps, 11x11⅝x2⅜" 75.00
Easter rabbit, 2-pc, 3 clips, 8½" 65.00
Easter rabbit w/basket, Made in USA, 2 clamps, 13x9¾x3½" 85.00
Easter rabbit w/basket, 7½" 115.00
Elephant baby on rocker, Dresden, 2-pc, w/clip, 5⅛" 65.00
Elephant w/trunk down, Made in USA 508, 3 clamps, 7x9⅛x3¾" ..55.00
Elephant w/trunk up, 2 clamps, 7⅜x10¾x2½" 65.00
Fisherman & fisherwoman, 6½", pr 150.00
Hen on nest, 2-pc w/clips, 3⅜" 45.00
Horse, Jaburg NYC, 4½" 65.00
Lovebirds, France, 11½" 115.00
Lovebirds, Loit, hinged, 4⅛" 45.00
Rabbit, hinged, 4" 35.00
Rabbit w/bk pack, 2-pc w/clip, 6" 65.00
Rabbits running (4), Germany, 2-pc, 4⅝" L 40.00
Reindeer, 2 clamps, 10⅛x11⅜x3¾" 175.00
Santa, 3" 25.00
Santa, 4¾" 65.00
Santa, 8" 150.00
Santa w/basket, dbl hinged, 9" 175.00
Santa w/pack on bk, holds doll, ...Cologne, 2 clamps, 8½" 150.00
Santa w/pack on bk, 2 clamps, 7x4x2⅛" 100.00
Santa w/pack on bk (old-style Santa), 2 clamps, 9x4¾x3¼" 125.00
Santa w/pack on bk & plane under arm, 2 clamps, 10x4¾x2¾" ...175.00
Santw/pack on bk & plane under arm, 2 clamps, 8x4½x2⅜" 150.00
Sheep, 4" 50.00
Squirrel w/nest, 6½" 100.00
Swan, 3 clamps, 8⅝x10x3¼" 30.00
Teddy bear, 2-pc, 5½" 110.00
Wild pig, 3¼" 50.00

Hard Candy Molds

Battleship in waves, TM-256, groove for stick, 2½x1¼" 55.00
Hand, TM-31, groove for stick, 1¾x1¼" 42.50

Lion, 3-part, TM-138, groove for stick, 1¾x1¼" 60.00
Locomotive, 3-part, TM-14, groove for stick, 3½x6" 125.00
Mary w/lamb, TM-244, groove for stick, 2x2" 80.00
Mouse, TM-37, groove for stick, 2¼x1¼" 90.00
Rat, TM-238, groove for stick, 2½x1" 80.00
Steamboat w/paddle wheel, groove for stick, 1¼x2¼" 90.00
Teddy bear, walnut, rctl, 2-part, makes 6, 1½x12" 130.00

Ice Cream Molds

American Eagle, pewter, 2-pc, hinged, 4½x4" 85.00
Banjo 65.00
Bassinet, 3-part 45.00
Calla lily, 3-part 145.00
Candle 125.00
Carnation, 3-part 145.00

Chick baby, E. & Co. NY, 3½", $50.00.

Christmas wreath, E&Co NY, hinged, 5¾" 55.00
Cornucopia 45.00
Cow, #659 ....50.00
Cupid in rose, E-959 ....50.00
Dove 45.00
Doves kissing, 3-part 145.00
Easter lily, 3-part 145.00
Father Christmas E&Co #166, 2-part, hinged, 5x2¼x3¼" 155.00
Fireman w/trumpet, S&Co #340, EX 150.00
Heart w/Cupid, E&Co, 3¾" 45.00
Hen 125.00
Lady w/bird, hinged, 5½" 35.00
Lobster, 3-part 145.00
Rose 45.00
Soldier, 5⅝" 45.00
Steamer fire engine, S&Co #497, 5" L, EX 130.00
Stork w/baby, #631 ....40.00
Stork w/baby, standing, E-1151 ....57.50
Strawberry, E-316 ....32.50
Teddy bear 125.00
Tiger, 3-part 145.00
Trunk 65.00
Turkey 45.00
Victorian girl, #286, 5" 55.00
Wishbone 65.00

Maple Sugar Molds

Beaver, hand cvd, EX detail, 5x9" 75.00
Birds, 5 in a row, EX detail, ¾x11⅞x1¾" 50.00
Fruit & foliage, hardwood, 2-part, 5½x8" 28.00
Heart w/face, hand cvd, in orig tin case, 1800s, 5½" 425.00
Hearts (2), varnished, 3x18" 125.00

Rabbit sitting, EX cvg, 1¼x6½x5" 55.00
Strawberry, deeply cvd pine, rctl, 1830s, 1¾x5½x9" 165.00

Miscellaneous

Cheese, tin, heart shape, tubular fr, 2¾x5⅞x5¾" 170.00
Cheese, tin, pierced circles, 3-ftd, w/lid, 3x5¼" dia 130.00
Cheese, tin w/arched ribbon hdl, 3-ftd, 3⅝x4½x5½" 120.00
CI, bird on a branch, oval, 5" 225.00
Copper, swirl design, pinpoint holes, 6⅝" 85.00
Pewter, 4-part, grapes/eagles & swags/rabbit/basket, 5x6" 250.00
Scottish shortbread, wood, cvd zigzag edge, 1¼x9½x7" 50.00
Tin, oval, domed lid w/wire hdl 38.00
Tin, overlapping circles/fluted sides, center post, 4x7x5" 50.00
Tin, pear, lt rust, 5¼x3½" 75.00
Tin, 6-pointed star, tube center, 2½x9" 32.00
Tin/copper, cabbage rose, 4¼x6⅝x4⅝" 125.00
Tin/copper, rose & leaves, fluted bottom, 4½x6⅝x4⅝" 125.00
Tin/copper, sheaf of wheat, scalloped, 4½x7x5¼" 55.00

Monmouth

The Monmouth Pottery Company was established in 1892 in Monmouth, Illinois. Their primary products were salt-glazed stoneware crocks, churns, jugs, bristol, spongeware, and brown glaze. In 1906 they were absorbed by a conglomerate called the Western Stoneware Company. Monmouth became their #1 plant and until 1930 continued to produce stoneware marked with their maple leaf logo. Items marked 'Monmouth Pottery Co.' were made before 1906; after the merger, 'Co.' was dropped and 'Ill.' was substituted. Western Stoneware Co. introduced a line of artware in 1926. The name chosen was Monmouth Pottery. Some stamps and paper labels add ILL to the name.

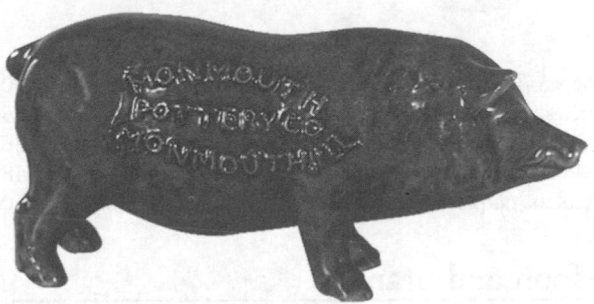

Pig, brown, marked Monmouth Pottery Co., Monmouth, ILL, $1,200.00.

Churn, Bristol glaze, 2-gal 250.00
Churn, Bristol glaze, 3-gal 250.00
Churn, Bristol glaze, 5-gal 250.00
Cooler, ice water; bl & wht sponge, w/lid & spigot, 8-gal 2,000.00
Crock, Albany slip, cobalt mk, 6-gal 400.00
Crock, Bristol glaze, 2 men in a crock stamp, 5-gal 600.00
Crock, Bristol glaze, 20-gal 100.00
Crock, cobalt on salt glaze, Albany slip int, 3-gal, $200 to 250.00
Crock, early dull Bristol glaze, cobalt stencil 300.00

Monot and Stumpf

The firm of Monot and Stumpf was organized in 1868, the merger of the E.S. Monot and F. Stumpf glassworks. It was located in Pantin, France. They produced fine art glass of various types until ca 1892, when the company reorganized and became known as the Cristallerie de Pantin.

Rose bowl, Pantin, pk opal, gold lustre int, 10-crimp, 4½" **118.00**
Salt cellar, Pantin, pk opal w/gold irid int, 10¼x2⅜" **65.00**
Vase, deep rose opal, ruffled, 3x5" **195.00**

Mont Joye

Mont Joye was a type of acid-cut French cameo glass produced by Cristallerie de Pantin in Paris around the turn of the century. It is accented by enamels. Our advisor for this category is Don Williams; he is listed in the Directory under Missouri.

Bowl, poppies on red, 12", +pr matching 12" vases **3,000.00**
Bowl, violets on lt gr frost, gilt accents, 4x9" **545.00**

Vase, gold oak leaves and silvered acorns on emerald green baluster form, light wear to rim, 25¼", $2,500.00.

Vase, acorns/leaves, gold/silver on textured emerald, 13x9" **1,000.00**
Vase, irises, mc w/gold spike leaves on textured frost, 20" **2,650.00**
Vase, scattered violets, scrolls at base on frost, 14x9" **865.00**
Vase, violets, gilt leaves/stems on clear pinched sides, 9" **485.00**
Vase, violets, purple w/gold on clear, 10" **400.00**

Moon and Star

Moon and Star was originally produced in the 1880s by John Adams & Company of Pittsburgh. In the 1960s, Joseph Weishar of Wheeling, West Virginia, owner of the Island Mould & Machine Company, reproduced some of the original molds and incorporated the pattern into approximately forty new and different items. Two of the largest distributors of this line were L.E. Smith of Mt. Pleasant, Pennsylvania, who pressed their own glass, and L.G. Wright of New Martinsville, West Virginia, who had theirs pressed by Fostoria, Fenton, and Westmoreland. Both companies carried a large and varied assortment of shapes and colors. Several other companies were involved in its manufacture as well, especially of the smaller items.

Over the years the glassware has been pressed in amberina (yellow shading to orange- or ruby-red), green, amber, crystal, light blue, and ruby. Pieces in ruby and light blue are most collectible and harder to find than the other colors, which seem to be abundant. Purple, pink, cobalt, amethyst, tan slag, and light green and blue opalescent were made, too, but on a lesser scale.

Current L.E. Smith catalogs contain a small assortment of pieces

that are still available in crystal, pink, cobalt (lighter than the old shade), and these colors with an iridized finish. A new color, teal green, was introduced in 1992, a water set in sapphire blue opalescent was pressed in 1993, and the new color in 1994 was cranberry ice. Items are currently being pressed in various colors by the Weishar Company, who adds their mark to the new glassware made primarily for collectors. Our values are given for ruby and light blue. For amberina, green, and amber, deduct 20%.

Ashtray, moon at rim, star in base, 6-sided, 5½" **15.00**
Butter dish, all over pattern, scalloped ft, 6x5½" **45.00**
Candle holders, allover pattern, flared & scalloped ft, 6", pr **35.00**
Compote, allover pattern, ftd, scalloped rim, 5½x8" **35.00**
Compote, allover pattern, scalloped rim, 7x10" **45.00**
Compote, allover pattern, w/lid, 8x10" **65.00**
Creamer & sugar bowl, open, disk ft, sm **28.00**
Decanter, bulbous w/allover pattern, plain neck, 32-oz, 12" **60.00**
Goblet, water; plain rim & ft, 5¾" **15.00**
Jelly dish, plain flat rim, disk ft, patterned lid, 6¾x3½" **35.00**
Nappy, allover pattern, crimped rim, 2¾x6" **18.00**
Relish bowl, 6 lg scallops form allover pattern, 1½x8" **25.00**
Salt cellar, allover pattern, scalloped, sm flat ft **8.00**
Shakers, allover pattern, metal lids, 4x2", pr **25.00**
Sherbet, plain rim & stem, 4¼x3¾" **15.00**
Soap dish, allover pattern, oval, 2x6" **12.00**
Sugar bowl, allover pattern, sm flat ft, w/lid, 5¼x4" **35.00**
Sugar shaker, allover pattern, metal lid, 4½x3½" **38.00**
Syrup, allover pattern, metal lid, 4½x3½" **38.00**
Toothpick holder, allover pattern, scalloped rim, ftd **10.00**
Tumbler, iced tea; no pattern at rim or on ft, 11-oz, 5½" **20.00**
Tumbler, juice; no pattern at rim or on disk ft, 5-oz, 3½" **12.00**
Tumbler, no pattern at rim or disk ft, 7-oz, 4½" **12.00**

Moorcroft

William Moorcroft began to work for MacIntyre Potteries in 1897. At first he was the chief designer but very soon took over their newly created art pottery department. His first important design was the Aurelian Ware, part transfer and part hand painted. Very shortly thereafter, around the turn of the century, he developed his famous Florian Ware, with heavy slip and done in mostly blue and white. Since the early 1900s there has been a sucession of designs, most of them very characteristic of the company. Moorcroft left MacIntyre in 1913 and went out on his own. He had already well established his name, having won prizes and gold medals at the St. Louis World's Fair as well as in Paris. In 1929 Queen Mary, who had been collecting his pottery, made him 'Potter to the Queen,' and the pottery was so stamped up until 1949. William Moorcroft died in 1945, and his son Walter ran the company until recent years. The factory is still in existence. They now produce different designs but continue to use the characteristic slipwork. Moorcroft pottery was sold abroad in Canada, the United States, Australia, and Europe as well as in specialty areas such as the island of Bermuda.

Moorcroft went through a 'Japanese' stage in the early teens with his lovely lustre glazes, Oriental shapes, and decorations. During the mid-teens he began to produce his most popular Pomegranate Ware, as well as Wisteria (often called 'Fruit'). Around that time he also designed the popular Pansy line as well as Leaves and Grapes. Soon he introduced a beautiful landscape series called variously Hazeldine, Moonlit Blue, Eventide, and Dawn. These wonderful designs along with Claremont (Mushrooms) seem to be the most sought after by collectors today. It would be possible to add many other designs to this list.

During the 1920s and 1930s, Moorcroft became very interested in highly fired Flambe (red) glazes. These could only be achieved through a very difficult procedure which he himself perfected in secret. He later passed the knowledge on to his son.

Dating of this pottery is done by knowledge of the designs, shapes, signatures, and marks on the bottom of each piece; an experienced person can usually narrow it down to a short time frame. Prices escalated for this 'rediscovered' pottery in the late 1980s but has now leveled off. This is true mainly for the pre-1935 designs of William Moorcroft, which is the era most sought after by collectors. Prices in the listings below are for pieces in mint condition unless noted otherwise; no reproductions are listed here. Advisors for this category are Wilfred and Dolli Cohen; they are listed in the Directory under California.

Bowl, anemones, flambe, 2¼x4¼" 150.00
Bowl, Claremont, toadstools in purple/gr/bl/yel, 12" L 1,995.00
Bowl, Claremont, toadstools on bl, hdls, 3x9½" 1,750.00
Bowl, clematis on gr, 1½x3¼" 100.00
Bowl, cornflowers, rose/bl/wine on sage gr to bl, ftd, 3x6" 1,000.00
Bowl, hibiscus, red/yel/bl on lt ground, 2½x10" 300.00
Bowl, hibiscus, 3 lg flowers on gr to bl, 3½x12" 550.00
Bowl, hibiscus on dk bl, 1¾x4½" 100.00
Bowl, hibiscus on gr, 1½x3¾" 80.00
Bowl, Moonlit Bl, landscape on dk bl, 3½x7½" 1,250.00
Bowl, orchids, mc on dk bl, 3x3" 165.00
Bowl, pansies, purple on bl/gr int, 3x9¾" 600.00
Bowl, pansies, wht/gr on gr, #993, 4⅝x8⅜" 635.00
Bowl, pomegranates, wine on gr to dk bl, 1¾x8¾" 550.00
Box, floral bouquet, red/yel/dk bl on shaded bl, label, 4½" dia ...245.00
Box, freesia, rose/yel on teal to cobalt, 3x6" dia 325.00
Box, spring flowers, red/yel/dk bl on teal/yel/dk bl, 3¾" 200.00
Candlesticks, wisteria, wht/yel/wine/rose on dk bl, 8½", pr 900.00

Charger, Moonlit Blue trees and landscape, green script mark, 5x13" diameter, $2,200.00.

Compote, lustre, berries, rose/bl/gr on cream, hdls, 7" 1,500.00
Cup & saucer, demitasse; 18th-C pattern, MacIntyre 450.00
Dish, blackberries, yel/pk/gr on lt gr to dk bl, 5½", +lid 300.00
Ginger jar, hibiscus, red/yel on dk bl, sgn Walter, 6" 185.00
Humidor, Caribbean, flying fish on teal to gr, 6½", NM 350.00
Jar, ginger; orange lustre, shouldered, 6" 150.00
Jar, leaves/fruit, mc on dk bl, lid w/finial, 3½x6" 290.00
Jar, pomegranates, red w/purple berries, #769, w/lid, 10" 950.00
Jar, wisteria, purple/red/yel/gr on dk bl, w/lid, #869, 10" 895.00
Lamp base, anemones, mc on gr to teal, 8½", +shade 450.00
Lamp base, cornflowers, yel/red/bl on lt bl/gr, bottle form 650.00
Lamp base, florals, gr on br w/bl at base, bottle form, 11" 650.00
Lamp base, orchid, mc on red-brn to dk bl flambe, bulbous, 10" 650.00
Lamp base, pomegranates, wine/purple on dk bl, 13x8", +shade .1,195.00
Pitcher, Gesso Faience, squeezebag decor/gold lines, 6½" 550.00
Plate, leaves & berries on bl flambe, 12" 650.00
Plate, Moonlit Bl, lg tree in foreground, 8½", NM 700.00
Vase, anemones, purple/bl/red on dk bl/gr, 6" 250.00
Vase, anemones, rose/wht/bls on bl-gr, 10x5" 450.00
Vase, anemones on dk bl, 4x4" 225.00

Vase, blackberries, violet/rose/gr/yel on dk bl, 6x5" 275.00
Vase, clematis, bl/lav/pk on bl to med gr, 6" 250.00
Vase, clematis, bl/red on shaded yel-gr, 7½" 300.00
Vase, Dawn, landscape/geometric band, bls/gold, 7½x6", NM .1,000.00
Vase, Flamminian, medallions on emerald gr, #1381, 5x10" 800.00
Vase, Florian, cornflowers/multiflora, bl/yel/gr, 3-hdl, 5" 800.00
Vase, Florian, irises, bl tones, heavy slip, MacIntyre, 7" 875.00
Vase, Florian, pansies, bl/yel/gr on lt to dk bl, slim, 12" 1,300.00
Vase, Florian, poppies, dk bl/wht, MacIntyre, 4" 600.00
Vase, Florian, poppies/forget-me-nots, MacIntyre, 7½" 1,450.00
Vase, Florian, tulip in gr/gold, MacIntyre, 7" 1,000.00
Vase, Florian, tulips, yel on gr w/cobalt accents, 7" 1,200.00
Vase, Florian, 5-color on lt & dk bl, stick neck, 5" 850.00
Vase, freesia, mc on dk bl, 5" 200.00
Vase, fruit/leaves, mc on dk bl, 6¼" 200.00
Vase, gr lustre, baluster, ca 1916, 8¾" 250.00
Vase, grapes/leaves, mc on red-brn, 6x5" 700.00
Vase, hibiscus, flambe, sgn Walter, 7" 300.00
Vase, hibiscus, red/yel/wine on ivory, 8" 275.00
Vase, leaves & berries, dk bl/wine/rust on brn to teal, 6" 275.00
Vase, leaves & fruit, mc on dk bl, 3½" 125.00
Vase, Moonlit Bl, aqua trees on cobalt, 4½" 950.00
Vase, Moonlit Bl, landscape on dk bl, shouldered, #65, 9" 1,600.00
Vase, Moonlit Bl, trees on dk bl, #M94, bulbous, 8½" 1,500.00
Vase, Moonlit Bl, turq trees on cobalt, shouldered, 7" 1,000.00
Vase, Moonlit Bl, turq trees on cobalt, 5x5" 1,100.00
Vase, orchids, red/yel/bl on bl, ca 1940s, 8½x4½" 425.00
Vase, pansies, purple/wht/mauve on cobalt, 5" 495.00
Vase, pansies, wht/yel/purple on dk bl, 6" 550.00
Vase, pomegranates, red on cobalt, flared-top cylinder, 10" 650.00
Vase, pomegranates, red on dk bl, flared cylinder, 13" 900.00
Vase, pomegranates, red/mc berries, silver flared top, 12" 1,100.00
Vase, pomegranates, rose/tan/lav/bl on dk bl, 8½x10" 1,100.00
Vase, pomegranates, Tudric sterling ftd base, 6½" 600.00
Vase, pomegranates on dk bl to brn, bulbous bottom, 9" 575.00
Vase, spring flowers on teal to cobalt, 7" 500.00
Vase, Tudor Rose, dk bl/wine roses on lt gr, 4x4", NM 625.00
Vase, wisteria, mc on dk bl, bulbous bottom, #74, 12" 850.00
Vase, wisteria, purple/bl/pk/yel on dk bl, shouldered, 9½" 550.00
Vase, wisteria, purple/rose/yel on dk bl, waisted neck, 13" 800.00
Vase, wisteria, yel/wine/plum on dk bl, wide cylinder, 11" 750.00

Moravian Pottery and Tile Works

Dr. Henry Chapman Mercer was an author, anthropologist, historian, collector, and artist. One of his diversified interests was pottery. In 1898 he established the Moravian Pottery and Tile Works in Doylestown, Pennsylvania, the name inspired by his study and collection of decorative stove plates made by the early Moravians. Because the red clay he used there proved to be unfit for tableware, he turned to the production of handmade tile which he himself designed. Though he never allowed it to become more than a studio operation, the tile works was nevertheless responsible for some important commercial installations, one of which was in the capitol building at Harrisburg.

Mercer died in 1930. Business continued in the established vein under the supervision of Mercer's assistant, Frank Swain, until his death in 1954. Since 1968 the studio has been operated by The Bucks County Commission, and tiles are still fashioned in the handmade tradition. They are marked 'Mercer' and are dated.

Candle sconce, Deer Riding Wolf, figures in relief, 11x4¼" 325.00
Tile, Birds of Tintern Abbey, dk gr on ivory, unmk, 5", NM 125.00
Tile, Centaur of Nuremberg, gr on ivory, unmk, 4½" 95.00

Tile, Knight of Nuremberg, gr on ivory, 4½" **95.00**
Tile, Lute, musician emerges from acanthus leaf, mc, 6¼x4½" ..**225.00**
Tile, Mayflower, bl **65.00**
Tile, pomegranate brocade, dk gr gloss, unmk, 4x3¾" **95.00**
Tile, Rain, Am Indian, rtcl, dk gr semimatt, 4"+fr, NM **165.00**
Tile, rampant lion, red clay & bl satin, unglazed, 4½" **85.00**
Tile, Spanish lion, blk gloss on orange arabesques, 8x6½" **495.00**
Tile, Zodiac symbol, fully glazed on red clay, unmk, 4" **100.00**

Morgan, Matt

From 1883 to 1885, the Matt Morgan Art Pottery of Cincinnati, Ohio, produced fine artware, some of which resembled the pottery of the Moors with intense colors and gold accents. Some of the later wares were very similar to those of Rookwood, due to the fact that several Rookwood artists were also associated with the Morgan pottery. Some examples were marked with a paper label, others with either a two- or three-line impression: 'Matt Morgan Art Pottery Co.,' with 'Cin. O.' sometimes added.

Charger, 2 owls on branch w/moon, Hirschfield, 1881, 11" **2,000.00**
Lamp vase, Oriental bird & grasses, Hirschfield, 1884, 7⅞" **400.00**
Tile, stylized poppies & leaves in relief, mk, 6" **175.00**
Vase, floral, gourd shape w/lid, 1880s, 5¼" **375.00**
Vase, 4 Morrish high-relief panels on bl w/gold, 19" **375.00**

Morgantown Glass

Incorporated in 1899, the Morgantown Glass Works experienced many name changes over the years. Today 'Morgantown Glass' is a generic term used to identify all glass produced there. Purchased by Fostoria in 1965, the factory was permanently closed in 1971. Our advisor for this category is Jerry Gallagher, longtime researcher of the company and author of *A Handbook of Old Morgantown Glass, Volume I*. He is listed in the Directory under Minnesota. See Clubs, Newsletters, and Catalogs for information concerning Mr. Gallagher's book, The Morgantown Collectors of America (a research society founded by him), and *The Morgantown Newscaster*, a triannual M.C.A. journal with research updates and reports of current trends.

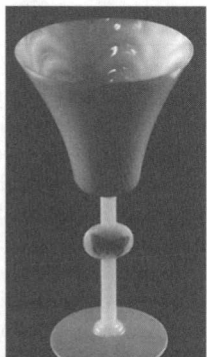

#8447 Unger goblet, Jade Green bowl and foot with Alabaster stem, honey bee, and butterfly enamel disk, very rare, $250.00.

Adair etch, crystal/gold; stem, goblet; #7604½ Heirloom, 10-oz ..**125.00**
Adam etch, crystal; stem, champagne; #7810 Monaco, 5-oz **38.00**
Adam etch, crystal; stem, goblet, #7810 Monaco, 9-oz **45.00**
Adonis etch, crystal; stem, goblet; #7604½ Heirloom, 9-oz **50.00**
Adonis etch, crystal/gr; stem, goblet; #7606½ Athena, 9-oz **110.00**
Adonis etch, gr; stem, parfait; #7604½ Heirloom, 5-oz **60.00**
Adonis etch, rose; stem, goblet; #7604½ Heirloom, 9-oz **65.00**

Adonis etch, topaz; stem, goblet; #7604½ Heirloom, 9-oz **65.00**
Am Beauty etch, crystal; jug, no lid, #19 Flemish, 34-oz **295.00**
Am Beauty etch, crystal; jug, no lid, #2 Arcadia, 54-oz **350.00**
Am Beauty etch, crystal; stem, champagne; #7695 Trumpet, 6-oz ..**48.00**
Am Beauty etch, crystal; stem, goblet; #7565 Astrid, 10-oz **68.00**
Am Beauty etch, crystal; stem, wine; #7668 Galaxy, 5-oz **48.00**
Am Beauty etch, crystal; stem, wine; #7695 Trumpet, 2½-oz **65.00**
Am Beauty etch, crystal; tumbler, iced tea; #7668 Galaxy, 12-oz .**45.00**
Am Beauty etch, crystal; tumbler, iced tea; #8701 Garrett, 14-oz .**45.00**
Am Beauty etch, crystal; tumbler, juice; #7668 Galaxy, 6-oz **34.00**
Am Beauty etch, crystal; tumbler, water; #9001 Billings, 8-oz **40.00**
Am Beauty etch, crystal; tumbler, water; #9715 Calhoun, 10-oz ..**42.00**
Am Beauty etch, rose; finger bowl, #2927, 4¼" **65.00**
Am Beauty etch, rose; jug, no lid, #39 Milton, 54-oz **325.00**
Am Beauty etch, rose; stem, goblet; #7565 Astrid, 10-oz **55.00**
Am Beauty etch, rose-amber; jug, w/lid, #39 Milton, 54-oz **425.00**
Aquaria etch, crystal/gr; stem, champagne; #7634 Oceana, 6-oz ...**87.50**
Aquaria etch, crystal/gr; stem, goblet; #7643 Oceana, 9-oz **95.00**
Arctic etch, crystal; stem, goblet; #7640 Art Moderne **135.00**
Arctic etch, crystal/blk; stem, goblet; #7640 Art Moderne **155.00**
Art Moderne, cobalt/crystal; stem, candlestick, #7640½, pr **335.00**
Art Moderne, cobalt/crystal; stem, cordial; #7640, 1½-oz **145.00**
Art Moderne, cobalt/crystal; stem, goblet; #7640, 9-oz **95.00**
Art Moderne, crystal/blk; stem, goblet; #7640, 9-oz **100.00**
Art Moderne, crystal/frost; stem, icer; sgn DC Thorpe, 2-pc **245.00**
Art Moderne, pastel/crystal; stem, goblet; #7640, 9-oz **90.00**
Baden etch, blk filament; stem, goblet; #7606½ Athena, 9-oz **95.00**
Baden etch, crystal/blk; jug, ftd; #49 Jubilee, 54-oz **385.00**
Baden etch, crystal/blk; tumbler, ftd; #7661 Camilla, 12-oz **75.00**
Baden etch, crystal/blk; tumbler, ftd; #7661 Camilla, 6-oz **55.00**
Barry #37, crystal/rose; jug, hdld/ftd, Palm Optic, 48-oz **335.00**
Barry #37, Meadow Gr cased Alabaster/gr; jug, hdld/ftd, 48-oz ...**595.00**
Barry #37, Meadow Gr/Jade; jug, hdld/ftd, 48-oz **495.00**
Bartley #7637, gr/cased Alabaster/gr; tumbler, ftd, 13-oz **95.00**
Biscayne etch, crystal/gold; stem, goblet; #7587 Kingsley, 9-oz **57.50**
Biscayne etch, crystal/gold; tumbler, bar; #9715, 2½-oz **68.00**
Bramble Rose etch, crystal; stem, champagne; #7577 Venus, 5½-oz .**58.00**
Bramble Rose etch, crystal; stem, goblet; #7577 Venus, 9-oz **58.00**
Bramble Rose etch, rose; plate, luncheon; #1500, 8½" **32.00**
Candlespheres, Old Amethyst, #8 Mars, pr **225.00**
Candlespheres, ruby, #8 Mars, pr **185.00**
Carlton, platinum Marco; bowl, flared, #4355 Janice, 13" **215.00**
Carlton, platinum Marco; stem, goblet; #7653 Cantata, 9-oz **78.00**
Carlton etch, crystal/blk; stem, goblet; #7606½ Athena, 9-oz **87.50**
Carlton etch, crystal/blk; stem, sherbet; #7606½, 5½-oz **65.00**
Carlton Frostie etch, crystal; punch bowl, #21, 12" **465.00**
Carlton Madrid, topaz/crystal; stem, goblet; #7665 Laura, 9-oz **65.00**
Carlton Milan, crystal; stem, goblet; #7668 Galaxy, 10-oz **32.50**
Cathay etch, crystal; stem, champagne; #7711 Callahan, 5½-oz ..**50.00**
Cathay etch, crystal; stem, goblet; #7711 Callahan, 9-oz **65.00**
Cherry Blossom etch, topaz; stem, champagne; #7577, 5½-oz **45.00**
Cherry Blossom etch, topaz; stem, goblet; #7577 Venus, 9-oz **60.00**
Corinth etch, crystal/gold; stem, goblet; #7654 Lorna, 9-oz **58.00**
Corinth etch, crystal/gold; stem, wine; #7654 Lorna, 3-oz **68.00**
Courtney #7637, crystal/DC Thorpe decor; stem, champagne; 5-oz .**195.00**
Courtney #7637, crystal/DC Thorpe decor; stem, claret; 4½-oz .**255.00**
Crinkle, amberina; tumbler, water; flat, #1962, 10-oz **68.00**
Crinkle, amethyst; San Juan, tankard; #1962, 54-oz, 9" **75.00**
Crinkle, amethyst; tumbler, ftd iced tea; #1962, 13-oz **27.50**
Crinkle, crystal; Tia Juana, juice/martini; #1962, 34-oz, 6½" **50.00**
Crinkle, gr; Ockner jug, #1962, 54-oz **72.00**
Crinkle, gr; tumbler, ftd iced tea; #1962, 13-oz **24.00**
Crinkle, lt bl frosted; tumbler, flat; #1962, 20-oz **38.00**
Crinkle, peacock bl; Ockner jug, #1962, 54-oz **98.00**

Crinkle, peacock bl; tumbler, ftd iced tea; #1962, 13-oz 27.50

Crinkle, peacock bl; tumbler, juice; flat, #1962, 6-oz 22.00

Crinkle, peacock bl; tumbler, water; flat, #1962, 10-oz 22.00

Crinkle, pk; sherbet, ftd, #1962, 6-oz 20.00

Crinkle, ruby; Ockner jug #1962, 54-oz 135.00

Crinkle, ruby; Owl tumbler, highball; flat, #1969, 16-oz 85.00

Crinkle, ruby; tumbler, zombie; flat, #1962, 20-oz 38.00

Eileen etch, crystal/gold #32 band; goblet, #7673 Lexington, 9-oz ..125.00

Elizabeth, azure; stem, goblet; #7630 Ballerina, 9-oz 100.00

Elizabeth, azure; stem, goblet; #7664 Queen Anne, 9-oz 125.00

Elizabeth, crystal; stem, wine; #7630 Ballerina, 2¾-oz 65.00

Fairwin, bl filament; stem, goblet; #7673 Lexington, 9-oz 110.00

Fairwin, bl filament; stem, juice; #7673 Lexington, 5-oz 75.00

Faun etch, crystal/blk; champagne, #7640 Art Moderne, 5½-oz .160.00

Faun etch, crystal/blk; stem, goblet; #7640 Art Moderne, 9-oz ...185.00

Fernlee, blk filament; stem, goblet; #7672 Octette, 9-oz 78.00

Fernlee, crystal/blk; stem, goblet; #7640 Art Moderne, 9-oz 135.00

Florence etch, crystal; stem, cocktail; #300 Touraine, 3-oz 45.00

Florence etch, crystal; stem, goblet; #300 Touraine, 9-oz 42.50

Floret etch, crystal; stem, goblet; #7684 Yale, 9-oz 85.00

Floret etch, crystal; stemmed icer & insert, #7589 Laurette 65.00

Fontinelle, blk filament; stem, goblet; #7620 Fontanne, 9-oz 165.00

Fontinelle, gr/crystal; stem, goblet; #7620 Fontanne, 9-oz 155.00

Golf Ball, cobalt/crystal; candlestick, 2 styles, #7643, 4", pr 225.00

Golf Ball, cobalt/crystal; candy dish, flat, #1212 Michael, 7" 325.00

Golf Ball, cobalt/crystal; stem, champagne; #7643, 5½-oz 48.00

Golf Ball, cobalt/crystal; stem, goblet; #7643, 9-oz 55.00

Golf Ball, crystal; pilsner, #7643, 10-oz, 9", rare 165.00

Golf Ball, pastel/crystal; stem, goblet; from $48 to 60.00

Golf Ball, rose/gr finial; candy dish, flat, #2938 Helga, 5" 685.00

Golf Ball, ruby/crystal finial; candy dish, #7858 Leora, 5½" 395.00

Golf Ball, ruby/crystal; candy dish, #9074 Maureen, 4½" 375.00

Golf Ball, ruby/crystal; candy dish, flat, #1212 Michael, 7" 315.00

Golf Ball, ruby/crystal; candy dish, flat, #2938 Helga, 5" 260.00

Golf Ball, ruby/crystal; compote, low, w/lid, #7643 Celeste 375.00

Golf Ball, ruby/crystal; stem, goblet; #7643 Celeste, 9-oz 50.00

Golf Ball, Stiegel/crystal; candy dish, LeRoy decor, #2938, 5" ...345.00

Guest set, Anna Rose; Palm optic, #25 Trudy, 2-pc 70.00

Guest set, Azure; Festoon optic, #25 Trudy, 2-pc 85.00

Guest set, Azure; Peacock optic, #24 Maria, 4-pc, rare 525.00

Guest set, Baby Bl opaque; Hollyhock decor, #23 Margaret 185.00

Guest set, Golden Iris; hdls, pulled spout, #23 Margaret 295.00

Guest set, Jade Gr opaque; #25 Trudy, 2-pc 85.00

Guest set, yel opaque bottle/blk tumbler, #25 Trudy 235.00

Hollywood, blk band; tumbler, highball; flat, #8701, 12-oz 48.00

Hollywood, red band; jug, cocktail; #548 Fairbanks, 36-oz 345.00

Kyoto etch, crystal/gr; stem, champagne; #7634 Tiburon, 6-oz ...120.00

Kyoto etch, crystal/gr; stem, goblet; #7634 Tiburon, 9-oz 145.00

Labelle etch, crystal/blk; stem, champagne; #7640 Art Moderne ..68.00

Labelle etch, crystal/gold band; stem, goblet; #7640 Art Moderne ..95.00

Lace Bouquet etch, crystal; stem, goblet; #7668 Galaxy, 10-oz 47.50

Lace Bouquet etch, crystal; stem, sherbet; #7668 Galaxy, 6-oz 37.50

LeMons, cobalt/gold; stem, goblet; #7640 Art Moderne, 9-oz 255.00

LeMons, cobalt/platinum; stem, goblet; #7640 Art Moderne, 9-oz .185.00

LeMons, rose/gold; stem, goblet; #7640 Art Moderne, 9-oz 275.00

LMX (El Mexicano), Hyacinth; Ockner jug, #1933, 54-oz 350.00

LMX (El Mexicano), Ice; candle holder, bulbous, 4", #1933, pr .280.00

LMX (El Mexicano), Ice; sherbet, ftd, #1933, 7-oz 25.00

LMX (El Mexicano), Rose Quartz; ice tub, #1933 ....295.00

LMX (El Mexicano), Rose Quartz; Ockner jug, #1933, 54-oz 340.00

LMX (El Mexicano), Rose Quartz; sherbet, ftd, #1933, 7-oz 57.00

LMX (El Mexicano), Rose Quartz; tumbler, ftd, #1933, 13-oz 68.00

LMX (El Mexicano), Seaweed; decanter, liquor; w/stopper, #1933 ..225.00

LMX (El Mexicano), Seaweed; relish, 3-part, #1933 ....115.00

Marilyn etch, crystal/gr; stem, goblet; #7636 Square, 5½-oz 120.00

Marilyn etch, crystal/rose; stem, champagne; #7636 Square, 5½-oz .135.00

Mayfair etch, crystal; stem, champagne; #7668 Galaxy, 6-oz 27.00

Mayfair etch, crystal; stem, goblet; #7668 Galaxy, 10-oz 38.00

Maytime etch, topaz; stem, champagne; #7664½ Vernon, 5½-oz ..40.00

Maytime etch, topaz; stem, goblet; #7664½ Vernon, 9-oz 50.00

Melon, alabaster/cobalt hdl; beverage set, #20069, 7-pc 850.00

Melon, frosted/blk hdl, Aurora etch; jug, #20069 ....695.00

Mikado etch, crystal; stem, champagne; #7711 Callahan, 6-oz 37.50

Mikado etch, crystal; stem, goblet; #7711 Callahan, 10-oz 48.50

Monroe #7690, cobalt or ruby/crystal; stem, champagne; 6-oz 75.00

Monroe #7690, cobalt or ruby/crystal; stem, goblet; 9-oz 87.50

Monroe #7690, Golden Iris/crystal; stem, cordial; 1½-oz 120.00

Monroe #7690, Old Amethyst/crystal; stem, cordial; 1½-oz 145.00

Monroe #7690, Old Amethyst/crystal; stem, goblet; 10-oz 115.00

Nantucket etch, crystal; stem, goblet; Queen Anne, 10-oz 95.00

Nantucket etch, crystal/gr; stem, goblet; #7654 Lorna, 9-oz 85.00

Nasreen etch, blk/filament; stem, sherbet; #7606½ Athena, 5½-oz .75.00

Nasreen etch, crystal/blk; tumbler, #9074 Belton, 9-oz 58.00

Nasreen etch, topaz/crystal; stem, claret; #7665 Laura, 5-oz 95.00

Old Bristol, cobalt w/opal disc-node; candlestick, 4", pr 380.00

Old Bristol, cobalt w/opal rim; plate, unknown #, 7½" 88.00

Old English #7678, cobalt/crystal; stem, champagne; 6½-oz 50.00

Old English #7678, cobalt/crystal; stem, goblet; 10-oz 68.00

Old English #7678, Stiegel Gr/crystal; stem, goblet; 10-oz 58.00

Old English #7678, Stiegel Gr/crystal; stem, iced tea; 12-oz 58.00

Old English #7678, Stiegel Gr/crystal; stem, sherbet; 6½-oz 48.00

Palm Optic, Alexandrite; stem, iced tea; #7667 Georgian, 12-oz ..195.00

Palm Optic, Anna Rose; stem, goblet; 37477 Venus, 9-oz 45.00

Palm Optic, Anna Rose/gr; stem, goblet; #7614 Hampton, 9-oz ...87.50

Palm Optic, Anna Rose/gr; stem, goblet; #7646 Sophisticate, 9-oz ...90.00

Palm Optic, Anna Rose/gr; stem, wine; #7614 Hampton, 3-oz 95.00

Palm Optic, Azure; ice bucket, SP metal rim/bail 385.00

Palm Optic, Azure; salver, ftd, unknown #, 7" 195.00

Palm Optic, Azure; stem, parfait; #7536 Alycia, 5½-oz 50.00

Palm Optic, crystal; stem, goblet; #7577 Venus, 9-oz 38.00

Palm Optic, crystal/Anna Rose; jug, #37 Barry, 48-oz 295.00

Palm Optic, Venetian Gr; stem, goblet; #7577 Venus, 9-oz 50.00

Palm Optic, 14k Topaz; stem, goblet; #7577 Venus, 9-oz 42.00

Paragon #7624, crystal/blk; stem, goblet; 9-oz 170.00

Paragon #7624, crystal/blk; stem, sherbet; 5½-oz 95.00

Paula #7675, Ritz Bl/crystal; stem, goblet; 10-oz 145.00

Paula #7675, Stiegel Gr/crystal; stem, goblet; 10-oz 125.00

Peacock Optic, gr or rose; stem, goblet; 37638 Avalon, 9-oz 45.00

Peacock Optic, gr; decanter, crystal stopper, #10½ Lynwood 395.00

Peacock Optic, gr; tumbler, bar; flat, #9051 Zenith, 1½-oz 85.00

Persian etch, crystal; marmalade jar, glass lid, #106 Willett 145.00

Persian etch, crystal; water bottle, #23 Largo 185.00

Picardy etch, crystal; champagne, #7646 Sophisticate, 5½-oz 38.00

Picardy etch, crystal; stem, goblet; #7646 Sophisticate, 9-oz 55.00

Pineapple Optic, amber; stem, goblet; #7644½ Vernon, 9-oz 45.00

Pineapple Optic, gr; stem, goblet; #7664½ Vernon, 9-oz 52.00

Pontinelle, blk filament; stem, candlestick, low, #7620, pr 495.00

Prairie Rose, crystal/gr; stem, cocktail; #6046 Kirby 32.00

Prairie Rose, crystal/gr; stem, goblet; #6046 Kirby 55.00

Priscilla, blk filament; stem, champagne; #7620 Fontanne, 6-oz ...95.00

Priscilla, blk filament; stem, goblet; 37620 Fontanne, 9-oz 130.00

Pygon #7623, crystal/blk; sherbet, 5-oz 85.00

Pygon #7623, crystal/frosted; champagne, sgn Thorpe, 5½-oz 155.00

Pygon #7623, crystal/frosted; wine, sgn Thorpe, 3½-oz 165.00

Pygon #7623, frosted; wine, Thorpe HP bird decor, 3½-oz 235.00

Reyer Thistle, crystal; stem, goblet; #7713 Scotia, 9-oz 55.00

Reyer Thistle, crystal; stem, sherbet; #7668 Galaxy, 5½-oz 34.00

Reyer Thistle, crystal; stem, wine; #7668 Galaxy, 2½-oz 45.00

Richmond etch, crystal; stem, goblet; #7570 Horizon, 10-oz 30.00
Richmond etch, crystal; stem, goblet; #7589 Laurette, 9-oz 35.00
Rosalie etch, crystal; bowl, console; #4355 Janice, 13" 225.00
Rosalie etch, topaz/crystal; stem, goblet; #7662 Majesty, 10-oz ...110.00
Rosamonde etch, crystal/Golden Iris, tumbler, #9074, 10-oz 65.00
Rosamonde etch, pnt crystal/Golden Iris, tumbler, #9074, 10-oz ..145.00
Saranac etch, crystal; stem, champagne; #7690 Monroe, 5½-oz ...48.00
Saranac etch, crystal; stem, goblet; #7690 Monroe, 10-oz 70.00
Sea Gulls enamel decor, jug, #545 Pickford, 60-oz 425.00
Sea Gulls enamel decor, tumbler, ftd, #9093, 12-oz 80.00
Shamrock etch, 2-Tone Laurel Line; jug; #40 Shannon, 48-oz ...345.00
Sharon etch, crystal/platinum; candlespheres; #8 Mars, pr 265.00
Sharon etch, crystal/platinum; vase, ball shape, #8 Luna 185.00
Sonoma etch, crystal; stem, champagne; #7659 Cynthia, 6-oz 58.00
Sonoma etch, crystal; stem, goblet; #7659 Cynthia, 10-oz 68.00
Sonoma etch, topaz; stem, goblet; #7659 Cynthia, 10-oz 85.00
Square #7636, champagne, DC Thorpe decor, 5½-oz 195.00
Square #7636, claret, DC Thorpe decor, 4½-oz 235.00
Square #7636, crystal; champagne, 5½-oz 160.00
Square #7636, crystal; goblet, 10-oz 235.00
Superba, blk/filament; champagne, #7664 Queen Anne, 6½-oz .145.00
Superba, blk/filament; goblet, #7664 Queen Anne, 10-oz 215.00
Superba, crystal/blk; champagne, #7654½ Legacy, 6½-oz 145.00
Superba, crystal/blk; goblet, #7654½ Legacy, 10-oz 225.00
Tinker Bell, Azure; tumbler, ftd, #9069, 12-oz 70.00
Tinker Bell, crystal; goblet, #7631 Jewel, 10-oz 155.00
Tinker Bell, crystal; guest set, #24 Maria, 4-pc, very rare 675.00
Tinker Bell, gr; vase, bud; ftd, #53 Serenade, 10" 345.00
Toulon gold stencil, rose; stem, champagne; #7604½, 6-oz 85.00
Toulon gold stencil, rose; stem, goblet, #7604½ Heirloom, 10-oz ..135.00
Toulon gold stencil, rose; stem, parfait; #7604½, 6-oz 150.00
Versailles, crystal; stem, goblet; #7688 Jamestown, 9-oz 55.00
Versailles, crystal; stem, goblet; #7711 Callahan, 10-oz 50.00
Victoria, crystal; goblet, #300 Touraine, 9-oz 55.00
Victoria Regina, crystal/blk; goblet, #7640 Art Moderne, 9-oz ...110.00
Virginia etch, amber; stem, goblet; #7614 Hampton, 9-oz 55.00
Virginia etch, crystal; stem, goblet; #7587 Hampton, 9-oz 45.00
Virginia etch, crystal; stem, goblet; #7711 Callahan, 10-oz 58.00
Yale #7684, cobalt or ruby; stem, goblet; 9-oz 125.00
Yale #7684, crystal; stem, goblet; 9-oz 100.00
Yale #7684, Stiegel Gr; stem, goblet; 9-oz 115.00

Continental Line

Ashley #4354, Golden Iris/crystal rim; basket, ftd, 10" dia 365.00
Clayton #4357½, Spanish Red; basket, 10" dia 375.00
El Greco #87, Ritz Bl; vase, flower; hdld, 11" 460.00
Electra #35½, Spanish Red, vase, flower; hdld, 10" 350.00
Irene #4356, amber/crystal rim; basket, 8-crimp, 10½" dia 365.00
Irene #4356, Ritz Bl/crystal; basket/bowl, 6-crimp, 10½" 325.00
Janet #4355, Stiegel Gr; basket/bowl, 8-crimp, 13" 340.00
Jennie #20, Aquamarine/crystal hdl; basket, bonbon; 4½" dia ..485.00
Jennie #20, crystal/ebony hdl; basket, bonbon; 4½" dia 475.00
Jupiter #71, Ritz Bl/crystal; vase, flower; Italian base, 6" 345.00
Lyndale #64, Confetti; kerosene lamp, Italian base, 6" 475.00
Naples #35½, Old Amethyst; vase, flower; Italian base, 12" 450.00
Neapolitan #64, blk amethyst; ivy ball, Italian base, 6" 400.00
Patrick #4358, all crystal; basket, flower; 8-crimp, 10" dia 345.00
Patrick #4358, Golden Iris; basket, flower; 8-crimp, 8" dia 395.00
Patrick #4358, Stiegel; basket, flower; 8-crimp, 6" dia 285.00
Roma #68, Indian Blk; vase, flower; Italian base, 10" dia 350.00
Trindle #4357, Old Amethyst; basket, 8-crimp, 9" dia 425.00
Vienna #71, Stiegel Gr; bowl, console; Italian base, 12" 785.00
Ziegfeld #61, Spanish Red; witch ball, Italian base, 8" 850.00

Silk-Screen Color Printing on Crystal

Manchester Pheasant, champagne, #7664 Queen Anne, 6½-oz .150.00
Manchester Pheasant, cocktail, #7664 Queen Anne, 3½-oz 165.00
Manchester Pheasant, goblet, #7664 Queen Anne, 10-oz 210.00
Manchester Pheasant, sherbet, #7664 Queen Anne, 6½-oz 135.00
Queen Louise, crystal/rose; stem, cocktail; #7614 Hampton, 6-oz .165.00
Queen Louise, crystal/rose; stem, goblet; #7614 Hampton, 9-oz .225.00
Queen Louise, crystal/rose; stem/wine; #7614 Hampton, 6-oz 190.00

Sunrise Medallion Etch

#37 Barry, Azure; jug, ftd, 48-oz 595.00
#37 Barry, crystal; jug, ftd, 80-oz 500.00
#45 Catherine, Azure; vase, bud; ftd, 10" 340.00
#45 Catherine, gr or rose; vase, bud; ftd, 10" 370.00
#53 Serenade, Azure; vase, bud; bulbous, ftd, 10" 425.00
#53 Serenade, rose; vase, bud; bulbous, ftd, 10" 400.00
#7630 Ballerina, Azure; stem, goblet; 9-oz 85.00
#7630 Ballerina, crystal; stem, goblet; 9-oz 65.00
#7630 Ballerina, gr; stem, goblet; 9-oz 70.00
#7630 Ballerina, rose; stem, goblet; 9-oz 75.00
#7630 Ballerina, topaz; stem, goblet; 9-oz 70.00
#7654½ Legacy, crystal/Moonstone; stem, champagne; 6-oz 155.00
#7654½ Legacy, crystal/Moonstone; stem, cocktail; 3-oz 155.00
#7654½ Legacy, crystal/Moonstone; stem, goblet; 9-oz 225.00
#7664 Queen Anne, Azure; stem, goblet; 10-oz 100.00
#7664 Queen Anne, crystal; stem, goblet; 10-oz 90.00

Moriage

The term 'moriage' refers to certain Japanese wares decorated with applied slipwork designs. There are several methods used to achieve the characteristic relief effect. The decorative devices may be designed separately and applied to the vessel, piped on in narrow ribbons of clay (slip-trailed), or built up by brushing on successive layers of liquified slip. See also Dragon Ware; Nippon.

Vase, allover floral decoration on green, 4½", $235.00.

Ashtray, floral, 4¾" 55.00
Cracker jar, cherry blossoms/branches, gilt florals, sqd 175.00
Cup & saucer, floral reserves, mc w/gold, mk 65.00
Humidor, EX slipwork, 7" 215.00
Rose bowl, turq & wht slipwork, jewels, ftd, 5¾" 275.00
Sugar shaker, roses on gr, bbl form 100.00
Vase, floral slipwork, panels w/birds, 12" 260.00

Mortars and Pestles

Mortars are bowl-shaped vessels used for centuries for the purpose of grinding drugs to a powder or grain into meal. The masher or grinding device is called a pestle.

Brass, flared rim, 4¾x5¾", +8¾" mortar	125.00
Brass, heavy, polished, ca 1800, 4x4", +pestle, EX	100.00
Brass, 13x12", +pestle	125.00
Burl wood, bowl shape, 7¼x5½"	140.00
Burl wood, rnd sides, 5⅛x5" dia	100.00
Porc, wht w/gold decor, Owens IL, 7", +7" pestle	30.00
Treenware, Lignum Vitae, trn, ftd, 7⅜x5", +8½" mortar	50.00
Trn wood, ftd, 5½x3⅞", trn 5⅝" pestle	65.00
Trn wood, heavy, no cracks & solid, ca 1860s, 8x5", +pestle	65.00
Wooden, primitive, 7x7"	40.00

Mortens Studio

Oscar Mortens was already established as a fine sculptural artist when he left his native Sweden to take up residency in Arizona. During the 1940s he developed a line of detailed animal figures which were distributed through the Mortens Studios, a firm he co-founded with Gunnar Thelin. Thelin hired and trained artists to produce Mortens' line, which he called Royal Designs. More than two hundred dogs were modeled and over one hundred horses. Cats and wild animals such as elephants, panthers, deer, and elk were made, but on a much smaller scale. Bookends with sculptured dog heads were shown in their catalogs, and collectors report finding wall plaques on rare occasions. The material they used was a plaster-type composition with wires embedded to support the weight. Examples were marked 'Copyright by the Mortens Studio' either in ink or decal. Watch for flaking, cracks, and separations. Crazing seems to be present in some degree in many examples. When no condition is indicated, the items listed below are assumed to be in near-mint condition, allowing for minor crazing.

Afghan, tan/charcoal face, 7x7", M	90.00
Beagle, recumbent	48.00
Beagle, standing, 4½x4½"	60.00
Boston Terrier, ivory mks on blk, standing, 6x6", M	75.00
Boxer, recumbent, 8" L	60.00
Boxer, standing, tan w/blk, 5½x5½"	75.00
Collie, standing, 6x7"	90.00
Dachshund, standing, lg	70.00
Dalmation, #112, sm	50.00
Doberman, standing, 6x7"	70.00
English Setter, #848	65.00
English Spaniel, standing, ivory w/blk, 5½x6½"	80.00
German Shepherd, standing, 7"	85.00
German Shepherd pup, 3½x3½"	35.00
Great Dane, recumbent, blk details on tan, 7½x6½"	75.00

Horse, black, grazing on grassy base, 4½x6½", $90.00.

Horse, wild, 6¾"	85.00
Lion, recumbent, 4x6"	135.00
Lynx	175.00
Mexican Chihuahua, sitting, tan w/blk details, 3x3½"	65.00
Pekingese, standing, 3½x4½"	95.00
Persian cat	48.00
Pointer, sitting, ivory w/blk spots, 4x4¾"	65.00
Spaniel pup, ivory w/blk spots, 3¾x3"	40.00
Springer Spaniel, 5"	65.00
St Bernard, 6½x8½"	100.00

Morton Pottery

Six potteries operated in Morton, Illinois, at various times from 1877 to 1976. Each traced its origin to six brothers who immigrated to America to avoid military service in Germany. The Rapp brothers established their first pottery near clay deposits on the south side of town where they made field tile and bricks. Within a few years, they branched out to include utility wares such as jugs, bowls, jars, pitchers, etc. During the ninety-nine years of pottery operations in Morton, the original factory was expanded by some of the sons and nephews of the Rapps. Other family members started their own potteries where artware, gift-store items, and special-order goods were produced. The Cliftwood Art Pottery and the Morton Pottery Company had showrooms in Chicago and New York City during the 1930s. All of Morton's potteries were relatively short-lived operations with the Morton Pottery Company being the last to shut down on September 8, 1976. For a more thorough study of the subject, we recommend *Morton's Potteries: 99 Years, Vols. I and II*, by Doris and Burdell Hall; their address can be found in the Directory under Illinois.

Morton Pottery Works — Morton Earthenware Co. (1877-1917)

Bank, acorn, gr, advertising Acorn Stove Co	50.00
Bean pot, yelware, ind, ¼-pt	20.00
Bowl, banded yelware, 15¼"	125.00
Coffeepot, brn Rockingham, ornate hdl, 5-pt	125.00
Jug, Dutch; brn Rockingham, 3-pt	65.00
Jug, Dutch; cobalt bl, rare, 3-pt	130.00
Jug, milk; brn Rockingham, 1-pt	50.00
Mug, banded yelware, 1-pt	85.00
Pie baker, yelware, 10" dia	100.00
Teapot, Rebecca, brn Rockingham, 5¼-pt	100.00

Cliftwood Art Potteries, Inc. (1920-1940)

Figurine, Billiken doll, brn, 11"	100.00
Figurine, Billiken doll, brn, 7½"	75.00
Figurine, lioness, Herbage Gr, 7x12"	50.00
Lamp, Boudoir, cobalt, #16, 6½"	24.00
Lamp, desk; w/elephant figure, natural colors, 8"	80.00
Lamp, doughnut shape w/clock insert, bl-mulberry, 8½"	150.00
Lamp, flattened bulb, bl-gray drip, #6, 16½"	75.00
Planter, cat, sitting, yel, 5½"	35.00
Planter, elephant w/howdah, cobalt & gr, 6½"	30.00
Planter, heron, turq matt, 6"	18.00
Planter, police dog, wht matt, 5x8½"	20.00
Vase, bl & wht drip, #114, 16"	75.00
Vase, fan shape w/hdls, brn drip, 9"	40.00
Vase, Grecian Urn, Old Rose, 6"	35.00
Vase, tree trunk form, gr, 9"	70.00
Wall pocket, tree trunk form, brn drip, rare, 8"	80.00

Midwest Potteries, Inc. (1940-1944)

Figurine, cat, recumbent, wht & gray, 3x8" 40.00
Figurine, cow creamer, wht & gold, 5" 20.00
Figurine, hen, wht & gold, 3¾" 18.00
Figurine, mountain goat, brn spray, 9½" 30.00
Figurine, Oriental man & woman shelf sitters, blk/wht/gold, pr ...25.00
Figurine, rooster, wht & gold, 5" 20.00
Figurine, wild turkey, brn/tan spray, 12" 30.00
Miniature, bird, bl & yel, 1½" 10.00
Miniature, frog, gr, 1" 10.00
Miniature, hen, gr/yel/wht, 1¼" 10.00
Miniature, rabbit, wht & pk, 1½" 12.00
Miniature, rooster, gr/yel/wht, 2" 10.00
Miniature, swan, wht matt, 2" 12.00
TV lamp, deer tan w/gold, 14", w/10" fawn 50.00
TV lamp, dogs, poodle, wht, 14", & pug, brn, 11" 60.00
TV lamp, owl, brn/wht/gray, 12" 60.00
TV lamp, Siamese cats, brn/wht, 13¼" adult & 8" kitten 50.00

Morton Pottery Company (1922-1976)

Davy Crockett, lamp, adult figure w/bear, gr & brn 75.00
Davy Crockett, lamp, boy figure w/bear, gr/brn/gray 100.00
Davy Crockett, planter, boy figure w/bear, gr/brn/gray 35.00
Flowerpot soaker, bird, bl & yel 18.00
Flowerpot soaker, calla lily, yel & gr 15.00
Flowerpot soaker, hound dog, brn/wht 20.00
Head vase, upswept hair, eyes closed, heart brooch, bl/wht/red 25.00
Head vase, 1920s style, wide-brimmed hat, wht glossy 50.00
Head vase, 1940s style w/pillbox hat, wht matt, #406 ....45.00
Spatterware, bowl, red/wht/bl, #600, nested set of 3 ....150.00
Spatterware, custard cup, gr/brn/wht, 5-oz 20.00
Spatterware, jug, ice box; brn/yel/gr w/sgraffito, w/lid 100.00
Spatterware, pitcher, milk; brn/yel/gr, w/advertising, 4½" 75.00
Spatterware, restaurant counter weiner warmer, mc, 3¾x8¾x7" 125.00
Spatterware, twin tea set w/tray, dk bl & gr over lt bl 150.00
Wall plaque, fish, mc 18.00
Wall plaque, fruit cluster, natural colors 20.00
Wall plaque, Lincoln head, brn 24.00
Wall plaque, mallard duck, mc 18.00
Wall plaque, rooster, natural colors 22.00
Wall plaque, shoe house, yel/gr/brn 20.00

American Art Potteries (1947-1961)

TV lamp, Afghan hounds, blk, 15", pr 75.00
TV lamp, birds on branch, planter base, mauve/bl spray, 11" 30.00
TV lamp, conch shell, yel/gr spray, 6" 25.00
TV lamp, fish (dbl) on rectangular base, gr/yel/wht, 6x9x3½" 25.00
Vase, blossoms encrusted on bulbous form, brn/yel spray, 12¾" ...45.00
Vase, ewer form, pk/gray/gold, 8½" 20.00
Vase, ostrich feather on cornucopia, gray/yel/wht spray, 10½" 30.00
Vase, ostrich feathers on urn form, brn/yel/gold, 10½" 45.00
Vase, ruffled tulip form, ivory/pk/purple spray, 9" 24.00
Wall pocket, apple w/3 leaves, red & gr 18.00
Wall pocket, bird on tree trunk, bl/tan spray 18.00
Wall pocket, flower blossom, mauve/gr 22.00
Wall pocket, pear shape, purple w/bl int 15.00

Mosaic Tile Co.

The Mosaic Tile Company was organized in 1894, in Zanesville,

Ohio, by Herman Mueller and Karl Langenbeck, both of whom had years of previous experience in the industry. They developed a faster, less-costly method of potting decorative tile, utilizing paper patterns rather than copper molds. By 1901 the company had grown and expanded with offices in many major cities. Faience tile was introduced in 1918, greatly increasing their volume of sales. They also made novelty ashtrays, figural boxes, bookends, etc., though not to any large extent. Until they closed during the 1960s, Mosaic used various marks that included the company name or their initials — 'MT' superimposed over 'Co.' in a circle.

Ashtray, ivory, 4x2" 35.00
Tile, Asian child's profile, mc, #3087, 5¾" 275.00
Tile, goose, 6" 90.00
Tile, Hercules & Waggoner, mc, MOSAIC/BB/D64/26, 6" 175.00
Tile, Hispano-Moresque decor, mc, 6" 70.00
Tile, Lincoln, bl & wht jasper type, hexagonal 40.00
Tile, mallard duck, 6", NM 75.00
Tile, Man That Pleased None, mc, MOSAIC/P73/29, 6" 175.00
Tile, sailing ship/waves, 4-color, 6x6", NM 375.00
Tile, Zodiac series, 6", ea 35.00

Moser

Ludwig Moser began his career as a struggling glass artist, catering to the rich who visited the famous Austrian health spas. His talent and popularity grew and in 1857 the first of his three studios opened in Karlsbad, Czechoslovakia. The styles developed there were entirely his own; no copies of other artists have ever been found. Some of his original designs include grapes with trailing vines, acorns and oak leaves, and richly enameled, deeply cut or carved floral pieces. Sometimes jewels were applied to the glass as well. Moser's animal scenes reflect his careful attention to detail. Famed for his birds in flight, he also designed stalking tigers — even elephants — all created in fine enameling.

Moser died in 1916, but the business was continued by his two sons who had been personally and carefully trained by their father. The Moser company bought the Meyr's Neffe Glassworks in 1922, and continued to produce quality glassware.

When identifying Moser, look for great clarity in the glass; deeply carved, continuous engravings; perfect coloration; finely applied enameling (often covered with thin gold leaf); and well-polished pontils. Our advisor for this category is Don Williams; he is listed in the Directory under Missouri. Items described below are enameled unless noted otherwise.

Card holder, green with florals and gold, signed, 3⅞", $500.00; Bowl, clear with applied acorns, 4" diameter, $285.00; Vase, orange with applied acorns, signed, #1020, 4¼", $480.00.

Bottle, scent; amethyst to clear, flower intaglios, mk, 7½" 700.00
Bottle, scent; amethyst to clear w/gold, amethyst top, 5x2" 225.00
Bowl, Alexandrite, appl 4-leg platform, 5x8" 200.00
Bowl, amber w/gold scrolls & floral swags, bl/gold ft, 4¾" 140.00
Bowl, dk amber, floral/bugs/appl grapes, sectioned/ftd, 9" 1,000.00

Bowl, sapphire bl, 3 appl snails/enameling, 3x9" 425.00
Box, amber, allover wht lace, purple/gold decor, 3½x6" 375.00
Box, amber w/bird on branch, flowers on base, ribbed, 4" dia 170.00
Box, amethyst, raised enamel top & sides, Karlsbad, 3x3½" 245.00
Box, cranberry w/gold & wht leafy scrolls, 6" dia 275.00
Box, sapphire, daisies/dots/scrolls, hinged, 3x5" 350.00
Carafe, amber w/mc flowers & wht ferns, 7" 175.00
Compote, emerald cut to amber w/wreath of flowers, 5x8" 150.00
Cordial, cranberry, gold & bl dots, wht branches & flowers 45.00
Creamer & sugar, amethyst w/flowers, silver rim & lid, 4½" 275.00
Decanter, amethyst to clear w/gold, flattened bulb, 7¾" 200.00
Finger bowl, cobalt, Amazon warrior frieze 165.00
Liqueur set, amethyst to clear w/gold, 2 cruets+2mugs+tray 500.00
Liqueur set, lime gr w/jewels & gold, 6 pcs on tray 495.00
Loving cup, emerald gr w/mc flowers & gold, 6" 225.00
Mug, Invt T'print, bl to clear w/enamel 140.00
Tankard, apple gr to clear w/poppy intaglios, 12¼" 765.00
Tumble-up, gr w/flowers, doll sz 475.00
Tumbler, amberina T'print w/gold, mc flowers/insects, 3¾" 275.00
Tumbler, gr w/appl lace & lacy gold, 3¾x2⅜" 235.00
Vase, amber, Amazon women frieze, bulbous, 5" 345.00
Vase, amber, elephants/trees frieze in gold/gr, 12x5" 1,300.00
Vase, cameo berry branches, violet-bl on frost, ftd, 9" 500.00
Vase, cameo elephants/palm trees on purple w/gold, 11½x8" ..2,000.00
Vase, cameo floral on lt gr to clear, ribbed cylinder, 14" 900.00
Vase, clear w/tulips intaglio, 6" 105.00
Vase, cranberry w/mc florals, 3-sided, 8" 990.00
Vase, cranberry w/much gold, ftd cylinder w/flared rim, 14" 200.00
Vase, cranberry w/portrait transfer, mk, 8½" 250.00
Vase, emerald gr, floral/2 wide gold bands, ribbed, 5¾x5" 200.00
Vase, gilt vines surrounds 6½x7" portrait on porc, 19" 500.00
Vase, gr w/jester in courtyard, ribbed/ruffled, 8" 250.00
Vase, gr w/mc florals & animals, sgn Cire, 13" 185.00
Vase, jack-in-pulpit; chartreuse to clear w/gold floral, 14" 250.00
Vase, lt alexandrite, faceted, mk Royalit, U-form, 6" 230.00
Vase, med bl w/floral, flat-sided disk w/cube hdls, 9½" 200.00
Vase, topaz w/etched gold Amazon warrior band, facets, 12x5" ..635.00

Moss Rose

Moss Rose was a favorite dinnerware pattern of many Staffordshire and American potters from the mid-1800s. In America the Wheeling Pottery of West Virginia produced the ware in large quantities, and it became one of their bestsellers, remaining popular well into the nineties.

Bone dish, unmk, gold edge 32.00
Butter pat, Meakin, EX 15.00
Cup & saucer, Meakin 25.00
Gravy boat, Meakin 35.00
Gravy tureen, w/underplate, Haviland 105.00
Mug, unmk, 3" 14.00
Plate, Powell Bishop, 9" 25.00
Platter, rectangular, Meakin, 14x10" 35.00
Sugar bowl, akimbo hdls, Meakin, w/lid 50.00
Tea set, Am, 14-pc 125.00
Tea set, child's; 15-pc 275.00
Toothbrush holder, scalloped top, Meakin, 5x2¾" 65.00
Tray, tiered, unmk 30.00

Mother-of-Pearl Glass

Mother-of-Pearl glass was a type of mold-blown satin art glass popu-
lar during the last half of the 19th century. A patent for its manufacture was issued in 1886 to Frederick S. Shirley, and one of the companies who produced it was the Mt. Washington Glass Company of New Bedford, Massachusetts. Another was the English firm of Stevens and Williams. Its delicate patterns were developed by blowing the gather into a mold with inside projections that left an intaglio design on the surface of the glass, then sealing the first layer with a second, trapping air in the recesses. Most common are the Diamond Quilted, Raindrop, and Herringbone patterns. It was made in several soft colors, the most rare and valuable is rainbow — a blend of rose, light blue, yellow, and white. Occasionally it may be decorated with coralene, enameling, or gilt. Watch for 20th-century reproductions, especially in the Diamond Quilted pattern. Our advisors for this category are Betty and Clarence Maier; they are listed in the Directory under Pennsylvania. See also Coralene.

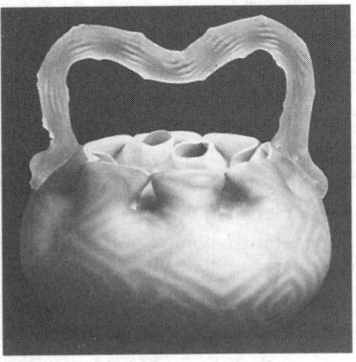

Basket, apricot Moire, pleated folds at rim, frosted handle, 19½", $550.00.

Basket, Herringbone, bl, crimped oval rim, camphor hdl, 9x9" ..450.00
Bonbon, Dmn Quilt, wht w/clear ribbons, Webb, 8½" L 550.00
Bottle, scent; Peacock Eye, wht, bulbous, 3¾" 635.00
Bowl, Dmn Quilt, bl w/mica, vaseline ft, berry pontil, 4x5" 235.00
Bowl, Dmn Quilt, rainbow, in Pairpoint SP Cupid fr, 6x6" 725.00
Bowl, Dmn Quilt, rainbow, triangular, ruffled, appl ft, 3x6" 1,250.00
Bowl, Dmn Quilt, wht w/brn & citron matsu-no-ke, 5x6" 550.00
Card tray, Zipper MOP, apricot, fluted, Stevens & Wms, 6½" dia .400.00
Condiment set, Ribbon, red, salt cellar/pepper/mustard+SP fr ...850.00
Creamer, Raindrop, bl, frosted hdl, 4½x3" 195.00
Ewer, Dmn Quilt, pk, ribbed body w/leaves, ruffled, 12" 800.00
Ewer, Herringbone, bl, HP/gold bird/floral, thorn hdl, 11" 150.00
Ewer, Herringbone, rainbow, fold-down rim, camphor hdl, 10" 1,200.00
Ewer, Herringbone, salmon, camphor hdl, 7½" 115.00
Finger bowl, Dmn Quilt, rainbow, +underplate, both mk Pat 900.00
Finger bowl, Dmn Quilt, rare amberina, 4½", +underplate 915.00
Lamp, Dmn Quilt, pk, ribbed/ruffled open-top shade, 17" 1,150.00
Pickle castor, Herringbone, bl, ornate fr w/owl figures 950.00
Pitcher, Dmn Quilt, pk w/asters, sqd mouth, squatty, 4½" 600.00
Pitcher, Herringbone, rainbow, fold-down crimped rim, 5" 1,250.00
Plate, Drape, pk, mk Pat, 7" 200.00
Rose bowl, Concentric Circles, rainbow, mk Pat, 2⅜x4⅜" 850.00
Rose bowl, Dmn Quilt, brn w/gold prunus & butterfly, Webb 450.00
Rose bowl, Dmn Quilt, rainbow, mk Pat, 4" H 200.00
Rose bowl, Herringbone, bl, pk int, crimped rim, Webb, 3½" 300.00
Rose bowl, Herringbone, pk, egg shape, 4-crimp, 3¾x3¼" 195.00
Rose bowl, Pinwheel, bl, 8-crimp, 5½x6" 235.00
Rose bowl, Ribbon, bl, 9-crimp top, 2⅝x3½" 265.00
Rose bowl, Ribbon, chartreuse gr, 8-crimp, 3x3½" 195.00
Rose bowl, Ribbon, chartreuse gr, 9-crimp, 2¾x3½" 245.00
Rose bowl, Ribbon, pk, ruffled, 2½" dia 250.00
Rose bowl, Rivulet, gr, ruffled & frosted ft, 3½x4¼" 250.00
Rose bowl, Rivulet, pk, 8-crimp, 2¾x4½" 195.00
Salt cellar, Raindrop, rainbow, SP rim, 2¼" 250.00
Tumbler, Dmn Quilt, apricot w/floral, 4" 235.00

Tumbler, Dmn Quilt, bl w/floral, 3¾" 125.00
Tumbler, Dmn Quilt, pk w/floral, 3¾" 135.00
Tumbler, Dmn Quilt, rainbow w/floral 700.00
Tumbler, Herringbone, apricot w/floral, 3¾" 135.00
Tumbler, Herringbone, pk, 3¾x2⅝" 195.00
Vase, Basketweave, shaded bl, bulbous bottom, Webb, 7x5" ...750.00
Vase, Coin Spot, pk, 3½x2¼" 325.00
Vase, Dmn Quilt, bl, decor at shoulder, irreg rim, appl ft, 7" ...350.00
Vase, Dmn Quilt, bl, fluted top, 8x3½" 250.00
Vase, Dmn Quilt, bl, in ornate silver ftd base w/leaves, 18" 525.00
Vase, Dmn Quilt, bl, tapered/ftd, waisted rim, 5½", pr 220.00
Vase, Dmn Quilt, bl to wht, Mt WA, dbl gourd, 9x4½" 450.00
Vase, Dmn Quilt, butterscotch, ruffled rim, 5½x4¾" 200.00
Vase, Dmn Quilt, pk, frosted ruffle, 5½" 158.00
Vase, Dmn Quilt, rainbow, 3-lobe top, long neck w/ring, 6" 900.00
Vase, Dmn Quilt, red w/floral & butterfly, tapered, 6" 195.00
Vase, Drape, pk, ruffled, 5¾x3⅝" 250.00
Vase, Flower & Acorn, bl, waisted neck, 7x6" 745.00
Vase, Flower & Acorn, wht, gold floral, Webb, 3½x5½" 650.00
Vase, Herringbone, apricot, knob neck/fan-crimped rim, 7" 120.00
Vase, Herringbone, bl, appl threading, Northwood, 8x2½" 450.00
Vase, Herringbone, bl, crimped rim, 9½" 130.00
Vase, Herringbone, bl, floral, ribbed body, camphor hdls, 9" ...150.00
Vase, Herringbone, rainbow, crimped fan top, ftd, 7" 350.00
Vase, Herringbone, yel, melon ribs, ruffled, 6x3" 175.00
Vase, Melon Rib Swirl, bl, ruffled top, ormolu ft, 7x3⅜" 195.00
Vase, Pompeian Swirl, gr to rose, Stevens & Wms, 5⅝" 750.00
Vase, Raindrop, bl, frosted & ruffled edge, 7½x4½" 175.00
Vase, Raindrop, butterscotch, ruffled top, 5x3⅞" 110.00
Vase, Raindrop, pk, pillow shape, Mt WA, 9½" 345.00
Vase, Ribbon, bl, bottle form, 5¼x3½" 110.00
Vase, Ribbon, bl, 5x6" 395.00
Vase, Ribbon, chartreuse gr, rectangular top, 2¾x3" 185.00
Vase, Ribbon, red w/gold florals, sq top, 3" 500.00
Vase, Snowflake, bl, dotted floral/butterfly/gilt, 7", pr 925.00
Vase, Swirl, pk w/rose o/l, Stevens & Wms, 11½x6" 950.00
Vase, Swirl, reverse amberina w/gold florals, 9½" 1,320.00

Mourning Collectibles

During the 18th and early 19th centuries, ladies made needlework pictures, samplers, paintings on ivory plaques, watercolor drawings, etc. to commemorate the death of a loved one. Elements contained in nearly all examples are the tomb, mourners, a weeping willow tree, and data relating to the deceased. Often plaits of hair were included. Today these are recognized and valued as a valid form of folk art. Our advisor for this category is Steve DeGenaro; he is listed in the Directory under Ohio. See also Hair Weaving.

Handkerchief, blk silk, 1880s, EX 60.00
Locket on chain, contains hair pc, gold mts, 1850s-80s 175.00
Memoriam card, flower litho, info inside, 1896, EX 10.00
Needlework, church/figure/cemetery, 1813, 23x28" 1,100.00
Needlework, embr silk, lady/urn/tombstone, 1800, 11" dia, ft .2,100.00
Needlework, silk, monument scene, ca 1799, 16x14" 2,185.00
Photo, postmortem, cabinet card sz, 1880s-90s, EX 22.50
Pin, watercolor on ivory in gold shell, ca 1900, M 250.00

Movie Memorabilia

Movie memorabilia covers a broad range of collectibles, from books and magazines dealing with the industry in general to the various promotional materials which were distributed to arouse interest in a particular film. Many collectors specialize in a specific area — posters, pressbooks, stills, lobby cards, or souvenir programs (also referred to as premiere booklets). In the listings below, a one-sheet poster measures approximately 27" x 41", three-sheet: 41" x 81", and six-sheet: 81" x 81". See also Autographs; Cartoon Art; Paper Dolls; Personalities; Sheet Music.

Book, Gone w/the Wind, motion picture edition, '39, EX 50.00
Book, Hollywood Babylon, Jayne Mansfield on jacket, '75, NM ...20.00
Book, King Rebel, John Huston, '65, dust jacket, NM 5.00
Book, Lassie-Forbidden Valley, Provost & Lassie cover, '59, EX ...15.00
Book, Mystery at Smuggler's Cove, Annette Funicello, '63, EX 5.00
Booklet, recipe; Royal Desserts, G Rogers, color, '40s, NM 20.00
Brochure, Gone w/Wind, Scarlett/Rhett cover, '39, 4-pg, 8x10" ..495.00
Calendar, Marilyn Monroe, salesman sample, nude photo, 1950 ..150.00
Camera, Roy Rogers, 620 Snap Shot, H George Co, VG 95.00

Campaign book, Columbia Studio's upcoming movies for 1934-35, 14x11", light wear and loose binding, $880.00.

Cigarette card, Carreras Ltd, De Havilland, England, NM 10.00
Cigarette card, Gold Leaf, Marlena Dietrich, German, fr, NM 20.00
Figurine, Marilyn Monroe, 7 Year Itch, M 450.00
Insert card, Accused, Loretta Young, '49, 36x14", VG 15.00
Insert card, Glass Menagerie, Douglas/Wyman, '50, 36x14", NM .30.00
Insert card, Houseboat, C Grant/S Loren, '58, 14x22", EX 22.00
Insert card, In This Corner, Scott Brady, '48, 14x22", EX 30.00
Insert card, Lost Tribe, Johnny Weissmuller, '49, 14x22", VG 35.00
Insert card, Sorrowful Jones, B Hope/L Ball, '49, 36x14", VG 55.00
Insert card, Sunset Pass, Zane Grey western, '46, 36x14", EX 48.00
Insert card, Torn Curtain, Hitchcock, '66, 36x14", NM 53.00
Lobby card, Doctor, You've...Kidding, Dee/Hamilton, set of 4 .....10.00
Lobby card, Ghostbusters, Murray/Aykroyd, '84, set of 8, M 25.00
Lobby card, Instanbul, Errol Flynn, '57, VG 20.00
Lobby card, Laughing Policeman, Matthau/Dern, '73, set of 8 ......25.00
Lobby card, My Bodyguard, Matt Dillon, '80, set of 8, NM 10.00
Lobby card, Sharkey's Machine, B Reynolds, '81, set of 8, NM 15.00
Lobby card, Splash, Daryl Hannah/Tom Hanks, '84, set of 8 ....10.00
Lobby card, War & Peace, Audrey Hepburn, '56, 8x10" 4.00
Magazine, Modern Screen, Ginger Rogers, 4/38, EX 18.00
Magazine, Modern Screen, Leigh cover, 6/40, EX 50.00
Magazine, Photoplay, Clark Gable as Rhett, 2/40, EX 85.00
Magazine, Photoplay, Garbo cover, 8/30, EX 55.00
Magazine, Sat Evening Post, Bonanza cast, color, 12/4/65, VG 10.00
Magazine, Screen Greats #9, Judy Garland/Mickey Rooney, EX ...25.00
Magazine, Screen Guide, V Leigh cover, 3/41, EX 50.00
Magazine cover, Motion Picture, Clara Bow, 11/32, EX 5.00
Magazine cover, Photoplay, Gary Cooper, color, 10/39, NM 20.00
Magazine cover, Photoplay, Joan Bennett, 7/35, NM 10.00
Magazine cover, True Romances, Hedy Lamarr, 9/39, NM 10.00
Photo, Greta Garbo dancing w/Robt Taylor, NM 7.00
Photo, Virginia Grey in sailor suit 7.00
Pin-bk button, Spanky, Hal Roach, Safety First, EX 38.00
Poster, Abbot & Costello Meet Invisible Man, '51, 14x36", M ..150.00
Poster, Brenda Star movie serial, '44, 1-sheet, EX 425.00

Poster, My Mother...Alien, Kim Basinger, color, '88, EX **25.00**
Poster, Painted Hills, Lassie, MGM, '51, 1-sheet, EX **80.00**
Poster, Santa Fe Rides, Bob Custer, ca '37, 1-sheet **350.00**
Poster, Snow White & 7 Dwarfs, re-release '75, 1-sheet, EX **30.00**
Poster, Staying Alive, John Travolta, color, '83, NM **25.00**
Poster, Thunderball, Sean Connery, 1-sheet, '65, NM **125.00**
Press book, Caesar & Cleopatra, Vivian Leigh cover, 26-pg **150.00**
Press kit, American Gigolo, Richard Gere, '80, M **8.00**
Press kit, Mommie Dearest, F Dunaway, '81, VG **10.00**
Press kit, No Small Affair, Demi Moore/Jon Cryer, '84 ....**11.00**
Pressbook, Close Encounters of the Third Kind, '78, VG **15.00**
Pressbook, Rocky III, '82, NM **10.00**
Program, Fantasia, '40, EX **40.00**
Program, Gone w/the Wind, '39, NM **155.00**
Promotion card, Shirley Temple & Mickey Mouse, 1930s **38.00**
Scrapbook, Bob Hope, 62-pg, 8½x11", EX **10.00**
Scrapbook, Dorothy Lamour, 46-pg, EX **20.00**
Scrapbook, Errol Flynn, 38-pg, 8½x11", EX **20.00**
Scrapbook, Gary Cooper, 54-pg, 8½x11", VG **10.00**
Scrapbook, Jan Sterling, 40-pg, 8½x11", EX **15.00**
Scrapbook, Lynn Barl, 36-pg, 8½x11", EX **10.00**
Scrapbook, Olivia De Havilland, 8½x11", VG **15.00**
Scrapbook, Richard Burton, 11x13", EX **10.00**
Scrapbook, Shelly Winters, 42-pg, 8½x11", EX **10.00**
Song book, Gene Autry, Cowboy Songs...Ballads, 94-pg, '38, VG .**10.00**
Song book, Kate Smith, young Kate on cover, '30, 63-pg, VG **15.00**
Still, Beneath the Planet of the Apes, color, set of 8 ....**40.00**
Still, Cinderfella, color, set of 2 ....**15.00**
Still, Devils' Bride, color, set of 8 ....**15.00**
Still, In Like Flint, color, set, of 6 ....**18.00**
Still, Night of Dark Shadows, set of 11 ....**20.00**
Still, Our Man Flint, color, set of 12 ....**36.00**
Theater ticket, Gone w/the Wind, 22¢ orig admission, M **20.00**
Title card, St Louis Kid, Jimmy Cagney, 1933, EX+ **125.00**
Window card, Cobweb, Widmark/Bacall/Boyer, '55, 14x22", NM .**11.00**
Window card, Destry, Audie Murphy, '54, 14x22", VG **25.00**
Window card, Gone w/the Wind, 1st reissue, '68, 22x14", M **41.00**
Window card, Jack...Beanstalk, Abbott/Costello, '52, 14x22", VG .**20.00**
Window card, Planet of Apes, Carlton Heston, '68, 14x22", M ...**52.00**
Window card, Wizard of Oz, full-color reissue, '71, 14x22", M **37.00**
Wristwatch, Marilyn Monroe, Bradley, MIB **65.00**

Mt. Washington

The Mt. Washington Glass Works was founded in 1837 in South Boston, Massachusetts, but moved to New Bedford in 1869 after purchasing the facilities of the New Bedford Glass Company. Frederick S. Shirley became associated with the firm in 1874. Two years later the company reorganized and became known as the Mt. Washington Glass Company. In 1894 it merged with the Pairpoint Manufacturing Company, a small Brittania works nearby, but continued to conduct business under its own title until after the turn of the century. The combined plants were equipped with the most modern and varied machinery available and boasted a working force with experience and expertise rival to none in the art of blowing and cutting glass. In addition to their fine cut glass, they are recognized as the first American company to make cameo glass, an effect they achieved through acid-cutting methods. In 1885 Shirley was issued a patent to make Burmese, pale yellow glassware tinged with a delicate pink blush. Another patent issued in 1886 allowed them the rights to produce Rose Amber, or amberina, a transparent ware shading from ruby to amber. Pearl Satin Ware and Peachblow, so named for its resemblance to a rosy peach skin, were patented the same year. One of their most

famous lines, Crown Milano, was introduced in 1893. It was an opal glass either free-blown or pattern-molded, tinted a delicate color and decorated with enameling and gilt. Royal Flemish was patented in 1894 and is considered the rarest of the Mt. Washington art glass lines. It was decorated with raised, gold-enameled lines dividing the surface of the ware in much the same way as lead lines divide a stained glass window. The sections were filled in with one or several transparent colors and further decorated in gold enamel with florals, foliage, beading, and medallions.

Our advisors for this category are Betty and Clarence Maier; they are listed in the Directory under Pennsylvania. See also Amberina, Cranberry; Salt Shakers; Burmese; Crown Milano; Royal Flemish; etc.

Biscuit jar, oak leaves/acorns on pnt Burmese, SP ft/hdls/lid, 5" ..**1,050.00**
Biscuit jar, yel mums on gr, paneled w/emb scrolls, SP mts **625.00**
Bowl, cameo griffins, rose on wht, 3½x8½" **525.00**
Bowl, Napoli, pond lilies on gr, 10", SP pond lily sgn base **2,250.00**
Box, Collars & Cuffs, collar form, floral/gilt, poppy finial **1,000.00**
Box, floral lid, 4-ftd SP Pairpoint bowl, 1¾x4½" **230.00**
Box, jewel; monk drinks wine on gr-pnt opal, sgn, 3x5½" dia ...**500.00**
Celery tray, cranberry to clear, Pat...1893, orig Pairpoint fr **425.00**

Creamer and sugar bowl, painted wild roses, silver-plated trim, 3½" to top of finial, $650.00 for the pair.

Creamer, emb/gilt flowers/scrolls/leaves, ribbed, SP mts **475.00**
Flower holder, floral on wht, mushroom shape, 2¾x5" **375.00**
Mustard pot, ribbed, glossy, silver top/hdl, 2¾" **625.00**
Pickle castor, Albertine, star mold, Pairpoint fr, 8½" **1,120.00**
Rose bowl, asters, bl/wht on brn to clear frost, scalloped, lg **1,300.00**
Shakers, mc florals, orig tops, pr **155.00**
Sugar shaker, apple blossoms, melon ribs, ornate emb lid **550.00**
Sugar shaker, floral, egg form, 4¼" **300.00**
Sweetmeat, floral/scrolls/gold on opal, ribbed, 5" dia **475.00**
Sweetmeat, lily of the valley on Dmn Quilt custard, 3" **900.00**
Tumbler, cameo leaves in arches, pk/wht on frost w/gold, 5" **600.00**
Vase, Delft, pk opal w/windmill & person, w/gold, 9x5½" **375.00**
Vase, Lava, blk w/mc abstracts, 8-rib, bulbous base, 9" **1,000.00**
Vase, Napoli, frog/bulrushes, mc w/gold, ribbed, 8½x5" **1,000.00**
Vase, Verona, floral, gold/blk/brn, long ruffled neck, sgn, 12" ..**1,200.00**

Mulberry China

Mulberry china was made by many of the Staffordshire area potters from about 1830 until the 1850s. It is a transfer-printed earthenware or ironstone named for the color of its decorations, a purplish-brown resembling the juice of the mulberry. Some pieces may have faded out over the years and today look almost gray with only a hint of purple. (Transfer printing was done in many colors; technically only those in the mauve tones are 'mulberry'; color variations have little effect on value.) Some of the patterns (Corean, Jeddo, Pelew, and Formosa, for instance) were also produced in Flow Blue ware. Others seem to have been used exclusively with the mulberry color. Our advisor for this category is Mary Frank Gaston; she is listed in the Directory under Texas.

Bochara, sauce tureen, John Edwards, w/lid & ladle 650.00
Calcutta, cup & saucer, handleless 160.00
Castle Garden, plate, medallion-floral border, 7⅞" 85.00
Corean, bowl, vegetable; w/lid, 9" 435.00
Corean, bowl & pitcher 985.00
Corean, creamer 165.00
Corean, cup & saucer 75.00
Corean, cup plate 55.00
Corean, gravy boat 275.00
Corean, pitcher, 1½-pt 225.00
Corean, pitcher, 1½-qt 425.00
Corean, pitcher, 1-qt 400.00
Corean, plate, 8" 50.00
Corean, plate, 9¾" 85.00
Corean, platter, Podmore Walker, 13x10½" 225.00
Corean, sauce bowl 35.00
Corean, sugar bowl, Clementson 350.00
Corean, teapot 600.00
Corean, wash bowl & pitcher 900.00
Corean, waste bowl, Podmore Walker 225.00
Cyprus, bowl, vegetable; Davenport, w/lid 375.00
Cyprus, creamer 250.00
Cyprus, platter, 12½" 160.00
Flora, creamer, Walker 150.00
Heath's Flower, platter, 14" 335.00
Hong, pitcher, 2-qt 500.00
Jeddo, bowl, vegetable; Adams, w/lid 535.00
Jeddo, creamer, Adams 215.00
Jeddo, cup & saucer, Adams 80.00
Jeddo, pitcher, Adams 2-qt 425.00
Jeddo, sugar bowl, Adams, open 195.00
Jeddo, teapot, Adams 475.00
Madras, soup plate, Doulton 30.00
Marble, creamer, child sz 200.00
Marble, creamer, 5½" 75.00
Marmota, platter, Ridgway, 9½x7¾" 120.00
Nankin, bowl, vegetable; Davenport, 8-sided, w/lid, lg 395.00
Nankin, creamer, Davenport 225.00
Ning-Po, creamer, Hall 275.00
Ning-Po, soup, Hall 95.00
Panama, creamer, Challinor 245.00
Passiflora, sauce tureen, w/lid & undertray 395.00
Pelew, bowl, vegetable; Challinor, w/lid 525.00
Pelew, cup & saucer, handleless; Challinor 50.00
Pelew, platter, Challinor, 18" 175.00
Pelew, teapot, Challinor 295.00
Rhone Scenery, cup & saucer, handleless 65.00
Rose, creamer, Walker 285.00
Rose, pitcher, Walker, 2-qt 375.00
Sydenhan, creamer 130.00
Tavoy, platter, 15" 130.00
Tavoy, teapot 275.00
Tippecanoe, cup plate, unmk, 4⅛", NM 35.00
Tivoli, teapot 325.00
Venture, creamer 95.00
Vincennes, bowl, vegetable; w/lid 395.00
Vincennes, creamer 225.00
Vincennes, cup & saucer, handleless; Alcock, ca 1860 ....75.00
Vincennes, plate, 8" 65.00
Vincennes, plate, 9½" 75.00
Vincennes, relish 195.00
Vincennes, sauce tureen 295.00
Washington Vase, bowl, vegetable; Podmore Walker, w/lid, 9¾" L .295.00
Washington Vase, bowl & pitcher, Podmore Walker 750.00

Washington Vase, creamer, Podmore Walker 215.00
Washington Vase, plate, Podmore Walker, 10" 80.00
Washington Vase, plate, Podmore Walker, 9" 75.00
Washington Vase, platter, Podmore Walker, 16" 295.00
Washington Vase, sauce tureen, rpr, w/ladle 595.00
Washington Vase, sugar pot, lion's head hdls 240.00
Washington Vase, teapot 525.00
Washington Vase, wash bowl & pitcher 750.00
Wreath, bowl, vegetable; w/lid, 11" 425.00

Muller Freres

Henri Muller established a factory in 1900 at Croismare, France. He produced fine cameo art glass decorated with florals, birds, and insects in the Art Nouveau style. The work was accomplished by acid engraving and hand finishing. Usual marks were 'Muller,' 'Muller Croismare,' or 'Croismare, Nancy.' In 1910 Henri and his brother Deseri formed a glassworks at Luneville. The cameo art glass made there was nearly all produced by acid cuttings of up to four layers with motifs similar to those favored at Croismare. A good range of colors was used, and some later pieces were gold flecked. Handles and decorative devices were sometimes applied by hand. In addition to the cameo glass, they also produced an acid-finished glass of bold mottled colors in the Deco style. Examples were signed 'Muller Freres' or 'Luneville.' Our advisor for this category is Don Williams; he is listed in the Directory under Missouri.

Cameo

Lamp, berry branches cut/pnt on wine/yel shade & base, 20" ..8,600.00
Lamp, floral on baluster base/10" dome shade, dbl o/l, 19" 9,000.00
Pitcher, berry leaves/2 beetles on gold opal, free-form, 6" 3,000.00

Vase/lamp base, exotic blossoms, buds and leafy vines, amber opalescent with brown over red-amber, signed, 9¾x9¾", $2,000.00.

Vase, bluebells, bl/gr on pastel mottle, flared rim, 13" 2,000.00
Vase, cockatoo in lg ring, lav on lime/bl, 14x10" 2,500.00
Vase, lady in forest, wine/gr/red on yel, shaped top, 12x6" 1,800.00
Vase, maple leaves/2 appl bugs, brn/yel on gr/orange, 5x5" 2,000.00
Vase, stylized fish/bubbles, red on frost w/foil, 6" 1,200.00
Vase, tiger lilies, lilac/pk opaque on gr texture, ftd, 13" 2,000.00
Vase, winter trees, cut/pnt on purple to yel, 7¾x3" 1,725.00

Miscellaneous

Chandelier, emb peacocks on lg+4 sm spheres, 4 arched arms ..3,500.00
Shade, mottled earth-tone frost bowl, 3 chain holes, 17" 900.00
Vase, butterscotch/orange/brn streaks, flecks of blk, 9x9" 485.00
Vase, gold mica & mottled autumn leaves in orange/gr, 8½" ..1,200.00
Vase, gold/gr & orange cluthra inclusions, pear form, 10" 600.00

Muncie

Muncie Pottery, established in Muncie, Indiana, by Charles O. Grafton, was produced from 1922 until about 1935. It is made of a heavier clay than most of its contemporaries; the styles are sturdy and simple. Early glazes were bright and colorful. In fact, Muncie was advertised as the 'rainbow pottery.' Later most of the ware was finished in a matt glaze. The more collectible examples are those modeled after Consolidated Glass vases — sculptured with lovebirds, grasshoppers, and goldfish. Their line of Art Deco-style vases bear a remarkable resemblance to the Consolidated Glass company's Ruba Rombic line. Vases, candlesticks, bookends, ashtrays, bowls, lamp bases, and luncheon sets were made. A line of garden pottery was manufactured for a short time. Items were frequently impressed with MUNCIE in block letters. Letters such as A, K, E, or D and the numbers 1, 2, 3, 4, or 5 often found scratched into the base are finishers' marks.

Ball refrigerator jug, orange peel, w/lid, 6½x6½" 65.00
Bottle, rnd, molded, matt dk gr, 4½" 85.00
Canoe, dk gr matt, w/insert, 11½" 275.00
Chamberstick, matt bl, 4" 85.00
Dutch shoe, matt gr/rose, 6½" L 150.00
Pinch bottle, trn, gloss dk gr/peachskin, 5½" 90.00
Vase, glossy blk, trumpet form, 12" 175.00
Vase, glossy yel, stick form, 8" 65.00
Vase, gr/rose, pillow form w/hdls, 9" 85.00
Vase, matt bl/rose, ruffled, hdls, 5½" 60.00

Vase, Ruba Rombic line, pink and white drip, 4½x6", $225.00.

Vase, Ruba Rombic style, gr over orange matt, #3A, 4" 250.00
Wall pocket, glossy dk bl, 6½" 115.00

Musical Instruments

The field of automatic musical instruments covers many different categories ranging from watches and tiny seals concealing fine early musical movements to huge organs and orchestrions which weigh many hundreds of pounds and are equivalent to small orchestras. Music boxes, first made in the early 19th-century by Swiss watchmakers, were produced in both disk and cylinder models. The latter type employs a pinned cylinder with tiny pins that lift the teeth in the comb of the music box (producing a sound much like many individual tuning forks), and music results. The value of a cylinder music box depends on the length and diameter of the cylinder, the date of its manufacture, the number of tunes it plays (four or six is *usually* better than ten or twelve), and its manufacturer. Nicole Freres, Henri Capt, LeCoultre, and Bremond are among the most highly regarded, and the larger boxes made by Mermod Freres are also popular. Examples with multiple cylinders, extra instruments (such as bells or an organ section), and those in particularly ornate cabinets or with matching tables bring significantly

higher prices. While smaller cylinder boxes are still being made, the larger ones (over 10" cylinders) typically date from before 1900. Disk music boxes were introduced about 1890 but were replaced by the phonograph only twenty-five years later. However, during that time, hundreds of thousands were made. Their great advantage was in playing inexpensive interchangeable disks, a factor that remains an attraction for today's collector as well. Among the most popular disk boxes are those made by Regina (USA), Polyphon, Mira, Stella, and Symphonion. Relative values are determined by the size of the disks they play, whether they have single or double combs, if they are upright or table models, and how ornate their cases are. Especially valuable are those that play multiple disks at the same time or are incorporated into tall-case clocks.

Player pianos were made in a wide variety of styles. Early varieties consisted of a mechanism which pushed up to a piano and played on the keyboard by means of felt-tipped fingers. These use sixty-five note rolls. Later models have the playing mechanism built in, and most use eighty-eight note rolls. Upright pump player pianos have little value in unrestored condition because the cost of restoration is so high. 'Reproducing' pianos, especially the 'grand' format, can be quite valuable, depending on the make, the size, the condition, and the ornateness of the case. 'Reproducing' pianos have very sophisticated mechanisms and are much more realistic in the reproduction of piano music. They were made in relatively limited quantities. Better manufacturers include Steinway and Mason & Hamlin. Popular roll mechanism makers include Ampico, Duo-Art, and Welte. The market for all types of player pianos has been weak for several years.

Coin-operated pianos (orchestrions) were used commercially and typically incorporate extra instruments in addition to the piano action. These can be very large and complex, incorporating drums, cymbals, xylophones, bells, and hundreds of pipes. Both American and European coin pianos are very popular, especially the larger and more complex models made by Wurlitzer, Seeburg, Cremona, Weber, Welte, Hupfeld, and many others. These companies also made automatically playing violins (Mills Violin Virtuoso, Hupfeld), banjos (Encore), and harps (Whitlock); these are quite valuable.

Mechanical organs range all the way from parlor pump organs and roll-operated reed organs to band organs found on carousels and giant fairground and dance hall organs. Pump organs made by Estey, Willcox, and others are often very ornate but also very common and bulky; as a result, the market is very limited. The more sophisticated roll-playing reed organs are collectible but still find a limited market due to the cost of restoration. They are very undervalued and have been for a long time. Carousel-type band organs, especially those made by well-known manufacturers such as Wurlitzer and Artizan, continue to sell well. The highest values are reserved for the larger Welte, Gavioli, Bruder, and other organs used in fairgrounds, dance halls, and private residences that incorporate hundreds of pipes. With a harder-to-find larger instrument, a good supply of rolls contributes much to its value, since in many cases rolls cannot be found.

Unless noted, prices given are for instruments in fine condition, playing properly, with cabinets or cases in well-preserved or refinished condition. In all instances, unrestored instruments sell for much less, as do those with broken or missing parts, damaged cases, and the like. On the other hand, particularly superb examples in especially ornate case designs and those that have been particularly well kept will often command more. Our advisor for mechanical instruments is Martin Roenigk; he is listed in the Directory under Connecticut. Fred Oster advises us on non-mechanical instruments; he is listed under Pennsylvania.

Key:
c — cylinder   d — disk

Mechanical

Box, Baker, Troll & Fils, 17¼" c, 12-tune, 31" case 2,400.00

Box, Bieling-Richier-Eisleben Polyphon, 15½" d, 10x21x19" .3,000.00
Box, Criterion, 12" d, cherry case, EX orig 1,450.00
Box, Criterion, 20½" d, oak case, upright, dbl comb 10,500.00
Box, Empress, dbl comb, 12" d, mahog 4-ftd case, 11x21x18" .2,400.00
Box, Imperial Symphonion 17⅝" upright, 2 c, EX 7,000.00
Box, Kalliope, 20½" d, upright, 12 bells, EX orig 7,500.00
Box, Mermod Freres, 11¼" c, 2½" d, 10-tune 1,500.00
Box, Mermod Freres Interchangeable, 4 13" c, rprs/rstr 5,000.00
Box, Perfection, 14" d, needs rstr 1,350.00
Box, Perfection 14" single c, 4 d, EX orig 1,800.00
Box, Polyphon, burled walnut, 24" d, coin-op, 79x33" 14,000.00
Box, Regina, upright, automatic changer, stain glass door, M .24,000.00
Box, Regina, 12" d, mahog cabinet 1,600.00
Box, Regina, 15½" changer, mahog case, EX 17,000.00
Box, Regina, 15½" curved front, oak case, coin-op, EX 16,500.00
Box, Regina, 15½" d, cvd mahog case, 10½x21x19", +60 d 5,700.00
Box, Regina, 15½" d, w/base, EX 4,200.00
Box, Regina, 15½" dbl comb, oak case, w/base cabinet, EX 5,500.00
Box, Regina, 20½" d, w/base cabinet, NM 7,500.00
Box, Regina, 20¾" d, walnut 29" case 4,500.00
Box, Regina #40, 15½" d changer, rosewood, art case, NM 6,800.00
Box, Regina Serpentine, 12" d, table model 1,750.00
Box, Stella, 17" d, mahog case, floor model, 42x29", EX 6,500.00
Box, Stella, 17¼" d, cvd mahog case, needs rstr 3,800.00
Box, Stella, 17¼" d, table model, dbl comb, mahog case, EX .5,000.00
Box, Stella Concert, 15½" d, w/table 4,000.00
Box, Swill Bells & Drum in Sight, 132" c, 8-tune, 24" 2,400.00
Box, Swiss, 13" c, 6-tune, Louis XV case, 43x29" 2,000.00
Box, Swiss Sublime Harmony Piccolo Zither, 18½" c, 10-tune ..3,700.00
Box, Symphonion, 25" d, upright, rstr, 90" 8,800.00
Box, Thornward, single comb, 15½" d, 12½x25x19" 2,500.00
Hurdy-Gurdy, Faventia, 11" c, 6-tune, HP 2-wheel cart 750.00

Piano, Cremona 25¢ Nickelodeon Style A, dark case with Arts and Crafts-style stained glass panels, ca 1918, with 75 paper rolls, 64x60", EX, $7,500.00.

Nickelodeon, Capital, oak case w/violin pipes & rolls, EX 8,000.00
Nickelodeon, Capitol, violin pipes, M rstr 11,000.00
Nickelodeon, Chicago Electric A Roll, EX 4,500.00
Nickelodeon, Coinola Keyboard, VG unrstr 3,800.00
Nickelodeon, National Eight, roll changer, 88-note, VG 7,000.00
Nickelodeon, Seeburg A, w/xylophone, NM 6,500.00
Nickelodeon, Seeburg C, art glass panels, ca 1910, rstr 6,500.00
Nickelodeon, Seeburg G look-alike, EX orig 11,000.00
Nickelodeon, Seeburg L, rstr, M 7,000.00
Nickelodeon, Western Electric, rstr 6,500.00
Orchestrion, Coinola C-2, EX 27,000.00
Orchestrion, Empress, art case, Lyon & Healy #17862, NM ...7,500.00

Orchestrion, Nelson-Wiggins, coin-op, oak case, 64x48" 9,775.00
Orchestrion, Nelson-Wiggins 5X, EX orig 11,000.00
Orchestrion, Seeburg G, w/9 instruments, rstr, M 35,000.00
Orchestrion, Seeburg K, eagle art glass, rstr 11,000.00
Orchestrion, Western Electric Special, all orig 10,000.00
Orchestrion, Wurlitzer B, EX orig 2,750.00
Organ, band; N Tonawanda Military, 18 brass trumpets, VG .20,000.00
Organ, band; Wurlitzer #150, EX 30,000.00
Organ, band; Wurlitzer #153, M 45,000.00
Organ, band; Wurlitzer #153, rstr 40,000.00
Organ, barrel; Frati, 38-key, w/trumpet/piccolo pipes, rstr 13,900.00
Organ, monkey; Gavioli, 41-key 7,500.00
Organ, monkey; Gavoli, 25-key 7,500.00
Organ, monkey; Molinari, 20-key 4,500.00
Organ, monkey; Molinari, 26-key, rstr, M 7,500.00
Organ, monkey; Taylor Co, late 1800s, VG, working 3,750.00
Organ, Wilcox & Wht Symphony, oak, w/shutters, rstr 1,500.00
Organette, Auerophone, EX 450.00
Piano, grand; Chickering, Stoddard, 1916, rstr 4,000.00
Piano, grand; Chickering Ampico, rfn, 1916, 68" 6,000.00
Piano, grand; Chickering Ampico 365, 77", EX orig 16,000.00
Piano, grand; Fisher Ampico, art case, harpsichord, 9-leg, EX 12,000.00
Piano, grand; Knabe Ampico, 64", M 3,500.00
Piano, grand; Steinway, w/Pianomation, 89", rstr 20,000.00
Piano, grand; Stroud Duo-Art, tubed sides, recent, NM 3,300.00
Piano, grand; Weber Duo-Art, mahog, 68", unrstr, G 900.00
Piano, push-up; Aeolian, 65-note, EX orig 225.00
Piano, upright; Ampico Marshall & Wendall, rstr 3,700.00
Piano, upright; Chickering Ampico, EX orig 1,500.00
Piano, upright; Fisher Marque Ampico, EX orig 1,100.00
Piano, upright; Steinway Duo-Art, rstr 6,000.00
Piano, Weber Grandezza, NM 17,500.00
Piano/orchestrion, Lion-Healy, w/pipes, EX 9,000.00
Piano/organ, Reproduco, walnut, EX orig 8,500.00
Pianocorder, Marantz, w/50 cassettes, EX 3,000.00
Rolmonica harmonica, MIB w/6 rolls 125.00
Violin, Mills Single Virtuoso, M 22,500.00

Non-Mechanical

Accordion, Huhner, Besh Ge Toors, EX in VG case 165.00
Banjo, Supertone label, 5-string, 36", EX 125.00
Drum, Excelsior, wood, gut snares, rope tension, 16x10", G 85.00
Drum, Porter Blanchard Concord NH, pnt/gilt, 1850s, 14x17", EX ..8,000.00
Fife, rosewood w/brass ends, Civil War Era, EX 65.00
Guitar, Dickerson, silver tortoise shell, electric, '40s, w/amp 300.00
Harmonica, Hoenig, early, 8", EX 35.00
Harmonica, Horner, Herb Shriner's Hoosier Boy, MIB 85.00
Harp, LVR Lewis, rosewood/parcel gilt, Gothic panels, 68" 3,800.00
Harp, Pleyel Wolff Paris, Fr Empire fruitwood & gilt, EX 1,500.00
Mandolin, Martin, rosewood, M in case 300.00
Organ, parlor; Story & Clark, Chicago, Victorian walnut, 77x50" ...300.00
Piano, baby grand; Baldwin, ebonized orig finish, 38x62x57" ..5,400.00
Pitch pipe, Chromatic Pitch Pipe, brass, 3", in pnt tin case 35.00
Saxaphone, True-Tone #213133, low pitch, NP, Pat 1914, EX ..265.00
Xylophone, JC Deagan, Chicago, dtd 1914, EX 850.00

Mustache Cups

Mustache cups were popular items during the late Victorian period, designed specifically for the man with the mustache! They were made in silverplate as well as china and ironstone. Decorations ranged from simple transfers to elaborately applied and gilded florals. To properly position the 'mustache bar,' special cups were designed for the 'left-ies.' These are the rare ones!

Blue Onion, 1800s **90.00**
Floral, bl on wht w/gold trim, Germany **60.00**
Pk lustre w/floral band, Germany, 4½" **45.00**
Roses, red on gr, Germany **55.00**
SP, cut/beaded decor, Eureka Silver, 1901, +saucer **115.00**

Nailsea

Nailsea is a term referring to clear or colored glass decorated in contrasting spatters, swirls, or loops. These are usually white but may also be pink, red, or blue. It was first produced in Nailsea, England, during the late 1700s but was made in other parts of Britain and Scotland as well. During the mid-1800s a similar type of glass was produced in this country. Originally used for decorative novelties only, by that time tumblers and other practical items were being made from Nailsea-type glass. See also Lamps; Witch Balls.

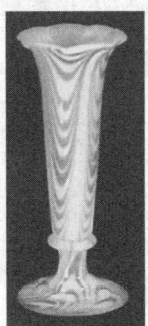

Vase, pink loopings on white, fluted top, footed, 6½", $235.00.

Decanter, bl-aqua w/wht herringbone loopings, 9⅜" **575.00**
Flask, pk loopings on milk glass, pontil scar, 7⅛" **150.00**
Flask, pk/lav/bl loopings on milk glass, teardrop form, 6¼" **210.00**
Flask, red herringbone loopings on pk-red, English, 6⅜" **165.00**
Flask, wht loopings on clear w/appl red threading overall, 6" **230.00**
Flask, wht opal swirls on canary yel, pontil scar, 6¾" **185.00**
Pocket flask, wht loopings on gr, pontil scar, oval, 6" **180.00**
Whimsey bellows, clear w/wht loopings, ped ft, 1880s, 13" **250.00**

Nakara

Nakara was a line of decorated opaque milk glass produced by the C.F. Monroe Company of Meriden, Connecticut, for a few years after the turn of the century. It differs from their Wave Crest line in several ways. The shapes were simpler; pastel colors were deeper and covered more of the surface; more beading was present; flowers were larger; and large transfer prints of figures, Victorian ladies, cherubs, etc. were used. Ormolu and brass collars and mounts complemented these opulent pieces. Most items were signed; however, this is not important since the ware was never reproduced. Our advisors for this category are Dolli and Wilfred R. Cohen; their address is listed in the Directory under California.

Bonbon, daisies/beaded scrolls on pk to yel, wire hdl, 6" dia **350.00**
Bonbon, roses/dots on pnt Burmese, ormolu rim/hdls, 6" W **575.00**
Box, Bishop's Hat, floral on bl, ormolu ft, 4¼" dia **485.00**
Box, Collars & Cuffs, pansies/beaded scrolls on bl to ivory **1,850.00**
Box, Crown mold, lg lilies, pk on gr, 5½x8½" **1,250.00**
Box, Crown mold, rose bouquet, mirror w/in, 5½x6" **1,000.00**
Box, floral, wht on dk bl & tan, hexagonal, 4" dia **495.00**

Box, floral on gr/pk shaded, plain mold, 2¾x3½" dia **350.00**
Box, ring; lady's portrait in wht on rose, unemb, 2x2¼" **695.00**
Hair receiver, violets/wht beads on pnt Burmese, ormolu mts **495.00**
Humidor, Tobacco, frog reading newspaper, metal lid, 6¾" **900.00**
Tray, bonbon; scrolls/beads, pk & wht on bl, ormolu collar **435.00**
Trinket bowl, floral/beading on pk, ornate ormolu hdls, 2x4" **175.00**

Vase, floral reserve on cobalt, ormolu mount and feet, 9½x6½", $2,250.00.

Vase, wild roses/scrolls on beige, 4-ftd ormlu base, 9" **795.00**

Napkin Rings

Napkin rings became popular during the late 1800s. They were made from various materials. Among the most popular and collectible today are the large group of varied silverplated figurals made by American manufacturers. Recently the larger figurals in excellent condition have appreciated considerably. Only those with a blackened finish, corrosion, or broken and/or missing parts have maintained their earlier price levels. When no condition is indicated, the items listed below are assumed to be all original and in very good to excellent condition. Check very carefully for missing parts, solder repairs, or marriages.

A timely warning: inexperienced buyers should be aware of excellent reproductions on the market, especially the wheeled pieces. However, these do not have the fine detail and patina of the originals and tend to have a more consistent, soft pewter-like finish. These are appearing at the large, quality shows at top prices, being shown along with authentic antique merchandise. Beware! For further information we recommend *Figural Napkin Rings* (Collector Books) by Lillian Gottschalk and Sandra Whitson.

Key:
gw — gold washed   SH&M — Simpson, Hall, &
R&B — Reed & Barton   Miller

Acorn & leaf on ea side of ring, rnd base, Toronto #129 ....**65.00**
Arab kneels, holds torch, oblong base, Tufts #1583 ....**225.00**
Bear reaches for honey bee on ring, tiered base, R&B #1470 ......**250.00**
Bird w/long tail perched on stem, leaf base, Meriden #202 ....**200.00**
Boy in harness pulls ring on wheels **500.00**
Boy scout saluting/standing beside ring **350.00**
Boy w/sleeves rolled pushes ring, Meriden #161 ....**350.00**
Boys kick on ea side of filigree ring, Meriden #332 ....**225.00**
Camel on oval ftd base, Meriden #269 ....**400.00**
Cat about to pounce, fly on ring, rnd base **200.00**
Cat looks thoughtful & leans against beaded ring **250.00**
Cat w/glass eyes, body forms ring **395.00**
Chair of tree limbs holds ring, rstr **125.00**
Cherries & leaves on side of ring, leafy base, Standard #732 ....**85.00**

Cherub, lg, ring on bk, octagonal base, SH&M #016 ....295.00
Cherub holds vase by ring, circular base, Rockford #178 ....350.00
Cherub in soldier hat w/sword sits on alligator 400.00
Cherub pulls bbl-shaped ring on branches 125.00
Cherub sits on leaves attached to ring 150.00
Cherub twins w/rings on bks, rectangular base, Tufts #1544 ....500.00
Cherub w/bow sits on stool, mug-like base, R&B #1501 ....500.00
Cherub w/spear rides on bk of fish, Meriden #157 ....200.00
Cherubs sits on ring, holds leash of prancing dog, Tufts #1543 ...300.00
Chick sits on wishbone, circular base, Meriden #552 ....65.00
Chick stands next to ring, Meriden #268 ....95.00
Chinese figure beside ring, oval ftd base, Meriden #158 ....395.00
Cockatoo rests on curved log base 95.00
Crane peers through grass, rnd ftd base, Meriden #207 ....175.00
Crocodile crawls w/ring on bk, unmk 195.00
Deer harnessed to ring resting on filigree sled, Toronto #11 ....250.00
Dog on haunches, carries ring on bk, Meriden #275 ....235.00
Dog w/glass eyes, sits, ring forms body, Wilcox #4311 ....500.00
Eagle holds knife rest, rectangular base, Rogers & Bro #203 ....500.00
Fawn peers over fence that juts from ring, Meriden #0282 ....300.00
Fox w/ring on bk, rectangular base, Derby #304 ....250.00
Foxes ea side of ring, detailed base, Middletown #119 ....250.00
Giraffe under palm tree, rectangular base, Racine #145 ....400.00
Goat harnessed to sled-like fr holding ring, Rogers & Bros #212 ..500.00
Grapes & leaves around ring, leafy base, Standard #701 ....85.00
Greenaway boy on horse, SHM #225 ....500.00
Greenaway boy sits sleeping before ring, Pairpoint 300.00
Greenaway boy w/whistle, Tufts #1622 ....400.00
Greenaway girl & boy by fence holder, rectangular base, Tufts ..500.00
Greenaway girl & boy w/pail, Tufts #1667 ....500.00
Greenaway girl in bonnet pushes ring, octagonal base, SH&M ..350.00
Greenaway girl on bench beside ring, rectangular base, Derby ...265.00
Greenaway girl pushes boy on sled, sq holder, SH&M #037 ....500.00
Greenaway girl sits on sm base beside ring, Derby #316 ....295.00
Greenaway girl w/gun, ftd sq base, SHM #205 ....500.00
Greenaway girl w/pigtails holds ring, no base, Rogers #280 ....295.00
Horse w/ring on bk, leaf base 200.00
Hummingbird on branch, leafy base, Toronto #1142 ....145.00
Jack & Jill climbing hill-shaped ring, Tufts #1667 ....500.00
Ladderback chair (rustic wood) holds ring in fr 125.00
Lady in hat & gown holds racquet, rectangular base 350.00
Leaves & logs ea side of bbl-form ring, R&B #625, EX 95.00
Lion roaring, attached to ring 295.00
Little Red Riding Hood w/basket, Pelton Bros #99 ....350.00
Mastiff dog w/paw on ball, flat rectangular base 250.00
Miner w/pick leans against triangular ring 135.00
Owl sits on ring, log base, Rogers #248 ....150.00
Peacock atop ring, tail down bk, Meriden #234 ....350.00
Pheasant leans on branch, flat octagonal base, Meriden #246 ....150.00
Rabbit, arched leaf fretwork forms holder, Cromwell #178 ....250.00
Rat on haunches beside ring, rectangular base 195.00
Rifles, 2 Xd sets, filigree ring between, Meriden #335 ....250.00
Rooster on shovel, flat base, Meriden #181 ....215.00
Sailor w/anchor, bud vase w/spout atop ring, R&B #1357 ....600.00
Sheep on raised patterned base, Barbour #15 ....250.00
Soldier in tunic stands before ring, Middletown #340 ....125.00
Squirrel blowing horn, glass eyes 250.00
Stag w/ring on bk, rectangular base, Meriden #204 ....500.00
Stork pulls rope attached to ring, oval base, R&B #1126 ....350.00
Swan rests before ring, oval ball-ftd base, R Smith #312 ....275.00
Turtle driven by cherub w/hat riding on bk, Pairpoint 500.00
Turtle on circular base supports ring, Meriden-Britania #193 .....195.00
Wheelbarrow holds ring, shield-shaped base, Tufts #1537 ....225.00
3-leaf clover supports ring, Pairpoint #6 ....65.00

Nash

A. Douglas Nash founded the Corona Art Glass Company in Long Island, New York. He produced tableware, vases, flasks, etc., using delicate artistic shapes and forms. After 1933 he worked for the Libbey Glass Company.

Bowl, Chintz, orange & yel, raised & scalloped rim, 7" 165.00
Goblet, gold w/orange/bl/violet irid, knob stem, sgn, 7" 250.00
Parfait, Chintz, bl lines alternate w/gr-threaded clear, 7" 200.00
Parfait, Chintz, gr verticals/bl threads, lt bl stem, 6" 125.00
Vase, Chintz, gold-silver stripes in bl, allover irid, 9x5" 600.00
Vase, Chintz, vertical silver stripes in red, 5½x5½" 1,500.00
Vase, red-brn pulled feathers on gr opal w/butterscotch, 11" ...1,850.00

Natzler, Gertrude and Otto

The Natzlers came to the United States from Vienna in the late 1930s. They settled in Los Angeles where they continued their work in ceramics, for which they were already internationally recognized. Gertrude created the forms; Otto formulated a variety of interesting glazes, among them volcanic, crystalline, and lustre. Our advisor for this category is Abby Malowanczyk; she is listed in the Directory under Texas.

Bowl, brn/blk metallic flakè, ftd/folded, rstr, 1¾x5" 450.00
Bowl, gr-yel gloss w/exposed red clay, 2x3½" 800.00
Bowl, yel gloss over concentric throwing ridges, 4x8" 1,900.00
Bowl, yel over slightly ribbed tan clay, 4" 460.00
Candle cup, pierced w/holes, Hebrew script, rust/brn, 5" 545.00
Vase, blk, cylindrical on sm ft, 5" 850.00
Vase, porous iron-gr under thick uneven copper w/tan runs, 9" ..920.00
Vase, yel/bl/brn flambe, wide cupped top, 5½x3" 1,500.00

New England Glass Works

Founded in 1818 by Deming Jarves in Boston, Massachussetts, the New England Glass Company produced cut, blown three-mold, free-blown, and pressed glass of the highest quality. They were recognized for their fine decorative accomplishments, using etching, gilding, and engraving to emphasize their wares. For more than fifty years, they produced prize-winning pressed glass dinnerware sets. Because they refused to compromise the quality of their product by using the cheaper lime-based glass that flooded the market in the 1860s, the company fell into financial trouble and by 1877 was forced to close. However, William Libbey, who had been the sales manager there since 1870, leased the premises and resumed operations with his father, Edward Drummond Libbey, as full partner. In 1892 the firm became known as The Libbey Glass Company. See also Amberina; Libbey.

Compote, amethyst, ribbon edge with wafer attachment, 1840-1860, 8x8½", NM, $8,800.00.

Champagne, Pineapple, flint, 5" 175.00
Jelly glass, canary, vintage eng, appl ft, 4⅛" 210.00
Mug, appl 2nd gather form ribs at base, eng wreath, att, 5" 825.00
Vase, canary, loop pattern, marble base, 11¼" 860.00
Whiskey, Pineapple, flint, 3" 145.00

New Geneva

In the early years of the 19th century, several potteries flourished in the Greensboro, Pennsylvania, area. They produced utilitarian stoneware items as well as tile and novelties for many decades. All failed well before the turn of the century.

Flowerpot, red-brn slip on buff, chip, 6" 145.00
Jar, red clay w/brn florals & foliage, appl hdls, 10" 825.00
Jug, red-brn slip w/stencil, glaze flakes, 9½" 210.00
Pitcher, red clay w/brn-brushed floral decor, 9⅝" 675.00

New Martinsville

The New Martinsville Glass Company took its name from the town in West Virginia where it began operations in 1901. In the beginning years, pressed tablewares were made in crystal as well as colored and opalescent glass. Considered an innovator, the company was known for their imaginative applications of the medium in creating lamps made entirely of glass, vanity sets, figural decanters, and models of animals and birds. In 1944 the company was purchased by Viking Glass, who continued to use many of the old molds, the animals molds included. They marked their wares 'Viking' or 'Rainbow Art.' Viking recently ceased operations and has been purchased by Kenneth Dalzell, President of the Fostoria Company. They, too, are making the bird and animal models. Although at first they were not marked, future productions are to be marked with an acid stamp. Dalzell/Viking animals are in the $50.00 to $60.00 range. Values for cobalt and red items are two to three times higher than for the same item in clear. See also Depression Glass; Glass Animals and Figurines.

Basket, Janice, blk, #4552, 11" 195.00
Basket, Janice, clear w/red hdl, 6½" 65.00
Bookend, clipper ship, pr 85.00
Bowl, Radiance, lt bl, etched decor, ftd, #4218/28, 10" 145.00
Bowl, Radiance, red, 7", w/gold filigree metal basket 145.00
Candle holder, Janice, lt bl, #4554, 5" 42.50
Candlesticks, Prelude, 2-light, pr 50.00
Celery, Janice, lt bl, 11" 60.00
Creamer, Radiance, amber 14.00
Cup, Radiance, amber 12.00
Punch cup, Radiance, red 15.00
Relish, Radiance, lt, bl, #4228, 8½" 65.00
Relish, Radiance, red, 2-part, 7" 45.00
Sherbet, Mt Vernon, amber, ftd, 4" 4.50
Tumbler, Mt Vernon, amber, 3½" 6.00
Wine, Mt Vernon, amber, ftd, 5" 6.00

Newcomb

The Newcomb College of New Orleans, Louisiana, established a pottery in 1895 to provide the students with first-hand experience in the fields of art and ceramics. Using locally dug clays — red and buff in the early years, white-burning by the turn of the century — potters were employed to throw the ware which the ladies of the college decorated.

Until about 1910 a glossy glaze was used on ware decorated by slip painting or incising. After that a matt glaze was favored. Soft blues and greens were used almost exclusively, and decorative themes were chosen to reflect the beauty of the South. 1930 marked the end of the matt-glaze period and the art-pottery era.

Various marks used by the pottery include an 'N' within a 'C,' sometimes with 'HB' added to indicate a 'hand-built' piece. The potter often incised his initials into the ware, and the artists were encouraged to sign their work. Among the most well-known artists were Sadie Irvine, Henrietta Bailey, and Fannie Simpson.

Newcomb pottery is evaluated to a large extent by two factors: design and condition. In the following listings, items are assumed matt unless noted otherwise. Our advisor for this category is David Rago; he is listed in the Directory under New Jersey.

Bowl, bellflowers under rim, AF Simpson, 1924, 2½x6¾" 1,100.00
Bowl, berries, pk/gr on bl, sgn P, 1916, 2½x6" 800.00
Bowl, floral at rim on bl to gr, S Irvine, 2½x6" 700.00
Bowl, poppies under rim, AF Simpson, 1925, 5x8" 1,300.00
Bowl vase, stylized floral band on flared neck, sgn, 2½x5" 800.00
Humidor, tobacco leaves/blossoms, Irvine, 1925, bulbous, 5½" ..2,100.00
Lamp, bl matt w/emerald gr at rim, wicker/silk shade, 14x11" .1,400.00
Mug, stylized band, bl/wht on bl gloss, Wood, sm rpr 900.00
Pitcher, wht ducks, Irvine, 1917, cylindrical, 4" 2,300.00
Plaque, trees, bl/gr on lt bl, Roman, 1906, 7¾" dia 3,500.00
Tile, bayou w/setting sun, Irvine, 1919, fr, 4" 1,500.00
Tile, tuxedo-clad frog w/banjo, mc, Nicholson, fr, 4½" 1,200.00
Trivet, lily-of-the-valley at rim on bl, Simpson, 4" dia 750.00
Trivet, moon/moss/trees, Arbo, 4¾" dia 1,400.00
Trivet, 4 wht flower clusters, Bailey, 1925, 5¾" dia 950.00

Vase, incised wisteria blossoms on glossy, M. LeBlanc, bulbous, early, 9x7½", $35,000.00.

Vase, band of lg cvd liles at top, glossy, Nicholson, 7x6" 4,000.00
Vase, bayou scene w/pk sky, Simpson, incurvate cylinder, 10" ...4,750.00
Vase, blk mottled gloss, 1916, 5¼x2½" 375.00
Vase, cherries, red/gr on bl, Irvine, 1922, 8½x4¾" 2,400.00
Vase, crocus blossoms on long stems on dk bl, A Mason, 9" 2,600.00
Vase, cvd mushrooms on rose over lt bl gloss, Nicholson, 10" .8,500.00
Vase, cypress trees/shoreline, bl & gr w/pk sky, NC, 6" 2,200.00
Vase, dandelions, cream on pale pk gloss, Irvine, 7x4" 1,750.00
Vase, floral band at rim, Bailey, tapered cylinder, 3½x3½" 865.00
Vase, floral band cvd on bl, AF Simpson, 3x5" 850.00
Vase, floral neck band on dk bl, Irvine, 1929, 5x5" 1,200.00
Vase, floral on shoulder, ca 1933, H Bailey, 6½x4½" 2,100.00
Vase, floral top band cvd on gr w/bl, Irvine, 8x3" 1,400.00
Vase, floral under collar rim, cvd on bl, Littlejohn, 4x4" 1,100.00
Vase, gr matt, hand thrown, ovoid, 4½" 375.00
Vase, gr matt over lt bl matt, mk N w/in C, 7x3½" 600.00
Vase, gr w/copper highlights, bulbous, 3x3½" 300.00

Vase, leaf band, stylized, ivory/gr on lt gr, stick neck, 6" 1,800.00
Vase, leaf/berry band at incurvate top on bl, Irvine, 8x3" 1,500.00
Vase, long-stem freesia, AF Simpson, 6½x3½" 1,400.00
Vase, long-stem irises on bl gloss, Bailey, bulbous, 9" 19,000.00
Vase, lotus band, 3-color on bl, Le Blanc, 7" 3,750.00
Vase, mint gr, mk NC, thrown by Meyer, 3" 300.00
Vase, moon/moss/oak trees, H Bailey, 1933, 5x6" 1,100.00
Vase, moon/moss/oak trees, Irvine, 1931, 5x3" 850.00
Vase, moon/moss/oak trees, Irvine, 1932, 5x5½" 2,100.00
Vase, moon/moss/oak trees, Irvine, 6½x6½" 3,250.00
Vase, moon/moss/tall pines, Irvine, 1929, 11x6½" 7,500.00
Vase, moss/lg oak trees, Simpson, bulbous, 1918, 5x5" 2,300.00
Vase, moss/oak trees, Irvine, 1931, 2½x2¾" 850.00
Vase, pine cones/needles on royal bl, Bailey, 1929, 8½x4½" ..3,000.00
Vase, thorny bands w/flowers on gloss, hdls, Morel, 4x4" 1,495.00
Vase, tooled neck band, 4 buttresses, bl/lav, Irvine, 4x3½" 1,200.00
Vase, tree scene, unusual, EX cvg, Bailey, 7x4" 3,750.00
Vase, trees, bl/gr on cream, impressionistic, Littlejohn, 4" 1,300.00
Vase, trees, dk bl on pk, glossy, Irvine, 1927, 3¼x4" 1,800.00
Vase, wht floral band on bl gloss, Summney, 3½x4", NM 1,600.00

Newspapers

People do not collect newspapers simply because they are old. Age has absolutely nothing to do with value. The key factor that determines value is the historic content in the issue. In most cases, the more important to American history the event is, the higher the value. If you spent time in your high school history class learning about that specific event, chances are it has a significant collector value in contemporary newspapers announcing the news. Editions lacking news of significant events in American history are referred to as 'atmoshpere' editions. Of the over 200 years in American history, perhaps as many as 98% of the dates fall into the 'atmosphere' edition category. Events of importance to local history — 'Big Blizzard Hits Area,' 'New Mayor Elected,' 'Hotel Burns Down,' etc. — usually do not interest the typical newspaper collector and also fall into the 'atmosphere' category.

The Newspaper Collectors Society of America offers a 20-page primer and price guide for collecting old and historic newspapers. To obtain your copy, send $2.00 and a self-addressed, stamped, business-size envelope to: NCSA, Box 19134-S, Lansing, MI 48901.

The NCSA also has an extensive web site on the Internet. The site contains over 200,000 words of information concerning old and historic newspapers and is a treasure trove for those conducting historic research. The web address is: http://www.serve.com/ephemera/historybuff.html. The e-mail address for the NCA is: ephemera@mail.serv.com.

1800-1820, Atmosphere editions 7.00
1821-1859, Atmosphere editions 5.00
1836, Texas declares independence 60.00
1845, Annexation of Texas 35.00
1846, Start of Mexican War 30.00
1846-1847, Major battles of Mexican War 20.00
1847, End of Mexican War 30.00
1848, Gold discovered in California 60.00
1859, John Brown's raid on Harper's Ferry 45.00
1860, Lincoln elected 1st term 150.00
1861, Lincoln's inaugural address 175.00
1861-1865, Atmosphere editions: Confederate titles 50.00
1861-1865, Atmosphere editions: Union titles 7.00
1861-1865, Major battles of Civil War 75.00
1862, Emancipation Proclamation 135.00
1863, Gettysburg Address 250.00
1865, April 29 edition of Frank Leslie's 350.00

1865, April 29 edition of Harper's Weekly 300.00
1865, Capture & death of J Wilkes Booth 100.00
1865, Fall of Richmond 100.00
1865, NY Herald, Apr 15 (Beware: reprints abound) 900.00
1865, Titles other than NY Herald, Apr 15 ....400.00
1866-1900, Atmosphere editions 4.00
1876, Custer's Last Stand 150.00
1881, Billy the Kid killed 200.00
1881, Garfield assassinated 50.00
1881, Gunfight at OK Corral 225.00
1882, Jesse James killed 200.00
1898, Sinking of Maine 40.00
1901, McKinley assassinated 60.00
1903, Wright Brother's flight 300.00
1906, San Francisco earthquake, other titles 30.00
1906, San Francisco earthquake, San Francisco title 500.00
1912, Sinking of Titanic 250.00
1915, Sinking of Lusitania 125.00
1927, Babe Ruth hits 60th home run 70.00
1927, Lindbergh arrives in Paris 75.00
1929, St Valentine's Day Massacre 150.00
1929, Stock market crash 90.00
1931, Al Capone found guilty 35.00
1931, Jack 'Legs' Diamond killed 35.00
1933, Machine Gun Kelley captured 35.00
1934, Baby Face Nelson killed 40.00
1934, Bonnie & Clyde killed 125.00
1934, Dillinger killed 150.00
1934, Pretty Boy Floyd killed 35.00
1937, Hindenbergh explodes 65.00
1941, Honolulu Star-Bulletin, Dec 7, 1st extra (+) 600.00
1941, Other titles, Dec 7, w/Pearl Harbor news 35.00
1948, Chicago Daily Tribune, Nov 3, Dewey Defeats Truman ...900.00
1961, Alan Shephard 1st astronaut in space 20.00
1961, Roger Maris hits 61st home run 25.00
1962, Death of Marilyn Monroe 30.00
1962, John Glenn orbits Earth 18.00
1963, JFK assassination, Nov 22, Dallas title 60.00
1963, JFK assassination, Nov 22, titles other than Dallas 8.00
1968, Assassination of Martin Luther King 12.00
1968, Assassination of Robert Kennedy 12.00
1969, Moon landing 22.00
1974, Nixon resigns 12.00

Nicodemus

Chester Nicodemus moved from Dayton, Ohio, to Columbus in 1930 and started teaching at the Columbus Art School. During this time he made vases and commissioned sculptures, water fountains, and limestone and wood carvings. In 1941 Chester left the field of teaching to pursue pottery making full time, using local red clay containing a large amount of iron. Known for its durability, he called the ware Ferro-stone. He made teapots and other utility wares, but these goods lost favor, so he started producing animal and bird sculptures, nativity sets, and Christmas ornaments, some bearing Chester's and Florine's names, as personalized cards for his customers and friends. Chester died in 1990.

His glaze colors were turquoise or aqua, ivory, green mottle, (pink) pussy willow, and golden yellow. The glaze was applied so that the color of the warm red clay would show through, adding an extra dimension to each piece. Examples are usually marked with his name incised in the clay, but paper labels were also used. Our advisor for this category is James Riebel; he is listed in the Directory under Ohio.

Ashtray, fraternity, 4" 25.00
Bookends, camel, pr 400.00
Bookends, dryad (kneeling nude), pr 250.00
Christmas card, not sgn by artist, sgn Chester & Florine 100.00
Christmas decoration 40.00
Coffeepot, ind 100.00
Figurine, bull, 7" 350.00
Figurine, cardinal, red 500.00
Figurine, collie, 6" 150.00
Figurine, colt, recumbent, 3½" 250.00
Figurine, dachshund 150.00
Figurine, horse, terra cotta, blk metallic details, mk, 12" 750.00
Figurine, kangaroo 250.00
Figurine, Madonna of the Flowers 150.00
Figurine, robin, 4½" 175.00
Figurine, St Francis, w/bowl 300.00
Figurine, St Francis, w/stand, no bowl, 14" 450.00

Flower holder, kneeling girl, curdled blue, 6¾", $150.00.

Nativity set, 9-pc 500.00
Pitcher, bl, 3" 50.00
Pitcher, mustard, sm 50.00
Planter, elephant 55.00
Pottery festival ornament, 1986-87, ea 50.00
Vase, hdls, 4" 125.00
Vase, mauve, hdls, w/sticker, 4" 160.00
Vase, w/fish & sea horse 400.00
Wall pocket, dbl cornucopia 350.00
Water fountain, boy w/frog, 21" 3,500.00

Niloak

During the latter part of the 1800s, there were many utilitarian potteries in Benton, Arkansas. By 1900 only the Hyten Brothers Pottery remained. Charles Hyten, a second generation potter, took control of the family business around 1902. Shortly thereafter he renamed it the Eagle Pottery Company. In 1909 Hyten and former Rookwood potter Arthur Dovey began experimentation on a new swirl pottery. Dovey previously worked for the Ouachita Pottery Company of Hot Springs and produced a swirl pottery there as early as 1906. In March 1910 the Eagle Pottery Company introduced Niloak, kaolin spelled backwards. During 1911 Benton businessmen formed the Niloak Pottery corporation. Niloak, connected to the Arts and Crafts movement and known as 'mission' ware, had a national representative in New York by 1913. Niloak's production centered on art pottery characterized by accidental, swirling patterns of natural and artificially colored clays. Many companies through the years have produced swirl pottery, yet none has achieved the technical and aesthetic qualities of Niloak.

Hyten received a patent in 1928 for the swirl technique. Although most examples have an interior glaze, some early Mission Ware pieces have an exterior glaze as well; these are extremely rare. Swirl/Mission Ware production continued steadily until the Depression when hard times and sagging sales caused Hyten to produce more traditional wares. In 1931 Niloak introduced Hywood Art Pottery, a glazed ware (sometimes similar in shape to Weller's Nile) of mostly hand-thrown vases. Soon thereafter, Niloak introduced castware as its primary production and renamed the line Hywood by Niloak. Throughout its existence, the company produced utilitarian items as well as artware. In 1934 Hyten's company found itself facing bankruptcy. Hardy L. Winburn, Jr., along with other Little Rock businessmen, raised the necessary capital and were able to provide the kind of leadership needed to make the business profitable once again. Both lines (Eagle and Hywood) were renamed 'Niloak' in 1937 to capitalize on this well-known name. The pottery continued in production until 1947 when it was converted to the Winburn Tile Company, which exists to this day in Little Rock. Be careful not to confuse the swirl production of the Evans Pottery of Missouri with Niloak. The significant difference is the dark brown matt interior glaze of Evans pottery.

Our co-advisors for this category are Lila and Fred Shrader (see the Directory under California) and David Edwin Gifford (see Arkansas), author of *The Collector's Encyclopedia of Niloak*.

Mission Ware

Ashtray, ind, 1x3" 55.00
Ashtray, 1¼x5" 135.00
Ashtray, 5½" 145.00
Bean pot, 5-color swirl, w/lid, 7¼" 350.00
Bottle, water; 8½" 350.00
Bowl, brn tones, 5¾x8" 400.00
Bowl, flat, str sides, 2¼x6½" 125.00
Bowl, flower; w/perforations, 4½x5" 175.00
Bowl, fruit; rolled rim, 3x9½" 225.00
Bowl, lg art mk, 2x4¾" 160.00
Box, cigarette; w/lid, 4½x3½" 245.00
Bud vase, stick neck w/flared base, 8¼" 175.00
Candlesticks, flared base, 10", pr 500.00
Candlesticks, inverted trumpet form, 8", pr 400.00
Carafe, cork-wrap stopper 350.00
Chamberstick, hdl, 4" 175.00
Clock, rnd center dial w/in rnd swirled shape, 4¼" 700.00
Compote, ped w/flared ft, w/lid, 6½" 390.00
Compote, ped w/flared ft, 5¾" 300.00
Cup, punch; 3¾" 70.00
Figurine, elephant, molded, unmk, 2" 600.00
Flower frog, 1½x3" 65.00
Humidor, w/lid, 6½" 350.00
Humidor, w/lid, 7½x5" 365.00
Jar, cigarette; w/lid, 3½x4½" 235.00
Jar, cylindrical w/trn finial, 4¼x2¾", NM 300.00
Jar, powder; w/lid, 3½x6" 285.00
Jardiniere, rnded body shape, 7" 400.00
Jardiniere, 5¾", w/ped: 8¼" overall 495.00
Lamp base, bull's-eye effect in swirl, 6½" 275.00
Lamp base, drilled & wired, 10½" 280.00
Match holder, w/striker grooves, 2½" 95.00
Mug, bbl shape, 4½" 150.00
Pin tray, 1¼x3¾" 80.00
Pitcher, bulbous, 1½-qt, 9" 245.00
Pitcher, cylindrical, 6½" 145.00
Planter, 4½" 150.00
Smoke set, 7x10" tray/humidor/lid/6½" jar/lid/ashtray 1,285.00

Stein/mug, mk Pat Pend'g, 4¼" 300.00
Tankard, cylindrical w/flared base, 13" 525.00
Tile, 4½x4½" 155.00
Tray, pin, 2x3¾" 79.00
Tray, rolled edge, cut-out hdls, 9x7" 400.00
Tumbler, 3½" 45.00
Tumbler, 4" 55.00
Vase, bud; 6" 125.00
Vase, bulbous, 5-color swirl, 5¼" 100.00
Vase, bulbous base, bull's-eye effect in swirl, 8¼" 180.00
Vase, bulbous w/long neck, flared rim, 6" 100.00
Vase, bulbous w/thick rim, mk/label, 4¼x5¼" 225.00
Vase, classic shape, 10¼" 250.00
Vase, cone shape w/flared ft, predominantly red, 9" 275.00
Vase, cone shape w/flared ft, 2" 125.00
Vase, cone shape w/flared ft, 8" 185.00
Vase, cylindrical, flared base, 9" 200.00
Vase, cylindrical, 10½" 375.00
Vase, cylindrical, 9x3½" 200.00
Vase, inverted cylinder, predominantly brn, 8¾" 175.00
Vase, pear shape, 7" 175.00
Vase, rose bowl, mini, 2" 65.00
Vase, shouldered form w/flat rim, common shape, 8" 190.00
Vase, wide flaring rim, 6¼x3¼" 225.00
Wall pocket, unmk, 8¼" 300.00
Wall pocket, 6½" 265.00

Miscellaneous

Ashtray, flat butterfly, high-gloss, 3x3½" 18.00
Ashtray/match box holder, Hywood, high-gloss, 5" 21.00
Bean pot, hdls, w/lid, high-gloss, mini, 2¾" 35.00
Bowl, appl hdls, Hywood, hand-thrown, Stoin glaze, 3x7" 75.00
Bowl, attached 7" Peter Pan figure looking in, high-gloss 45.00
Bowl, high-gloss, football shape & sz 110.00
Bowl, Hywood, hand-thrown, Stoin glaze, 3x6" 65.00
Bowl, petal ribbing, tab hdls, matt, 3x12" 75.00
Bowl, w/floral-shaped frog, matt, 1-pc, 9" 55.00
Candlestick, Hywood by Niloak, 8" 32.00
Cookie jar, tab hdls, matt, w/lid, 9" 85.00
Creamer, cow, high-gloss, 5" 55.00
Creamer & sugar bowl, Aladdin style, high-gloss, w/lid, unmk 45.00
Cup & saucer, floral emb, matt 39.00
Cup & saucer, Peacock Blue 40.00
Ewer, flared ped base, matt, 16" 65.00
Figurine, dog, retriever, matt, 4½" 35.00
Figurine, donkey, stubborn look, matt, 4" 45.00
Figurine, military tank, matt, 2½" 30.00
Figurine, razorback hog w/or w/o 'U of A,' matt 80.00
Figurine, turkey, high-gloss, 2¼" 22.00
Jug, slender, hand-thrown, high-gloss, 8" 55.00
Pitcher, ball shape, matt, 7½" 45.00
Pitcher, ball shape, w/stopper, matt, 7½" 55.00
Pitcher, hand-thrown, gloss, 8" 95.00
Planter, cactus decor, w/½" wedge ft, matt, 3x8x4" 38.00
Planter, elephant on lg ball, high-gloss 22.00
Planter, horn of plenty, high-gloss, 4" 30.00
Planter, kangaroo, high-gloss, 5" 27.00
Planter, pelican w/orig pnt, matt, 5½" 42.00
Planter, Scottie dog, high-gloss, 3½" 30.00
Plate, petal decor, matt, 10" 35.00
Relish dish, 3-part, pie-crust edge, gloss, 9x6" 35.00
Shakers, ball shape w/S&P hdls, high-gloss, 2½", pr 30.00
Shakers, Grecian urn, matt, 3" 35.00

Shakers, jug shape, high-gloss, 3" 22.00
Shakers, military tank; high-gloss, 2¾", pr 35.00
Strawberry jar w/ruffled collar, high-gloss, 10" 40.00
Teapot, Aladdin style, high-gloss, sticker 55.00
Teapot, tall & slender w/S-curve spout, matt, 9" 80.00
Toothpick holder, open-mouth frog, high-gloss, 2½" 25.00

Vase, high-gloss rust brown, wing handles, paper sticker, 7", $40.00.

Vase, fan w/ribbing & ped base, matt, 7" 30.00
Vase, horn of plenty, high-gloss, 8" 25.00
Vase, tree trunk texture & shape, matt, 7½" 35.00
Wall pocket, cup & saucer decor, high-gloss, 6" 52.00
Wall pocket, pitcher & bowl decor, matt, 8½" 65.00

Nippon

Nippon generally refers to Japanese wares made during the period from 1891 to 1921, although the Nippon mark was also used to a limited extent on later wares (accompanied by 'Japan'). Nippon, meaning Japan, identified the country of origin to comply with American importation restrictions. After 1921 'Japan' was the acceptable alternative. The term does not imply a specific type of product and may be found on items other than porcelains. For further information we recommend *The Collector's Encyclopedias of Nippon Porcelain* (there are three in the series) by our advisor, Joan Van Patten; you will find her address in the Directory under New York. In the following listings, items are assumed hand painted unless noted otherwise. Numbers included in the descriptions refer to these specific marks:

Key:
#1 — China E-OH	#5 — Rising Sun
#2 — M in Wreath	#6 — Royal Kinran
#3 — Cherry Blossom	#7 — Maple Leaf
#4 — Double T Diamond in Circle	#8 — Royal Nippon, Nishiki
	#9 — Royal Moriye Nippon

Ashtray, Am Indian in relief, rectangular, #2, 6½" 950.00
Ashtray, landscape decor w/red fox figure at side, #2, 6½" 475.00
Ashtray, moose portrait, 6-sided, #2, 6" 130.00
Ashtray, river landscape, triangular, #2, 4¾" 120.00
Basket, acorns in relief, twig hdl, #2, 7½" W 225.00
Basket vase, Gouda-style geometric decor, gr #2, 7" 200.00
Basket vase, landscape tapestry, #7, 8¾" 975.00
Bowl, exotic bird & flowers, gold rim, mk, 9¾" 115.00
Bowl, fruit in relief, gold hdls, #2, 7½" 200.00
Bowl, mc roses w/cobalt & gold, scalloped rim, #7, 7¾" 275.00
Bowl, pastoral scene, fancy border & hdls, #2, 9¾" 160.00
Bowl, woodland scene, plain flat rim, #2, 7¼" 110.00
Box, trinket; mc butterflies on wht, #2, 3¼" dia 85.00

Cake plate, camel scenic, gold hdls, #2, 11", +6 sm 250.00
Candlestick, bl butterfly/pk florals on wht w/gold, #2, 7½" 135.00
Candlestick, portrait, gold trim, sq base, #7, 5" 400.00
Candlesticks, geometric bands on cream, gr #2, 6¼", pr 215.00
Candlesticks, Wedgwood, cream on bl, rnd base, #2, 6", pr 650.00
Candy dish, hunt scene around rim, #7, 12" 300.00
Celery tray, mc floral reserves w/cobalt & gold, #7, 13¼" L 400.00
Chocolate pot, gold o/l on wht, gold hdl, 6-sided, #7, 9¾" 200.00
Chocolate pot, lg open flowers w/gold, #2, 9" +6 c/s 450.00
Chocolate pot, mc roses in band, much gold, ornate hdl, #7, 14" .275.00
Coffee set, AD; sampan scenic, mk, pot+5 c/s+shakers 425.00
Compote, mc florals, gold rim & hdls, #2, 10" 115.00
Cookie jar, florals w/many gold beads, gold hdls, #7, 7x8" 400.00
Cookie jar, roses w/cobalt & gold, 3-ftd, #2, 7" 225.00
Cracker jar, scenic reserve w/cobalt & gold, #7, 8½" 500.00
Creamer & sugar bowl, gold o/l on wht, #8, 3½", 4½" 125.00
Cruet, sampan scenic, flat-top stopper, #2, 7¼" 300.00
Cup & saucer, Doll Face, #5, 2⅛", 5" 70.00
Dresser tray, woodland scene, geometric border, #2, 11" L 200.00
Ewer, moriage florals, melon ribs, ruffled rim, #7, 9¼" 400.00
Ewer, portrait reserve w/cobalt & gold, bulbous, #7, 9" 650.00
Ferner, floral band, floral molded hdls, #2, 3¾x8½" 275.00
Ferner, gold lion decor on wht, rectangular, ftd, #7, 5½" 200.00
Ferner, lion's portrait, 3-ftd, #2, 5¾" 350.00
Ferner, moriage & pnt florals, #7, 8¾" 275.00
Ginger jar, exotic bird reserve, mk NIPPON, 7½" 325.00
Hair receiver, mc florals, #7, 4¾" dia 65.00
Humidor, bird in relief, #2, 7½" 1,500.00
Humidor, couple on open touring car, 'laced' details, #2, 7" 725.00
Humidor, dog, elk & landscape in relief, gr #2, 7½" 1,000.00
Humidor, fisherman w/catch in relief, #2, 7¼" 1,800.00
Humidor, hunting dogs in relief, brn tones, #2, 7½" W 1,200.00
Humidor, ostriches in desert, sq, #2, 6½" 525.00
Humidor, owls in relief, #2, 7¼" 950.00
Humidor, playing cards, #2, 4½" 400.00
Jar, landscape w/cobalt & gold, cylinder, w/lid, #7, 5½" 250.00
Lamp base, mc roses, gold base, #7, 18" 375.00
Match holder/ashtray, Wedgwood, cream on bl, #2, 3½" H 335.00
Matchbox, girl standing on moon crescent, mk NIPPON, 3" 275.00
Matchbox holder, dbl; florals on wht, hanging, #2, 6" L 165.00
Mug, Egyptian decor on brn, gold #2, 5" 250.00
Mug, moriage landscape, bl #7, 5½" 225.00
Nappy, roses w/gold beading, ruffled rim, bl mk, 6¼" 175.00
Pancake server, floral swags on wht, w/lid, mk, 8½" dia 125.00
Pitcher, mc roses w/cobalt & gold, unmk, 7¾" 600.00
Plaque, exotic bird on branch, #7, 11" 275.00
Plaque, flowers & wooded landscape in relief, #2, 10½" 1,000.00
Plaque, flowers in basket, gold rim, #2, 12" 250.00
Plaque, Indian chief's portrait, geometric border, #2, 7¾" 325.00
Plaque, lady's portrait, fancy gold border, Kinjo mk, 10" 500.00
Plaque, moose in landscape, #2, 15" 1,400.00
Plaque, owl on branch w/bl sky, #2, 9" 300.00
Plaque, pineapple & mixed fruits, rectangular, #2, 10¼" 625.00
Plaque, sampan scenic, gr rim, #2, 9" 225.00
Plaque, still life on table, #2, 12" 375.00
Plaque, winter scenic, #2, 10" 275.00
Plate, game bird, vining border, #2, 8½" 300.00
Potpourri jar, sampan scenic, gr #2, 5¾" 185.00
Punch bowl, swan scenic w/gold, #2, 9½", +6 3¾" cups 1,000.00
Rose bowl, grapes in relief, #2, 3½" H 275.00
Shaving mug, river scenic, earth tones, #7, 4" 145.00
Smoke set, man on camel in desert, #2, 3-pc 500.00
Stein, man on camel beside tent, gold hdl, #2, 7" 625.00
Stein, monk drinking, vintage border, #2, 7" 750.00

Sugar shaker, Deco-style florals on wht, gold hdl, #2, 5" 125.00
Sugar shaker, florals & gold on wht, 6-sided, #2, 5¼" 90.00
Talcum powder flask, florals w/gold, mk, 5" 150.00
Tankard, elk portrait, cylindrical, #2, 11", +4 4¾" mugs 1,500.00
Tea tile, Egyptian portrait, geometric rim, 8-sided, #2, 6¼" 175.00
Teapot, Deco-style florals, HP mk, 5½" pot+cr/sug+6 c/s 375.00
Tidbit tray, geometric florals, center hdl, 3-part, #2, 7" 110.00
Tray, roses on wht, Wedgwood rim & hdls, #2, 10½" L 250.00
Tray, Wedgwood, cream on bl, hdls, #2, 10" sq 325.00
Tumblers, violets on wht, mk, 4" 50.00
Urn, lady's portrait, much gold, bolted, #7, 12" 1,000.00
Urn, landscape reserve w/gold, ornate hdls, bolted, #2, 16" 1,500.00
Vase, castle tapestry w/gold, cylindrical, #7, 6¼" 600.00
Vase, children by river in relief, #2, 12½" 5,500.00
Vase, daffodils, rope trim, ring hdls, #2, 9½" 325.00
Vase, Deco-style floral reserves, gold hdls, #2, 8¾" 175.00
Vase, Deco-style florals divided by scenic band, #8, 11½" 225.00
Vase, exotic bird on floral branch, can neck, hdls, #2, 7½" 125.00
Vase, figures in field reserve, 3 angle hdls, #2, 12" 1,200.00
Vase, floral reserve in wht band w/gold, 6-sided stick, #7, 12" 275.00
Vase, floral tapestry, bottle form, #7, 8½" 675.00
Vase, game birds, cylindrical, #7, 15" 1,000.00
Vase, gold florals on cobalt, inverted cone w/hdls, #7, 4½" 250.00
Vase, lady's portrait, gold hdls, #7, 16" 1,600.00
Vase, lady's portrait reserve w/gold, sm hdls, #7, 12" 950.00
Vase, landscape in gold w/much gold thoughout, hdls, #2, 7½" .300.00
Vase, landscape w/cobalt & gold, cylindrical, #7, 6½" 450.00
Vase, man on camel scene, moriage trim on hdls, #2, 12½" 650.00
Vase, mc florals, much gold, lg ring hdls, bl #7, 7½" 325.00
Vase, mc florals w/gold, bulbous, ornate hdls, #7, 7¾" 425.00
Vase, moriage birds, bulbous, stick neck hdls, mk, 9½" 400.00
Vase, moriage birds on landscape, #7, 8½" 525.00
Vase, moriage dragon, angle hdls, gr #2, 12½" 300.00
Vase, moriage dragon, sm ring hdls, bottle neck, #2, 9½" 300.00
Vase, moriage florals, ftd trumpet form, #9, 9" 350.00
Vase, moriage florals, ornate hdls, bl #7, 8½" 350.00
Vase, moriage landscape in relief, #2, 9½" 550.00
Vase, Oriental figure in landscape, gold hdls, #8, 9½" 175.00
Vase, ostrich reserve, cobalt & gold, ring hdls, #2, 13" 550.00
Vase, poinsettias, angle hdls, #2, 8½" 175.00
Vase, portrait reserve w/gold, lg angle hdls, #7, 6½" 700.00

Vase, river landscape at sunset, ruffled rim, handles, green mark, 8¼", $250.00.

Vase, river scenic, bulbous, can neck, gold hdls, #2, 8¾" 200.00
Vase, river scenic band on yel, can neck, angle hdls, #2, 7" 110.00
Vase, river scenic w/cobalt & gold, wide angle hdls, #7, 8½" 425.00
Vase, river scenic w/house, loving cup shape, #2, 4¼" 125.00
Vase, river trapestry, many gold florals, hdls, #7, 6¼" 575.00
Vase, scenic reserve on Wedgwood body, cream on bl, #2, 9½" .500.00
Vase, swan scenic reserve, cobalt & gold, hdls, #7, 10" 450.00
Vase, swan scenic w/gold, gourd shape, hdls, #7, 12¼" 500.00

Vase, swans scenic, cylindrical, #2, 8"	1,200.00
Vase, Wedgwood, cream on bl, sm angle hdls, #2, 6¾"	500.00
Vase, Wedgwood, cream on lav w/floral reserve, #2, 16"	900.00
Vase, wht Deco-style roses, gold hdls, bottle neck, #7, 10½"	225.00
Wine jug, Am Indian in canoe, squat, gr #2, 8¾"	700.00

Nodders

So called because of the nodding action of their heads and hands, nodders originated in China where they were used in temple rituals to represent deity. At first they were made of brass and were actually a type of bell; when these bells were rung, the heads of the figures would nod. In the 18th century, the idea was adopted by Meissen and by French manufacturers who produced not only china nodders but bisque as well. Most nodders are individual; couples are unusual. The idea remained popular until the end of the 19th century and was used during the Victorian era by toy manufacturers.

Boy as statesman, wire glasses, Staffordshire type, 7"	155.00
Boy in clown outfit, Staffordshire, 7½"	165.00
Boy w/shamrock on hat, wire cane, bsk, 4"	85.00
Cat, pnt papier-mache, late 1800s, 7½", EX	465.00
Chicken driving pk car, celluloid	110.00
Girl in pajamas kneeling, compo	65.00
Juggler, seated, bsk, head & hands move, 6¾"	125.00
Lady carrying basket, Germany, 5"	110.00
Lady in rocker, smoking pipe, Germany, late 1800s	90.00
Man's head on book, jaw moves, bsk, toothpick holder	115.00
Old lady w/dog & staff, bronze, 1850s, 4½"	195.00
Old lady w/dog & staff, silver, Elkington, 1850s, 4½"	275.00
Old Scotsman street vendor, bronze, 19th C, 4½"	350.00
Oriental couple, delicate bsk, Germany, late 1800s, pr	275.00
Oriental lady, seated & holding mirror, Meissen, 4½"	125.00
Oriental man or lady, parian, 7", pr	195.00
Oriental mandarin, standing, Meissen, 4¾"	130.00
Rabbit pushing baby buggy, celluloid	95.00
Robed figure, 3-way type, Portugal, old, 10"	200.00
Turtle, compo & fiberboard, tail & head move, EX pnt, 5" L	65.00

German Comic Characters

During the early 1930s, Germany produced a collection of small figure dolls, approximately 2" to 4" high, representing the most popular comic strip and cartoon characters of that time. They were made of bisque with brightly painted details and clearly stamped with their appropriate names and 'Germany' on their backs. Generally, their movable heads were attached with an elastic string going through their bodies, hence the name 'nodders,' but there were some characters produced earlier that were frozen with no movable parts. The most popular ones came in boxed sets, but the lesser-known characters were sold separately, making them rarer and harder to find today. We have listed the most valuable characters from the series here; those not mentioned below are valued at $125.00 and under. Our advisor for German character nodders is Doug Dezso; he is listed in the Directory under New Jersey. He will answer questions (as long as an SASE is included) on German character nodders only.

Ambrose Potts	350.00
Aunt Mamie & Uncle Willie, ea	350.00
Auntie Blossom	150.00
Bill, Dock, Avery, Max or Pop Jenks, ea	200.00
Buttercup	250.00
Chubby Chaney	250.00
Corky	475.00
Ferina	350.00
Grandpa Teen	350.00
Happy Hooligan	600.00
Harold Teen	150.00
Junior Nebbs	500.00
Lillums	150.00
Little Annie Rooney, arm moves	250.00
Little Egypt	350.00
Lord Plushbottom	150.00
Ma & Pa Winkle, ea	350.00
Majory, Patsy, Lilacs or Josie, ea	400.00
Mary Ann Jackson	250.00
Min Gump	150.00
Mr Bailey	150.00
Mr Bibb	400.00
Mr Wicker	250.00
Mushmouth	350.00
Mutt or Jeff, ea	250.00
Nicodemus	350.00

Old Timer, $350.00.

Pat Fannigan	400.00
Pete the Dog	250.00
Rudy or Fanny Nebbs, ea	250.00
Scraps	250.00
Widow Zander	400.00
Winnie Winkle	150.00

Noritake

The Noritake Company was first registered in 1904 as Nippon Gomei Kaisha. In 1917 the name became Nippon Toki Kabushiki Toki. The 'M' in wreath mark is that of the Morimura Brothers, distributors with offices in New York. It was used until 1941. The tree crest mark is the crest of the Morimura family.

The Noritake Company has produced fine porcelain dinnerware sets and occasional pieces decorated in the delicate manner for which the Japanese are noted. Their Azalea pattern was produced exclusively for the Larkin Company, who gave the lovely ware away as premiums to club members and their home agents. From 1916 through the thirties, Larkin distributed fine china which was decorated in pink azaleas on white with gold tracing along edges and handles. Early in the thirties, six pieces of crystal hand painted with the same design were offered: candle holders, a compote, a tray with handles, a scalloped fruit bowl, a cheese and cracker set, and a cake plate. All in all, seventy different pieces of Azalea were produced. Some, such as the fifteen-piece child's set, bulbous vase, china ashtray, and the pancake jug, are quite rare. One of the earliest marks was the Noritake M in wreath with variations. Later the ware was marked 'Noritake, Azalea, Hand Painted, Japan.'

Another of their dinnerware lines has become a favorite of many collectors. Tree in the Meadow features a growing near a lake. There is usually a cottage in the distance. This line was made during the 1920s and 1930s and seems today to be in good supply. Various interesting forms are seen, and reassembling a complete set should be an enjoyable undertaking.

Authority Joan Van Patten has compiled two lovely books, *The Collector's Encyclopedia of Noritake, Vols. I and II,* with many full-color photos and current prices; you will find her address in the Directory under New York. In the following listings, examples are hand painted unless noted otherwise. Numbers refer to these specific marks:

Key:
#1 — Komaru   #3 — N in Wreath
#2 — M in Wreath

Azalea

Basket, mint; Dolly Varden, #193	195.00
Bonbon, #184, 6¼"	50.00
Bowl, #12, 10"	42.50
Bowl, deep, #310	68.00
Bowl, fruit; shell form, #188, 7¾"	385.00
Bowl, oatmeal; #55, 5½"	28.00
Bowl, vegetable; divided, #439, 9½"	295.00
Bowl, vegetable; oval, #101, 10½"	60.00
Bowl, vegetable; oval, #172, 9¼"	58.00
Butter chip, #312, 3¼"	145.00
Butter tub, w/insert, #54	48.00
Cake plate, #10, 9¾"	40.00
Candy bowl, #185	195.00
Candy jar, #313	695.00
Casserole, gold finial, w/lid, #372	540.00
Casserole, w/lid, #16	125.00
Celery/roll tray, #99, 12"	55.00
Cheese/butter dish, #314	135.00
Child's set, #253, 15-pc	2,500.00
Coffeepot, AD; #182	595.00
Compote, #170	98.00
Condiment set, #14, 5-pc	65.00
Creamer & sugar bowl, #122	158.00
Creamer & sugar bowl, #449, ind	395.00
Creamer & sugar bowl, #7	45.00
Creamer & sugar bowl, AD: open, #123	140.00
Creamer & sugar bowl, gold finial, #401	155.00
Cruet, #190	195.00
Cup & saucer, #2	17.50
Cup & saucer, AD; #183	150.00
Cup & saucer, bouillon; #124, 3½"	24.50
Egg cup, #120	60.00
Gravy boat, #40	48.00
Jam jar set, #125, 3-pc	155.00
Match/toothpick holder, #192	130.00
Mayonnaise set, scalloped, #453, 3-pc	495.00
Mustard jar, #191	60.00
Pickle/lemon set, #121	24.50
Pitcher, milk jug; #100, 1-qt	195.00
Plate, #4, 7½"	10.00
Plate, bread & butter; #8, 6½"	10.00
Plate, cream soup; #363	175.00
Plate, dinner; #13, 9¾"	28.00
Plate, grill; 3-compartment, #38, 10¼"	165.00
Plate, scalloped sq, salesman's sample	950.00
Plate, soup; #19, 7⅛"	25.00
Platter, #17, 14"	60.00
Platter, #186, 16"	475.00
Platter, #56, 12"	58.00
Platter, cold meat; #311, 10¼"	215.00
Refreshment set, #39, 2-pc	48.00
Relish, #194, 7⅛"	85.00
Relish, loop hdl, 2-part, #450	425.00
Relish, oval, #18, 8½"	20.00
Relish, 2-part, #171	58.00
Relish, 4-part, #119, rare, 10"	150.00
Saucer, fruit; #9, 5¼"	10.00
Shakers, #126, ind, pr	27.50
Shakers, bell form, #11, pr	30.00
Shakers, bulbous, #89, pr	30.00
Spoon holder, #189, 8"	115.00
Spoon holder, #339, 2-pc	35.00
Syrup, #97, w/underplate	135.00
Tea tile, #169, 6"	48.50
Teapot, #15	110.00
Teapot, gold finial, #400	495.00
Toothpick holder, #192	130.00
Vase, bulbous, #452	1,150.00
Vase, fan form, ftd, #187	185.00
Whipped cream set, #3, 3-pc	38.50

Tree in the Meadow

Basket, Dolly Varden	85.00
Bowl, berry; ind	12.00
Bowl, cream soup; 2-hdl	28.00
Bowl, oatmeal	10.00
Bowl, soup	15.00
Bowl, vegetable; 9"	35.00
Butter pat	15.00
Butter tub, open, w/drainer	30.00

Candy dish, Tree in Meadow, 5½", $400.00.

Celery dish	25.00
Cheese dish	45.00
Coffeepot	150.00
Compote	50.00
Condiment set, 5-pc	45.00
Creamer & sugar bowl, demitasse	40.00
Cup & saucer	25.00
Cup & saucer, demitasse	25.00
Egg cup	25.00
Gravy boat	40.00
Jam jar/dish, w/underplate	70.00
Lemon dish	15.00
Mayonnaise set, 3-pc	40.00
Mustard jar, w/lid & spoon	30.00

Plate, bonbon	33.00
Plate, dinner	25.00
Plate, grill	40.00
Plate, luncheon; sq	25.00
Plate, 6½"	10.00
Plate, 7½"	15.00
Platter, 10"	20.00
Platter, 14"	35.00
Relish, divided	20.00
Shakers, sm, pr	15.00
Spoon holder	40.00
Sugar shaker & pitcher	65.00
Syrup jug, w/underplate	50.00
Tea tile	25.00
Teapot, demitasse	150.00
Teapot, strap hdl	50.00
Waste bowl, from tea set	30.00

Miscellaneous

Ashtray, clown figure seated at side, #2, 5"	300.00
Ashtray, pipe & matches on sq shape, #2, 4½"	65.00
Ashtray, rabbit sits at side of bl lustre tray, #2, 2¾"	190.00
Ashtrays, Bridge set; card suit shapes, #2, 4-pc set	100.00
Basket dish, man on camel scene, gold center hdl, #2, 7½"	185.00
Bowl, exotic bird & flowers, red rim, hdls, #2, 6¾"	90.00
Bowl, floral center, orange & bl lustre, hdls, #2, 9¼"	60.00
Bowl, floral center, orange lustre, sq w/blk hdls, #2, 6½"	40.00
Bowl, lg Deco-style florals, hdls, red #2, 10¼"	90.00
Bowl, parrot on branch, wide bl border w/smooth rim, #2, 10"	65.00
Bowl, river scenic in flower fr, orange rim w/gold, #2, 9¾"	50.00
Bowl, sampan scenic w/heavy silver o/l trim, #2, 10"	100.00
Bowl, 2 irises, bl scalloped rim w/gold, hdls, #2, 10½"	60.00
Box, clown figural, head finial, ruffle forms lid, #2, 5½"	325.00
Cake plate, exotic birds on cream, pk rim w/gold, #2, 8¼"	45.00
Candlesticks, daisies on bl w/gold, sq ft, #2, 9", pr	225.00
Candy dish, gold etched florals, hdls, #2, 6"	100.00
Candy dish, Oriental landscape, basket hdl, #2, 7½"	65.00
Candy dish, vintage decor, boat shape, 2 hdls, #2, 9"	75.00
Chamberstick, orange lustre w/blk trim, ring hdls, #2, 4¾"	80.00
Cheese & cracker dish, lady finial, #2, 9" dia	215.00
Cheese dish, Deco-style flowers along sides, #2, 4x8x6"	100.00
Chocolate pot, florals on wht w/gold, #2, 9½", +4 c/s	225.00
Cigarette box, classic figures in reserve on lid, #2, 5½" L	140.00
Coaster, sailboat scenic, orange/bl lustre, #2, 4"	15.00
Compote, floral center, gold hdls & rim, ftd, #2, 9¾"	95.00
Compote, 3 ladies form stem of scalloped bowl, #2, 7"	400.00
Condensed milk container, Deco florals, gold hdls, #2, 5¼"	100.00
Condiment set, 3 yel building forms on tray, #2	125.00
Creamer & sugar bowl, berry; floral, gold lid, #2, 6½"	70.00
Creamer & sugar bowl, floral band on wht, w/lid, #2, 3"	50.00
Dresser box, lady figural, orange lustre dress, #2, 4½"	300.00
Dresser set, river scenic w/swans, gold trim, #1, 8-pc	375.00
Egg cup, river scenic w/windmill, #2, 3½"	30.00
Flower frog, fish figural, red #2, 4½"	250.00
Flower frog, toadstools on rnd base, #2, 3½"	160.00
Humidor, golfer in red, gr #2, 6½"	450.00
Humidor, lady & monkey silhouettes on yel, #2, 6½"	375.00
Humidor, owl in relief on brn, #2, 7"	475.00
Inkwell, lady figural, bl lustre dress, #2, 4½"	300.00
Jam jar, strawberries on yel, rose finial, #2, 5½"	75.00
Lemon dish, Deco-style cottage scene, yel rim, #2, 4¼"	50.00
Lemon dish, lemon in relief, #2, 6"	55.00
Lobster set, flower-form bowl, lobster on plate, #2, 10¾"	125.00

Mustard jar, river scenic w/swans, gold trim, #2, 2½"	35.00
Nappy, mixed pk & wht roses on pastel shaded, hdl, #2, 5"	40.00
Nut dish, nuts in relief, silver trim, #2, 8"	95.00
Open salt & pepper shaker, floral/orange lustre, #2, +tray	65.00
Pin dish, recumbent clown figural, #2, 4"	310.00
Plaque, Wedgwood style, classic figures on bl, #2, 5", pr	800.00
Plate, wild bird, fruit-basket border, #2, 8½"	90.00
Punch bowl, peacock reserve on pk w/gold, #2, 16", +8 cups	1,000.00
Relish dish, 2-lobe w/bird center hdl, floral decor, #2, 6"	115.00
Salt cellar, swan figural, #2, 2½" L, pr	55.00
Salt shaker, river scenic w/gold, bell shape, #2, 2½"	12.00
Sauce dish, bird & florals, gold lustre, #2, 4½", +spoon	40.00
Serving dish, mc floral on red, center hdl, 8-sided, #2, 5"	30.00
Smoke set, Deco florals on red w/gr band, #2, 4-pc	350.00
Snack set, Deco florals on cream, yel border, #2, 7½" tray	65.00
Sugar bowl, river scenic, angle hdls, red #2, 3½"	25.00
Syrup, orchids on wht w/gold, #2, 4½"	70.00
Syrup, river scenic w/gold, #2, 4½", +underplate	65.00
Toast rack, bl lustre w/red bird finial, #2, 5½" L	95.00
Trinket dish, river scenic, center hdl, #1, 2¼"	25.00
Vase, exotic bird figure beside trunk base, lustre, #2, 5¼"	250.00
Vase, floral band along ruffled rim, fan form, #2, 6½"	135.00
Vase, house & river landscape, earth tones, bulbous, #2, 8¾"	100.00
Vase, lg open flowers on pastel shaded, gold hdls, #2, 11¼"	165.00
Vase, peacock figural, #2, 5¼"	125.00
Vase, river scenic medallion on gr w/gold, tub hdls, #1, 10"	170.00
Vase, sampan scenic, gold ring hdls, #1, 10"	250.00
Vase, squirrel on branch in relief, #2, 5¼"	225.00
Wall pocket, dbl; exotic bird/florals, bl lustre trim, #2, 8"	150.00

Norse

The Norse Pottery was established in 1903 in Edgerton, Wisconsin, by Thorwald Sampson and Louis Ipson. A year later it was purchased by A.W. Wheelock and moved to Rockford, Illinois. The ware they produced was inspired by ancient bronze vessels of the Norsemen. Designs were often incised into the red clay body. Dragon handles and feet were favored decorative devices, and they achieved a semblance of patina through the application of metallic glazes. The ware was marked with model numbers and a stylized 'N' containing a vertical arrangement of the remaining letters of the name. Production ceased after 1913. Our advisor for this category is John Danis; he is listed in the Directory under Illinois.

Bowl, stylized animal handles, #14, 6x11" 1,200.00.

Candlestick, blk w/gold snake looped at base, #54, 12", pr	275.00
Mug, incised decor, blk w/bronze wash, #51, 5"	150.00
Vase, angle shoulder w/2 lg dragons as hdls, #6, 7½x14½"	1,500.00
Vase, geometrics at top, gold remains, #45, 4½"	95.00
Vase, groups of dots/elongations, gr on blk, #11, 5½x7½"	500.00
Vase, slash mks at shoulder, #43, 9x1¾"	100.00

Wall pocket, dmn shape w/lizards, #72, 11" 250.00

North Dakota School of Mines

The School of Mines of the University of North Dakota was established in 1890; but due to a lack of funding it was not until 1898 that Earle J. Babcock was appointed as director and efforts were made to produce ware from the native clay he had discovered several years earlier. The first pieces were made by firms in the east from the clay Babcock sent them. Some of the ware was decorated by the manufacturer; some was shipped back to North Dakota to be decorated by native artists. By 1909 students at the University of North Dakota were producing utilitarian items such as tile, brick, shingles, etc., in conjunction with a ceramic course offered through the chemistry department. By 1910 a ceramic department had been established, supervised by Margaret Kelly Cable. Under her leadership, fine artware was produced. Native flowers, grains, buffalo, cowboys, and other subjects indigenous to the state were incorporated into the decorations. Some pieces have an Art Nouveau — Art Deco style easily attributed to her association with Frederick H. Rhead, with whom she studied in 1911. During the twenties the pottery was marketed on a limited scale through gift and jewelry stores in the state. From 1927 until 1949 when Miss Cable announced her retirement, a more widespread distribution was maintained with sales branching out into other states. The ware was marked in cobalt with the official seal — 'Made at School of Mines, N.D. Clay, University of North Dakota, Grand Forks, N.D.' in a circle. Very early ware was sometimes marked 'U.N.D.' in cobalt by hand.

Bowl, buffalo prs, med bl on cream, sgn JM, 4x5" 850.00
Bowl, flower/leaf band, blk on brick, Huckfield, 3x4½" 375.00
Bowl, Indian motif, blk on red-orange, GLN/1931, 5x7½" 325.00
Bowl, mc bands on tan, sgn FC Huckfield, 3¼x2½" 275.00
Bowl, rose/lt gray-gr matt, closed rim, 3x4" 170.00
Bowl, tan birds/leaves, blk lines etc on red, Dorpat, 4" 425.00
Humidor, purple, sgn Summers, w/lid, 7" 275.00
Paperweight, wagon & oxen design 150.00
Planter/bookend, cvd/pnt ivy, gr tones, 3¾", NM 75.00
Tile, Rebekah Assemblies, seafoam gloss, 3½" dia 95.00
Tile, thunderbird, 1917, fr 385.00
Trivet, cvd bell flowers, bl on wht/tan, Huckfield, 5" dia 225.00
Vase, cream crackle, ftd U form, mk H136, 6x7½" 160.00
Vase, cvd cardinals/flowering branches on maroon, Lein, 6x5" ..375.00
Vase, cvd cowboys, med brn on dk brn, Anderson, 4x3½" 425.00
Vase, cvd cowboys on horsebk, lt on bk brn, Mattson, 6¾x4½" .1,500.00
Vase, cvd daffodils in 6 panels, 2-tone brn, Anderson, 8" 850.00
Vase, cvd geometrics, blk lines on dk bl, sg MT, 3¾x5½" 300.00
Vase, cvd leaves (EX work) on yel/gr matt, Sheppard, 7½" 850.00
Vase, cvd leaves at neck, tobacco brn matt, O'Brien, 8½" 475.00
Vase, cvd tulip on long stem, aqua gloss, Breacy, 9" 550.00
Vase, cvd tulips/buds on long stems, med gr matt, RM/31, 6" 425.00
Vase, cvd wheat sheaves on shaded lt brn matt, Huckfield, 5x2½" ..325.00
Vase, cvd 2-color floral band on pk matt, Huck/2540, 3x4¾" 325.00
Vase, dk bl to rose gloss, McHovell, 8½" 200.00
Vase, emb leafy plants, olive on brn matt, Hewes, 1948, 5x4" 400.00
Vase, emb women in ethnic costumes, brn/gr, Mattson, 3¾x4" .650.00
Vase, fish/hooks/waves at shoulder, bl/rust, sgn, 4½x4½" 800.00
Vase, gr to bl matt, teardrop form, 6½" 220.00
Vase, Indian motif, blk on brick/blk/ochre, Mattson, 4x4½" 300.00
Vase, long brn runs w/pk over aqua gloss, ribbed, Mattson, 7x6" ..400.00
Vase, prairie rose, M Cable, 7x6" 395.00
Vase, primitive deer, yel/blk on brick, Mattson, 3½x4" 550.00
Vase, ribbed w/emb gr/brn floral on brn, mk Prairie Rose, 3x5" ..250.00
Vase, rose & gr matt, 5x7½" 275.00

Vase, stamped Xs/stars/moon/tulips on gr-brn, Mattson, 10" 350.00
Vase, textured band of girls on brn matt, Summers, 6" 290.00
Vase, Viking ship, bl tones, Mattson, 3x3" 350.00
Vase, yel over peach matt, sgn Gooslaw, 4x7" 350.00

Northwood

The Northwood Company was founded in 1896 in Indiana, Pennsylvania, by Harry Northwood, whose father, John, was the art director for Stevens and Williams, an English glassworks. Northwood joined the National Glass Company in 1899 but in 1901 again became an independent contractor and formed the Harry Northwood Glass Company of Wheeling, West Virginia. He marketed his first carnival glass in 1908, and it became his most popular product. His company was also famous for its custard, goofus, and pressed glass. Northwood died in 1923, and the company closed. See also Carnival; Custard; Goofus; Opalescent; Pattern Glass.

Bowl, master berry; Barbella, Maiden's Blush, +4 ind 65.00
Bowl, master berry; Holly, clear w/ruby stain & gold, +2 sm 95.00
Bowl, master berry; Royal Ivy, rubena frost 125.00
Butter dish, Cherries, gr w/gold, mk, 6x7¾" dia 110.00
Butter dish, Pods & Posies, gr w/gold 140.00
Butter dish, Royal Ivy, rubena frost 275.00
Butter dish, Royal Oak, rubena frost 235.00
Celery vase, Leaf Umbrella, bl cased 325.00
Creamer, Cherries, gr w/gold, mk, 4¾x4" dia 75.00
Cruet, Royal Ivy, rainbow craquelle, orig stopper 725.00
Lamp base, Leaf Mold, pk & vaseline spatter, w/burner, mini 195.00
Pitcher, water; Cherry Lattice Decorated Ware, +4 tumblers 225.00
Pitcher, water; Leaf Mold, cased spatter, +6 tumblers 900.00
Pitcher, water; Leaf Mold, pk/wht spatter w/silver flecks 725.00
Pitcher, water; Royal Ivy, cased spatter 385.00
Pitcher, water; Royal Oak, rubena 400.00

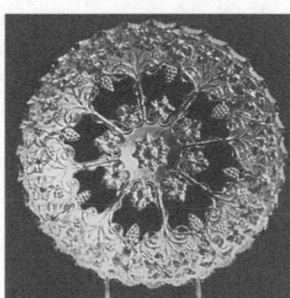

Plate, Grape Frieze, cobalt with heavy gold, 3-toed, ca 1906, 11", $235.00.

Rose bowl, bl & gr pull-ups on wht, appl ft, 8-crimp, 3¼" 300.00
Rose bowl, maroon pull-ups on chartreuse, pk int, 4x4½" 650.00
Shakers, Grape & Leaf, wht opaque w/gr leaves, pr 135.00
Shakers, Leaf Mold, red spatter on canary satin, pr 185.00
Shakers, Royal Ivy, rubena frost, pr 185.00
Spooner, Leaf Umbrella, cased spatter 175.00
Spooner, Peach, gr w/gold 115.00
Sugar bowl, Royal Ivy, rubena frost 200.00
Sugar shaker, Leaf Umbrella, cranberry spatter 365.00
Sugar shaker, Leaf Umbrella, yel cased 275.00
Sugar shaker, Swirl, cranberry 495.00
Syrup, Grape & Leaf, wht opaque 125.00
Syrup, Leaf Umbrella, cranberry, orig pewter lid 650.00
Syrup, Royal Ivy, rainbow craquelle 695.00
Syrup, Royal Ivy, rubena 450.00
Toothpick holder, Leaf Mold, cranberry, vaseline & wht 150.00

Toothpick holder, Leaf Umbrella, cranberry, rare 250.00
Toothpick holder, Royal Ivy, cranberry clear & frosted 150.00
Toothpick holder, Royal Ivy, rainbow craquelle 265.00
Toothpick holder, Royal Oak, rubena frost 150.00
Toothpick holder, Swirl, threaded rubena, str sides, 2¼" 125.00
Tumbler, Oriental Poppy, gr w/M gold 75.00
Tumbler, Teardrop & Flowers, bl w/gold 65.00
Vase, pull-up feathers, mauve on beige, bl int, 5x2⅞" 775.00
Vase, Twist, Chinese coral red, 10" 95.00

Norweta

Norweta pottery was produced by the Northwestern Terra Cotta Company of Chicago, Illinois. It was made for approximately ten years, beginning sometime before 1907. Both matt and crystalline glazes were employed, and terra-cotta vases were also produced. Not all were marked.

Candlesticks, 4-sided, lady/bldgs/owl, lt bl, 7", EX, pr 200.00
Doorstop, seated elf reading a book, 9x5" 350.00
Lamp, seminude atop ornate column, arm raised, 65", VG 1,500.00
Vase, Nouveau form, co-joined ladies, integral hdls, 16x20" ...1,200.00
Vase, royal bl gloss, flaring cylinder, 9½" 450.00

Nutcrackers

The nutcracker, though a strictly functional tool, is a good example of one to which man has applied ingenuity, imagination, and engineering skills. Though all were designed to accomplish the same end, hundreds of types exist in almost every material sturdy enough to withstand sufficient pressure to crack the nut. Figurals are popular collectibles, as are those with unusual design and construction. Patented examples are also desirable. Our advisor for this category is Earl MacSorley; he is listed in the Directory under Connecticut. For more information, we recommend *Ornamental and Figural Nutcrackers* by Judith A. Rittenhouse.

Black man's face on round base, cast iron, jaw opens, American, 1860-1900, 8¼", $1,000.00.

Dog, blk & wht porc enamel-plated CI, Am, 1900s, 5¾x11" 250.00
Dog, copper-plated CI, Am, 1900s, 5x11¾x2" 100.00
Dog, walking; copper-plated bronze, 1900s, 11¼x5¾x3⅝" 200.00
Elephant w/rider, brass, 1930-50s, 6⅝x2x1" 45.00
Fish, NP CI, gr glass eyes, English, 1930, 8½" 150.00
Fish, olive wood, Greek, 1950s, 8x2¼x1" 25.00
Girl w/hoop skirt, brass, screw-type, English, 1956, 3¾" 125.00
Lion head, wooden, glass eyes, Swiss or Tyrolean, 1900s, 9" 150.00
Man, bearded w/hat, wooden, Swiss or Tyrolean, 1900s, 8¾" 150.00
Nut vendor, wooden, mk Murren, 1850-1890, 8⅛" 200.00
Parrot, aluminum, gr & gold pnt, 1900-1950s, 10x2x5¼" 75.00
Peasant, standing, wooden, attached tray, Am, '30s, 12" 100.00

Peasant w/spectacles, wooden, Swiss or Scandinavian, 8¼" 100.00
Rabbit head, wooden/glass eyes, Swiss or Tyrolean, 1900s, 8⅛" .125.00
Sailor, CI, mk Tough Nut, English, 1897, 7¾x4¾x3⅛" 650.00
Skull & cross bones, NP CI, mk, English, 1928, 6" 100.00
Soldier, pnt CI, wooden base, Taiwan, 1990, 5x6½" 25.00
Squirrel, bronze, 1920-1930s, 5¾x9⅜x2½" 200.00
Squirrel on leaf, aluminum, blk pnt, 1950s, 11¾x8x10" 25.00
Superman figural, cvd wood, EX pnt 25.00
Whale, hand-wrought brass, mk HA PIND, ca 1900, 6¼x1x1½" ...100.00

Occupied Japan

Items marked 'Occupied Japan' are popular collectibles. They were produced during the period from the end of World War II until April 18, 1952, when the occupation ended. By no means was all of the ware exported during that time marked 'Occupied Japan'; some was marked 'Japan' or 'Made In Japan.' It is thought that because of the natural resentment felt by the Japanese toward the occupation, only a fraction of these wares carried the 'Occupied' mark. Even though you may find identical 'Japan'-marked items, because of its limited use, only those with the 'Occupied Japan' mark are being collected to any great extent. Values vary considerably, based on the quality of workmanship. Generally, bisque figures command much higher prices than porcelain, since on the whole they are of a finer quality.

For those wanting more information, we recommend *The Collector's Encyclopedia of Occupied Japan Collectibles* by Gene Florence; he is listed in the Directory under Kentucky. Our advisor for this category is Florence Archambault; she is listed in the Directory under Rhode Island. She represents the Occupied Japan Club, whose mailing address may be found in the Directory under Clubs, Newsletters, and Catalogs. All items described in the following listings are assumed ceramic unless noted otherwise.

Ashtray, Am Indian chief's head form 13.00
Ashtray, hand form, metal 10.00
Ashtray, Wedgwood type, 2½" 9.00
Bowl, salad; wood, 10" 25.00
Bowl, vegetable; apple decor, 8" 16.00
Candle holder, Mexican figural, 5" 35.00
Child's set, Disney character, 2-place, 9-pc 110.00
Christmas item, nativity figures, 2½", 7-pc set 80.00
Christmas item, reindeer, celluloid, 7x7½" 12.00
Christmas item, snow baby-like skier, 3½" 20.00
Cigarette box, Oriental man carries box w/dragon finial, 6⅜" 27.00
Cigarette lighter, metal, Aladdin lamp form, table sz 25.00
Cigarette lighter, metal, urn style, 3¼" 12.00
Cigarette lighter, metal gun form w/pearl hdls 30.00
Clicker, metal, chicken, 1½" 8.00
Coaster, mk Alcohol Proof, Isco 5.00
Creamer, floral w/gold, 3" 15.00
Creamer, lustre w/flowers, 1½" 9.00
Creamer, windmill form, 3" 12.00
Cup & saucer, blk & gold trim, Ucagco 15.00
Cup & saucer, blk & wht checkerboard border 12.00
Cup & saucer, demitasse; lacy flower on blk 14.00
Cup & saucer, demitasse; Oriental house scene 12.00
Cup & saucer, demitasse; wht w/floral decor & red panels 13.00
Cup & saucer, fancy gold trim, Shofu China, 2⅝" 10.00
Cup & saucer, pk w/floral int, Jyoto 12.00
Cup & saucer, red hearts & blk trim 10.00
Dinnerware, set for 12, w/gravy/4 platters/casserole, up to 500.00
Dinnerware, set for 4, w/creamer & sugar bowl, up to 250.00
Dinnerware, set for 6, w/gravy boat & sm platter, up to 300.00

Dinnerware, set for 8, w/gravy boat & 3 platters, up to 350.00
Doll, celluloid, Kewpie, 2¾" 20.00
Duck, celluloid, 4½" 22.00
Fan, paper, 8" spine 20.00
Figurine, American Indian chief, 5⅛" 16.00
Figurine, American Indian lady, 4¼" 7.00
Figurine, angel lying on bk holding bowl, 5½" 45.00
Figurine, angel on pk basket, 5" 45.00
Figurine, angel w/donkey, 4⅛" 30.00
Figurine, Blk fiddler, 5" 40.00
Figurine, Blk horn player, 6¼" 42.00
Figurine, boy playing accordion, mc, 5" 12.00
Figurine, boy playing tuba, mc, 4⅞" 12.00
Figurine, cellist lady & man, Maruyama, 3½" 22.00
Figurine, Cinderella & Prince Charming, Maruyama, 8¼" 125.00
Figurine, Colonial couple on sled w/dog, 5¾" 80.00
Figurine, Colonial man, bl coat, lt bl vest, 7" 35.00
Figurine, Colonial man w/flowers, lady w/basket, 8", pr 60.00

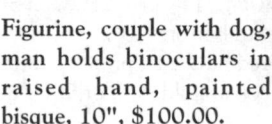

Figurine, couple with dog, man holds binoculars in raised hand, painted bisque, 10", $100.00.

Figurine, dog w/gr hat & pipe, brn highlights, 3½" 12.00
Figurine, girl on fence playing violin, mc, 4¼" 7.00
Figurine, girl w/doll, mc, 4¼" 14.00
Figurine, girl w/songbook, Ucagco, 5¾" 28.00
Figurine, hula girl, 4½" 20.00
Figurine, hunter in lilac hat, gr shirt, orange pants, 6⅛" 38.00
Figurine, lady seated w/book, yel hat, bl & red dress, 5¼" 25.00
Figurine, ladybug w/bat, blk jacket, 2¼" 7.00
Figurine, ladybug w/top hat & bass fiddle, 3" 7.00
Figurine, man playing flute, red hat, 5" 17.00
Figurine, old lady gnome, 3¾" 7.00
Figurine, Oriental lady on stair-step base, gold trim, 10" 25.00
Figurine, peacock w/plume tail, mc, 5" 18.00
Figurine, seated boy w/duck, mc, 4" 11.00
Furniture, bench, 1¾" 6.00
Furniture, piano, 1¾" 8.00
Jar, powder; bl w/wht floral reserve, oval, 2½" 12.00
Lamp base, courting couple, 6½", pr 75.00
Lamp base, musician & singer, 11½", pr 100.00
Mint dish, fish form, gold metal, 3-ftd 12.00
Mug, cannibal figure, hdl, 4¼" 37.00
Mug, face of winking man, 4" 38.00
Planter, bird beside house, 3" 9.00
Planter, boy beside cherry tree, 3⅝" 12.00
Planter, cat, blk & wht, pk highlights, 3⅝" 9.00
Planter, frog in weeds, 3⅝x3" 17.00
Planter, girl w/cart, 2⅝" 8.00
Planter, Scottie figural, 7" 20.00

Platter, apple decor, 15" 25.00
Shakers, baseball players, comical, pr 30.00
Shakers, bride & groom, pr 25.00
Shakers, graduates, pr 22.00
Shakers, tomato form, 3½", pr 20.00
Slide rule, MIB 35.00
Stein, people sitting at table, bl tones, 6" 20.00
Sugar bowl, birds on lustre glaze, w/lid 16.00
Teapot, aluminum, 9" 35.00
Toby mug, Gen McArthur, 5" 55.00
Toy, stork, celluloid, 9" 55.00
Tray, metal, leaf form, mk Economy, 5" 6.00
Tray, metal, souvenir of UN building, 2x4¾" 12.00
Umbrella, paper, 18" 28.00
Vase, bud; angel sitting at bottom, 5¼" 17.00
Vase, carriage scene, classic form, 3" 10.00
Vase, lg appl rose on bulbous form, 4¼" 17.00
Vase, pagoda in relief, ftd, sm hdls, 5¼" 26.00
Vase, swan form, mc, 5" 20.00
Wall plaque, flying duck, 6½", EX 28.00
Wall pocket, Colonial man & lady bust in gr window, 3⅝", pr 24.00

Ohr, George

George Ohr established his pottery around 1893 in Biloxi, Mississippi. The unusual style of the ware he produced and his flamboyant personality earned him the dubious title of 'the mad potter of Biloxi.' Though acclaimed by some of the critics of his day to be perhaps the most accomplished thrower in the history of the industry, others overlooked the eggshell-thin walls of his vessels, each a different shape and contortion, and saw only that their 'tortured' appearance contradicted their own sedate preferences.

Ohr worked alone. His work was typically pinched and pulled, pleated, crumpled, dented, and folded. Lizards and worms were often applied to the ware, each with detailed, expressive features. He was well recognized, however, for his glazes, especially those with a metallic patina. The ware was marked with his name, alone or with 'Biloxi' added. Ohr died in 1918. Our advisor for this category is Fer-Duc, Inc.; whose address is listed in the Directory under New York.

Bowl, bsk, pinched/folded-in rim, ftd, 2¾x5¾" 800.00
Bowl, clear glaze on orange clay, twisted/crushed, 1½x3" 350.00
Bowl, glazed in thirds (test?), raspberry int, folded, 4½" 2,100.00
Bowl, gr/brn speckled gloss, crushed/folded rim, 2¼x4¾" 900.00
Bowl, gun-metal, mahog int, paper thin, torn rim, 4½" 900.00
Bowl, red/bl/pk/gr sponging, irid gr int, pinched rim, 4" 2,600.00
Compote, khaki/brn speckled, pinched/tortured cup, 3x5" 1,000.00
Mug, gr mottle, incised greeting/dedication, 3¼" 700.00
Mug, pk gloss w/bl sponge & gr detail, twist/dents/inscription ..1,600.00
Pitcher, bl mottle gloss, thin w/lt twist, 3¼" 900.00
Pitcher, gun-metal lustre, pinched, leaning to 1 side, 3¼" 1,500.00
Pitcher, gun-metal w/orange int, paper thin, ftd/ruffled, 3" 1,000.00
Plaque, bird in hand, high relief, gr/brn on gr gloss, 5½" dia ...1,000.00
Puzzle mug, dk brn/blk metallic, rtcl, rabbit-head hdl, 3½" 650.00
Puzzle mug, gun-metal/olive, rope hdl, 3½x5" 400.00
Puzzle mug, gun-metal/yel/brn/gr mottle, misshapen 600.00
Teapot, purple/bl/gr mottled matt, left-handed, 4½x7" 3,250.00
Vase, blk/brn metallic gloss, bulbous w/can neck, 4½" 750.00
Vase, blk/brn pebbly metallic gloss, folded/crimped rim, 6x5" 900.00
Vase, bsk, cylinder w/rim & base twist, 7x3¾" 900.00
Vase, bsk, pleated incurvate body, crimped/folded rim, 4½" 1,000.00
Vase, bsk w/dk wash, dimpled body, ruffled rim, 5½x5¾" 1,200.00
Vase, buff bsk, deep in-body twist at shoulder, 5½x5½" 1,000.00

Vase, cobalt gloss, can neck w/crimped rim, bulbous, 7x5" **1,600.00**
Vase, deep bl/gr mottled gloss, bottle w/waisted neck, 9x3" **1,700.00**
Vase, dk pk matt, in-body twist, flared rim, 4x3¾" **3,200.00**
Vase, gr/blk/gun-metal on purple, cylinder, bun base, 8", EX ..**1,900.00**
Vase, gr/red/gun-metal flambe, orange/red int, hourglass, 8" ...**1,300.00**
Vase, gray-gr/speckled gun-metal, cylinder w/lg twist, 7", NM .**1,350.00**
Vase, gun-metal metallic blk/gr, ftd, waisted neck, 7x3½" **800.00**
Vase, gun-metal w/cvd bird panels, twisted/crumpled neck, 3½" .**800.00**
Vase, khaki w/gun-metal specks, lg dents, folded rim, 4x4" **1,400.00**
Vase, khaki/gun-metal mottle, 3 sides/3 ft, crimped, 3x5" **1,200.00**
Vase, mirred blk, boat-shape opening, 4½x5" **650.00**
Vase, mirror blk, folded rim, rpr chip, 5½x4" **750.00**
Vase, orange/gun-metal flambe, folded/crimped rim, 5x3½" ...**1,500.00**
Vase, peacock-feather dk bl w/pk, in-body twist, cup neck, 5" ..**1,300.00**
Vase, scroddled bsk, vertical in-body folds, folded rim, 6" **1,400.00**
Vase, silver 'metal shavings' texture, 4 pinches, 4x5½" **4,500.00**

Old Ivory

Old Ivory dinnerware was produced during the late 1800s by Herman Ohme, of Lower Salzbrunn in Silesia. The patterns are referred to by the numbers stamped on the bottom of many items. (Though not every piece is numbered, the vast majority bears the tiny blue fleur-de-lis/crown mark with Silesia or Germany beneath. Handwritten numbers signify something other than pattern.) Patterns #16 and #84 are the easiest to find and come in a wide variety of table items. Values are about the same for both patterns. Other floral designs include pink, yellow, and orange roses; holly; and lavender flowers — all on the same soft ivory background. The ware was not widely distributed; its two main distribution points were in Maine and, to a lesser extent, Chicago. Our prices are intended to represent a nationwide average, though you may have to pay a little more in some areas. Novice collectors should be aware of copy-cat versions from the turn of the century that are much heavier and of a coarser material. They are marked 'Old Ivory' without the blue trademark. They are not included in this listing.

Basket, #201, 3½x8½x5" **250.00**
Bowl, master berry; #15, +6 sm **295.00**
Butter dish, #16 or #84, w/insert, rare **625.00**
Cake plate, #16 or #84, open hdls, 10" **80.00**
Cake plate, #78, w/hdls, 10" **100.00**
Celery tray, #10, daisies, 11½" **85.00**
Chocolate pot, #75, yel roses **450.00**
Chocolate set, #16 or #84, serves 6 ....**850.00**
Chop plate, #11, 13" **185.00**
Cracker jar, #16 or #84, squatty, w/hdls **425.00**
Creamer & sugar bowl, #16 or #84, w/lid **195.00**

Cup and saucer, #15 (Poppies), $55.00.

Cup & saucer, #16 or #84, 3" **55.00**
Cup & saucer, chocolate, #7 ....**50.00**
Demitasse pot/teapot, #16 or #84 ....**425.00**
Mayonnaise, #16 or #84, w/undertray, gold & floral border **285.00**

Muffineer, #16 or #84, rare **450.00**
Plate, #82, 8" **85.00**
Plate, Holly, 6" **65.00**
Relish, #8, rectangular **85.00**
Shakers, #16 or #84, pr **135.00**
Shakers, #75, pr **95.00**
Spooner, #15, rare **300.00**
Tea tile, #16 or #84 ....**225.00**
Toothpick holder, #16 or #84 ....**250.00**
Tray, dresser; #15, mk, 12x6" **165.00**
Waste bowl, mk Silesia & Ohme **225.00**

Old Paris

Old Paris porcelains were made from the mid-18th century until about 1900. Seldom marked, the term refers to the area of manufacture rather than a specific company. In general, the ware was of high quality; characterized by classic shapes, colorful decoration, and gold application.

Urn, bsk figural finial, cameo reserve, rtcl collar, hdls, 18" **500.00**
Urn, estate scenes w/gold on mauve, head hdls, 1840s, 7½", pr ..**650.00**
Urn, portrait cameo, rtcl rim, figural finials, 18", pr **1,000.00**
Vase, courting scenes w/gold, urn shape, rstr, 10¼", pr **500.00**
Vase, floral shape, floral/cobalt panels w/gilt, 14", pr **500.00**
Vase, lg floral reserve on bl w/gilt, bulbous bottom, 13", pr **1,200.00**
Vase, Neoclassic, figures on blk w/gilt, red hdls, 21", pr **2,000.00**
Vase, Rococo Revival, lady in garden, cobalt/gold, 18", pr, EX ..**800.00**

Old Sleepy Eye

Old Sleepy Eye was a Sioux Indian chief who was born in Minnesota in 1780. His name was used for the name of a town as well as a flour mill. In 1903 the Sleepy Eye Milling Company of Sleepy Eye, Minnesota, contracted the Weir Pottery Company of Monmouth, Illinois, to make steins, vases, salt crocks, and butter tubs which the company gave away to their customers in each bag of their flour. A bust profile of the old Indian and his name decorated each piece of the blue and gray stoneware. In addition to these four items, the Minnesota Stoneware Company of Red Wing made a mug with a verse which is very scarce today.

In 1906 Weir Pottery merged with six others to form the Western Stoneware Company in Monmouth. They produced a line of blue and white ware using a lighter body, but these pieces were never given as flour premiums. This line consisted of pitchers (five sizes), steins, mugs, sugar bowls, vases, trivets, and mustache cups. These pieces turn up only rarely in other colors and are highly prized by advanced collectors. Advertising items such as trade cards, pillow tops, thermometers, paperweights, letter openers, postcards, cookbooks, and thimbles are considered very valuable. The original ware was made sporadically until 1937. Brown steins and mugs were produced in 1952.

Barrel, flour; orig paper label, 1920s **1,800.00**
Barrel, grapevine-effect banding **3,500.00**
Barrel, oak w/brass bands **4,500.00**
Butter crock, Flemish **625.00**
Calendar, 1904, NM **375.00**
Calendar, 1904, VG **150.00**
Cookbook, EX **185.00**
Cookbook, Indian on cover, Sleepy Eye Milling Co, 4¾x4" **300.00**
Cookbook, loaf of bread shape, EX **115.00**
Cookbook, loaf of bread shape, NM **210.00**
Coupon, for ordering cookbook **250.00**

Coupon, for ordering pillow top	200.00
Dough scraper, tin/wood, To Be Sure, EX	435.00
Fan, Indian chief, die-cut cb, 1900	220.00
Flour sack, cloth, mc Indian, red letters	345.00
Flour sack, paper, Indian in blk, blk lettering, NM	125.00
Ink blotter	125.00
Label, barrel end; mc Indian portrait, 16", NM	160.00
Label, barrel; Indian chief, Whilmann's Bros, 16" dia, EX	250.00
Label, egg crate; Indian chief in color, 1930s, 9x11"	32.00
Letter opener, bronze	900.00
Match holder, pnt	1,875.00
Match holder, wht	1,050.00
Mug, bl & gray, 4¼"	360.00
Mug, bl & wht, 4¼"	220.00
Mug, verse, Red Wing, EX	1,625.00
Paperweight, bronzed company trademk	560.00
Pillow cover, Sleepy Eye & tribe meet President Monroe	750.00
Pillow cover, trademk center w/various scenes, 22", NM	850.00
Pin-bk button, Indian, rnd face	350.00
Pitcher, #1, 4"	185.00
Pitcher, #2	250.00
Pitcher, #3	315.00
Pitcher, #3, w/bl rim	1,375.00
Pitcher, #4	400.00
Pitcher, #5	435.00
Pitcher, bl & gray, 5"	235.00
Pitcher, bl on cream, 8", M	345.00
Pitcher, gold & brn, 1981 Sesquicentennial	160.00
Pitcher, standing Indian, good color, #5 size	1,560.00
Plaque, plaster bust of Old Sleepy Eye in wood fr, 33x25"	385.00
Postcard, colorful trademk, 1904 Expo Winner	185.00
Ruler, wooden, 15"	500.00
Salt crock, Flemish, 4x6½"	600.00
Sheet music, in fr	300.00

Sign, Sleepy Eye Flour and Cereals, tin litho diecut, minor imperfections, 13½", $1,650.00.

Sign, self-fr tin, Old Sleepy Eye Flour, 20x24"	2,500.00
Spoon, demitasse; emb roses in bowl, Unity SP	105.00
Spoon, Indian-head hdl	125.00
Stein, bl & wht, 7¾"	625.00
Stein, brn, 1952, 22-oz	300.00
Stein, brn & wht	1,300.00
Stein, brn & yel, Western Stoneware	1,200.00
Stein, cobalt	1,000.00
Stein, Flemish	700.00
Stein, ltd edition, 1979-84, ea	125.00
Sugar bowl, bl & wht, 3"	750.00
Thermometer, front rpl	800.00
Vase, cattails, all cobalt	1,450.00
Vase, cattails, bl & wht, good color, 9"	800.00
Vase, cattails, brn on yel, rare color	1,500.00

Vase, Indian & cattails, Flemish, 8½"	470.00

O'Neill, Rose

Rose O'Neill's Kewpies were introduced in 1909 when they were used to conclude a story in the December issue of *Ladies' Home Journal*. They were an immediate success, and soon Kewpie dolls were being produced worldwide. German manufacturers were among the earliest and also used the Kewpie motif to decorate chinaware as well as other items. The Kewpie is still popular today and can be found on products ranging from Christmas cards and cake ornaments to fabrics and wallpaper.

Our advisor for this category is Denis C. Jackson who is listed in the Directory under Washington. In the following listings, 'sgn' indicates that the item is signed Rose O'Neill. Unsigned items are of little interest to collectors. Items marked 'Germany' are sometimes reproductions.

Box, 3 action Kewpies on lid, china, rnd, JC Bavaria	125.00
Clock, gr jasper, 3 action kewpies in relief, sgn, EX	395.00
Kewpie, bsk, Action, arms folded, 4½"	475.00
Kewpie, bsk, Confederate soldier, 4½"	475.00
Kewpie, bsk, driving chariot, minimum value	2,950.00
Kewpie, bsk, Gardener, 4"	450.00
Kewpie, bsk, Groom w/Bride, 4"	325.00
Kewpie, bsk, holding butterfly, 4"	525.00
Kewpie, bsk, holding pen, 3"	400.00
Kewpie, bsk, Hottentot (Blk), 3½"	440.00
Kewpie, bsk, in basket w/flowers, 3½"	750.00
Kewpie, bsk, Japan, 2"	50.00
Kewpie, bsk, Japan, 4"	70.00
Kewpie, bsk, Japan, 6"	130.00
Kewpie, bsk, jtd hips & shoulders, pnt shoes & socks, 4-5"	525.00
Kewpie, bsk, jtd hips & shoulders, 4"	485.00
Kewpie, bsk, jtd hips & shoulders, 9"	900.00
Kewpie, bsk, reading book, 3½"	825.00
Kewpie, bsk, Thinker, 4"	265.00
Kewpie, bsk, Traveler, 3½"	360.00
Kewpie, bsk, w/any article of clothing, 5"	300.00
Kewpie, bsk, w/any article of clothing, 9", minimum value	650.00
Kewpie, bsk, w/dog Doodle, 3½", minimum value	1,200.00
Kewpie, bsk, w/outhouse, 2½"	1,400.00
Kewpie, bsk, w/rabbit, 2½"	365.00
Kewpie, bsk, w/teddy bear, 4"	550.00
Kewpie, bsk, 1-pc body, jtd shoulders, bl wings, 12"	1,300.00
Kewpie, bsk, 1-pc body, jtd shoulders, bl wings, 2½"	110.00
Kewpie, bsk, 1-pc body, jtd shoulders, bl wings, 6"	200.00
Kewpie, bsk head, chubby jtd toddler body, glass eyes, 10"	3,600.00
Kewpie, bsk head, chubby jtd toddler body, glass eyes, 12"	4,900.00
Kewpie, bsk head, chubby jtd toddler body, glass eyes, 20"	7,900.00
Kewpie, bsk head, cloth body, glass eyes, 12", minimum value	2,600.00
Kewpie, bsk head, cloth body, pnt eyes, 10"	1,500.00
Kewpie, bsk head, cloth body, pnt eyes, 14"	1,800.00
Kewpie, celluloid, Blk, 5"	135.00
Kewpie, celluloid, jtd shoulders, 12"	260.00
Kewpie, celluloid, jtd shoulders, 5"	110.00
Kewpie, celluloid, Soldier or Action Kewpie, 4", minimum	100.00
Kewpie, celluloid, 2"	40.00
Kewpie, celluloid, 5"	85.00
Kewpie, celluloid, 9"	165.00
Kewpie, cloth, plain body, removable clothes, 15", M	550.00
Kewpie, cloth, plain body, removable clothes, 26", M	1,400.00
Kewpie, cloth w/mask face, Krueger, 15", M	450.00
Kewpie, cloth w/mask face, Krueger, 7-8", M	175.00

Kewpie, compo head & half arms, 13"	350.00
Kewpie, shoulder head, cloth or stockinette body, 6-7"	600.00
Kewpie Doodle Dog, bsk, 1½"	725.00
Paperweight, Kewpie in center	350.00
Soap, Kewpie figural, 4"	95.00
Talcum container, tin or celluloid, 7-8", EX	185.00

Onion Pattern

The familiar pattern known to collectors as Onion acquired its name through a case of mistaken identity. Designed in the early 1700s by Johann Haroldt of the Meissen factory in Germany, the pattern was a mixture of earlier Oriental designs. One of its components was a stylized peach, which was mistaken for an onion; as a result, the pattern became known by that name. Usually found in blue, an occasional piece may also be found in pink and red. The pattern is commonly associated with Meissen, but it has been reproduced by many others including Villeroy and Boch and Royal Copenhagen.

Blue Danube is a modern line of Onion-patterned dinnerware produced in Japan and distributed by Lipper International of Wallingford, Connecticut. One hundred twenty five items are available in porcelain; it is sold in most large stores with china departments.

Bowl, berry; Xd swords, 5¼"	40.00
Bowl, rim soup; England, late	20.00
Bowl, sq, Meissen in oval, #19, 8½", pr	200.00
Butter dish, scalloped edge, 7½" dia	350.00
Cache pot, gold borders, Meissen, 1890s, 5½"	225.00
Cheeseboard, 9½x6¼", G-	25.00
Coffeepot, graniteware	50.00
Coffeepot, 1800s, 9½"	375.00

Compote, 8½x9½" diameter, $325.00.

Cup & saucer, demitasse; twisted hdl, Meissen, ca 1860	60.00
Dish, leaf shape w/hdls, Xd swords, 3½"	75.00
Dish, shell shape, Meissen, 1900, 7¾", pr	220.00
Egg beater, star shape, wooden hdl	175.00
Masher, lg	175.00
Meat tenderizer, lg	295.00
Pestle	145.00
Pie crimper, wooden hdl	150.00
Plate, dinner; England, late	18.00
Plate, dinner; 1900s, 10½"	70.00
Plate, lattice edge, Meissen, 11½"	165.00
Plate, Meissen, 6¼"	28.00
Plate, Meissen, 9½"	59.00
Plate, sq, Meakin, 7"	30.00
Platter, scalloped oval, 1880s, Xd swords, 23x18"	500.00
Reamer, red, old, unmk Germany	100.00

Rolling pin, heavy, old, EX quality, 18"	300.00
Sauce boat, Hutschenreuther	75.00
Shaving mug, w/matching brush	75.00
Sugar bowl, Xd swords	190.00
Tea set, doll sz, 10-pc	165.00
Tureen, leaf finial & hdls, Meissen, w/lid, 13½"	600.00
Tureen, shell hdls, dome lid, 1900, 10½" H	650.00
Whisk	100.00

Opalescent Glass

First made in England in 1870, opalescent glass became popular in America around the turn of the century. Its name comes from the milky-white opalescent trim that defines the lines of the pattern. It was produced in table sets, novelties, toothpick holders, vases, and lamps.

Acorn Burrs (& Bark), bowl, sauce; bl	55.00
Alaska, banana boat, vaseline	275.00
Alaska, butter dish, vaseline	400.00
Alaska, creamer, bl	90.00
Alaska, creamer, emerald	80.00
Alaska, creamer, vaseline	85.00
Alaska, cruet, emerald	250.00
Alaska, pitcher, water; bl	395.00
Alaska, pitcher, water; vaseline	370.00
Alaska, shakers, bl, pr	120.00
Alaska, shakers, vaseline, pr	110.00
Alaska, spooner, bl	90.00
Alaska, spooner, vaseline	85.00
Alaska, sugar bowl, bl, w/lid	160.00
Alaska, sugar bowl, vaseline, w/lid	165.00
Alaska, tray, bl	200.00
Alaska, tumbler, vaseline	75.00
Arabian Nights, pitcher, water; bl	400.00
Arabian Nights, pitcher, water; wht	250.00
Arabian Nights, tumbler, cranberry	120.00
Argonaut Shell, butter dish, bl	310.00
Argonaut Shell, compote, jelly; vaseline	85.00
Argonaut Shell, cruet, wht	200.00
Argonaut Shell, spooner, bl	110.00
Argonaut Shell, sugar bowl, bl, w/lid	250.00
Argonaut Shell, tumbler, vaseline, rare	100.00
Beaded Ovals in Sand, bowl, master; gr	70.00
Beaded Ovals in Sand, butter dish, bl	285.00
Beaded Ovals in Sand, creamer, gr	80.00
Beaded Ovals in Sand, sugar bowl, bl	225.00
Beaded Ovals in Sand, tumbler, bl	95.00
Beatty Honeycomb, celery vase, bl	85.00
Beatty Honeycomb, mug, bl	55.00
Beatty Honeycomb, spooner, wht	60.00
Beatty Honeycomb, sugar bowl, bl	120.00
Beatty Rib, celery vase, bl	80.00
Beatty Rib, creamer, wht, ind	40.00
Beatty Rib, pitcher, water; bl	185.00
Beatty Rib, sugar bowl, bl	85.00
Beatty Rib, tumbler, wht	35.00
Beatty Swirl, butter dish, bl	170.00
Beatty Swirl, mug, bl	60.00
Beatty Swirl, pitcher, water; vaseline	190.00
Beatty Swirl, tray, water; bl	90.00
Beatty Swirl, tumbler, vaseline	45.00
Bubble Lattice, cruet, vaseline	170.00
Bubble Lattice, spooner, bl	60.00

Bubble Lattice, sugar bowl, wht 70.00
Bubble Lattice, tumbler, cranberry 110.00
Buttons & Braids, bowl, wht 35.00
Buttons & Braids, pitcher, water; bl 175.00
Buttons & Braids, pitcher, water; gr 175.00
Buttons & Braids, tumbler, bl 40.00
Buttons & Braids, tumbler, cranberry 90.00
Christmas Snowflake, tumbler, bl 110.00
Christmas Snowflake, tumbler, cranberry 125.00
Chrysanthemum Base Swirl, bowl, sauce; wht 25.00
Chrysanthemum Base Swirl, butter dish, bl 325.00
Chrysanthemum Base Swirl, pitcher, water; bl 395.00
Chrysanthemum Base Swirl, straw holder, bl 500.00
Chrysanthemum Base Swirl, sugar shaker, bl 200.00
Chrysanthemum Base Swirl, tumbler, bl 90.00
Circle Scroll, compote, jelly; bl 145.00
Circle Scroll, spooner, gr 80.00
Circle Scroll, sugar bowl, gr 225.00
Circle Scroll, tumbler, bl 90.00
Coin Spot, bowl, cranberry, master 70.00
Coin Spot, celery vase, gr 110.00
Coin Spot, compote, bl 60.00
Coin Spot, pitcher, water; gr 195.00
Coin Spot, pitcher, water; rubena 200.00
Coin Spot, pitcher, water; wht 125.00
Coin Spot, sugar shaker, gr 95.00
Coin Spot, sugar shaker, wht 100.00
Coin Spot, tumble-up, cranberry 275.00
Coin Spot, tumbler, cranberry 90.00
Criss Cross, bowl, sauce; wht, Consolidated 45.00
Criss Cross, pitcher, water; cranberry, Consolidated 1,200.00
Daisy & Fern, bottle, scent; cranberry 150.00
Daisy & Fern, mustard pot, bl 95.00
Daisy & Fern, pitcher, water; bl 250.00
Daisy & Fern, pitcher, water; wht 150.00
Daisy & Fern, shakers, cranberry, 2¾", pr 180.00
Daisy & Fern, sugar bowl, bl 125.00
Daisy & Fern, vase, cranberry 120.00
Diamond Spearhead, celery vase, wht 150.00
Diamond Spearhead, compote, gr, tall, rare 395.00
Diamond Spearhead, compote, jelly; vaseline 110.00
Diamond Spearhead, creamer, bl 195.00
Diamond Spearhead, cup & saucer, vaseline 110.00
Diamond Spearhead, mug, bl 65.00
Diamond Spearhead, pitcher, water; bl 700.00
Diamond Spearhead, pitcher, water; vaseline 475.00
Diamond Spearhead, pitcher, water; wht 395.00
Diamond Spearhead, spooner, gr 75.00
Diamond Spearhead, sugar bowl, bl, rare 250.00
Dolly Madison, creamer, gr 80.00
Dolly Madison, spooner, bl 80.00
Dolly Madison, spooner, wht 60.00
Dolly Madison, sugar bowl, bl, w/lid 150.00
Dolly Madison, tumbler, gr 95.00
Double Greek Key, butter dish, wht 175.00
Double Greek Key, celery vase, bl 165.00
Double Greek Key, creamer, bl 110.00
Double Greek Key, shakers, wht, pr 185.00
Double Greek Key, spooner, bl 100.00
Double Greek Key, sugar bowl, bl, w/lid 175.00
Double Greek Key, tumbler, bl 80.00
Drapery, bowl, master berry; wht 75.00
Drapery, creamer, bl 55.00
Drapery, pitcher, water; bl 165.00

Everglades, bowl, sauce; bl, oval 40.00
Everglades, butter dish, bl 360.00
Everglades, butter dish, vaseline 375.00
Everglades, compote, jelly; gr 90.00
Everglades, compote, jelly; vaseline 95.00
Everglades, creamer, bl 85.00
Everglades, pitcher, water; vaseline 395.00
Everglades, shakers, vaseline, pr 280.00
Everglades, sugar bowl, bl 195.00
Everglades, tumbler, bl 85.00
Fan, bowl, sauce; wht 25.00
Fan, butter dish, gr 395.00
Fan, creamer, gr 110.00
Fan, gravy boat, wht 40.00
Fern, finger bowl, bl 65.00
Fern, mustard pot, bl 140.00
Fern, pitcher, bl 250.00
Fern, pitcher, water; cranberry, 8½" 700.00
Fern, shakers, wht, pr 100.00
Fern, toothpick holder, cranberry, rare 450.00
Fern, tumbler, cranberry 100.00
Flora, butter dish, wht 150.00
Flora, compote, jelly; vaseline 140.00
Flora, creamer, vaseline 90.00
Flora, cruet, bl 650.00
Flora, pitcher, water; bl 495.00
Flora, shakers, wht, pr 200.00
Flora, spooner, vaseline 100.00
Flora, sugar bowl, bl, w/lid 135.00
Flora, toothpick holder, vaseline 450.00
Flora, toothpick holder, wht 250.00
Flora, tumbler, bl 85.00
Fluted Scrolls, butter dish, bl 150.00
Fluted Scrolls, cruet, bl 185.00
Fluted Scrolls, pitcher, water; bl 240.00
Fluted Scrolls, pitcher, water; vaseline 200.00
Fluted Scrolls, puff box, vaseline 60.00
Frosted-Leaf & Basketweave, butter dish, vaseline 250.00
Frosted-Leaf & Basketweave, creamer, vaseline or canary 135.00
Frosted-Leaf & Basketweave, spooner, bl 140.00
Frosted-Leaf & Basketweave, sugar bowl, bl 175.00
Gonterman Swirl, butter dish, amber 340.00
Gonterman Swirl, celery vase, bl 210.00
Gonterman Swirl, creamer, bl 175.00
Gonterman Swirl, cruet, bl 400.00
Hobnail, butter dish, bl 275.00
Hobnail, butter dish, wht 190.00
Hobnail, celery, vaseline, 6½" 100.00
Hobnail, creamer, vaseline 95.00
Hobnail, finger bowl, bl 65.00
Hobnail, syrup, rubena 350.00
Hobnail, tray, water; bl 175.00
Hobnail, tumbler, wht 70.00
Honeycomb & Clover, bowl, master berry; bl 85.00
Honeycomb & Clover, bowl, novelty, wht 35.00
Honeycomb & Clover, butter dish, bl 365.00
Honeycomb & Clover, tumbler, gr 75.00
Idyll, butter dish, gr 375.00
Idyll, creamer, gr 130.00
Idyll, spooner, bl 140.00
Idyll, sugar bowl, gr 200.00
Idyll, toothpick holder, bl 295.00
Idyll, tumbler, bl 90.00
Intaglio, bowl, novelty, bl 50.00

Intaglio, butter dish, bl 485.00
Intaglio, compote, jelly; wht 45.00
Intaglio, creamer, bl 60.00
Intaglio, cruet, vaseline 300.00
Intaglio, spooner, wht 35.00
Intaglio, sugar bowl, wht 60.00
Intaglio, tumbler, wht 40.00
Inverted Fan & Feather, compote, jelly; bl, rare 250.00
Inverted Fan & Feather, creamer, bl 225.00
Inverted Fan & Feather, creamer, wht 165.00
Inverted Fan & Feather, pitcher, water; wht 300.00
Inverted Fan & Feather, rose bowl, gr 90.00
Inverted Fan & Feather, tumbler, bl 90.00
Iris w/Meander, bowl, master berry; gr 85.00
Iris w/Meander, butter dish, bl 300.00
Iris w/Meander, compote, jelly; bl or vaseline 50.00
Iris w/Meander, creamer, bl 95.00
Iris w/Meander, pickle dish, wht 40.00
Iris w/Meander, pitcher, water; bl 390.00
Iris w/Meander, spooner, bl 95.00
Iris w/Meander, sugar bowl, gr, w/lid 145.00
Iris w/Meander, toothpick holder, wht 60.00
Iris w/Meander, tumbler, wht 45.00
Iris w/Meander, vase, vaseline 60.00
Jackson, candy dish, vaseline 50.00
Jackson, creamer, bl 60.00
Jackson, pitcher, water; bl 350.00
Jackson, spooner, vaseline 55.00
Jackson, sugar bowl, bl 120.00
Jackson, sugar bowl, vaseline 115.00
Jackson, tumbler, wht 35.00
Jewel & Flower, bowl, novelty, bl 50.00
Jewel & Flower, butter dish, bl 300.00
Jewel & Flower, creamer, wht 50.00
Jewel & Flower, cruet, vaseline 450.00
Jewel & Flower, pitcher, water; bl 500.00
Jewel & Flower, pitcher, water; vaseline 400.00
Jewel & Flower, spooner, bl 65.00
Jewel & Flower, tumbler, vaseline 80.00
Jeweled Heart, butter dish, bl 325.00
Jeweled Heart, compote, gr 150.00
Jeweled Heart, plate, bl, sm 45.00
Jeweled Heart, sugar bowl, gr, w/lid 180.00
Jeweled Heart, tumbler, gr 65.00
Lords & Ladies, butter dish, bl 90.00
Lords & Ladies, creamer, bl 65.00
Lustre Flute, bowl, sauce; bl 50.00
Lustre Flute, butter dish, bl 395.00
Lustre Flute, pitcher, bl 375.00
Lustre Flute, spooner, bl 95.00
Lustre Flute, tumbler, wht 60.00
Palm Beach, pitcher, water; vaseline 400.00
Palm Beach, spooner, vaseline 145.00
Palm Beach, sugar bowl, bl 200.00
Palm Beach, tumbler, bl 90.00
Palm Beach, wine, vaseline, rare 400.00
Paneled Holly, bowl, master berry; bl 195.00
Paneled Holly, butter dish, bl 400.00
Paneled Holly, shakers, bl, pr 260.00
Paneled Holly, spooner, wht 90.00
Paneled Holly, sugar bowl, bl, very rare 275.00
Paneled Holly, tumbler, wht 60.00
Poinsettia, bowl, fruit; bl 70.00
Poinsettia, pitcher, water; bl, either shape 450.00

Poinsettia, sugar shaker, gr 300.00
Poinsettia, syrup, cranberry, minimum value 450.00
Poinsettia, tumbler, bl 75.00
Princess Diana, butter dish, bl 100.00
Princess Diana, compote, bl, metal base 145.00
Princess Diana, pitcher, water; vaseline 115.00
Regal, butter dish, bl 195.00
Regal, celery vase, bl 150.00
Regal, celery vase, gr 175.00
Regal, pitcher, gr 225.00
Reverse Swirl, bottle, water; bl 145.00
Reverse Swirl, butter dish, vaseline 165.00
Reverse Swirl, cruet, cranberry 450.00
Reverse Swirl, custard cup, bl 50.00
Reverse Swirl, lamp, cranberry, mini 300.00
Reverse Swirl, pitcher, water; bl 250.00
Reverse Swirl, shakers, vaseline, pr 125.00
Reverse Swirl, sugar shaker, vaseline 140.00
Reverse Swirl, syrup, bl 180.00
Reverse Swirl, tumbler, bl 60.00
Reverse Swirl, tumbler, wht 30.00
Ribbed Spiral, creamer, vaseline 65.00
Ribbed Spiral, shakers, bl, pr 170.00
Ribbed Spiral, toothpick holder, bl 175.00
Ribbed Spiral, vase, vaseline, lg 80.00
Ruffles & Rings, bowl, nut; gr 35.00
Ruffles & Rings, rose bowl, bl 45.00
Scroll w/Acanthus, bowl, master berry; bl 55.00
Scroll w/Acanthus, butter dish, bl 370.00
Scroll w/Acanthus, compote, jelly; gr 60.00
Scroll w/Acanthus, shakers, gr, pr 195.00
Scroll w/Acanthus, sugar bowl, gr 150.00
Scroll w/Acanthus, toothpick holder, bl 285.00
Scroll w/Acanthus, tumbler, gr 75.00
Seaweed, butter dish, cranberry 395.00
Seaweed, pitcher, water; bl 350.00
Seaweed, sugar bowl, wht 135.00
Seaweed, syrup, wht 135.00
Shell, Beaded; sugar bowl, bl 225.00
Shell, Beaded; toothpick holder, gr 675.00
Shell, Beaded; tumbler, gr 115.00
Spanish Lace, bottle, barber; cranberry 250.00
Spanish Lace, bottle, scent; bl 190.00
Spanish Lace, bowl, vaseline, 6" 80.00
Spanish Lace, bride's basket, cranberry, 2 sizes 200.00
Spanish Lace, creamer, bl 140.00
Spanish Lace, cruet, bl 275.00
Spanish Lace, pitcher, water; bl, minimum value 250.00
Spanish Lace, pitcher, water; cranberry, minimum value 650.00
Spanish Lace, rose bowl, vaseline 70.00
Spanish Lace, shakers, pr 115.00
Spanish Lace, sugar shaker, cranberry 200.00
Spanish Lace, tumbler, vaseline 60.00
Stars & Stripes, pitcher, water; cranberry (+) 1,100.00
Stars & Stripes, tumbler, wht 70.00
Stripe, pitcher, bl 275.00
Stripe, shakers, bl, pr 100.00
Stripe, tumbler, bl 55.00
Sunburst on Shield, bowl, master berry; bl 140.00
Sunburst on Shield, cruet, bl, rare 450.00
Sunburst on Shield, pitcher, water; bl 600.00
Sunburst on Shield, spooner, bl 140.00
Sunburst on Shield, sugar bowl, vaseline 250.00
Sunburst on Shield, tumbler, bl 125.00

Swag with Brackets, pitcher, white opalescent, $145.00; Matching tumbler, $45.00.

Swag w/Brackets, bowl, master; vaseline **65.00**
Swag w/Brackets, bowl, sauce; gr **35.00**
Swag w/Brackets, butter dish, bl **195.00**
Swag w/Brackets, compote, jelly; bl **60.00**
Swag w/Brackets, creamer, bl **95.00**
Swag w/Brackets, creamer, vaseline **80.00**
Swag w/Brackets, shakers, vaseline, pr **200.00**
Swag w/Brackets, spooner, bl **95.00**
Swag w/Brackets, toothpick holder, gr **300.00**
Swag w/Brackets, tumbler, gr **75.00**
Swirl, pitcher, water; bl, minimum value **125.00**
Swirl, pitcher, water; cranberry, minimum value **250.00**
Swirl, sugar bowl, bl, w/lid **90.00**
Swirl, toothpick holder, gr **120.00**
Tokyo, compote, jelly; bl **55.00**
Tokyo, plate, wht **35.00**
Tokyo, sugar bowl, bl **140.00**
Tokyo, vase, gr **50.00**
Water Lily & Cattails, bowl, master berry; bl **70.00**
Water Lily & Cattails, relish, gr, hdls **90.00**
Water Lily & Cattails, spooner, amethyst **115.00**
Water Lily & Cattails, sugar bowl, gr **175.00**
Water Lily & Cattails, tumbler, bl **70.00**
Wild Bouquet, bowl, sauce; bl **60.00**
Wild Bouquet, butter dish, bl **495.00**
Wild Bouquet, compote, jelly; bl **160.00**
Wild Bouquet, compote, jelly; gr **130.00**
Wild Bouquet, creamer, gr **150.00**
Wild Bouquet, shakers, bl, pr **180.00**
Wild Bouquet, toothpick holder, gr **375.00**
Wild Bouquet, tumbler, bl, rare **125.00**
Wild Bouquet, tumbler, wht **40.00**
Windows (Swirled), celery vase, bl **90.00**
Windows (Swirled), mustard, cranberry **150.00**
Windows (Swirled), pitcher, water; cranberry, minimum value .**650.00**
Windows (Swirled), plate, cranberry, either sz **250.00**
Windows (Swirled), toothpick holder, bl **300.00**
Wreath & Shell, bowl, master berry; bl **95.00**
Wreath & Shell, bowl, novelty; vaseline **65.00**
Wreath & Shell, bowl, sauce; bl **37.00**
Wreath & Shell, butter dish, bl **250.00**
Wreath & Shell, celery vase, bl **180.00**
Wreath & Shell, pitcher, water; wht **150.00**
Wreath & Shell, rose bowl, bl **95.00**

Opaline

A type of semiopaque opal glass, opaline was made in white as well as pastel shades and is often enameled. It is similar in appearance to English bristol glass, though its enamel or gilt decorative devices tend to exhibit a French influence.

Box, wht w/high relief ebony cameo in gold fr, 3¾x4½" **160.00**
Vase, gr w/alabaster figural hdls, gilt trim, 14x6" **135.00**
Vase, wht w/gold band & HP floral spray, mini, 2¾x1" **60.00**
Vase, wht w/HP berries & leaves, bl ribbon & gold trim, 2½" **65.00**
Vase, wht w/lg floral branch, cylindrical, sgn FT, 18" **185.00**
Vase, wht w/portrait of boy (& girl), sgn Ahne, ftd, 12x5", pr **265.00**

Orientalia

The art of the Orient is an area of collecting currently enjoying strong collector interest, not only in those examples that are truly 'antique' but in the 20th-century items as well. Because of the many aspects involved in a study of Orientalia, we can only try through brief comments to acquaint the reader with some of the more readily available examples. We suggest you refer to specialized reference sources for more detailed information. See also specific categories.

Key:
Ch — Chinese   FV — Famille Verte
ctp — contemporary   gb — guard border
cvg — carving   hdwd — hardwood
drw — drawer   Jp — Japan
Dy — Dynasty   Ko — Korean
E — export   lcq — lacquer
FJ — Famille Juane   mdl — medallion
FN — Famille Noire   rswd — rosewood
FR — Famille Rose   tkwd — teakwood

Blanc de Chine

Figure, Guanyin, seated by table, holds scroll, rstr, 9" **1,450.00**

Figure, seated Guanyin (goddess of mercy), rockwork base, late 17th/early 18th century, minor restorations, 10", $850.00.

Figure, Guanyin on cushion, hollow molded, 19th C, 8¼" **1,840.00**
Teapot, molded as laughing Buddha, Quianlong period, 6" **435.00**
Vase, gu form, 8 Daoist immortals/florals, 18th C, 12" **1,750.00**

Blue and White Porcelain

Bowl, dragon & cloud, curving wall, Daoguang, 5¾" **1,850.00**
Bowl, florals/bands/shou medallion, late Choson Dy, 5¼" **1,150.00**
Deep dish, Buddha's hand w/citron branches, Kangxi, 8", 8 for ..**2,200.00**
Jar, ginger; flowering prunus, no lid, 18th C, 10½" **865.00**
Jar, pingmei design, dbl ring, no lid, Ch, 18th C, 8" **800.00**
Plaque, immortals & sages in garden, ca 1900, 71" H, pr **4,600.00**

Vase, cracked ice & prunus, trumpet form, Meiji/Taisho, 62", pr .**3,450.00**
Vase, dragon among clouds, ring neck, late Choson Dy, 16½" ..**3,750.00**
Vase, scrolls/cicada/dragons on pear form, ca 1900, 18", pr **3,700.00**
Water dropper, floral sprays/abstract lines, Choson Dy, 2½" **800.00**

Bronze

Bell, dinner; in cvd tkwd stand, 17½x10" **100.00**
Bird group, cockerel & hen, sgn Moriama, Meiji, 19⅜" **3,450.00**
Censer, dragon chasing pearl, sgn Yosiaki, Meiji, 20" **1,495.00**
Censer, lion's head w/open jaw, gold eyes, Meiji, 10¾" **488.00**
Study of Benten w/koto, sgn Toryusai, Meiji, 8¼" **2,500.00**
Study of hawk, wings out, wood base, Ganki, Meiji, 26¼" **8,050.00**
Study of huntsman w/birds in net, 3-pc casting, Meiji, 40" **1,955.00**
Study of lobster, naturalistic, EX patina, Meiji, 20" **4,300.00**
Study of warrior, jimbaori & armor, sgn Gyoko, Meiji, 13" **1,725.00**
Tsuba, circular dai cast w/scattered aoi, Tokugawa, 3" **1,380.00**
Vase, duck scene & blossoms w/gilt, trumpet neck, Meiji, 19" ...**800.00**
Vase, Phoenix/paulownia silver inlay w/gilt, Taisho, 7¼" **1,380.00**
Vase, wine vessel shape w/writhing dragon, Meiji, 23¼" **3,165.00**

Celadon

Celadon, introduced during the Ching Dynasty, is a green-glazed ware developed in an attempt to imitate the color of jade. Designs are often incised or painted on over glaze in heavy enamel applications.

Bowl, gray-gr, cvd lotus-petal band, ftd, Koryo Dy, 6¾" **545.00**
Brush pot, crackle glaze, ca 1900, 5" **375.00**
Censer, scrolling leaves, 3-leg, rtcl lid, Yuan Dy, 4¼" **690.00**
Cup, floral scrolls/leaves on wht slip, Koryo Dy, 3¾" **1,035.00**
Ewer, 8-lobed melon shape, strapwork hdl, Koryo Dy, 7¼" **2,070.00**
Jar, gray-gr crackle w/pnt carp/weeds, Choson Dy, 8" **1,150.00**
Jar, mortuary; yel-gr, scrolls/leaves, 5-lobe, Song Dy, 12" **1,100.00**
Jar, storage; crackled cinnamon-brn, ovoid, Choson Dy, 15" ..**1,035.00**

Censer, simple tripod form, finely reticulated domical gold lid chased with a nanakusa pattern and stamped junkin (pure gold), lozenge mark, signed Yozan, 20th century, 4⅛", $5,500.00.

Vase, birds/butterflies/etc, salamander hdls, rstr, 12", pr **600.00**
Vase, butterflies/birds, mc, hexagonal, Ch, 12", pr, NM **600.00**
Vase, cvd leaves on ftd pear form w/garlic head, Yuan, 9½" **2,300.00**
Water dropper, recumbent lion-dog form, copper red, Ko, 4⅛" ..**700.00**

Furniture

Armchair, cinnabar lcq, scrolled arms, ca 1800, 34", pr **4,600.00**
Cabinet, red lcq w/MOP inlay, Choson Dy, 59x31x17", pr **1,850.00**
Cabinet, water scenes w/MOP inlay, Choson Dy, 38x32x16", pr .**3,450.00**
Cabinet, 2-door, 2-drw, Huali, 18th C, 73½x41x19½" **2,300.00**
Chair, throne; red lcq, fu dogs & lions, Ch, ca 1800, 45" **5,175.00**
Chest, burlwood, 2-door, 3 rows of drws, Meiji, 12x22x12" **800.00**
Desk, scholar's; fitted top, drws, Choson Dy, 12x32x14" **490.00**

Screen, gilt/lcq flowers, 3-panel, ea: 62x17", Meiji **4,885.00**
Screen, table; porc inlaid rswd, triptych, 19th C, 27" H **1,380.00**
Shodana, cvd, sliding doors/staggered shelves, Meiji, 64" **1,150.00**
Stand, cvd rswd, sq top, 4-leg, Ch, 19x16x16½" **250.00**
Stand, cvd tkwd, rnd soapstone-insert top, 4-leg, Ch, 19", EX ...**250.00**
Stand, cvd tkwd, soapstone top, faux marble shelf, Ch, 28" **400.00**
Stand, cvd tkwd, 8-sided soapstone-insert top, 4-leg, Ch, 32" **525.00**
Stand, cvd wood w/blk pnt, soapstone-insert top, Ch, 37" **165.00**
Stool, Ch Huanghuali, cane seat, Ming Dy, 20x23x18" **460.00**
Stool, elmwood, 3-cushion-molded edge, 18th C, 19x22x22" ..**3,165.00**
Table, blk lcq w/floral, 3 cloisonne medallions, 18x45x20" **450.00**
Table, E, wood, cvd dragons & clouds, late 19th C, 47" dia ...**1,725.00**
Table, figured wood, plain aprons, Huanghuali, 32x49x16" **3,450.00**
Table, Kang; cinnabar lcq, cvd scholars, 19th C, 13x36x22" ..**2,875.00**
Tansu, keyakiwood, 2 drws over sliding doors, Meiji, 34x32x13" ..**1,840.00**
Tansu, lcq floral/diaper lozenges, 3-drw, Meiji, 35" **5,750.00**

Hardstones

Agate, butterscotch, belt hook, 2-section, 19th C, 3½" **630.00**
Agate & jadeite, belt buckle, gilt-metal mts, 19th C, 4" **375.00**
Jade, Quan Yin holding lotus, crane beside, 8½" **160.00**
Jade, spinach, vase w/mask decor, w/lid, 18th C, 5⅞" **1,495.00**
Jade, wht, belt hook, monkey, horse-head terminal, 19th C, 4" ...**635.00**
Jade, wht, belt slide, floriform, 19th C, mini, 2⅜" **515.00**
Jadeite, bl-gr w/wht inclusions/russet veins, bowl, 3¾" **800.00**
Jadeite, russet, belt hook, 2 conjoined bats, 1900s, 3⅝" **1,000.00**
Nephrite, celedon w/wht inclusions, dbl cup w/lid, 4⅝" **1,725.00**
Nephrite, gray-gr w/gr veins, boy w/branch, 18th C, 4" **1,725.00**
Nephrite, Ruyi scepter, lion & carp panels, animal mask, 11" .**1,850.00**
Nephrite, wht, recumbent water buffalo, 19th C, 3" **800.00**
Nephrite, wht, talisman, San Yang, 18th C, 2¾" **1,495.00**
Nephrite, wht, toggle, rtcl squirrel/grapes, 18th/19th C, 2¼" **750.00**
Nephrite, wht, toggle, 2 puppies w/branch, 18th/19th C, 1½" **430.00**
Rock crystal, water pot, phoenix-bird cvg, 19th C, 7¾" L **2,875.00**

Inro

Lcq, blk/gilt, pines/river, 5-case, 19th C, 4" **1,840.00**
Lcq, brn/gilt, 2 rats in cage, 5-case, 19th C, 3¼" **1,840.00**
Lcq, gilt, bird/cherry tree/garden, 5-case, 19th C, 4" **5,465.00**
Lcq, gold, temple veranda, 5-case, 4" **6,325.00**
Lcq, gold, w/5 pewter inlay dragonflies, 2-case, 19th C, 3" **4,025.00**
Lcq, gold & silver, Bukan/pine/tiger, sgn, 19th C, 3¾" **4,885.00**
Lcq, red, cockerels, flattened ovoid, 4-case, 19th C, 2⅞" **1,495.00**
Lcq wood w/gilt, chyrsanthemums, 2-case, 19th C, 3" **975.00**
Silver & coral, chrysanthemum & asagao, sgn, 19th C, 2½" ...**1,265.00**
Wood, Chinese scholars on pavilion terrace, 4-case, 19th C, 3" ..**635.00**

Lacquer

Lacquerware is found in several colors, but the one most likely to be encountered is cinnabar. It is often intricately carved, sometimes involving hundreds of layers built one at a time on a metal or wooden base. Later pieces remain red, while older examples tend to darken.

Box, blk w/MOP inlay, landscape/prunus/etc, 17th C, 16" L ...**2,100.00**
Box, flowering gilt branches, shell inlay, Meiji, 2⅝x5x4" **2,300.00**
Box, picnic; kite among pines, gilt/blk, Meiji, 7x4⅝x4" **1,600.00**
Box, rooster on drum w/shell & hardstone inlay, Meiji, 14" **4,600.00**
Box, scroll; kikko w/jashiji int, rstr, 19th C, 15¾" L **2,070.00**
Box, silver-mtd edges, cherry blossom gilt, Meiji, 4" L **3,450.00**
Bundai, pines/river in gilt & silver, Meiji, 8⅝x13x10¾" **4,600.00**
Case, watch; water scene w/tortoise-shell inlay, Meiji, 6" **2,000.00**

Kobako, chrysanthemums on ftd drum form, 19th C, 4½" dia ..**2,070.00**
Kobako, cranes/pines/Juji in gilt, 19th C, 3¾", NM **2,585.00**
Kobako, gold & silver valley scene, Meiji, 2x4½x3¼" **1,600.00**
Kobako, incense; mythical beasts/mc momiji, Meiji, 5½" L ..**18,500.00**
Kobako, open fans & landscape in gold, Meiji, 5¼" L **3,450.00**
Koro, woven cane in gilt & silver, 6-lobed, 19th C, 2⅞" **2,875.00**
Picnic set, mini tea-house form w/gilt & lcq, Meiji, 15" **2,300.00**
Sake cups, brocade & diaper bands w/inlay, 4", 4¾", 5⅛" **2,875.00**
Tea safe, E, w/pewter canisters, Ch, 1800s, 11x8" **300.00**

Netsukes

A netsuke is a miniature Japanese carving made with two holes called the himitoshi, either channeled or within the carved design. As kimonos (the outer garment of the time) had no pockets, the Japanese man hung his pipe, tobacco pouch, or other daily necessities from his waist sash. The most highly valued accessory was a nest of little drawers called an inro, in which they carried snuff or sometimes opium. The netsuke was the toggle that secured them. Although most are of ivory, others were made of bone, wood, metal, porcelain, or semiprecious stones. Some were inlaid or lacquered. They are found in many forms — figurals the most common, mythological beasts the most desirable. They range in size from 1" up to 3", which was the maximum size allowed by law. Many netsukes represented the owner's profession, religion, or hobbies. Scenes from the daily life of Japan at that time were often depicted in the tiny carvings. The more detailed the carving, the greater the value.

Careful study is required to recognize the quality of the netsuke. Many have been made in Hong Kong in recent years; and even though some are very well carved, these are considered copies and avoided by the serious collector. There are many books that will help you learn to recognize quality netsukes, and most reputable dealers are glad to assist you. Use your magnifying glass to check for repairs. In the listings that follow, netsukes are ivory unless noted otherwise; 'stain' indicates a color wash.

Artichoke shaker w/insect, screw-on stem cap, 1½" **150.00**
Ball, rtcl openwork rats w/inlaid eyes, stain, 1890s **425.00**
Child kneeling w/lg leaf having butterfly on bk, sgn, 1¼" **125.00**
Children (3) crouching w/drum, fan & fish, sgn, ¾x1¾" **275.00**
Dragon w/inlaid eyes coiled around pearl, Shuzan, 1890s **435.00**
Guardian lion, tightly coiled, sgn Masanao **375.00**
Jolly fat man w/disfigured mask, child by bag, 2nd on drum, 3" ..**465.00**
Lady w/child on bk & elder examine kettle, Kyokkosai **325.00**

Lion dancer with drum and bells beside child reaching for drumstick, sepia wash on details, signed Masatoshi, late 19th century, 1½", $500.00.

Monkey pries open shell, sgn Saimei **150.00**
Saramawashi entertainer w/monkey on shoulder **450.00**

Porcelain

Chinese export ware was designed to appeal to Western tastes and was often made to order. During the 18th century, vast amounts were shipped to Europe and on westward. Much of this fine porcelain consisted of dinnerware lines that were given specific pattern names. Rose Mandarin, Fitzhugh, Armorial, Rose Medallion, and Canton are but a few of the more familiar.

Bough pot, E, figural reserves, canted corners, 19th C, 8", pr ..**6,900.00**
Bough pot, E, Mandarin palette: flowers/etc, 19th C, 8¾" **1,375.00**
Bowl, blk/gold urn, gold berry finial, serpentine, 10" L **550.00**
Bowl, E, floral panels/prunus, florals w/in, 1800s, 5x18", EX **200.00**
Bowl, E, mc floral reserves, geometric border, rstr, 4½x10" **200.00**
Bowl, salad; Bl Fitzhugh, star crack, 9½" **500.00**
Bowl, vegetable; Bl Fitzhugh, mismatched lid, 9½" **230.00**
Bowl, vegetable; E, bl crest & border w/gold, w/lid, 12½" **635.00**
Bulb dish, FR, rectangular w/cut corners, Hongxian, 11" L **1,265.00**
Candle holders, lady w/lotus cup, gilt base, 19th C, 13", pr **2,300.00**
Charger, E, butterfly/floral, landscapes in rim, 1800, 14" **425.00**
Charger, FR, mtn landscape, Qianlong mk, 19th C, 21¼" **3,165.00**
Dish, bl & yel, dragon & pearl, Daoguang mk, 10" dia **5,460.00**
Ginger jar, FR, mille fleur theme, Daoguang mk, 19", pr **11,500.00**
Lantern, Ch, nobles in panels, rtcl, baluster, hex base, 12½" **260.00**
Mug, FR/E, people in reserve, bk: birds/flowers, 4½" **170.00**
Pitcher, E, Am eagle on pear form, mc w/gold, 18th C, 14" **3,750.00**
Plate, E, eagle & gilt monogram, rprs, 1800s, 7½" **485.00**
Plate, E, eagle decor, 1800s, rpr, 9⅛" **175.00**
Plate, E, eagle decor, 1800s, 8", NM **345.00**
Plate, E, floral center cavetto, bl/gold star border, 9" **100.00**
Plate, E, FR, central flora, scalloped floral rim, 1800s, 9" **80.00**
Platter, hot water; Bl Fitzhugh, 14¼" **500.00**
Platter, Rose Canton, Ch, 1800s, 14½" **680.00**
Punch bowl, E, Mandarin palette reserves, 18th C, 11⅜" dia **700.00**
Punch bowl, E, ships decor, rstr, 1800s, 10¼" dia **375.00**
Tea caddy, E, eagle decor, rim rpr, 1800s **200.00**
Teapot, E, mc florals w/gold, 5¼", EX **220.00**
Teapot, E, scrolls & flowers, red & blk w/gold, 1770s, 2¾", EX ..**150.00**
Tray, E, armorial, early 1800s, 11¼", NM **550.00**
Tureen, sauce; FR, floral sprays, w/lid & tray, 5¼x6½" **4,025.00**
Tureen, sauce; Rose Canton, landscapes/birds, 8½", +tray **925.00**
Tureen, soup; Rose Canton, Ch, 1800s, w/lid, 10½" **1,950.00**
Vase, battle scenes, Ko, 9½", pr **300.00**
Vase, E, mc garden flowers/birds, kylin hdls, 19th C, 23½" **500.00**
Vase, FN, writhing dragon, stick neck, 20th C, 17⅛" **1,380.00**
Vase, FR, diaper bands & gold, baluster, 19th C, 14" **2,185.00**
Vase, FR, scenic reserves, globular, long neck, 19th C, 9⅜" **460.00**

Pottery

Bowl, cizhou sgraffito flower decor Song Dy, 8⅛" **575.00**
Bowl, flower head w/in lotus lappets on gray, Choson Dy, 7⅝" ..**4,600.00**
Brush pot, wht, rtcl wanzi roundel/vajira bolts, late Choson, 5" ..**2,300.00**
Figurine, horse, amber & straw glazed, Tang Dy, 12¾" H **2,875.00**
Mortuary figure, court official, pnt details, Tang Dy, 13" **1,265.00**
Mortuary figure, official in peaked bonnet, pnt, Tang Dy, 28" ..**1,955.00**
Roof tile, 3 sections form dragon, mc details, Ming, 43", pr **2,300.00**
Teapot, terra cotta, squat melon form w/branch hdl, 1910 ....**60.00**
Vase, Guan-style crackleware, 8-sided, 18th C, 5¾" **920.00**

Rugs

The 'Oriental' or Eastern rug market has enjoyed a renewal of interest in recent years as collectors have become aware of the fact that some of the semiantique rugs (those sixty to one hundred years old) may be had at a price within the range of the average buyer.

Afgan, tree of life on ivory, 1950s, 78x42", EX **865.00**

Baluch, dmn lattice, rosettes/sm animals, 1910, 69x33", VG **285.00**
Baluch, hexagonal lattice on navy, 1900, 55x75", VG **230.00**
Baluch prayer, tree of life, S-motif border, 1890s, 53x45", EX **460.00**
Baluch prayer, tree of life on dk gold, 1910, 62x39", EX **375.00**
Beshir, 4 concentric dmn mdl, boteh border, 250x144", VG ...**3,450.00**
Ersari, 3 columns of 6 gulli-guls on rust, 1890s, 110x90", VG .**1,380.00**
Ersari Ensi, quartered garden plan, 1880s, 74x56", EX **375.00**
Ersari Ensi, 6 plant panels, dk bl on rust, 1880, 76x60", EX **500.00**
Ersari Torba, 2 mdls on rust, geometric borders, 46x17", EX **175.00**
Gendje, diagonal boteh stripes, 1880s, 96x45", VG **690.00**
Hamadan, overall Mina Khani floral lattice on red, 56x41", EX ..**400.00**
Heriz, gabled mdl+4 lg boteh on dk bl, 1925, 52x41", EX **1,495.00**
Heriz, lg bl/rose mdl on red, ivory/bl borders, 128x92", G **1,300.00**
Heriz, mdl on red, dk bl turtle border, 1920s, 130x120", EX **2,875.00**
Heriz, overall palmettes/rosettes/etc, 1910, 120x82", VG **2,500.00**
Karabagh, lg stepped mdl on navy w/flowers, 1910, 84x46", EX .**1,035.00**
Karabagh, lightning in 3 dmns on brn, dtd 1897, 72x50", VG ...**430.00**
Karabagh, staggered octagons on navy, 1880s, 74x34", VG **800.00**
Karabagh, staggered shield mdls on ivory, 1890s, 88x48", VG ..**1,265.00**
Karabagh, 2½ 4-lobe mdls on red, crab border, 70x52", VG **460.00**
Karachoph Kazak, lg 8-sided mdl+4sqs on red, 1875, 72x62", EX ..**1,495.00**
Karadja, palmettes/vines etc on navy, 1910, 130x74", EX **4,600.00**
Karadja, 3 mdls on red, dk bl border, 1925, 51x19", EX **300.00**
Karadja, 3 mdls/sm motifs on dk bl, 1910, 51x45", EX **630.00**
Karadja, 5 sq mdls etc on red, 1925, 134x38", EX **1,380.00**
Kazak, lg gabled sq mdl on red, 1875, 64x45", EX **1,610.00**
Kazak, 2 stepped dmn mdls on rust, 1875, 78x52", EX **800.00**
Kazak, 3 lg stepped polygons on red, 1880s, 120x72", EX **690.00**
Kazak, 4 lg stepped dmn mdls on bl, 1875, 90x52", VG **545.00**
Khamseh, lg hex mdl/birds on navy, 1925, 78x60", EX **690.00**
Kuba, rows of octagons on gold, 1875, 70x40", EX **575.00**
Kuba Kelim, staggered palmette mdls on red, rstr, 116x60" **490.00**
Kurd, allover arabesque leaves etc on navy, 1910, 135x44", EX ..**1,265.00**
Kurd, chevrons in narrow stripes, meander borders, 150x75" **865.00**
Kurd, dmn lattice, 4 narrow borders, 1900, 65x44", EX **285.00**
Kurd, 8 hexagons, mc on navy, red border, 1910, 78x52", EX **575.00**
Luri, staggered floral plants on dk bl, 1910, 59x50", VG **460.00**
NW Persian, 2 lg calyx mdls on rust, 1910, 78x32", EX **900.00**
NW Persian, 4 serrated dmn mdls on dk brn, 1910, 135x40", EX .**575.00**
NW Persian, 6 hexagonal mdls on red, 1910, 155x39", EX **1,725.00**
Perepedil, ram horn motifs/octagons on bl, 1910, 58x27", EX **800.00**
Qashqai, column w/4 dmn mdls on dk bl, 1890s, 116x31", G **460.00**
Qashqai, 3 red mdl/birds & flowers, 1900, 108x63", VG **575.00**
S Caucasian, hexagonal lattice, dmn border, 130x45", VG **1,150.00**
Serab, 3 stepped hexagonal mdls on rust, 1925, 88x36", G **1,150.00**

Shirvan, column of 5 Lesghi stars and mixed motifs, 4 colors on plum field, ivory octagon border, late 19th century, 72x51", EX, $1,150.00.

Shirvan, dmn lattice of flowering plants, 1880s, 60x48", EX ...**1,900.00**
Shirvan, lg/sm octagon mdls on dk bl, 1890s, 60x40", VG **630.00**
Shirvan, staggered ashik guls on navy, 1890s, 66x45", VG **575.00**
Shirvan, 5 lg hex mdls on dk bl, 1890s, 104x52", EX **2,400.00**
Shirvan prayer, boteh/geometric stripes, 1880s, 69x48", EX ...**2,300.00**
Shirvan prayer, dmn lattice of flower plants, 1880, 60x43", VG ...**460.00**
Shirvan prayer, hex lattice of hooked dmns, 1875, 74x34", EX .**1,495.00**
Tekke, 3 columns of sm chuval guls on rust, 1910, 48x40", EX ..**545.00**
Tekke, 5 columns of 12 guls on rust, 1825, 98x84", VG **575.00**
Tekke, 6 columns of 12 guls on rust, 1880s, 98x80", EX **2,000.00**
Yuruk prayer, rows of octagons/geometrics, 1910, 52x36", EX **345.00**

Snuff Bottles

The Chinese were introduced to snuff in the 17th century, and their carved and painted snuff bottles typify their exquisite taste and workmanship. These small bottles, seldom measuring over 2½", were made of amber, jade, ivory, and cinnabar; tiny spoons were often attached to their stoppers. By the 18th century, some were being made of porcelain, others were of glass with delicate interior designs tediously reverse painted with minuscule brushes sometimes containing a single hair. Copper and brass were used but to no great extent.

Agate, dk amber, monkey on horse cvg, ovoid, 1800-80 ....**400.00**
Amber, cinnamon w/veins, flattened ovoid w/butterfly, 1800s ...**400.00**
Amber, honey-brn, standing beauty reliefs, 1800-80 ....**1,600.00**
Amber, red-brn, boys in garden cvg, pear shape, 1800-80s **925.00**
Amethyst, peach form w/cvd leaves, stem stopper, 1800-80 ....**865.00**
Cranberry glass, 8-sided, faceted, jadeite stopper, 19th C **430.00**
Fossil limestone, mini shell forms w/carnelian patches, 1800s **460.00**
Glass, yel, cvd peonies on rocks, amethyst top, 19th C **1,265.00**
Gr jade, dragon cvd in relief, 2¾" **850.00**
Hornbill, cicada form, conforming stopper, EX **460.00**
Jade, wht w/gr veins, beauty w/kites relief, 1800-80, sm **550.00**
Jadeite, apple/gr/pale russet matrix, fish form, 19th C **750.00**
Jadeite, celadon w/dk gr veins, reserve cvg, 19th C **750.00**
Nephrite, pale celadon, pebble form, cvd bat, 19th C **285.00**
Nephrite, wht, flat circle w/cvd prunus, agate top, 1800-80 ....**3,150.00**
Porc, aquatic beasts/dgagons, coral glass top, late 19th C **635.00**
Porc, corncob form w/praying mantis on leaf, late 19th C **700.00**
Porc, FR, flattened baluster, late 19th C, pr **865.00**
Porc, FV, dragon & pearl, conical base, jade stopper, 1800s **3,450.00**
Rvpt figural scenes, sgn Ye Zhongsan, coral top, ca 1928 ....**1,265.00**

Textiles

Bedspread, pheasants/birds/flowers embr on silk, 92x75" **900.00**
Cape, priest's, cranes/clouds embr on peach silk, 1900, 57" **825.00**
Embroidered panel, water scene, Jp, 19x22" **188.00**
Jacket, silk brocade, embr flowers & bats **100.00**
Robe, dragon & jewels embr on purple brocade, 1800s, 56" **465.00**
Robe, gold dragons on bl silk, horse-hoof cuffs, 1800s **1,450.00**
Robe, priest's, Buddha on throne embr on satin, 1700s, 95", EX ..**700.00**
Robe, 9 dragons on bl silk, horse-hoof cuffs, Kesi, 19th C **3,150.00**

Woodblock Prints, Japanese

Framed prints are of less value because one can not inspect their condition or tell if they have borders or are trimmed.

Bamboo Garden, sgn Okiie Hashimoto, 1959, 64x53" **575.00**
Bar, lady w/bottles, sgn Kiyoshi Saito, 20th C, 58¾x43¾" **1,725.00**
Beauty w/handkerchief, sgn oju Kunisada, ca 1857, kakemono-e .**350.00**

Boy & cat, sgn Jun Sekino, 20th C, 67½x35¾" 750.00
Ikarugano-sato Horyu-ji Nara, Kiyoshi Saito, 20th C, 45½x61" .920.00
Karashishi & pup on rocks, sgn oju Hiroshige hitsu, kakemono-e ..550.00
Kubi kazari (necklace), sgn Joichi Hoshi, 20th C, 47x37" 1,265.00
Lattice Door, sgn Jun Sekino, 20th C, 75¾x57¼" 920.00
Maidens attending court lady, sgn Utamaro hitsu, oban tate-e ..1,095.00
Moss Garden, sgn Okiie Hashimoto, 1960, 77x54" 865.00
Ohashi-Evening Squall, sgn Hiroshige ga, oban tate-e, G 3,750.00
Sand Garden, stone path, sgn Okiie Hashimoto, 1959, 64x54" ..865.00
Wakashu dressed as komuso, sgn Utamoro hitsu, kakemono-e ...690.00

Miscellaneous

Box, boxwood butterfly shape w/MOP/horn/aogai inlay, Meiji, 6" .1,150.00
Boxwood study, tiger, blk stain, inlaid eyes, himotoshi, 2⅛" .16,000.00
Jug, Sumida, appl man & lg plant, enamel drip at rim, 5¼" 225.00
Kannon, gilt & lcq wood, holds kalasa, Tokugawa, 19" 1,265.00
Kikujido on chrysanthums, drilled w/himotoshi, 1800s, 2" 1,150.00
Traveling shrine, gilt & mc lcq, metal hardware, Edo, 7¼" 1,265.00
Tsuba, gilt copper, w/shells & sea plants, Tokugawa, 3" 975.00
Vase, mixed metal o/l copper, peonies/rocks, Meiji, 8" 800.00
Wood study, monkey/gingko hut, w/himotoshi, 19th C, 1½" 690.00
Wood study, 2 pups, inlaid eyes, legs form himotoshi, 19th C, 2" .2,070.00

Orrefors

Orrefors Glassworks was founded in 1898 in the Swedish province of Smaaland. Utilizing the expertise of designers such as Simon Gate, Edward Hald, Vicke Lindstrand, and Edwin Ohrstrom, it produced art glass of the highest quality. Various techniques were used in achieving the decoration. Some were wheel engraved; others were blown through a unique process that formed controlled bubbles or air pockets resulting in unusual patterns and shapes. Our advisor for this category is Abby Malowanczyk; she is listed in the Directory under Texas.

Decanter, sax player/cactus eng, clear/gr, Gate, 7" 200.00
Fish bowl, Graal, int fish/plants, Hald, 6x8¾", NM 865.00
Vase, Ariel, girl's head on cobalt layer, Ohrstrom, 7x5" 2,875.00
Vase, Ariel, smoky gray w/int wisps, Ohrstrom, 1955, 10" 1,400.00
Vase, burlap-woven tan/gr lines on clear, Hald, U-form, 9½" 800.00
Vase, eng child blows bubbles, Lindstrand #1382, 1935, 7x7" 210.00
Vase, eng man w/balloons & 2 children, Hald/Rossler, 1934, 4" ...400.00
Vase, eng nude dancer, 6-panel, topaz base, Lindstrand, 10" 345.00
Vase, eng nude dancer/flowers, Lindstrand, sqd U-form, 7¾" 400.00
Vase, eng nude girl on surfboard on waves, Lindstrand 750.00
Vase, eng nude in window, Lindstrand, #1361, orig 1935, 7" 500.00
Vase, Graal, int fish/seaweed, heavy, Hald, 7x6" 975.00
Vase, Kraka, int bl netting/bubbles, Palmquist, flattened, 9" 490.00
Vase, Kraka, int bl swags & bubbles, Palmquist, 1952, 13" 1,000.00
Vase, Xs, tan/gray-on-clear top, can base, Landberg, 6½" 750.00

Ott and Brewer

The partnership of Ott and Brewer began in 1865 in Trenton, New Jersey. By 1876 they were making decorated graniteware, parian, and 'ivory porcelain' — similar to Irish belleek though not as fine and of different composition. In 1883, however, experiments toward that end had reached a successful conclusion, and a true belleek body was introduced. It came to be regarded as the finest china ever produced by an American firm. The ware was decorated by various means such as hand painting, transfer printing, gilding, and lustre glazing. The company closed in 1893, one of many that failed during that depression. In

the listings below, the ware is belleek unless noted otherwise. Our advisor for this category is Mary Frank Gaston; she is listed in the Directory under Texas.

Basket, crisscross indents, gold leaves, twig hdl, mk, 4" 550.00
Bowl, Cactus, gold thistles inside & out, mk, 3¼x10½" 1,000.00
Bowl, dessert; bl int, shell ft, rare, 2x4" 250.00
Bowl, pk lustre int, gold rim, 3½" 130.00
Cake plate, Tridacna, gold decor, rare, 9½" 300.00
Cup & saucer, gold-paste flowers, thin 225.00
Cup & saucer, soup; gold-paste flowers & butterfly, thin 225.00
Cup & saucer, Tridacna, gold florals/etc, 2 hdls, 6" dia 250.00
Cup & saucer, Tridacna, lav lustre int, gold rim 125.00
Ewer, gold stylized leaves, cactus hdl, 8½" 1,200.00
Pitcher, irises etc, bamboo spout/neck, cactus hdl, 8" 1,400.00
Plate, pk & gold-paste flowers, ruffled, 9" 250.00
Ram's horn, wht lustre, red mk 2,000.00
Shell dish, purple lustre int, ftd, 2½x5¼" 275.00
Teapot, Tridacna, yel w/gold, wht loop hdl, mk, 4" 400.00
Tray, gold-paste orchid, sq, ruffled rim, 8¼" 450.00

Vase, gold-paste floral and leaf designs on white with gold trim, marked, 6½", $800.00.

Vase, leaves & butterfly, gold paste on matt, hdls, 5½" 600.00

Overbeck

The Overbeck Studio was established in 1911 in Cambridge City, Indiana, by four Overbeck sisters. It survived until the last sister died in 1955. Early wares were often decorated with carved designs of stylized animals, birds, or florals with the designs colored to contrast with the background. Others had tooled designs filled in with various colors for a mosaic effect. After 1937, Mary Frances, the last remaining sister, favored handmade figurines with somewhat bizarre features in fanciful combinations of color. Overbeck ware is signed 'OBK,' frequently with the designer's and potter's initials under the stylized 'OBK.'

Brooch, blond in full skirt, 4-color, 2" dia 250.00
Figurine, cat w/arched bk, 2x3½", NM 325.00
Figurine, man, standing, 5" 295.00
Figurine, Southern belle, elaborate detail, 4½" 300.00
Jardiniere, repetitive flowers, gr-brn on tan, 5x7", NM 4,400.00
Tumbler, grasshopper band, gr on yel, sgn EF, 4x3", 4 for 1,400.00
Vase, cvd bird medallions on gray gloss, 6½" 2,400.00
Vase, 4 panels w/sharp geometrics, bl/grn matt, sgn, 5x6" 1,400.00

Overlay Glass

Art glass having layers of more than one type or color of glass is sometimes called overlay or cased glass. Very often glassware of this type has applied decorations such as fruit, flowers, leaves, or ruffles (rigaree), such as is commonly identified with Stevens and Williams.

Bowl, peachblow w/yel swags & branches forming ft, 5x7"	600.00
Bowl, pk on wht w/appl 3-color floral/leaves/ft, 5½" H	625.00
Pitcher, clear w/gr leaves & red strawberry, amber hdl/ft, 5"	525.00
Pitcher, gold satin w/emb swirl ribs, frosted reeded hdl, 5"	175.00
Pitcher, orange to wht shaded, ruffled, clear hdl, 7¼"	165.00
Pitcher, rose to pk shaded, clear hdl, bulbous, 7¼"	185.00
Pitcher, wht w/appl pk floral/gr leaves/bl rim, amber hdl, 7"	200.00
Rose bowl, bl, HP florals w/gold, 8-crimp, 3½x4¼"	95.00
Vase, bl w/HP florals, much gold at top, wht int, 7x4½"	200.00
Vase, bl w/wht lacy decor & gold, 12x4½", pr	425.00
Vase, cream w/bl int, appl crystal ruffled leaf & rim, 5½"	145.00
Vase, pk w/red & wht spatter flowers, amber leaves/ft, 7"	350.00
Vase, pk/wht, clear wishbone ft, clear appl flowers, 4¾x3"	120.00
Vase, red, HP florals, cut scallops w/gold, gold hdls, 8½"	150.00

Overshot

Overshot glass is characterized by the beaded or craggy appearance of its surface. Earlier ware was irregularly textured, while 20th-century examples tend to be more uniform.

Pitcher, appl neck ring, twisted hdl, trefoil rim, 13"	275.00
Pitcher, gr w/amber shell hdl, Sandwich, ca 1875, 8¼"	235.00

Pitcher, heavy floral enamel decoration of white roses and blue forget-me-nots with green leaves on clear, 8", $265.00.

Pitcher, tankard; cranberry, clear reeded hdl, 9⅜x4½"	175.00
Pitcher, tankard; cranberry w/clear hdl, 7¼"	135.00
Pitcher, tankard; rubena, clear hdl, 9½"	175.00

Owens Pottery

J.B. Owens founded his company in Zanesville, Ohio, in 1891, and until 1907, when the company decided to exert most of its energies in the area of tile production, made several quality lines of art pottery. His first line, Utopian, was a standard brown ware with underglaze slip decoration of nature studies, animals, and portraits. A similar line, Lotus, utilized lighter background colors. Henri Deux, introduced in 1900, featured incised Art Nouveau forms inlaid with color. (Be aware that the Brush-McCoy Pottery acquired many of Owens' molds and reproduced a line similar to Henri Deux, which they called Navarre.) Other important lines were Opalesce, Rustic, Feroza, Cyrano, and Mission, examples of which are rare today. The factory burned in 1928, and the company closed shortly thereafter. Values vary according to the quality of the artwork and subject matter. Examples signed by the artist bring higher prices

than those that are not signed. For further information we recommend *Owens Pottery Unearthed* by Kristy and Rick McKibben and Jeanette and Marvin Stofft. The Stoffts are listed in the Directory under Indiana.

Aborigine, vase, geometrics on gr matt, squat bottle form, 5"	375.00
Eventide, vase, tan/gr trees on orange mottle, 8x6"	2,600.00
Feroza, vase, Nouveau swirls emb on brn-bronze, hdls, 9½"	600.00
Lotus, jardiniere, mushrooms, #230, 3"	210.00
Lotus, vase, irises, EX art, sgn, #1258, 7½"	600.00
Lotus, vase, lg iris, artist sgn, 8x6"	700.00
Lotus, vase, stylized leaf on lt gr to tan, 7x6"	450.00
Lotus, vase, toadstools, #235, 2-hdld mug form, 5"	400.00
Matt, vase, cvd daffodils on gr to tan, sgn GJ, 10x5"	450.00
Matt Gr, cider pitcher, emb stylized fruit tree, 11", +6 mugs	800.00
Matt Gr, tankard, emb Nouveau orange trees, 10"	325.00
Matt Gr, vase, buttressed top, tapering, #1158, 9½x4"	475.00
Matt Gr, vase, emb stylized flowers at wide base, 6¾x6½"	300.00
Matt Gr, vase, 4 spines, petal top, narrow neck, 6½"	200.00
Matt Lotus, vase, pansies, sqd w/doughnut neck, 5¾"	350.00
Matt Utopian, vase, daisy, sgn HE, ftd pillow form, 5"	175.00
Matt Utopian, vase, floral, elongated bottle form, 7½"	325.00
Matt Utopian, vase, leaves, Harry Eberlein, #1076, 13x7"	450.00
Matt Utopian, vase, lg clover buds, sgn, shouldered, 11"	400.00
Matt Utopian, vase, 2 lg pansies, artist sgn, 14½"	550.00
Mirror Blk, vase, emb purple grapes/gr leaves, #0220, 8½"	450.00
Mission, vase, red drips on gr, 11", in oak stand	900.00
Opalesce, vase, roses, copper/gold/gr on sandy ground, 11x4"	500.00
Tile, purple grapes on brn & yel, mk, 6"	175.00
Utopian, candlestick, floral, #958, 7"	150.00
Utopian, corn jug, sgn T Steel	350.00
Utopian, ewer, floral, 7"	275.00
Utopian, mug, cherries, sgn, 5"	125.00
Utopian, pitcher, wheat sprig, 5x8"	175.00
Utopian, silver o/l, clover blossoms, #752, 4½"	500.00
Utopian, vase, carnations, incurvate cylinder, 6½"	140.00
Utopian, vase, floral, #05, 11x4½"	250.00
Utopian, vase, floral, EX art, shouldered, 7½"	250.00
Utopian, vase, floral, sgn TS, pillow form w/4 ft, #821, 5"	150.00
Utopian, vase, floral, 3-sided petticoat shape, 3"	100.00
Utopian, vase, floral, 4 arched panel sides, 4"	125.00
Utopian, vase, floral, 4-sided base, 4"	125.00
Utopian, vase, floral w/silver o/l, ftd/long hdls, 9"	1,750.00
Utopian, vase, honeysuckle, sgn TR, 6"	175.00
Utopian, vase, leaves, twisted body, #117, 4½"	130.00
Utopian, vase, male lion, sgn MT, shouldered, 16x10"	4,000.00
Utopian, vase, orange/brn/yel drip gloss, #1072, 11"	250.00
Utopian, vase, pansies, deeply twisted, 5"	140.00
Utopian, vase, pansies, hdls, #879, 6"	120.00
Utopian, vase, pansies on long stems, EX art, sgn, #219, 8½"	280.00
Utopian, vase, Rembrandt portrait, sgn EP, 10x5"	1,500.00
Utopian, vase, sweet peas, 8"	200.00
Utopian, vase, tulips, EX art, 5"	150.00
Utopian, vase, tulips, 12"	275.00
Utopian, vase, wild roses, EX art, trumpet neck, 16"	600.00
Venetian, bowl, gold irid, undulating surface, 3¾x7"	300.00

Pacific Clay Products

The Pacific Clay Products Company got its start in the 1920s as a consolidation of several smaller southern California potteries. The main Los Angeles plant had been founded in 1890 to make kitchen stoneware, ollas, and similar items. Terra cotta and brick were later produced.

In 1932 Hostess Ware, a vividly colored line of dinnerware, was introduced to compete with Bauer's Ring Ware. Coralitos, a lighterweight, pastel-hued dinnerware line was first marketed in 1937, and a similar but less expensive line called Arcadia soon followed. Artware including vases, figurines, candlesticks, etc., was produced from 1932 to 1942, at which time the company went into war-related work and pottery manufacture ceased. A limited amount of hand-decorated dinnerware was also made. For further information we recommend *The Collectors Encyclopedia of California Pottery* (with 1995 values) by our advisor, Jack Chipman; he is listed in the Directory under California.

Bowl, Ring-style, 8½"	45.00
Chop plate, Ring-style, 12"	65.00
Coaster, Hostess Ware	15.00
Cocktail cup, Ring-style	60.00
Coffeepot, AD; hdl, w/lid	150.00
Creamer & sugar bowl, Hostess Ware, open, closed hdls, sm	50.00
Cup & saucer, coffee/tea; Hostess Ware, hdld	35.00
Cup & saucer, demitasse; Ring-style	35.00
Custard cup, early design	35.00
Dish, baking; clip-on wooden hdls, 8¾"	125.00
Figurine, bird, stylized, satin wht, circular in-mold mk, lg	80.00
Figurine, Pan, seated & playing pipes, rare	350.00
Goblet, Ring-style	100.00
Jar, Ring-style, w/lid, 5"	100.00
Pitcher, ball jug form, early	80.00
Pitcher, Ring, 2-qt	100.00
Plate, baby; bunny border, divided, 9"	100.00
Plate, Plaid, dinner sz	40.00
Relish tray, Ring-style, 4-part, wooden hdl	75.00
Shaker, Ring-style, pr	15.00
Shakers, Hostess Ware, sm, pr	15.00
Sugar bowl, demitasse; Ring-style, yel	25.00
Teapot, long spout, ftd	125.00
Teapot, Ring-style, turq, ftd, lg	150.00
Tray, Hostess Ware, Ring, 15"	90.00
Tumbler, 4"	22.00
Vase, bird motif, HP, stamped mk, ca 1939, 8¾"	60.00
Vase, low hdls, 5"	65.00

Paden City

The Paden City Glass Company began operations in 1916 in Paden City, West Virginia. The company's early lines consisted largely of the usual pressed tablewares, but by the 1920s production had expanded to include colored wares in translucent as well as opaque glass in a variety of patterns and styles. The company maintained its high standards of handmade perfection until 1949, when under new management much of the work formerly done by hand was replaced by automation. The Paden City Glass Company closed in 1951; its earlier wares, the colored patterns in particular, are becoming very collectible.

Paden City Glass is not always easily recognized by collectors or dealers, as it was almost never marked. It is believed this was so the glass could be sold to decorating companies. The company assigned both line numbers and names to many of its blanks or sets of glassware. Colors were sometimes given more than one name, and etchings were named as well. All this makes identification of items offered for sale through mail order difficult, and labels prepared by dealers are often confusing.

A review of literature available on Paden City reveals the following names for the company's plate etchings: Ardith; California Poppy; Cupid; Delilah Bird (Peacock Reverse); Eden Rose; Frost; Gazebo; Gothic Garden; Lela Bird; Nora Bird; Orchid (three variations); Peacock and Rose (Peacock and Wild Rose); Samarkand; Trumpet Flower; Utopia. Names given to cuttings made on Paden City blanks are York-

town and Lazy Daisy. It is not clear whether the names originated with Paden City or with secondary decorating companies.

Our advisors for this category are George and Mary Hurney; they are listed in the Directory under Illinois. (Note: their interest is only in Paden City glassware, not the pottery.) See also Glass Animals and Figurines; Kitchen Collectibles, Glass.

This list gives company line numbers with corresponding line names:

#69, #69½ — Georgian
#191 — Party
#210 — Regina
#215 — Hotcha
#220 — Largo
#221 — Maya
#300 — Wotta
#411 — Mrs B
#412 — Crow's Foot Square
#890 — Crow's Foot Round
#895 — Lucy
#991 — Penny
#994 — Popeye and Olive
#1503 — Trance

And, finally, a listing of colors with alternate names or descriptive phrases:

Amber — (dull)	Mulberry — amethyst
Cheriglo — (delicate) pink	Opal — opaque white
Cobalt Blue — Royal Blue	Primrose — (amber with reddish
Crystal — (clear, no tint)	tint)
Dark Green — forest green	Red — ruby
Dark Amber — (honey color)	Rose — (dark pink)
Light Blue — Copen, Neptune	Yellow — (pale, soft)

Bowl, berry; Crow's Foot, red, 5"	5.00
Bowl, console; Crow's Foot, amber, 3-ftd, 11½"	30.00
Bowl, console; Maya, bl, 3-ftd, 11½"	55.00
Bowl, Gothic Garden, pk, sq, ftd, 9"	95.00
Bowl, vegetable; Crow's Foot, red, oval	29.00
Candle holder, Royal Lace, gr, ruffled	70.00
Candlesticks, Crow's Foot, cobalt, mushroom, pr	95.00
Candlesticks, Nora Bird, pk, pr	120.00
Candy dish, Cupid, 3-part	150.00
Cheese & cracker, Crow's Foot, red	225.00
Cheese & cracker, Gazebo, bl, w/lid	210.00
Compote, Cupid, pk	80.00
Compote, Peacock & Wild Rose, gr	75.00
Cotton ball dispenser, bl, bunny form	70.00
Creamer, Penny Line	8.00
Cup, Popeye & Olive, red	10.00
Cup & saucer, Crow's Foot, red, sq	13.50
Goblet, Georgian, red, 9-oz	18.50
Goblet, Popeye & Olive, red	20.00
Ice bucket, Peacock & Wild Rose, gr	95.00

Ice tubs, Party Line: Pink, $30.00; Amber, $27.50.

Plate, Crow's Foot, amber, sq, 10¾" 19.00
Plate, Crow's Foot, amber, 8" 5.00
Plate, Crow's Foot, red, 9¼" 33.00
Plate, Crow's Foot, sq, hdls, 10⅜" 17.50
Plate, indented; Peacock & Rose, 10½" 55.00
Plate, Penny Line, 6" 4.00
Plate, Penny Line, 8" 6.00
Plate, salad; Rosemary, pk 6.50
Platter, Crow's Foot, amber, oval 10.00
Salver, cake; Orchid, ftd 27.00
Sandwich server, Lela Bird, center hdl 95.00
Sherbet, Georgian, red, stem 12.50
Sherbet, Penny Line, 6-oz 8.00
Sherbet, Popeye & Olive, red, 4¼" 18.00
Sherbet, Royal Lace 10.00
Tumbler, Ardith, amber, flat, 5⅛", 6 for 125.00
Tumbler, Crow's Foot, amber 38.00
Tumbler, Georgian, red, ftd V shape, 3½" 10.00
Tumbler, Penny Line, ftd, 10-oz 10.00
Tumbler, Penny Line, ftd, 8-oz 9.00
Tumbler, Popeye & Olive, red 15.00
Vase, Lela Bird, blk, 12" 285.00
Vase, Peacock & Wild Rose, pk, 10½" 140.00
Vase, Peacock Reverse, gr, 6" 145.00

Paintings on Ivory

Miniature works of art executed on ivory from the 1800s are assessed by the finesse of the artist, as is any fine painting. Signed examples and portraits with an identifiable subject are usually preferred. Note: when the dimensions fall before mention of the frame, they describe the size of the painting itself.

Portraits of a man and lady, in plain yellow gold frames, braided hair panels on backs, 18k Stockholm 1807 on frames, maker's marks: C.G.H., 2¾", $820.00 for the pair.

Child's portrait, EE Kaufer, oval gold case, 4⅛x3½" 250.00
Duchess de Montebello, lacy red gown, sgn Wyde, 2¾x3¾" 230.00
Lady in blk bonnet w/feathers, sgn, 1½x2", enamel fr 220.00
Lady in classical attire & laurel wreath, sgn, fr, 5½x3¾" 140.00
Lady in garden, sgn, in ivory & ebony fr, 4¾x3⅞" 165.00
Lady in lace bonnet, identified/1778, fr, 3¾x3¼" 275.00
Lady in lacy dress, ca 1840, orig ivory fr, 5x5" 165.00
Lady in lg flowered hat, inlaid/eng ivory fr, 5½x4¼" 225.00
Lady in plumed hat, sgn Cosway, brass fr, 4¼x3½" 165.00
Lady in purple bonnet, pk dress, 2x2¾", ornate metal fr 160.00
Lady in red cape, fancy brass fr, 1¾x2¼" 350.00
Lady w/gold earrings & necklace, 1¾x2¼" 150.00
Letizia, mother of Napoleon, 2½" dia, sq ebony fr 425.00
Man's portrait, sgn Williams, gilt case, 4½x3½" 85.00

Marie Antoinette, MIG, in Florentine fr, 5⅝" 110.00
Mary & Child, gilt brass & velvet fr, 5x3¼" 150.00
Napoleon, sgn, eng ivory fr, 5½x4¼" 110.00
Napoleon, sgn Major, inlaid ivory fr, 3⅝x3¼" 165.00
Napoleon in battle scene, fr, 5½x4½", pr 550.00
Young man, worn, 4x4", in leatherized case 140.00
2 ladies w/book, gilt fr w/easel bk, 2¾x2⅜" 500.00

Pairpoint

The Pairpoint Manufacturing Company was built in 1880 in New Bedford, Massachusetts. It was primarily a metalworks whose chief product was coffin fittings. Next door, the Mt. Washington Glassworks made quality glasswares of many varieties. (See Mt. Washington for more information concerning their artware lines.) By 1894 it became apparent to both companies that a merger would be to their best interest.

From the late 1890s until the 1930s, lamps and lamp accessories were an important part of Pairpoint's production. There were three main types of shades, all of which were blown: puffy — blown-out reverse-painted shades (usually floral designs); ribbed — also reverse painted; and scenic — reverse painted with scenes of land or seascapes (usually executed on smooth surfaces, although ribbed scenics may be found occasionally). Cut glass lamps and those with metal overlay panels were also made. Scenic shades were sometimes artist signed. Every shade was stamped on the lower inside or outside edge with 1) The Pairpoint Corp., 2) Patent Pending, 3) Patented July 9, 1907, or 4) Patent Applied For. Bases were made of bronze, copper, brass, silver, or wood and are always signed.

Because they produced only fancy, handmade artware, the company's sales lagged seriously during the Depression; and as time and tastes changed, their style of product was less in demand. As a result, they never fully recovered; consequently part of the buildings and equipment was sold in 1938. The company reorganized in 1939 under the direction of Robert Gundersen and again specialized in quality hand-blown glassware. Isaac Babbit regained possession of the silver departments, and together they established Gundersen Glassworks, Inc. After WWII, because of a sharp decline in sales, it again became necessary to reorganize. The Gundersen-Pairpoint Glassworks was formed, and the old line of cut, engraved artware was reintroduced. The company moved to East Wareham, Massachusetts, in 1957. But business continued to suffer, and the firm closed only one year later. In 1970, however, new facilities were constructed in Sagamore under the direction of Robert Bryden, sales manager for the company since the 1950s.

In 1974 the company began to produce lead glass cup plates which were made on commission as fund-raisers for various churches and organizations. These are signed with a 'P' in diamond and are becoming quite collectible. Our advisor for Pairpoint lamps is Daniel Batchelor; he is listed in the Directory under New York. See also Napkin Rings.

Glass

Bowl, bright bl w/lg clear pinwheel, 3½x11½", EX 490.00
Box, jewel; floral/gold scrolls on ivory, gilt mts, 4x7x4" 950.00
Candlesticks, Viscaria, teardrop stems, 9", pr 225.00
Ice bucket, eng polar bear, SP mts, 9x4¾" 325.00
Pokal, old English Hobnail cutting, domed lid w/finial, 14" 400.00
Smoke set, gilt metal tray w/ashtray, pot & matchbox, #4941 ....300.00
Vase, Ambero, frosted, int pnt w/grapes on yel-gr, 12x8" 1,800.00

Lamps

Chandelier, dragonflies & flowers on wht Lucca shade, 14" 8,000.00
Fairy, puffy poppy shade; frosted cut base 1,150.00

Puffy 10" sqd Torino shade w/roses; fluted rose-emb std **4,800.00**
Puffy 14" rose/butterfly Papillon shade; rtcl 'copper' std **8,000.00**
Puffy 15" grapes sgn shade; SP 3-arm foliate-etch std, 22" **8,000.00**
Puffy 8" apple blossom Stratford shade; gilt hex std **2,800.00**
Puffy 8" apple blossom/roses Stratford shade; mahog std, 15" ..**4,000.00**
Puffy 8" plaid linenfold shade w/lg flower clusters; mk std **2,600.00**
Puffy 8" rose tree & lattice shade; SP baluster std, 16" **2,500.00**
Puffy 8" roses/butterflies Papillon shade; acanthus std **5,000.00**
Puffy 8" roses/butterfly shade (NM); baluster std **3,100.00**
Rvpt 12" roses/lattice melon-rib Venice shade; rose-emb std ..**4,000.00**
Rvpt 14" iris Plymouth shade; gilt std w/sqd scalloped ft **3,000.00**
Rvpt 15" autumn Directoire shade; 3-shaft scroll-ft std **1,750.00**
Rvpt 16" 3-galleon Landsdowne shade sgn Chadd; 3-dolphin std .**5,000.00**
Rvpt 17" flamingos/trees Danver shade; ovoid std w/hex ft **3,000.00**
Rvpt 18" farmhouse Landsdowne shade sgn Fisher; mk std, 22" ..**3,350.00**
Rvpt 18" floral Danver beehive shade; mk mahog std, 24" **2,800.00**
Rvpt 18" jungle/birds Carlisle shade; 3-strap SP std **4,000.00**
Rvpt 20" sea gull Copley shade sgn Fisher; matching pnt std ..**5,500.00**

Pairpoint Limoges

Limoges china blanks were imported from France in strict accordance with Pairpoint specifications. They were decorated by Pairpoint in designs that ranged from simple to elaborate florals and scenes. These are easily identified. Look for the Pairpoint name over a crown with the Limoges name below. You may also find similar ware marked 'Pairpoint Minton.'

Box, jewel; wild roses on gr, kidney shape, 7½x6" **200.00**
Gravy boat, Dresden, mc floral, ornate hdl, +underplate **175.00**
Vase, spider mums, red/pk on gr, 8½" **200.00**

Paper Dolls

No one knows quite how or when paper dolls originated. One belief is that they began in Europe as 'pantins' (jumping jacks) and were frequently worn as part of the costume. By the late 1790s, they were being mass produced. During the 19th century, most paper dolls portrayed famous dancers and opera stars such as Fanny Elssler and Jenny Lind. In the late 1800s, the Raphael Tuck Publishers of England produced many series of beautiful paper dolls; retail companies used them as advertisements to further the sale of their products. Around the turn of the century, many popular women's magazines began featuring a page of paper dolls.

Most familiar to today's collectors are the books with dolls on cardboard covers and clothes on the inside pages. These made their appearance in the late 1920s and early thirties. The most collectible (and the most valuable) are those representing celebrities, movie stars, and comic-strip characters of the thirties and forties.

For further information we recommend *Collector's Guide to Magazine Paper Dolls* and *Tomart's Price Guide to Lowe and Whitman Paper Dolls* (Tomart Publications), both by our advisor Mary Young. Additional paper dolls are listed in *Schroeder's Collectible Toys, Antique to Modern*. When no condition is indicated, the dolls listed below are assumed to be in mint, uncut, original condition. Cut sets will be worth about half price if all dolls and outfits are included and pieces are in very good condition. If dolls were produced in die-cut form, these prices reflect such a set in mint condition with all costumes and accessories.

Key:
CS — cut set   CF — cut in folder

Amy Carter, Toy Factory, 14" doll & uncut outfits, MIB **25.00**

Ann Southern, Saalfield #301 Saalfield, 1943, uncut, VG **75.00**
Annette, 1956 Whitman, WDP, 1962, CF/EX **36.00**
Archies, 1987 Whitman 5 dolls & outfits, 1969, CF/NM **18.00**
Babes in Toyland, Whitman, 1961, uncut punch-out book, VG ..**30.00**
Baby Nancy Her Nursery & Clothes, Whitman, 1931, CS/EX **35.00**
Barbie & Ken, Sun Valley, #4338/7420, Whitman 1974, MIB **15.00**
Beverly Hillbillies, #1955 Whitman, 1964, uncut, M **70.00**
Brady Bunch, #1976 Whitman, 1973, uncut, M **50.00**
Buffy (Family Affair), #1985 Whitman, 1968, M **35.00**
Bugs Bunny & Honey Bunny, #1985-45 Golden, 1983, VG **8.00**
Captain Marvel 3 Famous Flying Marvels, Fawcett, 1945, VG **50.00**
Charlie's Angels Farrah Fawcett, Toy Factory, 1977, MIB **25.00**
Chitty-Chitty Bang-Bang, #1982 Whitman, 1968, CF/NM **18.00**
Debby Reynolds, #1956 Whitman, 1960, CF/NM **28.00**
Donny & Marie Osmond, #1991 Whitman, 1977, uncut, NM **20.00**
Elizabeth Taylor as Cleopatra, Blaise Pub, 1963, MIB **40.00**
Flintstones Pebbles, Wonder Book, 1974, G **12.00**
Fonzie (Happy Days), 14" doll, Toy Factory, 1976, M, sealed **26.00**
Gentle Gladys, Raphael Tuck, 9" doll/3 dresses/hat, ca 1900 ....**75.00**
Grace Kelly, #2049 Whitman, 2 dolls, uncut, 1955, EX **110.00**
Green Acres, Oliver & Lisa #1979 Whitman, 1967, CF/M **25.00**
Jane Russell, #4328, Saalfield, 1955, uncut, NM **75.00**
Jane Withers, #986, 1941, 3 cut/7 uncut pgs **45.00**
Lennon Sisters, #1995 Whitman, 1963, CF/NM **15.00**
Little Cherubs, Platt & Munk, 1921, EX **58.00**
Little Lulu, #1970 Whitman, 1971, CS/M **12.00**
Lois, #3967 Whitman 1941, wooden, uncut **30.00**
Nancy Reagan, Dover, 1983, (still available), NM **3.00**
Nanny & the Professor, #4213 Saalfield, 1970, NM **35.00**
Partridge Family, #5137 Artcraft, 1972, CS/NM **18.00**
Pat Boone, #1968 Whitman, 1959, uncut, EX **55.00**
Patience & Prudence, #2411 Lowe, 1957, VG **35.00**
Princess Diana, #1985-50 Golden Book, 1985, M **10.00**
Queen Elizabeth Coronation, Jack & Jill magazine, 6/1953, NM **6.00**
Rhonda Fleming, #4320 Saalfield, 1954, uncolored/uncut, NM ..**80.00**
Richard Burton as Mark Antony, Blaise Pub, 1963, MIB **40.00**

Roy Rogers and Dale Evans, Dusty, Whitman #1950, 1957, complete, uncut, NM, $125.00.

Sandra Dee, #4413 Saalfield, 1959, uncut, M **60.00**
Saturday Night Live, Gilda Radner, M **12.00**
Sesame Street Miss Piggy, Colorforms, uncut, M, sealed **15.00**
Shirley Temple, #1986 Whitman, 1976, uncut, EX **20.00**
Slumber Party, #4854 Merrill, 1943, uncut **75.00**
Tricia Nixon, #4248 Saalfield, 1970, M **35.00**
Tuesday Weld, #5112 Saalfield, 1960, cut, NMIB **25.00**
Welcome Back Kotter, Toy Factory, 1976, MIB (sealed) **25.00**
White House w/Tricia, Julie & Pat Nixon, #4475 Saalfield, 1969, NM ..**35.00**
Winter Girl Wendy/Summer Girl Sue, #2611 Saalfield, 1952, NM.**35.00**

Paperweights

All paperweights listed here are made totally of glass (including the lampwork flowers, fish, birds, snakes, lizards, and millefiori rods). The only elements that are not glass are the clay sulfides encased within some of the Baccarat and St. Louis weights. Today, antique weights (1845 to ca 1870s) and those made by contemporary artists attract the most attention and are the most expensive. Lower-priced 'gift' weights come from American glasshouses and studios, China, Murano, Italy, and Scotland. But because of the expenses involved in their manufacture (fuel, material, and labor), even they are not cheap. There is an international association of paperweight collectors with many state and regional chapters. (For information see Clubs, Newsletters, and Catalogs in the Directory.) Many books are currently available on the subject of paperweights. For the beginner we recommend *All About Paperweights* by L.H. Selmen.

Probably inspired by the work of Pierre Bigaglia (Venice), the French factories of Baccarat, Clichy, and St. Louis turned their attention to paperweight-making in the 1840s. They first made millefiori paperweights, the technique a revival of methods used in Alexandria, Damascus, Rome, and Byzantium before the time of Christ. (This art form had faded out but had been revived in 16th-century Venice.) The French Classic period was 1845 to 1860; English (Whitefriars and Bacchus) and American (Sandwich and New England) glasshouses followed their lead about ten years later. Gradually, as the paperweight's popularity declined, production began to wane; Clichy closed in the 1880s, as did a few American factories. Baccarat made weights as late as 1910; in the '20s and '30s, a worker by the name of Dupont revived the art. Then in the 1950s St. Louis and Baccarat sparked a renewal of interest in weight-making that is still going strong today. Some of the most desirable weights from American artists were made by the Banfords, Randall Grubb, Rick Ayotte, Chris Buzzini, Ken Rosenfeld, Gordon Smith, Paul Stankard, Charles Kaziun (d), Del (d) and Debbie Tarsitano, and the Trabuccos. From Scotland, Paul Ysart (d), Perthshire and Caithness/Whitefriars are also well known.

Note: Prices do not reflect the usual buyer's fee charged by most auction houses. Furthermore, there are many factors which determine value, particularly of antique weights. Auction-realized prices of contemporary weights are usually different from issue price; 'list price' may be for weights issued earlier and reduced for clearance or influenced by market demand and other factors. The competition for antique weights has been increasing dramatically over the last five years. New collectors entering the field have greatly influenced prices. As the numbers of collectors increase, available antique weights decrease per capita, forcing prices upwards. Since the 1930s antique paperweights have steadily increased in value making them one of today's best investments. The dimension given at the end of the description is diameter.

Key:
con — concentric
fct — faceted
gar — garland
grd — ground
jsp — jasper
latt — latticinio
mill — millefiori
o/l — overlay
pm — pastry mold
pwt — paperweight
sil — silhouette

Ayotte, Rick

Amazon parrot on branch w/tropical flowers on bl opaque, 3¾" ..850.00
Christmas cactus bouquet w/berries on clear, 3¾", NM 600.00
Loon on water/2nd diving for fish, magnum compound, 1995, 4".2500.00
Orange-red rose, 2¼" 300.00
Pk rose & leaves, 1995, mini, 2¼" 350.00
Toucan & foliage, 1981, ltd ed 50, 2⅝" 550.00
1995 Illusion series, lady slippers/carnations/etc, 4" 1350.00
2 layers of yel & wht petals w/yel stamen on gr leaves, 2⅜" 225.00
2 red roses & bud w/wht blossoms, ltd ed, 3½" 950.00
3 daffodils/wht buds & flowers/wht berries w/yel tips, 3½" 850.00
3 tree frogs/Flaming Sword flowers on gr w/red, ltd ed, 3½" 900.00

Baccarat, Antique

Antique Baccarat, red and white within a garland of alternate white and arrowhead canes, 2½", $1,400.00.

Close pack mill w/complex canes, not sgn or dtd, 3" 1,350.00
Close pack mushroom/squirrel sil/torsade w/star base, 3" 3,000.00
Con mill, 3 mc rings, panel fcts at base, 2" 175.00
Fct butterfly over clear w/in mc gar, 1 & 6 fcts, 3" 2,600.00
Fct pansy & bud on clear star-cut base, 2¾" 1,000.00
Mc gars on clear interlace/surround 6 starburst canes, 3" 850.00
Pansies bouquet, fcts & enameling, 3¼" 950.00
Pansy w/7 leaves & bud on clear star-cut grd, 2⅝" 375.00
Pope Pius IX etched, 6 & 1 fcts, 3¼" 385.00
Primrose & bud in gar on star-cut clear base, 3⅛" 2,800.00
Starburst cane centers 2 interlacing mc gars, 3¼" 3,500.00
Sulfide, Frederick Wilhelm IV, in star-cut base, 2¾", EX 600.00
Wht dbl clematis on clear star-cut grd, bubbles, 3⅛" 800.00
2 trefoil gars & 6 sil canes, fct o/l, 3¼" 8,500.00
5 sils, close-pack mill, dtd B1848, 2⅝" 2,600.00

Baccarat, Modern

Close con mc mill, 1968, 3" 550.00
Close pack mill w/Zodiac canes, stamped, 1970s, 3" 245.00
Purple & yel pansy w/leaves & bud on clear star-cut grd, 3" 300.00
Salamander on pebbly grd, 1972, 3" 700.00
Snake & flower on gr, 1970, 3⅛" 650.00
Sulfide, Abraham Lincoln, dbl o/l 325.00
Sulfide, Eisenhower, waffle-cut claret base w/6 & 1 fcts, 2¾" 190.00
Sulfide, Eleanor Roosevelt, dbl o/l 285.00
Sulfide, Harry Truman, dbl o/l 285.00
Sulfide, John F Kennedy 200.00
Sulfide, Mt Rushmore, dbl o/l 450.00
Sulfide, Pierre Laval 125.00
Sulfide, Queen Elizabeth II & Prince Philip 150.00
Sulfide, Theodore Roosevelt 65.00
Sulfide, Thomas Paine, dbl o/l 285.00
Sulfide, Will Rogers 65.00
Sulfide, Woodrow Wilson 65.00
Zodiac sils on carpet grd, 1971, 3" 600.00

Banford, Bobby

Pk flower, mc knotweeds & 6 pk buds on leafy bed, 3⅛" 600.00
Red flower/wht knotweeds/3 bl buds on leaves on cobalt, 2⅜" ...250.00
1 bl & 1 ruby flower w/buds on wht grd, veined leaves, 3½" 600.00
2 lg bl flowers/5 yel buds/2 knotweeds on clear, sgn, 3" 275.00
2 pk flowers/sm wht flowers/knotweed/yel buds in clear, 2¾" 300.00
2 purple flowers/sm pk & wht flowers/knotweed/leaves, 3⅛" 600.00
2 violets & bud w/gr leaves on star-cut base, 3⅛" 400.00

Banford, Bob

Pansy in center of Fr-style bouquet w/dragonflies, 4" 2,000.00
Red dahlia on leaves w/in mc torsade on muslin grd, 3¼" 800.00
2 lt bl flowers/2 buds/gr leaves, 1 & 6 fcts, sgn, 3¼" 425.00
2 Palagrines, buds & leaves on cobalt grd, 1995, 3¼" 600.00
2 pansies/3 buds & gr leaves on dmn-cut base, 3¼" 750.00

Banford, Ray

3 purple iris w/buds & leaves over dmn-cut base, 3⅛" 1,000.00
3 wht/4 yel-tipped orange roses in basket on cobalt, 3⅛" 1,000.00
4 Sandwich-style roses/buds on muslin bed, red & gr torsade 800.00

Buzzini, Chris

Coneflower bouquet w/thistle/lily/roses/etc, ltd ed 10, 3⅜"......1,500.00
Velvety stickweed & log, ltd ed 10, 1966, 3⅜" 1,200.00
3 Japanese cherry blossums w/buds, ltd ed, 3⅜" 750.00
3 red azaleas/2 purple crocus/lupine spray/foliage, 3½" 750.00
4 mixed flowers/buds & leaves, 1 & 12 fcts, 3¼" 1,200.00

Caithness

Barrier Reef, fish & plant life, ltd ed 635.00
Comet, clear w/wht tail on blk grd w/bl & wht, sgn, 3" 115.00
Moonflower on blk grd w/bl, bubbles, sgn, 3¼" 50.00
Scorpion & 2 cacti w/blooms on sandy grd, ltd ed 675.00

Clichy, Antique

Fct spaced mill w/mc canes & central pk & gr rose, 2½" 1,450.00
Mc scattered mill canes w/17 complex canes & wht lace, 2½" .1,600.00
Patterned mill on cobalt opaque, moss canes/floret ring, 2⅝" ...1,600.00
Patterned mill on turq opaque grd w/floret-cane ring, 2½" 2,250.00
Scattered mill on 'sodden snow' grd, 3⅛" 2,500.00
Spaced con canes w/mc combinations, 2¼" 1,350.00
Spaced con mill w/pk rose in clear base, 3¼" 1,650.00
Spaced mill w/19 complex canes, repolished, 2¼" 975.00

Donofrio, Jim

Donkey-tail cactus w/mc flowers/Indian pot/brn rocks, 3⅜" 450.00
Knife/tomahawk/beads/medicine pouch on pebbly grd, 3⅝" ...1,000.00
Pk flower & bud/2 rows of bl flowers/leaves, face root, 3⅛" 425.00
2 lizards/yel flower/bud on desert grd, 3½" 1,000.00
2 tree frogs on branch/2 bl flowers on sandy grd, 3½" 1,000.00

Ebelhare, Drew

Con mill design in stave basket, 2" 215.00
Pk & gr rose/buds/etc in stave basket on carpet grd, 2¼"..............230.00

Grubb, Randy

Jeannette's Garden, 2 dahlias/foxglove/etc, magnum, 3⅝".......1,200.00
Pk hibiscus blossom w/stems & leaves, 3¼"................................400.00
Raspberries on vine w/leaves, 3" 450.00
Violets/lilacs/wht knotweed w/in mill garland, 3⅛" 700.00
2 purple iris & bud w/foliage, 3"...400.00

Lundberg Studios

Lundberg, S; Daisy Cluster, mc daisies at varied levels 350.00

Lundberg, S; dk pulled swirls on bl irid, #6/74 ....110.00
Lundberg, S; purple hyacinth & bud on lily pads in bl water 320.00
Lundberg, S; red hibiscus & gr leaves 300.00
Lundberg, S; underwater plants/fish, beveled corners, 2¾x3" 450.00
Lundberg, S; water lilies on lily pads & bl water 300.00
Richter, L; world globe cut into bl irid, 3¼" 180.00
Salazar, Daniel; pk flower on bl w/6 sm rose canes, 2¾" 300.00
Salazar, Daniel; striped Peace rose & 9 gr leaves on clear 110.00
Salazar, Daniel; upright poinsettia on wht opaque, 3⅜" 85.00
Salazar, Daniel; 5 orchids on stem w/leaves/etc on blk, 3¾"........500.00

Maul, David Grant

Bl & wht striped petals on mauve grd, 3" 240.00
Flower & buds on blk grd, 1 & 6 fcts, 3" 280.00
Red & wht striped flower & buds on lt bl grd, 3" 240.00
Yel water lily w/red pistil/4 gr leaves, ftd, 4⅜" 350.00
2 buds & wht flower on royal bl grd, fct 6 & 1 ....280.00

New England Glass, Antique

Garlanded nosegay in gar on swirled wht latt grd, 2½" 375.00
Garlanded nosegay on swirled wht latt grd, tipped canes, 3" 500.00
Patterned mill on wht swirled latt grd, 4 & 8 fcts, 2⅝" 300.00
Poinsettia & 3 gr leaves on wht swirled latt, 3⅛" 775.00
Poinsettia on swirled wht latt grd, 4 & 12 fcts, 2½", NM 400.00
Poinsettia w/complex cane center on swirled wht latt, 3⅛" 775.00
4 pears/4 cherries/4 lg & 4 sm leaves, domed, 2⅞" 600.00
5 apples/4 cherries/leaves on wht latt cushion, 3¼" 995.00
5 pears/4 cherries/8 gr leaves on wht swirled latt, 2½" 470.00

Orient & Flume

Alexander, E; grapes & leaves on marvered frit surface, 3¾"........190.00
Alexander, E; 3 wht iris w/leaves on bl irid egg shape, 3½" 140.00
Beyers, S; angelfish in water scene, 3⅝" 370.00
Beyers, S; Monarch butterfly & flowers, 3½" 350.00
Beyers, S; Swallowtail butterfly/bl flowers 350.00
Held G; cherry blossom on irid grd, 3⅛" 300.00
Lilies & leaves eng on frosted surface, 3" 100.00
Sillars, B; water lily & pad on bl, 3⅛" 310.00

Parabelle

Clichy-type rose center cane w/close con mill on gr, 2⅞" 325.00
Clichy-type roses in 6 mc con mill rings, '89, 2⅞" 170.00
Close pack mill in stave basket, 1987, 3¼" 225.00
Cranberry canes amid gr & wht canes on carpet grd mill, 2¾" ...170.00
Pansy canes & Clichy-type roses in close pack piedouche, 3" ..1,250.00
Yel pansy w/in con mill mc canes, 2¾" 170.00
4 mc cane flowers w/leaves on wht stardust grd, 2⅛" 135.00

Perthshire

Center cane & 4 rows of mc canes, 2" 45.00
Central P cane amid mc patterned mill panels w/twists, 3" 100.00
Circlets & panels of mc canes, 1 & 6 fcts, 1990, 2¾" 90.00
Con mill design w/6 rows of canes around center cane, 2½" 90.00
Crown, 1990, 2⅛" 245.00
Crown w/top fct & wht flower, ltd ed 300, 1996, 2½" 265.00
Fct pk water lily/buds on bl, ltd ed 250, 1966, 2¾" 440.00
Flower sil cane in center of 4 mc cane panels, ltd ed, 3" 125.00
Mc mixed fruits & cherries on swirled wht latt, 1980, 2½" 300.00
Orange & purple canes in 4 sections w/mc canes, 1985, 3⅛" 95.00

Pentagonal patterned mill, 1980, 2⅞" 155.00

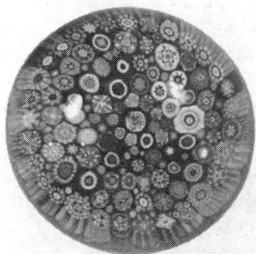

Perthshire, close pack multi-color complex canes within cane garland, signed and dated, 3⅜", $275.00.

Pk flower w/pattern mill & spiral twist, ltd ed , 1966, 3¼" 285.00
Pk rose buds on star-cut base, top & 16 side fcts, 1966, 3⅛" 785.00
Spoke pattern mc mill w/dbl mill gar, 3" 95.00
12 mc mill canes spaced on wht upset muslin grd, 2¾" 70.00
5 mc mill canes surrounded by latt twists, 1985, 2½" 50.00

Rosenfeld, Ken

Bl flowers w/yel stamens on wht grd, 1989, 3¾" 375.00
Chili peppers on natural grd, 3⅝" 400.00
Earth Grd Bouquet, 2 purple/1 yel/2 bl flowers w/bud, 3⅜" 375.00
Mixed crocuses, 3½" 500.00
Orchid Bouquet, 3 purple flowers on clear grd, sgn, 2⅞" 350.00
Radishes, carrots, asparagus & turnips, 3½" 300.00
Raspberry Bouquet, 5 red berries w/leaves on clear, 3¼" 300.00
Red rose/2 yel flowers/2 buds/wheat on bl grd, 1990, 3½" 600.00
Rose Bouquet, 1 yel/3 red roses w/bud & leaves on clear, 3" 250.00
Roses & bud on moss gr grd, 1989, 3½" 600.00
VA Bluebells, 5 flowers/3 buds on pk opaque, sgn, 3½" 250.00
2 pk/2 yel/4 purple flowers w/leaves on clear, sgn, 3½", NM 175.00
2 yel/2 bl/2 pk-striped flowers/2 buds on amethyst, 3⅜" 425.00
3 yel/4 purple flowers & 2 buds w/gr leaves, sgn, 2⅜" 225.00

Smith, Gordon

Mc ribbon snake/berries/flowers on sandy grd w/rocks, 3½" 800.00
Moorish idols among coral on reef, 3½" 800.00
Poisonous Strawberry Dart, creature/foliage/rocky grd, 3⅝" 900.00
10 dogwood flowers/5 berries/gr leaves on clear, sgn/dtd, 3" 375.00
2 peach blossoms/3 buds/3 gr leaves on clear, sgn/dtd, 3", NM ...375.00

St. Louis, Antique

Apple/2 pears/3 cherries/leaves/dbl swirl latt basket, 3½" 1,650.00
Dahlia w/stem, fcts, clear base, 3⅛" 4,800.00
Dancing couple sil amid close con mill, 3⅛" 5,500.00
Macedoine w/5 sil canes, 2¾" 2,000.00
Mc pattern mill on upset muslin grd, 2⅛" 750.00
Salmon/bl center cane/5 bl/wht canes in mc ring on clear, 2¼" .200.00
Scramble w/filigree & twists/3 complex canes/devil cane, 2¼" ...750.00
Scramble w/2 mill canes among color & latt twists, 2⅛" 325.00
Sulfide, Louis Napoleon Bonaparte III, crescent wreath, 3¼" 750.00

St. Louis, Modern

Dahlia on clear crystal, ltd ed 200, 1966, 3" 570.00
Dbl o/l close-pack mill mushroom on star-cut base, 3⅛" 500.00
Fct dbl o/l bouquet, 1975, 2⅞" 550.00
Memory, pk/wht/bl flowers on yel latt, ltd ed, 1993, 3⅝" 1,900.00
Persia, closepack w/complex canes, ltd ed 250, 1993, 3¼" 890.00
Princess, red rose/bud on bl carped grd, fcts, 1993, 3¼" 1,180.00

Sulfide, Cupid amid 5 bl & gr flowers on pk, 1 & 6 fcts, 3⅛" 230.00
2 yel Clichy-type roses & bud on bl opaque grd, 1976, 3⅛" 200.00
5-cane petal flower w/3 leaves/wht bud on yel grd, 3¼" 195.00
9 mc complex cane rings on wht latt piedouche, 1972, 3x3⅛" .1,000.00

Trabucco, Jon and David

Brn & wht frog on natural grd w/2 rocks, 3⅜" 550.00
Cherries on branch w/wht buds & blossoms on natural grd, 3⅜" .550.00

Trabucco, Victor

Blk & yel snake among rocks on natural grd, 3¼" 600.00
Swallowtail butterfly w/wht blossom/bud/blueberries, 3¾" H 950.00
2 purple violets & 2 buds w/gr tendrils, sgn/dtd, 3" 500.00
3 red & wht fuchsias w/stem & leaves, window panel, 4½" 950.00

Whitefriars

Bed of roses on rose translucent grd, 1 & 6 fcts, '82, 2⅞" 120.00
Con mill, pk/wht/red/bl rings, dtd 1848, 3¾" 400.00
Mc butterfly in pk & wht gar, 1 & 6 fcts, 1982, 3" 140.00
Pattern mill canes, 1 & 5 fcts, 1973, 3" 350.00
Red cane gar on carpet grd of wht canes w/bl centers, '72, 3" 250.00
Red/wht heart cane amid con mill on clear grd, 3¼" 180.00

Ysart, Paul

Mc butterfly in gr & wht gar on gr opaque grd, sgn, 3" 750.00
Purple flower w/gold aventurine, bubbles form gar, H cane, 3" ...400.00
Red fish on sandy fruit grd w/6 mill canes, H cane, 2⅞" 400.00
Scramble w/geometrically spaced bubbles, H cane, 3" 300.00
6 mc flowers & gr leaves in gr & wht gar on bl grd, 3" 750.00

Miscellaneous

Bacchus, 6 con mc mill rings w/wht/bl center cane, 3⅜" 1,200.00
Bohemian, close-pack mill on upset muslin grd, 1850s, 2½" ...1,300.00
Boudon de Saint-Amans, Shakespeare sulfide (facing left), 2½" .375.00
Cape Cod Glass Works, 3-color swirl, 1993, 3" 275.00
Correia, orchid on mottled translucent gr grd, ltd ed, 3" 125.00
French sulfide, royal couple on clear grd, bubbles, 2½" 90.00
Hacker, Harold; sulfide kitten on blk jsp grd, 2¾" 135.00
Manson, Wm; 6 dk amethyst cherries on leafy branch, 2⅞" 150.00
Smith, Carolyn; orange/red flower on lt gr pebbled grd, 2¼" 130.00
Stankard, Paul; Sippewisset bouquet on clear base, 1979, 3" ...2,800.00
Tarsitano, Debbi; lav rose w/bud/wht flowers on cobalt, 2¾" 300.00
Tarsitano, Delmo; mulberry clusters/leaves on cobalt, 3⅜" 900.00
Tarsitano, Delmo; salamander & flower on sandy grd, 3¼" 1,200.00
Val St Lambert, wht/red canes, red/wht/bl/yel rods, 1880s, 2⅝" .175.00
Whittemore, FD; yel SC jessamine w/bud/leaves on purple, 2¼" .425.00

Papier-Mache

The art of papier-mache was mainly European. It originated in Paris around the middle of the 18th century and became popular in America during Victorian times. Small items such as boxes, trays, inkwells, frames, etc., as well as extensive ceiling moldings and larger articles of furniture were made. The process involved building layer upon layer of paper soaked in glue, then coaxed into shape over a wood or wire form. When dry it was painted or decorated with gilt or inlays. Inexpensive 20th-century 'notions' were machine processed and mold pressed. See also Christmas; Candy Containers.

Cigar case, HP dancing couple/flute player, pouch w/in, 5½" L .200.00
Fire screen, HP decor on butterfly form, 1860s, 57" 375.00
Stork display pc, Germany, early, 25", NM 250.00
Table, tilt-top; MOP inlay, gold pnt decor, 29x15x18" 980.00
Wig stand, bust-length lady, pnt decor, late 1800s, 14½" 630.00
Wig stand, figural head, 16", EX 260.00

Parian Ware

Parian is hard-paste unglazed porcelain made to resemble marble. First made in the mid-1800s by Staffordshire potters, it was soon after produced in the United States by the U.S. Pottery at Bennington, Vermont. Busts and statuary were favored, but plaques, vases, mugs, and pitchers were also made.

Pitcher, George Washington figures in relief, American, 19th century, 10", $935.00.

Bust, classical female, highly detailed, no mk, 11", NM 140.00
Bust, Dryden, mk J&TR/290, 8" 90.00
Bust, French man, youthful appearance, marble base, 10" 95.00
Bust, Handel, mk R&L, 8" 100.00
Bust, lady, John Hancock, Copeland, dtd 1863, 11" 325.00
Bust, 18th-C lady, mk Gille, Jne Fab, 11¾", EX 350.00
Figurine, Apollo, Bavaria, Germany, 10¾" 65.00
Figurine, Bennington cross w/2 figures, 11¼" 110.00
Figurine, boy w/bucket pours water into shell, English, 11" 150.00
Figurine, classical goddess w/globe & calipers, 15½" 140.00
Figurine, hunter & dog, mk Minton, 14½" 300.00
Figurine, lady w/garland of roses by column, 18" 320.00
Figurine, Mercury, after Thorwaldson, ca 1850, 23¼" 1,400.00
Figurine, Mrs H Moore, seated lady, Minton, 6¾" 170.00
Figurine, Naomi & Her Daughter-in-Law, Minton, 12¼", EX ...185.00
Figurine, nude lady in shackles, Copeland, 18½" 700.00
Figurine, Queen Victoria (& Prince Albert), 7", NM, pr 325.00
Figurine, 2 owls on log, Matchmaking, 1871 registry mk, 7½" ...225.00

Parrish, Maxfield

Maxfield Parrish was a painter and illustrator who began his career in the last decade of the 19th century. His work remained prominent until the early 1940s. His most famous painting, *Daybreak*, was published in print form and sold nearly two thousand copies between 1910 and 1930. All prices are for framed prints except for those from the 1960s. See also magazines.

Ad, Arizona, thermometer for Em's Cafe, Neb, '40s, 7½x9½" ...170.00
Book, Dream Days, Grahame, 8 blk/wht plates & cover, '02, EX .135.00
Book, King Albert's Book, EX 115.00
Book, King of Hearts, spiral, G- 450.00
Book, Poems of Childhood, E Field, '55 edition, VG 135.00
Book, The Early Years, Skeeters, EX 225.00

Book, Wonderbook of Tanglewood Tales, 1st ed, EX 150.00
Book, Wonderbook of Tanglewood Tales, 2nd ed, EX 120.00
Calendar, Evening, complete, B/B, '47, med, NM 150.00
Calendar, Golden Hours, Edison/Mazda, cropped, fr, sm 250.00
Calendar, Lamplighter of Bagdad, Mazda, 14x19½", EX 725.00
Calendar, Old Glen Mill, B/B, '54, 17x21½", EX 300.00
Calendar, Peaceful Country, '63, 18x14", EX 175.00
Calendar, Peaceful Country, B/B, '63, 20x24½", VG 150.00
Calendar, Peaceful Country, B/B, '63, 32x16", EX 225.00
Calendar, Peaceful Valley, B/B, full pad, '55, M 175.00
Calendar, Quiet Solitude, B/B, '62, 32x16", M 425.00
Calendar, Sheltering Oaks, complete w/pad, '60, 14x18", EX 325.00
Calendar, Solitude, Edison/Mazda, fr, color, sm folio, NM 165.00
Calendar, Twilgiht, B/B, '61, 32x16", M 375.00
Calendar, Twilight, complete w/pad, '61, 18x14" 200.00
Calendar, Under Summer Skies, B/B, 32x16", EX 350.00
Calendar, Under Summer Skies, complete, '59, 14x18", EX 275.00
Calendar print, Old Glen Mill, B/B, '54, 17x22" 175.00
Calendar print, Peaceful Country, B/B, '63, 20x24½" 175.00
Calendar print, Quiet Solitude, B/B, '62, 14x18", EX 250.00
Calendar print, Venetian Lamplighter, Edison/Mazda, sm 150.00
Jell-O ad, The King & Queen Might Eat Thereof, 6x8", M 125.00
Jell-O booklet, Parrish color cover, 4½x6", M 40.00
Magazine article, 1st 40 Years Are the Hardest, w/2 prints, EX 70.00
Magazine cover, Classic Temple & Garden, LHJ, June '01, EX 45.00
Magazine cover, Collier's, Feb 3, '06, VG 70.00
Magazine cover, Florentine Fete, LHJ Dec 1920, 14½x9½" 130.00
Magazine print, w/Trumpets & Drum, blk/wht, '03 ....50.00
Playing cards, Contentment, pack of 48 (4 missing), o/w EX 90.00
Playing cards, Reveries, pack of 48 (4 missing), o/w EX 90.00
Playing cards, Spirit of the Night, EX, 7 for 80.00
Playing cards, Waterfall, complete (52) in case 250.00
Print, Canyon, fr, 12x15", NM 245.00
Print, Cleopatra, sm 425.00
Print, Daybreak, fr, 10x18" 175.00
Print, Dreaming, fr, 6x10" 230.00
Print, Dreaming, nude figure sits at tree, 10x18", EX 575.00
Print, Garden of Allah, fr, 15x30" 450.00
Print, Garden of Allah, matted, 9x18", EX- 150.00
Print, Hilltop, House of Art, period fr, superb color, 12x18", NM ..450.00
Print, Hilltop, lg 800.00
Print, Jell-O, King & Queen..., color, matted, 6x8", EX 60.00
Print, Lute Players, fr, 18x30" 750.00
Print, Pierro's Serenade, '08 Collier's Art Book, 9½x11¼" 150.00
Print, Prince Codadad, fr, 9x11", EX 150.00
Print, Rubaiyat, '17, 13x36", EX 550.00
Print, Skeeters, sm 250.00
Print, Solitude, sm 325.00
Print, Stars, fr, 10x6" 235.00

Print, Stars, in original frame, 20x12", NM, $695.00.

Print, Stars, 18x30", M 1,300.00
Print, Twilight, fr, 23x19" 235.00
Sheet music, Djer Kiss Waltz, some tears & wrinkles, color EX 90.00

Pate-De-Verre

Simply translated, pate-de-verre means paste of glass. In the manufacturing process, lead glass is first ground, then mixed with sodium silicate solution to form a paste which can be molded and refired. Some of the most prominent artisans to use this procedure were Almaric Walter, Daum, Argy-Rousseau, and Decorchemont. See also specific manufacturers.

Scarab, gray mottled w/amethyst, sgn Decorchemont, 3x4½" 850.00
Skull mask, dull gray-gr, sgn Poetavera, 7½" 500.00
Vase, 12-panel, cvd geometrics, bubbles, Decorchemont, 7x6" ..4,600.00

Pate-Sur-Pate

Pate-sur-pate, literally paste-on-paste, is a technique whereby relief decorations are built up on a ceramic body by layering several applications of slip, one on the other, until the desired result is achieved. Usually only two colors are used, and the value of a piece is greatly enhanced as more color is added.

Charger, nymphs in water landscape, white on green, signed Schenck, gilt trim, George Jones, ca 1875, 12" diameter, $550.00.

Vase, From the Fight, bound winged male, L Solon, 1875, 7" 600.00
Vase, nymph at sunset, Schenck, hdls, 8⅛" 600.00

Pattern Glass

Pattern glass was the first mass-produced fancy tableware in America and was much prized by our ancestors. From the 1840s to the Civil War, it contained a high lead content and is known as 'Flint Glass.' It is exceptionally clear and resonant. Later glass was made with soda lime and is known as non-flint. By the 1890s pattern glass was produced in great volume in thousands of patterns, and colored glass came into vogue. Today the highest prices are often paid for these later patterns flashed with rose, amber, canary, and vaseline; stained ruby; or made in colors of cobalt, green, yellow, amethyst, etc. Demand for pattern glass declined by 1915, and glass fanciers were collecting it by 1930. No other field of antiques offers more diversity in patterns, prices, or pieces than this unique and historical glass that represents the Victorian era in America.

Our advisor for this category is Darlene Yohe; she is listed in the Directory under Arkansas. For a more thorough study on the subject, we recommend *The Collector's Encyclopedia of Pattern Glass*, by Mollie Helen McCain, available from Collector Books. See also Bread Plates; Cruets; Historical Glass; Salt and Pepper Shakers; Salts, Open; Sugar Shakers; Syrups; specific manufacturers such as Northwood.

Note: Values are given for open sugar bowls and compotes unless noted 'w/lid.'

Actress, bowl, ftd, 7" 55.00
Actress, compote, 11x6" 125.00
Actress, marmalade, w/lid 115.00
Actress, tray, dresser 65.00
Admiral Dewey, See Dewey; See Also Greentown Dewey
Alabama, butter dish, ruby stained 145.00
Alabama, jelly compote 62.50
Alabama, shakers, pr 60.00
Allover Diamond, decanter, 1-pt 48.00
Allover Diamond, egg cup 22.00
Allover Diamond, tumbler 15.00
Almond Thumbprint, butter dish, non-flint 42.50
Almond Thumbprint, punch bowl, non-flint 75.00
Almond Thumbprint, tumbler, ftd 38.00
Amazon, celery vase, etched 36.00
Amazon, champagne 32.50
Amazon, creamer 38.00
Amberette, See Klondike
Apollo, cake stand, etched, 9" 48.00
Apollo, salt cellar 20.00
Arched Ovals, butter dish, gr 48.00
Arched Ovals, pitcher, water; gr 42.50
Arched Ovals, punch cup 7.50
Arched Ovals, wine 15.00
Argus, champagne, flint 70.00
Argus, egg cup 25.00
Argus, mug, appl hdl 75.00
Art, butter dish, ruby stained 130.00
Art, goblet 65.00
Art, plate, 10" 40.00
Art, tumbler 32.50
Ashburton, egg cup, dbl 98.00
Ashburton, goblet 45.00
Ashburton, tumbler, ale; flint, 5" 87.50
Ashburton, whiskey, hdld, flint 95.00
Atlas, goblet, ruby stained 68.00
Atlas, marmalade jar 48.00
Atlas, tray, water 72.50
Atlas, tumbler 27.50
Aurora, goblet 32.00
Aurora, mug, hdls, ruby stained 62.50
Aurora, waste bowl 30.00
Aurora, wine, ruby stained 48.00
Austrian, butter dish, canary 325.00
Austrian, tumbler 22.50
Balder, See Pennsylvania
Baltimore Pear, creamer 30.00
Baltimore Pear, pitcher, water 98.00
Baltimore Pear, plate, 9" 37.50
Bar & Diamond, shakers, pr 55.00
Bar & Diamond, tumbler 22.50
Barberry, plate, bl, 6" 48.00
Barberry, sugar bowl, shell finial 42.50
Barley, celery vase 22.50
Barley, goblet 35.00
Barley, honey dish, ftd, 3½" 12.50
Barley, sugar bowl, w/lid 40.00
Barrel Huber, See Huber
Basket Weave, creamer, bl 32.00
Basket Weave, mug, 3" 20.00
Basket Weave, waste bowl, vaseline 27.50

Beaded Band, butter dish	38.00
Beaded Band, pitcher, water	78.00
Beaded Band, relish, sm	15.00
Beaded Grape, celery tray	35.00
Beaded Grape, sugar bowl, gr, w/lid	55.00
Beaded Grape, wine	32.00
Beaded Grape Medallion, goblet, buttermilk	32.00
Beaded Grape Medallion, honey dish, 3½"	12.50
Beaded Grape Medallion, relish, w/lid	150.00
Beaded Grape Medallion, tumbler, ftd	48.00
Beaded Medallion, butter dish	45.00
Beaded Medallion, pitcher, water	115.00
Beaded Mirror, See Beaded Medallion	
Beaded Swirl, compote, high std, emerald gr	48.00
Beaded Swirl, creamer, flat	25.00
Beaded Swirl, egg cup, emerald gr	15.00
Beaded Tulip, bowl, oval, 9½"	24.00
Beaded Tulip, plate, 6"	24.00
Bearded Head, See Viking	
Bellflower, cordial, knob stem	120.00
Bellflower, egg cup	40.00
Bellflower, tumbler, bar	85.00
Bigler, celery vase	90.00
Bigler, champagne	100.00
Bigler, decanter, bar lip, 1-pt	60.00
Bird & Strawberry, cake stand	55.00
Bird & Strawberry, goblet, color highlights	295.00
Bird & Strawberry, pitcher, water	240.00
Bird & Strawberry, sugar bowl	55.00
Bleeding Heart, creamer, molded hdl	32.00
Bleeding Heart, goblet, knob stem	32.50
Bleeding Heart, pitcher, water	100.00
Block & Fan, biscuit jar, ruby stained	145.00
Block & Fan, cake stand, 10"	45.00
Block & Fan, waste bowl	35.00
Blue Jay, See Cardinal Bird	

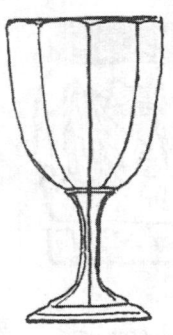

Bohemian

Bohemian, bowl, berry; boat shape, gr	55.00
Bohemian, mug, rose stained w/gold	80.00
Bow Tie, compote, 6½x8¼"	55.00
Bow Tie, goblet	65.00
Bow Tie, sugar bowl	37.50
Bow Tie, tumbler	60.00
Broken Column, banana stand	120.00
Broken Column, carafe	80.00
Broken Column, relish, oval, 11x5"	25.00
Buckle, salt cellar, flat, flint	32.50
Buckle, sugar bowl, w/lid, flint	95.00
Buckle w/Star, mustard jar, w/lid	80.00
Buckle w/Star, sauce bowl, flat, 4½"	12.00
Buckle w/Star, tumbler	55.00

Bull's Eye, carafe	50.00
Bull's Eye, cordial	78.00
Bull's Eye, mug, appl hdl, 3½"	100.00
Bull's Eye, salt cellar, ind	42.50
Bull's Eye, whiskey	78.00
Bull's Eye & Fan, custard cup	12.00
Bull's Eye & Fan, relish	22.50
Bull's Eye & Fan, sugar bowl, w/lid, amethyst stain	42.50
Bull's Eye & Fan, tumbler, pk stained	68.00
Bull's Eye Band, See Reverse Torpedo	
Bull's Eye in Heart, See Heart w/Thumbprint	
Bull's Eye w/Diamond Point, honey dish	35.00
Bull's Eye w/Diamond Point, wine	125.00
Button Arches, butter dish	58.00
Button Arches, pitcher, milk; ruby stained	110.00
Button Arches, plate, 7"	15.00
Button Arches, salt cellar, ruby stained	32.00
Button Band, bowl, 10"	32.00
Button Band, cordial	40.00
Button Band, wine	38.00
Cabbage Rose, butter dish	65.00
Cabbage Rose, champagne	48.00
Cabbage Rose, egg cup	42.00
Cabbage Rose, wine	40.00
Cable, champagne	235.00
Cable, goblet	90.00
Cable, tumbler, ftd	215.00
California, See Beaded Grape	
Cane, goblet, vaseline	42.00
Cane, spooner, apple gr	38.00
Cane, tray, water; bl	55.00
Cape Cod, bowl, hdls, 6"	38.00
Cape Cod, goblet	48.00
Cape Cod, pitcher, milk	60.00
Cape Cod, plate, 10"	45.00
Cape Cod, sauce dish, flat	18.00
Cape Cod, wine	36.00
Cardinal Bird, bowl, berry	68.00
Cardinal Bird, pitcher, water	160.00
Cardinal Bird, spooner	40.00
Cardinal Bird, sugar bowl, w/lid	60.00
Cathedral, bowl, bl, crimped rim	25.00
Cathedral, butter dish	45.00
Cathedral, relish tray, fish shape, vaseline	50.00
Cathedral, tumbler	25.00
Centennial, See Liberty Bell	
Chain, relish, 7½x5¼"	24.00
Chain, sugar bowl, w/lid	35.00
Chain & Shield, platter, oval	27.50
Chain w/Diamonds, See Washington Centennial	
Chain w/Star, creamer	27.50
Chain w/Star, goblet	28.00
Chain w/Star, jelly compote	18.00
Chain w/Star, pickle dish, oval	15.00
Chain w/Star, spooner	26.00
Chandelier, compote, high std, etched	88.00
Chandelier, salt cellar, master	32.00
Chandelier, tumbler, water; etched	42.50
Chandelier, violet bowl	42.50
Classic, butter dish, open log ft	245.00
Classic, creamer, collared base	120.00
Classic, goblet	285.00
Classic, plate, President Cleveland	185.00
Coin, See US Coin	

Colorado, custard cup, gr, lg 27.50
Colorado, mug 25.00
Colorado, plate, bl, 8" 72.50
Colorado, punch cup 17.50
Colorado, punch cup, gr 28.00
Columbian Coin, goblet, clear w/gold 62.50
Columbian Coin, mug, frosted coins 125.00
Columbian Coin, syrup, frosted coins 325.00
Columbian Coin, tumbler, gold coins 60.00
Comet, butter dish 195.00
Comet, goblet 88.00
Comet, whiskey, hdl 265.00
Compact, See Snail
Connecticut, celery vase 28.00
Connecticut, tumbler, lemonade; hdl 20.00
Cord & Tassel, goblet 38.00
Cord & Tassel, wine 45.00
Cord Drapery, pickle dish, amber 80.00
Cord Drapery, sugar bowl, gr, w/lid 185.00
Cord Drapery, wine 88.00
Cordova, finger bowl 20.00
Cordova, nappy, hdld, 6" 15.00
Cordova, pitcher, water 60.00
Cordova, punch cup 8.00
Cordova, tumbler 17.50
Cottage, champagne 75.00
Cottage, plate, 7" 22.50
Croesus, bowl, ftd, 4" 12.50
Croesus, bowl, gr, ftd, w/lid, 8" 125.00
Croesus, compote, amethyst, high std, w/lid, 7" 125.00
Croesus, pitcher, water; gr 200.00
Croesus, spooner 60.00
Croesus, sugar bowl, amethyst, w/lid 175.00
Crow's Foot, See Yale
Crown Jewels, See Chandelier
Crystal Wedding, creamer, etched 60.00
Crystal Wedding, nappy 27.50
Crystal Wedding, tumbler, ruby stained 48.00
Cube w/Fan, See Pineapple & Fan
Cupid & Venus, bowl, oval, 9" 35.00
Cupid & Venus, cake stand 55.00
Cupid & Venus, champagne 95.00
Cupid & Venus, cordial, 3½" 88.00
Cupid & Venus, marmalade 88.00
Cupid & Venus, spooner 35.00
Cupid & Venus, wine, 3¾" 85.00
Currant, goblet, buttermilk 22.50
Currant, relish 15.00
Currier & Ives, butter dish 60.00
Currier & Ives, pitcher, water; amber 140.00
Currier & Ives, saucer, bl 80.00
Currier & Ives, spooner 20.00
Currier & Ives, tray, 9½" dia 50.00
Currier & Ives, tumbler 42.50
Currier & Ives, wine, amber 50.00
Curtain, creamer 32.00
Curtain, sugar bowl, w/lid 40.00
Cut Log, cake stand, 10" 68.00
Cut Log, mug 22.50
Cut Log, salt cellar, master 68.00
Cut Log, tankard 75.00
Dahlia, bowl, bl 30.00
Dahlia, champagne, amber 75.00
Dahlia, creamer 20.00

Dahlia, pickle dish 22.50
Dahlia, plate, apple gr, 9" 35.00
Dahlia, sauce dish, flat of ftd 18.00
Dahlia, spooner, vaseline 57.50
Daisy & Button, bowl, amber, 9" 37.50
Daisy & Button, celery vase, bl 98.00
Daisy & Button, egg cup, bl 22.50
Daisy & Button, goblet, appl gr 48.00
Daisy & Button, match holder, vaseline 32.00
Daisy & Button, plate, bl, sq, 7" 22.00
Daisy & Button, sugar bowl, bl, w/lid 85.00
Daisy & Button, wine 28.00
Daisy & Button w/Crossbar, cake stand, bl 85.00
Daisy & Button w/Crossbar, goblet, amber 37.50
Daisy & Button w/Crossbar, wine 27.50
Daisy & Button w/Thumbprint Panels, cake stand 55.00
Daisy & Button w/Thumbprint Panels, goblet, amber stained 50.00
Daisy & Button w/Thumbprint Panels, shaker, amber stained 80.00
Daisy & Button w/V Ornament, butter dish, amber 82.50
Daisy & Button w/V Ornament, mug 25.00
Daisy & Button w/V Ornament, sherbet, vaseline 12.50
Daisy & Button w/V Ornament, toothpick holder, bl 42.50
Daisy & Button w/V Ornament, tumbler 15.00
Dakota, celery tray, clear 48.00
Dakota, compote, high std, 5" 65.00
Dakota, goblet, etched 38.00
Dakota, spooner, etched 35.00
Dakota, waste bowl, plain 47.50
Deer & Dog, creamer 20.00
Deer & Dog, sugar bowl, frosted dog finial 130.00
Deer & Dog, wine 80.00
Deer & Pine Tree, cake stand 125.00
Deer & Pine Tree, goblet 60.00
Deer & Pine Tree, mug, lg 40.00
Deer & Pine Tree, platter, 13x8" 62.50
Deer & Pine Tree, sugar bowl, w/lid 60.00

Delaware

Delaware, banana bowl, gr w/gold 60.00
Delaware, butter dish, rose w/gold 160.00
Delaware, creamer 50.00
Delaware, tumbler, gr w/gold 42.50
Dew & Raindrop, bud vase, 6" 27.50
Dew & Raindrop, punch cup 9.00
Dewey, creamer, w/lid 48.00
Dewey, parfait 48.00
Dewey, See Also Greentown, Dewey
Dewey, tumbler 48.00
Diagonal Band, cake stand 40.00
Diagonal Band, creamer 32.00
Diagonal Band, wine 25.00
Diamond Horseshoe, See Aurora
Diamond Medallion, See Grand
Diamond Point, spill holder, flint 50.00

Diamond Point, spill holder, gold rim, flint 125.00
Diamond Point, whiskey, hdl, flint 88.00
Diamond Quilted, creamer, amber 40.00
Diamond Quilted, relish, vaseline, leaf shape, 8" 15.00
Diamond Quilted, tumbler, amber 32.50
Diamond Thumbprint, ale glass, 6" 98.00
Diamond Thumbprint, butter dish 215.00
Diamond Thumbprint, compote, low std, 8" 70.00
Diamond Thumbprint, finger bowl 110.00
Diamond Thumbprint, pitcher, milk 465.00
Dinner Bell, See Cottage
Doric, See Feather
Double Leaf & Dart, See Leaf & Dart
Drapery, butter dish 42.50
Drapery, goblet 27.50
Drapery, pitcher, water; appl hdl 78.00
Egg in Sand, creamer 28.00
Egg in Sand, relish 12.50
Egyptian, butter dish 80.00
Egyptian, pickle dish 22.50
Egyptian, plate, 12" 88.00
Egyptian, sauce bowl, ftd 17.50
Egyptian, spooner 18.00
Elephant, See Jumbo
Emerald Green Herringbone, See Florida
Empress, celery vase 60.00
Empress, pitcher, water; gr w/gold 165.00
Empress, tumbler 35.00
Empress, tumbler, gr w/gold 50.00
Esther, cake stand, gr 110.00
Esther, celery vase, gr 100.00
Esther, cracker jar, ruby stained 215.00
Esther, creamer, gr 120.00
Esther, goblet 55.00
Esther, plate, ruby stained, 10" 75.00
Esther, tumbler, gr 88.00
Etched Dakota, See Dakota
Eureka, tumbler 28.00
Eureka, wine 32.00
Excelsior, cordial 45.00
Excelsior, pickle jar, w/lid 50.00
Eyewinker, banana stand 130.00
Eyewinker, butter dish 65.00
Eyewinker, celery vase, 6½" 60.00
Eyewinker, goblet 32.00
Eyewinker, sugar bowl, w/lid 55.00
Fairfax Strawberry, See Strawberry
Feather, butter dish 68.00
Feather, cordial 120.00
Feather, creamer, gr 75.00
Feather, honey dish 15.00
Feather, pickle dish 18.00
Feather, tumbler, gr 88.00
Festoon, marmalade 35.00
Festoon, plate, 8" 40.00
Fine Cut, cake stand 38.00
Fine Cut, plate, 10" 20.00
Fine Cut & Block, cordial 65.00
Fine Cut & Block, goblet, pk blocks 50.00
Fine Cut & Diamond, See Grand
Fine Cut & Feather, See Feather
Fine Cut & Panel, butter dish, vaseline 75.00
Fine Cut & Panel, cake stand, amber, 10" 60.00
Fine Cut & Panel, plate, amber, 6" 25.00

Fine Cut & Panel, plate, vaseline, 6" 22.50
Fine Cut & Panel, spooner 12.00
Fine Rib, egg cup, dbl, flint 36.00
Fine Rib, goblet, flint 78.00
Fine Rib, whiskey, bl, flint 120.00
Fingerprint, See Almond Thumbprint
Fishscale, celery vase 32.50
Fishscale, creamer 25.00
Flamingo Habitat, compote, w/lid, 6½" 98.00
Flamingo Habitat, goblet 35.00
Flamingo Habitat, tumbler 32.00
Flamingo Habitat, wine 45.00

Florida

Florida, bowl, gr, 7¾" 20.00
Florida, nappy 15.00
Florida, plate, 7½" 12.00
Florida, relish, 6" 12.50
Florida, tumbler, gr 42.00
Flower Pot, creamer, vaseline 90.00
Flower Pot, goblet 45.00
Flute, claret 25.00
Flute, whiskey, hdld 62.50
Frosted Circle, plate, 7" 22.50
Frosted Circle, wine 42.50
Frosted Leaf, celery vase 125.00
Frosted Leaf, goblet 120.00
Frosted Lion, See Lion
Frosted Ribbon, See Ribbon
Frosted Roman Key, champagne, flint 80.00
Frosted Roman Key, goblet, flint 55.00
Frosted Roman Key, sugar bowl, w/lid 85.00
Frosted Stork, sauce bowl 30.00
Frosted Stork, tray, 15⅛x11" 98.00
Galloway, butter dish 65.00
Galloway, goblet 60.00
Galloway, olive dish 22.00
Galloway, pitcher, milk; clear w/gold 65.00
Galloway, punch cup 12.50
Garfield Drape, goblet 40.00
Garfield Drape, pitcher, water 105.00
Garfield Drape, spooner 32.00
Gem, See Nailhead
Georgia, bonbon 28.00
Georgia, cake stand, 10" 55.00
Georgia, creamer 35.00
Georgia, spooner 35.00
Georgia, tumbler 32.50
Good Luck, See Horseshoe
Grand, goblet 32.00
Grand, pitcher, water 45.00
Grand, spooner 20.00

Grape & Festoon w/Shield, mug, 1⅞" 20.00
Grape & Festoon w/Shield, pitcher, water 75.00
Grape & Festoon w/Stippled Leaf, relish 18.00
Grape & Festoon w/Stippled Leaf, wine 45.00
Grasshopper, butter dish, amber 100.00
Grasshopper, salt cellar 50.00
Grasshopper, spooner, w/insect 55.00
Greek Key, pitcher, tankard, 1½-qt 245.00
Greek Key, punch cup 18.00
Greek Key, tumbler 80.00
Guardian Angel, See Cupid & Venus
Hairpin, champagne, flint 75.00
Hairpin, tumbler 55.00
Halley's Comet, creamer 42.00
Halley's Comet, tumbler 27.50
Hamilton, butter dish 70.00
Hamilton, egg cup 45.00
Hamilton, goblet, flint 55.00
Hand, butter dish 95.00
Hand, honey dish 15.00
Hand, tumbler 88.00
Hawaiian Lei, cup & saucer 40.00
Heart w/Thumbprint, finger bowl 42.50
Heart w/Thumbprint, shaker, orig top 48.50
Heart w/Thumbprint, wine, gr w/gold 140.00
Herringbone Band, See Ripple
Herringbone Buttress, See Greentown, Herringbone Buttress
Hickman, creamer, gr 38.00
Hickman, goblet 42.00
Hidalgo, goblet, frosted 24.00
Hidalgo, sugar bowl, w/lid 45.00
Hidalgo, tumbler 27.50
Hinoto, egg cup 40.00
Hinoto, wine 65.00
Holly, cake stand, 11" 135.00
Holly, pitcher, water 235.00
Holly, sugar bowl, w/lid 130.00
Holly Amber, See Greentown, Holly Amber
Honeycomb, butter dish, non-flint, clear w/gold 80.00
Honeycomb, champagne, flint 45.00
Honeycomb, honey dish, w/lid, non-flint 24.00
Honeycomb, mug, flint 30.00
Hops & Barley, See Wheat & Barley
Horn of Plenty, butter pat, flint 24.00
Horn of Plenty, champagne, flint 225.00
Horn of Plenty, decanter, flint, 1-qt 500.00
Horn of Plenty, plate, flint, 6" 110.00
Horn of Plenty, wine, flint 125.00
Horseshoe, bowl, oval, 9x6" 32.00
Horseshoe, cake stand 100.00
Horseshoe, creamer 45.00
Horseshoe, wine 300.00
Huber, celery vase 38.00
Huber, egg cup 30.00
Hummingbird, creamer 48.00
Hummingbird, tray, water 50.00
Hummingbird, wine 95.00
Idaho, See Snail
Illinois, finger bowl 25.00
Illinois, pitcher, water; sq 75.00
Illinois, plate, sq, 7" 27.50
Illinois, relish 15.00
Illinois, vase, emerald gr, 9½" 132.00
Iowa, decanter 38.00

Iowa, olive dish 18.00
Iowa, pitcher, water 50.00
Iris w/Meander, See Opalescent Glass
Ivy in Snow, creamer 22.00
Ivy in Snow, mug, ruby stained 48.00
Jacob's Ladder, compote, 5x10" 45.00
Jacob's Ladder, creamer 35.00
Jacob's Ladder, marmalade 10.00
Jersey Swirl, butter dish, bl 70.00
Jersey Swirl, salt cellar, canary 24.00
Jewel Band, pitcher, milk 48.00
Jewel w/Dewdrop, bowl, 7½" 24.00
Jewel w/Dewdrop, mug, 3½" 35.00
Jewel w/Dewdrop, sugar bowl, w/lid 65.00
Jewel w/Festoon, creamer 27.50
Jewel w/Festoon, sauce bowl 12.50
Jewel w/Moondrop, cake plate 55.00
Jewel w/Moondrop, tumbler 42.50
Jewelled Moon & Star, butter dish 70.00
Jewelled Moon & Star, platter 45.00
Job's Tears, See Art
Jumbo, butter dish, frosted elephant finial 675.00
Jumbo, creamer 165.00
Jumbo, goblet 695.00

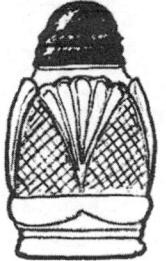

Kentucky

Kentucky, cup, gr 22.50
Kentucky, plate, sq, 7" 15.00
Kentucky, punch cup, gr 20.00
Kentucky, spooner 35.00
Kentucky, wine, gr 40.00
King's Crown, banana stand, ftd, ruby stained 150.00
King's Crown, compote, high standard, 8" 65.00
King's Crown, cordial 30.00
King's Crown, goblet, ruby stained 55.00
King's Crown, sugar bowl, 2¾" 32.00
King's Crown, tumbler, ruby stained 37.50
Klondike, celery vase, amber stained 140.00
Klondike, sauce dish, amber stain 75.00
Klondike, tumbler, amber stained 140.00
La Clede, See Hickman
Lace, See Drapery
Lawrence, See Bull's Eye
Leaf, See Maple Leaf
Leaf & Dart, pitcher, milk 140.00
Leaf & Dart, wine 28.00
Leaf Bracket, See Greentown, Leaf Bracket
Leaf Medallion, See Northwood, Leaf Medallion
Liberty Bell, bowl, ftd, 8" 100.00
Liberty Bell, compote, 8" 75.00
Liberty Bell, mug, mini 120.00
Liberty Bell, plate, closed hdls, 6" 78.00
Lily of the Valley, champagne 37.50
Lily of the Valley, honey dish 12.50

Lily of the Valley, pitcher, milk 95.00
Lincoln Drape, egg cup 70.00
Lincoln Drape, sugar bowl, w/lid, flint 120.00
Lion, butter dish, rampart finial 135.00
Lion, champagne 195.00
Lion, compote, low std, 8" 82.50
Lion, creamer 78.00
Log Cabin, butter dish 315.00
Log Cabin, creamer, 4½" 125.00
Log Cabin, pitcher, water 350.00
Long Spear, See Grasshopper
Loop, butter dish, flint 200.00
Loop, creamer, flint 38.00
Loop, goblet, flint 22.50
Loop, vase, flint, 9⅜" 80.00
Loop & Dart, goblet 35.00
Loop & Dart, spooner 35.00
Loop & Dart, sugar bowl, w/lid 45.00
Loop w/Stippled Panels, See Texas
Maine, cake stand, gr 60.00
Maine, mug 37.50
Maine, pitcher, water 100.00
Maine, tumbler, gr 50.00
Manhattan, creamer, ind 25.00
Manhattan, salt shaker, orig top 28.00
Maple Leaf, bowl, oval, ftd, 6x10" 60.00
Maple Leaf, tumbler 37.50
Maryland, bowl, berry; ruby stained 40.00
Maryland, celery vase 32.00
Maryland, plate, clear w/gold, 7" 30.00
Mascotte, cheese dish 67.50
Massachusetts, goblet 45.00
Massachusetts, pitcher, water 70.00
Medallion, cake stand, amber 50.00
Medallion, relish, amber, 7x5" 22.50
Medallion, sugar bowl, amber, w/lid 45.00

Melrose

Melrose, compote, 5¾x7½" 27.50
Melrose, wine 20.00
Michigan, butter dish, bl stained 185.00
Michigan, goblet 37.50
Michigan, relish, pk stained 22.50
Michigan, vase, 6" 18.00
Minerva, compote, 8½x8" 90.00
Minerva, honey dish 20.00
Minnesota, bonbon, 5" 17.50
Minnesota, goblet, ruby stained 55.00
Minnesota, nappy, 4½" 15.00
Minnesota, pitcher, tankard, ruby stained 215.00
Minor Block, See Mascotte
Mirror, See Galloway
Missouri, bowl, w/lid, 8" 55.00

Missouri, cordial, gr 60.00
Missouri, goblet 55.00
Missouri, mug, gr 48.00
Missouri, tumbler, gr 36.00
Moon & Star, champagne 70.00
Moon & Star, claret 45.00
Moon & Star, compote, high std, w/lid, 10" 70.00
Moon & Star, egg cup, flint 40.00
Morning Glory, champagne, flint 385.00
Morning Glory, wine, flint 95.00
Nail, decanter 37.50
Nail, pitcher, water 85.00
Nailhead, bowl, 6" 18.00
Nailhead, spooner 20.00
Nailhead, wine 38.00
Nestor, sauce dish, gr w/HP decor 40.00
Nestor, tumbler, gr 32.00
New England Pineapple, creamer, flint 275.00
New England Pineapple, pitcher, water 325.00
New England Pineapple, tumbler, gr 40.00
New Jersey, carafe, water 80.00
New Jersey, goblet 42.50
New Jersey, sauce bowl, ruby stained 30.00
O'Hara Diamond, bowl, berry, sm 12.00
O'Hara Diamond, cup & saucer, ruby stained 62.50
O'Hara Diamond, goblet 28.00
O'Hara Diamond, plate, 7" 22.00
O'Hara Diamond, tumbler 28.00
One Hundred & One, butter dish 65.00
One Hundred & One, goblet 50.00
One Hundred & One, sugar bowl, w/lid 48.00
One-O-One, See One Hundred & One
Oregon #1, bread plate 35.00
Oregon #1, mug 37.50
Oregon #1, relish 48.00
Oregon #1, tumbler 30.00
Orion, See Cathedral
Palmette, goblet 38.00
Palmette, sauce bowl, flat, 4" 17.50
Panelled Daisy, celery vase 36.00
Panelled Daisy, plate, sq, 9" 28.00
Panelled Forget-Me-Not, butter dish 45.00
Panelled Forget-Me-Not, mustard jar 42.50
Panelled Forget-Me-Not, spooner 27.50
Panelled Star & Button, salt cellar, master 15.00
Panelled Thistle, basket 75.00
Panelled Thistle, pitcher, milk 65.00
Panelled Thistle, rose bowl, 2¾x5" 45.00
Panelled Thistle, sugar bowl, w/lid 42.50
Pavonia, butter dish, ruby stained, flat, etched 135.00
Pavonia, creamer, eng 40.00
Pavonia, pitcher, lemonade 115.00
Pavonia, waste bowl, ruby stained 60.00
Pennsylvania, biscuit jar, gr 135.00
Pennsylvania, compote, jelly, high std 55.00
Pennsylvania, relish 10.00
Pennsylvania, tumbler, juice 12.50
Pigmy, see Torpedo
Pillow Encircled, sauce dish 12.50
Pillow Encircled, tumbler 30.00
Pineapple & Fan, tumbler, water; gr 58.00
Pineapple & Fan, vase, trumpet form, 10" 32.00
Pineapple Stem, See Pavonia
Pioneer, See Westward Ho

Pleat & Panel, cake stand, sq, 10" 65.00
Pleat & Panel, goblet 35.00
Plume, celery vase 35.00
Plume, sugar bowl 22.50
Polar Bear, goblet 100.00
Polar Bear, waste bowl 90.00
Popcorn, celery vase 20.00
Popcorn, wine 32.00
Portland, celery tray 20.00
Portland, jam jar, clear w/gold, SP lid 42.00
Portland, wine 25.00
Powder & Shot, egg cup, flint 60.00
Powder & Shot, honey dish, flint 12.50
Prayer Rug, See Horseshoe
Pressed Leaf, spooner 22.50
Pressed Leaf, sugar bowl, w/lid 45.00
Primrose, pickle dish 25.00
Primrose, plate, amber, 7" 20.00
Primrose, tray, water; 11" dia 32.00
Princess Feather, creamer 40.00
Princess Feather, goblet 45.00
Priscilla, creamer, ind 25.00
Priscilla, syrup, orig pewter lid 135.00
Psyche & Cupid, celery vase 30.00
Psyche & Cupid, creamer 65.00
Question Mark, bowl, oblong, 7" 20.00
Question Mark, celery vase 30.00
Question Mark, tumbler 20.00
Recessed Pillared Red Top, See Nail
Red Block, cheese dish 132.50
Red Block, goblet 36.00
Red Block, mug 57.50
Red Block, pitcher, water; 8" 165.00
Red Top, See Button Arches
Reverse Torpedo, cake stand, high std 88.00
Reverse Torpedo, goblet 90.00
Reverse Torpedo, tumbler 32.00
Ribbed Ivy, butter dish 90.00
Ribbed Ivy, egg cup 40.00
Ribbed Palm, champagne, flint 78.00
Ribbed Palm, wine, flint 75.00

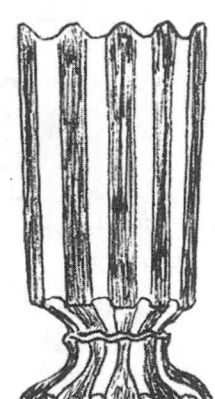

Ribbon

Ribbon, dresser bottle, w/stopper 110.00
Ribbon, platter, 13" 55.00
Ribbon Candy, butter dish, ftd 60.00
Ribbon Candy, creamer 32.00
Ribbon Candy, goblet 92.50
Ribbon Candy, sugar bowl, w/lid 45.00

Ripple, ice tub 55.00
Ripple, wine 35.00
Ripple Band, See Ripple
Rochelle, See Princess Feather
Roman Rosette, butter dish 50.00
Roman Rosette, shakers, pr 35.00
Rose in Snow, bottles, bitters; orig stopper 110.00
Rose in Snow, creamer, sq 40.00
Rose in Snow, mug, bl, lg 120.00
Rose in Snow, pitcher, water 125.00
Rose in Snow, pitcher, water; amber 160.00
Rose Sprig, pitcher, milk 45.00
Rose Sprig, relish boat, bl 22.00
Rose Sprig, wine 32.00
Rosette, jelly compote 20.00
Rosette, plate, 7" 17.50
Royal Ivy, See Northwood
Royal Oak, See Northwood
Ruby Thumbprint, See King's Crown
S-Repeat, tumbler, amethyst 42.50
S-Repeat, wine, gr 45.00
Sandwich Star, compote, low std, 8½" 62.50
Sandwich Star, decanter, bar lip, 1-pt 75.00
Sawtooth, champagne, knob stem, flint 60.00
Sawtooth, egg cup, non-flint 27.50
Sawtooth, goblet, flint 60.00
Sawtooth, tumbler, bar; non-flint 25.00
Sawtooth, wine, knob stem, non-flint 22.50
Sawtooth Band, See Amazon
Scalloped Daisy Red Top, See Button Arches
Scroll w/Flowers, sugar bowl, w/lid 55.00
Sedan, See Panelled Star & Button
Seneca Loop, See Loop
Shell & Jewel, pitcher, milk; bl 78.00
Shell & Jewel, sugar bowl, w/lid 45.00
Shell & Jewel, tumbler, amber 36.00
Shell & Tassel, creamer, sq 60.00
Shell & Tassel, oyster dish 225.00
Sheraton, relish, hdld, bl 22.50
Sheraton, wine 22.00
Shoshone, mug 25.00
Shoshone, spooner, amber 48.00
Shuttle, mug, amber 325.00
Shuttle, tumbler 48.00
Skilton, pitcher, water 50.00
Skilton, relish 18.00
Snail, bowl, ruby stained, 10" 55.00
Snail, custard cup 30.00
Snail, sauce bowl 16.00
Snail, wine 68.00
Spades, See Medallion
Spirea Band, butter dish 50.00
Spirea Band, creamer 25.00
Spirea Band, goblet, vaseline 38.00
Spirea Band, spooner, vaseline 32.50
Sprig, compote, high std, w/lid 68.00
Sprig, pickle dish 18.00
Sprig, sugar bowl 48.00
Sprig, tumbler 28.00
Sprig, wine 38.00
Star & Feather, creamer 35.00
Star & Feather, plate, amber, 7" 18.00
Star Rosetted, plate, 7" 12.00
Stars & Stripes, creamer 22.50

Stars & Stripes, wine 17.50
States, goblet, clear w/gold 38.00
States, nappy, hdls, clear w/gold 25.00
Stedman, spooner 17.50
Stippled Chain, egg cup 30.00
Stippled Chain, goblet 24.00
Stippled Forget-Me-Not, cup & saucer 40.00
Stippled Forget-Me-Not, sugar bowl, w/lid 40.00
Stippled Grape & Festoon, compote, low std, 8" 42.50
Stippled Grape & Festoon, goblet 35.00
Stippled Ivy, egg cup 28.00
Stippled Ivy, sugar bowl, w/lid 38.00
Stippled Panelled Flower, See Maine
Strawberry, spooner 35.00
Strawberry, wine 100.00
Strigil, bowl, flared rim, 9" 30.00
Strigil, punch cup 15.00
Sunk Honeycomb, goblet, ruby stained 47.50
Sunk Honeycomb, pitcher, water; ruby stained 88.00
Sunken Primrose, See Florida
Swan, mustard, amber 75.00
Swan, sugar bowl, w/lid 195.00
Tarentem's Thumbprint, pitcher, water; etched 45.00
Teardrop & Tassel, compote, 6" 30.00
Teardrop & Tassel, creamer 42.50
Teardrop & Tassel, See Also Greentown, Teardrop & Tassel
Tennessee, butter dish 58.00
Tennessee, cake stand, 9½" 40.00
Tennessee, goblet 42.50
Tennessee, mug 38.00
Texas, celery tray, rose stained 55.00
Texas, horseradish 45.00
Texas, vase, 6½" 27.50
Texas, wine, ruby stained 115.00
Theatrical, See Actress
Thousand Eye, cordial, gr 58.00
Thousand Eye, egg cup, bl 62.50
Thousand Eye, nappy, vaseline, 5" 48.00
Thousand Eye, plate, sq, 10" 27.50
Thousand Eye, plate, 10" 35.00
Three Face, cake stand 145.00
Three Face, celery vase 125.00
Three Face, champagne, saucer type 150.00
Three Face, claret, eng 260.00
Three Face, goblet, eng 135.00
Three Face, salt cellar 45.00
Three Face, sauce dish 25.00
Three Face, spooner 80.00
Three Face, sugar bowl, vaseline, w/lid 65.00
Three Panel, butter dish, vaseline 57.50
Three Panel, celery vase, amber, ruffled rim 58.00
Three Panel, goblet, bl 42.50
Three Panel, sugar bowl, bl, w/lid 55.00
Thumbprint, See Argus
Thumbprint Band, See Dakota
Thunderbird, See Hummingbird
Torpedo, cup & saucer 58.00
Torpedo, jelly compote, w/lid 40.00
Torpedo, pitcher, milk, 8½" 95.00
Torpedo, salt cellar, master 47.50
Tree of Life, See Portland
Tree of Life w/Hand, cake stand, frosted base, 11½" 88.00
Tree of Life w/Hand, spooner 38.00
Triangular Prism, spooner, flint 55.00

Tulip w/Sawtooth, creamer, flint 88.00
Tulip w/Sawtooth, goblet, flint 65.00
Two Panel, bowl, bl, oval, 7¾" 27.50
Two Panel, goblet, amber 30.00
Two Panel, pitcher, water; gr 65.00
US Coin, butter dish, frosted 475.00
US Coin, cake stand, frosted 435.00
US Coin, creamer, clear 365.00
US Coin, cruet, frosted 525.00
US Coin, epergne, clear 1,100.00
US Coin, epergne, frosted 700.00
US Coin, pickle dish, clear 215.00
US Coin, sugar bowl, clear, w/lid 235.00
US Coin, syrup, frosted 350.00
US Coin, toothpick holder, clear 200.00
US Coin, tumbler, ale; clear 265.00
US Coin, tumbler, frosted 225.00
US Coin, waste bowl, clear 235.00
Utah, compote, high std, w/lid, 6" 50.00
Utah, creamer 32.00
Utah, tumbler 17.50
Valencia Waffle, goblet, bl 32.00
Valencia Waffle, relish, amber, 9x5⅜" 22.50
Vermont, goblet, gr w/gold 52.50
Vermont, pitcher, water; gr w/gold 130.00
Viking, bowl, sq, 8" 48.00
Viking, compote, low std, w/lid, 9" 110.00
Viking, egg cup 40.00
Viking, spooner 28.00
Waffle, egg cup, flint 45.00
Waffle, sugar bowl, flint, w/lid 98.00
Waffle & Thumbprint, tumbler, whiskey; flint 95.00
Washington, cordial 145.00
Washington, goblet 115.00
Washington, wine 120.00

Washington Centennial

Washington Centennial, butter dish, ftd 100.00
Washington Centennial, egg cup 42.50
Wedding Bells, goblet 45.00
Wedding Ring, sugar bowl, w/lid 80.00
Wedding Ring, tumbler 82.50
Westward Ho, compote, high std, 8" 135.00
Westward Ho, marmalade, w/lid 188.00
Westward Ho, platter, 13" 165.00
Wheat & Barley, pitcher, water; amber 80.00
Wheat & Barley, shakers, pr 40.00
Wildflower, bowl, vaseline, sq, 8" 25.00
Wildflower, creamer, bl 37.50

Wildflower, relish, gr	27.50
Wildflower, tumbler, amber	42.50
Willow Oak, butter dish, bl	75.00
Willow Oak, creamer	35.00
Windflower, creamer	38.00
Windflower, sugar bowl, w/lid	55.00
Wisconsin, banana stand	72.50
Wisconsin, cup & saucer	48.00
Wisconsin, goblet	70.00
Wisconsin, relish	28.00
Wooden Pail, pitcher	100.00
Wooden Pail, sugar bowl, amethyst, mini	24.00
Wyoming, creamer	48.00
Wyoming, mug	40.00
X-Ray, marmalade, gr w/gold	75.00
X-Ray, rose bowl, emerald gr w/gold	70.00
Yale, compote, high std, w/lid	60.00
Yale, sugar bowl, w/lid	45.00
Yale, tumbler	20.00
Zipper, butter dish	42.50
Zipper, creamer	50.00
Zipper, spooner	20.00
Zipper, wine, ruby stained	40.00

Paul Revere Pottery

The Saturday Evening Girls were a social group of young Boston ladies who met to pursue various activities, among them pottery making. Their first kiln was bought in 1906, and within a few years it became necessary to move to a larger location. Because their new quarters were near the historical Old North Church, they chose the name Paul Revere Pottery. With very little training, the girls produced only simple ware. Until 1915 the pottery operated at a deficit; then a new building with four kilns was constructed on Nottingham Road. Vases, miniature jugs, children's tea sets, tiles, dinnerware, and lamps were produced, usually in soft matt glazes often decorated with incised, hand-painted designs from nature. Examples in a dark high gloss may also be found on occasion.

Several marks were used: 'P.R.P.'; 'S.E.G.'; or the circular device, 'Boston, Paul Revere Pottery' with the horse and rider.

The pottery continued to operate; and even though their product sold well, the high production costs of the handmade ware caused the pottery to fail in 1946.

Pitcher, rooster band above a second band with an inscribed verse, black and white on turquoise, SEG, #103, indistinct signature, 9¾", $2,200.00.

Bookends, sqs/geometrics/initials, SEG, 4x5x2½"	375.00
Bowl, rose feathered matt w/lt lustre, SEG, 3½x10"	150.00
Bowl, rosettes band on speckled bl, SEG/FL/#53, 1½x4¾"	300.00
Bowl, tortoise/hare band on bl/gr, Race Is Not to..., 5½"	2,400.00

Bowl, tree band, 5-color on bl, SEG/b-21/FL, 2½x6½"	1,000.00
Bowl, 3 little pigs on path, house, SEG/EG/1912, 2½x5½"	850.00
Box, sailing ship, brn/gr on gr/yel/bl, PRP, 1923, 4" dia	550.00
Candlestick, dk bl gloss, PRP, 6½"	175.00
Candlestick, gr, SEG, 6½"	95.00
Chamberstick, dk bl lustre, ribbed aqua int, PRP, 7½"	175.00
Chocolate pot, hen medallion, mc/bl, bl bands, SEG, rstr, 9"	650.00
Cup & saucer, demitasse; lotus band on buttercup, SEG, 2", 5"	275.00
Cup & saucer, lotus band on wht, 2½", 6", NM	230.00
Demitasse pot, lilies, wht/blk on yel/wht, SEG, +8 c/s, VG	600.00
Egg cup, chicks, yel on bl band on oatmeal, SEG, 1½"	170.00
Inkwell, tree scene on bl, sq, SEG, 2x3x3"	425.00
Jar, lotus band on ivory, blk-lined band on lid, SEG, 4¾x3"	400.00
Jar, swan/royal bl band on ivory, protruding top, SEG, 4½"	650.00
Jar, tree band, brn/wht/blk on mustard, SEG/FL 5-19, +plate	450.00
Nut dish, squirrel band on ivory, SEG/JG/1914, 3" dia	500.00
Paperweight, ship, brn/yel on dk bl octagon, SEG, EX	325.00
Pitcher, geese on navy band on wht, SEG, 5x3"	260.00
Pitcher, swans/lotus band on lt gr, SEG, 2¾"	490.00
Pitcher, tree scene band on tan, SEG, 4¼x4½"	425.00
Pitcher, tulip band, orange/brn/bl-gr on bl-gr, PRP, 7x7"	865.00
Plate, tulips on cream, geometric border, SEG, 6"	275.00
Plates, blk-lined wht rim band on steel bl, SEG, 7½", set of 4	150.00
Tea set, frothy wht blk-lined band on bl-gray, 15-pc	550.00
Tea set, yel matt, 6 c/s, 6 bread plates, PRP, sm rpr	225.00
Tile, bl, sq PRP, 5¼"	175.00
Tile, tree/mtn range, mc, PRP, 1938, 5¾x5¾"	345.00
Tile, Viking ship, mc, octagonal, SEG/SB/1916, 2½"	650.00
Tile, windmill on mustard yel, octagonal, SEG, 2½"	290.00
Trivet, tree band on bl, SEG/RL, 5½" dia	600.00
Trivet, tree reserve on bl w/blk banding, PRP, 1925, 6" dia	400.00
Trivet, tree scene, yel perimeter, PRP, 4½" dia	425.00
Trivet, wht swan, yel/bl sky on dk bl, 5½" dia	450.00
Trivet, wht w/bl rim outlined in blk, SEG/JL/5-19, 4¼"	100.00
Vase, Arts & Crafts band on rose, PRP, 4½x4"	900.00
Vase, blk lustre w/sponge texture, PRP, 4¾"	150.00
Vase, drip glaze in shades of bl, experimental, PRP, 7x5"	200.00
Vase, feathered steel gray, ivory int, SEG/RB/1917, 9x11"	450.00
Vase, lt bl, bulbous, PRP, 4¼x5"	70.00
Vase, scenic band on bl-gr, PRP, 1926, 9x4"	1,380.00
Vase, speckled/feathered dk bl over gray-bl lustre, PRP, 6¾"	175.00
Vase, tulip band, wht/bl w/blk outlines on gr, U-form, 5x4"	375.00

Pauline Pottery

Pauline Pottery was made from 1883 to 1888 in Chicago, Illinois, from clay imported from the Ohio area. Its founder was Mrs. Pauline Jacobus, who had learned the trade at the Rookwood Pottery. Mrs. Jacobus moved to Edgerton, Wisconsin, to be near a source of suitable clay, thus eliminating shipping expenses. Until 1905 she produced high-quality wares, able to imitate with ease designs and styles of such masters as Wedgwood and Meissen. Her products were sold through leading department stores, and the names of some of these firms may appear on the ware. Not all were marked; unless signed by a noted local artist, positive identification is often impossible. Marked examples carry a variety of stamps and signatures: 'Trade Mark' with a crown, 'Pauline Pottery,' and 'Edgerton Art Pottery' are but a few.

Bowl, wild roses w/gold, 3 lobes & hdls, 10x3¼", NM	995.00
Jar, swirling flower bands, mc/mustard on teal w/gold, 7", NM	350.00
Teapot, floral, gold trim, EX	450.00
Vase, ivory w/bl & gold arabesque decor, 5"	425.00

Peachblow

Peachblow, made to imitate the colors of the Chinese Peachbloom porcelain, was made by several glasshouses in the late 1800s. Among them were New England Glass; Mt. Washington; Webb; and Hobbs, Brockunier and Company (Wheeling). Its pink shading was achieved through action of the heat on the gold content of the glass. While New England's peachblow shades from deep crimson to white, Mt. Washington's tends to shade from pink to blue-gray. Many pieces were enameled and gilded. While by far the majority of the pieces made by New England had a satin (acid) finish, they made shiny peachblow as well. Wheeling glass, on the other hand, is rarely found in satin. In the 1950s Gundersen-Pairpoint Glassworks initiated the reproduction of Mt. Washington peachblow using an exact duplication of the original formula. Though of recent manufacture, this glass is very collectible. Our advisors for this category are Betty and Clarence Maier; they are listed in the Directory under Pennsylvania.

Bowl, Mt WA, floral, yel/wht w/gr vines, shallow, 6" 3,100.00
Bowl, Webb, gold prunus & butterfly, triangular top, 6x3" 295.00
Creamer, NE Glass, 12-rib, wht hdl, 1893 WF, 3¼" 550.00
Cruet, Wheeling, faceted amber stopper, petticoat form, 6" ...1,300.00
Cup, punch; Wheeling, amber loop hdl, acid, 2¼" 200.00
Finger bowl, Mt WA, daisies/leaves, scalloped gilt rim, 4½" ..4,200.00
Finger bowl, Mt WA, ruffled, acid, 2½x5¾" 1,200.00
Mustard pot, Wheeling, silver hinged lid, 2¾" 600.00
Pear, NE Glass, w/stem, 4½" L 135.00
Pitcher, Mt WA, tankard, acid, 7" 5,000.00
Pitcher, NE Glass, tankard, 8" 1,550.00
Pitcher, Sandwich, amber reeded hdl, crimped rim, acid, 8" 325.00
Pitcher, Stevens & Wms, gr rigaree & leaves, reeded hdl, 9" 875.00
Pitcher, Wheeling, amber hdl, sqd mouth, 4¾" 800.00
Pitcher, Wheeling, amber loop hdl, ind, 3" 500.00
Pitcher, Wheeling, Drape, sq mouth, clear reeded hdl, 4½" 300.00
Pitcher, Wheeling, sq top, amber hdl, 8x7" 2,200.00
Pitcher, Wheeling, tankard, amber hdl, acid, 9" 1,650.00
Plate, Gundersen, acid, 8" 375.00
Rose bowl, NE Glass, 7-crimp, 2½x2¾" 300.00
Rose bowl, World's Fair 1893 in gold, acid, 2½" 375.00
Shaker, NE Glass, Wild Rose, dents in lid, 4" 945.00
Shaker, Wheeling, bulbous, acid, 2½" 425.00
Spittoon, NE Glass, lady's, shiny, 2¾x5¼" 750.00
Spooner, NE Glass, sq top 700.00
Stocking darner, NE Glass, 5½" 150.00
Toothpick holder, NE Glass, sq top, 2¼" 550.00
Toothpick holder, NE Glass, tricornered 750.00
Tumbler, Mt WA, acid, 4" 1,250.00
Tumbler, NE Glass, 3½" 500.00
Tumbler, whiskey; NE Glass, bbl shape, 2½" 450.00
Vase, Gundersen, ruffled cornucopia, acid 525.00
Vase, jack-in-pulpit; Mt WA, folded/crimped rim, 12½" 4,000.00
Vase, lily; Gundersen, acid, 9½" 300.00
Vase, lily; Mt WA, acid, 10" 2,900.00
Vase, lily; NE Glass, 6½" 650.00
Vase, lily; NE Glass, 8" 850.00
Vase, Morgan; Wheeling, on amber base, 10" overall 1,765.00
Vase, Mt WA, floral, distended stick neck, acid, 7½" 2,700.00
Vase, Mt WA, ribbed, waisted neck, scalloped rim, 4¼" 3,000.00
Vase, Mt WA, stick neck, acid, 7¾" 2,250.00
Vase, Mt WA, trn-down rim, trumpet form, dome base, 8", pr ..3,450.00
Vase, Mt WA, 8 ribs, waisted neck, petal top, 4½" 1,840.00
Vase, Webb, birds & flowers w/gold, shiny, 5¼x3½" 500.00
Vase, Webb, bl int, ruffled rim, 6" 145.00

Vase, Webb, floral/ferns/gold leaves, amber branch hdls, 6x6" ...700.00
Vase, Webb, gold florals & butterfly, 3¾x2¾" 325.00
Vase, Webb, gold leaves & silver flowers, shiny, 5⅛x3¼" 295.00
Vase, Webb, gold prunus, propeller mk, 6¾x3⅜" 375.00
Vase, Webb, stick neck, pinched sides, 8¼" 295.00
Vase, Webb, stick neck, 4½" 125.00
Vase, Wheeling, ruffled & crimped rim, 17½" 4,750.00
Vase, Wheeling, stick neck, acid, 8¾x3" 950.00
Vase, Wheeling, stick neck, 10" 1,250.00
Vase, Wheeling, stick neck, 8½x4" 1,050.00
Vase, Wheeling, tapered, 6½" 525.00
Vase, Wheeling, teardrop shape, 9" 550.00
Vase, Wheeling, 4" 500.00
Wine glass, Gundersen, acid 200.00

Pearlware

Developed by Wedgwood in the late 1770s primarily for their dinnerware lines, pearlware was soon being made by many other Staffordshire potteries as well. Much of it made for export to America. It is characterized by its blue-white body, similar in appearance to true porcelain. During the first decade of the 1800s, pearlware with chinoiserie decorations and hand-painted flowers became popular. See also Leeds.

Bowl, mc figural transfer w/floral ground, ca 1800, 9½" 425.00
Bowl, simple brn sprig, brn border, lt ribbing, 3x6", EX 60.00

Coffeepot, simple floral swags and geometric panels, applied flower finial, 10", NM, $425.00.

Coffeepot, peafowl, rpr, 19th C, 10" 350.00
Cup plate, blk transfer scene, mc band, Wood, 3¾", NM 35.00
Egg standish, 6 cups/salt dip/tray, Wedgwood, 1800s, 10" L 425.00
Pitcher, band of leaves & stylized fruit, mc, 3¾" 60.00
Pitcher, emb hunting dogs in pk lustre/gr enamel, 5", VG 100.00
Pitcher, mc floral w/brn striping, wear/chips, 5" 75.00
Pitcher, Sailor's Farewell, blk transfer, 9½" 750.00
Plate, couple at beehive, bl transfer, feather edge, 5¾" 160.00
Plate, floral center, mc w/brn line border, flake, 8" 95.00
Plate, Oriental house & landscape, bl feather edge, 8" 175.00
Plate, Queen Anne's Rose design, pk border, 7⅜", NM 155.00
Teapot, mc floral sprays, bulbous, rstr, 6" 255.00
Teapot, pk lustre & gr molded decor, rpr, 7" 250.00

Peking Cameo Glass

The first glasshouse was established in Peking in 1680. It produced glassware made in imitation of porcelain, a more desirable medium to the Chinese. By 1725 multilayered carving that resulted in a cameo effect lead to the manufacture of a wider range of shapes and colors.

The factory was closed from 1736 to 1795, but glass made in Po-shan and shipped to Peking for finishing continued to be called Peking glass. See also Orientalia.

Belt buckle, red o/l, Daoist scene, rectangle, 19th C, 2¾" 860.00
Bowl, bright yel, lotus form w/peony branch panels, 6¼" 800.00
Bowl, peonies, turq on wht, bk: crane, late, 3x6¾" 175.00
Cup, yel, dragon panels in high relief, 19th C, 4½" 800.00
Jar, flowering vines, gr on opal wht, 5x5" 575.00
Vase, bl, dragon panels, stick neck, 19th C, 9⅛" 1,380.00
Vase, 2 birds/flowering tree, dk bl on wht, late, 10", pr 500.00

Peloton

Peloton glass was first made by Wilhelm Kralik in Bohemia in 1880. This unusual art glass was produced by rolling colored threads onto the transparent or opaque glass gather as it was removed from the furnace. Usually more than one color of threading was used, and some items were further decorated with enameling. It was made with both shiny and acid finishes.

Biscuit jar, pk w/mc strings, rstr SP, 7¾" to top of hdl 1,070.00
Bowl, wht gloss w/pastel strings, 6 shell ft, 4-point rim, 4" 300.00

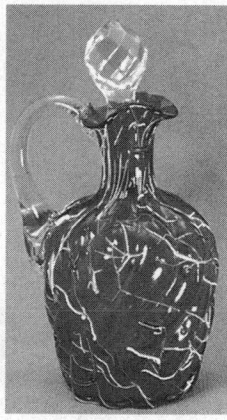

Cruet, multicolor stringing on cranberry, clear faceted stopper, $950.00.

Pitcher, clear w/mc strings, 6½x3¾" 145.00
Rose bowl, cased lilac, ribbed, appl crystal ft, 2¼" 200.00
Rose bowl, wht w/mc strings, shallow ribs, 2½x3½" 135.00
Sweetmeat, wht satin w/pastel strings, SP mts, 6½x5½" 600.00
Vase, lav-pk w/mc strings, pinched middle, 3¼x3⅞" 235.00
Vase, wht w/mc strings, ribbed w/tricorn top, 4x4¾" 295.00
Vase, wht w/pastel strings, ribbed, ruffled, ftd, 6½x6" 450.00
Vase, yel w/wht strings, hdls, 5" 100.00

Pennsbury

Established in the 1950s in Morrisville, Pennsylvania, by Henry Below, the Pennsbury Pottery produced dinnerware and novelty items, much of which was sold in gift shops along the Pennsylvania Turnpike. Henry and his wife, Lee, worked for years at the Stangl Pottery before striking out on their own. Lee and her daughter were the artists responsible for many of the early pieces, the bird figures among them. Pennsbury pottery was hand painted, some in blue on white, some in multicolor on caramel. Pennsylvania Dutch motifs, Amish couples, and barbershop singers were among their most popular decorative themes. Sgraffito (hand incising) was used extensively. The company marked their wares 'Pennsbury Pottery' or 'Pennsbury Pottery, Morrisville, PA.'

In October of 1969 the company closed. Contents of the pottery were sold in December of the following year, and in April of 1971, the buildings burned to the ground. Items marked Pennsbury Glenview or Stumar Pottery (or these marks in combination) were made by Glenview after 1969. Pieces manufactured after 1976 were made by the Pennington Pottery. Several of the old molds still exist, and the original Pennsbury Caramel process is still being used on novelty items, some of which are produced by Lewis Brothers, NJ. Production of Pennsbury dinnerware was not resumed after the closing. Our advisor for this category is Shirley Graff; she is listed in the Directory under Ohio. Note: prices may be higher in some areas of the country — particularly the East Coast, the southern states, and Texas.

Ashtray, Schmootzer's 30.00
Bookends, eagle, pr 200.00
Butter dish, Folkart, w/lid, 5x4" 45.00
Candlestick, Delft Toleware, 3¾" 40.00
Candlesticks, hummingbird, #117, 5", pr 250.00
Candy dish, Hex, heart shape, 6x6" 35.00
Canister set, tea, coffee, flour & sugar, Blk Rooster 550.00
Casserole, Blk Rooster, w/lid, 10¼x8¼" 100.00
Coffeepot, Red Rooster, 2-cup, 6" 40.00
Creamer & sugar bowl, Red Rooster, 4", pr 40.00
Desk basket, eagle 45.00
Figurine, barn swallow, #123, 6¼" 225.00
Figurine, cardinal, #120, 6½" 200.00
Figurine, ducklings, hand-mk Pennsbury, 6½" 295.00
Figurine, hummingbird, #119, 3½" 200.00
Figurine, wood duck, all wht, #114, 10" 300.00
Mug, Amish Couple 25.00
Mug, beer; Amish 30.00
Mug, beer; Gay Ninety 30.00
Mug, beverage; Red Rooster, 5" 25.00
Mug, coffee; Blk Rooster 20.00
Mug, coffee; Red Barn 20.00
Mug, Here's Looking at You 35.00
Mug, Swallow the Insult 35.00
Pitcher, Amish man, 5" 35.00
Pitcher, Folkart, mini, 2½" 30.00
Pitcher, Tulip, 4" 40.00
Plaque, eagle, 6" 30.00
Plaque, Toleware, brn, 5x7" 40.00
Plate, Bl Dowry, 10" 35.00
Plate, Daily Bread 60.00
Plate, Mother's Day, 1973 ....65.00
Pretzel bowl, Amish couple 75.00
Shakers, Amish, man & woman, mini pitcher form 30.00
Tile, Hex, 6" 30.00
Tray, Crested Birds, octagonal, 3x5" 30.00
Vase, Dartmouth insignia, 10" 30.00
Wall pocket, Blk Rooster 50.00
Wall pocket, clown & donkey, 6½" 95.00

Pens and Pencils

The first metallic writing pen was patented in 1809, and soon machine-produced pens with steel nibs gradually began replacing the quill. The first fountain pen was invented in 1830; but, due to the fact that a suitable metal for the tips had not yet been developed, they were not manufactured commercially until the 1880s. The first successful commercial producers were Waterman in 1884 and Parker with the Lucky Curve in 1888.

The self-filling pen of 1890 featured the soft, interior sack which filled with ink as the metal bar on the outside of the pen was raised and lowered. Variations of the pumping mechanism were tried until 1932 when Parker introduced the Vacumatic, a sackless pen with an internal pump. Our advisors for this category are Judy and Cliff Lawrence; they are listed in the Directory under Florida. For those seeking additional information, a catalog is published monthly by the Pen Fanciers, whose address can be found in the Directory under Clubs, Newsletters, and Catalogs. In the listings that follow, all pens are lever-filled unless otherwise noted.

Key:
AF — aeromatic filler	GPM — gold-plated metal
BF — button filler	GPT — gold-plated trim
CF — cartridge filler	HR — hard rubber
CPT — chrome-plated trim	NPT — nickel-plated trim
ED — eyedropper filler	PF — plunger filler
GFM — gold-filled metal	TD — touchdown filler
GFT — gold-filled trim	VF — vacumatic filler

Ballpoint Pens

Everhard Faber, 1945, brn/GF cap, EX **65.00**
Eversharp, CA, 1945, bl/GF cap, M **95.00**
Eversharp, CA, 1947, GFM, EX **125.00**
Eversharp, Skyline, CA, 1944, maroon w/striped cap, EX **50.00**
Eversharp, Skyline, CA, 1948, brn/gold striped cap, M **50.00**
Parker, Arrow, 1980, GFM, GFT, initials, EX **65.00**
Parker, T-Ball Jotter, 1959, sterling filigree, initals, EX **100.00**
Reynold's, #400, 1946, aluminum, EX **300.00**
Reynold's, Internat'l, 1945, aluminum, M **250.00**
Reynolds, Rocket, 1946, bl w/GFT, dried up, otherwise EX **80.00**
Sheaffer, Lady Sheaffer Stratowriter, 1948, bl, GFT, NM **75.00**
Sheaffer, Stratowriter, 1946, GFM, M **95.00**
Sheaffer, Wht Dot Tuckaway Stratowriter, 1948, maroon, GFT, M .**70.00**

Fountain Pens

Conklin, #2P Crescent Filler, 1922, blk chased HR, GFT, EX ...**140.00**
Conklin, #30 Crescent Filler, 1924, blk chased HR, GFT, EX ...**180.00**
Conway Stewart, #103, 1959, bl, GFT, AF, G **40.00**
Conway Stewart, #225M, 1925, red mottled HR, NPT, LF, EX .**225.00**
Conway Stewart, #286, 1938, blk, GFT, LF, EX **80.00**
Conway Stewart, #55, 1935, blk, GFT, LF, G **90.00**
Conway Stewart, 1940, emerald stripes, GFT, LF, NM **125.00**
Edison, Universal #6, 1925, red mottled HR, GFT, LF, EX **375.00**

Ideal, #452, 1928, sterling filigree, initialed, lever filler, G, $425.00.

Inkograph Stylographic, 1925, GFM, GFT, LF, NM **225.00**
Inkograph Stylographic, 1946, blk, GFT, LF, EX **40.00**
Mentmore, 1939, pk/blk marble, CPT, BF, EX **70.00**
Mont Blanc Masterpc, 1950, 14k gold, piston filler, EX **7,000.00**
Parker, #17 Super English, 1964, blk, GFT, AF, EX **100.00**
Parker, #2½ Lucky Curve, 1922, blk chased HR, GFT, BF, G **120.00**
Parker, #45, 1960, blk, stainless cap, CPT, CF, M **32.00**
Parker, #45, 1960, orange, stainless cap, GFT, AF, M **40.00**
Parker, #51, 1950, gray w/Lustraloy cap, GFT, AF, EX **55.00**
Parker, #51 Demi-Sz, 1953, Cordovan brn, GFM cap, GFT, AF, M .**150.00**
Parker, #51 Flighter, 1949, stainless steel, GFT, AF, G **170.00**

Parker, #51 Special, 1954, gray w/chrome cap, CPT, AF, EX **50.00**
Parker, #75 Spanish Treasure, 1954, sterling, AF, MIB **1,000.00**
Parker, Bl Dmn Duofold, 1944, pk/silver stripes, GFT, VF, EX ..**200.00**
Parker, Bl Dmn Vacumatic, 1943, silver pearl stripes, GFT, EX ...**80.00**
Parker, Bl Dmn Vacumatic, 1945, bl stripes, GFT, VF, EX **125.00**
Parker, Bl Dmn Vacumatic, 1945, blk, GFT, VF, M **200.00**
Parker, Bl Dmn 51, 1944, gray, GFM cap, GFT, VF, EX **155.00**
Parker, Bl Dmn 51, 1945, bl w/GFM cap, GFT, VF, EX **180.00**
Parker, Duofold, 1941, gr/gold/blk stripes, GFT, VF, G **40.00**
Parker, Duofold Jr, 1925, gr marbleized, GFT, BF, EX **125.00**
Parker, Duofold Jr, 1928, red, GFT, BF, EX **125.00**
Parker, Duofold Jr, 1931, lapis bl marble, GFT, BF, EX **200.00**
Parker, Duofold Special, 1931, blk, GFT, BF, Canada, EX **245.00**
Parker, English Duofold, 1945, blk, GFT, BF, EX **165.00**
Parker, Lady Duofold, 1931, blk & pearl marble, GFT, BF, EX **75.00**
Parker, Lucky Curve, 1921, GFM, BF, M **425.00**
Parker, VS, 1947, blk w/Lustraloy cap, GFT, BF, M **125.00**
Sheaffer, Craftsman, 1950, maroon, GFT, TD, M **30.00**
Sheaffer, Lifetime, 1934, gr jade marble, GFT, LF, EX **200.00**
Sheaffer, Lifetime, 1939, blk, man's, GFT, LF, EX **250.00**
Sheaffer, Lifetime Autograph, 1939, blk, 14k gold trim, LF, EX .**215.00**
Sheaffer, Lifetime Triumph Tuckaway, 1946, blk, GFT, PF, EX ...**85.00**
Sheaffer, Wht Dot Triumph Snorkel, 1953, blk, GFT, TD, EX **80.00**
Swan Self Filler, 1928, blk, GFT, LF, G **80.00**
Wahl, Gold Seal Signature, 1927, blk chased HR/GFT/LF, med sz, G .**250.00**
Wahl-Eversharp, Skyline, 1943, bl stripes, GFT, LF, EX **150.00**
Wahl-Oxford, 1932, red marble, GFT, LF, EX **60.00**
Waterman, French, 1979, blk, GFT, CF, EX **70.00**
Waterman, Ideal #12 POC, 1912, blk chased HR, ED, rare, G ...**300.00**
Waterman, Ideal #412½VS Baby Safety, sterling, 1909, ED, EX ..**225.00**
Waterman, Ideal #42½V Argent Safety, 1922, sterling, ED, EX ...**450.00**
Waterman, Ideal #452, 1928, sterling filigree, LF, G **350.00**
Waterman, Ideal #52, 1924, blk chased HR, NPT, LF, EX **125.00**
Waterman, Ideal #56, 1925, red ripple HR, GFT, LF, G **400.00**
Waterman, Ideal #7, 1935, Emerald Ray, GFT, LF, EX **425.00**
Waterman, Ideal #92, 1930, red-gold marble, GFT, LF, EX **200.00**
Waterman, 100 year Supersz, 1944, blk, GFT, LF, EX **350.00**
Waverly Cameron, 1939, blk, GFT, LF, EX **60.00**

Mechanical Pencils

Caran D'Arche Repeater, 1932, silver, EX **90.00**
Carter, 1928, lady's, bl marble, GFT, EX **55.00**
Parker, #51, 1944, gray w/GFM cap, GFT, EX **90.00**
Parker, Duofold, 1922, red enameled metal, GFT, G **70.00**
Parker, Duofold Jr, 1925, red, GFT, EX **150.00**
Parker, Duofold Jr, 1928, gr jade marbleized, GFT, EX **90.00**
Parker, Duofold Sr, 1928, red, GFT, EX **175.00**
Parker, Duofold Sr, 1929, Moderne Pearl/blk marble, GFT, EX .**175.00**
Parker, Duofold Sr, 1931, Moderne Pearl/blk marble, GFT, EX .**175.00**
Parker, Golf, 1933, sea gr pearl marble, GFT, EX **150.00**
Parker, Vacumatic, 1941, gold pearl stripes, GFT, initial, EX **90.00**
Sheaffer, #400, 1939, gold pearl stripes, GFT, G **12.00**
Sheaffer, Fineline, 1940, bl/MOP, GFT, M **40.00**
Sheaffer, Lifetime, 1920, ribbon ring, GFM, GFT, EX **20.00**
Sheaffer, Lifetime, 1925, lady's, gr jade marble, GFT, EX **45.00**
Sheaffer, Lifetime Crest, 1945, blk, GFM cap, GFT, initials, EX ..**70.00**
Sheaffer, Target, 1959, gr, GFT, M **30.00**
Sheaffer, Triumph, 1942, blk, GFT, M **75.00**
Sheaffer, Triumph, 1942, gr stripes, GFT, M w/sticker **95.00**
Sheaffer, Wht Dot, 1949, bl, GFT, initials, EX **15.00**
Sheaffer, Wht Dot, 1959, gr, GFT, M **30.00**
Sheaffer, 1939, gold pearl stripes, GFT, initials, EX **60.00**
Sheaffer, 1950, brn, GFT, EX **10.00**

Wahl-Eversharp, Command Performance, 1944, solid 14k gold, EX ..225.00
Waterman, Ideal, 1932, scarlet-gold marble, GFT, EX 50.00
Waterman, Ideal, 1934, Silver Ray, wht GFT, EX 125.00
Waterman, 1931, gold-red marble, GFT, EX 90.00

Sets

Chilton Wingflow, 1935, blk w/gold inlay, GFT, TD, MIB 1,000.00
Eversharp, Command Performance, 1944, solid 14k gold, LF, EX ..650.00
Parker, #51, 1950, blk w/GFM caps, GFT, VF, M 260.00
Parker, #51 Demi-Sz, 1948, blk w/Lustraloy cap, GFT, VF, M 200.00
Sheaffer, Lifetime Giftie Threesome, 1929, MIB w/bottle 1,000.00
Sheaffer, Snorkel Masterpc, 1953, solid 14k gold, TD, EX/G ..1,000.00
Sheaffer, Triumph Masterpc, 1945, solid 14k gold, LF, M 1,400.00
Wahl-Eversharp, #64, 1943, bl w/14k caps & trim, LF, EX 400.00
Wahl-Eversharp, #64 Skyline, 1943, bl, 14k trim, LF, M, +case .500.00
Wahl-Eversharp, Gold Award, 1943, sterling, GFT, LF, EX 300.00
Wahl-Eversharp, 1924, GFM, GFT, initialed, LF, NM 275.00
Waterman, 1955, gr w/stainless caps, alloy nib, CPT, CF, M 25.00

Personalities, Fact and Fiction

One of the largest and most popular areas of collecting today, if tradepaper ads and articles are any indication, is character-related memorabilia. Everyone has favorites, whether they be comic-strip personalities or true-life heroes. The earliest comic strip dealt with the adventures of the Yellow Kid, the smiling, bald-headed Oriental boy always in a nightshirt. He was introduced in 1895, a product of the imagination of Richard Fenton Outcault. Today, though very hard to come by, items relating to the Yellow Kid bring premium prices.

In 1902 Buster Brown and Tige, his dog and constant companion (more of Outcault's progenies), made it big in the comics as well as in the world of advertising. Shoe stores appealed to the younger set through merchandising displays that featured them both. Today items from their earlier years are very collectible.

Though her 1923 introduction was unobtrusively made through only one newspaper, New York's *Daily News*, Little Orphan Annie, the vacant-eyed redhead in the inevitable red dress, was quickly adopted by hordes of readers nationwide; and, before the demise of her creator, Harold Gray, in 1968, she had starred in her own radio show. She made two feature films, and in 1977 'Annie' was launched on Broadway.

Other early comic figures were Moon Mullins, created in 1923 by Frank Willard; Buck Rogers by Philip Nowlan in 1928; and Betty Boop, the round-faced, innocent-eyed, chubby-cheeked Boop-Boop-a-Doop girl of the early 1930s. Bimbo was her dog and KoKo her clown friend.

Popeye made his debut in 1929 as the spinach-eating sailor with the spindly-limbed girlfriend, Olive Oyl, in the comic strip *Thimble Theatre*, created by Elzie Segar. He became a film star in 1933 and had his own radio show that during 1936 played three times a week on CBS. He obligingly modeled for scores of toys, dolls, and figurines, and especially those from the thirties are very collectible.

Tarzan, created around 1930 by Edgar Rice Burroughs, and Captain Midnight, by Robert Burtt and Willfred G. Moore, are popular heroes with today's collectors. During the days of radio, Sky King of the Flying Crown Ranch (also created by Burtt and Moore) thrilled boys and girls of the mid-1940s. Hopalong Cassidy, Red Rider, Tom Mix, and the Lone Ranger were only a few of the other 'good guys' always on the side of law and order.

But of all the fictional heroes and comic characters collected today, probably the best loved and most well known is Mickey Mouse. Created in the late 1920s by Walt Disney, Micky (as his name was first spelled) became an instant success with his film debut, Steamboat Willie. His popularity was parlayed through wind-up toys, watches, fig-

urines, cookie jars, puppets, clothing, and numerous other products. Items from the 1930s are usually copyrighted 'Walt Disney Enterprises'; thereafter, 'Walt Disney Productions' was used.

For more information we recommend *Schroeder's Collectible Toys, Antique to Modern*, by Sharon and Bob Huxford. For those interested in Disneyanna, we recommend *Stern's Guide to Disney Collectibles; Character Toys and Collectibles* (there are two volumes); and *The Collector's Encyclopedia of Disneyana*. All are available from Collector Books. Our advisor for this category is Norm Vigue; he is listed in the Directory under Massachusetts. See also Autographs; Banks; Big Little Books; Cartoon Books; Children's Books; Comic Books; Cookie Jars; Dolls; Games; Lunch Boxes; Movie Memorabilia; Paper Dolls; Pin-Back Buttons; Posters; Puzzles; Rock 'N Roll Memorabilia; Toys.

Abbott & Costello, wristwatch, Bradley, MIB 65.00
Addams Family, bank, Thing figure, Filmways, 1964, MIB 125.00
Addams Family, Morticia hand puppet, NM 48.00
Alice in Wonderland, bank, ceramic, Leeds 75.00
Alvin & the Chipmunks, toothbrush, battery-op, VG 12.00
Amos & Andy, Weber City map, premium, NM in mailer 65.00
Atom Ant, Halloween costume, Ben Cooper, 1965, G 15.00
Bambi, Bambi Picture Book, Disney, 1942 authorized edition 65.00
Bambi, bookends, ceramic, Disney, pr 52.00
Bambi & Thumper, lamp, ceramic figures/plastic base, 1964, EX .20.00
Bambi & Thumper, planter, ceramic, Leeds 45.00
Batman, bicycle license plate, Marx, 1976, MIP 20.00
Batman, cave lamp, w/Batman figure & orig decal, 1966 ....60.00
Batman, comb, red in pouch w/insignia, 1960s, G 20.00
Batman, Escape Gun, plastic & rubber, 1966, 10", M on card 55.00
Batman, plate, Melaware, 1966 ....15.00
Batman, talking alarm clock, Janex, 1975, EX+ 45.00
Beany & Cecil, jack-in-the-box, Mattel, NM 85.00
Beany & Cecil, tea set, child's, serves 4, M on card 68.00
Ben Casey, coloring book, Saafield, 1963, M 25.00
Ben Casey MD, Nurses Kit, M, unused 40.00
Bert & Ernie, animated alarm clock, Bradley, 1980, NMIB 30.00
Betty Boop, Christmas cards, Popular Comics, KFS, 1951, MIB ...48.00
Betty Boop, doll, fur-trim negligee, 1984, 19", M 250.00
Betty Boop & Bimbo, ashtray, lustreware, 1930s 250.00
Big Bad Wolf, alarm clock, Ingersoll, 1933, MIB 650.00
Bing Crosby, color book, Saafield #4580, 1954, M 35.00
Blondie, paint set, tin box, Am Crayon, 1946, EX 15.00
Bobby Benson, enameled tie clasp, scarce premium, M 88.00
Buck Rogers, Big Big Book, Planetoid Bros, 1934, EX 100.00
Buck Rogers, Intergalactic Playset, MIB, sealed 40.00
Buck Rogers, pencil case, cb, EX graphics, 1936 ....75.00
Buck Rogers, pop-up book, Dangerous Mission, 1934, NM 400.00
Buck Rogers, Solar Scouts badge, M 95.00
Buck Rogers, Solar Scouts Buck knife, 1930s, NM 1,200.00
Buck Rogers, Strato-Kit, 1947, M in pkg 80.00
Buck Rogers, Sylvania Space Ranger Premium Kit, 1952, M in pkg ..155.00
Bugs Bunny, color book, Carrot Machine, Whitman #1087, '63, M ..9.00
Bugs Bunny, toothbrush, battery operated, 1973, MIB 25.00
Bugs Bunny & Pals, paper cups, 1950s, MIB 40.00
Bullwinkle, bank, plastic, 12", EX 30.00
Captain Gallant, coloring book, Lowe, 1956, NM 30.00
Captain Marvel, iron-on, 1940s, M in envelope 75.00
Captain Marvel, magic whistle, premium, M 95.00
Captain Marvel, party horn, 1946, unused 95.00
Captain Marvel, photo, 1942 premium, EX 70.00
Captain Marvel, tie clip, 1946, M on card 125.00
Care Bear, wristwatch, Bradley, 1983, MIB 40.00
Casper the Friendly Ghost, costume, pajamas, NMIB 35.00
Charlie Brown, color book, Saafield #4629, M 10.00

Charlie McCarthy, cb puppet, NM in orig mailer 40.00
Charlie McCarthy, radio game, coffee premium, '38, M in mailer ...45.00
Charlie's Angels, paint-by-number set, 1977, M 30.00
Charlie Tuna, lamp, compo figure, scarce, 1960s, NM 75.00
CHiPs, binoculars, MIB 20.00
Cinderella, apron pattern, JC Penney's premium, 1950s, M 35.00
Cinderella, bank, ceramic, Leeds 95.00
Cisco Kid, paper gun, premium, EX+ 18.00
Cisco Kid Club, ring, radio premium 175.00
Cookie Monster, animated alarm clock, M Bradley, EX 15.00
Dagwood & Blondie, doll stroller, tin litho, 1949, EX 65.00
Dale Evans, horseshoe pendant, on display card 15.00
Dale Evans, official cowboy hat, M 125.00
Daniel Boone, mug, milk glass, red enameling 30.00
Davy Crockett, electric 'oil' lamp, orig illus shade, M 195.00
Davy Crockett, lunch tray, tin litho, Disney, w/stand 70.00
Davy Crockett, plate, Oxford china 55.00
Davy Crockett, rubber boots, western style w/fringe, MIB 145.00
Davy Crockett, souvenir plate, Royal China, 9¼" 35.00
Davy Crockett, tie clip, MIB 25.00
Davy Crockett, wallet, plastic, savings bank premium, M 30.00
Davy Crockett, Wonder Book, 1955, EX 8.00
Davy Crockett, wristwatch, US Time, 1954, MIB 375.00
Dennis the Menace, bedspread, all-over graphics, EX 65.00
Dennis the Menace, curtains, comic strip illus, NM, pr 45.00
Dick Tracy, color book, Saalfield #399, 1946, NM 45.00
Dick Tracy, Girl's Division badge, radio premium 12.50
Dick Tracy, handcuffs, Ja-Ru, 1980s, M on card 12.00
Dick Tracy, Jr Membership certificate, 1940s, M 30.00
Dick Tracy, Jumbo Movie Viewer, 1955, M on card 46.00
Dick Tracy, magnifying glass, Laramie, 1979, M on card 5.00
Dick Tracy, pocket flashlight, orig fob, 1939 premium 88.00
Dick Tracy Club, Fingerprint File trading card set, M 350.00
Donald Duck, color book, w/nephews on cover, Whitman #1057, M .6.00
Donald Duck, crib toy, celluloid, 4", EX 98.00
Donald Duck, figure, bsk, w/accordion, head trn, Japan, 5", EX .195.00
Donald Duck, linen book, 1st Donald book, 1935, EX 150.00
Donald Duck, paper puppet, NBC Bread premium, unused 30.00
Donald Duck, pitcher, gold decor, Walt Disney, 6¼" 80.00
Donald Duck, planter, ceramic, Leeds 45.00
Donald Duck & Nephews, standee display, 1940s, 36", NM ...1,250.00
Donald Duck the Sailor, lamp base, Disney, 1960s, NM 50.00
Dopey, bank, ceramic, Leeds 135.00
Dopey, bsk figure, Walt Disney, 3" 38.00
Dopey, night light, tin litho & cb, NM 225.00
Dopey, planter, ceramic, Leeds 55.00
Dr Dolittle, Magic Set, Remco, 1967, M (EX box) 20.00
Duck Tales, backpack, bl, premium, M in pkg 15.00
Dukes of Hazzard, Colorforms, 1981, EX 18.00
Dumbo, pitcher, Disney, Am Pottery, 1950s, M 75.00
Elmer Fudd, vase, peeking around tree, Shaw Pottery, 1940s, M ..88.00
ET, bowl, plate & mug, MIB 10.00
Fearless Fosdick, Wildroot handbill, EX color, 1954 ....20.00
Felix the Cat, figural sterling pin, 1930s, M 135.00
Felix the Cat, figure, lead, Sullivan, 3" 150.00
Felix the Cat, jtd push-up figure, M 145.00
Felix the Cat, nodder, papier-mache, 5" 250.00
Felix the Cat, Orange Dry bottle cap, M 45.00
Felix the Cat, place card holder, celluloid figure, 1930s, 1¾" 45.00
Felix the Cat, rattle, tin litho, 1930s, NM 195.00
Felix the Cat, wind chimes, metal 15.00
Felix the Cat, yarn winder, 1920s, VG 45.00
Ferdinand the Bull, bsk figure, Japan, 4" 35.00
Ferdinand the Bull, hand puppet, compo head, EX 65.00

Ferdinand the Bull, pencil sharpener, 1930s, EX 25.00

Flash Gordon, Arresting Ray Gun, clicker pistol, King Features, Mars, MIB, $275.00.

Flintstones, bubble pipe, Fred figure, M 15.00
Flintstones, Fred wristwatch, w/rare Flintstone band, 1972, M ...160.00
Flintstones, puffy magnets, 1978, set of 8, 4", M 18.00
Flipper, paint book, Whitman, 1964, M 16.00
Frankenstein, Halloween costume, Universal Monster, 1980, MIB ...26.00
Garfield, alarm clock, battery-op, Nelsonic, MIB 30.00
Garfield, shoelace locks, figural, 1989, M on card 10.00
Gene Autry, wristwatch, animated Six Shooter, New Haven, MIB ...475.00
Goofy, gumball dispenser, 3", M on card 10.00
Goofy, wristwatch, runs bkwards, Helbros, 1972, MIB 600.00
Gumby, paddle ball, M in pkg 10.00
Happy Days, activity book, 1983, EX+ 5.00
Happy Days, Fonzie's Garage playset, Mego, 1977, M, sealed 50.00
Happy Hooligan, ashtray, lead, figural 75.00
Harold Teen, ukelele, 1930s, EX in orig case 165.00
Herby (from Smitty), tie, illus, EX 25.00
Hokey Wolf, tablet, 1961, 8x11", EX+ 15.00
Holly Hobbie, wristwatch, Bradley, 1978, M 45.00
Hopalong Cassidy, bicycle, M rstr 4,800.00
Hopalong Cassidy, binoculars, blk metal, 2 decals, EX 125.00
Hopalong Cassidy, hair barrette, silver color 25.00
Hopalong Cassidy, Hair Trainer bottle, portrait label, NM 40.00
Hopalong Cassidy, holster night light, orig card label, NM 350.00
Hopalong Cassidy, knife, folding, orig vinyl belt loop, M 135.00
Hopalong Cassidy, mat, bathroom; chenille, NM 165.00
Hopalong Cassidy, mug, milk glass, blk portrait on horse 35.00
Hopalong Cassidy, pencil case, tan, Hasbro, w/inserts, NM 110.00
Hopalong Cassidy, pin-bk button, Chicago Tribune 45.00
Hopalong Cassidy, pop-up book, unused, lg 45.00
Hopalong Cassidy, Publicity & Exploitation manual, '50s, EX 55.00
Hopalong Cassidy, Savings Club Teller Badge, M in cello 22.00
Hopalong Cassidy, scarf, 1950, M 78.00
Hopalong Cassidy, schoolbook cover, Bond Bread premium, M ...26.00
Hopalong Cassidy, wallet, ornate gold, no coin, MIB 325.00
Hopalong Cassidy, woodburning set, Wm Boyd on 13x16" box, EX ...175.00
Hopalong Cassidy, wristwatch, Good Luck From Hoppy, MIB ...300.00
Hopalong Cassidy, wristwatch, on saddle, M w/tags, NM box 500.00
Howdy Doody, Big Golden Book, In the Wild West, EX 35.00
Howdy Doody, ceiling shade, glass, colorful, NM 265.00
Howdy Doody, Clarabell hand puppet, googly eyes, NM 45.00
Howdy Doody, coloring book, 1951, NM 40.00
Howdy Doody, cup, Ovaltine, red plastic, Bob Smith, EX+ 30.00
Howdy Doody, handkerchief, sgn Bob Smith, NM 40.00
Howdy Doody, key chain ornament, photo w/moving eyes, 1940s ..45.00
Howdy Doody, pot holder, 1950s 30.00
Howdy Doody, puppet, terry cloth 25.00
Howdy Doody, rocking chair, orig bell on base 250.00
Howdy Doody, Sun Ray Camera, 1950, M on card 68.00
Howdy Doody, talking alarm clock, MIB 170.00
Howdy Doody, Welch juice bottle, w/lid 70.00
Huckleberry Hound, bank, Knickerbocker, M 25.00

Huckleberry Hound, club ring, metal, 1961, VG+ **45.00**
I Dream of Jeannie, Jeannie costume, Ben Cooper, 1974, MIB **30.00**
Incredible Hulk, roller skates, Larami, 1970s, MIB **28.00**
Jack Armstrong, Explorer telescope, radio premium, EX **55.00**
Jack Armstrong, whistle ring, radio premium, EX **68.00**
Jackie Gleason, wristwatch, Ralph Kramden on face, NM **45.00**
Jane Powell, color book, photo cover, Whitman #1861, 1957, M .**30.00**
Jeannette MacDonald, paint book, Merrill 33461, M **30.00**
Jerry Mahoney, wiffle ball, premium, MIB **75.00**
Jiminy Crickett, Soaky, VG **15.00**
Jimmy Allen, ID bracelet, radio premium **22.00**

The Katzenjammer Kids, Magic Drawing and Coloring Book, 1930s, 32 pages (some neatly colored), with original magic crayon in pouch, EX+, $75.00.

Katzenjammer Kids, bottle cap set, complete **75.00**
King Kong, jewelry box, Presents, 1990s, M **25.00**
Kit Carson, mug, milk glass, orange enameling **15.00**
Knight Rider, rubber stamp set, 1982, M on card **15.00**
Lassie, color book, photo cover, 1956, M **18.50**
Lassie, playset, Marx, 1992, MIB **60.00**
Laugh In, sleeping bag, illus characters, 1969, EX **75.00**
Laurel & Hardy, animated advertising fan, cb diecut, NM **55.00**
Laurel & Hardy, Dakin dolls, M w/tags, pr **60.00**
Leave It to Beaver, paperbk book, photo illus, 1960, M **15.00**
Lennon Sisters, color book, Whitman #1133, 1959, VG **8.00**
Li'l Abner, bank, can form, 1953 ....**50.00**
Li'l Abner, bowl, bright mc illus, 1968, M **25.00**
Li'l Abner, gloves, M in pkg w/cartoon images **50.00**
Li'l Abner, nut dish, 9 characters, 1968, NM **40.00**
Lilly Munster, Halloween costume, Ben Cooper, 1965, M in NM box **200.00**
Linus the Lionhearted, hand puppet, EX **30.00**
Little Lulu, paper mask, c Marjorie Buell, premium, M **30.00**
Little Lulu, valentines, Kleenex premium, uncut sheet, M **22.50**
Little Lulu, 3-D Valentines set, Kleenex premium **18.50**
Little Orphan Annie, cup, ceramic, Ovaltine **50.00**
Little Orphan Annie, ID bracelet, radio premium **24.00**
Little Orphan Annie, ROA manual, 1935 ....**35.00**
Little Orphan Annie, Sun Dial wristwatch, w/instructions, M ...**150.00**
Little Orphan Annie, tea set, lustreware, 15-pc **340.00**
Little Orphan Annie w/Sandy, ashtray, lustreware, Japan, 1930s ..**150.00**
Lone Ranger, Airbase, Kix premium, unused in orig mailer **160.00**
Lone Ranger, billfold, 1948, EX **100.00**
Lone Ranger, Branding Iron die-cut sign, 7½x5½", M **165.00**
Lone Ranger, color book, Whitman #1010, 1975, M **12.00**
Lone Ranger, crayon box, tin, w/crayons, 1950s, EX **65.00**
Lone Ranger, first aid kit, tin litho, 1938, sm, NM **90.00**
Lone Ranger, hairbrush, w/decal, dtd 1939, MIB **95.00**
Lone Ranger, Official Silver Bullet pencil, M **32.00**
Lone Ranger, paint book, 1941, EX **25.00**
Lone Ranger, pedometer, EX **28.00**
Lone Ranger, printer's plate, zinc on copper, tent ad, 7½x12" **50.00**
Lone Ranger, push-button puppet, 1968, 3¼", NM **30.00**
Lone Ranger, Safety Club badge, Smith Oil Co, 1938, NM **35.00**
Lone Ranger, signal siren flashlight, US Electric, 1950, MIB **200.00**
Lone Ranger, Silver's lucky horseshoe pin, EX **58.00**
Lone Ranger, store poster, Kix ad, 1947, M **225.00**
Lone Ranger, toothbrush holder, chalkware, 1940s, NM **89.00**

Lone Wolf, Arrow Membership badge, radio premium **19.00**
Lone Wolf, ring, radio premium **85.00**
Lone Wolf, Tribe manual, premium **40.00**
Ludwig Von Drake, squeeze toy, Dell, 1950s-60s, 7½", VG **50.00**
Mary Poppins, dot-to-dot book, 1973, M **12.50**
Mary Poppins, needlepoint kit, 3 pictures w/foam fr, M **45.00**
Maverick, cuffs & badge, M on card **28.00**
Max Headroom, wall clock, Coke advertising, 1987, MIB **20.00**
Mickey Mouse, alarm clock, Ingersoll, ca 1955 ....**125.00**
Mickey Mouse, alarm Clock, Phinney-Walker, 1950s, EX **75.00**
Mickey Mouse, Alphabet Book, 1936, NM **85.00**
Mickey Mouse, baby rattle, celluloid, 1930s, NM **150.00**
Mickey Mouse, belt & tie, 1940s, M on card **325.00**
Mickey Mouse, bottle cap, 1930s **25.00**
Mickey Mouse, bowl, Beetleware, 1930s, 5½", M **25.00**
Mickey Mouse, Bubble Buster gun, 1930s, 8", EX **175.00**
Mickey Mouse, charm, plastic, figural, 1930s **10.00**
Mickey Mouse, clock, 60th Anniversary, radio style, Seiko, MIB .**75.00**
Mickey Mouse, crib toy, celluloid, early **65.00**
Mickey Mouse, dot-to-dot color book, Whitman #1272, M **16.00**
Mickey Mouse, Dutch wooden shoes, HP, EX **95.00**
Mickey Mouse, fan, barrel shape, MIB **20.00**
Mickey Mouse, figure, jtd, celluloid, w/saxophone, 1930s **85.00**
Mickey Mouse, film strip, color, 1930, MIB **40.00**
Mickey Mouse, Globetrotters poster, 1930s **175.00**
Mickey Mouse, mini playing cards, WDE, 1930s, EX in case **65.00**
Mickey Mouse, MM Magazine, Dec 1937, NM **400.00**
Mickey Mouse, pencil box, pie-eyed Mickey, early, Dixon, NM ...**60.00**
Mickey Mouse, picture printing set, MIB **120.00**
Mickey Mouse, popcorn popper, tin, EX **250.00**
Mickey Mouse, rocking horse, pnt wood, early, EX **350.00**
Mickey Mouse, spinning top, 1930s, NM **145.00**
Mickey Mouse, tool chest, empty, NM **25.00**
Mickey Mouse, wristwatch, 50 Years w/Mickey, Bradley, MIB ...**125.00**
Mickey Mouse Club, felt hat w/ears, 1950s, M **22.50**
Mighty Mouse, alarm clock, tin litho, Japan, 1960s, EX **100.00**
Mighty Mouse, Soaky, EX **22.00**
Mohammad Ali, alarm clock, M **35.00**
Mork & Mindy, Colorforms, 1979, M **18.50**
Mork & Mindy, Magic Transfer set, 1979, M **13.50**
Mr Magoo, Birthday Bash party set, M, unpunched **15.00**
Mr Spock, wristwatch, Bradley, 1979, MIB **135.00**
Mr T, color & activity book w/pop-up picture, Golden, 1984, M ...**7.00**
Ms Pac Man, wristwatch, Bradley, MIB **35.00**
Muppet Babies, Shrinky Dinks, 1985, MIB **5.00**
Mutt & Jeff, celluloid figures, mc pnt, Japan, NM, pr **185.00**
Oscar the Grouch, wristwatch, Bradley, 1971, M **65.00**
Peanuts, Charlie Brown All-Star watch, MIB **55.00**
Peanuts, lampshade, all characters in night scene, 1965, M **30.00**
Peanuts, Peppermint Patty, figural ceramic bank, 1972, NM **22.00**
Peanuts, Snoopy bank, clear thick glass, 1966, 5½" **10.00**
Peanuts, Snoopy bike horn, 1966, G **10.00**
Peanuts, Snoopy clock, on bl dial w/butterfly, Equity, G **25.00**
Peanuts, Snoopy on Soccer Ball ceramic bank, 1966, NM **20.00**
Peanuts, Snoopy squeeze toy, as a golfer, NM **3.50**
Pee Wee Herman, wristwatch, flip-top, M in pkg **65.00**
Pepsodent Show Ticket, Bob Hope, 1947, unused **12.00**
Peter Pan & Tinkerbell, scarf, Disney, 1950s, lg, EX **38.00**
Pinocchio, pencil sharpener, Jiminy Cricket figure, wall mt, NM .**29.00**
Planet of the Apes, Dr Zaius bendee, M on card **21.50**
Planet of the Apes, Galen dangle toy, M in pkg **20.00**
Pluto, color book, Whitman #1070, M **6.00**
Pluto, planter, ceramic w/gold trim, Leeds **185.00**
Police Academy, Shrinky Dinks, MIB **8.00**

Popeye, book, Popeye & His Friends, hardcover, 1937, EX 20.00
Popeye, Christmas card, Hallmark, 1934, NM 20.00
Popeye, dime register bank, gr tin litho, EX 75.00
Popeye, egg cup, HP ceramic, 1930s, 3", NM 170.00
Popeye, flasher ring, M 30.00
Popeye, fly swatter, w/orig cut-out booklet & tag, 1936, M 165.00
Popeye, paint book, 1938, M 65.00
Popeye, pencil box, complete, 1933 ....78.00
Popeye, pillowcase, Popeye & Wimpy, Vogart, 1929, M 145.00

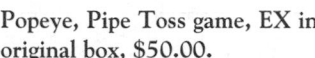
Popeye, Pipe Toss game, EX in original box, $50.00.

Popeye, Power Strength Test Toy, 1950s, M in pkg 68.00
Popeye, TV tray, tin litho, 1979, 17", M 35.00
Popeye, valentine, diecut, early 1930s 30.00
Porky Pig, book, PP Book of Tricks, 1942, M 90.00
Princess Diana, Color Me Princess book, Dell, 1982, VG 9.00
Princess of Power, talking toothbrush, NM 40.00
Raggedy Ann, popcorn tin, 24", VG 25.00
Raggedy Ann, wristwatch, Bobbs-Merrill, 1972, NM 95.00
Raggedy Ann & Andy, bookends, ceramic figural, 1971, NM 28.00
Red Ryder, suspenders, Pat 1941, EX 75.00
Red Ryder & Little Beaver, paint book, S Slesinger, 1947, M 40.00
Reddy Kilowatt, ashtray, glass 10.00
Reddy Kilowatt, pot holder, magnetic, M in pkg 25.00
Reg'lar Fellers, Gene Byrnes pencil box, NM 40.00
Reg'lar Fellers, paint set, 1932, MIB 85.00
Return of the Jedi, color book, Kenner #19350, 1984, M 6.00
Rifleman, rifle, from TV show, M 145.00
Rin-Tin-Tin, Major Swanson patch, unused 12.00
Robin Hood, mug, milk glass 12.00
Robin Hood, water gun, figural, 1973, NMIB 50.00
Rocketeer, slumber bag, M 25.00
Rocky & Bullwinkle, Circustime balancing toy, 1959, M on card .20.00
Rocky Jones, Space Ranger Wings, MOC 23.00
Ronald McDonald, wristwatch, wind-up, 1979, MIB 65.00
Rosemary Clooney, color book, Abbot #348, 1954, NM 25.00
Roy Rogers, bank, tin litho, wall hanging, 1950s, M 135.00
Roy Rogers, bedspread, tan w/red design, NM 210.00
Roy Rogers, book, Favorite Cowboy Songs, EX 10.00
Roy Rogers, coloring book, 1946, M, unused 30.00
Roy Rogers, gloves, leather, M, pr 110.00
Roy Rogers, lamp, compo figure on Trigger, orig shade 275.00
Roy Rogers, outfit, Yankee boy #916, child sz, MIB 165.00
Roy Rogers, postcard, full color 10.00
Roy Rogers, Tuck-A-Way Gun, M on card 60.00
Roy Rogers, wristwatch, Ingraham, 1951, M 225.00
Scooby Doo, rubber stamp set, 1982, M on card 10.00
Shadow, book, Eyes of the Shadow, hardcover, 1931, EX 125.00
Shirley Temple, Birthday Book, Dell, 1936, M 98.00
Shirley Temple, book, Now I Am Eight, M 32.00
Shmoo, drinking glass, orange pyro, Al Capp, 1949 ....35.00

Six Million Dollar Man, color book, Rand McNally, 1977, VG 9.00
Skippy, cereal bowl, Beetleware, 1933 ....22.00
Skippy, figure, celluloid, jtd arms, 5¼", EX 250.00
Smokey the Bear, blueprint to Gr Forests, 1954, unused 30.00
Smokey the Bear, pocket watch, 1976, MIB 200.00
Smokey the Bear, Soaky, M 18.00
Smurfs, musical top, litho tin, Ohio Art, 1982, MIB 20.00
Sneezy, figural soap, 1930s, M 135.00
Snow White, alarm clock, wind-up, orange plastic, Disney, NM ..60.00
Snow White, book, cut-out; w/dwarfs' house, 1937, 13x13", NM ...185.00
Snow White, handkerchief, Disney, 1930s, EX 30.00
Snow White, Jingle Club pin, WD, lg 60.00
Snow White, song book, many illustrations, Disney, 1938, EX ...55.00
Snow White, standee, 1940s, NM 950.00
Snow White, towels, linen, mc embr w/paper label, pr 125.00
Snow White & Dopey, music box, Schmid, M 48.00
Snuffy Smith, hand puppet, cloth w/rubber head, Gund, NM 20.00
Space Patrol, tablecloth, Reed 25.00
Spiderman, color Book, Whitman #1398, 1979, M 10.00
Spiderman, roller skates, red/blk/bl plastic, 1979, EX 15.00
Star Trek, color book, Whitman, 1978, VG 9.00
Strawberry Shortcake, alarm clock, 3-D, Bradley, 1982, MIB 18.00
Strawberry Shortcake, lamp, bsk figural, mk AGC, 1981, M 30.00
Strawberry Shortcake, wristwatch, Bradley, MIB 40.00
Superman, Acme film viewer, 1940, MIB 225.00
Superman, belt buckle, Lee, 1950 ....78.00
Superman, Colorforms, 1964, M, unused 40.00
Superman, coloring book, Missile Base Mystery, Whitman, 1977, M 10.00
Superman, pin-bk, Action Comics logo on reverse, 1940 ....85.00
Superman, pocket watch, Bradley, 1959 ....150.00
Superman, scrapbook, 1940 ....95.00
Superman, squirt gun, figural, Durham, 1960s-70s, EX 40.00
Superman, story & record set #2, 1947 ....65.00
Superman, vinyl binder, image on yel, M 35.00
Superman, wristwatch, ½-figure on rectangular dial, 1939, NM 350.00
Tarzan, book, Pan-Am, 1938 premium, EX 450.00
Tarzan, magic slate, 1968, EX 28.00
Tarzan, membership pin, Sons of Tarzan Club, celluloid, EX 58.00
Tarzan, sign, Ice Cream Cup, 1930s 400.00
Terry & the Pirates, color book, Saalfield #398, 1946, EX 40.00
Three Little Pigs, ashtray, lustreware, 1930s 90.00
Three Little Pigs, tea set, lustreware, 1930s, MIB 300.00
Tom & Jerry, sand pail, Ohio Art, 1970s, VG 30.00
Tom Mix, Big Big Book, VG/EX 48.00
Tom Mix, Glow in the Dark arrowhead compass, premium 70.00
Tom Mix, Humming Lariat, EX 95.00
Tom Mix, ID bracelet, Ralston Straight Shooters 65.00
Tom Mix, magnetic ring, radio premium, EX 100.00
Tom Mix, Tiger Eye ring, premium, 1950 ....185.00
Tonto, soap figure, Castile, MIB 50.00
Topo Gigio, bank, ceramic, nodding head, NM 38.00
Uncle Scrooge, color book, Dell #209, 1955, G 8.00
Welcome Back Kotter, Barbarino Halloween costume, MIB 18.50
Welcome Back Kotter, calculating wheel, 1976, M on card 12.50
Welcome Back Kotter, greeting cards, complete set, MIB 23.00
Winnie the Pooh, baby rattle, figural, VG 15.00
Winnie the Pooh, ceiling shade, colorful, 1960s, M 60.00
Winnie the Pooh, cloth apron, NM 10.00
Winnie the Pooh, pin-bk button, Disneyland, 3½" 5.00
Winnie the Pooh, wristwatch, 7 jewels, Sears, M 45.00
Wizard of Oz, night light, Scarecrow, 1989, MIB 25.00
Wonder Woman, color book w/doll on bk, Whitman, 1979, M 9.00
Woody Woodpecker, bank, ceramic 32.00
Yogi Bear, push-button puppet, Kohner, NM 13.50

Zorro, TV Junior Guide, 1958, EX 12.00

Peters and Reed

John Peters and Adam Reed founded their pottery in Zanesville, Ohio, just before the turn of the century, using the local red clay to produce a variety of wares. Moss Aztec, introduced about 1912, has an unglazed exterior with designs molded in high relief and the recesses highlighted with a green wash. Only the interior is glazed to hold water. Pereco (named for Peters, Reed and Company) is glazed in semi-matt blue, maroon, or cream. Orange was also used very early, but such examples are rare. Shapes are simple with in-mold decoration sometimes borrowed from the Moss Aztec line. Wilse Blue is a line of high-gloss medium blue with dark specks on simple shapes. Landsun, characterized by its soft matt multicolor or blue and gray combinations, is decorated either by dripping or by hand brushing in an effect sometimes called Flame or Herringbone. Chromal, in much the same colors as Landsun, may be decorated with a realistic scenic, or the swirling application of colors may merely suggest one. Vivid, realistic Chromal scenics command much higher prices than weak, poorly drawn examples. (Brush-McCoy made a very similar line called Chromart. Neither will be marked, and due to the lack of documented background material available, it may be impossible make a positive identification. Collectors nearly always attribute this type of decoration to Peters and Reed.) Shadow Ware is a glossy, multicolor drip over a harmonious base color. When the base is black, the effect is often iridescent.

Perhaps the most familiar line is the brown high-glaze artware with the 'sprigged'-type designs. Although research has uncovered no positive proof, it is generally accepted as having been made by Peters and Reed. It is interesting to note that many of the artistic shapes in this line are recognizable as those made by Weller, Roseville, and other Zanesville area companies. Other lines include Mirror Black, Persian, and an unidentified line which collectors call Mottled Colors. In this high-gloss line, the red clay body often shows through the splashed-on multicolors.

In 1922 the company became known as the Zane Pottery. Peters and Reed retired, and Harry McClelland became president. Charles Chilcote designed new lines, and production of many of the old lines continued. The body of the ware after 1922 was light in color. Marks include the impressed logo or ink stamp 'Zaneware' in a rectangle.

Bowl, Landsun, bl & wht, 2x6" 25.00
Bowl, Moss Aztec, pine cones & needles, #404, 4x7" 55.00
Bowl, Pereco, tan w/geometric decor, semimatt, #600, 3x9" 45.00
Bowl, Persian, brn w/geometric decor, #605, 2x5" 30.00
Candlestick, Moss Aztec, slim, 364, 8½" 65.00
Flower frog, Landsun, mushroom shape, lt brn, 2½x4" 35.00
Flower frog, Pereco, lily-pad shape, lt brn, 1½x4" 35.00
Flowerpot, Florentine, mc floral band & geometrics on beige, 4" .45.00
Ginger jar, Shadow Ware, gr drips on mirror blk, w/lid, 8½" 150.00
Hanging basket, Moss Aztec, grapes & vines, Ferrell, 10x9" 125.00
Jar, Landsun, variegated gr, #1, w/lid, 3" 80.00
Jar, Landsun, w/lid, 4" 100.00
Jardiniere, Moss Aztec, trees & geometrics, #218, 9x11" 175.00
Jardiniere, Persian, lions' heads, beige & brn, 7x7½" 125.00
Jug, Brn Ware, cavalier portrait, twisted body & hdl, 5½" 100.00
Letter holder, Brn Ware, floral, rectangular, 4½x8x3½" 110.00
Mug, Brn Ware, cavalier bust, waisted shape, 5½" 85.00
Pitcher, Brn Ware, floral, sq rim, slim, 9" 125.00
Vase, Brn Ware, cherries, pinched neck, bulbous, hdls, 6" 75.00
Vase, Brn Ware, crossed leaves, bulbous, sm angle hdls, 10½" ...150.00
Vase, bud; Marbleized, bl, yel & blk swirls on brn, 6½" 65.00
Vase, bud; Wilse Bl, 6-sided, 6" 40.00
Vase, Chromal, cabin, fence & mtn (realistic) scene, 8" 600.00

Vase, Chromal, cabin, mtns & moon, #5, 10" 700.00
Vase, Chromal, impressionistic lake/mtns, cylindrical, 9¾" 300.00
Vase, Chromal, mtn winter scene (vivid), 12" 900.00
Vase, Chromal, stylized landscape, 7½" 200.00
Vase, Florentine, mc floral on beige, fan form, #30, 6" 50.00
Vase, Landsun, gr, bl & brn geometric design, #45, 5" 60.00
Vase, Marbleized, mc swirls on brn, classic form, 11½" 175.00
Vase, Moss Aztec, flowers/leaves, sgn Ferrell, str sides, 8" 75.00
Vase, Moss Aztec, leaves w/trailing stems, #172, 8" 75.00
Vase, Shadow Ware, bl & yel drips on tan, bulbous, #780, 8" 150.00
Vase, Shadow Ware, gr drips on mirror blk, #772, 4" 90.00
Vase, Shadow Ware, yel & gold drips on brn, shouldered, 8" 150.00
Vase, Wilse Bl, bl w/blk specks, bulbous, 5½" 40.00

Pewabic

The Pewabic Pottery was formally established in Detroit, Michigan, in 1907 by Mary Chase Perry Stratton and Horace James Caulkins. The two had worked together since 1903, firing their ware in a small kiln Caulkins had designed especially for use by the dental trade. Always a small operation which relied upon basic equipment and the skill of the workers, they took pride in being commissioned for several important architectural tile installations.

Some of the early artware was glazed a simple matt green; occasionally other colors were added, sometimes in combination, one over the other in a drip effect. Later Stratton developed a lustrous crystalline glaze. (Today's values are determined to a great extent by the artistic merit of the glaze.) The body of the ware was highly fired and extremely hard. Shapes were basic, and decorative modeling, if used at all, was in low relief. Mary Stratton kept the pottery open until her death in 1961. In 1968 it was purchased and reopened by Michigan State University. Several marks were used over the years: a triangle with 'Revelation Pottery' (for a short time only); 'Pewabic' with five maple leaves; and the impressed circle mark.

Bowl, aqua/yel-gr/gold w/tan irid, flat shoulder, 4x6½" 700.00
Bowl, bl/gold/lav/tan lustre, aqua int, 2½x5" 250.00
Bowl, dk purple/gold/gray, Chinese gr/red int, 2½x4½" 275.00
Bowl, thick turq lustre drip on blk matt, 3¼x6½" 850.00

Pitcher, blue with green highlights, 7, $550.00.

Plate, cvd geese border, tan on bl w/overglaze lustre, rpr, 9" 400.00
Plate, squeeze-bag apples, red/yel on ivory crackle, 9" 375.00
Tile, fish, burgundy lustre on khaki crystalline matt, 2¾", M 150.00
Tile, satyr w/bow & arrow, turq satin, unmk, 6" 375.00
Trivet, bluebird on golden yel, hexagonal, self-fr, mk, 10" 450.00
Trivet, triangle mosaic tiles, hexagonal, label, 10" dia 450.00
Vase, aqua drip on tan/gray/rose w/mc irid, cylinder, 8½" 950.00
Vase, bl irid w/mc highlights, gourd form, 6½" 650.00
Vase, bl matt, cylinder w/waisted neck, 9x3¾" 650.00
Vase, bl/gold irid, spherical, 3" 550.00

Vase, bl/purple irid, 2¾x3½" **450.00**
Vase, dk/lt gr streaked, 5 maple leaf mk, 3¾x3½" **325.00**
Vase, gold/bl irid flambe, waisted neck/angle shoulder, 3¾" **450.00**
Vase, gray-gr w/pk luster overglaze, shouldered, 9¾x8" **1,700.00**
Vase, Persian Bl, feathered gloss, waisted neck, 5½x5¼" **300.00**
Vase, pocked/speckled 3-tone bl drip glaze, blk neck, 9¾x8" **850.00**
Vase, royal bl gloss w/lg patches of gold & gr lustre, 5x4" **550.00**
Vase, tan lustre drip w/mc irid highlights on bl matt, 4½x4" **550.00**
Vase, thick aubergine lustre mottle, shouldered, 3½x4½" **350.00**
Vase, thick bl gloss, teardrop form, 10x5¾" **475.00**
Vase, thick burgundy lustre drip on dk purple, 4½x2½" **420.00**
Vase, thick tan matt w/brn highlights, shouldered, 7" **190.00**
Vase, thick volcanic cobalt/sea-gr/blk irid, 6½x5½" **1,400.00**
Vase, turq drip on gray irid, irid red base/int, 4¼x4" **635.00**

Pewter

Pewter is a metal alloy of tin, copper, very small parts of bismuth and/or antimony, and sometimes lead. Very little American pewter contained lead, however, because much of the ware was designed to be used as tableware, and makers were aware that the use of lead could result in poisoning. (Pieces that do contain lead are usually darker in color and heavier than those that have no lead.) Most of the fine examples of American pewter date from 1700 to the 1840s. Many pieces were melted down and recast into bullets during the American Revolution in 1775; this accounts to some extent why examples from this period are quite difficult to find. The pieces that did survive may include buttons, buckles, and writing equipment as well as the tableware we generally think of.

After the Revolution makers began using antimony as the major alloy with the tin in an effort to regain the popularity of pewter, which glassware and china was beginning to replace in the home. The resulting product, known as britannia, had a lustrous silver-like appearance and was far more durable. While closely related, britannia is a collectible in its own right and should not be confused with pewter.

Key: tm — touch mark

Basin, eagle tm att Gersham Jones, ca 1780-1800, 8" **460.00**
Basin, eagle tm of Thomas Danforth III, ca 1810, 10¼" **1,265.00**
Basin, Love tm, wear & corrosion, 2x8" **200.00**
Beaker, Boardman & Hart tm, hdls, 3⅛" **345.00**
Beaker, church; TD&S Boardman imperfect tm, 5¼" **315.00**
Beaker, Munden & Grove tm, 4¼" **315.00**
Beaker, Timothy Boardman & Co, 5¼" **600.00**
Beaker, unmk Am, ca 1900, 5¼" **230.00**
Beaker, unmk Am, eng women at well scene, hdls, 19th C, 3" ...**115.00**
Bottle, nursing; unmk England, 18th C, sm rprs, 6½" **435.00**
Bowl, baptismal; unmk (Boardman Group), 5½x7⅞" **575.00**
Bowl, baptismal; unmk Am, ftd, mid-1800s, 3¾x6½" **260.00**
Bowl, broth; John Langford tm, ca 1740s, 3½x5¾" **460.00**
Box, tobacco; James Dixon & Son tm, Sheffield, 4¾x3" **85.00**
Candle holder, F Porter Westbrook tm, dents, 5¾" **160.00**
Chalice, unmk Boardman, early 1800s, 7", pr **550.00**
Chalice, unmk England, mid-1700s **235.00**
Chambersticks, unmk Am, early 19th C, 2½", pr **260.00**
Charger, B&Co tm, wear/scratches, 14¾" **335.00**
Charger, eagle/Samuel Danforth tm, deep dish, 11" **660.00**
Charger, John Duncomb tm, 18" **575.00**
Charger, Samuel Duncomb tm, eng initials, 16½" **230.00**
Charger, Thomas Swanson tm, 15" **315.00**
Coffeepot, Boardman & Hart tm, triple-belly, cut decor, 12" **525.00**
Coffeepot, Dixon & Son tm, melon ribs, wood hdl & finial, 12" ..**140.00**

Coffeepots: Cellew & Co. touch mark, ca 1830-60, minor pitting, 11½", $400.00; Samuel Simpson touch mark, ca 1835-52, 11½", NM, $500.00.

Coffeepot, H Homan tm, cast flower finial, 11" **220.00**
Coffeepot, unmk Beverly Group, lighthouse style, 10¼" **230.00**
Compote, unmk, hinged lid, 2-compartment int, dents, 8½x8" .**250.00**
Creamer, unmk Am, goblet shape, soldered rpr, 5¾" **100.00**
Dish, Blakslee Barnes tm, 11⅛" **285.00**
Flagon, Boardman & Co tm, 3-tiered finial, 2-qt, 12¾" **1,725.00**
Flagon, faint Continental tm on lid, ca 1800, 7¾" **425.00**
Flagon, faint tm (Fr), 18th C, 10" **175.00**
Flagon, faint tm on lid (Norman), 18th C, 12" **175.00**
Flagon, unmk Trask, 1800s, 12½" **450.00**
Ladle, ebonized wooden hdl, 14½" **85.00**
Ladle, Thomas Danforth Boardman tm, 13½" **260.00**
Lamp, Capen & Molineux NY tm, fluid burner, 7¾" **450.00**
Lamp, R Gleason tm, saucer base, whale-oil burner, 5¼" **500.00**
Lamp, Roswell Gleason tm, lozenge top, ca 1840s, 8" **350.00**
Lamp, unmk Am, burning fluid burner, rpr, 8"+burner, pr **375.00**
Measure, gill; unmk Boardman, no lid, 3⅛" **315.00**
Measure, Guernsey; A Carter tm, ca 1750, 7" **800.00**
Measure, Guernsey; John De St Croix tm, ca 1730, 5⅝" **950.00**
Measure, John Carr tm, bud baluster, w/lid, 18th C, 5" **515.00**
Measure, Minister Iron Co tm, 1 Half Pint, haystack type **45.00**
Measure, Pierre Goncert tm on lid, 18th C, 10½", EX **285.00**
Measure, shoulder type, late 1700s, 10¾" **175.00**
Measure, T&W Wilshire tm, bud baluster, w/lid, ca 1800, 8½" .**230.00**
Measure, tappet hen; Scotland, ca 1800, 7" **1,035.00**
Measure, unmk Am, baluster, lidless, rpr, ca 1800, 11" **545.00**
Measure, unmk Boardman, baluster, lidless, rpr, 5¼" **200.00**
Measure, unmk Boardman, inspector's initials IPS, ½-gal, 9" ..**1,100.00**
Measure, unmk Boardman, inspector's initials PL, lidless, 4" **800.00**
Measure, unmk England, bud baluster, w/lid, ½-gal, 11" **1,265.00**
Measure, unmk England, bud baluster, w/lid, 18th C, 6", EX **175.00**
Mug, Ingram & Hunt, minor rpr, 1-pt **315.00**
Mug, Robert Iles tm, tulip shape, 4¾", EX **375.00**
Mug, unmk, ca 1800, 1-qt, 6" **285.00**
Mug, unmk England, tulip shape, mid-1700s, rpr, 4¾" **115.00**
Pitcher, rum; unmk England, 1800s, minor dents, 8¼" **315.00**
Pitcher, water; Boardman Group tm, 11¼" **700.00**
Plate, angel tm, Continental, 9½", pr **225.00**
Plate, B Barnes Phila w/eagle tm, dents/scratches, 8" **165.00**
Plate, Boardman Group lion tm, 9⅜" **260.00**
Plate, Continental tm, eng decor, 18th C, 10" **65.00**
Plate, David Melville tm, 8⅛" **345.00**
Plate, eagle & Samuel Pierce tm, wear/scratches, 8" **360.00**
Plate, Edward Danforth tm, 8" **225.00**
Plate, Frederick Bassett, 8½" **315.00**
Plate, Gershom Jones anchor tm, rpr, 8⅜" **120.00**
Plate, Gershom Jones tm, late 1700s, 8¼" **545.00**

Plate, Jacob Whitmore tm, 8" 375.00
Plate, James Tisoe tm, armorial eng, 8-sided, 8¾" 500.00
Plate, John Watts tm, 9¼", pr 260.00
Plate, Joseph Danforth tm, 8" 260.00
Plate, lion (Boardman) tm, corroded bk, 9" 250.00
Plate, Parkes Boyd tm, 8" 500.00
Plate, partial Townsend tm, wear/pitting, 9¼" 95.00
Plate, Richard Austin lamb & dove tm, 8" 490.00
Plate, Thomas D Boardman, 7⅞" 200.00
Plate, unmk, ca 1800, 6⅞", pr 145.00
Plate, unmk, molded rim, 10¼" 100.00
Plate, unmk Am, ca 1800, 7¾", pr 105.00
Plate, William Billings tm, 8¼" 400.00
Plate, William Danforth tm, 7⅞" 288.00
Plate, William Kirby tm, hammered booge, 8⅞" 660.00
Platter, Samuel Danforth tm, 7⅞" 200.00
Porringer, cast heart hdl, 3¼" 195.00
Porringer, faint SG tm, cast crown hdl, 4¼" 275.00
Porringer, Samuel E Hamlin Jr tm, flower hdl, 4½" 850.00
Porringer, TD & SB tm (TD & S Boardman), flower hdl, 5½" ..750.00
Porringer, unmk (att Melville, RI), solid hdl, 5½" 550.00
Porringer, unmk (att Richard Lee), ca 1800, 2¼" 300.00
Porringer, unmk Boardman Group, modified basin, 1800s, 4¼" .200.00
Porringer, unmk England, goemetric hdl, 18th C, pitting, 5" 345.00
Porringer, unmk New England, cast initials on bk of hdl, 5½" ..230.00
Porringer, unmk New England, cast R on heart hdl, 1800s, 4¼" ...200.00
Porringer, unmk New England, crown hdl, early 1800s, 4¼" 175.00
Porringer, unmk New England, modified basin, 1800s, 4½" 260.00
Porringer, unmk New England, Old English hdl, 19th C, 4¼" ...175.00
Porringer, unmk PA, tab hdls, ca 1817-45, 5½" 750.00
Porringer, unmk RI, flower hdl, ca 1800, 5" 260.00
Sauce boat, Henry Joseph tm, fine 18th-C form, 4x7¼" ...925.00
Soup plate, 2 eagle tm, wear/split, 11" 195.00
Spoon, Thomas Danforth Boardman tm, 8" 150.00
Sugar bowl, Homan & Co, Cincinnati, cast flower finial, 7" 80.00
Syrup, unmk Am, 19th C, 6" 115.00
Tall pot, Boardman & Hart NY tm, rpr, 11" 300.00
Tall pot, eagle & R Gleason tm, minor pitting, 11" 250.00
Tall pot, unmk Am, lighthouse type, rprs, 10¼" 220.00
Tankard, Wm Eddon tm, sm rpr to lid, 1700s, 1-qt, 6¾" ..980.00
Teapot, Ashbil Griswold tm, 8" 375.00
Teapot, eagle/A Griswold tm, soldered rpr, 7" 275.00
Teapot, EB Mannings Pat June 5, 1862 Warranted, 8¾", EX 100.00
Teapot, English tm, pear shape, late 1700s, 7½" 575.00
Teapot, G Richardson Warranted tm, 9¼" 600.00
Teapot, LL Williams Philada tm, rpr hdl, 8¼" 275.00
Teapot, Sellew & Co Cincinnati, 6¼" 275.00
Teapot, unmk, New England or NY, modified pear shape, 6¾" ..260.00
Teapot, unmk Am, 7¼" 220.00
Teapot, unmk England, boat shape, wood hdl, 1800s, 6x10", EX ..175.00
Toddy plate, 2 lion tm, separation, 6½" 220.00
Tumbler, Thomas Danforth Boardman eagle tm, 2¾" 100.00

Pfaltzgraff

Pfaltzgraff has operated in Pennsylvania since the early 1800s making redware at first, then stoneware crocks and jugs, yellow ware and spongeware in the twenties, artware and kitchenware in the thirties, and stoneware kitchen items through the forties. To collectors, they're best known for their Gourmet Royal (circa 1950s), a high-gloss dinnerware line of solid brown with frothy white drip glaze around the rims, and their giftware line called Muggsy, comic-character mugs, ashtrays, bottle stoppers, children's dishes, a pretzel jar, a cookie jar, etc. It was

designed in the late 1940s and continued in production until 1960. The older versions have protruding features, while the features of later examples were simpy painted on.

For more information on Gourmet Royal dinnerware, we recommend *The Flea Market Trader* and *The Garage Sale and Flea Market Annual* (both published by Collector Books).

Beanpot, Yorktown, old, 2½-qt 36.00
Bowl, oval vegetable; Gourmet, 2-part, 12" 20.00
Bowl, soup/cereal; Gourmet, 5½" 6.00
Candle holder, Yorktown, 3" 17.50
Canister, Yorktown, Sugar, str sides, 6" 20.00
Casserole, Country Time, 2-qt 42.00
Cookie jar, Clown w/Drum 200.00
Cookie jar, Cookie Cop 550.00

Cookie jar, Derby Dan, marked Muggsy, $250.00 minimum value.

Cookie jar, Old Lady in the Shoe 165.00
Cookie jar, Train 175.00
Creamer, Gourmet 7.50
Cruet, Country Time 28.00
Cup & saucer, Gourmet 5.00
Drippings jar, Yorktown 16.00
Fork, Country Time, wood hdl 28.00
Gravy boat, Gourmet, loop hdl 17.50
Lazy Susan, Yorktown, 4-part, plastic base 22.50
Pitcher, Yorktown, 1-qt 17.50
Planter, donkey, 10" 17.50
Platter, Country Time, 12" 18.00
Souffle dish, Gourmet, 2-qt, 8½" 20.00
Teapot, Yorktown, sm 22.50

Muggsy

Ashtray 125.00
Canape holder, Carrie, lift-off hat holds toothpicks ...150.00
Cigarette server 125.00
Clothes sprinkler bottler, Myrtle, blk, from $225 to ...250.00
Clothes sprinkler bottler, Myrtle, wht 175.00
Cookie jar, character face, minimum value 250.00
Jar, utility; Handy Harry, hat forms lid 200.00
Mug, action figure 80.00
Mug, Blk action figure 125.00
Mug, character face 38.00
Shot mug, character face 50.00
Tumbler 65.00

Phoenix Bird

Blue and white Phoenix Bird china has been produced by various Japanese potteries from the early 1900s. With slight variations the design features the Japanese bird of paradise and scroll-like vines of Kara-Kusa, or Chinese grass. Although some of their earlier ware is unmarked, the majority is marked in some fashion. More than one hundred different stamps have been reported, with 'Made in Japan' the one most often found. Coming in second is Morimura's wreath and/or crossed stems (both having the letter 'M' within). The cloverleaf with 'Japan' below very often indicates an item having a high-quality transfer-printed design. Among the many categories in the Phoenix Bird pattern are several shapes; therefore (for identification purposes), each has been given a number, i.e. #1, #2, etc. Newer items, if marked at all, carry a paper label. Compared to the older ware, the coloring of the new is whiter and the blue more harsh; the design is sparse with more ground area showing. Although collectors buy even 'new' pieces, the older is of course more highly prized and valued.

For further information we recommend *Phoenix Bird Chinaware, Books I — IV*, written and privately published by our advisor, Joan Oates; her address is in the Directory under Michigan. Join Phoenix Bird Collectors of America (PBCA) and receive the *Phoenix Bird Discoveries* newsletter, an informative publication that will further your appreciation of this chinaware. See Clubs, Newsletters, and Catalogs for ordering information.

Bonbon dish, rattan hdl 65.00
Casserole #1, oval lid 75.00
Celery tray #1, 13½" L 95.00
Creamer & sugar bowl #1 ....75.00
Creamer & sugar bowl #27, str sides 35.00
Gravy boat #5, w/oval scalloped underplate 95.00
Hair receiver, 2-pc 45.00
Hostess tray #1, rnd 115.00
Jar, bath salts; w/mushroom lid 45.00
Jug, batter; teardrop lid 65.00
Matchbox holder, attached tray 150.00
Muffineer #1, 4¼" 95.00
Pickle dish #1 ....50.00
Plate, wicker encased, wicker hdl 35.00
Ramekin, w/4⅞" underplate 32.00
Salt dip #2, rnd, ftd 30.00
Sherbet, ped ft 25.00
Tea set, child's playset #2 ....125.00
Tea/toast #1, kidney shape 25.00
Toothpick holder #2 ....40.00

Phoenix Glass

Founded in 1880 in Monaca, Pennsylvania, the Phoenix Glass Company became one of the country's foremost manufacturers of lighting glass by the early 1900s. They also produced a wide variety of utilitarian and decorative glassware, including art glass by Joseph Webb, colored cut glass, Gone-with-the-Wind style oil lamps, hotel and bar ware, and pharmaceutical glassware. Today, however, collectors are primarily interested in the 'Sculptured Artware' produced in the 1930s and 1940s. These beautiful pressed and mold-blown pieces are most often found in white milk glass or crystal with various color treatments or a satin finish.

Phoenix did not mark their 'Sculptured Artware' line on the glass; instead, a silver and black or gold and black foil label in the shape of the mythical phoenix bird was used.

Quite often glassware made by the Consolidated Lamp and Glass Company of nearby Coraopolis, Pennsylvania, is mistaken for Phoenix's 'Sculptured Artware.' Though the style of the glass is very similar, one distinguishing characteristic is that perhaps 80% of the time Phoenix applied color to the background leaving the raised design plain in contrast, while

Consolidated generally applied color to the raised design and left the background plain. Also, for the most part, the patterns and colors used by Phoenix were distinctively different from those used by Consolidated.

In 1970 Phoenix Glass became a division of Anchor Hocking which in turn was acquired by the Newell Group in 1987. Phoenix has the distinction of being one of the oldest continuously operating glass factories in the United States. For more information refer to *Phoenix and Consolidated Art Glass, 1926-1980*, written by our advisor, Jack D. Wilson, who is listed in the Directory under Illinois. See also Consolidated Glass.

Key: mg — milk glass

Ashtray, slate gray bkground on mg, MOP flowers, 3" L 40.00
Bowl, Lacy Dew Drop, pk on mg, 8" sq 40.00
Bowl, Tiger Lily, pk frosted, 11½" 275.00
Candle holders, Strawberry, gr over mg, 4¼", pr 130.00
Compote, Moon & Star, pearl lustre on mg, 8" dia 45.00
Mold, Jell-O; Queen Anne, crystal, star shape 4.00
Sugar bowl, Lacy Dew Drop, bl wash, w/lid 60.00
Umbrella vase, Thistle, tan pearlized, 18" 450.00
Vase, Bachelor Button, gr bkground on satin mg, 7" 165.00
Vase, Bicentennial, crystal w/red, wht & bl pattern 50.00
Vase, Bittersweet, Reuben Line, lt bl wash, 9½" 175.00
Vase, Cosmos, aqua bkground, wht flowers on crystal, 7½" 150.00

Vase, Daisy, blue on milk glass, 9x9", $250.00.

Vase, Fern, crystal on bl, 7" 85.00
Vase, Freesia, Cedar Rose bkground on crystal, 8" 165.00
Vase, Lily, aqua on crystal, frosted pattern, tri-crimp, 8" 250.00
Vase, Madonna, tan pealized 200.00
Vase, Philodendron, amber, 1960s, 11" 45.00
Vase, Philodendron, brn shadow finish, 11½" 175.00
Vase, Pine Cones, no cones, aqua on crystal frost, rare, 6½" 235.00
Vase, Primrose, frosted design on bl, 8¾" 475.00
Vase, Thistle, bl on mg, MOP pattern, 18" 425.00
Vase, Wild Geese, mg on lt bl, 9½x12" 280.00
Vase, Wild Geese, red pearlized, 10" 275.00
Vase, Wild Geese, wht on tan, 9x11" 215.00
Vase, Zodiac, med bl on mg, frosted pattern, 10" 495.00
Vase, Zodiac, wht on peach, rare, 10½" 700.00

Phonographs

The phonograph, invented by Thomas Edison in 1877, was the first practical instrument for recording and reproducing sound. Sound wave vibrations were recorded on a tinfoil-covered cylinder and played back with a needle that ran along the grooves made from the recording, thus reproducing the sound. Other companies further improved Edison's invention; among them were Victor, Columbia, Zonophone, and Vitaphone. All Victor I's through VI's were originally available with brass bell, morning-glory, or wood horns. Wood horns are the most desirable, adding $1,000.00 (or more) to the value of a machine. Spring models were produced until 1929 (and later); after 1929, most were electric (though some electric-motor models were produced as early as 1910). Unless another condition is noted, prices are for complete, original phonographs in at least fine to excellent condition. Note: Edison coin-operated cylinder players start at $7,000.00 and may go up to $20,000.00 each. All outside horn Victor phonographs are worth at **least** $1,000.00 or more if in excellent original condition. Our advisor for this category is J.R. Wilkins; he is listed in the Directory under Texas. Unless noted, values are for examples in excellent condition, sold at popular, repeated buying prices.

Key:
mg — morning glory   rpd — reproducer
NP — nickel plated

Berliner Trademark, disc player **3,500.00**
Brunswick Model 117, Concert rpd, inside horn, floor model **200.00**
Busy Bee Grand, disc, Busy Bee rpd, red mg horn **500.00**
Columbia AB McDonald, cylinder, eagle rpd, 2 mandrels, EX .**1,250.00**
Columbia AG Grand, D rpd, 56" brass horn/5" mandrel, +stand, EX ...**1,500.00**
Columbia AJ, disc, Columbia rpd, brass bell horn, top wind ...**1,200.00**
Columbia AQ, cylinder, D rpd, sm horn, key wind **400.00**
Columbia AT, cylinder, D rpd, lg mg horn, EX **400.00**
Columbia AU, blk horn, open works, 7" turntable **500.00**
Columbia B Eagle, cylinder, eagle rpd/aluminum horn/key wind .**400.00**
Columbia BC 20th Century, 4" Higham rpd, 54" horn, 6" mandrel .**2,100.00**
Columbia BD Majestic, disc, mahog, analyzing rpd, mg horn ..**1,700.00**
Columbia BE Leader, Lyric rpd, brass bell horn, serpentine **500.00**
Columbia BF Peerless, Lyric rpd, 14" brass horn, oak case **650.00**
Columbia BK Jewel, Lyric rpd, brass bell/crane horn, oak case ...**450.00**
Columbia BN Improved Champion, Columbia rpd, oak horn .**1,500.00**
Columbia BO Invincible, Lyric rpd, oak horn & case **2,100.00**
Columbia BS Coin-op, Eagle rpd, 14" metal horn, VG **2,500.00**
Columbia Grafonola Mignon, Columbia rpd, inside horn, floor .**175.00**
Columbia Q, D rpd, blk horn, oak case, earphones **350.00**
Columbia Q, D rpd, cone horn, key wind **375.00**
Columbia Q Busy Bee, D rpd, blk cone horn, key wind **300.00**
Columbia Regent Desk, Columbia rpd, inside horn, desk cabinet **400.00**
Edison Amberola V, Dmn B rpd, inside horn, mahog, table model ...**450.00**
Edison Amberola VI, Dmn B rpd, inside horn, table model **350.00**
Edison Amberola 30, cylinder, Dmn C rpd, inside horn, oak **400.00**
Edison Amberola 50, cylinder, Dmn C rpd, inside horn, mahog ...**550.00**
Edison Amberola 75, cylinder, Dmn C rpd, inside horn, mahog ...**700.00**
Edison Concert A, cylinder, C rpd, 40" brass horn w/tripod **2,500.00**
Edison Concert C, cylinder, B rpd, 30" bell horn, +stand, M ..**2,500.00**
Edison Fireside, cylinder, K rpd, metal cygnet horn, complete ...**1,000.00**
Edison Fireside A, cylinder, Dmn B rpd, oak Music Master horn .**2,250.00**
Edison Fireside A, cylinder, K rpd, maroon Fireside horn **1,800.00**
Edison Fireside B, cylinder, Dmn B rpd, cygnet horn, 4 min, VG ...**1,000.00**
Edison Gem A, cylinder, C rpd, repro aluminum horn **400.00**
Edison Gem A, cylinder, early Gem rpd, cone horn, drip pan-A ..**950.00**
Edison Gem B, cylinder, C rpd, blk mg horn w/crane **500.00**
Edison Gem C, cylinder, C rpd, repro cone horn, early **500.00**
Edison Gem D Maroon, cylinder, K rpd, Fireside horn, w/crane ..**1,800.00**
Edison Home, cylinder, S rpd, metal cygnet horn **1,000.00**
Edison Home A Suitcase, cylinder, C rpd, bell horn, w/decal **475.00**
Edison Home D, cylinder, C rpd, 14" brass bell horn, decal **650.00**
Edison Home E, cylinder, O rpd, oak cygnet horn, oak case **2,000.00**
Edison Home G, cygnet horn **1,800.00**
Edison Opera, cylinder, L rpd, mahog cygnet horn, mahog case ..**4,000.00**
Edison Std A, cylinder, C rpd, blk/brass horn, banner **475.00**
Edison Std A Suitcase, cylinder, old-style rpd, 14" bell **550.00**

Edison Std B, cylinder, O rpd, 19" mg horn, 2/4-min **900.00**
Edison Std B, cylinder, 2-min, C rpd, 15" brass horn **450.00**
Edison Std D, cylinder, C rpd, 14" bell horn **500.00**
Edison Std G, cygnet horn **1,800.00**
Edison Triumph, cylinder, C rpd, 7" brass bell, 2-min **950.00**
Edison Triumph, cylinder, O rpd, oak cygnet horn, NM **2,500.00**
Edison Triumph D, cylinder, H rpd, 23" bell horn, 2/4-min **725.00**
Edison Triumph G, cylinder, opera case **4,000.00**
Eldridge R Johnson M, Victor type, rare, EX **2,800.00**
Heywood-Wakefield Perfektone, inside horn, wicker case **700.00**
Horn only, Columbia, all aluminum, 14" **150.00**
Horn only, Edison, brass bell, orig, 14" **125.00**
Mignonphone, cb horn in cover, camera type, complete **175.00**
Pathe Actuelle, cone horn, upright **700.00**
Pathe Coquet, Ebonite rpd, aluminum horn **425.00**
Puck Lyre, cylinder, floating rpd/aluminum horn/string drive **365.00**
Regina Hexaphone 104, Hexaphone rpd, oak built-in horn, rstr .**7,500.00**
Standard A, disc, Standard rpd, orig red mg horn **650.00**
Standard X, disc, Standard rpd, red flowered mg horn **650.00**
Victor D, disc, brass bell horn **1,750.00**
Victor E Monarch Jr, disc, Exhibition rpd, brass bell horn **1,000.00**
Victor I, disc, Exhibition rpd, 16" bell horn, 8" turntable **1,000.00**
Victor II, disc, Exhibition rpd, oak wood horn, oak case **2,500.00**
Victor II, disc, Exhibition rpd, 18" brass bell horn, oak **1,000.00**
Victor III, disc, Exhibition rpd, 16" brass bell horn, oak **1,750.00**
Victor IV, disc, Exhibition rpd, 20" brass bell horn, mahog **1,500.00**
Victor M Monarch, disc, Exhibition rpd, 30" bell horn, oak ...**1,500.00**
Victor MS Monarch Specialty, disc, Exhibition rpd, lg oak horn ..**2,500.00**
Victor O, disc, 8-petal mg horn, oak **1,200.00**
Victor P Premium, disc, Concert rpd, bell horn, wood-tone arm ...**1,200.00**
Victor R Royal, disc, Exhibition rpd, 9½" bell horn **1,000.00**
Victor Schoolhouse XXV, disc, orig oak horn, NM **2,500.00**
Victor V, disc, Exhibition rpd, oak horn **3,500.00**
Victor V, disc, metal horn **2,500.00**
Victor VI, disc, Exhibition rpd, mahog horn & case w/gold **5,000.00**
Victor VI, disc, metal horn **3,500.00**
Victor VI, disc, wood horn **5,000.00**
Victor Victrola VV-XI, disc, #2 rpd, inside horn **200.00**
Victor Victrola VV-50, disc, #2 rpd, inside horn, 1st portable **150.00**
Victor VV 8-30, disc, Orthophonic rpd, inside horn, credenza ...**600.00**
Victor VV-XIV, disc, inside horn, mahog case, upright **350.00**
Victor VV-XIV, disc, inside horn, oak case, upright **450.00**
Victor VV-XVI, disc, inside horn, mahog case, upright **450.00**
Victor VV-XVI, disc, inside horn, oak case, upright **550.00**
Victor Z, disc, Exhibition rpd, brass bell horn **1,200.00**
Zonophone A, disc, Concert rpd, brass horn, beveled glass **2,200.00**
Zonophone Parlor, disc, brass bell horn, rear crank **1,100.00**

Photographica

Photographic collectibles include not only the cameras and equipment used to 'freeze' special moments in time but also the photographic images produced by a great variety of processes that have evolved since the daguerrean era of the mid-1800s. For the most part, good quality images have either maintained or increased in value. Poor quality examples (regardless of rarity) are not selling well. Interest in cameras and stereo equipment is down, and dealers report that often average-priced items that were moving well are often completely overlooked. Though rare items always have a market, collectors seem to be buying only if they are bargain priced.

Our advisor for this category is John Hess; he is listed in the Directory under Massachusetts.

Albumens

Arapaho women (1 sits/1 stands), many ornaments, 1880s, 4x6" .250.00
Civil War Naval officer w/telescope, 3x3", EX 125.00
Friends school, Providence RI, Hacker, 1860s, 10x15", EX 70.00
Paddlewheeler Chattanooga, att JF Coonley, ca 1864, 17x14½" ..350.00
Saloon interior, Reno NV, much detail, 5½x8½", VG 50.00
Seminude Indian ladies (2), much jewelry, 1880s, 4x6" 250.00

Ambrotypes

An ambrotype is a type of photograph produced by an early wet-plate process whereby a faint negative image on glass is seen as positive when held against a dark background.

Half plate, boy & girl seated, tinted dress, gold-trim case 100.00
Half plate, 6-man boat crew, Lone Star Boat Club, EX 1,000.00
4th plate, man w/huge beard, face tinted, EX 35.00
4th plate, 2 boys w/puppy on table, EX in case 125.00
4th plate, 2 seated children, geometric wood fr, EX 35.00
4th plate, 2 sisters, finely dressed, w/fans, EX 35.00
4th plate, 3 friends in studio pose, EX 35.00

6th plate, occupational type, man sawing wood, some hand coloring, EX in leather case, $400.00.

6th plate, boy w/toy train on table, ruby glass, compo case 300.00
6th plate, girl (about 6 yrs old) in fancy dress w/bloomers 22.50
6th plate, girl w/parrot on hand, some tinting, w/full case 260.00
6th plate, Naval officer in full uniform, w/plumed helmet 90.00
6th plate, Union Zouave Soldier, chest-up view, w/case 350.00

Cabinet Photos

Cathedral, 250 Yrs Old, Albuquerque NM, Sanders, oversz 40.00
Miss Uno, circus performer w/monkey, Sword Bros, VG 16.00
Plantation Life, Blk man w/wheelbarrow, wht man on mule, 1880s .35.00
Sea captain in 'pea' jacket, ship beyond, primitive painting 12.50
Tacoma WA panoramic scene, wharf area, Rutter, 1891, oversz ..26.00
US Marine Corps soldier in 7-button frock, 1880s 50.00
7 Sutherland sisters, all w/very long hair, VG 16.50

Cameras

Among the earliest daguerrean cameras was the sliding box-on-a-box camera. It was focused by sliding one box in and out of the other, thus adjusting the distance of the lens to the ground glass. This was replaced on later models with leather bellows. These were the forerunners of the multilens cameras developed in the late 1870s, which were capable of recording many small portraits on a single plate. Double-lens cameras produced stereo images which, when viewed through a device called a stereoscope, achieved a 3-dimensional effect. In 1888 George Eastmann introduced his box camera, the first to utilize roll film. This greatly sim-

plified the process, making it possible for the amateur to enjoy photography as a hobby. Detective cameras, those disguised as books, handbags, etc., are among the most sought after by today's collectors.

Canon IVSB, red engraving on top plate, with Canon 50mm f/1.8 lens, 1952-55, NM, $225.00.

Contaflex Super, M 125.00
Diamond Jr, top loading, box type, ca 1898 ....80.00
Eastman Kodak Bullet, WD Teague, Bakelite, orig box, VG 40.00
Graflex National, 120 film, 1933, MIB w/directions 200.00
Icarette #501, EX 70.00
Jiffy Kodak Six 16, EX 35.00
Kodak #1 Autographic Kodak Jr, M in orig case 20.00
Zeiss Ikon accessory lenses, 35mm & 8mm w/filters, in case 100.00
Zeiss Ikon Contaflex IV, M 135.00

Carte De Visites

Among the many types of images collectible today are carte de visites, known as CDVs, which are 2¼" x 4" portraits printed on paper and produced in quantity. The CDV fad of the 1800s enticed the famous and the unknown alike to pose for these cards, which were circulated among the public to the extent that they became known as 'publics.' When the popularity of CDVs began to wane, a new fascination developed for the cabinet photo, a larger version measuring about 4½" x 6½". Note: A common portrait CDV is worth only about 50¢ unless it carries a revenue stamp on the back; those that do are valued at about $1.00 each.

Benjamin Franklin, oval portrait from painting, scarce 10.00
Blind man seated, dk tinted glasses, Victorian era 27.50
Buffalo Bill in buckskin coat, chest-up view, rare 195.00
Civil war officer w/hand on cvd chair, Chicago, VG 35.00
Civil War private in frock coat by pillar, EX 30.00
Confederate Army winter quarters at Centreville, Gardner, VG ..88.00
Farmer & 3 Gurnsey bulls, JW Black Boston, EX 18.00
Gen Fitzhugh Lee, Seldon & Emmis, VA, 1863, EX 160.00
Gen John Ellis Wool seated, Anthony/Brady 80.00
Gen Phillip H Sheridan w/signature, Anthony/Brady, EX 900.00
Gen Robert E Lee, Anthony/Brady, EX 160.00
Gen Tom Thumb & Wife, Commodore Nutt & Miss Minnie Warren, EX .15.00
Indian Wars Sergeant seated w/cavalry saber on lap, 1870s 30.00
Lincoln & family, based on Carpenter's painting, EX 20.00
Lucretia Coffin Mott, in Quaker bonnet, rare image, VG 50.00
Man riding 'boneshaker' wooden bicycle, full view, 1860s, EX 55.00
Mansion w/gambrel roof, Loomis, Boston 12.50
Mary Todd Lincoln, ¾-length view in blk, Ostendorf, EX 55.00
Miss Jennie Quibly, 20-yr-old midget, 28" high, 32 lbs, EX 25.00
Mrs Battersby Weight 700 lbs, seated lady w/crown, EX 50.00
Postmortem, sm girl on couch, JD Powers, EX 30.00
Union Gen Nathaniel Lion, standing, Anthony/Brady, EX 100.00
Union soldier stands in greatcoat by seated wife, JW Black 30.00
2 gamblers playing cards, close-up view, shows cards, 1860s 25.00
3 seamen in uniform, JT Green's Union Gallery, 1868, EX 25.00

Daguerreotypes

Among the many processes used to produce photographic images are the daguerreotypes (made on a plate of chemically treated metal) — the most-valued examples being the 'whole' plate which measures 6½" x 8½". Other sizes include the 'half' plate, measuring 4½" x 5½", the 'quarter' plate at 3¼" x 4¼", the 'sixth' plate at 2¾" x 3¼", the 'ninth' at 2" x 2½", and the 'sixteenth' at 1⅜" x 1⅝". (Sizes may vary slightly, and some may have been altered by the photographer.)

4th plate, college graduation class of 19 men, 1850s, EX **450.00**
4th plate, man in fine clothes, w/cane, EX, w/case **170.00**
4th plate, man's portrait, stamped Gurney, EX, w/case **225.00**
4th plate, man's portrait, tinted/gold highlights, EX, w/case **150.00**
6th plate, girl in highchair, w/magnifying case dtd 1853 ....**275.00**
6th plate, gold miner from waist up, EX **850.00**

6th plate, unidentified locomotive, mid-19th century, EX in cracked gutta percha case, $1,200.00.

6th plate, man in top hat, domed-topped mat, EX, w/compo case .**60.00**
6th plate, man signing document, EX, w/compo case **90.00**
6th plate, Mexican War Naval officer, Blumbe, EX **220.00**
6th plate, Military officer in full dress w/wife at side **400.00**
6th plate, mother & daughter, tinted, EX, w/compo case **50.00**
6th plate, phrenologist w/phrenological bust & book, w/case ..**1,600.00**
6th plate, postmortem of child, flower fr, EX **425.00**
6th plate, Robert Ross portrait, W Clark, London, 1847, G **50.00**
6th plate, violinist w/instrument, full compo case **300.00**
9th plate, girl w/dog on lap, w/case, EX **280.00**
9th plate, lady w/off-shoulder dress, G, w/leather case **100.00**
9th plate, mother w/infant, +thermoplastic case **60.00**

Photos

Blk Masons & Eastern Star, 9 ladies/12 men, ca 1910, 5x7", VG ..**150.00**
Salt print, John Hunt Morgan & wife, 7x5" oval **650.00**
Sepia tone, Lillian Gish, 1922, 7x9", EX **65.00**
Silverprint, Hindenburg Explosion, Internat'l News, 1937 ....**300.00**
11 Blk porters w/supervisors by train car, 1930s, 10x8" **225.00**

Stereoscopic Views

Stereo cards are photos made to be viewed through a device called a stereoscope. The glass stereo plates of the mid-1800s and photo prints produced in the darkroom are among the most valuable. In evaluating stereo views, the subject, date, and condition are all-important. Some views were printed over a thirty- to forty-year period; 'first generation' prices are far higher than later copies, made on cheap card stock with reprints or lithographs, rather than actual original photographs.

It is relatively easy to date an American stereo view by the color of the mount that was used, the style of the corners, etc. From about 1854 until the early 1860s, cards were either white, cream-colored, or glossy gray; shades of yellow and a dull gray followed. While the dull gray was used for a very short time, the yellow tones continued in use until the late 1860s. Red, green, violet, or blue cards are from the period between 1865 until about 1870. Until the late 1870s, corners were square; after that they were rounded off to prevent damage. Right now, quality stereo views are at a premium. Values are suggested for early cards in good to excellent condition.

Arriving at Lakehurst NJ, Keystone airplane series, G **15.00**
Baldwin, Early Dirigible in Flight, Keystone, G **15.00**
Bound for Klondike Gold Fields, Calikoot Pass, AK, Keystone **15.00**
Boxer Chief Undergoing...Death for His Crimes, Kilburn, 1902 ...**95.00**
Cabin Home, Blk family by log cabin, Kilburn, #445, 1880s, VG .**15.00**
Camping Out, California, Kilburn, ca 1880, VG **8.00**
Chicago Fire, PB Green, 1871, VG+, set of 8 ....**80.00**
Children in school yard, Dakota Territory, Newcombe, G **20.00**
Cincinnati & Covington Suspension Bridge, Mendenhall, G **12.00**
Donkey Train, Ute Pass Near Manitou, Weitfle, VG **20.00**
Fisk Singers, Blk singers, AC McIntyre, EX **55.00**
Fort Sumter, fort & harbor, EX **15.00**
GA log cabin, 6 Blk children, 1 girl w/wash, SG Havens, EX **40.00**
Galveston Flood, Blk lady & children, Brown, #1214b, 1900, VG ..**12.00**
Grand Masonic Ceremony, San Francisco, 1972, G **10.00**
Hon Wm Jennings Bryan on His Farm..., Underwood, 1900 ....**20.00**
House Building by Masai Women, Keystone, gray mt, EX **6.00**
Kotton, Kur, Koons & Kisses, Keystone #9522, 1890s, VG **20.00**
Looking Up 5th Ave, man w/camera on skyscraper, Keystone **42.50**
Martyrs, Lincoln & Garfield; w/mourning wreath, Underwood **22.50**
Near Fort Lowell, Tucson, AZ Territory, fort scene, 1878 ....**35.00**
Old Torpedo, Spanish Fort, New Orleans, Mugnier, VG **50.00**
Quincy market building, Boston, 1870s, EX **18.00**
Round Horn & 2 Wives, Indian chief & family, Goff, VG **200.00**
Sanitarium in Battlecreek, Murphy, VG+ **8.00**
Train wreck, Hartford CT, 1870s, EX **15.00**
Ute Braves of Kah-poh-tah Land, NM, O'Sullivan **50.00**
View of IA Capitol From Northeast, trolley scene, Baldwin, G **15.00**
2 Blk boys on balustrade, JA Bolles, 1870s, M **80.00**

Tintypes

Tintypes, contemporaries of ambrotypes, were produced on japanned iron and were not as easily damaged.

Full plate, Union officer in full dress, ¾-view, fr **500.00**
2¼x1¾", Blk man w/mustache, waist-up view, VG **17.50**
2¼x3¼", 3 men beside early bicycles, EX **17.50**
4th plate, sm boy beside Gothic Revival chair, tinted, EX **25.00**
4th plate, soldier in full dress w/Am flag, EX+, w/case **500.00**
4th plate, Union corporal, full-length, w/patriotic case **125.00**
4th plate, Union Naval officer, ¾-pose w/gold, compo case **150.00**
4th plate, Union sergeant casual portrait, VG **150.00**
4th plate, 3 children on platform by rose plant, tinted, EX **40.00**
4x2½", Indian Wars Zouave soldier, standing in full dress **165.00**
6th plate, African lady w/lg earrings, ribboned hair, w/case **50.00**
6th plate, African-AM GAR veteran in uniform, compo case ...**450.00**
6th plate, Civil War militia drummer stands w/drum **190.00**
6th plate, high-wheel bicyclist, proper attire, w/case **125.00**
6th plate, musicians playing rotary-valve horns, w/case **70.00**
6th plate, Union cavalryman w/saber & M1858 Remington revolver ...**325.00**
6th plate, Union soldier w/revolver, in MOP patriotic case **250.00**
6th plate, Union soldier w/Saxon rifle, wearing kepi, w/case **325.00**

Union Cases

From the mid-1850s until about 1880, cases designed to house these early images were produced from a material known as thermoplastic, a man-made material with an appearance much like gutta percha. Its innovator was Samuel Peck, who used shellac and wood fibers to create a composition he called Union. Peck was part owner of the Scoville Company, makers of both papier-mache and molded leather cases, and he used the company's existing dies to create his new line. Other companies, among them A.P. Critchlow & Company, Littlefield, Parsons & Company, and Holmes, Booth, & Hayden soon duplicated his material and produced their own designs. Today's collectors may refer to cases made of this material as 'thermoplastic,' 'composition,' or 'hard cases,' but the term most often used is 'Union.' It is incorrect to refer to them as gutta percha cases.

Sizes may vary somewhat, but generally a 'whole' plate case measures 7" x 9⅛" to the outside edges, a 'half' plate 4⅞" x 6", a 'quarter' plate 3¾" x 4¾", a 'sixth' 3⅛" x 3⅝", a 'ninth' 2⅜" x 2⅞", and a 'sixteenth' 1¾" x 2". Clifford and Michele Krainik and Carl Walvoord have written a book, *Union Cases*, which we recommend for further information. Another source of information is *Nineteenth Century Photographic Cases and Wall Frames* by Paul Berg; he is listed in the Directory under California.

16th plate, Indian Head Penny, K-617, G, w/portrait tintype **200.00**
4th plate, blk lacquer w/mc pnt & MOP inlay, EX, w/dag **100.00**
4th plate, Bountiful Harvest, K-47, w/portrait ambrotype **150.00**
4th plate, Geometric w/scrolled edge, K-84, w/portrait dag **150.00**
4th plate, Sir Roger deCoverly & Gypsies, K-29, EX **100.00**
6th plate, blk lacquer w/mc florals/gold/MOP inlay, EX **135.00**
6th plate, blk lacquer w/MOP inlay florals, rpr hinge **90.00**
6th plate, Bobby Shafto, K-135, w/2 portrait ambrotypes, EX **85.00**
6th plate, Clipper Ship & Fort, K-100, w/ambrotype **150.00**
6th plate, Deer & Pine Tree, K-167, couple ambrotype **150.00**
6th plate, Faithful Hound, K-142, w/portrait tintype **65.00**
6th plate, Farmer's Dream, K-138, EX w/portrait ambrotype **110.00**
6th plate, Fireman's Duty, K-118, w/lady & child ambrotype **175.00**
6th plate, Flower Bier, K-94, G, w/2 portrait ruby ambrotypes **85.00**
6th plate, Music Lesson, K-145, w/couple ambrotype, EX **110.00**
6th plate, Rebekkah at Well, K-155, w/2 ruby ambrotypes **200.00**
6th plate, Scroll, K-95, ca 1845, w/4 daguerreotypes **225.00**
6th plate, Spray of Strawberries, K-93, w/2 ruby ambrotypes **150.00**
6th plate, Volunteer Fireman, K-116, w/ruby ambrotype **175.00**
6th plate, Wreath of Fruit, K-180, w/ruby ambrotype **125.00**
9th plate, Cutout, K-335, w/lady's portrait ambrotype **300.00**
9th plate, Jardiniere of Roses, K-561, VG, w/4 tintypes **100.00**

Miscellaneous

Book, Am & Alfred Stieglitz..., 1st edition, 1934, EX **90.00**
Book, Man Ray Photographs 1920-34, JT Soby, 1934, NM **425.00**
Stanhope, alabaster bbl, Niagara Falls scene **30.00**
Stanhope, binoculars, ivory **65.00**
Stanhope, cross, bone, WWI, troups in trenches, ca 1914, EX **50.00**
Stanhope, inkwell, ivory, chalet form, German views **50.00**
Stanhope, pen, rhinestones, Lord's Prayer **45.00**
Stanhope, pipe, cvd wood, 6 Port Erin views, 1" L, EX **50.00**
Stanhope, scent bottle, brass, w/neck chain, 6 views, EX **155.00**
Stanhope, tape measure, bbl form w/ivory finial, 1 view **65.00**
Stereoptican, folding box type, ebonized w/cvg **140.00**
Viewer, folding, olive wood veneer case w/SP trim, 9" L **150.00**
Viewer, mahog w/beaded trim, table top, EX, +travel slides **385.00**

Piano Babies

A familiar sight in Victorian parlors, piano babies languished atop

shawl-covered pianos in a variety of poses: crawling, sitting, on their tummies or on their backs playing with their toes. Some babies were nude, and some wore gowns. Sizes ranged from about 3" up to 12". The most famous manufacturer of these bisque darlings was the Heubach Brothers of Germany, who nearly always marked their product; see Heubach for listings. Watch for reproductions. These guidelines are excerpted from one of a series of informative doll books by Pat Smith, published by Collector Books.

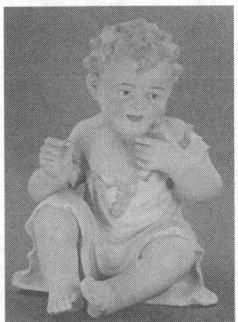

Baby in white gown with pink trim, repair to toe, 10½", $300.00.

Blk, bsk, 12", EX quality **925.00**
Blk, bsk, 12", med quality **495.00**
Blk, bsk, 16", EX quality, minimum value **1,085.00**
Blk, bsk, 16", med quality **1,000.00**
Blk, bsk, 4", EX quality **325.00**
Blk, bsk, 4", med quality **225.00**
Blk, bsk, 8", EX quality **525.00**
Blk, bsk, 8", med quality **300.00**
Bsk, molded hair, unjtd, molded-on clothes, 12", EX quality **895.00**
Bsk, molded hair, unjtd, molded-on clothes, 15", med quality **325.00**
Bsk, molded hair, unjtd, molded-on clothes, 4", EX quality **250.00**
Bsk, molded hair, unjtd, molded-on clothes, 4", med quality **150.00**
Bsk, molded hair, unjtd, molded-on clothes, 8", EX quality **725.00**
Bsk, molded hair, unjtd, molded-on clothes, 8", med quality **275.00**
Bsk, w/animal/pot/flowers/etc, 12", EX quality **950.00**
Bsk, w/animal/pot/flowers/etc, 16", EX quality, minimum **1,100.00**
Bsk, w/animal/pot/flowers/etc, 4", EX quality **295.00**
Bsk, w/animal/pot/flowers/etc, 8", EX quality **525.00**

Picasso Art Pottery

Pablo Picasso created some distinctive pottery during the 1940s, marking the ware with his signature.

Bowl, toreador & bull sillouette on wht, Madoura, 2¾x5" **4,750.00**
Plate, facial features, blk/gr/red/ivory, sgn Geo Ramie, 9" **1,400.00**
Plate, horse & rider edged in gr on wht, Madoura Fue, 8" **650.00**

Pickard

Founded in 1895 in Chicago, Illinois, the Pickard China Company was originally a decorating studio, importing china blanks from European manufacturers. Some of these early pieces bear the name of those companies as well as Pickard's. Trained artists decorated the wares with hand-painted studies of fruit, florals, birds, and scenics and often signed their work. In 1915 Pickard introduced a line of 23k gold over a dainty floral-etched ground design. In the 1930s they began to experiment with the idea of making their own ware and by 1938 had succeeded in developing a formula for fine translucent china. Since 1976 they have issued an annual limited edition Christmas plate. They are now located in Antioch, Illinois.

The company has used various marks. The earliest (1893-1894) was a double-circle mark, 'Edgerton Hand Painted' with 'Pickard' in the center. Variations of the double-circle mark (with 'Hand Painted China' replacing the Edgerton designation) were employed until 1915, each differing enough that collectors can usually pinpoint the date of manufacture within five years. Later marks included the crown mark, 'Pickard' on a gold maple leaf, and the current mark, the lion and shield. Work signed by Challinor, Marker, and Yeschek is especially valued by today's collectors. For further information we recommend *Collector's Encyclopedia of Pickard China* by Alan B. Reed, available from Collector Books. Our advisor for this category is Milt Steinfeld; he is listed in the Directory under New Jersey.

Bonbon, violets on gr w/gold, scalloped, hdls, 1893-1903, 5½" 85.00
Cake plate, river through farmland, Challinor 300.00
Creamer & sugar bowl, garden scene w/gold, Challinor 350.00
Creamer & sugar bowl, pilgrims & ship on matt, 1912-19 mk 225.00
Creamer & sugar bowl, Tulip Conventional, Tomasch, 1903-05 mk 250.00
Cup & saucer, poppies on cream w/gold, 1898-1903 mk 135.00
Hair receiver, purple flowers, pearlized 130.00
Mayonnaise, cornflowers w/gold, sgn CK, w/underplate 165.00
Mug, Poinsettia Conventional, sgn Tolley, 1910-12, 5" 250.00
Pitcher, cider; HP strawberries, sgn De Roy, mk, 5¾x7" 425.00
Pitcher, gooseberries/leaves/ribbons, sgn, bulbous, 6½" 300.00
Pitcher, lemonade; peacocks 350.00
Pitcher, lemonade; wide gold etched band 215.00
Pitcher, strawberries on maroon band w/blooms, 1893-1903 mk, 5" ..365.00
Plate, fruit & flowers in 5" medallion, sgn Gaspar, 10" 170.00
Plate, pk florals w/wide gold border, sgn Vober, 8½" 170.00
Plate, poppies, sgn Reury, 9" 90.00
Plate, strawberries w/gold, sgn DeRoy, 8½" 145.00
Stein, Arrow Maker, Indian portrait, sgn Jubasch, 1903-05, 7" ..950.00
Sugar bowl, violets on yel to gr, 1898-1903 mk, 6½" L 85.00
Teapot, floral w/gold on wht, sgn Wight, 1905-10 mk, 7½" 110.00
Tray, dresser; violets & gold on ivory, sgn Kries, 11x8" 225.00
Tray, hunting dogs in meadow, sgn Farrington, 1903-05 mk, 16" .2,500.00
Vase, Japanese lady w/comb, cylindrical, 1903-05 mk, 12" 1,800.00
Vase, rose medallion on patterned gold, 1922-25 mk, 8" 300.00
Vase, violets w/gold, sgn Brauer, bulbous, 1910-12 mk, 6¼" 195.00

Pickle Castors

Pickle castors, which were both functional and decorative, became popular after the Civil War, reaching their peak about 1885. By 1900 they had virtually disappeared from factory catalogs. Numerous styles were available. They consisted of a decorated, silverplated frame that held either a fancy clear pressed-glass insert or one of decorated colored art glass — the latter being popular in the more affluent Victorian households and more desirable with collectors today.

In the listings below, the description prior to the semicolon refers to the jar (insert), and the remainder of the line describes the frame. When no condition is indicated, the silverplate is assumed to be in very good to excellent condition; glass jars are assumed near-mint.

Key:
rsl — resilvered   3-D — three-dimensional

Amberina, melon shape; ftd fr w/florals/leaves/beads, Webster ...600.00
Amberina, swirled ribs, Libbey; ftd Meriden fr 465.00
Barley, clear; orig SP fr, +tongs 125.00
Bl, rows of dmn prisms/faceted blocks; fr w/emb birds etc 235.00
Bl Herringbone MOP, ornate fr w/owl figures 750.00
Cane, amber; fr w/rtcl 3-leaf hdl, +bird-ft tongs 300.00

Cane, Flemish bl; fr w/emb floral base, +tongs, 12" 350.00
Chry'mum Base Reverse Swirl, bl opal; fr: 3-D elephant heads ...550.00
Cranberry, clear rigaree, scalloped; ornate SP fr 495.00
Cranberry, vertical ribs; ftd Tufts fr w/side bail 425.00
Crown Milano, acorns/leaves w/gold; Pairpoint std w/gargoyle ..1,100.00
Daisy & Button, apple gr; ornate Wilcox SP fr, +tongs 300.00
Daisy & Button, sapphire bl; orig ftd SP fr 350.00
Daisy & Button, yel; fr w/rtcl scrolls, bird-ft tongs, 12" 350.00
Daisy & Button canoe, amber; Homan wheeled fr w/owls, +forks ..850.00
Daisy & Fern, bl opal; SP fr 470.00
Dmn Point, clear; ornate ftd Meriden fr, +tongs 185.00
Florette, pk cased; orig SP fr 395.00
Frosted panels w/storks; ornate fr w/arched hdl, +tongs 225.00
Frosted pumpkin w/bird finial; leaf-shaped fr, Wilcox #0675 ......395.00
Frosted w/wood texture & flowers; Poole fr, +tongs 350.00
Heart Arches w/HP florals on wht satin; mk fr 395.00
Hobnail, amber; Racine fr w/floral-emb lid, +fork 425.00
Invt T'print, apricot w/HP daisies, Mt WA; sgn Pairpoint fr 625.00
Invt T'print, bl, lavish HP floral, scalloped; SHM fr, rstr 625.00
Invt T'print, clear, squatty; fr w/rtcl ft & emb ferns, +tongs 475.00
Invt T'print, cranberry, HP floral; orig SP fr w/peacocks 450.00
Invt T'print, cranberry, HP floral; short ornate fr 450.00
Invt T'print, cranberry, M Gregory boy; Rockford #611 foxes fr .625.00
Invt T'print, cranberry, wht floral; floral fr, +bird-ft tongs 500.00
Invt T'print, cranberry; ornate rstr ftd fr, bud finial, +fork 575.00
Invt T'print, cranberry; rtcl floral/scroll-top fr, +tongs 300.00
Invt T'print, emerald w/floral; ornate fr w/rtcl berries, 11" 400.00
Invt T'print, med bl w/floral; ftd/hdl fr, bird-ft tongs, 12" 400.00
Invt T'print, royal bl, gold flowers; rib-base ftd fr, +tongs 350.00
Leaf Mold, yel & pk; ornate Derby fr w/owl & fan hdl finial 650.00
Mc spatter (cased); ornate Wilcox ftd fr 495.00
Peachblow w/floral; fr w/emb birds, ornate finial, 9" 500.00
Pk shaded satin Herringbone; ftd sq base ornate fr, Wm Rogers .750.00
Pk shaded satin w/HP floral; ftd fr, single bail, Tufts #3389 ....650.00
Pk to rose shaded, blown-out shells, HP florals; signed SP fr 425.00
Pk/opal rib optic; ftd orig fr, Pairpoint #688 ....650.00
Purple slag, waffle/panel mold; birds/fountain emb fr 375.00
Rubena bark texture w/coralene; low fr w/pickles, Derby #147 ...950.00

Sapphire blue with enameled floral decoration, ornate silver frame and tongs, 10½", M, $450.00.

Sapphire bl w/floral, cylindrical; simple fr, 10½", +tongs 250.00
Swirl, clear; low ftd Meriden fr w/hdls, no tongs 150.00
Swirl, cranberry w/HP florals; Benedict fr 495.00
Yel satin Quilt, cased, HP decor; orig ornate SP fr, EX 765.00
Yel to wht opal w/HP pk roses; Derby #405 fr w/birds, 12" 785.00
12-Panel w/etch wreath; fr w/rtcl trim, leaf hdl, +tongs 225.00

Pie Birds

A pie bird (pie funnel, pie vent, pie chimney) is placed on the center of the bottom crust and surrounded by filling with the top crust resting on the 'shoulders' of the pie bird. The arches of the pie bird allow steam to enter and exit out the top vent (to prevent juice run over) while the 'shoulders' hold the top crust up during baking (to avoid sogginess). Pie birds are open-bottomed, hollow, glazed inside and outside, have a top vent aperture and 99% have two arches at the base. From Victorian times to the present, pie funnels are used in deep-dish meat pies. No bottom crust is used, therefore, the 'shoulders' play an important roll in preventing sogginess. In the 1930s a blackbird pie vent was designed. They were so popular that many thousands were sold in England and exported from Japan. For about twenty years figural pie vents have been created in England to catch the baker's attention; animals (dogs, elephants, and frogs), occupational people (policemen and chefs), and whimsical clowns and Teddy bears have been produced. In the past three years, over one-hundred new U.S. made pie vents have flooded the collectibles market (holiday related is the new pie bird category). Incense burners, one-hole pepper shakers, and a dated brass toy bird whistle should not be mistaken for pie vents. No pie birds were made in Czechoslovakia.

Our advisors for this category are Alan Pedel (representing the English market; see England in the Directory) and Lillian Cole (listed under New Jersey).

Bear holding honey jar, caramel color, mk SB, England 30.00
Benny the Baker, mk pat Pend, Cardinal China, 5½" 85.00
Bird, bl & wht on wht base, mk Royal Worcester, 2-pc 65.00
Bird, blk w/yel beak, no mk, imported, new, 4" or 3½" 4.00
Bird, caramel color, mk Sunglow New Devon, England, 4¼" 55.00
Bird, cobalt, unmk (US), new, 4½" 12.00
Blackbird on log, mk Artone Pottery England 50.00
Blue Willow, rooster, goose, birds, new, ea 15.00
Canary, yel w/pk lips, Josef Original, 3½" 22.00
Chef, mk The Servex Chef on hat, Holland, 5" 100.00
Chef & Baker, wht, lg vent hole, unmk (Tauton, England), 3½", ea ..45.00
Chef & Baker, wht, tiny vent hole, unmk, imported/new, 3¾", ea 10.00
Chef w/pan, no arches, Josef or Lorrie Orig, imported, 3½" 40.00
Crow dressed as chef, holds pie, mk SB, England 30.00

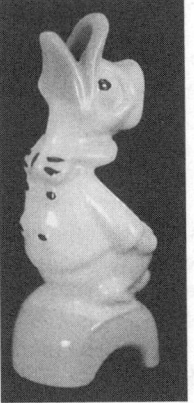

Donald Duck, marked Donald Duck and copyright Walt Disney, 4¾", $200.00.

Dragon, tin w/spines & horns, mk SB England, new 30.00
Funnel, TG Green advertising, England, 1992-present, 3" 15.00
Funnel, yelware, mk Kitchen Devil, England, new, 3" 12.00
Funnels, cream, unmk (England), various heights, ea 18.00
Granny Pie Baker, no arches, Josef or Lorrie Orig, imported, 3½" .40.00
Pillsbury, chick, pk or bl base 30.00
Repros, Taiwan, Chef or Mammy, red, yel & wht, new, 4½", ea ...10.00
Repros, Taiwan, Cleminson or Shawnee styles, tan bases, new, ea ..10.00
Rooster, mc, mk Cleminson or incised Cb 25.00
Songbird, bl, pk or cinnamon, 4½", ea 25.00
Songbird, blk or cream w/gold trim, ea 40.00

Pierce, Howard

Howard Pierce, having begun his studio pottery in 1941 in Claremont, California, was a talented artist who found a special niche in creating porcelain wildlife pieces. His formal training encompassed three years, one each at the Chicago Art Institute, California's Pomona College, and the University of Illinois. Howard, along with his wife, Ellen Van Voorhis, produced a large number of varied pieces over a half century.

While wildlife held a special interest for Mr. Pierce, his initial products were vases, wall pockets, bowls, jewelry, and other art and dinnerwares. Throughout his career, he took special interest in a variety of materials: polyurethane, which he discovered caused an allergic reaction for him, forcing him to discontinue its use; bisque in a Jasperware style, mostly in mint or pink glazes; porcelain bisques which he used to model animals and plants that were positioned in or near open areas of his high-gloss vases and candle holders; a lava treatment that he best describes as, '...bubbling up from the bottom'; gold leaf which is scarce today but should not be confused with 'Sears gold'; a rough-textured Mt. St. Helens glaze which he obtained by using some of the ash from the volcano when it erupted; and cement. By the time Mr. and Mrs. Pierce had moved to Joshua Tree, California, he was concentrating almost all his talents on animals and wildlife. He experimented with glazes, recording the glaze numbers in a book and on occasion incising that number into the bottom of a creation. His earliest mark is the 'Claremont, CA,' underglaze mark which most often included a stock number. Next he used a rubber stamp-type mark that read 'Howard Pierce Porcelain.' Later the word 'Porcelain' was dropped. Not all of his pieces are marked, especially the smaller two pieces in a three-piece set or the smaller item in a two-piece set. Near the end of 1992, due to failing health, Howard and Ellen Pierce destroyed all the molds they had ever created. When his health improved, Mr. Pierce began working a few hours a week making smaller pieces of his past work. He also was able to create a few new molds, but, again, they were smaller in size. The small pieces carry 'Pierce' in a stamp-like mark. Howard Pierce passed away in February, 1994. Our advisor for this category is Susan N. Cox; she is listed in the Directory under California.

Bowl, gondola shape, brn on wht, 5x9½" 20.00
Figurine, Blk boy & girl holding hands, 4½" 62.00
Figurine, cat, seated, sandstone, 14" 50.00
Figurine, ermine, standing, 1950s, 9" 155.00
Figurine, giraffe, brn agate, in-mold mk, 1950s, 10½" 40.00
Figurine, hippo, 'volcanic' brn, recent, 6" 40.00
Figurine, horse, brn w/tan & mottled tail, 9" 155.00
Figurine, owls in tree, lg 75.00
Figurine, partridge, stylized, brn, 1950s, lg 55.00
Figurine, roadrunner, wire legs, tail up, polyurethane 185.00
Figurine, rooster & hen, brn & wht, 1950s, 9¼, 7¾", pr 175.00
Figurine, squirrel, gray, 4" 25.00
Figurine, turtle, speckled brn on wht, 1950s, 5" 25.00
Figurine, water bird, wht w/brn bill & ft, 14" 65.00
Magnet, dolphin, brn, 3¼x1½" 30.00
Pencil holder, nude obese women, brn, 4¼" 40.00
Sign, Copper Mountain Campus, 4½x3½" 47.00
Sign, tree-bark surface, Howard Pierce Porcelain 110.00
Vase, bud; brn, stamp mk, 3½" 30.00
Vase, Deco girl w/in circular cutout, creche style, gr, sq 55.00
Vase, fish insert, creche style, gr, 8" 75.00
Wall pocket, jasperware, pk & tan w/5 wht deer, 8" L 160.00
Wall pocket, 3-color jasperware, plants, Claremont, 2½x4½" 40.00
Whistle, bird shape, brn, 3½" 20.00

Pietra-Dura

From the Italian Renaissance period, Pietra-Dura is a type of mosaic work used for plaques, table tops, frames, etc., that includes small pieces of gemstones, mother-of-pearl, and the like.

Panel, birds at fountain, gilt fr, 8¼x10¼" 225.00
Plaque, inlaid rooster & hen, 4¼x6⅜" 115.00

Pigeon Blood

Pigeon blood glass, produced in the late 1800s, may be distinguished from other dark red glass by its distinctive orange tint.

Creamer, Venecia, w/enamel decor 165.00
Mug, Tom & Jerry, gold trim, ca 1910, 6 for 200.00
Mustard pot, Torquay, w/hinged lid 110.00
Pitcher, Bulging Loops, water sz 410.00
Plate, ca 1900, 8" 145.00
Rose bowl, HP floral w/gilt, 5" dia 70.00
Syrup pitcher, Torquay 285.00
Tumbler, HP floral, int ribs 65.00
Wine, 6" 42.00

Pilkington

Founded in 1892 in Manchester, England, the Pilkington pottery experimented in wonderful lustre glazes that were so successful that when they were diplayed at exhibition in 1904, they were met with critical acclaim. The pottery soon attracted some of the best ceramic technicians and designers of the day who decorated the lustre ground with flowers, animals, and trees; some pieces were more elaborate with scenes of sailing ships and knights on horseback. Each artist signed his work with his personal monogram. Most pieces were dated and carried the company mark as well. After 1913 the company became known as Royal Lancastrian.

Their Lapis Ware line was introduced in the late 1920s, featuring intermingling tones of color under a matt glaze. Some pieces were very simply decorated while others were painted with designs of stylized leafage, scrolls, swirls, and stripes. The line continued into the thirties. Other pieces of this period were molded and carved with animals, leaves, etc., some of which were reminiscent of their earlier wares.

The company closed in 1938 but reopened in 1948. During this period their mark was a simple P within the outline of a petaled flower shape. Our advisor for this category is David Ehrhard; he is listed in the Directory under California.

Bookends, dolphin, 5½", pr 300.00
Bowl, Lapis, Wm S Mycock, geometric design 225.00
Tile, Apache dancer, set of 3 ....130.00
Vase, emb leaves, sang-de-boeuf flambe, stick neck, 7x5" 275.00
Vase, Lapis, GM Rogers, bulbous, bold design 195.00
Vase, matt gr, rnded shoulder, flared neck, emb decor 235.00
Vase, stylized upright feathers, blk on orange/yel, 13x6½" 900.00
Vase, Sunstone, copper-red crystalline w/blk 'soot,' 9½" 750.00

Pillin

Polia Pillin was born in Poland in 1909; many of her family were artisians and craftsmen. Except for a few weeks of formal instruction at the Hull House in Chicago, Pillin is self-taught in the arts. Her work has been shown in many exhibits, and she has received awards from the Los Angeles County Art Institute, Syracuse Museum, Los Angeles County Fair, and the California State Fair. First interested in oils and watercolors, she has carried the same Byzantine quality over to her pottery. All of her work is signed 'Pillin' or 'W&P Pillin,' both with the loop of the P extended in an arc over the remaining letters of her name.

Bowl, lady/rooster/horse, mc on lt bl & wht, 3½x5" 475.00
Box, lady w/bird, mc on gr/brn, 2x4" dia 375.00
Jug, blistered yel/brn gloss, sgn, 7¾x5" 275.00
Plate, horses 395.00
Vase, abstract figure on all 4 sides, 11½x3¾" 975.00
Vase, dbl portraits of girls & rooster on dk yel, pinched, 5" 275.00
Vase, gr/olive matt texture, wide gourd w/tiny neck, 13" 375.00
Vase, horse & 2 ladies, wht on peacock & rust, 9x7" 850.00
Vase, horses, lady w/balloons, mc on bl, can form, 4½" 375.00
Vase, horses, mc on wht to brn, pear form, 6" 350.00
Vase, lady w/birds, ball form, 6" 425.00
Vase, lt to dk brn crystalline, bulbous w/can neck, 8½" 270.00
Vase, lt to dk gr, glossy, bulbous w/sm opening, 6½" 200.00

Vase, orange speckled, bottle neck with flared lip, 9¼", $595.00; Plate, lady on horse, blue rim, 6", $295.00.

Vase, scarlet flambe gloss, spherical w/short neck, 9½x7" 425.00
Vase, 2 full-length ladies, mc on yel/brn, slim form, 15" 1,500.00

Pin-Back Buttons

Buttons produced up to the early 1920s were made with a celluloid covering held in place by a ring (or collet) to the back of which a pin was secured. Manufacturers used these 'cellos' to advertise their products. Many were of exceptional quality in both color and design. Sets of buttons were produced, featuring a variety of subjects. These were given away by tobacco, chewing gum, and candy manufacturers, who often packed them with their product as premiums. Usually the name of the button maker or the product manufacturer was printed on a paper placed in the back of the button. Often these 'back papers' are still in place today. Much of the time the button maker's was printed on the button's perimeter, and sometimes the copyright was added. Beginning in the 1920s, a large number of buttons were lithographed on tin; these are referred to as tin 'lithos.' Nearly all pin-back buttons are collected today for their advertising appeal or graphic design. There are countless categories to base a collection on.

The following listing contains non-political buttons representative of the many varieties you may find. All are celluloid unless described otherwise. Values reflect buttons in excellent, well-centered condition, with bright color and only the very slightest of wear, if any.

Armoured Cruiser Pennsylvania, ship at sea, sepia, 1¾" 15.00
Atlantic City 1911, swimming scene, mc on wht, 1¼" 30.00
Balloon Route Trolley Trip, Pacific Electric Ry, mc, 1¼" 35.00
Best Tracklayer Tractors, red/wht/bl, 1¼" 30.00
Bruce (Springsteen), portrait on blk, name in bl, 2" 8.00

Burgerville, I'm a Hamburger Lover, tin litho, red/wht/bl, 1⅜" 3.00
Can't Be Beat (Crescent Bicycles), red/wht/bl, ⅝" 8.00
Chiquita, The Living Doll, Cuban midget in gown, mc, 1¾" 95.00
Dayton-Moneyweight Scales, gr/blk/wht, 1¼" 20.00
Ducks Unlimited, 1975, sgn Maass, mc, 2¼" 25.00
Ducks Unlimited, 1980, sgn Maass, mc, 2¼" 20.00
Ducks Unlimited, 1985, sgn Hanson, mc, 2¼" 15.00
Earle Freeman Month at Kellogg's, red/blk/wht, 1¾" 20.00
Fleer's Bubble Gum, Junior Salesman's Club, red/wht/bl, 1¼" 15.00
Flying A Quality, Tide Water Oil Co, orange/blk/wht, 1¼" 12.00
Gen Robert E Lee, portrait, sepia, 2¼" 30.00
Grand Int Race, 3 cyclists photos on clover, 4-color, 1¼" 45.00
Great Lakes Exposition, 1937 Federal Day, bl on wht, ⅞" 8.00
Great Scott, Astronaut Scott Carpenter, red/wht/bl/blk, 1¾" 25.00
Jack Johnson Heavyweight Champion, boxing pose, blk/wht, 1¾" ...85.00
Kill the Rats, 3 Anti-Axis rats, blk/red/wht, 1¼" 45.00
King Edward VIII Coronation 1937, red/wht/bl/blk, 1¼" 25.00
Liberty Bell Bird Club, Farm Journal, mc/red rim, ⅞" 12.00
Liquor Dealer, 1906 Centennial, photo, blk on wht, 1¼" 25.00
Log Rollers, 1933 World's Fair, paper, blk on wht, 1" 15.00
Mac Tonight, McDonald's, yel/bl/blk/wht, 3" 12.50
Nabisco Golden Anniv, boy in rain outfit, red/yel/gold, 1¼" 20.00
Parrot Brand Biscuit A-B-C, parrot, Pat 1896, mc on wht, ⅞" 20.00
Rochester's Weekly Magazine, flags above waterfall, mc, 2¼" 45.00
Safety First, Spanky of Our Gang, Hal Roach, mc, 1¼" 50.00
Santa on phone at desk, store ad, mc on wht, 1¼" 50.00
Sophie Tucker for President, tin litho, blk/wht, 1⅜" 15.00
Stop Hitler, CIO, V in center, red/wht/bl, 1¼" 12.50
Studebaker, spoked wagon wheel, mk, ⅞" 30.00
Vote for Ferguson's Honey Bread, loaf, mc, ⅞" 15.00
Vote Yes for Sunday Movies, bl/wht, 1¼" 15.00
Washington, flag, ax & cherries, mc, 1½" 12.00
Wear Daisy Rubbers, daisy, mc, 1¼" 15.00
Wm Cody, photo w/facsimile signature, sepia, 1¼" 65.00

Pink Lustre Ware

Pink lustre was produced by nearly every potter in the Staffordshire district in the late 18th and first half of the 19th centuries. The application of gold lustre on white or light-colored backgrounds produced pinks, while the same over dark colors developed copper. The wares ranged from hand-painted plaques to transfer-printed dinnerware. Design features in the phrase immediately following the item (i.e. cup, plate, etc.) are in pink lustre unless otherwise specifically described within the line.

Cup & saucer, mc florals w/lustre vine band, NM 55.00
Cup plate, House pattern, 4" dia 45.00
Pitcher, cider; bbl form, ca 1815, 7" 850.00
Pitcher, emb leaves/landscape, female head on hdl, 6", VG 130.00
Pitcher, floral/vintage resist on pearlware, 5", VG 100.00

Pitcher, house among trees, landscape beyond, 5½", NM, $185.00.

Pitcher, mc oval reserves/sailing ship, pearlware, 9½", NM 650.00
Pitcher, Queen Caroline, emb/pnt floral border, 1820, 5¼" 600.00
Pitcher, stylized 4-color band w/lustre on pearlware, 7", VG 115.00
Pitcher, Wellington & Blucher on horsbk, 1800s, 5⅛" 450.00
Plate, Victoria & Albert, pk transfer w/mc, lustre rim, 8¾" 130.00
Sugar bowl, purple transfer genre scene, hdls, w/lid, 4½" 35.00
Watch pocket, 2 columns support shelf w/lion finial, 7½" 800.00

Pink Paw Bears

These charming figural pieces are very similar to the Pink Pigs described in the following category. They were made in Germany during the same time frame. The cabbage green is identical; the bears themselves are whitish-gray with pink foot pads. You'll find some that are unmarked while others are marked 'Germany' or 'Made in Germany.' In theory, the unmarked bears are the oldest, made prior to 1890 when the McKinley Tariff Act required imports to be marked with the country of origin. Those marked 'Made In' were probably produced after the revision of the Act in 1914.

1 by bean pot 135.00
1 by graphaphone 135.00
1 by honey pot 145.00
1 by top hat 110.00
1 in roadster (car identical to pk pig car) 165.00
1 on binoculars 150.00
1 peeking out of basket 135.00
1 sitting in wicker chair 150.00
2 in front of basket 135.00
2 in hot-air balloon 150.00
2 in purse 165.00
2 in roadster 150.00
2 on pin dish 120.00
2 peering in floor mirror 150.00
2 sitting by mushroom 125.00
2 standing in wash tub 150.00
3 in roadster 175.00
3 on pin dish 145.00

Pink Pigs

Pink Pigs on cabbage green were made in Germany around the turn of the century. They were sold as souvenirs in train depots, amusement parks, and gift shops. 'Action pigs' (those involved in some amusing activity) are the most valuable, and prices increase with the number of pigs. Though a similar type of figurine was made in white bisque, most serious collectors prefer only the pink ones. They are marked in two ways: 'Germany' in incised letters, and a black ink stamp 'Made in Germany' in a circle.

1 beside gr drum, wall-mt match holder 60.00
1 beside purse 75.00
1 beside shoe 75.00
1 beside stump, camera around neck, toothpick holder 120.00
1 beside waste basket 75.00
1 coming out of cup 95.00
1 coming out of suitcase 95.00
1 coming through gr fence, post at sides, open for flowers 95.00
1 driving touring car 165.00
1 going through purse 90.00
1 in buggy 110.00
1 in case looking through binoculars 145.00
1 in gr Dutch shoe 75.00
1 in gr suitcase bank, head 1 side, bk other, gold trim 110.00

1 in Japanese submarine, Japan imp on both sides 125.00
1 in jaws of trap, rare, unmk, 5" L 125.00
1 in money sack bank 85.00
1 in roadster 145.00
1 lg pig sitting behind 3" trough 95.00
1 napping on side, Schlite Pat, 5" L 98.00
1 on binoculars 95.00
1 on binoculars, gold trim 125.00
1 on chair 110.00
1 on gr trinket dish, leg caught in lobster claw 110.00
1 on keg playing piano 150.00
1 on shoulder of gr ink bottle 115.00
1 playing accordion on side of tray, wht bear ea side 150.00
1 playing piano 145.00
1 pushing head through wooden gate 95.00
1 putting letter in mailbox 95.00
1 reclining on horseshoe ashtray 70.00
1 riding train, 4½" 150.00
1 sits, holds orange Boston Baked Beans pot match holder 125.00
1 sits by high-top boot 110.00
1 sitting in bathtub 135.00
1 sitting on log, mk Germany 110.00
1 standing in gr tub 95.00
1 w/attached toothpick holder 75.00
1 w/front ft in 3-part dish containing 3 dice, 1 ft on dice 125.00
1 w/tennis racket stands beside vase, Lawn Tennis, 3¾" 95.00
1 wearing chef's costume, holds frypan, w/basket 95.00
2, mother & baby in bl blanket in tub, rabbit on board atop 110.00
2, mother in tub gives baby a bottle, lamb looks on, 4x3½" 115.00
2, 1 at telephone booth, 1 inside, 4½" 110.00
2 at confession, 4½" 90.00
2 at wishing well 110.00
2 behind trough, unmk 75.00
2 by eggshell 95.00
2 by lg gr telephone 95.00
2 dancing, in top hat, tux & cane 110.00
2 holding hands in roadster, 4½" L 160.00
2 in basket, Merry Squeelers, 3½x3" 90.00
2 in bed, Good Night on footboard, 4x3x2½" 145.00
2 in carriage 95.00
2 in love sit on lg log, 2 openings on tree stump, 7" L 105.00
2 in open car 145.00
2 in open trunk, 3¾" 95.00
2 in purse 95.00
2 on basket, head raising lid, plaque on front 110.00
2 on binoculars, gold trim 165.00
2 on cotton bale, 1 peers from hole, 1 over top 135.00
2 on seesaw on top of pouch bank 90.00
2 on top hat 95.00
2 on tray hugging, 3x4½" 90.00
2 sitting at table playing card game 'Hearts' 170.00
2 under toadstool 125.00
3, 1 on lg slipper playing banjo, 2 dancing on side 145.00
3, 2 sit in front of coal bucket, 3rd inside 125.00
3 at trough, 4½" L 98.00
3 dressed up on edge of dish 80.00
3 sm pigs behind oval trough, mk, 2¾x2½x1¾" 95.00
3 w/baby carriage, father & 2 babies, Wheeling His Own 125.00
3 w/carriage, mother & 2 babies, Germany 95.00

Pisgah Forest

The Pisgah Forest Pottery was established in 1926 near Mount

Pisgah in Arden, North Carolina, by Walter B. Stephen, who had worked in previous years at other locations — Nonconnah (Tennessee) and Skyland (North Carolina – 1913 until 1916). Stephen, who was born in the mountain region near Asheville, was known for his work in the Southern tradition. He produced skillfully-executed wares exhibiting an amazing variety of techniques. He operated his business with only two helpers. Recognized today as his most outstanding accomplishment, his Cameo line was decorated by hand in the pate-sur-pate style (similar to Wedgwood Jasper) in such designs as Fiddler and Dog, Spinning Wheel, Covered Wagon, Buffalo Hunt, Mountain Cabin, Square Dancers, Indian Campfire, and Plowman. Stephen is known for other types of wares as well. His crystalline glaze is highly regarded by today's collectors.

Many different stamps mark his wares, several of which contain the outline of the potter at the wheel and 'Pisgah Forest.' Cameo is sometimes marked with a circle containing the line name and 'Long Pine, Arden, NC.' Two other marks may be more difficult to recognize: 1) a circle containing the outline of a pine tree, 'N.C.' to the left of the trunk and 'Pine Tree' on the other side; and 2) the letter 'P' with short uprights in the middle of the top and lower curves. Stephen died in 1961, but the work was continued by his associates. Our advisor for this category is R.J. Sayers; he is listed in the Directory under North Carolina.

Bowl, Cameo, bl gloss, sgn Stephen, 1961, low 300.00
Creamer & sugar bowl, gr mottle, pk int, w/lid 35.00
Creamer & sugar bowl, turq, hdls, w/lid, sgn 45.00
Mug, Cameo, oxen pulling covered wagon, Stephen, 1949 ....175.00
Pitcher, forest gr & pk, 4" 40.00
Pitcher, milk; Cameo, bl w/wagon train, figure & dog 175.00
Pitcher, milk; gr w/pk int, 8" 65.00
Vase, aqua over violet gloss, classic form, 6" 80.00
Vase, aqua/gray-gr gloss, shouldered, 9½" 130.00
Vase, aqua/violet gloss, hdls, 1941, 6½x5" 90.00
Vase, bl/gr/wht crystalline w/gold highlights, 8" 500.00
Vase, brn crystalline, bulbous w/flared rim, Stephen, 6½" 300.00
Vase, butterscotch w/bl crystalline, 6" 200.00
Vase, Cameo, Indian life on mottled bl, baluster, 7½x4" 400.00
Vase, Cameo, men/oxen, bl/aqua gloss, Stephen, 10x5", NM 600.00
Vase, Cameo, men/wagons on lav/bl, sgn Stephen, drilled, 12" 475.00

Vase, caramel crystalline over white with blue showing through, embossed signature, 8", $1,200.00.

Vase, feathered sage gr gloss w/dk gr speckles, 7¾x5" 100.00
Vase, pk, hdld, Stephen, 1934, 6x5" 100.00
Vase, raspberry pk/gray speckled matt, 6¼x4" 275.00
Vase, silver/ivory crystalline, rose int, waisted, 6x4" 150.00
Vase, tobacco brn, pk int, 7½" 85.00
Vase, turq, rnd lip, 12", VG 150.00
Vase, turq w/pk int, 7", pr 120.00
Vase, wht arrowheads on dk brn, Nonconnah, 5x4¾" 600.00
Vase, wht snowflake crystalline on gray-bl, rose int, 5x4" 250.00
Vase, wht w/appl leaves, 8" 250.00

Pittsburgh Glass

As early as 1797, utility window glass and hollowware were being produced in the Pittsburgh area. Coal had been found in abundance, and it was there that it was first used instead of wood to fuel the glass furnaces. Because of this, as many as 150 glass companies operated there at one time. However, most failed due to the economically disastrous effects of the War of 1812. By the mid-1850s those that remained were producing a wide range of flint glass items including pattern-molded and free-blown glass, cut and engraved wares, and pressed tableware patterns. Our advisor for this category is Mark Vuono; he is listed in the Directory under Connecticut.

Bottle, bar; amethyst, 8-panel, appl lip, 10⅜" 1,300.00
Bottle, bar; Pillar Mold, appl lip & ring, 9½" 50.00
Bottle, dk aqua, jug shape w/appl hdl, 5½"+stopper 660.00
Bowl, cobalt, 21 vertical ribs, appl ft, 3x4¼" 1,045.00
Candlestick, stepped quatrefoil shape base, pewter insert, 8" 300.00
Candlesticks, pressed hexagonal base, gallery rim, 7", pr 365.00
Canister, 3 appl cobalt rings, appl finial, 9¾", EX 275.00
Compote, blown bowl w/pressed base, 12-panel, eng swags, 6¾" ..1,100.00
Compote, cobalt, 8 ribs, appl ft, wafer stem, 5x6" 2,975.00
Compote, deep bowl, wide ft, 7½x9⅛" 300.00
Compote, flared ft, folded lip, 3¼x5¾" 360.00
Creamer, aqua, threaded neck & lip, appl hdl, 4⅛" 1,485.00
Cruet, 13 vertical ribs, ewer form, w/stopper, 8½" 110.00
Decanter, blown & cut, 3 appl rings, 8⅜"+stopper 550.00
Goblet, vintage & sailboat eng, ftd, 5½" 990.00
Pan, cobalt, 8-panel tumbler mold, 1½x5¼" 660.00

Pillar Mold vase, flared and scalloped lip, bulbous body, 8", $200.00; Pillar Mold center bowl, wide flat lip, knopped baluster-shaped pedestal, large round foot, 8½x10", $375.00.

Pitcher, appl hollow hdl, flared lip, 7¾" 440.00
Pitcher, Pillar Mold, appl hdl, broken bubble, 8⅝" 145.00
Pitcher, vining foliage eng, bulbous, sm chip, 5⅝" 440.00
Pitcher, 12-Pillar Mold, pontil scar, 1840-60, 6" 300.00
Punch cup, paneled, appl hdl, flint, 2½" 20.00
Sugar bowl, amethyst, galleried rim, domed lid, 7¼", NM 990.00
Sugar bowl, aqua, galleried lip, domed lid, 6", NM 4,125.00
Sugar bowl, clear w/red & bl loopings, wht int, w/lid, 12" 2,970.00
Sugar bowl, dk violet bl, 8-rib, 10-rib lid, 6⅝" 3,900.00
Sugar bowl, Pillar Mold, appl ft & stem, 8-rib, w/lid, 10⅝" 600.00
Syrup, amber, Pillar Mold, 12-rib, hdl, pewter lid, 7" 2,650.00
Tumbler, cut decor, Washington sulfide in base, 3⅛" 4,000.00
Tumbler, eng floral swags & tassels, chip, 3⅜" 275.00
Tumbler, eng greyhound & flowers, cut flutes on base, 3¼" 3,355.00
Vase, clear w/appl fiery opal trim, appl ft & stem, 6" 3,500.00
Vase, Pillar Mold, wide ft, baluster stem, 9¾" 260.00
Wine, cut panels, strawberry dmns, fans, 4", 8 for 360.00

Wine, Pillar Mold, knop stem, flared bowl w/8 ribs, 4⅜" 275.00

Plastics

The term 'collectible plastics' is defined as those types produced between 1868 (when synthetic plastics were invented) and the period immediately following WWII. There are several, and we shall mention each one and attempt briefly to acquaint you with their characteristics:

1) Pyroxylin (Celluloid, Loalin, French Ivory, Pyralin). Chemical name: cellulose nitrate. Earliest form, invented in 1868 by John Wesley Hyatt; highly flammable; yellows with age; much used in toiletry articles. Fairly lightweight, many articles of pyroxylin were made by heating and molding thin sheets.

2) Cellulose Acetate (Tenite, Similoid). Made in attempt to produce a product similar to cellulose nitrate but without the flammability. Had limited use in the costume jewelry trade; most often encountered as car knobs and handles of the thirties and forties. Surfaces tend to crack with age and exposure to light. Always molded, never cast. Colors varied; imitation horn and marble were most popular; imitation coral is seen in molded 'floral' jewelry.

3) Casein Plastics (Ameroid, Galalith, Dorcasine, Casolith). Invented in 1904 using milk proteins. Use limited to buttons and buckles due to warping and lengthy curing time. Made in a wide range of colors; very easy to laminate or to carve from stock rods or sheets, but never molded.

4) Phenol Formaldehyde (Bakelite, Catalin, Marblette, Agatine, Gemstone, Durite, Durez, Prystal). Invented by L.H. Baekland in 1908; used extensively in the thirties. There are two major types: cast and molded. Molded types include Durez and Bakelite, dark-toned, wood flour-filled plastics that were used extensively for early telephones (still used when non-conductivity of heat and electricity is vital). The most popular name in cast phenolics was Catalin, trade name of the American Catalin Corporation of New York. Made in a wide range of colors; widely used for costume jewelry, cutlery handles, decorative boxes, lamps, desk sets, etc. Heavyweight material with a slightly 'greasy' feel; very hard but can be carved with files, grinding tools, and abrasive cutters. Buffs to high, durable polish. Cast phenolics were used primarily from 1930 to around 1950 when they proved too labor-intensive to be economical.

5) Urea Formaldehyde (Beetleware, Plaskon, Duroware, Hemocoware, Uralite). Invented around 1929, this was lighter in color than phenol formaldehyde, thus used for injection-molded products in pastel colors. Lightweight, not strong; shiny rather than glossy. It cannot be carved and was used mainly for cheap radio and clock cases, never for jewelry.

The period between the two World Wars produced acrylic resins such as Lucite and vinyl. Polystyrene made its appearance then, and furfural-phenols were in use in industrial applications. Though a great future was predicted for ethyl cellulose, by the late thirties it was still in the experimental phase. For most purposes the field of decorative plastics from the first half of the century can be narrowed down to the five major types listed above. Of these, cellulose acetate is rarely encountered. Casein is limited to button and belt buckle manufacture; urea is easily identifiable as a cheap, brittle material. Pyroxylin is the celluloid of which so many vanity sets were made. Molded phenolics such as Bakelite were dark in color and used for utilitarian objects; cast phenolics such as Catalin were used most notably for jewelry (please don't call it Bakelite), cutlery handles, desk sets, and novelties.

Dealers and collectors should be aware of '70s reproduction Marblette animal napkin rings (they have no eye rods and no age patina) and molded acrylic bracelets in imitation of carved Catalin ones (look for a seam line or lack of definition in carved areas). As prices rise, copies become more common. 1986 saw the mass production of inlaid polka-dot bracelets using old-stock findings but without the precision fit (or patina) of the originals.

In 1988 and continuing to the present, a large number of 'collage' pieces appeared in vintage clothing and antique stores on the West and East Coasts. These are over-sized, glued-together assemblages of old Catalin stock parts including buttons with the shanks filed off, poker chips, etc., made into brooches or pendants, sometimes hung on necklaces of re-strung Catalin beads. They can be recognized by their aesthetically jumbled, 'put-together' look; and although some may claim they are old, they are not.

Our advisor for this category is Catherine Yronwode, who also publishes an informative newsletter, *The Collectible Plastics;* she is listed in the Directory under California. Our thanks to Benjamin Rose for help with radio prices.

Bakelite

Cigarette box, half-cylinder, rotates open, dk brn	45.00
Clock, electric, alarm, Deco design, blk or dk brn	65.00
Clock, mantel, wind-up alarm, Deco design, dk brn	60.00
Inkwell, streamlined, blk, w/lid	25.00
Penholder, streamlined, blk	22.50
Radio, Majestic #55, dk brn, 1939	250.00
Radio, Silvertone Compact, Sears, dk brn, 1936-1937	250.00
Radio, Stewart Warner Varsity College, dk brn, 1938-1939	250.00
Roulette wheel, dk brn, 1930s	80.00
Roulette wheel, mc Catalin chips, wood rack, w/box, 1930s	200.00
Watch, lady's handbag; Westclox, blk, 2¾" dia	100.00

Catalin

Ashtray, marbleized lt gr, sq, 4½"	30.00
Barometer, Taylor, amber & dk gr, rectangular, 4"	45.00
Blotter, Carvacraft, Great Britain, amber/blk	45.00
Bottle opener, chrome plate, red, gr, or amber hdl	10.00
Bracelet, bangle; apple-juice clear, figural bk-cvg	175.00
Bracelet, bangle; apple-juice clear, floral bk-cvg	150.00
Bracelet, bangle; apple-juice clear, geometric bk-cvg	130.00
Bracelet, bangle; deep cvg, w/rhinestones	90.00
Bracelet, bangle; elaborate floral cvg, narrow	60.00
Bracelet, bangle; elaborate floral cvg, wide	85.00
Bracelet, bangle; lt geometric cvg, narrow	30.00
Bracelet, bangle; lt geometric cvg, wide	45.00
Bracelet, bangle; novelty, mc, figural or animal cvg	250.00
Bracelet, bangle; scratch cvd, narrow	22.00
Bracelet, bangle; scratch cvd, w/rhinestones	35.00
Bracelet, bangle; scratch cvd, wide	27.00
Bracelet, bangle; stylized floral cvg, narrow	28.00
Bracelet, bangle; stylized floral cvg, wide	45.00
Bracelet, bangle; uncvd, narrow	8.00
Bracelet, bangle; uncvd, wide	11.00
Bracelet, bangle; 12 inlaid polka dots, wide	225.00
Bracelet, bangle; 2-color stripes	80.00
Bracelet, bangle; 3-color stripes	100.00
Bracelet, bangle; 4-color (or more) stripes	150.00
Bracelet, bangle; 6 inlaid polka dots, narrow	200.00
Bracelet, cellulose acetate chain, 7 cvd figural charms	250.00
Bracelet, clamper; figural, animal, or novelty applique	250.00
Bracelet, clamper; inlaid geometric designs	200.00
Bracelet, clamper; stylized floral cvg	95.00
Bracelet, clamper; w/inlaid rhinestones	50.00
Bracelet, curved/flat links, deeply cvd	65.00
Bracelet, curved/flat links, uncvd	45.00
Bracelet, stretch; orig elastic, Catalin & metal	50.00
Bracelet, stretch; orig elastic, deeply cvd	65.00
Bracelet, stretch; orig elastic, mc, uncvd	50.00

Buckle, latch type, mc, novelty or figural applique	65.00
Buckle, latch type, mc, stylized floral or geometric, cvd	40.00
Buckle, latch type, mc, uncvd	25.00
Buckle, latch type, 1-color, novelty or figural	55.00
Buckle, latch type, 1-color, stylized floral or geometric	30.00
Buckle, latch type, 1-color, uncvd	8.00
Buckle, latch type, 1-color w/rhinestones, Deco	30.00
Buckle, slide type, mc, stylized floral or geometric, cvd	35.00
Buckle, slide type, mc, uncvd	20.00
Buckle, slide type, 1-color, stylized floral or geometric, cvd	9.00
Buckle, slide type, 1-color, uncvd	6.00
Butter mold, gr/amber/brn, floral cvg, 2½"	45.00
Buttons, card of 6, red or blk laminated, 1½" rod	18.00
Buttons, card of 6, scotty, fruit, or cvd floral figural	28.00
Buttons, card of 6, uncvd octagonal, amber, 1" dia	10.00
Cake breaker, CJ Schneider, red, gr, or amber hdl	4.00
Carving set, knife, fork, steel	30.00
Carving set, 3-pc w/wood wall rack	40.00
Checkers, red & blk, full set, in box	35.00
Cheese slicer, Scotty hdl, wood & chrome base	20.00
Chess set, hand cvd, red & blk, leather box	300.00
Chopsticks, ivory, pr	5.00
Cigarette box, chrome inserts, cylindrical, 4½"	45.00
Cigarette box, lt gr, wood bottom, rectangular, 5½x3¾"	40.00
Cigarette holder, imitation amber, sterling tip, orig case	25.00
Cigarette holder, long, mc or w/rhinestones	25.00
Cigarette lighter, Arco-Lite devil's head, red or blk	175.00
Cigarette lighter, mc stripes or inlay	45.00
Clock, New Haven, wind-up alarm, amber, Deco, 3⅝"	60.00
Clock, Sessions, electric alarm, scalloped case, 4¼" dia	60.00
Clock, Seth Thomas, wind-up alarm, maroon case, 3½"	60.00
Clock, Westclox, Moonbeam, electric flashing light alarm	90.00
Clothesline, Jigger, red anchors, 10 pins, metal box	10.00
Cocktail recipes, Ben Hur, mtd on drunk, red w/blk base	50.00
Cocktail recipes, Ben Hur, mtd on fighting roosters	45.00
Cork, Ben Hur, w/red fighting roosters, blk base	25.00
Corkscrew, chrome, red, gr, or amber hdl	12.50
Corn holder, Kob Knobs, diamond shape or lathe trn, 8 +box	50.00
Crib toy, Tykie Toy, boy, girl, clown, kitten, etc, ea	195.00
Crib toy, Tykie Toy, clown, loalin head/Catalin body	195.00
Crib toy, Tykie Toy, elephant, laolin head/Catalin body	195.00
Crib toy, Tykie Toy, 11 mc spools on string, 1940s	100.00
Crib toy, Tykie Toy, 12-1½" rings on 2⅞" ring, 1940s	100.00
Crib toy, Tykie Toy catalogue, 1946	35.00
Crib toy, Tykie Toy Tales (book about these toys), 1946	45.00
Dice, ivory or red, 2½", pr	15.00
Dice, ivory or red, ¾", pr	2.00
Dice cage, metal/red Catalin, blk Lucite base, w/dice	100.00
Dice cup, leather or cork lined	40.00
Dominoes, ivory or blk, full set, w/wood box	40.00
Dominoes, red or gr, full set, w/wood box	50.00
Drawer pull, 1-color, w/pnt inlay stripe	2.00
Drawer pull, 2-color, octagon, w/inlaid dot	3.00
Dress clip, mc inlaid Deco design	30.00
Dress clip, novelty, figural, animal, or vegetable	50.00
Dress clip, scratch cvd	25.00
Dress clip, stylized floral cvg	30.00
Dress clip, 1-color, w/rhinestones, Deco design	30.00
Earrings, lg drop style, pr	10.00
Earrings, novelty, figural, animal, or vegetable, pr	35.00
Earrings, stylized floral cvg, pr	15.00
Earrings, uncvd disks, pr	8.00
Egg beater, red, gr, or amber hdl	16.00
Flatware, chrome plate, 1-color hdl	2.00

Flatware, chrome plate, 3-pc matched place setting 8.00
Flatware, stainless, 1-color hdl 3.00
Flatware, stainless, 1-color hdl, leatherette box, 36-pc 180.00
Flatware, stainless, 1-color hdl, 3-pc matched place setting 10.00
Flatware, stainless, 2-color hdl 4.00
Flatware, stainless, 2-color hdl, wood box, 36-pc 250.00
Flatware, stainless, 2-color hdl, 3-pc matched place setting 15.00
Gavel, lathe turned, ivory 25.00
Gavel, lathe turned, red, blk, & ivory 35.00
Gavel, lathe turned, red, w/presentation box, dtd 1946 ....40.00
Ice cream scoop, stainless, red hdl 20.00
Inkwell, Carvacraft Great Britain, amber, dbl well 115.00
Inkwell, Carvacraft Great Britain, amber, single well 90.00
Knife, cvd red, gr, or amber hdl 6.00
Lamp base, brass & amber, Deco design, 10" 30.00
Lamp base, red, amber, & blk, Deco design, 8" 44.00
Letter opener, blk & amber stripes, Deco design 20.00
Letter opener, chrome/Catalin, Deco design 20.00
Letter opener, marbleized gr, dagger shape 20.00
Mah-Jong set, tiles, rails, 6-color, complete, w/box 150.00
Memo pad, Carvacraft Great Britain, amber 55.00
Nail brush, Ducky, duck shape, translucent eye rod 50.00
Nail brush, marbleized lt gr, 2½x1½" 9.00
Nail brush, Masso, amber octagon, 2" dia 9.00
Nail brush, turtle shape, dark amber, 3½" 20.00
Napkin ring, amber, red, or gr, 2" dia band 8.00
Napkin ring, animal or bird, no inlaid eye or ball on head 30.00
Napkin ring, chicken w/inlaid beak 35.00
Napkin ring, elephant w/ball on head 35.00
Napkin ring, lathe turned, amber, red, or gr, 1¾" dia 10.00
Napkin ring, Mickey Mouse or Donald Duck shape w/decal 60.00
Napkin ring, rabbit w/inlaid eye rod 40.00
Napkin ring, rocking horse or camel w/inlaid eye rod 72.00
Napkin ring, scotty, w/inlaid eye rod 40.00
Napkin ring set, 6-colors, 2" band, orig box 40.00
Necklace, cellulose acetate chain, animal figurals 300.00
Necklace, cellulose acetate chain, Deco dangling pcs 200.00
Necklace, cvd red & amber beads, 18" 65.00
Necklace, uncvd gr beads, 20" 40.00
Ozone generator, Air-Clear, dk amber, streamlined case 75.00
Pencil sharpener, Disney character decal, silhouette shape 45.00
Pencil sharpener, gun, tank, or plane shape w/decal 40.00
Pencil sharpener, orange, no decal, ¾x1" 8.00
Pencil sharpener, red, Mickey Mouse decal, ¾x1" 30.00
Pencil sharpener, scotty, red, cvd details, blk base 30.00
Pencil sharpener, scotty, yel, silhouette shape 20.00
Pencil sharpener, Trylon & Perisphere, 1939 World's Fair 50.00
Penholder, amber & blk striped, Deco design 35.00
Penholder, marbleized amber, Deco design 25.00
Penholder, Scotty, red w/blk base 45.00
Picture frame, amber & red Deco design, 6x7" 45.00
Picture frame, red, gr, or amber, sq, 6" 35.00
Pin, animal, resin wash w/glass eye, lg 150.00
Pin, animal, resin wash w/glass eye, sm 90.00
Pin, animal or vegetable, inlaid or appl in several colors, lg 210.00
Pin, animal or vegetable, inlaid or appl in several colors, sm 125.00
Pin, animal or vegetable, 1-color, lg 90.00
Pin, animal or vegetable, 1-color, sm 80.00
Pin, mc Deco design, lg 80.00
Pin, mc Deco design, sm 60.00
Pin, novelty or patriotic figural, resin wash/inlay/appl, lg 200.00
Pin, novelty or patriotic figural, resin wash/inlay/appl, sm 135.00
Pin, novelty or patriotic figural, 1-color, lg 95.00
Pin, novelty or patriotic figural, 1-color, sm 65.00

Pin, stylized floral cvg, lg 50.00
Pin, stylized floral cvg, sm 40.00
Pin, w/danglers, animal or vegetable, resin wash/inlay/appl 200.00
Pin, w/danglers, animal or vegetable, 1-color 135.00
Pin, w/danglers, geometric form, mc 60.00
Pin, w/danglers, geometric form, 1-color 50.00
Pin, w/danglers, novelty or patriotic, resin wash/inlay/appl 250.00
Pin, w/danglers, novelty or patriotic, 1-color 150.00
Pipe, amber & gr, bowl lined w/clay 30.00
Pitcher, glass, red, gr, or amber hdl, syrup size 18.00
Pocket watch, Debonaire, yel Deco case, 1⅞" dia 60.00
Poker chip rack, cylindrical, w/50 chips, 2½" 85.00
Poker chip rack, rectangular, w/200 chips, 4" 120.00
Powder box, amber & blk fluted cylinder, 2½" 50.00
Powder box, amber & gr fluted cylinder, 4" 60.00
Radio, AMC 'Peaktop,' amber, maroon trim 2,500.00
Radio, Emerson Cathedral (AU190), amber 1,200.00
Radio, Emerson Cathedral (AU190), bright red, very rare 13,000.00
Radio, Emerson Cathedral (AU190), gr marbled 2,200.00
Radio, Emerson College model, amber or gr, 1938 ....1,000.00
Radio, Emerson College model, red, 1938 ....1,200.00
Radio, Fada Streamliner, amber, amber knobs/bezel, 1941 ....1,000.00
Radio, Fada Streamliner, amber, red knobs/bezel, 1941 ....1,100.00
Radio, Fada Streamliner, red, amber knobs/bezel, 1941, rare 9,800.00
Radio, Kadette Klockette, amber, gr, or maroon, 1937 ....1,200.00
Radio, Kadette Klockette, red, 1937 ....1,500.00
Ring, inlaid Deco stripe design, 2-color 45.00
Ring, stylized floral cvg, 1-color 35.00
Ring, uncvd, 1-color 20.00
Ring, uncvd, 2-color 30.00
Ring case, hinged-lid style, amber or maroon 150.00
Ring case, open-top style, amber, red, or blk, Deco design 90.00
Safety razor, Schick Injector, amber hdl 18.00
Safety razor, Schick Injector, extra blades, orig box, 1939 ....45.00
Salad servers, Chase chrome, ivory, blk, or brn, pr 45.00
Salad servers, chrome, red, gr, or amber hdls, pr 12.00
Shakers, ball shape or half-cylinder shape, 1½", pr 30.00
Shakers, glass, in 3⅛" Catalin holder, pr 30.00
Shakers, mushroom shape, amber & ivory, 1⅞", pr 35.00
Shakers, stepped cylinder shape, 3½", pr 30.00
Shakers, Washington Monument, 3¼", pr 35.00
Shaving brush, red, gr, or amber 20.00
Shaving brush, red, gr, or amber, w/holder 40.00
Spatula, stainless, red, gr, or amber hdl 6.00
Spoon, iced tea, chrome, w/Catalin knob, 6-pc set 25.00
Spoon, slotted, stainless, red, gr, or amber hdl 5.00
Steering knob, chrome clamp 18.00
Stirrer, iced tea; Chase, chrome ball/mint leaf, 6-pc set 35.00
Stirrer, iced tea; shovel blade, Catalin hdl, 6-pc set 45.00
Strainer, red, gr, or amber hdl, 2¾" dia 5.00
Strainer, red, gr, or amber hdl, 5" dia 6.00
Swizzle stick, baseball-bat shape, amber or red 5.00
Swizzle stick holder, amber or red, Rheingold Lager decal 95.00
Thermometer, BT Co, amber & blk, 2¾" dia 45.00
Thermometer, Taylor, amber & dk gr, rectangular, 4" 45.00
Writing set, blk, amber, or gr marble, Deco, 5-pc, orig box 175.00

Celluloid

Bracelet, imitation tortoise w/inlaid rhinestones 40.00
Bracelet, snake w/inlaid rhinestones 48.00
Bridge marker, pnt ivoroid animal or figure, France 25.00
Bridge pencil holder, animal, pearlescent ivory on blk 70.00
Buttons, ivoroid or pearlescent, ¾" dia, card of 6 ....8.00

Carving set, ivoroid, knife/fork/steel, eng blade 30.00
Clock, Greek temple facade, wind-up alarm, ivoroid 50.00

Crib toy, rattle, winking moon face (possibly a Tykie Toy, but may be from another manufacturer), $250.00.

Dresser set, amberoid & gr marbleized, 7-pc 80.00
Dresser set, ivoroid, 10-pc, w/9" bevel glass mirror 110.00
Dresser set, ivory pearlescent or amberoid, 5-pc 60.00
Flatware, gr pearl on blk hdl, 3-pc set 9.00
Flatware, ivoroid hdl, table knife, fork, or spoon, ea 2.00
Hair receiver, ivoroid, pearlescent or amberoid, w/2-part lid 12.00
Manicure set, ivoroid, pearlescent or amberoid, 10-pc, +case 30.00
Manicure set, ivoroid, 18-pc, roll-up leather case 25.00
Manicure set, 4 mini-tools in coral-color tube, Germany 22.00
Manicure set, 4 mini-tools in tube holder w/pnt florals 35.00
Mirror, dresser; ivoroid, cut-out hdl, bevel glass, 8" 25.00
Mirror, dresser; ivoroid, oval bevel glass, 13" 35.00
Mirror, dresser; pearlescent or amberoid, bevel glass, 12" 28.00
Picture frame, easel bk, ivoroid, 2" dia 15.00
Powder box, ivoroid, pearlescent or amberoid 15.00
Shaving stand, ivoroid, 5-pc, w/razor 75.00

Lucite

Bottle, perfume; w/atomizer, rose inclusion 20.00
Bracelet, stretch, orig elastic, clear, bk-cvd 27.00
Picture frame, Deco, clear, sq, 6" 18.00
Purse, box style, clear, pearl, ivory, or tortoise 45.00
Shakers, translucent red, 4", pr 12.00

Playing Cards

Playing cards can be an enjoyable way to trace the course of history. Knowledge of the art, literature, and politics of an era can be gleaned from a study of its playing cards. When royalty lost favor with the people, Kings and Queens were replaced by common people. During the periods of war, generals, officers, and soldiers were favored. In the United States, early examples had portraits of Washington and Adams as opposed to Kings, Indian chiefs instead of Jacks, and goddesses for Queens.

Tarot cards were used in Europe during the 1300s as a game of chance, but in the 18th century they were used to predict the future and were regarded with great reverence.

The backs of cards were of no particular consequence until the 1890s. The marble design used by the French during the late 1800s and the colored wood-cut patterns of the Italians in the 19th century are among the first attempts at decoration. Later the English used cards printed with portraits of royalty. Eventually cards were decorated with a broad range of subjects from reproductions of fine art to advertising.

Although playing cards are becoming popular collectibles, prices are still relatively low. Complete decks of cards printed earlier than the first postage stamp can still be purchased for less than $100.00. Our advise for this category comes from the American Antique Deck Collectors Club, 52 Plus Joker; see Directory under Clubs, Newsletters, and Catalogs.

Key:
AC — ad card
C — complete
cts — courts
hc — hand colored
J — joker
OB — original box
SC — score card
std — standard
XC — extra card
WF — World's Fair

Advertising

Anheuser-Busch Spanish Am War 31, 1899, 52+Uncle Sam J, EX .500.00
Beechcraft, plane bks, dbl deck, MIB 17.50
Black Velvet, narrow nonstd, 1974, dbl deck, MIB/NMIB 20.00
Budweiser, narrow, Miss Budweiser plane, 52+4J, EX, OB 12.00
Canadian Club, narrow, 52C, VG-, VG box 22.00
Dixie Burning Oils, wide, Brn & Bigelow std, 52+J+XC, '40, MIB .10.00
Egg-O-See Cereal, wide, 1906, 52+special J+ad card, MIB 200.00
Fairchild Semiconductor, wide nonstd, 1968, 52+2J+XC, MIB 18.00
Falk, nonstd, product photo bks, 1955, 52, EX, torn box 28.00
Grant's Scotch Whiskey, narrow nonstd, 1928-40 ads, 54C, MIB 35.00
Herculese Buggy Co, wide, 52+Horse & Buggy J+SC, EX+, VG case ..248.00
Home Rubber, wide, Never Burn/Blow Out, 52+J+AC+SC, EX, OB .110.00
Iron Fireman, bl disk bks, ca 1960, M, no box 16.00
Jersey Whiskey, wide, ad-type bk, 52+2J+AC, G-, torn box 50.00
Jim Beam, KY Straight Bourbon, wht/blk, 52+2J, MIB 12.50
Kinney Bros, transformation, 1889, 43 of 52, EX- 350.00
Kissproof, narrow, Kissproof Girl, 52+J+AC, VG-, torn box 40.00
Kraftmaid, ad promos on cts, 52+2 special J, EX in G- box 55.00
Michelin, wide nonstd, Tire Guy cts, 52, VG- 17.00
Park Lane, narrow, tapestry bks, 1925, C, NMIB 40.00
Tiffany & Co, Harlequin, transformation, 1879, 42C, EX- 1,200.00
Time Magazine, wide, 1978 commemorative, 52+J+XC, MIB ...150.00
Vanity Fair, nonstd, 1986, 51 of 52+Maryanski J, MIB 42.00
Wayne Dog Food, hunting dog bks, 52+2J, EX, OB 17.50
Woman's World, wide, lady in lg hat, 52+J, G, torn box 30.00

Modern Decks

Aircraft Spotters II, wide, red bks, 1943, 52+J+XC, MIB 22.00
Almagated Meat Cutters, photos/bios, '52, 52+2J, G+, G box 22.00
Austria, Coronet, Patience, fantasy cts, dbl deck, MIB, sealed 22.00
China, dream of Red Mansions, nonstd, 52+2J, NMIB 17.00
Coolidge Dogs, dogs playing cards, dbl deck, EX/M, OB 25.00
Egypt, Tutankhamen, wide, mask on bk, M, broken box 30.00
Forcolar, No Revoke, 1947, dbl deck, ea 52+J+AC, ea NMIB 33.00
Germany, Happy Cards, 1966, 52+2J+XC, M, no box 15.00
Hermes, wide, Cassandre, 1950, 52+2 special J+XC, MIB 85.00
Israel, Jacob's Bible, nonstd, 1954, dbl deck, ea MIB 17.00
Miro, nonstd, Beranger, gold on cts, 1950, 52+2J, G 28.00
Montclair, planes w/V bkground, Arrco, 1940s, 52+J+AC, MIB ..14.00
Paul Webb, Full House, dbl decks, ea 52+J, EX, OB/NMIB 12.50
Russia, 150th Anniversary of Card Making, 1967, MIB 45.00
Swiss, Des Alchimestes, oversz, nonstd cts, 1967, 37C, NMIB 30.00
US, Politicards, Nixon administration spades, '72, EX, OB 12.50
US, Tiffany, repro transformation cts, dbl deck, ea MIB 20.00
Victory, nonstd, special cts, 1945, 52+J+special J, NMIB 88.00

Older Decks, Bridge or Whist

Arrow Bridgeway, bl lady w/dog, late '20s, 52+J+SC, EX, OB 20.00
Carson Pirie Scott, USPC, 1928, 52+J, EX in slipcase 22.00
Congress USPC, Minnehaha, MIB, sealed 70.00

Congress USPC, Rural Life, 1926, 42+J+AC+SC, MIB **15.00**
Criterion, gold edge, 1930s, 52+J+SC, NM **22.00**
Dondorf, Swiss costumes, scenic Aces, 1900, 52, NM, broken box **.55.00**
Dondorf, Whist, teens as cts, ca 1900, 52+J, G **10.00**
Dougherty, Tally Ho, 1930s, 52+J, VG, OB **33.00**
Goodall, Linette, linen grained, 1900s, 52+J+blank, MIB **28.00**
King Press, Imperial, red & bl bks, '20s, 104+2J+2XC, NMIB **26.00**

Older Decks, Narrow, Odd Sizes or Shapes

Black Cat, Cerraras, 1928, 42C, NM **60.00**
Colonial Period, Stevens, USPC-type cts, 1930s, 55C, MIB **62.00**
Crest Approach Forcing System, 1931, 52+J+SC+XC, EX-, VG box **..32.00**
NYCC, Elf, std faces, ca 1923, 2x3", MIB, sealed **28.00**
Parasol, Criterion (?), Deco silver & blk bks, 1930s, EX, OB **23.00**
Royal Revelers, antiprohibition, 1932, 52+J+SC, G+, G box **105.00**
Russel-Culbertson's Own, 1932, 52+booklet, EX, OB **25.00**
Waddington, circular, red & gold bks, 52+J+XC, VG+, G- box ...**10.00**

Older Decks, Wide

Am PCC Premier, bird bks, Henry VII J, 1890, 52+J, G, G- box **.67.00**
Am PCC Steamboats, gr bks, musician J, 1890s, 52+J, VG+, G- box **.82.00**
Bicycle #808, Racer #1, red bks, 52, VG **25.00**
Bicycle USPC #808, Cupid, red bks, 52", VG+, EX box **30.00**
Clemente Jacques, Excelsior, El Gallo theme, 1923, 40C, EX+ **35.00**
Congress USPC, Harbor, 1920s, 52+J+SC+2AC, NMIB **35.00**
Congress USPC, Viola, lady in fur, ca 1914, 52+J, VG-, G- box **..40.00**
Goodall, Victoria on gray, Monarch cts, 52C, EX+, slipcase **110.00**
Goodall Pasha, bl bks, pre-1900, 52+J, M in torn box **30.00**
Kalamazoo PCC, Oaken Bucket/Dreaming, 104+2J+2SC, G, w/case **.30.00**
Nat'l CC Owls, steamboat-type stock, 1895, 52+blank, G **55.00**
New Era USPC #46, European cts, ca 1895, 52, VG, G- box **125.00**
Playanlearn, Levis & Cook, Fr translations, 1918, 52C, OB **180.00**
Standard, Uncle Sam, pattern bk, 1925, 52+J+AC, EX, OB **16.50**
Tigers USPC, Tiger J, plaid bks, ca 1881, 52+J, NM+, VG box **.200.00**
Tourists USPC, bl pattern bks, ca 1920, 52+J, VG-, no box **80.00**

Pinups

Elvgren, lady in chair w/box of roses, 52+2J, M, no box **35.00**
Elvgren, South Seas, 52+2J, MIB **45.00**
Elvgren, 52 pinups on faces, pk bks, 52+J+XC, MIB **135.00**
Esquire, Vargas, redhead, 1944, 52+booklet, G, OB **10.00**
Fairchild swimsuit pinups, dbl deck, 52/52+J, VG/EX, ½ box **22.00**
Mac Person, Not...to Hoyle, dbl deck, ea 52+2J, EX+/EX- in box ...**40.00**
Quick on the Draw, dbl deck, 1847, 52+J+SC/52+SC, M/NM in box **.45.00**
Vargas, Comme ci Comme ca!, dbl deck, ea 52+J+XC, NMIB **..265.00**
Vargas, 52 pinups on faces, 52+special J+bio card, NMIB **135.00**
Winning Aces, dbl deck, 1948, ea 52+J+XC, VG- in box **22.00**

Souvenir and Expositions

Alaska-Yukon Expo, blk/wht photos, 1909, 52+J, NMIB **125.00**
Apollo 11, narrow, Eagle landing on moon, 1959, 52+2J, NMIB **.17.00**
CA, Waters, state seal w/poppies, ca 1900, 52+J+XC, NM, EX box **..45.00**
Chicago, narrow scenic, 1950s, dbl deck, ea MIB **26.00**
Hawaii, gr fr, gilt edge, 1901, 52+J+AC, EX+, NM box **62.00**
Hopi Boy, wide, Southwest Indians, 52+special J+J, VG in box **.630.00**
Iberian-Am Expo, Palao, 40C+fact card+booklet, EX, G- box **75.00**
Maine, State House bks, 1910, 52+scenic J+XC, G, OB **20.00**
MT & Yellowstone, photos, 1898, 51+J+XC, VG, G- box **87.50**
NY WF, color sketches, bl bks, 52+2J, M, no box **15.00**
O'Callaghan's Chicago, red border, 1930, 52+AC+booklet, MIB **..96.00**

Pan-Am Expo, aluminum, bison bks, 1901, 52+J, VG in case **725.00**
St Louis WF, Cupples, Jefferson/Napoleon, 52, G+ in case **66.00**
WA State, older A photos, 1899, 52+J+map C, VG+, unmk case **..55.00**
Yellowstone Park, bl rays, 53 photos, 52+J+SC, NMIB **28.00**

Transportation: Airline, Steamship, Railroad

Air India, 1st Class in red on wht, 52+J, MIB **12.50**
Bangor & Aroostock, older logo, 52+2J, MIB **10.00**
Braniff, Spanish & Portuguese translations, MIB **7.00**
Cathay Pacific, bl wave design on gold, MIB, sealed **10.00**
Coastwise, steamer bk, 1930s, 52+J+SC, EX, torn box **40.00**
Cotton Belt, wide, Blk girl w/watermelon, 52C, VG, OB **345.00**
Denver & Salt Lake Moffat Line, wide scenic, 1914, 52+J, MIB **..280.00**
French Line, wide, gr bks, 52+2J+XC, EX-, VG slipcase **28.00**
IL Central, Medallion, For 100 Yrs, 1951, M, sealed **25.00**
Knutsen, cargo ship bks, dbl deck, ea M in sealed paper box **20.00**
Milwaukee Rd, wide scenic, 53 photos, 1916, 52+J, VG-, G- box ...**55.00**
Savannah, 1935, 52+SC, NMIB **22.00**
Singapore, wide, girl in flower field, MIB, sealed **12.00**
Southern Pacific, narrow scenic, train, 1935, 52+J+SC, EX, OB **..35.00**
Southern Pacific, wide scenic, 52 photos, 52+J+SC+AC, MIB **22.50**
US Lines, red/bl bks, dbl deck, ea 52+J, ea VG in box **20.00**

Political

    The most valuable political items are those from any period which relate to a political figure whose term was especially significant or marked by an important event or one whose personality was particularly colorful. Posters, ribbons, badges, photographs, and pin-back buttons are but a few examples of the items popular with collectors of political memorabilia.

    Political campaign pin-back buttons were first mass produced and widely distributed in 1896 for the president-to-be William McKinley and for the first of three unsuccessful attempts by William Jennings Bryan. Pin-back buttons have been used during each presidential campaign ever since and are collected by many people. The most scarce are those used in the presidential campaigns of John W. Davis in 1924 and James Cox in 1920.

    Contributions for this category were made by Michael J. McQuillen, monthly columnist of *Political Parade*, which appears in *AntiqueWeek* newspapers; he is listed in the Directory under Indiana. Our advisor for this category is Paul J. Longo; he is listed under Massachusetts. See also Autographs; Broadsides; Historical Glass; Watch Fobs.

Drawing, Our Governor Growing As One Sided as Most, pen and ink, Thomas Nast, 21x14", EX, $700.00.

Badge, Democratic Nat'l Convention, Chicago, 1944, w/ribbon **..28.00**
Badge, McKinley, Protection, w/portrait, EX **35.00**
Badge, McKinley & Hobart Inaugurated Mar 4th 1897, brass, EX **..45.00**
Badge, McKinley/Roosevelt jugate, Nation's Choice, brass/mc **55.00**
Badge, Republican Nat'l Convention, Lincoln portrait, 1944 ......**28.00**
Badge, Timothy L Woodruff for Governor, sepia-tone, EX **35.00**

Badge, usher's, 1908 Republican Convention, bronze, 2-pc 30.00
Banner, Eisenhower-Nixon jugate, fabric, 36x48" 75.00
Belt buckle, LBJ in relief, metal rectangle, EX 15.00
Button, Dwight D Eisenhower, portrait, celluloid, easel bk, 9½" ..60.00
Button/stud, Cox, rooster diecut, I Will Crow..., 1920, ⅞", EX 20.00
Button/stud, Hoover, metal elephant shape, 1928, 1", EX 10.00
Button/stud, McKinley portrait on flag ground, 1896, ⅞", EX 22.00
Cigar, Wm H Taft portrait on band, 4½", M 40.00
Cigarette holder, Dewey, bl letters on wht, NM 20.00
Comb, Nixon & Nakasian, blk plastic, NM 15.00
Dollar token, Goldwater, 100 Common Sense, 1964 ....3.50
Freedom dollar, Goldwater portrait 5.00
Lapel stud, Cleveland/Stevenson, silk on tin, 1892 ....30.00
Light bulb, Republican elephant filament, working 25.00
Match cover, Nixon Now, red/wht/bl, M 2.00
Medal, Cleveland, Am's Tariff Reform Champion, w/ribbon, EX ..50.00
Medal, Gerald Ford Vice Presidential inaugural, bronze, M 7.50
Medal, John Fremont Born Jan 21, 1813, brass, 1856, M 35.00
Medal, Nixon inaugural, silver proof, Franklin Mint, 1973 ....65.00
Medal, Vote To Win w/Roosevelt (Franklin), aluminum, 1¼" ...15.00
Medallion, McKinley/Roosevelt jugate, brass, mechanical 45.00
Medallion, McKinley/Roosevelt/Bryan, brass, mechanical 45.00
Memorial, Andrew Johnson, text/details, ltd ed, 1901, 15x20" 25.00

Mirror, Franklin Delano Roosevelt, Daily & Sunday Times, celluloid, rare, $150.00.

Mirror, pocket, Theodore Roosevelt portrait, scarce 200.00
Mug, McKinley, Protection & Prosperity, glass, ornate lid 85.00
Pamphlet, Industrial Unionism, Debs campaign, EX 30.00
Pamphlet, J Monroe, Message From President..., 1818, 91-pg 45.00
Pennant, Hoover portrait, Chicago 1932 Convention, NM 100.00
Pin-bk, Bryan portrait, I Gave My Dollar..., 1900, 1¼", EX 100.00
Pin-bk, Bryan/Sewell jugate, NADC, shield ground, 1896, 1¼", EX 45.00
Pin-bk, Bryan/Sewell jugate, 16 to 1, 1896, ⅞", EX 25.00
Pin-bk, Carter for President, 1976, lg 4.00
Pin-bk, Coolidge, Keep Coolidge, 1924, ⅞", EX 25.00
Pin-bk, Coolidge/Dawes (name), 1924, ⅞", EX 15.00
Pin-bk, Coolidge/Dawes jugate, wht ground, 1924, ⅞", EX 40.00
Pin-bk, Cox portrait, Peace, Progress, Prosperity, 1920, ⅞", EX .175.00
Pin-bk, Cox/Roosevelt (names), 1920, ⅞", EX 35.00
Pin-bk, Davis portrait, 1924, ⅞", EX 125.00
Pin-bk, Davis portrait in wishbone, Victory, 1924, ⅞", EX 2,100.00
Pin-bk, Davis/Bryan (name), 1924, ⅞", EX 70.00
Pin-bk, Ford in Every Garage 6.00
Pin-bk, Geraldine Ferraro, 1st Woman Vice President 6.00
Pin-bk, Goldwater/Miller, celluloid, 1964, 3½" 15.00
Pin-bk, Harding (name), 1920, ⅞", EX 12.00
Pin-bk, Harding Coolidge (names), 1920, ⅞", EX 15.00
Pin-bk, Harding portrait, 1920, ⅞", EX 16.00
Pin-bk, Herbert C Hoover for President, celluloid 25.00
Pin-bk, Hoover portrait, red/wht/bl border, 1928, 1¼", EX 42.00
Pin-bk, Hoover/Curtis (names), 1928, ⅞", EX 12.00
Pin-bk, Hughes, Hughes, Willis, Merrick, 1916, ⅞", EX 20.00

Pin-bk, Hughes (name), 1916, ⅞", EX 12.00
Pin-bk, Hughes/Fairbanks jugate, blk/wht, 1916, ⅞", EX 48.00
Pin-bk, MacArthur, America's Hero, red/wht bl border 12.00
Pin-bk, MacArthur, Man of the Hour, red/wht/bl border, 1¼" 10.00
Pin-bk, McKinley, portrait on gold ground, 1900, ⅞", EX 20.00
Pin-bk, McKinley/Hobart jugate, blk/wht/red/bl, ⅞" 25.00
Pin-bk, McKinley/Roosevelt jugate, Full...Bucket, 1900, 1¼", EX .125.00
Pin-bk, Oliver North for President, M 3.00
Pin-bk, Parker, natural-color picture, 1904, 1¼", EX 50.00
Pin-bk, Parker, Uncle Sam's Wht Elephant shown, 1904, 1¾", EX ..50.00
Pin-bk, Parker/Davis jugate, Miss Liberty, 1904, 1¼", EX 185.00
Pin-bk, Richard Nixon for President, portrait, mc, EX 10.00
Pin-bk, Roosevelt, My Hat Is in the Ring, 1912, 1¼", EX 125.00
Pin-bk, Roosevelt portrait, Stand Pat, 1904, 1¼", EX 350.00
Pin-bk, Roosevelt/Fairbanks jugate, sepia, 1904, 1¼", EX 55.00
Pin-bk, Shirley Chisolm President, Catalyst for Change, M 3.00
Pin-bk, Smith (name), Hello Al, 1928, 1¼", EX 30.00
Pin-bk, Smith portrait, gr border, 1928, ⅞", EX 18.00
Pin-bk, Smith/Robinson (names), 1928, ⅞", EX 10.00
Pin-bk, Taft, natural-color portrait, 1908, 1¼", EX 30.00
Pin-bk, Taft (name), 1912, ⅞", EX 12.00
Pin-bk, Taft/Sherman, elephant ears jugate, 1908, 1¼", EX ...5,500.00
Pin-bk, Vote No for My Sake, boy in center, prohibition, ⅞" 15.00
Pin-bk, Willkie/McNary jugate, EX 35.00
Pin-bk, Wilson portrait, Safety First, 1916, ⅞", EX 27.00
Pin-bk, Wilson/Marshall jugate, Am First, 1912, ⅞", EX 35.00
Pocketknife, Carter/Mondale jugate, sm portraits, EX 10.00
Pocketknife, Hoover/Curtis jugate, sepia-tone hdls, VG 65.00
Pocketknife, Mr & Mrs Woodrow Wilson portraits, VG 55.00
Pocketknife, Reagan/Bush jugate, M 5.00
Poster, Harding/Coolidge jugate, 1920, 21x28", VG 70.00
Poster, Landon/Knox jugate, vignetted portraits, 1938, 21x14" 50.00
Poster, Taft litho, Enquirer Printing Co, OH, 1907, 22x17" 75.00
Print, H Greeley Candidate...for President of US, 24x17" 75.00
Razor, Taft/Sherman jugate, rare, EX 150.00
Ribbon, Bryan Day, Vice President, 1896, blk/wht, EX 35.00
Ribbon, For Liberty We Stand, MacArthur photo, red/wht/bl, EX ..50.00
Ribbon, Henry Clay, People's Welfare..., orange, 7", EX 275.00
Ribbon, Humphrey/Muskie jugate, red/wht/bl, plastic, NM 5.00
Ribbon, Ike 1952, wht on bl, EX 40.00
Ribbon, Lowden for Ever, portrait, blk/wht, EX 35.00
Ribbon, South Canton McKinley Club, portrait, blk/yel, EX 55.00
Scissors, Wilson portrait, Miss Liberty figure, WWI era 75.00
Script pin, Cleveland, brass, M on orig card 40.00
Spinner, mechanical; Bryan, US flag on reverse, EX 65.00
Stanhope, portraits of Garfield & family, EX 40.00
Stereo card, Wm McKinley funeral, solemn soldiers, 1901 ....5.00
Stevengraph, Centennial, G Washington portrait, NM 125.00
Sticker, Vote for Woman Suffrage Amendment, mc, 1915, EX 15.00
Ticket, general admission; JFK acceptance speech, NM 25.00
Ticket, Harrison/Tyler Grand Ball, coated stock, 3¼", EX 100.00
Ticket, 1907 dedication of McKinley Memorial, red/wht/bl 10.00
Token, Maj Gen'l WH Harrison...People's Choice..., brass, ⅞" ...40.00
Token, Webster Credit Current 1841, copper, EX 40.00
Transcript of 1858 Lincoln/Douglas debate, published 1860, EX .125.00
Watch, Spiro Agnew, Dirty Time, caricature, M 60.00
Watch fob, Cox sepia-tone insert, NM 300.00
Watch fob, Taft, bronze, rectangular, EX 28.00
Watch fob, WJ Bryan Our Next President 35.00

Pomona

Pomona glass was patented in 1885 by the New England Glass

Works. Its characteristics are an etched background of crystal lead glass often decorated with simple designs painted with metallic stains of amber or blue. The etching was first achieved by hand cutting through an acid resist. This method, called first ground, resulted in an uneven feather-like frost effect. Later, to cut production costs, the hand-cut process was discontinued in favor of an acid bath which effected an even frosting. This method is called second ground. Our advisors for this category are Betty and Clarence Maier; they are listed in the Directory under Pennsylvania.

Bowl, 1st ground, 3x4½" 275.00
Bowl, 2nd ground, cornflowers (no bl), 6¼" 77.50
Butter dish, 1st ground, acanthus leaf, gold stain, 4x8" dia 540.00
Celery vase, 1st ground, ruffled, 6¼" 370.00
Celery vase, 2nd ground, T'print w/cornflowers, 6½" 300.00
Champagne, 2nd ground, 5" 250.00
Creamer, 1st grind, scalloped trim, partial-stained hdl, 4" 300.00
Creamer, 2nd ground, cornflowers, pulled ft, 4" 100.00
Creamer, 2nd ground, cornflowers, ruffled, crimped base, 3" 225.00
Creamer, 2nd ground, pansies/butterfly, 2¾x5½" 300.00
Finger bowl, 1st ground, ruffled, 1¾x5½" 220.00
Finger bowl, 2nd ground, cornflowers, w/bl stain, 2½x5½" 150.00
Finger bowl, 2nd ground, T'print w/cornflowers & ivy, 4" 160.00
Pitcher, lemonade; 1st ground, 2 butterflies, w/bl stain, 12" 1,700.00
Pitcher, 1st ground, Invt T'print, sqd scalloped rim, 7" 200.00
Punch cup, 1st ground, cornflowers 145.00
Punch cup, 1st ground, Invt T'print 45.00
Punch cup, 2nd ground, cornflowers 110.00
Sugar bowl, 1st ground, cornflowers, 2½x6" 100.00
Toothpick holder, 1st ground, tricorner rim, scalloped trim, 2" ..200.00
Tumbler, lemonade; 1st ground, cornflowers, w/bl stain 350.00
Tumbler, lemonade; 2nd ground, Rivulet, w/hdl 185.00
Tumbler, 2nd ground, cornflowers, w/yel stain, 3¾" 145.00
Tumbler, 2nd ground, cornflowers, 3¾" 60.00
Tumbler, 2nd ground, Dmn Quilt, cornflowers, 4" 95.00
Vase, 1st ground, cornflowers, ruffled, appl base, 5½" 220.00

Porcelier

The Porcelier Company, originally from East Liverpool, Ohio, started business in the late 1920s and moved to Greensburg, Pennsylvania, in the early 1930s. The company flourished until the late 1940s and finally closed its doors due to labor disputes in 1954.

They produced an endless line of vitrified porcelain products including furniture coasters, electric appliances, dripolators, and light fixtures. These products were sold in many stores under a variety of names and carried over ten different types of marks and labels.

The prices below are for items in excellent undamaged condition. If you have any questions or information regarding Porcelier, please contact our advisor, Jim Barker; he is listed in the Directory under Pennsylvania. For more information we recommend *Collector's Guide to Porcelier China* by Susan Grindberg.

Drip pot, Dutch boy & girl 35.00
Drip pot, Hearth, 6-cup 35.00
Fixture, ceiling light; cowboy 145.00
Fixture, ceiling; half-bbl design 55.00
Percolator #120, electric 85.00
Percolator set #710, electric 145.00
Table lamp, Rose pattern 65.00
Teapot, Beehive w/Flower, 4-cup 45.00
Teapot, Flamingo, 8-cup 75.00
Teapot, Mexican, 4-cup 45.00

Teapot, Tree Trunk, 6-cup 48.00

Postcards

Postcards are distinguished from almost any other collectible due to the fact that nearly any topic can be found represented on cards! For this reason, postcard collecting is considered the 'all-encompassing hobby'! A German by the name of Emmanuel Herrman is credited for inventing the postcard, first printed in Austria in 1869. They were eagerly accepted by the Continentals and the English alike, who saw them as a more economical way to send written messages.

The first to be printed in the United States were on U.S. government postals. The Columbian Exposition of 1892-1893 served as the spark that ignited the postcard phenomenon. Souvenir cards by the thousands were sent to folks back home — expo scenes, transportation themes, animals, birds, and advertising messages became popular. There were patriotic themes, Black themes, and cards for every occasion and holiday. Scenics, cards with small-town railroad depots, and views of U.S. towns (especially photos) are very sought after.

Some of the earliest postcard publishers were Raphael Tuck, Nister, and Gabriel. Early 20th-century illustrators such as Frances Brundage and Ellen Clapsaddle designed cards that are especially collectible.

Although the postcard rage waned at the onset of WWI, they rank today among the most sought-after items of ephemera, second only to stamps.

Even though postcards may be sixty to ninety years old, they must be in excellent condition. As a worth-accessing factor, condition is second only to subject matter. When no condition is indicated, the items listed below are assumed to be in excellent condition whether used or unused. Our advisor for this category is Ronald D. Millard; he is listed in the Directory under Florida.

Key:
p/ — publisher   s/ — signed

Advertising, Am La France Fire Engine Co, Elmira NY, EX 10.00
Advertising, Bell Telephone, girl using phone, blk/wht, EX 20.00
Advertising, Daniel Webster Flour, 1915, EX 12.50
Advertising, Roosevelt Bears Put Out a Fire (book), mc, EX 20.00
Advertising, Yorkton Fair, Happy Pig, July...1910, EX 8.00
Black, Go It Dina, Tuck's Happy Little Coons series, EX 30.00
Black, Gold Dust Twins, Thanksgiving scene, 1913, EX 30.00
Black, Pick of the Pickaninnies, Ullman, 1907, G 80.00
Black, w/alligator, mc, wht border, G 6.00
Boileau, Philip; Calendar Girl, 1906, VG 75.00
Boileau, Philip; NY Fashions, Nat'l Cloak & Suit ad, 1910, G 45.00

Christmas, My Dear Little Friend, Santa at chimney, 1907 postmark, EX, $4.00.

Christmas, Blk Santa in early auto, 1910s 22.50
Christmas, children by tree, Prang, c 1880, G 8.00
Christmas, Father Christmas & children, Tuck, Series #136 ....12.00

Christmas, girl w/doll, Brundage, EX **27.00**
Christmas, Santa in red w/toys, ...Greetings, ca 1912, EX **15.00**
Christmas, 2 children w/book, Clapsaddle, ca 1907-15, G **12.00**
Clapsaddle, Washington's Birthday, divided bk, EX **12.50**
Comac, couple in water w/umbrella in rain, divided bk, EX **12.50**
Easter, children w/rabbit ears, undivided bk, G **8.00**
Exposition, Internat'l Auto & Motorcycle, Berlin, 1938, M **35.00**
Fantasy, Flying Fish Trip to Catalina Island, EH Mitchell, G **8.00**
Fantasy, girl (winged) in daisies, blk & wht, ca 1901-07, EX **20.00**
Fantasy, Little Old Man of the Woods, divided bk, G **20.00**
Fantasy, Nouveau girl w/cornflowers in hair, G **7.50**
Fantasy, old man's face made of twisted/turned ladies **15.00**
Halloween, Bring Your Nerve..., S Berg, 1913, EX **20.00**
Hold-to-light, Times Building, NY, p/Cupples, EX **45.00**
Linen, Roller Coaster, Riverview Beach, Pennsville NJ, G **6.00**
Marilyn Monroe, 3 faces, color **12.00**
Mutt & Jeff radio advertising, 1935, scarce, EX **35.00**
Novelty, Cupid w/woman New Year, silk add-on clothes, M **15.00**
Photo, baby w/teddy bear, blk & wht, divided bk, EX **8.00**
Photo, Chicago street scene, 1915, EX **6.00**
Photo, child & hot-air balloon, 1913 ....**18.00**
Photo, factory explosion scene in WI, blk & wht, 1911, EX **15.00**
Photo, Fire Dept & City Hall, Jamestown NY, 1912 ....**15.00**
Photo, Howdy Doody & Buffalo Bob Smith, 1952, NM **30.00**
Photo, Manchester OH, flood of 1907 ....**20.00**
Photo, Nantasket Beach MA, night scene w/autos & people, 1926 ..**6.00**
Photo, NY street scene in front of Hall of Records, 1908 ....**8.00**
Photo, pioneer home, Nebraska, couple in door, 1905 ....**15.00**
Photo, Sleepy Eye MN, Main Street, 1940s **8.00**
Photo, Steamer May Graham on St Joe River, MI, 1908 ....**30.00**
Photo, stern-wheeler Alabama, Rome GA, 1907 ....**25.00**
Photo, 2 children on rocking horse, early **25.00**
Risque, lady on ball, blk & wht w/tinted flowers, divided bk **10.00**
Schmucker, Samuel; Mermaid series, color, M **150.00**
Suffragette series #6, Uncle Sam Suffragee, c Dunston-Weller **75.00**
Transportation, Dignity & Impudence, comic, mc, divided bk **5.00**
Transportation, Farman Biplane, Tuck, Aviation series, EX **25.00**
Transportation, HMS Barnham photo, multiview deck, blk/wht, G .**12.00**
Tuck, Glorious California, series #3513, M, 6 for **25.00**
Valentine, Maid Was in the Garden, Tuck, divided bk, EX **8.00**
Valentine, pretty little girl, E Nister, divided bk, EX **20.00**
Valentines Day, Oh Come to Me Arms, Tuck, divided bk, EX **8.00**

Posters

Advertising posters by such French artists as Cheret and Toulouse-Lautrec were used as early as the mid-1800s. Color lithography spurred their popularity. Circus posters by the Strobridge Lithograph Co. are considered to be the finest in their field, though Gibson and Co. Litho, Erie Litho, and Enquirer Job Printing Co. printed fine examples as well. Posters by noted artists such as Mucha, Parrish, and Hohlwein bring high prices. Other considerations are good color, interesting subject matter and, of course, condition. The WWII posters listed below are among the more expensive examples; 80% of those on the market bring less than $50.00. See also Movie Memorabilia; Political.

Advertising

Alba Cigarettes, Blk man in yel turban, 47x31¼", EX **375.00**
Beatty's CA Grapine, girl w/rose, 20x15"+fr, G **150.00**
Clapp & Jones Steam...Engines, pumper, Phoenix Litho, 20x24" ..**650.00**
Jap Rose Soap, 2 children bathe doll, 35x31"+fr, G **400.00**
Johnson's Steam Fire Engines, steam engine, 1865, 16x21", G ...**400.00**

Kendall's Spavin Cure, lady w/horse & beagles, 28x22"+fr, NM ...**650.00**
Lily Starch, babies/fairies/gnomes/flowers, 28x12", VG **1,400.00**
Massillon Agricultural Works, horses/machinery/etc, 22x28", G- .**350.00**
Reliable Canned Goods, lady in store, Calvert, 22x13", G **1,600.00**
Superlative Cigarettes, girl w/pansies, 17x12"+fr, VG **200.00**
Surtro Bath, swimmers & spectators, 80x82", EX **2,100.00**
Wheeler & Wilson, mother/child/sewing machine, 1888, 40x30" **300.00**

Literary

Christmas Scribner's, poems/stories, Parrish cover, 22x14", EX ..**375.00**
Cuba in War Time, Cuban on horse, Remington, 11x15½", VG+ **488.00**
Harper's March, 1896, woman w/masks on wall, 18¼x10½", VG+ **230.00**
Harper's May, 1895, woman w/sheep, 17x13½", VG+ **258.00**
Harper's Round Table, men & gymnist, Penfield, 15¾x10½", NM ...**258.00**
New York Herald, winged woman, March 22, 1896, 46x30", EX ..**488.00**
NY Sunday World/Roosevelt's Romance, ca 1900, 17x22", EX ..**230.00**

Magic

Carter Sweeps Secrets of the Sphinx, Otis Litho, 1920, 28x40" .**425.00**
Carter the Great, Otis Litho Co, 1920s, 14x22", M **125.00**
Carter the Great Beats the Devil..., cb, 13x19½", EX **235.00**
George, Triumphant Am Tour, Otis Litho, 1920s, 1-sheet **225.00**
Houdini, ca 1925, 72x96", M **8,500.00**
Vanishing Woman, floating scene, linen bk, National, 28x21" ..**250.00**

Sports

France, skiers in red & blk against bl & wht slopes, 39x24", NM .**460.00**
Greyhound Racing, dogs jumping fence, 87x40", VG+ **345.00**
Jack Johnson, Champion of World, driving car, 1909 ....**600.00**
Monte Carlo Beach, Adam & Eve ski w/sea serpent, 32x47", EX ...**650.00**
New Hampshire, skier against shape of state, 32x20½", NM **200.00**
Vichy/Ses Sources, woman golfer in Paris, 1928, 39½x24½", NM .**2,000.00**

Theatrical

Billy the Kid, saloon scene, US Litho, 1907, 27½x20", VG **185.00**
Follies Bergere, linen bk, Jules Cheret, 49x34", EX **550.00**
George Thatcher's Minstrels, Blk baseball scene, 29x39½", VG ..**4,500.00**
Harlin Tarbell illus for vaudevillian Blk face, 27x20", G **170.00**
Human Hearts, winter scene, Russell Morgan, 1901, 42x80" **135.00**
Marguerite in Prison, Faust, Calvert, 3-sheet, EX **135.00**

Maurice Chevalier, man with tilted straw hat in blue inset, Charles Kiffer, Bedos & Co., Paris, 60x36", EX, $900.00.

Tile Club in Idle Hours, canal boat/train, Forbes, 22x28", VG ...**285.00**
3 of Brooklyn's Musical Drolls, multiple characters, 27x37", VG ..**225.00**

Travel

Air France, world map w/airline routes, 1935, 24¼x38½", NM ..**690.00**
Am Airlines to NY, image of NYC skyline, 40x30", NM **375.00**

Australia, Great Barrier Reef, fish w/coral, 1954, 39x25", EX+ ..860.00
Australia, kangaroo w/baby, 1954, 39½x24½", NM 488.00
Australia, koalas in tree, 1954, 38x23½", NM 200.00
Australian Nat'l Travel Assoc, blk swan, 38¼x24¾", NM 375.00
Austria: Land of Alpine Beauties, skiers, 39¼x24½", EX 126.00
Fly There by Swissair, winter couple w/skis, 40x25", NM 200.00
Holland for the Holidays, ship & dock, 39½x25", EX 290.00
Nice, Gulliver at Lilliput, 1912, 41¾x30", NM 315.00
Paris, 3 city landmarks w/birds, 1945, 38¾x24", VG+ 250.00

War

WWI, Enlist in the Navy, Miss Liberty & soldier, 39½x28", EX ...345.00
WWI, Fight, HC Christy, 30x20" 275.00

I Want You for the Navy,
Howard Chandler Christy,
1917, 41x27½", VG, $750.00.

WWI, Liberty Bonds, red handprint, JA St John, 20x30", EX 100.00
WWI, More Ships!, Am eagle soars over harbor, 58x39", VG+ .630.00
WWI, Over There! man waves to plane, 37x30", VG+ 230.00
WWI, Uphold Our Honor, Fight for Us, woman & flag, 42x28", NM, ..230.00
WWII, Assurance for Young Men of the Navy, 32x24" 95.00
WWII, Careless Word...Another Cross, Atherton, 1943, 27x22" ..120.00
WWII, Liberty Lives On, ship w/Miss Liberty, 40x26½", NM ...690.00
WWII, War Bonds, Squander Bug, Seuss, 14x46", EX 95.00
WWII, Xmas Overseas..., Santa w/helmet, Graves, 21x27" 15.00

Miscellaneous

Buffalo Bill, Strobridge, 1907, 1-sheet, EX 4,000.00
Montana Frank Wild West Show, 3-sheet, EX 990.00
Wanted, Patti Hearst linked to Symbionese Liberation Army, EX ..30.00

Pot Lids

Pot lids were pottery covers for containers that were used for hair dressing, potted meats, etc. The most desirable were decorated with colorful transfer prints under the glaze in a variety of themes, animal and scenic. The first and probably the largest company to manufacture these lids was F. & R. Pratt of Fenton, Staffordshire, established in the early 1800s. The name or initials of Jesse Austin, their designer, may sometimes be found on exceptional designs. Although few pot lids were made after the 1880s, the firm continued into the 20th century.

American pot lids are very rare. Most have been dug up by collectors searching through sites of early gold rush mining towns in California. Minor rim chips are expected and normally do not detract from listed values.

American

Chlorine Detergent...WE Hagan..., brn transfer, 2⅞", EX 350.00

Eugene Roussel Odontine...Philada, blk transfer, 2¾" sq, EX 175.00
Jules Hauel Perfumer..., purple transfer, 2¾", EX 195.00
Jules Hauel...Ambrosial Cream, purple transfer, 3½", EX 350.00
Jules Hauel...Ambrosial Cream, red transfer, 3½", EX 425.00
Occidental Tooth Paste..., blk transfer, 3¼", VG 275.00
Prepared by EH Sargent...Gums, blk transfer, 3⅜", w/base 525.00
Taylor's Saponaceous Compound, bl transfer, 4", EX 400.00
Taylor's Saponaceous Compound, blk transfer, 3⅜", EX 375.00
Taylor's Saponaceous Compound, lav transfer, 4", EX 450.00
Taylor's Saponaceous Compound, purple transfer, 3¼", VG 275.00
WA Batchelor's Dentifrice..., cobalt transfer, 2⅜x3⅝", EX 425.00
William's Swiss Violet..., gr/lav/blk transfer, 3¾", EX 200.00
Worsley's Saponaceous Shaving Compound..., blk transfer, 4", NM ..500.00

English

Albert Memorial, mc, 4", EX 90.00
Allied Gens FM Lord Raglan, RL Robert, mc, 4¾", EX 190.00
Bear on throne, lion/crowing rooster, mc, 3", EX 110.00
Bear Pit, bldg w/dome roof, World's Fair 1851, M 250.00
Bellevue, Pegwell Bay, lg estate, mc, 5", EX 140.00
Bride, mc, rare, 3", EX 160.00
Charing Cross, mc, 4", EX 90.00
Chin Chew River, mc transfer, Pratt, 5¼" 100.00
Dutch battle, windmill burning, Pratt, Wouvermann, 6" L 85.00
Edward Cook's Hygienic..., blk transfer, 1¾x2⅜", w/base 90.00
England's Pride, mc, rare, 4¾", EX 180.00
Examining the Nets, mc, hairline, 4", EX 150.00
Fish Barrow, mc, fancy emb border, 5" 130.00
Garden Terrace, mc, matching base, very rare, 2¼", EX 175.00
Grand Internat'l Bldg, mc, rare, 4", EX 240.00
Grand Internat'l Bldg 1851 Exhibition..., mc, rare, 5", EX 300.00
Hauling in the Trawl, 4", EX 140.00
Holborn Viaduct, mc, some crazing, 4" 60.00
Landing the Catch, mc, 4", EX 70.00
Late Prince Consort, mc, 4", EX 140.00
Lobster Fishing, Pegwell Bay, Tatnell & Son on bldg, 4", EX 85.00
Lobster Saucer, lobster/cat/fish, mc, 4½", EX 135.00
Marriage of Prince Edward & ...Alexandra, mc, rare, 4", EX 110.00
Pratt, cattle & ruined abbey, mc transfer, 4" dia 85.00
Pratt, Shrimpers, fisherman & children, mc transfer, 4⅛" 85.00
Pretty Kettle of Fishball, dogs & pot, mc transfer, Pratt, 4" 115.00
Rivals, mc transfer in wooden fr, Pratt, 6½" 85.00
Royal Harbour Ramsgate, 4", EX 70.00
Seashells, 4¼", VG 120.00
Shrimpers, mc, 4", EX 90.00
St Paul's Cathedral, mc, 4", EX 75.00
Strasburg, mc transfer, Pratt, 5", EX 80.00
Swinton's English Primrose..., cobalt transfer, 2⅝", w/base 185.00
Tam O'Shanter & Souter Johnny, mc, rare, 4", EX 150.00
Trafalgar Square, mc, 4", EX 65.00
Windsor Park: Returning From Hunting, emb edge, mc, 5", EX .180.00

Powder Horns and Shot Flasks

Though powder horns had already been in use for hundreds of years, collectors usually focus on those made after the expansion of the United States westward in the very early 1800s. While some are basic and very simple, others were scrimshawed and highly polished. Especially nice carvings can quickly escalate the value of a horn that has survived intact to as high as $400.00. Those with detailed maps, historical scenes, etc. bring even higher prices.

Metal flasks were introduced in the 1830s; by the middle of the century they were produced in quantity and at prices low enough that they became a viable alternative to the powder horn. Today's collector regards the smaller flasks as the more desirable and valuable, and those made for specific companies bring premium prices.

Flask, brass, att Dixon, vertical bands, pear shape, 7¾" 55.00
Flask, brass, G&JW Hawksley Sheffield, emb decor, 8½", EX 85.00
Flask, brass, peer shape w/eagle & shield, 6½x3¼" 40.00
Flask, brass violin shape, G&JW Hawksley Sheffield, 8", EX 60.00

Copper flask, embossed scrolls, marked G. & J.W. Hawksley, Sheffield, 8¼", VG, $60.00; Brass flask with embossed flags, cannon, anchors over crossed rifles and pistols, Colts Patent banner below, 6¾", VG, $500.00.

Flask, copper, Am Flask & Cap, emb Indian on horse, 9", EX 225.00
Flask, copper, Am Flask & Cap Co, emb shells, EX 50.00
Flask, copper, Dixon & Sons, emb basketweave & leaves, 8" 75.00
Flask, copper, Dixon & Sons, emb dead game & scrolls, 8½" 165.00
Flask, copper, Dixon & Sons, emb game, 10", EX 300.00
Flask, copper, Dixon & Sons, emb shell & bush, brass spout, 8" ...85.00
Flask, copper, Dixon & Sons, hunting scene medallion, 7", EX 95.00
Flask, copper, emb buffalo hunt scene, fox/deer heads, 8", EX 395.00
Flask, copper, emb bushes, 4¾" 35.00
Flask, copper, emb Indian w/rifle by tree, dtd 1851, 8", EX 240.00
Flask, copper, emb spaniel's head in sunburst, 8", G 125.00
Flask, copper, Hawksley, emb fox/grouse/rabbit, 8¼", EX 215.00
Flask, copper, Hawksley, emb pheasant & net, 8" 115.00
Flask, copper & brass, ear style, mk English made, 13½" 95.00
Flask, leather, Am Flask & Cap Co, emb stag & boar, EX 95.00
Flask, leather w/emb hanging game, brass tip, 8" 30.00
Flask, zinc, molded scene, brass tip, 6", G 25.00
Horn, artillery priming, pewter spout, wood plug, 18", VG 150.00
Horn, cvd, simple detail, 6¾" 60.00
Horn, cvd faceted spout, cvd plug, brass tacks, 17", EX 145.00
Horn, cvd mermaid/ship/bird, crude, 8½" 125.00
Horn, cvd name/1749, pine plug, rings on spout, 11¼" 330.00
Horn, eng coat-of-arms crests & flowers, fat plug, 7" 465.00
Horn, eng flags/fish/name/1835, 8½", EX 250.00
Horn, eng leaves & flowers, repro, 14", on oak stand 360.00
Horn, eng man/Indian/weaponry, sgn, dtd 1756, 15" 2,100.00
Horn, eng tip: name/PA/1816, pegged, cherry plug, 10" 900.00
Horn, incised & chip cvd, pine plug, pegged, 14" 165.00
Horn, trn wooden butt w/iron loop, cvd plug, 11⅜" 160.00

Pratt

Prattware has become a generic reference for a type of relief-molded earthenware with polychrome decoration. Scenic motifs with figures were popular; sometimes captions were added. Jugs are most common; but teapots, tableware, even figurines were made. The term 'Pratt' refers to Wm. Pratt of Lane Delph, who is credited with making the first examples of this type, though similar wares were made later by other Staffordshire potters. Pot lids and other

transfer wares marked Pratt were made in Fenton, Staffordshire, by F. & R. Pratt & Co. (See Pot Lids).

Jug, emb hunters & hounds, 5" 350.00
Jug, Miser, early 1800s, rpr, 5½" 175.00
Pitcher, cows & people in relief, mc w/pk lustre, 6⅛", NM 325.00
Pitcher, soldier w/rifle in relief, bl uniform, 7" 175.00
Pitcher, Sportive Innocence/Mischievous Sports, 5¾", EX 225.00
Plaque, Adam & Eve, mc, 7½", VG 300.00
Plate, thirsty soldier, mc transfer, 7½", EX 80.00
Snuff jar, hunt scene, bl w/mc decor, Reg 1856 ....245.00
Syrup, classical warriors on orange, att, 6¾" 120.00
Tea caddy, emb men/ladies, brn/yel/bl on cream, 4½", EX 225.00
Teapot, emb garlands/figures under arches, 2-color on cream, EX ...225.00
Toby jug, pearlware, underglaze enamels, w/lid, 1800s, 9½" 575.00

Precious Moments™

Known as 'America's Hummels,' Precious Moments™ are a line of well-known collectibles created by Samuel J. Butcher and produced by Enesco, Inc. These pieces have endeared themselves to many because of the inspirational messages they portray. Over 300,000 club members have joined the national club in thirteen years.

The collection was fifteen years old in 1993. Each piece is produced with a different mark each year. This mark, not the date, is usually the link to the value of the piece. Most mold changes result in increased values; and, when a piece is retired or suspended, its price increases as well. As an example, 'God Loveth a Cheerful Giver' retailed for $9.50 in 1980; it was retired in 1981 and has a secondary market price now of $800.00. The majority of the collection has increased in value from its original retail.

Rosie Wells Enterprises, Inc., our advisor for this category, has published the Precious Moments collector magazine, *Precious Collectibles*®, as well as a secondary market price guide. She has hosted International Conventions for Precious Moments™ collectors since 1983. Her address is in the Directory under Clubs, Newsletters, and Catalogs. Items listed below are assumed to be in mint condition with the original box.

A Special Delivery, girl w/baby, 521493, Vessel mk 40.00
Boy & Girl on Seesaw, E-1375A, Triangle mk 145.00
Clowns, thimbles, 100668, set of 2, Olive Branch mk 35.00
Collin, boy w/drum, 529214, Trumpet mk 22.00
Cubby, doll, groom, E-7267B, no mk 425.00
Grandfather, old man kneeling, 529516, G Clef mk 25.00
He Cleansed My Soul, girl in bathtub, 100277, Dove mk 65.00
He Leadeth Me, boy leading lamb, E-1377A, no mk 130.00
High Hopes, boy w/kite, 521957, Bow & Arrow mk 50.00
His Burden Is Light, Indian girl, E-1380G, no mk 135.00
I'm a Possibility, boy w/football, 100188, Olive Branch mk 80.00
Isn't He Precious, girl sweeping, 522988, Bow & Arrow mk 30.00
Jesus Is Born, angels in chariot, E-2801, Hourglass mk 325.00
Jesus Is Born, angels in chariot, E-2801, no mk 375.00
Jesus Is the Light, girl w/candle, E-1373G, no mk 135.00
Jesus Loves Me, fr, boy w/teddy, E-7170, Hourglass mk 65.00
Kristy, doll, 12" girl doll, E-2851, Cross mk 180.00
Let's Be Friends, 2 dogs hugging, 527270, Vessel mk 25.00
March, calendar girl, girl w/kite, 110019, Cedar Tree mk 55.00
Oh Holy Night, bell, angel w/violin, 522821, Bow & Arrow mk ..35.00
Onward Christian Soldiers, soldier, E-0523, Fish mk 65.00
Peace on Earth, choir boys, E-4725, no mk 120.00
Press On, girl ironing, E-9265, Fish mk 80.00
Puppy Love, 2 puppies, 520764, Flower mk 25.00

Silent Night, musical, tree, 15814, Dove mk **100.00**
Sitting Pretty, angel on stool, 104825, Cedar Tree mk **55.00**
Surrounded w/Joy, boy w/wreath, E-0506, Dove mk **80.00**
Thee I Love, boy carving tree, E-3116, Triangle mk **120.00**
Timmy, doll, jogger, E-5397, Cross mk **155.00**
To My Deer Friend, girl w/fawn, 100048, Olive Branch mk **100.00**
Unicorn, ornament, E-2371, Hourglass mk **60.00**
Wee Three Kings, plate, E-0538, no mk **55.00**
Winter's Song, plate, girl w/birds, 12130, Dove mk **65.00**

Pre-Columbian Artifacts

The term 'pre-Columbian' loosely refers to some time prior to 1492, when Columbus arrived in America. In particular, it indicates pre-1492 artifacts of Central and South America, some of which can be dated as early as 4000 B.C. Artifacts representing the cultures of the Inca, Maya, and Aztec Indians are avidly sought by the collector. These may be made of precious metals, hardstones, or pottery. Some were used in rituals and religious rites; some such as bowls and other utensils, though strictly utilitarian, nevertheless convey through form and decoration the craftsmanship of these early tribes.

Axe, copper, Aztec, 1300-1400 AD, 2" **145.00**
Bell, gold, metal clapper, Veraguas, 800-1100 AD, ¾" **450.00**
Belt, woven warriors, tassel, Huaural, 1100-1400 AD, 83" **300.00**
Bowl, Costa Rican, pottery, ribbed w/cvd designs, 3½x7" **85.00**
Bowl, pottery, mc pnt, ped ft, Veraguas, 2½" **95.00**
Bowl, pottery w/mc pnt, Aztec, 1300-1400 AD, 4¾" **725.00**
Cvg, jadeite kneeling figure, 5⅜" **45.00**
Figure, pottery, blk on wht, Chancay, 1100-1400 AD, 4½" **125.00**
Figure, pottery, hollow, w/bracelets & loincloth, 11" **415.00**
Incense burner lid, pottery, dog shape, hdl on bk, slip decor **295.00**
Jar, blkware, bird effigy, hdl, Peru, sm chip, 4½" **225.00**
Jar, brn clay w/blk burn mks, bird-shaped rim & hdl, 5½" **60.00**
Jar, clay, wavy red & blk lines, crescent shape, 6x5½" **120.00**
Jar, Costa Rican, pottery, mc pnt geometrics, 6x5" **138.00**
Jug, pottery, jaguar shape w/slip decor, 7⅛x9" **330.00**
Knife, mahog obsidian, finely flaked, Jalisco, 900 AD, 8", VG ...**150.00**
Necklace, gray ceramic beads, Sinu culture, 500-1500 AD, 28" **40.00**
Necklace, shell beads w/cvd owl pendant, Veraguas, 500 AD **475.00**
Pendant, bird form, soapstone, Colima, 100 BC-200 AD, sm **32.00**
Pendant, frog, gold w/circles, Veraguas, 800-1100 AD, 1¾" **2,000.00**
Pitcher, monkey idol, Chancay, Peru, 7", M **550.00**
Plate, redware, Aztec, 1300-1400 AD, 8½" **110.00**
Spear point, obsidian, stemmed style, Jalisco, 6½" **300.00**
Stirrup jar, buff pottery w/umber lizard ea side, 10x5¾" **400.00**
Textile, 11 lg woven birds, Chancay, 1100-1400 AD, 1¼x34" ...**200.00**
Water bottle, human w/fine features, Chancay, Peru, 8", M **550.00**
Whistle, pottery, fish shape, Veraguas, 800-1100 AD, 3½" **200.00**

Primitives

Like the mouse that ate the grindstone, so has collectible interest in primitives increased, a little bit at a time, until demand is taking bites instead of nibbles into their availability. Although the term 'primitives' once referred to those survival essentials contrived by our American settlers, it has recently been expanded to include objects needed or desired by succeeding generations — items representing the cabin-'n-cornpatch existence as well as examples of life on larger farms and in towns. Through popular usage, it also respectfully covers what are actually 'country collectibles.'

From the 1600s into the latter 1800s, factories employed carvers, blacksmiths, and other artisans whose handwork contributed to turning out quality items. When buying, 'touch marks,' a company's name and/or location and maker's or owner's initials, are exciting discoveries.

Primitives are uniquely individual. Following identical forms, results more often than not show typically personal ideas. Using this as a guide (combined with circumstances of age, condition, desire to own, etc.) should lead to a reasonably accurate evaluation. For items not listed, consult comparable examples. Authority Kathryn McNerney has compiled several lovely books on primitives and related topics: *Primitives, Our American Heritage; Collectible Blue and White Stoneware;* and *Antique Tools, Our American Heritage.* You will find her address in the Directory under Florida. See also Butter Molds and Stamps; Boxes; Copper; Farm Collectibles; Fireplace Implements; Kitchen Collectibles; Molds; Tinware; Weaving; Woodenware; and Wrought Iron.

Washboard roller, $65.00.

Bed warmer, brass & wrought iron w/punched star design, 49" ...**285.00**
Bed warmer, brass w/emb star decor, wood hdl, 12" dia, 44" L **275.00**
Bed warmer, brass w/eng florals, trn grpt hdl, 42", EX **325.00**
Bed warmer, brass w/eng starflower on lid, trn hdl, 44", EX **250.00**
Bed warmer, brass w/pierced & well-tooled motif, trn hdl, 43" ...**440.00**
Bed warmer, copper w/eng flowers & scrolls, wood hdl, 11" dia ..**225.00**
Bed warmer, copper w/eng pinwheels, 12½" dia, wood hdl, 40" .**250.00**
Bed warmer, tin w/brass trim, wood hdl, old blk pnt, 43" **125.00**
Candle mold, copper, 1-tube, arched ribbon hdl, 11x2x3" **195.00**
Candle mold, pewter, 18-tube, pine fr, 22" **900.00**
Candle mold, pewter, 24-tube, pine fr, 19x20", EX **1,200.00**
Candle mold, redware, 24-tube, pine fr, 24½" L **1,430.00**
Candle mold, tin, 12-tube, dbl-ear hdls, 11" **130.00**
Candle mold, tin, 12-tube, strap hdl, 11½x8½" **145.00**
Candle mold, tin, 12-tube, w/hdl, 10" **100.00**
Candle mold, tin, 18-tube, dk finish, rpl hdl, 11" **225.00**
Candle mold, tin, 24-tube, wood fr w/cut-out ends, 18x21" **1,375.00**
Candle mold, tin, 3-tube, appl ribbon hdl, 10x3⅝x2½" **110.00**
Candle mold, tin, 5-tube, arched base, scroll hdls, 9x9x3½" **270.00**
Candle mold, tin, 6-tube, gallery rim, arched hdl, 5x3x3⅝" **290.00**
Candle mold, tin, 6-tube, strap hdl, 10½x7x2⅜" **95.00**
Candle snuffer, iron, scissors type, Bernard Co Pat 1860 ....**65.00**
Cane rack, softwood, 22 1" dia holes, trn legs, 35x47x9" **100.00**
Churn, staved bbl shape w/iron bands, bl pnt, 24x11", G **375.00**
Cookie board, slate, wear & scratches, 18" dia+hdl **200.00**
Cookie mold, cornucopia, CI, 4x5¼" **165.00**
Cork extractor, wrought iron, box jtd, 9" **30.00**
Cranberry picker, pnt leaves & berries on tin & wood, 7x6x11½" ..**70.00**
Cutter, cheese/bread; CI blade in wooden box, 10x12x15" **145.00**
Dough box, dvtl, 3-brd top, trn ft, orig red, 28x42x28" **1,875.00**
Dough box, dvtl poplar, old red rpt, cut-out heart hdls, 30" **500.00**
Dough box, dvtl poplar, old yel pnt, w/lid, 31" L **350.00**
Dough box, poplar, dvtl case w/lid, 32" L **140.00**
Dough scraper, wrought iron, Brady & Son Lancaster PA, 4⅜" .**300.00**
Dough scraper, wrought iron, heart-shaped cutout, 5¼x4⅛" **200.00**
Fly chaser, CI, spring-wound, rnd ribbed base, 7½x5", EX **225.00**
Food chopper, wrought steel, heart cutout/trn wood hdl, 7x5" ...**350.00**

Foot warmer, oak & hardwood, old gr rpt, brass hdl, 1850, 8" **300.00**
Foot warmer, pierced tin, wood fr, wire latch, 6x9x7⅝" **190.00**
Hourglass, cvd wood, old blk & gold pnt, 6⅜" **95.00**
Kraut cutter, poplar, AJ Kuhn brand, dk patina, 25½x8" **100.00**
Kraut cutter, poplar, heart cutout on end, EX patina, 9¾" **385.00**
Kraut cutter, walnut, rnded ends, ram's horn key, 20x8" **50.00**
Lamp filler, brass/copper, Manning-Bowman, 9" **65.00**
Lamp filler, HP brass, Manning-Bowman, 8½" **210.00**
Lighting stand, arms adjust, tripod base, gr pnt, 1800, 40" **1,500.00**
Pump, Genuine Bay State, pnt/stencil, Breck & Son, 79" **200.00**
Rack, candle-drying; wooden post w/4 dowel rods, old pnt, 15" .**170.00**
Rack, drying; pine, leather hinges, 3-part, ea: 72x37" **125.00**
Rack, drying; pine, 2 folding sections, ea w/4 bars, 49x39" **40.00**
Rack, drying; wooden, 4 fold-out hinged sections, 60x30" **85.00**
Rack, drying; 3 dowel-rod bars, red rpt, 49x40" **55.00**
Rack, drying; 3-bar, cut-out ends, gray-wht wash, 53" L **220.00**
Rug beater, bentwood, Goodenough's Improved..., 41" **95.00**
Rug beater, wire dbl-heart shape w/trn hdl, 6" W, 14" overall **30.00**
Salt box, pine, wrought iron nails, old red pnt, 17x11" **415.00**
Skimmer, wrought iron & brass, 17¾" **80.00**
Sugar break/cutter, CI, pliers shape, R Timming & Sons, 9⅞" **80.00**
Sugar break/cutter, iron scissors type w/box joint, 9" **85.00**
Sugar break/cutter, iron w/banded decor, crescent blades, 9¾" ..**110.00**
Sugar break/cutter, iron w/scalloped designs, 9⅜" **160.00**
Washboard, National #197, cobalt enamelware **90.00**
Washboard, redware panel in wooden fr, nailed, 14x7" **525.00**

Prints

The term 'print' may be defined today as almost any image printed on paper by any available method. Examples of collectible old 'prints' are Norman Rockwell magazine covers and Maxfield Parrish posters and calendars. 'Original print' refers to one achieved through the efforts of the artist or under his direct supervision. A 'reproduction' is a print produced by an accomplished print maker who reproduces another artist's print or original work. Thorough study is required on the part of the collector to recognize and appreciate the many variable factors to be considered in evaluating a print. Prices vary from one area of the country to another and are dependent upon new findings regarding the scarcity or abundance of prints as such information may arise. Although each collector of old prints may have their own varying criteria by which to judge condition, for those who deal only rarely in this area or newer collectors, a few guidelines may prove helpful. Staining, though unquestionably detrimental, is nearly always present in some degree and should be weighed against the rarity of the print. Professional cleaning should improve its appearance and at the same time help preserve it. Avoid tears that affect the image; minor margin tears are another matter, especially if the print is a rare one. Moderate 'foxing' (brown spots caused by mold or the fermentation of the rag content of old paper) and light stains from the old frames are not serious unless present in excess. Margin trimming was a common practice; but look for at least ½" to 1½" margins, depending on print size.

When no condition is indicated, the items listed below are assumed to be in very good to excellent condition. See also Parrish, Maxfield.

Audubon, John J.

Audubon is the best known of American and European wildlife artists. His first series of prints, 'Birds of America,' was produced by Robert Havell of London. They were printed on Whitman watermarked paper bearing dates of 1826 to 1838. The Octavo Edition of the same series was printed in seven editions, the first by J.T. Bowen under Audubon's direction. There were seven volumes of text and prints, each 10" x 7", the first five bearing the J.J. Audubon and J.B. Chevalier mark, the last two, J.J. Audubon. They were produced from 1840 through 1844. The second and other editions were printed up to 1871. The Bien Edition prints were full size, made under the direction of Audubon's sons in the late 1850s. Due to the onset of the Civil War, only 105 plates were finished. These are considered to be the most valuable of the reprints of the 'Birds of America Series.'

In 1971 the complete set was reprinted by Johnson Reprint Corp. of New York and Theatrum Orbis Terrarum of Amsterdam. Examples of the latter bear the watermark G. Schut and Zonen. In 1985 a second reprint was done by Abbeville Press for the National Audubon Society.

Although Audubon is best known for his portrayal of birds, one of his less-familiar series, 'Vivaparous Quadrupeds of North America,' portrayed various species of animals. Assembled in corroboration with John Bachman from 1839 until 1851, these prints are 28" x 22" in size. Several octavo editions were published in the 1850s. In the following listing, all measurements are actual print size unless stated otherwise.

Am Coot, #305, Bowen, 1850s, 6½x10" **125.00**
Am Crossbill, #197, Havell, 1834, 26½x21" **1,100.00**
Am Crow, Bien **2,000.00**
Am Ptarmigan, #418, Havell, 17½x24" **1,380.00**
Baltimore Oriole, #217, Bien, 1858-60, 39x26" **3,000.00**
Barnacle Goose, #296, Havell, 1836, 25x38" **1,495.00**
Belted Kingfisher, Havell, #77, 34x25" **6,500.00**
Bl-Winged Yel Swamp Warbler, #111, Bowen, 1st ed, 1841, 20x13" .**135.00**
Black-Throated Bunting, #384, Havell, 1837, 20x13" **875.00**
Brazilian Caracara Eagle, #156, Havell, 39x26" **7,500.00**
Caracara Eagle, #4, Bowen, 1st ed, dbl matted, fr **450.00**
Cardinal, #203, Bowen, 1st ed, 6½x10" **700.00**
Common Am Skunk, Female/Young; #42, Bowen, 1844, 27x21¼" ..**3,500.00**
Connecticut Warbler, #99, Bowen, 1st ed, 1841, matted, fr **145.00**
Eared Grebe, #404, Havell, 1838, 25x38" **1,495.00**
Fish Crow, #226, Bowen, 1850s, 6½x10" **350.00**
Gannet, #326, Havell, 1836, 26x39½" **10,000.00**
Golden-Winged Woodpecker, #273, Bowen, 1850s, 6½x10" **125.00**
Great Am Hen & Young, #6, 26¾x39¾" sheet **25,000.00**
Great Auk, #341, Havell, 1836, 25x37½" **4,300.00**
Great White Heron, #281, Havell, 1835, 25½x38" **12,650.00**
Greenshank, #269, Havell, ca 1826-38, 18x25" **3,000.00**

Grey Fox, #21, from Viviparous Quadrupeds of North America, J.T. Bowen, 1843, 21x27", framed, $12,000.00.

Harlequin Duck, #297, Havell, 1836, 21½x31½" **2,760.00**
King Duck, #276, Havell, 1835, 26¼x38½" **4,500.00**
Long-Eared Owl, #37, Bowen, 1st ed, 1841, dbl matted, fr **200.00**
Maryland Marmot, lg folio **900.00**
Mountain Mockingbird, #139, Bowen, 1850s, 6½x10" **125.00**
Musk Ox, Males; #111, Bowen, 1847, 21⅝x27⅛" **2,000.00**
Northern Hare, #11, Bowen, 1843, 21x26" **2,000.00**
Osprey, #381, Amsterdam Edition, 39x26" **2,000.00**
Polar Bear, #91, Bowen, 1846, 18½x25" **6,000.00**
Red-Breasted Sandpiper, #315, Havell, 1836, 12¼x19½" **750.00**

Red-Cockaded Woodpecker, #389, Havell, 21½x14" **1,000.00**
Red-Shoulder Hawk, #56, Havell, 26x38" **15,000.00**
Rocky Mountain Neotoma, #29, Bowen, 18¾x26½" **500.00**
Rusty Grackle, #222, Bien, ca 1858-60, 39x26" **1,800.00**
Says Least Shrew, #70, Bowen, 1845, 21½x27" **230.00**
Swamp Hare, #37, Bowen, 1850s, 7x10" **250.00**
Virginia O'possum, #55, Bowen, 1850s, 7x10" **300.00**
White Ibis, #222, Havell, 1833, 26x28" **7,800.00**
White-Crowned Pigeon, #280, Bien, ca 1858-60, 39x26" **2,500.00**

Currier and Ives

Nathaniel Currier was in business by himself until the late 1850s when he formed a partnership with James Merrit Ives. Currier is given credit for being the first to use the medium to portray newsworthy subjects, and the Currier and Ives views of 19th-century American culture are familiar to us all. In the following listings, 'C' numbers correspond with a standard reference book by Conningham. Values are given for prints in very good condition; all are colored unless indicated black and white. Unless noted 'NC' (Nathaniel Currier), all prints are published by Currier and Ives. Our advisors for this category are John and Barbara Rudisill (Rudisill's Alt Print Haus); they are listed in the Directory under Maryland.

Abigail, NC, 1846, C-9, sm folio **85.00**
Accomodation Train, 1876, C-32, sm folio **400.00**

American Express Train, dated 1864, C-130, 18" folio, $12,000.00.

Am Farm Scenes/No 3, NC, 1853, C-133, lg folio **4,000.00**
Am Fireman, Prompt to the Rescue; 1858, C-154, med folio ..**1,300.00**
Am Forest Game, 1866, C-156, lg folio **1,000.00**
Am Prize Fruits, 1862, C-183, lg folio **1,900.00**
Arguing the Point, NC, 1855, C-265, lg folio **4,500.00**
Arkansas Traveler, 1870, C-270, sm folio **275.00**
Autumn Fruits, 1861, C-317, med folio **400.00**
Autumn in the Adirondacks, undtd, C-323, sm folio **400.00**
Autumn on Lake George, 1872, C-324, sm folio **250.00**
Bear Hunting, Close Quarters; undtd, C-447, sm folio **750.00**
Beautiful Persian, undtd, C-457, sm folio **75.00**
Beauty of New England, undtd, C-462, sm folio **350.00**
Beauty of the North, undtd, C-466, med folio **65.00**
Benjamin Franklin, Statesman..., NC, 1847, C-499, sm folio **500.00**
Between Two Fires, 1879, C-511, sm folio **225.00**
Bird's Nest, undtd, C-533, sm folio **125.00**
Blue Fishing, undtd, C-578, sm folio **950.00**
Boss of the Track, 1881, C-619, sm folio **200.00**
Brace of Meadow Larks, 1879, C-644, sm folio **200.00**
Brook Trout Fishing, 1872, C-704, sm folio **900.00**
Burning of Chicago, 1871, C-738, sm folio **450.00**
Camping in the Woods, Laying Off; undtd, C-774, lg folio **4,000.00**
Cares of a Family, NC, 1856, C-814, lg folio **3,500.00**
Catharine, NC, 1845, C-849, sm folio **90.00**

Caught on a Fly, 1879, C-864, sm folio **300.00**
Central Park, NY, The Bridge; undtd, C-950, sm folio **350.00**
Champion Pacer Direct, 1891, C-966, sm folio **300.00**
Champion Stallion Directum, 1893, C-975, sm folio **300.00**
Chicky's Diner, undtd, C-1029, sm folio **150.00**
Choice Bouquet, 1874, C-1041, sm folio **150.00**
City of New York, NC, 1855, C-1102, lg folio **3,000.00**
Clara, undtd, C-1127, sm folio **75.00**
Clipper Ship in a Hurricane, undtd, C-1154, med folio **2,000.00**
Clipper Ship in a Snow Squall, undtd, C-1157, sm folio **900.00**
Clipper Ship Red Jacket, undtd, C-1166, sm folio **850.00**
Coming in 'On His Ear,' 1875, C-1221, sm folio **200.00**
Cork Castle & Black Rock Castle, undtd, C-1253, sm folio **90.00**
Cozzen's Dock, West Point; undtd, C-1277, med folio **800.00**
Custer's Last Charge, 1876, C-1333, sm folio **350.00**
Darktown Yacht Club, Hard...Breeze; 1885, C-1439, sm folio **250.00**
Day Before Marriage, 1847, C-1459, sm folio **100.00**
Declaration, NC, 1846, C-1524, sm folio **95.00**
Declaration Committee, 1876, C-1530, sm folio **300.00**
Declaration of Independence, NC, undtd, C-1531, sm folio **200.00**
Disputed Heat, Claiming Foul; 1878, C-1587, lg folio **1,800.00**
Distanced!, 1878, C-1589, sm folio **225.00**
Dreadful Wreck of Mexico on Hempstead..., NC, undtd, C-1624 .**2,400.00**
Dutchman & Hiram Woodruff, 1871, C-1640, sm folio **700.00**
Easter Flowers, 1969, C-1655, sm folio **50.00**
Easter Offering, 1871, C-1659, sm folio **30.00**
Elizabeth, NC, 1846, C-1698, sm folio **95.00**
Emma, NC, 1849, C-1727, sm folio **90.00**
Enchanted Isles, 1869, C-1740, sm folio **90.00**
English Snipe, 1871, C-1744, sm folio **375.00**
English Winter Scene, undtd, C-1745, sm folio **525.00**
Express Train, 1870, C-1792, sm folio **2,000.00**
Family Pets, NC, undtd, C-1840, sm folio **100.00**
Farmer's Home, Autumn; 1864, C-1889, lg folio **2,000.00**
First Ride, NC, 1849, C-1987, sm folio **130.00**
Flowers, NC, undtd, C-2058, sm folio **100.00**
Flushing a Woodcock, undtd, C-2071, sm folio **400.00**
Fording the River, NC, undtd, C-2081, med folio **550.00**
Forest Scene, Summer; undtd, C-2086, sm folio **225.00**
Fruit & Flowers Piece, 1863, C-2160, med folio **400.00**
Fruits of Temperance, 1870, C-2195, sm folio **200.00**
Fruits of the Season, 1870, C-2198, sm folio **150.00**
Gap of Dunloe, undtd, C-2219, sm folio **95.00**
Geburts und Taufschein, undtd, C-2227, sm folio **75.00**
Gen Lewis Cass, NC, 1846, C-2288, sm folio **80.00**
Gen Shields at the Battle..., 1862, C-2294, sm folio **195.00**
Gen Tom Thumb, Smallest Man Alive; NC, 1849, C-2305, sm folio ...**150.00**
Getting a Hoist..., 1875, C-2365, sm folio **250.00**
Girl I Love, 1870, C-2376, sm folio **75.00**
God Bless Our Home, undtd, C-2392, sm folio **200.00**
Going to Pasture, Early Morning; undtd, C-2403, sm folio **200.00**
Got the Drop on Him, 1881, C-2455, sm folio **250.00**
Grand Horse St Julien, 1881, C-2488, sm folio **325.00**
Grand National Whig Banner, NC, 1844, C-2511, sm folio **200.00**
Grand Pacer Richball, 1890, C-2519, sm folio **300.00**
Great Salt Lake, Utah; undtd, C-2649, sm folio **400.00**
Group of Lilies, undtd, C-2670, sm folio **130.00**
Happy Home, NC, undtd, C-2713, sm folio **100.00**
Happy Little Pups, C-2717, sm folio **135.00**
Happy Mother, undtd, C-2720, sm folio **300.00**
Harbor for the Night, undtd, C-2724, sm folio **300.00**
Harvesting, The Last Load; undtd, C-2750, sm folio **325.00**
Haunted Castle, undtd, C-2756, sm folio **90.00**
Home of the Deer, undtd, 1871, C-2867, med folio **500.00**

Home of the Mississippi, 1871, C-2876, sm folio 575.00
Hooked, 1874, C-2928, sm folio 500.00
Horse Fair, undtd, C-2940, sm folio 300.00
Horse Shed Stakes..., 1877, C-2942, sm folio 250.00
Hues of Autumn on Racquet River, undtd, C-2982, sm folio 300.00
Hundred Leaf Rose, undtd, C-2986, sm folio 100.00
Husking, 1861, C-3008, lg folio 9,800.00
Hyde Park, Hudson River; NC, undtd, C-3010, sm folio 300.00
Imported Messenger, 1880, C-3042, sm folio 300.00
In the Mountains, undtd, C-3071, sm folio 275.00
Ingleside Winter, undtd, C-3112, sm folio 600.00
Italian Landscape, undtd, C-3139, sm folio 75.00
James K Polk, 11th President...; NC, undtd, C-3163, sm folio 125.00
Jane, undtd, C-3181, sm folio 80.00
John Adams, 2nd President of US; NC, undtd, C-3251, sm folio .175.00
John Tyler, 10th President..., NC, undtd, C-3281, sm folio 175.00
Jolly Dog, 1878, C-3287, sm folio 125.00
Julia, NC, undtd, C-3307, sm folio 80.00
King of the Forest, undtd, C-3333, sm folio 200.00
Kitties Among the Roses, 1873, C-3352, sm folio 150.00
Lake George NY, undtd, C-3407, sm folio 250.00
Lake of the Woods, undtd, C-3409, sm folio 225.00
Lakeside Home, 1869, C-3423, med folio 350.00
Leaders, 1888, C-3471, lg folio 1,000.00
Liberty, undtd, C-3486, sm folio 200.00
Lieutenant Gen Winfield Scott..., undtd, C-3495, sm folio 125.00
Life in New York..., undtd, C-3506, sm folio 350.00
Life in the Woods, Returning; 1860, C-3513, lg folio 3,500.00
Life of a Fireman, Ruins; NC, 1854, C-3520, lg folio 2,500.00
Lincoln Family, 1867, C-3546, sm folio 80.00
Lion Hunter, NC, undtd, C-3554, sm folio 165.00
Little Bo-Peep, undtd, C-3577, sm folio 150.00
Little Ellen, undtd, C-3614, sm folio 95.00
Little Fruit Bearer, undtd, C-3631, sm folio 100.00
Little Jamie, undtd, C-3642, sm folio 95.00
Little Mary & Her Lamb, 1877, C-3670, sm folio 150.00
Little May Blossom, undtd, C-3671, sm folio 85.00
Little Sister, undtd, C-3709, sm folio 95.00
Little Sisters, 1875, C-3710, sm folio 95.00
Little Students, undtd, C-3720, sm folio 150.00
Little Willie, undtd, C-3738, sm folio 90.00
Loss of a Steamship Swallow, NC, 1845, C-3779, sm folio 425.00
Lottie, undtd, C-3785, sm folio 75.00
Maggie, undtd, C-3864, sm folio 95.00
Maiden Rock, Mississippi River; undtd, C-3891, sm folio 500.00
Mama's Rosebud, 1858, C-3949, med folio 150.00
Marriage Certificate, NC, 1848, C-4000, sm folio 100.00
Mazeppa - Plate 1, NC, 1846, C-4092, sm folio 75.00
Merry Christmas, NC, undtd, C-4109, sm folio 400.00
Mill-Cove Lake, undtd, C-4123, sm folio 350.00
Mink Trapping, Prime; 1862, C-4139, lg folio 10,000.00
Miseries of a Bachelor, undtd, C-4151, sm folio 200.00
Moonlight, the Ruins; undtd, C-4184, sm folio 95.00
Moose & Wolves, A Narrow Escape; undtd, C-4185, sm folio ...300.00
Moosehead Lake, undtd, C-4186, sm folio 250.00
Mother's Dream, undtd, C-4233, med folio 125.00
Mother's Wing, 1866, C-4239, med folio 250.00
Mountain Rumble, undtd, C-4244, sm folio 175.00
My Boyhood's Home, undtd, C-4276, sm folio 200.00
My Gentle Dove, 1871, C-4300, sm folio 75.00
My Highland Boy, NC, undtd, C-4305, sm folio 95.00
My Little Favorite, undtd, C-4315, med folio 125.00
My Love & I, 1872, C-4343, sm folio 125.00
My Pet Bird, 1872, C-4348, med folio 175.00

Narrows From Stanten Island, NC, undtd, C-4380, sm folio 375.00
Naval Heroes of the US, Plate 3; NC, C-4399, sm folio 550.00
New Suspension Bridge, Niagara Falls; undtd, C-4432, sm folio .300.00
Niagara by Moonlight, undtd, C-4454, med folio 225.00
Niagara Falls, C-4457, med folio 350.00
Niagara Falls From Canada Side, undtd, C-4461, sm folio 225.00
Night by the Campfire, 1861, C-4472, med folio 575.00
Noontide a Shady Spot, undtd, C-4501, sm folio 175.00
Nosegay, 1870, C-4512, sm folio 100.00
October Landscape, undtd, C-4529, med folio 550.00
Old Farm Gate, 1864, C-4555, lg folio 1,400.00
Old Ford Bridge, undtd, C-4559, sm folio 225.00

The Old Homestead in Winter, after G.H. Durrie, dated 1864, C-4563, 18" folio, $6,500.00.

Old Mill in Summer, undtd, C-4571, sm folio 300.00
Old Oaken Bucket, 1872, C-4577, sm folio 225.00
On a Point, NC, 1855, C-4592, med folio 600.00
On the Coast of California, undtd, C-4598, sm folio 350.00
Pacing for a Grand Purse, 1890, C-4677, lg folio 1,500.00
Pair of Nutcrackers, undtd, C-4693, sm folio 200.00
Parson's Colt, 1879, C-4706, sm folio 225.00
Partridge Shooting, 1870, C-4718, sm folio 400.00
Path Through the Woods, undtd, C-4723, sm folio 175.00
Pennsylvania Railroad Scenery, undtd, C-4745, sm folio 750.00
Perry's Victory on Lake Erie, NC, undtd, C-4754, sm folio 650.00
Pigeon Shooting, Playing the Decoy; 1862, C-4780, lg folio ...2,975.00
Played Out, 1871, C-4794, sm folio 325.00
Pride of the Garden, 1873, C-4914, sm folio 175.00
Progress of Intemperance..., NC, 1841, C-4954, sm folio 125.00
Puzzled Fox, 1872, C-4984, sm folio 300.00
Quail Shooting, NC, 1852, C-4989, lg folio 3,000.00
Quails, NC, undtd, C-4992, sm folio 350.00
Queen of Beauty, undtd, C-4997, sm folio 75.00
Queen of the Ball, 1870, C-5007, sm folio 75.00
Raspberries, 1870, C-5065, sm folio 150.00
Rising Family, 1857, C-5151, lg folio 4,500.00
River Side, undtd, C-5163, sm folio 225.00
Roadside Mill, 1870, C-5175, sm folio 350.00
Rose, undtd, C-5206, sm folio 100.00
Roses of May, 1870, C-5215, sm folio 100.00
Safe Sailing, undtd, C-5292, sm folio 175.00
Scene on the Susquehanna, undtd, C-5415, sm folio 300.00
Scenery of the Catskills, undtd, C-5419, sm folio 300.00
Scholar's Rewards, 1874, C-5425, sm folio 225.00
See-Saw, undtd, C-5457, med folio 350.00
Shoeing the Horse, NC, undtd, C-5493, sm folio 375.00
Shooting on the Beach, undtd, C-5497, sm folio 1,225.00
Silver Cascade, Wht Mountains; undtd, C-5521, sm folio 275.00
Single, NC, 1845, C-5527, sm folio 175.00
Soldier's Adieu, NC, 1847, C-5593, sm folio 125.00
Soldier's Home..., 1862, C-5599, sm folio 125.00
Soldier's Memorial, 1863, C-5600, med folio 200.00

Source of the Hudson..., undtd, C-5627, sm folio 325.00
Spaniel, NC, 1842, C-5637, sm folio 275.00
Split Rock, St John River; undtd, C-5663, sm folio 275.00
Spring, NC, 1849, C-5671, sm folio 225.00
Squall Off Cape Horn, undtd, C-5680, sm folio 700.00
Stable Scene No 1, NC, undtd, C-5683, med folio 1,000.00
Stable Scene No 2, NC, undtd, C-5686, sm folio 500.00
Steamer Penobscot, 1883, C-5736, lg folio 1,600.00
Straw-Yard Winter, undtd, C-5837, med folio 975.00
Striped Bass, 1872, C-5844, sm folio 375.00
Summer Evening, undtd, C-4853, sm folio 175.00
Summer Fruits, 1861, C-5857, med folio 375.00
Summer Gift, 1870, C-5860, sm folio 150.00
Summer Ramble, undtd, C-5874, med folio 350.00
Sunday in the Olden Time, undtd, C-5883, sm folio 175.00
Sunnyside on the Hudson, undtd, C-4893, sm folio 275.00
Sunrise on Lake Sanarac, 1860, C-5895, lg folio 2,800.00
Surrender of Gen Lee..., 1865, C-5909, sm folio 250.00
Susan, NC, 1847, C-5918, sm folio 95.00
Sylvan Lake, undtd, C-5940, sm folio 200.00
Through to the Pacific, 1870, C-6051, sm folio 1,200.00
To the Memory of..., NC, 1846, C-6074, sm folio 50.00
Tomb of Washington..., undtd, C-6110, med folio 150.00
Trinket..., undtd, C-6152, sm folio 300.00
Trotting Cracks at the Forge, 1869, C-6169, lg folio 8,000.00
Two Watchers, undtd, C-6276, sm folio 125.00
Under Cliff, On the Hudson; undtd, C-6282, sm folio 250.00
Valley Forge VA, undtd, C-6355, sm folio 250.00
View of Astoria, LI; 1862, C-6388, med folio 1,200.00
View of Hudson River...Ruggle's House, 1846, C-6421, sm folio ..275.00
View on the Housatonic, 1867, C-6443, lg folio 1,400.00
Village Blacksmith, 1864, C-6462, lg folio 3,000.00
Virginia Water Windsor Park, undtd, C-6475, sm folio 125.00
Washington at Prayer, NC, undtd, C-6517, sm folio 125.00
Washington at Princeton, NC, 1846, C-6518, sm folio 475.00
Washington Columns..., undtd, C-6520, sm folio 350.00
Washington's Reception...at Trenton..., NC, C-6555, sm folio ..125.00
Water Jump at Jerome Park, 1877, C-6564, sm folio 465.00
Water Rail Shooting, NC, 1855, C-6567, sm folio 800.00
Watkins' Glen NY, undtd, C-6573, sm folio 350.00
Way to Happiness, NC, undtd, C-6583, sm folio 50.00
Wedding Day, NC, undtd, C-6599, sm folio 125.00
Well - I'm Blowed!, 1883, C-6613, sm folio 250.00
Western River Scenery, 1886, C-6620, med folio 925.00
White Squadron US Navy, 1893, C-6644, lg folio 1,200.00
Why Don't He Come?..., undtd, C-6653, sm folio 125.00
Wild Duck Shooting..., 1870, C-6671, sm folio 575.00
Wild West in Darktown, Buffalo Chase; 1893, C-6679, sm folio ..250.00
William Tell, Son's Head; undtd, C-6712, sm folio 95.00
Winter Morning, 1861, C-6740, med folio 2,100.00
Woodcock Shooting, 1870, C-6775, sm folio 550.00
Wooding Up on the Mississippi, 1863, C-6776, lg folio 9,500.00
Woodlands in Summer, undtd, C-6778, sm folio 250.00
Woodlands in Winter, undtd, C-6779, sm folio 450.00
Wreck of the Atlantic, C-6787, sm folio 300.00
Yacht Vesta..., undtd, C-6817, sm folio 425.00
Young Mother, NC, undtd, C-6860, sm folio 85.00
Young Sailor, NC, 1849, C-6867, sm folio 175.00
Zachary Taylor, Nation's..., NC, 1847, C-6874, sm folio 135.00

Fox, R. Atkinson

A Canadian who worked as an artist in the 1880s, R. Atkinson Fox moved to New York about ten years later, where his original oils were widely sold at auction and through exhibitions. Today he is best known, however, for his prints, published by as many as twenty print-makers. More than thirty examples of his work appeared on Brown and Bigelow calendars, and it was used in many other forms of advertising as well. Though he was an accomplished artist able to interpret any subject well, he is famous for his landscapes. Fox died in 1935. Our advisor for Fox prints is Pat Gibson whose address is listed in the Directory under California.

English Garden, fr, #57, 14x20" 95.00
Flanders Field, #76, 6x12" 95.00
Garden of Contentment, #78, fr, 12½x20½" 140.00
Garden of Love, orig fr, #42, 10x12" 140.00
Garden of Nature, fr, #189, 18x10" 145.00
Haven of Beauty, #204, 10x18" 145.00
Heart's Desire, #55, fr, 12¼x22¼" 175.00
His Last Cartridge, #51, 10x8" 165.00
Hunter's Paradise, #192, 4x5" 65.00
It's Only a Cottage, puzzle, #520 ....95.00
Land of Dreams, #14, fr, 10x8" 80.00
Love's Paradise, #13, 18x30" 275.00
Music of the Waters, #218, 20x16" 150.00
Reliable Guardian, #667, 10x12" 75.00
Spirit of Youth, #4, fr, 18x10" 150.00
Sunset Dreams, #23, fr, 9x15" 100.00

Gutmann, Bessie Pease

Delicately tinted prints of appealing children sometimes accompanied by their pets, sometimes asleep, often captured at some childhood activity are typical of the work of Gutmann; she painted lovely ladies as well and was a successful illustrator of children's books. Her career spanned the earlier decades of this century. Our advisor for this category is Earl MacSorley; he is listed in the Directory under Connecticut.

Bubbles, McCall's magazine cover, May 1912 ....125.00
Chuckles, #216 ....40.00
First Step, #815 ....125.00
Harmony, #802 ....125.00
His Majesty, #793 ....115.00
Home Builders, #655 ....125.00
Love's Blossom, #223, unfr, 14x11" 40.00
Miss Flirt, #217, unfr, 11x14" 40.00
Smelling, #18 ....125.00
Sunbeam, #730 ....175.00
Tasting, #21, sm 125.00
Television, #821, unfr, 14x21" 45.00
Tom Tom the Piper's Son, #219 ....150.00
Winged Aureole, #700 ....275.00
4 seasonal panels, Swift calendar, 1915 ....700.00

Icart, Louis

Louis Icart was a Parisian artist who immortalized the women of France through his etchings, which were widely distributed in the 1920s. Etchings from the thirties and forties are generally harder to find. Most etchings after 1925 have his embossed 'windmill' seal at the lower left. He also produced a few lithographs and about four hundred oil paintings. He did very vew watercolors and no bronzes. Many phony watercolors, sketches, and bronzes that look similar in subject to his popular etchings are being circulated. Also seen, especially in Florida, are cheap lithographic copies of his etchings with fake 'windmill' seals. A magnifier will reveal the dot-matrix printing process of these lithos (etchings never have dot patterns). Our Icart advisor is William Holland, author of *Louis Icart: The Complete Etchings;* and *The Collectible Maxfield Parrish*; he is listed in the Directory under Pennsylvania.

Autumn Swirls, 1924, 17x12", VG	1,495.00
Ballerina, 1935, 14x18", VG	2,185.00
Black Shawl, 1925, 16x12", EX	1,840.00
Bluebirds, 1925, 19x15", VG	1,400.00
D'Artagnan, 21x14", VG	1,380.00
Eve, 1928, 13x29", VG	1,400.00
Fair Dancer, 1939, 19x23", orig fr	1,610.00
Gossip, 1926, 17x13", VG	1,100.00
Hydrangeas, 1929, 16x20", orig fr	1,000.00
Lady of the Camelias, 17x21", EX	1,500.00
Laziness, 1925, 15x19", VG	1,500.00
Lilies, 1934, 28x19", EX	3,000.00
Look, 1928, 19x14", VG	1,265.00
Lounging, 1924, 14x17½", VG	1,725.00
Love's Blossom, 1937, 17x25", M	3,500.00
Madame Butterfly, 1927, 13x20", EX	1,495.00
Melody Hour, 1934, 23x19"	4,300.00
Mockery, 1928, 15x18", VG	1,400.00
My Model, 1921, 21¾x17", EX	2,875.00
On the Champs Elysees, 1938, 15¾x22", orig fr	1,900.00
Parasol, 1928, 18x15", VG	1,400.00
Perfect Harmony, 1932, 13x17", EX	3,250.00
Red Gate, 1925, 17¾x13", VG	1,600.00
Red Riding Hood, 1927, 21x14", VG	1,500.00
Smoke, 14x19", EX	1,800.00
Sofa, 1937, 17x26", orig fr	3,450.00
Spanish Nights, 1926, 22x14", VG	1,035.00
Swallows, 1926, 19x11", VG	1,400.00
Sweet Caress, 1924, 18x12", VG	1,600.00
Tou Tou, 1923, 14x10¾", NM	3,450.00
Treasures, 1924, 9x12", VG	900.00
Venus, 1928, 13¾x19", orig fr	1,500.00

Kurz and Allison

Louis Kurz founded the Chicago Lithograph Company in 1833. Among his most notable works were a series of thirty-six Civil War scenes and one hundred illustrations of Chicago architecture. His company was destroyed in the Great Fire of 1871, and in 1880 Kurz formed a partnership with Alexander Allison, an engraver. Until both retired in 1903, they produced hundreds of lithographs in color as well as black and white.

Battle of Atlanta, lg folio	240.00
Battle of Bull Run, lg folio	290.00
Battle of Cedar Creek, lg folio	285.00
Battle of Chattanooga, lg folio	290.00
Battle of Corinth, MS; lg folio	290.00
Battle of Franklin, TN, lg folio	290.00
Battle of Kenesaw Mountain, lg folio	290.00
Battle of Lookout Mountain, lg folio	290.00
Battle of Pea Ridge, lg folio	410.00
Battle of Princeton, lg folio	240.00
Battle of Williamsburg, VA; lg folio	290.00
Battle of Wilson's Creek, MO; lg folio	290.00
Capture of Fort Fisher, lg folio	260.00
Fort Pillow Massacre, lg folio	315.00

McKenney and Hall

Ca-Ta-He-Casa, Blk Hoof; Shawnee chief, 1838, lg folio	250.00
Chippewa Mother & Child, 1843, lg folio	250.00

Keeshewaa, Suak & Fox chief, 1838, lg folio	310.00

Ki-On-Twog-Ky (Cornplant), hand-colored, 1836, folio edition, 18x13", $1,050.00.

Lap Pa Win Soe, Delaware chief, 1837, lg folio	190.00
Little Crow, Sioux chief, Greenough, 1838, lg folio	200.00
Meeta Koosega/Pure Tobacco, Chippewa chief, 1837, lg folio	210.00
Nea Mathla, Seminole chief, 1838, lg folio	380.00
Ong Pa Ton Ga/Big Elk, Omaha chief, 1838, lg folio	230.00
Ongewae, Chippewa chief, 1843, lg folio	230.00
Ouatawapea or Col Lewis, Shawnee chief, 1838, lg folio	335.00
Pashenine, Chippewa chief, 1843, lg folio	280.00
Pashepaha/Stabber, Suak & Fox chief, 1838, lg folio	210.00
Pea Mus Ka, Suak & Fox chief, 1838, lg folio	240.00
Sha Ha Ka, Mandan chief, 1838, lg folio	230.00
Waapashaw, Sioux chief, Biddle, 1836, lg folio	200.00

Mucha, Alphonse

Mucha became famous for his beautiful Art Nouveau lithographs featuring Sarah Bernhardt and Job cigarette papers, which he issued in the 1890s. Born in Prague in 1860, he studied there as well as in Paris and for a time taught at the New York School of Applied Design for women before returning to Prague.

Biscuits Lefevre Utile-Flirt, young couple, 24½x10½"	3,500.00
Daybreak, 1899, 42x15"	6,900.00
Documents Decoratifs, 17 plates, Levey, 18x13", G	400.00
Gismonda, Les Maitres de L'Affice, 14x5½"	865.00
Job, brunette w/lit cigarette, 12x9¾"	1,495.00
Job, 58¾x40"	5,700.00
La Dam Aux Camelias, Sarah Bernhardt, 14¾x5¾"	1,100.00
La Plume, Sarah Bernhardt, 24x16½"	2,990.00
La Samartaine, Sarah Bernhardt, 14¾x5½"	1,265.00
Lorenzaccio, Sarah Bernhardt, '14x5½"	865.00
Lorenzaccio, Sarah Bernhardt, 1896, 39x15", VG	3,450.00
Lorenzaccio, Sarah Bernhardt, 80x30"	12,650.00
Morning Awakening, 1899, 42x15"	6,325.00
Nude (from Document Decoratifs), 1902, 14½x5", VG	1,000.00
Salome, 1897, 15x11¾"	1,380.00
Tete Byzantine-Brunette (fancy border), 1897, 16½x13½", VG	2,185.00
Winter, Spring, Summer, Autumn, 1900, 27¾x11½", set	13,225.00
Zodiac La Plume, maid in profile, 1896, 25¾x19"	10,350.00

Nutting, Wallace

Born in 1862, Nutting pursued many careers. His hand-tinted photographs of landscapes and interior scenes are prized by collectors today. He was also a writer, minister, farmer, and a furniture maker, designing reproductions of early American pieces. Collectors of his prints should be aware of rosy-hued, inconsistently bright or dark examples — especially large prints of *An Elaborate Dinner* and *A Chair for John;* these have been reproduced. Prices for large interior prints have recently been on the increase. Those with animals have risen at least 50% in the past few years, and prints with men are commanding extremely high prices. Those with babies and/or adolescent children bring very high prices as well. Our advisor for this category is Milt Steinfeld; he is listed in the Directory under New Jersey.

At Grandmother's, lg Fr stone house in Spring, 9½x7¼" **430.00**
Blockhouse Thru Blossoms, blockhouse on hilltop, 9¼x7¾" **165.00**
Blossom Pasture, cattle grazing, 13¼x5" **775.00**
Castle of St Angelo, lg rnd castle w/river & bridge, 6x4½" **475.00**
Dixville Shadows, road beside lake & mountains, 9½x7¼" **185.00**
Drying Apples, couple work beside fire, 9½x7½" **850.00**
English Door, path leads to rose-covered doorway, 4½x6¼" **250.00**
Flume Falls, rocky cliffs w/waterfalls, 6x9½" **750.00**
Hollyhock Cottage, red flowers beside cottage, 9½x7½" **170.00**
Life of the Golden Age, sheep graze beside lake, 13¼x4¾" **425.00**
New Life, sheep grazing in pasture, 6½x4½" **425.00**
Nova Scotia Idyl, dirt roads beside lake, 9¼x7¼" **185.00**
Old Home, mother & daughter beside fire, 13¼x5" **550.00**
On the Slope, sheep grazing on hillside, 13¼x6½" **600.00**
Original Dennison Plant, factory scene in Maine, 7½x9¼" **500.00**
Priscilla's Cottage, English cottage & garden, 9¼x7¼" **480.00**
Quilting, 1916, 12x16" **215.00**
Surf Off Swampscott, surf crashing rocky coast, 13¼x6¼" **825.00**
Sylvan Dell, wide stream w/trees in Fall, 4¾x12¾" **125.00**
Through the Orchard, lane w/blossoming trees, 9½x6" **175.00**
Tranquil Vale, man in boat fishing at sunset, 13½x5" **600.00**
Untitled, dirt roads thru trees & hills, 3¼x3¾" **110.00**
Untitled, flowering trees over canal, 4¾x3½" **100.00**
Untitled, woman in long dress, 3x6½" **200.00**
Village End, wide view of 2 rural homes, 13¼x7¼" **480.00**
What Shall I Answer?, woman on staircase, 7¼x12½" **400.00**

Prang, Louis

Battle of Kenesaw Mountain, lg folio **100.00**
Sheridan's Ride, October 19, 1864; lg folio **180.00**
Siege of Vicksburg, Assault on Fort Hill, fr, lg folio **395.00**

Yard Longs

Values for yard-longs are given for examples in **near mint** condition, full length, nicely framed, and with the original glass. To learn more about this popular area of collector interest, we recommend *Those Wonderful Yard-Long Prints and More,* Book 2, and *More Wonderful Yard-Long Prints,* Book 3, by our advisors W.D. and M.J. Keagy, and C.G. and J.M. Rhoden. They are listed in the Directory under Indiana and Illinois respectively. A word of caution: watch for reproductions; know your dealer.

Absence Cannot Hearts Divide, Pompeian Beauty, 1921, 28x7" .**125.00**
American Beauty Souvenir, Clay, Robinson & Co, 1910 ....**400.00**
Butterick pattern lady, 1930 ....**450.00**
Cupid's Festival, M Delecrolk **350.00**
Down on the Congo, c 1904, 2nd in series of 4 ....**350.00**
Euthymol Girl, 1907 ....**350.00**
Fruit, by J Califano, c 1903 ....**200.00**
Girl w/the Poppies, B Lichtman **300.00**
Indian Girl, Schlitz Malt Extract, 1909, minimum value **400.00**
Lady seated in wht gown w/shawl wrap, Blenner, 1912, 32x8" ...**125.00**
Mary Pickford, Pompeian Beauty, 1918, 28x7", EX **110.00**

Mother & Child, 1913 ....**350.00**
Our Feathered Pets, by Paul DeLongpre **300.00**
Pabst Malt Extract, 1903 ....**400.00**
Pigs in Clover, minimum value **500.00**
Pompeian Beauty, 1911 ....**300.00**
Selz Good Shoes, 1917 ....**450.00**

Spring Is Here, by Cambril, c 1907 by Gray Litho. Co. NY, from $150.00 to $250.00.

Sweetest Story Ever Told, Pompeian Beauty, 1920, 26x8", EX ...**125.00**
Temptation Candy Girl **400.00**
Water Lilies, by R LeRoy **200.00**
Yard of Wild Flowers **200.00**

Purinton

Founded in 1936 in Wellsville, Ohio, Purinton Pottery relocated in 1941 in Shippenville, Pennsylvania, and began producing hand-painted wares that are today attracting the interest of collectors of 'country-type' dinnerware. Using bold brush strokes of vivid color, simple yet attractive patterns such as Apple, Fruits, Tea Rose, and Pennsylvania Dutch were manufactured in tableware sets and accessory pieces. For more information we recommend *Purinton Pottery* by Susan Morris; she is listed in the Directory under Iowa. Our advisor for this category is Pat Dole; she is listed in the Directory under Alabama.

Bank, Uncle Sam **40.00**
Basket, Mountain Rose **45.00**
Basket, Pansy **45.00**
Bean pot, Apple **50.00**
Bean pot, Oriental, ind **30.00**
Bowl, cereal; Intaglio **17.00**
Bowl, dessert; Apple **15.00**
Bowl, vegetable; Intaglio **20.00**
Bowl, vegetable; Normandy Plaid **20.00**
Canister, coffee; Fruit, tall **30.00**
Canisters, Apple, sq, set of 4 ....**200.00**
Casserole, Pennsylvania Dutch, w/lid **75.00**
Coffeepot, Fruit, 8-cup **65.00**
Coffeepot, Ivy, 4-cup **30.00**
Coffeepot, Ivy, 6-cup **35.00**
Coffeepot, Ivy, 8-cup **50.00**
Cookie jar, Apple, oversz **100.00**
Cookie jar, Apple, sq, wooden lid **125.00**
Cookie jar, Intaglio, sq, wooden lid **125.00**
Cornucopia, Starflower **20.00**
Creamer, Fruit, mini **10.00**
Creamer, Ivy **10.00**
Creamer, Pennsylvania Dutch **30.00**
Creamer & sugar bowl, Apple, mini **30.00**
Creamer & sugar bowl, Apple, w/lid **25.00**
Creamer & sugar bowl, Ivy **25.00**
Cup, Plaid **12.00**

Cup, Sunflower	20.00
Cup & saucer, Intaglio	20.00
Dutch Jug, Apple, 5-pt	75.00
Flowerpot, Ivy, lg	30.00
Grill platter, Apple	45.00
Honey jug, Morning Glory	35.00
Honey jug, Petals	35.00
Honey jug, Shooting Star	35.00
Honey jug, Windflower	40.00
Jardiniere, Windflower	30.00
Jug, Dutch; Apple, 5-pt	75.00
Jug, Dutch; Chartreuse, 5-pt	70.00
Jug, Dutch; Fruit, 2-pt	30.00
Jug, Dutch; Ivy, 2-pt	30.00
Jug, Dutch; Normandy Plaid, 2-pt	35.00
Jug, Kent; Fruit	20.00
Jug, Kent; Ivy	20.00
Jug, Rebecca; Mountain Rose	45.00
Marmalade jar, Sunflower	60.00
Night bottle & tumbler, Apple & Pear	75.00
Oil & vinegar, Daisy, bl trim, tall	100.00
Oil & vinegar, Plaid, red, sq, pr	50.00
Plate, breakfast; Apple	15.00
Plate, breakfast; Sunflower	40.00
Plate, dinner; Apple	20.00
Plate, dinner; Intaglio	20.00
Plate, dinner; Maywood	20.00
Plate, dinner; Plaid	20.00
Plate, salad; Apple	10.00
Plate, salad; Pennsylvania Dutch	25.00
Platter, meat; Intaglio	30.00
Pour & shake set, Heather Plaid, 3-pc	75.00
Range set, Ivy, 3-pc	75.00
Relish, Apple, 3-compartment	58.00
Relish, Normandy Plaid, 3-compartment	45.00
Roll tray, Ingaglio	45.00
Shaker, Apple, jug form	10.00
Shaker, Ivy, jug form	10.00
Shakers, Apple, jug form, pr	20.00
Shakers, Apple, shake & pour, pr	75.00
Shakers, Heather Plaid, shake & pour, 3-pc set	75.00
Shakers, Palm Tree, shake & pour, pr	200.00
Shakers, range; Fruit, pr	42.00
Shakers, range; Ivy, pr	30.00
Tea & toast, Maywood	20.00
Tea & toast, Normandy Plaid	20.00
Teapot, Fruit, 4-cup	48.00
Teapot, Fruit, 6-cup	50.00
Teapot, Ivy, 6-cup	55.00
Teapot, Mountain Rose, 2-cup	45.00
Teapot, Oriental, 2-cup	35.00
Tumbler, Apple	30.00
Tumbler, Fruit	27.00
Tumbler, Intaglio, 6-oz	15.00

Purses

Beaded purses and bags represent an area of collecting interest that is very popular today. Purses from the early 1800s are often decorated with small, brightly colored glass beads. Cut-steel beaded purses were popular in the 1840s and remained stylish until about 1930. Mesh purses are also popular. In the 1820s the mesh that was used in their manufacture was woven. Chain-link mesh came into usage in the 1890s, followed by the enamel mesh bags carried by the flappers in the 1920s. Purses are divided into several categories by (a) construction techniques — whether beaded, embroidered, or a type of needlework; (b) material — fabric or metal; and (c) design and style. Condition is very important. Watch for dry, brittle leather or fragile material. For those interested in learning more, we recommend *Antique Purses, A History, Identification, and Value Guide, Second Edition,* by Richard Holiner; *More Beautiful Purses,* and *Combs and Purses,* both by Evelyn Haertigi of Carmel, California. Our advisor for this category is Veronica Trainer; she is listed in the Directory under Ohio.

Antique 14k yellow gold mesh studded with diamonds and sapphires, with cabochon sapphire clasp, approximately 6 troy ozs, $1,200.00.

Beaded, amber, dbl beaded fringe, lg, EX	175.00
Beaded, blk & red stripes, fringe, narrow SP fr, 7x10"	125.00
Beaded, facing birds, mc/clear openwork over bl fabric, 9x6"	75.00
Beaded, floral on blk, gold-plated mts, fringe, 11x7", EX	85.00
Beaded, floral on purple, NP brass mt, fringe, wear, 8½x7"	65.00
Beaded, floral wreath on wht & clear, SP mt, fringe, 10x7"	90.00
Beaded, gold, dmn form, fringe, V-form fr, 7x12"	155.00
Beaded, gold woven design w/gilt fr, 7x7½"	85.00
Beaded, mc floral, relief cherub on sterling fr, 9x13"	365.00
Beaded, mc floral tapestry, drawstring, 6x9"	135.00
Beaded, mc floral tapestry w/striped fringe, SP fr, 8x14"	200.00
Beaded, mc geometric design, much fringe, drawstring, 8x12"	200.00
Beaded, mc rug pattern, jeweled fr, 6x11"	300.00
Beaded, rows of bl on bl fabric, SP brass fr, 7x9"	80.00
Beaded, scenic tapestry w/jeweled fr, fringe, 7½x12"	250.00
Beaded, scrolls, blk/red on dk bl, drawstring, fringe, 8½"	90.00
Beaded, shield/scroll-like designs, mc, fringe, 10x7"	100.00
Beaded, stylized peacock on blk, silver filigree fr, 10½"	155.00
Brocade, silver w/gold-tone filigree compact & lipstick holder	110.00
Leather, alligator, dbl-compartment, strap adjusts, 12x9"	150.00
Leather, snakeskin, lt brn clutch type, 9x4½", EX	55.00
Lucite, clear w/gold tulle/sparkles, carryall, Wilardy, 4x7"	295.00
Lucite, marbleized brn w/piano fringe, teardrop clasp, mirror	45.00
Lucite, tortoise, swing hdls, carryall, Wilardy, 4x7"	225.00
Lucite, wht marbleized, envelope closure, w/carryall, Elgin	300.00
Lucite w/rhinestones, clutch type, 1950s, EX	45.00
Mesh, blk & wht floral, blk Whiting & Davis fr, 5½x6¾"	100.00
Mesh, blk/gold/silver floral, Whiting & Davis 2-tone fr, 5x7"	80.00
Mesh, enameled, cut fringe bottom, Mandalian, 4x7"	155.00
Mesh, German silver, ornate fr, 5¾x5¼"	115.00
Mesh, German silver w/gold emb floral fr, fringe, lg, EX	155.00
Mesh, gold-tone fr w/lg faux jewel, Germany, 4x5¼"	50.00
Mesh, mc Deco-style floral, fringe, Mandalian, 4¼x7"	100.00
Mesh, mc Deco-style geometrics, fringe, Mandalian, 5x9"	175.00
Mesh, mc floral, fringe, Whiting & Davis fr, 5x7"	90.00
Mesh, silver, ornate sterling Whiting & Davis fr, 3¾x6¼"	345.00

Mesh, silver, Whiting & Davis fr, finger ring, 1½x3½"	35.00
Plastic, wht marble, Hillary, NM	48.00
Reticule, beaded, floral pattern, 6x10"	115.00
Rhinestones allover, silk lining, Fr, 1930s, EX	195.00
Suede w/brass trim, telephone shape, gold letters, Fr, 7x10x5"	1,495.00
Velvet, blk w/ornate brocade design, chain hdl, India, 7x4"	35.00

Puzzles

'Jigsaw' puzzles have been around almost as long as games. The first examples were handcrafted from wood, and they are extremely difficult to find. Most of the early examples featured moral subjects just as the board games did. By the 1890s jigsaw puzzles had become a major form of home entertainment. During the Depression years jigsaw puzzles were set up on card tables in almost every home. The early wood examples are the most valuable.

Cube puzzles, or blocks, were often made by the same companies as the board games. Again, early examples display the finest quality lithography. While all subjects are collectible, some (such as Santa blocks) often command prices higher than games from the same period. As early as the 1920s, puzzle makers began to produce vast numbers of character-related puzzles, and because of the extreme interest shown today in collecting memorabilia featuring early stars of TV and movies, puzzles of this type are very appealing and their values are on the rise. Our advisor for this category is Norm Vigue; he is listed in the Directory under Massachusetts. In the listings all items are jigsaw puzzles unless noted otherwise.

Personalities, Movies, and TV Shows

Annie, jigsaw, Milton Bradley #4285, 1983, MIB, sealed	5.00
Bee Gees, photo, 1979, NM in EX box	22.50
Bonanza, jigsaw, Milton Bradley, 1964, 100-pc, 10x19", EX	25.00
Buzzy the Crow, jigsaw, Built-Rite, 1961, 70-pc, MIB	26.00
Captain Kangaroo, Fairchild, 1959, EX (G box)	10.00
Charlie's Angels, jigsaw, EX in box	15.00
Daktari, Whitman, 1967, 100-pc, 14x18", EX+	12.00
David Cassidy, photo cover box, 1972, lg, M	30.00
Dick Tracy, Jaymar, 1950s, NMIB	40.00
Dino, fr-tray, Hanna-Barbera, 8x10", VG (EX box)	18.00
Dracula, HG, 1975, NM in coffin-shaped box	32.00
Farrah Faucett, 1977, MIB, sealed	25.00
Flipper, Whitman, 1967, 100-pc, 14x18", NM	15.00
Frankenstein, Jaymar, 1963, 60-pc, EX (VG box)	40.00
Gene Autry, fr-tray, Whitman, 1947, 11¼x14½", EX	28.00
Gunsmoke, photo of James Arness/Amanda Blake, 1958, M, sealed	30.00
Hardy Boys, jigsaw, Am Publishing #1515, 1978, MIB, sealed	18.00

Hopalong Cassidy Puzzles, Milton Bradley, 1950, NMIB, set of 3, $90.00.

How the West Was Won, HG Toys #493-01, 1978, MIB, sealed	15.00
Howdy Doody, Is That You Clarabelle, fr-tray, 1952, EX	25.00
James Bond, Thunderball, 1965, boxed	30.00

King Kong atop trade center, HG, 1976, 14x10", EX in box	18.00
Magilla Gorilla, fr-tray, Whitman, 1964, 11x14", NM	25.00
Mickey Mouse, jigsaw, Parker Bros, 1950s, set of 4, EX in box	45.00
Our Gang, jigsaw, Wilder Mfg, Spanky as Caesar, NM	115.00
Peter Max, Read, 1970, MIB	75.00
Rin-Tin-Tin & His Friends, jigsaw, Jaymar, 1957, EX in box	15.00
Robin Hood, fr-tray, Built Rite, 1950s, EX	20.00
Roy Rogers, jr jigsaw, Whitman, set of 3, 1952, EX in box	80.00
Space Kidettes, fr-tray, Whitman, 1967, 11x14", EX	25.00
Star Trek, fr-tray, Whitman, 1978, 8x10", NM	16.00
Sword in the Stone, Disney, 1968, NM	15.00
Tom & Jerry, fr-tray, Whitman, 1959, 11x14", EX	22.00
Tommy Tortoise & Moe Hare, jigsaw, Built-Rite, '61, 70-pc, MIB	26.00
Welcome Back Kotter, fr-tray, 1977, sealed	12.50
Welcome Back Kotter, slide, photo illus, 1976, MOC	25.00
Zorro, 1965, NMIB	15.00

Miscellaneous

Ann Hathaway's Cottage, plywood, 1930s, 19½x16", EX in box	75.00
Basket of flowers, R Purrington, 214-pc, 1930s, EX in box	28.00
Boating at Night, att Ullman, plywood, 1910s, 6x8", EX	12.00
Canal in Venice, Ken-Way, plywood, 1930s, 12x9", EX	30.00
Country Side, Parker Bros, 1909, 12x7¼", EX in box	18.00
Cross Country Marathon, Milton Bradley, 1900s, EX in box	42.50
Dissected Map of the US, J Ottman Lithograph, 1910, EX	45.00
Eiffel Tower, plywood, Condor Toys, 1950s, 19½x15½", EX	45.00
Grazing Time, plywood, cows in pasture, 220-pc, 1930s, EX	20.00
Little Workers Picture Cubes, McLoughlin Bros, litho on wood, EX	550.00
Map of the US, plywood, McLoughlin Bros, ca 1900, 22x14", NMIB	100.00
Map of US w/Information, Saalfield, 1932, NMIB	35.00
Old Windmill at Sunset, plywood, Parker Bros, EX in box	85.00
Paddlewheel Boat City of Worcester, McLoughlin Bros, early G	200.00
Plastic Inlaid US Map, Hassenfeld Bros, 1967, VG	10.00
Schuykill River, wooden, 117-pc, early 1900s, 10x12", EX	20.00
United States, Parker Bros, 53-pc, 1915, 12x20", EX	20.00
WA Crossing Delaware, McLoughlin Bros, early, EX in box	300.00
Washington DC, jigsaw, Saalfield, 1932, NMIB	35.00
Wild Animals, jigsaw, Parker Bros, 1930, EX in box	40.00
Wild West Picture Puzzle, McLoughlin Bros, 1890, EX	375.00
Within US, Doepke, 1957, changeable block map, EX	20.00

Pyrography

Pyrography, also known as burnt wood, Flemish art or poker work, is the art of burning designs into wood or leather and has been practiced over the centuries in many countries.

In the late 1800s pyrography became the hot new hobby for thousands of Americans who burned designs inspired by the popular artists of the day including Mucha, Gibson, Fisher, and Corbett. Thousands of wooden boxes, wall plaques, novelties, and pieces of furniture that they purchased from local general stores or from mail-order catalogs were burned and painted. These pieces were manufactured by companies such as The Flemish Art Company of New York and Thayer & Chandler of Chicago, who printed the designs on wood for the pyrographers to burn.

This Victorian fad developed into a new form of artistic expression as the individually burned and painted pieces reflected the personality of the pyrographers. The more adventurous started to burn between the lines and developed a style of 'all-over burning' that today is known as Pyromania. Others not only created their own designs but even made the pieces to be decorated. Both these developments are particularly valued today as true examples of American folk art.

By the 1930s its popularity had declined and, like Mission furniture, was neglected by generations of collectors and dealers. The recent appreciation of Victoriana, the Arts and Crafts Movement, the American West, and the popularity of turn-of-the-century graphic art has rekindled interest in pyrography which embraces all these styles.

A new book, *The Burning Passion — Antique and Collectible Pyrography,* by Carole and Richard Smyth, our advisors for this category, is currently available from the authors; they are listed in the Directory under New York.

Key: hb — hand burned

Book rack, hb/pnt girl w/book, 5¾" W, extends to 15¾"L 150.00
Flatware box, factory burned/pnt poinsettias, Rogers, 9x11x5"....195.00
Frame, hb/pnt flower garland, Thayer-Chandler, 8" dia.................85.00
Gameboard, hb/pnt ea side/edges, Flemish Art, 15" sq (open).....200.00
Knife rack, hb Lizzie Borden w/axe, 5 hooks below, rare..............550.00
Magazine stand, 4-shelf, burned/pnt florals, Thayer-Chandler, 48"..800.00
Mirror, hand; hb/pnt lady's head w/flowing hair, 13¼"x6¾".......180.00
Nut bowl, hb/pnt squirrel on branch, Flemish Art Co #816, 5".....65.00
Panel, basswood, burned/pnt oranges, Thayer-Chandler, 16x30"..465.00
Plaque, cvd/burned/pnt strawberry basket, 3-ply, 12"dia 70.00
Plaque, hb orange cat w/bow, paper 1912 calendar, 5¾" dia..........50.00
Ribbon holder, hb/pnt Sunbonnet babies (3), 5x12" 160.00

Quezal

The Quezal Art Glass and Decorating Company of Brooklyn, New York, was founded in 1901 by Martin Bach. A former Tiffany employee, Bach's glass closely resembled that of his former employer. Most pieces were signed 'Quezal,' a name taken from a Central American bird. After Bach's death in 1920, his son-in-law, Conrad Vohlsing, continued to produce a Quezal-type glass in Elmhurst, New York, which he marked 'Lustre Art Glass.' See also that particular category. Examples listed here are signed unless noted otherwise.

Bowl, gold irid, ribbed/shouldered, 2x4" 175.00
Bowl, gold w/purple irid, stretched petal edge, 2½x6" 425.00
Finger bowl, red-gold irid, +stretch-border plate 275.00
Lamp, desk; gold/wht feathered lily shade; gooseneck std 450.00
Lamp, pulled motif, gr/gold on opal 9" shade/trumpet std 1,700.00
Shade, allover spider webbing, gold int, 6", pr 400.00
Shade, feathers, gold/gr on opal, gold int, 5½" 100.00
Shade, gold feathers w/gr outlines on opal, sgn, 6", pr 375.00
Vase, Agate, streaks of amber/bl/aqua/blk, trumpet neck, 6" ...1,600.00

Vase, blue iridescent with pulled and trailed white and gold designs, tall segmented form with wide mouth and circular foot, 12", $1,000.00.

Vase, bl irid, flared neck, angle shoulder, 8x4" 650.00
Vase, deep gold w/purple & bl highlights, 2x2½" 425.00

Vase, feathers, gr/gold on opal, trumpet w/3-fold rim, 8" 1,700.00
Vase, feathers & 3 appl reeded shells, gr/purple on wht, 5½" ..2,300.00
Vase, feathers+2 bands, gr/gold on ivory, squat base, 11" 1,500.00
Vase, gold irid, ruffled & stretched rim, 4½" 375.00
Vase, gold irid, 8x5" 450.00
Vase, jack-in-pulpit; leaves, gr/gold, folded gold rim, 12" 1,300.00
Vase, leaves, bl/orange spaced on opal w/gold threading, 6½" 550.00
Vase, marbleized earth tones, glossy, tapered, 7½" 650.00
Vase, pulled lines, gr/gold/wht, gold int, wide ruffle rim, 12" ...2,000.00

Quilts

Quilts, while made of necessity, nevertheless represent an art form which expresses the character and the personality of the designer. During the 17th and 18th centuries, quilts were considered a necessary part of a bride's hope chest; the traditional number required to be properly endowed for marriage was a 'baker's dozen'! Quilts were used not only for bed coverings but for curtains, extra insulation, and mattresses as well. American Colonial quilts reflect the English and French taste of our ancestors. They would include the classifications known as Lindsey-Woolsey and the Central Medallion applique quilts fashioned from imported copper-plate printed fabrics.

By 1820 spare time was slightly more available, so women gathered in quilting bees. This not only was a way of sharing the work, but also to show off their best work. The hand-dyed and pieced quilts emerged, and they are now known as Sampler, Album, and Friendship quilts. By 1845 American printed fabric was available.

In 1793 Eli Whitney developed the cotton gin; as a result, textile production in America became industrialized. Soon inexpensive fabrics were readily available, and ladies were able to choose from colorful prints and solids to add contrast to their work. Both pieced and appliqued work became popular. Pieced quilts were considered utilitarian, while appliqued work was shown with pride of accomplishment at the fair. Today many collectors prize pieced quilts and their intricate geometric patterns above all other types. Many of these designs were given names: Daisy and Oak Leaf, Grandmother's Flower Garden, Log Cabin, and Ocean Wave are only a few. Appliqued quilts involved stitching one piece — carefully cut into a specific form such as a leaf, a flower, or a stylized device — onto either a large one-piece ground fabric or an individual block. Often the background fabric was quilted in a decorative pattern.

Amish women scorned printed calicos as 'worldly' and instead used colorful blocks set with black fabrics to produce a stunning pieced effect. During the Victorian period the crazy quilt emerged. This style was formed by random pieces put together following no organized lines and was usually embellished by elaborate embroidery stitches. Fabrics of choice were brocades, silks, and velvets.

Another type of quilting, highly prized and rare today, is trapunto. These quilts were made by first stitching the outline of the design onto a solid sheet of fabric which was backed with a second having a much looser weave. White was often favored, but color was sometimes used for accent. The design (grapes, flowers, leaves, etc.) was padded through openings made by separating the loose weave of the underneath fabric; a backing was added and the three layers quilted as one.

Besides condition, value is judged on intricacy of pattern, color effect, and craftsmanship. Examine the stitching. Quality quilts have from ten to twelve stitches to the inch. In the listings that follow, examples rated excellent have minor defects. Values given here are auction results; retail may be somewhat higher. Our advisor is Suzi McLennan Anderson; she is listed in the Directory under New Jersey.

Key:
dmn — diamond   mp — machine pieced
embr — embroidery   ms — machine sewn
hs — hand sewn   X — cross
hq — hand quilted, quilting

Amish

Baskets, pastel on blk, lav border, ms binding, worn, 83x60" **500.00**
Blk w/dbl pk border, loss to bking, 64x84" **250.00**
Blocks, gold/gray/wine, str quilting, X in center, 80x83", NM **385.00**
Geometric design in gr & purple, 19th C, full sz, EX **1,840.00**
Sawtooth strips, some fading at edges, 63x84" **635.00**

Appliqued

Am eagle amid stars, red/wht/bl, late 1800s, 97x73" **1,600.00**
Carolina Lily, red/gr/orange cotton, early 20th C, 80x81", EX ...**575.00**
Floral w/eagle center, red/teal/yel calico, 1900s, 93x79" **475.00**
Iris, 12 flowers on wht, hs, 1930, 72x92", EX **400.00**
Mexican Rose, 4-color on wht, feather quilting, 78" sq, NM **550.00**
Pansy Bouquets, bl scalloped border, ca 1900, 74x88", EX **250.00**
Red poppies w/embr, dmn quilting, red border, 1930s, 68x80", EX ...**300.00**
Rose wreaths, red/gr/wht, line quilting, 19th C, 88x84", EX ...**1,035.00**
Roses, pk on wht, early 1800s, stains, 65x68" **400.00**
Sawtooth Quarter Fan, EX quilting, 1800s, discolored, 87x75", EX ...**375.00**
Tulips, mc on wht, circular quilting, 1940, 74x80", EX **325.00**
Vining tulips, ms w/embr, scalloped border, 86x70", EX **250.00**
9 floral medallions, gr/red/pk/yel, feather quilting, 93x83" **950.00**

Pieced

Autograph patch (no names), dk/lt calicos, hs, 77x68", EX **185.00**
Blocks, bl & wht w/embr tulips, EX quilting, 1940s, 78x80", NM ...**285.00**
Carpenter's Sq, red & wht, fine quilting, 78x78" **550.00**
Christian Cross, mc w/bl check binding, 1920s, 65x79", NM **225.00**
Churn Dash, mc mini prints, red sashing, 1880s, 70x82", EX **250.00**
Corn & Beans, mc calicos/red, hs, 1880s, 70x84", VG **225.00**
Corn & Beans, mixed indigo prints/wht/red, 1930s, 70x82", VG ..**235.00**
Cross Patch, red/wht/bl, circular quilting, 1900, 72x82", EX **265.00**
Dbl Irish Chain, red/wht cotton, red border, hs, 76x88", EX **485.00**
Dbl Wedding Ring, mc calicos/gr/lav, EX quilting, 80x82", M ...**415.00**
Dbl 9-Patch, old calicos, fine quilting, 84x71", EX **325.00**
Dmn in Sq, mc w/blk & gr border, PA, 80x82", NM **600.00**
Drunkard's Path, mc calicos, EX quilting, hs, 64x76", M **525.00**
Drunkard's Path, pk & wht, EX quilting, 1930, 70x78", VG **165.00**
Fans, mc prints/burgundy, dmn quilting, 1940s, 84" sq, EX **235.00**
Flower Basket, pk/bl/gr/lav on wht, EX quilting, 77x86", NM **500.00**
Flower Garden, mc prints, bl fences, 1930s, 76x86", EX **350.00**
Geometrical, orange/brn/wht cotton, early 20th C, 79x84", NM ..**700.00**
Grandmother's Flower Garden, gr & wht border, 104x82" **225.00**
Hexagons w/in Hexagon, mc calicos, machine bound, 90x77", NM ...**300.00**
Irish Chain, red/goldenrod/olive gray, sgn/1891, 90x80", EX **745.00**
Jacob's Ladder, mc calicos, hs, 1930, 68x80", EX **285.00**
Log Cabin, mc mini prints/lav, EX quilting, 1930, 62x78", M **465.00**
Log Cabin, mc silks w/red sqs, child sz, 53x58", VG **200.00**
Lone Star, mc prints w/bright bl, EX quilting, 1930s, 75x82", M ..**300.00**
Lone Star, red/yel/gr, dk gr border, PA, 80x78", NM **900.00**
Mosaic, mc triangles/point border, dmn quilting, 70x80", EX **200.00**
Oak Leaf, friendship type, Dakota territories/1887, 83x84" **400.00**
Ocean Waves, ginghams/chambrays/cottons, 1920s, 84x64", EX .**195.00**
Ocean Waves, red/wht mini prints, EX quilting, 1900, 67x82", EX ..**400.00**
OH Star, bright calicos, feed sack bking, 70x70", NM **335.00**
OH Star, red/bl/wht calico w/red & bl border, 89x76", EX **440.00**

Old Maid's Puzzle, earth tones, hs, 1880s, 80x80", EX **285.00**
Orchid 9-Patch, lav/mc on wht, circle quilting, '30, 70x80", EX .**375.00**
Pinwheel Skew variant, mc w/dk gr, PA, 94x84", NM **425.00**
Posey in Pot, mc prints/blk embr/gr ruffles, 1930, 72x80", EX **250.00**
Radiating ribs, 5x11x8" **50.00**
Rolling Stone, bl/blk/burgundy/gray calico, 1880, 62x88", EX **300.00**

**Star of Bethlehem,
1800s, 87x89", NM,
$900.00.**

Star of Bethlehem, gr/pk/yel/brn, 19th C, 42" sq **500.00**
Star of Bethlehem, mc calicos, EX quilting, 1920, 66x76", EX ...**185.00**
Star of Bethlehem, mc calicos, hs, 1880s, 84x86", EX **365.00**
Star of Bethlehem, 19th C, faded, 82x78" **315.00**
Stepping Stones, mc calicos, hs, 1900s, 72x80", NM **225.00**
String Stars, mc calicos, bl shirting, 1880s, 78x82", NM **265.00**
String Stars, mc prints/bl/cranberry, hs, 1900, 65x78", EX **285.00**
Thousand Pyramids, mc satins & gr sateen, 1850s, 80x72", EX ..**450.00**
Triangles w/in Dmn, calicos, muslin bk, wide border, 88x67", NM ..**350.00**
Triple Irish Chain, calicos/wht, EX quilting, '30, 78x100", NM .**450.00**
Turkey Tracks, rose/tan/pumpkin, dmn quilting, '20s, 65x82", VG ..**165.00**
Wild Goose Chase, wht w/red & gr, 20th C, 73x75", NM **225.00**
20 stars, pk calico & wht, on stretcher, 41x34" **220.00**
4-H Club Patch, friendship type, cottons, 1930s, 70x81", EX **200.00**
6-Point Star, mc prints w/red, EX quilting, 1900, 74x82", EX **200.00**
9-Patch, red/bl mini prints, circular quilting, 1900, lg, EX **200.00**

Quimper

Quimper is a type of pottery produced in Quimper, France. A tin enamel-glazed earthenware pottery with hand-painted decoration, it was first produced in the 1600s by the Bousquet and Caussy Factories. Little of this early ware was marked. By the late 1700s, three factories were operating in the area, all manufacturing the same type of pottery. The Grande Maison de HB, a company formed as a result of a marriage joining the Hubaudiere and Bousquet families, was a major producer of Quimper pottery. They marked their wares with various forms of the 'HB' logo; but of the pottery they produced, collectors value examples marked with the 'HB' within a triangle most highly.

Francois Eloury established another pottery in Quimper in the late 1700s. Under the direction of Charles Porquier, the ware was marked simply 'P.' Adolph Porquier replaced Charles in the 1850s, marking the ware produced during that period with an 'AP' logo. 'PB' (for Porquier-Beau) was used ca 1875 until 1900.

Jule HenRiot began operations in 1886, using molds he had purchased from Porquier. His mark was 'HR,' and until the 20th century he was in competition with The Grande Maison de HB. In 1926 he began to mark his wares 'HenRiot Quimper.' In 1968 the two factories merged. They are still in operation under the name Les Faenceries de Quimper. The factory sold in the fall of 1983 to Sarah and Paul

Janssens from the United States, making it the first time the owners were not French. For those interested in learning more about Quimper, we recommend *Quimper Pottery: A French Folk Art Faience* by Sandra V. Bondhus, our advisor for this category, whose address can be found in the Directory under Connecticut.

Bell, lady w/florals, bagpipe form, orig clapper, HQF, 3½" 130.00
Bonbon, lady/man/coat of arms, 3-part, HR Quimper, 8" dia 130.00
Bonbonniere, boys w/sailboat, Porqueir Beau mk, 2½x4½" sq ...950.00
Bowl, peasant man, scalloped, ca 1840s, unmk, 3½x12" 220.00
Bowl, red & bl roses, bl sponged rim, Quimper, 1½x7" 70.00
Box, powder; lady on rock w/ferns at sides, HQF, 2¼x3½" 60.00
Cake plate, lady & rose garland, HBQF, 12½" 80.00
Cake plate, Ordinaire, lady w/florals, HBQ, 11½" 130.00
Chamberstick, lady, floral garland, HQF, 6x6½", NM 140.00
Charger, sunburst & geometrics, HBQ, 12½" 120.00
Cigarette holder, camel in dessert, geometrics, HQF, 3x3", EX ..200.00
Compote, lady w/hands folded, garlands, HRQ, 5½x9½" 350.00
Coupe, man or lady, floral garlands, HRQ, 9", pr 300.00
Cruets, oil & vinegar; man/lady, sponged stoppers, HQF, 7", pr .160.00
Cup & saucer, geometrics, trefoil, 1800s, unsgn, 4", 5¼" 85.00
Cup & saucer, man w/walking stick, HBQF, flakes 20.00
Cup & saucer, peasant, florals, HRQF, 4¼", 5", set of 4 ....175.00
Figurine, lady w/sheaf & scythe, HRQ, 9", EX 300.00
Figurine, Lannk & Louisik, Modern Movement, HQF, rprs, 4", pr .110.00
Figurine, man w/bagpipes, lady w/distaff, HBQ, 5½", pr 250.00
Figurine, sailor curling rope, HBQ, 6", EX 100.00
Figurine, Ste Anne w/Child, mc w/gold, HQ, 12½", EX 135.00
Inkwell box, rose, stylized border, heart shape, HQF, 2x3" 140.00
Jar, cream w/Modern Movement palette, w/lid, HBQ, 5" hdl to hdl .25.00
Knife rest, lady & distaff, Croisille, HQF, #195, 3" 75.00
Ladle, florals, bold brush strokes on 5½" hdl, HBQF 65.00
Match holder, man w/pipe, latticework, unmk, flake, 3x3" 140.00
Match safe, lady, a la touche florals, wall hanging, HRQ, 3¼" ...150.00
Menu, lady w/basket, floral spray, HRQ, 7x5" 240.00
Mug, man & lady, HR, minor wear, 3", pr 130.00
Mustard pot, lady & evergreen, w/lid, HB Quimper, 3½" 55.00
Pipe, a la touche floral spray, unsgn, recent, 6" 70.00
Pitcher, cider; man w/walking stick, HQF, 6½", NM 170.00
Pitcher, lady, Ordinaire, sponged hdl, HQF, #439, 6" 85.00
Pitcher, lady & garlands, HQF, 8" 140.00
Pitcher, man, Ordinaire, sponged hdl, #4, 7½" 100.00
Pitcher, man & floral sprays, banded border, HQF, 7½", NM 110.00
Pitcher, man w/pipe & fir tree, orange bands, HBQF, 6" 85.00
Pitcher, sailor man w/baskets & nets, Pecheur, HBQ, 5" 130.00

Plate, Jeunes maries de Kerlouen (Newlyweds from Kerlouen), Decore Riche, blue on blue acanthus border, HR Quimper, 10", M, $600.00.

Plate, daisy & rose, 4-bl-dot design, broken fish mk, 7" 75.00
Plate, flower bouquet, pk w/bl band, HBQF, 9¼" 85.00
Plate, French verse, garland border, unmk, 1940s, 9¾" 90.00
Plate, lady, bud-&-dot border, cut corners, HQF, 8¼" 85.00
Plate, lady & florals, garland border, pierced, HQF, 10" 80.00

Plate, lady's portrait, Broderie Breton, HBQ, 9¼" 80.00
Plate, peasant lady, fish form, HQ, 10", NM 230.00
Plate, peasant lady in swirls, sponged rim, HQBF, 9½" 55.00
Plate, peasant man w/walking stick, gr w/mc trim, HBQ, 9¼" 85.00
Platter, courting couple, Decore Riche, HRQ, 11x7¼" 450.00
Platter, lady, a la touche border, scalloped, HQF, 11½x7½" 130.00
Platter, Naive, peasant couple, unsgn HB, 19½x14½" 925.00
Porringer, man, bl sponged hdls, pierced, HQ, 6½" 20.00
Ramekin, sunflower int, garland ext, heart shape, HQF, 2½" 45.00
Shoe, peasant man, 1 of pr, HQF, 3" 30.00
Snuff bottle, lady w/ermine tails, bagpipe form, HR, 3", NM 250.00
Snuff box, lady w/floral sprays, book form, HQF, 3" 200.00
Statue, St Vierge w/Christ Child, HRQ, #8, 12½" 240.00
Statue, Ste Anne w/child Mary at side, mc, HQF, #101, 13" 170.00
Sugar bowl, man & lady, dolphin hdls, HQF, #116, 7½" W 160.00
Tankard, butterfly, sponged & herringbone panels, HBQ, 6" 250.00
Teapot, lady, canteen type, HB Quimper, no lid/rpr, 9x10" dia ..180.00
Teapot, lady by bale/man w/branch, canteen form, HB, 11¾" ...650.00
Tureen, lady & florals on lid, w/lid, HQF, 6x8" 160.00
Tureen, lady & spruce tree on lid, hdls, w/lid, HBQ, 5½x7" 95.00
Vase, couple dancing/Crest of Brittany, Decor Riche, HQ, 15¼" ..925.00
Vase, lady w/basket, Decor Riche, cylindrical, HBQ, rstr, 6" 130.00
Vase, man & lady, horseshoe form, HB, 5½x4½" 575.00
Vase, pr of musicians, Decor Riche, HBQ, 15" 700.00
Vase, quintal; man w/flute, 5 openings, HQ, 6", NM 110.00
Wall pocket, lady & florals, bagpipe shape, HBQ, 7½" 160.00
Wall pocket, lady w/basket, envelope shape, HR, 5x4¼" 350.00
Wall pocket, man & lady, ermines, cornucopia form, HR, 8" 195.00
Wall pocket, portly man w/pipe, bagpipe form, HR Quimper, 8" ..200.00

Radford

Pottery associated with Albert Radford (1882-1904) can be categorized by three periods of production. Pottery produced in Tiffin, Ohio (1896-1899), consists of bone china (no marked examples known) and high-quality jasperware with applied Wedgwood-like cameos. Tiffin jasperware is often impressed 'Radford Jasper' in small block letters. At Zanesville, Ohio, Radford jasperware was marked only with an incised, two-digit shape number, and the cameos were not applied but rather formed within the mold and filled with a white slip. Zanesville Radford ware was produced for only a few months before the Radford pottery was acquired by the Arc-en-Ciel company in 1903. Production in Zanesville was handled by Radford's father, Edward (1840-1910), who remained in Zanesville after Albert moved to Clarksburg, West Virginia, where the Radford Pottery Co. was completed shortly before Albert's death in 1904. Jasperware was not produced in Clarksburg, and the molds appear to have been left in Zanesville, where some were subsequently used by the Arc-en-Ciel pottery. The Clarksburg, West Virginia, pottery produced a standard glaze, slip-decorated ware, Ruko; Thera and Velvety, matt glazed ware often signed by Albert Haubrich, Alice Bloomer, and other artists; and Radura, a semimatt green glaze developed by Albert Radford's son, Edward. The Clarksburg plant closed in 1912. Our advisor for this category is James L. Murphy; he is listed in the Directory under Ohio.

Jasper

Bowl, muses & vintage, fluted rim, imp mk 295.00
Letter holder, lady w/bow & target scene, bark trim, #61 ....500.00
Mug, vintage, gray, #25, 5" 165.00
Pitcher, tankard, vintage, lt bl, #26, 12" 200.00
Vase, angels, 6½" 200.00
Vase, bust of Washington, reverse: eagle, bark trim, #12, 7" 265.00

Vase, cherubs on flying eagles, #23, 9½" **475.00**
Vase, Gladstone bust ea side, twisted form, 3" **125.00**
Vase, lady w/dog, bk: Roman kneels, bark trim, #18, 7" **350.00**
Vase, running girl, deep bl, flat & twisted, #53, 3½" **100.00**
Vase, 3 horses in clouds pull chariot, bark trim, #16, 7" **295.00**

Miscellaneous

Candle holder, Ruko, floral, sgn/mk, rare, 7" **175.00**
Jardiniere & ped, griffins, blended, mk Owens/sgn Radford, 34" ..**695.00**
Vase, Radura, matt gr, 4-hdld, 10" **150.00**
Vase, Thera, lg floral, #1453, 12½x6" **700.00**
Vase, Velvety, matt gr w/wild roses, #7463, 10" **200.00**

Radios

Vintage radios are very collectible. There were thousands of styles and types produced, the most popular of which today are the breadboard and the cathedral. Consoles are usually considered less marketable, since their size makes them hard to display and store. For those wishing to learn more about antique radios, we recommend *The Collector's Guide to Antique Radios, Volumes I and II*, by Sue and Marty Bunis, available from your local bookstore or Collector Books. They are also the authors of *A Collector's Guide to Transistor Radios*. For information on novelty radios, refer to *Collector's Guide to Novelty Radios* by Marty Bunis and Robert Breed. Values are given for radios in near mint to mint condition.

Key:
pb — push button   SW — short wave
phono — phonograph   tbl/m — table model
s/r — slide rule

A-C Dayton Xl-15, wood, highboy, battery, console, 1923 ....**165.00**
Admiral 115-5A, plastic, magnified dial, pb, AC, tbl/m, 1938 .....**75.00**
Admiral 6T02, plastic, s/r dial, AC/DC, tbl/m, 1946 ....**35.00**
Air Castle 5050, right front dial, AC/DC, tbl/m, 1948 ....**30.00**
Air-Way #F, wood, 2-dial front panel, battery, tbl/m, 1923 ....**225.00**
Airline 62-77, Cathedral, wood, window dial, battery, 1933 ......**115.00**
Airline 84WG-2714A, wood, s/r dial, FM, phono, console, 1948 .**80.00**
Am Bosch, wood, window dial, AC, tbl/m, 1928 ....**135.00**
AMC 42N48-09, walnut, alarm clock, AM/FM, AC/DC, tbl/m, 1963 ..**15.00**
Amplex 3500-4, Cabinette, wood, 2-dial, battery, tbl/m, 1925 ...**325.00**
Aria 593, wood, curved grill w/vertical bars, AC/DC, tbl/m **95.00**
Arvin 444A, metal, midget, tubes, tbl/m, 1946 ....**80.00**
Arvin 5572, plastic, alarm clock, ftd, tubes, AC, tbl/m, 1958 ....**20.00**
Atwater Kent 456, Tombstone, wood, rnd dial, AC, 1936 ....**250.00**
Atwater Kent 55, metal, window dial, AC, tbl/m, 1929 ....**75.00**
Automatic 8-15, plastic, Deco, sq dial, tbl/m, 1937 ....**75.00**
Bendix 115, plastic, s/r dial, AC/DC, tbl/m, 1948 ....**275.00**
Browning-Drake 4-R, wood, 2-dial, lift top, tbl/m, 1925-37 ....**140.00**
Cameo 14N18-03, wood grain, 2 speakers, tubes, tbl/m, 1964 ......**10.00**
Cisco 9A5, plastic, sq dial, AC/DC, tbl/m, 1947 ....**75.00**
Clinton 1102, wood, rnd dial, tuning eye, console, 1937 ....**135.00**

Crosley #176 Travette, metal Deco-style case, 4-section grill, 2 octagonal knobs, table model, $110.00.

Crosley 22, walnut veneer, highboy, battery, console, 1929 ....**130.00**
Crosley 401, Bandbox Jr, metal, battery, tbl/m, 1928 ....**80.00**
Crosley 5-50, wood, thumbwheel dial, battery, tbl/m, 1926 ....**85.00**
Crosley 58TK, plastic, rnd dial, 2 knobs, AC/DC, tbl/m, 1948 .....**50.00**
Dewald 648, wood, 6-pb, 4 knobs, tbl/m, 1939 ....**65.00**
Emerson 368, walnut, 6-pb, SW, AC, console, 1940 ....**120.00**
Emerson 603, wood, s/r dial, phono, FM, AC, console, 1949 ....**75.00**
Espey 6547, wood, s/r dial, phono, AC, tbl/m, 1946 ....**30.00**
Fada 855, plastic, s/r dial, AC/DC, tbl/m, 1950 ....**45.00**
Federal 143, wood, lowboy, 2 dials, battery, console, 1925 ....**450.00**
Firestone 4-A-159, plastic, s/r dial, AC/DC, tbl/m, 1957 ....**20.00**
Freshman 5-F-4, mahog, 3 dials, battery, tbl/m, 1925 ....**100.00**
GE F-75, wood, SW, AC, console, 1937 ....**125.00**
GE K-62, wood, lowboy, window dial, 6-leg, AC, console, 1931 .**100.00**
GE 54, plastic, s/r dial, Deco-style tbl/m, 1940 ....**85.00**
General Motors 27C5L, plastic, sq dial, AC/DC, tbl/m, 1948 ......**45.00**
Gilfillan 20, mahog, lowboy, battery, console, 1926 ....**100.00**
Gloritone 99, Cathedral, wood, ½-rnd dial, 3 knobs, 1931 ....**225.00**
Grebe CR-8, wood, blk Bakelite panel, battery, tbl/m, 1921 ......**500.00**
Grunow 594, violin-shape, airplane dial, tbl/m, 1937 ....**70.00**
Hallicrafters EC-306, wood, phono, SW, AC, tbl/m, 1948 ....**40.00**
Howard 40, wood, lowboy, stretcher base, console, 1931 ....**135.00**
Jackson-Bell 38, wood, lowboy, 6-leg, console, 1932 ....**140.00**
Jewel 504, wood, s/r dial, 2 knobs, AC/DC, tbl/m, 1947 ....**40.00**
Kennedy 521, wood, lowboy, stretcher base, console, 1928 ....**175.00**
Knight 6C-225, plastic, s/r dial, AC/DC, tbl/m, 1947 ....**50.00**
Kodel 68B-151K, wood, oval dial, tuning eye, battery, tbl/m **60.00**
Lafayette D41, wood, airplane dial, SW, battery, tbl/m, 1938 ......**35.00**
Maguire 700E, wood, s/r dial, phono, AC, tbl/m, 1947 ....**30.00**
Majestic 400, plastic, s/r dial, AC/DC, tbl/m, 1941 ....**80.00**
Motorola, Winona, walnut, lift top, battery, tbl/m, 1926 ....**110.00**
Motorola #54, Catalin, vertical louvers, tbl/m, 1939, minimum .**550.00**
Philco 37-61, Tombstone, wood, rnd dial, SW, AC, 1937 ....**100.00**
Philco 42-345, wood, s/r dial, 6-pb, SW, AC, tbl/m, 1942 ....**50.00**
Philco 910, plastic, s/r dial, FM, AC, tbl/m, 1962 ....**25.00**
RCA C9-4, wood, rnd dial, tuning eye, SW, AC, console, 1935 .**175.00**
RCA T10-1, Tombstone, wood, airplane dial, SW, AC, 1936 ...**145.00**
RCA 5T1, Tombstone, wood, tuning eye, SW, AC, 1936 ....**125.00**
RCA 56X, plastic, dial w/red dot pointer, AC/DC, tbl/m, 1946 ...**35.00**
Silvertone 6437, wood, s/r dial, pb, SW, AC, console, 1940 ....**100.00**
Silvertone 8003, bl metal, midget, AC/DC, tbl/m, 1949 ....**75.00**
Sparton 20, wood, lowboy, lift top, phono, AC, console, 1932 ...**140.00**
Stewart-Warner 03-5C1, 2-tone wood, AC/DC, tbl/m, 1939 ....**40.00**
Truetone D-727, wood, tuning eye, pb, SW, tbl/m, 1937 ....**70.00**
US Radio 3092, wood w/inlay, AC/DC, tbl/m, 1933 ....**75.00**
Westinghouse H-350T7, plastic, AM/FM, AC/DC, tbl/m, 1951 ..**40.00**
Westinghouse WR-182, 2-tone walnut, SW, AC/DC, tbl/m, 1940 ..**50.00**
Wurlitzer Lyric SA-99, wood, lowboy, 6-leg, console, 1934 ....**145.00**
Zenith LP Zenette, Cathedral, 2-tone wood, window dial, 1931 ...**200.00**
Zenith 5-S-29, Tombstone, wood, rnd dial, SW, AC, 1936 ....**165.00**
Zenith 6-D-116, wood, rnd dial, SW, AC, tbl/m, 1936 ....**65.00**

Novelty

Avon Skin So Soft **35.00**
Blabber Mouse, AM only, NM **35.00**
Cabbage Patch Girl, Coleco, 1980s, EX **95.00**
Ghost Buster Slimer, MIB **45.00**
Hamburger Helper Helping Hand, MIB **45.00**
Heinz Ketchup Bottle, plastic, MIB **65.00**
Hershey's Syrup, MIB **75.00**
Lady Bug **35.00**
Lemon, MIB **15.00**
Michael Jackson, AM/FM, NM **25.00**

Planters Mr Peanut, EX	65.00
Polaroid 600 Filmpack Film, MIB	25.00
Raid Bug, MIB	225.00
Snoopy on doghouse, EX	40.00
Spaceman, Pulsates, 1977, NM	45.00
Statue of Liberty	40.00
Teacup & saucer, MIB	35.00

Transistors

Post-World War II baby boomers, now approaching their fiftieth year, are rediscovering prized possessions of youth, their pocket radios. The transistor wonders, born with rock 'n roll, were at the vanguard of miniaturization and futuristic design in the decade which followed their introduction to Christmas shoppers in 1954. The tiny receiving sets launched the growth of Texas Instruments and shortly to follow abroad, Sony and other Japanese giants.

The most desirable sets include the 1954 four-transistor Regency TR-1 and colorful early Sony and Toshiba models. Certain pre-1960 models by Hoffman and Admiral represented the earliest practical use of solar technology and are also highly valued. To avoid high tariffs, scores of two-transistor sets, boys' radios, were imported from Japan with names like Pet and Charmy. Many early inexpensive transistor sets could be heard only with an earphone. The smallest sets are known as shirt-pocket models while those slightly larger are called coat pockets. Early collectible transistor radios all have civil defense triangle markings at 640 and 1240 on the frequency dial and nine or fewer transistors. Very few desirable sets were made after 1963. Model numbers are most commonly found inside sets. Our advisor for this category is Mike Brooks; he is listed in the Directory under California and welcomes questions. Please include a SASE.

Admiral 909, All World	75.00
Airline Gen-1215A	50.00
Arvin 9577	100.00
Claricon 77A	100.00
Dumont 1210	40.00
Emerson 747, 838 or 839	125.00
GE 675	100.00
Global GR-715	160.00
Harpers 2TP-110	75.00
Hoffman KP706, Trans Solar	175.00
Magnavox AM-2	125.00
Mayfair ST-6J	55.00
Motorola 56T1	150.00
Motorola 7X24S	110.00
NEC NT-61	50.00
Olson RA-315	40.00
Packard Bell 6RT-2	60.00
Penney's 6TP408	80.00
Philco T4	50.00
Raytheon T-100-1	200.00
RCA-7-BT-9J	200.00
Realtone TR-870, Satellite	65.00
Realtone TR1088	125.00
Regency TR-1, red	400.00
Regency TR-7	70.00
Ross RE-700, Micro	50.00
Silvertone 213	30.00
Sonora 610	150.00
Sony TR-8	150.00
Toshiba 3TP-315Y	75.00
Toshiba 5TR-193	175.00
Truetone DC 3090	70.00

Truetone D3614A	150.00
Victoria 602, VIP	40.00
Westinghouse H-694P8	35.00
Windsor 6T-220	80.00
York TR-121	20.00

Zenith Royal 20, plastic case, 8 transistors, chrome front grill area with vertical bars, Made in Hong Kong, AM, battery operated, 3x2⅜x1¼", M, $30.00.

Zenith Royal 56, Sun Charger	125.00
Zohar MTR-201	30.00

Railroadiana

Collecting railroad-related memorabilia has become one of America's most popular hobbies. The range of collectible items available is almost endless, considering the fact that more than 175 different railroad lines are represented. Some collectors prefer to specialize in only one, while others attempt to collect at least one item from every railway line known to have existed. For the advanced collector, there is the challenge of locating rarities from short-lived railroads; for the novice there are abundant keys, buttons, passes, and playing cards. Among the most popular specializations are dining-car collectibles — flatware, glassware, dinnerware, etc., in a wide variety of patterns and styles.

Almost anything from the Rock Island Line has become very collectible, and good lanterns are appreciating on today's market. The Denver & Rio Grande Railroad lantern manufactured by Handlan-Buck, top marked and with a red cast (embossed) melon globe, now commands about $1,400.00. Lantern prices are based on the scarcity of the railroad, the color and shape of the globe, and whether the railroad name is embossed rather than being simply acid etched. Note: Two-color lantern globes are now being reproduced.

Since we've mentioned reproductions, collectors should be made aware that there is a spittoon currently out of Taiwan that is brass, about 12" high, could be in two sections, and has a pinched waist. The wording 'Union Pacific Railroad' and a train are embossed on the front and the back. Unscrupulous dealers are passing these off as old and asking exorbitant prices. Buyer beware! To continue this sad story, railroad police badges have given the trade the jitters; so many are reproduced (so well!). Remember the 11th commandment: Know Thy Dealer. (Prices stated below are for authentic badges.)

For a more thorough study, we recommend *Railroad Collectibles, Third Revised Edition*, by Stanley L. Baker, available at your local library or bookstore. Because prices are so volatile, the best pricing sources are often monthly or quarterly 'For Sale' lists. Two you may find helpful may be ordered from Golden Spike, P.O. Box 422, Williamsville, NY 14221, and Grandpa's Depot and Caboose, 1616 17 St., Suite 267, Denver, CO 80202. Our advice for the dinnerware section comes from Shrader's Antiques (see Directory, California), while Grandpa's Depot (see Colorado) advises us for the remainder.

Key:

BL — bottom logo	SL — side logo
BS — bottom stamped	SM — side mark
FBS — full back stamp	TL — top logo
NBS — no bottom stamp	TM — top mark
NTL — no top logo	

Dinnerware

Plate, Illinois Central, Limited Service, 10", $350.00.

Ashtray, C&O, Chessie, TL, NBS, 4½" dia **95.00**
Ashtray, C&O, Silhouette, TM, BS, 7x3" **110.00**
Ashtray, C&O, Staffordshire, TL, BS, 3¾" dia **95.00**
Ashtray, N&W, Dogwood, NBS, 3¾" dia **75.00**
Ashtray, NYNH&H, Indian Tree, BS, 4¼" dia **48.00**
Bowl, berry; C&NW, Depot Ornaments, NBS, 5½" **35.00**
Bowl, berry; CMStP&P, Traveler, NBS, 5" **35.00**
Bowl, berry; GN, Oriental, NBS, 5" **52.00**
Bowl, berry; MP, Eagle, TL, BS, 5" **65.00**
Bowl, berry; SP, Prairie Mtn Wildflowers, BS, 5" **65.00**
Bowl, berry; T&P, Eagle, TL, NBS, 5½" **85.00**
Bowl, berry; UP, Historical, TL, BS, 5¼" **132.00**
Bowl, bouillon; C&O, Geo Washington, w/hdls, SL, NBS **175.00**
Bowl, bouillon; CMStP&P, Traveler, NBS, 3¾" **35.00**
Bowl, bouillon; N&W, Cavalier, SL, NBS, 3¾" **48.00**
Bowl, bouillon; RDG, Stotesbury, w/hdls, +saucer (BS) **128.00**
Bowl, bouillon; SOO, Regent, hdls, BS **125.00**
Bowl, bouillon; SP, Prairie Mtn Wildflowers, NBS, 3¾" **55.00**
Bowl, bouillon; WP, Feather River, SL, NBS, 3¾" **65.00**
Bowl, cereal; CRI&P, LaSalle, TL, BS, 6½" **110.00**
Bowl, cereal; NP, Monad, TL, NBS, 6½" **65.00**
Bowl, cereal; NYNH&H, Merchants, BS, 6½" **28.00**
Bowl, cereal; Pullman, Indian Tree, TM, NBS, 6¼" **95.00**
Bowl, cereal; SR, Piedmont, BS, 6" **35.00**
Bowl, salad; WP, Feather River, TL, NBS, 6" sq **195.00**
Bowl, soup; N&W, Cavalier, TM, NBS, 7¾" **65.00**
Butter pat, ATSF, California Poppy, BS, 3½" **110.00**
Butter pat, ATSF, California Poppy, NBS, 3½" **32.00**
Butter pat, B&O, Centenary, BS, 3½" **75.00**
Butter pat, C&O, Charlottesville, NTL, NBS, 3½" **65.00**
Butter pat, CB&Q, Violets & Daisies, BS, 3½" **110.00**
Butter pat, CB&Q, Violets & Daisies, NBS, 3½" **31.00**
Butter pat, D&H, Vermont, TL, NBS, 3½" **128.00**
Butter pat, D&RGW, Blue Adam, NBS, 3½" **28.00**
Butter pat, N&W, Cavalier, TL, NBS, 4" **100.00**
Butter pat, NYC, Hyde Park, BS, 3" sq **185.00**
Butter pat, NYNH&H, Indian Tree, BS, 3½" **235.00**
Butter pat, Pullman, Indian Tree, TM, NBS, 3½" **100.00**
Butter pat, SP, Prairie Mtn Wildflowers, NBS, 3" **100.00**
Butter pat, UP, Historical, TL, BS, 3" **265.00**
Butter pat, UP, Winged Streamliner, NBS, 3¼" **35.00**
Celery dish, NYC, Mercury, TM, BS, 9½x4½" **65.00**
Celery dish, SAL, Miami, TM, NBS, 11x5" **235.00**
Chocolate pot, ATSF, California Poppy, BS, w/lid **260.00**
Coffeepot, ATSF, Mimbreno, BS, w/lid, 5½" **275.00**
Compote, GN, Pacific Coast, 3" ped, TM, NBS, 8" **225.00**
Creamer, ATSF, California Poppy, no hdl, NBS, 3" **85.00**
Creamer, NYC, Dewitt Clinton, hdl, SL, BS, 4½" **55.00**
Creamer, PRR, Keystone, no hdl, SM, NBS, 2½" **75.00**
Creamer, Pullman, Indian Tree, no hdl, SM, NBS, 2½" **85.00**

Creamer, SP, Sunset, hdl, SL, NBS, 3½" **155.00**
Creamer, StL&SF, Denmark, hdl, NBS, 3¼" **42.00**
Cup & saucer, B&O, Centenary, BS **135.00**
Cup & saucer, C&O, Chessie, SL, NBS **175.00**
Cup & saucer, CM&StP, Olympian (Haviland), TM, NBS **110.00**
Cup & saucer, CMStP&P, Olympian (Lenox), TM, NBS **85.00**
Cup & saucer, demi; ARR, McKinley, SL, NBS **650.00**
Cup & saucer, demi; C&NW, Wild Rose, NBS **210.00**
Cup & saucer, demi; C&O, Silhouette (Martha), saucer BS **395.00**
Cup & saucer, demi; CB&Q, Violets & Daisies, NBS **65.00**
Cup & saucer, demi; PRR, Broadway, NBS **195.00**
Cup & saucer, demi; SP&S, American, NBS **85.00**
Cup & saucer, demi; UP, Challenger, TM, NBS **185.00**
Cup & saucer, demi; UP, Desert Flower, BS **72.00**
Cup & saucer, demi; UP, Winged Streamliner, TM, NBS **72.00**
Cup & saucer, FH, Trend, NBS **28.00**
Cup & saucer, GN, Mountains & Flowers, BS **135.00**
Cup & saucer, NYC, Dewitt Clinton, TM, BS **110.00**
Cup & saucer, NYC, Mercury, TL, BS **85.00**
Cup & saucer, SP, Harriman Blue, SL & TL, NBS **265.00**
Cup & saucer, SP, Prairie Mtn Wildflowers, FBS **95.00**
Cup & saucer, WP, Feather River, SL, NBS **385.00**
Egg cup, CN, Toronto, SL, NBS, dbl **160.00**
Egg cup, FEC, Mistic, NBS, dbl **42.00**
Egg cup, Pullman, Indian Tree, SM, NBS, sm **140.00**
Egg cup, UP, Desert Flower, BS, sm **60.00**
Egg cup, UP, Portland Rose, NBS, sm **285.00**
Gravy boat, ACL, Carolina, NBS, sm **12.00**
Gravy boat, CB&Q, Violets & Daisies, NBS **95.00**
Gravy boat, L&N, Green Leaf, NBS **80.00**
Gravy boat, NYC, Platinum Blue, SL, BS **110.00**
Hot food cover, CMStP&P, Galatea, NBS, 5½" **175.00**
Hot food cover, CMStP&P, Traveler, NBS **95.00**
Hot food cover, PRR, Keystone, SL, NBS, 5½" **135.00**
Ice cream shell, ATSF, Bleeding Blue, tab hdl, TL, NBS **245.00**
Ice cream shell, ATSF, Mimbreno, tab hdl, FBS **185.00**
Ice cream shell, B&A, Berkshire, tab hdl, TL, NBS **220.00**
Mustard, C&NW, Coach & Four, slotted lid, NBS, 3" **155.00**
Mustard, C&O, Geo Washington, slotted lid, SM, BS, 2¾" **240.00**
Pitcher, N&W, Dogwood, NBS, 6½" **35.00**
Plate, ATSF, Adobe, TL, NBS, 9½" **85.00**
Plate, C&NW, Flambeau, no center scene, NBS, 9½" **25.00**
Plate, C&NW, Flambeau, The 400, info on reverse, 10½" **500.00**
Plate, CMStP&P, Traveler, FBS, 9½" **185.00**
Plate, CRI&P, Golden State, TL, BS, 6" **98.00**
Plate, D&H, Champlain, TL, NBS, 9" **125.00**
Plate, divided; CMStP&P, Traveler, 9½" **185.00**
Plate, divided; SP, Prairie Mtn Wildflowers, FBS, 12x8" **145.00**
Plate, IC, Creole, TL, NBS, 7¼" **75.00**
Plate, IC, Pirate, NBS, 10" **168.00**
Plate, service; MP, State Capitols, TM, BS, 10½" **322.00**
Plate, service; MP, State Flowers, TM, BS, 10¾" **225.00**
Plate, SMStP&P, Traveler, NBS, 9½" **155.00**
Plate, SP, Montello, FBS, 6¼" **75.00**
Platter, GTW, Blue & Gold, TL, BS, 6x8½" **145.00**
Platter, KCS, Flying Crow, TL, NBS, 11x8" **585.00**
Platter, L&N, Regent, NBS, 8½x5½" **90.00**
Platter, PRR, Broadway, BS, 11½x8" **55.00**
Platter, SP, Sunset, TL, BS, 10½x7" **165.00**
Relish dish, WAB, Meridale, NBS, 7½x3½" **28.00**
Sherbet, ATSF, Mimbreno, ped ft, NBS **7.00**
Sherbet, B&O, Derby, ped ft, BS **102.00**
Sherbet, B&O, Gold Band, ped ft, NBS **15.00**
Sherbet, D&RG, Prospector, ped ft, SL, NBS **58.00**

Sherbet, UP, Winged Streamliner, ped ft, SL, NBS 48.00
Sugar bowl, ATSF, California Poppy, w/lid, NBS 112.00
Teapot, ATSF, California Poppy, NBS, w/lid 145.00
Teapot, CB&Q, Violets & Daisies, w/lid, NBS 122.00
Teapot, CRI&P, Sage Green, w/lid, SL, BS 345.00
Teapot, UP, Winged Streamliner, w/lid, SL, NBS 158.00
Tray, NYC, Dewitt Clinton, TL, BS, 8½x5½" 155.00

Glass

Ashtray, B&O, clear glass w/bl logo & Capitol dome, 4½" 25.00
Ashtray, GN, entwined wht letters, BS, 4" dia 18.00
Ashtray, Pullman, oval, fits onto passenger car wall, mk 40.00
Ashtray, RI, clear, blk bearskin logo 18.00
Ashtray, SF, wht center logo on clear, oval, 5¼" L 18.00
Bottle, milk; MOPAC, buzz saw logo, qt 60.00
Champagne, SF, Hock style, stemmed, 5" 60.00
Cocktail set, UP, mixer+2 roly poly 2½" tumblers, logo 35.00
Cordial, SF, stemmed, 4" 60.00
Cruet, GN, older frosted goat logo 165.00
Double shot, SF, str sides, weighted base, 2-oz, 2½" 50.00
Goblet, UP, stemmed, tall 18.00
Martini set, UP, frosted logo, pitcher+2 glasses+stirrer 45.00
Mug, BN, gr name, blk slogan, 1972 ....12.00
Pitcher, water; M&StL, SP fr, Albert Pick & Co, 1928 ....365.00
Playing cards, D&RGW, 53 views, M in worn box 25.00
Roly poly, EL, dtd 1969, 2¾" 10.00
Shot glass, UP, name in wht, 2½" 14.00
Tumbler, Erie, amethyst, slant sides, 3¼x3" 38.00
Tumbler, Frisco, bl logo on side, 5" 15.00
Tumbler, SF, SM, 5½x2½" 14.00
Tumbler, SR, diesel engine & Southern Serves South, 3½" 14.00
Tumbler, UP, shield logo, str sides, 4½" 10.00
Wine, IC, frosted dmn logo, stemmed 17.50
Wine, SF, Santa Fe in script, 4½" 25.00

Keys

A companion to the switch locks would be the switch keys (that fit in the same lock) or similar keys that have straight bits and open box car locks (requiring 'car' keys). Switch keys and/or car keys are brass with hollow barrels and round heads with holes for attaching to a key ring. In order to be collectible, the head must be marked with a name, initials, or a railroad with 'switch' generally designated by 'S' and 'car' as 'C' markings. Railroad, patina 'not polished,' and a manufacturer other than Adlake all affect the price and collectibility.

A new precedent was set in 1995 when a Denver and South Park 'car' key went at a Missouri auction for $2,500.00. The key was marked DSP&P (an early Colorado road that quit in 1898), brass, and had a hollow barrel and straight bit. Switch keys that only recently brought $15.00 to $17.00 are now bringing $30.00.

Switch, ATSF, Adlake 30.00
Switch, B&O, Adlake 30.00
Switch, BR, Adlake 30.00
Switch, C&N, Adlake 30.00
Switch, D&RGW, Adlake 30.00
Switch, GNRy, brass 35.00
Switch, IHB, Adlake, cut brass, NM 30.00
Switch, MKT, Adlake 30.00
Switch, MOPAC, Adlake 30.00
Switch, MOPAC, Slaymaker, brass 40.00
Switch, TH&B, Adlake 30.00

Lamps

Hand, GTW on side, steel/brass, 4 lenses, 12", VG 85.00
Inspector's, BR&P on brass plate, Dietz Ideal, VG 95.00
Inspector's, NYCS on clear globe, unmk Dietz Acme, EX 65.00
Inspector's, Wabash, Dietz Acme, unmk globe, rpt, EX 85.00
Switch stand, Armspear Mfg, 4 lenses, EX 165.00
Switch stand, unmk Adlake, sq top, bell bottom, 4 lenses 90.00
Switch stand, unmk Adlake, 4-toed, 4 lenses, lt rust 75.00
Switch stand, unmk Armspear, 2 red lenses, Pat 1915, EX 85.00
Vertical, Adlake, red & clear lenses, steel, worn pnt, sm 50.00
Wall candle, unmk, brass, removable glass chimney, 1907 ....50.00

Lanterns

Before 1920 kerosene brakemen's lanterns were made with tall globes, usually 5⅜" tall. These are the most desirable and are usually found at the top of the price scale. Short globes from 1921 through 1940 normally measure 3½" in height, except for those manufactured by Dietz, which are 4" tall. (Soon thereafter, battery brakemen's lanterns came into widespread useage; these are not popular with collectors and are generally not railroad marked.)

All should be marked with the name or initials of the railroad. Look on the top, the top apron, or the bell base (if it has one). Globes may be found in these colors (listed in order of popularity): clear, red, amber, aqua, cobalt, and two-color.

Lantern, marked Wm Porter Maker, H&J Sangsters Patent June 1851, brass, with original presentation globe with etched steam locomotive engraving, 13", M, $2,500.00.

AT&SF, Adlake Reliable, mk clear 5⅜" globe, Pat 1909, EX 155.00
B&O, Adams & Westlake, twist-off pot, Pat 1895, VG 125.00
BR&P, Dietz #39 std w/clear tall mk globe, EX 400.00
C of G, Adams & Westlake Adlake No 100 Kero, Pat 1913, EX .150.00
C&A, Adams & Westlake, mk 5⅜" globe, rprs, Pat 1909 ....150.00
C&EI, Adams & Westlake, etched red 5⅜" globe, cleaned 175.00
C&IM, Handlan, w/Adlake 300 pot/burner, red 4½" globe, '28 ...65.00
CCC&StL, Adams & Westlake bell bottom, Pat 1909, complete ..150.00
CRR on dome, Adlake Reliable, red tall unmk globe 365.00
CStPM&O, Adams & Westlake, mk clear 5⅜" globe, rprs, 1909 ..195.00
D&H, Adlake & Westlake, fancy logo on clear globe, 1909, EX ..300.00
D&H, TM on apron, bell bottom, mk clear globe, tall, complete 350.00
D&H on apron, Adlake Reliable, clear globe, tall, EX 350.00
D&I, Adams & Westlake Reliable, clear Macbeth 5⅜" globe 265.00
D&RG, Dietz, bell bottom, wood hdl, clear etched globe 250.00
D&SL, Adams & Westlake, TM, tall unmk melon globe, Pat 1909 .350.00
EJ&E, Adlake Reliable, bell bottom, Pat 1913, EX 185.00
GN, Adams & Westlake Reliable, mk clear globe, Pat 1913, EX ..175.00
GT, Adams & Westlake Reliable, red Dietz Vulcan globe, VG 85.00
ICR, ET Wright, clear 5½" globe, Pat 1908, EX 125.00

KCS, Adlake Reliable, bell bottom, clear 5⅜" globe, 1913 ....**250.00**
L&A, Handlan, tall flat dome, amber 4½" globe, EX **85.00**
L&N, Dressel, unmk clear globe, flat verticals, 3½" globe **50.00**
LV, Armspear, red cast 6" globe, complete, EX **165.00**
ME Central, Dietz Vesta, bl tall unmk globe **285.00**
MOPAC, Adams & Westlake, red 5⅜" globe, Pat 1895, EX **175.00**
N&W, Armspear, red cast 5⅜" globe, Pat 1913, complete **165.00**
NYC, Dietz #6 bell bottom, 6" clear globe, dings/pinhole **65.00**
NYNH&H, Dressel, unmk clear 3¼" globe, flat verticals, EX **75.00**
PC&StL, brass top w/twist-off bell, clear unmk globe, VG **150.00**
PRR Keystone, Adlake Kero, red K globe, Pat 1923, EX **65.00**
PRR Keystone Casey, clear tall mk globe, Pat 1903 ....**275.00**
RI, Adams & Westlake, mk apron, blk pnt, tall globe, Pat 1909 ...**250.00**
RI, Adams & Westlake Adams, mk red cast globe, Pat 1909, EX .**185.00**
SF, Adams & Westlake, mk 5⅜" globe, Pat 1895, VG **150.00**
SF, emb mk on bell bottom, clear mk globe, tall, G **300.00**
SPCo, Dietz Steel Clad, clear mold-blown 6" globe, complete ...**350.00**
StL&SW, Handlan-Buck, dome top, vertical ribs, clear globe **250.00**
TX & Pacific, Adlake Kero, short red mk globe, TM **80.00**
Unmk, Adlake Reliable, bell bottom, compact fr, Pat 1913 ....**60.00**
Unmk, Dietz No 39 Standard, bell bottom, Vulcan 5⅜" globe **60.00**
WC, Adams & Westlake, Soo Line 5⅜" red etched globe, EX ...**200.00**

Linens and Uniforms

Apron, CA Zephyr printed over Pullman logo **17.00**
Blanket, Burlington Rte, tan wool w/maroon logo, twin sz **275.00**
Blanket, Pullman, bl-gray wool, EX **175.00**
Blanket, Pullman, cinnamon, full sz, EX **160.00**
Blanket, Pullman, cinnamon, woven-in logo, twin sz **125.00**
Blanket, Pullman, cross-stitch pattern, wool, EX **150.00**
Blanket, Soo Line, wool, lg logo **225.00**
Headrest cover, SCL, yel/gr, beach scene **17.50**
Headrest cover, SR, khaki, lg logo, button-down style **17.00**
Jacket, cook's, C&NW, w/logo on front, M **15.00**
Jacket, waiter's, NYC, Empire State Express, wht w/bl lapels **18.00**
Napkin, C&O, bl thread on wht, 18" sq **7.00**
Napkin, FW&DC, wht w/red sewn letters in corner **10.00**
Napkin, RG, wht on wht, speed letters, G- **7.00**
Napkin, SF, old script, wht on wht, 19½" sq **10.00**
Napkin, UP, yel, bl or pk, ea **7.00**
Pants, waiter's, Milwaukee, purple stripe, EX **12.00**
Pants, waiter's, RG, yel stripe, EX **5.00**
Pillowcase, Pullman, overstamped BN, twin sz **10.00**
Sheet, CA Zephyr imprinted over Pullman, berth sz **15.00**
Sheet, Pullman, twin sz, EX **12.00**
Tablecloth, Amtrak, wht, stamped NRPC, 31x45" **10.00**
Tablecloth, Burlington Rte, wht-on-wht logo, 43x45" **35.00**
Tablecloth, FEC Ry Car 90 (Henry Flager's car), 65x67" **50.00**
Tablecloth, NYC, 2-tone rust w/wht letters, 40x43" **18.00**
Tablecloth, RG, plum color, speed letters in corner, 40" sq **18.00**
Tablecloth, SCL, wht on wht logo, VG **25.00**
Tablecloth, UP, pk, 31½x46", EX **12.00**
Towel, CA Zephyr, red stripe, G **15.00**
Towel, dish drying; BR, bl on wht, G **10.00**
Towel, hand; BR, EX **10.00**

Locks

Brass switch locks (pre-1920) were made in two styles: heart-shaped and Keen Kutter style. Values for the heart-shaped locks are determined to a great extent by the railroad represented and just how its name appears on the lock. Most in demand are those with large embossed letters; if the letters are small and incised, demand is minimal.

For instance, one from the Union Pacific line (even with heavy embossed letters) may go for only $45.00, while the same from the D&RG railroad could go easily sell for $250.00. Old Keen Kutter styles (brass with a 'pointy' base) from Colorado & Southern and Denver & Rio Grande could range from $600.00 to $1,200.00.

Steel switch locks (circa 1920 on) with the initials of the railroad incised in small letters — for example BN, L&H, and PRR — are usually valued at $20.00 to $28.00.

Brass heart-shaped locks, PRRCO, Fraim, 1911, Keystone on shackle, $150.00; N&WRy Co, FS Hdw. Co., 1924, $100.00.

C of GA, Adlake, steel, w/chain, EX **27.50**
C&W RY, Handlan Buck, brass, heart shape, early, +unmk key .**200.00**
CM&StP RR, brass, heart shape, early, +mk brass key **155.00**
CRI&P Signal Use Not Oil But Use Plenty Graphite **45.00**
D&RG, brass, scarce, sm, +sm brass key **400.00**
SCL, Master Lock Co, heavy steel, w/chain & key, unused **65.00**
SP, Yale & Towne padlock **50.00**
VGN, steel, w/chain & key **88.00**

Silverplate

The value of a hollow ware item is affected by where the logo and/or railroad name was stamped; a side-marked piece is much preferred to one with the mark on the bottom. Note: Some railroad silver from early private cars has recently surfaced. Marks such as Denver & Salt Lake car 101 (called the 'Pheasant') and FECRy's 'Alicia' (Henry Flagler's car) are good examples and might today be considered 'museum quality' by railroadiana buffs.

Bowl, melon; MOPAC, BS, 1946, 7½" dia **75.00**
Bowl, MOPAC, deep, BS, 7" dia, EX **55.00**
Bread tray, MOPAC, Reed & Barton, BS, 13" L **85.00**
Butter icer, Pullman, Meriden, BS, early, 10" dia **250.00**
Coffeepot, T&P, Reed & Barton, BS, 10-oz **150.00**
Compote, T&P, BS, 4½x6½" **225.00**
Condiment holder, Frisco, 3-hole, Reed & Barton **85.00**
Creamer, MOPAC, flip lid, 1927 BS, 6-oz **75.00**
Creamer, T&P, pagoda finial, Reed & Barton, BS, 10-oz **125.00**
Finger bowl, GN, pierced sides, dtd 1924 ....**75.00**
Finger bowl, SF, hand chased, emb florals, 1910s, 4½" **350.00**
Finger bowl, UP, attached tray, 1947 ....**95.00**
Fork, cocktail; CCC&StL, Commonwealth **22.00**
Fork, place; BR, Modern **12.00**
Fork, place; Fred Harvey, Albany, International **18.00**
Fork, place; Pullman, Roosevelt, BS/TM **15.00**
Fork, place; UP, Savoy, International, BS **20.00**
Gravy boat, UP, 4-oz, G **75.00**
Gravy ladle, Pullman, Roosevelt, 7½" L **100.00**
Hot food cover, UP, BS, 1951, 5½" **95.00**
Knife, luncheon; PA RR, Broadway, TM **15.00**
Knife, luncheon; Pullman, Roosevelt **15.00**
Knife, place; BR, Belmont **15.00**
Knife, place; BR, Modern **12.00**
Knife, place; CA Zephyr **15.00**

Knife, place; SF, Cromwell 18.00
Knife, viande; New Haven, Hutton, TM 15.00
Menu holder, ACL, Deco-style piercing, SM/BS, 1940 ....125.00
Menu holder, UP, half-moon shape, BS, 1954 ....125.00
Mustard holder, UP, w/glass insert, BS, 1948, 4-oz 85.00
Place fork, ACL, Zephyr 12.00
Place set, Fred Harvey, Albany, knife/fork/spoon, BS 40.00
Place set, SF, Albany, knife/fork/spoon, BS 40.00
Sherbet, GN, ped ft, 1946 ....100.00
Sherbet, New Haven, stemmed, BS, 4" 50.00
Spoon, demitasse; NYC, Century, BS 20.00
Spoon, grapefruit; MP, Devon, Wallace, TM 15.00
Spoon, iced tea; BR, Modern 12.00
Spoon, iced tea; CA Zephyr 15.00
Spoon, iced tea; MP, Century 12.00
Spoon, iced tea; NYC, Century 12.00
Spoon, iced tea; SF, Albany 15.00
Spoon, serving; BR, Belmont, TM 18.00
Spoon, serving; SF, Albany 15.00
Spoon, serving; UP, Westfield, Meriden, BS 20.00
Spoon, soup; CA Zephyr 15.00
Spoon, soup; GN, Hutton, TM 15.00
Sugar bowl, BR, pagoda finial, R&B, 6-oz 125.00
Sugar bowl, MOPAC, compote style, BS, Wallace, w/lid, 9-oz 95.00
Sugar bowl, Pullman, w/lid, BS, 1925, 7-oz 150.00
Sugar bowl, Pullman, w/lid, BS, 1933, 10-oz 75.00
Syrup, UP, attached tray, 1947, 4-oz 95.00
Tray, change; Milwaukee, premerger BS, Wallace, 12-oz, 6¼" 65.00
Tray, change; UP, BS, 1946, 6½" dia 95.00
Tray, MOPAC, buzz saw logo, silver on copper, 1937 BS, 11" 55.00
Tray, Pullman, oval, BS, 1938, 10" 85.00
Tray, Pullman, Wallace, BS, 1924, 10", G 50.00
Tray, RI, Wallace, BS, 1927, 12", G 50.00
Tray, serving; Pullman, dtd 1929, 14x11" 125.00
Tray, T&P, eagle logo on top, BS, 1946, 7" dia 125.00
Tureen, soup; RI, peaked finial, Wallace, BS, 1927, +tray 175.00

Miscellaneous

Annual passes are skyrocketing in popularity (as opposed to trip or one-time passes, which are not very desirable in the field of pass collecting). Their values are contingent upon the specific railroad, its length of run (whether it was a short one or a major line), and their appearance. Many were tiny works of art lettered with fancy calligraphy and decorated with vignettes.

Timetables are climbing rapidly in popularity, and pins with the names of railroad companies are very good right now. On the other hand, 'Brotherhood' pins (or any item) hold little interest for collectors. Watch for reproduction signs; most are small in size, about 5" x 12", on aged cardboard under glass in black frames. These will read 'Public Telephone,' 'Waiting Room,' etc.

Badge, Berkshire RR Street Railway, blue enameling on nickel silver, $85.00.

Badge, Amtrak Conductor, gold w/color logo 30.00
Badge, breast; CCC&StL Police Sergeant, silver eagle on seal ...285.00
Badge, C&S Police, silver w/dk bl enamel & eagle atop, 2x3" 350.00
Badge, CC&StL (Big 4) Police, silver w/fancy base & eagle, G ..285.00
Badge, CRI&P Police, silver star w/knobs, blk letters 125.00
Badge, employee ID: Ry Express Agency, celluloid, '20s, 1½" 5.00
Badge, Engineer, incised letters in nickel, pin-bk, 3" L 35.00
Badge, Erie RR Police, silver shield w/blk letters 225.00
Badge, hat; D&RGW Parlor Car Conductor, anodized gold w/blk, M .70.00
Badge, hat; D&RGW Pullman Conductor, anodized gold w/blk, NM .65.00
Badge, hat; D&RGW Trainman, silver/blk, M 85.00
Badge, hat; FJ&G Motorman, brass patina, scarce 125.00
Badge, NP Freight Conductor, blk enamel on silver 85.00
Badge, Pullman Porter, emb blk letters on anodized silver, G 65.00
Badge, Reading Police, silver w/lg eagle atop, screw bk 225.00
Badge, Rio Grand Southern Police, silver w/blk, 1¾x2½" 450.00
Badge, SAL Trainman emb in brass on anodized blk, M 75.00
Badge, SF Baggage Man, silver w/cross logo & blk pnt 65.00
Badge, Sleeping Car Porter emb in brass on anodized brass, M 95.00
Badge, Trainman, blk letters on nickel, screw-bk, ¾x3", M 28.00
Baggage label, Burlington Rte, Serving Wartime Am, WWII, 3½x4" .20.00
Baggage label, C&NW, employee-owned logo on blk, 2x3" 5.00
Baggage label, SP, orange/red peel-off, 2½" 5.00
Baggage label, Streamlined Zephyr, lt bl/silver, 3¼" dia 10.00
Bandana, Union Pacific Golden Spike Days 25.00
Bench, C&M & B&M pierced in oak bks, 37x92", VG orig 400.00
Bill, freight; NV Copper Belt, 1930, 5x8" 5.00
Blotter, Blue Valley Creamery, locomotive & cars, 3x5" 10.00
Blotter, BR, Glacier National Park, 4x9", M 10.00
Blotter, Milwaukee, lg diesel #79A in bl, 3½x6½", EX 10.00
Blotter, MOPAC, red buzz saw logo, 3x9", unused 10.00
Blotter, NP, Great Big Baked Potato, baked potato form 22.00
Blotter, Santa Fe, Serving Am in War & Peace, 4x8¾", M 15.00
Blueprint, Rio Grand Western, driving springs, 1902, 9x12" 5.00
Blueprint, UP Depot building, CO, 1972, 24x27" 10.00
Book, Basalt, C&R Danielson, 1965, w/jacket, sgn/#d edition 75.00
Book, Colorado Midland, Cafky, 1965, w/jacket, sgn/#d edition .175.00
Book, Colorado Road, H Wagner, author sgn, M w/dust jacket ..150.00
Book, Giant's Ladder, Boner, 1962, w/map of 1924 D&SLRy 100.00
Book, Hear the Train Blow, Beebe/Clegg, 1952, w/dust jacket 45.00
Book, Mansions on Rails, Beebe, 1959, 382-pg, w/jacket 125.00
Book, Pike's Peak by Rail, Hollenbeck/Russell, 1962, w/jacket 15.00
Book, Portrait of Silver Lady, 1972, w/jacket & dust box 195.00
Book, Railroad Men, E Hubbard/Roycrofters, 1913, 8-pg, 4x5½" .25.00
Book, Rails Around Gold Hill, Cafky, 1955, w/jacket & map 175.00
Book, Rails That Climb, Bollingo, 1950, 402-pg, w/jacket 50.00
Book, Silver San Juan, Ferrel, 1973, w/jacket, sgn/#d edition 200.00
Book, Stairway to the Stars, Abbot, 160-pg, w/map packet 75.00
Book, Switzerland Trail, Crossen, 1962, w/jacket/maps, sgn/#d ..150.00
Booklet, B&O, Regulations of Relief Dept, 1889, 63-pg, 4½x7" ..10.00
Booklet, C&S, Picturesque CO, 1910, 7x10", M 40.00
Booklet, CM, Through the Rockies, 27 pictures, 7x10" 75.00
Booklet, RI, CO...Under Turquoise Sky, scenic cover, 1921, 6x9" ...30.00
Booklet, Swiss Federal Railway, w/map, 1932, 49-pg, 5x8" 7.50
Bottle, seltzer; Fred Harvey, silvered spritzer top, 12" 155.00
Brochure, BR, Nebraska Zephyr, brn/blk, 1947, 3x6" 10.00
Brochure, C&A joint w/MOPAC & T&P, bargain fares, 1936, 3x6" .7.00
Brochure, C&S, Rocky Mtn Nat'l Park, 1916, 20-pg, 4x8" 40.00
Brochure, D&RGW, Engine 168 Presented to CO Springs, 1938, 6x9" ..10.00
Brochure, D&RGW, Evolution of Power, 1923, 4-pg, 5x9" 10.00
Brochure, D&RGW, Through the Rockies..., 78-pg, 8x10" 10.00
Brochure, Erie RR 100th Anniversary, 1951, M 15.00
Brochure, Fred Harvey, Indian Detour, bl cover, 1929, 9x14" 35.00
Brochure, Olympian, red/blk, shows schedules, 1941, 3x6" 10.00

Brochure, Ranier Nat'l Park, color cover, 1938, 4x8" **17.00**
Brochure, RG Motorway, Pike's Peak, ca 1923, 4x8", EX **10.00**
Builder's plate, D&SL, emb letters on CI, 1947, 7x31" **150.00**
Bumper sticker, WP, WP Lives, silver/orange, 4x5", unused **5.00**
Calendar, NP, Gentle Boxcar, 2-sided, 1964, 6x8" **5.00**
Calendar, PA RR, Army/Navy game, 1955, NM **90.00**
Calendar, SP, 12 blk/wht locomotive pictures, 1987, 10x12" **10.00**
Calendar top, CB&Q, Burlington Zephyr, 1934 ....**75.00**
Chisel, C&NW, 18" **10.00**
Coal scuttle, D&RG, galvanized **75.00**
Coat hanger, Pullman, wooden **12.00**
Contract/lease, CM, printed booklet form, 1899, 15-pg, 5x8" **15.00**
Coupons, bond; Rio Grand Southern, 1900, 1x2½" **5.00**
Dater die, RG, brass, complete w/orig dater machine **250.00**
Flyer, SP, Automated Buffet Car, yel sheet, dbl sided, 5x6" **4.25**
Fusee box, UP, galvanized, red/blk pnt, 24x18½x5", EX **50.00**
Globe, BR, clear, tall **67.50**
Globe, cobalt, top & bottom flange, fits early Dietz, 5" **50.00**
Globe, unmk, gr, short **40.00**
Hammock, berth; gr cord & mesh, 61", EX **65.00**
Hat, Amtrak, w/gold Conductor badge, M **60.00**
Lapel pin, CO & Southern, brass skeleton **25.00**
Lapel pin, Erie logo on brass **22.50**
Magazine, IL Central Gulf News, 1972, 33-pg, 9x12", EX **3.50**
Magazine, Railway Journal, 1943, 25-pg, EX **7.00**
Magazine cover, IL Central, brn leather, 9x10", G **50.00**
Magazine cover, IL Central, Panama Ltd, brn leather, 9x12", G ..**50.00**
Map, BYD&RG, Denver, 1909, 3¼x9", opens to 14" **20.00**
Map, Mexican Centry RR, 1903, 22x27", M **70.00**
Map, Moffat Road, 1-sheet, 1911, 9x15", VG **15.00**
Map, Pacific Electric, blk/wht, 1930, 17x24" **15.00**
Menu, D&RG, Around the Circle color scene, 1915, 5½x10" **50.00**
Menu, Fred Harvey, CA Limited, 1931, 5½x8", EX **30.00**
Menu, Fred Harvey, Final Rail Fan Tour, 1938, 9x12" **25.00**
Menu, Rio Grande, Broiler Special, purple, 1950s **10.00**
Menu, Silverton Northern, heavy wht stock, 5½x9" **40.00**
On-board card, SP, Pacific Limited, economy lunches, 3¼x5" **10.00**
Paperweight, CM&StP, locomotive form, 6" **145.00**
Pass, annual; ATSF, 1912 ....**15.00**
Pass, annual; ATSF Eastern Lines, 1910 ....**15.00**
Pass, annual; B&O, 1913 ....**15.00**
Pass, annual; C&A, 1910 ....**15.00**
Pass, annual; CB&Q, 1910 ....**15.00**
Pass, annual; Grand Rapids & IN, 1917 ....**15.00**
Pass, annual; TX & Gulf Ry, bl, emb blk letters, 1909 ....**45.00**
Pass, Fred Harvey, Eating House, reduced employee rate, 1921 ....**22.00**
Pass, presidential; CM&PS, 1911 ....**17.00**
Pass, presidential; GN, printed, JR Hulen Vice President, '37 ......**17.00**
Photo, D&RGW, Roosevelt banner on observation car, 2½x3½" .**10.00**
Photo, President T Roosevelt in Royal Gorge, GL Beam, 1905 ....**65.00**
Postcard, Fred Harvey **2.50**
Poster, CO Midland, Pan Am-Pacific & Canadian/CA Expo ad, M ..**25.00**
Poster, D&RG, $20 round trip: Denver to Salt Lake, 10x13½" **25.00**
Ruler, D&RGW, prospector on clear plastic **10.00**
Scales, Ry Express, CI, weighs up to 60 lbs, scarce, 1950s **150.00**
Schedule/brochure, C&NW MN 400, orange cover, 1937, 4x8" ..**10.00**
Shipping order, CM, red circle logo, 1910, unissued, 3½x4½" **10.00**
Sign, Baggage Room, rolled steel, mc pnt, 12x21" **175.00**
Sign, car; Dining Car Is Opposite Direction, 5x7" **17.00**
Sign, car; Food Services This Way/Other Way, 2-sided, 5x7" **10.00**
Sign, car; Meal Service Car Forward, w/steel grommet, 8x9" **10.00**
Sign, car; Quiet Is Requested/Have You Forgotten, 5x9" **15.00**
Sign, Diner, stainless steel, blk letters, 2¼x14", EX **45.00**
Sign, Railway Express, mc pnt on tin, 6x40", EX **125.00**

Sign, RI, heavy steel, lt wear & rust, 11x27" **45.00**
Sign, Rock Island Hotel, pnt wood, 2-sided, 14x45", EX **250.00**
Spittoon, NC&StL, CI, 5½x9" dia, EX **115.00**
Stove, caboose; D&RGW, complete w/grates & mk lids, NM **800.00**
Sugar pack, Fred Harvey logo, ind **2.00**
Swizzle stick, GN, wht plastic w/bl letters **2.00**
Swizzle stick, Grand Central Terminal, bl glass, 6½" **10.00**
Ticket, CC&O, 4-part, paper, passenger's, 2¼x10¼" **5.50**
Ticket, Silverton Northern, hard stock, 1¼x2¼" **7.00**
Tie, Amtrak, maroon w/blk & wht logos **5.00**
Time certificate, Silver City, Deming & Pacific, 1893, 3x6" **20.00**
Timetable, B&W-D&RG, Curecanti logo, 1918 ....**15.00**
Timetable, CA Zephyr, bright orange cover, 1949, 4-pg **20.00**
Timetable, Cedar Rapids & IA City, blk/wht, 3½x6½" **5.00**
Timetable, D&RG joint w/WP, dk red cover, 1925, 54-pg **20.00**
Timetable, D&RGW joint w/WP, dk gr cover, 1911, 10", VG **50.00**
Timetable, Frere Marquette, gr, 1950, VG **10.00**
Timetable, IL Central, 1923, EX **17.50**
Timetable, Queen & Crescent Rte, 1902, EX **47.50**
Timetable, RI, 2 Express Trains Ea Way, horseshoe logo, 1886 ....**75.00**
Timetable, SF Big System, KS City via SF Rte, blk/wht, 1888, EX ...**50.00**
Timetable, Southwest Limited, blk/wht, 1948, EX **10.00**
Timetable, Suburban West, blk/wht, 1939, 3x6" **5.00**
Timetable, UP, Overland Rte in shield logo, 1906, VG **48.00**
Timetable, Wabash, mc flag logo, 1941, G **10.00**
Timetable/brochure, RGW, bl cover, dmn logo, 1899, 38-pg, EX ..**100.00**
Toilet paper holder, UP, silvered metal, pre-1935, EX **65.00**
Toothpick, Fred Harver signature logo on wrapper **2.00**
Uniform, conductor's, IL Traction System, pre-1937, EX **175.00**
View book, D&SL, Over the Moffat Road..., 1906, 10x15", VG ..**40.00**
Voucher, treasurer's, Denver, Leadville & Gunnison, 1898, 7x8" ..**10.00**
Whistle, brass, 3-chime, CI pigtail, Pat 1877, 18½x5½" dia **665.00**

Razors

As straight razors gain in popularity, prices of those razors also increase. This carries with it a lure of investment possibilities which can encourage the novice or speculator to make purchases that may later prove to be unwise. We recommend that before investing serious money in razors, you become familiar with the elements which make a razor valuable. As with other collectibles, there are specific traits which are desirable and which have a major impact on the price of a piece.

The following information is based on the book *The Standard Guide to Razors* by Roy Ritchie and Ron Stewart (available from R&C Books, P.O. Box 151, Combs, KY 41729, @ $9.95 +$2.50 S&H, autographed). It describes the elements most likely to influence a razor's collector value and their system of calculating that value. (Their book is a valuable reference guide to both the casual and serious collector of razors.)

There are four major factors which determine a razor's collector value. These are: the brand and country of origin, the handle material, the art work found on the handles or blades, and the condition of the razor. Ritchie and Stewart freely admit that there are other factors that may come into play with some collectors, but these are the major players in determining value. They have devised a system of evaluation which is based on these four factors.

The most important factor is the value placed on the brand and country of origin. This is the price of a common razor made by (or for) a particular company. It has plain handles, probably made of plastic, no art work except perhaps a simple blade etch and is in collectible condition. It is the beginning value. Hundreds of these values are provided in the 'Listings of Companies and Base Values' chapter in the book.

The second category is that of handle material. This covers a wide range of materials, from fiber on the low end to ivory on the high end. The collector needs to be able to identify the different handle materials when he sees them. This often takes some practice, since there are some very good plastics that can mimic ivory quite successfully. Also, the difference between genuine celluloid and plastic can become significant when determining value. A detailed chart of these values is supplied in the book. The listing below can be used as a general guide.

The third category is the most subjective. Nevertheless, it is an extremely important factor in determining value. This category is artwork, which can include everything from logo art to carving and sculpture. It may range from highly ornate to tastefully correct. Blade etching as well as handle artistry are to be considered. Perhaps what some call the 'gotta have it' or the 'neatness' factors properly fall into this category. You must determine just where your razor falls in evaluating it in this category. Again, this book provides a more complete listing of considerations than is used here.

Finally, the condition is factored in. The book's scales run from 'parts' (10% +) to 'Good' (150% +/-). Average (100% +/-) is classified as 'Collectible.'

Samplings from charts:

Chart A: Companies and Base Value:

Abercrombie & Finch, NY	11.00
Aerial, USA	20.00
Boker, Henri & Co, Germany	12.00
Brick, F, England	9.00
Case Mfg Co, Spring Valley, NY	35.00
Chores, James	8.00
Dahlgren, CW; Sweden	12.00
Diane, Japan	10.00
Electric Co, NY	14.00
ERN, Germany	11.00
Faultless, Germany	10.00
Fox Cutlery, Germany	8.00
Golden Rule Cutlery, Chicago	11.00
Griffon XX, Germany	9.00
Henckels, Germany	15.00
Holley Mfg Co CT	27.00
International Cutlery Co NY/Germany	8.00
IXL, England	14.00
Jay, John; NY	10.00
KaBar, Union Cut Co, USA	28.00
Kanner, J; Germany	6.00
Kern, R&W; Canada/England	9.00
LeCoeltre, Jacque; Switzerland	12.00
Levering Razor Co, NY/Germany	18.00
McIntosh & Heather, OH	12.00
Merit Import Co, Germany	7.00
National Cut Co, OH	11.00
Oxford Razor Co, Germany	10.00
Palmer Brothers, Savannah, GA	20.00
Primble, John; India Steel Works, Louisville, KY	22.00
Queen City, NY	30.00
Quigley, Germany	8.00
Rattler Razor Co, USA	25.00
Robeson Cut Co, USA	25.00
Salamander Works, Germany	11.00
Soderein, Ekilstuna, Sweden	11.00
Taylor, LM; Cincinnati, OH	14.00
Tower Brand, Germany	10.00
Ulmer, Germany	10.00
US Barber Supply, TX	11.00
Vinnegut Hdw Co, IN	11.00

Vogel, ED; PA	8.00
Wade & Butcher, England	24.00
Weis, JH; Supply House, Louisville, KY	15.00
Yankee Cutlery Co, Germany	11.00
Yazbek, Lahod, OH	9.00
Zacour Bros, Germany	8.00
Zepp, Germany	7.00

Chart B, as described below, is an abbreviated version of the handle materials list in *The Standard Guide to Razors*. It is an essential category in the use of the appraisal system developed by the authors.

Ivory	550%
Tortoise Shell	500%
Pearl	400%
Stag	400%
Bone	300%
Celluloid	250%
Compostion	150%
Plastic	100%

Chart C deals with the artistic value of the razor. As pointed out earlier, this is a very subjective area. It takes study to determine what is good and what is not. Taste can also play a significant role in determining the value placed on the artistic merit of a razor. The range is from superior to nonexistent. Categories generally are divided as follows:

Superior	550%
Good	400%
Average	300%
Minimal	200%
Plain	100%
Nonexistant	0%

Chart D is also very subjective. It determines the condition of the razor. You must judge accurately if the appraisal system is to work for you.

Good 150%

Does not have to be factory mint to fall within this cagegory. However, there can be no visible flaws if it is to be calculated at 150%.

Collectible 100%

May have some flaws that do not greatly detract from the artwork or finish.

Parts 10%

Unrepairable, valuable as salvageable parts.

Razors may fall within any of these categories, ie. collectible + 112%.

Now to determine the value of your razor, multiply A times B, then multiply A times C. Add your two answers and multiply this sum times D. The answer you get is your collector value. See the example below.

(a) Brand and Origin Base Value	(b) Handle Material % Value	(c) Artwork % Value	(d) Condition % Value	(e) Collector Value
Wade & Butcher England $24.00	Iridescent Pearl Handles 24 x 400% $96.00	Carved handles 24 x 350% $84.00	Cracked handle at pin Collectible- 80%	$96+$84=$180 $180 x 80%= **$144.00**

Reamers

Reamers have been made in hundreds of styles and colors and by as many manufacturers. Their purpose is to extract the juices from lemons, oranges, and grapefruits. The largest producer of glass reamers was McKee, who pressed their products from many types of glass — custard; delphite and Chalaine blue; opaque white; Skokie green; black; caramel and white opalescent; Seville yellow; and transparent pink, green, and clear. Among these, the black and the caramel opalescents are the most valuable.

The Fry Glass Company also made reamers that are today very collectible. The Hazel Atlas Crisscross orange reamer in pink often brings in excess of $300.00; the same in blue, $275.00. Hocking produced a light blue orange reamer and in the same soft hue, a two-piece reamer and measuring cup combination. Both are considered rare and very valuable with currently quoted estimates at $400.00 and up for the former and $800.00 and up for the latter. In addition to the colors mentioned, red glass examples — transparent or slag — are rare and costly.

Among the most valuable ceramic reamers are those made by American potteries. The Spongeband reamer by Red Wing is valued in excess of $500.00; Coorsite reamers with gold or silver trim are worth $300.00 and up. Figurals are popular — Mickey Mouse and John Bull may bring $600.00 to $1,000.00. Others range from $55.00 to $350.00. Fine china one- and two-piece reamers are also very desirable and command very respectable prices.

A word about reproductions: A series of limited edition reamers is being made by Edna Barnes of Uniontown, Ohio. These are all marked with a 'B' in a circle. Other repoductions have been made from old molds. The most important of these are: Anchor Hocking two-piece two-cup measure and top, Gillespie one-cup measure with reamer top, Westmoreland with flattened handle, Westmoreland four-cup measure embossed with orange and lemons, Duboe (hand-held darning egg), and Easley's diamonds one-piece.

Our advisor for this category is Dee Long; she is listed in the Directory under Illinois. For more information concerning reamers and reproductions, contact our advisor or the National Reamer Collectors Association (see Clubs, Newsletters, and Catalogs). Be sure to include an SASE when requesting information.

Ceramic

Puddinhead figural, yellow and green hat, 6¼", $150.00.

Baby's Orange, orange shape, 2 hdls, child's, 2-pc	150.00
Clown figural, gr/orange/blk/wht, Japan, 7½"	80.00
Clown figural, maroon/gr/blk/wht, Japan, 6½"	75.00
Clown figural, purple/bl/wht, 6"	50.00
Cottage form, tan w/gr trim, Japan, 5½"	60.00
Cowboy tumbler w/reamer, no hdl	300.00
Duck figural cup w/reamer top, decal, Japan, 2¾"	85.00
Elephant figural, Japan, 2-pc, 4¼"	200.00
Grapefruit shape, yel, lg, 3-pc	120.00

Jack & Jill, 2 hdls, child's	100.00
Leaf base, gr & tan w/orange trim, brn hdl, 4¼"	40.00
Mexican w/cactus figural, Japan	250.00
Orange form, gr leaves, Japan, 4½"	42.50
Orange shape, clown-head reamer, 3-pc	120.00
Pear form, wht w/gr leaves & gold	58.00
Pear form, yel & orange w/gr leaves, Japan, 4½"	50.00
Pig clown figural	250.00
Pitcher form, bl & wht w/cows, 5", 2-pc	125.00
Pitcher form, floral, Nippon, 3", 2-pc	175.00
Pitcher form, floral design, 5", 2-pc	60.00
Pitcher form, rust leaves, dk bl trim, 3½"	45.00
Pitcher form, yel lustre, 4"	40.00
Royal Rudolstadt, floral, 2-pc	200.00
Simple 2-spout style, wht, France, 3¼"	20.00
Smiley face, orange	50.00
Teapot form, child on horse, Goebel, baby's	110.00
3 chicks w/umbrella, 2 hdls, child's, 2-pc	100.00

Glass

Anchor Hocking, gr, Circle, pitcher w/reamer top	70.00
Anchor Hocking, gr, orange reamer, loop hdl	20.00
Anchor Hocking, gr clambroth, tab hdl	125.00
Cambridge, cobalt, sm tab hdl	300.00
Cambridge, crystal, sm tab hdl	25.00
Child's, pnt dog, 2-pc	95.00
Easley's, wht opal, sq	200.00
Federal, amber, tab hdl	15.00
Federal, amber, 6-sided cone, vertical hdl	275.00
Federal, pk, ribbed sides, loop hdl	30.00
Fenton, gr opaque pitcher/reamer	800.00
Fenton, red, pitcher w/reamer top	1,100.00
Fleur-de-Lis, milk glass, emb lettering	85.00
Glasbake, crystal, McKee on hdl	75.00
Hazel Atlas, cobalt, Crisscross	275.00
Hazel Atlas, gr, pitcher, mk A&J, 4-cup	35.00
Hazel Atlas, gr, pitcher w/reamer top, 2-cup	30.00
Hazel Atlas, yel, pitcher w/reamer top, 2-cup	200.00
Jeannette, delphite, sm	75.00
Jeannette, pk, Hex Optic, bucket form	45.00
Jeannette, ultramarine, Jennyware	110.00
Lindsay, pk	400.00
Orange Juice Extractor, blk	375.00
Paden City, pk, Party Line, cocktail shaker w/reamer top	65.00
Paden City, pk, pitcher w/reamer top	85.00
Radnt, crystal	115.00
RE-GO, wht opal	650.00
Sunkist, caramel butterscotch	325.00
Sunkist, lt pk	60.00
Sunkist, milk glass, Westmoreland Glass	25.00
Sunkist, Seville yel	55.00
Sunkist, Thatcher Glass Co, milk glass	35.00
Sunkist Junior, clambroth, mechanical	75.00
US Glass, milk glass, pitcher w/reamer top, 2-cup	150.00
US Glass, pk, pitcher set, 3-pc	275.00
US Glass, yel, pitcher form	700.00
Valencia, milk glass, emb lettering	100.00

Records

Records of interest to collectors are often not the million-selling hits by 'superstars.' Very few records by Bing Crosby, for example, are of any more than nominal value, and those that are valuable usually don't even have his name on the label! Collectors today are most interested in records that were made in limited quantities, early works of a performer who later became famous, and those issued in special series or aimed at a limited market. Vintage records are judged desirable by their recorded content as well; those that lack the quality of music that makes a record collectible will always be 'junk' records in spite of their age, scarcity, or the obsolescence of their technology.

Records are usually graded visually rather than by audio quality, since it is seldom if ever possible to first play the records you buy at shows, by mail, at flea markets, etc. Condition is one of the most important value-assessing factors. For example, a truly mint-condition Elvis Presley 45 of Milk Cow Blues (Sun 215) has a potential value of over $1,000.00. If that same 45 had a sticker on it that was one-eighth of an inch square, it could lose up to half of that value! To be judged mint, a record and sleeve must be in original, unsealed condition. It must show absolutely no evidence of use. Excellent condition is a rating applied to a record that may show slight signs of wear and use but will have almost no audible defect.

While the value of most 78s does not depend upon their being in appropriate sleeves or jackets (although a sleeveless existence certainly contributes to damage and deterioration!), this is not the case with many 45s, most EPs (extended play 45s), and LPs (long-playing 33⅓s). Often, common and otherwise minimally valued 45s might be collectible if they are in appropriate 'picture sleeves' (special sleeves that depict the artist/group or other fanciful or symbolic graphic and identify the song titles, record label, and number), e.g. many common records by Elvis Presley, The Beatles, and The Beach Boys. In order for most EPs and LPs to be saleable, they *must* be in their original jackets and in nice condition — indeed, excellent or better — unless they are very scarce and sought-after. Sleeves may show marginal deterioration but no repairs, pen or pencil marks, stickers, or physical damage. A Good record has both visual and audible distractions but is still playable. Sleeves will show ring wear but will not be physically damaged, and Fair indicates a record that is both visually and audibly distracting, one that has obvious damage — no skips, but possible 'play through' scratches. It can still be usable. Sleeves will show heavy ring wear and some minor physical damage. A Poor record may or may not play. Sleeves are faded, torn, marked, or otherwise damaged beyond pleasurable viewing.

Many promo records being discarded by radio stations today are finding their way into collections. These may say 'Not for Sale,' 'Audition Copy,' 'D.J.,' etc. These radio station versions are sometimes different than commercial issues and sometimes more sought after than their commercial twins. Promos by certain 'hot' artists, such as Elvis Presley and The Beach Boys are usually premium disks.

Our advisor for this category is L.R. Docks, author of *American Premium Record Guide*, which lists 60,000 records by over 7,000 artists, now in its fourth edition. He is listed in the Directory under Texas. In the listings that follow, prices are suggested for records that are in excellent condition.

Key:
Bru — Brunswick   Para — Paramount
Ch — Champion   Orch — Orchestra
Col — Columbia   Vi — Victor
Edi — Edison   Vo — Vocalion

Blues, Rhythm and Blues, Rock 'N Roll, Rockabilly

Accents, Wiggle Wiggle, Bru 55100, 78 rpm 20.00
Allen, Danny; Teenage Blues, Valley 101, 78 rpm 10.00
Anderson, Bill; City Lights, TNT 9015, 45 rpm 30.00
Appell, Dave; Applejack, President 1013, 45 rpm 10.00
Arp, James; Let It Rock, Vellez 1515, 45 rpm 15.00

Baker, Charlie; You Crack Me Up, Mun Rab 106, 45 rpm 20.00
Banks, Dick; Dirty Dog, Liberty 55145, 45 rpm 15.00
Beatniks, Blue Angel, Key-Lock 913, 45 rpm 15.00
Belew, Carl; Cool Gator Shoes, Decca 30947, 45 rpm 10.00
Billy the Kid, Apron Strings, Kapp 261, 45 rpm 15.00
Blake, Tommy; I Dig You Baby, Sun 300, 45 rpm 150.00
Blazer Boy, Mornin' Train, Imperial 5199, 45 rpm 30.00
Breedlove, Jimmy; That's My Baby, Atco 6094, 45 rpm 10.00
Brooks, Chuck; Spinning My Wheels, Dub 2844, 45 rpm 15.00
Brown, Danny; Standing on the Corner, Earth 702, 45 rpm 10.00
Bryan, Wes; Tiny Spaceman, United Artist 102, 45 rpm 10.00
Burke, Buddy; That Big Old Moon, Bullseye 1002, 45 rpm 20.00
Byrnes, Edd; Kookie, Warner Bros 1309, LP 15.00
Cadillacs, Down the Road, Josie 778, 45 rpm 30.00
Carr, Cathy; Ivory Tower, Fraternity 1005, LP 30.00
Carroll, Jimmy; Big Green Car, Fascination 2000, 45 rpm 30.00
Cash, Johnny; Country Boy, Sun 112, EP 20.00
Charles, Bobby; Later Alligator, Chess 1609, 45 rpm 15.00
Charmers, Magic Rose, Allison 921, 45 rpm 12.00
Chavis, Boozoo; Boozoo Stomp, Imperial 5374, 45 rpm 20.00
Checkers, Night Curtains, King 4581, 45 rpm 60.00
Chelmars, Confess, Select 712, 45 rpm 12.00
Clear Waters, Boogie Woogie Baby, Atomic H 203, 45 rpm 20.00
Climbers, My Darlin' Dear, J&S 1652, 45 rpm 40.00
Cochran, Eddie; Skinny Jim, Crest 1026, 45 rpm 50.00
Copeland, Ken; Fanny Brown, Lin 5017, 45 rpm 20.00
Craddock, Billy 'Crash'; Birddoggin', Colonial 721, 45 rpm 15.00
Curtis, Don; Rough Tough Man, Kliff 104, 45 rpm 50.00
Cymbal, Johnny; Mr Bass Man, Kapp 3324, LP 30.00
Davis, Link; Grasshopper Rock, Nucraft 2026, 45 rpm 10.00
Davison, Jimmie; Froggie Went a-Courtin', Target 861, 45 rpm 8.00
Dean, Bobby; Hot Rod Daddy, Arcade 195, 45 rpm 15.00
Dickens, Jimmy (Little); Raisin' the Dickens, Col 1047, LP 30.00
Dixon, Floyd; Red Cherries, Aladdin 3144, 45 rpm 20.00
Douglas, Mel; Cadillac Boogie, San 1506, 45 rpm 30.00
Draper, Rusty; Pink Cadillac, Mercury 70921, 45 rpm 8.00
Dudley, Dave; Rock 'N Roll Nursery Rhyme, King 4933, 45 rpm .10.00
Eagles, Please Please, Mercury 70391, 45 rpm 12.00
Echoes, Ding Dong, Gee 1028, 45 rpm 12.00
El Dorados, Boom Diddle Boom, Vee Jay 263, 45 rpm 15.00
Elmore, Johnny; War Chant Boogie, Jar 105, 45 rpm 15.00
England, Hank; Truck Driving Buddy, Process 148, 45 rpm 10.00
Everly Bros, Bird Dog, Cadence 1350, 78 rpm 30.00
Fabian, Hold That Tiger, Chancellor 5003, LP 40.00
Fats Domino, Cheatin', Imperial 5220, 45 rpm 20.00
Fender, Freddy; Wasted Days...Nights, Duncan 1001, 45 rpm 15.00
Fisher, Sonny; Sneaky Pete, Starday 190, 45 rpm 50.00
Five Dollars, Yellow Moon, Fortune 845, 45 rpm 15.00
Flamingos, Blues in a Letter, Chance 1162, 45 rpm 400.00
Ford, Tennessee Ernie; Sixteen Tons, Capitol 3262, 78 rpm 10.00
Four Blazes, Mood Indigo, United 114, 45 rpm 10.00
Four Seasons, Bermuda, Gone 5122, 45 rpm 20.00
Frazier, Calvin; Track Down, Checker 908, 45 rpm 10.00
Gilley, Mickey; Suzy-Q, Astro 104, 45 rpm 20.00
Gipson, Wild Child; Uncle John, Hit 2002, 45 rpm 30.00
Glasser, Dick; Crazy Alligator, Col 41472, 45 rpm 12.00
Gordon, Rosco; Weeping Blues, Flip 227, 45 rpm 40.00
Guitar Dave, Zoro, Central 291, 45 rpm 8.00
Gunter, Arthur; Honey Babe, Excello 2058, 45 rpm 20.00
Haley, Bill & the Comets; Sundown Boogie, Essex 374, 45 rpm ...30.00
Harmon, Bob; Kentucky Home Boogie, Decca 29872, 45 rpm 10.00
Harris, Ray; Greenback Dollars, Sun 272, 45 rpm 15.00
Hawkins, Dale; Liza Jane, Checker 934, 45 rpm 10.00
Hewitt, Ben; Whirlwind Blues, Mercury 71612, 45 rpm 15.00

Hill, Jaycee; Romp Stompin' Boogie, Epic 91105, 45 rpm 20.00
Hobeck, Curtis; China Rock, Lu 508, 45 rpm 20.00
Holly, Buddy; Peggy Sue, Coral 61885, 78 rpm 75.00
Hooker, John Lee; Blue Monday, De Luxe 6004, 45 rpm 30.00
Hooker, John Lee; Down Child, Modern 923, 45 rpm 12.00
Houston, Joe; Sabre Jet, Bayou 004, 45 rpm 15.00
Husky, Ferlin; Born To Lose, Capitol 1204, LP 20.00
Ink Spots, Melody of Love, King 1336, 45 rpm 15.00
Ivan, Frankie Frankenstein, Coral 65607, 45 rpm 15.00
Jack & Jill, Party Time, Caddy 110, 45 rpm 10.00
James, Bill; School's Out, Mun Rab 104, 45 rpm 10.00
James, Sonny; Honey, Capitol 988, LP 15.00
Jennings, Waylon; Jole Band, Bru 55130, 45 rpm 75.00
Jive Bombers, Bad Boy, Savoy 1508, 45 rpm 8.00
Johnson, Buddy; Rock 'N Roll, Mercury 20209, LP 30.00
King, BB; Other Night Blues, RPM 311, 45 rpm 30.00
King Crooners, School Daze, Excello 2187, 45 rpm 20.00
Kinks, Long Tall Sally, Cameo 308, 45 rpm 40.00
Lannis, Louisiana; Tongue Twister Boogie, Snowcap 1125, 45 rpm .20.00
Lee, Harry; Rockin' on a Reindeer, Igloo 101, 45 rpm 60.00
Lewis, Jerry Lee; Great Balls of Fire, Sun 281, 78 rpm 20.00
Lightnin' Slim, Rooster Blues, Excello 8000, LP 30.00
Little Richard, Tutti-Fruitti, Specialty 561, 45 rpm 8.00
Lonesome Drifter, Eager Boy, K 5812, 45 rpm 175.00
Lord, Bobby; Pie Peachie Pie Pie, Col 21498, 45 rpm 15.00
Louis, Joe Hill; Dorothy May, Checker 763, 45 rpm 150.00
Love, Billy; Drop Top, Chess 1508, 435 rpm 30.00
Mack, Bill; Play My Boogie, Imperial 8177, 45 rpm 30.00
Marathons, Peanut Butter, Arvee 428, LP 30.00
Marquees, Wyatt Earp, Okeh 7098, 45 rpm 15.00
Mayfield, Percy; Lonesome Highway, Specialty 439, 45 rpm 12.00
McVoy, Carl; Tootsie, Hi 2001, 45 rpm 12.00
Mercy Baby, Mercy Blues, Ace 535, 45 rpm 10.00
Midnights, Hear My Plea, Music City 762, 45 rpm 20.00
Minors, 'Jerry'; Celeste 3007, 45 rpm 100.00
Mitchell, Billy; Bald Head Woman, Atlantic 974, 45 rpm 20.00
Monotones, Tattle Tale, Hull 743, 45 rpm 15.00
Moore, Merrill; Bartender's Blues, Capitol 2386, 45 rpm 8.00
Morrison, Jim; Ready To Rock, Arctic 5001, 45 rpm 75.00
Mullican, Moon; Cherokee Boogie, King 965, 45 rpm 12.00
Nelson, Ricky; Stood Up, Imperial 5483, 78 rpm 20.00
Nix, Willie; Nervous Wreck, Chance 1163, 45 rpm 150.00
Noel, Sid; Flying Saucer, Aladdin 3331, 45 rpm 15.00
Olson, Rocky; Kansas City, Chess 1723, 45 rpm 10.00
Orlandos, Cloudburst, Cindy 3006, 45 rpm 40.00
Paragons, Florence, Winley 215, 45 rpm 15.00
Parakeets, Teenage Rose, Atlas 1071, 45 rpm 40.00
Patton, Pat; Flip Kitten, King 4942, 45 rpm 10.00
Perkins, Carl; Levi Jacket, Col 41379, 45 rpm 12.00
Pico Pete, Hot Dog, Jet 100, 45 rpm 12.00
Platters, Give Thanks, Federal 12153, 45 rpm 75.00
Scott, Sandy; Shake It Up, Choice 5606, 45 rpm 20.00
Temptations, Birds & Bees, Parksway, 803, 45 rpm 15.00
Walker, Jackie; Peggy Sue, Imperial 5473, 45 rpm 15.00
Whitman, Slim; Cattle Call, Imperial 8281, 45 rpm 10.00
Williams, Hank; Ramblin' Man, MGM 3219, LP 70.00

Country and Western

Allen, Jules; Home on the Range, Vi 21627, 78 rpm 8.00
Ashley, Clarence; Little Sadie, Col 15522-D, 78 rpm 60.00
Autry, Gene; TB Blues, Ch 45073, 78 rpm 20.00
Banjo Joe, Engineer Joe, Col 15238-D, 78 rpm 15.00
Baxter, Johnny; I Want My Rib, Superior 2811, 78 rpm 30.00

Bill Palmer Trio, Duck Foot Sue, Bluebird 1825, 78 rpm 20.00
Boone County Highballers, Darned, Col 15132-D, 78 rpm 25.00
Brooks, Billy; Freight Train Blues, Col 15614-D, 78 rpm 30.00
Butcher, Dwight; Pistol Pete, Vi 23819, 78 rpm 35.00
Carolina Buddies, Mistreated Blues, Col 15770-D, 78 rpm 25.00
Carson, Bert; My Red Haired Lady, Superior 2520, 78 rpm 20.00
Cartwright Bros, Kelly Waltz, Col 15220-D, 78 rpm 10.00
Cedar Creek Sheik, Ford V-8, Bluebird 6939, 78 rpm 25.00
Colt Bros, In 1992, Melotone 12449, 78 rpm 8.00
Cook, Herb; Arkansas Sweetheart, Col 15729-D, 78 rpm 15.00
Cox & Hobbs, Alabama Blues, Gennett 7080, 78 rpm 50.00
Davis Trio, Sleepy Hollow, Para 3238, 78 rpm 20.00
Denmon, Morgan; Naomi Wise, Okeh 45075, 78 rpm 12.00
Duncan Boys, Kentucky Stomp, Supertone 9676, 78 rpm 30.00
Earl & Bell, On the Oregon Trail, Vo 15014, 78 rpm 8.00
Ferguson, John; Railroad Daddy, Challenge 159, 78 rpm 15.00
Fruit Jar Guzzlers, Kentucky Bootleggers, Para 3113, 78 rpm 50.00
Greene, Amos; Memphis Yodel, Supertone 9671, 78 rpm 18.00
Hammond, John; Little Birdie, Gennett 6256, 78 rpm 20.00
Harris, JD; Cackling Hen, Okeh 45024, 78 rpm 20.00
Highlanders, Tennessee Blues, Para 3200, 78 rpm 50.00
Hopkins, Doc; Methodist Pie, Broadway 8337, 78 rpm 10.00
Hutchens, John; I Got Mine, Ch 15503, 78 rpm 10.00
Jones Bros, Little Green Valley, Melotone 12179, 78 rpm 8.00
Justice, Dick; Cocaine, Bru 395, 78 rpm 20.00
Kelly Bros, Stormy Hawaiian Weather, Vi 23853, 78 rpm 30.00
Lancaster, GE; Tennessee Yodel, Superior 2538, 78 rpm 40.00
Lewis, Archie; Miss Handy Hanks, Ch 16677, 78 rpm 30.00
Love, John (Daddy); Blue Days, Bluebird 6583, 78 rpm 20.00
Mack, Bill; Play My Boogie, Imperial 8174, 78 rpm 10.00
Maddux Family, Stone Rag, Decca 5393, 78 rpm 7.00
Maple City Four, Roll Dem Bones, Supertone 9193, 78 rpm 8.00
Martin, John; Hobos Pal, Superior 2658, 78 rpm 30.00
McFarlane, JD; Devil in the Wood Pile, Okeh 45027, 78 rpm 20.00
McPherson, Whitey; Brakeman Blues, Vo 04245, 78 rpm 10.00
Miller, John; Highway Hobo, Superior 2839, 78 rpm 25.00
Moore, John; Columbus Prison Fire, Broadway 8188, 78 rpm 12.00
Nichols Bros, Dear Old Tennessee, Vi 23596, 78 rpm 60.00
Norris, Land; Groundhog, Okeh 40096, 78 rpm 20.00
Padgett, Jack; Boogie Woogie Gal, Talent 729, 78 rpm 15.00
Pine Ridge Boys, Railroad Boomers, Bluebird 8671, 78 rpm 8.00
Price, William; Little Birdie, Challenge 332, 78 rpm 8.00
Red Mountain Trio, Dixie, Col 15462-D, 78 rpm 15.00
Ritter, Tex; Lady Killin' Cowboy, Decca 5076, 78 rpm 15.00
Rodgers, Jimmie; Home Call, Vi 23681, 78 rpm 80.00
Scott, Jimmie; Rocky Road, Star Talent 781, 78 rpm 10.00
Short Bros, Whistling Coon, Okeh 45206, 78 rpm 15.00
Simmons, Bill; Rocky Mountain Blues, Vi 23603, 78 rpm 20.00
Steen, Joe; Railroad Jack, Ch 16258, 78 rpm 15.00
Stone, Jimmie; Midnight Boogie, Imperial 8137, 78 rpm 10.00
Swamp Rooters, Swamp Cat Rag, Bru 556, 78 rpm 20.00
Tennessee Ramblers, Fiddlers Contest, Bru 257, 78 rpm 15.00
Texas Night Hawks, Possum Rag, Okeh 45363, 78 rpm 30.00
Tubb, Ernest; My Mother Is Lonely, Bluebird 8966, 78 rpm 100.00
Vass Family, Deep Blue Sea, Decca 5432, 78 rpm 10.00
W Virginia Coon Hunters, Greasy String, Vi 20862, 78 rpm 30.00
White, George; Livin' in the Mountains, Okeh 45432, 78 rpm 10.00
Wooten, Kyle; Lumber Camp Blues, Okeh 45511, 78 rpm 50.00

Jazz, Dance Bands, Personalities

Alabama Fuzzy Wuzzies, Congo Stomp, Ch 15415, 78 rpm 250.00
Astaire, Fred; Slap That Bass, Bru 7856, 78 rpm 10.00
Barbecue Pete, Avenue Strut, CH 15904, 78 rpm 50.00

Beery, Noah; One Little Drink, Bru 4828, 78 rpm 10.00
Bobby's Revelers, Heebie Jeebies, Silvertone 3551, 78 rpm 75.00
Broadway Rastus, Rock My Soul, Para 12764, 78 rpm 100.00
Calloway, Cab (Orch); Old Yazoo, Bru 6400, 78 rpm 12.00
Carmichael, Hoagy (Orch); Stardust, Gennett 6311, 78 rpm 100.00
Cellar Boys, Barrel House Stomp, Vo 1503, 78 rpm 200.00
Coleman, EL; Steel String Blues, Okeh 8216, 78 rpm 50.00
Cotton Pickers, Shoo Shoo Boogie Boo, Bru 4447, 78 rpm 15.00
Crosstown Ramblers, River Bottom Guide, Ch 15030, 78 rpm 60.00
Davis, Wilmer; Gut Struggle, Vo 1034, 78 rpm 100.00
Dixie Daisies, St Louis Blues, Banner 0839, 78 rpm 12.00
Dixie Jazz Band, Dixie Drag, Oriole 1396, 78 rpm 15.00
Dixie Stompers, Jackass Blues, Harmony 166-H, 78 rpm 15.00
Dudley, Roberta; Krooked Blues, Sunshine 3001, 78 rpm 300.00
Finley, Bob (Orch); Doin' the Campus Crawl, Cameo 9101, 78 rpm ..10.00
Freidman, Al (Orch); Speedy Boy, Ed 52244, 78 rpm 20.00
Glascoe, Percy; Stomp 'Em Down, Col 14088-D, 78 rpm 30.00
Goodman, Benny (Orch); Jungle Blues, Bru 4013, 78 rpm 15.00
Gray, Glen (Orch); My Dance, Decca 387, 78 rpm 10.00
Hall's Jazz Band, Dallas Blues, Okeh 40437, 78 rpm 20.00
Harlem Trio, Fuzzy Wuzzy, Herwin 93012, 78 rpm 200.00
Henderson, Fletcher (Orch); Chattanooga, Ajax 17017, 78 rpm .30.00
Hines, Earl (Orch); Panther Rag, QRS 7093, 78 rpm 200.00
Hudson Trio, Twelfth Street Rag, Famous 3024, 78 rpm 10.00
James, Corky (Blackbirds); Bugahoma Blues, Bell 1182, 78 rpm ..250.00
Jolson, Al; April Showers, Bru 6502, 78 rpm 30.00
Kay, Dolly; Seven or Eleven, Col A3828, 78 rpm 10.00
King, Frances; She's Got It, Okeh 40854, 78 rpm 15.00
Lang, Eddie (Orch); Eddie's Twister, Okeh 40807, 78 rpm 20.00
Lawrence, Sarah; Don't Love Me, Oriole 894, 78 rpm 50.00
Lill's Hot Shots, Drop That Sack, Vo 1037, 78 rpm 120.00
Lumberjacks, Whoopee Stomp, Lincoln 3059, 78 rpm 10.00
Mapp, Eddie; Riding the Blues, QRS 7078, 78 rpm 200.00
McKinney's Cotton Pickers, Cherry, Vi 21730, 78 rpm 30.00
Miller, Glenn (Orch); Blues Serenade, Col 3052-D, 78 rpm 50.00
Moonlight Revelers, Alabama Shuffle, Grey Gull 1775, 78 rpm ..50.00
Moskowitz, Joseph; Operatic Rag, Vi 17978, 78 rpm 20.00
New Orleans Five, Memphis Blues, Oriole 371, 78 rpm 15.00
Niles, Tom (Orch); Amos & Andy, PNY-34033, 78 rpm 60.00
Original Memphis Five, Indiana Stomp, Col 480-D, 78 rpm 15.00
Pacific Coast Players, Jazzing Around, Radiex 1326, 78 rpm 12.00
Preer, Evelyn; Muddy Water, Banner 1972, 78 rpm 8.00
Ramblers, Lonely Eyes, Romeo 315, 78 rpm 8.00
Rhythm Aces, Jazz Battle, Bru 4244, 78 rpm 100.00
Rocky Mountain Trio, Freakish Blues, Gennett 3002, 78 rpm 15.00
Rubinoff, Dave; Fiddlin' the Fiddle, Perfect 14483, 78 rpm 10.00
Seminole Syncopators, Blue Grass Blues, Okeh 40228, 78 rpm ..120.00
Simms, Howard; Pensacola Joe, Harmograph 841, 78 rpm 50.00
Snodgrass, Harry; Maple Leaf Rag, Bru 3239, 78 rpm 10.00
Spencer Trio, John Henry, Decca 1873, 78 rpm 10.00
Sullivan, Joe; Gin Mill Blues, Col 2876-D, 78 rpm 40.00
Troy Harmonists, Great Scott, Perfect 108, 78 rpm 75.00
University Six, Dustin' the Donkey, Harmony 134-H, 78 rpm 12.00
Virginians, Low Down, Vi 21680, 78 rpm 10.00
Washington, Buck; Old Fashion Love, Col 2925-D, 78 rpm 40.00
West, Mae; Easy Rider, Bru 6495, 78 rpm 15.00
Williams, Mary Lou; Clean Pickin', Decca 1155, 78 rpm 12.00
Yankee Six, Jimtown Blues, Okeh 40348, 78 rpm 50.00

Scarce and Unusual Labels

Ajax (Canada) 4.00
Autograph (March Lab, Chicago) 4.00
Black Patti (Chicago Record Co) 50.00

Chautauqua (Washington DC) 10.00
Dandy 4.00
Domestic (Philadelphia) 3.00
Edison (Long-playing 24-minute) 10.00
Edison (Long-playing 40-minute), 12" 15.00
Edison (sample), 12" 20.00
Flexo (Pacific Coast Record Corp), flexible, sm 6.00
Homestead (Chicago Mail Order) 4.00
Meritt (Kansas City) 25.00
National (Iowa City) 2.00
Paramount (12000 and 13000 series) 4.00
QRS (Cova Recording Co, NY) 5.00
RCA Victor Picture Discs 10.00
Rialto (Rialto Music House, Chicago) 10.00
Sunrise (RCA Victor product) 20.00
Sunshine (Los Angeles, CA) 10.00
Up-To-Date 25.00
Victor V-38000 to V-38146, inclusive 3.00
Yerkes 4.00

Red Wing

The Red Wing Stoneware Company, founded in 1878, took its name from its location in Red Wing, Minnesota. In 1906 the name was changed to the Red Wing Union Stoneware Company after a merger with several of the other local potteries. For the most part they produced utilitarian wares such as flowerpots, crocks, and jugs. Their early 1930s catalogs offered a line of art pottery vases in colored glazes, some of which featured handles modeled after swan's necks, snakes, or female nudes. Other examples were quite simple, often with classic styling. After the addition of their dinnerware lines in the 1935, 'Stoneware' was dropped from the name, and the company became known as Red Wing Potteries, Inc. They closed in 1967. For further study we recommend *Red Wing Stoneware, An Identification and Value Guide,* and *Red Wing Collectibles* by Dan and Gail DePasquale and Larry Peterson, available at your bookstore or from Collector Books. Our advisor for the general dinnerware lines is Doug Podpeskar; he is listed in the Directory under Minnesota. Karen Silvermintz (see Texas) and Charles Alexander (see Indiana) advise on the Town and Country dinnerware.

Key:
c/s — cobalt on stoneware   RW — Red Wing
MN — Minnesota   RWUS — Red Wing Union
NS — North Star   Stoneware

Commercial Art Ware and Miscellaneous

Vase, #679, 12½", $95.00.

Ash receiver, donkey figural, head bk to accept ashes, 4¾" 100.00
Ashtray, mini flowerpot center, advertising 300.00
Bank, bear form, Hamm's Beer, 1960s 225.00
Bust, President McKinley, sgn bk 295.00
Figurine, cow w/nursing calf on base, brn 475.00
Figurine, reclining draped lute player w/doe, maroon, #2507 ......195.00
Jardiniere, emb floral panels, #105, 6½" 32.00
Sewer pipe, advertising 50.00
Toothpick holder, gopher on stump form 120.00
Trivet, yel, 1858-1958 ....70.00
Vase, charcoal gray w/wht spatter, waisted, 12" 65.00
Vase, elephant-head hdls, mustard gloss, 6x5" 24.00
Vase, emb classical figure, 4-sided, loop hdls, #1161, 9" 85.00
Vase, emb floral on yel gloss, flared rim 9" 70.00
Vase, mustard-brn & gr matt, squat body, long neck, 10x6" 100.00
Vase, Roman scene emb, gr gloss, 2-hdld jug shape, 10" 65.00
Vase, wide ribs w/floral-emb terminals, hdls, #186, 9" 90.00
Wall clock, Mammy 125.00

Cookie Jars

Bob White, unmk 125.00
Carousel, unmk 900.00
Crock, wht 60.00
Dutch Girl, yel w/brn trim 140.00
Friar Tuck, cream w/brn, mk 195.00
Friar Tuck, gr, mk 295.00
Friar Tuck, yel, unmk 175.00
Grapes 225.00
Grapes, cobalt or dk purple, ea 450.00
Jack Frost, unmk 750.00
King of Tarts, mc, mk 975.00
King of Tarts, pk w/bl & blk trim, mk 950.00
King of Tarts, wht, unmk 675.00
Peasant design, emb/pnt figures on brn 85.00
Pierre (chef), brn, unmk 195.00
Pierre (chef), gr, unmk 350.00
Pierre (chef), pk, mk 450.00
Pineapple, yel 200.00

Dinnerware

Blossomtime, plate, Concord shape, 7" 3.50
Bob White, bowl, salad; bird int, 12" 60.00
Bob White, butter dish, ¼-lb 75.00
Bob White, casserole, w/lid, 2-qt 45.00
Bob White, cup & saucer 20.00
Bob White, hors d'oeuvres bird 40.00
Bob White, pitcher, water; sm 45.00
Bob White, plate, 10½" 12.50
Bob White, shakers, quail form, pr 40.00
Bob White, sugar bowl, w/lid 25.00
Bob White, teapot 100.00
Bob White, tumbler, rare, 4-oz 125.00
Capistrano, bowl, berry; 5½" 8.00
Capistrano, plate, salad; 8" 8.00
Capistrano, plate, 6½" 5.00
Country Garden, gravy boat 22.00
Country Garden, plate, 8" 10.00
Crazy Rhythm, creamer & sugar bowl 25.00
Damask, butter dish 15.00
Fantasy, plate, 10½" 10.00
Hearthside, plate, 6" 4.00
Lexington Rose, pitcher, water 65.00

Lotus, casserole, w/lid 28.00
Lotus, cup & saucer 10.00
Lotus, plate, 10½" 10.00
Lotus, plate, 7½" 7.00
Lute Song, bowl, divided oval 20.00
Lute Song, butter dish 32.00
Lute Song, casserole 25.00
Lute Song, cup & saucer 10.00
Lute Song, platter, 13" 20.00
Lute Song, teapot 65.00
Magnolia, chop plate 16.00
Magnolia, saucer 2.00

Orleans, French casserole, $45.00.

Pepe, bowl, divided vegetable 25.00
Pepe, plate, 10" 12.50
Pitcher, water; lg 85.00
Pompeii, cup & saucer 8.00
Pompeii, plate, 7½" 6.00
Random Harvest, coffeepot, tall 25.00
Random Harvest, gravy boat 35.00
Random Harvest, plate, 10" 12.50
Round-Up, bowl, cereal 60.00
Round-Up, bowl, divided vegetable 95.00
Round-Up, butter dish 200.00
Round-Up, casserole, lg 195.00
Round-Up, casserole, 1-qt 120.00
Round-Up, creamer 50.00
Round-Up, cup & saucer 55.00
Round-Up, pitcher, water; lg 150.00
Round-Up, plate, 10½" 35.00
Round-Up, plate, 6½" 20.00
Round-Up, plate, 7½" 20.00
Round-Up, relish, 3-compartment 95.00
Smart Set, beverage server, w/stand 160.00
Smart Set, bread tray 75.00
Smart Set, casserole, blk lid, 2-qt 70.00
Smart Set, casserole, 4-qt 150.00
Smart Set, cruet, w/stopper 100.00
Smart Set, cup & saucer 38.00
Smart Set, marmite, w/lid 32.00
Smart Set, pitcher, water; 14" 125.00
Smart Set, plate, 10" 35.00
Smart Set, plate, 6" 12.00
Smart Set, teapot 200.00
Tampico, cup & saucer 12.50
Tampico, mug, coffee 45.00
Tampico, platter, 13¼" 20.00
Village Green, bowl, cereal 15.00
Village Green, butter dish, w/lid 25.00

Village Green, gravy boat, w/tray 25.00
Village Green, shakers, pr 20.00
Village Green, warmer 18.00

Stoneware

Bean pot, Albany slip, Boston style, RWUS, 1-gal 200.00
Bean pot, Ambany slip, Boston style, NS, 1-gal 125.00
Bean pot, wht w/Albany slip top, bail hdl, RWUS, 1-qt 75.00
Bowl, beater; Albany slip, RW 25.00
Bowl, paneled, bl sponging on wht, rare 235.00
Bowl, Saffron Grape, zigzags emb on rim, RWUS 125.00
Bowl, wht w/bl bands at rim 75.00
Chamber pot, bl bands on wht, unsgn 135.00
Churn, #2/red wing on wht, RWUS, 2-gal 235.00
Churn, #3/parrot, molded seam, MN, 3-gal 2,750.00
Churn, #5/bird, c/s, RW, 5-gal 1,150.00
Churn, #8/birch leaves, c/s, unsgn, 8-gal 365.00
Churn, molded seam, 2 elephant-ear leaves/#3/oval, c/s, MN, 3-gal .600.00
Cooler, #10/birch leaf, c/s, MN, 10-gal 385.00
Cooler, #4/dbl leaves, c/s, unmk, 4-gal 400.00
Cooler, #6/butterfly, RW, 6-gal 1,750.00
Cooler, #6/daisy, c/s, RW, 6-gal 1,600.00
Cooler, #6/detailed flower/Ice Water, c/s, RW, 6-gal 4,500.00
Crock, #25/2 leaves, cobalt on wht, RWUS, 25-gal 450.00
Crock, #3, drop-8 design, c/s, 3-gal 275.00
Crock, #4/dbl P, c/s, MN, 4-gal 350.00
Crock, #4/2 elephant-ear leaves, c/s, RWUS, 4-gal 75.00
Crock, butter; high style, Albany slip, MN, 1-gal 70.00
Crock, butter; low style, Albany slip, MN, 10-lb 70.00
Crock, butterfly/#10, c/s, unmk, 10-gal 225.00
Crock, 2 elephant-ear leaves/#20, c/s, ca 1900, 20-gal 200.00
Jar, butter; Albany slip, high style, NS, ½-gal 40.00
Jar, butter; Albany slip, low style, RW, 5-lb 40.00
Jar, pantry; red wing/cobalt bands on wht, 5-lb 375.00
Jar, preserve; Albany slip, wall stamp, RW, 1-gal 385.00
Jar, wax sealer; Albany slip, RW, 1-qt 55.00
Jug, beehive; #3/birch leaves on wht, RWUS, 3-gal 225.00
Jug, beehive; #4/birch leaves, c/s, hand-trn, RWUS, 4-gal 415.00
Jug, bl bands on wht, cone top, MN, 1-gal 375.00
Jug, common, Albany slip, ball top, MN, ½-gal 150.00
Jug, common, Albany slip, dome top, MN, 1-gal 115.00
Jug, common, Albany slip, funnel top, MN, 1-gal 85.00
Jug, fancy, wht w/bl band & brn top, MN, 1-pt 665.00
Jug, fancy, wht w/brn ball top, RW, ½-gal 175.00
Jug, fancy, wht w/brn ball top, RW, ½-pt 180.00
Jug, fancy, wht w/brn ball top, RW, 2-gal 250.00
Jug, molded seam, Albany slip, bail hdl, MN, ½-gal 235.00
Jug, molded seam, wht, bail hdl, MN, 1-qt 125.00
Jug, molded seam, wht, bail hdl, MN, ½-gal 100.00
Jug, molded seam, wht, bail hdl, RW, 1-qt 130.00
Jug, shoulder; #3/birch leaves on wht, molded, MN, 3-gal 110.00
Jug, shoulder; #5/birch leaves on wht, std top, 5-gal 130.00
Jug, shoulder; brn & salt glaze, cone top, 2-gal 265.00
Jug, shoulder; brn & salt glaze, dome top, RW, 1-gal 200.00
Jug, shoulder; brn & salt glaze, dome top, 2-gal 135.00
Jug, shoulder; brn & salt glaze, funnel top, MN, 1-gal 85.00
Jug, shoulder; brn & salt glaze, funnel top, ½-gal 130.00
Jug, shoulder; brn & salt glaze, std top, 1-gal 125.00
Jug, shoulder; brn top, red wing on wht, 1930s, 1-gal 175.00
Jug, shoulder; wht, cone top, RW, ½-gal 100.00
Jug, shoulder; wht, standard top, RW, ½-gal 45.00
Jug, shoulder; wht, std top, MN, 1-qt 85.00
Pipkin, Albany slip, unsgn 88.00

Pitcher, Cherryband, blue on white, ca 1916, $200.00.

Pitcher, bl mottled, fancy hdl, RWUS 325.00
Pitcher, mustard; wht, MN, 1-qt 85.00
Pitcher, Spongeware & Saffron, RWUS, lg 195.00
Spittoon, salt glaze, unsgn 200.00
Success filter, bands decor, c/s, incised decor, MN, 4-gal 850.00
Umbrella stand, bl & wht sponging 835.00
Wash bowl & pitcher, emb lily, bl & wht 635.00

Town and Country

Produced by Red Wing for one year only in the late 1940s, Town and Country was designed by Eva Zeisel as an informal or semiformal dinnerware. Irregular, often eccentric shapes characterize the line, as handles of pitchers and serving pieces are usually extensions of the rim. Bowls and platters are free-form comma shapes or appear tilted, with one side slightly higher than the other. Although the ware is unmarked, it is recognizable by its distinctive shapes and glazes. White is often used to complement interiors of bowls and cups, Bronze (metallic brown) enjoys favored status, while gray is unusual. Other colors include rust, dusk blue, sand chartreuse, peach, and forest green.

Bean pot, rust, w/lid 400.00
Bowl, mixing; dusk bl 100.00
Bowl, vegetable; sand, 8" 35.00
Bowl, 5" 15.00
Casserole, marmite, chartreuse, ind 35.00
Creamer, rust 35.00
Creamer & sugar bowl, w/lid, minimum value 50.00
Cruets, oil & vinegar; mixed colors, orig stoppers, sm, pr 150.00
Cup & saucer, forest gr w/wht int 27.50
Pitcher, peach, 3-pt 125.00
Pitcher, sand, 2-pt 85.00
Plate, bronze, 10" 45.00
Plate, gray, 8" 15.00
Plate, 10½" 20.00
Plate, 6½" 7.50
Platter, peach, comma shape, 9" 35.00
Shaker, lg 25.00
Shakers, Shmoo shape, bronze, pr 65.00
Shakers, Shmoo shape, single-color other than bronze, pr 45.00
Sugar bowl, bronze, w/lid 65.00
Syrup, chartreuse 95.00
Teapot, sand 250.00

Redware

The term redware refers to a type of simple earthenware produced by the Colonists as early as the 1600s. The red clay used in its production was abundant throughout the country, and during the 18th and 19th centuries redware was made in great quantities. Intended for utilitarian purposes such as everyday tableware or use in the dairy, redware was simple in design and decoration. Glazes of various colors were used, and a liquid clay referred to as 'slip' was sometimes applied in patterns such as zigzag lines, daisies, or stars. Plates often have a 'coggled' edge, similar to the way a pie is crimped or jagged, which is done with a special tool. In the following listings, EX (excellent condition) indicates only minor damage. Our advisor for this category is Barbara Rosen; she is listed in the Directory under New Jersey. See also Shenandoah.

Bank, brn runs, ovoid, minor chips, 4¼" 275.00
Bank, unglazed turnip shape, button-like knob on top, 3½x3" 60.00
Bowl, amber w/brn flecks, 9⅝", EX 150.00
Bowl, milk; amber w/brn flecks & dk brn daubs, 3¾x10½" 65.00
Bowl, milk; yel slip rim, deep, wear/scratches, 7x15" 330.00
Bowl, str & wavy lines in yel slip, dk brn sponging, 7¾" 465.00
Bowl, 3-line yel slip, coggled edge, shallow, 10" 400.00
Charger, 3-color slip, old rim rpr, 11½" 635.00
Creamer, cream-colored slip w/brn flecks, att Baecher, 5¼" 1,485.00
Creamer, olive & brn mottle, 4¼" 330.00
Cup, gr-brn mottle, tooled decor, att Baecher, 3½" 440.00
Cup, orange w/brn spots, strap hdl, sm chips, 2⅝" 30.00
Figurine, poodle w/basket, mid-1800s, rpr, 6½x6" 925.00
Flowerpot, brn splotches, yel slip dots, w/saucer, 3½" 45.00
Flowerpot, cream mottle, attached saucer base, 4⅜x7" 1,650.00
Jar, cream w/brn & gr brushed arches & lines, 7" dia 1,375.00
Jar, dk brn, scrolled dbl-ear hdls, tooled flowers, 6½" 1,400.00
Jar, dk reddish w/brn splotches, 5½" 55.00
Jar, gr w/amber spots, sm chips, 7¼" 140.00
Jar, gr w/orange spots & brn horizontal stripes, 7¾" 165.00
Jar, lt gr w/amber spots, flared lip, hairline, 8" 50.00
Jar, mustard speckled, ovoid, chips, 9" 400.00

Jar, ovoid, splotched glaze, 9", EX, $800.00.

Jar, preserving; amber w/brn spots, strap hdl, 8⅜" 300.00
Jar, preserving; orange w/dk brn spots, 8¼", EX 350.00
Jar, shiny clear w/brn flecks & sponging, ovoid, 7" 250.00
Jar, shiny clear w/dk orange & brn splotches, w/lid, 6⅜" 300.00
Jug, brn flecks w/gr & amber spots, ovoid, 7¾", EX 110.00
Jug, cream slip w/gr & running brn, Southern, 3½" 300.00
Jug, gr-amber w/brn flecks, ovoid, tooled shoulder, 6¾" 375.00
Jug, lt gr w/amber spots, incised lines at shoulder, 8½" 135.00
Jug, manganese splotches, 19th C, 5¾" 400.00
Jug, shiny blk, ribbed strap hdl, ovoid, lt wear, 6¼" 200.00
Jug, shiny clear w/red-tan & dk brn splotches, ovoid, 9¼" 500.00
Loaf pan, personalized name in yel slip, rectangular, 15", EX ..1,500.00
Loaf pan, 3-line yel slip, coggled rim, 13" 425.00
Loaf pan, 3-line yel slip, coggled rim, 17", EX 525.00
Loaf pan, 4-line yel slip, coggled rim, 15½", VG 195.00
Mold, Turk's head, clear w/brn edge sponging, 2½x7" 125.00
Mold, Turk's head, dk brn sponging, spiral fluting, 7¼" 75.00
Mold, Turk's head, yel slip rim, gr & brn daubs, 8¾", EX 85.00

Mug, child's, mc floral enamel, blk rim, 2¼" 85.00
Mug, 2-tone gr, Stahl, 1938, EX 60.00
Pie plate, Apple Pie in yel slip, 10" dia, EX 700.00
Pie plate, yel slip w/gr center design, wear, 7¾" 285.00
Pie plate, 3-line yel slip, coggled rim, flakes, 12½" 550.00
Pie plate, 3-line yel slip, coggled rim, minor wear, 8" 495.00
Pie plate, 3-line yel slip, coggled rim, wear/flakes, 9" 360.00
Pie plate, 6-line yel slip, wear/chips, 8½" 250.00
Pitcher, amber w/brn splotches, ovoid, strap hdl, 9½", EX 40.00
Pitcher, cream w/brn & gr, 3-spout, rpr hdl, att Everley, 7" ...935.00
Plate, initials in yel slip, 9" 500.00
Plate, 3-line yel slip, coggled rim, wear, 8⅞" 330.00
Plate, 3-line yel slip, coggled rim, 9" 495.00

Regal China

Located in Antioch, Illinois, the Regal China Company began its business in 1938. Products of interest to collectors are James Beam decanters, cookie jars, salt and pepper shakers, and similar novelty items. The company closed its doors sometime in 1993. The Old Mac-Donald Farm series listed below is especially collectible. Prices are based on excellent gold trim. (Gold trim must be 90% intact or deductions should be made for wear.) See also Decanters.

Alice in Wonderland

Cookie jar 3,200.00
Creamer, White Rabbit 600.00
Pitcher, King of Hearts, milk sz 650.00
Shakers, matching colors, rare, pr 675.00
Shakers, Tweedledee & Tweedledum, pr 850.00
Shakers, wht w/gold trim, pr 675.00
Sugar bowl, White Rabbit, w/lid 600.00
Teapot, Mad Hatter 2,500.00

Cookie Jars

Cat 425.00
Churn Boy 275.00
Clown, gr collar 675.00
Davy Crockett 550.00
Diaper Pin Pig 525.00
Dutch Girl, peach trim 800.00
FiFi Poodle 650.00
Fisherman 650.00
French Chef 375.00
Goldilocks 375.00
Hobby Horse 250.00
Hubert Lion 775.00
Humpty Dumpty, red wall 325.00
Little Miss Muffett 385.00
Majorette 325.00
Oriental Lady w/Baskets 600.00
Peek-a-Boo 1,500.00
Quaker Oats 125.00
Three Bears 285.00
Toby Cookies 750.00
Tulip 300.00
Uncle Mistletoe 850.00

Old McDonald's Farm

Butter dish, cow's head 220.00

Canister, flour, cereal, coffee; med, ea 220.00
Canister, pretzels, peanuts, popcorn, chips, tidbits; lg, ea 300.00
Canister, salt, sugar or tea; med, ea 220.00
Canister, soap or cookies; lg, ea 300.00
Cookie jar, barn 275.00
Creamer, rooster 110.00
Grease jar, pig 175.00
Pitcher, milk 400.00
Shakers, boy & girl, pr 75.00
Shakers, churn, gold trim, pr 90.00
Shakers, feed sacks w/sheep, pr 195.00
Spice jar, assorted lids, sm, ea 100.00
Sugar bowl, hen 125.00
Teapot, duck's head 250.00

Shakers

A Nod to Abe, 3-pc 225.00
Bendel, bears, wht w/pk & brn trim, pr 100.00
Bendel, bunnies, wht w/blk & pk trim, pr 135.00
Bendel, kissing pigs, gray w/pk trim, lg, pr 375.00
Bendel, love bugs, burgundy, lg, pr 165.00
Bendel, love bugs, gr, sm, pr 65.00
Cat, pr 225.00
Clown, pr 450.00
Dutch Girl, pr 275.00
FiFi, pr 450.00
Fish, C Miller, pr 60.00
French Chef, pr 350.00
Goldilocks, wht w/gold trim, pr 175.00
Humpty Dumpty, pr 140.00
Peek-a-Boo, peach trim, rare, lg, pr 575.00
Peek-a-Boo, red dots, lg, pr 500.00
Peek-a-Boo, red dots, sm, pr 220.00
Peek-a-Boo, wht solid, lg, pr 400.00
Peek-a-Boo, wht solid, sm, pr 200.00
Peek-a-Boo, wht w/burgundy trim, rare, sm, pr 350.00
Peek-a-Boo, wht w/gold trim, lg, pr 450.00
Pigs, pk, mk C Miller, 1-pc 95.00
Tulip, pr 50.00

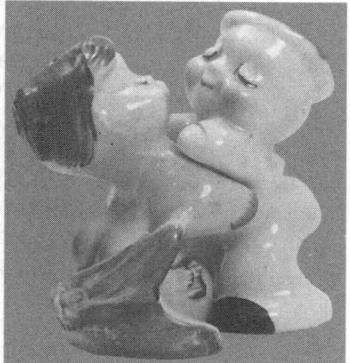

Van Telligen shakers, sailor and mermaid huggies, $195.00 for the pair.

Van Telligen, bears, brn, pr 20.00
Van Telligen, boy & dog, blk, pr 95.00
Van Telligen, boy & dog, wht, pr 60.00
Van Telligen, bunnies, solid colors, pr 22.00
Van Telligen, ducks, pr 30.00
Van Telligen, Dutch boy & girl, pr 40.00
Van Telligen, Mary & lamb, pr 55.00
Vermont Leaf People, 3-pc 125.00

Miscellaneous

Banks, kissing pigs, Bendel, lg, pr 425.00
Creamer & sugar bowl, cat form, ea 175.00
Creamer & sugar bowl, Tulip 100.00
Teapot, Tulip, tall 125.00

Relief-Molded Jugs

Early relief-molded pitchers (ca 1830s-40s) were made in two-piece molds into which sheets of clay were pressed. The relief decoration was deep and well defined, usually of animal or human subjects. Most of these pitchers were designed with a flaring lip and substantial footing. Gradually styles changed, and by the 1860s the rim had become flatter and the foot less pronounced. The relief decoration was not as deep, and foliage became a common design. By the turn of the century, many other types of pitchers had been introduced, and the market for these early styles began to wane.

Watch for recent reproductions; these have been made by the slip-casting method. Unlike relief-molded ware which is relatively smooth inside, slip-cast pitchers will have interior indentations that follow the irregularities of the relief decoration. Values below are for pieces in excellent condition. Our advisor for this category is Kathy Hughes; she is listed in the Directory under North Carolina.

Key: Reg — Registered

Apostle, wht, Meigh, 1842, 9⅞" 525.00
Ariadne, Samuel Alcock & Co, ca 1850, 9" 500.00
Barley, gr, Dudson, Apr 25, 1861, 8" 175.00
Beaded Medallions, parian, unmk, 19th C, 7" 125.00
Bullrushes on bl-gray, Ridgway & Abington, Reg Mar 7, 1848, 9" .175.00
Equestrian hunters, grapevines, lt gr, branch hdl, unmk, 6" 125.00
Goddess w/7 cherubs, wht, Copeland & Garrett, 19th C, 9" 350.00
Gothic Floral, bl/brn/wht, Beech & Hancock, 7/14/1862, 8" 200.00
Jousting Jug, Ridgway, Reg Sept 1, 1840, 7¼" 375.00
Julius Ceasar, gray, appl laurel wreath, Meigh, 1839, 8¼" 450.00
Musical instruments, WT Copeland, ca 1855, 10" 400.00
Pan (w/lid), buff, Wm Ridgway & Co, ca 1830, 7¼" 250.00
Tam-O'-Shanter, Wm Ridgway & Co, Reg Oct 1, 1835, 8¼" 295.00
Two Drivers, gray, Minton, ca 1849, 7⅞" 575.00

Restraints

Since the beginning of time, many things from animals to treasures have been held in bondage by hemp, bamboo, chests, chains, shackles, and other constructed devices. Many of these devices were used to hold captives who awaited further torture, as if the restraint wasn't torturous enough. The study and collecting of restraints enables one to learn much about the advancement of civilization in the country or region from which they originated. Such devices at various times in history were made of very heavy metals — so heavy that the wearer could scarcely move about. It has only been in the last sixty years that vast improvements have been made in design and construction that afford the captive some degree of comfort. Our advisor for this category is Joseph Tanner; he is listed in the Directory under Washington.

Key:
bbl — barrel
d-lb — double lock button
K — key
Kd — keyed
lc — lock case
NST — non-swing through
ST — swing through
stp — stamped

Foreign Handcuffs

Australian, Saf Lock, ST, takes pin-tumbler K in side, stp 140.00
Deutsche Polizei, ST, middle hinge, folds, takes bbl-bit K 80.00
East German, aluminum, single lg hinge, ST, bbl key 50.00
East German, heavy steel, NP single lg hinge, NST, bbl key 80.00
English, Chubb, NST, hi-security 10-slider lock mechanism 275.00
English, Chubb Arrest, steel, ST, multi-bit solid K 225.00
English, Latrobe, aluminum alloy, center chain, ST, dbl-bit K ...160.00
French Lapegy, ST, aluminum alloys, takes flat bitted K 75.00
French Revolved, oval, ST, takes 2 Ks: bbl & pin tumbler 150.00
German, 3-lb steel set, 2⅝" thick, center chain, bbl K 175.00
German Clejuso, oval design, ST, dbl-cuff weight, 22-oz 100.00
German Clejuso, sq lc, adjusts/NST, d-lb on side, bbl K 100.00
German Darby, adjusts, well finished, NST, sm 120.00
German Hamburg 8, non-adjust NST, center bar/post w/K-way ..250.00
Hiatt, English Darby, like US CW Darby, stp Hiatt & #d 75.00
Hiatt, solid state, 2 separate cuffs joined bk to bk, stp/#d 165.00
Hiatt English non-adjust screw K Darby style, uses screw K 100.00
Hiatt Figure 8, swings open to insert/withdraw wrists 125.00
Italian, stp New Police, modern Peerless type, ST, sm bbl K 35.00
Plug 8, remove plug before inserting external threaded K 200.00
Spanish, stp Alcyon/Star, modern Peerless type, flat K 65.00
Spanish, stp Alcyon/Star, modern Peerless type, ST, sm bbl K 45.00

Foreign Leg Shackles

East German, aluminum, lg hinge, cable amid 4 cuffs, bbl key 80.00
German Clejuso, sq lc, adjusts/NST, d-bl on side, bbl K 125.00
German Clejuso Darby type, adjusts/NST/plated, uses screw K ..160.00
Hiatt English combo manacles, handcuff/leg irons w/chain 275.00
Hiatt English non-adjust screw K Darby style, uses screw K 100.00
Hiatt Plug leg irons, same K-ing as Plug-8 cuffs, w/chain 225.00

U.S. Handcuffs

Adams, teardrop lc, bbl Kd, NST, usually not stp 170.00
American Munitions, modern/rnd, sm bbl Kd, ST bow, stp 45.00
Bean Giant, sideways figure 8, solid center lc, dbl-bit K 400.00
Bean Patrolman, kidney-bean form, d-lb on lc, NST, stp T 100.00
Bean-Cobb, sm rnd lc, removable cylinder, d-lb, NST, 1899 ....80.00
Cavenay, looks like Marlin Daley but w/screw K, NST 160.00
Civil War padlocking type, various designs w/loop for lock 170.00
Colt, modern ST bow, sm bbl Kd, stp w/Colt & Co name 150.00
Flash Action Manacle, like Bean Giant w/ST, K-way center 200.00
Flexibles, steel segmented bows, NST Darby type, screw K 150.00
H&R Super, ST, shaft-hinge connector takes hollow titted K ...100.00
Harvard, takes sm bbl K, ST, stp Harvard Lock Co 65.00
Judd, NST, used rnd/internally triangular K, stp Mattatuck 120.00
Lilly Hand Iron, 2" strap iron (8" L), oval bands, NST, sq K 400.00
Marlin Daley, NST, bottle-neck form, neck stp, dbl-titted K 200.00
Mattatuck, NST, propeller-like K-way, stp Mattatuck/etc 90.00
Palmer, 2" steel bands, 2 K-ways (top & center), NST stp 300.00
Peerless, ST, takes sm bbl K, stp Mfg'ered by Peerless Co 40.00
Peerless, ST, takes sm bbl K, stp Mfg'ered by S&W Co 75.00
Phelps, NST, twist chain between cuffs, Tower look-alike 200.00
Pratt combo, 1 cuff connects w/nipper/claw, ST, mk Pratt 225.00
Providence Tool Co, stp, NST, Darby screw K style 120.00
Rankin, steel NST, mk screw K 225.00
Romer, NST, takes flat K, resembles padlock, stp Romer Co 250.00
S&W 94 Maximum Security, ST, takes Ace-type K, stp S&W 80.00
Strauss, ST, takes lg solid bitted K, stp Strauss Eng Co 85.00
Tower, NST, bottom K, solid/flat-fitted K goes in cuff edge 100.00
Tower bar cuffs, cuffs separate by 10-12" steel bar 120.00

Tower Dbl-Lock, NST, takes bbl-bitted K, usually stp Tower 60.00
Tower Detective Pinkerton, NST, sq lc, bbl-bitted K, no stp 120.00
Tower Single Lock, NST, bbl-bit K, K-way slanted on lc, sm 70.00
Tower-Bean, NST, sm rnd lc, takes tiny bbl-bitted K, stp 75.00
Tri-lock, heavy polymer & stainless steel, ST, triple lock 60.00
Walden 'Lady Cuff,' NST, takes sm bbl K, lightweight, stp 250.00

U.S. Leg Shackles

American Munitions, as handcuffs 55.00
Civil War or prison ball & chain, padlocking or rivet type 250.00
Cloc spike, 30" L, opening for ankle w/padlock & 2 spikes 500.00
H&R Supers, as handcuffs 400.00
Harvard, as handcuffs 75.00
Judd, as handcuffs 135.00
Leg lock brace, metal brace, ankle to knee, lever locked 225.00
Oregon boot, break-apart shackle on above-ankle support 400.00
Palmer, as handcuffs but w/detachable chain, NST 400.00
Providence Tool Co, stp, NST 150.00
Strauss, as handcuffs 125.00
Tower, bottom K, as handcuffs 100.00
Tower ball & chain, leg iron w/chain & 6-lb to 50-lb ball 200.00
Tower Dbl-Lock, as handcuffs 90.00
Tower Detective, as handcuffs 150.00

Various Other Restraining Devices

African slave Darby-style cuffs, heavy iron/chain, handmade 130.00
African slave Darby-style leg shackles, heavy/hand forged 160.00
African slave padlocking or riveted forged iron shackles 135.00
Argus iron claw, twist T to open & close 40.00
Darby neck collar, rnd steel loop opens w/screw K 150.00
English figure-8 nipper, claws open by lifting top lock tab 80.00
Gale finger cuff, knuckle duster, non-K, mk GFC 125.00
German nipper, twist hdl opens/closes cuff, stp Germany/etc 75.00
Jay Pee, thumb cuffs, mk solid body, bbl K 15.00
Mighty-Mite, thumb cuffs, solid body, ST, mk, bbl K 75.00
Phillips nipper, claw, flip lever on top to open 80.00
Thomas Nipper, claw, push button on top to open 80.00
Tower Lyon, thumb cuffs, solid body, NST, dbl-bit center K 150.00

Reverse Painting on Glass

    Verre eglomise is the technique of painting on the underside of glass. Dating back to the early 1700s, this art became popular in the 19th century when German immigrants chose historical figures and beautiful women as subjects for their reverse glass paintings. Advertising mirrors of this type came into vogue at the turn of the century.

General Lafayette and General Jackson,
each on horseback, Chinese, 19th century,
each 15x12"+frame, $990.00 for the pair.

Martin Van Buren, mc portrait on gr, orig fr, 12x9½" 715.00
Napoleon, portrait, mc on gr, flaking, fr, 11½x10" 275.00
Oriental landscape w/10 figures, fr, 20x32" 715.00
Panel, couple seated under tree, 4⅛x5⅜"+wood fr 50.00
Summer, landscape, oval inner fr, 9½x7" 350.00

Rhead

Associated with many companies during his career — Weller, Vance Avon, Arequipa, A. E. Tile, and finally Homer Laughlin China — Frederick Hurten Rhead organized his own pottery in Santa Barbara, California, ca 1913. Admittedly more of a designer than a potter, Rhead hired help to turn the pieces on the wheel but did most of the decorating himself. The process he favored most involved sgraffito designs inlaid with enameling. Egyptian and Art Nouveau influences were evidenced in much of his work. The ware he produced there was often marked with a logo incorporating the potter at the wheel and 'Santa Barbara.'

Candlesticks, geometrics, wht/royal bl enamel inlay, 6", pr 1,400.00
Tile, cvd Grecian woman, 7-color, Santa Barbara, 6", NM 600.00
Vase, dk bl gloss, bulbous w/3 closed rim hdls, 3¼x3¼" 200.00

Richard

Richard, who at one time worked for Galle, made cameo art glass in France during the 1920s. His work was often multilayered and acid cut with florals and scenics in lovely colors. The ware was marked with his name in relief. Our advisor for this category is Don Williams; he is listed in the Directory under Missouri.

Vase, cottage among trees, mountain and lake beyond, amethyst and lavender on gray, 8", $1,250.00.

Cameo

Atomizer, leaves, raspberry/pk, wafer ft, sgn, 7" 785.00
Bowl, floral, dk bl on yel, boat form, 2¾x3¾" 285.00
Vase, landscape, red on orange, baluster, 23" 3,000.00
Vase, orchids/2 bees, bl-blk on tangerine, distended neck, 8" 950.00
Vase, scenic w/bldgs, slim/ftd, 17" 1,750.00
Vase, trees/house, cut/HP, bulbous, 3½" 485.00
Wall pocket, thistles, brn on yel, spear form, 7x1½" 650.00

Ridgway

As early as 1792, the Ridgway brothers, Job and George, produced fine quality earthenwares in Shelton, Staffordshire, marking their products 'Ridgway, Smith, & Ridgway' and later 'Job & George Ridgway.'

Around 1800 the brothers split, and each had his own firm, both in Shelton. They were joined in the business by various members of the Ridgway family, and in fact their descendants still operate there today.

The two firms created by the split were the Bell Works and the Cauldon Pottery. Bell produced stone china and earthenware decorated with blue transfer printing. Their mark was 'J. & W. Ridgway' or 'J. & W.R.' (John and William) until 1848 when 'William Ridgway' was used. The Cauldon Pottery made earthenware, stone china, and high-quality porcelains fine enough to win them the distinction of being appointed potters to the Queen. From 1830 their wares attest to this fact, bearing the Royal Arms mark with 'J.R.' within the crest. In 1840 '& Co.' was added. Most examples of Ridgway's wares found today are transfer-printed historical scenes. See also Staffordshire, Historical; and Flow Blue.

Biscuit jar, Coaching Days, brn rattan hdl, 6½" 235.00
Bowl, Coaching Days, 10" 55.00
Coffeepot, Coaching Days, 8" 110.00
Cup & saucer, Coaching Days 38.00
Cup & saucer, Royal Vista 25.00
Mug, Mormon Sq, Salt Lake City, 4½" 45.00
Pitcher, Coaching Days, 5½" 70.00
Pitcher, Coaching Days, 7½" 85.00
Pitcher, stoneware, bl w/emb band, HP florals, 1835, 11" 180.00
Plaque, Taking Up the Mails, yel, 12" 135.00
Plate, chop; Coaching Days, 13½" 135.00
Plate, Coaching Days, 10" 45.00
Punch bowl, flowers & birds, blk transfer w/mc, 7x16" 135.00
Teapot, Coaching Days, 5½" 175.00
Tray, Coaching Days, oval, 12" 75.00
Vase, Coaching Days, 5" 70.00

Riviera

Riviera was a line of dinnerware introduced by the Homer Laughlin China Company in 1938. It was sold exclusively by the Murphy Company through their nationwide chain of dime stores. Riviera was unmarked, lightweight, and inexpensive. It was discontinued sometime prior to 1950. Colors are mauve blue, red, yellow, light green, and ivory. On rare occasions, dark blue pieces are found, but this was not a standard color. For further information we recommend *The Collector's Encyclopedia of Fiesta* (1996 values) by Sharon and Bob Huxford, available from Collector Books.

Batter set, complete 240.00
Batter set, ivory, w/decals, complete 155.00
Bowl, baker; 9" 20.00
Bowl, cream soup; w/liner, ivory 70.00
Bowl, fruit; 5½" 10.00
Bowl, nappy; 7¼" 22.00
Bowl, oatmeal; 6" 32.00
Bowl, utility; ivory 48.00
Butter dish, cobalt, ¼-lb 215.00
Butter dish, colors other than cobalt or turq, ¼-lb 110.00
Butter dish, turq, ¼-lb 220.00
Butter dish, ½-lb 115.00
Casserole 95.00
Creamer 11.00
Cup & saucer, demitasse; ivory 55.00
Jug, open, ivory, 4½" 90.00
Jug, w/lid 115.00
Pitcher, juice; mauve bl 185.00
Pitcher, juice; yel 100.00

Plate, deep	20.00
Plate, 10"	42.00
Plate, 6"	8.00
Plate, 7"	10.00
Plate, 9"	15.00
Platter, closed hdls, 11¼"	20.00
Platter, cobalt, 12"	58.00
Platter, 11½"	18.00
Platter, 15"	50.00
Sauce boat	22.00
Saucer	3.50
Shakers, pr	18.00
Sugar bowl, w/lid	17.50
Teacup	10.00
Teapot	110.00
Tidbit, ivory, 2-tier	75.00
Tumbler, hdl	58.00
Tumbler, hdl, ivory	125.00
Tumbler, juice	45.00

Robertson

Fred H. Robertson, clay expert for the Los Angeles Brick Company and son of Alexander Robertson of the Roblin Pottery, experimented with crystalline glazes as early as 1906. In 1934 Fred and his son George established their own works in Los Angeles, but by 1943 they had moved operations to Hollywood. Though most of their early wares were turned by hand, some were also molded in low relief. Fine crackle glazes and crystallines were developed. Their ware was marked with 'Robertson,' 'F.H.R.,' or 'R.,' with the particular location of manufacture noted. The small pottery closed in 1952.

Chamberstick, rose matt, dish base, hdl, 2¼x5¾"	125.00
Plaque, 3-D berries/poppies on red clay, no mk, 2½x3"	250.00
Plate, gazelle, dk bl on turq, wht rim, Hollywood, 11"	500.00
Vase, crystalline mottled celadon/lt bl flambe, FHR/LA, 7x3"	900.00

Robj

Robj was the name of a retail store that operated in Paris for only a few years, from about 1925 to 1931. Robj solicited designs from the best French artisans of the period to produce decorative objects for the home. These objects were produced mostly in porcelain but also in glass and earthenware. The most well known are the figural bottles which were particularly popular in the United States. However, Robj also produced tea sets, perfume lamps, chess sets, ashtrays, bookends, humidors, powder jars, cigarette boxes, figurines, lamps, and milk pitchers. Robj objects tend to be whimsical, and all embody the Art Deco style. Items listed below are ceramic unless noted otherwise. Our advice for this category comes from Randall Monsen and Rod Baer, their address is listed in the Directory under Virginia.

Bottle, scent; Oriental figure sitting, no lid	60.00
Bottle, Scotsman in uniform, mc, 10½", VG	250.00
Box, powder; clear/frosted glass, Deco emb, 1¼" dia	850.00
Cocktail shaker, golfer figural, bl & wht	1,250.00
Console set, 4 seated nude boys support 10" bowl, +pr vases	1,200.00
Decanter, peasant girl figural, 10"	250.00
Decanter, Professor	360.00
Inkwell, Blackamoor in gold/wht robe holds well, no lid, 6"	275.00
Inkwell, Boy Scout figural	365.00

Roblin

In the late 1800s, Alexander W. Robertson and Linna Irelan established a pottery in San Francisco, combining parts of their respective names to coin the name Roblin. Robertson was responsible for potting and firing the ware, which often reflected his taste for classic styling. Mrs. Irelan did much of the decorating, utilizing almost every method but favoring relief modeling. Mushrooms and lizards were her favorite subjects. Vases were a large part of their production, all of which were made from native California red, buff, and white clays. The ware was well marked with the firm name or the outline of a bear. Roblin Pottery was destroyed in the earthquake of 1906.

Napkin ring, 2 braided bands/monogram, dk red clay, 1¾x2"	70.00
Plate, cvd frog/dragonfly on hammered brn matt, Irelan, 7"	700.00
Vase, bsk, barrel shape, 2½"	100.00
Vase, bsk, cylindrical, w/provenance, 1⅜x1¼"	100.00
Vase, decorative band on yel crackled gloss, 2¾x2¼"	450.00
Vase, flecked terra cotta & cocoa-brn bsk, 3"	150.00

Rock 'N Roll Memorabilia

Memorabilia from the early days of rock 'n roll recalls an era that many of us experienced firsthand; these listings are offered to demonstrate the many and various aspects of this area of collecting. Items indicated by this symbol (+) have been reproduced. Beware! Many are so well done even a knowledgeable collector will sometimes be fooled.

Our advisor for Elvis memorabilia is Rosalind Cranor, author of *Elvis Collectibles* and *Best of Elvis Collectibles* (Overmountain Press); she is listed in the Directory under Virginia. The remainder is under the advisement of Bob Gottuso, author of Beatles and Kiss sections in *Garage Sale Gold* by Tomart; see Pennsylvania.

Aerosmith, promo pen, Pump, X-rated, 1990-91 world tour	15.00
Andy Gibb, doll, 10", MIB	35.00
Andy Gibb, flip book, Shadow Dancin', 3x3¾"	24.00

Beatles, compact, brass, unused makeup, M, $450.00.

Beatles, balloon, various colors, M, sealed in pkg	75.00
Beatles, belt, bl, red or blk w/repeating faces in silver, NM	90.00
Beatles, binder, vinyl, 3-ring, EX	90.00
Beatles, bobbin' head dolls, 8", EX, set of 4 (+)	325.00
Beatles, bracelet, portrait medallion on chain, EX	65.00
Beatles, cake nodders, 1966, set of 4 (+)	35.00
Beatles, canvas print, sold at Shea Stadium, August 1965	45.00
Beatles, Carefree stockings, M in pkg w/faces	100.00
Beatles, coloring book, Saalfield, unused, NM	65.00
Beatles, flag, Die Beatles, Germany	25.00
Beatles, game, Flip Your Wig, complete in EX box	150.00

Beatles, hair bow, M on photo card, sealed 250.00
Beatles, harmonica, Hohner, NMIB 90.00
Beatles, headband, Better Wear, M in pkg, sealed 45.00
Beatles, necklace, silver w/flasher portrait, UK 125.00
Beatles, pillow, group portrait w/guitars, Nordic House, 12", EX ..150.00
Beatles, sheet music, Here, There & Everywhere, photo cover 10.00
Beatles, sheet music, Please Please Me 10.00
Beatles, signatures of all 4 on 3x6" sheet of paper 1,600.00
Beatles, sneakers, Wing Dings, unused, MIB 450.00
Beatles, soaky bottle, Paul or Ringo, NM, ea 100.00
Beatles, ticket, 1966 Boston concert 45.00
Beatles, wristwatch, 1988, MIB 60.00
Beatles, Yel Submarine, Corgi, MIB 550.00
Beatles, Yel Submarine clothes hanger 125.00
Beatles, Yel Submarine Pop-Out Book, 1968, NM 45.00
Bee Gees, puffy stickers, 1979, set of 6 (4 styles) 5.00
Bill Haley & Comets/Platters/Chuck Berry, program, 1956, 24-pg ..45.00
Blondie, ashtray, Parallel Lines, photo on hexagon, 3¼" 35.00
Blondie, International Fan Club Book, #2, 1981 ....9.00
Blondie, promotional scarf, Parallel Lines album, 48", M 25.00
Bo Diddley/L Michaels, poster, Squiggly Trinity, '67, 14x20" 60.00
Bobby Darin, iron-on picture patch, 3½" sq, M in pkg 12.00
Bobby Sherman, paint/color/activity book, 1971, M 22.00
Bon Jovi, backstage pass, 1987 ....4.00
Boy George, doll, LJN, 1984, 12", MIB 135.00
Brenda Lee, coupon, ad for ice cream sandwiches, M 10.00
Connie Francis, program booklet 12.00
Cream, concert ticket, w/Butterfield Blues, 1967, M 40.00
Culture Club, cup, plastic, Boy George picture, hdl, 5¼" 20.00
Dave Clark Five, concert program 20.00
Dave Clark Five, tour book, lg format, 1964 ....38.00
David Bowie, concert program, 1983, M 10.00
David Cassidy, paint/color/activity book, 1971, M 28.00
Def Leppard, pencil holder, Pyromania, metal, 1984 ....18.00
Donny & Marie Osmond, brunch bag, vinyl, EX+, w/thermos 70.00
Donny & Marie Osmond, TV playset, VG (no box) 45.00
Doors, concert ticket, ca 1967, unused 60.00

Elvis Presley, pitcher and 4 mugs, fired-on decoration, $100.00.

Elvis Presley, ashtray/coaster, blk & wht, 1956, 3½", EX 340.00
Elvis Presley, beach hat, blk cloth/wide wht band, w/tag, '56 .....110.00
Elvis Presley, bedsheet piece, w/certificate of authenticity 25.00
Elvis Presley, billfold, many colors, mk, 1956, EX, ea 575.00
Elvis Presley, bolo tie, 1956, EX 250.00
Elvis Presley, diary, 1956, mk, EX 560.00
Elvis Presley, dog tag key chain, MOC 160.00
Elvis Presley, EP Game, Teenage-Games, 1956, complete, EX ..1,350.00
Elvis Presley, French purse, 1956, mk, EX 600.00
Elvis Presley, guitar, Emenee, plastic, w/case, 1956, M 1,700.00

Elvis Presley, guitar, Lapin Products, 1986, M in pkg 60.00
Elvis Presley, Hallmark Christmas ornament, 1992, MIB 20.00
Elvis Presley, heart necklace, Love Me Tender, gold, '56, MOC ...315.00
Elvis Presley, hound dog, stuffed, 10", EX 445.00
Elvis Presley, promo kit, Tickle Me, w/actual leathers, $50 to 65.00
Everly Brothers, chocolate tin, 1950s, EX 95.00
Fleetwood Mac, back stage pass, Tusk, 1982 ....5.00
Frankie Avalon, iron-on picture patch, 3½" sq, M in pkg 12.00
Freddy & the Dreamers, button, I Love, blk/wht/red, 3½" 18.00
Gene Pitney w/Buckinghams, concert program, 1960s, M 25.00
Grateful Dead, concert poster, blk/wht, NY, 1980, 28x22" 70.00
Grateful Dead, concert poster, German tour, 1982, 24x33½" 65.00
Grateful Dead, concert poster, mc, NY City, Oct 1980, 24x18" .140.00
Grateful Dead, concert poster, Summit concert II, 1986, 20x14" ..100.00
Jefferson Airplane, poster, Other Half, 1967, 14x20", M 50.00
Kinks, concert ticket, w/Taj Mahal & Sha-Na-Na, 1969, M 35.00
Kiss, backstage pass, Japan tour, laminated 15.00
Kiss, bracelet & pin set, metal ID, England, 1970s, scarce 75.00
Kiss, bust of band, ceramic, authorized, 1978, rare 225.00
Kiss, calendar, Eric Carr pictured, 1986, M, sealed 30.00
Kiss, dolls, Mego, set of 4, M in EX boxes 500.00
Kiss, game, On Tour, EX/NM 35.00
Kiss, guitar pick, used by G Simmons, in fr w/2 ticket stubs 50.00
Kiss, gum cards, series I, complete set of 66, EX 50.00
Kiss, Halloween costume of Gene, Paul, Ace or Peter, ea 50.00
Kiss, interview picture disk collection, M in holder 50.00
Kiss, jacket, flame pattern, 1978, M, unused 90.00
Kiss, jeans jacket w/full-sz bk patch, 1970s, EX 25.00
Kiss, lapel pin, blk & gold on sterling, 2¾", on '77 card 35.00
Kiss, magazine cover, Crazy, 1978, EX 17.00
Kiss, Marvel comic w/poster #2, M 48.00
Kiss, necklace, 3-D logo in silver on gold finish 10.00
Kiss, patch, entire band, Dynasty Promo, 4x3", NM 8.00
Kiss, pendant, heavy silver-tone metal w/Gene's head & logo 35.00
Kiss, poster 'put ons,' self adhesive, '76, 8½x9¾", M 12.00
Kiss, puzzle, Destroyer, complete, w/box 30.00
Kiss, puzzle, Gene Simmons, MIB 30.00
Kiss, tour program, World Tour '77 & '78, EX 50.00
Knickerbockers, concert program, 1960s, M 25.00
Led Zeppelin, book, portraits, orig lg sz 40.00
Led Zeppelin, button, concert promo, 1977, 3" dia, M 18.00
Led Zeppelin, concert poster, blk on gray, 17x22" 70.00
Led Zeppelin, patch, promo for album, MIE, 4x3½", M 8.00
Lee Michaels/Rod Stewart, concert poster, Singer, '70, 14x22" ...75.00
Madonna, backstage pass from concert 10.00
Mama Cass, Showbiz Baby doll 60.00
Marie Osmond, dress pattern, M in pkg 5.00
Michael Jackson, Beat It outfit for doll, M on card 18.00
Michael Jackson, doll, Grammy Awards, 12", MIB 45.00
Michael Jackson, doll, Thriller, 12", MIB 45.00
Michael Jackson, Human Nature pop folio (pocket folder), NM ..12.00
Michael Jackson, Peel-Away Stickers, M on card 10.00
Mick Jagger, paperback promo cover, Performance 15.00
Monkees, book, Who's Got the Button?, hardcover 14.00
Monkees, eyeglasses, 1960s, w/tag 35.00
Monkees, finger puppets, Remco, 1970, M 25.00
Monkees, flasher ring 15.00
Monkees, guitar, Mattel, 1966, 24", M 90.00
Monkees, ID bracelet, M 38.00
Monkees, lunch pail, vinyl, w/thermos, NM 300.00
Monkees, Monkee Mobile, 3" diecast figures, Husky, VG 50.00
Monkees, playing cards, photo illus, 1966, MIB 35.00
Monkees, poster, World Tour, Philadelphia, 1986 ....7.00
Monkees, talking hand puppet, Mattel, 1966, mute, EX 45.00

Monkees, wax pack, unopened, 1960s 15.00
Monkees, writing tablet, photo front, unused, 8½x11" 40.00
Mother Earth, concert poster, Kaleidoscope, 14½x21½", M 15.00
Pat Boone, charm bracelet, w/records/shoes/photo/TV 30.00
Paul Revere & the Raiders, concert program, 1960s, M 25.00
Paul Revere & the Raiders, model kit, M, sealed 350.00
Poison, first aid kit, Unskinny Bop, pill form, filled 24.00
Police, concert program, 1983, M 10.00
Prince Lovesexy, concert program, 1988, M 10.00
REM, poster, M in tube 35.00
Rolling Stones, belt buckle, silver metal, 1970s, M 25.00
Rolling Stones, button, blk/wht, England, 1964 ....25.00
Rolling Stones, concert program, Hawaii, 1973, M 15.00
Rolling Stones, key ring, 1983, M on tongue card w/photos 9.00
Rolling Stones, poster, Steelwheels Tour, mc, 1989, 15x19" 15.00
Rolling Stones, self-sticking tongues, set of 36 on orig card 3.00
Rolling Stones, sheet music, Stupid Girl, photo cover, 1966 ....5.00
Rolling Stones, tour itinerary & photos, August 1972 ....20.00
Rolling Stones, wall clock, Musidor, 1983, 12x21", MIB 25.00
Sex Pistols, patch, concert promotional, 1976, 3x2", M 8.00
Sha-Na-Na, concert program, 1980s, M 10.00
Steppenwolf, concert poster, blk/wht, 1968, 14x21", M 20.00
Supertramp, concert program, 1983, M 10.00
The Who, feature in Crawdaddy Rock Magazine, 1968 ....15.00
Three Dog Night, concert poster, John Mayall, 1970s 20.00
Tom Petty, poster, M 35.00
Van Halen, binoculars, w/Van Halen logo 15.00
Van Halen, concert program, 1986, M 10.00
Van Halen, key chain, brass-colored metal, M 8.00
Warrant, mug, Cherry Pie, ceramic 14.00

Rockingham

In the early part of the 19th century, American potters began to prefer brown- and buff-burning clays over red because of their durability. The glaze favored by many was Rockingham, which varied from a dark brown mottle to a sponged effect sometimes called tortoise shell. It consisted in part of manganese and various metallic salts and was used by many potters until well into the 20th century. Over the past two years, demand and prices have risen sharply, especially in the east. For further information we recommend *Collector's Guide to Rockingham, The Enduring Ware*, by Mary Brewer. See also Bennington.

Bottle, molded arch design w/female busts, 7¾x3½x2½" 130.00
Bowl, mixing; 10½", EX 85.00
Bowl, shallow, 2½x9" 50.00
Bowl, tub shape, 6¼" 200.00
Crock, cherub heads form hdls, 5x6¾" 75.00
Dog, seated, EX molded detail, 10" 200.00
Dog, seated, primitive, 10¼" 140.00
Frame, brn Bennington-type glaze, sm chip, oval, 7x8" 200.00
Pie plate, lt wear, 9¾" 85.00
Pie plate, 11" 135.00
Pitcher, ferns in relief, 10" 200.00
Pitcher, hanging game in relief, 11" 250.00
Pitcher, tulips in relief, 7" 100.00
Pitcher, 19th C, 11½" 345.00
Pitcher, 6¼" 50.00
Platter, octagonal, 12¾" 250.00
Platter, octagonal, 14¾" 350.00
Soap dish, rectangular w/flared top edge, 2⅜x7¾x5⅝" 65.00
Spittoon, molded shells at rim, 4x7¾", EX 35.00
Teapot, molded Chinamen, paneled, prof rpr to lid, 9¾" 95.00

Teapot, Rebekah at the Well, paneled, 7¾" 85.00
Toby bottle, 9⅝" 110.00
Toby pitcher, 7⅛" 130.00

Rogers, John

John Rogers (1829-1904) was a machinist from Manchester, New Hampshire, who turned his hobby of sculpting into a financially successful venture. From the originals he meticulously fashioned of red clay, he had bronze master molds made from which plaster copies were cast. He specialized in five different categories: theatrical, Shakespeare, Civil War, everyday life, and horses. His large detailed groupings portrayed the life and times of the period between 1859 and 1892. When no condition is indicated, examples are assumed to be in very good to excellent condition. Our advisor for this category is George Humphrey; he is listed in the Directory under Maryland.

Balcony 1,500.00
Bushwacker 2,000.00
Charity Patient 650.00
Chess 825.00
Country Post Office 750.00
Fairy's Whisper, ca 1881 ....1,400.00
Fetching the Doctor 750.00
First Ride 725.00
Football, inscr, 16x11" 1,000.00
Hide & Seek 2,000.00
Home Guard 800.00
Matter of Opinion 600.00
Neighboring Pews 475.00
Peddler at the Fair 800.00
Picket Guard 750.00
Politics 700.00
Referee 600.00
Rip Van Winkle at Home, 18½" 425.00
School Days 600.00

The Shaughraun and Tatters, marked John Rogers, New York, $700.00.

Slave Auction 2,000.00
Speak for Yourself John 600.00
Traveling Magician, ca 1877 ....750.00
Washington 1,250.00
Watch on the Santa Maria 750.00
Weighing the Baby, Pat 1875, 21" 600.00
Wounded Scout, ca 1864 ....750.00

Rookwood

The Rookwood Pottery Company was established in 1879 in

Cincinnati, Ohio. Its founder was Maria Longworth Nichols Storer, daughter of a wealthy family who provided the backing necessary to make such an enterprise possible. Mrs. Storer hired competent ceramic workers who through constant experimentation developed many lines of superior art pottery. While in her employ, Laura Fry invented the air-brush-blending process for which she was issued a patent in 1884. From this, several lines were designed that utilized blended backgrounds. One of their earlier lines, Standard, was a brown ware decorated with under-glaze slip-painted nature studies, animals, portraits, etc. Iris and Sea Green were introduced in 1894 and Vellum, a transparent mat-glaze line, in 1904. Other lines followed: Ombroso in 1910 and Soft Porcelain in 1915. Many of the early artware lines were signed by the artist. Soon after the turn of the 20th century, Rookwood manufactured 'production' pieces that relied mainly on molded designs and forms rather than freehand decoration for their esthetic appeal. The Depression brought on financial difficulties from which the pottery never recovered. Though it continued to operate, the quality of the ware deteriorated, and the pottery was forced to close in 1967.

Unmarked Rookwood is only rarely encountered. Many marks may be found, but the most familiar is the reverse 'RP' monogram. First used in 1886, a flame point was added above it for each succeeding year until 1900. After that a Roman numeral added below indicated the year of manufacture. Impressed letters that related to the type of clay utilized for the body were also used — G for ginger, O for olive, R for red, S for sage green, W for white, and Y for yellow. Artware must be judged on an individual basis. Quality of the artwork is a prime factor to consider. Portraits, animals, and birds are worth more than florals; and pieces signed by a particularly renowned artist are highly prized. Our advice for this category comes from Fer-Duc Inc., whose address is listed in the Directory under New York.

Black Opal

Vase, floral, H Wilcox, #839B, 1925, 9⅜" 1,100.00
Vase, floral, stylized, H Wilcox, #2065, 1924, 7¾" 950.00
Vase, floral, trailing, L Epply, #2785, 1925, 13⅝" 2,000.00

Cameo

Bowl, dogwood blossoms on pk, 1888, #228B, 10½" 200.00
Bowl, floral on tan shaded, S Toohey, 1893, #198W, 2x7" 100.00
Cup & saucer, wht floral, H Wilcox, 1887, #291, 3", 5" dia 230.00
Pitcher, dogwood blossoms, AR Valentien, 1887, #335B, 7", NM .350.00
Pitcher, honeysuckle, A Van Briggle, 1888, #246, 8¼" 475.00
Pitcher, mums, mc on brn to cream, 1887, #48, 6½" 70.00
Plate, apple blossoms, unsgn, wht clay, 1887, #317B, 9¼" 250.00
Vase, orange blossoms w/gold, G Young, 1888, #403W, 4½" 700.00

Iris

Vase, apple blossoms, C Steinle, 1906, #935E, 6⅛" 950.00
Vase, barn swallows in flight, Schmidt, #935C, 9" 4,300.00
Vase, calla lilies on wht, C Schmidt, 1906, #905, 15" 5,750.00
Vase, cherry blossoms, wht, E Lincoln, 1909, #900D, 6¼" 1,200.00
Vase, chrysanthemums, John D Wareham, 1902, #905B, 14½" .8,000.00
Vase, clover & honey bees, C Schmidt, 1902, no #, 6½" 1,600.00
Vase, clover blossoms, R Fechheimer, 1904, #614F, 6" 500.00
Vase, crane in grasses, K Shirayamadani, 1907, #907F, 7" 4,100.00
Vase, crocus, wht, C Schmidt, 1904, #904E, 6⅜" 1,300.00
Vase, crocus on blk to gr, C Schmidt, 1908, #904CC, 10⅜" .17,000.00
Vase, daisies, C Steinle, 1909, #1655F, 6¼" 1,100.00
Vase, dandelions, I Bishop, 1903, #926E, 6" 450.00
Vase, daylilies, wht, C Schmidt, 1907, #950C, 9¾" 3,300.00
Vase, dragon coiled at shoulder, OG Reed, 1896, #743C, 6⅝" .1,300.00

Vase, fish, ET Hurley, 1906, #902D, 6⅝", NM 3,700.00
Vase, fish & ribbons, L Asbury, 1898, #762C, 5⅝" 5,250.00
Vase, floral, S Sax, 1906, #951E, 7⅛", EX 500.00
Vase, floral on gray, I Bishop, 1906, #950E, X mk, 7¼", NM 550.00
Vase, hydrangeas, A Valentien, 1904, #940B, 12⅜" 9,750.00
Vase, iris & 2 buds, C Lindeman, 1909, #1278E, 8¼" 1,100.00
Vase, irises on blk to gray, C Schmidt, 1903, #907E, 8½" 9,250.00
Vase, irises on wht, S Sax, 1903, #901BB, 9¾" 2,000.00
Vase, Japanese irises on blk, C Schmidt, 1909, #951C, 14" ...14,500.00
Vase, milkweeds, C Schmidt, 1903, #907C, 13¾" 17,000.00
Vase, peacock feathers on blk, C Schmidt, 1908, #950C, 9¾" ..11,000.00
Vase, pine cones, R Fechheimer, 1901, #786D, 8¼" 1,300.00
Vase, Queen Anne's lace, S Sax, 1906, #935C, 8¼" 2,600.00
Vase, Virginia creepers, F Rothenbusch, 1905, #905D, 7⅝" ...1,400.00

Limoges

Bowl, bat in weeds, 4-color w/gold, M Rettig, ftd, 1883, 2x5" 150.00
Ewer, Oriental swallows & grasses, M Rettig, 1883, #101, 11" ...750.00
Jar, floral, A Valentien, 1885, #142C, 5½" 950.00
Jar, tea; bamboo & butterfly, NJ Hirschfield, 1883, #97, 5⅛" 600.00

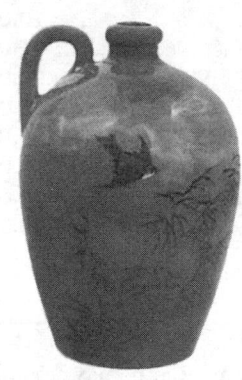

Jug, bird flying in landscape, brown, white, and gold on blue-green to green, signed A.R. Valentien, #12A, 1884, 8", $1,000.00.

Jug, bird soars among rushes, AR Valentien, 1884, #61, 4½" 325.00
Jug, butterfly over rushes, A Valentien, 1884, #61, 5" 325.00
Jug, cherry blossoms, Myer Asch, 1883, #61, 5" 400.00
Jug, perfume; clouds/grasses/bird, M Rettig, 1884, #60, 4⅝" 300.00
Jug, perfume; dragonfly/grasses, M Rettig, 1883, #61, 4¾" 350.00
Jug, spiders/web/cattails, A Humphreys, 1882, anchor mk, 5" 300.00
Plate, bird, pie-crust rim, AM Bookprinter, 1885, #87, 6½" 160.00
Plate, butterfly, pie-crust rim, Rettig, 1885, #87, 6½" 160.00
Shell dish, birds & flowers w/gold, MHP, 1882, #222, 2½x8½" ...80.00
Tankard, dogwood blossoms on cobalt, ETK, 1882, 9½", EX 850.00
Teapot, birds soar among rushes, AR Valentien, 1884, #69, 6" ..950.00
Vase, bats & full moon, M Longworth Nichols, 1882, 6½x9" .2,000.00
Vase, butterfly/grasses/clouds, unsgn, 1885, #90C, 4⅛" 300.00
Vase, geese in flight/grasses, A Valentien, 1882, #65R, 9¾" ...2,000.00
Vase, ships at night, MFG, pocket form, 1882, rpr, 4⅛" 375.00

Mat

Note: Both incised mat and painted mat are listed here. Incised mat descriptions are indicated by the term 'cvd' within the line; the others are for the hand-painted mat ware.

Mug, Arts & Crafts geese in flight, A Pons, 1907, #587C, 5" 600.00
Vase, Arts & Crafts leaves, M Mitchell, 1904, #914F, 4⅞" 1,000.00
Vase, Arts & Crafts peacock feather, Toohey, '03, #30ZD, 5⅜" .550.00
Vase, berries & leaves, CS Todd, 1919, #977, 10⅞" 900.00
Vase, cvd buds at shoulder on gr, Duell, 1908, 8¾" 900.00
Vase, cvd floral, dk brn, H Wenderoth, 1882, 7½" 170.00

Vase, cvd lg floral, pk on gr, Pons, #1098, 1907, 3x5", NM 350.00
Vase, cvd/pnt mushrooms, E Barrett, 1930, #8926, 9" 475.00
Vase, Deco-style leaves, W Hentschel, 1929, #892C, 8⅞" 800.00
Vase, floral, K Shirayamadani, 1938, #913C, 9¼" 1,700.00
Vase, floral, M McDonald, 1925, #1357D, 8⅞" 550.00
Vase, floral, W Hentschel, 1926, #931, 4¾" 500.00
Vase, iris blossoms, JW Pullman, 1927, #30E, 8½" 375.00
Vase, moths in band, W Hentschel, 1912, #1356C, 11" 700.00
Vase, repeating florals, W Hentschel, 1913, #1343, 4⅞" 950.00
Vase, stylized florals, mc on aqua, Barrett, 1925, #614F, 7" 300.00
Vase, swells & waves, K Shirayamadani, 1902, #927E, 6¾", NM ..2,300.00
Vase, tulips, mc on gray, A Sprague, 1901, #51DZ, 5⅛" 1,400.00
Vase, 3 dogs, J Jensen, 1934, mk S (special shape), 3⅞" 2,100.00
Wall pocket, lilies, bl, 1920, #1397, 11" 325.00

Porcelain

Bowl, Deco deer & blossoms, J Jensen, 1946, #2813C, 3x13½" ..1,000.00
Vase, berried branches, A Conant, 1919, #233, 8" 1,000.00
Vase, birches along water, ET Hurley, 1945, #6197C, 8½" 6,500.00
Vase, birds & berries, S Sax, 1917, #2065, 7½" 1,700.00
Vase, birds in 3 scenic panels, A Conant, 1919, #2103, 5½" ..2,800.00
Vase, blossoms & leaves, J Harris, 1939, #924, 6" 400.00
Vase, butterflies/flowers/trees, A Conant, 1921, #2547, 9½" ..6,500.00
Vase, cascading flowers, S Sax, Jewel, '22, #356F, 5½x2¾" 750.00
Vase, Chinese Plum, bleeding hearts, Shirayamadani, '26, 10" ...7,000.00
Vase, Chinese Plum, blossoms, HE Wilcox, 1926, #2825A, 16½" ...18,000.00
Vase, Chinese Plum, floral, S Sax, 1923, #77C, 5½" 2,100.00
Vase, Chinese Plum, floral, S Sax, 1933, #2918B, rpr, 11" 2,900.00
Vase, Chinese Plum, pansies/blossoms, Wilcox, '24, #2105, 5" ..850.00
Vase, exotic birds/flowers, Hentschel, 1925, #2246C, 14½" 2,100.00
Vase, fish, wht on butterfat texture, J Jenson, Jewel, '34, 5" 350.00
Vase, floral wreath at shoulder, L Epply, Jewel, '19, 5½" 1,000.00
Vase, florals w/gold, S Sax, 1920, #1091D, 6½" 800.00
Vase, jonquils & buds, Shirayamadani, 1926, #494B, 5" 3,250.00
Vase, lg blossoms, L Holtkamp, 1945, #2781, 7" 450.00
Vase, lg blossoms, MH McDonald, EX art, 1939, #902D, 7½" ...800.00
Vase, lg parrot, Shirayamadani, Jewel, 1930, 9" 2,750.00
Vase, magnolias on branches, L Holtkamp, 1949, #2984A, 16" .900.00
Vase, peacock feathers on cream, S Sax, Jewel, 1917, 7" 925.00
Vase, stylized female nudes, J Jensen, 1937, #904D, 8½" 2,000.00
Vase, stylized fish & waves, J Jensen, 1945, #C184E, 7" 600.00
Vase, stylized floral, WE Hentschel, 1920, #943E, 7" 1,000.00
Vase, vertical & horizontal ribs, S Sax, 1927, #2942, 6" 700.00
Vase, vertical lines on curdled ground, L Holtkamp, '57, 6" 400.00
Vase, wide & narrow stripes, L Holtkamp, '51, #6933, 12" 350.00

Sea Green

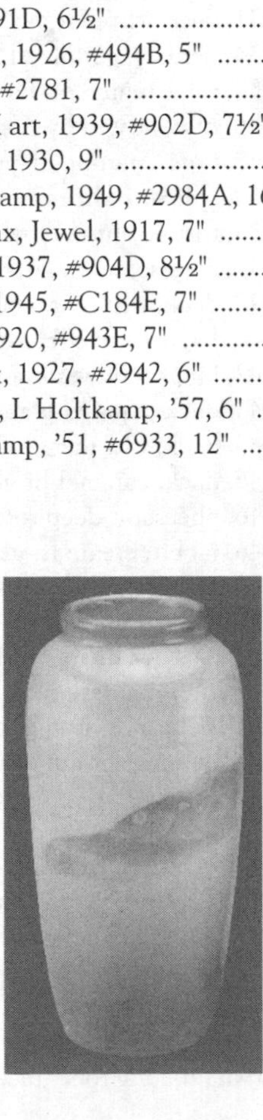

Vase, fish, E.T. Hurley, #904E, 1906, 6⅝x3", $2,300.00.

Vase, flock of geese, AR Valentien, 1896, #745A, 11" 4,000.00
Vase, floral, C Baker, 1896, #379, 9", NM 3,500.00
Vase, floral, S Coyne, 1901, #922, X mk, 5½" 550.00
Vase, grasshopper in cattails, M Daly, 1895, #496A, 12½" 1,200.00
Vase, hyacinths, S Coyne, 1901, #915C, prof rpr, 7" 1,600.00
Vase, iris/bud/dragonfly, C Baker, 1895, #786D, 8¼" 900.00
Vase, irises on gr, S Laurence, 1902, #932B, 14½" 7,000.00
Vase, lilies of the valley, E Lincoln, 1905, #926D, 7" 1,100.00
Vase, rose spray on thorny branches, Coyne, 1901, #920, 5¾" .1,725.00
Vase, sea gulls & choppy seas, S Laurence, 1902, #892B, 10⅜" .4,600.00
Vase, sea gulls & clouds, ET Hurley, 1900, #46, 9¼" 2,600.00
Vase, tulips on dk gr, S Laurence, 1901, #926C, 8⅛" 1,600.00
Vase, 3 robins in tree, ET Hurley, 1899, #883E, X mk, 5¾" 1,000.00

Standard

Jardiniere, dragons, unsgn Shirayamadani, 1899, #S1476, 11" ..2,200.00
Jug, berries & leaves, Dibowski, 1889, #677, 8½" 400.00
Jug, whiskey; Am Indian, ET Hurley, 1898, #512B, 9⅛" 3,400.00
Jug, whiskey; corn, silver o/l, OG Reed, 1892, #677, 11" 3,100.00
Mug, boy's portrait, AM Valentien, twist hdl, 1890, #328B, 6" ..650.00
Mug, hops, E Felten, 1901, #587C, X mk, 4⅝" 275.00
Mug, wheat, E Lincoln, 1900, #837, 5" 325.00
Pitcher, floral, mc, ER Felton, 1899, #838F, 5", NM 100.00
Vase, Am Indian, MA Daly, 1899, #786C, 9⅜", NM 3,500.00
Vase, berries, S Toohey, 1895, #715D, 6⅞" 600.00
Vase, clover blossoms, C Lindeman, 1903, #745C, 5⅝", NM 325.00
Vase, clover blossoms, K Shirayamadani, 1889, #48CE, rpr, 7" ..275.00
Vase, clover blossoms, L Perkins, 1893, #468D, 7¼", NM 375.00
Vase, daffodils, CA Baker, 1894, #503B, rpr, 7" 275.00
Vase, daffodils, Coyne, #903B, 1901, 10x6" 1,265.00
Vase, daisies on pillow form, G Young, 1886, #90C, 3⅞" 325.00
Vase, floral, K Hickman, 1899, #860, 6⅛" 350.00
Vase, floral, MA Daly, 1901, #922B, 10⅝" 1,000.00
Vase, floral branches, K Shirayamadani, #589D, 11½", NM 450.00
Vase, lg blossoms & stems, J Swing, 1903, #922D, 7" 300.00
Vase, lotus blossoms, A Valentien, 1886, #197R, 28⅞" 4,100.00
Vase, nasturtiums, G Young, 1897, #740, 7⅞" 2,200.00
Vase, orange blossoms, E Noonan, 1904, #916E, 4" 200.00
Vase, quince, silver o/l, K Shirayamadani, 1890, #507S, 15⅜" ..24,000.00
Vase, roses, A Sprague, 1893, #534C, 6¾", +provenance 1,300.00
Vase, roses, W Klemm, 1901, #712, 4¾", +provenance 400.00
Vase, teasel, L Linderman, 1902, #917E, 5¾" 475.00

Tiger Eye

Creamer, entwined tracery, chestnut on brn, sgn MR, #211 ....350.00
Jug, water; dragonfly & mums, M Daly, 1885, rpr, 8½" 500.00
Vase, daisies on red to brn, AR Valentien, 1885, #142B, 6" 200.00

Vellum

Candlestick, winged dragon on gr, L Epply, 1909, #922G, 7" 500.00
Lamp, wisteria, K Shirayamadani, 1904, #907C, complete, 14" ..5,250.00
Plaque, Arts & Crafts landscape, Asbury, '12, 3¾x7½"+fr 1,700.00
Plaque, landscape, L Asbury, 1918, 9¼x14⅜"+fr 4,700.00
Plaque, marine scene, Ed Diers, 1913, 8¼x10½"+fr 3,900.00
Plaque, mountain scenic, F Rothenbusch, 1927, 9⅞x11⅞" 7,750.00
Plaque, snowy mtns & pines, E Diers, 1919, 9¼x14½" 4,400.00
Plaque, snowy pines & stream, S Coyne, 1915, 5⅛x8⅛" 2,500.00
Plaque, tree-lined lake, C Schmidt, 1919, 8½x10¾" 4,300.00
Plaque, view of ocean through sand, S Cox, 1913, 8½x10¾" .3,700.00
Plaque, winter landscape on porc, S Coyne, 1922, 7⅞x9⅞" ...4,600.00
Plaque, Winter Sunset, shoreline, Coyne, fr, 5x9" 2,185.00

Vase, Arts & Crafts evergreens, ET Hurley, #2060, 7⅝" 1,700.00
Vase, berry band, ET Hurley, 1922, #2236, 5⅜" 350.00
Vase, birches, bl/pk/lav, ET Hurley, 1942, #1721, rpr, 6¼" 600.00
Vase, birches & meadow, Ed Diers, #1358D, 1923, 8¾x4" 2,400.00
Vase, birches & water, ET Hurley, 1944, #6869, 9" 2,300.00
Vase, Cincinnati riverfront, E Diers, 1907, #907#, 9⅛" 3,600.00
Vase, daisies, L Epply, 1906, D30F, X mk, 6⅛" 500.00
Vase, Deco florals, L Epply, 1930, #2933, 11¾" 2,500.00
Vase, dogwood blossom band, K Van Horne, 1910, #939D, 7⅝" .500.00
Vase, ducks in flight, wht on bl-gr band, Asbury, 1908, 8x6" ..2,600.00
Vase, floral, att F Rothenbusch, 1932, #295E, 7⅛" 500.00
Vase, floral, mc on peach w/bl neck, CST, 1916, #912, 7" 600.00
Vase, floral, MG Denzler, 1917, #47C, 6⅛" 550.00
Vase, floral on bl to pk, Rothenbusch, 1915, #951E, 7½", NM ..450.00
Vase, oak leaves, S Coyne, 1904, #31DZ, 5⅜" 750.00
Vase, orchid, C Schmidt, 1905, #30E, 6" 1,000.00
Vase, Oriental fruit blossoms, ET Hurley, 1916, #2033C, 12⅜" .700.00
Vase, pines reflecting, ET Hurley, 1916, #1660D, 9¼" 3,000.00
Vase, scenic landscape, bl on gr, L Epply, 1912, #892C, 9" 1,000.00
Vase, tree scene, L Asbury, 1914, #1658E, 8" 1,700.00
Vase, tree scene panorama, Rothenbusch, rpr drill hole, 10" 800.00
Vase, tree-lined lake, ET Hurley, 1940, #30E, 8⅜" 2,400.00
Vase, trees reflecting, C Schmidt, 1917, #950B, 13" 3,900.00
Vase, trees reflecting, E Diers, 1927, #2032E, 7⅝" 2,000.00
Vase, trees/hillside, F Rothenbusch, '14, #2039, 11½", EX 400.00
Vase, Venetian harbor on gr, C Schmidt, 1925, #808, rpr, 8" ...3,400.00
Vase, wild roses, E Diers, 1908, #917C, 7⅞" 900.00
Vase, wild roses, F Rothenbusch, 1908, #12789E, X mk, 8⅞" 550.00
Vase, wild roses, F Rothenbusch, 1914, #1369D, 9" 800.00
Vase, 2 fish among seaweed & foam, Hurley, 1906, #951C, 10" ...4,100.00

Wax Mat

Mask, Art Deco face, L Abel, 1931, #6244, 9½" 1,900.00
Vase, bold floral, Delia Workman, 1928, 5" 500.00
Vase, delicate floral, J Harris, 1929, #2309, 7" 375.00
Vase, floral, mc on curdled bl, S Coyne, 1934, #892C, 9" 475.00
Vase, floral, thorny stems, MH McDonald, 1926, #2672, 8" 600.00
Vase, floral branches, K Jones, 1923, #356F, 6½" 325.00
Vase, lilies/wisteria/tulips, Shirayamadani, '37, #2932, 14" 5,500.00
Vase, repeating florals, C Covalenco, 1925, #614B, 15" 1,800.00
Vase, stylized floral, E Barrett, 1924, #2672, 8" 650.00
Vase, stylized floral, J Jensen, 1928, #927E, 7" 425.00
Vase, stylized floral, J Wesley Pullman, 1930, #6200D, 7x6" 600.00
Vase, stylized floral on triangles, E Barrett, '24, #1918, 9" 750.00

Miscellaneous

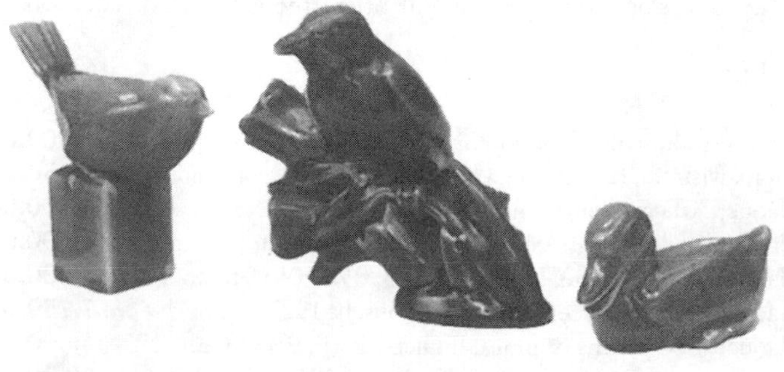

Figurines: Sparrow on block, 1946, green hi-glaze, #6383, 4", EX, $50.00; Bird on flower branch, blue hi-glaze, 1942, #6837, 5", $125.00; Duck, 1946, caramel hi-glaze, #6064, 3", $100.00.

Ashtray, 1929, frog w/open mouth, blk hi-glaze, #6097, 3" 170.00
Ashtray, 1938, rook on tray, lt bl mat, #1139, 7½" W 180.00
Ashtray, 1943, clown w/legs wide on sq tray, S Toohey, #6026 ..275.00
Ashtray, 1943, owl at side, gr mat, #1084, 5" 200.00
Ashtray, 1944, fox at side, wht, #2647, 6" 135.00
Basket, 1925, gr mat, #2059, 6" 60.00
Bookends, sphinx, 1920, gr mat, #2503, 7⅛", pr 700.00
Bookends, 1919, elephant, gunmetal gray, #2444D, pr 325.00
Bookends, 1922, rook, olive, gr & brn mat, #2275, 5x5½", pr 300.00
Bookends, 1923, rook seated, brn mat, #2275, 5x5½", pr 220.00
Bookends, 1924, peacock on throne, yel, #3345, 5", pr 325.00
Bookends, 1929, collie, gray mat, #2779, 6", pr 425.00
Bookends, 1937, 3 blind mice, tan mat, #6641, 4", NM, pr 600.00
Bookends, 1938, elephant, trunk up, wht mat, #6124, 7", pr 325.00
Bookends, 1943, owl on book, wht mat, #2655, 5½", pr 250.00
Bookends, 1943, rook, wht mat, #2275, 5x5½", pr 240.00
Bookends, 1946, hound, gr hi-glaze, #2998, 6", M, pr 120.00
Bowl, 1923, curved leaves w/buds, bl mat, #2529, 2½x12" 140.00
Bowl, 1929, Oriental style, 5-ftd, yel mat, #2802, 4x8" 160.00
Box, 1927, mother & child, bl/gray mat, #2456, 2x4x3" 240.00
Bust, 1930, lady, greenware, w/stand, #2026, 7½x7" 200.00
Butter dish, 1930s, Blue Ship, #M-13, 3½" 450.00
Candlestick, 1941, nude reclining, wht mat, #2595, 5" 250.00
Candlesticks, 1922, organic decor, gr, #1193, 7", pr 275.00
Centerpc, 1921, flower basket form, HP by C Steinle, #2521 ..1,250.00
Clock, 1950, figure of boy beside, wht hi-glaze, #7053, 7" 300.00
Creamer & sugar bowl, 1949, yel hi-glaze, #547, 3", 3½" 45.00
Ewer, 1959, Bengal Brn, RE Menzel, S (special shape), 7" 375.00
Figurine, 1924, dog, wht mat, #2777, 5" 325.00
Figurine, 1924, monkey, brn mat, #2677, 4x4½" 275.00
Figurine, 1928, nude seated, wht mat, #2868, 4½" 425.00
Figurine, 1929, swan on water, bl & wht, #6021, 4" 230.00
Figurine, 1931, Deco elephant, L Abel, #6256, 6¼" 800.00
Figurine, 1931, deer, wht mat, #6170, 6½" 200.00
Figurine, 1934, donkey, gunmetal, #6241, 6" 200.00
Figurine, 1934, nude seated on base, wht mat, #2868, 4x4" 210.00
Figurine, 1935, nude seated by frog, ivory mat, #6521, 4½" 225.00
Figurine, 1939, horse, gunmetal gr, #6140, 6½" 300.00
Figurine, 1939, pelican, wht mat, #6149, 6" 225.00
Figurine, 1939, turtle, wht mat, #1686, 4½" 300.00
Figurine, 1939, 2 geese, wht mat, #1555, 4" 250.00
Figurine, 1940, duck, wht mat, #6064, 3½" 100.00
Figurine, 1941, donkey, sgn MH McDonald, wht mat, #6216, 6" ..400.00
Figurine, 1942, bird on flower branch, bl hi-glaze, #6837, 5" 125.00
Figurine, 1943, duck, aqua hi-glaze, #6064, 3" 100.00
Figurine, 1945, duck, wht mat, #6064, 3" 100.00
Figurine, 1946, duck, caramel hi-glaze, #6064, 3" 100.00
Figurine, 1946, pheasant, deep rose, #2832, 8½" 200.00
Figurine, 1946, rabbit, cream hi-glaze, #6160, 3" 120.00
Figurine, 1949, polar bear, wht mat, #6124, 4" 375.00
Figurine, 1949, polar bear, wht mat, #6484, 4" 425.00
Flower frog, 1921, satyr sitting on tortoise, #2336, 7" 150.00
Flower frog, 1925, floral design, aqua hi-glaze, #2702, 6¼" 45.00
Flower frog, 1926, bird on stump, aqua hi-glaze, #2710, 6" 125.00
Humidor, 1930, copper-dust crystalline, #6136, 4⅛" 550.00
Lamp, 1918, cvd pine needles, gr mat, #1134P, 14" 750.00
Lamp, 1920s, blk w/mc floral bottom, #2613, partial label 500.00
Letter holder, 1941, molded stamp w/Franklin, bl hi-glaze, 3x4" .170.00
Paperweight, 1928, fruit basket, mc, #6020, 3½" 210.00
Paperweight, 1935, grapes, rose, #6388, 6" L 145.00
Pitcher, 1945, wht mat, #1944, 10" 160.00
Tile, cherub among blossoms, mc, #93 W2, 2x14x1½" 1,600.00
Tile, Faience, emb grapes, #82, 7⅞x7⅞" 650.00
Tile, Grecian maid, long robe, mc, 8-tile panel, 33x17", pr 5,750.00

Tile, 1924, bird w/flowers, mc, #3124, 6" sq 300.00
Tile, 1949, parrot, gr/red/yel hi-glaze, #2048, 6" sq 145.00
Tray, 1908, geometrics at rim, bl over gr mat, #1305, 6" dia 50.00
Tray, 1924, peacock feathers, pk mat, #1668, 7" 65.00
Tray, 1924, swan figural, bl mat, #1213, 5½" W 170.00
Tray, 1927, nude reclines at side, aqua hi-glaze, #2595, 4½" 225.00
Tray, 1935, frog at side, ivory mat, #2765, 6" 200.00
Tray, 1954, 2-tiered, gray/brn hi-glaze, #S22028, 11x12" dia 60.00
Trivet, 1922, bird on branch, mc on turq w/wht, #2349, 6" dia ..220.00
Trivet, 1929, sea gull, aqua & wht, #2351, 5" dia 185.00
Vase, bud; 1954, lily & leaf form, gr hi-glaze, #6591, 5" 55.00
Vase, 1894, Aerial Bl, St Francis, Horsfall, #273, 6¾" 12,000.00
Vase, 1911, Arts & Crafts, hdls, brn mat, #1807, 4½x5" 130.00
Vase, 1912, tasseled hdl ends, dk brn & dk red mat, #2928, 15" .210.00
Vase, 1918, solid blk w/bl int, #2442, 15⅞" 425.00
Vase, 1918, swans swimming, bl mat, #2097, 3½" 180.00
Vase, 1919, aqua hi-glaze, #2496, orig label, 27½" 600.00
Vase, 1919, Arts & Crafts decor, pk mat, #1811, 5½x7½" 125.00
Vase, 1919, Chinese plum over mc florals/trees, #943D, 8" 500.00
Vase, 1919, emb florals, dk purple mat, #2493, 11½" 225.00
Vase, 1919, emb florals at base, tan on wht, #2478, 7½" 130.00
Vase, 1919, French Red, leaves, S Sax, #1656E, X mk, 7⅜" 600.00
Vase, 1921, French Red, peacocks, S Sax, #2372, 16¼" 31,000.00
Vase, 1922, classic form, curdled blk mat, #2032C, 12" 180.00
Vase, 1923, emb bluebells at neck, brn & bl mat, #2111, 6" 300.00
Vase, 1923, emb florals, bl mat, #2118, 6½" 160.00
Vase, 1923, 5-sided w/rook decor, bl mat, #1795, 5" 180.00
Vase, 1924, blk hi-glaze, #1357C, 11" 130.00
Vase, 1925, emb geometrics at waist, hdls, bl mat, #2768, 4" 100.00
Vase, 1926, faint geometric decor at rim, pk mat, #2112, 6½" ...105.00
Vase, 1926, sqs on shoulders, gray & gr mat, #2312, 6½" 130.00
Vase, 1927, Arts & Crafts decor, pk mat, #2283, 5½" 115.00
Vase, 1927, hdls, lt gr & pk mat, #77-C, 5½" 125.00
Vase, 1928, emb birds & flowers, lt bl mat, #6032, 11" 150.00
Vase, 1928, geometrics, hdls, gr on pk mat, #2741, 5¾x3½" 60.00
Vase, 1930, clover, purple mat, #6029, 6" 250.00
Vase, 1930, flower panels, brn mat, #6147, 6½" 250.00
Vase, 1930, 5 daisy-like blossoms, brn mat, #3380, 6½" 170.00
Vase, 1932, deer & flora, bulbous, gr hi-glaze, #6053, 7½" 150.00
Vase, 1932, deer & flora, wht mat, #6053, 7½" 80.00
Vase, 1934, Deco-style deer, aqua hi-glaze, #6214, 4½" 140.00
Vase, 1934, emb florals at top, wht mat, #6363, 5½" 80.00
Vase, 1935, emb mistletoe, wht mat, #6545, 4x4½" 80.00
Vase, 1936, Oxblood, #6197C, 8⅞" 450.00
Vase, 1940, bulbous, ivory mat, #778, 10" 80.00
Vase, 1942, cvd overlapping leaves, yel mat, #6704, 5½" 180.00
Vase, 1943, classic form, med bl hi-glaze, #614D, 10½" 150.00
Vase, 1944, zebras & bands, brn hi-glaze, #6739, 10½" 160.00
Vase, 1945, sq hdls, bl crystalline, #6887, 4½" 150.00
Vase, 1946, 3 geese in flight, bulbous, lt pk, #6831, 6" 140.00
Vase, 1948, emb lg blooms & leaves, bulbous, bl, #6833, 6" 110.00
Vase, 1954, brn hi-glaze, #6436, 4" 45.00
Vase, 1954, cloverleaves on neck, gr hi-glaze, #6953, 4x8" 100.00
Vase, 1956, tapered cylinder, bl hi-glaze, #950CP, 9½" 80.00
Vase, 1959, Cirrus, #7157, 17¾" 200.00
Wall pocket, 1920, Arts & Crafts, rose mat, #2008, 7½" 200.00

Rorstrand

The Rorstrand Pottery was established in Sweden in 1726 and is today Sweden's oldest existing pottery. The earliest ware, now mostly displayed in Swedish museums, was much like old Delft. Later types were hard-paste porcelains that were enameled and decorated in a peas-

ant style, Contemporary pieces are often described as Swedish Modern. Rorstrand is also famous for their Christmas plates.

Beaker, sculpted flowers in relief, pk/gray, sgn, 4½" 350.00
Urn, majolica, fruit/scrolls/mask, figural hdls, 20", EX 525.00
Vase, blk matt w/olive & brn streaks, bottle neck, 13½" 550.00
Vase, Deco-style figures, 8" 185.00
Vase, sgraffito fish, 1950s, 8" 465.00

Rose Mandarin

Similar in design to Rose Medallion, this Chinese export porcelain features the pattern of a robed mandarin, often separated by florals, ladies, genre scenes, or butterflies in polychrome enamels. It is sometimes trimmed in gold. Elaborate in decoration, this pattern was popular from the late 1700s until the early 1840s.

Bowl, fruit; 1800s, 10" L, +underplate 1,850.00
Brush box, 1840, 7¾" L, EX 875.00
Cache pot, 1800, 4½", w/underplate 525.00
Coffeepot, w/lid, 1800s, 11" 1,500.00
Dish, 1840s, sq, 9", pr 1,800.00
Garden seat, 1800S, 18½" 2,975.00
Pilgrim flask, lizard hdl, bk: peacocks, 1840, 10", pr 3,500.00
Plate, central panel, gold border w/4 panels, 1800s, 8½" 200.00
Platter, 1800s, 8½x11½" 285.00
Punch bowl, 1800s, hairlines, 14¼" 1,265.00

Temple jar, paneled courtyard scenes, brass-bound rim, hinged lid, foo dog finial, 1830s, 16½", $2,475.00.

Temple jar, foo dog finial, 4 appl dog heads, 1830, 17" 2,500.00
Temple jar, 1800s, 24" 3,850.00
Vase, 1800s, 23", pr 3,850.00
Wash basin, 1800s, 17", +water bottle, 16", both VG 1,200.00

Rose Medallion

Rose Medallion is one of the patterns of Chinese export porcelain produced from before 1850 until the second decade of the 20th century. It is decorated in rose colors with panels of florals, birds, and butterflies that form reserves containing Chinese figures. Pre-1850 ware is unmarked and is characterized by quality workmanship and gold trim. From about 1850 until circa 1860, the kilns in Canton did not operate, and no Rose Medallion was made. Post-1860 examples (still unmarked) can often be recognized by the poor quality of the gold trim or its absence. In the 1890s the ware was often marked 'China'; 'Made in China' was used from 1910 through the 1930s.

Bowl, butterflies, 10¾" L 440.00
Bowl, salad; 19th C, 9¾" 1,150.00

Bowl, serving; w/lid, late, 10¼" 345.00
Bowl, serving; 19th C, 8¼" sq 425.00
Bowl, shaped rim, 19th C, 4¾x10½" 750.00
Bowl, vegetable; w/lid, 1800s, 9½" L 635.00
Bowl, vegetable; 19th C, 9½" 350.00
Box, rectangular, w/lid, 3x6x3½" 500.00
Brush box, rectangular, divided interior, w/lid, 7½" 300.00
Charger, 19th C, 14" dia 375.00
Cup & saucer, bouillon; w/lid 115.00
Cup & saucer, mk China 35.00
Dish, sq, late 19th C, 9¼" 285.00
Garden seat, 19th C, 18½" 2,550.00
Pitcher, gilt rim, 8-sided baluster, 19th C, 7" 325.00
Pitcher, late, 8¾" 100.00
Plate, central scene w/in floral border, 19th C, 10" 145.00
Plate, exotic birds & butterflies, 8", EX 85.00
Plate, monogram, 19th C, 9½" 125.00
Plate, soup; 19th C, 9¾" 110.00
Plate, 19th C, 9½", set of 6 ....425.00
Platter, late 19th C, 14", pr 475.00
Platter, well & tree; w/landscape panels, 19th C, 16¾", EX 400.00
Platter, 19th C, 13¼x10½" 300.00
Platter, 19th C, 15¼" 385.00
Platter, 19th C, 18" 650.00
Platter, 19th C, 20", EX 575.00
Platters, nesting set of 4, monogram, 12" to 16¼" 2,415.00
Punch bowl, gilt bronze mts: rtcl rim/ft, dragon hdls, 17" 1,600.00
Punch bowl, late 19th C, lt wear, 5⅞x14½" 550.00
Punch bowl, scene in base, 19th C, 6½x16" 1,725.00
Punch bowl, 19th C, 13½" 1,500.00
Sauce boat, 19th C, 8", +undertray 600.00
Shrimp dish, gilt rim, 19th C, 10½" 575.00
Soap dish, w/insert, 2½x6x4½" 325.00
Teapot, in wicker cozy, 7", EX 200.00
Teapot, 7¾", +c/s 275.00
Temple jar, w/lid (rpr), 19th C, 17½" 1,840.00
Tureen, soup; w/monogram, 19th C, 14½" 3,225.00
Vase, flared rim, shouldered, 19th C, 14½x6", pr 865.00
Vase, now lamp, ca 1900, 14" 190.00
Vase, w/lid (sm chips), 19th C, 8½" 800.00

Roselane

Founded in California in 1938 by William and Georgia Fields, the Roselane company at first produced only figurines for the local florist. But by the forties they offered candle holders, wall pockets, vases, and a line of modernistic animals mounted on wooden bases. In the fifties their 'Sparklers' became popular — small stylized animal and bird figures with rhinestone eyes. (Today these are worth from $10.00 to $25.00, depending on size.) The company closed in 1977. A variety of marks was used; all incorporate the Roselane name.

Bowl, fish design, turq & blk, w/stand, 13" dia 65.00
Dealer sign, Roselane, deep aqua, glossy, 3x12½" 175.00
Dish, brn & gr, sq, #106 ....25.00
Figurine, Basset hound, Sparkler, 3¼x1¼" 12.00
Figurine, fawn, stylized, on ½-dome base, 5" 28.00
Figurine, owl, Sparkler, brn, 7" 18.00
Figurine, owl, Sparkler, 3" 12.00
Figurine, pug dog, Sparkler, 4" 15.00
Figurine, quail, metallic w/walnut base 55.00
Sculpture, elephant, stylized, brn lustre, wood base, 8" 125.00
Vase, Chinese Modern, emb decor base, ftd, 9¾" 25.00

Rosemeade

Rosemeade was the name chosen by the Wahpeton Pottery Company of Wahpeton, North Dakota, to represent their product. The founders of the company were Laura A. Taylor and R.J. Hughes, who organized the firm in 1940. It is most noted for small bird and animal figurals, either in high gloss or a Van Briggle-like matt glaze. The ware was marked 'Rosemeade' with an ink stamp or carried a 'Prairie Rose' sticker. The pottery closed in 1961. Our advisor for this category is Bryce L. Farnsworth; he is listed in the Directory under North Dakota.

For more information refer to *Collector's Encyclopedia of the Dakota Potteries* by Darlene Hurst Dommel.

TV lamp, pheasant, $400.00.

Ashtray, Internat'l Peace Garden Monument 110.00
Ashtray, state shape, Alabama 35.00
Ashtray, state shape, Georgia 100.00
Ashtray, state shape, Vermont 75.00
Ashtray, state shape, Wyoming 45.00
Ashtray/figurine, fawn 160.00
Ashtray/figurine, fox 240.00
Ashtray/figurine, mouse 140.00
Ashtray/figurine, turkey 110.00
Bank, fish 170.00
Bank, rhino 670.00
Bank, Theodore Roosevelt cabin 320.00
Bell, elephant 200.00
Bell, peacock 285.00
Bookends, buffalo, pr 480.00
Bookends, wolfhounds, blk, pr 210.00
Creamer & sugar bowl, duck figurals, wht 90.00
Figurine, Indian God of Peace 200.00
Figurine, mountain goat, lg 320.00
Figurine, Mt Rushmore 225.00
Figurine, zebra 350.00
Figurines, geese, gray, pr 90.00
Figurines, seals, blk, set of 3 ....45.00
Figurines, tiger kittens, pr 310.00
Hors d'oeuvre, pheasant on tray 140.00
Pitcher, ball shape 25.00
Pitcher, Ewald Bros, cow heads in relief, lg 170.00
Plaque, meadowlark 240.00
Plaque, sunfish 180.00
Plaque, walleye 200.00
Shakers, bull & cow, tan, pr 240.00
Shakers, chickens, cartoon-like, bl, pr 40.00
Shakers, cocks, fighting, pr 90.00
Shakers, coyotes, howling, pr 300.00
Shakers, dogs' heads (bloodhounds), pr 40.00
Shakers, dogs' heads (fox terriers), pr 30.00
Shakers, dogs' heads (Scotties), pr 50.00

Shakers, fish (brn trout), pr 350.00
Shakers, fish (Northern Pike), pr 270.00
Shakers, fish (trout), pr 390.00
Shakers, gophers, tall, upright, pr 90.00
Shakers, Indian God of Peace, pr 525.00
Shakers, Paul Bunyan & Babe the Blue Ox, pr 160.00
Shakers, pheasant roosters, striding, pr 100.00
Shakers, pheasants, golden, pr 200.00
Shakers, Prairie Rose, pr 40.00
Vase, bud; pk speckled 25.00
Vase, bud; turq, tall 30.00
Vase, Koala bear in tree, tall 190.00
Wall pocket, Indian God of Peace 375.00
Wall pocket, leaf shape 30.00

Rosenthal

In 1879 Phillip Rosenthal established the Rosenthal Porcelain Factory in Selb, Bavaria. Its earliest products were figurines and fine tablewares. The company has continued to operate to the present decade, manufacturing limited edition plates.

Cracker jar, floral, wide gold hdls 90.00
Figurine, angelfish, yel w/blk, T Heidenreich, 14x10" ..595.00
Figurine, Balinese dancer leans on Buddha, Holzerdefanti, 16" ..1,600.00
Figurine, beaver, wht, sgn Professor Gaul, 15" 375.00
Figurine, elephant on stand, #726, 3" 98.00
Figurine, frog on lily pad, sgn HH Stone, porc, 1¼x2⅛" ..50.00
Figurine, mother doe w/suckling fawn, Roehring, 1954, 12" ..495.00
Figurine, seated nude, legs to side, pastels, Fritz, 6½x8" ..285.00
Figurine, seated seminude w/apple, Heindenreich, #532, 8x6½" .460.00
Figurine, snail, gray/wht w/bl & wht swirl, sgn ES, 3½x2" ..130.00
Figurine, standing nude, cream matt, Obennaien, 1931, 17" ..285.00
Jar, lg Oriental character, cobalt on brn tones, 8½" 250.00
Mug, cascading grapes w/gold, sgn, 5¼" 140.00
Vase, blk gloss w/long striated blk matt neck, Wirkkala, 9" ..115.00

Roseville

The Roseville Pottery Company was established in 1892 by George F. Young in Roseville, Ohio. Finding their facilities inadequate, the company moved to Zanesville in 1898, erected a new building, and installed the most modern equipment available. By 1900 Young felt ready to enter into the stiffly competitive art pottery market. Roseville's first art line was called Rozane. Similar to Rookwood's Standard, Rozane featured dark blended backgrounds with slip-painted underglaze artwork of nature studies, portraits, birds, and animals. Azurean, developed in 1902, was a blue and white underglaze art line on a blue blended background. Egypto (1904) featured a matt glaze in a soft shade of old green and was modeled in low relief after examples of ancient Egyptian pottery. Mongol (1904) was a high-gloss oxblood red line after the fashion of the Chinese Sang de Boeuf. Mara (1904), an iridescent lustre line of magenta and rose with intricate patterns developed on the surface or in low relief, successfully duplicated Sicardo's work. These early lines were followed by many others of highest quality: Fujiyama and Woodland (1905-06) reflected an Oriental theme; Crystalis (1906) was covered with beautiful frost-like crystals. Della Robbia, their most famous line (introduced in 1906), was decorated with designs ranging from florals, animals, and birds to scenes of Viking warriors and Roman gladiators. These designs were accomplished by sgraffito with slip-painted details. Very limited but of

great importance to collectors today, Rozane Olympic (1905) was decorated with scenes of Greek mythology on a red ground. Pauleo (1914) was the last of the artware lines. It was varied — over two hundred glazes were recorded — and some pieces were decorated by hand, usually with florals.

During the second decade of the century until the plant closed forty years later, new lines were continually added. Some of the more popular of the middle-period lines were Donatello, 1915; Futura, 1928; Pine Cone, 1931; and Blackberry, 1933. The floral lines of the later years have become highly collectible. Pottery from every era of Roseville production — even its utility ware — attest to an unwavering dedication to quality and artistic merit.

Examples of the fine art pottery lines present the greatest challenge to evaluate. Scarcity is a prime consideration. The quality of artwork varied from one artist to another. Some pieces show fine detail and good color, and naturally this influences their values. Studies of animals and portraits bring higher prices than the floral designs. An artist's signature often increases the value of any item, especially if the artist is one who is well recognized. For further information consult *The Collector's Encyclopedia of Roseville Pottery, First and Second Series,* by Sharon and Bob Huxford, available at your local library or bookstore.

Apple Blossom, jardiniere (#302) & pedestal (16½"), gr 850.00
Artcraft, jardiniere, 4 buttresses, 4" 300.00
Aztec, vase, geometric decor on bl, unmk, 10½" 350.00
Azurean, vase, floral, sgn Leffler, #822/7, 15½" 1,100.00
Azurean, vase, landscape, bulbous, unmk, 9" 1,850.00
Baneda, bowl, hdls, 3½x9" 225.00
Baneda, vase, hdls, 10x8" 700.00
Baneda, vase, red, hdls, 9½x4¼" 550.00
Bank, beehive, tan & brn mottle, unmk, 3" 185.00
Bank, buffalo, brn on cream, unmk, 3x6" 175.00
Bank, pig, gr & cream, unmk, 2½x5" 135.00
Bittersweet, basket, #807-8, 8½" 100.00
Bittersweet, planter, #828-10, 10½" 95.00
Bittersweet, vase, hdls, #884-8, 8" 100.00
Blackberry, jardiniere, 6" 400.00

Blackberry vases: Large 2-handled form, 12½" (rare size), from $900.00 to $1,200.00; Squat 2-handled form, 4x6" diameter, $325.00.

Blackberry, vase, pear shape, sm hdls at top, 5x4" 300.00
Bleeding Heart, hanging basket, floral, 8" W 200.00
Bleeding Heart, vase, squat w/hdls, 4" 70.00
Bottle, monkey, elbows on knees, unmk, 6" 135.00
Bushberry, dbl bud vase, #158, 4½" 130.00
Bushberry, dbl cornucopia, #155-8, 6" 100.00
Bushberry, pitcher, cider; bulbous, #1325, 8½" 300.00
Bushberry, vase, conical, 4" 50.00
Carnelian I, bowl, hdls, 3x9" 45.00
Carnelian I, vase, angle hdls, 10" 135.00
Carnelian II, planter, hdls, paper label, 3x8" 75.00
Carnelian II, vase, cone top/bulb base, bar hdls, 12" ..700.00
Carnelian II, vase, pk/gr drip glaze, shaped scroll hdls, 10" ..250.00
Carnelian II, vase, trumpet neck, low hdls, unmk, 10" ..125.00

Cherry Blossom, jardiniere, 8x10" 400.00
Cherry Blossom, vase, spherical, hdls, 5" 425.00
Cherry Blossom, vase, spherical w/sm neck hdls, 8" 600.00
Chloron, vase, emb floral, integral hdls, 9" 400.00
Clemana, bowl, floral on bl, #281-5, 4½x6½" 85.00
Clemana, vase, floral, bulbous, #756-9, 9½" 200.00
Clematis, bookends, bl, #14, 5½", pr 175.00
Clematis, console bowl, floral, angle hdls, #458-10, 14" L 115.00
Columbine, bookend planter, floral on bl, #8, 5" 150.00
Columbine, vase, floral on bl, angle hdls, #17-7, 7½" 125.00
Corinthian, vase, concave ribs, emb floral band, unmk, 8½" 90.00
Corinthian, wall pocket, concave ribs, floral band, unmk, 8" 165.00
Cosmos, flower frog, floral, unmk, 3½" 65.00
Cosmos, vase, floral, hdls, ftd, #956-12, 12½" 300.00
Creamware, candlestick, Good Night, w/girl, shield bk, 7" 350.00
Cremona, vase, floral/leaves on sqd form, 10½" 210.00
Crocus, vase, floral, bl on blk, unmk, 9" 400.00
Crocus, vase, floral, wht on bl, sgn GS, 9" 375.00
Crystalis, candlestick, flared base, Mongol seal, 9" 850.00
Crystalis, vase, shouldered, bottle neck, unmk, 11" 1,375.00
Crystalis, vase, spacecraft form, 3 hdls at can neck, EX glaze ...1,000.00
Crystalis, vase, tan/mustard, integral hdls, 4" 700.00
Dahlrose, hanging basket, floral band, unmk, 7½" 165.00
Dahlrose, window box, floral band, unmk, 6x11½" 175.00
Della Robbia, vase, bellflowers/brn band on mustard, 9x6" 5,500.00
Della Robbia, vase, chrysanthemums, sgn, 8¼x5" 7,000.00
Dogwood I, bowl, floral, ink stamp, 4" 65.00
Dogwood I, vase, floral, ink stamp, 7" 135.00
Dogwood II, dbl bud vase, 8" 150.00
Dogwood II, vase, floral, unmk, 14½" 325.00
Donatello, bowl, unmk, 5" 45.00
Donatello, comport, impressed mk, 9½" 155.00
Donatello, dbl bud vase, fluted posts, hdls, 7" 300.00
Early Pitcher, Bridge, unmk, 6" 135.00
Early Pitcher, Goldenrod, unmk, 9½" 115.00
Early Pitcher, Poppy, #11, 9" 135.00
Early Pitcher, Wild Rose, unmk, 9½" 115.00
Egypto, bowl, lobed rim/body, 3¼x8¾" 250.00
Egypto, ewer, emb Nouveau foliage, integral hdl at lip, 7½" 300.00
Egypto, pitcher, emb geometrics, 10½x5" 375.00
Egypto, pitcher, stylized floral/line motif, 11" 250.00
Egypto, vase, arching panels framed in relief, 5½" 400.00
Egypto, vase, swirling vines, 6½" 550.00
Falline, vase, brn, cylinder w/wide base, low hdl, 12" 650.00
Falline, vase, ear-shaped hdls, ftd, gr/brn/bl, unmk, 6" 250.00
Falline, vase, gourd shape, low hdls, 12½" 500.00
Ferella, bowl w/built-in flower frog, brn, 9½" 375.00
Ferella, console bowl, red, 6x12½" 650.00
Ferella, flowerpot, brn, 5" 450.00
Ferella, vase, brn, hdls, 5" 350.00
Ferella, vase, red, hdls, 6" 425.00
Florane, bowl, 10" 32.50
Florane, sand jar, 12" 115.00
Florentine, ashtray, emb grapes, unmk, 5" 55.00
Florentine, dbl bud vase, emb grapes, unmk, 4½" 65.00
Foxglove, tray, floral on brn, impressed mk, 8½" 85.00
Foxglove, vase, 4 buttressed hdls, 14" 250.00
Freesia, console bowl, floral on bl, 3469-14, 16½" L 135.00
Freesia, flowerpot & saucer, #670-5, 5½" 100.00
Fuchsia, candlestick, #1133-5, 5½" 150.00
Fuchsia, console bowl, low hdls, #351-10, 3½x12½" 150.00
Fuchsia, hanging basket, brn, hdls, 6" dia 400.00
Fuchsia, vase, hdls, #893-6, 6" 135.00
Fudji, vase, Oriental floral, twisted sq shape, 10" 1,375.00

Fudji, vase, Oriental stylized multicolor decoration on tan bisque, 8½", $1,100.00.

Fudji, vase, floral, ogee sides, 11", NM 950.00
Fudji, vase, Nouveau florals, elongated gourd form, 11x3" 3,750.00
Futura, hanging basket, 7" 325.00
Futura, vase, #388, paneled cone on rnd base, 9" 300.00
Futura, vase, #403, cone top, petticoat body, hdls, 7" 550.00
Futura, vase, #427, ovoid w/thistle on pk, rnd base, 8" 450.00
Futura, vase, #429, cream & gray w/short buttresses, 9" 450.00
Futura, vase, #430, 4-sided w/curved planes, 4-ftd, 9" 550.00
Futura, vase, #435, 3 stacked rings at waist, 10" 600.00
Futura, vase, #438, teasel on tan, hdls, 15½" 700.00
Futura, vase, #483, lt bl V-panels on stepped base, 9" 225.00
Holland, mug, Dutch boy, unmk, 4" 50.00
Holland, powder jar, Dutch figure, unmk, 3" 90.00
Imperial I, basket, #7, 9" 115.00
Imperial I, vase, low angle hdls, unmk, 10" 150.00
Imperial II, vase, med bl w/tan flambe, 11" 350.00
Imperial II, wall pocket, red/bl gloss, 6" 375.00
Ixia, jardiniere (#640) & pedestal (17"), NM 1,100.00
Ixia, vase, floral, low hdls attach to base, #856-8, 8½" 85.00
Jonquil, bowl, floral, low hdls, unmk, 3" 175.00
Jonquil, crocus pot, attached saucer, unmk, 7" 350.00
Jonquil, vase, pear form w/hdls, 5" 125.00
Juvenile, cake plate, ducks on gr band, unmk, 9½" 175.00
Juvenile, creamer, Santa Claus, ink stamp, 3½" 175.00
Juvenile, cup & saucer, ducks on gr band, 2", 5½" 135.00
Juvenile, fat puppies on gr band, unmk, 3½" 115.00
Juvenile, mug, cat on band, mk, 3" 135.00
Juvenile, mug, dogs on bl band, 2-hdld, 3" 85.00
Juvenile, plate, pigs on band, mk, 8" 200.00
Juvenile, sugar bowl, nursery-rhyme decor, unmk, 3" 115.00
La Rose, vase, floral swags, ink mk, 4" 75.00
La Rose, wall pocket, floral swags, unmk, 9" 175.00
Luffa, jardiniere, floral on brn, 5½" base dia 325.00
Luffa, lamp, floral on bl to gr, sm angle hdls, unmk, 9½" 450.00
Magnolia, candlestick, #1146-2 ½, 2½" 45.00
Magnolia, vase, angle hdls, #91-8, 8" 125.00
Mara, vase, floral relief at shoulder, stems to base, 10½" 2,100.00
Matt Green, hanging basket, unmk, 9" 175.00
Matt Green, planter w/liner, #510, 4" 135.00
Ming Tree, basket, twig hdl, #509-12, 13" 225.00
Ming Tree, bowl, rectangular, twig hdls, #526-9, 4x11½" 50.00
Ming Tree, conch shell, #563, 8½" 45.00
Mongol, mug, 3-hdld, 6" 775.00
Mongol, vase, long trumpet neck, 16" 975.00
Morning Glory, basket, wht, highly arched hdl, 10½" 600.00
Morning Glory, vase, hdls, 14½" 1,200.00
Morning Glory, vase, wht, hdls 4x7" 450.00
Moss, console bowl, 14" L, +pr short candlesticks 290.00
Moss, vase, #259, 4x5" 120.00
Mostique, jardiniere, 9" 250.00
Mostique, vase, incurvate, 15" 400.00
Mostique, vase, incurvate, 8" 70.00
Mostique, vase, incurvate w/hdls, 8½" 250.00
Olympic, pitcher, Ulysses at Table of Circle, mk, 7" 2,150.00

Orian, vase, aqua/bl, shoulder-to-base hdls, 10½" 140.00
Panel, see Rosecraft Panel
Pauleo, gunmetal blk over red, #119, 16" 2,000.00
Pauleo, vase, gold mottling, classic form, unmk, 17½" 1,150.00
Pauleo, vase, maroon, bulbous, unmk, 9" 550.00
Peony, bookend, on L shape, #11, 5½" 185.00
Peony, dbl candle holder, #115-3, 5" 55.00
Persian, candlestick, floral on wht, unmk, 8½" 135.00
Persian, jardiniere, floral, paper label, 5" 190.00
Pine Cone, bowl, gr, #426-6" 150.00
Pine Cone, console bowl, gr, #323-15" 240.00
Pine Cone, jardiniere (11" dia) & ped (#405), gr, $1,000 to 1,200.00
Pine Cone, vase, brn, sm branch hdl, #278-4" 180.00
Pine Cone, vase, gr, #490, 8½" 200.00
Pine Cone, vase, gr, branch hdls, #842, 8½" 200.00
Pine Cone, vase, gr, hdls, flat sided, #121-7 ....175.00
Poppy, ewer, slim form, #880-8, 18½" 450.00
Poppy, jardiniere, sm ring hdls, #335-6, 6½" 115.00
Raymor, cornucopia vase, blk/gray froth, 6" 70.00
Raymor, gravy boat, brn, #190, 9½" 30.00
Raymor, pitcher, water; wht, #189, 10" 125.00
Rosecraft Black, comport, unmk, 4x11" 115.00
Rosecraft Black, ginger jar, paper label, 8" 225.00
Rosecraft Hexagon, candlestick, flared ft, 8" 140.00
Rosecraft Hexagon, vase, 6" 135.00
Rosecraft Panel, lamp base, foliage on gr, X1F8, 10" 235.00
Rosecraft Panel, vase, foliage on dk gr, flaring rim, 10" 225.00
Rosecraft Panel, vase, 4 panels w/branches & berries, 8x7" 275.00
Rozane, ewer, floral, slim, RPCO mk, #875/x, 7½" 165.00
Rozane, pitcher, daffodils, #828, 8½" 210.00
Rozane, vase, floral, integral hdls, #872, RPCO mk, 5½" 185.00
Rozane, vase, silver o/l floral, #580, 5" 475.00
Rozane Light, pillow vase, floral, 6½" 300.00
Rozane Light, tankard, ear of corn, J Imlay, 10" 400.00
Rozane Light, vase, floral, M Timberlake, classic form, 15" 950.00
Rozane Light, vase, lg spray of roses, sgn J Imlay, 15" 600.00
Rozane 1917, basket, simple hdl, bl glaze, mk, 11" 135.00
Rozane 1917, bowl, ftd, tub hdls, 5" 80.00
Rozane 1917, bowl, incurvate rim, gr glaze, 3" 55.00
Russco, dbl bud vase, dk gr/yel crystalline, 8½" 120.00
Silhouette, box, floral reserve, #740, 4½" 45.00
Silhouette, vase, floral reserve, trumpet neck, #789-14, 14" 225.00
Snowberry, basket, integral hdl, #1BK-12, 12½" 165.00
Snowberry, vase, hdls, #IRB-6, 6" 90.00
Sunflower, candlesticks, 4x3", pr 280.00
Sunflower, vase, bulbous, hdld, 9½x7" 800.00
Sunflower, vase, hdls, 6x5" 475.00
Sunflower, vase, sm rim-to-width hdls, 5x5" 350.00
Sunflower, wall pocket, 7½x6" 700.00
Teasel, vase, low hdls attach to base, #887-10, 10" 200.00
Teasel, vase, spherical w/tab hdls, 4" 120.00
Topeo, console bowl, bl, 13" W 220.00
Topeo, vase, bl/gr, shouldered, 12" 475.00
Topeo, vase, dk red, spherical, 6" 230.00
Tourist, vase, 8" 750.00
Tourist, window box, 7x12" 2,000.00
Tourmaline, candlestick, wide flared base, bl, paper label, 5" 45.00
Tourmaline, vase, emb decor, ftd, sm hdls, unmk, 8" 85.00
Velmoss Scroll, bowl, #C7, unmk, 3" 85.00
Velmoss Scroll, vase, 8" 230.00
Victorian Art, vase, fruit/foliage on bl-gray, 11x8" 450.00
Victorian Art, vase, scarabs on bl-gray, 8x6" 375.00
Vista, basket, unmk, 12" 300.00
Vista, flowerpot, 6x7" 300.00

Vista, jardiniere, 10" 500.00
Vista, vase, cylindrical w/2 vertical hdls, 12" 550.00
Vista, vase, swollen cylinder, 19½" 1,100.00
Water Lily, cookie jar, 10½" 450.00
Water Lily, vase, hdls, #78-9, 9" 135.00
Wincraft, cornucopia, floral, #221-8, 9x5" 55.00
Wincraft, vase, floral, #274-7, 7" 85.00
Windsor, vase, orange mottle, spherical w/hdls, 7" 260.00
Windsor, vase, rust leaves on bl, #554-10" 400.00
Wisteria, vase, hdls, 10" 650.00
Wisteria, vase, shoulder hdls, 4x7" 350.00
Woodland, vase, floral, twisted, 10½" 850.00
Woodland, vase, stylized Persian floral, sgn HS/ET, 9" 750.00
Woodland, vase, stylized stems, slim gourd form, 11" 950.00
Zephyr Lily, cornucopia, #203, 6" 70.00
Zephyr Lily, fan vase, #205-6, 6½" 85.00

Rowland and Marsellus

Though the impressive back stamp seems to suggest otherwise, Rowland and Marsellus were not Staffordshire potters but American importers who commissioned various English companies to supply them with the transfer-printed historical ware that had been a popular import item since the early 1800s. Plates (both flat and with a rolled edge), cups and saucers, pitchers, and platters were sold as souvenirs from 1890 through the 1930s. Though other importers — Bawo & Dotter, and A. C. Bosselman & Co., both of New York City — commissioned the manufacture of similar souvenir items, by far the largest volume carries the R. & M. mark, and Rowland and Marcellus has become a generic term that covers all 20th-century souvenir china of this type. Their mark may be in full or 'R. & M.' in a diamond. Though primarily made with blue transfers on white, other colors may occasionally be found as well. Our advisor for this category is David Ringering; he is listed in the Directory under Oregon.

Key:
r/e — rolled edge　　　　　　v/o — view of
s/o — souvenir of

Creamer, Plymouth, marked as Burbank, $35.00.

Cup & saucer, Brooklyn, s/o 95.00
Cup & saucer, Lewis & Clarke Expo 95.00
Cup & saucer, mush; Take ye a cupp o'kindnesse..., gr 45.00
Cup & saucer, Pittsburgh, s/o 95.00
Cup & saucer, Yale, s/o 95.00
Fern pot, w/stand, lady's portrait by British artist, 11½" 460.00
Plate, Asbury Park NJ, v/o, 9" 35.00
Plate, Battle of Lake Erie, fruit & flower border 50.00
Plate, Boston MA, v/o, 9" 35.00
Plate, Bunker Hill Monument, fruit & flower border 50.00
Plate, Butte MT, s/o, r/e 70.00
Plate, Cape Cod, fisherman's portrait, 9" 35.00

Plate, coupe; Am Poets, 7 portraits, 10" 50.00
Plate, coupe; Cooperstown NY, s/o, 6" 40.00
Plate, coupe; Fresno CA, 5 scenes, 6" 40.00
Plate, coupe; Harrisburg, s/o, 10" 50.00
Plate, coupe; Minneapolis MN, s/o, 10" 50.00
Plate, coupe; New Bedford MA, s/o, 5 scenes, 6" 35.00
Plate, coupe; Salem MA, witch & 5 scenes, v/o, 6" 40.00
Plate, coupe; Tuscon AZ, 5 scenes, v/o, 6" 40.00
Plate, coupe; Washington DC, v/o, 6" 35.00
Plate, coupe; Yale, s/o, 10" 50.00
Plate, Decator IL, s/o, r/e 65.00
Plate, Flint MI, v/o, 9" 35.00
Plate, Haverhill (MA), s/o, r/e 60.00
Plate, Horseshoe Curve, fruit & flower border 50.00
Plate, Lookout Mountain, TN, s/o, r/e 60.00
Plate, Lynn MA, 9" 35.00
Plate, New Library at Boston, fruit & flower border 50.00
Plate, Omaha NB, v/o, 9" 35.00
Plate, Pilgrim Hall, fruit & flower border 50.00
Plate, Portland OR, s/o, r/e 70.00
Plate, Ride of Paul Revere, fruit & flower border 50.00
Plate, Sacramento CA, v/o, 9" 35.00
Plate, Valley Forge (PA), 1777-78, r/e 55.00
Plate, Whirlpool Rapids, fruit & flower border 50.00
Plate, Zanesville OH, s/o, r/e 60.00
Sugar bowl, Plymouth, Am pilgrims 55.00
Tumbler, Ottawa Canada 75.00
Tumbler, Tacoma WA, s/o 75.00
Tumbler, Thousand Islands, v/o 75.00

Royal Bayreuth

Founded in 1794 in Tettau, Bavaria, the Royal Bayreuth firm originally manufactured fine dinnerware of superior quality. Their figural items, produced from before the turn of the century until the onset of WWI, are highly sought after by today's collectors. Perhaps the most abundantly produced and easily recognized of these are the tomato and lobster pieces. Fruits, flowers, people, animals, birds, and vegetables shapes were also made. Aside from figural items, pitchers, toothpick holders, cups and saucers, humidors, and the like were decorated in florals and scenic motifs. Some, such as the very popular Rose Tapestry line, utilized a cloth-like tapestry background. Transfer prints were used as well. Two of the most popular are Sunbonnet Babies and Nursery Rhymes (in particular, those decorated with the complete verse).

Caution: Many pieces were not marked; some were marked 'Deponiert' or 'Registered' only. While marked pieces are the most valued, unmarked items are still very worthwhile. Our advisors for this category are Larry Brenner from New Hampshire and Dee Hooks from Illinois; they are listed in the Directory under their home states.

Figurals

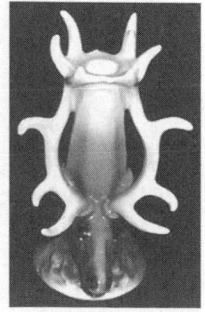

Candlestick, elk, tall,
blue mark, $875.00.

Ashtray, Devil & Cards, 2 cards, bl mk 325.00
Ashtray, elk, bl mk 185.00
Ashtray, shell, bl mk 80.00
Bowl, berry; tomato, bl mk 40.00
Bowl, conch shell, bl mk, 6" dia 60.00
Bowl, lobster & leaf, bl mk, med 125.00
Box, oyster & pearl, bl mk, 4½x2½" 450.00
Candlestick, monkey, gr, bl mk 3,900.00
Candlestick/match holder, clown, red, bl mk, tall 1,800.00
Candy dish, Devil & Cards, bl mk, 6½" 500.00
Candy dish, lobster, bl mk, 5½" 180.00
Creamer & sugar bowl, grapes, MOP, bl mk 275.00
Cup & saucer, demitasse; Devil & Die, unmk 125.00
Cup & saucer, demitasse; orange, bl mk 250.00
Cup & saucer, demitasse; oyster & pearl, bl mk 350.00
Humidor, clown lady, red, bl mk 950.00
Humidor, murex shell, bl mk 725.00
Marmalade, orange, w/lid, bl mk, lg 675.00
Match holder, elk head, bl mk, wall type 500.00
Match holder, Santa, red striker on bk, bl mk 5,200.00
Mug, beer; Devil & Cards, bl mk, commemorative 150.00
Mug, beer; elk, bl mk, tall 495.00
Mug, shaving; elk, bl mk 550.00
Mustard, grapes, yel, bl mk 150.00
Mustard, murex shell, bl mk 90.00
Mustard, tomato, bl mk 80.00
Nappy, poppy, red, bl mk 75.00
Nut bowl, poppy, lav pearlized, unmk, master sz 250.00
Nut cup, poppy, red, bl mk, sm 75.00
Pitcher, apple, bl mk, lemonade sz 875.00
Pitcher, apple, bl mk, water sz 695.00
Pitcher, apple, yel, bl mk, cream sz 200.00
Pitcher, bell ringer, bl mk, cream sz 325.00
Pitcher, bird of paradise, bl mk, cream sz 450.00
Pitcher, bull, rust, bl mk, cream sz 300.00
Pitcher, butterfly, open wings, bl mk, cream sz 375.00
Pitcher, cat, blk, bl mk, cream sz 250.00
Pitcher, chick, bl mk, cream sz 350.00
Pitcher, chimpanzee, bl mk, cream sz 600.00
Pitcher, clown, red, bl mk, cream sz 350.00
Pitcher, crow, blk w/red beak, bl mk, cream sz 195.00
Pitcher, dachshund, bl mk, milk sz 400.00
Pitcher, Devil & Cards, bl mk, cream sz 235.00
Pitcher, Devil & Cards, bl mk, milk sz 325.00
Pitcher, duck, bl mk, cream sz 300.00
Pitcher, eagle, bl mk, milk sz 450.00
Pitcher, elk, bl mk, cream sz 200.00
Pitcher, elk, bl mk, milk sz 350.00
Pitcher, fish head, unmk, cream sz 210.00
Pitcher, fish head, unmk, milk sz 375.00
Pitcher, grapes, purple, bl mk, cream sz 120.00
Pitcher, lamplighter, bl mk, cream sz 300.00
Pitcher, lamplighter, bl mk, milk sz 400.00
Pitcher, lemon, bl mk, cream sz 285.00
Pitcher, lobster, bl mk, milk sz 300.00
Pitcher, lobster, bl mk, water sz 500.00
Pitcher, lobster, gr mk, cream sz 150.00
Pitcher, melon, bl mk, water sz 1,500.00
Pitcher, monkey, gr, bl mk, milk sz 850.00
Pitcher, mountain goat, bl mk, cream sz 335.00
Pitcher, orange, bl mk, cream sz 295.00
Pitcher, orchid, bl mk, water sz 2,500.00
Pitcher, owl, gr & yel, bl mk, cream sz 600.00
Pitcher, owl, unmk, cream sz 400.00

Pitcher, pansy, gr mk, cream sz 225.00
Pitcher, parakeet, unmk, cream sz 225.00
Pitcher, parrot, bl mk, milk sz 400.00
Pitcher, pelican, bl mk, water sz 815.00
Pitcher, pelican, pk, unmk, cream sz 300.00
Pitcher, perch, bl mk, cream sz 450.00
Pitcher, pig, gray, bl mk, cream sz 600.00
Pitcher, platypus, Deponiert, cream sz 1,100.00
Pitcher, poodle, gray, bl mk, cream sz 225.00
Pitcher, poppy, red, bl mk, milk sz 275.00
Pitcher, rooster, mc, bl mk, cream sz 400.00
Pitcher, rose, pk & wht, bl mk, cream sz 325.00
Pitcher, Santa w/pack as hdl, bl mk, cream sz 2,500.00
Pitcher, shell w/coral hdl, bl mk, cream sz 60.00
Pitcher, shell w/sea horse hdl, bl mk, cream sz 550.00
Pitcher, shell/sea horse hdl, unmk, cream sz 285.00
Pitcher, St Bernard, bl mk, water sz 750.00
Pitcher, St Bernard, unmk, water sz 700.00
Pitcher, tomato, bl mk, water sz 500.00
Salt cellar, Devil & Cards, bl mk, master 295.00
Shakers, cherries, bl mk, pr 175.00
Shakers, coachman, bl mk, pr 500.00
Shakers, conch shell, unmk, pr 75.00
Shakers, grapes, purple, bl mk, pr 125.00
Shakers, lobster, bl mk, pr 220.00
Shakers, lobster & leaf, bl mk, pr 225.00
String holder, rooster, bl mk 375.00
Sugar bowl, murex shell, bl mk 100.00
Sugar bowl, pansy, bl mk, w/lid 350.00
Sugar bowl, poppy, bl mk, w/lid 150.00
Tea strainer, pansy, purple, bl mk 395.00
Teapot, pansy, bl mk 650.00
Teapot, pansy, gr mk, EX 650.00
Teapot, poppy, bl mk 300.00
Teapot, tomato, bl mk 250.00
Toothpick holder, elk, bl mk 225.00
Toothpick holder, murex shell, bl mk 90.00
Wall pocket, grapes, MOP, unmk, lg 250.00
Wall pocket, grapes, purple, bl mk, lg 275.00
Wall pocket, pansy, pearlized, bl mk 500.00
Wall pocket, peach w/leaves, bl mk 600.00

Nursery Rhymes

Bell, Jack & the Beanstalk, wooden clapper, bl mk 325.00
Bowl, Jack & Jill, bl mk, 5¾" 110.00
Box, Little Jack Horner, kidney shape, bl mk 135.00
Cake plate, Ring Around the Rosies, bl mk 265.00
Candlestick, Little Boy Blue, bl mk 235.00
Candy dish, Little Miss Muffett, rolled rim 90.00
Hair receiver, Ring Around the Rosies, bl mk 365.00
Pin dish, Jack & the Beanstalk, bl mk 115.00
Pitcher, Little Miss Muffett, bl mk, milk sz 215.00
Plate, Jack & Jill, bl mk, 7½" 175.00
Plate, Little Jack Horner, bl mk, 7¾" 115.00

Scenics and Action Portraits

Bell, peacock, bl mk 245.00
Bowl, bird/turkeys/man, 3x10" 200.00
Bowl, wheat girl w/chickens, bl mk, 9½" 395.00
Box, Snow Babies, unmk, 3½x3¾" dia 150.00
Candlestick, Brittany Girls, bl mk, 6", pr 350.00
Candlestick, Snow Babies, saucer shape w/hdl 225.00

Candlestick, storks on gr, bl mk 100.00
Charger, boy w/donkeys, bl mk, 13" 300.00
Cracker jar, Arab scene, bl mk 395.00
Cup & saucer, Beach Baby, bl mk 215.00
Cup & saucer, man w/turkeys, bl mk 100.00
Dresser tray, goose girl, bl mk 495.00
Ewer, hunter w/dogs, bl mk, 4½" 180.00
Hair receiver, girl w/turkey, bl mk 130.00
Match holder, Arab scene, bl mk 95.00
Match holder, frog & bee on red, bl mk, wall type 400.00
Pitcher, Beach Baby, bl mk 215.00
Pitcher, man in boat fishing, bl mk, water sz, 7" 300.00
Pitcher, water; cavaliers toasting, bl mk 275.00
Shakers, HP ivory floral, bl mk, pr 250.00
Stick pin holder, man hunting w/dogs, bl mk 215.00
Sugar bowl, Snow Baby, bl mk 235.00
Tea set, child's, boy w/donkey, bl mk, serves 2 ....250.00
Vase, Arab on horse, bl mk, mini 100.00
Vase, Babes in Woods, hdls, bl mk, #154 ....310.00
Vase, muff lady, cobalt, bl mk, 6½" 400.00

Sunbonnet Babies

Tray, babies hanging laundry, blue mark, 8x11¼", $700.00.

Bell, babies fishing, bl mk 385.00
Cake plate, babies cleaning, hdls, bl mk, lg 275.00
Chamber stick, babies fishing, ring hdl, bl mk 375.00
Mug, babies washing, bl mk, lg 300.00
Pitcher, babies fishing, bl mk, cream sz 335.00
Pitcher, babies mending, bl mk, cream sz 250.00
Plate, babies cleaning, bl mk, 6" 210.00
Plate, babies ironing, bl mk, 7½" 200.00
Rose bowl, babies washing, bl mk 375.00
Sugar bowl, babies washing, bl mk, w/lid 385.00
Toothpick holder, babies fishing, bl mk, 3½x2x2" 500.00
Tumbler, babies cleaning, bl mk, 3½" 375.00

Tapestries

Basket, Rose Tapestry, sterling trim, bl mk, 4½" 900.00
Basket, Rose Tapestry, 2-color on gr, #1011, bl mk 435.00
Basket, Rose Tapestry, 3-color, #1087, bl mk, 5½" 550.00
Bowl, Rose Tapestry, 3-color, bl mk, lg 995.00
Box, powder; Rose Tapestry, bl mk 225.00
Cake plate, Rose Tapestry, 3-color, open hdls, bl mk 395.00
Candy dish, Rose Tapestry, 3-color, rococo edge, bl mk, 8" 300.00
Cup & saucer, chocolate; Rose Tapestry, 3-color, bl mk 325.00
Cup & saucer, demitasse; Rose Tapestry, 3-color, bl mk 295.00
Hair receiver, Rose Tapestry, 3-color, bl mk, 3" 250.00
Hatpin holder, Rose Tapestry, 3-color, bl mk 465.00
High-top shoe, Rose Tapestry, bl mk 600.00
Match holder, highland sheep, bl mk, wall sz 500.00
Nappy, Rose Tapestry, orange, #1128 ....175.00
Nut set, Rose Tapestry, #1037, bl mk, master+6 cups 1,400.00

Pin dish, Rose Tapestry, 3-color w/gold rim, bl mk, 4¾" 110.00
Pitcher, brn & wht cows, bl mk, mini 185.00
Pitcher, Colonial Curtsey scene, bl mk, 4" 265.00
Pitcher, Highland Goats, bl mk, cream sz 355.00
Pitcher, Highland Sheep, bl mk, cream sz 295.00
Pitcher, Rose Tapestry, bl mk, cream sz, 3" 275.00
Pitcher, Rose Tapestry, corset shape, bl mk, milk sz, 6" 385.00
Pitcher, The Bathers, bl mk, cream sz 285.00
Planter, cow scenic, gold hdls, ruffled, bl mk 250.00
Planter, Rose Tapestry, bl mk 200.00
Plaque, lady on horse, bl mk, 9½" 770.00
Plate, Rose Tapestry, bl mk, 4½" 155.00
Rose bowl, Rose Tapestry, bl mk 285.00
Toothpick holder, goats grazing, ftd, bl mk 295.00
Toothpick holder, lady w/horse, bl mk 410.00
Tray, Highland Sheep, bl mk, #1058, 8x11" 600.00
Tumbler, castle & forest scene, bl mk 245.00
Vase, castle scene, bl mk, 4" 325.00
Vase, cavalier making toast, bl mk 220.00
Vase, Rose Tapestry, 2-color, bl mk, #1185 ....345.00
Vase, stag in stream, bl mk 550.00
Wall pocket, Rose Tapestry, 3-color, bl mk, lg 1,100.00

Royal Bonn

Royal Bonn is a fine-paste porcelain, ornately decorated with scenes, portraits, or florals. The factory was established in the mid-1800s in Bonn, Germany; however, most pieces found today are from the latter part of the century.

Ewer, floral, gold serpent hdls mk, 12½" 400.00
Vase, emb floral, wht on gr mottle, leaf hdls, bulbous, 13" 350.00

Vase, lady's portrait, signed Wiskner, 8", $975.00.

Vase, lady on lt brn/gold mottle, ornate hdls/cup top, 4½" 265.00
Vase, portrait, artist sgn, hdld urn form, 14" 450.00
Vase, purple & yel iris, gold hdls, 7½" 200.00
Vase, roses, sgn FM, 2 animal-head hdls, pear form, 14" 350.00
Vase, roses on gr, 8½" 275.00
Vase, stylized leaves, mc, dbl gourd, #40-3298/9, 8¾" 175.00
Vase, wht hydrangeas, lg hdls from ruffled rim to base, 14" 450.00
Vase, Worcester-style floral w/gold, hdls, ped ft, 12x6¼" 175.00

Royal Copenhagen

The Royal Copenhagen Manufactory was established in Denmark in about 1775 by Frantz Henrich Muller. When bankruptcy threatened in 1779, the Crown took charge. The fine dinnerware and objects of art produced after that time carry the familiar logo, the crown over three wavy lines. See also Limited Edition Plates.

Bowl, Flora Danica, Leuciscus Idus Van Anpus, #358, 5½x8¾" .1,495.00

Compote, Blue Fluted, half-lace, #634, 7x11" 276.00
Figurine, boy & girl kiss, #2162, 8" 180.00
Figurine, boy at lunch, #865 ....175.00
Figurine, boy w/calf, #772 ....290.00
Figurine, boy w/gourd, #4539 ....225.00
Figurine, boy w/horn, #3689 ....105.00
Figurine, boy w/2 calves, #1858, 7½x9" 475.00
Figurine, boy w/2 wht geese, mk, 7x4¾" 195.00
Figurine, children playing, #1568, 4½" 200.00
Figurine, children reading, #1567, 3⅞" 150.00
Figurine, cow w/calf, #800, 10½" 240.00
Figurine, girl w/calf, #779 ....280.00
Figurine, girl w/doll, #1938, 5" 280.00
Figurine, girl w/goose, #528, 7½" 250.00
Figurine, goat lady, #694 ....350.00
Figurine, koala bear, #5402 ....275.00
Figurine, milkmaid, #899, 11½" 425.00
Figurine, nude on rock, #4027 ....195.00
Figurine, October, #4532 ....275.00
Figurine, Pan on ped, #433 ....285.00
Figurine, Pan playing pipes, #1736 ....235.00
Figurine, Pan riding bear, #1804, rare 585.00
Figurine, Pan w/goat, youthful, #1012/498, 5" 265.00
Figurine, polar bear, #320 ....50.00
Figurine, rooster, ca 1961, #1127, 3¼x5½" 70.00
Figurine, Sandman, #1145 ....165.00
Figurine, 2 girls in garden, #1316 ....325.00
Pickle dish, Flora Danica, Lalix Reticulata, 9½x7¾" 400.00
Pitcher, hobnail on olive/cream matt mottle, tube neck, 8" 460.00
Plaque, lg fish relief in brns/dk bl, #21792, 5x10½" 480.00
Plate, Flora Danica, Gobius Niger, #3549, 10" 400.00
Plate, Flora Danica, Thymallus Vulgaris, rtcl/shaped rim, 10" 600.00
Platter, Flora Danica, Nephrops Norvegicus, #3520, 14x8½" .1,150.00
Sauce boat, Flora Danica, fish/aquatic flora, #3556, 9½" 1,035.00
Vase, flowers/dragonfly, pastels on wht to bl, 10x9" 375.00

Royal Copley

Royal Copley is a decorative type of pottery made by the Spaulding China Company in Sebring, Ohio, from 1942 to 1957. They also produced two other major lines — Royal Windsor and Spaulding. Royal Copley was primarily marketed through five-and-ten cent stores; Royal Windsor and Spaulding were sold through department stores, gift shops, and jobbers. Items trimmed in gold are worth 25% to 50% more than the same item with no gold trim.

For more information we recommend *Royal Copley* and *More About Royal Copley* by Leslie and Marjorie Wolfe, edited by our advisor for this category, Joe Devine; he is listed in the Directory under Iowa. These books have been brought back by popular demand and include updated values.

Ashtray, lily pad w/bird, gr stamp, 5" 10.00
Ashtray, straw hat w/bow, emb mk, 5" 15.00
Bank, pig, paper label, lg, 7½" 55.00
Bank, pig, paper label, red, 4½" 35.00
Bank, rooster, paper label, 7½" 60.00
Bowl, bird perched on side, gr stamp, 4" 12.00
Creamer, leaf, hdl, gr stamp, 3" 18.00
Figurine, dancing lady, gray top w/yel skirt, paper label, 8" 75.00
Figurine, dog, paper label, 6½" 20.00
Figurine, dove, paper label, 5" 15.00
Figurine, kingfisher, paper label, 5" 30.00
Figurine, rooster, wht, paper label, lg, 8" 75.00
Figurine, sea gull, paper label, 8" 35.00

Figurine, thrush, mc, paper label, 6½" 16.00
Figurine, woodpecker, gr stamp or raised letters, 6¼" 15.00
Lamp, dancing girl, orig shade 90.00
Lamp, figurine; Oriental boy w/jug, orig shade 40.00
Lamp base, cocker spaniel, 10" 75.00
Open vase/planter, bird in flight, paper label, 7¼" 25.00
Pitcher, daffodil, gr stamp, 8" 48.00
Pitcher, floral decal, hdl, gold stamp, 6" 15.00
Pitcher, Pome Fruit, gr stamp, 8" 48.00
Planter, barefooted boy, paper label, 7½" 20.00
Planter, big apple, emb mk, 5½" 30.00
Planter, birdhouse w/bird, paper label, 8" 60.00
Planter, clown, 8¼" 50.00
Planter, coach form, gr stamp, 3¼x6" 16.00
Planter, dog pulling wagon, paper label, 5¾" 35.00
Planter, dog w/string bass, paper label, 7" 90.00
Planter, double spray, paper label, 4½" 12.00
Planter, duck & mailbox, paper label, 6¾" 50.00
Planter, girl w/wheelbarrow, paper label, 7" 28.00
Planter, gloved lady, emb mk, 6" 35.00
Planter, kitten w/cello, paper label, 7½" 60.00
Planter, Peter Rabbit, paper label, 6½" 40.00
Planter, pigtail girl, emb mk, 7" 30.00
Planter, pony, emb mk, 5¼" 18.00
Planter, rooster, paper label, 8" 35.00
Planter, salmon, jumping, paper label, 6½x11½" 60.00
Planter, salt box, emb mk, 5½" 30.00
Planter, teddy bear, paper label, 6¼" 45.00
Planter, teddy bear, paper label, 8" 50.00
Planter, teddy w/mandolin, paper label, 6¾" 60.00
Planter, Tony, paper label, 8¼" 48.00
Planter/wall pocket, Chinese girl w/big hat, emb mk, 7½" 28.00
Plaque/planter, dogwood, paper label, 4½" 15.00
Plaque/planter, mill scene, sgn in script, 8" 50.00
Sugar bowl, leaf, hdld, gr stamp, 3½" 18.00
Vase, bud; parrot, mc, gr stamp or raised letters, 5" 16.00
Vase, cornucopia, floral decal, 8¼" 25.00
Vase, fish, paper label, 6" 45.00
Vase, harmony, paper label, 7½" 12.00
Vase, ivy decor, ftd, paper label, 8" 12.00
Vase, mare & foal, emb mk, 8½" 38.00
Vase, philodendron, ftd, paper label, 7½" 12.00
Vase, trailing leaf & vine, paper label, 8½" 15.00
Vase/planter, horse head, paper label, 6¼" 28.00
Vase/planter, kitten on stump, paper label, 6½" 32.00
Vase/planter, Oriental-style fish, ftd, paper label, 5½" 15.00

Royal Crown Derby

The Royal Crown Derby company can trace its origin back to 1848. It first operated under the name of Locker & Co. but by 1859 had become Stevenson, Sharp & Co. Several changes in ownership occured until 1866 when it became known as the Sampson Hancock Co. The Derby Crown Porcelain Co. Ltd. was formed in 1876, and these companies soon merged. In 1890 they were appointed as a manufacturer for the Queen and began using the name Royal Crown Derby.

In the early years considerable 'Japan ware' decorated in Imari pattern using red, blue, and gold in Oriental patterns was popular. They excelled in their ability to use gold in the decoration, and some of the best flower painters of all time were employed. Nice vases or plaques signed by any of these artists will bring thousands of dollars: Gregory, Mosley, Rouse, Gresley, and D'esir'e Leroy. We have observed porcelain plaques decorated with flowers signed by Gregory selling at auction for

as much as $12,000.00. If you find signed pieces and are not sure of your values, it would be best if possible to have it appraised by someone very knowledgeable regarding current market values.

As is usual among most other English factories, nearly all of the vases produced by Royal Crown Derby came with covers. If they are missing, deduct 40% to 45%. There are several well-illustrated books available from antique book sellers to help you learn to identify this ware. The back stamps used after 1891 will date every piece except dinnerware. The company is still in business, producing outstanding dinnerware and Imari-decorated figures and serving pieces. They also produce custom (one only) sets of table service for the wealthy of the world. The advisors for this category are Henry and Geneva Tyler, who are listed in the Directory under Florida.

Vase, florals on cream ground, molded florals at neck on gilded yellow, domed lid, ca 1889, 12", $925.00.

Bowl, serving; Japan pattern, Imari palette, oval, 1800s, 10" 200.00
Cigarette lighter, Imari pattern, 3½" 65.00
Vase, floral/scrolls, mc/gold on cream, hdls, 8" 135.00

Royal Doulton, Doulton

The range of wares produced by the Doulton Company since its inception in 1815 has been vast and varied. The earliest wares produced in the tiny pottery in Lambeth, England, were salt-glazed pitchers, plain and fancy figural bottles — all utility-type stoneware geared to the practical needs of everyday living. The original partners, John Doulton and John Watts, saw the potential for success in the manufacture of drain and sewage pipes and during the 1840s concentrated on these highly lucrative types of commercial wares. Watts retired from the company in 1854, and Doulton began experimenting with a more decorative product line. As time went by, many glazes and decorative effects were developed, among them Faience, Impasto, Silicon, Carrara, Marqueterie, Chine, and Rouge Flambe. Tiles and architectural terra cotta were an important part of their manufacture. Late in the 19th century at the original Lambeth location, fine artware was decorated by such notable artists as Hannah and Arthur Barlow, George Tinworth, and J.H. McLennan. Stoneware vases with incised animal drawings, gracefully shaped urns with painted scenes, and cleverly modeled figurines rivaled the best of any competitor.

In 1882 a second factory was built in Burslem which continues even yet to produce the famous figurines, character jugs, series ware, and table services so popular with collectors today. Their Kingsware line, made from 1899 to 1946, featured flasks and flagons with drinking scenes, usually on a brown-glazed ground. Some were limited editions, while others were commemorative and advertising items. The Gibson Girl series, twenty-four plates in all, was introduced in 1901. It was drawn by Charles Dana Gibson and is recognized by its blue and white borders and central illustrations, each scene depicting a humorous or poignant episode in the life of 'The Widow and Her Friends.' Dickensware, produced from 1911 through the early 1940s, featured illustrations by Charles Dickens, with many of his famous characters. The Robin Hood series was introduced in 1914; the Shakespeare series #1, portraying scenes from the Bard's plays, was made from 1914 until World War II. The Shakespeare series #2 ran from 1906 until 1974 and was decorated with featured characters. Nursery Rhymes was a series that was first produced in earthenware in 1930 and later in bone china. In 1933 a line of decorated children's ware, the Bunnykin series, was introduced; it continues to be made to the present day. About 150 'bunny' scenes have been devised, the earliest and most desirable being those signed by the artist Barbara Vernon. Most pieces range in value from $60.00 to $120.00.

Factors contributing to the value of a figurine are age, color, and detail. Those with a limited production run and those signed by the artist or marked 'Potted' (indicating a pre-1939 origin) are also more valuable. After 1920 wares were marked with a lion — with or without a crown — over a circular 'Royal Doulton.' Our advisor for this category is Nicki Budin; she is listed in the Directory under Ohio.

Animals and Birds

Dog, Airedale, #1022, lg	700.00
Dog, Bulldog, brn & wht, HN1047, wht, sm	195.00
Dog, Bulldog, seated, DA22	50.00
Dog, Cairn, K-11	75.00
Dog, Cocker Spaniel, HN1036, 5¼x7⅜"	165.00
Dog, Corgi, #2558, med	250.00
Dog, Dachshund, brn, #1139, lg	525.00
Dog, Dachshund, HN1128, med	150.00
Dog, Doberman, #2645, med	180.00
Dog, English Cocker Spaniel, red, #1137, med	120.00
Dog, English Setter, #1049, lg	95.00
Dog, Irish Setter, #1055, med	150.00
Dog, Pekinese, #1012, sm	120.00
Dog, Pekinese, seated, K-6	95.00
Kitten, HN2580, HN2581 or HN2584, ea	85.00
Penguin & chick, K-20	250.00
Tern, HN1196	295.00

Bunnykins

Figurine, Aussie Surfer, #133	95.00
Figurine, Bedtime, yel, #103	125.00
Figurine, Billy Bunnykins, D6001, early	2,800.00
Figurine, Cheerleader, yel, #143	85.00
Figurine, Harry the Herald, #155	200.00
Figurine, John Bull, limited edition, #134	150.00
Figurine, Master Potter, #121	85.00
Figurine, Mountie, limited edition, #135	350.00
Figurine, Mr Bunnybeat, #16	65.00
Figurine, Rise & Shine, #11	50.00
Figurine, Sleepytime	50.00
Figurine, Springtime, #7	355.00
Figurine, Tally Ho, #12	55.00
Figurine, Touchdown, #29	50.00

Character Jugs

'Ard of 'Earing, lg	1,150.00
'Ard of 'Earing, mini	850.00
'Arriet, mini	75.00
'Arriet, sm	85.00
'Arry, D6249, mini	75.00
'Arry, sm	85.00
Apothecary, D6581, mini	65.00

Aramis, D6454, sm	80.00
Aramis, D6641, lg	145.00
Athos, D6439, lg	145.00
Auld Mac, D5823, lg	135.00
Auld Mac, D5824, sm	55.00
Auld Mac, D6253, gr jacket, mini	45.00
Bacchus, D6505, sm	50.00
Beefeater, D6206, ER, lg	100.00
Beefeater, D6233, ER, sm	75.00
Beefeater, D6233, GR, sm	60.00
Beefeater, D6251, GR, mini	55.00
Blacksmith, D6385, mini	65.00
Blacksmith, D6571, lg	150.00
Bootmaker, D6586, mini	55.00
Captain Cuttle, D5842, lg	95.00
Cardinal, D6063, A, sm	75.00
Cavalier, D6173, sm	60.00
Dick Turpin, D6528, horse hdl, lg	145.00
Dick Turpin, D6535, horse hdl, sm	70.00
Dick Turpin, D6542, horse hdl, mini	55.00
Don Quixote, D6460, sm	50.00
Falconer, D6533, lg	135.00
Falconer, D6547, mini	45.00
Falstaff, D6287, lg	135.00
Falstaff, D6519, mini	45.00
Farmer John, D5788, lg	160.00
Farmer John, D5789, sm	70.00
Fortune Teller, D6503, sm	325.00
Friar Tuck, D6321, lg	450.00
Gaoler, D6570, lg	150.00
Gaoler, D6584, mini	55.00
Gondolier, D6589, lg	575.00
Gondolier, D6595, mini	325.00
Gone Away, D6531, lg	145.00
Granny, D6384, sm	50.00
Granny, toothless, D5521, lg	850.00
Guardsman, D6772, mini	55.00
Gunsmith of Williamsburg, D6587, mini	55.00
Henry V, D6671, decal hdl, lg	150.00
Izaak Walton, D6404, anniversary, lg	140.00
Jarge, D6288, lg	350.00
Jarge, D6295, sm	195.00
Jester, D5556, sm	125.00
John Barleycorn, D5735, sm	70.00
John Peel, D5731, sm	70.00
Johnny Appleseed, D6372, lg	325.00
Lawyer, D6498, lg	130.00
Lobster Man, D6620, sm	55.00
London Bobby, D6744, lg	125.00
Long John Silver, D6386, sm	50.00
Lumberjack, D6613, sm	70.00
MacBeth, D6667, lg	135.00
Mad Hatter, D6602, sm	80.00
Mikado, D6507, sm	325.00

Monty (Field Marshal Montgomery), D6202, large, $100.00.

Mr Micawber, D5843, odd sz	165.00
Mr Micawber, D5843, sm	75.00
Mr Micawber, D6143, tiny	95.00
Neptune, D6548, lg	125.00
Neptune, D6552, sm	50.00
North American Indian, D6611, lg	125.00
North American Indian, D6614, sm	50.00
Old Charley, D5420, lg	125.00
Old King Cole, D6037, sm	125.00
Parson Brown, D5486, lg	140.00
Parson Brown, D5529, sm	50.00
Pied Piper, D6462, sm	50.00
Poacher, D6464, sm	50.00
Porthos, D6440, lg	145.00
Regency Beau, D5669, lg	950.00
Robin Hood, feather, D6205, lg	125.00
Robin Hood, feather, D6234, sm	55.00
Robinson Crusoe, D6539, sm	60.00
Sairey Gamp, D5451, lg	125.00
Sairey Gamp, D5528, sm	50.00
Sairey Gamp, D6045, mini	45.00
Sairey Gamp, D6146, tiny	95.00
Sam Johnson, D6289, lg	275.00
Sam Johnson, D6296, sm	195.00
Sam Weller, D5841, odd sz	175.00
Sancho Panza, D6461, sm	50.00
Santa, red, wht & gr hdl, D6840, lg	325.00
Santa, wreath hdl, D6794, lg	275.00
Scaramouche, D6558, lg	675.00
Scaramouche, D6561, sm	435.00
Simon the Cellarer, D5616, sm	70.00
Smuggler, D6619, sm	60.00
Tam O'Shanter, D6640, mini	50.00
Tony Weller, D5530, sm	60.00
Town Crier, D6044, mini	85.00
Town Crier, sm	100.00
Trapper, D6609, lg	145.00
Trapper, D6612, sm	50.00
Vicar of Bray, D5615, lg	195.00
Viking, D6502, sm	110.00
Walrus & Carpenter, D6604, sm	60.00

Figurines

A Courting, HN2004	485.00
A La Mode, HN2544	165.00
Adrienne, HN2304, bl	175.00
All Aboard, HN2940	165.00
Anthea, HN1527	850.00
Antoinette, HN2326	140.00
Ascot, HN2356	185.00
At Ease, HN2473	195.00
Autumn Breezes, HN1913	225.00
Autumn Breezes, HN1934	195.00
Autumn Breezes, HN2147, blk	350.00
Bachelor, HN2319	250.00
Ballad Seller, HN2266	275.00
Ballerina, HN2116	295.00
Bell O' the Ball, HN1997, 1947-79, 6"	295.00
Bess, HN2002	275.00
Blithe Morning, HN2021	195.00
Bridget, HN2070	325.00
Broken Lance, HN2041	495.00
Camelia, HN2222	275.00

Carolyn, HN2112	300.00
Carpet Seller, HN1464	340.00
Celeste, HN2237	225.00
Cherie, HN2341	100.00
China Repairer, HN2943	175.00
Christmas Time, HN2110	365.00
Cissie, HN1809	120.00
Clare, HN2793	165.00
Clockmaker, HN2279	325.00
Cookie, HN2218	175.00
Coppelia, HN1952	575.00
Country Lass, HN1991	125.00
Daffy Down Dilly, HN1712	375.00
Daphne, HN2268	165.00
Delight, HN1772, 1st version	195.00
Diana, HN2468	135.00
Doctor, HN2858	295.00
Duchess of York, HN3086	535.00
Dulcie, HN2305	175.00
Easter Day, HN2039	325.00
Eleanor of Provence, HN2009	600.00
Ermine Coat, HN1981	275.00
Fleur, HN2368	185.00
Flower Seller's Children, HN1342	650.00
Forest Glade 'Giselle,' HN2140	375.00
Forget-Me-Not, HN1813	455.00
Gaffer, HN2053	345.00
Gay Morning, HN2135	275.00
Geisha, HN1223	1,200.00
Genevieve, HN1962	275.00
Genie, HN2989	165.00
Giselle, HN2139	395.00
Good Day Sir, HN2896	135.00
Goody Two Shoes, HN1905	455.00
Gossips, HN2025	350.00
Granny's Heritage, HN2031	495.00
Gypsy Dance, HN2230, 2nd version	300.00
He Loves Me, HN2046	195.00
Heart to Heart, HN2276	425.00
Helmsman, HN2499	250.00
Her Ladyship, HN1977	300.00
Hinged Parasol, HN1579	575.00
Honey, HN1909, pk	375.00
Hurdy Gurdy, HN2796	750.00
Invitation, HN2170	125.00
Irene, HN1621	350.00
Ivy, HN1768	125.00
Janet, HN1916	210.00
Janice, HN2165	425.00
Jolly Sailor, HN2172	650.00
Jovial Monk, HN2144	235.00
June, HN2027	575.00
Kate Hardcastle, HN2028	600.00
Kathy, HN3305	110.00
La Sylphide, HN2138	475.00
Lady Charmian, HN1949, 1st version	250.00
Lambing Time, HN1890	195.00
Leisure Hour, HN2055	395.00
Lilac Time, HN2137	320.00
Lisa, HN2310	150.00
Lunchtime, HN2485	155.00
Lydia, HN1908	150.00
Margaret, HN1989	395.00
Masque, HN2554	275.00

Maureen, HN1770 ....350.00
Megan, HN3306 ....115.00
Mendicant, HN1365 ....275.00
Midinette, HN2029 ....295.00
Midsummer Noon, HN2033 ....600.00
Milkmaid, HN2057 ....150.00
Minuet, HN2015 ....275.00
Miss Demure, HN1402, 7½" 225.00
Miss Muffett, HN1936 ....190.00
Miss Muffett, HN1937 ....195.00
My Pretty Maid, HN2064 ....450.00
Old Mother Hubbard, HN2314 ....295.00
Omar Kayyam, HN2247 ....165.00
Orange Lady, HN1953, 8¾" 265.00
Pamela, HN1469, gr 1,050.00
Pantalettes, HN1362 ....395.00
Paula, HN2906 ....125.00
Pearly Boy, HN2035 ....175.00
Peggy, HN2038 ....110.00
Penelope, HN1901 ....375.00
Philippa of Hainault, HN2008 ....600.00
Polka, HN2156 ....335.00
Polly Peachum, HN550, 1st version 385.00
Potter, HN1493 ....450.00
Pretty Polly, HN2768 ....165.00
Prized Possessions, HN2942 ....450.00
Professor, HN2281 ....175.00
Prue, HN1996 ....350.00
Punch & Judy Man, HN2765 ....285.00
Puppet Maker, HN2253 ....450.00
Queen of the Ice, HN2435 ....195.00
Roseanna, HN1926, rose-to-bl dress, rose bouquet, 8" 375.00
Rosebud, HN1983 ....450.00
Royal Canadian Mounted Police, HN2547, 1973 ....750.00
Sibell, HN1695, gr dress 595.00
Skater, HN2117 ....350.00
Spring Morning, HN1922 ....225.00
St George & Dragon, HN2051, 1950-85, 7¼" 500.00
Stitch in Time, HN2352 ....200.00
Stop Press, HN2683 ....165.00
Suitor, HN2132 ....365.00
Summer's Day, HN2181 ....275.00
Sunday Morning, HN2184 ....325.00
Suzette, HN1487, pk 295.00
Suzette, HN2026, color variation 250.00
Sweet & Twenty, HN1298 ....285.00
Sweet Sixteen, HN2231 ....200.00
Sweeting, HN1935 ....135.00
Tall Story, HN2248 ....250.00
Tea Time, HN2255 ....155.00
Thank You, HN2732 ....165.00
Tinkle Bell, HN1677 ....120.00
Top O' the Hill, HN1833, gr version, 7½" 225.00
Top O' the Hill, HN2127, yel 200.00

Town Crier, HN2119,
$300.00.

Tuppence Bag, HN2320 ....165.00
Uncle Ned, HN2094 ....395.00
Uriah Heep, HN2101 ....100.00
Veronica, HN1517, rose-shaded dress, lav hat, 8¼" 365.00
Victoria, HN2471 ....225.00
Votes for Women, HN2816 ....220.00
Wendy, HN2109 ....95.00
Young Master, HN2872 ....225.00

Flambe

Bowl, Sung, red & bl mottle, F Moore monogram, Noke, 6⅛" 300.00
Figurine, cat, 5¼" 80.00
Figurine, dog of Fo, #48 ....175.00
Figurine, dragon, veined, ca 1973, 10½" L 900.00
Figurine, elephant, trunk raised, Sung, 5½" 200.00
Figurine, elephant, 7½" L 170.00
Figurine, fox, seated, 9½" 500.00
Figurine, fox, 4½" 80.00
Figurine, goose, 6⅛" 115.00
Figurine, Great Horned Owl, veined 450.00
Figurine, penguin, 6" 250.00
Figurine, penguin on base, 9" 1,000.00
Figurine, rabbit, 4½" L 80.00
Figurine, rhinoceros, 1973, 17" L 1,000.00
Figurine, salmon, leaping 750.00
Figurine, tiger, 14" 475.00
Pitcher, mottled red & bl, SP trim, ca 1900, 8¼" 500.00
Vase, Chang, wht & yel crackle over flambe, Titanian, 7¾" 1,350.00
Vase, country house, 11" 200.00
Vase, farming landscape in underglaze blk, 20th C, 8½", pr 200.00
Vase, mottled red/bl/gr, Fred Moore monogram, ca 1930, 10", pr 400.00
Vase, red & yel mottle, H Nixon monogram, ca 1930, 6¾" 250.00
Vase, red mottle, Noke, early 20th C, 7¼" 325.00
Vase, sheep in landscape, Noke, ca 1925, 8" 500.00
Vase, shepherd & sheep landscape, ca 1895, 5¾" 500.00
Vase, Sung, bl & red mottle, F Allen monogram, ca 1935, 6½" 550.00
Vase, Sung, farm scene, A Eaton, Noke, ca 1920, 13¾" 850.00
Vase, veined, bulbous, mid-20th C, 16¾" 750.00

Series Ware

Ashtray, Ships A, trading ketch & 2 sloops, mc, D2872, 5¼" sq 150.00
Bowl, Gypsies, 5" 160.00
Bowl, salad; Bayeux Tapestry, Battle of Hastings, D2873, 6" 98.00
Candlestick, King Arthur's Knights, mc, D2961, 1924, 6½" 110.00
Candlestick, Ships A, profile view, mc, D2872, 1934, 6½" 145.00
Chop plate, Under the Greenwood Tree, 13½" 270.00
Creamer, Nursery Rhymes A, Little Man, 1905, 3¼" 98.00
Cup & saucer, Australia Gum Trees A, mc, D5506 ....75.00
Cup & saucer, Mad Hatter 125.00
Loving cup, King Arthur's Knights, mc, D-2961, 6" 385.00
Mug, King Arthur's Knights, mc, D2961, dtd 1921, 5½" 265.00
Mug, Moreton Hall, court scene, D1898 ....135.00
Pitcher, Eglington Tournament, knights charging, D2792, 13½" 550.00
Pitcher, Egyptian A, blk & wht figures on red, D3619, 7½" 335.00
Pitcher, Gondoliers, couple in gondola, D3039, 7⅛" 315.00
Pitcher, Jackdaw of Rheims, sgn Noke, D2532, 4" 275.00
Pitcher, Jacobean, Ye Little Bottle, mc, D1011, 7¾" 350.00
Pitcher, Shakespeare, Ophelia, milk sz, 7" 150.00
Plate, Am Buildings C, US Capitol, dk bl/wht, 10" 135.00
Plate, Australia Gum Trees, Gum Trees & Settlement, mc, 10½" 75.00
Plate, Australian Views, Koala Bears, TC1060, 10⅜" 90.00
Plate, Canadian Maple Tree, Rose & Thistle, D4653, 10⅜" 135.00

Plate, Canadian Views, Lake Louise & Victoria, TC1066, 10½" .65.00
Plate, Canadian Views, Niagara Falls, D6476, 10½" 75.00
Plate, Castles & Churches, Rochester Castle, mc, D6308, 10⅜" .110.00
Plate, Castles & Churches, Windsor Castle, litho, 10⅜" 95.00
Plate, Coaching Days, coach going up hill, E2768, 5⅝" 60.00
Plate, Falconry, 3 Ladies Galloping..., D3696, 10¼" 135.00
Plate, Flowers, Fruit & Trees, Poplars at Sunset, 1925, 9¼" 75.00
Plate, Flowers: Nasturtiums, D3786, dtd 1915, 8½" 135.00
Plate, Flowers: Prunus A, wht on cobalt, 8½" 145.00
Plate, Gibson Widow & Friends, She Finds Consolation, 10½" ...95.00
Plate, Gondoliers, lady w/fan & gentleman, D3039, 10½" 165.00
Plate, Haystacks, church beyond, D2538, 1907, 10⅝" 165.00
Plate, Historic United States, MacDonnough's Victory, 9⅝" 215.00
Plate, Home Waters, barges at pier, Grace, 1913, 8¼" 60.00
Plate, Jackdaw of Rheims, Many a Knight..., E3305, 8" 50.00
Plate, Nautical History B, Sir Francis Drake, D2737, 1907, 8" 50.00
Plate, Nursery Rhymes, Little Old Woman, 7" 85.00
Plate, Old English Inns, Bears Head, D6072, 10½" 80.00
Plate, Professionals, Parson, D3303, 1924, 10⅜" 130.00
Stein, Night Watchman, front view, D4746, 5" 95.00
Teapot stand, Old Moreton Hall, Acanthus leaf border, D3858 ...75.00
Toothpick holder, Woodland, mc transfer, D5815, 1938, 2½" ...110.00
Tray, sandwich; Australia Gum Trees A, D5506, 1935, 5¼" dia ..80.00
Tray, sandwich; Countryside, A Village, mc, D3467, 14½x6¼" ..150.00
Tumbler, Nursery Rhymes, Little Bo Peep 95.00
Vase, Rembrandt Ware, oval portrait, A Eaton, ca 1900, 13½" ..1,250.00

Stoneware

Bibelot, bird at side, mc, Lambeth, ca 1925, 5¾" 250.00
Biscuit jar, cows & sm girls, H Barlow, SP trim, 1878, 6½" 1,750.00
Biscuit jar, deer scene, H Barlow, SP trim, ca 1879, 8¼" 950.00
Biscuit jar, geese & grasses, F Barlow, SP trim, 1881, 7" 800.00
Biscuit jar, goats frieze/floret border, H Barlow, 1877, 6¾" 800.00
Biscuit jar, leaves, SP rim & lid, Lambeth, 1878, 8" 230.00
Biscuit jar, sheep, H Barlow, SP trim & lid, ca 1873, 8½" 850.00
Bowl, salad; Art Union of London, MV Marshall, ca 1900, 7¾" .250.00
Candlesticks, foliage, E Simmance, early 1900s, 7⅜", pr 350.00
Cup, hounds, Hannah Barlow, 3-hdld, SP trim, 1876, 6½" 450.00
Inkwell, baby figural, Suffragette Movement, ca 1908, 3⅜" 450.00
Jug, donkeys, H Barlow, ca 1891, 8½" 850.00
Jug, monks scenes, Lambeth, 7¾" 115.00
Mug, hounds in panels, H Barlow, 3-hdld, late 1800s, 6" 1,200.00
Pepper shaker, advertising, brn & tan salt glaze, 4½" 90.00
Pitcher, emb Indian faces, face as spout, 1893, 5¾" 325.00
Pitcher, exotic bird, Titanian Ware, ca 1925, 7¼" 225.00
Pitcher, horses & children, H Barlow, ca 1883, 8¾" 700.00
Pitcher, hunters relief, wht/tan/brn, missing lid, ca 1900, 6" 325.00
Pitcher, leaf/floral bands, wht/brn/bl, spout w/emb face, 9" 225.00
Pitcher, leaves & floral medallions, FC Roberts, 1882, 9¾" 300.00
Pitcher, lions frieze, Hannah Barlow, 1877, 8⅞" 1,000.00
Salt cellar, pig figural, Titanian Ware, SP trim, 1925, 4" 275.00
Tankard, rabbits, H Barlow, pewter trim, 1878, 5" 900.00
Vase, appl cherry blossoms/birds/fish, wht/brn on tan, 6" 300.00
Vase, bud; Art Union of London, E Simmance, 1902, 8¼" 150.00
Vase, cats band, scroll & leaf border, H Barlow, 1885, 6⅝" 800.00
Vase, cows & goats grazing, Hanna Barlow, ca 1895, 8¼" 800.00
Vase, deer grazing, leaf & flower border, EE Stormer, 1891, 7" ...700.00
Vase, dragon in relief, E Simmance, ca 1879, rstr, 15¼" 2,000.00
Vase, emb florets, incised foliage, F Butler, 1879, 11" 450.00
Vase, florals & leaves, E Simmance, ca 1895, 8½" 300.00
Vase, horses grazing, Hannah Barlow, 1878, 16⅝" 3,000.00
Vase, pigs on stippled ground, H Barlow, 1895, 12" 850.00
Vase, Silicon, acanthus/foliate bands, 3-color on tan, 9" 325.00

Vase, Waning of Honeymoon, 2 rabbits at sides, 1895, 6½" ...1,350.00
Watch stand, dragon w/fr on bk, sgn, unmk, 19th C, 5⅛" 300.00

Toby Jugs

Best Is Not Too Good, D6107 ....425.00
Double XX (Man on Barrel), D6266 ....350.00
Falstaff, D6063 ....95.00
Fat Boy, D6264 ....260.00
Honest Measure, D6108, 4¼" 125.00
Jolly Toby, D6109 ....125.00
Mr Micawber, D6262 ....250.00
Old Charley, D6069 ....250.00
Sairey Gamp, D6263 ....225.00
Sherlock Holmes, D6661 ....125.00
Winston Churchill, D6171, lg 150.00
Winston Churchill, D6172, sm 115.00
Winston Churchill, D6175, mini 95.00

Miscellaneous

Flowerpot, stylized flower/leaf bands, pk/wht on gr, 15x17" 1,000.00
Ginger jar, Chang, wht crackle w/mc drip, Nixon, Noke, 11½" ..6,000.00
Vase, Arts & Crafts-style flowers, lav/gray on brn, #79, 11x5" ...250.00
Vase, faience, butterflies, M Denley, ca 1883, 10⅝" 350.00
Vase, faience, leaves & vegetables on gr, Lambeth, ca 1900, 13" ..150.00
Vase, Impasto Ware, floral on brn, F Allen, 17½", EX 900.00
Vase, landscape, sgn Prince, bone china, ca 1928, 10" 200.00
Vase, Luscian Ware, lady in landscape, L Johnson, 1895, 9" 850.00
Vase, stylized flowers/grapes, bl/gr on bl flambe, 9x3½" 350.00

Royal Dux

The Duxer Porzellan Manufactur was established by E. Eichler in 1860. Located in what is now Duchcov, Czechoslovakia, the area was known as Dux, Bohemia, until WWI. The war brought about changes in both the style of the ware as well as the mark. Prewar pieces were modeled in the Art Nouveau or Greek Classical manner and marked with 'Bohemia' and a pink triangle containing the letter 'E.' They were usually matt glazed in green, brown, and gold. Better pieces were made of porcelain, while the larger items were of pottery. After the war the ware was marked with the small pink triangle but without the Bohemia designation; 'Made in Czechoslovakia' was added. The style became Art Deco, with cobalt blue a dominant color.

Vase with maids clinging to sides, lobster climbing up base, #862, 21½", $1,900.00.

Basket, stylized floral/berries on brn/yel, Xd hdls, 8" 150.00
Centerpc, maid/2 children support shell bowl, glossy, 20x16" .1,000.00
Figurine, Art Deco harem dancer, cobalt & gold, 14" 475.00

Figurine, elephant, lt gr/gray w/gold, #736, 13x16" 125.00
Figurine, girl sits on stone pedestal, reads book, #2374, 16" 650.00
Figurine, girl sitting beside bowl, triangle mk, 5x5" 150.00
Figurine, lady on bench, man beside, basket at ft, 17x10x7" ...1,500.00
Figurine, maid bends over water lily, w/gold, #332, 11½" 600.00
Figurine, nude: Morning Dew (& similar), 2-tier ped, 14", pr 750.00
Figurine, peasant w/pouch & bag (& maid w/teapot), 21", pr .1,000.00
Figurine, Roman maid (& male), w/lg basket, 6", pr 500.00

Royal Flemish

Royal Flemish was introduced in the late 1880s and was patented in 1894 by the Mt. Washington Glass Company. Transparent glass was enameled with one or several colors and the surface divided by a network of raised lines suggesting leaded glasswork. Some pieces were further decorated with enameled florals, birds, or Roman coins. Our advisors for this category are Betty and Clarence Maier; they are listed in the Directory under Pennsylvania.

Biscuit jar, mc panels, lion on shield, gold scrolls, 5x7½" 3,750.00
Ewer, lad spears winged creature, much gold, rnd body, 11" 4,950.00
Ginger jar, gold winged dragon, 7" 1,900.00
Pickle castor, gold wild roses, emb scrolls; ornate fr 750.00
Sugar shaker, Queen Anne's Lace, clear satin, ovoid 825.00
Vase, boy/griffin, bk: cherub/dragon, hdld bottle w/lid, 17" 6,500.00
Vase, gold dragons & stars, ornate collar, muted reds, 8" 2,750.00
Vase, Guba ducks/gold moon/stars, crown-rim stick neck, 16" .6,100.00
Vase, lg snow geese against sun, dragons on neck band, 15" 8,500.00
Vase, mums & wild roses w/gold, sgn, 14" 4,250.00
Vase, pansies, wine on frost, much gold, bulb neck, 8x8" 1,385.00
Vase, 3 circle medallions w/gold lines, allover flowers, 12" 3,000.00

Royal Haeger, Haeger

In 1871 David Henry Haeger, a young son of German immigrants, purchased a brick factory at Dundee, Illinois, and began an association with the ceramic industry that his descendants have pursued to the present time. David's bricks had rebuilt Chicago after their great fire in 1871. By 1914 they had ventured into the field of commercial artware. Vases, figurines, lamp bases, and gift items in a pastel matt glaze carried the logo of the company name written over the bar of an 'H.' From 1929 to 1933, they produced a line of dinnerware which they marketed through Marshall Fields. Ware produced before the mid-thirties sometimes is found with a paper label; these are of special interest. 'Royal Haeger,' their premium line designed in 1938 by Royal Hickman, is highly desirable with collectors today. The mark 'Royal Haeger' (in raised lettering) was used during the thirties and forties; later a paper label in the shape of a crown was used.

Fast becoming popular with today's collectors is the Earth Graphic Wraps line, first introduced in the mid-'70s. These one-of-a-kind pieces are decorated with rough, raised formations on backgrounds of marigold, white, fern, and brown, in both matt and glossy finishes.

The Macomb plant, built in 1939, primarily made ware for the florist trade. A second plant, built there in 1969, produces lamp bases. For those interested in learning more about the subject, we recommend *Collecting Royal Haeger* by our advisors, Lee Garmon and Doris Frizzell; both are listed in the Directory under Illinois.

Cigarette lighter, #813H, 10" H 15.00
Clock, Chinese pagoda style, Royal Haeger, 9½" 75.00
Cookie jar, Keebler Elf (orig HP) 75.00
Cookie jar, pig, standing, Bartlow Bros Inc, Korn Top 80.00

Cradle, musical, fully working, R-613, 6" L 95.00
Earth Graphic Wraps, candle holders, lg, 5½", pr 40.00
Earth Graphic Wraps, jardiniere, hdld, #5000, 10" opening, 12" dia .65.00
Earth Graphic Wraps, pitcher, squat, #8188, 8" 35.00
Earth Graphic Wraps, pot, hdld, #8207, 6½" opening, 9" dia 55.00
Earth Graphic Wraps, vase, #4170, 12" 30.00
Figurine, angelfish w/mermaid on bk, R-347, 14" 65.00
Figurine, Cocker Spaniel pup, ea 15.00
Figurine, giraffe & young, R-740, 15" 125.00
Figurine, racing horse, dbl, R-408, 10" 65.00
Figurine, St Frances, R-1231, 10½" 20.00
Figurine, Cocker Spaniel dog, R-7355 ....65.00
Flower block, jeweled lady, R-571, 15½" 35.00
Fountain, portable, electric, complete, R-8030, 13" 250.00
Planter, Rudolf Red-Nose Reindeer, R-766, 9½" 65.00
Poodle lamps, complete w/orig shade, 32" (including finial), pr .500.00
Tile, Leda & Swan, oval, #883, 10" L 25.00
TV lamp, Madonna, #3806, 11½" 35.00
TV lamp, Red Bull, wooden base, sm 75.00
Vase, macaw on branch, cylindrical, R-425, 16" 150.00
Vase, swan, solid base, R-36, 16" 45.00
Wall mask, Comedy or Tragedy, R-1198 or R-1199, 11", ea 25.00
Wall pocket, swan w/wings spread, R-517 ....35.00

Royal Rudolstadt

The hard-paste porcelain that has come to be known as Royal Rudolstadt was produced in Thuringia, Germany, in the early eighteenth century. Various names and marks have been associated with this pottery. One of the earliest was a hay-fork symbol associated with Johann Frederichvon Schwarzburg-Rudolstadt, one of the first founders. Variations, some that included an 'R,' were also used. In 1854 Earnst-Bohne produced wares that were marked with an anchor and the letters 'EB.' Examples commonly found today were made during the late 1800s and early twentieth century. These are usually marked with an 'RW' within a shield under a crown and the words 'Crown Rudolstadt.' Items marked 'Germany' were made after 1890.

Chocolate pot, pk roses/gold trim, gr/wht flowers, 10" 275.00
Ewer, floral w/gold on yel, gold hdl about neck, 10½" 135.00
Ewer, fruit reserve on gr w/gilt florals, sgn, ornate, 14" 300.00
Figurine, girl in rocker, HP pastels, crown mk, 7½" 135.00
Lamp, Delft, windmill pnt on globe, 23" 700.00
Tea set, golliwoggs dancing, child sz, 13-pc 295.00
Teapot, roses, pk on wht w/gold, mk, ind 115.00
Vase, floral on yel, hdls, 12" 110.00

Royal Vienna

In 1719 Claude Innocentius de Paquier established a hard-paste porcelain factory in Vienna where he made highly ornamental wares similar to the type produced at Meissen. Early wares were usually unmarked; but after 1744, when the factory was purchased by the Empress, the Austrian shield (often called 'beehive') was stamped on under the glaze. In the following listings, values are for hand-painted items unless noted otherwise. Decal-decorated items would be considerably lower.

Note: An influx of Japanese reproductions on the market have influenced values to decline on genuine old Royal Vienna. Buyer beware! On new items the beehive mark is over the glaze, the weight of the porcelain is heavier, and the decoration is obviously decaled. Our advisor for this category is Madeleine France; she is listed in the Directory under Florida.

Box, portrait on cobalt w/much gold, bl mk, 2x4" dia 325.00
Candlesticks, HP portraits on maroon & gold, 5½", pr 675.00
Cup, Hector, Paris & Flitera on red, sgn Hept, 3", +saucer 235.00
Demitasse pot, garden w/ladies, +cr/sug, 4 c/s, 15" tray 925.00
Mug, Rosina, lady's portrait, sgn Gorref, 2", +bowl saucer 175.00
Plaques, 3 Grecians reserve, ornate corners, fr, 17x22", pr 2,500.00
Plate, La Bella Temperia: lady in chair, gold/gr border, 9½" 635.00
Plate, lady on bench, 2nd w/basket, doves at ft, Wagner, 9½" 875.00
Plate, Marie de Medicis, jeweled/gilt border, 1800s 525.00
Plate, quail in landscape, gold/wine border, mk, lg 150.00
Teapot, lady/cherubs in garden, allover gold, ftd, rstr, 5" 225.00
Urn, lovers in reserve on bl w/gilt, hdls, late, 17" 500.00

Vases, allegorical scenes on cobalt, signed Jackl, raised fired gold mark, blue beehive mark, 14", $2,500.00 for the pair.

Vase, lady's portrait, artist sgn, maroon luster & gold, 9¾" 1,050.00
Vase, 2 maids on wine w/gold, sgn, hdls, lg sq base, 12" 500.00

Roycroft

Near the turn of the century, Elbert Hubbard established the Roycroft Printing Shop in East Aurora, New York. Named in honor of two 17th-century printer-bookbinders, the print shop was just the beginning of a community called Roycroft, which came to be known worldwide. Hubbard became a popular personality of the early 1900s, known for his talents in a variety of areas from writing and lecturing to manufacturing. The Roycroft community became a meeting place for people of various capabilities and included shops for the production of furniture, copper, leather items, and a multitude of other wares which were marked with the Roycroft symbol, an 'R' within a circle below a stylized cross. Hubbard lost his life on the Lusitania in 1915; production in the community continued until the Depression.

Interest is strong in the field of Arts and Crafts in general and in Roycroft items in particular. Copper items are evaluated to a large extent by the condition of the original patina that remains. In the listings that follow, values reflect the worth of items retaining their original patina unless condition is otherwise described. Our advisor for this category is Bruce Austin; he is listed in the Directory under New York.

Key: h/cp — hammered copper

Andirons, openwork wrought iron w/twists & curliques, 27" ..1,600.00
Armchair, #028, 2-slat bk, mk, all orig, 38x25x22" 2,700.00
Ash stand, mahog w/h/cp top, mk, 32" 650.00
Ashtray, #623, h/cp, 1½x4¼" 125.00
Bean pot & jug, ceramic, brn 60.00
Bell, h/cp, shaped brass hdl, 3x2" 300.00
Bench, lower shelf w/keyed tenons, rfn top, 20x42" 5,000.00
Book, Ballads of a Bookworm, Browne, sgn Hubbard/#d, 9x6" ..125.00
Book, Essay on Self Reliance, Emerson, leather cover, in box 150.00
Book, Hubbard, ...Catalog of Books & Things, Hunter cover 70.00
Book, Legacy I & II, sgn by Hubbard, 7x4½", EX 150.00
Book, Little Journeys...Great Musicians, sgn Hubbard, 1901 ....50.00

Book, Little Journeys...Great Scientists, Hubbard, hardcover 50.00
Book, Story of Passion, Bacheller, hand illumination, 8x6" 40.00
Bookends, #1902, tooled leather w/daisies & leafy border, 5" 500.00
Bookends, #305, h/cp, lg emb poppy, rnd top, rivets, 6x5" 450.00
Bookends, #307, h/cp, repousse peacock, 4½x6" 200.00
Bookends, #309, h/cp, rings riveted to face, 5¼x4" 300.00
Bookends, h/cp, foliage on framework, center cutout 175.00
Bookends, h/cp, galleon in circle, rnd/folded tops, 5x5½" 250.00
Bookends, h/cp w/emb floral, dk patina, 4¼x4¾" 175.00
Bookends, h/cp w/riveted Gothic brass design, 4¾x4x3½" 850.00
Bookends, h/cp w/sm floral, 1 w/cut-out center, 8½x6" 100.00
Bookstand, Little Journey's, 3-shelf, metal tag, 26x26x14" 600.00
Bowl, fruit; #C-804, h/cp, floral in center, 1¼ x8½" 175.00
Bowl, h/cp & SP, scalloped/notched, 6½" 125.00
Bowl, h/cp w/vertical ray motif, flared, rfn, 4½x12" 225.00
Bowl, like #214, h/cp, flared rim, rfn, 1¾x5½" 80.00
Box, cigarette; h/cp w/brass wash, hammered edge band, 5" 250.00
Bracelet, child's, hammered silver w/sm floral & orb mk, EX 170.00
Candlestick, h/cp, w/hdl, rfn, 1½x4½" 100.00
Candlesticks, h/cp, bobeche on rod stds, 6½", pr 375.00
Candlesticks, h/cp, twist stems, 12½", pr 475.00
Chamberstick, #404, h/cp, w/hdl, 1¾x5½" 150.00
Chandelier, #065½, 4 shades (center 1 missing), rfn 3,250.00
Creamer, gr/red geometric & Roycroft orb, Buffalo, 4½", EX 200.00
Creamer & sugar bowl, brn/gr on wht 600.00
Crumb scraper set, #811, h/cp w/emb floral 80.00
Desk set, #716, h/cp w/emb floral, blotters/opener+4 pcs 650.00
Ewer, h/cp, lg curved hdl, 3 neck rings, long spout, 6" 650.00
Frame, h/cp w/emb sq flowers ea corner, 12x10" 600.00
Humidor, #611, h/cp, flower on lid & front, rfn, 6x4½" 375.00
Humidor, copper, acid etched, 4½x3½" dia 175.00
Ink blotter, h/cp, rocker type, 2x4¾" 30.00
Inkwell, h/cp, flower on lid, sq, no liner, 1¾x3" 125.00
Kettle, h/cp, 3-ftd, 3x4¾" 60.00
Lamp, dome shade w/mica panels, sq base, 14½x8" 1,800.00
Lamp, h/cp & mica sq shade, sq std/base, 14½" 3,000.00
Letter holder, #704, h/cp w/shaped rims, sm floral, 4x5" 90.00
Match holder, h/cp, lg sq base, 3¼x5" 50.00
Pamphlet, Friendships Garland or the..., 1899, 8x5" 80.00
Pin, lapel; gold-plated w/blk onyx bkground, ¾x½" 400.00
Pipe knocker, #617, h/cp, wood knocker center, 2½x7" 125.00
Plant basket, h/cp, bk: strap w/curliques, 10x3x4" 150.00
Plate, #805, h/cp w/emb floral, worn patina, 10" 300.00
Plate, h/cp, rfn, 8" 100.00
Sconce, h/cp, curled corners, shaped bk, 12x6x3" 300.00
Sconce, h/cp, no mk, 10x2¾", pr 425.00
Sconce, h/cp, raised rectangle over socket, no mk, 10", pr 300.00
Shakers, dk gr/red geometrics on cream, Buffalo, 3", pr 450.00
Teacup, gr/red geometrics & Roycroft orb, Buffalo 100.00
Tray, #824, h/cp, octagonal, hdld, 17" 350.00
Tray, #826, h/cp, octagonal, rfn, 12" 200.00
Tray, like #806, h/cp, hdls, rfn, 19" 350.00
Vase, Am Beauty, h/cp, long trumpet neck, 14½" 3,250.00
Vase, Am Beauty #201, h/cp, rfn, 19x8" 2,000.00
Vase, brass wash, tooled flowers/bells, can neck, 9¾x3½" 450.00
Vase, h/cp, cylinder w/flared base, 10½" 1,900.00
Vase, h/cp w/band of sqd flowers at shoulder, cleaned, 6" 900.00
Vase, h/cp w/silver Arts & Crafts design, cylindrical, 6" 1,500.00
Vase, h/cp w/tooled floral & circles on linear band, 9½" 1,000.00

Rozenburg

Some of the most innovative and original Art Nouveau ceramics were created by the Rozenburg factory at The Hague in The Netherlands between 1885 and 1916. Some pieces are similar to Gouda. Rozenburg also made highly prized eggshell ware, so called because of its very thin walls; this is eagerly sought after by collectors. T.A.C. Colenbrander was their artistic leader, with Samuel Schellink and J. Kok designing many of the eggshell pieces.

Bowl, Nouveau floral, ped ft, earthenware, 4¼x7¼" 425.00
Cup & saucer, Nouveau floral, octagonal, Van Rossum 535.00
Plaque, 5 flowers on bl, cobalt rim, 1890s, rstr, 18" 575.00
Tile, windmill, pastoral, pictorial fr, sgn Gabriel 485.00

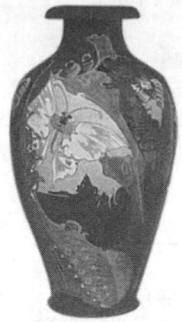

Vase, stylized butterflies and floral panels, multicolor on dark green, restoration at base, 1901, 21½", $1,980.00.

Vase, stylized lotus, naturalistic colors, #669, 6½x6¾" 575.00
Vase, sunflowers, 5-color, bulbous w/hdls, eggshell, 11" 2,300.00

Rubena

Rubena glass was made by several firms in the late 1800s. It is a blown art glass that shades from clear to red. See also Art Glass Baskets; Cruets; Sugar Shakers; Salts; specific manufacturers.

Bottle, scent; frosted, clear cut stopper w/gold, 6x2½" 75.00
Celery vase, Invt T'print, 6" 85.00
Jug, Invt T'print, clear hdl, Hobbs & Brockunier, 4" 155.00
Pitcher, Coin Spot, opal, 8" 85.00
Pitcher, HP mc florals, bulbous, clear reeded hdl, 9¼" 195.00
Tumbler, reversed colors, HP florals, 3¾x2¾" 55.00
Vase, gnome picks flowers (Mary Gregory style), 6x2½" 120.00

Rubena Verde

Rubena Verde glass was introduced in the late 1800s by Hobbs, Brockunier, and Company of Wheeling, West Virginia. Its transparent colors shade from red to green. Our advisor for this category is Mike Roscoe; he is listed in the Directory under Michigan. See also Art Glass Baskets; Cruets; Sugar Shakers; Salts.

Bowl, allover floral enameling, appl rigaree, 11½" L 265.00
Bride's basket, Hobnail, wht opal; Tufts SP fr, 12½" H 785.00
Creamer, appl vaseline leaves, vaseline hdl & ft, 4¾x3" 135.00
Cruet, Invt T'print, vaseline hdl, faceted stopper, 6½" 525.00
Pitcher, Honeycomb, 8" 215.00
Rose bowl, HP florals & gold scrolls, 8-crimp, 4x4¼" 75.00

Ruby Glass

Produced for over one hundred years by every glasshouse of note in this country, ruby glass has been used to create decorative items such as

one might find in gift shops, utilitarian bottles and kitchenware, figurines, and dinnerware lines such as were popular in the Depression era. For further information and study, we recommend *Ruby Glass of the 20th Century* by our advisor, Naomi Over; she is listed in the Directory under Colorado.

Bank, owl figural, Anchor Hocking, 1981, 7" 265.00
Boat, Daisy & Button, LG Wright, 6" L 15.00
Candlestick, metal stem, 8½" 55.00
Candlestick, swan neck, Viking, 6¼" 30.00
Creamer & sugar bowl, rnd, Anchor Hocking, 1940s 12.50
Cup & saucer, Sandwich, Indiana 38.00
Cup & saucer, sq, Anchor Hocking, 1940s 7.50
Goblet, Indiana Glass, 9-oz 32.00
Leaf plate, stem hdl, 8½" 45.00
Marmalade, Eyewinker, LG Wright, 8¾" 38.00
Paperweight, apple, Viking, 3¾" 25.00
Paperweight, strawberry form 18.00
Pie shell, Pyrex, 9½" 55.00
Pitcher, Blenko, #3750, 16-oz 22.50
Pitcher, trumpet neck, bulbous body, 6¾" 40.00
Plate, Bubble, Anchor Hocking, 1960, 9⅜" 12.00
Saucer, Rock Crystal, McKee 18.00
Sherbet, Anchor Hocking 7.50
Tray, att Anchor Hocking, 14" dia 30.00
Tumbler, Hobnail, Anchor Hocking, 1930s, 4½" 8.50
Vase, Hoover, Anchor Hocking, 9" 20.00
Vase, slim form, Viking, 16" 15.00
Vase, swan hdls, Venetian, 12" 135.00

Ruby-Stained Glass

Ruby-flashed or ruby-stained glass was made through the application of a thin layer of color over clear. It was used in the manufacture of some early pressed tableware and from the Victorian era well into the 20th century. These items were often engraved on the spot with the date, location, and buyer's name. Our advisors for this category are Bill and Marilyn Moore; they are listed in the Directory under Washington.

Bowl, berry; Frost Crystal, master+4 sm ind 14.00
Bowl, berry; Punty Band, in SP basket, 4¼" 55.00
Bowl, berry; Ruby T'print, boat shape, master+4 sm ind 150.00
Celery, Sunk Honeycomb 42.50
Compote, Ruby T'print, etched leaves & vines, 8x8½" 195.00
Creamer, Arched Ovals, Lakemont Park, 1908, 2¾" 25.00
Creamer, Buttons & Arches, Gloria 1907, 2½" 22.00
Creamer, Heart Band, Union City, 4" 22.00
Creamer, Ruby Thumbprint, mini, 3" 34.00
Creamer, Sunk Honeycomb, 6¼" 30.00
Mug, Bordered Elipse, 3⅛" 30.00
Mug, Buttons & Arches, Hot Springs AR, 2¾" 22.00
Mug, Fleur-de-Lis, gold trim, 3¼" 32.00
Mug, Lacy Medallion, Edna, 1900, 3¾" 26.00
Mug, Lacy Medallion, 1900, 3¾" 30.00
Mug, Punty Band, Eldorado Springs MO, 3½" 34.00
Mug, Scalloped Daisy, 1918, 2½" 25.00
Mug, Sunk Honeycomb, inscribed & dtd 1897, 3" 24.00
Pitcher, Hobnail w/T'print, 7" 62.00
Pitcher, Plume, Worlds Fair 1893, To Mama, 5½" 55.00
Pitcher, Sheaf & Block, 7½" 60.00
Punch cup, Buttons & Arches, Jericho Springs MO, 2¼" 21.00
Punch cup, Lacy Medallion, Terre Haute St Fair, 1899 ....25.00
Punch cup, Masonic Temple 1893, 2¾" 25.00
Punch cup, Ruby T'print, 2¼" 22.50

Shakers, Punty Band, dtd 1902, 3", pr **58.00**
Spooner, Buttons & Arches, Asbury Park, 1900, 4" **32.00**
Spooner, Fleur-de-Lis, gold trim, 4" **54.00**
Spooner, Ruby T'print, etched leaves, 4" **42.50**
Sugar bowl, Triple Triangle, w/lid, 6⅜" **62.00**
Tankard, etched decor & name, pewter top, 6¼" **95.00**
Toothpick holder, Beaded Swag, inscribed, dtd 1908, 2" **26.00**
Toothpick holder, Buttons & Arches, inscribed, 2¼" **22.00**
Toothpick holder, Punty Band, Betty From Kate, 1901, 2¼" **30.00**
Toothpick holder, Red Shield, inscribed, Carthage Fair, 2½" ...**20.00**
Toothpick holder, Scalloped Daisy, inscribed, dtd 1907, 2½" ...**22.50**
Tumbler, Baby T'print, inscribed, 3½" **30.00**
Tumbler, Button Arches, Lancaster PA w/gold striping, 4x3" ...**23.00**
Tumbler, Dmn & Sunburst Variant, 4" **36.00**
Tumbler, Red Shield, Ohio State Fair, 1920, 3¾" **22.00**
Wine, Bull's Eye, May 1908, 4" **28.00**
Wine, Buttons & Arches, Manchester NH 1915, 4" **25.00**

Rugs

Hooked rugs are treasured today for their folk-art appeal. It was a craft that was introduced to this country in about 1830 and flourished its best in the New England states. The prime consideration is not age but artistic appeal. Scenes with animals, buildings, and people; patriotic designs; or whimsical themes are preferred. Those with finely conceived designs, great imagination, interesting color use, etc., demand higher prices. Condition is, of course, also a factor. Marked examples bearing the stamps of 'Frost and Co.,' 'Abenakee,' 'C.R.,' and 'Ouia' are highly prized. Note: the rugs listed here are rag unless noted otherwise. See also Orientalia, Rugs.

Black and white cat within flower border, early 1900s, 22x42", condition and color EX, $1,495.00.

Basket of flowers w/2 birds on hdl, mc, 1900s, 32x50" **225.00**
Cat, gray on lt gray dmn, bl/blk/purple border, 17x36" **385.00**
Cat on cushion, mc w/blk border, 24x40", EX **525.00**
Duck hunting scene w/EX detail, 26x36" **385.00**
Fireplace scene w/chair/cat/clock/etc, mc, 27x35", EX **270.00**
Fish scale center, mc w/blk border, 27x147", EX+ **995.00**
Flagstone design, mc solids & blk, 36" dia **85.00**
Floral w/peacock tail border, mc, wear, 28x48" **250.00**
Frost & Co, lion pattern, mc, 1900s, mtd, 26x54", NM **575.00**
Frost & Co, lion pattern, 19th C, 33½x62½", EX **485.00**
Geometric heart design, mc, Am, 19th C, 28x49", EX **1,100.00**
Geometric linear design, mc, worn, 35x50" **250.00**
Geometric mc shells, ca 1900, rebacked, 28x62" **1,265.00**
Grenfell, ladies & dogs in landscape, mtd, 26x40", EX **435.00**
Grenfell, mallard duck, flying, 12x18" **150.00**
Grenfell, polar bear on iceberg, 22x31" **850.00**
Hand in heart, mc stripes, brn border, 22x45" **330.00**
Heards/dmns/circles/etc, mc, PA, 23x40" **415.00**
Horse & jockey, mc on gray, 26x47", EX **575.00**
Ivy trellis w/roses, mc on gray, 22x37", VG **140.00**
Marbleized design w/gr border, 26x40", EX **110.00**
Mary & lamb w/stone wall & flowers, blk border, 21x35" **135.00**

Pansies in lg reserve, floral border, 25x40" **90.00**
Rag/yarn, flower basket w/flower border, mc on brn, 28x40" ...**225.00**
Rag/yarn, lion, mc w/pk tongue, wear/fading, 28x40" **110.00**
Rag/yarn, mc geometric decor w/triangle & dmns, 31x49", EX ...**80.00**
Rectangles w/18 college names in red, 33x56", EX **250.00**
Tumbling blocks, mc solids & stripes, 27x52", EX **150.00**
Vines, mc on beige & olive, banded border, 39x63" **500.00**
4 concentric medallions, 4-color on gray, 22x43", EX **200.00**

RumRill

George Rumrill designed and marketed his pottery designs from 1933 until his death in 1942. During this period of time, four different companies produced his works. Today the most popular designs are those made by the Red Wing Stoneware Company from 1933 until 1936 and Red Wing Potteries from 1936 until early 1938. Some of these lines include Trumpet Flower, Classic, Manhattan, and Athena, the Nudes.

For a period of months in 1938, Shawnee took over the production of RumRill pottery. This relationship ended abruptly and the Florence Pottery took over and produced his wares until the plant burned down. The final producer was Gonder. Pieces from each individual pottery are easily recognized by their designs, glazes, and/or signatures. It is interesting to note that the same designs were produced by all three companies. They may be marked RumRill or with the name of the specific company that made them. Our advisors for this category are Wendy and Leo Frese; they are listed in the Directory under Texas.

Bookends, eagle figural, blk, pr **200.00**
Bowl, Snowdrop (wht on gr), #231, 12" **125.00**
Ewer, Apple Blossom (rose on gr), #184, 7" **50.00**
Ewer, Marigold (yel), #295, 10" **45.00**
Ivy ball, Dutch Blue, #600, 10" **150.00**
Ivy ball, wht, #600, 10" **75.00**
Pitcher, Goldenrod (orange over gr), #52, 8¾" **75.00**
Planter, Eggshell (wht), #303, 11½" **50.00**
Planter, turq, #338, 13" **60.00**
Urn, Pompeian (wht w/brn), w/lid, #252, 14" **100.00**
Vase, Dutch Blue (bl w/wht stippling), #215, 6" **125.00**
Vase, Horizon (bl on tan), #195, 10½" **95.00**
Vase, Jade (gr), #302, 6" **30.00**
Vase, Lilac (gr on lav), #308, 10" **95.00**
Vase, Neoclassic, lt bl, #666 ....**175.00**

Ruskin

This English pottery operated near Birmingham from 1898 until 1935. Its founder was W. Howson Taylor, and it was named in honor of the reknown author and critic, John Ruskin. The earliest marks were 'Taylor' in block letters and the initials 'WHT,' the smaller W and H superimposed over the larger T. Later marks included the Ruskin name.

Bowl, beige/ivory speckle, ftd, 2x5", NM **50.00**
Candlesticks, bl-gr gloss, lt bl rim ring, 1919, 6½", pr **115.00**
Inkwell, mauve flambe, rnd, w/lid, #1007, 2x3" **175.00**
Vase, squeeze-bag stems w/sm buds, gr on teal, 10x5½" **350.00**

Russel Wright Dinnerware

Russel Wright, one of America's foremost industrial designers, also designed several lines of ceramic dinnerware, glassware, and aluminum ware that are now highly sought-after collectibles. His most popular dinnerware then and with today's collectors, American Modern, was manufactured by the Steubenville Pottery Company from 1939 until 1959. It was produced in a variety of solid colors in assortments chosen to stay attune with the times. Casual (his first line sturdy enough to be guaranteed against breakage for ten years from date of purchase) is relatively easy to find today — simply because it has held up so well. During the years of its production, the Casual line was constantly being restyled, some items as many as five times. Early examples were heavily mottled, while later pieces were smoothly glazed and sometimes patterned. The ware was marked with Wright's signature and 'China by Iroquois.' It was marketed in fine department stores throughout the country. After 1950 the line was marked 'Iroquois China by Russel Wright.' For those wanting to learn more about the subject, we recommend *The Collector's Encyclopedia of Russel Wright Designs* (with updated values) by our advisor, Ann Kerr. She is listed in the Directory under Ohio.

American Modern

To calculate values for items in American Modern, add 100% to the suggested prices in the following listings for examples in these colors: White, Bean Brown, Cantaloupe, and Glacier Blue.

Bowl, lug soup	15.00
Bowl, vegetable	22.00
Butter dish	185.00
Carafe (stoppered jug)	165.00
Celery dish	25.00
Coaster/ashtray	15.00
Coffeepot, AD	75.00
Coffeepot, 8x8½"	150.00
Cup & saucer	15.00

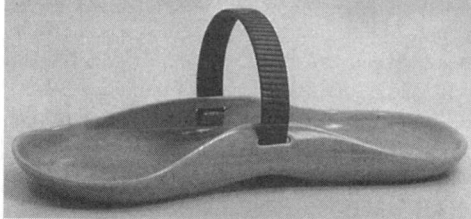

Divided relish, 10", $75.00.

Hostess set, plate & cup	85.00
Pickle dish	16.00
Pitcher, water	100.00
Plate, bread & butter; 6¼"	5.00
Plate, dinner; 10"	10.00
Plate, salad; 8"	12.00
Ramekin, ind, w/lid	150.00
Relish rosette	150.00
Salad fork & spoon	90.00
Shakers, pr	14.00
Sugar bowl, w/lid	14.00
Teapot, 6x10"	75.00

Casual

In Casual, Brick Red and Aqua items go for around 200% more than any other color, while those in Avocado Yellow are priced lower than suggested values.

Asbestos pad	40.00
Bowl, fruit; restyled, 5¾"	8.00
Bowl, gumbo, flat	35.00
Bowl, salad; 10"	30.00

Bowl, soup; restyled, 18-oz	10.00
Butter dish, ½-lb	75.00
Casserole, deep, 4-qt, 8"	65.00
Casserole, open, 10"	40.00
Coffeepot, w/lid	85.00
Cookware, 6-qt	175.00
Creamer, restyled	15.00
Creamer, stacking	12.00
Cup & saucer, AD	85.00
Cup & saucer, coffee	12.00
Gravy bowl, 12-oz, 5¼"	12.00
Gravy stand, 7½"	15.00
Lid for gravy bowl, ladle slot, 6¾"	20.00
Lid for water pitcher	30.00
Lid for 4-qt casserole	20.00
Mug, restyled, 9-oz	75.00
Percolator	175.00
Pitcher, water; restyled, 2-qt	150.00
Plate, dinner; 10"	10.00
Plate, luncheon; 9½"	8.00
Plate, party; w/cup	75.00
Platter, oval, 14½"	30.00
Shakers, stacking, pr	12.00
Sugar bowl, lg family sz	18.00
Sugar bowl, stacking, 4"	12.00

Glass

Unless otherwise described, values are given for glassware in Coral and Seafoam; other colors are 10% to 15% less.

American Modern, chilling bowl, rare, 12-oz, 3x5½"	75.00
American Modern, cocktail, 3-oz, 2½"	25.00
American Modern, cordial, 2"	38.00
American Modern, dbl old-fashioned, rare	45.00
American Modern, dessert dish, 2"	40.00
American Modern, goblet, 4"	40.00
American Modern, pilsner, rare, 7"	100.00
American Modern, sherbet, 2½"	25.00
American Modern, tumbler, iced tea; 13-oz	30.00
American Modern, tumbler, juice; 4"	30.00
American Modern, tumbler, water; 4½"	30.00
American Modern, wine, 3"	25.00
Eclipse, old-fashioned	15.00
Eclipse, shot glass	10.00
Flair, tumbler, iced tea; 14-oz	65.00
Flair, tumbler, juice; 6-oz	50.00
Flair, tumbler, water; 11-oz	50.00
Pinch, tumbler, iced tea; 14-oz	35.00
Pinch, tumbler, juice; 6-oz	35.00
Pinch, tumbler, red, any sz	125.00
Pinch, tumbler, water; 11-oz	35.00
Snow glass, bowl, salad/vegetable; rnd	165.00
Snow glass, bowl, vegetable; oval, w/lid	175.00
Snow glass, candle holders, pr	200.00
Snow glass, plate, salad	65.00
Snow glass, shakers, pr	110.00
Snow glass, sugar bowl, w/lid	85.00
Snow glass, tumbler, iced tea; 14-oz	150.00
Snow glass, tumbler, juice; 5-oz	150.00

Highlight

Bowl, oval vegetable; Wht, Pepper or Blueberry, ea	60.00

Bowl, soup/cereal; Citron or Nutmeg, 2 szs, ea 25.00
Butter dish, White, Pepper or Blueberry, ea 175.00
Creamer, Citron or Nutmeg, ea 25.00
Gravy boat, Citron or Nutmeg, ea 30.00
Mug, White, Pepper or Blueberry, ea 35.00
Plate, bread & butter; Citron or Nutmeg 8.00
Plate, dinner; White, Pepper or Blueberry, ea 30.00
Relish server, Citron or Nutmeg, ea 55.00
Sugar bowl, White, Pepper or Blueberry, ea 30.00

Spun Aluminum

Russel Wright's aluminum ware may not have been especially well accepted in its day — it tended to damage easily and seems to have had only limited market appeal — but today's collectors feel quite differently about it, as is apparent in the suggested values noted in the following listings.

Baine Marie server 400.00
Bowl 75.00
Candelabrum 200.00
Casserole 85.00
Cheeseboard 85.00
Cooking item, ea 100.00
Gravy boat 125.00
Ice bucket 75.00
Serving accessory, sm 115.00

Spaghetti set, 3-piece, $400.00.

Vase, 12" 110.00
Vase/flowerpot, sm 85.00

Sterling

Bowl, bouillon; 7-oz 12.00
Bowl, onion soup; 10-oz 20.00
Bowl, soup; 6½" 15.00
Coffee bottle 95.00
Creamer, ind, 3-oz 12.00
Cup, demitasse; 3½-oz 55.00
Pitcher, water; 2-qt 65.00
Plate, bread & butter; 6¼" 5.00
Plate, dinner; 10¼" 12.00
Platter, oval, 10½" 17.00
Teapot, 10-oz 65.00

Miscellaneous

Bauer, bowl, orange to wht, canoe shape, 24" L 750.00
Bauer, candle-holder bowl, wht, cup ea end, 18" W 850.00
Bauer, flowerpot, sq, 312A, 4½" 300.00
Bauer, vase, #2A, 8½" 375.00
Bauer, vase, #6A, 10½" 800.00
Bauer, vase, blk metallic (rare glaze), ovoid, 5x4" 425.00
Bauer, vase, oval, #18A, 12" 900.00

Bauer, vase/planter, #16A, 7½" 600.00
Brochure, minimum value 35.00
Display sign, Iroquis Cookware, minimum, EX 300.00
Flair, bowl, oval vegetable; deep 13.00
Flair, tumbler 15.00
Home Decorator, creamer 10.00
Home Decorator, cup & saucer 10.00
Home Decorator, plate, dinner 5.00
Ideal Adult Kitchen Ware, bowl, salad 16.00
Ideal Adult Kitchen Ware, decanter, juice 25.00
Ideal Adult Kitchen Ware, tumbler, 2 szs, ea 25.00
Ideal Child's Dishes, boxed set 150.00
Ideal Child's Dishes, serving item, ea 20.00
Mary Wright, Country Garden, plate 75.00
Mary Wright, cup & saucer 100.00
Meladur, cup, 7-oz 8.00
Meladur, plate, dessert; 6¼" 5.00
Meladur, plate, dinner; 9" 8.00
Residential, bowl, oval vegetable; shallow 12.00
Residential, creamer & sugar bowl, w/lid 25.00
Residential, lug soup 12.00
Stainless, fork 70.00
Stainless, knife 100.00
Stainless, soup spoon 70.00

Russian Art

Before the Revolution in 1917, many jewelers and craftsmen created exquisite marvels of their arts, distinctive in the extravagant detail of their enamel work, jeweled inlays, and use of precious metals. These treasures aptly symbolized the glitter and the romance of the glorious days under the reign of the Tsars of Imperial Russia. The most famous of these master jewelers was Carl Faberge (1852-1920), goldsmith to the Romanovs. Following the tradition of his father, he took over the Faberge workshop in 1870. Eventually Faberge employed more than five hundred assistants and set up workshops in Moscow, Kiev, and London as well as in St. Petersburg. His specialties were enamel work, clockwork automated figures, carved animal and human figures of precious or semiprecious stones, cigarette cases, small boxes, scent flasks, and his best-known creations, the Imperial Easter Eggs — each of an entirely different design. By the turn of the century, his influence had spread to other countries, and his work was revered by royalty and the very wealthy. The onset of the war marked the end of the era. Very little of his work remains on the market, and items that are available are very expensive. But several of his contemporaries were goldsmiths whose work can be equally enchanting. Among them are Klingert, Ovchinnikov, Smirnov, Ruckert, Loriye, Cheryatov, Kuzmichev, Nevalainen, Adler, Sbitnev, Third Artel, Wakewa, Holmstrom, Britzin, Wigstrom, Orlov, Nichols, and Plincke. Most of them produced excellent pieces similar to those made by Faberge between 1880 and 1910.

Perhaps the most important bronze Russian artist was Eugenie Alexandrovich Lanceray (1847-87). From 1875 until 1887, he modeled many equestrian groups of falconers and soldiers ranging in height from about 20" to 30". Some of them bear the Chopin foundry mark; they are presently worth from $4,000.00 up. Other excellent artists were Schmidt Felling (19th century), who specialized in mounted figures of cossacks wearing military uniforms, and Nicholas Leiberich (late 19th century), who also specialized in equestrian groups. Most of the pieces made by the above artists were signed and had the foundry mark (Chopin, Woerfell, etc.).

Russian porcelain is another field where Imperial connections have undoubtedly added to the interest of collectors and museums worldwide. The most important factories were: Imperial Russian Porcelain, St. Petersburg (or Petrograd or Leningrad, 1744-1917); Gardner, Moscow (1765-1872); Kuznetsoff, St. Petersburg and Moscow (1800-1900); Korniloff, St. Petersburg (1800-1900); and Babunin, St. Petersburg (1800-1900).

Beaker, silver, chased swags/birds, Moscow, 1780-84, 3⅛" 515.00
Beaker, silver, chased town vignettes/florals, IYEZ mk, 3" 200.00
Beaker, silver, repousse birds/scrolls, 3-ftd, w/lid, 1762 ....1,100.00
Beaker, vodka; silver-gilt & niello, mk F Ja, Moscow 425.00
Bowl, vegetable; 84 std silver, St Petersburg, 1829, 14" L 800.00
Bowl fr, silver w/orig glass bowl, Faberge hallmks, 4x12" 2,875.00
Box, silver-gilt & enamel, circular, K Faberge, 1910, 2" 3,500.00
Candelabra, ormolu w/circular malachite base, 1800s, pr 8,000.00
Chalice, silver/plique-a-jour, Klingert, 1800, mk 875, 4½" 995.00
Cigarette case, silver-gilt, chased troika, 1895, 4¼" 300.00
Cup, dbl; egg form, silver-gilt w/enamel, Moscow, 1900s, 2½" .6,495.00
Cup & saucer, demi; silver-gilt/enamel, Moscow, 1900s, +spoon ..2,585.00
Cup & saucer, demi; silver vermeil w/tooled decor, lt wear 200.00
Cup & saucer, 84 std silver w/enamel, Moscow, 1895, 2⅜" 800.00
Cvg, seated pug dog, agate, gold-mt ruby eyes, Faberge, 1900 .6,750.00
Easter egg, floral garlands on lt bl, late 1800s, 12cm, pr 750.00
Egg, enameled silver, opens like locket, MMy 1914, 3⅝" 1,250.00
Egg, Shroud of Christ, St Petersburg, late 18th C, 10cm 1,350.00
Egg, silver-gilt, chased florals, Viktor Aarne, 2½" L 425.00
Egg, St Alexandra, St Petersburg Imperial Factory, 1880s, 9cm ..1,800.00
Egg, St Mark by lion's head, St Petersburg, late 1800s, 10cm ..1,800.00
Egg, St Vladimir w/sword, St Petersburg, late 1800s, 12cm 2,250.00
Egg, 84 std silver w/floral enamel, Moscow, 1910s, 2⅝" 1,495.00
Egg, 84 std silver-gilt w/floral enamel, Moscow, 1900, 2" 1,495.00
Egg, 925 std silver w/enamel florals, post-revolution mk, 2" 635.00
Icon, Christ Pantocrator, 84 std silver-gilt, Okhlad, 1875, 4" 750.00
Icon, St Elijah, pnt & gilt on wood, Kiev, ca 1750, 12x10" 635.00
Kovsh, silver-gilt w/shaded enamel, Moscow, 1900s, 6¾" 2,300.00
Kovsh, silver-gilt/enamel vines & rosettes, Ovchinnikov, 4" 465.00
Kovsh, silver-gilt/pnt floral, sgn Klingert, 1900, 9½" 3,750.00
Kovsh, 84 std silver w/enamel, fleur-delis, Moscow, 1900s, 3⅝" ..1,150.00
Kovsh, 84 std silver-gilt/floral enamel, Moscow, 1910s, 4" 1,495.00
Kovsh, 84 std silver/enamel foliage, Moscow, 1910s, 4⅞" 2,050.00
Kovsh, 916 std silver-gilt w/enamel, att Klingert, 2¾" 520.00
Salt, enameled, 3 ball ft, mk GK, 1x1½", +spoon mk GK 300.00
Salt cellar, enamel on silver, TK Gustav Klingert/triangle 300.00
Shoe horn, St Petersburg, 84 std silver w/enamel hdl, 4¾" 865.00
Snuff box, 84 std silver w/niello decor, Moscow, 1820s, 2½" 800.00
Tea set, mc birds & flowers w/gold, porc, Popov/1850s, 5-pc ..1,150.00
Teapot, enamel on silver, att St Petersburg, 6½" 3,800.00
Teaspoons, champleve/gilt-silver, Tiffany, ca 1900, 12 for 925.00
Triptych, Christ Pantocrator, 84 std silver, 1900s, 4", +case ...1,495.00
Triptych icon, enamel on silver w/worn gilt, mini, 3x4½" 500.00
Vase, nephrite, gold eagle medallion mt, cylindrical, 5¾" 525.00
Vase, silver, scroll/leaf repousse, sgn HC, 6½" 200.00

Sabino

Sabino art glass was produced by Marius-Ernest Sabino in France during the 1920s and '30s. It was made in opalescent, frosted, and colored glass and was designed to reflect the Art Deco style of that era. In 1960 using molds he modeled by hand, Sabino once again began to produce art glass using a special formula he himself developed that was characterized by a golden opalescence. Although the family continued to produce glassware for export after his death in 1971, they were never able to duplicate Sabino's formula.

Bottle, scent; Frivolities, ladies & swans, 6¼" 85.00

Bottle, scent; nudes bathing, bl opal, Sabino-Paris, 5½" 225.00
Figurine, Argentina 900.00
Figurine, Barbarian fish 50.00
Figurine, cat 25.00
Figurine, Chabot, fish 100.00
Figurine, cherub, sm 40.00
Figurine, dove, head down or up, sm 24.00
Figurine, Egyptian goddess 85.00
Figurine, gazelle, 4x6" 65.00
Figurine, Isadora Duncan 750.00
Figurine, kneeling nude surrounded by 3 doves, label, 6" 350.00
Figurine, La Carpe 2,800.00
Figurine, lady & doves 350.00
Figurine, nude w/graceful cloak, 9½" 400.00
Figurine, pekingese 25.00
Figurine, snail 27.50
Figurine, Tanagra 325.00
Figurine, woodpecker 60.00

Luminors with chrome bases: L'Idole, nude in lotus position, opalescent, engraved mark, electrified, 6½", $2,000.00; Elephant mother and calf, fiery opalescent, engraved mark, electrified, 7¼", $2,250.00.

Mask, Triton 2,275.00
Plate, Birth of Star, 3 nude maids drift around rim, 12" 650.00
Powder box, Petalia, med 150.00
Tray, sea urchun, lg 85.00
Tray, swallow, sm 35.00
Vase, Abondance 4,500.00
Vase, Algues Marines 365.00
Vase, Art Decoratifs, dancing nude on ea of 4 sides, 10" 2,750.00
Vase, Beehive 195.00
Vase, Deco nudes w/hands joined encircle vase, 10" 1,875.00
Vase, groups of bees/geometrics, aqua opaque, 6½x6½" 500.00
Vase, La Danse 1,500.00
Vase, Manta Ray 400.00
Vase, Ovals & Pearls 265.00
Vase, rows of jutting sqs, opal, tumbler form, 5½", EX 385.00
Vase, turq, 6 lg concave dahlias, ca 1930, 7½x7½" 1,650.00
Vase, 8 dancing maids in flowing gowns, ovoid, 1930s, 14" 2,750.00

Salesman's Samples and Patent Models

Salesman's samples and patent models are often mistaken for toys or homemade folk art pieces. They are instead actual working models made by very skilled craftsmen who worked as model-makers. Patent models were made until the early 1900s. After that, the patent office no longer required a model to grant a patent. The name of the inventor or the model-maker and the date it was built is sometimes noted on the patent model. Salesman's samples were occasionally made by model-makers, but often they were assembled by an employee of the company.

These usually carried advertising messages to boost the sale of the product. Though they are still in use today, the most desirable examples date from the 1800s to about 1945.

Many small stoves are incorrectly termed a 'salesman's sample'; remember that no matter how detailed one may be, it must be considered a toy unless accompanied by a carrying case, the indisputable mark of a salesman's sample.

Tooled leather saddle, highly decorated, fully equipped, fleece lined, marked M. E. French Maker, Montrose, Colo., 8" L, NM, $2,500.00.

Barrel dolly, CI & brass, 17½x8x4½", VG 375.00
Bathtub, CI, claw ft, NM 85.00
Canoe, Old Town labels, worn bl-gr pnt, 48", EX 2,000.00
Chair, folding lounge; Pat 1927, EX 85.00
Chair, PA pnt decor, plank seat, 3-spindle bk w/crest, 14" 250.00
Clothes wringer, Horse Shoe Brand, 11" L 195.00
Clothesline, Nu-Way, Elgin IL, 1930s, EX 185.00
Floor sweeper, Bissell's Jr, complete w/case, NM 42.50
Fry pan, CI, Penn Stoves, EX 32.00
Furnace, Coleman's Furnace, 10x8x5", EX 150.00
Hitching post, jockey, CI, 10½" 485.00
Pan, graniteware, Stewart Ware, EX 90.00
Pump, Cincinnati Co, wood/CI, pnt: Water Purifier, 11", VG ...250.00
Saddle, tooled leather, unmk, EX 300.00
Sifting machine, S Harris, Pat...1862...1868, 3¼x8x3", EX 200.00
Stock pen, wood, folds into case, Pat Sept 29 1891, 24" L 165.00
Teakettle, tin, bail hdl, Germany 30.00
Waffle iron, Stover Jr, NM 125.00
Wringer, Gem Wringer, CI & wood, Am Wringer Co, 15", VG 80.00
Wringer, Horseshoe Brand, wood/CI/rubber, 15" 85.00

Salt Shakers

The screw-top salt shaker was invented by John Mason in 1858. In 1871 when salt became more refined, some ceramic shakers were molded with pierced tops. 'Christmas' shakers, so called because of their December 25, 1877, patent date, were fitted with a rotary agitator designed to break up any lumps in the salt. There are four types: Christmas Barrel (rare in cranberry and amethyst); Christmas Panel (rare in colors); Christmas Pearl (opaque, pearly white with painted decor); and Octagon Waffle (clear, thick glass made in three sizes with a rotary agitator, sometimes having undated tops). The dated tops and patented agitators were produced by Dana K. Alden of Boston, who contracted with various glasshouses to make the glass bodies. The Christmas Barrel and Christmas Panel patterns were produced by Boston and Sandwich (though the Christmas Barrel was made elsewhere as well). Alden contracted with Mt. Washington to make the Christmas Pearl pattern, and Waffle Octagon was made by several glass factories, McKee and Federal among them. Both of the latter patterns were made as late as 1900. Identical shakers which have no agitator or dated top are the companion peppers; these fetch about 30% less than the salts on today's markets.

Today's Victorian salt shaker collectors' interest primarily encompasses art glass, decorated cranberry and ruby, and custard and colored opalescent examples. (See also specified categories.) If you would like to learn more about Victorian glass salt shakers, we recommend *The World of Salt Shakers, Second Edition,* (updated 1996) by Mildred and Ralph Lechner; their address may be found in the Directory under Virginia. (Mildred and Ralph deal only in Victorian shakers; please do not contact them with questions pertaining to novelty types.) In the following listings, prices are for single shakers unless noted 'pair.' Values are for old, original shakers. Some of these may have been reproduced, and this will be noted in the description.

Alden (Sheaf & Block), ruby-stained crystal, ca 1893, 3" **55.00**
Banded Shells, gr opaque, emb shells, 1890, 1⅞" **46.00**
Beaded Bottom, bl opaque, ca 1898-1900, 3" **37.00**
Beaded Dahlia, pk cased, ca 1894-1900, 2⅝" **70.00**
Beaded Oval Mirror, bl opaque slag, ca 1890, 3¼" **60.00**
Beads & Bulges, cranberry, ca 1894-1900, 3⅜" **85.00**
Beatty Rib, bl opal, vertical ribs, 1889-90, 2⅞" **60.00**
Big Owl, wht opal, blown & pressed, on base, 1884-91, 5½" **138.00**
Block (Duncan's), clear w/ruby stain, ca 1887, 2⅜" **45.00**
Block & Star, bl opaque, ca 1955-56, 2¼" **23.00**
Bow & Flower, wht opaque opalware, ca 1901-08, 2¾" **21.00**
Bow & Tassel, wht opaque opalware, ca 1899-1901, 3⅛" **18.00**
Bulge Bottom, wht opaque opalware, ca 1894-97, 2¼" **34.00**
Bulging Loops, pk opaque, triple cased, 1895-1904, 3⅛" **75.00**
Bulging Petal, bl opaque, 1894-1898, 2⅛" **42.00**
Cane Woven, custard opaque, ca 1901-04, 2½" **50.00**
Cathedral Panel, pk opaque, ca 1894-1900, 3" **40.00**
Christmas Pearl, wht opal w/pnt bkground, 1884-93, 3⅜" **80.00**
Clear over cranberry, twisted panels, ca 1956-59, 2¼" **55.00**
Clover Leaf, bl opaque, ca 1894-1900, 3⅛" **38.00**
Coinspot, cranberry opal, ca 1900, 3½" **80.00**
Cone, bl opaque, satin or cased, 1894-1904, 2⅞" **60.00**
Corn, custard opaque, ca 1894-1901, 3⅛" **55.00**
Cotton Bale, bl opaque, 1894-1895, 2⅝" **35.00**
Creased Bale, pk opaque, ca 1894-1900, 3" **38.00**
Criss Cross, cranberry opal, 1894-1895, 3⅛" **80.00**
Dbl Deck, wht opaque, ca 1897-1902, 2¾" **35.00**
Ear, gr opaque, ca 1894-1900, 3" **35.00**
Eye Winker, ca 1889-1895, 3" (+) **30.00**
Fern Leaf, wht opaque opalware w/gold, ca 1901-07, 3" **14.00**
Fish, pk cased, ca 1894-1900, 3⅛" **50.00**
Florette, lt gr opal, ca 1894-1989, 2¼" **100.00**
Flower & Rib, pk cased, ca 1894-1900, 3½" **65.00**
Flower Bouquet, bl opaque, 1891, 3" **42.00**
Flowered Scroll, clear w/amber stain, ca 1893, 2⅝" **70.00**
Georgian, royal bl, ftd, ca 1931-39, 3⅜" **45.00**
Grape, Four Leaf, crystal w/goofus, ca 1899-1906, 3½" **36.00**
Guttate, variegated pk to wht, 2-pc metal lid, 1894-1900, 3" (+) .**55.00**
Heart, variegated pk to wht opaque, ca 1894-97, 2⅞" **60.00**
Horseshoe & Aster, vaseline, 1890-91, 3½" **90.00**
Jeweled Moon & Star, crystal w/amber stain, ca 1896, 3" **36.00**
Lacy Scroll, yel cased, 2-pc metal lid, ca 1895, 3⅜", pr **285.00**
Lantern, wire-hdld lid, ca 1904, 4" **40.00**
Leaf Dbl, variegated purple opaque, ca 1895-1901, 3⅝" **90.00**
Liberty Bell, hdld lid, bell form, 1875-77, 2¼" **100.00**
Little Shrimp, custard, ca 1895-1901, 1½" **65.00**
Log & Star, Bellaire Goblet Co, 1890, 2⅞" **22.00**
Marble Glass Box, off-wht & chocolate slag, 1890-91, 2⅞" **140.00**
Melon, Nine Rib, cranberry, Kopp, ca 1895-1900, 1⅞" **180.00**
Panelled Four Dot, variegated pk opaque to wht, 1894-96, 2¼" ...**50.00**
Pansy Six, pigeon blood, 6 emb pansies, 1895-1900, 2½" **90.00**
Periwinkle, variegated yel opaque, ca 1896-1903, 2½" **86.00**

Pineapple, variegated pk opaque & wht, ca 1894-1898, 3" 48.00
Pleated Skirt, pk opaque, 1891, 1¾" 42.00
Pointed Rib, bl opaque, ca 1896-1902, 2⅞" 40.00
Polka Dot, cranberry opal, bulbous, ca 1955, 2⅜" 55.00
Quilt, bl opaque, 1894-1898, 2½" 43.00
Red Block & Lattice, clear w/ruby stain, ca 1892-94, 3⅛" 65.00
Reverse Swirl, cranberry opal, orig screw-on lid, 2½" 110.00
Rhea-D, wht opaque opalware, ca 1889-1900, 2¾" 30.00
Rib & Scroll, lime gr opaque, ca 1904-1905, 3" 46.00
Ribbon Band, pk cased, ca 1896-1903, 3½" 50.00
S-Repeat, gr w/gold (+) (originals flouresce, repros don't) 35.00
Scroll, Gaudy, opaque wht opalware, ca 1900-08, 2½" 13.00
Scroll & Net, pk cased, ca 1897-1903, 3" 50.00
Scroll in Scroll, bl opaque, ca 1896-1901, 2¼" 34.00
Seashell, off-wht & chocolate slag, ca 1890, 3⅜" 87.00
Spider Web, pk opaque cased, ca 1894-97, 2⅜" 40.00
Square S, bl opaque, ca 1890, 3¼" 45.00
Sunk Daisy, clear w/ruby stain, ca 1890-1901, 2⅞" 50.00
Sunset, pk opaque, ca 1894-97, 2⅞" 46.00
Swirl & Leaf, pk opaque, triple cased, ca 1894-1900, 3" 65.00
Swirl Fenton, pastel pk opaque, ca 1954, 3⅛" 24.00
Three Face, clear/frosted, ftd, ca 1878-85, 2⅝" (+) 125.00
Thrush, wht opaque opalware, ca 1890, 2¾" 135.00
Torquay, pigeon blood, bulging base, ca 1897-1899, 3⅛" 105.00
Triple Bud, variegated pk, ca 1895-1901, 3" 85.00
Triple Rib, bl, ca 1895-1902, 3" 47.00
Twisted Leaf, pk opaque, triple cased, ca 1894-1900, 2⅞" 60.00
Two-Way Swirl, cranberry, ca 1895-1901, 3¼" 71.00
Wildflower, vaseline, bulbous bottom, 1874, 3⅛" 40.00
Zippered Block, clear w/ruby stain, ca 1890-97, 2⅞" 47.00

Novelty

Those interested in novelty shakers will enjoy *Salt and Pepper Shakers, Volumes I, II, III, and IV*, by Helene Guarnaccia, and *The Collectors Encyclopedia of Salt and Pepper Shakers, Figural and Novelty, Volumes I and II*, by Melva Davern. Both are available at your local library or from Collector Books. Note: 'Mini' shakers are no taller than 2". Instead of having a cork, the user was directed to 'use tape to cover hole.' Our advisor for novelty salt shakers is Judy Posner; she is listed in the Directory under Pennsylvania. See also Regal; Rosemeade; Occupied Japan; Shawnee; other specific manufacturers.

Advertising, Borden's Elsie & her twins, set 95.00
Advertising, Esso gas pump, plastic, pr 45.00
Advertising, Evinrude outboard motors, w/stands, pr 150.00
Advertising, Firestone tires, pr 75.00
Advertising, Greyhound bus, metal, M, pr 95.00
Advertising, Hamm's Beer, bear figurines, made in Brazil, 5", pr ...150.00
Advertising, Marathon Mile-Maker Gas Pumps, pr 55.00
Advertising, Mr Peanut, ceramic, 1992, Taiwan, 5", pr 35.00
Advertising, Philgas tanks, pr 35.00
Advertising, Seagrams 7, plastic, pr 35.00
Animal, basset hound, pr 26.00
Animal, boxer dog w/collar, pr 25.00
Animal, camel w/2 humps, Enesco, pr 22.00
Animal, cat on 8-ball, brn w/pk necktie, pr 10.00
Animal, dinosaur, realistic, pr 60.00
Animal, dog family on tricycle, pr 32.00
Animal, donkey pulls cart w/2 bbls (shakers) 12.00
Animal, dove, Poinsettia Studios, pr 48.00
Animal, horse's head, brn, pr 12.00
Animal, kitten boxing, pr 15.00
Animal, monkey family on tricycle, pr 38.00

Animal, monkey on phone (2 pcs), set 18.00
Animal, spotted fawns, 1 recumbent, 1 standing, pr 26.00
Anthromorphic, walking egghead, 3-pc nester set 75.00
Character, angry baseball player & umpire, pr 60.00
Character, Charlie & Homer, Walter Lantz, pr 245.00
Character, chef w/rolling pin & table, pr 65.00
Character, Colonial man & lady, wht w/gold, pr on base 38.00
Character, cop & hooker, metal, pr 32.00
Character, cowboy riding spotted rearing horse, pr 60.00
Character, English Bobby, pr 24.00
Character, musical notes on stand, 3-pc set 30.00
Character, Queen of Hearts, Relco, pr 45.00
Character, soldier & princess embrace, pr 35.00
Character, Tom Sawyer & Huckleberry Finn, pr 85.00
Comic, pup w/nodding spring tail, pr 35.00
Comic, worm in pear (or apple), pr 18.00
Disney, Donald Duck, gold trim, pr 85.00
Disney, Donald Duck's Nephews, pr 195.00
Disney, Grumpy & Sneezy, Tokyo Disneyland, pr 175.00
Disney, Mowgli & baby elephant, Enesco, pr 295.00

Pinocchio, bright colors, EX details, unmarked, $150.00 for the pair.

Mini, cowboy boots, pr 28.00
Mini, hay wagon & barn, pr 35.00
Mini, ink bottle & ink spot, pr 40.00
Mini, Liberty Bell & Declaration of Independence, pr 32.00
Mini, satchel & suitcase, pr 28.00
Mini, thread & thimble, pr 28.00
Nursery rhyme, Goldilocks, Relco, pr 45.00
Nursery rhyme, Man in Moon, head stacks on body, 2-pc set 125.00
Nursery rhyme, Miss Muffett & spider, Poinsettia Studios, pr 95.00
Nursery rhyme, Mother Hubbard & dog, Poinsettia Studios, pr 95.00
Nursery rhyme, Peter Pumpkin Eater, Poinsettia Studios, pr 95.00
Vegetable people, farmer man & lady, pr 42.00

Salts, Open

Before salt became refined, processed, and free-flowing as we know it today, it was necessary to serve it in a salt cellar. An innovation of the early 1800s, the master salt was placed by the host and passed from person to person. Smaller individual salts were a part of each place setting. A small silver spoon was used to sprinkle it onto the food.

If you would like to learn more about the subject of salts, we recommend *5,000 Open Salts*, written by William Heacock and Patricia Johnson, with many full-color illustrations and current values. Our advisor for this category is Chris Christensen; he is listed in the Directory under California. In the listings below, the numbers refer to *Open Salts* by Johnson and Heacock and *Pressed Glass Salt Dishes* by L.W. and D.B. Neal. Lines with 'repro' within the description reflect values for reproduced salts.

Key:
EPNS — electroplated nickel silver   HM — hallmarked

Animals, Figurals, and Novelties

Bird & Berry, amber or bl, McKee, HJ-931M, old	55.00
Bird & Berry, unmk Degenhart, HH-933, colors, minimum	25.00
Chicken, covered, milk glass, Westmoreland, HJ-949	20.00
Duck, covered, clear, red beak, HJ-1012	45.00
Duck, pressed, heavy, HJ-4677	45.00
Elk pulling sleigh, mk 800 silver	525.00
Rabbit, covered, clear, mk Vallerystahl, HJ-3750	55.00
Sleigh, Fostoria, HJ-3735, ca 1940	45.00
Squirrel on stump, various colors, Boyd, HJ-929-930, repro	10.00
Swan, Crown Tuscan, Cambridge, HJ-036, 1970s repro	20.00
Swan, str neck, Crown Tuscan, Cambridge, HJ-935	100.00
Swan, str neck, gr, pk, or amber, Cambridge, HJ-935	35.00
Swan pulling cart, bl carnival, HJ-941, 1970s repro	25.00
Swan pulling cart, clear, HJ-941 shape, ca 1890	65.00
Turtle, amber, bl, or milk glass, HJ-4475, 3¼"	60.00
Wheelbarrow, Nile Gr, Greentown, HJ-4669	300.00

Art Glass

Crown Milano, HJ-46	185.00
Daum Nancy, flowers, mk, HJ-11	1,500.00
English Victorian, bl ruffled rigaree, SP fr, HJ-96 style	230.00
English Victorian, cranberry ruffled, clear rigaree, HJ-1312	115.00
Millefiori, rnd, HJ-609, ca 1890	375.00
Monot Stumpf, HJ-19 to HJ-22, ea	110.00
Mt Washington, decor, HJ-35 to HJ-44, ea	110.00
Quezal, mk, HJ-18, 1" dia	250.00
Steuben, bl, mk Aurene, HJ-14, 2" dia	400.00
Steuben, Calcite, ped, HJ-34	300.00
Tiffany, ruffled, bl, HJ-30 or HJ-31, ea	500.00
Tiffany, ruffled, sgn LCT Favrille, HJ-32	200.00
Webb, bl, lily design, HJ-85	1,200.00
Webb, cranberry, acorn design, HJ-84	1,300.00
Webb, 3-color, HJ-27	1,600.00

China and Porcelain

Austrian, HP, mk HJ-1272	12.00
Austrian or French, HP, HJ pg 78, ind, ea	12.00
Elfinware, allover florals, German, HJ-1270	35.00
Elfinware, basket, German, HJ-1246 to HJ-1249, ea	15.00
Elfinware, basket, German, HJ-1253	15.00
French, mk Sampson, HJ-1786, ca 1880, repro of Chinese	125.00
Goss, mini ancient salt cellar, HJ-2029	45.00
Haviland, factory decor, HJ-1397 to HJ-1400, ea	30.00
KPM, dbl, boy between 2 bowls, HJ-1155 or HJ-1156, ea	275.00
KPM, dbl, w/cherub, mk, HJ-1107	295.00
Lenox, silver o/l, HJ-1815	45.00
Limoges, HP, mk, HJ-1275	12.00
Meissen, scroll ft decor, HJ-1812 to HJ-1814, ea	125.00
Meissen, sq, HJ-1595, ind	55.00
Nippon, HP, ped ft, HJ-1484 to HJ-1485, ea	18.00
Nippon, HP buckets, HJ-1446 to HJ-1457, ind, ea	14.00
Pickard, sq, HJ-1569	55.00
Royal Bayreuth, claw, poppy, or grapes, HJ pg 89, ind, ea	75.00
Royal Bayreuth, sheep, ped ft, HJ-1666	95.00
Royal Copenhagen, oval, HJ-1672, ca 1920	25.00
Royal Worcester, HJ-1861, ca 1870	150.00

Cut Glass

Amber, ped ft, English, ca 1880, master, pr	250.00

Amber flashed, ped ft, hdls, English, HJ-2060, master	175.00
Amethyst, etched, Hawkes, HJ-2038	65.00
Bl cut to clear, ped ft, HJ-67	110.00
Clear, etched, rnd, Hawkes, HJ-3268 to HJ-3269, ea	27.00
Clear, oval, Hawkes, HJ-3209	45.00
Clear, oval on ped, shell shape, Fr, HJ-3727, 4⅞"	195.00
Clear, ped ft, mk Libbey	65.00
Clear, rnd, nappy style, HJ-3170	55.00
Cranberry, rnd, Moser type, HJ-305	85.00
Cranberry, serrated top edge, rnd, HJ-304	65.00
Daisy & Button, oval, HJ-3214	20.00
Daisy & Button, rnd tub, HJ-2853	25.00
Fan & Dmn, HJ-3416 or HJ-3417, ea	15.00
Heart, club, spade, dmn, HJ-3033 to HJ-3034, 4 for	195.00
Zippered, HJ-3088 to HJ-3089, ea	10.00

Lacy Sandwich Glass

Avon, HJ-3506, repro	10.00
French, amber, HJ-2117, ca 1900, repro, VG	75.00
Lafayette Boat, sgn Pairpoint, ca 1980, repro	15.00
Metro Museum of Art, vaseline, bl, etc, repro, ea	15.00
Neal BF-1C, vary rare, HJ-3462	225.00
Neal BS-3, violet-bl, 3" L, EX	335.00
Neal BT-5, bl opal, 3⅝" L, EX	900.00
Neal CN-1A, minor chips, scarce, 7⅛" L	125.00
Neal EE-1A, sm chips, 3" L	125.00
Neal EE-3B, Scrolled Eagle, clear	150.00
Neal EE-3B, Scrolled Eagle, fiery opal, 3¼" L, EX	450.00
Neal NE-3, rare, 3" L	175.00
Neal RP-18A, cobalt (unlisted), sm chips/check, 3"	225.00
Neal SD-4E, 3⅛" L	175.00
Neal SL-1, cobalt, sm chips, rare, 3" L	325.00
Neal SN-1, cobalt, edge flakes, scarce, 3" L	150.00

Pottery and Faience

Adams, HM, HJ-1849, ca 1902	110.00
Niloak, rnd, HJ-1735, 1½"	45.00
Quimper, dbl, w/dog, HJ-1134	105.00
Quimper, pr of shoes, HJ-1162, ca 1940	35.00
Royal Doulton, HP animals, HJ-1859, ca 1890	75.00
Royal Doulton, pyramid shape, HJ-1870, ca 1873	140.00
Satsuma, various shapes, HJ-1931 to HJ-1933, ca 1970s, ea	20.00
Wedgwood, HM, HJ-1871, ca 1900	145.00

Pressed Glass, Clear

Amazon, HJ-2568, ind	12.00
American, HJ-2574, ind	10.00
Applied Bands, HJ-2934	25.00
Arched Leaf, HJ-3530	30.00
Atlanta, HJ-2758, ind	55.00
Banded Star, HJ-2939	50.00
Beaded Acorn Medallion, HJ-3533	45.00
Bearded Head, HJ-3636	50.00
Bow Tie, HJ-2548, ind	25.00
Candlewick, HJ-2642	10.00
Dmn Point Discs, HJ-2930	18.00
Dmn Rosettes, HJ-3407	30.00
English Hobnail, master	10.00
Fancy Arch, HJ-3058	30.00
Fandango, HJ-2673	25.00
Frosted Eagle, HJ-2967, ind	45.00

Grasshopper, HJ-3573 ....45.00
Hartford, HJ-2972, ind 20.00
Hawaiian Lei, HJ-2577, ind 12.00
Jersey Swirl, HJ-3387, ind 10.00
Lady Hamilton, HJ-2954 ....15.00
Liberty Bell, HJ-2689 ....55.00
Loop & Dart, ped ft, HJ-2955 ....45.00
Mardi Gras, HJ-2534 ....10.00
Marjorie, HJ-2676 ....15.00
Moon & Star, ped ft, ind 45.00
Noonday Sun, HJ-2591, ind 20.00
Picket, HJ-2792 ....15.00
Pillows, HJ-2697 ....35.00
Scroll w/Flowers, HJ-3352 ....30.00
Snail, HJ-2656, ind 25.00
Sprig in Snow, HJ-2966 ....25.00
Stippled Scroll, HJ-3538 ....35.00
Tree of Life, 'Salt,' ped ft, HJ-3581 ....95.00
Urn, Heisey, HJ-2969, ind 45.00
Urn, Heisey, master 65.00
Washington Centennial, HJ-3510 ....45.00
3-Face, HJ-4428, old 45.00
3-Face, HJ-4430 to HJ-4431, repro, ea 10.00

Pressed Glass, Colored

Applied Bands, amber flashed, HJ-2100 ....55.00
Atterbury, color repro 10.00
Bagware, HJ-449 ....15.00
Basketweave, milk glass, mk Atterbury, HJ-4466, master 45.00
Basketweave, milk glass, mk Atterbury, HJ-4482, ind 45.00
Beatty Rib, bl opal, HJ-196 ....35.00
Beatty Rib, wht opal, HJ-196 ....25.00
Brazilian, gr, HJ-335 ....55.00
Chippendale, amber, ped ft, HJ-596 ....35.00
Eyewinker, repro 6.00
Fish figural, milk glass, HJ-4464, master 100.00
Flemish, amber or gr, HJ-507 ....22.00
Gr opaline, sgn Baccarat, HJ-491 ....75.00
Illinois, ruby stained, HJ-298 ....70.00
King's Crown, ruby stained, HJ-2776 ....65.00
Lady Caroline, bl, English, HJ-127 ....105.00
Leaf & Rib, HJ-505, ind 18.00
Lords & Ladies, bl, English, HJ-137 ....75.00
Lords & Ladies, canary, English, HJ-137 ....55.00
Moon & Star, all colors are repros 8.00
Sq Hobnail, canary opal, HJ-197 ....65.00
Tree of Life, bl, HJ-2952, ind 40.00
Tree Stump, Xd logs, milk glass, HJ-4473 ....55.00
Triangle, bl, gr, amethyst, or canary, HJ-442 ....24.00
William & Mary, rose, English, HJ-568 ....55.00
Wreath & Shell, bl opal, HJ-444 ....110.00
3-Panel, bl, HJ-429, ind 18.00
3-Panel, canary or gr, HJ-564 ....25.00

Silverplate

Babies, Art Nouveau, gold-washed bowl, English, HJ-4283 ....150.00
Boat shape on ped ft, cobalt liner, Am, HJ-661, VG 45.00
Crackle glass, cranberry flashed, Victorian fr, VG 150.00
Crackle glass in Victorian fr, HJ-4215 to HJ-4217, VG, ea 85.00
Dolphin holds shell, Pairpoint, HJ-4382, master, VG 110.00
Heart shape, 3 ball ft, Wilcox, worn, HJ-4067 ....15.00
Lattice holder, clear liner, ind 20.00

Lattice holder, cobalt liner, HJ-653, ind, VG 15.00
Oval, cranberry liner, ftd lattice holder, HJ-317, VG 65.00
Oval, 4-ftd, clear liner, English, HJ-3945, VG 40.00
Oval lattice, gr liner, Derby, HJ-378, VG 85.00
Overshot cranberry glass liner, sq fr, HJ-4215 to HJ-4217, ea 150.00
Rams' heads, rnd, Whiting, HJ-4252, VG 55.00
Rnd bowl w/kangaroo, EPNS, Australia, HJ-4305, VG 35.00
Shell w/dolphin legs, HJ-4278, VG 15.00
Tulip on leaf, Am, HJ-4155, VG 30.00
Victorian holder, clear liner, hdl, HJ-3918, EX 65.00
Wolf-like dogs w/bowl on bk, Meriden, HJ-4322, VG 125.00

Sterling

Albert Cole, medallion, HJ-4208, ca 1850 ....200.00
American, Lenox insert, lattice holder, HJ-3856 .....35.00

Austria-Hungary, ca 1840,
3x4¼", $225.00.

Austria-Hungary, cut/flashed bowl, sterling ped, HJ-106 ....225.00
Austria-Hungary, wht opal cut-bk bowl, sterling ped, HJ-138 ....150.00
Chinese, mini house w/shaker set, HJ-4743 ....195.00
English, boxed set of 2, apostle spoon, HJ-4794 ...200.00
French, ornate, HM, matching spoon, HJ-3937, ind 125.00
German, basket, ped ft, HM 800, HJ-4228 ....95.00
German, cobalt liner, lattice holder, HJ-642, ind 45.00
German, oval, ftd, cobalt liner, HJ-724 ....55.00
German, swan, HH 800, matching spoon, HJ-4299, ca 1890 ....95.00
Gorham, medallion, ped ft, HJ-3976, ca 1870 ......150.00
Gorham, rnd, ornate lattice, cranberry liner, HJ-323, 1890s 140.00
Kerr, Art Nouveau, ped ft, cobalt liner, HJ-702, 1880 ....95.00
Reed & Barton, ped ft, HJ-4226, ca 1900, master, pr 250.00
Russian, chair, HM, dtd, HJ-4737 ....450.00
Russian, HP over sterling, 3 ball ft, HJ-2004 ....450.00
Russian, rnd, ftd, HM, HJ-4053, ca 1893, ind 65.00
Steiff, chased, w/pepper, HJ-4385, 1918 ....150.00
Steiff, salt & pepper set, high relief, HJ-4385, 1918 ....150.00
Tiffany, fish, matching spoon, HJ-4324 ....125.00
Viking, HP, HM, matching spoon, HJ-2002 to HJ-2005, ea 125.00

Other Types

Bl opal, dbl, ped ft, Fr, HJ-144, ca 1910 ....65.00
Bl slag, tureen shape, Sowerby, HJ-385 ....85.00
Intaglio, HP animals/etched butterfly, HJ-156 or HJ-157, ea 55.00
Intaglio, pnt animal center, HJ-160 ....45.00
Intaglio, 2 in jeweled tree holder, HJ-90 ....95.00
Plique-a-jour, Viking HM, HJ-83 ....650.00
Shell on sterling ped, English HM, HJ-202 ....35.00
Threaded glass, gr, 'Salt,' sterling rim, HJ-377 ......125.00
Venetian glass, swans 30.00

Samplers

American samplers were made as early as the the colonial days;

even earlier examples from 17th-century England still exist today. Changes in style and decorative motif are evident down through the years. Verses were not added until the late 17th century. By the 18th century, samplers were used not only for sewing experience but also as an educational tool. Young ladies, who often signed and dated their work, embroidered numbers and letters of the alphabet and practiced fancy stitches as well. Fruits and flowers were added for borders; birds, animals, and Adam and Eve were popular subjects. Later houses and other buildings were included. By the 19th century, the American Eagle and the little red schoolhouse had made their appearances.

Many factors bear on value: design and workmanship, strength of color, the presence of a signature and/or a date (both being preferred over only one or the other, and earlier is better), and, of course, condition.

ABCs, silk on homespun, sgn/1832, fr, 10x19" 385.00
ABCs/Adam & Eve/tree/serpent, homespun, undtd, 6½x5½" ...465.00
ABCs/birds/lions/flower urns/deer, sgn/1837, 17x17", EX 1,000.00
ABCs/crowns/house/etc, homespun, sgn/1843, fr, 20x19" 660.00
ABCs/fancy flower border, sgn/1832, fr, 17x18" 2,990.00
ABCs/flowers, homespun, sgn/1835, worn/rprs, 19x18" 300.00
ABCs/flowers/church, wool on canvas, sgn, OH, 18x22" 715.00
ABCs/flowers/strawberry border, homespun, sgn/1823, fr, 12x10" ..350.00
ABCs/house/flower baskets/bird/tree, sgn/1830, 17" sq, EX 1,500.00
ABCs/house/tree/turkey/etc, sgn/OH/1833, 19x20", EX 1,500.00
ABCs/lines, homespun, sgn, fr, 9x7" 195.00
ABCs/verse/family record, homespun, ca 1827, fr, 19x13" 385.00
ABCs/verse/flowers/etc, homespun, sgn, fading/wear, 11x17" 165.00
ABCs/verse/geometrics/flowers, homespun, sgn/1850, 20x16" ...1,045.00
ABCs/verse/house/trees, sgn/1820, fading, fr, 17x17" 1,850.00
ABCs/verses/strawberry border, homespun, sgn/1832, 18x18" .2,970.00
ABCs/vine border, homespun, sgn/OH/1824, fr, 21x12" 1,925.00
ABCs/vine border, homespun, sgn/1792, wear, 14x12", G 660.00
Adam & Eve/Quakers/birds/flowers, sgn/1817, rprs, 17x13" 1,100.00
Adam & Eve/serpent, wool on needlepoint canvas, 1853, 23x21" .525.00
Alphanumerics, homespun, sgn/1818, fading, fr, 16x12" 250.00
Alphanumerics/deer/flowers, sgn/1846, 8½x8½" 500.00
Birds/animals/lion/rabbits, homespun, sgn/1795, fr, 19x19" 385.00
Farmhouse & farmer in field, sgn/1821, 10x7" 2,500.00
Flower baskets/flower border, homespun, sgn/1824, fr, 24" sq 880.00
Flowering tree/rooster/birds/flowers/etc, sgn/1811, 13x15" 500.00
Landscape/verse/dbl vine border, homespun, sgn/OH/1834, 21x24" ..4,000.00
Mother/child/trees/birds, sgn/1796, 12x11", EX 865.00
Stag/flowers, wool & silk on homespun, sgn/1841, fr, 14x14" 450.00
Verse/butterflies, homespun, sgn/1835, mahog fr, 23x18" 770.00
Verse/flowers/birds/border, sgn/1838, 17x17" 400.00
Verse/flowers/trees/birds/fancy border, sgn/1800s, 17x13", G ..1,855.00
Verse/flowers/vine border, linen, sgn/1834, 16x14" 400.00
Verse/lion/unicorn/birds/etc, sgn/1828, fr, 18x16" 600.00
Verse/weeping willows/house/flowers/etc, sgn/1832, 16x19", G ..425.00

Sandwich Glass

The Boston and Sandwich Glass Company was founded in 1820 by Deming Jarves in Sandwich, Massachusetts. Their first products were simple cruets, salts, half-pint jugs, and lamps. They were attributed as being one of the first to perfect a method for pressing glass, a step toward the manufacture of the 'lacy' glass which they made until about 1840. Many other types of glass were made there — cut, colored, snake-skin, hobnail, and opalescent among them. After the Civil War, profits began to dwindle due to the keen competition of the Western factories which were situated in areas rich in natural gas and easily accessible sand and coal deposits. The end came with an unreconcilable wage dispute between the workers and the company, and the factory closed in

1888. See also Cup Plates; Lacy Glass; Salts, Open; other specific types of glass.

Bottle, bar; canary, 8-panel, long neck, att, 11½" 600.00
Candlestick, clambroth columnar base, bl opaque socket, 9¼" ..1,300.00
Candlestick, violet-bl, hexagonal, att, 7½" 350.00
Candlesticks, canary, petal sockets, looped bases, 7", pr, EX 225.00
Candlesticks, canary, 6-sided sockets/stems/bases, 9½", pr 1,600.00
Decanter, cobalt, ribbed, tam-o'-shanter stopper, 1850s, 6¾" 175.00
Jar, bear figural, amethyst, chips, 3¾" 250.00
Jar, bear figural, clambroth, mk FB Strouse NY, 3¾", EX 515.00
Lamp, canary, 8-panel font, monument base, brass collar, 10" 550.00
Pitcher, overshot/craquelle, ice bladder w/rigaree, 14" 425.00
Spoon holder, Lyre, clear opal, ca 1850s, 4¾", EX 545.00
Sugar bowl, bl opaque, Gothic Arch, sm chips, 5¼" 1,375.00
Tumbler, lemonade; appl pk threading & hdl, 5½", 6 for 200.00
Vase, Pillar Mold, hexagonal base, 8-rib bowl, 10⅝", pr 220.00
Vase, spill, dk electric bl, hexagonal body & base, 4⅞", NM 255.00

Sarreguemines

Sarreguemines, France, is the location of Utzschneider and Company, founded in 1770, producers of majolica, transfer-printed dinnerware, figurines, and novelties which are usually marked 'Sarreguemines.'

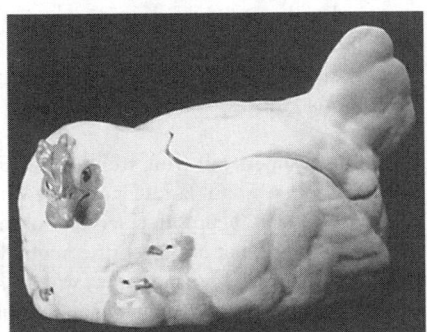

Container modeled as a hen with nesting chicks, 5¾" H, $250.00.

Butter dish, strawberries w/tan & gr leaves 165.00
Charger, portrait: parents & nanny w/baby, faience, 14" 450.00
Jam pot, strawberries on dk gr, w/underplate 85.00
Oyster plate, pk to brn wells w/bl & gr, 9¼" 140.00
Pitcher, clover in dmn decor on dk gr, turq int 85.00
Pitcher, man's face, 3½" 75.00
Plate, fruit, mk, 6⅞" 55.00
Plate, peasant scene 48.00
Stein, tavern scene, hinged lid, mk, 1-liter, 9" 195.00

Satin Glass

Satin glass is simply glassware with a velvety matt finish achieved through the application of an acid bath. This procedure has been used by many companies since the 20th century, both here and abroad, on many types of colored and art glass. See also Mother-of-Pearl; Webb.

Ewer, apricot w/florals & scrolls, ribbed, camphor hdls, 10" 125.00
Ewer, pk w/floral, camphor hdl, leaf ft, 10", pr 225.00
Mug, wht w/pk & gold looping, frosted reeded hdl, 3½" 145.00
Rose bowl, pk w/florals & gold foliage, 8-crimp, 3x3½" 75.00
Rose bowl, Shell & Seaweed, pk w/asters & vines, scalloped 175.00
Rose bowl, yel w/cherub & vines, 3¾" 135.00
Rose bowl, yel w/violets, scalloped, 3¾" 125.00

Vase, bl, partial floral decor, egg form, scalloped rim, 7½" **85.00**
Vase, pk w/floral, ftd, 13½" **100.00**
Vase, pk w/floral & butterflies, ribbed/ftd, branch hdl, 14" **160.00**
Vase, yel cased, stick neck, 7½x3½" **90.00**

Satsuma

Satsuma is a type of fine cream crackle-glaze pottery or earthenware made in Japan as early as the 17th century. The earliest wares, made at the original kiln in the Satsuma province, were enameled with only simple florals. By the late 18th century, a floral brocade (or nishikide design) was favored, and similar wares were being made at other kilns under the direction of the Lord of Satsuma. In the early part of the 19th century, a diaper pattern was added to the florals. Gold and silver enamels were used for accents by the latter years of the century. During the 1850s, as the quality of goods made for export to the western world increased and the style of decoration began to evolve toward becoming more appealing to the Westerners, human forms such as Arhats, Kannon, geisha girls, and samurai warriors were added. Today the most valuable pieces are those marked 'Kinkozan,' 'Shuzan,' 'Ryuzan,' and 'Kozan.' The genuine Satsuma 'mon' or mark is a cross within a circle — usually in gold on the body or lid, or in red on the base of the ware. Character marks may be included.

Caution: Much of what is termed 'Satsuma' comes from the Showa Period (1926 to the present); it is not true Satsuma but a simulated type, a cheaper pottery with heavy enamel. Collectors need to be aware that much of the of the 'Satsuma' today is really Satsuma style and should not carry the values of true Satsuma. Our advisor for this category is Norma Angelo; she is listed in the Directory under New York.

Basket, ladies/men, gilt trim, rtcl hdl, 4 ft, 3x3" dia **150.00**
Bowl, dessert; seasonal landscapes on sepia, Meiji, 4¾" **275.00**
Censer, legendary figures in reserves, lion hdls, Meiji, 22" **1,440.00**
Censer, procession at Nikko shrine, metal lid, Meiji, 3¾" **350.00**
Figurine, girl in gold brocade robe, w/dog, 7" **200.00**
Incense burner, foo dog finial & hdls on cobalt, ca 1900, 10" **125.00**
Jar, landscape/birds/figures in panels, 6-sided, Meiji, 3⅝" **3,500.00**
Jar, 4 scenic panels w/gold on cobalt, Meiji, 6⅛" **1,800.00**
Punch bowl, panels of Samurai/saints/geishas, gilt, 5x12" **2,000.00**
Teacup & saucer, beauties/children, mc/gilt, Meiji, 12 for **480.00**
Teacup & saucer, seated bijin on gilt-pnt sepia, Meiji, 4 for **160.00**
Teapot, child entertains family, bk: parade, melon ribs, 2" **125.00**
Vase, outdoor scene w/figures, bk: indoor, stick neck, 5½" **160.00**
Vase, panels: saints/geishas, gold flowers etc, mk, 3" **200.00**
Vase, saints/dragons, gilt floral etc, mk w/X & seal, 3½", pr **275.00**
Vase, 2 portrait panels: Samurai/children, gold scrolls, 17" **1,200.00**
Vase, 5 of 8 Daoist Immortals, pear shape, Meiji, 14½" **3,000.00**
Vase, 7 Lucky Gods & attendants, waisted, Meiji, 7¼" **1,850.00**

Scales

In today's world of pre-measured and pre-packaged goods, it is difficult to imagine the days when such products as sugar, flour, soap, and candy first had to be weighed by the grocer. The variety of scales used at the turn of the century was highly diverse; at the Philadelphia Exposition in 1876, one company alone displayed over three hundred different weighing devices. Among those found today, brass, cast-iron, and plastic models are the most common. Fancy postal scales in decorative wood, silver, marble, bronze, and mosaic are also to be found.

A word of caution on the values listed: these values range from a low for those items in fair to good condition to the upper values for items in excellent condition. Naturally, items in mint condition could com-

mand even higher prices, and they often do. Also, these are **retail** prices that suggest what a collector will pay for the object. When you sell to a dealer, expect to get much less. These estimated values have been prepared by a committee of the International Society of Antique Scale Collectors under the direction of Robert Stein and George Mallis. The values noted are averages taken from various auction and other catalogs in the possession of the Society members. Among these, but not limited to, are the following: Joel L. Malter & Co., Inc., Encino, CA; *Collectors Journal of Ancient Art*, Joel L. Malter & Co., Inc.; Nobody's Bizness But Our Own, Storrs, CT; Craig A. Whitford Numismatic Auctions; *Auktion Alt Technic*, Auction Team, Koln, Germany; *Waaqgen Auktion Essen*, Auktion Karla W. Schenk-Behrens, Essen, Germany.

Bowers and Merena Auctions held a large public auction of scales which involved over 250 items in November of 1995. The auction catalog and prices realized may still be available for collectors. Those interested should call Bowers and Merena in New York City at 800-458-4646 to ascertain availability and price for this catalog. Those seeking additional information concerning antique scales are encouraged to contact the International Society of Antique Scale Collectors, whose address can be found in the Directory under Clubs, Newsletters, and Catalogs.

Key:

ap — arrow pointer	h — hanging
bal — balance	hcp — hanging counterpoise
bm — base metal	hh — hand held
br — brass	l+ — label with foreign coin
Brit — British	values
Can — Canadian	lb w/i — labeled box with
Col — Colonial	instructions
CW — Civil War	lph — letter plate or holder
cwt — counterweight	pend — pendulum
Engl — English	PP — Patent Pending
eq — equal arm	st — sterling
Euro — European	tt — torsion type
FIS — Fairbanks Infallible	ua — unequal arm
Scale Co.	wt — weight

Dayton platform scale, 'Moneyweight' marquee, very rare, 32", EX restored, $800.00.

Analytical (Scientific)

Am, eq, mahog w/br & ivory, late 1800s, 14x16x8", $200 to **400.00**

Apothecary (Druggist)

Am, tt bal, 2 marble pans/oak base, 1880s, 8x15x8", $150 to **250.00**

Assay

Am, eq, mahog box w/br & ivory, plaque/drw, 1890s, $250 to ...**350.00**

Coin: Equal Arm Balance, American

Blk japanned metal, eagle on lid, late 19th C, $125 to 225.00
Col, oak 6-part box, Col moneys, Boston, 1720-75, $600 to ...1,200.00
Post Col to CW, oak 6-part box, lt+, 1843, $400 to 1,000.00

Coin: Equal Arm Balance, English

Charles I, wooden box w/11 Briot wts, 1640s, $900 to 1,500.00
1-pc wood box, rnd wts, label, Freeman, 1760s, $250 to 450.00
6-pc oak box, coin wts label, Thos Harrison, 1750s, $200 to 450.00

Coin: Equal Arm Balance, French

Solid wood box, 12 sq wts, J Reyne, Bourdeau, 1694, $400 to .1,000.00
Solid wood box w/recesses, 5 sq wts, A Gardes, 1800s, $250 to ..800.00
1-pc oval box, nested/fractional wts, label, 1700s, $250 to 400.00
1-pc oval box, no wts, label of Fr/Euro coins, 1700s, $150 to 250.00
1-pc walnut box, nested wts, Charpentier label, 1810, $275 to ..675.00

Coin: Equal Arm Balance, Miscellaneous

Amsterdam, 1-pc box, 32 sq wts, label, late 1600s, $1,000 to ..2,800.00
Cologne, full set of wts & full label, late 1600s, $1,200 to 2,800.00

Counterfeit Coin Detectors, American

Allender Pat, lb w/i, cwt, Nov 22, 1855, 8½", $350 to 750.00
Allender PP, rocker, labeled box, cwt, 1850s, 8½", $450 to 750.00
Allender PP, space for $3 gold pc, lb w/i, cwt, 1855, $350 to 750.00
Allender PP, space for $3 gold pc, no box or cwt, 1855, $275 to ..375.00
Allender Warranted, rocker, no box or cwt, 1850s, $250 to 475.00
McNally-Harrison Pat 1882, rocker, cwt, JT McNally, $275 to ..500.00
McNally-Harrison Pat 1882, rocker, cwt & box, FIS, $400 to 750.00
McNally-Harrison...1882, rocker, CI base, no cwt/box, $250 to .400.00
Thompson, Z-formed rocker, Berrian Mfg, 1877 Pat, $175 to 350.00

Counterfeit Coin Detectors, English

Folding, Guinea, self rising, labeled box, 1850s, $150 to 250.00
Folding, Guinea, self rising, wooden box, pre-1800, $175 to 275.00
Rocker, simple, no maker's name or cb, end cap box, $85 to 125.00
Rocker, w/maker's name & cb, end cap box, $120 to 150.00

Diamond

Am, eq w/carat wts, 5" box, Kohlbusch, ca 1900, $175 to 225.00

Postal

In the listings below an asterisk (*) was used to indicate that any one of several manufacturers' or brand names might be found on that particular set of scales. Some of the American-made pieces could be marked Pelouze, Lorraine, Hanson, Kingsbury, Fairbanks, Troemner, IDL, Newman, Accurate, Ideal, B-T, Marvel, Reliance, Victor, Liberty, Gem, Superior, Landers-Frary-Clark, Chatillon, Triner, American Bank Service, or Weiss. European/U.S.-made scales marked with an asterisk (*) could be marked Salter, Peerless, Pelouze, Sturgis, L.F.&C., Alderman, G. Little, or S&D. English-made scales with the asterisk (*) could be marked Josh. & Edmd. Ratcliff, R.W. Winfield, S. Mordan, STS (Samuel Turner, Sr.), W.&T. Avery, Parnall & Sons, S&P, or H.B. Wright. There may be other manufacturers as well.

Brit/Can Bal, eq, br or CI on base, *, 4"-15", $100 to 750.00

Engl Bal, eq/Roberval, gilt or st, on stand, *, 3"-8", $500 to 2,500.00
Engl Bal, eq/Roberval, plain to ornate, *, 3"-8", $100 to 2,500.00
Engl Spring, candlestick, br or st, *, 3½"-15", $100 to 500.00
Engl Spring, CI, br or NP fr, Salter, ozs/lbs, 7"-10", $25 to 200.00
Engl Steelyard, ua, 1- or 2-beam, h lph, *, 4"-15", $100 to 1,500.00
Euro pend, gravity, br, CI or NP fr on base, oz/grams, $75 to 350.00
Euro pend, gravity, 2-arm, bm, br or NP, *, 6"-9", $50 to 300.00
Euro/US Spring, br or NP, pence/etc, h or hh, *, 4"-17", $10 to ...100.00

Postal scale, steelyard principle, Buffalo (manufacturer), base embossed 'Property of U.S. P.O. Service,' cast iron with gold and blue lettering, brass tray and weight arm, 1890, 6¾", EX, $110.00.

US pend, gravity, metal, pnt face, ap, hcp, sm, $20 to 100.00
US Spring, pnt base metal, *, 2½"-8", $10 to 80.00
US Spring, pnt bm, *, mtd on inkstand, 2½"-8", $75 to 250.00
US Spring, pnt bm, rnd glass-covered face, *, 8"-10", $25 to 100.00
US Spring, SP, oblong base, *, 2½"-8", $100 to 200.00
US Spring, st, oblong base, *, 2½"-8", $200 to 500.00
US Steelyard, ua, CI, *, 5"-13" beam, 4½"-12" base, $25 to 100.00

Schafer and Vater

Established in 1890 by Gustav Schafer and Gunther Vater in the Thuringia region of southwest Germany, by 1913 this firm employed over two hundred workers. The original factory burned in 1918 but was restarted, and production continued until WWII. In 1972 the East German government took possession of the building and destroyed all of the molds and the records that were left.

You will find pieces with the impressed mark of a nine-point star with a script 'R' inside the star. On rare occasions you will find this mark in blue ink under glaze. The items are sometimes marked with a four-digit design number and a two-digit artist mark. In addition or instead, pieces may have 'Made in Germany' or in the case of the Kewpies, 'Rose O'Neil copyright.' The company also manufactured items for sale under store names and those would not have the impressed mark.

Schafer and Vater used various types of clays. Items made of hardpaste porcelain, soft-paste porcelain, jasper, bisque, and majolica can be found. The glazed bisque pieces may be multicolored or have a colored slip wash applied that highlights the intricate details of the modeling. Gold accents were used as well as spots of high-gloss color called jewels. Metallic glazes are coveted. You can find the jasper in green, blue, pink, lavender, and white. New collectors gravitate toward the pink and lavender shades.

Since Schafer and Vater made such a multitude of items, collectors have to compete with many cross-over collections. This includes collections of shaving mugs, hatpin holders, match holders, figurals, figural pitchers, Kewpies, tea sets, bottles, naughties, etc.

Reproduction alert: In addition to the crudely made Japanese copies, some English firms are beginning to make figural reproductions. These seem to be well marked and easy to spot. Our advisor for this category is Dawn Ricker; she is listed in the Directory under Michigan.

Ash keeper, frog 175.00

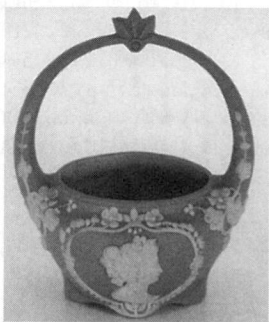

Basket, pink cameo on blue, 5", $175.00.

Bottle, A Good Sip, brn, 5" 150.00
Bottle, A Wee Bit of Scotch, 4½" 100.00
Bottle, Apache Dancer, 6" 225.00
Bottle, apple or pear w/smiling face, ea 125.00
Bottle, baker, I Am Always Full, 6" 275.00
Bottle, baker, Let's Have Another, 9½" 325.00
Bottle, bear, 6½", +tray & shots 575.00
Bottle, bowler or hunter, bent-neck flask, 6", ea 175.00
Bottle, camel 125.00
Bottle, Don't Let Thy Nose..., 4" 135.00
Bottle, Drinkometer, Boy Wanted 275.00
Bottle, Drinkometer, doctor, Use It Daily 175.00
Bottle, Drinkometer, doctor w/cane 225.00
Bottle, Dutchman in bbl, brn, 6½" 200.00
Bottle, Falstaff, bl, 6½" 300.00
Bottle, Firewater, brn, 4½" 195.00
Bottle, Firewater, mc, 5½" 245.00
Bottle, Having a Barrel of Fun, mk, 7½" 240.00
Bottle, His Master's Breath 100.00
Bottle, I Won't Be Long Now 150.00
Bottle, Indian, brn, 8½" 275.00
Bottle, Indian, w/tray & shots 500.00
Bottle, Indian face, mc 225.00
Bottle, Merry Xmas, bent-neck flask 225.00
Bottle, Mr Cocktail, brn, 8" 250.00
Bottle, Never Drink the Water, 5½" 140.00
Bottle, nightcap, bent-neck flask, 6" 175.00
Bottle, nightcap man (prosit), bl 175.00
Bottle, nightcap-Xmas, bent-neck flask 225.00
Bottle, Oh, You Kid, 5½" 175.00
Bottle, Old Scotch 90.00
Bottle, Old Scotch-Little Scotch, mc, 8" 250.00
Bottle, One of the Boys, 6" 185.00
Bottle, One of the Boys, 7" 210.00
Bottle, Poison, brn, 5½" 190.00
Bottle, Poison, brn, 8" 300.00
Bottle, Poison, snake & skull, w/shots 550.00
Bottle, policeman w/hand up, mc, 7½" 200.00
Bottle, Prohibition, mc, 5½" 175.00
Bottle, sailor, bl, 6½" 225.00
Bottle, Scotchman on bottle, bl, 7" 225.00
Bottle, Scotchman w/bagpipe, mc, 5½" 150.00
Bottle, Tango dancer, 6" 225.00
Bottle, Turkey Trot, 6" 225.00
Bottle, Uncle Sam on bottle, 7" 160.00
Bottle, Wet or Dry, brn, 4½" 200.00
Bowl, cameo, cutouts, mc w/gold 300.00
Box, Colonial girl w/fan 275.00
Box, googly girl in chair 335.00

Candle holder, cameo, metallic glaze 275.00
Cup & saucer, cameo w/jeweling, jasper 325.00
Figurine, boy pulling rickshaw 190.00
Figurine, Deco dog, orange 225.00
Figurine, dog chasing girl w/cat 240.00
Figurine, googly boy or girl, 9", ea 500.00
Figurine, googly boy whispering to girl 225.00
Figurine, Kewpie soldier standing 400.00
Hatpin holder, bear hugging tower 400.00
Hatpin holder, Deco face w/jeweling 350.00
Hatpin holder, Egyptian head, metallic 425.00
Hatpin holder, roses on tower 150.00
Hatpin holder, strawberries on tower 225.00
Match holder, Can't Eat, I'm in Love 160.00
Match holder, Everybody's Doing It! 175.00
Match holder, Now Shall I W-Wag It 140.00
Match holder, Scratch My Back! 150.00
Match holder, Scratch Your Match on My... .... 225.00
Match holder, Waiting for the Smack 150.00
Nodder, big-eyed monk 250.00
Nodder, Egyptian girl 200.00
Nodder, ghost, bl 600.00
Nodder, man smoking pipe 350.00
Nodder, monk sticking out tongue 375.00
Nodder, pig dressed as doctor 325.00
Nodder, Waiting for the Tide 225.00
Pin dish, Deco lady, metallic glaze 275.00
Pitcher, cow, sitting 250.00
Pitcher, girl holding out apron, 6½" 340.00
Shaving mug, Deco lady 400.00
Shaving mug, scuttle, topsy turvy 350.00
Tea set, English lady & butler, fanciful 2,000.00
Vase, Deco woman doing back bend figural 390.00
Vase, Egyptian woman figural 190.00
Vase, girl sits & smiles on crescent moon 750.00

Scheier

The Scheiers began their ceramics careers in the late 1930s and soon thereafter began to teach their craft at the University of New Hampshire. After WWII they cooperated with the Puerto Rican government in establishing a native ceramic industry, an involvement which would continue to influence their designs. In the fifties they retired and moved to Mexico; they currently reside in Arizona.

Bowl, abstract linear int, brn/tan, gunmetal ext, 7" 230.00
Bowl, brn speckled, flaring/ftd, mk YE, 3½x6¼" 175.00
Bowl, brn speckled, pk int, flaring/ftd, 4½x5" 175.00
Bowl, brn-speckled tan w/int spiral, turq ext, 3x16" ... 145.00
Bowl, copper crystalline flambe, str-sided, ftd, 3½x7" .. 250.00
Bowl, cvd leaf abstract on yel/bl/brn mottle, 3½x6" .. 500.00
Bowl, cvd/blk-lined fish on deep bl, brn base, tan int, 4x8" .. 500.00
Bowl, emb swirl center, brn-speckled gr flambe, 12½" .. 200.00
Bowl, robin's egg bl gloss, thin-walled, ftd, 3¾x5½" .. 250.00
Bowl, tan w/brn speckles, turq int, U-form, 3" 145.00
Bowl, 4 cvd stick figures on azure, brn-speckled wht int, 4¾" .. 200.00
Cup, linear decor on yel, 3x4" 170.00
Pitcher, ribbed, brn-speckled cocoa gloss, 1948, 10½" .. 150.00
Plate, caramel swirl gloss w/blk & gr speckles, 10" ... 150.00
Plate, cvd abstract deer band, navy on lt salmon gloss, 6¾" .. 225.00
Plate, dk bl-speckled aqua gloss, red clay, 8", set of 4 .. 125.00
Tile, 2 invt fish people cvd on brn-speckled blk, early, 6" .. 70.00
Vase, abstract fish etc, brn on speckled tan matt, 5¼x5½" .. 400.00

Vase, caramel-speckled over ivory-tan, brn base, 5½x5" 150.00
Vase, cvd humans raise fish etc above heads, brn/bl, 6" 400.00
Vase, cvd stylized humans on brn, ovoid w/flared neck, 7" 435.00
Vase, gunmetal & olive, short flaring neck, 5" 300.00

Schlegelmilch Porcelain

Authority Mary Frank Gaston, who is our advisor, has completed four volumes of *The Collector's Encyclopedia of R.S. Prussia* with full-color illustrations and current values. Mold numbers appearing in some of the listings refer to these books. You will find Mrs. Gaston's address in the Directory under Texas.

Key:
BM — blue mark   SM — steeple mark
GM — green mark   RM — red mark

E.S. Germany

Fine chinaware marked 'E.S. Germany' or 'E.S. Prov. Saxe' was produced by the E.S. Schlegelmilch factory in Suhl in the Thuringia region of Prussia from sometime after 1861 until about 1925.

Basket, lady & child reserve w/gold & lustre, mk, 7" 125.00
Bowl, boat scene, dmn shape, hdls, mk, 6½x6½" 55.00
Bowl, lady w/flowers, pierced border, open hdls, mk, 11¾" 275.00
Bowl, 4 portrait medallions, Hortense, 10⅜" 395.00
Bun tray, girl w/ponytail portrait, floral medallions, 12" 175.00
Cake plate, Gibson girl portrait on bl w/gold, mk, 10½" 435.00
Candlesticks, lilies, wht on gr, mk, 5", pr 90.00
Candlesticks, purple floral, mk, 4⅝", pr 125.00
Candy dish, 4 portrait medallions, Recamier, 7" 225.00
Chamberstick, bl flowers, cobalt inner border, mk, 2x6" 115.00
Cup & saucer, Queen Louise portrait reserve on red, mk 175.00
Cuspidor, roses, mk 395.00
Ewer, lady smelling rose, mk, 17" 695.00
Pitcher, milk; flower, pk on turq, brn mk, 4½" 225.00
Plate, bird on branch, smooth rim, mk, 6" 35.00
Plate, girl w/wheat & sickle, gold stencilling, mk, 10" 85.00
Plate, lady & cherub, turq & gold trim, open hdls, mk, 10" 195.00
Plate, mc roses on cream shaded, smooth gold rim, mk, 8½" 45.00
Plate, portrait w/flowers & gold, scalloped, hdls, mk, 9½" 145.00
Relish, poppies on cream w/gold rim, open hdls, mk, 8x3½" 65.00
Tankard, Easter lilies, cobalt trim, mk, 10½" 595.00
Vase, chickens & daisies, ornate/pierced gold hdls, mk, 7½" 550.00
Vase, figures in court scene, slim, mk, 7½" 195.00
Vase, Indian portrait reserve/florals, uptrn hdls, mk, 6" 300.00
Vase, lady's portrait, gold tub hdls, mk, 7½" 300.00
Vase, lady w/doves (4 portraits), 3 gold hdls at base, mk, 14" ..1,100.00
Vase, lady w/roses portrait, much gold & beading, 11½", pr 750.00
Vase, Madame DuBoise, ornate gold hdls, mk, 7" 250.00
Vase, woman w/letter in reserve on red w/gold, mk, 9¼" 450.00

E.S. Prussia

Chocolate set, mc roses w/gold, lustre finish, mk, 10-pc 500.00
Match holder, lady w/daisy crown, hanging, unmk 110.00
Vase, man w/roses, gold trim, mk, 8" 500.00

R.S. Germany

In 1869 Reinhold Schlegelmilch began to manufacture porcelain in Suhl in the German province of Thuringia. In 1894 he established another factory in Tillowitz in upper Silesia. Both areas were rich in resources necessary for the production of hard-paste porcelain. Wares marked with the name 'Tillowitz' and the accompanying 'R.S. Germany' phrase are attributed to Reinhold. The most common mark is a wreath and star in a solid color under the glaze. Items marked 'R.S. Germany' are usually more simply decorated than R.S. Prussia. Some reflect the Art Deco trend of the 1920s. Certain hand-painted floral decorations and themes such as 'Sheepherder,' 'Man with Horses,' and 'Cottage' are especially valued by collectors — those with a high-gloss finish or on Art Deco shapes in particular. Not all hand-painted items were painted at the factory. Those with an artist's signature but no 'Hand Painted' mark indicate that the blank was decorated outside the factory.

Bowl, floral, looped inside hdl, mk, 6x12" 30.00
Bowl, gr & wht floral, scalloped edge, 3 sm ft, mk 45.00
Bowl, lilies, mk, 9¼" 65.00
Bowl, roses, tricorner, 3-hdl, mk 95.00
Bowl, roses, 12-sided, mk, 10" 75.00
Cake plate, gold flowers/trim on wht, blown-out carnations, mk ..250.00
Cake set, daisies on cream to gr, mk, 1 lg plate+6 sm 145.00
Charger, cotton plant, mk 175.00
Chocolate set, dogwood & pine decor, mk, tall pot+4 c/s 295.00
Cup & saucer, chocolate; sweet peas w/gold, mk 250.00

R.S. Germany ewer, lady's portrait in reserve, ornate handle, gold trim, 9½", $275.00.

Humidor, horse & dog, artist sgn, mk 800.00
Mustard pot, house scene, mk 110.00
Plate, floral, mk, 7½" 35.00
Plate, floral, mk, 9" 40.00
Plate, lilacs on wht, gr & pk, gold trim, mk, 11¼" 110.00
Toothbrush holder, roses w/gold, hanging, mk 125.00
Trivet, peafowls & dogwood trees, mk 150.00

R.S. Poland

'R.S. Poland' is a mark attributed to Reinhold Schlegelmilch's factory in Tillowitz, Silesia. It was in use for a few years after 1945.

Bowl, berry; crowned cranes, mk, 5¾" 800.00
Bowl, poppies, heart mold, mk, 3x10¼" 265.00
Cake plate, floral, floral border, hdls, 10" 135.00
Creamer, violets on cream w/gold, ftd, angle hdl, mk, 4½" 85.00
Planter, floral band w/gold, ped ft, 6¾x6½" dia 235.00
Planter, floral medallions, mk, 5½x7½" 235.00
Server, lav & orange roses, center hdl, mk, 11" dia 515.00
Talcum shaker, roses on cream shaded, 3 hdls at base, mk 250.00
Vase, brn & wht peacocks, gold trim, mk, 13" 900.00
Vase, lady, sheep & cottage scene, ornate gold hdls, mk, 10" 635.00
Vase, man w/cow, farm scene beyond, classic form, mk, 9" 1,100.00
Vase, mill scene & ladies w/sheep, gold hdls, mk, 10" 635.00

R.S. Prussia

Art porcelain bearing the mark 'R.S. Prussia' was manufactured by Reinhold Schlegelmilch from the late 1870s to the early 1900s in a Germanic area known until the end of WWI as Prussia. The vast array of mold shapes in combination with a wide variety of decorations is the basis for R.S. Prussia's appeal. Themes can be categorized as figural (usually based on a famous artist's work), birds, florals, portraits, scenics, and animals.

Bell, mc flowers, ruffled rim, twig hdl, unmk, 3½" 285.00
Bell, pk roses, shiny, unmk 250.00
Bell, tiny florals, pleated, mk 135.00
Bowl, berry; mc roses w/turq, carnation mold, mk, +5 sm 650.00
Bowl, berry; pk roses w/gold, RM, 10½",+6 sm 715.00
Bowl, berry; point & clover mold, RM, +4 sm 475.00
Bowl, Dice Thrower, point & clover mold, RM, 4¾x9½" 400.00
Bowl, dogwood flowers, pearlized, ftd, RM, 6" 90.00
Bowl, floral, pearlized, icicle border, RM 395.00
Bowl, floral center, 4 portrait reserves, Tiffany border, 9" 450.00
Bowl, floral w/gold, RM, 10½" 250.00
Bowl, fruit int w/bl trim & much gold, RM, 10½" 300.00
Bowl, lilies & dogwoods, mold #182, 9½" 150.00
Bowl, mill scene on yel w/gold, mk, 11" 500.00
Bowl, Mme LeBrun w/hat, lily mold, 9½" 850.00
Bowl, pk poppies & cobalt florals, mk, 3x10¼" 965.00
Bowl, roses, yel on pk to yel, mk, 10" 175.00
Bowl, roses & wild flowers, 3-ftd, 6½" dia 95.00
Bowl, roses on wht w/gold, RM, 10" 325.00
Bowl, roses w/gold, mold #82, 11" 220.00
Bowl, snowball & roses, blk border, mk, lg 200.00
Bowl, snowballs/roses, cobalt/gold, point & clover mold, mk, 10" ..595.00
Bowl, wht & gr floral, satin, RM, 5¼" 35.00
Bowl, 5-color floral on wht w/gold, lily mold, 10" 325.00
Cake plate, basket of orange roses, mk 225.00
Cake plate, Dice Players, RM, 10½" 750.00
Cake plate, florals, sunflower mold, RM, 11" 250.00
Cake plate, flowers reflecting in water, open hdls, mk, 11" 175.00
Cake plate, Hidden Image, blown-out mold, RM, 11" 450.00
Cake plate, irises, mk, 11" 250.00
Cake plate, poppies w/gold, iris mold, RM 600.00
Cake plate, roses & lt gold lilies w/dk gold, mk, 12" 300.00
Cake plate, roses on purple to yel, hdls, mk, 11" 175.00
Cake plate, swallows/chickens/duck/water/lilies, mk, 10" 1,000.00
Cake plate, tulips & shadow lilies w/gold, scalloped, RM, 12" 325.00
Chocolate pot, dogwood, ribbed & pearlized lustre, RM, +6 c/s .675.00
Chocolate pot, roses, mc on yel, ftd, mk 295.00
Chocolate pot, roses on wht w/gold, RM 325.00
Coffeepot, mc florals, mk 575.00
Cracker jar, emb florals & roses, hdls, unmk, 7" 125.00
Cracker jar, poppies, mold #509A 300.00
Cracker jar, wht forget-me-nots & gr foliage on wht, mk 200.00
Cracker jar, 3-fruit decor, mk 425.00
Creamer & sugar bowl, Deco-type swan w/gold trim, mk 375.00
Creamer & sugar bowl, dogwood, pearlized, RM 145.00
Creamer & sugar bowl, floral, carnation mold, unmk 325.00
Creamer & sugar bowl, roses, mold #502 ....350.00
Creamer & sugar bowl, swan scenic w/gold, RM 450.00
Creamer & sugar bowl, winter scene on satin, RM, NM 550.00
Cup & saucer, demitasse; cottage scene, mk 150.00
Cup & saucer, demitasse; lily of the valley, cream/gr, RM 125.00
Mustache cup, purple & wht flowers w/gold, mk, w/saucer, lg 165.00
Mustard pot, swans, unmk 150.00
Mustard pot, wht roses w/gold, mk, lg 90.00

Pitcher, roses, wht w/gold on ivory & gr, mk, water sz 425.00
Pitcher, tankard; hanging baskets, RM, 13" 900.00
Pitcher, tankard; red & yel roses, carnation mold, RM, 13½" 895.00
Plate, poppies w/gold, mk, 8¾" 75.00
Plate, roses w/gold thorns on cobalt w/gold border, mk, 9" 225.00
Pomander, roses 125.00
Shaving mug, iris variation, orig beveled mirror, mk 250.00
Shaving mug, mc florals on gr, made w/o soap shelf, RM 225.00
Sugar bowl, floral decor, w/lid 145.00
Tea set, pk flowers, unmk, ftd pot+4 c/s, child sz 595.00
Teapot, flowers on cobalt, SM, sm flake 425.00
Tray, bun; iris variant, unmk, 13½x7" 135.00
Tray, card; red roses, rectangular, mk, 5½" 110.00
Tray, dresser; pk roses on gr w/gold, RM, 11½x7" 185.00
Tray, floral, mk, 12¼x9" 125.00
Tray, florals, wht on gr to brn, oval, hdls, mk, 11" 90.00
Tray, Melon Eaters, unmk, 12x7¾" 1,200.00
Tray, relish; Man in Mountain, mk, 8x3¾" 300.00
Tray, roses on pearlized, carnation mold, RM, 11½x7½" 285.00
Vase, cottage scene on gr tones, scalloped, mk, 9½" 850.00
Vase, florals on cobalt, SM, 9" 600.00
Vase, mill scene, jeweled ped ft, hdls, mk, 10" 795.00

R.S. Suhl, E.S. Suhl

Porcelains marked with this designation are attributed to Reinhold Schlegelmilch's Suhl factory.

Box, floral, w/beveled mirror, mk 200.00
Teapot, dogwood, +cr & sug 310.00
Vase, Melon Boys, mk, 9" 1,200.00
Vase, sunflowers on brn, hdls, mk, 6¾" 110.00
Wall plaque, daisies, 10½" 125.00

R.S. Tillowitz

R.S. Tillowitz-marked porcelains are attributed to Reinhold Schlegelmilch's factory in Tillowitz, Silesia.

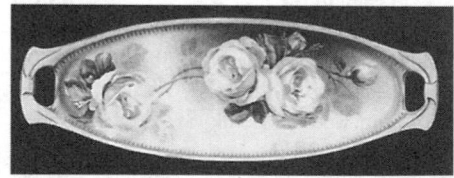

R.S. Tillowitz tray, 3 large roses, 13½" long, $135.00.

Bowl, pheasants, scalloped rim, open hdls, oval, mk, 10" 225.00
Cake set, fuchsia on gr w/tan shadows, open hdls, 7-pc 350.00
Creamer & sugar bowl, roses on cream to gr, w/lid 50.00
Gravy boat, wht flowers on shaded cream, mk 70.00
Mint dish, floral, mk, 7½x5" 100.00
Pitcher, pk floral garland at neck on wht, mk, 8½" 65.00
Plate, cherries, mk, 11" 60.00
Plate, poppies on gr, mk, 6" 25.00
Plate, stylized butterfly border w/gold, gold hdls, mk, 7" 35.00
Tray, magnolias, w/gold, mk, 8¾x4" 55.00

Schneider

The Schneider Glass Company was founded in 1914 at Epinay-sur-Seine, France. They made many types of art glass, some of which sandwiched designs between layers. Other decorative devices were applique and carved work. These were marked 'Charder' or 'Schneider.' During the twenties commercial artware was produced with Deco motifs cut by acid through two or three layers and signed 'LeVerre Francais' in script or with a section of inlaid filigrane. Our advisor for this category is Don Williams; he is listed in the Directory under Missouri. See also Le Verre Francais.

Bowl, 4 cobalt ribs on clear, bubbles, 4½x13½" 250.00
Compote, orange/pk/lav mottle on purple ft, 6x8½" 325.00
Compote, wht/pk mottle w/blk amethyst stem & striped ft, 12" .635.00
Compote, yel w/cobalt mottling, blk-amethyst ft, 4¼x15" 460.00
Compote, yel/orange on purple stem w/rnd ft, 7½" 460.00
Pitcher, clear w/amber to red elongated mottling, ftd, 15" 750.00
Vase, blown into Majorelle ribbed basket w/appl leaves, 7x15" .2,200.00
Vase, clear w/orange/purple streaks & bubbles, appl hdls, 6" 690.00
Vase, clear-cased swirls of gr/orange/amber, shouldered, 10" 230.00
Vase, lt topaz w/appl amethyst shoulder ring, 8½x8½" 400.00
Vase, mottled w/striped stem, iron base w/appl berries, 16" 1,100.00
Vase, orange-red w/burgundy mottle, blown into ftd iron mt, 8" .800.00
Vase, random bl splotches on red, flared rim, 13½" 985.00
Vase, red w/yel & amber mottling, blown into wire fr, 8½" 690.00
Vase, splotches/swirls, brns/orange to bl at bun ft, 24" 800.00

Schoolhouse Collectibles

Schoolhouse collectibles bring to mind memories of a bygone era when the teacher rang her bell to call the youngsters to class in a one-room schoolhouse where often both the 'hickory stick' and an apple occupied a prominent position on her desk. Our advisor for this category is Kenn Norris; he is listed in the Directory under Texas.

Bell, desk; cast brass, CI base, 3½" 28.00

Book, The Practical Speller, Draughon's Practical Business College Co., copyright 1890, VG, $8.00.

Book, McGuffey's New Fifth Eclectic Reader, 1866, EX 35.00
Book, Our New Friends (Dick & Jane), 1946, VG 45.00
Bookmark, advertising; yel flowers on lt cb, 1⅞x5⅞" 12.00
Counting fr, red, wht & bl beads, 1870-80s, 10½x13" 75.00
Desk, child's, hardwood w/dk reddish varnish, 34x19x14" 55.00
Desk, master's, butternut/pine, fold-down lid, on fr, 38x31" 550.00
Desk, master's, cherry, lift-lid, fitted int, rfn, 34x38x27" 685.00
Desk, master's, cherry, lift-lid, rstr, 32x21x19" 175.00
Desk, master's, hardwood, 1-brd lift-lid, rfn, 33x38x26" 330.00
Ink jar, ceramic, wire lock, Sanford's Ink, 9" 125.00
Learning wheel, Presidents of USA, 1930s, 10" dia 25.00
Learning wheel, spells over 1,500 words, 8½" 15.00
Lunch box, heavy cb, riveted corners, leather strap, 7½x5½" 32.00
Lunch box, pressed & pnt tin, wood & wire hdl, 7¼x4½" 30.00
Multiplication/addition table, paper on cb, 7x9¼" 18.00
Paste jar, metal lid, Evans' School Glue, 9" 42.00
Pencil sharpener, autombile form, sheet metal, Japan, 1¾" 28.00
Pencil sharpener, clock form, sheet metal, Germany 18.00

Pencil sharpener, pistol form, CI, Germany 18.00
Pencil sharpener, saxaphone, gold pnt, Germany 35.00
Pencil sharpener, Scottie shape, celluloid, 1½" 35.00
Pencil sharpener, tank form, mottled gr, 1⅞" 18.00
Penmanship booklet, 22 pgs drill exercises, c 1870, 7x8½" 10.00
School register, daily records, c 1891, 9x11¾" 10.00
Sewing cards, used w/colored thread, ca 1894, 4x5½" 25.00
Slate, cb, ABCs, 1940s, 7¼x10½" 10.00
Slate, dbl, folds both ways, wire-bound fr, 8½x12½" 33.00
Spelling board, ca 1930, EX 35.00
Stamping outfit, Excelsior ABC Marker, orig box, 3¾x12½" 12.00
Vocabulary cards, animals, fill-in sentences on bk, 5½x9", ea 5.00

Pencil Boxes

Among the most common of school-related collectibles are the many classes of pencil boxes. Generally from the period of the 1870s to the 1940s, these boxes were made in many hundred different styles. Materials included tin, wood (thin frame and solid hardwood), and leather; later fabric and plastics were used. Most pencil boxes were in a basic, rectangular configuration, though rare examples were made to resemble other objects. These included rolling pins, ball bats, and nightsticks. Pencil boxes are still to be found at reasonable prices, though collectors have lately noticed this field. All boxes listed below are in very-good to near-mint condition. Our advisors for pencil boxes are Sue and Lar Hothem, authors of *School Collectibles of the Past*; they are listed in the Directory under Ohio.

Advertising, cb, Fort Pitt Shoes, giant pencil type, 11½" 25.00
Advertising, cb, Kinney Shoes, giant pencil type, 11¾" 25.00
Advertising, cb, Wright Dept Stores, giant pencil type, 10" 25.00
Japanned w/butterflies, Eberhard Faber #324, 3¾x8" 35.00
Oak, top & side, ¼" thick, inscr circle around lock, 8" 15.00
Tin, advertising on inside, lift-top, gr & gold box, 7¾" 10.00
Wooden, dbl-level, slide-top, pencil dtd 1906, 9½" 30.00
Wooden, dbl-level, slide-top, rose decal, 9¼" 28.00
Wooden, lift-lid, dovetailed corners, brass-lined holes, 8⅝" 18.00
Wooden, Nursery Rhymes, lithographed scenes, 7⅞" 20.00
Wooden, Oriental motif, raised medallion, 7¾" 18.00
Wooden, solid, w/sliding top, ruler on side, 12" (rare sz) 45.00
Wooden, 1-level, slide-top, 9¼" 24.00
Wooden, 4-level, 1 compartment ea, floral decor, 9¼" 70.00

Schoop, Hedi

Swiss-born Hedi Schoop started her ceramics business in North Hollywood in 1940. With a talented crew of about twenty decorators, she produced figurines, figure-vases, console sets, TV lamps, and other decorative housewares — much of which was accented with gold or platinum trim. Schoop's pottery closed after a fire destroyed the building in 1958. Marks are impressed or printed. For further information we recommend *The Collector's Encyclopedia of California Pottery* by our advisor, Jack Chipman; he is listed in the Directory under California.

Bowl, console; kneeling girl inside, much gold 150.00
Bowl, crimped acorn shape 65.00
Bowl, Oriental style w/dragons 65.00
Cookie jar, Darner Doll 350.00
Figurine, Conchita, 13" 135.00
Figurine, dancers, armx Xd above head, wht w/gold, 11", pr 135.00
Figurine, Dutch girl, 10½" 85.00
Figurine, girl w/accordion, 11" 95.00
Figurine, girl w/hip basket, lg hat, 13" 125.00

Figurine, Oriental boy w/oboe (& girl), gold trim, 10½", pr **125.00**
Figurine, Orientals w/buckets, pr **125.00**
Figurine, peasant lady w/bowl overhead, 14" **85.00**
Figurine, Repose, seated lady w/bowl in lap, silver-bl, 1949 ....**225.00**
Figurine, rooster, lg **150.00**
Planter, cat w/pk bow, tooled fur, 6" **65.00**
TV lamp, Comedy & Tragedy **350.00**
Vase, stylized rooster, gr w/irid copper, 14" **100.00**

Schramberg

The Schramberg factory was founded in 1820 as 'Vechtritz & Faist'; in 1883 it became a branch of Villeroy & Boch Schramberg. In 1912 Mr. Meyer bought the factory, and it existed as Schramberger Majolika Fabrik (SMF) until 1989.

Most of the patterns were named. Perhaps the most widely available is the Gobelin pattern. This name is stamped on the bottom of the piece along with a number that corresponds to the painter who executed it. If there is also a pressed number on the piece, it is the number of the form.

Little is known about the designers who worked for Schramberg. Perhaps the most well known is Eva Zeisel who worked at Schramberg from the fall of 1928 and continued there for nearly two years. Zeisel was involved in all areas from design and manufacturing to merchandising. Our advisor for this category is Cheryl Goyda; she is listed in the Directory under Pennsylvania.

Basket, G5, SMF, 4" **45.00**
Candle holder, floral, 4-color, 4", ea **50.00**
Creamer, G2, Wheelock **20.00**
Planter, G3, SMF, 3¾" **60.00**
Planter, G6, SMF, 4½" **60.00**
Syrup, floral, SMF, 4½" **25.00**
Tray, floral, #54, SMF **30.00**
Vase, floral, blk & orange, SMF, 6½" **55.00**
Vase, floral, Wheelock, 4¼" **25.00**
Vase, G1, 8-color, 7" **70.00**
Vase, G4, 7-color, #57, 4½" **45.00**
Vase, G4, 7-color, hdls, 9" **85.00**

Scouting Collectibles

Boy Scouts

Scouting was founded in England in 1907 by a retired Major General, Lord Robert Baden-Powell. Its purpose is the same today as it was then — to help develop physically strong, mentally alert boys and to teach them basic fundamentals of survival and leadership. The movement soon spread to the United States, and in 1910 a Chicago publisher, William Boyce, set out to establish Scouting in America. The first World Scout Jamboree was held in 1911 in England. Baden-Powell was honored as the Chief Scout of the World. In 1926 he was awarded the Silver Buffalo Award in the United States. He was knighted in 1929 for distinguished military service and for his Scouting efforts. Baden-Powell died in 1941. For more information you may contact our advisor, R.J. Sayers, author of *Guide to Scouting Collectibles*, whose address (and ordering information regarding his book) may be found in the Directory under North Carolina.

Armband, 1957 Nat'l Jamboree Staff, red on wht felt **25.00**
Badge, Asst Scoutmaster, type 1, lt gr, sq **65.00**
Badge, Eagle Scout, type 1, no BSA on tan sq, 1918-24 ....**100.00**

Badge, Eagle Scout, 1942, M **80.00**
Badge, Field Scout, on tan sq, 1930, EX **30.00**
Badge, Junior Asst Scoutmaster, tan sq, 1930 ....**18.00**
Badge, Scout Executive, on gr wool, 1930s **45.00**
Badge, Scoutmaster, type 1, full gr First Class, sq **125.00**
Badge, Senior Patrol Leader, tan sq, 1930 ....**15.00**
Bank, Scout in camp, mechanical, 1970 reproduction **25.00**
Bank, Scout stands w/staff, money in pack, 1920 ....**50.00**
Bar, service; Lone Scout, bronze, 1915-24 era **15.00**
Book, Cubbing, The Boy's Cubbook; 1st ed, brn cover, 1930, EX ..**10.00**
Book, souvenir; BSA Official, 1957 Nat'l Jamboree **6.50**
Bust, Baden-Powell, metal or plaster, full-face, 8" **125.00**
Camera, Official Boy Scout Kodak, gr, bellows **75.00**
Camera, Seneca Boy Scout Camera, in litho box **40.00**
Certificate, Eagle Scout, emb, 1930-60 ....**5.00**
Compass, BSA, Litenite, floating dial, glows in dark, 1918-24 .....**22.00**
Figure, Barclay 1930 Scout set of 4 Scouts, ea set **100.00**
Figure, Iron Scout, Scout saluting, khaki gr, 1930 ....**20.00**
Figurine, Scout, ceramic, varied poses, 1950, set of 4 ....**20.00**
Figurine, Scout, molded lead, 1930s, set of 5 ....**20.00**
Game, Boy Scout Progress Game, w/box & board, 1912 ....**90.00**
Game, Boy Scout Target Ball, Parker Bros, 1912 ....**50.00**
Game, Kiddie Camper, Scouts in camp, marbles, 1920 ....**150.00**
Game, Scout Tin Pins, mc litho box, w/pins, 1920 ....**60.00**
Game, Scouts in Camp, 22 stand-up figures, w/box **150.00**
Games, Game of Scouting, 50 cards (complete), litho box, 1930 .**45.00**
Handbook, Official...for Boys, Baden-Powell/Seton, 1st ed, '10 ..**200.00**
Hatpin, BSA, Eagle Scout, type 1, flat bkground pnt **70.00**
Jacket, BSA, standard issue w/4 billows pockets, 1918-24, EX **50.00**
Knickers, 1932-era Cub Scout, bl, VG **25.00**
Lantern, folding; BSA, 1925-32 ....**10.00**
Lantern slide, Baden Powell in full uniform, 1930, sm version **30.00**
Neckerchief, BSA, 1937 World Jamboree, felt, 3" (+) **38.00**
Neckerchief, 1957 Nat'l Jamboree, any variation **8.00**
Patch, BSA Eagle, tan, type 1, 1924 ....**225.00**
Patch, Patrol Leader's, gr felt bars on tan sq, 1918-24 era **10.00**

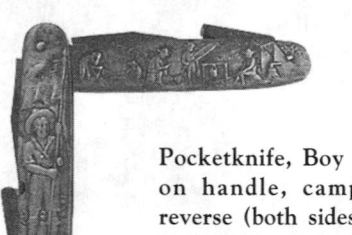

Pocketknife, Boy Scout with flag on handle, camping scene on reverse (both sides shown), larger knife blade missing, G, $30.00.

Pocketknife, Shrade #1066, 2-blade, bone hdl, 1975-80 ....**5.00**
Ring, BSA, Eagle Scout, sterling, rope fretwork, 1925-32 ....**99.00**
Uniform, BSA, gr, V-neck, collar type, 1937-45 era **7.00**
Uniform, type 1, WWI, snap color, bellows pockets, 1913-20 ....**150.00**
Uniform, type 2, open lapel type, 1920-27 ....**65.00**
Uniform, type 3, shirt/breeches/belt, all 1930 ....**50.00**
Yearbook, Rockwell cover, D Appleton & Co, 1928 ....**7.00**

Girl Scouts

Collecting Girl Scout memorabilia is a hobby that is growing nationwide. When Sir Baden-Powell founded the Boy Scout Movement in England, it proved to be too attractive and too well adaped to youth to limit its great opportunities to boys alone. The sister organization, known in England as the Girl Guides, quickly followed and was equally successful. Mrs. Juliette Low, an American visitor to England and a personal friend of the father of Scouting, realized the tremendous future of the movement for her own country, and with the active and friendly cooperation of the Baden-Powells, she founded the Girl Guides in America, enrolling the first patrols in Savannah, Georgia, in March 1912. In 1915 National Headquarters were established in Washington, D.C., and the name was changed to Girl Scouts. The first National Convention was held in 1914, and each succeeding year has shown growth and increased enthusiasm in this steadily growing army of girls and young women who are learning in the happiest ways to combine patriotism, outdoor activities of every kind, skill in every branch of domestic science, and high standards of community service. Today there are over 400,000 Girl Scouts and more than 22,000 leaders. Mr. Sayers is also our Girl Scout advisor.

Badge, GSA, Thanks medal, 10k gold w/bl ribbon, 1930 ....**50.00**
Badge, Life Saving, sterling Maltese cross, 1916 ....**300.00**
Bookends, Girl Scout, compo, 1940, pr **15.00**
Bracelet, GSA, brass links w/gr emblem, ca 1960, NM **12.00**
Camera, GSA Official, Falcon, 1940 ....**30.00**
Camera, Official GSA, Univex, 1937, EX **50.00**
Catalog, GSA Official, uniforms, 1930s era **15.00**
Compact, unofficial, bronze, 1½" sq w/mirror **20.00**
Cookie cutters, GSA, gr hdls, 1950, complete set **20.00**
Doll, compo, Brownie uniform, 1930, 13" **65.00**
Doll, Girl Scout, stuffed type, 1940s, VG **30.00**
Emblem, Girl Scout Hospital Aide **15.00**
First aid kit, Johnson & Johnson, gr sq, 1940 ....**15.00**
Handbook, GSA Official, tan cover, 1920 ....**25.00**
Insignia, Official GSA Eaglet pin, type 2, 1920s **200.00**
Insignia, Official Thanks medal, 10k gold, still in use **65.00**
Pin, Mariner, 1940 ....**15.00**
Sash, merit badge; w/15 badges from 1930 era **35.00**
Sewing kit, gr cover, w/contents, 1930-40 ....**15.00**
Uniform, GSA, dk gr, complete, 1940 ....**30.00**
Uniform, GSA, khaki, full dress, 1920 era **100.00**
Uniform, GSA, speckled gr, complete, 1930 era **45.00**
Uniform, GSA Brownie, w/middy & bloomers, 1918, EX **200.00**
Whistle, dk gr, wooden ball, 1940, VG **25.00**
Whistle, GSA Official, cylinder, 1920s **20.00**
Wings, Brownie, 1926 ....**15.00**

Scrimshaw

The most desirable examples of the art of scrimshaw can be traced back to the first half of the 19th century to the heyday of the whaling industry. Some voyages lasted for several years, and conditions on board were often dismal. Sailors filled the long hours by using the tools of their trade to engrave whale teeth and make boxes, pie crimpers (jagging wheels), etc., from the bone and teeth of captured whales. Eskimos also made scrimshaw, sometimes borrowing designs from the sailors who traded with them.

Beware of fradulent pieces; fakery is prevelant in this field. If you're in doubt, it's best to deal with reputable people who guarantee the items they sell. There are also many carved teeth that are actually made of plastic. A listing of these plastic items has been published by the Kendall Whaling Museum in Sharon, Massachusetts. Our advisor for this category is John Rinaldi; he is listed in the Directory under Maine. See also Powder Horns.

Basket, open-cvd whalebone, wood inlay, 19th C, 5½x9¾x7" ..**2,275.00**
Busk, 4 panels w/4 flags/ships/lady/plant/misc, 1850s, 14¾" **1,090.00**
Clock tower, 2 cvd teeth/wood base/tortoise inlay, 1850s, 9x7½" ..**4,985.00**

Cradle, cvd whale panbone, mini, 4¾x5¼" **850.00**
Crimper, Nantucket style, made entirely from bone, 1850s, 7" ...**200.00**
Crimper, Nantucket style w/ebony band spacer, 19th C, 5½" **225.00**
Crimper, swan neck & head, sinusoid hdl, 4⅝" **2,100.00**
Crimper, whale bone w/ivory wheel, 5¾" **200.00**
Fid, whalebone w/polyhedron knob & dmn cuts on shaft, 19th C, 5" ...**55.00**
Necklace, graduated whale ivory beads, 29", EX **725.00**
Pointer, whale ivory lady's leg hdl on bone shaft, 19th C **525.00**
Swift, whalebone & viory, red/gr/blk stain, 19th C, 26" **2,850.00**
Tooth, Am frigate & British ship, bk: sailing ship, 1840s, 6¼" .**4,250.00**
Tooth, couple/flowers birds, bk: cottage/etc, mc, 1840s, 6" **1,750.00**
Tooth, HMS Fisgard 1846 (frigate), cottage scene, 5¾", VG **950.00**
Tooth, HMS Fisgard 1847 (frigate port view), home scene, 5½" .**1,275.00**
Tooth, inscribed w/name/dtd 1839, whaling scene/scrolls, 6" ..**3,275.00**
Tooth, Liberty w/flag, sailor/lady dancing, 1850s, 5¾", pr **2,700.00**
Tooth, M Cunha, frigate battle scene, Captain Cook..., mc, 7" ..**1,270.00**
Tooth, M Cunha, ornate scene: Inauguration of WA, mc, 7¼" ..**1,175.00**
Tooth, mc Am chip protrait, mtd husser on bk, 19th C, 6¼" ..**3,300.00**
Tooth, sailor w/hat, soldier w/sword/flag, mid-1800s, 6" **875.00**
Tooth, shailing ship ea side, mc stain, 1850s, 5x2½" **1,275.00**
Tusk, pin-prick cvg: fine lady, acrobat, red stain, 1860s, 14" **985.00**

Sebastians

Sebastian miniatures were first produced in 1938 by Prescott W. Baston in Marblehead, Massachusetts. Since then more than six hundred have been modeled. These figurines have been sold through gift shops all over the country, primarily in the New England states. In 1976 Baston withdrew his Sebastians from production. Under an agreement with the Lance Corporation of Hudson, Massachusetts, one hundred designs were selected to be produced by that company under Baston's supervision. Those remaining were discontinued. In the time since then, the older figurines have become very collectible. Price is determined by three factors: 1) in production/out of production; 2) labels — color of oval label, i.e. red, blue, green, etc.; Marblehead label, a green and silver palette-shaped label used until 1977; or no label; 3) condition. If there is no label and the varnish coat is quite yellowed, then it is considered to be of the Marblehead era. Dates are merely copyright dates and have no particular significance in regard to value. (Signed) 'P.W. Baston' should only have impact on price when the signature is an actual autograph. Most pieces are manufactured with an imprinted 'P.W. Baston' on the base. Baston died in 1984; the miniatures are now being done by P.W. Baston, Jr.

Peace & Brotherhood, Sebastian Remembers America series, P.W. 'Woody' Baston, 1988, $45.00.

Adams Academy, w/steeple **150.00**
America's Home Town, Smith's **60.00**
America Salutes Desert Storm, bronze **60.00**
Basketball Hall of Fame **35.00**
Best in the Midwest, paperweight **85.00**
Budding Philatelist, pnt **40.00**

Cavalry 500.00
Charles Dickens, bl label 35.00
Chiquita Banana 300.00
Eastern Star 75.00
Egg Rock Light 55.00
Elizabeth Monroe 115.00
Family Feast 135.00
First at Bat 35.00
First Days of Fall 37.50
First Kite 35.00
For You 40.00
George & Hatchet 400.00
Hanna Dustin, paperweight 250.00
Hanna Dustin, pen stand 300.00
Hood Co Cigar Store Indian 500.00
Horizon Girl 300.00
Ice Sleigh, St Paul Carnival 5.00
Iron Master's House 500.00
Jack & Jill, bl label 35.00
Jimmy Fund III, Ice Hockey 40.00
John Monroe 115.00
Juliet, Marblehead era 40.00
Little Sister, bl label 40.00
Mrs Obocell 400.00
Nabisco Buffalo Bee 500.00
Old Woman in Shoe, Jell-O 375.00
Paul Revere, Masons 225.00
Prince Philip 200.00
Princess Elizabeth 200.00
Romeo, Marblehead era 70.00
Ronald Reagan, Young Republican 85.00
Rub-a-Dub-Dub, bl label 40.00
Secrets, Marblehead label 350.00
Sir Frances Drake 250.00
Soap Box Derby 45.00
Swanboat, Masons 300.00
Trick or Treat, SMCS 45.00
Uncle Mistletoe, Lance label 200.00
Uncle Sam, Marblehead era 50.00
White House, gold 100.00
Wickford Weavers 300.00

Sevres

Fine-quality porcelains have been made in Sevres, France, since the early 1700s. Rich ground colors were often hand painted with portraits, scenics, and florals. Some pieces were decorated with transfer prints and decalcomania; many were embellished with heavy gold. These wares are the most respected of all French porcelains. Their style and designs have been widely copied, and some of the items listed below are Sevres-type wares.

Cup, ram's head, gilt-decorated classical relief, 1800s, 5¼" **1,495.00**
Cup & saucer, demitasse; Crown of Napoleon on pk w/gold, mk .**395.00**
Cup & saucer, floral band w/gilt, 1800s, 5x4¾" **150.00**
Ewer, courting scene w/gold scrolls & florals, sgn, 11½" **175.00**
Figurine, Deco lady, floral gown/figured bl cloak, 20th C, 12½" ..**1,725.00**
Figurine, dogs/wolf battle, on plinth, parian, 1898, 12x18" **1,150.00**
Jar, fleur-de-lis/garlands, gilt-bronze mts, 1800s, 4x3" **575.00**
Jewelry casket, courting scenes/gilt on lt bl, 13" L **550.00**
Plate, couple in garden w/lamb, sgn, 9¼" **195.00**
Plate, lovers in landscape, 1900, 9½", set of 12 ....**2,600.00**
Plate, Napoleon III, w/gilt, 1844, 9½", set of 8 ....**400.00**

Plate, tropical bird in landscape, mc/gilt, 1700s, 9½" **345.00**
Sconce, gilt brass, porc insert w/couple reserve, 14", pr **475.00**
Urn, courting pr/scrolls on wht, sgn Leo, ormolu mts, 11" **450.00**
Urn, lovers/gilt on wht, pear form, ormolu mts, 24", pr **3,750.00**
Vase, cherubs on Celeste Bleu, jeweled bronze dore, 37½", pr ...**2,800.00**
Vase, floral band on wht, krater shape, hdls, ftd, 1809, 13" **2,000.00**
Vase, florette decor teardrop form w/gilt bronze mts, 9", pr **900.00**
Vase, lady/cherub, sgn Delys, w/lid, 13", EX **1,450.00**

Sewer Tile

Whimsies, advertising novelties, and other ornamental items were sometimes made in potteries where the primary product was simply tile.

Bank, pig, seated, OH, 9¾" **300.00**
Bowl, oblong w/4 ft, mk Elwood/1949, 17½", VG **85.00**
Dog, molded/tooled details, OH, 17" **195.00**
Dog, seated, OH, 10" **85.00**

Fish, EX details, 10", $125.00.

Lion on rectangular base, OH, 10", EX **225.00**
Match holder, stump form, OH mk, 5½" **12.00**
Owl, gray mottle w/blk pnt details, 6¾" **240.00**
Owl, wht clay eyes, mk DC 1935, 8¾" **360.00**
Pig, full body, mk Nat'l Sewer Pipe...Akron OH, 14" **1,300.00**
Rabbit on 6½" oval nest w/eggs, EX **225.00**

Sewing Items

Sewing collectibles continue to intrigue collectors, and fine 19th-century and earlier pieces are commanding higher prices due to increased demand and scarcity. Complete needlework boxes and chatelaines in original condition are rare. But even though they may be incomplete, as long as boxes contain fittings of the period and the chains of the chatelaine are intact and contemporary with the style and the individual holders original and matching the brooch, they should be considered prime additions to any collection. As 19th-century items become harder to find, new trends in collecting develop. Among them are needlebooks, many of which were decorated with horses, children, beautiful ladies, etc. Some were giveaways printed with advertisements of products and businesses. Even early pins are collectible; the earliest were made in two parts with the round head attached separately. Pin disks, pin cubes, and other pin holders make interesting additions to a sewing collection as well.

Tape measures are now popular. Victorian figurals command premium prices. Early wooden examples of transferware and Tunbridge ware have gained in popularity as have figurals of vegetable ivory, celluloid, and other early plastics. From the 20th century, tatting shuttles made of plastics as well as bone, brass, sterling, and wood decorated with Art Nouveau, Deco, and more modern designs are in demand; so are darning eggs, stillettos, and thimbles. Because of the decline in the popularity of needlework after the 1920s (due to increased production of machine-made items), a variety of novelty-type items were made in an attempt to regain consumer interest, and many collectors today find them appealing.

Watch for reproductions. Sterling thimbles are being made in Holland and in the U.S. and are available in many designs from the Victorian era. But the originals are usually plainly marked, either in the inside apex or outside on the band. Avoid testing gold and silver thimbles for content; this often destroys the inside marks. Instead, research the manufacturer's mark; this will often denote the material as well. Even though the reproductions are well finished, they do not have the manufacturers' marks. Many thimbles are being made specifically for the collectible market; reproductions of porcelain thimbles are also found. Prices should reflect the age and availability of these thimbles. Our advisor for this category is Marjorie Geddes; she is listed in the Directory under Oregon. See also Mauchline Ware.

Basket, cvd whalebone w/wooden base, oval, 1850s, 9¼x6¾" ...1,500.00
Basket, fine coiled rye straw bound w/splint, 5⅝x12" dia 45.00
Box, bentwood w/mc pnt floral decor, Scandinavian, 6x9¾x6" .475.00
Box, gr vinegar grpt on wood, 19th C, 9½" H, EX 1,950.00
Clamp, brass, bird form, worn fabric cushion, 4½" L 195.00
Clamp, brass, bird spring clamp top, cushion below, 5¼" 260.00
Clamp, CI, blk pnt, swivel mechanism to hold fabric, 4½" 85.00
Clamp, iron, dove form 345.00
Clamp, SP, bird form, w/heart key/clamp, Pat 1852, 1940s repro .95.00
Clamp, SP brass, bird form w/open heart key 175.00
Clamp, wrought iron, bird form, PA, 10¼" 275.00
Cutter, buttonhole; brass/iron pliers type, R Heinisch, 10" 65.00
Cutter, buttonhole; brass/iron pliers type, Wynn-Timmins, 8" 85.00
Cutter, buttonhole; CI/brass, Compton, 10" L 50.00
Cutter, buttonhole; wrought iron, spade-shaped blade, 4¼" 75.00
Darner, blk glass w/wht loopings, pontil scar, 2½" 85.00
Darner, cobalt glass w/wht & yel herringbone ribs, 5" 165.00
Darner, mc spatter glass, clear cased, open end, 6" L 145.00
Darner, mc spatter glass, clear cased, open end, 7⅝" 110.00
Darner, mc splotches in milk glass, 1890-1920, 3¾" 120.00
Emery, bean pod form, gr satin, 2¼" 65.00
Kit, WWI era, US Army, soft leather w/emb eagle 20.00
Lace bobbin, Midlands, bone, fairing 125.00
Measure, bone, castle form, brick details, wind-up, 1½" 345.00
Measure, celluloid, ad for Boot Worker's Union, spring type, M ..65.00
Measure, celluloid, ad for John Deere, spring type, EX 65.00
Measure, celluloid, ad for Lydia Pinkham, spring type, lg 70.00
Measure, celluloid, baseball player figural, spring type, Japan 265.00
Measure, celluloid, bear (walking) figural, spring type, Japan 125.00
Measure, celluloid, Blk man w/cigar figural, spring type 185.00
Measure, celluloid, bulldog's head, spring type, Japan, MIB 215.00
Measure, celluloid, chariot form, spring type, Germany 195.00
Measure, celluloid, Dagwood's dog figural, spring type, Japan 150.00
Measure, celluloid, dog & doghouse figural, spring type, Germany ..150.00
Measure, celluloid, dog w/puppy figural, spring type, Japan 110.00
Measure, celluloid, Donald Duck figural, spring type, Japan 450.00
Measure, celluloid, elephant (sitting) figural, spring, Germany ..265.00
Measure, celluloid, flower basket form, spring type, Japan 90.00
Measure, celluloid, fruit basket form, spring type, Japan 85.00
Measure, celluloid, girl w/flowers figural, Japan 115.00
Measure, celluloid, girl w/muff figural, Japan 125.00
Measure, celluloid, girl w/2 baskets figural, Japan 100.00
Measure, celluloid, house w/red roof form, Japan 95.00
Measure, celluloid, Indian's head, Japan 125.00
Measure, celluloid, Indian w/tomahawk figural, Japan 110.00
Measure, celluloid, jester's head, Japan 195.00

Measure, celluloid, kangaroo, Japan 115.00
Measure, celluloid, Scottie dog & stump, Japan 125.00

Measure, celluloid ship, red and white, 2x2¼", $125.00.

Measure, celluloid, ship form, red, Japan 125.00
Measure, celluloid, squirrel w/nut figural, spring type, Japan 120.00
Measure, celluloid/metal, ad for Lewis Lye, spring type, EX 25.00
Measure, celluloid/metal, ad for Sears...Plows, spring type 60.00
Measure, metal, clock form, wind-up, Germany 115.00
Measure, metal, coffee grinder form, wind-up, Germany 95.00
Measure, metal, donkey figural, wind-up, Germany 210.00
Measure, metal, hat form, wind-up, Germany 195.00
Measure, metal, poodle figural, wind-up, Germany 300.00
Measure, plastic, covered wagon form, 1¾" 135.00
Needle case, bone, flat w/beading, ca 1850, 3½" 245.00
Needle case, celluloid, rolling pin form, bl, 4¼" 125.00
Needle case, cvd bone, fish form, steel rivets 300.00
Needle case, treenware, trn urn shape, 6 holes, 4⅜x1¾" 200.00
Needle case, vegetable ivory, egg shape w/pierced decor 65.00
Pattern, devil costume, Butterick, 1921, M in orig pkg 40.00
Pincushion, compo-head Dutch doll, felt clothes, 5½" 60.00
Pincushion, red wool boot shape w/clear glass beaded bird, 6½" ..65.00
Pincushion, red wool heart w/beaded bird, 1900s, 6x6¼" 145.00
Pincushion, trn & cvd treenware, velvet cushion, 6⅛x3⅜" 190.00
Ribbon threader, gilt metal w/scroll design 65.00
Scissors, embroidery; sterling, emb daisies, 3½", EX 165.00
Stand, mahog w/bone inlays, sliding drw, bone finials, 7½", EX .300.00
Tatting shuttle, brass, eng Mother 145.00
Tatting shuttle, sterling, script initials 195.00
Thimble, china, mc band w/gold trim, Meissen 1st ltd ed 130.00
Thimble, china, pnt roses, gold trim, modern 10.00
Thimble, gold filled, Stern Bros 45.00
Thimble, gr glass, Mary Gregory-style figure, Italy, modern 18.00
Thimble, pewter, scenic, Battersea Ltd, England 20.00
Thimble, sterling, bridge/tower scene, Pat '81 ....100.00
Thimble, sterling, emb cherubs, Simons 250.00
Thimble, sterling, harbor scene/scrolls, star in cap 95.00
Thimble, sterling, identifiable floral, Simons 65.00
Thimble, sterling, Ketchum & McDougal, Salem witch 950.00
Thimble, sterling, mini-paneled, Simons 35.00
Thimble, sterling, paneled, SBC (Stern Brothers) mk 40.00
Thimble, sterling, scrolls & stripes in border, unmk 32.00
Thimble, sterling, Stitch in Time, Simons 450.00
Thimble case, leather, plush lined, unmk 50.00
Thimble case, SP/brass, bucket form 125.00
Thimble case, sterling & gold acorn form, Tiffany 285.00
Thimble stand, turtle, w/post, rectangle, SP, modern, 1x2¼" 45.00

Sewing Machines

The fact that Thomas Saint, an English cabinetmaker, invented the first sewing machine in 1790 was unknown until 1874 when Newton Wilson, an English sewing machine manufacturer and patentee, chanced on the drawings included in a patent specification describing methods of making boots and shoes. By the middle of the 19th century, several patents were granted to American inventors, among them Isaac M. Singer, whose machine used a treadle. These machines were ruggedly built, usually of cast iron. By the 1860s and '70s, the sewing machine had become a popular commodity, and the ironwork became more detailed and ornate.

Though rare machines are costly, many of the old oak treadle machines (especially these brands: Davis, Home, Household, National, New Home, Singer, Weed, Wheeler & Wilson, and Willcox & Gibbs) have only nominal value. Machines manufactured after 1875 are generally very common as most were mass produced. Values for these later sewing machines range from $50.00 to $100.00. Refer to *Toy and Miniature Sewing Machines* by Glenda Thomas for more information. Our advisor for this category is Peter Frei; he is listed in the Directory under Massachusetts.

Child's, Artcraft Junior Miss, floral decor on red, 1950s **75.00**
Child's, Artcraft Metal Products Little Mother, EX in box **85.00**
Child's, Britains Petite, battery-op, 1980s, M in plastic case **40.00**
Child's, Casige, florals on blk, MIG, pre-WWII, 7½" **95.00**
Child's, Casige, gr metallic pnt, MIG-British Zone, 6½" **75.00**
Child's, Crystal Little Queen, battery-op, 5½x3½x6¾" **30.00**
Child's, Delta Specialty Am Girl, wood base, 1930s, 5¼x4" **125.00**
Child's, Dolly Dressmaker, battery-op, TN, 1940s-50s, NM **200.00**
Child's, Muller No 15, EX **245.00**
Child's, New Home Little Worker, Pat 1911-12 ....**175.00**
Child's, Romance, metal, belt driven, rpl base, EX **150.00**
DW Clark, latest Pat June 8, 1858 ....**1,400.00**
Fetter & Jones **2,000.00**
McLean & Hooper **4,000.00**
New Home, Orange MA, 1903, EX **185.00**
Pratt's, Ladies' Companion, Pat Feb & March 1857/Feb '58 ...**6,000.00**
Shaw & Clark, latest Pat Feb 16, 1864 ....**900.00**
Singer, ca 1880, EX **165.00**
Singer, Featherweight #211, blk w/case & attachments **300.00**
Wheeler-Wilson, treadle, walnut case, attachments, EX **700.00**
Willcox & Gibbs, early, sm **125.00**

Shaker Items

The Shaker community was founded in America in 1776 at Niskeyuna, New York, by a small group of English 'Shaking Quakers.' The name referred to a group dance which was part of their religious rites. Their leader was Mother Ann Lee. By 1815 their membership had grown to more than one thousand in eighteen communities as far west as Indiana and Kentucky. But in less than a decade, their numbers began to decline until today only a handful remain. Their furniture is prized for its originality, simplicity, workmanship, and practicality. Few pieces were signed. Some were carefully finished to enhance the natural wood; a few were painted.

Although other methods were used earlier, most Shaker boxes were of oval construction with overlapping 'fingers' at the seams to prevent buckling as the wood aged. Boxes with original paint fetch triple the price of an unpainted box; number of fingers and size should also be considered.

Although the Shakers were responsible for weaving a great number of baskets, their methods are not easily distinguished from those of their outside neighbors, and it is nearly impossible without first-hand knowledge to positively attribute a specific example to their manufacture. They were involved in various commercial efforts other than woodworking — among them sheep and dairy farming, sawmilling, and pipe and brick making. They were the first to raise crops specifically for seed

and to market their product commercially. They perfected a method to recycle paper and were able to produce wrinkle-free fabrics. Our advisor for this category is Nancy Winston; she is listed in the Directory under New Hampshire. Standard two-letter state abbreviations have been used throughout the following listings.

Key:
bj — bootjack
CB — Canterbury
EF — Enfield
NL — New Lebanon

PH — Pleasant Hill
ML — Mt. Lebanon
SDL — Sabbathday Lake
WV — Watervliet

Armchair rocker, tiger and bird's-eye maple, original red stain, splint seat, 4-slat back, New Lebanon, ca 1830, 46", $6,000.00.

Armchair, #1, orig pnt & taped seat, ML, child's, 28", EX+ **1,750.00**
Armchair, #5, maple, varnish, red/blk tape seat, ML/1880, 39" ..**2,200.00**
Armchair, #5, maple, varnish, tape seat, ML, 1880, 36" **1,000.00**
Basket, maple splint, hickory hoop swing hdl, 1850s, 11x10" **600.00**
Basket, maple/ash splint, dbl-wrapped rim, NL, 1840s, 15x14" ...**100.00**
Basket, splint, dbl-wrapped rim, sq base, 1850s, 11x10", EX **100.00**
Basket, work; blk ash splint, hickory hdls, NL, 1840, 23x30" ..**1,200.00**
Basket, work; maple splint, hickory wrap, side hdls, 15x21" **400.00**
Bed, maple/pine, gr-bl pnt, on rollers, rstr, 34x73x36" **700.00**
Bench, apple; pine/maple, 3-leg, paring platform/peg/pail, NL ...**700.00**
Bench, foot; pine, varnish/decal, ML, ca 1900, 7x12x12" **345.00**
Bench, pine, orig brn pnt, mortised/wedged, EF, 1840s, 163" L ..**550.00**
Bench, pine/oak, orig bl-gr pnt top/salmon base, 37" L **200.00**
Bench, visitor's, walnut, orig stain, ML, 26x91", EX **800.00**
Book, Millennial Praises, Hancock, 1813, slipcased **325.00**
Book, Sacred Role, calfskin bound, CB, 1843 ....**325.00**
Book, song; leather bound, EF/WV/NL compendium, 1840s ...**5,750.00**
Bootscraper, CI, 3 wrought edges w/bolting holes, 11x25" **125.00**
Bottle, Extract of Wormwood, blown, aqua, wax sealed, ML, 6" ..**250.00**
Box, bentwood, lapped seams/copper tacks, EF, 1919, 4½" **350.00**
Box, blanket; pine, yel stain, brass hdls, NL, 1850s, 32" L **450.00**
Box, butternut, dvtl, ivory heart escutcheon, EF, 4x10x7" **1,550.00**
Box, candle; maple/birch, varnished, dvtl, sliding lid, CB **400.00**
Box, document; poplar, orig red, brass hinges, 1840, 14" L **400.00**
Box, dough; poplar, yel stain, shaped hdls, dvtl, 12x31x14" **500.00**
Box, letter; tiger maple, dvtl, orig finish, 4x11x7" **1,000.00**
Box, pine, orig red pnt, nailed, leather hinges, NL, 4x6x12" **250.00**
Box, pine, paper label: Garden Seeds...Near Albany NY **1,050.00**
Box, sewing; hexagonal w/poplarware needle case, emery/scissors ..**400.00**
Box, 1-finger, pine/hardwood, Harvard type, iron tacks, 6½" L ..**110.00**
Box, 3-finger, maple/pine, lt varnish, 4½" L **400.00**
Box, 3-finger, maple/pine, natural, sm splits, 6¼" L **200.00**
Box, 3-finger, maple/pine, orig gray pnt, 7⅛" L, EX **350.00**
Box, 3-finger, maple/pine, orig lt varnish, 5¾" L **400.00**
Box, 3-finger, maple/pine, orig yel wash, split, 13⅛" L **680.00**
Box, 3-finger, old olive gr pnt, 19th C, 4¼x10¾", EX **975.00**

Box, 3-finger, pine/hardwood, copper tacks, 6" L 330.00
Box, 4-finger, maple/pine, natural, copper nails, 4¼x10¼" 500.00
Box, 4-finger, maple/pine, orig orange pnt, 4⅛x10⅛" 6,600.00
Box, 4-finger, maple/pine, orig red pnt, ME, 1830, 3¼x8¾" ..1,500.00
Box, 4-finger, maple/pine, varnish, 8⅞" L 350.00
Box, 4-finger, maple/pine, yel pnt traces, oval, 10¼" L 500.00
Box, 4-finger, maple/pine, yel stain/varnish, 6⅜" L 700.00
Box, 4-finger, old varnish, copper tacks, 13½" L 715.00
Box, 5-finger, maple/pine, yel pnt, 5½x13¼" 1,500.00
Box, 5-finger, w/lid, 19th C, 6¾x15" 2,185.00
Candlestand, cherry w/figure, trn shaft/spider legs, ML, 18" dia .900.00
Candlestand, cherry/birch, orig varnish, 1830s, 24x16" dia 2,500.00
Carrier, maple/pine, 3-finger, hickory hoop hdl, 7x11" L 1,750.00
Carrier, sewing; oak, 4-finger, lined, SDL, 11" L, +tools 600.00
Carrier, tool; birch, brass screws, 3-finger-hole hdl, 27" 350.00
Chair, #1, maple, lt varnish, plush rpl seat, ML, 27½" 900.00
Chair, boudoir; maple, dk stain, 2-color tape seat, ML, 28" 500.00
Chair, side; #1, ladderbk, birch/cane seat, EF, 1830, 42" 3,200.00
Chair, side; #15, maple, orig finish, tilts missing, WV, 1830s 450.00
Chair, side; #19, maple, cane seat, tilters, CB, 1830s, 41" 4,200.00
Chair, side; #3, cherry, tilters, splint seat, ML, 36", 4 for 2,750.00
Chair, side; birch, red stain, caned seat, EF, 1830s, rstr 1,800.00
Chair, side; maple, red wash, tape seat, CB, 1830s, 41", EX ...1,400.00
Chair, side; maple, yel pnt, splint seat, WV, 1830s, 39" 800.00
Chair, side; maple/birch, rush seat, EF, 1840s, 41" 900.00
Chair, side; maple/birch, varnish, rush seat, 3-slat, 39" 600.00
Chair, side; maple/butternut, tape seat, NL, 1830s 800.00
Chair, side; tiger maple/maple/birch, rush seat, NL, 1850, 39" .1,200.00
Chest, pine, orig stain, breadbrd ends, dvtl, NL, 14x26x15" 850.00
Chest, pine/birch, red stain, 6-drw, EF, 1840s, 44x35x18" 1,500.00
Chest, storage; pine/cherry, orig red, CI hdls, NL, 22x38x21" .1,200.00
Cloak, sister's, gray wool, 2 interior pockets, SDL, long 325.00
Cloak, sister's, red wool, silk lined, 2 pockets, CB 900.00
Cloak, sister's, violet dyed wool/cream silk brocade, CB 650.00
Coffeepot, tin, side hdl, tin-supported spout, MA, 1870s, 14" 300.00
Colander, tin, hanging ring, CB tag on base, 4x11½" 175.00
Counter, tailoring; pine, orig red pnt, 3-drw, CB, 1840s, 52" ..8,000.00
Cradle, birch w/orig red stain, nailed/screwed sides, 37" 550.00
Cupboard, chimney; pine, 3-shelf int/panel door, 84x15x11" .4,500.00
Cupboard, hanging; pine, orig red pnt, 1 panel door, 30x24x9" .4,100.00
Cupboard, pine, orig red, 2-door/3-shelf, SDL, 1820s, 75x32" .2,800.00
Cupboard, pine, 2-door/5-shelf, pnt traces, EF, 1840, 85x38" ..3,000.00
Cupboard, walnut, 2 panel doors over 2 drws, OH, 89x46x21" ..3,250.00
Desk, traveling; walnut, lift lid, brass hinges, 1-drw, 1880s 400.00
Doll, bsk, glass eyes, orig dress/cloak/bonnet, 12½" 750.00
Dust pan, tin w/steel bands, hanging loop, 17x16½" 100.00
Duster, maple & wool, trn w/sm knob, varnished, MA, 14½" 125.00
Flax wheel, maple/oak, dk patina, stamped FW, 44¼x36" 375.00
Flax wheel, maple/oak, natural, stamped SR AL, 1840, 34" 500.00
Footstool, maple, dk stain, ML trademk decal, 1880s, 7x12" 300.00
Footstool, maple, orig dk stain, ML, 1880s, 7½x11½" 150.00
Footstool, maple, taped/sawdust filled, ML, 1870s, 9x13x10" 450.00
Footstool, pine, dk brn pnt over red stain, bj ends, 1840s, sm 350.00
Fruit press, oak/maple, steel colander/tin drainer, 1840s, 38" 400.00
Keg, staved pine, orig bl-gray pnt, att, 15x17" 685.00
Measure, bentwood, 2-finger, copper tacks, oval, 5⅜" 115.00
Measure, maple, steel braces, nailed lap, EF, 6x12½" dia 150.00
Measure, oak/pine, SDL stencil trademk, 6½x11½" dia 200.00
Mop, maple & cotton, trn hdl, natural patina, 40" 125.00
Pail, pine, bl pnt over orange wash, w/lid, CB, 10x7" dia 800.00
Pail, pine, orig yel pnt, CI bail plates, w/lid, 12x9" dia 1,800.00
Pail, pine w/steel bands, swing hdls, w/lid, EF, 13x10" dia 325.00
Plane, carpenter's; maple, cast-steel blade, CB, 1850s, 22" L 150.00
Print, Elder Frederick Evans at Home, Harper's Weekly, 1870 ...135.00

Rack, drying; birch, pnt traces, pegged, shoe ft, 25x21" 200.00
Rack, drying; hickory, EX natural patina, EF, 41" 330.00
Rack, drying; pine, old gray-wht pnt, SDL, 3-part, ea: 39x45" 250.00
Rack, towel; cherry, shoe ft, 3 bars, mortised/pinned, 37x30" 715.00
Rake, maple/oak, orig gr pnt, bent hickory brace, 50" L 200.00
Rocker, #1, maple, dk stain, orig taped bk/canvas seat, ML, 28" .700.00
Rocker, #2, dk stain, orig taped seat/bk, ML, 1880s, 34½" 350.00
Rocker, #3, maple/tiger maple, taped seat, 2-slat, ML, 34½" 450.00
Rocker, #4, maple, dk stain, 3-slat, ML, 1870s, 33" 550.00
Rocker, #4, maple, orig stain, blk/red tape seat, 34" 600.00
Rocker, #4, red stain, red/blk woven seat (poor), ML, 35" 385.00
Rocker, #5, maple w/dk stain, taped seat, 1870s, 38" 650.00
Rocker, #6, maple, orig bl/tan tape seat, ML, 1870s, 42½" 1,250.00
Rocker, #7, maple, dk stain, twine seat, ML, 1870s, 41" 900.00
Rocker, #7, maple, dk stain/rfn, taped seat, ML, 1880s, 43" 750.00
Rocker, #7, maple, ebony pnt, splint seat/bk, ML, 1880s, 43" 500.00
Rocker, #7, maple, orig stain, tape seat/bk, ML, 41" 900.00
Rocker, #7, maple, restained, rstr shawl bar, tape seat, ML 950.00
Rocker, elder's ladderbk, maple/tiger maple, NL, 1830s, 45" ..4,000.00
Rug, cotton, 4-color graduating oval stripes, 65x44" 650.00
Rug, cotton & wool, 3-color stripes, 83x56" 400.00
Rug whip, maple/steel wire, ML paper label, 27½" 275.00
Scoop, bentwood w/trn hdl, varnish, copper tacks, 5¾" dia 80.00
Shelf, hanging; cherry; dvtl, 4-tier, CI brackets, 29x28x8" 2,300.00
Shoes, leather, hand-sewn heel/soles, sq toes/laces, 1850, pr 25.00
Shovel, maple, red stain, 1-pc cvd hdl, shaft & scoop, 41x12" 450.00
Sieve, herb; pine, natural, 3-color dyed horsehair (plaid) 350.00
Sock-drying form, poplar, CB, set of 5 ....125.00
Stand, work; birch/pine/poplar, 1-drw, 1840s, 27x17x16½" 1,100.00
Stand, work; cherry/butternut/pine/poplar, 2-drw, NL, 1830s .3,500.00
Stand, work; maple/pine, 2 dvtl drws, tripod, 1830s 15,000.00
Stand, work; maple/tiger maple/pine, stain, 2-drws, 1830s 15,000.00
Stool, 2-step; pine, orig red pnt/varnish, cutouts, 23x16x13" ..2,900.00
Stool, 2-step; pine, red varnish, dbl-C arched end, 9x12x9" 350.00
Stool, 3-step; pine, brn over gray, tenon/mortised, 27x17x18" ...900.00
Swift, maple, orig varnish, trn thumbscrews, MA, 1870s, 22" L .275.00
Table, trestle; cherry/butternut/poplar, trn legs, NL, 88" L ...32,500.00
Table, work; birch, orig stain, rnded drop leaves, 31x15" 800.00
Table, work; cherry/pine, red top, 2-drw/2-brd top, 24" L 600.00
Table, work; cherry/pine, varnish, 1 door, 1830s, 28x30x21" ..1,500.00
Table, work; cherry/pine, 2-drw, dvtl, 2-brd/rpt, 21" L 600.00
Table, work; maple w/2-brd pine top, orig red, 50" L 1,500.00
Table, work; maple/pine, orig red pnt, 2-brd top, SDL, 1840s 450.00
Table, work; pine, orig red, 1-drw, nailed, 2-brd, 32" L 500.00
Trunk, dome top, leather w/brass beads, NL, 1860s, 13x27x16" .200.00
Wood bin, poplar w/old worn pnt, trn pegs ea end, 38x35x19" .495.00
Wool wheel, birch/maple/hickory, wash finish, sgn FW, 60x80" .250.00
Yarn winder, maple, hand-held form, 4 arms on disk w/hdl 200.00
Yarn winder, maple, red rpt, trn/splayed legs, 4-arm wheel, 48" ..400.00

Shaving Mugs

Between 1865 and 1920, owning a personalized shaving mug was the order of the day, with the occupationals enjoying their greatest popularity. Most men having occupational mugs would frequent the barber shop several times a week where their mugs were clearly visible for all to see in the barber's rack. As a matter of fact, this display was in many ways the index of the individual town or neighborhood.

During the first twenty years, blank mugs were almost entirely imported from France, Germany, and Austria and were hand painted in this country. Later on, some china was produced by local companies. It is noteworthy that American vitreous china is inferior to the imported Limoges and is subject to extreme crazing.

Artists employed by the American barber supply companies were for the most part extremely talented and capable of executing any design the owner required, depicting his occupation, fraternal affiliation, or preferred sport. When the mug was completed, the name and the gold trim always added in varying degrees, depending on the price paid by the customer. This price was determined by the barber who added his markup to that of the barber-supply company. As mentioned above, the popularity of the occupational shaving mug diminished with the advent of World War I and the introduction by Gillette of the safety razor. Later followed the blue laws forcing barber shops to close on Sundays, thereby eliminating the political and social discussions for which they were so well noted.

Occupational shaving mugs are the most sought after of the group which would include those with sport affiliations. Fraternal mugs, although desirable, do not command the same price as the occupationals. Occasionally, you will find the owner's occupation together with his fraternal affiliation. This combination could add anywhere between 25% to 50% to the price, which is dependent on the execution of the painting, rarity of the subject, and detail. Some subjects can be done very simply; others can be done in extreme detail, commanding substantially higher prices. It is fair to say, however, that the rarity of the occupation will dictate the price. Mugs which have lost the gold through wear lose between 20% and 30% of their value immediately. This would not apply to the gold trim around the rim, but to the loss of the name itself. Our advisor for this category is Burton Handelsman; he is listed in the Directory under New York.

Advertising, Holzager Antiseptic Shaving Soap, glass, 1908 ....**35.00**
Bulldog HP on side, gold hdl **25.00**
Butterflies & lily pads, name in gold **65.00**
Copper lustre w/orange & bl bands, EX **65.00**
Floral, mk Bonn Germany **40.00**
Fraternal, Knights of Pythias, T&V Limoges **110.00**
Fraternal, Loyal Order of Moose, moose head, Germany, Eisemann .**95.00**

Fraternal, Masons, exceptional detail and gold, $900.00.

Fraternal symbols & name in gold w/stripes, T&V Limoges, 3½" .**75.00**
Gibson girls transfer, ceramic, gold trim, EX **45.00**
Mirror on side of open mug w/bl trim, Germany, US Pat, EX **75.00**
Occupational, brewer, barrel wagon & horses, EX **500.00**
Occupational, bricklayer, 5 men at work, EX **650.00**
Occupational, cabinetmaker, man at lg machine, T&V Limoges ..**325.00**
Occupational, carpenter, man working, building tools, gold trim **750.00**
Occupational, coalman, truck w/mechanical dump, Austria ...**1,500.00**
Occupational, fisherman scene, gold name & trim, T&V Limoges ..**500.00**
Occupational, harness maker, man at work, gold name, EX **1,100.00**
Occupational, mail carrier, man w/letters **1,750.00**
Occupational, trainman, men working on steam engine **750.00**
Patriotic, eagle w/banner, HP name in gold, EX **65.00**

Shawnee

The Shawnee Pottery Company operated in Zanesville, Ohio,

from 1937 to 1961. They produced inexpensive novelty ware (vases, flowerpots, and figurines) as well as a very successful line of figural cookie jars, creamers, and salt and pepper shakers.

They also produced three dinnerware lines, the first of which, Valencia, was designed by Louise Bauer in 1937 for Sears & Roebuck. A starter set was given away with the purchase of one of their refrigerators. Second and most popular was the King Corn line. It was produced from 1946 to 1954, when the colors were changed to a lighter yellow for the kernels and darker green for the shucks. This variation was called Queen Corn. (Our values are for yellow corn prices unless white is noted in the description.) Their third dinnerware line, produced after 1954, was called Lobsterware. It was made in either black, brown, or gray; lobsters were usually applied to serving pieces and accessory items.

For further study we recommend these books: *The Collector's Guide to Shawnee Pottery* by our advisors, Janice and Duane Vanderbilt, who are listed in the Directory under Indiana; and *Shawnee Pottery, An Identification and Value Guide*, by Jim and Bev Mangus, who are listed in Ohio.

Cookie Jars

Basketweave, hexagon shape, mk USA, minimum value **50.00**
Cottage, mc, mk USA 6, minimum value **650.00**
Drum Major, gold trim, mk USA 10, minimum value **500.00**
Dutch Boy, dbl stripes, mk USA, minimum value **175.00**
Dutch Boy, decals & gold trim, mk USA, minimum value **250.00**
Dutch Boy, Great Northern, mk Great Northern 1025, minimum value .**250.00**
Dutch Boy, patches, gold trim, mk USA, minimum value **275.00**
Dutch Girl, cold pnt, mk USA, minimum value **75.00**
Dutch Girl, decals & gold trim, mk USA, minimum value **250.00**
Dutch Girl, pnt under glaze, mk USA, minimum value **75.00**
Dutch Girl, tulips, mk USA, minimum value **100.00**
Elephant, pk, mk Shawnee 60, minimum value **150.00**
Fernware, octagonal shape, mk USA, minimum value **75.00**
Fruit Basket, gold trim, mk Shawnee 84, minimum value **200.00**
Jo Jo the Clown, gold trim, mk Shawnee 12, minimum value **500.00**
Little Chef, brn cold pnt, mk USA, minimum value **60.00**
Little Chef, cream color, mk USA, minimum value **80.00**
Muggsy, decals & gold trim, mk Pat Muggsy USA, minimum value ..**550.00**
Owl, gold trim, mk USA, minimum value **225.00**
Puss 'N Boots, mk Pat Puss 'N Boots, minimum value **150.00**
Sailor Boy, blk hair, gold trim, mk USA, minimum value **500.00**
Sailor Boy, blond hair, gold trim, mk USA, minimum value **500.00**
Sitting Elephant, cold pnt, mk USA, minimum value **75.00**
Smiley the Pig, plums, mk USA, minimum value **325.00**
Smiley the Pig, red cold pnt, mk USA, minimum value **50.00**
Smiley the Pig, shamrocks w/gold trim, mk USA, minimum value ...**325.00**
Smiley the Pig, strawberries w/gold trim, mk USA, minimum value .**700.00**
Smiley the Pig, tulips, mk USA, minimum value **200.00**
Winnie the Pig, bl collar, mk USA, minimum value **225.00**
Winnie the Pig, clover bud w/gold trim, mk USA, minimum value ..**500.00**
Winnie the Pig, red collar w/gold trim, minimum value **350.00**

Corn Line

Bowl, cereal; mk #94 ....**45.00**
Bowl, fruit; mk #92 ....**40.00**
Bowl, mixing; mk #5, 5" **25.00**
Bowl, mixing; mk #8, 8" **35.00**
Butter dish, mk #72 ....**50.00**
Casserole, mk #73, sm **50.00**
Casserole, mk #74, lg **50.00**
Cookie jar, mk #66 ....**200.00**
Creamer, gold trim, mk USA **60.00**
Creamer, mk #70 ....**25.00**

Mug, #69 ....45.00
Pitcher, wht corn, gold trim, mk USA 100.00
Plate, mk #68, 10" 30.00
Platter, 12, mk #96 ....45.00
Relish dish, mk #79 ....17.00
Shakers, lg, pr 25.00
Shakers, sm, pr 17.00

Snack set, 4 mugs and 4 plates,
MIB, $435.00.

Sugar bowl, wht corn, mk USA 30.00
Teapot, mk #75, 30-oz 70.00
Teapot, wht corn, gold trim, mk USA, 30-oz 120.00

Kitchenware

Casserole, fruit, gold trim, mk Shawnee 83 ....135.00
Coffeepot, Pennsylvania Dutch, mk USA 52 ....150.00
Creamer, Elephant, decals & gold trim, mk Pat USA 200.00
Creamer, Puss 'N Boots, all wht, mk Pat Puss 'N Boots 50.00
Creamer, Puss 'N Boots, decals w/gold, mk Pat Puss 'N Boots 250.00
Creamer, Smiley the Pig, peach flower, mk Pat Smiley 50.00
Creamer, Snowflake, mk USA 17.00
Creamer, tilt; Pennsylvania Dutch, mk USA 10 ....80.00
Jug, Fernware, octagonal shape, mk USA 50.00
Jug, Snowflake, ball shape, mk USA 50.00
Lobster, hors d'oeuvres holder, 25 holes 150.00
Lobster, snack jar, #925 ....250.00
Lobster, spoon holder 175.00
Pitcher, Boy Blue, mc w/gold trim, mk Shawnee 46 ....175.00
Pitcher, Charlie Chicken, wht w/gold trim, mk Chanticleer 250.00
Pitcher, fruit, mk Shawnee 80 ....70.00
Pitcher, Smiley the Pig, peach flower, mk Pat Smiley 125.00
Pitcher, Smiley the Pig, red flower w/gold, mk Pat Smiley 210.00
Pitcher, Sunflower, mk USA 80.00
Salt box, Fernware, yel, mk USA 80.00
Shakers, Charlie Chicken, gold trim, sm, pr 55.00
Shakers, Charlie Chicken, lg, pr 30.00
Shakers, chef, sm, pr 15.00
Shakers, Dutch boy & girl, Great Northern, lg, pr 200.00
Shakers, Farmer Pig, sm, pr 25.00
Shakers, flowerpot w/gold trim, sm, pr 40.00
Shakers, fruit, gold trim, mk USA 8 , pr 55.00
Shakers, fruit, sm, pr 15.00
Shakers, jug shape, bl, lg, pr 30.00
Shakers, milk can, paper sticker, sm, pr 18.00
Shakers, Muggsy, gold trim, lg, pr 150.00
Shakers, owl, gold trim, sm, pr 50.00
Shakers, Swiss boy & girl, gold trim, lg, pr 75.00
Shakers, watering can, gold trim, sm pr 55.00
Shakers, wheelbarrow, gold trim, sm, pr 55.00
Shakers, Winnie & Smiley, clover bud, lg, pr 115.00
Shakers, Winnie & Smiley, clover bud, sm, pr 65.00
Shakers, Winnie & Smiley, decals & gold trim, lg, pr 150.00

Sugar bowl, bucket shape, decals w/gold trim, mk USA 75.00
Sugar bowl, cottage, mk USA 8 ....200.00
Sugar bowl, Sunflower, mk USA 40.00
Teapot, clover bud w/gold, mk USA 175.00
Teapot, cottage, mc, mk USA 7 ....300.00
Teapot, elephant, yel, bl or gr, mk USA, ea 100.00
Teapot, emb rose, solid gold, mk USA 200.00
Teapot, Granny Ann, matt finish w/gold, mk Pat Granny Ann USA ..225.00
Teapot, red flower, mk USA 40.00
Teapot, Tom Tom, gold trim, mk Tom the Piper's Son Pat USA ...250.00
Utility jar, gr basketweave, mk USA 80.00
Valencia, ashtray 17.00
Valencia, bowl, mixing; 9" 23.00
Valencia, bowl, punch or salad; 12" 47.00
Valencia, coffee cup, AD 37.00
Valencia, coffeepot, regular 16.00
Valencia, egg cup 12.00
Valencia, pie server, 9" 60.00
Valencia, plate, 9¾" 15.00
Valencia, waffle set, 5-pc 55.00

Miscellaneous

Bank, bulldog 130.00
Bank, Howdy Doody, mk USA Bob Smith 375.00
Bank, tumbling bear 125.00
Clock, pyramid shape, medallion finish 110.00
Clock, trellis design 100.00
Figurine, puppy dog, decals w/gold trim 110.00
Figurine, raccoon, decals w/gold 110.00
Figurine, Spanish dancers, pr 40.00
Figurine, squirrel, decals w/gold trim 110.00
Figurine, tumbling bear 60.00
Lamp base, Champ the Dog 20.00
Match holder, Fernware, mk USA 80.00
Planter, auto w/8-spoke rims, gold trim, mk USA 506 ....24.00
Planter, dog & jug, mk USA 610 ....10.00
Planter, high-heel shoe, emb decor, mk USA 12.00
Planter, kitten & basket, mk Shawnee USA 2026 ....30.00
Planter, pixie & wheelbarrow, yel & brn, unmk 15.00
Planter, poodle on bicycle, mk USA 712 ....32.00
Planter, squirrel & stump, gold trim, mk Shawnee 664 ....20.00
Sock darners, people shape, mk USA 75.00
Toastie Susan, pk or turq 90.00

Shearwater

Since 1928 generations of the Peter, Walter, and James McConnell Anderson families have been producing figurines and artwares in their studio at Ocean Springs, Mississippi. Their work is difficult to date. Figures from the twenties and thirties won critical acclaim and have continued to be made to the present time. Early marks include a die-stamped 'Shearwater' in a dime-sized circle, a similar ink stamp, and a half-circle mark. Any older item may still be ordered in the same glazes as it was originally produced, so many pieces on the market today may be relatively new. However, the older marks are not currently in use. Currently produced Blacks and pirates figurines are marked with a hand-incised 'Shearwater' and/or a cypher formed with an 'S' whose bottom curve doubles as the top loop of a 'P' formed by the addition of an upright placed below and to the left of the S. Many are dated, '93, for example. These figures are generally valued at $35.00 to $50.00 and are available at the pottery or by mail order. New decorated and carved pieces are very expensive, starting at $400.00 to $500.00 for a 6" pot.

Bowl, bl w/rings, 3½x6½" base, 3½" opening	60.00
Candle holder, tan & matt gr, mk, 5¼"	45.00
Cup & saucer, Oriental decor, gr	35.00
Teapot, dusty gr, hand trn, appl hdl & spout, mk, 6"	65.00
Vase, cvd fish on bl gloss, sgn Anderson, 1930, rim crack, 9"	800.00
Vase, Deco style w/emb pelicans on lav w/brn flecks, 7"	475.00
Vase, Ming gr, early mk, 8x5¼"	75.00

Sheet Music

Sheet music is often collected more for its colorful lithographed covers, rather than for the music itself. Transportation songs (which have pictures or illustrations of trains, ships, and planes), Ragtime and Blues, Comic characters (especially Disney), Sports, Political, and Expositions are eagerly sought after. Much of the sheet music on the market today is valued at under $5.00; some of the better examples are listed here. Values are given for examples in excellent to near-mint condition unless otherwise noted. Our advisor for this category is Jeannie Peters; she is listed in the Directory under Ohio.

After the Ball, Movie: Babe Ruth Story, 1920	10.00
America, Movie: West Side Story, 1957	5.00
As Long As I'm Dreaming, Movie: Welcome Stranger, 1947	5.00
Bad & Beautiful, photo cover: K Douglas & L Turner, 1953	5.00
Because of You, photo cover: Al Roberts, 1913	5.00
Bluebirds in the Moonlight, Movie: Gulliver's Travel, 1937	10.00
Buttons & Bows, photo cover: Hope & Russell, 1948	5.00
Chicago, sgn by Fred Fisher, 1922	35.00
Cold, Cold Heart, Hank Williams, 1951, EX	7.00
Cossack Love Song, George Gershwin, 1926	10.00
Darktown Strutters' Ball, photo cover: Elsie White, 1917	30.00
Don't Cry Swanee, photo cover: Al Jolson, 1923	10.00
Dreamer w/a Penny, Musical: All for Love, 1949	5.00
Fairy Tales, Musical: Buddies, 1919	10.00
Forever, photo cover: Little Dippers, 1960	5.00
Ghost Riders in the Sky, sgn photo: Vaughn Monroe	10.00
Goodnight Nurse, photo cover: Mae West, 1912	15.00
Have a Heart, Musical: Ziegfield Follies, 1916	10.00
How Do You Do?, Movie: Song of the South, Disney, 1946	10.00
I Don't Want...Your Yard, photo cover: Cherrie Simpson, 1894	15.00
I'll Have Vanilla, photo cover: Eddie Cantor, 1934	10.00
I Love You From Coast to Coast, photo cover: V Lopez, 1936	5.00
I'm Happy That's All, photo cover: Eva Tanguay, 1911	15.00
I Want To Be Free, photo cover: Elvis Presley, 1957	17.00
I Want You, I Need You, Movie: I'm No Angel, 1933	10.00
If I Only Had a Brain, Movie: Wizard of Oz, 1939	25.00
In Dixie Land w/Dixie Lou, photo cover: Bunny Gray, 1912	10.00
It's Raining Sundrops, Movie: West Point Story, 1950	8.00
Jennie, Musical: Girl of My Heart, 1921	10.00
Katrina, Movie: Adventures of Ichabod Crane/Mr Toad, 1949	10.00
Later Tonight, Movie: Wintertime, 1943	10.00
Little April Shower, Movie: Bambi, Disney, 1942	10.00
Love & Learn, Movie: That Girl From Paris, 1936	8.00
Magic Is the Moonlight, Movie: Bathing Beauty, 1944	5.00
Maybe This Is Love, Musical: Three Cheers, 1928	10.00
Me & My Shadow, photo cover: Sophie Tucker, 1927, VG	7.00
Mona, photo cover: Bob Hope, 1938	5.00
Morning Glory, photo cover: Katherine Hepburn, 1933	20.00
My Cabin of Dreams, photo cover: Benny Goodman, 1937	10.00
My Mother Would Love You, Movie: Panama Hattie, 1942	5.00
My Old Flame, photo cover: Mae West, 1934	11.00
New Moon, Irving Berlin, Movie: New Moon, 1919	15.00
Oh Helen!, photo cover: Sophie Tucker, 1918	10.00

On the Avenue, Inaugural March for 1909, 1909	30.00
One Hundred Rifles, photo cover: R Welch & J Brown, 1969	22.00
One Song, Disney cover: Snow White, 1937, EX	15.00
Over the Rainbow, sgn photo cover: Judy Garland, 1939	400.00
Raindrops Keep...Head, Movie: Butch...Sundance Kid, 1969	5.00
Rose in the Bud, Movie: Battle of the Sexes, 1907	5.00
School Days, Movie: Star Maker, 1936	10.00
Shuffle Off to Buffalo, Movie: Forty Second Street, 1932	5.00
So This Is Love, Movie: Cinderella, Disney, 1949	10.00

Some of These Days, by Shelton Brooks, Sophie Tucker cover, 1937, NM, $10.00.

Song of the South, Movie: Song of the South, Disney, 1946	10.00
St Louis Blues, photo cover: L Armstrong, renewed 1942, VG	7.00
Take Me Out to the Ballgame, Norworth & Von Tilzer, 1908	30.00
That's Amore, sgn photo cover: Dean Martin, 1953	5.00
They're All My Friends, George M Cohan	15.00
Tiny Bubbles, sgn photo cover: Don Ho, 1966	5.00
Twenty Four Hours a Day, Movie: Sweet Surrender, 1935	10.00
Washington Post March, John Philip Sousa, 1889	20.00
Weary River, photo cover: Richard Barthelmess, 1929	5.00
When I Marry Mr Snow, Rodgers & Hammerstein II, 1945	5.00
Where Am I?, Movie: Stars Over Broadway, 1935	5.00
Who's Afraid...Big Bad Wolf?, photo cover: Mickey Mouse, 1934	20.00
Why Don't You Love Me?, sgn photo cover: Hank Williams, 1950	5.00
With All My Heart, photo cover: Rudy Vallee, 1930	5.00
You & I, Theme Song of Maxwell House Coffee-Time, 1941	10.00
You Are Love, Movie: Show Boat, 1927	5.00
You'd Better Love Me, Musical: High Spirits	5.00
You Gave Me Your Heart, Movie: Blood & Sand, 1922	10.00
Zip-A-Dee-Doo-Dah, Movie: Song of the South, Disney, 1946	10.00

Shelley

In 1872 Joseph Shelley became partners with James Wileman, owner of Foley China Works, thus creating Wileman & Co. in Stoke-on-Trent. Twelve years later James Wileman withdrew from the company, though the firm continued to use his name until 1925 when it became known as Shelley Potteries, Ltd. Like many successful 19th-century English potteries, this firm continued to produce useful household wares as well as dinnerware of considerable note. In 1896 the beautiful Dainty White shape was introduced, and it is regarded by many as synonymous with the name Shelley. In addition to the original Dainty 6-Flute design, other lovely shapes were produced: 12-Flute, 14-Flute, Oleander, Queen Anne, and the more modern shapes of Vogue, Regent, and Eve.

Though often overlooked, striking earthenware was produced under the direction of Frederick Rhead and later Walter Slater and his son Eric. Many notable artists contributed their talents in designing unusual, attractive wares: Rowland Morris, Mabel Lucie Attwell, and Hilda Cowham, to name but a few.

In 1966 Allied English Potteries acquired control of the Shelley

Company, and by 1967 the last of the exquisite Shelley China had been produced to honor remaining overseas orders. In 1971 Allied English Potteries merged with the Doulton group. Our advisors for this category are Lila and Fred Shrader; they are listed in the Directory under California.

Key: MLA — Mabel Lucie Attwell   QA – Queen Anne

Ashtray, Dainty Pink, 5" dia **38.00**
Ashtray, Finleighs (over) Brighton w/flags, 5" dia **32.00**
Ashtray, Maytime (Chintz), 3½" sq **24.00**
Bowl, cereal; Begonia, 6-flute, 6¼" **42.00**
Bowl, cereal; Bridal Rose, Oleander shape, 6¼" **38.00**
Bowl, cereal; Oleander, 6-flute, 6¼" **45.00**
Bowl, cream soup; Harebell, Oleander shape, w/underplate **65.00**
Bowl, cream soup; Regency, 14-flute, w/underplate **55.00**
Bowl, flat soup; Duchess, 7½" **25.00**
Bowl, flat soup; Rose & Red Daisy, 6-flute, 7½" **52.00**
Bowl, fruit; Drifting Leaves, 5¼" **22.00**
Bowl, fruit; Indian Peony, 5¼" **26.00**
Bowl, fruit; Rose & Red Daisy, 6-flute, 5¼" **35.00**
Bowl, rimmed soup; Dainty Blue, 6-flute **75.00**
Bowl, rimmed soup; Dainty White, 6-flute **28.00**
Bowl, rimmed soup; Rose Spray, Oleander shape **65.00**
Bowl, rimmed soup; Rosebud, 6-flute **65.00**
Bowl, vegetable; Archway of Roses, oval, 9" **135.00**
Bowl, vegetable; Begonia, 6-flute, w/lid, 9½" dia **285.00**
Bowl, vegetable; Begonia, 6-flute, 9" **145.00**
Bowl, vegetable; Dainty White, 6-flute, w/lid, 9½" **150.00**
Bowl, vegetable; Dainty White, 6-flute, 9" **95.00**
Box, coronation of George V, June 1911, w/lid, 2" dia **90.00**
Box, crested ware, pearl lustre, British flags, w/lid, 3½x4½" **55.00**
Box, Wild Anenome, 6-flute, w/lid, 4½" dia **135.00**
Butter dish, Regency, 6-flute, w/lid, 7½" dia **135.00**
Butter dish, Rosebud, 6-flute, oblong, w/lid **135.00**
Butter dish, Stocks, 6-flute, w/lid, 7½" dia **145.00**
Butter pat, Bridal Rose **45.00**
Butter pat, Bridal Rose, 6-flute **55.00**
Butter pat, Campanula **45.00**
Butter pat, Celandine, 6-flute **45.00**
Butter pat, Georgian **35.00**
Butter pat, Rose & Red Daisy **42.50**
Butter tub, Harmony Drip Ware, w/lid & underplate **150.00**
Cake plate, Glorious Devon, 6-flute, tab hdls, 9" sq **110.00**
Cake plate, Pansy (lg), 6-flute, ped ft, 8" **195.00**
Cake plate, Regency, 6-flute, ped ft, 8" **175.00**
Candle holder, Blue Rock, 6-flute, 3¾" **125.00**
Candle holder, Maytime, 4¼" **165.00**
Candy dish, Rose Trousseau, 14-flute, 4" dia **45.00**
Candy dish, rust, blk & gold Deco, 4½" dia **65.00**
Candy dish, Windflower, 6-flute, tab hdls, 5½" sq **45.00**
Chamber set, pitcher+bowl+candlestick+3 pcs utility ware **385.00**
Children's ware, bowl, cereal; MLA, Fisherman Joe, 5½" **130.00**
Children's ware, chamberstick, Teddy Bears at play, finger ring .**110.00**
Children's ware, egg cup, Hilda Cowham, toy train scene **62.00**
Children's ware, feeding dish, Baby's Plate, rhymes, 6x9" **110.00**
Children's ware, mug, Puff-Puff **55.00**
Children's ware, plate, MLA, Boo-Boos on horsie, 7" **125.00**
Children's ware, plate, Puff-Puff, 7" **75.00**
Chocolate pot, Bands & Lines, Regent shape, 4-cup **155.00**
Chocolate pot, Harmony Drip Ware, 6½" **135.00**
Chocolate pot, Hedgerow w/gold, 6-cup **145.00**
Coffeepot, Anenome Bunch, Regent shape, 8-cup **195.00**
Coffeepot, blk matt w/much gold trim, QA shape, 8-cup **350.00**
Coffeepot, Bridal Rose, 6-flute, 6-cup **250.00**

Coffeepot, Celandine, 6-flute, 8-cup **245.00**
Coffeepot, Mode shape, bl & wht (Deco), 8-cup **210.00**
Coffeepot, Rose Pansy Forget-Me-Not, 6-flute, 6-cup **199.00**
Coffeepot, Woodland, 6-cup **165.00**
Comport, Intarsio, w/ped & 3 S-curve supports, 8" **395.00**
Condiment set, Dainty Blue, 6-flute, shakers+mustard+lid+tray ..**255.00**
Creamer, Hibiscus, 6-flute, med sz **34.00**
Creamer & sugar bowl, Archway of Roses, QA shape, w/lid **175.00**
Creamer & sugar bowl, Blue Iris, Mode shape, med **75.00**
Creamer & sugar bowl, Blue Rock, 6-flute, med **75.00**
Creamer & sugar bowl, Bridal Rose, 6-flute, ind, w/tray **135.00**
Creamer & sugar bowl, Harmony Drip Ware, Mode shape, med ..**55.00**
Creamer & sugar bowl, Lily of the Valley, 6-flute, w/lid, lg **145.00**
Cup & saucer, Banded Bridal Rose, Henley shape **50.00**
Cup & saucer, blk w/Summer Glory inside cup, Oleander shape ..**65.00**
Cup & saucer, Blocks (Deco), Vogue shape **125.00**
Cup & saucer, Blue Daisy (Chintz) **60.00**
Cup & saucer, Blue Poppy, 6-flute **59.00**
Cup & saucer, Blue Rock, 14-flute **56.00**
Cup & saucer, Daffodil Time **52.00**
Cup & saucer, Dainty Floral (flower molded into hdl), 6-flute ...**110.00**
Cup & saucer, Dainty White **50.00**
Cup & saucer, demitasse; Begonia, 6-flute **54.00**
Cup & saucer, demitasse; blk matt w/pnt flowers & rich gold **55.00**
Cup & saucer, demitasse; Daffodil Time **45.00**
Cup & saucer, demitasse; Garland of Flowers, QA shape **75.00**
Cup & saucer, demitasse; Georgian, Mocha shape **48.00**
Cup & saucer, DuBarry, Gainsborough shape **49.00**
Cup & saucer, Harebell, farmer sz **85.00**
Cup & saucer, Maytime (Chintz), Ripon shape w/gold ped & hdl .**60.00**
Cup & saucer, Pansy, 14-flute, sm **55.00**
Cup & saucer, Pansy, 6-flute, lg **60.00**
Cup & saucer, Polestar, 14-flute **50.00**
Cup & saucer, Rose Arches, QA shape **95.00**
Cup & saucer, scenics, Henley shape **55.00**
Egg cup, Bridal Rose, 6-flute, lg **75.00**
Egg cup, Campanula, 6-flute, sm **45.00**
Egg cup, Dainty Blue, 6-flute, lg **95.00**
Egg cup, Dainty White, lg **28.00**
Egg cup, Harmony Drip Ware, sm **38.00**
Ginger jar, Harmony Ware, w/lid, 9½" **195.00**
Hatpin holder, crested ware, Wileman, 5½" **57.00**
Horn, Blue Rock, 6-flute, w/hdl, 4¾" **100.00**
Horn, Shamrocks, 6-flute, no hdl, 4¾" **80.00**
Jam container, Rose Spray, 6-flute, w/lid & underplate **122.00**
Menu plaque, floral decor, Wileman, 5x7" w/support **110.00**
Mustard container, Bridal Rose, 6-flute, w/lid, 2½" **95.00**
Napkin rings, Blue Rock, set of 4 ....**275.00**
Pitcher & bowl, utility ware, cream w/bl striping, Wileman **175.00**
Plate, Bridal Rose, 6-flute, 12¾x9½" **175.00**
Plate, chop; Blue Rock, 6-flute, 13" **190.00**
Plate, chop; DuBarry, 13" **145.00**
Plate, Dainty Blue, 6-flute, 6" **30.00**
Plate, Dainty Blue, 6-flute, 8" **45.00**
Plate, Golden Harvest, 10½" **40.00**
Plate, Heron, 10½" **55.00**
Plate, Primrose, 6-flute, 6" **22.00**
Plate, Primrose Chintz, 8" **40.00**
Plate, Regency, 6-flute, platinum trim, 10½" **65.00**
Plate, Regency, 6-flute, 10½" **55.00**
Plate, Regency, 6-flute, 6" **22.00**
Plate, Sheraton, 8" **30.00**
Platter, Duchess, 14x12" **95.00**
Platter, Sheraton, 12x10" **98.00**

Pudding mold, star shape, utilitarian ware, 6½" at base **75.00**
Relish dish, Primrose, Oleander shape, 5x9" **110.00**
Shakers, Bridal Rose, 6-flute, pear shape, 4", pr **135.00**
Shakers, Maytime, cylindrical, 3¾", pr **125.00**
Tankard, Cloisello, lion's head detail on hdl, 7" **225.00**
Tea & toast set, Blue Rock, 6-flute cup, 6x9" plate **110.00**
Tea & toast set, Regency, 6-flute cup, 8" dia plate **65.00**
Tea & toast set, Rosebud, 6-flute cup, 8" dia plate **85.00**

Teapot, unnamed pattern of yellow bouquets on white, 5¼", $135.00; Store sign, gold on yellow, 2¾x3¾" oval, $110.00.

Teapot, Begonia, 6-flute, 8-cup **250.00**
Teapot, Blue Rock, 6-flute, 8-cup **295.00**
Teapot, Drifting Leaves, 8-cup **165.00**
Teapot, Wild Anenome, 6-flute, 4-cup **195.00**
Toast rack, Dainty Pink, 6-flute, 3-bar **165.00**
Toast rack, Indian Peony, 5-bar **85.00**
Tray, dresser; Festival of Empire, tab hdls, 6x9" **385.00**
Tray, sandwich; Blue Rock, 6-flute, tab hdls, 11½x4½" **175.00**
Tray, sandwich; Regency, 6-flute, tab hdls, 13½x6" **95.00**
Tray, triple; Heavenly Blue, 6-flute, gold hdl, sm **195.00**
Tray, triple; Rosebud, 6-flute, w/hdl, lg **225.00**
Vase, bulbous w/narrow neck, flared collar, hdls, 10" **75.00**
Vase, Cloisello, cylindrical, 6" **95.00**
Vase, Lustre Ware w/plums & leaves on blk, 6¼" **135.00**
Vase, pansy ring; Maytime, 6¼" dia **155.00**

Shenandoah

The Shenandoah Valley, extending from Virginia to Pennsylvania, is well known for the fine pottery made there from the early 1800s until the turn of the century. It is characterized by bright, clear glazes in a variety of colors or in combination. Many small potteries were involved. Items marked 'Bell' indicate one of the larger companies.

Butter crock, redware, cobalt brushed decor, J Bell, 6½", EX ..**1,650.00**
Creamer, redware, cream w/gr, tooled rings, att, 6" **550.00**
Cuspidor, redware, cream w/gr & brn, att, 6¾", EX **440.00**
Figurine, lamb, redware, gr w/coleslaw, att Bell family, 2½", EX ..**935.00**
Flowerpot, redware, cream w/brn & gr, w/saucer, att, 8" **1,045.00**
Jar, redware, cream w/bl & brn, tooled decor/hdls, att, 6" **195.00**
Jug, redware, cream w/gray-gr mottle, tooling, att, 6" **1,425.00**
Mold, Turk's head, redware, brn runs, John Bell, rpr, 7" **850.00**
Pitcher, redware, cream w/brn & gr, tooling, att, 6" **2,750.00**
Pitcher, redware, cream w/brn & olive, att, 10", EX **1,150.00**
Pitcher, redware, dk brn runs, strap hdl, John Bell, 5⅜" **2,200.00**
Salt cellar, redware, cream w/gr & brn, att, 3" **1,045.00**
Spill holder, redware, brn mottle, John Bell Waynesboro, 4⅛" .**1,045.00**
Sugar bowl, redware, brn speckled, flower hdl, w/lid, att, 5" **1,750.00**

Silhouettes

Silhouette portraits were made by positioning the subject between a bright light and a sheet of white drawing paper. The resulting shadow was then traced and cut out, the paper mounted over a contrasting color and framed. The hollow-cut process was simplified by an invention called the physiognotrace, a device that allowed tracing and cutting to be done in one operation. Experienced silhouette artists could do full-length figures, scenics, ships, or trains freehand. Some of the most famous of these artists were Charles Peale Polk, Charles Wilson Peale, William Bache, Doyle, Edouart, Chamberlain, Brown, and William King. Though not often seen, some silhouettes were completely painted or executed in wax. Examples listed here are hollow-cut unless another type is described and assumed to be in excellent condition unless noted otherwise.

Key:
bk — backing	p — profile
c/p — cut and pasted	wc — watercolor
fl — full length	

Family, fl, 5 people, giltwood fr, 12x19" **750.00**
Lady, fl, ink bodice & dress, fr, 7x6" **275.00**
Lady, fl, well-detailed dress, fr, 5¼x4½" **360.00**
Lady, p, c/p, gold details, fr, 5½x4½" **225.00**
Lady in chair, c/p, pen & ink label, Edouart, fr, 10x8¼" **225.00**
Lady w/ornate hairdo, p, pen/ink/wc, rpr tear, fr, 8x6" **250.00**
Man, p, c/p, blk lacquer fr w/gilt, 5x4¼" **415.00**
Man, p, in worn bl & wht paper fr, 5½x4¼" **195.00**
Man, p, ink & ink wash on paper, John Wass, fr, 6x5" **165.00**
Man, p, pencil/ink/wc, fr, 5⅜x4½" **200.00**
Man (& lady), p, wc clothing, identified, 3¾x2¾", pr **545.00**
Man & lady, p, identified, 1804, fr, 6x5", pr **125.00**
Man w/top hat & long coat, fl, c/p, pnt details, fr, 17x12" **225.00**
Youth, p, ink on paper, fr w/gold, 6½x6" **245.00**

Silver

Coin Silver

During colonial times in America, the average household could not afford items made of silver, but those fortunate enough to have accumulations of silver coins (900 parts silver/100 parts alloy) took them to the local silversmith who melted them down and made the desired household article requested. These pieces bore the owner's monogram and often the maker's mark, but the words 'Coin Silver' did not come into use until 1830. By 1860 the standard was raised to 925 parts silver/75 parts alloy and the word 'Sterling' was added. Our advisor for Coin Silver is Betty Bird; she is listed in the Directory under California.

Key:
gw — gold washed	t-oz — troy ounce

AC Benedict, NY; ladle, scalloped oval/beaded hdl, 1833-39, 12" ..**220.00**
Blynn & Baldwin, julep cup, eng OH State...Premium, 1850, 4" .**440.00**
Charters, Cann & Dunn, NY; tea set, chased trim, 1850, 4-pc .**1,300.00**
D Kinsey & Co, tablespoon, rattail hdl, 1850-60, 8" **45.00**
E Kinsey, Cincinnati; ladle, eng monogram, 8" **225.00**
EM Eoff, NY; tray, ftd, foliate hdls, eng floral/scrolls, 26" **2,300.00**
FM (Frederick Marquand), soup ladle, 1799-1882, 7-t-oz **375.00**
Gorham, RI; tazza, fluted at center, swing basket hdl, 9" **690.00**
Gorham, RI; tea/coffee, emb scrolls/flowers, 1865, 4-pc **1,840.00**
Gorham, RI; tray, ftd, oval, 9", 10-t-oz **460.00**
Gorham, RI; water pitcher, inscribed, minor dents, 11" **865.00**
Hayden & Whieldon, butter knife, Oriental, 1803-55, 7⅛" **40.00**
Hildeburn & Bros...Phila; julep cup, dents, 3⅜" **220.00**
HL Bean, teaspoon **20.00**

J Curry, Phila; presentation cup, emb fruit band, 1831-50, 7" 990.00
J&I Cox, NY; tongs, shell jaws, 1831-33, 6¾" 95.00
JB Jones, Boston; spoon, shell/scroll, monogram, set of 12 ....250.00
JG Joseph, Cincinnati; spoon, 9", EX, 4 for 375.00
John McMullin, Phila, creamer, ca 1800, 6½" 315.00
Lincoln & Reed, Boston; cream pitcher, 1830s, 8½", 21-t-oz 525.00
PL Krider, PA; ewer, eng cartouch/foliage, baluster, 1850, 10" ...285.00
T&S, soup ladle, Sheaf of Wheat 750.00
Tompkins & Black, punch ladle, Tuskin, 20" 395.00
Unmk, teaspoon, rattail hdl, 5¾", 4 for 200.00
Unmk (MA), porringer, cast hdl, 5¼" 600.00
W Gale & Son, coffeepot, eng floral bands/beading, 13" 865.00
W Gale & Son, NY; creamer & sugar bowl, appl vintage, 1858 .800.00
W Miller, spoon, 1810, 9" 35.00
WT Stark, spoon, 9" 25.00

Flatware

Silver flatware is being collected today either to replace missing pieces of heirloom sets or in lieu of buying new patterns, by those who admire and appreciate the style and quality of the older ware. Prices vary from dealer to dealer; some pieces are harder to find and are therefore more expensive. Items such as olive spoons, cream ladles, lemon forks, etc., once thought a necessary part of a silver service, may today be slow to sell; as a result, dealers may price them low and make up the difference on items that sell more readily. Many factors enter into evaluation. Popular patterns may be high due to demand though easily found, while scarce patterns may be passed over by collectors who find them difficult to reassemble. If pieces are monogrammed, deduct 25% (rare, ornate patterns) to 35% (common, plain pieces). Our advisor for this category is Rick Spencer; he is listed in the Directory under Utah. (See also Tiffany, Silver.)

Acanthus, bouillon, Jensen 45.00
Acanthus, caviar knife, Jensen 85.00
Acanthus, knife, Jensen, 9" 70.00
Acorn, bonbon spoon, Jensen 95.00
Acorn, cocktail fork, Jensen 60.00
Acorn, cold-cut fork, Jensen 75.00
Acorn, dinner knife, Jensen 85.00
Acorn, fish fork, Jensen 85.00
Acorn, iced-tea spoon, Jensen 75.00
Acorn, lemon fork, Jensen 75.00
Avalon, chocolate muddler, International, 1990 ....75.00
Avalon, cold-meat fork, International, 1900 ....75.00
Avalon, sugar tongs, International, 1900 ....47.50
Beaded, cream soup spoon, Jensen 75.00
Beaded, knife, Jensen, 9" 65.00
Beaded, soup spoon, oval, Jensen 75.00
Bridal Rose, berry spoon, Alvin, lg 275.00
Bridal Rose, fish slice, Alvin 495.00
Bridal Rose, sugar spoon, Alvin 95.00
Brocade, butter spreader, International, 1950 ....20.00
Brocade, fork, International, 1950, 7¼" 20.00
Buttercup, cheese scoop, Gorham, 1899 ....125.00
Buttercup, fork, Gorham, 1899, 7" 25.00
Buttercup, iced-tea spoon, Gorham, 1899 ....25.00
Buttercup, luncheon fork, Gorham, 1899 ....25.00
Buttercup, rnd soup spoon, Gorham, 1899 ....30.00
Buttercup, sugar tongs, Gorham, 1899 ....60.00
Cactus, bouillon spoon, Jensen 50.00
Cactus, citrus spoon, Jensen 65.00
Cactus, dinner fork, Jensen, 7⅝" 110.00
Chantilly, bonbon, Gorham, 1895 ....40.00

Chantilly, butter spreader, Gorham, 1895 ....20.00
Chantilly, ice-cream fork, Gorham, 1895 ....35.00
Chantilly, master butter spreader, Gorham, 1895 ....75.00
Chantilly, meat fork, Gorham, 1895 ....95.00
Chantilly, salad fork, Gorham, 1895, 5¾" 25.00
Chantilly, soup ladle, Gorham, 1895 ....300.00
Charles II, berry spoon, Dominick & Haff, lg 250.00
Charles II, butter pick, Dominick & Haff 100.00
Chrysanthemum, berry spoon, Durgin, lg 250.00
Chrysanthemum, gravy ladle, Durgin 225.00
Chrysanthemum, ice-cream knife, Durgin 575.00
Chrysanthemum, seafood fork, Durgin 35.00
Courtship, butter spreader, International, 1936 ....15.00
Dresden, asparagus server, Whiting 275.00
Dresden, berry spoon, Whiting 95.00
Dresden, iced-tea spoon, Whiting 325.00
Dresden, sugar shell, Whiting 50.00
Eloquence, asparagus server, Lunt 135.00
Eloquence, dinner knife, Lunt 35.00
Eloquence, pie server, Lunt 125.00
Eloquence, teaspoon, Lunt 14.00
Fairfax, fork, Gorham, 1910, 7¾" 25.00
Fontaine, master butter spreader, International 30.00
Fontana, iced-tea spoon, Towle, 1957 ....20.00
Fontana, 4-pc place setting, Towle, 1957 ....105.00
French Provincial, lemon fork, Towle, 1949 ....13.00
French Provincial, teaspoon, Towle, 1949 ....12.00
Frontenac, citrus spoon, International 50.00
Frontenac, cold-meat fork, International 105.00
Frontenac, lettuce fork, International 150.00
Frontenac, olive spoon, International 100.00
Frontenac, pastry tongs, International 350.00
Frontenac, sauce ladle, International 55.00
Frontenac, tablespoon, International 52.00
Georgian, bonbon, Towle, 1898 ....95.00
Georgian, bouillon spoon, Towle, 1898 ....30.00
Georgian, luncheon fork, Towle, 1898 ....45.00
Georgian, luncheon knife, Towle, 1898 ....40.00
Georgian, tablespoon, Towle, 1898 ....75.00
Georgian, teaspoon, Towle, 1898 ....25.00
Grand Colonial, cream soup spoon, Wallace 18.00
Grand Colonial, luncheon fork, Wallace 20.00
Grande Baroque, butter spreader, Wallace, 1941 ....24.00
Grande Baroque, citrus spoon, Wallace, 1941 ....30.00
Grande Baroque, demitasse spoon, Wallace, 1941 ....20.00
Grande Baroque, master butter spreader, Wallace, 1941 ....28.00
Grande Baroque, pie/cake server, Wallace, 1941 ....35.00
Grande Baroque, salad-serving fork, Wallace, 1941 ....125.00
Grande Baroque, sugar shell, Wallace, 1941 ....30.00
Grande Baroque, tablespoon, Wallace, 1941 ....65.00
Irving, chocolate spoon, Wallace 35.00
Irving, long pickle fork, Wallace 32.00
Irving, luncheon fork, Wallace 20.00
Joan of Arc, bonbon, International 28.00
Joan of Arc, buffet fork, International, 8⅞" 65.00
Joan of Arc, dessert spoon, International 28.00
Joan of Arc, dinner knife, International 28.00
Joan of Arc, infant spoon, International 22.00
Joan of Arc, pastry fork, International 20.00
Joan of Arc, sauce ladle, International 30.00
Joan of Arc, tomato server, International 60.00
Jonquil, olive spoon, Unger 95.00
Jonquil, pickle fork, Unger 95.00
King Richard, gravy ladle, Towle, 1932 ....65.00

King Richard, teaspoon, Towle, 1932 ....15.00
Lancaster, beef fork, Gorham 65.00
Lancaster, cheese scoop, Gorham 150.00
Lancaster, lettuce fork, Gorham 75.00
Lancaster, slotted vegetable spoon, Gorham 275.00
Lily, bonbon, Whiting, 1902 ....110.00
Lily, bouillon spoon, Whiting, 1902 ....40.00
Lily, gravy ladle, Whiting, 1902 ....225.00
Lily, master butter spreader, Whiting, 1902 ....100.00
Lily, poultry shears, Whiting, 1902 ....275.00
Lily, preserve spoon, Whiting, 1902, 6⅛" 135.00
Lily, sardine fork, Whiting, 1902 ....150.00
Louis XV, bonbon, Whiting, 1891 ....35.00
Louis XV, chocolate spoon, Whiting, 1891 ....22.00
Louis XV, dinner fork, Whiting, 1891 ....40.00
Louis XV, ice-cream spoon, Whiting, 1891 ....35.00
Louis XV, punch ladle, Whiting, 1891 ....400.00
Louis XV, sardine fork, Whiting, 1891 ....48.00
Louis XV, sauce ladle, Whiting, 1891 ....28.00
Louis XV, stuffing spoon, Whiting, 1891 ....275.00
Louis XV, sugar tongs, Whiting, 1891 ....65.00
Louis XV, tablespoon, Whiting, 1891 ....40.00
Lyric, cream soup spoon, Gorham, 1940 ....20.00
Lyric, master butter spreader, Gorham, 1940 ....19.00
Mazarin, dinner fork, Dominick & Haff 40.00
Mazarin, luncheon fork, Dominick & Haff 30.00
Mazarin, sugar tongs, Dominick & Haff 95.00
Meadow Rose, jelly server, Wallace 28.00
Meadow Rose, steak-carving fork, Wallace 22.00
Meadow Rose, sugar spoon, Wallace 28.00
Meadow Rose, teaspoon, Wallace 12.00
Mt Vernon, fork, Lunt, 1905, 7¼" 18.00
Mt Vernon, ice-cream fork, Lunt, 1905 ....30.00
Mt Vernon, sugar tongs, Lunt, 1905 ....35.00
Mt Vernon, teaspoon, Lunt, 1905 ....10.00
Orange Blossom, demitasse spoon, Alvin 25.00
Orange Blossom, tablespoon, Alvin 65.00
Orange Blossom, teaspoon, Alvin 32.00
Prelude, baby fork, International, 1939 ....15.00
Prelude, bonbon, International, 1939 ....30.00
Prelude, coffee spoon, International, 1939 ....16.00
Prelude, tablespoon, International, 1939 ....38.00
Pyramid, cream ladle, Jensen 155.00
Pyramid, oval soup spoon, Jensen 95.00
Repousse, cream ladle, Kirk 45.00
Repousse, iced-tea spoon, Kirk 30.00
Repousse, pickle fork, Kirk 28.00
Repousse, pie server, Kirk 250.00
Richelieu, citrus spoon, International 35.00
Richelieu, cold-meat fork, International 75.00
Richelieu, dessert spoon, International 35.00
Rose, berry spoon, Stieff 150.00
Rose, bonbon, Stieff 75.00
Rose, cold-meat fork, Stieff, 7½" 48.00
Rose, dinner knife, Stieff 30.00
Rose, lemon fork, Stieff 22.00
Rose, lettuce fork, Stieff 95.00
Rose, master butter spreader, Stieff 30.00
Rose, olive spoon, Stieff 55.00
Rose, pickle fork, Stieff 20.00
Rose, preserve spoon, Stieff, 8¼" 55.00
Rose, salad fork, Stieff 25.00
Rose, tablespoon, pierced, Stieff 55.00
Rose Point, berry spoon, Wallace 100.00

Rose Point, cocktail fork, Wallace 16.00
Rose Point, dinner knife, Wallace 26.00
Rose Point, iced-tea spoon, Wallace 26.00
Rose Point, master butter spreader, Wallace 30.00
Rose Point, tomato server, Wallace 68.00
Royal Danish, cream soup spoon, International 30.00
Royal Danish, dessert spoon, International 30.00
Royal Danish, luncheon fork, International 20.00
Royal Danish, pie/cake server, International 35.00
Royal Danish, steak-carving set, International 65.00
Royal Danish, sugar spoon, International 18.00
Sea Rose, fork, Gorham, 1958, 7⅜" 21.00
Sea Rose, tablespoon, Gorham, 1958 ....40.00

Sir Christopher, partial flatware service, Wallace, approximately 35 troy ounces of weighable silver, $600.00.

Sir Christopher, butter spreader, Wallace, 1936 ....18.00
Sir Christopher, cheese cleaver, Wallace, 1936 ....25.00
Sir Christopher, dinner knife, Wallace, 1936 ....35.00
Sir Christopher, ice-cream fork, Wallace, 1936 ....24.00
Sir Christopher, lemon fork, Wallace, 1936 ....30.00
Sir Christopher, sugar spoon, Wallace, 1936 ....30.00
Sir Christopher, teaspoon, Wallace, 1936 ....13.00
Strasbourg, cream ladle, Gorham 65.00
Strasbourg, jelly server, Gorham 50.00
Strasbourg, luncheon knife, Gorham 25.00
Strasbourg, meat fork, Gorham 95.00
Strasbourg, punch ladle, solid, Gorham 175.00
Strasbourg, sugar tongs, Gorham 65.00
Versailles, bouillon, Gorham, 1888 ....40.00
Versailles, gravy ladle, Gorham, 1888 ....125.00
Versailles, ice-cream fork, Gorham, 1888 ....50.00
Versailles, meat fork, Gorham, 1888 ....150.00
Versailles, pie server, Gorham, 1888 ....300.00
Violet, chocolate spoon, Wallace 35.00
Violet, iced-tea spoon, Wallace 35.00
Violet, salad fork, Wallace 35.00
Violet, salad-serving fork, Wallace 125.00
Wedgwood, bouillon, International 22.00
Wedgwood, cake server, International 35.00
Wedgwood, ice-cream fork, International 28.00
Wedgwood, master butter spreader, International 25.00
Wild Rose, bonbon, International 28.00
Wild Rose, cold-meat fork, International 50.00
Wild Rose, cream soup spoon, International 22.00
Wild Rose, luncheon knife, International 25.00
Wild Rose, salad fork, International 25.00
William & Mary, cream ladle, Lunt 22.00
William & Mary, olive spoon, Lunt 22.00

William & Mary, tablespoon, Lunt **32.00**

Hollow Ware

Until the middle of the 19th century, the silverware produced in America was custom made on order of the buyer directly from the silversmith. With the rise of industrialization, factories sprung up that manufactured silverware for retailers who often added their trademark to the ware. Silver ore was mined in abundance, and demand spurred production. Changes in style occurred at the whim of fashion. Repousse decoration (relief work) became popular about 1885, reflecting the ostentatious preference of the Victorian era. Later in the century, Greek, Etruscan, and several classic styles found favor. Today the Art Deco styles of this century are very popular with collectors.

In the listings that follow, manufacturer's name or trademark is noted first; in lieu of that information, listings are by country. Weight is given in troy ounces. See also Tiffany, Silver.

A Stone, bowl, hammered/emb long-stem rose repeats, 10" **2,400.00**
A Stone, gravy boat w/undertray, helmet form, monogram **825.00**
A Stone, sauce boat, repousse floral, 7" L **1,150.00**
Allan Alder, salad bowl, hdl is rim extension, 12" **800.00**
Allan Alder, serving dish, shallow/oval, 10", pr **920.00**
Austrian, 800 standard; sugar box, eng scrolls, 4 scroll ft **800.00**
B Starr, loving cup, ornate leaf-mold C hdls, 9¼" **1,450.00**
Bailey, Banks & Biddle; candy compote, rtcl floral borders **140.00**
Bailey, Banks & Biddle; fruit stand, rtcl/octagonal, 12" **400.00**
Bucellati, hot milk jug, spiral fluted, 3-leg base, 5" **460.00**
Bucellati, hot water urn on lampstand, spiral fluting, 16" **2,500.00**
Chinese Export (CJ Co), vase, basket form, rtcl/eng mums, 16" .**1,150.00**
Churchill-Treadwell, sugar urn, 1800s, 11", 16-t-oz **835.00**
Continental, box, emb busts of Napoleon I/Marie Louise, 12" **2,300.00**
Continental, candelabrum bases, appl lion masks, 1800s, 11", pr ..**1,380.00**
Continental, dessert plate, hand-chased berries, 1880s, 8½" **75.00**
Continental, dish, figures in classical borders, 8½" **290.00**
Continental, pitcher, emb shell/floral bands, lyre hdl, 13" **725.00**
Continental, roll tray, rtcl urn/floral motifs, 19th C, 14" **500.00**
Continental, 13 standard; beaker, lion ft, rtcl, ornate, 14" **2,000.00**
Continental, 833 standard; biscuit box, bright cut, 1809, 3" ...**1,150.00**
D Dupuy, creamer, bright cut, scroll hdl, rpr, 5½" **1,495.00**
D Dupuy, Phila; cream jug, 1800, rpr, 7", 5-t-oz **1,150.00**
Danish, vinaigrette, heart form, crown on lid, 3¼" **230.00**
Dominick & Haff, butter dish, floral-emb crown lid, w/liner ...**1,150.00**
Dominick & Haff, water pitcher, fluted lower body, 1884, 8" **750.00**

Edward Barnard & Sons, Ltd., London, wine cooler, 1901-02, 29 troy oz., 7¾", $1,200.00.

EJ Greenberg, tea set, paw ft, gadroon/shell rim, 4-pc **1,600.00**
Ferd-Fuchs & Bros, plate, hexagonal, 13" **465.00**
Garreau, cruet stand, paw ft, emb Grecian figures, 1820, 12" ..**1,100.00**
Geo Jensen, dish, Blossom, 4 openwork areas on rim, #28, 6" **700.00**
Geo Jensen, master nut stand, leaf-molded octagonal base **625.00**
Geo Jensen, pitcher, Grapevine, #407A, 9x5" **3,700.00**

Geo Jensen, tray, Blossom, openwork hdls, #SP, 10" dia **1,100.00**
Geo Jensen, tureen, floral finial, wood hdls, Neilsen, 11" **2,600.00**
German, 800 standard; creamer, bust of Napoleon form, 3" **750.00**
German, 800 standard; tea/coffee+tray, emb putti etc, 4-pc **4,000.00**
Gorham, bowl, emb bars & floral swags, 2¼x10" **175.00**
Gorham, candlesticks, panels of shells/scrolls, 1913, 12", pr **2,000.00**
Gorham, center bowl, ribbed, ftd, 3½x12" **275.00**
Gorham, compote, scroll border, 6x11½" **400.00**
Gorham, fruit stand, scalloped, reeded border, 13¼" L **385.00**
Gorham, goblet, wine; blossom form, 5½", 32-t-oz, 8 for **600.00**
Gorham, tea set, invt pear w/eng scrolls, 5-pc, 89-t-oz **1,700.00**
Gorham, vegetable dish, C-scroll floral-emb rim, 1905, 10" L ...**175.00**
Grimminger, tea/coffee, ovoid w/wood finials/hdls, 5-pc **1,495.00**
Hamilton-Inches, punch bowl, inscribed, Bacchus masks, 16" ..**2,585.00**
Harleux, cruet stand, rtcl rim, scroll supports, 1850, 12" **575.00**
Hester Bateman, tea caddy, fluted/str sides w/ivory finial **2,185.00**
Hester Bateman, teapot, fluted/str sided, ivory finial, rpr **1,100.00**
Hodgson-Kennard, compote, scalloped, ribbed ft, 15-t-oz **200.00**
Howard & Co, fruit stands, rtcl scroll/shell border, 11½", pr **475.00**
Howard & Co, tray, quatrelobed, vintage border/ft, 15" **800.00**
International, coffeepot, Prelude **475.00**
International, vase, Orchid, 11" **525.00**
J Bridge, mustard pot, Geo IV, half-gadrooned, floral band **400.00**
J Chartier, att; saucepan, Queen Anne, 1702, mini **385.00**
J Craig, sauce tureen, Geo III, hoof ft, emb scrolls, 5x11" **2,500.00**
J Edwards, teapot stand, thread-mold border, 1795, 7" L **400.00**
J Lawrence, vinaigrette, eng floral, Burmingham, 1822 ....**180.00**
J Parker-E Wakeling, salver, 3 shell/claw ft, 1770, 10" **850.00**
J Priest, candlesticks, floral decor, 1752, 10", set of 4 ....**7,100.00**
Jacobi-Jenkins, soup tureen, allover repousse, w/lid, 11" H **2,800.00**
JE Caldwell, roll tray, plain w/shell hdls, 12" **140.00**
Joseph Angell Sr & Jr, ftd salver, bead/shell rim, 12" **100.00**
Joseph Jr-Nathaniel Richardson, sugar urn, 8½", 8-t-oz **1,495.00**
JR Armiger, water pitcher, allover repousse, 8½" **1,600.00**
Kalo, bowl, oval w/4-petal wide rim, monogram, 9-t-oz **315.00**
Kalo, bowl, 5-lobe rim, monogram, 9½" **750.00**
Kalo, chamberstick, hammered, 6-t-oz **635.00**
Kalo, child's cup, hammered, emb rabbit, 3" **425.00**
Kalo, pipkin, hammered, cvd hardwood hdl, #121, 8-t-oz **690.00**
Kalo, stamp box, hammered w/bead band, wood knob, 2½" dia .**650.00**
Kalo, tray, hammered, 3-lobe ends, 5½x14" L **500.00**
Kalo, vase, hammered, 4-lobe, incurvate, 3½" **475.00**
Kirk & Sons, bowl, emb fruit & flowers, stippled rays, 9" **600.00**
Kirk & Sons, candelabra, 5-light, repousse, 14", pr **1,500.00**
Kirk & Sons, porringer, emb florals, rtcl/eng hdl, 1850 ....**575.00**
Kirk & Sons, tea/coffee, chased bands, masks on hdls, 6-pc ..**10,350.00**
L Maciel, service plate, shaped flower/foliage-chased rim, 11" **280.00**
LA Crichton, cake basket, shell form, 3 dolphin ft, 10x14" **6,000.00**
LeBolt, candlesticks, hammered, wide base, 8x5", pr **1,300.00**
LeBolt, compote, hammered w/5 lobes, flaring base, mk, 6" **425.00**
London hallmks for 1801-02, teapot, eng birds, 13-t-oz **715.00**
London hallmks for 1807-09, creamer w/ball ft, 4.3-t-oz **220.00**
Los Castillo, silent butler, hammered, orchid finial, 4-ftd **575.00**
M Linwood, vinaigrette, moss agate lid inset, 1¼" **500.00**
Maciel, tea/coffee+tray, scroll borders, stepped lids, 4-pc **1,100.00**
Mapin-Webb, salver, Geo II, shell/mask border, hoof ft, 20" ...**1,450.00**
Moulton Family, MA, porringer, 1880, 5½", 8-t-oz, EX **1,365.00**
Odiot, teapot, floral cartouch, ped ft, 1850s, 7" **750.00**
Old Newbury Crafters, bowl, faceted floral form, hammered, 11" ...**430.00**
Pairpoint, tray, cast angular hdls, eng floral, 19th C, 25" **350.00**
Persian, box, rtcl lid w/thistles & leaves, oval, 6½" **475.00**
Petterson Studio, bowl, hammered, 2x6" **225.00**
R Hennel, can, emb florals/scrolls, pear shape, 1870, 5" **575.00**
R Sawyer, creamer, emb 'horns,' bright-cut band, 1806, 4¾" **300.00**

R&D Hennell, coffeepot, Geo III, bright cut, rpr, 12" 920.00
R&W Wilson, butter dish, cow finials, emb scenes, 7", pr 2,800.00
R&W Wilson, sugar stand, octagonal w/beaded edge, urn finial 500.00
Reid & Sons, salver, Chpndl style, Geo V, molded border, 16" ...1,150.00
Richard Comyns, castor, plain baluster, Geo II taste, 8", pr 575.00
Rogers, tea set, floral garlands/finials, 2 pots, cr/sug 850.00
Roggatz, sugar chest, vintage legs, dolphin finial, 5x6" 635.00
Shreve & Co, candlesticks, slim baluster, 13½", pr 1,800.00
Shreve & Co, tea/coffee, urn form, peaked lids, 11" pot, 5-pc 690.00
Shreve-Crump-Low, punch ladle, 7.5-t-oz 195.00
Spanish, platter, oval w/emb rim, 1800s, 10" 690.00
Towle, tray, Seville, 20x15" 500.00
V Juarez, fruit bowl, scalloped, 3 ball ft, 1958, 10" 190.00
Wallace, tea service, Washington, 5-pc, 68-t-oz 1,200.00
Whiting, cream & sugar, gw liners, 2¾" 150.00
Whiting, pitcher, emb/eng florals, helmet shape, 10" 485.00
Wilkinson, Henry & Co; coaster, rtcl border, eng crest 1,000.00
Wm B Kerr, plate, ethnically diverse children, 1927, 6½" 115.00
Wm Shaw, can, emb florals/leaves, ftd pear shape, 1765, 5" 575.00
Wortz-Voorhis, service plate, scroll/flower bud rim, 11" 230.00

Silver Lustre Ware

Much of the ware known as silver lustre was produced in the 1800s in Staffordshire, England. This type of earthenware was entirely covered with the metallic silver glaze. It was most popular prior to 1840 when the technique of electroplating was developed and silverplated wares came into vogue. Later in the century, artisans used silver lustre to develop designs on vases and other decorative ware.

The process for decorating pottery with the silver-resist method involved first coating the design or that portion of the pattern that was to be left unsilvered with a water-soluble solution. The lustre was applied to the entire surface of the vessel and allowed to dry. Before the final firing, the surface was washed, removing only the silver from the coated areas. This type of ware was produced early in the 1800s by many English potteries, Wedgwood included.

Creamer, Loop Rib base, gadroon top border, 4x5" 80.00
Jug, sporting; bl transfer, ca 1815, 6¼", EX 450.00
Jug, sporting; bl transfer w/mc, ca 1815, 5½", EX 600.00
Pitcher, Cossack Battle Scene in bl, rstr, 5" 165.00
Pitcher, floral/dog/bird on pearlware, 6", VG 100.00
Pitcher, mc florals, ca 1815, 8⅜", M 1,250.00
Pitcher, Oriental courtyard scenes, ca 1815, 6¾" 350.00
Pitcher, 3 emb/silver zigzag bands, red striping, 5", EX 65.00
Shaker, Toby figural, minor wear, 5" 95.00
Teapot, bird-head terminal hdl, ribbed bottom, 6x10" 250.00
Vase, grapevines, urn form w/sq ft, ca 1815, 13", EX 950.00

Silver Overlay

The silver overlay glass made during the 1800s was decorated with a cut-out pattern of sterling silver applied to the surface of the ware.

Bottles with similar scrolling overlay designs: Teal green, 2½", $250.00; Ruby, 3¼", $275.00.

Bottle, clear w/floral/foliage o/l, 1900s, +stopper, 12" 175.00
Bottle, scent; emerald gr w/heavy swirling o/l, 4" 325.00
Bottle, scent; gr, ornate o/l, bulbous, 5" 265.00
Bowl, banana; floral/scrolls o/l, scalloped/ftd, 12½" L 80.00
Decanter, perfume; clear, leaf/scroll o/l, monogram, 7", pr 175.00
Loving cup, rainbow satin, o/l apple blossoms & hdls, 4" 1,550.00
Pitcher, clear, geometric o/l, faceted stopper, 5½" 150.00
Vase, cranberry, scrolls o/l, fluted rim, 4½" 275.00
Vase, red-amber cased to opal wht, much floral o/l, 10" 800.00

Silverplate

Silverplated hollow ware is fast becoming the focus of attention for many of today's collectors. Pricing is based on pieces in excellent condition. Serving pieces are priced to reflect the value of examples in complete original condition; knives must retain their original blades. If pieces are monogrammed, deduct 25% (rare, ornate patterns) to 35% (common, plain pieces). Our advisor for this category is Rick Spencer; he is listed in the Directory under Utah. See also Railroadiana, Silverplate.

Key:
gw — gold wash   hh — hollow handle

Flatware

Arbutus, 1908, Wm Rogers, fruit spoon 8.00
Arbutus, 1908, Wm Rogers, sauce ladle 15.00
Arbutus, 1908, Wm Rogers, soup ladle 65.00
Arbutus, 1908, Wm Rogers, strawberry fork 18.00
Berkshire, 1897, beef fork 17.00
Berkshire, 1897, bouillon spoon 16.00
Berkshire, 1897, cocktail fork 12.00
Berkshire, 1897, dinner knife, hh 27.00
Berkshire, 1897, ice-cream spoon 25.00
Berkshire, 1897, jelly knife 25.00
Berkshire, 1897, teaspoon 7.00
Berwick, 1904, baby-food pusher 38.00
Berwick, 1904, dinner knife, hh 32.00
Berwick, 1904, soup spoon, oval 18.00
Berwick, 1904, strawberry fork 35.00
Berwick, 1904, sugar tongs 36.00
Berwick, 1904, teaspoon 10.00
Blenheim, preserve spoon 12.00
Blenheim, salad fork 6.00
Bride, 1909, Holmes & Edwards, soup spoon, rnd 12.00
Bride's Bouquet, Alvin, bouillon soup 40.00
Bride's Bouquet, Alvin, cream ladle 26.00
Bride's Bouquet, Alvin, ice cream fork 38.00
Bride's Bouquet, Alvin, soup spoon, oval 12.00
Bride's Bouquet, Alvin, sugar tongs 40.00
Carlton, 1898, cocktail fork 6.00
Carlton, 1898, punch ladle, solid hdl 95.00
Carnation, Wm Rogers, fruit spoon 18.00
Carnation, Wm Rogers, iced-tea spoon 25.00
Charter Oak, 1906, 1847 Rogers, bottle opener, hh 150.00
Charter Oak, 1906, 1847 Rogers, cheese knife, hh 150.00
Charter Oak, 1906, 1847 Rogers, cocktail fork 22.00
Charter Oak, 1906, 1847 Rogers, ind butter spreader 22.00
Charter Oak, 1906, 1847 Rogers, pie/ice-cream slice, hh 70.00
Charter Oak, 1906, 1847 Rogers, salad fork, 5¾" 40.00
Charter Oak, 1906, 1847 Rogers, soup spoon, rnd 26.00
Columbia, 1892, 1847 Rogers, cocktail fork 16.00

Columbia, 1892, 1847 Rogers, fruit spoon 15.00
Columbia, 1892, 1847 Rogers, lettuce spoon, lg 80.00
Columbia, 1892, 1847 Rogers, luncheon fork 12.00
Columbia, 1892, 1847 Rogers, luncheon knife, hh 25.00
Columbia, 1892, 1847 Rogers, oyster ladle 70.00
Columbia, 1892, 1847 Rogers, salad-serving set 150.00
Floral, 1902, Wallace, pickle fork 35.00
Floral, 1902, Wallace, salad fork 28.00
Floral, 1902, Wallace, soup spoon, rnd 20.00
Floral, 1902, Wallace, strawberry fork 45.00
Florette, 1909, butter knife, twisted 12.00
Florette, 1909, dinner fork 7.00
Florette, 1909, olive server, long hdl 28.00
Flower de Luce, 1904, demitasse spoon, gw 12.00
Flower de Luce, 1904, fruit knife, hh 20.00
Flower de Luce, 1904, pickle fork, long hdl 20.00
Glenrose, Wm A Rogers, dinner knife, hh 27.00
Glenrose, Wm A Rogers, gravy ladle 28.00
Glenrose, Wm A Rogers, pickle fork, short hdl 24.00
Glenrose, Wm A Rogers, teaspoon 15.00
Gloria, Grenoble, bonbon tongs 35.00
Gloria, Grenoble, soup spoon, oval 15.00
Gloria, Grenoble, tablespoon 14.00
Gloria, Grenoble, teaspoon 10.00
Hanover, 1901, bouillon spoon 8.00
Hanover, 1901, fish-serving fork 55.00
Hanover, 1901, jelly slice 32.00
Hanover, 1901, pie fork 16.00
Hanover, 1901, soup ladle 80.00
Hanover, 1901, sugar tongs 25.00
Hanover, 1901, teaspoon 6.00
Holly, 1906, EEH Smith, dinner fork 25.00
Holly, 1906, EEH Smith, dinner knife, hh 55.00
Holly, 1906, EEH Smith, pickle fork, long hdl 500.00
Holly, 1906, EEH Smith, soup ladle, med 300.00
Holly, 1906, EEH Smith, teaspoon 25.00
La Concorde, 1910, Wm Rogers, butter knife, twisted ...15.00
La Concorde, 1910, Wm Rogers, demitasse spoon 9.00
La Concorde, 1910, Wm Rogers, strawberry fork 30.00
La Concorde, 1910, Wm Rogers, sugar spoon 8.00
La Vigne, 1908, dinner knife, hh, rare 90.00
La Vigne, 1908, iced-tea spoon 80.00
La Vigne, 1908, tablespoon 10.00
Modern Art, 1904, Reed & Barton, berry spoon 55.00
Modern Art, 1904, Reed & Barton, cold-meat fork 28.00
Modern Art, 1904, Reed & Barton, ice-cream fork 35.00
Modern Art, 1904, Reed & Barton, sugar tongs 30.00
Moselle, 1906, World Silver, cocktail fork 28.00
Moselle, 1906, World Silver, cream ladle 65.00
Moselle, 1906, World Silver, gravy ladle 80.00
Moselle, 1906, World Silver, mustard ladle 175.00
Moselle, 1906, World Silver, salad-serving set 300.00
Mystic, dinner fork, hh 12.00
Mystic, tomato server 38.00
Narcissus, Oxford, cold-meat fork 20.00
Narcissus, Oxford, dinner fork 10.00
Narcissus, Oxford, olive fork, short hdl 16.00
Narcissus, Oxford, sugar shell 8.00
Narcissus, Oxford, teaspoon 5.00
Orange Blossom, dinner knife, hh 38.00
Orange Blossom, fruit spoon 7.00
Orange Blossom, ice-cream fork 25.00
Orange Blossom, pastry server 38.00
Orange Blossom, salad fork 15.00

Orange Blossom, teaspoon 8.00
Pearl, 1898, Reed & Barton, fish server, eng blade 95.00
Raphael, 1896, cocktail fork 15.00
Raphael, 1896, cold-meat fork 40.00
Raphael, 1896, pastry fork 40.00
Raphael, 1896, pie/cake server 65.00
Sharon, 1910, 1847 Rogers, beef fork 13.00
Sharon, 1910, 1847 Rogers, preserve spoon 20.00
Sharon, 1910, 1847 Rogers, punch ladle, hh 140.00
Sharon, 1910, 1847 Rogers, salad fork 16.00
Siren, berry spoon 35.00
Siren, demitasse spoon 10.00
Siren, ice-cream slice 55.00
Thistle, 1905, EEH Smith, berry spoon 600.00
Thistle, 1905, EEH Smith, master butter spreader 20.00
Thistle, 1905, EEH Smith soup spoon, oval 16.00
Venice (Orient), 1904, beef fork 14.00
Venice (Orient), 1904, ice-cream spoon 15.00
Venice (Orient), 1904, iced-tea spoon 10.00
Venice (Orient), 1904, tablespoon 8.00
Vintage, 1904, 1847 Rogers, cake fork server 95.00
Vintage, 1904, 1847 Rogers, chocolate spoon 40.00
Vintage, 1904, 1847 Rogers, cream ladle 28.00
Vintage, 1904, 1847 Rogers, food pusher 60.00
Vintage, 1904, 1847 Rogers, fruit knife, hh 35.00
Vintage, 1904, 1847 Rogers, ice-cream fork 55.00
Vintage, 1904, 1847 Rogers, ind butter spreader 18.00
Vintage, 1904, 1847 Rogers, tomato server 145.00
Wildwood, 1908, Oneida, berry spoon 28.00
Wildwood, 1908, Oneida, cream ladle 22.00
Wildwood, 1908, Oneida, fruit spoon 6.00
Wildwood, 1908, Oneida, salad fork 14.00

Hollow Ware

Champagne bucket, appl ribbing, Gorham, 8" 200.00
Lobster server, lobster figural, ruffled rim, Wilcox, 8x5" ...150.00
Taper jacks, w/snuffer, 5", pr 185.00
Tea set, emb florals/etched ferns, pot/cr/sug/spooner, Tufts ...225.00
Tea/coffee, bulbous forms, 4 pcs on 19" tray, Christofle ...1,265.00
Teakettle, melon ribbed, fruit finial, 14" on stand 165.00
Tray, eng/rtcl foliage, appl border, hdls, 30" 350.00
Tray, Modern Art, 1904, Reed & Barton, 12" dia 80.00
Vegetable stand, shell corners, cast feet, 19th C, pr ...1,150.00
Venison cover, eng armorial, C-scroll foliate hdl, 18" L ...160.00
Wine cooler, campana form w/ornate shells & scrolls, 10½" ...575.00
Wine coolers, gadroon/shell edges, ornate hdls, pr ...1,500.00

Sheffield

Candelabra, 2-arm, baluster std, Boulton, 1800, 20", pr ...1,400.00
Candelabra, 2-arm, floral border, 20", pr 345.00
Candelabra, 3-arm, half-fluted stds, Boulton, 1810, 26", pr ...1,600.00
Candlesticks, reeded borders, wavy bands, ca 1790, 12", pr ...500.00
Candlesticks, reeded std/base, w/etched shades, 18", pr ...775.00
Coffeepot, plain baluster w/gadroon border, 1820, 9½", EX ...700.00
Hot water urn, crest/wreath, lion-mask hdls, bombe form, 17" ...650.00
Hot water urn, reeded lid/sides, sq ball-ftd base, 18" ...625.00
Mug, floral/scroll emb on ft, pear shape, Wm Shaw, 1765, 5" ...260.00
Plate, eng Earl's coronet, gadrooned border, RG/SG, 10" ...150.00
Platter, armorial, beaded edge, Walker-Knowles, 16x12" ...575.00
Platter, armorial eng, shell/floral border, dome lid, 21" ...1,000.00
Platter, well & tree; fancy cast/trn wood hdls, scroll ft, 24" ...525.00
Tea urn, Empire style, lion mask/ring hdls, on plinth, 17" ...400.00

Tray, eng crest, ivory bar hdls, 19th C, 17" 250.00
Tureen, soup; reeded hdls, scroll legs, Roberts-Cadman 1,000.00
Urn, crest, lion mask/loose ring hdls, ped base, 10", pr 1,000.00
Wine cooler, campana form, reeded bracket hdls, 1810, 10" 500.00
Wine coolers, half-gadrooned, female mask hdls, 9x9½", pr ...1,350.00
Wine coolers, scroll/shell band, crest, Fenton-Creswick, 9", pr .1,800.00

Slag Glass

Slag glass is a marbleized opaque glassware made by several companies from about 1870 until the turn of the century. It is usually found in purple or caramel (see Chocolate Glass), though other colors were also made. Pink is rare and very expensive. It was revived in recent years by several American glasshouses, L.E. Smith, Westmoreland, and Imperial among them.

Blue, basket, cherries/leaves in relief, crimped/ruffled, 9" 75.00
Blue, humidor, drum shape, cap-shaped finial, 6½x5¼" 250.00
Pink, Invt Fan & Feather, bowl, master berry 800.00
Pink, Invt Fan & Feather, butter dish, 7x7⅝" 1,300.00
Pink, Invt Fan & Feather, creamer 425.00
Pink, Invt Fan & Feather, cruet 1,400.00
Pink, Invt Fan & Feather, jelly compote, scalloped rim, 4½x5" ...550.00
Pink, Invt Fan & Feather, pitcher, 7½" 1,200.00
Pink, Invt Fan & Feather, punch cup 265.00
Pink, Invt Fan & Feather, sauce dish, ball ft, 2½x4½" 265.00
Pink, Invt Fan & Feather, sauce dish, shell ft, 2⅜x4" 600.00
Pink, Invt Fan & Feather, shakers, rare, pr 1,200.00
Pink, Invt Fan & Feather, spooner, 4¼" 425.00

Pink, Inverted Fan and Feather sugar bowl, with lid, 7¼", $900.00.

Pink, Invt Fan & Feather, toothpick holder 650.00
Pink, Invt Fan & Feather, tumbler, 4" 435.00
Purple, Beads & Bark, vase, novelty 50.00
Purple, candy dish, Indiana Glass, ftd 55.00
Purple, Flute, celery vase 85.00
Purple, Jenny Lind, compote, 7¾x8½" 165.00
Purple, oil lamp, emb spears, clear font, 13" 145.00
Purple, Oval Medallion, spooner 85.00
Purple, Panel & Waffle mold, compote, w/lid, 8x8' 80.00
Purple, Panel & Waffle mold, vase, ftd, scalloped, 8" 48.00
Purple, plate, lattice edge, 13" 85.00
Purple, Scroll w/Acanthus, creamer & sugar bowl 100.00
Purple, Scroll w/Acanthus, spooner 75.00
Purple, vase, paneled sides, 8" 90.00
Red, vase, mc/gold decor at top, 7" 60.00

Smith Bros.

Alfred and Harry Smith founded their glassmaking firm in New Bedford, Massachusetts. They had been formerly associated with the Mt. Washington Glass Works, working there from 1871 to 1875 to aid in establishing a decorating department. Smith glass is valued for its excellent enameled decoration on satin or opalescent glass. Pieces were often

marked with a lion in a red shield. Our advisors for this category are Betty and Clarence Maier; they are listed in the Directory under Pennsylvania.

Bowl, gold prunus, beaded rim, melon ribs, 2¾x6" 380.00
Bowl, lotus blossom/gilt on cream w/bl swirls, 3½x6" 425.00
Bowl, pansies, bl edge w/wht dots, melon ribs 2¼x4" 225.00
Cracker bbl, Art Nouveau girl in medallion 1,250.00
Cracker bbl, daisies/red traceries w/gold, glass lid, 8" 800.00
Cracker bbl, lotus/leaves on bl-marbled tan, melon ribs 800.00
Decanter, iris stalks, gold on ivory, faceted/squat body, 11" 600.00
Humidor, pansies on cream, melon-ribbed cover, 6½x4" 850.00
Rose bowl, asters on cream, 2¼x3" 285.00
Salt cellar, gold prunus on bl, beaded top 100.00
Shaker, lay-down egg, violets on tan, souvenir, 3" 300.00
Sweetmeat, pansies, melon ribs; metal rim/bail/cover, 2½x4" 350.00
Vase, daisies, dotted enamel rim, spherical, 4" 175.00
Vase, daisies on clear swirl mold, 7" 565.00
Vase, floral on bl, beaded top, melon ribs, 3¾x4" 225.00
Vase, pond lilies on pk, wine trim, 7" 195.00
Vase, wisteria, lav on shaded apricot, 3 dents to body, 4½" 375.00

Snow Babies

During the last quarter of the 19th century, snow babies — little figurals in white snowsuits — originated in Germany. They were made of sugar candy and were often used as decorations for Christmas cakes. Later on they were made of marzipan, a confection of crushed almonds, sugar, and egg whites. Eventually porcelain manufacturers began making them in bisque. They were popular until WWII. These tiny bisque figures range in size from 1" up to 7" tall. Quality German pieces bring very respectable prices on the market today. Beware of reproductions. Our advisor for this category is Linda Vines; she is listed in the Directory under New Jersey.

Babies, 1 pulling another on sled, Germany, 2" 165.00
Babies, 2 dancing the cha-cha, Germany, 2" 125.00
Baby hiding under snow ledge, snow bear on top, Germany, 2" ..175.00
Baby holding soccer ball on shoulder, Germany, 2" 125.00
Baby inside igloo, Santa on top, Germany, 2" 150.00
Baby inside igloo, Santa on top, Japan, 2" 50.00
Baby on red or silver airplane, Germany, 2" 125.00
Baby playing musical instrument, Germany, 2" 110.00
Baby riding snow bear, Germany, 2½" 150.00
Baby sitting, snow on hands & ft, Germany, early, 2" 150.00
Baby standing or sitting, Germany, 1" 40.00
Baby w/seal & red ball, Germany, 2" 125.00
Bear playing w/colorful ball, Germany, 1" 65.00
Child, no snow, pushing lg snowball, Germany, 2" 125.00
Child skater (girl or boy), snow on sweater & hat, Germany, 2" ..110.00
Children (2) walking down brick wall, Germany, 2½" 75.00
Penguins (3) walking down brick wall, Germany, 2½" 75.00
Pixies (2) sit on hobby horse, wood stick legs, Germany, 2" 125.00
Santa atop elephant, Germany, 2" 175.00
Santa driving yel car, toys in bk, Germany, 2" 125.00
Santa riding on snow bear, Germany, 2½" 175.00
Santa riding yel train, pixie in bk, Germany, 3" 150.00
Snow angel sits w/arms out, pk wings, loop in bk, Germany, 1½" ..200.00
Snow cat, dog or rabbit, Germany, 1", ea 60.00
Snowman sitting, red hat w/pompon, Germany, 1½" 75.00

Snuff Boxes

As early as the 17th century, the Chinese began using snuff. By the early 19th century, the practice had spread to Europe and America. It was used by both the gentlemen and the ladies alike, and expensive snuff boxes and bottles were the earmark of the genteel. Some were of silver or gold set with precious stones or pearls, while others contained music boxes. In the following listings, the dimension noted is length. See also Orientalia, Snuff Bottles.

14k yellow gold enameled with white roses on a black background, 1800s, 3" long, $1,000.00.

Horn w/eng flowers/couple/inscription, oval, 3" 165.00
MOP lid, tortoise sides, silver base, oval, 1780s, 3½" 400.00
Musical, blk lacquer w/shepherd boy, 1¼x4¾", VG 345.00
Neillo on 800 silver w/strapwork on lid, 'wicker' sides, 3" 315.00
Porc, HP couples dancing at ball on red, Continental, 3½" 450.00
Silver, chased decor w/ornaments & soldier's head, German, 3" ..195.00
Silver, chased sides, cut corners, Czech, ca 1820s, 3½" 175.00
Silver-mtd tortoise shell & compo w/inset portrait, 3" 345.00
Sterling, incised design, NM London, 1813, ¾x1¾x3" 235.00
Whale's tooth, cvd Georgian lovers/monks/lady bathers, 6½" ..1,900.00

Soap Hollow Furniture

In the Mennonite community of Soap Hollow, Pennsylvania, the women made and sold soap; the men made handcrafted furniture. Rare today, these pieces were stenciled, grain painted, and beautifully decorated with inlaid escutcheons. These pieces are becoming very sought after. When well kept, they are very distinctive and beautiful. The items described in these listings were recently sold through Merle S. Mishlers Auctions, RD 2, Hollsopple, Pennsylvania. All are in excellent condition unless otherwise noted. Our advisors for this category represent DLK Nostalgia and Collectibles; they are listed in the Directory under Pennsylvania.

Chest, blanket; feathers on mustard & brn, MB/1897, EX 1,100.00
Chest, blanket; grpt w/blk lid, fruit/florals w/gold, 1882 ....2,900.00
Chest, blanket; maroon w/gold stencil, rnd escutcheon, 1856 .2,000.00
Chest, blanket; rose decals, blk & brn graining, LK/1890, EX .5,000.00
Chest, 4 lg/2 sm drws w/decor, enamel pulls, sgn, 1851, EX+ ..4,600.00
Chest, 4 lg/3 sm drws, stencil, enamel pulls, sgn, 1883, EX+ ...5,400.00
Chest of drws, bk brd, hidden lock, stencil, sgn HS, 1879, EX ...5,500.00
Chest of drws, brn grpt w/stencil, pnt pulls, 1883, EX+ 5,400.00
Chest of drws, floral decals/fruit/gilt stencil/grpt, MH/1879, EX ..2,750.00
Chest of drws, redwood, 1841, EX 750.00
Chest of drws, stenciling w/decals, dk brn, fancy bk brd, EX ...7,200.00
Cradle, gilt stencils, mustard trim, maroon grpt, EX 1,100.00
Cupboard, corner; maroon w/blk, stencil, 1856, EX 11,500.00
Dresser, Empire style, columns on 3 drws, sgn HF, 1874, EX ...2,200.00
Frame, gilt eagles, stenciled, blk, EX 1,050.00
Rope bed, cherry, red & brn finish, rare, EX 2,300.00
Stand, bed side; rpt mustard brn, EX 400.00

Soapstone

Soapstone is a soft talc in rock form with a smooth, greasy feel from whence comes its name. It is also called Soo Chow Jade and composed basically of talc, chlorite, and magnetite. In colonial times it was extracted from out-croppings in large sections with hand saws, carted by oxen to mills, and fashioned into useful domestic articles such as footwarmers, cooking utensils, inkwells, etc. During the early 1800s, it was used to make heating stoves and kitchen sinks. Most familiar today are the carved vases, bookends, and boxes made in China during the Victorian era.

Candle holder, gray, trapezoidal, 1½x2½x2½" 125.00
Censer, dragon-mask/ring hdls, dragon finial, 3-leg, 8" 165.00
Figure, Arhat seated, cat at side, 18th C, 5¼" 165.00
Figure, Lohan w/dbl-gourd bottle, 1800s, 2" 85.00
Foot warmer, oblong, heavy wire bail, EX 50.00
Horse, rearing, flying mane, red-brn, 12x9" 165.00
Lamp, urn w/floral & bird cvgs, brass base, 10", + shade 425.00
Screen, goggle-eye goldfish/seaweed, blk/pk/gr, 7½x5½" 60.00
Vase, daisies/leaves, vintage rim, blk soapstone base, 11" 85.00
Vase, dbl; brn, joined by floral cvg, 3x6" 125.00

Soda Fountain Collectibles

The first soda water sales in the United States occurred in the very late 1790s in New York and New Haven, Connecticut. By the 1830s soda water was being sold in drug stores as a medicinal item, especially the effervescent mineral waters from various springs around the country. By this time the first flavored soda water appeared at an apothecary shop in Philadelphia.

The 1830s also saw the first manufacturer (John Matthews) of devices to make soda water. The first marble soda fountain made its appearance in 1857 as a combination ice shaver and flavor-dispensing apparatus. By the 1870s the soda fountain was an established feature of the neighborhood drug store.

The fountains of this period were large, elaborate marble devices with druggists competing with each other for business by having fountains decorated with choice marbles, statues, mirrors, water fountains, and gas lamps.

In 1903 the fountain completed its last major evolution with the introduction of the 'front' counter service we know today. (The soda clerk faced the customer when drawing soda.)

By this time ice cream was a standard feature being served as sundaes, ice cream sodas, and milk shakes. Syrup dispensers were just being introduced as 'point-of-sale' devices to sell various flavorings from many different companies. Straws were commonplace, especially those made from paper. Fancy and unusual ice-cream dippers were in daily use, and they continued to evolve reaching their pinnacle with the introduction of the heart-shaped dipper in 1927.

This American business has provided collectors today with an almost endless supply of interesting and different articles of commerce. One can collect dippers, syrup dispensers, glassware, straw dispensers, milk shakers, advertising, and trade catalogs.

Collectors need to be made aware of decorating pieces that are fantasy items: copper ice-cream cones, a large copper ice-cream dipper, and a copper ice-cream soda glass. These items have no resale value. Our advisors for this category are Joyce and Harold Screen; they are listed in the Directory under Maryland. See also Advertising.

Bottle, crockery, Dr Swett's Root Beer, brn & cream 50.00
Bottle, flavor; acid etched 35.00
Bottle, seltzer; Nehi Bottling Co, gr glass, w/spigot, EX+ 100.00
Bottle, syrup extract; James Tufts, paper label, 1-pt, EX 40.00
Bottle, syrup extract; John Matthews, paper label, 1-pt 50.00
Bottle, syrup; Cherry Smash, label under glass, w/cap 300.00
Can, tin, Sugar Rolled Ice Cream Cones, EX 45.00

Carton, Borden's Vanilla Ice Cream, Elsie's face, 2-qt, EX **5.00**
Container, Borden's Malted Milk Candy, glass, emb metal lid, 9" **100.00**
Container, Johnston's Hot Fudge, stoneware, electric, EX **100.00**
Container, malted milk; Borden's, pnt label, tin lid **250.00**
Container, malted milk; common names, aluminum, knob lid, EX ...**60.00**
Container, tin, Perfector Chocolate Syrup, ½-gal, EX **300.00**

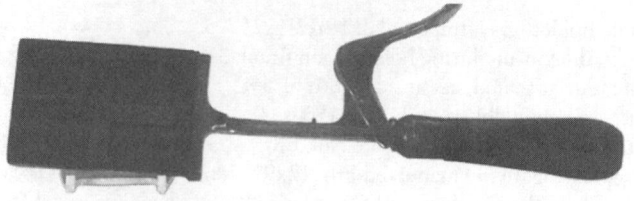

Dipper, The Mayer, used for ice-cream sandwiches, 11½", $550.00.

Dipper, banana split; Gilchrist **450.00**
Dipper, banana split; United **650.00**
Dipper, Cold Dog, cylinder **750.00**
Dipper, Gilchrist #31, NP brass, wood hdl, sz 8-30 ....**35.00**
Dipper, Gilchrist #33, NP brass, wood hdl, sz 6 ....**110.00**
Dipper, Sky High **950.00**
Dipper, tin, key-operated, early **18.00**
Dispenser, Buckeye Root Beer, blk, missing pump, 11½x8", VG ..**400.00**
Dispenser, Buckeye Root Beer, ceramic, urn shape, wht pump ...**900.00**
Dispenser, Buckeye Root Beer, mug in oval, w/pump, 16", VG ...**1,200.00**
Dispenser, Cherry Fizz, 3 color transfers, w/pump, 16", VG **3,000.00**
Dispenser, Cherry Julep, ball shape w/orig pump, 14x9" dia, G ..**650.00**
Dispenser, Cherry Smash, 3 cherries on front, orig pump, 16", VG ..**925.00**
Dispenser, Fowler's Cherry Smash, 5¢ on side, orig pump **1,400.00**
Dispenser, Grape Julep, ball shape, w/pump, 14x9" dia, VG **750.00**
Dispenser, Grape Kola, porc, figure-8 shape, complete, 20", EX ..**1,500.00**
Dispenser, Green River Soda, 2 bottles on top **300.00**
Dispenser, Howell's Orange Julep, orig pump, 14x9" dia, VG **700.00**
Dispenser, Jersey-Creme, Perfect Drink, 15x7½", EX **750.00**
Dispenser, Lash's Orangeade, gr glass, EX **250.00**
Dispenser, Massey's Root Beer, bbl form, 15x8x8", VG **900.00**
Dispenser, Miners, Beef Malt, bull's-head figural **450.00**
Dispenser, Mission Orange, glass bbl w/blk glass base, 13", VG ..**125.00**
Dispenser, Mission Real Fruit Juice, lime gr glass/metal, 12", VG ..**125.00**
Dispenser, NuGrape, glass bowl w/milk glass base, 11½", VG **45.00**
Dispenser, Ver-ba, porc, w/pump, 15x8x8", EX **700.00**
Dispenser, Ward's Lemon Crush, lemon form, w/pump, 13", EX **850.00**
Dispenser, Ward's Orange Crush, orange form, no pump, 10", G ...**500.00**
Dispenser, Ward's Orange Crush, orange form, w/pump, 16", VG ..**800.00**
Display, compo ice-cream cone, 2-pc, early, 24", EX **375.00**
Fan pull, Cheer Up Soda, cb diecut, bottle shape, EX **18.00**
Hat, soda jerk's, Kist Beverages, wht paper, 1950s, EX **4.00**
Hat, soda jerk's, Orange Crush, paper, Crushy figure, NM **6.00**
Ice-cream mold, pewter, eagle, 3-pt **600.00**
Ice-cream mold, pewter, fish form, 2-pt **350.00**
Ice-cream mold, pewter, rose **30.00**
Jar, Horlick's Malted Milk, label under glass, orig lid **275.00**
Jug, syrup; stoneware, J Hungerford Smith **110.00**
Magazine, Soda Fountain, 1905, EX **40.00**
Magazine, Soda Fountain, 1915, EX **30.00**
Magazine, Soda Fountain, 1925, EX **15.00**
Magazine, Soda Fountain, 1935, EX **7.00**
Magazine, Soda Fountain, 1940, EX **5.00**
Mechanical pencil, White's Dairy & Ice Cream Co, working **15.00**
Mixer, Arnold, wht porc & CI base, 4 NP cups, EX orig **95.00**

Mixer, Hamilton-Beach, brass & copper, marble base, 19x6x8", G ..**125.00**
Mixer, Hamilton-Beach, marble & polished brass, 14", EX **250.00**
Mug, Frostie Root Beer, thick glass **17.50**
Mug, MODOX emb on glass **150.00**
Mug, Richardson Root Beer, thick glass **18.00**
Name plate, metal, James W Tufts, dmn shape **300.00**
Name plate, metal, John Matthews, rnd **300.00**
Name plate, metal, Robert M Green & Sons **75.00**
Opener, Orange Crush, chrome plated, Crushy & bottle, 1920s, sm ..**15.00**
Rack, ice-cream cone; metal, holds 24, 4x27½x10", G **30.00**
Stereoview card, showing early sofa fountain, ca 1890, EX **60.00**
Straw dispenser, glass, Aztec pattern, horizontal **500.00**
Straw dispenser, glass, Heisey, horizontal **600.00**
Straw dispenser, SANI-SERV, mechanical, horizontal **250.00**
Straw holder, panelled glass w/metal lid **350.00**
Straw holder, Rex pattern, glass w/glass lid **450.00**
Straw holder, Sani Straw, Pat 1917, M **125.00**
Table, bent wire w/oak top, 25" dia, EX **100.00**
Table, ice-cream; marble top, bent-wire base, 36x20", G+ **150.00**
Trade catalog, James Tufts, 1885, EX **250.00**
Trade catalog, John Matthews, 1891, EX **300.00**
Trade catalog, Liquid Carbonic, 1910, EX **75.00**

Spangle Glass

Spangle glass, also known as Vasa Murrhina, is cased art glass characterized by the metallic flakes embedded in its top layer. It was made both abroad and in the United States during the latter years of the 19th century, and it was reproduced in the 1960s by the Fenton Art Glass Company.

Vasa Murrhina was a New England distributor who sold glassware of this type manufactured by a Dr. Flower of Sandwich, Massachusetts. Flower had purchased the defunct Cape Cod Glassworks in 1885 and used the facilities to operate his own company. Since none of the ware was marked, it is very difficult to attribute specific examples to his manufacture. See also Art Glass Baskets; Fenton.

Bottle, scent; gold w/mica, bl & gold butterflies, dome cap, 5" ...**325.00**
Bowl, cranberry w/mica, 3 scroll ft, emb heads & stars, 3¾" **145.00**
Bowl, 3-color, leaf form w/crimped sides, 2½x7" **195.00**
Candlestick, mc w/gr aventurine, ruffled ft, clear hdl, 5½ **75.00**
Candlestick, mc w/gr aventurine & gold, clear base, 5¼x3½" **60.00**
Candlesticks, spatter w/gr mica, hollow baluster, 8", pr **150.00**
Creamer, bl w/silver mica, emb swirls, clear hdl, 4⅞x3⅛" **195.00**
Ewer, purple o/l, clear edge/thorn hdl, 7½" **325.00**
Fairy lamp, cranberry swirl w/silver mica, Clarke base, 3½" **175.00**
Pitcher, bl w/mica, emb swirls, 4⅝x3½" **195.00**
Rose bowl, bl & wht spatter w/mica, 8-crimp, 3⅛x3⅝" **85.00**
Rose bowl, mc spatter w/mica, 3⅝x3½" **100.00**
Rose bowl, rose-red w/mica, wht int, 8-crimp, 3⅜x3⅜" **95.00**
Tumbler, Invt T'print, orange & wht spatter w/mica, 3¾" **50.00**
Vase, bl o/l w/mica, clear hdl, ewer form, 6¾x2¾" **65.00**
Vase, bl o/l w/silver mica, thorn hdl, ewer form, 7½" **110.00**
Vase, bl w/silver mica, conical w/5" neck, 8" **100.00**
Vase, mc spatter w/mica, wht int, sq top, 5¼x4¼" **65.00**
Vase, rose-pk w/silver mica, wht int, wishbone ft, 6¼x3¾" **95.00**

Spatter Glass

Spatter glass, characterized by its multicolor 'spatters,' has been made from the late 19th century to the present by American glasshouses as well as those abroad. Although it was once thought to have been made entirely by workers at the 'end of the day' from bits and pieces of leftover scrap, it is now known that it was a standard line of production. See also Art Glass Baskets.

Carafe, 3-color w/wht ovals, appl ft, 9x5", +matching tumbler ...**295.00**
Cruet, bl & wht, clear hdl, heart-shaped stopper, 8¾" **145.00**
Jam jar, gr & wht w/wht egg-shape designs, leaf finial, 6x3" **75.00**
Jam jar, mc w/wht oval designs, w/lid, 6¾x3¼" **65.00**
Jam jar, yel/brn/wht/pk w/clear leaf finial, 6½x3½" **80.00**
Pitcher, Invt T'print, cranberry/wht, hexagonal neck, 8½" **175.00**
Pitcher, red & wht cased, w/clear ribbed hdl, 8¼" **165.00**
Vase, mc w/pulled ruffled top, clear thorn hdls, squatty, 11" **95.00**
Vase, yel & wht w/HP bird & flowers, clear hdls, 7x4½" **175.00**
Vase, 4-color, wht int, 7½x3¼" **110.00**

Spatterware

Spatterware is a general term referring to a type of decoration used by English potters beginning in the late 1700s. Using a brush or a stick, brightly colored paint was dabbed onto the soft-paste earthenware items, achieving a spattered effect which was often used as a border. Because much of this type of ware was made for export to the United States, some of the subjects in the central design — the schoolhouse and the eagle patterns, for instance — reflect American tastes. Yellow, green, and black spatterware is scarce and highly valued by collectors.

In the descriptions that follow, the color listed after the item indicates the color of the spatter. The central design is identified next, and the color description that follows that refers to the design. Our advisor is Diane Patalano; she is listed in the Directory under New Jersey.

Bowl, bl, Adam's Rose, red & gr, 5" dia, VG **225.00**
Bowl, sauce; gr, tulip, 4-color, Davenport, 5" dia, EX **600.00**
Creamer, bl, cow & calf form, brn/yel, rstr, no lid, 4⅜" **715.00**
Creamer, bl, peafowl, 4-color, paneled, 6¼" **385.00**
Creamer, bl, rooster, 4-color, 4½" **650.00**
Creamer, bl, star, red, 5⅛", NM **275.00**
Creamer, purple & bl rainbow, hexagonal paneled shape, 4½" ..**950.00**
Creamer, rainbow, paneled, 5⅝" **275.00**
Creamer, red, peafowl, 4-color, leaf hdl, rprs, 4½" **330.00**
Creamer, red, peafowl on branch, 4-color, paneled, 6" **525.00**

Creamer, Schoolhouse pattern in red and green, back and rim with red spatter, repaired handle, 4", $1,200.00.

Cup & saucer, bl, carnation, red w/gr leaves, NM **700.00**
Cup & saucer, bl, memorial tulip, 3-color, 4½" **750.00**
Cup & saucer, bl, open tulip, bl & gr, EX+ **500.00**
Cup & saucer, blk & brn rainbow, thistle, 3-color, NM **1,400.00**
Cup & saucer, purple, Adam's Rose, red & gr, EX+ **400.00**
Cup & saucer, purple, holly berries, red & gr, EX+ **275.00**
Cup & saucer, purple, open tulip, 3-color, EX+ **675.00**
Cup & saucer, purple/blk rainbow, alternating stripes, NM **350.00**
Cup & saucer, red, Adam's Rose, red & gr, EX **450.00**
Cup & saucer, red & bl, Adams Rose, red & gr, NM **500.00**
Cup & saucer, red & gr rainbow, alternating stripes, Adams **350.00**
Cup & saucer, red & purple, rainbow, memorial tulip, 3-color ...**800.00**
Pitcher, bl, tulip, 4-color, paneled, hairline, 6¾" **825.00**
Pitcher, bl, 4-part flower, red & gr, paneled, rpr, 11¼" **330.00**

Plate, bl, eagle & shield, bl transfer, 7", EX **400.00**
Plate, bl, open tulip, 3-color, 8⅜", NM **650.00**
Plate, bl, peafowl, 4-color, flake, 11" **575.00**
Plate, bl, peafowl, 4-color, molded edge, 9½", NM **385.00**
Plate, bl, peafowl, 4-color, sm flakes, 8¾" **385.00**
Plate, bl, profile tulip, bl/red/gr, 8⅜" **850.00**
Plate, bl, thistle, red & gr, wear, 8¼" **775.00**
Plate, bl, tulip, red/bl/gr/blk, 8¼", NM **600.00**
Plate, bl, tulip, 4-color, Thos Walker, 8⅝", EX **385.00**
Plate, bl, 6-pointed star, 3-color, 7", NM **450.00**
Plate, bl & gr rainbow, alternating bands, 6⅛" **325.00**
Plate, gr, Christmas balls, yel & red, 8⅜", NM **4,000.00**
Plate, purple, acorn, 4-color, flakes, 9⅜" **1,600.00**
Plate, purple, peafowl, 4-color, rpr, 9½" **300.00**
Plate, red, dahlia, 3-color, Barber & Till, 9⅜" **385.00**
Plate, red, peafowl, 3-color, 10½", VG **220.00**
Plate, red, peafowl, 4-color, edge wear, 9¼" **600.00**
Plate, red, peafowl on branch, 4-color, 8¾", NM **800.00**
Plate, red, profile tulip, bl/red/gr, 5¼" **450.00**
Plate, red, tulip, 5-color, wear/chips, 8⅜" **360.00**
Plate, red, 6-pointed star, 3-color, 9½" **600.00**
Plate, red & bl rainbow, dahlia, 3-color, 8⅜" **900.00**
Plate, red & bl rainbow, peafowl, 3-color, 8" **3,200.00**
Plate, red & bl sponged rim, 8½" **90.00**
Plate, red & gr rainbow, alternating concentric bands, 6" **450.00**
Plate, red/bl/gr, flower, Adams Tunstall, 9½" **60.00**
Plate, yel, morning glory, 3-color, 6½" **600.00**
Platter, red, Adam's Rose, red & gr, 13½x10⅛" **1,500.00**
Saucer, bl, peafowl, 3-color **230.00**
Soup plate, bl, peafowl, 4-color, 10" **1,600.00**
Soup plate, purple, 4-color, prof rpr, 9⅜" **275.00**
Soup plate, rainbow, bull's eye, red & purple, 10½" **1,200.00**
Soup plate, red, rose, 4-color, impressed N, 9½" **660.00**
Sugar bowl, bl, peafowl, 4-color, prof rpr, 8¼" **385.00**
Sugar bowl, bl, peafowl, 4-color, 5¼", NM **1,000.00**
Sugar bowl, red, peafowl, 4-color, mismatched lid, 4¼" **275.00**
Sugar bowl, red, prof rpr, 4½" **85.00**
Sugar bowl, red, rooster, 4-color, mismatched lid, 4¾" **385.00**
Sugar bowl, red, rose & flowers, w/lid, 4¾", EX **275.00**
Sugar bowl, red & bl rainbow, paneled, prof rpr, w/lid, 8" ...**275.00**
Sugar bowl, red & purple rainbow, w/lid, 4½" **1,200.00**
Tea bowl, purple, flying eagle, blk transfer **385.00**
Tea bowl, red & yel rainbow, mini, EX **165.00**
Tea bowl & saucer, bl, rose, 3-color **600.00**
Tea bowl & saucer, bl, schoolhouse, red & gr, hairline **220.00**
Tea bowl & saucer, bl, tulip, 4-color, NM **445.00**
Tea bowl & saucer, gr, peafowl, 4-color, NM **415.00**
Tea bowl & saucer, red, eagle, bl transfer w/mc pnt **385.00**
Tea bowl & saucer, red, peafowl, 4-color **465.00**
Tea bowl & saucer, red, peafowl, 4-color, near match **225.00**
Tea bowl & saucer, red, rooster, 4-color, NM **1,500.00**
Tea bowl & saucer, red, schoolhouse, 3-color, rpr **600.00**
Tea bowl & saucer, yel, thistle, red & gr, EX **600.00**
Teapot, bl, fort, 3-color, paneled, prof rpr, 8½" **1,000.00**
Teapot, gr, morning glory, 3-color, chips, 6¼" **500.00**
Toddy, bl & purple rainbow w/bull's-eye center, 5" **360.00**
Waste bowl, bl, peafowl, 4-color, wear, 6½" **1,300.00**
Waste bowl, gr, Christmas balls, red & yel, 2¾x4⅞" **1,800.00**

Spode-Copeland

The Spode Works was established in 1770 in England by Josiah Spode I and continued to operate under that title until 1843. Their earliest products were typical underglaze blue-printed patterns. After 1790 a translucent porcelain body was the basis for a line of fine enamel-decorated dinnerware. Stone China was introduced in 1805, often in patterns reflecting an Oriental influence. In 1833 William Taylor Copeland purchased the company, having been Spode's business partner. Copeland continued the business in much the same tradition as the Spode-Copeland partnership. Spode was the Royal Potter for years, providing many exquisite items for the Royal Families. They employed paintresses to decorate the merchandise by hand. Most of the Spode-Copeland wares were marked with one of several variations that incorporate the firm's name, making identification possible. The Spode Company merged with Worcester Royal Porcelain Company in 1976 and became Royal Worcester Spode Limited. This company was then purchased by Derby International in 1988. The two firms separated in 1989. The holding company is the Porcelain and Fine China Companies Limited, a division of Derby International. Spode china is still being manufactured today at exactly the same location where Josiah Spode I began in 1770. Robert Copeland, a descendent of William Taylor Copeland, resides in England. He writes books and gives lectures on Spode. Our advisor for this category is Don Haase; he is listed in the Directory under Washington.

Bowl, cereal; Patricia **28.00**
Bowl, cream soup; Aster 35.00
Bowl, cream soup; Wicker Dale, w/underplate 45.00
Bowl, dessert; Dresden Rose Savoy 62.00
Bowl, fruit; Billingsley Rose 28.00
Bowl, fruit; Wicker Dale 28.00
Bowl, rice; Wicker Dale, 4" 25.00
Bowl, rim soup; Chinese Rose, 7" 45.00
Bowl, rim soup; Italian, 8½" 65.00
Bowl, rim soup; Tower, bl; 10½" 75.00
Bowl, vegetable; Camilla, bl, oval, 9" 75.00
Bowl, vegetable; Rome, oval, 1805, 8" 295.00
Bowl, vegetable; Ruins, oval, 1880, 8" 295.00
Bowl, vegetable; Wicker Dale, oval, 10¼" 85.00
Bowl, vegetable; Wicker Dale, 8" sq 80.00
Butter dish, Tower, pk, sq, w/lid 120.00
Butter pat, Tower, pk 25.00
Butter tub, Tower, bl, 1815 ....355.00
Cake stand, Tower, pk, 3x9½" 100.00
Casserole, Fleur-de-Lis, India Red 135.00
Chocolate pot, Trade Winds, sailing ships 110.00
Chop plate, Patricia, 13" 145.00
Coffeepot, Dresden Rose Savoy, 8-cup 295.00
Coffeepot, Fleur-de-Lis, Indian Red, 6-cup 145.00
Coffeepot, Tower, bl, 8-cup 195.00
Creamer & sugar bowl, Aster, w/lid, lg 110.00
Creamer & sugar bowl, Tower, pk, w/lid, lg 120.00
Creamer & sugar bowl, Wicker Dale, w/lid, sm 95.00
Cup & saucer, bouillon; Patricia 35.00
Cup & saucer, demitasse; Old Salem 35.00
Cup & saucer, demitasse; Shanghai, bone china 55.00
Cup & saucer, demitasse; Tower, bl 39.00
Cup & saucer, Irene, bone china 69.00
Cup & saucer, Moss Rose 35.00
Cup & saucer, Tower, bl 39.00
Cup & saucer, Tower, pk 39.00
Cup & saucer, Wicker Dale 39.00
Egg cup, Gainsborough 32.00
Foot bath, Tower, bl 1,595.00
Gravy, Tower, bl, w/base 295.00
Honey pot, Wicker Dale, VG 45.00
Lazy Susan, Tower, pk 495.00

Muffin dish, Tower, pk, domed lid 125.00
Mug, George Washington, Copeland 135.00
Pitcher, Herrings Hunt, gr trim, 8" 135.00
Pitcher, milk; Wicker Dale, 5½" 67.50
Pitcher, parian, Independence, w/WA & flags, Copeland, 8" 150.00
Plate, bread & butter; Buttercup 25.00
Plate, bread & butter; Tower, pk 28.00
Plate, bread & butter; Wicker Dale 28.00
Plate, dinner; Aster 39.00
Plate, dinner; Castle, 1815 ....195.00
Plate, dinner; Filigree 165.00
Plate, dinner; Mayflower 39.00
Plate, dinner; Romney 35.00
Plate, dinner; Rosebud Chintz 35.00
Plate, dinner; Tower, pk, 10½" 42.00
Plate, dinner; Wicker Dale 38.00
Plate, luncheon; Famille Rose 35.00
Plate, luncheon; Wicker Dale, 8" 35.00
Plate, salad; Chelsea Garden, bone china 49.00
Plate, salad; Jewell 28.00
Plate, salad; Tower, pk 32.00
Plate, salad; Wicker Dale 30.00
Plate, The Poore Knight, 10" 150.00
Platter, Florence, 17" 155.00
Platter, Imari, octagonal, Copeland, 1850s, 18½" 375.00
Platter, Lucano, med bl, 18th C, 18¼" 400.00
Platter, Tower, pk, 14½" 155.00
Platter, turkey; Tower, bl, 24" 495.00
Platter, Wild Flower, 17" 165.00
Potpourri vase, pattern #967, paw ft, rtcl lid, 6" 875.00
Sauce boat, Fleur-de-Lis, bl, w/underplate 85.00
Sink, bathroom; Tower, bl 850.00
Strainer, platter; Grasshopper, med bl transfer, oval, 13" 350.00
Teapot, Billingsley Rose, 6-cup 145.00
Teapot, Rose Bud Chintz, 8-cup 185.00
Teapot, Wicker Dale 200.00
Tureen, soup; bl transfer figures/sheep/bldgs, 12", +plate/ladle ...800.00
Tureen, soup; Venetian scene, 19th C, 14" 715.00

Spongeware

Spongeware is a type of factory-made earthenware that was popular during the last quarter of the 19th century. It was decorated by dabbing color onto the drying ware with a sponge, leaving a splotched design at random or in simple patterns. Sometimes a solid band of color was added. The vessel was then covered with a clear glaze and fired at a high temperature. Blue on white is the most preferred combination, but green on ivory, orange on white, or those colors in combination may also occasionally be found.

Bowl, blue and white, 6x13", $275.00.

Bowl, emb arched panels & pattern bl sponging, 3¾x8⅜" 130.00
Bowl, emb arched panels w/bl pattern sponge bands, 6x12" 150.00
Bowl, flowing brn & bl sponging, 3½x7¼", EX 40.00
Bowl, mixing; bl /wht, vertical ribs, stoneware, 4x10⅛" 95.00

Bowl, vegetable; bl/wht, oval, 2⅛x10x6¾" **50.00**
Bowl w/spout, pattern brn & bl sponging, emb swirls, 4x9" **70.00**
Jar, red/bl/brn mottled sponging, cylindrical, 7½x7¾" **90.00**
Pitcher, bl/wht, bulbous w/emb scrolls, flared rim, 6⅝" **75.00**
Pitcher, water; pattern bl sponging w/emb flower, 9x5¾" **350.00**
Pitcher, water; pattern gr sponging, bl bands, bbl form, 8½" **75.00**
Plate, bl/wht, 10⅜" **50.00**
Platter, bl/wht, emb scrolls, scalloped, 13⅜x9¼", EX **110.00**
Soap dish, bl/wht, rectangular, 5x3⅝" **125.00**

Spoons

Souvenir spoons have been popular remembrances since the 1890s. The early hand-wrought examples of the silversmith's art are especially sought and appreciated for their fine craftsmanship. Commemorative, personality-related, advertising, and those with Indian busts or floral designs are only a few of the many types of collectible spoons. In the following listings, spoons are entered by city, character, or occasion. Our advisor for this category is Margaret Alves; she is listed in the Directory under Connecticut.

Key:
B — bowl   FF — full figure
BR — bowl reverse   GW — gold wash
emb — embossed   H — handle
eng — engraved   HR — handle reverse

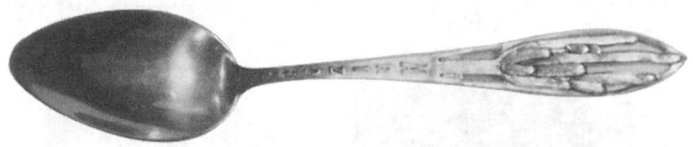

Arizona on handle, cactus finial, plain bowl, demitasse, $12.00.

Arkansas Traveler & car on H; stainless, demitasse **5.00**
Boston & Old Meeting House w/cutout on H; plain B **30.00**
Boston on shaft; hub finial; Old South Church emb in B **20.00**
Catalina Island CA scene in B; fish FF H; plain HR **30.00**
Catalina Island on shaft; old Abe finial H; plain B **25.00**
CO, miners & veggies on H; Denver building in B; bronco HR ...**35.00**
Colorado Springs in B; cowboy & steer on BR; flower H **32.00**
Duluth eng in GW B; FF Indian H **45.00**
Fort Pitt & crown in B; fort cut-out finial on twist H; 5½" **37.00**
Ft Gibbon AK in B; Eureka & His Rocker on H; ornate HR, demi ...**37.50**
Gatlinburg TN in B; Christus & head emb on H; stainless **6.00**
Grand Canyon AZ in B; Hermit Rest & scene on H; sterling **30.00**
Hawaii & Pineapple on H; plain B; demitasse **18.00**
Holly leaves & berries emb in B; plant on H; Whiting, bonbon ...**98.00**
ID seal & scenes on H & HR; plain B; sugar shell **22.50**
IN w/ears of corn on H; Soldiers & Sailors monument in B **22.50**
Jacksonville eng in B; oranges/leaves/flowers emb on H; 6" **24.00**
Kansas City MO city scene in B; simple H **22.50**
Lincoln's Home finial H; Lincoln Nat'l Monument in B; Gorham ...**55.00**
Little Red Red Riding Hood, sterling **25.00**
Los Angeles eng in B; roses & leaves on H; demitasse **14.00**
Lucy eng on scrolled H; dtd 1902 on HR; plain B; Wallace **30.00**
Mackinac Island eng in B; FF Indian H; demitasse **22.00**
Mary Poppins, teaspoon **5.00**
McCabe's Fortieth Jubilee **10.00**
Merry Christmas/Happy New Year/etc on H; emb scene in B **28.00**
Mexico on shaft; HP fort finial; plain B; demitasse **24.00**

Miami FL on shaft; Royal Palm & tree on finial; plain B **30.00**
Monaco eng in B; pnt shield finial; long spiral H **25.00**
Morman Temple in GW B; simple H; plain HR **22.00**
National Cash Register **25.00**
New Jersey & state seal on H; State House Trenton in B **24.00**
New Orleans in B; St Louis Cathedral & Sugar Bowl emb on H ..**30.00**
New Westminster BC in B; Fraser River Salmon & salmon on H ...**37.50**
Orient Bicycle, demitasse **25.00**
Panama CA Expo & cut-out scene on H; plain B **48.00**
Pittsburgh state seal & Wm Pitt on H; plain B; Watson **22.50**
Presbyterian College Durant OK & building in B; OK on H **25.00**
Rapid City MI, Largest Chair in the World **10.00**
Rio de Janiero w/enameled shield & 1565-1965 on H; plain B **18.00**
Salt Lake City, Temple Square B; state seal on H; 5" **27.50**
San Francisco & scene in GW B; bear & seal on H; Shreve & Co ..**22.00**
San Gabriel Mission Pasadena CA in B; symbols on H & HR **35.00**
Sioux City eng in B; corn cutout on H; Watson, 6" **25.00**
Statue of Liberty & goldenrod on H; plain GW B **40.00**
Twig H; leaf GW B; Knowles, sterling **32.00**
Utah seal & 1896 emb on H; plain B; demitasse **20.00**
Virginia on H; Mt Vernon Washington's Mansion in B; demitasse ...**25.00**
Washington DC & Capitol on H; WA Monument on HR **24.00**
Yellowstone & bear emb on H; plain B; Watson **27.50**

Sporting Goods

When sports cards became so widely collectible several years ago, other types of related memorabilia started to interest sports fans. Now they search for baseball uniforms, autographed baseballs, game-used bats and gloves, and all sorts of ephemera. Although baseball is America's all-time favorite, other sports have their own groups of interested collectors. Our advice for this category comes from Paul Longo Americana. Mr. Longo is listed in the Directory under Massachusetts. See also Target Balls.

Key: LOA — letter of authenticity

Award, 1985 Player of the Year, Dan Marino, 11", LOA, EX **500.00**
Badge, pass; Indianapolis 500, 1948, M **85.00**
Baseball, inscr, 1,000th hit by Cleon Jones, 1973, EX **300.00**
Baseball, official Am League, sgn, Babe Ruth, EX **2,000.00**
Baseball, official Am League, sgn, Rabbit Maranville, LOA, NM .**2,000.00**
Baseball, official Am League, sgn, Ray Schalk, LOA, EX **1,500.00**
Baseball, official Nat'l League, sgn, J Robinson, NM **1,500.00**
Baseball, sgn Bo Jackson **35.00**
Baseball, sgn Bobby Richardson, Feeney **35.00**
Baseball, sgn by 1949 Boston Braves (23 total), NM **175.00**
Baseball, sgn by 1970 NY Mets (29 total), EX **300.00**
Baseball, sgn by 1978 Red Sox team (23 total), NM **100.00**
Baseball, sgn Tom Seaver **35.00**
Baseball, sgn Yogi Berra & Whitey Ford, Rawlings **125.00**
Basketball, signed by 1989 Boston Celtics (16 total), NM **275.00**
Bat, H&B pro model, game used, sgn Ernie Banks, LOA, NM .**4,000.00**
Bat, Louisville Slugger 125, sgn Lou Brock, cracked **130.00**
Bat, Spalding T-5, early 1900s, EX **95.00**
Book, 1860 (1st) Beadle's Baseball Guide, VG **1,400.00**
Calendar, St Louis Cardinals, 1943, VG **250.00**
Christmas card, sgn Babe Ruth, EX **1,200.00**
Christmas card, sgn Michael Jordan, 1990-91, team caroling, EX ...**400.00**
Contract, between Babe Ruth & 1930 NY Yankees, EX **29,900.00**
Football, Don Shula sgn & dtd, record 325 wins, NM **3,000.00**
Football helmet, leather, Michigan style, 1940s, adult sz, EX **150.00**
Glove, batting; sgn Dave Winfield, game-used **125.00**

Glove, batting; sgn Wade Boggs, game-used **95.00**
Glove, catcher's, Johnny Bench by Rawlings, #MJ60, M **40.00**
Glove, fielder's, split finger, Bill Doak, Rawlings, 1930s, EX **50.00**
Golf club, wooden shaft, Ernest Jones Special, VG **125.00**
Hat, sgn Tom Seaver, worn St Patrick's Day, gr, LOA, EX **300.00**
Helmet, batting; sgn Jose Cruz of Astros, game-used **125.00**
Helmet, batting; sgn Reggie Jackson of Angels, game-used **500.00**
Helmet, sgn by 1993 NY Giants, NM **250.00**
Jacket, NY Mets manager Bud Harrelson, name sewn on bk, EX ..**250.00**
Jacket, warm-up; John Starks, EX **200.00**
Jersey, home; 1985 Angels, sgn Reggie Jackson, EX **1,000.00**
Jersey, home; 1992-93 Pistons, sgn Isiah Thomas, LOA, EX **650.00**
Jersey, home; 1994 Dodgers, sgn Delino DeShilds, game-used **300.00**
Jersey, road; Charles Oakley, NM **350.00**
Jersey, road; 1990 Orioles, sgn Cal Ripkin Jr, LOA, EX **2,000.00**
Jersey, 1970s Bengals, sgn Ken Anderson, game used **450.00**
Key chain, motorcycle AMA Gypsy tour, 1940 ....**50.00**
Medallion, Man of War, Louisville Am Legion commemorative, '29 ..**50.00**
Photo, inscr, Bill Dickey to Jake Powell, 8x10", EX **300.00**
Photo, inscr, Joe DiMaggio, Burke orig, 8x10", NM **1,000.00**
Photo, inscr, Lou Gehrig, Burke orig, EX **5,000.00**
Photo, inscr, Red Ruffing to Jake Powell, 1938, 8x10", EX **300.00**
Photo, panoramic; 1905 World Series, 36x8", VG **1,000.00**
Photo, sgn, Pie Traynor in uniform, 16x20" **750.00**
Photo, team; sgn, 1955 Cleveland Indians, 19x14½", EX **500.00**
Photo, team; York PA, baseball, 1919, EX **90.00**
Photo, team; 1913 Cleveland Indians, 13x8", VG **1,500.00**
Photo, team; 1949 World Champion NY Yankees, 32x21", EX .**400.00**
Pin, promo; Tyson vs Holyfield, enamel on metal, 3" **3.50**
Poster, Ali vs Evangelista, 1977, 22¾x14½", NM **400.00**
Poster, Milwaukee Braves, promo for 1954 baseball cards **100.00**
Press pin, 1913 Phil Athletics, gr & gold ribbon, VG **2,500.00**
Press pin, 1927 NY Yankees, NM **2,000.00**
Program, Globetrotters vs All Stars, 1950, NM **125.00**
Program, NY Knicks, 1st game, 1946, vs Chicago Stags, EX **700.00**
Program, NY Rangers, Madison Sq Garden, color cover, '42 ....**95.00**
Program, souvenir; Harlem Globetrotters, 1954, M **30.00**
Program, 1st for Madison Square Garden, 1925, EX **575.00**
Program, 1889 World Series, NY Nat'l Team vs Brooklyn, EX ..**1,265.00**
Program, 1940-41 Bruins vs Maple Leafs, sgn by 17 Bruins **460.00**
Program, 1963 Old Timers Day, sgn by 32 Old Timers, EX **600.00**
Program, 1978 NY Yankees vs Boston Red Sox, sgn by Yankees, EX ..**350.00**
Ring, 1971 Pitts World Series Championship, dmn/14k gold ..**3,000.00**
Scorecard, 1875 Boston vs Philadelphia, EX **1,000.00**
Sticker, football; Rose Bowl, 1934 ....**20.00**
Tennis ball, sgn Arthur Ashe, yel Wilson **140.00**
Tennis racket, wood & metal, 1920s, EX **50.00**
Ticket, baseball; Lee Center NY, ca 1895 ....**20.00**
Ticket, boxing; Coney Island, amateur bout, 1927, unused **22.00**
Ticket, Indianapolis 500, 1946 ....**40.00**
Ticket, Stanford football game, CA Memorial Stadium, 1932 ......**15.00**
Ticket stub, 1962 opening day, Houston Colt 45's vs Cubs, NM **300.00**
Trade stimulator, Catch Ball, ca 1918, 36", EX **1,380.00**
Trophy, Spaulding, catcher on top of lg baseball, 20", EX **2,990.00**
Trophy, Victor; presented to Archie Moore, 1971, 19", NM **300.00**
Uniform, home; Derrick Coleman, Rookie year, LOA, EX **2,000.00**
Uniform, road; flannel, Gary Gentry, 1971, LOA, EX **1,600.00**
Uniform, road; flannel, Jerry Grote, 1971, LOA, EX **1,600.00**
Yearbook, Red Grange, Illinois College, 1926, EX **150.00**

St. Clair

The St. Clair Glass Company began as a small family-oriented operation in Elwood, Indiana, in 1941. Most famous for their lamps, the family made numerous small items of carnival, pink and caramel slag, and custard glass as well. Later, paperweights became popular production pieces; many command considerably high prices on today's market. Weights are stamped and usually dated, while small production pieces are often unmarked. For further information we recommend *St. Clair Glass Collector's Book* by Bonnie Pruitt, available from our advisor Ted Pruitt, who is listed in the Directory under Indiana.

Apple, plain **95.00**
Ashtray, flower, sm **70.00**
Bell, Christmas, lg **115.00**
Bell, mc florals, 4½" **42.00**
Bird, lg **95.00**
Bird, sm **40.00**
Bottle, scent; carnival glass **95.00**
Bowl, pk slag, ruffled rim, clear ped ft **175.00**
Candle holder, floral paperweight base **85.00**
Covered dish, dolphin **100.00**
Creamer & sugar bowl, Grape & Cable, red carnival, lg **200.00**
Cruet, paperweight base & stopper, lg **150.00**
Doorstop, Little Bo Peep, sm **525.00**
Figurine, Scottie, blk amethyst **340.00**
Figurine, Scottie, caramel **200.00**
Inkwell, Sprig **110.00**
Insulator, red **200.00**
Lamp, mc floral hexagonal base w/air bubbles, 24", pr **440.00**
Miniature, pepper **75.00**
Miniature, strawberry **100.00**

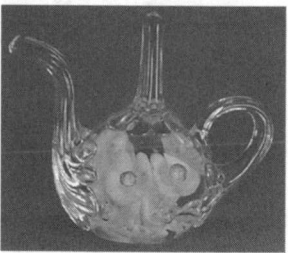

Paperweight, teapot form, 4½", $90.00.

Paperweight, assassinated presidents, set of 4 ....**525.00**
Paperweight, bird, cobalt or clear **75.00**
Paperweight, bl floral **44.00**
Paperweight, elephant, sulfide **155.00**
Paperweight, floral, controlled bubbles, lg **145.00**
Paperweight, Kewpie, sulfide, windowed **185.00**
Paperweight, rose, windowed & etched **1,350.00**
Paperweight, window flower, Paul St Clair **200.00**
Paperweight, windowed & ribboned, Ed St Clair **400.00**
Pear, lg. **95.00**
Pear, carnival glass, lg **100.00**
Plate, Christmas **25.00**
Plate, Kewpie **225.00**
Plate, Lyndon B Johnson **25.00**
Ring holder, bl paperweight **30.00**
Ring holder, teapot form, paperweight base **85.00**
Ring post, floral paperweight base **55.00**
Shot glass, Fez, from $150 to **200.00**
Toothpick holder, Daisy & Button **30.00**
Toothpick holder, flower paperweight base, ruffled rim **75.00**
Toothpick holder, Indian Maiden, caramel, from $150 to **200.00**
Toothpick holder, Invt Fan & Feather, red carnival **25.00**
Toothpick holder, Nixon, Bob St Clair **40.00**
Toothpick holder, Santa **135.00**

Toothpick holder, sheaf of wheat 45.00
Toothpick holder, swans 45.00
Tumbler, Invt Fan & Feather 35.00
Vase, paperweight base 85.00
Wine, Pinwheel 45.00

Staffordshire

Scores of potteries sprang up in England's Staffordshire district in the early 18th century; several remain to the present time. (See also specific companies.) Figurines and groups were made in great numbers; dogs were favorite subjects. Often they were made in pairs, each a mirror image of the other. They varied in heights from 3" or 4" to the largest, measuring 16" to 18". From 1840 until about 1900, portrait figures were produced to represent specific characters, both real and fictional. As a rule these were never marked.

The Historical Ware listed here was made throughout the district; some collectors refer to it as Staffordshire Blue Ware. It was produced as early as 1820, and because much was exported to America, it was very often decorated with transfers depicting scenic views of well-known American landmarks. Early examples were printed in a deep cobalt. By 1830 a softer blue was favored, and within the next decade black, pink, red, and green prints were used. Although sometimes careless about adding their trademark, many companies used their own border designs that were as individual as their names.

This ware should not be confused with the vast amounts of modern china (mostly plates) made from early in the century to the present. These souvenir or commemorative items are usually marketed through gift stores and the like. (See Rowland and Marcellus.) Our advisor for Historical Staffordshire is William Kurau; he is listed in the Directory under Pennsylvania. See also specific manufacturers.

Key:
blk — black   l/b — light blue
gr — green   m/b — medium blue
d/b — dark blue   m-d/b — medium dark blue

Figures and Groups

Boy (& girl) w/mule, 8", pr 300.00
Cat, blk spots, bl ribbon collar, no base, 8", facing pr 690.00
Cat, reddish-tan w/blk spots, glass eyes, no base, 5x6", pr 800.00
Cobbler at work, dog beneath stool, 6½" 150.00
Country boy sits on stump w/lamb at side, 8½" 200.00
Cow, recumbent, 1700s, 4½x6½" 635.00
Deer, recumbent, licking its bk, mc on bl base, #182, 3" 130.00
Deer, spotted, 6x5", EX, pr 1,300.00
Dog family, group of 3, on cobalt plinth, 6½x7½" 750.00
Dog w/Prince (& Princess of Wales), 9½x8½", pr (1 VG) 1,500.00
Exotic bird on tall naturalistic base, 10", facing pr 1,700.00

Figurine, musicians with harp and concertina, 17", $225.00.

Gentleman serenading lady, 7" 345.00
Highlander w/felled deer, EX details, 15" 300.00
Hunter (& Setter at Point), Walton, 5", pr, G 700.00
John Soloman Rarey (trainer) & horse Cruiser, 9", EX 400.00
King & Queen of Sardinia, 13", EX 275.00
Lady mourning beside an urn on pk column, 18th/19th C, 9½" .160.00
Leopard, tan w/red-brn spots, recumbent, 2x4¼" 575.00
Lion, 1 paw on yel ball, gr/ochre base, rstr, 3" 1,100.00
Llama, wht w/mc basket & flowers, flaw, 7½" 325.00
Man & lady riding goats, mc, crazing, 13" 425.00
Man w/rifle by cannon, 2nd w/pipe before castle, 9" 300.00
Nell (& Jobson), ca 1830, 6½", pr 270.00
Pigeon, 2" 60.00
Poodle, gold lustre decor, 10", EX, facing pr 325.00
Poodle, on cobalt plinth, 3¼", facing pr 345.00
Prodigal's Return, father & son, 14" 225.00
Ram, recumbent, 1700s, 4x6" 750.00
Ram (& ewe), bocage, att Walton, 4¾", VG, pr 500.00
Saint Sebastian, man in loincloth by tree, 10" 325.00
Sheep, gr plinth, 2½", facing pr 250.00
Sheep, recumbent, 2½x3¼", facing pr 115.00
Spaniel, copper lustre spots, sm hairlines, 9½", pr 350.00
Spaniel, cream w/rust spots, 4¾x5", facing pr 460.00
Spaniel, orange/gray/blk/gold, 4½", EX 70.00
Spaniel, pk base w/gr flowers, 8x7", EX, facing pr 3,200.00
Spaniel, wht w/red-brn spots, 7½", facing pr 635.00
Spaniel, wht w/reddish-brn spots, 10", facing pr 525.00
St Bernard, mc w/gold, appl glass eyes, 10", pr 500.00
St Bernard, standing, 13", facing pr 325.00
Swan, 3½" 60.00
Turkish musician, Rockingham, rstr, 5½", pr 75.00
Vase, spill; couple w/wheat bundles ea side, coleslaw, 8" 90.00
Vase, spill; cow & calf by tree & stream, mc w/gold, 11¼" 425.00
Vase, spill; fisherman & lady w/nets & catch by tree, 8" 120.00
Vase, spill; Highland lad & lassie by tree, 13½" 200.00
Vase, spill; huntsman, maid & hound, 11" 200.00
Vase, spill; lady w/flowers by tree trunk w/serpent, 15" 750.00
Vase, spill; ram (& ewe), 4½", pr 635.00
Vase, spill; Robin Hood, 2 men (1 seated), w/dog, 15" 175.00
Vase, spill; shepherd w/crook & dog by tree trunk, 6" 100.00
Venus & Cupid on ornate base, brn & gr details, rstr, 4½" 185.00
Whippet & rabbit, 7x7", pr 575.00
Young man w/horse, 6½" 200.00
Zebra, gr & blk details, line & chip, 6¼" 80.00

Historical

Basket, Brooklyn Ferry, d/b, vine leaf border, RSW, 5x10" 3,000.00
Basket, East Comes, Isle of Wight, d/b, Wood, 3½x11½", NM ..1,200.00
Basket, fruit; Harvard College, m/b, 11", EX 700.00
Bowl, Boston Antheneum, d/b, Ridgway, 2x4¾", EX 635.00
Bowl, Boston Antheneum, d/b, Stevenson, 1820s, rpr, 12½" 635.00
Bowl, fisherman, river & castle, d/b, 5½", NM 175.00
Bowl, Franklin's Tomb, d/b, Wood, shallow, rpr, 6¾" 200.00
Bowl, porridge; Castle Huntley Perthshire, d/b, Wood, 6½" 140.00
Bowl, Quebec/Buenos Ayres, d/b, Davenport, rpr, 4x11¼" sq .1,700.00
Bowl, tea dregs; Basket of Flowers, m-d/b, 3⅜x5½" 90.00
Bowl, tea dregs; City Hall NY, d/b, rose border, Stubbs, rprs, 6" .150.00
Bowl, tea dregs; Landing of Lafayette, d/b, Clews, rprs, 3x5½" ...180.00
Bowl, vegetable; Arms of MA, d/b, Mayer, 1½x7⅞" 3,250.00
Bowl, vegetable; castle view, flower border, d/b, w/lid, 12" 750.00
Bowl, vegetable; Dorney Court Buckinghamshire, d/b, Wood, 10" ..325.00
Bowl, vegetable; fruit, d/b, w/lid, ca 1830s, 11¼" 750.00
Bowl, vegetable; Landing of Lafayette, d/b, Clews, 9⅜", NM 500.00

Bowl, Wadsworth Tower, d/b, shell border, Wood, 1½x8⅜" ..1,000.00
Cake stand, Chinoiserie...2 Hunters...w/Deer..., d/b, 4x12", NM ..325.00
Coffeepot, Lafayette at Tomb...Franklin, d/b, rpr, 12" 625.00
Creamer, Boston State House, d/b, Rogers, 4¾", EX 430.00
Cup, handleless; B&O RR, d/b, Diorama border series, 2 chips ..160.00
Cup & saucer, Am Eagle on Urn, d/b, Clews, EX+ 250.00
Cup & saucer, B&O RR, d/b, Diorama, NM 500.00
Cup & saucer, Exchange Coffee House Boston, m-d/b, Wood, NM .550.00
Cup & saucer, handleless; Basket of Flowers, d/b, oversz 185.00
Cup & saucer, handleless; Castle Toward, d/b, Hall 195.00
Cup & saucer, handleless; Lafayette at Franklin's Tomb, d/b 360.00
Cup & saucer, Nile River, m/b, pyramids in border, flake 125.00
Cup plate, Athecus, brn, Adams, 4", EX 65.00
Cup plate, beehive, d/b, Stevenson & Williams, 3⅝" 185.00
Cup plate, British Am, pk, Davenport, 1850s, 4" 175.00
Cup plate, Castle Forres Aberdeenshire, d/b, Wood, 3¾" 80.00
Cup plate, Castle Garden, Battery, NY, d/b, 3⅝" 330.00
Cup plate, Commerce, mulberry, Alcock, 4" 75.00
Cup plate, Dunraven Glamorgan, d/b, Wood, 3¾", EX 75.00
Cup plate, Faker's Rock, Oriental scenery, d/b, Hall, 4¼" 86.00
Cup plate, Fishers, m/b, Cork, Edge & Malkin, 3⅞" 45.00
Cup plate, Franklin's Tomb, d/b, rpr, 3⅝" 185.00
Cup plate, Lady of Lake, m/b, Careys, 3⅞" 130.00
Cup plate, Landing of Gen Lafayette, d/b, Clews, rpr, 4⅜" 115.00
Cup plate, Mendenhall Ferry, d/b, eagle/scroll border, 5¼" 215.00
Cup plate, Pomerania, blk, 4", VG 32.00
Cup plate, Sandy Hill, blk, Clews, 3¾" 125.00
Cup plate, Seasons, pk, Adams, 4" 55.00
Cup plate, St Catherine Hill...Guilford, d/b, Clews, 4½", NM ...150.00
Cup plate, Tyrolean, gr, Ridgway, 4", EX 45.00
Cup plate, Wm Penn's Treaty, brn, Thos Green, 3⅞" 125.00
Cup plate, Woodlands...Phila, d/b, eagle border, Stubbs, rprs, 3¼" ...75.00
Cup plate, 2 Sailboats & Rowboat, d/b, Wood, rstr, 3½" 100.00
Custard cup, Landing of Lafayette, d/b, Clews, rstr, 2¾" 200.00
Custard cup, Wadsworth Tower, d/b, Wood, 2¼", NM 375.00
Ladle, Upper Ferry Bridge...Schuylkill, d/b, Stubbs, 10" 1,100.00
Leaf dish, Blind Boy, m-d/b, serrated border, 5¾", EX 200.00
Pitcher, Duke of Wellington/Lord Hill, d/b, oval, 6", VG 310.00
Pitcher, Field Sports...Hunting for Pheasants, d/b, 6" 500.00
Pitcher, Franklin, pk, Davenport, 10¼" 400.00
Pitcher, Franklin's Tomb, d/b, Wood, rstr, 6¾" 425.00
Pitcher, Franklin's Tomb, d/b, Wood, 5⅝", NM 350.00
Pitcher, Landing of Fathers, m-d/b, Wood, rstr hdl, 6½" 650.00
Pitcher, NY City Hall/NY Hospital..., d/b, Stevenson, 8½" 800.00
Pitcher, Residence...Richard Jordan, l/b, 6¾" 700.00
Pitcher, Schenectady on Mohawk River, pk, Jackson, 6½", EX .300.00
Pitcher, Wells Cathedral..., d/b, Hall, minor rstr, 9¾" 650.00
Plate, Albany, d/b, Davenport Cities series, 10" 325.00
Plate, Arms of RI, d/b, Mayer, Arms of States series, 8¾", NM ..475.00
Plate, Baltimore & OH RR, d/b, Wood, 10", EX 635.00
Plate, Baltimore & OH RR (inclined), d/b, Wood, wear, 9⅛" 400.00
Plate, Baltimore Exchange, d/b, fruit/flower border, 10" 435.00
Plate, Bank of US Phila, d/b, eagle border, Stubbs, 10⅛" 400.00
Plate, Barrington Hall, d/b, Stevenson, 8⅞" 195.00
Plate, Beehive, d/b, RSW, 6⅛" 85.00
Plate, Beehive, d/b, RSW, 8¼" 155.00
Plate, Boston State House, d/b, Rogers, chipped rim, 10" 175.00
Plate, Boston State House, d/b, Wood, ca 1830s, 9¾" 130.00
Plate, Boston State House, m-d/b, Wood, 6½" 140.00
Plate, Cadmus, d/b, Wood, 10½" 425.00
Plate, Cashiobury Hertfordshire, d/b, grapevine border, 8⅜" 125.00
Plate, Cathedral at York, d/b, grapevine border, Wood, 6½" 140.00
Plate, Catskill Mtn House US, maroon, Adams, 10⅛" 175.00
Plate, Chief Justice Marshall steamboat, d/b, Wood, 8¼", VG ...430.00

Plate, Chief Justice Marshall...Tory Line, d/b, Wood, 8¼" 700.00
Plate, Christ Church Oxford, m-d/b, Ridgway, 9⅞", NM 90.00
Plate, Church in...NY, d/b, eagle border, Stubbs, rprs, 6⅛" 400.00
Plate, City Hall NY, d/b, Ridgeway, rprs, 9¾" 85.00
Plate, City of Albany, d/b, Wood, minor stain, 10" 415.00
Plate, City of Albany State of NY, d/b, Wood, 10" 720.00
Plate, Commodore MacDonnough's Victory, d/b, Wood, wear, 8¼" 200.00
Plate, Commodore MacDonnough's Victory, d/b, Wood, wear, 9¼" 170.00
Plate, Commodore MacDonnough's Victory, d/b, Wood, 6½" ...250.00
Plate, Commodore MacDonnough's..., d/b, pk lustre rim, 8½" ...350.00
Plate, Cowes Harbor, d/b, Wood, 6¼" 345.00
Plate, Dam & Water Works... (side-wheeler), d/b, Henshall, 10" ...425.00
Plate, Dartmouth, d/b, Wood, 8⅛" 330.00
Plate, Death of the Bear, m-d/b, Spode, 9⅞" 425.00
Plate, English manor, unidentified, crocus border, m-d/b, 7" 85.00
Plate, Erie Canal...Late Governor, d/b, flakes, 8½" 175.00
Plate, Esholt House Yorkshire, d/b, grapevine border, 10¼", NM ..150.00
Plate, gazelle, d/b, Quadrupeds series, 7⅝" 250.00
Plate, Gen Jackson Hero of New Orleans, blk w/pk lustre, 8¾" ..1,155.00
Plate, Gunston Hall, Norfolk Hall, d/b, sm stain, 7½" 90.00
Plate, Hindu Temple, d/b, Rogers, 8¾", VG 65.00
Plate, Hospital Near Poissy France, d/b, Hall, 6½" 155.00
Plate, Hunter & Spaniel w/Ducks, d/b, 10¼", NM 300.00
Plate, Jenny Lind, purple, 10" 40.00
Plate, Junction of Sacandaga & Hudson Rivers, l/b, Clews, 7" 70.00
Plate, Lafayette at Tomb of Washington, d/b, 10", NM 640.00
Plate, Landing of Fathers at Plymouth, d/b, Wood, 10⅛" 230.00
Plate, Landing of Lafayette, d/b, Clews, 8⅞" 325.00
Plate, Landing of Lafayette at Castle Garden..., d/b, Clews, 8" ...260.00
Plate, leopard, d/b, Wood Zoological series, 7¾" 375.00
Plate, Less Painful To Learn in Youth..., blk, 8-sided, 7½", EX 60.00
Plate, Marine Hospital Louisville KY, d/b, Wood, 9⅛" 440.00
Plate, Muhamadan, Mosque & Tomb, d/b, Hall, 10" 120.00
Plate, Mosaic Tracery, d/b, Clews, stain, 8¼" 120.00
Plate, Nahant Hotel...Boston, d/b, Stevenson & Wms, 8½", VG ...285.00
Plate, NY Battery, d/b, vine border, 7⅜" 375.00
Plate, Oriental transfer, d/b, Wood, 9¼" 165.00
Plate, Park Theater NY, d/b, Stevenson & Wms, 9¾", NM 250.00
Plate, Philadelphia Fairmount (no sheep), ca 1825, 10¼" 275.00
Plate, Plains Hill Surrey, d/b, Ralph Hall, 10" 135.00
Plate, Reverend J Wesley medallion, blk w/mc trim, 7" 200.00
Plate, river scene w/fisherman, d/b, Clews, 8⅞" 170.00
Plate, Robinson Crusoe, blk w/mc, 8-sided, stain, 8¼" 35.00
Plate, Ross Castle Monmouthshire, d/b, grapevine border, 6½" .145.00
Plate, St Paul's School London, d/b, Adams, 8", EX 85.00
Plate, toddy; Am & Independence, d/b, Clews, 5⅝" 165.00
Plate, toddy; Cottage in Woods..., d/b, Wood Fr Views, 5⅝" 85.00
Plate, toddy; Culzean Castle, d/b, Stevenson, 5¼" 125.00
Plate, toddy; fisherman & buildings, d/b, flower border, 5½" 100.00
Plate, toddy; Ship Under Full Sail, d/b, Wood, rstr, 5¾" 100.00
Plate, toddy; Ship Under Half Sail, d/b, Wood, rprs, 5¼" 135.00
Plate, Union Line, d/b, Wood, wear/chips, 9" 300.00
Plate, Union Line, d/b, Wood, 10⅛" 325.00
Plate, University Building, d/b, Clews, 7¾", EX 115.00
Plate, Upper Ferry Bridge...Schuylkill, d/b, Stubbs, 8¾" 250.00
Plate, Vevay (IN), m-d/b, fruit & flower border, Henshall, 6⅝" ...600.00
Plate, View Near Philadelphia, d/b, Davenport, 10" 550.00
Plate, View of Liverpool, d/b, Wood, prof rstr, 10" 375.00
Plate, Washington, d/b, Davenport Cities series, 7⅝" 275.00
Plate, Welcome Lafayette...Glory, d/b, Clews, wear, 8¾" 635.00
Plate, William Penn's Treaty, brn, Thomas Green, 10⅞" 140.00
Plate, Winter View of Pittsfield MA, d/b, Clews, 10½" 375.00
Plate, Woodlands Near Phila, d/b, eagle border, rstr, 3¾" 70.00
Platter, Almshouse NY, d/b, Ridgway Beauties..., hairline, 14¾" ...600.00

Platter, Am & Independence, d/b, states border, Clews, rpr, 11½" .360.00
Platter, Angus Seats series, m-d/b, Ridgway, 12¾" 400.00
Platter, Castle Prison St Albans..., d/b, Hall, rstr, 10⅝" 550.00
Platter, Christianburg...Africa, d/b, Wood, prof rstr, 18¾" 850.00
Platter, Cornwall Terrace, d/b, Adams, 19¼" 1,100.00
Platter, Detroit, d/b, worn/scratched, 18½" 385.00
Platter, Eddistone Light House, d/b, shell border, 9⅝" 1,100.00
Platter, Gyrn Flintshire Wales, d/b, Ralph Hall, 17⅛" 925.00
Platter, Jedburgh Abbey Roxburgshire, d/b, Adams, 17", EX 475.00
Platter, Landing of Gen Lafayette, d/b, Clews, rprs, 17" dia 935.00
Platter, Mid-Eastern scene, purple, 17" 275.00
Platter, New Haven Connecticut, mulberry, Jackson, 10¾" 285.00
Platter, Niagara From Am Side, d/b, Wood, 14¾", EX 1,800.00
Platter, NY From Heights Near Brooklyn, d/b, Stevenson, 16" ..1,600.00
Platter, Ontario Lake Scenery, l/b, Heath, 15½" 180.00
Platter, Parkland Scene, d/b, Chetham & Robinson, 14½x11" ..200.00
Platter, Picturesque Views Newburgh Hudson River, l/b, 18", NM ..380.00
Platter, Residence of Late Richard Jordan..., pk, 15⅝x13" 800.00
Platter, river view, well & tree type, d/b, 21⅝", NM 700.00
Platter, St George's Chapel, d/b, Adams, 16¾" 750.00
Platter, St Paul's Church Boston, d/b, Ridgway, rpr, 9½" 325.00
Platter, States...Mansion...Lake w/Swans, d/b, Clews, 17" 4,000.00
Platter, Temple of Friendship, d/b, Henshall, 20½" 1,200.00
Platter, Wesleyan Methodist Schools..., blk, d/b border, 13½" ...250.00
Platter, Zoological...Camel Cage, brn, Clews, 11" 275.00
Punch bowl, Capitol WA, d/b, Tams-Anderson-Tams, 5¼x11¾" ..2,250.00
Sauce boat, Batalha Portugal, d/b 195.00
Soup, English manor, unidentified, d/b, Adams, mini, 3¾", EX .125.00
Soup, Fairmont Near Phila, d/b, eagle border, Stubbs, 10", EX ...250.00
Soup, View du Chateau a Menonville, d/b, Wood, 9⅛" 180.00
Soup, Villa in Regents Park London, d/b, 10", NM 145.00
Strainer, platter; Far Eastern Scenery, m/b, line, 12⅞" 300.00
Strainer, platter; Wild Rose border, m/b, oval, 12⅞", NM 375.00
Sugar bowl, MacDonnough's Victory, d/b, chip, 6⅞" 660.00
Sugar bowl, Rural Estates, d/b, shell hdls, sm rpr 395.00
Teapot, Eagle (on shell), brn, Hall, 7", EX 275.00
Teapot, Eagle Over Panel, d/b, Davenport, rstr, 6½x12¼" 550.00
Teapot, India Wharf & Broad St Stores, d/b, Wood, 1820, 6¼" ...800.00
Teapot, Lafayette at Tomb of Franklin, d/b, crack, 8¾" 700.00
Teapot, Landing of Lafayette, d/b, Clews, rstr, 7½x12" 450.00
Tureen, gravy; Gubbins Hertfordshire, d/b, Wood, 8", +tray 275.00
Tureen, gravy; Hindoo Village, d/b, Hall, 8¾" 325.00
Tureen, gravy; Pass in Catskill Mtns, d/b, Wood, 8", +tray 550.00
Tureen, soup; Boston Mails..., blk, Edwards, w/lid, rpr, 9x5" 600.00
Tureen & stand (1-pc), Shells, m-d/b, staple rpr, w/lid, 6¾" 200.00
Underplate, Eddistone Light House, d/b, rtcl, 9¼" 925.00
Underplate, Priory, l/b, 6½" 105.00
Wash bowl, Arms of Maryland, d/b, Mayer, 4½x12⅝" 2,500.00
Wash bowl & pitcher, Clew's Select Views, d/b 1,850.00
Wash bowl & pitcher, Views of Erie Canal..., d/b, Wood, NM ..1,700.00
Wash pitcher, Upper Ferry Bridge..., d/b, eagle border, 10" 825.00

Miscellaneous

Creamer, cow & milkmaid, mc w/blk details, rstr, 5½" 450.00
Creamer, Toby, mc & lustre, 5¼" 195.00
Cup, handleless; Wood's Rose, purple flower/gr ferns, Wood 45.00
Cup plate, Belzoni, pk, Enoch Wood & Sons, 3⅞" 50.00
Cup plate, Canova, pk & gr, Mayer, 3⅞" 40.00
Cup plate, Swiss Scenery, blk, 3¾" 50.00
Incense burner, cottage, mc, 6¾" 220.00
Inkwell, spaniel seated on cushion, mc w/gold, 4" 400.00
Mug, cricket game, red transfer, 2⅞" 130.00
Mug, Farmer's Arms/Winter/Poem Extolling..., blk w/gold, 5" ...150.00

Mug, Franklin's Maxims, He That Goes a Borrowing..., 2⅜" 110.00
Pastille burner, cottage w/2 brick chimneys, rstr, 5x4½" 350.00
Pitcher, Tyrolese, brn, Jones, 7" 145.00
Plate, Feather, red transfer, Wood & Challinor, 7" 35.00
Platter, wild rose border, m-d/b, well & tree type, 20⅝" 600.00
Quill holder, cat in bonnet, blk & gr trim, 4½", EX 110.00
Soup, Amaryllis, pk, JH&Co, 10¼" 35.00
Soup, Valencia, purple, Job & John Jackson, 10½", NM 45.00
Teapot, scenic, pk transfer, oval, ftd, 6" L 110.00
Tumbler, Biltmore House, brn w/mc enamel, 4" 25.00
Tureen, Fisherman, bl & brn, 6x8x5", w/lid/plate/ladle 275.00

Stained Glass

There are many factors to consider in evaluating a window or panel of stained glass art. Besides the obvious factor of condition, intricacy, jeweling, beveling, and the amount of selenium (red, orange, and yellow) present should all be taken into account. Remember, repair work is itself an art and can be very expensive. Our advisor for this category is Carl Heck; he is listed in the Directory under Colorado.

Lamps

Bigelow-Kennard, candle shield, frog on gridwork, 6x12" 200.00
Bigelow-Kennard, 18" sunflower shade, segments are petals 9,700.00
Chandelier, fruit border w/birds etc, shaped dome, 24", EX 750.00
Chandelier, gridwork w/floral apron, irreg border, 22", VG 400.00
Chandelier, shaped dome w/grapevine border, 23" 750.00
Duffner-Kimberly, 15" sqd shade: lappets/flowers; sqd std 1,950.00
Duffner-Kimberly, 16" floral/arches shade; std w/4 paw ft 8,000.00
Duffner-Kimberly, 18" 4-side shade; std w/4 Pharoah ft, 30" ...7,500.00
Duffner-Kimberly, 19" geometric dome shade; simple std, EX .1,500.00
Duffner-Kimberly, 22" poppy shade; std w/emb climbing poppy ..14,500.00

Suess, 22" red-mottled peonies shade with yellow centers and green leaves on white ground form shade, bronzed-metal telescoping base in Tiffany style, 29" tall, EX, $7,000.00.

Wilkinson, 21½" mums shade w/crown; bronze urn std, 27" ...3,250.00
Wilkinson (att), 20" floral-band shade; metal foliate-cast std .1,450.00

Windows

Laurel wreath, fleur-de-lis, ribbons, 55x61" 440.00
Prairie School, clear/wht/amber, 2 panes, ea 30x14" 650.00
Prairie School, 3 upright geometric stalks, 20x25", EX, pr 550.00
Prairie School, 3-color geometrics, in oak door, 31x16" 200.00
Stylized design in slag glass w/faceted ruby center, 35x25" 230.00

Stanford

The Stanford Pottery Co. was founded in 1945 in Sebring, Ohio. One of the founders was George Stanford, a former manager at Spaulding

China (Royal Copley). They continued in operations until the factory was destroyed by a fire about 1961. They produced a Corn Line, similar to that of the Shawnee Company, that is today becoming very collectible. Most examples are marked (either Stanford Sebring Ohio or with a paper label), so there should be no difficulty in distinguishing one from the other.

In addition to their Corn Line, they produced planters and figurines, many of which were black trimmed with gold, made to be sold as pairs or sets. Wall pockets and vases were made as well. In 1949 they introduced a line called Tomato Ware, consisting of a cookie jar, grease jar, salt and pepper shakers, creamer and sugar bowl, mustard jar, marmalade jar, etc. These were shaped as bright red tomatoes with green leaves and stems (often used as lid finials), and were marketed under the name 'The Pantry Parade.' Our advisor for this category is Joe Devine; he is listed in the Directory under Iowa.

Corn Line, butter dish	45.00
Corn Line, casserole, 8" L	35.00
Corn Line, cookie jar	85.00
Corn Line, creamer & sugar bowl	45.00
Corn Line, pitcher, 7½"	55.00
Corn Line, plate, 9" L	30.00
Corn Line, relish tray	35.00
Corn Line, shakers, sm, pr	25.00
Corn Line, shakers, 4", pr	25.00
Corn Line, spoon rest	25.00
Corn Line, teapot	60.00
Planter, drum major or majorette, ea	15.00
Planter, Dutch Boy or girl by tulip, blk w/gold trim, ea	15.00
Tomato Ware, casserole, w/lid, 6x9"	55.00
Tomato Ware, cookie jar, 8"	60.00
Tomato Ware, creamer	25.00
Tomato Ware, grease jar, w/lid	30.00
Tomato Ware, marmalade jar	25.00
Tomato Ware, mustard jar	25.00
Tomato Ware, pitcher, 6½"	50.00
Tomato Ware, sugar bowl	25.00
Wall pocket, bird, bl & cobalt w/gold trim	28.00

Stangl

Stangl Pottery was one of the longest-existing potteries in the United States, having as its beginning in 1814 the Sam Hill Pottery, becoming the Fulper Pottery which gained eminence in the field of art pottery (ca. 1860), and then coming under the aegis of Johann Martin Stangl. The German-born Stangl joined Fulper in 1910 as chemical engineer, left for a brief stint at Haeger in Dundee, Illinois, and rejoined Fulper as general manager in 1920. He became president of the firm in 1928. Although Stangl's name was on much of the ware from the late twenties onward, the company's name was not changed officially until 1955. J.M. Stangl died in 1972; the pottery continued under the ownership of Wheaton Industries until 1978, then closed. Stangl is best known for its extensive Birds of America line, styled after Audubon; its brightly colored, hand-carved, hand-painted dinnerware; and its great variety of giftware, including its dry-brushed gold lines. For more information we recommend *Stangl Pottery* by Harvey Duke; for ordering information refer to the listing for Nancy and Robert Perzel, Popkorn Antiques (our advisors for this category), in our Directory under New Jersey.

Birds

#3250D, Gazing Duck	100.00
#3250F, Quacking Duck	100.00
#3274, Penguin	500.00

#3275, Turkey	550.00
#3276, Bluebird	70.00
#3276D, Bluebirds, pr	160.00
#3285/3286, Hen & Rooster, shakers, old style, pr	125.00
#3286, Hen, shaker, early	65.00
#3286, Hen, shaker, late	45.00
#3400, Lovebird, early	100.00
#3401, Wren, old style, tan	250.00
#3401, Wren, revised	60.00
#3401D, Wrens, revised pr	100.00
#3402, Oriole, revised	65.00
#3404D, Lovebirds, revised pr	125.00
#3405, Cockatoo, pk	45.00
#3405D, Cockatoos, old, pr	190.00
#3405D, Cockatoos, revised pr	125.00
#3406, Kingfisher, teal	75.00
#3406D, Kingfishers, teal, pr	130.00
#3407, Owl	350.00
#3408, Bird of Paradise	100.00
#3432, Running Duck, brn	450.00
#3443, Flying Duck, teal	250.00
#3444, Cardinal, pk	85.00
#3444, Cardinal, red matt	125.00
#3445, Rooster, gray	200.00
#3445, Rooster, lt yel	175.00
#3446, Hen, gray	175.00
#3446, Hen, yel	180.00
#3447, Prothonatary Warbler	75.00
#3449, Paraquet	150.00
#3450, Passenger Pigeon	1,200.00
#3454, Key West Quail Dove, single wing up	300.00
#3491, Hen Pheasant, Antique Gold	100.00
#3491, Pheasant hen	200.00
#3492, Pheasant Cock	200.00

#3582, Parakeets, green, 7", $175.00 ($225.00 if in blue).

#3589, Indigo Bunting	70.00
#3590, Carolina Wren	175.00
#3591, Brewers Blackbird	130.00
#3594, Red-Faced Warbler	75.00
#3596, Grey Cardinal	85.00
#3597, Wilson Warbler	50.00
#3598, Kentucky Warbler	60.00
#3599D, Hummingbirds	300.00
#3635, Gold Finch group	200.00
#3750D, Western Tanagers, red matt	380.00
#3754D, White Wing Crossbills, red matt	350.00
#3758, Magpie Jay	900.00
#3810, Blackpoll Warbler	150.00
#3813, Evening Grosbeak	125.00
#3850, Yel Warbler	100.00
#3852, Cliff Swallow	135.00
#3868, Summer Tanager	550.00
#3922, European Finch	900.00

Miscellaneous

Amber Glo, bowl, 8" 20.00
Amber Glo, coffee server 50.00
Amber Glo, cruet, w/stopper 25.00
Amber Glo, gravy boat, w/undertray 20.00
Americana, tray, 7" 8.00
Animal, elephant, Antique Gold, 5" 100.00
Animal, rabbit, #3245 ....250.00
Antique Gold, leaf bowl, #5137, 13" 32.00
Ashtray, pansy, brn & golden yel, 4" 10.00
Ashtray, pansy, pk & red, 4" 18.00
Ashtray, pheasant, oval, #3926 ....25.00
Ashtray, poppy, 4" 20.00
Ashtray, Scotty, Granada Gold, #2089 ....60.00
Blueberry, bowl, 10" 40.00
Blueberry, bowl, 12" 65.00
Blueberry, cup 10.00
Carnival, bread tray, #420 ....25.00
Carnival, plate, 8" 7.00
Country Garden, bowl, divided vegetable 35.00
Country Garden, bowl, fruit 10.00
Country Garden, bowl, 8" 30.00
Country Garden, butter dish 30.00
Country Garden, cup & saucer 16.00
Country Garden, jug, ½-pt 15.00
Country Garden, lug soup 12.00
Country Garden, pitcher, 1-pt 25.00
Country Garden, plate, 10" 18.00
Country Garden, plate, 8" 14.00
Country Life, bowl, flat soup; single mallard 100.00
Country Life, chop plate, barn 300.00
Country Life, plate, rooster, 10" 100.00
Country Life, plate, w/farmer, 11" 200.00
Country Life, sugar bowl, rooster, w/lid 50.00
Festival, chop plate, Terra Rose, 14¼" 50.00
Festival, goblet, Terra Rose, ftd, 5¾" 25.00
Festival, plate, Terra Rose, 6¼" 6.00
Flora, bowl, vegetable; rnd, 8" 25.00
Flora, plate, salad 10.00
Flowerpot, red horizontal stripes, 3" 10.00
Flowerpot, red vertical stripes, 4" 12.00
Fruit, bowl, cereal; 5½" 15.00
Fruit, bowl, fruit; 5½" 13.00
Fruit, bowl, soup; 7½" 20.00
Fruit, cruet 35.00
Fruit, pitcher, ½-pt 15.00
Fruit, plate, serving; metal hdl, 10" 8.00
Fruit, plate, 10" 22.00
Fruit, plate, 6" 7.00
Fruit, plate, 8" 20.00
Fruit, sugar bowl, w/lid 18.00
Fruit & Flowers, cup 12.00
Fruit & Flowers, gravy boat 25.00
Fruit & Flowers, plate, 10" 20.00
Fruit & Flowers, plate, 8" 15.00
Garland, creamer 8.00
Garland, cup & saucer 14.00
Garland, plate, 8" 10.00
Golden Blossom, bowl, divided vegetable 25.00
Golden Blossom, pitcher, 2-qt 25.00
Golden Harvest, bowl, divided vegetable 32.00
Golden Harvest, bowl, fruit; 5½" 8.00
Golden Harvest, chop plate, 12" 20.00

Golden Harvest, creamer & sugar bowl, w/lid 15.00
Golden Harvest, cup & saucer 18.00
Golden Harvest, egg cup 10.00
Golden Harvest, plate, 10" 12.00
Golden Harvest, plate, 6" 4.00
Golden Harvest, shakers, pr 15.00
Golden Harvest, teapot 50.00
Granada Gold, dbl pear dish, #3782 ....18.00
Holly, creamer 18.00
Holly, mug, 2-cup 40.00
Holly, plate, dinner 30.00
Kiddieware, bowl, Pony Trail 150.00
Kiddieware, cup, Indian Campfire 100.00
Kiddieware, feeding dish, Our Barnyard Friends, 3-part dish 95.00
Kiddieware, Kiddie set, Mealtime, special cup+3-part dish 120.00
Kiddieware, plate, Little Bo Peep or Little Boy Blue, ea 100.00
Kiddieware, plate, Little Quackers, redware 150.00
Magnolia, chop plate, 12" 20.00
Mug/ashtray, S Toby, Parson, 1930s 200.00
Orchard Song, bread tray 23.00
Orchard Song, coaster 5.00
Orchard Song, server, center hdl, 10" 6.00
Oyster, plate, pk, turq, gr 250.00
Pig bank, w/bl tulip decor, #10768 ....130.00
Planter, horse head, Terra Rose, gr, 13" 400.00
Provincial, bowl, fruit; 5½" 8.00
Provincial, gravy boat, w/underplate 25.00
Provincial, plate, dinner 15.00
Sculptured Fruit, bowl, 10" 35.00
Star Flower, cup & saucer 15.00
Terra Rose, pitcher, gr, 1-pt 15.00
Terra Rose, warmer, gr 10.00
Thistle, bowl, 8" 25.00
Thistle, chop plate, 12½" 28.00
Thistle, creamer & sugar bowl, w/lid 26.50
Thistle, cup & saucer 12.00
Thistle, fruit; bowl, 5½" 10.00
Thistle, plate, 8" 10.00
Thistle, relish 25.00
Thistle, shakers, pr 16.00
Thistle, skillet, hdld, 8" 35.00
Town & Country, bowl, soup/cereal; bl, 5½" 40.00
Town & Country, cheese & cracker, bl dustpan shape 100.00
Town & Country, chop plate, bl 65.00
Town & Country, coffeepot, bl 100.00
Town & Country, mold, bl, fluted, 6" 45.00
Town & Country, plate, bl, 10" 45.00
Town & Country, plate, bl, 8" 35.00

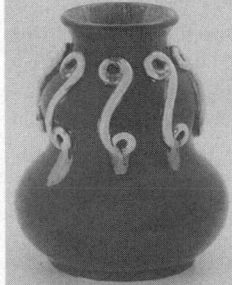

Tropical Ware, vase, aubergine and celadon green with applied white scrolls, #2024, 7½", $125.00.

Trumpet Flower, cigarette box, rectangular 25.00
Tulip, bowl, fruit 12.00
Water Lily, teapot, mini 35.00

White Dogwood, bowl, 8" 30.00
White Dogwood, lug soup 15.00
Wig stand, blond, wood base 275.00
Wig stand, brunette, ceramic base 250.00

Stanley Tools

The Stanley company was founded in Connecticut in 1854, and over the years has absorbed more than a score of tool companies already in existence. By the second decade of the 20th century, having long since solidified their position as *the* source for tools of the highest grade, the company enjoyed worldwide prestige. Through both World Wars, they were recognized as one of the nation's premier producers of wartime goods. Industrial arts classes introduced baby boomers to Stanley tools and provided yet another impetus to expansion and recognition. Overall, the company's growth and development has kept an easy pace along with the economy of the nation, and it continues today as a leader in the field of tool production.

Two facters to consider when evaluating a tool are these: age and condition. One of their earliest trademarks (1854-1857) is 'A. Stanley,' found only on rulers. In the early twenties, their now-familiar 'sweetheart' trademark, the letters SW and a heart shape within the confines of a modified rectangle, was adopted. They continued to use this trademark until it was discontinued in 1933. Many other variations were used as well, some of which contain a patent date. A study of these marks will help you determine the vintage of your tools. Condition is extremely important, and though a light cleaning is acceptable, you should never attempt to 'restore' a tool by sanding, repainting, or replacing parts that may be damaged or missing. Tools listed below are for those in average 'as found' condition, ranging from very good to excellent.

For more information, we recommend *Antique and Collectible Stanley Tools*, written by our advisor, John Walter, who is listed in the Directory under Ohio.

Display tool caddy, wooden with black lettering, 1970s, 20x36", EX, $20.00.

Brace, bit; #918, NP steel, wood hdls, 1909-14, 6-14" 30.00
Chisel, 4-square; #1150, steel shank, wood hdl, 1925-35, 6 szs 25.00
Divider, angle; #31, rosewood w/steel blades, 1911-17, 8" 100.00
Drill, breast; #742, CI, 2-speed, 1911-60, 16" 20.00
Gauge, marking & cutting; #60, NP CI, 1874-97, 7" 75.00
Hammer, tack; #4, NP CI, 1870, 12" 50.00
Knife, razor blade; #199, aluminum, 1936-50, 6" 5.00
Level, carpenter's; w/plumb, #13, wood/brass, 1867-92, 24-30" 25.00
Level, pocket; #42, brass, 1859-1917, 3" 50.00
Mitre box, #2358, bl enameled CI, 1932-82, 5" capacity, 20" 100.00
Plane, block; #65, CI, type #1, 1898-1902, 7" 150.00
Plane, jack; #5, CI, wood hdl & knob, type #2, 1969-72, 14" 250.00
Plane, smooth; #37, CI & wood, type #1, 1867-69, 13" 500.00
Rule, carpenter's; #30, wood w/brass trim, 1859, 2-fold, 6" 500.00
Rule, zigzag; #014, yel enameled hardware, 1917, 48" 50.00
Saw, bead; #1, 1936-42, 10" 50.00
Screwdriver, #20, NP steel blade, wood hdl, 1909-54, many szs 10.00
Spoke shave; #52, CI, 1870-1947, 10" 15.00

Square, mitre; wood, steel blade, brass trim, 1870, 8-12" 50.00
Tape measure, #6386, NP steel, 1937-50, 6" 30.00

Statue of Liberty

Long before she began greeting immigrants in 1886, the Statue of Liberty was being honored by craftsmen both here and abroad. Her likeness was etched on blades of the finest straight razors from England, captured in finely detailed busts sold as souvenirs to Paris fairgoers in 1878, and presented on colorfully lithographed trade cards, usually satirical, to American shoppers. Perhaps no other object has been represented in more forms or with such frequency as the universal symbol of America. Liberty's keepsakes are also universally accessible. Delightful souvenir models created in 1885 to raise funds for Liberty's pedestal are frequently found at flea markets, while earlier French bronze and terracotta Liberties have been auctioned for over $100,000.00. Some collectors hunt for the countless forms of 19th-century Liberty memorabilia, while many collections were begun in anticipation of the 1986 Centennial with concentration on modern depictions. Our advisor for this category is Mike Brooks; he is listed in the Directory under California.

Admission ticket, Liberty Platform, 1886 ....35.00
Booklet, Rays From Liberty's Torch, 1890 ....50.00
Bookmark, fabric, Bartholdi Souvenir, 1886 ....25.00
Bottle, American Dry Co Seltzer 30.00
Bottle, Liberty Maraschino Cherries, ca 1940 ....12.00
Cigarette photo card, Virginia Brights, 1886 ....18.00
Coffeepot, mc image on enameled metal, 11" 250.00
Cup, sterling, Windsor Club, 1907, 2" 22.00
Engraving, dedication ceremony, Am Bank Note Co, 1883, 5½x4" ..110.00
Fob, sterling, Lindbergh NY-Paris 40.00
Hanukkah, menorah, Liberty figural candle holders, M Anson .1,800.00
Lamp base, wht metal figure, clock in base, 1885, 20", EX 300.00
Lamp clock, bronze figural, Souvenir of NY, United Clock, 18" ...145.00
Lithograph, Gaget-Gauthier Foundry, Paris, 1883 souvenir 80.00
Match holder, Arnold Automatic Steamer 200.00
Medal, Columbian Exposition, 1893 ....60.00
Medal, Democratic Nat'l Convention, NY, 1924 ....30.00
Medal, Greenberg & Bro Clothiers, 1892 ....37.50
Medal, World Liberty Penny, July 18, 1918 ....30.00
Model, CI figure w/nickeled silver flame, rare, 40", EX 11,000.00
Model, plastic, Max Voight, Phila, 1918, 72", EX 880.00
Painting, rvpt scene, 22x15", EX 100.00
Photo album, celluloid image on front, velvet bk, 10x8", EX 275.00
Photograph, Bartholdi, Falk Studios, NY, 1880s 150.00
Photograph, Liberty nearing completion, 1886 ....85.00
Postcard, Bon Voyage, harbor scene w/Liberty in distance, EX 15.00
Program, souvenir; Oct 28, 1886 ....200.00
Ribbon, silk, Paris Exposition, 1878 ....100.00
Smoking stand, figural, copper-plated cast metal, EX 150.00
Spoon, Liberty figural hdl, SP, 5¾", EX 77.00
Statue, bronze, sgn, EX details, 16" 125.00
Statue, cast metal on marble base, June 13, 1885 ....1,000.00
Statuette, porc, Benedicting, modern 25.00
Stereo card, head of Liberty, Paris, 1880 ....75.00
Trade card, Eagle Pencils 60.00

Steamship Collectibles

For centuries, ocean-going vessels with their venturesome officers and crews were the catalyst that changed the unknown aspects of our world to the known. Changing economic conditions, unfortunately, have now placed the North American shipping industry in the same jeopardy as the American passenger train. They are becoming a memory. The surge of interest in railroad collectibles and the railroad-related steamship lines has lead collectors to examine the whole spectrum of steamship collectibles. Our advisors for this category are Lila and Fred Shrader; they are listed in the Directory under California.

Key:
BS — back stamped   SM – side mark
NBS — no back stamp   TL — top logo
SL — side logo   TM — top mark

Dinnerware

Ashtray, Goodrich Steam Lines, TL, 5½" dia	**19.00**
Ashtray/match holder, Bowring Steamship Co Ltd, TM/BS, 1-pc	**110.00**
Bowl, cereal; Am Banner Line, TM: AB in flag, 6"	**29.00**
Bowl, cereal; Hellenic Lines Ltd, TL, 6½"	**22.00**
Butter pat, Clipper Line, TL w/gold band	**12.00**
Butter pat, North German Lloyd, TL, Bauscher	**35.00**
Butter pat, Union Castle Line, TM, Ashworth Bros	**39.00**
Butter pat, US Bureau of Fisheries (USBF), TL	**35.00**
Creamer, Eastern Steamship Lines Inc, SM, BS, Buffalo, 4"	**45.00**
Creamer, Moore & McCormack, SL, 3¼"	**65.00**
Cup & saucer, demitasse; Am Mail Line, SL & TL	**75.00**
Cup & saucer, demitasse; North German Lloyd, SL & TL, Bauscher	**55.00**
Cup & saucer, demitasse; White Star Line, wht/turq/brn, SL & TL	**165.00**
Egg cup, Buffalo & Cleveland, SL, lg	**65.00**
Egg cup, Union Castle Line, SM, sm	**38.00**
Pitcher, Bowring Steamship Co, SM, Sutherland, 7"	**110.00**
Plate, Am Mail Line, TL, Buffalo, 7"	**45.00**
Plate, Bibby Line, gr & blk stripes, TL, 9½"	**35.00**
Plate, Cunard, Gentlemen's Cabin, transfer, Staffordshire, 9"	**95.00**
Plate, Merchants & Miners Trans Co, TM: M&MMT Co, 7½"	**65.00**
Plate, Red Star Line, wht w/turq & brn, TM, 8"	**65.00**
Platter, Standard Oil in gr on wht w/gr pinstripes, 10x8"	**135.00**
Teapot, Cunard, tan/blk stripes on lt tan cube form, BS, 5" sq	**185.00**

Miscellaneous

Ashtray, SS France, cobalt glass w/ship & 'France'	**10.00**
Ashtray, United Fruit Line, glass w/UFL logo etched on glass	**32.00**
Baggage label, Cunard	**5.00**
Booklet, Cunard, Berengaria, color cover, 1920, 8x11"	**25.00**
Booklet, Matson, HI Highlights bamboo, silk cord, '35, 7x8½"	**35.00**
Bridge pad, RMS Laconia, enamel crest, 4 aces, 3x5½", EX	**40.00**
Brochure, Alcoa, Caribbean cruise, 1959	**7.50**
Brochure, Am Export Lines, Mediterranean cruise, 1967	**7.50**
Brochure, Holland-Am, S Am/Caribbean cruises, 1959/60, 8x9"	**7.50**
Brochure, Matson, HI Holiday, fold-out 12 panels, 1938	**12.00**
Condiment set, Hamburg Am Line, silver fr w/glass s/p+mustard	**165.00**
Cuff links & tie bar, HMS Queen Elizabeth, ca 1930	**95.00**
Deck plans, Am Export Lines, Constitution, Independence, 1958	**7.50**
Deck plans, Italian Line, Raffallo & Michaelangelo, 1966	**7.50**
Globe, Hammond's 12, steamship routes, wear, 14", VG	**200.00**
Hat ribbon, French Line SS Normandie, red w/gold lettering	**90.00**
Invitation, SS Independence, cocktails w/captain, 1964	**7.50**
Menu, cocktail; New Amsterdam, blk cover, 1947, 4½x7"	**7.50**
Menu, Farrell Lines, SS Red Jacket, printed, 1981, 5¼x9"	**3.50**
Menu, French Line, dbl fold, 1924, 7x9"	**6.00**
Menu, Matson Lines SS Monterey, farewell dinner, 1960	**10.00**
Menu, Royal Viking, Mexican dinner, 1986, 8¼x11"	**7.50**
Party favor, N German Lloyd, 3" celluloid face w/crepe paper, '37	**25.00**
Passenger list, Heian Maru, 1930s	**10.00**

Passenger list, Leviathan, portrait cover, 1926	**20.00**
Passenger list, Queen Elizabeth, 1948	**9.00**
Playing cards, Matson Lines, dbl deck, MIB	**18.00**
Playing cards, N German Lloyd, Norddetscher Lloyd Bremen, MIB	**35.00**
Postcard, LASSCO w/balloon ride ad on address on side, 1920s	**10.00**
Program, entertainment, K-Y Steamer, Japanese, 1930s	**9.00**
Sign, Holland Am, Dutch girl, celluloid/paper/tin, 10x14"	**67.50**
Ticket folio, Cunard Line, w/related paper items, 1928	**40.00**
Timetable, Am Steamship, deck plans, 1914, EX	**24.00**
Tip tray, Cunard, Aquatania chromo litho, ca 1915, M	**145.00**
Whistle, CI/brass/copper, Lunkenheimer, 17"+stand	**175.00**

Steins

Steins have been made from pottery, pewter, glass, stoneware, and porcelain, from very small up to the four-liter size. They are decorated by etching, in-mold relief, decals, and occasionally they may be hand painted. Some porcelain steins have lithophane bases. Collectors often specialize in a particular type — faience, regimental, or figural — while others limit themselves to the products of only one manufacturer. Our advisor for this category is Ron Fox; he is listed in the Directory under New York. See also Mettlach.

Key:
L — liter   PUG — print under glaze
lith — lithophane   tl — thumb lift
POG — print over glaze

Character steins, all porcelain and modern (but made from old original molds by Schierholz), left to right: Uncle Sam, ½-L, M, $360.00; Von Moltke, ½-L, M, $360.00; Masquerade Lady, ½-L, $365.00.

Ceramic, Budweiser girl, made in Italy, 1973, 1-L, 4 for	**1,275.00**
Character, baby, porc, Schierholz, modern, ½-L	**300.00**
Character, Bismark, porc, mc, rpr helmet finial, 1950s, 1-L	**145.00**
Character, bowling ball, porc, Schierholz, hairline, ½-L	**175.00**
Character, clown, porc, Schierholz, modern, ½-L	**385.00**
Character, cucumber, porc, Schierholz, modern, ½-L	**400.00**
Character, devil, porc, E Bohne/Sohne, ½-L	**800.00**
Character, drunken monkey, porc, mk RPM, ca 1950, ½-L	**200.00**
Character, drunken monkey, porc, Schierholz, ½-L	**600.00**
Character, dwarf on toadstool, Schierholz, modern, ½-L	**360.00**
Character, elephant, porc, Schierholz, ear rpr, ½-L	**770.00**
Character, Frederich III, porc, Schierholz, modern, ½-L	**400.00**
Character, Funnel Man, pottery, Reinhold Hanke, ½-L, EX	**190.00**
Character, Gentleman Rabbit, porc, Schierholz, 1980s, ½-L	**495.00**
Character, Gooseman, porc, lith, lip rpr, ½-L	**525.00**
Character, Gooseman, porc, Shierholz, 1980s, ½-L	**320.00**
Character, Indian, porc, E Bohne Sohne, ¼-L, NM	**400.00**
Character, knight, stoneware, bl salt glaze, sm rpr, .2-L	**175.00**
Character, man w/cigar, pottery, Eckhardt & Engler, rpr, ½-L	**220.00**
Character, military monkey, pottery, modern, ½-L, NM	**80.00**

Character, monk, pottery, mk Original King, modern, ½-L 60.00
Character, monk, stoneware, salt glaze, flake, ½-L 230.00
Character, Munich Child, porc, lith, .2-L 300.00
Character, Munich Child, porc, Martin Pauson, rpr, ½-L 300.00
Character, Munich Child, pottery, inlay rpr, ½-L 220.00
Character, Mushroom Lady, porc, Schierholz, modern, ½-L 255.00
Character, Nurnberg Tower, pewter, missing finial, ½-L 200.00
Character, Nurnberg Tower, pottery, missing finial, ½-L 185.00
Character, Nurnberg Tower, stoneware, pewter lid, 1-L, NM 360.00
Character, owl, pottery, Merkelbach & Wick, ½-L 255.00
Character, owl, stoneware, mk MWG, bl salt glaze, ½-L, EX 160.00
Character, owl, stoneware, rpr on base, ½-L, EX 600.00
Character, ram, pottery, Merkelbach & Wick, ½-L 330.00
Character, rich man, pottery, #722, ½-L, NM 145.00
Character, Sad Radish, porc, Schierholz, rpr, ½-L 286.00
Character, skull, porc, att E Bohne Sohne, ½-L 575.00
Character, skull on book, porc, E Bohne Sohne, .3-L 745.00
Character, skull on book, porc, E Bohne Sohne, ½-L, EX 335.00
Character, Uncle Sam, porc, Shierholz, orig, ½-L 2,695.00
Character, workman, pottery, modern, sm rpr, ½-L 30.00
Earthenware, relief/glazed: Art Nouveau/bats, rare, ½-L 850.00
Faience, buildings, Bayreuth, ca 1780, rprs, 1-L, VG 175.00
Faience, florals, Schrezheim, late 1700s, 1-L, EX 780.00
Faience, St George & dragon, Potsdam, late 1700s, 1-L, EX 330.00
Glass, blown, cranberry, pewter o/l & lid, ½-L 495.00
Glass, blown, cut, frosted, gold enamel, pewter lid, ½-L, NM 150.00
Glass, blown, etched: stag, pewter lid, loose hinge, .4-L 160.00
Glass, blown, faceted, dwarf tl, glass lid, .3-L, NM 110.00
Glass, blown, faceted, worn SP lid w/man rowing, ½-L 130.00
Glass, blown, frosted & enameled, porc inlaid lid, ½-L 320.00
Glass, blown, HP: Franz Joseph, prism lid, ½-L 188.00
Glass, blown, wht o/l on clear, glass inlaid lid, ½-L, NM 165.00
Glass, pressed, relief: ram/monkey/cat, prism lid, .3-L 165.00
Glass, wht cased, HP crest & crown, metal lid, ½-L 330.00
Military, pottery, Regt Nr 32...Westphal, pewter lid, ½-L 230.00
Occupational, porc, baker transfer, lith, ½-L 360.00
Occupational, porc, barrel strap maker transfer, lith, ½-L 825.00
Occupational, porc, fireman transfer, pewter lid, 1-L 575.00
Occupational, pottery, farmer transfer, pewter lid, 1-L 200.00
Occupational, stoneware, blacksmith, pewter lid, ½-L, NM 250.00
Porc, HP: flowers, pewter lid w/tear, ca 1860, 1½-L 265.00
Porc, HP: student's society, pewter lid, 1931, ½-L, NM 240.00
Porc, relief: cupid, pewter lid, #8644, ½-L 230.00
Porc, relief: Kanar Zucht/Vogelschutz Ver Koburg, rpr, ½-L 140.00
Porc, transfer: artillery soldiers, lith, ½-L, NM 100.00
Porc, transfer: XIV Deutscher...Munchen 1893, lith, rare, 1-L ...798.00
Pottery, etched: drinking scene, pewter lid (torn), #3013, ½-L ..100.00
Pottery, etched: Kraft & Gremulth, Remy, inlaid lid, ½-L 198.00
Pottery, POG: student's society, pewter lid, rpr strap, ½-L 110.00
Pottery, relief: Chief Hollow Horn, mc, Gerz 027, ½-L 105.00
Pottery, relief: festival scene, mc, pewter lid, 1-L 145.00
Pottery, relief: Lee Monument/Old Creole Home, ½-L 165.00
Pottery, relief: Prussian eagle/crests, rpr pewter lid, ½-L 120.00
Pottery, relief: soldiers, pewter lid, ½-L 110.00
Pottery, transfer: Erinnerung an Munchen, music box, 1-L, EX ..175.00
Pottery, transfer: GAR 1861-65, no lid, 2", M 67.50
Regimental, porc, Bayr Inft...Erlangen, wreath tl, ½-L 385.00
Regimental, porc, Comp Pionier Battl...1898-1900, ½-L, NM ...300.00
Regimental, porc, Feld Artl...Pirna 1903-05, Saxon tl, ½-L 550.00
Regimental, porc, Feld Artl...Wesel, lion tl, 1897-99, ½-L 300.00
Regimental, porc, Fuss Artl...Strassburg, griffin tl, ½-L 285.00
Regimental, porc, Garde Gren...Charlottenberg, eagle tl, ½-L, EX ..300.00
Regimental, porc, Inft Regt...Neubreis, lith, no lid, ½-L 140.00
Regimental, porc, Inft...Freiburg, griffin tl, 1905-07, ½-L 175.00

Regimental, porc, no regiment, eng 1899-1901 on lid, ½-L 150.00
Regimental, porc, Regt...Darmstadt, lion tl, 1902-04, ½-L 415.00
Regimental, porc, Schw Reiter...Landshut, 1898-01, ½-L 465.00
Regimental, porc, 1 Esk Leib...Potsdam, 1875-78, ½-L 580.00
Regimental, porc, 4 Feld Artl Regt Augsburg, 1895-87, ½-L 330.00
SP, Art Nouveau, Goosman of Nurnburg under hdl, worn, 1½-L ..155.00
Stoneware, Bevo Fox figural, Thewalt, ½-L 185.00
Stoneware, bl Delft design, Ceramarte, ½-L 350.00
Stoneware, Clydesdale Hofbrau, Ceramarte, hammered lid, ½-L ..175.00
Stoneware, etched: Souvenir...St Augustine, alligator hdl, ½-L .220.00
Stoneware, Grant's Farm, Ceramarte, red boxes/bbls, ½-L 150.00
Stoneware, lead glaze: Art Nouveau, pewter lid, #2108, ½-L 150.00
Stoneware, relief: bowling & dwarfs, pewter lid, 2½" L 175.00
Stoneware, relief: Columbus reserve, R Hanke, ½-L 525.00
Stoneware, relief: dwarfs, Whites Utica, no lid, 1-L 200.00
Stoneware, relief: Regensburg, Gambrinus, pewter lid, 1-L 105.00
Stoneware, relief: Zeppelin, aluminum lid from Zeppelin, ½-L, EX ..500.00
Stoneware, relief: 3-wheel bicycle scenes, salt glaze, ½-L 330.00
Stoneware, relief: 5 figures in panels, pewter lid, ½-L 92.50
Stoneware, salt glaze: Art Nouveau, Merkelbach, #2112, ½-L 300.00
Stoneware, transfer & enamel: Marzi & Remi, #2023, rpr, ½-L .220.00
Stoneware, transfer & enamel: Munich child, ½-L 175.00
Stoneware, transfer & enamel: target shooting, pewter lid, ½-L .185.00
Stoneware, transfer & enamel: Turkish Munich Child, ½-L 385.00
Stoneware, transfer & enamel: XI Teutches Turnfest 1908, ½-L .415.00
Third Reich, porc, flak scene, no lid, body M, ½-L 230.00
Third Reich, porc, 7 Comp IR Regensburg 1934-35, ½-L 400.00
Third Reich, pottery, Labor Co 1934-35, metal lid, ½-L 240.00
Third Reich, pottery, solders in gask masks, rpl lid, ½-L 195.00
Third Reich, stoneware, Erinnerung am Deinstzeit, ½-L 380.00
Third Reich, stoneware, Flak Abt 195, 1941, rpr lid, ½-L 440.00
Third Reich, stoneware, incised: Labor Co, 1935-36, ½-L 200.00
Third Reich, stoneware, Marine Flakbrigade..., rpr lid, ½-L 450.00
Third Reich, stoneware, Unteroffiziers Korps, 1938, ½-L 415.00
Third Reich, stoneware, VEI Munchen/Munich Child, 1934, 1-L .350.00
US Military, pottery, Air Transport...1949, pewter lid, ½-L 330.00
US Military, pottery, Munich Military Post, 1921-37 mk, 1-L 70.00

Steuben

Carder Steuben glass was made by the Steuben Glass Works in Corning, New York, while under the direction of Frederick Carder from 1903 to 1932. Perhaps the most popular types of Carder Steuben glass are Gold Aurene which was introduced in 1904 and Blue Aurene, introduced in 1905. Gold and Blue Aurene objects shimmer with the lustrous beauty of their metallic iridescence. Carder also produced other types of 'Aurenes' including Red, Green, Yellow, Brown, and Decorated, all of which are very rare. Aurene also was cased upon Calcite glass. Some pieces had paper labels.

Other types of Carder Steuben include Cluthra, Cintra, Florentia, Rosaline, Ivory, Ivorene, Jades, Verre de Soie; there are many more.

Frederick Carder's leadership of Steuben ended in 1932, and the production of colored glassware soon ceased. Since 1932 the tradition of fine Steuben art glass has been continued in crystal.

Our advisor for this category is Thomas P. Dimitroff; he is in the Directory under New York. In the following listings, examples are signed unless noted otherwise.

Key: ACB — acid cut back

Basket, Bl Aurene, berry prunts, #1468, 11" 1,800.00
Basket, Bl Aurene on Calcite, swirled prunts on hdl, #5069, 8" ..2,500.00
Bonbon, Gold Aurene, triangular rim, ring hdl, #2670, 6½" 635.00

Bookends, gazelle, #7399, 6¾" 450.00
Bottle, cologne; bl, flower stopper, 5½" 350.00
Bottle, Gold Aurene, bell form w/ball stopper, #8181, 4¾" 600.00
Bottle, scent; Bl Aurene, cup rim, conical stopper, #3423, 5" .1,500.00
Bottle, scent; Bl Aurene, shouldered sq, #2759, 3¾" 900.00
Bottle, scent; Gold Aurene, blk stopper w/flower, #3245, 6" 400.00
Bottle, scent; Verre de Soie, #1988, 6" 350.00
Bottle, scent; Verre de Soie, ribs, Pk Cintra stopper, 4½" 425.00
Bouillon cup, Gold Aurene w/rtcl silver holder & tray 250.00
Bowl, Acanthus, crystal ACB, #8549 ....350.00
Bowl, amethyst, draped, #3030 ....225.00
Bowl, Aurene, hexagonal, sgn, #6241, 7" 675.00
Bowl, Bl Aurene, wide flared rim, #2606, 4½x11" 865.00
Bowl, centerpc; cranberry w/swirled ribs, #6509, 12" 250.00
Bowl, centerpc; Grotesque, Ivory, #7535, 12" 250.00
Bowl, Cluthra, pk to wht, shouldered, #6906, 5½x11" 1,000.00
Bowl, Cluthra, rose, #6169 ....425.00
Bowl, console; Bristol Yel, clear ft, rolled edge, 13" 175.00
Bowl, emerald, mold-blown ribs, ped ft, 9x5½" 275.00
Bowl, Florentia, 5-petal blossom, gr on frost, #6785, 4x14" 2,600.00
Bowl, Gold Aurene, wide flaring rim, 5x12" 850.00
Bowl, Gold Aurene & Calcite, ped ft, 3¾x9¾" 350.00
Bowl, Gold Aurene w/reddish irid, #2618, 4¼" H 275.00
Bowl, Gr Jade, lobed, #6200, 2¼x15¾" 250.00
Bowl, Grotesque, lt antique gr w/bubbles, #7307, 12" L 325.00
Bowl, Ivorene, 8-ruffle rim, 4x12" 400.00
Bowl, lg appl scroll ft, #7910, 1942, 7x9" 430.00
Bowl, Mirror Blk on Alabaster, dbl-etched Nedra, #6078, 6¾" .1,265.00
Bowl, Pomona Gr, lt ribbing, trn-down rim, #6002, 5x14" 230.00
Bowl, Rosaline, sgn Carder, 2½x5" 275.00
Bowl, Strawberry Mansion, Federalist eagle, Carder, 4¾" 375.00
Bowl, Verre de Soie w/aquamarine edging, #5195, 4x10" 195.00
Bowl vase, Cluthra, pk/wht swirls w/trapped bubbles, 5x8" 865.00
Bowl/cake plate, Rosaline, #3579 ....250.00
Candlestick, Bristol Yel, ribbed/flanged, floral/vine ft, 7" 225.00
Candlestick, Gold Aurene on Calcite, ringed trumpet base, 6" ..210.00
Candlestick, Pomona Gr, 2-knop slim baluster, #2596, 12" 250.00
Candlesticks, amethyst crystal, #3100, pr 450.00
Candlesticks, Bl Aurene on Calcite, wide top, #3581, 6", pr ...2,000.00
Candlesticks, Celeste Bl, Optic, ribbed, #2956, 15", pr 800.00
Candlesticks, Gold Aurene, twist stem, #686, 8", pr 1,400.00
Candlesticks, Mat-Su-No-Ke, Celeste Bl & crystal, #3304, 10", pr.850.00
Candlesticks, Pomona Gr, 2-knop ribbed std, #2959, 10", pr 500.00
Candlesticks, Spanish Gr, random bubble/threading, 15", pr 650.00
Candlesticks, Verre de Soie w/cobalt threads, 5", pr 425.00
Champagne, Strawberry Mansion, eng eagle, mk, 4½" 500.00
Cocktail, bl ft & lightly ribbed bowl, twist topaz stem, 4½" 100.00
Compote, amber, hollow stem & ball connector, #6002, 6x6" ...325.00
Compote, amethyst, #1983 ....350.00
Compote, Bl Aurene, shallow w/shaped stem, #2642, 8x6" 750.00
Compote, Gold Aurene on Calcite, in Poole SP cherub-std ft ...800.00

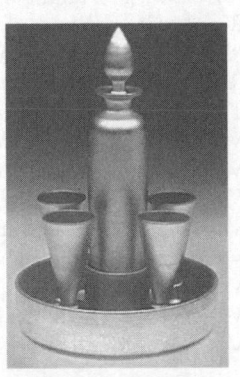

Cordial set, Gold Aurene, 8¾" cylindrical decanter, with 4 conical glasses on 6¼" diameter tray, each piece signed and numbered #2025, $3,250.00.

Cordial, Gold Aurene, twist stem, 3½" 300.00
Cordial, Rosaline & Gr Jade, Alabaster stem & ft, 6", 3 for 175.00
Cordial, Spanish Gr, threaded, prunts on knopped stem, #6359 ...50.00
Creamer & sugar bowl, Pomona Gr, topaz hdls, swirled, #6139 ..375.00
Dish, Gold Aurene, wide flat rim, #2361, 1x6½" 160.00
Ewer, Gold Aurene, stick neck, angle hdl, #2773, 5½" 750.00
Flower frog, Gold Aurene, red highlights, 2½x4" 95.00
Goblet, Bristol Yel w/blk threading, ribbed, #8381, 9" 40.00
Goblet, Cerice Ruby Swirl w/crystal stem & ft, #6474, 5¼" 150.00
Goblet, crystal w/Cintra stem, #1317 ....200.00
Goblet, Gold Aurene w/EX irid, twist stem, #2361, 6" 250.00
Goblet, Gold Ruby, cone-shape bowl, clear knop stem, 7" 175.00
Goblet, gr ft & flared/ribbed bowl w/clear twist stem, 8½" 125.00
Goblet, Oriental Poppy, gr stem & ft, 8" 1,095.00
Goblet, teardrop in ball stem, #7877, 5¾", set of 4 ....375.00
Goblet, topaz w/gr ped ft & appl trails, #6303, set of 12 ....1,500.00
Jar, Bristol Yel w/blk threads, Macy's label, #6887, w/lid 450.00
Lamp base, gold irid cylinder neck/bulb bottom, leafy metal ft ...300.00
Lamp base, Gr Jade, etched mums/leaves, w/fittings, 12x7" 865.00
Lamp shade, Gold Aurene, fleur-de-lis mk, 5", EX 125.00
Luncheon set, Alabaster wheel-cut floral on Rosaline, 14-pc 800.00
Nappy, Jade Gr, Alabaster hdl, folded-in sides, #1226, 5½" 120.00
Parfait, Rosaline w/Alabaster ft, sgn Carder, #5130, 7½" 325.00
Parfait, Rosaline w/Alabaster knobbed ft, #1060, 6" 120.00
Salt cellar, Gold Aurene, #567, 1¾x4¾" 250.00
Sherbet, Gold Aurene w/bl highlights, stick stem, #2680, 4" 100.00
Stocking darner, Bl Aurene, 6" 550.00
Stocking darner, feathers, gold on Calcite, att, 6¼" 750.00
Stocking darner, Gold Aurene, sgn Carder, 6" 450.00
Stocking darner, Gr Jade, 6½" 300.00
Stocking darner, hooked motif, gold on Calcite, att, 6" 600.00
Stocking darner, oil spots on Calcite, att, 6½" 500.00
Vase, ACB, Gr Jade, matzu pattern, global, 7" 750.00
Vase, ACB, Gr Jade to Alabaster w/3-repeat birds, #6148, 9" .1,050.00
Vase, ACB lotus/leaves on Plum Jade w/scrolls, 7x7" 2,250.00
Vase, amber, ribbed, #7377 ....200.00
Vase, amber, 3-branch tree trunk form, #2743, 6" 275.00
Vase, Antique Gr, ribbed optic, #2105 variant, 13½" 225.00
Vase, Aurene/Calcite, ruffled rim, #184, 8" 375.00
Vase, Bl Aurene, #2683, 10" 2,100.00
Vase, Bl Aurene, #2812, 4x4" 650.00
Vase, Bl Aurene, appl scroll shoulder hdls, base chip, 12" ...1,150.00
Vase, Bl Aurene, classic form, #2683, 10½" 1,700.00
Vase, Bl Aurene, shouldered w/sm can neck, #2794, 5" 650.00
Vase, Bl Aurene, splotched irid, ribbed ovoid, 4" 485.00
Vase, blk, 3 3-sided cones on rnd base, #5873, 10½" 800.00
Vase, Bristol Yel, twist ribs, 3-lobe flared top, #6441, 12" 400.00
Vase, Brn Aurene, gold heart-leaves, flared neck, #270, 7¾" ..8,000.00
Vase, bud; Bl Aurene, #2551, 8¼" 560.00
Vase, bud; Gold Aurene w/bl irid, #2556, 8¾" 150.00
Vase, bud; Rosaline w/Alabaster ft, #5228, 13½" 350.00
Vase, Celeste Bl, swirled, rectangular, #6199, 9x5¾" 200.00
Vase, Cluthra, amethyst, classic form, 10" 1,050.00
Vase, Cluthra, bl/crystal, bulbous, #2683, 6" 1,100.00
Vase, Cluthra, gr, classic form, 8" 600.00
Vase, Cluthra, Pomona Gr, #2683, 10" 1,000.00
Vase, Cluthra, rose, #6169 ....425.00
Vase, Cluthra, wht, #2683, 10" 900.00
Vase, Cluthra, wht, classic form, 8" 800.00
Vase, cornucopia; sq ped, 6" 235.00
Vase, crystal crackle, appl decor, #6382 ....250.00
Vase, dk amber, diagonal ribs, similar to #6031, 10" 210.00
Vase, emerald gr w/silver thread crackle, lion's head decor, 9" ...175.00
Vase, Flemish Bl Dmn Quilt, wide threaded band, #6777, 10" ...175.00

Vase, Flemish Bl w/swirl, #6212 ....350.00
Vase, Florentia, pk floral & collar wrap, #6781, 7x7" 1,150.00
Vase, Gold Aurene, dented body, long petal neck, #65, 6" 425.00
Vase, Gold Aurene, flared rim, #6991, 8½x8¼" 775.00
Vase, Gold Aurene, flared rim & ft, #2907, 6" 550.00
Vase, Gold Aurene, flared/ruffled U-form, #162, 3½" 525.00
Vase, Gold Aurene, squat w/dimpled body, long neck, #132, 5" .490.00
Vase, Gold Aurene, 3-prong stump form, #1744, 6¼" 550.00
Vase, Gold Aurene, 6-ruffle rim on trumpet form, #723, 7½" 490.00
Vase, Gold Aurene on Calcite, flared ftd V-form, 8x10" 575.00
Vase, Gold Aurene w/millefiori wht buds & gr leaves, 9½" 2,750.00
Vase, gr, Dmn Optic, fan form w/ball stem & threading, 8x7" ...225.00
Vase, Gr Aurene w/gold leaves w/swirled tips, gold int, 7x7" ..2,800.00
Vase, Gr Jade, 3 thorny stumps w/common base, 6" 210.00
Vase, gr to wht, 3-prong, crystal ft, #6873 ....1,100.00
Vase, Grotesque, amethyst to clear, #7090, 1920, 11" 575.00
Vase, Grotesque, clear to gr, 11" 375.00
Vase, Grotesque, emerald gr to clear, 9" 295.00
Vase, Grotesque, ruby to clear, #7090, 9" 350.00
Vase, Ivorene, classic form, #2683, 8½x8½" 490.00
Vase, Ivorene, lg ribbed/flared top, #7565, 10" 550.00
Vase, Ivorene, 3-lily, #7595, 12½" 1,000.00
Vase, Ivory, #913, 6" 350.00
Vase, leaves/pulled vines, gold on Gr Aurene, #508, 8" 3,500.00
Vase, Lt Bl Aurene, feathers on gourd neck/shoulder, 6½" 850.00
Vase, Mirror Blk, 3 triangular tubes on oval, #6873, 10" 700.00
Vase, Moss Agate, bubbles/aventurine in gold-amber, 6x4" 5,500.00
Vase, Oriental Poppy, #6030, 7" 1,840.00
Vase, Oriental Poppy, flat cone on twisted opal ft, 10", pr 3,400.00
Vase, Pegasus, horse eng sgn Waugh, ftd U-form, #8206, 7" 635.00
Vase, pk to wht Cluthra, crystal hdls, #8515 ....1,050.00
Vase, Pomona Gr, rectangular, swirled, #6199, 9" 150.00
Vase, Pomona Gr, swirled, #6030, 7" 175.00
Vase, Rosalene & Alabaster, #5228, 13½" 295.00
Vase, topaz, urn form, lid w/pear finial, 14" 750.00
Vase, topaz w/Pomona Gr stem/ft, ribbed fan form, #6287, 8½" .200.00
Vase, Verre de Soie, classic form, ftd, 4¾" 175.00
Wine, Gold Aurene, twist stem, 4½" 250.00

Stevengraphs

A Stevengraph is a small picture made of woven silk resembling an elaborate ribbon, created by Thomas Stevens in England in the latter half of the 1800s. They were matted and framed by Stevens, usually with his name appearing on the mat or, more commonly, the trade announcement on the back of the mat. He also produced silk postcards and bookmarks, all of which have 'Stevens' woven in silk on one of the mitered corners. Anyone wishing to learn more about Stevengraphs is encouraged to contact the Stevengraph Collectors' Association, whose address can be found in the Directory under Clubs, Newsletters, and Catalogs.

Buffalo Bill Cody, Nate Salsbury, and Indian Chiefs, original matt and 8x7" frame, $375.00.

Are You Ready, rowing teams, fr, G 220.00
Coventry, 2 blk & wht scenes, fr, pr 110.00
Crystal Palace, inside, fr 385.00
Dick Turpin's Last Ride on His Blk Bess, Hogarth, VG 150.00
First Innings, G 300.00
First Touch, fr, VG 330.00
God Speed the Plough, G 150.00
Good Old Days, coach & 4, matted & fr, 7½x10½", M 195.00
Mrs Cleveland, VG 135.00
Queen Victoria Jubilee 1837-1887, unfr 55.00
Rescue at Sea, fr, VG 220.00
Start, NM 175.00
Victoria, Queen of Empire on Which the Sun Never Sets, unfr .195.00
Water Jump, fr, G 220.00
Wellington & Blucher, G 165.00

Miscellaneous

Bookmark, Dr Guthrie 50.00
Bookmark, Garibaldi, United Italy 50.00
Bookmark, Gen Grant, Richmond 1865 ....50.00
Bookmark, Happy Birthday 85.00
Bookmark, Happy Christmas 50.00
Bookmark, Many Happy Returns 50.00
Bookmark, Princess Alexandra & Prince Albert 50.00
Bookmark, To My Son, G 40.00
Postcard, Shakespeare's Birthplace 45.00

Stevens and Williams

Stevens and Williams glass was produced at the Brierly Hill Glassworks in Stourbridge, England, for nearly a century, beginning in the 1830s. They were credited with being among the first to develop a method of manufacturing a more affordable type of cameo glass. Other lines were also made — silver deposit, alexandrite, and engraved rock crystal, to name but a few. Our advisor for this category is Don Williams; he is listed in the Directory under Missouri.

Biscuit bbl, wht w/pk int, 3 appl variegated leaves, 8x6" 395.00
Bowl, bl, pk int, ruffled, clear wishbone ft, 7½x4½" 265.00
Bowl, bl striped satin, box-pleated top, 4¼x4⅛" 200.00
Bowl, cameo floral on moss agate craquelle, 3¾x8½" 4,900.00
Bowl, cameo mums, orange/wht on pk, 3 camphor ft, 4½x6" 950.00
Bowl, gr w/pk int, appl mc leaves, amber ft, 3x5¼" 150.00
Bowl, Silveria, foil/red shading/gr threading, 4x8", EX 2,000.00
Finger bowl, bl to clear, fruit intaglio, 6", +8" plate 265.00
Finger bowl, gr to clear, vintage intaglio, 4¾", +plate 265.00
Pitcher, Swirl MOP, yel-amber to raspberry w/gold floral, 8" 865.00
Rose bowl, bl frost w/bl opaque stripes, pleated, 4½x4" 135.00
Rose bowl, brn to gold o/l, box-pleated top, 3½x4¼" 225.00
Rose bowl, gold prunus on brn shaded, pleated top, 5¼x3½" 435.00
Rose bowl, rose/pk swirls on leaf-shaped gr base, 5¾" dia 450.00
Rose bowl, Swirl MOP, rust/caramel alternate, bl int, 4½" 800.00
Rose bowl, wht w/pk int, 3 appl amber/gr acanthus leaves, 4½" .250.00
Tumbler, gr & wht stripes alternate w/clear, silver band, 5" 110.00
Vase, lt amber w/appl pear & plum, gr leaves, bl ft, 6x5" 350.00
Vase, peach o/l w/appl acorns/etc, clear ruffled rim, 9" 195.00
Vase, pulled swirls, red/gr/topaz on opal, shouldered, 8" 1,200.00
Vase, red/pk o/l, 2 appl amber pears etc, T-hdls/X ft, 10" 500.00
Vase, rose o/l w/appl amber scallops & mc leaves, 7½" 275.00
Vase, Silveria, red/gold/silver w/gr veins, twisted, 6x6" 3,000.00
Vase, Swirl MOP, bl shaded to rose, long neck, 7½" 800.00
Vase, Swirl MOP, dk gr & rose, bl int, 18¼x7" 1,600.00

Vase, Swirl MOP, gr to red, 5⅜x5¼"	**750.00**
Vase, turq w/combed bl swirls, dbl gourd w/hdls, 9"	**550.00**
Vase, wht w/appl acorns & leaves, pk int, 9x5½"	**200.00**
Vase, wht w/appl amber hdl/flower, pk int, pleated top, 11"	**225.00**
Vase, wht w/appl mc leaves, pk int, amber rim, 7½x5"	**225.00**

Stickley

Among the leading proponents of the Arts and Crafts movement, the Stickley brothers — Gustav, Leopold, Charles, Albert, and John George — were at various times and locations separately involved in designing and producing furniture as well as decorative items for the home. (See Arts and Crafts for further information.) The oldest of the five Stickley brothers was Gustav; his work is the most highly regarded of all. He developed the style of furniture referred to as Mission. It was strongly influenced by the type of furnishings found in the Spanish missions of California — utilitarian, squarely built, and simple. It was made most often of oak, and decoration was very limited or non-existent. The work of his brothers display adaptations of many of Gustav's ideas and designs. His factory, the Craftsman Workshop, operated in Eastwood, New York, from the late 1890s until 1915, when he was forced out of business by larger companies who copied his work and sold it at much lower prices. Among his shopmarks are the early red decal containing a joiner's compass and the words 'Als Ik Kan,' the branded mark with very similar components, and paper labels.

The firm known as Stickley Brothers was located first in Binghamton, New York, and then Grand Rapids, Michigan. Albert and John George made the move to Michigan, leaving Charles in Binghamton (where he and an uncle continued the operation under a different name). After several years John George left the company to rejoin Leopold in New York. (These two later formed their own firm called L. & J.G. Stickley.) The Stickley Brothers Company under Albert's sole direction produced furniture that featured fine inlay work, decorative cutouts, and leaned strongly toward a style of Arts and Crafts with an English influence. It was tagged with a paper label 'Made by Stickley Brothers, Grand Rapids,' or with a brass plate or decal with the words 'Quaint Furniture,' an English term he chose to refer to his product. In addition to his furniture, he made metal furnishings as well.

The workshops of the L. & J.G. Stickley Company first operated under the name 'Onondaga Shops.' Located in Fayetteville, New York, their designs were often all but copies of Gustav's work. Their products were well made and marketed, and their business was very successful. Their decal labels contained all or a combination of the words 'Handcraft' or 'Onondaga Shops,' along with the brothers' initials and last name. The firm continues in business today. Our advisor for this category is Bruce Austin; he is listed in the Directory under New York. Note: When only one dimension is given for tables, it is length. Values are for furniture with excellent original finish unless noted otherwise.

Gustav Stickley

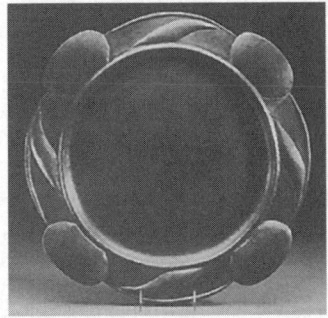

Gustav Stickely hammered repousse copper serving tray, #346, marked, 21" diameter, $2,500.00.

Armchair, #310½, 3-slat bk, leather seat, decal/label	**950.00**
Armchair, #344, child's, 3-slat bk, mk, rfn, new leather	**425.00**
Ashtray, hammered copper, 4 lg dimples in rim, mk, 5¾" dia	**325.00**
Ashtray, 4 raised hearts on lg flat rim, mk, 5¾"	**325.00**
Bed, #922, wide/narrow slat in head & ftbrd, brand, dbl, EX	**4,250.00**
Book, Craftsman Homes, floor plans illus, 1909, 11x8½"	**225.00**
Bookcase, #523, 2 6-pane doors, keyed tenons, brand, 44x41"	**5,000.00**
Bookcase, #700, 1-door w/3 long panes & ldgl, decal, 58x35"	**8,000.00**
Bookcase, #715, 1 door w/16 panes of glass, label, 65x35"	**4,500.00**
Bookcase, #717, 2-door, ea w/8 panes, label, 56x48x13"	**4,000.00**
Bookcase, #719, 2-door, ea w/12 panes, brand, old rfn, 55x60"	**4,500.00**
Bookcase, #719, 2-door, ea w/12 panes, brand, 57x60"	**7,500.00**
Bookcase, like #716, 2-door, ea w/8 panes, mk, rfn top, 56"	**2,300.00**
Bookcase, 3-door ea w/12 panes, lt int, decal, 56x73", EX	**14,000.00**
Candlestick, #233, copper, hdls form heart, electric, 9"	**1,000.00**
Cellarette, #86, flip-top, 1-drw, decal, rfn, 43x24x18", VG	**2,000.00**
Chair, cube; #335, 6-slat sides/bk, unsgn, rfn, new leather	**2,500.00**
Chair, desk; #398, short H-bk, brand, new leather, 32"	**600.00**
Chair, lady's Morris; #367, 20-spindle sides, decal, 36"	**6,500.00**
Chair, office; #361, swivel base, no mk, new leather, 35"	**2,200.00**
Chair, side; #1289, 5 tapered slats, unsgn, rfn, new seat	**650.00**
Chair, side; #1291, rabbit-ear posts, 38x17x15"	**450.00**
Chair, side; #354, V-bk w/5 slats, label, all orig, 35"	**500.00**
Chair, side; #358, H-bk w/rush seat, brand, 39", pr	**1,000.00**
Chair, side; #374, tall 10-spindle bk, base: 7 ea side, decal	**4,250.00**
Chair set, #306½, 3-slat bk, decal, 2 arms+4 sides	**2,800.00**
Chair set, #306½, 3-slat bk, decal, 36", 4 sides	**3,000.00**
Chair set, #370, ladderbk, sgn, orig leather, 4 side+1arm	**1,800.00**
Chamberstick, hammered copper, riveted hdl, drilled, 9"	**300.00**
Chest, bridal; iron straps, cedar lined, corner mts, 41" L	**9,000.00**
China cabinet, #815, 2-door, ea w/8 panes, sgn, 64x40"	**6,500.00**
China cabinet, #902 (possible prototype), no mk, rfn, 64x33"	**4,750.00**
China cabinet, 1-door w/16 panes, label, 58x36"	**5,000.00**
Clock, rectangular case, brass face, Seth Thos mvt, 14", EX	**6,000.00**
Clock, tall case; #86, copper face, decal, 80x26x15", NM	**12,000.00**
Costumer, #53, dbl posts, iron hooks, 72x13x22"	**2,400.00**
Desk, #705, drop-front, 1-drw, red decal, 52x26x14"	**2,200.00**
Desk, #709, 5-drw, decal, rfn, 30x28x48"	**1,700.00**
Desk, #710, 2-drw ea side center drw, decal, rfn, 48", VG	**1,500.00**
Desk, #721, ash, slab sides, drop-front, sgn, 39x29", VG	**425.00**
Desk, #728, drop-front, 1-drw, hammered hdw, decal, 48x26x15"	**700.00**
Dresser, #905, 2-drw over 3, lg mirror, decal, 66x48", EX	**4,000.00**
Footstool, #300, arched sides, unsgn, old rfn, worn leather	**800.00**
Footstool, #301, 1-slat front/bk, 2 ea side, decal, 17x19x16"	**600.00**
Footstool, #302, monk's, flaring ft, decal, 4½x12x12"	**650.00**
Hall seat, #224, slab sides, panel bk, lift seat, sgn, 48"	**9,000.00**
Lamp, floor; #500, harp std w/Quezal lily shade, 58"	**3,000.00**
Lamp, orig lined wicker shade, tiered sq base, mk, 19x16"	**1,500.00**
Lantern, #205, cut-out hearts, hammered copper/glass, 8x5½"	**900.00**
Lantern, #673, sq w/sq cutouts, rpl glass, 8½x7x7"	**750.00**
Lantern, newel-post; rtcl hearts, rtcl cone top, no mk, 19"	**3,750.00**
Magazine stand, #79, slab sides w/½-rnd cutouts, mk, 40"	**1,300.00**
Magazine stand, 4-shelf, tree of life cvd on sides, 43"	**700.00**
Music cabinet, #70, 10 panes of 4 ldgl sqs in door, sgn, 46"	**7,500.00**
Music stand, #670, 4-shelf, tapered posts, label, 39x22x15"	**2,500.00**
Rocker, #2603, 4-slat bk, open arms, unsgn, rstr/rfn, G	**300.00**
Rocker, #311½, 5-slat bk, open arms, sgn, rfn, new leather	**450.00**
Rocker, #323, 5-slat sides, unsgn, rfn, new leather, 40"	**2,500.00**
Rocker, sewing; 2-slat bk, rush seat, decal, 31"	**200.00**
Rug, drugget in honeycomb pattern, dk gr on oatmeal, 72x36"	**600.00**
Server, #802, 2-drw, copper hdw, mk, rfn, 38x42x18"	**2,100.00**
Server, #818, 3-drw, decal, rfn, 48"	**3,000.00**
Settle, #212, V-bk w/12 slats, decal, 47", EX	**3,000.00**
Settle, #226, 4-slat sides, decal, rpl leather, 29x60x31"	**6,500.00**

Table, #466, arched X-stretchers, rfn, unsgn, 30" dia 1,800.00
Table, #53T, cut corners, inset Grueby tile, sgn, 17" sq 8,000.00
Table, #603, X-base, label/brand, rfn top, 18" dia, G 400.00
Table, #611, cut-corner top, lower shelf, brand, 24" sq 2,300.00
Table, #637, trestle, decal, rfn top, 29x48x30" 1,000.00
Table, #650, 1-drw, label, 30x36x24" 900.00
Table, #668, arched X-stretchers, unsgn, rfn, 44" dia 1,500.00
Table, dining; #632, 5-leg, 7 leaves/case, decal, 53½" dia 4,500.00
Table, library; #619, leatherette top (VG), decal, 66", VG 5,500.00
Table, library; #657, 12 spindles ea side, label, rfn, 48" 2,500.00
Table, library; #659, 13 spindles ea side, decal, 54" 8,000.00
Table, tea; #604, arched X-stretchers, label, rfn, 26x20" 600.00
Telephone stand, #605, sq lower shelf, unsgn, 30x14x14" 600.00
Tray, hammered, hdls, rfn, mk, 16" 1,100.00
Umbrella stand, #100, wide slats, tapering, unsgn, 24x12" 1,800.00

L. & J.G. Stickley

Armchair, #408, 6 side slats, slat bk, cleaned, 32x27x25" 3,000.00
Armchair, #422, 6-slat bk, mk, varnished, new leather, 38" 600.00
Armchair, Onondaga, arms/legs form right angle, new leather ...800.00
Armchair, wing-bk, bow arms, lg corbels, decal, new leather ..2,000.00
Bookcase, 2-door, ea w/3 sq panes at top, unsgn, 54x48" 2,750.00
Bookcase, 2-door, ea w/4 sm sqs at top, decal, 55x50x12" 4,500.00
Bookstand, #45, arched X-rails, solid bk, decal, 45x21x12" 2,500.00
Catalog, Work of..., Fayetteville NY, 9½x7" 100.00
Chair, Morris; #411, fixed-bk, mk, new fabric, cleaned finish .1,800.00
Chair, Morris; #471, 6-slat sides, decal, new leather, 37" 2,800.00
Chair, Morris; #498, 5-slat sides, decal, new leather, 41" 5,000.00
Chair, Morris; #831, bk adjusts, open arms, decal, rfn, VG 1,500.00
Chair set, #804, 2-slat bk, drop-in seat, sgn, 5 sides+arm 1,600.00
Chair set, #940, 3-slat bk, wood seat, decal, VG, 6 for 2,200.00
China cabinet, #746, 2-door, 12 sm panes in top of ea 6,500.00
China cabinet, #761, arch to door & side panels, mk, 60x36" .5,500.00
Costumer, corbelled X-base, sq/tapered pole, decal, 72" 750.00
Desk, #503, book shelf ea side w/2 slats front/bk, 44" 650.00
Desk, #611, 5-drw, 2 sm drw in top gallery, branded, 42" 1,400.00
Dresser, #94, 9-drw, panel sides, top rfn, mk, 53x39x19" 4,500.00
Footstool, #391, 18x19x14", VG 250.00
Footstool, #394, no mk, 16x20x16" 750.00
Footstool, #396, arched sides, through tenons, unsgn, rfn 375.00
Magazine stand, #46, 4-shelf, 3-slat sides, unsgn, rfn, 42" 1,500.00
Magazine stand, #47, 4-shelf, slab sides, decal, 42x18" 1,700.00
Mirror, #65, curved top, thru tenons, sgn, 27x40", VG 2,000.00
Rocker, #404, open arms, unsgn, rfn/1 rocker rpl, new leather ...800.00
Rocker, #837, 4-slat bk, tenons through arms, sgn, new leather .650.00
Rocker, Onondaga, 6-slat bk, narrow butted arms, new vinyl 600.00
Server, #741, 3-drw, decal, 44" 2,000.00
Settle, Onondaga, 15-slat bk, 4 extended posts, 72" 7,500.00
Smoker's cabinet, #26, 1-door, top overhangs, decal, 29" 2,500.00
Table, dining; #716, 5 posts on X-base, sgn, 48" dia 4,000.00
Table, drop-leaf; rnd leaves form oval top, sgn, open: 64" 1,400.00
Table, library; #505, arched apron, decal, rfn, 48" 800.00
Table, library; #530, 1 long drw, lower shelf, sgn, rfn, 36" 900.00
Table, library; #531, lower shelf, 1-drw, decal, rfn, 48" 1,000.00
Table, trestle; #593, decal, minor stains to top, 48" 1,000.00
Table, trestle; #595, shaped ftbrds, decal, rfn, 54" 1,700.00

Stickley Bros.

Armchair, #559½, 2 horizontal slats/5 vertical, label, VG 800.00
Armchair, #816½, 5-slat bk/sides, unsgn, rfn, new leather 400.00
Bench settle, #3715, 3-slat sides, label, rpl leather, 78" 3,750.00
Chair, office; #311, 5-slat bk, swivels, unsgn, new vinyl 1,100.00

Chair, side; #602½, 2-slat bk ea w/heart cutout, rfn 500.00
Chair, side; 5-spindle bk, 2-spindle stretchers, new leather 300.00
Chair set, #373½, 2-slat bks, new leather, 5 for 1,000.00
Chair set, #379½, 3-slat bks, tagged, rfn, 1 arm+5 sides 1,400.00
Chair set, tacked bk cushion, curved bk, att, 6 for 650.00
Chamberstick, hammered copper, trumpet form w/hdl, 9", VG ..400.00
Costumer, sq post on 4-leg ped base, 4 hooks, no mk, 68" 350.00
Desk, kneehole; 1 long drw, 1 ea side, tag, 42", G 425.00
Desk, 2 drw in arched gallery, shaped ends, unsgn, 36", G 750.00
Dresser, 6-drw, caned/cut-out gallery bk, decal, rfn, 52x34" ...1,000.00
Jardiniere, #302, hammered copper w/Arts & Crafts motif, 14" .1,500.00
Magazine stand, #4074, mahog, 3-shelf w/trough top, sgn, 30" ...750.00
Magazine stand, #4702, 3-spindle sides, metal tag, 31x26x12" ...650.00
Magazine stand, #4843, 5-shelf, 2-spindle sides, #d, 42x14" 800.00
Mirror, #7507, rectangular fr w/through tenons, 27x39", EX 700.00
Mirror, 2 slats ea side, peaked crest, att, no hooks, 22x40" 650.00
Pedestal, #133, sq, widens toward base, metal tag, 34" 800.00
Plant stand, #131, arch apron/X base, unsgn, rfn, 34x14" sq 950.00
Rocker, #715, 3-slat sides, metal tag/label, new leather, 32" ...1,800.00
Rocker, #790, bk: 3 slats over leather insert (rpl), unsgn 600.00
Rocker, 6-slat sides, unsgn, rpl rocker, new leather, 38" 900.00
Server, 1-drw, top overhangs, copper hdw, no mk, 37x34x21" ..1,000.00
Settle, even-arm, 7-slat bk, 2 ea side, mk, new leather, 50" 2,500.00
Sideboard, #8869, 2 sm drw over 2, cabinet door ea side, 60" ..2,600.00
Table, #130, through tenons, X-stretcher, mk, 40" dia, VG 1,000.00
Table, drop-leaf; w/gate leg, tag, 36" dia 1,500.00
Table, game; gr felt fold-up top, metal tag, open: 29x36x36" ..1,600.00
Table, lamp; rnd lower shelf, metal tag, 29x24" 1,100.00
Table, library; #2530, 2-drw, copper/brass hdw, no mk, rfn 1,100.00
Table, library; #2784, 1-drw, 3-slat sides, tagged, 40" 850.00
Table, serving; #2618, removable glass top tray, tag, 27" W 750.00
Table, 3-slat sides, lower stretcher, tag, 30x31x18", VG 900.00
Tea cart, spoked wheels, glass tray, hdls, no mk, 27x18x22" 600.00
Tray, #36, hammered copper, 4 lg recesses w/emb circles, 14" .1,300.00
Umbrella stand, rack ea side 4-shelf center, drw atop, mk 475.00
Vase, #11, hammered copper, doughnut neck band, 11" 700.00
Vase, #98, hammered copper, dent to base, 7" 230.00
Vase, hammered copper, 3-hdld loving cup form, 6x6", EX 175.00

Stiegel

Baron Henry Stiegel produced glassware in Pennsylvania as early as 1760, very similar to glass being made concurrently in Germany and England. Without substantiating evidence, it is impossible to positively attribute a specific article to his manufacture. Although he made other types of glass, today the term Stiegel generally refers to any very early ware made in shapes and colors similar to those he is known to have produced — especially that with etched or enameled decoration. It is generally conceded, however, that most glass of this type is of European origin. Our advisor for this category is Mark Vuono; he is listed in the Directory under Connecticut.

Bottle, tulip w/crowned GIII eng, ½-post neck, 9¼" 160.00
Chestnut flask, clear, checkered dmns, sm, stain, 6⅞" 1,100.00
Chestnut flask, lt amethyst w/dk swirls, checkered dmns, 7¼" .2,500.00
Creamer, emerald gr, 11-dmn, cylindrical, appl hdl, 3⅝" 700.00
Mug, tulip eng, oversz, 6¼" 525.00
Pocket bottle, amethyst, Daisy & Dmn above 30 ribs, 4¾" 130.00
Salt cellar, modified dmn pattern, pontil scar, 2½x3¼" 325.00
Salt cellar, 20-dmn, dbl ogee bowl, ftd, 3x2¼" 100.00
Sugar bowl, amethyst, 11-dmn, appl ft, pontil scar 2,500.00
Sugar bowl, cobalt, 11-dmn pattern, w/lid, 6⅝x4½" 7,000.00

Tumbler, bird on branch eng, 3⅛" 165.00
Tumbler, eng rim decor, ribbed base, 3⅝" 160.00
Tumbler, lovebirds in star eng, 5½" 185.00

Stocks and Bonds

Scripophily (scrip-awfully), the collecting of 'worthless' old stocks and bonds, gained recognition as an area of serious interest around the mid-1970s. Today there are an estimated 5,000 collectors in the United States and 15,000 worldwide. Collectors who come from numerous business fields mainly enjoy its hobby aspect, though there are those who consider scripophily an investment. Some collectors like the historical significance that certain certificates have. Others prefer the beauty of older stocks and bonds that were printed in various colors with fancy artwork and ornate engravings. Even autograph collectors are found in this field, on the lookout for signed certificates.

Many factors help determine the collector value: autograph value, age of the certificate, the industry represented, whether it is issued or not, its attractiveness, condition, and collector demand. Certificates from the mining, energy, and railroad industries are the most popular with collectors. Other industries or special collecting fields include banking, automobiles, aircraft, and territorials. Serious collectors usually prefer only issued certificates that date from before 1910. Unissued certificates are usually worth one-fourth to one-tenth the value of one that has been issued. Inexpensive issued common stocks and bonds dated between the 1930s and 1980s usually retail between $1.00 to $10.00. Those dating between 1890 and 1930 usually sell for $10.00 to $50.00. Those over one hundred years old retail between $25.00 and $100.00 or more, depending on the quantity found and the industry represented. Some stocks are one of a kind while others are found by the hundreds or even thousands, especially railroad certificates. Autographed stocks normally sell anywhere from $100.00 to $1,000.00. A formal collecting organization for scripophilists is known as The Bond and Share Society with an American chapter located in New York City.

Our advisor for this category is Warren Anderson; he is listed in the Directory under Utah. In many of the following listings, two-letter state abbreviations immediately follow company name. All are in fine condition unless noted otherwise.

Key:
cp — coupon   U — unissued
I/C — issued/cancelled   vgn — vignette
I/U — issued/uncancelled

Adelle Mining & Concentrating Co, CO/1898, cabin vgn, I/U ...**40.00**
AK Exploration & Mining, AK Territory/1935, banner title, I/C ...**25.00**
AL & Chattanooga RR, 1869, $1,000 bond, train vgn, I/U **125.00**
Am Sumatra Tobacco, 1921, eagle vgn, gr print, I/C **27.50**
Am Voting Machine Co, ME/1917, torch vgn, bl border/seal, I/U .**20.00**
Angelus Mill & Mining, AZ Territory/1903, 3 vgns, I/U **25.00**
Anglo-CA Gold Mining Co, England/1852, scrolling title, I/U ...**75.00**
Anita Mining, SD/1902, bold title, $25 bond, vgn, I/U, 15x16" ...**25.00**
Atlantic Fruit & Sugar Co, 1924, $1,000 bond, vgn, ABNCo, I/C **40.00**
AZ Victory Copper Mines Corp, DE/1925, banner title, I/U **20.00**
Bank of Orange County, NY/1862, stock, lady vgn, bl, I/U **70.00**
Bell Mining, ID/1908, goddess vgn, bold title, I/U **25.00**
Bonanza Gold Mining & Milling, CO/1905, gold border/seal, I/U ..**35.00**
Canada Southern Railway, 187_, bond, map vgn, unissued **35.00**
Cedar Falls & MN RR, 1895, $100 bond, train vgn, I/U **125.00**
Chicago & Alton RR, IL/1899, $1,000 bond, vgn, ABNCo, I/C ..**40.00**
Cincinnati & Springfield Railway, 1871, $1,000 bond, vgn, I/C ..**95.00**
Comet Mining Co of UT, France/1883, bond, lg title/2 vgns, I/U **.85.00**
Commercial Motor Body Corp, DE/1917, banner title, I/U **25.00**

Conway's Theatre Ticket Offices Inc, DE/1919, angel vgn, I/U ...**25.00**
Gold Hill Consolidated, ME/1914, miners in tunnel vgn, I/U **25.00**
Golden Anchor Mining Co, AZ Territory/1906, goddess vgn, I/U **50.00**
Grand Rapids/IN RR, MI/IN/1860, train/steamer vgns, purple, I/C ..**50.00**
Gray Eagle Gold Mining CO, AZ Territory/1909, eagle vgn, I/U .**25.00**
Gulf/CO/Santa Fe Railway, TX/1928, train vgn, ABNCo, I/C **30.00**
Homestake Extension Mining, AZ Territory/1905, 3 vgns, I/U **30.00**
Ingersoll Warner Mercantile, KS/1906, Indians/train vgn, I/U **30.00**
Internat'l Railroad, TX/1874, $1,000 bond, sgn G Grow, I/U **150.00**
KY & TN RR, 1872, $1000 bond, train vgn, Nat'l Bank Note, I/C .**95.00**
Lahontan Mines, NV/1918, 2 mining vgns, gold border, I/U **20.00**
Louisville Railway, KY/1895, 2 vgns, gr border, I/C **35.00**
MA & NM Consolidated Mining, MA/1882, $100 bond, lg vgn, I/U .**60.00**
Manhattan Pine Nut Extension Mining, NV/1908, 3 vgns, I/U ...**35.00**
Marquette Mining Co, CO/1926, eagle/flag/shield vgn, I/U **15.00**
MI/UT Consolidated Mines, UT/1920, bold title, gold seal, I/U ..**20.00**
Mobil & Girard RR, AL/1866, $500 bond, train vgn, w/stamp, I/C ..**40.00**
Mohawk & Malone Railway, NY/1902, 2 vgns, ABNCo, coupons, I/U ..**35.00**
Montezuma Milling & Transportation, AZ Territory/1909, vgn, I/U **30.00**

Mutual Benefit Life Insurance, New Jersey, 1865, $50.00 scrip dividend certificate, pelican vignette, gray, black, and red inks, NM, $40.00 minimum value.

MS Valley Co, MS/1890, train vgn, early, I/C **85.00**
Nat'l Gold & Silver Mining Co, SD/1919, 3 vgns, I/U **25.00**
Nat'l Mines & Products, WY/1921, eagle vgn, SBNCo, I/U **15.00**
OH & PA Railroad, 1855, 5 vgns, ornate border, I/C **80.00**
PA Canal Co, PA/1870, $1,000 bond, lg vgn, bl print, I/C **125.00**
Park City Mining & Smelting, CO/1922, goddess vgn, ABNCo, I/C ..**25.00**
Parrot Silver & Copper, MT/1901, parrot/silver bar vgn, I/C **15.00**
Penobscot & Kennebec RR, 1856, $400 bond, train vgn, I/C **70.00**
Ray Hercules Copper Co, ME/1916, photo miners vgn, ABNCo, I/U ..**25.00**
Rico Mining Co, CO/1915, somewhat plain, RBNCo, I/C **20.00**
Seyler-Humphrey Gold Mining Co, SD/1906, 3 vgns, gold seal, I/U ...**25.00**
Sunset-Eclipse Gold Mining, WY/1902, blk on wht, I/U **35.00**
Superior-Alta Mining Co, UT/1904, minor vgn, banner title, I/U ..**35.00**
Tonopah & Mount Butler Gold Mining, AZ Territory/1903, I/U ...**30.00**
Treasure Gold Mining Co, AZ Territory, 1910, 3 vgns, I/U **25.00**
Tunkey Mining, DE/1917, DE seal vgn, SBNCo, I/U **15.00**
TX Crude Oil, TX/1919, 6" gusher vgn, I/U **25.00**
United Petroleum, CO/1917, train in oil field vgn, RMBNCo, I/U ..**15.00**
Upper Potomac Steamboat Co, VA/1875, $100 bond, vgn, I/U ...**55.00**
Whitewater Oil Mining & Refining, CO/1902, title banner, I/U .**25.00**
Woodburn Oil Crop, DE/1932, eagle vgn, ABNCo, I/U **7.00**

Stoneware

There are three broad periods of time that collectors of American pottery can look to in evaluating and dating the stoneware and earthenware in their collections. Among the first permanent settlers in America were English and German potters who found a great demand for their individually turned wares. The early pottery was produced from red and yellow clays scraped from the ground at surface levels. The earthenware made in these potteries was fragile and coated with lead glazes that periodically created health problems for the people who ate or drank from it. There was little stoneware available for sale until the early 1800s, because the clays used in its production were not readily available in many areas and transportation was prohibitively expensive. The opening of the Erie Canal and improved roads brought about a dramatic increase in the accessibility of stoneware clay, and many new potteries began to open in New York and New England.

Collectors have difficulty today locating earthenware and stoneware jugs produced prior to 1840, because few have survived intact. These ovoid or pear-shaped jugs were designed to be used on a daily basis. When cracked or severely chipped, they were quickly discarded. The value of handcrafted pottery is often determined by the cobalt decoration it carries. Pieces with elaborate scenes (a chicken pecking corn, a bluebird on a branch, a stag standing near a pine tree, a sailing ship, or people) may easily bring $1,000.00 to $12,000.00 at auction.

After the Civil War there was a need and a national demand for stoneware jugs, crocks, canning jars, churns, spittoons, and a wide variety of other pottery items. The competition among the many potteries reached the point where only the largest could survive. To cut costs, most potteries did away with all but the simplest kinds of decoration on their wares. Time-consuming brush-painted birds or flowers quickly gave way to more simply executed swirls or numbers and stenciled designs. The coming of home refrigeration and Prohibition in 1919 effectively destroyed the American stoneware industry. See also Bennington, Stoneware.

Churn, #3/flower basket, c/s, Haxstun...NY, 1880s, 15", EX 2,700.00
Churn, #4/flowers, c/s, N Clark & Co Lyons, 1840s, 18", EX 300.00
Churn, #4/flowers (2), c/s, J Fisher & Co..., rpr, 16½" 200.00
Churn, #4/leaf, c/s, Haxstun & Co...NY, 1880s, 17" 375.00
Churn, #6/flower basket, c/s, WH Farrar Geddes, 19½", EX ...1,600.00

Churn, #6/leaping stag with tree beyond, cobalt on salt glaze, J. Burger Jr., Rochester, N.Y., 20", EX, $6,000.00.

Cooler, #10/flower basket, c/s, att Purdy, Mogadore OH, 21", EX ..3,850.00
Cooler, floral branch, c/s, Cyrus Felton, ear hdls, w/lid, 20" 4,100.00
Crock, #1/flower, c/s, AO Whittemore Havana, 7½", EX 140.00
Crock, #1/flower, c/s, LH Yeager...PA, ovoid, 7", VG 180.00
Crock, #1/flower, c/s, M Tyler Albany, ovoid, 1830, 9", EX 180.00
Crock, #1/flower, c/s, Wm E Warner West Troy, 1870s, 7", EX .100.00
Crock, #2/bird on stump, c/s, Brady & Ryan, 1885, 9½", VG 475.00
Crock, #2/bird on twig, c/s, NY Stoneware..., 9½", EX 350.00
Crock, #2/chicken pecking, c/s, Brady & Ryan, 9½", NM 900.00
Crock, #2/flower, c/s on cinnamon clay, att Geddes, 9" 80.00
Crock, #2/flowers (2), c/s, T Harrington Lyons, rpr, 12" 290.00
Crock, #2/flowers on stump, c/s, Brady & Ryan..., 9½", EX 550.00
Crock, #2/long-tailed bird, c/s, Haxstun...NY, 9½", EX 1,200.00
Crock, #2/1844, c/s, West Troy Pottery, 1884, 9½", EX 300.00
Crock, #3/bird on branch, c/s, stain/line, 1880s, 10½" 210.00
Crock, #3/chicken pecking corn, c/s, Ottman Bros, 3-gal, EX 700.00
Crock, #3/chicken/trees/grass, c/s, Athens, 1892, 10" 1,800.00
Crock, #3/flower, c/s, Orcut & Montague Troy, 1825, 13", EX ..325.00
Crock, #3/flower, c/s, T Harrington Lyons, 10", EX 150.00
Crock, #3/grapes, c/s, OL & AK Ballard...VT, 10½", NM 280.00
Crock, #4/bird on plume, c/s, EB Gates, 11½", VG 300.00
Crock, #4/bird on stump, c/s, Adam Caire..., 1885, rstr, 11½" ..325.00
Crock, #4/chicken pecking, c/s, att Brady & Ryan, rstr, 11½" 425.00

Crock, #4/dbl tulip, c/s, WE Welding Brantford Ont, 11½", EX ...200.00
Crock, #4/flower, c/s, John Burger Jr..., 1880s, 4-gal 270.00
Crock, #4/hen pecking corn, c/s, unsgn, chips, 11½" 675.00
Crock, #4/lg eagle, c/s, WJ Seymour..., ca 1855, 11", VG+ 450.00
Crock, #4/stag & landscape, c/s, Ft Edward, rstr, 11½" 3,500.00
Crock, #5/bird in wreath, c/s, NY Stoneware..., 12½", EX 2,300.00
Crock, #5/flower (ornate), c/s, 1880s, rstr, 12" 200.00
Crock, #5/flowers, c/s, Fort Edward Stoneware...NY, 12" 360.00
Crock, #6/bird & flower (lg), c/s, NA White & Son, 6-gal, EX ..1,650.00
Crock, #6/flowers, c/s, Hubbell & Chesebro Geddes, rstr, 14" 425.00
Crock, cake; #2/dbl flower, c/s, WA MacQuoid...NY, 6" 750.00
Jar, #2/flower, c/s, NY Stoneware Co, 11" 100.00
Jar, #2/standing deer, c/s, Edmunds & Co, prof rpr, 12" 1,500.00
Jar, #2/triple flower, c/s, Hubbell & Chesebro Geddes, 10½", EX ...300.00
Jar, #2/wreath, c/s, CW Braun Buffalo NY, 1880s, 11½", EX 160.00
Jar, #3/flower & foliage band encircles jar, c/s, 14½" 475.00
Jar, #3/flowers/tulips, c/s, J Hamilton...Greensboro PA, 14" 300.00
Jar, foliage (brushed), c/s, w/hdl, 7x8¾" 415.00
Jar, preserving; #1½/plume, c/s, Satterlee & Mory, 10" 210.00
Jar, preserving; #1/flower, c/s, Edmunds & Co, 9½", NM 200.00
Jar, preserving; #1/flower, c/s, Havana, prof rpr, 9" 170.00
Jar, preserving; #1/plume, c/s, 1870, chip, 10" 180.00
Jar, preserving; #2/dbl flower, c/s, HM Whitman Havana, 12", EX ..250.00
Jar, preserving; #2/dbl flower, c/s, T Harrington..., 11½", EX 150.00
Jar, preserving; #2/floral, c/s, JB Magee Ithaca, 1855, 11" 150.00
Jar, preserving; #2/floral, c/s, Macumber-Tannahill, rstr, 11" 140.00
Jar, preserving; #2/geometrics, c/s, Haxstun Ottman..., 11½" 150.00
Jar, preserving; #2/triple-flower, c/s, Lyons, chip, 11½" 250.00
Jar, preserving; #4/bird on twig, c/s, NY Stoneware..., 14", EX ...525.00
Jar, preserving; bird (primitive), c/s, sm chips, 7½" 185.00
Jar, preserving; c/s, Cowden & Wilcox, narrow mouth, 9¾" 90.00
Jar, preserving; cherries, c/s, 6½", NM 1,700.00
Jar, preserving; cornstalk & snake, c/s, chipped lid, 8⅜" 1,265.00
Jar, preserving; pinwheel/stripes, c/s, Jas Hamilton, 9½" 600.00
Jar, preserving; rose, c/s, Hamilton & Jones...PA, 7¼" 195.00
Jar, preserving; scroll label: Jas Hamilton & Co...PA, c/s, 8" 250.00
Jar, preserving; shield/foliage (stencil), c/s, 8⅜" 360.00
Jar, preserving; snake (brushed), c/s, 7½", EX 2,100.00
Jar, preserving; 3 stars/stripes, c/s, Hamilton & Jones, 9¾" 580.00
Jug, #1/bird on plume, c/s, NY Stoneware..., stain, 11½" 225.00
Jug, #1/bird on twig, c/s, West Troy Pottery, 1870s, 11½", EX ...375.00
Jug, #1/flower, c/s, P Mugler...NY, 1850s, 11", NM 525.00
Jug, #1/flower (lg/dk), c/s, Cowden & Wilcox, 1870s, 11" 675.00
Jug, #1/Littlefield Bros Grocers in script, c/s, 1870s, 11½" 140.00
Jug, #1/snowflake stencil, c/s, FH Cowden, 1-gal, 10½", EX 170.00
Jug, #2/A Bertzold Buffalo NY in script, c/s, 1900s, 14", EX 110.00
Jug, #2/bird on plume, c/s, JC Waeld..., 1860s, 2-gal, NM 300.00
Jug, #2/dbl plume, c/s, Nichols & Boynton...VT, 1850s, 11" 350.00
Jug, #2/flower, c/s, Cowden & Wilcox, 1870s, 14" 425.00
Jug, #2/flower, c/s, CW Braun Buffalo NY, 1880, 14", NM 120.00
Jug, #2/flower, c/s, WH Farrar Geddes, 1850s, 13½" 200.00
Jug, #2/I Seymour & Co Troy, c/s, ovoid, ca 1827, 13", EX 150.00
Jug, #2/long-tailed bird, c/s, NY Stoneware..., 13½", NM 600.00
Jug, #2/stylized flower, c/s, CF Pharris Geddes, 13½" 425.00
Jug, #2/tornado, c/s, WH Farrar Geddes, 1850s, 14", EX 270.00
Jug, #2/vine, beehive form, c/s, DS Gifford..., 2-gal 230.00
Jug, #2/1862 & dots, c/s, OL & AK Ballard...VT, 1860s, 14" 925.00
Jug, #3/triple flower, c/s, Pottery Wks...NY, 1870s, 15" 350.00
Jug, Albany slip, U S Treasury Mucilage Wm Davis Boston, 9", EX ..150.00
Jug, Albany slip w/sgraffito label: Louis Zable...KY, 13½" 45.00
Jug, bird, incised & c/s, I Seymour Troy, ovoid, 2-gal, 14" 2,300.00
Jug, bird on twig, c/s, Fort Edward Pottery, 1½-gal, 13", EX 600.00
Lid, squiggles, c/s, 1850s, chip on hdl, 12" dia 80.00
Match safe, Bristol glaze, sm fracture, ca 1900s, 3" 70.00

Pail, batter; Albany slip, bail hdl, no lid, chips, 10" **65.00**
Pail, batter; bl accents on ears/hdl/spout, Binghamton, 9", EX ...**250.00**
Pitcher, flower, c/s, 2 long drips of Albany slip, 10¾" **415.00**

Store

Perhaps more more than any other yesteryear establishment, the country store evokes the most nostalgic feelings for folks old enough to remember its charms — barrels for coffee, crackers, and big green pickles; candy in a jar for the grocer to weigh on shiny brass scales; beheaded chickens in the meat case outwardly devoid of nothing but feathers. Today mementos from this segment of Americana are being collected by those who 'lived it' as well as those less fortunate! Our advisor for this category is Charles Reynolds; he is listed in the Directory under Virginia. See also Advertising; Scales.

Spool cabinet, Royal Society, 1-glass front-drawer vertical case, 35½x19x19½", some loss to trim, $300.00.

Automatic cashier, Brandt, solid brass, Pat 1896 ....**650.00**
Box, banana; wood w/metal hdls, EX litho & advertising, EX **120.00**
Box, biscuit; tin & glass, colorful lid **125.00**
Box, biscuit; wood, hinged lid, Currier & Ives scene, 22" L **175.00**
Cabinet, bean; oak w/brass tags & hdls, 15x21x12", VG+ **250.00**
Cabinet, oak floor model for spools of ribbon, 48x32x26", EX ...**900.00**
Case, curved front, table-top, 28x18x6", VG **300.00**
Case, glass w/oak fr, Sun Mfg on brass plaque, 42x49x27", EX ...**750.00**
Case, hardwood/pine, red stain, 6-pane door, 33x18x6" **500.00**
Case, oak fr, glass top, 2 step-bk shelves, 40x48x23" **360.00**
Case, poplar, glass on 3 sides, hinged door, shelves, 34" H **150.00**
Coffee bin, pine w/orig stencil, 33" H **550.00**
Coffee bin, wooden w/worn surface, stenciled label, 24" **425.00**
Cookie jar, rnd glass canister w/hinged lid, counter-top **115.00**
Counter, scrubbed poplar, open base, 5 drws, 33x75x20", EX **445.00**
Desk, 12 sm drws, kneehole, 3 sm drw & 2 panel do, 31x74" ...**1,500.00**
Display, figural straight razor, iron & wood, rpt, 32x4", G **250.00**
Ice chipper, CI w/wooden hdl, Peerless, 2¼x10¾" **12.50**
Jar, candy; glass, early, 24", EX **750.00**
Jar, glass, paneled sides, w/lid, 12¼x5¾" dia **40.00**
Mannequin, compo, 1940s, 25", M **350.00**
Mannequin, compo, 1940s, 32", M **325.00**
Mannequin, compo man w/jtd arms, counter-top, 1930s, 24" **750.00**
Pigeon holes, ash & poplar, 20 holes, dk finish, 24x18x7" **140.00**
Register, receipt; McCaskey, oak, 34½x23x20½", EX **250.00**

Stoves

Antique stoves' desirability is based on two criteria: their utility and their decorative value. It's the latter that adds an 'antique' premium to the basic functional value that could be served just as well by a modern stove. Sheer age is usually irrelevant. Decorative features that enhance desirability include fancy, embossed ornamentation, nickel-plated trim, mica windows, ceramic tiles, and (in cooking stoves) water reservoirs and high warming closets rather than mere high shelves. The less sheet metal and the more cast iron, the better. Look for crisp, sharp designs in preference to those made from worn or damaged and repaired foundry patterns. Stoves with a pastel porcelain finish can be very attractive; blue is a favorite, white is least desirable. Chrome trim dates a stove to circa 1933 or later and is a good indicator of a post-antique stove. Though purists prefer the earlier models trimmed in nickel rather than chrome, there is now considerable public interest in these post-antique stoves as well, and some people are willing to pay a good price for these appliance-era 'classics.'

Among stove types, base burners (with self-feeding coal magazines) are the most desirable. Then come the upright, cylindrical 'oak' stoves, kitchen ranges, and wood parlors. Cannon stoves approach the margin of undesirability; laundries and gasoline stoves plunge through it.

There's a thin but continuing stream of desirable antique stoves going to the high-priced Pacific Coast market. Interest in antique stoves is least in the Deep South. Demand for wood/coal stoves is strongest in areas where firewood is affordable and storage of it is practical. Demand for antique gas ranges has become strong, especially in metropolitan markets, and interest in antique electric ranges is starting to surface. The market for antique stoves is so limited and the variety so bewildering that a consensus on a going price can hardly emerge. They are only worth something to the right individual, and prices realized depend very greatly on who happens to be in the auction crowd. Even an expert's appraisal will usually miss the realized price by a substantial percent.

In judging condition look out for deep rust pits, warped or burnt-out parts, unsound firebricks, poorly fitting parts, poor repairs, and empty mounting holes indicating missing trim. Search meticulously for cracks in the cast iron. Our listings reflect auction prices of completely restored, safe, and functional stoves, unless indicated otherwise.

Base Burners

Art Amherst #15, NP trim, tiles, 11" urn, 50x25x28" **1,875.00**
Burdett-Smith #44, swivel top, tiles, 38" **1,200.00**
Favorite #30, Piqua OH, fancy CI, mica windows, 52"+14" urn .**2,000.00**
Germer, Erie PA, Radiant Home 7K, tiles/NP/mica, 1897, G, 62" **1,000.00**
Michigan Stove, Art Garland #400, gargoyles/NP/mica, 1889, rstr ..**9,800.00**
Ransom Art Denmark 315, Albany..., tiles/NP/mica, 1898, VG .**4,500.00**
Weir Glenwood #6, NP trim, mica windows, 1909, 68" **875.00**

Box Stoves

A Belanger Barge #34, scrollwork, CI, 1905, sm **200.00**
Bussey & McLeod Ajax 18, ornate CI, 1897, 53 lbs, very sm **250.00**
E Eaton #24, Amherst NH, schoolhouse type, 24x38x16" **435.00**
Shaker, 1-pc cast body, wrought latch, 1800s, 21x35x14" **350.00**

Franklin Stoves

Acme #18 Orient 1890, 6 tiles, mica windows, fancy **395.00**
H Ransom Ben Franklin Air Tight, CI fireplace, Pat 1850 ....**250.00**
Home Franklin #2, CI fireplace, dtd 1850, 31x36" **200.00**
Magee Ideal #3, CI fireplace, 2 side trivets, 1892, 32x28" **250.00**
Muzzy & Co Villa Franklin, folding doors, 1830s, 30"+4" urn **175.00**
Southard Robertson Sunny hearth #2, 1850s, 35x20x29½" **275.00**
Walker & Pratt Good Cheer #22, fireplace, 1850s, 32x27x31" ..**300.00**
Walker & Pratt Laconia, ornate CI, NP ft rail, 1890s, 35" **125.00**
Wyer & Noble, CI/brass-trim fireplace, very old, rstr/EX **2,000.00**

Laundry Stoves

Sweetwater Stove Co, Sweetwater Tenn, 2-hole, CI, 1930, VG ..**25.00**
Walker & Pratt #14, holds irons, Pat 1874, 25x24x24" **500.00**

Parlor

The term 'parlor stove' as we use it here is very general and encompasses at least eight distinct types recognized by the stove industry: cottage parlor, double-cased airtight, circulator, cylinder, oak, base burner, Franklin, and the fireplace heater.

Bangor Comfort #23, oval w/dome top, Pat 1875, 33"+10" urn ..**185.00**
Burdett Smith & Co #44, sq, tiles, mica door, 38"+8" urn **350.00**
Fuller-Warren-Morrison Floral #2, CI, 1853, 45x22x17" **1,250.00**
GW Eddy Forest #3, ornate CI, Pat 1854, 28"+6" urn **275.00**
Ilion #3, ornate CI, rnd body, claw ft, 1853, 27"+11" urn **600.00**
Ilion #5, ornate CI, ca 1853, 33"+13" 2-pc urn **500.00**
JH Shear, Albany NY #4, CI, columns, 56", EX **2,000.00**
Low & Hicks Reverse Air-Tight #4, cathedral front, 29"+11" urn ..**325.00**
Modern Glenwood Wood Parlor, slide top, 1900s, 45x28x24½" ...**325.00**
Perry Dandy #12, swivel dome top w/8" lid, 45"+7" urn **200.00**
Pratt & Wentworth Peerless, tip-up dome, 1840s, 37x19x25" **135.00**
Somersworth #20, tip-up dome top, 1850s, 29x30x29" **300.00**
Stanley's Pat No 2, CI, EX detail, 33½" **440.00**
Warnick & Leibrandt Union Airtight, ornate CI, 1851, 26" **250.00**
Wood/Bishop Royal Clarion #14, mica door, oven, 1890s, 50" ..**225.00**
2-column, JH Shear #2, Albany NY, CI, 56" **850.00**
4-column, AJ Coffin #4, ornate CI, 1840s, 47"+10" urn **1,450.00**

Ranges (Gas)

Cribben-Sexton Universal, 4-burner, gr/cream, high oven, '27, VG ...**375.00**
Detroit Jewel, 4-burner, blk/NP, glass oven door, 1918, VG **500.00**
Magic Chef, 6-burner/2-oven, warming closet, 1932, EX **2,500.00**
Magic Chef, 6-burner/2-oven, warming closet, 1937, rstr **6,000.00**
Weir Insulated Glenwood, 6-burner/2-oven, wht, 1932, rstr ...**4,125.00**

Ranges (Gas, Wood, and Coal Combination)

Magee New Republic, 1929, M, rstr **5,000.00**

Ranges (Wood and Coal)

Cribben-Sexton Universal, bl porc, high closet/no reservoir ...**2,750.00**
Home Comfort, gray graniteware, reservoir, warming ovens, NM ..**1,000.00**
Kalamazoo, tan enamel, 1937, EX **315.00**
Portland Atlantic Grand, ornate bk shelf, 12x20x18", EX **2,125.00**
Portland Ideal Atlantic 8-20, ornate CI, bk shelf, 1850s **1,550.00**
Quick Meal, bl porc, EX **3,125.00**
Taunton Quaker Standard #8-20, NP trim, trivets, shelf, 1890s .**850.00**
Weir Glenwood C #280, dbl-shelf bk, no trivets, 1900s **1,000.00**
Weir Glenwood E, ornate CI, ca 1890, oven: 11x20x22" **815.00**
Wood/Bishop Home Clarion, CI, 1907, oven: 12x19x19" **750.00**
Wood/Bishop New Clarion #8, low closet, 1882, 32x28x46" ..**1,875.00**
Wood/Bishop Popular Clarion, scrolling, trivets, 1890s **1,050.00**

Stove Manufacturers' Toy Stoves

Buck's Jr Range, St Louis MO, new body/pnt/recast parts, 26" ...**850.00**
Bucks Jr #2, CI w/NP trim, ca 1900, 23x22", EX orig **1,760.00**
Charter Oak #503, GF Filley, St Louis MO, 14x12x25", EX **2,050.00**
Dainty, Reading Stove Works, PA, 7x13x8", VG **150.00**
Great Majestic Jr, Majestic Mfg, 31x16x23", M **5,650.00**

Karr, Qualified, bl porc w/NP, Belleville IL, 1925, EX **2,500.00**
Karr Range, Belleville IL, bl porc, old model, 21½x13x9" **3,100.00**
Little Eva T Southard, NYC, 8½x14x11", G **350.00**
Little Fanny, CI, minor rust, EX **300.00**
Little Willie, CI, EX **75.00**
Royal American, Bridgeford, Louisville KY, 14x12x10", G **950.00**

Toy Manufacturers' Toy Stoves

Arcade Hotpoint range, pnt CI, tan & gr, VG **150.00**
Arcade Roper, pnt CI & sheet metal w/silver trim, 6", EX **100.00**
Arcade Roper, range, pnt CI, gas type, door opens, 4½", EX **70.00**
Bing, cook stove, bl steel, brass trim, 16½", VG **600.00**
Crescent, cook stove, bl steel, brass trim, 16½", VG **600.00**
Eagle, cook stove, CI & steel, 6-burner, 11", EX **110.00**
Eagle, Hubley, Lancaster PA, NP, recast parts **450.00**
Eclipse, CI, EX **175.00**
Kenton Royal, CI & steel, 4-burner, ornate, 10", VG **100.00**
Kenton Royal, pnt CI & steel, 4-burner, no pipe, rpt, 10", VG **45.00**
Little Giant, unmk/unidentified, 7½x8½x11", EX orig **675.00**
Novelty, Kenton Hdwe, bl pnt/NP trim, rfn, 13x6½x8½" **600.00**
Pet, The; Young Bros, Albany NY, 10½x6x8½" **165.00**
Rival, J&E Stevens, Cromwell CT, 14x9x16", M, +2 kettles ..**1,350.00**
Rival, J&E Stevens, Cromwell CT, 1895, 13x7½x18½", G **240.00**
Royal, plated CI, stovepipe, shield shape, 16", G **85.00**
Triumph, Kenton Hdwe, OH, 14x8½x19", G **195.00**

Strawberry Soft Paste and Lustre Ware

Strawberry lustre is a general term for pearlware and semiporcelain decorated with hand-painted strawberries, veins, tendrils, and pink lustre trim. Strawberry soft paste is decorated creamware without the pink lustre trim. Both types were made by many manufacturers in England in the 19th century, most of whom never marked their ware.

Coffeepot, dome lid, soft paste, 12", NM **1,800.00**
Cup & saucer, pearlware, pk/red int bands, EX **325.00**
Plate, pearlware, wide pk/red rim bands, #8, 8" **425.00**
Plate, soft paste, Davenport, ca 1810, 6½" **185.00**
Sauce boat, lustre, 6" **175.00**
Teapot, baluster form, 11¼" **850.00**
Teapot, squat, 1820s, 6", VG **525.00**
Teapot, vine border, ftd, 11", EX **600.00**

Stretch Glass

Stretch glass, produced from 1916 until after 1930, was made in an effort to emulate the fine art glass of Tiffany and Carder. The glassware was sprayed with a metallic salts mix while hot, then reshaped, causing a stretch effect in the iridescent finish. Pieces which were not reshaped had the iridized finish without the stretch, as seen on Fenton's #222 lemonade set and #401 guest set. Northwood, Imperial, Fenton, Diamond, Lancaster, and the United States Glass Company were the largest manufacturers of this type of glass. See also specific companies.

Basket, wht, Imperial, 10" **60.00**
Bowl, amber, Jeannette, 3⅞x10" **40.00**
Bowl, bl, ribbed int, ftd, 9½" **60.00**
Bowl, gr, flared rim, 10" **40.00**
Bowl, olive; pk, frost/flower decor, gold rim, Imperial, 7" **45.00**
Bowl, purple, rolled rim, collar base, Vineland, 2¼x9½" **35.00**
Bowl, russet, ftd, 9½" **65.00**

Bowl, tangerine, Fenton, #857	75.00
Bowl, topaz, Northwood, 3x13"	70.00
Bowl, wht, HP florals, Lancaster, 3x9¾"	50.00
Candlesticks, bl, Northwood, #695, 8½", pr	75.00
Candlesticks, Dmn, gr, wht enameled decor, 9", pr	80.00
Candlesticks, russet, Northwood, #695, 8½", pr	85.00
Compote, amberina, Imperial, 4½x6"	150.00
Compote, Dmn, bright gr, zipper notch stem, 5½x6½"	65.00
Compote, gray, scalloped, Imperial, 8½"	65.00
Guest set, bl, Fenton, #401, 2-pc	65.00
Guest set, pk, Fenton, #200	125.00
Plate, bl, EX irid, Imperial, 8¾"	19.00
Plate, gold trim, 7½"	15.00
Plate, wht, Colonial Panel, 7"	10.00
Server, topaz, center hdl, US Glass	50.00
Sugar bowl, vaseline, Fenton #3	32.00
Tumbler, bl, Fenton, #222	32.00
Vase, jade gr, US Glass, 8½"	70.00

String Holders

Today, if you want to wrap and secure a package, you have a variety of products to choose from: cellophane tape, staples, etc. But in the 1800s, string was about the only available binder; thus the string holder, either the hanging or counter type, was a common and practical item found in most homes and businesses. Chalkware and ceramic figurals from the 1930s and 1940s contrast with the cast and wrought iron examples from the 1800s to make for an interesting collection. Our advisor for this category is Charles Reynolds; he is listed in the Directory under Virginia.

Ceramic, cat's head	55.00
Ceramic, elephant & leaves	60.00

Cast iron, beehive form, advertising Walker's Soap, $475.00.

Ceramic, porter, Fredricksburg	200.00
Ceramic, puppy's head	70.00
Ceramic, Scottie dog's head	90.00
Chalkware, housewife, MIB	35.00
Chalkware, Mammy, 8"	275.00
CI, ball form, hinged, ornate bkplate & curved arm, 13" L	95.00
CI, beehive form, NM	38.00
CI, oval ceiling type, arms to hold string & bags	525.00
Pottery, Colonial lady, gr trim, Japan	30.00
Pottery, kitten w/pk ball of yarn, Japan	30.00
Pottery, Mammy in plaid dress, Made in Japan	150.00
Tin/CI, bottle shape, Anheuser-Busch's Malt-Nutrine	2,100.00

Sugar Shakers

Sugar shakers (or muffineers, as they were also called) were used during the Victorian era to sprinkle sugar and spice onto breakfast muffins, toast, etc. They were made of art glass, in pressed patterns, and in china. See also specific types and manufacturers. Our coadvisors for this category are Jeff Bradfield and Dale MacAllister; they are listed in the Directory under Virginia.

Acorn, wht opaque w/decor	150.00
Argus Swirl, Peach Bloom	225.00
Big Windows, bl opal	325.00
Blown Twist, vaseline opal	275.00
Bulging Loops, bl cased, glossy	350.00
Challinor's Forget-Me-Not, bl opaque	160.00
Chrysanthemum Base Swirl, cranberry	350.00
Coin Dot, cranberry opal	200.00
Coin Spot, bl opal, ring neck	165.00
Coin Spot, cranberry	225.00
Cone, pk cased, tall	200.00
Cranberry w/cut decor, cylindrical, sterling pear-form top, 6"	175.00
Daisy & Fern, bl opal, wide waist	225.00
Daisy & Fern, wht opal	160.00
Hobb's Invt T'print, bl, tapered	100.00
Hobb's Optic, cranberry, ring neck	275.00
Hobnail, amber	75.00
Horseshoe, amber	75.00
Invt T'print, amber, tapered	100.00
Invt T'print, cranberry, tapered	175.00
Many Lobes, wht satin w/EX decor	110.00
Parian Swirl, cranberry	250.00
Quilted Phlox, amethyst	225.00
Reverse Swirl, bl opal	250.00
Reverse Swirl, vaseline opal	275.00
Ribbed Lattice, bl opal	225.00
Ribbed Lattice, cranberry opal	275.00
Ribbed Pillar, pk & wht spatter	175.00
Ring Neck, pk & wht spatter, brass top, 4¾", EX	160.00
Rope Ribs, amber	95.00
Spanish Lace, cranberry opal	350.00
Spanish Lace, vaseline opal	275.00
Tepee	85.00
Tomato, ornate top, Mt WA	300.00
Venetian Dmn, cranberry	250.00
Windows, bl opal	295.00

Sunderland Lustre

Sunderland lustre was made by various potters in the Sunderland district of England during the 18th and 19th centuries. It is characterized by a splashed-on application of the pink lustre, which results in an effect sometimes referred to as the 'cloud' pattern. Some pieces are transfer printed with scenes, ships, florals, or portraits.

Chamber pot, verse 'Marriage'/other blk transfers w/mc, EX	565.00
Creamer, cow figural, mottled lustre, ca 1825, 6½" L, pr	250.00
Pitcher, Sailor's Farewell/Fortune Hunter, 19th C, 9½"	350.00
Pitcher, Success to the Coal Trade/Tars..., rpr/chips, 6"	115.00
Plaque, Thou God Seest..., blk transfer, wear, 6" dia	195.00
Watch holder, grandfather clock form, ca 1825, 10¾", EX	900.00
Wine, wht band w/mc florals, copper lustre trim, wear, 4"	125.00

Surveying Instruments

The practice of surveying offers a wide variety of precision instruments primarily for field use, most of which are associated with the recording of distance and angular measurements. These instruments were primarily made from brass; the larger examples were fitted with tripods and protective cases. These cases also held accessories for the instruments, and these can sometimes play a key part in their evaluation. Instruments in complete condition and showing little use will have much greater values than those that appear to have had moderate or heavy use. Instruments were never polished during use, and those that have been polished as decorator pieces are of little interest to most avid collectors. Our advisor for this category is Dale Beeks; he is listed in the Directory under Iowa.

5½" light mountain transit, Eugene Dietzgen Co., Chicago, IL, 9¼" external focus telescope, 3½" compass, 2 vernier, black and lacquered brass, ca 1927, $375.00.

Alidade, US Coast survey style, Buff & Buff, ca 1920, +box 350.00
Compass, Alexander Magarey NY, brass, ca 1850s, pine case 575.00
Compass, E&GW Blunt, 1850s, eng 5¾" needle, 7" vanes 500.00
Compass, EA Kutz NY, 1850s, 6" needle, EX in box 850.00
Compass, Heisely & Son Harrisburg, 1812, 6" needle 850.00
Compass, Loring & Churchill Boston, 1860s, 5⅛" needle 850.00
Compass, plain; A Megary NY, 1840s, 5" needle, 8x13¾" 700.00
Compass, Richard Patten NY, 14½" mahog case 700.00
Compass, S Thaxter & Son Boston, brass, 1850s, 5", +box 700.00
Compass, vernier, B Pike & Sons NY, ca 1850, 6" 450.00
Compass, vernier, HM Poole MS, brass, 1860s, 6", +box 1,050.00
Compass, vernier, W&LE Gurley NY, ca 1875, 5" needle 600.00
Compass, vernier, Wm J Young & Sons, 1875, 5¾" needle 700.00
Compass/level, Adams London, 1750s, 19" scope, 6¼" needle ..1,250.00
Level, Chas Schott Nashville, brass, 1850s, 14½", +case 415.00
Level, convertible wye, Keuffel & Esser NY, ca 1912, 3¼" 175.00
Level, dumpy, Buff & Buff Boston, ca 1912, 15½" scope 200.00
Level, dumpy, David White WI, 1930s, 5" scope, 12" 125.00
Level, dumpy, Keuffel & Esser NY, ca 1913, 17½" scope 200.00
Level, Stackpole & Bro NY, brass, tripod base, 1850s, +case 470.00
Level, wye, architect's, Eugene Dietzgen Chicago & NY, 11½" ..200.00
Level, wye, architect's, W&LE Gurley, ca 1920, 12" scope 275.00
Level, wye, engineer's, Brandis NY, 1920s, 17½" scope 225.00
Level, wye, engineer's, Queen & Co Phila, ca 1900, 20" scope ..225.00
Level, wye, engineer's, W&LE Gurley NY, 1890s, 18¾" scope ..250.00
Level, wye, Iszard-Warren Phila, ca 1909, 12" scope 275.00
Level, wye, Keuffer & Esser, 1889, 21½" scope, 22" 450.00
Level, wye, Stackpole & Bro NY, 1850s, 17½", w/box 450.00
Level, wye, Troughton & Simms, 1880s, 15" scope, 3" compass .600.00
Level trier, Buff & Buff, cast base, ca 1945, 19x4½", NM 150.00
Level/transit, E Dietzgen Chicago, 1940s, 12" scope, +box 100.00
Theodolite, Bausch & Lomb NY, 1915, 11¾" scope, 6½" dia 700.00
Theodolite, triangulation; CL Berger & Sons, 10", M 1,400.00
Theodolite, Troughton & Simms, ca 1875, 10¼" scope 900.00
Transit, Buff & Buff, 1910, 11½" scope, 6¼" 300.00
Transit, Buff & Buff Boston, ca 1912, 11½" scope, 6¼" 400.00
Transit, Fauth & Co WA DC, 1900s, 10½" scope 600.00
Transit, Heller & Brightly, 1900s, 11½" scope, 6½" 750.00
Transit, Keuffel & Esser, twisted fr, ca 1909, 10½" scope 500.00

Transit, mountain; W&LE Gurley, 1890s, 8" scope 750.00
Transit, Queen & Co, ca 1900, 10¼" scope 500.00
Transit, solar; CL Berger & Sons, Saegmuller attachment, '05 ..2,000.00
Transit, W&LE Gurley, 1853, 12" scope, 5" vial, EX 450.00
Transit, Young & Sons Phila, ca 1904, 9½" scope, 6" 500.00

Swarovski Crystal

The Swarovski family has been perfecting the glassmaker's art in Wattens, Austria, since 1895. Collectible figurines and desk items were introduced in 1977, and the Swarovski Collectors Society (SCS) was created in 1987. Featuring lead content of 30%+, these 'Silver Crystal' limited edition decorative accessories have attracted a following of over 200,000 dedicated collectors worldwide. Some designs were distributed regionally, making persuit of retired items an interesting challenge that spans the globe. Most items have an etched mark on the underside. The first mark was a block-style SC. In 1989 the mark was changed to a Swan. Marks on larger items also include the name Swarovski. SCS figurines are further identified with the year and designer's initials. The periodical *Swan Seekers News*, published by Maret Webb, our advisor for this category, is available if you want more information about retired Swarovski items. Her address is listed in the Directory under Arizona. Prices listed below reflect the presence of complete original packing and enclosures, without which prices are compromised 10% to 35%.

do1x861, Lobebirds, minimum 2,500.00
do1x881, woodpeckers, minimum 1,330.00
do1x891, turtledoves, minimum 700.00
do1x901, dolphins, minimum 850.00
do1x911, seals, minimum 360.00
do1x921, whales, minimum 340.00
do1x931, elephant, minimum 750.00
do1x941, kudu, minimum 360.00
scsren1, cactus 240.00
003-0168678, birthday cake 130.00
003-8901707, dolphin brooch, minimum 105.00
52505, Trimlite bee 100.00
7551nr100, gold butterfly 840.00
7600nr120, candle holders, pr 275.00
7607nr000001, eagle, minimum 5,400.00
7621nr000002, toucan 140.00
7621nr000003, owl 110.00
7621nr000004, parrot, minimum 110.00
7622nr70, rhinoceros 110.00
7628nr80, whale, sgn 185.00
7634nr52, cat, med 300.00
7640nr100001, Dumbo, 1993 ....240.00
7645nr100, falcon head, lg 1,030.00
7650nr32, sparrow, lg 130.00
7652nr45, rabbit, lg 175.00
7670nr32, bear, mini 180.00

Swastika Keramos

Swastika Keramos was a line of artware made by the Owens China Co., of Minerva, Ohio, around 1902-04. It is characterized either by a coralene type of decoration (similar to the Opalesce line made by the J.B. Owens Pottery Company of Zanesville) or by the application of metallic lustres, usually in simple designs. Shapes are often plain and handles squarish and rather thick, suggestive of the Arts and Crafts style.

Pitcher, metallic gold & burgundy to gr drip glaze, 13" 160.00

Pitcher, silver oil-spot panels fr w/gold swastikas, 10" 300.00
Vase, clouds/cactus, red/gold lustre, att Lessell, 12" 300.00
Vase, gr w/variegated old lines, mk, 8" 200.00

Syracuse

Syracuse was a line of fine dinnerware and casual ware which was made for nearly a century by the Onondaga Pottery Company of Syracuse, New York. Early patterns were marked O.P. Company. Collectors of American dinnerware are focusing their attention on reassembling some of their many lovely patterns. In 1966 the firm became officially known as the Syracuse China Company in order to better identify with the name of their popular chinaware. Many of the patterns were marked with the shape and color names (Old Ivory, Federal, etc.), not the pattern names. By 1971 dinnerware geared for use in the home was discontinued, and the company turned to the manufacture of hotel, restaurant, and other types of commercial tableware.

Apple blossom, plate, 8" 20.00
Arcadia, creamer & sugar bowl, w/lid 70.00
Arcadia, cup & saucer 28.00
Arcadia, gravy boat 65.00
Avalon, plate, salad; gold trim 17.50
Avalon, plate, 10" 25.00
Bombay, coffeepot, ivory w/gold trim 95.00
Bombay, rim soup, gold trim 26.00
Bracelet, plate, 10¼" 35.00
Bracelet, platter, 12" 55.00
Bracelet, rim soup, 8¾" 36.00
Briarcliff, bowl, vegetable; w/lid 130.00
Briarcliff, cream soup 25.00
Briarcliff, platter, 12" 57.50
Clover, bowl, cereal; 5½" 16.00
Clover, cup & saucer 24.00
Clover, plate, salad; 8" 16.00
Coralbel, cup & saucer 24.00
Coralbel, plate, 10¼" 30.00
Coralbel, soup 25.00
Coronet, plate, salad 20.00
Diane, coffeepot 230.00
Gardenia, plate, salad 17.50
Indian Tree, bowl, cereal 20.00
Jefferson, bowl, vegetable; oval 47.50
Jefferson, gravy boat 67.50
Jefferson, platter, 14" 78.00
Lady Mary, bowl, vegetable; oval 45.00
Lady Mary, plate, dinner; 9¾" 22.00
Lyric, bowl, vegetable; ftd 55.00
Lyric, platter, 16" 78.00
Meadow Breeze, plate, bread & butter 20.00
Minuet, plate, salad 17.50
Orchard, plate, dinner 25.00
Orleans, cup, bouillon 12.00
Orleans, gravy boat 65.00
Orleans, platter, 14" 55.00
Royal Court, plate, 10¼" 50.00
Sharon, plate, dinner 27.50
Sherwood, bowl, vegetable; w/lid 130.00
Sherwood, plate, salad 17.50
Sherwood, rim soup 36.00
Silhouette, plate, 10½" 30.00
Singing Cowboys, chop plate 38.00
Singing Cowboys, mug 25.00

Singing Cowboys, plate, 6½" 15.00
Singing Cowboys, plate, 7½" 18.00
Singing Cowboys, platter, oval 38.00
Singing Cowboys, rim soup 24.00
Stansbury, bowl, vegetable; w/lid 125.00
Stansbury, cream soup; w/underplate 30.00
Stansbury, gravy boat 67.50
Stansbury, plate, salad; 8" 16.00
Stansbury, platter, 12" 50.00
Suzanne, bowl, dessert; 7" 18.00
Suzanne, gravy boat 75.00
Suzanne, rim soup 32.00
Victoria, cup & saucer 36.00
Victoria, platter, 12x9" 70.00
Virginia, bouillon w/underplate 12.00
Whitby, plate, salad; 8" 22.00

Syrups

Values are for old, original syrups. Beware of reproductions! See also various manufacturers and specific types of glass. Our coadvisors are Jeff Bradfield and Dale MacAllister; they are listed in the Directory under Virginia.

Acorn, bl, decor 225.00
Acorn, pk, wht hdl 275.00
Big Windows, bl opal swirl 525.00
Bubble Lattice, bl opal 500.00
Bulging Loops, pk cased 435.00
Button Arches, ruby stain 250.00
Coin Spot, bl opal, ring neck 240.00
Coin Spot, rubena opal, SP top, clear reeded hdl 150.00
Coin Spot, 9-Panel; bl opal 225.00
Coin Spot, 9-Panel; wht opal 175.00
Coin Spot & Swirl, bl 150.00
Cone, bl, tall 295.00
Cone, pk satin, tall 295.00
Cone, yel, squatty 295.00
Coreopsis, pigeon blood 325.00

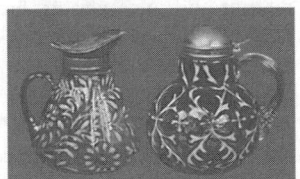

Daisy and Fern, blue opalescent with blue handle, tin lid, 5½", $250.00; Spanish Lace, cranberry opalescent, clear reeded handle, silverplated lid, 5½", $500.00.

Empress 145.00
Fern, cranberry opal 500.00
Fleur-de-Lis 115.00
Florette, pk satin 275.00
Flower & Pleat 195.00
Guttate, pk cased (+) 325.00
Herculese Pillar, bl 175.00
Invt T'print, amber 175.00
Invt T'print, bl, Hobbs 150.00
Iris, milk glass w/gold 135.00
Medallion Sprig, rubena 650.00
Reverse Swirl, bl opal 350.00
Scalloped Swirl, ruby stain 600.00
Utopia Optic, cranberry w/gold & enamel 375.00
Valencia, amber 195.00

Tamac Pottery

At the close of World War II, finding jobs almost nonexistent for homecoming military men, Leonard Tate and Allen Macauley decided to take advantage of an offer made by the state of Oklahoma who was trying to encourage industry by offering free factory sites for new businesses. Their wives had both worked as designers for the same company, so the foursome decided to combine efforts and past experiences and thus formed 'Tamac' pottery, a conglomeration of the two last names.

The company was organized in September 1946, in Henry and Zoma Tate's garage (they were Leonard Tate's parents) in Perry, Oklahoma; production was very limited. They expanded in 1948 and were able to produce over three hundred pieces of earthenware daily.

The Tates and Macauleys were directly responsible for all phases of Tamac production: designing and making the molds, mixing the Oklahoma and Kansas clays, final processing and shipping. They had customers in every state as well as foreign countries, and they operated an outlet store as well.

About seventy various pieces of Tamac pottery were produced, mainly buffet/dinnerware. Other 'specialty' pieces included candle holders, ashtrays, vases, and table centerpieces. One of their most popular sellers was the barbeque line, designed for casual entertaining and backyard dining. It consisted of tray-like plates with unique coffee mugs having nontraditional handles.

Six colors were produced, each with a 'frosted' rim of a different color. The six colors were: Frosty Pine, Avocado, Frosty Fudge, Honey, Raspberry, and Butterscotch. The Frosty Pine and Avocado (both with dark green bases) are the most readily available. Few items, mainly 'specialty' pieces, were manufactured in Raspberry.

In 1950 the Macauleys sold their shares to the Tates. The business expanded and by 1952 required bank financing which proved impossible to obtain. As a result, the plant was sold in September of that year to Earl, Raymond, and Bettye Bechtold. (Earl was a brother to Zoma Tate.) With only eight employees, the pottery produced about 250,000 pieces a year, shipping their product to ten states and four foreign countries, those being Canada, Australia, Germany, and Belgium. Most of their sales, however, were made at the plant itself. The motto of the pottery was 'See it Made.'

Raymond Bechtold was the active manager of the business and added more than thirty-five pieces to the line, among them the juice pitcher and juice glasses, breakfast plate and mug, covered casserole, decanter and goblet set, teapot, demitasse line, chocolate pitcher, and bud vase. These items are now among the most sought after. Bechtold also experimented with new colors in the accessory and floral lines such as Raspberry, Sky Blue, and Bronze. Only Raspberry was popular, and the others were quickly phased out.

Raymond Bechtold assumed full control of the pottery in 1960 and operated it until February 1965, when he sold it to Mrs. Lenita Moore. Mrs. Moore's mother had been a long-time employee of the plant and was the active manager. The pottery operated until 1970 when it closed and the final auction was held. The building still stands and is used for storage.

Tamac pottery can easily be identified by its unique design and the stamp on the bottom of each piece: 'TAMAC Perry, Okla USA.' Some earlier pieces carry the etched 'TAMAC' mark.

Our advisors for this category are Bob and Dondee Klein. They are listed in the Directory under Oklahoma.

Ashtray, bridge	8.00
Ashtray, Oklahoma	15.00
Ashtray, rnd	15.00
Ashtray, 3-corner	8.00
Bird, 3-dimensional, any color, ea	30.00
Bowl, centerpc; dish garden	20.00

Bowl, centerpc; S-shape	17.50
Bowl, serving; 2-qt	18.00
Bowl, serving; 4-qt	30.00
Butter dish, no lid	9.00
Candle holder, dbl	25.00
Candle holder, single	18.00
Casserole, w/lid, 2-qt	30.00
Chocolate pot, tall & thin	55.00
Coffee cup, hdls	5.00
Coffee mug, w/finger insert	9.00
Creamer, demitasse	10.00
Creamer, 8-oz	8.00
Cup, demitasse	12.00
Decanter, wine; w/stopper	60.00
Goblet, wine; 6-oz	13.00
Pitcher, juice; 24-oz	15.00
Pitcher, 2-qt	25.00
Pitcher, 4-qt	35.00
Planter vase, no tray, 5x6" dia	20.00
Planter vase, w/tray & drain hole	15.00
Plate, barbecue; 15"	12.00
Plate, dinner; 10"	8.00
Platter, turkey; 18"	35.00
Saucer	3.00
Saucer, demitasse	7.00
Sugar bowl, w/lid	10.00
Teapot, short & squat	50.00
Toothpick holder	7.00
Tumbler, juice; 4-oz	10.00
Tumbler, 16-oz	8.00
Vase, free-form, 5½"	25.00
Violet planter, w/tray & drain hole	17.00
Wall vase/pocket, 5"	12.50

Target Balls

Prior to 1880 when the clay pigeon was invented, blown glass target balls were used extensively for shotgun competitions. Approximately 2¾" in diameter, these balls were hand blown into a three-piece mold. All have a ragged hole where the blowpipe was twisted free. Target balls date from approximately 1840 (English) to World War I, although they were most widely used in the 1870-1880 period. Common examples are unmarked except for the blower's code — dots, crude numerals, etc. Some balls are embossed in a dot or diamond pattern so they were more likely to shatter when struck by shot, and some have names and/or patent dates. When evaluating condition, bubbles and other minor manufacturing imperfections are acceptable; cracks are not. The prices below are for mint condition examples.

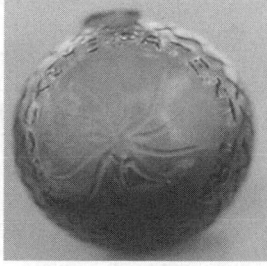

For Hockey's Patent Trap, green, English, $500.00.

Amber w/emb ribs, horizontal or vertical	150.00
Bogardus' Glass Ball Pat'd April 10 1877, amber, Am	350.00
Bogardus' Glass Ball Pat'd April 10 1877, other than amber, Am	800.00

CTB Co, blk pitch, Pat dates on bottom, Am 250.00
Dmn Quilt w/plain center band, ground top, Am 150.00
Dmn Quilt w/shooter emb in 2 panels, clear, English 300.00
Dmn Quilt w/shooter emb in 2 panels, gr or purple, English 300.00
Great Western Gun Works, Pittsburgh, amber, Am 900.00
Gurd & Son, London, Ontario, amber, Canadian 500.00
Ilmenau (Thur) Sophiehutte, amber, Dmn Quilt, Germany 425.00
Ira Paine's Filled Ball Pat Oct 23 1877, amber, Am 250.00
Ira Paine's Filled Ball Pat Oct 23 1877, other than amber, Am ..800.00
NB Glass Works Perth, other than pale gr, English 200.00
NB Glass Works Perth, pale gr, English 100.00
Plain, amber w/mold mks 65.00
Plain, clear w/mold mks 1,000.00
Plain, cobalt w/mold mks 150.00
T Jones, Gunmaker, Blackburn, pale bl, English 150.00
WW Greener, St Mary's Works, various colors, English, ea 250.00

Related Memorabilia

Ball thrower, dbl; old red pnt, ME Card, Pat...78, 79, VG 900.00
Clay birds, Winchester, Pat May 29 1917, 1 flight in box 100.00
Pitch bird, blk DUVROCK 1.00
Shell, dummy, w/single window, any brand 35.00
Shell, dummy shotgun, Winchester, window w/powder, 6" 125.00
Shell set, dummy, Gamble Stores, 2 window shells, 3 cut out 125.00
Shell set, dummy, Winchester, 5 window shells 175.00
Shell set, dummy shotgun, Peters, 6 window shells+full box 175.00
Shotshell loader, rosewood/brass, Parker Bros, Pat 1884 ....50.00
Target, Am sheet metal, rod ends mk Pat Feb 8 '21, set 25.00
Target, blk japanned sheet metal, Bussy Patentee, London 50.00
Target, BUST-O, blk or wht breakable wafer 20.00
Trap, DUVROCK, w/blk pitch birds 250.00
Trap, MO-SKEET-O, w/birds 150.00

Tea Caddies

Because tea was once regarded as a precious commodity, special boxes called caddies were used to store the tea leaves. They were made from various materials: porcelain, carved and inlaid woods, and metals ranging from painted tin or tole to engraved silver. Our advisor for this category is Tina Carter; she is listed in the Directory under California.

Lacquered wood w/mc floral decor, dome top, 2-part, 8" 225.00
Mahog, English, 1800s, 7¼x12", EX 230.00
Mahog w/brass lion mask hdls, fitted int, Georgian 375.00
Mahog w/inlay, English, early 1800s, 4½x4½", EX 385.00
Mahog w/inlay, English, 19th C, 4¾x7½", VG 495.00
Mahog w/line inlay, fitted interior, English, 10" L 335.00

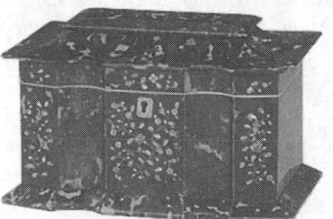

Regency mahogany with mother-of-pearl inlay, hinged pagoda-shaped lid, base with 2 compartments and floral inlay, early 1800s, 5½x8x6", $1,400.00.

Rosewood w/ivory escutcheon, English, 19th C, 5¾x7¼", EX ...350.00
Rosewood w/nacre inlay, 2 interior lids, English, 8" 415.00
SP, floral repousse, rectangular bombe shape, English, 1800s 450.00
Veneer w/bands, English Sheraton, 1790 ....500.00

Wood veneer (G), glass insert, 2 compartments 225.00
Wooden casket shape w/brass lock & hinges, 19th C, 5x8x4½" .150.00
Wooden w/inlay & marquetry banding, fitted interior, 10" 285.00

Tea Leaf Ironstone

Tea Leaf Ironstone became popular in the 1880s when middle-class American housewives became bored with the plain white stone china that English potters had been exporting to this country for nearly a century. The original design has been credited to Anthony Shaw of Longport, who decorated the plain ironstone with a hand-painted copper lustre design of bands and leaves. Originally known as Lustre Band and Sprig, the pattern has since come to be known as Tea Leaf Lustre. It was produced with minor variations by many different firms both in England and the United States. By the early 1900s, it had become so commonplace that it had lost much of its appeal.

Items marked Red Cliff are reproductions made from 1950 until 1980 for this distributing and decorating company of Chicago, Illinois. Hall China provided many of the blanks.

Our advice for this category comes from Home Place Antiques, whose address is listed in the Directory under Illinois.

Baker, Wilkinson, 9½x6¾" 30.00
Bone dish, scalloped, Meakin, EX 75.00
Bone dish, scalloped edge, Wilkinson, EX 75.00
Bowl, crimped edge, Wilkinson, 9½" sq, 3⅜" tall 75.00
Bowl, vegetable; Cable style, Burgess, w/lid, EX 245.00
Bowl, vegetable; Fish Hook, bracket ftd, Meakin, w/lid, 11x7", EX ...195.00
Bowl, vegetable; Pagoda, ribbed, hdls, w/lid, Wedgwood, 11x7" .225.00
Bowl, vegetable; Sunburst, ftd, w/lid, Shaw, 11½x5½", EX 225.00
Butter dish, Fish Hook, w/drain, Meakin, EX 165.00
Butter dish, simple, w/drain, Wedgwood, 5½" sq 165.00
Butter dish, vertical ribbing w/leaf finial, Mellor-Taylor, sq 140.00
Butter pat, Anthony Shaw & Sons, VG 16.00
Butter pat, ribbed, scalloped edge, Mellor-Taylor, sq 16.00
Butter pat, rnd, Meakin, 3¼", EX 15.00
Coffeepot, Bamboo, Meakin, 9", EX 225.00
Creamer, Bamboo, Meakin, 6½", EX 165.00
Cup & saucer, Adams Microtex, EX 35.00
Cup & saucer, Chelsea type, Johnson Bros, 3½x2⅝", EX 85.00
Cup & saucer, Morning Glory, Tunstall 85.00
Cup & saucer, str sided, Meakin, 2¾", EX 85.00
Cup plate, Wilkinson, 3¼" 50.00
Pitcher, milk; Bamboo, Meakin, 7½" 265.00
Plate, gold lustre, Bridgewood, 7" 12.00
Plate, Meakin, 8" 15.00
Plate, Meakin, 9¾" 35.00
Plate, Morning Glory, Portland shape, Elsmore & Forster, 6⅞" ...45.00
Plate, Red Cliff, 8¼" 10.00
Plate, soup; flanged, gold lustre, Meakin, 8¾" 30.00
Plate, Wedgwood, 9" 22.00
Plate, Wilkinson, 8" 16.00
Platter, Mellor-Taylor, 12x9½" 65.00
Platter, Wedgwood, 13x9½" 60.00
Platter, Wedgwood, 14x10¼" 65.00
Sauce dish, rnd, Meakin, 4¾" 18.00
Sauce dish, scalloped, sq, gold lustre, Powell Bishop, 4½" 12.00
Sauce tureen, no lid, Gothic hdl, Burgess 50.00
Shaving mug, leaf on hdl, 12-sided, Shaw 185.00
Shaving mug, Meakin, 3¼x3½" 230.00
Sugar bowl, Bamboo, Grindley, EX 95.00
Sugar bowl, Fish Hook, w/lid, Meakin, 7" 85.00
Sugar bowl, gold lustre, w/lid, unmk, EX 48.00

Teapot, Fish Hook, Meakin, 8½" 200.00
Toothbrush holder, Fish Hook, Meakin 165.00
Wash bowl, Meakin, 14¾", EX 235.00

Teapots

The custom of drinking tea has resulted in the production of many tea-related collectibles; the most popular is the teapot. The first teapots were manufactured in the Chinese village of Yixing during the late 16th century and were no bigger than the tiny cups previously used for tea drinking. Amazingly these same tiny teapots are still being used today.

A wide range of teapots can be found by the avid searcher; those most readily available today were produced from about 1870 to the present. Almost every pottery and porcelain manufacturer in Europe as well as in America have produced teapots. Some are purely functional, others decorative and whimsical. Refer to various manufacturers' names for further listings. Our advisor for this category is Tina M. Carter, listed in the Directory under California. Her book, *Teapots*, is available at bookstores or direct from the author.

Automobile, gr glaze, no mk, 8" L 300.00
Barge, brn, emb mk, S Derbyshire, England, lg 75.00
Barge, raised floral design on brn, 'A Present...,' 1800s, 10" 1,000.00
Bone china, bl/wht/gold, SYP, Wedgwood, England, ca 1905-06 .125.00
Brn earthenware, Sadler, England, floral & gold decor 50.00
Buff sharkskin, tan, slip decor, unmk Japan, ca 1920 ....32.00
Bunny figural, mk England, ca 1960, 6-cup 45.00
Cat figural, paw spout, blk/gray/cream, US Zone Germany, 9" 60.00
Charles & Diana, brn pottery, Wales CM, 2½" 78.00
China, bees/leaves on cream, bee finial, Occupied Japan, 6x5" 38.00
China, dk brn w/gold floral & beadwork, Tunstall England, 6x9" .32.00
China, set in basket, mk China, ca 1930 ....100.00
Copper, ball ft, Art Deco style, China 38.00
Dbl spout, earthenware, slip decor, ca 1890 ....85.00
Dog figural, sitting on haunches, upraised legs form spout 48.00
Electroplated nickel silver, Sheffield, England, wood hdl 40.00
Elf figural, HP, label E&R, Western Germany 50.00
Ellgreave, Wood & Sons, England, ironstone w/floral 38.00

English, H.J. Wood, ceramic lady figural, many color variations, in production from 1930s to 1970s, 8½", $95.00. (A similar teapot was made by Shawnee.)

Fitz & Floyd, Christopher Columbus, ltd ed, recent 90.00
Flow bl, man seated, legs outstretched, conical hat, 8x9" 50.00
Gr lustre, HP, Royal Hanover, Germany, 6½" 75.00
Horizontal lines, bulbous, Susie Cooper, England 65.00
HP decor, mk Wade, +matching cr/sug 55.00
Humpty Dumpty, Lingard, England, ca 1930 ....75.00
Iced Tea dispenser, brn, USA, 2-pc 175.00
Jasperware, bl/wht, Wedgwood, dtd 20th C, 6-cup 190.00
John Bull figural, wht porc 90.00
Lipton's, oval & ribbed, Fraunfelter, ca 1930 ....40.00
Ming Tea Co, Made in Japan, w/label, 1½-cup 20.00

Pyrex mk, blown glass, etched flowers, 6-cup 60.00
Red & wht marbleized o/l w/gold bands, 7x4½" 235.00
Rococo style, HP gold, appl flowers, mk Italy, 10" 38.00
Rudolph the Red Nosed Reindeer, Japan, +cr/sug 65.00
Snow White w/Dwarfs, musical, Walt Disney Productions 50.00
Souvenir, cobalt, Washington DC, Germany, mini 28.00
Spode's Tower, bl/wht transfer, London shape, England, VG 50.00
Tank, gr w/silver details, Made in England, 8½" L 200.00
Tea for Two, man in tux hdl, girl in gown forms pot, Japan 45.00
Torquay, scene & motto, Watcombe, England, 1½-cup 45.00
Weller, majolica, wooded scene, mk USA, ca 1930, VG 52.00
WWII, Esc to US by Royal Navy or Allied Fleets, brn, England ..45.00

Teco

Teco artware was made by the American Terra Cotta and Ceramic Company, located near Chicago, Illinois. The firm was established in 1886 and until 1901 produced only brick, sewer tile, and other redware. Their early glaze was inspired by the matt green made popular by Grueby. 'Teco Green' was made for nearly ten years. It was similar to Grueby's yet with a subtle silver-gray cast. The company was one of the first in the United States to perfect a true crystalline glaze. The only decoration used was through the modeling and glazing techniques; no hand painting was attempted. Favored motifs were naturalistic leaves and flowers. The company broadened their lines to include garden pottery and faience tiles and panels. New matt glazes (browns, yellows, blue, and rose) were added to the green in 1910. By 1922 the artware lines were discontinued; the company was sold in 1930.

Values are dictated by size and shape, with architectural and organic forms being more desirable. Teco is usually marked with a vertical impressed device comprised of a large 'T' to the left of the remaining three letters.

Ashtray, gr, crimped sides, Gates design, 4½" dia 150.00
Bookends, maid w/jug in oval reserve, cream/orange, 7" 600.00
Bookends, seated gargoyle w/prominent wings, ivory matt, 8½" ...1,700.00
Bowl, gr, #C108, 3¾x4½" 175.00
Bowl, gr, #80, 2½x7", NM 400.00
Bowl, gr/blk matt, #317, 2½x8", NM 400.00
Bowl, med gr w/charcoal, cream int, 4 sq buttress legs, 12" 4,750.00
Bowl, rust/brn metallic crystalline, 4x6", NM 500.00
Box, med gr w/charcoal, slightly domed lid, 1½x4" dia 500.00
Pitcher, gold to brn crystalline, #56, 4" 525.00
Pitcher, gr, stylized organic hdl, incurvate, #294, 9x5" 400.00
Planter, cream w/orange, 8 architectural ft, 24" L, EX 850.00
Vase, aventurine, stick neck, wide bun bottom, 5½" 200.00
Vase, aventurine, teardrop w/flared rim, 4x3¾" 450.00
Vase, bl, cone w/sm rim & 4 V-shape bottom fins, sm rpr, 8½" ...1,900.00
Vase, brn, cylinder w/2 full-length closed buttresses, 6¼" 650.00
Vase, brn, squat inkwell shape, 2x3" 275.00
Vase, dk gr, swollen cylinder w/collar rim, #60D, 17" 2,600.00
Vase, dk gr mottle w/gunmetal, rpr, 17x8" 1,300.00
Vase, gr, blade leaves/flowers, cylinder w/ring rim, 8¾", NM 750.00
Vase, gr, bulbous base, flared neck, 4-petal rim, #233, 5" 400.00
Vase, gr, bulbous w/cylinder neck, #362, 3½" 275.00
Vase, gr, classic form, #64B, no mk, 11½x4¾" 425.00
Vase, gr, daffodils/leaves, #60B, flake to base, 8x4" 600.00
Vase, gr, Grecian shape w/lg integral loop hdls, #297, 6x9" 750.00
Vase, gr, ovoid w/flared rim & closed shoulder hdls, #407, 8½" ..1,300.00
Vase, gr, scalloped/flared rim, #233, 5x4" 375.00
Vase, gr, shouldered/squat w/long 4-lobe neck, #182, 16", NM ...1,000.00
Vase, gr, waisted neck, flared rim, 5½" 200.00
Vase, gr, 2 sm neck-to-width buttress hdls, #A402, 6¾x4" 1,000.00

Vase, gr, 3-sided cylinder, 8x4" **800.00**
Vase, gr, 4 integral hdls form open 'windows' at neck, 13" **14,950.00**
Vase, gr, 4 long buttresses around tall neck, 6½x3" **1,300.00**
Vase, gr, 4-sided w/buttress rim hdls, 9x4¼" **2,100.00**
Vase, gr, 4-sided w/4 open integral hdls at rim, #184, 9" **2,300.00**
Vase, gr w/charcoal, twisted shoulder hdls, #257, rpr, 12" **1,400.00**
Vase, gr w/gun-metal, 4 rim-to-base open buttresses, 7½x4" ...**1,800.00**
Vase, gr w/gun-metal gray, lg integral hdls, #297, 5½x8½" **425.00**
Vase, lt gr, conical w/bulbous neck, 9x4½" **700.00**
Vase, pumpkin, in-mold sqd hdls, #427, 8½" **900.00**
Vase, robin's egg bl, #G60, simple form, 25x12", EX **850.00**
Vase, tan, dbl gourd w/4 rnded open buttresses, #287, 6½" **1,200.00**

Teddy Bear Collectibles

The story of Teddy Roosevelt's encounter with the bear cub has been oft recounted with varying degrees of accuracy, so it will suffice to say that it was as a result of this incident in 1902 that the teddy bear got his name. These appealing little creatures are enjoying renewed popularity with collectors today. To one who has not yet succumbed to their obvious charms, one bear seems to look very much like another. How to tell the older ones? Look for long snouts, jointed limbs, large feet and felt paws, long curving arms, and glass or shoe-button eyes. Most old bears have a humped back and are made of mohair stuffed with straw or excelsior. Cute expressions, original clothes, a nice personality, and, of course, good condition add to their value. Steiff bears in mint condition may go for a minimum of $100.00 per inch (for a small bear) up to $200.00 per inch (for one 20" high or larger). These are easily recognized by the trademark button within the ear. For further information we recommend *Teddy Bears, Annalee's & Steiff Animals*, by Margaret Fox Mandel, available from Collector Books. See also Toys, Steiff.

Key: jtd — jointed

Bears

Am, blond bristly mohair, all orig, ca 1910, 20" **575.00**
Am, cotton plush, glass eyes, jtd, 1940s, 23", EX **900.00**
Am, golden mohair, ca 1910, 15", NM **675.00**
Bing, Buddie, tan mohair, button eyes, jtd, 1915, 12", EX **1,800.00**
Clemens, tan mohair, felt pads, glass eyes, 17", M **250.00**
Clemens, tan mohair, sm hump, glass eyes, jtd, 9", M **95.00**
Clemens, tan mohair, yel chest plate, jtd, squeaker, 11", EX **55.00**
German, battery-op talker, brn synthetic, plastic eyes, 20", EX ..**155.00**
German, pull-string talker, shaggy brn synthetic, glass eyes, 18" **150.00**
Hermann, tan mohair, bent arms, glass eyes, rpl pad, 17", EX **285.00**
Hermann, tan mohair, hump, growler, no eyes, jtd, old, 11", EX ...**200.00**
Hermann, Zotty type, frosted mohair, hump, glass eyes, 12", NM **155.00**
Ideal, beige mohair, glass eyes, orig sailor dress, early, 29" **1,600.00**
Merrythought, Paddington, England, 20", M **175.00**
Schuco, brn mohair, glass eyes, gold crown/Berlin banner, 3" **150.00**
Schuco, gold mohair, orig ribbon, 3½", M **175.00**
Schuco, gold mohair, yes/no, jtd, orig ribbon, 5", EX, $500 to **675.00**
Schuco, Golliwog, 2-faced, cinnamon, 5" **950.00**
Schuco, Golliwog, 2-faced, tan mohair, yes/no, jtd, 3¾", M **635.00**
Schuco, long dense gold mohair, yes/no, 1930s, 13" **1,700.00**
Schuco, tan mohair, beaded eyes, jtd, no ID, 3½", EX **125.00**
Schuco, Tricky, gold mohair, yes/no, 1930s, 15", M **2,500.00**
Steiff, apricot, shoe-button eyes, w/button, 1907, 16", M **2,500.00**
Steiff, clown outfit, mohair, button eyes, 1904, 14", VG+ **805.00**
Steiff, gold mohair, glass eyes, claws, 1940s, no ID, 8", EX **250.00**
Steiff, gold mohair, glass eyes, printed button, 1920s, 19", G ..**2,300.00**

Steiff, long gold mohair, jtd, w/button, 1905, 13", M **1,200.00**
Steiff, tan mohair, sheared snout, ribbon, all ID, '80s, 7½", M ...**145.00**
Steiff, wht, glass eyes, jtd limbs, 1920s, 14", M **2,600.00**
Unknown, brn mohair, glass eyes, growler, on wheels, 1950s, 26" ..**365.00**
Unknown, brn mohair, glass eyes, jtd, long snout, 11", EX **125.00**
Unknown, brn/cream mohair, soft fill, growler, 20", EX **125.00**
Unknown, mohair, floss nose/mouth, jtd, squeaker, 1920s, 12" ..**500.00**
Unknown, mohair, hump, glass eyes, long nose, jtd, 20" **550.00**
Unknown, tan mohair, amber eyes, laughing type, voice, 18", EX ...**165.00**
Unknown, Zotty type, glass eyes, straw stuffed, 11", EX **40.00**

Telephones

Since Alexander Graham Bell's first successful telephone communication, the phone itself has undergone a complete evolution in style as well as efficiency. Early models, especially those wall types with ornately carved oak boxes, are of special interest to collectors. Also of value are the candlestick phones from the early part of the century and any related memorabilia.

Automatic Electric, beige, 3-slot iron pay phone, 1950s, EX **120.00**
Automatic Electric, blk, 3-slot iron pay phone, 1950s, rstr **200.00**
Automatic Electric, chrome, 3-slot iron pay phone, 1950s, EX ..**250.00**
Candlestick, Conn Tel & Elec Co Inc, 11½" **110.00**
Dean Electric, crank-type wall mt, walnut, w/shelf, 26" **245.00**
Harrison Internat'l Telephone Co, wall type, 32", VG **385.00**
Kellogg, oak, wall style, rfn, 24", EX **235.00**
Kellogg, Pat'd 1905, tall wall type w/writing desk, NM **325.00**
New England Bell, 2-box, walnut, wall type, EX **500.00**
Northern Electric, beige, 3-slot iron pay phone, 1950s, rstr **135.00**
Northern Electric, oak case, w/crank, wall type **250.00**
Stromberg, pk, wall type, 1950s-60s, rstr **25.00**
Stromberg Carlson, candlestick, oil-can shape, 1898 ....**375.00**

Western Electric, black candlestick style, 1915, 11¼", VG with scratches and paint wear, $125.00.

Western Electric, metal wall phone, dial, 1920s **75.00**
Western Electric, NP candlestick, pony receiver, NM **250.00**

Blue Bell Paperweights

First issued in the early 1900s, bell-shaped glass paperweights were used as 'give-aways' and/or presented to telephone company executives as tokens of appreciation. The paperweights were used to prevent stacks of papers from blowing off the desks in the days of overhead fans. Over the years they have all but vanished — some taken by retiring employees, others accidently broken. The weights came to be widely used for advertising by individual telephone companies; and as the smaller companies merged to form larger companies, more and more new paperweights were created. They were widely distributed with the opening of the first transcontinental telephone line in 1915. The bell-shaped paperweight embossed 'Opening of Trans-Pacific Service, Dec. 23,

1931,' in peacock blue glass is very rare, and the price is negotiable. In 1972 the first Pioneer bell paperweights were made to sell to raise funds for the charities the Pioneers support. This has continued to the present day. These bell paperweights have also become 'collectibles.' For further study we recommend *Blue Bell Paperweights, 1992 Revised Edition*, and its accompanying *1995 Addendum* by Jacqueline C. Linscott; she is listed in the Directory under Florida.

Bell System Ches & Pot Tel Co & Assoc Companies, ice bl	550.00
Bell Telephone System, cobalt	225.00
Break-Up of the Bell System, bl opaline swirl	50.00
Compliments of Millville Kiwanis Club, ice bl	800.00
Missouri & Kansas Telephone Co, peacock	125.00
Nevada Bell (silver etched), blk	75.00
Pacific Bell (gold etched)/Nevada Bell (silver etched), blk	500.00
Pays 7% Mountain States Telephone, peacock	200.00
Region 10 Assembly, bl	100.00
Southern Bell Telephone & Telegraph Co, cobalt w/gold letters	175.00
Western Electric Co, cobalt	200.00

Related Memorabilia

Directory, New England, 1907	30.00

Fan, American Telephone & Telegraph..., Bell System, cardboard with wooden handle, cream and blue, 12x8" diameter, EX, $35.00.

License holder, Compliments of S Bell..., fishing scene, cb	5.00
Sign, Am Telephone & Telegraph, paper, Weavers of Speech, EX	100.00
Sign, New England Telephone & Telegraph, cb, bl/wht, 20x8"	145.00
Sign, Public...Bell System, porc flange, 2-sided, 1921, 18", NM	250.00

Telescopes

Antique telescopes were sold in large quantities to sailors, astronomers, voyeurs, and the military but survive in relatively few numbers because their glass lenses and brass tubes were easily damaged. Even scarcer are antique reflecting telescopes, which use a polished metal mirror to magnify the world. Telescopes used for astronomy give an inverted image, but most old telescopes were used for marine purposes and have more complicated optics that show the world right-side up. Spyglasses are smaller, hand-held telescopes that collapse into their tube and focus by drawing out the tube to the correct length. A more compact instrument, with three or four sections, is also more delicate, and sailors usually preferred a single-draw spyglass. They are almost always of brass, occasionally of nickel siver or silver plate; and usually covered with leather, or sometimes a beautiful rosewood veneer. Solid wood barrel spyglasses (with a brass draw tube) tend to be early and rare. Before the middle of the 1800s, makers put their names in elaborate script on the smallest draw tube, but as 1900 approached, most switched to plain block printing. British instruments from WWI are commonly found, by a variety of makers but sharing a format of a 2" objective, 30" long with three draws extended, tapered main tube, and sometimes with low- and high-power oculars and a beautiful leather

case. U.S. Navy WWII spyglasses are quite common but have outstanding optics and focus by twisting the eyepiece, which makes them weatherproof. The Quartermaster (Q.M.) 16x spyglass is 31" long, with a tapered barrel and a 2½" objective. The Officer of the Deck (O.D.D.) is a 23" cylinder with a 1½" objective. Very massive, short, brass telescopes are usually gunsights or ship equipment and have little interest to most collectors. World War II marked the first widespread use of coated optics, which can be recognized by a colored film on the objective lens. Collectible post-WWII telescopes include early refractors by Unitron or Fecker and reflectors by Cave or Questar. Modern spotting scopes often use a prism to erect the image and are of great interest if made by the best makers, including Nikon and Zeiss. Several modern makers still use lacquered brass, and many replica instruments have been produced.

A telescope with no maker's name is much less interesting than a signed instrument, and 'Made in France' is the most common mark on old spyglasses. Dollond of London made instruments for two hundred years and is probably the most common name on antiques, but because of their important technical innovations and very high quality, Dollond telescopes are always valuable. Bardou, Paris, telescopes are also very high quality. Bardou is another relatively common name, since they were a prolific maker for many years and their spyglasses were sold by Sears. Alvin Clark and Sons were the most prolific early American makers in operation from the 1850s to the 1920s, and their astronomical telescopes are of great historical import.

Spyglasses are delicate instruments that were subject to severe use under all weather conditions. Cracked or deeply scratched optics are impossible to repair and lower the value considerably. Most lenses are doublets, two lenses glued together, and deteriorated cement is common. This looks like crazed glaze and is fairly difficult to repair. Dents in the tube and damaged or missing leather covering can usually be fixed. The best test of a telescope is to use it, and the image should be sharp and clear. Any accessories, eyepieces, erecting prisms, or quality cases can add significantly to value. The following prices assume that the telescope is in very good to fine condition and give the objective lens (obj.) diameter, which is the most important measurement of a telescope.

Our advisor for this category is Peter Abrahams, who studies and collects telescopes and other optics. Please contact, especially to exchange reference material. Mr. Abrahams is listed in the Directory under Oregon.

Key:
obj — objective lens	ODD — Officer of the Deck

Angelo Oeregni, vellum bbl, 3-draw, ca 1700, 32", EX	800.00
Bardou & Son, Paris, 4-draw, 50 mm obj, leather cover, 36"	220.00
Bate, London, leather covered, 1-draw, early 1800s, 31", EX	500.00
Bausch & Lomb, 1-draw, 45 mm obj, wrinkle pnt, 17"	90.00
Brashear, 3½" obj, brass, tripod, w/eyepcs	3,800.00
Cary, London (script), 2" obj, tripod, w/3 eyepcs	2,200.00
Clark, Alvan, 4" obj, iron mt on wood legs, 48"	4,000.00
Dallmeyer, London (script), 2½" obj, SP, 5-draw, 49"	450.00
Dollond, London (block), 2-draw, 2" obj, leather cover	220.00
Dollond, London (script), 2-draw, 2" obj, leather cover	300.00
Dollond, London (script), 3" obj, brass, 40", on tripod	2,500.00
France of Made in France, 30 mm obj, 3-draw, lens cap	80.00
Gilbert & Wright, London, wooden bbl, 1-draw, 18th C, EX	700.00
Lincoln, London, 10-sided wooden bbl, 1-draw, 41", EX	1,000.00
McAlister (script), 3½" obj, brass, 45", tripod	3,000.00
Mogey, 3" obj, brass, 40", on tripod, w/4 eyepcs	2,000.00
Queen & Co (script), 70 mm obj, 6-draw, wood veneer, 50"	650.00
Questar, 3½" dia reflecting, on astro mt, 1950s	1,200.00
Ramsden, London, wooden bbl, 1-draw, EX optics, 18th C, 46"	1,200.00

Short, James; 3" dia reflecting, brass cabriole tripod **2,500.00**
Tel Sct Regt Mk 2 S, many makers' names, UK, WWI **120.00**
Unitron, 4" obj, wht, 60", on tripod, many accessories **1,800.00**
US Navy, Bu Ships, Mk II, 10-Power, 1943, ODD **80.00**
US Navy, Made in France, brass, rope work on body, 3-draw, 29" .**200.00**
USN Quarter Master Mk II, 16-Power, 31", EX in box **275.00**
Vion, Paris, 40-Power, 3-draw, 40 mm obj, leather cover, 22" **95.00**
W&T Tulley Isington, London, brass, tripod, w/2 extra eyepcs .**2,000.00**
Wollensak Mirroscope, 1950s, 2" dia, 12" L, leather case **300.00**
Wood bbl, rnd taper, 1½" obj, sgn, 1800s **300.00**
Wood bbl, 8-sided, 1½" obj, 1700s, 30" **1,500.00**
Zeiss Asiola, 60 mm obj prism spotting scope, pre-WWII **450.00**

Televisions

Many early TVs have escalated in value in the last few years. Pre-1943 sets (usually with only one to five channels) are often worth $500.00 to $5,000.00. Unusually styled small-screen wooden 1940s TVs are 'hot'; but most metal, Bakelite, and large-screen sets are still shunned by collectors. 1950s color TVs with 16" or smaller tubes are valuable; larger color sets are not. Our advisor for this category is Harry Poster, author of *Poster's Radio & Television Price Guide 1920-1990, 2nd Edition;* he is listed in the Directory under New Jersey.

Admiral, 20X11, sq lines, Bakelite 10" tabletop **95.00**
Air King, A-1000, 10" wooden tabletop, 1948 ....**100.00**
Arvin, 15-550, lg color console, 15" rnd picture tube, 1954 ....**450.00**
Bendix, 235M1, push-button tuner, 10" mahog tabletop, 1949 ....**75.00**
CBS-Columbia, 20M, metal tabletop, 20" screen, 1950 ....**15.00**
Crosley, AC10, wooden console, 4-legged, 21" screen, 1965 ....**10.00**
DeWald, ET-140, sq tabletop, 14" rectangular picture tube, 1950 .**20.00**
Emerson, 614, Bakelite tabletop, 10" porthole-look screen, 1950 .**95.00**
Hallicrafters, 514, lid hides screen, hdl, 7" portable, 1948 ....**200.00**
Meck, XC-703, 7" leatherette-covered portable, lid & hdl **175.00**
Motorola, VT-105, 1st 10" tabletop model, 1948 ....**175.00**
National, TV-10W, 10 wooden tabletop, 1949 ....**150.00**
Olympic, TV-104, 10" wooden tabletop, 1948 ....**75.00**
RCA, CT-100, color, 1st production TV, 15" rnd screen, 1954 .**500.00**
RCA, 9PC41, buffet-style projection, channel 1 tuner, 1949 ....**45.00**
Scott, 800BT, projection, pop-up screen, scarce, 1949 ....**350.00**
Sentinel, 816C, color console, 21" screen, 1956 ....**75.00**
Sony, TV-120, transistorized, sq lines, 12" portable, 1961 ....**20.00**
Sparton, 16A211, wooden, color console, 15" rnd screen, 1955 .**350.00**
Sylvania, 172K, 21" corner console w/Halolight, bookcase, 1952 ..**125.00**
Tele-Tone, TV-307, 16" wooden console, sq lines, 1950 ....**35.00**
Transvision, 10BL, built-in magnifier, 10" set, 1948 ....**200.00**
Westinghouse, H-655, 17" console, lg tuner, 1951 ....**35.00**
Zenith, C-4007, 24" console, Space Command remote, 1959 ....**25.00**
Zenith, 37T99, 16" w/porthole-look screen, 1948 ....**75.00**

Teplitz

Teplitz, in Bohemia, was an active art pottery center at the turn of the century. The Amphora Pottery Works was only one of the firms that operated there. (See Amphora.) Art Nouveau and Art Deco styles were favored, and much of the ware was hand decorated with the primary emphasis on vases and figurines. Items listed here are marked 'Teplitz' or 'Turn,' a nearby city. Our advisor for this category is Jack Gunsaulus; he is listed in the Directory under Michigan.

Basket, facing couple w/clasped hands figural, Wahliss, 6½" **125.00**
Creamer, HP drummer boy w/house/fence/trees, Stellmacher, 3¾" ..**70.00**

Pitcher, appl cherries, branch hdl, Wahliss, 1899, 11" **175.00**
Pitcher, emb ornate body w/florals & gold, snake hdl, 9¼" **165.00**
Pitcher, Greenaway-style children & chick, Stellmacher **115.00**
Vase, Crown Oak Ware, stick neck w/integral hdls, 9" **150.00**
Vase, florals/gold/butterflies on cobalt to bl, Wahliss, 14" **650.00**
Vase, leaf-shape panels, spider-web ground, #1636, 5½" **1,300.00**
Vase, rtcl flowers, stems form panels below, Stellmacher, 8" **350.00**
Watering pot, leopard on gr mottle, Stellmacher, 6x9" **230.00**

Terra Cotta

Terra cotta is a type of earthenware or clay used for statuary, architectural facings, or domestic articles. It is unglazed, baked to durable hardness, and characterized by the color of the body which may range from brick red to buff.

Bust of Louis XIV, long curling hair, draped cape around shoulders, raised on socle base, 19th century, 26", $1,870.00.

Bust, Eros, stamped R Ruggeri on faux marble base, 15" **125.00**
Garden urn, emb thistles, Portland Stoneware #362, 24x27" **400.00**
Sculpture, draped nude on craggy ped, Fr, 1880, 34" **1,300.00**

Thermometers

Few objects man has invented have been so eloquently expressed both functionally and artistically as the ubiquitous thermometer. Developed initially by Galileo as a scientific device, thermometers slowly evolved into decorative objet d'art, functional household utensils, and eye-catching advertising specialties. Most American thermometers manufactured early in the 20th century were produced by Taylor (Tycos), and today their thermometers remain the most plentiful on the market. Decorative thermometers manufactured before 1800 are now ensconced in the permanent collections of approximately a dozen European museums. Because of their fragility, few devices of this era have survived in private collections. Nowadays most antique thermometers find their way to market through estate sales.

Insofar as sheer beauty, uniqueness, and scientific accuracy, decorative thermometers are far superior to the ordinary and inexpensive versions which carry advertising. Decorative thermometers run the gamut from plain tin household varieties to the highly ornate creations of Tiffany and Bradley and Hubbard. They have been manufactured from nearly every conceivable material — oak, sterling, brass, and glass being the favorites — and have tested the artistry and technical skills of some of America's finest craftsmen. Ornamental models can be found in free-hanging, wall-mounted, or desk/mantel versions. The largest collection of decorative thermometers — some six hundred specimens — is housed at the Thermometer Collectors Club of America headquarters in Sacramento, California.

Thermometer prices are based on age, ornateness, and whether mercury or alcohol is used as the filler in the tube. A broken or missing tube will cut at least 40% off the value. (Only one company in the world makes replacement tubes.) Virtually all American-made thermometers available today as collectors' items were made between 1875 and 1940. The golden age of decoratives ended in the early 1940s as modern manufacturing processes and materials robbed them of their natural distinctiveness.

Key:
br — brass
F&C — Fahrenheit & Celsius
F&R — Fahrenheit & Reamer
hyg — hygrometer
mrc — mercury

pmc — permacolor
R&C — Reamer & Celcius
sc — scales
stl — stainless

Alexandre, desk, scimitar figural, br sc/mrc, 9" 430.00
Amadio, F, Corn Hill, desk, ivory pillar/compass, mrc, 1890, 10" ..850.00
Anonymous, cvd wood squirrel, glass R sc, mrc, 1905, 10" 850.00
Anonymous, desk, alabaster w/eagle, br R&C sc, mrc, 1895 ....875.00
Anonymous, desk, br conquistador figural, brass sc, mrc 490.00
Anonymous, desk, love scene, silver metal, br R&C sc, mrc, 8" .830.00
Anonymous, pendant, sterling case, ivory F sc, mrc, 1880, 5" .1,250.00
Anonymous, wall, giltwood fr, ivory, F sc, mrc, 1790, 10x3½" ..3,100.00
Bearskin Ltd, wall, metal clip, rnd mrc, 1930, 3x4" 750.00
Capendium, desk, handmade br/porc fr, F&C sc, rnd mrc, 4" 850.00
Casella London, wall, maxi/minimum, 2 units, wood, plastic sc .260.00
Cheshire Silversmiths, desk, br candelabra, mrc, 1875, 10" 4,500.00
Clark, desk, ivory ped, crown, mrc, 1904, 7" 295.00
Creswel, travel, ivory case/mirror, removable sc, mrc, 2½" 2,800.00
CW Wilder...NH, desk, Deco women, br F sc, mrc, 8" 900.00
Desk, picture fr w/glass, mrc, 1902, 7" 180.00
Diamond, wall, br F sc on wood, rare, 7½x1½" 400.00
Dollard London, desk, sterling, br sc, mrc, 1908, 6" 750.00
Freeborn, desk, bronze w/lead decor/br sc, mrc, 8" 130.00
G Cooper, desk, bell shape w/cupola, sterling, dial, 2x3" 400.00
Gloucenter Scientific, stl case, glass front, pmc, 42" 1,200.00
Heath & Wing, figural calendar, br w/porc sc, mrc, 1870 ....930.00
Hohmann Maurer Co, steel F&C sc & bk, mrc, 12" 80.00
J Waldstein, wall, br R sc on wood, mrc, 1900s, 10½" 920.00
Nova Products, desk, rnd, glass encased, dial sc, Pat 1923 ....75.00
Pairpoint, desk, sterling picture fr, mrc, 1907, 5" 450.00
Phila Therm Co, hygrometer, br sc, rotating bezel, 1928 ....30.00
Reau, desk, sq incline base, floral top, mrc, 1895 ....180.00
Slouche, desk, alabaster ped, paper sc inset, mrc, 8x2½" 95.00
Standard, wall, ivory F sc on ebony, mrc, 9" 625.00
Taylor, hanging, pnt wood, red spirit, 6x24" 50.00
Thermindex Switzerland, desk, Bakelite stand, F sc, 5" 530.00
Tycos, maxi/minimum, japanned tin/br, mrc, T-5452, 8" 125.00
VJD Inc, wall, clip, F br sc, mrc tube, 4" 1300.00
W Pratt, desk, wood inlays, ivory sc, mrc, 1900, 6" 75.00
Warren Foundries, wall, umbrella w/dragon hdl, br sc, mrc, 12" .220.00
WG Loveday, wall, Clearside, F metallic sc, 5" dia 400.00
Whitehead & Hoag, Lambrecht's Polymeter, wall, mrc, 9" 1200.00
Zeradatha, desk, cast metal, dial w/rotate sc, 1926, 7" 75.00

1000 Faces China

So named because of its many hand-painted faces, much of this chinaware was made during the '30s through the '50s (some even earlier). Though many pieces are unmarked, others are marked 'Made in Japan.' There are two primary patterns, 'Black Face' and the 'Gold' pattern, and variations exist. Both designs employ many colors. Dinner plates usually are decorated with an outer-most 'ring of color' (two or three hues) containing a simple design which is often flowers. The inner ring is usually comprised of many colors radiating from the center circle which may be done in a primary color (red, for instance) with a

design such as a dragon or clouds painted in gold. 'Black Face' is distinguishable by its range of colors — primarily red, white, and yellow with some green and blue — and the black hand-painted faces. The 'Gold' pattern is also multicolored but is dominated by the gold throught the design, and the faces themselves are gold as well. Other variations include '1000 Men in Robes' and '1000 Faces' with black or blue rims on the saucers and cups. These pieces seem to be very scarce. In the listings that follow, all items are marked 'Made in Japan' (MIJ) unless noted otherwise. Our advisor for this category is Suzi Hibbard; she is listed in the Directory under California.

Cup & saucer, Blk Face 40.00
Cup & saucer, demitasse; Gold 25.00
Cup & saucer, Gold 35.00
Plate, Blk Face, 10" 45.00
Plate, 6" 10.00
Shakers, pr 18.00
Snack set, 8½" L 45.00
Soup set, Blk Face, 3-pc 75.00
Sweetmeat set, Gold, 15-pc, serves 6 ....150.00
Sweetmeat set, w/lacquer box, 6", 5-pc 75.00
Tea set, Blk Face, 15-pc, serves 6 ....150.00
Tea set, Gold, 15-pc, serves 6 ....125.00
Teapot, Gold, dragon spout, 7" 50.00

Tiffany

Louis Comfort Tiffany was born in 1848 to Charles Lewis and Harriet Young Tiffany of New York. By the time he was eighteen, his father's small dry goods and stationery store had grown and developed into the world-renowned Tiffany and Company. Preferring the study of art to joining his father in the family business, Louis spent the next six years under the tutelage of noted artists. He returned to America in 1870 and until 1875 painted canvases that focused on European and North African scenes. Deciding the more lucrative approach was in the application of industrial arts and crafts, he opened a decorating studio called Louis C. Tiffany and Co., Associated Artists. He began seriously experimenting with glass, and eschewing traditionally painted-on details, he instead learned to produce glass with qualities that could suggest natural textures and effects. His experiments broadened, and he soon concentrated his efforts on vases, bowls, etc., that came to be considered the highest achievements of the art. Peacock feathers, leaves and vines, flowers and abstracts were developed within the plane of the glass as it was blown. Opalescent and metallic lustres were combined with transparent color to produce stunning effects. Tiffany called his glass Favrile, meaning handmade.

In 1900 he established Tiffany Studios and turned his attention full time to producing art glass, leaded-glass lamp shades and windows, and household wares with metal components. He also designed a complete line of jewelry which was sold through his father's store. He became proficiently accomplished in silverwork and produced such articles as hand mirrors embellished with peacock feather designs set with gems and candlesticks with Favrile glass inserts.

Tiffany's work exemplified the Art Nouveau style of design and decoration, and through his own flamboyant personality and business acumen he perpetrated his tastes onto the American market to the extent that his name became a household word. Tiffany Studios continued to prosper until the second decade of this century when due to changing tastes his influence began to diminish. By the early 1930s the company had closed.

Serial numbers were assigned to much of Tiffany's work, and letter prefixes indicated the year of manufacture: A-N for 1896-1900, P-Z for 1901-1905. After that, the letter followed the numbers with A-N in use from 1906-1912; P-Z from 1913-1920. O-marked pieces were made especially for friends and relatives; X indicated pieces not made for sale.

Our listings are primarily from the auction houses in the East where Tiffany sells at a premium. All pieces are signed unless noted otherwise.

Glass

Bowl, Aqua Pastel, opal cased to bl-gr w/wht striping, 2⅜x5" 430.00
Bowl, bl irid, ribbed herringbone, #1925, 3x8" 1,265.00
Bowl, bl irid, sharply pinched rim sections, 1x2½" 150.00
Bowl, bl/pk/gold irid w/clear spokes, stretched, 3½x7½" 750.00
Bowl, eng ivy, lady bugs intaglio on ribbed gold, 5x12" 1,725.00
Bowl, flower; lily pads, gr in gold irid, 13½", +frog 2,000.00
Bowl, gold w/mc irid, ribbed, scalloped, 3x7½", NM 400.00
Bowl, leaf pads/vines, gr/gold, folded rim, 12", EX 900.00
Bowl, Pk Pastel, wide pk stretched rim over opal wht, 2½x9" 865.00
Bowl, Yel Pastel, yel triangles on clear, scalloped, 1½x7½" 800.00
Bowl vase, bl irid, raised veins, 4½x5" 925.00
Bowl vase, gold, 10-rib, undulating rim, 3½x5½" 750.00
Compote, bl irid, stretched/ruffled wide flaring rim, 4½x6" ...1,300.00
Compote, floriform; gold, wide stretched petal rim, 4½x9" 690.00
Compote, gold w/mc irid, #7587, 4x8" 425.00
Compote, gold w/mc irid, flared/shallow, slim ped ft, 5x5½" 475.00
Compote, intaglio ivy vine on gold, cupped/folded ft, 3½x8¾" ..1,495.00
Compote, lt gr w/aqua, ped ft w/ball under fluted bowl, 7" 600.00
Compote, Pk Pastel, 10 opal stripes on rose, clear std, 2¼x5" 690.00
Dish, bl irid w/EX color, ribbed/fluted, X305, 1½x4" 200.00
Dish, gold w/mc irid, deeply pinched rim, 1x3" 150.00
Jar, Pk Pastel, Dmn Quilt, gilt-bronze lid #137, 4" 865.00
Pitcher, intaglio purple grape band on bl irid, 8½" 3,220.00
Plate, gold, 8-rib, deep scallops, 6" 200.00
Plate, pulled design w/cvd pontil, purple on amber irid, 8½" ..1,495.00
Punch cup, gold irid w/gr lily pads & vines, appl hdl 675.00
Sherbet, gold w/mc irid, prunts on bowl & ft, 3½" 270.00
Tumbler, vertical stripes, pk/wht, swollen center, 5½" 235.00

Vase, blue iridescent with everted rim and tripod feet, swirled pewter motif around neck, #02950, 5", $2,860.00.

Vase, bl irid, appl scroll hdls at shoulder, ftd, 4x5½" 900.00
Vase, bl irid, pulled hdls, ped ft, sgn/#d, mini, 3" 850.00
Vase, bl irid, 10-rib, ovoid, 4¾" 800.00
Vase, bl irid trumpet form on SP copper glass-inlay ft, 17½" ...4,800.00
Vase, bud; leaves, gr on gold, flared lip, rnd ft, 10" 1,000.00
Vase, Cypriote, textured gold/mc irid, flared cylinder, 11" 2,300.00
Vase, diagonals of gold irid spots on rippled gold, 6x6" 1,840.00
Vase, feathers, tan/wht w/violet highlights on yel, 10½" 1,600.00
Vase, feathers at base, gr/gold w/wht top, ovoid, 2½" 650.00
Vase, floral, bl irid on blk, bl irid int, cylindrical, 15" 5,750.00
Vase, floral/swirled irid shapes on electric bl, 9½x7" 6,300.00
Vase, floriform; amber irid, bulb w/wide mouth, stem ft, 4½" 575.00
Vase, floriform; bl irid, ribbed swollen lily, 13" 2,500.00
Vase, floriform; feathered cone cup, gold/gr/wht, 12½" 5,750.00
Vase, floriform; feathered cup/stem, long folds in rim, 13" 13,800.00
Vase, floriform; feathers, gr on wht, gold int, flared rim, 5" 800.00
Vase, floriform; Gr Pastel w/wht striations, clear ft, 11" 1,375.00

Vase, floriform; leaves, brn/wht on amber, bulbous top, 12" 6,900.00
Vase, floriform; str-rim cup w/leafy base, gold/gr/wht, 15" 7,500.00
Vase, gold, 10-rib, appl disk ft, trumpet form, 9¾" 800.00
Vase, gold irid trumpet in enameled brass base, #151, 13" 1,000.00
Vase, gold w/bl, violet & orange irid, ribbed, shouldered, 2" 300.00
Vase, gold w/mc irid, appl stemmed teardrops, 4" 425.00
Vase, gold w/mc irid, bottle form w/stick neck, #394L, 6" 650.00
Vase, gold w/mc irid, dbl-gourd form, #9935B, 7" 950.00
Vase, gold w/mc irid, ribbed, waisted, K539, 3" 400.00
Vase, gold w/mc irid, slim inverted trumpet form, 5" 400.00
Vase, gold w/mc irid, 3-ftd pot shape, 1½" 400.00
Vase, gold w/orange & bl irid, ribbed, long neck, 3½" 550.00
Vase, gold w/orange & violet irid, can neck, shouldered, 6½" 800.00
Vase, gold w/orange & violet irid, swollen cylinder, 3½" 325.00
Vase, gold w/violet & lt bl irid, gourd form w/sm hdls, 3" 400.00
Vase, gr irid w/mc highlights, sqd shoulders, #5008N, 8" 2,300.00
Vase, heart vines, gr on cobalt, bulbous, 2¾" 1,495.00
Vase, hooked bands, silver/bl on blk, shouldered, #2003E, 4½" ..2,700.00
Vase, hooked mid-band, gold/bl irid, U-form, 2½" 325.00
Vase, hooked shoulder band, purple/gr irid on emerald, 5x5" ..2,875.00
Vase, hooked/pulled 'leaves,' royal bl/wht/lt orange, 6½" 1,700.00
Vase, intaglio floral on gold, leafy neck band, #7540G, 9" 2,700.00
Vase, irid swirls, lt gr/royal bl on silvery gray, 8x7" 2,990.00
Vase, leaf/vine at shoulder on blk, 7x6" 2,760.00
Vase, leaves on gold trumpet form; bronze base, 18" 975.00
Vase, leaves/stems under rim on gold/mc irid swirls, 14x10" ...5,500.00
Vase, marbleized rust red, appl irreg outlines, ovoid, 8½" 5,750.00
Vase, millefiori, wht w/yel centers & gr leaves on gold, 2½" ...1,380.00
Vase, paperweight, cased amber irid w/whorls, 6½x5" 11,500.00
Vase, paperweight, gold irid w/int leaves/wht flowers, 5x5" 5,175.00
Vase, pk opal/gold irid, clear ft, fluted trumpet form, 13" 900.00
Vase, red irid, flared can neck, angle shoulder, 6" 3,450.00
Vase, swirls at shoulder, lav/pk/bl on yel irid, 3" 1,100.00
Vase, Tel el Amarna, red w/silver-bl lip/ft, zigzag band, 4" 5,400.00
Vase, tomato red cased to yel w/EX irid, 2⅝" 1,495.00
Vase, trailed swirls/feathers, rainbow irid on gold, 6x8" 4,350.00
Vase, vines/flowers, wht/gr on amber irid, cut/appl, 16" 9,200.00
Vase, vines/7 flowers w/appl centers, gr/wht on gold, 11¾" 3,450.00
Vase, wht irid w/gold-lit gr irid collar, disk ft, 3x4" 550.00
Vase, wht opal w/pastel highlights, tiny shoulder hdls, 3" 500.00

Lamps

Lamp prices seem to be getting stronger, especially for leaded lamps with lighter colors (red, blue, and purples). Bases that are unusual or rare have brought good prices and added to the value of the more common shades that sold on them. Bases with enamel or glass inserts are very much in demand. Our advisor for Tiffany lamps is Carl Heck; he is listed in the Directory under Colorado.

Key: c-b — counter-balance

Base, bronze, paneled std on lappet-emb bun w/5 ball ft, 10" 750.00
Base, cast as roots, 4 dbl-prong legs, #189, 29" 9,500.00
Base, cushion ft w/emb scrolls & leaves, #366, 22" 4,000.00
Base, Greek urn w/4 straps becoming legs, #181, electrified 2,400.00
Base, sqd baluster cast w/4 Virtues, #557, 21" 1,500.00
Base, 2 uprights support arch w/socket, #488, 19½" 5,175.00
Base, 5-ftd cushion base w/emb scrolls/pods, #26872, 19" 5,500.00
Candle, floral-pnt mesh screen shade; paw-ftd dish base, 13" ..1,725.00
Candle, gold glass cup, swirled base, slim std, 20", pr 3,400.00
Candle, ribbed dbl-bulb opal shade; 3-arm cup/pencil std, 24" .1,600.00
Chandelier, ldgl 18" lemon leaf shade w/turtle-bk finial, EX ...9,500.00
Desk, bead-fr turtle-bk tile shade; jeweled bun base, 14½" 5,000.00

Floor, damascene 10" bl irid (rare) shade; harp std #682 ....**6,850.00**
Floor, damascene 10" dome shade in harp fr; #428 3-leg std **4,500.00**
Floor, linenfold 9½" shade (several cracks); std #622, EX **2,800.00**
Harp, feathered 7" gr/gold/opal shade; #418 std, 12" **2,650.00**
Harp, gold cased 7" dome shade; 16-rib std #419, 13½" **2,750.00**
Lantern, pod form 14" gold shade w/int yel & gr flowers **13,800.00**
Lily, 10-light, gold shades sgn; layered lily pad std w/gilt **14,500.00**
Lily, 12-light, gold shades sgn; #1063 layered lily pad std **18,400.00**
Lily, 12-light (9 authentic); lily pad std #25889, 20" **14,900.00**
Lily, 3-light, gold shades; 3-stem std #319, 13" **3,500.00**
Lily, 3-light (1 sgn); gadrooned dished rnd base, 12" **2,000.00**
Lily, 6-light, organic stem/tendril hook w/central urn, #4159 .**9,200.00**
Lily, 7-light, 7 upright sgn shades; #29721 ribbed std **8,000.00**
Linenfold, 19" 12-panel emerald gr shade; #533 std **11,500.00**
Mushroom, wht 8" dome shade; hooked/pulled #87071 base, 14" ..**10,000.00**
Nautilus, shell shade; bronze base #29630, 14x17½" **3,500.00**
Nautilus, shell w/gilt edge; jeweled gilded #23596 base, 13½" ...**5,500.00**
Nautilus, shell w/silver rim; cushion-ftd std #797 ....**3,500.00**
Sconce, feathered tulip shade; rnd bronze wall mt, 8x4x7", pr ..**4,000.00**
Sconce, 2 tulip shades w/feathering; 2-arm wall mt, 13", pr **9,200.00**
Shade, ball form w/allover leaves, gold on amber, 12½" **4,100.00**
Shade, gold, 10-rib bell form, sgn, 5", set of 4 ....**2,000.00**
Shade, ldgl 14" acorn-band dome **4,600.00**
Table, ldgl 14" acorn-band shade; 3-arm std #444, 21" **5,000.00**
Table, ldgl 14" daffodil shade; mushroom std #337, 18" **14,950.00**
Table, ldgl 15" allover roses cone shade; tree std #554 ....**59,700.00**
Table, ldgl 16" acorn-band shade; alligatored std #585, 21" **5,175.00**
Table, ldgl 18" acorn-band shade; simple #532 std **6,900.00**
Table, ldgl 18" clematis shade; std #2-6878 w/tendrils **29,000.00**
Table, ldgl 18" dogwood shade; tendrils on ftd std #800 ....**23,000.00**
Table, ldgl 18" swirling oak leaf shade; #553 std **8,625.00**
Table, ldgl 20" daffodil shade; paneled stick std #532, 32" **27,600.00**
Table, ldgl 20" Russian cone shade; gilded std #531, 27" **19,550.00**
Table, ldgl 20" 7-dragonfly shade; gilded twisted #443 std **26,450.00**
Table, ldgl 22" peony shade; ribbed/foliate #638 std **51,700.00**
Table, ldgl 22" tulip shade; std #573 w/gr patina, 28" **41,400.00**
Table, ldgl 24" lotus-ribbed shade; paneled std #7283, 26" **23,000.00**
Table, mesh screen 16" maple-leaf emb shade (worn); #338 std **19,000.00**

Metal Work

Items are bronze unless noted otherwise.

Blotter, Modeled, #1115, 3x5½", EX **110.00**
Blotter ends, Pine Needle, w/orig blotter, #998, 12x19", EX **130.00**
Bowl, cast leaves/scroll hdls, oval, rolled rim, 19" **745.00**
Bowl, copper w/stylized clover, gr w/gold outlines, 1½x10" **100.00**
Bowl, gilt metal, #406, 4x8", +undertray #1721, 12" dia **175.00**
Bowl, pie-crust edge, gold dore, #1713, 1½x4½", EX **50.00**
Box, jewel; Pine Needle, gold patina, #816, 3x4x6½" **1,035.00**
Box, jewel; sarcophagus on 4 ball ft, gilded, #1666, 8" L **2,990.00**
Box, Pine Needle, 2½x7x7", VG **1,300.00**
Box, stamp; Zodiac, compartmented, hinged lid, #414, 3¾" **260.00**
Candelabrum, 4-branch, blown-in glass in base & cups, 15" ...**3,500.00**
Candlestick, jeweled cup on 3-leg std, rnd base, 10" **2,185.00**
Candlesticks, blown-in gr glass liners, #H26522, 10", pr **2,200.00**
Candlesticks, cup in 3-prong cage, 4-strap paw-ft std, 12", pr ..**2,000.00**
Candlesticks, 2 cups in 3-finger basket, trefoil base, 9", pr **2,500.00**
Candlesticks, 3-part base, ea w/4 'toes,' 13", VG, pr **1,495.00**
Clock, geometrics/border recesses, gr/gold patina, #360, 6½" ..**1,725.00**
Compote, rtcl floral/red jewels, artichoke stem, #1668, 5x9" **800.00**
Compote, twisted wire/mc enamel on wide flat rim, #519, 3x8" .**325.00**
Desk set, Am Indian, rocker blotter/inkwell/pen tray+4 pcs **1,495.00**
Desk set, Modeled, letter rack/blotter/clock/tray/calendar **1,500.00**

Desk set, Venetian, gold patina, inkstand/pen tray/letter clip **635.00**
Desk set, Zodiac, blotter ends/rocker+pen tray/box/paper clip ..**1,600.00**
Desk set, Zodiac, letter rack/pen tray/inkwell/box+5 pcs **2,100.00**
Flask, 18k gold, hinged screw-on cap, #17814, 4¼x2½" **1,100.00**
Frame, abalone, some gr/red polychrome, #1145, 12x9" **1,800.00**
Frame, Adam, gilded, #1610, 12x8" **2,500.00**
Frame, Adam, gilded, #1786, 9½" **1,725.00**
Frame, dbl; Grapevine, 2 oval reserves, gilded, #953, 7" **2,185.00**
Frame, emb neoclassical foliage, gilded, #1611, 12x8" **2,185.00**
Frame, Grapevine, #948, 8" **1,950.00**
Frame, Grapevine, 12" **3,200.00**
Frame, Pine Needle, #916, 14" **4,800.00**
Frame, Zodiac, #942, 8" **1,950.00**
Frame, Zodiac, gilded, #926, 14x12", M **2,300.00**

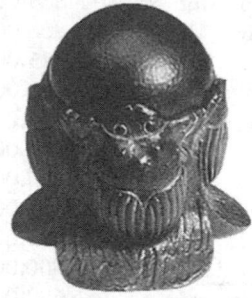

Inkstand, 3 upright cast bronze scarabs at base of hinged cover, opens to blue favrille flower form inkwell, signed LCT Favrille, #29234, 4¼x4¼", $8,000.00.

Letter opener, 4 enamel rectangles, #359, 11" **350.00**
Letter rack, Pine Needle, 2-section, #1008, 6x2½x10" **550.00**
Matchbox holder, Modeled, #112, 3½x4½", EX **110.00**
Mirror, lily pad base, twisting vine fr, #25890, rnd, 18" **14,950.00**
Note pad, Modeled, #1120, 7½x4½", EX **110.00**
Paperweight, owl, w/gilt, 3" **1,000.00**
Tray, Byzantine, 2 red/4 turq beads, #879, 4¼x2¾", EX **175.00**

Pottery

Vase, blk/brn/gold/bl wash on cream, can neck w/hdls, 9" **1,900.00**
Vase, blk/brn/gr matt, can neck, 14½x9" **1,100.00**
Vase, bronze-clad w/emb daffodils, gr int, 13x7" **2,875.00**
Vase, bsk, gr int, tapering, sqd, 9" **700.00**
Vase, bud; bronze-clad w/emb tulips, 2½" **1,600.00**
Vase, floral vines emb on bsk, can neck, squat body, 3x4" **1,150.00**
Vase, gr shades w/crystalline, dk gr/brn/bl int, 15x10", NM **900.00**
Vase, lt/dk gr, cylinder neck, hand-thrown, 6x3¾", VG **350.00**
Vase, poinsettia band emb on gr/blk matt, 10x12", EX **1,300.00**
Vase, water lilies emb on wht bsk, ftd sphere, rpr, 5" **180.00**
Vase, wide base w/frogs supports water lily top, rpr, 7x9" **650.00**
Vase/lamp base, lime/gr irid mottle, shouldered, 16x10" **600.00**

Silver

Bonbonniere, hdl is Eros w/flaming torch, rtcl stem, 13" **3,100.00**
Bowl, centerpc; acanthus, chased lip, ftd/hdls, 7x25x14" **3,200.00**
Bowl, centerpc; allover emb/chased fruit & flowers, 5x14" L .**3,700.00**
Bowl, trophy; bombe form w/scroll bands, ram's heads, 6x9" **3,165.00**
Candlesticks, Corinthian column, stepped sq base, 12", pr **1,840.00**
Carving set, hammered hdls, 3-pc **400.00**
Coffeepot, AD; etched arabesque/column panels, #7054, 10" .**1,725.00**
Compote, grape/leaf-molded border & base, 7½" dia **525.00**
Condiment set, 3 owls, graduated szs (lg: 4½"), w/gilt **1,495.00**
Ewer, allover emb floral, 2 cartouches, floral finial, 8" **625.00**
Mug, band of children on parade, eng child's name, 3¼" **300.00**
Pitcher, water; emb/chased ivy, beaded border, EC Moore, 9½" ..**3,165.00**

Porringer, emb floral, floral-eng hdl, 9-troy-oz 725.00
Teapot, eng bands, bud finial, Wm Gale, 8" 1,150.00
Tray, roll; thread-mold border, oval, 11½" 180.00
Trophy, Masonic, dtd 1919, 11" 260.00
Vase, pierced florals, serpentine edge, tapered/ftd, 9¾" 650.00
Vase, trumpet form w/petal rim, 13½" 500.00
Water pitcher, scroll/foliate bands, cylinder neck, 7" 1,600.00

Miscellaneous

Hatpin, gold irid glass ball on long shaft, 9¼" 400.00
Pendant, turtlebk w/lead surround & twisted gilt metal fr, 4" 300.00
Tea screen, 3 ldgl 9x4" apple blossom/spider-web panels 7,800.00
Vase, floriform; apricot opal blossom, gr leaf-decor ft, 12" 5,175.00

Tiffin Glass

The Tiffin Glass Company was founded in 1887 in Tiffin, Ohio, one of the many factories composing the U.S. Glass Company. Its early wares consisted of tablewares and decorative items such as lamps and globes. Among the most popular of all Tiffin products was the black satin glass produced there during the 1920s. In 1959 U.S. Glass was sold, and in 1962 the factories closed. The plant was re-opened in 1963 as the Tiffin Art Glass Company. Products from this period were tableware, hand-blown stemware, and other decorative items.

Those interested in learning more about Tiffin glass are encouraged to contact the Tiffin Glass Collectors' Club, whose address can be found in the Directory under Clubs, Newsletters, and Catalogs. See also Black Glass; Glass Animals.

Bottle, seltzer; La Fleure, ftd, #185 ....18.50
Bowl, cereal; Thistle, pk 20.00
Bowl, Twilight, heart shape, hdl, 7" 85.00
Bowl, Twilight, wishbone shape, ftd, 6½" 135.00
Candle holders, gr satin, scalloped base, 9¼", pr 70.00
Candlesticks, June Night, dbl, pr 125.00
Candy dish, Lois, gr, conical, w/lid, #345 ....95.00
Champagne, Cherokee Rose, #17403 ....18.00
Champagne, Classic 22.50
Champagne, Dogwood, pk 20.00
Champagne, Fontaine, Twilight, tall 35.00
Champagne, Fuchsia, #15803 ....18.00
Champagne, June Night, #17358, 5½-oz 22.50
Champagne, Persian Pheasant, 5½-oz 27.50
Champagne, Shawl Dancer 42.50
Cocktail, Arcadian, pk/crystal, #024, 3-oz 35.00
Cocktail, Cordelia 13.00
Cocktail, Dmn Optic, vaseline/amber 45.00
Cocktail, Fuchsia 20.00
Cocktail, Paulina, crystal/gr, ftd, #185½, 3-oz 35.00
Cocktail, Persian Pheasant, 5¼" 27.50
Cocktail, Spiral Optic, crystal/gr, 6" 20.00
Cordial, Arcadian, pk/crystal, #24, 1½-oz 75.00
Cordial, Cerice 27.50
Cordial, Cherokee Rose, 1-oz 55.00
Cordial, June Night, #17358 ....45.00
Cordial, Persian Pheasant 55.00
Creamer & sugar bowl, Fuchsia, #5902 ....65.00
Cup, Thistle, pk 20.00
Cup & saucer, Flanders, ftd 47.50
Cup & saucer, Fontaine, Twilight, blown 125.00
Finger bowl, La Fleure, yel, ftd, #8185 ....37.50
Flower arranger, Twilight, 13⅝" 125.00

Goblet, iced tea; June Night, ftd, #17358 ....27.50
Goblet, iced tea; Shawl Dancer, conical 20.00
Goblet, water; Cherokee Rose, #17403 ....25.00
Goblet, water; Classic, ftd, 14-oz 90.00
Goblet, water; Dogwood, pk 25.00
Goblet, water; Eternally Yours 15.00
Goblet, water; Fontaine, Twilight 45.00
Goblet, water; Fuchsia, #15803 ....22.50
Goblet, water; Psyche, crystal w/gr stem 45.00
Parfait, Cherokee Rose, #17399 ....48.00
Plate, Byzantine, 8½" 12.00
Plate, Cherokee Rose, 8" 18.50
Plate, Fontaine, Twilight 30.00
Plate, Fuchsia, #8833, 8⅛" 22.50
Plate, June Night, fancy edge, 8" 22.50
Plate, La Fleure, yel, 7¼" 15.00
Plate, Persian Pheasant, pk, 8" 24.00
Plate, Thistle, pk, luncheon sz 14.00
Relish, Cherokee Rose, 3-part, 6½" 48.00
Saucer, La Fleure, yel 5.00
Sherbet, Byzantine, tall 20.00
Sherbet, Cherokee Rose, #17403, tall 20.00
Sherbet, Coronada, tall 18.00
Sherbet, Fuchsia, #15083, 4⅛" 18.00
Sherbet, Persian Pheasant, 7" 20.00
Sherry, June Night, #17403, 2-oz 45.00
Sugar bowl, Flanders, yel, flat 75.00
Sugar bowl, Juno, yel 37.50
Tumbler, iced tea; Classic, #354, 12-oz 60.00
Tumbler, juice; Arcadian, pk/crystal, ftd, #185, 5-oz 45.00
Tumbler, juice; Persian Pheasant, 5-oz 18.00
Tumbler, juice; Wisteria, #17394 ....25.00
Tumbler, old fashioned; Psyche, crystal/gr, ftd, 4-oz 45.00
Vase, blk satin, gold decor, 7¾" 75.00
Vase, bud; Cherokee Rose, 8" 45.00
Vase, bud; Fuchsia, #14185, 10½" 42.50
Wine, Byzantine 35.00
Wine, Dogwood, pk 25.00

Tiles

Though originally strictly functional, tiles were being produced in various colors and used as architectural highlights as early as the Ancient Roman Empire. By the 18th century, Dutch tiles were decorated with polychrome landscapes and figures. During the 19th century, there were over a hundred companies in England involved in the manufacture of tile. By the Victorian era, the use of decorative tiles had reached its peak. Special souvenir editions, campaign and portrait tiles, and Art Nouveau motifs with lovely ladies and stylized examples from nature were popular. Today all of these are very collectible. See also specific manufacturers.

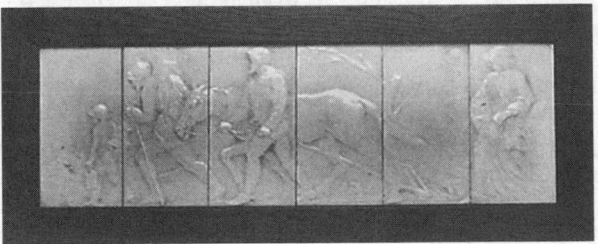

Low 6-tile frieze of men plowing a field, cream color, late 1800s, 12x36" and frame, $400.00.

Atlantic, galleon in high seas, mc, mk, 8" 375.00
Beaver Falls, Dutch Renaissance portrait, gr majolica, 6", pr 450.00
Beaver Falls, man's profile in relief under bl majolica, 4¼" 295.00
Beaver Falls, Renaissance child, sgn B, burgundy majolica, 6" 325.00
CA Art, knight on horsebk, salmon, 6" 95.00
CA Art, peacock on trellis w/mc grapes, unmk, 12x8" 625.00
Chilcote, Chas; stylized dolphin/bubbles, bl on dk gr, 5½" dia ...425.00
Claycraft, mission courtyard w/palms (excised), mc, mk, 8x16" .750.00
Enfield, bumble bee, blk gloss on gr matt, 3" 420.00
Enfield, Don Quixote, buff bsk, 4" 55.00
Enfield, Horseman of St Omer, charging left, 9" 225.00
Enfield, October, scorpion, brn matt, self-fr, 3¾x3" 90.00
Franklin, bear on mtn silhouette on raspberry-red, 2¾" 125.00
Franklin, blk silhouette profile w/lantern, 8¾" 225.00
Internat'l, Industry, woman at spinning wheel, brn/beige, 6" 175.00
Kensington, lady's portrait, brn/gr mottle, fr, 6" 170.00
Linnwood, Deco flowers, sheer wht matt, mk, 6" 225.00
Low, Dante (& Beatrice), gr gloss, orig wide fr, 6", pr 450.00
Low, Dutch Renaissance man on gr majolica, mk, 8" 395.00
Low, Nathan Hale, yel majolica, mk, 1885, 7¼x5¼" 240.00
Low, seasons, solid colors, 6x3", set of 4 ....575.00
Matawan, stylized quatrefoil, yel/wht on turq, mk, 7" dia 150.00
Minton, Elfin holding an egg, 6" 95.00
Minton, Much Ado About Nothing, mc, 6" 90.00
Mueller (att), 12-tile scenic w/trees, 18x24" 1,400.00
Mueller Mosaic, sea horses, blk on orange, unmk, 4" 225.00
Muresque, brn & wht mission, bl sky, self-fr, mk, 4x12" 400.00
Muresque, ship on high seas, mc, mk, #95, 6", NM 250.00
Pardee, Dutch lady selling milk from tile, Delft style, 6" 85.00
Plymouth, Richard Sparrow house, red clay/wht, mk, 1937, 5¾" ..225.00
Robertson, Calvin Coolidge, royal bl, 4½x2⅞", NM 125.00
San Jose, flamingos in water, mc on bl/gr, 8" 375.00
SS Tile Co, stylized flower, blk on red crystalline, 6" 200.00
Trenton, boy's head in profile, olive gloss, Broome, fr, 6" 150.00
Trenton, Dutch Renaissance man & lady portraits, 6"+fr, pr 475.00
Trenton, fireplace surround, acanthus leaves, brn/bl, 16-pc 850.00
Trenton, lady w/flowers in hair, man w/wavy hair, 6", pr 395.00
Trenton, shepherdess w/sheep, lt burgundy majolica, unmk, 18x6" .375.00
US Encaustic, Dutch boy w/umbrella, amber majolica, 6¼" 175.00
US Encaustic, lady w/sticks on bk, golden majolica, 6"+fr 275.00
Wise, Wm; Country Pursuits, seated girl w/fawns, blk/wht 75.00
Wise, Wm; highland cattle, blk/buff 100.00

Tinware

In the American household of the 17th and 18th centuries, tinware items could be found in abundance, from food containers to foot warmers and mirror frames. Although the first settlers brought much of their tinware with them from Europe, by 1798 sheets of tin plate were being imported from England for use by the growing number of American tinsmiths. Tinwares were often decorated either by piercing or painted designs which were both freehand and stenciled. (See Toleware.) By the early 1900s, many homes had replaced their old tinware with the more attractive aluminum and graniteware.

In the 19th century, tenth wedding anniversaries were traditionally celebrated by gifts of tin. Couples gave big parties, dressed in their wedding clothes, and reaffirmed their vows before their friends and family who arrived bearing (and often wearing) tin gifts, most of which were quite humorous. Anniversary tin items may include hats, cradles, slippers and shoes, rolling pins, etc. See also Primitives and Kitchen Collectibles.

Anniversary, hat, pnt decor, 4¾" 150.00
Anniversary, helmet, pierced visor, brass point, 7" 65.00

Baby bottle, strap hdl, tapered sides, tin tube w/in, 4x2½" 180.00
Box, sm strap hdl on front of hinged lid, 5x6" dia 55.00
Box, stamped line decor, hinged lid, 5⅛x6½x5" 20.00
Cake pans, sq w/crimped rim, graduated set of 3, 8", 7", 6" 80.00
Cheese sieve, dmn shape, pierced designs, ftd, lg 350.00
Cheese sieve, heart shape, punched design, 7¾" 275.00
Coffeepot, emb floral band, strap hdl, wood finial, 5½x3½" 70.00
Coffeepot, punchwork tulip decor, 11" 500.00
Coffeepot, rib-emb spout, copper bottom, wood finial, 9x5½" 70.00
Coffeepot, rnd w/tapered sides, hinged lid, 10½x6¼" 95.00
Coffeepot, stick spout, strap hdl, tapered, hinged lid, 8¾" 30.00
Colander, heart shape, 3 punched hex-like designs, 14" dia 480.00
Colander, star-punched bottom, dmn-punched sides, 3½x9½" 75.00
Colander, strap hdl, ftd, 4¾x11½" dia 30.00
Egg poacher, triple, w/spring 32.00
Flour sifter, Ernshaw, scoop shape w/hdl 125.00
Grater, arched fishscale-type cutters, rectangular, 13¼" L 50.00
Horn, field; flares from mouthpc, oval hdl, 56" L, EX 155.00
Lamp filler, long curved spout w/scroll decor, 5x8½" L 50.00
Lunch carrier, stacked oblong, top hdl, 4-pc 110.00
Lunch kettle, lid holds water, w/tray+2 rnd cans, mk, 6x6x9" 55.00
Measure, 1-Gill through 1-Qt emb on side, cone shape, 6¾" 30.00
Oil can, conical top, curved spout w/brass tip, 12" 35.00
Pail, wire loop on lid, wire hdl, 4½x6" 20.00
Pail, worn wht pnt w/blk smoked graining, w/lid, 7x9½" 100.00
Plate warmer, 4 high arched legs, stenciled decor, 26x13x11" 550.00
Rolling pin, all narrow grooves, wood hdls, rare 395.00
Sconce, crimped detail, EX patina, 12¾", pr 225.00
Sconce, oval reflector bk, crimped-edge drip stand, 12x7x4" 225.00
Sconce, punchwork decor, early, 14½", pr 350.00
Spice box, punched lid, 3 compartments+1 for grater, 6¾" 55.00
Squirrel cage, arched top, rotating wheel, mc pnt, 13x18x10" 300.00

Sugar shaker, 4", $35.00.

Taper stick, emb heart pan w/scalloped rim, 2¼x3" dia 60.00
Teakettle, curved spout, arched ribbon hdl, brass knob, 10½" 65.00
Tinder lighter, w/candle socket on lid, 4" 275.00

Tobacciana

Tobacciana is the generally accepted term used to cover a field of collecting that includes smoking pipes, cigar molds, cigarette lighters, humidors — in short, any article having to do with the practice of using tobacco in any form. Perhaps the most valuable variety of pipes is the meerschaum, hand carved from hydrous magnesium, an opaque white-gray or cream-colored mineral of the soapstone family. (Much of this is today mined in Turkey which has the largest meerschaum deposit in the world, though there are other deposits of lesser significance around the globe.) These figural bowls often portray an elaborately carved mythological character, an animal, or a historical scene. Amber is sometimes used for the stem. Other collectible pipes are corn cob (Missouri Meerschaum) and Indian peace pipes of clay or catlinite. (See American Indian Art.)

Chosen because it was the Indians who first introduced the white man to smoking, the cigar store Indian was a symbol used to identify tobacco stores in the 19th century. The majority of them were hand carved between 1830 and 1900 and are today recognized as some of the finest examples of early wood sculptures. When found they command very high prices.

For further information on lighters, refer to *Collector's Guide to Cigarette Lighters* by James Flanagan. Our advisor for this category is Chuck Thompson; he is listed in the Directory under Texas. Chris Rossiter assisted with pipe listings; you will find him listed in the Directory under Wisconsin. See also Advertising; Snuff Boxes.

Tobacconist's figure, reclining Turk, carved and painted wood, American, late 1800s, 20x46½", $2,000.00.

Baseball card, Jack Knight, Piedmont Cigarettes, 1911, EX 55.00
Cigar mold, CI, hinged, ftd, Pat 1871, ⅞x5⅝x1" 45.00
Cigarette case, brass, envelope shape w/NY 1939 NY 'postmk' 75.00
Cigarette case, SS Empress of Scotland, Lucite/brass 115.00
Cigarette case, sterling, James E Blake Co, ca 1910, sm 195.00
Cigarette holder, meerschaum, horses, amber stem, Austria, M .155.00
Cutter, cigar; Abercrombie Royal Standard, metal/wood, EX 350.00
Cutter, cigar; JG Hutchinson & Co, CI, 8½x15x4", G 150.00
Cutter, plug; Brighton, CI lady figural, 7x10x3", G 70.00
Cutter, plug; Brighton #3, elf figural, 13" L, VG 250.00
Cutter, plug; Evans Terry, CI, counter top, 1914, NM 150.00
Dispenser, man in turban by humidor, dispenses from mouth 285.00
Figure, Indian w/headdress, mc pnt, ca 1860, 53", EX+ 2,000.00
Figure, man w/cigar package, cvd wood, 63", VG 750.00
Humidor, winking Scotsman's head, pottery, 5½x3½" 125.00
Lighter, Budweiser bottle form, orig label, 2¾", EX 25.00
Lighter, cast zinc Blk dandy w/cigar bundle, mc, 1880s, 31" 3,000.00
Lighter, cigar; Wireless, Eldridge Man No 12, Chicago, NM 385.00
Lighter, Evans, 14k gold plated, 3-pc 150.00
Lighter, Lucky Strike Cigarettes, gr tin, EX 15.00
Lighter, Robeson, celluloid desk top, Sticklight 50.00
Lighter, Ronnie, metal, nude mermaid, table type 95.00
Lighter, Ronson, bartender mixing drink at bar, 6¾" 1,150.00
Lighter, Ronson, brass, dog figural 100.00
Lighter, Ronson, chrome, 12" lady on blk metal base 550.00
Lighter, Ronson, pencil type, MIB 50.00
Lighter, Ronson Rozenthal Plaza, 5-pc 250.00
Lighter, Sweetheart, pocket sz 25.00
Lighter, Windsor, nude boy w/box, table type 15.00
Lighter, Zippo, slim line, MIB 20.00
Lighter, Zippo type, Automobile Club of S CA, NM 18.00
Lighter combo case, Evans, gold-tone, filigree 48.00
Lighter/music box, Perry Como Kraft Music Hall, pocket, MIB 85.00
Matchbook holder, National Cigars, NP brass 28.00
Tamp, whalebone, cvd as Naughty Nellie leg, 3" 250.00

Pipes

Clay, General Pershing in peaked cap bowl, England, 7" 12.00
Clay, head of General Gordon, mk England, 6" 17.00
Clay, lady in fancy hat bowl, reed mouthpc, Fr, 1840s 50.00
Clay, Madame Curie-shaped bowl, English made, 5½" 12.00
Clay, plain bowl w/Castle Derry, Made in Cork Ireland, 6" 7.00
Clay, plain bowl w/tall ship in relief, Cork Ireland, 5½" 6.00
Meerschaum, boy & horse, amber stem, 7", EX 150.00
Meerschaum, boy beside stone wall, amber stem, 7", EX 150.00
Meerschaum, cvd rope work, silver stem, horn mouthpc 200.00
Meerschaum, man w/beard & hat, birch stem, horn mouthpc, 8¾" ..475.00
Meerschaum, nautical figure-head mermaid, 1850s 165.00
Meerschaum, nude lady, amber stem, 9½" 350.00
Meerschaum, Victorian lady's head, SP & amber stem, 4½" 150.00
Meerschaum, Yellow Kid, sgn/dtd, Outcult 1896, M 1,400.00
Porc, lady's arm holding stein bowl, stem horn, flex hose, 16" 175.00
Porc, occupational type, farmer plowing, name under scene 75.00
Porc, Regimental, Danish King, 12" 175.00
Porc, Regimental, Prussian soldiers HP on bowl, helmet lid 385.00
Porc, 16th-C lady's portrait, long birch stem, red mouthpc 175.00
Wood, boot bowl, stem protrudes from heel, birch stem, '20s 45.00
Wood, bull's head, ivory horns, amber eyes glow when lit, '50s 65.00
Wood, burled bowl & reservoir, birch stem, NP trim, Czech 45.00
Wood, cvd bearded 17th-C man, birch mouthpc, 1890s, 12" 275.00
Wood, cvd scene, fake 1812 date, silver lid, birch stem 45.00

Toleware

The term 'toleware' originally came from a French term meaning 'sheet iron.' Today it is used to refer to paint-decorated tin items, most popular from 1800 to 1850s. The craft flourished in Pennsylvania, Connecticut, Maine, and New York State. Early toleware has a very distinctive look. The surface is dull and unvarnished; background colors range from black to cream. Geometrics are quite common, but florals and fruits were also favored motifs. Items made after 1850 were often stenciled, and gold trim was sometimes added.

American toleware is usually found in practical, everyday forms — trays, boxes, and coffeepots are most common — while French examples might include candlesticks, wine coolers, jardinieres, etc. Be sure to note color and design when determining date and value, but condition of the paint is the most important worth-assessing factor. In the listings that follow, the dimension given for boxes and trays indicates length. Unless noted otherwise, values are for examples with average wear.

Canister, tea; floral, 4-color on worn brn japanning, 6½" 330.00
Coffeepot, floral, mc on asphaltum, PA, early 19th C, 10", EX .1,495.00
Coffeepot, floral, mc on blk, PA, early 19th C, 8½", EX 575.00
Deed box, floral, gold on bl japanning, mini, 2x3x2" 150.00
Deed box, floral, mc on brn japanning, dome top, 10", EX 600.00
Deed box, floral on brn japanning w/wht band, 6½" 165.00
Deed box, florals & commas, mc on blk japanning, dome top, 9" .335.00
Dust pan, orig red pnt w/silver vintage stencil, 6" 28.00
Food warmer, yel stripes/gold stencil on blk, brass burner, 9" 175.00
Lunch pail, floral, gold on red, wear, 4x5" dia 160.00
Match holder, floral, 3-color on dk brn, w/trefoil crest, 7" 50.00
Needle case, floral, 2-color on blk japanning, 9" 50.00
Sander, orig decor, pierced star on top, 3x2⅞" dia 85.00
Snuff box, sailing ship, mc on yel, hinged lid, 1x1⅝x3" 175.00
Sugar bowl, feathers, mc on blk japanning, flakes, 4x4¼" 125.00
Sugar bowl, floral, 2-color on dk brn japanning, 3¾" 140.00
Tea caddy, floral, mc on dk brn japanning, wear, 6⅝" 100.00
Tea caddy, floral, 4-color on blk japanning, 5½" 85.00
Tea caddy, house, gold stencil on blk, 8" 40.00
Tray, apple; gold floral on gr japanning, mini, 1¼x4" sq 100.00
Tray, bread; floral, mc on dk brn japanning w/gold, 12⅜" L 300.00

Tray, bread; floral, 4-color on blk w/yel rim, EX color, 13" L 360.00
Tray, floral, 3-color on blk japanning, 8-sided, 18" 140.00

Tools

Before the Civil War, tools for the most part were handmade. Some were primitive to the point of crudeness, while others reflected the skill of those who took pride in their trade. Increasing demand for quality tools and the dawning of the age of industrialization resulted in tools that were mass produced. Factors important in evaluating antique tools are scarcity, usefulness, and portability. Those with a manufacturer's mark are worth more than unmarked items. When no condition is indicated, the items listed here are assumed to be in excellent condition. Our advisor for this category is Jim Calison; he is listed in the Directory under New York. See also Keen Kutter; Stanley; Winchester.

Auger, spiral, dbl-twist bl on trn hdl w/wrought eye, 21", G 12.00
Awl, cobbler's, brass ferrule, trn wood hdl, assorted set of 8 ....20.00
Axe, broad; steel edge, 13½" 55.00
Bevel, IJ Robinson, brass & rosewood, Pat 1970, 6" 275.00
Carriage jack, oak, iron teeth, minimum value 100.00
Chisel, Greenlee, 1" blade, 14" long 24.00
Coachmaker's bitstock, metal, thumb latch quick-release, 1845-50 .70.00
Digger, post-hole; clamshell shovels, split hdl 25.00
Drafting set, 9-pc, orig fitted felt-lined wooden case, ca 1900 ....50.00
Drawknife, Hart Mfg, 18½" 18.00
Gauge, bevel; W Creson Phila, 9¾" blade, EX 25.00
Hog scraper, galvanized steel w/wood hdl, dbl headed, 5" L 5.00
Hoof knife, farrier's, wooden hdl, Italian 9.00
Level, Universal Star, EX 220.00

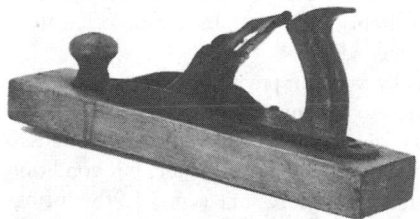

Molding plane, wood and iron, Rosenbloom, Cincinnati, Ohio, 10", $65.00.

Plane, floor; maple, 36" 85.00
Plane, jack; Slotworks #15 on toe, maple, rpl hdl, 16x3", EX 25.00
Plane, molding; J&L Denison, pre-1845 mk, EX 35.00
Plane, plow; adjustable, cherry w/brass fittings, minimum value .150.00
Plane, plow; rosewood w/brass fittings, 12" 55.00
Plane, rabbet; cherry, notched to fit wood 65.00
Plumb bob, Dietzgen, brass, 14-oz, mk, 14" 30.00
Rasp, farrier's, Nicholson 4-in-Hand, dbl end, 8", EX 16.00
Reamer, wooden, t-hdl, tapered bit, threaded tip, 9" 12.00
Router, Millers Falls #77, EX 48.00
Scribe, timber; brass & iron, Germany, 6⅛" 35.00
Witchet, combined hardwoods, brass-lined throat, dbl blades 250.00
Wrench, auto; mk Ford 1 T-1917, 5½" 8.00
Wrench, buggy; CI, str shaft, 1 closed & 3 open sockets 8.00

Toothbrush Holders

Most of the collectible toothbrush holders were made in prewar Japan and were modeled after popular comic-strip and Disney characters. Since many were made of bisque and decorated with unfired paint, it's not uncommon to find them in less-than-perfect paint, a factor you

must consider when attempting to assess their values. Our advisor for this category is Marilyn Cooper, author of *Pictorial Guide to Toothbrush Holders*; she is listed in the Directory under Texas.

Bear in jacket, 2 holes, Japan, 5½" 90.00
Black chef, rare 500.00
Boy w/violin, dog at ft, Goldcastle/Japan, 5½" 70.00
Cat w/bass fiddle, 2 holes, Japan, 6", EX 150.00
Clown, open arms, stands behind dish, Germany, 4⅜" 230.00
Cowboy, Japan, 4½" 80.00
Dachshund, 2 holes, Japan, 5¼" 80.00
Donald Duck, long bill, arm around pillar, Disney, Japan, NM ..1,500.00
Donkey, 1 hole, Goldcastle/Japan, 5¾", G 85.00
Dutch boy w/hands on hips, 3 holes, Japan, 5¼" 70.00
Dutch children kissing, 2 holes, Japan, 6¼" 55.00
Girl in red bonnet holds blk & wht dog, Japan, 5¼" 80.00
Penguin, 3 holes, Japan, 5½", EX 90.00
Skeezix, K-USA, metal, 6" 160.00
Skippy, jtd arm holds brush, bsk, scarce, 5⅝", NM 225.00
Snow White, Maw England, 1938 ....225.00
3 Little Pigs w/instruments, Walt Disney, prewar Japan, NM 195.00

Toothpick Holders

Once common on every table, the toothpick holder was relegated to the china cabinet near the turn of the century. Fortunately, this contributed to their survival. As a result, many are available to collectors today. Because they are small and easily displayed, they are a very popular collectible. They come in a wide range of prices to fit every budget. The rare ones have been reproduced and, unfortunately, are being offered for sale right along with the originals. These 'repros' should be priced in the $10.00 to $30.00 range. Unless you're sure of what you're buying, choose a reputable dealer. In addition to pattern glass, you'll find examples in china, bisque, art glass, and various metals. Toothpick holders in the listings that follow are glass unless noted otherwise. Some toothpick holders have been reproduced. Beware of reproductions. Values here are for originals. Our advisor for this category is Judy A. Knauer; she is listed in the Directory under Pennsylvania.

Agata, sqd rim, VG mottling, 2¼" 650.00
Atlas 30.00
Beatty Rib, amethyst, scarce 55.00
Bird's Basket, amber 30.00
Bohemian, cranberry w/gold 225.00
Bulging Loops, gr 85.00
Capitol 34.00
Chrysanthemum Sprig, custard w/gold & decor 300.00
Cone, gr 70.00
Cranberry, ball shape w/clear shell base, polished pontil 145.00
Cut Block, ruby stain 110.00
Delaware, gr w/EX gold 75.00
Empress, gr w/gold 250.00
Esther, gr w/gold 90.00
Fiber Bundle, milk glass 30.00
Frasier, cranberry w/enamel 75.00
Geneva, custard w/decor 250.00
Harvard, gr 35.00
Illinois 35.00
Iris w/Meander, bl opal 90.00
Jefferson Colonial, gr 68.00
Kansas 60.00
Kentucky, gr w/gold 140.00

Leaf Mold, cranberry spatter 225.00
Minnesota 30.00
New Hampshire, rose blush 65.00
Ohio Star 60.00
Paneled Sprig, wht opal 85.00
Pennsylvania, clear w/gold 40.00
Pleat & Bow, milk glass w/bl flowers 35.00
Radiant, etched 40.00
Reverse Swirl, dk bl & wht spatter 125.00
Reverse Swirl, wht opal 85.00
Ribbed Lattice, cranberry opal 295.00
Ribbed Sprial, bl opal 95.00
Ribbed T'print, custard w/pnt rose buds 90.00
Rip Van Winkle, gr opaque, Portieux 80.00
Rising Sun, rose blush 48.00
Scroll Band, ruby stain 80.00
Serpent, milk glass 60.00
Shell & Seaweed, wht opaque w/gold 85.00
Summit, ruby stain 195.00
Truncated Cube, ruby stain 50.00
Twist, bl opal 105.00
Valise, amber 50.00
Vermont, custard w/gr trim, old 95.00
X-Ray, amethyst w/gold 150.00

Torquay Pottery

Torquay is a unique type of pottery made in the South Devon area of England as early as 1867. At the height of productivity, at least a dozen companies flourished there, producing simple folk pottery from the area's natural red clay. The ware was both wheel-turned and molded and decorated under the glaze with heavy slip resulting in low-relief nature subjects or simple scrollwork. Three of the best-known of these potteries were: Watcombe (1867-1962); Aller Vale (in operation from the mid-1800s, producing domestic ware and architectural products); and Longpark (1890 until 1957). Watcombe and Aller Vale merged in 1901 and operated until 1962 under the name of Royal Aller Vale and Watcombe Art Pottery.

A decline in the popularity of the early classical terra-cotta styles (urns, busts, figures, etc.) lead to the introduction of painted and glazed terra-cotta wares. During the late 1880s white clay wares, both turned and molded, were decorated with colored glazes (Stapleton ware, grotesque molded figures, ornamental vases, large jardiniers, etc.). By the turn of the century, the market for art pottery was diminishing, so the potteries turned to wares decorated in colored slips (Barbotine, Persian, Scrolls, etc.).

Motto wares were introduced in the late 19th century by Aller Vale and taken up in the present century by the other Torquay potteries. This eventually became the 'bread and butter' product of the local industry. This was perhaps the most famous type of ware potted in this area because of the verses, proverbs, and quotations that decorated it. This was achieved by the sgraffito technique — scratching the letters through the slip to expose the red clay underneath. The most popular patterns were Cottage, Black Cockerel, Multi-Cockerel, and a scrollwork design called Scandy. Other popular decorations were Kerswell Daisy, ships, kingfishers, applied bird decorations, Art Deco styles, Egyptian ware, and many others. Aller Vale ware may sometimes be found marked 'H.H. and Company,' a firm who assumed ownership from 1897 to 1901. 'Watcombe Torquay' was an impressed mark used from 1884 to 1927.

Our advisors for this category are Jerry and Gerry Kline; they are listed in the Directory under Ohio. If you're interested in joining a Torquay club, the address of The North American Torquay Society is given under Clubs, Newsletters, and Catalogs.

Wash set, parrot design, 9" pitcher and 15" diameter bowl, $395.00.

Art Pottery

Bottle vase, colored scrolls on cream, B-1, Aller Vale, 6" 275.00
Butter dish, Kingfisher, unmk, 5½" 145.00
Candle holder, bl flower, Lemon & Crute, 1918-20, 6" 100.00
Candlestick, Tintern Abbey, Longpark, 8⅛" 250.00
Figure, cat, gr, Watcombe, 8½" 950.00
Hot water pot, pewter o/l on gr, Watcombe, 1901-20 ....235.00
Jam jar, Jazz, unmk Watcombe, 4" 65.00
Loving cup, commemorative, Tommy Adkins, God Bless, 4½" ..275.00
Pitcher, Clematis, Watcombe, 1902-15, 6" 115.00
Pitcher, Daffodil, unmk Watcombe, 7" 145.00
Pitcher, Fish & Coral, Dartmouth, 7" 100.00
Pitcher, Rose on Trellis, Watcombe, 1920-45, 5¾" 150.00
Vase, Barbotine, Aller Vale, 2⅝" 90.00
Vase, Crocus, Longpark, 1930-40, 7½" 200.00
Vase, Daffodil on gr, 3-hdl, Longpark, 8" 250.00
Vase, floral, mk Watcombe Porcelain, 1878-83, 6" 245.00
Vase, Ladybird on gr, 2-hdl, Aller Vale, 8" 350.00
Vase, Scroll, Aller Vale, 1890-1910, 4" 95.00
Vase, Scroll, unmk, 5¾" 87.00
Vase, Windmill, 2-hdl, Watcombe, 6" 250.00

Devon Motto Ware

Ashtray, Cottage, Watcombe, 'Stitch in Time...,' 3¼" sq 50.00
Basket, Cockerel, oval, 'Homemade Preserves,' 5" 125.00
Biscuit barrel, Cottage, Watcombe, 'Help Yourself,' 6" 300.00
Bottle, scent; Bathes Orig Devonshire Violets, unmk, 3½" 60.00
Bottle, scent; Devon Lav, unmk, 3" 45.00
Bottle, scent; Violets, sealed, cork top 40.00
Bowl, Scrolls, Watcombe, 'There's More in Kitchen...,' 3x8" 175.00
Caldron, Thistle, Longpark, 'Lang May Yer Lum Reek,' 3" 60.00
Chamberstick, Blk Cockerel, Longpark, 'Be the Day...,' 5½" 175.00
Chamberstick, Cottage, 'Pleasant Dreams,' 3½" 65.00
Cheese dish, Cottage, Watcombe, 'Help Yourself...,' 6½x5¼" ...250.00
Condiment holder, w/shakers, egg cup & mustard, 3½" 225.00
Creamer, Cockerel, 'Help Yerzel...,' 2¼" 45.00
Creamer, Multi-Cockerel, Longpark, 'Elp Yerzels...,' 2¾" 65.00
Creamer & sugar bowl, Shamrock, Longpark, motto, ea 2½" 75.00
Cup, child's, unmk Royal Torquay, 'You're Very Welcome,' 1¼" .38.00
Cup & saucer, Blk Cockerel, unmk Watcombe, 'Guid Morn...,' 2½" ..65.00
Dog dish, Scandy, unmk, 'Love Me, Love My Dog,' 5" dia 155.00
Egg cup, Cottage, Royal Watcombe, 'Lands End...,' 1¾" 30.00
Egg cup, Cottage, Royal Watcombe, 'New Laid,' 1935-62, 2¾" ...37.50
Egg cup, Swan, Watcombe, 'Laid To Day,' saucer base, rare 135.00
Hatpin holder, Shamrock, Aller Vale, 4¾" 225.00
Inkwell, Scandy, Aller Vale, 'Us Be Always Glad...,' 2x2½" 90.00
Inkwell, Scandy, Longpark, 'Us Be Always..,' 1¾" 95.00
Jam dish, Cottage, Watcombe, 'Say Little But Think...,' 3" 55.00
Jug, puzzle; Kerswell Daisy, Aller Vale, 'Here Gentlemen...' 250.00
Match striker, Thistle, Longpark, 'Ilka Dog Has...,' 3" 105.00
Muffineer, Cottage, Watcombe, 'Heaven Send Thee...,' 4½x7" .265.00

Mug, child's, Cottage, Royal Watcombe, 'Hope on Hope...,' 2½" ..60.00
Mug, Cottage, Watcombe, 'Rolling Stone Gathers...,' 3¼" 60.00
Mug, shaving; Multi-Cockerel, Longpark, motto, 4" 300.00
Mug, shaving; Sailboat, Longpark, 'Rolling Stone...,' 4" 230.00
Mustard pot, Cottage, 'I Improve...,' 1¾x2½" 55.00
Pitcher, Cottage, unmk Watcombe, 'May You Find...,' 5½" 145.00
Pitcher, Cottage, Watcombe, 'Masters Two Will...,' 2¼" 45.00
Pitcher, Scandy, unmk, 'Don't Shiver...,' 5¾" 110.00
Pitcher, Scandy, unmk Exeter, 'Do the Work That's...,' 9¼" 235.00
Pitcher, Thistle, Longpark, 'Help Yersel...,' 2½" 40.00
Plate, Cottage, 'Time & Tide Wait...,' 6½" 65.00
Plate, Cottage, Watcombe, 'Contrivise Is Better...,' 5" 60.00
Plate, Cottage, Watcombe, 'Sweep Before Your...,' 4½" 48.00
Plate, Cottage, Watcombe, 'The Only Way to...,' 1920-45, 7¼" ..90.00
Sugar bowl, Blk Cockerel, Longpark, 'Be Aisy w/...,' 4" dia 60.00
Teapot, floral, unmk Hart & Moist, 'Now Ladies All I...,' 4½" 90.00
Teapot, Scandy, Watcombe, 'Du-ee Drink a Cup...,' 3¾" 130.00
Tile, Cottage, Watcombe, 'Daunt'ee Waste...,' 6½" dia 125.00
Tile, Cottage, Watcombe, 'They Also Serve...,' 4¾" 75.00
Tile, curling iron; Scandy, Longpark, w/motto, 7½x5" 275.00
Toast rack, Watcombe, 'Help Yourself to Toast,' 5x3½" 175.00
Tray, dresser; Cottage, Watcombe, unusual motto, 7½x11" 300.00
Tray, dresser; Scandy, Longpark, unusual motto, 7½x11" 300.00
Vase, udder; Scandy, Aller Vale, motto, 3½" 125.00

Toys

The prices shown in this edition reviews auction reports, known sales, and sales lists. We have shown prices of toys in various conditions and noted which toys sold with boxes. To get the most out of this guide, when you see the same toys with different prices, you must consider these important factors. On occasion, a toy will bring a much higher than normal price at auction. This is 'auction fever.' Sometimes a collector simply wants to add a toy to his collection, and to him price is not as important as availability.

Toys can be classified into at least two categories: early collectible toys with an established history, and the newer toys. The antique toys are easier to evaluate. A great deal of research has been done on them, and much data is available. The newer toys are just beginning to be studied; relative information is only now being published, and the lack of production records makes it difficult to know how many may be available. Often warehouse finds of these newer toys can change the market. This has happened with battery-operated toys and to some extent with robots. Review past issues of this guide. You will see the changing trends for the newer toys. All toys become more important as collectibles when a fixed period of manufacture is known. When we know the numbers produced and documentation of the makers is established, the prices become more predictable.

The best way to learn about toys is to attend toy shows and auctions. This will give you the opportunity to compare prices and condition. The more collectors and dealers you meet, the more you will learn. There is no substitute for holding a toy in your hand and seeing for yourself what they are. If you are going to be a serious collector, buy all the books you can find. Read every article you see. Knowledge is vital to building a good collections. Study all books that are available. These are some of the most helpful: *American Toy Cars and Trucks* by Lillian Gottschalk; *Toy Autos 1890-1939*, the Peter Ottenheimer Collection; *Collecting the Tin Toy Car, 1950-1970*, by Dale Kelley; *Arcade Toys* by Al Aune; *The Art of the Tin Toy* by David Pressland; *Lehmann Toys* by Cieslik; *The History of Martin Mechanical Toys* by Marchand; *Mechanical Toys* by Spilhaus; *American Antique Toys* by Barenholtz, McClintock, and Holland; *American Clockwork Toys* by Whitton; *The George Brown Sketchbook* by Edith Barenholtz; *Toy Dreams* by Kitahara; *Collecting*

Toys, Collecting Toy Soldiers, and *Collecting Toy Trains, An Identification & Value Guide #3*, by Richard O'Brien; *Occupied Japan Toys With Prices* by David Gould and Donna Crevar-Donaldson; *Evolution of the Pedal Car and Other Riding Toys, 1844-1970s*, by Neil Wood; *Toys of the Sixties, A Pictorial Guide*, by Bill Bruegman; and *Fisher-Price, A Historical, Rarity & Value Guide, 1931-1963*, by John Murray and Bruce Fox. Other informative books (published by Collector Books) are *Schroeder's Collectible Toys, Antique to Modern*, by Sharon and Bob Huxford; *Motorcycle Toys, Antique & Contemporary*, by Sally Gibson-Downs and Christine Gentry; *Mego Toys* by Wallace M. Chrouch; *Collector's Encyclopedia of Disneyana* by David Longest and Michael Stern; *Stern's Guide to Disney Collectibles* by Michael Stern; *Modern Toys, American Toys, 1830-1980*, by Linda Baker; *Character Toys and Collectibles, Antique and Collectible Toys* and *Toys, Antiques & Collectibles*, both by David Longest; *Collector's Guide to Tootsietoys* by David Richter; *Collectible Male Action Figures* by Paris and Susan Manos; *Matchbox Toys, 1948-1993*, and *Diecast Toys and Scale Models*, both by Dana Johnson. *The Dictionary of Toys Sold in America, Vol. I & II*, by Earnest and Ida Long are good for identification and dating.

Our advisor for all toys except Farm Toys, Guns, Steiff, Toy Soldiers, and Trains is Jon Thurmond; he is listed in the Directory under Missouri. In the listings that follow, toys are listed by manufacturer's name if possible, otherwise by type. Condition is given when known. Measurements are given when appropriate and available; if only one dimension is noted, it is the greater one — height if the toy is vertical, length if it is horizontal. See also Children's Things; Personalities. For toy stoves, see Stoves.

Key:
b/o — battery operated   NP — nickel plated
cl — celluloid   w/up — wind-up
jtd — jointed

Company or Country of Manufacturer

AC Williams, Dbl-Decker Bus, CI, NP wheels, 7¾", G 210.00
AC Williams, Fageol Bus, CI, nickel windows, 1929, 7¾", VG .250.00
AC Williams, Ford Coupe, CI, NP grille, snap-apart, 6¾", EX ..750.00
AC Williams, Ford Model A, CI, rubber tires, 5¼", NM 400.00
AHI, Fred & Barney Car, b/o, 1974, very rare, NM 250.00
Alps, Accordion Player Hobo, b/o, plush monkey on cymbals, MIB .525.00
Alps, Antique Gooney Car, b/o, 4 actions, 1960s, MIB 150.00
Alps, Banjo Bunny, celluloid bunny on stump, 8", NM in G box ..225.00
Alps, Butterfield Stagecoach, litho tin, wheels stuck, 13", G 50.00
Alps, Dice Throwing Monkey, b/o, 1960, MIB 100.00
Alps, Frankie the Roller Skating Monkey, b/o, 12", MIB 245.00
Alps, Mambo the Drumming Elephant, b/o, 1950, NM 140.00
Alps, Mexicalli Pete, b/o, clothed monkey w/bongos, 10", EX+ ...90.00
Alps, Teddy the Drummer, b/o, 1970, MIB 75.00
Arcade, see also Farm toys
Arcade, Army Tank, CI, shoots balls, 1937, 7½", MIB 2,200.00
Arcade, Buick Coupe, CI, NP driver, 1927, 8½", VG 4,000.00
Arcade, Car Carrier, CI, NP wheels, 3 cars, 1932, 24½", VG .2,500.00
Arcade, Chevy Utility Stake Truck, CI, NP driver, 9", EX 950.00
Arcade, Delivery Truck, CI, rubber tires, 8⅜", EX 5,500.00
Arcade, Express Truck, CI, NP driver, 1929, 8½", VG 1,650.00
Arcade, Fire Pumper, CI, NP wheels, orig decals, 6¾", NM 475.00
Arcade, Model A Wrecker, CI, orig stickers, 7", NM 600.00
Arcade, Monocoupe, CI, NP wheels & props, ca 1929, 5½", EX ..475.00
Arnold, Format Coupe 2900, lt gauge steel, 10", NM in G- box ..300.00
Arnold, German Submarine, tin, w/all accessories, EX 495.00
Arnold, Mac 700 Motorcycle, litho tin, 2-lever control, EX+ .1,250.00
ATC, Air Carousel, litho tin & celluloid, lever action, 6", EX ..118.00
Automatic Toy, Mystery Alpine Express, litho tin, 20", EX in box ...230.00

Automatic Toy, Spiral Speedway, 2 buses on track, 1950s, MIB .200.00
Baldwin, Hen Laying Egg, hand crank, 1950, NM 75.00
Bandai, Am Cars Set, b/o, pnt/litho tin, 7", G+ in torn box 140.00
Bandai, Dump Truck, b/o, 1960, MIB 125.00
Bandai, Snorkel Pumper Fire Engine, b/o, 1970, MIB 100.00
Bell Mfg, Dancing Dan, b/o, plastic, 1940s, 15", NMIB 280.00
Bing, Ford Model T Phaeton, litho tin, lady driver, 6½", EX 465.00
Bing, Ford Model T Sedan, tin w/metal wheels, 1925, 6½", EX .425.00

Bliss, horse-drawn sand and gravel wagon, paper litho on wood, 9¾x21", EX, $325.00.

Buddy L, Wrigley's Spearmint Railway Express, 1938, EX 385.00
Carette, Limousine, litho tin, rpt tin driver, 9", EX- 1,975.00
Carpenter, Dr's Cart, CI, spoke wheels, 1 horse, 10", G 75.00
Champion Hardware, Ford Coupe, CI, NP wheels, 7½", EX 375.00
Chein, Army Cannon Truck, srping-loaded cannon, 8", NM 185.00
Chein, Broadway Trolley, litho tin w/up, ca 1935, EX+ 275.00
Chein, Clown, tin w/up, ca 1930, 5½", EX 275.00
Chein, Ferris Wheel, litho tin w/up, 16½", EX 175.00
Chein, Mr Rabbit, tin litho rabbit on wheels, 5½", EX 125.00
Chein, Racer #3, yel litho tin, w/driver, ca 1925, 6½", VG 265.00
Chein, Touring Car, w/driver & passengers, litho tin w/up, VG+ ..165.00
Chein, Trolley, Broadway #270, litho tin floor toy, VG+ 70.00
CK, Acrobat & Clown on Highbar, tin, 12", G in box 65.00
CM, Bleating Pig, celluloid, HP features, 5½", EX in box 135.00
Cragstan, Crapshooting Monkey, NMIB 90.00
Cragstan, Shuttling Dog Train, b/o, 1950s, EX 100.00
Cragstan, Trumpet Playing Monkey, b/o, plush & litho tin, MIB 275.00
Daishin, Happy Naughty Chimp, b/o, 1960, MIB 125.00
Daiya, Army Tank, b/o, brn litho tin, no guns, 8½" 75.00
Daiya, Fairy Land Train #0741, b/o, 3 actions, 1950s, NM 70.00
Dayton, Hillclimber Fire Engine, metal, 14½", VG 625.00
Dent, Auto Dump Truck, CI, NP driver, 1920s, 8", EX 1,800.00
Dent, Breyer's Ice Cream Delivery Van, CI, 1932, EX 2,100.00
Dent, Coach Bus, CI, NP wheels, 1925, 7⅝", EX 1,300.00
Dent, Coast-to-Coast Bus, CI, brass pattern, 15½", EX 2,900.00
Dent, Fire Chief Car, spoke wheels, open tiller, 5", EX 250.00
Dent, Ford Cabin Aeroplane, NP wheels & props, 11¼", M ...6,000.00
Dent, Lucky Boy Glider, CI, NP, 4¼", NM 600.00
Dent, Road Sweeper, CI, gear-driven, 1930s, 7¾", EX 3,700.00
Epoch, Roger Rabbit Bobber, b/o, moves w/sound, 15", MIB 800.00
Fisher-Price, Chick Cart, #407, NM 55.00
Fisher-Price, Happy Helicopter, #498, EX 195.00
Fisher-Price, Jumbo Jitterbug, #422, EX 225.00
Fisher-Price, Kriss Kricket, #678, VG 100.00
Fisher-Price, Musical Duck, #795, EX 100.00
Fisher-Price, Running Bunny Cart, #304, NM 90.00
Fisher-Price, Tailspin Tabby, cloth ears, paddle, #400, VG 125.00
Freidag, Checker Cab, CI, license plate, 1920s, 7½", EX 4,000.00
Freidag, Coach Bus, NP wheels, 8⅞", G 675.00
FYT/Taiwan, Diesel Locomotive, b/o, 1975, MIB 40.00
G Levy, Carnival Bell Ringer, tin figure, 1930s, EX 330.00

G Levy, Pot Ball Clown, litho tin, many actions, 9½", EX+ ...1,025.00
Gescha, Manrovier Tank, lever activated, 8", NM (G box) 165.00
Graham, Ladder Truck, CI, snap-apart, 1933, 5", EX 250.00
Gunthermann, Bicycle, litho tin w/pnt tin figure, 8", EX 1,650.00
Gunthermann, Boy on Steer, litho tin, ca 1920, 6½", G- 550.00
Gunthermann, Buick Convertible, tin w/compo driver, 11", EX .345.00
Gunthermann, Jack Sprat, rpt tin, 1910s, 6½" 460.00
Gunthermann, Rabbit w/Cymbals, 9½", EX 375.00
Gunthermann, Wright Bros Type Airplane, litho tin pilot, 7", EX .1,000.00
H Katz, Coney Island Giant Dip, 19", EX+ in G box 3,300.00
Haji, Apache Rider, litho tin, 7", G (orig box) 40.00
Haji, Strutting My Fair Dancer, b/o, litho tin & vinyl, MIB 250.00
Hess, Boy on Sled, litho tin w/cast wheels, 6¾", VG 450.00
Hong Kong, Battleship, b/o, plastic, 1970, MIB 55.00
Hong Kong, Reversible Race Car, b/o, 1970, NM 35.00
Hong Kong, Warpath Willie, b/o, 1970, MIB 65.00
Huber, Steam Roller, CI, orange w/pnt driver, 7¾", EX+ 403.00
Hubley, see also Farm Toys
Hubley, Ahrens-Fox Fire Engine, spoke wheels, 3½", VG 350.00
Hubley, Borden's Milk Truck, CI, rubber tires, 3⅝", NM 450.00
Hubley, Bremen, airplane, NP wheels/props/pilots, 7", VG 1,100.00
Hubley, Coal Truck, CI, NP wheels, open cab, 6⅝", NM 1,100.00
Hubley, Elgin Street Sweeper, CI, moving parts, 8¾", EX 3,900.00
Hubley, Fire Pumper, CI, driver, 3 horses, 1948, 10", EX 105.00
Hubley, Fire Truck, CI, spoke wheels, 5½", pnt chips o/w VG 50.00
Hubley, H-21 Am Eagle, CI, red & bl, 1960, MIB 100.00
Hubley, Harley-Davidson Motorcycle, CI, NP wheels, 7", EX ..1,400.00
Hubley, Ladder Truck, CI, NP tires & driver, 1929, 13", NM 950.00
Hubley, Lindy plane, gray, rubber tires, NP props, 11", EX 2,200.00
Hubley, Panama Steam Shovel, CI, bl & silver, 8⅝", EX 1,000.00
Hubley, Road Roller, CI, NP driver, 1930s, 7¾", EX 550.00
Hubley, Steam Shovel Truck, CI, NP wheels & shovel, 4", EX ..220.00
Ichiko, Russian Taxi, b/o, litho tin, 9", EX 225.00
Ideal, Phantom Raider, b/o, 1963, NMIB 325.00
Illco, VW Fire Chief Car, b/o, 1970, MIB 50.00
Irwin, Super Racing Car, plastic, rubber tires, 1950s, NMIB 180.00
Irwin, Whistling Boy, plastic, NMIB 125.00
Ives, Clown on Velocipede, clockwork, 1870s, EX 11,000.00
Ives, Dumping Coal Wagon, CI, Blk driver w/mule, 13", VG 725.00
Japan, Balloon Vendor, b/o, tin, 11", EX in EX box 170.00
Japan, Brave Eagle, b/o, Indian plays drum, 12", MIB 125.00
Japan, Twin Racing Cars, b/o, litho tin, remote, NMIB 500.00
K, Circus Trailer, litho tin, 18", NMIB 625.00
K, Jolly Bear the Drummer Boy, b/o, 7", NMIB 250.00
Kenton, Airmail, CI, NP motor/wheels/prop, 7" wingspan, VG .475.00
Kenton, Buckeye Ditch Digger, CI, chain drive, 1930, 9", EX 875.00
Kenton, Fire Patrol Truck, CI, rubber tires, 4 firemen, 9", EX .1,400.00
Kenton, Gas & Oil Truck, CI, C-style cab, 11¼", VG 1,650.00
Kenton, Jaeger Cement Mixer, CI, NP cylinder, 7⅜", M 2,400.00
Kenton, Ladder Truck, CI, rubber tires, driver, 9", VG 800.00
Kenton, Overland Circus Truck, CI, driver & hippo, 7¼", EX ..1,300.00
Kilgore, Blue Streak Roadster, CI, rubber tires, 6", EX 500.00
Kilgore, Sea Gull, CI, orange w/NP wheels & props, 8", EX 1,300.00
Kilgore, Tat, airplane, CI, red & yel w/NP wheels & prop, NM ..7,500.00
Kingsbury, Golden Arrow, tin racer w/driver, 20", EX 925.00
Kingsbury, Panama Truck, sheet metal w/CI driver, 13", EX 525.00
KO, Air Mail Helicopter, b/o, action & sounds, MIB 225.00
KO, Circus Boat, litho tin & vinyl, friction, 7", NM in EX box .140.00
KT, Auto Cycle, prewar, camouflaged, 5¾", NM in VG+ box ...305.00
Lehmann, Climbing Monkey, string activated, Pat 1892, 8", VG+ ..175.00
Lehmann, Express, man & 2-wheeled cart, tin w/up, 6", VG+ ...350.00
Lehmann, Hansom Cab, driver+2, litho tin w/up, 5½", EX 2,200.00
Lehmann, Quack-Quack Duck Cart, litho tin w/up, 7", MIB 775.00
Lehmann, Tut-Tut, man in open car, tin litho w/up, 7", NM .2,000.00

Lindstrom, Am Railway Express w/Trailer, litho tin, 16", EX 675.00
Lindstrom, Betty, litho tin girl in pants & apron, 8", EX+ 150.00
Lindstrom, Dancing Dutch Boy, litho tin, 1930s, 8", NMIB 300.00
Lindstrom, Dancing Lassie, litho tin girl, 8", EX+ 155.00
Lindstrom, Greatest Show on Earth, elephant w/wagon, 1930, EX .1,700.00
Lindstrom, Santa Claus, litho tin, 8", G 120.00
Lindstrom, Skeeter Duck #55, moves in S pattern, 9½", NMIB .135.00
Linemar, Army Radio Jeep, b/o, 4 actions, 1950s, 7", NM 225.00
Linemar, Auto Dockyard Crane, 1950, VG+ 75.00
Linemar, Barber Bear, b/o, plush w/litho tin, 11", NMIB 525.00
Linemar, Bubble Blowing Popeye, litho tin, 12", EX in box 1,150.00
Linemar, Busy Secretary, litho tin, 1950s, 7", NM 250.00
Linemar, Calypso Joe, native girl w/tom-toms, 6", EX 125.00
Linemar, Camera Shooting Bear, clothed bear, 11", MIB 450.00
Linemar, Cary the Crow, litho tin, EX 100.00
Linemar, Cat w/Vacuum Cleaner, litho tin, 3½", NMIB 150.00
Linemar, G-Man Patrol Car, b/o, remote, 8½", MIB 484.00

Linemar, Gym-Toys Acrobat, Donald Duck figure, wind-up, MIB, $650.00.

Linemar, Nutty Nibs, b/o, litho tin native, 12", EX in VG box ..750.00
Linemar, Police Car, b/o, remote, 8½", NMIB 297.00
Linemar, Snake Charmer, b/o, litho tin, 7", M in EX box 550.00
Linemar, Sneezing Bear, b/o, litho tin, 9", EX in box 440.00
Linemar, Spanking Bear, b/o, litho tin & plush, 10", NMIB 575.00
Linemar, Suzie the Cashier Bear, b/o, clothed plush, 9", EX 725.00
Lionel, Mickey Mouse Hand Car, orange car, 1930s, 8", NMIB ..1,600.00
Lionel, Peter Rabbit Chick-Mobile, 1930s, 10", EX in G box 900.00
Lionel, Santa Car, Mickey Mouse in gift bag, MIB 1,500.00
Lupor, City Taxi, litho tin, rubber tires, NMIB 170.00
Martin, El Diablo, cloth-dressed man, HP body, 8", EX 1,900.00
Martin, Le Pochard, HP tin, 1900s, 8", EX in orig box 975.00
Marusan, Tugboat, b/o, litho tin, 1950s, 13", EX in VG box 140.00
Marx, Amos Walker, litho tin w/up, 10½", EX 450.00
Marx, Army Transport Truck, pressed steel, 13½", NM 250.00
Marx, Blondie's Jalopy, litho tin w/up, 16¾", EX 2,600.00
Marx, Brightlite Filling Station, litho tin, 9½", NM 525.00
Marx, Carousel Truck, litho tin w/up, w/horses, 7½", NMIB 135.00
Marx, City Coal Truck, silver litho tin w/up w/red bed, 13", G 95.00
Marx, Dapper Dan Coon Jigger, tin litho w/up, 11", NMIB 900.00
Marx, Dump Truck, pressed steel/NP grille, 10½", G+ 60.00
Marx, Flippo the Jumping Dog, litho tin w/up, 4", EX+ in box ..300.00
Marx, Fred Flintstone on Dino, plush/litho tin, 19", EX in box ..750.00
Marx, Joe Penner & His Duck, litho tin w/up, 8", EX 650.00
Marx, Moon Mullins & Kayo Handcar, tin w/up, 6", EX in box .990.00
Marx, Nutty Mad Car, litho tin, crazy actions/noise, 9", MIB 675.00
Marx, Range Rider, litho tin, rocker base, 1938, EX 350.00
Marx, Sleek Coupe w/Trailer, litho tin, 22½", EX 850.00
Marx, Steam Roller, pressed steel, chrome-plated, 11⅜", EX 60.00
Marx, Twirling Tail Donald, plastic w/up, Disney, 6½", EX 85.00
Mego/Japan, Doodle the Poodle, b/o, 1960, MIB 75.00
Mego/Japan, Flippity Flyer, b/o, 1970, MIB 100.00
Mettoy, Tractor, gr, tin, 7½", NMIB 100.00
Mettoy, Train Engine, tin, friction, 1950s, 6", NM 115.00

Minic, Breakdown Lorry, tin, w/up, NMIB 500.00
Minic, Ford Saloon, bl tin, 3½", NM in EX+ box 150.00
Minic, Royal Mail Van, red tin w/decals, 3½", EX 110.00
Minic, Taxi, blk tin, meter & spare, 4", NMIB 275.00
Minic, Transport Express Van, bl tin w/decals, 3½", NM 80.00
Minic, Vauxhall Cabriolet, bl tin, rubber tires, 5", EX 130.00
Minic, Vauxhall Tourer Convertible, gr & blk tin, 5", NMIB 180.00
Modern Toys, Santa in Sleigh, b/o, litho tin, 17", EX 200.00
Moko, Limousine, butler driver, 8", NM+ 1,250.00
MT, Broadway Trolley, b/o, litho tin, 1950s, EX 95.00
MT, Bubble Blowing Lion, b/o, litho tin, 7", NM in EX box 171.00
MT, Circus Clown, litho tin, cloth & rubber, 5", NMIB 300.00
MT, Good-Time Charlie, b/o, 1960, NM 110.00
MT, Santa Copter, b/o, 1960, missing prop o/w MIB 100.00
MT, Sparky the Seal, b/o, plush over tin, 8", MIB 130.00
MT, Tom & Jerry Helicoter, b/o, bump & go, EX 325.00
MT, Walking Gorilla, b/o, remote, NMIB 1,600.00
Mueller Kadeder, Zeppelin Go Round, pnt tin, 10½", VG 770.00
Nifty, Barney Google & Spark Plug, 1920s, 7", VG 950.00
Nylint, Pump-Mobile, litho tin cowboy, 8½", EX+ in box 528.00
Ohio Art, Alpine Cable Car Ride, litho tin, 2 cars, NM 115.00
Ohio Art, Donald Duck Watering Can, litho tin, 1930s, EX 275.00
Ohio Art, Mickey Mouse Washing Machine, w/Minnie, 7½", NMIB .1,100.00
Orobor, Garage w/Autos, 2-car garage w/cars, 6" autos, G+ 2,000.00
PN, Thunderbird, litho tin w/compo driver, 13", NM in VG box ..150.00
PN #900, Police Cycles, 2 side-by-side, 7", EX in EX box 575.00
Pratt & Letchworth, Hansom Cab, CI, brn horse, 1890s, 11", G ..450.00
Ranger Steel, Mechanical Billiard Table, 2 men, EX in G box ...375.00
Red Box/Hong Kong, Supreme Blender, b/o, 1976, MIB 35.00
Remco, Flying Dutchman, b/o, orig box 225.00
Richman Toys, Batmobile, Limited Edition, remote, 21", MIB ..400.00
S&E, Drinking Captain, b/o, 1950s, MIB 180.00
S&E, Rabbits & Carriage, b/o, mama pushes baby in buggy, MIB ..475.00
Sajo, Atomboat, tin boat, Harbor Command on roof, 11", NMIB ..200.00
San, Bubbling Boy, litho tin, 8", NMIB 210.00
San, Smoking Bunny, b/o, walks w/pipe lit, tin & cloth, 9", MIB .250.00
Sankyo Toys, Atom Speedboat, NMIB 210.00
Schuco, Charlie Chaplin, tin, cloth outfit, 6½", EX in box 275.00
Schuco, elephant, yes/no, missing tail cover, 1950, 5", NM 550.00
Schuco, Grand Prix Racer, w/up, Schuco key, NM+ in VG box .475.00
Schuco, hedgehog (from Noah's Ark), 2", EX 65.00
Schuco, Hopsa Monkey w/Mouse, clothed, plush, 5", NMIB 300.00
Schuco, Mercedes Benz #1225, EX in box 120.00
Schuco, Mercedes Police Car, b/o, pnt & litho tin, 8½", VG 400.00
Schuco, Micro-Jet #1030, red tin, Schuco key, 5½", EX+ 110.00
Schuco, Mirakocar 1001, red tin body, 4½", EX+ in box 150.00
Schuco, mouse, Mikifex, w/up w/orig key, 3½" L, NM 150.00
Schuco, Mouse in Convertible, Sonny 2005, tin, 5¾", G 220.00
Schuco, owl (from Noah's Ark), 2½", MIB 175.00
Schuco, penguin (from Noah's Ark), 1950, 2½", M 95.00
Schuco, Porsche Formel II Micro-Racer #1037, friction, NMIB .100.00
Schuco, rabbit, orig ribbon, ca 1950, 3½", M 225.00
SH, Old Tyme Town Car, b/o, 1950, NM 95.00
SKK, Circus Train, friction, 15", NMIB 90.00
Skoglund & Olson, Gasoline Truck, CI, rear duals, 10½", EX .2,200.00
Sonco, Funland Cup Ride, b/o, EX 200.00
Strauss, Alabama Coon Jigger (Tombo), litho tin w/up, 10", G .600.00
Strauss, Dizzie Lizzie Car, litho tin w/up, 8", NMIB 375.00
Strauss, Jenny the Balky Mule, litho tin w/up, 1920s, 9", EX 550.00
Strauss, Lux-a-Cab, mk 48, driver, 4 litho doors, 8½", EX 1,050.00
Strauss, Twin Trolleys, litho tin w/up, non-working, VG 200.00
Technofix, Motorcycle, litho tin, red cycle w/rider, 7", NM 270.00
Technofix, Racing Cycle, litho tin, metal front wheels, 7", VG .140.00
Technofix/US Zone, Mini Race Car, w/2 Porsches, MIB 450.00

Tipp, Racer #32, litho tin w/molded driver, 16", EX 2,900.00
TN, Atom Motorcycle, litho tin, rider dismounts, 11½", VG 250.00
TN, Battleship Destroyer, litho tin, 8", G 50.00
TN, Clown Magician, litho tin & cloth, 7", EX+ in EX+ box 600.00
TN, Golden Jubilee Car, b/o, 4 actions, 1950s, NM 185.00
TN, Miss Friday the Typist, b/o, tin litho, 8", EX in EX box 200.00
TN, Musical Clown, b/o, plays London Bridge on xylophone, NMIB .775.00
TN, Pete the Talking Parrot, b/o, repeats messages, 17", EX+ 375.00
TN, Shutter Bug, b/o, takes pictures, litho tin, MIB 695.00
TN/Japan, Gorilla, b/o, remote, 9½", NMIB 340.00
Tonka, Army Tractor, 1964, EX 85.00
Tonka, Fire Pumper #5, hoses/ladder/hydrant, 1953, 17½", M ...245.00
Tonka, Marine Service, semi truck, no boats, 1961, EX 150.00
Tonka, Mobil Dragline, 1960, EX 125.00
Tonka, Parcel Delivery Metro Van, 1954, EX 195.00
Tonka, Thunderbird Express, 1959 semi truck, EX 195.00
Toy Biz, Batmobile, b/o, radio controlled, 1989, MIB 95.00
Toyland Toys, Arty the Trapeze Artist, celluloid, 12", MIB 150.00
TPS, Ball-Playing Giraffe, litho tin, clockwork, 8½", EX+ 430.00
TPS, Big League Hockey Player, litho tin, clockwork, EX 325.00
TPS, Candy Loving Canine, litho tin, 6", NM 220.00
TPS, Circus Cyclist, litho tin, cloth outfit, 6½", NMIB 900.00
TPS, Circus Seal, plush w/tin ft, 6½", EX in box 80.00
TPS, Cleo Clown Training Dog, litho tin, NM in EX+ box 350.00
TPS, Climbo the Climbing Clown, litho tin, 7", NMIB 425.00
TT, Central Express Car, mk Super Express, litho tin, 6", MIB ..105.00
Unique Art, GI Joe & His Jouncing Jeep, mk 5-4065, 1941, 8", EX .250.00
Unique Art, Lincoln Tunnel, 24", NM (EX box) 700.00
Unique Art, Musical Kiddie-Go-Round, litho tin, 11", EX+ in box ..325.00
Unique Art, Police Cycle, litho tin, metal wheels, 8", G- 145.00
Unique Art, Sky Rangers, litho tin, 1930s, EX+ in box 400.00
US Hardware, Oarsmen In Racing Scull, CI, 9 men, 15", VG .5,500.00
US Zone, Boby, monkey on trike, litho tin, 4", NMIB 225.00
US Zone, Hand-Standing Clown, well detailed, 5", NM 350.00
US Zone, Jumbo the Elephant, olive gr, orange & yel, VG 150.00
US Zone, Lasso Cowboy, litho tin, 6", EX+ in EX box 195.00
US Zone, Tick-Tack Express, friction, 2 buses, 18", EX in box ..225.00
Usagayi, Camouflage Soldier Cycle, litho tin, friction, 8", EX 225.00
Vindex, Delivery Cycle, CI, NP hdlbars, rubber tires, 9", EX ..5,000.00
Vindex, P&H Power Excavator, CI, dumps by hand, 10½", NM ..7,500.00
W Germany, Arabian Trotter, compo & tin, 1955, 6", NMIB ...180.00
W Germany, Hurricane Motor Launch, litho tin, 7", VG in box .25.00
Wells, Inverted Clown, litho tin, clockwork, EX in box 225.00
Wells, Stake Truck, litho tin, balloon tires, 10½", EX+ 275.00
Wilkins, Fire Pumper, bronzed CI, 2 horses & men, 18", G 3,450.00
Wilkins, Panama Wagon, CI, 2 horses, orig driver, 19", G 475.00
Wolverine, Crane, litho tin, 1947, 18", NM in G box 180.00
Wolverine, Diving Submarine, w/litho guns, 1940, EX 150.00
Wolverine, Loop De Loop, litho carnival scene, MIB 575.00
Wolverine, Mystery Car, litho tin & wood, 13½", VG 175.00
Wolverine, Neck & Neck, litho tin horse race, 1950s, 27", NMIB ..225.00
Wolverine, Ski Jumper, litho tin, 1930s, EX+ in VG box 250.00
Wolverine, Sunny Andy Kiddie Kampers, litho tin, 14", EX+ 350.00
Wyandotte, Ambulance, plastic, friction, 1940s, 9", NM 150.00
Wyandotte, chicken, tin, push down, lays marble egg, 8" 85.00
Wyandotte, Man on the Flying Trapeze #516, 9", EX+ in box ...225.00
Wyandotte, Red Ranger Ride 'Em Cowboy, litho tin, 7", EX 95.00
Wyandotte, Super Shovel, EX 140.00
Y, Begging Puppy, 1960s, G 25.00
Y, Blushing Cowboy, 4 actions, 1960s, NM 125.00
Y, Blushing Willie, 1960, 10", EX 60.00
Y, Boxing Dog, litho tin & plush, 6", MIB 85.00
Y, Bubble Blowing Elephant, plush-covered litho tin, 7", MIB ...125.00
Y, Child Indian in War Paint, 1950, MIB 130.00

Y, Cragstan One-Armed Bandit, 1960s, MIB 275.00
Y, Cragstan Two-Gun Sheriff, b/o, 5 actions, 1950s, EX in box .200.00
Y, Drumming Bear, walks, lighted eyes, 12½", NMIB 1,600.00
Y, Happy Hound Dog, b/o, 6 actions, 1950s, rare, EX 225.00
Y, Non-Stop Boat, b/o, litho tin, MIB 375.00
Y, Pelican w/Fish in Mouth, b/o, 4 actions, 1960s, EX 90.00

Farm Toys

Combine, Vindex, Case, CI, working head, 12¼", NM 5,700.00
Disk, Am Precision, Allis Chalmers, pnt couplers, '50s, 6", VG ...80.00
Disk Harrow, Am Precision, Allis Chalmers, 1950s, 9", G 65.00
Engine, gas; Vindex, John Deere, working pulley & flywheel, EX .1,050.00
Hay loader, Vindex, Case, CI, revolving chains & teeth, 9", EX ..5,200.00
Manure spreader, Vindex, John Deere, CI, working, 9¼", NM 2,500.00
Plow, 3-bottom; Vindex, Case, CI, NP discs, 10¼", NM 3,200.00
Plow, 3-bottom; Vindex, Case, red w/gr spokes, 10", EX 1,200.00
Roller w/rake, Hubley, Huber, 8", EX 400.00
Steam roller, Hubley, Huber, orange, 8", G 200.00

Thresher, Arcade, painted cast iron, EX, $350.00.

Thresher, Vindex, John Deere, CI, 15", rare, NM 3,700.00
Tractor, Am Precision, Allis Chalmers Model C, 7½", EX 140.00
Tractor, Arcade, Allis Chalmers, CI, tin scoop, 7⅛", EX 525.00
Tractor, Arcade, CAT, CI, NP chain tracks, 1929, 5⅜", EX ..1,600.00
Tractor, Arcade, Farmall Regular, red, 6", VG 350.00
Tractor, Arcade, Ford 9N, CI driver, gray, 7", VG 270.00
Tractor, Arcade, Fordson, CI, NP driver, 5¾", VG 375.00
Tractor, diesel; Arcade, CAT, pnt CI, driver, 7", EX 1,600.00
Tractor, diesel; Arcade, CI, 1937, driver, 7⅝", VG 1,400.00
Tractor, Hubley, Allis Chalmers Model WC, driver, 7", VG 160.00
Tractor, Hubley, Avery, blk, 4¼", VG 170.00
Tractor w/earth hauler, Arcade, Allis Chalmers Model U, 8", EX ..180.00
Tractor w/earth hauler, Arcade, 14", VG 340.00
Tractor & dump, Arcade, Allis Chalmers, rubber tires, 8", EX ...110.00
Wagon, Arcade, CI w/NP wheels & wire hitch, 6¼", VG 220.00
Wagon, Vindex, John Deere, CI, 2 blk horses, 7½", EX 1,700.00
Wagon, Whitewater Farm; Vindex, CI, 2 horses, 7½", EX 3,400.00

Guns: Cast-Iron Cap Guns (Caution: Some reproductions exist.)

In years past, virtually every child played with toy guns, and the survival rate of these toys is minimal, at best. The interest in these charming toy guns has recently increased considerably, especially western-styled, as collectors discover their scarcity, quality, and value. Toy gun collectibles encompass the early and the very ornate figural toy guns and bombs. The more realistic ones had recognizable character names, gleaming finishes, faux jewels, dummy bullets, engraving and colorful grips. This section will cover some of the most popular cast iron and die-cast toy guns from the past hundred years.

Our advisor is James Schleyer, internationally recognized collector and appraiser of toy guns. He has authored numerous books, articles, and newsletters on antique toy guns and holsters and is the former newsletter editor for the Toy Gun Purveyors, an international club that fostered the collecting of these valuable and rare toys. Mr. Schleyer's address is listed in the Directory under Virginia. Please include a SASE when requesting information.

Am, Kilgore, revolving cylinder, 1940, 9⅜", VG 350.00
Army 45 Auto, Hubley, 1945, 6½", M 135.00
Atta Boy, single shot, 1935, 4", G- 50.00
Bango, jewels, Stevens, England, 1940, 7½", VG 80.00
Big Bill, single shot, Kilgore, 1935, 4⅞", M 65.00
Big Horn, reverse cylinder, Kilgore, 1940, 8⅝", M 500.00
Big Scout, single shot, Stevens, 1930, 9⅜", VG 150.00
Billy the Kid, single shot, Stevens, 1940s, 6¾", G- 120.00
Border Patrol, automatic, Kilgore, 1935, 4½", VG 65.00
Buc-A-Roo, single shot, Kilgore, 1940, 7¾", M 100.00
Buffalo Bill, single shot, Kenton, 1930, 13½", rare, VG 550.00
Buffalo Bill, single shot, Stevens, 1890, 11¾", rare, G- 235.00
Bulldog, single shot, Hubley, 1935, 6", G 35.00
Bunker Hill, single shot, National, 1925, 5¼", M 95.00
Captain, automatic, Kilgore, 1940, 4¼", VG 65.00
Champ, automatic, star medallion, Hubley, 1940, 5", EX 100.00
Chief, single shot, Dent, 1935, 7½", VG 110.00
Colt, single shot, Stevens, 1900, 5½", EX 75.00
Colt Detective Special, Hubley Authentic Gun Replicas, MIB ..375.00
Cowboy, Hubley, 1940, 8", VG 85.00
Cowboy King, Stevens, 1940, 9", M 350.00
Dick, automatic, Hubley, 1930, 4⅛", VG 45.00
Doughboy, automatic, Kilgore, 1920, 4⅞", VG 100.00
Eagle, single shot, Hubley, 1935, 8½", VG 155.00
G-Man, automatic, Kilgore, 1935, 6", rare, M 185.00
Gene Autry, Dummy, 1940, 8⅜", rare, M 325.00
Gene Autry, eng, Kenton, 1940, 6½", rare, VG 500.00
Gene Autry, repeater, NP, Kenton, 1940, 8¾", VG 220.00
Invincible, Kilgore, 1935, 5¼", G- 45.00
Lasso Em Bill, revolving cylinder, Kilgore, 1930, 9", EX 275.00
Lawmaker, NP, Kenton, 1940, 8¾", rare, M 250.00
Lone Eagle, revolving cylinder, Kilgore, 1930, 5¼", EX 150.00
Mohican, single shot, Dent, 1930, 5¼", EX 85.00
National Automatic, National, 1915, 3¾", G- 25.00
Officer's Pistol, automatic, Kilgore, 1940, 5", rare, M 350.00
Pawnee Bill, Stevens, 1940, 7⅝", VG 235.00
Peacemaker, gold, Stevens, 1940, 8½", M 175.00
Pirate, dbl bbl, Hubley, 1940, 9⅜", M 145.00
Presto, automatic, Kilgore, 1940, 5⅛", VG 65.00
Rodeo, single shot, Hubley, 1940, 7", EX 50.00
Roy Rogers, CI, Kilgore, 1940, 10¼", rare, EX 950.00
Scout, single shot, Stevens, 1890, 7", VG 75.00
Six Shooter, revolving cylinder, Kilgore, 1940, 6½", VG 85.00
Spitfire, automatic, Kilgore, 1940, 4⅝", EX 90.00
Texan, revolving cylinder, 1940, 9¼", M 175.00
Texan Jr, Hubley, 1940, 8⅛", VG 70.00
Trooper Safety, repeater, Kilgore, 1925, 10¼", M 145.00
Warrior, repeater, NP, Kilgore, 1920s, 9", EX 175.00
Wild West, single shot, Kenton, 1920s, 11½", rare, M 285.00
101 Ranch, single shot, Hubley, 1930, 11½", VG 245.00
2 Time, rubber band, Kenton, 1929, 9¼", VG 155.00
2-in-1, rubber band, Stevens, 1930, 9¼", VG 150.00
49-er, Stevens, 1940, 9", M 350.00

Guns: Diecast and Miscellaneous Toy Guns

Alan Ladd, Geo Schmidt, rare, 10¼", EX 325.00
Army 45 Auto, Hubley, 6½", M 85.00
Atomic Disintegrator, space gun, Hubley, 8", VG 285.00
Bonanza, revolving cylinder, Leslie-Henry 44, 10½", M 175.00
Bronco, revolving cylinder, Kilgore, 9½", VG 75.00

Buck'n Bronc, Geo Schmidt, 10½", EX 115.00
Buckle Gun, derringer, Mattel, 3", VG 95.00
Champion, Leslie-Henry, 9", VG 75.00
Cowboy, gold, revolving cylinder, Hubley, 12", rare, EX 250.00
Cowboy, revolving cylinder, Hubley, 12", M 165.00
Cowhand 250, Nichols, 8½", VG 70.00
Coyote, Hubley, 8¼", M 85.00
Dale Evans, jewels, Geo Schmidt, rare, 10½", VG 285.00
Davy Crockett, Flintlock Buffalo Rifle, Hubley, 25", EX 145.00
Deputy, BB, copper grips, Schmidt, sm, 8½", EX 75.00
Fanner 'Shootin' Shell,' bullets, Mattel, 9", M 150.00
Fanner 45 'Shootin' Shell,' Mattel, rare, 11¼", EX 285.00
Fanner 50, NP, Mattel, 10⅝", EX 125.00
G-Man, Sparkling Machine Gun, tin, Marx, 26", VG 145.00
Gene Autry, NP, Leslie-Henry, 9", M 165.00
Gene Autry, revolving cylinder, bullets, Leslie-Henry 44, EX 135.00
Grizzly, revolving cylinder, gold, Kilgore, 10¼", M 225.00
Hawkeye, automatic, Kilgore, 4¼", M 45.00
Hopalong Cassidy, cameo grips, Geo Schmidt, 9", EX 300.00
Hopalong Cassidy, gold, Wyandotte, 9", M 400.00
Hopalong Cassidy, Wyandotte, 9", VG 285.00
Indian Scout Rifle, bullets, Mattel, 30", M 210.00
Lone Ranger, antique bronze, Actoy, 10", VG 175.00
Lone Ranger, tin w/jewel, clicker, Marx, 8", M 75.00
Maires Leg, Winchester Lever-Pistol, Marx, 14", EX 135.00
Marshal, revolving cylinder, bullets, Halco, 10½", M 175.00
Maverick, Leslie-Henry, 10½", VG 130.00
Maverick 45, revolving cylinder, Halco, 11", VG 225.00
Model 61, revolving cylinder, steel-bl finish, Nichols, rare, M ...325.00
Mountie, automatic, Kilgore, 6", M 50.00
Mustang 500, NP, Nichols, 12¼", EX 165.00

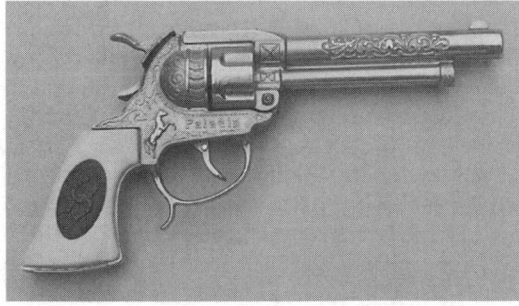

Paladin, Leslie-Henry, nickel finished, very rare character, M, $235.00.

Pioneer, blk grips w/compass, Hubley, 10¼", EX 130.00
Rebel Scattergun, dbl-bbl, Marx, 21", rare, M 500.00
Red Ranger, Wyandotte, 7¾", VG 45.00
Remington 35, revolving cylinder, bullets, Hubley, 8¼", EX 60.00
Ric-O-Shay, revolving cylinder, bullets, Hubley, 12¼", M 175.00
Roy Rogers, copper grips, Geo Schmidt, 10¼", EX 175.00
Roy Rogers, gold, Leslie-Henry, 9", EX 325.00
Roy Rogers, revolving cylinder, eng, Kilgore, 10", M 385.00
Stallion 38, revolving cylinder, bullets, Nichols, 9½", EX 115.00
Stallion 45 Mk II, revolving cylinder, bullets, Nichols, 12", M ..275.00
Texan Jr, diecast, Hubley, 9", VG 40.00
Thundergun, eng, NP, Marx, 12½", M 225.00
Wagon Train, antique bronze, Leslie-Henry 44, 11¼", VG 125.00
Wells Fargo, NP, Actoy, 11", M 155.00
Wild Bill Hickok, Leslie-Henry, 9", VG 75.00
Wild Bill Hickok, Leslie-Henry 44, 11¼", EX 120.00
Winchester Saddle Gun, Mattel, 33", M 185.00

Wyatt Earp, Buntline Special, Actoy, 11", M 155.00
45 Colt, revolving cylinder, ivory grips, NP, Hubley, 14", VG ...125.00

Guns: Early-Style Figural Guns and Bombs (Caution: Reproductions exist.)

Admiral Dewey Bomb, CI, Grey Iron, 1900, 1¾", EX 285.00
Butting Match, CI, Ives, 1885, 5", EX 275.00
Cannon, Kenton, CI, 1900, 4⅞", VG 450.00
Chinese Must Go, CI, Ives, 1880, 4¾", G- 375.00
Clown on Powder Keg, CI, Ives, 1890s, 3¾", VG 385.00
Dbl-Face Man, CI, Ives, 1890, 1⅝", VG 125.00
Devil's Head Bomb, CI, Ives, .22 Blank, 1880, 2¼", VG 250.00
Dog's Head Bomb, CI, Ives, 1880, 2⅛", EX 230.00
George Washington Bomb, CI, 1900, 1¼", EX 285.00
Hobo Bomb, CI, Ideal, 1890s, 2", G- 100.00
Liberty Bell Bomb, CI, 1876, 2⅜", EX 155.00
Lightening Express, Kenton, CI, 1900, 5", EX 575.00
Punch & Judy, CI, Ives, 1880s, 5¼", VG 700.00
Sea Serpent, CI, Stevens, 1890, 3½", EX 900.00
Yel Kid Bomb, CI, Grey Iron, 1900, 1½", VG 155.00

Pedal Cars and Ride-On Toys

#503 Am Fire Chief truck, all orig, EX 125.00
Am National Jordan Roadster, bl w/yel pinstripe, blk fenders, 40" ..3,750.00
BMC Station Wagon, gr pressed steel, silver hubs, 40", EX+ 950.00
Coaster Craft, red pnt w/rear flared fender, red wheels, M 225.00
Dip Side Champion, pedal car, 1950s, rstr 450.00
Gendron Fire Chief's Car, blk & red w/rear tool box, 50" 2,000.00
John Deere #4430, rstr 325.00
Keystone, car, blk & red w/yel trim, butterfly fenders, 43" 550.00
Murray, Atomic Missile, bl & gray pressed steel, 48", NM 1,500.00
Murray T-Bird, dusty rose pressed steel, hard rubber tires, 32" ..1,610.00
Racer, contemporary aluminum body w/side exhaust, 61" 1,500.00
Scooter, gr pnt w/wood footrest, 12x2¾" pneumatic tires, VG ...150.00
Speed Racer, single seat, center hdl pushes to power, 41" 345.00
Steelcraft Mack Dump Truck, red flat-bed w/yel pinstripe, 44" ...1,250.00
Toledo Buick Roadmaster, red & gr w/yel pinstripe, 48" 3,100.00
Triang, R&S Special Race Car, #6 on red pressed steel, 50" 575.00

Penny Toys

Airplane, tin litho w/open cockpit & pilot, 4", EX 120.00
Beetle, on wheels, legs move, Germany, 3", EX 80.00
Boat Tail Racer, red w/goggled driver, Germany, 3", EX 260.00
Boy in Highchair, tin, bottom becomes table, 3", VG 182.00
Cannon, spring-loaded tab shoots cannon, Germany, 2¼", EX 40.00
Carousel, tin litho, Meier/Germany, 1900s, 2½", G 230.00
Dancing couple, pnt wood, Germany, 3½" 30.00
General Omnibus, tin litho w/driver, Fischer/Germany, VG 366.00
Man w/Wheelbarrow, tin litho, pipe in mouth, striding, 3", EX .120.00
Sand Pail, tin litho, children at play, bail hdl, 2½", EX 72.00
Squirrel Cage Whistle, tin litho, whistles & spins, 4½" 165.00
Taxi Cab, tin litho, open car, inertia drive, 3¼", VG+ 275.00
Touring Car, tin litho, w/driver, w/up, Germany, 4", EX 150.00

Pipsqueaks

Pipsqueak toys were popular among the Pennsylvania Germans. The earliest had bellows made from sheepskin. Later cloth replaced the sheepskin, and finally paper bellows were used.

Cat, compo & mohair, glass eyes, silent, 5", G 100.00

Cat seated, pnt papier-mache, rpl bellows, 1880s, 7", NM 920.00
Cat w/kitten, pnt papier-mache, cloth bellows, late 19th C, 6" ..315.00
Cat w/kitten, pnt papier-mache, rpl bellows, 1880s, 7½" 465.00
Cat w/2 kittens, striped flocking, animated mouth, 7", VG 450.00
Chickens in coop, pnt cb & papier-mache, 1880s, 6x4x5", G 545.00
Cockatoo, pnt papier-mache, wood/cloth bellows, 8½" 400.00
Dbl-sided moon face, pnt papier-mache, cloth bellows, 3x2¾" ..715.00

Goat, hide covered with nodding head and squeaker, on painted wood platform with iron wheels, 10½", VG, $700.00.

Goose, papier-mache, mc pnt, spring legs, squeaks, rprs, 6" 150.00
Horse in cage, dapple-gray flannel coat, glass eyes, 9", EX 475.00
Monkey, pnt papier-mache, wood/leather bellows, 4", EX 350.00
Parrot on stump, papier-mache, squeaks, EX color, 4" 145.00
Ram, wood, papier-mache, wooly coat, tin horns, silent, 5" 150.00
Robin on spring & tree trunk, wood/leather bellows, 5x7", NM .860.00
Rooster, papier-mache, orig pnt, silent, EX color, 6¼" 90.00
Rooster, pnt papier-mache/wood, wire spring legs, 13", VG 375.00
Rooster, tin/cb, orig chromolitho, clucks, Stanley, 8", EX 30.00
Rooster in cage, litho paper & wood, 8¼x7x6⅞", VG 140.00
Rooster in house, cloth & feather bird, 6½", VG 200.00
Sheep in cage, wood & paper, silent, 5¾" 150.00
St Bernard w/sleeping child, wood/leather bellows, 4x7", VG .1,000.00

Pull Toys

Bear Pulling Bell, on wheels, compo bear, 7", EX in box 160.00
Cart & 2 figures, CI/steel, 3 bells, rpl axle, 10", VG 385.00
Cow, wood & compo w/wht leather, glass eyes, Germany, 11" ...195.00
Elephant, papier-mache w/orig gray flocking, head nods, 8½" ...195.00
Ewe & lamb, wood & papier-mache w/wooly coats, 5" L 300.00
Goats w/girls on wheeled platform, pnt tin, Am, 6", VG 500.00
Horse, cloth covered, hair for mane & tail, 12½", EX 275.00
Horse, wood & papier-mache, dapple gray pnt, Germany, 8", VG ..55.00
Horse, wood & papier-mache w/mohair covering, 18", EX 250.00
Horse & clown on wagon, steel/CI, worn pnt, bell ringer, 10" ...165.00
Horse & jockey, wood & papier-mache, orig mc pnt, rpr, 6¾" 65.00
Reindeer, tin litho, 4-wheeled platform, Germany, 4", EX 220.00
Roosters (3), pnt papier-mache, wire spring legs, 1880s, 8x10" ..925.00
Sheep, wood/papier-mache/wool, glass eyes/bell, Germany, 7" ...635.00
Tabby Cat, cloth covered, glass eyes, 4 tin wheels, 8", G+ 130.00

Robots

Astro-Scout, Yonezawa, tin litho, friction, 9", EX in box 1,800.00
Atom Robot, KO, bump-&-go action, 1960s, 6½", EX+ 380.00
Fighting Robot, SH, arms swing/chest lights up, 11½", NMIB ...440.00
Gold Robot, Linemar, tin litho, remote control, 6", NMIB 4,100.00
Lavender Robot, Modern Toys, b/o, 14¾", VG 3,500.00
Lost in Space Robot, Remco, bl version, MIB 650.00
Moon Robot, Yonezawa, dk gray, 10¾", EX- in box 3,000.00
Mr Robot, Cragstan, red/blk/clear plastic, b/o, 11", G 225.00
Piston Action Robot, TN, Robby type, remote control, 8¼", NMIB ..1,750.00

Robby Robot Bulldozer, San, friction, 6½", EX **350.00**
Smoking Spaceman, Linemar, mouth puffs smoke, 12", EX **1,900.00**
Space Fighter Robot, SH, b/o, 1960, MIB **195.00**
Space Walk Man, China, w/lights & gun sound, b/o, 12", MIB **60.00**
Television Spaceman, Alps, TV screen in chest, b/o, 13", MIB ..**1,100.00**
Venus Robot, KO, plastic, b/o, remote control, 5½", MIB **170.00**

Schoenhut

Our advisor for Schoenhut Toys is Keith Kaonis, who has collected these toys for nearly twenty years. Because of his involvement with the publishing industry (currently *the Inside COLLECTOR, Antique DOLL World,* and during the eighties, *Collectors' SHOWCASE*), he has visited collections across the United States, produced several articles on Schoenhut toys, and served a term as president of the Schoenhut Collectors' Club. Keith is listed in the Directory under New York.

Value ranges represent items in only fair condition (by the low end) up to those in good to very good condition, i.e., very minor scratches and wear, good original finish, no splits chips, no excessive paint wear or cracked eyes, and, of course, completeness. Animals with painted eyes in fair condition are represented by the low side of the range; use the high side to evaluate glass-eyed animals in very good condition.

Humpty Dumpty Circus Clowns and Other Personnel

Clowns with two-part heads (a cast face applied to a wooden head) were made from 1903-1915 and are most desirable — condition always is important. There have been nine distinct styles in fourteen different costumes recorded. Only eight costume styles apply to the two-part headed clowns. The later clowns, ca. 1920, had one-part heads whose features were pressed and they were no longer tied at the wrists and ankles.

Black Dude, reduced sz, $300 to **600.00**
Black Dude, 1-part head, purple coat, $250 to **800.00**
Black Dude, 2-part head, blk coat, $500 to **800.00**
Chinese Acrobat, 1-part head, $300 to **600.00**
Chinese Acrobat, 2-part head, rare, $500 to **1,000.00**
Clown, early, G, $150 to **500.00**
Clown, reduced sz, 1926-35, $75 to **150.00**
Gent Acrobat, bsk head, rare, $300 to **600.00**
Gent Acrobat, 1-part head, $500 to **900.00**
Gent Acrobat, 2-part head, very rare, $800 to **1,200.00**
Hobo, reduced sz, $300 to **600.00**
Hobo, 1-part head, $200 to **500.00**
Hobo, 2-part head, curved-up toes, $700 to **1,200.00**
Hobo, 2-part head, facet toe ft, $400 to **800.00**
Lady Acrobat, bsk head, $300 to **500.00**
Lady Acrobat, 1-part head, $200 to **400.00**
Lady Rider, bsk head, $250 to **500.00**
Lady Rider, 1-part head, $200 to **400.00**
Lady Rider, 2-part head, very rare, $700 to **1,200.00**
Later, ca 1916-20, $100 to **250.00**
Lion Trainer, bsk head, rare, $350 to **600.00**
Lion Trainer, 1-part head, $250 to **500.00**
Lion Trainer, 2-part head, early, very rare, $600 to **1,200.00**
Ring Master, bsk, ca 1912-14, $450 to **650.00**
Ring Master, 1-part head, $200 to **450.00**
Ring Master, 2-part head, early, very rare, $500 to **1,200.00**

Humpty Dumpty Circus Animals

Humpty Dumpty Circus animals with glass eyes, ca. 1903-1914, are more desirable and can demand much higher prices than the later painted-eye versions. As a general rule, a glass-eye version is 30% to 40% more than a painted-eye version. (There are exceptions.) The following list suggests values for both GE (glass eye) and PE (painted eye) versions and reglects a low PE price to a high GE price.

There are other variations and nuances of certain figures: Bulldog – white with black spots or brindle (brown), open-and closed-mouth zebras and giraffes; ball necks and hemispherical necks on some animals such as the pig, leopard, and tiger to name a few. These points can affect the price and should be judged individually.

Arabian camel, glass eyes, open mouth, 8", G, $450.00; Giraffe, glass eyes, leather ears, cord tail, 11", VG, $700.00.

Alligator, GE/PE, $200 to **650.00**
Arabian Camel, 1 hump, GE/PE, $250 to **750.00**
Bactrian Camel, 2 humps, GE/PE, $200 to **1,500.00**
Brown Bear, GE/PE, $200 to **900.00**
Buffalo, cloth mane, GE/PE, $300 to **700.00**
Buffalo, cvd mane, GE/PE, $200 to **1,200.00**
Bulldog, GE/PE, $400 to **1,600.00**
Burro (made to go w/chariot & clown), GE/PE, $200 to **700.00**
Cat, GE/PE, rare, $600 to **3,000.00**
Cow, GE/PE, $250 to **1,000.00**
Deer, GE/PE, $300 to **1,000.00**
Donkey, GE/PE, $75 to **200.00**
Donkey w/blanket, GE/PE, $90 to **300.00**
Elephant, GE/PE, $90 to **300.00**
Elephant w/blanket, GE/PE, $200 to **500.00**
Gazelle, GE/PE, rare, $700 to **3,000.00**
Giraffe, GE/PE, $200 to **700.00**
Goat, GE/PE, $150 to **400.00**
Goose, PE only, $200 to **600.00**
Gorilla, PE only, $1200 to **2,500.00**
Hippo, GE/PE, $300 to **1,000.00**
Horse, brn, saddle & stirrups, GE/PE, $150 to **400.00**
Horse, wht, platform, GE/PE, $125 to **400.00**
Hyena, GE/PE, very rare, $1,000 to **3,700.00**
Kangaroo, GE/PE, $400 to **1,400.00**
Leopard, GE/PE, $350 to **800.00**
Lion, cloth mane, GE, $500 to **1,200.00**
Lion, cvd mane, GE/PE, $250 to **2,000.00**
Monkey, 1-part head, PE only, $250 to **450.00**
Monkey, 2-part head, wht face, $300 to **900.00**
Ostrich, GE/PE, $200 to **850.00**
Pig, 5 versions, GE/PE, $200 to **900.00**
Polar Bear, GE/PE, $500 to **1,800.00**
Poodle, cloth mane, GE only, $300 to **600.00**
Poodle, GE/PE, $125 to **300.00**
Rabbit, GE/PE, very rare, $1,000 to **4,000.00**
Rhino, GE/PE, $250 to **1,200.00**
Sea lion, GE/PE, $400 to **1,000.00**
Sheep (lamb) w/bell, GE/PE, $200 to **750.00**
Tiger, GE/PE, $250 to **900.00**
Wolf, GE/PE, very rare, $600 to **4,000.00**
Zebra, GE/PE, $250 to **1,000.00**
Zebu, GE/PE, rare, $1,000 to **3,000.00**

Humpty Dumpty Circus Accessories

There are many accessories: wagons, tents, ladders, chairs, pedestals, tight rope, weights, and more.

Menagerie tent, early, ca 1904, $1,800 to	**2,500.00**
Menagerie tent, later, ca 1914-20, $1,200 to	**2,000.00**
Oval lithographed tent, 1926, $3,000 to	**4,000.00**
Side show panels, 1926, pr, $3,000 to	**4,000.00**

Steiff

Margaret Steiff began making her felt stuffed toys in Germany in the late 1800s. The animals she made were tagged with an elephant in a circle. Her first teddy bear, made in 1903, became such a popular seller that she changed her tag to a bear. Felt stuffing was replaced with excelsior and wool; when it became available, foam was used. In addition to the tag, look for the 'Steiff' ribbon and the button inside the ear. For further information we recommend *Teddy Bears and Steiff Animals*, a full-color identification and value guide by Margaret Fox Mandel, available from Collector Books or your public library. See also Teddy Bears.

Bambi, w/tags & buttons, raised letters, 6", M	**75.00**
Bessy the Cow, w/udders, orig collar & bell, 1950s, 9", M	**300.00**
Boar, plastic tusks, no ID, 1950s, 8", VG	**160.00**
Camel on Wheels, felt & mohair, ear button, 1913, 9¾", VG	**1,200.00**
Cat Hand Puppet, plush w/glass eyes, 1950s, 8½", EX	**75.00**
Cockie Spaniel Hand Puppet, plush, w/tag, 1950s, M	**125.00**
Diggey Badger, standing, w/tags & buttons, 4", M	**125.00**
Donkey, mohair, blk mane, straw stuffed, button eyes, 8½x11"	**175.00**
Duck, w/button & tag, 1950s, 5", M	**85.00**
Floppy Kitty, asleep, w/tags & buttons, 1950s, M	**150.00**
Foxy Hand Puppet, plush, w/tag, 1950s, M	**155.00**
Froggy Hand Puppet, plush, w/tag & button, 1950s, M	**125.00**
Gaty Alligator Hand Puppet, plush, w/tag, 1950s, M	**165.00**
Golden Age of Circus Set, 6 animals, ear button, 5 wagons, MIB	**3,000.00**
Goose, w/button & tag, 4½", M	**145.00**
Jocko, w/tags & buttons, 1950s, 12", M	**295.00**
Lady Bug on Wheels, mohair, 1950s, 19", M	**495.00**
Leo the Lion Hand Puppet, plush w/tag & button, M	**150.00**
Lion, laying, mohair, glass eyes, ear button, 1950s, 15", EX	**250.00**
Lion, standing, w/button, 4", EX	**125.00**
Lion on Wheels, ca 1920, 26", G+, from $1,450 to	**1,800.00**
Mimic Dally Dalmatian Arm Puppet, plush, w/tag, 1950s, M	**395.00**
Molly Dog, sitting, w/tags & buttons, 10½"	**550.00**
Nagy Beaver, w/tags & buttons, 1950s, 4", M	**145.00**
Niki Rabbit, w/tags & buttons, 1950s, 7", M	**496.00**
Paddy Walrus, w/tags & buttons, 1950s, 5", M	**250.00**
Pomeranian on Wheels, w/tags & buttons, 4", M	**145.00**
Raudi the Dog, orig collar & tag, VG	**145.00**
Spidey, mohair, glass eyes, w/tags & buttons, 1960s, 4", M	**595.00**
Squirrel w/Nut, red, w/tags & buttons, 7", M	**135.00**
Tiger, laying, w/tags & buttons, 1950s, 12", M	**285.00**
Zebra, standing, velvet, w/tags & buttons, 1950s, 5", M	**150.00**

Toy Soldiers and Accessories

Unique to this country are what are called 'Dimestore' soldiers; they were made by various companies from the 1930s and until sometime in the 1950s. The most common are Barclay, Manoil, and Jones (hollow cast lead); Grey Iron (cast iron); and Auburn (rubber). They're about 4" to 4½" high. They were sold in Woolworth's and Kresge's 5 & 10 Stores (most for just five cents), hence the name 'Dimestore.' Marx made tin soldiers for use in target gun games; these sell for about $4.00.

Condition is most important as these toys were made to play with. They're most often found with much of the paint worn off. In the listings that follow, prices are for examples in excellent condition which means they show very little wear. Please remember that these pieces are only representative. There were over six hundred made, plus a number of others by minor makers such as Tommy Toy and All-Nu, all of which are higher priced. Serious collectors should to refer to *Collecting Toys* (1993) or *Toy Soldiers* (1992), both by Richard O'Brien, Books Americana, Inc. Reference numbers are those used in O'Brien's books and are considered the standard for the hobby. Another very popular toy soldier has been made by Britains of England since 1893. They are smaller and more detailed than 'Dimestores,' and variants number in the thousands. O'Brien's 'Toy Soldier' book has over two hundred pages devoted to Britains and other foreign makers.

Britains, #1436 Italian Infantry marching at the slope in foreign dress with pith helmets, 1936-41, rare, EX in EX- box, $800.00.

Auburn Rubber, bugler, early version,	**25.00**
Auburn Rubber, Marmon-Harrington tank, 3¼"	**38.00**
Auburn Rubber, soldier, gun tip intact, early version	**49.00**
Auburn Rubber, soldier, plane shooter	**55.00**
Auburn Rubber, soldier marching, port arms, early version	**19.00**
Barclay, #1 cannon, 1st Barclay toy made	**68.00**
Barclay, AA gunner, brn	**14.00**
Barclay, AA gunner, cast helmet	**25.00**
Barclay, AA gunner (podfoot), red	**98.00**
Barclay, aircraft carrier, 2 orig planes	**135.00**
Barclay, Army truck, open bed, no decals, ca 1960	**15.00**
Barclay, Austin Coupe, metal wheels, ca 1931	**39.00**
Barclay, aviator (podfoot), brn	**19.00**
Barclay, Barclay, navy officer, long stride	**21.00**
Barclay, beer truck, red & wht tires, no barrels, mk #376	**45.00**
Barclay, boy	**15.00**
Barclay, boy, red & tan	**17.00**
Barclay, boy skater	**12.00**
Barclay, brakeman	**7.00**
Barclay, bugler, brn	**18.00**
Barclay, bugler, gr	**21.00**
Barclay, bull, brn & blk	**15.00**
Barclay, cadet, short stride, tiny flaw	**18.00**
Barclay, conductor	**9.00**
Barclay, delivery van	**29.00**
Barclay, engineer	**9.00**
Barclay, firefighter w/hose	**28.00**
Barclay, girl, rare	**16.00**
Barclay, girl in rocker	**19.00**
Barclay, girl skater, bl	**21.00**
Barclay, groom	**21.00**
Barclay, hobo	**9.00**
Barclay, Indian on horse	**30.00**
Barclay, knight w/shield	**20.00**

Barclay, machine gunner 17.00
Barclay, male passenger 12.00
Barclay, marine 20.00
Barclay, marksman, gr 19.00
Barclay, monoplane, single engine 99.00
Barclay, navy officer, short stride 15.00
Barclay, newsboy 9.00
Barclay, officer, brn 21.00
Barclay, old man w/cane 16.00
Barclay, plane (sm Lindy-type), tin prop, metal wheels 85.00
Barclay, policeman 9.00
Barclay, porter w/whisk broom 20.00
Barclay, redcap 9.00
Barclay, Santa (sm) on red sled 39.00
Britains, #101, Band...in State Dress, 12-pc, NMIB 475.00
Britains, #115, Egyptian Cavalry, MIB 250.00
Britains, #2, Royal Horse Guards, 1935, 5-pc, Whisstock box 170.00
Britains, #24, 9th Queen's Royal Lancers, 5-pc, NMIB 200.00
Britains, #312, Grenadier Guards, 8-pc, NMIB 180.00
Britains, #35, Royal Marines, 1940, 8-pc, EX in Whisstock box .200.00
Britains, #47, Skinner's Horse, 5-pc, EX in G box 180.00
Britains, #80, 1st Bombay Lancers, 1910, 15-pc, G in G- box 850.00
Courtenay, Archbishop of Sens, position 4, sgn, EX 375.00
Courtenay, Edward, The Black Prince, position H6, VG 750.00
Courtenay, King Edward III, position 6, sgn, EX 550.00
Courtenay, King John of France, position 1, sgn, EX 400.00
Courtenay, Vicomte Rochechouart, position 12, VG 400.00
Dinky, #150D, driver 28.00
Dinky, #152 B, reconaissance car 85.00
Dinky, #160B, gunner, seated 22.00
Dinky, #603, army private 13.00
Dinky, #612, commando jeep, all metal, MIB 55.00
Dinky, #621, 3-ton Army wagon, M 65.00
Dinky, #642, pressure refueler, EX 75.00
Dinky, #666, Corporal missile, MIB 450.00
Dinky, #680, Ferret scout car, MIB 40.00
Dinky, #692, Leopard tank, MIB 80.00
Dinky, #822, M-3 halftrack, NM 75.00
Dinky, #826, Berliet wrecker, M 175.00
Grey Iron, cowboy, NM 26.00
Grey Iron, girl skater, ca 1920s, very scarce 145.00
Grey Iron, gunner, EX 9.00
Grey Iron, pirate boy 'Ji' 34.00
Grey Iron, US Doughboy charging, early version 16.00
Grey Iron, US machine gunner, prewar 20.00
Manoil, cadet, NM 28.00
Manoil, carpenter sawing lumber, NM 37.00
Manoil, cow grazing, NM 15.00
Manoil, farmer sharpening scythe, NM 26.00
Manoil, flagbearer, skinny, NM 32.00
Manoil, hound, NM 24.00
Manoil, lady w/pie, NM 31.00
Manoil, observer, NM 34.00
Manoil, tommy gunner, NM 28.00

Trade Signs

Trade signs were popular during the 1800s. They were usually made in an easily recognizable shape that one could mentally associate with the particular type of business it was to represent, especially appropriate in the days when many customers could not read!

Boot w/spur, bootmaker, metal, w/ornate bracket 1,045.00

Bootmaker, boots, red & blk pnt wood, 19th C, 36", EX 460.00
Eyeglasses, pnt wood & glass, 13x39", VG 1,500.00
Fireman's stovepipe parade hat, pnt wood, 28", NM 9,800.00
Ice cream cone, copper/stainless steel, 34x13", VG+ 225.00
Mortar & pestle, cvd wood, gilt pnt, 19th C, 38" 430.00
Pig (realistic), pnt tin, 19th C, 16x35" 3,100.00
Pocket watch, CI & zinc, G mc pnt, 19th C, 36" 865.00
Pretzel, cvd wood, old gold pnt, 20½" L 1,000.00
Rampant lion/3 stars relief-cvd on dmn shape, rpt, 33" 165.00
Shoes, pnt wood, Am, late 1800s, 47½" 630.00
Slide rule, pnt wood, 13x77x2", VG 200.00
Stagecoach scene, Tally-Ho-Rest (tavern), pnt wood, 28x34" ...2,585.00
Tavern name/eagle in shield, pnt wood, late 1700s, 62x27" 5,175.00

Tramp Art

'Tramp' is considered a type of folk art. In America it was primarily made from the end of the Civil War through the 1930s, though it employs carving and decorating methods which are much older, originating mostly in Germany and Scandinavia. 'Trampen' probably refers to the itinerant stages of Middle Ages craft apprenticeship. The carving techniques were also used for practice. Tramp art was perpetuated by soldiers in the Civil War and primarily practiced where there was a plentiful and free supply of materials such as cigar boxes and fruit crates. The belief that this work was done by tramps and hobos as payment for room or meals is generally incorrect. The larger pieces especially would have required a lengthy stay in one place.

There is a great variety of tramp art, from boxes and frames which are most common to large pieces of furniture and intricate objects. The most common method of decoration is chip carving with several layers built one on top of another. There are several variations of that form as well as others such as 'Crown of Thorns,' an interlocking method, which are completely different. The most common finishes were lacquer or stain, although paints were also used. The value of tramp art varies according to size, detail, surface, and complexity. The new collector should be aware that tramp art is being made today. While some sell it as new, others are offering it as old. In addition, many people mistakenly use the term as a catchall phrase to refer to other forms of construction — expecially things they are uncertain about. Our advisor is Matt Lippa; he is listed in the Directory under Alabama.

Box, even pyramiding, lady's photo on top, gold pnt, sm 160.00
Box, lift-top, ped ft, EX chromos under lid/base, varnish 195.00
Box, rectangular pyramiding, EX finish, mirror under lid 275.00

Shaving box, notch-carved wooden strips applied overall, razor and leaf design on front, brass-hinged lid, 9x16½x9½", EX, $325.00.

Box, traveling; complex cvgs, brass hdl, mirror, 8-sided 625.00
Cabinet, corner; chip-cvd, 1-brd front, overhang top, 1890s 235.00
Chest, 3-drw, ceramic knobs, overhang top, mini 450.00
Clock case, fretwork crest w/cvd flag/sword, 2-drw, varnish 1,850.00
Comb box, notch-cvd layered rosettes, porc knobs, 10x9x4½" 85.00
Corner shelf, cut-out shapes in bl, 2-shelf, lt gr pnt 325.00

Frame, shield shape w/pyramiding on gold base, varnished 235.00
Frame, sq & hex pyramids, orig finish, rpl mirror 425.00
Frame, triangular stick style w/mirrors, gold pnt 150.00
Frame, 8 steep layers, smooth top layer, EX patina 170.00
Medicine cabinet, crest & pyramid medallions, mirror, lg 1,100.00
Plant stand, layered X stretcher, lollipop finial, mustard pnt 400.00

Traps

Though of interest to collectors for many years, trap collecting has gained in popularity over the past ten years in particular, causing prices to appreciate rapidly. Traps are usually marked on the pan as to manufacturer, and the condition of these trademarks are important when determining their value. Grading is as follows:

Good: one-half of pan legible.
Very Good: legible in entirety, but light.
Fine: legible in entirety, with strong lettering.
Mint: in like-new, shiny condition.

Our advisor for this category is Boyd Nedry; he is listed in the Directory under Michigan. Prices listed here are for traps in fine condition.

Acme, Shann Mfg Co, mousetrap 20.00
Alaskin, The Wolf Trap, dbl coil spring 95.00
Alexander Crosby & Sons, pan model 35.00
Ampco, self-setting gopher trap 18.00
Auto Set, wood snap, rat trap 8.00
Baby Stinky, metal, fly trap 20.00
Basic, wood snap, mousetrap 6.00

Bear trap, ca 1900, 8x19", EX, $185.00.

Better Mouse Trap, McGill Co, wood snap 7.00
Blake & Lamb, #2 dbl long spring 15.00
Bullock, automatic self-setter 250.00
Clayton, killer trap 135.00
Cooper #2, clutch trap 65.00
Cortland #1, dbl jaw, dogless, single spring 100.00
Crago #7, clutch trap 650.00
CW Choghill, fruit jar fly trap 35.00
Death Grip, Brooklin MI, mole trap 45.00
Delusion, tin & wood, self-setting mousetrap 45.00
Diamond #21, single long spring 8.00
Dwight #0, dogless, single spring 350.00
Easy Setting, wood, 4-hole choker, mousetrap 22.00
Eclipse #2 under spring 40.00
Economy #2, dbl long spring 34.00
Elechik #1½", coil spring 25.00
Electrocuter, blk plastic, mousetrap 40.00
Evans Mouse & Fish, brass 300.00
EZ Trap, Toledo OH, mole trap 35.00
Family Mousetrap, self-set live trap 30.00
Fut-Set, metal, rat trap 15.00
Gabriel Fish & Game 80.00
Gibbs Gladiator, metal, rat trap 20.00

Gibbs King Bee #1 ....20.00
Gibbs Two Trigger 8.00
Good, wood snap, mousetrap 9.00
Handforged #5, bear trap 250.00
Helfrich #750, coil spring 95.00
Herters #41AX, bear trap 535.00
Holdfast, wood snap, mousetrap 6.00
Jillson, brass, spear type, rat trap 135.00
Katch Kwik, wood snap, rat trap 15.00
Kliflock, killer trap 50.00
Kwik Grip #1, coil spring 7.00
Lastword, Booth Mfg Co, mousetrap 30.00
Little Giant, fly trap 25.00
Master Built, wood snap, mousetrap 5.00
Mouse Buffet, fruit jar, mousetrap 20.00
Never Miss, wood snap, rat trap 10.00
Newhouse, gopher trap 8.00
Newhouse #1, long spring 15.00
Newhouse #4, dbl spring 35.00
Newhouse #4½, dbl long spring, wolf trap 125.00
Newhouse #6, Oneida Community NY, bear trap 750.00
Northwoods #1½, coil spring 4.00
Old Tom, Detroit MI, fruit jar, mousetrap 25.00
Oneida Community #12, w/teeth, under spring 50.00
Orvis Glass Minnow Trap 85.00
Out-O-Sight, wood snap, mousetrap 15.00
Phillips Specialties, gopher trap 32.00
PS&W #4, dbl long spring 35.00
Quigley, Van Camp Hwd Co, wood snap, mousetrap 10.00
Rice Improved Conibear 20.00
Roy, gopher trap 18.00
Runway, metal, mousetrap 22.00
Stand-By, wood snap, rat trap 8.00
Step-Ease Better, wood snap, mousetrap 8.00
Stop Thief #2, killer trap 15.00
Teeter, gopher trap 35.00
Terror, metal snap, mousetrap 40.00
Unique, plastic, coon trap 20.00
Victor, selective action, wood snap, rat trap 6.00
Wiggington Mouse Destroyer, wht plastic 20.00
Wire cage, dome shape, live mousetrap 25.00
Woodward Death Clamp, 4" sz 40.00
X-Terminator, plastic, live mousetrap 6.00
Yankee, Plymouth MI, mole trap 50.00
Ymir, mink & martin trap 20.00

Trivets

Although strictly a decorative item today, the original purpose of the trivet was much more practical. They were used to protect table tops from hot serving dishes, and irons heated on the kitchen range were placed on trivets during use to protect work surfaces. The first patent date was 1869; many of the earliest trivets bore portraits of famous people or patriotic designs. Florals, birds, animals, and fruit were other favored motifs. Watch for remakes of early original designs. Some of these are marked Wilton, Emig, Wright, Iron Art, and V.M. for Virginia Metalcrafters. However, many of these reproductions are becoming collectible in the '90s. Expect to pay considerably less for these than for the originals, since they are abundant.

Brass

Heart & dmn cutouts, 3 trn ft, 9" L 95.00

Heart shape, 3 cylindrical ft, polished top, 7½" 110.00
Man O' War racehorse 70.00
Rnd w/rtcl top, 7½" dia 25.00
Tilt-top tea table form, 6 heart cutouts in center, 12" 400.00
4 hearts & 2 dmns, 8¾" 120.00

Cast Iron

Floral w/star hdl, 9" 72.50
George Washington portrait, 9½" L 75.00
Midget, 4" dia 65.00
8-point star w/2 hearts & 2 birds, pnt traces, 8¾" 70.00

Wrought Iron

Hand shape, ftd, lt rust, 9" 170.00
Heart shape, appl legs, 7¾" 270.00
Heart shape, appl rnd ft, 5¼" 140.00
Heart shape w/scrollwork, scrolled hdl, sq ft, 10" 190.00
Heart shape w/scrollwork, trn wood hdl, 10½" 160.00
Rectangle of 4 crimped bars, flattened ft, 8¼" 55.00
Shield shape, ftd, 6¾" 35.00
Shield shape, long iron hdl w/ball finial, 11⅞" 55.00
Shield shape, trn wood hdl, 11⅜" 70.00
Shield shape w/sides bent down to form ft, 10½" 45.00

Trolls

    The first trolls to come to the United States were molded after a 1952 design by Marti and Helena Kuuskoski of Tampere, Finland. The first trolls to be mass produced in America were molded from wood carvings made by Thomas Dam of Denmark. As the demand for these trolls increased, several U.S. manufacturers were licensed to produce them. The most noteworthy of these were Uneeda Doll Company's Wishnik line and Inga Dykins Scandia House True Trolls. Thomas Dam continued to import his Dam Things line. Today trolls are enjoying a renaissance as baby boomers try to recapture their childhood. As a result, values are rising.

    The troll craze from the '60s spawned many items other than troll dolls such as wall plaques, salt and pepper shakers, pins, squirt guns, rings, clay trolls, lamps, Halloween costumes, animals, lawn ornaments, coat racks, notebooks, folders, and even a car.

    In the '70s, '80s, and '90s new trolls were produced. While these trolls are collectible to some, the avid troll collector still prefers those produced in the '60s. Remember trolls must be in mint condition to receive top dollar. For more information we recommend *Collector's Guide to Trolls, ID and Values*, by Pat Peterson. Our advisor for this category is Roger Inouye; he is listed in the Directory under California.

Cow with white hair and blue eyes, Dam Things, 3½", $45.00.

Blue Ugly, elephant, blk rabbit fur hair, poseable head, 3½" 25.00
Caveman, gr eyes, yel hair, Dam, 1964, 12" 135.00

Cheerleader, vinyl pnt body, plastic eyes, Dam, 1964, 2½" 18.00
Common, 10" 50.00
Common, 12" 60.00
Common, 15" minimum 80.00
Common, 2½-3", minimum 15.00
Common, 4", from $20 to 25.00
Common, 7", from $30 to 40.00
Dbl-Nik Clown, red & wht hair, wht shoes, red & wht costume ..55.00
Doll-face, side-glancing eyes, curly coarse hair, 7" 20.00
Fuzz ball, bl mohair, wood eyes, Made in Sweden, 5" 25.00
German character, nodder, gray body, inset eyes, paper sticker 60.00
Giraffe, amber gold eyes, blond hair, mk Dam, 12" 100.00
Girl w/accordion, A/S NyForm, #118, gray hair, gapped teeth 50.00
Good Night, amber eyes, (blk around right), pk hair, Wishnik, 5" .20.00
Guardian, brn body, dk amber eyes, shield protects chest, 7" 40.00
Here Comes the Judge, gold eyes, orange hair, Judge's shirt, 6" 50.00
Horse, softer vinyl, 1990 Limited Edition, Dam, 6½" 70.00
Hula-Nik, yel eyes, gold hair, hula skirt, Wishnik, 5" 30.00
Iggy-normous, sailor, amber eyes, blond mohair, 1964, Dam, 12" ...150.00
Lion, nodder, soft dk hair, inset eyes, 4x6½" 50.00
Pencil holder, bl w/gold-trim uniform, gray beard, blk hat, 4" 2.00
Robin Hood, bow, quiver w/arrows, red hair, brn eyes, mk Russ 9.00
Rock-Nik, brn eyes, gr hair, cb guitar, Hong Kong, 5" 20.00
Seal, brn body, wht chest, dk amber eyes, Norfin, 6½" 50.00
Shekter, monkey w/lace diaper, wht hair, inset amber eyes, 3" 40.00
Troll car, rare 98.00
Turtle, gr shell, bank, Norfin, 4" 50.00
Whale, plastic, bl eyes, blk w/gray chest, Norfin, 5" 50.00
Wiley Fox, w/international passport, mohair, plastic eyes, 7" 60.00
Wooden body, pnt eyes, rope arms, 7" 14.00

Trunks

    The first use of the term 'trunk' can be traced back to Egyptian times, when hollowed-out tree sections were used to transport goods of commerce. In the the days of steamboat voyages, stagecoach journeys, and railroad travel, trunks were used to transport clothing and personal belongings.

    The most desirable trunks are flat-tops, 24" to 38" long, from the late 1800s, preferably in restored condition. Embossed dome-tops (rounded on top to better accommodate milady's finery) from the 1880s, 24" to 38" long, in complete original condition are very desirable as well. On the other hand, ca 1870s flush tin trunks, even in mint condition, inspire very little collector interest.

    Unless the trunk is complete (retaining all original trays and compartments), its value is considerably lessened. If parts are absent or broken, the trunk is judged incomplete. All interiors differ; some had upper-lid compartments, others did not. Our advisor is Doris Harroff; she is listed in the Directory under Indiana.

Dome-top, emb decor, 1880s, 24" to 38", complete, $75 to 175.00
Flat-top, orig, 1880-1900, 24" to 38", complete, $75 to 125.00
Flat-top, orig, 1880-1900, 24" to 38", complete, rstr, $300 to 425.00
Leather trim w/brass tacks on pine, 19x10x9" 110.00
Stagecoach, flat or dome, pre-1860s, 24" to 38", rstr, up to 475.00

Tuthill

    The Tuthill Glass Company operated in Middletown, New York, from 1902 to 1923. Collectors look for signed pieces and those in an identifiable pattern. Condition is of utmost importance, and examples with brilliant cutting and intaglio (natural flowers and fruits) combined fetch the highest prices.

Bowl, cosmos/hobstars, 3¼x8" 150.00
Bowl, intaglio mums/leaves, shaped rim, 4½x9" 345.00
Bowl, vintage intaglio w/in hobnail gallery, oval, 9¾" 575.00
Bread tray, vintage intaglio, hobstars, 9¾x7" 750.00
Cake plate, hobstars, X-hatching, X-cut fans, low std, 10" 400.00
Compote, hobstars/X-hatching/fans, notched rim, rayed base, 6" ...235.00
Plate, wild rose intaglio, 8¼" 275.00
Vase, flashed hobstars in ped ft, fan form, 11½" 900.00

Typewriters

The first commercially successful typewriter was the Sholes and Glidden, introduced in 1874. By 1882 other models appeared, and by the 1890s dozens were on the market. At the time of the First World War, the ranks of typewriter-makers thinned, and by the 1920s only a few survived.

Collectors informally divide typewriter history into the pioneering period, up to about 1890; the classic period, from 1890 to 1920; and the modern period, since 1920. There are two broad classifications of early typewriters: (1) Keyboard machines, in which depression of a key prints a character and via a shift key prints up to three different characters per key; (2) Index machines, in which a chart of all the characters appears on the typewriter; the character is selected by a pointer or dial and is printed by operation of a lever or other device. Even though index typewriters were simpler and more primitive than keyboard machines, they were none-the-less a later development, designed to provide a cheaper alternative to the standard keyboard models that were selling for upwards of $100.00. Eventually second-hand keyboard typewriters supplied the low-price customer, and index typewriters vanished except as toys. Both classes of typewriters appeared in a great many designs.

It is difficult, if not impossible, to assign standard market prices to early typewriters. Unlike postage stamps, carnival glass, etc., few people collect typewriters, so there is no active marketplace from which to draw stable prices. Also, condition is a very important factor, and typewriters can vary infinitely in condition. A third factor to consider is that an early typewriter achieves its value mainly through the skill, effort, and patience of the collector who restores it to its original condition, in which case its purchase price is insignificant. Some unusual-looking early typewriters are not at all rare or valuable, while some very ordinary-looking ones are scarce and could be quite valuable. No general rules apply. When no condition is indicated, the items listed below are assumed to be in excellent, unrestored condition. Our advisor for this category is Mike Brooks; he is listed in the Directory under California.

Blinkensderfer Electric, 1903 ....2,000.00
Boston, index 2,000.00
Crandall 400.00
Crown, index 500.00
Edland, index 750.00
Fitch 700.00
Ford 900.00
Hall, index, EX 700.00
McCool #Z 350.00
Mignon Model 4, index, EX 195.00
Niagara, index 875.00
O'Dell's, rnd, 1890 ....975.00
Oliver #9, overhead, 1912 ....295.00
Peoples, index 250.00
Rapid 450.00
Royal #10, 1922, EX 50.00
Smith-Corona #4, portable, 1920s, EX in case 50.00
Standard Visible Writer, old upright keys, NM 85.00
World, index, EX 200.00

Uhl Pottery

Founded in Evansville, Indiana, in 1849 by German immigrants, the Uhl Pottery was moved to Huntingburg, Indiana, in 1908 because of the more suitable clay available there. They produced stoneware — Acorn Ware jugs, crocks, and bowls — which were marked with the acorn logo and 'Uhl Pottery.' They also made mugs, pitchers, and vases in simple shapes and solid glazes marked with a circular ink stamp containing the name of the pottery and 'Huntingburg, Indiana.' The pottery closed in the mid-1940s. Those seeking additional information about Uhl pottery are encouraged to contact the Uhl Collectors' Society, whose address is listed in the Directory under Clubs, Newsletters, and Catalogs.

Ashtray, acorn, brn 250.00
Ashtray, pig, blk 175.00
Bowl, batter; bl, 8" 95.00
Bowl, mixing; reverse pyramid, bl, 9" 75.00
Bowl, salad; bl, 9" 95.00
Casserole, bl, #528, mk, 5-pt 70.00
Cookie jar, yel, #522 ....80.00
Dog feeder, wht, #130 ....110.00
Flowerpot, bl, ribbed, 5" 75.00
Frog, gr, 6" 260.00
Jar, Acorn Ware, 8-gal 95.00
Jug, Acorn Ware, brn/wht, 2-gal 45.00
Jug, Acorn Ware, brn/wht, 5-gal 70.00
Jug, Baseball, wht, mini 75.00

Jug, blue ball form, 6½", $125.00.

Jug, Egyptian, bl, #125, 25-oz 75.00
Jug, Elephant, blk 60.00
Jug, Football, brn, 3-oz 45.00
Jug, Merry Christmas, pk/gr, 1941 ....275.00
Jug, Ring, peach, 1-oz 145.00
Jug, Square, brn/wht, 2-oz 25.00
Mug, coffee; pk, mk, 8-oz 55.00
Pitcher, Grape, bl, 1-qt 225.00
Pitcher, Grape, bl, 2-qt 185.00
Pitcher, Grape, bl, 3-qt 195.00
Pitcher, Lincoln, bl, 2-qt 500.00
Plate, chop; gr, 14" 80.00
Roaster, self basting, bl, 11" 195.00
Shoe, Dutch, pk, #2 mk 45.00
Shoe, military boot, blk 60.00
Shoe, slipper, gr 45.00
Stein, tan, mk, 3-oz 125.00
Teapot, bl, #131, 2-cup 285.00
Teapot, bl, #143, 8-cup 260.00
Teapot, yel, #132, 4-cup 140.00
Vase, bl, cut flower, #114, 10" 75.00
Vase, bl, cut flower, mk, #123, 8" 85.00
Vase, bud; wht, 3" 65.00

Vase, pk, cut flower, mk, #113, 8" 55.00

Unger Brothers

Art Nouveau silver of the highest quality were produced by Unger Brothers, who operated in Newark, New Jersey, from the early 1880s until 1909. In addition to tableware, they also made brushes, mirrors, powder boxes, and the like for milady's dressing table as well as jewelry and small personal accessories such as match safes and flasks. They often marked their products with a circle seal containing an intertwined 'UB' and '925 fine sterling.' In addition to sterling, a very limited amount of gold was also used. Note: This company made no pewter items; Unger designs may occasionally be found in pewter, but these are copies. Items dated in the mark or signed 'Birmingham' are English (not Unger).

Bud vase, Love's Dream 250.00
Cuff links, lady figural, pr 195.00
Hand mirror & brush, Nouveau lady 275.00
Match safe, Cupid kissing woman 185.00
Mustache comb, nude 135.00
Pin, gargoyle, gold wash w/ruby eyes 365.00
Smoking tray, women waft up from pipe smoke 375.00
Vanity set, He Loves Me, mirror+2 brushes+jar w/cut lid, 1904 ..**1,300.00**

Universal

Universal Potteries Incorporated operated in Cambridge, Ohio, from 1934 to 1956. Many lines of dinnerware and kitchen items were produced in both earthenware and semiporcelain. In 1956 the emphasis was shifted to the manufacture of floor and wall tiles, and the name was changed to the Oxford Tile Company, Division of Universal Potteries. The plant closed in 1976. Our advisor for this category is Ted Haun; he is listed in the Directory under Indiana.

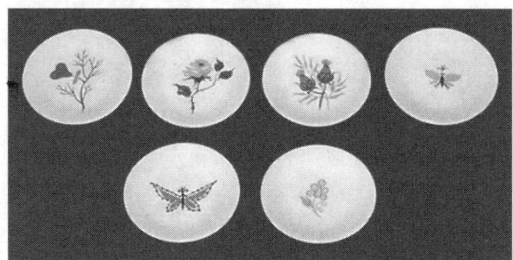

Set of 6 coasters, in original box (not shown) labeled 'Fascination,' $65.00.

Ballerina, bowl, soup 6.00
Ballerina, chop plate 15.00
Ballerina, gravy boat 10.00
Bittersweet, bowl, soup; 7¼" 15.00
Bittersweet, cup & saucer 14.00
Bittersweet, pitcher, w/lid, low 40.00
Bittersweet, plate, salad; 7" 12.00
Bittersweet, platter, oval, 13½" 28.00
Calico Fruit, pepper shaker 20.00
Calico Fruit, refrigerator jug, w/lid 35.00
Cattail, bowl, mixing; 6" 15.00
Cattail, bowl, 7" 10.00
Cattail, cookie jar 75.00
Cattail, cup & saucer 10.00

Cattail, scales, metal 35.00
Cattail, teapot 20.00
Woodvine, bowl, mixing; 4" 19.00
Woodvine, bowl, mixing; 7½" 22.00
Woodvine, pitcher, milk; 6½" 38.00
Woodvine, sugar bowl, w/lid 18.00

University City

Located in University City, Missouri, this pottery opened for only five years (1910-1915), but because of the outstanding potters associated with it, produced notable artware. The company's founder was Edward Gardner Lewis, and among the well-known artists he employed were Adelaide Robineau, Frederick Rhead, Taxile Doat, and Julian Zsolnay.

Vase, mustard crystalline, sgn TD, spherical, 2x2½" 300.00
Vase, pk/wht flambe gloss, bottle form, Robineau, 8", EX **2,700.00**
Vase, snowflake crystals, gold/pk on cream, ftd, rpr, 7x4" **1,300.00**
Vase, yel/red crystalline, sgn TD, 3¾x3¾x2½" 500.00
Vase, 2 rows lg cvd Zs on dk gray, flaring cylinder, 8½x4½" 950.00

Val St. Lambert

Since its inception in Belgium at the turn of the 19th century, the Val St. Lambert Cristalleries has been involved in the production of high-quality glass, producing some cameo. The factory is still in production. Our advisor for this category is Don Williams; he is listed in the Directory under Missouri.

Bottle, scent; frosted sapphire bl w/allover patterning, 5½" 75.00
Candlesticks, full-length cut panels, hex base, 9", pr 200.00
Vase, cameo acorns/oak leaves, yel-gr on clear w/gold, 9" 325.00
Vase, cameo boat/trees, gr on bl/gr, flattened ovoid, 6" 800.00
Vase, cameo poppies, purple on frost, bulbous, 7½" 525.00

Valentien Pottery

Albert and Anna Marie Valentien were artists who produced pottery in California from 1911 until 1912. Albert also worked for T.J. Wheatley, and both were once associated with the Rookwood pottery. They designed both plain and sculptural ware made in solid matt colors as well as vellum-type glazes.

Vase, emb floral, speckled shaded gray matt, long neck, 9", EX .**1,600.00**
Vase, stylized floral on microcrystalline matt gr, 5x4" **1,700.00**

Valentines

Handmade valentines date back to the mid-1700s in the United States; as time went on, increased interest resulted in other types of Valentine cards being made. Today valentine collectors are not the only ones who buy; valentines are often considered a desirable addition to other collections as well — Black memorabilia, advertising, transportation memorabilia, Walt Disney, cartoon and movie characters, etc. Besides examples representing these areas, 3-dimensionals and mechanical valentines (1860s to the present) are becoming highly prized by many collectors. One of the least favorite categories of valentines to collect are the Penny Dreadfuls. They can date from the 1800s. They reflected every facet of life, occupation, and often poked fun at someone's looks. These were usually done with a wood block and originally hand colored. As with all categories of valentines, Penny Dreadfuls can fit into anyone's collection. Please remember there are six qualifying specifications to consider when evaluating a valentine card: age, size, category, manufacturer, artist signature, and condition. Our advisor for this category is Katherine Kreider; she is listed in the Directory under California and Pennsylvania.

Key:
AS — artist signed   mch-flt — mechanical-flat

Am flag, w/child, mch-flt, MIG, 5¼x2", EX 25.00
Blk Cherub fan, mch-flt, Tuck, 10¾x8¾", EX 200.00
Blk messenger, mch-flt, Tuck, 1900s, 9½x5", EX 75.00
Bonnet ladies, mch-flt, MIG, 5x4", EX 35.00
Candy container, heart, 1925, ½x2", VG 5.00
Choked to Death, celluloid, 13½x10½", VG 75.00
Cinderella Valentine booklet, USA, 6½x3¾", VG 15.00
Civil War tent draped in Am flag, mch-flt, 7x5", EX 350.00
Comic, Flappers, 24 set, 1930s, 5x6½", EX 40.00
Comic, Hit 'Em Hard booklet, complete, 1940s, 8½x5½", EX 20.00
Comic, Occupational, flat, USA, 1930s, 9½x6", VG 2.00
Dapper Dan, mch-flt, MIG, 1920s, 11½x6¼", EX 125.00
Dimensional baby grand piano, 1920s, 9x11", NM 275.00
Dimensional observation car, Tuck, 8½x5½x3", EX 200.00
Dimensional pipe organ, MIG, 9½x8¾x6", VG 25.00
Dimensional wooden speed boat, AS, 1940s, 10½x10x2", EX 75.00
Hold-to-light fountain, 1930s, MIG, 11x8x3", EX 125.00
Hold-to-light log cabin, 1920s, MIG, 10x9½x4½", EX 125.00
Kaleidoscope, mch-flt, MIG, 1927, 7x4", EX 35.00
Little Dutch Maiden, flat, Bavaria, 5½x4½", EX 50.00
Love-O-Gram, Mickey Mouse caricature, 4½x13", EX 50.00
Manuscript valentine, hand colored, 1845, 8x5", NM 350.00
Monoplane, flat, HLW, MIG, 1915, 3¼x3¼", NM 95.00
Oh Boy Gum, flat, Rust Craft, USA, 4x5", NM 125.00
Paint booklets, Carrington, complete, 6¾x5", EX 20.00
Paper doll sailor, mch-flt, MIG, 9½x3½", VG 10.00

Penny Dreadful, Ugly, Fat and Forty, early 1900s, 8¾x6½", EX, $40.00.

Penny Dreadful, rubber neck, 1900s, 8¾x6½" 35.00
Playing cards, Art Deco, flat, Carrington, 1940s, NM 45.00
Pocketknife, novelty, USA, 7¼x13", EX 50.00
Puzzle purse, handmade, 1800s, 6x6", EX 1,500.00
Sailboat w/lollipop, plastic, 1950s, 5½x6x1¼", EX 40.00
Sailor's valentine, handmade, 1800s, 6½x4¾", EX 250.00
Scherenschnitte, uncolored, handmade, 5½x4½", EX 150.00
Silhouette couple, Art Deco, flat, USA, 7x4½", EX 15.00
Tute Fruite, flat, 1930s, 6x4½", EX 125.00
Valentine cachet, Loveland CO, 1947, EX 10.00
Valentine writer, rare, 1800s, 7x4", VG 125.00
Watch paper, handmade, rare, 1800s, 2x2", EX 250.00
Whitney, greeting card, 1920s, 6x6", EX 5.00

Whitney, 1800s, 3¾x3", EX 20.00

Van Briggle

The Van Briggle Pottery of Colorado Springs, Colorado, was established in 1901 by Artus Van Briggle, whose early career had been shaped by such notables as Karl Langenbeck and Maria Nichols Storer. His quest for several years had been to perfect a completely flat matt glaze, and upon accomplishing his goal, he opened his pottery. His wife, Anne, worked with him, and they, along with George Young, were responsible for the modeling of the wares. Their work typified the flow and form of the Art Nouveau movement, and the shapes they designed played as important a part in their success as their glazes. Some of their most famous pieces were Despondency, Lorelei, and Toast Cup. Increasing demand for their work soon made it necessary to add to their quarters as well as their staff. Although much of the ware was eventually made from molds, each piece was carefully trimmed and refined before the glaze was sprayed on. Their most popular colors were Persian Rose, Ming Blue, and Mustard Yellow.

Van Briggle died in 1904, but the work was continued by his wife. New facilities were built; and by 1908, in addition to their artware, tiles, gardenware, and commercial lines were added. By the twenties the emphasis had shifted from art pottery to novelties and commercial wares. As late as 1970, reproductions of some of the early designs continued to be made. Until about 1920 most pieces were marked with the date and shape number; after that the AA mark was used.

Bowl, floral shoulder band, dk bl/wine, recent, 6½", +frog 100.00
Bowl, ivy leaves, lt bl, #211, dtd 1903, 2½x5½" 450.00
Bowl, moths, bl/aqua, 8½", +flower frog 150.00
Bowl, moths, dk bl/purple, ca 1920, 8½", +duck flower frog 225.00
Bowl vase, dmn/circle shoulder band, bl over tan, 1919, 3x6" 325.00
Bowl vase, leaves, bl, #510, pre-1920, 4½x7" 275.00
Bowl vase, leaves/stems, bl/aqua, incurvate, recent, 4½" 80.00
Candlestick, Mtn Craig Brn w/gr, #446, 9x3½" 175.00
Chamberstick, gr, hdld vase form w/saucer base, 1914, 6" 225.00
Conch shell, bl/wine, recent, 9x4" 50.00
Mug, fraternity; Greek letters, gold on purple, ca 1907, 5" 275.00
Night light, owl figure, creamy wht, pre-1920, needs wiring 250.00
Pitcher, copper clad, ca 1907-12, 4" 800.00
Plaque, Little Star, mustard brn gloss 65.00
Plate, poppy (lg/swirling), lt gr, dtd 1902, 8½" 1,100.00
Vase, butterfly (lg), lt pomegranate, #668, 1915, 3¾x4" 350.00
Vase, daffodils, Persian Rose, gourd form, #841, 6¼x2½" 125.00
Vase, daffodils at shoulder, lt bl/lav, post-1930, 9" 160.00
Vase, dragonflies (3), gr to brn, #837, dtd 1914, 3½x5" 400.00
Vase, dragonflies at neck, bl w/exposed clay, #498, 1907, 6½" .2,000.00
Vase, floral, bl-gray/caramel, ca 1920s-30s, spherical, 3" 200.00
Vase, floral, Persian Rose, #645, 4½x3¼" 80.00
Vase, floral spray, bl/aqua, pillow form, recent, 4½" 50.00
Vase, flower/leaf on long stem, dk gr/brn matt, 1930s, 5½" 90.00
Vase, flowers on long stems, bl/aqua, ca 1920s, 11½" 220.00
Vase, flowers on long stems, dk gr, #7, dtd 1902, 7" 2,100.00
Vase, Indian heads (3 in relief), gray-bl/rose, EX mold, 12" 750.00
Vase, Indian heads (3 in relief), lt bl/aqua matt, 1930s, 11" 375.00
Vase, irises on long stems, 3-color, #161, 1903, 9½x3¾" 4,000.00
Vase, leaves, bl/aqua, ca 1930s, 5½" 80.00
Vase, leaves, integral hdls, bl over rose, ca 1930s, 9" 120.00
Vase, leaves, Persian Rose, #654, 4x3½" 90.00
Vase, leaves (twisted), dk bl/burgundy, shouldered, 1930s, 7" 250.00
Vase, leaves (veined/swirling), gr, EX mold, #8, 1902, 6x4" 2,400.00
Vase, leaves swirl at base, dk bl/wine, 1920s-30s, 13½" 270.00
Vase, lilies on long stems, red on sheer gr, #204, 4x4" 950.00

Vase, Lorelei, mustard yel, post-1930s, 11" **750.00**
Vase, Lorelei, yel matt, #17, 1907-12, sm base rpr, 9½" **3,750.00**
Vase, oak leaf/acorn, bl/aqua, ca 1920s, 5½x3½" **190.00**
Vase, oak leaf/acorn, mint gr, ca 1917, 5½x3½" **550.00**
Vase, plain, bl/aqua, trumpet neck, petal rim, 1930s, 6" **60.00**
Vase, plain, carnation-pk, rough texture, #410, 1906, 10x8" **500.00**
Vase, poinsettia/berries, bl-gr, hdls, #663, 10x3½" **1,000.00**
Vase, spiderwort, lime gr, #695, ca 1908, 4x4½" **650.00**

Vance Avon

Although pottery had been made in Tiltonville, Ohio, since about 1880, the ware manufacturered there was of little significance until after the turn of the century when the Vance Faience company was organized for the purpose of producing quality artware. By 1902 the name had been changed to the Avon Faience company, and late in the same year it and three other West Virginia potteries incorporated to form the Wheeling Potteries Company. The Avon branch operated in Tiltonville until 1905 when production was moved to Wheeling. Art pottery was discontinued.

From the beginning, only skilled craftsmen and trained engineers were hired. Wm. P. Jervis and Frederick Hurten Rhead were among the notable artists responsible for designing some of the early artware. Some of the ware was slip decorated under glaze, while other pieces were molded with high-relief designs. Examples with squeeze-bag decoration by Rhead are obviously forerunners of the Jap Birdimal line he later developed for Weller. Ware was marked 'Vance F. Co.'; 'Avon F. Co., Tiltonville'; or 'Avon W. Pts. Co.'

Jar, slip-trailed roses, pk/gr on wht, mk Avon, 16", VG **1,300.00**
Vase, dk gr/brn/blk squeeze-bag motif, firing crack, 6x3" **300.00**
Vase, raised stylized lines, blk on olive/orange gloss, 6x6" **375.00**

Vaseline

Vaseline, a greenish-yellow colored glass produced by adding uranium oxide to the batch, was produced during the Victorian era. It was made in smaller quantities than other colors and lost much of its popularity with the advent of the electric light. It was used for pressed tablewares, vases, whimseys, souvenir items, oil lamps, perfume bottles, drawer pulls, and doorknobs. Pieces have been reproduced, and some factories still make it today in small batches. Vaseline glass will flouresce under an ultraviolet light.

Bottle, cologne; flint, att NE Glass, 4½" **225.00**
Bowl, Wildflower, 7½x7½" **30.00**
Candlesticks, flint, NE Glass, 1890s, 10¼x5" dia **200.00**
Celery tray, Daisy & Button, Hobbs & Brockunier, 2x14" L **125.00**
Goblet, Wildflower, 5" **30.00**
Pitcher, opal hobnails, sq mouth, clear ribbed hdl, 7" **95.00**
Sugar bowl, Starburst & Pinwheel, w/lid **45.00**

Verlys

Verlys art glass, produced in France after 1931 by the Holophane Company of Verlys, was made in crystal with acid-finished relief work in the Art Deco style. Colored and opalescent glass was also used. In 1935 an American branch was opened in Newark, Ohio, where very similar wares were produced until the factory ceased production in 1951. French Verlys was signed with one of three mold-impressed script signatures, all containing the company name and country of origin. The American-

made glassware was signed 'Verlys' only, either scratched with a diamond-tipped pen or impressed in the mold. There is very little if any difference in value between items produced in France and America. Though some seem to feel that the French should be higher priced (assuming it to be scarce), many prefer the American-made product.

In June of 1955, about sixteen Verlys molds were leased to the A.H. Heisey Company. Heisey's versions were not signed with the Verlys name, so if an item is unsigned it is almost certainly a Heisey piece. The molds were returned to Verlys of America in July 1957. Our advisor for this category is Don Frost; he is listed in the Directory under Oregon.

Ashtray, Swallow, crystal etched, 4¾" **85.00**
Bowl, Birds & Bees, clear/frosted, 2¼x11⅝" **350.00**
Bowl, Birds & Bees, Directorie bl, 2¼x11⅝" **450.00**
Bowl, Crysanthemum, 10⅛x6¼" **385.00**
Bowl, Pine Cone, bl, mk, 6" **185.00**
Bowl, Poissons, fish, bl & opal, fish form hdls, 3¾x19¼" **1,500.00**
Bowl, 3 molded orchids, frosted, shallow, 14" **395.00**
Box, Poppies, clear/frosted, 13½" **325.00**

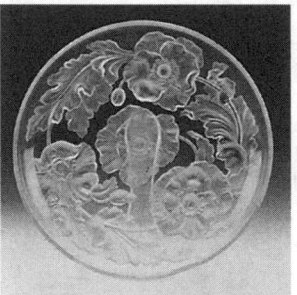

Bowl, Poppies, clear and frosted, 2¾x13½", $325.00.

Charger, Birds & Dragonflies, 12" **350.00**
Vase, Alpine Thistle, opal, shouldered, 9" **625.00**
Vase, Lovebirds, clear/frosted, paper label, 6¾x4½" **225.00**
Vase, Mandarin, emb Oriental figure, gray wash, 9½" **400.00**
Vase, mermaid, shouldered, Directoire bl, 1 of 2 forms, 11" **1,350.00**
Vase, Thistle, topaz, 9¾" **750.00**
Vase, woman of the field, bk: woman of the night, U-form, 8" ...**600.00**

Vernon Kilns

Vernon Potteries Ltd. was established by Faye G. Bennison in Vernon, California, in 1931. The name was later changed to Vernon Kilns; until it closed in 1958, dinnerware, specialty plates, and figurines were their primary products. Among its wares most sought after by collectors today are items designed by such famous artists as Rockwell Kent, Walt Disney, Don Blanding, Jane Bennison, and May and Vieve Hamilton. Authority Maxine Nelson has compiled a lovely book *Collectible Vernon Kilns*, with full-color photos, current prices, and an index; you will find her listed in the Directory under California.

Anytime, creamer **8.00**
Anytime, pitcher, 1-pt, 7" **12.00**
Arcadia, tidbit **30.00**
Barkwood, bowl, salad; 10½" **25.00**
Barkwood, casserole, ind, 4" **12.00**
Barkwood, coffee server, w/stopper **25.00**
Barkwood, egg cup, dbl **10.00**
Barkwood, shakers, pr **10.00**
Barkwood, teapot, 11" **25.00**
Barkwood, tumbler, 14-oz **12.00**
Beverly, coffeepot, AD; 2-cup **85.00**

Brown-Eyed Susan, bowl, chowder; tab hdls	12.00
Brown-Eyed Susan, casserole, w/lid	45.00
Brown-Eyed Susan, chop plate, 12"	25.00
Brown-Eyed Susan, tumbler, 14-oz	20.00
Chintz, teapot	60.00
Delores, bowl, serving; oval	25.00
Delores, chop plate, 12"	30.00
Delores, plate, bread & butter; 6½"	6.00
Delores, plate, dinner; 10½"	15.00
Early California, shakers, pr	15.00
Fantasia, bowl, mushroom, HP, #120	295.00
Fantasia, bowl, Sprite, pk, #125, 3x10½"	300.00
Fantasia, bowl, winged nymph, HP, #122, 2½x12"	490.00

Fantasia figurines: Donkey Unicorn, #16, $450.00; Centaurette, reclining, #17, $600.00; Unicorn, sitting, #14, $350.00.

Fantasia, figurine, satyr, 4½"	250.00
Fantasia, shakers, mushrooms, pr	120.00
Fantasia, vase, Pegasus, bl, #127	700.00
Fantasia, vase, winged nymph, HP, #123	450.00
Frontier Days, bowl, 9"	45.00
Frontier Days, chop plate, 14"	150.00
Frontier Days, flat soup	55.00
Gingham, bowl, chowder; tab hdls	15.00
Gingham, butter dish	21.00
Gingham, chicken pie, w/lid, ind	25.00
Gingham, cup & saucer, jumbo	35.00
Gingham, mug	18.00
Gingham, plate, 9½"	9.00
Gingham, sugar bowl, w/lid	12.00
Homespun, bowl, flat soup	15.00
Homespun, bowl, mixing; 6"	22.50
Homespun, butter dish	25.00
Homespun, casserole, hdls, rnd, w/lid	45.00
Homespun, coaster, 4½"	25.00
Homespun, coffee server	35.00
Homespun, cup & saucer	12.00
Homespun, egg cup	18.00
Homespun, pitcher, 2-qt, 11¼"	40.00
Homespun, plate, 10½"	15.00
Homespun, plate, 9½"	10.00
Homespun, platter, 12½"	17.50
Homespun, sugar bowl, w/lid	12.00
Homespun, syrup, drip-cut top	45.00
Honolulu, shakers, pr	30.00
Lei Lani, bowl, chowder	45.00
Lei Lani, cup & saucer, demitasse	32.00
Lei Lani, plate, 10½"	40.00
Lei Lani, plate, 9½"	35.00
Lei Lani, shakers, pr	40.00
Mayflower, lug soup, 6"	12.00
Moby Dick, chowder, cobalt, open	65.00
Organdie, bowl, chowder; 6"	7.00
Organdie, bowl, oval, 10"	10.00
Organdie, chop plate, 12"	22.00

Organdie, coaster, 4½"	18.00
Organdie, cup & saucer	6.00
Organdie, cup & saucer, demitasse	20.00
Organdie, pitcher, disk, scarce, 2-qt	65.00
Organdie, pitcher, streamline, 1-pt, 6"	20.00
Organdie, plate, 7½"	6.00
Organdie, plate, 9½"	10.00
Organdie, platter, oval, 12"	15.00
Organdie, syrup	35.00
Organdie, tidbit, 3-tier	35.00
Plate, souvenir of state, $12 to	25.00
Raffia, cup & saucer	5.00
Raffia, plate, 10"	8.00
Raffia, platter, oval, 13"	15.00
Shadows, bowl, chowder	12.00
Tam O'Shanter, bowl, divided vegetable	30.00
Tam O'Shanter, bowl, salad; ind, 5¼"	15.00
Tam O'Shanter, carafe, w/stopper	35.00
Tam O'Shanter, casserole, hdls, w/lid	35.00
Tam O'Shanter, mug, coffee	22.00
Tam O'Shanter, plate, 7½"	8.00
Tam O'Shanter, platter, oval, 12"	22.00
Tam O'Shanter, platter, oval, 14"	28.00
Tam O'Shanter, tumbler, 5"	20.00
Tickled Pink, shakers, pr	20.00
Winchester '73, platter, 12"	125.00

Vistosa

Vistosa was produced from about 1938 through the early forties. It was Taylor, Smith, and Taylor's answer to the very successful Fiesta line of their nearby competitor, Homer Laughlin. Vistosa was made in four solid colors: mango red, cobalt blue, light green, and deep yellow. 'Pie crust' edges and a dainty five-petal flower molded into handles and lid finials made for a very attractive yet nevertheless commercially unsuccessful product. For further information, we recommend *Collector's Guide to Lu-Ray Pastels* by Kathy and Bill Meahan (Collector Books). Our advisor for this category is Ted Haun; he is listed in the Directory under Indiana.

Bowl, salad; ftd	160.00
Bowl, 5¾"	8.00
Bowl, 8½"	24.00
Cake plate	25.00
Chop plate, 13"	18.00
Chop plate, 15"	35.00
Creamer	20.00
Cup & saucer	15.00
Egg cup	22.50
Gravy boat	90.00
Pitcher, cobalt or red, ea	75.00
Plate, salad; 7"	8.00
Plate, 7"	7.00
Plate, 9"	10.00
Shakers, pr	32.00
Sugar bowl, w/lid	25.00
Teapot	95.00

Volkmar

Charles Volkmar established a workshop in Tremont, New York, in 1882. He produced artware decorated under the glaze in the manner of the early barbotine work done at the Haviland factory in Limoges, France. He relocated in 1888 in Menlo Park, New Jersey, and together with J.T. Smith established the Menlo Park Ceramic Company for the production of art tile. The partnership was dissolved in 1893. From 1895 until 1902, Volkmar located in Corona, New York, first under the name Volkmar Ceramic Company, later as Volkmar and Cory, and for the final six years as Crown Point. During the latter period he made art tile, blue under-glaze Delft-type wares, colorful polychrome vases, etc. The Volkmar Kilns were established in 1903 in Metuchen, New Jersey, by Volkmar and his son. Wares were marked with various devices consisting of the Volkmar name, initials, or 'Crown Point Ware.'

Bowl, fruit; volcanic purple, lt gr int, flared, 1916, 4x10½" **400.00**
Panel, landscape, soft grs in vellum, unmk, 2 tiles: 5½" ea **325.00**
Tile, Hispano-Moresque, mc w/floral sections, mk, 6" **650.00**
Tile, rabbit family, yel on gr, V mk, 6"+fr **875.00**
Vase, barbotine florals, wht/pk/gr on blk mottle, 6½x3½" **325.00**
Vase, bl/gr streaky matt w/gloss band at ft, bottle neck, 6x5" **285.00**
Vase, cvd leaves w/extended tips on gr matt, 5¾x4" **750.00**

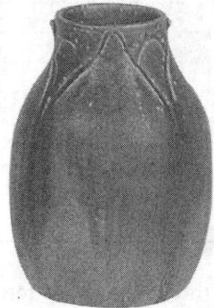

Vase, green matt with raised and carved stylized leaves at top, marked, 5¾x4", $600.00.

Vase, gr matt, squat w/flaring neck, faceted base, 3½x4½" **150.00**
Vase, leathery speckled gr matt, shouldered cylinder, 7¾x5" **400.00**
Vase, sang-de-boeuf/wht flambe, orange peel texture, 1949, 5" ..**400.00**

Volkstedt

There were several porcelain factories in and around Volkstedt, Province of Thuringia, the original and earliest one established in 1762 by George Heinrich Macheleid. Others soon followed, producing many fine porcelain figures and groups in the Scheib-Alsbach, Potschappel, and Sitzendorf style. The 'crossed hayforks' mark was used from 1787 to 1800 by Christian Nonne; it was later modified with the addition of a crown by R. Ekhart (1906-08). An 'M' crossed by a 'V' with a crown was used from 1907-47 by Muller, who used an oval-shaped diamond with an 'M,' 'V,' and a crown from 1910-1960. The Greiner Bros. mark was a double crossed 'G' and a crown, in use from 1850-1920.

Figurine, boy & girl at table, appl florals, mk **80.00**
Figurine, girl in floral dress w/goose, after Canova, 6" **180.00**
Figurine, lady sits w/lute, man holds book, 9x9½" **1,100.00**
Figurine, lady w/2 children & goat, lacy skirts, 1915 mk, 8" **300.00**
Figurine, Tea Time, ladies at table, 7x8" **295.00**
Plaque, gr jasper w/wht floral Baroque fr, ca 1874, 9x10½" **465.00**

Wade

The Wade Group of Potteries originated in 1810 with a small, single-oven pottery near Chesterton, just west of Burslem, England. This pottery, first owned by a Henry Hallen, was eventually taken over by

George Wade who had opened his own pottery in the latter part of the 19th century, on Hall Street, Burslem. In the early 19th century, George Wade combined the two businesses into one pottery — the George Wade Pottery, located on High Street, Burslem. This pottery was named the Manchester Pottery; it still stands and is in business today.

Both the original Hallen Pottery and the newer George Wade Pottery specialized in pottery items for the textile industry, then booming in northern England. In 1906 Wade's son, George Albert Wade, joined the company, and in 1919 the pottery name was changed to George Wade and Son Ltd.

George Wade's brothers, Albert and William, had interests in two other potteries, Wade Heath & Co. Ltd., founded in 1867 as Wade, Colclough and Lingard (changed to Wade & Co. in 1887 and to Wade Heath & Co. Ltd. in 1927) and J.& W. Wade & Co., founded in the late 19th century with a name change also in 1927, to A.J. Wade & Co. Together the potteries manufactured decorative tiles, teapots, and other related dinnerware. In 1938 Wade Heath took over the Royal Victoria Pottery, also in Burslem, and began producing a wide range of figurines and other decorative items. The A.J. Wade & Co. pottery ceased production in 1970 but the main building was not sold and reopened recently as The Pottery Store. The Royal Victoria Pottery is still in production but is now referred to as Hill Top.

In 1947 a new pottery was opened in Portadown, Northern Ireland, to produce both industrial ceramics and Irish porcelain giftware. In 1958 all the Wade potteries were amalgamated, becoming the Wade Group of Potteries. The most recent addition to the group is Wade (PDM) Limited, a marketing arm for the advertising ware made by Wade Heath at the Royal Victoria Pottery. Wade (PDM) Limited was incorporated in 1969. In 1989 the Wade Group of Potteries was bought out by Beauford Engineering. With this takeover, Wade Heath and George Wade & Son Ltd. were combined to form Wade Ceramics. Wade (Ireland) Ltd. and Wade (PDM) Ltd. became subsidiaries of Wade Ceramics. In 1990 Wade (Ireland) Ltd. changed its name to Seagoe Ceramics Limited. In April, 1993, Seagoe Ceramics Limited ceased the production of table and giftware to concentrate on industrial ceramics. The pottery, although still owned by Beauford, is no longer part of the Wade Group.

For those interested in learning more about Wade pottery, we recommend *The World of Wade* and *The World of Wade Book 2* by Ian Warner and Mike Posgay; Mr. Warner is listed in the Directory under Canada.

Blk & Wht Scotch Whisky Ashtray, 5" sq **15.00**
Disney Figurine, Dwarf, 1981-86, ea **180.00**
Disney Figurine, Snow White, 1981-86 ....**200.00**
Gilbey's Wine Barrels, Port, Irish or Scotch, 5¾", ea **28.00**
Gilbey's Wine Barrels, Sherry, Gin, Scotch or Port, 4¾", ea **24.00**
Johnnie Walker Ashtray, 5" sq **25.00**
NatWest Piggy Bank, Annabel **40.00**
NatWest Piggy Bank, Baby Woody **30.00**
NatWest Piggy Bank, Maxwell, Lady Hillary or Sir Nathaniel, ea .**50.00**
San Francisco Mini Mansions, brn, ea **90.00**
San Francisco Mini Mansions, Cable Car **140.00**
San Francisco Mini Mansions, pk or wht, ea **80.00**
San Francisco Mini Mansions, yel or bl, ea **65.00**
Scotty (Caddy) Teapot, 5¼" **135.00**
Scotty (Caddy) Teapot, 5¾" **150.00**
Tankard, Veteran Car, 1-pt **22.00**
Tankard, Veteran Car, ½-pt **18.00**
Tetley Tea Gaffer Money Box **45.00**
Wade (Ireland) Ltd Donkey & Cart Vase **45.00**
Wade (Ireland) Ltd Leprechaun on Acorn **90.00**
Wade (Ireland) Ltd Leprechaun on Pig **60.00**
Wagon Train Plaque, Seth Adams or Flint McCollough, ea **95.00**
World of Survival, Am Cougar, 4" **600.00**

World of Survival, Elephant, 6" 550.00
World of Survival, Polar Bear, 4½" 400.00
World of Survival, Rhinoceros, 4½" 350.00
Worthington 'E' Water Jug 40.00

Wallace China

Dinnerware with a Western theme was produced by the Wallace China Company, who operated in California from 1931 until 1964. Artist Till Goodan designed three lines, Rodeo, Pioneer Trails, and Boots and Saddle, which they marketed under the package name Westward Ho. When dinnerware with a western theme became so popular just a few years ago, Rodeo was reproduced, but the new trademark includes neither 'California' or 'Wallace China.'

Our advisor for this category is Marv Fogleman; he is listed in the Directory under California. If you'd like to learn more about this company, we recommend *The Collector's Encyclopedia of California Pottery* by Jack Chipman.

Boots and Saddle, ashtray, 5½", $55.00.

Boots & Saddle, cup & saucer 85.00
Boots & Saddle, pitcher, lg 395.00
Boots & Saddle, plate, 10½" 75.00
Boots & Saddle, platter, sgn Goodan, 15" 175.00
Boots & Saddle, shakers, pr 135.00
Chuck Wagon, coffee cup 30.00
El Rancho, cup & saucer 40.00
El Rancho, cup & saucer, demitasse 50.00
El Rancho, plate, 9½" 65.00
El Rancho, sugar bowl, w/lid 75.00
Pioneer Trails, cup, 7-oz 45.00
Rodeo, plate, 10½" 90.00
Rodeo, plate, 13" 175.00
Rodeo, shakers, 5", ea 75.00
Westward Ho, ashtray, longhorn 40.00
Westward Ho, plate, dinner; longhorn 65.00
Westward Ho, plate, Little Buckaroo, VG 125.00

Walley

The Walley Pottery operated in West Sterling, Massachusetts, from 1898 to 1919. Never more than a one-man operation, Walley himself handcrafted all his wares from local clay. The majority of his pottery was simple and unadorned. Though it was usually glazed in matt green, on occasion you may find high- and semi-gloss green as well as matt glazes in blue, cream, brown, and red. The most rare and desirable examples of his work are those with applied or relief-carved decorations. Some pieces are marked 'WJW.'

Bowl vase, curdled/lt irid bl semigloss, 4½" 550.00

Mug, high-relief horned demon, speckled gr matt, rpr, 7½" 650.00
Vase, brn w/streaks of red & blk, shoulder/base width, 6x4" 550.00
Vase, chestnut w/gr & dk brn, dbl shoulder bulge, 9", NM 1,000.00

Walrath

Frederick Walrath was a studio potter who worked from around the turn of the century until his death in 1920. He was located in Rochester, New York, until 1918 when he became associated with the Newcomb Pottery in New Orleans, Louisiana.

Bowl, stylized trees, mustard on brn matt, 2½x5" 1,265.00
Flower frog, couching nude, gr matt, rtcl base, mk, 5¾x5" 300.00
Flower frog, kneeling nude on mushroom, ivory, no mk, 6" 125.00
Inkwell/pen holder, angel on raised base, gr, 7½x5¾" 500.00
Mugs, Arts & Crafts leaves/bands, yel-gr/olive, 5½", 4 for 900.00
Paperweight, nude w/long hair, lt gr/tan/gray matt, 4½" 400.00
Tile, stylized floral ea corner, 3-color, wide oak fr, 6" 950.00
Vase, crystals, lt gr/cream/brn flambe, shouldered, 9½x5" 3,750.00
Vase, floral, dk red/bl on dk bl crystalline, 1911, 6¾x4" 475.00
Vase, flowers/leaves, bl/pk/khaki on brn, 4½x3¾" 900.00
Vase, leaf band, bl-gray w/yel dots on slate gray, 4¾x3½" 950.00

Walrich

This small pottery operated in Berkeley, California, from 1922 until about 1930. They designed their own molds and developed their own glazes and are well known for their formula for a particularly outstanding shade of blue. Porcelain as well as earthenware clays were utilized, and in addition to artware vases, figurines were also made. Their trademark was a vase enclosed within a circle with the name of the pottery and its location in letters around the inner perimeter.

Tile, brn tree in field, yel sun, mk, 5½" sq 575.00
Tile, galleon, yel on bl gloss, 6" dia 50.00
Tile, trees/bushes/lake/mtns, 5-color, glossy, oak fr, 5" 475.00
Vase, chartreuse mottled matt, 4-sided, sgn GR Wall, 7½x5" 275.00

Walter, A.

Almaric Walter was employed from 1904 through 1914 at Verreries Artistiques des Freres Daum in Nancy, France. After 1919 he opened his own business where he continued to make the same type of quality objets d'art in pate-de-verre glass as he had earlier. His pieces are signed A. Walter, Nancy H. Berge Sc.

Bird, yel on gr leafy base w/2 brn pine cones, 3¼x2" 1,050.00
Buddha, in lotus position, lt amber, 6¾" 1,725.00
Dish, earth tones, oval rim, flared sqd base, sgn Finot, 8" 500.00
Night light, berried ribs, dome shade/cover, 5¾", EX 4,800.00
Paperweight, stag beetle, rust/blk on yel/gr base, Berge, 3" 1,495.00
Pendant, beetle emb on turq & frost, oval, 2⅛" 400.00
Seal, gray-gr on dk gr plinth, Mercier, 6" 1,600.00
Tray, beetle beside U-shape depression, SGN Berge, 4" 2,400.00
Tray, bumble bee on rim of shield shape, 4" 2,300.00
Vase, berry band under rim, conical w/flaring base, 6½" 2,600.00

Wannopee

The Wannopee Pottery, established in 1892, developed from the reorganization of the financially insecure New Milford Pottery Company of New Milford, Connecticut. They produced a line of mottled-glazed pottery called 'Duchess' and a similar line in porcelain. Both were marked with the impressed sunburst 'W' with 'porcelain' added to indicate that particular body type.

In 1895 semiporcelain pitchers in three sizes were decorated with relief medallion cameos of Beethoven, Mozart, and Napoleon. Lettuce-leaf ware was first produced in 1901 and used actual leaves in the modeling. Scarabronze, made in 1895, was their finest artware. It featured simple Egyptian shapes with a coppery glaze. It was marked with a scarab, either impressed or applied. Production ceased in 1903.

Vase, brn gloss, concave cylinder w/3 diagonal appl hdls, 8" **220.00**
Vase, gr/brn streaks w/irid, cylinder neck, snake hdls, 27" **300.00**
Vase, Scarabronze, caramel, 6 integral shoulder hdls, 20x12" ..**2,100.00**

Warwick

The Warwick China Company operated in Wheeling, West Virginia, from 1887 until 1951. They produced both hand-painted and decaled plates, vases, teapots, coffeepots, pitchers, bowls, and jardinieres featuring lovely florals or portraits of beautiful ladies done in luscious colors. Backgrounds were usually blendings of brown and beige, but ivory was also used as well as greens and pinks. Various marks were employed, all of which incorporate the Warwick name. For a more thorough study of the subject, we recommend *Warwick, A to W*, a supplement to *Why Not Warwick* by our advisor, Donald C. Hoffmann, Sr.; his address can be found in the Directory under Illinois. In an effort to inform the collector/dealer, Mr. Hoffmann now has a video available that identifies the company's decals and their variations by number.

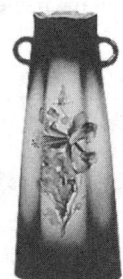

Vase, Verona, brown w/floral decoration, 11¾", $145.00.

Vase, Maria, brn, floral, A-40, 10½" **210.00**
Vase, Maria, charcoal, floral, C-6, 10½" **235.00**
Vase, Maria, pk, Hilda type w/flower, H-1, 10½" **265.00**
Vase, Maria, wht, w/birds, D-1, 10½" **275.00**
Vase, Monroe, brn, Anna Potaka, A-17, 10½" **265.00**
Vase, Monroe, brn, floral, A-27, 10½" **235.00**
Vase, Monroe, wht, birds, D-1, 10½" **280.00**
Vase, Narcis #1, brn, floral, A-27, 8½" **220.00**
Vase, Narcis #1, brn, portrait, A-17, 8½" **250.00**
Vase, Narcis #1, charcoal, nude, C-1, 8½" **285.00**
Vase, Narcis #2, brn, floral, A-27, 6¾" **240.00**
Vase, Narcis #2, red, floral, E-2, 6¾" **240.00**
Vase, Orchid, brn, floral, A-27, 10¼" **235.00**
Vase, Orchid, pk, portrait, H-1, 10¼" **290.00**
Vase, Orchid, wht, birds, D-1, 10¼" **275.00**
Vase, Oriental, charcoal, floral, C-6, 11" **295.00**
Vase, Oriental, red, floral, E-2, 11" **290.00**
Vase, Pansy, brn, floral, A-23, 4" **100.00**
Vase, Pansy, charcoal, floral, C-6, 4" **100.00**
Vase, Pansy, red, floral, E-2, 4" **95.00**

Vase, Pansy, yel/gr, portrait, K-1, 4" **125.00**
Vase, Parisian, charcoal, nude, C-1, 4" **255.00**
Vase, Parisian, pk, Hilda type, H-1, 4" **275.00**
Vase, Peerless, brn, floral, A-40, 9½" **230.00**
Vase, Peerless, tan matt, portrait, M-1, 9½" **260.00**
Vase, Penn, brn, floral, A-40, 9½" **230.00**
Vase, Penn, charcoal, floral, C-6, 9½" **240.00**
Vase, Poppy, brn, floral, A-27, 10½" **260.00**
Vase, Poppy, charcoal, floral, C-6, 10½" **280.00**
Vase, Poppy, wht, w/roses, no RLC, 10½" **285.00**
Vase, President, matt, nut decor, M-4, 11½" **245.00**
Vase, President, matt, pine cones, M-64, 11½" **260.00**
Vase, Queen, charcoal, floral, C-6, 12" **285.00**
Vase, Regency, brn, floral, A-27, 11½" **275.00**
Vase, Regency, charcoal, floral, C-6, 11½" **290.00**
Vase, Regency, russet, floral, 11½" **290.00**
Vase, Roberta, red, fisherman, E-3, 10" **300.00**
Vase, Roberta, tan matt, acorns, M-4, 10" **310.00**
Vase, Roman, brn, floral, A-40, 11½" **270.00**
Vase, Rosalie, brn, floral, A-27, 9½" **200.00**
Vase, Rosalie, brn, floral, A-6, 9½" **200.00**
Vase, Rosalie, charcoal, floral, C-6, 9½" **230.00**
Vase, Rosalie, matt, nuts, M-1, 9½" **260.00**
Vase, Rosalie, pk, portrait, H-1, 9½" **275.00**
Vase, Rosalie, wht, birds, D-1, 9½" **280.00**
Vase, Rose, brn, floral, A-6, 8" **150.00**
Vase, Rose, red, floral, E-2, 8" **180.00**
Vase, Rose, red, portrait, E-1, 8" **190.00**
Vase, Royal #1, brn, portrait, A-17, 10" **300.00**
Vase, Royal #2, brn, floral, A-27, 8" **285.00**
Vase, Senator #1, brn, floral, A-27, 15" **200.00**
Vase, Senator #1, matt, nut, M-4, 15" **215.00**
Vase, Senator #1, red, floral, E-2, 15" **230.00**
Vase, Senator #2, brn, floral, A-23, 13½" **200.00**
Vase, Senator #2, matt, nuts, M-64, 13½" **225.00**
Vase, Senator #2, pk, Hilda type, H-1, 13½" **290.00**
Vase, Thelma, brn, floral, A-23, 9½" **230.00**
Vase, Tobio Jug #1, brn, floral, A-027, 7¾" **140.00**
Vase, Tobio Jug #1, brn, floral, A-6, 7¾" **150.00**
Vase, Tobio Jug #1, brn, monk, A-36, 7¾" **135.00**
Vase, Tobio Jug #1, pk, portrait, H-1, 7¾" **235.00**
Vase, Tobio Jug #1, wht, birds, D-1, 7¾" **215.00**
Vase, Tobio Jug #1, yel/gr, floral, K-2, 7¾" **250.00**
Vase, Tobio Jug #2, brn, floral, A-6, 7" **145.00**
Vase, Tobio Jug #2, brn, portrait, A-17, 7" **185.00**
Vase, Tobio Jug #2, red, floral, E-2, 7" **195.00**

Wash Sets

Before the days of running water, bedrooms were standardly equipped with a wash bowl and pitcher as a matter of necessity. A 'toilet set' was comprised of the pitcher and bowl, toothbrush holder, covered commode, soap dish, shaving dish, and mug. Some sets were even more elaborate. Through everyday usage, the smaller items were often broken, and today it is unusual to find a complete set.

Porcelain sets decorated with florals, fruits, or scenics were produced abroad by Limoges in France; some were imported from Germany and England. During the last quarter of the 1800s and until after the turn of the century, American-made toilet sets were manufactured in abundance. Tin and graniteware sets were also made.

Buffalo, Chrysanthemum, pitcher/bowl **265.00**
English, bl-gr florals, pitcher/bowl/pot/toothbrush holder **375.00**

Ironstone w/cobalt & gold, mk Warwick, 6-pc set 275.00
Knowle-Taylor-Knowles, child's, wht w/gold, pitcher/bowl 65.00
Old Paris, floral & scrollwork panels on wht, pitcher/bowl 575.00
Royal Coronaware, floral, blk w/mc trim, 15¼" dia, 2 pcs 265.00
Yellowware, wht band w/blk stripes, pitcher/bowl/tumbler 120.00

Watch Fobs

Watch fobs have been popular since the last quarter of the 19th century. They were often made by retail companies to feature their products. Souvenir, commemorative, and political fobs were also produced. Of special interest today are those with advertising, heavy equipment in particular. Some of the more pricey fobs are listed here, but most of those currently available were produced in such quantities that they are relatively common and should fall into a price range of from $3.00 to $10.00. Our advisor for this category is Tony George; he is listed in the Directory under California.

Abraham Fur Co, St Louis 150.00
Adams Road Machinery, emb machine on silver-tone, Metal Arts .18.00
Buick Motor Cars, mc enamel, 1920s 45.00
Buy It Because It's a Studebaker, car on silver-tone, 1930s 60.00
Caterpillar Diesel Engines, brass 48.00
Caterpillar Tractor, brass 45.00
Chrysler logo, brass 12.00
Dickinson County, KS, 1916 ....50.00
Dodge Brothers Motor Vehicles, 3-color enamel 95.00
Eastland, emb train scene on silver-tone, 1920s 80.00
EC Simmons, logo shaped w/gr enameled face 120.00
Fordson Tractor 40.00
Fraternal Order of Eagles 45.00
Gallion Tandem Rollers 20.00
Gardner Denver, jackhammer 40.00
Gisholt Machine Co, emb machines on silver-tone, 1930s 40.00
Gooch's Best Macaroni, silver-tone metal diecut, 1915 ....65.00
Great Seal of US, bronze 22.50
Green River Whiskey 60.00
Grove Am Equipment Co, emb crane, bronze metal, 1960s 8.00
Harley-Davidson Motorcycles 195.00
Indian Motorcycles, sterling arrow shape 195.00
Jamestown Expo, 1907 ....120.00
JD Adams 160.00
John Deere, MOP, EX 70.00
Keen Kutter EC Simmons Cutlery & Tools, enameling 125.00
Land-Belt Speeder, shovel crane emb on bronze-tone, 1950s 15.00
Mack Trucks, bulldog emb on bronze-tone metal, 1960s 18.00
Marion Power Shovel Co, emb machine on silver-tone, 1960s 12.00
Masonic emblem, lg, w/lg link gold-filled chain 75.00
Mexican Border Service, 1916 ....30.00
Shapleigh Hardware 80.00
State Farm Insurance, enamel 70.00
Stevens Detroit, bronze elephant diecut, Whitehead & Hoag 32.00
Wabco, emb heavy machinery on bronze metal, 1970s 10.00
Walters & Dunbar, Chicago Livestock Commission 125.00
Yellowstone Park, longhorn steer 150.00

Watches

First made in the 1500s in Germany, early watches were actually small clocks, suspended from the neck or belt. By 1700 they had become the approximate shape and size we know today. The first watches produced in America were made in 1810. The well-known

Waltham Watch Company was established in 1850. Later, Waterbury produced inexpensive watches which they sold by the thousands.

Open-face and hunting-case watches of the 1890s were often solid gold or gold-filled and were often elaborately decorated in several colors of gold. Gold watches became a status symbol in this decade and were worn by both men and women on chains with fobs or jeweled slides. Ladies sometimes fastened them to their clothing with pins often set with jewels. The chatelaine watch was worn at the waist, only one of several items such as scissors, coin purses, or needle cases, each attached by small chains.

Most turn-of-the-century watch cases were gold-filled; these are plentiful today. Sterling cases, though interest in them is on the increase, are not in great demand. Our advise for this category comes from Maundy International Watches, Antiquarian Horologists, price consultants, and researchers for many watch reference guides and books on Horology. Their firm is a leading purveyor of antique watches of all kinds. They are listed in the Directory under Kansas. For character-related watches, see Personalities.

Key:

adj — adjusted	k/s — key set
brg — bridge plate design	k/w — key wind
d/s — double sunk dial	l/s — lever set
fbd — finger bridge design	mvt — movement
g/f — gold-filled	o/f — open face
g/j/s — gold jewel setting	p/s — pendant set
h/c — hunter case	r/g/p — rolled gold plate
HCI#P — heat, cold,	s — size
isochronism & position	s/s — single sunk dial
adjusted	s/w — stem wind
j — jewel	w/g/f — white gold-filled
k — karat	y/g/f — yellow gold-filled

Am Watch Co, 0s, 7j, #1891, 14k, h/c, Am Watch Co 625.00
Am Watch Co, 12s, 17j, #1894, 14k, o/f, Royal 350.00
Am Watch Co, 12s, 21j, #1894, 14k, h/c 675.00
Am Watch Co, 16s, 11j, #1872, p/s, silver h/c, Park Road 425.00
Am Watch Co, 16s, 15j, #1899, y/g/f, h/c 250.00
Am Watch Co, 16s, 16j, #1884, 5-min, 14k, Repeater 5,000.00
Am Watch Co, 16s, 17j, #1888, Railroader 625.00
Am Watch Co, 16s, 19j, #1872, 14k, h/c, Am Watch Woerd's Pat ...3,250.00
Am Watch Co, 16s, 21j, #1888, o/f, 14k, Riverside Maximus .1,475.00
Am Watch Co, 16s, 21j, #1899, y/g/f, l/s, o/f, Crescent St 400.00
Am Watch Co, 16s, 21j, #1908, y/g/f, o/f, Grade #645 ....280.00
Am Watch Co, 16s, 23j, #1908, o/f, 18k, Premier Maximus, MIB ...10,000.00
Am Watch Co, 16s, 23j, #1908, y/g/f, o/f, adj, RR, Vanguard 325.00
Am Watch Co, 16s, 23j, #1908, y/g/f, o/f, Vanguard Up/Down ..725.00
Am Watch Co, 18s, #1857, silver h/c, Samuel Curtiss k/w 3,450.00

American Watch Company, 18 size, 11 jewels, #1857, coin silver, key set, key wind, PS Bartlett, Waltham Mass, 2nd or 3rd run, $225.00.

Am Watch Co, 18s, 11j, #1857, k/w, 1st run, PS Barlett 900.00
Am Watch Co, 18s, 11j, #1857, silver h/c, k/w, DH&D 1,425.00

Am Watch Co, 18s, 11j, #1857, silver h/c, k/w, s/s, Ellery, EX ...350.00	Hamilton, #947 (mk), 18s, 23j, 14k, h/c, orig/sgn, EX 7,450.00
Am Watch Co, 18s, 15j, #1877, k/w, RE Robbins 395.00	Hamilton, #950, 16s, 23j, y/g/f, o/f, l/s, sgn d/s 575.00
Am Watch Co, 18s, 15j, #1883, y/g/f, 2-tone, Railroad King 675.00	Hamilton, #965, 16s, 17j, 14k, p/s, h/c, brg, scarce 1,100.00
Am Watch Co, 18s, 17j, #1883, y/g/f, o/f, Crescent Street 175.00	Hamilton, #972, 16s, 17j, y/g/f, g/j/s, o/f, d/s, l/s, adj 200.00
Am Watch Co, 18s, 17j, #1892, HC, Canadian Pacific Railway .900.00	Hamilton, #974, 16s, 17j, 20-yr, y/g/f, o/f, s/s 150.00
Am Watch Co, 18s, 17j, #1892, y/g/f, o/f, Sidereal, rare 1,950.00	Hamilton, #992, 16s, 21j, y/g/f, o/f, adj, d/s, dbl roller 285.00
Am Watch Co, 18s, 17j, 25-yr, y/g/f, o/f, s/s, PS Bartlett 180.00	Hamilton, #992B, 16s, 21j, y/g/f, o/f, l/s, Bar/Crown 400.00
Am Watch Co, 18s, 21j, #1892, y/g/f, o/f, d/s, Crescent St 325.00	Hampden, 12s, 17j, w/g/f, o/f, thin model, Aviator 150.00
Am Watch Co, 18s, 21j, #1892, y/g/f, o/f, Grade #845 ....325.00	Hampden, 16s, 17j, o/f, adj 100.00
Am Watch Co, 18s, 21j, #1892, y/g/f, o/f, Pennsylvania Special ..1,775.00	Hampden, 16s, 17j, y/g/f, h/c, s/w 225.00
Am Watch Co, 18s, 7j, #1857, silver case, k/w, CT Parker 2,250.00	Hampden, 16s, 21j, g/j/s, y/g/f, NP, h/c, Dueber, ¾-mvt 280.00
Am Watch Co, 6s, 7j, #1873, y/g/f, h/c, Am Watch Co 195.00	Hampden, 16s, 21j, o/f, adj, dbl roller, Special Railway 350.00
Auburndale Watch Co, 18s, 7j, k/w, l/s, Lincoln 1,000.00	Hampden, 16s, 7j, gilded, NP, ¾-mvt 100.00
Aurora Watch Co, 18s, 11j, o/f, k/w, h/c 550.00	Hampden, 18s, 15j, k/w, mk on mvt, Railway 800.00
Aurora Watch Co, 18s, 15 ruby j, y/g/f, s/w 600.00	Hampden, 18s, 15j, s/w, gilded, JC Perry 250.00
Ball (Elgin), 18s, 17j, o/f, silver, Official RR Standard 525.00	Hampden, 18s, 15j, silver, k/w, h/c, Hayward 240.00
Ball (Hamilton), 16s, 21j, #999, g/f, o/f, l/s 365.00	Hampden, 18s, 15j, y/g/f, damascened, h/c, Dueber 200.00
Ball (Hamilton), 16s, 23j, #998, y/g/f, o/f, Elinvar 900.00	Hampden, 18s, 21j, y/g/f, g/j/s, h/c, New Railway 280.00
Ball (Hamilton), 18s, 19j, #999, g/f, o/f, l/s 450.00	Hampden, 18s, 21j, y/g/f, o/f, d/s, l/s, N Am Railway 325.00
Ball (Hampden), 18s, 17j, o/f, adj, RR, Superior Grade 1,650.00	Hampden, 18s, 23j, y/g/f, d/s, adj, New Railway 365.00
Ball (Illinois), 12s, 19j, w/g/f, o/f 250.00	Hampden, 18s, 23j, 14k, h/c, Special Railway 950.00
Ball (Waltham), 16s, 17j, y/g/f, o/f, Commercial Std 225.00	Hampden, 18s, 7-11j, k/w, gilded, Springfield Mass 240.00
Ball (Waltham), 16s, 21j, o/f, Official Standard 365.00	Howard, E; 16s, 15j, s/w, 14k h/c, Series V, L sz 1,500.00
Columbus, 18s, 11-15j, k/w, k/s 550.00	Howard, E; 18s, 15j, h/c, silver case, k/w, Series I, N sz 2,400.00
Columbus, 18s, 15j, o/f, l/s 240.00	Howard, E; 18s, 15j, h/c, 14k case, k/w, Series II, N sz 2,650.00
Columbus, 18s, 15j, y/g/f, o/f, Jay Gould on dial 625.00	Howard, E; 18s, 15j, 18k h/c, k/w, Series II, N sz 3,400.00
Columbus, 18s, 21j, y/g/f, h/c, train on dial, Railway King 625.00	Howard, E; 18s, 17j, 25-yr, y/g/f, o/f, orig case 675.00
Columbus, 18s, 23j, 14k h/c, Columbus King 1,800.00	Howard, E; 6s, 15j, s/w, 18k h/c, Series VIII, G sz 1,200.00
Columbus, 6s, 11j, 14k h/c 495.00	Howard (Keystone), 12s, 23j, 14k, h/c, brg, Series 8 ....650.00
Cornell, 18s, 15j, s/w, JC Adams 625.00	Howard (Keystone), 16s, 17j, y/g/f, o/f, Series 9 ....295.00
Cornell, 18s, 15j, silver h/c, k/w, John Evans 540.00	Howard (Keystone), 16s, 21j, y/g/f, o/f, RR Chronometer II 525.00
Dudley, 12s, #1, 14k, o/f, flip-bk case, Masonic 3,450.00	Howard (Keystone), 16s, 23j, y/g/f, o/f, Series 0, jeweled bbl 695.00
Elgin, 10s, 18k, h/c, k/w, k/s, s/s, Gail Borden 775.00	Illinois, 0s, 7j, 14k, l/s, h/c 325.00
Elgin, 12s, 15j, 14k, h/c 550.00	Illinois, 12s, 17j, y/g/f, o/f, d/s 95.00
Elgin, 12s, 17j, 14k, h/c, GM Wheeler 550.00	Illinois, 16s, 17j, y/g/f, o/f, d/s, Bunn, EX 225.00
Elgin, 16s, 15j, doctor's, 4th model, 14k, 2nd sweep hand 1,650.00	Illinois, 16s, 17j, 14k h/c, RR King 900.00
Elgin, 16s, 15j, 14k, h/c 725.00	Illinois, 16s, 19j, y/g/f, o/f, d/s, 60-hr, Sangamo Special 1,095.00
Elgin, 16s, 21j, g/f, 3 fbd, grade #72-91, scarce 1,975.00	Illinois, 16s, 21j, g/j/s, h/c, Burlington 295.00
Elgin, 16s, 21j, y/g/f, g/j/s, o/f, BW Raymond 325.00	Illinois, 16s, 21j, o/f, d/s, Santa Fe Special 395.00
Elgin, 16s, 21j, y/g/f, g/j/s, 3 fbd 395.00	Illinois, 16s, 21j, o/f, s/s, Bunn Special 325.00
Elgin, 16s, 21j, y/g/f, o/f, l/s, RR, Father Time 295.00	Illinois, 16s, 23j, y/g/f, o/f, d/s, RR, Bunn Special, 60 hrs 700.00
Elgin, 16s, 23j, up/down indicator, BW Raymond 850.00	Illinois, 16s, 23j, y/g/f, stiff bow, o/f, Sangamo Special 795.00
Elgin, 17s, 7j, k/w, orig silver case, Leader 185.00	Illinois, 18s, 11j, #1, silver, k/w, Alleghany 150.00
Elgin, 18s, 11j, silver, h/c, k/w, gilded, MG Odgen 285.00	Illinois, 18s, 11j, #3, o/f, s/w, l/s, Comet 250.00
Elgin, 18s, 15j, o/f, d/s, k/w, silveroid, RR, BW Raymond 1st run 950.00	Illinois, 18s, 11j, Forest City 225.00
Elgin, 18s, 15j, silver h/c, Penn RR dial, BW Raymond k/w mvt ..2,250.00	Illinois, 18s, 15j, #1, adj, y/g/f, k/w, h/c, gilt, Bunn 825.00
Elgin, 18s, 15j, 14k, k/w, k/s, h/c, HL Culver 1,300.00	Illinois, 18s, 15j, #1, k/w, k/s, silver h/c, Stuart 775.00
Elgin, 18s, 17j, silveroid, BW Raymond 285.00	Illinois, 18s, 15j, k/w, k/s, gilt, Railway Regulator 675.00
Elgin, 18s, 21j, y/g/f, o/f, Father Time 325.00	Illinois, 18s, 15j, s/w, silveroid 95.00
Elgin, 18s, 23j, y/g/f, o/f, 5-position, RR, Veritas 485.00	Illinois, 18s, 17j, g/j/s, adj, B&O RR Special (Hunter), h/c 1,375.00
Elgin, 6s, 11j, 14k, h/c 400.00	Illinois, 18s, 17j, h/c, s/w, NP, coin silver, Bunn 425.00
Elgin, 6s, 15j, 20-yr, y/g/f, h/c, s/s 150.00	Illinois, 18s, 17j, o/f, d/s, adj, silveroid case, Lakeshore 225.00
Fredonia, 18s, 11j, y/g/f, h/c, k/w 425.00	Illinois, 18s, 17j, o/f, s/w, 5th pinion, Miller 325.00
Hamilton, #4992B, 16s, 22j, o/f, steel case 280.00	Illinois, 18s, 21j, g/j/s, g/f, o/f, A Lincoln 340.00
Hamilton, #910, 12s, 17j, 20-yr, y/g/f, o/f, s/s 125.00	Illinois, 18s, 21j, g/j/s, o/f, adj, B&O RR Special 1,495.00
Hamilton, #912, 12s, 17j, y/g/f, o/f, adj 125.00	Illinois, 18s, 21j, 14k, g/j/s, h/c, Bunn Special 1,250.00
Hamilton, #920, 12s, 23j, 14k, o/f 525.00	Illinois, 18s, 23j, g/j/s, Bunn Special 625.00
Hamilton, #922MP, 12s, 18k case, Masterpiece (sgn) 1,100.00	Illinois, 18s, 24j, g/j/s, adj, o/f, Chesapeake & Ohio 2,400.00
Hamilton, #925, 18s, 17j, y/g/f, h/c, s/s, l/s 240.00	Illinois, 18s, 24j, g/j/s, Bunn Special 825.00
Hamilton, #928, 18s, 15j, y/g/f, o/f, s/s 160.00	Illinois, 18s, 26j, g/j/s, o/f, Ben Franklin USA 6,500.00
Hamilton, #933, 18s, 16j, h/c, NP, low serial # 1,400.00	Illinois, 18s, 26j, 14k, Penn Special 6,500.00
Hamilton, #938, 18s, 17j, 10k, y/g/f, adj 750.00	Illinois, 18s, 7j, #3, Interior 175.00
Hamilton, #940, 18s, 21j, NP, coin silver, o/f 325.00	Illinois, 18s, 7j, #3, silveroid, America 140.00
Hamilton, #946, 18s, 23j, y/g/f, o/f, g/j/s, EX 625.00	Illinois, 18s, 9-11j, o/f, k/w, s/s, silveroid case, Hoyt 150.00

Illinois, 8s, 13j, ¾-mvt, Rose LeLand, scarce 275.00
Ingersoll, 16s, 7j, wht base metal, Reliance 45.00
Lancaster, 18s, 7j, o/f, k/w, k/s, eng silver case 150.00
Marion US, 18s, h/c, k/w, k/s, ¾-plate, Asa Fuller 350.00
Marion US, 18s, 15j, NP, h/c, s/w, Henry Randel 400.00
Melrose Watch Co, 18s, 7j, k/w, k/s 375.00
New York Watch Co, 18s, 7j, silver, h/c, k/w, Geo Sam Rice 375.00
New York Watch Co, 19j, low sz #, wolf's teeth wind 1,775.00
Patek Philippe, 12s, 18j, 18k, o/f 2,400.00
Patek Philippe, 16s, 20j, 18k, h/c 3,400.00
Rockford, 16s, 17j, y/g/f, h/c, brg, dbl roller 225.00
Rockford, 16s, 21j, #515, y/g/f 275.00
Rockford, 16s, 21j, g/j/s, o/f, grade #537, rare 800.00
Rockford, 16s, 23j, 14k, o/f, mk Doll on dial/mvt 2,250.00
Rockford, 18s, 15j, o/f, k/w, silver case 325.00
Rockford, 18s, 17j, silveroid w/mc dial, fancy mvt/hands 275.00
Rockford, 18s, 17j, y/g/f, o/f, Winnebago 275.00
Rockford, 18s, 21j, o/f, King Edward 525.00
Seth Thomas, 18s, 17j, #2, g/j/s, adj, Henry Molineux 650.00
Seth Thomas, 18s, 17j, Edgemere 150.00
Seth Thomas, 18s, 25j, g/j/s, g/f, Maiden Lane 2,600.00
Seth Thomas, 18s, 7j, ¾-mvt, bk: eagle/Liberty model 150.00
South Bend, 12s, 21j, dbl roller, Grade #431 ....225.00
South Bend, 12s, 21j, orig o/f, d/s, Studebaker 175.00
South Bend, 18s, 21j, g/j/s, h/c, Studebaker 925.00
South Bend, 18s, 21j, 14k, h/c 995.00
Swiss, 18s, 18k, h/c, 1-min, Repeater, High Grade 5,250.00

Waterford

The Waterford Glass Company operated in Ireland from the late 1700s until 1851 when the factory closed. One hundred years later (in 1951) another Waterford glassworks was instituted that produced glass similar to the 18th century wares — crystal glass, usually with cut decoration. Today Waterford is a generic term referring to the type of glass first produced there.

**Lismore decanter, $177.50;
Matching cordials, $45.00 each.**

Bowl, scalloped, oval, 11" 460.00
Candelabra, 2-arm, prisms, crystal chains, sq ped, 21", pr 1,250.00
Champagne, Eileen 75.00
Champagne flute, Curraghmore, 8-oz 98.00
Decanter, Dmn Point, sgn, 13" 250.00
Decanter, Lismore, 9½" sq 265.00
Egg bowl, w/lid, 6" 95.00
Figurine, fish 95.00
Goblet, water; Eileen 75.00
Vase, Lismore, 10" 235.00

Watt Pottery

The Watt Pottery Company was established in Crooksville, Ohio, on July 5, 1922. From approximately 1922 until 1935, they manufactured hand-turned stone containers — jars, jugs, milk pans, preserve jars, and various sizes of mixing bowls, usually marked with a cobalt blue acorn stamp. In 1936 production of these items was discontinued, and the company began to produce kitchen utilityware and ovenware such as mixing bowls, spaghetti bowls and plates, canister sets, covered casseroles, salt and pepper shakers, cookie jars, ice buckets, pitchers, bean pots, and salad and dinnerware sets. Most Watt ware is individually hand painted with bold brush strokes of red, green, or blue contrasting with the natural buff color of the glazed body. Several patterns were produced: Apple, Autumn Foliage, Cherry, Dutch Tulip, Morning Glory, Rio Rose, Rooster, Tear Drop, Starflower, and Tulip, to name a few. Much of the ware was made for advertising premiums and is often found stamped with the name of the retail company.

Tragedy struck the Watt Pottery Company on October 4, 1965, when fire completely destroyed the factory and warehouse. Production never resumed, but the ware they made has withstood many years of service in American kitchens and is today highly regarded and prized by collectors. The vivid colors and folk art-like execution of each cheerful pattern create a homespun ambiance that will make Watt pottery a treasure for years to come.

For further study we recommend *Watt Pottery, An Identification and Price Guide,* by our advisors for this category, Sue and Dave Morris, who are listed in the Directory under Iowa. For the address of the *Watt's News* newsletter, see the section on Clubs, Newsletters, and Catalogs.

Apple, bean pot, #76, w/lid 175.00
Apple, bowl, #04 ....65.00
Apple, casserole, ribbed, #601, w/lid 125.00
Apple, grease jar, #01, w/lid 325.00
Apple, mug, #121 ....175.00
Apple, pie plate, #33, w/advertising 125.00
Apple, pitcher, #17, w/ice lip 225.00
Apple, sugar bowl, #98, w/lid 400.00
Autumn Foliage, baker, #96, w/lid 90.00
Autumn Foliage, bowl, mixing; #8 ....35.00
Autumn Foliage, mug, #121 ....150.00
Autumn Foliage, pie plate, #33, w/advertising 125.00
Autumn Foliage, pitcher, #15 ....65.00
Autumn Foliage, shakers, hourglass form, pr 175.00
Banded, casserole, bl/wht bands, w/lid, 8" dia 55.00
Basketweave, bowl, mixing; #7, gr 30.00
Cherry, cookie jar, #21, w/lid 250.00
Cherry, salt shaker, bbl shaped 90.00
Cherry, spaghetti bowl, #39 ....125.00
Dutch Tulip, bowl, mixing; #8 ....110.00
Dutch Tulip, casserole, #67, w/lid 250.00
Dutch Tulip, cheese crock, #80, w/lid 475.00
Dutch Tulip, pitcher, #15, w/advertising 225.00
Eagle, bowl, mixing; #6, ribbed 125.00
Goodies jar, #76, w/lid 275.00
Kitch-N-Queen, bowl, mixing; #8, ribbed 30.00
Morning Glory, bowl, mixing; #9 ....100.00
Morning Glory, cookie jar, #95, w/lid 400.00
Morning Glory, pitcher, #96, w/ice lip 375.00
Rio Rose, bowl, berry; 4" dia 25.00
Rio Rose, pitcher, #17 ....190.00
Rio Rose, spaghetti bowl, 13" 80.00
Rio Rose (cut leaf), cup & saucer 90.00
Rio Rose (cut leaf), plate, dinner; 8½" 45.00

Rooster, bowl, mixing; #8 ....65.00
Rooster, creamer, #62 ....225.00
Rooster, ice bucket, w/lid 275.00
Rooster, pitcher, #15, w/advertising 145.00
Starflower, bowl, cereal; #74 ....25.00
Starflower, casserole, #18, tab hdls, ind 125.00
Starflower, mug, #501, bbl shape 90.00
Starflower, pitcher, #17 ....135.00
Starflower, shakers, bbl shape, pr 175.00
Tear Drop, bean server, #75, ind 20.00
Tear Drop, bowl, #06, ribbed 40.00
Tear Drop, casserole, #66, w/lid 85.00
Tear Drop, pitcher, #15 ....60.00
Tulip, bowl, deep mixing; #64 ....85.00
Tulip, casserole, #600, ribbed, w/lid 250.00
Tulip, cookie jar, #503, w/lid 375.00
Tulip, creamer, #62 ....225.00
Tulip, pitcher, #17, w/ice lip 300.00
White Daisy, bread plate, 6½" 55.00

Wave Crest

Wave Crest is a line of decorated opal ware (milk glass) patented in 1892 by the C.F. Monroe Co. of Meriden, Connecticut. They made a full line of items for every room of the house, but they are probably best known for their boxes and vases. Most items were hand painted in various levels of decoration, but more transfers were used in the later years prior to the company's demise in 1916. Floral themes are common; items with the scenics and portraits are rarer and more highly prized. Many pieces have ornately scrolled ormolu and brass handles, feet and rims attached. Early pieces were often signed with a black mark; later a red banner mark was used, and occasionally a paper label may be found. However, the glass is quite distinctive and has not been reproduced, so even unmarked items are easy to recognize. Our advisors for this category are Dolli and Wilfred Cohen; they are listed in the Directory under California. Note: There is no premium for signatures on Wave Crest. Values are given for hand-decorated pieces (unless noted 'transfer') that are *not* worn.

Ash receiver, emb scrolls w/floral, ormolu hdld ped ft, 3¾" 200.00
Atomizer, bl apple blossoms on ball shape, orig hardware 250.00
Biscuit jar, apple blossoms on tulip mold 350.00
Biscuit jar, emb scrolls/ribs, flowers ea side, metal mts 350.00
Biscuit jar, pastel ferns on squat shape w/melon ribs 350.00
Biscuit jar, Puffy, HP florals, heavily emb, 8x5½" 575.00
Biscuit jar, wild roses/emb scrolls, sqd, SP rim & mts 275.00
Bottle, scent; Puffy, HP forget-me-nots, sq 350.00
Box, Baroque Shell, pk rose bud on lid, ormolu mts, 7" dia 900.00
Box, Baroque Shell, violets/tracing, sq reserve on yel, 7" dia 895.00
Box, emb wild roses & scrolls, daisies on pk, 5¾" dia 450.00
Box, floral on pk, emb icicles around dome lid, 4½" dia 425.00
Box, lg robin on lid, 5¾x6½" sq 1,850.00
Box, pk roses w/lav on scrollwork, 6x4¾" sq 735.00
Box, Puffy, forget-me-nots, red on tan, 3" dia 200.00
Box, Swirl, floral bouquet on lt yel, 4" dia 275.00
Box, Swirl, forget-me-nots on pk, 2½x3" dia 250.00
Box, Swirl, forget-me-nots on tan & opal, 2½x3" dia ..250.00
Box, Swirl, lotus on gr & beige w/allover floral, 6½" dia 1,000.00
Box, Swirl, poppies/leaves on wht, hinged, 4x6½" dia 550.00
Box, wild rose/emb scrolls on bl, paw-ftd ormolu base, 5" sq 600.00
Finger bowl, deer in forest transfer 195.00
Humidor, Cigars, emb scrolls/floral, HP floral on gr/bl 895.00
Humidor, Tobacco, florals, pk on bl, 5½" 800.00

Ice bucket, wild roses on bl, ornate lid & hdl, 6¼" dia 1,020.00
Jar, dancing storks on pastel spiral panels, gilt mts, 5½" 1,150.00
Pickle castor, Swirl, toadstools/flowers, SP fr 395.00
Sugar shaker, pk florals w/wht dots 295.00
Sugar shaker, Swirl, pk/gold scrolls on yel w/gray tracing 500.00
Tray, pin; Puffy, daisies on wht, ormolu hdls, 2x3" 125.00
Vase, floral/dk gr scrolls on cream, long neck, ormolu ft, 9" 595.00
Vase, irises on yel, heavily emb, beaded top, 9¾" 550.00
Vase, wild roses, emb bl scrolls, 9" 550.00

Weapons

Among the varied areas of specialization within the broad category of weapons, guns are by far the most popular. Muskets are among the earliest firearms; they were large-bore shoulder arms, usually firing black powder with separate loading of powder and shot. Some ignited the charge by flintlock or caplock, while later types used a firing pin with a metallic cartridge. Side arms, referred to as such because they were worn at the side, include pistols and revolvers. Pistols range from early single-shot and multiple barrels to modern types with cartridges held in the handle. Revolvers were supplied with a cylinder that turned to feed a fresh round in front of the barrel breech. Other firearms include shotguns, which fired round or conical bullets and had a smooth inner barrel surface, and rifles, so named because the interior of the barrel contained spiral grooves (rifling) which increased accuracy. For further study we recommend *Modern Guns, Tenth Edition* and *Pocket Guide to Rifles*, both by Russell Quartermous and Steve Quartermous, available at your local bookstore. All weapons but swords are under the advisement of Steve Howard, see the Directory under California. See also Militaria.

Key:
bbl — barrel	mag — magazine
cal — caliber	mgn — magnum
conv — conversion	mod — modified
cyl — cylinder	oct — octagon
f/l — flintlock	o/u — over/under
f/s — full stock	p/b — patch box
ga — gauge	perc — percussion
hdw — hardware	/s — stock
h/s — half stock	

Carbines

Winchester Model 1892 Eastern, 38 caliber, straight stock, hard rubber butt plate, EX, $1,500.00.

Ball & Williams (Ballard Pat), 44 cal, 22" oct-to-rnd bbl, EX 825.00
Gallagher's Pat Standard, steel hdw, p/b, G 1,045.00
Hall-North 1843, 52 cal, walnut/s, 1851 on block, EX 990.00
Joslyn 1862, brass hdw, inspector's mks, VG 1,265.00
Maynard 2nd Model, perc, 50 cal, 1865 on trigger plate, VG ..1,100.00
Palmer, bolt-action, 50 cal, US & EG Lamson & Co on lock, VG .1,595.00
Sharps & Hankins 1862 Cavalry, walnut/s, 19" rnd bbl, G 660.00
Sharps New 1859, perc, 52 cal, 22" rnd bbl, p/b, walnut/s, EX ..1,375.00
Springfield 1873 Trapdoor, 45-70 cal, 22" bbl, VG 750.00
Starr, perc, 54 cal, 31" rnd bbl, walnut/s, VG 1,045.00

Muskets

Danish, 80 cal, smooth bore 41½" bbl, f/s, 1700s, EX **400.00**
F/l Committee of Safety, 89 cal, B Horner on lock, 47", VG **450.00**
Harpers Ferry 1842, perc, 69 cal, walnut/s, w/bayonet, G **550.00**
Harpers Ferry 1842, perc, 69 cal, 42" bbl & bayonet, VG **880.00**
Potsdam, perc, f/s w/brass mts, mk 1824 41" bbl, EX, +bayonet ..**500.00**
Revolutionary War era, 46½" oct-to-rnd bbl, iron hdw, 60" **880.00**

Pistols

Allen & Wheelock, perc, 4" oct-to-rnd bbl, walnut grip, G **275.00**
Am Arms, 22 & 32 cal 3" bbls swivel, brass fr, VG **400.00**
Continental Arms pepperbox, 22 cal, 5-shot bbl, G **200.00**
European perc, 36 cal, folding trigger, 4" damascus bbl, G **85.00**
Johnson, perc, US & 1854 on lock, walnut/s, rprs, 14", VG **475.00**
North 1816 f/l, 54 cal, 9" bbl, 15", G **880.00**
Waters 1836 f/l, 54 cal, 1837 & eagle head on lock, 14", VG **880.00**
Woodwards, 30 cal, swivel breech, SP traces on fr, 2½" bbl **165.00**

Revolvers

Colt, single action, 38 WCF cal, worn SP fr, 5½" bbl, VG **1,250.00**
Colt, single action, 41 cal, rubber grip, 4¾" bbl, EX **2,500.00**
Colt 1851 Navy, perc, 36 cal, 7½" bbl, G **660.00**
Colt 1860 Army, perc, 44 cal, 8" bbl, G **635.00**
E Whitney pocket, perc, 28 cal, 3½" bbl, G **275.00**
London Pistol Co, perc, 31 cal, wood grip, 5" bbl, VG **325.00**
Moore's Pat Belt, single action, 32 cal rimfire, 5" bbl, VG **350.00**
Reid knuckle duster, 22 cal, worn SP on brass, 1866 on strap **275.00**
Savage Navy, perc, 36 cal, 6-shot, 7⅛" bbl, VG **450.00**
Smith & Wesson 1st model dbl action, 32 cal, 3" bbl, EX **165.00**
Starr 1858 DA Army, perc, 44 cal, rprs/rpl, 11½" **750.00**
Whitney Navy, perc, 36 cal, eng cyl, 7½" bbl, VG **500.00**

Rifles

A Davidson & Co, perc, maple/s w/silver inlay, 44" bbl, VG ..**1,800.00**
Hall 1819 f/l, walnut/s, 2nd production/dtd 1837, NM **2,650.00**
JP Sauer & Son, single shot, 32 cal, eng fr, 25¾" bbl, G **495.00**
KY, perc, curly maple f/s, mc RW Booth..., 35" bbl, 52", EX **685.00**
KY by A Angstadt, perc, 38 cal, brass hdw, 45" oct bbl, G **880.00**
KY f/l, curly maple f/s, brass p/b, rpr, 43" bbl, 59", VG **825.00**
Mid Eastern Snaphaunce, ornate eng & inlaid steel & brass, VG .**300.00**
OH-style h/s, perc, 40 cal, curly maple/s, dbl triggers, VG **330.00**
Springfield 1863 Type I, perc, 58 cal, walnut/s, bayonet, EX ...**1,925.00**
West PA, f/l, curly/s, silver cheek pc, eng p/b, 44" bbl, VG **1,875.00**
Winchester 63, 22 long cal, VG **500.00**
Winchester 64, lever action, 30 WCF cal, blued finish, EX **660.00**
Wm G Schrekengost, perc, 32 cal, maple/s, tulip p/b, 37" bbl .**2,500.00**
Wm Lloyd, perc, curly maple/s w/inlay, brass p/b, 42" bbl, EX ...**1,650.00**

Shotguns

AH Box A Grade, early style 12 ga, 30" bbls, EX **500.00**
Browning Over/Under Grade 1, 12 ga, 28" bbls, EX **1,200.00**
Eastern Arms, single shot, 410 ga, 26" bbl, EX **125.00**
H Pieper, 12 ga, full side lock w/dbl triggers, mk bbls, G **125.00**
LC Smith Field Grade by Hunter Arms, 12 ga, 30" bbls, VG **250.00**
Mauser 98, w/Weaver K2.5 scope, reblued, poor wood **225.00**
Parker Bros, 12 ga, hammerless, Std grade, dbl bbls, EX **500.00**
Parker Deluxe, 12 ga, #2 fr, 30" steel bbls, VG **750.00**
Parker GH, 12 ga, 20" dbl bbls, reblued, EX **2,100.00**
Parker VH, 12 ga, str English-style/s, 30" bbls, EX **600.00**

Savage-Fox Sterlingworth, 16 ga, 30" bbls, rfn, EX **250.00**
Winchester 12 Deluxe, 12 ga, 32" bbl w/Simmons rib, EX **450.00**
Winchester 97, pump action, 12 ga, 30" rnd bbl, full choke, EX ..**500.00**

Swords

All swords listed below are priced 'with scabbard,' unless otherwise noted.

Am Milita officer's, eagle pommel, 30" str blade, VG **250.00**
Am Militia High Grade, eagle pommel, 1810s, 32" blade, EX .**1,900.00**
Ames 1840, musician's, 2-section scabbard w/brass tip, 35" **195.00**
Ames 1860 NCO, 32" blade, missing scabbard, EX **165.00**
Confederate Heavy Cavalry, cast brass hilt, 36" blade, EX **1,450.00**
French Naval officer's, monster-head hilt, 29" blade, EX **250.00**
N Star 1812 Contract Saber, 33½" curved blade, EX **500.00**
N Star 1818 noncommissioned officer's, 25¾" blade, VG **450.00**
Prussian officer's presentation, 33" Damascus gilded blade **2,200.00**
Standard 1850 regulation foot officer's, 30" etch blade, EX **1,450.00**
US 1850 Presentation Grade field officer's, Solingen, 37", VG ..**700.00**
US/N Starr 1818 Contract saber, 32" curved blade, EX **400.00**

Weather Vanes

The earliest weather vanes were of handmade wrought iron and were generally simple angular silhouettes with a small hole suggesting an eye. Later copper, zinc, and polychromed wood with features in relief were fashioned into more realistic forms. Ships, horses, fish, Indians, roosters, and angels were popular motifs. In the 19th century, silhouettes were often made from sheet metal. Wooden figures became highly carved and were painted in vivid colors. E.G. Washburne and Company in New York was one of the most prominent manufacturers of weather vanes during the last half of the century. Two-dimensional sheet metal weather vanes are increasing in value due to the already heady prices of the full-bodied variety. Originality, strength of line, and patination help to determine value. When no condition is indicated, the items listed below are assumed to be in excellent condition.

Key:
fb — full-bodied   f/fb — flattened full-bodied

Leaping stag, gilt copper, attributed to Harris and Co., Boston, 1800s, 32", EX, $17,000.00.

Banner, cast & wrought iron, 17", EX **375.00**
Beaver, copper, primitive style, 1900s, rprs, 33" L **195.00**
Chicken silhouette, sheet steel, old pnt, 51" H **130.00**
Cod fish, gilt copper, New England, late 1800s, 30", EX **6,325.00**
Cod fish, gilt copper, 30", G **750.00**
Eagle, copper, 48" w/46" wingspan, EX **1,950.00**
Eagle, copper w/gilt traces, full body, 28x29" on base **600.00**

Eagle, cvd wood, gilt pnt, age cracks, 19th C, 16" **1,265.00**
Eagle, zinc w/gilt & verdigris, 15", EX **1,035.00**
Horse & rider, copper, old yel pnt, late 1800s, 31" **1,500.00**
Horse running, copper, verdigris surface, late 1800s, 28½" **865.00**
Horse running, copper w/cast-zinc head, 27x33", EX **7,500.00**
Horse running, gilt copper, late 1800s, 41", EX **2,070.00**
Horse running, gilt copper w/verdigris, rpl head, 29" **750.00**
Horse running, gilt zinc & copper, Am, late 19th C, 33" **690.00**
Horse running, zinc & copper, 19th C, 30", VG **1,035.00**
Horse silhouette, cut-out pine, weathered, 33", on wooden base .**110.00**
Horse silhouette, sheet steel, old gray pnt, 1900s, 28" L **385.00**
Roadster, zinc, low relief w/CI & copper base w/arrow, 21x22" **75.00**
Rooster, copper, fb w/sheet comb & tail, late 1800s, 21" **860.00**
Schooner, cvd wood, Frank Adams/Martha's Vinyard, 1930s, 34" .**975.00**
Windmill, wood & metal, old mc pnt, concrete base, 27" H **45.00**

Weaving

Early Americans used a variety of tools and a great amount of time to produce the material from which their clothing was made. Soaked and dried flax was broken on a flax brake to remove waste material. It was then tapped and stroked with a scutching knife. Hackles further removed waste and separated the short fibers from the longer ones. Unspun fibers were placed on the distaff on the spinning wheel for processing into yarn. The yarn was then wound around a reel for measuring. Three tools used for this purpose were the niddy-noddy, the reel yarn winder, and the click reel. After it was washed and dyed, the yarn was transferred to a barrel-cage or squirrel-cage swift and fed onto a bobbin winder.

Today flax wheels are more plentiful than the large wool wheels since they were small and could be more easily stored and preserved. The distaff, an often-discarded or misplaced part of the wheel, is very scarce. French spinners from the Quebec area painted their wheels. Many have been stripped and refinished by those unaware of this fact. Wheels may be very simple or have a great amount of detail, depending upon the owner's ethnic background and the maker's skill.

Clock winder, 4 trn winder arms, 3 splayed legs, 40½" **100.00**
Comb, flax or wool; wrought w/6½" spikes, 22x26x1⅛" **125.00**
Stool (weaver's), 2-slat, splint seat, New England, 40" **165.00**
Swift, cvd whalebone & ivory, reptile cvd base, mid-1800s, NM .**1,500.00**
Swift, whale bone, whale ivory & baleen, cvd 4-leg base, 18" ..**3,450.00**
Swift, wooden umbrella shape w/bbl-shaped clamp, 25x17", VG .**125.00**
Tape loom, maple w/red traces, decorative details, 22x11" **850.00**
Wheel, hard & soft wood, trn & chip-cvd details, 61x72" **450.00**
Wheel, hardwood, EX trn details, rfn, 39", EX **325.00**
Wheel, hardwood, trn/chip-cvd details, 37", EX **400.00**

Webb

Thomas Webb and Sons have been glassmakers in Stourbridge, England, since 1837. Besides their fine cameo glass, they have also made enameled ware and pieces heavily decorated with applied glass ornaments. The butterfly is a motif that has been so often featured that it tends to suggest Webb as the manufacturer. Our advisor for this category is Don Williams; he is listed in the Directory under Missouri. See also specific types of glass such as Alexandrite, Burmese, Mother of Pearl, and Peachblow.

Bottle, scent; wht satin, gold & mc enamel, silver lid, 5½" **295.00**
Bowl, aqua to cream w/clear appl garlands & berries, 4½" **245.00**
Ewer, gr to off-wht satin, gold/gr apples, gold leaves, 9" **425.00**

Rose bowl, bl satin w/flowers/vines, tooled camphor ft, 4½" **65.00**
Rose bowl, gold flowers & butterfly, 2½" **380.00**
Rose bowl, pk, scalloped rim, 3 appl leaves form ft, 3½" **160.00**
Rose bowl, pk satin w/forget-me-nots & berries, pear form, 4" **150.00**
Rose bowl, red w/zipper motif, crimped edge, 2" **170.00**
Sweetmeat jar, aqua w/gold florals, SP trim, 5¼x3⅜" **300.00**
Vase, bl shaded satin, bird/florals/lg butterfly, 8x6" **425.00**
Vase, Bronze Glass, mirror-lustre cobalt irid, 11½" **230.00**
Vase, coral satin w/heavy gold prunus & 2 bees, 5x2¾" **200.00**
Vase, floriform; rubena, ribbed, ftd, mk MIE, 4¾" **165.00**
Vase, gold satin w/gold floral/butterfly, 5x3" **245.00**
Vase, golden yel w/gold prunus & butterfly, 6⅝x3⅜" **300.00**
Vase, pk satin, floral/gilt on tan, stick neck/flat sides, 10" **250.00**
Vase, pk/wht satin stripes, ruffled w/bulbous bottom, 8x4" **400.00**

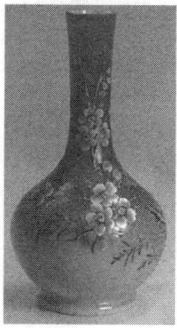

Vase, roses on pink to orange, 11½", $385.00.

Vase, rose to gr satin, cream int, 9x4½" **395.00**
Vase, turq-gr to yel satin w/gold prunus/butterfly, 4½" **100.00**
Vase, yel cased satin w/mc bird, mk, 9½" **415.00**
Vase, yel satin, gourd form, 11" **285.00**
Vase, yel satin w/gold florals & butterfly, stick neck, 5" **225.00**

Cameo

Bottle, lay-down; floral, wht on citron, att, 3½" **900.00**
Bottle, scent; rectangle w/wht floral on X-cut clear, 6x6x2" **1,250.00**
Bottle, scent; wild roses on 4 sides, wht on citron, 5½" **2,750.00**
Bowl, cherry branches, lt bl on bl, 1¾x5" **650.00**
Cup & saucer, prunus/buds/butterfly, red on clear, 2¾x5" **550.00**
Decanter, cherry blossoms, pk/wht on yel, silver mts, 9½" **5,175.00**
Decanter, lg leaves/flowers, wht on lt bl, silver mts, 8½" **1,300.00**
Lamp, floral, red on wht, U-form shade, squat ftd base, 9" **4,050.00**
Lamp base, butterflies/fern fronds, wht on red, squatty, 8½" **700.00**
Rose bowl, rose/buds cascade from rim, wht on citron **1,450.00**
Vase, allover floral, wht on citron, gold portrait, 4" **1,200.00**
Vase, azaleas, bk: butterfly/bee, wht on med bl, 6" **1,850.00**
Vase, cascading floral, wht/red on citron, stick neck, 10" **2,750.00**
Vase, cherry blossoms, bk: bee, wht on yel, 9" **1,100.00**
Vase, cherub/floral, wht on emerald gr, sgn Woodall, 3x2½" ..**7,500.00**
Vase, floral/butterfly, red & wht on frost, 9x6" **1,495.00**
Vase, floral/butterfly, wht on opal cased to pk/amber, 7" **2,300.00**
Vase, lg flower stalk, brn-washed wht on ivory, long neck, 11" ..**1,700.00**
Vase, lilies/leaves, amber on clear, wide trumpet form, 9" **490.00**
Vase, phlox on long stems/butterflies, wht on bl, 3" **1,050.00**
Vase, trumpet flowers/butterfly, wht on peachblow, 12x6" **3,500.00**
Vase, vines/florals, bk: butterfly, wht on red, 4¾" **1,035.00**
Vase, wild roses/berries, bk: butterfly, lt on med bl, ftd, 5" **1,300.00**

Wedgwood

Josiah Wedgwood established his pottery in Burslem, England, in

1759. He produced only molded utilitarian earthenwares until 1770 when new facilities were opened at Etruria for the production of ornamental wares. It was there he introduced his famous Basalt and Jasperware. Jasperware, an unglazed fine stoneware decorated with classic figures in white relief, was usually produced in blues; but it was also made in ground colors of green, lilac, yellow, black, or white. Occasionally three or more colors were used in combination. It has been in continuous production to the present day and is the most easily recognized of all the Wedgwood lines. Jasper-dip is a ware with a solid-color body or a white body that has been dipped in an overlay color. It was introduced in the late 1700s and is the type most often encountered on today's market.

Though Wedgwood's Jasperware was highly acclaimed, on a more practical basis his improved creamware was his greatest success. Due to the ease with which it could be potted and because its lighter weight significantly reduced transportation expenses, Wedgwood was able to offer 'chinaware' at affordable prices. Queen Charlotte was so pleased with the ware that she allowed it to be called 'Queen's Ware.' Most creamware was marked simply 'Wedgwood.' ('Wedgwood & Co.' and 'Wedgewood' are marks of other potters.) From 1769 to 1780, Wedgwood was in partnership with Thomas Bentley; artwares of the highest quality may bear the 'Wedgwood & Bentley' mark indicating this partnership. Moonlight Lustre, an allover splashed-on effect of pink intermingling with gray, brown, or yellow, was made from 1805 to 1815. Porcelain was made, though not to any great extent, from 1812 to 1822. Bone china was produced before 1822 and after 1872. These types of wares were marked 'WEDGWOOD' (with a printed 'Portland Vase' mark after 1872). Stone china and Pearlware were made from about 1820 to 1875. Examples of either may be found with a printed or impressed mark to indicate their body type. During the late 1800s, Wedgwood produced some fine parian and majolica. Creamware, hand painted by Emile Lessore, was sold from about 1860 to 1875. From the 20th century, several lines of lustre wares — Butterfly, Dragon, and Fairyland (designed by Daisy Makeig-Jones) — have attracted the collector and, as their prices suggest, are highly sought after and admired.

Nearly all of Wedgwood's wares are clearly marked. 'WEDGWOOD' was used before 1891, after which time 'ENGLAND' was added. Most examples marked 'MADE IN ENGLAND' were made after 1905. A detailed study of all marks is recommended for accurate dating. See also Majolica.

Key:
WW — Wedgwood   WWMIE — Wedgwood Made in
WWE — Wedgwood England   England

Vase, Fairyland Lustre, Castle on a Road, pattern Z5125 on shape #2442, WWE, ca 1920, 7½", $4,000.00.

Basket, Creamware, openwork, WW, 3x9½", NM 350.00
Biscuit box, Jasper, lt gr, acorn finial, England, 8" 375.00
Biscuit jar, Jasper, 3-color, classical figures, WW, 5⅛" 750.00
Biscuit jar, Jasper, 3-color, scrolls/etc, SP trim, WW, 5" 865.00
Bowl, centre; Dragon Lustre, MOP int, WWE, Z-4829, 8¾" 690.00
Bowl, Dragon Lustre, MOP int, 8-sided, WWE, Z-4829, 4¾" 285.00
Bowl, Fairyland Lustre, Leapfrogging Elves, WWE, Z-4968, 3⅞" ..1,000.00

Bowl, Fairyland Lustre, Moorish scene, WWE, Z-5125, 8" 1,250.00
Bowl, Fairyland Lustre, Poplar Trees, WWE, 11" 3,680.00
Bowl, Hummingbird Lustre, flying geese, WWE, Z-5927, 10" 535.00
Bowl, Jasper, yel, lion masks, SP, WWE, 8½", +servers 600.00
Bowl, lobster; Creamware, ocean transfer, WW, ca 1864, 10" ...250.00
Bowl, Powder Bl Lustre, fish, MOP int, WWE, ca 1925, 4⅝" 430.00
Box, Basalt, Cupid Sharpening Arrow, oval, WWE, 2" 95.00
Box, Jasper, crimson, w/lid, WWE, ca 1900, 3" 575.00
Box, Jasper, dk bl, WWE, ca 1981 ....120.00
Box, Jasper, Portland Bl, Camilla, WWE 50.00
Box, Jasper, royal bl, MIE, 4⅝" dia 130.00
Box, Lustre, bird & turtle decor, MOP int, WW, Z-4829, 3¼" ..400.00
Bust, Ariadne, Basalt, silver-gilt mtd base, WW, 2¼" 345.00
Bust, George Moore, Carrara, sgn EW Wyon, WW, ca 1859, 14¼" .430.00
Bust, Milton, Basalt, mid-19th C, Etruria mk, 13¼" 920.00
Cake plate, Jasper, lt bl, MIE, 9½" 65.00
Candlestick, Jasper, dk bl, WWE, 6" dia 255.00
Chocolate pot, Jasper, dk bl, classical figures, WWE, 7½" 325.00
Cigarette lighter, Jasper, sage gr, vintage decor, MIE 40.00
Coffeepot, Basalt, Rosso Antico, mc flowers, WW, 8" 450.00
Coffeepot, Basalt, Sacrifice, 19th C, 6¾" 450.00
Creamer, Caneware, classical relief, WW, ca 1800, 3½" 400.00
Creamer, Creamware, Eastern Flowers 78.00
Creamer, Jasper, dk bl, vintage decor, WW, 1¼x3" 145.00
Creamer & sugar bowl, Jasper, terra cotta, WWE 200.00
Cup, melba; Butterfly Lustre, orange, MOP int, WWE, 6 for ..1,725.00
Cup & saucer, demitasse; Jasper, cobalt, Boston shape, WWE ...100.00
Cup & saucer, Jasper, dk bl, pear shape, WWE 95.00
Cup & saucer, Jasper, sage gr, classic figures, WWE 100.00
Figure, Basalt, infant pointing, free-form base, WW, 5" L 900.00
Goblet, Moonlight Lustre, WW, ca 1815, 3⅝" 230.00
Inkstand, Basalt, pnt flowers, canted corners, WWE, 5¾x8" 600.00
Inkstand, moonstone body, dbl well, K Murray, WWE, '35, 10" ..375.00
Jar, cigarette; Jasper, sage gr, WWE 155.00
Jar, jam; Jasper, cobalt, SP trim, WW, 4½" 265.00
Jug, Doric; Jasper, lilac, figures, pewter lid, WW, 1870s, 6" 515.00
Jug, Jasper, dk bl, Etruscan, England, 6¼" 230.00
Matchbox, Jasper, crimson, WWE, 3½x2" 500.00
Matchbox, Jasper, lt bl, oblong, w/striker, WW 265.00
Mug, Jasper, dk bl, classic figures/medallion, SP rim, WW, 5" 125.00
Mug, Moonlight Lustre, WW, ca 1815, 3" 230.00
Napkin rings, Bone China, Clementine, WWE, 4 for 70.00
Nautilus shell, Bone China, on coral stand, ca 1878, 4" 265.00
Pitcher, Jasper, bleeding gr, Franklin & Washington, WWE, 3¾" .325.00
Pitcher, Jasper, crimson, rope twist hdl, WWE, ca 1900, 5¼" 500.00
Pitcher, Jasper, lt bl, satyr's head at spout, WW, 1895, 2¾" 300.00
Pitcher, Jasper, sage gr, classical figures, WWE, 6⅜x3¾" 155.00
Pitcher, Jasper, 3-color, bellflowers, WW, 1850s, 4¼" 500.00
Pitcher, tankard; Jasper, cobalt, WWE, 4" 100.00
Pitcher, tankard; Jasper, gr, ladies & cherubs, WWE, 6½" 175.00
Pitcher, tankard; Jasper, olive gr, MIE, 7¼" 250.00
Plaque, Fairyland Lustre, Enchanted Palace, WWE, fr: 11x14" ..975.00
Plaque, Jasper, dk bl, classical figures, WW, 4⅜x5⅝"+fr 315.00
Plaque, Jasper, 3-color, ...Achilles, WW, fr, 8½x23" 2,075.00
Plaque, Jasper, 3-color, classical figures, WW, 4x10½"+fr 725.00
Plaque, Jasper, 3-color, Hercules..., WW, fr, 8½x23¼" 1,800.00
Plate, Creamware, Knave of Clubs, tan rim, WWE 125.00
Platter, Botanicals, brn transfer w/pk & gold, WW, 18" 900.00
Potpourri, Jasper, dk bl, w/lid, WW, ca 1886, 3½" 460.00
Punch bowl, Fairyland Lustre, Poplar Tree, WWE, Z-4968, 11" .5,000.00
Ring tree, Jasper, lt bl, cherubs, WWE, 2½" 200.00
Sugar bowl, Jasper, lt gr, w/lid, WWE, 3" 130.00
Tea & coffee set, Jasper, pk, WWE, 1970, mini, 2 pots+4 pcs 175.00
Tea set, Caneware, trn bodies, WW, ca 1800, 2⅞" pot+cr/sug ...700.00

Tea set, Jasper, royal bl, MIE, 3-pc 650.00
Teapot, Basalt, Capri, ca 1840, lg 525.00
Teapot, Drabware, smear glaze, spaniel finial, WW, NM 325.00
Teapot, Jasper, lilac, Brewster, ca 1870 ....465.00
Teapot, Jasper, lt gr, WWE, 4½" 200.00
Tray, Jasper, lt bl, Churchill, MIE, 4¼" 78.00
Tray, Jasper, lt bl, Spade, WWE 42.50
Tray, pin; Jasper, dk bl, Muse, WW, 4¼" 130.00
Urn, Jasper, dk bl, drum base, WW, 1850s, 14¼", pr 1,200.00
Vase, Basalt, Arcadian, 5" 235.00
Vase, bud; Jasper, dk bl, Cameo, WWE, 5" 125.00
Vase, bud; Jasper, terra cotta, Arcadian, MIE, 5" 100.00
Vase, Drabware, WW, 5" 225.00
Vase, Fairyland Lustre, Willow, #2410, WWE, Z-4968, 8" 2,250.00
Vase, Ivory Vellum, mc florals, elephants, WW, 1890s, 10", NM .250.00
Vase, Jasper, dk bl, stick form, WW, ca 1867, 7¼" 235.00
Vase, Jasper, lt bl, Apollo & 9 Muses, WW, 1861, 8¼" 285.00
Vase, Jasper, lt bl, ram's head & flowers, WWE, 10¼x3⅜" 265.00
Vase, Jasper, 3-color, w/lid, WW, 19th C, 13¾" 3,000.00
Vase, spill; Jasper, dk bl, MIE, ca 1930, 3" 95.00

Weil Ware

Max Weil came to the United States in the 1940s, settling in California. There he began manufacturing dinnerware, figurines, cookie jars, and wall pockets. American clays were used, and the dinnerware was all hand decorated. Weil died in 1954; the company closed two years later. The last backstamp to be used was the outline of a burro with the words 'Weil Ware — Made in California.' Many unmarked pieces found today originally carried a silver foil label; but you'll often find a four-digit handwritten number series, especially on figurines. For further study we recommend *The Collector's Encyclopedia of California Pottery* by our advisor, Jack Chipman. He is listed in the Directory under California.

Figurine, boy w/wheelbarrow, #4005 ....45.00
Figurine, girl, flower vase under right arm, 2nd in skirt, 10" 40.00
Figurine, girl, tall/slim, basket at waist, HP floral, 11" 45.00
Figurine, girl, ½-rnd flower vase ea side, appl roses, 10" 38.00
Figurine, girl sits between flower vases, HP floral, #4028, 9" 40.00
Figurine, 18th-C lady, fancy updo, appl roses/cvd lace, #1729, 14" ..90.00
Wall pocket, Oriental girl 40.00

Weller

The Weller Pottery Company was established in Zanesville, Ohio, in 1882, the outgrowth of a small one-kiln log cabin works Sam Weller had operated in Fultonham. Through an association with Wm. Long, he entered the art pottery field in 1895, producing the Lonhuda Ware Long had perfected in Steubenville six years earlier. His famous Louwelsa line was merely a continuation of Lonhuda and was made in at least five hundred different shapes until 1924. Many fine lines of artware followed under the direction of Charles Babcock Upjohn, art director from 1895 to 1904: Dickens Ware (1st Line), under-glaze slip decorations on dark backgrounds; Turada, featuring applied ivory bands of delicate openwork on solid dark brown backgrounds; and Aurelian, similar to Louwelsa, but with a brushed-on rather than blended ground. One of their most famous lines was 2nd Line Dickens, introduced in 1900. Backgrounds, characteristically caramel shading to turquoise matt, were decorated by sgraffito with animals, golfers, monks, Indians, and scenes from Dickens novels. The work is often artist signed. Sicardo, 1903, was a metallic lustre line in tones of rose, blue, green, or purple with flowing Art Nouveau patterns developed within the glaze.

Frederick Hurten Rhead, who worked for Weller from 1903 to 1904, created the prestigious Jap Birdimal line decorated with geisha girls, landscapes, storks, etc., accomplished through application of heavy slip forced through the tiny nozzle of a squeeze bag. Other lines to his credit are L'Art Nouveau, produced in both in high-gloss brown and matt pastels, and 3rd Line Dickens, often decorated with Cruikshank's illustrations in relief. Other early artware lines were Eocean, Floretta, Hunter, Perfecto, Dresden, Etched Matt, and Etna.

In 1920 John Lessel was hired as art director, and under his supervision several new lines were created. LaSa, LaMar, Marengo, and Besline attest to his expertise with metallic lustres. The last of the artware lines and one of the most sought after by collectors today is Hudson, first made during the early 1920s. Hudson, a semimatt glazed ware, was beautifully artist decorated on shaded backgrounds with florals, animals, birds, and scenics. Notable artists often signed their work, among them Hester Pillsbury, Dorothy England Laughead, Ruth Axline, Claude Leffler, Sarah Reid McLaughlin, E.L. Pickens, and Mae Timberlake.

During the thirties Weller produced a line of gardenware and naturalistic life-sized figures of dogs, cats, swans, geese, and playful gnomes. The Depression brought a slow, steady decline in sales, and by 1948 the pottery was closed. For a more thorough study we recommend *The Collector's Encyclopedia of Weller Pottery* by Sharon and Bob Huxford, available at your local library or from Collector Books.

Hudson vases all with floral decoration: Daisies, signed Leffler, 11", $900.00; Multicolor blossoms, signed Allsbury, 12", $850.00; Dogwood blossoms and buds, signed England, 13", $700.00.

Aurelian, jug, ear of corn, 5¼x5½" 250.00
Aurelian, lamp, floral, spherical w/sm ft, E Abel, 12" 850.00
Aurelian, vase, birds, EX art, Ed Abel, bulbous, 11" 1,400.00
Aurelian, vase, irises, Madge Hurst, #557, 7x7", NM 375.00
Aurelian, vase, pansies, cylindrical, 7" 250.00
Aurelian, vase, roses, Hattie Mitchell, spherical, 5½" 475.00
Baldin, vase, apples, bulbous, unmk, 5½" 165.00
Barcelona, oil jar, florals & stripes on tan, unmk, 25½" 1,100.00
Barcelona, vase, floral on tan, hdls, mk, 6½" 200.00
Blue & Decorated, vase, blue jay on limb, 13½", NM 700.00
Blue & Decorated, vase, pastel floral band at top, 9" 250.00
Blue & Decorated, vase, 2 birds on branch, cylindrical, 8½" ...1,000.00
Blue Drapery, wall pocket, floral, unmk, 9" 185.00
Blue Ware, jardiniere, 2 angels, unmk, 8½" 250.00
Bonito, candle holders, floral on cream, 1½", pr 80.00
Bonito, vase, floral, sgn Pillsbury, ear hdls, 10" 225.00
Bonito, vase, tiger lily, str sides, narrowing at base, 9" 200.00
Breton, vase, floral band on gr matt, 9x6" 200.00
Brighton, parrot on high perch, EX color, 14x9" 1,600.00
Brighton, parrot on high perch, mc gloss, 8" 700.00
Brighton, woodpecker on pedestal, bright colors, 9" 290.00
Burntwood, plate, Pildey Picnic, Zanesville, 1910, 7" 200.00
Burntwood, vase, stylized flowers, 9x4½" 200.00
Burntwood, vase, 6-sided, mk, 5" 110.00
Cameo, vase, wht flowers on turq, hdls, unmk, 5" 30.00
Candis, hanging basket, gr w/gr wash on wht, unmk, 5½" 85.00
Chase, vase, fox hunt scene on bl, hand mk, 6½" 300.00

Chase, vase, hunt scene on bl, cylindrical, mk, 9" 400.00
Chengtu, urn, Chinese Red, mk, 5½" 75.00
Chengtu, vase, Chinese Red, classic shape, 13" 210.00
Claywood, candle holder, floral panels, brn/tan, unmk, 5" 75.00
Claywood, spittoon, floral panels, brn/tan, unmk, 4½" 135.00
Coppertone, bowl, frog perched on side, 14¾", +flower frog 450.00
Coppertone, bowl vase, hdls, 7x8" 250.00
Coppertone, cigarette urn, frog on lily pad, 4x4½" 425.00
Coppertone, dish, w/frog clutching tan/brn blossom, 4x5½" 300.00
Coppertone, vase, bulbous w/2 frog hdls, 8x9" 800.00
Coppertone, vase, flaring sides, 6x5" 200.00
Coppertone, vase, trumpet form, 6½" 170.00
Darsie, flowerpot, tassels on ivory, mk, 5½" 25.00
Dickens II, jug, Blue Hawk (Indian in headdress), 6" 450.00
Dickens II, mug, fish, fish hdl, 5" 200.00
Dickens II, mug, monk drinking ale, 6" 140.00
Dickens II, tobacco jar, Turk's head, 7½" 850.00
Dickens II, vase, Black Heart (Indian chief), Dunlavy, 9" 2,000.00
Dickens II, vase, bust portrait, man w/wht hat, #664, 10½" 325.00
Dickens II, vase, duck/lake, pillow form, 5¼" 200.00
Dickens II, vase, female golfer, teardrop form, 7½" 900.00
Dickens II, vase, Ghost Bull (Indian in headdress), 7½" 475.00
Dickens II, vase, male golfer, cylindrical, 10" 1,400.00
Dickens II, vase, monk w/lute on brn & olive, 11" 400.00
Dickens III, loving cup, Norse ship, 4" 260.00
Dickens III, vase, cavalier portrait, bl on bl, 14½" 650.00
Eocean, Late Line; vase, florals at shoulder, 8" 290.00
Eocean, tankard, grapes, Mitchell, #580, 12½" 950.00
Eocean, vase, blossoms/buds, 12x4" 270.00
Eocean, vase, fish/swirls of water, sgn ER, ovoid, 8" 1,100.00
Eocean, vase, jonquil, tall rectangular shape, 8" 325.00
Eocean, vase, lg floral, pear shape, 6½" 220.00
Eocean, vase, nasturtiums, EX color, 8x7" 425.00
Eocean, vase, pansy, invt cone w/waisted neck & sm hdls, 4½" .220.00
Eocean, vase, pr of storks, sgn Chilcote, 4-sided, 10½" 3,000.00
Eocean, vase, wht stork on wht to gray, cylindrical, 6½" 400.00
Eocean, vase, 3 long-stem carnations, shouldered, 10½" 750.00
Eocean Rose, vase, long-stem roses, EX art, Wm Stemm, 13" 900.00
Etna, vase, frog at shoulder, 4" 500.00
Etna, vase, lg roses/thorny stems, 14x5" 450.00
Flemish, vase, lg magnolias, incurvate cylinder, 18" 375.00
Florenzo, pillow vase, floral on cream, mk, 4" 45.00
Floretta, vase, floral, petal rim, shoulder hdls, #41, 7" 300.00
Floretta, vase, grapes in reserve on brn, bulbous, 12" 200.00
Forest, jardiniere, woodland scene, unmk, 4½" 115.00
Forest, pitcher, woodland scene, glossy, 5" 175.00
Glendale, vase, dbl bud; bird amid 2 stump forms, unmk, 7" 275.00
Gloria, ewer, floral on brn, mk, #G-12, 9" 45.00
Greora, jar, coppery rust w/gr striations, w/lid, 6" 275.00
Greora, vase, orange/gr, bulbous, 3" 60.00
Hobart, pelican, gr, 5½" 80.00
Hobart, vase, dbl bud; nude amid trunk forms, pk, mk, 10" 400.00
Hudson, tile, seaside castle, sgn Timberlake, fr, 6" 4,500.00
Hudson, vase, blk-lined floral clumps, Pillsbury, 12½" 650.00
Hudson, vase, dogwood band, S Timberlake, 7" 250.00
Hudson, vase, dogwood on bl, sgn DL, 7" 325.00
Hudson, vase, floral band w/butterfly, cylindrical, 9" 500.00
Hudson, vase, floral clusters on pk to gr, Hood, ovoid, 7" 300.00
Hudson, vase, floral sprig on dk bl to pk, Timberlake, 9" 450.00
Hudson, vase, lg daisies/buds, EX art, Leffler, 11x5" 900.00
Hudson, vase, lg floral spray, EX art, McLaughlin, 12" 900.00
Hudson, vase, lg iris, EX art, McLaughlin, cylindrical, 9" 700.00
Hudson, vase, lg irises on bl to lt yel, Timberlake, 10" 800.00
Hudson, vase, lg morning glories on bl to gr, Pillsbury, 9½" 550.00

Hudson, vase, lilies of the valley, EX art, Pillsbury, 7x6" 700.00
Hudson, vase, lily of the valley on bl to cream, 7x3" 200.00
Hudson, vase, pansies, sgn JL, 6" 325.00
Hudson, vase, rose on lt bl to cream, 7½" 200.00
Hudson, vase, wild rose branch, EX art, England, 13x5" 700.00
Hudson Perfecto, vase, sm florals, 6x6" 200.00
Hunter, vase, duck swimming, jug form, hand mkd, 7" 525.00
Ivoris, basket, emb floral, mk, 5" 50.00
Ivoris, covered jar, emb floral, mk, 5" 50.00
Ivory, planter box, classic figures, unmk, 5" 120.00
Jap Birdimal, pitcher, geisha girl on lt bl, 11½" 900.00
Jap Birdimal, pitcher, stylized trees, sgn Rhead/LRS, 4" 700.00
Jap Birdimal, vase, girl in knee-length robe, VMH, 6½" 600.00
Jap Birdimal, vase, 3 fish, bl/blk/wht on gray-gr, LS, 6" 850.00
Knifewood, vase, daisies/butterflies on blk, 4½" 130.00
Knifewood, vase, exotic bird, slim, mk, 9" 225.00
L'Art Nouveau, bud vase, poppies/maid, sqd, 8x2½" 2,500.00

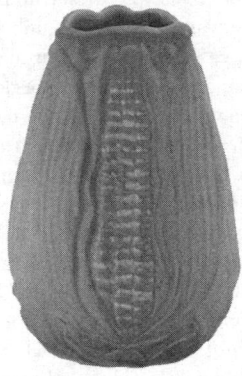

L'Art Nouveau, vase, formed as ear of corn, 4½", $175.00.

L'Art Nouveau, vase, 2 emb ladies, sqd, 16x6" 600.00
La Sa, vase, river scene, slim trumpet form, 7½" 375.00
Lawn ornament, frog w/sprinkler holes, 8½x10" 2,600.00
Lawn ornament, squirrel eating acorn, rstr ears, 12x12", EX ...2,300.00
Lonhuda, loving cup, angel/clouds, EX art, 2-hdl, 5½" 1,000.00
Lonhuda, vase, floral, hdls are rim extensions, 4½" 180.00
Louwelsa, Blue; vase, lg jonquil, cylindrical, 9" 750.00
Louwelsa, clock, floral, Rococo shape, 10x11½" 1,200.00
Louwelsa, mug, full-face Indian, sgn Sulcer, 6" 400.00
Louwelsa, mug, lg full-face Indian, LJB, EX art, 6" 900.00
Louwelsa, vase, clover, long neck, bun base, sgn, 13" 500.00
Louwelsa, vase, floral, bulbus, 10½" 300.00
Louwelsa, vase, Indian chief, EX art, initialed, 13" 1,800.00
Louwelsa, vase, lg long-stem mums, Haubrich, 16x8" 1,500.00
Louwelsa, vase, palm fronds, E Abel, 15" 1,200.00
Louwelsa, vase, palms, 5" 140.00
Louwelsa, vase, pansies/vines, 8½" 200.00
Louwelsa, vase, roses/buds, EX art, sgn HM, 12" 700.00
Lustre, vase, purple/gr/gold irid, 6-sided, 8½" 120.00
Malverne, candle holder, floral, mk, 2" 45.00
Marbleized, compote, 8" 60.00
Marbleized, jardiniere, 9x20" 650.00
Marvo, vase, dbl bud; foliage, gr/brn, unmk, 5" 85.00
Marvo, vase, foliage, brn, trumpet form, 11½" 100.00
Matt, lg leaves/pods, gray on lt gray, 3 sm hdls, 9½" 650.00
Melrose, console bowl, floral on pk, mk, 5x8½" 100.00
Muskota, bowl, 3 3-D flying wht geese on 1 side, 6½x10" 425.00
Muskota, flower frog, frog on lily pad, 4½" 230.00
Muskota, flower frog, Leda & the Swan, 7" 450.00
Muskota, flower frog, nude boy, 4" 300.00
Novelty, camel, lying down, gr, 4" 90.00

Novelty, flower frog, nude dancer w/drape, wht, 8½" 210.00
Patricia, urn, duck-head hdls, mk, 4½" 45.00
Pearl, bowl, pearls & roses on cream, 3" 65.00
Roma, candelabrum, floral on cream, 5-light, mk, 8" 200.00
Roma, vase, dbl bud; floral on tan, mk, 8½" 100.00
Rosemont, vase, bluebird on branch on blk, mk, 10½" 375.00
Scandia, bud vase, geometrics, 7½x3½" 125.00
Senic, vase, river landscape, mk, #S-2, 6½" 37.50
Sicard, bowl, emb Nouveau whiplash stems etc, 4x8" 450.00
Sicard, floral, twisted ovoid, EX glaze, 4½" 600.00
Sicard, poppies, concave cylinder, 9x4¼" 950.00
Sicard, vase, cyclamen, ovoid, 7" 600.00
Sicard, vase, fleur-de-lis, waisted dbl gourd, 10" 1,500.00
Sicard, vase, floral, EX detail/color, 12" 2,200.00
Sicard, vase, florals on dotted ground, waisted gourd, 9" 220.00
Sicard, vase, lg floral on red w/purple & gold, no mk, 4½" 750.00
Sicard, vase, Nouveau flowers, purple/bl/gr, sgn, 8½" 1,000.00
Silvertone, vase, floral, pear form w/flared rim, 7" 200.00
Silvertone, vase, lg lilies, trumpet form, 12" 325.00
Softone, vase, dbl bud; pk, mk, 9" 25.00
Stellar, vase, bl stars on wht matt, 5½x6½" 650.00
Sydonia, console bowl, bl speckled to gr, mk, 6x17" 75.00
Sydonia, planter, bl speckled to gr, mk, 4" 40.00
Turada, oil lamp base, orig fittings, 7x11" 450.00
Turada, vase, flattened egg form, 4-ftd, 6" 160.00
Velva, vase, floral on brn, sm hdls, ftd, mk, 9" 65.00
White & Decorated, vase, bluebird/branch, cylindrical, 7" 500.00
White & Decorated, vase, floral, ovoid, 8" 230.00
White & Decorated, vase, pendant floral band at top, 9" 350.00
White & Decorated, vase, wide poppy band, rose/pk/bl, 9½" 350.00
Woodcraft, candle lamp, owl atop tangle of branches, 13½" 400.00
Woodcraft, dish, fox & cubs on side, 5" H 290.00
Woodcraft, squirrel figure, 13½" L 850.00
Woodcraft, vase, tree trunk w/owl, squirrel on side, 18" 1,000.00
World's Fair, dish, LA Purchase, gray matt, 5" dia 50.00
Xenia, vase, poppies, wine/gr on gray-bl, waisted, 11x5" 800.00
Xenia, vase, stylized roses, red/pk/gr on dk gr matt, 11x8" 2,600.00
Zona, teapot, fruit branch, twig hdl, +cr/sug 225.00
Zona, umbrella stand, maids in purple dresses hold garlands 650.00

Western Americana

The collecting of Western Americana encompasses a broad spectrum of memorabilia and collectibles. Examples of various areas within the main stream would include the following fields: weapons, bottles, photographs, mining/railroad artifacts, cowboy paraphernalia, farm and ranch implements, maps, barbed wire, tokens, Indian relics, saloon/gambling items, and branding irons. Some of these areas have their own separate listings in this book. Western Americana is not only a collecting field but is also a collecting *era* with specific boundries. Depending upon which field the collector decides to specialize in, prices can start at a few dollars and run into the thousands.

Our advisor for this category is Bill Mackin, author of *Cowboy and Gunfighter Collectibles* (order from the author); he is listed in the Directory under Colorado.

Bit, hand-tooled silver w/foliate motif, 1940, 8x5" 85.00
Chaps, shotgun type w/fringe, illegible mk, ca 1890, EX 385.00
Chaps, white angora wooly type w/basketweave belt, 1920s, M ..1,200.00
Coat, angora 'wooly,' 1890, sm man's 250.00
Cuffs, leather w/brass star-design studs, ca 1900, pr 250.00
Gun belt, Edward H Bohlin, silver mtd Budcadero, EX 1,840.00
Hat, cowboy's, Plainsman's style, nutria, early 1900s, EX 250.00

Hat, cowboy's, 10-gallon Stetson, 8½" crown, 1920s, EX 1,200.00
Ore bags, buffalo hide, sgn WF (Wells Fargo) & Co, EX 550.00
Pendleton blanket, geometrics, fringe, 1930, 78x74" 135.00
Program, Buffalo Bill Wild West show, fr 450.00
Quirt, blk & orange horsehair, finely hitched, 1920s, EX 350.00
Quirt, natural mc shades of horsehair, finely hitched, 1890s 440.00
Reata, braided rawhide, CA made, 60' 300.00
Saddle, John Clark, Portland half-seat, EX 3,300.00
Saddle, unmk, half-seat, ca 1890, EX 1,045.00
Spurs, Buermann, CA style w/jingle bobs chains, pr 275.00
Spurs, Buermann, Cowpuncher's Favorites, str shanks, pr 155.00
Spurs, Buermann, Cross L style, str shank, pr 165.00
Spurs, Buermann, Hercules, bronze, drop shank, pr 285.00

Spurs, Buermann 'Roosevelt' model, 1910, EX, $6,200.00.

Spurs, CA, silver inlay, silver & gold buckles, 1940 ....495.00
Spurs, Mexican, silver inlay bottle opener, Colonial, pr 550.00
Spurs, str shank, chased rowels, pr 225.00
Stagecoach foot warmer, tin & wood, 9½x9x6" 250.00

Western Pottery Manufacturing Company

This pottery was originally founded as the Denver China and Pottery Company; William Long was the owner. The company's assets were sold to a group who in 1905 formed the Western Pottery Manufacturing Company, located at 16th Street and Alcott in Denver, Colorado. By 1926, 186 different items were being produced, including crocks, flowerpots, kitchen items, and other stoneware. The company dissolved in 1936.

Seven various marks were used during the years, and values may be higher for items that carry a rare mark. Numbers within the descriptions refer to specific marks, see the line drawings. Prices may vary depending on demand and locale. Our advisors for this category are Cathy Segelke and Pat James; they are listed in the Directory under Colorado.

Churn, #2, hdl, 4-gal, M 75.00
Churn, #2, hdl, 5-gal, M 65.00

Churn, #2, no lid, 5-gal, G 80.00
Crock, #4, bail lip, 4-gal, G 55.00
Crock, #4, hdl, no lid, 8-gal, M 90.00
Crock, #4, ice water; bl/wht sponge pnt, 3-gal, NM 30.00
Crock, #4, 2-gal, M 32.00
Crock, #4, 6-gal, EX 72.00
Crock, #4b, 20-gal, M 200.00
Crock, #4b, 22x17½", 15-gal, NM 150.00
Crock, #5, bail lip, 1½-gal, M 45.00
Crock, #5, no lid, 6-gal, M 70.00
Crock, #6, wire hdl, 10-gal, NM 100.00
Crock, #6, 2-gal, NM 30.00
Crock, #6, 3-gal, M 40.00
Crock, #6, 4-gal, M 50.00
Crock, #6, 5-gal, NM 60.00
Foot warmer, #6, M 50.00
Jug, #6, brn/wht, 1-gal, EX 25.00
Jug, #6, brn/wht, 5-gal, M 75.00
Rabbit feeder, #1, EX 25.00
Rabbit waterer, #1, M 25.00

Westmoreland

Originally titled the Specialty Glass Company, Westmoreland began operations in East Liverpool, Ohio, producing utility items as well as tableware in milk glass and crystal. When the company moved to Grapeville, Pennsylvania, in 1890, lamps, vases, covered animal dishes, and decorative plates were introduced. Prior to 1920 Westmoreland was a major manufacturer of carnival glass and soon thereafter added a line of lovely reproduction art-glass items. High-quality milk glass became their speciality, accounting for about 90% of their production. Black glass was introduced in the 1940s, and later in the decade ruby-stained pieces and items decorated in the Mary Gregory style became fashionable. By the 1960s colored glassware was being produced, examples of which are very popular with collectors today. Early pieces were marked with a paper label; by the 1960s the ware was embossed with a superimposed 'WG.' The last mark was a circle containing 'Westmoreland' around the perimeter and a large 'W' in the center. The company closed in 1985, and on February 28, 1996, the factory burned to the ground. See also Animal Dishes with Covers; Carnival Glass. Note: Though you may find pieces very similar to Westmoreland's, their Della Robbia has no bananas among the fruits relief.

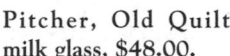

Pitcher, Old Quilt, milk glass, $48.00.

Appetizer set, Panelled Grape, milk glass, 3-pc 60.00
Ashtray, English Hobnail, red 18.00
Ashtray, Old Quilt, milk glass, 4½" 12.50
Banana stand, Doric, milk glass 30.00
Basket, Panelled Grape, milk glass, oval, 6" 25.00
Basket, pansy; Della Robbia, crystal w/stain 35.00
Basket, pansy; milk glass, #757 ....22.00
Bell, cameo pattern, milk glass, no decor 18.00

Bonbon, Princess Feather, hdld 18.00
Bowl, Beaded Grape, Golden Sunset, 7" 30.00
Bowl, Beaded Grape, milk glass, ftd, w/lid, #1884, 9" 45.00
Bowl, Beaded Grape/Roses & Bows, milk glass, 4" sq 37.50
Bowl, Della Robbia, crystal w/gold fruit, 13½" 65.00
Bowl, Dolphin, milk glass, ftd shell form 35.00
Bowl, Doric, milk glass, oval, 12" 35.00
Bowl, fruit; Old Quilt, milk glass, ftd, crimped, 9" 45.00
Bowl, grapefruit; Princess Feather, amber, 6¾" 17.50
Bowl, Irish Waterford, ruby stain, 6" 18.00
Bowl, Old Quilt, milk glass, octagonal, ftd, 7½" 25.00
Bowl, Panelled Grape, milk glass, #1881, 8" 40.00
Bowl, Panelled Grape, milk glass, lipped, 12" 95.00
Bowl, Panelled Grape, milk glass, lipped, 9" 45.00
Bowl, Panelled Grape, milk glass, oval, 10" 50.00
Bowl, Ring & Petal, milk glass, octagonal 45.00
Box, chocolate; Panelled Grape, milk glass, w/lid 40.00
Box, Old Quilt, milk glass, w/lid, sq, #41 ....35.00
Box, puff; Panelled Grape, milk glass w/gold, w/lid 45.00
Candelabrum, Panelled Grape, milk glass, 3-light 200.00
Candlestick, American Hobnail, milk glass 15.00
Candlestick, Dolphin, milk glass, 4" 15.00
Candlestick, Lotus, 2-way, milk glass 25.00
Candlesticks, Beaded Grape, milk glass, pr 22.50
Candlesticks, Doric, milk glass, lace edge, pr 22.00
Candlesticks, Thousand Eye, milk glass, 5¼", pr 38.00
Candy dish, Panelled Grape, milk glass, ruffled, 3-ftd 25.00
Candy dish, Panelled Grape, mint gr, ftd, 8" 55.00
Candy jar, Swirl & Ball, gr marble, w/lid 45.00
Candy/jelly dish, Princess Feather, milk glass, w/lid 35.00
Cheese dish, Old Quilt, milk glass 55.00
Cheese dish, Panelled Grape, milk glass, rnd 50.00
Cocktail, Panelled Grape 15.00
Cocktail, Thousand Eye 12.00
Compote, American Hobnail, milk glass, 5¾x6" 22.50
Compote, Beaded Grape, milk glass, bl grapes & gold, w/lid 40.00
Compote, Della Robbia, crystal w/amethyst stain 24.00
Compote, Della Robbia, crystal w/dk stain, 5¼" 35.00
Compote, Dolphins, gr, 7" 110.00
Compote, Old Quilt, Antique Bl opaque, low, ftd 35.00
Compote, Open Lace, milk glass, ftd, milk glass 80.00
Compote, Panelled Grape, Brandy Wine Bl, w/lid, 7" 30.00
Creamer, Panelled Grape, milk glass, lg 22.00
Creamer & sugar bowl, Maple Leaf, milk glass 25.00
Creamer & sugar bowl, Old Quilt, milk glass, lg 30.00
Creamer & sugar bowl, Old Quilt, milk glass, sm 22.00
Creamer & sugar bowl, Panelled Grape, milk glass, w/lid, sm 25.00
Cruet, Princess Feather 24.00
Cup, Beaded Edge, red 10.00
Cup, demitasse; English Hobnail 14.00
Cup & saucer, Panelled Grape, milk glass 25.00
Egg cup, chick, milk glass w/red HP details 15.00
Epergne, Panelled Grape, milk glass, 12" bowl, 8" vase 250.00
Goblet, water; Colonial, Bermuda Bl 12.00
Goblet, water; Della Robbia, milk glass 16.00
Goblet, water; Della Robbia, red stain 35.00
Goblet, water; Old Quilt, milk glass 15.00
Goblet, water; Panelled Grape, amber 15.00
Goblet, water; Panelled Grape, bl opal 25.00
Goblet, water; Panelled Grape, milk glass 20.00
Goblet, water; Princess Feather 10.00
Goblet, water; Princess Feather, amber, 5⅞" 12.50
Goblet, wine; Della Robbia, milk glass, 8" 17.50
Hat, English Hobnail, sm 15.00

Honey dish, Beaded Grape, milk glass, w/lid, 5" **25.00**
Honey dish, Beaded Grape/Roses & Bows, milk glass, w/lid, 5" **40.00**
Honey dish, Old Quilt, milk glass, w/lid **28.00**
Jardiniere, Old Quilt, milk glass, ftd, 6½" **48.00**
Jardiniere, Panelled Grape, milk glass, ftd, 6½" **37.00**
Pitcher, Colonial, Bermuda Bl **65.00**
Pitcher, Panelled Grape, milk glass, 1-qt **40.00**
Plate, Beaded Edge, milk glass, HP fruit, 7" **15.00**
Plate, Beaded Edge, milk glass, HP fruit, 8½" **18.00**
Plate, Beaded Edge/Zodiac, 14½" **45.00**
Plate, coupe soup; Beaded Edge, milk glass, apples, 7½" **15.00**
Plate, coupe soup; Beaded Edge, milk glass, birds, 7½" **22.50**
Plate, Della Robbia, crystal w/lt stain, 9" **30.00**
Plate, Forget-Me-Not, milk glass, 8" **15.00**
Plate, Lattice Edge, milk glass, 11" **18.00**
Plate, Lotus, gr, 9" **18.50**
Plate, Panelled Grape, milk glass, 8½" **24.00**
Plate, Princess Feather, 8" **17.50**
Plate, sandwich; Della Robbia, bl & gold w/lustre, 14" **85.00**
Plate, sandwich; Della Robbia, red stain, 14" **65.00**
Plate, torte; Christmas bouquet & holly, milk glass, 14½" **210.00**
Plate, 3 kittens, milk glass **35.00**
Punch bowl, Fruit, w/ladle & 12 cups **200.00**
Punch bowl, Panelled Grape, milk glass, w/base & ladle **485.00**
Relish, Panelled Grape, 3-part **40.00**
Rose bowl, American Hobnail, lilac opal, 4½" **15.00**
Sauce boat, Panelled Grape, milk glass, w/tray **65.00**
Shakers, Old Quilt, milk glass, flat, pr **25.00**
Shakers, Panelled Grape, milk glass, ftd, 4", pr **24.00**
Shakers, Princess Feather, amber, ftd, pr **30.00**
Shakers, Princess Feather, pr **30.00**
Shell compote, Dolphins, bl opaque, 8" **75.00**
Sherbet, Old Quilt, milk glass **19.00**
Sherbet, Panelled Grape, amethyst **20.00**
Sherbet, Panelled Grape, milk glass **16.00**
Sherbet, Thousand Eye, low **12.00**
Sherbet/champagne, Princess Feather, amber, 4⅝" **12.50**
Sugar bowl, Princess Feather, amber **15.00**
Tumbler, juice; Princess Feather, 5-oz **20.00**
Vase, bud; Roses & Bows, milk glass **25.00**
Vase, English Hobnail, milk glass, fan form **15.00**
Vase, Panelled Grape, Golden Sunset, 9" **35.00**
Vase, Panelled Grape, milk glass, ftd, 11½" **50.00**

Wheatley, T. J.

In 1880 after a brief association with the Coultry Works, Thomas J. Wheatley opened his own studio in Cincinnati, Ohio, claiming to have been the first to discover the secret of under-glaze slip decoration on an unbaked clay vessel. He applied for and was granted a patent for his process. Demand for his ware increased to the point that several artists were hired to decorate the ware. The company incorporated in 1880 as the Cincinnati Art Pottery, but until 1882 it continued to operate under Wheatley's name. Ware from this period is marked 'T.J. Wheatley' or 'T.J.W. and Co.,' and it may be dated.

Bowl, broad leaves, tips form rim, gr matt, #681, 2½x9" **425.00**
Bowl, heavily emb dogwood, thick gr matt, 3x7½" **350.00**
Bowl vase, 4 appl leaves curl at rim, WP/#114, 6x8", NM **700.00**
Bust, Dante, gr matt, no mk, 12x15" **550.00**
Candlesticks, gr matt, Roman column form, 12", VG, pr **225.00**
Tile, grotesque face, olive gr/tan/brn, in A&C oak fr, 7½" **700.00**
Tile, lion in relief, brick red & gr, unmk, 7¾", EX **125.00**

Vase, broad upright leaves on dk gr w/teal, 14x7" **2,100.00**
Vase, gr matt, incurvate cylinder, 10" **250.00**
Vase, lg appl grapevine in high relief on gr, 12", NM **1,100.00**
Vase, lg leaves/pussy willows, flowing gr matt, ovoid, 12½" **1,500.00**
Vase, long leaves/bud, feathered gr matt, buttress hdls, 20" **3,000.00**
Vase, molded upright leaves, variegated gr matt, 14", NM **2,000.00**
Vase, overlapping upright leaves, gr matt, #648, 4¼x5½" **350.00**
Vase, textured gr matt, 4 twisting rim-to-width hdls, 7x8½" **450.00**
Vase, thick gr mottle matt, 4 hdls at waisted neck, 12", NM ...**2,500.00**
Vase, 6 wide leaves alternate w/scrolled rim hdls, gr, 12x9" **1,840.00**

Whieldon

Thomas Whieldon was regarded as the finest of the Staffordshire potters of the mid-1700s. He produced marbled and black Egyptian wares as well as tortoise shell, a mottled brown-glazed earthenware accented with touches of blue and yellow. In 1754 he became a partner of Josiah Wedgwood. Other potters produced similar wares, and today the term Whieldon is used generically.

Creamer, cow figural w/gilt decor, 5x7½", EX **100.00**
Pitcher, cauliflower form, cream/gr, ca 1790, 6", EX **250.00**
Plate, tortoise shell, yel/gr, scalloped emb-panel rim, 9" **350.00**

Plate, green splotches on brown mottle, shaped and molded rim, 9", $325.00.

Sugar caster, translucent colors, rstr, 18th C, 4¼" **80.00**
Tea caddy, brn running glaze, no lid, 3⅜" **275.00**
Teapot, brn glaze, crabstock hdl & spout, rstr, 7½" **500.00**
Teapot, brn tortoise shell, paw ft, bird finial, prof rpr, 5" **1,045.00**
Teapot, cabbage leaf mold, hexagonal, ca 1760, rstr, 5" **400.00**
Teapot, cauliflower form, w/lid, ca 1800, 8¼", EX **350.00**

Wicker

Wicker is the basket-like material used in many types of furniture and accessories. It may be made from bamboo cane, rattan, reed, or artificial fibers. It is airy, lightweight, and very popular in hot regions. Imported from the Orient in the 18th century, it was first manufactured in the United States in about 1850. The elaborate, closely-woven Victorian designs belong to the mid- to late 1800s, and the simple styles with coarse reedings usually indicate a post-1900 production. Art Deco styles followed in the twenties and thirties. The most important consideration in buying wicker is condition — it can be restored, but only by a professional. Age is an important factor, but be aware that 'Victorian-style' furniture is being manufactured today.

Armchair, sq bk w/curved arms, uphl seat, wht pnt, 33" **150.00**
Armchair rocker, natural willow & rattan, cushion seat, 38" **265.00**
Armchair rocker, ornate fan-bk, curlicues, wht pnt, 39" **285.00**

Armchair rocker, platform type w/openwork & curlicues, wht pnt .575.00
Baby buggy, old wht rpt, steel fr, Gendron label, 44" L, G 90.00
Chair, continuous arms, openwork bk, apron, wht pnt, 36x32" ..215.00
Chair, photographer's, high bk w/curlicues, apron, 42" 375.00
Chair, side; tight machine weave, apron, uphl seat, 32" 200.00
Chair, tight Deco dmn-like weave, apron, 37" 170.00
Doll coach, print wallpaper, wood hdl & wheels, 20x19½x10" ..200.00
Footstool, tight weave w/braid, latticed sides, 12x20x12" 165.00
Lamp, Eiffel tower-shape base, fringed shade, 60", VG 400.00
Lamp, floor; sqd openwork flaring base, 24" shade, EX 700.00
Ottoman, cabriole legs, pnt gold, Heywood-Wakefield, 15x18" .150.00
Potty chair, lg wooden knobs on arms, old, EX 145.00
Rocker, sewing; tight weave, side pocket, wht pnt, 34x18" 150.00

Rocking chair, ram's horn-shaped top rail, reeded back with basketweave strip, braided armrests, petal-shaped seat, American, late 1800s, EX, $550.00.

Settee, curlicues across bk & below cane seat, pnt, 32x36" 425.00
Settee, curved arms, much openwork, apron, wht pnt, 40x50x20" .375.00
Sofa, tight weave, metal springs, uphl, wht pnt, 86" 300.00
Stroller, Victorian, doll sz, 26x37", w/parasol 300.00
Table, coffee; tight weave w/shelf, 1940s, 16x20x16", EX 80.00
Table, wooden inset top w/tight-weave apron, oval, 37" L 165.00

Will-George

In 1934, after years of working in the family garage, the Will George company was founded by William and George Climes in Los Angeles. They manufactured high-quality artware of porcelain and earthenware. Both brothers, motivated by their love of art pottery, had extensive education and training in manufacturing and decoration. In 1940 actor Edgar Bergen, a collector of pottery, developed a relationship with the brothers and invested in their business. With this new influx of funds, the company relocated to Pasadena. Our advisor for this category is Marty Webster. He is listed in the Directory under Michigan.

Figurine, artist holding a palette, mc, 8" 75.00
Figurine, boy holding frog, on base, mc, 9" 95.00
Figurine, cardinal on branch, 10" 65.00
Figurine, cardinal on branch, 12½" 95.00
Figurine, eagle on rock, wht & brn, 10" 85.00
Figurine, flamingo, head facing bk, 10" 75.00
Figurine, flamingo, head up & facing bk, 7½" 40.00
Figurine, girl holding doll, on base, mc, 9" 95.00
Figurine, mallard duck w/spread wings, 7x11" 65.00
Figurine, monk, brn bsk, 4½" 30.00
Figurine, parrot on branch, mc, 14" 110.00
Pitcher, chicken form, mc, 7" 125.00
Tumbler, chicken figural, mc, 4½" 50.00

Wine, chicken figural, mc, 5" 55.00

Willets

The Willets Manufacturing Company of Trenton, New Jersey, produced a type of belleek porcelain during the late 1880s and 1890s. Examples were often marked with a coiled snake that formed a 'W' with 'Willets' below and 'Belleek' above. Not all Willet's is factory decorated. Items painted by amateurs outside the factory are worth considerably less. In the listings below, all items are belleek unless noted otherwise. Our advisor for this category is Mary Frank Gaston. You will find her address in the Directory under Texas.

Cup & saucer, demitasse; cream w/dragon hdl, 1895 mk 45.00
Hatpin holder, floral w/silver o/l, 4½", NM 85.00
Mug, 6-figure drinking scene w/gold on gr, mk, 5⅝" 95.00
Pitcher, purple grapes w/mc leaves, serpent mk, 6½" 295.00
Stamp box, bouquet on gr lid, emb decor, 2½x1⅝x1½" 160.00
Vase, dragonflies & cattails on blk matt, ca 1905, 8" 285.00
Vase, lion portrait, brn mk, ca 1885, 8" 375.00
Vase, roses, red & wht on shaded brn, shouldered, 11½" 375.00

Willow Ware

Willow Ware, inspired no doubt by the numerous patterns of the blue and white Nanking imports, has been popular since the late 18th century and has been made in as many variations as there were manufacturers. English transfer wares by such notable firms as Allerton and Ridgway are the most sought after and the most expensive. Japanese potters have been producing Willow-patterned dinnerware since the late 1800s, and American manufacturers have followed suit. Although blue is the color most commonly used, mauve, black, and even multicolor Willow Ware may be found. Complementary glassware, tinware, and linens have also been made. In addition to 'Allerton' and 'Ridgway,' both companies used the possessive forms of their names in marking their wares (i.e. Allerton's, Ridgway's). For further study we recommend the book *Blue Willow*, with full-color photos and current prices, by Mary Frank Gaston. You will find her address in the Directory under Texas. In the following listings, if no manufacturer is noted, the ware is unmarked. See also Buffalo.

Butter dish, English, marked, 8" diameter, $150.00.

Ashtray, oval, 7¼" 30.00
Ashtray, Please Don't Burn Our Home, oval, 6" 40.00
Baker, Japan, blk 35.00
Bowl, berry; Japan, blk 9.00
Bowl, flat soup; England 18.00
Bowl, flat soup; Ridgway 22.00
Bowl, fruit; Japan, 5" 5.00
Bowl, Royal, pk, 5¾" 5.00
Bowl, Royal, 5½" 3.50
Bowl, soup; Homer Laughlin 12.00
Bowl, vegetable; Allerton, w/lid 165.00
Bowl, vegetable; Homer Laughlin, oval 30.00

Bowl, vegetable; Made in Japan, oval, 8½" 30.00
Bowl, vegetable; Staffordshire, w/lid 160.00
Bowl, vegetable; Steventon, sq, w/lid 350.00
Butter dish, Allerton 190.00
Butter pat, Booth's, sq, 3" 25.00
Cake plate & server, Moriyama 120.00
Canister set, Japan, bbl shape 275.00
Canisters, old, 4 for 275.00
Carafe, wine 125.00
Condiment set, Japan 200.00
Creamer, Grindley, ind 20.00
Creamer & sugar bowl, Booth's, ind 65.00
Creamer & sugar bowl, Japan, oval 40.00
Creamer & sugar bowl, John Steventon 65.00
Cup & saucer, Allerton 50.00
Cup & saucer, demitasse; Japan 12.00
Cup & saucer, Japan, blk 12.00
Demitasse set, Japan, 15-pc 165.00
Dresser box, Booth's, 4x5" 135.00
Gravy boat, Ridgway 60.00
Gravy boat w/attached underplate, Allerton 75.00
Lamp, hurricane; complete 95.00
Lamp, kerosene; complete, 9" 125.00
Lamp, w/reflector, Japan, 8" 95.00
Mug, inside decal, Japan 20.00
Mug, Japan 15.00
Mustard pot w/attached underplate & spoon, Japan 70.00
Pie plate, Maastricht, 9¾" 55.00
Pitcher, Allerton 135.00
Pitcher, Booth's, 7" 120.00
Plate, Booth's, 8" 18.00
Plate, Carter & Hall, luncheon sz, 8 for 200.00
Plate, England, salad sz 13.00
Plate, Homer Laughlin, 7" 6.00
Plate, Japan, blk, luncheon sz 12.00
Plate, Japan, dinner sz 12.00
Plate, Maastricht, 6" 10.00
Plate, Ridgway, 10½" 22.00
Plate, Royal, luncheon sz 7.00
Plate, Royal, pk, 7¼" 7.00
Plate, Royal, 6" 3.00
Plate, Steventon, England, salad sz 15.00
Platter, England, stoneware, 14x7" 225.00
Platter, England, 17x14" 300.00
Platter, Homer Laughlin 30.00
Platter, Japan, oval, 12½x9" 35.00
Platter, Japan, 12¾" 25.00
Pudding mold, England, red, set of 3 for 75.00
Salad fork & spoon, Japan paper label 25.00
Shakers, Japan, bbl shape, pr 20.00
Shakers, w/wood tops & bottoms, pr 20.00
Teapot, Gibson, wood trim 100.00
Teapot, Sadler 150.00
Toothpick holder, unmk 85.00
Tureen, Japan, red, electric, w/ladle 185.00

Winchester

The Winchester Repeating Arms Company lost their important government contract after WWI and of necessity turned to the manufacture of sporting goods, hardware items, tools, etc., to augment their gun production. Between 1920 and 1931, over 7,500 different items, each marked 'Winchester Trademark U.S.A.,' were offered for sale by thousands of Winchester Hardware stores throughout the country. After 1931 the firm became Winchester-Western. Unless noted otherwise, values are for examples in EX condition. Our advisor for this category is James Anderson; he is listed in the Directory under Minnesota. See also Knives.

Advertising screen, Toonerville Trolley scene entitled *The Powerful Katrinka Helps the Hammer Demonstration*, complete in three 38x18" panels, overall size: 48x60", EX, $2,200.00.

Ad folder, on gun oil, 4-pg, 3½x8", EX 25.00
Axe, Michigan pattern, WM302, EX 95.00
Baseball bat, #2700, EX 380.00
Battery, C-cell, #1311, EX 15.00
Book, Winchester, The Gun That Won the West, Williamson, EX ..46.00
Calendar, salesman's store; 1926, VG+ 425.00
Camp stove, EX 75.00
Can, gun oil, red & wht top, EX 10.00
Can, pellets, .177 cal, 500 count, M 14.00
Can opener, CI, WRA mk, VG 75.00
Catalog, pocket; fishing, M 50.00
Catalog, Western; 1963, M 9.00
Decal, Jr Rifle Corp, Pro Marksman 47.50
Diploma, Jr Rifle Corps, dtd 1921, EX 75.00
Fly rod container, aluminum, mk Winchester Trade Mk, 39", VG 85.00
Golf club, wood-shaft driver, Winchester Pickwick #6425, EX ..175.00
Golf club (Brassie), EX 175.00
Grain scales, brass 325.00
Hack saw, W48, EX 65.00
Hammer, nail; W611½, 16-oz, EX 75.00
Hatchet, box; WCBO, EX 50.00
Ice skates, shoe type, EX 90.00
Knife, Fr cook's, nickel-silver bolsters, 8", VG+ 45.00
Knife, pocket; ebony hdl, 2-blade trapper, #2641, VG+ 175.00
Lapel pin, Jr Rifle Corp, bronze, M 45.00
Light, Bull's Eye, NP, 2 D-cell batteries, EX+ 25.00
Light, head-band type, complete, VG+ 50.00
Lure, Tahoe spoon, #9492, VG+ 75.00
Lure (spinner), #9624, EX 55.00
Marble, 100th Anniversary, show horse & rider, M 10.50
Nippers, W5, 3 szs, EX, ea 40.00
Pencil, pull-out bullet form, M 85.00
Pin-bk button, Century of Achievement, horse & rider, 3", M 10.00
Pin-bk button, Jr Rifle Corp, bl & gold, EX 35.00
Plane, bull nose; W75, 4", EX 75.00
Plane, corrugated bottom, 9", EX 100.00
Plane, smooth; W3, 8", EX 95.00
Pliers, slip-joint; #2106, 6", VG 50.00

Plug, multiwobbler, EX 300.00
Plug, 5-hook, EX 700.00
Plug, 5-hook, MIB 1,200.00
Printing block, wood, 3", EX 15.00
Punch, prick; W115, ⅜", EX 40.00
Razor, safety; w/papers, NMIB 125.00
Razor, straight; #8530, EX 90.00
Razor, straight; Fr-ivory hdl, #8625, VG+ 70.00
Reel, #4350 ....135.00
Reel, casting; #2392, EX 165.00
Reel, casting; #4253, EX 165.00
Reel, casting; #4390, EX 130.00
Roller skates 65.00
Scissors, #9016, G 35.00
Score sheet, Jr Trapshooting, EX 25.00
Screwdriver, #7100, smallest, VG 35.00
Screwdriver, #7124, 5" 30.00
Screwdriver, #7127, 10", G+ 30.00
Sign, Blk men surprised by skunk, paper, EX 325.00
Spatula, #7646 ....75.00
Square, steel; W10, 12", EX 75.00
Stick pin, shotgun shell, bl, EX 75.00
Target ball, cobalt bl, EX+ 150.00
Target disk, Western, M 7.50
Tie bar, golden spike shape, well mkd, M 10.00
Waffle iron, #W36 ....295.00
Washer wringer, EX 200.00
Wrench, monkey; Coe's pattern 85.00
Wrench, monkey; WB12, 12", EX 50.00
Wrench, open-end; #1628, 9", VG 34.00

Windmill Weights

Windmill weights were used to protect the windmill's plunger rod from damage during high winds by adding weight that slowed down the speed of the blades.

Bull, Boss Bull, old worn pnt, 32-lb 1,800.00
Bull, Fairbury (mk), CI, worn pnt, 38-lb 1,095.00
Crescent, Eclipse A13, Fairbanks Morse & Co, 10½" 165.00
Horse, long-tailed, Dempster, old blk pnt, 37-lb, 21½" 1,000.00

Horse, bob-tailed, Dempster, old worn paint, 17", $350.00.

Rooster, Elgin, mk 10FT No 2, old wht rpt, 16" 525.00
Rooster, Elgin A20, pnt traces, 20" on wooden base 1,265.00
Rooster, Hummer, old pnt, ca 1900, 8⅝x9⅞x1¾", EX 500.00
Squirrel, Elgin Co, old worn pnt, 60-lb 2,500.00

Winfield

The Winfield Pottery was founded in 1929 in Pasadena, California.

The artware and giftware items they made were marked Winfield, Pasadena, sometimes with the date added. In 1946 the line of more than four hundred shapes was licensed to the American Ceramic Products Company of Santa Monica who began using the Winfield trade name on their semiporcelain dinnerware. The Winfield Pottery from then on marked their output 'Gabriel.' Both companies closed during the early 1960s.

Bowl, cereal; Blue Pacific 18.00
Bowl, cereal; Passion Flower 18.00
Bowl, fruit; Green Bamboo, 5" 15.00
Bowl, fruit; Passion Flower 15.00
Casserole, Passion Flower, dbl hdls, EX 22.50
Creamer, Passion Flower 15.00
Cup & saucer, Blue Pacific 10.00
Cup & saucer, Passion Flower 10.00
Plate, Bird of Paradise, 10" 15.00
Plate, Bird of Paradise, 6" 5.00
Plate, Bird of Paradise, 8" 7.00
Plate, Blue Pacific, 10" 18.00
Plate, Blue Pacific, 6" 6.00
Plate, Blue Pacific, 8" 10.00
Plate, Green Bamboo, 10" 20.00
Plate, Green Bamboo, 8" 10.00
Plate, Passion Flower, 10" 15.00
Plate, Passion Flower, 8" 10.00
Plate, Tiger Lily, 10" 20.00
Sugar bowl, Passion Flower, w/lid 22.50

Wire Ware

Very primitive wire was first made by cutting sheet metal into strips which were shaped with mallet and file. By the late 13th century, craftsmen in Europe had developed a method of pulling these strips through progressively smaller holes until the desired gauge was obtained. During the Industrial Revolution of the late 1800s, machinery was developed that could produce wire cheaply and easily; and it became a popular commercial commodity. It was used to produce large items such as garden benches and fencing as well as innumerable small pieces for use in the kitchen or on the farm. Beware of reproductions. Our advisor for this category is Rosella Tinsley; she is listed in the Directory under Kansas.

Basket, egg gathering; hexagonal, wire in circles, top hdl 65.00
Basket, fryer; twisted hdl, table rest, ca 1900s, 8" dia 22.00
Basket, onion; like potato boiler, no ft or hdl 110.00
Bench, garden; mesh weave, old rpt, 38" 120.00
Broom holder, heavy wire w/fancy designs, wall mt 45.00
Carpet beater, braided design, oval shape w/wooden hdl 28.00
Compote, fancy, sm rnd scalloped base, lg bowl top 125.00
Cream whip, blk tinned wire, spiral base, ca 1890, 1-pc, 16" 30.00
Dish drainer, looped wire & ft, oblong, 19x18" 42.50
Fly cover, screen wire, dk tin hand, wooden knob, 8½" 50.00
Fruit jar holder, looped wire, w/bail hdl 18.00
Ladle, ornate, lamp chimney cleaner at hdl end 28.00
Napkin holder, twisted, easel bk, standing 70.00
Plate lifter, adjustable slide, ca 1890s, rare, 18" 75.00
Rolling pin holder, heavy wire, hangs vertically 50.00
Settee, dmn woven, iron fr, 37" 275.00
Soap dish, spiral bk, twisted wire 75.00
Soap dish, twisted wire, w/toothbrush holders at top 70.00
Sponge holder, twisted wire, oblong, curved bottom, wall mt 110.00
Tea ball, screen wire, tin banding, lock fastener, 2¼" oval 28.00
Trivet, twisted, ftd, some rust, 1¼x9" dia 55.00

Trap, 6x17", $30.00.

Utensil rack, heavy wire, fancy bk, 6 hooks, wall mt 125.00
Vegetable washer, oval wire, 2-pc, EX 60.00

Witch Balls

Witch balls were a Victorian fad touted to be meritorious toward ridding the house of evil spirits, thus warding off sickness and bad luck. Folklore would have it that by wiping the dust and soot from the ball, the spirits were exorcised. It is much more probable, however, considering the fact that such beautiful art glass was used in their making, that the ostensive Victorians perpetrated the myth rather tongue-in-cheek while enjoying them as lovely decorations for their homes.

Blown, blk amethyst, sheared opening 1 end, 1870-90, 4¼" 85.00
Free-blown, teal bl, tooled mouth, Am, 1850-80, 3¾" 160.00
Nailsea, bl w/wht loopings, sheared mouth, 5" dia 550.00
Nailsea, pk & wht opaque loopings on clear, Am, 1850-80, 5" ..675.00
Pattern molded, electric bl, 16-rib swirl, 1850-80, 6¾" 375.00

Wood Carvings

Wood sculptures represent an important section of American folk art. Wood carvings were made not only by skilled woodworkers such as cabinetmakers, carpenters, etc., but by amateur 'whittlers' as well. They take the form of circus-wagon figures, carousel animals, decoys, busts, figurines, and cigar-store Indians. Oriental artists show themselves to have been as proficient with the medium of wood as they were with ivory or hardstone. See also Carousel Animals; Decoys; Tobacciana.

Bird, gesso cvd w/mc pnt, mtd on wrought bracket, 10½" L 325.00
Bird, mc pnt, sgn E Pierce, 3½", EX 95.00

Black figure with top hat, old paint, 19th century, 10¼", $800.00.

Bluebird, mc pnt body, copper wire legs & ft, 6x6x2½"+base 300.00
Cardinal bird, pnt wood, iron legs & ft, cork base, 7x7x3" 150.00
Cat, seated, open front legs, orig gray & wht pnt, 1800s, 5½" ..1,650.00
Dog, standing, nicely worn, 3⅝x4¾" 145.00
Penguin, folky, mc pnt, att Chas Hart, MA, 20" 350.00

Pig, worn blk pnt, cvd inserted tail, 10¼" L 220.00
Rabbit, EX details, on base, 15½" 575.00
Rooster, EX mc pnt, Schimmel type, 4⅜x3⅛x1", EX 200.00
Rooster, mc pnt, att Schimmel, 9" 1,200.00
Santa Claus, cigar-store type w/mc pnt, 1900s, 60" 660.00
Shoe, high-top, 1800s, wear, 17" L 1,840.00
Sunfish, orig pnt, metal fins, sgn, 9" 85.00
Trout, alligatored pnt, mtd on brd, 1800s, 33" 2,800.00

Woodenware

Woodenware (or treenware, as it is sometimes called) generally refers to those wooden items such as spoons, bowls, food molds, etc., that were used in the preparation of food. Common during the 18th and 19th centuries, these wares were designed from a strictly functional viewpoint and were used on a day-to-day basis. With the advent of the Industrial Revolution which brought it new materials and products, much of the old woodenware was simply discarded. Today original hand-crafted American woodenwares are extremely difficult to find. See also Mauchline Ware.

Bowl, ash burl, curved/flared sides, rfn, 2⅜x7½" 440.00
Bowl, ash burl, EX figure, scrubbed, red traces, 8½x20" 990.00
Bowl, ash burl, EX figure & patina, scrubbed, 7x18x20" 2,750.00
Bowl, ash burl, red stain, scrubbed interior, 4½x16" 850.00
Bowl, ash burl, trn detail, bulbous lip, 2½x8½" 495.00
Bowl, ash burl w/dk stain stripe, age cracks, 4½x5¾" 385.00
Bowl, burl, trn, 1800s, 14" dia 800.00
Bowl, butter; maple, 6¾x21½" 130.00
Bowl, EX patina, tool mks, rim hdl, 10½x13¾" 110.00
Bucket, staved, truncated sides, wooden bands & lid, 11x11" 140.00
Bucket, sugar; staved, old red pnt, w/lid, 14½x15" 195.00
Bucket, sugar; staved, w/lid & bentwood hdl, EX old pnt, 10x10" ..365.00
Butter paddle, cherry wood, hand cvd, oblong, 4" hdl 50.00
Butter paddle, curly maple, dished curved blade, 9¾" 250.00
Butter paddle, maple, lt natural patina, 10½" 75.00
Butter print wheel, scrubbed, 5½" 175.00
Butter scraper, cvd w/thin blade 30.00
Cheese drainer, cradle shaped, pegged sides, 1840s 245.00
Cookie board, man & dog, 27½x9" 100.00
Cookie board, 3 animals, 5x14½" 115.00
Cutting board, pig shape, worn red pnt, 9¼x7¼" 35.00
Dipper, maple w/burl bowl, hook hdl, 1-pc, 18¼" 575.00
Doughnut cutter, EX patina 75.00
Egg cup, Lehn type, trn, w/pnt decor, ped base, 2¾x2⅛" 975.00
Jar, bail hdl, w/lid, crack, 4½" 260.00
Jar, burl w/G trn detail, acorn finial, old varnish, 10" 440.00
Jar, Pease, minor crack in lid, 6¾" 330.00
Jar, Pease, w/lid, 5¼" 225.00
Jar, poplar, orig red-brn & yel sponging, 11" 2,100.00
Jar, poplar w/brn & yel sponging, rpr, 7½" dia 330.00
Keg, stave, bung hole on side, old brn pnt, 8¾" 165.00
Mortar & pestle, ash burl w/EX figure & patina, 7" 600.00
Noggin, grooved sides, hand cvd, 1-pc, 5¾", EX 185.00
Noggin, rfn, 10¾" 80.00
Noodle board, pine, 19½" dia+3¼" hdl 95.00
Pie board, soft wood, oval, 15⅛x23¾" (including hdl) 50.00
Rolling pin, maple, rnd knob hdl 1 end, 1880s, 1-pc, 18½" 40.00
Scoop, cranberry; flat bottom, 15¼x10½x5" 225.00
Scoop, cvd shovel shape, 8¾x3¼" 45.00
Spoon, hand cvd, tablespoon sz 20.00
Spoon, strainer; pierced oval shape, 16" L 60.00
Trencher, hewn, rectangular, 4¾x21½x12½" 190.00

Woodworking Machinery

Vintage cast-iron woodworking machines are monuments to the highly skilled engineers, foundrymen, and machinists who devised them, thus making possible the mass production of items ranging from clothespins, boxes, and barrels to decorative moldings and furniture. Though attractive from a nostalgic viewpoint, many of these machines are bought by the hobbyist and professional alike, to be put into actual use — at far less cost than new equipment. Many worth-assessing factors must be considered; but as a general rule, a machine in good condition is worth about 65¢ a pound (excluding motors). A machine needing a lot of restoration is not worth more than 35¢ a pound, while one professionally rebuilt and with a warranty can be calculated at $1.10 a pound. Modern, new machinery averages over $3.00 a pound. Two of the best sources of information on purchasing or selling such machines are *Vintage Machines — Searching for the Cast Iron Classics*, by Tom Howell, and *Used Machines and Abused Buyers* by Chuck Seidel from *Fine Woodworking*, November/December 1984. Prices quoted are for machines in good condition, less motors and accessories. Our advisor for this category is Mr. Dana Martin Batory; he is listed in the Directory under Ohio. No phone calls, please.

American Saw Mill Machinery Company, 1931

Band saw, Monarch Line, #X25, 30" built-in ball-bearing motor ..770.00
Jointer, Monarch Line, #XII, ball-bearing, 16" 1,200.00
Planer, Monarch Line, single surface, 30" 2,600.00
Sander, Monarch Line, #X8, ball-bearing drum & disk 560.00

Blue Star Products, 1939

Band saw, #1200, 12" floor model 85.00
Lathe, #1001, 72" bed, 12" swing 60.00
Table saw, #800, 8" 95.00

Boice-Crane Power Tools, 1937

Band saw, #800, 14" 100.00
Drill press, #1600, 15" 75.00
Lathe, #1100, gap bed 50.00
Scroll saw, #900, 24" 75.00

Crescent Machine Company, 1921

Band saw, 36" 975.00
Mortiser, hollow chisel 525.00
Universal Wood-Worker, #59, 5 machines in 1 ....2,050.00

Defiance Machine Works, 1910

Band saw, 28" 520.00
Table saw, #2, hand feed, 20" 650.00
Table saw, #2, power feed, 20" 1,100.00

Gallmeyer & Livingston Company, 1927

Band saw, Union, 20" 390.00
Jointer, Union, motor on arbor, 8" 370.00
Table saw, Union #7, 7" 210.00

G.N. Goodspeed Company, 1876

Boring machine, upright 225.00

Planer, New & Improved, Pony, 24" 900.00
Table saw, 12" 200.00

Greenlee Bros. & Company, 1925

Tenoner, #530, sash, door & cabinet, ball-bearing 1,530.00

Hoyt & Brother Company, 1888

Band saw & resawing machine, #1194, 20" 1,700.00
Cutoff saw, overhung, traversing, 14" 650.00
Joiner, Perfection, 8" 450.00
Mortiser & borer, #2 ....780.00
Planer, matcher & surfacer, New Combined, #2, 24" 5,200.00
Sandpapering machine, The Boss, #5, 24" 1,600.00
Scroll saw, #1 ....300.00
Shingle machine, Grand Mogul, 2-block, automatic feed 2,210.00
Table saw, #2, 14" 800.00
Wood shaper, dbl spindle 850.00

J.A. Fay & Egan Company, 1900

Jointer, New #2, 16" 1,550.00
Jointer, New #2, 24" 1,700.00
Jointer, New #2, 30" 1,820.00
Jointer, New #4, extra heavy, 16" 1,625.00
Jointer, New #4, extra heavy, 20" 1,690.00
Jointer, New #4, extra heavy, 24" 1,885.00
Jointer, New #4, extra heavy, 30" 2,275.00
Molder, #1½, 4-sided, 4" 1,050.00
Molder, #2, 4-sided, 6" 1,500.00
Mortiser, #2, hollow chisel, automatic horizontal 1,500.00
Mortiser, #5, dbl hollow chisel, horizontal 1,100.00
Planer, #2½, dbl-belted surface, med sz 1,850.00
Saw, rip; #2, Improved Standard 1,175.00
Saw, rip; #2, self-feeding, lg 1,775.00
Saw, rip; #3, self-feeding, X-lg 2,400.00

J.D. Wallace Company, 1940s

Band saw, 16" 210.00
Grinder & sander, disk; Wonder, 16" 165.00
Jointer, 4" 15.00
Lathe, 6x24" 115.00
Saw, circular (table saw); Universal, 7" 75.00
Saw, circular; plain, 7" 65.00

L. Power & Co., 1888

Mortiser & borer, #2 ....780.00
Shaper, single spindle, reversible 585.00
Table saw, self-feeding, 14" 715.00

Ober Manufacturing Company, 1889

Rip saw, self-feeding, 14" 725.00
Saw, swing cut-off, 18" 275.00
Shaper, saw & jointer combination 400.00

Oliver Machinery Company, 1922

Band saw, #17, 30" 925.00
Shaper, #483, high speed, dbl spindle 1,300.00
Table saw, #32, Variety, 12" 500.00

Parks Ball Bearing Machine Company, 1925

Jointer, H-133, Ideal, 12" **400.00**
Sanding machine, H-165, Economy, 24" **230.00**
Saw, H-97, swing cut-off, Alert, 12" **225.00**

P.B. Yates Machine Company, 1917

Planer, #160, dbl surface, 20" **1,235.00**
Saw, #232, swing cut-off, 16" **260.00**

S.A. Woods Machine Company, 1876

Circular resawing machine, Joslin's Improved, 50" **2,275.00**
Planer, panel; Improved, 20" **520.00**
Planer, Pat Improved, shop surface, 30" **1,430.00**

Sprunger Power Tools, 1950s

Band saw, 14" **60.00**
Jigsaw, 20" **40.00**
Lathe, gap bed, 10" **50.00**
Table saw, tilt arbor, 10¼" **75.00**

Worcester Porcelain Company

The Worcester Porcelain Company was deeded in 1751. During the first or Dr. Wall period (so called for one of its proprietors), porcelain with an Oriental influence was decorated in underglaze blue. Useful tablewares represented the largest portion of production, but figurines and decorative items were also made. Very little of the earliest wares were marked and can only be identified by a study of forms, glazes, and the porcelain body, which tends to transmit a greenish cast when held to light. Late in the fifties, a crescent mark was in general use, and rare examples bear a facsimile of the Meissen crossed swords. The first period ended in 1783, and the company went through several changes in ownership during the next eighty years. The years from 1783-1792 are referred to as the Flight period. Marks were a small crescent, a crown with 'Royal,' or an impressed 'Flight.' From 1792-1807 the company was known as Flight and Barr and used the trademark 'F&B' or 'B,' with or without a small cross. From 1807-1813 the company was under the Barr, Flight, and Barr management; this era is recognized as having produced porcelain with the highest quality of artistic decoration. Their mark was 'B.F.B.' From 1813-1840 many marks were used, but the most usual was 'F.B.B.' under a crown to indicate Flight, Barr, and Barr. In 1840 the firm merged with Chamberlain, and in 1852 they were succeeded by Kerr and Binns. The firm became known as Royal Worcester in 1862. The production was then marked with a circle with '51' within and a crown on top. The date of manufacture was incised into the bottom or stamped with a letter of the alphabet, just under the circle. In 1891 Royal Worcester England was added to the circle and crown. From that point on each piece is dated with a code of dots or other symbols. After 1891 most wares had a blush-color ground. Prior to that date it was ivory. Most shapes were marked with a unique number.

During the early years they produced considerable ornamental wares with a Persian influence. This gave way to a Japanesque influence. James Hadley is most responsible for the Victorian look. He is considered the 'best ever' designer and modeller. He was joined by the finest porcelain painters. Together they produced pieces with very fine detail and exquisite painting and decoration. Figures, vases, and tableware were produced in great volume and are highly collectible. During the 1890s they allowed the artists to sign some of their work. Pieces signed on the face by the Stintons, Baldwyn, Davis, Raby, Austin, Pow-

ell, Sedgley, and Rushton (not a complete list) are in great demand. The company is still in production. There is an outstanding museum on the company grounds in Worcester, England.

The advisors on this category are Henry and Geneva Tyler in Florida. Note: most pieces had lids or tops (if there is a flat area on the top lip, chances are it had one), if missing deduct 30 to 40%.

Key: ug — underglaze

Bowl, floral bouquets/butterflies, ug bl, 1st period, 6" **150.00**
Bowl, Japan pattern, Imari palette, ca 1820, 13" L **2,000.00**
Bowl, service; Queen Charlotte, oval, unmk, ca 1800, 11½", pr ...**950.00**
Candlesticks, 3-D boy (girl), tree std, rock base, 11", pr **650.00**
Charger, sgraffito decor, A Binns, earthenware, 1881, 17", pr **500.00**
Compote, boy (girl) beside bowl, J Hadley, 1885, 8¼", pr **1,000.00**
Creamer & sugar bowl, mc floral w/gold, w/lid, #1253 ....**225.00**
Cup & saucer, bl forget-me-nots w/gold, ca 1913-40 ....**145.00**
Cup & saucer, handleless; emb/ug bl floral, 1st period **460.00**
Ewer, gold motif on ivory, ornate scrolled hdl, #1138, 8" **300.00**
Ewer, mc florals w/gold, salamander hdl, mk, 9¼" **395.00**
Figurine, Babes in the Woods, 6¼x2¾" **175.00**
Figurine, boy w/harmonica & dog, June of series, 6½" **175.00**
Figurine, boy w/squirrels, October of series, 7¾" **175.00**
Figurine, dancing girl, ivory w/gold, Hadley, 1885, 9½" **500.00**
Figurine, Happy Days, #3435 ....**1,250.00**
Figurine, L'Allegro, pk floral w/gold, late 19th C, 16" **400.00**
Figurine, lady water carrier, sgn, #637, 6½" **275.00**
Jardiniere, lions' heads & swags w/gold, 1888, 7⅛" **400.00**
Jug, floral, pk & bl w/gold, bamboo hdl, 10¼" **250.00**
Jug, floral w/gold, mask spout, ca 1890, 9¾" **425.00**
Jug, 1951 Bicentenary Commemorative, mask spout, 4⅞" **75.00**
Mug, floral sprig, ug bl, pinched cylinder, 1st period, 5" **285.00**
Mug, floral/butterflies, ug bl, 1st period, 6" **500.00**
Plate, animals/figures, J Rushton, jewels, 1862, 9", 6 for **1,250.00**
Plate, Harrington: cottage, sgn GH Evans, 10½" **100.00**
Plate, peaches/cherries, dk bl/pk/gilt floral border, 8½" **250.00**
Sauce boat, Oriental figures in medallions w/gold, 1770, 7½" **950.00**
Shrimp dish, Queen Charlotte, shaped rim, unmk, ca 1800, 8", pr .**950.00**
Sweetmeat stand, 3-shell form, floral/gold, late 1700s, 4¾" **800.00**
Vase, bird & floral w/gold, pierced border, hdls, 1885, 10⅞" **500.00**
Vase, bud; gold florals in relief on ivory, #1049, 4" **30.00**
Vase, floral & strawberry sprays, fan form, ca 1881, 6¾" **600.00**
Vase, floral on cream, urn form w/hdls, 1893, 4½x4" **75.00**
Vase, floral w/gold, ftd, stick neck, ram-head hdls, #1600, 12" ...**425.00**
Vase, floral w/gold, pierced hdls, ca 1890, 10¾" **650.00**

Vase, flying swans on blue, signed Baldwyn, shape #1572, ca 1904, 10½", $4,000.00.

Vase, landscape panels, jewels, w/inset, 1892, 4" **600.00**
Vase, nautilus shell, gilt & bronze decor, ca 1893, 8⅛" **500.00**
Vase, parrots, rtcl neck/hdls, bottle form, imp mk, 17x7" **1,200.00**
Vase, tropical birds, gold hdls, SP rings, 1891, 11" **600.00**

World's Fairs and Expos

Since 1851 and the Crystal Palace Exhibition in London, World's Fairs and Expositions have taken place at a steady pace. Many of them commemorate historical events. The 1904 Louisiana Purchase Exposition, commonly known as the St. Louis World's Fair, celebrated the 100th anniversary of the Louisiana Purchase agreement between Thomas Jefferson and Napoleon in 1803. The 1893 Columbian Exposition, known as The Chicago World's Fair, commemorated the 400th anniversary of the discovery of America by Columbus in 1492. (Both of these fairs were held one year later than originally scheduled.) The multitude of souvenirs from these and similar events have become a growing area of interest to collectors in recent years. Many items have a 'crossover' interest into other fields: i.e., collectors of postcards and souvenir spoons eagerly search for those from various fairs and expositions. For additional information collectors may contact World's Fairs Collectors Society (WFCS), whose address is in the Directory under Clubs, Newsletters, and Catalogs, or our advisor, D.D. Woollard, Jr. His address is listed in the Directory under Missouri.

Key:
T&P — Trylon & Perisphere   WF — World's Fair

1876 Centennial, Philadelphia

Book, Centennial Diary 1876, 22 pgs, cover split o/w EX 20.00
Book, History of Centennial..., McCabe, 300 illus, 6x9", EX+ 75.00
Cloth, eagle above Memorial Hall, 25x19", NM 85.00
Cloth, Flags of the Nations, mc, 24x15", EX 85.00
Cup, china, mc view Centennial Memorial Bldg, 3½", EX 95.00
Medallion, wood, emb of Gen Hawley, Pres of...Expo, 2½", EX ...75.00
Print, mc view of NY Bldg, w/sm mat, 15½x11½", EX 25.00

1893 Columbian, Chicago

Badge, brass, Chicago: Souvenir...Expo 1893, EX 15.00
Bell, brass, wood hdl, Liberty Bell w/expo mks, 2½", EX 35.00
Book, Chicago WF 1893, photo record, pub 1980, 116 pgs, NM ..15.00
Booklet, Simmons Saw & Mfg Co, shows their exhibit etc, EX 10.00
Cup, china, Govt Bldg scene, mk England, gold trim, 2½", EX 60.00

Disk, hand-painted view of Fisheries Building on glass, 2⅛", NM, $7.00.

Goblet, glass, gr, etched Louella & WF 1893, rare, 3" 60.00
Medal, aluminum, Landing scene design, Chicago facts on bk, VG .10.00
Medal, Treasury Dept, 33mm brass, US Govt Bldg design, VG+ 8.00
Paperweight, glass, Ferris Wheel, Dia 264 Ft view, EX 85.00
Plaque, cast brass, landing scene, 7½x9¼", EX 88.00
Plate, china, expo bldgs, Wedgewood, 8½", ea 55.00
Pocketknife, brass hdls, Columbus bust, Expo bldgs, 3¼", EX 100.00
Ring, sterling silver, 'Gorham' Spanish inscription 80.00

Scissors, embroidery; steel, sailing vessel, Graef & Schmid 85.00
Shaker, egg shaped, frosted milk glass, Col 1893 Exhibition, EX ..100.00
Ticket, Admit Bearer, Washington, EX 12.50
Ticket, Chicago Day, w/stub, EX 17.50
Trade card, Merrick's Spool Cotton, Horticultural Bldg scene, EX ..15.00
Watch fob, 4-part, brass, spread eagle on bk, 1⅛", EX+ 85.00
Watch fob & chain, braided hair, brass ends, expo scene, 7" 85.00

1898 Trans-Mississippi

Badge, pin-bk, brass, mk Souvenir, emb Govt Bldg, EX 30.00
Book, Snap Shots of the T-M Expo, 40 pgs, 7x9", VG 20.00
Medallion, brass, heart shape, emb Nebraska Bldg, EX+ 22.50
Poster, panoramic view of expo, red lettering, 29x42", EX+ 175.00
Spoon, fair bldg in bowl, lady's figure on hdl, 5½", EX 35.00
Trade card, mc, Boston Rubber Shoe Co, 3½x5½", EX 7.50

1901 Pan American

Book, Souvenir of...P-A Expo, J Bayne pub, 50 full-pg views, NM ..22.50
Charm, buffalo shape, celluloid, not mk, sm 5.00
Coin, elongated; design of Electric Tower, EX 15.00
Envelope, mc design of US Govt Bldg, lt blemish o/w EX 15.00
Frying pan, missing thermometer in hdl, 5½" 12.50
Kewpie doll, celluloid, mk Pan-Am on ft, movable arms, 3", EX ..40.00
Napkin ring, aluminum, buffalo design, mk Pan-Am 1901, 1½" ..20.00
Pan, brass, curved hdl, Electric Tower design, mk, 2" dia, EX 20.00
Paperweight, glass; Govt Bldg mc view, mk Empire Art, EX 40.00
Playing cards, expo scenes, 2 ladies on bk, NM (w/case) 70.00
Poster stamps, expo scenes, from 1" sq to 1x2", ea 2.00
Ribbon, woven silk, Electric Tower in gray, 6x9" mat, EX 60.00

1904 St. Louis

Bookmark, multicolored celluloid, Scruggs, Vanderboort & Barney Dry Goods, 5x2", NM, $62.50.

Badge, employee; nickel, w/serial number, 1½" dia 100.00
Booklet, RI Bldg, mc cover, 35-pg, EX 12.50
Cup, collapsible, aluminum, Cascade Gardens, 2½", EX 40.00
Jar, dresser; milk glass, US Govt Bldg decal, 3x3½", EX 60.00
Mirror, pocket; mc view of Palace of Transportation, 2", EX 75.00
Plate, china, mc scene of Palace Liberal Arts, 6¼", EX 40.00
Pocketknife, emb views on aluminum hdl, 2¾" 75.00
Puzzle, steel ball maze, mc expo design, 3" sq, rare, EX 75.00
Stein, Festival Hall & Cascades, German, expo mk, EX 150.00
Vase, ceramic, cobalt, Souvenir of...1904, mk Austria, 4", EX 50.00

1909 Alaska Yukon Pacific

Handkerchief, silk, bird's-eye view of fair, mc, 15" sq, EX 40.00
Pin-bk, children, Children's Day June 5, mc, NM 25.00
Plate, china, Oregon State Bldg, mc transfer, 8" 90.00

Silk, 5 views, blk print on lt brn, 18" sq, fr 50.00
Tumbler, copper gilt on metal, 3 expo scenes & logo, 3½" 25.00

1915 Panama Pacific

Award ribbon, emb lettering & seal of expo, 3½x7", NM 50.00
Book, Art of the Expo, 91 pgs, photographic illus, 6x9", EX 35.00
Book, Colortypes of the PPIE, 32 pgs mc views, 9x6¼", EX 17.50
Booklet, GE Co at PPIE, 12-pgs, GE exhibit, 8x11", EX 12.50
Cup, collapsible, aluminum, emb N&S Am, PPIE 1915 SF, 2½" dia .32.50
Mailing folder, 22 mc views in strip form, 4x6", EX 12.50
Pan, metal, Tower of Jewels emb, Official Souvenir, 2¼", EX 15.00
Pin-bk, LA County Day, gr/wht/orange, orig paper labels, EX 22.50
Print, Festival Hall, mk c 1913 by PPIE, 6½x8½", EX 12.50
Table cover, scalloped edges, overview of expo, 16x25", EX 35.00

1926 Sesquicentennial

Ashtray, metal, Liberty Bell emb, mk, 5½x3¼", EX 15.00
Book, Flags of Am, expo edition, 32 pgs, 8x5½", EX 12.50
Book, Official Souvenir View; Cartinell, 32 pgs, soft cover, EX ...15.00
Certificate of membership, impressed seal, rare, 11x8½", EX 30.00
Invitation, Opening Ceremonies, Liberty Bell/Am flag design, EX ..30.00
Key, metal, head shaped like Liberty Bell, mk, 2¼", EX 15.00
Mailing folder, 18 views, lt cover wear, 6x4½", EX 12.50
Train schedule, NYC Day, list of events, EX 10.00

1933 Chicago

Tapestry, overview of fair, 25x41", M, $75.00.

Blotter, Johnson Gasoline & Oils, fair bldgs pictured 15.00
Book, Official Book of the Fair, 1933, 104-pg 22.50
Book, Official Guide (1933), 176-pg, w/map 15.00
Candle holders, metal w/emb bldgs, 4", pr 30.00
Letter sheet w/matching envelope, fair bldgs pictured 30.00
Medal, bronze, Official, AU, 1½" dia 25.00
Pillow cover, fair bldgs on satin, 15" sq, M 40.00
Pin-bk, cello, World Champion Log Rollers, 1" 15.00
Tape measure, cello, Temple of Jehol & Globe design, 1½" 50.00

1939 New York

Ashtray, metal, NY WF 1940 emb, T&P in center, 4½", EX 22.50
Ashtray, syrocco wood base, emb T&P design & date, 3" sq, EX .25.00
Bandana, Boy Scout; scout, eagle & T&P pictured, 30", EX 125.00
Book, Official Guide, illus, 1st edition, 256 pgs, 5x8", EX 22.50
Book, picture; Frank Buck's Jungle, Buck & animals, 1940, EX 25.00
Booklet, Firestone, illus, tires being made, 48 pgs, EX 10.00
Brochure, Routes to WF, T&P design, schedule, map, info, EX 7.50
Catalog, Masterpcs of Art Official Illus, 258 pgs, 7x9", EX 15.00
Coin, elongated, T&P design w/date, World of Tomorrow, EX 10.00
Fan, paper, wood hdl, WF views, mk Pavilion Japan NY WF, G ..65.00
Handkerchief, silk or rayon, mc views of WF, 18" sq, VG 35.00

Lamp base, wht w/gold trim, T&P shape, mk, EX 100.00
Mailing folder, G Washington on front, 18 fair views, EX 12.50
Mailing folder, T&P on front, 18 views of fair, EX 12.50
Medal, brass, T&P design w/date, Rockefeller Center on bk, EX 7.50
Pin, Heinz in emb letters, pickle shape, gr, 1¼", EX 5.00
Pitcher, china, cream, bust of G Washington, 4½", EX 30.00
Playing cards, T&P design, globe w/NY WF lettered, M, sealed ...40.00
Sheet music, Rising Tide, T&P pictured, lyrics by Stillman, EX ..30.00
Souvenir, Statue of Liberty, metal, T&P design, WF mks, EX 50.00
Spoons, demi; G Washington hdl, T&P & flags in bowls, set of 6 ..85.00

1939 San Francisco

Book, Famous Guide to SF & WF, 144 pgs, illus, 5x7", EX 17.50
Book, Official Guide, 116-pgs, illus, fold-out map, EX 20.00

Compact, brushed brass, mirror in lid, made by Clarice Jane, MIB, $30.00.

Mailing folder, Treasure Island Night & Day, 14 mc views, EX 10.00
Map of SF, aerial view of expo, unfolds to 20" sq, EX 5.00
Plate, china, Bay Bridge & Tower design, mk Homer Laughlin, EX ..100.00
Ticket, souvenir; w/stub, 5x2½", residue on bk o/w EX 10.00

1964 New York

Book, Guide, 1964-65, 312 pgs, Time-Life, illus, EX 12.50
Bumper sticker, I've Seen NY State at Fair 1964-65, 4x8", NM ...15.00
Dish, glass, mc fair scenes, 4x4½", NM 10.00
Flash card set, mc scenes w/WF info, 28 cards, 3½x6", EX 22.50
Greeting card, mc Transportion & Travel Bldg scene, 3x5", EX 5.00
Key chain, brass medallion, design & info on Unisphere, EX 15.00
Pin, metal, open works of Unisphere, 1¾" dia, NM 22.50
Record, 33⅓ rpm, Triumph of Man, mc fold-out jacket, EX 12.50
Shakers, shape of Unisphere, silver colored, 2", EX, pr 17.50
Tray, metal, mc scene of Unisphere, rnd, 12", EX 12.50

Wright, Frank Lloyd

Born in Richland Center, Wisconsin, in 1869, Wright became a pioneer in architectural expression, developing a style referred to as 'prairie.' From early in the century until he died in 1959, he designed houses whose rooms were open, rather than divided by walls in the traditional manner. They exhibited low, horizontal lines and strongly projecting eaves, and he filled them with furnishings whose radical aesthetics complemented the structures to perfection. Several of his homes have been preserved to the present day, and collectors who admire his ideas and the unique, striking look he achieved treasure the stained glass windows, furniture, chinaware, lamps, and other decorative accessories made by Wright.

Chair, side; slanted plank bk extends to block ft, no mk 9,000.00
Chair set, 2 arm+4 sides, new Wright uphl, 31" 2,000.00
Headbrd, #2000, Taliesin design on edge, full sz, EX 800.00
Magazine, Architectural Forum, 1938, devoted to his work 175.00
Nightstand, mahog w/Greek Key border, 1-drw, mk, 26x21x18" .700.00
Server, mahog, 2 doors left & 2 4-drw banks, bk shelf, 66" 1,100.00

Sofa, Heritage Henredon, even arms, Taliesin trim, re-uphl ...2,100.00
Stand, mahog w/Greek Key border, ink stamp, 24x24x20", pr ..1,000.00
Stool, mahog cube w/tapered base, cushion top, 1955, VG 1,100.00
Table, coffee; drop sides, Taliesin trim, sgn, 60" L, EX 2,000.00
Table, dining; copper inlay, Xd base w/in 4 legs, 54" dia 1,500.00
Table, mahog, V-supports, sq top, 1-drw, no mk, rstr, 18x36" .3,200.00
Table, side; lower shelf w/drw, Taliesin design, mk, EX 1,100.00

Wrought Iron

Until the middle of the 19th century, almost all the metal hand forged in America was made from a material called wrought iron. When wrought iron rusts it appears grainy, while the mild steel that was used later shows no grain but pits to an orange-peel surface. This is an important aid in determining the age of an ironwork piece.

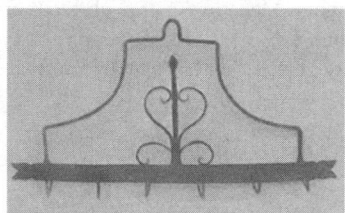

Utensil rack, scrolled and twisted details, 22½" long, EX, $275.00.

Axe holder, fish shape, from Conestoga wagon, 3½x9½" 4,900.00
Axe holder, scroll design, from Conestoga wagon, 4x7x4⅜" 225.00
Candle snuffer, scissors type, 6¾" 55.00
Fork, wedding; inlaid, cut-out heart, 29" 750.00
Fork, 2-tine, J Schmidt 1844 on hdl, 17" 210.00
Fork, 2-tine, sgn FBS Canton O, Pat Jan 26 86, 16⅜" 70.00
Fork, 3-tine, rnd loop finial hdl, 26" L 75.00
Kettle lamp, trunnion-mtd font, center wick support, 7" 495.00
Ladle, appl 5½" bowl, flattened hdl w/crown finial, 22" 100.00
Lighting stand, candle-socket counterbalance, tripod base, 33" .450.00
Lighting stand, tripod w/arch legs, sheet-metal top, 51x15" 550.00
Lighting stand w/candle socket & 2nd spring-loaded socket, 22" ..360.00
Rack, utensil; scrolled & twisted details, 22½" L 275.00
Rush light holder, w/candle-socket counterbalance, 8", VG 175.00
Salamander, 3½" rnd blade, 20" hdl w/mushroom-shape top 50.00
Spatula, notches on flattened hdl, 3" blade, 15" L 65.00
Spatula, trn wood hdl, mk C Heisler, 1¾" W, 12" L 85.00
Spatula, 2¾x2½" blade mk J English, ornate 14" hdl 200.00
Spear, fish; 11-prong, socket collar, mk Ideal, 8x15" 105.00
Spear, fish; 6-prong, wraparound collar, 4x11" 95.00
Strap hinge, fleur-de-lis design, 15x18" 75.00
Sugar nippers, simple tooled detail, 9" 175.00
Thumb latch, w/thumb plate, 12¼" 170.00
Thumb latch, w/thumb plate, 14⅝" 200.00

Yellow Ware

Ranging in color from buff to deep mustard, yellow ware which almost always has a clear glaze can be slip banded, plain, Rockingham decorated, flint enamel glazed, or mocha decorated. Mocha-decorated pieces are usually the most expensive and desirable. The majority of pieces are plain and do not bear a manufacturer's mark. Yellow ware which was primarily produced in the United States, England, and Canada was popular from the mid-19th century to the early 20th century. A utilitarian ware, it was first domestically produced in New York, New Jersey, Pennsylvania, and Vermont. With more than thirty active potteries, East Liverpool, Ohio, became the center for yellow ware pro-

duction. After experiencing several years of dramatic price increases, the market has begun to stabilize. Note: Because this was a utilitarian type of everyday pottery, yellow ware is often found with signs of heavy use and damage; this would of course decrease its value. For further information we recommend *Collecting Yellow Ware, An Identification and Value Guide*, written by our advisor, John Michel, and Lisa S. McAllister. Mr. Michel's address is in the Directory under New York.

Baking dish, oval w/extended lip, 12¼", NM 235.00
Bed pan, bl seaweed, wht band, brn stripes, 8¼" 100.00
Bowl, bl seaweed, wht band, brn stripes, 3½x7", NM 385.00
Bowl, gr seaweed, wht band, brn stripes, 4⅝x10⅛", EX 350.00
Bowl, mixing; bl & wht stripes, Warrented Fireproof, 6x12" 85.00
Bowl, mixing; bl & wht stripes on deep golden yel, 6x13", EX ...100.00
Chamber pot, seaweed, bl w/dk brn stripes, OH, 2⅛" 385.00
Chamber pot, wht band, 1850s 95.00
Colander, milk-pan shape, lg holes, 1880s, 11" 550.00
Colander pie plate 13" 500.00
Cookie jar, emb floral decor, ca 1900-40, lg 135.00
Creamer, cow, plain yel, minimum value 2,000.00
Custard cup, cone shape w/lip, 2½" 32.00
Custard cup, rnd shape, common type, 4" 22.00
Egg cup, plain, 2¼" 32.00
Flowerpot & saucer, 1900-30 ....150.00
Jar, wht band & brn stripes, cylindrical, w/lid, 6x8¾" 195.00
Ladle, rare, 10", minimum value 750.00
Mold, ear of corn, 8½" 235.00
Mold, pinwheel 100.00
Mold, rabbit shape, brn w/Turk's head hdls, 8⅝" 75.00
Mug, bl seaweed, wht band w/stripes, 3⅝" 275.00
Mug, brn & wht stripes, near-match lid, 5⅝" 385.00
Mug, brn stripes, wht band, ribbed hdl, late, 4" 60.00

Mustard pot, incised blue lines, ca 1850-1900, EX, $350.00.

Pepper pot, bl bands, English, 1870-1900 ....575.00
Pie plate, 8" 75.00
Pitcher, bl & teal seaweed, wht band, brn stripes, 7½", EX 495.00
Pitcher, blk seaweed, wht band, bl & wht stripes, w/lid, 6¼" 935.00
Plate, bread; Westward Expansion, 6¼" 150.00
Salt cellar, bl seaweed, wht band w/bl stripes, 2¼x3", EX 440.00
Shakers, bl, dk brn & wht stripes, 4", pr 990.00
Spice jar, emb wheat, 3¾" 195.00
Tea bowl & saucer, English, ca 1900 ....150.00
Teapot, emb basketweave, Jeffords, Pat Nov 13, 1879 ....500.00
Teapot, tapered hexgon, 6" 215.00
Vase, ribbed & flared, 1900s, 8" 70.00

Zanesville Art Pottery

In 1900 the Zanesville Roofing Tile Company changed its name to the Zanesville Art Pottery Company and began the manufacture of standard glaze art pottery as well as cobalt blue jardinieres. David

Schmidt (1847-1922) was president of the concern during its twenty years of operation, and Albert Radford was general manager for a short time about 1901. The plant burned in 1901, possibly due to arson, and again in 1910 but was rebuilt both times. In 1920 the plant was sold to S.A. Weller and became Weller Plant No. 3. All identified pieces of the company's art pottery are impressed 'La Moro' with a shape number. Our advisor for this category is James L. Murphy; he is listed in the Directory under Ohio.

Loving cup, clover sprig, standard glaze, 3-hdl, 6" 150.00
Tankard, monk in profile, shades of gr, #881, 15" 900.00
Vase, clover, standard glaze, cylindrical, 15" 200.00
Vase, poppies, sgn M, La Moro, swollen cylinder, 15x5" 300.00

Zanesville Glass

Glassware was produced in Zanesville, Ohio, from as early as 1815 until 1851. Two companies produced clear and colored hollowware pieces in five characteristic patterns: 1) diamond faceted, 2) broken swirls, 3) vertical swirls, 4) perpendicular fluting, 5) plain, with scalloped or fluted rims and strap handles. The most readily identified product is perhaps the whiskey bottles made in the vertical swirl pattern, often called globular swirls because of their full, round bodies. Their necks vary in width; some have a ringed rim and some are collared. They were made in several colors; amber, light green, and light aquamarine are the most common. Our advisor for this category is Mark Vuono; he is listed in the Directory under Connecticut.

Bottle, cornflower bl, 24-rib swirl, wear, 8¼" 5,175.00
Bottle, globular, amber, 24-rib swirl, stain, 7¼" 660.00
Bottle, globular, amber, 24-rib swirl, 7⅝", NM 1,450.00
Bottle, globular, aqua, 24-rib swirl, potstones, 7½" 300.00
Bottle, globular, olive-amber, 24-rib swirl, potstone, 9½" 1,045.00
Bottle, lt bl, 24-broken-rib swirl, stain, 8¼" 600.00
Chestnut flask, amber, 10-dmn, flared lip, 4¾" 3,400.00
Chestnut flask, amber, 10-dmn, sheared mouth, 4⅝" 1,200.00
Chestnut flask, aqua, 10-dmn, potstones, 5¼" 600.00
Chestnut flask, aqua, 10-dmn, sheared mouth, 5" 1,235.00
Chestnut flask, dk amber, 10-dmn, 4⅝" 495.00
Chestnut flask, dk amber, 20-dmn, blister, 5¼" 165.00
Chestnut flask, dk amber, 24 vertical ribs, 6½" 300.00
Chestnut flask, dk amber, 24-broken-rib swirl, 6⅝" 2,100.00
Chestnut flask, dk red-amber, 10-dmn, wear, 4⅞" 250.00
Chestnut flask, golden amber, 24 vertical ribs, stain, 4¾" 275.00
Chestnut flask, olive-amber, 24-rib swirl, 5", EX 165.00
Chestnut flask, olive-yel, 10-dmn, 5⅜", NM 2,400.00
Salt cellar, blown, amber, 24 vertical ribs, ground lip, 3" 770.00
Vase, aqua, 19-rib swirl, appl ft, hdls, att, 6", NM 465.00

Zell

The Georg Schmider United Zell Ceramic Factories has a long and colorful history. Affectionately called 'Zell' by those who are attracted to this charming German-Dutch type tin-glazed earthenware, this ware came into production in the latter part of the last century.

While Zell has created some lovely majolica-like ware, it is the German-Dutch scenes that are collected with such enthusiasm. Typical scenes are set against a lush green background with windmills on the distant horizon. Into the scenes appear typically garbed girls (long dresses with long white aprons and lowland bonnet head-gear) being teased or admired by little boys attired in pantaloon-type trousers and

short rust-colored jackets. There are variations on this theme and occasionally a collector may find an animal theme or even a Kate Greenaway-like scene.

A similar ware in both theme, technique and quality, but bearing the mark Haag or Made in Austria is included in this listing.

While Zell produced a wide range of wares and even quite recently (1970s) introduced an entirely hand-painted hen/rooster ware, it is this early charming German-Dutch theme ware that is coveted and collected in increasing numbers by devoted collectors. Our advisors for this category are Fred and Lila Shrader; they are listed in the Directory under California.

Bowl, rim soup; Zell, Kate Greenaway-like scene, 8½" 65.00
Bowl, vegetable; Zell, boys strolling near harbor, 6x9½" 90.00
Candlestick, Zell, Dutch scenery: windmills & harbor, 9" 110.00
Creamer, Haag, animals at play, 3½" 35.00
Cup & saucer, Zell, children on road w/windmills & harbor 45.00
Pitcher, Made in Austria, children cross stream, motto, 9" 65.00
Plate, Zell, boys tease girls on road w/windmills & harbor, 7½" 65.00
Vase, Haag, bears at play in forest, slender, 7" 50.00

Zsolnay

Only until the past decade has the production of the Zsolnay factory become more correctly understood. In the beginning they produced only cement; industrial and kitchenware manufacture began in the 1850s, and in the early 1870s a line of decorative architectural and art pottery was initiated which has continued to the present time.

The city of Pecs (pronounced Paach) is the major provincial city of southwest Hungary close to the Yugoslav border. The old German name for the city was Funfkirchen, meaning 'Five Churches.' (The 'five-steeple' mark became the factory's logo in 1878.)

Although most Americans only think of Zsolnay in terms of the bizarre, reticulated examples of the 1880s and 1890s and the small 'Eosine' green figures of animals and children that have been produced since the 1920s, the factory went through all the art trends of major international art potteries and produced various types of forms and decorations. The golden period, circa 1895-1920, is when its Art Nouveau (Sezession in Austro-Hungarian terms) examples were unequaled. Vilmos Zsolnay was a Renaissance man devoted to innovation, and his children carried on the tradition after his death in 1900. Important sculptors and artists of the day were employed (usually anonymously) and married into the family, creating a dynasty.

Nearly all Zsolnay is marked, either impressed 'Zsolnay Pecs' or with the 'five steeple' stamp. Variations and form numbers can date a piece fairly accurately. For the most part, the earlier ethnic historical-revival pieces do not bring the prices that the later Sezession and second Sezession (Deco) examples do. Our advisor for this category is John Gacher; he is listed in the Directory under Rhode Island.

Ewer, simple stylized floral medallion on curdled pk/wht, 12" 110.00
Figurine, chicken, cubistic, irid gr/gold/bl, 7⅞" 600.00
Figurine, very stylized, holding bowl on head, wht/blk, 8½" 300.00
Figurine, woman w/water jar, red flambe, #8678/30/48, 15" 750.00
Vase, appl scrolls form 8 curled hdls, vivid mottle, 12" 2,400.00
Vase, bl/gr irid, emb folds issue from side, irregular rim, 12" 550.00
Vase, brick red craquelle w/bl irid crevices, 5½" 250.00
Vase, marbleized red/blk lustre, flared rim, 13x6" 600.00
Vase, mosaic crackle glaze in red on mustard, bottle neck, 7" 175.00
Vase, Nouveau floral, red/bl irid, ovoid, 3½" 750.00
Vase, 3-D lady sits on shoulder, tan w/strong irid, 9½" 600.00

Advisory Board

The editors and staff take this opportunity to express our sincere gratitude and appreciation to each person who has in any way contributed to the preparation of this guide. We believe the credibility of our book is greatly enhanced through their efforts. See each advisor's Directory listing for information concerning their specific areas of expertise.

You will notice that at the conclusion of some of the narratives the advisor's name is given. This is optional and up to the discretion of each individual. Simply because no name is mentioned does not indicate that we have no advisor for that subject. Our board grows with each issue and now numbers nearly 450; if you care to correspond with any of them or anyone listed in our Directory, you must send a SASE with your letter. If you are seeking an appraisal, first ask about their fee, since many of these people are professionals who must naturally charge for their services. Because of our huge circulation, every person who allows us to publish their name runs the risk of their privacy being invaded by too many phone calls and letters. We are indebted to every advisor and very much regret losing any one of them. By far, the majority of those we lose give that reason. Please help us retain them on our board by observing the simple rules of common courtesy. Take the differences in time zones into consideration; some of our advisors tell us they often get phone calls in the middle of the night. For suggestions that may help you evaluate your holdings, see the Introduction.

AAA Antique Shop
Nappanee, Indiana

Peter Abrahams
Lake Oswego, Oregon

Charles and Barbara Adams
Middleboro, Massachusetts

Jay Adams
Clifton, New Jersey

Geneva D. Addy
Winterset, Iowa

Charles Alexander
Indianapolis, Indiana

Margaret Alves
Shelton, Connecticut

James Anderson
New Brighton, Minnesota

Suzy McLennan Anderson
Holmdel, New Jersey

Tim Anderson
Provo, Utah

Warren R. Anderson
Cedar City, Utah

Norma Angelo
Bemus Point, New York

Dorothy Malone Anthony
Fort Scott, Kansas

John Apple
Racine, Wisconsin

Dick and Ellie Archer
St. Augustine, Florida

Una Arnbal
Ames, Iowa

Bruce A. Austin
Pittsford, New York

Rod Baer
Vienna, Virginia

Wayne and Gale Bailey
Dacula, Georgia

Mrs. Lillian Baker, Fellow IBA
Cambridge, England
Gardena, California

Roger Baker
Woodside, California

Robert Banks
Brookeville, Maryland

Jim Barker
Bethlehem, Pennsylvania

Kit Barry
Brattleboro, Vermont

Henry Bartsch
Rockaway, Oregon

Mark Bassett
Lakewood, Ohio

Daniel J. Batchelor
Oswego, New York

Dana Martin Batory
Crestline, Ohio

Joyce Bee
Sandy, Oregon

D.R. Beeks
Mt. Vernon, Iowa

Scott Benjamin
LaGrange, Ohio

Phyllis and Tom Bess
Tulsa, Oklahoma

Robert Bettinger
Mt. Dora, Florida

John E. Bilane
Union, New Jersey

Betty Bird
Mt. Shasta, Georgia

Brenda Blake
York Harbor, Maine

Clarence H. Bodine, Jr.
New Hope, Pennsylvania

Sandra V. Bondhus
Unionville, Connecticut

Clifford Boram
Monticello, Indiana

Dick and Waunita Bosworth
Kansas City, Missouri

Jeff Bradfield
Dayton, Virginia

Larry Brenner
Manchester, New Hampshire

William J. Brinkley
McLeansboro, Illinois

Mike Brooks
Oakland, California

Jim Broom
Effingham, Illinois

David L. Brown
Victoria, British Columbia, Canada

Rick Brown
Newspaper Collector's Society of America
Lansing, Michigan

Nicki Budin
Worthington, Ohio

Richard M. (Dick) Bueschel
Mt. Prospect, Illinois

Robert C. Butz
Newbury Park, California

Jim Calison
Wallkill, New York

Carol and Jim Carlton
Englewood, Colorado

Fran Carter
Coos Bay, Oregon

Tina M. Carter
El Cajon, California

Cerebro
East Prospect, Pennsylvania

Jackie Chamberlain
Wickenburg, Arizona

Mick and Lorna Chase
Cookeville, Tennessee

Pat and Chris Christensen
Costa Mesa, California

Jack Chipman
Venice, California

Cimini, Joan
Belmont, Ohio

Debbie and Randy Coe
Lafayette, Oregon

Wilfred and Dolli Cohen
Santa Ana, California

Lillian M. Cole
Flemington, New Jersey

Marilyn Cooper
Houston, Texas

J.W. Courter
Kevil, Kentucky

Susan Cox
El Cajon, California

Rosalind Cranor
Blacksburg, Virginia

Ron Damaska
New Brighton, Pennsylvania

Auction Houses

We wish to thank the following auction houses whose catalogs have been used as sources for pricing information. Many have granted us permission to reproduce their photographs as well.

A-1 Auction Service
P.O. Box 540672, Orlando, FL 32854; 407-839-0004. Specializing in American antique sales

Absolute Auction & Realty, Inc.
Robert Doyle
P.O. Box 658, 348 Main St., Beacon, NY 12524. Antique and estate auctions the 4th Friday of every month at their gallery.'Do your antiq'n in Beacon, 27 shops, 2 auction galleries'

Alex G. Malloy, Inc.
P.O. Box 38, South Salem, NY 10590; 203-438-0396. Specializing in ancient and medieval coins, antiquities, numismatic literature; 4 mail bid auctions per year

America West Archives
Anderson, Warren
P.O. Box 100, Cedar City, UT 84721; 801-586-9497. Publishes 26-page illustrated catalog 6 times a year that includes auction section of scarce and historical early western documents, letters, autographs, stock certificates, and other important ephemera, Subscription: $15 per year

Andre Ammelounx
The Stein Company
P.O. Box 136, Palatine, IL 60078; 708-991-5927 or (Fax) 708-991-5947. Specializing in steins, catalogs available

Anthony J. Nard & Co.
US Rt. 220, Milan, PA 18831
717-888-9404 or
(Fax) 717-888-7723

Arman Absentee Auctions
16 Sixth St, Stamford, CT 06905; 203-928-5838. Specializing in American glass, historical Staffordshire, English soft paste, paperweights

The Arts & Crafts Emporium
434 N. La Brea Ave.
Los Angeles, CA 90036
213-935-3777

Bertoia & Brady Auctions
2413 Madison Ave., Vineland, NJ 08360; 609-692-4092

Bider's
241 S. Union St., Lawrence, MA 01843; 508-688-4347 or 508-683-3944. Antiques appraised, purchased, and sold on consignment

Brian Riba Auctions Inc.
P.O. Box 53, Main St., S. Glastonbury, CT 06073; 203-633-3076

Butterfield & Butterfield
220 San Bruno Ave., San Francisco, CA 91043; 415-861-7500 or (Fax) 415-861-8951. Also located at: 7601 Sunset Blvd., Los Angeles, CA 90046; 213-850-7500 or (Fax) 213-850-5843. Fine Art Auctioneers and Appraisers since 1865

Cerebro
P.O. Box 327, E. Prospect, 17317; 717-252-2400 or 800-69-LABEL. Specializing in antique advertising labels, especially cigar box labels, cigar bands, food labels, firecracker labels; Holds semiannual auction on tobacco ephemera; Consignments accepted

Charles E. Kirtley
P.O. Box 2273, Elizabeth City, NC 27096; 919-335-1262. Specializing in World's Fair, Civil War, political, advertising and other American collectibles

Cherry Land Auctions
Ronald D. Millard
P.O. Box 4086, Tequesta, FL 33469; 407-743-0010. Specializing in postcard mail auctions

Cincinnati Art Gallery
635 Main St., Cincinnati, OH 45202; 513-381-2128. Specializing in American art pottery, American and European fine paintings, watercolors

Col. Doug Allard
P.O. Box 460, St. Ignatius, MT 59865-0460; 406-745-2951 or (Fax) 406-745-2961

Collector's Auction Services
326 Seneca St., Oil City, PA 16301; 814-677-6070. Specializing in advertising, oil and gas, toys, rare museum and investment-quality antiques

Collector's Sales & Service
P.O. Box 4037
Middletown, RI 02842; 401-849-5012 or (Fax) 401-846-6156

Country Girls Estate & Appraisal Service
P.O. Box 144, Saddle RIver, NJ 07458

David Rago
P.O. Box 3592, Station E, Trenton, NJ 08629; 609-397-9374. Gallery: 17 S. Main St., Lambertville, NJ 08530. Specializing in American art pottery and Arts & Crafts

Dunbar's Gallery
Leila and Howard Dunbar
76 Haven St., Milford, MA 01757; 508-634-8697 or (Fax) 508-634-8698

Dunning's
755 Church Road
Elgin, IL 60123; 708-741-3483 or 312-664-8400

Dynamite Auctions
Franklin Antique Mall & Auction Gallery
1280 Franklin Ave., Franklin, PA 16323; 814-432-8577 or 814-786-9211

Du Mouchelles
409 Jefferson Ave., Detroit, MI 48226

Early American Numismatics
Dana Linett, President
P.O. Box 2442, La Jolla, CA 92038

Early Auction Co.
123 Main St., Milford, OH 45150

Freeman Fine Arts
1808 Chestnut St.
Philadelphia, PA 19103; 215-563-9275 or (Fax) 215-563-8236

Garth's Auctions Inc.
2690 Stratford Rd., Box 369, Delaware, OH 43015; 614-362-4771

The Glass Menagerie, bimonthly newsletter
Susan Candelaria, Editor
5440 El Arbol, Carlsbad, CA 92008

Glass-Works Auctions
James Hagenbuch
102 Jefferson, East Greenville, PA 18041; 215-679-5849. America's leading auction company in early American bottles and glass

Greenberg Auctions
7566 Main St., Sykesville, MD 21784. Specializing in trains: Lionel, American Flyer, Ives, Marx, HO

Guernsey's
136 E. 73rd St., New York, NY 10021; 212-794-2280. Specializing in carousel figures

Hake's Americana & Collectibles
Specializing in character and personality collectibles along with all artifacts of popular culture for over 20 years. To receive a catalog for their next 3,000-item mail/phone bid auction, send $5 to Hake's Americana, P.O. Box 1444M, York, PA 17405

Hanna-Whysel Auctioneers & Appraisers
Steven Whysel
3403 Bella Vista Way, Bella Vista, AR, 72714; 501-855-9600. Antiques and art auctions

Harmer Rooke Galleries
32 E. 57th St, 11th Floor
New York, NY 10022; 212-751-1900 or (Fax) 212-758-1713

Horst Auctioneers
Horst Auction Center
50 Durlach Rd. (corner of Rt. 322 & Durlach Rd., West of Ephrata), Ephrata, Lancaster County, PA 17522; 717-859-1331 or 717-738-3080. Voices of Experience

Jack Sellner
Sellner Marketing of California
P.O. Box 308, Fremont, CA 94536; 415-745-9463

James D. Julia
P.O. Box 210, Showhegan Rd., Fairfield, ME 04937

James R. Bakker Antiques, Inc.
James R. Bakker
370 Broadway, Cambridge, MA 02139; 617-864-7067. Specializing in American paintings, prints and decorative arts

John Toomey Gallery
818 North Blvd., Oak Park, IL 60301; 708-383-5234 or (Fax) 708-383-4828. Specializing in furniture and decorative arts of the Arts & Crafts, Art Deco and Modern Design movements; Modern Design Expert: Richard Wright

Joy Luke Fine Arts Brokers and Auctioneers
The Gallery
300 East Grove St., Bloomington, IL 61701; 309-828-5533

Ken Farmer Realty & Auction Company
1122 Norwood St., Radford, VA 24141; 703-639-0939 or (Fax) 703-639-1759

Kerry & Judy's Toys
7370 Eggleston Rd., Memphis, TN 38125-2112; 901-757-1722. Specializing in toys, 1900-1960s; Consignments always welcome

Kit Barry Ephemera Auctions
68 High St., Brattleboro, VT 05301; 802-254-3634. Tradecard and ephemera auctions, fully-illustrated catalogs with prices realized; Consignment inquiries welcome

Kurt R. Krueger
160 N. Washington St., P.O. Box 275, Iola, WI 54945-0275

L.R.'Les' Docks
Box 691035, San Antonio, TX 78269-1035. Providing occasional mail-order record auctions, rarely consigned; the only consignments considered are exceptionally scarce and unusual records

Litchfield, Auction Gallery
425 Bantam Rd., P.O. Box 1337, Litchfield, CT 06759; 203-567-3126 or (Fax) 203-567-3266

Lloyd Ralston Toys
447 Stratford Rd.
Fairfield, CT 06432

Manion's International Auction House, Inc.
P.O. Box 12214, Kansas City, KS 66112; 913-299-6692 or (Fax) 913-299-6792

Maritime Auctions
R.R. 2, Box 45A, York, ME 03909; 207-363-4247

McMasters Doll Auctions
P.O. Box 1755, 5855 Glenn Highway Rd., Cambridge, OH 43725; 614-432-4320 or (Fax) 614-432-3191

Mid-Hudson Auction Galleries
One Idlewild Ave., Cornwall-on-Hudson, NY 12520; 914-534-7828 or (Fax) 914-534-4802

Monsen & Baer, Annual Perfume Bottle Auction
Monsen, Randall; and Baer, Rod
Box 529, Vienna, VA 22183; 703-938-2129 or (Fax) 703-242-1357. Cataloged auctions of perfume bottles; Will purchase, sell, and accept consignments; Specializing in commercial, Czechoslovakian, Lalique, Baccarat, Victorian, crown top, factices, miniatures

Neal Auction Company
4038 Magazine St., New Orleans, LA 70115; 504-899-5329 or 1-800-467-5329 or 504-897-3803

Noel Barrett Antiques & Auctions
P.O. Box 1001, Carversville, PA 18913; 215-297-5109 or (Fax) 215-297-0457

New England Absentee Auctions
16 6th St., Stamford, CT 06905; 203-975-9055. Specializing in Quimper pottery

Nostalgia Co.
21 S. Lake Dr., Hackensack, NJ 07601; 201-488-4536

Phillips
406 E. 79th St.
New York, NY 10021

The Political Gallery
5335 N. Tacoma, Suite 24, Indianapolis, IN 46220; 317-257-0863 or (Fax) 317-254-9167. Publishes quarterly catalogs

Postcards International
P.O. Box 2930, New Haven, CT 06515-0030; 203-865-0814 or (Fax) 203-495-8005

Refinders
737 Barberry Rd., Highland Park, IL 60035; 708-831-1102 or 708-831-1160. Refinders will find your wants from 1860-1960

Rex Stark Auctions
49 Wethersfield Rd., Bellingham, MA 02019

Richard A. Bourne Co. Inc.
Estate Auctioneers & Appraisers
Box 141, Hyannis Port, MA 02647
617-775-0797

Richard Opfer Auctioneering, Inc.
1919 Greenspring Dr., Timonium, MD 21093; 301-252-5035

Roan, Inc.
Box 118, R.D. 3, Cogan Station, PA 17728

Ron Fox Auctions
Ron Fox
83 Morris St., Brentwood, NY 11717; 516-231-0633 or (Fax) 516-952-7719. Specializing in steins; Auctions with illustrated catalogs and video tapes

Skinner, Inc.
Auctioneers & Appraisers of Antiques and Fine Arts
The Heritage on the Garden, 63 Park Plaza, Boston, MA 02116; 617-350-5400 or (Fax) 617-350-5429. Second address: 357 Main Street, Boston, MA 01740; 508-779-6241 or (Fax) 508-779-5144

Smith & Jones, Inc.
12 Clark Lane; Sudbury, MA 01776; 508-443-5517 or (Fax) 508-443-8045. Specializing in Dedham dinnerware, Buffalo china and important American art pottery. Full-color catalogs available

Soldiers Trunk
60 Craigs Rd., Windsor, CT 06095; 203-688-0580. Specializing in American and foreign military items; 4 catalog issues for $20

Sotheby Parke Bernet, Inc.
980 Madison Ave., New York, NY 10021

Steffen Historical Militaria
Roger S. Steffen
14 Murnan Rd., Cold Springs, KY 41076; 606-431-4499. Specializing in quality militaria, military art, rare books, antique firearms

Tradewinds Auctions
Henry and Nancy Taron
24 Magnolia, Ave., Manchester-By-The-Sea, MA 01944

Treadway Gallery, Inc.
2029 Madison Rd., Cincinnati, OH 45208; 513-321-6742 or (Fax) 513-871-7722. Specializing in American Art Pottery; American and European art glass; European ceramics; Italian glass; fine American and European paintings and graphics; and furniture and decorative arts of the Arts & Crafts, Art Nouveau, Art Deco and Modern Design Movements. Modern Design expert: Thierry Lorthioir. Members: National Antique Dealers Association, American Art Pottery Association, International Society of Appraisers, American Ceramic Arts Society, Ohio Decorative Arts Society, Art Gallery Association of Cincinnati.

Weschler's
Adam A. Weschler & Son
905 E. St. N.W., Washington, DC 20004

Willis Henry Auctions
22 Main St., Marshfield, MA 02050

Directory of Contributors

When contacting any of the buyers/sellers listed in this part of the Directory by mail, you must include an SASE (stamped, self-addressed envelope) if you expect a reply. As hectic as our lifestyles are, the time it saves them is probably worth more to them than the price of a stamp. Not only that, but trying to decipher someone's handwritten name and address can be very frustrating. Sometimes even zip codes are unreadable, and even more time is required to double check zip code numbers. And in the end, if 'Rosen' becomes 'Rirer' and 'Ave. 5' becomes 'Ave. S,' even if the person you contacted was gracious enough to answer you, you probably won't ever know he did. Many of these people are professional appraisers and there will be a fee for their time and service. Find out up front. Include a clear photo if you want an item identified. Most items cannot be described clearly enough to make an identification without a photo.

If you call and get their answering machine, when you leave your number so that they can return your call, tell them to call back collect. And please take the differences in time zones into consideration. 7:00 AM in the midwest is only 4:00 AM in California! And if you're in California, remember that even 7:00 PM is too late to call the east coast. Most people work and are gone during the daytime. Even some of our antique dealers say they prefer after-work phone calls. Don't assume that a person who deals in a particular field will be able to help you with related items. They may seem related to you when they are not.

Please, we need your help. This book sells in such great numbers that allowing their names to be published can create a potential nightmare for each advisor and contributor. Please do your part to help us minimize this, so that we can retain them on our board and in turn pass their experience and knowledge on to you through our book. Many of our people tell us that even with the occasional problem, they feel that the good outweighs the bad and makes all their hard work worthwhile.

Alabama

Dole, Pat
9825 Red Mill Rd.
Birmingham, 35215; 205-833-9853.
Specializing in Purinton pottery

Donnelly, Ron
Saturday Heroes
6302 Championship Dr., Tuscaloosa, 35405. Specializing in Big Little Books, movie posters, premiums, western heroes, Gone with the Wind, character collectibles, early Disney; Inquiries require SASE; No free appraisals

Lippa, Matt; and Schaaf, Elizabeth
Artisans
P.O. Box 256, Mentone, 35984; 205-634-4037. Specializing in folk art, quilts, painted and folky furniture, tramp art, whirligigs, windmill weights; E-mail: artisans@vistech.net or http://www.vistech.net/users/artisans

Luckey, Carl
Carl F. Luckey Communications
R.R. 4, Box 301, Lingerlost Trail, Killen, 35645. Freelance writer specializing in art, antiques, and collectibles. No telephone calls will be accepted; SASE required for correspondence

Arizona

Chamberlain, Jackie
Jackie Chamberlain Antiques
P.O. Box 20842, Wickenburg, 85358. Specializing in holiday collectibles, antique reference books, pewter ice-cream molds, rare out-of-print books. Holiday slide program available for rent

Chase Collectors Society
Van Hook, Barry L.
2149 Jibsail Loop, Mesa, 85202-5524; 602-838-6971. Publishes (6 issues per year) newsletter, *Art Deco Reflections* (sample copy: $1); Membership: $5

Ellwood, J.M.
7077 E. Main #4, Scottsdale, 85251; 602-947-9679. Specializing in cast-iron banks, toys, irons, trivets, doorstops and miscellaneous cast iron

Schaut, Jim and Nancy
Aquarius Antiques
P.O. Box 10781, Glendale, 85318; 602-878-4293. Specializing in Automobilia, racing memorabilia, auto toys; Authors of *American Automobilia*, 1994

Webb, Maret
Swan Seekers Network
4118 E. Vernon Ave., Phoenix, 85008-2333; 602-957-6294 or (Fax) 602-957-1631. Business hours: 9:00 a.m. - 5:00 p.m., M.S.T., Mon. – Fri.; Publishes *Swan Seekers News* and *Swan Seekers Marketplace* periodicals ($28 in US per year, $38 foreign); Specializing in Swarovski crystal

Arkansas

Dryden, James
Dryden Pottery
P.O. Box 603, Hot Springs National Park, 71902; 501-627-4201. Specializing in hand-thrown artware vases, mugs, ovenware, etc.

Gifford, David Edwin
Arkansas Pottery Research
P.O. Box 7617, Little Rock, 72217; 501-664-0902. Historian/author/collector of Arkansas art pottery from 1905 to 1932; Seeking all information and company literature on the Ouachita Pottery, Niloak Pottery, and Camark Pottery companies as well as quality pieces marked Ouachita Hot Springs, Niloak Patent Pend'G, LeCamark or Hywood Art Pottery; Will answer queries — LSASE please

Whysel, Steven
Hanna-Whysel, Inc., Auctioneers & Appraisers
Antiques & Decorative Arts Center, 119 W. Emma, Springdale, 72764; 501-751-5115 (Auctions and Appraisals: 501-751-5775 or 501-273-7770). Specializing in Art Nouveau, art, and full line

Yohe, Darlene
Timberview Antiques
P.O. Box 343, Stuttgart, 72160; 501-673-3437. Specializing in American pattern glass, historical glass, Victorian pattern glass, carnival glass, and custard glass

California

Baker, Mrs. Lillian
15237 Chanera Ave., Gardena, 90249; 213-329-2619. Author Collector Books on antique, collectible, and high-fashion costume jewelry, hatpins and hatpin holders, miniatures

Baker, Roger
Baker's Lady Luck Emporium
Box 620417, Woodside, 94062. Specializing in Saloon Americana — advertising, gambling, bar bottles, cigar lighters, match safes, bowie knives (1830-1900), dirks, daggers, cowboy hats, spurs, chaps, saddles, barber items: bottles, shaving mugs, razors

Berg, Paul
P.O. Box 8895, Newport Beach, 92620; Author of *Nineteenth Century Photographica Cases and Wall Frames*

Brooks, Mike
7335 Skyline, Oakland, 94611; 510-339-1751. Specializing in typewriters, transistor radios, early televisions, Statue of Liberty

Bueschel, Richard M.
414 N. Prospect Manor Ave., Mt. Prospect, 60056-2046; 847-253-0791. Specializing in saloon, coin-operated machines, trade catalogs

Butz, Robert C.
Collector's Wedgwood
P.O. Box 462, Newbury Park, 91319. Specializing in Wedgwood

Carter, Tina M.
882 S. Mollison, El Cajon, 92020; 619-440-5043. Specializing in teapots, tea-related items, tea tins, children's and toy tea sets, coffeepots, etc.; Book on teapots available. Send $16 (includes postage) or $17 for CA residents, Canada: add $5, to above address

Chipman, Jack
California Spectrum
P.O. Box 1079, Venice, 90294-1079. Specializing in California ceramics; author of *Collector's Encyclopedia of California Pottery*, autographed copies available from author for $24.95+$3.50 postage and handling+(CA) tax of $2.35

Christensen, Pat and Chris
1067 Salvador St., Costa Mesa, 92626. Specializing in open salts

Cohen, Wilfred and Dolli
Antiques & Art Glass
P.O. Box 27151, Santa Ana, 92799; 714-545-5673 (best to phone after 6:00 p.m. Pacific time). Specializing in Wave Crest (C.F. Monroe), Victorian Era art and pattern glass (salt shakers, toothpick holders, syrups, cruets, sugar shakers, tumblers, biscuit jars, table and pitcher sets), art and cameo glass open salts, custard, ruby-stained, burmese, peachblow and amberina, pottery by Moorcroft (pre-1935 only), Buffalo (Deldare and Emerald ware), and Polia Pillin; Please include SASE for reply.

Cox, Susan N.
237 E. Main St., El Cajon, 92020; 619-447-0800. Specializing in California pottery and Frankoma

Dolan, Maryanne
138 Belle Ave., Pleasant Hill, CA 94523. Specializing in vintage clothing

Ehrhard, J. David
Psycho-Ceramic Restorations
1064½ Hillhaven Ave., Tujunga, 91042. Specializing in restoration of ceramics, collects Susie Cooper and British pottery, Mabel Lucie Attwell

Enge, Delleen
Franciscan Dinnerware Matching Service
323 E. Matilija, Ste. 112, Ojai, 93023

Escoe, Adrienne S., Member
Glass Knife Collectors Club
4448 Ironwood Ave., Seal Beach, 90740; 310-598-1585; Specializing in glass knives; E-mail: escoebliss@earthlink.net

Fogleman, Marv
Marv's Memories
1814 W. Carriage Dr., Santa Ana, 92704. Specializing in Western Dinnerware, Metlox, Mikasa, and Franciscan

George, Tony
22431-B160 Antonio Pkwy., #252, Rancho Santa Margarita, 92688; 714-589-6075. Specializing in watch fobs

Giacomini, Mary Jane
P.O. Box 404, Ferndale, CA 95536-0404; 707-786-9464. Author of *American Bisque, A Collector's Guide With Prices*; Specializing in American Bisque pottery, cookie jars

Gibson, Pat
38280 Guava Dr., Newark, 94560; 510-792-0586. Specializing in R.A. Fox

Harrison, Gwynne
P.O. Box 1, Mira Loma, 91752-0001; 909-685-5434. Specializing in Autumn Leaf (Jewel Tea)

Hibbard, Suzi
WanderWares
2570 Walnut Blvd. #20, Walnut Creek, 94596; Specializing in Dragonware, 1000 Faces china, Oriental china. Inquiries should be accompanied by SASE; Computer correspondence: hmbk24a@prodigy.com

Howard, Steve
101 1st St., Suite 404, Los Altos, 94022; 510-484-4488. Specializing in antique American firearms, bowie knives, Western Americana, old advertising, and vintage gambling items

Inouye, Roger
765 E. Franklin Ave., Pomona, 91766; 909-623-1368. Specializing in Trolls

Kreider, Katherine
Kingsbury Antiques
4555 N. Pershing Ave., Suite 33-138, Stockton, 95207; 209-467-8438. Author of *Valentines With Values*, over 600 color photos and informative text ($19.95+2.90 S&H); Please send check to Kingsbury antiques, P.O. Box 7957, Lancaster, PA 17604-7957. If ordering from PA please include correct sales tax. No free appraisals

Main Street Antique Mall
237 E Main Street
El Cajon, 92020; 619-447-0800

Maurer, Oveda L.
Oveda Maurer Antiques
34 Greenfield Ave., San Anselmo, 94960; 415-454-6439. Specializing in 18th-century and early 19th-century American furniture, lighting, pewter, hearthware, glass, folk art, and paintings

Nelson, Maxine
4140 N. 78th St. Apt. 2255, Scottsdale, AZ 85251 Specializing in Vernon Kilns; author of *Collectible Vernon Kilns*; Autographed copies available from the author for $24.95+$2.50 postage & handling (CA sale tax: $1.93); SASE appreciated for inquiries

Paper Pile Quarterly
Ada Fitsimmons, Editor
P.O. Box 337, San Anselmo, 94979; 619-322-3525. Sales- and features-magazine serving paper collectors and dealers since 1980, quarterly cataloged sales and large advertising section; Subscription: $17 per year (shipped 1st class)

Pardini, Dick
3107 N. El Dorado St., Dept. SAPG, Stockton, 95204-3412; 209-466-5550 (recorder may answer). Specializing in California Perfume Company items dating from 1886 to 1928 and 'go-with' related companies: buyer and information center. Not interested in items that have Avon, Perfection, or Anniversary Keepsake markings. California Perfume Company offerings must be accompanied by a photo, Xerox copy, or sketching along with a condition report and, most important, price wanted. Inquiries require large SASE; not necessary if offering items for sale

Roller, Gayle
P.O. Box 222, San Marcos, 92079-0222. Specializing in Hagen-Renaker

Sanford, Steve and Martha
230 Harrison Ave., Campbell, 95088; 408-978-8408. Specializing in Brush McCoy

Shrader, Fred and Lila
Shrader Antiques
2025 Hwy. 199, Crescent City, 95531; 707-458-3525. Specializing in railroad, steamship and other transportation memorabilia; Shelley china, Buffalo china, Niloak, and Zell

Stella's Collectibles
Memory Lanes Antique Mall
20740 S. Figueroa St., Carson, (Space 214) 90745; 310-316-7198; Julie's Antiques, Long Beach (Space 24); Santa Monica Antique Market (Space 113); Westchester Faire Mall (Space 320-326); Enchanted Treasures, Lake Elsinore (Space 25). Specializing in quality glass, china, and figurines

Thornton, Don
1345 Poplar Ave., Sunnyvale, 94087. Specializing in egg beaters; author of *Beat This: The Eggbeater Chronicles* ($28.95 including postage and handling)

Webb, Frances Finch
1589 Gretel Lane, Mountain View, 94040. Specializing in Kay Finch ceramics

Yronwode, Catherine
6632 Covey Rd., Forestville, 95436; 707-887-2424. Specializing in pre-1950 collectible plastic

Zeder, Audrey
6755 Coralite St. S., Long Beach, 90808 (appointment only). Specializing in British Royal Commemorative Souvenirs (mail-order catalog available); Author (Wallace-Homestead) of *British Royal Commemoratives*

Canada

Brown, David L.
Stevengraph Collectors Assn.
2103-2829 Arbutus Rd., Victoria, British Columbia, V8N 5X5; 604-477-9896. Specializing in Stevengraphs

Melis, Mirko
Marcelle Antiques
P.O. Box 53039, 5100 Erin Mills Pkwy., Mississauga, Ontario, L5M 4Z5; 905-689-1648. Specializing in American and European art glass, Russian works of art (enamels, porcelains, silver, etc.), English and Continental glass and china, member of Antique Appraisal Association of America, Inc., and AADA (Associated Antique Dealers of America, Inc.)

Old China Patterns Limited
1560 Brimley Rd., Unit 1, Scarborough, Ontario, MIP369; 416-299-8880 or (Fax) 416-299-4721. Specializing in discontinued china dinnerware, matching service (since 1966), charter member I.A.D.M.

Warner, Ian
P.O. Box 93022, 499 Main St. S., Brampton, Ontario, L6Y 4V8; 905-453-9074 or (Fax) 905-453-2931. Specializing in Wade porcelain and Swankyswigs, author of *The World of Wade*, Co-author: Mike Posgay

Colorado

Carlton, Carol and Jim
8115 S. Syracuse St., Englewood, 80112; 303-773-8616. Specializing in Broadmoor, Coors and other Colorado pottery

Heck, Carl
Carl Heck Decorative Arts
Box 8416, Aspen, 81612; 970-925-8011. Specializing in original Tiffany lamps, art glass, windows and chandeliers; Also reverse painted and leaded glass table lamps, stained and beveled glass windows, bronzes, paintings, etc.; Buy and sell; Fee for written appraisals. Please include SASE for reply

Mackin, Bill
Author of *Cowboy and Gunfighter Collectibles*; available from author: 1137 Washington St., Craig, 81625; 303-824-6717, Paperback: $25; Other titles available; Specializing in old and fine spurs, guns, gun leather, cowboy gear, Western Americana (Collection in the Museum of Northwest Colorado, Craig)

Over, Naomi L.
8909 Sharon Lane, Arvada, 80002; 303-424-5922. Specializing in ruby glassware, author of *Ruby Glass of the 20th Century*, available from author for $24.50 soft bound or $32.50 hard bound (includes shipping and handling); Naomi will attempt to make photo identifications for all who include a SASE with correspondence

Segelke, Cathy; and James, Pat
Hillrose, 970-847-3758 (Cathy) or 970-847-3759 (Pat). Specializing in crocks, Western Pottery Mfg. Co. (Denver, CO)

Toohey, Marlena
703 S. Pratt Pky., Longmont, 80501; 303-678-9726. Specializing in black glass; Book available from author for $20 (includes shipping and handling)

White, John 'Grandpa'
Grandpa's Depot
1616 17th St., Suite 267, Denver, 80202; 303-628-5590 or (Fax) 303-628-5547. Specializing in railroad-related items, catalogs available

Winther, Jo Ellen
8449 W. 75th Way, Arvada, 80005; 800-872-2345 or 303-421-2371. Specializing in Coors

Connecticut

Alves, Margaret
84 Oak Ave., Shelton, 06484; 203-924-4768. Specializing in spoons: plated, sterling, silver, pre-1920s

Bondhus, Sandra V.
Box 100, Unionville, 06085; 860-678-1808. Author of *Quimper Pottery: A French Folk Art Faience*; Specializing in Quimper pottery

FDS Antiques, Inc.
62 Blue Ridge Dr., Stamford, 06903-4923. Publishes *The 'No Nonsense' Antique Mall Directory*, a directory of antique malls, centers, and multi-dealer co-ops; Over 4,700 listings listed according to state

Harned, Denise
P.O. Box 330373, Elmwood, 06133-0373. Author of *Griswold Cast Collectibles*; Specializing in Griswold cast iron and aluminum

Kilbride, Mrs. Richard J.
81 Willard Terrace, Stamford, 06903; 203-322-0568. Has available for sale: *Art Deco Chrome, The Chase Era*, and *Art Deco Chrome, Book 2, A Collector's Guide, Industrial Design in the Chase Era*

MacSorley, Earl
823 Indian Hill Rd., Orange, 06477; 203-387-1793 (after 7:00 p.m.). Specializing in nutcrackers, Bessie Pease Gutmann prints, figural lift-top spittoons

Postcards International
Shapiro, Marty
P.O. Box 2930, New Haven, 06515-0030; 203-865-0814 or (Fax) 203-495-8005. Specializing in vintage picture postcards

Roenigk, Martin
Mechantiques
26 Barton Hill, E. Hampton, 06424; 203-267-8682. Specializing in mechanical musical instruments, music boxes, band organs, musical clocks and watches, coin pianos, orchestrions, monkey organs, automata, mechanical birds and dolls, etc.

Thalberg, Bruce
Mountain View Dr., Weston, 06883; 203-227-8175. Specializing in canes and walking sticks: novelty, carved, and Black

Van Deusen, Hobart D.
28 The Green, Watertown, 06795; 203-945-3456. Specializing in Canton, SASE required when requesting information

Vuono, Mark
306 Mill Rd., Stamford, 06903; 203-357-0892 (10 a.m. to 5:30 p.m. E.S.T.). Specializing in historical flasks, blown 3-mold glass, blown American glass

District of Columbia

Durham, Ken and Jackie
(By appointment)
909 26 St. N.W., Suite 502, Washington, D.C. 20037. Specializing in counter-top arcade machines, trade stimulators, and vending machines; 16-page illustrated list: $2; Send SASE for free list of books on coin-operated machines. http://www.olg.com

England

Pedel, Alan
Hidden Treasures
Marwood Lee, Barnstaple, Devon, EX31 4EB; 011-44-271-75166 (anytime). Specializing in pie birds and most other collectibles

Florida

Archer, Dick and Ellie
Artiques
419 Sevilla Dr., St. Augustine, 32086; 904-797-4678. Specializing in Victorian silverplate: figurals, fancy hollow ware, and collectibles

Bettinger, Robert
P.O. Box 333, Mt. Dora, 32757; 352-735-3575. Specializing in American art pottery

Cohen, Joel
Cohen Books & Collectibles
P.O. Box 810310, Boca Raton, 33481; 407-487-7888. Specializing in Disneyana

deCourtivron, Gael
Cocaholics
4811 Remington Dr., Sarasota, 34234; 941-355-2652 or 813-359-2652. Specializing in Coca-Cola memorabilia

Dodds, Rebecca
Silver Flute
Box 39644, Ft. Lauderdale, 33339. Specializing in jewelry

Elsner, Dr. Robert
29 Clubhouse Lane, Boynton Beach, 33436; 407-736-1362. Specializing in antique barometers and nautical instruments

France, Madeleine
P.O. Box 15555, Ft. Lauderdale, 33318; 305-584-0009. Specializing in top-quality perfume bottles: Rene Lalique, Steuben, Czechoslovakian, DeVilbiss, Baccarat, Commercials; French dore bronze and decorative arts

Hudson, Hardy
Our Antiques Market
5453 Lake Howell Rd., Winter Park, 32792; 407-657-2100 from 11:00 a.m. to 6:00 p.m. Specializing in majolica, American art pottery (buying one piece or entire collections); Also buying Weller (garden ornaments, birds, Mammy, Hudson or animal related), better Roseville, Overbeck, Kay Finch animals

Lawrence, Judy and Cliff
1169 Overcash Dr., Dunedin, 34698. Specializing in fountain pens and mechanical pencils; No free appraisals

Linscott, Jacqueline C.
3557 Nicklaus Dr., Titusville, 32780. Specializing in Blue Bell paperweights; Author of *1992 Revised Edition, Blue Bell Paperweights*, and *1995 Addendum*, complete with history, illustrations, and price guide; Available from author for $17 (includes postage and handling)

Linscott, Len
Line Jewels-Insulators
3557 Nicklaus Dr., Titusville, 32780. Specializing in glass insulators and other telephone items. SASE required

McNerny, Kathryn
118 Creek Hollow Lane, Middleburg, 32068. Author (Collector Books) on blue and white stoneware, primitives, tools

Millard, Ronald D.
Cherry Land Auctions
P.O. Box 4086, Tequesta, 33469; 407-743-0010. Specializing in postcard mail auctions

New World Maps, Inc.
Charles R. Neuschafer
1123 S. Broadway, Lantana, 33462-4522; 407-586-8723. Buys and sells antique and collectible maps, specializing in 20th-century road maps; Columnist for *Paper Collectors Marketplace* and member of International Map Dealers Association

Parker, Alton B.
6127 Dartmouth Dr., Bradenton, 34207-4730; 813-756-0386. Specializing in Azalea china, Depression Glass, Roseville pottery

Posner, Judy
November-April: 4195 S. Tamiami Trail, #183SC, Venice 34293; 941-497-7149. May-October: R.D. 1, Box 273SC, Effort, PA 18330; 717-629-6583. Specializing in figural pottery, salt and peppers, Black memorabilia, Disneyana, character and advertising collectibles, cookie jars; Buy, Sell, Collect; Appraisals: $25

Supnick, Mark
2771 Oakbrook Manor, Ft. Lauderdale, 33332. Author of *Collecting Hull Pottery's Little Red Riding Hood* ($12.95 postage paid). Specializing in American pottery

Tyler, Henry
13 Bellevue Dr.,
Treasure Island, 33706

White, Douglass
Classic Interiors & Antiques
2042 N. Rio Grande, Suite E, Orlando, 32804; 407-839-0004. Specializing in Fulper, Arts & Crafts furniture

Wise, Raphael C.
The Collector's Stop
12018 Suellen Circle, West Palm Beach, 33414; 407-793-0986. Specializing in Wedgwood Jasper Ware, Rosenthal, Moorcroft, Buffalo Deldare and Emerald Ware, Heisey, contemporary paperweights, English porcelains

Georgia

Bailey, Wayne and Gale
P.O. Box 173, Dacula, 30211; 770-963-5736. Specializing in Goebels (Friar Tuck)

Bird, Betty
Memory Land & Antiques, Etc.
107 Ida St, Mt. Shasta, 96067; 916-926-4331. Specializing in coin silver and open salts

Glenn, Walter
Geode Ltd.
3393 Peachtree Rd., Atlanta, 30326; 404-261-9346. Specializing in Frankart

Hartley, Glenn, Sr.
Fire Mark Circle of the Americas
2859 Marlin Dr., Chamblee, 30341-5119; 404-451-2651. Specializing in fire marks, Methodist, Masonic, Foremost Dairies, Goodyear

Joiner, John R.
Aviation Collectors
173 Green Tree Dr., Newnan, 30265; 404-502-9565. Specializing in commercial aviation collectibles

Illinois

Ammelounx, Andre
The Stein Auction Company
P.O. Box 136, Palatine, 60078; 708-991-5927 or (Fax) 708-991-5947. Specializing in steins, catalogs available

The Barrel Antique Mall
5850 S St. Road, I-55 Exit 90, Springfield, 62707; 217-585-1438

Brinkley, Wm. J.
Brinkley Galleries
401 S. Washington Ave., McLeansboro, 62859. Specializing in Meissen, Dresden, European porcelains, American porcelains (Cybis)

Broom, Jim
Box 65, Effingham, 62401. Specializing in opalescent pattern glassware

Bueschel, Richard M. (Dick)
414 N. Prospect Manor Ave., Mt. Prospect, 60056-2046; 847-253-0791 or (Fax) 847-253-7919. Specializing in coin machines, trade catalogs, pre-prohibition saloon, prohibition speakeasy, screen doors, fretwork, advertising folding chairs, food can openers. Author of books relating to coin-operated machines and saloon collectibles (available from author)

Danis, John
11028 Raleigh Ct., Rockford, 61115; 815-963-0757 or (Fax) 815-877-6042. Specializing in R. Lalique; Norse pottery

Feldman, Arthur M.
Arthur M. Feldman Gallery
1815 St. Johns Ave., Highland Park, 60035; 708-432-8858. Specializing in Judaica and antiques

Frizzell, Doris
Doris' Dishes
5687 Oakdale Dr., Springfield, 62707; 217-529-3873. Specializing in Royal Haeger, and Depression Glass; Co-author (Collector Books) of Royal Haeger book

Garmon, Lee
1529 Whittier St., Springfield, 62704; 217-789-9574. Specializing in Royal Haeger, Royal Hickman, glass animals; Co-author (Collector Books) of *Glass Animals and Figural Flower Frogs of the Depression Era*

Griffith, Woody
Chicago, 312-975-1957. Specializing in DeVilbiss, perfumes, perfume lamps

Hall, Doris and Burdell
B&B Antiques
210 W. Sassafras Dr., Morton, 61550-1245. Authors of *Morton's Potteries: 99 Years* (Vols. I and II); Specializing in Morton pottery, American dinnerware, early American pattern glass, historical items

Haussmann, Richard A., Past President, Aurora Historical Society
Aurora, 60507

Hilst, Randy
1221 Florence #4, Pekin, 61554; 309-346-2710. Specializing in general line including fishing and hunting collectibles

Hoffmann, Pat and Don, Sr.
1291 N. Elmwood Dr., Aurora, 60506; 708-859-3435. (After November 1996 this area code will be changed to 630). Authors of *Warwick, A to W*, a supplement to *Why Not Warwick?*; video regarding Warwick decals currently available. Specializing in Warwick china

The Home Place Antiques
Durham, William; Galaway, William
615 S. State St., Belvidere, 61008; 815-544-0577. Specializing in Tea Leaf ironstone and white ironstone

Hooks, Dee
Dee's China Shop
P.O. Box 142, Lawrenceville, 62439-0142; 618-943-2741. Specializing in R.S. Prussia, Royal Bayreuth, Haviland, other fine china

Hopp, Dennis Carl
Midcentury
642½ W. Addison, Chicago, 60613; 312-549-5405. Specializing in 20th-century design, glass, pottery, enamels, metal, art

Hurney, George and Mary
Glass Connection (Mail-order only)
312 Babcock Dr., Palatine, 50067; 847-359-3839. Specializing in Depression Glass and Paden City glass (not advising on pottery)

The Illinois Antique Center
320 S.W. Commercial St.
Peoria, IL 61602

International Society of Antique Scale Collectors
Bob Stein, President
176 W. Adams, Suite 1706, Chicago, 60603; 312-263-7500. Publishes *Equilibrium* Magazine; President's newsletter; Annual membership directory; Out-of-print catalogs; Annual convention

John Toomey Gallery
818 N. Blvd, Oak Park, IL 60301

Long, Dee
112 S. Center, Lacon, 61540. Specializing in reamers

Lotton, Charles
Lotton Art Glass
1938 177th St., Lansing, 60438; 708-474-4022. Specializing in art glass

Lubliner, Larry
Refinders mail/telephone auction
737 Barberry Rd., Highland Park, IL 60035; 708-831-1102 or 708-831-1160. Refinders will find your wants from 1860-1960

Martin, Jim
R.R. 1, 1091 215th Ave., Monmouth, 61462; 309-734-2703. Specializing in Old Sleepy Eye, Monmouth pottery, Western Stoneware

Meyer, Larry
4001 Elmwood, Stickney, 60402; 708-749-1564. Specializing in fire grenades and extinguishers

Miller, Larry; and Strickfaden, Dick
218 Devron Circle, E. Peoria, 61611-1605. Specializing in German and Czechoslavakian Erphila

Ochsner, Grace
Grace Ochsner Doll House
1636 E. County Rd. 2700, Niota, 62358; 217-755-4362. Specializing in piano babies, bisque German dolls

Owen, Larry and Sally
Specializing in Morten Studio dogs, etc.

Pollack, Frank and Barbara (Appointment only)
1214 Green Bay Rd., Highland Park, 60035; 708-433-2213. Specializing in American country antiques and art

Randy's Ol' Time Collectibles
Illinois Antique Center
308 S.W. Commercial, Peoria, 61602; 309-346-2710. Specializing in general line, including hunting and fishing collectibles

Rastello, Lisa
Milkweed Antiques
5N531 Ancient Oak Lane, St. Charles, 60175; 708-377-4612. Specializing in Depression-Era collectibles

Rhoden, Joan and Charles
Memories/Rhoden's Antiques
605 N. Main, Georgetown, 61846; 217-662-8046. Specializing in Heisey and other Elegant Glassware, general line antiques. Co-authors of Those Wonderful Yard-Long Prints and More, and More Wonderful Yard-Long Prints, and Yard-Long Prints, Book III, illustrated value guides

Rodrick, Tammy
1509 N. 300th St., Sumner, 62466. Specializing in antiques and collectibles

Spencer, Dick
Glass and More (Shows only)
1203 N. Yale, O'Fallon, 62269; 618-632-9067. Specializing in Cambridge, Fenton, Fostoria, Heisey, etc.

Spiess, Greg
230 E. Washington, Joliet, 60433; 815-722-5639. Specializing in Odd Fellows lodge items

Stifter, Donna & Craig
P.O. Box 6514, Naperville, 60540; 630-717-7949. Specializing in Pepsi-Cola, Coca-Cola and other soda-pop brand collectibles

Stretch Glass Society
Attention: Joanne Rodgers
P.O. Box 573, Hampshire, 60140. Membership: $12 per year; quarterly newsletter, annual convention

TV Guide Specialists
Box 20, Macomb 61455
309-833-1809

Waite, Jim
112 N. Main St., Farmer City, 61842; 800-842-2593. Specializing in Sebastians

Weldi-Skinner, Mary
1656 W. Farragut Ave., Chicago, 60640. Specializing in American and European art pottery, designer collectibles

Wells, Rosalie J. 'Rosie'
R.R. 1S, E. Wells Dr., Canton, 61520; 1-800-445-8745. Publishes The Ornament Collector™, Precious Collectibles®, and Collectors' Bulletin™. She also publishes the Weekly Collectors' Gazette and annual price guides for Precious Moments® Collectibles, Hallmark Ornament Collectibles, and Hallmark's Merry Miniatures. Rosie has hosted eight International Conventions for Precious Moments Collectors and also hosts the semiannual Midwest Collectibles Fest, held in St. Charles, IL, each March and October. For Hot Tips call 1-900-420-3713 ext. 307 for Precious Moments® and ext. 306 for Hallmark ornament news. In Canada: 1-900-451-5323 ext. 101 for Hot Tips on Precious Moments® news, Hallmark ornaments and other popular limited edition collectibles and ornaments. Rosie also offers a touchtone 900 line (1-900-740-7575) for callers to record Voice Ads to reach American collectors. Call 'Rosie' at 309-668-2211 for information on limited edition collectibles.

Westover, Elaine; Treasurer/ Membership information
Abingdon Pottery Collectors Club
210 Knox Hwy. 5, Abingdon, 61410. 309-462-3267. Specializing in collecting and preservation of Abingdon pottery

Wilson, Jack D.
P.O. Box 81974, Chicago, 60681-0974; 312-282-9553. Specializing in Phoenix and Consolidated glass; Buying Ruba Rombic; Author of Phoenix & Consolidated Art Glass: 1926-1980

Yester-Daze Glass
c/o Illinois Antique Center
320 S.W. Commercial St., Peoria, 61604; 309-347-1679. Specializing in glass from the 1920s, '30s and '40s; Fiesta; Hall; Pie Birds; Sprinkler Bottles; and Florence figurines

---

Iowa

Beeks, Dale
P.O. Box 117, Mt. Vernon, 52314; 319-895-0506. Specializing in instruments of science technology & medicine. Also surveying instruments & microscopes

---

Indiana

AAA Antique Shop
US 6 West, Nappanee, 46550; 219-773-4912. Specializing in trunks

Alexander, Charles
221 E. 34th St., Indianapolis, 46205; Specializing in American dinnerware

Boram, Clifford
Antique Stove Information Clearinghouse
Monticello; Free consultation by phone only: 219-583-6465

Crossroads Antique Mall
311 Holiday Square, Seymour, 47274; 812-522-5675. Open 7 days a week

Edwards, Bill
620 W. 2nd, Madison, 47250. Author (Collector Books) on carnival glass

Fred, James A.
Antique Radio Labs
R.R. 1, Box 41, Cutler, 46920; 317-268-2214. Specializing in radios made from 1922 to 1950

Garrett, Jerry and Sandi
Jerry's Antiques (Shows only)
1807 W. Madison St., Kokomo, 46901; 317-457-5256. Specializing in Greentown glass, old postcards

Gilley's Antique Mall and Collectibles
1209 W. Main (US 40), Plainfield, 46168; 317-839-8779. Open daily from 10 a.m. to 5 p.m., features booths with over 250 dealers; Outdoor summer weekend flea market

Haun, Ted
2426 N. 700 East, Kokomo, 46901; 317-628-3640. Specializing in American pottery and china, '50s items, Russel Wright designs

Heiss, Virginia
7777 N. Alton Ave., Indianapolis, 46268; 317-875-6797. Specializing in Muncie, AMACO, Brandt Steele, Marblehead, Kenton Hills

Keagy, William and June
P.O. Box 106, Bloomfield, 47424; 812-384-3471. Co-authors of Those Wonderful Yard-Long Prints and More, More Wonderful Yard-Long Prints, and Yard-Long Prints, Book III, illustrated value guides

McQuillen, Michael J. P.O. Box 11141, Indianapolis, 46201-0141; 317-322-8518. Writer of column, Political Parade, which appears monthly in AntiqueWeek newspapers; Specializing in political campaign memorabilia; Collector and dealer

Old Storefront Antiques
P.O. Box 357, Dublin, 47335; 317-478-4809. Specializing in country store items, tins, primitives, pharmaceuticals, advertising, etc.; Active in mail order with catalogs available; Information requires LSASE

Pruitt, Ted
3382 W. 700 N., Anderson, 46011. St. Clair Glass Collector's Book, available ($15 ea) from Ted at above address

Scowden, Virgil
Williamsport, 47993; 317-762-3408 or 317-762-3178. Antiques museum, general line, tours

Slater, Thomas D.
The Political Gallery
1325 W. 86th St., Indianapolis, 46260; 317-257-0863. Specializing in political and sports memorabilia

Stofft, Marvin and Jeanette
Marnette Antiques
Tell City, 47586; 812-547-5707.
Specializing in Ohio art pottery,
buy and sell; no phone appraisals,
SASE required

Swayzee Antique Mall
115 N. Washington St., Swayzee,
46986; 317-922-7903

Uebelhor, Tom
Secretary/Treasurer of Uhl Collectors Society
233 E. Timberlin Lane, Huntingburg, 47542; 812-482-9575. Contact for membership and newsletter information

Vanderbilt, Duane and Janice
4040 W. Over Dr., Indianapolis,
46268; 317-875-8932. Authors
(Collector Books) of *Collector's
Guide to Shawnee Pottery*

Webb's Antique Mall
over 400 Quality Dealers
200 W. Union St.,
Centerville, 47330

Wright, Bill
325 Shady Dr., New Albany, 47150.
Specializing in knives: Bowie, hunting, military, and pocketknives

Iowa

Addy, Geneva D.
P.O. Box 124, Winterset, 50273;
515-462-3027

Arnbal, Una
Woodland Antiques
242 Trail Ridge Rd., Ames,
50014; 515-292-1005. Specializing in china, glass, Lomonosov
figurines, Danish collector plates

DeGood, Hal and Meredith
The Baggage Car
3100 Justin Dr., Suite B, Des
Moines, 50322; 515-270-9080. Specializing in Hallmark collectibles;
publishers of Hallmark newsletter

DeLozier, Loretta
1101 Polk St., Bedford, 50833;
712-523-2289. Author (Collector
Books) of *Collector's Encyclopedia of
Lefton China, Identification & Values*; Specializing in Lefton china

Devine, Dennis; Norman; and Joe
D & D Antique Mall
1411 3rd St., Council Bluffs, 51503;
712-323-5233 or 712-328-7305.
Specializing in furniture, phonographs, collectibles, general line.
Joe Devine: Royal Copley collector

Jaarsma, Ralph
De Pelikaan Antieks
812 Washington St., c/o Red Ribbon Antique Mall, Pella, 50219.
Specializing in Dutch antiques

Morris, Susan
P.O. Box 656, Panora, 50216; 515-755-3161. Specializing in Watt pottery and Purinton pottery; Author
of *Watt Pottery — An Identification
and Value Guide* and *Purinton Pottery
— An Identification and Value Guide*

Nichols, Harold J.
632 Agg, Ames, 50010; 515-292-9167. Author of *McCoy Cookie Jars
from the First to the Last*; Specializing in Roseville, Weller, McCoy

Picek, Louis
Main Street Antiques
110 W. Main St., Box 340, West
Branch, 52358. Specializing in folk
art, country Americana, the unusual

Westmoreland Glass Society
Jim Fisher, President
513 5th Ave., Coralville, 52241;
319-354-5011. Membership: $15
(single) or $25 (household)

Kansas

Anthony, Dorothy Malone
World of Bells Publications
802 S. Eddy, Fort Scott, 66701;
316-223-3404. Specializing in
publishing and selling books on
all types of small bells

Maundy International
P.O. Box 13208-GG, Shawnee
Mission, 66282; 1-800-235-2866.
Specializing in watches — antique
pocket and vintage wristwatches

McCormick, John and Marilyn
P.O. Box 3174, Shawnee, 66226;
913-441-0793. Specializing in
Gonder pottery

Rash, Jim
135 Alder Ave., Pleasantville,
08232; 609-646-4125. Specializing in advertising, cereal, and cartoon figures

Smies, David
Pops Collectibles
Box 522, 315 So. 4th, Manhattan, 66502; 913-776-1433. Specializing in coins, stamps, cards,
tokens, Masonic collectibles

Snyder, Charlie and Rose
Charlie's Collectables
R.R. 4, Box 79, Independence,
67301; 316-331-6259. Specializing in cookie jars and accessories,
salt and pepper shakers, pottery

Street, Patti
Currier & Ives Newsletter
P.O. Box 504, Riverton, 66770;
316-848-3529

Tinsley, Rosella
105 15th St., Osawatomie, 66064;
913-755-3237. Specializing in
primitives, kitchen, farm, woodenware, and miscellaneous
(phone calls only)

Winslow, Ralph
4008 W. 100 Terrace, Overland
Park, 66207. Specializing in Dryden Pottery

Kentucky

Courter, J.W.
3935 Kelley Rd., Kevil, 42053;
502-488-2116. Specializing in
Aladdin lamps; Author of *Aladdin
— The Magic Name in Lamps*, softbound, 180 pages; and *Aladdin Electric Lamps*, hardbound, 229 pages

Florence, Gene
Box 7186H, Lexington, 40522.
Author (Collector Books) on
Depression Glass, Occupied
Japan, Elegant Glass, Kitchen

Hornback, Betty
Betty's Antiques
707 Sunrise Lane, Elizabethtown,
42701; 502-765-2441. Specializing in Kentucky Derby and horseracing memorabilia

Johnson, Wes, Sr.
RFD, Glenview, 40025. Specializing in Cracker Jack: toys, point of
sale, packages, etc.; Checkers
Confection, Schoenhut toys, Victor Toy Oats, Universal Theatre
(Chicago), old toys; Please
include SASE

Ritchie, Roy B.
P.O. Box 384, Hindman, 41822;
606-785-5796. Author of *Standard
Knife Collector's Guide* and *Standard
Guide to Razors*; Specializing in
razors and knives, all types of cutlery

Stewart, Ron
P.O. Box 151, Combs, 41729;
606-436-5917. Author of *Standard Knife Collector's Guide* and
Standard Guide to Razors; Specializing in razors and knives, all
types of cutlery

Willis, Roy M.
Heartland of Kentucky Decanters
and Steins
P.O. Box 428, Lebanon Jct., 40150.
Huge selection of limited edition
decanters and beer steins — open
showroom. Include large selfaddressed envelope (two stamps)
with correspondence. Fee for
appraisals. Decanter price guide (listings only, no pictures): $5.00 PPD

Maine

Blake, Brenda
Box 555, York Harbor, 03911; 207-363-6566. Specializing in egg cups

Hathaway, John
Hathaway's Antiques
3 Mills Rd., Bryant Pond, 04219;
207-665-2124. Specializing in
fruit jars; Mail order a specialty

Rinaldi, John
Nautical Antiques and Related Items
Box 765, Dock Square, Kennebunkport, 04046; 207-967-3218.
Specializing in nautical antiques,
scrimshaw, naval items, paintings,
etc.; Annual Fall catalog: $5

Zayic, Charles S.
Americana Advertising Art
P.O. Box 57, Ellsworth, 04605;
207-667-7342. Specializing in
early magazines, early advertising
art, illustrators

Maryland

Banks, Robert
18901 Gold Mine Court,
Brookeville, 20833. Specializing in
American flags of historical significance and exceptional design

Ezell, Elaine; & Newhouse, George
Cruets Cruets Cruets
P.O. Box 1609, Pasadena, 21123-1609; 410-255-6777. Specializing in
cruets, glass, porcelain and pottery

Greenberg, Bruce C., Ph. D.
7566 Main St., Sykesville, 21784. Specializing in toy trains; author of comprehensive publications on Lionel, American Flyer, and Ives trains

Humphrey, George C.
4932 Prince George Ave., Beltsville, 20705; 301-937-7899. Specializing in John Rogers groups

Meadows, John, Jean and Michael
Meadows House Antiques
919 Stiles St., Baltimore, 21202; 410-837-5427. Specializing in antique wicker, furniture (rustic, twig, and old hickory), quilts and tramp art

Michels, John
Jamm Enterprises
1658 Hardwick Rd., Baltimore, 21286; 410-825-3636. Specializing in watch holders and small clocks

Rudisill's Alt Print Haus
Rudisill, John and Barbara
P.O. Box 199, Worton, 21678; 410-778-9290. Specializing in Currier & Ives

Screen, Harold and Joyce
2804 Munster Rd., Baltimore, 21234; 410-661-6765 (after 6:00 p.m. E.S.T.). Specializing in soda fountain 'tools of the trade' and paper: catalogs, *Soda Fountain Magazine*, etc.; E-mail: sodaftn@ aol.com

Yalom, Libby
The Shoe Lady
P.O. Box 7146, Adelphi, 20783; 301-422-2026. Specializing in glass and china shoes; Author of book

Massachusetts

Adams, Charles and Barbara
Middleboro, 02346; 508-947-7277. Specializing in Bennington (brown only)

Dunbar's Gallery
Leila and Howard Dunbar
76 Haven St., Milford, 01757; 508-634-8697 or (Fax) 508-634-8698. Specializing in advertising and toys

Frei, Peter
P.O. Box 500, Brimfield, 01010; 1-800-942-8968. Specializing in sewing machines (pre-1875, non-electric only), adding machines, typewriters, and hand-powered vacuum cleaners; SASE required with correspondence

Hess, John A.
Fine Photographic Americana
P.O. Box 3062, Andover, 01810. Specializing in 19th-Century photography

Dedham/CKAW Antiques
Kaufman, James D.
248 Highland St., Dedham, 2026; 800-283-8070. Specializing in Dedham and Chelsea Keramic Art works

Longo, Paul J.
Paul Longo Americana
Box 5510, Magnolia, 01930; 508-525-2290. Specializing in political pins, ribbons, banners, autographs, old stocks and bonds, baseball and sports memorabilia of all types

MacLean, Dale
183 Robert Rd., Dedham, 02026; 617-326-3010 or 617-329-1303 (evenings). Specializing in Dedham and Dorchester potteries

Mallis, A. George
788 Stony Hill Rd., Wilbraham, MA 01095-02202. Specializing in antique scales

Morin, Albert
668 Robbins Ave. #23, Dracut, 01826; 508-454-7907. Specializing in miscellaneous Akro Agate and Westite

Owings, K.C., Jr.
Antiques Americana
Box 19, N. Abington, 02351; 617-857-1655. Specializing in Civil War, Revolutionary War, autographs, documents, books, antiques

Vigue, Norm
62 Bailey St., Stoughton, 02072; 617-344-5441. Buying and selling TV, western, cartoon-show collectibles, animation art and 1-sheets, radio cereal premiums, and board games

Wellman, BA
88 State Rd W. Homestead Farms #2, Westminster, 01473-1435. Specializing in **all** areas of American ceramics, dinnerware, and figurines; with Video Book Identification and price guides available on Ceramic Arts Studio

Williams, Neil
73 Jamestown Dr., Springfield, 01108; 413-739-7797. Specializing in Planters Peanuts

Michigan

Brown, Rick
Newspaper Collectors' Society of America
Box 19134-S, Lansing, 48901; 517-887-1255. Specializing in newspapers

Gunsaulus, Jack
Gray's Gallery/Jack's Corner Bookstore
583 W. Ann Arbor Trail, Plymouth, 48170. Specializing in porcelain, books, jewelry, glass

Haas, Norman
264 Clizbe Rd., Quincy 49802; 517-639-8537. Specializing in American art pottery

Iannotti, Dan
212 W. Hickory Grove Rd., Bloomfield Hills, 48302-1127; 810-335-5042. Specializing in modern mechanical banks; Member of The Mechanical Bank Collectors of America

Krupka, Rod
2615 Echo Lane, Ortonville, 48462; 810-627-6351. Specializing in lightning rod balls

Kurella, Elizabeth M.
The Lace Merchant
Box 222, Plainwell, 49080; 616-685-9792. Publisher of newsletter and books on lace and linens. Specializing in lace and linens

Marsh, Linda K.
1229 Gould Rd., Lansing, 48917. Specializing in Degenhart glass

Martin, Karen
1020 Erie Rd., Erie, 48133; 393-838-4639. Specializing in Barbie dolls

Nedry, Boyd W.
728 Buth Dr., Comstock Park, 49321; 616-784-1513. Specializing in traps (including mice, rat, and fly traps) and trap-related items

Newbound, Betty
4567 Chadsworth, Commerce, 48382. Author (Collector Books) on Blue Ridge dinnerware, milk glass, wall pockets, and figural planters and vases; Specializing in collectible china and glass

Nickel, Mike
A Nickel's Worth
P.O. Box 456, Portland, 48875; 517-647-7646. Specializing in Roseville art pottery and juvenile pieces, Weller, Rookwood, Kay Finch, Ceramic Arts Studio, Josef, and Florence figurines

O'Callaghan, Tim
46878 Betty Hill, Plymouth, 48170; 313-459-4636. Specializing in dime-store soldiers, also Ford Motor Co., and 'Old Ironsides' (USS Constitution) memorabilia

Oates, Joan
685 S. Washington, Constantine, 49042; 616-435-8353. Specializing in Phoenix Bird chinaware

Ricker, Dawn V.
39145 Marne, Sterling Heights, 48313; 810-566-0891. Specializing in Schafer & Vater, Royal Bayreuth, Orrefors, Kosta, Royal Haeger; Please include good photograph and SASE when requesting information

Webster, Marty
2756 Kimberly Rd., Ann Arbor, 48104; 313-665-2030. Specializing in California porcelain and pottery

Minnesota

Anderson, James
Box 120704, New Brighton, 55112; 612-484-3198. Specializing in old fishing lures and reels, also tackle catalogs, posters, calendars, Winchester items

Gallagher, Jerry
420 1st Ave. N.W., Plainview, 55964; 507-534-3511. Specializing in Morgantown research; matching service for Morgantown, Heisey, Fostoria, Cambridge, Duncan, and Tiffin. Publisher of *A Handbook of Old Morgantown Glass and Price Guide* ($35+$4 shipping & handling), Morgantown 1931 catalog reprint (sold out), *Morgantown Colors* placard ($4 post paid), and *The Morgantown Newscaster*, triannual research journal of the Morgantown Collectors of America, Inc. (subscription: $18 per year)

Harrigan, John
1900 Hennepin, Minneapolis, 55403; 612-872-0226 or (in winter) 407-732-0525. Specializing in Battersea (English enamel) boxes

Ketcham, Steve
Steve Ketcham Antiques
(Shows and mail order only)
Box 24114, Edina, 55424; 612-920-4205. Specializing in early American bottles; early Red Wing stoneware (no art pottery or dinnerware); advertising signs, trays, trade cards, pocket mirrors, etched beer and shot glasses. Please include SASE for reply

Nelson, C.L.
Box 222, Spring Park, 55384; 612-473-5625. Specializing in 18th-, 19th- and 20th-century English pottery and porcelain, among others: Gaudy Welsh, ABC plates, relief-molded jugs, Staffordshire transfer ware

Podpeskar, Doug
624 Jones St., Eveleth, 55734-1631; 218-744-4854. Specializing in Red Wing dinnerware. Prefers letters with clear photos of items to be identified along with SASE for return

---

Missouri

Bine, John and Judy
I-70 Antique Mall
32 San Carlos Dr., St. Charles, 63303; 314-940-0878. Specializing in elegant and Depression-era glassware, pottery

Bosworth, Dick and Waunita
Kansas City Trade Winds
7307 N.W. 75th St., Kansas City, 64152. Specializing in American art pottery, Parrish prints, art glass, Arts & Crafts furniture, lighting

Clapp, Barbara
Nana's Antique Mall
1001 Daniel Dr., Mt Vernon, 65712; 417-466-2646. Specializing in pottery and glass

International Rose O'Neill Club
Contact Karen Stewart
P.O. Box 668, Branson, 65616. Dues: $7 (single) or $10 (family) includes newsletter *Kewpiesta Kourier*, published quarterly

Old World Antiques
1715 Summit, Kansas City, 64108
Branch Location: 4436 State Line Rd., Kansas City, 66103. Specializing in 18th- and 19th-century furniture, paintings, accessories, clocks, chandeliers, sconces, and much more

Roberts, Brenda
Country Side Antiques
R.R. 2, Marshall, 65340. Specializing in Hull pottery and general line. Author of *Collectors Encyclopedia of Hull Pottery, Roberts' Ultimate Encyclopedia of Hull Pottery* and *The Companion Guide to Robert's Ultimate Encyclopedia of Hull Pottery*, all with accompanying price guides; SASE required

Siegel, Brenda and Jerry
Tower Grove Antiques
3308 Meramec, St. Louis, 63118; 314-352-9020. Specializing in Ungemach pottery

Scott, John and Peggy
Scotty's Antiques
4640 S. Leroy, Springfield, 65810; 417-887-2191. Specializing in Depression-era glassware and pottery

Smith, Pat
Independence
Author (Collector Books) of doll book series

Stout, Elizabeth M.
152 Highway F., Defiance, 63341; 314-987-2223. Specializing in calendar plates

Tarrant, Jenny
Holly Daze Antiques
4 Gardenview, St. Peters, 63376. Specializing in early holiday items, Halloween, Christmas, Easter, etc.; Always buying Halloween collectibles (except masks and costumes) and German rabbits and Santas

Thurmond, Jon and Carolyn
Collectorholics
15006 Fuller, Grandview, 64030; 816-322-0906. Specializing in 1950s-1980s character, space, and unusual toys

Wiesehan, Doug
D & R Farm Antiques
4535 Hwy. H, St. Charles, 63301. Specializing in salesman's samples and patent models, antique toys, farm toys, metal farm signs

Williams, Don
P.O. Box 147, Kirksville 63501; 816-627-8009 (between 8 a.m. and 6 p.m.). Specializing in art glass; SASE required with all correspondence

Woollard, D.D., Jr.
11614 Old St. Charles Rd., Bridgeton, 63044; 314-739-4662. Specializing in World's Fair & Exposition memorabilia

---

Nebraska

Larsen, Robert V.
3214 19th St., Columbus, 68601. Specializing in old hatpins and hatpin holders

Neely, Nancee P.
16592 Hascall, Omaha, 68130; 402-330-7033. Specializing in Fairing boxes

---

New Hampshire

Brenner, Larry
Brenner Antiques
1005 Chestnut St., Manchester, 03104; 603-625-8203. Specializing in Royal Bayreuth

Winston, Nancy
Willow Hollow Antiques
RFD 1, Box 550, Northwood, 03261; 603-942-5739. Specializing in Shaker baskets, primitives, country smalls, paper Americana, toys

---

New Jersey

Adams, Jay (Mail order only)
245 Lakeview Ave., Suite 208, Clifton, NJ 07011; 201-365-5907. Specializing in Depression-era china and glass

Anderson, Suzy McLennan
Heritage Antiques & Appraisal Services
65 E. Main St., Holmdel, 07733; 908-946-8801 or (Fax) 908-946-1036. Specializing in American furniture and decorative accessories

Bilane, John E. (Mail order only)
2065 Morris Ave., Apt. 109, Union, 07083. Specializing in antique glass cup plates

Cole, Lillian M., Editor of *Piebirds Unlimited* Newsletter
14 Harmony School Rd., Flemington, 08822; 908-782-3198. Specializing in pie birds, pie funnels, pie vents

Dezso, Doug
864 Paterson Ave., Maywood, 07607-2119; 201-488-1311. Specializing in nodders (German), glass candy containers, Tonka

Doorstop Collectors of America
Doorstopper newsletter
Jeanie Bertoia
2413 Madison Ave., Vineland, 08630; 609-692-4092. Membership: $20 per year, includes 2 newsletters and convention. Send 2-stamp SASE for sample

George, Dr. Joan M.
ABC Collector's Circle
67 Stevens Ave., Old Bridge, 08857. Specializing in educational china (particularly ABC plates and mugs)

Litts, Elyce
P.O. Box 394, Morris Plains, 07950; 201-361-4087. Author (Collector Books) of *Collector's Encyclopedia of Geisha Girl Porcelain*

Lockwood, Howard J.
Box 191, Fort Lee, 07024; 201-692-9780. Specializing in Italian glass of the 20th century

Meschi, Edward J.
129 Pinyard Rd., Monroeville, 08343; 609-358-7293 or (Fax) 609-358-7293. Specializing in Durand art glass, Icart etching, Maxfield Parrish prints, Rookwood pottery, occupational shaving mugs, oil paintings, and other fine arts

Patalano, Diane. I.S.A.
P.O. Box 144, Saddle River 07458. Specializing in banks, Black americana, cookie jars, furniture, spatterware, various antiques and collectibles

Perzel, Robert and Nancy
Popkorn
4 Mine St. (near Main St.), P.O. Box 1057, Flemington, 08822; 908-782-9631. Specializing in Stangl dinnerware, birds, and artware; Depression Glass

Poster, Harry
Vintage TVs
Box 1883, S. Hackensack, 07606; Days: 201-794-9606; 24-Hour Fax: 201-794-9553; Phone: 201-410-7525. Writes *Poster's Radio and Television Price Guide*; Specializes in vintage televisions, transistor radios, 3-D stereo cameras

Rago, David
17 S. Main St., Lambertville, 08530; 609-397-9374. Specializing in Arts & Crafts, art pottery

Rash, Jim
135 Alder Ave., Egg Harbor Township, 08234; 609-646-4125. Specializing in advertising dolls

Rosen, Barbara
6 Shoshone Trail, Wayne, 07470. Specializing in figural bottle openers and antique dollhouses

Steinfeld, Milt
633 Westfield Ave., Box 457, Westfield, 07091. Specializing in collectible glass and china, Victorian silverplate, and other small collectibles

Vines, Linda L.
Yesterday Once More
P.O. Box 721, Upper Montclair, 07043; 201-748-4990. Specializing in Snow Babies, all holidays (Christmas, Easter, Halloween), dolls, toys, and Steiff

Visakay, Stephen
Vintage Cocktail Shakers (By appointment)
P.O. Box 1517, W. Caldwell, 07007-1517. Specializing in vintage cocktail shakers.

New Mexico

Hardisty, Don
Artistic Restorations
3020 E. Majestic Ridge, Las Cruces, 88011; 505-522-3721 or (Fax) 505-522-7909. Specializing in Bossons, Hummels, and postcards; Don's Collectibles carries a full line of current issues and most discontinued Bossons and Hummel figurines of all marks

Manns, William
P.O. Box 6459, Santa Fe, 87502; 505-995-0102. Co-author of *Painted Ponies*, hard-bound edition (226 pages), available from author for $39.95+$5 shipping; Specializing in carousel art and western antiques

New York

Angelo, Norma
Box 133, High Acres Ct., Bemus Point, 14712. Specializing in Oriental porcelain; Please include SASE when requestion information; No free appraisals

Austin, Bruce A.
1 Hardwood Hill Rd., Pittsford, 14534; 716-387-9820 (evenings); 716-475-2879 (week days). Specializing in clocks and Arts & Crafts furnishings and accessories

Batchelor, Daniel J.
R.R. 10, Box 1010, Oswego, 13126. Specializing in Pairpoint, Handel, Bradley and Hubbard lamps; Photo and SASE required with all correspondence

Calison, Jim
Tools of Distinction
Wallkill, 12589; 914-895-8035. Specializing in antique and collectible tools, buying and selling

Dimitroff, Thomas P.
Dimitroff's Antiques (Appointment only)
140 E. First St., Corning, 14830; 607-962-6745. Specializing in Steuben and cut glass

Doyle, Robert A.
Absolute Auction & Realty, Inc.
P.O. Box 658, 348 Main St., Beacon 12524. Antique and estate auctions the 4th Friday of every month at their gallery. 'Do your antiq'n in Beacon, 27 shops, 2 auction galleries'

Fer-Duc Inc.
Ferrara, Joseph
Box 1303, Newburgh, 12550; 914-565-5990. Specializing in American art pottery (Ohr, Rookwood, Zanesville), 19th- and 20th-century American paintings

Fox, Ron
Ron Fox Auctions
83 Morris St., Brentwood, 11717; 516-231-0633 or (Fax) 516-952-7719. Specializing in steins; Auctions with illustrated catalogs and video tapes

Gerson, Roselyn
P.O. Box 40, Lynbrook, 11563; 516-593-8746. Author/collector specializing in unusual, gadgetry, figural compacts and vanity bags/purses

Greguire, Helen
Helen's Antiques
103 Trimmer Rd., Hilton, 14468; 716-392-2704. Specializing in graniteware (any color), carnival glass lamps and shades, carnival glass lighting of all kinds; Author (Collector Books) of *The Collector's Encyclopedia of Graniteware, Colors, Shapes & Values*, (updated values, $28.45 postage paid); Second book on graniteware now available (same price); Also available is *Carnival in Lights*, featuring carnival glass, lamps, shades, etc. ($13.45 postage paid, all available from author); Also interested in unusual and rare toasters and author of new book on toasters and related items

Handelsman, Burton
18 Hotel Dr., White Plains, 10605; 914-428-4480 (home) and 914-761-8880 (office). Specializing in occupational shaving mugs, accessories

Herley, Patrick J.
P.O. Box 606, E. Setauket, 11733; 516-928-6052. Specializing in Goss china

Jordan, Ruth E.
Meridale, 13806; 607-746-2082. Specializing in cut glass, American Brilliant period

Kaonis, Keith, Publisher
Inside Collector and *Doll World*
60 Cherry Lane, Huntington, 11743; 516-351-0982. Specializing in Schoenhut toys

Laun, H. Thomas and Patricia
Little Century
215 Paul Ave., Syracuse, 13206; 315-437-4156. Summer residence: 35109 Country Rte. 7, Cape Vincent, 13618; 315-654-3244. Specializing in firefighting collectibles

Malitz, Lucille
Lucid Antiques
Box KH, Scarsdale, NY 10583; 914-636-7825. Specializing in lithophanes, kaleidoscopes, stereoscopes, medical and dental antiques

Malloy, Alex G.
Alex G. Malloy, Inc.
P.O. Box 38, South Salem, 10590; 203-438-0396. Specializing in ancient and medieval coins; antiquities, numismatic literature

Meisel, Louis K. and Susan P.
Meisel Decorative Arts Gallery
133 Prince St., New York City, 10012. Specializing in Clarice Cliff, pond sailboats, nautical and scientific instruments, toy and model airplanes, and pinups (original art)

Michel, John and Barbara
Americana Blue
200 E. 78th St., 18E, New York City, 10021; 212-861-6094. Specializing in yellow ware, cast iron, and tramp art

Owens, Lowell
Owens' Collectibles
12 Bonnie Ave., New Hartford, 13413. Specializing in beer advertising

Rifken, Blume J.
Author of *Silhouettes in America — 1790-1840 — A Collector's Guide*. Specializing in American antique silhouettes from 1790 to 1840

Safir, Charlotte F.
1349 Lexington Ave., 9-B, New York City, 10128; 212-534-7933. Specializing in cookbooks, children's books (out-of-print only)

Schleifman, Roselle
Ed's Collectibles/The Rage
16 Vincent Rd., Spring Valley, 10977; 914-356-2121. Specializing in Duncan & Miller, Elegant Glass

Smyth, Carole and Richard
Carole Smyth Antiques
P.O. Box 2068, Huntington, 11743; 516-673-8666. Authors of *The Burning Passion — Antique and Collectible Pyrography*, available from authors at above address for $19.95+$3 postage (New York State residents add 8.5% sales tax)

Steinbock, Nancy
Nancy Steinbock Posters
518-438-1577. Specializing in posters: travel, war, literary, advertising

Tuggle, Robert
105 W. St., New York City, 10023; 212-595-0514. Specializing in John Bennett, Anglo-Japanese china

Van Kuren, Jean and Dale
Ruth's Antiques, Inc.
9060 Main St., Clarence, 14031; 716-632-1630. Specializing in Buffalo pottery, chocolate molds, Noritake Azalea, general line

Van Patten, Joan F.
Box 102, Rexford, 12148. Author (Collector Books) of books on Nippon and Noritake

North Carolina

Degenhardt, Richard K.
Sugar Hollow Farm
124 Cypress Point, Hendersonville, 28739; 704-696-9750. Author of *Belleek, The Complete Collectors' Guide and Illustrated Reference*, 1st and 2nd editions. Specializing in Belleek (The only Belleek is the Irish. Established by legal action in 1929)

Hughes, Kathy (Mrs. Paul)
Tudor House Galleries
1401 E. Blvd., Charlotte, 28203; 704-377-4748. Specializing in relief-molded jugs, 18th- and 19th-century English pottery and 19th-century oil paintings

Iannantuoni, Jean-Paul
P.O. Box 563072, Charlotte, 28256-3072; 704-547-9951 (Monday-Thursday from 7:00 p.m. to 10:00 p.m. EST, Saturday and Sunday from 1:00 p.m. to 8:00 p.m.). Specializing in Royal Doulton secondary market

Kirtley, Charles E.
P.O. Box 2273, Elizabeth City, 27096; 919-335-1262. Specializing in monthly auctions and bid sales dealing with World's Fair, Civil War, political, advertising, and other American collectibles

Sayers, R.J.
Southeastern Antiques & Appraisals
14 Longbranch Rd., Pisgah Forest, 28768. Specializing in Boy Scout collectibles, Pisgah Forest pottery, primitive American furniture; Author of *Guide to Scouting Collectibles*, *Revised 1996 Edition*, available from author for $26.95+$4 postage

North Dakota

Farnsworth, Bryce
1334 14½ St. South, Fargo, 58103; 701-237-3597. Specializing in Rosemeade pottery; If writing for information, please send a picture if possible, also phone number and best time to call

Ohio

Baker, Shirley and John
Shirley's Collectibles
673 W. Twp. Rd. 118, Tiffin, 44883; 419-447-9875. Specializing in Tiffin glass

Bassett, Mark
P.O. Box 771233, Lakewood, 44017. Specializing in Cowan, American and European art pottery, Art Deco.

Batory, Mr. Dana Martin
402 E. Bucyrus St., Crestline, 44827. Specializing in antique woodworking machinery, old and new woodworking machinery catalogs. In order to prepare a definitive history on American manufacturers of woodworking machinery, Dana is interested in acquiring by loan, gift, or photocopy, any and all documents, catalogs, manuals, photos, personal reminiscences, etc., pertaining to woodworking machinery and/or their manufacturers. NO phone calls please.

Benjamin, Scott
411 Forest St., LaGrange, 44050; 216-355-6608. Specializing in gas globes; Co-author of *Gas Pump Globes* and several other related books, listing nearly 4,000 gas globes with over 400 photos, prices, rarity guide, histories, and reproduction information (currently available from author); Also available: *Petroleum Collectibles Monthly* magazine, please inquire

Blair, Betty
Golden Apple Antiques
216 Bridge St., Jackson, 45640; 614-286-4817. Specializing in art pottery, Watt, cookie jars, chocolate molds, general line

Budin, Nicki
Curio Cabinet
679 High St., Worthington, 43085; 614-885-1986. Specializing in Royal Doulton

Business Recollections, Antiques and Collectibles
Nada Sue Knauss
1211 Potter Rd, Weston, 43569; 419-669-4735. Specializing in pottery, postcards

China Specialties, Inc.
19238 Dorchester Circle, Strongsville, 44136; 216-238-2528. Specializing in Autumn Leaf

Cimini, Joan
63680 Centerville-Warnock Rd., Belmont, 43718. Specializing in Imperial glass; Candlewick matching service

Cincinnati Auction Gallery
635 Main St., Cincinnati, 45202; 513-381-2128. Specializing in American art pottery (especially Rookwood), American and European fine paintings, watercolors

Collectors of Findlay Glass
P.O. Box 256, Findlay, 45840. An organization dedicated to the study and recognition of Findlay glass; *The Melting Pot* Newsletter published quarterly; Convention held annually; Membership: $10 per year

Collings, Sam and Becky
Hardtimes Glassware
202 Brook Dr., Brookfield, 44403; 216-448-8986. Specializing in Depression glass

Deason, Betty
419-447-4482. Specializing in dolls, old cards, everything

DeGenaro, Steve
P.O. Box 5662, Youngstown, 44504. Specializing in post-mortem photos, mourning collectibles

Distel, Ginny
Distel's Antiques
4041 S.C.R. 22, Tiffin, 44883; 419-447-5832. Specializing in Tiffin glass

Ebner, Rita and John
Cracker Barrel Antiques
4540 Helen Rd., Columbus, 43232. Specializing in door knockers, cast-iron bottle openers, Griswold

Ferguson, Maxine
1380 Bussemer, Zanesville, 43701.

Forsythe, Ruth A.
Box 327, Galena, 43021. Author of *Made in Czechoslovakia*, books I and II; SASE required

Graff, Shirley
4515 Grafton Rd., Brunswick, 44212. Specializing in Pennsbury pottery

Guenin, Tom
Box 454, Chardon, 44024. Specializing in antique telephones and antique telephone restoration

Hamlin, Jack & Treva
R.R. 4, Box 150, Kaiser St., Proctorville, 45669; 614-886-7644. Specializing in Currier and Ives by Royal China Co.

Harnish, Jerry
110 Main St., Bellville, 44813; 419-886-4782. Specializing in G.I. Joe

Hothem, Lar
Hothem House
Box 458, Lancaster, 43130. Specializing in books about Indians and artifacts

Huffman Antiques
Mary Huffman
3143 S SR 53, Tiffin 44883; 419-447-5938. Specializing in general line

Kao, Fern Larking
P.O. Box 312, Bowling Green, 43402; 419-352-5928. Specializing in jewelry, sewing implements, ladies' accessories

Kerr, Ann
P.O. 437, Sidney, 45365; 513-492-6369. Author (Collector Books) of *Collector's Encyclopedia of Russel Wright Designs*; Specializing in work of Wright; Interested in 20th-century decorative arts

Kier, Don and Anne
2022 Marengo St., Toledo, 43614; 419-385-8211. Specializing in general glass and china, 19th-century antiques, autographs, Brownies, Royal Bayreuth

Kitchen, Lorrie
Toledo, 419-478-3815. Specializing in Depression-era glass, Hall china, Fiesta, Blue Ridge, Shawnee

Klender, James and Grace
Town & Country Antiques & Collectibles
P.O. Box 447, Pioneer, 43554; 419-737-2880. Specializing in Depression glass, and general line

Kline, Mr. and Mrs. Jerry and Gerry
Members of North American Torquay Society and Torquay Pottery Collectors' Society
604 Orchard View Dr., Maumee, 43537; 419-893-1226. Specializing in collecting Torquay pottery

Mathes, Richard
P.O. Box 1408, Springfield, 45501-1408; 513-324-6917. Specializing in buttonhooks

Moore, Carolyn
445 N. Prospect, Bowling Green, 43402. Specializing in primitives, yellow ware, graniteware, collecting stoneware

Murphy, James L.
1023 Neil Ave., Columbus, 43201; 614-297-0746. Specializing in Radford, Vance Avon

National Imperial Glass Collectors' Society, Inc.
P.O. Box 534, Bellaire 43906. Dues: $15 per year (plus $1 for each additional member in the same household); Quarterly newsletter; Convention every June

Nelson, Norman
2267 E. Erie, Lorain, 44052; 216-288-4977. Specializing in jukeboxes

Osentosk, Randy
902 Dryden, Toledo, 43612; 419-478-6822. Specializing in toys, strange and unusual things that should not exist

Patchin, Erma
3425 E-F Rd, Swanton, 43558; 419-826-8661. Specializing in miscellaneous antiques

Peters, Jeannie L.
Mt. Washington Antiques
3742 Kellogg, Cincinnati, 45226; 513-231-6584. Specializing in sheet music

Pierce, David
27544 Black Rd., P.O. Box 248, Danville, 43014; 614-599-6394. Specializing in Glidden pottery; Fee for appraisals

Radel, Erle and Janice
Rapids Renovations & Antiques
Grand Rapids. Specializing in furniture and fine jewelry, (collectors only) Labino art glass

Rees, Debbie
Zanesville.
Specializing in Watt, Roseville juvenile and other Roseville pottery, Zanesville area pottery, cookie jars, and Steiff

Riebel, James; Krause, Terry
Pottery Peregrinators
Zanesville, 614-452-7687. Specializing in American art pottery, Nicodemus, and carnival glass

Roscoe, Mike
3351 Lagrange, Toledo, 43608; 419-244-6935. Specializing in toys, advertising, coin-operated machines, furniture, and miscellaneous

Trainer, Veronica
Bayhouse
Box 40443, Cleveland, 44140; 216-871-8584. Specializing in beaded and enamelled mesh purses

Tucker, Dan
Toledo, 419-478-3815. Specializing in Depression-era glass, Hall china, Fiesta, Blue Ridge, Shawnee

Vroman, Bill & Judy
739 Eastern Ave., Fostoria, 44830; 419-435-5443. Collectors of Jewel Tea or Autumn Leaf, Buying-Selling all types of fine antiques

Walker, Bunny
Box 502, Bucyrus, 44820; 419-562-8355. Specializing in Steiff teddy bears, penny toys, pottery

Walter, John
The Old Tool Shop
208 Front St., Marietta, 45750; 614-373-9973. Specializing in all types of antique tools

Whitmyer, Margaret and Kenn
Box 30806, Gahanna, 43230. Author (Collector Books) on children's dishes. Specializing in Depression-era collectibles

Wilkins, Juanita
The Bird of Paradise
Lima. Specializing in R.S. China, Old Ivory china, colored pattern glass, lamps, and jewelry

Young, Mary
Box 9244, Wright Brothers Branch, Dayton, 45409; 513-298-4838. Specializing in paper dolls; Author of several books

Oklahoma

Bess, Phyllis and Tom
14535 E. 13th St., Tulsa, 74108; 918-437-7776. Authors of *Frankoma Treasures*, and *Frankoma and Other Oklahoma Potteries*. Specializing in Frankoma and Oklahoma pottery

Klein, Bob and Dondee
1002 Walnut Court, Guthrie, 73044; 405-282-6545. Specializing in Tamac pottery

McIntosh, Charles and Peggy
Mac's Glass, Dolls & Toys
201-C Seminole, Coweta, 74429; 918-486-6103. Specializing in Depression-era glassware, Fisher-Price toys, vintage Barbies, and other collectible Barbies

Moore, Art and Shirley
2145 S. Norfolk Ave., Tulsa, 74114; 918-747-4164. Specializing in Lu Ray Pastels, Depression glass

Scott, Roger R.
4250 S. Oswego, Tulsa, 74135; 918-742-8710 or (Fax) 918-583-1226. Specializing in Victor and RCA Victor trademark items along with Nipper

Willis, Ron L.
2110 Fox Ave., Moore, 73160. Specializing in militaria

Oregon

Abrahams, Peter
1948 Mapleleaf Rd., Lake Oswego, 97034; 503-636-2988 (or e-mail: telscope@europa.com). Specializing in telescopes, binoculars, microscopes. Peter studies and collects optics: telescopes, binoculars, hand magnifiers, and microscopes and especially seeks reference material on these subjects, including books, catalogs, repair manuals, and histories

Bartsch, Henry
Antique Registers
2050 N. Hwy. 101, Rockaway Beach, 97136; 503-355-2932. Specializing in antique cash registers; Co-author of *Antique Cash Registers 1880-1920*. Written insurance appraisals are provided by Mr. Bartsch for a $25 fee; Please include register's model, serial number, condition and 3 keeper photographs.

Bird, Leah and Walt
Bird's Nest
P.O. Box 4502, Medford, 97501; 541-779-3028. Specializing in vintage clothing (pre-1940s), beaded and mesh purses, buttons

Brown, Marcia
Sparkles
6959 Pinehurst, Central Point, 97502; 503-826-3039. Specializing in rhinestone jewelry

Carter, Fran (Appointment only)
Box 3220, Coos Bay, 97420; 503-888-5780. Specializing in estate sales

Coe, Debbie and Randy
Coes Mercantile
Lafayette School House Mall #2, 748 3rd (Hwy. 99W), Lafayette, 97127; Specializing in Elegant and Depression glass, art pottery

Couts, Rick and Melissa
Intellasearch
1361 N. 4th St., Lakeview, 97630; 1-800-947-5390. Specializing in America's antiques and collectibles data base service

Cox, Billy & Thelma, Owners
Medford Antique Mall
1 West 6th St., Medford 97501

Davis, Patricia M.
4326 NW Tam-O-Shanter Way, 'Claremont,' Portland, 97229

Geddes, Marjorie
P.O. Box 5875, Aloha, 97007; 503-649-1041. Specializing in sewing items, open salts, Florence ceramics, California figurines, miscellaneous small and elegant collectibles

Hirshman, Susan and Larry
Everyday Antiques
542 Siskiyou Blvd., Ashland, 97520; 541-482-9411. Specializing in china, glassware, kitchenware

Main Antique Mall
30 N. Riverside, Medford, 97501; Quality products and services for the serious collector, dealer, or those just browsing

Miller, Don and Robby
P.O. Box 508, Talent, 97540; 503-535-1231 Specializing in milk bottles, TV Siamese cat lamps, seltzer bottles, red cocktail shakers.

Morris, Thomas G.
Prize Publishers
P.O. Box 8307, Medford, 97504. Author of *The Carnival Chalk Prize*, Books I and II, pictorial price guides on carnival chalkware figures with brief histories and values for each

Ringering, David
Belle Ringer Antiques
1480 Tumalo Dr. S.E., Salem, 97301; 503-585-8253. Specializing in Rowland & Marsellus and other souvenir/historical china with scenes of buildings, parks, and other tourist attractions of the 1890s-1930s. Feel free to contact David if you have any questions about Rowland & Marsellus or other souvenir china. He will be happy to answer questions about souvenir china

Roberts, Fred and Marilyn
Bah Humbug Collectibles
2663 Aldersgate Rd., Medford, 97504; 541-776-3826. Specializing in Hummels

Pennsylvania

Barker, Jim
Toastermaster Antique Appliances
P.O. Box 41, Bethlehem, 18016; 610-439-0751. Specializing in electric toasters (1905-1950) and any other small electric appliances, fans, Porcelier, Royal Rochester, etc.

Barrett, Noel
Rosebud Antiques
P.O. Box 1001, Carversville, 18913; 215-297-5109. Specializing in toys

Bodine, Clarence H., Jr., Proprietor
East/West Gallery
41B Ferry St., New Hope, 18938. Specializing in antique Japanese woodblock prints, netsuke, inro, tsuba

Cerebro
P.O. Box 327, East Prospect, 17317; 717-252-2400 or 800-69-LABEL. Fax: 717-252-3685. Specializing in antique advertising labels, especially cigar box labels, cigar bands, food labels, firecracker labels

Damaska, Ron
738 9th Ave., New Brighton, 15066; 412-843-1393. Specializing in Fry cut glass, match holders, oil lamps, silver; SASE required when requesting information

DLK Nostalgia & Collectibles
P.O. Box 5112, Johnstown, 15904. Specializing in corkscrews and openers, Art Deco, clocks, toys, breweriana, robots, battery-operated toys, sculptures, lamps, collectibles and nostalgia

Garvin, Joann
P.O. Box 182, Beaver Falls, 15010; 412-843-3999. Specializing in Fiesta

Gottuso, Bob
Bojo
P.O. Box 1403, Cranberry Township, 16066-0403; Phone/Fax: 412-776-0621. Specializing in Beatles, Elvis, Kiss, Monkees, licensed rock 'n roll memorabilia

Goyda, Cheryl
Box 192, E. Petersburg, 17520; 717-569-7149. Specializing in SMF/Wheelock Black Forest and Czechoslovakian pottery

Hagenbuch, James
Glass-Works Auction
102 Jefferson, East Greenville, 18041; 215-679-5849. America's leading auction company in early American bottles and glass

Hain, Henry F., III
Antiques & Collectibles
2623 N. Second St., Harrisburg, 17110; 717-238-0534. Lists available of items for sale

Hinton, Michael C.
246 W. Ashland St., Doylestown, 18901; 215-345-0892. Owns/operates Bucks County Art & Antiques Company and Chem-Clean Furniture Restoration Company; Specializing in quality restorations of a wide range of art and antiques from colonial to contemporary; Catalog of paintings and frames available

Holland, William
William Holland Fine Arts
1708 E. Lancaster Ave., Paoli, 19301; 610-648-0369 or (Fax) 610-647-4448. Specializing in Louis Icart etchings and oils, Art Nouveau and Art Deco items; Author of *Louis Icart: The Complete Etchings* and *The Collectible Maxfield Parrish*

Irons, Dave
Dave Irons Antiques
223 Covered Bridge Road, Northampton, 18067; 610-262-9335. Author of *Irons By Irons* (soft-cover); Available from author, (over 1,600 irons pictured, contains current information and price ranges, collecting hints, news of trends, and information for proper care of irons); Specializing in pressing irons, country furniture, primitives, quilts, accessories

Kamm, George
George Kamm Paperweights
24-SP Townsend Ct., Lancaster, 17603; 717-872-7858. Specializing in antique and contemporary paperweights — color brochure published bimonthly; $5 annual fee (refundable); Sample on request (#10 SASE required)

Knauer, Judy A.
National Toothpick Holder Collectors' Society
1224 Spring Valley Lane, West Chester, 19380; 610-431-3477. Specializing in toothpick holders and Victorian glass

The Krauses
Krause, Gail
97 W. Wheeling St., Washington, 15301; 412-228-5034. Author of book on Duncan glass

Kreider, Katherine
Kingsbury Antiques
P.O. Box 7957, Lancaster, 17604-7957; 717-892-3001. Author of *Valentines With Values*, available post-paid by sending $22.90 ($24.09 Pennsylvania residents); No free appraisals. Stop by Booth #315 at Black Angus, in Adamstown (new section) and talk about valentines.

Kurau, William
Box 457, Lampeter, 17537; 717-464-0731. Specializing in historical Staffordshire; SASE required when requesting information

Lindsay, Ralph
P.O. Box 21, New Holland, 17557. Specializing in target balls. SASE required with correspondence

Maier, Clarence and Betty
Mail order: The Burmese Cruet
Box 432, Montgomeryville, 18936; 215-855-5388. Specializing in Victorian art glass.

Marks, Mariann Katz
1416 Main, Honesdale, 18431. Author (Collector Books) of *Majolica Pottery, Second Series*; Specializing in collecting, buying, and selling American and English majolica of the Victorian period; LSASE required for mail-order list; Enclose photo and price wanted with offers to sell

Merchants Square Mall
Jim & Annetta Vitez, Managers
1901 S. 12th St., Allentown, 18103; 610-797-7743

Oster, Frederick
Frederick W. Oster Fine Violins
1529 Pine St., Philadelphia, 19102; 215-545-1100 or (Fax) 215-735-3634. Specializing in rare and antique instruments of the violin family, as well as antique stringed and wind instruments

Posner, Judy
May-October: R.D. 1, Box 273SC, Effort, 18330; 717-629-6583 or November-April: 4195 S. Tamiami Trail, #183SC, Venice, FL 34293; 941-497-7149. Specializing in figural pottery, salt and peppers, Black memorabilia, Disneyana, character and advertising collectibles, cookie jars. Buy, Sell & Collect; Appraisals: $25

Rosso, Philip J. and Philip Jr.
Wholesale Glass Dealers
1815 Trimble Ave., Port Vue, 15133; 412-678-7352. Specializing in Westmoreland glass

Weiser, Pastor Frederick S.
55 Kohler School Rd., New Oxford, 17350; 717-624-4106. Specializing in frakturs and other Pennsylvania German documents

Rhode Island

Dumont, Louise
579 Old Main St., Coventry, 02816; 401-828-2799. Winter address: 319 Hawthorne Blvd, Leesburg, FL 34748; 904-787-6060. Specializing in cookie jars, Abingdon

Gacher, John
The Zsolnay Store
152 Spring St., Newport, 02840; 401-841-5060. Specializing in Zsolnay, Fischer, Amphora, and Austro-Hungarian art pottery

The Occupied Japan Club
c/o Florence Archambault
29 Freeborn St., Newport, 02840-1821. Publishes bimonthly newsletter, *The Upside Down World of an O.J. Collector*; SASE required when requesting information

South Carolina

Roerig, Fred and Joyce
R.R. 2, Box 504, Walterboro, 29488; 803-538-2487. Specializing in cookie jars; Authors of *Collector's Encyclopedia of Cookie Jars, an Illustrated Value Guide*, publishers of *Cookie Jarrin' with Joyce: The Cookie Jar Newsletter*

Tennessee

Chase, Mick and Lorna
Fiesta Plus
380 Hawkins Crawford Rd., Cookeville, 38501; 615-372-8333. Specializing in Fiesta, Franciscan, Metlox, other American dinnerware

Grist, Everett
6503 Slater Rd., Suite 11, East Ridge, 37412-3355; 615-855-4032. Specializing in covered animal dishes and marbles

Hudson, Murray
Murray Hudson Antiquarian Books & Maps
109 S. Church St., Box 163, Halls, 38040; 901-836-9057 or Fax: 901-836-9017. Specializing in antique maps, globes and books with maps, atlases, explorations, travel guides, geographies, surveys, etc.

Kerry & Judy's Toys
7370 Eggleston Rd., Memphis, 38125-2112. Specializing in Western Hartlands

Roberts, Mindy
Angel & Trump Antiques
P.O. Box 382663, Germantown, 38183; 901-748-0907

Texas

Cooper, Marilyn
8408 Lofland Dr., Houston, 77055; 713-465-7773. Specializing in figural toothbrush holders, Pez

Dockery, Rod
4600 Kemble St., Ft. Worth, 76103; 817-536-2168. Specializing in milk glass; SASE required with correspondence

Docks, L.R. 'Les'
Shellac Shack; Discollector
Box 691035, San Antonio, 78269-1035. Author of *American Premium Record Guide*. Specializing in vintage records

Frese, Leo and Wendy
Three Rivers Collectibles
Box 551542, Dallas, 75355; 214-341-5165. Specializing in Rum-Rill, Red Wing pottery and stoneware, Hull

Gaston, Mary Frank
Box 342, Bryan, 77806. Author (Collector Books) on china and metals

Gibbs, Carl, Jr.
P.O. Box 131584, Houston, 77219-1584; 713-521-9661. Author of *Collector's Encyclopedia of Metlox Potteries*, autographed copies available from author for $24.95 plus $3 shipping and handling.

Malowanczyk, Abby and Wlodek
Collage-20th Century Classics
3017-B Routh St., Dallas, 75201; 214-880-0020 or (Fax) 214-351-6208. Specializing in architect-designed furniture and decorative arts from the modern movement

Norris, Kenn
Schoolmaster Auctions
P.O. Box 4830, 208 Kerr St., Sanderson, 79848; 915-345-2640. Specializing in school-related items, barbed wire, related literature, and L'il Abner

Pringle, Joyce M.
Antiques and Moore
3708 W. Pioneer Pkwy., Arlington, 76013. Specializing in Boyd, Summit, and Mosser glass

Smith, Allan
1806 Shields Dr., Sherman, 75092; 903-893-3626. Specializing in children's lunch boxes, Coca-Cola, Dr. Pepper, Pepsi Cola, RC Cola, and western stars' items

Thompson, Chuck
Chuck Thompson & Associates
P.O. Box 11652, Houston, 77293. Send LSASE for free list of Chuck's tobacciana publications; Thompson specializes in smokers' ashtrays with and without advertising imprints. His research includes ashtrays designed for homes, automobiles, ocean liners, hotels, trains, and any place where 'ash receivers' were provided to accommodate smokers

Tucker, Richard and Valerie
Argyle Antiques
P.O. Box 262, Argyle, 76226; 817-464-3752. Specializing in windmill weights, shooting gallery targets, figural lawn sprinklers, cast-iron advertising paperweights and other unusual figural cast iron

Turner, Danny and Gretchen
Running Rabbit Video Auctions
P.O. Box 701, Waverly, 37185; 615-296-3600. Specializing in marbles

Waddell, John
2903 Stan Terrace, Mineral Wells, 76067. Specializing in buggy steps

Wilkins, James R.
Olden Year Musical Museum
Box 381951, Duncanville, 75138-1951; 214-298-5587. Specializing in music boxes, phonographs, grind organs, nickelodeons

Woodard, Dannie
The Aluminist
P.O. Box 1347, Weatherford, 76086; 817-594-4680. 6 issues per year; Back issues or sample copy: $2 each

Utah

Anderson, Tim
Box 461, Provo, 84603. Specializing in autographs; Buys single items or collections — historical, movie stars, US Presidents, sports figures, and pre-1860 correspondence. Autograph questions? Please include photocopies of your autographs if possible and enclose a SASE for guaranteed reply.

Anderson, Warren R.
America West Archives
P.O. Box 100, Cedar City, 84721; 801-586-9497. Specializing in old stock certificates and bonds, western documents and books, financial ephemera, autographs, maps, photos; Author of *Owning Western History*, with 75+ photos of old documents and recommended reference guide (available for $18 soft cover or $28 hardback, postpaid, from author)

Spencer, Rick
Salt Lake City, 801-973-0805. Specializing in silverware, Old McDonald by Regal, Shawnee, Van Telligen, salt and pepper shakers. No free appraisals

Vermont

Barry, Kit
68 High St., Brattleboro, 05301; 802-254-3634. Author of *Reflections 1* and *Reflections 2*. Specializing in advertising trade cards and ephemera in general

Virginia

Bradfield, Jeff
Jeff's Antiques
90 Main St., Dayton, 22821; 540-879-9961. Also located in Pat's Antique Mall (I-81), Exit 227, Verona, and Rolling Hills Antique Mall, I-81, Exit 247B, Harrisburg. Specializing in candy containers, toys, postcards, sugar shakers, lamps, furniture, pottery, and advertising items

Cranor, Rosalind
P.O. Box 859, Blacksburg, 24063. Specializing in Elvis collectibles; Author of *Elvis Collectibles* and *Best of Elvis Collectibles*, currently available from author for $19.95+$1.75 postage each

Flanigan, Vicki
Flanigan's Antiques
P.O. Box 1662, Winchester, 22604. Specializing in antique dolls and hand fans

Friend, Terry
839 Glendale Rd., Galax, 24333; 703-236-9027 after 9:30 p.m. E.S.T. Specializing in coffee mills; SASE required

Haigh, Richard
10607 Baypines Lane, Richmond, 23233; 804-741-5770. Specializing in Locke Art, Steuben

Harold, James P.
2200 Columbia Pike, Arlington, 22204-4422. Specializing in pink lustre ware

Lechner, Mildred and Ralph
Box 554, Mechanicsville, 23111; 804-737-3347. Author (Collector Books) on glass salt shakers; Specializing in art and pattern glass salt shakers circa 1870-1940; Directors of Antique and Art Glass Salt Shakers Society Club, 1991-92; **Please note:** Mildred and Ralph have absolutely **NO** involvement or dealings concerning novelty salt shakers or their values

MacAllister, Dale
P.O. Box 46, Singers Glen, 22850; Specializing in sugar shakers and syrups

Monsen, Randall; and Baer, Rod
Monsen & Baer
Box 529, Vienna, 22183; 703-242-1357. Specializing in perfume bottles, Roseville pottery, Art Deco

Reynolds, Charles
Reynolds Toys
2836 Monroe St., Falls Church, 22042; 703-533-1322. Specializing in limited-edition mechanical and still banks, figural bottle openers

Schleyer, Jim
Toy Gun Purveyers
Box 243-S, Burke, 22015. Specializing in toy guns

Tutton, John
1967 Ridgway Rd., Front Royal, 22630; 540-635-7058. Specializing in milk bottles

Washington

Frost, Donald M.
Country Estate Antiques (Appointment only)
14800 N.E. 8th St., Vancouver, 98684; 360-604-8434. Specializing in fine glass

Haase, Don (Mr. Spode)
D&D Antiques
P.O. Box 818, Mukilteo, 98275; 206-348-7443. Specializing in Spode-Copeland China; E-mail: mrspode@aol.com or mrspode@msn.com

Jackson, Denis C., Editor
The Illustrator Collector's News
P.O. Box 1958, Sequim, 98382; 206-683-2559. Copy of recent sample: $3. Specializing in old magazines & illustrations such as: Rose O'Neill, Maxfield Parrish, pinups, Marilyn Monroe, Norman Rockwell, etc.

Moore, Bill and Marilyn
Mukilteo, 296-290-9055, Specializing in ruby-stained glass

Payne, Sharon A.
Antiquities & Art
9104 163rd Ave. NE, Granite Falls, 98252; 360-691-4847. Specializing in Cordey

Rothe, Linda
10020A, Main St. #422, Bellevue, 98004; Specializing in Black Americana

Weldin, Bob
Miner's Quest
W. 3015 Weile, Spokane, WA 99208; 509-327-2897. Specializing in mining antiques and collectibles (mail-order business)

Wheeler-Tanner Escapes
Tanner, Joseph and Pamela
3024 E. 35th Ave., Spokane, 99223; 509-448-8457. Specializing in handcuffs, leg shackles, balls and chains, restraints and padlocks of all kinds (including railroad) locking and non-locking devices; Also Houdini memorabilia: autographs, photos, posters, books, letters, etc.

Whitaker, Jim and Kaye
Eclectic Antiques
P.O. Box 475 Dept. S, Lynnwood, 98046. Specializing in Josef Originals and motion lamps; SASE required

West Virginia

Fostoria Glass Society of America, Inc.
Box 826, Moundsville, 26041. Specializing in Fostoria glass

Wisconsin

Apple, John
John Apple Antiques
1720 College Ave., Racine, 53403; 414-633-3086. Specializing in brass cash registers and parts

Fortney, Daniel
Suite 713, Chalet at the River, 823 N. 2nd St., Milwaukee, 53203. Specializing in china and glass

Knapper, Mary
Phoneco, Inc.
207 E. Mill Rd., P.O. Box 70, Galesville, 54630; 608-582-4124. Specializing in telephones, antique to modern

Matzke, Gene
Gene's Badges & Emblems
2345 S. 28th St., Milwaukee, 53215; 414-383-8995. Specializing in police badges, leg irons, old police photos, fire badges (old), patches, old handcuffs, and memorabilia

Rice, Ferill J.
302 Pheasant Run, Kaukauna, 54130. Specializing in Fenton art glass

Rossiter, Chris
Box 264, Cleveland, 53015; 414-693-8086. Specializing in pipes (especially porcelains) also collecting toys and English military

Washburn, Cara
Washburn Antiques
N. 8527 Lakeside Rd., Willard, 54493; 715-267-7322 (M-F). Specializing in glass

Clubs, Newsletters, and Catalogs

Abingdon Pottery Collectors Club
Elaine Westover, Membership and Treasurer
210 Knox Hwy. 5, Abingdon, IL 61410; 309-462-3267. Specializing in collecting and preservation of Abingdon pottery

ABC Collectors' Circle
Dr. Joan M. George
67 Stevens Ave., Old Bridge, NJ 08857. Specializing in ABC plates and mugs

Akro Agate Collectors Club and *Clarksburg Crow* newsletter
Roger Hardy
10 Bailey St., Clarksburg, WV 26301-2524; 304-624-4523 (evenings) or West End Antiques, 97 Milford St., Clarksburg, WV 26301; 304-624-7600 (week days). Annual membership fee: $20

The Aluminist
Dannie Woodard, Publisher
P.O. Box 1346, Weatherford, TX 76086. Subscription: $12 (for 6 issues)

America West Archives
Anderson, Warren
P.O. Box 100, Cedar City, UT 84721; 801-586-9497. 26-page illustrated catalogs issued 6 times a year; Has both fixed-price and auction sections offering early western documents, letters, stock certificates, autographs, and other important ephemera; Subscription: $15 per year

American Antique Deck Collectors 52 Plus Joker Club
Clear the Decks, quarterly publication
Ray Hartz, President
P.O. Box 1002, Westerville, OH 43081; 614-891-6296. Specializing in antique playing cards

American Bell Association, Int., Inc.
c/o The Bell Tower
P.O. Box 19443, Indianapolis, IN 46219. Dorothy Malone Anthony, past president

Antique & Art Glass Salt Shaker Collectors' Society (AAGSSCS)
2832 Rapidan Trail, Maitland, FL 32751

Antique & Collectors Reproduction News
Antiques Coast to Coast
c/o Lorna Bambrook
Box 71174, Des Moines, IA 50325; 515-270-8994 or (subscriptions only) 800-227-5531. Monthly newsletter, subscription: $32 per year in US; $41 in Canada

Antique Advertising Association of America (AAAA)
P.O. Box 1121, Morton Grove, IL 60053; 708-466-0904. Publishes *Past Times* Newsletter; Subscription: $35

Antique Bottle & Glass Collector Magazine
Jim Hagenbuch, Publisher
102 Jefferson St., P.O. Box 180, East Greenville, PA 18041. Published monthly for $3 per copy and $19 annual subscription ($22 in Canada)

Antique Bowie Knife Collectors Assn.
Roger Baker, Member
Box 620417, Woodside, CA 94062

Antique Comb Collectors Club International
Antique Comb Collector Newsletter
Belva Green, Editor
3748 Sunray Dr., Holiday, FL 34691-3239; 813-942-7554

Antique Journal
Michael F. Shores, Publisher; Jeffrey Hill, Editor/General Manager
1684 Decoto Road, Suite #166, Union City, CA 50191-8592

Antique Purses Catalog: $4
Bayhouse
P.O. Box 40443, Bay Village, OH 44140; 216-871-8584. Includes colored photos of beaded and enameled mesh purses.

Antique Radio Club of America
81 Steeplechase Rd., Devon, PA 19333

Antique Souvenir Collectors' News
Gary Leveille, Editor
P.O. Box 562, Great Barrington, MA 01230

Antique Stove Association
Clifford Boram, Secretary
417 N. Main St., Monticello, IN 47960. Inquiries should be accompanied by SASE and marked 'Urgent' in red

Antique Telephone Collectors Association
Box 94, Abilene, KS 67410; 913-263-1757. An international organization associated with the Museum of Independent Telephony

Antique Trader Weekly
Julie Hoppensteadt, Editor
P.O. Box 1050, Dubuque, IA 52004-1050. Featuring news about antiques and collectibles, auctions and events; Listing over 165,000 buyers and sellers in every edition; Subscription: $32 (52 issues) per year; Toll free for subscriptions only: 800-334-7165

Antique Wireless Association
Ormiston Rd., Breesport, NY 14816

Appraisers National Association
120 S. Bradford Ave., Placentia, CA 92670; 714-579-1082. Founded in 1982 by Dr. David Long, Ph.D., President of the College for Appraisers, to provide for a standardization of educational requirements for certification of its appraiser members and assure the public that A.N.A. appraisers not only have a broad range of knowledge in personal property valuation, but are held to the highest ethical and professional standards in the industry

Alex G. Malloy, Inc.
P.O. Box 38, South Salem, NY 10590; 203-438-0396. Specialized catalogs on antiquities, and ancient and medieval coins

Arkansas Pottery Collectors' Society
P.O. Box 7617, Little Rock, AR 72217

Arts & Crafts Quarterly
17 S. Main St., Lambertville, NJ 08530; 609-397-9374

Ashtray Journal, a Newsletter for Ashtray Collectors
Chuck Thompson
Box 11652, Houston, TX 77293. For collectors of smokers' ashtrays, from inexpensive advertising ashtrays to valuable works of art; Subscribers receive free ads in bimonthly newsletter; Subscription: $14.95 per year; Sample: $3.95

Association of Coffee Mill Enthusiasts
c/o John E. White, Treasurer
5941 Wilkerson Road, Rex, GA 30273; Annual dues: $30, covers cost of quarterly newsletter and copy of membership roster.

Autograph Times
2303 N. 44th St., #225, Phoenix AZ 85008; 602-947-3112 or (Fax) 602-947-8363. Subscription: $15 (U.S.) per year

Autographs of America
Tim Anderson
P.O. Box 461, Provo, UT 84603; 801-226-1787 (please call in the afternoon). Free sample catalog of hundreds of autographs for sale

Avon Times (National Newsletter Club)
c/o Dwight or Vera Young
P.O. Box 9868, Dept P., Kansas City, MO 64134. Inquiries should be accompanied by large SASE

Beatlefan
P.O. Box 33515, Decatur, GA 30033. Subscription: $15 (U.S.) for 6 issues or $18 (Canada and Mexico)

The Beer Stein Journal
Gary Kirsner, Publisher
P.O. Box 8807, Coral Springs, FL 33075; 305-344-9856 or (Fax) 305-344-4421. Published quarterly; Subscriptions: $20 per year in USA

Black Memorabilia Illustrated Sales List
Judy Posner
May-October: R.D. 1, Box 273 SC, Effort, PA 18330; 717-629-6583 or November-April: 4195 S. Tamiami Trail, #183SC, Venice, FL 34293; 941-497-7149. Send $2 and LSASE. Buy-Sell-Collect

Bojo
P.O. Box 1403, Cranberry Township, PA 16066; Send $2 for 20 pages of Beatles, toys, dolls, jewelry, autographs, Yellow Submarine Items, etc.

Boyd's Art Glass Collectors Guild
P.O. Box 52, Hatboro, PA 19040-0052

Boyd's Crystal Art Glass
Jody & Darrell's Glass Collectibles Newsletter
P.O. Box 180833, Arlington, TX 76096-0833. Publishes 6 times a year. Subscription includes an exclusive glass collectible produced by Boyd's Crystal Art Glass. LSASE for current subscription rates. Sample copy of newsletter: $3

British Royal Commemorative Souvenirs Mail Order Catalog
Audrey Zeder
6755 Coralite St. S, Long Beach, CA 90808

Buckeye Marble Collectors Club
437 Meadowbrook Dr., Newark, OH 43055

The Buttonhook Society
Box 287, White Marsh, MD 21162. Publishes bimonthly newsletter *The Boutonneur*, which promotes collecting of buttonhooks and shares research and information contributed by members

California Perfume Company
For information contact Dick Pardini
3107 North El Dorado St., Dept. SAPG, Stockton, CA 95204-3412. Information requires large SASE; not necessary when offering items for sale

Candy Container Collectors of America
P.O. Box 352, Chelmsford, MA 01824-0352
Or contact: Jeff Bradfield
90 Main St., Dayton, VA 22821

The Cane Collector's Chronicle
Linda Beeman
15 2nd St. N.E., Washington, D.C. 20002; $30 for 4 issues

The Carousel News & Trader
87 Parke Ave. W., Suite 206, Mansfield, OH 44902. A monthly magazine for the carousel enthusiast. Subscription: $22 per year; Sample: $3

The Carousel Shopper Resource Catalog
Box 47, Dept PC, Millwood, NY 10546; Only $2 (+50¢ postage); A full-color catalog featuring dealers of antique carousel art offering single figures or complete carousels, museums, restoration services, organizations, full-size reproductions, books, cards, posters, auction services and other hard-to-find items for carousel enthusiasts

Central Florida Insulator Collectors
557 Nicklaus Dr., Titusville, FL 32780

Ceramic Arts Studio Catalog Reprints
BA Wellman
88 State Road W., Homested Farms #2, Westminster, MA, 01473-1435. Also available: Video Book identification and price guides for Ceramic Arts Studio

Ceramic Arts Studio Collector's Association
P.O. Box 46, Madison, WI 53701; 608-241-9138. Publishes newsletter, *CAS Collector*, a 22-page bimonthly; Annual membership: $15; Sample copy: $3; Inventory record and price guide also available

Character and Advertising Collectibles Illustrated Sales List
Judy Posner
May-October: R.D. 1, Box 273SC, Effort, PA 18330; 717-629-6583, or November-April: 419 S. Tamiami Trail, #183SC, Venice, FL 34293; 941-497-7149. Send $2 and LSASE. Buy-Sell-Collect

Chase Collectors Society
c/o Barry L. Van Hook
2149 W. Jibsail Loop, Mesa, AZ 85202-5524; 602-838-6971. Publishes newsletter *Art Deco Reflections*, Membership: $10, Sample copy of newsletter: $1

Chicagoland Antique Amusements Slot Machine & Jukebox Gazette
Ken Durham, Editor
909 26 St., N.W., Suite 502, Washington, DC 20037. 20-page newspaper published twice a year; Subscription: 4 issues for $10; Sample: $5; Send SASE for free list of books; http://www.olg.com

Coin-Op Newsletter
Ken Durham, Publisher
909 26th St. N.W., Suite 502, Washington, D.C. 20037. Subscription (10 issues): $24 per year; Sample: $5; Send SASE for free list of books; http://www.olg.com

The Cola Clan
Alice Fisher, Treasurer
2084 Continental Drive N.E., Atlanta, GA 30345

Collectors of Findlay Glass
P.O. Box 256, Findlay, OH 45840. An organization dedicated to the study and recognition of Findlay glass; Newsletter *The Melting Pot*, published quarterly; Convention held annually; Membership: $10 per year

The Compact Collectors Chronicles
Roselyn Gerson
P.O. Box S, Lynbrook, NY 11563. Publishes *Powder Puff* Newsletter, which contains articles covering all aspects of compact collecting, restoration, vintage ads, patents, history, and articles by members and prominent guest writers; Seeker and sellers column offered free to members

Cookie Jars and Go Withs Illustrated Sales List
Judy Posner
May-October: R.D. 1, Box 273SC, Effort, PA 18330; 717-629-6583 or November-April: 4195 S. Tamiami Trail, #183SC, Venice, FL 34293; 941-497-7149. $2 and LSASE; Buy-Sell-Collect

Cookie Jarrin' With Joyce: The Cookie Jar Newsletter
R.R. 2, Box 504, Walterboro, SC 29488

The Copley Courier
1639 N. Catalina St., Burbank, CA 91505

Creamers Newsletter
P.O. Box 11, Lake Villa, IL 60046-0011. Subscription: $5 per year (issued quarterly)

Currier & Ives Catalog
Rudisill's Alt Print Haus
P.O. Box 199, Worton, MD 21678. Please include LSASE

Currier & Ives China by Royal Newsletters
c/o Jack and Treva Hamlin
R.R. 4, Box 150, Kaiser St., Proctorville, OH 45669; 614-886-7644. 2 different newsletters and book soon to be available

Currier & Ives Quarterly Newsletter
c/o Patti Street
P.O. Box 504, Riverton, KS 66770; 316-848-3529. Subscription: $12 per year (includes 2 free ads)

Czechoslovakian Collectors Guild International
P.O. Box 901395, Kansas City, MO 64190

The Dedham Pottery Collectors Society Newsletter (quarterly publication)
Jim Kaufman, Publisher
248 Highland St., Dedham, MA 02026; 800-283-8070. Subscription: $18

Depression Glass Daze
Teri Steel, Editor/Publisher
Box 57, Otisville, MI 48463; 313-631-4593. The nation's market place for glass, china, and pottery

Disneyana Illustrated Sales List
Judy Posner
May-October: R.D. 1, Box 273SC, Effort, PA 18330; 717-629-6583, or November-April: 4195 S. Tamiami Trail, #183SC, Venice, FL 34293; 941-497-7149. Send $2 and LSASE. Buy-Sell-Collect

Docks, L.R. 'Les'
Shellac Shack
Box 691035, San Antonio, TX 78269-1035. Send $2 for a 72-page catalog of 78s that Docks wants to buy, the prices he will pay, and shipping instructions

Doorstop Collectors of America
Doorstopper Newsletter
Jeanie Bertoia
2413 Madison Ave., Vineland, NJ 08630; 609-692-4092. Membership: $20 per year, includes 2 newsletters and convention; Send 2-stamp SASE for sample

Dragonware Club
c/o Suzi Hibbard
2570 Walnut Blvd. #20, Walnut Creek, CA 94596. Inquiries should be accompanied by SASE; All contributions welcome; Computer correspondence: hmbk24a@prodigy.com

Drawing Room of Newport
Gacher, John
152 Spring St., Newport, RI
02840; 401-841-5060. Book on
Zsolnay available

Eggcup Collector's Corner
67 Stevens Ave., Old Bridge, NJ
08857. Issued quarterly; Subscriptions: $18 per year (checks made out to Joan George). Sample copies: $5

The Elegance of Old Ivory Newsletter
Box 1004, Wilsonville, OR 97070

Fenton Art Glass Collectors of
    America, Inc.
Williamstown, WV 26187

Fiesta Collector's Quarterly
    Newsletter
19238 Dorchester Circle,
Strongsville, OH 44136. Subscription: $12 per year

Figural Bottle Opener Collectors
c/o Nancy Robb
3 Avenue A, Latrobe, PA 15650.
Please include SASE

Fire Mark Circle of Americas
Glen Hartley, Sr.
2859 Marlin Dr., Chamblee, GA
30341-5119; 404-451-2651. Specializing in fire marks, Methodist, Masonic, Foremost Dairies, Goodyear

Florence Collector's Club Newsletter
Rita Bee, Editor; Beth Dunigan,
Publisher; c/o Florence Collector's Club Membership Chairman
P.O. Box 122, Richland, WA
99353. 6 issues per yr for $20

Fostoria Glass Society of America, Inc.
P.O. Box 826, Moundsville, WV
26041

Frankoma Family Collectors
    Association
c/o Nancy Littrell
P.O. Box 32571, Oklahoma City,
OK 73123-0771. Membership
dues: $25; Includes quarterly
newsletter, annual convention

Friar Tuck Collectors Club
P.O. Box 173, Dacula, GA
30211; 770-963-5736. Quarterly
newsletter, annual convention,
write or call for membership
application and information

Friends of Degenhart
c/o Degenhart Museum
P.O. Box 186, Cambridge, OH
43725; 614-432-2626. Membership:
$5 ($10 for family) includes *Heartbeat* Newsletter (printed quarterly) and free admission to museum

H.C. Fry Society
P.O. Box 41, Beaver, PA 15009.
Founded in 1983 for the sole purpose of learning about Fry glass; Publishes *Shards*, quarterly newsletter

GAR Post 20 Mem. Assn.
Richard A. Haussmann, Chaplain
P.O. Box 1865, Aurora, 60507

George Kamm Paperweights
24-SP Townsend Court, Lancaster, PA 17603; 717-872-7858.
Specializing in antique and contemporary paperweights; Color brochure published bimonthly, $5 annual fee (refundable); Sample on request (requires #10 SASE)

Glass Knife Collector's Club
Wilbur Peterson
711 Kelly Dr., Lebanon, TN 37087

Goofus Glass Gazette
c/o Leon Travis
9 Lindenwood Ct., Sterling, VA
20165-5646. Subscription: $20
per year; Sample: $5

Gonder Pottery Collectors' Newsletter
c/o John and Marilyn McCormick
P.O. Box 3174, Shawnee, KS 66226

Grandpa's Depot & Caboose
John 'Grandpa' White
1616 17th St., Suite 267, Denver,
CO 80202; 303-628-5590 or (Fax)
303-628-5547. Publishes catalogs
on railroad-related collectibles

The Hagen-Renaker Collector's
    Club Newsletter
c/o Jenny Palmer
13975 Litzen Rd., Copemish, MI
49625. Subscription: $20 per year;
Sample copy: $4

Hake's Americana & Collectibles
Specializing in character and personality collectibles along with
artifacts of popular culture for
over 20 years. To receive a catalog for their next 3,000-item
mail/phone bid auction, send $3
to: Hake's Americana; P.O. Box
1444M, York, PA 17405

Hall China Collector's Club
    Newsletter
300 W. York Dr., Terre Haute, IN
47802; 812-234-3870. Subscription:
$13 per year (published quarterly)

Head Hunters Newsletter
c/o Maddy Gordon
P.O. Box 83H
Scarsdale, NY 10583. Subscription:
$20 yearly for 4 quarterly issues

How To Open and Operate a
Home-Based Antiques Business;
How To Recognize and Refinish
    Antiques for Pleasure and Profit
Jacquelyn Peake, author
P.O. Box 591
Ashland, OR 97520
or Globe Pequot Press
P.O. Box 833, Old Saybrook, CT
06475. Available at $15.95 for the
first-mentioned volume, $14.95 for
the latter

Ice Screamer
c/o Duvall Sollers
P.O. Box 132, Monkton, MD
21111. Published bimonthly;
Dues: $15 per year; Annual convention held in late June

The Illustrator Collector's News
    (TICN)
Denis C. Jackson, Editor
P.O. Box 1958, Sequim, WA
98382; Fax 206-683-2559. Subscription: $17 per year; $3 for
sample copy of bimonthly publication; Publishes price and identification guides on various
illustrators and magazines, write
for further information

Indiana Historical Radio Society
245 N. Oakland Ave., Indianapolis, IN 46201

International Association of Calculator Collectors, *International*
Calculator Collector Newsletter
Guy Ball, Co-Editor
14561 Livingston St., Tustin, CA
92680-2618. Subscription: $8 per
year ($12 foreign), published
quarterly

International Association of R.S.
    Prussia, Inc.
Frances Coy, Secretary 212
Wooded Falls Rd., Louisville, KY
40243. Membership: $20 per
household; Yearly convention

International Club for Collectors
    of Hatpins & Hatpin Holders
    (ICC of H&HH)
Lillian Baker, Founder
15237 Chanera Ave., Gardena,
CA 90249; 213-329-2619.
Monthly *Points* Newsletter and
Pictorial Journal

International Nippon Collectors
    Club (INCC)
c/o Phil Fernkes
112 Oak Ave N., Owatonna, MN
55060. Publishes newsletter 6 times
a year; Holds annual convention

International Perfume and Scent
    Bottle Collectors Association
Randall B. Monsen, President
P.O. Box 529, Vienna, VA 22183
or (Fax) 703-242-1357. Membership: $35 (USA) or $48 (Foreign);
Newsletter published quarterly

International Rose O'Neill Club
Contact Karen Stewart
P.O. Box 668, Branson, MO
65616. Publishes quarterly
newsletter *Kewpiesta Kourier*.
Dues: (includes newsletter) $7
(single) or $10 (family)

International Society of Antique
    Scale Collectors
Bob Stein, President
176 West Adams, Suite 1706,
Chicago, IL 60603; 312-263-7500.
Publishes *Equilibrium* Magazine;
Quarterly President's Newsletter;
Annual membership directory and
out-of-print scale catalogs; Holds
annual convention

Iron Talk
Jimmy Walker, Editor
P.O. Box 68, Waelder, TX 78959.
Journal of antique pressing irons;
News of prices, patents, markets,
collectibles, collectors, history,
reference, advice and much more;
One-year bimonthly subscription:
$25 in U.S. (Texans add $1.94
tax); $30 foreign

Kitchen Antiques & Collectibles
    News Newsletter
Kollectors of Old Kitchen Stuff
Dana & Darlene DeMore, Editors
4645 Laurel Ridge Dr., Harrisburg, PA 17110; 717-545-7320.
Subscription: $24 per year for 6
issues of *Kitchen Antiques & Collectibles News*

The Lace Merchant
Elizabeth M. Kurella, Publisher
Box 222, Plainwell, MI 49080;
616-685-9792

The Lady's Gallery
Color-glossy magazine of fashion, decorative arts, and collectibles. Subscription: $23.95 (US, 6 issues) per year; Call 216-871-4479 for further information

The Laughlin Eagle
Joan Jasper, Publisher
Richard Racheter, Editor
1270 63rd Terrace S., St. Petersburg, FL 33705. Subscription: $14 (4 issues) per year; Sample: $4

License Plate Collectors Hobby Magazine
Drew Steitz, Editor
P.O. Box 222
East Texas, PA 18046; Phone or Fax 610-791-7979. Bimonthly publication with many photographs, classifieds, etc.; $18 pr year (1st class, U.S.); Sample: $2

Line Jewels, NIA #255
3557 Nicklaus Dr., Titusville, FL 32780

Mabel Lucie Attwell Catalogs
J. David Ehrhard
10642½ Hillhaven Ave., Tujunga, CA 91042

Majolica International Society
Suite #103, 1275 First Ave., New York, NY 10021. Dues: $30 per year, entitles member to attend annual meeting and to receive the quarterly newsletter *Majolica Matters*

Majolica Mail Order Catalog
Items from the collection of Mariann Katz Marks
P.O. Box 750, Honesdale, PA 18431. Please send LSASE for majolica listing

Marble Collectors' Society of America
Claire Block, Secretary
P.O. Box 222, Trumbull, CT 06611. Publishes *Marble Mania*; Gathers and disseminates information to further the hobby of marbles and marble collecting; $12 adds your name to the contributor mailing list ($21 covers 2 years)

Marble Collectors Unlimited
P.O. Box 206, Northboro, MA 01532

Mason's Ironstone Collectors Club
c/o Susan Hirshman
542 Siskiyou Blvd., Ashland, OR 97520. Dues: $25 per year (includes 6 newsletters)

Mid-West Open Salt Society
Dave Dillingham
2620 Middlebelt Rd., W. Bloomfield, MI 48324

Mike's General Store
52 St. Anne's Rd., Winnepeg, Manitoba, Canada R2M 2Y3; 204-255-3464. Catalog subscription: $6 per issue or next 4 issues for $20

Miniature Bottle Club of the Great Lakes
39145 Marne, Sterling Heights, MI 48313; 810-566-0891. Dues $5 per year; 4 meetings per year

Morgantown Collectors of America
Jerry Gallagher
420 1st Ave. N.W., Plainview, MN 55964; 507-534-3511. *The Morgantown Newscaster*, triannual journal for research of Morgantown Glass only; affiliated with no club; Subscription: $18 per year; *Morgantown Colors* placard: $4 postpaid; *A Handbook of Old Morgantown Glass, Volume I*, (A Guide to Identification and Shape): 256 pages, includes 8 color plates, 1,800+ illustrations, and price guide, $35+$4 insured shipping and handling; Order autographed copies from the author at above address; SASE required for answers to queries

Mt. Washington Art Glass Society
P.O. Box 24094, Fort Worth, TX 76124-1094. Publishes *MWAGS Review*, to educate, inform and provide helpful information to anyone interested in art glass; Holds annual convention; Subscription/membership: $20 per individual or $25 for 2 persons in 1 household

Murray Hudson Antiquarian Books and Maps
109 S. Church St., Box 163, Halls, TN 38040; 800-748-9946 or 901-836-9057; Fax: 901-836-9017. Buyer and seller of antiquarian maps (especially pocket, wall, U.S. Civil War, and railroad maps) and books with maps (atlases, travel guides, geographies, gazetteers, explorations, land surveys, etc.), especially of Southeastern and Southwestern U.S. prior to 1900; Also world globes, map jigsaw puzzles and gameboards prior to 1950; Contact for catalog

Mystic Lights of the Aladdin Knights Newsletter
c/o J.W. Courter; 3935 Kelley Rd., Kevil, KY 40253; 502-488-2116. Information requires LSASE

The Nelson McCoy Express
Jean Bushnell, Editor
3081 Rock Creek Dr., Broomfield, CO 80020; 300-469-8309

Index

ABC Plates 1
Abington 1-2
Abino.............................73
Adams.............................2
Adams Rose, Early and Late ...2-3
Advertising 3-10;36,77-78,
    101-102,135,193,223-224,399,
    402,403,463,472,548,561-562
Advertising, See Also
    Automobilia; Coca-Cola;
    Keen Kutter; Soda Fountain
    Collectibles; Winchester
Advertising Cards 10-11
Advertising Dolls 11-12
African Art 12-13
Agata 13
Akro Agate 13-15
Aladdin Lamps 282
Alamo Pottery 15
Alaska Yukon-Pacific
    Exposition 566-567
Albumen Prints 388
Alexander-Kins 173-175
Alexandrite 15
Alhambra China 15-16
Alice in Wonderland 432
Almanacs 16;235
Aluminum 16-17;252,460
AMACO American Art Clay
    Co........................17
Amberina..............................17
Ambrotypes 388
American Art Potteries..........329
American Bisque 18
American Character
Dolls 167-168
American Encaustic Tiling
    Co..........................18-19
American Folklore
    Miniatures 261
American Indian Art 19-23
American Indian Art, See Also
    Eskimo Artifacts
Amethyst Glass 23-24
Amphora 24
Andirons...........................196,456
Angle Lamps 282-283
Animal Dishes with
    Covers 24-25; 155,236

Animal Dishes with Covers, See
    Also Greentown
Animation Cels and
    Drawings..........................98-99
Anna Pottery 25
Annalee Dolls........................168
Ansonia 115,116
Antiquities 25-26
Anton Lang; See Lang, Anton
Apothecary (Druggist) Bottles .59
Apple Peelers..........................276
Appliances, Electric 26; 33,402
Arcade Toys 529
Arequipa..............................26-27
Argy-Rousseau, G...................27
Armand Marseille Dolls..168-169
Armchairs...............108,191,456,
                477,506, 507,559
Armoires..............................220
Arranbee Dolls 169
Art Deco 27-28
Art Deco, See Also Bronzes;
    Chase; Frankart; Etc.
Art Glass Baskets....................28
Art Glass Baskets, See Also
    Specific Categories
Art Nouveau..........................28
Arts and Crafts....................28-30
Arts and Crafts, American
    Indian 19
Ashtrays..............15,16,43,49,86,
    105,181,210,230,245,253,261,
    274,341,345,347,420,421,441,
                443,515
Atlases 302
Atomizers.............................148
Attwell, Mabel Lucie 30;482
Audubon Prints..............407-408
Aunt Jemima 49,50
Aurene 503-505
Austrian Glass 30
Austrian Ware........................30;464
Autographs..........................30-32
Autographs, See Also
    Rock 'N Roll
Automobilia 32
Autumn Leaf......................32-34
Aviation 34;400
Aviation, See Also Militaria

Avon 34-35
Ayotte, Rick 363
Azalea 344
Baccarat 35;363
Badges.......35;32,34,136,194,223,
        316,400-401,423,473,474
Bakelite 397
Ball Fruit Jars 212
Ballpoint Pens 378
Banks....35-39;18,68,432,449,480
Barber Shop Collectibles.....39;59
Barber Shop Collectibles, See
    Also Bottles; Razors; Shaving
    Mugs
Barbie Dolls and Related
    Dolls 169-170
Barbie Gift Sets and Related
    Accessories 170
Barnum and Bailey 112
Barometers 39-40
Barovier Glass......................266
Barware 40;105
Basalt 40
Basalt, See Also Wedgwood
Base Burners 510
Baskets....40-41;16,20,29,143,477
Batchelder 41
Battersea 41
Bauer 41-42
Bavaria 42
Beatles 436-437
Bed Warmers 406
Beds 108,214
Bedspreads 279
Beer Cans 42-43
Bellaire, Marc 43
Belleek, American 43-44
Belleek, Irish 44-45
Bells 45;105,194,443
Belsnickle 111
Belton Dolls..........................170
Benches 191,214-215,477
Bennett, John 45
Bennington 45-46
Bernard Leach; See Leach, Bernard
Beswick 46
Big Little Books..................47-48
Bing and Grondahl 48;290-291
Binoculars..........................48-49

Birdcages..........................49
Bisque 49;246,390
Bisque, See Also Heubach;
    Nodders
Bitters Bottles......................59-60
Black Americana...........49-50;37
                183-185
Black Cats 50-52
Black Glass 51
Black Glass, See Also Bottles;
    L.E. Smith; Tiffin
Blades and Points, American
    Indian 20
Blanc de Chine......................354
Blanket Chests, Coffers, Trunks
    and Mule Chests..................215
Blankets, Navajo 20-21
Bliss 167
Blotters 423
Blown Glass.............51-52;60,503
Blown Glass Bottles and
    Flasks 60
Blown Three-Mold Glass 52
Blue & White Porcelain .354-355
Blue and White Stoneware.52-53
Blue Bell Paperweights....518-519
Blue Onion, See Onion Pattern
Blue Ridge, 53-54
Blue Ridge Mountain Boys by
    Paul Webb 261
Bluebird China....................54-55
Boch Freres 55
Boehm 55-56
Bohemian Glass......................56
Book Flasks 46
Book of Knowledge Banks........37
Bookcases..........................215,506
Bookends 56;29,105,210,
                441,455,517
Bookends, See Also Glass
    Animals and Figurines
Bookmarks 505
Books..........................47-48,49,135,
        196,221,235-236,331,366,
        390,423,456,472,473,477
Bootjacks & Bootscrapers ...56-57
Boru, Sorcha..........................57
Bossons Artware..................57-58
Bottle Openers 58

Bottles, Cologne or Perfume; See Bottles, Scent

Bottles, Scent 35;52,60-61, 145-146,280-281, 487,504,528,553

Bottles and Flasks......58-63;2,27, 68,119,146,148,253, 396,436, 469,490,501,569

Box Stoves 510

Boxes 63-64;29,89,118,180, 181,186,270,330,477-478

Boy Scouts 473

Boyd Crystal Art Glass 64-65

Bracelets 21,268,269,397

Bradley and Hubbard.........65,178

Brass..............65-66;45-58, 85,177,262,538-539

Brastoff, Sascha 66

Brayton, Laguna 66-67

Bread Plates and Trays 67

Breweriana, See Advertising; Beer Cans

Brides' Baskets and Bowls ...67-68

Bristol Glass................................68

British Royalty Commemoratives............68-69

Broadmoor...........................69-70

Broadsides..................................70

Bronzes 70-71;355

Brooches 269

Brouwer 71

Brownies by Palmer Cox...................71-72;111

Bru Dolls..................................170

Bruce Fox Aluminum.............252

Brush...72

Brush-McCoy 72-73

Buck Rogers......................47,379

Buddy Lee 12

Buffalo Pottery 73-74

Buggy Steps 74-75

Bunnykins.................................451

Bureaus, See Chests

Burmese 75;187,283

Buster Brown 4

Butter Molds and Stamps....75-76

Butter Pats 74,502

Buttonhooks.................................76

Byrdcliffe 76

C.D. Kenny...................................4

Cabat.....................................76-77

Cabbage Patch Dolls.......170-171

Cabinets...........................215,506

Calculating Devices 77

Calendar Plates.........................77

Calendars 77-78;5,7, 32,119,271,349,366

Caliente 78

California, Designed by Royal Hickman...................252-253

California Faience 78

California Perfume Company......................78-79

Calling Cards, Cases, and Receivers 79

Camark 79

Cambridge Glass 79-84;227

Cambridge Pottery 84

Cameo...........84-85;146-147,148, 155,220,286,288,333,435,553

Cameras 388,473,474

Canary Ware 85

Candelabra 85

Candle Holders and Candlesticks 85;29,46,51, 86,105,114,134,183,233, 243,254,342,456,466, 504,512,523,558

Candle Molds 406

Candlestands 215,478

Candlewick..........................86-87

Candy Baskets and Containers..87-88;110,145,243

Canes.....................................88-89

Canisters...................52,275,433

Canton...89

Capo-Di-Monte 89

Carbines....................................551

Cardinal Tuck (Red Monk) ...231

Carlton Ware 90

Carnival Collectibles 90

Carnival Glass....................90-97

Carousel Figures 97

Carte De Visites 388

Cartoon Art 98-99

Cartoon Books............................99

Cartoon Characters, See Cartoon Art; Personalities

Cash Registers 99-100

Cast Iron................100;56,57,58, 121-122,177,178,274, 307,347,512, 539,562

Cast Kitchen Ware................274

Castor Sets...............................100

Catalin 397-398

Catalina Island...............100-101

Catalogs....................101-102;32, 196-197,491,561

Caughley Ware 102

Caughley Ware, See Also Coalport

Celadon 355

Celebrity Dolls 171

Celluloid..................289,398-399

Centennial Exposition 566

Ceramic Art Company ...102-103

Ceramic Arts Studio, Madison.......................103-104

Chairs 108,191,215-216,478, 506,507,560,567

Chairs (Barber).........................39

Chalkware..................104-105;90

Chandeliers 283

Character Jugs 451-452

Chase Brass and Copper Company.....................105-106

Checkerboards......................;221

Cheese Molds 322

Chelsea 106

Chelsea Dinnerware 106

Chelsea Keramic Art Works ..106

Cherry Seeders 276

Chests 191,216,490

Chicago Crucible 106-107

Chicago World's Fair..............567

Children's Books 107;47-48, 71,99,124-125,135

Children's Dishes 1,54,107, 109,179

Children's Furniture 166

Children's Things 107-109; 117,414,448,477,482

Children's Things, See Also Dollhouses and Furnishings, Games, Puzzles, Toys

China Cabinets 191

China Dolls 171

Chocolate Glass 109

Chocolate Molds 321

Christening Gowns 279

Christmas Collectibles ...109-112; 210-211,340,347,402-403

Chrysanthemum Sprig, Blue ..112

Churns....276,322,431,557-558

Cinderella........................173,380

Circus Collectibles 112

Clambroth 112-113

Clarice Cliff.............................113

Cleminson 113,392

Clewell 113-114

Clews 114

Clifton 114

Cliftwood Art Potteries, Inc. .328

Clocks..............114-116;7,27,191

Cloisonne 116

Clothes Sprinkler Bottles .276,385

Clothing & Accessories 117;19

Cluthra..............117-118;503-505

Coaching Days 435

Coalport....................................118

Coca-Cola 118-121

Cocktail Shakers 40,105,275

Coffee Grinders................121-122

Coffeepots, Biggins, and Boilers..........................189,234, 351,376,384,525

Coin Pattern............................203

Coin-Operated Machines .122-124

Colanders..........................234,525

Coleco Dolls 171

Columbian Exposition, Chicago 566

Comic Books 124-125

Compacts..............................125;68

Compasses 513

Consolidated Lamp and Glass...........................125-126

Continental Line.....................327

Cookbooks 126-127,349

Cookie Cutters 127-128

Cookie Jars...........128-129;2,18,49, 52,66,72,113,254,287,293,300, 308-309,385,412,430,432,455,479

Cookie Jars, See Also Abingdon; American Bisque; McCoy; Metlox; Red Wing

Cookie Molds 100

Cooper, Susie............................129

Coors 129-130

Copper 130-131;456,552-553

Copper Lustre 131

Coralene Glass 131

Cordey 132

Corkscrews................................132

Corn Line.................479-480;499

Cornstick Pans 274
Cosmos............................132-133
Cottageware............................133
Covered Dishes............68,253,318
Covered Dishes, See Also Animal
   Dishes with Covers
Coverlets........................133-134
Cowan 134
Cracker Jack..................134-136
Cradles..........................21,108
Cranberry 136-137;283
Creamware............................137
Creamware, See Also Leeds
Crested China 233
Crib Toys............................397
Cribbage Boards 185
Crocks..........................46,52,53,
   322,431,508,558
Crown Milano..........137-138;464
Crown Point Ware, See Volkmar
Cruets 138;50,306
Cup Plates, Glass..............138-139
Cup Plates, See Also Pairpoint;
   Staffordshire
Cupboards........................108,478
Cupboards, See Also Pie Safes
Currier and Ives by
   Royal 139-140
Currier & Ives Prints.......408-410
Custard 140-142
Cut Glass 142-144;145-146
   248,289-290,464
Cut Overlay Glass 144
Cut Velvet 144
Cybis..............................144-145
Czechoslovakian
   Collectibles 145-146
D'Argental 146-147
Daguerreotypes 389
Dairy Bottles..........................61
Dam Things..........................539
Darners......................476,504
Daum Nancy..........................147
Davenport 147-148
Davenport, See Also Flow Blue;
   Mulberry
Davy Crockett 75,380
Dazey Churns 276
De Vez 148
De Vilbiss 148

Decanters 148-152;52,143,
   144,260,261,436,553
Decoys 152-153
Dedham, See Also Chelsea
   Keramic Art Works
Dedham Pottery 153-154
Degenhart........................154-155
Delatte 155
Deldare 73-74
Delft 155-156
Denver 156
Denver White 156-157
Depression Glass 157-164
Derby 164
Desert Sands..................164-165
Desks 191-192,217,472,506
Devon Motto Ware.........528-529
Dick Tracy..................47,99,380
Disney.............98-99,107,463,545
Distlefink 113
Documents 165-166
Documents, See Also Autographs
   Stocks & Bonds
Dolls 167-177;12,21,474
Donald Duck 47,222,380
Door Knockers........................177
Doorstops 177-178
Doranne of California 128,129
Dorchester Pottery 178-179
Dorflinger 179
Doulton, See Royal Doulton
Dr. Pepper..............................5
Dragon Ware....................179-180
Dresden................................180
Dresser Accessories 180-181;
   148,399
Dressers................................217
Dry Sinks........................217-218
Dryden................................181
Duncan and Miller..181-182; 227
Durand 182-183
Durant Kilns 183
E.S. Germany and E.S.
   Prussia 470
Earrings................268,269,397
Easy Day Automatic Clothes
   Washer..................................78
Eegee Dolls..................171-172
Effanbee Dolls......................172
Egg Beaters 274-275

Egg Cups 183-184;189-190,
   226,246,482,528
Egg Timers..............................231
Elfinware 184-185;464
Elks (Fraternal Order) 211
Elvis Presley..........................437
Epergnes................................185
Erphila 185
Eskimo Artifacts.............185-186
Extinguishers 194
Fairings 186
Fairy Lamps..........................283
Fans..186
Fans, Electric..........................26
Fantasia..................................544
Farm Collectibles 186-187
Farm Collectibles; See Also
   Cast Iron; Woodenware;
   Wrought Iron
Farm Toys................................532
Father Christmas.............111-112
Fenton 187-188;227
Fiesta 188-191
Fifties Modern 191-192
Finch, Kay....................192-193
Findlay Onyx 193
Fire Marks..............................193
Firefighting Collectibles .193-195
Fireglow 195
Fireplace Implements 196
Fireplace Implements, See Also
   Wrought Iron
Fisher, Harrison 196
Fisher-Price..........................530
Fishing Collectibles.........196-197
Flags of the United
   States............................197-198
Flambe 453
Flasks................61-62;60,336,569
Flatware........................397-398,
   484-486,487-488
Floradine................................193
Florence Ceramics............198-199
Florentine Cameo...................199
Flow Blue..........................199-201
Flower Frogs....................134,441
Flower Frogs..........See Also Glass
   Animals and Figurines
Flue Covers 201-202
Folk Art 202;563

Foot Warmers..........................407
Fostoria 202-208;227-228
Fox Prints 410
Frakturs........................206-207
Frames..................207;29,523,538
Frankoma 210-211
Frances Ware....................207-208
Francie Dolls..........................169
Franciscan 208-210
Frankart 210
Franklin Stoves....................510
Fraternal Organizations..211-212;
   479,548
Fraunfelter 212
Friar Tuck (Brown Monk) 231
Fruit jars..............................212
Fry....................................212-213
Fulper 213-214
Furniture..........214-220;108,355,
   477-478,490,559-560,567-568
Furniture, See Also Specific
   Categories
G.A.R. Memorabilia 223
Galle..............................220-221
Gambling Memorabilia 221
Game Calls 221
Gameboards 221
Games..........221-222;71,135,473
Gas Globes and Panels....223-224
Gaudy Dutch....................224-225
Gaudy Ironstone......................225
Gaudy Welsh..........................225
Geisha Girl....................225-226
German Comic Character
   Nodders 343
German Porcelain 226
Ginny Dolls..........................177
Girl Scouts 473-474
Gladding McBean and
   Company 227
Glass Animals and
   Figurines 227-229,513
Glass Knives 229
Glass Shoes..........................230
Glidden................................230
Goebel..........................230-231
Goetting & Co. 78
Goldscheider 231
Golliwoggs 184
Gonder 231-232

Gone-With-the-Wind and
   Banquet Lamps 283
Goofus Glass 232
Goss and Crested
   China 232-233;464
Gouda 233
Grand Feu 233-234
Grandfather Clocks, See Tall
   Case Clocks
Graniteware 234-235
Grateful Dead 437
Graters 234,276
Green Opaque 235
Greenaway, Kate 235-236;337
Greentown Glass.............236-237
Gregory, Mary 305-306
Grenades (Fire-Related) .194-195
Griswold 274
Grueby.............................237-238
Guns, See Weapons
Guns (Toy) 532-534
Gustavsberg 238
Gutmann Prints......................410
Haag.....................................569
Hagen-Renaker 238
Hagenauer 238-239
Hair Weaving..........................239
Half Dolls 172
Hall.................................239-242
Hall Pieces.............................218
Hallmark................................242
Halloween 242-243
Halloween Costumes; See
   Personalites, Fact and Fiction
Hampshire 243-244
Handcuffs...............................434
Handel...................................244
Hard Candy Molds..........321-322
Hardstones (Oriental) 355
Harker 244-245
Harlequin 245-246
Hatpin Holders 246-247;469
Hatpins 247
Hats 117,316
Haviland...................247-248;464
Hawkes 248
Head Vases......................248-249
Heisey......................249-252;228
Herend 252
Heubach 252;172

Hickman, Royal Arden...252-253
Higgins..................................253
Highboys...............................218
Highchairs 108
Hinze Ambrosia.......................78
Hires.......................................5-6
Historical Glass 253-254;67
Historical Glass, See Also Bread
   Plates and Trays
Hobbs, Brockunier & Co. 254
Hogscrapers 86
Holly Amber 236-237
Holt Howard...........................254
Homer Laughlin 254-255
Hopalong Cassidy...................380
Horsman Dolls 172-173
Howdy Doody........................380
Hubley 530
Hull 253-254
Humidors 50,342,456
Hummels 257-259;291
Humpty Dumpty Circus..535-536
Hutschenreuther 259
Icart Prints......................410-411
Ice Cream Molds 322
Ideal Dolls.............................173
Imari 259-260
Imperial German 316
Imperial Glass 260-261;228
Imperial Glass, See Also
   Candlewick; Carnival Glass;
   Stretch Glass
Imperial Porcelain 261
Implement Seats 186-187
Indian Tree 261-262
Indian Ware 114
Ink Bottles 62
Inkwells and Inkstands..........262;
           398,436,528
Inro 355
Insulators.......................262-263
Irons 263-264
Ironstone..........264-265;516-517
Italian Glass 265-266
Ivory 266-267
Jack-in-the-Pulpit Vases.........267
Jack-O'-Lanterns 242-243
Jackson, Michael 437
Jacquard Coverlets 134
Japanese Lustreware 267

Japanese Militaria..................317
Jasperware...............246,417-418
Jervis 267
Jewel Tea, See Autumn Leaf
Jewelry 267-269;25,69
Jewelry and Adornments
   American Indian 21
Josef Originals........................269
Judaica 270
Jugtown.................................270
Jukeboxes 122-123
K.P.M. Porcelain......270-271;464
Kayzerzinn Pewter 271
Keeler, Brad 271
Keen Kutter.......271-272;277,548
Kelva 272
Ken Dolls 169
Kenton 530
Kenton Hills 272
Kentucky Derby Glasses..272-273
Kerosene Lamps..............283,284,
             285-286
Kettles............................65,131
Kew Blas 273
Kewpies 350-351
Keys 421
King's Rose 273-274
Kiss.......................................437
Kitchen Collectibles 274-276;
            480,525
Kitchen Collectibles, See Also
   Graniteware; Reamers
Kitchen Kraft.................191,245
Knives.............................276-278
Kosta....................................278
Kugels 112
Kurz and Allison.....................411
L.E. Smith 228-229
L.G. Wright........................24,25
Labels 278-279;423
Labino...................................279
Lace, Linens, and
   Needlework 279-280;422
Lacy Glassware 280
Ladies' Home Journal 300
Lalique............................280-281
Lamps 281-286;15,27,28,29,65,
   105,126,133,146,192,210,213,
   244,253,310,324,348,361362,
   384,415,421,450,456,498,506,

Lamps continued..522-523,550,561
Lang, Anton 286
Lanterns.......................195,233,
      283-284,421-422,473
Lavender Salts, Goetting & Co.;
   See California Perfume Co.
Le Verre Francais....................286
Leach, Bernard 286-287
LeCamark, See Camark
Led Zeppelin..........................437
Leeds, Leeds Type...................287
Lefton China...................287-288
Legras 288
Lenox 288-289;464
Letter Openers...................289;398
Li'l Abner 381
Libbey............................289-290
License Plates 32
Life Magazines 300
Lighters 105,347,397,526
Lightning Rod Balls................290
Limited Edition Plates 290-292
Limoges.................292;439,479
Lithophanes 292
Little Orphan Annie 37,47
            99,299,381
Little Red Riding Hood...........72
           128,293
Liverpool 293
Lladro 293-294
Lobby Cards...........................331
Lobmeyer 294
Locke Art 294
Locks 294-296;422
Loetz 296
Log Cabin Syrup........................6
Lomonosov Porcelain.............296
Lone Ranger 124,381
Longwy 297
Lonhuda.................................297
Look Magazines 300
Lotton 297
Lotus Ware 297-298
Lowboys................................218
Loy-Nel-Art............................310
Lu Ray Pastels........................298
Lucite 413
Lunch Boxes.............298-299;136
Lures 197
Lustreware 382

Lux Pendulettes......................115

Madame Alexander.........173-175

Maddux of California......299-300

Madoura.................................390

Magazine Covers 196,366

Magazine Stands.....................220

Magazines 300-301;69, 331,491

Magic 403

Maize 290

Majolica 301-302

Malachite Glass......................302

Mammy.................38,49,50,129

Mantel Lustres.......................302

Maple Sugar Molds.................322

Maps and Atlases 302-303; 424

Marblehead............................303

Marbles.............................303-305

Marine Collectibles................305

Marine Collectibles, See Also
   Scrimshaw; Steamship;
   Telescopes; Tools

Martin Bros...........................305

Marvel Electric Silver Cleaner.78

Marx 167,531

Mary Gregory 305-306

Mason Fruit Jars.....................212

Mason's Decoys 152-153

Mason's Ironstone 306

Masons (Fraternal
   Order)........................211,548

Massier 306

Mastercrafters Clocks 115

Match Holders ...306-307;29,179, 254,293,301,318,350,469

Match Safes 307

Mattel 175

Mattel Dolls, See Also Barbie
   Dolls and Related Dolls

Mauchline Ware 307-308

McCoy.............................308-310

McCoy, J.W...........................310

McKee 310;24,25

McKee, See Animal Dishes with
   Covers; Depression Glass;
   Kitchen Collectibles; Reamers

McKenney and Hall...............411

McLoughlin Bros...................414

Measures 234,384

Measures (Sewing) 476

Mechanical Banks 37

Medals 316,317,401

Medical Collectibles 310-311

Medicine Bottles 62-63

Meerschaum 526

Meissen.....................311,351,464

Menus 424,502

Mercury Glass........................311

Meriden 391

Merrimac 311

Metlox 311-314

Mettlach 314-315

Michael Jackson 437

Mickey Mouse 47,98,222, 381,414

Microscopes 315

Midwest Potteries, Inc............329

Midwestern Glass 315-316

Militaria 316-318;503

Militaria, See Also Weapons

Milk Glass 318-319;67, 284,558-559

Millefiori 319

Mineral Water & Soda Bottles .63

Miniature Lamps 284

Miniatures 319

Minton 319-320;525

Minton, See Also Majolica

Mirror Almond and Mirror
   Brown 256-257

Mirrors 320,399

Mission Ware 340-341

Mix, Tom 47,382

Mixers 276

Mocha 320-321

Molds..........321-322;234,432,491

Mollye 175

Monkees 437-438

Monmouth.............................322

Monot and Stumpf..........322-323

Mont Joye 323

Moon and Star.......................323

Moorcroft.........................323-324

Moravian Pottery and Tile
   Works 324-325

Morgan, Matt 325

Morgantown Glass 325-327

Moriage.................................327

Moriage, See Also Dragon
   Ware; Nippon

Mortars and Pestles 327-328

Mortens Studio.......................328

Morton Pottery 328-329

Mosaic Tile Co.......................329

Moser....................................329-330

Moss Rose 330

Mother-of-Pearl
   Glass 330-331;68

Motion Lamps 284-285

Mourning Collectibles 331

Movie Memorabilia.........331-332; 30-32,362,414,481

Movie Memorabilia, See Also
   Autographs

Moxie.......................................7

Mt. Washington 332;17, 138,376,464

Mucha Prints 411

Muffin Pans 235,274

Muggsy 385

Mulberry China...............332-333

Muller Freres.........................333

Muncie..................................334

Music Boxes 334-335

Musical Instruments........334-335

Muskets.................................552

Mustache Cups................335-336

Nailsea..................................336

Nailsea, See Also Lamps

Nakara 336

Napkin Holders 275

Napkin Rings 336-337;398

Nash......................................337

National Cash Registers....99-100

Natzler, Gertrude and Otto....337

Necklaces............................21,268

Needle Cases 476

Needlework 280,331

Netsukes 356

New England Glass
   Works 337-338; 17,138,364,376

New England Glass Works, See
   Also Amberina; Libbey;
   Paperweights

New Geneva 338

New Martinsville.............338;229

New York World's Fair............567

Newcomb 338-339

Newspapers 339;69

Nickelodeons.........................335

Nicodemus 339-340

Niloak..............................340-341

Nipper.......................................9

Nippon 341-343;464

Nodders 343;469

Noritake 343-345

Norse 345-346

North Dakota School of
   Mines 346

Northwood 346-347

Norweta 347

Nostalgia Line 314

Nozzles 195

Nude Stems 82-83

Nutcrackers 347

Nutting Prints 411-412

O'Neill, Rose 350-351

Occupied Japan 347-348

Odd Fellows (Fraternal
   Order)........................211-212

Ohr, George 348-349

Old Ivory 349

Old McDonald's Farm.....432-433

Old Paris 349

Old Sleepy Eye 349-350

Onion Pattern 351

Onyx 193

Opalescent Glass............351-354

Opaline 354

Orchestrions 335

Organs 335

Orientalia 354-358

Ornaments 110-111

Orphan Annie, See Little
   Orphan Annie

Orrefors................................358

Ott and Brewer......................358

Overbeck 358

Overlay Glass 358-359

Overshot 359

Owens Pottery 359

Pacific Clay Products 359-360

Paden City.....................360-361; 229,426

Paintings on Ivory 361

Pairpoint.................361-362;391

Pairpoint Limoges..................362

Pan-American Exposition 566

Panama-Pacific Exposition.....567

Paper Dolls 362
Paperweights 363-365;237,
253,457,495
Paperweights, See Also Glass
Animals and Figurines
Papier-Mache....365-366;242-243
Parian Ware..............................366
Parlor Stoves..............................511
Parrish, Maxfield.............366-367
Pate-De-Verre 367
Pate-Sur-Pate...........................367
Pattern Glass 367-375;100,
138,283,285,391,462-463,
464-465,512,514,527-528
Paul Revere Pottery................375
Pauline Pottery 375
Peachblow 376;68
Peanuts 381
Pearlware 376
Pedal Cars and Ride-On
Toys 534
Peking Cameo Glass 376-377
Peloton 377
Pencil Boxes 472
Pencil Sharpeners...........398,472
Pennsbury 377
Penny Toys 534
Pens and Pencils.............377-379
Pepsi-Cola 7-8
Perfection 78
Personalities, Fact and
Fiction........379-384;18,30-32,
98-99,124-125,128-129,
184,222-223,242,299,300-301,
331-332,362,414,426-429,481
Personalities, See Also
Autographs; Games, Movie
Memorabilia; Puzzles; Toys
Peters and Reed 383
Pewabic 383-384
Pewter...........................384-385
Pfaltzgraff 385
Phoenix Bird 385-386
Phoenix Glass..........................386
Phonographs...................386-387
Photographica 387-390;403,
424,495,501
Piano Babies 390
Pianos 335
Picasso Art Pottery.................390

Pickard 390-391
Pickle Castors 391
Pie Birds 391-392
Pie Safes...................................218
Pierce, Howard 392
Pietra-Dura 393
Pigeon Blood 393
Pilkington 393
Pillin 393
Pin-Back Buttons 393-394;
34,69,223,401
Pincushions 476
Pink Lustre Ware....................394
Pink Paw Bears 394
Pink Pigs.........................394-395
Pins 268,269,398
Pinups 400
Pipes 22,526
Pipsqueaks 534
Pisgah Forest 395
Pistols......................................552
Pitchers and Bowls; See
Wash Sets
Pittsburgh Glass..............396;285
Planters....................72,104,181,
309,348,450,480
Planters Peanuts......................8-9
Plastics...................396-399;184
Plated Amberina 18
Playboy Magazines..................300
Playing Cards ...399-400; 366,502
Pocketknives 69,401
Poison Bottles...........................63
Political 400-401
Pomona 401-402
Popeye 47,299,381-382
Poppets by Metlox..................314
Porcelier...................................402
Porringers................................385
Postcards.......402-403;69,196,350
Posters..403-404;112,331-332,424
Pot Lids....................................404
Powder Horns and Shot
Flasks 404-405
Prang, Louis 412
Pratt 405
Pre-Columbian Artifacts........406
Precious Moments...........405-406
Premiums; See Personalities, Fact
and Fiction

Presley, Elvis............................437
Primitives 406-407
Prints.......407-412;29,69,366-367
Pull Toys..................................534
Purinton 412-413
Purses.............................413-414
Puzzles 414
Pyrography 414-415
Queen's Rose 273-274
Quezal 415
Quilts 415-416
Quimper 416-417;464
R.S. Germany, R.S. Poland, R.S.
Prussia, Etc. 470-471
Racks 407,478
Radford 417-418
Radios..................418-419;398
Railroadiana 419-424;184,400
Ranges 511
Razors 424-425;398,562
RCA Victor 9
Reamers 425
Records 426-429
Red Goose Shoes 9-10,38
Red Wing 429-431
Redware...........................431-432
Reed and Barton 336-337
Regal China 432-433
Registering Banks 37
Reissner, Stallmacher & Kessel;
See Amphora; Teplitz
Relief-Molded Jugs 433
Restraints 433-434
Reverse Painting on
Glass 434-435;244
Reverse-Painted Lamps 285
Revolvers 552
Rhead.......................................435
Richard 435
Ridgway 435
Rifles 552
Ringling Brothers 112
Rings 268-269
Riviera 435-436
Roasters 196,235,274
Robertson 436;525
Robinson-Ransbottom 128,129
Robj 436
Roblin 436
Robots 534-535

Rock 'N Roll
Memorabilia 436-437
Rockers 108,478,506,
507,559-560
Rockingham 438
Rogers, John 438
Rogers, Roy.............125,129,382
Rolling Pins 275,276,351
Rolling Stones 438
Roly Poly Tobacco Tins 10
Ronson.....................................526
Rookwood 438-442
Rorstrand 442
Rose Mandarin 442
Rose Medallion 442-443
Rosebud 130
Roselane 443
Rosemeade 443-444
Rosenthal.................................444
Roseville..........................444-446
Roulette Wheels.....................221
Rowland and
Marsellus 446-447
Roy Rogers.............125,129,382
Royal Bayreuth.........447-449;464
Royal Bonn..............................449
Royal Copenhagen 449;
291-292,464
Royal Copley...................449-450
Royal Crown Derby................450
Royal Doulton,
Doulton 450-454;464
Royal Dux 454-455
Royal Flemish 455
Royal Haeger, Haeger.............455
Royal Rudolstadt 455
Royal Vienna 455-456
Roycroft 456
Rozenberg........................456-457
Ruba Rombic 126
Rubena.....................................457
Rubena Verde 457
Ruby Glass 457
Ruby-Stained Glass.........457-458
Rugs.........458;22-23,192,356-357
RumRill 458
Ruskin 458
Russel Wright
Dinnerware.................458-460
Russian Art 460-461;465

Sabino................................461
Salesman's Samples and Patent
   Models......................461-462
Salopian..............................102
Salt Cellars, See Salts, Open
Salt Shakers.....462-463;50,54,57,
   104,154-155,181,190,254,
   275-276,288,341,346,348,
   398,433,443-444,480,559
Salts, Open................463-465;52
Samplers......................465-466
San Francisco World's Fair.....567
San Ildefonso Pottery...............22
Sandwich Glass..............466;464
Sandwich Glass, See Also Cup
   Plates; Salts, Open
Santas........111,112,168,312,321
Sarreguemines.......................466
Sarsaparilla Bottles..................63
Satin Glass.....................466-467
Satsuma..........................467;247
Saturday Evening Post
   Magazines......................300
Savoi Et Cie...........................78
Scales............................467-468
Scarlett O'Hara.....................174
Schafer and Vater...........468-469
Scheier.........................469-470
Schierholz......................502-503
Schlegelmilch Porcelain .470-471
Schneider......................471-472
Schoehnut...............175,535-536
Schoolhouse Collectibles.......472
Schoop, Hedi...................472-473
Schramberg...........................473
Schuco.........................518,531
Scouting Collectibles......473-474
Scrimshaw...........................474
Sebastians....................474-475
Secretaries...........................218
Sesquicentennial Exposition..567
Seth Thomas Clocks.......115-116
Settees.........................218,560
Sevres..................................475
Sewer Tile............................475
Sewing Items...................475-476
Sewing Items, See Also
   Mauchline Ware
Sewing Machines............476-477
Sextants..............................305

SFBJ Dolls.....................175-176
Shackles...............................434
Shaker Items...................477-478
Shaving Mugs..........471,478-479
Shawnee.........................479-480
Shearwater.....................480-481
Sheet Music......................481;72
Sheffield Silverplate........488-489
Shelf Clocks...................115-116
Shelf Sitters.........................104
Shelley..........................481-483
Shelves................................218
Shenandoah..........................483
Shirley Temple.................176,382
Shooting Gallery Targets.........90
Shot Flasks...........................405
Shotguns..............................552
Shrine (Fraternal Order)........212
Sideboards...........................218
Signs, See Advertising;
   Coca-Cola
Silhouettes...........................483
Silk-Screen Color Printing on
   Crystal...........................327
Silver..........483-487;465,523-524
Silver Lustre Ware.................487
Silver Overlay.......................487
Silverplate........487-489;100,391,
           422-423,465
Simon & Halbig.....................176
Skillets...............................274
Skipper Dolls........................170
Slag Glass............................489
Sleepy Eye, See Old Sleepy Eye
Slot Machines........................123
Smith Bros...........................489
Smith, L.E......................228-229
Snow Babies..........................489
Snow White.....................299,382
Snuff Bottles........................357
Snuff Boxes....................489-490
Soap Hollow Furniture...........490
Soapstone.............................490
Soda Fountain
   Collectibles.................490-491
Soda Fountain Collectibles, See
   Also Advertising
Sofas..............................192,218
Spangle Glass........................491
Spatter Glass..............491-492;476

Spatterware...........................492
Spirits Bottles........................63
Spode-Copeland..............492-493
Spongeware.....................493-494
Spoons.......................494;69,423
Sporting Goods........494-495;403
Sports Illustrated Magazines...300
St. Clair.........................495-496
St. Louis World's Fair.............566
Staffordshire..........496-498;1,184
Staffordshire, See Also Clews
Stained Glass.........................498
Stands...............218-219,478,506
Stanford.........................498-499
Stangle.........................499-501
Stanhopes...........................390
Stanley Tools........................501
Statue of Liberty...................501
Steamship Collectibles ..501-502;
               184,400
Steiff.........................536;465,518
Steins.........502-503;314-315,350
Steins, See Also Mettlach
Stereoscopic Views.................389
Sterilizers............................39
Steuben.........................503-505;464
Stevengraphs.........................505
Stevens and Williams.....505-506
Stickley.........................506-507
Stiegel.........................507-508
Stocks and Bonds...................508
Stone Artifacts, American
   Indian...........................23
Stone Artifacts, See Also
   Antiquities
Stoneware.......508-509;46,52-53,
        322,431,454,503
Stools................219,478,506,507
Store.............................510;512
Stoves.........................510-511
Straw Dispensers and Holders .491
Straw Holders........................276
Strawberry Soft Paste and Lustre
   Ware...........................511
Stretch Glass...................511-512
String Holders...................512;50
Sugar Shakers...........512;193,346
Sulfide Marbles...............304-305
Sunbonnet Babies...................448
Sunderland Lustre..................512

Sunrise Medallion Etch..........327
Surveying Instruments 512-513
Swarovski Crystal...................513
Swastika Keramos.............513-514
Sweet 16, Goetting & Co.; See
   California Perfume, Co.
Swords................................552
Syracuse..............................514
Syrup Tins...............................6
Syrups...............514;190,276,346
Tablecloths..................34,280,422
Tables......................192,219,478,
        491,507,560,568
Tall Case Clocks....................116
Tamac Pottery.......................515
Target Balls....................515-516
Tarzan.............................47,382
Tea Caddies..........................516
Tea Leaf Ironstone...........516-517
Teakettles..............65,131,235
Teapots ..517;42,51,54,69,74,133,
   180,190,230,235,241,246,288,
   289,302,360,385,413,417,480,
   483,498,511,540,555,559,561
Teco................................517-518
Teddy Bear Collectibles.........518
Telephones.....................518-519
Telescopes.....................519-520
Televisions...........................520
Teplitz................................520
Terra Cotta...........................520
Terri Lee.........................176-177
Theorems on Paper or
   Velvet...........................202
Thermometers.................520-521
Thermometers, See Also
   Advertising
Thermoses.....................298-299
Thimbles..........................69,476
Third Reich....................316-317
Thousand Faces China...........521
Three-Face Glass...................374
Tiffany...............521-524;464,465
Tiffin Glass.....................524;229
Tiles................524-525;18,41,69,
   237,324-325,329,338,
   375,441-442,457,529,545
Timetables...........................424
Tintypes..............................389
Tinware.........................525;322

Tinware, See Also Kitchen
    Collectibles; Primitives
Toasters 26,196
Tobacciana......................525-526
Toby Jugs 454
Toleware.......................526-527
Tom Mix.......................47,382
Tomato Ware 499
Toodles Dolls.........................177
Tools.............................527;23,
    272-272,501,561-562
Toothbrush Holders 527;113
Toothpick Holders....527-528;17,
    50,75,154-155,193,
    346-347,449,458,495-496
Torquay Pottery 528-529
Town and Country.................431
Toy Soldiers and
    Accessories 536-537
Toys.......................529-537;119,
    134-136,166-167,511,518
Toys, See Also Cracker Jack;
    Personalities
Trade Signs............................537
Trade Stimulators 123-124
Tramp Art 537-538
Trans-Mississippi Exposition..566
Transferware, See ABC Plates;
    Pink Lustre; Silver Lustre;
    Staffordshire, Miscellaneous
Transistor Radios...................419
Traps.....................................538
Tree in the Meadow.......344-345
Trenton 525
Trivets 538-539;338,375
Trolls 539
Trunks 539

Turner, See Creamware
Tuthill 539-540
TV Guide Magazines..............301
TV Lamps 299
Tykie Toys 397
Typewriters 540
Uhl Pottery 540-541
Uneeda 177
Unger Brothers 541
Union Cases 389-390
Universal 541
University City.......................541
US Coin Pattern 374
Utopian Ware........................359
Vacuum Cleaners 26
Val St. Lambert 541
Valencia................................480
Valentien Pottery 541
Valentines 541-542;403
Van Briggle 542-543
Van Erp 29-30
Van Halen 438
Van Telligen..........................433
Vance Avon 543
Vaseline 543
Vendors 121,124
Venini Glass....................265-266
Verlys...................................543
Vernon Kilns..................543-544
Viking...................................229
Vistosa 544
Vistosi Glass 266
Vogue....................................177
Volkmar 544-545
Volkstedt 545
Wade 545-546
Waffle Irons...........................274

Wagner 274
Wall Pockets.............50,392,417
Wallace China 546
Walley 546
Walrath 546
Walrich 546
Walter, A..............................546
Wannopee......................546-547
Wardrobes 219
Warwick 547
Wash Sets 547-548;264
Washboards 407
Washstands 219-200
Watch Fobs....................548;401
Watches 548-550
Waterford 550
Watt Pottery 550-551
Wave Crest 551
Weapons...................551-552;23
Weather Vanes 552-553
Weaving 553;478
Webb 553;376,464
Webb, See Also Alexandrite;
    Burmese; Mother of Pearl;
    Peachblow
Wedgwood 553-555;516-517
Weil Ware 555
Weller...........................555-557
Western Americana 557
Western Pottery Manufacturing
    Company.....................557-558
Westite 15
Westmoreland................558-559;
    24,25,229
Wheatley, T.J. 559
Whieldon..............................559
Whiting and Davis 413,414

Wicker............................559-560
Will-George..........................560
Willets 560
Willow Ware................560-561;
    73-74,239
Winchester...................561-562
Winchester; See Also Knives
    Weapons
Windmill Weights..................562
Winfield................................562
Wire Ware.......................562-563
Witch Balls...........................563
Wolverine.............................532
Wood Carvings......................563;
    75-76,88-89
Woodblock Prints,
    Japanese.....................357-358
Woodenware 563
Woodworking Machinery 564
Worcester Porcelain
    Company 565;392,464
World's Fairs and
    Expos 566-567;400
Wright, Frank Loyd.........567-568
Wright, L.G......................24,25
Wristwatches, See Also
    Personalities
Wrought Iron 568;86,539
Yard-Long Prints 412
Yellow Ware 568
Zanesville Art Pottery.....568-569
Zanesville Glass 569
Zaneware, See Peters and Reed
Zeisel Designs..................241-242
Zell..569
Zsolnay..................................569

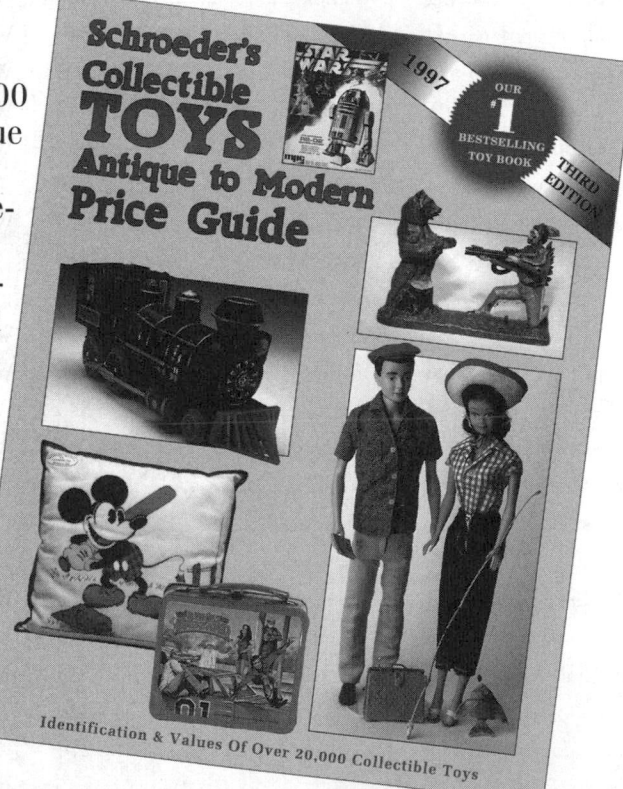